THE ENCYCLOPAEDIA OF ISLAM

THE ENCYCLOPAEDIA OF ISLAM

NEW EDITION

PREPARED BY A NUMBER OF
LEADING ORIENTALISTS

EDITED BY

**P. J. BEARMAN, TH. BIANQUIS, C. E. BOSWORTH,
E. VAN DONZEL AND W. P. HEINRICHS**

UNDER THE PATRONAGE OF
THE INTERNATIONAL UNION OF ACADEMIES

VOLUME XI

W — Z

LEIDEN
BRILL
2002

The preparation of this volume of the Encyclopaedia of Islam was made possible in part through grants from the Research Tools Program of the National Endowment for the Humanities, an independent Federal Agency of the United States Government; the British Academy; the Oriental Institute, Leiden; Académie des Inscriptions et Belles-Lettres; and the Royal Netherlands Academy of Sciences.

The articles in this volume were published in double fascicules of 112 pages, the dates of publication being:

2000: Fascs. 179-180, pp. 1-112

2001: Fascs. 181-186, pp. 113-448

2002: Fascs. 187-188, pp. 449-575

ISBN 90 04 12756 9

PRINTED IN THE NETHERLANDS

AUTHORS OF ARTICLES IN THIS VOLUME

For the benefit of readers who may wish to follow up an individual contributor's articles, the Editors have listed after each contributor's name the pages on which his or her signature appears. Academic affiliations are given (for a retired scholar, the place of his/her last known academic appointment).

In this list, names in square brackets are those of authors of articles reprinted or revised from the first edition of this *Encyclopaedia* or from the *Shorter Encyclopaedia of Islam*. An asterisk after the name of the author in the text denotes an article reprinted from the first edition which has been brought up to date by the Editorial Committee; where an article has been revised by a second author his or her name appears within square brackets after the name of the original author.

F. Adanir, University of Bochum. 215
C. Adle, Centre National de la Recherche Scientifique, Paris. 471
Feroz Ahmad, University of Massachusetts, Boston. 321
Virginia Aksan, McMaster University, Hamilton, Ontario. 131, 321
R.M.A. Allen, University of Pennsylvania. 251
C. Alvarez de Morales, C.S.I.C., Granada. 15
A.A. Ambros, University of Vienna. 552
Edith G. Ambros, University of Vienna. 132, 205, 251, 319, 350, 519
R. Amitai, Hebrew University, Jerusalem. 18
Meropi Anastassiadou, Institut Français d'Etudes Anatoliennes, Istanbul. 283
A. Arazi, Hebrew University, Jerusalem. 13, 158
Françoise Aubin, Centre d'Etudes de Recherches Internationales, Paris. 122
A. Ayalon, Tel Aviv University. 126
the late D. Ayalon, Hebrew University, Jerusalem. 27
Roswitha Badry, University of Freiburg. 569
Eva Baer, Jerusalem. 425
M.A. al-Bakhit, Āl al-Bayt University, Mafraq, Jordan. 460
Çiğdem Balim, University of Manchester. 163
M.L. Bates, The American Numismatic Society, New York. 148
Tiziana Battain, University of Trieste. 457
M. Bazin, University of Reims. 267
A. Bazzana, University of Lyons. 426
Peri Bearman, Harvard University. 358
the late A.F.L. Beeston, University of Oxford. 302
M.A.J. Beg, Cambridge. 151
P. Behnstedt, University of Heidelberg. 280
Doris Behrens-Abouseif, University of London. 69
H. Bell, Oxford Academy for Advanced Studies. 13
A. Ben Abdesselem, Institut National des Langues et Civilisations Orientales, Paris. 133, 145
H. Bencheneb, Paris. 544
J.P. Berkey, Davidson College, Davidson, North Carolina. 463
Lidia Bettini, University of Florence. 523, 558
Th. Bianquis, University of Lyons. 181, 190, 320, 383, 392, 547
Sheila S. Blair, Boston College. 298, 467
Kh.Y. Blankinship, Temple University, Philadelphia. 311
F.C. de Blois, Royal Asiatic Society, London. 184, 210, 223, 497, 513
J.M. Bloom, Boston College. 298
M. Boivin, Ecole des Hautes Etudes en Sciences Sociales, Paris. 518
C.E. Bosworth, University of Manchester. 2, 16, 34, 52, 100, 101, 130, 134, 135, 136, 144, 148, 178, 179, 184, 202, 205, 214, 220, 221, 224, 227, 235, 238, 246, 255, 288, 290, 294, 297, 301, 302, 312, 333, 334, 336, 337, 343, 358, 362, 366, 371, 387, 394, 426, 432, 440, 447, 458, 459, 463, 464, 483, 485, 487, 516, 522, 540, 559, 565, 571, 575
Annabelle Böttcher, Free University, Berlin. 299
W.C. Brice, University of Manchester. 14, 32, 271, 386
J.T.P. de Bruijn, University of Leiden. 361, 393
Kathleen R.F. Burrill, Columbia University. 162, 202
R.D. Burrowes, University of Washington. 276
Y. Callot, University of Tours. 14, 32
Sheila R. Canby, British Museum, London. 264
S. Carboni, Metropolitan Museum of Art, New York. 554
A. Carmona, University of Murcia. 78, 192
M.G. Carter, University of Oslo. 173, 459
B. Catlos, University of Toronto. 160
Jacqueline Chabbi, University of Paris. 442
Khalifa Chater, Bibliothèque Nationale, Tunis. 490
E. Chaumont, Centre National de la Recherche Scientifique, Aix-en-Provence. 219, 299
H.E. Chehabi, Boston University. 574
W.C. Chittick, State University of New York, Stony Brook. 39
P.M. Cobb, University of Notre Dame. 464
P.M. Costa, University of Bologna. 6
M. Côte, University of Aix-en-Provence. 139, 147, 366
J. Couland, University of Paris. 176
Patricia Crone, Institute for Advanced Study, Princeton. 312
Seta B. Dadoyan, American University of Beirut. 282
R. Dankoff, University of Chicago. 360
R.E. Darley-Doran, Winchester. 171, 200, 231
G. Dávid, Eötvos Loránd University, Budapest. 142, 492, 546
Randi Deguilhem, IREMAM, Aix-en-Provence. 92
F.M. Denny, University of Colorado, Boulder. 121, 210
D. DeWeese, Indiana University, Bloomington. 118
A. Dietrich, University of Göttingen. 343
E. van Donzel, Leiden. 178, 234, 281, 293
Nelly van Doorn-Harder, Valparaiso University, Valparaiso, Indiana. 530, 537
Anne-Marie Eddé, University of Reims. 191, 391
H. Eisenstein, University of Vienna. 130
Mohamed El Mansour, University Mohamed V, Rabat. 133, 201, 202, 388
W. Ende, University of Freiburg. 47, 398, 530
G. Endress, University of Bochum. 246
Sibel Erol, New York University. 257
J. van Ess, University of Tübingen. 165
T. Fahd, University of Strasbourg. 404
Suraiya Faroqhi, University of Munich. 257, 301, 341, 495, 545
Halima Ferhat, University of Rabat. 356, 566

Maribel Fierro, C.S.I.C., Madrid. 15, 103, 249, 425
R. Firestone, Hebrew Union College, Los Angeles. 254, 354, 373
Barbara Flemming, University of Leiden. 362
G.S.P. Freeman-Grenville, Sheriff Hutton, York. 106, 108, 283, 445, 450
M. Gaborieau, Centre National de la Recherche Scientifique, Paris. 120, 358, 406, 536
D. Gazagnadou, University of Paris. 268
G.J.H. van Gelder, University of Oxford. 151, 153, 184, 247
E. Geoffroy, University of Strasbourg. 236, 406, 524
Ali Gheissari, University of San Diego. 239, 309
Cl. Gilliot, University of Aix-en-Provence. 152, 266
Geneviève Gobillot, University of Lyons. 562
G. Goodwin, Royal Asiatic Society, London. 267
Molly Greene, Princeton University. 204
D. Gril, University of Aix-en-Provence. 212
[A. Grohmann, Vienna]. 270
A.J. Gully, University of Exeter. 319
the late U. Haarmann, Free University, Berlin. 175
Wael B. Hallaq, McGill University, Montreal. 389
H. Halm, University of Tübingen. 103, 129, 405
J. Hämeen-Anttila, University of Helsinki. 382
C. Hamès, Centre National de la Recherche Scientifique, Paris. 443, 470
Shah Mahmoud Hanifi, University of Michigan, Ann Arbor. 494
I. Hasson, Hebrew University, Jerusalem. 522, 551
A. Havemann, Free University, Berlin. 359
G.R. Hawting, University of London. 311, 312
S. Heidemann, University of Jena. 392, 452, 455
W.P. Heinrichs, Harvard University. 37, 52, 53, 313, 364, 472
C.J. Heywood, University of London. 290
C. Holes, University of Oxford. 47
[E. Honigmann, Brussels]. 488
M.B. Hooker, Australian National University, Canberra. 99, 493
D. Hopwood, University of Oxford. 26
J.O. Hunwick, Northwestern University. 9, 99, 124
Halil İnalcik, Bilkent University, Ankara. 197
Svetlana Ivanova, National Library, Sofia. 150, 208, 517
Mawil Y. Izzi Dien, University of Wales, Lampeter. 23, 58, 208
P. Jackson, University of Keele. 174
Renate Jacobi, Free University, Berlin. 129, 548, 571
J. Jankowski, University of Colorado. 253
J.J.G. Jansen, University of Leiden. 57
Penelope C. Johnstone, University of Oxford. 145, 152, 225, 486
F. de Jong, University of Utrecht. 185
W.E. Kaegi, University of Chicago. 292
O. Kahl, Sheffield. 496
J.G. Katz, Oregon State University. 468
Barbara Kellner-Heinkele, Free University, Berlin. 341
H. Kennedy, University of St. Andrews. 128
P.F. Kennedy, New York University. 564
R.G. Khoury, University of Heidelberg. 36, 101, 180, 559, 565
Abdelfattah Kilito, University Mohamed V, Rabat. 52, 352
Hilary Kilpatrick, Lausanne. 423
D.A. King, University of Frankfurt. 508
E. Kohlberg, Hebrew University, Jerusalem. 162, 483
G.C. Kozlowski, DePaul University, Chicago. 97
P.G. Kreyenbroek, University of Göttingen. 316
Remke Kruk, University of Leiden. 32
V. Lagardère, Centre National de la Recherche Scientifique, Lyons. 141
Ann K.S. Lambton, Kirknewton, Northumberland. 87, 194, 286, 309, 473
W. and Fidelity Lancaster, Orkney. 160
J.M. Landau, Hebrew University, Jerusalem. 357
H. Landolt, Institute of Ismaili Studies, London. 218
A. Layish, Hebrew University, Jerusalem. 81
O.N.H. Leaman, University of Kentucky. 217
M. Lecker, Hebrew University, Jerusalem. 19, 220, 475, 476, 496, 559, 566
F. Leconte, Lycée Berthelot, Châtellerault. 228
S. Leder, University of Halle. 103, 354, 552
F. Leemhuis, University of Groningen. 6, 148, 247
G. Leiser, Vacaville, California. 494
J. Lentin, University of Paris. 465
Y. Lev, Bar-Ilan University, Ramat-Gan. 171
[G. Levi Della Vida, Rome]. 284
[E. Lévi-Provençal, Paris]. 491
B. Lewis, Princeton University. 569
L. Lewisohn, University of London. 23
Chang-Kuan Lin, National Cheng-chi University, Taipei. 216
P. Lory, Ecole Pratique des Hautes Etudes, Paris. 113, 221
P.E. Losensky, Indiana University, Bloomington. 53, 59, 567
R.D. McChesney, New York University. 95
N. McHugh, Fort Lewis College, Durango, Colorado. 6, 125
W. Madelung, University of Oxford. 243, 250, 474, 481
D. Mallet, Institut Français d'Etudes Arabes, Damascus. 438
[G. Marçais, Paris]. 24
C. Melville, University of Cambridge. 432
Rana von Mende-Altayli, Berlin. 256
[Th. Menzel]. 138
J.W. Meri, University of California, Berkeley. 529
F. Mermier, Centre National de la Recherche Scientifique, Lyons. 277
Y. Meron, Jerusalem. 159
Françoise Michaux, University of Paris. 246
[V. Minorsky, Cambridge]. 238
L. Molina, University of Granada. 355
G. Monnot, Ecole Pratique des Hautes Etudes, Paris. 177
J.E. Montgomery, University of Cambridge. 460
Shireen Moosvi, Aligarh Muslim University. 439
D.O. Morgan, University of London. 293
J.-M. Mouton, University of Paris. 423
W.W. Müller, University of Marburg. 380
M. Muranyi, University of Bonn. 572
Sachiko Murata, State University of New York, Stony Brook. 137
R. Murphey, University of Birmingham. 153, 215, 331
Mustapha Naimi, University Mohamed V, Rabat. 21
Husayn Nassar, Cairo University. 384
I.R. Netton, University of Leeds. 37, 49
E. Neubauer, University of Frankfurt. 251, 351, 428, 517, 574
G. Nonneman, Lancaster University. 547
H.T. Norris, University of London. 385
Claudia Ott, University of Erlangen. 234
Aylin Özman, Hacettepe University, Ankara. 342
D. Panzac, IREMAM, Aix-en-Provence. 4
L. Paul, University of Göttingen. 491
J.R. Perry, University of Chicago. 444
Esther Peskes, University of Bonn. 45
R. Peters, University of Amsterdam. 63, 172, 510

T. Philipp, University of Erlangen. 393
Ch. Picard, University of Toulouse. 226
Élizabeth Picard, Centre National de la Recherche Scientifique, Aix-en-Provence. 403
R. Pinilla-Melguizo, University of Cordoba. 14, 15, 18
I. Poonawala, University of California, Los Angeles. 390
A. Popovic, Centre National de la Recherche Scientifique, Paris. 322, 446
D.S. Powers, Cornell University. 75
Cristina de la Puente, University of Madrid. 17
Ghada al-Hijjawi al-Qaddumi, Safat, Kuwait. 263, 571
B. Radtke, University of Utrecht. 56, 112
Abdul-Karim Rafeq, College of William and Mary, Williamsburg, Virginia. 334, 367
F.J. Ragep, University of Oklahoma. 556
Munibur Rahman, Oakland University, Rochester, Michigan. 25
S.A. al-Rashid, King Saud University, Riyadh. 16
W. Raven, University of Frankfurt. 161
S. Reese, Xavier University, New Orleans. 539
Anne Regourd, Centre National de la Recherche Scientifique, Paris. 10, 405
S. Reichmuth, University of Bochum. 338
A.K. Reinhart, Dartmouth College, Hanover, New Hampshire. 101
Y. Richard, University of Paris. 484
M.E.J. Richardson, University of Manchester. 513
A. Rippin, University of Victoria, British Columbia. 56, 152, 237, 249, 349, 351, 406
C.F. Robinson, University of Oxford. 143
E. Rogan, University of Oxford. 159
Fátima Roldán Castro, University of Seville. 109
F. Rosenthal, Yale University. 345
A. Rouaud, Centre National de la Recherche Scientifique, Paris. 248, 456, 481
U. Rudolph, University of Zurich. 7
Y. Sabar, University of California, Los Angeles. 425
Abdulaziz Sachedina, University of Virginia. 534
Noha Sadek, University of Lyons. 371
T. Saguchi, Kanazawa. 347
Mondher Sakly, University of Sfax. 169
J.-F. Salles, University of Lyons. 397
J. Samsó, University of Barcelona. 462, 508
F. Sanagustin, University of Lyons. 382
T. Sato, University of Tokyo. 223
Emilie Savage-Smith, University of Oxford. 399
A. Savvides, Aegean University, Rhodes. 214, 333, 384, 426
Ayman F. Sayyid, Egyptian National Library. 33
W. Schmucker, University of Bonn. 245
G. Schoeler, University of Basel. 376, 402
R. Seesemann, University of Bayreuth. 538
R. Sellheim, University of Frankfurt. 48, 317, 549
B. Semmoud, University of Artois. 51
J. Sesiano, Ecole Polytechnique Fédérale, Lausanne. 31
[C.F. Seybold, Tübingen]. 21
Ursula Sezgin, University of Frankfurt. 164
C. Shackle, University of London. 2, 125
R. Shaham, Hebrew University, Jerusalem. 300
Irfan Shahîd, Georgetown University, Washington, D.C. 369, 461
B. Shoshan, Ben Gurion University of the Negev. 3
Mohammad Yusuf Siddiq, Zayed University, Dubai. 237
Hussein Sirriyeh, Leeds University. 476
G.R. Smith, University of Manchester. 48, 225, 236, 269, 274, 292, 342, 381, 524, 572
S. Soucek, Princeton University. 225
J.L. Spaulding, Kean College, Union, New Jersey. 11
F.H. Stewart, Hebrew University, Jerusalem. 174
N. Stillman, University of Oklahoma, Normal. 242
W. Stoetzer, University of Leiden. 28, 181, 200, 377, 509
Jacqueline Sublet, Centre National de la Recherche Scientifique, Paris. 346
R. Talmon, University of Haifa. 349
H.G.B. Teule, University of Nijmegen. 262
the late G.R. Tibbetts, Oxford. 105, 108, 110, 369
Amin Tibi, University of Oxford. 355, 427, 466, 516, 559
[J. Tkatsch]. 5
Shawkat M. Toorawa, Cornell University. 105, 106, 108, 369
Houari Touati, Centre National de la Recherche Scientifique, Paris. 533
[A.S. Tritton, London]. 572
J.F. Troin, University of Tours. 24
Abdel-Magid Turki, Centre National de la Recherche Scientifique, Paris. 396
D. Urvoy, University of Toulouse. 142
B. Utas, Uppsala University. 135
[V. Vacca, Rome]. 485
D.M. Varisco, Hofstra University, Hempstead, New York. 487
Chantal de La Véronne, Centre National de la Recherche Scientifique, Paris. 183, 239
C.H.M. Versteegh, University of Nijmegen. 378, 379, 434
K.S. Vikør, University of Bergen. 213, 466
the late F. Viré, Centre National de la Recherche Scientifique, Paris. 109, 183, 283, 294, 458
J.O. Voll, Georgetown University, Washington, D.C. 451
E. Wagner, University of Giessen. 127, 281
D. Waines, University of Lancaster. 370, 381, 486
P.E. Walker, University of Chicago. 209
Wiebke Walther, University of Tübingen. 387, 477
B.G. Weiss, University of Utah. 7
[A.J. Wensinck, Leiden]. 213
I. Wilks, Ceredigion, Wales. 138
R. Wisnovsky, Harvard University. 253
Christine Woodhead, University of Durham. 57, 163, 202, 254
O. Wright, University of London. 492
M.E. Yapp, University of London. 198, 363
E. Yarshater, Encyclopaedia Iranica, New York. 555
Neguin Yavari, Institute of Ismaili Studies, London. 222
S. Yerasimos, University of Paris. 335, 337
[G. Yver, Algiers]. 146
Muhammad Qasim Zaman, Brown University. 188, 258
Th. Zarcone, Centre National de la Recherche Scientifique, Paris. 115, 296, 452, 535
[K.V. Zettersteen, Uppsala]. 129
E.J. Zürcher, University of Leiden. 332, 363
A. Zysow, Harvard University. 422

ABBREVIATED TITLES
OF SOME OF THE MOST OFTEN QUOTED WORKS

Abu 'l-Fidā', *Taḳwīm* = *Taḳwīm al-buldān*, ed. J.-T. Reinaud and M. de Slane, Paris 1840

Abu 'l-Fidā', *Taḳwīm*, tr. = *Géographie d'Aboulféda, traduite de l'arabe en français*, vol. i, ii/1 by Reinaud, Paris 1848; vol. ii/2 by St. Guyard, 1883

Aghānī[1] or [2] or [3] = Abu 'l-Faradj al-Iṣfahānī, *al-Aghānī*; [1]Būlāḳ 1285; [2]Cairo 1323; [3]Cairo 1345-

Aghānī, Tables = *Tables alphabétiques du Kitāb al-aghānī*, rédigées par I. Guidi, Leiden 1900

Aghānī, Brünnow = *The XXIst vol. of the Kitāb al-Aghānī*, ed. R.E. Brünnow, Leiden 1883

ALA = *Arabic Literature of Africa*, ed. R.S. O'Fahey and J.O. Hunwick, Leiden 1993-

ʿAlī Djewād = *Memālik-i ʿOthmāniyyenīn taʾrīkh we djughrāfiyā lughātī*, Istanbul 1313-17/1895-9

ʿAlī Mubārak, *Khiṭaṭ* = ʿAlī Mubārak, *al-Khiṭaṭ al-tawfīḳiyya al-djadīda li-Miṣr al-Ḳāhira wa-mudunihā wa-bilādihā 'l-ḳadīma wa-'l-shahīra*, 20 vols., Būlāḳ 1304-6

Anbārī, *Nuzha* = *Nuzhat al-alibbāʾ fī ṭabaḳāt al-udabāʾ*, [1]Cairo 1294; [2]Stockholm, etc. 1963

ʿAwfī, *Lubāb* = *Lubāb al-albāb*, ed. E.G. Browne, London-Leiden 1903-6

Babinger, *GOW* = F. Babinger, *Die Geschichtsschreiber der Osmanen und ihre Werke*, 1st ed., Leiden 1927

Baghdādī, *Farḳ* = *al-Farḳ bayn al-firaḳ*, ed. Muḥammad Badr, Cairo 1328/1910

Balādhurī, *Futūḥ* = *Futūḥ al-buldān*, ed. M.J. de Goeje, Leiden 1866

Balādhurī, *Ansāb* = Balādhurī, *Ansāb al-ashrāf*, i, ed. M. Hamid Allāh, Cairo 1960; iii, ed. ʿAbd al-ʿAzīz al-Dūrī, Beirut 1978; iv A, ed. Iḥsān ʿAbbās, Beirut 1979; iv B and v, ed. M. Schlössinger and S.D.F. Goitein, Jerusalem 1936-39

Barkan, *Kanunlar* = Ömer Lûtfi Barkan, *XV vc XVI inci asırlarda Osmanlı Imparatorluğunda ziraî ekonominin hukukî ve malî esasları, I. Kanunlar*, Istanbul 1943

Barthold, *Four studies* = V.V. Barthold, *Four studies on the history of Central Asia*, tr. by V. and T. Minorsky, 3 vols., Leiden 1956-63

Barthold, *Turkestan* = W. Barthold, *Turkestan down to the Mongol invasion*, London 1928 (GMS, N.S. V)

Barthold, *Turkestan*[2] = *ibid.*, revised edition, London 1958

Barthold, *Turkestan*[3] = *ibid.*, revised and enlarged ed., London 1968

Blachère, *HLA* = R. Blachère, *Histoire de la littérature arabe*, 3 vols., Paris 1952-64

de Blois, *Persian literature* = F. de Blois, *Persian literature, a bio-bibliographical survey, begun by the late C.A. Storey*, vol. v, London 1992-

Brockelmann, I, II = C. Brockelmann, *Geschichte der arabischen Literatur (GAL)*, zweite den Supplementbänden angepasste Auflage, Leiden 1943-49

Brockelmann S I, II, III = *GAL*, Erster (zweiter, dritter) Supplementband, Leiden 1937-42

Browne, *LHP* = E.G. Browne, *A literary history of Persia*, 4 vols., London and Cambridge 1902-24

Browne, ii = *A literary history of Persia, from Firdawsi to Saʿdi*, London 1908

Browne, iii = *A history of Persian literature under Tartar Dominion*, Cambridge 1920

Browne, iv = *A history of Persian literature in modern times*, Cambridge 1924

Caetani, *Annali* = L. Caetani, *Annali dell'Islam*, Milan 1905-26

Camb. hist. Iran = *The Cambridge history of Iran*, 7 vols., Cambridge 1968-91

Camb. hist. Ar. lit = *The Cambridge history of Arabic literature*, ed. A.F.L. Beeston *et alii*, 4 vols., Cambridge 1983-92

Chauvin, *Bibliographie* = V. Chauvin, *Bibliographie des ouvrages arabes et relatifs aux Arabes*, Lille 1892

Clauson, *Etymological dictionary* = Sir Gerard Clauson, *An etymological dictionary of pre-thirteenth century Turkish*, Oxford 1972

Creswell, *Bibliography* = K.A.C. Creswell, *A bibliography of the architecture, arts and crafts of Islam to 1st Jan. 1960*, Cairo 1961

Ḍabbī = *Bughyat al-multamis fī taʾrīkh ridjāl ahl al-Andalus*, ed. F. Codera and J. Ribera, Madrid 1885 (BAH III)

Damīrī = *Ḥayāt al-ḥayawān* (quoted according to titles of articles)

Dawlatshāh = *Tadhkirat al-shuʿarāʾ*, ed. E.G. Browne, London-Leiden 1901

Dhahabī, *Ḥuffāẓ* = al-Dhahabī, *Tadhkirat al-ḥuffāẓ*, 4 vols., Hyderabad 1315 H.

Dictionnaire arabe-français-anglais = *Dictionnaire arabe-français-anglais (langue classique et moderne)*, Paris 1963-

Djuwaynī = *Taʾrīkh-i Djihān-gushā*, ed. Muḥammad Ḳazwīnī, Leiden 1906-37 (GMS XVI)

Djuwaynī-Boyle = *The history of the World conqueror*, by ʿAṭā-Malik Djuwaynī, trans. J.A. Boyle, 2 vols., Manchester 1958

Doerfer, *Elemente* = G. Doerfer, *Türkische und mongolische Elemente im Neupersischen*, Wiesbaden 1963-

Dozy, *Notices* = R. Dozy, *Notices sur quelques manuscrits arabes*, Leiden 1847-51

Dozy, *Recherches*[3] = *Recherches sur l'histoire et la littérature de l'Espagne pendant le moyen-âge*, third edition, Paris-Leiden 1881

Dozy, *Suppl.* = R. Dozy, *Supplément aux dictionnaires arabes*, Leiden 1881 (anastatic reprint Leiden-Paris 1927)

EMA[1] = K.A.C. Creswell, *Early Muslim architecture*, 2 vols., Oxford 1932-40

EMA[2] = K.A.C. Creswell, *Early Muslim architecture*, 2nd ed., London 1969-

Fagnan, *Extraits* = E. Fagnan, *Extraits inédits relatifs au Maghreb*, Alger 1924

Farhang = Razmārā and Nawtāsh, *Farhang-i djughrāfiyā-yi Īrān*, Tehran 1949-53

Firishta = Muḥammad Ḳāsim Firishta, *Gulshan-i Ibrāhīmi*, lith. Bombay 1832

Gesch. des Qor. = Th. Nöldeke, *Geschichte des Qorāns*, new edition by F. Schwally, G. Bergsträsser and O. Pretzl, 3 vols., Leipzig 1909-38

Gibb, *HOP* = E.J.W. Gibb, *A history of Ottoman poetry*, 7 vols., London 1900-9

Gibb-Bowen = H.A.R. Gibb and Harold Bowen, *Islamic society and the West*, London 1950-57

Goldziher, *Muh. St.* = I. Goldziher, *Muhammedanische Studien*, 2 vols., Halle 1888-90

Goldziher, *Vorlesungen* = I. Goldziher, *Vorlesungen über den Islam*, Heidelberg 1910

Goldziher, *Vorlesungen*[2] = 2nd ed., Heidelberg 1925
Goldziher, *Dogme* = *Le dogme et la loi de l'Islam*, tr. F. Arin, Paris 1920
Gövsa, *Türk meshurları* = Ibrahim Alaettin Gövsa, *Türk meşhurları ansiklopedisi*, Istanbul 1946
Ḥādjdjī Khalīfa, *Djihān-nümā* = Istanbul 1145/1732
Ḥādjdjī Khalīfa = *Kashf al-ẓunūn*, ed. Ş. Yaltkaya and Kilisli Rifat Bilge, Istanbul 1941-43
Ḥādjdjī Khalīfa, ed. Flügel = *K. al-ẓ.*, Leipzig 1835-58
Ḥamd Allāh Mustawfī, *Nuzha* = *Nuzhat al-ḳulūb*, ed. G. Le Strange, Leiden 1913-19 (GMS XXIII)
Hamdānī = *Sifat Djazīrat al-ʿArab*, ed. D.H. Müller, Leiden 1884-91
Hammer-Purgstall, *GOR* = J. von Hammer(-Purgstall), *Geschichte des Osmanischen Reiches*, Pest 1828-35
Hammer-Purgstall, *GOR*[2] = *ibid.*, 2nd ed., Pest 1840
Hammer-Purgstall, *Histoire* = *ibid.*, trans. by J.J. Hellert, 18 vols., Bellizard [etc.], Paris [etc.], 1835-43
Hammer-Purgstall, *Staatsverfassung* = J. von Hammer, *Des Osmanischen Reichs Staatsverfassung und Staatsverwaltung*, 2 vols., Vienna 1815 (repr. 1963)
Houtsma, *Recueil* = M. Th. Houtsma, *Recueil des textes relatifs à l'histoire des Seldjoucides*, Leiden 1886-1902
Ḥudūd al-ʿālam[1] = *Ḥudūd al-ʿālam. The regions of the world*, translated by V. Minorsky, London 1937 (GMS, N.S. XI)
Ḥudūd al-ʿālam[2] = *ibid.*, 2nd revised and enlarged ed., London 1970
Ibn al-Abbār = *K. Takmilat al-Ṣila*, ed. F. Codera, Madrid 1887-89 (BHA V-VI)
Ibn al-Athīr, ed. Tornberg = Ibn al-Athīr, *al-Kāmil fi 'l-tawārīkh*, ed. C.J. Tornberg, 12 vols., Leiden 1851-76
Ibn al-Athīr, ed. Beirut = *ibid.*, Beirut, 13 vols., 1385-7/1965-7
Ibn al-Athīr, trad. Fagnan = *Annales du Maghreb et de l'Espagne*, tr. E. Fagnan, Algiers 1901
Ibn Bashkuwāl = *K. al-Ṣila fi akhbār a'immat al-Andalus*, ed. F. Codera, Madrid 1883 (BHA II)
Ibn Baṭṭūṭa = *Voyages d'Ibn Batouta*, Arabic text, ed. with Fr. tr. by C. Defrémery and B.R. Sanguinetti, 4 vols., Paris 1853-58
Ibn Baṭṭūṭa, tr. Gibb = *The travels of Ibn Baṭṭūṭa*, Eng. tr. H.A.R. Gibb, 3 vols., Cambridge 1958-71
Ibn al-Faḳīh = *Mukhtaṣar K. al-Buldān*, ed. M.J. de Goeje, Leiden 1886 (BGA V)
Ibn Ḥawḳal = *K. Ṣūrat al-arḍ*, ed. J.H. Kramers, Leiden, 1938-39 (BGA II, 2nd edition)
Ibn Ḥawḳal-Kramers-Wiet = Ibn Hauqal, *Configuration de la terre*, trans. J.H. Kramers and G. Wiet, Beirut 1964, 2 vols.
Ibn Hishām = *Sira*, ed. F. Wüstenfeld, Göttingen 1859-60
Ibn ʿIdhārī = *K. al-Bayān al-mughrib*, ed. G.S. Colin and E. Lévi-Provençal, Leiden 1948-51; vol. iii, ed. E. Lévi-Provençal, Paris 1930
Ibn al-ʿImād, *Shadharāt* = *Shadharāt al-dhahab fi akhbār man dhahab*, Cairo 1350-51 (quoted according to years of obituaries)
Ibn Isḥāḳ, tr. Guillaume = *The life of Muḥammad, a translation of Isḥāq's (sic)* Sīrat Rasūl Allāh, tr. A. Guillaume, Oxford 1955
Ibn Khaldūn, *ʿIbar* = *K. al-ʿIbar wa-dīwān al-mubtada' wa 'l-khabar, etc.*, Būlāḳ 1284
Ibn Khaldūn, *Muḳaddima* = *Prolégomènes d'Ebn Khaldoun*, ed. E. Quatremère, Paris 1858-68 (*Notices et Extraits* XVI-XVIII)
Ibn Khaldūn-Rosenthal = *The Muqaddimah*, trans. from the Arabic by Franz Rosenthal, 3 vols., London 1958
Ibn Khaldūn-de Slane = *Les prolégomènes d'Ibn Khaldoun*, traduits en français et commentés par M. de Slane, Paris 1863-68 (anastatic reprint 1934-38)
Ibn Khallikān = *Wafayāt al-aʿyān wa-anbā' abnā' al-zamān*, ed. F. Wüstenfeld, Göttingen 1835-50 (quoted after the numbers of biographies)
Ibn Khallikān, ed. ʿAbbās = *ibid.*, ed. Iḥsān ʿAbbās, 8 vols., Beirut 1968-72
Ibn Khallikān, Būlāḳ = *ibid.*, ed. Būlāḳ 1275
Ibn Khallikān-de Slane = *Kitāb Wafayāt al-aʿyān*, trans. by Baron MacGuckin de Slane, 4 vols., Paris 1842-71
Ibn Khurradādhbih = *al-Masālik wa 'l-mamālik*, ed. M.J. de Goeje, Leiden 1889 (BGA VI)
Ibn Ḳutayba, *al-Shiʿr* = Ibn Ḳutayba, *Kitāb al-Shiʿr wa 'l-shuʿarā'*, ed. de Goeje, Leiden 1900
Ibn al-Nadīm, *Fihrist* = Ibn al-Nadīm, *K. al-Fihrist*, ed. G. Flügel, 2 vols., Leipzig 1871-2
Ibn al-Nadīm, tr. Dodge = *The Fihrist of al-Nadīm*, tr. B. Dodge, 2 vols., New York and London 1970
Ibn Rusta = *al-Aʿlāḳ al-nafīsa*, ed. M.J. de Goeje, Leiden 1892 (BGA VII)
Ibn Rusta-Wiet = *Les Atours précieux*, traduction de G. Wiet, Cairo 1955
Ibn Saʿd = *al-Ṭabaḳāt al-kubrā*, ed. H. Sachau *et al.*, Leiden 1905-40
Ibn Taghrībirdī = *al-Nudjūm al-zāhira fī mulūk Miṣr wa 'l-Ḳāhira*, ed. W. Popper, Berkeley-Leiden 1908-36
Ibn Taghrībirdī, Cairo = *ibid.*, ed. Cairo 1348 ff.
Idrīsī, *Maghrib* = *Description de l'Afrique et de l'Espagne*, ed. R. Dozy and M.J. de Goeje, Leiden 1866
Idrīsī-Jaubert = *Géographie d'Édrisi*, trad. de l'arabe en français par P. Amédée Jaubert, 2 vols., Paris 1836-40
Iṣṭakhrī = *al-Masālik wa 'l-mamālik*, ed. M.J. de Goeje, Leiden 1870 (BGA I) (and reprint 1927)
Justi, *Namenbuch* = F. Justi, *Iranisches Namenbuch*, Marburg 1895
Juynboll, *Handbuch* = Th.W. Juynboll, *Handbuch des islāmischen Gesetzes*, Leiden 1910
Kaḥḥāla, *Nisā'* = ʿUmar Riḍā Kaḥḥāla, *Aʿlām al-nisā' fī ʿālamay al-ʿArab wa 'l-Islām*, 5 vols., Damascus 1379/1959
Khʷāndamīr = *Ḥabīb al-siyar*, Tehran 1271
Kutubī, *Fawāt*, ed. Būlāḳ = Ibn Shākir al-Kutubī, *Fawāt al-wafayāt*, 2 vols., Būlāḳ 1299/1882
Kutubī, *Fawāt*, ed. ʿAbbās = *ibid.*, ed. Iḥsān ʿAbbās, 5 vols., Beirut 1973-4
LA = *Lisān al-ʿArab* (quoted according to the root)
Lambton, *Landlord and peasant* = A.K.S. Lambton, *Landlord and peasant in Persia, a study of land tenure and revenue administration*, London 1953
Lane = E.W. Lane, *An Arabic-English lexicon*, London 1863-93 (reprint New York 1955-6)
Lane-Poole, *Cat.* = S. Lane-Poole, *Catalogue of oriental coins in the British Museum*, London 1877-90
Lavoix, *Cat.* = H. Lavoix, *Catalogue des monnaies musulmanes de la Bibliothèque Nationale*, Paris 1887-96
Le Strange = G. Le Strange, *The lands of the Eastern caliphate*, 2nd ed., Cambridge 1930
Le Strange, *Baghdad* = G. Le Strange, *Baghdad during the Abbasid caliphate*, Oxford 1924
Le Strange, *Palestine* = G. Le Strange, *Palestine under the Moslems*, London 1890
Lévi-Provençal, *Hist.Esp.Mus.* = E. Lévi-Provençal, *Histoire de l'Espagne musulmane*, new ed., 3 vols., Leiden-Paris 1950-53
Lévi-Provençal, *Chorfa* = E. Lévi-Provençal, *Les historiens des Chorfa*, Paris 1922
MAE = K.A.C. Creswell, *The Muslim architecture of Egypt*, 2 vols., Oxford 1952-9

Makkarī, *Analectes* = *Nafh al-ṭīb fī ghuṣn al-Andalus al-raṭīb (Analectes sur l'histoire et la littérature des Arabes de l'Espagne)*, Leiden 1855-61
Makkarī, Būlāķ = *ibid.*, ed. Būlāķ 1279/1862
Marquart, *Ērānšahr* = J. Marquart, *Ērānšahr nach der Geographie des Ps. Moses Xorenacʿi*, Berlin 1901
Marquart, *Streifzüge* = J. Marquart, *Osteuropäische und ostasiatische Streifzüge, Ethnologische und historisch-topographische Studien zur Geschichte des 9. und 10. Jahrhunderts (c. 840-940)*, Leipzig 1903
Maspero-Wiet, *Matériaux* = J. Maspéro et G. Wiet, *Matériaux pour servir à la géographie de l'Egypte*, Cairo 1914 (MIFAO XXXVI)
Masʿūdī, *Murūdj* = *Murūdj al-dhahab*, ed. C. Barbier de Meynard and Pavet de Courteille, 9 vols., Paris 1861-77; ed. and tr. Ch. Pellat, *Les prairies d'or*, 7 vols. text and 4 vols. translation, Paris-Beirut 1962-89 (cited according to paragraph)
Masʿūdī, *Tanbīh* = *K. al-Tanbīh wa 'l-ishrāf*, ed. M.J. de Goeje, Leiden 1894 (BGA VIII)
Mayer, *Architects* = L.A. Mayer, *Islamic architects and their works*, Geneva 1956
Mayer, *Astrolabists* = L.A. Mayer, *Islamic astrolabists and their works*, Geneva 1958
Mayer, *Metalworkers* = L.A. Mayer, *Islamic metalworkers and their works*, Geneva 1959
Mayer, *Woodcarvers* = L.A. Mayer, *Islamic woodcarvers and their works*, Geneva 1958
Mez, *Renaissance* = A. Mez, *Die Renaissance des Islams*, Heidelberg 1922
Mez, *Renaissance*, Eng. tr. = *The renaissance of Islam*, translated into English by Salahuddin Khuda Bukhsh and D.S. Margoliouth, London 1937
Mez, *Renaissance*, Spanish trans. = *El renacimiento del Islam*, translated into Spanish by S. Vila, Madrid-Granada 1936
Miquel, *Géographie humaine* = A. Miquel, *La géographie humaine du monde musulman jusqu'au milieu du 11e siècle*, 4 vols., Paris-The Hague 1973-88
Mīrkhʷānd = *Rawḍat al-ṣafā*, Bombay 1266/1849
Miskawayh, in *Eclipse of the ʿAbbasid caliphate* = Miskawayh, *Tadjārib al-umam*, in *The eclipse of the ʿAbbasid caliphate*, ed. and tr. H.F. Amedroz and D.S. Margoliouth, 7 vols., Oxford 1920-21
Muķaddasī = *Aḥsan al-taķāsīm fī maʿrifat al-aķālīm*, ed. M.J. de Goeje, Leiden 1877 (BGA III)
Munadjdjim Bashi = *Ṣaḥāʾif al-akhbār*, Istanbul 1285
Nallino, *Scritti* = C.A. Nallino, *Raccolta di scritti editi e inediti*, Roma 1939-48
ʿOthmānli müʾellifleri = Bursali Meḥmed Ṭāhir, *ʿOthmānli müʾellifleri*, Istanbul 1333
Pakalın = Mehmet Zeki Pakalın, *Osmanlı tarih deyimleri ve terimleri sözlüğü*, 3 vols., Istanbul 1946 ff.
Pauly-Wissowa = *Realenzyklopaedie des klassischen Altertums*
Pearson = J.D. Pearson, *Index Islamicus*, Cambridge 1958; S I = *Supplement, 1956-60*
Pons Boigues = *Ensayo bio-bibliográfico sobre los historiadores y geógrafos arábigo-españoles*, Madrid 1898
PTF = *Fundamenta philologiae turcica*, ed. J. Deny *et alii*, 2 vols., Wiesbaden 1959-64
Rypka, *Hist. of Iranian literature* = J. Rypka *et alii*, *History of Iranian literature*, Dordrecht 1968
Ṣafadī = *al-Wāfī bi 'l-wafayāt. Das biographische Lexikon des Ṣalāḥaddīn Ḫalīl ibn Aibak aṣ-Ṣafadī*, ed. H. Ritter, S. Dedering *et alii*, 22 vols., Wiesbaden-Beirut-Damascus 1962-
Samʿānī, *Ansāb*, fasc. = *K. al-Ansāb*, facsimile edition by D.S. Margoliouth, Leiden 1912 (GMS, XX)
Samʿānī, ed. Ḥaydarābād = *ibid.*, ed. M. ʿAbd al-Muʿīd Khān *et alii*, 13 vols., Ḥaydarābād 1382-1402/1962-82
Santillana, *Istituzioni* = D. Santillana, *Istituzioni di diritto musulmano malichita*, Roma 1926-38
Sarkīs = Sarkīs, *Muʿdjam al-maṭbūʿāt al-ʿarabiyya*, Cairo 1346/1928
Schwarz, *Iran* = P. Schwarz, *Iran im Mittelalter nach den arabischen Geographen*, Leipzig 1896-
Sezgin, *GAS* = F. Sezgin, *Geschichte des arabischen Schrifttums*, 9 vols., Leiden 1967-84
Shahrastānī = *al-Milal wa 'l-niḥal*, ed. W. Cureton, London 1846
Sidjill-i ʿOthmānī = Meḥmed Thüreyyā, *Sidjill-i ʿOthmānī*, Istanbul 1308-16
Snouck Hurgronje, *Verspr. Geschr.* = C. Snouck Hurgronje, *Verspreide Geschriften*, Leiden 1923-27
Sources inédites = Comte Henry de Castries, *Les sources inédites de l'histoire du Maroc*, première série, Paris [etc.] 1905-, deuxième série, Paris 1922
Spuler, *Horde*[1] = B. Spuler, *Die Goldene Horde, die Mongolen in Russland*, 1st ed., Leipzig 1943
Spuler, *Horde*[2] = *ibid.*, 2nd ed., Wiesbaden 1965
Spuler, *Iran* = B. Spuler, *Iran in früh-islamischer Zeit*, Wiesbaden 1952
Spuler, *Mongolen*[1] = B. Spuler, *Die Mongolen in Iran*, 1st ed., Leipzig 1939
Spuler, *Mongolen*[2] = *ibid.*, 2nd ed., Berlin 1955
Spuler, *Mongolen*[3] = *ibid.*, 3rd ed., Berlin 1958
Storey = C.A. Storey, *Persian literature: a biobibliographical survey*, London 1927-
Survey of Persian art = ed. by A.U. Pope, Oxford 1938
Suter = H. Suter, *Die Mathematiker und Astronomen der Araber und ihre Werke*, Leipzig 1900
Suyūṭī, *Bughya* = *Bughyat al-wuʿāt*, Cairo 1326
TA = Muḥammad Murtaḍā b. Muḥammad al-Zabīdī, *Tādj al-ʿarūs* (quoted according to the root)
Ṭabarī = *Taʾrīkh al-rusul wa 'l-mulūk*, ed. M.J. de Goeje *et al.*, Leiden 1879-1901
Taeschner, *Wegenetz* = Franz Taeschner, *Das anatolische Wegenetz nach osmanischen Quellen*, 2 vols., Leipzig 1924-6
Taʾrīkh Baghdād = al-Khaṭīb al-Baghdādī, *Taʾrīkh Baghdād*, 14 vols., Cairo 1349/1931
Taʾrīkh Dimashk = Ibn ʿAsākir, *Taʾrīkh Dimashk*, 7 vols., Damascus 1329-51/1911-31
Taʾrīkh-i Guzīda =Ḥamd Allāh Mustawfī al-Ķazwīnī, *Taʾrīkh-i guzīda*, ed. in facsimile by E.G. Browne, Leiden-London 1910
TAVO = *Tübinger Atlas des Vorderen Orients*, Wiesbaden
Thaʿālibī, *Yatīma*, ed. Damascus = Thaʿālibī, *Yatīmat al-dahr fī maḥāsin ahl al-ʿaṣr*, 4 vols., Damascus 1304/1886-7
Thaʿālibī, *Yatīma*, ed. Cairo = *ibid.*, ed. Muḥammad Muḥyī al-Dīn ʿAbd al-Ḥamīd, 4 vols., Cairo 1375-7/1956-8
Tomaschek = W. Tomaschek, *Zur historischen Topographie von Kleinasien im Mittelalter*, Vienna 1891
Weil, *Chalifen* = G. Weil, *Geschichte der Chalifen*, Mannheim-Stuttgart 1846-82
Wensinck, *Handbook* = A.J. Wensinck, *A handbook of early Muhammadan Tradition*, Leiden 1927
Wensinck, *Concordances* = A.J. Wensinck *et alii*, *Concordances et indices de la tradition musulmane*, 7 vols., Leiden 1936-79
WKAS = *Wörterbuch der klassischen arabischen Sprache*, Wiesbaden 1957-
Yaʿķūbī = *Taʾrīkh*, ed. M.Th. Houtsma, Leiden 1883
Yaʿķūbī, *Buldān* = ed. M.J. de Goeje, Leiden 1892 (BGA VII)
Yaʿķūbī-Wiet = *Yaʿķūbī. Les pays*, trad. par Gaston Wiet, Cairo 1937

Yāḳūt, ed. Wüstenfeld = *Muʿd̲j̲am al-buldān*, ed. F. Wüstenfeld, 5 vols., Leipzig 1866-8

Yāḳūt, ed. Beirut = *ibid.*, 5 vols., Beirut 1374-6/1955-7

Yāḳūt, *Udabāʾ* = *Irs̲h̲ād al-arīb ilā maʿrifat al-adīb*, ed. D.S. Margoliouth, Leiden 1907-31 (GMS)

Zambaur = E. de Zambaur, *Manuel de généalogie chronologie pour l'histoire de l'Islam*, Hanover (anastatic reprint Bad Pyrmont 1955)

Zinkeisen = J. Zinkeisen, *Geschichte des osmanische Reiches in Europa*, Gotha 1840-83

Ziriklī, *Aʿlām* = K̲h̲ayr al-Dīn al-Ziriklī, *al-Aʿlām ḳāmūs tarād̲j̲im li-as̲h̲har al-rid̲j̲āl wa ʾl-nisāʾ al-ʿArab wa ʾl-mustaʿribīn wa ʾl-mustas̲h̲riḳīn*, 10 vols., Damascus 1373-8/1954-9

Zubayrī, *Nasab* = Muṣʿab al-Zubayrī, *Nasab Ḳuray s̲h̲*, ed. E. Lévi-Provençal, Cairo 1953

ABBREVIATIONS FOR PERIODICALS ETC.

AARP = *Art and Archaeology Research Papers.*
AAS = *Asian and African Studies.*
Abh. A. W. Gött = *Abhandlungen der Gesellschaft der Wissenschaften zu Göttingen.*
Abh. K. M. = *Abhandlungen für die Kunde des Morgenländes.*
Abh Pr. Ak. W. = *Abhandlungen der preussischen Akademie der Wissenschaften.*
Afr. Fr. = *Bulletin du Comité de l'Afrique française.*
AI = *Annales Islamologiques.*
AIEO Alger = *Annales de l'Institut d'Études Orientales de l'Université d'Alger* (N.S. from 1964).
AIUON = *Annali dell'Istituto Universitario Orientale di Napoli.*
Anz. Wien = *Anzeiger der [kaiserlichen] Akademie der Wissenschaften, Wien. Philosophisch-historische Klasse.*
AO = *Acta Orientalia.*
AO Hung. = *Acta Orientalia (Academiae Scientiarum Hungaricae).*
APAW = *Abhandlungen der preussischen Akademie der Wissenschaften.*
ArO = *Archiv Orientální.*
ARW = *Archiv für Religionswissenschaft.*
ASAE = *Annales du Service des antiquités de l'Égypte.*
ASI = *Archaeological Survey of India.*
ASI, NIS = *ibid.*, New Imperial Series.
ASI, AR = *ibid.*, Annual Reports.
AÜDTCFD = *Ankara Üniversitesi Dil ve Tarih-Coğrafya Fakültesi Dergisi.*
BAH = *Bibliotheca Arabico-Hispana.*
BASOR = *Bulletin of the American Schools of Oriental Research.*
BEA = *Bulletin des Études Arabes, Alger.*
Belleten = *Belleten* (of *Türk Tarih Kurumu*).
BÉt. Or. = *Bulletin d'Études Orientales de l'Institut Français de Damas.*
BFac. Ar. = *Bulletin of the Faculty of Arts of the Egyptian University.*
BGA = *Bibliotheca geographorum arabicorum.*
BIE = *Bulletin de l'Institut d'Égypte.*
BIFAO = *Bulletin de l'Institut Français d'Archéologie Orientale du Caire.*
BiOr = *Bibliotheca Orientalis.*
BJRUL = *Bulletin of the John Rylands University Library, Manchester.*
BRAH = *Boletín de la Real Academia de la Historia de España.*
BSE = *Bol'shaya Sovetskaya Éntsiklopediya* (Large Soviet Encyclopaedia) 1st ed.
BSE[2] = *ibid.*, 2nd ed.
BSL[P] = *Bulletin de la Société de Linguistique de Paris.*
BSMES or *BRISMES* = *British Society for Middle Eastern Studies Bulletin*, continued as *British Journal of Middle Eastern Studies.*
BSO[A]S = *Bulletin of the School of Oriental [and African] Studies.*
BTLV = *Bijdragen tot de Taal-, Land- en Volkenkunde [van Nederlandsch Indië].*
BZ = *Byzantinische Zeitschrift.*
CAJ = *Central Asiatic Journal.*
CHIr = *Cambridge History of Iran.*
COC = *Cahiers de l'Orient contemporain.*
CSCO = *Corpus Scriptorum Christianorum Orientalium.*
CT = *Cahiers de Tunisie.*
EI[1] = *Encyclopaedia of Islam*, 1st edition.
EIM = *Epigraphia Indo-Moslemica.*
EIr = *Encyclopaedia Iranica.*
ERE = *Encyclopaedia of Religions and Ethics.*
EW = *East and West.*
GaP = *Grundriss der arabischen Philologie.*
GGA = *Göttingische Gelehrte Anzeigen.*
GIPh = *Grundriss der iranischen Philologie.*
GJ = *Géographical Journal.*
GMS = *Gibb Memorial Series.*
Gr. I. Ph. = *Grundriss der Iranischen Philologie.*
Hdb d. Or = *Handbuch der Orientalistik.*
HUCA = *Hebrew Union College Annual.*
IA = *Islâm Ansiklopedisi.*
IBLA = *Revue de l'Institut des Belles Lettres Arabes*, Tunis.
IC = *Islamic Culture.*
IFD = *Ilahiyat Fakültesi Dergisi.*
IHQ = *Indian Historical Quarterly.*
IJMES = *International Journal of Middle Eastern Studies.*
ILS = *Islamic Law and Society.*
IOS = *Israel Oriental Studies.*
IQ = *The Islamic Quarterly.*
Iran JBIPS = *Iran, Journal of the British Institute of Persian Studies.*
Isl. = *Der Islam.*
JA = *Journal Asiatique.*
JAfr S. = *Journal of the African Society.*
JAL = *Journal of Arabic Literature.*
JAnthr. I = *Journal of the Anthropological Institute.*
JAOS = *Journal of the American Oriental Society.*
JARCE = *Journal of the American Research Center in Egypt.*
JASB = *Journal of the Asiatic Society of Bengal.*
JBBRAS = *Journal of the Bombay Branch of the Royal Asiatic Society.*
JE = *Jewish Encyclopaedia.*
JESHO = *Journal of the Economic and Social History of the Orient.*
JIMMA = *Journal of the Institute of Muslim Minority Affairs.*
JIS = *Journal of Islamic Studies.*
J[R] Num. S. = *Journal of the [Royal] Numismatic Society.*
JNES = *Journal of Near Eastern Studies.*
JPak. HS = *Journal of the Pakistan Historical Society.*
JPHS = *Journal of the Punjab Historical Society.*
JPOS = *Journal of the Palestine Oriental Society.*
JQR = *Jewish Quarterly Review.*
JRAS = *Journal of the Royal Asiatic Society.*
J[R]ASB = *Journal and Proceedings of the [Royal] Asiatic Society of Bengal.*
JRGeog. S. = *Journal of the Royal Geographical Society.*
JSAI = *Jerusalem Studies in Arabic and Islam.*
JSFO = *Journal de la Société Finno-ougrienne.*
JSS = *Journal of Semitic Studies.*
JTS = *Journal of Theological Studies.*
KCA = *Körösi Csoma Archivum.*
KS = *Keleti Szemle* (Oriental Review).
KSIE = *Kratkie Soobshčeniya Instituta Étnografiy* (Short communications of the Institute of Ethnography).
LE = *Literaturnaya Éntsiklopediya* (Literary Encyclopaedia).
MDOG = *Mitteilungen der Deutschen Orient-Gesellschaft.*
MDPV = *Mitteilungen und Nachrichten des Deutschen Palästina-Vereins.*
MEA = *Middle Eastern Affairs.*
MEJ = *Middle East Journal.*
Méms. DAFA = *Mémoires de la Délégation Française en Afghanistan.*
MES = *Middie East Studies.*
MFOB = *Mélanges de la Faculté Orientale de l'Université St. Joseph de Beyrouth.*

MGMN = *Mitteilungen zur Geschichte der Medizin und Naturwissenschaften.*
MGWJ = *Monatsschrift für die Geschichte und Wissenschaft des Judentums.*
MIDEO = *Mélanges de l'Institut Dominicain d'Études Orientales du Caire.*
MIE = *Mémoires de l'Institut d'Égypte.*
MIFAO = *Mémoires publiés par les membres de l'Institut Français d'Archéologie Orientale du Caire.*
MMAF = *Mémoires de la Mission Archéologique Française au Caire.*
MME = *Manuscripts of the Middle East.*
MMIA = *Madjallat al-Madjma' al-'Ilmī al-'Arabī,* Damascus.
MO = *Le Monde oriental.*
MOG = *Mitteilungen zur osmanischen Geschichte.*
MSE = *Malaya Sovetskaya Éntsiklopediya* (Small Soviet Encyclopaedia).
MSFO = *Mémoires de la Société Finno-ougrienne.*
MSL[P] = *Mémoires de la Société Linguistique de Paris.*
MSOS Afr. = *Mitteilungen des Seminars für Orientalische Sprachen, Afrikanische Studien.*
MSOS As. = *Mitteilungen des Seminars für Orientalische Sprachen, Westasiatische Studien.*
MTM = *Millī Tetebbü'ler Medjmū'asi.*
MUSJ = *Mélanges de la Faculté orientale de l'Université St.-Joseph.*
MW = *The Muslim World.*
NC = *Numismatic Chronicle.*
Nak. W. Gött = *Nachrichten von der Gesellschaft der Wissenschaften zu Göttingen.*
NZ = *Numismatische Zeitschrift.*
OC = *Oriens Christianus.*
OLZ = *Orientalistische Literaturzeitung.*
OM = *Oriente Moderno.*
PEFQS = *Palestine Exploration Fund. Quarterly Statement.*
Pet. Mitt. = *Petermanns Mitteilungen.*
PO = *Patrologia Orientalis.*
PPUAES = *Publications of the Princeton University Archaeological Expedition to Syria.*
PTF = *Philologiae Turcicae Fundamenta,* Wiesbaden 1959-.
QDAP = *Quarterly Statement of the Department of Antiquities of Palestine.*
QSA = *Quaderni de Studi Arabi.*
RAAD = *Revue de l'Académie Arabe de Damas.*
RAfr. = *Revue Africaine.*
RCAL = *Rendiconti de l'Academia dei Lincei.*
RCEA = *Répertoire chronologique d'Épigraphie arabe.*
REJ = *Revue des Études Juives.*
Rend. Lin. = *Rendiconti della Reale Accademia dei Lincei, Classe di scienze morali, storiche e filologiche.*
REI = *Revue des Études Islamiques.*
RHR = *Revue de l'Histoire des Religions.*
RIMA = *Revue de l'Institut des Manuscrits Arabes.*
RMM = *Revue du Monde Musulman.*
RMMM = *Revue des Mondes musulmans et de la Mediterranée.*
RN = *Revue Numismatique.*
RO = *Rocznik Orientalistyczny.*
ROC = *Revue de l'Orient Chrétien.*
ROL = *Revue de l'Orient Latin.*
ROMM = *Revue de l'Occident musulman et de la Mediterranée.*
RSO = *Rivista degli studi orientali.*
RT = *Revue Tunisienne.*
SB. Ak. Heid. = *Sitzungsberichte der Heidelberger Akademie der Wissenschaften.*
SB. Ak. Wien = *Sitzungsberichte der Akademie der Wissenschaften zu Wien.*
SBBayer. Ak. = *Sitzungsberichte der Bayerischen Akademie der Wissenschaften.*
SBPMS Erlg. = *Sitzungsberichte der Physikalisch-medizinischen Sozietät in Erlangen.*
SBPr. Ak. W. = *Sitzungsberichte der Preussischen Akademie der Wissenschaften zu Berlin.*
SE = *Sovetskaya Étnografiya* (Soviet Ethnography).
SO = *Sovetskoe Vostokovedenie* (Soviet Orientalism).
Stud. Ir. = *Studia Iranica.*
Stud. Isl. = *Studia Islamica.*
S.Ya. = *Sovetskoe Yazîkoznanie* (Soviet Linguistics).
TBG = *Tijdschrift van het Bataviaasch Genootschap van Kunsten en Wetenschappen.*
TD = *Tarih Dergisi.*
THITM = *Türk Hukuk ve İktisat Tarihi Mecmuasi.*
TIE = *Trudî instituta Étnografiy* (Works of the Institute of Ethnography).
TM = *Turkiyat Mecmuası.*
TOEM/TTEM = *Ta'rīkh-i 'Othmānī* (*Türk Ta'rīkhi*) *Endjümeni medjmū'asî.*
UAJb = *Ural-altäische Jahrbücher.*
Verh. Ak. Amst. = *Verhandelingen der Koninklijke Akademie van Wetenschappen te Amsterdam.*
Versl. Med. Ak. Amst. = *Verslagen en Mededeelingen der Koninklijke Akademie van Wetenschappen te Amsterdam.*
VI = *Voprosî Istoriy* (Historical Problems).
WI = *Die Welt des Islams.*
WI, n.s. = *ibid.*, new series.
Wiss. Veröff. DOG = *Wissenschaftliche Veröffentlichungen der Deutschen Orient-Gesellschaft.*
WO = *Welt des Orients.*
WZKM = *Wiener Zeitschrift für die Kunde des Morgenländes.*
ZA = *Zeitschrift für Assyriologie.*
ZAL = *Zeitschrift für Arabische Linguistik.*
ZATW = *Zeitschrift für die alttestamentliche Wissenschaft.*
ZDMG = *Zeitschrift der Deutschen Morgenländischen Gesellschaft.*
ZDPV = *Zeitschrift des Deutschen Palästinavereins.*
ZfN = *Zeitschrift für Numismatik.*
ZGAIW = *Zeitschrift für Geschichte der Arabisch-Islamischen Wissenschaften.*
ZGErdk. Birl. = *Zeitschrift der Gesellschaft für Erdkunde in Berlin.*
ZS = *Zeitschrift für Semitistik.*

LIST OF TRANSLITERATIONS

SYSTEM OF TRANSLITERATION OF ARABIC CHARACTERS:

Consonants

ء	ʾ (except when initial)	ز	z	ق	ḳ
ب	b	س	s	ك	k
ت	t	ش	sh	ل	l
ث	th	ص	ṣ	م	m
ج	dj	ض	ḍ	ن	n
ح	ḥ	ط	ṭ	ه	h
خ	kh	ظ	ẓ	و	w
د	d	ع	ʿ	ي	y
ذ	dh	غ	gh		
ر	r	ف	f		

Long Vowels

ا ى	ā
و	ū
ي	ī

Short Vowels

ـَ	a
ـُ	u
ـِ	i

Diphthongs

ـَوْ	aw
ـَيْ	ay
ـِيّ	iyy (final form ī)
ـُوّ	uww (final form ū)

ة a; at (construct state)

ال (article), al- and 'l- (even before the antero-palatals)

PERSIAN, TURKISH AND URDU ADDITIONS TO THE ARABIC ALPHABET:

پ	p	ژ	zh	ٹ	t́	ڑ	ŕ
چ	č	ك or گ	g (sometimes ñ in Turkish)	ڈ	d́	ں	ṇ

Additional vowels:

a) Turkish: e, i, o, ö, ü. Diacritical signs proper to Arabic are, in principle, not used in words of Turkish etymology.
b) Urdu: ē, ō.

For modern Turkish, the official orthography adopted by the Turkish Republic in 1928 is used. The following letters may be noted:

c = dj	ğ = gh	j = zh	k = k and ḳ	t = t and ṭ
ç = č	h = h, ḥ and kh	ş = sh	s = s, ṣ and th	z = z, ẓ, ḍ and dh

SYSTEM OF TRANSLITERATION OF THE RUSSIAN ALPHABET:

а	a	е	e	к	k	п	p	ф	f	щ	shč	ю	yu
б	b	ж	ž	л	l	р	r	х	kh	ы	ï	я	ya
в	v	з	z	м	m	с	s	ц	ts	ь	ʾ	ѣ	ě
г	g	и	i	н	n	т	t	ч	č	ъ	ʿ		
д	d	й	y	о	o	у	u	ш	sh	э	é		

ADDENDA AND CORRIGENDA

VOLUME I

P. 511[b], **ANKARA**, *add to Bibl.*: T.M. Cross and G. Leiser, *A brief history of Ankara*, Vaccaville, Calif. 2000.

P. 1131[b], **BAYHAKĪ**, *add to Bibl.*: F. Bertotti, *L'opera dello storico persiano Bayhaqī*, Naples 1991: Julie S. Meisami, *Persian historiography to the end of the twelfth century*, Edinburgh 1999, 79-108.

VOLUME III

P. 455[b], **HIND BINT ʿUTBA**, *add to Bibl.*: Renate Jacobi, *Portrait einer unsympathetischen Frau: Hind bint ʿUtba, die Feindin Mohammeds*, in *WZKM*, lxxxix (1999), 85-107.

P. 885[b], **IBN AL-MUKAFFAʿ**, *add to Bibl.*: J.D. Latham, art. *Ebn al-Moqaffaʿ*, in *EIr*, viii, 39-43 (includes material expanding the same author's ch. in *CHAL, II, ʿAbbasid belles-lettres*, Cambridge 1990, 48-77, and making certain corrections to it); Mirella Cassarino, *L'aspetto morale e religioso nell'opera di Ibn al-Muqaffaʿ*, Soveria Mannelli (Catanzaro) 2000.

P. 1117[a], **ILEK-KHANS** or **KARAKHĀNIDS**, *add to Bibl.*: Reşat Genç, *Karahanlı devlet teşkilatı (XI. yüzyil)*, Istanbul 1981; M.N. Fedorov, *Notes on the Qarākhānids and their coinage – I*, in *Suppl. to the Oriental Numismatics Society Newsletter*, no. 165, London 2000, 1-52; *Notes . . . – II*, in *Suppl. . . .*, no. 168, London 2001, 1-48.

VOLUME V

P. 486[b], **AL-KURDJ**, l. 16, *add*: Concerning the etymology of the name, Pers. *gurdj* and *gurdjī* are ultimately identical with Grk. *Ibēres*. The Armenian *virkh* for "Georgians" shows that the original form was **vīr*. An Arm. form without the pl. suffix *-kh* is *vrastan* "Georgia", with normal loss of *i* in a non-final syllable, cf. Pers. *gurdjistān*, older *gurdjastān*. Pers. *gurdjī* shows the normal development of O Pers. *vi-* to NP *gu-* and palatalisation of the velar before *i*, *gurdj* being a back formation. European designations like Ital. *Georgia* are transformations by popular etymology of *gurdjī*, possibly from a Class. Ar. *djirdjī* so far unattested. Georgian *kartvelebi*, *sakartvelo*, etc. originally designated only the area around Tbilisi, so that **vīr* is probably the original name of the Georgians. (F. Thiesen)

VOLUME VII

P. 445[b], **MUḤAMMAD MURTAḌĀ**, *add to Bibl.*: Ziriklī, *Aʿlām*[2], vii, 297-8; Kaḥḥāla, *Muʾallifīn*, xi, 282-3; ʿAbd al-Raḥmān al-Ahdal, *al-Nafas al-yamānī*, Ṣanʿāʾ 1979, 239-52; Kattānī, *Fihris al-fahāris*, Beirut 1402/1982, i, 527-43, ii, 621-4; M.M. al-Dimyāṭī, *Muʿdjam asmāʾ al-nabātāt al-wārida fī Tādj al-ʿarūs li ʾl-Zabīdī*, Cairo 1966; Ḥ. al-Djāsir, *Naẓarāt fī kitāb Tādj al-ʿarūs min djawāhir al-Ḳāmūs li ʾl-Sayyid Muḥammad Murtaḍā al-Zabīdī*, al-Riyāḍ 1987; H.Ṭ. Shalāsh, *al-Adwiya wa ʾl-adwāʾ fī muʿdjam Tādj al-ʿarūs*, Baghdād 1408/1987; Ḥ. Naṣṣār, *al-Muʿdjam al-ʿarabī*, Cairo 1408/1988, ii, 604-40; R.L. Lārī, *ʿAllāma Sayyid Murtaḍā Bilgrāmī Zabīdī. Ḥayāt awr ʿilmī kārnāma*, Lakhnaw 1990; S. Reichmuth, *Murtaḍā az-Zabīdī (d. 1791) in biographical and autobiographical accounts . . .*, in *WI* (1999), 64-102.

P. 1007[a], **NĀṢIR-I KHUSRAW**, *add to Bibl.*: Alice C. Hunsberger, *Nasir Khusraw: the ruby of Badakhshan. A portrait of the Persian poet, traveller and philosopher*, London and New York 2000.

VOLUME VIII

P. 64[a], **NĪSHĀPŪRĪ**, *add to end of first paragraph*: The alleged text of the *Saldjūḳ-nāma*, indifferently published by Ismāʿīl Afshār at Tehran in 1322/1953 is, in the opinion of A.H. Morton, the work of Abu ʾl-Ḳāsim Ḳāshānī (whose literary activity seems to span the years between 699/1300 and 716/1316), and is quite closely related to the section on the Saldjūḳs in the *Djāmiʿ al-tawārīkh* of Rashīd al-Dīn Faḍl Allāh [*q.v.*]. Mr Morton is producing a critical text, based on the R.A.S. Pers. ms. 22b, of an anonymous history of the Saldjūḳs dedicated to Sultan Ṭoghril III b. Arslan and apparently written during his reign. This seems to be one of the later works exploiting the original *Saldjūḳ-nāma* (if this was indeed its actual name) of Ẓahīr al-Dīn, and the editor believes that his final text, which will take into account readings from parallel historical sources, will be as close as we are likely to get to the text of the original *Saldjūḳ-nāma*.

VOLUME X

P. 164[b], **ṬĀLIB ĀMULĪ**, *add to Bibl.*: Mireille Schnyder, *Die "Wunderfügnisse" der Welt. Zur Bedeutung von Metapher und Vergleich in der deutschen und persischen Dichtung des 17. Jahrhunderts*, Bern/Frankfurt a.M., etc. 1992, 167-81.

P. 530[a], **ṬĪNA**, *replace beginning of second paragraph, ll. 43-55, with*: As a technical term of philosophy, *ṭīna* is used in some early Arabic translations from the Greek, and in the first period of Arabic philosophical writing, to render the basic meaning of Greek ὕλη, Ar. *hayūlā* [*q.v.*], as "matter, material substrate" (synonymously with *mādda*), especially in the sense of the Aristotelian Prime Matter, the substratum of the forms of the primary bodies or στοιχεῖα (*usṭuḳussāt*, *ʿanāṣir*), while *hayūlā* renders the general usage of ὕλη as of "matter relative to form". See e.g. *ṭīna* for ὕλη in Ibn al-Muḳaffaʿ's introduction to the *Organon* (*al-Manṭiḳ li-Ibn al-Muḳaffaʿ*, ed. M.T. Dānishpazhūh, Tehran 1978, 4,4); in an early version of Aristotle's *De anima*, 403b18, ed. ʿA. Badawī,

P. 644[a], **TUNISIA**. II. HISTORY. (a) The pre-Islamic period, *add to Bibl.*: arts. C. Nicolet, *Les guerres puniques* and J. Desanges, *L'Afrique romaine et libyco-berbère*, in Nicolet, *Rome et la conquête du monde méditerranéen*, ii, Paris 1993; Cl. Lepelley, *L'Afrique*, in F. Jacques, *Rome et l'intégration de l'Empire*, ii, Paris 1998; A. Mahjoubi, *Villes et structures urbaines de la province romaine d'Afrique*, Tunis 2000.

opposite
P. 770, **ʿŪD**, Fig. 1, 3rd col., l. 10, *for* 8182/6561, *read* 8192/6561.
P. 787ª, **ʿUḲAYLIDS**, *add to Bibl.*: 1. Sources. Ibn al-Ḳalānisī; Sibṭ Ibn al-Djawzī; Ibn al-ʿAdīm. 2. Studies. Th. Bianquis, *Damas et la Syrie sous la domination fāṭimide*, 2 vols. Damascus 1987-9, i, 154-6, ii, 601-15; H. Kennedy, *The ʿUqaylids of Mosul*, in *Actas del XII Congreso de la U.E.A.I.*, Malaga n.d.; Bianquis, *Raḥba et le Diyār Muḍar, de la fondation de la ville à la conquête seljoucide*, in *BEO*, xli-xlii (1989-90), 23-53.
P. 824ª, **ʿUMAR** b. **ḤAFṢŪN**, l. 4, *for* [see BARBASHTURU] *read* [see BUBASHTRU, in Suppl.].
P. 833ª, **ʿUMAR KHAYYĀM**, l. 3, *for* 28, 32, *read* 28, 33.
P. 836ᵇ, **ʿUMĀRA** al-**YAMANĪ**, *add to Bibl.*: P. Smoor, *ʿUmâra's elegies and the lamp of loyalty*, in *AI*, xxxiv (2000), 467-564; idem, *ʿUmâra's odes describing the Imam*, in *AI*, xxxv (2001), 1-78.
P. 846ᵇ, **UMAYYADS**, l. 14 from below, *add to Bibl.*: al-Balādhurī, *al-Ansāb al-ashrāf*, complete ed. S. Zakkār and Ziriklī, 13 vols. Beirut 1996.
P. 928ᵇ, **UṢŪL**, l. 5 from bottom, for *ḥarf/djarr*, read *ḥarf djarr*.

VOLUME XI
P. 2ª, **VIDJAYANAGARA**, l. 6, *for* (1568-1614) *read* (1586-1614); l. 18, *for* Srī Rāya III's *read* Srī Ranga Rāya III's; *and add to Bibl.*: H. Heras, *The Aravidu dynasty of Vijayanagara*, Madras 1927; B.A. Saletore, *Social and political life in the Vijayanagara empire (A.D. 1346-A.D. 1646)*, 2 vols. Madras 1934; N. Venkataramanayya, *Studies in the history of the Third Dynasty of Vijayanagara*, Madras 1935; R. Sewell, *A forgotten empire – Vijayanagara*, repr. New Delhi 1962; N. Karasimha, *Towards a new formation. South Indian society under Vijaynagara rule*, Delhi 1992; S. Subrahmanyam, *Agreeing to disagree. Burton Stein on Vijayanagara*, in *South Asia Research*, xvii (Autumn 1997), 127-39.
P. 246ᵇ, **YAḤYĀ** b. al-**BIṬRĪḲ**, l. 10, *for* and literature of the Rūm of his time, *read* and writing system of the Rūm of his time.
in *Bibl.*, l. 2, *add* pp. 290-1 to references in Flügel's edition.
P. 309ª, **YAZDĪ**, ll. 9 and 14, *for* Ḍirgham al-Dawla Ḳashḳāʾī, *read* Ḍaygham al-Dawla Ḳashḳāʾī.
P. 333ᵇ, **YERLIYYA**, l. 13, *for page reference in* U. Heyd, *Ottoman documents on Palestine, 1522-1615*, Oxford 1960, *read* 68-9.
ll. 18-21, *replace* al-Muḥibbī, *Khulāṣat* . . . al-Ṭabbākh, *Iʿlām*, iii, 129) *with* al-Muḥibbī, *Khulāṣa*, ii, 129, iii, 156, 299, 427-8, iv, 449-50; al-Murādī, *Silk*, i, 106-7, ii, 63; al-Ghazzī, *Nahr al-dhahab*, iii, 266, 279; al-Ṭabbākh, *Iʿlām*, iii, 219).
P. 334ª, ll. 37-8, for *1154-1175/1762-1741*, read *1154-1175/1741-1762.*
P. 355ᵇ, **YŪSUF** b. **ʿĀBID** al-**IDRĪSĪ**, l. 3, *for the deathdate of* 992/1584, *read* after 1036/1627.

V

VAN [see WĀN].
VARDAR [see WARDAR].
VARNA [see WARNA].
VEYSEL [see ʿĀSH̲ĪḲ WEYSEL, in Suppl.].
VIDIN [see WIDIN].
VIDJAYANAGARA, the name of a mediaeval Hindu power which covered large parts of the Deccan from the mid-14th century to the later 17th century and which is relevant to this Encyclopaedia because of the incessant warfare between its Rādjās (some sixty of whom, from various, distinct lineages, issued royal inscriptions claiming sovereignty over India south of the Krishna river) and the Muslim sultanates of the Deccan. It appears in Indo-Muslim sources as Bidjanagar.

The name Vidjayanagara, meaning "City of victory", was that of the state's original capital on the upper Tungabhadrā river. Its ruins lie at Hampī in the Bellary Division in the western part of the modern Karnataka State of the Indian Union (lat. 15° 20′ N., long. 76° 25′ E.); for the mediaeval city and its buildings, see HAMPĪ. The kingdom arose from the ruins of four great Hindu dynasties which had ruled the territories south of the Vindhya range on the eve of the first Muslim penetration of the Deccan by the Dihlī Sultan ʿAlāʾ al-Dīn K̲h̲aldjī in 693/1294 [see KHALDJĪs]. A Hindu reaction came in the time of the Sultan Muḥammad b. Tug̲h̲luḳ [q.v.], when an infant Hindu state arose in the Andhra coastlands along the Bay of Bengal. The ancient Hindu Hoysala kingdom was overthrown by Vidjayanagara in 1346, but expansion by the new state was challenged in the south by the existence of the recently-established Muslim-sultanate of Madura on the Malabar coast [see MAʿBAR]. Nevertheless, this last ephemeral independent sultanate was extinguished by the Vidjayanagara Rādjās in ca. 779/1377, and the Malabar region held by Hindu rulers until the short-lived Muslim conquest in the later 11th/17th century by the Mug̲h̲al emperor Awrangzīb [q.v.].

To the north, the sultanate of the Bahmanids [q.v.], much more powerful than Madura had been, formed a barrier against both Vidjayanagara and the other main Hindu state of the eastern Deccan, Warangal [q.v.]. The Bahmanids conquered Warangal by 830/1425 but were never able to subdue Vidjayanagara. Warfare between the two powers was frequent, with the Rayčūr [q.v.] *doʾāb*, the land between the Tungabhadrā and Bhīma rivers, which Muḥammad b. Tug̲h̲luḳ had overrun, being the main bone of contention. The Bahmanids attacked Telingāna [q.v.] in 763/1362, and there were several wars over the next decades between Muḥammad I Bahman S̲h̲āh (759-76/1358-75) and his successors, such as Tādj al-Dīn Fīrūz S̲h̲āh (800-25/1397-1422), and the Rādjās of Vidjayanagara, with Fīrūz S̲h̲āh frequently allied with the Hindu Velama ruler of Warangal. However, there were also periods of peace, with a rough balance of power emerging in the Deccan, as Muslim powers suspicious of Bahmanid expansion, such as those to the north, K̲h̲āndes̲h̲, Gudjarāt and Mālwā, gave tacit support to Vidjayanagara, and there was also some cultural interaction; Fīrūz S̲h̲āh took a Vidjayanagara princess in marriage. But it was an ignominious defeat at the hands of Dēvarāya I at Panagal in 822/1419 which led to Fīrūz S̲h̲āh's enforced abdication in 825/1422. His successor Aḥmad I S̲h̲āh wrought a condign revenge on both Vidjayanagara and its recent ally Warangal in 827/1424 and then on the former in 836/1433. According to the Muslim historian Firis̲h̲ta, Dēvarāya II, the greatest ruler of the Sangama line of Vidjayanagara recruited Muslim archers and cavalrymen for his army (an inscription of 1430 says that this ruler had 10,000 Turuśka, i.e. Muslim, lit. "Turkish", horsemen in his forces), and in 1433 used his armies to invade the Bahmanid lands. The historian ʿAbd al-Razzāḳ al-Samarḳandī led a mission to Vidjayanagara in 846-7/1443 and describes the splendour of the capital and its court and the flourishing state of the kingdom, and especially of its ports on the Bay of Bengal (*Maṭlaʿ al-saʿdayn*; cf. S.H. Hodivala, *Studies in Indo-Muslim history*, i, 1939, 410 ff.). The Bahmanid sultanate had a resurgence of power later in the 9th/15th century under Muḥammad III S̲h̲āh and his able minister Maḥmūd Gāwān [q.v.], and the latter in campaigns of 873-6/1469-72 captured Goa, which had in previous decades passed into the orbit of Vidjayanagara, and brought Bahmanid authority to the coastal region of Konkar [q.v. in Suppl.] on the shores of the Arabian Sea. Yet after Maḥmūd Gāwān's death in 886/1481, the Bahmanid sultanate fell into chaos and by 934/1528 dissolved into five local Muslim sultanates of the Deccan.

Vidjayanagara, too, was plunged into confusion towards the end of the 15th century but was rescued after 1509 by the energetic Tūluva line of Rādjās. By now a new factor was appearing on the coastlands of the Arabian Sea in the shape of the Portuguese, established at Goa and elsewhere, and it was also now that Vidjayanagara's main Muslim enemy became the ʿĀdil S̲h̲āhs of Bidjapur [q.vv.]. The ʿĀdil S̲h̲āh Ismāʿīl was decisively defeated near Rayčūr in 926/1520 by Krishnadēvarāya, and his forces again worsted in 946/1539. In the middle years of the century, Rāmarāya successfully kept at bay not only the ʿĀdil S̲h̲āhs but also the Niẓām S̲h̲āhs and Ḳuṭb S̲h̲āhs [q.vv.], until he was in turn defeated in 972/1565 by a coalition of four Muslim sultanates at the villages of Rakshasa and Tangadi, usually called the battle of Tālīkoṭa [q.v.], when Rāmarāya was killed and Vidjayanagara sacked and deprived of its glory.

The Vidjayanagara state survived for another century

under the Āravidū line of rulers, but with diminished territory and revenues, and with the capital at first transferred south-eastwards to Penukondā, safer from Muslim attacks. Though deprived of its northern provinces, it was still strong under Venkata II Rāya (1568-1614), who ruled from a capital at Čandragiri, allied with the Portuguese, received various foreign embassies and was in direct correspondence with Philip II of Spain. It was Venkata III who in 1639 allowed the English East India Company to build a fort at the village of Madras, which was named Fort St. George [see MADRAS]. But by now, Muslim pressure was being strongly felt, with the ʿĀdil Shāhs extending southwards into Mysore [see MAHISUR] and then eastwards into Karnātaka, and the Ḳuṭb Shāhs pushing towards the Bay of Bengal and the Coromandel coast. The then Vidjayanagara capital of Vellore was captured, and Srī Rāya III's territories shrank almost to nothing; he is last mentioned in an inscription of 1678. After Awrangzīb extinguished the sultanates of the ʿĀdil and Ḳuṭb Shāhs, the remaining Vidjayanagara territories in the extreme southwestern tip of the Deccan peninsula passed briefly under Mughal rule.

In modern times, apart from two or three British pioneers, the history of Vidjayanagara has until recently largely been written by Hindu Indian writers, and these have often regarded Vidjayanagara as the guardian of the Hindu heritage in South India, with a historic mission of resistance to Islam; in this same tradition, Vidjayanagara has sometimes been regarded by them not only as a mediaeval Indian state but also as the precursor of the Marāthā confederacy [see MARĀTHĀS].

Bibliography: Majumdar (general ed.), *The history and culture of the Indian people. VI. The Delhi Sultanate*, Bombay 1960, 271-325; *VII. The Mughul Empire*, Bombay 1974, 486-501; Habib and Nizami (eds.), *A comprehensive history of India, V. The Delhi Sultanat (A.D. 1206-1526)*, Delhi etc. 1970, 1028-1103; H.K. Sherwani and P.M. Joshi (eds.), *History of medieval Deccan (1295-1724)*, Ḥaydarābād 1973, i, 79-139; B. Stein, *Vijayanagara* (= *The New Cambridge history of India*, I.2), Cambridge 1989, with full bibl. See also HIND. IV. History. (C.E. BOSWORTH)

VIZE [see WIZE].

VODINA [see WODINA].

VOIVODE [see WOYWODA].

VOLGA RIVER [see ITIL].

VOLGA TATARS [see ḲAZAN; TURKS. I. History].

VOLOS [see ḲULUZ, in Suppl.].

VOYNUḲ [see WOYNUḲ].

W

WĀ-SŌKHT, or "bitter repudiation (sc. of the beloved)", a term of Perso-Urdu literary criticism which has two senses. First, it denotes a theme intrinsic to Persian love poetry which came to be prominently exploited for its own sake in the 10th/16th-century Persian *ghazal* by such *sabk-i hindī* poets as Waḥshī (d. 991/1553), although the exclusive association with the latter suggested by Shiblī (*Shiʿr al-ʿadjam*, 3, 16) is to be questioned (P. Losensky, *Welcoming Fighānī*, Costa Mesa 1998, 82). Later, the term *wā-sōkht* was used in the Urdu poetry of the 18th and 19th centuries to describe a stanzaic poem devoted to the theme of repudiating the beloved. Like other such distinctive Urdu developments, this minor genre seems to have originated with the innovative poet Sawdā [*q.v.*], who uses *muthamman* stanzas each concluding with a Persian verse. But *musaddas* stanzas were preferred by later exponents of the *wā-sōkht*, who notably include Mīr Muḥammad Taḳī, Djurʾat and Muʾmin [*q.vv.*]. A standardised semi-narrative structure incorporating the inevitable *sarāpā* came to characterise the final phase of the *wā-sōkht* which was developed by minor poets of the later Lakhnaʾū school, such as Baḥr, Rikkat and Shawḳ [*q.v.*]. Maximal exploitation of the inherently limited scope of the *wā-sōkht* was achieved in the two extended examples by Amānat (d. 1275/1858 [*q.v.*]), of 117 and 307 *musaddas* stanzas respectively.

Bibliography: *Wā-sōkht az Āghā Ḥasan Amānat*, ed. Mīrzā Naṣīr Bēg, Lahore 1964, 1-49.

(C. SHACKLE)

WABĀʾ (A., from *wabiʾa* "to be contaminated", said of a region or land affected by the plague), the mediaeval Arabic term for "epidemic, pestilence", and theoretically distinguished from *ṭāʿūn*, from *ṭaʿana* "to pierce, stab", in the more specific sense of "plague". In mediaeval Arabic medical treatises, one encounters the phrase "every *ṭāʿūn* is a *wabāʾ*, but not every *wabāʾ* is a *ṭāʿūn*". While it appears that the distinction had been kept in the early Hidjrī centuries, it is doubtful, however, whether later Muslim writers always used the two terms with the precise distinction in mind, and it has been shown that considerable confusion existed in the usage of terminology.

1. In the mediaeval Islamic world up to the 10th/16th century.

Epidemics of smallpox and measles, and possibly of typhus, tuberculosis, cholera and dysentery, had been known since early Islam, yet the available information is too sparse and vague to enable precise knowledge of specific cases. Mediaeval Muslim medicine, under Greek influence, considered as the cause of such epidemics the pestilential corruption of the environment, particularly the air (miasma).

Enough material has survived to show that medical writers in early Islamic centuries understood *ṭāʿūn* to mean both the bubonic plague and the swellings of the lymph glands so characteristic of this disease. Relying on Greek and Latin sources, and parallel to the classical notion of the "black death", they speak of the "black *ṭāʿūn*", the worst kind of plague, one of the prominent signs of which is the appearance of dark blotches under the skin. The 7th/13th-century author Muḥyī al-Dīn al-Nawawī [*q.v.*], for example, speaks of "tumours . . . accompanied by a fiery inflammation", of "palpitation of the heartbeat and nausea", all symptoms which accord with modern medical data collected on the bubonic plague. The physician Ibn al-Nafīs [*q.v.*] identified buboes with plague infection. The Andalusian historian Ibn al-Khaṭīb [*q.v.*], a contemporary of the Black Death (see below), stands out in his opposition to the view of the jurists and his insistence on the factor of contagion in spreading the plague.

The plague is a virulent and extremely lethal epidemic illness, which appeared in world history in the form of great cycles of periodic infection known as pandemics. The bacilli, known as *Pasteurella pestis*, are carried by fleas (*Xenopsylla cheopis*) into populations of wild rodents, where the plague can find a permanent reservoir. It is agreed that the factors which led to outbreaks of plague were an epizootic in the rodents, especially in rats, which would destroy the hosts for the fleas and cause the latter to pass to humans. When an infected flea bites a human, plague bacilli multiply and accumulate in the lymph glands and create buboes (hence: bubonic plague). As the disease progresses, the body's temperature rises and the pulse dramatically increases. In plagues attested in history, a large percentage of cases of infections resulted in fatality within two weeks at the most. A mortality rate of up to 70% made bubonic plague a disastrous disease. Complications could draw the plague bacilli into the lungs, causing the highly contagious and absolutely fatal pneumonic plague which prevails mainly in the winter months and causes death rapidly. A septicaemic variety of plague results from the introduction of the bacillus into the bloodstream and is a very acute plague form, since death can occur within hours. Plague infection spread primarily along communication and trade routes, both by land and sea. Contrary to the assertion of some scholars, there seems no ground for the suggestion that populations could develop natural immunity to the plague.

A plague recorded for the years A.D. 573-4 is of interest since it occurred immediately after what is commonly held to have been the date of Muḥammad's birth. It appears to have been part of the pandemic which began with the so-called Plague of Justinian in 541 and continued for two centuries up to 131/749. The geographical origin of this pandemic is unclear, and the mediaeval Muslim ascription of it to an African plague reservoir should be treated with caution. One should also note the so-called Plague of S͟hīrawayh (6/628), named after the Sāsānid emperor S͟hīrawayh or S͟hīrūy Kawād͟h II, who perished in this outbreak, as being the first recorded case of plague in the Muslim era. A decade later, in Syria and ʿIrāḳ in 17-18/638-9, the Plague of ʿAmwās in Palestine [see ʿAMWĀS] was the first plague to strike the newly-established Muslim empire. It appears to have been of devastating proportions in terms of the mortality it caused; many thousands of Arabs and the conquered population perished. Plague then occurred in the Muslim Near East between 49/669 and 131/749, about a dozen times in Syria and ʿIrāḳ, of which the so-called "Plague which snatches people away [in droves]" (*ṭāʿūn al-d͟jārif*) in 67/687 in ʿIrāḳ, and then that of 126/743-4, which persisted almost continuously until 131/749, were particularly devastating. Thereafter, there appears to have been a respite in the incidence of plague until it struck Bag͟hdād in 301/913-14. Later, sporadic outbreaks are difficult to identify because of the dubious terminology.

The second pandemic in the mediaeval Islamic world is known as the Black Death. It appeared in Mongolia—where plague had been endemic for a long time—*ca.* 732/1331, and reached Islamic territories in 748/1347, most likely by the overland route through Turkestan and the Black Sea region. It was as devastating to the Near Eastern populations as to the European ones, and although no accurate mortality data are available, modern research has suggested a population decline of between 25% and 33%. From the available sources, it appears that Egypt and Syria were the regions primarily affected. In addition to high mortality there was large-scale flight from infected areas which aggravated the situation. Cultivated land was abandoned and famine developed. Urban centres suffered as well, since economic activity drastically declined and various functions were suspended. In Ibn K͟haldūn's poetic phrase, "It was as if the voice of existence in the world had called out for oblivion and restriction and the world responded to its call". There were frequent recurrences until as late as the 19th century. For Egypt, close to 50 recurrences of either *wabā'* or *ṭāʿūn* have been recorded for the period between 1348 and 1517. For Syria, the number is about 25. Among the effects of this phenomenon, one should point out the almost certain lack of demographic recovery until modern times.

Theological belief and a normative scheme of behaviour with regard to the plague arose and were incorporated into *ḥadīt͟h* [*q.v.*] and other kinds of literature, such as the genre of treatises on the plague. Juristic literature furnished not only legal precedents, which set limits to intellectual discussion and communal behaviour in the context of epidemics, but also an aetiological explanation of the plague, methods of prevention and treatment. Theological explanations contradicted the medical ones of an infected environment (see above) by claiming that disease comes directly from God, hence no infection should be feared. Accordingly, plague was a divine punishment inflicted on impious Muslims and unbelievers. A special kind of lore developed around demons (*d͟jinn* [*q.v.*]) as the agents of the plague. However, if a pious Muslim survived the ordeal, he would be rewarded in the afterlife. In traditions ascribed to the Prophet, death from the plague is one of the means of gaining the status of *s͟hahīd* [*q.v.*] or martyr. It was maintained that plague was a form of the divine mercy (*raḥma*), and that a pious Muslim should suffer an epidemic patiently, trusting in God's will and not trying to foil it. Such views explain the dicta prohibiting flight from stricken places.

Bibliography: M.W. Dols, *The Black Death in the Middle East*, Princeton 1977; idem, *The general mortality of the Black Death in the Mamluk empire*, in A.L. Udovitch (ed.), *The Islamic Middle East, 700-1900*, Princeton 1981, 397-428; B. Shoshan, *Notes sur les épidémies de peste en Egypte*, in *Annales de démographie historique* (1981), 387-404; L.I. Conrad, *The plague in the early medieval Near East*, Ph.D. diss, Princeton Univ., unpubl.; idem, *Ṭāʿūn and wabā'*, in *JESHO*, xxv (1982), 268-307; Dols, *Al-Manbiji's "Report of the Plague". A treatise on the plague of 764-65/1362-64 in the Middle East*, in D. Williman (ed.), *The Black Death. The impact of the fourteenth century plague*, Binghamton 1982, 65-75; Conrad, *Plagues in the Islamic world*, in *Dict. of the Middle Ages*, ix, New York 1978, 684-6; idem, *Die Pest und ihr soziales Umfeld im Nahen Osten des frühen Mittelalters*, in *Isl.*, lxxiii (1996), 80-112.

(B. SHOSHAN)

2. In the Ottoman Empire.

The development, in the course of the 16th century, of the vast Ottoman Empire does not seem to have affected the presence and proliferation of the plague, firmly established in the Ancient World since the mid-14th century and persisting there until the time of its disappearance in the early 20th century. Identifying the disease with certainty, establishing the chronology, geographical extension and intensity of epidemics of the plague over four centuries across this immense territory, is a task which has not as yet been tackled. However, publications currently available make it possible to sketch the major aspects of the presence and effects of the plague, with the following proviso: the available information becomes more thorough and reliable the closer our own time is approached, and data is less complete and less certain the further one travels from towns and coastal regions. From the early 16th to the mid-19th century, the plague was virtually always present in at least one of the Ottoman provinces, spreading periodically over a much larger area, even the whole of the Empire. While the mortality rate of the disease was always very high—an average of three fatalities for every four patients—its intensity varied considerably: in some cases it would cause only a few deaths, then return to the same area some years later and wipe out a quarter of the population within weeks.

The 16th century is the period in which lacunae are most apparent. It is possible, however, to point to a huge pandemic in the years 1572-89, at which time the plague is found to have affected, with a few brief interruptions, the Near East as well as Egypt, Anatolia, the Balkans and North Africa. On the other hand, the plague was much in evidence during the whole of the 17th century, as is shown by these two examples: in Algiers it is recorded in 1600-2, 1605, 1606-9, 1611-3, 1620-4, 1626-7, 1630, 1639-44, 1647, 1649, 1654-61, 1665, 1673, 1675-6, 1680-3, 1686, 1689-95, 1697-1702, thus every other year on average. Cairo was affected, to a degree sufficient to have drawn the attention of the chroniclers, in 1601-3, 1619, 1620-6, 1642-4, 1667-8, 1671, 1696, thus 18 years in total. The plague was still rife in the 18th century; in 100 years, 68 years of pestilence have been recorded in Istanbul, 57 in Aegean Anatolia, 44 in Egypt, 42 in Albania-Epirus, 41 in Bosnia, 33 in Syria, 18 in Bulgaria, 45 in the Regency of Algiers and 19 in that of Tunis. Improved sources of information reveal that these epidemic instances were of limited intensity and that the deadly epidemics, those which could wipe out between one-tenth and one-third of the population of an urban area, the large cities in particular, occurred only rarely, once in each generation on average. This was the case in 1705, 1726, 1751, 1778 and 1812 in Istanbul, 1713, 1741, 1762, 1781 and 1818 in Salonica, 1718, 1733, 1762, 1787, 1812 and 1837 in Aleppo. The beginning of the 19th century was a continuation of the 18th with two great pandemics which ravaged almost the whole of the Empire in 1812-19 and 1835-38. Then, in the years 1840-44, the plague seems to have disappeared from the Ottoman Empire, with the exception of limited outbreaks in Cyrenaica in 1856-59 and in ʿIrāḳ in 1856-9, 1874-7 and 1891-2. It emerged again in 1894, persisting for more than half a century, in African and Asian territories which were formerly Ottoman.

The plague was above all a disease affecting various species of wild rodents, which played a decisive role in the perpetuation of the disease according to a complex process, in which their fleas participated, in what used to be called the natural centres of the plague. In terms of the Ottoman Empire, this refers to Persian Kurdistan, the Libyan desert and the ʿAsīr [*q.v.*] massif between Yemen and Ḥidjāz. It was from these zones that the disease spread, always carried by rodents, over vast territories and long periods of time, thus forming, in the 17th and 18th centuries, temporary centres, notably in Albania-Epirus, Moldavia-Walachia, Istanbul, Anatolia and Egypt. In these centres, the epizootic disease was communicated, fortuitously, to humans through the intermediary of fleas. On becoming an epidemic disease it would subsequently be diffused, by land and sea, throughout the whole of the Empire, carried by couriers, merchants, sailors, nomads, soldiers and fugitives—any travellers, in fact.

It is difficult to evaluate precisely the demographic effects of the plague. However, the 16th century seems to have enjoyed a fairly long epidemic remission, accounting for the relative prosperity of the population observed in Anatolia and the Near East. This came to an end in the 1580s, and the 17th and 18th centuries show an increase in the frequency of the disease, probably responsible for a stagnation of the Ottoman population taken as a whole. In its more severe manifestations, the plague also damaged economies, disrupting harvests in the countryside and commercial and industrial activities in the towns. The plague was thus one of the decisive factors behind the problems and weaknesses of the Ottoman Empire in the 18th century.

The beliefs and the behaviour of Muslims when confronted by epidemics of the plague were determined in the Middle Ages, and works of this era, especially those of Ibn Ḥadjar al-ʿAsḳalānī in the 15th century, were regarded as authoritative in succeeding centuries. The situation changed from the early 19th century onward, with the appearance in the Near East, in 1820, of a new epidemic disease—cholera, originating in Bengal, which, spreading from Mecca, was to add its effects to those of the plague. The change came about through the influence of the Europeans resident in the Levant, who successfully applied the techniques of protection in use in Europe, and especially through the awareness on the part of rulers of Muslim states of the importance of the demographic factor in military, fiscal and economic spheres. Traditional resignation to divine will was replaced, at least in the higher echelons of the state, by a conception which sought to reconcile the *Sharīʿa* with modern science and the interests of the state. From the 1830s onward, the Ottoman Empire, Egypt, Tunisia and Morocco, equipped themselves with sanitary authorities and regulations, placing quarantine stations on maritime and terrestrial frontiers. These innovations were achieved with the aid of Westerners, diplomats and doctors, who saw an opportunity to enhance their influence. The rapidity of the results obtained, such that no cases of plague were recorded in the Ottoman Empire after 1844, resulted as much from the efforts of local sanitary institutions as from natural extinction of the temporary centres of the previous centuries. Later recurrences of the plague, few and of limited scope, were energetically combatted.

Bibliography: J.N. Biraben, *Les hommes et la peste en France et dans les pays européens et méditerranéens*, 2 vols. Paris 1975-6; M. Dols, *The second plague pandemic and its recurrences in the Middle East: 1347-1894*, in *IJMES*, xxii (1979), 162-89; D. Panzac, *La peste dans l'Empire ottoman 1700-1850*, Louvain 1985 (abridged Turkish ed., *Osmanlı imparatorluğu'nda veba (1700-1850)*, Istanbul 1997); idem, *La population de l'Empire ottoman. Cinquante ans (1941-1990) de publications et de recherches*, Aix-en-Provence 1993; Sadok Boubaker, *La peste dans les pays du Maghreb: attitudes face au fléau et impacts sur les activités commerciales (XVe-XVIIIe siècles)*, in *Revue d'Histoire maghrébine*, lxxix-lxxx (1995), 311-41; Gülden Sarıyıldız, *Hicaz karantina teşkilâtı (1865-1914)*, Istanbul 1996; S. Speziale, *Oltre la peste. Sanità, popolazione e società in Tunisia e nel Maghreb (XVIII-XX secolo)*, Cosenza 1997.

(D. Panzac)

WABĀR, in Arabian lore a district and tribe localised in the southern part of the Arabian peninsula. Al-Bakrī, *Muʿdjam*, ed. Wüstenfeld, 835, and Yāḳūt, *Buldān*, ed. Wüstenfeld, iv, 896, give the name as an indeclinable *faʿāli* form, Wabār[i], with the irregular *nisba* Abārī.

1. In Arabian lore and history.

The Wabār are mentioned by the historians alongside the ʿĀd, Thamūd [*q.vv.*] and other extinct tribes like the Djadīs and Ṭasm [*q.v.*] as peoples of Arabia, now vanished (*al-ʿArab al-bāʾida*), accounted by some genealogists as being among the "true, original" Arabs (*al-ʿArab al-ʿarbāʾ* or *al-ʿāriba*), and described as such by e.g. al-Hamdānī and al-Ṭabarī. The latter, i, 221, tr. W.M. Brinner, *The History of al-Ṭabarī*, ii, *Prophets and patriarchs*, Albany 1987, 20, and al-Masʿūdī, *Tanbīh*, 184, and *Murūdj*, iii, 288-90 = § 1161, number the Wabār among the extinct Arab tribes and give their genealogy.

The statements of the Arab geographers and historians about the history of the Wabār are strongly saturated with legend. The stories current among the Arabs are given by Ibn al-Faḳīh, 37-8, whose statements are combined from several sources, al-Bakrī (*op. cit.*), and much more fully Yāḳūt (iv, 896; a brief synopsis in the *Lisān*, still more briefly in the *Ḳāmūs* and a little more fully in the *Tādj*, *s.v.*). Yāḳūt quotes various authorities, including Hishām Ibn al-Kalbī, Muḥammad b. Isḥāḳ, Ibn al-Faḳīh, and other direct and indirect sources. His statements (iv, 897) agree almost word for word with those of Ibn al-Faḳīh. Al-Ḳazwīnī (*ʿAdjāʾib*, ed. Wüstenfeld, ii, 41) and later writers are based on Yāḳūt. The same characteristic features are common to the authors and compilers mentioned. These include the purely legendary elements: that the name of the land goes back to an ancestor Wabār, who flourished at the time of the confusion of tongues (so al-Masʿūdī, *Tanbīh*, 184; al-Ṭabarī, i, 221, 250), that after the fall of the ʿĀd (cf. Ibn Saʿd, *Ṭabaḳāt*, i/1, 20), the previous inhabitants of Wabār, the Djinn, took possession of the land (so also al-Hamdānī, *op. cit.*, 154, 223; al-Ṭabarī, i, 221), and men lived there no longer but only half-men (*nasnās*), beings who had only half a head, one eye, one hand and one leg (Yāḳūt, ii, 263, tells the same story of al-Shiḥr), that no one dared enter this land, and that its mysterious inhabitants destroyed the crops of the adjoining lands between al-Shiḥr and Yaman. A feature which is developed in the legend, on older models, is the story that Wabār was a particularly fertile land, rich in water and fruit-trees and especially in palms (so also al-Masʿūdī, *Murūdj*, iii, 276, 288-9 = §§ 1150, 1161); al-Nābigha's mention of palms in the land of Wabār (in Ahlwardt, *The Divans*, etc., London 1870, 112, from Yāḳūt) was taken as evidence that the land was fertile and inhabited (cf. al-Bakrī, *loc. cit.*, with Yāḳūt, iv, 898). The mentions of Wabār in poetry are, of course, not independent evidence, but repeat as a rule only the conventional notions of the great antiquity and fall of the people and the isolation of their land (cf. also Yāḳūt, iv, 897).

What arouses interest in these fables and may be of use are the geographical ideas at the bottom of them. According to some of these statements, the broad land of Wabār stretched from al-Shiḥr to Ṣanʿāʾ, in general to the eastern frontier of Yaman; according to others, it comprised the whole territory between Nadjrān and Ḥaḍramawt; lastly, according to others, it was the territory between the "sands of Yabrīn" (*rimāl Yabrīn*) and Yaman (see also al-Djawharī). From these topographical hints, which in spite of their differences together give a rough general picture, it can be deduced that the portion of the South Arabian desert, of the Rubʿ al-Khālī or Dahnāʾ, north of the Mahra [*q.vv.*] country, was called Wabār by the Arabs, but this geographical name was also understood in a wider sense and extended to the whole Dahnāʾ. The part called Wabār adjoined in the east the desert area of al-Aḥḳāf (dunes) which lay north and west of Ḥaḍramawt. C. Landberg (*Études sur les dialectes de l'Arabie méridionale*, Leiden 1901, i, 160) says, on the authority of information received from local people, that in the expression *ahl al-aḥḳāf* the place-name, according to South Arabian ideas, refers not only to the district of al-Aḥḳāf but also to caves in which the Arabian troglodytes live (cf. Yāḳūt, i, 154, on the different topographical clues for this district).

It is impossible to accept Ritter's (*Erdkunde*, xiii, 315) identification of the Wabār with the Βανούβαροι, who are mentioned by Ptolemy in connection with the Thamūd and are to be located in the northern half of the west coast of Arabia (the first component of the name is obviously connected with *Banū*). Ritter's comparison (xii, 271, 392) of Wabār in al-Idrīsī (ed. Jaubert, i, 156) is also to be rejected. Nevertheless, although the records are clothed in the form of legend, it does not follow that the whole story is a pure invention, but only that we have here the memory of an ancient people which has become a legend; similar things are to be found in the history of most nations. There is a series of fabulous stories associated with the whole of Southern Arabia between Yaman and ʿUmān, a region little known to Arab scholars and littérateurs.

Various ruined sites and buildings have been noted by European travellers. Thus H.St.J. Philby saw in 1917, at al-Sayḥ in the Aflādj oasis, the ruins of a large building called by the locals Ḳuṣayrat ʿĀd and regarded in local tradition as the capital of a king whose capital was at "Wubār" further south, on the border with Ḥaḍramawt (*The heart of Arabia*, London 1922, ii, 99 ff.). Al-Ṭabarī, i, 221, locates the land Abār between Yamāma and al-Shiḥr in the Ḥaḍramawt, and the geographers generally regard the oasis of Yabrīn as marking the northern edge of Wabār.

Bibliography: Given in the article.

(J. Tkatsch*)

2. Modern attempts to locate the site.

As emerges from 1. above, it seems hardly possible to locate the site of Wabār from the written and oral sources. Archaeological research, on the other hand, did not produce any specific results until 1992, when much publicity was given to the supposed discovery of the ancient city of "Ubar" (i.e. Wabār) at al-Shisar in northern Dhofar or Ẓafār [*q.v.*] (Sultanate of Oman), a site well known to the local inhabitants as the last watering point before the vast expanse of the sands of the Rubʿ al-Khālī. It was also suggested that Wabār could be identified with the *Omanum emporium*, a trading settlement mentioned by Ptolemy.

At the time of the present writer's first visit to the site in July 1980, al-Shisar had no permanent dwellings, except for a fortlet built in 1955 by the Sultan of Oman for a small detachment of soldiers. A small cultivated area, with palm trees, vegetables and seasonal crops, covered an area of about half a km^2. The main concern of the garrison was clearly to guard a perennial spring which could be reached at the bottom of a steep descent, some 15 m below ground, in a large cave exposed by the collapse of a limestone dome. The mouth of the cave was in the past encompassed by a stone enclosure, irregularly rectangular in plan, measuring about 60 × 70 m and reinforced at almost regular intervals by small towers. The collapse of the cave mouth, which is still in progress, has some time ago caused the destruction of a large portion of the western side of the enclosure.

On the archaeological discovery at al-Shisar, any firm judgement would be premature, since a detailed scientific report is not yet available. The identification with the *Omanum emporium* is dubious in light of recent extensive work on Ptolemy's *Geography*, which points to the interpretation of the term *emporium* as referring exclusively to coastal market towns; and even the Bedouin who accompanied Bertram Thomas when he crossed the Empty Quarter, and who recounted the legend that Wabār was a great city buried beneath the sands, were indicating an area far to the northwest of al-Shisar. Hence the small size and the architectonic features of the enclosure found at al-Shisar do not seem to offer any evidence for its identification with a major pre-Islamic trading town. According to popular belief in the area, the ruin could be related to a stronghold built by the ruler of Ḥadramawt, Sultan Badr b. Ṭuwayriḳ, around the middle of the 10th/16th century (see on him, R.B. Serjeant, *The Portuguese off the South Arabian coast*, Beirut 1974, index of proper names).

Bibliography: G.M.B. Jones, *On the incense trail. From the Empty Quarter to the Indian Ocean*, in *Minerva*, iii/4 (July-August 1992), 14-17; M.C.A. Macdonald, *Wabar*, in the section *Archaeology and artifacts of the Arabian Peninsula* by R. Boucharlat, in J.M. Sasson (ed.), *Civilizations of the Ancient Near East*, ii, New York 1995, 1351; and for a popular account of the search for "Ubar" and its identification with al-Shisar, N. Clapp, *The road to Ubar. Finding the Atlantis of the sands*, London, Boston and New York 1998.

(P.M. Costa)

WAD MADANĪ, a city in the Republic of Sudan (1993 pop., 220,000), located on the left bank of the Blue Nile 136 km/85 miles southeast of the capital Khartoum [see AL-KHURṬŪM], and the main urban centre of the Djazīra region (the area between the Blue and White Niles). It is adjacent to the headquarters of the Djazīra irrigation scheme at Barakāt.

The name is derived from Muḥammad b. Madanī (*fl.* late 17th century), known as Wad (i.e. Walad) Madanī, a prominent religious scholar and teacher of the Mālikī legal handbook *al-Risāla* by Ibn Abī Zayd al-Ḳayrawānī [*q.v.*]. His tomb, a simple brick *ḳubba* in which his successors were also buried, is located in the oldest quarter of the town, named al-Madaniyyīn. Wad Madanī developed into a large settlement during the 18th century and, in the aftermath of the Turkish-Egyptian conquest of the Fundj [*q.v.*] kingdom in 1821, it supplanted Sinnār as a regional administrative and commercial centre. It also continued to be a major centre of Islamic scholarship and training during the 19th and 20th centuries, with the schools of the Madaniyyīn family, of Muḥammad al-Izayriḳ (d. *ca.* 1883), and of ʿAlī al-Būshī (d. 1929). These schools stressed study of the Ḳurʾān and jurisprudence over Ṣūfism (Muḥammad wad Madanī himself is known as *al-Sunnī*), befitting the city's development into a major commercial entrepôt.

Bibliography: For a biography of Muḥammad b. Madanī, see Muḥammad al-Nūr b. Ḍayf Allāh, *K. al-Ṭabaḳāt*, ed. Yūsuf Faḍl Ḥasan, ²Khartoum 1974, 329-32; H.C. Jackson, *Two Gezira families*, in *Sudan Notes and Records*, iii (1920), 94-109 includes an account of the Madaniyyīn; Muḥammad al-Izayriḳ is remembered by one of his pupils in Babikr Bedri, *The memoirs of Babikr Bedri*, tr. Yousef Bedri and G. Scott, London 1969, 11-14.

(N. McHugh)

WAʾD AL-BANĀT (A.), "the disposal by burying alive of newborn daughters", refers to the practice in pre-Islamic times of burying newborn girls immediately after birth. The concept occurs with strong disapproval in the Ḳurʾān in LXXXI, 8, in the form *al-mawʾūda*, but according to mediaeval *tafsīr*, the practice is alluded to also in LX, 12 (believing women who do not kill their children), XVI, 58/59; XLIII, 17 (anger and grief for the birth of a daughter), and in VI, 151, XVII, 31 (the killing of children for fear of poverty). According to the *ḥadīth*, the practice was explicitly forbidden by the Prophet (see Wensinck, *Concordances*, s.v. *w-ʾ-d*). From two traditions where *al-ʿazl* [*q.v.*] "coitus interruptus" is called respectively *al-waʾd al-khafī* "the hidden burying alive" (Muslim, *nikāḥ*, 141; Ibn Mādja, *nikāḥ*, 61; Ibn Ḥanbal, vi, 361, 434) and *al-mawʾūda al-ṣughrā* "the lesser buried alive one" (Abū Dāwūd, *nikāḥ*, 48; Ibn Ḥanbal, iii, 33, 51, 53) it may be concluded that, more generally, the practice was probably a primitive sort of population control, though "gendered". In modern Islam, the issue of the prohibition of infanticide has played an important role in the debate on the legality of family planning (see Abdel Rahim Omran, *Family planning in the legacy of Islam*, London 1992, 86-89 and *passim*); the opponents argue that *ʿazl* or any practice that prevents pregnancy is to be equated with *waʾd*, whilst the proponents maintain that contraception merely prevents pregnancy and involves no killing and that only *abortus provocatus* is covered by the prohibition of *waʾd* and that *ʿazl* was permitted by the Prophet.

(F. Leemhuis)

AL-WAʿD WA 'L-WAʿĪD (A.), "the Promise and the Threat", represents one of the "Five Principles" (*al-uṣūl al-khamsa*), which since the time of Abu 'l-Hudhayl [*q.v.*] have been considered characteristic of Muʿtazilī theology. With this slogan, the Muʿtazila expressed their conviction that not only the unbelievers had to face damnation on the Day of Judgement but that Muslims who had committed a grave sin (*kabīra* [see KHAṬĪʾA]) without repentance were also threatened by eternal hellfire.

The starting-point of this dogma was the exegesis of certain Ḳurʾānic statements. These stress, on the one hand, that God has "promised" Paradise to the believers (e.g. IX, 72) and Hell to the unbelievers (e.g. IX, 68) (in both cases the verb *waʿada* is used), i.e. He has made a binding declaration of intent. On the other hand, the Ḳurʾān declares that certain grave sins will be punished by eternal damnation. Thus it says in e.g. IV, 10 that "Those who devour the property of the orphan unjustly, . . . will in the end roast in a hellish blaze" (cf. also IV, 30; LXXXII, 14, *et al.*).

The Muslims of the early period were nonetheless of the opinion that these "verses of threat" were not addressed to them. They were apparently convinced that, due to their adherence to Islam, they automatically belonged to the "People of Paradise" (*ahl al-djanna*), thinking that such warnings could only be meant for the unbelievers, characteristically called the "People of the Fire" (*ahl al-nār*). This certainty of salvation, however, crumbled during the first century of the Hidjra. Various religious movements (Khāridjites, Ḳadarīs and ascetics) contributed to this process, since they, for a wide variety of reasons, thought that eternal punishment was not precluded in the case of sinful Muslims.

These discussions apparently influenced the opinions of the Muʿtazilīs. The Ḳadarī model was decisive here; for, just like the adherents of the Ḳadariyya, the Muʿtazila were of the opinion that individuals determine their actions themselves and are, therefore, to be held responsible for their good and bad deeds. In addition, the Muʿtazila stressed the principle of

Divine justice. The latter is manifest in the fact that God reliably keeps the promises and threats which He has made in the Ḳurʾān. These declarations were formulated in a general way (*ʿāmm*[an]) and should not be relativised by interpreting them in a particular way (*khāṣṣ*[an]) by having them refer to this or that group (such as the unbelievers). The Muʿtazila concluded that God will punish all individuals, including Muslims, who have committed a grave sin by eternal hellfire. Thus there is no way out for the grave sinner, unless he sincerely repents of his crime (*al-tawba wādjiba*; cf. ʿAbd al-Djabbār, *Mughnī*, xiv, 335 ll. 2 ff.). If he does, the Prophet will make intercession (*shafāʿa* [*q.v.*]) on his behalf on the Day of Judgement, at which point the sinner can expect God's forgiveness. For justice is binding on both sides: on the sinner who must repent to find forgiveness (*inna 'l-maghfira bi-sharṭ al-tawba*; cf. *Mutashābih al-Ḳurʾān*, 596 l. 13), and on God who is obliged to accept this repentance (*ḳabūl al-tawba wādjib; Mughnī*, xiv, 337 ll. 6 ff.).

This dogma was internally consistent, but hardly won acceptance outside the school. This was achieved rather by another scenario about the fate of man in the Hereafter, which was developed by the Murdjiʾa and became predominant in many varieties of Islam. According to it, no believer has to expect eternal punishment in Hell. His own belief (and the Prophet's intercession) guarantee for him that he will at most suffer a temporal punishment in Hell and in the end enter Paradise. This optimistic basic attitude was adopted by the two Sunnī schools of theology, the Ashʿariyya and the Māturīdiyya. But it met with approval also among the Shīʿīs, for, even though the Imāmī theologians followed the Muʿtazila in many other respects, they rejected the adoption of the Muʿtazilī principle of *al-waʿd wa 'l-waʿīd*.

Bibliography: G.F. Hourani, *Islamic rationalism. The ethics of ʿAbd al-Jabbār*, Oxford 1971, 121 ff.; D. Gimaret, *La doctrine d'al-Ashʿarī*, Paris 1990, 487 ff.; S. Schmidtke, *The theology of al-ʿAllāma al-Ḥillī*, Berlin 1991, 223 ff.; J. van Ess, *Theologie und Gesellschaft im 2. und 3. Jahrhundert Hidschra*, i-vi, Berlin-New York 1991-6, index s.v. *waʿīd*; P. Sander, *Zwischen Charisma und Ratio. Entwicklungen in der frühen imāmitischen Theologie*, Berlin 1994, 205 ff.; U. Rudolph, *Al-Māturīdī und die sunnitische Theologie in Samarkand*, Leiden 1997, 343 ff.

(U. Rudolph)

WAḌʿ AL-LUGHA (A.), literally "the establishment of language," a phrase which reflects a view of the nature of language that pervades the classical Muslim linguistic sciences (*al-ʿulūm al-lughawiyya*) and the non-linguistic science most concerned with linguistic matters, *ʿilm uṣūl al-fiḳh* (the science of the methodology of jurisprudence). Language (*lugha*), in that view, was essentially a code made up of patterned vocal sounds or vocables (*alfāẓ*) and their meanings (*maʿānī*). This code was understood to have emerged out of a primordial establishment of the vocables *for* their meanings. Hence the application of the term *mawḍūʿ* to vocables and *mawḍūʿ lahu* to meanings. Considered from the semiotic point of view, vocables were considered to be "signs" (*adilla*) and meanings "things signified" (*madlūlāt*).

Classical Muslim learning attributes to a Muʿtazilī thinker, ʿAbbād b. Sulaymān, and to his followers the belief that vocables signified their meanings by virtue of a natural affinity between vocable and meaning. The term *waḍʿ* connotes a rejection of this view. To the extent that the adherents of the concept of *waḍʿ* contended with the view of the school of ʿAbbād, they repeated the debate among the ancient Greeks between the proponents of *thesis* and the proponents of *physis*. These positions are thus also discussed by Islamic philosophers (see e.g. al-Fārābī, *Sharḥ al-ʿIbāra*, ed. W. Kutsch and S. Marrow, Beirut 1960, 50-1). However, ʿAbbād's view soon became extinct among the Muslims as the concept of *waḍʿ* assumed the character of an orthodoxy. The correlations between vocables and their meanings were seen as entirely rooted in the primordial *waḍʿ*. Disagreement lingered as to the identity of the agent or agents of *waḍʿ*—some thought God to be the establisher of the code, others assigned this role to primordial human society—but resolution of the debate was not considered necessary. What was important to all parties was the non-natural *posited* character of the code.

Although the meanings of vocables could change over time, the term *waḍʿ* was reserved for the original, primordial assignment of vocables to meanings. All subsequent change occurred within an already established *lugha* and came under the heading of *ʿurf* or *iṣṭilāḥ*, not *waḍʿ* in the strict sense. *Waḍʿ* produced the basic language or code in relationship to which all subsequent semantic development amounted to extension, accretion or modification, and not true invention. In principle, all original meanings, including meanings which have become rare, remain part of the ongoing code and can assume relevance in the interpretation of texts.

In the *uṣūl al-fiḳh* works, features of the language such as ambiguity, synonymity, and figurative usage were defined in terms of *waḍʿ* and thus seen as built into the basic language. For example, an ambiguous expression was considered to be a vocable that had been subjected to multiple establishments. Eagerness to explain in full detail how the primordial *waḍʿ* gave rise to all the multifarious components of language prompted in the late 8th/14th century the formation of a special "science of *waḍʿ*" (*ʿilm al-waḍʿ*). The seminal work in this science was a short treatise by ʿAḍud al-Dīn al-Īdjī [*q.v.*] entitled *al-Risāla al-waḍʿiyya*, upon which numerous commentaries, supercommentaries and glosses were written. Eventually, manuals summarising the doctrines of this science appeared.

The science of *waḍʿ* broke the *lugha* down into its meaning-laden components, which included not merely words as such but also constituents of words, such as forms, radicals, and suffixes, and syntactic combinations of words, such as construct phrases, attributive phrases and whole sentences. The *waḍʿ* of each component was then classified with reference to a complex taxonomy that consisted of six basic types of *waḍʿ*. The notion of types of *waḍʿ* was first adumbrated in al-Īdjī's treatise, although the full development of the six types was the work of subsequent commentators.

Bibliography: 1. Sources. Yūsuf b. Aḥmad al-Didjwī, *Khulāṣat al-waḍʿ*, Cairo 1333/1915; Abu 'l-Layth al-Samarḳandī, *Sharḥ ʿalā al-Risāla al-waḍʿiyya*, Cairo 1329/1911; ʿAbd al-Khāliḳ al-Shubrāwī, *al-Minḥa al-ilāhiyya fī 'l-ḳawāʿid al-waḍʿiyya*, Cairo n.d.

2. Studies. B.G. Weiss, *ʿIlm al-waḍʿ. An introductory account of a later Muslim philological science*, in *Arabica*, xxxiv (1987), 339-56; idem, *The search for God's Law. Islamic jurisprudence in the writings of Sayf al-Dīn al-Āmidī*, Salt Lake City 1992, 117-50.

(B.G. Weiss)

WADAʿ, Wadʿ (A., collective, sing. *wadaʿa* or *wadʿa*), shells of the gasteropod *Cypraea*, cowrie shells, most commonly *Cypraea moneta* or *Cypraea annulus*, used in India and widely in West Africa as money

down to the early 20th century. They were also
known in Egypt as *kawda* (or *kūda*, see G. Wiet, *Le
traité des famines de Maqrizi*, in *JESHO*, v [1962], 62),
reflecting the word's Hindi, and ultimately Sanskrit,
origin as *kauri*, whence the English "cowrie". Cowries
were also used as money in ancient China and widely
in India. They have been used even more widely as
ornaments, as fertility symbols, and in Arabia as a
protection against the evil eye.

1. Usage in the economies of the Indian
subcontinent and sub-Saharan Africa.

The two varieties of cowrie can be found over a
wide range in the Indian Ocean and the Pacific,
but the principal source of those used as currency
(*C. moneta*) was the Maldive Islands [*q.v.*]. The monetary use of the cowrie in India remains understudied.
While gold and silver were the media of interregional
and international trade, cowries along with copper
coinage played an important role in rent and taxation, and in the development of a textile industry.
Although huge numbers must have been in circulation in the heyday of their usage in the 17th and
18th centuries, the way in which their importation
and circulation were linked to the importation and
circulation of precious metals is poorly understood. It
is clear, however, that the cowrie-rupee ratio was relatively stable down to the late 18th century, when competition from much-increased copper circulation caused
the cowrie to drop sharply against the rupee. Bengal
and Orissa remained strongholds of the cowrie well
into the early 19th century when, according to Perlin,
"rapid inflation—connected with the collapse of the
old manufacturing system and the region's changing
colonial status—drove them from general use".

It is not known how cowries first reached West
Africa, though they may have crossed the Sahara in
small quantities in Carthaginian or Roman times. The
earliest references to the importation of cowries in
Arabic sources are al-Bakrī (writing in 460/1067-8),
who mentions cowries as being imported into Kūg̲h̲a
(*K. al-Masālik wa 'l-mamālik*, ed. de Slane, Algiers 1857,
179), and al-Zuhrī (mid-6th/12th century), who says
that cowries were imported into Zāfun [Diafunu]
(*K. al-D̲j̲aʿrāfiyā*, ed. Hadj-Sadok, in *BÉt. Or.*, xxi [1968],
127), but neither says that cowries were being used
as currency. The first mention of cowries as currency
is provided by al-ʿUmarī, who lists cowries as one of
a number of currency items in use, all of which were
valued by reference to a locally-woven cloth called
dandī (*apud* al-Munad̲j̲d̲j̲id, 23).

He also reports that in Mali (which he calls Takrūr
[*q.v.*]) the currency consisted of cowries and that the
merchants who imported them made big profits on
them. Ibn Baṭṭūṭa (iv, 122) confirms the use of cowries
in central Mali and in Gao on the eastern edge of
the empire, and gives the exchange rate as 1,500
cowries to the *mit̲h̲kāl* of gold. Compared with later
exchange rates, these cowries were very expensive.
This may reflect the long and difficult route they must
have taken from the Maldives to the Mediterranean,
and across the Sahara on camel back. In the Maldives,
where Ibn Baṭṭūṭa had seen them at source, 400,000
could be purchased for one *mit̲h̲kāl*, and on occasion
up to one million. In *ca.* 1510 Leo Africanus reported
an even higher exchange rate at Timbuktu: 400 to
the *mit̲h̲kāl*, but this may either be a simple error or
reflect a famine rate; in a known period of famine,
1617-19, the exchange rate was 500 to the *mit̲h̲kāl*.
Otherwise, in the Middle Niger area the rate from
the 16th to the 19th century remained relatively stable at about 3,000 cowries to the *mit̲h̲kāl*. Even in

1853 the German traveller Heinrich Barth reported
a rate of 3-4,000 to the *mit̲h̲kāl* in Timbuktu.

To the east of this region in Hausaland, cowries
may have been in use as early as the 16th century.
Anania reports the use of "small very white sea shells"
as money in Katsina, and says they are "as used by
all these blacks" (*L'universale fabrica del mondo*, ³Venice
1582, tr. in D. Lange and S. Berthoud, in *Cahiers
d'histoire mondiale*, xiv [1972], 335). Cowries were to
become central to the trading activities of the Hausa
states where gold, which was plentiful in the 16th
century, became progressively scarcer and was superseded by the Maria Theresa silver thaler [see SIKKA. 3]
by the 19th century. Cowries suffered from galloping
inflation in the late 19th century in Hausaland and
elsewhere in West Africa, and in the early years of
the 20th century were gradually edged out by colonial currencies in silver and copper. Although cowries
had been used in Kanem [*q.v.*] in the 14th century,
they seem not to have been used in its successor state
Bornu [*q.v.*] until very late on. Under S̲h̲ayk̲h̲ ʿUmar
b. Muḥammad al-Amīn al-Kānimī, cowries were introduced for petty transactions in 1848-9, while larger
transactions were carried out with the Maria Theresa
thaler. East of Lake Chad, cowries were not used, nor
were they acceptable north of Timbuktu or Agades.

Until the 19th century, the Sahelian regions immediately to the south of the Sahara were supplied from
North Africa. One of the earliest routes was overland from Bengal to the Mediterranean and thence
through Egypt, while some evidently went through
Venice and across to North African ports. The evidence,
however, is fragmentary, and the mechanics of the
trade quite unknown. Following the Portuguese discovery of a sea route to Asia via the Cape of Good Hope
in 1499, European ships of various nations began
shipping cowries back to Europe, often as ballast, and
re-exporting them to African ports. Pétis de la Croix
(1697) notes cowries being imported from France to
Tripoli for transportation southwards, and evidence
from the late 18th century points to Mogador (al-
Ṣawīra [*q.v.*]) in Morocco as a point of importation
of cowries from Europe for the trans-Saharan trade.
European merchants were also importing cowries to
ports on the West African coast such as Accra, Whydah
and Lagos, and to ports in the Bights of Benin and
Biafra. In these coastal regions cowries were used for
the purchase of slaves, and constituted the basic trans-
actional currency. By the 1830s cowries imported via
Europe to the coast were being traded up the river
Niger and supplying some of the Hausa states.

As a currency, cowries had both advantages and disadvantages. They are handsome objects, extremely hard
wearing and impossible to counterfeit. Being brought
into their area of use from far away, there was little
danger of an over-supply leading to inflation, though
this did happen on the West African coast from the
late 1850s when importation of *C. annulus* from Zanzibar flooded the market. On the other hand, cowries
were heavy to transport and tedious to count. The
latter problem was partially solved by the fabrication
of units containing multiples of cowries. On the West
African coast 40 cowries made one "string", while 5
strings made one "bunch" and 50 bunches made one
"head". In Hausaland, cowries were counted in fives,
and a rush sack or "mat" containing 20,000 cowries
was the standard unit, weighing about 50 pounds (or
more if there was a preponderance of larger *annulus*
shells), which was one man's head load. In the
Bambara (or Bamana) area of the upper Niger, there
was a peculiar system of counting cowries in which

the unit was ten, but the hundred of cowries was only 80 actual cowries, a thousand was ten "hundreds", ten thousand was ten lots of a "thousand" and 100,000 was only eight lots of "ten thousand"; thus 100,000 was in fact only 64,000 shells, while 10,000 was only 8,000 shells, 1,000 was actually 800 and 100 was only 80. It has been suggested that this way of reckoning was aimed at providing the petty trader with a discount, but it may also represent the remnants of an older indigenous counting system.

Bibliography: (1). India. Sushil Chandra De, *Cowery currency in India*, in *Orissa Hist. J.*, i/1 (1952), 1-10, i/2 (1952), 10-21; J. Heiman, *Small change and ballast: cowrie trade and usage as an example of Indian Ocean economic history*, in *South Asia*, n.s. iii (1980), 48-69; F. Perlin, *Money-use in late pre-colonial India and the international trade in currency media*, in J.F. Richards (ed.), *The imperial monetary system of Mughal India*, Delhi 1987, 232 ff.

(2). Africa. (a) Sources. J.G. Jackson, *An Account of Timbuctoo and Housa . . . by El Hadge Abd Salam Shabeeny*, London 1820; E. Daumas, *Le grand désert. Itinéraire d'une caravane du Sahara au pays des nègres, royaume de Haoussa*, 4th ed. Paris 1860; Leo Africanus, *Description de l'Afrique*, tr. A. Epaulard, 2 vols., Paris 1956; Ṣalāḥ al-Dīn al-Munadjdjid, *Mālī ʿind al-Djughrāfiyyīn al-muslimīn*, i, Beirut 1963; G. Nachtigal, *Sahara and Sudan*, tr. A.G.B. Fisher and H.J. Fisher, 4 vols., London 1971-87; H. Barth, *Travels and discoveries in Northern and Central Africa . . . in the years 1849-1855*, repr. London 1965; R. Mauny, *Tableau géographique de l'ouest africain au moyen âge*, Dakar 1961. (b) Studies. A.M.H. Kirk-Greene, *The major currencies of Nigerian history*, in *J. Hist. Soc. Nigeria*, ii/1 (Dec. 1960), 132-50; M. Hiskett, *Materials relating to the cowry currency of the Western Sudan*, in *BSOAS*, xxix (1966), 122-42, 339-66; S.O. Johansson, *Nigerian currencies: manillas, cowries and others*, 2nd ed. Nörrkoping 1967; V. Magalhães-Godinho, *L'économie de l'empire portugais aux XVe et XVIe siècles*, Paris 1969; Marion Johnson, *The cowrie currencies of West Africa*, in *J. African Hist.*, xi (1970), 17-49, 331-53; J. Hogendorn and M. Johnson, *The shell money of the slave trade*, Cambridge 1986; D. Lange, *Un document de la fin du XVIIe siècle sur le commerce transsaharien*, in *2000 ans d'histoire africaine. Le sol, la parole, l'écrit*, Paris 1981, 673-84; A. Félix Iroko, *Les cauris en Afrique occidentale du Xe au XXe siècle*, doctoral diss., Univ. of Paris-Sorbonne 1987; idem, *Les marchards vénitiens et le commerce des cauris entre le XIIIe et le XVe siècle*, in *Africa* [Rome], xvv/3 (1990), 480-4; J.O. Hunwick, *Islamic financial institutions: theoretical structures and aspects of their application in sub-Saharan Africa*, in E. Stiansen and Jane Guyer (eds.), *Currencies, credit and culture: African financial institutions in historical perspective*, Uppsala 1998 (Research report of the Nordiska Afrikainstitutet). (J.O. Hunwick)

2. Definition in the Arabic sources.

The ensemble of information on shells called *wadʿa* in *LA*, vi, 4795, and *TA*, v, 533-4, allows us to identify with certainty that cowries or porcelain-shells are here envisaged; whether large or small, they come from the sea and are thrown up by it and left (hence their name, from the verb *wadaʿa* "to leave, let") on the beaches, and not fished up. They have a split like a date stone and are hollow, with a kind of fleshy worm inside or, as may also be found, a tiny organism like a moth (*al-ḥalama*), a parasite. They are remarkable for their whiteness and hardness like a stone, but they can, however, be pierced. Their brilliance is vaunted by poets. The link with the Indian subcontinent is noted by Ibn al-Bayṭār, ed. L. Leclerc, 188-9, tr. 404-5 no. 2272, repeated by the Rasūlid al-Malik al-Muẓaffar Yūsuf, *al-Muʿtamad fi 'l-adwiya al-mufrada*, Beirut 1370/1951, 544, being called "the bracelet of Sind" (*siwār al-Sind*). The lexica also show that the *wadʿa* could also be called *kharaz*. In a famous verse of Imruʾ al-Ḳays, cited in *LA*, i, 617, we have *ka-anna ʿuyūn al-waḥsh ḥawl khibāʾinā * wa-arḥulinā al-djazʿ alladhī lam yuthakkab*, with *djazʿ* defined as *kharaz yamānī*. The term appears in the lexicon of the Constantinois region of former French Algeria in fairly recent times, as "a variegated sea shell, shaped like a grain of coffee with a split in the middle (porcelain of the sea)" (M.A. Cherbonneau, *Définition lexicographique de plusieurs mots usités dans le langage de l'Afrique septentrionale*, in *JA*, xiii (Jan. 1859), 63-70, at 67: *w.d.ʿ, oudé*).

The term *wadʿa* can nevertheless be used in Arabic for all sorts of other shells, cf. E. Doutté, *Magie et religion dans l'Afrique du Nord*, Paris 1903, 82); the problems raised by a systematic translation of *wadʿa* by "cowrie" were discussed by Th. Monod, using evidence from al-Bakrī and Ibn Baṭṭūṭa, in his *Sur quelques coquilles marines du Sahara et du Soudan*, in *La vie dans la région désertique Nord-tropicale de l'Ancien monde*, vi (1938), 147-78, at 172-3, noting the term's usage for shells in general.

3. Usage for divination in the Arab world.

Divination by cowrie shells is not apparently treated in *ḥadīth*; Ibn Ḥanbal mentions it rather as a protective amulet (*ḥirz*), cf. Wensinck, *Concordances*, vii, 168. The lexica, such as *LA* and *TA*, say, s.v., that it protects from the evil eye. Judy F. Pugh mentions that amongst the Muslim artisans of Benares, divination by means of cowrie shells thrown on to the ground traditionally represents an orthodox form of divination (*Divination and ideology in the Banaras Muslim community*, in K.P. Ewing (ed.), *Sharīʿat and ambiguity in South Asian Islam*, Berkeley, etc. 1988, 295). Nevertheless, it is currently condemned in North Yemen, including by students of *ḥadīth*, as a kind of *tandjīm* or *faʾl* or as a practice of the *ʿarrāf*.

It is difficult to ascertain how old such practices are. The cowrie retains its protective function, as a *ḥirz*, till today, cf. Lane, *Manners and customs*, ch. XI, and is used on animals to ward off the evil eye, cf. A. Fodor, *Amulets from the Islamic world*, in *Catalogue of the exhibition held in Budapest in 1988*, in *The Arabist (Budapest)*, ii (1990), no. 5, 214-15, 248, 296-8, 341. Today, cowries are either worn round the neck or carried in a pocket as at Ṣanʿāʾ. The cowrie also has medical uses, essentially as a dessicating or detersive agent (Ibn al-Bayṭār, *loc. cit.*; al-Malik al-Muẓaffar Yūsuf, *loc. cit.*). There are descriptions of divination by cowrie shells in travel literature, but these accounts are recent. Also, the relevant knowledge is transmitted orally, and there are no known treatises on it; could this be from the poor image, in orthodox eyes, of the practice, since this form of divination is strongly perceived as charlatanry (*shaʿwadha*)? It has been, and still is, often connected with such groups as the Gypsies and the Ṣulayb or Ṣlēb (for the latter, see ṣulaib, ṣulayb, in *EI*[1] and *EI*[2] respectively, and B. Vernier, *Quédar, carnets d'un méhariste syrien*, Paris 1938, 244). It is practised by wandering or nomadic persons, who follow round their clientèle, showing the close link between this form of divination and monetary gain. Probably originating far from the towns, it has been carried thither (Gypsies in the Ghūṭa of Damascus; in Yemen, Bedouin from the region of Maʾrib practising in Ṣanʿāʾ or at Ridāʿ near Dhamār). The essentially feminine nature of its practitioners may have contributed to its controversial image. The exiguous material is complemented below by material gained by the author's personal observation in Yemen in 1999, at Ṣanʿāʾ and Ridāʿ.

In general, the "instruments" of divination are a jumble of objects, in which shells (cowries are not always precisely noted here) may be dominant—porcelains of the genus *Cypraea annulus*; murex; shells from the *Olividiae* family, probably of the genus *Oliva*—or may not be dominant quantitatively (Emily Said-Ruete, *Mémoires d'une princesse arabe*, Paris 1891, 328; Vernier, *op. cit.*, 103-4; they may often be mixed with inanimate objects or objects formed from organic matter, such as whitened bones or fragments of bone, pieces of money, stones or a rosary, *maṣbaḥa*). One wonders, accordingly, what each element represents. On the other hand, the contents of the basket containing all these objects may be of a homogeneous nature, with a limited number of shells. They are not thrown or allowed to fall on the earth, but may be used in a basket, which keeps them from contact with the dust and defines the area used; and the way in which an object falls is taken into account in the interpretation. According to the author's observations in Yemen, the person seeking guidance chooses a shell and puts it on the pile held in the diviner's hands, and the latter either lets it fall directly or throws it down. The operation of throwing down is repeated from three to five times until the solution to the problem emerges. It is difficult to classify definitively the various configurations that may emerge, given the polysemy of the various elements involved, their symbolic value, and the number of shells involved and their positions, and this large number of variables makes any clear decision almost impossible to attain. Hence the diviner resorts to external factors, such as discovering the reason for the enquirer's resort to this form of divination, or whether the enquirer is a stranger (hence involved in travelling) or whether a love affair is involved (probably to be connected with a daughter of the enquirer's paternal or maternal uncles, the favoured choices for marriage), etc. The actual juxtaposition of the objects thrown may also have significance.

In Yemen, these consultations are not preceded by any perceptible Ḳurʾānic recitation (*tilāwa*). It seems that the problems of the enquirer are evaluated through psychological means and through observation. The presence of a rosary, manipulated in the first place with the shells, may signify the presence of God over the proceedings, but there also exist practitioners who claim to be guided by the *d̲j̲inn*. In general, we lack sufficient material to disengage any fixed lines of procedure, but it seems that this form of divination is inspired by a varied technique of psychology and of manipulation of the divinatory objects, as is clearly apparent in Black Africa, as shown by Amar Samb for Dakar (*Les systèmes de divination en Afrique noir, l'exemple du Sénégal*, in *Notes africaines*, no. 184 (Oct. 1984), 73-4).

4. Usage for divination in Sub-Saharan Africa.

Throwing down cowry shells is not considered historically as being Islamic in origin (Ch. Monteil, *La divination chez les Noirs de l'Afrique occidentale française*, in *Bull. du Comité d'études historiques et scientifiques de l'AOF*, xiv/1-2 (Jan.-June 1931), 53; Samb, *op. cit.*, 73). It nevertheless exists in Black Africa, even though it is at the same time considered as being connected with superstition, paganism or even with what is accursed. Although those who throw down cowries for divinatory purposes are most often Muslims, the interpretation is done with reference to a polytheistic religious context or one of a monotheism connected with the earth (animism). How far it has a place within Islam and the animist religions is hard to define; moreover, its practitioners usually make reference to a popular Islam whose contours are hard to fix precisely.

Divination here rests basically on the principle that it is God who is speaking through the cowries, and these last are inseparably His mouthpiece and His ear. Nevertheless, anthropomorphisation of the shells, or their symbolic value, do not permit one to adopt unreservedly the symbolism of the female vulva that is ordinarily associated with them (see in general here, E.G. Gobert, *Le pudendum magique et la problème des cauris*, in *Rev. Afr.*, xcv [1951], 5-62); furthermore, the colour white, that of God in dreams, may also be the symbolic element visualised.

Bibliography (in addition to references given in the article): For section 2: M. Piamenta, *Dictionary of post-classical Yemeni Arabic*, Leiden 1991, part 2, 520, s.vv. *wadʿ*, *tiwiddāʿ*, *muwaddaʿ*.

For sections 3 and 4: M.D.W. Jeffreys, *Cowry, vulva, eye*, in *Man*, xlii (Sept.-Oct. 1942), 71, 120; idem, *Cowry and vulva again*, in *ibid.*, xliii (Nov.-Dec. 1943), 121, 144; A. Hauenstein, *Quelques formes de divination parmi les Wobé et les Guéré de Côte d'Ivoire*, in *Anthropos*, lxxi (1976), 473-507; W. Bascom, *Sixteen cowries. Yoruba divination from Africa to the New World*, Bloomington and London 1980; Silvie Fainzang, *"L'intérieur des choses." Maladie, divination et reproduction sociale chez les Bisa du Burkina*, Paris 1986, 204; Hauenstein, *Mélanges ethnologiques*, in *Zeitschr. für Ethnologie*, cxii/1 (1987), 105-24; Marie Boutroy and Maguy Vautier, *Le chant des cauris*, Paris 1999, 79. One should note the work of M.L. Rodriguez de Areia, *Les symboles divinatoires. Analyse socio-culturelle d'une technique de divination des Cokwe de l'Angola* (Ngombo ya cisuka), Coimbra 1985, for the interest of its approach. Thanks are extended to André Julliard, CNRS, for information on Black Africa.

(Anne Regourd)

WADĀĪ (various renderings of this non-Arabic name, including, in al-Tūnisī, the above one and Waddāī and al-Wāday), conventionally Wadai in English, Ouadai in French, an upland region lying to the west of the Sudanese province of southern Dār Fūr [*q.v.*], now falling mainly within the Republic of Chad [see Čad, in Suppl.] but with its eastern fringes in the Sudan Republic.

1. History.

Wadai was one of several Islamic African kingdoms to arise at the dawn of the modern era in the comparatively fertile highlands west of the Nile valley and east of Lake Chad. This zone was inhabited by a mosaic of ethnic groups; many spoke Nilo-Saharan languages, and among these was Boro Mabang, the tongue that defined the ethnic core of Wadai. Islam first entered this polyethnic highland world at the close of the Middle Ages as one of the powerful, prestigous and exotic things accessible to a community only through a powerful chieftain capable of opening roads abroad to diplomacy and trade. Of these chieftains there were many, fierce rivals of each other, one of whom would eventually emerge victorious as the founding monarch of each realm. The earliest legendary history of Wadai is inextricably linked to that of its eastern neighbor, Dār Fūr. When during the 16th century the first Dād̲j̲ū-speaking dynasty of Dār Fūr was overthrown, Wadai welcomed refugees from the east and as suzerains sponsored the formation of a small subordinate Dādjū realm of Dār Sila. By the close of the century, however, the same Tundjur conquerors who had ousted the Dādjū had also annexed Wadai as a tributary dependency of their realm, whose capitals at Uri and ʿAyn Farah in northern Dār Fūr attracted visitors from both the Nile and the Mediterranean. In the middle of the 17th century, Tundjur rule everywhere gave way to new dynasties of kings who claimed Arab ancestry and enjoyed the support of Arabic-speaking pastoralists. In Wadai a leader named ʿAbd al-Karīm repudiated ties with Dār Fūr and founded the historical ruling house of his kingdom. In Dār Fūr, too, the Tundjur were overthrown, but the new Kayra monarchs were reluctant to cede authority over Wadai. There followed more than a century of inconclusive but occasionally bitter struggle between the two great formerly Tundjur realms. Finally, at the close of the 18th century, a *détente* was achieved that allowed each rival an imperial age; henceforth Dār Fūr would expand eastwards toward the Nile, while Wadai struck westward to annex a huge empire that soon absorbed the kingdom of Bagirmi [*q.v.*] and touched the shores of Lake Chad.

ʿAbd al-Karīm and his successors were absolute rulers. While viewed as defenders and propagators of Islam, they also led the nation's secret rainmaking rituals on a sacred mountain near the capital of Wara. If not actually "adored as pharaohs", as disparaging Islamic tradition said of their predecessors the Tundjur kings, they were nevertheless surrounded by the full panoply of regalia and restraints that characterise sacral kingship in Africa. The king was served by a complicated array of titled officials, who typically combined one or more duties at court with a military or territorial command elsewhere in the kingdom; since high officials were not allowed to leave the presence of their royal master, however, their functions in the kingdom at large were carried out by trusted agents. Vital to the system was a large corps of confidential messengers who conveyed a steady flow of information or commands between capital and countryside. Each courtier or agent served only at his master's pleasure; competition for official favour was intense and career permanence uncertain. While most of the highest officials were Boro Mabang speakers chosen from the kingdom's dominant ethnic group, a lord might also choose for positions of trust a slave, a eunuch, a capable individual from a lesser ethnic community, or even a foreigner; the cadre of courtiers was therefore fairly cosmopolitan. As Wadai expanded during the 19th century there arose a new category of imperial proconsuls entitled *ʿaḳīds*, who differed from older royal courtiers not only in the great diversity of their ethnic origins but also in that they were allowed to absent themselves for extended periods from the presence of the king. Youths were gathered at the capital as a corps of pages to receive training in statecraft for future government service. Imperial officialdom derived part of its coherence from an intricate network of carefully-arranged marriages, the design of which was entrusted to senior female members of the royal family. Since the women assigned to these liaisons nursed the next generation of leadership, the women's quarters of the palace complex often seethed with dynastic intrigue.

The heartland of Wadai was divided into four provinces corresponding to the cardinal points of the compass; these provinces, in turn, were subdivided for administrative purposes according to the homelands of the diverse ethnic communities who inhabited them. Superimposed upon this tidy arrangement of provinces and districts was an extensive network of royal estates directly responsible to the seneschal of the king's demesne; similar, though smaller, arrays of holdings were assigned to the Queen Mother, and perhaps other very important individuals. Most forms of wealth originated from the land, and an elaborate system of taxation in kind gathered the government's portion of everything produced. Some tax goods were conveyed to Wāra to support the court community, while others were stored in royal magazines near their points of origin to feed an army on campaign or relieve a hungry populace in time of famine.

Recognising the importance of local trade among the subjects, the government allowed the payment of taxes in diverse forms by setting the rates at which, for example, a tax levied in grain might also be paid in cattle, salt or iron ingots; thus the king in effect regulated the market value of all commodities. The king supported a bodyguard from his own estates, and each fiefholding official was required to do likewise; collectively, these forces comprised the professional army of Wadai. On campaign they would be joined by a legion of lightly-armed volunteers whose task it was to dispatch enemy wounded or rescue their own, and above all to loot and pillage for the king in return for a share of the booty. Wars were undertaken for diverse reasons of state, but particularly numerous were the raids launched southward to seize slaves from among the neighbouring small-scale communities who were not Muslims and had no kings, people derogatively dubbed "Kirdi".

Wadai reached its apogee under Sultan Muḥammad S̲h̲arīf (1834-58), who opened relations with the Sanūsiyya [*q.v.*] brotherhood. Mediterranean commercial ties increased dramatically under his sons ʿAlī (1858-74) and then Yūsuf (1874-98), who spent his later years adroitly deflecting the acquisitive ambitions of the Sudanese Mahdists [see AL-MAHDIYYA], based in Dār Fūr. After 1898 the kingdom lapsed into a long struggle for the throne among rival princes backed by diverse court factions, Dār Fūr, the Sanūsiyya, and by the French, who assumed control in the capital in 1909.

Bibliography: Muḥammad b. ʿUmar al-Tūnisī, Fr. tr. N. Perron, *Voyage au Ouadây, par le Cheikh Mohammed Ebn Omar el-Tounsy*, Paris 1851; G. Nachtigal, *Sahârâ und Sûdân*, Eng. tr. A.G.B. Fisher and H.J. Fisher, iv, *Wadai and Dar Fur*, London 1971-87; H. Carbou, *La région du Tchad et du Ouadai*, 2 vols. Paris 1912; M.-J. Tubiana *et alii*, *Abd el-Karim, propagateur de l'Islam et fondateur du royaume du Ouaddai*, Paris 1973; R.S. O'Fahey and J.I. Spaulding, *Kingdoms of the Sudan*, London 1974; L. Kapteijns and J. Spaulding, *After the millennium. Diplomatic correspondence from Wadai and Dar Fur on the eve of colonial conquest, 1885-1916*, East Lansing, Mich. 1988.

(J.L. SPAULDING)

2. Languages.

Great linguistic diversity characterises the Wadāī region in eastern Chad [see ČAD, in Suppl.]. The official languages of the Republic of Chad are Standard Arabic and French. Maba is reported to be spoken by some of its neighbours as a second language, although the principal *lingua franca* of the region is Chadian Arabic [see S̲H̲UWA. 2 and SŪDĀN, Bilād al-. 3].

Like Maba itself, most of the other languages of eastern Chad have been classified as Nilo-Saharan (NS), which is a phylum of diverse languages stretching from Egypt in the northeast [see NŪBA] to Tanzania in the southeast (the Maasai language) and to Mali in the west (Songhay [*q.v.*], although the NS classification of Songhay has recently been challenged).

The Maba language is associated with the historical kingdom of Wadāī, where it was spoken at the royal court (see 1. above). Maba flourishes in the vicinity of the town of Abéché in eastern Chad. It has also been attested in the Republic of the Sudan (see Doornbos [1983] and Bell [1998]).

The term "Maba" is primarily the self-name of an ethnic group (see 1. above). Wadāī seems originally to have been a term that was used by the western and northern neighbours of the Maba such as the Arabs, the Bagirmi, the Hausa, the Kanuri and the Daza (see Edgar [1989]). Neighbours to the east of Wadāī, such as the Masalit, often use the term "Bargū" (or "Borgū") to refer to the Maba people. The Maba language has also been designated by this term (e.g. in the Republic of the Sudan, see Bell [1998]).

Although the Maba language is occasionally cited as "Ouaddaïen", emphasising the close relationship between the terms Maba and Wadāī, the Maba people normally use their own expression which may be glossed as "the language of the Maba". Edgar transcribed this expression as /bùrá mábàŋ/ with marking for tone, high /á/ and low /à/. The phrase may be analysed as follows: /bùrá/ "the language" + /mábà/ "the Maba" + /ŋ/ "of" ("the language of the Maba"). The phrase has also been transcribed as follows: /bora mábaŋ/ by Doornbos (1983), /boro mabaŋ/ by Spaulding (see 1. above), and /burā mabā/ (transliterated from the Arabic characters of Abū Naẓīfa [1994]).

The genitival element "of" is represented above by a velar nasal consonant /ŋ/ (= /n͟g/). This sound occurs frequently in Maba, e.g. as the second consonant in the word for "three": /koŋāl/. It appears from Perron's 1851 publication that al-Tūnisī represented /ŋ/ in Maba words by a special Arabic-based letter *kāf* with three dots above it, a symbol that might be referred to as a "*ŋāf*".

A full adaptation of Arabic alphabetic characters to the phonology of Maba has recently been published by Abū Naẓīfa (1994). Inspired by the *Ad͟jamī* or *ʿAd͟jamī* script of Hausa [*q.v.*], he proposed an Arabic-based system with 11 new consonantal characters. His solution to the problem of /ŋ/ was a single dot just under the upper stroke of the Arabic consonant *kāf*. He proposed an interesting set of characters for the pre-nasalised stops of Maba (/mb/, /nd/, /ng/ and /nd͟j/) by placing a dot under the *mīm*, the *dāl*, the *g͟hayn* and the *d͟jīm* respectively. In the case of *d͟jīm*, this resulted in two dots horizontally side-by-side. This system is inventive rather than consistent with attempts elsewhere to achieve a standardised set of symbols in *ʿAd͟jamī* scripts for non-Arabic languages, e.g. at the Institut d'Études et de Recherches pour l'Arabisation in Rabat or at the Khartoum International Institute for Arabic Language.

Maba is closely related to several other languages of Wadāī, and together they are known as the Maban group. Most speakers of the Maba, Marfa, Karanga and Kibet languages live in eastern Chad, but about half of the speakers of the southerly Aiki or Runga language extend across the border of Wadāī into the Central African Republic, probably reflecting their historical interest in trade with the south. The majority of the speakers of the closely related Masalit language are to be found in the Republic of the Sudan.

The Wadāī region also has a number of NS languages which are more distantly related to Maba. A Dad͟ju language geographically separates the Maban languages of northern Wadāī from Maban languages such as Kibet and Aiki in southern Wadāī. Dad͟ju speakers are also present in and around the town of Abéché. Contiguous with Dad͟ju and Aiki on the Sudanese border are the speakers of Sinyar and Fongoro. A close relative of these two languages, the Bagirmi language of western Chad, was associated with the historical kingdom of Bagirmi [*q.v.*], which was defeated by the kingdom of Wadāī in the early 19th century. Immediately to the northeast of Wadāī is the heartland of the Tama group of languages, including Sungor, Mararit and Tama. Just to the north of Wadāī are speakers of Amdang, which is related to Fūr, a language associated with the historical sultanate of Dār Fūr in the Sudan. Amdang is also known as Mimi and this is a source of considerable confusion, since linguistic informants have identified certain other languages as "Mimi", one of these being a Maban group language (for a summary of the problem, see Doornbos [1983]). Saharan languages of northern and western Chad are also attested in Wadāī. These include Zaghawa, Daza [see TUBU. 2], Kanembu and Kanuri [*q.v.*] to the north and west of Wadāī.

In addition to the NS languages enumerated above, several languages of the Hamito-Semitic or Afro-Asiatic (AA) phylum are found in this region. Apart from Arabic, the AA phylum is represented in southwestern Wadāī by some of the so-called Chado-Hamitic languages, especially Kajakse, but also Birgit and Mubi.

AA is distinguished from NS by a number of typological features, most prominent of which is a particular system of grammatical gender (masc./fem.), as in Arabic. According to Roth (1979), when the Maba speak Chadian Arabic, the system of agreement for grammatical gender often tends to disappear, since their own NS language does not possess this feature.

When al-Tūnisī sojourned in Wadāī early in the 19th century, he noted that it was not necessary for him to learn to speak "Ouadayen", since Arabic was so widely used. He noted that the expression for "interpreter" was *k͟has͟hm al-kalām* "the mouth of speech". He also reported that instruction in Islamic law and religion was provided by an Arab scholar in Wāra, the capital of Wadāī at that time. While some of the Arabic loan-words in his published Maba vocabulary could be suspected to have resulted from the bias of an Arab investigator, a number of Arabic loan-words must already have been in use, e.g. the Arabic term *malik* used in the citation below instead of a Maba term such as *kolik* "king".

/Mélik manik Kalak ni*na* tounyou-ny/ (/*n*/=/ŋ/)
Roi de nous Dieu vie donne-lui

The transliteration and literal translation come from Perron (1851). The sense of the sentence is thus: "God, give life to our King!" Today, when Chadian Arabic is the principal *lingua franca* of Wadāī, it is not surprising to observe that Arabic has had a major impact on Maba and that a high proportion of the Maba vocabulary consists of Arabic loan-words.

The Sahelian belt embracing Wadāī is a celebrated route for pilgrims travelling between West Africa and Mecca, sometimes over a period of many years. Pilgrims and traders bring with them a great number of different languages. Among these are languages such as Hausa (AA), which is widely used as a *lingua franca*, and also Fulfulde which represents Niger-Kordofanian (NK), a third great phylum of African languages characterised by eleborate systems of noun classes and geographically spread from Senegal to South Africa.

An on-going summary of rough data on the languages of Wadāī and estimates of numbers of speakers may be extracted from the *Ethnologue: Chad* on the internet [http://www.sil.org/Ethnologue/countries/Chad.html] by focusing on the following relevant languages (spelled and classified as presented there): AA: Arabic, Chadian Spoken; Arabic, Standard; Kajakse, Mubi, Birgit. NK: Fulfulde, NS—*Maban group*: Karanga, Mimi, Kendeje, Surbakhal, Kibet, Runga, Maba, Marfa, Masalit, Massalat. NS—*other groups: Tama-Sungor*: Sungor, Tama, Mararit; *Dadju*: Dadju [Saaronge], Dadju [Dar Sila]; *Bongo-Bagirmi*: Sinyar, Fongoro [in the *Ethnologue: Sudan*]; *Fur*: Fur, Amdang [Mimi]; *Saharan*: Teda, Daza, Kanembu, Kanuri, Bideyat, Zaghawa.

Bibliography: Muḥammad b. ʿUmar al-Tūnisī, *Voyage au Soudan Oriental, le Ouday*, tr. and ed. N. Perron and E.-F. Jomard, Paris 1851; A.N. Tucker and M.A. Bryan, *Linguistic analyses*, London 1966; H. Jungraithmayr, *How many Mimi languages are there?*, in *Africana Marburgensia*, iv/2 (1971), 62-70; J. Cabot (ed.), *Atlas pratique du Tchad*, Paris 1972; A. Roth, *Esquisse grammaticale du parler arabe d'Abbéché, Tchad*, Paris 1979; P. Doornbos and M.L. Bender, *Languages of Wadai-Darfur*, in M.L. Bender (ed.), *Nilo-Saharan language studies*, East Lansing, Mich. 1983, 42-79; P. Nougayrol, *Introduction à la langue des Aiki*, Paris 1989; J.T. Edgar, *A Masalit grammar with notes on other languages of Darfur and Wadai*, Berlin 1989; idem, *Maba-group lexicon*, Berlin 1991; idem, *First steps toward proto-Maba*, in *African languages and cultures*, iv/2 (1991), 113-33; ʿAbd Allāh Muḥammad Ādam Abū Naẓīfa, *al-Aṣwāt wa-rumūzuhā fī Burā Mabā, lughat (al-Wadāī–al-Barḳū)*, Beirut 1994; H. Barth, *Burā Mabā, lughat (al-Wadāī–al-Barḳū)*, ed. Abū Naẓīfa, tr. Muḥammad ʿAbd al-Dīn ʿUthmān, Beirut 1994 (the Arabic tr. was based on relevant portions of the English version of Barth's *Sammlung und Bearbeitung central-afrikanischer Vokabularien/Collection of vocabularies of central-African languages*, 2nd ed. by A.H.M. Kirk-Greene, London 1971; Barth's original German edition appeared in Gotha 1862-6 in 3 vols.); B. Grimes (ed.), *Ethnologue* [Chad], 13th ed., Dallas 1996; H. Bell, *The Nuba Mountains. Who spoke what in 1976?*, Bergen 1998, localities 15 and 18 [http://www.hf.uib.no/smi/sa/tan/nuba.html].

(H. Bell)

al-**WAḌḌĀḤ** [see DJADHĪMA AL-ABRASH].

WAḌḌĀḤ al-YAMAN, sobriquet ("person of outstanding handsomeness amongst the Yemenis") of a minor Umayyad poet of the Ḥidjāzī school, ʿAbd al-Raḥmān b. Ismāʿīl b. Kulāl al-Khawlānī, d. *ca.* 90/707.

Two of the earliest sources on him, Muḥammad b. Ḥabīb's *K. Asmāʾ al-mughtālīn*, 273, and al-Balādhurī's *Ansāb al-ashrāf*, fol. 656a, state that one of his ancestors stemmed from the *Abnāʾ al-Furs*, the Persian soldiers and officials sent out to Yemen to aid Sayf b. Dhī Yazan against the Abyssinians, but there are contradictory traditions on his Yemeni ancestry which are late and clearly of a romantic nature.

The only episodes of his life mentioned in the sources concern his amorous adventures. One links him tragically with a lady of the *Abnāʾ* also, Rawḍa bt. ʿAmr. The other is much more elaborated and seems to have been at the origin of his assassination, sc. his liaison with Umm al-Banīn bt. ʿAbd al-ʿAzīz b. Marwān, wife of the Umayyad caliph al-Walīd I b. ʿAbd al-Malik. Several divergent traditions exist on this, but these do not necessarily lead to Ṭāhā Ḥusayn's scepticism about the poet's very existence. One tradition describes how Waḍḍāḥ was discovered in Umm al-Banīn's rooms concealed in a chest, and was forthwith buried alive in it by her husband and master's slaves; this was transmitted by ʿĪsā b. Daʾb, a specialist in romantic tales, as the *K. Waḍḍāḥ wa-Umm al-Banīn*, according to the *Fihrist*, ed. Cairo n.d., 426, and included in the *Miʾat layla wa-layla*, with Waḍḍāḥ as a great martyr for love (tr. M. Gaudefroy-Demombynes, Paris 1982, 69-75). The most credible tradition (from al-Ḥirmāzī and Ibn Zabāla, in *Ansāb, loc. cit.*) is more prosaic and as such does not seems to have aroused the interests of the anthologists so much: that Waḍḍāḥ eulogised the caliph's wife against his express orders on the eve of her making the Pilgrimage and became linked with her on her return to Damascus, so that al-Walīd, on hearing about this, ordered Waḍḍāḥ's killing.

These traditions seem to have relegated the poet himself and his work to the background of attention. Transmitters and anthologists, unlike the musicians and singers, seem not to have appreciated his talent as a pioneer in the shaping of the tradition of courtly love poetry into its definitive form, with its two essential themes of the poet's attitude to the phenomenon of love and the encounter of lovers. In his poems on the first theme, the poet appears as a *fatā*, vowed to love and pleasure, and the attainment of the beloved appears as an inevitable consequence of the poet's persistence; in a poem on the second theme, we have a dialogue between the two lovers.

Bibliography: Muḥammad b. Ḥabīb, *K. Asmāʾ al-mughtālīn fi ʾl-Djāhiliyya wa ʾl-Islām*, in *Nawādir al-makhṭūṭāt*, ii, Cairo 1395/1975, 273; Balādhurī, *Ansāb al-ashrāf*, ms. Reisülküttâp Aşir Efendi, nos. 597-8, ii, fols. 656a-b; al-Zubayr b. Bakkār, *al-Akhbār al-muwaffakiyyāt*, Baghdād 1972, 209; Ḳālī, *Dhayl al-amālī*, Cairo 1926, 100; *Aghānī*[3], vi, 209-41; al-Sarī al-Raffāʾ, *al-Muḥibb wa ʾl-maḥbūb wa ʾl-mashmūm wa ʾl-mashrūb*, Damascus 1407/1986, i, 144, 209; Abū ʿAlī al-Fārisī, *Sharḥ K. al-Ḥamāsa*, Beirut n.d., i, 176, ii, 316, iii, 202; Washshāʾ, *al-Ẓarf wa ʾl-ẓurafāʾ*, Beirut 1407/1986, 133; Ḳurṭubī, *Bahdjat al-madjālis*, Beirut 1402/1982, i, 276; al-Muʿāfā b. Zakariyyāʾ, *al-Djalīs al-ṣāliḥ al-kāfī*, Beirut 1413/1993, i, 581-2; Thaʿālibī, *Thimār al-ḳulūb*, Cairo 1965, 96, 109, 110; Zamakhsharī, *Rabīʿ al-abrār*, Beirut 1412/1992, ii/1, 438, § 46; Sarrādj, *Maṣāriʿ al-ʿushshāḳ*, Beirut 1378/1958, ii, 192 ff.; Ibn Ḳudāma al-Maḳdisī, *K. al-Tawwābīn*, Beirut 1406/1986, 149-50; Ibn Manẓūr, *Mukhtaṣar taʾrīkh Dimashḳ*, Damascus 1329, ii, 298-302; Ibn Khallikān, *Wafayāt*, ed. ʿAbbās, ii, 45-6, vii, 69; Ṣafadī, *Wāfī*, xviii, Wiesbaden 1988, 117-20; Ibn Shākir al-Kutubī, *Fawāt al-wafayāt*, Cairo 1951, i, 529-32, § 211; Dāwūd al-Anṭākī, *Tazyīn al-aswāḳ bi-tafṣīl ashwāḳ al-ʿushshāḳ*, Beirut 1413/1993, ii, 11-12; Mughulṭāy, *K. al-Wāḍiḥ al-mubīn fī dhikr man ustushhida min al-muḥibbīn*, Stuttgart 1936, 108-12; Blachère, *HLA*, iii, 651-3, J.-C. Vadet, *L'esprit courtois en Orient dans les cinq premiers siècles de l'Hégire*, Paris 1968, 110-11; Sezgin, *GAS*, ii, 433; Ṭāhā Ḥusayn, *Ḥadīth al-arbiʿāʾ*, Cairo 1962, 227-34; idem, *Min taʾrīkh al-adab al-ʿarabī. I. al-ʿAṣr al-djāhilī wa ʾl-ʿaṣr al-islāmī*, Beirut 1970, 536-44; ʿAfīf ʿAbd al-Raḥmān, *Muʿdjam al-shuʿarāʾ*, Beirut 1417/1996, 280, § 1941.

(A. Arazi)

WĀDĪ (a.), pls. *awdiya*, *awdāʾ*, etc., in Syrian colloquial *widyān* (see A. Barthélemy, *Dictionnaire arabe-français. Dialectes de Syrie*, Paris 1935-54, 889), in the Arab lands in general, a river valley. The conventional English spelling is wadi.

1. In the Arabian peninsula.

In desert terrain, a wadi is usually dry, but may carry seasonal water, or occasional floods (*sayl*), which are often a mixture of water, mud and stones. These desert valleys are very different in both topography and gradient from those in lands of higher and more regular rainfall; for while it is easy to follow the valley of a stream which is always visible, it is often difficult to map the course of the Arabian wadis, in long stretches of which water rarely, if ever, appears on the surface.

The greater part of the rainfall which is carried, either on or below the surface, along the wadis of central Arabia, falls on the high western rim of the massif in the Negeb or Negev [see AL-NAḲB], Ḥidjāz, ʿAsīr and Yemen, and flows east-north-eastwards in sympathy with the general slope of the plateau.

In the higher reaches of these wadis, the pattern of drainage is so complex and firmly incised that it was evidently established during periods of higher rainfall in the Pleistocene epoch. At such times, the more powerful streams, which flowed to the Red Sea down the well-watered western slopes, "captured" some of the drainage on the east side of the watershed, notably in the case of the headwaters of the Wādī al-Ḥamḍ. During these pluvial episodes, lakes of water accumulated, the overflows from which incised the deep valleys of some wadis, notably in the case of the Wādī Ḥaḍramawt which rises in the Ramlat al-Sabʿatayn, now a sand-basin but apparently once a lake. The same phenomenon can be traced in the overflows from the former lake basins of Anatolia, and from the high plain at the head of the Samaria gorge in Crete.

In their middle courses the Arabian wadis are characterised not by surface streams in clear-cut meanders, as in valleys of temperate latitudes, but by subterranean flow under broad shallow depressions in the sand, the gentle side-slopes of which are barely perceptible. When the water flow is near enough to the surface to be reached by wells or through the roots of data-palms, oases may be established, as at al-Ḳaṣīm [*q.v.*] in the middle course of the Wādī al-Rumma. In central Arabia in general, the greater part of the underground reserve consists of "fossil water" which accumulated during wetter episodes of the Quaternary and Holocene epochs; the annual rainfall serves as a supplement which raises the level of the water-table.

The terminus of such great wadis as al-Rumma and al-Dawāsir, where they meet the Gulf, is not marked by deltas or estuaries, but simply by the upwelling of freshwater springs through the coastal sands, as in the district of al-Hufūf [*q.v.*], or through the bedrocks under the seawater of the Gulf itself.

Through the convenience of their oasis wells, the wide wadis of Arabia and Syria are often followed by roads of trade or pilgrimage: the Wādī 'l-Sirḥān, for example, leads from Jordan to central Arabia, and the Wādī Rumma is used in part by the Darb Zubayda [*q.v.* in Suppl.], the Pilgrim Road from ʿIrāḳ to Mecca. The flash-floods of the narrow mountain wadis, however, make them hazardous for travellers; but these flows used to be controlled for purposes of irrigation in the Negeb, for instance, and in the Yemen where they filled the great reservoir of Mārib [*q.v.*].

Bibliography: W.C. Brice (ed.), *The environmental history of the Middle East since the last Ice Age*, London 1978. (W.C. BRICE)

2. In North Africa.

Here, the form *oued* is usual in French usage. In the Maghrib, it denotes all watercourses, including the great perennial rivers, like the Oued Chélif in Algeria; it can equally at times designate, in very arid regions, low-lying areas where there is a total lack of any flow. This is why, in the Great Western Erg/Grand Erg Occidental, to the north of Tinimoun and towards lat. 29° 30' N., long. 0° 30' E., it is used to designate the streams running amongst the dunes (*faydj* [see FUYŪDJ]). The term has acquired a more restricted meaning in physical geography for denoting the watercourses in arid regions, which may have a seasonal flow in semi-arid areas but are spasmodic or temporary in the most desert-like areas.

Bibliography: J. Brunhes, *L'irrigation dans l'Espagne et dans l'Afrique du Nord*, Paris 1902; J. Despois, *L'Afrique du Nord*, 3Paris 1964; H. Isnard, *Le Maghreb*, Paris 1966; Despois and R. Raynal (eds.), *Géographie de l'Afrique du Nord-Ouest*, Paris 1967. (Y. CALLOT)

3. In Muslim Spain.

In al-Andalus, this term, through the intermediacy of the Hispano-Arabic dialect word *wád*, gave rise to a large number of toponyms in the Iberian peninsula beginning with "Guad" and "Guadi". In al-Andalus, *wādī* was used not only for smaller, seasonal watercourses which dried up in summer but also for more important ones which might also be described by the word *nahr* "river". It nevertheless seems that, in the peninsula, *wādī* had a toponymical signification whereas *nahr* was a more generic one. The word also appears in many toponyms which have lost any connection with water, such as the towns Wādī 'l-Ḥidjāra [*q.v.*] = Guadalajara, Wādī Āsh [*q.v.*] = Guadix, and such geographical accidents as Wādī 'l-Raml = Guadarrama. Finally, al-Wādī denoted districts (*iḳlīm*) belonging respectively to Seville and Cordova, and, as a second element, also denoted in mediaeval Arabic historiography the name of one of the gates in the wall of Cordova, Bāb al-Wādī, the present fortress Alcalá del Río, Ḳalʿat al-Wādī, and a *munya* set up by al-Manṣūr at Cordova, Dhāt al-Wādiyayn "that of the two rivers".

Many of the Spanish toponyms beginning with "Guad" are followed by pre-Islamic names adapted into Arabic, e.g. "Anas" > Wādī Āna = Guadiana; "Acci" > Wādī Āsh = Guadix; "Salsum" > Wādī Shawsh = Guadajoz; etc. One frequently finds others which are Arabic in their totality with the second term a qualifying adjective, e.g. Guadalimar < Wādī 'l-Aḥmar "Red river", or a substantive, e.g. Guadarromán < Wādī 'l-Rummān "River of the pomegranates". Moreover, some archaic orthographical forms of "Guad-" survive, such as Huad-, Gud-, Got-, Güid-, Güit-, Güed-, Hüet-, Od-, Oid-, etc.; apocopated forms, such as Guaira alongside Guadaira (Seville) or Gurrazar (Toledo); and even contaminated forms like Guandatillo (Soria) or Agua Rocín (Jaén), in which Agua is in reality a reflex of *Wādī*.

Bibliography: *EI*[1], art. *Guad . . . Guadi . . .* (C.F. Seybold); E. Terés, *Materiales . . . Nómina fluvial*, esp. 29-50, 235-79 (= J. Zanón, *Indices*). (R. PINILLA-MELGUIZO)

WĀDĪ 'L-ʿAḲĪḲ [see AL-ʿAḲĪḲ].

WĀDĪ ĀSH, a town of al-Andalus, modern Guadix, now in the province of Grenada [see GHARNĀṬA] 60 km/37 miles northwest of the province's capital, chef-lieu of a *partido judicial* and seat of the diocese of Guadix-Baza, with a population of *ca.* 20,000, perhaps twice what it had in Islamic times.

The name goes back to a pre-Islamic toponym, perhaps Iberian, *Acci*, rendered *Āsh* by the Arabs, prefixed by the element *Wādī* [see WĀDĪ. 3.], applied not only to the town and the river on which it stood but also to the surrounding region. Sometimes the forms Wādī 'l-Ashā(t) and W. Yāsh are found, or, for the town only, Madīnat Āsh and M. Banī Sām, a name which Simonet thought went back to the Yemeni tribe of Sām(ī) established there. In Castilian texts, one finds

Guedix and above all Guadiex, which evolved into the modern Guadix.

It was a Roman settlement (*Colonia Iulia Gemella Acci*) and then a Visigothic one, and then immediately formed part of Islamic Spain with the arrival of the Arabs, whilst becoming a centre of opposition to the Umayyad state till the time of ʿAbd al-Raḥmān III; the *ḥuṣūn Wādī Āsh* are mentioned by Ibn Ḥayyān in connection with the *amīr*'s campaign of 913-14 in the *kūra* of Ilbīra. In the period of the Taifas [see MULŪK AL-ṬAWĀʾIF. 2.], Guadix formed part of the Zīrid kingdom of Granada, as also its neighbour Baza (Basṭa), both of these being involved together in clashes with Granada and the Taifa of Almeria (al-Mariyya). After being under Almoravid and Almohad control, it passed in 1232 to the Naṣrids of Granada, and from 1238 formed part of their kingdom. This was the period of Guadix's greatest florescence, especially under the rule of the Banū Ashkīlūla, being at that time a focus of rebellion against the authority of Granada. Its role continued to be important under the Naṣrids, until El Zagal, one of the claimants to power in the internecine conflicts, ceded it to the Catholic monarchs in 1489, it already having paid tribute to them since 1433.

The district of Guadix included, according to Simonet, many settlements and fortresses. The town itself was built round the citadel (*alcazaba*), whose remains, going back to the 10th century and forming a complete enceinte, dominated the *madīna* and the suburbs. It had a rich agricultural hinterland, with a *secano* (dry-farming region) very rich in cereals (wheat, barley and millet), above all in the region of the Sened (modern Marquesado del Cenete), and there were irrigated lands along the river fringes (the Vega), with vegetables and fruit. There were, further, mines in the region, stock-rearing and hunting, plus a flourishing silk industry and trade. Famous persons from Guadix included the poets Ibn al-Ḥaddād [*q.v.*] and Ibn al-Nizār, the *ʿulamāʾ* Ibn Djābir and Abū Hāshim Khālid b. Zakariyyāʾ [*q.v.*] and the mystic al-Shushtarī.

Bibliography: 1. Sources. ʿUdhrī, *Tarṣīʿ al-akhbār*, ed. al-Ahwānī, 3, 86, 89; Ibn Ḥayyān, *Muktabis*, ed. Antuña, 116, 112, and v, ed. Chalmeta, 66, tr. Viguera and Corriente, 63; ʿAbd Allāh b. Buluggīn, *Tibyān*, Span. tr. Lévi-Provençal and García Gómez, 109-10, 133-6, Eng. tr. Amin T. Tibi, *The Tibyān*, Leiden 1986, index; Rushāṭī, *Iktibās al-anwār*, ed. Molina and Bosch, 90; Ibn Saʿīd, *Mughrib*, ii, 140-1; Ibn al-Khaṭīb, *Iḥāṭa*, i, 507, ii, 30, iv, 270; idem, *Aʿmāl*, 304, 337; Ḥimyarī, *Rawḍ*, 193/233; Makkarī, *Nafḥ*, ed. ʿAbbās, i, 149-50, iv, 519-22 = *Analectes*, i, 142.

2. Studies. F.J. Simonet, *Descripción del Reino de Granada*, 98-101; P. Madoz, *Diccionario geográfico*, Madrid 1846-50, ix, 40-5; E. Terés, *Materiales. . . . Nómina fluvial*, 462-3 (J. Zanón, *Indices*); Rachel Arié, *L'Espagne musulmane au temps des Nasrides*, Paris 1973, index; L. Asenjo, *Guadix*, Granada 1983; M.C. Jiménez, *La Granada islámica*, Granada 1990, 276-7.

(C. ALVAREZ DE MORALES and R. PINILLA-MELGUIZO)

AL-**WĀDĪʾĀSHĪ**, SHAMS AL-DĪN MUḤAMMAD B. DJĀBIR al-Kaysī al-Andalusī al-Tūnisī (673-749/1274-1348: not to be confused with his slightly younger contemporary, the blind poet and grammarian from Almeria Muḥammad b. Aḥmad b. ʿAlī b. Djābir al-Hawwārī), the North African author of a *Barnāmadj*.

Al-Wādīʾāshī was born in Tunis, where he died during the plague. He travelled twice to the East, visiting also al-Andalus, and combining commerce with study. Ibn al-Ghammāz, Ibn ʿAbd al-Rafīʿ, Badr al-Dīn Ibn Djamāʿa, al-Ghubrīnī and the grammarian Abū Ḥayyān were among his 180 teachers; Ibn Khaldūn, Ibn Marzūḳ al-Djadd, Ibn al-Khaṭīb and Ibn Farḥūn were his pupils. He contributed to the diffusion of the works of Ibn Taymiyya, al-Tūnī, Ibrāhīm al-Djaʿbarī al-Khalīlī, Ibn Djamāʿa, al-Būṣīrī, al-Ḥarrālī and Ibn Nubāta. His works dealt mainly with *ḥadīth* (*Arbaʿūn ḥadīth*[an]); he also wrote a biography of Ḳāḍī ʿIyāḍ as well as *Taḳyīd ʿalā ʾl-Ḳaṣīda al-ʿarūḍiyya al-musammāt bi ʾl-Maḳṣad al-djalīl fī ʿilm Khalīl li-Abī ʿAmr b. al-Ḥādjib*, *Urdjūza fī taʿbīr al-ruʾyā* and a *dīwān* of his poetry. But he is mainly known for his *Barnāmadj*, a monumental work (ed. M. Maḥfūẓ, Beirut 1980; [2]Beirut 1982; ed. M. al-Ḥabīb, Tunis 1981) and one of the sources of Ibn al-Ḳāḍī's [*q.v.*] *Durrat al-ḥidjāl* (see J.Mª Fórneas, in *Al-Andalus–Magreb*, [1993], 89-101).

Bibliography: 1. Sources. Ṣafadī, *Wāfī*, ii, 283, no. 717; Ibn al-Khaṭīb, *Iḥāṭa*, iii, 163-5; Ibn Khaldūn, *al-Taʿrīf*, tr. A. Cheddadi, [2]Paris 1980, 46; Ibn Farḥūn, *Dībādj*, ii, 299-301; Ibn al-Djazarī, *Ghāya*, ii, 106, no. 2882; Ibn Ḥadjar, *al-Durar al-kāmina*, iv, 33, no. 3618; Ibn al-Ḳāḍī, *Durrat al-ḥidjāl*, ii, 102-3, no. 535; Makkarī, *Nafḥ*, v, 200-2; Makhlūf, *Shadjarat al-nūr*, i, 210, no. 733.

2. Studies. Pons Boigues 326, no. 279; Brockelmann, S II, 371; Ziriklī, vi, 68, vii, 35; Kaḥḥāla, ix, 146, xi, 230; J.Mª Fórneas, in *al-And.*, xxxviii (1973), 1-67, xxxix (1974), 301-61; Benchekroun, *La vie intellectuale marocaine*, 519. (MARIBEL FIERRO)

WĀDĪ ʾL-DAWĀSIR [see AL-DAWĀSIR].

WĀDĪ ḤALFĀ or simply ḤALFĀ, a town of the northern Nilotic Sūdān (lat. 21° 46' N., long. 31° 17' E.), the administrative centre of the Ḥalfā District of the modern Republic of the Sudan. It lies just south of the frontier with Egypt. It was formerly on the Nile, some 10 km/6 miles north of the Second Cataract, and formed the northern terminus of the Sudan Railway from the capital Kharṭūm, with a pre-1964 steamboat service taking passengers down the Nile to al-Shallāl and the Egyptian railway system. It played little active role in the Sudanese Mahdiyya of the 1880s and 1890s, the centre of the movement being further south, except for the advance from Dongola on Egypt in summer 1889 of Mahdist forces under ʿAbd al-Raḥmān al-Nudjūmī, abruptly halted on 3 August by the crushing of the Mahdist expedition at Toski (Ṭūshkī) north of Wādī Ḥalfā and the killing of its commander [see AL-MAHDIYYA, at Vol. V, 1250a-b].

What remains of Wādī Ḥalfā now lies on the eastern shore of Lake Nuba, the extension into the Sudan of Lake Nasser, formed behind the Aswān High Dam, constructed after the Nile Waters Agreement of 1959 between President ʿAbd al-Nāṣir [*q.v.* in Suppl.] of Egypt and General Ibrāhīm ʿAbbūd of the recently-independent Sudan Republic, which divided the water which was to accumulate between the two countries. Some 502,000 Nubians of the Wādī Ḥalfā lands which were to be inundated, were compulsorily resettled on the upper Atbara river in Kassala Province [see KASALA] of the eastern Sudan, with their settlement there eventually known as Ḥalfā al-Djadīd "New Ḥalfā" [see NŪBA. 4]. The high-handed action of the Sudan government in expelling these people from their ancestral homes, with no voice in where they were to be resettled, provoked in 1960 widespread rioting in Wādī Ḥalfā itself, Kharṭūm and other towns of the Sudan against the ʿAbbūd régime. The region of Wādī Ḥalfā is rich in antiquities of the ancient civilisations of Nubia [see NŪBA. 2 (a)], and in the 1970s it saw extensive rescue archaeological work before the flooding of the Nile valley there.

Bibliography: P.M. Holt, *A modern history of the Sudan, from the Funj Sultanate to the present day*, London 1965, 72, 74, 188-90 and index; K.D.D. Henderson, *Sudan Republic*, London 1965, 135-8 and index.

(C.E. Bosworth)

WĀDĪ ḤANĪFA, a valley of Nadjd [*q.v.*], now in Saudi Arabia, named after the tribe of Ḥanīfa [see ḤANĪFA B. LUDJAYM], who in pre-Islamic and early Islamic times occupied the region.

It runs in a northwestern to southeastern direction to the east of the massifs of central Nadjd, rising on the crest of the Djabal al-Ṭuwayḳ [see AL-ṬUWAYḲ, DJABAL] and following to the west of modern al-Riyāḍ. The wadi is *ca.* 150 km/90 miles long and 300 to 600 m wide, and cuts through various gaps in the ridges of the region. After reaching the region of al-Khardj [*q.v.*], it becomes known as the Wādī al-Sahbā' [see AL-SAHBĀ'] and is thereafter largely traceable to the shores of the Gulf near the Ḳaṭar peninsula. In the rainy season, the Wādī Ḥanīfa is joined by several affluent wadis and is filled with water, but outside such times it transports a considerable subterranean flow which is drawn upon by various oases in the vicinity of al-Riyāḍ.

In pre- and early Islamic times, the town of al-Yamāma [*q.v.*] was situated in the wadi, but now consists of only a small group of hamlets; the town was probably destroyed by violent floods, whereas al-Dir'iyya and al-Riyāḍ [*q.vv.*] stand above the flood level. The Wādī Ḥanīfa remains today, as it was in earlier times, a well-cultivated area.

Bibliography: H.St.J.B. Philby, *Arabia of the Wahhabis*, London 1928, 68-79; Naval Intelligence Division. Admiralty Handbooks, *Western Arabia and the Red Sea*, London 1946, 29, 233; W.C. Brice, *A systematic regional geography. Southwest Asia*, London 1966, 271; 'Abd Allāh b. Khamīs, *Mu'djam al-Yamāma*, 2 vols. al-Riyāḍ 1978, i, 348-53. See also AL-'ARAB, DJAZĪRAT. iii, at Vol. II, 538b.

(S.A. al-Rashid)

WĀDĪ 'L-ḤIDJĀRA, Spanish form Guadalajara, currently the capital of a homonymous province situated to the northeast of Madrid. Although it is difficult to define the limits of this region during the mediaeval period with absolute precision, it may be stated that its territory corresponds to the zones enclosed between the river Tagus to the east and the river Jarama, which traverses the Sierra Guadarrama, to the west. The principal axis of communication of the region is the valley of the Henares, comprising the Arabic toponym of Wādī 'l-Ḥidjāra "river [or valley] of stones". The city of Guadalajara is situated on the banks of this river, as are other strongholds such as Alcalá de Henares (Ḳal'at 'Abd al-Salām), the Complutum of the Roman period, Alcolea (Ḳulay'a) and Atienza (Atīnsa), the most northerly point of the region. This zone also formed a part of the "Middle March" (*al-thaghr al-adnā* [see AL-THUGHŪR. 2.]) of which the political and military capital was Toledo (Ṭulayṭula [*q.v.*]). This zone constituted an important site for its defence, being a frontier region and a necessary transit point for armies seeking to move from northeast to south and to defend without too much difficulty the untamed mountains of the Central System. Originating on the right bank of the Henares, there had been since the Roman period a highway linking the cities of Toledo and of Saragossa. Among the principal routes of al-Andalus, mentioned by al-Iṣṭakhrī in the 4th/10th century, is the Cordova-Toledo-Guadalajara-Saragossa route.

Following the conquest, attributed by the sources to Ṭāriḳ b. Ziyād [*q.v.*], Guadalajara appears sporadically in Arabic texts which refer to it as a town of secondary importance, both politically and culturally. From this time onward, the little Roman settlement of Arriaca becomes known as Wādī 'l-Ḥidjāra or, to a lesser extent, Madīnat al-Faradj, from the anthroponymy of the family of the Banu 'l-Faradj, a Berber family which governed the region and was descended from the Banū Sālim, another family which gave its name to the town of Medinaceli (Madīnat Sālim). Both the history of the town and that of its circumscription seem to be strongly influenced by its frontier status, since the chronicles mention numerous walled fortresses, always in connection with various military events taking place in different periods. Thus the region exerts considerable interest in its role as a favoured refuge for dissidents intent on pursuing their aims or as a site for warfare against the Christians. For example, in 151/768, during the reign of the Umayyad *amīr* 'Abd al-Raḥmān I (138-72/756-88), the Berber chieftain Shaḳya al-Miknāsī, who had rebelled and taken control of the region of Mérida (Marīda), sought refuge with the government troops of Cordova in the fort of Sopetran. A century later, in 245/860, Mūsā b. Mūsā b. Ḳasī who had been independent governor of the "Upper March" during the last years of the reign of 'Abd al-Raḥmān II (206-38/822-52) and who no longer recognised the sovereignty of Muḥammad, the new Umayyad *amīr* of Cordova, confronted his stepson Izrāḳ b. Mantīl b. Salīm, governor of Guadalajara in an episode related by the sources in the style of an epic. Mūsā b. Mūsā b. Ḳasī was defeated and then killed by the governor who remained loyal to the Umayyads of Cordova. Despite this, the three sons of Mūsā b. Mūsā b. Ḳasī continued to defy Cordova, being finally defeated after a series of prolonged battles at the end of the reign of Muḥammad (238-73/852-86).

During this period and in the reign of his son 'Abd Allāh b. Muḥammad (275-300/888-912), there was a perceived need for defensive measures against the growing menace of the increasingly powerful Christian kingdoms. As a result, not only were the defensive systems of the "Upper Frontier" consolidated, but there was also a series of military constructions in the region between Toledo and Atienza. Sites fortified included Madrid (Madjrīṭ), Talamanca (Ṭalamanka), Canales (Ḳanālish), Olmos (Wūlmūsh) and Calatalifa (Ḳal'at al-Khalīfa). From this period onward and with the support of the populace of this turbulent region, these fortresses were to prove vital for the defence of al-Andalus, as is illustrated both by the historical chronicles and the bio-bibliographical dictionaries, where details are to be found of numerous local *'ulamā'* who died in combat. It is known that during the amīrate of 'Abd Allāh, at the end of the 3rd/9th century, troops from Wādī 'l-Ḥidjāra participated in the *djihād* against Alfonso III. Later, the caliph 'Abd al-Raḥman III al-Nāṣir (300-50/912-61) exerted effective military control over the region of Guadalajara. On this topic, Ibn Ḥayyān relates that the caliph deposed its governor, a member of the family of the Banū Sālim who had long controlled this region, and appointed a member of the Umayyad family in his place. During this period, this frontier zone was the site of the battle in which the Muslims triumphed over the king of León.

In the aftermath of the fall of the caliphate of Cordova, Wādī 'l-Ḥidjāra became a territory coveted by the Taifa [see MULŪK AL-ṬAWĀ'IF. 2.] kingdoms of

Saragossa and Toledo with which it shared frontiers. The population of Guadalajara was divided between supporters of the Banū Hūd of Saragossa represented by Sulaymān al-Mustaʿīn and the Dhu 'l-Nūnid sovereign of Toledo al-Maʾmūn, in a series of confrontations lasting from 435/1043 to the death of al-Mustaʿīn in 439/1047. During these conflicts, each party sought the aid of Christian sovereigns: Ferdinand I of Castile on the side of Toledo, and Garcia of Pamplona in support of Saragossa. The son of al-Mustaʿīn, Aḥmad al-Muḳtadir, pursuing an expansionist policy, succeeded in taking political and military control of the region of Guadalajara which ultimately became part of the greatly extended territory of his Taifa kingdom.

The impression that is gained of Wādī 'l-Ḥidjāra as being a military frontier region, with the role of protecting cities of greater political importance, is that reflected by the Arab and Christian sources, although the latter seem to be unaware of the exact date of its reconquest; for a long time this was attributed, without historical foundation, to Alvar Fañez. In spite of everything, it is known that it took place in the time of Alfonso VI, and was probably simultaneous with the reconquest of Toledo in 478/1085. A Christian document dated 1107 bears the signature of "un alkad de Medina et de Guadalajara". At a later time, in 1133 Alfonso VII granted the town a *fuero* in which he expressed his intention of repopulating the region, thus countering the dispersal of population suffered by the zone after its reconquest.

The activities of the *ʿulamāʾ* of Guadalajara and their family ties are reasonably well known, being detailed in the biographies of sixty scholars contained in bio-bibliographical compilations between the 3rd/9th and the first half of the 6th/12th century. For the most part they were Hispano-Roman converts, some of whom adopted Arabic *nisba*s reflecting their professional links with families installed in the region. It is also known that numerous Berber families had settled in the region, including the Banu 'l-Faradj and the Banū Masʿada; the latter was the origin of several *ʿulamāʾ*. The interests of the *ʿulamāʾ* of Guadalajara seem to have coincided with those of the other *ʿulamāʾ* of al-Andalus, and special dedication is observed to the study of *ḥadīth*, of *fiḳh* and of Ḳurʾānic readings. The role of scholars of Cordova in the training of the intellectual élite of Guadalajara was crucial, with Muḥammad b. Waḍḍāḥ playing a particularly significant part; in fact, the first *ʿulamāʾ* of the region, from the ascetic Muḥammad b. Bāligh to the *ḳāḍī* Muḥammad b. ʿAzra, studied with Ibn Waḍḍāḥ. In the 5th/11th century, there is observable an increase in the number of *ʿulamāʾ* dedicating themselves to literature and grammar, and even to poetry. It is in this period that the *faḳīh* and writer ʿAbd al-Malik b. Ghuṣn al-Khushanī al-Ḥidjārī makes his appearance. All of the written corpus of the *ʿulamāʾ* of Guadalajara has been lost, with the exception of a few verses and fragments of the geographical work composed by ʿAbd Allāh b. Ibrāhīm al-Ḥidjārī, preserved in Ibn Saʿīd's *al-Mughrib*.

Bibliography: 1. Geographical sources. Iṣṭakhrī, 41-4, 47; Ibn Ḥawḳal, ed. Kramers, 75-6, 81; Muḳaddasī, 30, 223, 235, 247; Bakrī, *The geography of al-Andalus and Europe from the book "al-Masālik wa-l-mamālik"*, ed. A.A. El-Hajji, Beirut 1387/1968, 62; Idrīsī, *Los caminos de al-Andalus en el siglo XII*, ed. and tr. J. Abid Mizal, Madrid 1989, 72-3 (text), 343 no. 510 (tr.); Ḥimyarī, *al-Rawḍ al-miʿṭār*, ed. ʿAbbās, Beirut 1975, 606, tr. in E. Lévi-Provençal, *La Péninsule ibérique au Moyen-âge d'après le* Kitāb al-rawḍ al-miʿṭār, Leiden 1938, 234 no. 185; Yāḳūt, *Buldān*, Beirut 1986, v, 343; P. Madoz, *Diccionario geográfico-estadístico-histórico de España y sus posesiones de ultramar*, Madrid 1846-50, i, 372, s.n. Alcalá de Henares, viii, 637-8 s.n. Guadalajara.

2. Historical sources. Ibn Ḥayyān, *Muḳtabis*, v, ed. P. Chalmeta, index; Ibn ʿIdhārī, *Bayān*, ed. Colin and Lévi-Provençal, Leiden 1948-51, Fr. tr. E. Fagnan, *Histoire de l'Afrique du Nord et de l'Espagne*, Algiers 1901-4, ii, 18, 117, 159, 271, 291, 316, 471; *Una descripción anónima de al-Andalus*, ed. and tr. L. Molina, Madrid 1983, i, 54, 58, 129-30, ii, 60, 65, 137-8; *Fatḥ al-Andalus*, ed. Molina, Madrid 1994, 23.

3. Bio-bibliographical dictionaries. For this type of source, see M. Marín's study of the *ʿulamāʾ* of Guadalajara, *Ulemas en la Marca Media*, in *Estudios onomástico-biográficos de al-Andalus*, Madrid, vii (1995), 203-29.

4. Studies. E. Lévi-Provençal, *España musulmana hasta la caída del Califato de Córdoba*, in *Historia de España*, ed. Menéndez Pidal, iv, Madrid 1950, index; idem, *Instituciones y vida social e intelectual*, in *ibid.*, v, 71, 191; L. Torres Balbás, *Arte hispanomusulmán*, in *ibid.*, 628-30, 643; F. Cantera Burgos, *Sinagogas españolas*, Madrid 1955, 160-2, 179-80, 225-7; F. Cantera and C. Carrete, *Las juderías medievales en la provincia de Guadalajara*, Madrid 1975; J.-C. García López, *La Alcarria en los dos primeros siglos de su reconquista*, Guadalajara 1973; B. Pavón Maldonado, *Alcalá de Henares medieval. Arte islámico y mudéjar*, Madrid-Alcalá de Henares 1982; idem, *Guadalajara medieval. Arte y arqueología árabe y mudéjar*, Madrid 1984; J. Vallvé, *La división territorial de la España musulmana*, Madrid 1986, 310-13; P. Ballesteros San José, *Sobre la conquista cristiana de Guadalajar y Sigüenza*, in *Actas del I encuentro de historiadores del Valle de Henares (nov. 1988)*, Alcalá de Henares 1988, 67-74; J. Valiente Malla and M.A. Cuadrado Prieto, *Las torres de Atienza*, in *ibid.*, 631-42; E. Manzano Moreno, *La frontera de al-Andalus en época de los Omeyas*, Madrid 1991, 54-5, 150-5, 160, 294, 318, 328, 333, 347, 372-4; M. Makki, *The political history of al-Andalus*, in S.A. Jayyusi (ed.), *The legacy of Muslim Spain*, Leiden 1992, 8, 29-30, 74; M.J. Viguera Molíns (ed.), *Los Reinos de Taifas. Al-Andalus en el s. XI*, in *Historia de España*, viii*, Madrid 1994, chs. of Viguera, M.L. Ávila Navarro and Pavón Maldonado.

(CRISTINA DE LA PUENTE)

(AL-)**WĀDĪ 'L-KABĪR**, Guadalquivir, the name given by the Arabs to the ancient *Betis* river in Southern Spain. It has remained in Spanish toponymy through the Spanish-Arabic dialect form Wād al-Kibīr. According to the Arab sources, it is also called al-Nahr al-Akbar or al-Nahr al-Aʿẓam (the Great River), Nahr Ḳurṭuba (River of Cordova) and Nahr Ishbīliyā (River of Seville), but it is seldom called Nahr Bīṭī/Bīṭa (Betis River). In poetry sometimes it is called Nahr Ḥimṣ (River of Ḥimṣ), that is, River of Seville. The history of this river goes back to Roman times, where it played a major role within the Roman Baetica, or southern Hispania. After the Islamic conquest, its ancient Latin name was changed to the Arabic one (al-)Wādī 'l-Kabīr (the Great River), possibly due to its extensive flow, which the Muslim conquerors compared with North African small streams that they knew previously.

Wādī 'l-Kabīr was, and still is at present, one of the most important rivers in the Iberian Peninsula, and the southernmost of them all. It flows through the heart of al-Andalus, from northeast to southwest, through the modern Andalusia. Its course is 560 kms long. It begins at the Cañada de Aguas Frías, among the Pozo Alcón and Cazorla mountains, but according to Arab writers, the course begins west of Baza (Basṭa), in a place called Fatḥ/Fadjdj al-Daylam, today Peña Negra at the Sierra de Cazorla, while other written sources speak of a place in the Sierra de Segura (Shaḳūra).

This river flowed through what were some of the most important cities and districts in al-Andalus such as the districts of Úbeda (Ubbadha [*q.v.*]), Andújar (Andūdjar), Córdoba (Ḳurṭuba [*q.v.*]) and Seville (Ishbīliyā [*q.v.*]). Further downstream, it waters the marshes (Las Marismas, al-Marā'im), finally meeting the Atlantic Ocean near Sanlúcar de Barrameda (Shalūḳa, Barr al-Mā'ida).

Many smaller rivers feed the course of the Guadalquivir, some of which still keep the Arab prefix "Guad" [see WĀDĪ. 3]. Its left bank takes in the waters from the Guadalimar (Wādī 'l-Aḥmar), Jándula (Shandula), Guadalmellato (Wādī Armillāt), Guadiato (Wādī Ātuh ?), and Guadiamar (Wādī Yanbar) rivers, among others. On its right bank the Guadiana (Wādī Yāna) Menor, Guadalbullón (Wādī 'l-Bulyūn), Guadajoz (Wādī Shawsh), Genil (Wādī Shanīl, the most important of these tributaries) and Guadaira (Wādī Ayra) are its main affluents.

In Antiquity, it seems that there were boats sailing along most of its course: Strabo speaks of big ships sailing to Hispalis (Ishbīliyā) and how small boats could sail to Corduba (Ḳurṭuba). Then, in the Muslim period, navigation continued to Seville, but only smaller boats could travel between Seville and Cordova, along the route mentioned by al-Idrīsī as *ṭarīḳ al-Wādī* ("the way of the river"). The river is very often mentioned by the Arab writers. The bridge (*ḳanṭarat al-Wādī*), made by the Romans, still links both sides of the city of Cordova, being the only stone bridge which spanned al-Wādī 'l-Kabīr during Arab times. Al-Wādī 'l-Kabīr was often hymned by the Arab poets, and al-Zuhrī compares it to the rivers Tigris, Euphrates, Nile and Jordan.

Bibliography: 1. Sources. Idrīsī, *Nuzha* (= *Descript. de l'Afr. et de l'Esp.*, 196); Dimashḳī, *Cosmographie*, 112, 246-139, 353; Abu 'l-Fidā', *Taḳwīm al-buldān*, tr. ii, 235-8, 248, 249-69; *Crónica del Moro Rasis*, éd. Gayangos, 61, 62; Bakrī, *al-Masālik wa 'l-mamālik*, index; Zuhrī, *Dja'rāfiyya*, index; *Akhbār madjmū'a*, ed. Lafuente, 102; *Fatḥ al-Andalus*, ed. Molina, 45-6; *Dhikr bilād al-Andalus*, ed. Molina, index; 'Umarī, *Masālik*, and Maḥallī, *Tuḥfa* (= Fagnan, *Extraits*, 100-1, 137-8, 142-3); Ḳazwīnī, *Āthār al-bilād*, ii, 370 (= Roldán-Castro, *El Occid. de al-And.*, 149); Rushāṭī-Ibn al-Kharrāṭ, *Iḳtibās*, ed. Molina and Bosch, 76, 179.

2. Studies. *EI*[1], art. *Guadalquivir* (C.F. Seybold); P. Madoz, *Diccionario geográfico*, Madrid 1846-50, index; Terés, *Materiales... Nómina fluvial*, 399-402 (Zanón, *Indices*); Aguirre and Jiménez, *Introd. al-Jaén islámico*, Jaén 1979, 50-51; Arenillas and Sáenz, *Guía física de España. 3. Los ríos*, [2]Madrid 1995, 216-37; M. Ribes, *El Guadalquivir*, Cordova 1984; H. Pérès, *La poésie andalouse en arabe classique*, index; Mazzoli-Guintard, *Un pont sans pareil...*, in *Châteaux, routes et rivières*, Périgord 1998, 11-27.

(R. PINILLA-MELGUIZO)

WĀDĪ 'L-KHAZNADĀR, the site of a battle in 699/1299 between the Mamlūks and the Īlkhānid Mongols [*q.vv.*], in the plain to the north of Ḥimṣ. The exact location of this site, also referred to as Madjma' al-Murūdj, has not been identified. This was the only time the Mongols were victorious over the Mamlūks in a major field battle.

Angry at the recent Mamlūk incursion to Mārdīn and interference in Mongol-controlled Anatolia, and urged on by Mamlūk renegades at his court, the Īlkhān Ghāzān [*q.v.*] ordered the call-up of some 13 *tūmāns* [*q.v.*], but only five out of every ten soldiers was to report, each bringing five horses. Crossing the Euphrates in the autumn, the Īlkhān and his army passed Ḥalab and Ḥamā and entered the plain of Ḥimṣ. They soon encountered the Mamlūk army, which arrived at the battlefield in an exhausted state, further suffering from other problems. The young sultan, al-Nāṣir Muḥammad b. Ḳalāwūn [*q.v.*], enjoyed only nominal command, and real control was in the hands of the *amīrs* Salār and Baybars al-Djāshnakīr; the latter, however, became ill and did not participate in the fighting. The contemporary Abu 'l-Fidā' (*Mukhtaṣar*, Cairo 1325/1407, iv, 43), describes the poor morale, discipline, organisation and supply system of the Mamlūk army. Contact between the two armies was made on Wednesday, 27 Rabī' I 699/22 December 1299 (cf. the Mamlūk sources). As the Mongols were dispersed to pasture the horses and fetch water, Ghāzān drew up those troops as he could, ordering the soldiers in the centre to dismount and shoot on foot, with the horses lying down before them as a protective barrier. The Mamlūks attacked first, their right pushing back the Mongol left under Ḳutlū-Shāh, who then joined the Īlkhān in the centre with some troops. The Mamlūk attack in this sector was repulsed. With time, the dispersed Mongol soldiers joined their ruler, and after hard fighting the superior numbers of his army helped decide the battle; some Mamlūk sources specifically mention the defeat of the Mamlūk left. The Mamlūk army retreated in disarray, making their way to Egypt while suffering depredations by the local hillsmen. Mongol raiders swept through Palestine, reaching as far as Gaza, Hebron and Jerusalem. Ghāzān himself advanced as far as Damascus, whose notables submitted to him. After several weeks, the Īlkhān withdrew, and following him the entire Mongol force. By spring, the Mamlūks had reoccupied Syria.

Bibliography: 1. Sources. Rashīd al-Dīn, *Djāmi' al-tawārīkh*, ed. 'A. 'Alīzāda, Baku 1957, iii, 332-9 (= K. Jahn (ed.), *Geschichte Ġāzān-Ḫān's aus dem Ta'rīḫ-i-mubārak-i-ġāzānī*, London 1940, 124-31); Waṣṣāf, *Ta'rīkh*, Bombay 1269/1852-3, 372-9; Het'um (Hayton), *La Flor des Estoires de la Terre d'Orient*, in *RHC, docs. arméniens*, ii, Paris 1906, 191-3; Baybars al-Manṣūrī, *al-Tuḥfa al-mulūkiyya fī dawlat al-turkiyya*, ed. 'A.Ṣ. Ḥamdān, Cairo 1407/1987, 156-9; K.V. Zetterstéen (ed.), *Beiträge zur Geschichte der Mamlūkensultane*, Leiden 1919, 58-62; Maḳrīzī, *Sulūk*, ed. M.M. Ziyāda, Cairo 1934-73, i, 886-8.

2. Studies. D.P. Little, *An introduction to Mamlūk historiography*, Wiesbaden 1970, *passim* (with analysis of all the Mamlūk sources for the battle); J.A. Boyle, in *Camb. hist. Iran*, v, 387-9; J.M. Smith, Jr., *'Ayn Jālūt: Mamlūk success or Mongol failure?*, in *Harvard Jnal. of Asiatic Studies*, xliv (1985), 324-30; A.P. Martinez, *Some notes on the Īl-Xānid army*, in *Archivum Eurasiae Medii Aevi*, vi (1986 [1988]), 165-78; S. Schein, *Gesta Dei per Mongolos 1300: the genesis of a non-event*, in *Eng. Hist. Review*, xciv (1979), 805-19; R. Amitai, *Mongol raids into Palestine (A.D. 1260-1300)*, in *JRAS* (1987), 236-55. (R. AMITAI)

WĀDĪ 'L-ḲURĀ, or "the valley of villages", a once prosperous region including several valleys in northern Ḥidjāz [*q.v.*], four or five days' journey from Medina. From beginning to end the valley was made of villages arrayed one after the other (*ḳurā manẓūma*).

According to one opinion, the Wādī 'l-Ḳurā extended between Madā'in Ṣāliḥ (i.e. al-Ḥid̲j̲r [*q.v.*], ancient Ḥegrā) in the north and al-Badāyiʿ (southeast of al-ʿUlā) in the south; the central settlement in Wādī 'l-Ḳurā during the first centuries of Islam, Ḳurḥ [*q.v.*], should be identified with modern al-Mibyāt (or rather al-Mābiyyāt) south of al-ʿUlā (A.A. Nasif, *The identification of the Wādi 'l-Qurā and the ancient Islamic site of al-Mibyāt*, in *Arabian Studies*, v [1979], 1-19; cf. Ḥ. al-D̲j̲āsir, *Laysa 'l-Ḥid̲j̲r Madā'in Ṣāliḥ*, in *al-ʿArab* [Riyāḍ], xiii [1978-9]), 3-13). However, according to another opinion, Wādī 'l-Ḳurā traversed a much larger area, joining the sea south of al-Wad̲j̲h; Ḳurḥ, according to the latter opinion, should be located at modern al-K̲h̲urayba (or K̲h̲uraybat al-ʿUlā) which is the northern part of al-ʿUlā (al-D̲j̲āsir, *Taʿlīḳāt ʿalā 'l-mawāḍiʿ fī s̲h̲iʿr al-Aḥwaṣ al-Anṣārī. iii*, in *Jnal. of the Institute of Arabic Manuscripts*, xxxvi [1992], 249-86, at 252-4; idem, *Riḥla ilā bilād al-ʿUlā*, in *al-ʿArab*, xii [1977-8], 161-85, at 183-4).

Ḳurḥ was also known as al-Ṣaʿīd and Ṣaʿīd Ḳurḥ. According to Lug̲h̲da al-Iṣfahānī (3rd/9th century), the market of Wādī 'l-Ḳurā was called al-Ṣaʿīd. The mosque in Ṣaʿīd Ḳurḥ was built where the Prophet Muḥammad once led his Companions in prayer. His place of prayer (*muṣallā*) was later demarcated with bones and stones (al-Fīrūzābādī, *al-Mag̲h̲ānim al-muṭāba fī maʿālim Ṭāba*, ed. al-D̲j̲āsir, Riyāḍ 1389/1969, 336).

In ancient times, i.e. in legendary history, the Wādī 'l-Ḳurā and the adjacent areas belonged to the T̲h̲amūd and the ʿĀd [*q.vv.*]. The Jews who came there later dug subterranean conduits and planted palm trees. Wādī 'l-Ḳurā was (from a tribal point of view) in the territory of tribal groups belonging to the Ḳuḍāʿa [*q.v.*]. Other tribal groups living in the same area were of the G̲h̲aṭafān and the Fazāra [*q.vv.*] (a subdivision of the former tribe). Two expeditions against the Fazāra at the time of the Prophet were carried out in the vicinity of Wādī 'l-Ḳurā. As for the G̲h̲aṭafān, the Jews of Wādī 'l-Ḳurā had a treaty with a G̲h̲aṭafānī group, the T̲h̲aʿlaba b. Saʿd b. D̲h̲ubyān (*Ag̲h̲ānī*[3], iii, 271). Another treaty, between the Jews and the ʿUd̲h̲ra [*q.v.*], prescribed for the latter a portion of the annual crops. In return, they defended the villages of Wādī 'l-Ḳurā, driving away from them other tribes of the Ḳuḍāʿa. The assigned portion of the ʿUd̲h̲ra amounted to one-third of the harvest, while two-thirds remained in the hands of the Jewish agriculturalists. When Muḥammad conquered Wādī 'l-Ḳurā (7 A.H.), he received half of the Jews' share, i.e. one-third of the total, while the Jews kept one-third to themselves. Upon the expulsion of the Jews (or rather of some of them) by ʿUmar b. al-K̲h̲aṭṭāb, they received in cash the estimated value of their share, sc. 90,000 dīnārs. ʿUmar then offered the ʿUd̲h̲ra an additional sixth of the crops in return for one-sixth of the value, i.e. 45,000 dīnārs. They accepted, becoming the owners of one-half of Wādī 'l-Ḳurā. One-third of the remaining half was included in the charitable endowments of the Prophet, while one-sixth of the same half belonged to all the Muslims (al-Māwardī, *al-Aḥkām al-sulṭāniyya*, tr. E. Fagnan, Algiers 1915, 362).

At least four indigenous Arabs, all of whom belonged to tribal groups of the Ḳuḍāʿa, are reported to have received from the Prophet grants of land in Wādī 'l-Ḳurā. Two were members of the ʿUd̲h̲ra, one was probably of the Balī, while another was of the Ḥārit̲h̲ b. Saʿd Hud̲h̲aym.

There is no unanimity in the sources on whether or not ʿUmar expelled the Jews of Wādī 'l-Ḳurā. However, the fact that many Companions received from him grants of land in Wādī 'l-Ḳurā indicates that part of the original Jewish inhabitants were driven out. One Jewish family which remained is specified. When Muḥammad alighted in Wādī 'l-Ḳurā, the sons of the Jew ʿArīḍ (or ʿUrayḍ) served him a dish of *harīs*[*a*] (i.e. ground meat and ground wheat fried in much fat). He granted them a portion from the annual crops of Wādī 'l-Ḳurā (perhaps rewarding them for a co-operation of sorts). Several centuries later there was a large Jewish community in Wādī 'l-Ḳurā. In the 4th/10th century, Ḳurḥ, said by al-Muḳaddasī to have been predominantly Jewish (*wa 'l-g̲h̲ālibu ʿalayhā' l-yahūdu*), was at the apogee of its prosperity. He wrote: "And the region (*nāḥiya*) of Ḳurḥ is called Wādī 'l-Ḳurā. Apart from Mecca, no town in the Ḥid̲j̲āz today is higher in rank, is in better repair, more populated, or has more merchants, wealth and fine qualities than it" (see also J. Mann, *The responsa* . . ., in *JQR*, N.S. vii [1916-17], 457-90, at 489).

Several prominent Muslims are known to have owned estates in Wādī 'l-Ḳurā. They included ʿUt̲h̲mān b. ʿAffān, ʿAlī b. Abī Ṭālib (who had several estates there), Usāma b. Zayd and ʿAbd Allāh b. ʿUmar b. al-K̲h̲aṭṭāb [*q.v.*], whose land was cultivated by his own slaves and by those belonging to his wife (Ibn Zand̲j̲awayh, *K. al-Amwāl*, ed. S̲h̲.D̲h̲. Fayyāḍ, Riyāḍ 1406/1986, iii, 1257-8). Muʿāwiya I [*q.v.*] reportedly initiated a large irrigation project in Wādī 'l-Ḳurā including watering places (*ʿuyūn*). Part of Muʿāwiya's estate in Wādī 'l-Ḳurā was bought from a Jew, while another part was made productive by Muʿāwiya himself. One has to bear in mind that significant pilgrim roads passed through or near Wādī 'l-Ḳurā, hence the *raison d'être* of the estates was probably the provision of food to the pilgrims.

The development of new irrigation projects, and the maintenance of old ones, required expert knowledge in water engineering. Irrigation experts were probably found among the slaves brought to Wādī 'l-Ḳurā in the early days of Islam. ʿUmar b. Dāwūd b. Zād̲h̲ān (better known as ʿUmar al-Wādī), a *mawlā* of ʿUt̲h̲mān b. ʿAffān, was the first in a distinguished line of musicians who lived in Wādī 'l-Ḳurā. At the same time ʿUmar was also a *muhandis* or "one who determines the measures and proportions of subterranean channels for water". This link by *walā'* with ʿUt̲h̲mān went back to ʿUmar's grandfather, Zād̲h̲ān (*Ag̲h̲ānī*[3], vii, 85) who was presumably a Persian slave employed in ʿUt̲h̲mān's estate in Wādī 'l-Ḳurā.

In the 3rd/9th century, the Ḳuḍāʿa were still dominant in the area. According to Lug̲h̲da, Wādī 'l-Ḳurā and its surroundings belonged to the ʿUd̲h̲ra, the Balī, the Saʿd Allāh and the D̲j̲uhayna (all of whom were subdivisions of the Ḳuḍāʿa). Groups of the Balī, the ʿUd̲h̲ra (many of whom were absorbed by the Balī) and the D̲j̲uhayna can still be found in the same area, in addition to groups of the ʿAnaza and the Ḥarb [*q.vv.*].

Bibliography (in addition to references given in the article): Balād̲h̲urī, *Futūḥ*; Ṭabarī; Wāḳidī; and Yāḳūt, index; the relevant entries in the geographical dictionary in Samhūdī, *Wafā' al-wafā*, ed. M.M. ʿAbd al-Ḥamīd, Cairo 1374/1955, repr. Beirut 1401/1981; Lug̲h̲da al-Iṣfahānī, *Bilād al-ʿarab*, ed. Ḥ. al-D̲j̲āsir and Ṣ.A. al-ʿAlī, Riyāḍ 1968, index; Masʿūdī, *Murūd̲j̲*, ed. Pellat, index; A.A. Nasif, *al-ʿUlā, an historical and archaeological survey with special reference to its irrigation system*, Riyāḍ 1988.

(M. Lecker)

WĀDĪ NŪN, the form of more recent times for the earlier Wādī Nūl, a great plain of southwestern

Morocco lying between the Anti-Atlas and its Saharan outliers some 35 km/20 miles from the Atlantic. The plain is formed from the silt carried down by a number of watercourses, of which the chief are the Wādī Ṣayyād and the Wādī Umm al-ʿAs̲h̲ar, which unite to form the Wādī Āsāka, which last runs through a defile into the Atlantic just south of what was the Spanish enclave of Ifni.

The Wādī Nūn contains a number of oases with large villages (Awgelmīm or Glaymīm, Ḳṣābī, Tīlīwīn, Fask, Dubiyān, Tig̲h̲mart, Asrīr, Waʿrūn, Abbūda, etc.). which in the past served as trading centres for the Saharan nomads. The local inhabitants are Arabophone Berbers, belonging for the most part to the Lamṭa with some Maʿḳil lineages and to the sociopolitical groups (*laff* [*q.v.*]) of the Takna, but some to the Ayt Baʿamrān and the Ak̲h̲sās. An element present from mediaeval Islamic times has been that of the Ḥarāṭīn [see ḤARṬĀNĪ], and there was a Jewish community until the 20th century.

The region has owed its historic importance to several factors. It is in Morocco one of the rarer groups of oases which through the centuries has communicated in the south with the Mauritanian Adrar and Senegal, and in the southeast, with the Niger bend. It is also at the exit of the easiest route between the desert and the northern slope of the Atlas, a natural route which runs onwards as far as al-Suwayra [*q.v.*] or Mogador. Finally, its proximity to the Atlantic Ocean has enabled its inhabitants at various times to enter into commercial relations with Europe and to act as a corridor for the exporting of the rich products of the Western Sūdān.

The pre-Islamic history of the region is obscure, but its population must have been Berber, of the groups Illmmidn (which in the language of the Iznagn or Ṣanhād̲j̲a [*q.v.*] would mean "those who have learnt to act together"), i.e. the Lamṭa, and the distinct Iwillimmidn or Lamtūna. In the first Islamic century, Lamṭa Berbers controlled the settlements of the Wādī Nūl, and it was probably the ephemeral rule of ʿAbd Allāh b. Idrīs II in the Sūs [*q.v.*] which brought them for the first time into contact with the Islamic faith. They were probably at this time essentially nomadic, but acquired a significant town, Nūl Lamṭa, which seems to have occupied the site of the later villages of Asrīr Tig̲h̲mart. It was a great entrepôt, where the famous shields of antelope hide (*lamṭ*) were made, and from it caravans set out to cross the Sahara for Mauritania and the Western Sūdān. It was probably this commercial role of the region which at an early date attracted a Jewish colony.

In the 5th/11th century, Nūl Lamṭa rose to prominence when the Almoravids [see AL-MURĀBIṬŪN] conquered the Wādī Nūl basin, and *ca.* 494/1101 established a celebrated mint there, and the high quality of its gold dīnārs attests the economic importance of the place and its importance to the Almoravids. Amongst the towns of the Great Atlas and the Anti-Atlas, Nūl and Ag̲h̲māt [*q.v.*] now consolidated their metropolitan position, with Nūl in third position after Sid̲j̲ilmāsa and Ag̲h̲māt and in front of Fās and Marrākus̲h̲. Imposing fortresses of the Almoravids above Nūl and Tag̲h̲ad̲j̲id̲j̲t still attest this importance. Al-Idrīsī describes the large size of the encampments there of the Iwillimmidn. The mint of Nūl Lamṭa continued to operate until 543/1148-9, two years after the death of the last Almoravid Isḥāḳ b. ʿAlī b. Yūsuf b. Tās̲h̲ufīn, and its continued cultural significance is shown by mentions of scholars there, such as ʿAbd Allāh b. Abī Bakr al-Samkānī who studied there in 663/1264-5 with S̲h̲ayk̲h̲ Abū Sulaymān Dāwūd al-Ḥaḥāʾī, who is said to have taught Ibn ʿAbd al-Barr's *K. al-Kāfī*.

The advent of the Almohads [see AL-MUWAḤḤIDŪN] did not prevent Nūl Lamṭa and other nearby towns like Tag̲h̲ad̲j̲id̲j̲t and Tagawst from retaining their vigorous independence against outside incursions. Hence ʿAbd al-Muʾmin sent his commander Abū Ḥafṣ with three corps of troops against the Wādī Nūn, wreaking complete destruction there in 549/1154-5, with massacres and deportations. Nevertheless the three towns later revived: al-Marrākus̲h̲ī, Ibn Saʿīd and Ibn K̲h̲aldūn attest the continuing importance of Nūl Lamṭa and Tagawst, whilst Tag̲h̲ad̲j̲id̲j̲t survived under an Almohad governor.

In 615/1218 the invasions of the Maʿḳil Arabs reached Wādī Nūn, and one of their component tribes, the D̲h̲awū Ḥassān, soon clashed there with the indigenous Illmmidn and Iguzuln. Allying with whoever paid them most, the incomers gradually overlaid the power of the Lamṭa, and with the subsequent conflict of the D̲h̲awū Ḥassān and the Marīnids [*q.v.*] over control of the region, Nūl Lamṭa declined in favour of Tagawst (the modern Ḳṣābī), and it was under the name Tagawst that the Europeans long knew the Wādī Nūn region.

From 1405, expeditions began under Portuguese, Spanish and other European navigators from the Canary Islands to the African coast, in a century when the existence of the confederation of the Takna is first attested. These expeditions were to secure slaves for the agricultural exploitation of the Islands, and constituted the celebrated *entradas*, several of which reached the gates of Tagawst and resulted in the foundation of a number of Spanish fortresses. One of them, San Miguel de Saca, which only lasted, however, for a very short time, was quite close to the Wādī Nūn, at the mouth of the Āsāka. These expeditions were perhaps preceded or accompanied by Christian missions. In 1525 Tagawst venerated the relics of a Portuguese from the Order of the Hermits of St. Augustine, who had lived in this region. It was a period when the Hilālī Arab tribe [see HILĀL] of the Awlād ʿĀmir apparently secured control over Tagawst, although the mass of cultivable land remained in the hands of the indigenous Illmmidn and Igulzuln.

The foundation of the Saʿdian dynasty [see SAʿDIDS] in the 10th/16th century resulted in the expulsion of the Christians and the people of Nūn supplied *gīs̲h̲* contingents to the sovereigns who had liberated Muslim soil. But very soon, it seems, their oases began to lose their position as starting-points for caravans. The S̲h̲orfā [see S̲H̲URAFĀʾ] came from Tāgmādārt in the upper Darʿa, and it was by this route naturally that they brought to Marrākus̲h̲ the booty of their conquests on the Niger.

This fact no doubt explains why the people of the Wādī Nūn very soon disowned this dynasty, as well as why they were always at more or less open enmity with the Fīlālīs, who for similar reasons favoured the route by Tāfīlālt. In the 17th and 18th centuries, the Wādī Nūn seems to have belonged to the marabout state of Tāzarwālt [*q.v.*], founded by Abū Ḥassūn al-Samlālī (Bū Dmiʿa). He and his successors in every case maintained very regular commercial relations with the country south of the desert. In their reign, European ships frequently came to the coast of the Sūs to carry away merchandise brought down by the caravans. This was a period of prosperity for the Wādī Nūn, which, towards the beginning of the 19th century, formed a practically independent state under

Shaykh Bayrūk, the capital of which, Awgelmīm, soon supplanted Tagawst.

The sultans, however, became disturbed at this direct trade between Europe and the southern provinces of the empire; they were losing all the profit from it. In the second half of the 18th century, Sīdī Muḥammad b. ʿAbd Allāh closed the southern ports to merchant ships and forced them henceforth to come to Mogador, which he had just founded. Tāzarwālt and Wādī Nūn had to send their caravans there and pay heavy taxes on the articles exported. All their efforts, and especially those of Bayrūk and his sons, were in the direction of direct relations with the European governments, in order to place their commerce under European protection and to lead ships to disobey the sultan's orders by founding on the coast a port where the customs duties were lower than those at Mogador. The way was paved for this policy by the old relations of the Jews of the Wādī Nūn with the European merchants and by the numerous shipwrecks which took place in this district at the end of the 18th century, which gave Bayrūk an opportunity to discuss his plan with Christians. He tried first of all in 1835-6 to interest England and then France in 1837-53; finally, after his death in 1859, his sons began negotiations with Spain, which enabled this nation to get, by the treaty of Tetouan, the concession of a fishing station on the coast. So far, these attempts had yielded no appreciable result; the commercial strength of the Ulād Bayrūk seemed rather precarious, and the coast of the Wādī Nūn, moreover, did not afford sufficient shelter for ships. It was only in 1876 that Mackenzie built a factory on Cape Juby, soon followed by Curtis, who settled near Awgelmīm in the Wādī Areksīs. These marked the beginning of a series of explorations and experiments which disturbed sultan Mawlāy al-Ḥasan so much that in 1886 he decided upon an expedition to the south. This ended in the submission of Tāzarwālt and of the Wādī Nūn and in the departure of the English merchants. The marabout *shaykh* Māʾ al-ʿAynayn [*q.v.*], whose anti-foreign influence was increasing in the western Sahara, undertook to put a stop to any Christian enterprise on these coasts. It was not till four years after his death, in 1916, that Spain established herself on Cape Juby and a German submarine landed a mission to seek an alliance with his son Mawlāy Aḥmad al-Hība, who was directing the opposition of the tribes in the Anti-Atlas against the French advance; this last effort led to nothing [see AḤMAD AL-HĪBA, in Suppl.].

By the first half of the 20th century, the process of desertification and migrations of the local populations towards the Atlantic plains and the cities, combined with the disappearance of the trans-Saharan commerce, made the Wādī Nūn chiefly significant for stock-rearing (camels, horses, cattle and, especially, sheep and goats), although agriculture included some cereals, vines, figs, oranges, pomegranates and dates. By then, the markets of Awgelmīm and Tighmart were only of local significance. The most notable were the fairs (*mūsem, amuggār*) of Asrīr, Ḳṣābī and Awgelmīm where the settled population and pastoralists exchanged products.

Bibliography: 1. Sources. These include geographers like Yaʿḳūbī, Ibn Ḥawḳal, Bakrī, Idrīsī, the *K. al-Djaʿrāfiyya*; historians like Ibn Khaldūn, *K. al-ʿIbar* and *Muḳaddima*, and Ibn ʿIdhārī's *Bayān*; and hagiographers like Ibn al-Zayyāt, *K. al-Tashawwuf ilā 'l-taṣawwuf*, ed. A. Faure, Rabat 1958. Because of the region's contacts with Europe, the accounts of European travellers, captives, visitors, etc. are important; for these, see the *EI*[1] art., and add Th. Monod and P. de Cenival, *Description de la côte d'Afrique de Ceuta au Sénégal par Valentin Fernandès (1506-1507)*, Paris 1938.

2. Studies. P. Marty, *Les Tekna de la Mauritanie*, Paris 1915; F. de la Chapelle, *Les Tekna du Sud-Ouest marocain*, Paris 1929; idem, *Esquisse d'une histoire du Sahara occidentale*, in *Hespéris* (VIIe Congrès de l'IHEM), xi (1930), 35-96; R. Montagne, *Les Berbères et le Makhzen dans le Sud du Maroc*, Paris 1930; De la Chapelle and de Cenival, *Possessions espagnoles sur la côte occidentale d'Afrique. Santa Cruz de Mar Pequeña et Ifni*, in *Hespéris* (1935), 2-3e trim., 19-77; V. Monteil, *Notes sur les Tekna du Sud-Ouest marocain*, Rabat 1948; M. Naimi, *La politique des chefs de la confédération Takna face à l'expansionisme commercial européen*, in *Rev. de l'hist. maghrébine*, Tunis, no. 35-6 (1984), 151-73; idem, *Nomades et sedentaires dans l'évolution de l'ensemble confédéral Takna*, in *BESM*, nos. 159-61 (1986), 231-45; idem, *Frontière climatique et mode de vie présaharien: Wad Nun, Bani et As Sagya Al Hamra au siècle des Murabitun*, in *L'Homme et le dromadaire en Afrique*, Agadir 1990, 139-52; idem, *American expansionist aims in south western Morocco during the nineteenth century*, in *The Atlantic connection, 200 years of Moroccan relations*, Rabat 1991, 105-16; idem, *The evolution of the Takna confederation caught between coastal commerce and trans-Saharan trade*, in C.R. Pennell (ed.), *Tribe and state. In honour of David Montgomery Hart*, Wisbech, Cambs. 1991, 213-38; idem, *Le pays Takna, commerce et etnicité avant la constitution confédérale*, in *Le Maroc et l'Atlantique*, Fac. des Lettres, Rabat Univ. 1992, 121-46; idem, *Le pouvoir makhzan dans le Sous*, in *Rev. Maroc-Europe*, no. 6 (1994), 85-94; idem, *Nul Lamta ou l'éveil du sens étiologique*, in *Le nom géographique: patrimoine et communication*, Rabat 1994, 45-85; idem, *Nul Lamta, tableaux édifiants*, in *Hespéris*, xxxiii (1995), 83-118. (MUSTAPHA NAIMI)

WĀDĪ RĪGH [see MAGHRĀWA. B. 4].

WĀDĪ YĀNA or **ĀNA**, or NAHR YĀNA/ĀNA, the classical Anas, Span. Guadiana, Port. Odiana, a great river of the south-central and southwestern parts of the Iberian peninsula.

It rises in the southeastern part of the central Meseta, in the Serranía de Cuenca [see ḲŪNKA], as the Záncara and Gigüela rivers, and flows westwards and then southwards to the Atlantic, with a course of 578 km/360 miles. Its last part, below Pomarão, forms part of the modern boundary between Spain and Portugal; only this section, and a little further upstream to Mertola, is navigable. Along its middle reaches are a series of seasonal lakes and marshes, *los Oyos del Guadiana* "the Eyes of the Guadiana", known in ancient times as "the re-born Guadiana", i.e. after the summer drought. Arabic authors noted the disappearance and re-appearance of the river, and al-Idrīsī calls it *al-nahr al-ghaʾūr* "the disappearing, subterranean river". Other names for the river in historical and geographical sources are Nahr Uḳlīsh ("of Uclès"), N. [Ḳalʿat] Rabāḥ ("of Calatrava"), N. Mārida ("of Merida") and N. Baṭalyaws ("of Badajoz"), from the towns along its banks.

Bibliography: F.J. Madoz, *Diccionario geográfico*, Madrid 1846-50, ix, 27. (C.F. SEYBOLD*)

WADĪʿA (A.), noun from the root *wadaʿa* which can denote the opposing meanings or *aḍdād* [*q.v.*], of both depositing an object with and accepting it from a person. It is also the term given to the legal contract that regulates depositing an object with another person, whether real or supposed. Strictly speaking, *īdāʿ* is the actual act, while the form I verb *wadaʿa* refers to the actual relationship, since *wadīʿa* is in reality the noun for the object of the contract (*maḥall al-ʿaḳd*).

The depositor (*mūdiʾ*) is thus a person who deposits an object or property with the *mūdaʿ*. Although the relationship falls within the area of contract when it involves tangible material matters, it is difficult to conceptualise as a contract when it involves non-material intangibles, such as acts of behaviour or personal or trade secrets.

According to the Ḥanafī school, the contract (*īdāʿ*) is defined as authorising another party to safeguard one's property by either declaration (*ṣarāḥat*[an]) or indication (*dilālat*[an]). The same basic conditions (*shurūṭ*) governing a standard contract apply to *wadīʿa*. This includes the sanity (*ʿaḳl*) of the contracting parties and their majority (*bulūgh*). However, the Ḥanafīs do not stipulate the adulthood of both parties and accept that a minor who has permission to trade (*ṣabī maʾdhūn*) is able to deposit his property freely. Another condition is that the object of the contract should be legal (*māl mutaḳawwim*). Accordingly, the statement made by Otto Spies in *EI*[1], iv, 1080, that "only *māl* can be deposited" applies once it is understood that the *māl* is not the focus of the condition but that the legality of the *māl* is involved. Thus wine is not legally an item of property for an ordinary Muslim but, if it is owned by a newly-converted Muslim it is considered as legal. The final, standard contractual condition required for *īdāʿ* is the offer by the depositor (*mūdiʿ*) and acceptance by the depositary (*mūdaʿ*). The obligations of the depositary dictate that he/she should safeguard the object to the best of his/her ability. When liability is to be assessed by the court, the safekeeping expected would be that normally accepted for similar objects. Liability can only be granted to the depositor if negligence or transgression (*taʿaddī*) is proved.

This occurs:

1. If he deposit the thing with a third person, for the depositing is based on the personal confidence which the depositor has placed in a definite individual known to him, Ibn Abī Laylā alone allows the depositary to deposit again. Opinions differ regarding further depositing with members of the family. Members of the family are considered to be such persons who live with the depositary and belong to his household: wife, children, parents, servants. The Shāfiʿī jurists follow *ḳiyās* and forbid further depositing, while the Ḥanafīs and Mālikīs who follow *istiḥsān* allow it. According to all schools, however, the depositary may deposit again in face of pressure from a higher power in order to save the thing deposited. As cases of this kind, examples are given of shipwreck, fire, inundation and enemy raids.

2. If the depositary uses the thing or derives advantage from it, e.g. if he wears the deposited clothes or rides the mule, unless he is trying thereby to avoid damage.

Contemporary applications of *wadīʿa* are numerous. Many may not have existed in the early days of Islam, but the same principles apply to them. The contract may also be circumstantially concluded in situations such as sporting facilities that provide lockers for clothes and an attendant to safeguard valuables. The responsibility in this case and in all similar cases comes under the rule of *wadīʿa* unless the parties involved declare their non-acceptance of liability in one way or another (al-Sanhūri, iv, 679).

According to al-Sanhūrī, *wadīʿa* is one of the named contracts (*ʿuḳūd musammāt*) which are contracts that are popularly known by a specific term. A distinguishing feature of the *īdāʿ* contract is that it is like *wakāla* [*q.v.*] in being a voluntary contract (*ʿaḳd tabarruʾ*) which converts into a trade contract (*ʿaḳd muʿāwaḍa*) once payment is stipulated. However, the contract is unlike the *wakāla* contract since it is one that involves an actual task, namely, safekeeping of the goods. The *wadīʿa*, however, in the same way as the *wakāla*, is a mutually-agreed contract that does not require a specific formality apart from *īdjāb* and *ḳabūl* [see BAYʿ]. It is also like *wakāla* in the way that it gives an obligation to only one party.

It is also important to highlight the differences between *īdāʿ* and the sale contract which involves the exchange of goods rather than their deposit. The difference between the two probably represents the most basic practical element that distinguishes the Islamic notion of the role of money from that of the modern banking system. The *wadīʿa* in Islamic law is simply a depositing process which produces no benefit or ownership for the depositary vis-à-vis the object, whereas sale is a contract which leads to full ownership of the object and its benefits. Money in Islam is considered to be only a medium of value and not an independent value generator. All schools of Islamic law agree that money can be the deposited object (*maḥall al-īdāʿ*), while almost no-one considers that it can be an object of sale.

Distinguishing the *wadīʿa* contract from other contracts is important in modern commercial life because it represents the legal basis for many forms of transactions within the Islamic banking system. The difference between *wadīʿa* and the loan (*ḳarḍ* [see ḲIRĀḌ]) contract is particularly important, since they represent the two forms of contracts paradoxically used as a basis for modern Islamic banking. The concept of *wadīʿa* is often used as justification for *muḍāraba* [*q.v.*] which represents the heart of Islamic interest-free banking. According to *muḍāraba*, the savings are advanced to an enterpreneur on a mutually-agreed percentage. The net profit would then be shared between the bank and the depositor or *mūdiʿ*. No violation (*taʿaddī*) is present here because the consent of the depositor is given and the contract carries the attributes of mutual responsibility in both the risk and the profit. However, it may be observed that, according to the strict principles of *īdāʿ*, a violation of safekeeping may occur when the bank actually uses the money to derive corporate benefit. As a consequence of this objection, the relationship between the bank and its customers should be viewed as a *ḳarḍ* contract rather than *īdāʿ*. For unlike the *īdāʿ*, a loan contract permits both using the object and providing a replacement should the object perish. Both of these processes represent a daily practice with current accounts and in all other banking transactions and loans. The lack of transparency of such relationships is only a part of the criticism of interest free-banking. Others maintain that the structure of the bank is inherently the same as that of an ordinary bank, only with a change in terminology, for example, the deposit account is called *ḥisāb al-wadāʾiʿ*. Nevertheless, although Islamic banking may appear similar to orthodox banking, it is very different in essence. The primary difference stems from the risk to which the *wadīʿa* is exposed in the two systems. In the *muḍāraba*, there is a clear element of risk that threatens the deposited money, whereas in ordinary banking no risk is involved. At this juncture, it may be correct to conclude that Islamic banking is metaphorically using the word *wadāʾiʿ* (pl. of *wadīʿa*) to describe capital invested, whereas money deposited in the ordinary banking system, although also called *wadāʾiʿ*, carries only a historical reference to the term since it is inconsistent with original Islamic terminology.

Bibliography: ʿAbd al-Razzāḳ al-Sanhūrī, *al-Wasīṭ fī sharḥ al-ḳānūn al-madanī*, Beirut 1952, iv, 12, vii, 675-776; Muhammad Uzair, *Some conceptual and practical aspects of interest free banking*, in *Studies in Islamic economics*, ed. Khurshid Ahmad, Leicester 1980, 44-8; Wahba al-Zuḥaylī, *al-Fiḳh al-islāmī wa-adillatuh*, Beirut 1985, v, 37-52; Waqar Masood Khan, *Towards an interest free Islamic banking*, Leicester 1985, 28-33; ʿAlī Aḥmad al-Sālūs, *al-Muʿāmalāt al-māliyya al-muʿāṣira fī mīzān al-fiḳh al-islāmī*, Kuwait 1986, 31-36; Muṣṭafā Aḥmad al-Zarḳa, *al-Maṣārif, muʿāmalatuhā, wadāʾiʿuhā wa-fawāʾiduhā*, in *Ḳirāʾāt fi ʾl-iḳtiṣād al-islāmī*, Djudda 1987, 321-51; *EI*[1] art. (O. Spies).

(Mawil Y. Izzi Dien)

WADJD (a.), a term in the terminology of Ṣūfī mysticism meaning "ecstasy, rapture". Al-Tahānawī states that *wadjd* "refers to a divine influx of inspiration which strikes the inner being of the Ṣūfī, generating either sadness or joy in him. It may also change his condition in some way, making him absent from his personal qualities by means of a vision of God" (*Kashshāf iṣṭilāḥāt al-funūn*, Bibl. Indica, Calcutta 1862, 1454).

The term derives from the root *w-dj-d*, with a range of meanings including "to find, obtain, experience, be moved by passion". Hence we have such *maṣdar*s as the *wadjd* under consideration and *widjdān* "feeling, sentiment, ecstasy". See further on this range of meanings, F. Jabre, *Essai sur le lexique de Ghazālī*, Beirut 1970, 270.

In the period of classical Ṣūfism, the development of *wadjd* as a technical term was bound up with scholastic discussions on moral theory which flourished in the Ṣūfī school of Baghdād. Ibn ʿAṭāʾ's (d. 309/921) celebrated dispute with al-Djunayd (d. 298/910 [*q.v.*]) on whether *wadjd* is characterised by the presence of joy or grief in the mystic is perhaps the most famous in this regard. Whereas al-Djunayd declared that ecstasy means "dissociation, severance (*inḳiṭāʿ*) from one's personal qualities while one's essence is graced with joy", Ibn ʿAṭāʾ agreed only partially with this definition, replacing the word "joy" by "grief" (al-Tahānawī, *loc. cit.*; L. Massignon, *The Passion of al-Ḥallāj, mystic and martyr of Islam*, tr. H. Mason, Princeton 1982, i, 92). Another member of this school, al-Kharrāz (d. 277/890 or 286/899 [*q.v.*]), said in his *K. al-Ṣifāt*, in which he analysed the experience of proximity to God (*ḳurb*), describing the various stations traversed by the mystic to attain that degree, that *wadjd* is the first station experienced by those who have proximity to God. Al-Kharrāz's understanding of *wadjd* has been described by P. Nwyia as not so much "ecstasy" as "instasy", a communion with oneself in order to find (*wadjada*) the word of God within and so be delighted (*Exégèse coranique et langage mystique*, Beirut 1970, 254, 259).

Many of the same ontological connotations of *wadjd* figure in the enigmatic meditations on annihilation of al-Djunayd, who explains that *wadjd* and *wudjūd* belong to the final degree of the three stages of annihilation of the selfhood in the divine (*fanāʾ* [see baḳāʾ wa-fanāʾ]). The concept of existing as a kind of annihilation of self was also often emphasised in later mediaeval Ṣūfism, and figures in the expositions of the spiritual stations [see ḥāl] of the mystical ascent to perfect love by most of the Ṣūfī authors, often with great intricacy. See e.g. on these, C. Ernst, *The stages of love in early Persian Sufism*, in L. Lewisohn (ed.), *Classical Persian Sufism, from its origins to Rūmī*, London 1993, 448-51.

Wadjd was also intimately connected with the practice of musical audition, *samāʿ* [*q.v.*], and al-Ghazālī states that "Singing produces a state in the heart which is called *wadjd*. In its turn, *wadjd* causes the bodily limbs to move, whether the movement is non-rhythmic and the emotion be disorderly, or a rhythmic movement, in which case it is called clapping and dancing" (*Iḥyāʾ ʿulūm al-dīn*, Cairo 1346-52/1927-33, ii, 237). Thus the highest state of ecstasy is called *wudjūd* or "existence" itself, to be found through *samāʿ*. Al-Ghazālī's philosophical analysis of the nature and place of *wadjd* among the mystico-psychological states experienced by Ṣūfīs during their concerts of *samāʿ* played a central role in subsequent debates on the legality of music and the place of ecstasy in the contemplative disciplines in Islam. An entire book of the *Iḥyāʾ* is devoted to the defence of *samāʿ*, the *K. Ādāb al-samāʿ wa ʾl-wadjd*, thus indicating the important place which rapture had always played in Islamic spirituality. He also enumerates seven reasons why listening to poetry is more conducive to rapture than hearing the cantillation of the Ḳurʾān, substantially because hearers are too habituated to this last to be further stirred by it. Concerning the place of ecstasy in Muslim spiritual life, he says that listening to poetry arouses yearning (*shawḳ* [*q.v.*]) in the lover of God, leading to mystical states (*aḥwāl*) which are called ecstasy (*Iḥyāʾ*, ii, 246-7). At the end of this Book, al-Ghazālī proffers his own definition, based on the opinions of Dhu ʾl-Nūn al-Miṣrī [*q.v.*] and others, that "ecstasy consists in a mystical state which is the fruit of *samāʿ*, it is an infusion of a true, original divine nature, which, following upon *samāʿ*, the listener 'found' (*yadjiduhu*) in himself" (*ibid.*, ii, 258).

Bibliography (in addition to references in the article): S. Rizvi, *Music in Muslim India*, in *IC*, xv (1941), 331-40; Djawād Nūrbakhsh, essay *Samāʿ*, in his *Dar kharābāt*, London 1982, Eng. tr. *In the tavern of ruin*, London 1990; J. During, *Musique et mystique dans les traditions de l'Iran*, Louvain 1989; A. Gribetz, *The* samāʿ *controversy: Sufi vs. legalist*, in *St. Isl.*, lxxiv (1991), 43-62; A. Shiloah, *Music in the world of Islam, a socio-cultural study*, Aldershot 1995; M. Sells, *Early Islamic mysticism. Sufi, Qurʾan, Miʿraj, poetic and theological writings*, New York 1996; Nadjīb Māyil Harawī, *Andar ghazal-i khʷīsh nahān khʷāham gashtan: samāʿ-nāmahā-i fārsī*, Tehran n.d.

(L. Lewisohn, shortened by the Editors)

WADJDA, conventionally Oujda, a town of eastern Morocco, 14 km/8 miles from the Algerian frontier in the southern part of the Angad plain. Despite its eccentric position, Wadjda is today the eighth largest town of Morocco, with 352,000 inhabitants in 1994. It has a strategic situation as a crossroads of the route from Fās to Orania and the axis of the route from the high plateaux to the Mediterranean; it has been fought over all through the centuries, and destroyed and rebuilt repeatedly.

1. Pre-modern history.

It was founded in 384/994 by Zīrī b. ʿAṭiyya, head of the great Zenāta Berber tribe of the Maghrāwa [*q.v.*]. In the course of the Ṣanhādja-Zenāta struggles, the latter had been pushed back into the extreme Moroccan west, where they became firm partisans of the Umayyads in Cordova. Zīrī was, with his tribe, authorised to occupy the region of Fās, but feeling insecure in that region and that town, and wishing to be nearer to the central Maghrib homeland of his tribe, he moved to Wadjda, installed there a garrison and his possessions, appointing one of his relatives as governor. According to al-Bakrī, in the mid-5th/11th century, a new quarter with a wall was allegedly added to the primitive core; the Great Mosque remained, however, outside these two urban centres.

In the time of Almoravid expansion, Yūsuf b. Tāshufīn occupied it in 472/1079, and in the next century, it came under Almohad control, with its fortifications repaired and strengthened under Muḥammad al-Nāṣir (*Rawḍ al-ḳirṭās*, 203, tr. 194). However, it was after the ʿAbd al-Wādids were installed at Tlemcen/Tilimsān that Wadjda, "the avenue of the frontier which separates the central from the far Maghrib", according to Ibn Khaldūn, began to play an important strategic role. In 670/1271, the Marīnid Abū Yūsuf Yaʿḳūb, having defeated Yaghmurāsan [*q.v.*] near Wadjda, totally destroyed the town. In 695/1296 Abū Yaʿḳūb Yūsuf seized the town, destroyed what remained of its fortifications, then rebuilt the ruined parts, with a palace, citadel and great mosque (probably the existing one) and began the eight-years' siege of Tilimsān. In 714/1314 Wadjda resisted the Marīnid Abū Saʿīd ʿUthmān's attack, but twenty-one years later was seized by Abu 'l-Ḥasan ʿAlī and its defences dismantled. Once again, under the Marīnids, with both Wadjda and Tilimsān in their hands, the Arab tribes of the region espoused the cause of the dispossessed ʿAbd al-Wādids and came to besiege Wadjda.

From the 16th to the 19th century, Wadjda was the locus for many changes of fortune in the struggles between the Turks of Algiers and the sultans of Morocco, coming within the sultans' realm in times of peaceful progress, but when the sultans were weak and their land troubled, Wadjda became attached to the province of Tlemcen and dominated by the Turks, according to L. Voinot. One of the few times when Sharīfian authority was in fact firmly established was under Mawlāy Ismāʿīl (1082-1139/1672-1727), who transplanted at Wadjda Arabs brought from south of Marrakesh, made them into a *gīsh/djaysh*, strengthened the town's defences, built numerous *ḳaṣba*s in the vicinity and organised the tribes of the plain. But after his death, the Turks reappeared and trouble was renewed. Finally, in 1795 a Sharīfian army took possession of the town again and permanently incorporated it into the Moroccan empire, with an *ʿāmil* installed there to represent the sultan.

In 1844, after the battle of Isly, it was temporarily occupied by French forces in reprisal for the sultan of Morocco's aid to the *amīr* ʿAbd al-Ḳādir [*q.v.*]. French troops reappeared there in 1859, and it was definitively occupied in 1907, even before the Protectorate was installed (1912). Since then, the form Oujda has been the sole one in use, including by the Moroccan administration. (G. Marçais*)

2. The modern city.

The modest small town of 6,466 inhabitants (1910) occupied by the French army was smaller than its neighbour, the Spanish *presidio* Melilla (12,000 people in 1908). Hence Oujda became the focus of an intense colonisation, esentially of "Pieds Noirs" from Algeria, French and then Spanish. In 1936, with the population at 34,500, the town had almost as many outsiders as Moroccans. The Jewish community (whether of Moroccan, Algerian or French origin) was important and active, owning 30% of the commercial enterprises as recorded in 1934, but after 1948, and especially after 1955, it emigrated massively. In 1951, just before independence, Oujda had over 80,000 people, including many Algerians amongst the third of non-Moroccans. The ebb and flow of populations continues now to affect the town, as in the past: the Algerian element was swollen during the 1954-62 Algerian war, brutally reduced after Algeria's achievement of independence, whilst in 1975 35,000 Moroccan refugees arrived there during the latent Algero-Moroccan war before being redistributed over other parts of Morocco, 6,500 of them remaining, however, at Oujda. The more gradual departure of Europeans left only a few hundred by 1982 (Guitouni).

The colonial period made Oujda an important military centre, with many camps and barracks, and also a great railway junction, second only to Casablanca for its freight traffic. Part of the old medina was destroyed to accommodate a new road network, and a new medina built to the north-north-east. A "European" town grew up to the west, mainly between the railway station and the medina, whilst precarious suburbs for rural immigrants grew up round the peripheries. Traffic with Algeria was heavy, and Oujda did not suffer from its distance from the administrative capital Rabat nor from its distance from Casablanca, since the ports of Orania could be used.

But after Moroccan independence in 1956, Oujda found itself in a cul-de-sac, with the Algerian frontier closed and with reverberations from the Moroccan-Algerian conflict. Each time the frontier has been reopened there has been a great surge of persons crossing (2 million in 1991) in search of the contraband goods smuggled out from Melilla. Service and transport businesses, hotel, industrial and financial activities have prospered, but the town has little industrial enterprise (only 4,000 employed) and has suffered from huge rural influxes as mines have closed in its southern hinterland; administrative and military functions (since Oujda is the chef-lieu of a *wilāya*) do not suffice to provide resources for a vastly swollen population (that will reach over 400,000 by the end of the 20th century).

The town has largely spread over the surrounding gardens and orchards and has extended its tentacles along the main roads, especially along that eastwards to Bukane and Algeria. Although well endowed with the fifth largest airport in Morocco and the fifth largest university centre, and being the main commercial centre for the eastern part of the country, Oujda suffers from its position away from the main centres of the country on the Atlantic seaboard and from the cyclical changes of fortune with regard to the Algerian border (last closed on 28 August 1994). It awaits a revived role as a stopover town when international exchanges between the countries of the Maghrib are reactivated.

Bibliography: For the mediaeval Arabic sources, see the *EI*[1] art., section 1. Of modern ones, see A. Bernard, *Les confins algéro-marocains*, Paris 1911; L. Voinot, *Oujda et l'amalat*, Oran 1912; H. Saladin, from de Beaulincourt, *Les monuments d'Oujda*, in *Bull. archéologique* (1910), 224 ff.; G. Marçais, *Manuel d'art musulman*, ii, 481, 558-9; J.L. Miège, *Le Maroc et l'Europe (1830-1894)*, Paris 1963; D. Nordman, *La notion de frontière en Afrique du Nord, mythes et réalités (1830-1912)*, diss. Montpellier III, 1975; M. El Arabi, *Les quartiers périphériques de la ville d'Oujda*, diss. Tours, 1981; Y. Katan, *Oujda, une ville frontière du Maroc*, Paris 1990; J. Fremeaux, *Les trois occupations d'Oujda par l'armée française*, in *Revue Maghreb-Europe*, Rabat, no. 5 (1993); Miège, *Pour une histoire d'Oujda dans la deuxième moitié du XIXème siècle*, in *ibid.*; A. Guitouni, *Le Nord-Est marocain. Réalités et potentialités d'une région excentrée*, Oujda 1955.

(J.F. Troin)

WADJHĪ [see MATHNAWĪ. 4].

WĀDJIB [see FARD].

WAFĀ, the pen-name of various minor Persian poets of the 18th-19th centuries. They include:

1. Muḥammad Amīn, b. 1110/1698-9 in Īličpūr (Eličpur) in the western Deccan, d. 1193/1779-80. His ancestors belonged to Iṣfahān, from where his father, Ḥakīm Muḥammad Taḳī Khān, migrated to India during the reign of Awrangzīb (1658-1707), and rose to a respectable position under Nawwāb Āṣaf Djāh (d. 1748), governor of the Deccan in the time of the Mughal Emperor Farrukhsiyar (1713-19). Muḥammad Amīn received his education from his father, and dedicated his time to the pursuit of poetry and epistolography (Ḳudrat Allāh Gopāmawī, Natāʾidj al-afkār, Bombay 1136/1957, 756-7).

2. Mīrzā Sharaf al-Dīn ʿAlī Ḥusaynī, called Āḳāsī Beg, b. 1137/1724-5 in Ḳumm, d. 1200/1785-6 (see Rieu, Catalogue of Persian manuscripts in the British Museum, suppl., no. 344). He came from a respected family of sayyids, and was one of the custodians of the Imāmzāda Fāṭima in Ḳumm. According to Luṭf ʿAlī Beg Ādhar (Ātashkada, ed. Sayyid Djaʿfar Shahīdī, Tehran (?) 1337/1958, 423), he went to India towards the latter part of Nādir Shāh's reign and stayed there for some thirty years. In 1180/1766-7 he returned to Persia, and from there went on the Pilgrimage to Mecca. He has left a dīwān containing poems in the traditional forms (Ethé, Cat. Pers. mss. India Office, i, no. 1718).

3. Muḥammad Ḥusayn Farāhānī, d. 1209/1794-5 at Ḳazwīn (cf. ʿAbd al-Razzāḳ Dunbulī, Nigāristān-i Dārā, ed. Khayyāmpūr, Tabrīz 1342/1963, 147). He belonged to Farāhān, a village of Ḳumm. Most of his ancestors had been ministers during their lifetimes, and he, too, served in that capacity under Zand and Ḳādjār rulers. As minister, he made efforts towards promoting education (Muḥammad Muʿīn, Farhang-i Fārsī, vi, Tehran 1371/1992, 2214). Dunbulī credits him with a dīwān of poems comprising some 4,000 verses, and also states that he composed a mathnawī in the metre of Niẓāmī's Haft paykar (ibid., 147).

4. Mīrzā Muḥammad ʿAlī Zawāraʾī, b. 29 Ṣafar 1195/25 February 1781 in Iṣfahān, d. reportedly 1245/1829-30 (Gulčīn-i Maʿānī, Tārīkh-i tadhkirahā-yi Fārsī, ii, Tehran 1363/1984, 116-17). He received his education in Iṣfahān and achieved competency in natural sciences, medicine, jurisprudence, and the art of poetry. He was among the intellectuals of Fatḥ ʿAlī Shāh Ḳādjār's reign, and moved in the company of the monarch's poet-laureate, Fatḥ ʿAlī Khān Ṣabā (see Sayyid Aḥmad Dīwān Begī, Ḥadīḳat al-shuʿarāʾ, iii, ed. ʿAbd al-Ḥusayn Nawāʾī, Tehran 1366/1987, 2005). According to Gulčīn-i Maʿānī, he composed a tadhkira of poets and poetry named Maʾāthir al-Bāḳiriyya, which was completed in 1245/1829-30 (ibid., 110).

5. Shaykh Muḥammad Bāḳir Tammāmī, b. 1278/1861-2 (Mīrzā Ḥasan Ḥusaynī Fasāʾī, Fārsnāma-yi Nāṣirī, ii, Tehran 1313/1895, 28). His father, Shaykh Abu 'l-Ḳāsim Shīrāzī, who wrote poetry under the pen-name Ṣafā, held the title of Shaykh al-Islām, which was passed on to his son Muḥammad Bāḳir by orders of the ruling monarch Nāṣir al-Dīn Shāh (see Dīwān Begī, ibid., 2007). Muḥammad Bāḳir's date of death is not known but, according to Muḥammad Ḥusayn Rukn-zāda Ādamiyyat, author of Dānishmandān u sukhan-sarāyān-i Fārs (iv, Tehran 1340/1961, 820), he was still alive in 1313/1895-6.

6. Mīrzā Ḥasan ʿAlī Shīrāzī, popularly known as Mīrzā Buzurg, b. 1224/1809-10. He studied under his father, Mīrzā Sayyid ʿAlī, who was a poet employing Niyāz as his pen-name. After studying medicine, he went to India in 1259/1838-9, and soon afterwards visited Mecca and Medina and travelled to Europe, where he stayed in Paris and London to complete his medical studies. On returning to India, he took up residence in Calcutta, teaching and practising medicine. In 1276/1859-60 he set out on a pilgrimage to Mashhad, but died en route in Bombay (Fārsnāma-yi Nāṣirī, ii, 119-20). According to this last, 122, he was the author of some 15,000 verses.

7. Abu 'l-Ḳāsim Shīrāzī, known as Mudarris. He was among the learned élite of Shīrāz; well versed in many rational and traditional sciences and was the author of a dīwān containing Persian poems and Arabic ḳaṣīdas (Shaykh Mufīd Dāwar, Tadhkira-yi mirʾāt al-faṣāḥat, ed. Muḥammad Ṭāwūsī, Shīrāz 1371/1992, 692-3; Fārsnāma-yi Nāṣirī, ii, 935).

8. Mīrzā Mahdī Ḳulī, known as Wafā Ashrafī, descended from a Georgian family which had settled in Persia during Ṣafawid times and was employed as confidential secretary to Manūčihr Khān Muʿtamad al-Dawla, who served as governor of Iṣfahān from 1838 until his death in 1847 (Madjmaʿ al-fuṣaḥāʾ, ii/3, 1091; Ḥadīḳat al-shuʿarāʾ, iii, 2004).

9. Mīrzā Muḥammad ʿAlī Kāshānī, a member of the nobility and a man of learning having special knowledge in medicine. He was employed in government service as head of the postal department in Zandjān (Ḥadīḳat al-shuʿarāʾ, iii, 2018).

Bibliography: Given in the text, but see also Maḥmūd Mīrzā Ḳādjār, Safīnat al-Maḥmūd, i, ed. Khayyāmpūr, Tabrīz 1346/1968, 224-5, 228; ʿAbd al-Ḥakīm Ḥākim, Tadhkira-yi mardum-i dīda, ed. Sayyid ʿAbd Allāh, Lahore 1961, 112-14; Mīrzā Furṣat Shīrāzī, Āthār al-ʿAdjam, Bombay 1354/1935, 510-11; Maʿṣūm Shīrāzī (Maʿṣūm ʿAlī Shāh), Ṭarāʾiḳ al-ḥaḳāʾiḳ, iii, ed. Muḥammad Djaʿfar Maḥdjūb, Tehran (?) n.d., 250-1; Muḥammad ʿAlī Muʿallim Ḥabībābādī, Makārim al-āthār, ii, Iṣfahān 1343/1963-4, 440-2; Muḥammad ʿAlī Tabrīzī (Mudarris), Rayḥānat al-adab, iv, Tabrīz (?) 1331/1952, 296-7; Muḥammad ʿAlī Mudjāhidī (Parwāna), Tadhkira-yi sukhanwarān-i Ḳumm, Ḳumm 1370/1991, 344-8.

(MUNIBUR RAHMAN)

WAFD (A., lit. "delegation"), the name of a nationalist political party in modern Egypt, whose heyday was for some three decades after 1918, petering out as an effective force in the 1950s.

It gained its name from the delegation which began to be formed in Egypt in September 1918 in order to make Egypt's demands for independence known at the Peace Conference in Paris. The leading member of the Wafd was Saʿd Zaghlūl [q.v.]. The delegation had a meeting with Sir Reginald Wingate, Egyptian High Commissioner, at which they demanded complete independence and asked for permission to go to London to put Egypt's case to the British government. At the same time, the Egyptian delegation (al-wafd al-miṣrī) was formed also under the leadership of Zaghlūl. The British refused to give permission for the Wafd to visit London and later deported Zaghlūl and three colleagues. This move led to the outbreak of a general rebellion throughout Egypt in 1919. It was not organised by Zaghlūl and the Wafd, but they came to represent the Egyptian people and to embody their demands for independence.

The British in an attempt to calm the situation sent out the Milner Mission to Egypt in December 1919. It was greeted with strikes and demonstrations and was boycotted by most Egyptians on the demand of the Wafd. The Mission realised that it had to make concessions and dropped the idea of the protectorate and offered to talk about the aspirations of the Egyptians. The Wafd replied that they would only accept complete independence.

Negotiations dragged on, prolonged by splits amongst the Egyptians over the role of the Wafd. Some politicians, including ʿAdlī Pas̲h̲a, tended to moderation, while Zag̲h̲lūl and his associates remained intransigent. The British tried to deal with the moderates but again realised that any move would fail which did not include the Wafd. Even so, no compromise was reached and Zag̲h̲lūl was again deported. The British reluctantly agreed to end the protectorate in 1922 and Egypt was declared a quasi-independent state.

Egyptian politicians set about drawing up a constitution for the country without the cooperation of the Wafd. However, elections were soon held in which the Wafdist leaders back from exile took part. The Wafd won a crushing victory at the polls and in January 1924 Zag̲h̲lūl formed the first Wafdist government.

The Wafd was organised formally on hierarchical lines. It became a political party in 1924 on coming into government. The original statutes of 1918 declared that the Wafd had been formed for one objective, sc. the achievement of the complete independence of Egypt. The organisation would be headed by a president who had wide authority, with a central committee which would have branches country-wide. The committee's main task was to collect funds, and consequently it deliberately recruited provincial notables who would help in that task. Students were also recruited into the party and they played a significant part in its activities. The secretary of the Wafd, Muṣṭafā al-Naḥḥās [*q.v.*], relied to a great extent on the support of students. They took part in demonstrations, in boycotts and in electioneering. The formation of labour unions also helped in the activities of the party.

Women played an important role in political activities, demonstrating and protesting. In 1920 the Wafdist Women's Central Committee was formed under the leadership of the prominent Egyptian feminist Hudā al-S̲h̲aʿrāwī. They took the lead in boycotting British goods in 1922 and struggled equally for their own voting rights. They believed that the fight for independence had to be accompanied by the fight for equality.

From 1924 to 1936 and until the beginning of the Second World War, Egyptian politics consisted of a three-way contest for power and authority between the King, the British and the politicians, the latter often being members of the Wafd. It was the leading political party of the period, and won every election which was not rigged against them. It was felt by many Egyptians that the Wafd was the real representative of the people.

On Zag̲h̲lūl's death in 1927, al-Naḥḥās took over the leadership of the Wafd and played a prominent role in Egyptian politics until 1952. He signed the 1936 Anglo-Egyptian Treaty, not, however, negotiated by him, which formalised relations between Britain and Egypt. The Treaty still withheld complete independence with its reserved points, and the Wafd had consequently to suffer some unpopularity. The 1930s were a period when more extreme political groupings were emerging, such as the Ik̲h̲wān al-Muslimūn [*q.v.*] and the Miṣr al-Fatāt, with Fascist tendencies. The Wafd tried to keep pace by forming it own paramilitary youth movement, the Blue Shirts.

On the outbreak of war in 1939, the British were keen to preserve Egypt within the Allied camp, although there were some Egyptians who believed that only by helping the Axis to expel the British would they gain complete independence. As the Axis forces approached Alexandria, the British felt they had to have a prime minister who would work with rather than against them. In February 1942 the British Ambassador, Miles Lampson (later Lord Killearn) forced King Fārūḳ to appoint the Wafdist leader Muṣṭafā al-Naḥḥās as prime minister. The Egyptians never forgave this insult, nor did they forget the fact that a Wafdist had been willing to co-operate with the occupier. This contributed to the decline in popularity of the Wafd, although it won elections held in 1942 and tried to regain support by introducing social measures such as free education and greater public health.

The last act of the Naḥḥās government was to host a conference of Arab states in Alexandria in 1944 which led eventually to the foundation of the Arab League. Elections in 1944 were boycotted by the Wafd, and politics in Egypt staggered on under the impact of the loss of Palestine. In January 1950 new elections were won by the Wafd. A very low turnout demonstrated indifference and frustration, and the minority vote obtained by the Wafd showed just how far it had fallen in public esteem. Al-Naḥḥās led his fourth government for only two years until he was overthrown by the Free Officers' coup of July 1952. The Wafd was disbanded in 1953, to return in a new guise in 1976 when Anwar al-Sādāt [*q.v.*] allowed the reformation of political parties. It gained some support, but never threatened the power of the official government party. It was disbanded for a time in protest against al-Sādāt's anti-party moves and re-formed after his death. In 1984 the Wafd won 58 seats. During the election, it had campaigned with the Ik̲h̲wān. It claimed to be the party of small businessmen and to be the sole heir of the 1952 revolution. In the 1987 elections, it ran alone and won 35 seats. Finally, in the 1990 elections the Wafd decided on a boycott because it had unsuccessfully demanded certain concessions. The Wafd remains a pale shadow of its predecessor.

Bibliography: M. Deeb, *Party politics in Egypt: the Wafd and its rivals*, London 1979; J.J. Terry, *Cornerstone of Egyptian political power: the Wafd 1919-1952*, London 1982. P.J. Vatikotis, *The history of modern Egypt from Muhammed Ali to Mubarak*, London 1991.

(D. Hopwood)

WĀFIDIYYA (a.), a collective formation from *wāfid* "one who comes, makes his way, in a delegation or group", in the Mamlūk Sultanate applied to troops of varying ethnic origins who came to Egypt and Syria to join the Sultanate's military forces.

There is no better proof for the superiority of the Mamlūk socio-military system over any other military form during a great part of Islamic history than the attitude of the Mamlūk Sultanate to the Mongol warriors and others, such as Kurds, K̲h̲ʷārazmians, etc. who, for this or that reason, sought and found refuge within its boundaries as *Wāfidiyya*.

The mainly Turkish Mamlūks considered the Mongols to be their next of kin and as belonging to the same ethnicity as they themselves (*min d̲j̲ins wāḥid*). They had the highest regard for their warlike qualities. Quite probably, the Mongols had an impact on the structure of Mamlūk society, although the degree and dimension of that impact have still to be studied more systematically (it has been proven, however, that the Mamlūks were never judged according to the *Yāsa* [*q.v.*], the Mongol law). Furthermore, the greatest influx of the Wāfidiyya Mongols took place during the reigns of two sultans: Baybars al-Bundukdārī (658-77/1260-77), a great admirer of the Mongols, and al-ʿĀdil Kitbughā (694-6/1295-7), who was himself an Oirat Mongol. Baybars even let part of them join the élite corps, the Baḥriyya regiment. However, the influx of these Mongols frightened him: "I fear there is something suspect in their coming from all sides" (al-Maḳrīzī, *Sulūk*, v, 515 ll. 1-6; Ibn ʿAbd al-Ẓāhir, ed. Ṣadaḳa, 105). A measure which he took to neutralise them was to disperse them within much bigger numbers of the Royal Mamlūks (*yufarriḳuhum kull djamāʿa bayna adʿāfihā min al-mamālīk al-sulṭāniyya*, Ibn ʿAbd al-Ẓāhir, 59, l. 1).

Baybars is said to have appointed from amongst them commanders from the rank of Amīr of a Hundred downwards (*ibid.*, 58 l. 19; al-Maḳrīzī, *Khiṭaṭ*, ii, 117; Sato, *State and rural society*, 101). Yet it seems that no *specific* Wāfidī Mongol appointed to that high rank by Baybars has been noted till now by any scholar. The only Wāfidī Amīr of a Hundred noted by the present writer in the reign of that sultan was a Kh^{w}ārazmian, who was related to him by marriage (see Ayalon, *Wāfidīya*, 93 n. 26a. On the Kh^{w}ārazmian and Kurdish *Wāfidīya*, who preceded the Mongols, see *ibid.*, 94-7).

Sultan Kitbughā had to conform to the Mamlūk policy towards the Wāfidiyya, who arrived in 695/1296 in huge numbers (10,000 according to some versions, 18,000 according to others). First of all, he returned to the older policy of separating the leaders from their soldiers, by letting only the leaders enter Egypt and forcing the rest to stay in Syria, settling many of them in its devastated coastal area, as was the case with the earlier Wāfidiyya newcomers. Of their chiefs (numbering between 113 and 300, according to different accounts), only their head, Ṭurghāy, a son-in-law of the Īl-Khānid Hülegü [*q.v.*] received the medium rank of Amīr of Forty (Zetterstéen (ed.), *Beiträge zur Geschichte der Mamlukensultane*, Leiden 1919, 38 l. 21; Ibn Taghrībirdī, *Nudjūm*, ed. Cairo, viii, 60 l. 6). Kitbughā did try, during his short reign, to raise the status of his compatriots, but failed because of the stubborn antagonism of the Royal Mamlūks. It is also stated that one of the two major reasons of his deposition was his favourable attitude to his fellow-Oirats. The Oirats continue to play a political role until the early part of al-Nāṣir Muḥammad b. Ḳalāwūn's third reign (709-41/1309-40). Subsequently, they were on the decline, and in 733/1333 we find them or their descendants as attendants or servants (*atbāʿ*) to the Mamlūks in the Cairo citadel (*Sulūk*, ii, 83 ll. 8-13).

The wide, and usually unbridgeable, gap separating the Mamlūks and non-Mamlūks arriving in the Sultanate, even when the non-Mamlūks belonged to the most highly-appreciated military stock, is well illustrated in the case of the Oirats. Kitbughā and Salār, both of them belonging to that ethnic group, and who arrived in the Sultanate as slaves, rose to the highest ranks, whereas the head of many thousands of Oirats, who arrived there as free men, did not rise above the rank of a medium *amīr*, in spite of his close family connection with one of the greatest Mongol Khāns.

After the influx of the Oirats, the Wāfidiyya migration greatly dwindled until it disappeared for good. At that period, when migration no longer posed any danger to the Mamlūks, they became more generous in bestowing the rank of Amīr of a Hundred on a very small number of immigrants belonging to that category.

Bibliography: D. Ayalon, *The Wafidiyya in the Mamluk kingdom*, in *IC*, (1951), 89-104; idem, *The European-Asiatic steppe: a major reservoir of power for the Islamic world*, in *Procs. of the 25th Congress of Orientalists, Moscow 1960*, Moscow 1963, ii, 47-52; idem, *The Great Yāsa of Chingiz Khan—a reexamination. Part C. The position of the Yāsa in the Mamlūk Sultanate*, in *SI*, xxxvi (1972), 113-58, and esp. 124, 134-7, 141-5, 147; R. Amitai-Preiss, *Mongols and Mamlūks. The Mamlūk-Īlkhānid war, 1260-1281*, Cambridge 1995, index s.v. Wāfidiyya; Tsugitake Sato, *State and rural society in medieval Islam. Sultans, Muqtaʿs and Fellahun*, Leiden 1997, 92, 95, 99-104, 235, 252, 258.

(D. Ayalon)

WĀFIR ("the ample, abundant"), the name of an Arabic poetic metre, the first metre of the second circle in al-Khalīl's classification [see ʿARŪḌ] of which the commonest pattern (*wāfir*-1) is:

⏑ – ⏖ – | ⏑ – ⏖ – | ⏑ – – ‖ ⏑ – ⏖ – | ⏑ – ⏖ – | ⏑ – –

The two consecutive short syllables alternate with one long syllable (48% of all variable positions in al-Mutanabbī's *wāfir* poems taken together are filled with a long syllable, 52% with two short syllables), but the incidence of double short syllables in the second foot of each hemistich appears to be higher than in the first foot (unpublished scansion data).

Occasionally, the first syllable is lacking in opening lines of the poem, a phenomenon called *kharm*, examples of which are al-Nābigha, no. 31; ʿAntara, nos. 1, 12; Ṭarafa, no. 7; Zuhayr, no. 5 (ed. W. Ahlwardt, *The divans of the six ancient Arabic poets*, London 1870); two *Mufaḍḍaliyyāt* poems: nos. 13, 35 (ed. Ch. J. Lyall, Oxford 1921); and four poems in the *Ḥamāsa* of Abū Tammām: nos. 116, 159, 188, 696 (al-Marzūḳī, *Sharḥ dīwān al-ḥamāsa*, ed. Aḥmad Amīn and ʿAbd al-Salām Hārūn, Cairo, 1951-3).

Throughout the first 300 years of Arabic poetry, the use of the *wāfir* metre appears to be fairly constant: up to 10% of the poems originating from what D. Frolov calls "the metrical school of al-Ḥīra", and up to 20% of the compositions by poets from the "Bedouin metrical school" (see his *Notes on the history of ʿArūḍ in al-Andalus*, 91, 93). Frolov's data may be compared with those in the graph in J. Bencheikh, *Poétique arabe*, 225.

In a discussion of the aesthetic value of different metres, Ḥāzim al-Ḳarṭādjannī [*q.v.*] places this metre, together with *kāmil*, after *ṭawīl* and *basīṭ* (see his *Minhādj al bulaghāʾ wa-sirādj al-udabāʾ*, ed. Muḥammad al-Ḥabīb Ibn al-Khōdja, ^{3}Beirut 1986, 268).

Two truncated (*madjzūʾ*) *wāfir* types, labelled *wāfir*-2 (⏑ – ⏖ – | ⏑ – ⏖ – ‖ ⏑ – ⏖ – | ⏑ – ⏑⏑ –) and *wāfir*-3 (⏑ – ⏖ – | ⏑ – ⏖ – ‖ ⏑ – ⏖ – | ⏑ – – –), are occasionally found. Examples in the work of ʿUmar b. Abī Rabīʿa (P. Schwarz, *Der Diwan des ʿUmar Ibn Abi Rebiʿa*, Leipzig 1901-9) are nos. 47, 166, 219, 284, 301, 317, 340, 366, 375, 404, 407 for *wāfir*-2; and 104, 110, 298, 347 for *wāfir*-3. The metrical irregularities in nos. 104, 166, 298 (Schwarz, *op. cit.*, iv, 179) can perhaps be explained as a mixture of metres, due to the similarity between the truncated *wāfir* and *hazadj*.

In modern poetry, *wāfir* continues to be used, albeit sparingly (S. Moreh, *Modern Arabic poetry 1800-1970*, 219, has six poems in *wāfir* or a *wāfir*-like metre in a sample of 759 modern poems). Badr Shākir al-Sayyāb (1926-64 [*q.v.* in Suppl.]) mixes *wāfir* and *radjaz* in his poem *Fi ʾl-maghrib al-ʿarabī* (see S.K. Jayyusi, *Trends and movements in modern Arabic poetry*, Leiden 1977, ii, 729).

Bibliography: G.W. Freytag, *Darstellung der arabischen Verskunst*, Bonn 1830, 133-4, 203-11;

Muḥammad b. Abī S̲h̲anab, *Tuḥfat al-adab fī mīzān as̲h̲ʿār al-ʿarab*, Algiers 1906, 32-5; J. Bencheikh, *Poétique arabe*, ²Paris 1989, 203-53; W.F.G.J. Stoetzer, *Theory and practice in Arabic metrics*, Leiden 1989, 150; D. Frolov, *Klassičeskiy arabskiy stik̲h̲*, Moscow 1991, 171-84; idem, *Notes on the history of ʿArūḍ in al-Andalus*, in *Anaquel de Estudios Árabes*, vi (1995), 87-110; B. Paoli, *Aux sources de la métrique arabe*, in *BÉt.Or.*, xlvii (1995), 183-215. (W. Stoetzer)

WAFḲ (A.), lit. "harmonious arrangement", the construction of magic squares.

One of the most impressive achievements in Islamic mathematics, in any case the most original one, is the development of general methods for constructing magic squares. A magic square of order n is a square with n cells on its side, thus n^2 cells on the whole, in which different natural numbers must be arranged in such a way that the sum of each row, column and main diagonal is the same. As a rule, the n^2 first natural numbers are actually written in, which means that the constant sum amounts to $\frac{1}{2}n(n^2+1)$. If, in addition, the squares left when the borders are successively removed have themselves this magic property, the square is called a *bordered* square. If any pair of broken diagonals (that is, which lie on either side of, and parallel to, a main diagonal and together have n cells) shows the constant sum, the square is called *pandiagonal*. Then there are *composite* squares: when the order n is a composite number—say $n = r \cdot s$ with r, $s \geq 3$—the main square can be divided into r^2 subsquares of order s; these subsquares, taken successively according to a magic arrangement for the order r, are then filled successively with sequences of s^2 consecutive numbers according to a magic arrangement for the order s, the result being then a magic square in which each subsquare is also magic.

Squares are usually divided into three categories: *odd-order* (or *odd*) squares are those with n odd, that is, $n = 3, 5, 7, \ldots$, and generally $n = 2k+1$ with k natural; squares are of *evenly-even* order if n, even, is divisible by 4, thus $n = 4, 8, 12, \ldots, 4k$; finally, *oddly-even* squares have their order n even but divisible by 2 only, whence $n = 6, 10, 14, \ldots, 4k+2$. There are general methods of construction, which depend upon the type of magic square considered (standard, bordered, pandiagonal) and the category to which the order n belongs. Those for standard magic squares may, however, not apply for the smallest orders $n = 3$ and $n = 4$, which are particular cases. Those for bordered squares suppose that $n \geq 5$. (Since no square of order 2 is possible, no square of order 4 is bordered.) Finally, those for pandiagonal squares of odd order are generally not directly applicable if n is divisible by 3, and there are no rules for constructing oddly-even squares since pandiagonal squares of this category do not exist.

Information about the beginning of Islamic research on magic squares is lacking. It may have been connected with the introduction of chess into Persia. Initially, the problem was a purely mathematical one; thus, the ancient Arabic designation for magic squares is *wafḳ al-aʿdād*, that is, "harmonious arrangement of the numbers". We know that treatises were written in the 9th century, but the earliest extant ones date back to the 10th century; one is by Abu 'l-Wafāʾ al-Būzd̲j̲ānī (d. 387/997 or 388/998) and the other is a chapter in Book III of ʿAlī b. Aḥmad al-Anṭākī's (d. 376/987) *Commentary on Nicomachos' Arithmetic* (see *Bibl.*). It appears that, by that time, the science of magic squares was already established: the construction of bordered squares of any order was known; standard magic squares could be formed for small orders (up to $n = 6$), and this was applied to the formation of composite squares. (Although methods for standard magic squares are easier to *apply* than methods for bordered ones, the latter are easier to *discover*.) The 11th century saw the discovery of several ways to construct standard magic squares, in any event for odd and evenly-even ones (see Sesiano, *Un traité médiéval*, and *L'Abrégé*): the much more difficult case of $n = 4k+2$, which Ibn al-Hayt̲h̲am (d. *ca.* 430/1040) could solve only with k even (Sesiano, *Herstellungsverfahren* (I)), was probably not settled before the second half of the 11th century. At the same time, pandiagonal squares were being constructed for squares of evenly-even and of odd order, provided in the latter case that the order was not divisible by 3. (Little attention seems to have been paid, however, to the sum of the broken diagonals; these squares were considered of interest because their construction characteristically required the use of chess moves and because the initial cell, say the place of 1, could be chosen at random within the square.) Treatises on magic squares are numerous in the 12th century, and later developments tend to be improvements or simplifications of existing methods. From the 13th century on, magic squares were increasingly associated with magic proper and used for divinatory purposes. Consequently, many texts merely picture squares and mention their attributes. Others do, however, keep the general theory alive even if their authors, unlike earlier writers, cannot resist adding various fanciful applications.

The link between magic squares and magic as such has to do with the association of each of the twenty-eight Arabic letters with a number (the units, the tens, the hundreds and one thousand). Thus it was sometimes possible to put in e.g. the first row a sequence of numbers equivalent to the letters of a proper name or the words of a sentence and then complete the square so as to produce the same sum in each line. But this involved a completely different kind of construction, which depended upon the order n and the values of the n-given quantities. The problem is mathematically not easy, and led in the 11th century to interesting constructions for the cases from $n = 3$ to $n = 8$ (Sesiano, *Un traité médiéval*). However, once again the subtle theory ended up mostly in a set of practical recipes and then a wider readership was gained at the expense of scholarship.

This development was unfortunate for Europe, where by the late Middle Ages only two sets of squares associated with the seven known celestial bodies had been learned of through Arabic astrological and magic texts—whence the name—and without any indication as to their construction. (Whereas as early as the 12th century some methods of construction had reached India and China, and also Byzantium, as can be seen from the treatise on magic squares written *ca.* 1300 by Manuel Moschopoulos.) Thus the extent of Islamic research remained unknown for quite a long time; indeed, a very long time, since it has only recently been assessed and its importance recognised.

Some examples of constructions

The smallest magic square is the square of order 3 (fig. 1). By constructing successive borders to this square, Islamic mathematicians found a general method of forming bordered squares of any odd order, which is explained by the two 10th-century authors mentioned above. Let n be the given odd order ($n = 9$ in fig. 2). Starting next to a corner cell, e.g. the lower right one, write in the first odd and even numbers alternately along the adjacent side lines until the mid-

2	9	4
7	5	3
6	1	8

Fig. 1

10	16	14	12	*75*	*76*	*78*	*80*	8
15	24	28	26	*61*	*62*	*64*	22	*67*
13	27	34	36	*51*	*52*	32	*55*	*69*
11	25	35	38	45	40	*47*	*57*	*71*
9	23	33	43	41	39	*49*	*59*	*73*
77	*63*	*53*	42	37	44	29	19	5
79	*65*	*50*	*46*	31	30	*48*	17	3
81	*60*	*54*	*56*	21	20	18	*58*	1
74	*66*	*68*	*70*	7	6	4	2	*72*

Fig. 2

	2			9			4	
	7			5			3	
	6			1			8	

Fig. 3

11	18	13	74	81	76	29	36	31
16	14	12	79	77	75	34	32	30
15	10	17	78	73	80	33	28	35
56	63	58	38	45	40	20	27	22
61	59	57	43	41	39	25	23	21
60	55	62	42	37	44	24	19	26
47	54	49	2	9	4	65	72	67
52	50	48	7	5	3	70	68	66
51	46	53	6	1	8	69	64	71

Fig. 4

22	47	16	41	10	35	4
5	23	48	17	42	11	29
30	6	24	49	18	36	12
13	31	7	25	43	19	37
38	14	32	1	26	44	20
21	39	8	33	2	27	45
46	15	40	9	34	3	28

Fig. 5

dle lines are reached. Write the next (odd) number in the adjacent (middle) cell, then put the following one in the corner cell diagonally opposite (that is, in the starting line), the next one in the middle-line cell diagonally opposite, the one after that in the other upper corner cell; and finally, arrange the subsequent numbers along the two adjacent side lines as before (lines with numbers of the same parity facing each other). At this point, half of the border cells are occupied. Fill in each of the remaining blank cells with the complement to $n^2 + 1$ of the number in the opposite cell, horizontally or vertically (diagonally for the corners). Repeat this procedure until the central square of order 3 is reached, and fill it with the remaining numbers as in Fig. 1.

It was mentioned above that composite squares were also known in the 10th century. Thus the above square of order 3 is used by both authors to build the smallest possible composite square of odd order (figs. 3 and 4).

The most common method for standard magic squares of odd order, already known in the 11th century and found in a set of three squares transmitted to Europe in the Middle Ages, is that of Fig. 5. Starting with 1 below the central cell, proceed with the consecutive numbers diagonally downwards as far as the side of the square; then move from the cell which would be reached outside the square to the corresponding cell in the main square and proceed diagonally downwards as before. When, after a sequence of n numbers, an occupied cell stands in the way, drop down two cells and continue as before.

The easiest method for constructing evenly-even squares was known in the 11th century as well, and two squares (of order 4 and 8) constructed by this method were also transmitted to Europe. Divide the square into subsquares of order 4 and put dots in each of their main diagonals (fig. 6). Then, count the cells from the first (for Arabs, the upper right) corner and write in the corresponding number whenever the cell contains a dot. When this has been done and the lower left corner has been reached, go backwards, count the cells once again and put the corresponding number in every unoccupied one (fig. 7).

For an oddly-even square, thus with $n = 4k + 2$, put

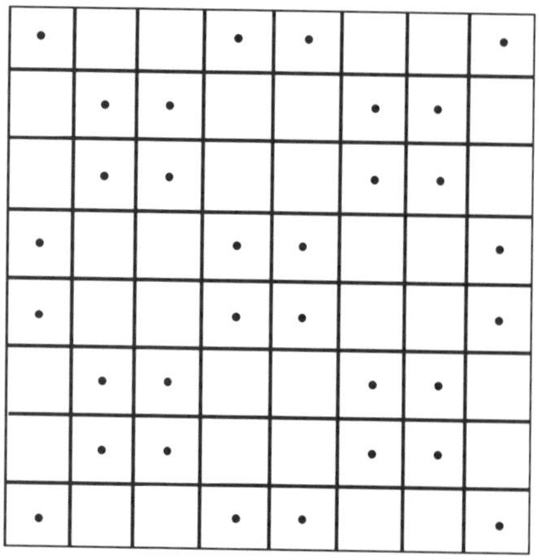

Fig. 6

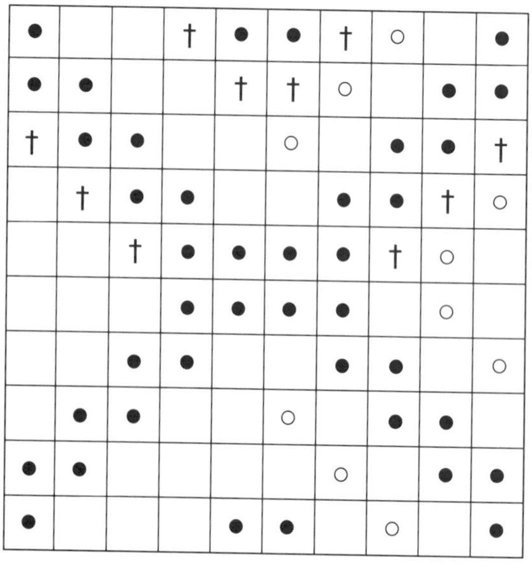

Fig. 8

8	*58*	*59*	5	4	*62*	*63*	1
49	15	14	*52*	*53*	11	10	*56*
41	23	22	*44*	*45*	19	18	*48*
32	*34*	*35*	29	28	*38*	*39*	25
40	*26*	*27*	37	36	*30*	*31*	33
17	47	46	*20*	*21*	43	42	*24*
9	55	54	*12*	13	51	50	*16*
6	*2*	*3*	61	60	*6*	*7*	57

Fig. 7

○→ ←●

10	92	93	97	6	5	94	8	99	1
20	19	83	84	86	85	17	88	12	11
80	29	28	74	75	26	77	23	22	71
61	69	38	37	65	66	34	33	62	40
51	52	58	47	46	45	44	53	49	60
41	42	43	57	56	55	54	48	59	50
31	32	68	67	35	36	64	63	39	70
21	79	78	24	25	76	27	73	72	30
90	89	13	14	15	16	87	18	82	81
100	2	3	4	96	95	7	98	9	91

←†

Fig. 9

8	*11*	*14*	1
13	2	7	*12*
3	*16*	*9*	6
10	5	4	*15*

Fig. 10

16	*51*	*54*	9	8	*59*	*62*	1
53	10	15	*52*	*61*	2	7	*60*
11	*56*	*49*	14	3	*64*	*57*	6
50	13	12	*55*	*58*	5	4	*63*
32	*35*	*38*	25	24	*43*	*46*	17
37	26	31	*36*	*45*	18	23	*44*
27	*40*	*33*	30	19	*48*	*41*	22
34	29	28	*39*	*42*	21	20	*47*

Fig. 11

124	36	107	92	101	131
6	85	115	100	94	191
194	72	135	50	137	3
5	62	75	134	123	192
196	175	69	110	40	1
66	161	90	105	96	73

Fig. 12

dots in the main diagonal and in $k-1$ broken diagonals of the first quarter and reproduce them symmetrically in the three other quarters; next, write crosses in a broken diagonal of the first quarter and reproduce them symmetrically in the upper left quarter; then, write ciphers in another broken diagonal of the first quarter and reproduce them symmetrically in the lower right quarter (fig. 8). Fill in the cells which are empty and those which have a dot as in the case of an evenly-even square. In order to fill the remaining cells, count from the other upper angle for the ciphers and from the other lower angle for the crosses (fig. 9). This method is described by al-Kharaḳī (d. 533/1138-9) as above, and with the same symbols (Sesiano, *Herstellungsverfahren (III)*).

Another common method of constructing squares of order 4 used chess moves (fig. 10): starting with 1 in the corner, 2 is placed by a knight's move (a move of two cells in one direction and one cell in the other), 3 by a queen's move (a move to the next cell diagonally), 4 by a knight's move again, whilst 5 to 8 are symmetrically located in the rows in descending order. To complete the square, the complement to $n^2 + 1 = 17$ of each of these numbers is written in the corresponding bishop's cell, that is, two cells diagonally away. The result is a pandiagonal square. This method was extended in the early 11th century to the construction of squares with the order $n = 4k$ (fig. 11). Divide the square into subsquares of order 4; next, fill half of the cells in each of the k^2 subsquares (taken in any order) with series of eight consecutive numbers as above, and then put in each bishop's cell (reached by moving two cells diagonally within the *same* subsquare) the complement to $n^2 + 1$ (to 65 in fig. 11, where $n = 8$). If, as in this example, the subsquares are initially taken in their natural order, the resulting square will be pandiagonal.

Our final example (fig. 12) is taken from an 11th-century text (*L'Abrégé*). The numerical values of the words *salām ʿalā Muḥammad wa-ʿalā ālihi djamīʿan* occupy the first row and the whole square has been completed so as to produce their sum as a magic constant.

Bibliography: *Kitāb Abi 'l-Wafāʾ al-Būzdjānī fī tartīb al-ʿadad al-wafḳ fī 'l-murabbaʿāt*, ms. Istanbul, Ayasofya 4843, fols. 23b-31b, 38a-56b; *al-Maḳāla al-thālitha min Sharḥ ʿAlī b. Aḥmad b. Muḥammad al-Anṭākī li-kitāb Nīḳūmākhūs*..., ms. Ankara, Saib 5311, fols. 1a-36a (edition of these two treatises in preparation); J. Sesiano, *Un traité médiéval sur les carrés magiques*, Lausanne 1996; idem, *L'Abrégé* enseignant la disposition harmonieuse des nombres, *un manuscrit arabe anonyme sur la construction des carrés magiques*, in *De Bagdad a Barcelona. Estudios sobre historia de las ciencias exactas*, ed. J. Casulleras and J. Samsó, Barcelona 1996, i, 103-57; idem, *Herstellungsverfahren magischer Quadrate aus islamischer Zeit (I)*, in *Sudhoffs Archiv*, lxiv (1980), 187-96; idem, *Herstellungsverfahren magischer Quadrate aus islamischer Zeit (III)*, in *ibid.*, lxxiv (1995), 193-226. (J. Sesiano)

AL-**WAFRĀNĪ** [see AL-IFRĀNĪ].

WĀḤA (A., pl. *wāḥāt*), oasis.

1. In the Middle East.

An oasis is a locality with access to water and cultivable soil in an area which is generally barren and parched. Perennial streams such as the Nile or Tigris-Euphrates, which flow from well-watered mountains through desert valleys, support continuous chains of oases. Other watercourses, which are seasonal, irregular or subterranean, can sometimes be tapped by wells to provide enough water for more isolated settlements, as at Tarīm and Shibām [*q.vv.*] in the Wādī Ḥaḍramawt, and in the district of al-Ḳaṣīm [*q.v.*] on the Wādī Rumma in central Arabia.

Underneath the sand-filled wadis of Arabia there are subterranean reservoirs of "fossil water" which accumulated during pluvial phasis of the Pleistocene period. These permanent reserves of water are supplemented by seasonal rainfall and surface or underground flow from nearby hills, so that the water-table is seasonally raised. In scattered oases, shallow wells operated by hand or animal power reach only the superficial water which is regularly replenished; but more widely the modern petrol-driven deep tube-wells pump from the "capital" stores of fossil water which cannot be restored. The water-table may then fall permanently beyond the reach of the hand-wells.

Throughout the Middle East, another common situation for oases is in the narrow piedmont zone where the long mountain ranges meet the sands of the great desert basins. Just there, the streams fed by the winter rains and snow-melt of the mountains spread out over "dry deltas" of deposited silt, and are thereafter lost in the desert sands. These locations, with fresh water and fertile soil, are ideal for oasis settlement.

In Persia and ʿUmān, the water supply at such sites is often improved by driving tunnels (*ḳanāts*, *kārīz* [see ḲANĀT]) into the foothills. Chains of such oases below mountain ranges provide, at convenient intervals, shelter, water and provisions for staging posts, and were followed by many of the great roads of commerce, pilgrimage and imperial control, e.g. by the section of the highway to Khurāsān and Central Asia under the southern slopes of the Elburz ranges of northern Persia, or by the ancient Spice Road from Aden to Gaza along the oases under the high western edge of the Arabian massif.

The relations between the oasis-dwellers and the travellers or nomads who visited them took many forms. Sometimes the Arabian tribes owned the oases and staffed them with servants; sometimes they left them empty, and only called twice a year to fertilise and to harvest the date-palms; elsewhere, the oasis dwellers were dominant, and the nomads begged permission to enter. Certainly, the nomadic economy was heavily reliant on access to the oasis markets and seasonal fairs.

The systems of water-rights and land-holding in the oases also vary greatly. Jean Brunhes in his classic work contrasted in these respects the stony Mzāb [*q.v.*] and the sandy Sūf in sub-montane Algeria: in the first, the well was the unit of ownership; in the second, the palm-tree, for the land was without value until a settler dug a hole in the sand deep enough to reach the ubiquitous water-table and to plant and tend a date-grove. Often a complex arrangement of rights to stream-flow for purposes of irrigation depended on crude but effective sun-calendars and shadow-clocks.

Until the 20th century, the political allegiance of oases was often shifting and uncertain. When the Middle East was divided up after the end of Ottoman rule, the frontiers were frequently only crudely defined and loosely controlled [see TAKHṬĪṬ AL-ḤUDŪD]. Small neutral zones were established in al-Tawal, and between Saudi Arabia and Kuwait, so that tribes from either side could have access to their wells. However, with the exploration for mineral oil, the precise definition of political borders has become of much greater concern; the neutral zones have vanished, and the political allegiance of e.g. the oases of al-Buraymī [*q.v.*] is a matter of grave dispute.

Bibliography: J. Brunhes, *L'irrigation dans l'Espagne*

et dans l'Afrique du Nord, Paris 1902; C.M. Doughty, *Travels in Arabia Deserta*, Cambridge 1888; D. Van der Meulen, *The wells of Ibn Saud*, London 1957.

(W.C. BRICE)

2. In North Africa.

In geographical terminology applied to the Maghrib, the equivalent of the term *wāḥa* is an area with dense vegetation, but not necessarily of trees, in a natural environment where most of the land surface is unsuitable for cultivation, attesting an additional supply of water. This can be natural, such as a spring or a wadi/oued [see WĀDĪ], sometimes stored up in a dam. It can also be artificial, by means of a well or bore-hole. The distinction is at times not easy to make when a natural supply is improved by man, e.g. by excavating adits, as with the foggaras of the Algerian Sahara, to increase the flow of a spring which has become rather feeble.

An oasis can have a vegetation of spontaneous growth, but more often it is occupied by men who practise there a form of agriculture which is, to a greater or lesser degree, mechanised and which often waters its plots of land through irrigation canals or waterwheels. This mechanisation allows one to distinguish "traditional" oases, little mechanised, where an intensive type of market gardening is carried out, often on a declining basis, and "modern" oases, often more recent and installed around bore holes or artesian wells, sometimes using greenhouses. These may function concurrently with the first type for the utilisation of water.

Bibliography: J. Brunhes (see 1. above); J. Despois, *L'Afrique du Nord*, [3]Paris 1964; H. Isnard, *Le Maghreb*, Paris 1966; Despois and R. Raynal (eds.), *Géographie de l'Afrique du Nord-Ouest*, Paris 1967.

(Y. CALLOT)

WAḤAM (A.) also *waḥām*, *wiḥām*, with the more general term *shahwa* "longing", also in use, denotes "pregnancy craving".

In Arab culture, like in many others, pregnancy cravings traditionally received attention, but this only appears to a very limited extent in Arabic medical works of the Greek tradition. Ibn Sīnā does not pay attention to the phenomenon, not even in discussions about the pregnant woman's [loss of] appetite (*Ḳānūn*, Beirut 1993, ii, 1647). ʿArīb b. Saʿīd al-Ḳurṭubī, *K. Khalḳ al-djanīn*, Algiers 1956, 40 cites Galen on the pregnant woman's craving to eat clay, which apparently comes under "bad (in the sense of harmful) appetite", *shahwa radīʾa*), a complaint for which treatment is prescribed. Al-Baladī, *K. Tadbīr al-ḥabālā*, Baghdād 1980, 135-6, also treats "harmful appetites" very cursorily, as one in a long range of minor pregnancy complaints.

In the popular view, however, pregnancy cravings were considered very important, and there was a threatening and magical aspect to them. Thwarting a pregnant woman's craving for a particular kind of food was considered harmful to the foetus. The view is found in al-Djāḥiẓ's story about al-Kindī (*Bukhalāʾ*, Cairo 1358/1939, 143-4), who threatens to hold his tenants responsible if a woman in his house miscarries after having been refused a share of their food. Al-Kindī's view is obviously seen as a ridiculous exaggeration, but there is sufficient evidence that paying attention to pregnancy cravings was, and is, part of the social code, cf. the verb *waḥḥama* "to slaughter a camel in order to satisfy a woman's craving"; also e.g. ʿAbd al-Laṭīf al-Baghdādī, *K. al-Ifāda*, London 1964, 234, fol. 58b). Observations by anthropologists made during the last century and modern lexicological sources show that the aspect generally emphasised was—and is—that refusing a pregnant woman the food she craves will result in a birthmark (*shahwa* "appetite") on the child in the shape of the food in question. This belief is not restricted to the Arab world, but used to be widespread also in Europe and, for instance, in the West Indies. An example from the Arab cultural sphere is that of a birthmark in the form of a grape that swelled up when grapes were in season (Winifred S. Blackman, *The Fellāḥīn of Upper Egypt*, London etc. 1927, 62). That this provided pregnant women with a means to exercise power otherwise unheard of in this particular cultural context, is illustrated, for instance, by the fuss made by a pregnant black concubine in Luxor (in 1860) with a craving for olives (Lady Duff Gordon, *Letters from Egypt (1862-1869)*, London 1969, 174-5).

Bibliography (in addition to references in the article): Doctoresse Legey, *Essai de folklore marocain*, Paris 1926, 78-9; J. Desparmet, *Coutumes, institutions, croyances des indigènes de l'Algérie. I. L'enfance, le mariage et la famille*, Algiers 1939, 283-4; Nefissa Zerdoumi, *Enfant d'hier . . . l'éducation de l'enfant en milieu traditionnel algérien*, Paris 1970, 65-9; R. Kruk, *Pregnancy and its social implications in mediaeval and traditional Arab society*, in *Quaderni di studi arabi 5-6 (1987-88). Atti del XIII congresso dell'Union européenne d'arabisants et d'islamisants*, Venice 1986, 418-30.

(REMKE KRUK)

AL-**WĀḤĀT** (pl. of *wāḥ* "oasis", this being a transcription of Coptic *ouah* denoting cultivated lands within the deserts, as already noted by Yāḳūt), the name of a series of oases in the western desert of Upper Egypt.

E. Amélineau, in his *Géographie de l'Egypte à l'époque copte* (Paris 1893), had great difficulty in identifying the names of the oases with the modern names, and the Arabic texts are equally ambiguous. According to Yāḳūt, *Buldān*, ed. Beirut, v, 341-2, they were three districts (*kuwar*) stretching southwards into the western desert parallel to the Nile valley. The first was opposite Fayyūm and extended to the latitude of Aswān; this was the largest oasis, with numerous villages and palm groves which produced the best dates in Egypt. The second was smaller and less populous. The third was the smallest and contained a town called Santariyya. The population of the oases was of Lawāta Berber stock. In the 9th/15th century al-Maḳrīzī mentions four oases: *al-dākhila* "the interior one", the pair of *al-khāridjatān*[i] "the exterior ones" and the oasis of Bahnasā, these yielding a total revenue of 25,000 dīnārs in the year 585/1190 (i.e. the Ayyūbid period). At the time of *al-rawk al-nāṣirī* [see RAWK], sc. in 715/1315, they were not included amongst the provinces of Egypt; the sultan did not appoint a governor and they were administered by those who held them as *iḳṭāʿ*s. In his notice, al-Maḳrīzī, before passing from the "interior" to the "exterior" oases, speaks of the town of Santariyya, this being the older Islamic name of the oasis known since the end of the 10th/16th century as Sīwa [*q.v.*], the classical oasis of Amon. Al-Bakrī is the only geographer, in addition to the later al-Maḳrīzī, who gives the dual form *al-wāḥatān*[i] *al-khāridjatān*[i]; it may be that *al-wāḥāt al-khāridja* were composed of two distinct urban groupings of settlements. The most important settlement here was Irīs, the modern Bārīs. The oasis of Bahnasā, different from its homonym of the Baḥr Yūsuf (= the ancient Oxyrhynchus; see on it AL-BAHNASĀ), is the oasis known today as *al-wāḥa al-baḥriyya* and there is also the *wāḥat al-farāfira* [see AL-FARĀFRA]. The first of these two was formerly called thus because it was connected with the town of the same name in the Nile valley by a road to the Nile 200 km/130 miles long. There are main towns called al-Ḳaṣr in Farāfra and in Da<u>kh</u>la.

These oases (*al-baḥriyya, al-farāfira, al-dā<u>kh</u>ila* and *al-<u>kh</u>āri<u>dj</u>a*: conventionally, Bahariya, Farafra, Dakhla and Kharga) today form one of the 26 governorates of Egypt with the name of al-Wādī al-<u>Dj</u>adīd, having an area of 45,800 km^2 and a population of 132,000, including three administrative centres, three towns and 134 villages.

On the rather complicated dialectology of the oases, see P. Behnstedt and M. Woidich, *Die ägyptischen Oases—ein dialektogischer Vorbericht*, in *ZAL*, viii [1982], 39-71 (includes texts).

Bibliography (in addition to references in the text): Masʿūdī, *Murū<u>dj</u>*, iii, 50-2 = §§ 894-5; Ibn Duḳmāḳ, *Intiṣār*, v, 11-12; Maḳrīzī, *<u>Kh</u>iṭaṭ*, i, 87, 234-7; ʿAlī Mubārak Pa<u>sh</u>a, *al-<u>Kh</u>iṭaṭ al-<u>dj</u>adīda*, xvii, 30-1; Muḥammad Ramzī, *al-Ḳāmūs al-<u>dj</u>u<u>gh</u>rāfī li 'l-bilād al-miṣriyya*, ii/4, 241-5, 256-7; H. Maspéro and G. Wiet, *Matériaux pour servir à la géographie de l'Egypte*, IFAO, Cairo 1914, 219-25; A. Fakhry, *The Oases of Egypt. I. Siwa Oasis*, Cairo 1973, *II. Bahrīyah and Farafra Oases*, Cairo 1974.

(AYMAN F. SAYYID)

WAHB, BANŪ, a family of officials in caliphal service, especially noted as secretaries and viziers to the ʿAbbāsids during the 3rd/9th and early 4th/10th centuries.

The majority of sources state that the family came from Wāsiṭ and were of Nestorian Christian origin before converting to Islam, nevertheless claiming a pure Arabic origin going back to the Yemeni tribe of Balḥāri<u>th</u> of Na<u>dj</u>rān. The Wahbīs thus belong to the tradition of servants of the caliphs with Nestorian backgrounds who were prominent in the administrations of the 3rd/9th century (cf. L. Massignon, *La politique islamo-chrétienne des scribes nestoriens de Deïr Qunna à la cour de Bagdad au IXe siècle de notre ère*, in *Vivre et Penser*, 2nd ser. [1942], 7-14). This role of the Wahbīs seems to go back to late Umayyad times, from which they passed into ʿAbbāsid service and then were particularly associated with the Barmakīs. Wahb served <u>Dj</u>aʿfar b. Yaḥyā [see BARĀMIKA] and then al-Maʾmūn's minister al-Faḍl b. Sahl [*q.v.*].

1. Sulaymān b. Wahb, Abū Ayyūb, began as a secretary to al-Maʾmūn and then acted for such generals as Mūsā b. Bu<u>gh</u>ā and Aytā<u>kh</u> in the reign of al-Wā<u>th</u>iḳ, thereby beginning a link with the Turkish military élite which was to run all through his career. At this time, his brother al-Ḥasan also was a secretary of the vizier Ibn al-Zayyāt [*q.v.*]. Sulaymān was twice *ʿāmil* or financial intendant of the province of Egypt under al-Mutawakkil, apparently deriving rich pickings from the office. In the short reign of al-Muhtadī (255-6/859-60) he served as the caliph's last vizier at a time when all real power in the state had passed to the Turkish military classes and the vizierate had likewise reached a low ebb. Under al-Muʿtamid he became briefly vizier again in 263/877 and again in 264/878, at a time of intrigues and rivalries with another secretary and vizier, al-Ḥasan b. Ma<u>kh</u>lad b. al-<u>Dj</u>arrāḥ [see IBN MA<u>KH</u>LAD], also of Christian origin. But Sulaymān was soon afterwards dismissed, unable to satisfy the financial exigencies of al-Muʿtamid and his brother the regent al-Muwaffaḳ, and died in prison in Ṣafar 272/July-August 885. He had, nevertheless, been the *mamdūḥ* of such leading poets of the time as Abū Tammām and al-Buḥturī [*q.vv.*].

2. ʿUbayd Allāh b. Sulaymān, son of the preceding, and also with long secretarial experience, shared in his father's disgrace, but had the support of the newly-nominated heir to the throne, al-Muwaffaḳ's son al-Muʿtaḍid [*q.v.*], and in Ṣafar 278/June 891 became al-Muʿtamid's last vizier and then, when al-Muʿtamid died the next year, vizier to the new caliph al-Muʿtaḍid, remaining in office till his own death in Rabīʿ II 288/April 901. ʿUbayd Allāh was closely concerned with the re-imposition of caliphal power in <u>Dj</u>ibāl by military force and with various administrative reforms, and was the patron of the two brothers of the Banu 'l-Furāt [see IBN AL-FURĀT] in their efforts to secure a greater inflow of tax revenues for the state by the strict supervision of provincial agents. ʿUbayd Allāh achieved a great contemporary reputation for his honest conduct and justice, and was favoured by the caliph's addressing him by his *kunya*; also, he seems wisely to have restrained al-Muʿtaḍid from putting blatantly anti-Umayyad, pro-<u>Sh</u>īʿī measures into force, fearing the effects on public order.

3. al-Ḳāsim b. ʿUbayd Allāh, Abu 'l-Ḥusayn, son of the preceding, succeeded as vizier when his father died and acted as al-Muʿtaḍid's minister until the caliph himself died in Rabīʿ II 289/March-April 902, and was the first vizier to the new caliph al-Muktafī [*q.v.*] until his own death in <u>Dh</u>u 'l-Ḳaʿda 291/October 904. Al-Ḳāsim had served at his father's side, but was of lower calibre: less scrupulous, more concerned with lining the pockets of himself and his protégés, and brutal with those he regarded as hostile or potentially so. Thus he secured the execution of the governor of Fārs Badr al-Muʿtaḍidī [*q.v.* in Suppl.], of the captive Ṣaffārid *amīr* ʿAmr b. al-Lay<u>th</u> [*q.v.*], of the poet Ibn al-Rūmī [*q.v.*], who had satirised the Banū Wahb, and various others, often against the will of his young master. He was planning to move against the surviving brother of the Banu 'l-Furāt, ʿAlī, but fell ill and died before he could achieve this. Although only a mediocre administrator, al-Ḳāsim was an able courtier and managed to raise the prestige of the office of vizier to a new height as the directing power in the state. He received great honours from the caliph, including the new honorific title of *Walī al-Dawla* "Friend, Protector of the State" (which was to appear on coins), and one of his daughters married a son of al-Muktafī. His death, however, meant the eclipse of the family's influence for nearly a generation and the ensuing ascendancy of persons like ʿAlī b. al-Furāt, involving *inter alia* an increase in <u>Sh</u>īʿī influence in the state, and new figures like the latter's rival ʿAlī b. ʿĪsā [*q.v.*].

4. al-Ḥusayn b. al-Ḳāsim, son of the preceding, succeeded ʿUbayd Allāh b. Muḥammad al-Kalwa<u>dh</u>ānī as al-Muḳtadir's penultimate vizier in Ramaḍān 319/September 931, and filled the office for eight months till Rabīʿ II 320/May 932. He relied on Furātid support against the influence of ʿAlī b. ʿĪsā and the powerful commander-in-chief Muʾnis al-Muẓaffar [*q.v.*], and, like his father, received from the caliph an honorific title, *ʿAmīd al-Dawla* "Mainstay of the State", which appears on coins. He endeavoured to restore the disastrous state of the caliphal finances, but fell from power, having been perhaps the last vizier to attempt to retain for the vizierate a measure of its former independence.

5. Muḥammad b. al-Ḳāsim, brother of the preceding, became vizier to al-Ḳāhir in <u>Sh</u>aʿbān 321/July 933 in succession to Ibn Muḳla [*q.v.*] and at the time of Muʾnis's fall and death, but served for only two-and-a-half months till his dismissal in <u>Dh</u>u 'l-Ḳaʿda 321/October 933.

Bibliography: 1. Sources. These include the historians Yaʿḳūbī, Ṭabarī, Masʿūdī, Hilāl al-Ṣābiʾ, Ibn al-Djawzī, Ibn al-Athīr, Ibn al-Tiḳṭaḳā, etc.; the works on secretaries and viziers by Djahshiyārī, Ṣūlī, Ibn al-Abbār, etc.; and scattered references in *adab* collections like the *Aghānī*, Tanūkhī's *Nishwār al-muḥāḍara* and *al-Faradj baʿd al-shidda*, and Ibn Ḥamdūn's *Tadhkira*. There is a biography of Sulaymān b. Wahb in Ibn Khallikān, ed. ʿAbbās, ii, 415-18, tr. de Slane, i, 596-600.

2. Studies. H.F. Amedroz, *Tales of official life in the "Tadhkira" of Ibn Hamdun*, in *JRAS* (1908), 418-30; H. Bowen, *The life and times of ʿAlī ibn ʿĪsà, "The Good Vizier"*, Cambridge 1928, 25-6, 45 ff., 57-66, 291-3, 301-3, 312-15, 327, 331-2; Zambaur, *Manuel*, 6-7; D. Sourdel, *Le vizirat ʿabbāside*, Damascus 1959-60, i, 300 ff., 312-15, 326-57, 463-7, 476-8, with a genealogical table of the Banū Wahb at 745.

(C.E. BOSWORTH)

WAHB B. **MUNABBIH**, ABŪ ʿABD ALLĀH, Yemeni narrator and author-transmitter from South Arabia. He was of Persian origin, having been born at Dhimar, two days' march from Ṣanʿāʾ in the year 34/654-5. Information about his conversion to Islam in the year 10 A.H. is unreliable. More probably the details concerned his father Munabbih, of whom it was said that "he converted to Islam at the time of the Prophet and that he was a good Muslim" (Ibn Ḥadjar, *Tahdhīb*, xi, 167). He lived with his five brothers at Ṣanʿāʾ, and Hammām was the eldest of them. The most reasonable date for the brother's death seems to be 101 or 102/719-20, and the least probable is 132, when compared with that of Wahb (see below). He left a *Ṣaḥīfa* with almost 140 translations and commentaries; these were published by R.F. ʿAbd al-Muṭṭalib in 1406/1986, following a manuscript from the Dār al-Kutub in Cairo, which corrects and expands the edition by Ḥamīdullāh, who followed mss. from Berlin and Damascus.

The other brothers were Ghaylān, ʿAbd Allāh, Maʿḳil (who predeceased Wahb) and ʿUmar, all unremarkable except that the last two used to transmit the traditions of Wahb, who was correctly recognised as a great authority in the field of biblical traditions; many varied quotations have come to light to document this aspect of his work and to show that he had inherited the knowledge of the two great converts Kaʿb al-Aḥbār and ʿAbd Allāh b. Salām (al-Dhahabī, *Ḥuffāẓ*, i, 100; and Ibn al-Faḳīh, 34, ll. 9 ff., where such praise astonished even Ibn ʿAbbās himself). He can be classified like his brothers, Hammām, Ghaylān and Maʿḳil, as one of the *ṭābiʿūn*.

The question arises whether he was a member of the *Ahl al-Kitāb* before his conversion to Islam (*Fihrist*, 22), or more precisely, whether he was Jewish (Ibn Khaldūn, *Muḳaddima*, Beirut 1961, 589, ll. 6 ff., and others before him). The oldest sources do not mention this question, and by contrast the facts are unverified since his father had converted long before the birth of his son. He was therefore probably born a Muslim. Al-Thaʿlabī, 192, speaks of an alleged meeting with Muʿāwiya; al-Masʿūdī, *Murūdj*, Cairo 1346/1927-8, ii, 152, recounts that al-Walīd had sent him an inscription discovered at Damascus to decipher.

He acted as a judge in Ṣanʿāʾ, and one day during the governorate of ʿUrwa b. Muḥammad he beat an official (*ʿāmil*), whom people had complained about, with a stick until he drew blood. The statement is also attributed to him that, in accepting the role of a judge, he had lost the gift of seeing the future in his dreams; but as in many similar statements one

must see here only an attempt to distract attention from his duties (see below, especially the introduction of the *Akhbār al-ḳuḍāt* of Wakīʿ [*q.v.*], ed. Cairo 1947-50, on the problems and dangers involved in being a judge, which stopped more than one Muslim from taking up this responsibility). Similarly, there are many details given about his life which accord well with his ascetic behaviour (see for example al-Dhahabī, *Ḥuffāẓ*, i, 100; Ibn Saʿd, v, 395; Ibn Ḥadjar, *Tahdhīb*, xi, 167). There are also many exhortations of all sorts in this vein attributed to him which were later questioned, according to later books where they are also reported. Wahb is thought to have originally adopted *ḳadar*, or the doctrine of freewill, but later to have rejected it, since it was contradictory to all the revealed writings. It is not recorded in which period of his life he was sent to prison, probably because of this belief and because of his contact with the People of the Book (see below). Perhaps it took place at the end of his life, for it is known that he died from the consequences of a flogging to which the governor of Yemen, Yūsuf b. ʿUmar al-Thaḳafī, had condemned him in 110/728 or 114/732.

There can no longer be any doubt about the books attributed to the author. Their contents were transmitted orally, taught or set down in writing, partly at least in his own lifetime, and later by particular members of his family. A literature belonging generally to the biblical heritage as disseminated by Judaeo-Christian scholarship (in Yemen and Ḥidjāz, and, especially, in Medina) was formed quite early. It was called biblical but was within Islam. It was disseminated by the philosophers and by others from the same Judaeo-Christian milieux chiefly in Arabia, and then supplemented by posterity.

Wahb, especially because of the books bearing his name which have come down to us and also because of the importance accorded to him by later authors, can be regarded as one of the most important intellectual heirs of this group of people. He handed down a method of approaching the biblical texts properly so-called which can again be found in his successors and in authors as serious as Ibn Ḳutayba, who in his work reserves a place of honour for Ibn Munabbih (in his *Maʿārif*, and especially in his *ʿUyūn al-akhbār*, see Vajda, Lecomte, and especially a recent thesis of Said Karoui from Heidelberg) in the work of this author on the Bible. There are a very large number of quotations regarding his fame to be found in many of the historical books of al-Ṭabarī (his *History* and his *Commentary*), of al-Masʿūdī, of al-Thaʿlabī, etc.; these concern the list of books that deal with the contents of the first book attributed to him (see Khoury, *Wahb*, 227-46). The title of this book as assigned to it by posterity is *K. al-Mubtadaʾ wa-ḳiṣaṣ al-anbiyāʾ*, but it varies according to different authors. It starts with the beginning of creation (*badʾ al-khalḳ*) and encompasses the history of the prophets, from Adam to the arrival of the Prophet of Islam (see MUBTADAʾ. 2).

The most ancient sources which bear witness to the circulation of this material under the name of the author are from the *Ḥadīth Dāwūd* ("The History of David"), which is an Arabic papyrus now kept in Heidelberg, the oldest of its kind in Islam. It was published by the present writer in 1972 (see Khoury, *Wahb*, 34-115) with a translation into German. The original condition in which this papyrus was found showed it to be much ravaged by worms and chronic wear and tear, to the point that certain pages are only half intact and certain lines have only a few words or even odd letters preserved. It was almost completely restored thanks to the parallel version in the *K. Badʾ al-k͟halk wa-ḳiṣaṣ al-anbiyāʾ* of ʿUmāra b. Wat͟hīma al-Fārisī, who made a copy not only of this history but also of others from a more or less original version by Wahb, transmitted by his grandson Idrīs b. Sinān, and by his son ʿAbd al-Munʿim b. Idrīs (d. 228/842, a year before the papyrus was written). It had been kept in the private library of Ibn Lahīʿa, the judge of Egypt, as this man's disciple and transmitter shows, who extended the initial material without changing the structure of the text. For this reason, in this book of ʿUmāra [*q.v.*, see also WAT͟HĪMA] we have a conflation of the oldest and the most weighty versions about biblical narratives from the first two centuries A.H. What is remarkable in the history of these texts is that we have more accuracy in the *isnād*, for where the papyrus sometimes uses simply *ḳāla*, ʿUmāra mentions the name of Wahb, who appears to be a primary source for this voluminous book. Unfortunately for us, only the second part is preserved, from Moses to the arrival of the Prophet Muḥammad (for this, see the ed. of Khoury, *Les légendes prophétiques*, 158-85, Arabic text 1-389; for David, see 102-26).

To these sources should be added information about the biblical world contributed by Ibn His͟hām but referring to the same grandson mentioned above (see further below). A *K. al-Isrāʾīliyyāt* (Ḥād͟jd͟jī K͟halīfa v, 40) is attributed to Wahb, but this does not seem to have been known in the literature of the first century of Islam (Khoury, *Wahb*, 205, 247-57); it probably relates to stories arising out of those in the preceding book. As for the *Ḳiṣaṣ al-ak͟hyār* (Ḥād͟jd͟jī K͟halīfa, iv, 518), this title can refer only to the same theme, and it points to evidence of how similar materials could have been able to circulate under different titles, given that the first of them was lost in transmission.

Under the rubric of biblical history, a translation by Wahb of the Psalms of David deserves to be mentioned, the *K. Zabūr Dāwūd . . . Tard͟jamat Wahb b. Munabbih* (Ibn K͟hayr, *Fahrasa*, 294). According to the multiple sources consulted (see Khoury, *Wahb*, 207, 258-63), it is less of a translation than a publicising of motifs adopted by David, popularising the Psalms to which he or posterity has added all sorts of material, and these were sometimes (at least partly) Islamicised. There are even three different titles, *Ḥikmat Wahb*, *Ḥikmat Luḳmān* and *Mawʿiẓa li-Wahb* (Ibn K͟hayr, 291-2, 294; Khoury, *op. cit.*, 206-7, 263-72), all of which relate to the same character and which, together with the traditions of the Psalms, could be considered under the same rubric of *Ḥikam* and *Mawāʿiẓ*, where David and Luḳmān (b. ʿĀd) enjoyed a place of privilege.

It is also worth mentioning here a *K. al-Ḳadar* which he wrote and later regretted (Ibn Saʿd, v, 395; Ibn Ḳutayba, *Maʿārif*, ed. ʿUkās͟ha, 625, 9; al-K͟hallāl, fol. 91b, ll. 3 ff.). According to Abū Nuʿaym, *Ḥilya*, iv, 24, ll. 17 ff., he even denied the existence of any material on *ḳadar* (see Khoury, 206, 270-2). In any case, there is a biblical ambience in the traditions attributed to him which are favourable to these ideas. However, it may not be possible to find in these texts the definite statement of such an ideology, which would perhaps have brought disgrace on the author and could have cost him his life.

Alongside the biblical section, which all these titles denote, is another which concerns the pre-Islamic Arab period; this established a true bridge between the biblical world and the Yemeni Arab past. It is the *K. al-Mulūk al-mutawwad͟ja min Ḥimyar wa-ak͟hbārihim wa-ḳiṣaṣihim wa-ḳubūrihim wa-as͟hʿārihim*, and according to Ibn K͟hallikān, *Wafayāt*, iii, 671, Ibn Ḳutayba is said to have seen a version of it himself. In any case, the presence of material on the same theme was attested by the *K. al-Tīd͟jān* of Ibn His͟hām, who referred to Wahb as his primary source, through the intermediary of the same grandson, and from him Asad b. Mūsā [*q.v.* in Suppl.]. He found it in the library of the judge of Egypt, who received him and opened his house to him as a disciple (see Khoury, *Asad b. Mūsā*, 23). In the first part of this book Wahb is found everywhere as the only authority; these are the pages containing the beginning of the biblical world, where the indication of names and dates, etc. points to certain, detailed knowledge; and it was to this world that the author wanted to connect Yemen, with a view to enhancing the worth of this country to the bosom of Islam, to Meccan and then to North Arabian roots, and to the centre of rivalries which had built up between north and south.

In the second part of Ibn His͟hām's book it is noticeable that the name of Wahb is mentioned increasingly less often, eventually disappearing altogether in the last part. The global tone which dominates this book resides in its distinctively biblical character, and this distinguishes it entirely from the book of ʿAbīd (or ʿUbayd) b. S͟harya [see IBN S͟HARYA], *Ak͟hbār ʿAbīd b. S͟harya fī ak͟hbār al-Yaman wa-as͟hʿārihā wa-ansābihā* (ed., with Ibn His͟hām's *K. al-Tīd͟jān*, Ḥaydarābād 1347/1928-9). In that book we are dealing with a story-teller who becomes the *samīr* of Muʿāwiya in Damascus, and fills out his stories mainly with poetry. This becomes the dominant element and confirms historical narrations (on this subject see Khoury, *Kalif, Geschichte und Dichtung*, esp. 213 ff.).

The last group of books attributed to Wahb is purely Islamic. Firstly, the *Mag͟hāzī Rasūl Allāh* (Ḥād͟jd͟jī K͟halīfa, v, 646). the only confirmation of which is the piece on the papyrus preserved in Heidelberg and published by Khoury, *Wahb*, 118-75, with a German translation. It is astonishing that Ibn Isḥāḳ, who was so dependent on Wahb for biblical history, as for example al-Ṭabarī clearly shows in his two important books (see above), should not take any account of Wahb in the Islamic field. It is as if Ibn Munabbih, far from the school of Medina and its founder al-Zuhrī, had been banished. It is true that he did not always use the *isnād*, which had not actually been imposed in his period, but he knew of it and used it from time to time, when it applied to writers who took little notice of rigid rules. What is more, the *isnād* was not always used wisely by the teachers of Medina, as has already been shown (see e.g. Khoury, *Wahb*, 276 ff.).

The events to be found there include the beginnings of Islam and the conversion of Zurāra b. Asʿad and his son Asʿad; the meeting at al-ʿAḳaba; the council held by Ḳuraysh at the *Dār al-nadwa*; the migration to Medina; and, finally, the campaign of ʿAlī against the tribe of K͟hat͟hʿam. In addition to these items concerning the *mag͟hāzī*, we have a small number of traditions which cover aspects of the life of the Prophet (see Khoury, *op. cit.*, 282-4). Ḥād͟jd͟jī K͟halīfa, ii, 382, also mentions a *Tafsīr Wahb*, and at iv, 387, another reference concerns the caliphs, sc. *Taʾrīk͟h al-K͟hulafāʾ*, or *Futūḥ*, but of these there is no trace.

It is easy to see which of the many aspects of the traditions attributed to Ibn Munabbih are covered, but it is difficult to say exactly what was actually put into writing in the lifetime of the author. The essential point is that the teaching of the master was fixed in writing during the 2nd/8th century, since certain versions were preserved in Ibn Lahīʿa's library by the Egyptian transmitters or settlers in Egypt, as confirmed by the papyrus and, especially, by the book of ʿUmāra b. Wat̲h̲īma.

As for later authors, they often altered certain traditions which they attached to his name, which means that not all of the alterations may have come from him. In any case, in his *K. al-Tīd̲j̲ān* he showed a real knowledge of the Bible, even if this was not extensive, in certain citations from the text (see Khoury, *Quelques reflexions*, 553 ff., esp. 555-6). What was circulated with these biblical and extra-biblical studies was a common Semitic reservoir of great antiquity, and this was often disseminated orally, especially outside the Judaeo-Christian dogmatic centres; this has been very ably noted by H. Schwarzbaum in his book on biblical and extra-biblical stories (see *Bibl.*). In short, Wahb is an important representative of the expansion of the historical perspective. His writings embodied a truly universal vision of history, comprising: 1. ancient biblical history; 2. pre-Islamic Yemeni history; 3. Islamic history of the prophet; and 4. history of the caliphate.

Bibliography (in addition to references given in the article): 1. Sources. Abū Bakr Aḥmad b. Muḥammad al-K̲h̲allāl, *al-D̲j̲āmiʿ li-ʿulūm Aḥmad b. Ḥanbal*, ms. B.L. Or. 2675; C.H. Becker, *Papyri Schott-Reinhardt*, i, Heidelberg 1906; Nabia Abbott, *An Arabic papyrus in the Oriental Institute. Stories of the Prophets*, in *JNES*, v (1946), 169-80; *Wahb b. Munabbih*, ed. R.G. Khoury (monograph and ed. of two papyri on the *Mag̲h̲āzī* and the History of David), Wiesbaden 1972; idem, *Les légendes prophétiques dans l'Islam depuis le Ier-IIIe siècle H.*, Wiesbaden 1978 (with ed. of the *K. Badʾ al-k̲h̲alḳ wa-ḳiṣaṣ al-anbiyāʾ* of ʿUmāra b. Wat̲h̲īma al-Fārisī).

2. Studies. V. Chauvin, *La récension égyptienne des 1001 nuits*, Brussels 1899; Cl. Huart, *Wahb b. Munabbih et la tradition judéo-chrétienne au Yémen*, in *JA*, sér. 10, iv (1904), 331 ff.; G. Vajda, *Observations sur quelques citations bibliques chez Ibn Qutayba*, in *REJ*, xcix (1935), 68-80; R. Blachère, *Regards sur la littérature narrative en arabe, Ier/VIIe siècle*, in *Semitica*, vi (1956), 75-86; G. Lecomte, *Les citations de l'Ancient et du Nouveau Testament dans l'œuvre d'Ibn Qutayba*, in *Arabica*, v (1958), 34-46; idem, *Ibn Qutayba, l'homme, son oeuvre, ses idées*, Damascus 1965; Khoury, *Asad b. Mūsā*, Wiesbaden 1976; H. Schwarzbaum, *Biblical and extra-biblical legends in Islamic folk-literature*, Walldorf-Hessen 1982; Khoury, *Les sources islamiques de la Sīra avant Ibn His̲h̲ām*, in *Colloque de Strasbourg*, Paris 1983, 7-29; idem, *Kalif, Geschichte und Dichtung. Der jemenitischer Erzähler ʿAbīd ibn Šarya am Hofe Muʿāwiyas*, in *ZAL*, xxv (1993), 204-18; S. Karoui, *Die Rezeption der Bibel in der frühislamischen Literatur am Beispiel der Hauptwerke von Ibn Qutayba*, Heidelberg 1997; Khoury, *L'importance des plus vieux mss arabes historiques sur papyrus, conservés à Heidelberg*, in *QSA*, xv (1997), 5-20.

(R.G. Khoury)

WAHBIYYA [see AL-IBĀḌIYYA].

WAḤDA (A.), "unit, unity".

1. As a term in grammar.

Here the genitive construct *ism al-waḥda* is variously rendered in Western grammars as *nomen unitatis* "noun of unity", "unit noun", "noun of individuality", and "singulative" (but on the last of these, see below).

The *ism al-waḥda* forms the counterpart to the *ism al-d̲j̲ins* or *nomen generis* "generic noun" and is derived from it by adding the feminine ending *-at^{un}*. If the generic noun refers to something which exists in units, the *ism al-waḥda* denotes such a unit; if the referent is homogeneous, the unit noun denotes a separate piece. Thus *naml^{un}* "ant(s)" vs. *namlat^{un}* "one ant" and *ḥadīd^{un}* "iron" vs. *ḥadīdat^{un}* "a piece of iron". The same grammatical feature exists in a number of other Semitic languages (Hebrew, Aramaic, Accadian, Mehri) and even in Berber. A related phenomenon in Arabic is the *ism al-marra* or *nomen vicis* derived from the verbal noun to denote a one-time action: *ibtisām^{un}* "smiling" vs. *ibtisāmat^{un}* "one smile". In the first form of the verb the *ism al-marra* follows the pattern *faʿlat^{un}*, even though not all verbal nouns have the form *faʿl^{un}*. One can, however, argue that *faʿl^{un}* is the default verbal noun, since it is always used with secondary denominative verbs of the first form (e.g. *kabadahū kabd^{an}* "he hit him in the liver").

The pair "generic noun—unit noun" should not be confused with the pair "collective—singulative", and words like *naml^{un}* should not be called collectives, as they frequently are. Generic nouns denote the genus and are not number-sensitive with regard to their referent: *akaltu tamr^{an}* may be said by a date-eater regardless of whether he ate one, two, or many dates. Collectives, in contrast, denote a plurality seen as a unit. The singulative is never derived from the collective by adding *-at^{un}*. As a matter of fact, in many cases it is the collective that is derived from the singulative (by adding the same ending *-at^{un}*, thus in participial forms like *muqātil^{un}* "fighter" vs. *muqātilat^{un}* "fighting force", *nisba*s like *ṣūfiyy^{un}* "Ṣūfī" vs. *ṣūfiyyat^{un}* "Ṣūfīdom", and *faʿʿāl* forms like *nad̲j̲d̲j̲ār^{un}* "carpenter" vs. *nad̲j̲d̲j̲ārat^{un}* "carpenters" [as a group, guild]). There is a variety of other lexical and morphological means to express this contrast. One should include here also the names of tribes/nations and other groups of people, from which the individual is derived by means of the *nisba: al-Rūm^{u}* "the Byzantines" vs. *Rūmiyy^{un}* "one Byzantine" and *d̲j̲und^{un}* "army" vs. *d̲j̲undiyy^{un}* "soldier". Some grammars consider these *nisba*s a separate type of *nomen unitatis* (e.g. Corriente, 81, with precedent among the mediaeval grammarians). While collectives/singulatives always denote sentient beings, generic and unit nouns never denote human beings, but otherwise are semantically fairly spread out (see the categories introduced by Ullmann, *Nomen generis*, 19-46). The only overlap between the two classes exists with (large) animals; as a result animal names may—quite unpredictably—be singulars (*kalb^{un}*), collectives (*ibil^{un}*), or generic nouns (*baḳar^{un}*). Synchronically, this variation in usage defies explanation, and animal nomenclature can be very intricate.

While collectives are mainly treated as feminines, generic nouns are mostly used as masculines, although feminine singular and plural forms of attributive adjectives are not rare either. The latter are best explained as *ad sensum* constructions: the generic nouns are felt to function like plurals of the unit nouns. Note that some mediaeval grammarians and lexicographers had no qualms calling the generic noun a plural of the unit noun (e.g. al-Farrāʾ [d. 200/822] according to al-Astarābādī, *S̲h̲arḥ al-Kāfiya*, repr. Beirut n.d., ii, 178 l. 18). This is also the reason why the generic noun is more specifically termed *ism al-d̲j̲ins al-d̲j̲amʿī* "the plural-like generic noun" to distinguish it from the wider meaning of *ism al-d̲j̲ins*, which is "common noun" as opposed to *ism al-ʿalam* "proper name" (see A. Fischer, *Terminologie*, for questions of nomenclature). But this is clearly a secondary development, due to contamination with the collective.

Both the generic noun and the unit noun can be put in the dual and plural. While unit nouns pose no problem in this respect (*s̲h̲ad̲j̲aratān*ⁱ "two [individual] trees", *s̲h̲ad̲j̲arāt*ᵘⁿ "several [individual] trees"), the semantics of the dual and plural of generic nouns have not yet been fully investigated (even Ullmann is somewhat reticent about the semantic side of these forms in his collection of pertinent references, *Nomen generis*, 50-2). In many instances the connotation is clearly that of "kind": *s̲h̲ad̲j̲arān*ⁱ "two kinds of trees", *as̲h̲d̲j̲ār*ᵘⁿ "[different] kinds of trees". This tallies well with the original meaning of the generic noun. But in other cases the connotation is rather that of "group" (the examples adduced by Ullmann, 50, for *buyūḍ*ᵘⁿ presuppose the meaning "kinds of eggs" in some cases and "clutches of eggs" in others). In still other cases the plural of the generic noun (e.g. *riyāḍ*ᵘⁿ) seems to serve as a plural for the unit noun (*rawḍat*ᵘⁿ), but that is difficult to prove and needs further study. In Modern Standard Arabic it is clearly felt to be so (personal survey).

Bibliography: M. Ullmann, *Das arabische Nomen generis*, Göttingen 1989 (= Abh. d. Akad. d. Wiss. in Göttingen, philol.-hist.Kl., 3. Folge, Nr. 176) (fundamental); idem, *Adminiculum zur Grammatik des klassischen Arabisch*, Wiesbaden 1989, 1-13; A. Fischer, *Die Terminologie der arabischen Kollektivnomina*, in *ZDMG*, xciv (1940), 12-24.

Grammars. Wright, i, 147; H. Reckendorf, *Die syntaktischen Verhältnisse des Arabischen*, Leiden 1898, 22-3; H. Fleisch, *Traité de philologie arabe*, i, Beirut 1961, 301-4; R. Blachère and M. Gaudefroy-Demombynes, *Grammaire de l'arabe classique*, [3]Paris 1952, 93; W. Fischer, *Grammatik des klassischen Arabisch*, [2]Wiesbaden 1987, 49-50; F. Corriente, *Gramática árabe*, [2]Madrid 1983. (W.P. HEINRICHS)

2. As a term in philosophy.

Here it conveys the ideas of oneness, unity, union, isolation and solitude (cf. in this last regard the title of Ibn Bād̲j̲d̲j̲a's [*q.v.*] *Tadbīr al-mutawaḥḥid*, and cf. also Ibn Sīnā's usage of *wāḥidiyya* as a synonym of *waḥda*, whereas *waḥdāniyya* conveys rather the idea of "unicity, uniqueness": see A.-M. Goichon, *Lexique de la langue philosophique d'Ibn Sina*, Paris 1938, s.vv. *waḥda*, *wāḥidiyya* and *waḥdāniyya*).

Waḥda is best translated in theological and philosophical contexts as oneness or unity. It does not occur in the Ḳur'ān, and is the equivalent of the Aristotelian μονάς. In Arabic, *waḥda* contrasts directly with *kat̲h̲ra*, *takat̲h̲t̲h̲ur* "multiplicity, plurality" (for an early philosophical discussion of *waḥda* vs. *kat̲h̲ra*, or *wāḥid* vs. *kat̲h̲īr*, see al-Fārābī, *K. al-Wāḥid wa 'l-waḥda*, ed. Muhsin Mahdi, Casablanca 1989). Al-G̲h̲azālī in his treatise on the Most Beautiful Names of God, *al-Maḳṣad al-asnā*, defines the divine name *al-Wāḥid* as follows: "The one who can neither be divided nor duplicated... God Most High is one in the sense that it is impossible for His essence to be arranged into parts... it belongs to none but God to be absolute unity" (tr. D.B. Burrell and Nazih Daher, Cambridge 1992, 130-1) (for a discussion of the theological treatment of the name *al-Wāḥid*, and other names meaning "the One", see D. Gimaret, *Les noms divins en Islam*, Paris 1988, 191-200). The modality of the Unity or Oneness of God precipitated much debate in mediaeval Islamic theology, particularly as theologians grappled with the problems arising from the idea that God had attributes.

In Islamic mystical philosophy and theosophy, perhaps the best known articulation of the term *waḥda* was in the phrase *waḥdat al-wud̲j̲ūd* "the oneness of being" or "unity of existence" [see WAḤDAT AL-S̲H̲UHŪD]. Whilst Ibn al-ʿArabī does not seem actually to have used the phrase himself in his own authenticated writings, there is no doubt that it represents his philosophical and theological perspective. As a counter to this, the phrase *waḥdat al-s̲h̲uhūd* "the unity of witnessing [only God]" came into being amongst more orthodox opponents of Ibn al-ʿArabī's monism, such as Aḥmad Sirhindī [*q.v.*] (see Y. Friedmann, *Shayk̲h̲ Aḥmad Sirhindī*, Montreal and London 1971, 59-60, and TAṢAWWUF. 2). But in Ṣūfism in general, the matter and definitions of *waḥda* could be very complex, and a work like the *K. Iṣṭilāḥāt al-Ṣūfiyya* of ʿAbd al-Razzāḳ al-Kās̲h̲ānī (d. 730/1330 [*q.v.*]) is full of gnomic utterances about *kat̲h̲ra* and *waḥda* (cf. *ibid.*, ed. and tr. Nabil Safwat and D. Pendlebury, *A glossary of Sufi technical terms...*, London 1991).

Bibliography (in addition to references in the article): Soheil M. Afnan, *A philosophical lexicon in Persian and Arabic*, Beirut 1969, s.v.; I.R. Netton, *Allah transcendent. Studies in the structure and semiotics of Islamic philosophy, theology and cosmology*, London 1989, 256-320. (I.R. NETTON)

WAḤDAT AL-WUD̲J̲ŪD [see WAḤDAT AL-S̲H̲UHŪD].

WAḤDAT AL-S̲H̲UHŪD (A.), with WAḤDAT AL-WUD̲J̲ŪD, two technical terms of Ṣūfī mysticism.

Waḥdat al-s̲h̲uhūd "the oneness of witnessing" is a doctrine established by S̲h̲ayk̲h̲ Aḥmad Sirhindī [*q.v.*] in response to *waḥdat al-wud̲j̲ūd* "the oneness of being" or "the unity of existence", a term that by his day was identified with the position of Ibn al-ʿArabī [*q.v.*; see also TAṢAWWUF. 2.]. Most of the secondary literature has assumed that there really is a specific, recognised doctrine known as *waḥdat al-wud̲j̲ūd* established by Ibn al-ʿArabī and that *waḥdat al-s̲h̲uhūd* really does offer an alternative or a corrective to that doctrine. Given the history of the expression and the contexts in which it appeared, however, this assumption is difficult to sustain. The various attempts by scholars to explain *waḥdat al-wud̲j̲ūd* by employing labels such as "pantheism" or "esoteric monism" succumb to the same assumption and fail to clarify what exactly was at issue in the texts. In fact, *waḥdat al-wud̲j̲ūd* was more an emblem than a doctrine, and if Ibn al-ʿArabī was considered its founder, this simply indicates that his writings mark Ṣūfism's massive entry into the theoretical discussions of *wud̲j̲ūd* that before him had been the almost exclusive preserve of the philosophers and the *mutakallimūn*.

The underlying issue is how Islam's first principle—*tawḥīd* [*q.v.*], the assertion that there is no god but God—is to be understood. Sirhindī makes this explicit by employing the terms *tawḥīd-i s̲h̲uhūdī* and *tawḥīd-i wud̲j̲ūdī* interchangeably with *waḥdat-i s̲h̲uhūd* and *waḥdat-i wud̲j̲ūd*. The specific form taken by the discussion goes back to the early adoption of the term *wud̲j̲ūd* to render the Greek idea of "being" or "existence" and is complicated by the literal sense of the verb, as exemplified by Ḳur'ānic usage (e.g. "He *finds* God", XXIV, 39). The difficulty arises the moment *wud̲j̲ūd* is ascribed to God, given that it can also be ascribed to everything other than God. If God is *wud̲j̲ūd*, then nothing else can be considered *wud̲j̲ūd* in the same sense. It is precisely the status of the "others" that needs to be clarified, and this is a basic issue in *Kalām*, philosophy, and much of theoretical Ṣūfism.

The authors of the early Ṣūfī manuals, such as al-Ḳus̲h̲ayrī, al-Sarrād̲j̲, and Hud̲j̲wīrī, had the Ḳur'ānic meaning of the term *wud̲j̲ūd* in mind when they discussed it along with *wadjd* and *tawādjud* and considered it a stage on the path in which the "finder" (*wādjid*) is aware only of God. Ibn al-ʿArabī follows this usage when he defines *wudjūd* as "finding the Real in ecstasy" (*widjdān al-ḥaḳḳ fi 'l-wadjd*) (*Iṣṭilāḥāt al-ṣūfiyya*, in *Rasāʾil Ibn ʿArabī*, Ḥaydarābād 1948, 5; *al-Futūḥāt al-makkiyya*, Cairo 1911, ii, 133.12, 538.1). *Wudjūd* in this sense is often difficult to differentiate from *fanāʾ* [*q.v.*]. In Anṣārī's classic *Manāzil al-sāʾirīn*, *wudjūd* is made the ninety-sixth of the one hundred stages of the path to God and defined as "achieving the reality of the thing" (*al-ẓafar bi-ḥaḳīḳat al-shayʾ*). In these discussions, *shuhūd* frequently plays a role, and it is not always clear that "witnessing" God means anything other than "finding" God. In offering definitions of *wudjūd*, al-Ḳushayrī provides an early example of many verses that use the two terms as rhymes: "My 'finding' [*wudjūdī*] is that I absent myself from *al-wudjūd*/with what appears to me through *al-shuhūd*" (*Risāla*, Cairo 1972, 249). Here, the second *wudjūd* can mean both the awareness of self and the "existence" of the self as seen independent from God, while *shuhūd* clearly means witnessing God. This interpretation is confirmed by al-Djunayd's definition of *mushāhada*, a term that is often used interchangeably with *shuhūd*: "Finding the Real along with losing you" (*wudjūd al-ḥaḳḳ maʿa fuḳdānika; ibid.*, 279). These authors frequently discuss the subtle differences between *shuhūd* and *kashf* "unveiling", and Ibn al-ʿArabī can employ both these terms as synonyms for *wudjūd* (see indexes of Chittick, *The Sufi path of knowledge*, Albany 1989; idem, *The self-disclosure of God*, Albany 1997). In Ibn al-ʿArabī's voluminous discussions of *wudjūd*, the philosophical/theological meaning usually, but not always, dominates over the Ṣūfī sense of experiential finding, without excluding it.

In tracing the history of the expression *waḥdat al-wudjūd*, we need to distinguish two basic usages. In the earliest instances, it means *waḥdat al-wudjūd al-ḥaḳḳ*, "the oneness of the real *wudjūd*", and indicates the self-evident fact that God's *wudjūd* is the one and only true *wudjūd*. Gradually, it comes to designate a distinctive perspective on the whole of reality, though interpretations of what this perspective implies can disagree sharply. The expression itself is not used by Ibn al-ʿArabī, even though his name eventually became associated with it. He should not be called its supporter unless it is explained in a way that corresponds with his teachings (cf. Chittick, *Imaginal worlds*, Albany 1992, ch. 1). However, these teachings are not easy to explain without distortion, since he speaks from diverse standpoints in keeping with various stations of knowledge achieved on the Ṣūfī path. Some, but not all, of these stations demand that God's absolute *wudjūd* be seen as obliterating the relative *wudjūd* of all else. For example, he sometimes speaks of *ahl al-djamʿ wa 'l-wudjūd* "the people of bringing together and finding", whom he also calls the "people of One Entity" (*ahl ʿayn wāḥida; Futūḥāt*, iii, 447.18; cf. Chittick, *Self-disclosure*, 183-4). In the Ṣūfī lexicon, *djamʿ* is contrasted with *farḳ* "separation", and it denotes seeing all things as brought together through God's reality. The people of bringing together and finding have been so overcome by the vision of God that they see no separation between him and the things. In effect, they say "All is He" (*hama ūst*)—the ecstatic and poetical exclamation found as early as Anṣārī and said in the later debates to be the position of *waḥdat al-wudjūd*. But Ibn al-ʿArabī does not consider this sort of vision the highest stage on the path to God, because it amounts to seeing with one eye; with the other eye the true Ṣūfī must also see that all is not He.

If the term *waḥdat al-wudjūd* had any significance for Ibn al-ʿArabī's own position, it would have been discussed in the writings of those of his disciples who wrote about theoretical issues, especially Ṣadr al-Dīn Ḳūnawī and ʿAfīf al-Dīn al-Tilimsānī [*q.vv.*]. Ḳūnawī does in fact use it on two occasions, but it arises naturally in the course of discussions of *waḥda* and *wudjūd*, and he attaches no special importance to it. In three works of al-Tilimsānī seen by the present writer, the closest he comes to it is *waḥdāniyyat al-wudjūd* (*Sharḥ al-asmāʾ al-ḥusnā*, commentary on the name *al-samīʿ*). Perhaps more significantly, in *Sharḥ fuṣūṣ al-ḥikam*, the earliest of the many commentaries written on this famous book, al-Tilimsānī says concerning a passage from the first chapter that Ibn al-ʿArabī is employing philosophical language to allude to *al-tawḥīd al-wudjūdī*. In the passage itself, Ibn al-ʿArabī has made the unremarkable statement that *wudjūd* brings together all "existent things" (*mawdjūdāt*). In the one work of his so far printed, *Sharḥ manāzil al-sāʾirīn*, al-Tilimsānī often uses the expression *al-djamʿ wa 'l-wudjūd*, defining it, in a phrase reminiscent of al-Djunayd's definition of *mushāhada*, as "the manifestation [*ẓuhūr*] of the Real's *wudjūd* through the annihilation [*fanāʾ*] of the creature's *wudjūd*" (ed. Tunis 1989, 462).

What might be considered the earliest instances in which the term *waḥdat al-wudjūd* designates a distinct position are found in the writings of Ibn al-ʿArabī's fellow-Murcian Ibn Sabʿīn (d. 669/1270 [*q.v.*]), who was much more conversant with the philosophical tradition. In the most explicit of these, he writes that the ignorant and the common people are dominated by multiplicity, while "the elect *ʿulamāʾ* are dominated by the root [*aṣl*], which is *waḥdat al-wudjūd*" (*Rasāʾil Ibn Sabʿīn*, Cairo 1965, 194; see also 38, 189, 264, 266). He may be saying here that *waḥdat al-wudjūd* is a doctrinal position; more likely, he is simply asserting that the elect see all things in terms of *tawḥīd*, while the common people see dispersion and incoherence. What is new here is not the idea but the expression, and it is not surprising in the context, given the centrality of the term *wudjūd* to philosophy. That this specific expression had no special significance for him is suggested by the fact that he does not mention it in his major work, *Budd al-ʿārif*, though he does insist that *wudjūd* is one (Beirut 1978, esp. 228, 303). Another early use of the term is found in two headings of one of the popularising Persian works of ʿAzīz al-Dīn Nasafī, *Kashf al-ḥaḳāʾiḳ* (written in 680/1281-2), where it designates a doctrine having four different formulations at the hands of two groups of Ṣūfīs, "the people of the fire" (*ahl-i nār*) and "the people of the light" (*ahl-i nūr*; see H. Landolt, *La paradoxe de la "face de dieu": ʿAzīz-e Nasafī (VIIᵉ/XIIIᵉ siècle) et le "monisme ésotérique" de l'Islam*, in *St. Ir.*, xxv [1996], 163-92). The folk of the fire see that the one, true *wudjūd* burns away all "others", while the folk of the light see that the "others" are rays of *wudjūd*'s light; these two perspectives correlate with *fanāʾ* and *baḳāʾ*. Again, the expression is new but not the ideas.

Perhaps the most telling of the early uses of *waḥdat al-wudjūd* is by Ḳūnawī's disciple Saʿīd al-Dīn Farghānī [*q.v.*], who employs it many times in both the Persian and Arabic versions of his commentary on Ibn al-Fāriḍ's *al-Tāʾiyya*. In this work, which is one of the most detailed and sophisticated discussions of the relevant theoretical issues in this period, *waḥdat al-wudjūd* is the complement of *kathrat al-ʿilm* and provides a philosophical basis for *fanāʾ* and *baḳāʾ*. God's *wudjūd* is one through its necessity, while God's knowledge is many through its objects; thus the oneness of God's *wudjūd* and the many-ness of His knowledge are the two principles through which he gives existence to the cosmos (*Mashārik al-darārī*, Tehran 1979, 344; *Muntahā 'l-madārik*, Cairo 1293/1876, i, 357). On the side of creation, the soul (*nafs*) manifests the many-ness of knowledge, while the spirit (*rūḥ*) manifests the oneness of *wudjūd* (*Mashārik* 359; *Muntahā*, ii, 17). Farghānī is careful to point out that *wudjūd* does not simply mean "existence", but also the habitude (*malaka*) of *wadjd*, that is, finding (*yāft*) one's inner connection to the world of the spirit's oneness (*Mashārik*, 364-5). In the Arabic passage that corresponds to this discussion, he offers what is perhaps the earliest example of the term *waḥdat al-shuhūd*; he tells us that the traveller, finding his own spirit, is attracted to "the world of the oneness of true witnessing" (*ʿālam waḥdat al-shuhūd al-ḥakīkī; Muntahā*, ii, 21). When the traveller reaches the advanced stages of the path, he undergoes annihilation of the soul, and this is accompanied by a subsistence in which he achieves the witnessing (*shuhūd*) of *waḥdat al-wudjūd*. This prepares him for the annihilation of the spirit, which yields a subsistence that is accompanied by the witnessing of *kathrat al-ʿilm*. Both modes of subsistence can be called *djamʿ* (*Mashārik*, 186; *Muntahā*, i, 226). At a still higher stage, he achieves *maḳām djamʿ al-djamʿ*, in which the two earlier stations are harmonised. In the highest stage, *aḥadiyyat al-djamʿ*, which is exclusive to Muḥammad, the two perspectives are seen to be the same (*Mashārik*, 395-96; *Muntahā*, ii, 45). The fact that the earlier, Persian version of this work was based on Ḳūnawī's lectures suggests that Ḳūnawī employed these terms in the same way that Farghānī does. Nonetheless, the term *waḥdat al-wudjūd* itself has not yet gained a special significance, because Farghānī does not always carry it over into the enlarged and thoroughly revised Arabic version of the work.

Despite these usages of the term *waḥdat al-wudjūd*, it is rarely found in the early texts, and apparently it does not become an issue until Ibn Taymiyya [*q.v.*], who mentions it in the titles of two treatises and attacks it violently, claiming that it asserts the identity of God and creation and that it is nothing but the well-known heresies *ḥulūl* ("incarnationism") and *ittiḥād* ("unificationism"). The major commentators on Ibn al-ʿArabī's *Fuṣūṣ*—Mu'ayyid al-Dīn Djandī, ʿAbd al-Razzāḳ Kāshānī, and Dāwūd al-Ḳayṣarī—do not mention it, but, by the 9th/15th century, it was controversial. Djāmī in *Nafaḥāt al-uns* (completed in 883/1478) writes that the exchange of letters between ʿAlā' al-Dawla Simnānī and Kāshānī in the early 8th/14th century had to do with *waḥdat al-wudjūd*, and this has led modern scholars to treat the debate in the same terms, even though the two authors do not mention *waḥdat al-wudjūd* in the letters, nor, it seems, in any of their other writings (see H. Landolt, *Der Briefwechsel zwischen Kāšānī und Simnānī über* Waḥdat al-Wuǧūd, in *Isl.*, 1 [1973], 29-81).

Sirhindī's reaction to *waḥdat al-wudjūd* occurs in the context of its relatively new-found fame and its general ascription to Ibn al-ʿArabī. He objects to it, he says, because a large number of his contemporaries were employing it as a pretext to avoid observing the rulings of the Sharīʿa (e.g. *Maktūbāt*, Dihlī 1964, no. 43). In explaining its meaning, he demonstrates little acquaintance with the writings of Ibn al-ʿArabī or the major figures who discussed the issues. By insisting that a correct interpretation of *waḥdat al-wudjūd* demands that it mean *waḥdat al-shuhūd*, he was saying that the *wudjūd* of the world is not identical with the *wudjūd* of God in every sense—despite the current rhetoric of "All is He"—and that if certain genuine Ṣūfīs had considered the *wudjūd* of God and the world to be the same, this goes back to their witnessing, not to the actual situation. At least partly because *wudjūd* in his understanding had none of the earlier connotations of finding, he felt it necessary to insist that seeing God in all things goes back to the viewer and does not offer a final explanation of the nature of reality. In any case, most Ṣūfī theoreticians in India ignored or dismissed his objections, while others felt it necessary to point out that he really did not disagree with Ibn al-ʿArabī (e.g. Shāh Walī Allāh, in his well-known *Fayṣala-yi waḥdat al-wudjūd wa 'l-shuhūd*). It is only in the modern period that Sirhindī has been elevated to special rank by historians of Islamic India (see Y. Friedmann, *Shaykh Aḥmad Sirhindī. An outline of his thought and a study of his image in the eyes of posterity*, Montreal and London 1971).

Finally, we should keep in mind that the Muslim authors themselves had no interest in the history of ideas in the modern sense. For Sirhindī, *waḥdat al-wudjūd* was a living issue, and it was not important to know exactly how it had come upon the scene. He saw that his contemporaries ascribed the expression to Ibn al-ʿArabī and, like Ibn Taymiyya, he thought that they understood it to mean the absolute identity of God and creation. Thus although his interpretation of *waḥdat al-wudjūd* exhibits no understanding of the subtleties of Ibn al-ʿArabī's position or of the various meanings that had been given to the term over the centuries, it does reflect the status of ongoing debates on *tawḥīd*, the most basic of theoretical issues in Islamic thought.

Bibliography (in addition to references given in the article): For various meanings given to the term *waḥdat al-wudjūd* in the sources and the secondary literature, see Chittick, *Rūmī and* Waḥdat al-wudjūd, in *Poetry and mysticism in Islam*, Cambridge 1994, 70-111. On Sirhindī, see J.G.J. ter Haar, *Follower and heir of the Prophet: Shaykh Aḥmad Sirhindī (1564-1624) as mystic*, Leiden 1992. For a good summary of Ibn Taymiyya's understanding of *waḥdat al-wudjūd*, see M.U. Memon, *Ibn Taimīya's struggle against popular religion*, The Hague 1976.

(W.C. Chittick)

WAHHĀBIYYA, a term used to denote (a) the doctrine and (b) the followers of Muḥammad b. ʿAbd al-Wahhāb (1115-1206/1703-92 [see IBN ʿABD AL-WAHHĀB]).

The term is derived from Muḥammad b. ʿAbd al-Wahhāb's father's name "ʿAbd al-Wahhāb" and was originally used by Muḥammad b. ʿAbd al-Wahhāb's opponents to denounce his doctrine as mere personal opinion. Probably the first appearance the term made is in the title of the *K. al-Ṣawāʿiḳ al-ilāhiyya fī 'l-radd ʿalā 'l-Wahhābiyya* (first ed. Bombay 1306/1888-9) of Sulaymān b. ʿAbd al-Wahhāb (d. 1208/1793-4) who up to 1190/1776 had strongly opposed his brother's teachings. Muḥammad b. ʿAbd al-Wahhāb and his followers called themselves *al-Muwaḥḥidūn* "those who profess the unity of God". Nevertheless, *al-Wahhābiyya* (and the derivation *Wahhābī/Wahhābiyyūn*) became the most widespread term for Muḥammad b. ʿAbd al-Wahhāb's doctrine and followers. In the 20th century it was also used by followers and sympathisers of the movement, like Sulaymān b. Saḥmān (d. 1930) in his *K. al-Hadiyya al-saniyya wa 'l-tuḥfa al-wahhābiyya al-nadjdiyya* (Cairo 1344/1926) or Muḥammad Rashīd Riḍā [*q.v.*] in his *al-Wahhābiyyūn wa 'l-Ḥidjāz* (Cairo 1344/1926).

1. The 18th and 19th centuries.

(a) *The doctrine*

The Wahhābiyya came into being by the middle of the 18th century in an oasis settlement in the centre of the Arabian Peninsula. In 1153/1740 Muḥammad b. ʿAbd al-Wahhāb began to proclaim publicly his teachings in Ḥuraymilā [*q.v.*] in the province of al-Miḥmal in Nadjd [*q.v.*].

In Nadjd, Ḥanbalism [see ḤANĀBILA] had for centuries been the dominant *madhhab* and Muḥammad b. ʿAbd al-Wahhāb was educated in its tradition. Yet, when he began to appear in public, his teachings were vehemently rejected as dissent from the Ḥanbalī *madhhab* by local Ḥanbalī scholars (e.g. his brother Sulaymān, then *ḳāḍī* in Ḥuraymilā, ʿAbd Allāh al-Muways (d. 1175/1761), *ḳāḍī* in Ḥarma/Sudayr, Sulaymān b. Suḥaym, Ḥanbalī scholar from al-Riyāḍ [*q.v.*]) as well as Ḥanbalī scholars from the eastern coastal province of al-Ḥasā [*q.v.*] (e.g. Muḥammad b. ʿAbd al-Raḥmān b. ʿAfāliḳ (d. 1164/1751), ʿAbd Allāh b. Fayrūz (d. 1175/1761-2), and Muḥammad b. ʿAbd Allāh b. Fayrūz (d. 1216/1801-2)). The conflict between representatives of the Ḥanbalī *madhhab*—e.g. the Ḥanbalī *muftī* in Mecca Muḥammad b. Ḥumayd al-ʿĀmirī (1235-95/1820-78) and Ḥasan b. ʿUmar al-Shaṭṭī al-Dimashḳī al-Baghdādī (1205-74/1791-1858)—and the Wahhābiyya was to continue also in the 19th century.

The very core of Muḥammad b. ʿAbd al-Wahhāb's teachings was made up of a concept of *tawḥīd* [*q.v.*] and its opposite *shirk* [*q.v.*], on which he based a radical criticism of his contemporaries' religious behaviour. He asserted that the overwhelming majority of Muslims, not only in Nadjd but in the whole Muslim world, had fallen into a state of religious ignorance no better than that of the *Djāhiliyya* [*q.v.*]. The reason for this he saw in the ignorance of the real meaning of *tawḥīd* as prescribed by God and exemplified by His prophet Muḥammad. Still at Ḥuraymilā, Muḥammad b. ʿAbd al-Wahhāb composed the *K. al-Tawḥīd alladhī huwa ḥaḳḳ allāh ʿalā ʾl-ʿabīd*, a thematically arranged collection of Ḳurʾānic verses and *ḥadīth*s which were to become the basic material for his argumentation (for a survey of its imprints and a bibliography of Muḥammad b. ʿAbd al-Wahhāb's writings cf. al-Ḍubayb). According to him, *tawḥīd* had a threefold meaning: *tawḥīd al-rubūbiyya*, *tawḥīd al-ulūhiyya* and *tawḥīd al-asmāʾ wa ʾl-ṣifāt*. Whereas he only touched upon the third category (the unity of God's attributes as laid down in the Ḳurʾān without interpretation) (e.g. *al-Masʾala al-thāmina*, in *TN*, 432), which was later more specified by his descendants (e.g. ʿAbd al-Raḥmān b. Ḥasan b. Muḥammad b. ʿAbd al-Wahhāb, in *MT*, 158, 176; ʿAbd al-Laṭīf b. ʿAbd al-Raḥmān, in *MRMN*, iii, 319 ff.), he elaborated in detail on the categories *tawḥīd al-rubūbiyya* and *tawḥīd al-ulūhiyya* (for abbreviations used in this section, see *Bibl.*).

Tawḥīd al-rubūbiyya (profession of the unity of God with regard to his divinity) in his definition was the mere verbal profession that God is the only, almighty creator and lord of the world. *Tawḥīd al-ulūhiyya*, which he also called *tawḥīd al-ʿibāda* (*al-Djawāhir al-muḍīʾa*, in *MRMN*, iv, 1-8, esp. 5; *Kashf al-shubuhāt*, in *MT*, 73-92, esp. 75), was the profession of the unity of God by serving God alone and proof of *tawḥīd al-rubūbiyya* through the deeds of the believer. According to him, *tawḥīd al-ulūhiyya* was the decisive dimension of *tawḥīd*, and only its fulfillment formed the distinctive mark between *islām* and *kufr*. Equating *tawḥīd* with the first religious duty, he subjected the behaviour of his fellow-Muslims to an examination according to his criteria concerning *tawḥīd*, and stated that most of them were not to be considered as Muslims because of their continued violation of their most eminent duty towards God. The proof for his accusation he saw in the expression of religious feelings through practices which he considered to be *shirk*. Among these he counted the following unless these were exclusively directed at God: *duʿāʾ* (prayer of invocation [*q.v.*]), *istiʿāna* (seeking help), *istighātha* (appeal for aid), *dhabḥ* (slaughter), *nadhr* (dedication vow [*q.v.*]), *khawf* (fear), *radjāʾ* (hope), *tawakkul* (trust [*q.v.*]), *ināba* (authorisation), *maḥabba* (love), *khashya* (fear), *raghba* (wish), *rahba* (fright), *taʾalluh* (devotion to religious service), *rukūʿ* (bending of the body), *sudjūd* (prostration), *khushūʿ* (submission), *tadhallul* (self-abasement) and *taʿẓīm* (glorification) (*al-Risāla al-tāsiʿa*, in *MT*, 128-30). Any act of devotion which displayed religious affection expended on human beings or objects like the veneration of tombs and entombed persons considered as saints, or veneration of places considered to possess supernatural powers, were therefore an offence against *tawḥīd*, thus *shirk*. The consequences he drew from his definition of *tawḥīd* were that a person guilty of neglecting *tawḥīd al-ulūhiyya* and thus offending against the first religious duty was to be regarded as a *mushrik* and thus outside Islam, even if he verbally confessed the unity of God and fulfilled the other religious duties. "It is well known that the Messenger of God summoned men to *tawḥīd* many years before he called on them to [obey] the pillars of Islam. And it is also well known that [the message of] *tawḥīd* which was brought by Djibraʾīl is the most important religious duty (*aʿẓam farīḍa*), more important than *ṣalāt*, *zakāt*, *ṣawm* and *ḥadjdj*. How is it possible that someone who rejects one of the pillars of Islam becomes an unbeliever, even if he acts in accordance with what the Messenger of God taught, whereas someone who refuses to profess *tawḥīd*, which is the religion of the messengers of God from Nūḥ to Muḥammad, does not become an unbeliever only because he utters the formula *lā ilāhᵃ illā llāhᵘ*?" (*Risāla fī ḥaḳīḳat al-islām*, in *MRMN*, iv, 41-6, esp. 45).

This doctrine of *tawḥīd* formed the fundament on which he based the rules for correct behaviour in belief. Attainment of knowledge about *tawḥīd* (*al-Risāla al-ʿāshira*, in *TN*, 309-12, esp. 311) and refraining from *shirk* had to be accompanied by combat of those who did not act according to the rules of *tawḥīd*, who were thus regarded as not being Muslims and became subject to *takfīr* (*al-Masʾala al-thālitha*, in *TN*, 405-7; *al-Risāla al-sādisa wa ʾl-ʿishrūn*, in *ibid.*, 360-93, esp. 372; *Risāla ukhrā fī kalimat al-tawḥīd*, in *MRMN*, iv, 36-40, esp. 37; for later Wahhābī scholars' statements on this topic, see e.g. *Hadiyya*, 46, 60, 67). By claiming that *tawḥīd* was the most neglected religious duty, Muḥammad b. ʿAbd al-Wahhāb criticised the long-established consensus of the Sunnī *madhāhib* which had accepted the mere uttering of the *shahāda* as fulfillment of the Muslim's first religious duty. He argued that the rules of *tawḥīd* as prescribed by God had become corrupted during the course of history, from the time of the Revelation until the 12th century of the Hidjra due to negligence by generations of religious scholars who had thus wrongly guided the *ʿāmma*, and he asserted that only the direct approach of the Ḳurʾān and the Sunna could again reveal its true meaning. In this matter, he saw himself not bound to any scholarly tradition but independently revealing the lost meaning of *tawḥīd* in an age of *djāhiliyya* to which everybody except himself had fallen victim (*al-Risāla al-ūlā*, in *TN*, 209-24, esp. 211; *al-Risāla al-ʿāshira*, in *ibid.*, 309-10).

The allegiance to *taḳlīd* [*q.v.*] of the *madhhab* authorities was unambiguously rejected by him, even though he did not claim the right to *idjtihād* [*q.v.*]. He argued that the direct approach of the Ḳurʾān and Sunna was not bound to the rigorous demands made on a *mudjtahid* on the part of the Sunnī *madhāhib* because God's prescriptions for mankind had been clearly and for all times revealed to all believers in His book and the Sunna of His Prophet. But the *madhāhib*'s *fiḳh* had alienated the *umma* from His clear will; as the Ḳurʾān and Sunna had been the sole sources for right guidance of the early Islamic community (*al-awwalūn*), their example was incumbent also on the later generations (*al-mutaʾakhkhirūn*) (*al-Risāla al-ūlā*, 218). The question of *idjtihād* was further discussed by disciples of Muḥammad b. ʿAbd al-Wahhāb (ʿAbd Allāh b. Muḥammad b. ʿAbd al-Wahhāb (*Hadiyya*, 35-53) and Ḥamad b. Nāṣir b. Muʿammar (*R. al-Idjtihād wa 'l-taḳlīd*, in *MRMN*, ii/3, 2-30; see below), who denied any claim for *idjtihād muṭlaḳ* on the part of Wahhābī scholarship but made indispensable the control of *madhhab* decisions in the light of the Ḳurʾān and Sunna; *madhhab* views must be checked on the basis of the Ḳurʾān and Sunna and must be refused if not in accordance with them. These criteria had to be applied to all *madhhab* authorities, including their founders, who had themselves stated that they were not infallible or more authoritative than the Ḳurʾān and Sunna (*R. al-Idjtihād*, 3). *Taḳlid* is allowed only for the ignorant masses, unable to obtain sufficient knowledge, or for scholars with only a limited education (*R. al-Idjtihād*, 6). Although they professed to follow Ḥanbalism in the *furūʿ* (*Hadiyya*, 39), they rejected *taḳlīd* of the *madhhab*'s authorities including Ibn Taymiyya and Ibn Ḳayyim al-Djawziyya [*q.vv.*] (*Hadiyya*, 51), to whom they often refered in their writings with the aim of strengthening their argumentation.

Muḥammad b. ʿAbd al-Wahhāb did not elaborate on a definition of *bidʿa* (innovation [*q.v.*]), apart from rejecting any *bidʿa* as aberration (*ḍalāla*) (*al-Risāla al-tāsiʿa*, in *TN*, 299-308, esp. 306). Probably as a result of the dogmatic dispute with the movement's adversaries, the Wahhābī concept of *bidʿa* was put into more concrete terms by his son ʿAbd Allāh (*Hadiyya*, 48 ff.). According to him, *bidʿa* generally is what happened after the 3rd century (*Hadiyya*, 48), a span of time including in his definition the age of the pious predecessors (*al-salaf al-ṣāliḥ*) as well as the four *imāms* and their immediate disciples (*Hadiyya*, 37). A distinction between *bidʿa ḥasana* and *bidʿa sayyiʾa* as accepted by the *madhāhib* is basically inadmissible, unless the term *bidʿa ḥasana* is applied exclusively to the practice of the pious predecessors, which may be divided into the categories *wādjiba, mandūba* and *mubāḥa*; anything else is *bidʿa sayyiʾa*, divisible into the categories *makrūha* and *muḥarrama*. Cases of *bidʿa* not concerning religious matters ("*mā lā yuttakhadh*[u] *dīn*[an] *wa-ḳurbat*[an]", *Hadiyya*, 51) may be exempted from this rule as long as they are not mixed up with religious matters (thus drinking coffee is allowed). The consequences of *bidʿa* are not to be confused with *takfīr* resulting from *shirk*. *Bidʿa* is an offensive against the *Sharīʿa* but does not make the believer an unbeliever. Yet *bidʿa* may lead to *shirk*. Invoking God through referring to the rank of the Prophet or pious men to gain access to Him (*tawassul*) is *bidʿa sayyiʾa*, whereas addressing the Prophet or pious men in their graves in the days of *barzakh* [*q.v.*] with the aim to obtain their intercession (*shafāʿa* [*q.v.*]) is *shirk*. The miracles of saints (*karāmāt al-awliyāʾ*) are not to be denied, and their right guidance by God is acknowledged whenever they act according to the *Sharīʿa*; yet swearing an oath by them with the aim of glorification is *shirk*. These rules also apply to the Prophet, who must not be venerated in a special manner; a visit to his grave is allowed in the course of visiting his mosque for prayer but, as a main objective, it is forbidden.

Neither Muḥammad b. ʿAbd al-Wahhāb nor his immediate disciples elaborated specifically on a theory of government and state. Muḥammad b. ʿAbd al-Wahhāb focused on a vision of *djamāʿa* [*q.v.*] which stressed the principle of *al-amr bi 'l-maʿrūf wa 'l-nahy ʿan al-munkar* as the individual's duty to fight *shirk* (*Risāla ukhrā*, 37), to refuse obedience to rulers and religious authorities not acting in accordance with the prescriptions for *tawḥīd* and to perform *hidjra* if necessary. Only in the 19th century did Wahhābī scholars define the functions of the imāmate in their writings (cf. ʿAbd al-Raḥmān b. Ḥasan b. Muḥammad b. ʿAbd al-Wahhāb, in *MRMN*, ii/2, 3-13), based on principles which drew from Ibn Taymiyya (cf. Laoust, 527; *ʿUnwān*, ii, 113).

(b) *Development until 1234/1818-19 (the first Wahhābī-Suʿūdī state)*

Muḥammad b. ʿAbd al-Wahhāb continued to propagate publicly his teachings after he was forced to leave Ḥuraymilā, first in al-ʿUyayna and, after being expelled from there also, from 1157/1744 or 1158/1745 onwards in al-Dirʿiyya [*q.v.*], then controlled by the local *raʾīs* Muḥammad b. Suʿūd (d. 1179/1765 [*q.v.*]). With Ibn Suʿūd's support, there developed the community of *Muwaḥḥidūn*, defining itself through commitment to the rules of *tawḥīd* according to the teachings of Muḥammad b. ʿAbd al-Wahhāb and the exclusion and combat of those not accepting them. By means of *daʿwa* (letters, envoys) and armed campaigns against neighbouring settlements (first attack 1159/1746 on al-Riyāḍ) the community's sphere of influence gradually extended at the local level. Under the leadership of ʿAbd al-ʿAzīz b. Muḥammad b. Suʿūd (1179-1218/1765-1803) it accomplished—settlement by settlement, tribal segment by tribal segment—the voluntary or enforced subjection of the provinces of Nadjd, sc. Sudayr in 1177/1763-4, al-Washm in 1181/1767-8, al-ʿĀriḍ [*q.v.*] after the fall of al-Riyāḍ in 1187/1773, al-Khardj [*q.v.*] and al-Aflādj [*q.v.*] in 1199/1785, al-Ḳaṣīm [*q.v.*] after the surrender of ʿUnayza [*q.v.*], and finally in 1202/1788, Wādī 'l-Dawāsir [*q.v.*] and Djabal Shammar [*q.v.*] in 1205/1790-1.

In the emerging state governed from al-Dirʿiyya, Muḥammad b. ʿAbd al-Wahhāb, bearing the title of *shaykh*, acted as the highest religious authority, teacher and supervisor of instruction in Wahhābī doctrine, and, according to Ibn Bishr [*q.v.*] (*ʿUnwān*, i, 143), he acted as *ḳāḍī*, *imām* and *khaṭīb*. The rulers of the Āl Suʿūd [*q.v.*], bearing the titles of *amīr* and *imām*, directed the state administration, appointing *ḳuḍāt*, *aʾimma* and *umarāʾ* in the settlements and for the tribes, collecting taxes (*zakāt*) from settled people and Bedouin, imposing punitive measures on the forcibly subjugated sections of the population, such as destruction of the agricultural infrastructure, and confiscation of property for the *bayt al-māl* or payment of ransom for captives and possessions.

By the death of Muḥammad b. ʿAbd al-Wahhāb in Dhu 'l-Ḳaʿda 1206/June 1792, the Wahhābī-Suʿūdī state had already begun to transcend the boundaries of Nadjd into al-Ḥasā, which was subjugated in 1207-8/1792-3, and it had launched the first attacks against the regions of Ḳaṭar [*q.v.*] and northern ʿUmān [*q.v.*].

According to Ibn Bishr (*ʿUnwān*, i, 93), Muḥammad

b. ʿAbd al-Wahhāb was succeeded first by his son Ḥusayn (d. 1224/1809), then by his son ʿAbd Allāh (1165-1242/1752-1827, d. in Cairo), both of them acting as *ḳuḍāt* in al-Dirʿiyya, while ʿAbd Allāh seems to have been more important as a scholar (author of *Djawāb ahl al-sunna fī naḳḍ kalām al-shīʿa wa 'l-zaydiyya* (*MRMN*, iv, 47-221), *al-Kalimāt al-nāfiʿa fi 'l-mukaffarāt al-wāḳiʿa* (*MT*, 229-96), numerous legal treatises (*MRMN*, i) and a *risāla* written on the occasion of the Wahhābī seizure of Mecca in 1803 (*Hadiyya*, 35-52)), directing the Wahhābī *madjālis* and instructing the heir-apparent Suʿūd b. ʿAbd al-ʿAzīz (1218-29/1803-14) and his son ʿAbd Allāh (1229-33/1814-18). Later sources (Āl al-Shaykh, 33; al-Bassām, i, 49) mention ʿAbd Allāh as the direct successor of Muḥammad b. ʿAbd al-Wahhāb. Several other descendants of Muḥammad b. ʿAbd al-Wahhāb (called Āl al-Shaykh) represented Wahhābī scholarship by the beginning of the 19th century: his sons ʿAlī (d. after 1233/1818 in Cairo) and Ibrāhīm (d. after 1251/1835 in Cairo), his grandson Sulaymān b. ʿAbd Allāh (1200-33/1786-1818, temporarily *ḳāḍī* in Wahhābī-occupied Mecca, author of *Taysīr al-ʿazīz al-ḥamīd, sharḥ Kitāb al-tawḥīd* (Beirut ²1970), *al-Tawḍīḥ ʿan tawḥīd al-khallāḳ fī djawāb ahl al-ʿIrāḳ* (first ed. Cairo 1901), *Awthaḳ ʿurā 'l-īmān* (*MT*, 178-92), *Ḥukm muwālāt ahl al-ishrāk* (*MT*, 192-208), *Ḥukm al-safar ilā bilād al-shirk* (*MT*, 209-13)), and other grandsons ʿAlī b. Ḥusayn (d. 1257/1841 or later, *ḳāḍī* in al-Dirʿiyya) and ʿAbd al-Raḥmān b. Ḥasan (1193-1285/1779-1869, *ḳāḍī* in al-Dirʿiyya). Important scholars of other descent were 1) Ḥusayn b. Ghannām (d. 1225/1811 [*q.v.*]), author of the first history of the Wahhābī community *Rawḍat al-afkār wa 'l-afhām li-murtād ḥāl al-imām* and *al-Ghazawāt al-bayāniyya wa 'l-futūḥāt al-rabbāniyya* (first ed. Bombay 1919; adapted prose version by N. al-Asad under the title *Taʾrīkh Nadjd*, Cairo 1961); 2) Ḥamad b. Nāṣir b. Muʿammar (d. 1225/1811), Wahhābī envoy to Mecca in 1211/1797, author of *al-Fawākih al-ʿidhāb fi 'l-radd ʿalā man lam yaḥkum bi 'l-sunna wa 'l-kitāb* (*Hadiyya*, 53-98), *R. al-Idjtihād wa 'l-taḳlīd* (*MRMN*, ii/3, 2-30) and other tracts (*MRMN*, ii/3), *ḳāḍī* in al-Dirʿiyya, and from 1220/1805 until his death, *ḳāḍī* and supervisor of the regulations for *ḳuḍāt* in Mecca; 3) ʿAbd al-ʿAzīz al-Ḥusayn (1154-1237/1741-1822), *ḳāḍī* in al-Washm, envoy to Mecca; 4) ʿAbd al-ʿAzīz b. Ḥamad b. Ibrāhīm (d. 1240/1825), envoy to the Imām of Ṣanʿāʾ under Suʿūd b. ʿAbd al-ʿAzīz and to Egypt 1230/1815, author of *al-Masāʾil al-sharʿiyya ilā ʿulamāʾ al-Dirʿiyya* (*MRMN*, iv, 564-84); 5) ʿUthmān b. ʿAbd al-Djabbār b. Shabāna (d. 1242/1826-7), *ḳāḍī* in ʿAsīr [*q.v.*], Raʾs al-Khayma [*q.v.*] and Sudayr; and 6) ʿAbd Allāh b. ʿAbd al-Raḥmān Abū Buṭayn (1194-1282/1780-1865), *ḳāḍī* in al-Ṭāʾif after 1220/1805, author of numerous treatises (*MRMN*, ii/3, 96-257).

The last decade of the 18th century was marked by increasing hostility between the Sharīf of Mecca, Ghālib b. Musāʿid (1202-28/1788-1813), and al-Dirʿiyya. Since the emergence of the Wahhābī movement, the relationship with the rulers of Mecca had been tense, and scholarly disputations between Meccan *ʿulamāʾ* and Wahhābī delegations (two of them in 1185/1771 and 1204/1790 led by ʿAbd al-ʿAzīz al-Ḥuṣayn) had not resulted in détente. In 1205/1791 Ghālib started off military activities against southern Nadjd, and the ensuing skirmishes lasted up to a peace treaty in 1212/1798, only to be broken in 1217/1802-3 by the Wahhābīs, who finally overran al-Ḥidjāz and took over al-Ṭāʾif (Dhu 'l-Ḳaʿda 1217/February-March 1803) and Mecca (Muḥarram 1218/April 1803). The first occupation of Mecca lasted only two-and-a-half months until Ghālib in Rabīʿ I 1218/June-July 1803 recaptured the town, but at the beginning of 1220/April 1805 the Wahhābīs took Medina and in Dhu 'l-Ḳaʿda 1220/January-February 1806 Mecca for the second time.

Wahhābī rule over the Ḥaramayn, which lasted until the turn of the year 1227/28 (1812/13), became one of the most disputed periods of Wahhābī history (cf. Daḥlān): the destruction of highly venerated tombs and mausoleums (cemetery of Maʿlā in Mecca) and domes erected at the birthplaces of the Prophet, of ʿAli b. Abī Ṭālib, Abū Bakr al-Ṣiddīḳ and Khadīdja bt. Khuwaylid [*q.vv.*]; the banning of the annual Pilgrimage caravans from Syria and Egypt; and the compulsory instruction of *ʿulamāʾ* and *ʿāmma* in Wahhābī doctrines, were the most striking examples of the collision of the Wahhābī interpretation of Islam with the majority view in the Muslim world. In a *risāla* written on the occasion of the conquest of Mecca (see above) in which he took part, ʿAbd Allāh b. Muḥammad b. ʿAbd al-Wahhāb elucidated the main points at issue: abolition of taxes considered to be unlawful (*mukūs/rusūm*); destruction of all utensils for consuming tobacco and prohibition of smoking it (cf. also Burckhardt, 284, 303); destruction of all places of *hashshāshīn* and immorality; destruction of all domes on graves and further buildings taken as places for worship of others than God; compulsion of all believers—no matter to which *madhhab* they might belong—to perform each *ṣalāt* collectively behind one *imām* (belonging to one of the four *madhāhib*); distribution of the writings of Muḥammad b. ʿAbd al-Wahhāb among the *ʿulamāʾ* and of a summary of their main contents among the *ʿāmma*, to be studied under supervision; interference in the ritual practices of the *madhāhib* when considered as incorrect (e.g. in the case of *ṣalāt* as performed by the Ḥanafī and the Mālikī *madhhab*s where, from the Wahhābī point of view, the moment of *ṭumaʾnīna* in *iʿtidāl* after *rukūʿ* and in *djulūs* between the *sadjadāt* was not properly observed); destruction of books that might lead to *shirk*, like the *K. Rawḍ al-rayāḥīn* (of al-Yāfiʿī, d. 768/1366-7 [*q.v.*]) or that might cause disturbance to people's beliefs, like books on *ʿilm al-manṭiḳ*; abolition of the special position of the *ahl al-bayt* in society (the doctrine of *kafāʾa* [*q.v.*] in marriage, for which no basis in the Ḳurʾān and Sunna can be found, kissing their hands which might lead to *shirk*, etc.); prohibition of various *bidaʿ*: publicly using the *subḥa* [*q.v.*] or rosary, raising the voice at the place of *adhān* [*q.v.*] other than for the *adhān* (Ḳurʾanic verses, prayers to the Prophet, *dhikr*), *tadhkīr* and *tarḥīm*, reading *ḥadīth*s from Abū Hurayra before the Friday sermon, gathering to hear *mawlid al-nabī* recitations, believing this to be a pious deed, gathering for *rawātib al-mashāyikh* like the *rātib al-Sammān* or the *rātib al-Ḥaddād* which even contain *shirk*, recitation of *fawātiḥ* for the *mashāyikh* after the five daily prayers which might lead to *shirk*. The Ṣūfī path (*al-ṭarīḳa al-ṣūfiyya*) and the purification of the inner dimension from sinful acts is not rejected, as long as the adherent of Ṣūfism sticks to the *Sharīʿa* (as understood by the Wahhābīs).

After the seizure of Medina, the treasures amassed in the Prophet's grave were taken by the Wahhābīs (for the discussion on this topic, cf. al-Alūsī, 55-6), yet the grave itself, after unsuccessful attempts to destroy its cupola, remained untouched (cf. Burckhardt, 281, 331-2); domes and buildings erected on other graves were destroyed.

In the first decade of the 19th century, the Wahhābī-Suʿūdī state increased its *daʿwa* activities also outside the Arabian Peninsula (e.g. in Tunisia and Morocco, cf. E. Pröbster, *Die Wahhabiten und der Maghrib*, in *Islamica*, vii [1935], 65-112 and in Syria, cf. H. Fleischer, *Briefwechsel zwischen den Anführern der Wahhabiten und dem Paša von Damascus*, in *ZDMG*, xi [1857], 427-43) and reached the peak of territorial expansion. South of al-Ḥidjāz, the Wahhābīs established dominance over ʿAsīr through their vassal Muḥammad b. ʿĀmir Abū Nuḳṭa al-Rufaydī and raided the Yemeni ports of al-Luḥayya and al-Ḥudayda [*q.vv.*] in 1225/1810. In the east, they subjugated Ḳaṭar and al-Baḥrayn and the Ḳawāsim [*q.v.*] tribes of northern coastal ʿUmān; in the south, they controlled the oasis of al-Buraymī [*q.v.*] and occasionally collected *zakāt* from the Sultan of Masḳaṭ [*q.v.*]. At the same time, they raided into al-ʿIrāḳ, where in Dhu 'l-Ḳaʿda 1216/March 1802 they overran the Shīʿī sanctuary of Karbalāʾ [*q.v.*] for the first time (second time in 1223/1808) and pillaged the tomb of al-Ḥusayn [*q.v.*]. Continuous quarrels with the southern ʿIrāḳī Muntafiḳ [*q.v.*], vassals of the Ottoman *wālī* in Baghdād, the Wahhābī hegemony over al-Ḥidjāz and Wahhābī influence on tribes in southern Syria (the only organised military campaign directed against Syrian territory was the raid on al-Muzayrīb and Buṣrā in Ḥawrān [*q.v.*] in 1225/1810), challenged the Ottoman Empire on several fronts simultaneously. In 1222/1807 Muḥammad ʿAlī [*q.v.*], Ottoman *wālī* of Egypt, was ordered to prepare a military campaign against the Wahhābīs, which was not, however, begun until 1226/1811, when Egyptian troops landed at Yanbuʿ [*q.v.*]. In Dhu 'l-Ḳaʿda 1227/November 1812 Medina, and in Muḥarram 1228/January 1813 Mecca, were taken from the Wahhābīs. Driven back to Nadjd, the Wahhābīs met with a crushing defeat at the hands of the Egyptian troops when in Dhu 'l-Ḳaʿda 1233/September 1818 al-Dirʿiyya was taken and reduced to ruins in Shaʿbān 1234/May-June 1819. Measures were taken against the Wahhābī-Suʿūdī state aimed at destroying its infrastructure, as well as at annihilating the power of its religious and political élites through executions (among others, ʿAbd Allāh b. Suʿūd, 1234/1818 in Istanbul; Sulaymān b. ʿAbd Allāh b. Muḥammad b. ʿAbd al-Wahhāb, 1233/1818 and his brother ʿAlī, 1234/1819 in al-Dirʿiyya) and deportations to Cairo (including an estimated total of 400 sons and grandsons of Muḥammad b. ʿAbd al-Wahhāb and leading members of the Āl Suʿūd, cf. Mengin ii, 151 ff.).

(c) *Development until the end of the 19th century (the second Wahhābī-Suʿūdī state)*

When the Egyptian troops left Nadjd in 1819 the territories of the former Wahhābī-Suʿūdī state returned to the rule of local *ruʾasāʾ*. In the struggle for re-establishment of a central political authority, Turkī b. ʿAbd Allāh b. Muḥammad b. Suʿūd succeeded between 1235/1820 and 1240/1824 in establishing himself in power at al-Riyāḍ as the new capital.

The political revival was soon after followed by the reconstruction of Wahhābī scholarship, in which ʿAbd al-Raḥmān b. Ḥasan, grandson of Muḥammad b. ʿAbd al-Wahhāb, who had been deported to Cairo, played the major role when he in 1241/1825-6 returned to Nadjd, taking over the office of senior religious authority in al-Riyāḍ. Until his death in 1285/1869, he worked as a *ḳāḍī*, as teacher of a whole generation of Wahhābī scholars and *ḳuḍāt* and as author of commentaries on the *Kitāb al-Tawḥīd* (*K. Fatḥ al-madjīd fī sharḥ K. al-Tawḥīd* (first ed. Cairo 1929), *K. Ḳurrat ʿuyūn al-muwaḥḥidīn fī taḥḳīḳ daʿwat al-anbiyāʾ wa 'l-mursalīn* (*MT*, 297-542)), refutations of anti-Wahhābī tracts (*Bayyān al-maḥadjdja fi 'l-radd ʿalā 'l-ladjdja* (*MRMN*, iv, 223-85), *al-Ḳawl al-nafis fi 'l-radd ʿalā Dāwūd b. Djirdjīs*, *al-Maḳāmāt radd*[an] *ʿalā ʿUthmān b. ʿAbd al-ʿAzīz b. Manṣūr al-Nāṣirī* (ms. al-Riyāḍ), *Bayān kalimat al-tawḥīd wa 'l-radd ʿalā 'l-Kashmīrī ʿAbd al-Maḥmūd* (*MRMN*, iv, 319-64), *al-Mawrid al-ʿadhb al-zulāl fī kashf shubah ahl al-ḍalāl* (*MRMN*, iv, 287-318)) and numerous other treatises.

Under the reign of Turkī b. ʿAbd Allāh, the Wahhābī-Suʿūdī state was able to regain parts of its former territories outside Nadjd when in 1245/1829-30 al-Ḥasā was retaken from the Banū Khālid, al-Ḳaṭīf and Raʾs al-Khayma [*q.vv.*], as well as al-Baḥrayn, swore allegiance; after a military expedition against ʿUmān in 1248/1832-3 Sultan Saʿīd, ruler of Masḳaṭ, paid an annual tribute. Yet the Wahhābī-Suʿūdī state could not regain its initial political stability because of internal rivalries for the imāmate which led to the assassination of Turkī b. ʿAbd Allāh at the hands of Mashārī b. ʿAbd al-Raḥmān b. Mashārī b. Suʿūd by the end of 1249/1834. The usurpation of power by Mashārī, whose reign lasted only forty days, seems to have been sanctioned in the absence of Turkī's son Fayṣal from al-Riyāḍ by the Āl al-Shaykh. Fayṣal b. Turkī on his return to al-Riyāḍ established himself as the new *imām*, to whom allegiance was sworn in early 1250/1834 by ʿAbd al-Raḥmān b. Ḥasan and other Wahhābī scholars. Fayṣal's rule was soon challenged in 1252/1836, when Muḥammad ʿAlī of Egypt, in the course of expanding his regional hegemony in the Arabian Peninsula, equipped an army under Ismāʿīl Pasha nominally led by Khālid b. Suʿūd, a brother of the late *amīr* ʿAbd Allāh b. Suʿūd, who had been deported to Egypt in 1234/1819. In Ṣafar 1253/May 1837 the Egyptian troops, with Khālid as a figure-head to win over the sympathies of the Nadjdī population, entered al-Riyāḍ, which Fayṣal b. Turkī had given up the previous year. In 1254/1838 Fayṣal surrendered to the Egyptians and was brought to Cairo. ʿAbd al-Raḥmān b. Ḥasan, together with other members of the Āl al-Shaykh, escaped from the new régime by moving to al-Ḥawṭa [*q.v.*] and al-Ḥarīḳ in southern Nadjd, where they kept themselves beyond the reach of Khālid b. Suʿūd until his power declined when the Egyptians withdrew their troops from Nadjd in 1256/1840. The expulsion of Khālid b. Suʿūd, whose rule was never recognised as legitimate by the Wahhābī scholars, seems to have been the prime mover for ʿAbd al-Raḥmān b. Ḥasan to support ʿAbd Allāh b. Thunyān b. ʿAbd Allāh b. Ibrāhīm b. Thunyān b. Suʿūd, who in 1257/1841 defeated Khālid and established himself in al-Riyāḍ as the new ruler. In 1258/1842 the Āl al-Shaykh returned to al-Riyāḍ after five years' exile in southern Nadjd.

But the struggle for the imāmate flared up again in 1259/1843, when Fayṣal b. Turkī returned from his imprisonment in Cairo, and, strongly supported by the Āl Rashīd [*q.v.*] of Djabal Shammar, moved against ʿAbd Allāh b. Thunyān and regained power with the approval of ʿAbd al-Rahmān b. Ḥasan. At the beginning of his second reign, he resumed a tradition seemingly established by his father Turkī to which he had stuck already at the beginning of his first reign in 1250/1834. In his capacity as *imām* of the Wahhābī community, he addressed himself to the population in a letter in which he called his subjects to *tawḥīd* and to the careful observance of all religious duties, emphasising the payment of *zakāt*, and in which he stressed the importance of the principles of *djamāʿa*, *djihād* and *al-amr bi 'l-maʿrūf wa 'l-nahy ʿan al-munkar*. He ordered the letter to be read aloud in all mosques and for this to be repeated every two months. For a period of 23 years up to his death in 1282/1865, Fayṣal remained the undisputed *imām* of the Wahhābī-Suʿūdī state. Under his second reign, a stable dominance was established over central and southern Nadjd, al-Ḥasā and al-Ḳaṭīf, whereas rule over the province of al-Ḳaṣīm and its main settlements Burayda and ʿUnayza [*q.vv.*] was precarious at best; the Djabal Shammar under Ṭalāl b. ʿAbd Allāh b. Rashīd (1264-84/1847-67) enjoyed a semi-autonomous status whilst remaining politically loyal to the Wahhābī-Suʿūdī state and paying *zakāt*. Relationships of political loyalty expressed by payment of *zakāt* were established with al-Baḥrayn, with the coastal shaykhdoms of northern ʿUmān and with the Sultan of Masḳaṭ. The Wahhābī-Suʿūdī state, for its part, expressed a formal loyalty to the Ottoman Empire by payment of an annual tribute via the Sharīf of Mecca.

In al-Riyāḍ, ʿAbd al-Raḥmān b. Ḥasan Āl al-Shaykh was in 1264/1848 joined by his son ʿAbd al-Laṭīf (1225-93/1810-76), who had been deported to Egypt in 1234/1819 and had since lived in Cairo. Like his father, he worked as a *ḳāḍī* in al-Riyāḍ, where he became a teacher in the Wahhābī *madjālis* and author of numerous treatises and refutations (*Taʾsīs al-taḳdīs fī ʾl-radd ʿalā Dāwūd b. Djirdjīs* (first ed. Bombay 1892), *Tuḥfat al-ṭālib wa ʾl-djalīs fī ʾl-radd ʿalā Ibn Djirdjīs, Miṣbāḥ al-ẓalām fī ʾl-radd ʿalā man kadhaba ʿalā ʾl-shaykh al-imām, Rasāʾil* (*MRMN*, iii, iv). Another prolific Wahhābī scholar and author of this period was ʿAbd Allāh Abū Buṭayn, who had been a renowned representative of Wahhābī scholarship before the fall of al-Dirʿiyya (see above) and then became *ḳāḍī* and teacher in ʿUnayza and Shaḳrāʾ/al-Washm (*Rasāʾil wa-masāʾil*, in *MRMN*, iv, 466-541; *Risāla fī taʿrīf al-ʿibāda* (*MT*, 217-27), *Taʾsīs al-taḳdīs fī kashf talbīs Dāwūd b. Sulaymān b. Djirdjīs, al-Intiṣār li-ḥizb Allāh al-muwaḥḥidīn wa ʾl-radd ʿalā ʾl-mudjādil ʿan al-mushrikīn, Mukhtaṣar Badāʾiʿ al-fawāʾid li-Ibn al-Ḳayyim, Ḥāshiya nafīsa ʿalā sharḥ al-Muntahā, Taʿlīḳāt ʿalā sharḥ al-durra al-muḍiyya sharḥ ʿaḳīdat al-Safārīnī*). Other noteworthy scholars were Ḥamad b. ʿAtīḳ (1227-1301/1812-83, *ḳāḍī* in al-Khardj and al-Aflādj, author of *Ibṭāl al-tandīd sharḥ Kitāb al-Tawḥīd* (Cairo 1367, Alexandria 1380, al-Riyāḍ 1389), *Bayān al-nadjāḥ wa ʾl-fakāk, al-Difāʿ ʿan ahl al-sunna wa ʾl-atbāʿ*), Muḥammad b. ʿAbd Allāh b. Salīm (1240-1323/1825-1905, *ḳāḍī* and teacher in Burayda), Muḥammad b. Maḥmūd (1250-1333/1834-1915, *ḳāḍī* in Wādī ʾl-Dawāsir, Ḍurmā and al-Riyāḍ).

Fayṣal b. Turkī's second reign was the longest period of uninterrupted development for the Wahhābī-Suʿūdī state in the 19th century. Soon after his death in Radjab 1282/December 1865, a fight for the imāmate began among his sons (ʿAbd Allāh, Suʿūd, Muḥammad and ʿAbd al-Raḥmān), when Suʿūd b. Fayṣal rebelled against his elder brother ʿAbd Allāh, who had been recognised as the legitimate *imām* at his father's death. Suʿūd's claim to rule was uncompromisingly condemned by ʿAbd al-Raḥmān b. Ḥasan and his son ʿAbd al-Laṭīf. When ʿAbd al-Raḥmān b. Ḥasan died in 1285/1869, ʿAbd al-Laṭīf b. ʿAbd al-Raḥmān became the senior Wahhābī scholar, and had to face a worsening of the fraternal strife concerning the imāmate when Suʿūd in 1287/1870 seized al-Ḥasā. Suʿūd's victory led ʿAbd Allāh to apply for help from Midḥat Pasha [*q.v.*], the Ottoman *wālī* of Baghdād. Yet Suʿūd advanced against al-Riyāḍ and captured the town in early 1288/1871. His usurpation of power was acknowledged as a legitimate take-over of the imāmate by ʿAbd al-Laṭīf b. ʿAbd al-Raḥmān for the sake of the Wahhābī community's preservation. When Ottoman troops entered al-Ḥasā in Rabīʿ II 1288/June-July 1871 ʿAbd Allāh b. Fayṣal, to whom the Ottomans seemingly had promised the appointment as *ḳāʾim-maḳām* [*q.v.*] of Nadjd joined them, vehemently condemned by ʿAbd al-Laṭīf b. ʿAbd al-Raḥmān for having deliberately handed over Muslim territory to *mushrikūn*. Yet ʿAbd al-Laṭīf b. ʿAbd al-Raḥmān's claim that *djihād* for the liberation of al-Ḥasā from the Ottomans was incumbent on the Wahhābī-Suʿūdī state was frustrated by the political weakness of Suʿūd, who was expelled from al-Riyāḍ by his uncle ʿAbd Allāh b. Turkī. In Radjab 1288/September-October 1871 ʿAbd Allāh b. Fayṣal renounced his cooperation with the Ottomans and returned to al-Riyāḍ, where ʿAbd Allāh b. Turkī placed the imāmate in his hands with the approval of ʿAbd al-Laṭīf b. ʿAbd al-Raḥmān. But in 1290/1873 he lost power for a second time to Suʿūd, who was once again acknowledged by ʿAbd al-Laṭīf b. ʿAbd al-Raḥmān as *imām* of the Wahhābī-Suʿūdi state. When Suʿūd died in Dhu ʾl-Ḥidjdja 1291/January 1875, ʿAbd al-Raḥmān b. Fayṣal took over the imāmate, which he returned in 1293/1876 to his brother ʿAbd Allāh, who was installed for the third time as ruler of the Wahhābī-Suʿūdī state and was once again acknowledged as the legitimate *imām* by ʿAbd al-Laṭīf b. ʿAbd al-Rahmān.

At this point there ended the fraternal strife over the imāmate which had split the population in their support of the various pretenders to power. Although the formal continuance of the Wahhābī-Suʿūdī state had been secured by ʿAbd al-Laṭīf b. ʿAbd al-Raḥmān through legitimation of each new ruler in al-Riyāḍ, the foundations of the state had been severely weakened not only through the definitive loss of al-Ḥasā to the Ottomans but also through the strengthening of movements for autonomy in other regions. In 1293/1876 ʿAbd Allāh b. Fayṣal had to face an upheaval against his authority in Burayda which was supported by the *amīr* of Djabal Shammar, Muḥammad b. Rashīd (1289-1315/1872-97). From this time onwards, the relationship between the Āl Rashīd and al-Riyāḍ openly deteriorated, with the Āl Rashīd gradually extending their territory at the cost of ʿAbd Allāh's power.

In Dhu ʾl-Ḳaʿda 1293/December 1876 ʿAbd al-Laṭīf b. ʿAbd al-Raḥmān died and was succeeded by his son ʿAbd Allāh (1265-1339/1849-1921) as senior Wahhābī scholar. The weakening of the Wahhābī-Suʿūdī state became obvious when in the years 1299-1301/1882-4 ʿAbd Allāh b. Fayṣal lost several battles against Ibn Rashīd and was at the same time challenged by the sons of his late brother Suʿūd. In 1305/1888 Ibn Rashīd advanced against al-Riyāḍ; ʿAbd Allāh and his brother ʿAbd al-Raḥmān were taken prisoners and brought to Ḥāʾil [*q.v.*] in Djabal Shammar, while in al-Riyāḍ an *amīr* on the part of Ibn Rashīd was installed.

After the brother's return to al-Riyāḍ in Rabīʿ I 1307/October-November 1889, ʿAbd Allāh b. Fayṣal died. ʿAbd al-Raḥmān b. Fayṣal tried to establish himself as new ruler, but in 1309/1891-2 Ibn Rashīd advanced again against al-Riyāḍ, seized it, destroyed the city walls and castles and installed Muḥammad b. Fayṣal b. Turkī (d. 1311/1894) as vassal *amīr*. The Wahhābī-Suʿūdī state had at this point ceased to exist.

ʿAbd al-Raḥmān b. Fayṣal fled with his son ʿAbd al-ʿAzīz to Ḳaṭar and then to al-Kuwayt. ʿAbd Allāh b. ʿAbd al-Laṭīf was brought to Ḥāʾil, where he remained for approximately a year and then returned to al-Riyāḍ, where he seemingly worked as a teacher. Other Wahhābī scholars who had to witness the decline of the Āl Suʿūd's power continued their occupations under the new ruler, such as Ḥasan b.

Ḥusayn b. ʿAlī b. Ḥusayn b. Muḥammad b. ʿAbd al-Wahhāb (1266-1341/1850-1922, *ḳāḍī* in al-Aflādj, al-Madjmaʿa and al-Riyāḍ), Saʿd b. Ḥamad b. ʿAtīḳ (1279-1349/1862-1930, *ḳāḍī* in al-Aflādj) and ʿAbd al-ʿAzīz b. Muḥammad b. ʿAlī b. Muḥammad b. ʿAbd al-Wahhāb (d. 1319/1901, *ḳāḍī* in Sudayr and al-Riyāḍ).

Although the Wahhābī community in the 19th century lacked its initial expansionist zeal and had to face setbacks even in its very heartland of Nadjd, Wahhābī ideas gained influence in other regions of the Islamic world [see IṢLĀḤ]. Details of this process are not well known. The second half of the century brought forth fierce anti-Wahhābī polemics and refutations, of which the most important were written by Aḥmad b. Zaynī Daḥlān (1232-1304/1817-86 [*q.v.*]) and Dāwūd b. Sulaymān b. Djirdjīs al-Baghdādī al-Khālidī (1231-99/1816-82) (*Ṣulḥ al-ikhwān min ahl al-īmān wa-bayān al-dīn al-ḳayyim fī tabriʾat Ibn Taymiyya wa-Ibn al-Ḳayyim*, Bombay 1306/1889; *al-Minḥa al-wahbiyya fī radd al-wahhābiyya*, Bombay 1305/1888; *Ashadd al-djihād fī ibṭāl daʿwat al-idjtihād*, Bombay 1305/1888). Their writings prove the growing importance of Wahhābī teachings for others than the community itself and the need felt by its opponents to reject them. Frankly pro-Wahhābī voices were scarce. One open supporter of the Wahhābī cause was the Indian scholar Muḥammad Bashīr al-Sahsawānī (d. 1326/1908), who opposed Daḥlān for his anti-Wahhābī attacks (*Ṣiyānat al-insān ʿan waswasat al-shaykh Daḥlān*, Dihlī 1890). Another Indian scholar, Sayyid Aḥmad Brēlwī (d. 1246/1831 [*q.v.*]), held tenets similar to Wahhābī teachings. However, the actual dimensions of Wahhābī influence in India [see KARĀMAT ʿALĪ for a person with a pseudo-Wahhābī background] and its spreading in other parts of the Islamic world in the 19th century remain as subjects for research.

Bibliography: *Madjmūʿat al-rasāʾil wa ʾl-masāʾil al-nadjdiyya*, 4 vols., Cairo 1346-49/1928-30 (abbr. *MRMN*); *Madjmūʿat al-tawḥīd al-nadjdiyya*, ed. M.R. Riḍā, Cairo 1346/1928 (abbr. *MT*); ʿUthmān b. Bishr, *ʿUnwān al-madjd fī taʾrīkh Nadjd*, 2 vols., Mecca 1349/1930 (abbr. *ʿUnwān*); *al-Hadiyya al-saniyya wa ʾl-tuḥfa al-wahhābiyya al-nadjdiyya*, ed. Sulaymān b. Saḥmān, repr. Mecca 1973; Ḥusayn b. Ghannām, *Taʾrīkh Nadjd*, ed. N. al-Asad, [2]Beirut-Cairo 1985 (abbr. *TN*); *K. Lamʿ al-shihāb fī sīrat Muḥammad b. ʿAbd al-Wahhāb*, ed. A.M. Abū Ḥākima, Beirut 1967; F. Mengin, *Histoire de l'Egypte sous le gouvernement de Mohammed-Aly*, 2 vols., Paris 1823; J.L. Burckhardt, *Notes on the Bedouins and Wahábys*, London 1830; Ibrāhīm b. Ṣāliḥ b. ʿĪsā, *ʿIḳd al-durar fī mā waḳaʿa fī Nadjd min al-ḥawādith fī ākhir al-ḳarn al-thālith ʿashar wa-awwal al-rābiʿ ʿashar*, ed. ʿAbd al-Raḥmān b. ʿAbd al-Laṭīf Āl al-Shaykh, al-Riyāḍ n.d.; idem, *Taʾrīkh baʿd al-ḥawādith al-wāḳiʿa fī Nadjd wa-wafayāt baʿḍ al-aʿyān wa-ansābuhum wa-bināʾ baʿḍ al-buldān min 700 ilā 1340*, ed. Ḥamad al-Djāsir, al-Riyāḍ 1966; Aḥmad b. Zaynī Daḥlān, *Khulāṣat al-kalām fī umarāʾ al-balad al-ḥarām*, Beirut n.d.; Maḥmūd Sh. al-Ālūsī, *Taʾrīkh Nadjd al-ḥadīth*, [2]Cairo 1929; ʿAbd al-Raḥmān b. ʿAbd al-Laṭīf Āl al-Shaykh, *Mashāhīr ʿulamāʾ Nadjd wa-ghayrihim*, al-Riyāḍ 1392/1972; ʿAbd Allāh al-Bassām, *ʿUlamāʾ Nadjd khilāl sittat ḳurūn*, 3 vols., Mecca 1398/1978; A.M. al-Ḍubayb, *Āthār al-shaykh Muḥammad b. ʿAbd al-Wahhāb: sidjill bibliyūghrāfī li-mā nushira min muʾallafātihi wa-li-baʿḍ mā kutiba ʿanhu*, al-Riyāḍ 1982; R.W. van Diffelen, *De geloofsleer der Wahhabieten*, Leiden 1927; H. Laoust, *Essai sur les doctrines sociales et politiques de Takī-d-dīn Aḥmad b. Taimīya*, Cairo 1939; R.B. Winder, *Saudi Arabia in the nineteenth century*, London-New York 1965; ʿAbd al-Raḥmān ʿAbd al-Raḥīm, *al-Dawla al-suʿūdiyya al-ūlā*, Cairo 1969; ʿAbd al-Fattāḥ Abū ʿUlayya, *al-Dawla al-suʿūdiyya al-thāniya*, al-Riyāḍ 1969; idem, *Muḥāḍarāt fī taʾrīkh al-dawla al-suʿūdiyya al-ūlā*, al-Riyāḍ 1983; R. Peters, *Idjtihād and taqlīd in 18th and 19th century Islam*, in *WI*, xx (1980), 131-45; M. Crawford, *Civil war, foreign intervention, and the question of political legitimacy: a nineteenth century Saʿūdī qāḍī's dilemma*, in *IJMES*, xiv (1982), 227-48; ʿAbd Allāh al-ʿUthaymīn, *Taʾrīkh al-mamlaka al-ʿarabiyya al-suʿūdiyya*, n.p. 1984; idem, *al-Shaykh Muḥammad b. ʿAbd al-Wahhāb: ḥayātuhū wa-fikruhū*, al-Riyāḍ 1986; Bakrī Shaykh Amīn, *al-Ḥaraka al-adabiyya fī ʾl-mamlaka al-ʿarabiyya al-suʿūdiyya*, [5]Beirut 1986; M. Cook, *The expansion of the first Saudi state: the case of Washm*, in *The Islamic world: from classical to modern times (Essays in honour of Bernard Lewis)*, ed. C.E. Bosworth *et al.*, [3]Princeton 1991, 661-99; idem, *On the origins of Wahhābism*, in *JRAS*, series 3, vol. ii (1992), 191-202; idem, *The provenance of the Kitāb Lamʿ al-shihāb fī sīrat Muḥammad b. ʿAbd al-Wahhāb*, in *Journal of Turkish Studies*, x (1986), 79-86; E. Peskes, *Muḥammad b. ʿAbdalwahhāb (1703-92) im Widerstreit. Untersuchungen zur Rekonstruktion der Frühgeschichte der Wahhābīya*, Beirut 1993; eadem, *The Wahhābiyya and Sufism in the eighteenth century*, in F. de Jong and B. Radtke (eds.), *Islamic mysticism contested. Thirteen centuries of controversies and polemics*, Leiden 1999, 145-61. (ESTHER PESKES)

2. The 20th century.

The development of the Wahhābiyya in the 20th century is marked, from 1902 onwards, by the establishment of the third Saudi-Wahhābī state in the Arabian Peninsula under the leadership of the Imām (later also Sultan and King) ʿAbd al-ʿAzīz b. ʿAbd al-Raḥmān Āl Suʿūd (d. 1953), known as "Ibn Suʿūd/Saʿūd" [see ʿABD AL-ʿAZĪZ, in Suppl., and AL-SUʿŪDIYYA, AL-MAMLAKA AL-ʿARABIYYA].

The restoration of Saudi power in Nadjd [*q.v.*] was accompanied by a revival there of Wahhābī doctrine and its propagation, especially among the Bedouin tribes. As a result, a religious and paramilitary movement, called the Ikhwān [*q.v.*], succeeded in the settlement of a great number of nomadic tribesmen in cantonments called *hidjra* [see AL-HIDJAR], which at the same time were intended to form agricultural communities. To some extent, the *hidjar* promoted the homogenisation, based on Wahhābī principles, of the population of Nadjd as well as some of the adjacent territories conquered by Ibn Suʿūd (for these developments until 1936, see Kostiner in *Bibl.*).

The revolt of many of the Ikhwān, beginning in 1927, was the result of a conflict between pristine Wahhābism, as conceived by the Ikhwān, and Ibn Suʿūd's political pragmatism, which the latter tried to justify in religious terms by the principles of *idjtihād* and *maṣlaḥa* [*q.vv.*]. The suppression of their revolt (in 1929-30) did not mean the total eclipse of the Ikhwān but their subordination under the state and, later on, their partial transformation into units of the National Guard or a "religious police" called *muṭṭawwiʿūn* [see MUTAṬAWWIʿA]. More recently, the memory of both their rôle in the dissemination of Wahhābī doctrine and of their revolt against Ibn Suʿūd seems to inspire certain oppositional circles within the Kingdom and abroad.

With the conquest of the Ḥidjāz [*q.v.*] in 1924-5 and the elimination of Hāshimite rule there [see HĀSHIMIDS], the pilgrimage to Mecca [see ḤADJDJ and MAKKA] and the *ziyāra* [*q.v.*] to Medina [see AL-MADĪNA] came under Wahhābī control. The religious policy of the new rulers, and in particular their suppression of practices considered as *bidaʿ* [see BIDʿA] as well as the destruction of mausolea and tombstones at the cemetery of Baḳīʿ al-Gharḳad [*q.v.*] and elsewhere, gave rise to heated agitation in many parts of the Muslim world. Likewise, the intervention of Wahhābīs in traditional practices of the pilgrimage led to serious clashes and even international crises, one of the first and most famous ones being the so-called *maḥmal* incident of 1926 [see MAḤMAL]. These events resulted in serious tensions between Saudi Arabia and a number of Muslim countries such as Egypt and Iran (see Boberg and Kramer, in *Bibl.*). As for Iran, the strife over pilgrimage issues and the control of the Ḥaramayn [*q.v.*] flared up again after the Islamic revolution there of 1978-9 (see the annual surveys by M. Kramer, in *Middle East contemporary survey*, Boulder, Col., etc., esp. from vol. xi [1987] onwards).

With a few exceptions, the leading Ḥidjāzī families of scholars and merchants, most of whom had earlier been closely linked with the Hāshimites, were eventually won over by Ibn Suʿūd and adopted, at least externally, Wahhābī doctrine and practices. To the dismay of many Nadjdī *ʿulamāʾ*, however, the enforcement of Wahhābī norms has been restrained, in the Ḥidjāz and elsewhere, by both tacit local resistance and governmental consent. In addition, there has been a more or less constant influx of foreigners from a great number of Muslim and non-Muslim countries and with differing social and cultural backgrounds: specialised expatriates, asylum seekers, religious students, etc. Their presence, together with local traditions, has militated against a total assimilation of Saudi society to the Wahhābī way of life. Finally, the gradual erosion of Wahhābī values must also be seen in connection with the affluence resulting from oil wealth and a number of social developments related to it (Grandguillaume, in *Bibl.*).

Consequently, the religious discourse and daily practice (not only in the Ḥidjāz) in one way or another has come under the influence of the norms and values of the Salafiyya [*q.v.*] and similar trends (which in the past may have themselves been inspired by the Wahhābiyya). The frame of mind of many intellectuals, civil servants and technocrats in the country is dominated by the principles of reformism [see IṢLĀḤ. i] and may be described as a kind of "neo-Wahhābiyya" (Schulze in *Bibl.*, index, 500, 505). This process of partial moderation has been strengthened, from the 1950s onwards, even by the immigration of members of the Muslim Brotherhood [see AL-IKHWĀN AL-MUSLIMŪN] and related groups who, coming to Saudi Arabia as political refugees, have served there as advisers, school teachers and in other capacities.

Nevertheless, ultra-orthodox Wahhābī principles and practices are upheld to a considerable extent. Representatives of this current, such as Shaykh ʿAbd al-ʿAzīz b. Bāz (until his death in May 1999 Grand Mufti and president of the Board of Senior Scholars, *Hayʾat kibār al-ʿulamāʾ*, established in 1971) make their influence felt, e.g. by issuing *fatwā*s [*q.v.*] as well as by shaping the structure and curricula of the Islamic University in Medina, an institution founded in 1961 (Schulze, index, 494, and Nādjī Muḥammad al-Anṣārī, *al-Taʿlīm fi ʾl-Madīna al-Munawwara*, Cairo 1414/1993, 610-40). In addition, Wahhābī *ʿulamāʾ* (including members of Muḥammad b. ʿAbd al-Wahhāb's family, known as the Āl al-Shaykh) still play an important rôle in the deliberations of the Mecca-based Muslim World League (*Rābiṭat al-ʿālam al-islāmī*), a Pan-Islamic organisation founded in 1962 (Schulze, esp. 181 ff., and see AL-RĀBIṬA AL-ISLĀMIYYA). To their embarrassment, however, some of their religious opinions and legal rulings are adopted by militant zealots and used in agitation against what the latter see as a betrayal of religious principles by a régime claiming Wahhābī legitimacy. The ideology of the rebels who seized the *ḥaram* of Mecca in November 1979 is a case in point (see Kechichian, in *Bibl.*, also Schulze, 369-74).

In spite of the opposition of many *ʿulamāʾ* to legal reform, a continuous process of modernist legislation characterised by a pragmatic approach can be observed in Saudi Arabia. There are even indications of the emergence of a legislative authority outside the control of the Wahhābī *ʿulamāʾ* (see Layish, in *Bibl.*). In line with this development, the promulgation in 1992 of three statutes or basic laws (*niẓām*, sing.), including one concerning the establishment of a *madjlis al-shūrā* [see MADJLIS; SHŪRĀ], are to be seen as a further step away from the traditional Wahhābī position of denying the need for any constitution beyond the Ḳurʾān and the Sunna of the Prophet (Teitelbaum, in *Bibl.*).

In the course of the 20th century, the Wahhābiyya have been rehabilitated in the eyes of many Sunnī Muslims all over the world. In particular from the second half of the 1920s onwards, prominent Salafīs and Arab nationalists such as Rashīd Riḍā [*q.v.*], Shakīb Arslān [*q.v.*], Muḥibb al-Dīn al-Khaṭīb [*q.v.* in Suppl.] and others have been instrumental in this development. There are, however, authors of different persuasions (including, of course, Ṣūfīs and Shīʿīs) who have continued to criticise Wahhābī doctrine and practice. (For bibliographical surveys of this literature, see ʿAlī, *Muʿdjam*, in *Bibl.*, and Āl Salmān, who in addition quotes Wahhābī refutations of these works, *Kutub*, i, 250-87.)

Wahhābī authors tend to describe the history of their movement in general, and with regard to the 20th century in particular, as an almost unremitting success story. In this connection, they are prone to exaggerate the *direct* influence of the Wahhābiyya, from the 18th century to the present, on more or less similar reform movements in West Africa, India and elsewhere (see e.g. the works of Djumʿa and Ḍāhir, which nevertheless are useful surveys, and also Q. Ahmad and Kaba, in *Bibl.*).

Bibliography: 1. Works in Arabic. In addition to a number of publications already mentioned in section 1 above, such as al-Bassām, *ʿUlamāʾ Nadjd*, Āl al-Shaykh, *Mashāhīr*, and Amīn, *al-Ḥaraka*, see Ḥāfiẓ Wahba, *Djazīrat al-ʿarab fi ʾl-ḳarn al-ʿishrīn*, Cairo 1935; Muḥammad al-Fiḳī, *Athar al-daʿwa al-wahhābiyya fi ʾl-iṣlāḥ al-dīnī wa ʾl-ʿumrānī fī djazīrat al-ʿarab*, Cairo 1935; Muḥammad ʿAbd Allāh Māḍī, *al-Nahaḍāt al-ḥadītha fī djazīrat al-ʿarab*, pt. 1, *Fi ʾl-Mamlaka al-ʿArabiyya al-Suʿūdiyya*, [2]Cairo 1952; Fahd al-Mārik, *Lamaḥāt ʿan al-taṭawwur al-fikrī fī djazīrat al-ʿarab fi ʾl-ḳarn al-ʿishrīn*, Damascus 1962; Kamāl Djumʿa, *Intishār daʿwat al-Shaykh Muḥammad ibn ʿAbd al-Wahhāb khāridj al-djazīra al-ʿarabiyya*, [2]Riyāḍ 1981; Khayr al-Dīn al-Ziriklī, *Shibh al-djazīra fī ʿahd al-malik ʿAbd al-ʿAzīz*, 4 vols., [2]Beirut 1985; ʿAbd al-ʿAzīz b. Bāz, *Fatāwā wa-tanbīhāt wa-naṣāʾiḥ*, 2nd (enlarged) ed. Cairo 1989; idem *et al.*, *Fatāwā islāmiyya*, 3 vols., Beirut 1988; idem *et al.*, *Fatāwā hayʾat kibār al-ʿulamāʾ*, 2 vols., Cairo n.d. [1990]; Rifʿat Sayyid Aḥmad, *Rasāʾil Djuhaymān al-ʿUtaybī, ḳāʾid al-muktaḥimīn li ʾl-masdjid al-ḥarām bi-Makka*, Cairo 1988; al-Sayyid ʿAbd Allāh Muḥammad ʿAlī, *Muʿdjam mā allafahu ʿulamāʾ al-umma al-islāmiyya li ʾl-radd ʿalā khurāfāt al-daʿwa al-wahhābiyya*, in *Turāthunā* (quarterly, Beirut), iv/4 (no. 17), Shawwāl 1409/

1989, 146-78; Muḥammad Kāmil Ḍāhir, *al-Daʿwa al-wahhābiyya wa-athāruhā fi 'l-fikr al-islāmī al-ḥadīth*, Beirut 1993; Muḥammad Khayr Ramaḍān Yūsuf, *Dalīl al-muʾallafāt al-islāmiyya fi 'l-Mamlaka al-ʿArabiyya al-Suʿūdiyya, 1400-1409 h.*, Riyāḍ 1413/1993; Abū ʿUbayda Mashhūr b. Ḥasan Āl Salmān, *Kutub ḥadhdhara minhā 'l-ʿulamāʾ*, 2 vols., Riyāḍ 1995.

2. Works in Western languages. For literature published until the late 1980s, see H.-J. Philipp, *Saudi Arabia/Saudi Arabien, bibliography on society, politics, economics*, 2 vols., Munich etc. 1984, 1989, index s.v. "Wahhabiyya" (vol. i, 367 f., ii, 560); J.S. Habib, *Ibn Saʿud's Warriors of Islam*, Leiden 1978; W. Ende, *Religion, Politik und Literatur in Saudi-Arabien*, in *Orient* (Hamburg), xxii (1981), 377-90, xxiii (1982), 21-35, 378-93, 524-39; G. Grandguillaume, *Valorisation et dévalorisation liées aux contacts de cultures en Arabie Saoudite*, in P. Bonnenfant (ed.), *La Péninsule Arabique d'aujourd'hui*, ii, Paris 1982, 623-54; A. Al-Yassini, *Religion and state in the Kingdom of Saudi Arabia*, Boulder and London 1985; A. al-Azmeh, *Wahhabite polity*, in I.R. Netton (ed.), *Arabia and the Gulf*, London and Sydney 1986, 75-90; J.A. Kechichian, *The role of the Ulama in the politics of an Islamic state. The case of Saudi Arabia*, in *IJMES*, xviii (1986), 53-71; idem, *Islamic revivalism and change in Saudi Arabia. Juhaymān al-ʿUtaybī's "Letters" to the Saudi people*, in *MW*, lxxx (1990), 1-16; A. Layish, *Saudi Arabian legal reform as a mechanism to moderate Wahhābī doctrine*, in *JAOS*, cvii (1987), 279-92; M. Kramer, *Tragedy in Mecca*, in *Orbis*, xxxii (1988), 231-47; R. Schulze, *Islamischer Internationalismus im 20. Jahrhundert. Untersuchungen zur Geschichte der Islamischen Weltliga*, Leiden 1990; D. Boberg, *Ägypten, Naǧd und der Ḥiǧāz*, Bern etc. 1991; J. Kostiner, *The making of Saudi Arabia, 1916-1936*, New York and Oxford 1993; J. Teitelbaum, arts. "Saudi Arabia", in *Middle East Contemporary Survey*, xvi (1992), 668-701, see also xvii (1993), 575-600, and xviii (1994), 548-82. Concerning similar reform movements outside Arabia, see e.g. Q. Ahmad, *The Wahabi movement in India*, Calcutta 1966; L. Kaba, *The Wahhabiya. Islamic reform and politics in French West Africa*, Evanston, Ill. 1974; C. Hock, *Fliegen der Seelen der Heiligen? Muslimische Reform und staatliche Autorität in der Republik Mali seit 1960*, Berlin 1999. (W. Ende)

WAHĪBA, Āl, a large ʿUmānī tribe with both settled and pastoralist sections, whose grazing *dār* covers a large area of the Sharḳiyya region to the south-east of the Djabal Akhḍar extending to the Arabian sea coastline, and including most of so-called Wahība Sands (though locally this sand-sea is known simply as "the sands", and tribes other than the Āl Wahība, notably the Djanaba, also live in it). The Āl Wahība are Hinawīs, and form part of a natural Sharḳiya-Hinawī alliance (which also includes the Ḥirth, Ḥadjriyyīn, and Ḥabs). There are four main tribal divisions: Bin Ḥayya, Hal Anfarri, Yaḥāḥīf, Hal Musallam, and the sheikhly section, Āl Bū Ghufayla, permanently settled at al-Aflādj. Each of these main divisions has a large number of sub-divisions. The Yaḥāḥīf, a semi-autonomous division, are alone said to account for more than half the numerical strength of the Āl Wahība.

Some sections of the Āl Wahība are more or less permanently settled in the towns and villages on the fringes of the sands (notably Sanaw, Bādiya, Barzamān, al-Mintirib), and in the wadis to the west (Wādī Andam, Wādī Ḥalfayn). Here many of the Āl Wahība are involved in agriculture and palm cultivation. In 1986, it was estimated that the nomadic, pastoralist population of the sands was 450-500 families, or about 2,700-3,000 souls, most of these being Āl Wahība. Some members of the tribe are semi-nomadic, summering in the villages on the northern fringe of the sands, and wintering in the sands with their animals. In the sands, the social structure is based on the mobile *farīḳ*, usually consisting of between one and five families who camp together, often in a loose assemblage of rugs and coverings simply draped over the branches of the proposis trees (*ghāf*) which abound in central and eastern sands. Goats and sheep are kept, as are camels by nearly all families, though usually in small numbers. The female camels bred by the Āl Wahība (particularly the *banāt farḥa* breed) are renowned as racing camels, and much in demand in ʿUmān and neighbouring countries such as Ḳaṭar where camel-racing is popular.

Bibliography: D. Chatty, *The Bedouin of Central Oman*, in *Jnal. of Oman Studies*, vi (1983), 149-62; J.C. Wilkinson, *Water and tribal settlement in South-East Arabia. A study of the Aflāj of Oman*, Oxford 1977; J.R.L. Carter, *Tribes in Oman*, London 1982; Wilkinson, *The Imamate tradition of Oman*, Cambridge 1987; *Jnal. of Oman Studies special report no. 3. The scientific results of the Royal Geographical Society's Oman Wahiba Sands project 1985-7*, Muscat 1988.

(C. Holes)

WĀḤIDĪ, a sultanate and confederation of tribes occupying the territory about 320 km/200 miles to the east of Aden [see ʿADAN], forming a delta shape from the Indian Ocean shore in the south, stretching north about 208 km/130 miles to the region of Bayḥān [*q.v.*], and flanked by the ʿAwlaḳī states in the west and the Ḳuʿayṭī sultanate in the east (see e.g. map in Johnston, *Steamer Point*). Its administrative capital was latterly Mayfaʿa near the impressive pre-Islamic fortifications of Naḳab al-Ḥadjar, whose pre-Islamic name, MYFʿT, it took, in the centre of the sultanate, while nearby ʿAzzān remained the home of the Wāḥidī ruling family (*dawla*) and Ḥabbān in the west the commercial capital. Other important towns included Biʾr ʿAlī (by 1961 incorporated into the one sultanate, but previously independent and whose ex-sultan was alive then), the pre-Islamic incense port of Cana (Ḳanā), on the south coast, and al-Ḥawṭa, a centre of religious visitations, between Mayfaʿa and Ḥabbān.

The name Wāḥidī is traditionally derived from one ʿAbd al-Wāḥid, a Ḳurashī (or Ḥimyarī) chief who gained control of the area, probably about the beginning of the 19th century, and established his residence in Ḥabbān (*Arab tribes*, 100). Local tradition and a passage from Bal-Faḳīh al-Shiḥrī's *Taʾrīkh* (see Serjeant, 40-1), however, relates that this is the oldest *dawla* in Southern Arabia and places ʿAbd al-Wāḥid about two centuries earlier. His inscribed tomb is reputed to be in the *djāmiʿ* mosque in Ḥabbān. In the 1880s, the sultanate appears to have split into three, with Biʾr ʿAlī and Balḥāf on the southern coast becoming independent of the ruler of Ḥabbān and ʿAzzān (*Arab tribes*, 102). When the Protectorate treaties were signed in 1888 and 1890, four separate treaties were ratified between the British government and states covering the area of the later sultanate: the "Shaykh" of ʿIrḳa (on the southern coast) (1888), the "Shaykhs" of Ḥawra (a short distance inland) (1888), the "Sultans of the Wāḥidī tribe" of Biʾr ʿAlī (1890) and the "Chiefs of the Wāḥidī tribe of Balḥāf" (1888) (*Arab tribes*, 180-6, with the texts of the treaties).

From 1937 the sultanate formed a part of the British-administered Eastern Aden Protectorate, but in late 1961, having joined the Federation of Arab Amirates of the South whose other member states belonged to the Western Aden Protectorate, it joined the latter grouping of states (Burrowes, *Dictionary*, 377, dates accession to 1962). After entry into the Federation, the then Sultan Nāṣir b. ʿAbd Allāh al-Wāḥidī was given the portfolio of agriculture and fisheries in the Federal Government and the sultanate administered by the State Secretary, Amīr Muḥammad b. Saʿīd. The sultanate ceased to exist in 1967, when the British handed over power to the National Liberation Front in South Arabia.

The Wāḥidī sultanate had some large areas of fertile agricultural land and its main produce was dates, grain crops and vegetables. Wādī Djirdān in the north remains famous for its high-quality honey, this high quality said to result from the abundance of *ʿilb* (pl. *ʿulūb*) trees (*Zizyphus spina Christi* Willd.) in the area.

Bibliography: Government of Bombay, *An account of the Arab tribes in the vicinity of Aden*, Bombay 1909; R.B. Serjeant, *Two tribal cases (documents) (Wāḥidī Sultanate, South-West Arabia)*, in *JRAS* (1951), 40-1; C.H. Johnston, *The view from Steamer Point*, London 1964; R.D. Burrowes, *Historical dictionary of Yemen*, Lanham and London 1995. (G.R. Smith)

al-**WĀḤIDĪ**, Abu 'l-Ḥasan ʿAlī b. Aḥmad b. Muḥammad b. ʿAlī b. Mattūya al-Mattūyī (Mattuwī) al-Naysābūrī al-Shāfiʿī, Arab philologist and Ḳurʾān scholar.

He was descended from a family of merchants from Sāwa [*q.v.*] who were very likely originally Christians. He was born in Naysābūr (Nīshāpūr), and died there after a long illness in advanced age in Djumādā II 468/January-February 1076, highly venerated as *ustādh ʿaṣrihī* "the master of his age". Still a boy, he took part in teaching sessions on *adab* and *naḥw*, and attended classes in the large law schools of his native city. Finally, he joined Abū Isḥāḳ al-Thaʿlabī [*q.v.*] (the form Thaʿālibī is also transmitted), the Ḳurʾān interpreter and authority on the biography of the Prophet, and associated himself with the pupils of Abu 'l-ʿAbbās al-Aṣamm [*q.v.*], the great local authority in the field of Tradition and Shāfiʿī law (Sezgin, i, 186). Of his students may be mentioned al-Maydānī [*q.v.*] and ʿAbd al-Ghāfir al-Fārisī (451-529/1059-1135). Just like other scholars he enjoyed the special favour and protection of the famous Saldjūḳ minister Niẓām al-Mulk [*q.v.*], who as a young man had taken part in al-Wāḥidī's sessions, and of the latter's brother Abu 'l-Ḳāsim ʿAbd Allāh b. ʿAlī b. Isḥāḳ *al-faḳīh al-adjall*.

Among al-Wāḥidī's works which have been preserved, the first to be mentioned are the *shaykh al-tafsīr* and the *imām ʿulamāʾ al-taʾwīl*'s highly-esteemed studies on the Ḳurʾān. Following a lecture given by his teacher Abū Ṭāhir al-Ziyādī (d. 410/1019) in 409/1018, he composed a terse philological commentary, entitled *al-Wadjīz fī maʿānī 'l-Ḳurʾān al-ʿazīz* (Cairo 1305/1887, repr. Beirut 1981). For the time being he put aside a detailed commentary, which he had already begun; he finally finished it five decades later in Radjab 461/May 1069 under the title *al-Wāsīṭ bayna 'l-maḳbūd ('l-Wadjīz) wa 'l-basīṭ ('l-Basīṭ) fī tafsīr al-Ḳurʾān al-ʿaẓīm* (for old mss. of parts of it, see Chester Beatty 4609, 5041, 5204). In the meantime he had published three *madjmūʿāt* on questions concerning the *tafsīr* (cf. Ahlwardt 750; *al-Mawrid*, xvii 4 [1409/1988], 292-304). It has to be checked whether the material of these three *madjmūʿāt* is to be found in his *Djāmiʿ al-bayān fī tafsīr al-Ḳurʾān* which has been preserved, or in *Ḥirār al-maʿānī* or in *al-Ḥāwī li-djamʿ al-maʿānī*, or whether they have been taken up into his third great commentary. So far it is not known when he started this third extensive commentary, entitled *al-Tafsīr al-basīṭ*, nor whether and when he completed it (for old manuscripts of parts of it, see Chester Beatty 3731, 3736, 5105). Particularly in demand was and still is his *Asbāb al-nuzūl* on the occasions in which singular sūras and verses were revealed (for the various recensions, see Ahlwardt, i, 180-1, no. 463-4; *G. des Q.*, ii, 183; for old manuscripts, see Chester Beatty 3733, 4522; latest prints Cairo 1411/1990, Beirut 1411/1991).

Like his teacher al-Thaʿlabī, al-Wāḥidī composed a *K. al-Maghāzī*, which seems to have been preserved (cf. R. Şeşen, *Nawādir al-makhṭūṭāt al-ʿarabiyya*, Beirut 1402/1982, iii, 57).

As grammarian, lexicographer and rhetorician he made a special name for himself with his commentary on the *Dīwān* of al-Mutanabbī [*q.v.*] (Sezgin, ii, ix, index). For the *al-Wasīṭ fi 'l-amthāl* falsely ascribed to him, see mathal.1.iii; Sellheim, in *Oriens*, xxxi (1988), 82-94, xxxii (1990), 468-9.

Bibliography: Brockelmann, I², 524, S I, 730; Sarkīz, 1905; Ziriklī, *Aʿlām*, Beirut 1979, iv, 255; Kaḥḥāla, *Muʾallifīn*, vii, 26-7; idem, *al-Mustadrak ʿalā Muʿdjam al-muʾallifīn*, Beirut 1406/1985, 471-2; idem, *Muʿdjam muṣannifī 'l-kutub al-ʿarabiyya fi 'l-taʾrīkh wa 'l-tarādjim wa 'l-riḥalāt*, Beirut 1406/1986, 335-6; M.ʿA. Mudarris, *Rayḥānat al-adab*, ²Tabrīz n.d. [*ca.* 1348/1969], vi, 285-6; Dihkhudā, *Lughat-nāma*, Tehran 1325/1947, vol. A/1, 406; *ibid.*, 1342/1963, vol. ʿA/2, 83-4; *ibid.*, 1345/1966, vol. W, 41; cf. the catalogues of manuscripts in libraries of Tehran, Mashhad, etc. by Dānish Pazhūh and others; Djawdat M.M. al-Mahdī, *al-Wāḥidī wa-manhadjuhū fi 'l-tafsīr*, Cairo 1978.

The main sources are: Bakharzī, *Dumyat al-ḳaṣr*, Nadjaf 1391/1971, ii, 255-6; ʿAbd al-Ghāfir al-Fārisī, *Siyāḳ Taʾrīkh Naysābūr*, in *The histories of Nishapur*, facs. ed. R.N. Frye, The Hague 1965, fols. 66b ll. 16-67a l. 6; 113a ll. 13-21, cf. H. Jaouiche, *Register der Personen- und Ortsnamen*, Wiesbaden 1984, 40; Samʿānī, *al-Taḥbīr fi 'l-muʿdjam al-kabīr*, Baghdād 1395/1975, ii, 377-8; Yāḳūt, *Udabāʾ*, v, 97-102 (with citations from ʿAbd al-Ghāfir!); Ibn al-Ḳifṭī, *Inbāh al-ruwāt ʿalā anbāh al-nuḥāt*, Cairo 1371/1952, ii, 223-5 (with citations from al-Bakharzī!); Ibn Khallikān, s.v. (on the problem of the *nisba*); Dhahabī, *Siyar aʿlām al-nubalāʾ*, Beirut 1405/1984, xviii, 339-42; idem, *al-ʿIbar*, Kuwait 1961, iii, 267; Ṣafadī, *Wāfī*, xx (in press); Yāfiʿī, *Mirʾāt al-djanān*, Ḥaydarābād/Deccan 1338/1919, iii, 96-7; Subkī, *Ṭabaḳāt al-Shāfiʿiyya al-kubrā*, Cairo 1386/1967, v, 240-3; Asnawī, *Ṭabaḳāt al-Shāfiʿiyya*, Baghdād 1391/1971, ii, 538-9; Ibn al-Djazarī, *Ghāyat al-nihāya fī ṭabaḳāt al-ḳurrāʾ*, Leipzig-Cairo 1351/1932, i, 523; Ibn Ḳāḍī Shuhba, *Ṭabaḳāt al-Shāfiʿiyya*, Ḥaydarābād/Deccan 1398/1978, i, 277-9; Ibn Taghrībirdī, *al-Nudjūm al-zāhira*, Cairo 1353/1935, v, 104; Suyūṭī, *Bughya*, 327-8 (Cairo 1384/1965, ii, 145); idem, *Ṭabaḳāt al-mufassirīn*, Leiden 1839, 23; Ṭāshköprüzāda, *Miftāḥ al-saʿāda*, Cairo n.d. [*ca.* 1388/1968], ii, 66-7; Ibn al-ʿImād, *Shadharāt*, iii, 330; Khʷānsārī, *Rawḍāt al-djannāt*, ²Tehran 1367/1948, 463; Ismāʿīl Pasha, *Hadiyyat al-ʿārifīn*, Istanbul 1951, i, 692.

(R. Sellheim)

WAHM (a., pl. *awhām*), lit. "notion", "supposition", in particular also "false notion", "delusion". In non-technical parlance the negative meaning of thinking something to be the case, contrary to fact, is preponderant; sometimes it comes close to *sahw* "inadvertency", "inadvertent omission". In later texts it may acquire the meaning of "hallucination" and "spectre" (see Dozy, s.v.).

1. In philosophy the term denotes "estimation", the "estimative faculty" (also *al-ḳuwwa al-wahmiyya*), and the "notion" resulting from the activity of this faculty (the plural is used with this last meaning, rarely also the second). *Wahm* belongs to the "internal senses" (*al-ḥawāss al-bāṭina*, see ḤISS), and in Ibn Sīnā it refers to the highest quasi-mental faculty in animals, that which allows a sheep to recognise the notion (*maʿnā*) "enemy" in a wolf and run away. Goichon and Afnan, following Mediaeval Latin usage, translate the term as "estimative faculty". It is rather close to *khayāl/takhayyul* "imagination" [see TAKHAYYUL, in Suppl.] and as a result, in Mediaeval Latin translations one finds it rendered as *estimatio, imaginatio, intellectus* and *opinio*.

Rahman found that nothing in Greek corresponded directly to *wahm* but that it was "a differentiation of Aristotle's "phantasia" (φαντασία) through Stoic influences". According to Morewedge, "there is no doubt that the concept was not directly borrowed from Aristotle" (324). Goichon concurs with this, while Wolfson espoused the idea of borrowing from the Greek. Walzer notes the problems that the Arabs had in finding an agreed rendition of the Greek word for "representation" (φαντασία): *Wahm*, as the chosen translation for φαντασία, was popular with such early translators as Usṭāth [*q.v.*] and Ibn Nāʿima who respectively translated Aristotle's *Metaphysics* and the so-called *Theology of Aristotle* [see UTHŪLŪDJIYĀ] for al-Kindī. Walzer (385) points out that there is a diversity of terminology "in Abū ʿUthmān al-Dimashqī's summary of Ḥunayn b. Isḥāq's translation of Galen's *Peri ēthōn*, which includes *taṣawwur, tawahhum*, and the curious hybrid *takhayyul fi 'l-wahm*". Al-Kindī used the transliteration *fanṭāsiyā* and also *tawahhum*; al-Fārābī, relying on later translators, usually renders "representation" by *takhayyul* (e.g. *al-Madīna al-fāḍila*, ch. i, 14; cf. Walzer, 385), which became the standard equivalent. For al-Fārābī, the delusionary character of *tawahhum* is prominent; commenting on Aristotle's *De Interpretatione* 21a, 32-3, "al-Fārābī is... misled by the translator's choice of *tawahhum* [imagination, with a suggestion that what is so imagined is mere fantasy] for δόξα, a word elsewhere rendered as *iʿtiqād* [belief]". He comments: "... that is to say, if a thing is said to be imagined it is excluded from existence. For our imagining it means that we picture it in our mind without its existing. If we raise in our minds something which exists we do not imagine it but know it" (Zimmermann, 156-7 and n. 1). Similarly, in Ibn Sīnā's *Dānish-nāma-i ʿAlāʾī*, *wahm* "refers to the ability to have a mental experience of an event in contrast to the actual happening of that event" (Morewedge, 321). But mostly, *wahm* is a technical term in the "psychological epistemology" of Ibn Sīnā whereby it "is an internal sense belonging to the animal soul" (*ibid.*), see above.

Morewedge (322) points out that *wahm* "has frequently been used in Persian to designate a mental power from which a being can cause entities to emanate by mere thought".

2. In mysticism [see Suppl.].

Bibliography: 1. Arabic and Persian sources. The sections on psychology in Ibn Sīnā, *Dānish-nāma-i ʿAlāʾī* (see also P. Morewedge, *The Metaphysica of Avicenna (Ibn Sīnā). A critical transl., comm. and analysis of the fundamental arguments in the Dānish-Nāma-i ʿalāʾī (The Book of Scientific Knowledge)*, New York 1973, Glossary, s.v. *wahm*), *K. al-Nadjāt* and *K. al-Shifāʾ* (see also F. Rahman, *Avicenna's De Anima*, London 1959); Kindī, *Rasāʾil al-Kindī al-falsafiyya*.

2. Dictionary entries and studies. Dozy, s.v. *wahm*; S.M. Afnan, *A philosophical lexicon in Persian and Arabic*, Beirut 1969, s.v. *wahm*; A.M. Goichon, *Lexique de la langue philosophique d'Ibn Sīnā (Avicenne)*, Paris 1960; H. Daiber, *Bibliography of Islamic philosophy*, 2 vols. Leiden 1999, ii, 538, s.v. *wahm*; R. Walzer, *Al-Farabi on the Perfect State: Abū Naṣr al-Fārābī's* Mabādiʾ ārāʾ ahl al-madīna al-fāḍila, Oxford 1985; F.W. Zimmerman, *Al-Fārābī's Commentary and Short Treatise on Aristotle's De Interpretatione*, Oxford 1981, 1987; H.A. Wolfson, *Goichon's three books on Avicenna's philosophy*, in *MW*, xxxi (1941); idem, *The internal senses in Latin, Arabic, and Hebrew philosophic texts*, in *Harvard Theological Review*, xxviii (1935), 69-133; H. Gätje, *Die "inneren Sinne" bei Averroes*, in *ZDMG*, cxv (1965), 255-93; Deborah Black, *Estimation* (wahm) *in Avicenna. The logical and psychological dimensions*, in *Dialogue, Canadian Philosophical Review*, xxxii/2 (1993), 219-58.

(I.R. NETTON)

WAHRĀN, the Arabic name for the North African coastal town conventionally known as Oran, the chief port of western Algeria (lat. 35° 45' N., long. 0° 38' W.). It is dominated by the Djebel Murdjadjo (400 m/1,312 feet) and sheltered within one of the large bays of the southwestern Mediterranean. In its hinterland lie vast, semi-arid plains, with the Great Sebkha [see SABKHA] in its western part.

It was founded by Muslims from Umayyad Spain in 290/903, not far from the bay of Marsā al-Kabīr, which was probably the ancient Portus Divini mentioned in the *Itinerarium* of Antoninus, and just a short time before the disintegration of the Khāridjite state centred on Tāhert [see RUSTAMIDS], which had controlled the roadsteads of the port. This was the period of Spanish Umayyad-Fāṭimid conflict. The former, with the support of Berber confederations like those of the Īfran and the Maghrāwa [*q.vv.*], the latter with the support of the Zīrids [*q.v.*], endeavoured to impose their political domination and to control the routes bringing gold from the Sūdān. Hence Wahrān was destroyed and rebuilt on two occasions, in 297/910 and 342/954. Yūsuf b. Tāshufīn conquered it in 473/1081, and the Almoravids kept control there till 539/1145. Like other Mediterranean coastal towns, it suffered through the Almoravids' deflection of the gold route to Marrakesh, and possibly—like the Ḥammādid capital Bidjāya/Bougie—from incursions of the Normans. Under the succeeding Almohads and then the ʿAbd al-Wādids (whose founder Yaghmurāsan [*q.v.*] was recognised by the last Almohads as ruler of the central Maghrib), Wahrān's commercial connections with Muslim Spain increased, thanks to the twin ports of Wahrān itself and Marsā al-Kabīr. The ʿAbd al-Wādids made it, together with Hunayn [*q.v.* in Suppl.] further west, the main maritime outlet for their unified kingdom based on their inland capital Tilimsān/Tlemcen and stretching from the Wadi Moulouya to the south of Kabylia.

In the 4th/10th century, Ibn Ḥawḳal described Wahrān as a lively place exporting great quantities of wheat, and in the next century, al-Bakrī described Marsā Wahrān as a great harbour, sheltered from all the winds; al-Idrīsī was struck by the continuous traffic in and out of it. The Almohad sultan ʿAbd al-Muʾmin had his fleet constructed at Marsā al-Kabīr, a port which Leo Africanus was later to describe in his *Description of Africa* as unparalleled in the world. Wahrān had lively markets (al-Idrīsī) and was surrounded by gardens with windmills (al-Bakrī); Leo again, at the opening of the 16th century, praised its building and estimated its population at 6,000 hearths, say *ca.* 30,000 inhabitants, sedentary Muslims as well as Jews, some autochthonous and other immigrants from Muslim Spain who had arrived in waves since the setting-up of the Inquisition in Spain in 1391. The town had spread beyond its original site to suburbs on the Karguenta plateau on the other side of the Ra'ṣ al-ʿAyn defile. Its prosperity was linked with that of Tilimsān, but was nevertheless now an independent maritime city and, like other Mediterranean coastal places, practised corsair marauding to compensate for periods of economic recession.

Encouraged by ʿAbd al-Wādid decline and the Mamlūks' deflection of the trans-Saharan trade routes towards the Nile valley, the armies of Castile undertook a Reconquista along the coastlands of the Maghrib. In 910/1505 Marsā al-Kabīr was seized, followed by Pedro Navarro's entry into Wahrān and its agricultural hinterland on 17 May 1509. Massacres (of 4,000, according to Marmol) and deportations took place under Cardinal Ximenes. As at Bidjāya, the population of Wahrān fell, down to 3,500, almost half of these being troops; the town was closed to Muslims, there were forcible conversions and the remaining Jews were expelled. It was near the port that the Spanish defeated and killed the corsair captain Urūdj [*q.v.*], who had made himself master of Algiers, and in 1543 restored the ʿAbd al-Wādid Abū ʿAbd Allāh to his throne in Tilimsān and made him their vassal. A new state was founded and organised around Algiers by Urūdj's brother Khayr al-Dīn Barbarossa [*q.v.*], and the ʿAbd al-Wādids expelled from their capital by Ṣalāḥ Reʾīs. An expedition of Count Alcaudete, the Spanish governor in Wahrān, ended in disaster at Mustaghānim [*q.v.*] (965/1558). Thereafter, Wahrān remained for over two centuries (except for an interval 1708-32 when the Turks recaptured it) a *presidio*, to which the fort of Santa Cruz overlooking the town remains, together with the fort of San Andrea, and Burdj al-Ḥawḍī and the Canastel and Spanish gates, bear witness. The Spanish presence created beyond a reduced agricultural region, compared with that which Ximenes described as a paradise, a no-man's land, the *bled el baroud* or "land of warfare", left to tribal allies like those of the Banū ʿĀmir, *Los Moros de Paz*, a hinterland left to nomadism and semi-nomadism.

Maritime activity in the port revived somewhat under the *bey* Bū Shalagham in 1120/1708, but after the Spanish, led by the Count of Montemar, regained the undefended town 24 years later, it was reduced to being a port for landing provisions for the increasingly isolated garrison. It had hardly more than 12,000 inhabitants, even after its recapture in 1206/1792 by the Bey of Mascara, the Ḳul-Oghlu [*q.v.*] Muḥammad al-Kabīr, 2,000 people having perished in the previous year from a terrible earthquake. Muḥammad al-Kabīr made Wahrān the capital of the Western Beylik, undertook rebuilding and moved in population, Muslims and Jews, from other towns of the region. To the *plaza de Oran*, dominated by the *ḳaṣba* (now in an advanced state of ruin) was added on the right bank of the Wādī 'l-Rāhī the new Jewish quarter, and two great streets, each 700 m long, along the plateau of the village of Karguenta. Corsair activity revived on a reduced scale, together with external trade, shared with Arzew and Rachgun, especially with nearby Gibraltar and Spain, until the blockade of Algeria which preceded the French occupation of 4 January 1831.

The French army occupied a town largely deserted by its 10-12,000 inhabitants, with the exception of the 3,000 Jews who remained or quickly returned, and now with less than 500 Muslims. According to Rozet, *Voyage dans le Régence d'Alger*, Paris 1833, the soldiers demolished fine houses, seeking wood for the fires of their kitchens. The Oran population, like that of Mustaghānim, had fled to the towns of the interior or the urban centres founded by the Amīr ʿAbd al-Ḳādir [*q.v.*]. The deserted houses were occupied by troops or by all sorts of adventurers who came in their wake, or were the object of speculation. Like the *funduḳs*, the mosques served as quarters for the troops (those of the Pasha and Sīdī Ḥawārī) or were transformed into churches (that of the Barrānīs), whilst the old mosque, called after Muḥammad al-Kabīr, was used as baths for the soldiers. Destructions by the army, or subsequently authorised, caused a diminution in the Muslim patrimony and the Spanish fortifications, already much reduced by the earthquake leaving substantially the Pasha and Sīdī Ḥawārī mosques, the Bey's palace and that of his favourite wife, several tombs, occasionally some houses in varying states of preservation, and the Burdj al-Aḥmar and the Burdj al-Marsa, two towers probably built by the Marīnid Abu 'l-Ḥasan in 748/1347.

By virtue of the Desmichels treaty of 6 January 1834, the town received a consul of ʿAbd al-Ḳādir, a sign of his sovereignty over the Algerian West recognised by the incomers and one which continued till 1841 in Oran and Mustaghānim. Even after ʿAbd al-Ḳādir's surrender, the original, autochthonous population of Oran, including its Jews, did not return to its former level till 1872, whilst the Muslims remained a minority there till the eve of independence, being numbered in the census of 1954 at 104,000 compared with 171,000 Europeans. Thus the town remained, till 1962, the most European in Algeria, with its expansion due to its role as the metropolitan centre of the Algerian West. It absorbed the revenues of extensive colonial landed domains and functioned as the second port of Algeria which, whilst sharing the export of primary products with the other ports of Orania, retained a monopoly of imported products. There were also concentrated there the few industries of the region and the services necessary for the functioning of the colonial agricultural enterprises. The operation of the port and viticulture played large roles in the demographic pattern of Oran and its region. The dockyards and the colonisation of the Oran plateau attracted Algerians and Europeans, and especially Spaniards, after 1870 when there was a boom in vine-growing. The great influx of Algerians from the 1930s onwards arose less from the attractive power of the town of Oran than from the worsening rural crisis conditions and the mechanisation of farming on the plateau, so that from 25,000 in 1926 there were rises of 45,000 in 1936 and 85,000 in 1948.

Communal segregation was a permanent feature of the growth of Oran's population in the colonial period. On the eve of World War II, the 46,000 Algerians (24% of the population) occupied up to four-fifths of the Madina Jdida (see below) and the southern and southwestern suburbs (al-Hamri, Medioni, etc.), and in 1954, it was only there and in the recently-established encampments around the town (Victor Hugo, Petit Lac, Planteurs, etc.) that they were in a majority. In the European part of the town, Algerians were virtually absent from the central quarters—even those that were proletarian in social structure, such as Saint-Pierre—and the middle-class extensions of the town centre, and a minority in the working-class quarters, except for Saint-Antoine, one of the rare mixed quarters of Oran.

From 1845 onwards, the expansion projects of the colonial town on the Karguenta plateau entailed the regrouping of some 2,000 Algerians there in one stretch of land. In 1880, when the European town had spread over the plateau, forming what became progressively the new town centre, the 9,000 Algerians remained concentrated almost wholly in what the Europeans called the "village nègre" and which the Algerians were to name Madina Jdida, in opposition to the old town and in deference to the Islamic urban tradition, even though neither its regular plan nor the architecture of its buildings conformed to this tradition. The urban life which developed there included the commercial and artisanal specialisation of streets, a concentration of mosques and *ḥammāms*, a *maḥkama*, *zāwiyas* (those of Sīdī Ḳaddūr and Sīdī Bilāl), but also the reformist *madrasa* al-Falāḥ and its offshoots in the suburbs of al-Hamri and Medioni. A form of urban life emerged there, with the oldest immigrants, now Oulad el-bled, contrasted with the *barrānīs*, newly-arrived rural immigrants, making the Madina Jdida, also called *madīnat al-ḥaḍar*, the *ʿāṣima* or capital of Muslim Oran and its rural hinterland.

The disturbances in the wake of the famines of the 1940s and the war for independence greatly swelled the Muslim population, which became a slight majority (210,000 out of a total of 400,000), concentrated on the marginal peripheries, whether planned, or spontaneous like the bidonvilles, and in the now saturated Madina Jdida and the southern and southwestern suburbs. The war brought about a violent cleavage, not between Muslim and Christian, as during the Spanish period, but between the indigenous population and the colons, beneficiaries of the colonial period and jealous of their privileges.

The substitution of Algerians in the 40,000 houses freed by the exodus of Europeans before and after independence has forcibly homogenised the communal landscape. At present, the town centre alone has over a hundred mosques and a large number of prayer rooms. Despite an influx of over 100,000 immigrants from the countryside and from the towns of Orania and Morocco, it was not till *ca.* 1970 that Oran recovered its population level of 400,000. The traditional enlarged family has begun to burst forth. A wage-earning class has developed considerably in the industrial zones of Arzew, Hassi Ameur and Essania since the 1970s, and new public housing in the Z.H.U.N. (*zones d'habitat urbain nouveau*) have made possible a spreading-out of the population. There is now an agglomeration of 1,170,000 inhabitants over 6,500 ha^2 beyond the 1962 perimeter, swallowing up the population groups around that perimeter and with extensions both eastwards and westwards. Liberalisation has, as in other large towns and cities, made the choice of habitat more selective and has extended unplanned zones of habitation, where fundamentalist Islamic ideas have even more appeal than in the town itself, where a vote of 39% for the Islamist candidate in the 1995 presidential election reveals the immense frustrations of a population still deeply attached to Islam.

Bibliography: 1. The pre-1831 period. (a) Sources. In addition to those given in the *EI*[1] art., see Leo Africanus, tr. Épaulard, Paris 1956, index. (b) Studies. In addition to those given in the *EI*[1] art. see F. Braudel, *Les Espagnols en Algérie*, in *Histoire et historiens d'Algérie*, Paris 1931; G. Marçais, *La Berbérie musulmane et l'Orient au Moyen-Age*, Paris 1946; R. Le Tourneau, *Les villes musulmanes de l'Afrique du Nord*, Algiers 1957; Ch.-E. Dufourcq, *L'Espagne catalane et le Maghrib au XIIIe et XIVe siècle*, Paris 1966; Ch.A. Julien, ed. Le Tourneau, *Histoire de l'Afrique du Nord*, Eng. tr. *History of North Africa*, London 1970; Jamil Abun-Nasr, *A history of the Maghrib in the Islamic period*, Cambridge 1987.

2. The post-1831 period. R. Lespès, *Oran, étude de géographie et d'histoire urbaines*, Paris 1938; Y. Lacoste, A. Nouschi and A. Prenant, *L'Algérie, passé et présent*, Paris 1960; M. Coquery, *L'extension récente des quartiers musulmans d'Oran*, in *Bull. de l'Assoc. des géogrs. français*, nos. 302-8 (1962); B. Semmoud, *Croissance urbaine, mobilité et changement social dans l'agglomération oranaise*, Cahiers du GREMAMO, no. 12 (1995), Paris VII-D Diderot.

(G. Marçais-[B. Semmoud])

al-**WAHRĀNĪ**, Abū ʿAbd Allāh Muḥammad b. Muḥriz b. Muḥammad, Rukn al-Dīn, Arabic prose writer. He was born in Oran, but spent a good part of his life in Egypt and then Syria, where he died at Dārayyā near Damascus in 575/1179. He wrote *maḳāmāt*, *rasāʾil* and *manāmāt* (stories of dreams). In one of his epistles he states that he had written a history of the Almohads, but no trace of this has so far been found. However, in the works of his which have survived, there are reflections on the state of the world in his time, on the Maghrib of the Almohads, on Sicily after its reconquest by the Normans, and on Ayyūbid Egypt and Syria.

There emerges from his writings that he lived off the generosity which he received from the great men of his time, and towards the end of his life he held the office of *khiṭāba*, delivering sermons at the Friday worship. Seeking gifts of money is a favourite theme of his epistles addressed to Ṣalāḥ al-Dīn al-Ayyūbī [*q.v.*] and to various viziers and judges. His panegyrics were mainly in prose, but he also composed numerous satires against his enemies, his rivals, and even against himself, displaying verve and humour, as well as erotic and scatological motifs which recall Ibn Sukkara, Ibn al-Ḥadjdjādj and Abu 'l-Muṭahhar al-Azdī [*q.vv.*]. If this *ṭarīḳ al-hazl* ("light-hearted treatment") of his subjects, dominates his œuvre, there is also a lyric strain when he describes his miserable state as an author and complains that the pursuit of *adab* does not give him a living.

Although a great admirer of al-Ḥarīrī [*q.v.*], al-Wahrānī did not imitate his style. His *maḳāmāt* are rather a gallery of comic portraits, sketching, by a few touches, a burlesque and grotesque picture. Another of his frequent traits is his use of prosopopeia, putting words in the mouths of minarets, or his own mule, complaining of hunger (an indirect method of solliciting help for himself!). In his stories of dreams, he speaks both of his contemporaries and persons of the past, the most developed one being one in which he describes the resurrection of the dead. In a story which recalls al-Maʿarrī's *Risālat al-Ghufrān*, al-Wahrānī finds himself in the Afterlife with various other writers who, although suffering the pangs of Judgement Day, still keep up their trivial and paltry quarrels. Providing an occasion for al-Wahrānī to settle his accounts, this eschatological dream, much admired by Ibn Khallikān, is one of his finest compositions.

Bibliography: Al-Wahrānī's writings have been gathered together by Ibrāhīm Shaʿlān and Muḥammad Naghsh as *Manāmāt al-Wahrānī wa-maḳāmātuhu wa-rasāʾiluhu*, Cairo 1968; a *maḳāma* on Fās was published by Saʿīd Aʿrāb in *al-Baḥth al-ʿilmī*, vi (1965).

There are notices of the author in Ibn Khallikān, ed. ʿAbbās, iv, 385-6; Ṣafadī, *Wāfī*, iv, 386-9; Ziriklī, *Aʿlām*, vii, 19. See also Brockelmann, S I, 489.

(Abdelfattah Kilito)

WAHRIZ, son of Kāmdjār, a Persian general of Khusraw Anūsharwān (A.D. 531-79 [see kisrā]). The name would apparently stem from MP *vēhrēz* "having a good abundance", see Nöldeke, *Gesch. der Perser und Araber*, 223 n. 2, and Justi, *Iranisches Namenbuch*, 340, but was in origin a title, since the Byzantine historian Procopius names the commander of the Sāsānid emperor Kawād's expedition into Georgia and Lazica (early 5th century) as having the title Ouarizēs (< **wahriz*); see daylam, at Vol. II, 190a.

In response to an appeal *ca.* 570, via the Lakhmids [*q.v.*], from Sayf b. Dhī Yazan, the leader of a Yemeni national movement against Abyssinian rule there, the Persian emperor despatched a force under the aged Wahriz. The story in the Arabic sources that these 800 troops were condemned prisoners released specially from prison for this do-or-die expedition is a later, folkloric detail; the force was much more probably one of Daylamī mercenaries. It sailed from the head of the Gulf around the Arabian shores to Yemen, landed there, fought its way to the capital Ṣanʿāʾ, killed the Abyssinian governor Masrūḳ, son of Abraha [*q.v.*], and installed Sayf b. Dhī Yazan as the Persians' vassal ruler in Yemen. After an attempted Abyssinian revanche, Wahriz returned to Yemen and finally installed the dead Sayf's son Maʿdī Karib as ruler in Ṣanʿāʾ, thus inaugurating a period of some 60 years' Persian dominance in Yemen. Wahriz is said to have died in Yemen shortly before Anūsharwān's own death.

Bibliography: Ibn Hishām, *Sīra*, 41-6, tr. Guillaume, 30-4; Dīnawarī, Cairo 1960, 64; Yaʿḳūbī, *Historiae*, i, 187, 227; Ṭabarī, iii, 948-58, 984, 988, tr. Nöldeke, *op. cit.*, 223-37, 257-8, 263-4, tr. C.E. Bosworth, *The History of al-Ṭabarī*, v, *The Sāsānids, the Lakhmids and Yemen*, Albany 1999, 239-52, 289, 294; Ḥamza al-Iṣfahānī, Beirut 1961, 114; Masʿūdī, *Murūdj*, see ed. Pellat, indices, vii, 759-60; Bosworth, in *Camb. hist., Iran*, iii/1, 606-7. See also al-yaman. 3.(a).

(C.E. Bosworth)

WAḤSH (a.), an adjective meaning "wild, desolate, uninhabited" (*al-dār al-waḥsh(a)* "the desolate abode", both with and without gender agreement), but more frequently a collective noun meaning "wild animals". The relative adjective (and the singulative) is *waḥshī*; the "wild ass" (*recte* "onager") is thus either *ḥimār al-waḥsh* or *al-ḥimār al-waḥshī*. The most common plural is *wuḥūsh* "kinds of wild animals", as one typically finds it in the title of the *kutub al-wuḥūsh*, lexicographical studies dealing with wild animals (name of the male and the female, age groups, etc.); see the relevant monographs by Ḳuṭrub (d. 206/821 [*q.v.*]) and al-Aṣmaʿī (d. 213/828 [*q.v.*]), ed. R. Geyer, in *SBAW Wien*, Phil.-hist. Kl., cxv (1888), 353-420. The opposite of *waḥshī* is *ahlī* "domesticated". Non-domesticated wild animals can nevertheless become tame; al-Djāḥiẓ makes this point about the animals kept in "wild-life enclosures" (sing. *ḥayr al-wuḥūsh*, see ḥāʾir), as maintained by caliphs and governors (*Ḥayawān*, ed. Hārūn, iv, 422; he mentions those of al-Muʿtaṣim and al-Wāthiḳ).

Waḥshī forms an opposition also with *insī*, the relative adjective, and singulative, of the collective noun *ins* "mankind". As adjectives they are used to denote the two sides of certain things in relationship to the human body: the one that points toward the human body is called *insī* and that which points away from it is called *waḥshī*; this refers to body-parts occurring in pairs (thus the *insī* side of the arm faces toward the rump, the *waḥshī* side away from it, cf. al-Aṣmaʿī, *Khalḳ al-insān*, ed. A. Haffner, in *Texte zur arabischen Lexikographie*, Leipzig 1905, 206, 207, 227), and also *inter alia*, to the two halves of the nib of the reed-pen [see ḳalam].

Since *insī* is a counterpart not only to *waḥshī* but also to *djinnī*, relative adjective and singulative of *djinn* "jinn-kind", it is not unlikely that the two terms referring to non-human beings influenced each other. This may explain the fact that the metathesised form *ḥūshī* (if it is that; or else < **wuḥūshī?*), usually listed as a synonym of *waḥshī*, has a distinctly jinnic connotation: it is said to be a relative adjective derived from *al-Ḥūsh* [*q.v.*], a land of the jinn ("beyond Yabrīn" [Yāʿḳūt, *Buldān*, ed. Beirut, ii, 319a], i.e. in the Rubʿ al-Khālī), whence come the *ḥūshī* camels, jinn-owned stallions that allegedly sire offspring among herds belonging to men. It should be noted that *ḥūsh* in itself, not the *nisba*, also refers to camels, often glossed as *mutawaḥhisha* "feral". (Note that Abu ʾl-ʿAlāʾ al-Maʿarrī uses the term metaphorically, together with two other camel terms, to denote the ease and frequency of certain rhymes: *dhulul* "docile", *nufur* "recalcitrant", and *ḥūsh* "untamed" rhymes, see *Luzūmiyyāt*, ed. I. al-Abyārī and Ṭ. Ḥusayn, Cairo 1378/1959, i, 45.) This being the case, one might suggest that the place name *al-Ḥūsh* was erroneously extracted from phrases like *bilād al-ḥūsh* and *rimāl al-ḥūsh*, which really meant "the land" or "the sands of the feral camels". The general area in which this land is located (broadly speaking between Yabrīn and al-Shiḥr) tallies well with the strong probability that the one-humped camel was dometicated in the desert areas of southern Arabia. The *ḥūsh* may even be a faint memory of truly wild camels, which today no longer exist. Al-Damīrī [*q.v.*] speaks of *ibil waḥshiyya* and *ibil al-waḥsh* "wild camels", which are allegedly the remnants of the camels of ʿĀd and Thamūd (*Ḥayāt al-ḥayawān*, [4]Cairo 1389/1969-70, i, 23, ll. 20-1), and Wabār [*q.v.*], the area in which the *ḥūsh* camels are predominantly found, is the former land/city of the ʿĀd [*q.v.*] that, after their destruction, was given by God to the jinn. Cf. R. Bulliet, *The Camel and the wheel*, [2]New York and Oxford 1990, 48.

For *waḥshī/ḥūshī* as a term of literary criticism, see the following entry.

Bibliography: Given in the article.

(W.P. Heinrichs)

WAḤSHĪ (a.) and **ḤŪSHĪ** (a.), synonymous terms in literary criticism denoting words that are uncouth and jarring to the ear due to their being archaic and/or Bedouinic (often including the criterium of cacophony). It is thus mostly used in the context of "modern" poetry [see muḥdathūn, in Suppl.]; and it mostly refers to single words rather than to any contextual obscurity (ʿAbd al-Ḳāhir al-Djurdjānī says this explicitly: *Dalāʾil*, ed. M.M. Shākir, Cairo 1404/1984, 44, l. 4). It is not, however, an exclusively poetic phenomenon. Al-Djāḥiẓ speaks of speech in general, when he says that the wording should be neither "plebeian, base, vulgar" (*ʿāmmī, sāḳiṭ, sūḳī*) nor "strange, uncouth" (*gharīb, waḥshī*); unless, in the latter case, he adds, the speaker is a Bedouin (*badawiyy^{an} aʿrābiyy^{an}*), as *waḥshī* speech is understood by *waḥshī* people, just as *sūḳī* jargon (*raṭāna*) is understood by *sūḳī* people (*Bayān*, ed. ʿAlī Abū Mulḥim, [2]Beirut 1412/1992, i, 135). From this we can deduce that (a) there is a golden mean between the all too colloquial, on the one hand, and the all too archaic, on the other, and that (b) for the Ancients and the

Bedouin, the *waḥshī* may be natural and thus not reprehensible. This latter point is taken up again by Ḳudāma [*q.v.*], who says that the Ancients used *waḥshī* words not by conscious search and affectation (*taṭallub, takalluf*) but according to their wont and the nature of their speech (*li-ʿādatihi wa-ʿalā sadjiyyati lafẓihi*) (*Naḳd al-shiʿr*, ed. S.A. Bonebakker, Leiden 1956, 100). Ibn Sinān al-Khafādjī (d. 466/1074) gives it a slightly different slant by putting the "naturally gifted Bedouin" (*al-badawī ṣāḥib al-ṭabʿ*)—who could be a contemporary—in the place of the Ancient and contrasting him with the "effect-seeking sedentary" (*al-ḳarawī al-mutakallif*); the latter knows these words only from the study of books (*Sirr al-faṣāḥa*, ed. ʿAbd al-Mutaʿāl al-Ṣaʿīdī, Cairo 1389/1969, 63). A finely-tuned scale of acceptability with regard to *gharāba* and *ibtidhāl* ("triteness"), based on a tripartite structure of language users (*ʿArab, khāṣṣat al-muḥdathīn, ʿāmmat al-muḥdathīn*) is offered by Ḥāzim al-Ḳarṭādjannī (d. 684/1285 [*q.v.*]) (*Minhādj al-bulaghā'*, ed. M. al-Ḥ. Belkhodja, Tunis 1966, 385-6; since the first part of the *Minhādj*, dealing with *lafẓ*, is missing in the unique ms., this passage has been culled from Bahā' al-Dīn al-Subkī, *ʿArūs al-afrāḥ fī sharḥ Talkhīṣ al-Miftāḥ*, and printed in an appendix; al-Subkī calls it a *mulakhkhaṣ*).

In spite of all this discussion, there was a popular misconception that the use of *waḥshī* words equalled *faṣāḥa* [*q.v.*]. Ibrāhīm b. al-Mahdī (d. 224/839 [*q.v.*]), the highly cultured ʿAbbāsid prince, is quoted as having said to his secretary ʿAbd Allāh b. Ṣāʿid: "Be careful not to seek out the *waḥshī* in speech, desiring to acquire eloquence; for that is the worst kind of inability to express oneself (*fa-inna dhālika huwa 'l-ʿiyyu 'l-akbar*); take that which is easy while avoiding the words of the *hoi polloi*" (*apud* Ibn Rashīḳ, *ʿUmda*, ed. M.M. ʿAbd al-Ḥamīd, Cairo 1383/1963-4, i, 265-7). Ibn Sinān al-Khafādjī recounts a *madjlis* in which one of the people present called Ibn Sinān's teacher, Abu 'l-ʿAlā' al-Maʿarrī, a possessor of *faṣāḥa*, because much of his work was unintelligible even to the literati (!). And a few centuries later, Ṣafī al-Dīn al-Ḥillī (d. *ca.* 752/1351 [*q.v.*]) was accused of being a less than perfect poet, because he did not use *gharīb* words in his poetry, an accusation against which he wrote a well-known poem with a satirical beginning, see Vol. VIII, 803b.

For Ibn Ṭabāṭabā (d. 322/934), finally, all this is just a matter of the art of the poet; if he is good, he can turn the distasteful and *waḥshī* into something pleasant and likeable, and the pleasant and likeable into something *waḥshī* and strange (*ʿIyār al-shiʿr*, ed. al-Māniʿ, Riyāḍ 1405/1985, 202).

Bibliography: Given in the article.

(W.P. Heinrichs)

WAḤSHĪ BĀFḲĪ (or **YAZDĪ**), Persian poet of the mid-10th/16th century. Contemporary sources give his name as either Shams al-Dīn Muḥammad (*Maykhāna*) or Kamāl al-Dīn (*ʿArafāt*). Waḥshī was born in the village of Bāfḳ, located between Yazd and Kirmān, sometime around 939/1532-3. After being tutored in poetry by his brother Murādī and the local poet Sharaf al-Dīn ʿAlī Bāfḳī, the young Waḥshī moved to Yazd and the nearby palace-complex in Taft and lived there for most of the rest of his life. Although Waḥshī wrote a few poems dedicated to the Ṣafawid Shāh Ṭahmāsp I [*q.v.*], most of his enconiums were addressed to the local rulers of Kirmān, Kāshān, and especially to the hereditary governors of Yazd, Ghiyāth al-Dīn Mīr-i Mīrān and his son Khalīl Allāh, descendants of Shāh Niʿmat Allāh Walī [*q.v.*] and in-laws of the Ṣafawid royal house. Probably as a result of excessive drinking, Waḥshī died in Yazd in 991/1583.

Although Waḥshī never ventured far from his birthplace, his poetry was widely known during his lifetime and has been admired by both contemporary and modern critics. Awḥadī Balyānī (*ʿArafāt*) considered Waḥshī the greatest rival of Muḥtasham Kāshānī, the poet laureate of Ṭahmāsp's court. Waḥshī is especially important for his role in the development of the *maktab-i wuḳūʿ*, "the school of the incident" or "realist style", which employed simple, colloquial language to describe and analyse the everyday incidents and emotions of profane love affairs. The unusually scornful way in which Waḥshī often addressed the beloved was dubbed *wā-sūkht* [see wā-sōkht]. These features are found chiefly in Waḥshī's *ghazal*s and *tarkīb-band*s, the genres in which he achieved his greatest fame. His *dīwān* also contains *ḳaṣīda*s, *tardjīʿ-band*s, *rubāʿī*s, and *ḳiṭʿa*s. In addition to several short, untitled works, Waḥshī's *mathnawī*s include *Khuld-i barīn*, *Nāẓir wa Manẓūr*, and *Farhād wa Shīrīn*. The last of these remained unfinished at Waḥshī's death and was twice "completed" in the Ḳādjār period by Wiṣāl-i Shīrāzī and Ṣābir-i Shīrāzī.

Bibliography: For a list of *tadhkira* sources, see Dh. Ṣafā, *Tārīkh-i adabiyyāt dar Īrān*, Tehran 1364 *sh.*/1985, v/2, 761. The most important of these sources are collected and quoted at length by Ḥ. Nakhaʿī in his introduction to Waḥshī's *Dīwān*, Tehran 1339 *sh.*/1960 (including the otherwise unpublished notice from Awḥadī Balyānī's *ʿArafāt al-ʿāshiḳīn*). See also Fakhr al-Zamānī Ḳazwīnī, *Tadhkira-yi Maykhāna*, ed. A. Gulčīn-i Maʿānī, Tehran 1340 *sh.*/1961, 181-97. Among the secondary sources, see Browne, *LHP*, iv, 238-40; Rypka, *Hist. of Iranian literature*, 296-7; Uways Sālik Ṣadīḳī, *Ashʿār-i čāp nashuda-yi Waḥshī*, in *Madjalla-yi Dānishkada-yi Adabiyyāt wa ʿUlūm-i Insānī-yi Dānishgāh-i Tihrān*, xviii (1350 *sh.*/1971), 105-16; and A. al-Khūlī, *Waḥshī al-Bāfiḳī*, Cairo 1978. Waḥshī's works have often been published; for a full listing, see *Fihrist-i kitābhā-yi čāpī-yi Fārsī*, i, cols. 1274-75 (*Khuld-i barīn*), cols. 1592-93 (*Dīwān*), and ii, col. 2413 (*Farhād wa Shīrīn*).

(P.E. Losensky)

WAḤY (a.), a term of the Ḳur'ān, primarily denoting revelation in the form of communication without speech. Cognates in other Semitic languages include Palmyrene Aramaic *twḥyt'* (*tawḥītā*) "decree [of the government]" and Mehri *hewḥū* "to come to someone's help".

In the Ḳur'ān, *waḥy* is presented as an exceptional modality of God's speaking to His creatures. This *waḥy* forms a concept of inspiration and communication without linguistic formulation, conveying the will of God, as in VII, 117: "And We suggested/put the idea into the head (*awḥaynā*) to Moses: 'Cast thy staff'. And lo, it forthwith swallowed up their lying invention". On other occasions, it conveys the speech of God to be shared as a message, as in XVIII, 27: "Recite what has been revealed (*ūḥiya*) to thee of the Book of thy Lord". This *waḥy* contains a prompting into action for its recipient (see T. Izutsu, *God and man in the Koran*, Tokyo 1964, 180), a doctrine held in common with a Biblical motif and reflected in the prophetic stories as retold in the Ḳur'ān (VII, 160, Moses; XX, 77, Moses; XXVI, 52, Moses; XXVI, 63, Moses; X, 87, Moses and Aaron told to take certain houses in Egypt for prayer; XXVIII, 7, Moses' mother told to suckle her child and then cast him into the sea; XX, 38; XXI, 73; XXIII, 27; XCIX, 5).

Prophets are not the only recipients of *waḥy*: the bees (XVI, 68) and heaven and earth (XLI, 12) are also spoken of. Nor is God the only source of *waḥy*: the satans among humans and *d̲j̲inn* also inspire via *waḥy*, cf. VI, 121: "The Satans inspire (*yūḥūna*) their friends to dispute with you; if you obey them, you are idolaters". But it is *waḥy* which inspires the prophets, cf. IV, 163: "We have revealed (*awḥaynā*) to thee as We revealed (*awḥaynā*) to Noah and the prophets after him, and We revealed (*awḥaynā*) to Abraham, Ishmael, Isaac, Jacob, and the Tribes, Jesus and Job, Jonah and Aaron, and Solomon, and We gave (*ātaynā*) to David Psalms ..." (see also XII, 109; XVI, 43; XXI, 7; XLII, 3, 51, in which a spirit, *rūḥ*, is the agent).

Arthur Jeffery (*The Qur'an as Scripture*, in *MW*, xl [1950], 190-2) argued that *waḥy* has the basic sense of internal prompting, which is to be understood as guidance in a general way (as in XVI, 123, for example: "Then We revealed [*awḥaynā*] to thee: 'Follow thou the creed of Abraham, a man of pure faith and no idolater'"), but that it becomes combined in the Ḳur'ān with an external sense such that the message itself is also a product of *waḥy*, e.g. VI, 19: "Say: 'God is witness between me and you, and this Ḳur'ān has been revealed [*ūḥiya*] to me that I may warn you thereby, and whomsoever it may reach'"; see also XXI, 45. This identification of the literal message as the product of *waḥy* is fully developed in a passage such as XXIX, 45 which associates "the Book" with *waḥy*: "Recite what has been revealed (*ūḥiya*) to thee of the Book". XLII, 7 speaks of an Arabic Ḳur'ān as the product: "And so we have revealed (*awḥaynā*) to thee an Arabic Ḳur'ān". In this usage, the word may be seen to be functionally equivalent to *tanzīl*, the word frequently used with the image of a literal "bringing down" of a message.

In dealing with *waḥy*, it has been common for scholars to resort to ideas of historical development in Muḥammad's thought (e.g. Jeffery, *Scripture*, 193, 201, in which "internal" inspiration is early, reflecting an idea native to Arabs and "external" revelation is later, that being a scriptural notion). Thus a separation is seen between a notion of internal "inspiration", similar to that claimed by the poets and which is argued to belong to Muḥammad's early conceptions, and a firm sense of revelation from outside which is seen to emerge later in Muḥammad's career as the distinction between himself and poets became clearer to him. Even Izutsu (*God and man*, 180), who normally wishes to assign single meanings to words throughout the Ḳur'ān, speaks of the non-technical (and even pre-technical) versus the technical: a prompting to action (for example, in VII, 117 with Moses and the rod) in which "the words do not count", versus a process in which the words are everything (as in XIII, 30, with the combination of "recite" and "reveal", and emphasised further in LXXV, 16, although that passage does not speak of *waḥy* explicitly).

Waḥy, one may rightly conclude, is a difficult term in the Ḳur'ān. The search for a single meaning for the word has proved frustrating to scholarship, for the situations in which it is used do not seem to allow for a unified schematic of its use. The relationship of *waḥy* to *tanzīl* only makes the picture more complex, for the semantic range of the latter word appears to duplicate that of the former to a fair extent. While the desire is to see *waḥy* as meaning "inspiration", problems arise there too, given the complexity of the relationship to *ilhām* [*q.v.*], individual communication by God, as well as the importance of the "external" sense of the process within *waḥy* as compared to "inspiration" which is expected to be an internal non-verbal process (which, of course, it is at times in the Ḳur'ān).

"Inspiration", it is worthy of note, is a reflection of cultural values and has different meanings in different settings. The modern tolerance of the artistic temperament and its inspiration is a continuation of the Platonic (and other) idea of inspiration as a type of madness. However, the prophet of the Near East relied on inspiration to give advice, first to the ruler, then in later times to the public at large. The Ḳur'ān shares in a Near Eastern value of inspiration, one transformed through the history of Islam in the desire to protect Muḥammad (and the Arabic language) from contemporary and necessarily secular (since prophecy had ceased) ideals of "inspiration".

Muslim perceptions and understandings of the process of revelation are contained in the *sīra* and *ḥadīt̲h̲* literature and are intimately connected to the life of Muḥammad such that his biography is reflective of and shaped by certain understandings of how revelation occurs. The material may be summarised as follows.

The beginning of revelation consisted in dreams anticipating real events (Ibn His̲h̲ām, 151; al-Ṭabarī, *Tafsīr*, xxx, 138; Ibn Saʿd, i/1, 129). Also afterwards, such dream visions are said to have occurred. When ʿĀ'is̲h̲a was under suspicion, she hoped that God would reveal her innocence to Muḥammad in a dream vision (Aḥmad b. Ḥanbal, vi, 197; al-Buk̲h̲ārī, *Tafsīr*, on sūra XXIV, *bāb* 6).

The first revelation in which D̲j̲ibrīl [*q.v.*] appeared to Muḥammad took place on Mount Ḥirā', when the angel said to him, "I am D̲j̲ibrīl". Thereupon Muḥammad hastened to K̲h̲adīd̲j̲a, crying, "Wrap me up", an allusion to Ḳur'ān, LXXIII, 1, or LXXIV, 1).

The first portions of the Ḳur'ān revealed was sūra XCVI, when the angel, in the month of Ramaḍān, during the retreat, showed him a piece of cloth, on which this sūra was written, saying, "Recite!" When Muḥammad protested that he could not read, the angel pressed him so strongly that he nearly suffocated. At the third repetition, the angel pronounced the verses which Muḥammad then retained.

After this there came a pause (*fatra* [*q.v.*]) in revelation. During this time Muḥammad was in such a depression that the thought of suicide came upon him (al-Ṭabarī, i, 1150; Ibn His̲h̲ām, 156, 166; Ibn Saʿd, i/1, 131). The pause ended with the revelation of Ḳur'ān, LXXIV, or XCIII.

The angel who transmitted revelation was visible to Muḥammad and to others (al-Buk̲h̲ārī, *Faḍā'il al-Ḳur'ān, bāb* 1; Ibn His̲h̲ām, 154, cf. 156; Abū Nuʿaym, *Dalā'il al-nubuwwa*, Ḥaydarābād 1320, 69). To some extent the ascension [see MIʿRĀD̲J̲] and the night journey may also be reckoned as revelations. Visions are also mentioned in the Ḳur'ān. LIII, 4-18, is the central focus here, with the idea of seeing someone or something typically identified as D̲j̲ibrīl (see also LXXXI, 22-5). In other parts of the Ḳur'ān, however, revelation is said to have taken place by audition as in LXXV, 18. These auditory experiences become a major element in *sīra* and especially *ḥadīt̲h̲*, and the accounts may be classified in a variety of ways.

(a) *How they were perceived by Muḥammad*

1. "Sometimes it comes as the ringing of a bell; this kind is the most painful. When it ceases, I retain what was said. Sometimes it is an angel who speaks to me as a man, and I retain what he says" (al-Buk̲h̲ārī, *Bad' al-waḥy, bāb* 2; *Bad' al-k̲h̲alḳ, bāb* 6;

Muslim, *Faḍā'il*, no. 87; al-Tirmidhī, *Manāḳib, bāb* 7; al-Nasā'ī, *Iftitāḥ, bāb* 37; Mālik, *Muwaṭṭa'*, ch. on *wuḍū' li-man mass al-Ḳur'ān*, no. 7; Aḥmad b. Ḥanbal, ii, 222, vi, 158, 163, 256 ff.).

2. In a different form of this tradition, Muḥammad says, "Sometimes it approaches me in the form of a young man (*al-fatā*) who hands it down to me" (al-Nasā'ī, *Iftitāḥ, bāb* 37).

3. The Apostle of God heard a sound like the humming of bees near his face; thereupon Ḳur'ān, XXIII, 1 ff. was revealed to him (al-Tirmidhī, *Tafsīr*, on sūra XXIII, no. 1; Aḥmad b. Ḥanbal, i, 34).

4. The Apostle of God used to move his lips from pain as soon as the revelation began. After the revelation of LXXV, 16, however, he listened until Djibrīl had withdrawn; thereupon he recited what he had heard (al-Bukhārī, *Tawḥīd, bāb* 43; al-Nasā'ī, *Iftitāḥ, bāb* 37; al-Ṭayālisī, no. 2628).

5. ". . . on the authority of ʿAbd Allāh b. ʿUmar: I asked the Prophet: 'Do you perceive the revelation?' He answered, 'Yes, I hear sounds like metal being beaten [cf. no. 1 above]. Then I listen and often I think I will die (of pain)'" (Aḥmad b. Ḥanbal, ii, 222).

(b) *How they were perceived by others*

1. Even on cold days, sweat appeared on his forehead (al-Bukhārī, *Bad' al-waḥy, bāb* 2; *Tafsīr* on sūra XXIV, *bāb* 6; Muslim, *Faḍā'il*, no. 86; Aḥmad b. Ḥanbal, vi, 58, 103, 197, 202, 256 ff., cf. iii, 21, and cf. further, above (a) 1.).

2. Muḥammad covers his head, his colour grows red, he snores as someone asleep, or rattles like a young camel; after some time he recovers (*surriyya ʿanhu*) (al-Bukhārī, *Ḥadjdj, bāb* 17; *ʿUmra, bāb* 10; *Faḍā'il al-Ḳur'ān, bāb* 2; Muslim, *Ḥadjdj*, no. 6; Aḥmad b. Ḥanbal, iv, 222, 224).

3. Muḥammad's colour grows livid (*tarabbada lahu wadjhuhu*: Muslim, *Ḥudūd*, nos. 13, 14; *Faḍā'il*, no. 88; Aḥmad b. Ḥanbal, v, 317, 318, 320 ff., 327; *mutarabbid*: al-Ṭabarī, *Tafsīr*, xviii, 4; *tarabbud djildihi*: Aḥmad b. Ḥanbal, i, 238 ff.; *tarabbada li-dhālika djasaduhu wa-wadjhuhu*: al-Ṭayālisī, no. 2667).

4. He falls into a lethargy or a trance (*subāt*) (Aḥmad b. Ḥanbal, vi, 103).

5. "Thereupon the Apostle of God sat down, turning towards him [ʿUthmān b. Maẓʿūn]. When they talked, the Apostle of God let his gaze swerve towards heaven; after a while he looked down to his right side and turned away from his companion, following his gaze and began to shake his head as if he tried to understand what was said to him, while ʿUthmān sat looking on. When Muḥammad had reached his aim, his gaze turned anew towards heaven, etc." (Aḥmad b. Ḥanbal, i, 318).

6. "When Muḥammad received a revelation ... this caused him much pain, such that we perceived it. That time he separated himself from his companions and remained behind. Thereupon he covered his head with his shirt, suffering intensely, etc." (Aḥmad b. Ḥanbal, i, 464).

"When the Apostle of God received a revelation, he began to cover his face with his shirt. When he swooned, we took it away, etc." (Aḥmad b. Ḥanbal, vi, 34; cf. above (b) 2.).

7. Zayd b. Thābit said, "I was at Muḥammad's side when the *sakīna* [*q.v.*] came upon him. His thigh fell upon mine so heavily that I feared it would break. When he recovered, he said to me, 'Write down', and I wrote down Ḳur'ān, IV, 97" (Aḥmad b. Ḥanbal, v, 184, 190 ff.; Abū Dāwūd, *Djihād, bāb* 19).

8. ʿAbd Allāh b. ʿAmr said, "*Sūrat al-mā'ida* was revealed to the Apostle of God while he was riding on his camel. The beast could not bear him any longer so he had to descend from it" (Aḥmad b. Ḥanbal, ii, 176). A similar tradition is transmitted from Asmā' bt. Yazīd (Aḥmad b. Ḥanbal, vi, 455, 458); another tradition of the same type is found in Ibn Saʿd, i/1, 131.

(c) *The circumstances under which revelation came upon Muḥammad*

1. Muḥammad is directly or indirectly asked for his opinion or decision when the answer is revealed to him. Examples include the use of perfumes during the *ʿumra* (al-Bukhārī, *Ḥadjdj, bāb* 17 [see above (b) 2.]); excuses for staying at home during an expedition (Abū Dāwūd, *Djihād, bāb* 19; Aḥmad b. Ḥanbal, v, 184); whether evil may proceed from good (Aḥmad b. Ḥanbal, iii, 21; al-Ṭayālisī, no. 2180); whether Muḥammad's wives were allowed to relieve a want near a town (Aḥmad b. Ḥanbal, vi, 56); whether ʿĀ'isha was guilty or not (al-Bukhārī, *Tafsīr*, on sūra XXIV, *bāb* 6; Aḥmad b. Ḥanbal, vi, 103, 197); whether divorce can be demanded in the case of adultery witnessed by one witness (al-Ṭayālisī, no. 2667); and concerning *ẓihār* (al-Ṭabarī, *Tafsīr*, xviii, 2). It is to be noted that the contents of these revelations are not always communicated and, if they are, they are not necessarily a part of the Ḳur'ān (cf. Nöldeke-Schwally, *Gesch. des Qor.*, i, 256-61); examples include Muḥammad's answers to the above questions regarding evil and his wives, as well as issues related to fornication (Aḥmad b. Ḥanbal, v, 317, 318, 320 ff., 327) and the permission of *liʿān* (al-Ṭayālisī, no. 2667).

2. Revelation comes upon Muḥammad while he is riding [see above (b) 8.] (al-Ṭabarī, *Tafsīr*, xxvi, 39), while his head is being washed (*ibid.*, xviii, 2), while he is at the table, holding a bone in his hand (Aḥmad b. Ḥanbal, vi, 56) and while he is on the pulpit (*ibid.*, iii, 21).

In Classical Muslim theology ". . . revelation as such was not the object of a consistent theory; for this we have to wait until the time of the philosophers. . . ." (J. van Ess, *Verbal inspiration? Language and revelation in classical Islamic theology*, in S. Wild (ed.), *The Qur'ān as text*, Leiden 1996, 189; the entire article, 177-94, is a perceptive overview of the implications of the topic, written in anticipation of vol. iv of his *Theologie und Gesellschaft im 2. und 3. Jahrhundert Hidschra*, Berlin 1997). The philosophical challenge [see e.g. NAFS] did, then, produce a theological reaction. Al-Īdjī (d. 756/1355) and his commentator al-Djurdjānī (d. 816/1413) combat the views of philosophers, according to whom it is a charisma peculiar to the prophets that "they see the angels in their corporeal forms and hear their speech by revelation; it is not to be rejected that, when they are awake, they see what the common people see when they are asleep; that is, they see persons who speak poetical words to them, which point to ideas corresponding to what really happens, since their soul is free from bodily occupations and can easily come into contact with the divine world (*ʿālam al-ḳuds*). Often this peculiarity becomes in them a settled faculty which is easily working". This theory of revelation is, according to al-Īdjī, misleading, not being in harmony with the views of the philosophers themselves, according to whom the angels cannot be seen, being merely psychic beings who do not produce audible speech, a property which belongs especially to corporeal beings. So the theory of the philosophers explains revelation as the imagining of what has no basis in reality, as little as what comes from the lips of ailing and lunatic people. Yet if any of us should command and prohibit on our own authority what is salutory and sensible, we would not, on account thereof, be a prophet. How much less, then, would be a prophetic utterance based upon imaginings which have no foundation and are often contrary to reason? (*Kitāb al-Mawāḳif*, ed. Soerensen, Leipzig 1848, 172 ff.).

Bibliography (in addition to sources mentioned in the article): Wensinck, *Handbook*, 162b, 163a, for all the tradition material; F. Buhl, *Das Leben Muhammeds*, Leipzig 1930, 134 ff.; T. Andrae, *Die Person Muhammeds*, Uppsala, 1917, 311; O. Pautz, *Muhhameds Lehre von der Offenbarung*, Leipzig 1898; J.L. Kugel, *Poetry and prophecy. The beginnings of a literary tradition*, Ithaca 1990, esp., but not only, M. Zwettler, *A mantic manifesto: the sūra of the "The Poets" and the Qur'anic foundations of prophetic authority*, 75-119; N. Kirmani, *Offenbarung als Kommunikation. Das Konzept* waḥy *in Naṣr Hāmid Abū Zayds* Mafhūm an-naṣṣ, Frankfurt am Main 1996; S. Wild, *"We have sent down to thee the book with the truth . . .". Spatial and temporal implications of the Qur'ānic concepts of nuzūl, tanzīl, and 'inzāl*, in idem (ed.), *The Qur'an as text*, Leiden 1996, 137-53, on the relationship between the various concepts surrounding "revelation". See also ḲUR'ĀN and MUḤAMMAD.

(A.J. Wensinck-[A. Rippin])

WĀ'IL [see BĀHILA; BAKR B. WĀ'IL].

WĀʿIẒ (A., pl. *wuʿʿāẓ*), preacher, mostly preacher who admonishes, to be distinguished from *ḳāṣṣ* [*q.v.*] and *mudhakkir*. This distinction, however, is only clearly made from the 4th/10th century onwards. It is the preacher's task to give sermons conveying admonishments (*waʿẓ, mawʿiẓa*), the public performance of which is called *madjlis al-waʿẓ* or *madjlis al-dhikr*. In contrast to the *khuṭba* [*q.v.*], it can be held at any place and time. Etymologically, the Arabic root *w-ʿ-ẓ* is related to Hebrew *y-ʿ-ṣ*. A *yoʿeṣ* is a king's adviser, mostly in wordly affairs (Baumgartner, *Hebräisches und Aramäisches Lexikon*, s.v. *y-ʿ-ṣ*); in Hebrew, the term lacks the aspect of religious warning. In the Ḳur'ān, the root *w-ʿ-ẓ* and its derivations (*waʿẓ, mawʿiẓa*) in most cases contain a warning. Consequently, the Ḳur'ān commentaries explain *mawʿiẓa* with *ʿibra*. The form II of the root *dh-k-r, dhakkara, mudhakkir*, and the form V *tadhakkara*, have the somewhat weaker nuance of "admonishing, to be admonished". However, the root may also indicate "good advice" (*nuṣḥ, naṣīḥa*) and "right guidance" (*irshād*). Finally, *waʿẓ* can also mean *waṣiyya*, the spiritual testament which a father gives to his son. In old Arabic poetry the root is also used in the sense of admonition.

1. In classical Islam.

The *wāʿiẓ* often carried a stick and sat on a stool (*kursī*). His public could consist of huge masses of people, as in the case of Ibn al-Djawzī (see below), but also of individuals, such as rulers, before whom he would stand in a *maḳām*; in principle, his sermon was addressed to everybody. From the 5th/11th century onwards, the function of *wāʿiẓ* becomes institutionalised. Thus Niẓām al-Mulk [*q.v.*] introduced it at the Niẓāmiyya in Baghdād. Consequently, the *wāʿiẓ* was often used for political and ideological purposes, as in discussions between schools of law and dogmatic movements, especially in Baghdād.

Themes of warning sermons were the transitoriness of the world and of life; the motif *ubi sunt qui ante nos in mundo fuere*, the threat of death; the weakness of the soul; the call to penance and to renunciation of the world (*zuhd*). In this way, the soul was to be shaken up and to judge itself, man was to become his own warning preacher. It is thus understandable that it should be the adherents of the pietistic-mystical movements who were active as *wuʿʿāẓ*.

In addition to the pious traditions found in the Ḳur'ān, *ḥadīth* and the *ḳiṣaṣ al-anbiyā'*, rhymed prose (*sadjʿ*), *badīʿ* [*q.vv.*] and poetry were often used as rhetorical means. Such means could also serve love poetry, re-interpreted in a mystical, Ṣūfī sense, which in the listener's soul was meant to kindle a longing for the only real beloved, God. Criticism of the *wuʿʿāẓ* was directed against an exaggerated use of this kind of poetry, against the use of weak traditions and of stories which only incite wordly interests. Famous warning preachers are above all known from Baghdād. To the 3rd/9th century belongs Manṣūr b. ʿAmmār (d. 225/839-40; see van Ess, *Theologie und Gesellschaft*, iii, 102-4), and to the 5th and 6th/10th and 11th centuries belongs the Ḥanbalī theologian Ibn ʿAḳīl (d. 513/1119 [*q.v.*]). ʿAbd al-Ḳādir al-Djīlānī (d. 561/1161 [*q.v.*]), whose name is connected with the Ḳādiriyya, was also famous as a preacher. The polymath Ibn al-Djawzī (d. 597/1200 [*q.v.*]), finally, was the most famous of them all. Ibn Djubayr [*q.v.*] has left an account of the overwhelming influence of his sermons.

Texts of sermons, in particular of those held before rulers and dating from relatively early times, were transmitted by al-Djāḥiẓ (d. 255/868-9), Ibn Ḳutayba (d. 276/889) and Ibn ʿAbd Rabbihi (d. 328/940). Abū Ṭālib al-Makkī (d. 386/996) and Muḥammad al-Ghazālī (d. 555/1111) [*q.vv.*] enter into a critical discussion on specific aspects of the *wuʿʿāẓ* phenomenon; in the 8th/14th century, criticism is taken up again in Mamlūk Egypt by Ibn al-Ḥādjdj (d. 785/1383 [*q.v.*]). The most detailed opinion on the function and task of the preacher and his sermons is given by Ibn al-Djawzī. Not only did he collect information on famous preachers of the past but he also assembled his own sermons into monographs, such as *Ṣayd al-khāṭir* and *Kitāb al-Mudhish*, and provided them with instructions for correct usage.

Bibliography: 1. Sources. Djāḥiẓ, *Bayān*, ed. Hārūn, see *fihris al-khuṭab*; Ibn Ḳutayba, *ʿUyūn*, Cairo 1925, i, 333-57; Ibn ʿAbd Rabbihi, *ʿIḳd*, ed. Amīn *et alii*, iii, 140-228; Abū Ṭālib al-Makkī, *Ḳūt al-ḳulūb*, tr. R. Gramlich, *Die Nahrung des Herzen*, Wiesbaden 1992-5, indices s.v. Prediger, Predigt; Ghazālī, *Iḥyā'*, ii, *kitāb* 19, *bāb* 3 (= ii, 337); Ibn al-Djawzī, *K. al-Ḳuṣṣāṣ wa 'l-mudhakkirīn*, ed. M. Swartz, Beirut 1971, ed. K. al-Sāmarrā'ī, Riyāḍ 1403; idem, *Talbīs Iblīs*, Cairo 1928, 123-5; idem, *K. al-Mudhish*, Beirut n.d.; idem, *Ṣayd al-khāṭir*, ed. ʿAṭā', Cairo n.d.

2. Studies. J. Pedersen, *The Islamic preacher, wāʿiẓ, mudhakkir, qāṣṣ*, in *Ignaz Goldziher memorial volume*, Budapest 1948, i, 226-51; Angelika Hartmann, *Islamisches Predigtwesen im Mittelalter: Ibn al-Ǧawzī und sein "Buch der Schlussreden"*, in *Saeculum*, xxxviii (1987), 336-66; G. Makdisi, *The rise of humanism in classical Islam and the Christian West*, Edinburgh 1990, 182-200; R. Gramlich, *Weltverzicht. Grundlagen und Weisen islamischer Askese*, Wiesbaden 1997, esp. 103-51.

(B. Radtke)

2. In modern times.

In the second half of the 20th century, the introduction of cassette tapes began to influence the nature of sermons. Popular preachers now take into consideration that their words are audiotaped by their public on simple cassette recorders, and, sometimes, widely distributed. These cheap cassettes have gained for a number of preachers a popularity only comparable to the popularity of pop stars in the West.

Some preachers have taken the distribution of the cassettes on which their sermons were registered into their own hands, and the sale of such cassettes may have become a modest source of income to them and their staff. However this may be, sermons by popular preachers are offered for sale almost everywhere in towns and villages in the Muslim world. Often, cassettes containing sermons are dated and numbered. This makes it possible to find out whether a preacher has been absent from the pulpit, for reasons of health or imprisonment. *Waʿẓ* can thus be a political manifestation.

The distribution on cassette tapes means that sermons are not only available in a written form (and hence in formal Classical Arabic), but also in the form in which they were actually delivered. Printed sermon collections usually "adapt the language of the sermon to the needs of the printed page", which, at least, means "replacing colloquial words by classical ones". It would be a matter of surprise if this would not have happened in the past as well. The modern cassettes, however, make the observation of the stylistic technique of "code-switching" a distinct possibility.

Although Islam is "a lay religion par excellence" (Snouck Hurgronje), not everybody is allowed to preach a sermon from the pulpit of the mosque. A preacher is usually referred to as *shaykh* but this is a general, deferential title that also is used in many other settings. Not every address by a preacher is a sermon. Dependent on the social context, his words may be referred to as a *muḥāḍara* "lecture" or *dars* "lesson".

The authority of the preacher depends on his knowledge, and on the recognition of this knowledge by his audience. Formal, Azhar-type training in Ḳurʾān and *Sharīʿa* is not always deemed to be sufficient: "Specialists in modern technical ways of knowing, and new prestigious branches of science, presume the right to displace traditional scholars" as preachers.

Bibliography: Translations of an example of a 19th century sermon may be found in E.W. Lane, *Manners and customs*..., ed. Paisley and London, 1896, ch. III, 100-2; of a 20th century sermon in G. Kepel, *The Prophet and Pharaoh*, Eng. tr. London 1985, 177-86. The most authoritative, modern study of a *wāʿiẓ* is P.D. Gaffney, *The Prophet's pulpit. Islamic preaching in contemporary Egypt*, Berkeley, etc. 1994. See also the chapters on the popular preachers Shaykh Kishk and Shaykh Muḥammad Mutawallī al-Shaʿrāwī in J.J.G. Jansen, *The neglected duty*, New York 1986. (J.J.G. Jansen)

WAḲʿA-NÜWĪS, the title of the late Ottoman official historian.

The post of official historian, *weḳāyiʿ-nüwīs*, later *waḳʿa-nüwīs* ("events/event-writer"), in the Ottoman empire dates from the early 18th century. It was a position attached to the Ottoman central administration, which provided for a series of officially-appointed writers to compile a continuous, approved narrative of recent Ottoman history as a formal historical record, to be routinely printed and made available. The post continued in existence for two hundred years, until 1922, virtually the end of the Ottoman empire.

The term *weḳāyiʿ-nüwīs* is known to have been used of some individual historians from the early 17th century, and continued on an *ad hoc* basis as a general designation for an official charged with recording the events of a military campaign or an embassy. The official historian's recording function may also have been foreshadowed by a possible duty of the late 16th-century court historiographer, the *shehnāmedji* [*q.v.*], to keep a regular daybook (see Djemāl al-Dīn Meḥmed Ḳarṣlī-zāde, *Āyīne-i ẓürefā/ʿOthmānlı taʾrīkh we müwerrikhleri*, Istanbul 1314/1896, 41-2). However, there is no clear continuity between the early court historiographers and the 18th-century office of *waḳʿa-nüwīs* (cf. L.V. Thomas, *A study of Naima*, New York 1972).

Naʿīmā [*q.v.*] is generally recognised as the first *waḳʿa-nüwīs*, commissioned around 1110/1698-9 by the Grand Vizier ʿAmūdja-zāde Ḥüseyin Köprülü [*q.v.*] to write a history of the Ottoman state from the *hidjrī* millennium (*ca.* 1591-2) onwards. It is likely, however, that a formal post was not instituted until the appointment in 1126/1714 of Rāshid [*q.v.*]. A general pattern emerged whereby each *waḳʿa-nüwīs* was expected to continue the narrative from where his predecessor had finished (sometimes several years prior to the time of writing), while also compiling notes on contemporary events for his own use or that of a successor. All relevant government departments were instructed to make their records available for consultation by the *waḳʿa-nüwīs* once they were no longer current. Drafts were submitted annually to the sultan, and could be published only with his approval.

Appointees were either members of the *ʿulemāʾ* or, more usually, of the *khʷādjegān*, section chiefs, within the Ottoman central bureaucracy. They were required to be learned, literary and loyal; an interest in history was an additional qualification. They tended to hold the post for only a few years in the middle of a bureaucratic or *ʿulemāʾ* career, often in addition to their existing post; few left any historical work other than that required of them as *waḳʿa-nüwīs*, and some are shadowy figures about whom little is known.

Consequently, the prestige of the office and its product fluctuated, particularly towards the end of the 18th century, as shown by a series of short-term appointments and complaints by appointees of poor remuneration and limited access to relevant documents. Significantly, the leading Ottoman historian of the mid-19th century, Aḥmed Djewdet Pasha [*q.v.*], *waḳʿa-nüwīs* from 1855 to 1866, chose to rewrite the history of the period 1774 to 1825. His successor, Luṭfī Efendi [*q.v.*], in post 1866-1907, compiled the last *waḳʿa-nüwīs* history, a basic chronicle of the period 1826-79. New developments in Ottoman historical writing after the *Tanẓīmāt* era rendered the traditional recording function of the official historian obsolete before the end of the empire. The last *waḳʿa-nüwīs*, ʿAbd al-Raḥmān Sheref, in post 1907-22, combined presidency of the newly-formed *Taʾrīkh-i ʿOthmānī Endjümeni*, an academic history society, with the writing of school textbooks. (For further information, see also individual entries on ʿIzzī; Enwerī; ʿĀṣim; Esʿad Efendi; and Taʾrīkh, Ottoman and modern Turkish, section 3/i "official historians".)

Bibliography: For an extended discussion of the post and its holders, with bibliography and references, see Bekir Kütükoğlu, *İA* art. *Vekāyinüvīs*, of which the present article is a much abridged summary.
(Christine Woodhead)

WAKĀLA (A.), verbal noun of the verb *wakala*, a technical term of Islamic religion, and more generally, of commercial practice and law. It means to commission, depute or authorise a person to act on behalf of another. It is a term far from easy to encapsulate in one meaning since it carries a variety of legal, and theological concepts. One of the attributes of God, given in the Ḳurʾān and *ḥadīth* is *al-Wakīl*, which indicates protection and sustenance, while according to al-Sarakhsī, the word indicates the entrusting (*ḥifāẓ*) of another person's property.

The concept of *wakāla* is significant in Islamic law as a practical mechanism by which all forms of contracts may be activated. According to Ḥanafī law, it is the basis of all forms of contractual partnership. For validity, the following basic rules are required, many of which are the same as expected in general contracts:

1. The condition of contract validity (*ṣiḥḥa*) requires that both parties must be able to dispose of their property, that the object of *wakāla* must be definite and legal, and that the obligation and acceptance of both parties (*īdjāb, ķabūl*) are clearly manifest.

2. The authorisation may be specific or general within the configuration which will be explained below.

3. The *wakāla* contract is like that of *wadīʿa* [*q.v.*], representing a voluntary contract which would be converted into a commercial contract if fees are stipulated.

4. No responsibility is incured on the proxy (*wakīl*) except in case of negligence (*tafrīṭ*) or intentional transgression (*taʿaddī*).

5. The contract can be terminated at the behest of either party or, like any other contract, by the death, insanity or legal incompetency of either of them.

Wakāla contracts may vary according to the nature of the economic operation that is governed. According to the requirement of the contract, *wakāla* can be either general (*ʿāmma*) to cover all forms of transactions and deals, or special (*khāṣṣa*) which is restricted to a particular disposition, for example a *wakāla* for selling cannot be valid in a transaction for letting. Muslim scholars differ regarding the legitimacy of the *wakāla* if it is drawn up in general and unlimited terms. Although the Ḥanafī and Mālikī schools accept this kind of *wakāla*, both Shāfiʿīs and Ḥanbalīs restrict the legitimacy of such contracts to what is stipulated. The reason that they give for rejecting general *wakāla* is that it can lead to great deception (*gharar*). This is probably why all the schools of Islamic law accept the prevalent custom (*ʿurf*) as a guide to control the deputed action. Accordingly, if the deputy violates custom and sells an object with great loss (*ghabn fāḥish*), his action can only be valid if confirmed by his client.

Agents can also be limited within certain logistic stipulations such as price bid, and quality and condition of the good or object. This *wakāla*, which is restricted by its *modus operandi*, is termed a *wakāla mukayyada*, its opposite being the unrestricted *wakāla muṭlaka*. When the timing of the contract is important, the contractors may opt for a time restriction on the *wakāla*. The *wakāla muwakkata* is the form of *wakāla* which is restricted by a time designated in the contract setting it up.

Due to the religious nature of Islamic law, *wakāla* as a legal mechanism extends itself to cover religious practices, too. It is part of the lawyer's undertaking to assess the validity of the *wakāla* in matters such as the pilgrimage (*ḥadjdj*), although, according to Ibn Ķudāma, *wakāla* is not valid in matters that specifically target or involve the personality of individuals (*ʿayn al-mukallaf*) such as testimony (*shahāda*), oaths (*aymān*), and pledges (*nudhūr*), or in rituals that individuals may find physically possible to perform, in contrast to those that may represent potential impossibilities such as *ḥadjdj*. The personality of the two parties is also an important element that differentiates *wakāla* from other contracts. The most important legal consequence of the personal aspect of *wakāla* is that it involves an inbuilt mechanism that terminates the contract once one of the two contractors dies.

Al-Sanhūrī, following the French terminology, cited *wakāla* as one example of the nominated contracts (*ʿuķūd musammāt*), which are contracts popularly known by a specific usage term. The nature of a representation contract as a "nominated contract" has apparently caused some confusion in French law and in the Arabic legal systems that have inherited its legacy. This confusion has resulted from the distinctive nature of the *wakāla*'s subject (*maḥall al-ʿaķd*) when compared with other contracts' subjects. The nature of the *wakāla*'s subject is a legal action (*taṣarruf ķānūnī*) or *acte juridique*, whereas all other contracts involves material action or *acte matériel*. The confusion arises in the classification of the contracts of professional persons such as lawyers, medical doctors and teachers which are considered by French law to be a deputisation contract rather than commission (*muķāwala*) contract. According to al-Sanhūrī, this is an unfounded assumption, based purely on personal grounds, because the subjects of all these contracts are legal actions and not material ones. However, al-Sanhūrī's statement generalises by treating each of these professions as one, despite the difference in their provided services. From an Islamic legal perspective, it is the service which represents the decisive factor whether the contract is one of deputation or commission. Accordingly, lawyers' services would be within the *wakāla* definition, whereas teachers' and medical doctors' employment falls within the spectrum of commission or an employment contract. The critical factor, in all contracts in Islamic law, is the nature of what the individual is offering and not the name of the profession. In Islamic law, all professions are ruled by the rules of professional contract (*ʿaķd al-ṣunnāʿ*), which are contracts that consider the provided service as the main guideline when problems concerning responsibility are raised.

A similar confusion about the position of *wakāla* arises in modern Arabic legal systems. Various definitions of *wakāla* seem to be affected by prevalent practical use within commercial life. Often the term is extended to include the supplier who is not necessarily an agent. In countries like Bahrain, Kuwait, Saudi Arabia and the UAE, it is important to examine each individual law separately in order to decide whether the actual basis constitutes *wakāla*.

Bibliography: Bukhārī, *Ṣaḥīḥ*, Istanbul 1315, 60-6; *LʿA*, Beirut n.d., xi, 735-6; ʿAbd al-Razzāķ al-Sanhūrī, *al-Wasīṭ fī sharḥ al-ķānūn al-madanī*, Beirut 1952 iv, 1, vii, 372; A.L. Udovitch, *Partnership and profit in mediaeval Islam*, Princeton 1970, 100; Wahba al-Zuḥaylī, *al-Fiķh al-islāmī wa-adillatuh*, Damascus 1985, iv, 157, v, 74-5; Sarākhsī, *Mabsūṭ*, Beirut 1986, xix, 2; Ibn Ķudāma, *al-Kāfī*, Beirut 1988, ii, 239-56; idem, *Mughnī*, ed. Ḥilū and Turkī, Cairo 1408/1988-9, 200; S.E. Ryner, *The theory of contracts in Islamic law*, London 1991, 101; Mohammad deen Napiah, *The theory of the contract of (al-wakalah)*, Ph.D. thesis, Glasgow Caledonian University 1995, unpubl., 57-65, 165.

For the use of *wakāla* in architecture, see ĶAYSARIYYA; KHĀN. (MAWIL Y. IZZI DIEN)

WAĶĀR, MĪRZĀ AḤMAD SHĪRĀZĪ, Persian poet of the Ķādjār period, born in 1232/1817 in Shīrāz, died there in 1298/1881. Waķār was the oldest of six sons of the poet Wiṣāl-i Shīrāzī, and under his father's tutelage, he became expert in Shīʿī and Ṣūfī lore, calligraphy and classical poetry. After his father's death, Waķār travelled to India in 1265/1848-9 and published an annotated, lithograph edition of Rūmī's *Mathnawī* during his year-long residence in Bombay. He spent most of the rest of his life in Shīrāz, supported by income from writing, calligraphy, and government stipends. He went to Tehran in 1274/1857-58 on family business and again around 1281/1864 and 1290/1873. Although he was well received at the Ḳādjār court and met Nāṣir al-Dīn Shāh, he was ill at ease in the capital city. His five brothers (especially Wiṣāl's third son Muḥammad Dāwarī) and two sons were all also capable poets.

In his many works of poetry and prose, Waḳār adheres to the models and style of the classical writers of the 5th-7th/11th-13th centuries. Containing more than 25,000 verses, his *dīwān* (first vol. printed Tabrīz 1348 *sh*./1969) includes all the traditional genres, but it is in the *ḳaṣīda* that Waḳār shows his real mastery. These poems are addressed to many members of the Ḳādjār court, in particular the governors of Fārs province (see Nawābī, 69-74). Imitating earlier masters, including Farrukhī, Manūčihrī, Sanā'ī and Anwarī [*q.vv.*], Waḳār's *ḳaṣīda*s are noted for their descriptions of the seasons and for an often personal, epistolary tone. His accounts of earthquakes in Shīrāz are frequently cited. Waḳār composed three *mathnawī*s. *Bahrām wa Bihrūz*, a didactic romance about the conflict between two brothers, remains unpublished. *Rumūz al-imāra* (Shīrāz 1331/1913) is a verse translation of ʿAlī's letter to the governor of Egypt in the metre of the *Shāh-nāma*. In the manner of Rūmī's *Mathnawī*, Waḳār's *Mūsā wa Khiḍr* (Shīrāz 1361 *sh*./1982) tells the story of these two prophets, digressing frequently into commentary and parallel tales. Among Waḳār's prose works, *Andjuman-i dānish* (Shīrāz 1366 *sh*./1987) consists of anecdotes intermixed with poetry in the style of Saʿdī's *Gulistān*. *Rūzmah-i Khusrawān-i Pārsī* (Shīrāz 1356 *sh*./1977) is an account of the legendary kings of ancient Iran. Also in the historical vein is Waḳār's long prose work on the martyrdom of Imām Ḥusayn, *ʿAshara-yi kāmila* (Shīrāz 1361 *sh*./1982). Waḳār penned a number of shorter prose epistles; these are unpublished, except for his commentary on six chronograms by Muḥtashim-i Kāshānī [*q.v.*].

Bibliography: Waḳār's published literary works are given in the body of the article above. Among the *tadhkira*s, see Riḍā Ḳulīkhān Hidāyat, *Madjmaʿ al-fuṣaḥā*, ed. M. Muṣaffā, Tehran 1336-41 *sh*./1957-62, vi, 1132-53; Mīrzā Ḥasan Fasā'ī Shīrāzī, *Fārsnāma-yi Nāṣirī*, repr. Tehran 1340 *sh*./1961, ii, 66-7; and Maʿṣūm ʿAlīshāh Shīrāzī, *Ṭarā'iḳ al-ḥaḳā'iḳ*, ed. M.J. Maḥdjūb, Tehran 1339-45 *sh*./1960-6, iii, 372-4. Aḥmad Dīwān Baygī Shīrāzī, *Ḥadīḳat al-shuʿarā'*, ed. ʿA. Nawā'ī, Tehran 1364-6 *sh*./1985-7, iii, 2028-40, and Shaykh Mufīd Dāwar, *Mir'āt al-faṣāḥa*, ed. M. Tāwūsī, Shīrāz 1371 *sh*./1992, 698-701, are especially useful for their editors' annotations and bibliographies. Among secondary works, see Browne, *LHP*, iv, 225, 300, 319; Rypka, *Hist. of Iranian literature*, 331-2; and especially, M. Nawābī, *Khāndān-i Wiṣāl-i Shīrāzī*, Tabrīz 1335 *sh*./1956, 51-119, which offers the fullest account of Waḳār's life and works. (P.E. Losensky)

WAḲF (a.), in Islamic law, the act of founding a charitable trust, and, hence the trust itself. A synonym, used mainly by Mālikī jurists, is *ḥabs*, *ḥubus* or *ḥubs* (in French often rendered as *habous*). The essential elements are that a person, with the intention of committing a pious deed, declares part of his or her property to be henceforth unalienable (*ḥabs*, *taḥbīs*) and designates persons or public utilities as beneficiaries of its yields (*al-taṣadduḳ bi 'l-manfaʿa*, *tasbīl al-manfaʿa*). The Imāmī Shīʿa distinguish between *waḳf* and *ḥabs*, the latter being a precarious type of *waḳf* in which the founder reserves the right to dispose of the *waḳf* property.

I. In Classical Islamic law
II. In the Arab lands
1. In Egypt
2. In Syria [see Suppl.]
3. In North Africa to 1914
4. In Muslim Spain
5. In the modern Middle East and North Africa
III. In Persia
IV. In the Ottoman empire to 1914
V. In Central Asia
VI. In Muslim India to 1900
VII. In Southeast Asia
VIII. In sub-Saharan Africa

I. In Classical Islamic Law

Not mentioned in the Ḳur'ān, it derives its legitimacy primarily from a number of *ḥadīth*s. The first one is related on the authority of Ibn ʿUmar and is included, in various versions, in the main *ḥadīth* collections:

> ʿUmar had acquired land in Khaybar and came to the Prophet to consult him in this matter saying: "O Messenger of God, I have acquired land in Khaybar which is more precious to me than any property I have ever acquired." He [Muḥammad] said: "If you want, make the land itself unalienable and give [the yield] away as alms (*in shi'ta ḥabbasta aṣlahā wa-taṣaddakta bihā*)." He (Ibn ʿUmar) said: Thereupon ʿUmar gave it away as alms [in the sense] that the land itself was not to be sold, inherited or donated. He gave it away as alms for the poor, the relatives, the slaves, the *djihād*, the travellers and the guests. And it will not be held against him who administers it if he consumes some of it(s yield) in an appropriate manner or feeds a friend who does not enrich himself by means of it (Ibn Ḥadjar al-ʿAsḳalānī, *Bulūgh al-marām*, Cairo n.d., no. 784).

Another *ḥadīth* often quoted in favour of the legitimacy of the *waḳf* is included in the *Ṣaḥīḥ* of Muslim: "The Messenger of God said: 'When a man dies, only three deeds will survive him: continuing alms, profitable knowledge and a child praying for him'" (*ibid.*, no. 783). Further, there is a report by Djābir that all companions of the Prophet who were financially capable of doing so, had made *waḳf*s (Ibn Ḳudāma, *al-Mughnī*, v, 598-9).

1. Origins.

In the legal discussions of the 2nd and early 3rd century A.H. we find several legal institutions that in the later legal doctrine were subsumed under the heading of *waḳf* and left their traces in that doctrine (see Schacht, *Early doctrines*). The terminology was probably fluid in the very beginning and was systematised only later. The first institution is that of *al-ḥabs fī sabīl Allāh*, the donation of horses, weapons, slaves for the sake of *djihād* or houses for sheltering the warriors at the frontier. The second one (*ḥabs mawḳūf*, *ṣadaḳa mawḳūfa*) is a kind of temporary endowment for a limited number of people that after their extinction reverts to the founder or his heirs. The word *mawḳūf* here has the original legal meaning of "suspended" and only later did it acquire the meaning of "made into a *waḳf*". This type of *waḳf* has survived in Mālikī doctrine. Thirdly, there was the permanent *waḳf* (called *ṣadaḳa muḥarrama* by the early Shāfiʿīs), usually in favour of the poor, or in favour of certain classes of relatives and descendants or even clients (*mawālī*) and then, after their extinction, to the poor. Its validity was contested, especially by Abū Ḥanīfa. Finally, there were permanent *waḳf*s in favour of mosques or public utilities. It seems that *waḳf*s in favour of one's relatives or descendants (*waḳf ahlī*) were very common in the early period and that the *waḳfs* in favour of mosques and public utilities (*waḳf khayrī*) were secondary.

At the beginning of this century, C.H. Becker (in *Isl.*, ii [1911]) argued that the institution of charitable *waḳf* was influenced by the *piae causae* in Byzantine law. His view was widely shared (see e.g. Heffening, art. *Waḳf* in *EI*[1], and J. Schacht, *Droit byzantin et droit musulman*, in *Fondazione A. Volta, atti dei convegni*, xii [1957], 213-15, where the older literature is quoted). Apart from the obvious structural similarities between both institutions (elaborated by A. d'Emilia, *Comparazione*), Becker's arguments were that, according to al-Maḳrīzī, there were only *waḳfs* of urban real estate in Egypt during the first three centuries of Islam, and that this state of affairs, in accordance with Byzantine law, was the same regarding Coptic pious endowments in this period. Cl. Cahen (*Réflexions sur le waqf ancien*, 37-56), however, showed that the evidence put forward by Becker was not convincing. If al-Maḳrīzī's observation is reliable, Cahen argued, this applies only to Egypt. Elsewhere, there is no indication of such a restriction, and, in fact, *waḳfs* of rural property were widespread in early Islam. This seriously weakens the argument of Byzantine influence on the development of the Islamic doctrine of *waḳf*. Moreover, the fact that, in Egypt, *waḳfs* were restricted to urban property in the early centuries of Islam may stem from the fact that the rural population of Egypt at that time was predominantly Christian. Finally, Cahen pointed out that, in early Islam, *waḳfs* in favour of relatives and descendants were predominant and not those in favour of religious institutions.

The immediate spread and popularity of the *waḳf* derives from the fact that it served social and economic needs. It was a means to protect an estate against confiscation by the state or against disintegration as a result of *Sharīʿa* succession. Moreover, it could be used to circumvent the rules of Islamic succession and keep property as much as possible within the agnatic group. At the same time it could provide a regular income for one's relatives and descendants in order to protect them from want. With regard to mosques and public utilities, there were two types, each serving its own purpose: there were *waḳfs* consisting of the mosque or the utility itself (school, bridge, fountain) and there were *waḳfs* generating the income for the maintenance and operation of these utilities. Finally, *waḳfs* provided relief for the poor.

2. Founding a *waḳf*.

(a) *The founder* (al-wāḳif, al-muḥabbis)

The founder of the *waḳf* must have the general capacity to act and contract (*ahliyyat al-adāʾ*), i.e. he must be adult, sound of mind, capable of handling financial affairs (*rashīd*), a free person and not under interdiction for prodigality or bankruptcy. Being a Muslim is not required; in principle, *waḳfs* founded by *dhimmīs* are valid. In addition, the founder must be sound of body to be legally capable of performing gratuitous acts. For if a person founds a *waḳf* during his last illness (*maraḍ al-mawt*), it is subject to the restrictions with regard to bequests (*waṣiyya* [*q.v.*]), that is, its value may not exceed one-third of the estate. In Mālikī law, finally, a married woman would need her husband's authorisation if the value of the *waḳf* exceeds one-third of her property, as in the case of gifts.

(b) *The object* (al-mawḳūf, al-muḥabbas)

The goods that are made into *waḳf* must be goods that are not excluded from legal traffic and can be the object of a valid contract (*māl mutaḳawwim*). This means that (1) people have control over them (hence not a fish in the sea or a runaway slave); (2) their use is lawful (hence not musical instruments or objects used for worship in other religions, such as crucifixes, nor impure goods like wine and pork); (3) they are not otherwise excluded from legal traffic (hence not public domains; *waḳf* property or an *umm walad* [*q.v.*]). These are general requirements that are applicable to all contracts involving the transfer of property.

In addition, there are some other requirements that are specific regarding the founding of a *waḳf*. Only physical goods (*ʿayn*) that are clearly defined and exist at the moment that the *waḳf* is founded can be made into a *waḳf*. A debt or "one of the houses owned by me" (if the founder owns more than one house) cannot validly constitute the object of a *waḳf*. Furthermore, the founder must be entitled to dispose of the intended object of the *waḳf*. He cannot make a *waḳf* of another person's property or his own property if it has been pledged. The previous conditions are mentioned by all the law schools with the exception of the Mālikīs. *Waḳfs* must be perpetual, but there is controversy on the implications of this principle with regard to the object of the *waḳf*. Goods whose use consists in their consumption cannot be dedicated to *waḳf*, but most schools allow movable goods that wear out by their use. Some jurists have argued that even silver and gold coins can be made into a *waḳf*. The Ḥanafīs, however, are stricter in this respect. Their basic rule is that only immovable property (both *ʿushr* and *kharādj* land) can be the object of *waḳf*. Only in exceptional cases do they allow that movable goods are made into a *waḳf*. These exceptions are:

1. Movable goods that follow immovable property, such as the slaves, animals, and agricultural tools belonging to a rural estate;

2. Movable goods that are mentioned in certain *ḥadīths* as valid objects of *waḳf*, such as horses and weapons for *djihād*; this is Abū Yūsuf's opinion;

3. Movable goods that people are accustomed to dedicate to *waḳf*, such as shovels, pickaxes and biers, to be used in graveyards, copies of the Ḳurʾān, to be read in mosques or schools, and cooking pots to be used in public kitchens for the poor; this view, ascribed to Muḥammad al-Shaybānī, has become the authoritative one within the Ḥanafī school.

(c) *The beneficiaries*

Both persons and public utilities, such as mosques, schools, bridges, graveyards and drinking fountains, can be the beneficiaries of a *waḳf*. Beneficiaries of the first type can be one or more individuals ("*Fulān ibn Fulān*", "my children", "my male offspring") or collectivities ("travellers", "the poor of this town"). The jurists note that in the case of *waḳfs* in favour of public utilities the actual beneficiaries are all Muslims, or the Muslims of a certain region or the inhabitants of a town, who collectively have the right to use these utilities. Modern legislation distinguishes between charitable *waḳfs* (*waḳf khayrī*) dedicated to pious causes (public utilities, the poor) and family *waḳfs* (*waḳf ahlī*) made in favour of one's relatives and descendants. Classical doctrine does not make this distinction and the two types of *waḳf* are governed by the same rules. There can be two groups of beneficiaries who are entitled at the same time, e.g. if the founder has stipulated that half of the proceeds go to the poor and half to his children. Usually, several subsequent classes of beneficiaries are mentioned. A very common clause is to designate first one's sons and unmarried daughters, then one's agnatic grandsons and unmarried agnatic granddaughters, then one's agnatic great-grandsons and unmarried agnatic great-granddaughters, and so on. In such cases, no class becomes entitled until the previous one is entirely extinct.

A valid dedication must satisfy the following conditions:

1. The immediate beneficiaries (i.e. the first class of beneficiaries) must exist at the time of the foundation of the *waḳf* and be identified or identifiable. The designation of an unborn child as the immediate beneficiary of a *waḳf* is therefore invalid. Only the Mālikīs hold that beneficiaries that do not yet exist may be designated. The proceeds are saved until he is born. If this does not occur, they return to the founder or his heirs.

2. The beneficiaries must be capable of acquiring property. This excludes slaves and *ḥarbīs*, but not *dhimmīs*. The scholars disagree on whether a *musta'min* can be a beneficiary. Regarding *waḳfs* in favour of public utilities, their users are regarded as the beneficiaries.

3. The purpose of the *waḳf* must be lawful. Therefore, a *waḳf* for the building and maintenance of churches, synagogues and monasteries is null and void, even if made by *dhimmīs*. However, some jurists point out that *waḳfs* in favour of churches and monasteries may be valid if they serve specific functions not related to worship, e.g. offering hospitality to the poor or travellers.

There is controversy on the validity of a *waḳf* in favour of the founder. Most jurists hold that such a stipulation is invalid. They argue that founding a *waḳf* implies the transfer of the right to dispose of and the right to use the *waḳf* property. Retaining (part of) the right to use it is in conflict with this principle. The Ḥanafīs, however (with the exception of Muḥammad al-Shaybānī), assert that such a *waḳf* is valid on the strength of the *ḥadīth* about ʿUmar quoted above, since he stipulated that the *waḳf*'s administrator was entitled to "eat" from its proceeds, and it is well known that he himself was its first administrator. The Ḥanbalīs interpret this *ḥadīth* in a more restricted sense: they regard a stipulation to the effect that the founder can use the *waḳf*'s proceeds during his lifetime as valid, but not his designation as a beneficiary.

The Ḥanafīs, with the exception of Abū Yūsuf, hold that it is required for the validity of a *waḳf* that the designation of the beneficiaries should include a final class whose existence is regarded as perpetual, such as the poor. Otherwise, they argue, the perpetuity of the *waḳf*, which is an essential element, is jeopardised. According to the other law schools and Abū Yūsuf (whose opinion became the prevailing one within the Ḥanafī school), the absence of such a designation does not affect the validity of the *waḳf*, since it is not known that the Companions included such stipulations when founding *waḳfs*. As a consequence the jurists have discussed what happens to the *waḳf* after the extinction of the last beneficiaries, or after the institution for which the *waḳf* has been founded, has been destroyed and cannot function anymore. Some argue that the *waḳf*, being perpetual, remains operative and that it must be determined who are the most appropriate new beneficiaries. According to Abū Yūsuf, it is an implied stipulation that the poor are the new beneficiaries since the founding of a *waḳf* is intended as a charity. The Ḥanbalīs and most Shāfiʿīs hold that the proceeds of the *waḳf* are to be spent on the founder's heirs. They also base their view on the implicit notion of charity in *waḳfs*, but add on the strength of several *ḥadīths* that the best charity is charity in favour of one's relatives. The Mālikīs distinguish between a perpetual and a temporary *waḳf*. After the extinction of the beneficiaries of the first type, the *waḳf* is continued in favour of the poor among the founder's closest agnates, or, in their absence, to the poor in general. If the *waḳf* was founded in favour of a public utility that has been destroyed and is beyond repair, the Mālikīs hold that a similar destination must then be sought for its proceeds. As for the temporary *waḳf* founded in favour of a limited number of individuals, for their lifetime or for a certain period, this type reverts to the founder or his heirs upon extinction.

(d) *The act of founding*

A *waḳf* is founded by a declaration of the founder. Although not required by law, this declaration would normally be recorded in a document (*waḳfiyya*, *rasm al-taḥbīs*; for the oldest example now known, dating from the end of the 2nd century A.H., see al-Shāfiʿī, *K. al-Umm*, Cairo 1321, iii, 282-3). The general theory of *fiḳh* regarding declaration of intent applies. If the wording of the declaration is obvious and unambiguous (*ṣarīḥ*), the declaration alone is constitutive, otherwise, i.e. if the declaration is indirect (*kināya*), circumstantial evidence pointing to the intent of founding a *waḳf* is required, e.g. the use of additional words, such as "it shall not be sold, given away or inherited". There are small differences between the various law schools, but as a rule expressions containing the words *waḳf*, *ḥabs* and *tasbīl* and their derivatives are regarded as unambiguous. In exceptional cases a *waḳf* can be founded by acts implying the intention. If for instance a person builds a mosque and allows other persons to pray in it or if he establishes a graveyard and lets other persons bury their dead in it, then this is regarded as tantamount to founding a *waḳf*. This is based on the principle that certain acts are by custom regarded as an expression of the intent to perform a certain legal act. Only the Shāfiʿīs always require a verbal declaration.

There are certain stipulations that are regarded as being contrary to essential characteristics of the *waḳf* and their inclusion would make the *waḳf* null and void. Some such stipulations have already been discussed: *waḳfs* dedicated to an unlawful aim or those for which the founder has been designated as beneficiary. There are, however, several others. These are related to two principles: the immediate effect of the act of founding a *waḳf* (*tandjīz*) and its perpetual character. All jurists except the Mālikīs agree that founding a *waḳf* to be effective at a future point of time (*muḍāf*), or making it dependent on an uncertain condition (*muʿallaḳ*), renders the act void. There is only one exception: all law schools allow that a person founds a *waḳf* by testament, effective upon his death. This, then, is governed by rules of testament (*waṣiyya* [*q.v.*]). Stipulations that the *waḳf* is founded for a limited period or that the founder may revoke it or sell or give away its property, are regarded by all jurists except the Mālikīs as contrary to the required perpetuity of the *waḳf* and invalidate its founding.

(e) *Conditions of irrevocability* (luzūm)

The Mālikīs, Ḥanafīs (with the exception of Abū Yūsuf), the Imāmī Shīʿa and some Ḥanbalīs hold, in analogy with gifts, that a *waḳf* is not binding and irrevocable until the property has actually been transferred to the beneficiaries or the administrator. If, before the property has been handed over, the founder dies or loses his right of disposal over the property as a result of bankruptcy or serious illness, the *waḳf* is void. Regarding public utilities, transfer of property is assumed to have taken place as soon as the founder lets the public use them. The Imāmī Shīʿa, however, require also in this case that the property be actually handed over to the administrator. Those who do not require transfer of property argue that the aforementioned *ḥadīth* from ʿUmar does not mention it as a condition and that founding a *wakf* is more like the freeing of a slave (an act which does not require this transfer) than making a gift.

There is also a difference of opinion on the question of whether it is required for the irrevocability of the *wakf* that the immediate beneficiaries, at least if they are defined, accept their rights. For most law schools, their acceptance is not a condition for the irrevocability, but, as in the case of bequests, a condition for acquiring their rights. The Shāfiʿīs, however, hold in analogy with bequests that the *wakf* is only binding and irrevocable after the immediate beneficiaries have accepted. Those beneficiaries that acquire their rights after the *wakf* has been founded, do not have to accept expressly. However, they may reject it, after which they forfeit their rights.

3. The legal effects.

All law schools hold that establishing a *wakf* is a valid and irrevocable act. Only Abū Ḥanīfa asserted that a *wakf* is only irrevocable if the founder establishes it as from the moment of his death or if it is affirmed by a *ḳāḍī*'s sentence. (For the discussion and arguments of both parties, see al-Kāsānī, *Badāʾiʿ al-ṣanāʾiʿ*, vi, 318-19; Ibn Ḳudāma, *al-Mughnī*, v, 598-600.) If a person founds a *wakf* during his lifetime, Abū Ḥanīfa holds that the *wakf* remains his property and he may revoke the *wakf* by alienating its property. After his death, the property reverts to his heirs. Establishing a *wakf* during one's lifetime is, in Abū Ḥanīfa's view, nothing else than a vow to donate the proceedings of the *wakf* property to the beneficiaries at the moment of one's death. This opinion, however, was not followed by his companions Muḥammad al-Shaybānī and Abū Yūsuf, who held, like the jurists of the other legal schools, that establishing a *wakf* is an irrevocable and binding act. In order to dispel all doubts about the binding character of a *wakf*, Ḥanafī practice was for the founder to have recourse to judicial proceedings. The standard procedure was that the founder, after having handed over the *wakf* property to the administrator, would reclaim it alleging that the *wakf* was revocable according to Abū Ḥanīfa's doctrine. The judge then would establish the irrevocability of the *wakf* by giving judgement according to the doctrine of Muḥammad al-Shaybānī and Abū Yūsuf and finding for the defendant.

The majority of the jurists base their opinion that establishing a *wakf* is a legally valid act on the *ḥadīth*s that have been mentioned at the beginning of this article. Abū Ḥanīfa, however, argues that *wakf*s may not infringe upon the rights of one's heirs and quotes a *ḥadīth* transmitted by Shurayḥ to the effect that after the revelation of the verses of succession Muḥammad said: "No *wakf*s to the detriment of the Ḳurʾānic shares of inheritance" (*lā ḥabs ʿan al-farāʾiḍ*). Moreover, he adduces a *ḥadīth* transmitted by ʿAbd Allāh b. Zayd (not included in the main collections; for the text, see Ibn Kudāma, *al-Mughnī*, v, 598) according to which the Prophet sold land that had been made *wakf*. And as to the examples of the Companions, he alleges that these instances may date from before the revelation of the verses of inheritance.

The irrevocability of the act of founding a *wakf* implies for all law schools except the Mālikīs (for whom the founder remains the owner of the goods, albeit without any of the powers of ownership) that the founder ceases to be the owner of the object of the *wakf*. Since Islamic law confers legal personality only on natural persons, the jurists had to come to grips with the problem of who becomes the new owner of the *wakf* goods. In order to answer this question, they made use of two analogies leading to two different solutions. As we have seen above, most law schools compare founding a *wakf* with making a gift or other gratuitous legal act. For them, the beneficiaries become the new owners, although their ownership is a restricted one, not including the right of disposal. As in the case of gifts, they regard the actual transfer of property and the taking possession by the beneficiaries or the administrator as the moment when the founder's property right ceases to exist and the *wakf* becomes irrevocable. Some jurists, however, compare it with the act of freeing a slave (*ʿitḳ*) and are of the opinion that the ownership, immediately upon the declaration, is transferred to God. On this theoretical issue, advocates of both views can be found within each law school, except for the Mālikīs.

Since a *wakf* is founded in perpetuity, the goods belonging to it need maintenance. If the goods are exploited by renting it out, maintenance must be paid from the proceeds, before the beneficiaries get their shares. If the beneficiaries of the *wakf* only have the right to use it, they themselves are liable for the maintenance of the goods. If they are negligent, the *ḳāḍī* is entitled to take appropriate measures, e.g. evicting the users of a house and renting it out in order to generate money for its maintenance. The same applies to *wakf*s consisting of e.g. slaves or animals. Horses dedicated as a *wakf* to the *djihād*, are the responsibility of the *Bayt al-Māl*.

What happens to the *wakf* if the *wakf* goods are seriously damaged or destroyed? One could think of a ruined house or mosque, a mosque in a region left by its inhabitants, trees that have died or a horse no longer fit for warfare. Now, if the damage to the goods is the result of a tort, there is no problem. The administrators or the beneficiaries can claim compensation, which then belongs to the *wakf* and must be used to repair or replace the goods. However, if the damage is not caused by human activity, there is a great deal of controversy among the jurists. The Shāfiʿīs and the Imāmī Shīʿa hold that the *wakf* remains in existence as long as there are goods left that can be used or exploited in whatever way. Solely if the remaining goods can only be used by consuming them do they accept that the *wakf* ends and that these goods become the property of the beneficiaries. The other law schools accept under certain conditions that the remaining goods be sold and that new *wakf* property be acquired with the proceeds of the sale (*istibdāl*). The Mālikīs allow this only with regard to movable goods that are unfit for their intended use. The Ḥanbalīs are more permissive in this respect. They regard *istibdāl* as lawful if the goods of the *wakf* have been damaged or destroyed to the extent that they can no longer be used for their intended exploitation. Unlike the other law schools, the Ḥanafīs first pose the question of whether or not the founder has stipulated for himself or for the future administrators the power to practice *istibdāl*. Although Muḥammad al-Shaybānī argued that such a stipulation is void, Abū Yūsuf's view, which prevailed among the Ḥanafīs, is that such a clause is perfectly valid, except with regard to mosques. If the founder has failed to introduce such a clause, or has even expressly forbidden *istibdāl*, the *ḳāḍī* may still allow it, if he deems it in the interest of the *wakf*. However, he can only act with the authorisation of the caliph or sultan.

4. Administration of the *waḳf*.

Especially if there is more than one beneficiary, the founder will usually make arrangements for the administration of the *waḳf* by appointing an administrator (*nāẓir, mutawallī, ḳayyim*) and laying down rules for the appointment of his successors. According to most law schools, the founder is entitled to administer the *waḳf* himself during his lifetime. Only the Mālikīs do not allow this, since they require for the validity of the *waḳf* that the founder actually hand over the property to the beneficiaries or the administrator. If the founder has not made arrangements, the jurists disagree as to who is entitled to appoint an administrator. According to Abū Yūsuf, the founder, being the person closest to the *waḳf*, is entitled to administer it. During his lifetime he has the right to appoint an administrator. By testament he may transfer this right to his testamentary executor (*waṣī*). The other jurists hold that, in this case, the *ḳāḍī* is responsible for the administration of the *waḳf* and that it is he who must appoint an administrator. However, if the number of beneficiaries is limited and identifiable, the Mālikīs, most Ḥanbalīs and the Imāmī Shīʿa are of the opinion that the beneficiaries have the right to administer the *waḳf* because they have rights to the *waḳf* property, either because they are regarded as the virtual owners of the *waḳf* (Ḥanbalīs and the Imāmī Shīʿa) or because they own the right to use and exploit (*milk al-manfaʿa*) the *waḳf* property (Mālikīs). An administrator must accept his appointment. The approval of the beneficiaries is not required (except according to those who hold that the beneficiaries, under certain conditions, are entitled to administer the *waḳf*, if such conditions obtain).

The administrator must have the capacity to act and contract. According to all law schools except the Ḥanafīs, he must be Muslim and male. In addition he must be trustworthy (*amīn*) and have the necessary skills. The Shāfiʿīs and some Ḥanbalīs require that he should be *ʿadl* [*q.v.*].

His duties are, in the first place, the maintenance and the exploitation of the *waḳf* property. He decides on the repairs that have to be carried out and on how the property is made profitable. Finally, he distributes the proceeds among the beneficiaries. He is entitled to take a remuneration for his activities. His position is similar to that of a guardian over a minor or an insane person, and like him, the administrator of a *waḳf* is under supervision of the *ḳāḍī*.

5. Extinction of the *waḳf*.

A *waḳf* is intended to last forever. Nevertheless the jurists envisage several situations that may result in its termination:

1. When the goods of the *waḳf* perish. In the event the goods are destroyed or damaged, to the extent that they can no longer be used or exploited in the way envisioned by the founder, Muḥammad al-Shaybānī held that the *waḳf* becomes extinct and that the remains of the goods revert to the founder or his heirs. The other jurists assert, however, that no possibility of alternative use or exploitation must be left unexplored before the *waḳf* comes to an end, and they carry this to great lengths. In principle, *waḳfs* consisting of land cannot become extinguished.

2. A *waḳf* can be declared null and void by the *ḳāḍī* if it does not satisfy the conditions of validity, or if the founder has introduced stipulations contrary to the essence of the notion of *waḳf*.

3. A *waḳf* becomes null and void if the founder apostatises from Islam.

4. According to the Mālikīs, if a *waḳf* is made in favour of a limited number of beneficiaries for their lifetime or for a certain period, it becomes extinct when the last of them has died or when the period for which the *waḳf* has been founded has expired. The *waḳf* property then returns to the founder or his heirs.

5. Under Mālikī law, a *waḳf* can be cancelled by the founder if he has stipulated that the property will return to him or may be sold by him in case he needs it.

Bibliography: 1. Legal texts. Dasūḳī, *Ḥāshiya ʿalā al-Sharḥ al-kabīr*, Cairo n.d., iv, 75-97; Hilāl al-Raʾy b. Yaḥyā, *K. Aḥkām al-waḳf*, Ḥaydarābād 1936; Ḥillī, *Sharāʾiʿ al-Islām*, Nadjaf 1969, ii, 211-21; ʿUmar Ḥilmī, *Itḥāf al-akhlāf fī aḥkām al-awḳāf*, Istanbul 1307/1889-90, Eng. tr. C.R. Tyser and D.G. Demetriades, *A gift to posterity on the law of Evqaf*, [2]Nicosia 1922; Ibn Ḳudāma, *al-Mughnī*, Beirut 1993, v, 597-649; Muḥammad Ḳadrī, *Ḳānūn al-ʿadl wa 'l-inṣāf li 'l-ḳaḍāʾ ʿalā mushkilāt al-awḳāf*, Cairo 1893, French tr. U. Pace and V. Sistro, *Code annoté du wakf*, Alexandria 1946; Kāsānī, *Badāʾiʿ al-ṣanāʾiʿ*, Beirut 1986, vi, 218-22; Aḥmad b. ʿAmr al-Shaybānī al-Khaṣṣāf, *K. Aḥkām al-awḳāf*, Cairo 1904; Ramlī, *Nihāyat al-muḥtādj ilā sharḥ al-Minhādj*, Beirut 1984, v, 358-404; Shaykhzāde, *Madjmaʿ al-anhur*, Istanbul 1401, i, 663-76.

2. Studies. A. Akgündüz, *Islam hukukunda ve Osmanlı tatbikatında vakıf müessesesi*, [2]Istanbul 1996; C.H. Becker, *Zur Entstehung der Waqfinstitution*, in *Isl.*, ii (1911), 404 ff.; Cl. Cahen, *Réflexions sur le waqf ancien*, in *SI*, xiv (1961), 37-56; H. Cattan, *The law of Waqf*, in *Law in the Middle East*, ed. M. Khadduri and H. Liebesny, Washington D.C. 1955, i, 203-22; A. d'Emilia, *Il waqf ahli secondo la dottrina di Abu Yusuf*, in *Pubbl. Ist. di Diritto Romano . . . del'Università di Roma*, ix (1938), 67-87; idem, *Per una comparazione fra le piae causae nel diritto canonico, il charitable trust nel diritto inglese e il waqf khairi nel diritto musulmano*, in *Scritti di diritto islamico. Raccolti a cura di Francesco Castro*, Rome 1976, 237-77; M. Gil, *The early waqf foundations*, in *JNES*, lvii (1998), 125-40; J. Luccioni, *Le habous ou wakf (rites malékite et hanéfite)*, Algiers 1942; O. Pesle, *La théorie et la pratique des habous dans le rite malékite*, Casablanca 1941; D.S. Powers, *The Maliki family endowment: legal norms and social practices*, in *IJMES*, xxv (1993), 379-406; D. Santillana, *Istituzioni di diritto musulmano malechita*, Rome 1938, ii, 412-51; J. Schacht, *Early doctrines on waqf*, in *Fuad Köprülü armağanı*, Istanbul 1953, 443-52; P.C. Hennigan, *The birth of a legal institution. The formation of the Waqf in the third century A.H. Ḥanafī legal discourse*, Ph.D. diss., Cornell Univ. 1999, unpubl.; N.A. Stillman, Waqf *and the ideology of charity in medieval Islam*, in I.R. Netton (ed.), *Studies in honour of Clifford Edmund Bosworth. 1. Hunter of the East*, Leiden 2000, 357-72.

(R. Peters)

II. In the Arab Lands

1. In Egypt.

The earliest pious foundations in Muslim Egypt seem to be gifts for charitable purposes rather than *awḳāf* as subsequently known. This was the case with the foundation of the first mosque built by ʿAmr b. al-ʿĀṣ in the first year of the Arab conquest (Ibn Duḳmāḳ, i, 62-3). On the return of the Arab troops from Alexandria in 21/641, Ḳaysaba b. Kulthūm, one of the *ahl al-rāya*, donated to the community a piece of land which he owned for the foundation of a mosque. The mosque personnel was paid by the *Bayt al-Māl*. Other plots were similarly donated for communal use, e.g. to establish a market for cattle. Al-Ḳalḳashandī attributes the earliest charitable *wakf* in Egypt based on the alienation of treasury land (*Bayt al-Māl*) to al-Layth b. Saʿd during the governorship of ʿAmr b. al-ʿĀṣ (Ibn Duḳmāḳ, iv, 38), but it is not clear that this was a *wakf* proper.

The earliest known document dealing with a genuine charitable *wakf* of agricultural land in Egypt dates from the ʿAbbāsid period; the founder, the financial official Abū Bakr Muḥammad b. ʿAlī al-Mādharāʾī, alienated the pond called Birkat al-Ḥabash together with the orchards around it for charitable purposes (the ponds of Cairo became waterless when the flood began to recede in the fall; they were then used for agricultural purposes). The revenue was to be used to operate a hydraulic complex and to buy food for the poor. The text of this *wakf*, dated 307/919, is published as a résumé by Ibn Duḳmāḳ (i, 55-6; Amīn, *Awḳāf*, 37-8). Another document from the Ikhshīdid period (dated 355/965) refers to a hydraulic complex known as *Biʾr al-Waṭāwīṭ* consisting of waterwheels and a well, which were endowed for charitable use (al-Maḳrīzī, *Khiṭaṭ*, ii, 135).

Al-Maḳrīzī states that the earliest pious *wakfs* were based on the alienation of commercial buildings, mainly apartment houses (*ribāʿ*), and that no land was alienated in the early period of the governors and their successors; even Ibn Ṭūlūn's foundations of a mosque, a hospital and an aqueduct were financed only with the revenue of apartment buildings (*ibid.*, ii, 295). The previous examples, however, show that during the ʿAbbāsid period pious and family endowments did include agricultural land (*ibid.*, ii, 114).

The origins of a central *wakf* administration cannot be precisely defined. Al-Ḳalḳashandī attributes, in rather vague terms, the origin of the *dīwān al-aḥbās* to the time of ʿAmr b. al-ʿĀṣ (*Ṣubḥ al-aʿshā*, iv, 38). During the Umayyad period, an institution for *wakf* administration was already well established, as the case of the *ḳāḍī* Tawba b. al-Namir (115-20/733-8) demonstrates; he supervised the *awḳāf*, ensuring that the charitable funds (*ṣadaḳa*) reached their destination and preventing abuses. Upon his death this *dīwān* had already become an important institution (Halm, 47-8). A similar *dīwān* was later created in Baṣra, which suggests that the Egyptian one might be the first in Islamic history. Half a century later, when another *ḳāḍī*, Ismāʿīl b. Ilyasaʿ (164-7/781-3), tried to apply the principle, accepted in the Ḥanafī *madhhab*, according to which a *wakf* is not irrevocable, he provoked a great controversy which eventually led to his dismissal; the Shāfiʿī *madhhab* prevailed in Egypt from the outset.

During the ʿAbbāsid period, some *ḳāḍīs* of Fusṭāṭ carried out strict inspections of the *awḳāf* properties on a monthly basis. The judge was free to administer according to his own discretion the funds donated to the *dīwān* without specific conditions, provided that they were spent *fī sabīl Allāh*, i.e. for any charitable purpose. The *ḳāḍīs* were also in charge of controlling the *awḳāf* of the *ahl al-dhimma*.

The Fāṭimids modified the *wakf* administration. The caliph al-Muʿizz ordered in 363/974 that the *aḥbās* funds be transferred to the *Bayt al-Māl* and that the beneficiaries should prove their claims (al-Maḳrīzī, *Khiṭaṭ*, ii, 295). He also cancelled the alienation of agricultural land, which al-Ḥākim, however, shortly afterwards reintroduced. The *wakfs* were then subject to a kind of tax farming (*ḍamān*); an individual would administer the *wakf* estate and collect its revenue, against a fixed yearly amount which would settle the claims of the beneficiaries and leave a balance for the *Bayt al-Māl*. With these funds, the Fāṭimid state used to support all types of philanthropic foundations, in particular those whose assets were exhausted. The tax farming system had the side-effect that the tax farmer (*ḍāmin*) might neglect the property in order to realise a maximum profit for himself. Ibn Mammātī, who witnessed the *wakf* bureaucracy during the late Fāṭimid and early Ayyūbid periods, criticised the renting-out of alienated estates because it deprived the *wakf* of investment opportunities and allowed the major profit to be reaped by the tenant. A large and detailed *wakfiyya* in the name of the Fāṭimid vizier al-Ṣāliḥ Ṭalāʾiʿ b. Ruzzīk [*q.v.*], preserved in a Mamlūk-period copy, is the only known Fāṭimid *wakfiyya* and the oldest example of this type; it refers to an agricultural estate alienated in a private *wakf* to the benefit of the family of Ibn Maʿṣūm, a descendant of the Shīʿī Imām Mūsā al-Kāẓim [*q.v.*] (Cl. Cahen, Y. Rāġib and A. Taher).

The state control over the *awḳāf* by the *dīwān al-aḥbās* did not exclude the role of the *ḳāḍī*, however, who was directly in charge of the inspection of the premises. The Fāṭimid *ḳāḍīs* of al-Fusṭāṭ and al-Ḳāhira used to inspect yearly the religious buildings in both cities.

With the *iḳṭāʿ* system introduced by the Ayyūbids, important changes occurred in the situation of the *awḳāf*. Land that was previously dedicated to philanthropic purposes was given as *iḳṭāʿ* to officers and state servants, who were to collect its *kharādj*, and this was often detrimental to the philanthropic services which this land originally financed. Following the overthrow of the Fāṭimids, Ṣalāḥ al-Dīn, endeavouring to cope with Crusader threats, alienated on a large scale land of the *Bayt al-Māl* in order to pay ransoms of Muslim prisoners of war and to support religious foundations and various philanthropic services aiming at consolidating Sunnī Islam. An important number of *madrasas* and a major *khānaḳāh* were created, sustaining communities of scholars and Ṣūfīs, including Muslim migrants to Egypt. According to Muḥammad Amīn, however, the Ayyūbid mode of creating pious endowments should not be described as based on *wakf* but rather on *irṣād*, the difference being that *wakf* implies the alienation of privately-owned property for a pious or other purpose, whereas *irṣād* involves the use of public funds, excluding a private involvement in the transaction, to sustain public or philanthropic services (*Awḳāf*, 54, 64). The *irṣād* was supposed to assume charges which were part of the *Bayt al-Māl*'s expenditures (Abū Zahra, 23).

The large quantity of *wakf* documents from the Mamlūk period to be found in Egyptian archives and their ongoing publication allows a much better view of the role of the *wakf* during this period than previously.

The Mamlūk *wakf* system consisted to a large extent of *irṣād*, referred to as *wakf*, thus blurring the line between the *Bayt al-Māl* and the sultan's private property. The Mamlūk establishment thus acquired the benefit of fulfilling a charitable act at the expense of the state. Scholars of the Ḥanafī *madhhab*, and mostly during the Ottoman period, did not consider the alienation of *Bayt al-Māl* funds as a true, sound *wakf*. In 789/1387 Sultan Barḳūḳ, who favoured the Ḥanafī *madhhab*, tried to liquidate some of the great *wakfs* established by his predecessors on the ground that they were from the outset illicit because they were based on the alienation of *Bayt al-Māl* land. The jurists, however, did not authorise him to liquidate *wakfs* serving pious works (al-Maḳrīzī, *Sulūk*, Cairo 1970-73, iii/1, 345). The Shāfiʿīs preferred to tolerate *wakfs* financed by *Bayt al-Māl* estates despite their doubtful status, as long as they supported the religious foundations which were, *per se*, entitled to funds from the public treasury.

The Mamlūks introduced their own reforms of the *wakf* system. During the reign of Baybars, the *wakf* administration was divided into three parts. A distinction was made between *aḥbās* and *awḳāf*. The latter included the *awḳāf ḥukmiyya* and the *awḳāf ahliyya*, whereas the *aḥbās* consisted of the *rizaḳ aḥbāsiyya*. The *awḳāf ḥukmiyya* were supervised by the S̲h̲āfiʿī chief *ḳāḍī* and included urban buildings in al-Ḳāhira and al-Fusṭāṭ (Miṣr) whose revenue served purely philanthropic functions such as the support of the Holy Cities and the poor and the payment of ransoms for Muslim prisoners of war. The *awḳāf ahliyya* included the great foundations of sultans and *amīr*s, such as *madrasa*s, *k̲h̲ānaḳāh*s, *kuttāb*s and funerary complexes; they were supported by urban and agricultural estates, both in Egypt and Syria, and their revenue was to serve combined charitable and private purposes by sustaining a religious institution and securing an income to the founder and his clan.

The *rizḳa* (meaning income) according to al-Nābulusī, Ibn Duḳmāḳ and Ibn al-D̲j̲īʿān, is a special kind of endowment based on the alienation of treasury land for the benefit of individuals, rather than institutions, for providing specific services. This system seems to have originated in the late Ayyūbid period (Michel, 108). The *rizaḳ aḥbāsiyya* established under the Mamlūks had as their main purpose the provision of services to the rural areas. Individuals were directly endowed with agricultural land which provided them with an income, often coupled with the condition that they maintain or serve some religious or philanthropic institution in the villages. The *rizaḳ* provided for the salaries of the religious personnel of the mosques and *zāwiya*s, for craftsmen and employees, such as the guardians of fields and villages, and building craftsmen. They also provided funds for the purchase of agricultural tools. These services included Christian villages as well (Halm, 52-3; Michel, 111-12). The supervision of the *rizaḳ* came within the Great *Dawādār*'s sphere of competence. N. Michel sees the *rizḳa* as a local Egyptian, non-religious institution, which originally was not ruled by religious law and was thus distinct from *wakf*. Over the course of time, however, the *rizaḳ aḥbāsiyya* were mistaken for *wakf* and acquired their legal status as irrevocable and exempted of taxes (Michel, 114).

Al-Ḳalḳas̲h̲andī writes that the *naẓar al-aḥbās al-mabrūra*, i.e. the general supervision of the pious endowments in the early 15th century, was either in the hands of the Sultan himself or delegated to his deputy or to the Great *Dawādār*, mostly to the latter. In the Baḥrī Mamlūk period, however, the supervision of the great pious *wakf*s was assumed either by an *amīr* or by the S̲h̲āfiʿī *ḳāḍī 'l-ḳuḍāt*.

Notwithstanding the role of a central *wakf* administration, the Mamlūk *ḳāḍī* was involved with *awḳāf* at the court level, where every *wakfiyya* had to be registered in several copies, of which one remained in the *ḳāḍī*'s archives.

From the outset, the Mamlūk sultans made full use of *wakf* possibilities. Their religious foundations were often part of ambitious urban projects which are still visible in the present Old City of Cairo. For their endowments, they allocated far more investments (land or commercial structures) than necessary for the upkeep of the religious foundation in order to produce a substantial surplus for themselves and their descendants. Such measures became necessary under the *iḳṭāʿ* system, which in principle gave the *amīr*s and state servants only a life-time usufruct of the land or other assets, excluding inheritance, not to mention confiscations and extortions ordered by the sultans. As a result of the large-scale use of *wakf*, it became a source of income not only for the religious and teaching establishments but also for an important number of administrators and other employees.

The main beneficiaries of Mamlūk *awḳāf* were, in addition to the founders and the religious and educational foundations of all types, the water supply, hospitals, the Holy Cities (including Hebron and Jerusalem), and various services related to the Pilgrimage and its infrastructure, including the *kiswa* for the Kaʿba. There were also public kitchens, like the ones sponsored by Sultan Barḳūḳ in Hebron and by Ḳāʾitbāy in Mecca and Medina. In times of plague, washing and burying the dead and providing coffins and shrouds were also provided for by pious endowments. Ḳāʾitbāy included in his endowment for the Holy Cities two ships to carry wheat from Egypt. Military institutions such as the arsenal (*k̲h̲izānat al-silāḥ*) and fortifications might also be maintained by *wakf* in the Mamlūk period.

At this time, all kinds of movable objects or chattels could be alienated, not only books, utensils and furniture for the religious foundations but also slaves or animals. Although discussions about the *wakf* of cash did take place in Mamlūk Egypt, no such *wakf* is so far known prior to the Ottoman era (Amīn, *Awḳāf*, 100). The Mamlūk élite also made use of the family *wakf*s, i.e. those whose beneficiaries were the family and the clan. Sultan al-Nāṣir Muḥammad remunerated his *amīr*s by making family *wakf*s for them and their descendants. In his own family endowment deed, he stipulated explicitly that his daughters should get the same share as his sons, thus circumventing the inheritance law (M. Amīn, appendix to Ibn Ḥabīb, ii, 378).

Some family *wakf*s included a simultaneous charitable share, consisting of donations to religious foundations, sometimes tied to specific services, such as to increase the number of students or raise the salaries, to add a fountain or buy candles, etc. The Azhar mosque and the hospital of Ḳalāwūn were among the institutions that, over the centuries, regularly acquired such endowments both in the Mamlūk and Ottoman periods.

The Mamlūk chroniclers repeatedly criticised *wakf* abuses by the ruling establishment. A device used by sultans and *amīr*s to acquire *wakf* property was simply to invalidate the *wakf* on legal grounds, either justifiably or not. The most famous case of *wakf* confiscation in the Mamlūk period was that of D̲j̲amāl al-Dīn al-Ustādār (al-Maḳrīzī, *K̲h̲iṭaṭ*, ii, 70-1). Sultan Barsbāy, who demolished *wakf* shops to build his own *madrasa* in their place, is reported to have made a fair offer to the tenants without pressurising them (idem, *Sulūk*, iv/2, 636-7; *K̲h̲iṭaṭ*, ii, 330). The *wakf* properties accumulated over generations represented a significant share of Egypt's resources and at the same time a great temptation to the rulers. Whenever the Mamlūk state was in need of liquid funds, especially in times of war or other crises, the tapping of the *wakf* resources was inevitable.

The urban *mawḳūfāt* in the Mamlūk and Ottoman periods included apartment houses (*rabʿ*), commercial buildings of various types (*ḳayṣāriyya, wakāla, funduḳ, k̲h̲ān*), shops, food stalls (*masmaṭ*), factories (sugar, soap, starch, glass, textiles, tanneries, etc.), ovens for hatching chickens, mills, bakeries, oil presses and baths. In the Ottoman period, the coffee-house became one of the most lucrative *wakf* investments.

The *awḳāf* were a major concern for the Ottoman conquerors of Egypt and one of the first issues which Selīm I [*q.v.*] tackled once he entered Cairo. According to legend, Selīm decided to conquer Egypt after having tested the Egyptian *ʿulamāʾ* and finding them corrupt enough to authorise the liquidation of the Azhar endowments for a good bargain. A decree dated Rabīʿ II 923/May 1517, i.e. the year of the Ottoman conquest, affirms, however, Selīm's intention to respect the pious endowments established by the Mamlūks (ʿAfīfī, *Awḳāf* 256-7). In 928/1522 a *nāẓir al-awḳāf* was appointed from Istanbul to control the *waḳf*s of Egypt and to reform the religious institutions so that they included Turkish scholars and Ṣūfīs. According to the *Ḳānun-nāme* of Süleymān the Magnificent, the *waḳf*s of the Mamlūk sultans were to be inspected by the *daftardār* and controlled by the authorities in Istanbul. Later, this office was replaced by the *nāẓir al-nuẓẓār*, who was appointed from the governor's entourage. The *awḳāf* of the *Ḥaramayn* came similarly under Ottoman control. The supervision of the great pious *waḳf*s, however, remained on the whole in the hands of local *amīr*s and beys. Those of the Holy Cities were sometimes controlled by Ottoman *agha*s of the Dār al-Saʿāda in Istanbul. Also, *awḳāf* were now no longer exempt from taxes, as had been the case in the Mamlūk period.

Owing to the continuous sale of treasury land in the Mamlūk period, the Ottomans found that almost half of Egypt's agricultural land had been alienated as *waḳf*. They abolished the *iḳṭāʿ* system, ordered a new cadaster, dissolved the *dīwān al-aḥbās* and investigated existing *waḳf*s in order to cancel all those of dubious origins or which were lacking proper documents. These measures helped them increase considerably the treasury land.

Giving supremacy to the Ḥanafī *madhhab*, the Ottomans stressed the distinction between *waḳf* and *irṣād*, a distinction that not had much relevance under the Mamlūks because of the prevalence of the Shāfiʿī *madhhab* at that time (K. Cuno, *Irṣād*). The alienation of treasury land under the Ottomans needed therefore to be authorised by the sultan or his governor (Nahal, 69). Due to the resistance of the *ʿulamāʾ*, however, the Ottomans were cautious when dealing with pious endowments inherited from their predecessors, which they preferred to maintain as long as they fulfilled philanthropic purposes. Thus *rizaḳ aḥbāsiyya* were also investigated but largely tolerated, even when their origin was suspect, as long as they secured an income for the needy. They were called *waḳf irṣādī* or simply *irṣād* (Michel; Cuno).

The separation of military and judicial powers by the Ottomans limited the encroachments of the ruling establishment in *waḳf* issues. The Ottoman *ḳāḍī* was independent of the *wālī* and had a greater administrative authority than his Mamlūk predecessor, including also some of the *muḥtasib*s' competence. He was expected to appoint or dismiss the *nāẓir*s, to examine their reports, to control rural and urban *waḳf* employees, to check that the stipulations were followed and the beneficiaries' interest secured, and also to implement regulations pertaining to the neighbourhood. Because of the importance of the *waḳf*s' resources, however, the Ottoman governors of Egypt nevertheless did interfere in *waḳf* matters, as on the occasion when the supervisors of all great *waḳf*s were compelled to purchase quantities of copper in order to get rid of a surplus sent from Istanbul.

The Ottoman governors of the 10th/16th and the 11th/17th centuries created important charitable *waḳf*s in Egypt, some of which also included a private share for the founder. Their *awḳāf* involved the foundation of new religious institutions mostly favouring the Ḥanafī *madhhab*; but most of all they endowed, upgraded and often transformed existing ones. Special attention was devoted to saints' tombs and shrines. Al-Azhar's prestige as a teaching institution increased during this period. The governors' *waḳf*s included an important number of commercial buildings of the *wakāla* type, built in the port cities and in Būlāḳ, Cairo's port, to facilitate the transport of goods to Istanbul and to provide at the same time funds for philanthropic works. The Pilgrimage infrastructure and its caravan benefited. Sultan Djaḳmaḳ and Ḳāʾitbāy's endowments for the Holy Cities (*dashīsha kubrā*) were enlarged by Selīm I and Süleymān the Magnificent; Murād III made a new endowment called the *dashīsha ṣughrā*, and Meḥemmed IV's wife also alienated agricultural land in Egypt for the Holy Cities. The Ottomans thus supported the *Ḥaramayn* mainly with the *waḳf* revenue of Egyptian land. Following Ḳāʾitbāy's example, Süleymān and Murād III endowed ships for the transportation of wheat from Egypt to Mecca and Medina (Behrens-Abouseif, *Qāytbāy's foundation*, 67). The Ottomans made use of the cash *waḳf*, albeit on a small scale (eadem, *Adjustment*, 217).

The military aristocracy of the Ottoman period became increasingly involved from the 11th/17th century onwards in the creation of large private *waḳf*s in Cairo for the benefit of the founder's own clan or household, which had a great impact on the upgrading and revitalising of their urban neighbourhoods. Notables of the religious establishment and the merchant class also created such endowments, which included the large number of *sabīl-maktab*s built all over Cairo during the Ottoman period. The Black Eunuchs of the Imperial Harem, whose careers often ended in Cairo, also figure among the founders of great private *waḳf*s which included a philanthropic share; that of ʿOthmān Agha in the early 11th/17th century, however, was purely charitable and of particular urban importance for the city of Cairo (Behrens-Abouseif, *Tanneries*).

Shortly after coming to power, Muḥammad ʿAlī abolished the *iltizām* [*q.v.*] or tax-farming system applied by the Ottomans. He also tried to prohibit the creation of new *waḳf*s by a decree of 9 Radjab 1262/3 July 1846, which was never implemented, however, and was even revoked by his successor ʿAbbās I. Following the overthrow of the *mamlūk*s, his son Ibrāhīm, who became the governor of Upper Egypt, confiscated all *waḳf* land there. Muḥammad ʿAlī assumed, moreover, control of the *rizaḳ aḥbāsiyya* all over Egypt, compensating their beneficiaries only partly, but did not interfere with *waḳf* of urban properties. In 1835 he established a general *waḳf* administration which was abandoned three years later, apparently because of the *ʿulamāʾ*'s opposition (Sékaly, 96, 410, 450, 628; Baer, 169). Muḥammad ʿAlī himself did alienate large agricultural estates (23,000 *faddāns*) in a *waḳf* for educational institutions in his hometown of Kavala or Ḳawāla [*q.v.*]. As a result of his confiscations, pious foundations established prior to Muḥammad ʿAlī's reign deteriorated, and primary education provided by the *maktab*s (*kuttāb* [*q.v.*]) was left without income (Baer, 149). The resulting desperate situation of the pious foundations prompted the Khedive Ismāʿīl later to allocate 10,000 *faddān*s for the benefit of mosques that were left without resources; moreover, he made vast endowments for the educational system of Egypt. In the second half of the century, the alienation of agricultural land increased due to the Khedives' and other high officials' endowments. These were similar to those of their Mamlūk and Ottoman predecessors, sc. a combination of a charitable and a family *wakf*, and their importance for education and health care and other philanthropic institutions was great. The Muḥammad ʿAlī family also returned to the Mamlūk tradition, abandoned by the Ottomans, of erecting lavish funerary foundations which were supported by *wakf*.

During the 19th century the great landowners of the Muḥammad ʿAlī family and other notables made extensive use of family endowments with agricultural land in order to regulate inheritance matters and safeguard properties against fragmentation. Paradoxically, the opposite result was achieved. Due to the perpetual nature of the endowment leading to an increasing number of beneficiaries over generations, the property was infinitely split up, as the critics of the family or *ahlī wakf* have always emphasised. The result was that the beneficiaries, left with an insignificant income, lost interest in their *wakfs*, leaving the supervisor free to handle it according to his own interests (Baer, 167).

In 1864 Ismāʿīl ordered that the *wakf* administration established by ʿAbbās I in 1851 should acquire the status of a ministry which would assume greater control over the pious *wakfs*, and he introduced severe punishment for usurpation and abuses. To achieve this, he needed the authorisation of the Porte to act on behalf of the Ottoman Chief *Ḳāḍī*, who continued to be the *de jure* official authority in Egyptian *wakf* matters, including those of the *Ḥaramayn*. In 1884, two years after the British occupation of Egypt, the Khedive Tawfīḳ abolished the *Wakf* Ministry and replaced it by an independent administration under his own direct supervision (Sékaly 111-12; Baer, 171), a measure necessary in order to prevent Christian officials, now in control of the ministries, from dealing with the Muslims' pious endowments and getting involved with *S̲h̲arīʿa* issues. The British, however, did not approve of the way in which the new body functioned, and in 1913 Lord Kitchener re-installed the *Wakf* Ministry with the consent of the Porte, under the condition, however, that it would be allowed to maintain a certain autonomy including the budget. During the late 19th century the Khedive's control of the *awḳāf* was indisputable, assuming the traditional competencies of the Ottoman Chief *Ḳāḍī*, from whom he still needed an authorisation (Sékaly, 109). This went on until World War I when the *de jure* Ottoman authority was finally also abolished.

The problems of abuse of the *wakf* system in Egypt have been virtually the same for all periods of Egypt's pre-modern history. Ever since Ibn Mammātī's comments in the 6th/12th century, the subject of *wakf* abuse was a regular issue in the chronicles and often a major political issue setting rulers against *ʿulamāʾ*. The tremendous accumulation of assets in *wakf* properties made it inevitable that the rulers, whether due to pressing circumstances or simply to greed, would turn to these resources. The success of the *ʿulamāʾ*'s resistance varied. The Mamlūk sultans managed to a great extent to manipulate judges according to their own will; Ottoman ones were more independent.

In order to safeguard his *wakf* against abuses, every *wakf* founder formulated strict stipulations, which often included that no *wakf* property should be rented for more than three years, neither should it be sold or exchanged (*istibdāl*). The stipulations limiting or excluding the trade of *wakf* property did not imply, however, the total blocking of an endowment. A *wakf* could always be enlarged through the addition of new investment estates by the founder himself, his successors or any other person. Sometimes, however, the status of religious foundations changed through such enlargements: a mosque would become a *madrasa*, a *madrasa* for the S̲h̲āfiʿī *mad̲h̲hab* would be enlarged to also include Ḥanafī teaching or Ṣūfī service as well, a mere *masd̲j̲id* might acquire the status of a *d̲j̲āmiʿ*; such transformations, however, did not remain undisputed. Although all important endowments stipulated that the revenue should be spent in the first place on maintaining the premises, over the course of time the alienated estates fell into disrepair, thus becoming less lucrative. The supervisor had no choice but to take rescue initiatives. These included the sale of the dilapidated estate in order to cover the restoration expenses or to acquire other assets instead (*istibdāl*). Such initiatives, which necessarily contradicted the founder's stipulations, had to be authorised by the *ḳāḍī*, who would need an assessment of the estate's dilapidated condition. For this purpose he had to summon a consortium of master-masons, jurists, *wakf* administrators and witnesses. Such assessments, however, were often fabricated, or the building might even be demolished overnight when a powerful person was involved (al-Maḳrīzī, *Sulūk*, ii, 320-1; *K̲h̲iṭaṭ*, ii, 69).

Long-term lease contracts were another solution to the problem of *wakf* decay. This allowed the tenant himself to carry out the necessary repairs and restorations, and to subtract the expenditures gradually from the rent. The long term often implied subrenting the estate and freezing the rent for a long period, while it gave the tenant a proprietor-like status. Sultan Barḳūḳ, who was in need of funds for his army but was not authorised to dissolve his predecessor's *awḳāf*, allowed his *amīr*s to rent *wakf* land on extended terms and exploit it to their profit; they subrented it in order to make a profit from the balance (al-Maḳrīzī, *Sulūk*, iii, 345 ff.).

The *ḥikr* [*q.v.* in Suppl.] was a long-term lease of land only, giving the tenant the right to own and alienate the buildings on it. He could then replace dilapidated *wakf* buildings by new ones and alienate them in a *wakf* of his own. As a result, several *wakfs* could be involved in the same plot. The Mamlūk sultans often participated as share-holders in commercial structures within the city that belonged to older *wakfs*; this offered them lucrative investment opportunities for their own *wakfs*, while they could rescue an old one from total decay. The *k̲h̲uluww* was a device that evolved during the reign of Sultan al-G̲h̲awrī and was vividly discussed among the jurists of the time. It was a form of rent that gave the tenant the right to act like a proprietor, i.e. in selling, bequeathing and alienating his rights in the property (ʿAfīfī, *Asālīb*, 116).

Bibliography: 1. Primary sources (not including documents). Ibn Duḳmāḳ, *K. al-Intiṣār li-ʿiḳd al-amṣār*, Būlāḳ 1314/1896-7; Ibn Mammātī, *K. Ḳawānīn al-dawāwīn*, ed. A.S. Suryāl ʿAṭiyya, Cairo 1943; Maḳrīzī, *K̲h̲iṭaṭ*, Būlāḳ 1270/1853-54; ʿAlī Mubārak, *al-K̲h̲iṭaṭ al-d̲j̲adīda al-tawfīḳiyya*, Būlāḳ 1306/1888; Kindī, *K. al-Wulāt wa-k. al-ḳuḍāt*, ed. R. Guest, London 1912; Ḳalḳas̲h̲andī, *Ṣubḥ*, Cairo 1914-28.

2. General. M.M. Amīn, *Catalogue des documents d'archive du Caire de 239/853 à 922/1516*, Cairo 1981; idem and L.A. Ibrahim, *al-Muṣṭalaḥāt al-miʿmāriyya fī 'l-wat̲h̲āʾiḳ al-mamlūkiyya/Architectural terms in Mamluk documents*, Cairo 1990; G. Baer, *A history of landownership in modern Egypt 1800-1950*, London 1962; J. Escovitz, *The office of Qāḍī al-Quḍāt in Cairo under the Baḥrī Mamlūks*, Berlin 1984; H. Halm, *Ägypten*

nach den mamlukischen Lehenregistern. I. Oberägypten und das Fayyūm, Wiesbaden 1979; G.H. El-Nahal, *The judicial administration of Ottoman Egypt in the 17th century*, Chicago 1979; Ibrāhīm Ghānim al-Bayyūmī, *al-Awḳāf wa 'l-siyāsa fī Miṣr*, Cairo 1998.

3. Studies on the *waḳf* system. M. Abū Zahra, *Muḥāḍarāt fī 'l-waḳf*, Cairo 1972; M. ʿAfīfī, *Asālīb al-intifāʿ al-iḳtiṣādī bi 'l-awḳāf fī Miṣr fi 'l-ʿaṣr al-ʿuthmānī*, in *AI*, xxiv (1988), 103-38; idem, *al-Awḳāf wa 'l-ḥayāt al-iḳtiṣādiyya fi 'l-ʿaṣr al-ʿUthmānī*, Cairo 1991; M.M. Amīn, *al-Awḳāf wa 'l-ḥayāt al-idjtimāʿiyya fī Miṣr 648-923/1250-1517*, Cairo 1980; D. Behrens-Abouseif, *Egypt's adjustment to Ottoman rule. Institution, waqf and architecture in Cairo (16th-17th centuries)*, Leiden 1994; D. Crecelius, *The organization of waqf documents in Cairo*, in *IJMES*, ii (1971), 266-77; idem, *Index of waqfiyyat from the Ottoman period preserved at the Ministry of Awqaf and the Dar al-Watha'iq in Cairo*, Cairo 1992; K.M. Cuno, *Ideology and juridical discourse in Ottoman Egypt. The uses of the concept of* Irṣād, in *ILS*, v/3 (1998), 1-27; Y.M. Delavor, *Le waqf et l'utilité économique de son maintien en Egypte*, Paris 1923; S. Denoix, *Pour une exploitation d'ensemble d'un corpus: les waqfs mamelouks du Caire*, in R. Deguilhem (ed.), *Les waḳfs dans l'espace islamique, outil de pouvoir socio-politique*, Damascus 1995, 29-44; L. Fernandes, *Notes on a new source for the study of religious architecture during the Mamluk period. The Waqfīya*, in *Al-Abḥāth*, xxxiii (1985), 3-12; ʿA. Ibrāhīm, *Silsilat al-dirāsāt al-wathāʾiḳiyya. I. al-Wathāʾiḳ fī khidmat al-āthār*, in *K. al-Muʾtamar al-thānī li-āthār al-bilād al-ʿarabiyya*, Cairo 1959, 205-87; M. Ḳadrī, *Ḳānūn al-ʿadl wa 'l-inṣāf li 'l-ḳaḍāʾ ʿalā mushkilat al-awḳāf*, Cairo 1928; N. Michel, *Les rizaq aḥbāsiyya. Terres agricoles en mainmorte dans l'Egypte mamelouke et ottomane, étude sur les Dafātir al-Aḥbās ottomans*, in *AI*, xxx (1996), 105-98; C.F. Petry, *A Geniza for Mamluk studies? Charitable trust (waqf) documents as a source of economic and social history*, in *Mamluk Studies Review*, ii (1998), 51-60; H. Rabie, *Some financial aspects of the waqf system in medieval Egypt*, in *al-Madjalla al-Taʾrīkhiyya al-Miṣriyya*, xviii (1971), 1-24; I. Salāma, *Ālāf al-fadādīn al-mawḳūfa ʿalā 'l-taʿlīm*, in *al-Miṣrī*, 9 August 1952; A. Sékaly, *Le problème des waqfs en Egypte*, Paris 1929, repr. from *REI* (1929).

4. Editions of *waḳf* texts and studies, including *waḳf* excerpts. M.M. Amīn, *Wathāʾiḳ waḳf al-sulṭān Ḥasan b. Muḥammad b. Ḳalāwūn ʿalā maṣāliḥ al-ḳubba wa 'l-masdjid wa 'l-madāris*, Cairo 1986, also as appendix in his ed. of al-Ḥasan b. Ḥabīb, *Tadhkirat al-nabīh fī ayyām al-Manṣūr wa-banīh*, iii, Cairo 1986, 341-450; idem, *Wathāʾiḳ waḳf al-sulṭān al-Nāṣir Muḥammad b. Ḳalāwūn*, as appendix in his ed. of al-Ḥasan b. Ḥabīb, *Tadhkirat al-nabīh*, ii, Cairo 1982, 231-448; idem, *Wathāʾiḳ min ʿaṣr salāṭīn al-mamālīk*, Cairo 1982; idem, *Wathāʾiḳ waḳf al-sulṭān Ḳalāwūn ʿalā 'l-bīmāristān al-manṣūrī*, in his ed. of al-Ḥasan b. Ḥabīb, *Tadhkirat al-nabīh*, i, Cairo 1976, 295-396; idem, *Un acte de fondation de waqf par une chrétienne*, in *JESHO*, xviii/1 (1975), 43-52; Cl. Cahen, Y. Rāgib and A. Taher, *L'achat et le waqf d'un grand domaine égyptien par le vizir fatimide Ṭalāʾiʿ b. Ruzzīk*, in *AI*, xiv (1982), 59-126; D. Crecelius, *The Waqfiyyah of Muhammad Bey Abu al-Dhahab I*, in *JARCE*, xv (1978), 125-46; A. Darrag, *L'acte de waqf de Barsbay*, Cairo 1963; U. Haarmann, *Mamluk endowment deeds as a source for the history of education in late medieval Egypt*, in *Al-Abḥāth*, xxviii (1980), 31-46; C. Hein, *Die Stiftungs- und Kaufurkunde des Amīrs Mitqāl al-Ānūkī*, in M. Meinecke (ed.), *Die Restaurierung der Madrasa des Amīrs Sābiq ad-Dīn Mitqāl al-Ānūkī und die Sanierung des Darb Qirmiz in Kairo*, Mainz 1980, 145-74; ʿA. Ibrāhīm, *Naṣṣān[i] djadīdān[i] min wathāʾiḳ al-amīr Ṣarghitmish*, in *Madjallat Kulliyyat al-Ādāb (al-Ḳāhira)* (= *MKAḲ*), xxvii (1969), 143-210; idem, *Min al-wathāʾiḳ al-ʿarabiyya fi 'l-ʿuṣūr al-wusṭā, wathīḳat istibdāl*, in *MKAḲ*, xxv (1963) 1-38; idem, *al-Maktaba al-mamlūkiyya*, Cairo 1962; idem, *Wathīḳat waḳf Masrūr b. ʿAbd Allāh al-Shiblī*, in *MKAḲ*, xxi/2 (1959), 133-73; idem, *Wathīḳat al-amīr Ḳarāḳadjā al-Ḥasanī*, in *MKAḲ*, xviii/2 (1956), 183-251; ʿI.B.M. Abū Ghāzī (ed.), *Wathāʾiḳ al-sulṭān al-Ashraf Ṭūmānbāy: dirāsa wa-taḥḳīḳ li-baʿḍ wathāʾiḳ al-waḳf wa 'l-bayʿ wa 'l-istibdāl*, Cairo 1978; ʿA.M. al-Imām, *al-Āthār wa 'l-amlāk al-miʿmāriyya li-ʿAbd al-Bāḳī al-Djurbadjī bi-Madīnat al-Iskandariyya*, Cairo 1993; idem, *Masdjid Ibrāhīm Tarbāna bi 'l-Iskandariyya (1097/1685)—dirāsa athariyya wathāʾiḳiyya*, in *Madjallat Kulliyyat al-Ādāb* (*Sūhādj*), xvi (1994), 276-564; A.M. El-Masry, *Die Bauten von Ḫādim Sulaimān Pascha (1468-1548) nach seinen Urkunden im Ministerium für Fromme Stiftungen*, Berlin 1991; R.S.R. al-Ḳaḥṭānī, *Awḳāf al-Sulṭān al-Ashraf Shaʿbān ʿalā 'l-Ḥaramayn*, Riyāḍ 1994; L.A. Mayer, *The buildings of Qaytbay as described in the endowment deed*, London 1938; A. Moberg, *Zwei ägyptische Waqf-Urkunden aus dem Jahre 691/1292*, in *MO*, xii (1918), 1-64; S.L. Mustafa, *Schule, Mausoleum und Kloster des Farağ ibn Barqūq in Kairo*, Glückstadt 1982; idem, *Die Moschee des Farağ ibn Barqūq in Kairo*, Glückstadt 1972; M. Salati, *Un documento di epoca mamelucca sul waqf di ʿIzz al-Din Abu 'l-Makarim Hamza b. Zuhra al-Husayni al-Ishaqi al-Halabi (ca. 707/1307)*, in *Annali di Ca' Foscari*, xxx/3 (1994); A.A. al-ʿUmarī, *Dirāsāt fī wathāʾiḳ Dāwūd Bāshā wālī Miṣr*, Cairo n.d.; A.M. ʿUthmān, *Wathīḳat waḳf Djamāl al-Dīn al-Ustādār*, Cairo 1983; R. Veselý, *An Arabic diplomatic document from Egypt. The endowment deed of Maḥmūd Pasha dated 974/1567*, Prague 1971; idem, *Trois certificats délivrés pour les fondations pieuses en Egypte au XVIe siècle*, in *Oriens*, xxi-xxii (1968-9), 248-99; G. Winkelhane and K. Schwarz, *Der Osmanische Statthalter Iskender Pascha (gest. 1571) und seine Stiftungen in Ägypten und am Bosphorus*, Bamberg 1985.

5. Case studies of *waḳf*. M. ʿAfīfī, *al-Awḳāf wa 'l-milāḥa 'l-baḥriyya fi 'l-baḥr al-aḥmar fi 'l-ʿaṣr al-ʿuthmānī*, in R. Deguilhem (ed.), *Les waqfs dans l'espace islamique, outil de pouvoir socio-politique*, Damascus 1995, 87-100; D. Behrens-Abouseif, *Qāytbāy's investments in the city of Cairo. Waqf and power*, in *AI*, xxxii (1998), 1-12; eadem, *An industrial complex in Ottoman Cairo. The tanneries of Bab al-Luq*, in D. Crecelius (ed.), *Dirāsāt fī taʾrīkh Miṣr al-iḳtiṣādī wa 'l-idjtimāʿī fi 'l-ʿaṣr al-ʿuthmānī*, Cairo 1996, 1-8; eadem, *The waqf of a Cairene notable in early Ottoman Cairo. Muhibb al-Dīn Abū al-Ṭayyib, son of a physician*, in Deguilhem (ed.), *Les waqfs*, 123-32; eadem, *Sultan Qāytbāy's foundation in Medina, the* Madrasah, *the* Ribāṭ *and the* Dashīshah, in *Mamluk Studies Review*, ii (1998), 61-72; eadem, *The Takiyyat Ibrahim al-Kulshani in Cairo*, in *Muqarnas*, v (1988), 43-60; Crecelius, *The waqf of Muhammad Bey Abu al-Dhahab in historical perspective*, in *IJMES*, xxiii (1991), 89-102; idem, *Incidences of waqf in three courts of Cairo (1640-1802)*, in *JESHO*, xxix (1986), 176-89; idem, *Ḥawliyyāt awḳāf Dumyāṭ fī awākhir al-ḳarn al-thāmin ʿashar*, in *MKAḲ* (special issue), lvii (February 1993), 151-77; L. Fernandes, *The foundation of Baybars al-Jashankir. Its waqf, history and architecture*, in *Muqarnas*, iv (1987); eadem, *The evolution of a Sufi institution in Mamluk Egypt. The khanqah*, Berlin 1988; eadem, *Mamluk politics and education. The evidence of two fourteenth century waqfiyyas*, in *AI*, xxiii (1987), 87-98; J.C. Garcin and M.A. Taher, *Un*

ensemble de waqfs du IX/XVe siècle en Egypte. Les actes de Jawhar al-Lālā, in R. Curiel and R. Gyselen (eds.), *Itinéraires d'Orient. Hommages à Claude Cahen*, Bures-Sur-Yvette 1994, 309-24; Garcin and Taher, *Les waqfs d'une madrasa au Caire au XVe siècle. Les propriétés urbaines de Ğawhar al-Lālā*, in Deguilhem (ed.), *Les waqfs*, 151-86; eidem, *Enquête sur le financement d'un waqf égyptien. Les comptes de Jawhar al-Lālā*, in *JESHO*, xxxviii/3 (1995), 262-305; A. Raymond, *Les grands waqfs et l'organisation urbaine à Alep et au Caire à l'epoque ottomane (XVIe-XVIIe siècle)*, in *BÉt.Or.*, xxxi (1979), 113-28; Veselý, *De la situation des esclaves dans l'institution du waqf*, in *ArO*, xxxii (1964), 345-53; J. Williams, *The Khanqah of Siryaqus. A Mamluk royal religious foundation*, in A.H. Green (ed.), *In quest of an Islamic humanism. Arabic and Islamic studies in memory of Mohamed al-Nowaihi*, Cairo 1986, 109-22; M. Zakarya, *Deux palais du Caire médiéval. Waqf et architecture*, Paris 1983.

(Doris Behrens-Abouseif)

2. In Syria [see Suppl.].

3. In North Africa to 1914.

i. *Public endowments.* The Marīnid [*q.v.*] sultans created public endowments (*waḳf k͟hayrī*) for mosques, *zāwiya*s, hospitals and, especially, *madrasa*s. They built at least six *madrasa*s in the period between 721/1321 and 756/1356, designating revenue-producing properties as endowments to pay the salaries of teachers and the expenses of students. These assets included stores (*ḥānūt*s) used for commerce and crafts, houses, apartments, stables, public baths, mills, orchards, public ovens, inns, halls, factories for weaving and soap-making, and arable land. Marīnid support for *madrasa*s was an aspect of their internal politics. At the beginning of their reign, they sought to check the influence and power of Fāsī notables and religious leaders and to foster a new religious élite that would support their rule. This they accomplished by building *madrasa*s and supporting the religious personnel associated with them. *Waḳf* inscriptions served as an instrument of Marīnid propaganda.

The Marīnids were careful to demonstrate that they owned the assets that they designated as endowments. According to the chroniclers, the sultans purchased the properties that they used to create or support public endowments; surviving *waḳfiyya*s specify that each endowed asset had been purchased from a named owner. However, revenues generated by public endowments were taxed, and proceeds were kept in the Public Treasury, usually located in the central mosque. The sultans apparently considered the funds in the Public Treasury as their private property, which could be used to purchase new properties and to endow them as a *waḳf k͟hayrī*, e.g. for the maintenance of a tomb. Some *muftī*s maintained, however, that endowment assets acquired in this manner had been confiscated and that the endowments were therefore illegal.

Abu 'l-Ḥasan (*r.* 731-49/1331-48) built *madrasa*s in Fez, Meknès, Salé, Tangier, Anfa, Azemmour, Safi, Ag͟hmāt, Marrakesh, and al-ʿUbbād. According to the chronicler Ibn Marzūḳ, the sultan regarded the construction of these *madrasa*s as signs of his respect for religious knowledge and of his personal piety and as a reflection of the glory of his reign. The assets assigned by Abu 'l-Ḥasan for the maintenance of the *madrasa* of the Dār al-Mak͟hzan in Fez (which had been built by his father) may be considered typical: the village of Abū Zayd; the Ḥammām al-Sulṭān in the K͟harrāṭīn quarter; the Ḥammām of Darb al-Ṭawīl; the constructions above the two aforementioned *ḥammām*s; the yearly rent of three large houses; sixteen shops; seven-eighths of the Inn of Darb al-G͟hurabā'; the mill located on the spring of Ḳammīma; a large oven in Fās D͟jadīd together with two shops connected to it and constructions above them; and a shop located outside the *madrasa*.

The Marīnids also endowed books and created public libraries, located in mosques or *madrasa*s. Abū Yūsuf (*r.* 656-85/1258-86) acquired books from al-Andalus and deposited them in the Madrasa al-Ṣaffārīn which he had constructed in 684/1285. The sultans were aware of the needs of the scholars who taught in the *madrasa*s, with whom they consulted before ordering that a manuscript be copied. In 728/1327, Abu 'l-Ḥasan endowed the *K. al-Tamhīd* of Ibn ʿAbd al-Barr and *al-Bayān wa 'l-taḥṣīl* of Ibn Rus͟hd al-D͟jadd [*q.v.* in Suppl.] for the use of *madrasa* students attached to Andalusian mosques. Other endowed books included: al-Ṭabarī, *D͟jāmiʿ al-bayān*; al-Ḳāḍī ʿIyāḍ, *Mas͟hāriḳ al-anwār*; al-Ḳurṭubī, *Tafsīr*, and Ibn al-G͟hallāb, *K. al-Taʿrīf*. In the middle of the 8th/14th century, Abū ʿInān (*r.* 749-59/1348-58) built a library attached to the Ḳarawiyyīn mosque, one room of which was devoted exclusively to copies of the Ḳur'ān. The sultan also nominated a clerk who was responsible for keeping a record of the books as they were put into use, and provided endowment revenues for the maintenance of the library. At the end of the century, Ibn K͟haldūn [*q.v.*] sent a copy of his *K. al-ʿIbar* from Egypt to Fez as a *waḳf* to be deposited in the library of the Ḳarawiyyīn mosque.

The management of *waḳf* resources was a position of great responsibility, to be undertaken only by persons of unquestioned integrity. A supervisor (*nāẓir*), specifically appointed for this task, was entrusted with the administration of these funds under the supervision of the *ḳāḍī*. This office, like others, was often inherited. Improper management of a public endowment caused a major scandal in 8th/14th-century Fez. Abu 'l-Faḍl al-Mazdag͟hī, scion of a distinguished family, served as *k͟haṭīb* of the Ḳarawiyyīn mosque for thirty consecutive years. In consideration of his personal wealth and stature, al-Mazdag͟hī was entrusted with the *waḳf* revenues deposited in the Ḳarawiyyīn. He reportedly invested the money in different economic enterprises, purchasing real estate and hoarding grain, in anticipation of a bad harvest when prices would rise. When it became apparent that he would not be able to return the money, he asked the Sultan Abu 'l-Ḥasan for "three charges of gold". Stung by the discovery that the *k͟haṭīb* had betrayed his confidence and that of the community, the sultan fasted for three consecutive days, after which he consulted with his religious advisers, who recommended that he draw upon his private resources to replace monies lost by private individuals and members of the community. The properties acquired by the *k͟haṭīb* were sold and the revenues were used to replace the lost *waḳf* revenues. Al-Mazdag͟hī was reinstated as *k͟haṭīb*, but died soon thereafter in Fez.

Marīnid endowments had a significant impact on many aspects of urban life and contributed to the urbanisation of Moroccan towns and cities. Public endowments attracted teachers, staff and students to urban centres, thereby increasing the demand for food, shelter, and clothing; the purchase, sale and rental of real estate added capital to the economy. But the heavy reliance on a single sector of the economy, sc. real estate, meant that the daily operation of the endowment system was sensitive to economic fluctuations. It was not difficult for individuals to misuse the system through embezzlement, extortion or theft, and it was therefore necessary for the agents of the legal system to play an active role in the regulation of endowments.

Beginning in the early 11th/17th century, members of the Turkish ruling élite in Algiers created family endowments (see below) in which they designated the poor of Mecca and Medina (*al-Ḥaramayn*) as the ultimate beneficiaries. As the family lines came to an end, these assets accumulated in what came to be known as the *Wakf al-Ḥaramayn*. To facilitate the supervision of these individual endowments, local governors issued orders for the compilation of the "*wakfiyya* of Algiers" sometime between 1101 and 1125/1689-90 and 1713-14; this measure was designed to ensure that the ultimate beneficiaries of the city's many familial endowments would know of their existence. Supervision of the affairs of the *Ḥaramayn* was entrusted to four people, two officers of the Turkish *odjak* in Algiers and two indigenous Algerians. This was part of a new policy designed to instill confidence in the safety of endowment assets and trust in their proper administration, and to promote a political, administrative and economic atmosphere conducive to the creation of additional endowments. During the second half of the 17th century and the first half of the 18th, administrators of the *Ḥaramayn* used surpluses left over after meeting regular expenses to purchase additional assets. Between 1078/1667-8 and 1250/1834, the number of properties controlled by the *Ḥaramayn* increased from 182 to 1,748, an average annual increase of 9.6%. To deal with the problem of old properties that had fallen into ruin, Muslim jurists and judges adopted a flexible approach to the interpretation of *wakf* law, giving their approval to legal instruments that served the material interests of the *wakf*, including perpetual leases (*ʿanā*ʾ; *djalsa*), and exchanges (*muʿāwaḍa*) that made it possible for *wakf* administrators to relinquish one asset and receive another in its place. In most cases, the rental value of the incoming asset was higher than that of the outgoing property. Exchange transactions were used to expand and improve the water system, to establish industrial enterprises, and to build or reconstruct mosques and *zāwiya*s. The new policy facilitated the recycling of urban property and the re-allocation of urban space, thereby contributing to the development of Algiers (see Hoexter, *Endowments*).

ii. *Family endowments*. The specific terms of a family endowment are set out in an endowment deed, a legal instrument drafted with great care in an effort to eliminate any possible ambiguity. In the words of the Fāsī jurist al-Mawāsī (d. 896/1491), "Legal documents are predicated upon the removal of all ambiguities and summary statements . . . even if this causes them to run on at great length" (al-Wansharīsī, *Miʿyār*, vii, 346). Unlike the Ḥanafīs, the Mālikīs do not allow a founder to designate himself or herself as the initial beneficiary. The founder customarily begins by designating the first generation of beneficiaries, usually one or more children, and indicating whether or not males and females are to be treated equally. Next, the founder indicates what happens to the revenues belonging to a beneficiary of the first generation upon his or her death. If that beneficiary leaves a child, his or her share reverts to that child; if the beneficiary dies without a child, his or her share reverts to the surviving beneficiaries of the first generation or their descendants. In this manner, the entitlement of extinct branches reverts to the surviving branches of the lineal descent group.

Referring to the second generation of beneficiaries, the founder generally indicates that the revenues are "for their descendants *and* their descendants' descendants" (emphasis added). Such phrasing was understood by the jurists as signifying that entitlement now applies to anyone who qualifies as either a descendant (*ʿaḳib*) of the founder or a descendant of a descendant; thus two (or more) generations of lineal descendants may qualify as beneficiaries simultaneously. Such an endowment is characterised as being *muʿaḳḳab* ("for a descent group").

A founder who does not want an endowment to become *muʿaḳḳab* must use some particle, word or phrase conventionally understood as signifying that entitlement does not pass from the first to the second generation of beneficiaries (or from the second to the third, etc.) until all members of a given generation have died out. The founder may use the particle *thumma* ("then"), as in the phrase, "then for their descendants", or the phrase one [generation] after the other (*awwal^an fa-awwal^an*)". The revenues in an endowment of this type are distributed exclusively among the members of a single generation. As the members of a single generation of beneficiaries die, the revenues accumulate in the hands of the surviving members of that generation until the longest-lived member eventually controls the entire endowment. Upon his or her death, the revenues are divided *per capita* among the next generation of beneficiaries, whereupon the process begins again.

When a line of beneficiaries dies out completely, the revenues revert to the charitable purpose specified by the founder, usually a mosque or some other religious institution (see below).

ii. (a) *Social practice*. Any family endowment rests upon the presumed charity or piety of its founder, as specified in an endowment created "for the poor among my children and my children's children", or "for the needy of so-and-so's family" (*ibid*., vii, 484), or for the founder's "needy relatives on both his father's and mother's sides" (*ibid*., vii, 478), or for the town's lepers (*ibid*., vii, 186).

By creating an endowment for a pious purpose, the founder hoped to earn a divine reward in the next life, a hope that is expressed in common formulae that appear in testamentary endowments, e.g. the founder indicates that he or she is seeking "the face of God the Almighty and the abundance of His momentous reward". This formula invariably is followed by the citation of Ḳurʾān, XVIII, 30, "Surely We leave not to waste the wage of him who does good works" (al-Wansharīsī, vii, 80).

A family endowment may be created for many reasons: as an act of piety; as a legal fiction to prevent revocation of a sale or to secure property whose ownership is contested; to avoid confiscation; as an act of loving kindness toward a dying husband; etc. Whatever the founder's motive, the endowment serves to keep property intact, to assure the entitlement of beneficiaries for the duration of the object and to regulate the transmission of usufructory rights from one generation to the next. Not only does the institution accord a founder the freedom to make decisions denied him by Islamic inheritance law [see FARĀʾIḌ; MĪRĀTH], but the creation of a family endowment also gives a proprietor a legal means to remove all or part of a patrimony from the effects of that law.

The creation of an endowment for the benefit of one's children and descendants—regarded as a pious act—reduces the quantum of property available as an inheritance for the founder's ascendents, collaterals, and spouse or spouses, thereby limiting its fragmentation through inheritance.

Founders who created an endowment for sons and their lineal descendants to the exclusion of daughters and their descendants frequently stipulated that, if the line of males came to an end, the endowment was to revert to a daughter or her female descendants (*ibid.*, vii, 80, 223). The specification of females as secondary beneficiaries of familial endowments suggests that Muslim society in the Marīnid period was not as rigidly patriarchal as is often asserted. Indeed, the family endowment frequently was used to supplement the rights of females. Family endowments customarily were created for the benefit of the founder's children, male and female (*ibid.*, vii, 9). It is true that a founder more often than not invoked the Ḳur'ānic principle that a son was to receive twice the share of a daughter. But the founder's ability to define a descent strategy made it possible to circumvent this provision if so desired (*ibid.*, vii, 281). The stipulation of equality between males and females could be applied to the founder's grandchildren and subsequent descendants, as, for example, in a deed specifying that the revenues of the endowment were to be divided "equally among [the founder's] male and female children and grandchildren" (*ibid.*, vii, 141).

In a study of 101 disputes relating to family endowments, seventy-five cases were identified in which both a founder and a beneficiary are mentioned. Of these endowments, 75% were created by fathers and mothers on behalf of their children and, less frequently, grandchildren. Fathers outnumber mothers as founders by a ratio of six to one. The remaining 25% of the endowments were created for someone other than the founder's children and lineal descendants (Powers, *The Maliki family endowment*, 386-8).

The institution commonly was used by males to support the interests of other males. In the same sample, fathers were three times as likely to create an endowment for sons as for daughters. By contrast, mothers appear to have been more even-handed.

Twelve percent of the endowments created by parents for the benefit of their children specify that the children were minors at the time the endowment was created, suggesting that it was common for a parent to establish a family endowment soon after he or she married and produced offspring. This practice points to a desire on the part of proprietors to make *de facto* arrangements for the ultimate devolution of their property while they were in the prime of life, a phenomenon that required founders to make special provisions for the inclusion of unborn children in the endowment (al-Wans̲h̲arīsī, vii, 223, 229, 269, 442). If a man had two or more wives, his calculations were more complex. Some husbands favoured the offspring of one wife over those of another; others treated sons of co-wives equally (*ibid.*, vii, 278, 281).

Because a testamentary endowment takes effect only upon the founder's death, the founder retains control of his property throughout his lifetime. This advantage is offset by two disadvantages: the endowment is limited to one-third of the estate and it may not be made in favour of an heir. The latter restriction entails that a testamentary endowment may not be created for the benefit of a son or daughter, thereby posing a dilemma for the founder who wants to maintain control of his property until he dies, but also wishes to designate one or more children as beneficiary. Because the prohibition on bequests to heirs does not apply to a grandchild whose father is alive, one way to solve the dilemma is to designate a currently living or unborn grandchild as the initial beneficiary. Since a minor grandchild is subject to the authority of its father, the latter would exercise effective control of the endowment revenues. Naming an unborn grandchild or great-grandchild as an endowment beneficiary also gives the founder an opportunity to privilege the offspring of one branch of the family over another (*ibid.*, vii, 311).

When a designated family line becomes extinct, the endowment revenues revert to a public institution. Commonly, a founder specifies that the revenues are to revert to "the Muslim poor" (*ibid.*, vii, 49) or to "the poor and indigent" (*ibid.*, vii, 60). Some made very particular designations, e.g. "the poor and the indigent in Granada and al-Bīra" (*ibid.*, vii, 463), or "the poor and indigent who reside in the mausoleum of S̲h̲ayk̲h̲ Abu 'l-ʿAbbās al-Sabtī" (*ibid.*, vii, 343), or "lepers" (*ibid.*, vii, 186). One founder stipulated that upon the extinction of the designated line, the revenues were to be used to support students, ransom captives and to manumit slaves (*ibid.*, vii, 438).

The most common way to insure the perpetuity of an endowment was to designate a religious institution such as a mosque, school or Ṣūfī convent—or the personnel associated with such an institution—as the ultimate beneficiary (*ibid.*, vii, 46, 281, 452, 459). In a testamentary endowment created on 5 Rad̲j̲ab 791/30 June 1389, the founder stipulated that when the descendants died out, the revenues were to revert to the D̲j̲āmiʿ al-Ṣābirīn inside the Victory Gate of Fez for the purchase of olive oil and carpets and for the repair of the mosque itself; any surplus revenues were to be used to feed the poor Ṣūfīs and *murābiṭūn* associated with the mosque (*ibid.*, vii, 312). Other founders designated as the ultimate beneficiary "the muezzin in a Friday mosque" (*ibid.*, vii, 202), or "whoever recites [the Ḳur'ān] over the graves of the founder and his relatives" (*ibid.*, vii, 141).

There are no constraints on the size of endowments created *inter vivos*, and we find individuals who designated part or all of their property as a familial endowment (*ibid.*, vii, 80, 432). In the 9th/15th century, the Zayyānid Sultan Abū ʿAbd Allāh Muḥammad designated as an endowment for a religious scholar immovable property that included gardens, lands prepared for sowing and a bath (*ibid.*, vii, 248-9). More commonly, however, a founder would designate a discrete piece of property or a fraction thereof as a familial endowment: residential property such as a room (*bayt*), house (*dār*) or compound (*rabʿ*); non-residential property such as a shop, bakery or mill; agricultural property such as gardens, orchards and olive groves; unspecified village properties; and even entire villages. It was not uncommon for a founder to designate a share of a piece of property as a familial endowment, e.g. half a house, one-fourth of a jointly-held compound, half of an unspecified share in several shops, two-thirds of a well-known strip of land, or one feddan of land (*ibid.*, vii, 45, 49, 75, 202, 226, 423, 446). It is likely that, over the course of time, considerable segments of the urban and rural landscape were being converted from private property into endowment property.

ii. (b) *Disputes.* Unaware of both the gender and number of his or her lineal descendants, the founder of an endowment would formulate a descent strategy designed to regulate its smooth functioning for every possible combination of male and female children and descendants. In an effort to avoid any ambiguity that might upset the subsequent functioning of the endowment, the notary who drafted the deed acted with great care. But even the most carefully drafted deed could not anticipate every potential dispute over control of the endowment. Such disputes typically were of two types: an external challenge to the endowment by persons who did not qualify as beneficiaries; or an internal struggle for control of the revenues among the beneficiaries themselves. A dispute over control of an endowment might arise during the lifetime of the founder, or, more commonly, one or more generations after his or her death (*ibid.*, vii, 261-2, 311-21, 435, 452-3); such disputes might last for several generations (Powers, *Court case*, 229-54).

The tendency for disputes to arise one or more generations after the death of both the founder of the endowment and the witnesses to the deed meant that written records played a critical role in the resolution of disputes. For this reason, an endowment deed was customarily deposited in a family archive for safekeeping, and it would pass from one generation of beneficiaries to the next. In the event of a dispute, the deed, together with other important documents, would be presented to the judicial authorities (al-Wan<u>sh</u>arīsī, vii, 80-2). In one case, a woman produced an endowment deed in an effort to secure her status as a member of the first set of beneficiaries. The deed was torn, and this fact cast doubt on the validity of the endowment. Although the *muftī* to whom the case was referred suspected that someone had tampered with the document, he accepted it as legitimate in its current state; he also warned that whoever had torn the document would suffer disgrace in both this world and the next (*ibid.*, vii, 455). Another strategy of a person who exercised physical possession of an endowment deed was to frustrate the claims of potential beneficiaries by refusing to make the document available. Such behaviour typically manifested itself in connection with the transfer of entitlement from one generation of beneficiaries to the next (*ibid.*, vii, 278-81).

Many *muftī*s refrained from issuing a judicial opinion until they had seen a certified transcription of the original endowment deed (*ibid.*, vii, 29-30, 228-9). On occasion, the *muftī*s complained about the summary nature of the transcription (*ibid.*, vii, 81). It was only when a *muftī* was presented with an accurate transcription of the endowment deed that the interpretative task could begin in earnest. No matter how carefully the notary had formulated the deed, how detailed the descent strategy specified therein, and how long the resulting document, the subsequent pattern of births, deaths and marriages within the family frequently resulted in ambiguous situations that required the intervention of either a judge, or if the case was difficult, a *muftī*. Asked to determine the exact intention (*irāda, ḳaṣd*) of the founder at the time of the endowment's creation, the jurists generally assumed that this intention was accessible in the words preserved in the endowment deed, irrespective of the passage of time or the changed circumstances of the endowment beneficiaries. They treated the founder's words as sacred and immutable, comparing them to God's words as preserved in the Ḳur'ān. One Andalusī jurist wrote:

"The words of the founder are like the words of the Divine Lawgiver. Their sense must be followed with respect to both the unambiguous meaning of the texts (*nuṣūṣ*) and the preponderant meaning of ambiguous texts (*ẓawāhir*)" (*ibid.*, vii, 285). In response to the contention that the revenues of a testamentary endowment created for both currently alive and unborn persons should be frozen until all of the potential beneficiaries had come into existence, the Fāsī jurist al-Maz<u>dj</u>aldī (d. 864/1459-60) said, "This [conclusion] is not required by either the founder's words or his intention" (*ibid.*, vii, 23).

Viewed from the perspective of the nature of the relationship between litigants, endowment disputes fall into three categories:

(1) *Beneficiaries versus the founder's heirs and agnates.* Unlike inheritance law, which imposes compulsory rules for the division of property among a wide group of male and female heirs in a manner that tends to fragment property, endowment law enables a proprietor to allocate usufructory entitlements to specified people in specified amounts, to regulate the transmission of those entitlements from one generation of beneficiaries to the next and to insure the physical and economic integrity of an estate or a piece of property. The wide gap separating these two sets of legal norms, sc., inheritance and endowments, may be illustrated by comparing the group composed of the beneficiaries of a familial endowment with the group composed of the founder's heirs. While most beneficiaries are also heirs, many heirs do not qualify as beneficiaries. A man who establishes an endowment for his children and lineal descendants effectively disinherits his spouse, siblings, cousins, uncles and nephews, to mention just a few. Because they have been disinherited, these "outsiders" have an obvious material interest in challenging the validity of the endowment; a successful challenge will result in the property's redesignation as inheritable property. As heirs, the spouse, siblings and other relatives stand to inherit a fractional share of the estate.

Endowments created from jointly-held property frequently resulted in disputes between the endowment beneficiaries and the founder's other heirs. The relationship between endowment beneficiaries and others could be complicated if the relative amount of endowed and unendowed portions of jointly-held property was unknown, e.g. due to carelessness on the part of the notary who formulated the endowment deed (*ibid.*, vii, 45-6, 49, 72, 432).

(2) *Founders and their children.* As noted, Mālikī jurists do not permit the founder of an *inter vivos* family endowment to serve as the initial beneficiary. This means that the numerous advantages of the endowment system vis-à-vis the inheritance laws are offset by the requirement that the founder immediately relinquish physical control of the property, a requirement that runs counter to the natural human desire to retain effective control of property until one dies. Many proprietors circumvented this obstacle by creating an endowment while their children were either unborn or minors. The law allows a founder who creates an endowment for a minor child to exercise control of the property on behalf of the child; when the child reaches the age of legal majority, the founder is obligated to convey the property (*ḥiyāẓa*) to the young adult. In practice, many founders ignored these regulations, spending the endowment revenues on their own interests and continuing to exercise *de facto* control of the endowment even after a child had reached the age of legal majority. This irregularity exposed the endowment to subsequent challenge and possible nullification (*ibid.*, vii, 202-3).

When the object of an endowment was a house in which the founder resided, the founder was obligated to vacate the premises for one year; failure to observe this rule could result in nullification of the endowment. In practice, many founders ignored the rule. A founder's failure to observe the one-year rule could result in litigation setting parent against child (*ibid.*, vii, 202, 218, 260-2, 426).

(3) *Disputes over transmission of entitlement from the beneficiaries of the first generation to those of the second and subsequent generations.* Questions relating to the timing of economic transfers surface again at the moment when endowment revenues are transferred from the first generation of beneficiaries to the second and subsequent generations. At this stage, three issues appear repeatedly: [a] the determination of whether or not an endowment becomes *muʿaḳḳab* (see above); [b] in the event that it does, the criterion according to which the revenues are to be divided among the qualifying beneficiaries; and [c] the definition of the lineal descent group for which the endowment had been created.

[a] The first issue has important consequences for the division of revenues among the founder's lineal descendants: If an endowment does become *muʿaḳḳab*, the revenues, in theory, are to be divided among all of the founder's living lineal descendants irrespective of their generation; if it does not become *muʿaḳḳab*, the revenues are controlled by the members of the oldest generation. In practice, a younger generation of descendants often contended that the endowment had become *muʿaḳḳab*, while the surviving members of an older generation insisted that it had not. In disputes of this nature, one or more paternal uncles might try to prevent the inclusion of their nephews in the division of the endowment revenues (*ibid.*, vii, 248-57, 486-8).

[b] If it is determined that an endowment does in fact become *muʿaḳḳab*, there remains the determination of the criterion according to which the revenues are to be divided among the qualifying beneficiaries. Some authorities maintained that they should be divided on a *per capita* basis, while others held that the judge should allocate the revenues according to need, as determined by his independent reasoning (*ibid.*, vii, 358). Need was defined by a number of variables, including family size, financial resources and degree of the beneficiary's relationship to the founder (*ibid.*, vii, 88, 358, 396, 462, 478, 484). In their discussions of this issue, the jurists manifest an explicit concern for the notion of equity (*ibid.*, vii, 359).

[c] The third recurring issue relates to the principle of agnation, as reflected in the definition of kinship terms. The term *walad* was defined by Mālik b. Anas as "a man's sons and daughters and his son's children, males to the exclusion of females". An uninterrupted line of Mālikī jurists defined the word *ʿaḳib* as "the descendants of a person who are not separated from him (or her) by a female link" (*ibid.*, vii, 281-5). Thus a female may qualify as a member of an agnatic lineal descent group, but she does not transmit this status to either her sons or daughters. If a man creates a family endowment for his son and the latter's lineal descendants, the principle of agnation will progressively exclude from the resulting lineal descent group both female *and* male cognatic descendants of the founder. These cognates are referred to as "the children of daughters" (*awlād al-banāt*).

We repeatedly find "the children of daughters" seeking inclusion in a lineal descent group established by a founder, and, significantly, a series of *muftī*s interpreted the terms of a particular endowment in such a manner as to validate their claims. This approach to the issue of gender was made possible by the *muftī*s' adoption of a literalist approach to statutory interpretation, as illustrated by a case referred to the Cordovan jurist Ibn Rus̲h̲d (d. 520/1126 [*q.v.*]). A man created an endowment for his two concubines, stipulating that when both had died, the endowment was to revert to his two paternal cousins, Aḥmad and al-Ḥasan, and to "their descendants and their descendants' descendants". The two concubines died; Aḥmad died leaving no descendants; and al-Ḥasan produced at least three generations of lineal descendants, including a grandson whose mother was al-Ḥasan's daughter, and a great-grandson whose mother was al-Ḥasan's agnatic granddaughter (his son's daughter). Although neither of these two persons was agnatically related to al-Ḥasan, both sought inclusion as beneficiaries of the endowment. Ibn Rus̲h̲d ruled that the grandson qualified but that the great-grandson did not. He reasoned that al-Ḥasan's daughter is his agnatic descendant and that her son qualifies as the "descendants' descendant" mentioned in the deed. The great-grandson, on the other hand, did not qualify as a beneficiary because the founder had not specified "the descendant of a descendant's descendant" (al-Wans̲h̲arīsī, vii, 463-4; Powers, *Fatwās*, 313).

iii. *Algeria 1820-1914.* The 19th century was a turning point for Muslim family endowments. Observers of early modern Muslim society have noted the rapid rate at which religious endowments proliferated throughout the Muslim world. By the beginning of the century, one-half of the land in Algeria and one-third in Tunisia had been reportedly transformed into endowment land (Köprülü, *L'Institution du vakouf*, 3). Over the course of the century, the *ʿulamāʾ* came into conflict with Muslim and non-Muslim rulers who wanted to weaken their power and gain access either to the revenues generated by religious endowments or to endowment property itself. In Algeria, the endowment system frustrated French efforts to purchase land on the open market. From Algeria to India, endowments in the 19th century increasingly were viewed as an obstacle to economic welfare and social progress.

Inspired by Western social and economic theories, modern advocates of reform—Muslim and non-Muslim—marshalled economic, moral, religious and legal objections to the *waḳf* system. These objections were directed exclusively at family endowments, which, so the argument ran, were solely responsible for retarding a given nation's social and economic development by sequestering large quantities of its capital resources. Despite the fact that the overwhelming majority of Muslim scholars have always accepted family endowments, advocates of reform now cited the opinions of early Muslim jurists who had opposed the institution, and they asserted that objections to the institution had persisted through the centuries.

To exploit the colony's important agricultural and mineral resources, France settled increasing numbers of its civilians in the Algerian countryside. The settlers clashed almost immediately with the Muslim population over the issue of access to, and control of, land. It was essential that the government should facilitate the colonists' acquisition of land and assure them of their rights. To this end, the French endeavoured to elaborate a new system of property law that favoured the colonists.

In the period immediately following the occupation of Algiers, Muslims sold large amounts of *habous* property to Europeans, who were ignorant of the fact that such property was inalienable. Other Muslims, presumably the endowment beneficiaries, subsequently entered claims to the property on the strength of endowment deeds in their possession. These litigations created considerable turmoil (Mercier, *Code*, 90). Although the French ceased to be duped as they grew more familiar with the system of endowments, the *habous* system continued to remove large amounts of land from the free market, thereby posing a serious, ongoing obstacle to "economic progress".

Initially, the French tried to mitigate the effects of *habous* by legislative means. The Ordinance of 1 October 1844 declared the sale of endowment property by Muslim beneficiaries to European settlers to be legally binding (*ibid.*, 90-1). According to Article Three of this ordinance, "No conveyance of immovable property agreed upon by a native in favour of a European may be contested [merely] on the ground that immovables are inalienable according to Muslim law" (Sautayra and Cherbonneau, *Droit musulman*, ii, 414). This provision was extended, by the Decree of 30 October 1858, to sales between natives. Now, "the provisions of Article Three of the Ordinance of 1 October 1844 . . . will apply to past and future transactions between a Muslim and a Muslim, and between a Muslim and a Jew" (*ibid.*). To the chagrin of the French, most Muslims ignored this legislative decree and refused to sell endowment land.

French settlers pressured their leaders to create better conditions for European entry into the Algerian land market. In response, the French government enacted a legislative decree on 26 July 1873 that was intended to resolve the land problem by declaring that all land in Algeria was henceforth subject to French law. Known as the *Loi Warnier*, the decree stated that "the establishment of immovable property in Algeria, its conservation, and the contractual transmission of immovables and property rights, irrespective of the [legal status] of the proprietor, will henceforth be subject to French law". Article Seven of this decree left Muslims subject to their own laws in matters of personal status and inheritance—a provision that was to be of critical importance (*ibid.*, i, i).

Like its predecessors, the *Loi Warnier* proved inadequate, in part because the divisions and categories of French law do not correspond exactly with those of Islamic law. Most French jurists maintained that family endowments were subject to the law of property, while Muslims viewed them as subject to the law of succession (Henry and Balique, *La doctrine coloniale*, 15-6). French jurists soon became embroiled in a controversy over the proper interpretation of the *Loi Warnier*. One group held that the law abolished religious endowments, basing its argument on Article One, para. 2, which states, "All property rights (*droits réels*) . . . based upon Muslim law that are contrary to French law are hereby abolished". These jurists reasoned that an endowment was a property right, that it was contrary to French law, that it was included within the scope of Article One, and that it had therefore been abolished. Other French jurists came to the opposite conclusion. They referred to Article Seven of the law, which not only states that nothing had been derogated from the Muslim law of inheritance but also makes no distinction between successions regulated by the law of inheritance and those regulated by family endowments. This latter group reasoned that family endowments, which would permit a person to transmit property to the next generation according to his or her own wishes, constituted a special case (*ordre spéciale*) of inheritance. Therefore, they insisted, the legal status of family endowments should be determined, not by Article One of the *Loi Warnier*, but by Article Seven. Their view was validated by the Court of Algiers in a decree issued on 23 March 1874. Accordingly, family endowments remained within the jurisdiction of the Muslim courts (Sautayra and Cherbonneau, *Droit musulman*, ii, 413-4).

French jurists understood the economic and political interests of colonialism, and many served those interests, consciously or unconsciously, by advocating changes that facilitated the new system of land tenure. Specifically, they argued against the aforementioned view confirmed by the Court of Algiers on 23 March 1874. Between 1885 and 1904, E. Zeys, E. Mercier, and M. Morand published a series of studies of *habous* that collectively developed the following three-fold argument: (1) historically, public endowments antedated family endowments; (2) family endowments deviated from the pious and humanitarian goals of public endowments and thus were, from an Islamic perspective, not only immoral but also illegal; and (3) family endowments and inheritance were mutually exclusive and incompatible institutions. French colonial scholarship, virulent in its opposition to family endowments (see especially Zeys, *Traité élémentaire*, ii, 185-6; Mercier, *Code*, 14, 27, 43-5, 129-34; Morand, *Etudes*, 226, 228-30, 233, 249-50, 264-6; for other French studies of *habous* published between 1886 and 1904, see Henry and Balique, *La Doctrine coloniale*, 118-21), prevailed in much of the Western scholarly literature during the course of the 20th century, resulting in a serious misunderstanding of both Islamic legal history and the social dynamics of Muslim societies (see *EI*[1] art. *Waḳf*).

Bibliographie: 1. Sources. K͟halīl b. Isḥāḳ, *Muk͟htaṣar*, Paris 1900; Abu 'l-Ḥasan ʿAlī al-D̲j̲aznāʾī, *Ẓahrat al-ās (la fleur du myrte) traitant de la fondation de la ville de Fès*, ed. and tr. A. Bel, Algiers 1923; Muḥammad b. Muḥammad al-Ṭarābulusī al-Mag͟hribī, known as al-Ḥaṭṭāb, *Mawāhib al-d̲j̲alīl li-s͟harḥ muk͟htaṣar al-K͟halīl*, [Libya] 1969; Muḥammad b. Aḥmad Ibn Marzūḳ, *al-Musnad al-Ṣaḥīḥ al-ḥasan fī maʾāt͟hir wa-maḥāsin mawlānā Abi 'l-Ḥasan*, ed. M.J. Viguera, Algiers 1981, Spanish tr. eadem, *El Musnad: hechos memorables de Abū l-Ḥasan, sultan de los Benimerines*, Madrid 1977; Abu 'l-ʿAbbās Aḥmad al-Wans͟harīsī, *al-Miʿyār al-mug͟hrib wa 'l-d̲j̲āmiʿ al-muʿrib ʿan fatāwā ahl Ifrīkiya wa 'l-Andalus wa 'l-Mag͟hrib*, 13 vols., Rabat 1981-3; Abū ʿAbd Allāh Muḥammad al-Anṣārī, known as al-Raṣṣāʿ al-Tūnisī, *S͟harḥ ḥudūd al-Imām al-akbar . . . Abī ʿAbd Allāh b. ʿArafa*, [Morocco] 1412/1992.

2. Studies. E. Sautayra and E. Cherbonneau, *Droit musulman: du statut personnel et des successions*, 2 vols. Paris 1873-4; E. Zeys, *Traité élémentaire de droit musulman algérien*, 2 vols. Algiers 1885-6; E. Mercier, *Le code du hobous ou ouakf selon la législation musulmane*, Constantine 1899; M. Morand, *Etude sur la nature juridique du habous*, in *Revue Algérienne*, xx (1904), 85-93, 127-54; repr. in *Etudes de droit musulman algérien*, Algiers 1919, 210-66; A. Bel, *Inscriptions arabes de Fès*, in *JA* (mars-avril 1917), 303-29; (juillet-août), 81-170; (septembre-octobre), 215-67; (juillet-août 1918), 189-276; (novembre-décembre), 237-399; (janvier-fevrier 1919), 5-87; O. Pesle, *La théorie et la pratique des habous dans le rite malékite*, Casablanca 1941; F. Köprülü, *L'Institution du vakouf. Sa nature juridique et son évolution historique*, in *Vakıflar Dergisi*, ii/3 (1942); E. Tyan, *Le Notariat et le régime de la preuve par écrit dans la pratique du droit musulman*, Beirut 1959; J. Schacht, *Sur quelques manuscrits de la bibliothèque d'al-Qarawiyyin*, in *Etudes d'orientalisme dédiés à la mémoire de E. Lévi-Provençal*, Paris 1962, i, 271-84; M. del Carmen Villanueva Rico, *Casas, mezquitas y tiendas de los habices de las iglesias de Granada*, Madrid 1966; C.-R. Ageron, *Les Algériens musulmans et la France: 1871-1919*, 2 vols. Paris 1968; J. Wakin, *The function of documents in Islamic law*, Albany 1972; M. Shatzmiller, *Un texte relatif aux structures politiques*

mérinides. Le cas du Ḫaṭīb Abū 'l-Faḍl al-Mazdaġī (746/1345), in *REI* (1977), 310-19; eadem, *Wakf khayri in fourteenth-century Fez. Legal, social and economic aspects*, in *Anaquel de estudios arabes*, ii (1991), 193-217; J.-R. Henry and F. Balique, *La doctrine coloniale du droit musulman algérien. Bibliographie systématique et introduction critique*, Paris 1979; A. Layish, *The Mālikī family waqf according to wills and waqfiyyāt*, in *BSOAS*, xlvi (1983), 1-32; S. Ferchiou, *Le système habus en Tunisie: logique de transmission et idéologie agnatique*, in *Hériter en pays musulman*, ed. M. Gast, Paris 1987, 57-74; Omar Benmira, *al-Nawāzil wa 'l-mudjtamaʿ: al-bādiya al-maghribiyya fī ta'rīkh al-Maghrib al-wasīṭ, al-ḳarnān al-rābiʿ ʿashar wa 'l-khāmis ʿashar*, Ph.D. diss. Muḥammad V University, Rabat 1989, unpubl.; D.S. Powers, *Orientalism, colonialism, and legal history. The attack on Muslim family endowments in Algeria and India*, in *Comparative Studies in Society and History*, xxxi (1989), 535-71; idem, *A court case from fourteenth century North Africa*, in *JAOS*, cx (1990), 229-54; idem, *Fatwās as sources for legal and social history. A dispute over endowment revenues from fourteenth-century Fez*, in *al-Qanṭara*, xi (1990), 295-341; idem, *The Maliki family endowment, legal norms and social practices*, in *IJMES*, xxv (1993), 379-406; Y. Reiter, *Islamic endowments in Jerusalem under British Mandate*, London 1996; M. Hoexter, *Endowments, rulers and community. Waqf al-Haramayn in Ottoman Algiers*, Leiden 1998. (D.S. Powers)

4. In Muslim Spain.

The term *waḳf* is generally replaced in al-Andalus by *ḥubus* or *ḥubs* (pl. *aḥbās*). The root *ḥ-b-s* as used in this sense appears in one of the *ḥadīth*s which is cited to trace the institution back to the Prophet: *ḥabbis aṣlahā wa-sabbil thamaratahā*. The Spanish Arabism *habiz* is assumed to have been derived from *aḥbās* pronounced with a variation in timbre (*imāla*), i.e. *aḥbīs*, and not from the word *ḥabīs*. The oldest Arabic texts use this term to denote property intended for charitable use and converted into a non-transferable right, but it is one which is not recognised in the Andalusī juridical texts concerning mortmain.

Matters concerning this institution occupy numerous pages of Andalusī works of *fiḳh* (see *Bibl.*), and these describe *taḥbīs* as the process by means of which during his lifetime the founder (*muḥabbis*) renounces ownership of property, and such property remains permanently withdrawn from any commercial transaction (*ḥubus muʿabbad*) and is converted from an item of personal estate to the real estate of a family or an institution. An essential clause states that the *muḥabbis* entrusts the property to a third party who will take possession (*ḥawz wa-ḳabḍ*) of it on condition that the usufruct is passed on for the immediate or longer term benefit of the needy, or for a charitable cause.

The Andalusīs have always maintained that, in accordance with the teaching of the school of Mālik, their goods and chattels may become the property of a charitable foundation. Thus among the *awḳāf* about benevolent giving, there are found gifts of books "which are to be available for those who are seeking knowledge, so that they may copy them, compare them or study them" (al-Djazīrī [d. 585/1189], *Maḳṣad*, 288). Normally, such works or pamphlets were deposited in mosques or *madrasa*s, but they have also been known to have been kept in an individual's house if necessary. Hārūn b. Sālīm (d. 238/852-3) was one such individual, and he set up a *waḳf* with his books in the house of Aḥmad b. Khālid (Ibn al-Faraḍī, *Ta'rīkh*, ed. Codera, no. 1528).

In al-Andalus it was common to arrange more specifically for goods and chattels or animals to be *aḥbās*, and these could be used in the cause of *djihād*, such as swords and other military equipment, slaves, beasts of burden, horses, etc. The horse would be marked on the hindquarters with a distinctive sign to show that it was *muḥabbas*, and then it was frequently placed in the hands of a horseman whose valour and prowess in combat were recognised.

The majority of *aḥbās khayriyya* or charitable foundations of a public nature, were based on goods and chattels. Most of the mosques, hospitals and cemeteries were built in this way or equipped with private funds. It is also the case that houses were sometimes set up as *aḥbās* for particular individuals to live in, such as pious women who were living alone, the *imām* of the mosque, pilgrims, etc. The running of such establishments was made possible by patrimonial funds granted as *aḥbās*: farmlands, property for letting, commercial establishments (kilns, bathhouses), and the income from them was allocated to such religious or charitable institutions.

But not all the mosques had access to sufficient *aḥbās* to meet their needs. Ibn al-Imām was therefore consulted about the person in charge of a mosque who was supplementing his salary with different *aḥbās*. All the property which was called *aḥbās al-dīwān* in al-Andalus was let out to individuals (*mutaḳabbilūn*) by means of a contract in which the amount (*ḳabāla*) to be paid each year was specified. The intermediary or agent charged with the task of reaching an agreement with the tenants was called the *dallāl*. All those who were in possession of property in any location belonging to the *aḥbās* were summoned once a year, eight days after the *ʿīd al-aḍḥā*, to draw up a corresponding contract for the following year. In order to avoid the situation whereby the tenant of *muḥabbasa* land would eventually claim the ownership for himself, in al-Andalus it was recommended that it not be leased out to the same person for more than four years.

If there was a drop in income it was usual for the tenants to approach the *ḳāḍī* with a request for a reduction in the amount they were liable to pay. The causes most commonly pleaded by the farmers were plagues and damage caused by the passage of troops (e.g. during the sieges suffered by Cordova in the 5th/11th century). The tenants in charge of bathhouses pleaded scarcity of water at their disposal, or particular difficult circumstances in which they found themselves, such as trying to heat these establishments with wet wood during a period of persistent rain. Then the *ḳāḍī* would send along witnesses to assess for themselves the alleged damage, and a reduction in the total sum to be paid as rent was made on the grounds of gracious remission (*isti'lāf*).

Since their task was the good business management (*naẓar*) of the *aḥbās*, the *fuḳahā'* were in the habit of allowing such remissions to ensure that there would always be candidates willing to rent the property, seeing that they were vying with each other to profit from some of these contracts. There was a fear that the land would remain unoccupied, as is evident from numerous reports of *muftī*s consulted on this subject in Andalusia. However, other *ʿulamā'* deplored the fact that the tenants abused the custom, and that they accepted these contracts in the sure knowledge that they would be granted the exemptions requested and that the result would be that it would in fact become an implicit clause in any contract in question.

Numerous *aḥbās khayriyya* were established by members of the Andalusī aristocracy. In 364/975 this was the way that caliph al-Ḥakam II [*q.v.*] set up a foundation with rents from the shops in the market of Cordova, which were used to pay the salaries of the teachers whom he had appointed to teach the Ḳurʾān to the sons of the poor. He also instituted as a *ḥubus* for the recently enlarged mosque in Cordova the revenue derived from a quarter of all the rural properties he had inherited from his father, the caliph ʿAbd al-Raḥmān III, properties which were spread throughout all regions of al-Andalus. He appointed his *ḥād̲j̲ib*, Sayf al-Dawla D̲j̲aʿfar, to collect, account for and administer these *ḥubus*. This famous eunuch, an officer of al-Ḥakam II, in turn set up important *aḥbās* for which Ibn al-Mas̲h̲s̲h̲āṭ (Ibn al-Abbār, *Takmila*, ed. Codera, no. 384) was appointed *nāẓir*.

In al-Andalus an essential tool for legally avoiding the application of the Islamic rules of inheritance was the *wakf ahlī*, an allocation to the descendants of the founder, on the condition that if they disappeared it would revert to needy persons or to charitable causes. It was frequently established with the aim of preventing the fragmentation of the family inheritance and ensuring that it remained economically viable. In addition it could prevent the transmission of property to women, although that would have been considered *makrūh* by the Andalusī *ʿulamāʾ*. It was also used to defend the inheritance from confiscation, such as was decreed by higher authority with relative frequency. They would declare that the owners of the property concerned were guilty of infringement, or were lacking in loyalty towards authority. The celebrated formularies of Ibn al-ʿAṭṭār (d. 399/1009) and of al-D̲j̲azīrī provided models of deeds authenticated by a notary of *istirʿāʾ* or of *taḳiyya*, in which a person would testify that he was going to set up a foundation in mortmain, not as a meritorious gesture before God, but as a means of avoiding being forced by authority to relinquish it.

The high number of *aḥbās* which are known to have been instituted in favour of descendants of the founder shows that the Andalusīs must frequently have thought them a good means of providing security against poverty for their successors. But this did not always yield the good results anticipated, for the heirs might not receive with the land the money necessary for running it. It has been shown that sometimes they ran the risk of incurring severe hardship, for they were prevented from selling any part of the land to obtain liquid assets. In such cases, the Andalusī *muftī*s were consulted about the possibility of disposing of some of this property. However, according to Ibn al-ʿAṭṭār (*Wat̲h̲āʾiḳ*, 176), the founder could decree that, if any of the beneficiaries of the *ḥubus* were to find himself in a state of need (it would have to be properly certified, unless he had stipulated that the heir would simply have to be believed if he claimed to be in a state of poverty, and that he would not have to have his statement attested), he could sell his portion and thus be relieved from his penury.

In Andalusī works about notorial formularies, there are various models of deeds of constitution for a *ḥubus* (*wat̲h̲īḳat taḥbīs, ʿaḳd ḥubus*). In these models the verbs *ḥabbasa* and *waḳḳafa* are used in the same document; the one indicates that the property has been placed outside the commercial channels, and the second states that it has been established exclusively for a specific purpose. It was within the power of the founder to designate a person to be in charge of the foundation and to be responsible for the aims that he had envisaged for it. If this person were to die, or prove to be unfit for such a mission, it was the duty of the *ḳāḍī* to find someone to be a substitute for him.

The most delicate clause was perhaps the one in which the *muḥabbis* designated the tenants to benefit from the property in question. The Andalusī authors of *wat̲h̲āʾiḳ* advise that the drafter of the document should question the grantor about his intentions in the matter. The founder could institute that the male descendants would be paid a double portion, or that all the descendants would have equal portions; or he could decide that the sons would be included in the division of profits during the lifetime of their father, or only after his decease, etc.

The Andalusī *ʿulamāʾ* discussed whether the expression "in favour of my children (*awlādī*) and their children" included the sons of daughters. Ibn Abī Zamanīn was of the opinion that the female line of descent should not be included, but other *fuḳahāʾ* expressed the opposite opinion; for this question they were followed by Ibn Rus̲h̲d al-D̲j̲add. On the basis of one of these decisions, the *ḳāḍī* Muḥammad b. Isḥāḳ b. al-Salīm (d. 367/978) was able to pronounce judgement in favour of the inclusion of the female line of descent for beneficiaries of a specific *ḥubus*. The jurist Muḥammad b. ʿAbd al-Malik b. Ayman (d. 330/942) instituted a *ḥubus* in favour of an unborn child. No-one really thought it was licit, but nevertheless the *ḳāḍī*s Muḥammad b. Isḥāḳ (already mentioned) and Ibn Zarb (d. 381/991) pronounced a judgement in favour of mandatory compliance with the clause.

As indicated in the formularies of Ibn al-ʿAṭṭār and of Ibn Mug̲h̲īt̲h̲ (d. 459/1067), several copies of the *taḥbīs* documents were in existence. One assumes that there were as many as there were interested parties. But it does not appear that the original was placed in an archive at the disposal of those who needed it. This absence of central archives is proved by the fact that al-D̲j̲azīrī (297) included a model of a deed authenticated by a notary for an instance where the heirs of the *ḥabus* had lost the original deed of constitution, and they had to acknowledge that they had received just such a deed from their father. It is obvious that if a copy of it had been kept in an archive, it would not have been necessary to draw up this new document because the original deed had been lost. Although we know that in Egypt in 363/974 al-Muʿizz directed that the deeds of constitution of the *awḳāf* should be deposited in the *bayt al-māl*, there is nothing to reassure us that this custom was also followed in al-Andalus. It is surprising that, in the model supplied by al-D̲j̲azīrī, it was the heirs who had to apply probatory force to the clauses which appeared in the deed of constitution by the request of the founder. These were clauses which the heirs might consider unfavourable, such as for example if the sons of the daughters were included among the beneficiaries (for a lawsuit which is particularly interesting on this point, see Ibn ʿIyāḍ, *Mad̲h̲āhib*, 192-6).

From the time when the founder drew up the deed before witnesses he renounced ownership of the property in question, which then had to be formally taken over by a third party. If the *ḥubus* was in favour of the children and these were minors, he could remain as administrator (providing this fact was sufficiently publicised) or designate someone else to be in charge of the administration of the property. He was, however, obliged to have a document drawn up in front of witnesses, stating that he undertook to hand over to them the revenue or profits which the property in question had produced since the time of the *taḥbīs* when they reached majority. If he instituted a *wakf* agreement on a house in which he was still living, he would have to leave it and go live in another.

The witnesses would have to attest that the house in question was empty of tenants and furniture, and closed up from the outside when the *ḥubus* was established. For the founder to be able to come and live again in that house, or use it as reserve space, a year would have to elapse, otherwise the *ḥubus* was not valid.

Generally, the Andalusī deeds of *taḥbīs* designated with great precision the ultimate recipient of the *ḥubus*, like for example the lepers' quarter on the other side of the river in Cordova, the maintenance of a certain bridge, the payment of the salary of the *imām* and other servants of a mosque, or repairs to the mosque, or the purchase of matting or oil for the lamps in the sanctuary, etc. However, there probably had to be a certain number of foundations devoted to charity where the revenue did not have such a specific destination, since we know that these funds under the control of the *ḳāḍī* were used many times for a purpose which was considered useful to the community, such as combatting the enemies of religion.

The various political systems in al-Andalus have always included a *ṣāḥib al-aḥbās*, a curator or administrator general of mortmain property, whose mission was to prevent the disappearance of real estate, or the alteration of its status, i.e. the purposes for which it had been intended, the beneficiaries designated and the actual location of the building (even if there was a proposal to exchange the property for another on a better site). This official was responsible to the treasury (*māl al-aḥbās*), made up of the revenue of the charitable bequests detailed for the mosques and other public institutions or good causes. In his *Taʾrīkh ʿUlamāʾ al-Andalus*, Ibn al-Faraḍī (d. 403/1013 [*q.v.*]) gave him the title of *nāẓir fi 'l-awḳāf* (*or fi 'l-aḥbās*), which appears to indicate that the term *ṣāḥib* came into general use after the 4th/10th century. This would leave the title *nāẓir fi 'l-aḥbās* to designate the representative of the *ḳāḍī* in each location, whose task it was to supervise the mainmort property, and to engage and pay the servants of the mosque. The title *nāẓir* was also given to the administrator of a specified *wakf*. Ibn al-Faraḍī also reports that the *nāẓir fi 'l-awḳāf* could sometimes carry out his tasks jointly with another office-bearer. This fact was established in his *Taʾrīkh* concerning two characters whose biography he was writing.

Given that controlling the *aḥbās* was one of the tasks of the *ḳāḍī* (or according to the expression of Ibn Sahl, the *dīwān al-ḳuḍāt*), this term denoted the person who was entrusted with attending to it on his behalf. This was one of the most important tasks of the administration (the names of dozens of people who have held it figure in the *Taʾrīkh*), and it gave rise to the appearance of the name of Ibn Ṣāḥib al-Aḥbās. The testimony of such a personality was worthy of trust and was a determining factor in the litigations surrounding such property. Certain lawsuits were conducted against those who were accused of embezzlement while carrying out their job (see e.g. Ibn al-Faraḍī, no. 1360).

The treasury of the *aḥbās* was of great economic importance as early as the time of ʿAbd al-Raḥmān I [*q.v.*]; it was reported that this treasury was the source of the 200,000 dīnārs necessary for the construction of the first great mosque in Cordova in 170/786. This treasury at Cordova was kept in the *maḳṣūra* of the great mosque, in the *bayt māl al-muslimīn*, and would have formed the most significant part of the revenues held there. The expression *bayt al-māl* [*q.v.*] is often interpreted as "the treasury of the charitable foundations", thus implying that all its income came from the *awḳāf*. The value of dīnārs arising from the *aḥbās* kept in the great mosque of Cordova and placed in the hands of the *ḳāḍī* was always very important, and it gave rise to clashes with the religious and political authorities, because at certain points in time the latter wished to use these funds for purposes which their guardians did not always consider appropriate.

The situation where it was impossible to transfer the *ḥubus* from its original location to another property was maintained by the *fuḳahāʾ* of al-Andalus, except for when it was necessary to proceed with the extension of a mosque. This initially prevented the caliph al-Nāṣir from enlarging his palace at the expense of some real estate (*madjshar*) which was a charitable foundation for lepers. Later, however, he produced a very advantageous exchange for the *ḥubus*, thanks to a very timely *fatwā* from Muḥammad b. Yaḥyā b. Lubāba, who authorised the exchange, basing his opinion (he disagreed with Mālik) on that of the ʿIrāḳīs, who were obliged to respect the original location of the *ḥubus* except where a mosque was concerned.

The *ʿulamāʾ* posed the question of what to do if the property about which the *ḥubus* had been instituted could not be found. One case which frequently came up in al-Andalus was that of property allocated to an institution situated in an area which in the interim had been seized by the enemy. In this hypothesis, the judgement was always that the property should go to a worthy public cause. Sometimes the Andalusī *ʿulamāʾ* considered that some of the causes for which specific *aḥbās* had been detailed were illicit. Numerous consultations recorded in the *Miʿyār* of al-Wansharīsī [*q.v.*], all dating from the Naṣrid period, have as their subject the legality of the *aḥbās* instituted in favour of the "Night of the Birth of the Prophet". The revenue from these was paid to the *imām*, so that he would organise a public prayer on the said night. An equivalent amount was also distributed to the *fuḳarāʾ*, who enlivened the celebrations with their singing and dancing. The *fuḳahāʾ* were unanimous in disapproving of the innovation of these festivities, and they stipulated that these legacies should be used for some other charitable purpose. The *ḥubus* which benefitted them was called a *fuḳarāʾ al-waḳt*. These were brotherhoods which existed in the Naṣrid period, and their members devoted themselves wholeheartedly to music and dance, and they were without question supported by a section of the population; nevertheless they were not considered legitimate.

The *ahl al-dhimma* [*q.v.*] of al-Andalus also instituted *aḥbās* in favour of their successors, probably because they wanted to obtain the same advantages as the Muslims were looking for from that institution. In order to do this they had to respect the norm, according to which the ultimate goal of the foundation had to comply with the precepts of Islam; an example of this was a *ḥubus* set up by a Jew in Lorca with the aim of benefitting the poor of the Muslim community of that city. There was also the case of another Jew who had set up a *ḥubus* in favour of the mosque of Cordova.

The transfer of the property rights of Christian churches constituted a very important problem in the period between the 4th/10th and the 6th/12th centuries, judging by the numerous legal opinions which have been preserved concerning such problems. The discussion by the Andalusī *fuḳahāʾ* about the *aḥbās* of the Christians focused on two questions. Were their churches (and the properties attached to them) to be regarded as real *aḥbās*? Were the foundations instituted by the *dhimmīs* in their lifetime irreversible? Ibn ʿAttāb (d. 462/1070), a Cordovan *muftī*, affirmed in a *fatwā* received by Ibn Sahl that these *aḥbās* did not prevent their founder from cancelling them and disposing of the property by sale. Then again Ibn ʿAttāb maintained that the land where the churches were built could equally well be sold, despite the fact that it was recognised that they were the *aḥbas* of the Christians. However, Ibn Sahl adds his contribution by citing this opinion, which is contrary to that of Ibn al-Ḳāsim, who forbade the sale of churches.

Now it is known that in al-Andalus the Christians sold their churches throughout the entire 2nd/8th century. But despite all that, and applying the doctrine of Ibn al-Ḳāsim, the *fuḳahāʾ* denied al-Manṣūr the chance of buying the property attached to churches. Many other *fuḳahāʾ*, however, defended the idea that according to the legislation of the *ahl al-dhimma*, these properties were not non-transferable, and the Christian *muḥabbis* had the chance to retract. Indeed, they maintained that in any case, Muslim legal authority should not be involved in the internal problems of that community, nor consequently protect in a coercive way such property from any further changes by sale or exchange. Besides, it was considered that since this property was not dedicated to Allāh, Muslims did not have to defend the principle that it was inalienable; the norms which protected the *aḥbās* drew their validity from the fact that they were dedicated to Allāh, whereas those of the Christians were dedicated to their idols. However, the question was resolved in a specially expeditious way. When the Almoravids expelled the Christians from al-Andalus, their churches were converted into mosques, and the property attached to Christian sanctuaries was then either turned into *aḥbās* for the new mosque, or even incorporated directly into the *bayt al-māl*.

Mediaeval Castilian legislation also recognised (perhaps in imitation of that of the institution of the *wakf ahlī*) the right to decide that certain property could not be transferred by the heir, who is obliged to pass them on in their entirety to his successor, with the same conditions of non-transferability. This right, called the *mayorazgo*, was introduced by Alphonso X to his subjects in the 13th century. The expression "the non-transferability of property" (*vinculación de bienes*), which was used to describe this institution, is reminiscent of the technical term *taḥbīs*. The Castilian institution, like the Islamic one, was very strict, since even the work and improvements brought about in a property which fell into this category were considered non-transferable.

After the Christian conquest, some of the Andalusī *aḥbās* were returned to the church, as was the case in Seville in the 13th century, or at Granada in 1501. For after the conversion or expulsion of the Muslims, the churches were considered the legitimate heirs to the possessions of the mosques and religious retreat houses. Others remained attached to mosques and were administered by the Mudéjar [*q.v.*] authority as designated by the Christian monarchs; this is well established, e.g. for Elche in 1281. Eventually some were divided up between the new conquerors, as happened in Murcia in 1272 after the Mudéjar rebellion.

Bibliography: Ibn al-ʿAṭṭār, *al-Wathāʾiḳ wa 'l-sidjillāt*, ed. P. Chalmeta and F. Corriente, Madrid 1983, 171-85, 203-7, 232-7, 586-96, 620-34; Aḥmad b. Mughīth al-Ṭulayṭulī, *al-Muḳniʿ*, ed. F.J. Aguirre Sádaba, Madrid 1994, 224-5, 323-8, 334-5; Djazīrī, *al-Maḳṣad al-maḥmūd*, ed. A. Ferreras, Madrid 1999, 284-98; Muḥammad b. ʿIyāḍ, *Madhāhib al-ḥukkām*, ed. M. Bencherifa, Beirut 1990, 192-207 (Span. tr. D. Serrano, Madrid 1998, 347-64); Ibn Hishām al-Azdī al-Ḳurṭubī, *al-Mufīd li 'l-ḥukkām*, ms. Granada, fols. 83b-88b; Wansharīsī, *al-Miʿyār al-muʿrib*, Rabat-Beirut 1981, vii; Ibn ʿIdhārī, *al-Bayān al-mughrib*, ii, 234, iii, 98, 104; *Dhikr bilād al-Andalus*, ed. L. Molina i, 115; M.ʿA. Khallāf, *Taʾrīkh al-Ḳaḍāʾ fī 'l-Andalus*, Cairo 1980, 65 ff.; idem, *Wathāʾiḳ fī aḥkām ḳaḍāʾ ahl al-dhimma*, Cairo 1980, 65 ff.; Mª C. Villanueva, *Habices de las mezquitas de la ciudad de Granada y sus alquerías*, Madrid 1961. Ana Mª Carballeira is working on a doctoral thesis at Madrid concerning the *aḥbās* in al-Andalus up to the Amoravid period.

(A. CARMONA)

5. In the modern Middle East and North Africa.

i. *The impetus for reform*

In the 20th century, public criticism of the *wakf*'s ill-effects on economy and society increased due to the following reasons:

(1) The severance of the judicial link between the *wakf* and the founder's heirs reduced their interest in the property.

(2) The tying-up of the *wakf* by freezing its ownership withdrew it from both private and national economic cycles. In some countries (like Egypt) this entailed a serious setback of the agrarian system, with manifold economic, social and political implications.

(3) The exclusive concentration of the *wakf* administration in the hands of the *mutawallī*, without effective supervision by the *Sharīʿa* court and the beneficiaries, especially with respect to *wakf khayrī*, could encourage deviations from proper management.

(4) The original purpose of the *wakf* could cease to exist in the course of time, or its functions could be taken over by state agencies.

The objectives of reform are economic, social and political: restoration of the *wakf* property to the economic cycle; accommodation of *wakf* law to the inheritance rules so as to prevent the deprivation of females and cognates of their inheritance rights; redivision of *wakf* landed property within the framework of agrarian reform; and (in Egypt) the undermining of the position of traditional leadership closely bound up with the agrarian system.

Juristic basis for the reforms has been provided mostly by the "eclectic" method (*takhayyur, talfīk* [*q.v.*]), *siyāsa sharʿiyya* [*q.v.*], and the technical distinction between family (*dhurrī* or *ahlī*) *wakf* and that for charitable purposes (*khayrī*).

Relevant legislation: Algeria—Law No. 91-10 (*awḳāf*), 1991; Egypt—Law No. 48 (*wakf* rules), 1946 and its amendment by law No. 87 of 1947; Law No. 180 (abolition of non-charitable *wakf*), 1952, and a decree of September 14, 1952; Law No. 247 (supervision of *awḳāf khayriyya*), 1953 (amended by Law No. 30, 1957); Law No. 549 (abolition of *ḥikr*), 1953; Law No. 525 (requisition of *wakf ahlī* administered by the Waqf Ministry), 1954; Law No. 152 (exchange of agricultural lands endowed for charitable purposes), 1957 (amended by Law No. 51, 1958); Law No. 29 (*Wakf* of Southern Province), 1960; *Israel*—The Absentees' Property (Amendment No. 3) (release and use of *wakf*) Law, 5725-1965; *Jordan*—Waḳf Law No. 25, 1946, replaced successively by Law of Awḳāf and Muslim Affairs, No. 45, 1962 and No. 26, 1966, and amended by Law No. 36, 1982; *Kuwait*—Decree concerning Application of Waḳf Rules in Sharīʿa Courts of April 5, 1951; Decree No. 257 (establishment of Secretariat General for Awḳāf), 1992; *Lebanon*—Law of Family Wakf, 1947; *Libya*—Law No. 10 (establishment of General Board for Awḳāf), 1971; Law No. 74 (principles of *awḳāf*), 1972; Law No. 16 (abolition of noncharitable *waḳf*), 1973; *Palestine*—Order of the Supreme Muslim Council, 1921; *Saudi Arabia*—The Administrative Regulations of the S̲h̲arīʿa Courts, No. 109, 1962; *Syria*—Decree No. 753, 1921; Decree No. 76 (abolition of family *waḳf*) amended by decree No. 97, both of 1949; Decree No. 128 concerning *waḳf k̲h̲ayrī*, 1949; Law No. 204, 1961; *Turkey*—Act No. 6219, 1954; *United Arab Emirates*—Waḳf Decree, 1980; *Yemen*—The Aden Mohammadan Waḳf Ordinance, 1939; Waḳf Law No. 78, 1976 amended by Law No. 15, 1978 and replaced by Waḳf Law no. 23, 1992.

ii. *Egypt, Lebanon and Syria*

Until the military coups, reforms were confined to supervision of the *waḳf* administration by means of governmental agencies, and moderate substantive amendments in the *waḳf* itself.

In Egypt (1946) and Lebanon (1947), the validity of the family *waḳf* was limited in time; a *waḳf k̲h̲ayrī* could be either temporary or perpetual; the founder could revoke his *waḳf* and recover it for himself, and after him, for the beneficiaries; the exclusion of legal heirs from their rights to entitlement was prohibited; and the founder's stipulations designed to restrict the freedom of the beneficiaries with respect to marriage, place of residence, or the raising of credit were deemed null and void.

The circumvention of the *s̲h̲arʿī* inheritance rules were frustrated through "obligatory entitlement" to close relatives with respect to two-thirds of the estate; the founder could grant his or her orphaned grandchildren an entitlement equal to what would have been due to their parent had he or she been alive at the time of the founder's death.

Waḳf property was to be managed, wherever possible, by the beneficiaries; the administration of a *waḳf k̲h̲ayrī*, in default of an administrator, was vested in the Ministry of Awḳāf; the consideration of sold *waḳf* property (*amwāl al-badal*) was to be invested in constructive projects, and *awḳāf* irretrievably neglected were to be abolished.

The actual effect of these reforms was slight because most of them were related to future, rather than existing, *awḳāf*, and royal ones were excluded from most of these reforms.

In Syria, under the French Mandate the Contrôl Général des Wakfs was established in 1921, but no reforms beyond *waḳf* registration were introduced.

The military régimes in Syria and Egypt introduced radical reforms in the *waḳf* to the point of its complete abolition. Syria, in 1949, abolished both the family *waḳf* and the *mus̲h̲tarak* (partly *d̲h̲urrī* or *ahlī* and partly *k̲h̲ayrī*) *waḳf*, and prohibited the foundation of such *awḳāf* in future. The family *waḳf* was to be registered, in full ownership, in the name of the founder, and if not alive, in that of the beneficiaries. The administration of the public *awḳāf* was transferred to a special Ministry. In case of *id̲j̲āratayn* (prolonged lease), the *waḳf* was to be sold and its consideration distributed among the beneficiaries. A founder's stipulations intended to exclude legal heirs from the estate were invalidated.

The function of *mutawallī* (administrator) of both family and public *awḳāf* was abolished, and the management was vested in the Ministry of Awḳāf which could allocate entitlement to charitable purposes regardless of the founder's stipulations.

Under the 1961 Law, the Ministry of Awḳāf was authorised to administer the *awḳāf k̲h̲ayriyya*, includ-

ing those that had been abolished, family *awḳāf* of which there were no longer any beneficiaries, *waḳf g̲h̲ayr ṣaḥīḥ* (of the *mīrī* category), *waḳf* with no specification of beneficiaries, and *waḳf al-Ḥaramayn* [see AL-ḤARAMAYN].

The Egyptian Law No. 180 of 1952 prohibited the creation of family *awḳāf* in future, and abolished *waḳf* existing property, which was to revert to the founder, and if not alive, to the existing beneficiaries according to their shares in entitlement or *amwāl al-badal*.

Under Law No. 525 of 1954, the Ministry of Awḳāf was authorised to expropriate family *awḳāf* under its direct administration, and to compensate beneficiaries out of the *amwāl al-badal* of *awḳāf k̲h̲ayriyya*.

Under Law No. 247 of 1953, the Ministry of Awḳāf was to administer all *awḳāf k̲h̲ayriyya* (except those whose *nāẓir*s were their founders) and allocate their proceeds to whatever public purpose it deemed appropriate, regardless of the founder's stipulations.

Between 1952-4, *ḥikr* [*q.v.* in Suppl.] (long-term lease of dilapidated *awḳāf*) on *awḳāf ahliyya* and *k̲h̲ayriyya* was abolished. In 1960 the lessee was given the option to buy the property from the *waḳf*, failing which it would be sold by auction.

Under Law No. 152 of 1957, the full ownership of all agricultural lands pertaining to *awḳāf k̲h̲ayriyya* was nationalised to be distributed within the framework of the agrarian reform. Their former *nāẓir*s were to receive bonds, and on their redemption after 30 years the capital was to be invested in development projects.

Under Law No. 29 of 1960, the founder may dedicate property to charitable purposes and allocate entitlement to himself. In the presence of close relatives, the *waḳf* is valid only with respect to one-third of the estate.

iii. *Palestine, Jordan and Israel*

In Palestine under the Mandate, the British established the Supreme Muslim Council (1921) with a view to replacing the Ottoman Ministry of Awḳāf. In 1937, the Council's Waḳf committee was relieved of its functions, and the *waḳf* properties were transferred to a government-appointed commission. The attempts during the Mandate to convert Muslim *awḳāf* into secular trusts failed.

After the incorporation of the West Bank into the Hashemite Kingdom in 1951 [see AL-URDUNN. 2(c)], the government's policy was aimed at strengthening the state control in the management of the *awḳāf*. In 1951, the 1921 Order establishing the Supreme Muslim Council was abrogated and the 1946 Waḳf Law was extended to the West Bank and Jerusalem. A Waḳf Council, presided over by the Ḳāḍī 'l-Ḳuḍāt, was established under that law, to be replaced, with minor changes, by the 1962 and 1966 Waḳf laws and amended by that of 1982; it controls the management of the *awḳāf* and its budget. No reform, however, has been introduced in the actual institution of the *waḳf*.

In Israel, the vast majority of the Muslim *awḳāf* became absentee property after their administrators had left Israel for the Arab states. The management and entitlement of absentee beneficiaries were vested in a Custodian. Holy places were administered by the Ministry of Religious Affairs, on behalf of the Custodian, by means of Muslim advisory boards. The income was allocated to Muslim religious services and social welfare. The consideration of properties that had been transferred to a governmental development authority were invested in the establishment of educational and social institutions and projects for the benefit of the Muslim community.

Under 1965 law, the Custodian may transfer the family *waḳf* to the beneficiaries' full ownership; *waḳf khayrī* is to be transferred to Muslim boards of trustees empowered to own and dispose of it at will, to use the income for social and cultural purposes regardless of the founder's stipulations, and to use the *amwāl al-badal* to establish institutions for the same purposes. The *waḳf* properties in East Jerusalem, under Israeli rule, have been exempted from the status of "absentee properties". The powers of the Council of Waḳf and Muslim Affairs and the General Director of the Muslim Waḳf Department—as defined in Jordanian law—were delegated to the Sharīʿa Court of Appeal in East Jerusalem.

The Palestinian authority appointed a general director of the *awḳāf* in the West Bank and East Jerusalem, who holds, since the early 1990s, the office of President of the Supreme Muslim Authority.

iv. *Saudi Arabia and Yemen*

No statutory legislation relating to *awḳāf* except certain minor provisions with no substantive significance, has taken place, but *ḳāḍīs* may resort here, as in other aspects of the law, to a school other than the Ḥanbalī one in case the relevant doctrine in the latter may cause hardship and is opposed to the public interest.

The Saudi Ministry of Awḳāf supervises the administration of the *waḳf khayrī*. The 1962 regulations prescribe that, upon the extinction of beneficiaries, income shall pass to charitable purposes and a *nāẓir*, preferably the Director of the Awḳāf, be appointed by court. The Ministry allocates the income of the *waḳf* in accordance with the founders' stipulations. Foreigners are prohibited from transmitting the income abroad.

Endowments on a large scale have been founded in favour of *ribāṭs* [*q.v.*] (hostels for the poor) by pilgrims from all over the Muslim world; these *ribāṭs* are managed by *nāẓirs*.

The 1939 Ordinance restored the validity of the family *waḳf* in the Aden colony, following its invalidation by the British Privy Council in 1894.

The Yemenite 1992 law prohibits an endowment exceeding one-third of the estate in the presence of a heir. Poor descendants of the founder have priority over other poor. Upon the extinction of a beneficiary, the founder may replace him by another one. A family *waḳf* is deemed void unless the beneficiary enters the category of a charity, or is physically disabled and has nobody to maintain him.

Family *awḳāf* contradicting the provisions of this law are deemed null and void unless endorsed by a *Sharīʿa* court or the founder's heirs, or forty years have elapsed since their establishment. The beneficiaries and the court may abolish a family *waḳf*, whereupon the ownership reverts to the beneficiaries according to their shares in entitlement. A beneficiary's heirs take their share in entitlement according to inheritance rules. In case of dispute between the beneficiaries concerning entitlement in and matters pertaining to division of a *waḳf* that has been revoked, the court will apportion entitlement according to the rules of inheritance or, in case of obscurity, *per capita* among the existing beneficiaries, male and female; the division of the property will be according to their shares in the entitlement.

Waḳf in favour of visions (*ḥaḍarāt*), commemoration (*iḥyāʾ*) of the nights, birthdays of saints (*mawālid*), of holy men (*awliyāʾ*) and of tombs (*ḳubūr*) is void.

Disposition of a *waḳf* is permissible only with the approval of the Ministry of Awḳāf and Guidance. The Ministry is in charge of the public *awḳāf* and supervises the administration of *awḳāf* pertaining to mosques by private *mutawallīs*.

v. *Kuwait and the United Arab Emirates*

Under the Kuwaiti 1951 Decree, the founder's poor relatives have precedence in a *waḳf khayrī*. In *awḳāf khayriyya* or *mushtaraka* where the founder has not stipulated otherwise, supervision is invested in the General Awḳāf Department. The founder may revoke any part of a family or charitable *waḳf* (excluding mosques).

Where a family *waḳf* is in a state of dilapidation, or the beneficiaries are numerous, the share of each being insignificant, the *waḳf* expires and reverts to the ownership of the founder or—if dead—to the beneficiaries. The family *waḳf* terminates with the expiry of the beneficiaries or the period specified by the founder; the ownership thereof reverts to the founder, his heirs, and—in their absence—to some public charity. The 1992 Law provides for the establishment of a General Secretariat for the Awḳāf and a Board of Awḳāf, the chairman of which is the Minister of Awḳāf.

In the United Arab Emirates, the 1980 decree abolished the existing family *waḳf* and prohibited its creation in the future.

vi. *Turkey*

In 1926, Turkey abolished the family *waḳf* and nationalised the public ones. Agricultural properties (exchanged for urban properties) were distributed within the framework of agrarian reform. In 1935, *idjāratayn* and *muḳāṭaʿa* (= *ḥikr* [*q.v.* in Suppl.]) were abolished and the establishment of new ones was prohibited. Lessees were made owners of the properties in return for monetary compensation. *Waḳf* institutions were replaced by charity associations. Public *awḳāf* were transferred to public ownership (known as "foundations") to be administered either directly by the foundations (*mazbut*) or by *mütevellis* under the control of the foundations (*mülhak*). The Türkiye Vakıflar Bankası was established under a 1954 Act in order economically to utilise the capital of these foundations. The Bank may lend against securities and immovable assets, establish or participate in partnerships and insurance, buy and sell real estate, and perform all kinds of banking transactions and services.

vii. *Libya and Algeria*

During Italian rule over Libya, some reforms were introduced in the administration of the *waḳf* (decree of 1939), but the institution itself remained intact. No substantial changes occurred during the British rule and under King Idrīs al-Sanūsī. Prior to the military coup, the bulk of *khayrī* endowments belonged to the Sanūsī order [see SANŪSIYYA] and served its lodges (*zāwiya*). Colonel Gaddafi/Ḳadhdhāfī outlawed the order and confiscated its *awḳāf*.

The 1971 law provides for the establishment of a General Board for Awḳāf to administer *awḳāf* in favour of charitable purposes or those whose beneficiaries are not known. The Board supervises the *awḳāf* in favour of the *zāwiyas* and tombs and the administration of family ones. The 1972 law, drafted along the pattern of the Egyptian 1946 law, introduced moderate reforms regarding the *waḳf*. The 1973 law abolished the *waḳf ahlī*. The founder may revoke his *waḳf* and resume the ownership himself provided he has retained the right to do so, failing which the *waḳf* reverts to the beneficiaries. *Amwāl al-badal* following expropriation for public purposes or sale due to dilapidation are to revert to the beneficiaries.

Under the Algerian 1991 law, the founder may revoke his own stipulations. The *ḳāḍī* may do so on grounds of damage to the *waḳf* and its beneficiaries. No renunciation of entitlement is permissible in respect to public *awḳāf* except in favour of a charitable purpose. A family *waḳf* for a specified period is deemed null and void. On the extinction of the descendants, a *waḳf* is to revert to the Waḳf Authority. This applies also to landed and movable property endowed in favour of associations and institutions when the endowment becomes extinct. *Waḳf* properties nationalised by virtue of 1971 law with a view to being distributed within the framework of the agrarian reform, are to be revived in favour of the original purposes, failing which they are to revert to the Waḳf Authority.

viii. *The decline of the waḳf in modern times*

Some of the main factors for the flourishing of the *waḳf* in Muslim society over the past centuries have ceased to exist in modern times:

(1) The extension of freedom of testation in modern legislation has diminished the incentive for using the family *waḳf* for circumventing Islamic law of inheritance with a view to preventing the fragmentation of the agnatic patrimony.

(2) The concern for social welfare, economic and development enterprises, and investments in infrastructure, which was partly the function of the *waḳf khayrī* in pre-modern times, have become the responsibility of the state and other agencies in modern times.

(3) The religious motive which also played an important role in traditional society as an incentive to found *awḳāf*, especially in favour of pious institutions and charity, seems to have diminished in modern society.

(4) Practical considerations, such as the desire to secure property from expropriation and exemption from taxes, and to prevent encumbrance and loss of property as a result of indebtedness, which often traditionally prompted the foundation of *awḳāf*, can be satisfied nowadays by legal devices that do not entail the negative repercussions.

(5) The reforms introduced in the *waḳf* to the point of complete abolition also diminish the incentive to endow.

Bibliography: J.N.D. Anderson, *Recent developments in sharīʿa law. IX. The waqf system*, in *MW*, xlii (1952), 257-76; G. Baer, *A history of landownership in modern Egypt, 1800-1950*, London 1962, ch. iv; idem, *Studies in the social history of modern Egypt*, Chicago 1969, ch. 5; idem, *The waqf as a prop for the social system (sixteenth-twentieth centuries)*, in *ILS*, iv (1997), 264-97, with important bibl.; A. Layish, *The family waqf and the* sharʿī *law of succession in modern times*, in *ibid.*, 352-88, with important bibl.; idem, *The Muslim waqf in Israel*, in *AAS*, ii (1965), 41-76; Y. Reiter, *Islamic awqāf in Jerusalem under British Mandate*, London 1996; idem, *Islamic institutions in Jerusalem*, London 1997; *Varia Turcica. XXVI. Le waqf dans le monde musulman contemporain (XIXᵉ-XXᵉ siècles)*, Istanbul 1994; H. Bleuchot, *Notice sur les "awqâf" libyens de 1969 à 1978*, in *Annuaire de l'Afrique du Nord*, xviii (1979), 397-400 (with important bibl.); Miriam Hoexter, *Waqf studies in the twentieth century: the state of the art*, in *JESHO*, xli (1998), 474-95, with important bibl.

(A. Layish)

III. In Persia

Precise details of the extent of *awḳāf* in Persia and their value at different periods and in different places are not available and the effect of the spread of *awḳāf* on the economy of the country has yet to be worked out. Moreover, what was typical of one district at one point in time cannot be taken as typical of others at all times. Government offices no doubt contain records of *awḳāf* but these are not generally available. Shrines also presumably have records of *awḳāf* constituted in their favour. Many surviving *waḳfiyya*s are held in private hands and some have been published. Some also survive in the form of inscriptions in mosques and other charitable buildings; historical works, especially local histories, biographical works and collections of state documents also contain information on *awḳāf*. Much of what follows is based on state documents and *waḳfiyya*s and does not necessarily reflect practice as opposed to theory. The available information on *awḳāf* for some districts, notably Yazd, Ḳum, Kirmān and, for the Ṣafawid period, Iṣfahān, is richer than elsewhere.

As stated in I. above, there are differences in the legal regulations governing *awḳāf* between Sunnī and Shīʿī theory and minor differences between the different rites. Under both Sunnī and Shīʿī governments in Persia, the constitution of *awḳāf* by rulers and their officials was common, and also by private individuals, both rich and poor, but it is the foundations by rulers and prominent persons of which the sources for the most part speak. The classical legal theory, whether Sunnī until the 10th/16th century or Shīʿī from the 10th/16th century onwards, remained normative, but in practice there were often modifications or deviations, especially in respect of the type of land which could be made into *waḳf*. The stipulation that property to be made into *waḳf* must be in the full legal possession of the founder was in theory observed, and sometimes it is specifically mentioned in the documents that the property had been legally bought by the founder. It is, however, doubtful whether all the *awḳāf* constituted by rulers were in fact made out of crown property [see khāliṣa] or had been legally bought and not usurped; similarly some of the property of powerful individuals made into *awḳāf* may, at some stage, have been usurped.

In practice, there does not appear to have been any restriction on the type of land made into *waḳf*. As well as landed estates, water rights, water mills, real estate, bazaars, shops and houses were also constituted into *awḳāf*, and, more rarely, rights of usufruct (A.K.S. Lambton, *Continuity and change in medieval Persia*, New York 1988, 148-9). Jean Aubin noted that Öldjeytü [*q.v.*] authorised Inal Khātūn in a decree (*nishān*) dated to the equivalent of 31 July 1305 to constitute over half of the village of Kalkhurān, which Ghazan Khān [*q.v.*] had given her for her upkeep (*ikhrādjāt*), into *waḳf* for Shaykh Ṣafī and his descendants. Ten years later, Öldjeytü constituted the remainder of the village into *waḳf* for the Shaykh, who later nevertheless managed to sell it to the descendants of the *ṣāḥib dīwān* Shams al-Dīn Djuwaynī, to whom it had originally belonged (*La propriété foncière en Azerbaydjan sous les Mongols*, in *Le Monde iranien et l'Islam*, iv [1976-7], 99-101). Books, carpets and other objects were frequently made into *waḳf* for mosques and *madrasa*s.

The great majority of charitable *awḳāf* were constituted for the benefit of mosques, *madrasa*s and *khānaḳāh*s, and their revenue devoted to purposes such as the support of the *ʿulamāʾ*, feasts and the feeding of the poor on religious festivals, the holding of religious assemblies, *rawḍa-khʷānī*s and so on. Many were also made for the upkeep of charitable buildings such as hospitals, caravansarais, water storage tanks and drinking-fountains. The first call on the funds of a *waḳf* was the development and upkeep of the property itself, and then, unless exemption had been granted by a special *farmān*, the payment of government taxes, after which came the payment of the wages of the servants of the foundation for which the *waḳf* had been constituted and the *mutawallī*, who was usually entitled to one-tenth of the revenue, though in some cases it was stipulated in the *wakf-nāma* that he should be paid more or less than this. Landed property held as *wakf* was often leased; some *wakfiyya*s laid down that the term of the lease should not exceed three years (see also Lambton, *Landlord and peasant in Persia*, repr. London 1969, 234-5. For expenditure of the revenue from G̲h̲azan K̲h̲ān's foundations, see Ras̲h̲īd al-Dīn, *Tārīk̲h̲-i mubārak-i g̲h̲āzānī*, ed. K. Jahn, London 1940, 316-18, and for Ras̲h̲īd al-Dīn's foundations, see *Wakf-nāma-i Rabʿ-i Ras̲h̲īdī*, ed. M. Minovi and Īrad̲j̲ Afs̲h̲ār, Tehran 1977-8, 42-4; and see Lambton, *Awqāf in Persia, 6th-8th/12th-14th centuries*, in *ILS*, iv/3, [1997], 316-18).

With the fragmentation of the caliphate and the rise of semi-independent dynasties, the conquered territories, whether belonging to Muslims or non-Muslims, fell to the conquerors and their military auxiliaries. The extent to which existing *awḳāf* continued to function varied and is not well documented. Many were probably usurped; and others decayed over time and fell out of operation.

From the early years of the semi-independent dynasties, the importance of *awḳāf* is attested by the existence of a *dīwān-i awḳāf* or a special office in charge of *awḳāf* [see DĪWĀN. iv, at Vol. II, 333b]. For political and financial reasons, control over *awḳāf* was important for rulers. First, *wakfī* land, unless specially exempted, was liable to taxation and its prosperity therefore contributed to state revenue. Secondly, the constitution of *awḳāf* gave prestige and opportunities of patronage to its founders and wealth to the administrators and beneficiaries.

For the Ṭāhirid, Būyid, Ṣaffārid, Sāmānid and G̲h̲aznawid periods, information on *awḳāf* is sparse, and such *awḳāf* as were constituted were probably of a modest nature. Under the Sāmānids there was a separate *dīwān* for *awḳāf* (Nars̲h̲ak̲h̲ī, *Tārīk̲h̲-i Buk̲h̲ārā*, ed. M. Riḍawī, Tehran AHS 1317/1938-9, 31; Barthold, *Turkestan*, 229). Nars̲h̲ak̲h̲ī mentions a number of *awḳāf* made by Amīr Ismāʿīl b. Aḥmad (279-95/892-907) (16-17, 33-4), all apparently of a modest nature. Much *wakfī* land was seemingly held by the *ʿulamāʾ* as *mutawallī*s [see SĀMĀNIDS. 1, at Vol. VIII, 1029a].

Under the Sald̲j̲ūḳs [see SALD̲J̲ŪḲIDS], there was probably an increase in *wakfī* land and in the control exercised over it by the state. The spread of *madrasa*s [*q.v.*], apart from anything else, and the foundation of mosques and other charitable buildings, is likely to have contributed to an increase of *awḳāf*. Māfarrūk̲h̲ī states that Niẓām al-Mulk [*q.v.*] constituted innumerable estates into *wakf* for a *madrasa* which he had built in the Dar Das̲h̲t quarter of Iṣfahān and that its annual revenue was over 10,000 dīnārs (*Maḥāsin Iṣfahān*, ed. Sayyid D̲j̲alāl al-Dīn Tihrānī, Tehran n.d., 104-5). Ḥusayn b. Muḥammad b. Abi 'l-Riḍā Āwī states that when he was writing (*ca.* 729/1328-9), the *madrasa* was still in existence but its *awḳāf* had been misappropriated (*Tard̲j̲uma-i Maḥāsin Iṣfahān*, ed. ʿAbbās Iḳbāl, Tehran AHS 1328/1949-50, 142, and see IṢFAHĀN. 1, at Vol. IV, 101b). It is probable that Niẓām al-Mulk's foundations were made partly with government funds (see further Lambton, *Continuity and change*, 43).

General supervision over *awḳāf* was exercised by the *wazīr*, the head of the *dīwān-i aʿlā* (see DĪWĀN. iv, and Lambton, *The internal structure of the Saljuq empire*, in J.A. Boyle (ed.), *Camb. hist. Iran*, v, 263, also in Lambton, *Theory and practice in medieval Persian government*, Variorum, London 1980), but immediate supervision was probably usually exercised by the *ḳāḍī al-mamālik* (cf. a document dated Muḥarram 457/Dec. 1064-Jan. 1065 for the chief *ḳāḍī* of the empire, in the *Muns̲h̲aʾāt Evog̲h̲li Ḥaydar*, in H. Horst, *Die Staatsverwaltung der Grosselǧūqen und Ḫōrazmšāhs (1038-1231)*, Wiesbaden 1964, 147-8). The *mutawallī* of an important *wakf* or group of *awḳāf* was probably often appointed by the state and, even if named in the *wakfiyya*, was given a document of appointment. If not a *ḳāḍī*, he was usually a member of the religious classes (Lambton, *The internal structure of the Saljuq empire*, 276).

The extent of the control exercised by the *dīwān-i awḳāf al-mamālik* over *awḳāf*, especially with regard to provincial *awḳāf*, is not entirely clear. Practice varied. In general, it seems that the provincial *ḳāḍī al-ḳuḍāt* was appointed by the *ḳāḍī al-mamālik* and had charge of provincial *awḳāf*, but the general supervision of provincial *awḳāf*, like most other aspects of the administration, was delegated to the provincial governor or *muḳtaʿ*. For example, the document issued by Sand̲j̲ar's *dīwān* appointing Tād̲j̲ al-Dīn Abu 'l-Makārim *raʾīs* of Māzandarān (although he is called *raʾīs*, his office was clearly that of governor), instructs him to investigate the condition of *awḳāf* and to see that their proceeds were expended on the objects for which they had been constituted (*ʿAtabat al-kataba*, 24) and he or his deputy was to remedy any disorders in their administration, remove any *mutawallī* or person in charge (*mutaṣarrif*) who committed peculation and as far as possible to revivify those *awḳāf* which had decayed (*ibid.*, 24, 28, 29; see also Lambton, *The administration of Sanjar's empire as illustrated in the ʿAtabat al-kataba*, in *BSOAS*, xx, [1957], also in eadem, *Theory and practice in medieval Persian government*, 383-4).

However, in some cases the *awḳāf* of a particular district were expressly placed outside the control of the *dīwān-i awḳāf-i mamālik*. In a document appointing Abū Saʿd Muḥammad b. Ismāʿīl as *ḳāḍī* of Nawḳān and the villages of Ṭūs which belonged to it, the *dīwān* is forbidden to interfere in the office of *mutawallī* of the *awḳāf*, "which from ancient times had been in the name of his (Abū Saʿd's) forebears" (*ʿAtabat al-kataba*, 33).

Such documents as have survived suggest that the main concern of the Sald̲j̲ūḳ government was to ensure that *wakf* revenue was expended as laid down in the relevant *wakfiyya* and to prevent encroachment on *awḳāf* by unauthorised persons. A document issued by Sand̲j̲ar's *dīwān* appointing Mad̲j̲d al-Dīn (who already had the title if not the office of *ḳāḍī al-ḳuḍāt*) as *ḳāḍī* of various branches of the military establishment, states that he was to look into large and small *awḳāf*, to enquire into their produce, to stop any damage being done to them, and to prevent encroachment upon them or their seizure by those who would devour them; also, he was to act in accordance with the conditions laid down by their founders and see that their produce was expended on the proper purposes (*ibid.*, 59). With the weakening of the central administration towards the end of the Great Sald̲j̲ūḳ period, it is not unlikely that irregularities in the administration of *awḳāf* occurred (see further Lambton, *Landlord and peasant in Persia*, 68-9).

It seems that in some cases the term *mutawallī* is used in the documents in the general sense of an official placed in charge of the *awḳāf* of a district, each of which had its own *mutawallī*. Thus a document in the collection *al-Muk̲h̲tārāt min al-rasāʾil* (ed. Īrad̲j̲ Afs̲h̲ār, Tehran AHS 1355/1976) issued by the *dīwān* of Maḥmūd b. Muḥammad (511-25/1118-31 [*q.v.*]) reappointing Muntad̲j̲ab al-Dīn Abu 'l-Ḳāsim Ismāʿīl b. ʿAbd al-ʿAzīz over the *awḳāf* of Iṣfahān and its districts (which had been constituted for the Friday mosques, other mosques, shrines, hospitals, *ribāṭs*, and other purposes), instructs him to carry out this office as formerly and to expend the produce of the *awḳāf* as laid down by the founders and to restrain the hands of those who would encroach upon them. No-one was to interfere with him or his deputies; complete control over *wakfī* affairs was vested in him. The *sipahsālār* Alp Ṭog̲h̲rïl Bilge Beg Abū Saʿīd Mawdūd b. Artuḳ was to listen if any of Muntad̲j̲ab al-Dīn's children or deputies had recourse to him and was not to send any *g̲h̲ulāms* to the *wakfī* estates except at the request of a deputy of the *dīwān-i awḳāf*. A certain Muḥammad b. Abi 'l-K̲h̲ayr, who had misappropriated a sum from the estates of the *wakf* for the Ḥaramayn, was to be summoned. The sum was to be recovered and Muḥammad b. Abi 'l-K̲h̲ayr punished. Tād̲j̲ al-Dīn Abu 'l-Ṭālib al-Ḥusayn b. Zayd b. al-Ḥusayn was not to interfere in the *awḳāf* of Iṣfahān and its neighbourhood or their produce or revenue and if, before the arrival of this *farmān*, he had taken anything from the *awḳāf*, it was to be immediately extracted from him to the last *man* [see MAKĀYĪL and MAWĀZĪN for this unit of weight] and any *wakf* in his possession was to be surrendered. The *mutawallīs* and peasants of the *awḳāf* were placed under the orders of Muntad̲j̲ab al-Dīn (278-9). A similar situation may have existed in other major mosques and shrines, and certainly did so in the Ṣafawid period and later (see below) when there was a *mutawallī* appointed by the government over the shrine or mosque in charge of the administration of its *awḳāf* made at different times, each, or some of which, may have had its own *mutawallī*.

Under the K̲h̲ʷārazms̲h̲āhs, the situation with regard to *awḳāf* was probably broadly similar to that which had prevailed under the Sald̲j̲ūḳs. A diploma (*mans̲h̲ūr*) for the *ḳāḍī al-ḳuḍāt* K̲h̲alaf al-Makkī renewed his charge of *awḳāf* properties which had been in the possession of his trusted agents (*muʿtamidān*) and of the *tawliyat* of the *awḳāf* of the mosques and *madrasas* which had been in the care of former *ḳāḍīs*, and at his request the accountant of the *dīwān*, who had been in charge of the *wakfī* accounts, was recalled and all affairs connected with the administration of the *awḳāf*, their development and their protection from the hands of those who would encroach upon them, were entrusted to him (Bahā' al-Dīn Bag̲h̲dādī, *al-Tawassul ilā 'l-tarassul*, ed. Aḥmad Bahmanyār, Tehran AHS 1315/1936-7, 51-4, and cf. the document appointing K̲h̲alaf al-Makkī *ḳāḍī* of the empire in succession to his father, *ibid.*, 61, 72). Another (undated) document in the same collection illustrates the interest of the government in ensuring that *wakfī* property was in good condition. It states that the village of Sakān Ak̲h̲sak (?), which was *wakf* for the K̲h̲ātūn Bahā' *madrasa* and one of the most important *wakfī* properties of K̲h̲ʷārazm, was beginning to fall into decay owing to the incompetence of the *mutawallī* (*ibid.*, 86). Accordingly, the sultan had decided to appoint the *wazīr* Naṣīr al-Dīn as *mutawallī* of the *wakf* and to give him full control over it. He was to arrange its affairs through deputies (*nā'ibān*) so that it might quickly return to a prosperous condition and its revenue be spent as the founder had laid down; and a suitable *mudarris* was to be appointed (*ibid.*, 87-9). This case is unusual in that the newly-appointed *mutawallī* was a *wazīr* and not a *ḳāḍī*.

In Fārs, various of the semi-independent Sald̲j̲ūḳ governors, notably Ḳarača Sāḳī, who was the virtual ruler of Fārs in the early years of the 6th/12th century, and Zāhida K̲h̲ātūn, the wife of Boz-Aba, who ruled the province after the death of her husband in 541/1146-7, were active in the constitution of property into *awḳāf*. The latter spent all the money, treasure and jewels which she had inherited from her ancestors and from Boz-Aba on the purchase of large villages to make into *wakf* for the *madrasa* which she built in S̲h̲īrāz. The Atabegs of Fārs continued this tradition (see further Lambton, *Continuity and change in medieval Persia*, 150). The rulers of other Sald̲j̲ūḳ succession states, notably the Ḳutlug̲h̲ K̲h̲ānids (Ḳarā K̲h̲iṭā'iyān) of Kirmān [*q.v.*] made many charitable foundations and constituted *awḳāf* for them (see further *ibid.*, 151, and eadem, *Awqāf in Persia*, 310-13).

Terken K̲h̲ātūn, who ruled Kirmān after the death of her husband Ḳuṭb al-Dīn Muḥammad in 655/1257 until her death in 681/1282, made numerous villages and estates into *awḳāf* for mosques, shrines, hospitals and lesser charitable purposes. These are recorded in the *Tārīk̲h̲-i S̲h̲āhī-yi Ḳarā K̲h̲iṭā'iyān* (ed. Muḥammad Ibrāhīm Bāstānī Pārīzī, Tehran AHS 1355/1976-7), the anonymous author of which states that records of the *awḳāf* of Kirmān had been kept in the provincial *dīwāns* (93). Piety may have been her primary motive, but it may be that she needed the public support which such foundations gave. She is stated to have claimed her dowry (*ṣadāḳ*) on her husband's death and with the 10,000 dīnārs to which it amounted to have bought land which she made into *awḳāf* for the *madrasa* and tomb complex which she built in Bardasīr (*ibid.*, 100). It seems likely that many, if not all, of her *awḳāf* were made out of her personal property. She had a private *dīwān* (*dīwān-i k̲h̲āṣṣ*) separate from the state or public *dīwān* and owned considerable resources (*ibid.*, 232). Her sons, Sulṭān Ḥad̲j̲d̲j̲ād̲j̲ and Soyurg̲h̲atmis̲h̲, also made many charitable foundations out of their inherited estates and private property (Naṣīr al-Dīn Muns̲h̲ī, *Simṭ al-ʿulā*, ed. ʿAbbās Iḳbāl, Tehran AHS 1328/1949-50, 39-40, 58). Terken K̲h̲ātūn designated herself as *mutawallī* of some of the foundations she constituted, including the numerous properties she made into *wakf* for the Friday mosque outside Bardasīr (*Tārīk̲h̲-i S̲h̲āhī-yi Ḳarā K̲h̲iṭā'iyān*, 244-5). In some of her smaller foundations, especially those made for slaves and slave-girls, her children were designated *mutawallī*. This was also the case of the mill (in Bahrāmd̲j̲ird) which she had bought and repaired and made into *wakf* for the shrine in the village of Ardas̲h̲īr in D̲j̲uwayn (*ibid.*, 225-6). The office of *mutawallī* of the *awḳāf* of the Friday mosque which she built at the New Gate of Bardasīr in 673/1274-5 was entrusted to "the ruler who was on the throne of Kirmān and (thereafter) to his/her children" (*ibid.*, 235-6). Some of Terken K̲h̲ātūn's *awḳāf* were for administrative affairs and public welfare. In 673/1275 she made the village of Ṣūfiyān in Rūdān into *wakf*, stipulating that thirty men should reside there to protect the road and escort caravans. The leader of the troop was to receive 5,000 *mans* of grain annually by way of wages and each of the thirty soldiers 2,000 *mans*, two-thirds to be paid in winter and one-third in summer (*ibid.*, 235). Whether Ṣūfiyān belonged to Terken K̲h̲ātūn or to the *dīwān* is not stated (see further, Lambton, *Awḳāf in Persia*, 310-13).

During the Mongol invasions, much *wakfī* land which lay in the path of the invading hordes must have suffered devastation, but so far as it escaped its status appears to have been little changed. From an early date there was a department of *awḳāf* in the Ilk̲h̲ānate. When Hülegü [*q.v.*] charged Naṣīr al-Dīn Ṭūsī [*q.v.*] with the establishment of an observatory at Marāg̲h̲a, the building of which was begun in 657/1259, he appointed him over the *awḳāf* of the empire. Naṣīr al-Dīn also held this office under Abaḳa [*q.v.*] and finally died when on a tour of inspection of *awḳāf* in ʿIrāḳ. He appointed in each locality an official responsible for the administration of *awḳāf*, allowing him to keep one-tenth of the *waḳfī* revenue for his salary. The *dīwān*'s share of the revenue was to be sent to Marāgha for the observatory (Hassan Mahmud ʿAbdel-Latif, *Naṣīr al-Dīn Ṭūsī (d. 1274) and his Tajrīd al-iʿtiḳād*, Ph.D. thesis, London University 1977, unpubl., 70 ff.). Tegüder Aḥmad, who succeeded Abaḳa in 680/1282, appointed Kamāl al-Dīn ʿAbd al-Raḥmān al-Rafīʿī *mutawallī* of the *awḳāf* of the empire, and ordered the proceeds of all *awḳāf* to be expended as laid down by their founders with the cognisance of Kamāl al-Dīn and the great *imāms* and *ʿulamāʾ*. The proceeds of the *awḳāf* for the Ḥaramayn were to be collected annually and sent to Baghdād at the time of the pilgrimage (Waṣṣāf, *Tārīkh*, ed. M.M. Iṣfahānī, lith. Bombay 1269/1852-3, 100). Under Ghazan Khān (694-703/1295-1304) there was probably an attempt to tighten control over the administration of *awḳāf*. It would seem, however, that Ghazan was not over-scrupulous in observing the legal prescription that property to be made into *waḳf* must be the personal property of the founder. When the Ḳāḍī Ṣāʾin Simnānī was executed after interrogation by the *yarghu* [*q.v.*] in 700/1301, his estates and property were added to the *khāliṣāt* and registered in the *awḳāf* registers of the royal tomb (Waṣṣāf, 419-20). However, Rashīd al-Dīn states that the property made into *awḳāf* for the complex which Ghazan made in the Shanb-i Ghāzān in Tabrīz, had all been in his full and legal possession and this had been corroborated by *fatwā*s (*Tārīkh-i mubārak-i ghāzānī*, 215).

Al-ʿUmarī, quoting information given to him by Niẓām al-Dīn Abu 'l-Faḍāʾil Yaḥyā al-Ṭayyārī, who had been a secretary to Abū Saʿīd, the last Īlkhān (716-36/1316-35), states that "no one interfered with them (*awḳāf*) either in the reign of Hülegü or his successors. Every *waḳf* was in the hands of its *mutawallī* and whoever had authority over it. Whatever might be said with regard to any damage (*naḳṣ*) to the affairs of *awḳāf* [in Persia], such damage was entirely due to abuses committed by those in charge of the *awḳāf* and not to anyone else" (K. Lech, *Das mongolische Weltreich. Al-ʿUmarī's Darstellung der mongolischen Reiche im seinem Werk Masālik al-abṣār fī mamālik al-amṣār*, with tr. and comm., Wiesbaden 1968, Arabic text, 92). This may have been an accurate statement as regards the central government, but there was much usurpation of property in general, including *awḳāf*, by Mongol officials and others. Ḥamd Allāh Mustawfī states that in Shīrāz there were over 500 charitable foundations, which had innumerable *awḳāf*, but the revenues of few of them reached their proper purposes (*Nuzhat al-ḳulūb*, Persian text, 116). He also alleges that the Pishkil Darra district of Ḳazwīn, which was *waḳf* for the Friday mosque of Ḳazwīn, had been usurped by the Mongols (*ibid.*, 67). Waṣṣāf asserts that most of the *awḳāf* of the empire and the buildings which they served were in a state of ruin and their revenues misappropriated, but he states that Kürdüdjin, the daughter of Tash Möngke and Abish Khātūn, to whom the last Īlkhān Abū Saʿīd had given the taxes of Fārs on a permanent contract (*bar sabīl-i muḳāṭaʿa-yi abadī*) three years after his accession, paid particular attention to the buildings of her forebears, increased their *awḳāf* and devoted their revenues to their proper purposes (*Tārīkh*, 624-5).

In spite of the fact that many *awḳāf* may have been devastated during the Mongol invasions and others usurped during the Īlkhānate, there appears to have been a proliferation of *awḳāf* during the period. One reason for this was probably the prevailing insecurity of tenure which led men to seek to safeguard their property from confiscation and to secure its continued enjoyment, or at least part of it, by themselves and their descendants by constituting it into *waḳf*. Both Ghazan Khān and Öldjeytü founded many *awḳāf*. Their motives were various; some of Ghazan's benefactions were clearly prompted by charity (see Lambton, *Awqāf in Persia*, 315 ff.), and some by a desire to secure the possession of property to his descendants, as when he laid down that his *īndjū* lands should be constituted into *waḳf* for the sons of his chief wife Bulughan Khātūn, or, if she had no sons, for the sons of his other wives and their male descendants (Rashīd al-Dīn, *Tārīkh-i mubārak-i ghāzānī*, 331). Al-Kāshānī mentions that Ghazan gave orders for a *dār al-siyāda* to be built in every province in Persia and for estates and villages to be made into *waḳf* for them, so that the annual income of each would be 10,000 dīnārs (*Tārīkh-i Uldjāytū*, ed. Mahin Hambly, Tehran AHS 1348/1969, 93-4). Rashīd al-Dīn confirms that Ghazan made such buildings in Iṣfahān, Shīrāz, Baghdād and various other towns (*ibid.*, 215). However, most of Ghazan Khān's *awḳāf*, and also Öldjeytü's, were for the benefit of foundations in their respective capitals, Tabrīz and Sulṭāniyya.

In spite of, or perhaps because of, the dislocation of traditional life under Mongol rule, many officials and private individuals acquired enormous wealth, some of which came from trade and possibly from money-lending. Much of it appears to have consisted of, or been invested in, land and real estate and to have been constituted into *waḳf*. The most outstanding case is that of Rashīd al-Dīn Faḍl Allāh Hamadānī [see RASHĪD AL-DĪN ṬABĪB]. Most of his *awḳāf* were for the benefit of the Rabʿ-i Rashīdī, the quarter which he built in Tabrīz; but he also constituted *awḳāf* for foundations in Yazd, Hamadān, Shīrāz and Kirmān. Lists of the properties which he made into *waḳf* for these foundations, which included mosques, *madrasa*s, *khānaḳāh*s, and hospitals, and *awḳāf* for his children and various holy men, are set out in the *Waḳf-nāma-i Rabʿ-i Rashīdī*, dated 709/1309-10, and include property in Yazd, Hamadān, Sharrāh, Tabrīz, Shīrāz, Iṣfahān and Mawṣil. Property in the first four places had also apparently been made into *waḳf* by Rashīd al-Dīn at an earlier date, for which special *waḳfiyya*s had been drawn up (Lambton, *Awqāf in Persia*, 317-18). As a convert to Islam, the support of the *ʿulamāʾ* was important for him and this he might have expected to gain as a result of his charitable foundations.

Among private individuals who constituted their property into *awḳāf*, the example of Sayyid Rukn al-Dīn Muḥammad and his son Shams al-Dīn Muḥammad of Yazd is notable. Sayyid Rukn al-Dīn disposed of a great deal of property—shares in *ḳanāt*s [*q.v.*], land and real estate in Yazd—and he also apparently had considerable capital available with which he purchased new property with a view to making it into *awḳāf*. His foundations and those of his son and their *awḳāf* are set out in the *Djāmiʿ al-khayrāt*, dated 748/1347-8 (ed. Muḥammad Taḳī Dānishpazhūh and Iradj Afshār, in *FIZ*, ix [AHS 1345/1966-7], and a revised edition in Afshār, *Yādigārhā-yi Yazd*, ii, Tehran AHS 1354/1975-6, 391-557; see also YAZD). An interesting feature of Shams al-Dīn Muḥammad's *awḳāf* is the inclusion of pensions (*idrārāt*) which he held on various funds among the property which he made into *waḳf* (*Djāmiʿ al-khayrāt*, 174, 203, 213, 214, 216). Rukn al-Dīn Muḥammad, Shams al-Dīn's father, had also had a pension drawn on the revenue of Yazd, part of which he had inherited from his forefathers and part from the *sayyids* and *imāms* of Yazd. After his death, it passed to Shams al-Dīn (*ibid.*, 140; see also Lambton, *Awqāf in Persia*, 213-15). Al-ʿUmarī states that *idrārāt*, which consisted of money or villages, were the property of their holders, who could dispose of them like landed estates, sell them, give them away, or constitute them into *waḳf* (*Das mongolische Weltreich*, Arabic text, 95-6. See also Naṣīr al-Dīn Ṭūsī, *Madjmūʿa-yi rasāʾil az taʾlīfāt-i Khʷādja Naṣīr al Dīn Ṭūsī*, ed. M. Riḍawī, Tehran AHS 1336/1957, 31).

Many of the *awḳāf* constituted during the Īlkhānate disappeared over time. On Rashīd al-Dīn's fall, the revenue of the *awḳāf* which he had made for the Rabʿ-i Rashīdī was withheld from expenditure on its proper purposes and his estates taken for the *dīwān* (Ḥāfiẓ Abrū, *Dhayl-i djāmiʿ-i tawārīkh-i rashīdī*, ed. Khān Bābā Bayānī, Tehran AHS 1350/1971, 129). The Ghiyāthiyya *awḳāf* or some of them, made by his son Ghiyāth al-Dīn Muḥammad, appear to have still been in existence in 1073/1662 (Lambton, *Landlord and peasant*, 113-14). There is also mention of Ghāzānī *awḳāf* in the 10th/16th century (Iskandar Beg Munshī, *Tārīkh-i ʿĀlamārā-yi ʿAbbāsī*, Tehran AHS 1334/1956, i, 148).

The Tīmūrids in Bukhārā, Harāt and elsewhere, and the Ṣafawids in Iṣfahān, followed the practice of Ghazan and Öldjeytü in founding magnificent buildings in their capitals and constituting valuable *awḳāf* for them. Perhaps partly as a result of the increasing number of royal foundations, the *ṣadārat* was expanded and separated from the wazīrate and the office of *ṣadr* [*q.v.*] regularised (see documents in the *Sharaf-nāma* of ʿAbd Allāh Marwārīd, in H.R. Roemer, *Staatsschreiben der Timuridenzeit*, Wiesbaden 1952). Maria E. Subtelny has drawn attention to the proliferation of *awḳāf* in Khurāsān under the Tīmūrids, especially Ḥusayn Mīrzā Bayḳara (*A Timurid educational and charitable foundation: the Ikhlāṣiyya complex of ʿAlī Shīr Nawāʾī in 15th century Herat and its endowment*, in *JAOS*, ix [1991], 38-61). Khʷāndamīr notes that in the reign of Ḥusayn Mīrzā Bayḳara [see ḤUSAYN (Mīrzā b. Manṣūr b. Bayḳara)] the spread of *awḳāf* in Khurāsān was such that two or three persons were needed to carry out the office of *ṣadr* (*Ḥabīb al-siyar*, Tehran AHS 1333/1954-5, iv, 321). Tīmūr apparently constituted a number of properties into *waḳf* for the Ṣafawid family (Lambton, *Landlord and peasant*, 112 n. 1), and the early Ṣafawid shāhs, notably Ṭahmāsp I (930-84/1524-76 [*q.v.*]), made property into *waḳf* for the Ṣafawid shrines in Ḳum [*q.v.*] and elsewhere. A document for the appointment of the *mutawallī* of the shrine of Sittī Fāṭima in Ḳum issued by the Aḳ Ḳoyunlu Yaʿḳūb Beg in 884/1479 mentions earlier appointments by Tīmūr and Shāhrukh (see H. Busse, *Untersuchungen zum islamischen Kanzleiwesen*, Cairo 1959, 56-7). Some of the *awḳāf* for the Ṣafawid shrine at Ardabīl [*q.v.*] also predated the assumption of royal power by the Ṣafawids.

Although the Tīmūrid and Ṣafawid periods were characterised by royal foundations, there was also much constitution of *awḳāf* by provincial governors, officials and private individuals. The motive for many of these foundations was probably local patriotism, but their founders were probably also influenced in many cases by the hope of obtaining local support as public benefactors. In Yazd, important *awḳāf*, were founded by the Tīmūrid governor Amīr Čaḳmaḳ and his wife Bībī Fāṭima and later by Muḥammad Taḳī Khān, who as governor of Yazd under the Afshārids, Zands and Ḳādjārs, exercised a considerable degree of independence [see YAZD]. Under the Ṣafawids, there was probably an increase in family *awḳāf*, made in the hope of ensuring the enjoyment of their revenues by the founder and his family and of preventing, or at least lessening, the interference of the government in the administration of the property so constituted. A typical example is the *waḳf-nāma* of Ghiyāth al-Dīn ʿAlī al-Ghiyāthī dated Ramaḍān 951/Nov.-Dec. 1544 (*Mawḳūfāt-i Ghiyāth al-Dīn ʿAlī al-Ghiyāthī*, ed. Karāmat Raʿna Ḥusaynī, in *Madjalla-yi Dānishkada-yi Adabiyyāt wa ʿUlūm-i Insānī* (Tehran), xvi/4 [Farwardīn 1348/ March 1969], 465-76). The founder relinquished ownership of the endowed properties and took them over again as *mutawallī* (*ibid.*, 471).

Ismāʿīl Ṣafawī [*q.v.*], the first Ṣafawid shāh, among his early acts appointed Shams al-Dīn Gīlānī *ṣadr* and put him in charge of the *awḳāf* of the empire (Khʷāndamīr, iv, 468). In the reign of Shāh Ṣafī (1076-1105/1666-94 [see SULAYMĀN SHĀH]), the office of *ṣadr* was divided; the *ṣadr-i khāṣṣa* administered and generally supervised *awḳāf* in the *khāṣṣa* provinces and the *ṣadr-i mamālik* those in the provinces under governors. The *ṣadr-i khāṣṣa* had additional functions in connection with those *awḳāf* of which the shāh was the *mutawallī*, including the appointment of administrators (*mubāshirān*) over them, deputy *mutawallīs* (*mutawalliyān-i djuzw*) and overseers (*nāẓirān*). In the case of *sharʿī awḳāf* (i.e. those constituted by private individuals), neither the *ṣudūr* nor *sharʿī* judges were to interfere with whomsoever the founder had designated as *mutawallī* (Mīrzā Rafīʿā, *Dastūr al-mulūk*, ed. Muḥammad Taḳī Dānishpazhūh, in *MDAʿUI*, xvi/1-2 [Ādhar 1317/November 1968], 66). The *awḳāf* in Iṣfahān, Yazd, Abarḳūh, Kāshān, Ḳum, Sāwa, Māzandarān, Astarābād, Giraylī, Ḥadjdjilar, Kabūddjāma, Naṭanz, Ardistān, Nāʾīn, Ḳumisha, Kamara and Maḥallāt, Farāhān, Gulpāyāgān, Dilidjān, Khʷānsar, Djāpalak, Barwarūd (?), Firaydan, Rārā, Mizdadj and Kuyar were under the *ṣadr-i khāṣṣa* (Mīrzā Rafīʿā, *loc. cit.*), who presumably appointed officials to take charge of the *awḳāf* in these districts (cf. the document appointing Muḥammad Mufīd *mustawfī* of the *awḳāf* of Yazd dated 1077/1667, in Muḥammad Mufīd, *Djāmiʿ-i mufīdī*, ed. Afshār, Tehran AHS 1340/1961-2, iii, 752-4). The precise relation of the *ṣadr-i khāṣṣa* to the *wazīr* of the Fayḍ Āthār department, also called the *wazīr-i mawḳūfāt*, who was in charge of the agriculture of the Maḥāll (the districts round Iṣfahān) and the repair of buildings in the Maḥāll and of gardens which were *waḳf* (apart from certain named gardens which were under the *nāẓir*), is not clear (Mīrzā Rafīʿā, in *MDAʿUI*, xvi/3, 321).

The Ṣafawid shāhs made extensive *awḳāf* for various shrines [see IMĀMZĀDA] and appointed *mutawallīs* for them. Shāh Ismāʿīl I allegedly took possession of estates in Maymand which had been made into *waḳf* for the Shāh Čirāgh mosque in Shīrāz, and vested the office of *mutawallī* in his children (Fasāʾī, *Fārs-nāma-i nāṣirī*, lith., Tehran 1313/1895, ii, 305). During the disorders after the fall of the Ṣafawids, they were usurped by Mīrzā Abū Ṭālib, the *kalāntar* of Shīrāz. Nādir Shāh [*q.v.*] restored them to the shrine in 1142/ 1729-30 (*ibid.*, i, 104). Misappropriation of *awḳāf* was not uncommon. The *wazīr* Ḳāḍī Djahān is alleged to have converted certain *waḳf* villages into his private property. After he had retired to Ḳazwīn, this came to the ears of Shāh Ṭahmāsp, who ordered him to be deprived of their possession and the equivalent of the revenue due from them to be recovered. However, because of Ḳāḍī Djahān's age and weakness, the shāh forgave him and granted him a sum of money as a *soyurghal* (Ḥasan Rūmlū, *Ahsan al-tawārīkh*, ed. C.N. Seddon, Baroda 1931, i, 375-6).

Ṭahmāsp I constituted *awḳāf* for the shrine of Shāh ʿAbd al-ʿAẓīm in Ray according to a *farmān* dated 960/1153 (Shihābī, *Waḳf dar Islām*, Tehran AHS 1343/1964, 72). His sister Shāhzāda Sulṭānum constituted *awḳāf* for the Čahārdah Maʿṣūm (sc. the twelve *imāms*, the prophet Muḥammad and Fāṭima, the wife of ʿAlī b. Ṭālib) and appointed as *mutawallī* Ṭahmāsp and whichever of his sons should become shāh after him. Ṭahmāsp appointed Mīr Kamāl al-Dīn Astarābādī his deputy (*nāʾib al-tawliya*) (Iskandar Munshī, i, 111-12). The latter, during Ṭahmāsp's reign, was also, with Mīr Abu 'l-Ḳāsim Iṣfahānī, joint *mutawallī* of the shrine of the Imām Riḍā at Mashhad; he undertook the *tawliya-i sunnatī* and Mīr Abu 'l-Ḳāsim the *tawliya-i wādjibī*. The first concerned the administration of *soyurghals* and what was given from the *khāṣṣa* administration for the expenses of the shrine on public feasts (*shīlān*) and for allowances for the servants of the shrine, *sādāt*, and others, while the *wādjibī tawliya* was concerned with the revenue of the *awḳāf* of the shrine and from vows (*ibid.*, i, 149). The most numerous *awḳāf* constituted by a ruling shāh belong to the reign of Shāh ʿAbbās I [*q.v.*]. R.D. McChesney has examined the *awḳāf* of Shāh ʿAbbās in detail and attempted an assessment of their political and economic aspects (*Waqf and public policy: the waqfs of Shāh ʿAbbās, 1011-1023/1602-1614*, in *Asian and African Studies*, xv [1981], 165-90). The best known of these foundations is that made, according to Iskandar Beg Munshī, in 1015/1606-7 or 1016/1607-8 when he constituted all his private estates (*djamīʿ-i amlāk wa raḳabāt-i muktasab-i khāṣṣa-i khᵘud*), "the just value of which was 100,000 *tūmān-i shāhī-yi ʿirāḳī* and the produce of which after the deduction of what was needed for their cultivation was, using a medium conversion rate, nearly 7,000 *tūmāns*", together with various buildings in Iṣfahān and the neighbourhood into *waḳf* for the Čahārdah Maʿṣūm. He vested the office of *mutawallī* in himself and thereafter in the reigning monarch. According to the terms of the *waḳf-nāma* drawn up by Shaykh Bahāʾ al-Dīn, the revenue of the *waḳf*, after the deduction of the dues of the *mutawallī* (*ḥaḳḳ al-tawliya*) was to be expended at the discretion of the *mutawallī* and according to the exigencies of the time (Iskandar Beg Munshī, i, 536). Mīrzā Raḍī, the *ṣadr*, was appointed the shāh's deputy in charge of the administration of the *waḳf* (*ibid.*, 64). According to Shihābī, most of the founders of *awḳāf* for the shrine of the Imām Riḍā at Mashhad after this designated the reigning shāh as the *mutawallī*. The shāh's deputy in the management of the *awḳāf* of the shrine was called the *mutawallī-bāshī* and later the *nāʾib al-tawliya* (*Waḳf dar Islām*, 60. On Shāh ʿAbbās's foundations, see also ʿAbd al-Ḥusayn Sipintā, *Tārīkhča-yi awḳāf dar Iṣfahān*, Iṣfahān AHS 1346/1967-8, 41 ff., 331 ff.).

Shāh Sulṭān Ḥusayn, the last of the Ṣafawids, constituted property into *waḳf* for the Madrasa-i Sulṭānī (Madrasa-i Mādar Shāh, now known as the Madrasa-i Čahār Bāgh) in Iṣfahān in 1122/1711-12 and designated himself as *mutawallī* and thereafter the reigning shāh (Sipintā, 120-32). He made the taxes and dues of the property so constituted into a permanent *soyurghal* for the administration of the *madrasa* (*ibid.*, 131).

The office of *mutawallī* of the shrines which had *awḳāf-i tafwīḍī* (i.e. *awḳāf* constituted by the reigning shāh) was influential and profitable. Mīrzā Rafīʿā describes the duties of the *mutawallīs* of the shrine of the Imām Riḍā in Mashhad, the shrine of Fāṭima, the sister of the Imām Riḍā, in Ḳum, the shrine of ʿAbd al-ʿAẓīm in Rayy, the Ṣafawid shrines in Ḳum, and the Ṣafawid shrine in Ardabīl and the respect in which the *mutawallīs* were held at the royal court (*MDAʿUI*, xvi/1-2, 66-9). Shihābī gives a list of the properties made into *waḳf* for the shrine of Shāh ʿAbd al-ʿAẓīm (*Waḳf dar Islām*, 72-3). He states that Mīrzā Ḥabīb Allāh, the grandson of Shaykh ʿAlī Karakī, was appointed *mutawallī* of the shrine of Fāṭima at Ḳum by Ṭahmāsp, while the *tawliyat* of the shrine at Māhān was given to another grandson, Mīr Sayyid Murtaḍā. Another of Shaykh ʿAlī's descendants, Mīrzā Ibrāhīm, *shaykh al-islām* of Ray, became *mutawallī* of the shrine of ʿAbd al-ʿAẓīm; his descendants still held that office in the 19th century. Yet another of Shaykh ʿAlī's sons, Sayyid Aḥmad, and his descendants after him, held the office of *mutawallī* of the shrine of Ṣafī al-Dīn at Ardabīl (*ibid.*, 74). Shāh ʿAbbās II (1052-77/1642-67 [*q.v.*]) redistributed the offices of *mutawallī* of the major shrines in an attempt to break up the large fortunes which their holders accumulated (Chardin, *Voyages*, ed. Langlès, Paris 1811, vi, 63-5), reorganised the administration of the *awḳāf-i tafwīḍī* (Muḥammad Ṭāhir Ḳazwīnī, *ʿAbbās-nāma*, ed. Ibrāhīm Dihgān, Arāk AHS 1329/1950-1, 223-4) and appointed Mīrzā Masʿūd Djābirī *wazīr-i awḳāf*. J.B. Fraser was informed by the *mudjtahid* Mīrzā ʿAbd al-Djawād that the revenues of the shrine of the Imām Riḍā from property and land in every province of Persia amounted in the reign of Shāh Sulṭān Ḥusayn to 15,000 *khurāsānī tūmāns*. In later years, his informant told him, there had been usurpation and the rents were ill-paid so that the revenue was probably not more than 2,000 or 2,500 *khurāsānī tūmāns* (*Narrative of a journey into Khorasan in the years 1821 and 1822*, London 1825, 455).

Although the richest and most extensive *awḳāf* in the Ṣafawid period were those made by the shāhs, there were also numerous *awḳāf* constituted by individuals, some affluent (for example Muḥammad Beg Begdilu (d. 1021/1612-13), a man of wealth and substance who made his landed estates into *waḳf* (Iskandar Munshī, ii, 608), but many less so, who were influenced not only by personal gain but by religious feeling and pietas (cf. the case of a certain Ḥādjdjī Yār Beg, a tanner of Iṣfahān, Luṭf Allāh Hunarfar, *Gandjīna-i āthār-i tārīkhī-i Iṣfahān*, Iṣfahān AHS 1344/1961-2, 541-3).

When the Afghāns took Iṣfahān on the fall of the Ṣafawids, they usurped much *waḳfī* property and made it into *khāliṣa* [*q.v.*]; and many records were destroyed (Shaykh Djābir Anṣārī, *Tārīkh-i Iṣfahān wa Ray*, Iṣfahān AHS 1322/1943, 35). Under Nādir Shāh, many *waḳfī* properties were resumed in Iṣfahān, if not elsewhere, and included in the Nādirī registers (*ibid.*, 37-8; see also Mīrzā Muḥammad Kalāntar-i Fārs, *Rūznāma*, ed. ʿAbbās Iḳbāl, Tehran 1946, 13). ʿĀdil Shāh revoked Nādir's regulations and ordered the *awḳāf* to be returned to their *mutawallīs*. However, a good deal of confusion prevailed and it is not clear to what extent this took place (*ibid.*). Karīm Khān, according to Sipintā, made an abortive attempt to rectify affairs (343). Further decay and confusion occurred in the famine years of 1871-2 (Shaykh Djābir Anṣārī, 51-2).

The Ḳādjār period was not notable for the constitution of *awḳāf*. One of the most important was that made for the Sipahsālār Madrasa in Tehran. The building was begun in 1819 by Amīn al-Dawla Ḥādjdjī Muḥammad Ḥusayn Khān Ṣadr-i Iṣfahān, who designated himself first as *mutawallī* and thereafter the ruling shāh

(Shihābī, 40). He died two years later before the building was completed. His brother Yaḥyā Khān Mushīr al-Dawla continued the work but also died before it was completed. It was finally finished by the shāh's *mutawallīs* (Shihābī, 38-9; for the text of Muḥammad Ḥusayn Khān's *waḳfiyya*, see Sipintā, 408-20).

In 1854 a Ministry of Pensions and *Awḳāf* was founded. In 1863 it was announced in the official gazette, *Rūznāma-i dawlat-i ʿāliya-yi Īrān*, that those in charge of all *awḳāf* both in districts near the capital and in the provinces were to send their accounts, duly attested by a *mudjtahid*, to the Ministry of Pensions and *Awḳāf*. Anyone who failed to do so would be deprived of office (no. 535, 17 Radjab 1279/1863). After the grant of the Constitution [see DUSTŪR. iv] the duties of the department of *awḳāf*, which came under the Ministry of Education, were set out in Article 6 of the Law of 28 Shaʿbān 1328/1910 and in the Supplementary Law of 19 Djumādā II 1329/1911 (Sipintā, 11). The legal position was in due course laid down in the Civil Code (see Lambton, *Landlord and peasant*, 230 ff.).

Bibliography (in addition to references given in the article): ʿAbd al-Wahhāb Ṭarāz, *Kitābča-yi mawḳūfāt-i Yazd*, ed. Īradj Afshār, in *FIZ*, x (AHS 1341/1962), 95-123; Muḥammad b. Hindūshāh Nakhdjiwānī, *Dastūr al-kātib fī taʿyīn al-marātib*, ed. A.A. Alizade, i/1-2, ii, Moscow 1964-76; anon, *Astarābād-nāma*, ed. Masīḥ Dhabīḥī, separate publication of *FIZ*, no. 12, Tehran AHS 1348/1969; Sayyid Ḥusayn Mudarrisī Ṭabāṭabāʾī, *Turbat-i pākān*, 2 vols., Ḳum 1395-6/1975-6.

In recent years a number of texts and studies of *awḳāf* have been published. Among them are the following: Īradj Afshār, *Waḳf-nāma-i si dih dar Kāshān*, in *FIZ*, iv (AHS 1335/1956-7), 112-22; Ḥusayn Shahshahānī, *Khulāṣa az waḳf-nāma-i masdjid-i Mīr ʿImād wa farmānhā-yi salāṭīn ki dar ān bāḳī mānda ast*, in *FIZ*, v/1 (AHS 1336/1957), 23-5; A.D. Papazyan, *Persidskie dokumentī matenadarana II (1601-1650 vv.)*, Erevan 1959; Muḥammad Taḳī Dānishpazhūh, *Du farmān marbūṭ bi shahr-i Ray*, in *Rāhnamā-yi Kitāb*, vii/1 (AHS 1343/1964), 140-5; M.T. Musevi, *Orta esr Azerbaijan tarikhine dair Fars dilinde yazilmish senedler*, Baku 1965; Muḥammad ʿAlī Hidāyatī, *Āstāna-i Ray. Madjmūʿa-i asnād wa farāmīn*, Tehran AHS 1314/1965-6; Afshār, *Waḳf-nāma-i āb-i Furāt az ʿahd-i Shāh Ṭahmāsp*, in *FIZ*, xiv (AHS 1346/1967-8) 313-18; Musevi, *Baku tarikhine dair orta esr senedleri*, Baku 1967; Mohamed Khadr, *Deux actes de waqf d'un Qaraḫānide d'Asie Centrale*, in *JA*, cclv (1967), 305-39, see also C.E. Bosworth, *À propos de l'article de Mohamed Khadr, Deux actes de waqf d'un Qaraḫānide d'Asie Centrale*, in *JA*, cclvii (1968), 449-53; Muḥammad Ibrāhīm Bāstānī Pārīzī, *Safar-i Shāh ʿAbbās bi Kirmān*, in *Bar-rasīhā-yi tārīkhī*, iii/1 (AHS 1347/1968) 31-52; Ibrāhīm Nabawī Ḥāʾirī, *Mawḳūfāt-i Ḥaḍrat-i Rasūl wa Ḥaḍrat-i Riḍā dar Astarābād wa Gurgān*, Nadjaf AHS 1347/1968-9; Farhang Djahānpūr, *Farāmīn-i pādishāhān-i ṣafawī dar mūza-i brītāniyā*, in *Bar-rasīhā-yi tārīkhī*, iv/4 (AHS 1348/1969), 140-2, 225-7, 234-5; Afshār, *Rashīd al-Dīn Faḍl Allāh wa Yazd*, in *Īrānshināsī*, ii/1 (1970), 23-33; idem, *Awḳāf-i rashīdī dar Yazd*, in *FIZ*, xvi-xvii (AHS 1349/1970-1); B. Fragner, *Zu einem Autograph des Mongolenwesirs Rašīd al-Dīn Fażullāh, der Stiftungsurkunde für das Tabrizer Gelehrten-Viertel Rabʿ-i Rašīdī*, in W. Eilers (ed.), *Festgabe deutscher Orientalisten zur 2500 Jahrfeier Irans*, Stuttgart 1971, 35-46; Ḥusayn Mudarrisī Ṭabāṭabāʾī, *Kitābča-i thabat-i mawḳūfāt wa khāliṣadjāt-i kishwar dar dawra-i nāṣirī*, in *Rāhnamā-i kitāb*, xviii/4-6 (AHS 1354/1975), 435-42; Afshār, *Waḳfiyya kadjadjī*, repr. from *FIZ*, xxi (AHS 1354/1976), 1-38; idem, *Sanadī dar bāra-i buḳʿa-i Shaykh Murshid-i Kāzirūnī*, in *Āyanda*, v/1-3 (AHS 1358/1979-80), 137-47; Fragner, *Repertorium persischer Herrscherurkunden*, Freiburg im Breisgau, 1980; E. Ehlers and Mustafa Momeni, *Religiöse Stiftungen und Stadtentwicklung das Beispiel Taft/Zentraliran*, in *Erdkunde Archiv für wissenschaftliche Geographie*, xliii (1989), 16-26; Ḳudrat Allāh Rawshanī (Zaʿfarānlū), *Waḳf-nāma-i āb-i khiyābān-i Mashhad*, in *FIZ*, xxviii (AHS 1369/1990), 320-5; Maḥmūd Rūḥ al-Amīnī, *Waḳf bar khamsa-i mustariḳa*, in *Āyanda*, viii/7-12 (AHS 1371/1992-3).

(ANN K.S. LAMBTON)

IV. IN THE OTTOMAN EMPIRE TO 1914

The understanding and interpretation of the role of *waḳf* in the Ottoman empire has radically changed since the opening of the vast Ottoman archival holdings in Turkey and the successor states, to which should be added the considerable number of Ottoman documents held in European libraries and archives (e.g. the Archives d'Outre-Mer in Aix-en-Provence which represent one of the more important holdings in Europe for Ottoman Algeria). The increased accessibility, especially from the 1970s onwards, for the international scholarly community to study portions of the Ottoman imperial and provincial archives—and the *waḳf* documents within them—in addition to the ongoing publication of archival catalogues in Turkish, Arabic, the Slavic languages, English, etc. (Kenderova, 1984; Lewis; Bilici, 1997; Faroqhi, 1999, 54-5, 60-61, 96; Temimi; Ivanova and Ivanova; bibliographical references cited within manuscript and library catalogues published by Başbakanlık and IRCICA; relevant library and archive internet sites), represents no less than a revolution in research on Ottoman *waḳf*. Furthermore, Ottoman *waḳf* foundation deeds themselves (*waḳfiyye* and *kitāb al-waḳf*) and associated documents are gradually being published under the auspices of the General Directorate of Waḳfs in Ankara (i.e. the foundation document of the Ottoman sultan, Meḥemmed the Conqueror, published in 1938 and the deeds published in the *Vakıflar Dergisi*), by Waḳf Ministries in the former Ottoman provinces (such as the Lālā Muṣṭafā Pasha *waḳfiyya* published by the Syrian Waḳf Ministry in Damascus) and by other organisations.

Access to this primary material has drastically changed methodological approaches to the study of Ottoman *waḳf* which, heretofore, had almost exclusively relied upon Islamic legal compendia (*aḥkām al-awḳāf*, *fatwā* collections and legal studies) or Western interpretations of it (i.e. Mercier), overwhelmingly giving a normative or interpretative view (Heffening). Barkan and Ayverdi's research, based on the data of a mid-10th/16th-century *taḥrīr* [*q.v.*], was the first to have systematically and quantitatively studied Ottoman *waḳf* at a given time and place. Since then, quantitative statistical analyses on predetermined aspects of a corpus of documents related to Ottoman *waḳf*, combined with qualitative evaluations drawn not only from *waḳf* endowment deeds (the above-mentioned *kitāb al-waḳf* and the *waḳfiyye*) but also from the *ḥudjdjat al-waḳf*, have been published (Raymond; Saidouni; Bakhit; Hénia; Roded; Shuval), revealing trends related to the identities and status of endowment founders and the administrators of the foundations, properties owned by *waḳf*, renters of this property, beneficiaries of the revenues, etc. Some publications on Ottoman *waḳf* have also analysed archival data juxtaposed with information from the legal domain, such as the *aḥkām al-awḳāf* or *fatwā* collections (Rafeq; Reilly; Cuno; Deguilhem, 1988).

An overall picture of Ottoman foundations which comes closer to reality is made possible by understanding *waḳf* as a dynamic and very diversified institution which partially developed on-the-ground in reaction to altering circumstances but which responded, at least to a certain extent, to predefined structures. Both the changing as well as the continuous practices of *waḳf* were reflected in the juridico-administrative Ottoman tribunal and bureaucratic records (which, though seemingly of formulaic language, expressed nonetheless changing circumstances), but also within the corresponding legal normative framework articulated in *fiḳh* [*q.v.*] (Hüsnü) and *ḳānūn* [*q.v.*] (A. Çetin, 221-7). In other words, the primary sources have indisputably shown that, far from being static or in "mortmain", foundation properties were not, in fact, inalienable and often changed hands not only through the legal mechanism of *istibdāl, irṣād* (Deguilhem, 1988) and other legalised means, but also simply as an integral part of the economy, in line with market demands. The economics and politics of Ottoman *waḳf* were based upon a flexible but stable system that had long since produced an institution capable of interacting and responding to individual, family, community and state needs.

Waḳf was omnipresent in all levels of Ottoman society, urban and rural, both in the form of individually functioning units and as separate parts of a basic single institutional system. Studying the institution *in situ* from the vantage point of the data found in endowment deeds, in the *ḥudjdjat al-waḳf* and in documents inscribed in *waḳf* and other registers (i.e. the *taḥrīr*, the *daftar mufaṣṣal*, etc.) reveals the extreme multiplicity of functions that were initiated, established and activated by *waḳf* networks in the Ottoman world (for an overview and state-of-the-art survey of *waḳf* research up until the end of the 1990s, see Hoexter, *Waqf studies*, and Bilici, 1997), over which the imperial authority attempted to exercise supervision with varying degrees of success over the centuries.

To grasp the ubiquitous character of the Ottoman foundations, one may say that the three most striking traits of the Ottoman *waḳf* were its widespread vertical and horizontal use throughout all socio-economic strata of society; its capacity to adapt to individual, group and state needs within Islamic as well as within Ottoman Christian (Abou Nohra; Ghazzal; Davie; Slim; Saliba—see for these references, *Bibl.*, below) and Jewish communities (Yazbak, 55-6, 60, 214-15, 217-18; Shaham; Gerber, *The Jews*); and, finally, its longevity—not only of the institution itself but also of the abundant individual *waḳfs* (although, of course, many also disappeared), whether endowed in the Ottoman period or founded during Ayyūbid or Mamlūk times but which continued to operate during the centuries of Ottoman rule (their longevity perceived, for example, via a comparative study of 10th/16th-century *tapu taḥrīr* registers which surveyed the existing *milk* [*q.v.*] and *waḳf* properties in relation to 20th-century *waḳf* liquidation documents).

From the early years of the empire, even while taking into account the regional differences across its vast Asian, African and European territories, the institution of *waḳf* continued to assume its traditional dual and complementary role within both urban and rural Ottoman contexts by simultaneously creating and financing religious, political, social, charitable, cultural and spiritual networks through the establishment of a continuous "permanent" economic linkage between *waḳf* beneficiaries and their corresponding revenue-producing assets, in addition to the personnel working for the endowments (Hütteroth and Abdelfattah, esp. map 4 showing regional *waḳf* links between late 10th/16th-century Egypt, Syria and the Ḥaramayn [*q.v.*]; Hoexter, *Endowments*, esp. for links between 17th-19th-century Algeria and the Arabian Holy Cities). *Waḳf* was the infrastructural core around which many aspects of Ottoman civilisation expressed itself.

Ottoman endowments included the *khayrī, dhurrī/ahlī* and *mushtarak waḳfs* (identifiable according to the *waḳf*'s immediate line of beneficiaries); the politically influential pilgrimage foundations—including the *dashīsha* (Afifi 1991, 1995) and Ḥaramayn foundations (which contributed towards the financing of more than just the Arabian Holy Cities: Hoexter, *Endowments*; Heywood; Faroqhi, 1994, 4, 76-8, 80-4, 87-9, 182; the sultanic imperial *humāyūn* [*q.v.*] (Barnes) *waḳfs* (to which also individuals contributed who were not associated with the sultanic household: Faroqhi, 1995, 97); the *irṣād* (Cuno) *waḳfs*, as well as a plethora of foundations which simultaneously incorporated elements from several of the above categories. Boundaries between the types of *waḳf* were not impermeable and differences between them should often be sought in terms of nuances.

For instance, revenues from the *irṣād waḳfs*, founded mostly by imperial family members and personalities close to the sultan, were presumably and frequently created for the general welfare (*maṣlaḥa* [*q.v.*]), but a considerable part of the *irṣād* shares in Egypt, during the latter centuries of the empire, were also distributed in the form of inheritable allocations (females not being excluded) to individual members of the *ʿulamāʾ* and the military institution. This was also a common enough characteristic of the other types of *waḳfs* mentioned above, especially the *khayrī* ones, but also the sultanic and Ḥaramayn endowments in that *waḳf* revenues were routinely used to create, modify or maintain local, regional or empire-wide political alliances. A striking example is the poor relief soup kitchen (*ʿimāret* [see KHAYR]) endowed, as an imperial *waḳf*, by Khürrem Sulṭāne [*q.v.*], wife of Süleymān Ḳānūnī, which, from its founding in 1552 until the end of the Ottoman period, catered to both the poor and wealthy in Jerusalem; being inscribed as a beneficiary of this *ʿimāret* became, in fact, a sign of political importance (Peri). Continuing to use the *irṣād* endowments as a comparative measure, juridical works and chronicles show that this type of Ottoman *waḳf* (recently studied by Cuno) was often founded with property belonging to the state (*bayt al-māl*), a feature obviously also shared with the imperial foundations. On a similar note, research in the Ottoman archives likewise documents the fact that private individuals constituted *waḳf* in Ottoman times not only with their private property, as the normative texts would have it, but also with *mīrī* [*q.v.*] state properties; in the 19th century, the *mīrī* property would, in this situation, have been held with a *sanad al-tābū* contract (Deguilhem, 1991, 70-4).

The Ottoman world was profoundly shaped by the foundations, each of which was administered as a separate unit by one or several *mutawallī*, supervised by a *nāẓir(a)* who, depending upon the size of the endowment, may have had an accountant (*muḥāsib*) and other personnel under his or her authority. By the 18th and, more especially, throughout the 19th century, the administration of *waḳf* became a veritable profession with some individuals managing ten or more foundations at a time. Aside from the individual administrators, the management of *waḳfs*, both in the provinces and in Istanbul, increasingly became concentrated and institutionalised, on one level, within the hands of local mosque officials (*imām*s and *mu'adhdhin*s) and, on another level, permanently associated with such positions as—to cite just a few among myriad examples—the offices of the Grand Vizier, the *shaykh al-islām* [*q.v.*], the inspector of the Ḥaramayn foundations, the Chief Black Eunuch, etc.

Revenue-generating properties belonging to *waḳf* in Ottoman times whose incomes subsidised the endowments' beneficiaries were located within urban centres, in the cities' immediate surroundings and outlying hinterlands, as well as sometimes in very remote rural regions. *Waḳf* assets consisted of all types of commercial and residential properties that were usually rented in order to create funds for the foundation beneficiaries. Such properties included the *bayt, dār, maghzan, dukkān, ḳahwa, ḥammām, ḳayṣāriyya, khān, bedestān*, parts of or an entire *sūḳ*, etc. *Waḳf* assets also consisted of agricultural real estate which equally yielded revenues for the foundations through rent contracts or by payment in kind from different types of gardens (*djunayna, ḥākūra*) and orchards (*bustān* [*q.v.*]) located within or close to urban centres in addition to parts of or entire villages and tracts of rural agricultural land such as the *ḥānūt, mazra'a* [*q.v.*], *čiftlik* [*q.v.*], *rizḳa aḥbāsiyya* in Ottoman Egypt, etc. Furthermore, as in previous periods, endowment wealth in the Ottoman realm also included moveable properties (*manḳūlāt*) amongst assets belonging to a *waḳf*, such as books, Ḳur'ān holders, etc. as well as animals, in particular, those used for pious purposes such as for the Pilgrimage (horses, camels). Nomadic communities living in the Ottoman empire used this type of foundation, putting a part of their animals into *waḳf*, as a means of keeping a portion of their properties within the family.

It is now a well-documented fact that sums of cash were also widely possessed by Ottoman *waḳf*s. By the mid-10th/16th century, cash holdings in fact already represented a substantial part of Ottoman *waḳf* assets (Barkan and Ayverdi) which, in the 18th and 19th centuries, represented, in some ways, the precursors of the Ottoman banking system. Foundation administrators lent out the cash at interest, often via specifically named money changers, members of the *ṣarrāf* profession, so indicated in the foundation document, with the purpose of creating liquid assets for the endowment. Ebu 'l-Su'ūd (1545-74 [see ABU 'L-SU'ŪD]), *sheykh al-islām* under Süleymān the Magnificent, was one of the Ottoman religious authorities to have pronounced *fatwā*s on the legality of monetary *waḳf*, whereas his contemporary, Meḥmed Birgewī (1520-73), opposed the practice. Since the cash *waḳf* (*waḳf al-nuḳūd*) produced money for the endowments through interest, it was the object of controversy even before Ottoman times (Mandaville; Yediyıldız, 116-20, 144-9; Bilici, *Les waqfs monétaires*; Cizakca). Towards the end of the Ottoman era, during the second half of the 19th and the beginning of the 20th centuries, some *waḳf* administrators placed money with the Ottoman Bank as a means of fructifying capital both on their own behalf as well as in the name of a *waḳf*, including endowments founded for Ṣūfī orders such as the Mewlewiyye (Eldem, 288-9).

Many public leaders—sultans but also local governors and bureaucrats as well as all types of notables at all hierarchical levels—marked their political power, often transforming and modifying the character and topography of cities and towns in the process, thanks to proceeds coming from *waḳf* assets, by establishing and subsidising religio-educational structures (*djāmi'*, *masdjid* [*q.v.*], *madrasa* [*q.v.*], *dār al-Ḳur'ān, dār al-ḥadīth*; Ṣūfī lodges and places of assembly (*zāwiya, khānḳāh, ribāṭ, tekke* [*q.vv.*]); poor relief sites such as soup kitchens or places giving other sorts of assistance (*'imāret* and the *takiyya madrasa* frequently used for giving poor relief in the Arab provinces); mausolea which often served as social gathering places (*turba* [*q.v.*]), medical dispensaries (*bīmāristān* [*q.v.*]); and public infrastructural services in the form of bridges, irrigation systems, fortresses, lighthouses, water conduits, aqueducts, water fountains, etc., in urban and rural areas alike.

During the expansionist periods of the empire, especially in the 9th/15th and 10th/16th centuries, *waḳf* was an important political instrument for the Islamisation of newly-conquered localities and frontier areas. To this end, the endowments funded convent-type structures (*ribāṭ*) situated in areas near or bordering on the *dār al-ḥarb* [*q.v.*], notably in the European Ottoman provinces where Ṣūfīs and other Muslims lived, worked the land, engaged in commerce and eventually colonised regions as a concrete means of increasing the expanse of lands belonging to the realm. As part of the Islamisation programme, which was closely tied to the legitimisation efforts of the sultanate, income from sultanic *waḳf*s and associated endowments within all the Ottoman provinces also funded the construction and maintenance of buildings intended for Islamic ritual and teaching (as mentioned above) and, during the early days of the empire, was sometimes involved in the transformation of churches, cathedrals and other already existing edifices into places for use by the Islamic community (Barkan, 1942; Inalcik, 1980, 1990).

Waḳf networks in Ottoman lands were the essential infrastructural link in the transmission of knowledge, since the construction and patronage of places for ritual observances and institutionalised learning, i.e. the mosques and religious schools mentioned above, were almost exclusively subsidised by *waḳf*; this was equally true for many libraries, both public (associated with mosques, Ṣūfī lodges or schools) and private. By way of a famous example, Meḥemmed the Conqueror, immediately upon annexing Konya to his empire in the middle of the 9th/15th century, recorded, in the *waḳf* registers, the magnificent 7th/13th-century manuscript collection there which had formerly belonged to the Ṣūfī Ṣadr al-Dīn al-Ḳūnawī, son-in-law of Ibn 'Arabī [*q.v.*] (Faroqhi, 1999, 46). Although this endowed library counted spectacular manuscripts amongst its holdings, other more modest libraries throughout the different provinces, including those owned by private individuals, were very common (Kenderova, 1999, for an endowed collection in the Balkans). Some of these private libraries were maintained for the active use of scholars and students, while others undoubtedly simply represented a form of capital, the manuscripts not necessarily being read. The *sālnāma*s or late Ottoman almanacs sometimes give lists of the endowed libraries and their contents.

Throughout the empire's territories and through the course of the centuries, *waḳf*-financed utilities ranged from extremely impressive and influential foundation complexes, which continue to function up until today (one of the many outstanding ones is the mid-10th/16th-century Süleymāniyye complex built by Mi'mār Sinān: Necipoglu), to much more modest but still functioning structures, all of them reaching deeply into the society of their time, so that almost everyone living in the empire was affected at some point, during his or her life, by *waḳf* networks which criss-crossed local, regional and international as well as confessional boundaries.

That endowments were often used as a political instrument by the sultans, by members of the harem and the imperial family, by persons who occupied bureaucratic, religious, military and other official positions at all levels, in addition to individuals in their private capacity, should not overshadow the fact that many *waḳfs* were also founded for pious, religious and charitable purposes and that, in fact, one purpose did not always exclude the other. As dispensers of justice toward the community, the Ottoman sultans and members of their extended households, as well as the average Muslim, undertook poor relief, via the agency of *waḳf*, as one of their responsibilities. Thus, for example, in 1570, Muṣṭafā Čelebi Efendi, a son of the *defterdār* [*q.v.*], Murād Čelebi Efendi, established a large *waḳf* in Istanbul which, according to his *waḳfiyye*, was for the salvation of his soul (an invocation often referred to in the foundation documents). This *waḳf*, similar to so many others, distributed, among other things, water "obtained from pure snow" to the poor and passers-by in Istanbul during the three hottest months of the year (Sauvan, 242). The fact that this water was of such high quality lent an even greater importance to the charity-giving.

The existence of the huge sultanic *waḳf* should not overshadow the fact that modest endowments, sometimes constituted from extremely limited assets, such as a very small plot of cultivated land or a tiny room in a *dār*, *khān* or other building, or even a portion of the above, were also very frequently established as *waḳf*. These modest or middle-sized endowments made by small property owners in the Ottoman empire were often of the *mushtarak* type and thus represented the method of simultaneously enacting a good deed through conferring largesse (even though of a limited amount) on a public or needy beneficiary while, at the same time, ensuring the transmission of family wealth from generation to generation according to specific inheritance strategies which did not necessarily exclude females. Certain *waḳf* strategies sometimes even favoured females both as beneficiaries and administrators of endowments (Garcin; Doumani).

Primary research has also dismantled the misconception of *waḳf* as a secure tax shelter. Ottoman administrative records reveal that both buildings and agricultural properties belonging to the foundations were indeed subject to taxes. Work by Barkan clearly demonstrates that *waḳf* and freehold lands (calculated together as a unit) contributed rather more than 13% in the form of taxes to the overall revenue budget for the Ottoman empire in 1527-28 (Barkan, 1953-4, 277; figures given by Inalcik, 1997, 82-3); in a like manner, Hütteroth and Abdulfattah (98) have shown that endowment properties were subject to the *ʿushr māl al-waḳf* tax in late 10th/16th-century Palestine. But, since the information on taxes levied upon foundations in the Ottoman empire has not yet been sufficiently researched so as to establish substantial quantitative data, it is difficult to evaluate the differences between the types and frequency of taxes imposed on endowment assets in relation to other types of property. Yet, in view of the fact that so many private individuals chose to establish *waḳf* as a means to pass on their properties to future generations instead of simply allowing their assets to be inherited according to Ḳurʾānic inheritance precepts [see FARĀʾIḌ], presumably indicates that *waḳf* property taxes were less onerous than those imposed on non-*waḳf* assets.

Archival work has also been done on the *waḳfs* owned by the guilds [see ṢINF. 3] in the Ottoman empire. Often used as a type of solidarity fund for guild members but also for other individuals associated or not with the guild, this type of endowment was frequently bestowed with cash assets which were lent out at interest. Aside from the endowments founded by individual craftsmen for the benefit of their guild, research has shown that, contrary to normative *waḳf* law where only an individual person may create a foundation, entire guilds also established *waḳf* for their common use (Akarli; Faroqhi, 1995, esp. 97, 102-8, who has studied *waḳf* registers, now held in the manuscript division of Milli Kütüphane in Ankara, from late 18th-century Bursa).

Another collective use of *waḳfs* in the empire was regarding those that were founded for the benefit of an urban quarter (*maḥalla* [*q.v.*]). The assets of the neighbourhood *waḳfs*, similar to those of the guild endowments, were mostly but not exclusively held in the form of currency, which was bestowed in *waḳf* by the quarter's inhabitants or by other individuals; revenue also accrued to this type of foundation by renting the real estate owned by that *waḳf*. The foundation's properties were therefore collectively owned by the quarter, and this *waḳf* acted as a safety net in times of need by the residents of that quarter. In particular, the neighbourhood *waḳf* often helped defray taxes imposed upon a quarter's population as an ensemble as well as assisting neighbourhood inhabitants for their material needs. Although further primary research needs to be conducted on this type of endowment, it seems that the neighbourhood *waḳf* was usually managed by the *sheykh* of the *maḥalla* or by another notable of the quarter.

As the Ottoman centuries went by, huge amounts of buildings and agricultural lands increasingly belonged to the endowments but, for the time being, it is impossible to assess, with any real certainty, the extent of *waḳf* holdings in the Ottoman lands. Nonetheless, 19th and 20th-century studies generally estimate *waḳf* properties to comprise approximately three-quarters of buildings and arable land in the empire. Without being quantitatively specific, it is abundantly clear that *waḳf* represented enormous assets in the Ottoman empire and were an integral part of the economy and the real estate market. Apart from the sultanic and associated *waḳfs*, over which the Ottoman state exercised some centralised control from at least the mid-9th/15th century (although local *mutawallīs* and *nāẓirs* of the sultanic endowments usually held considerable decision-making powers), periodic attempts were made by the state to extend its administration over the other foundations. But, it was only in the late 18th century under sultan Selīm III's reform programme, the Niẓām-i Djedīd [*q.v.*], and especially after the crushing of the Janissaries in the summer of 1826, that the imperial power succeeded in incorporating important endowments under its control. As a first measure, just a few months after the destruction of the Janissaries, the central government created the Ministry of *Waḳf* in October 1826 which, in the next few years, increasingly took over the administration of the influential and wealthy endowments attached to the offices of the Grand Vizier, the *sheykh al-islām*, the *reʾīs al-küttāb* [*q.v.*], the inspector of the Ḥaramayn foundations, the Chief Admiral, the Chief Black Eunuch and others. The subsequent *Tanẓīmāt* [*q.v.*] reorganisations widened and, to some extent, enforced regulatory legislation over the management of *waḳf* and its assets. Ascertaining the real extent of state interventionary powers regarding the control over *wakf* is somewhat problematical; yet it is indisputable that the 19th-century Ottoman empire and the Young Turks régime progressively created the infrastuctural apparatus to incorporate management of the endowments within its centralised administration (Barnes, 87-153; Yerasimos).

The end date for this section, 1914, does not in any way reflect a chronological rupture in the history of Ottoman *wakf*; the hostilities of World War I did not specifically affect the endowments in the empire. A much more significant date was 1924 when, along with the abolition of the caliphate and the Ministry of *S͟herīʿat*, *wakf* administration and its properties were incorporated within the secular state apparatus of Muṣṭafā Kemāl's Turkish Republic.

Bibliography: J. Abou Nohra, *Contribution à l'étude du rôle des monastères dans l'histoire rurale du Liban: recherche sur les archives du couvent St. Jean de Kinshara 1710-1960*, diss., University of Strasbourg 1983, unpubl.; M. ʿAfīfī, *al-Awḳāf wa 'l-ḥayāt al-iḳtiṣādiyya fī Miṣr fī ʿaṣr al-ʿut͟hmānī*, Cairo 1991; idem, *al-Awḳāf wa 'l-malāḥa al-baḥriyya fī 'l-Baḥr al-Aḥmar fī 'l-ʿaṣr al-ʿut͟hmānī*, in R. Deguilhem, 1995, 88-100; E. Akarli, *Gedik, implements, masterships, shop usufruct and monopoly among Istanbul artisans, 1750-1850*, in *Wissenschaftskolleg Jahrbuch* (1985-6), 223-32; G. Baer, *Women and Waqf. An analysis of the Istanbul Tahrir of 1546*, in *AAS*, xvii (1983), 9-27; idem, *The Waqf as a prop for the social system (sixteenth-twentieth centuries)*, in *ILS*, iv (1997), 264-97; M.A. Bakhit, *Safad et sa région d'après des documents de waqf et des titres de propriété 780-964 (1378-1556)*, in *Revue des Mondes Musulmans et de la Méditerranée (REMMM)*, lv-lvi (1990), 101-23; Ö.L. Barkan, *Les fondations pieuses comme méthode de peuplement et de colonisation*, in *Vakıflar Dergisi*, ii (1942), 59-65; idem, *Osmanlı imparatorluğu bütçelerine dair notlar*, in *İstanbul Üniversitesi İktisat Fakültesi Mecmuası*, xv (1953-4), 239-329; idem and E.H. Ayverdi, *İstanbul vakıflari tahrir defteri, 943 (1546) tarihli*, Istanbul 1970; J.R. Barnes, *An introduction to religious foundations in the Ottoman empire*, Leiden 1986; F. Bilici, *Les waqfs monétaires à la fin de l'empire ottoman et au début de l'époque républicaine en Turquie: des caisses de solidarité vers un système bancaire moderne*, in Bilici 1994, 51-9; idem (ed.), *Le waqf dans le monde musulman contemporain (XIXe-XXe siècles)*, Istanbul 1994 (*wakf* in Anatolia, the Balkans, the Arab provinces and Central Asia); idem, *Recherches sur les waqfs ottomans au seuil du nouveau millénaire*, in *Arab Historical Review for Ottoman Studies (AHROS)*, xv-xvi (1997), Zaghouan (Tunisia), 81-96 (detailed, essential up-to-date survey of available Ottoman archival material as well as a state-of-the-question); A. Çetin, *Osmanlı Başbakanlık Arşivi kilavuzu*, Istanbul 1979; O. Çetin, *Dawr al-awḳāf al-ʿut͟hmāniyya al-k͟hayriyya fī 'l-mud͟jtamaʿ al-ʿut͟hmānī*, in *AHROS*, xv-xvi (1997), 49-55; M. Cizakca, *Cash waqfs of Bursa, 1555-1823*, in *JESHO*, xxxviii (1995), 247-61; K. Cuno, *Ideology and juridical discourse in Ottoman Egypt. The uses of the concept of Irṣād*, in *ILS*, v (1998), 1-28; M. Davie, *Le millet grecque-orthodoxe de Beyrouth, 1800-1940. Structuration interne et rapport à la cité*, Ph.D. thesis, Sorbonne, U. Paris IV, 1993, unpubl.; R. Deguilhem, *The loan of murṣad on waqf properties*, in F. Kazemi and R.D. McChesney (eds.), *A way prepared. Essays on Islamic culture in honor of Richard Bayly Winder*, New York 1988, 68-79; eadem, *Waqf documents: a multi-purpose historical source—the case of 19th century Damascus*, in D. Panzac (ed.), *Les villes dans l'empire ottoman: activités et sociétés*, Paris 1991, 67-95, 191-203; eadem (ed.), *Le waqf dans l'espace islamique. Outil de pouvoir socio-politique* (esp. concerns *wakf* in the Arab provinces, including the Mag͟hrib), Damascus 1995; S. Denoix, *Formes juridiques, enjeux sociaux et stratégies foncières* (sc. of collectively-owned assets including Ottoman *wakf*), in *Biens communs, patrimoines collectifs et gestion communautaire dans les sociétés musulmanes*, in *REMMM*, lxxix-lxxx (1997), 9-22 (many of the articles in this issue deal with Ottoman *wakf*); B. Doumani, *Endowing family. Waqf, property devolution, and gender in Greater Syria, 1800 to 1860*, in *Comparative Studies in Society and History*, xl (Jan. 1998), 3-41; E. Eldem, *A history of the Ottoman Bank*, Istanbul 1999; S. Faroqhi, *Seyyid Gazi revisited. The foundation as seen through sixteenth and seventeenth century documents*, in *Turcica*, xiii (1981), 90-122; eadem, *Men of modest substance. House owners and house property in seventeeth-century Ankara and Kayseri*, Cambridge 1987; eadem, *Pilgrims and sultans. The Hajj under the Ottomans*, London-New York 1994; eadem, *Ottoman guilds in the late eighteenth century. The Bursa case*, in eadem, *Making a living in the Ottoman lands 1480-1820*, Istanbul 1995, 93-112; eadem, *Approaching Ottoman history. An introduction to the sources*, Cambridge 1999, esp. 54-5, 60-1, 96, 129; J.-Cl. Garcin, *Le waqf est-il la transmission d'un patrimoine?*, in J. Beaucamp and G. Dagron (eds.) *La transmission du patrimoine. Byzance et l'aire méditerranéenne. Travaux et mémoires du Centre de Recherche d'Historie et Civilisation de Byzance*, Paris 1998, 101-9; H. Gerber, *The Waqf institution in early Ottoman Edirne*, in *AAS*, xvii (1983), 29-45; idem, *The Jews and the Islamic endowment institution in the Ottoman empire* (in Hebrew), in *Sefunot*, N.S., ii, no. 17 (1983), 105-31; Z. Ghazzal, *Lecture d'un waqf maronite du Mont Liban au XIXe siècle*, in Deguilhem, 1995, 101-12; N. Hanna, *Construction work in Ottoman Cairo (1517-1798)*, in *Suppl. aux AI*, iv, Cairo 1984, esp. 17-23; H. Hatemi, *Önceki ve bugünkü türk hukukunda vakıf kurma muamelesi*, Istanbul 1969; W. Heffening, art. *Wakf*, in *EI*[1], A. Hénia, *Pratique habous, mobilité sociale et conjoncture à Tunis à l'époque moderne (XVIIIe-XIXe siècle)* in Deguilhem, 1995, 71-100; C. Heywood, *The Red Sea trade and Ottoman waqf support for the population of Mecca and Medina in the later seventeenth century*, in A. Temimi (ed.), *La vie sociale dans les provinces arabes à l'époque ottomane*, iii, Zaghouan 1988, 165-84; M. Hoexter, *Waqf studies in the twentieth century. The state of the art*, in *JESHO*, xli (1998), 474-95; eadem, *Endowments, rulers and community. Waqf al-Ḥaramayn in Ottoman Algiers*, Leiden 1998; Ḥ. Ḥüsnü, *Aḥkām-i evḳāf*, Istanbul 1321/1903; W.-D. Hütteroth and K. Abdulfattah, *Historical geography of Palestine, Transjordan and Southern Syria in the late sixteenth century*, Erlangen 1977; H. Inalcik, *The hub of the city. The Bedestan of Istanbul*, in *Internat. Jnal. of Turkish Studies*, i (1980), 1-17; idem, *Istanbul, an Islamic city*, in *JIS*, i (1990), 1-23; idem, *An economic and social history of the Ottoman empire 1300-1600*, i, Cambridge 1997; S. Ivanova and Z. Ivanova, *Nineteenth-century waqf archives preserved in the Oriental Department of the National Library St. Cyril and Methodius*, in Bilici, 1994, 185-98 (on *wakf* documents in Sofia and elsewhere in Bulgaria for the duration of the Ottoman presence); *JESHO*, xxxviii (1995) (special issue on *wakf*); S. Kenderova, *Inventory of the documents in [the] Arabic language kept in the Oriental Department of the Cyril and Methodius National Library in Sofia (XIII-XX c.)*, Sofia 1984; eadem, *Les lecteurs de Samakov au XIXe siècle*, in *REMMM*, lxxxvii-lxxxviii (1999), 61-75 (on *wakf* archives in Sofia); A. Layish, *Waqfs and Sufi monasteries in the Ottoman policy of colonization. Sultan Selim I's waqf of 1516 in favour of Dayr al-Asad*, in *BSOAS*, l (1987), 61-89; R. van Leeuwen, *Waqfs and urban structures. The case of Ottoman Damascus*, Leiden 1999; B. Lewis, *Studies in the Ottoman archives—I*, in *BSOAS*, xvi (1954), 469-501; F. Lopasic, *Islamisation of the Balkans with special reference to Bosnia*, in *JIS*, v (1994), 163-86; J. Mandaville, *Usurious piety. The cash waqf controversy in the Ottoman empire*, in *IJMES*, x (1979), 289-308; E. Mercier, *Le Code de Habous*, Constantinople 1899, V. Moutaftchieva, *Le vakif—un aspect de la structure socio-économique de l'empire ottoman (XV*[e]*-XVII*[e] *s.)*, Sofia 1981; Gülru Necipoglu, *The Süleymaniya complex in Istanbul. An interpretation*, in *Muqarnas*, iii (1986), 92-117; N. Öztürk, *Türk yenileşme çerçevesinde vakıf müessesesi*, Ankara 1995; O. Peri, *Waqf and Ottoman welfare policy. The poor kitchen of Hasseki Sultan in eighteenth-century Jerusalem*, in *JESHO*, xxxv (1992) 167-86; A.-K. Rafeq, *City and countryside in a traditional setting. The case of Damascus in the first quarter of the eighteenth century*, in T. Philipp, *The Syrian land in the 18th and 19th centuries*, Stuttgart 1992, 295-332; A. Raymond, *Artisans et commerçants au Caire au XVIII*[e] *siècle*, Damascus 1973, repr. Damascus and Cairo 1999; J. Reilly, *Rural waqfs of Ottoman Damascus. Rights of ownership, possession, and tenancy*, in *AO*, li (1990), 27-46; R. Roded, *Quantitative analysis of waqf endowment deeds. A pilot project*, in *Osmanlı Araştırmaralar*, ix (1989), 5-76; N. Saidouni, *Les biens waqf aux environs d'Alger à la fin de l'époque ottomane*, in Bilici, 1994, 99-117; S.M. Saliba, *Une famille, un couvent: Deir Mar Challita Mouqbès, 1615-1878*, in *Chronos*, Balamend (Lebanon), iii (2000), 93-138; Y. Sauvan, *Une liste des fondations pieuses* (waqfiyya) *au temps de Sélim II*, in *BEO*, xxviii (1975), 231-58; R. Shaham, *Christian and Jewish waqf in Palestine during the late Ottoman period*, in *BSOAS*, liv (1991), 460-72; T. Shuval, *La ville d'Alger vers la fin du XVIII*[e] *siècle. Population et cadre urbain*, Paris 1998; S. Slim, *Le métayage et l'impôt au Mont-Liban XVIII*[e]*-XIX*[e] *siècles*, Beirut 1987; A. Temimi, *Sommaires des registres arabes et turcs d'Alger*, Tunis 1983; *Vakıflar Dergisi*, Ankara (dates from 1938 onwards); R. Veselý, *De la situation des esclaves dans l'institution du waqf*, in *ArO*, xxxii (1964), 345-53; M. Yazbak, *Haifa in the late Ottoman period, 1864-1914*, Leiden 1998; B. Yediyıldız, *Institution du Vakf au XVIII*[e] *siècle en Turquie—étude socio-historique*, Ankara 1985; S. Yerasimos, *Les waqfs dans l'aménagement urbain d'Istanbul au XIX*[e] *siècle*, in Bilici, 1994, 43-9; Th. Zarcone, *Waqfs et confréries religieuses: l'influence de la réforme des waqfs sur la sociabilité et la doctrine mystique*, in Bilici, 1994, 237-48.

(Randi Deguilhem)

V. In Central Asia

Since in Islamic times the region governed from such Transoxanian cities as Bukhārā and Samarḳand often included the southern banks of the upper Oxus river course, it is convenient to consider here also what is now northern Afghānistān.

(a) *The pre-Mongol period*

One of the earliest, if not the earliest, known *waḳf* foundations was established by the Sāmānid Ismāʿīl b. Aḥmad (d. 295/907) at Bukhārā. The date of the original deed was 254/868, but it was redrafted in 676/1277 and the surviving version written during the reign of the Manghit Amīr Ḥaydar (1215-42/1800-26); according to this last, the foundation supported both the family mausoleum and the descendants of Ismāʿīl.

The Ḳarākhānid or Ilek-Khānid Tamghāč Bughrā Khān founded *waḳfs* for a hospital (*bīmāristān*) in Radjab 458/May-June 1066 and for a college (*madrasa*) at some unknown date in Samarḳand. In the course of listing the properties abutting the Ḳarākhānid endowments, other *waḳf*-supported institutions are mentioned: the Masdjid-i Dāwūd; the Congregational Mosque; the tomb (*mashhad*) of "al-Ṭarkhān" and his daughter "al-Khātūn"; and a student scholarship fund (M. Khadr, 318-19, 325; ilek-khāns, at Vol. III, 1115b).

A second known Ḳarākhānid *waḳf* is that of Arslan Khān Muḥammad b. Sulaymān (495-?523/1102-?1129) for a "*madrasa* for jurists" in Bukhārā. The documentation on it includes a reference to it in the version of Narshakhī that has survived (R.N. Frye, *The History of Bukhara*, Cambridge, Mass. 1954, 30) and a lawsuit of unknown date seeking restitution of grain and money embezzled from the *waḳf* income.

(b) *The Mongol period*

A family endowment (*waḳf-i awlād*) from 698/1299 by ʿAbd al-Raḥīm b. Muḥammad b. ʿAbd Allāh Istīdjābī (Isfīdjābī) for his son Ḳuṭb al-Dīn Yūsuf and then his male descendants in Bukhārā and for the upkeep of the mosque and shrine of a local saint, Khᵂādja Khamana, is the first known *waḳf* from Transoxania in the Mongol period. The *waḳfiyya* exists in its Arabic original with an accompanying contemporary Persian translation. The endowment included the village of Khamana in the district (*tūmān*) of Sāmdjān, including its own canal (*nahr-i khāṣṣ*). One unusual feature of this *waḳf* was the assignment of the income of specific amounts of land (rather than a percentage of the endowment income or fixed amounts of money) to pay the salaries of the mosque officials and for the specific requirements of the *waḳf*.

(c) *The post-Mongol era: the Bākharzī* waḳf *foundation*

The 726/1326 *waḳf* founded by Shaykh Yaḥyā in memory of his grandfather, the Ṣūfī *shaykh* Sayf al-Dīn Bākharzī, established a pattern of large *waḳf* complexes associated with the shrine of a religious figure, a pattern which is a characteristic feature of the urban landscape of the region. Major architectural complexes, usually with a shrine as the focal point, underwritten by extensive *waḳf* endowments that were in turn administered by family dynasties, are a recurrent feature of the socio-economic history of the cities of Central Asia. These entities were vehicles for the transfer of some part of the agricultural surplus of the surrounding countryside into the city and its commercial life. As managers of agricultural lands as well as the principal commercial structures (markets, stores, warehouses, stables, mills and baths), the families that controlled these shrine and educational complexes used their positions to perpetuate themselves as well as to influence government policy on economic and social matters.

The Bākharzī *waḳf* is also an example of how *waḳf* was used as a source of development capital in Bukhārā as it was in Iṣfahān (R.D. McChesney, *Waqf and public policy. The waqfs of Shāh ʿAbbās 1011-1023*, in *Asian and African Studies*, xv [1981], 165-90) and Istanbul [*q.v.*, at Vol. IV, 226-9] in order to revive local economies. The foundation document, a scroll of nearly 1,000 lines, detailed a vast agricultural expanse, including an area outside the Ḳarshī Gate of Bukhārā estimated at more than 100 km^2. These lands, which were intended to support a mosque and *khānaḳāh* complex as well as the tomb of Sayf al-Dīn Bākharzī, were situated amidst extensive ruins. At the same time, on its own lands the document speaks of newly-planted vineyards, orchards and vegetable gardens. When Ibn Baṭṭūṭa recalled his stay at the *khānaḳāh* in 1333, only seven years after the foundation was established, he mentions vast agricultural *waḳfs* belonging to it and its ability to feed "all comers" (*Riḥla*, tr. Gibb, iii, 27-8, tr. iii, 554).

Like many of the large foundations of the time,

the Bāk͟harzī foundation was very long-lived. The surviving documents pertaining to the foundation include a grant in 1745 of two parcels of irrigated land totalling four hectares, and a record of the restoration (*taʿmīr wa marammat*) of the *waḳfiyya* itself by the *k͟haṭīb* of Fatḥābād, the location of the tomb, al-Ḥād͟jd͟j Mīr Maḳṣūd Dahbīdī.

(d) *Tīmūrid* waḳf*s*

The advent of the Tīmūrid era in Central Asia brought an efflorescence of large *waḳf* foundations. Those published or described include:

1. A *waḳf* of 785/1383 involving much irrigated land in the Samarḳand region.

2. Tīmūr's *waḳf* for the shrine of S͟hayk͟h Aḥmad-i Yasawī. The document, purporting to be Tīmūr's original *waḳfiyya* for the shrine in Turkistān, has been called a "crude forgery" by O.D. Ček͟hovič, but it is more than likely that Tīmūr did endow the shrine when it was built, or at least encouraged others to do so. In 1866, Mīr Ṣāliḥ Begčurin described the *waḳf* of the shrine complex (which at the time included a mosque, a *madrasa*, and a staff of eight, not including the *madrasa* teachers) as comprising two inns and a caravanserai, this last, donated in 1820, with 80 shops producing 100 *tilla*s of income used for upkeep of the shrine.

3. The endowments for the library, *madrasa, k͟hānaḳāh*, and mosque of K͟hʷād͟ja Muḥammad Pārsā (d. 822/1420), one of Bahāʾ al-Dīn Naḳs͟hband's chief disciples.

4. The *waḳf*s for Ulug͟h Beg's *madrasa* and observatory in Samarḳand (both built in 823/1420, according to Ḥāfiẓ Ābrū, *Ẕubda*, Tehran 1372/1993, 743-4) and his *madrasa* in Buk͟hārā (undated). Although modern scholars have not yet studied in any detail the endowments for the two great *madrasa*s founded by Tīmūr's grandson, there is a considerable amount of archival material on them in the Uzbek State Archives; see R.D. McChesney, *Waqf in Central Asia*, Princeton 1991, 37 n. 31, for secondary sources on the *madrasa*s.

5. The 868/1464 *waḳf* of Ḥabība Sulṭān Bīgum, daughter of the Tīmūrid *amīr* D͟jalāl al-Dīn Suhrāb for the mausoleum called ʿIs͟hrat-K͟hāna in Samarḳand, the tomb of K͟hāwand Sulṭān Bīgī.

6. Ḥusayn Bāyḳarā's endowment with commercial properties and a large canal at the rediscovered alleged tomb-site of ʿAlī b. Abī Ṭālib east of Balk͟h in 885/1480-1 (see McChesney, *op. cit.*).

7. The *waḳf* foundation of K͟hʷād͟ja ʿUbayd Allāh Aḥrār [see AḤRĀR, in Suppl.] in Samarḳand for the complex called Muḥawwaṭa-i Mawālī" in the area called Kamāngarān. It held properties throughout Central Asia right up to the Soviet period, and was established principally as a family trust (*waḳf-i awlād*) (see McChesney, *Central Asia. Foundations of change*, Princeton 1997, 98-109, for the development of the foundation during the 17th century).

8. The endowment of Mīr ʿAlī S͟hīr Nawāʾī [*q.v.*] (before 886/1481-2) on behalf of an educational complex including a congregational mosque, *madrasa, k͟hānaḳāh*, hospital and bath outside Harāt. See M.E. Subtelny, *A Timurid educational and charitable complex. The Ikhlāṣiyya complex of ʿAlī Shīr Navāʾī in 15th century Herat and its endowment*, in *JAOS*, cxi [1991], 38-61, and eadem, *The* Vaqfīya *of Mīr ʿAlī Shīr Navāʾī as apologia*, in *Jnal. of Turkish Studies*, xv [1991], 257-86.

(e) *The Shībānid and Tuḳāy-Tīmūrid periods, 10th-11th/16th-17th centuries*

When the revivers of the Činggisid k͟hānate, the Abu 'l-K͟hayrid S͟hībānids [*q.v.*], ousted the last of the Tīmūrids from Central Asia and northern Afg͟hānistān, they and their 11th/17th-century successors, the Tuḳāy-Tīmūrids (D͟jānids, As͟htark͟hānids) similarly used the financial instrument of *waḳf* to establish and fund their own public works.

9. One of the earliest is the extensive endowment for a pair of *madrasa*s in Samarḳand dedicated in the name of S͟hībānī K͟hān (d. 916/1510) and established by his daughter-in-law Mihr Sulṭān K͟hānum, probably before 926/1520.

10. In D͟jumādā II 947/October 1540, an *amīr* named Kamāl al-Dīn Ḳanāḳ (Ḳiyāḳ, Ḳunāḳ) set up a large *waḳf* to support an educational-cultic complex of congregational mosque, *madrasa*, ablution stations and *ribāṭ* inside Balk͟h in the Čuḳur Mūsā S͟hayk͟h quarter. Like many *waḳf*s to follow in the course of the century, this large public *waḳf* was in fact a "mixed" one, as it made provisions for both the founder's descendants and public institutions. In this case, the future generations were to receive 10% of the income (after expenditure on building maintenance) in accordance with the Ḳurʾānic rules on the *farāʾiḍ* [*q.v.*]. The document also refers to four other mosques which Kamāl al-Dīn had already endowed and three mosques which his brother had likewise built and endowed. The 947/1540 endowment makes it clear that Kamāl al-Dīn envisioned the earlier foundations as part of the new endowment. The stipulations provide for paying the salaries of the employees of the seven mosques and furnishing felt carpets, woven reed mats, and lamp oil from the income of the new endowment. However, Kamāl al-Dīn explicitly prohibits use of the income from the 1540 endowment for building repairs on the other seven mosques. Presumably the earlier endowments were expected to cover that expense. The document itself also provides evidence of one approved judicial procedure for making a *waḳf* at the time. The settlor declares that he has handed over the property to an appointed trustee and then taken it back, a formal device which establishes the *ḳāḍī*'s role as arbiter. The latter then affirms the binding nature of the endowment and records its permanent nature in the present document called a *sid͟jill*.

The pattern of large *waḳf*s jointly supporting public institutions and the private interests of future generations of the founder's family continued during these two centuries. In Buk͟hārā, one of the more notable *waḳf*-founding families was the D͟jūybārīs. From their origins as keepers of the Čār (Čahār) Bakr shrine in the western Buk͟hāran suburbs and beneficiaries of its endowments, the family emerged as one of the wealthiest and most influential families in Central Asia, and preserved both its wealth and influence for several centuries, in large part through the purchase of real estate, conversion of those purchases into *waḳf* and designating as beneficiaries not only the *madrasa*-mosque complexes that they built but also succeeding generations of the family. There are many unpublished endowment deeds of the family in the Uzbek State Archives, which taken together establish the long-term economic influence of the family in Central Asia. On the family's origins, see F. Schwarz, *From scholars to saints. The Bukharan Shaykhs of Ğūybār and the ziyārat to the Four Bakr*, in *Iz Istorii kul'turnogo naslediya Buk͟harī*, vi, Buk͟hārā 1998. On the building and endowment activities of the family, see McChesney, *Economic and social aspects of the public architecture of Bukhara in the 1560's and 1570's*, in *Islamic art*, ii [1987], 217-42, and idem, *Central Asia. Foundations of change*, 109-14.

In the 11th/17th century, besides additions made to the large endowments of the preceding centuries (e.g. Nadr Dīwān-Begī Arlāt's dramatic expansion and endowment of Kh^wādja Aḥrār's tomb area on the southern side of Samarḳand with a large *madrasa*, and several large *waḳfs* of books for the Ulugh Beg *madrasa* in Bukhārā), there were new projects in Samarḳand (the Shīr Dār and Ṭillākār *madrasas* on the Rīgistān built by another leading *amīr*, Yalangtūsh Bī Alčīn); in Bukhārā (Nadr Dīwān Begī's *madrasa* and *khānaḳāh* and ʿAbd al-ʿAzīz Khān II's two *madrasas*; and in Balkh (the two *madrasas* of father and son, Nadhr Muḥammad), all of which generated major new endowments.

Throughout the century, the issue of *waḳf* also touches on the relations between the Tuḳāy-Tīmūrids in Bukhārā and the Tīmūrid rulers of India. A tradition about the endowment of the Gūr-i Amīr complex in Samarḳand had persisted through the centuries. Muḥammad Sulṭān (d. 805/1403), grandson of Tīmūr, was believed to have founded a *waḳf* for his *madrasa*, one of the buildings of the complex, the terms of which local residents believed they knew as late as 1101/1690. Because of the importance of the tombs there to such Tīmūrid epigoni as the Mughals ruling in India, efforts, ultimately unsuccessful, were made by the latter late in 1102/1690-1 to re-capitalise the *waḳf* with cash sent from Kābul and to revive the terms of what was believed to be the original endowment.

(f) *The Manghit period (mid-18th to early 20th centuries)*

The great bulk of surviving *waḳf* documents date to the late 18th, 19th and early 20th centuries. This is in part due to the usual effects of time on paper documents and in part to the project of the Manghit *amīr*, Shāh Murād b. Dāniyāl ("Amīr-i Maʿṣūm", 1199-1215/1785-1800), either as an act of piety or perhaps to ensure the government had a record of *waḳfs* in Bukhārā, to have many *waḳfiyyas* re-copied. As a consequence, many foundations are only known through these late copies. Another factor was the arrival of the Russians, who were interested in the tax potential of the regions that they had conquered. In 1886, the Governor-General ordered that all *waḳf* deeds should be presented for inspection, with the threat of their nullification if these documents were not brought forward. At that time, the authorities tallied 7,509 *waḳfs* in the territories under Russian direct administration based on the documents presented, with a slightly different count in an earlier publication: 2,909 *waḳfs* in Turkestan, 1,326 in Syr Darya, 1,076 in Fergana, 507 in Zarafshan, 1,177 in Khojent, 382 in Namangan, 297 in Samarḳand and 282 in Margelan for a total of 7,956 separate foundations. To these numbers should then be added the thousands of *waḳfs* in the khānates of Bukhārā and Khīwa.

But the practice of document preservation and duplication is well attested long before the time of Shāh Murād. On the reverse of the 947/1540 *waḳfiyya* is a note specifying how many copies were to be made of the document and where they were to be kept—two in Bukhārā, one at a private house in Samarḳand and a fourth in Shahr-i Sabz. In Balkh, there were to be three copies, one kept by the settlor himself, the other two to be kept by two named *ḳāḍīs*. Inside the body of the document is a further stipulation that, every ten years, the *mutawallī* was to make a fresh copy of the *waḳfiyya*.

After the Soviet Revolution of 1917, *waḳf* property was officially abolished. The extent to which it persisted as social practice even under official prohibition has yet to be studied. While the institution was being swept away, its records were being preserved. The establishment of the Central State Historical Archives in Tashkent and the accumulation of manuscript works (both books and single documents) by the Academies of Sciences in the new Soviet Republics meant the history of *waḳf* in Central Asia, if not the institution itself, would be preserved.

The extensive documentary record for *waḳf* has great potential for historians of Central Asia. The *waḳfiyyas* are rich in topographic, toponymic and architectural information. The Ḳarākhānid ones, for example, specify the structural elements of *khāns* (caravanserais) in 5th/11th-century Samarḳand. These may then be compared with later deeds in which caravanserais or comparable commercial structures (*tīms*) are described. What is true for individual buildings is also true for topography and toponomy. The 947/1540 *waḳf* in Balkh details the layout of three of the city's quarters (Sallākh-khāna, Āsiyābād, and Čukur Mūsā Shaykh). In the light of the virtual disappearance of all traces of the mediaeval and early modern internal plan of the city, this record is invaluable. Similarly, from the corpus of Djūybārī endowments deeds, complemented by property sales records, whole streets of Bukhārā may be reconstructed as they existed in the 10th/16th century. Suburban topography and toponomy may likewise be recovered from *waḳf* documents when agricultural properties (orchards, vineyards, fields and farms) form the income-producing part of a foundation.

The documents are also a major source for economic history. Already one study has used *waḳf* documents to establish wage and price trends in Bukhārā in the 10th/16th century (E.A. Davidovič, *Istoriya denezhnogo obrashčeniya srednevekovoi Srednei Azii*, Moscow 1983, 281-91). Currency and units of account in use (*rāyidj al-waḳt*), types of land tenure, institutional budgets, wages and prices in historical context, all may be studied through these materials. The cash *waḳf*, controversial in the 10th/16th century but apparently routine by the 19th century, also emerges from the documentary records.

Social history, too, finds a wealth of data in *waḳf* records. The owners and tenants of property which bounded *waḳf* property, or tenants on *waḳf* property itself are often identified by name thereby indicating property ownership and tenancy by gender, occupation and ethnicity.

The "Ḥaramayn *waḳf*", that is, endowments made to help support institutions in Mecca and Medina or related to the Pilgrimage, has a venerable history in Central Asia. Tīmūr's spiritual guide, Amīr Sayyid Baraka, who is buried alongside him in the Gūr-i Amīr, was reportedly an official of the Ḥaramayn *waḳf*. According to Kh^wāndamīr, writing more than 100 years later, Sayyid Baraka had been sent from Mecca to Balkh in 771/1369-70 to inspect Ḥaramayn *waḳf* lands in the Balkh region when he first came to Tīmūr's attention (*Ḥabīb al-siyar*, Tehran 1333/1954, pt. 3, vol. iii, 415-16). There are archival records of numerous endowments, many of them from the early 20th century, that continued the tradition of founding *waḳfs* to benefit the Holy Cities. One of the more unusual properties donated to the Ḥaramayn *waḳf* by the Manghit *Amīr* ʿAbd al-Aḥad (1886-1910) is a room (*ḥudjra*) in the Muḥammad Naẓar Parwānačī *madrasa*, suggesting that *madrasa* rooms, originally the object of an endowment, had been transformed into an income-generating piece of property that could then be made into *waḳf*.

Bibliography: 1. Sources. Information on Central Asian *waḳfs* may be found in several kinds of records: in *shurūṭ* literature (e.g. the *waḳf* for a hospital founded by the Ḳarākhānid Ibrāhīm b. Naṣr Tamghāč Bughrā Khān, given by M. Khadr and Cl. Cahen,

Deux actes de waqf d'un Qaraḫānide d'Asie Centrale, in *JA*, cclv/2 (1967), 305-34, found in the *Ghurar al-shurūṭ wa-durar al-sumūṭ* of al-Righdamūnī); in a dynamic documentary tradition which includes original foundation charters and/or later updated recensions of the original decrees, in governmental decrees (*farāmīn, manāshīr, aḥkām*) regulating the operation of a foundation; in court records of litigation (*mukhāṣama, daʿwā*); in other property records: sale affidavits (*iḳrārāt, ḳibāladjāt*), ownership transfers (*tamlīk-nāmas*), wills (*taraka-nāmas*) and bequests (*waṣiyyat-nāmas*); and in many genres of literature (histories, biographies, geographies/cosmographies).

The known collections of Central Asian *waḳf* documents include more than 2,000 *waḳf* deeds, virtually all from Bukhārā, in Tashkent in Fond I-323 of the Uzbek State Archives (ms. catalogue by I. Miradïlov, *Kollektsiya vakufnïkh dokumentov*); several hundred *waḳf* deeds and related documents in the Fond Vakfname at the Institute of Oriental Studies of Uzbekistan (O.D. Čekhovič, *Sobranye vostočnïkh aktov Akademii Nauk Uzbekistana*, in *Istoričeskie Zapiski*, no. 26 (1948), 306-11; idem, *Novaya kollektsiya dokumentov po istorii Uzbekistana*, in *ibid.*, no. 36 (1951), and G.A. Džuraeva (Juraeva), *Dokumental'noe nasledie Uzbekistana (Vakfname Instituta Vostokovedeniya Ak. Nauk Respublika Uzbekistana)*, n.d., unpubl. paper); at least 75 *waḳf-namas* in Samarḳand, at the Uzbek State Historical Museum (K.D., *Inventarnaya kniga rukopisnïkh dokumentov feodal'nogo-kolonial'nogo perioda Uzbekskogo Gosudarstvennogo Istoričeskogo Muzeya*, Samarḳand, n.d., unpubl. catalogue), an unknown number in Bukhārā at the Bukharan State Library and the Bukharan State Art and Architecture Museum (see B. Kazakov, *Kollektsiya istoričeskikh dokumentov Bukharskogo Gosudarstvennogo Arkhitekturno-Khudožestvennogo Muzeya-Zapovednika*, in *Iz istorii kul'turnogo naslediya Bukharï*, Tashkent 1990, 62-8), and an unknown number in Dushanbe, Tadjikistān at the Firdawsī State Public Library, the Institute of Oriental Studies, and the Aḥmad Donish Institute of History (see on these, A.A. Egani and Čekhovič, *Regestï Sredneaziatskikh Aktov*, in *Pis'mennye pamiyatniki vostoka. Ežegodnik(i) 1974-1979*, Moscow 1981-7).

Many more documents pertaining to *waḳf* in the area that came under Russian direct administration after 1865 (e.g. Samarḳand, Farghāna, Tashkent) are to be found in other fonds of the Uzbek archives, especially Fond no. 1 "Kantselariya Turkestanskogo General-Gubernatora", no. 17, "Sïr-Dar'inskoe Oblastnoye Pravlenye", no. 18, "Samarkandskoye Oblastnoye Pravlenye", no. 19, "Ferganskoye Oblastnoye Pravlenye", and no. 26 "Upravlenye Kush-Begi Emira Bukharskogo". See Z.I. Agafonova and N.A. Khalfin, *Putevoditel'* (Tsentral'nyi Gosudarstvennyi Istoričeskii Arkhiv UzSSR), Tashkent 1948. The collection of 19th-century Khīwan documents, including many *waḳfiyyas* was moved from Leningrad (St. Petersburg) to the Uzbek Central State Historical Archives in Tashkent in 1962 (subsequent to the publication of the Agafonova-Khalfin guide) and was added to Fond I-125, "Kantselariya Khana Khivinskogo" (Yu.È. Bregel', *Arkhiv Khivinskikh Khanov*, in *Narodï Azii i Afriki* (1966), no. 1, 67-76, and idem, *Dokumentï Arkhiva Khivinskogo Khanov po istorii i ètnografii Karakalpakov*, Moscow 1967, 10-11). No doubt much more *waḳf* material from Central Asia is to be found in other archival holdings in the former Soviet Union.

2. Studies. These are given in the article.

(R.D. McChesney)

VI. In Muslim India to 1900

In their operation as institutions, *awḳāf* in India resembled similar organisations in Muslim West Asia. At the same time, a number of forces unique to the subcontinent gave South Asian endowments a distinctive history. Several Indian historical circumstances gave them characteristics that made them diverge from patterns in the structure of *awḳāf* found in territories farther west. Muslims in the subcontinent were always a minority—influential certainly, but a minority none the less. Muslim-dominated states spread throughout South Asia in temporal fits and starts. During the crucial period of Mughal hegemony, a cash economy greatly enhanced the revenues available to the state, thus changing the complexion of patronage for individuals as well as establishments. Finally, the relatively early date, the late 18th century, at which British imperialism began to shape Muslim customs meant that Indian *awḳāf* were hybrids of a sort not found elsewhere in the Islamic world.

Inscriptional evidence concerning South Asian endowments is limited. Existing collections of epigrapha have not picked up information on endowments or widely disseminated it. Dedicatory carvings frequently employ terms other than *waḳf*: *inʿām* might be used in one inscription, *lā kharadj* in another, and sometimes even Hindu terms such as *devutter* will appear. During the Mughal period in Bengal, the expansion of Islamic institutions was underwritten by revenue abatements known as *sanads* (R. Eaton, *The rise of Islam and the Bengal frontier*, Berkeley, etc. 1993). Historical chronicles which often amount to panegyrics to one or another ruler make but perfunctory mention of *awḳāf*. They restrict themselves to the notice that a sultan established endowments or that he seized and redistributed the endowments of his predecessor (P. Jackson, *The Delhi Sultanate*, Cambridge 1998). When we look at the great dynastic histories dealing with the Mughals in India, mention of *awḳāf* virtually ceases.

Climate and vermin have meant that few, if any deeds of endowments, *waḳf-nāmas*, have survived. Also, documents have had a tendency to disappear when they proved inconvenient to the needs of later generations. While we know that a number of *awḳāf* were established for the maintenance of the Tādj Maḥall [*q.v.*], not a single document concerning them has come down to us (W. Begley and Z. Desai, *The Taj Mahal*, Seattle 1989; Irfan Habib, *The agrarian system of Mughal India*, Bombay 1963). Endowments in South Asia, therefore, cannot provide the material for the kinds of analysis of particular ruling groups such as the Mamlūks (C. Petry, *The civilian elite of Cairo in the later Middle Ages*, Princeton 1981), or of institutions such as the *mazar-i sharīf* (R. McChesney, *Waqf in Central Asia*, Princeton 1991).

We know that the Dihlī Sultanates tried to use the *iḳṭāʿ* as the basis for supporting their military and fiscal élites. In West Asia, e.g. in Saldjūḳ Persia, *awḳāf* were sometimes part of an effort to convert prebendary tenures (*iḳṭāʿāt*) into possessions (see III. above). In any case, the complications of revenue collection and control over access to agricultural surpluses in India meant that few attempts to secure absolute possession of some bit of territory were likely to endure. Though India's population was always big when compared to that of the rest of the world, land remained open for cultivation well into the 20th century. The crops that the land produced and the people who produced them were far more important than the ownership of mere real estate. Also, many cities and towns served as the capitals of states. Rulers, even within the same dynasty, tended to shift from place to place, taking their courtiers with them. Thus the farms and houses that usually provided the incomes of *awḳāf* had a somewhat fluid place in the lives of those notables who were in the position to establish an endowment (G. Kozlowski, *Muslim endowments and society in British India*, Cambridge 1985).

The reign of the Mughal emperor Akbar coincided roughly with the influx of silver brought by Europeans to purchase Indian goods (J. Richards, *The Imperial monetary system of Mughal India*, Delhi 1987; idem, *The Mughal empire*, Cambridge 1993). Irfan Habib has reckoned that by 1600, 85% of the Mughal revenue demand was collected in coin. While cash *awḳāf* were known in the Ottoman empire (see IV. above), they do not seem to have been extensively used in Mughal India. Rather, the Mughals made use of a number of other chancery terms for what were grants of revenue or the right to collect revenue, e.g. *wadjh-ī milk*, *waẓīfa* and *inʿām*. Prebends known as *madad-ī maʿāsh* were very common. The holders of *inʿām* and *madad-ī maʿāsh* grants over several generations later claimed to British officials that their prebendary holdings were actually *awḳāf* and should therefore be exempt from most kinds of sale, as well as immune from seizure for debt (Kozlowski, *op. cit.*, 39-40).

For their part, the Mughal rulers' reliance on stipends may have arisen from their need to bring within their own imperial orbit the religious figures and institutions which had been patronised by the lines of sultans who had preceded them (Kozlowski, *Imperial authority, benefactions and endowments* (awqāf) *in Mughal India*, in *JESHO*, xxxviii [1995], 355-70). Religious scholars, the tomb-shrines of saints (P. Currie, *The shrine and cult of Muʿīn al-Dīn Chishtī of Ajmer*, Delhi 1989) and *madrasa*s were scattered all over India. The sultanates not only of Dihlī, but also of Bengal, Gudjarāt, Djawnpūr and the Deccan, offered support for places of prayer, schools and mausoleums as well as for the various functionaries attached to them. The task of the Mughals was somehow to reconcile these important places and people to their authority. The most flexible way of accomplishing that feat was through the distribution of rights to cash generated by produce and manufactured goods. In such an environment, the permanence associated with a *wakf*, though usually more theoretical than realistic, may have made them seem unsuitable to the dynamic process of forging Mughal legitimacy. Unlike the experience in the Ottoman empire, imperial notables and local leaders do not seem to have turned to endowments as ways of anchoring their material assets as well as their status. In Mughal politics, assertions of independence almost invariably took the form of armed rebellion. Rather, the nobility, including the women of the imperial household, built many of the mosques that later generations were to associate with Mughal grandeur. Nobles or imperial sisters, cousins, aunts and wives provided the financial wherewithal for edifices such as the Maḥabbat Khān mosque of Peshawar, the somewhat misnamed Bādshāhī of Lahore and some of the greater mosques of Old Dihlī (S. Blake, *Shahjahanabad*, Cambridge 1991, 53 ff., and Kozlowski, *Private lives and public piety*, in G. Hambly (ed.), *Women in the medieval Islamic world*, New York 1998, 469 ff.).

In theory, the *ʿulamāʾ* should have had an important role in the administration of endowments. In certain places and periods (M. Hoexter, *Endowments, rulers and community*, Leiden 1998), the learned classes did have considerable authority over *awḳāf*. In 18th-century Egypt, the *ʿulamāʾ* were themselves prodigious founders of endowed establishments (see II.1. above), but in India, the role of religious functionaries was residual. They seem to have held power over endowments only in the last resort. Though celebrated for the compilation of Ḥanafī *fiḳh* known as the *Fatāwā-yi ʿĀlamgīrī*, when it came to *awḳāf*, the scholars of Mughal India simply repeated what had come down to them. Unlike the work of Ottoman scholars such as Ebu 'l-Suʿūd, they do not seem to have made any original contributions to the legal theory of endowments.

With the growing influence of British law, the configuration of economic, political and social forces in Mughal India changed in a number of formal as well as informal ways. In part through ignorance and in part through design, British notions of land ownership gradually became the crucial economic fact of India. The cash that the mortgaging of land could produce greatly increased seizures for unpaid loans. Likewise, the British-sponsored law courts enforced highly-textual notions of inheritance. For Muslims, that meant literal enforcement of Ḳurʾānic injunctions regarding inheritance, which made a division of property among a number of heirs almost inevitable. The subdivision of landed property also led inexorably to the fragmentation of material assets and the loss of family prestige. This was countered to some extent by creating a *wakf* which allowed donors to stipulate how the income of dedicated property was to be disbursed. The donors themselves as well as their children could receive the income of an undivided estate apportioned as seemed best according to the notions of honour in leading families. An estate owner who left only wives and daughters would know that, if the usual Ḳurʾānic inheritance rules applied, the share of his property that would have gone to sons would be distributed among male first cousins, and daughters and wives would not get any markedly bigger portion. An endowment, by contrast, allowed for the transmission of the income of an intact inheritance.

When faced with legal suits regarding *awḳāf*—often lodged by individuals who claimed that the endowment violated their Ḳurʾānic rights—British judges of the 1870s and 1880s issued conflicting judgements. In 1894, the Privy Council under the leadership of Lord Hobhouse issued a ruling in the case of *Abdul Fata Mahommed Ishak (and others) v. Russomoy Dhur Chowdhry (and others)* stating that a *wakf* had to be a "charitable and religious trust" (Kozlowski, *Muslim endowments*, 144 ff.) In that way, British judges and Indians trained in British law schools created, in effect, a Muslim law of endowments.

At the same time that British judicial functionaries were encountering *awḳāf* that to their minds looked suspiciously like attempts by Muslims to avoid the strictures of their own law, administrative officials were gradually drawn into managerial oversight over large establishments that had public religious as well as educational purposes. Despite some regulations that forbade official involvement in the management of Hindu, Muslim and Sikh institutions, local officers could not sometimes avoid attempts to settle muddles that led to widespread discontent. Attempts to ensure "good order" often gave rise to thorough transformations of some institutions. Thus the Hughli Imāmbārá was altered by the involvement of imperial officials. The building had been a shrine where the rites of Imāmī Shīʿism had been performed. A few boys, both Muslim and Hindu, had studied Persian there. The organisation eventually became Hughli College, with a curriculum of "modern" subjects and a student body including both Muslims and non-Muslims. Perhaps the most significant effect that the involvement of British administrators had was to implant the message that efficient management was a slogan under which campaigns against the custodians of particular, big endowments could be launched. The assets of any given *waḳf* could look to a politician, including politically-inclined *ʿulamāʾ*, like an important financial resource for any "reform" project he had in mind.

By 1900, *awḳāf* had become an issue in India's emerging political arena. Various associations and religious scholars, together with a variety of would-be politicians, lined up to have their say on the issue of endowments. In particular, the opinion of Lord Hobhouse in *Abdul Fata Mahommed Ishak, etc.*, became a focal point for controversy. With the exception of a few who argued that Hobhouse was right about Muslim law, most criticised the view as an erroneous interpretation of *fiḳh*. Moreover, critics argued that the inability to secure continuity in their undivided estates by means of *waḳf* placed the Muslim gentry of India in peril. That side of the debate over Muslim endowments gradually disappeared from the press and other venues for public discussion, but the larger and more public Muslim endowments, however, have remained matters of great interest and debate to the present day (cf. J. Malik, *The colonialisation of Islam*, New Delhi 1996).

Bibliography: Given in the article.

(G.C. Kozlowski)

VII. In Southeast Asia

The institution of *waḳf* (various local spellings, inc. *waqf, wakaf, wakap, wagf*, etc.) has undergone considerable change here as a result of reformulations by English and Dutch colonial laws. There are only minimal references in the historical texts (Malay and Javanese) and little evidence as to how the *waḳf* operated in pre-European Southeast Asia except for the odd mention in accounts of Arab trading practice. However, in the 19th and 20th centuries the institution has a prominent part in the *S̲h̲arīʿa* (Syariah) as administered in the European possessions. Each has to be considered separately.

(i) *British Burma.* The religion of Burma is Buddhism. Islam is the religion of minority Muslim immigrants, and of border peoples incorporated within the boundaries of the state of Burma (e.g. the Arakanese, Rohyinga). The main immigration dates from the 1880s, and the Indian Muslims made up about 1% of the total population or about 20% of the Indian migrant population by World War II. Islamic law was allowed to Muslims for succession, inheritance, marriage and any "religious usage or institution" (Burma Laws Act, 1898. § 13). This included *waḳf*, and the latter was further defined in the Mussalman Waḳf Validating Act of 1913, and Act of British India. There were no particularly Burmese features [see zerbadis and section VI. Muslim India, above].

(ii) *The Straits Settlements and the Malay State. Ca.* 1880-1952 to 1957, legal policy in respect of *waḳf* was uneven in these territories. In the Straits Settlements (then comprising Singapore, Penang and Malacca) a *waḳf* was always defined in terms of the English law on charities. Many *waḳf*, perfectly good in *S̲h̲arīʿa* terms, were refused for breaches of the technical rules on charitable trusts. The only exception in the long and complex precedent was that gifts for the relief of poverty were always allowed. On the other hand, gifts for "religious purposes", such as the construction of mosques, schools, the provision of books and food for students were often disallowed, and generally restricted. The courts were not applying the *S̲h̲arīʿa* at all. There was no legislation except for the Muslim and Hindu Endowments Ordinance (1905) which was solely concerned with administrative matters. In the Malay States, the position was rather more complicated. The problem was that the dates for the reception of English law were uncertain and always a matter of later legal dispute. In addition, the Malay States were classed as "Federated" and "Unfederated" and this had important consequences for the *S̲h̲arīʿa.* Broadly speaking, in the Unfederated States the *S̲h̲arīʿa* was rather sheltered from British re-organisation and administration. The main issue, so far as *waḳf* was concerned, was the consistent attempt by Malay sultans to control the use of *waḳf* for private or family benefit. A *waḳf* would only be allowed if it were for a clear religious or public benefit. In addition, however, the courts in both the Federated and Unfederated Malay States were, from about 1900, increasingly required to implement principles of English law, including laws on charitable trusts. The result was a partial assimilation of *waḳf* to the English trust and a large scale importation of Anglo-Indian laws on the subject into the Malay States. Family *waḳf*s were almost unknown from the 1920s onwards, and even the incidence of public *waḳf* was much reduced. The assimilation of the *waḳf* to the English trust had the effect of much reducing the confidence of Muslim donors in the institution.

(iii) *Singapore, 1950s-present, and Malaysia, 1950s-1988.* In preparation for independence (Malaysia in 1957, Singapore in 1965), the constituent states all passed legislation promoting the *S̲h̲arīʿa.* These are the Administration of Islamic (or Muslim) Law Enactments. While there are variations amongst them, they all provide for the establishments of a "Muslim Fund" (*Bait-ul-Mal*) the main purpose of which is to administer *waḳf* property through an Islamic religious Council (*Majlis Ulama Islam*). The following description, which is typical of all the legislation, is taken from the Singapore Act of 1966. The Majlis administers all *wakaf 'am, waḳf, wakaf khas, nazr 'am* and all trusts of any description for the benefit of Muslims "to the extent of any property affected thereby and situated in the state". The Majlis has the power to appoint a *mutawali* (manager) to manage any *waḳf* or *nazr 'am* and it may remove any existing trustee where there has been mismanagement, or where it would otherwise be to the advantage of the *waḳf* or *nazr 'am.*

The Act provides for restrictions on the creation of Muslim charitable trusts. No *waḳf* or *nazr* may involve more than one-third of the property of the person making the same by will. All *waḳf khas* and *nazr* must be validated or ratified by the President of the Majlis or, if it was made during a fatal illness, it must be in writing and witnessed by two adult Muslims, of whom one has to be a Kathi or Naib (Assistant) Kathi. In any case, the Act cannot render valid any will, death-bed gifts, *waḳf* or *nazr* which are invalid under Muslim law. The income of any *waḳf* or *nazr* is to be applied in accordance with the provisions of the instrument or declaration which creates the *waḳf* or *nazr.* Where there is no specific provision for expenditure, the income forms part of the Fund. Subject to an impossibility of performance or changed circumstances, the property and assets effected by a lawful *waḳf* or *nazr 'am* does not form part of the fund but is held as a segregated fund and applied in pursuance of the *waḳf* or *nazr 'am.* Where there has been a lapse of time or changed circumstances so that the provisions of a *waḳf* or *nazr 'am* cannot be carried out, the Majlis may prepare an alternative scheme, as analogous as possible to that in the original. It may also direct that the property and assets be added to and form part of the Fund. All questions as to validity or as to the meaning and construction of documents or declarations affecting a Muslim charitable trust are to be decided according to Muslim law. However, where in the opinion of the Majlis, the meaning of any instrument or declaration is obscure, the Majlis may request the Court to construe it and must act in accordance with the construction. In its construction the Court must apply Muslim law.

The Majlis is obliged to comply with stringent requirements in respect of its financial dealings. It must produce an annual report, together with a balance sheet for the Fund, an income and expenditure account, and a list of properties and investments. These documents are all subject to audit by the Director of Audit or a Public Officer authorised by him. In addition, the Majlis must also publish an annual list of all the properties subject to any trust, *wakf* or *nazr* which do not form part of the Fund. This list is also subject to audit. The Majlis must also prepare and submit to the Minister estimates for each ensuing year in respect of all income or property receivable and disposable. These estimates may be approved by the Minister or they may be amended by him.

One point may be emphasised, sc. the reference to "Muslim" (or "Islamic") law. In Singapore still and in pre-1988 Malaysia, this reference is (a) to Anglo-Muhammadan precedents from India or the Straits, and (b) to the standard textbooks of the S̲h̲āfiʿī school. At the lower levels of the *S̲h̲arīʿa* courts, it is the latter which prevails, but in the higher levels and in the secular courts, it is the Anglicised precedent. In addition, the *S̲h̲arīʿa* courts are also developing their own precedent, so that in the official law reports for both Malaysia and Singapore classical *fiḳh* now appears in an English form and the doctrine of precedent, unknown as such in *S̲h̲arīʿa*, has come to apply in *wakf* as in other matters.

(iv) *Malaysia* [*q.v.*] *1988-present.* In June 1988 the Malaysian Constitution was amended (Art. 121 (1A)) so as to reserve matters of *S̲h̲arīʿa* for the religious courts. The intention was to oust the jurisdiction of the secular courts on any matter of Islam within the jurisdiction of the *S̲h̲arīʿa* courts. This includes *wakf.* At about the same time, most states in Malaysia introduced additional detailed legislation on Islamic family law and also on the administration of Islamic law. The effect of this legislation is to elaborate and reinforce the administration of the classical *wakf*, but at the same time, the statutes have also increasingly introduced English law technical classifications. *Wakf*, for example, is equated with a "charitable trust", other terms used include "domicile", "conveyance", "vesting", "cyprès", and so on. In addition, the reported cases (jurisprudence) interpreting the legislation refer to the complex Indian or Anglo-Indian precedent.

The main features are that the motive must be religious, that the dedication must be permanent and that the usufruct must be utilised for the good of mankind. However, there are also several points of contrast with the English trust as well as similarities. Thus the motive in *wakf* is always religious, but this need not be the case in trust. In *wakf*, the property belongs to God and the dedication is thus permanent. In trusts, on the other hand, the perpetuity rules are crucial. In a trust, a settlor may take an interest, but this is not the case in *wakf* except for Ḥanafīs. On the other hand, both *wakf* and trust laws agree that the subject-matter is any property capable of being owned. Perhaps the major distinction is that the *mutawali* is not a "trustee"; Islam does not recognise an intermediate vesting as in the case of a trustee. But, on the other hand, the duties laid on the *mutawali* do come close to those laid on trustees, particularly in financial matters.

While all the Malaysian legislation refers to the "Islamic law" as to determining the validity of an individual *wakf*, it is difficult to see how this reference can be sustained given the complete reformulation of *wakf* as a "charitable trust". This trend, of course, was present in the Straits Settlements in the 1920s and 1930s, and now seems to have come to fruition.

(v) *Indonesia* [*q.v.*]. In the former Netherlands East Indies, Islam was heavily controlled and the *S̲h̲arīʿa* was allowed very little recognition as a law for Muslims. It was not until 1882 that a Muslim Court (*Priesterraad*) was established, but with a very limited jurisdiction, which included *wakf.* The 1882 regulation and later amendment in 1937 was purely procedural, providing only for the administration of and accounting for *wakf*; this remains the position today. "The Compilation of Islamic Law" (implemented by Presidential Instruction No. 1/1991), Book iii (§§ 215-228) defines *wakf* as a "legal act . . . which institutionalises assets for religious purposes or other public needs in accordance with the teachings of Islam". The eighteen sections of Book iii are, after this definition, wholly procedural. Assets must be durable and of value according to the standard S̲h̲āfiʿī textbooks. Assets must also be free from claim by any other person and the assets are held and administered under the supervision of an officer appointed by the Minister of Religion. The *nadzin* (legal person administering) must be an Indonesian national, an adult, "emotionally and spiritually healthy", and must be registered by the local office of the Ministry of Religion. Reports and accounts of administration must be provided. Alteration of the use of assets may be approved for the public benefit or if the original purpose has become impossible. Detailed data are as yet only slowly becoming available, but the future of *wakf* seems assured.

(vi) *The Philippines* [*q.v.*]. *Wakf* undoubtedly existed in the Muslim South, but equally certainly was heavily overlaid with customary rules. This is certainly the case in the 1977 Muslim Code of the Philippines (Presidential Decree No. 1083) where *wakf* is mentioned twice. It is defined in Art. 173 as constituting "communal property" along with customary heirlooms and ancestral property. It is described as "charitable trust property" and must be administered or disposed of in accordance with "Muslim law, *ada* (*adat*) and special provisions of the law". The administrator is a "trustee" (Art. 174 (2) (3)) who is appointed by the *S̲h̲arīʿa* Circuit Court. The terms of the Code are quite clear; *wakf* is a charitable trust (as in Malaysia) and the *mutawali* is a trustee. Further, room is left for customary forms of *wakf.* The second mention of *wakf* in the Code is in Art. 104 which allows for the creation of a *wakf* ("*waqf-bil-wasiya*") by will but amounting up to one-third of the estate only, unless allowed by the heirs (Art. 106). Detailed data are as yet lacking.

Bibliography: 1. Up to 1980. M.B. Hooker, *Islamic law in South East Asia*, Kuala Lumpur 1984.

2. From 1980. (a) Malaysia: the primary source is the legislation. A good example is the Administration of Islamic Law (Federal Territory) Enactment, No. 505/1993, Part vi. For imported Anglo-Indian

precedent, see D.S. Mulla, *Principles of Mahomedan law*, 16th ed., Bombay 1968. (b) Indonesia: the primary source is the *Compilation of Islamic law* (Presidential Instruction No. 1/1993), Book iii. See also Suhardi (Hj Imam), *Hukum wakaf di Indonesia*, Yogyakarta 1985, which gives examples of registered *waḳf*s.

(M.B. Hooker)

VIII. In sub-Saharan Africa

Unlike the Middle East and North Africa, in most of sub-Saharan Africa before the 20th century the *waḳf* institution was little used as an instrument for endowing mosques, colleges, and other religious establishments. The reasons for this are not entirely clear, but the lack in most parts of Africa of building stone and the consequent impermanence of structures may have been a contributory factor. In West Africa and the Nile valley, the institution of the *madrasa* [*q.v.*] was itself lacking, even in such considerable centres of learning as Timbuktu, and no ruler saw fit to endow one. Learning was imparted on a purely individual, non-institutional basis.

Only in Zanzibar under the Bū Saʿīdī dynasty (1804-1964 [see bū saʿīd]) was land regularly set aside as *waḳf*, and this was not for the construction of religious buildings but to create inalienable areas in the N'gambo, the non-élite quarter of the city. This was typically where ex-slaves were settled, and the plots of land were made into *waḳf* by their élite owners for the benefit of the poor and needy, or in some cases for the benefit of sons or daughters. The institution was bureaucratised by the British in the 20th century, and a Wakf Department was created. Many *waḳf* dedications were invalidated by the British, resulting in the loss of such land and the imposition of land rents and even house rents on the poorest segment of the population, despite protests from *waḳf* dedicators and the poor of N'gambo.

Muslim rulers in West Africa, however, did establish endowments outside the region, notably in the Ḥid̲j̲āz and Egypt. During his pilgrimage of 903/1497 Askiya *al-ḥād̲j̲d̲j̲* Muḥammad of Songhay [*q.v.*] purchased gardens in Medina for the use of West African pilgrims. In the late 10th/16th century Mai Idrīs Alawma of Bornu purchased a house and a date grove in Medina, and placed slaves in it as an act of piety. Much earlier, in the mid-7th/13th century, a *madrasa* had been established in Cairo for Kānemī students, and although this is not stated, it is likely that this was a *waḳf*. In 1251/1837-8 a *waḳf* was established by Muḥammad ʿAlī Pas̲h̲a to support the *riwāḳ* of Sinnār at the request of a Sudanese *s̲h̲ayk̲h̲*, and clearly for the benefit of Sudanese students.

There are two domains other than real estate for which there is literary or documentary evidence of the *waḳf* institution in sub-Saharan Africa: slaves and books. In his questions to al-Mag̲h̲īlī [*q.v.*], Askiya *al-ḥād̲j̲d̲j̲* Muḥammad raised the matter of royal slaves who were inherited by succeeding rulers and never sold or given away, and wanted to know if this was lawful. Al-Mag̲h̲īlī sanctioned the custom, invoking the *ḥubus* (the North African equivalent of *waḳf*) institution to justify it (J.O. Hunwick, *S̲h̲arīʿa in Songhay*, Oxford 1985, 86, 88). In 19th-century Timbuktu, individuals made slaves into *waḳf*s for their descendants; documents preserved in the Centre Aḥmad Bābā there show, for example, a woman making a slave woman into a *waḳf* for her male and female children (doc. 3851/ii), and another in which a woman makes a slave woman a *waḳf* exclusively for her daughter and the daughter's female descendants (doc. 3851/ix). Again in Timbuktu, in the 10th/16th century Askiya *al-ḥād̲j̲d̲j̲* Muḥammad made a *waḳf* of sixty *d̲j̲uzʾ* (two complete copies) of the Ḳurʾān for the Great Mosque of Timbuktu (al-Saʿdī, *Taʾrīk̲h̲ al-Sūdān*, in Hunwick, *Timbuktu and the Songhay Empire*, Leiden 1999, 83). In Lamu [*q.v.*] on the East African coast there is evidence that, in the nineteenth century, not only were copies of parts of the Ḳurʾān endowed in perpetuity but an array of other Arabic texts.

If the *waḳf* proper was not generally an instrument for endowing land and buildings, another institution which resembled it in some ways was widespread in Sahelian Africa in the 9th/15th to the 12th/18th centuries, and possibly earlier; it also appears to have been unique to this area. It consisted of the granting by a ruler of a piece of land, and sometimes taxation rights over people, together with exemption from payment of taxes and fines, and certain other privileges (notably freedom from harassment and the hospitality demands of royal officials) to religious scholars and favoured notables. Such endowments are known from the kingdom of Sinnār on the Blue Nile, from Dār Fūr, from Kānem-Bornu, and (though marginally) from Songhay. In the case of religious scholars and holy men, these grants were made in order to encourage them to settle in the sultan's domains, and often to perform religious services for him. These are only occasionally designated as *waḳf*s (see Spaulding, *Public documents*, 182-3; O'Fahey, *Endowment, privilege and estate*, 339); more usually they are called *d̲j̲ah* or *ṣadaḳa* in the Sudanese kingdoms (the estate granted being called *ḥākūra*). While the documents making such grants do not always state that land is alienated in perpetuity, as one would expect in a true *waḳf*, they were effectively titles to land that extended to descendants, and were often confirmed and reconfirmed by succeeding sultans; indeed, those that have been published were discovered in the personal archives of the families concerned in the 20th century, indicating their continuing validity in the eyes of their owners. In Kānem-Bornu and Songhay, where the documents grant privilege without land, they are called respectively *maḥram* and *ḥurma*, terms that indicate that the grantee's person and property were inviolate.

Bibliography: H.R. Palmer, *Sudanese memoirs*, Lagos 1928, iii, 3-27; J.O. Hunwick and R.S. O'Fahey, *Some waqf documents from Lamu*, in *Bull. of Information (Fontes Historiae Africanae)*, vi (1981), 26-43; O'Fahey, *Land in Dār Fūr. Charters and related documents from the Dār Fūr Sultanate*, Cambridge 1985; J. Spaulding and M.I. Abū Sālim (eds.), *Public documents from Sinnār*, East Lansing, Mich. 1989; Hunwick, *Studies in the Taʾrīk̲h̲ al-Fattāsh. II. An alleged charter of privilege issued by Askiya al-Ḥājj Muḥammad to the descendants of Mori Hawgāro*, in *Sudanic Africa*, iii (1992), 133-48; Hamidu Bobboyi, *Relations of the Bornu ʿUlamāʾ with the Sayfawa rulers. The role of the maḥrams*, in *ibid.*, iv (1993), 175-204; Abdul Sheriff (ed.), *The history and conservation of Zanzibar Stone Town*, London 1995; O'Fahey, *Endowment, privilege and estate in central and eastern Sudan*, in *ILS*, iv (1997), 334-51.

(J.O. Hunwick)

WAK̲H̲ĀN, a region in the heart of Inner Asia, to the south of the Pamir [*q.v.*] range, essentially a long and narrow valley running east-west and watered by the upper Oxus or Pand̲j̲a and the Wak̲h̲ān Daryā, its southernmost source.

The length of Wak̲h̲ān along the Oxus is 67 miles and of the Wak̲h̲ān Daryā (from Langar-kis̲h̲ to the Wak̲h̲d̲j̲īr pass) 113 miles. Afg̲h̲an sources put the distance from Is̲h̲kās̲h̲im to Sarḥadd at 66 *kurōh* (= 22 *farsak̲h̲*s).

To the south of Wakhān rises the wall of the Hindū Kush, through which several passes lead to the lands of the upper Indus. The main pass (12,460 feet) of Baroghil leads into Čitrāl. The northern wall of Wakhān is the Wakhān range, the peaks of which reach a height of 23,000 feet. In the west, Wakhān stretches to the bend of the Oxus, where the river entering the boundaries of Shughnān [*q.v.*] turns northwards. In the east Wakhān (through the high valley of Wakhdjīr) is adjoined by Chinese possessions and Lake Čaḳmaḳ Tīng.

Wakhān has historically formed part of the mountain barrier separating Central Asia from northern India. By the 1895 Russo-Afghan Agreement (see below), the frontier was defined as running: (*a*) in the lower part of Wakhān, up the course of the Oxus as far as Langar-kish where the two sources of the Oxus meet: the river Wakhān from the south-east (from the Little Pāmīr) and the river Pāmīr from the north-east (from the Great Pāmīr); (*b*) from Langar-kish the frontier follows the course of the Pāmīr river to its source (Lake Zor-kul or Victoria); (*c*) more to the east again, the frontier runs by a zigzag line towards the south to China (near the Beyik pass). Afghan territory therefore comprises the left bank of the Oxus, all the valley of the Wakhān Daryā, the land on the left bank of the Pāmīr river and a small part of the upper course of the Aḳ Su (including Lake Čaḳmaḳ Kul).

The Afghan part of Wakhān contains seven districts, namely from west to east: Warg, Ūrgand, Khandūd, Ḳalʿa-yi Pandja, Bābā-Tangī, Nirs-wa-Shalak and Sarḥadd (this last-named village is at the foot of the Baroghil pass at a height of 11,350 feet), as well as the thinly-populated territory of the Little Pāmīr (watered by the Wakhān Daryā).

On the Afghan side, there are in Wakhan 64 villages and on the Russian 27 ones. The indigenous population (Wakhīs) belongs to the race of Iranian mountaineers (*Ghalča*), very often with blue eyes, a feature which had struck the Chinese as early as the 6th century; there are also Kirghiz Turkish nomads. The Wakhī language is an Eastern Iranian one, with archaic features, spoken by some 10,000 persons (see J.R. Payne, *Pamir languages*, in R. Schmitt (ed.), *Compendium linguarum iranicarum*, Wiesbaden 1989, 417-44; ĪRĀN. iii. Languages, in Suppl.).

From the 7th century, Wakhān is continually mentioned in the early Chinese sources under the names of Hu-mī, Po-ho, etc. (cf. Marquart, *Ērānšahr*, 243, and Chavannes, *Documents sur les Tou-kiue occidentaux*, index). Hiuen-Tsang mentions the greenish eyes of the people of Ta-mo-si-tʾie-ti (a form not yet satisfactorily explained) and its capital Hun-tʾo-to (= Khandūd) with its great Buddhist *vihāra*. In 747 Wakhān was the theatre of the operations of the famous Chinese general Kao-sien-tse against the Tibetans (cf. Chavannes, 152-3). Among Arab authors, al-Iṣṭakhrī (< al-Balkhī) several times mentions Wakhān as a land of infidels, as the place from which musk comes and where the Oxus rises (see al-Iṣṭakhrī, 279, 280, 296; Ibn Rusta, 91). Al-Masʿūdī, *Murūdj*, i, 213, and *Tanbīh*, 64, applies the term "Türk" to all the inhabitants of the upper Oxus: the Awkhān (اوخان, read: وخان), Tubbat (Tibetans) and Ayghān (?). As to the Iranian Wakhīs, the term "Türk" can only refer to their ruling dynasty (cf. Markwart, *Wehrot und Arang*, Leiden 1938, 101-2). More detailed information is supplied by the Persian geographical work *Ḥudūd al-ʿālam*, tr. Minorsky, 121, comm. 366-7, which calls Wakhān the residence of the king and capital of the land (*shahr*) of Sikāshim (it ought probably to be emended to *Ishkashim, the capital of Wakhān). At Kh-mdādh (*Khundād) are the temples (*but-khāna*) of the Wakhīs, and "to its left" was a fortress occupied by the Tibetans. Samarḳandāḳ was regarded as the remotest frontier of the dependencies of Transoxiana; it had Hindu, Tibetan and Wakhī inhabitants (probably the Sarḥadd of the present day).

In the struggle for political and strategic positions in Central Asia, which Kipling calls in *Kim* "the Great Game", Wakhān played a significant role. After the October 1872 Anglo-Russian Agreement tacitly recognised the Amīr of Kābul's territories as extending up to the Oxus, the Russians in February 1873 conceded Afghan control of Badakhshān [*q.v.*] and Wakhān. But after 1891, Russia attempted to explore and annex the Wakhān area and thereby acquire a common frontier with British India, provoking a vigorous reaction from Britain. Hence the March 1895 Russo-Afghan Agreement conceded all lands north of the Oxus to Russia and all of them south, as far west as Khodja Ṣāliḥ, to Afghānistān; ʿAbd al-Raḥmān Khān [*q.v.*] now somewhat reluctantly assumed control of the Wakhān corridor or "panhandle" of Afghānistān, which thus became a buffer against Russian designs on India.

The former British Indian frontier with the Wakhān corridor is now shared by Pākistān in the west and [Āzād] Kashmīr in the east; its extreme eastern tip is contiguous with the People's Republic of China (Sinkiang or Xinjiang Uighur Autonomous Region; the boundary was not actually delimited by surveyors on the ground until 1964). When, after the Second World War, the Communists took over in Sinkiang, Kirghiz who lived on the Chinese side of the Russo-Turkish border fled for refuge in the eastern part of Wakhān and settled around Buzai Gumbad under their leader Raḥmān Gul; in the 1980s, they finally emigrated to Turkey. In contemporary Afghānistān, the corridor comes within the *wilāyat* or province of Badakhshān. The parts of Wakhān north of the corridor formerly came within the Gorno-Badakhshan Oblast of the Soviet Tajikistan SSR, and are now in the independent Tajikistan Republic.

Bibliography: J. Wood, *A journey to the source of the River Oxus*, ²London 1876; G.N. Curzon, *The Pamirs and the source of the Oxus*, London 1898, 32 and map; S.M. Khan (ed.), *The life of Abdur Rahman, Amir of Afghanistan*, London 1900, ii, 145, 288; Count Bobrinskoy, *Gortsî verkhoviev P'andja*, Moscow 1908; Prince Masalsky, *Turkestan*, St. Petersburg 1913, 99-102 (vol. xix of the series *Russia* by P.P. Semenov); *Tādjīkistān*, Tashkent 1925, *passim* (collection of memoirs by Korženewsky, Barthold, Semenov, etc., on the Soviet Republic of Tajikistan); Burhān al-Dīn Khān Khūshkakī, *Kattaghan wa-Badakhshān*, Russ. tr. Tashkent 1926, 149-70; Sir Aurel Stein, *Serindia*, Oxford 1921, i, ch. iii, 60-71 (old Chinese references); idem, *Innermost Asia*, Oxford 1928, ii, 863-71 (antiquities: Zangibār near Ḥiṣār, Zamr-i ātash-parast near Yamčīn); idem, *On ancient tracks past the Pamirs*, in *The Himalayan Journal*, iv (1932) (separate print, 1-26); J. Humlum *et alii*, *Afghanistan, étude d'un pays aride*, Copenhagen 1959, 162; J. Mouchet, *La vallée du Wakhan*, in *Afghanistan*, xxv/1 (1972), 78-87; L. Dupree, *Afghanistan*, Princeton 1973, 5-6, 405, 424. See also SHUGHNĀN. (V. MINORSKY-[C.E. BOSWORTH])

WAKHSH, a district of Central Asia and the name of a river there. The Wakhsh Āb is a right-bank tributary of the Oxus, flowing down from the Alai range of mountains to the south of Farghāna. Geiger and Markwart thought that the Greek name

"Ὦξος came from Wa<u>kh</u>s<u>h</u>, the tributary thus giving its name to the great river (see Markwart, *Wehrot und Arang*, 3 ff., 89; Barthold, *Turkestan down to the Mongol invasion*, 65; and ĀMŪ DARYĀ).

In early mediaeval times, the Wa<u>kh</u>s<u>h</u> district must have had a population which included remnants of the Hephthalites, such as the Kumīd<u>j</u>īs [*q.v.*] and also Turks, the Ḳarluḳ being mentioned by Ibn Rusta, 92. The geographers describe it as a prosperous region where horse-rearing was important; at that time (4th/10th century), the part of Wa<u>kh</u>s<u>h</u> along the left bank of the river came within the province of <u>Kh</u>uttal(ān) [*q.v.*]. The name still survives today as that of the Wa<u>kh</u>s<u>h</u> river (called in its upper course the Sur<u>kh</u>āb), at present coming within the independent Tajikistan Republic.

Bibliography: See also *Ḥudūd al-ʿālam*, tr. Minorsky, 71, 120, comm. 198, 209, 361-3; Markwart, *Wehrot und Arang*, Leiden 1938, 53-5, 57-60, 75-8, 89-90; Le Strange, *The lands of the Eastern Caliphate*, 434-6, 437-9. (C.E. BOSWORTH)

WAKĪʿ, MUḤAMMAD b. <u>KH</u>ALAF b. Ḥayyān Ṣadaḳa al-Ḍabbī (d. 24 Rabīʿ I 306/4 September 918), historian, expert in *ḥadī<u>th</u>*, geography, Ḳurʾānic verse-numbering and other subjects.

His best-known work is *A<u>kh</u>bār al-Ḳuḍāt*, a biographical dictionary of *ḳāḍī*s, with a preface on the nature of judgeship. The work is arranged first regionally—according to the *amṣār*—then chronologically. His aim in the work is to provide "information about [*ḳāḍī*s] and their rulings; the way in which they were appointed; their genealogies and tribes; their methods; those who transmitted reports from them and samples of those reports" (i, 5). Wakīʿ's extensive introductory section has reports from the Prophet condemning bribery and covering other themes that became standard in *Adab al-Ḳāḍī* literature, e.g. the difficulties of being a *ḳāḍī*, that one ought not to judge when angry, etc. Some of the entries, e.g. on <u>Sh</u>urayḥ [*q.v.*] (ii, 189 ff.), are practically intellectual biographies, with extensive lists of judicial rulings that may help trace the earliest stages of Islamic positive law. Much of Wakīʿ's information comes from sources now lost to us, such as Abū <u>Th</u>awr [*q.v.*]. His other works on the numbering of Ḳurʾānic verses, on geography, on archery, and on technical subjects such as weights and measures, do not survive.

Little is known of his life, except that he was born and died in Ba<u>gh</u>dād, and served as *ḳāḍī* in Ahwāz, or "all the districts of Ahwāz" (*kuwar Ahwāz kulluhā*). He moved in literary circles, as well as religio-legal ones, and was an associate of Abu 'l-Farad<u>j</u> al-Iṣfahānī [*q.v.*]. He is reported to have been laconic in speech, but to have had an "easy" style in his writing.

Bibliography: See Sezgin, *GAS*, i, 376 and biographical sources cited there, to which add Yāḳūt, *Ir<u>sh</u>ād*, iii, 848; Ibn al-Nadīm, *Fihrist*, ed. Tad<u>j</u>addud, 127, tr. Dodge, i, 250; Ba<u>gh</u>dādī, *Hidāya*, ii, 25 (garbled); *A<u>kh</u>bār al-ḳuḍāt*, ed. ʿAbd al-ʿAzīz Muṣṭafā al-Marā<u>gh</u>ī, 3 vols. Cairo 1369/1950. (A.K. REINHART)

WAKĪʿ B. AL-<u>D</u>JARRĀḤ B. MALĪḤ al-Ruʾāsī, Abū Sufyān, famous ʿIrāḳī traditionist, b. Kūfa 129/746, where his father was head of the *bayt al-māl*, d. at Fayd [*q.v.* in Suppl.] on the Pilgrimage route in 197/812.

He was schooled in the Islamic sciences, above all *ḥadī<u>th</u>*, through his father, and transmitted not only from this last but also from many ʿIrāḳī and non-ʿIrāḳī scholars of the 2nd/8th century, such as Ismāʿīl b. Abī <u>Kh</u>ālid, ʿIkrima b. ʿAmmār, al-Aʿma<u>sh</u>, al-Awzāʿī and Mālik, amongst the long list given by Ibn Ḥad<u>j</u>ar, *Tahd<u>h</u>īb*, xi, 124-5, together with another list of the scholars who transmitted from him, 125-6. His fame was so great that he was considered to be the foremost of the *muḥaddi<u>th</u>ūn* of his age, despite the errors of transmission attributed to him. In general, he seems to have made an impression on more than one great scholar through his intellectual honesty, which is said to have left his integrity intact *vis-à-vis* the ruling power, probably in allusion to the offer of a post as judge which Hārūn al-Ra<u>sh</u>īd reportedly made to him but which he refused out of piety and fear lest the job should involve him in dependence to the state. His attitude is further explicable by his well-known asceticism.

Although Wakīʿ had a legendary memory and was said never to have been seen with a book in his hand, several works of his are known: *Tafsīr al-Ḳurʾān*, *al-Sunan*, *al-Maʿrifa wa 'l-taʾrī<u>kh</u>*, *al-Muṣannaf* (cited by Ibn Hanbal, i, 308, and Ibn Ḥad<u>j</u>ar, *Iṣāba*, i, 434) and also a book on *zuhd*, preserved in the Ẓāhiriyya, Damascus, see Sezgin, i, 97 no. 2.

Bibliography: 1. Sources. Abū Nuʿaym al-Iṣbahānī, *Ḥilya*, viii, 368-80; Bu<u>kh</u>ārī, *Taʾrī<u>kh</u>*, iv/2, 179; <u>Dh</u>ahabī, *Mīzān al-iʿtidāl*, Cairo 1382, 335-6; idem, *Ḥuffāẓ*, Cairo 1375, 306-9; Ibn Abī Ḥātim, *<u>D</u>jarḥ/Taḳdima*, i, 219-32; Ibn Abī Yaʿlā, *Ḥanābila*, Cairo 1952, 391-2; Ibn Ḥad<u>j</u>ar, *Tahd<u>h</u>īb*, xi, 123-31; Ibn Ḥibbān, *Ma<u>sh</u>āhīr*, 173; Ibn al-Nadīm, *Fihrist*, 226; al-<u>Kh</u>aṭīb al-Ba<u>gh</u>dādī, xiii, 466-81; Ḳura<u>sh</u>ī, *<u>D</u>jawāhir*, Ḥaydarābād 1332, ii, 208.

2. Studies. Kaḥḥāla, *Muʾallifīn*, xiii, 166; Ziriklī, *Aʿlām*, ix, 135; Sezgin, *GAS*, i, 96-7; R.G. Khoury, *ʿAbd Allāh Ibn Lahīʿa, juge et grand maître de l'école égyptienne*, Wiesbaden 1956, 144-5. (R.G. KHOURY)

AL-**WĀḲIʿA** [see AL-ḲURʾĀN].

AL-**WĀḲIDĪ**, MUḤAMMAD B. ʿUMAR b. Wāḳid, historian from Medina, also expert in *fiḳh*, author and often-quoted authority on early Islamic history (*sīra*, *ma<u>gh</u>āzī*, *ridda*, *futūḥ*), b. 130/747-8, d. 12 <u>Dh</u>u 'l-Ḥid<u>j</u>dja 207/28 April 822. He is of paramount importance for early Arabic historiography on account of the quantity and quality of the information which he passed on in the literature, and for the nature of his methodology.

The outlines of his biography are given by his pupil and secretary Ibn Saʿd (vii/2, 77 and v, 314-321). Al-Wāḳidī was a client of the Sahm, a sub-tribe (*baṭn*) of Aslam. ʿAbd Allāh b. Burayda al-Aslamī, *ḳāḍī* of Marw (d. 115/733), is mentioned as patron of a man who was probably al-Wāḳidī's grandfather. His mother is said to have been the granddaughter of a Persian who was a merchant, and a singer at Medina (*Aghānī*[3], viii, 322). In 180/796-7 he settled at Ba<u>gh</u>dād, were he was appointed at some later date *ḳāḍī* of ʿAskar al-Mahdī, i.e. al-Ruṣāfa, at the eastern side of the city. According to Ibn Saʿd, the caliph al-Maʾmūn appointed him to this office when he came from <u>Kh</u>urāsān. Since al-Maʾmūn returned to Ba<u>gh</u>dād only in 204/819, al-Wāḳidī's appointment would have been three years before his death. Ibn al-Nadīm (*Fihrist*, ed. Tad<u>j</u>addud, 111) and, depending on him, Yāḳūt (*Ir<u>sh</u>ād*, vii, 56) mention that Hārūn al-Ra<u>sh</u>īd had already appointed him to the judgeship. The appointment by al-Maʾmūn may therefore have been a re-appointment after an interruption for a certain period of time. However, al-Wakīʿ (*A<u>kh</u>bār al-ḳuḍāt*, iii, 270-1) mentions al-Wāḳidī as being only in al-Maʾmūn's service.

Al-Wāḳidī was known for a somewhat excessive generosity, and this habit, as well as a failed transaction in the grain trade (see al-Khaṭīb al-Baghdādī, iii, 4), seems to have had a lasting impact on his life, since he was henceforth encumbered by debts. He even left debts when he died, and these were settled by al-Ma'mūn, who acted as his executor. A richly colourful and lively account allegedly told by al-Wāḳidī himself (Ibn Sa'd, v, 314-19) tells how he came to enjoy the patronage of Yaḥyā b. Khālid al-Barmakī, to whom he owed the particular favour of the caliph Hārūn al-Rashīd and, subsequently, of his son 'Abd Allāh al-Ma'mūn: When Hārūn came, together with Yaḥyā b. Khālid, to Medina on one of his pilgrimages, al-Wāḳidī served them as a guide. Subsequently, he left for Baghdād, and thence to al-Raḳḳa, the residence of Hārūn at that time (and until 192/808). Here he succeeded after much difficulty in coming into contact with Yaḥyā, who honoured him and interceded with the caliph for him, showing al-Wāḳidī special attention and generous support.

In consequence of this patronage, we may conclude, al-Wāḳidī's work at Baghdād exceeded that of an average *muḥaddith* in respect to the range of facilities to which he had access. Ibn Sa'd points out his expertise of early Islamic history, his acquaintance with contradicting doctrines concerning *ḥadīth* and *fiḳh* (*aḥkām*) and knowledge of opinions which were generally approved; "and he explained all this in books which he excerpted (*istakhradja*), composed (*waḍa'a*) and transmitted formally (*ḥaddatha bihā*)." Both of these traits, the attempt to evaluate the information he received, and the extensive use and production of books, are characteristic of his work. The huge amount of written materials ("books") which were in his possession was impressive. He is said to have left six hundred bookcases, each one weighing as much as two men (*Fihrist*, 111, line 6; *Ta'rīkh Baghdād*, iii, 6). The importance and quantity of this material was renowned, and Ibn al-Nadīm mentions that he had two slave boys writing for him day and night. Equally famous were the number and variety of his own writings. Aḥmad b. Ḥanbal, although he did not quote al-Wāḳidī because of his critical stance concerning al-Wāḳidī's reliability, attached great importance to his books, read them and used to take notes from them (*Ta'rīkh Baghdād*, iii, 15).

Among the experts on *ḥadīth* of the 3rd/9th century, censure of al-Wāḳidī's untrustworthiness prevailed, unjustifiably in the view of al-Dhahabī (*Siyar a'lām al-nubalā'*, ix, 469). The most substantial—and influential—rebuke was advanced by Yaḥyā b. Ma'īn (d. 233/847), who discovered the use of false ascription in his material (Ibn Abī Ḥātim al-Rāzī, *al-Djarḥ wa 'l-ta'dīl*, iv/1, 21). He was also blamed, mostly by Aḥmad b. Ḥanbal, for applying the technique of combining several traditions into one tradition, which he introduced by a collective *isnād*, instead of presenting each tradition separately together with its proper *isnād*, although this usage was already established by older authorities. Nevertheless, the *ḥadīth* experts denied al-Wāḳidī's authority in this field, and although examples for the precision and extent of his memory are given, scepticism prevailed. This attitude is, however, characteristic only of the circles of *muḥaddithūn* of the 3rd/9th century, whereas later, due to the indispensability of al-Wāḳidī as a historian, a general condemnation was no longer tolerated. Ibn Sayyid al-Nās, for instance, saw the distrust as caused by the fact that al-Wāḳidī handled a huge amount of traditions, which would naturally encompass some strange materials (*'Uyūn al-athar*, Cairo 1406/1986, i, 29). The leaning towards a moderate Shī'ī viewpoint ascribed to al-Wāḳidī by Ibn al-Nadīm is not corroborated in his writings, although it is noticeable that he has quite a number of traditions that report that the Prophet lay on 'Alī's lap when he was dying.

Al-Wāḳidī's work survives in the *Kitāb al-Maghāzī* (ed. J. Marsden Jones, London 1966), the only book of his which is preserved in a *K. al-Ridda* attributed to him (ed. M. Ḥamīdallāh, Paris 1989, and Yaḥyā al-Djabbūrī, Beirut 1990), and in many quotations throughout historical literature. The manuscript which serves as basis for the edition of the *Maghāzī* is a copy of a recension made by Muḥammad b. al-'Abbās Ibn Ḥayyawayh (d. 382/992), as Brockelmann already noted (S I, 207). In this text, al-Wāḳidī is repeatedly quoted (*ḳāla*), and in some instances (e.g. 74,690) Ibn Ḥayyawayh refers to 'Abd al-Wahhāb b. Abī Ḥayya, the librarian (*warrāḳ*) of al-Djāḥiẓ (d. 319/931; *Ta'rīkh Baghdād*, xi, 28-9), from whom he had received authorisation for the transmission of this text. The *Maghāzī* represents some of the particularities of al-Wāḳidī's work as an historian. As already observed by Caetani, al-Wāḳidī's accounts reflect, in comparison with others, coherent, straightforward and historically reasonable reports (*Annali*, ii, 1545, vi (Indices), 198-9). More than any other authority in this field before him, he attempted to establish the chronology of the military campaigns (cf. Ella Landau-Tasseron, *Processes of redaction: the case of the Tamīmite delegation to the Prophet Muḥammad*, in *BSOAS*, xlix [1986], 253-70, at 269). In pursuit of this goal, he sometimes became entangled in contradictions (Marsden Jones, Introd. (Arabic) to the *Maghāzī*, 32-3). After presenting the details of an event, he generally adds short remarks explaining his preference of a certain version which he has chosen from different accounts, such as "and this is the most certain" etc. (*ibid.*, 34). His technique of personal inquiry is also referred to in various accounts. He states that he used to ask the descendants of the participants at the military campaigns of the time of the Prophet for their knowledge of events and places. It is also said that he used to go out to the locations themselves in order to gain a personal impression of the topography (*Ta'rīkh Baghdād*, iii, 6). It may be in this context that we have to understand al-Wāḳidī's remark that he retained more in his memory than in his books, possibly referring here not only to the power of his memory but also hinting at the information he had brought to light through personal inquiry and inspection.

Another typical trait of his work is the use of combined reports. It has been argued that al-Wāḳidī presents new texts in so far as they did not exist in this form in any earlier source, but that they actually follow earlier sources which can be reconstructed (M. Lecker, *Wāqidī's account of the status of the Jews in Mecca*, in *JNES*, liv [1995], 27-8). On the other hand, the fusion of various accounts into one may have a direct impact on the contents of reports in that it results in combining different events into one (cf. Landau-Tasseron, *op. cit.*, 262-3). This may even be discovered when al-Wāḳidī does not indicate a combined report (G. Schoeler, *Charakter und Authentie der muslimischen Überlieferung über das Leben Mohammeds*, Berlin-New York 1996, 137-40). Al-Wāḳidī also presents materials that betray their origin from Ibn Isḥāḳ, whom he does not quote. Against the allegation that he plagiarises Ibn Isḥāḳ it has been argued that both authors drew on a common corpus of material (Marsden Jones, *Maghāzī literature*, in *Camb. hist. of Ar. lit. To the end of the Umayyad period*, 349; against this view, Schoeler, *op. cit.*, 141). Evidence gained from the comparison of historical texts shows that al-Wāḳidī had a variety of sources at his disposal (see Lecker, *The death of the Prophet Muḥammad's father: did Wāqidī invent some of the evidence?*, in *ZDMG*, cxlv [1995], 9-27).

As Ibn al-Nadīm explains, Ibn Saʿd composed his books from al-Wāḳidī's orderly arranged collections (*taṣnīfāt*), and we may suppose that for his *Ṭabaḳāt*, Ibn Saʿd mainly used materials from a work of al-Wāḳidī carrying this same title. A *K. al-Ṭabaḳāt* of al-Wāḳidī seems to have been used by Khalīfa b. Khayyāṭ (*Ṭabaḳāt*, ed. al-ʿUmarī, Introd., 28), and Ibn ʿAbd al-Barr refers to it as his source. Al-Wāḳidī's *K. al-Ridda* is quoted by Ibn Hadjar al-ʿAskalānī in his *Iṣāba*, but the *K. al-Ridda*, which is extant (see above), does not contain al-Wāḳidī's material only but also quotes Ibn Isḥāḳ. To the traces of his works noted by Jones and Sezgin, one may add the quotations from al-Wāḳidī's *al-Futūḥ*, *al-Kāmil*, and *al-Mubāyaʿāt* in Ibn Ḥadjar's *Iṣāba*. A *Taʾrīkh al-Wāḳidī*, the contents of which are hard to establish with certainty, may also have been in the hands of Ibn Abi 'l-Ḥadīd, who quotes al-Wāḳidī several times (*ḳāla*, *dhakara*, *rawā*) on various matters and once mentions his *Taʾrīkh* (xvi, 279); his son Muḥammad transmitted this work from his father, according to al-Samʿānī (*Ansāb*, Beirut 1988, v, 567).

Legendary accounts about the early Islamic conquests ascribed to al-Wāḳidī, like the *Futūḥ al-Shām* (ed. W. Nassau Less, 3 vols., Calcutta 1854-62), which served Simon Ockley as a source for his *History of the Saracenes*, London 1718, and the *Futūḥ Diyār Rabīʿa wa-Diyār Bakr* (tr. as *Geschichte der Eroberung von Mesopotamien und Armenien von Mohammed ben Omar al-Wakedi* by B.G. Niebuhr, ed. A.D. Mordtmann, Hamburg 1847, also known as *Futūḥ al-Djazīra wa 'l-Khābūr wa-Diyārbakr wa 'l-ʿIrāḳ*, ed. Ḥarfūsh, Damascus 1996, and the *Kitāb Futūḥ Miṣr wa 'l-Iskandariyya*, ed. Hamaker, Leiden 1825), are of later origin and their ascription to al-Wāḳidī is false (cf. F. Rosenthal, *A history of Muslim historiography*, ²Leiden 1968, 186-193). For titles and manuscripts of the legendary *futūḥ* literature ascribed to al-Wāḳidī, see Brockelmann, I, 141-2, S I, 207-8; Sezgin, i, 294-7.

Bibliography: In addition to the literature given in the article, see A.A. Duri, *The rise of historical writing among the Arabs*, Princeton 1983, 37-40.

(S. LEDER)

AL-**WĀḲIFA** or AL-WĀḲIFIYYA, a Shīʿī sect (*firḳa*) whose adherents maintained that the seventh Imām Mūsā al-Kāẓim (d. 183/799 [*q.v.*]) had not died but that God had carried him out of sight (*rafaʿahū ilayhi*), and awaited his return as the Mahdī [*q.v.*]. By their Twelver Shīʿī (Imāmī) opponents they were called *al-wāḳifa* ("the ones who stand still" or "those who stop, put an end to [the line of Imāms]", because they let the succession of imāms end with him and contested the transfer of the imāmate to his son ʿAlī al-Riḍā [*q.v.*].

The sect is mentioned by Twelver Shīʿī as well as Sunnī heresiographers (al-Nawbakhtī, *Firaḳ al-Shīʿa*, ed. H. Ritter, Istanbul 1931, 68 = Saʿd b. ʿAbd Allāh al-Ḳummī, *al-Maḳālāt wa 'l-firaḳ*, ed. M.Dj. Mashkūr, Tehran 1963, 90; pseudo-Nāshiʾ al-Akbar, ed. J. van Ess, Beirut 1971, 47; al-Ashʿarī, *Maḳālāt*, ed. Ritter, Wiesbaden 1963, 28; al-Shahrastānī, ed. Cureton, 127); the Imāmī authors of *ridjāl* books (al-Kashshī, al-Ṭūsī, al-Nadjāshī) identify many men as Wāḳifīs in order to disqualify them as transmitters of traditions. Several Wāḳifīs, mainly Kūfans, defended the occultation (*ghayba* [*q.v.*]) of the Seventh Imām in special treatises of which only the titles are still extant (listed by Klemm, in *WO*, xv, 126-7); the youngest of these authors, al-Ḥasan b. Muḥammad b. Samāʿa al-Kūfī, died in 263/876-7. Towards the end of the 3rd/9th century the sect seems to have merged with the Twelver Shīʿa or Ithnā ʿAshariyya [*q.v.*].

Bibliography: V. Klemm, *Die vier sufarāʾ des Zwölften Imam. Zur formativen Periode der Zwölferšīʿa*, in *WO*, xv (1984), 126-43; H. Halm, *Shiism*, Edinburgh 1991, 31-3.

(H. HALM)

WAKĪL [see WAKĀLA].

AL-**WAḲḲASHĪ**, ABU 'L-WALĪD HISHĀM B. AḤMAD b. Hishām al-Kinānī al-Waḳḳashī al-Ṭulayṭulī (408-89/1017-96), Andalusī scholar in both the traditional and speculative sciences from Waḳḳash, modern Huecas in the province of Toledo.

He was a pupil of al-Ṭalamankī [*q.v.*]. Nominated judge in Talavera by the Dhu 'l-Nūnid rulers of Toledo, he later settled in Denia where he died. Abu 'l-Ṣalt Umayya [*q.v.*] of Denia was his pupil. Al-Waḳḳashī was praised for his vast knowledge extending to many fields: *handasa*, mathematics, logic, *fiḳh*, *uṣūl*, *iʿtiḳādāt*, grammar, lexicology, poetry, history (especially *ayyām* and *ansāb al-ʿarab*). He wrote on *al-ḳadar wa 'l-Ḳurʾān* and *tanbīhāt wa-rudūd ʿalā kibār al-taṣānīf al-taʾrīkhiyya wa 'l-adabiyya*, such as *tahdhīb al-Kunā li-Muslim*, *Mukhtaṣar li-Kitāb al-Ḳabāʾil li-Muḥammad b. Ḥabīb*, *Sharḥ al-Muwaṭṭaʾ* and *Nukat al-Kāmil li 'l-Mubarrad* (the last-mentioned together with Ibn al-Sīd al-Baṭalyawsī; it has been edited by Ẓuhūr Aḥmad Azhar, Balāhūr (Pakistan) 1401/1980; see also Razzūḳ, in *Mawrid*, iii/1 [1974], 250, and al-Faḥḥām, in *RIMA*, xxix [1985], 75). The *Mukhtaṣar al-fiḳh* attributed to al-Waḳḳashī in Brockelmann, I, 384, and S I, 662, is the work of another scholar, al-Ṭulayṭulī. Al-Waḳḳashī's most famous work is the *ḳaṣīda* he wrote on the occasion of the conquest of Valencia by El Cid (see R. Menéndez Pidal, *Sobre Aluacaxí y la elegía árabe de Valencia*, in *Homenaje a F. Codera*, Saragossa 1904, 393-409; A.R. Nykl, *La elegía árabe de Valencia*, in *Hispanic Review*, viii [1940], 9-17). He was suspected of *iʿtizāl* and of being critical of religious revelation (see M. Asín Palacios, in *al-And.*, iii [1935], 368-74; Pérès, *Poésie*, 456).

Bibliography: 1. Sources. Ṣāʿid, *Ṭabaḳāt*, ed. Blachère, 74/136-7 (ed. Bū ʿAlwān, 178-9); Abū Muḥammad al-Rushāṭī and Ibn al-Kharrāṭ al-Ishbīlī, *al-Andalus fī "Kitāb Iḳtibās al-anwār" wa-fī "Ikhtiṣār Iḳtibās al-anwār"*, ed. E. Molina López and J. Bosch Vilá, Madrid 1990, 91-2, 196; Ibn Bashkuwāl, ed. Codera, no. 1323; Dhahabī, *Siyar*, xix, 134-6, no. 71; Suyūṭī, *Bughya*, ii, 327-8, no. 2099; Maḳḳarī, *Nafḥ*, iv, 137, no. 619.

2. Studies. Pons Boigues, 167, no. 127; Kaḥḥāla, xiii, 147-8; Brockelmann, I, 461; Cl. Sarnelli, in *AIUON*, N.S. xiv (1964), 617; M. Fierro, in *Historia de España R. Menéndez Pidal*, viii/1, Madrid 1994, 439.

(MARIBEL FIERRO)

WAḲT [see ZAMĀN].

WĀḲWĀḲ, WAḲWĀḲ, WĀḲ WĀḲ, WĀḲ AL-WĀḲ, AL-WĀḲWĀḲ (A.), a name, possibly onomatopoeic, of uncertain origin, found in mediaeval Islamic geographical, zoological and imaginative literature. One of the most mystifying place names in the geographical literature, it refers variously to an island or group of islands, inhabited by a dark-skinned population who speak a distinct language; a people or race; and a tree producing human-fruit. There is also the cuckoo bird, onomatopoeically known as Wāḳwāḳ.

1. The island or islands of Wāḳwāḳ.

(a) *Introduction*

There are many stories connected with it but none

of them help to identify the place with certainty and there is no suitable equivalent toponym. European scholars have equated Wāḳwāḳ with nearly every island and peninsula in the Indian Ocean, and some with places in the Pacific. The general impression is that Wāḳwāḳ is a coastal country (*arḍ*, *bilād*) or island (*d̲j̲azīra*) on the shores of one of these oceans.

Ferrand's summary of the material in the 1st edition of the *Encyclopaedia of Islam* was extremely full but Ferrand took his texts too literally. Reducing Wāḳwāḳ to a definite two locales, and equating these with Madagascar and Sumatra, is perhaps going a little too far. After all, both places were adequately provided with names by most geographers and both were well known to the Arabs. Moreover, they were certainly aware of the distinctions between the Zand̲j̲ and their neighbours and would consequently not have mistaken the Zand̲j̲ for Malagasy or Bushmen populations (Ferrand in *EI*[1], IV, 1108).

Nevertheless, the texts do require careful examination, with note taken of their chronology. Thus al-Masʿūdī deserves particular credence for both his early date and also his being the only one of the Arab geographers actually to have visited Zanzibar and to have been well informed about the East African coastlands; and other early sources, as well as al-Masʿūdī, such as Ibn al-Faḳīh and Buzurg b. S̲h̲ahriyār (see below) do refer to an African Wāḳwāḳ (however it is spelt).

The island of Wāḳwāḳ has been given many identifications by European scholars over the past two centuries. Habicht, in his edition of the *Thousand and one nights* in 1825 (i, 299), decided on Japan. Langlès (*Voyage de Sindbad*, 147) thought it was the islands of Southeast Asia. Reinaud (Introduction to *La Géographie d'Aboul-Feda*, 1840, pp. cccv, cccxv) favoured Africa, i.e. Madagascar. De Slane, in his translation of the *Prolegomena* of Ibn K̲h̲aldūn (i, 95 n. 3), believed it to be the Seychelles, but Rosenthal in the notes to his translation (i, 99 n. 29) thought that the context pointed rather to Madagascar or the East African coastlands; Ibn K̲h̲aldūn himself probably had as little idea of its position as any of the European scholars.

The appearance of Buzurg b. S̲h̲ahriyār's *ʿAd̲j̲āʾib al-Hind* in 1883 almost doubled the amount of information available to help scholars better identify Wāḳwāḳ. Devic himself (Buzurg, tr. 169) said that Wāḳwāḳ most probably belonged to the neighbourhood of the Malayan Archipelago but that it was too vaguely defined to be able to identify precisely. Lane (*Arabian Nights*, 1247 n. 32) held similar views, and suggested that Wāḳwāḳ was "All the islands which they (sc. the Arab geographers) were acquainted with on the East and South-East of Borneo". De Goeje reverted to the Japan theory on the basis of Ibn K̲h̲urradād̲h̲bih's text, stating that the connection with Africa was only the fault of Ptolemy, while Ferrand attempted (*Madagascar et les îles Uâq-Uâq*, in *JA* [1904], 489-509) to prove that it was Madagascar and that the Far Eastern one was due to Ptolemy. Later (*Les îles Râmny, Lâmery, Wâkwâk, Ḳomor des géographes arabes et Madagascar*, in *JA* [1907], 450-506) he discovered that some passages must refer to the Far East, probably Sumatra, and finally (*Le Wâqwâq, est-il le Japon?*, in *JA* [1932], 193-243) he proved that there were definitely two Wāḳwāḳs, sc. Madagascar and Sumatra. Thus Ferrand intimated that the Wāḳwāḳs are the two areas of Malay culture on each side of the Indian Ocean and that the attack on Ḳanbalū, described by Buzurg (*ʿAd̲j̲āʾib al-Hind*, ed. al-S̲h̲ārūnī, 142-3; *Captain Buzurg*, tr. Freeman-Grenville, 103; Tibbetts, *Arabic texts on South-East Asia*, 171 n. 14), was a description of a Sumatran expedition to the African coast.

Ferrand's views were validated in J. Faublé and M. Urbain-Faublée, *Madagascar vu par les auteurs arabes avant le XI*[e] *siècle*, in *Studia*, xi (1963), 445-62. Viré (see below) has argued for an Indian Ocean-wide identification (as has Miquel, *Géographie humaine*, ii, 511-13). More recently, Allibert has argued for an approach that incorporates information from imaginative literature (see below), and Toorawa (see *Bibl.*) for one that brings the Mascarene islands into Wāḳwāḳ's fabular cartography. In actual fact, all the theories seem to be right, although the less definite they make their identifications, the better. The theories of Devic and Lane, who make Wāḳwāḳ some ill-defined place in Southeast Asia, and those of Viré and Allibert, who find evidence for Wāḳwāḳ in several places on the Indian Ocean littoral simultaneously, appear to be the most defensible.

(b) *The waters around the Wāḳwāḳ islands*

The usual names given to the waters around Wāḳwāḳ were *Baḥr al-Hind* and *al-Baḥr al-Hindī* [*q.vv.*] the "Indian Sea", *Baḥr al-Zand̲j̲* [*q.v.*] and the less common *Baḥr al-Ḥabas̲h̲ī*, the "Sea of the Blacks", and *Baḥr Fāris* [*q.v.*], the "Persian Sea". The uncertainty about this sea's name is underscored by the very name of the waters further south into which the *Baḥr al-Hind* appears to melt: the *Baḥr al-Ẓulma* (or *Ẓulumāt*) [see AL-BAḤR AL-MUḤĪṬ], the "Sea of Obscurity". Al-Idrīsī writes that "In it are a number of islands, some of which are visited by merchants, others of which are not by virtue of the difficulty of access, the [terrifying] power of the[ir] waters [for navigation], the unpredictability of the winds, and the savagery of their peoples who maintain no contact with any of their known neighbouring populations" (*Opus geographicum*, ed. Cerulli *et al.*, i, 87). Mariners driven off course were said to be tossed forever in this sea, said to join *al-Baḥr al-Ẓiftī*, the "Black Sea" or "Sea of Pitch" in Northern Asia, reminiscent of the "Gravelly Sea" described by Mandeville in his *Travels* (*The tales of Sir John Mandeville*, tr. Moseley, Harmondsworth 1983, 169). Indeed, one scholar has corresponded certain of Mandeville's descriptions with those of al-Idrīsī (C. Deluz, *Le livre de Jehan de Mandeville. Une géographie du XIV*[e] *siècle*, Louvain-la-Neuve 1988, 75-86).

(c) *Two Wāḳwāḳs?*

The first author to speak of two Wāḳwāḳs is Ibn al-Faḳīh (A.D. 902), referring to "Wāḳwāḳ al-Ṣīn", "the Wāḳwāḳ of China", and "Wāḳwāḳ al-Yaman", the Wāḳwāḳ of Yemen" (Ibn al-Faḳīh, at 55, page references here and elsewhere to G. Ferrand, *Relation de voyages et textes géographiques arabes, persans et turcs relatifs à l'Extrême-Orient du VIII*[ème] *au XVIII*[ème] *siècles*, 2 vols. with continuous pagination, Paris 1913-14, with actual translation of the texts in question given in the book, repr. Frankfurt 1986). Little interpretive attention has been paid to Yemen as a possible location as other sources speak either of great sailing distances or of its being "south of ʿIrāḳ". Ferrand equated this Wāḳwāḳ of the South with al-Masʿūdī's Wāḳwāḳ near Sofāla, which he claims as Madagascar (see *EI*[1], IV, 1105); but there is no clue that Ibn al-Faḳīh's Wāḳwāḳ was in Africa. Judging from the number of texts placing Wāḳwāḳ in Southeast Asia (see Ferrand, *Le Wâqwâq, est-il le Japon?*), there is no reason why this should not be the location of Wāḳwāḳ. It is possible that Ibn al-Faḳīh, confused by the conflicting statements that he had before him, came to the conclusion (as did Ferrand) that the only solution was that there was more than one Wāḳwāḳ. Until the time when the Ptolemaic theory of the eastern extension of Africa came to confuse the topographical picture of South Africa and Southeast Asia, Ibn al-Faḳīh is the only author who produces more than one Wāḳwāḳ.

(G.R. Tibbetts and Shawkat M. Toorawa)

(d) *The African Wāḳwāḳ?*

Mediaeval geographers and travellers mention Wāḳwāḳ in connection with East Africa in a confusing number of ways. Thus these sources state that the isles of Wāḳwāḳ are situated in the Larwī sea which washes the western coast of India and the lands inhabited by the Zandj (al-Yaʿḳūbī, at 49). The Wāḳwāḳ of the south is different from that of China (Ibn al-Faḳīh, at 55). The lands of Sofāla [*q.v.*] and of Wāḳwāḳ are situated in the extremity of the sea of the Zandj (al-Masʿūdī, at 108). The land of Wāḳwāḳ is contiguous to that of Sofāla; there are two towns in it, D.d.w. (Dārū? Waru? [see Daunicht, 190-1]) and B.n.h.na (Nabhana?), miserable and sparsely populated (al-Idrīsī, at 183). The town of D.ghd.gha (Daghdagha?), inhabited by a hideous and deformed dark-skinned population, is next to the land and island of Wāḳwāḳ (*ibid.*, at 184). Wāḳwāḳ is situated in the land of the Zandj (Ibn al-Wardī, at 425), to the east (= south) of Sofāla on the same southern (= western) shore of the Indian Ocean which extends without interruption to the end of the tenth section of the first clime, at the place where the Indian Ocean flows out of the Encompassing Sea (Ibn Khaldūn, at 460). The islands of Wāḳwāḳ are near the last islands of Dībādjāt al-Dum (= the Laccadives and Maldives [*q.vv.*]) (Buzurg b. Shahriyār, at 586). The Wāḳwāḳ of the land of the Zandj is vast, fertile and prosperous (Ibn al-Wardī, at 425). The gold of Wāḳwāḳ of the south is of inferior quality compared with that of the Wāḳwāḳ of China (Ibn al-Faḳīh, at 55). There is much gold in the Wāḳwāḳ of the land of the Zandj (al-Masʿūdī, at 108; Ibn al-Wardī, at 425). The natives of the Wāḳwāḳ of the land of the Zandj have no ships, but the merchants of ʿUmān come to trade with them and get slaves in exchange for dates (Ibn al-Wardī, at 425; cf. also al-Idrīsī, at 183). They know neither cold nor rain (Ibn al-Wardī, at 425). Of all these authorities, only al-Masʿūdī actually visited the East African coastlands, as was noted above, section 1(a). What he writes stands out from other confused items of information (his account of the Zandj gives many examples of his accuracy, including Bantu words which are recognisable as such); he realised that Sofāla and the Wāḳwāḳ were below, i.e. south of, the Zandj country, in a region where one today finds speakers of click languages.

However, as Tolmacheva (*The African Wāq-Wāq. Some questions regarding the evidence*, in *Fontes historiae africanae*, xi-xiii [1986-7], 9-15) has asserted, in spite of the great number of Arabic texts (and the often derivative Persian and Turkish ones) that speak of Wāḳwāḳ, very few speak of an African connection. In her important re-interpretation of al-Masʿūdī's account (*Murūdj*, § 847), Tolmacheva sees no direct evidence for an (African) Wāḳwāḳ connected to Sofāla and the Zandj. She believes that although al-Masʿūdī's words seem to place the Zandj capital in Wāḳwāḳ, the only explicit statement concerning Wāḳwāḳ in this passage is that it is located in the farthest reaches of the sea, possibly but not unambiguously the Sea of the Zandj. For Tolmacheva, the presumption of a link between Wāḳwāḳ and the Zandj accounts for al-Idrīsī's erroneous link, and for all subsequent mediaeval and modern placement of Wāḳwāḳ in Africa. This is corroborated by the fact that al-Masʿūdī traveled to both the East and to East Africa, and yet never mentions two Wāḳwāḳs, nor a "southern" one. He also at no point characterises Wāḳwāḳ or its inhabitants. Against her arguments, however, is the undoubted fact that al-Masʿūdī *does* mention an East African Wāḳwāḳ.

With regard to the references to the *arḍ al-Wāḳwāḳ* in Arabic literature, Tolmacheva has source-critically divided these into three groups: (1) al-Masʿūdī (*Murūdj*, i, 233, iii, 6-7 = §§ 246, 847-8, see also Pellat's indices, vii, 750); (2) al-Idrīsī, whose accounts are partly derivative from, but give greater precision to, al-Masʿūdī's accounts, and who is the "true generator" of a specifically African Wāḳwāḳ—yet who was, it must be admitted, entirely dependent on informants, unlike al-Masʿūdī (on al-Idrīsī, see now the translation by Viré); and (3) the weakest group, comprising the late, often redundant compilations of Ibn al-Wardī, al-Ḥimyarī, Ibn Saʿīd al-Maghribī (in spite of the originality of some of his material), and even Ibn Khaldūn's passing remarks, all of which are derivative from al-Idrīsī's accounts.

According to al-Idrīsī, Wāḳwāḳ is the fourth and southernmost of the divisions of the eastern African coast. Like the name of his first division Bilād al-Barbarā or Barābara (perpetuated in the northern Somali town of Berberā [*q.v.*]), the word Wāḳwāḳ might be the onomatopoeic rendering of the name for click-speakers. Of the towns mentioned by al-Idrīsī, B.n.h.na could be the modern Inhambane in southern Mozambique, the present Portuguese spelling of which would be better represented in speech by *Nyambana*, or the Moluccan Amboina. If it is true that identifications of Wāḳwāḳ with East African coastal toponyms, or indeed any toponyms, rely on linguistic and ethnonymic arguments rather than on textual ones and must always be treated with prudence, such linguistic and ethnonymic arguments cannot be disregarded.

(e) *The Wāḳwāḳ attack on Ḳanbalū*

A question to be resolved is the attack by Wāḳwāḳ ships on Ḳanbalū in A.D. 945 mentioned in the sources. Buzurg b. Shahriyār's description of the attack by a fleet of 1,000 ships may be regarded as literary hyperbole. It was quite possibly made from Sumatra or Java, but this does not prove, of course, that Sumatra was Wāḳwāḳ. To the inhabitants of Ḳanbalū the attackers came from an unknown island in the east beyond the range of their knowledge. Recent archaeological excavations now also support the argument that Ḳanbalū was Mkumbuu on the island of Pemba, where, significantly, a 10th-century mosque has now been located. It would have held some 600 worshippers, suggesting that in its heyday it was by far the largest and most important trading centre yet discovered in eastern Africa. Ferrand was right in dismissing de Goeje's suggestions that these ships were Japanese, but his proposal that they were Sumatran, based on philological arguments, is rivalled by Madagascar, where the language, Malagasy, is related to Indonesian ones, and where outrigger canoes, *ngalawa*, were used in numbers (and still are; but they are too small to have carried sufficient food and water for a voyage across the Indian Ocean). Very recently, Fāṭimid coins, as yet unpublished, have been recovered in Diego Suarez bay at the northern tip of Madagascar [see further madagascar].

It thus seems that, on the whole, Wāḳwāḳ referred to a country just beyond one's reach in the general direction of the east. Thus it appears as a well-populated land east of China, about which one heard stories but which was never really reached in any numbers. Similarly, it is applied in Southeast Asia to some island a little off the usual path of Arab traders. Thus stories of islands a little off the route, as well as a few legendary tales, became attached to Wāḳwāḳ. As new ground was explored, Wāḳwāḳ retreated eastwards, always to be the last island in the east until Sīdī Čelebi in the 10th/16th century was able to place it anywhere but south of the islands of Timor. Daunicht (*Der Osten nach der Erdkarte al-Ḫuwārizmīs*, Bonn 1970, ii, 172-274) has made a fascinating case for identification with the Moluccas, Irian Jaya, and northwestern Australia (where three Islamic coins from Kilwa have been found, in company with tamarisk trees, not native to Australia).

(G. Ferrand-[G.S.P. Freeman-Grenville and Shawkat M. Toorawa])

(f) *Wāḳwāḳ and the Far East*

One group of stories relating to Wāḳwāḳ is based on a passage from Ibn Khurradādhbih (69-71) where he places Wāḳwāḳ east of China and says it is a country producing much gold, mentioning golden dog chains (? leads) and monkey collars. This is one of the standard stories passed down from author to author. The ingenuity of the natives and the fact that it was a prosperous country east of China caused de Goeje to identify it with Japan (*Le Japon connu des arabes*, 295). De Goeje's identification was based partly on the description given by Ibn Khurradādhbih and partly on his identification of the word Wāḳwāḳ with an early Chinese name for Japan, *Wo-kuo*, in Cantonese *Wo-kwok*, of which Wāḳwāḳ is an acceptable rendering. The description of the people of Wāḳwāḳ, given in one passage of Buzurg's *ʿAdjā'ib al-Hind* (ed. Shārūnī, 135), where the great size of the towns and islands is mentioned, is even more reminiscent of Japan. Although Ibn Khurradādhbih's story is the only original one mentioning the prosperous country, there are several texts which state that Wāḳwāḳ is east of China. Some are merely quoting from Ibn Khurradādhbih but others add a little.

In his 4th/10th-century encyclopaedia, the *Mafātīḥ al-ʿulūm*, al-Khʷārazmī (ed. Van Vloten, 217), writes that Kandiz is the most easterly town in the world and is situated at the extremity of China and Wāḳwāḳ. He describes the world as a bird, with China as its head and Wāḳwāḳ beyond it. Ibn ʿAbd al-Ḥakam (d. 257/871) describes the world as a bird in *Futūḥ Miṣr wa 'l-Maghrib*, ed. C.C. Torrey, New Haven 1922, stating that the right wing is ʿIrāḳ, beyond which is a people called Wāḳ, and beyond whom another called Wāḳ Wāḳ, and beyond them people known only to God (19), disassociating Wāḳwāḳ from China. The story of the world as a bird is a very common one in Arabic literature and very early appears as a story from ʿAbd Allāh b. ʿAmr b. al-ʿĀṣ in Ibn al-Faḳīh and Ibn ʿAbd al-Ḥakam. It is obvious that, at this very early stage, Wāḳwāḳ was regarded as a land not simply in the extreme east but at the edge of the known.

(g) *Southeast Asia*

Another group of stories mentions a primitive people with whom the Arab sailors trade. Stories of this kind give locations for Wāḳwāḳ in Southeast Asia, mentioning it in connection with Zābadj, Ḳumār or Ṣanf. Such stories come mainly from Buzurg b. Shahriyār's *ʿAdjā'ib al-Hind* and from other writers who copied this work. They have the appearance of sailors' tales. The ship in the first story (Buzurg, 8) comes across al-Wāḳwāḳ on the way to Zābadj or in the direction of Zābadj. In a similar tale found later in the same work (190), it is between Sribuza and China. In yet another case it is beyond the end of Dībādjāt al-Dum (the Maldives) (Buzurg, 163). The *Mukhtaṣar al-ʿadjā'ib* of Ibn Waṣīf Shāh (38) also prefers to put Wāḳwāḳ in Southeast Asia; in one place it makes it the home of a Māhārādja and in another "in the Sea of Ṣanf" (Čampa) (39). In the latter account, it has been mixed up with a story about a volcano which, according to other authors, is definitely about Southeast Asia. Al-Bīrūnī, from whom one would expect a clear account, says Wāḳwāḳ belongs to Cambodia (Ḳumār), and mixes earlier accounts of Wāḳwāḳ and Ḳumār so that, in spite of his unrivalled knowledge of India, it is certain that he had no clear idea himself of the location of Wāḳwāḳ. These stories about primitive peoples could equally well refer to the coast of Africa where such peoples could be found.

(h) *The Indian Ocean littoral*

Viré, who believed the word Wāḳwāḳ to be onomatopoeic, and who relied in part on Ibn al-Faḳīh (tr. Massé, 9) and his identification of three (*pace* Viré), not just two Wāḳwāḳs, posits that Wāḳwāḳ definitively refers in all instances to small-statured, dark-skinned populations that inhabit three distinct areas on the Indian Ocean littoral: the Akkas and Negrillos in Africa, the Negritos in Malaya in Southeast Asia, and the Lapons, Samoyeds and Manchus in the Arctic and sub-Arctic regions of northern Asia (Viré, 35 n. 1). More recently, Allibert (*Wakwak: végétal, minéral ou humain? Reconsidération du problème*, in *Études Océan Indien*, xii (1991), 171-89), whose research has focused on the Wāḳwāḳ tree and its human-fruit (see below), has persuasively argued for a Southeast Asian location of both the tree and island(s).

Allibert, taking his lead from the observations of Miquel and Bremond (*Mille et un contes de la nuit*, Paris 1991), has attempted to demonstrate that islands of women in geographical and imaginative literature and the islands of Wāḳwāḳ are one and the same thing (*L'Île des femmes dans les récits arabes*, in *Études Océan Indien*, xv, 261-7). This is consonant with Allibert's call for an integrated and coherent approach to the Wāḳwāḳ issue. He shows, to his mind unequivocally, that the fruit of the Wāḳwāḳ tree is the Southeast Asian coconut and that Wāḳwāḳ is thus the vehicle of an ancient mythology inscribed in the story of the human-fruit and woman-island. The evidence for his argument is, like Ferrand before him, primarily linguistic, but has virtue. He reflects at length on the *rāndj* of al-Masʿūdī, which he ties to various accounts in the geographies about palms and coconuts. He goes on to explain the mythological dimension by making the equation, "botanical reality + animal or human and/or geographical reality = mythical term", which for him translates into: "coconut palm + Austronesian population = Wāḳwāḳ fruit".

2. Living organisms bearing the name of Wāḳwāḳ.

One early story usually connected with Wāḳwāḳ mentions a tree named Wāḳwāḳ with fruit having a human appearance (a coconut, divested of its coir, has "eyes"), and another early story a strange race who utter the cry "*Wāḳ, Wāḳ!*"

(a) *The "race"*

In an early story which appears in its full form in Ibn Waṣīf Shāh (26), a kind of animal is mentioned which from the description appears to be a baboon. The name *wakwak* or *wahwah* is given to a species of gibbon in Malay, for it is an onomatopoeia for its cry, just as it could be for the bark of a baboon. In his *EI*[1] art., Ferrand showed that *wak-wak* or *vak-vak* is a name given by the Bantus to baboons and to Bushmen.

(b) *The tree*

The tree with the human-fruit first appears in Arabic in the *K. al-Badʾ wa ʾl-taʾrīkh* of al-Muṭahhar al-Maḳdisī [*q.v.*] (89) at the end of the 4th/10th century. Here we have a short note saying that the tree was called Wāḳwāḳ and grew in India. A fuller account of this tree is given in Buzurg (65-6) (quoting Muḥammad b. Bābishād), where the tree is not named but is stated to come from the land of Wāḳwāḳ. However, the story itself must have been common in the Near East, for it appears much earlier in a Chinese text, the *T'ung-tien* of Tu Huan, which was written between A.D. 766 and 801 and is of Middle Eastern provenance. According to this work, the story was told to Tu Huan's father, who had been captured and taken to the Middle East, where he stayed between 751 and 762, as a story emanating from Arab sailors, who sailed toward the West. The story given by Tu Huan resembles that of Buzurg almost word-for-word, except that the tree in his account bears a crown of small children instead of fruit with human faces. Hence, in spite of the more factual representation of the story given by Buzurg in the *ʿAdjāʾib al-Hind*, the "little humans" seem to be part of the original story. The story is given throughout by many writers, but is embellished in various ways. The "little humans" on landing on the ground are said to utter the cry "Wāḳ, Wāḳ", which seems an alternative version borrowed from the second tale. A full version is given in the 6th/12th-century *K. al-Djughrāfiyā* written in Spain. The story is also given in one version of Friar Odoric's travels (Sir Henry Yule and H. Cordier, *Cathay and the way thither*, London 1915, ii, 138-9). It differs in detail, but only in as much as the Arabic accounts differ from each other. In Ibn al-Wardī's 9th/15th-century account, the women-fruit cry out praise to the Creator (*al-Khallāḳ*). This is reminiscent of an account about ʿĀʾisha who, on her deathbed, is reported to have wished she were a leaf or a tree uttering the praises of God (Ibn Saʿd, viii, 51).

There is a very early attestation of a tree the fruits of which are corporeal in Arabic. In Ḳurʾān, XXXVII, 60/62, 62/64, mention is made of the tree of Zaḳḳūm, with heads of demons where fruit should be. This motif would have been known to all the authors writing about the Wāḳwāḳ tree. The possibility that this description informed the many later accounts of the Wāḳwāḳ tree cannot be excluded. Al-Djāḥiẓ had mentioned that the Wāḳwāḳ are the product of a cross between plants and animals and is cited by al-Damīrī, *Ḥayāt al-ḥayawān al-kubrā* (Cairo 1336, ii, 123) to that effect.

In his account, Marwazī (*Sharaf al-Zamān Ṭāhir Marvazī on China, the Turks and India* [= *Ṭabāʾiʿ al-ḥayawān*], ed. and tr. V. Minorsky, London 1942, 60, cf. 160, writes: "I have read in the *Kitāb al-Baḥr* ("Book of the sea") that in the island of Wāq-Wāq, where ebony grows, there is a tribe whose nature is like that of men in all their limbs, except the hands, instead of which they have something like wings, which are webbed like the wings of a bat. They, both males and females, eat and drink while kneeling. They follow the ships asking for food. When a man makes for them, they open these wings and their flight becomes like that of birds, and no one can overtake them." This account is noteworthy both for its conflation of tree, human and bird, and for its evocation of the bat, *waṭwāṭ* in Arabic.

Eva Baer, *Sphinxes and harpies in medieval Islamic art*, Jerusalem 1965, has catalogued examples of Wāḳwāḳ tree motifs in mediaeval Islamic art, and writes that the earliest depiction is to be found on a slab attributed to one of the Ghaznawid palaces but probably datable to a little later (66-8, figs. 82-6). She observes also that the decorative designs reflect the talking or Wāḳwāḳ tree of the Alexander Romance. It is widely found in manuscripts of the "Wonders of the World" genre, especially the works of al-Ḳazwīnī. This talking tree is the transformed oracular Tree of the Sun and Moon which is reputed to have told Alexander of his approaching death (see Phyllis Ackerman, *The talking tree*, in *Bulletin of the American Institute for Persian Art and Archaeology*, iv/2 [1935], 67-72). In an Old French poem on the legend of Alexander, young women are born with and wilt with the flowers of a tree: they cannot leave the shade of these trees without dying (see *King Alisaunder*, ed. Smithers, Early English Texts Society, Old Series, ccxxvii (1952) and ccxxxvii (1957), and the unpublished Anglo-Norman *Roman de toute chevalerie* on which it is based).

The Wāḳwāḳ tree is described, and depicted, in the introductory passages to the first Ottoman work describing the New World, the anonymous 10th/16th-century *Tārīkh-i Hind-i gharbī* (T.D. Goodrich, *The Ottoman Turks and the New World. A study of* Tarih-i Hind-i Garbi *and sixteenth-century Ottoman Americana*, Wiesbaden 1990, 58). This account relies in large part on al-Ḳazwīnī and, although it does not place the tree in the New World, gives the impression that it is to be found there (see Toorawa, *Where women grow on trees. An Arab-Islamic tree in the New World*, forthcoming).

The tree also makes an appearance in the Turkish shadow-play tradition, scholars of which have attributed its origin to the legend of the tree whose fruits are shapely women. But, as İ. Başgöz (*The Waqwaq tree in the Turkish shadow-play theatre Karagöz and the story of Esther*, in A. Levy, *The Jews of the Ottoman Empire*, Princeton, N.J. 1994, 552-3) points out, it appears rather to be inspired by the execution by hanging, from a particular tree (*Platanus orientalis*), of Janissaries in 1826, in a re-enactment of an earlier such execution (1066/1655-6). The latter became known as "the vakvak incident" (*waḳʿa-i wāḳwāḳiyye*). Başgöz shows further that another possible source is the final act in the story of Esther and Haman in the Old Testament (554-5). A comment made by Ewliyā Čelebi in his *Seyāḥat-nāme* (*The intimate life of an Ottoman statesman, Melek Ahmed Pasha (1588-1662)*, tr. R. Dankoff, Albany 1991, 74-5) is contemporary, but apparently unrelated. He notes that dead *celalis* lying beneath the trees of a meadow "ador[n] the plain like the Tree of Vakvak".

The tree was long ago identified as the *ʿushar* (*Calotropis syriaca*) by de Goeje, when he connected Wāḳwāḳ with Japan. The story does appear in Japanese literature, but almost certainly comes from the Chinese of Tu Huan, which again comes from the Arabs, so it cannot be used to strengthen de Goeje's theory. The description given by Buzurg's *ʿAdjāʾib al-Hind* resembles that of the *ʿushar*, which is a tree of the Middle East and Africa. Ferrand claimed that this tree could not be the *ʿushar* and suggested the Pandanus tree on philological grounds, for it is called *vakwa* in Madagascar, thus using it to strengthen his own Madagascar theory. The fruit of the Pandanus may bear little resemblance to the fruit of the story but is attested in a Filipino story of related interest.

An argument might, in fact, be made for identifying Wāḳwāḳ with the Philippines. In addition to its numerous islands, "dark"-skinned population, and distinct language (actually several dozen), there are in Philippine mythology creatures reported to be pretty-faced, fair-skinned maidens who drape their wings over the branches of trees in the heart of the jungle while they sleep out the day, their long hair thrown over their faces (M.D. Ramos, *Creatures of Philippine lower mythology*, Quezon City 1990, 127). They are called *aswang* in Tagalog, Bikol and several other languages, and *wakwak* in Surigao. In one account, the *aswang/wakwak* is depicted as tying a skirt round her when flying, and "beating her buttocks with a magical pandanus streamer" (Ramos, 128, citing B. Malinowski, *Argonauts of the Western Pacific*, New York 1961, 242). The *wakwak* are said to live in trees, and to call out "Kakak! Kakak!" (Ramos, *Creatures*, 133, citing F.X. Lynch, *An mga Asuwang. A Bikol belief*, in *Philippine Soc. Sc. and Hum. Rev.*, xiv (Dec. 1949), 420) or other similar sounds.

(G.R. Tibbetts and Shawkat M. Toorawa)

3. Wāḳwāḳ in imaginative literature and the imaginaire.

There is a convincing piece of evidence that Wāḳwāḳ is simply the name given to the conceptual limit of the known world in the statement made by Ḥasan al-Baṣrī's eventual guide, the Shaykh ʿAbd al-Ḳuddūs, in the *Thousand and One nights*—Ḥasan is trying to reach Wāḳwāḳ in order to get back his wife who has fled to her home with their two sons (Lane, *The Arabian nights' entertainment*, 796): "My son, relinquish this most vexatious affair; you could not gain access to the Islands of Waqwaq even if the Flying Jinn and the wandering stars assisted you, since between you and those islands are seven valleys, seven seas and seven mountains of vast magnitude."

There is a similar quest for a spouse in the 8th/14th-century *Sīrat Sayf b. Dhī Yazān*, when King Sayf is urged by his wronged and distraught wife to pursue her and her son: "'You seized me first, then afflicted me with grief and deserted me to take other women. But what has been has been. If you have any valor and resolve, and if you truly love me, then pursue me to the City of Maidens in the islands of Waq al-Waq.' With that she clasped her son beneath her garment at her breast and vanished through the air . . ." (*The adventures of Sayf Ben Dhi Yazan, an Arab folk epic*, tr. L. Jayyusi, Bloomington 1996, 241). Lane noted the similarities between the *Thousand and one nights*' story of Ḥasan and the Bird-Maiden and the romance of Sayf b. Dhī Yazān, in particular the beautiful women with wings of feather who fly like birds (Lane, 1246 n. 16).

In one Persian tale, the fruits of a tree ripen, fall to the ground, mature into men's heads, and then one of the fruits greets the king respectfully (see *The Palace of the Nine Pavilions* [Bodl. ms Caps. Or. A. 4.], in *The three dervishes and other Persian tales and legends*, tr. R. Levy, Oxford 1947, 160).

Ibn Ṭufayl's [*q.v.*] description in his philosophical-allegorical tale, *Risālat Ḥayy b. Yaḳẓān* (ed. Saʿd, Beirut, 117), famously speaks of an island below the equator where people are born without mother or father, and where there is a tree which bears women as fruit. This is analysed by F. Malti-Douglas, *Woman's body, woman's word. Gender and discourse in Arabo-Islamic writing*, Princeton 1991, 85-96.

Yāḳūt, a systematic recorder of geographical information, observes that Wāḳwāḳ is only to be found in fables and superstitions (*khurāfāt*) (*Muʿdjam al-buldān*, ed. Wüstenfeld, vi, 936). This appearance in fables and superstitions has extended, seven centuries later, even further than Yāḳūt could ever have imagined; thus the Islands of Wāḳwāḳ now appear as a "card" in the Arabian Nights "expansion" of a fantasy game called "Magic".

Just as it provided material for Ibn Ṭufayl and for "Magic", so too has Wāḳwāḳ been used in modern Arabic literature. In what might at first appear to be a more traditional appropriation/appearance, it figures in a 1975 short story by the Moroccan writer, Mustafa al-Masannawi, *Abdullah Samsa in Waqwaq Island* (in M. Shaheen, *The modern Arabic short story. Shahrazad returns*, London 1989, 114-18). This post-modern, Borgesian-Kafkaesque tale, divided into ten numbered sections of unequal length, and accompanied by five appendices, evokes Wāḳwāḳ in a number of ways. In section three, a description is quoted from *The great Pharaonic encyclopaedia*, and section seven consists of "An extract from a radio broadcast from the Island of Waqwaq". In 1997 the Palestinian poet ʿI. al-Manāṣira published a volume titled *Lā athiḳu bi-ṭāʾir al-waḳwāḳ*, Jerusalem 1999 (title poem, 20-32).

Finally, one may invoke the contemporary Egyptian colloquial expression *il ḥāga-di ma-tiḥṣal-sh walā fi bilād wāʾ il-wāʾ* "these things don't happen, not even in Wonderland", which makes of Wāḳwāḳ a place of wonderment somewhere beyond the horizon (M. Hinds and El-Sayyid Badawi, *A dictionary of Egyptian Arabic, Arabic-English*, Beirut 1986, 921).

(Shawkat M. Toorawa)

Bibliography (in addition to references in the article): Ferrand's articles are reprinted in *Études sur la géographie arabo-islamique*, ii, Frankfurt 1986. See also the collection of other studies of his in *Études sur la géographie islamique*, Frankfurt 1986. M.J. de Goeje, *Le Japon connu des Arabes* = Excursus F, in P.A. van der Lith, *Livre des merveilles de l'Inde*, 295-307; G.R. Tibbetts, *A study of the Arabic texts containing material on South-East Asia*, London 1979, Appx. 1, Wāqwāq; Buzurg b. Shahriyār, *Livre des merveilles de l'Inde*, ed. Van der Lith, Fr. tr. L.M. Devic, Leiden 1883-6; Eng. tr. G.S.P. Freeman-Grenville, *Captain Buzurg ibn Shahriyar of Ram Hormuz. The book of the wonders of India, mainland, sea and islands*, London-The Hague 1981, 39, 101, 103; idem, *Some thoughts on Buzurg ibn Shahriyar al-Ramhormuzi: the Book of the wonders of India*, in *Paideuma*, xxviii (1982); *K. ʿAdjāʾib al-Hind*, ed. Y. al-Shārūnī, London 1990; H.N. Chittick and R.I. Rotberg (eds.), *East Africa and the Orient*, New York 1975, with numerous relevant articles; F. Viré, *L'Océan indien d'après le géographe Abû Abd-Allâh Muhammad Ibn Idrîs al-Hammûdî al-Hasanî dit Al-Šarîf AL-IDRISI (493-560 H/1100-1166). Extraits traduits et annotés du «Livre de Roger»*, in P. Ottino (ed.), *Études sur L'Océan indien*, St. Denis de la Réunion 1979, 13-45; S.M. Toorawa, *Wâq al-wâq. Fabulous, fabular Indian Ocean (?) island(s)*, in *Emergences*, x/2 (Dec. 2000) 387-402; and recent information on excavations on Pemba and Zanzibar kindly supplied by M.C. Horton.

(G.S.P. Freeman-Grenville, G.R. Tibbetts and Shawkat M. Toorawa)

4. As a zoological term.

Here, *wāḳwāḳ*, *waḳwāḳ* and *waḳūḳ* are onomatopoeic masc. nouns denoting a member of the Cuculides family of birds and imitating their cries (Fr. "coucou", Eng. "cuckoo", Ger. "Kuckuck"); the pl. ought to be *waḳāwīḳ*, but this is never found in the texts. With this general name, members of the Cuculides (*waḳwāḳiyyāt*) also have numerous local names, according to region: *ḥamām ḳawwāl*, *ṭāṭawī*, *ṭakūk*, *ḳawḳal*, *kukur*, *kukum*, *kunkur* and *hūhū*. The Arabic-speaking lands distinguish five species of cuckoo: (a) the Common cuckoo (*Cuculus canorus*), with two sub-species *C.c. canorus* and *C.c. telephonus*; (b) the Great spotted cuckoo (*Clamator glandarius*); (c) the Pied crested or Jacobin cuckoo (*Clamator jacobinus*), with the sub-species *C.c. serratus*; (d) the Collared cuckoo (*Cuculus torquatus*); and (e) the Large-heeled cuckoo (*C. senegalensis aegyptius*).

Bibliography: Damīrī, *K. Ḥayāt al-ḥayawān al-kubrā*, Cairo 1937, ii, 390; A. Malouf, *Muʿdjam al-ḥayawān*, Cairo 1932, 77-9; E. Ghaleb, *al-Mawsūʿa fī ʿulūm al-ṭabīʿa*, Beirut 1936, ii, 648; F. Hue and R.D. Etchecopar, *Les oiseaux du Proche et Moyen Orient*, Paris 1970, 394-5. (It is surprising that neither Djāḥiẓ, *Ḥayawān*, nor Ḳazwīnī, *ʿAdjāʾib al-makhlūḳāt*, mention the cuckoo under any one of its names.)

(F. Viré)

WALAD [see saghīr].

WALĀTA, conventionally Oualata, an important Saharan caravan town in mediaeval Islamic times, now a small town in the southeastern region of modern Mauritania, the Ḥawḍ or Hodh (lat. 17° 15' N., long. 6° 55' W.).

For its history, see mūrītāniyā, at Vol. VII, 625a-b.

WALĀYA (a.). For the use of this term in Shīʿism, see wilāya. 2.

WALBA, a district of the *kūra* of Niebla in the southwestern part of al-Andalus, the modern Huelva. The name appears in various forms in the Arabic sources, such as Wānyu in al-ʿUdhrī (5th/11th century) and Wāniba (Yāḳūt), both going back to Latin Onuba.

Its political history is closely linked with that of Niebla [see labla], even though it was for a while, in the time of the Taifas, separated from Niebla. This was, in fact, a period of prosperity and security for the people there. This was due to the actions of ʿAbd al-ʿAzīz al-Bakrī who, in 403/1012, in the midst of the civil wars of that time, made himself the ruler of a little principality embracing Walba and the island of Saltés. Soon afterwards, in 414/1023-4, Abu 'l-ʿAbbās Aḥmad al-Yaḥṣubī arose in Niebla to form a second *ṭāʾifa* in similar fashion within the ancient *kūra*. The ʿAbbādid al-Muʿtaḍid [*q.v.*], ruler of the neighbouring *ṭāʾifa* of Seville, altered this state of affairs in his greed to acquire new territories, which he achieved in 443/1051-2. Out of prudence, ʿAbd al-ʿAzīz decided to cede Huelva and shut himself up in Saltés, but he could only maintain this for a short while under pressure from the Sevillan ruler, and had in the end to abandon it. Out of all the versions in the chronicles of the period, the most probable seems to be that of Ibn Saʿīd, who says that al-Bakrī marched on Cordova and definitively established himself there. It was in this capital that his son, the famous historian and geographer Abū ʿUbayd, received his education along the traditional lines of the age.

The island of Saltés considered itself as naturally linked with Huelva. It was not a separate district, and was in fact—as al-Idrīsī said in the 6th/12th century—less than a mile from Huelva and separated from it by a narrow neck of the sea only a stone's throw wide. Numerous historians stress its commercial importance, iron-working and falconry being amongst its main activities. Al-Ḥimyarī (9th/15th century) mentioned the traces of Antiquity there and attributed to it the advantages of both a maritime and a continental town.

Bibliography: Abū ʿUbayd al-Bakrī, *al-Masālik wa 'l-mamālik*, ed. al-Ḥayyī, Beirut 1968; Ibn Saʿīd, *al-Mughrib*, ed. Ḍayf, Cairo 1978, i, 346-7; Ḥimyarī, *Rawḍ*, ed. and tr. Lévi-Provençal; A. Jiménez Martin, *Huelva monumental*, Huelva 1980; Mª L. Pardo, *Huelva y Gibraleón (1282-1495). Documentos para su historia*, Huelva 1980; A. González Gómez, *Huelva en la Edad Media. Un enclave frontero*, Huelva 1986; F. Roldán Castro, *Niebla musulmana (siglos VIII-XIII)*, ²Huelva 1997; R. Amador de los Rios, *Catálogo de los monumentos históricos y artísticos de la provincia de Huelva*, ²Huelva 1997. (Fátima Roldán Castro)

WĀLĪ (a., pl. *wulāt*), from the root *w-l-y* "to be near something", hence "to be in charge of something", comes to mean "person in authority, governor, prefect, administrator manager", with the *maṣdar* of *wilāya* for his office and/or sphere of competence. The word occurs once in the Ḳurʾān, XIII, 12/11, applied to God in the sense of "patron, protector". See on aspects of the function of the governor in mediaeval Islamic times, amīr. A near-synonym is *ḥākim* "one who exercises power, jurisdiction, etc." Under the Ottomans, the *wālī*, also termed *pasha* [*q.v.*], was the governor of a province, *eyālet* or *wilāyet*; see Pakalın, i, 577-8.

In contemporary North Africa and the Middle East as far east as Afghānistān, various terms are employed for the administrative divisions of the province, including *wilāya*, *muḥāfaẓa*, *imāra*, *liwāʾ* and *ustān* in Arabic and Persian usage, and *il* in modern Turkey, with corresponding titles for their governors like *wālī*, *muḥāfiẓ*, *amīr*, etc. (Ed.)

WALĪ (a., pl. *awliyāʾ*), indicates a friend of God or a saint, often also a mystic in general.

1. General survey
2. In North Africa
3. In the Arab lands of the Fertile Crescent [see Suppl.]
4. In Turkey, the Balkans, the Caucasus and Ādharbāydjān
5. In Central Asia
6. In Muslim India
7. In Southeast Asia and Indonesia
8. In Chinese Islam
9. In West Africa
10. In Chad and the Nilotic Sudan

1. General survey.

Walī is a *faʿīl* form of the root *w-l-y* with the meaning of "to be near". The one who is near is also a friend, he possesses friendship (*wilāya* [*q.v.*]) (more rarely *walāya*; for a discussion of these two forms, see Corbin, *En Islam iranien*, iii, 9-10; Chodkiewicz, *Sceau*, 34). But in some way, the *walī* also acquires his friend's, i.e. God's, good qualities, and therefore he possesses particular authority, forces, capacities and abilities. In the Ḳurʾān, the adjective *walī* is also applied to God, Who is the believers' friend (II, 257). Ḳurʾān and *ḥadīth* do not know the concept of exceptional, blessed people who are close to God, but by the 2nd/8th century it seems to have been accepted (van Ess, *Theologie*, ii, 89-90; Radtke-O'Kane, *The concept of sainthood*, 109-10; Radtke, *Drei Schriften*, ii, 68-9). In many aspects, its origin is obscure; ancient Christian and Jewish elements can be recognised (Mach, *Der Zaddik*, 134-46). Stories about the wonderful deeds of God's friends also seem to have been collected and transmitted at an early stage, among others by Ibn Abi 'l-Dunyā (d. 281/894 [*q.v.*]). He wrote the *Kitāb al-Awliyāʾ*, the earliest compilation on the theme of God's friends; Abū Nuʿaym al-Iṣfahānī (d. 948/1038 [*q.v.*]) made use of it in his *Ḥilyat al-awliyāʾ*. Ibn Abi 'l-Dunyā's work does not show any method or explanation, but some writings dating from the second half of the 3rd/9th century had already passed the stage of pure compiling. The Baghdādī Ṣūfī Abū Saʿīd al-Kharrāz (d. probably 286/899 [see AL-KHARRĀZ]) wrote a short treatise *Kitāb al-Kashf wa 'l-bayān*. Dealing with a number of questions concerning the theme of *awliyā'*/*wilāya*, he discusses (1) the relation between the friends of God and the Prophet, and opposes the opinion of mystics, whose names he does not mention, according to whom the friend of God is higher in rank than the Prophet; (2) the question whether the friend of God receives inspiration (*ilhām*); and (3) the distinction between the miracles of the prophets (*āyāt*) and those of God's friends (*karāmāt*).

Further writings, which not only deal in much greater detail with the themes treated by al-Kharrāz but already develop the entire concept of the friend of God and friendship with God, came from al-Ḥakīm al-Tirmidhī (d. between 295/907 and 300/912 [*q.v.*]). Later authors, such as Ibn al-ʿArabī (see below), would in principle only develop further the questions first raised by al-Ḥakīm al-Tirmidhī. Basically, they are dealt with in his famous treatise *Sīrat al-awliyā'*, also known as *Khatm al-awliyā'* or *Khatm al-wilāya*. Next to this main work there exist two other writings by al-Tirmidhī on the theme of the friend of God. One is called *al-Farḳ bayn al-āyāt wa 'l-karāmāt*, the first monograph on the possibility of miracles worked by God's friends and their relation with the miracles of the prophets. After an introduction, which is based on proofs taken from Holy Scripture and on psychological observations, but does not show any knowledge of scholastic-rational proofs, al-Tirmidhī adduces more than sixty stories on friends of God from early times. The greater part is also found in the works of Ibn Abi 'l-Dunyā and of Abū Nuʿaym al-Iṣfahānī. The other work by al-Tirmidhī on the theme is his autobiography *Bad' sha'n Abī ʿAbd Allāh*. It is the first autobiography of a Muslim mystic before al-Ghazālī's *Munḳidh min al-ḍalāl*.

The *Sīrat al-awliyā'* begins with the fundamental distinction between two classes of friends of God, the *walī ḥaḳḳ Allāh* and the *walī Allāh*. If the *walī ḥaḳḳ Allāh* wants to come near to God on the mystical path, he can only achieve this by observing the obligations of the divine legal order (*ḥaḳḳ*) with all his inner power, while the *walī Allāh* reaches his aim through divine grace. The former is obliged to walk on the path encumbered with all sorts of hardships: he is a *sālik*, while the latter is exempted from this toil; he is attracted to God by God and is a *madjdhūb* [*q.v.*]. In later Ṣūfism, this opposition, represented here for the first time in a systematic way, was to play an important role. Other terms used by al-Ḥakīm al-Tirmidhī for the two classes of mystics are *muhtadī* (rightly guided) and *mudjtabā* (elected).

For al-Tirmidhī, the path, i.e. the journey to God, means a delving into the inner self on the one hand and the ascent to God through the macrocosmos on the other, it is a journey to heaven (*miʿrādj* [*q.v.*]). The ascent of the *walī ḥaḳḳ Allāh* must stop at the end of the created cosmos, God's throne. He can attain God's proximity, but not God Himself; he is only admitted to God's proximity (*muḳarrab*). It is the *walī Allāh* who reaches God. Ascent beyond God's throne means to traverse consciously the realms of light of the divine names which, in gnostic tradition, are grouped hierarchically around God's unknowable essence. When the *walī Allāh* has traversed all the realms of the divine names, i.e. has come to know God in His names as completely as possible, he is then extinguished in God's essence. His soul, his ego, is eliminated and he is in God's hands. When he acts, it is God Who acts through him. And so the state of extinction means at the same time the highest degree of activity in this world.

The friend of God, therefore, is recognisable in the world because of a number of external characteristics: (1) when people see him, they are automatically reminded of God; (2) anyone who advances towards him in a hostile way is destroyed; (3) he possesses the gift of clairvoyance (*firāsa*); (4) he receives divine inspiration (*ilhām*); (5) he can work miracles (*karāmāt* [*q.v.*]) like walking on water (*al-mashy ʿalā 'l-mā'*) and shortening space and time (*ṭayy al-arḍ*); and (6) he associates with al-Khaḍir [*q.v.*] (for this list, see Radtke, *Drei Schriften*, ii, 82, § 80; Radtke-O'Kane, *The concept of sainthood*, 124-5; for further miracles, see Radtke, *Miracles*, where an analysis of al-Tirmidhī's *Farḳ* is given). This list of themes from now on forms a constant element of the discussion on God's friends and friendship with God.

In this way the friend of God not only knows that he is indeed God's friend—this question is raised at the very beginning of the *Sīrat al-awliyā'*—but he can also be sure of eternal bliss. This is communicated to him through good tidings from God (*bushrā*), for, though he is not sinless (*maʿṣūm*) like the Prophet, he is preserved from sin (*maḥfūẓ*). The good tidings can be transmitted to him in dreams or by divine inspiration (*ilhām*). In his autobiography, al-Tirmidhī imparts a number of such dreams.

Divine inspiration of a friend of God is never in contradiction to the Prophet's revelation (*waḥy*) or law, for notwithstanding the high blessing he has received, his spiritual rank is lower than that of the Prophet. His life and its stages come about in the external and internal imitation of the Prophet, he is the latter's real heir, for God's friends, contrary to a *ḥadīth* of the Prophet, are the true heirs of the prophets (*al-awliyā' warathat al-anbiyā'*).

Just as in the case with Muḥammad, who is the seal of prophecy or of the prophets (*khatm al-nubuwwa*/*al-anbiyā'*), and as such the last and most complete of them, there exists a hierarchy among God's friends. Indications for this idea are already found in the 2nd/8th century, but here, too, al-Tirmidhī is the first of whom it can be said that he gives the broad outlines of a systematic presentation. Forty elected *awliyā'*—other names are *ṣiddīḳīn*, *abdāl* [*q.v.*], *umanā'* and *nuṣaḥā'*—after the Prophet's death took over control of the world, each one of them exercising it in temporal succession. The fact that they exist is a guarantee for the continuing existence of the world. Among them is a group of seven who are especially blessed. As runners-up of creation, the forty friends of God form, after the prophets, the second spiritual hierarchy of the cosmos. In the same way as in the prophets' hierarchy, there is within the friendship with God or among the friends of God a highest, perfect one, the seal (*khatm al-wilāya; khātam*/*khātim al-wilāya*/*al-awliyā'*); as is clear from his autobiography, al-Tirmidhī considered himself as this highest friend of God.

Al-Tirmidhī's new creation of *khatm al-wilāya*, in particular, had a wide effect. The concept was taken up and further developed by Ibn al-ʿArabī, and through him it entered later Ṣūfism. But for almost three centuries, al-Ḥakīm al-Tirmidhī's systematic position vis-à-vis *walī* and *wilāya* remained without successor in Ṣūfī mystical writings. The concept *khatm al-wilāya* was avoided, the comparison with the Prophet being shunned. With the exception of the *Kashf al-maḥdjūb* by the Persian Hudjwīrī (d. *ca.* 465/1072 [*q.v.*]), which is based on al-Tirmidhī, the authors of the basic handbooks speak only briefly of the theme of the friend of God. Among them, mention should be made of al-Kalābādhī (d. *ca.* 380/990 [*q.v.*]), of Abū Naṣr al-Sarrādj (d. 378/988 [*q.v.*]), of Abū Ṭālib al-Makkī (d. 386/996 [*q.v.*]), of Abū Nuʿaym al-Iṣfahānī and of al-Ḳushayrī (d. 465/1072 [*q.vv.*]) (for details, see Chodkiewicz, *Sceau*, 41-64). It is discussed whether the friend of God can work miracles, can be recognised while in this world, and can know that he himself is a friend of God. The wording often seems to have been borrowed verbatim from al-Tirmidhī without the authors mentioning him; this is the case with al-Ḳushayrī's *Risāla*. ʿAbd al-Ḳādir al-Djīlānī (d. 561/1166 [*q.v.*]), the progenitor of the Ḳādiriyya, also borrowed extensively from al-Tirmidhī's *Sīrat al-awliyāʾ* (*Drei Schriften*, i, introd., 7-9). Al-Tirmidhī's presentation of the hierarchy of the saints is taken over and slightly modified by ʿAmmār al-Bidlīsī (d. between 590/1194 and 604/1207), the teacher of Nadjm al-Dīn Kubrā (d. 617/1220 [see KUBRĀ, NADJM AL-DĪN]; he uses in particular the concept of *khatm al-wilāya* for the first time since al-Tirmidhī (Badeen, *Bidlīsī*). Rūzbihān-i Baḳlī (d. 606/1209 [*q.v.*]) not only wrote an autobiography, like Ḥakīm al-Tirmidhī, but also knew a highly developed hierarchy of God's friends. The theological-scholastical literature (for a summary, see Gramlich, *Wunder*, 94-110; Fakhr al-Dīn al-Rāzī's Ḳurʾān commentary is particularly detailed) discusses above all whether miracles worked by saints can stand up to intellectual scrutiny. The Muʿtazilīs denied them, whereas the Ashʿarīs in general admitted them. The scholastic arguments have survived until today and still serve to justify the miracles worked by saints (Radtke, *Traditionalismus*, 243-50).

Until modern times, the discussion has been shaped by Ibn al-ʿArabī, who in substance adopted al-Ḥakīm al-Tirmidhī's basic themes about the *walī*. In the *Futūḥāt makkiyya* (ch. lxxiii) and in a smaller work (*Tirmidiana minora*, 277-8), he comments on a section of al-Tirmidhī's *Sīrat al-awliyāʾ*. It is true that the commentary does not contribute anything to the understanding of al-Tirmidhī's text; the latter is for Ibn al-ʿArabī only a peg on which he can hang his own system and develop it. As is the case with al-Tirmidhī, the theory of the *walī* is entirely embedded in an Islamic cosmological and prophetological system (for the latter, see the works by Nyberg, Afifi, Chodkiewicz and Chittick). Two ways of al-Tirmidhī's doctrine are substantially elaborated upon by Ibn al-ʿArabī. One is that the hierarchy of God's friends is fundamentally differentiated [see ḲUṬB], the other that the concept of *khatm al-wilāya* is expanded, because Ibn al-ʿArabī introduces various kinds of *wilāya* [*q.v.*] (Chodkiewicz, *Sceau*, 65-78). Via Saʿd al-Dīn al-Ḥammūʾī (d. 649/1252 [*q.v.*]), who belonged to Ibn al-ʿArabī's school, the latter's doctrines reached such authors as ʿAzīz-i Nasafī (d. *ca.* 700/1300) in the Persian-speaking regions. A renaissance of the *khatm al-wilāya* doctrine can be observed particularly in the 18th and 19th centuries. Aḥmad al-Tidjānī (d. 1230/1815), the founder of the Tidjāniyya [*q.v.*], and Muḥammad ʿUthmān al-Mīrghanī (d. 1268/1851), the founder of the Khatmiyya, adopted for themselves the title *khatm al-wilāya*, to which the latter order owes its name [see MĪRGHANIYYA]. It is not only during his lifetime that the friend of God possesses extraordinary powers. After his death, too, he acts as a mediator with God; his help can be sought (*tawassul, istighātha*). His tomb confers blessings (*baraka*), which can also be obtained through pilgrimage. The aim of the latter is to obtain blessings through the friend of God (*tabarraka*). For this reason, everywhere in the Islamic world there arose centres for the veneration of saints. For opponents of Ṣūfism such as Ibn Taymiyya (d. 728/1328 [*q.v.*]) and the Wahhābīs, these practices are an abomination, because the latter see in them a form of idolatry (*shirk*). While expanding their territory, the Wahhābīs destroyed the tombs of saints wherever they were able.

Stories about the lives of outstanding friends of God lived on among their disciples, and especially in their families. Some time after the death of the friend of God, they were collected in biographies, from which arose Islamic hagiography [see MANĀḲIB]. The first of these lives of saints are written in Arabic, but they have only been preserved in Persian translation, as in the case of Ibn Khafīf (d. 371/982 [*q.v.*]) and of Abū Isḥāḳ Kāzarūnī (d. 426/1033 [*q.v.*]). These lives often have little historical value. The authors, mostly members of the saint's family, of his school or of his order, are concerned with the glorification of the saint by proving that he possessed extraordinary blessings and powers.

It is not only movements such as the Salafiyya [*q.v.*] and the Wahhābiyya which, inside the framework of Islamic theology, have formed a front against the veneration and theory of saints. Since the 19th century, proponents of the *walī* concept have also had to assert themselves against the attacks of Western rationalism. Convincing answers are not yet at hand (Radtke, *Traditionalismus*, esp. 255-7).

Bibliography: 1. Sources. Ibn Abi ʾl-Dunyā, *K. al-Awliyāʾ*, in *Madjmūʿat rasāʾil*, Cairo 1354/1935; Abū Nuʿaym al-Iṣbahānī, *Ḥilyat al-awliyāʾ*, Cairo 1351 ff./1932 ff.; Abū Saʿīd al-Kharrāz, *K. al-Kashf wa ʾl-bayān*, ed. Ḳ. al-Sāmarrāʾī, Baghdād 1967; al-Ḥakīm al-Tirmidhī, *K. Khatm al-awliyāʾ*, ed. O. Yaḥyā, Beirut 1965; idem, *K. Sīrat al-awliyāʾ*, ed. B. Radtke, in *Drei Schriften*, i, 1-134, Beirut 1992; idem, *al-Farḳ bayn al-āyāt wa ʾl-karāmāt*, ms. Ankara, Ismail Saib i, 1571, fols. 152b-177b; idem, *Badʾ shaʾn Abī ʿAbd Allāh*, ed. Yaḥyā, in Tirmidhī, *Khatm*, 14-32, facs. and German tr. in Radtke, *Tirmidiana minora*, 244-77, Eng. tr. in Radtke and O'Kane, *Concept of sainthood*, 15-36. Handbooks. Hudjwīrī, *Kashf al-mahdjūb*, ed. V. Zhukovsky, repr. Tehran 1336/1958, 265 ff., tr. Nicholson, *The Kashf al-mahjūb. The oldest Persian treatise on Sufism*, Leiden-London 1911, 210-41; Kalābādhī, *al-Taʿarruf li-madhhab ahl al-taṣawwuf*, ed. Arberry, Cairo 1934, tr. idem, *The doctrine of the Sufis*, [2]Cambridge 1977, ch. 26; Sarrādj, *K. al-Lumaʿ fi ʾl-taṣawwuf*, ed. Nicholson, Leiden-London 1914, 315-32, Ger. tr. R. Gramlich, *Schlaglichter über das Sufitum*, Stuttgart 1990, 449-68; Abū Ṭālib al-Makkī, *Ḳūt al-ḳulūb*, Cairo 1932, Ger. tr. Gramlich, *Die Nährung der Herzen*, Wiesbaden 1992-95, index, s.v. *Gottesfreund*; Ḳushayrī, *Risāla*, many eds., Ger. tr. Gramlich, *Das Sendschreiben al-Qušayrīs*, Wiesbaden 1989, index, s.v. *Gottesfreund*; ʿAmmār al-Bidlīsī, *Zwei mystische Schriften*, ed. E. Badeen, forthcoming Beirut; Ibn al-ʿArabī, *al-Futūḥāt al-makkiyya*, Cairo 1329-1911. Lives of saints. Abu ʾl-Ḥasan al-Daylamī, *Sīrat-i Ibn Khafīf*, ed. Annemarie Schimmel, Ankara 1955; F. Meier, *Die Vita des Scheich Abū Isḥāq al-Kāzarūnī*, Leipzig 1948; Muḥammad b. Munawwar, *Asrār al-tawḥīd fī maḳāmāt al-Shaykh Abī Saʿīd*, ed. Muḥammad Shafīʿī-i Kadkanī, Tehran 1366-7, Eng. tr. J. O'Kane, *The secrets of God's mystical oneness*, New York 1992; ʿAzīz al-Dīn Nasafī, *K. al-Insān al-kāmil*, ed. M. Molé, Tehran-Paris 1962, 313-25; Ibn Taymiyya, *al-Furḳān bayna awliyāʾ al-Raḥmān wa-awliyāʾ al-Shayṭān*, Cairo 1366/1947; idem, *Ḥaḳīḳat* *ma<u>dh</u>hab al-ittiḥādiyyīn*, in *Ma<u>dj</u>mūʿat al-Rasāʾil wa ʾl-masāʾil*, iv, Cairo n.d., 1 ff.

2. Studies. H. Corbin, *En Islam iranien*, esp. iii, Paris 1972; M. Chodkiewicz, *Le sceau des saints*, Paris 1986; J. van Ess, *Theologie und Gesellschaft im 2. und 3. Jahrhundert Hidschra. Eine Geschichte des religiösen Denkens im frühen Islam*, i-vi, Berlin-New York 1991-7; B. Radtke and J. O'Kane, *The concept of sainthood in early Islamic mysticism*, London 1996; Radtke, *Drei Schriften des Theosophen von Tirmi<u>d</u>*, i, Beirut-Stuttgart 1992, ii, Beirut-Stuttgart 1996; R. Mach, *Der Zaddik in Talmud und Midrasch*, Leiden 1957; Radtke, *Tirmi<u>d</u>iana minora*, in *Oriens*, xxxiv (1994), 242-98; idem, *Al-Ḥakīm al-Tirmidhī on miracles*, in *Les Saints et leurs miracles*, forthcoming Paris; Gramlich, *Die Wunder der Freunde Gottes*, Wiesbaden 1987; idem, *Die schiitischen Derwischorden Persiens*, Wiesbaden 1965-81, ii, 160-5 (on the hierarchy of saints); C. Ernst, *Ruzbihan Baqli*, London 1996; Radtke, *Zwischen Traditionalismus und Intellektualismus. Geistesgeschichtliche und historiografische Bemerkungen zum Ibrīz des Aḥmad b. al-Mubārak al-Lamaṭī*, in *Built on solid rock. Festschrift für Ebbe Knudsen*, Oslo 1997, 240-67; H.S. Nyberg, *Kleinere Schriften des Ibn al-ʿArabī*, Leiden 1919, 103-20; A. Afifi, *The mystical philosophy of Muhyid-din Ibnul-ʿArabi*, Cambridge 1939; W. Chittick, *The Sufi path of knowledge*, Albany 1989; Jamil M. Abun-Nasr, *The Tijaniyya. A Sufi order in the modern world*, London 1965; Radtke, *Lehrer-Schüler-Enkel. Aḥmad b. Idrīs, Muḥammad ʿUṯmān al-Mīrġanī, Ismāʿīl al-Walī*, in *Oriens*, xxxiii (1992), 94-132; I. Goldziher, *Die Heiligenverehrung im Islam*, in *Muh. Stud.*, ii, 275-378; Grace Martin Smith and C.W. Ernst (eds.), *Manifestations of sainthood in Islam*, Istanbul 1993; H.-Ch. Loir et Cl. Gilliot (eds.), *Le culte des saints dans le monde musulman*, Paris 1995.

(B. Radtke)

2. In North Africa.

The saint (*walī*, also *sayyid* or *ṣāliḥ*) has played an essential role in the religious and social life of the Ma<u>gh</u>rib for more or less a millennium.

Historical development. Historically speaking, the first figures of ascetics, popularly admired and with followings, appear in Ifrīḳiya in the 4th-5th/10th-11th centuries (cf. H.R. Idris (ed.), *Manâqib d'Abû Ishâq al-Jabnyânî et de Muhriz b. Khalaf*, Paris 1959). But we depend here on few written sources, and the phenomenon may well be older. The outstanding, prominent figures here appear rather to the west of that region. Abū Yaʿzā (or Yaʿazzā, d. 572/1177) was the typical illiterate, charismatic and miracle-mongering saint (see Y. Lobignac, *Un saint berbère, Moulay Ben Azza*, in *Hésperis*, xxxi [1944], and E. Dermenghem, *Le culte des saints dans l'Islam maghrébin*, Paris 1954, ²1982). His contemporary Ibn Ḥirzihim (d. 559/1163) was more cultivated but had nevertheless a very popular reputation.

Abū Madyan (d. 594/1197) was a spiritual disciple of these preceding two saints, and was the first figure in Ma<u>gh</u>ribī Ṣūfism to exercise an influence beyond his own region. This Andalusī went to the East where he may have met some of the great masters, e.g. ʿAbd al-Ḳādir al-<u>Dj</u>īlānī. On returning, he settled at Bougie and formed a circle of disciples, headed for the Almohad court of Yaʿḳūb al-Manṣūr at Marrakesh, and died en route at Tlemcen, whose patron saint he became (see ABŪ MADYAN and A. Bel, *Sidi Bou Medyan et son maître Ed-Daqqâq à Fès*, in *Mélanges René Basset*, Paris 1923, i, 30-68; C. Addas, *Abū Madyan and Ibn ʿArabī*, in *Muhyiddin Ibn ʿArabi, a commemorative volume*, Shaftesbury 1993). One of his disciples was the saint from the Rīf ʿAbd al-Salām Ibn Ma<u>sh</u>ī<u>sh</u> [see ʿABD AL-SALĀM], who was rather sparsely noticed in his lifetime but had a posthumous fame through his being recognised as a master and a "pole" by Abu ʾl-Ḥasan al-<u>Sh</u>ā<u>dh</u>ilī [*q.v.*]. It is with this last (d. 656/1258 in Upper Egypt), and especially his disciples of the 8th-9th/14th-15th centuries [see IBN ʿAṬĀʾ ALLĀH and <u>SH</u>Ā<u>DH</u>ILIYYA, with *Bibls.*] that the Ṣūfism of the brotherhoods appeared and enjoyed a spectacular rise in the Ma<u>gh</u>rib.

Among the main saints of the ensuing period, one may note the heads of brotherhoods like the Fāsī Aḥmad al-Zarrūḳ (d. 899/1494), educated in Egypt, but exercising his reformist influence first in Morocco and then Libya (see A.F. Khushaim, *Zarruq the Sufi*, Tripoli 1976). Also within the <u>Sh</u>ā<u>dh</u>iliyya was Abū ʿAbd Allāh Muḥammad al-<u>Dj</u>azūlī [*q.v.*], who returned to Morocco after a long trip to the East and then began a life as a hermit. But his preaching, his reputation as a thaumaturge and his <u>Sh</u>arīfī birth ensured him a prodigious success. He died *ca.* 869/1465 and his body, after several delays, was buried at Marrakesh, where he became one of the city's seven patron saints. The Ṣūfī tradition was periodically given fresh life by notable personalities such as Muḥammad b. Nāṣir from southern Morocco, or the <u>Sh</u>ā<u>dh</u>ilī Abū Ḥāmid al-ʿArabī al-Darḳāwī (d. 1823 [see DARḲĀWA]), whose influence spread all over the western and central Ma<u>gh</u>rib. Aḥmad al-Ti<u>dj</u>ānī (1737-1815 [*q.v.*]) was initiated into many orders before founding at ʿAyn Māḍī near Laghouat in what is now Algeria his own *zāwiya*, which spread especially into Morocco and then into Sudanic Africa (see J.M. Abun-Nasr, *The Tijaniyya, a Sufi order in the modern world*, London 1965). Another type of active, organising saint was al-Sanūsī (*q.v.*, and also K.S. Vikør, *Sufi and scholar on the desert edge. Muhammad ben ʿAlī Sanūsī*, London 1995). More recently still, the charisma and the activity of Aḥmad b. ʿAlīwa of Mustaghānim (d. 1934) marked his age, although he was rather too late to become a *walī* in the traditional sense (see IBN ʿALĪWA, and M. Lings, *A Moslem saint of the twentieth century, Shaikh Ahmad al-ʿAlawī*, London 1961, Fr. tr. *Un saint musulman du 20ᵉ siècle, le cheikh Ahmad al-ʿAlawī*, Paris 1984).

Characteristics. This development of the *walī*'s role over a millennium, coupled with the great geographical and social diversity (town vs. village) and cultural traditions (Berber, Bedouin), produced a great diversity of images of saints. Hagiography nevertheless allows us to discern a certain number of dominant types found in one region or another or at one time or another. The most current profile is of the pure, ascetic Sunnī, refusing all ostentation. The quality and amount of his education matters little, and even when he is a scholar, it is not his doctrinal works or poetry which attach the hearts of his disciples to him. On the other hand, he is clearly charismatic, and his miracles (*karāmāt*) are innumerable but stereotypical: reading people's thoughts, cures, bilocations, visions, etc. He is often the head of a brotherhood. But other profiles exist at the side of this one. Hence the popularity of the ecstatic and eccentric saint (*ma<u>dj</u><u>dh</u>ūb*); <u>Sh</u>ū<u>dh</u>ī and his pupil Ibn al-Marʾa (d. 611/1214; cf. Dermenghem, *op. cit.*) or ʿAlī al-Ṣanhā<u>dj</u>ī (10th/16th century) and his pupil ʿAbd al-Raḥmān al-Ma<u>dj</u><u>dh</u>ūb (d. 976/1569; see A.L. de Premare, *Sîdî ʿAbder-Rahmân al-Medjdûb*, Paris-Rabat 1985) remain till today popular figures. Moreover, the antinomian saint, who hides his interior states with a veil of conduct which may be habitually shocking, illustrates the *malāmatī* tradition in the Ma<u>gh</u>rib; thus Aḥmad Abu ʾl-ʿAbbās b. al-ʿArūs, one of the patron saints of Tunis (d.

868/1463; cf. Brunschvig, *Ḥafṣides*, ii) has remained famous for his provocative behaviour and his outrageous sayings. Sometimes saints have been warriors, *murābiṭūn*, who have died as martyrs. One should also note that Maghribī sainthood is by no means confined to men, and certain women have marked the memories of the faithful; some of the tombs of female saints are very frequently visited. Nor are saints exclusively Muslim; Jewish saints may be respected well beyond their own communities of origin and vice-versa. Popular sainthood, bursting out of a framework of the brotherhoods, sometimes shows very old features probably stemming from a pre-Islamic "shamanism"; thus the ʿIsāwiyya claim to stem from the Shādhilī-Djazūlī master Muḥammad b. ʿĪsā al-Mukhtār (d. 931/1524; cf. R. Brunel, *Essai sur la confrérie religieuse des Aïssaouas au Maroc*, Paris 1926), although this last would probably have been surprised to have been present at the therapeutic rituals, of animist inspiration, practised by certain branches of the brotherhood. An analogous remark can be made in regard to ʿAlī b. Ḥamdūsh and the Moroccan brotherhood of the Ḥamdūshiyya (see V. Crapanzano, *The Hamadsha, a study in Moroccan ethnopsychology*, Berkeley, etc. 1973).

This extreme veneration for saints stems from the basic, cosmic function attributed to *awliyāʾ*. These last are viewed as active members of the spiritual hierarchy of friends of God, and it often happens that great saints are seen attributing to themselves the function of *ḳuṭb* [*q.v.*] (Ibn Mashīsh, al-Shādhilī, etc.). The saint assures for his close retainers and adepts not only his spiritual guidance and strength but also material prosperity, and he is an intercessor with the supernatural world. His presence diffuses *baraka* or spiritual blessing, which his entourage tries to acquire for aims often far removed from purely spiritual ones (health, social success, etc.) through practices common to magic: whence the recitation for secular aims of ejaculatory prayers (*ḥizb*) taught by the saints. Thus within the Djazūlī current, the connection with the saint is lightened to the far limit of its strictly mystical dimension. The diffusing of *baraka* is made possible by a fairly simple allegiance and devotional rites like recital of the litanies of the *Dalāʾil al-khayrāt*, without there being any question of asceticism or a long spiritual journey. One should further note how the development of Sharīfism has played a certain role in the tone of Maghribī sainthood, especially from Marīnid times onward; Idrīsid Sharīfī origins are therefore attributed to Ibn Mashīsh, al-Shādhilī and al-Djazūlī. The spreading of *baraka*, according to such masters as al-Djazūlī, can be effected not only through the spiritual successors of Muḥammad, which the saints are, but also by his genealogical descendants.

The *walī*'s role as protector of a place may be considerable. Certain patron saints are well known, such as Ibn ʿArūs for Tunis, Abū Madyan for Tlemcen, Mawlāy Idrīs for Fās, etc. But one should also take into account thousands of minor, local saints whose tombs remain visible in villages or the quarters of towns, little-known, anonymous, sometimes even legendary. Even though history can find hardly anything to say about them, their presence and their social efficacity can be immense. They remain, in effect, very much alive at their tomb, to the point that the person's name most often serves to denote the place. The rituals can be purely private, but the patronal festivals (*mawsim*, *mawlid* [*q.vv.*]) give rise to massed groups with Ḳurʾān recitations, *dhikr*s, processions and fairs. Among the most important should be mentioned those of Mawlāy Idrīs at Fās, of Muḥammad b. ʿĪsā at Meknès and Ibn Mashīsh in the Rīf. But basically, it is not really necessary for the saint to have been really buried in the spot in question, as shown by the number of *maḳām*s of ʿAbd al-Ḳādir al-Djīlānī in the Maghrib, who in any case never went to the Maghrib. Protection and intercession are drawn and raised by the effect of the rites rather than by a sanctity attached to the place itself.

Bibliography (in addition to works cited in the article): 1. Sources. Aḥmad Bābā, *Nayl al-ibtihādj*, Fās 1917; Bādisī, *al-Maḳṣad*, tr. G. Colin, in *Archives marocaines*, xxvi-xxvii (1926); Ghubrīnī, *ʿUnwān al-dirāya*, Algiers 1970; Ibn al-ʿArabī, *Rūḥ al-ḳuds*, Damascus 1964, Eng. tr. R.W. Austin, *The Sufis of Andalusia*, London 1971, Fr. tr. G. Leconte, *Les Soufies d'Andalousie*, Paris 1995; Ibn ʿAṭāʾ Allāh, *Laṭāʾif al-minan*, Fr. tr. E. Geoffroy, *La sagesse des maîtres soufis*, Paris 1998; Ibn ʿAyyād, *al-Mafākhir al-ʿaliyya fī 'l-maʾāthir al-shādhiliyya*, Cairo 1355/1937; Ibn Maryam, *Bustān al-ʿārifīn*, ed. Ben Cheneb, Algiers 1908; Ibn al-Ṣabbāgh, *Durrat al-asrār wa-tuḥfat al-abrār*, Eng. tr. E. Douglas, *The mystical teachings of al-Shadhili*, Albany 1993; Leo Africanus, *Description*, tr. Epaulard; Tādilī, *al-Tashawwuf ilā ridjāl al-taṣawwuf*, ed. A. Toufiq, Rabat 1984, Fr. tr. M. de Fenoyl, *Regards sur le temps des Soufis*, Casablanca 1995.

2. Studies. Lévi-Provençal, *Historiens des Chorfa*, Paris 1922; idem, *Religion, culte des saints et confréries dans le Nord marocain*, Paris 1926; H. de Castries, *Les sept patrons de Marrakech*, in *Hésperis* (1924); J. Berque, *Al-Yousi. Problèmes de la culture marocaine au XVIIe siècle*, The Hague 1958; J.S. Trimingham, *The Sufi orders in Islam*, Oxford 1971; D. Eickelman, *Moroccan Islam. Tradition and society in a pilgrimage center*, Austin 1976; P. Shinar, *L'Islam maghrébin contemporain: essai de bibliographie sélective 1830-1970*, Aix-en-Provence 1983; M. Kably, *Société, pouvoir et religion au Maroc à la fin du Moyen-Âge*, Paris 1986; F. Colonna, *Présence des ordres mystiques dans l'Aurès aux XIXe et XXe siècles*, in A. Popovic and G. Veinstein (eds.), *Les ordres mystiques dans l'Islam*, Paris 1986; R.S. O'Fahey, *Enigmatic saint. Ahmad ibn Idris and the Idrisi tradition*, London 1990; H. Touati, *Entre Dieu et les hommes: lettrés, saints et sorciers au Maghreb (XVIIe siècle)*, Paris 1994. There is also information, often rather old and partial but still useful, in C. Depont and X. Coppolani, *Les confréries religieuses musulmanes*, Algiers 1884, repr. Paris 1987; L. Rinn, *Marabouts et Khouan*, Algiers 1884; E. Montet, *Le culte des saints dans l'Afrique du Nord et plus spécialement au Maroc*, Geneva 1909; E. Westermarck, *Ritual and belief in Morocco*, London 1926; E. Michaux-Bellaire, *Les confréries religieuses au Maroc*, in *Archives Marocaines*, xxvii (Rabat 1927); G. Drague, *Esquise d'histoire religieuse du Maroc: confréries et zaouiyas*, Paris 1951.

(P. Lory)

3. In the Arab lands of the Fertile Crescent [see Suppl.].

4. In Turkey, the Balkans, the Caucasus and Ādharbāydjān.

Saints play an important role here, especially in connection with the cults which have grown up around their tombs (*ziyāra*). Between the Turks of the Balkans and Anatolia, and those in Central Asia, despite the distance separating them, the concept of the saint and the organisation of pilgrimages displays no fundamental differences. This concept of sainthood derives its originality from the syncretic character of Turkish Islam, which has incorporated certain beliefs and practices from earlier cults, such as animism, shamanism,

Buddhism, Zoroastrianism and Christianity (in the study of the phenomenon of sainthood, it is not always easy to separate the various regions of the Turkish world, but for a detailed consideration of the situation in Central Asia, see 5. below).

These elements are particularly discernible in the saints of the 10th to the 14th centuries before being opposed by the *ʿulamāʾ*, the representatives of orthodoxy. They nevertheless maintained themselves in certain out-of-the-way parts of Central Asia, especially in rural areas and amongst nomads of the whole Turkish world (e.g. amongst the Yürüks, Ta<u>kh</u>ta<u>dj</u>îs [*q.vv.*] and ʿAlewīs in Anatolia). One may note e.g. that the earliest Turkish saints, such as Aḥmad Yasawī and Ḥā<u>dj</u><u>dj</u>ī Bektā<u>sh</u> Walī [*q.vv.*], performed miracles reminiscent of those of Central Asian shamans (changing into birds and totemistic creatures like the crane or deer; raising a man to life from his bones; etc.). Such saints were generally to be found amongst the Bektā<u>sh</u>ī, Yasawī and Ḳalandarī holy men. On the other hand, the Turkish saint often corresponded to the usual image of the Muslim holy man, often the founder or an adept of Ṣūfī orders like the Naḳ<u>sh</u>bandiyya, Ḳādiriyya, <u>Kh</u>alwatiyya, etc. One should bear in mind, too, that in the Turkish world sainthood is the product of two factors: the ideal of the holy war, *<u>dj</u>ihād*, marked by the spirit of *<u>gh</u>azw*, and Ṣūfism. This is understandable in the light of the fact that the Turkish world, over long centuries, was the object of campaigns of Islamisation conducted by Ṣūfīs, rather than by the *ʿulamāʾ*, being at the origin of the conversion of some pagan rulers to Islam.

As well as the Arabic term *walī*, and the Persian *<u>sh</u>āh* and *pīr*, saints in the Turkish world are denoted by Turkish terms like *baba* in Anatolia, *ata* in Central Asia (both meaning "father"), as well as *eren* or *ermi<u>sh</u>* (< *ermek* "to reach, attain") or *yatîr* ("one who settles down") in Anatolia. Saints' tombs are denoted by terms of Arabic or Persian origin alluding to the idea of pilgrimage (*mazār, ziyāratgāh*), tomb (*ḳabr, maḳbar*) or domed mausoleum (*gunbad, ḳubba*). But such tombs are also denoted by terms usually used for dervish convents, or a particular part of it (*tekke* in the Balkans, *langar* "refectory" and *ribāṭ* in Central Asia), or by a quality of the saint (*pīr* "venerable, respectable", in Ā<u>dh</u>arbāy<u>dj</u>ān).

Saints of the Turkish world may be classified into three categories. The first includes the *<u>gh</u>āzīs*, heroes of the Islamisation process and martyrs for the faith; the second, saints from the Ṣūfī milieu; and the third, the great figures of Islam and certain rulers.

The most representative types of the first in the regions under consideration are Abū Ayyūb al-Anṣārī (7th century [*q.v.*]), killed beneath the walls of Constantinople, Sayyid Baṭṭāl <u>Gh</u>āzī, who fought the Christians in Anatolia, and Ḳîzîl Deli Sulṭān, who converted Western Thrace to Islam. Religious figures and warriors who fought the Tsarist and Soviet Russians from the 18th to the early 20th century have also been canonised (the Imāms Manṣūr U<u>sh</u>urma and <u>Sh</u>āmil [*q.vv.*] in the Caucasus, Ḳurbān Murād in Turkmenistan, etc.) or against Kemālist Turkey in the 20th century (<u>Sh</u>ey<u>kh</u> Esʿad and ʿAbd al-Ḥakīm Arwāsī in Istanbul). Others in this category added the qualities of the Ṣūfī to their work of Islamisation, such as Ṣarî Ṣaltuḳ in Turkey and the Balkans, Ḥā<u>dj</u><u>dj</u>ī Bektā<u>sh</u>, his disciple Ḥā<u>dj</u><u>dj</u>îm Sulṭān, and Abdāl Mūsā, in Anatolia, ʿO<u>th</u>mān Baba in the Balkans, etc.

In the second, most important category, which includes the Ṣūfīs, one finds, in one group, those engaged in Islamisation and the fight against the infidels (a process which came to an end in Turkey in the 15th-16th centuries, but which continued in Central Asia up to the opening of the 20th century), and in the other group, those Ṣūfīs wholly occupied by their spiritual mission. These last include the founders of the great *ṭarīḳas* of the Turkish world plus their pupils and spiritual descendants: the Naḳ<u>sh</u>bandī Emīr Bu<u>kh</u>ārī at Istanbul; the <u>Kh</u>alwatīs Merkez Efendi and Ḳo<u>dj</u>a Muṣṭafā Pa<u>sh</u>a and the Ḳādirī Ismāʿīl Rūmī at Istanbul; Mawlānā <u>Dj</u>alāl al-Dīn Rūmī at Ḳonya; Ḥā<u>dj</u><u>dj</u>ī Bektā<u>sh</u> Walī in Anatolia; etc.

In the third category are to be found both Biblical figures (Daniel's tomb at Tarsus in southern Turkey), figures from the Ḳurʾān or Islamic history (tombs of <u>Kh</u>iḍr in several places, etc.), and theologians. Amongst the rulers around whom a cult grew up, one might mention the Ottomans Bāyezīd II and ʿAbd al-Ḥamīd II [*q.vv.*] in Turkey.

In numerous cases, the spots chosen for a Muslim saint's tomb could be either exceptional places already sacred from pagan times (hill tops, springs, grottoes, large rocks, etc.) or ruins of sanctuaries connected with pre-Islamic religious cults. Most of the mausolea in Eastern Turkestan were built on a spot where there had previously been Buddhist monasteries or funerary monuments (Kuhmarī Mazār and Kum Rabāt Pādi<u>sh</u>āhîm at <u>Kh</u>otan). Likewise, ancient Christian churches and monasteries were used in the Balkans and Anatolia (Ṣarî Ṣaltuḳ at Babaeski in Thrace, <u>Kh</u>iḍr at Samarḳand). A Nestorian saint who has become a Muslim one in Kirghizistan has even been identified.

As for saints' tombs connected with the *<u>gh</u>āzī* tradition, these tend to be in strategically situated and protected places connected with the saint's military functions: the summits of hills (Göz<u>dj</u>ü Baba in Istanbul and Muḥyī al-Dīn Abdāl in Eastern Thrace) or defiles (*derbend*) (Ḳîzîl Deli Sulṭān (Derbendī) in Western Thrace).

However, there are also in the Turkish world a certain number of towns which have always attracted saints and where tombs are very numerous. There exist pilgrims' guides for such towns, rich in historical details for the historical researcher: Istanbul (cf. <u>Kh</u>o<u>dj</u>azāde Aḥmed Ḥilmī, *Ẓiyāret-i ewliyā*, Istanbul 1325/1907-8), Bursa (cf. Meḥmed <u>Sh</u>ems el-Dīn, *Yādigār-i <u>Sh</u>emsī*, Bursa 1332/1913-14), Bu<u>kh</u>ārā (cf. Nāṣir al-Dīn al-Ḥanafī al-Bu<u>kh</u>ārī, *Tuḥfat al-zāʾirīn*, Novo-Bu<u>kh</u>ārā 1910), Samarḳand (cf. Muḥammad ʿAbd al-<u>Dj</u>alīl Samarḳandī, *Ḳandiyya*, ed. Īra<u>dj</u> Af<u>sh</u>ār, in *Du risāla dar tārī<u>kh</u>-i mazārāt wa <u>dj</u>u<u>gh</u>rāfiyā-yi Samarḳand*, Tehran 1367 *<u>sh</u>.*/1988).

On the architectural plane, there are several features which distinguish tombs of Turkish saints from those of the rest of the Islamic world. One might cite e.g. the remarkable height (sometimes 20 m) of the cenotaphs of certain Central Asian saints, the presence there of customs inherited from the steppe peoples like a tall mast with a horse's tail at its top and the presence of arms (axes, halberds, etc.) near the tombs of dervish *<u>gh</u>āzīs* in Anatolia.

The main saints' tombs with an active cult around them today are: in Turkey, those of Ḥā<u>dj</u><u>dj</u>ī Bektā<u>sh</u> (Hacıbektaş), Mawlānā <u>Dj</u>alāl al-Dīn (Ḳonya), Abū Ayyūb al-Anṣārī (Istanbul) and Ḥā<u>dj</u><u>dj</u>ī Bayram Walī (Ankara); and in the Balkans, that of Aywaz Dede (Bosnia). The faithful, and especially women, who make up the greater part of the visitors to these shrines, address themselves directly to the saints or else through the intermediacy of the custodians of the shrines, hoping for their intercession (*<u>sh</u>afāʿa* [*q.v.*]) with God on their behalf. The reasons for such pleas are various: illness, sterility, social success, etc. The offerings (money, cereals or beasts) given to the custodians are in the western Turkish world called *adak* (Tkish. *adamak* "to make a vow"), *nedhr* (Ar. *nadhara* "to vow, dedicate") and sometimes *niyāz* (Pers. "vow, supplication") (in Central Asia, one finds, additionally, *ṣadaḳa* (Ar. "pious gift") and the composite term *nadhr-niyāzmanlik*).

Denounced by the *ʿulamāʾ*, and above all, by the Wahhābiyya [*q.v.*], the cult of saints was subsequently dismantled by the Soviets and the Kemālists, but has nevertheless survived and is at present enjoying a remarkable resurgence in both Turkey and Central Asia.

Bibliography: Lāmiʿī Čelebi, *Terdjüme-yi Nefeḥāt ül-uns*, Istanbul 1270/1854; Cl. Huart, *Les saints des derviches tourneurs*, Paris 1918; Fuʾād Köprülü, *Türk edebiyyatinda ilk mütesawwiflar*, Istanbul 1919, ²Ankara 1966; F.W. Hasluck, *Christianity and Islam under the Sultans*, 2 vols. Oxford 1929; Abdülbaki Gölpinarlı (ed.), *Vilâyet-nâme, menâkib-ı Hünkâr Hacı Bektaş-i Velî*, Istanbul 1958; Hikmet Tanyu, *Ankara ve çevresinde adak ve adak yerleri*, Ankara 1967; J.-P. Roux, *Les traditions des nomades de la Turquie méridionale. Contribution à l'étude des représentations religieuses des sociétés turques d'après les enquêtes effectuées chez les Yörük et les Tahtaci*, Paris 1970; V.N. Basilov, *Kul't svyatikh v Islame*, Moscow 1970; M. Balaev, *Mugäddäslärä pärästish galiglarinin kharaktari vä täzahür formalari*, in *Ateizm mäsäläläri*, Baku 1975; Masami Hamada, *Islamic saints and their mausoleums*, in *Acta Asiatica* (Tokyo), xxxiv (1978); Ahmed Yaşar Ocak, *Türk halk inanclarında ve edebiyatında evliya menkabeleri*, Ankara 1984; M. Balivet, *Derviches turcs en Romanie latine. Quelques remarques sur la circulation des idées au XVᵉ siècle*, in *Byzantinische Forschungen*, xi (1987); Evstratios Zenginē, *O Bektasismos stē Dytiki Trakē. Symbolē stēn istoria tēs diadoseōs tou Mousoulmanismou ston elladiko hōro*, Thessalonica 1988; Ocak, *Kültür tarihi kaynaği olarak menâkibnâmeler, metodolojik bir yaklaşım*, Ankara 1992; Baha Tanman, *Settings for the veneration of saints*, in R. Lifchez (ed.), *The dervish lodge. Architecture, art and Sufism in Ottoman Turkey*, Berkeley and Los Angeles 1992, 141-67; N. Clayer and A. Popovic, *[Le culte des saints] dans les Balkans*, and *Le culte d'Ajvatovica et son pélerinage annuel*, in Ch. Loir and E. Guillot (eds.), *Le culte des saints dans le monde musulman*, Paris 1995; Gölpinarlı, *Otman Baba vilayet-nâmesi*, in *Jnal. of Turkish Studies*, xix (1995); Th. Zarcone, *L'hagiographie dans le monde turc*, in Denise Aigle (ed.), *Saints orientaux*, Paris 1995; idem, *[Le culte des saints] en Turquie et en Asie Centrale*, and *Le mausolée de Hacï Bektâsh Velî en Anatolie centrale (Turquie)*, in *Le culte des saints dans le monde musulman*; Liliana Masulovic-Marsol, *Tombes des saints musulmans et guérison: une approche anthropologique*, in *Cimetières et traditions funéraires dans le monde islamique*, Ankara 1996. See also the *Bibl.* to 5. below.

(Th. Zarcone)

5. In Central Asia.

The veneration of saints in Central Asia, as elsewhere in the Muslim world, has usually been approached as a syncretic phenomenon fraught with "survivals" from pre-Islamic times, and as a "concession", in popular religion, either to a presumed indigenous attachment to deep-rooted non-Islamic practices, or to the psychological rigours, deemed unpalatable to the masses, of an austere monotheism. For Central Asia the weight of Soviet, Sovietological, nationalist, and antiquarian scholarship has left this approach deeply entrenched, with the result that antecedents for the veneration of Muslim saints in Central Asia are typically located, though unconvincingly, in Buddhist, Christian, Zoroastrian, "shamanist" or "national" traditions. The rich sources on the historical development of doctrine and practice focused on the *awliyāʾ* have been less often studied.

Early and fundamental doctrinal formulations regarding the *awliyāʾ* had, with al-Ḥakīm al-Tirmidhī (d. *ca.* 300/910 [*q.v.*]), a Central Asian locus; while al-Tirmidhī's formulations remained somewhat controversial, a more mainstream defence of the saints and their *karāmāt* was offered by the Bukhāran al-Kalābādhī (d. 385/995), and still later the Khʷārazmian Nadjm al-Dīn al-Kubrā (d. 618/1221) discussed the marks, qualities and stages of *walāya* [*q.v.*]. Doctrinal writings of later Central Asian Ṣūfīs have hardly begun to be explored; of pivotal importance in shaping and refining the Central Asian consensus on the notion of the *walī* were the writings of the Naḳshbandī *shaykh* Khʷādja Muḥammad Pārsā (d. 822/1419), especially his *Faṣl al-khiṭāb*, which became a basic work in Central Asian *madrasa* curricula down to the present century.

The *walī* is encountered only abstractly through doctrinal formulations, but is met more directly through hagiographical narratives inspired by his or her charismatic person or legacy; it is there that we often find the principal doctrinal issues and controversies regarding the *awliyāʾ* addressed in polemical contexts. The perennial issue of the relationship between *walāya* and *nubuwwa*, for instance, was injected into the rivalry between the Naḳshbandī and Yasawī orders by the 10th/16th-century Yasawī Ṣūfī Ḳāsim Shaykh of Karmīna, who criticised Naḳshbandī claims that the silent *dhikr* was superior to the vocal *dhikr*. Equating the former with *walāya* and the latter, through its public character, with *nubuwwa*, Ḳāsim Shaykh reportedly argued that, although sainthood is superior to prophethood, when those two qualities are combined in a single person (as in Muḥammad), it would be absurd, when *walāya* is found in one person and *nubuwwa* in another, for the saint to claim primacy over the prophet; hence Naḳshbandī partisans should not exalt their "hidden" and silent *dhikr* over the public "mission" of the *dhikr-i djahr* (Mīr Musayyab Bukhārī, *Kitāb-i maḳāmāt-i mashāʾikh*, ms. St. Petersburg University No. 854, fol. 520a).

Similarly, the much-discussed question of whether the saints are known to the world is cast in concrete political terms by Sayyid Manṣūr, another Yasawī *shaykh* of 10th/16th-century Transoxania, in a hagiographical narrative that assumes the equivalence between "*shaykh*" and "saint". Asked by a local ruler to serve as the *shaykh* in his domains (and implicitly his legitimiser), Sayyid Manṣūr agreed on condition that the ruler would publicly affirm his saintly status by exhibiting the external signs of deference and consultation; this was necessary, he explained to the ruler, because the public does not know the saints whom God creates, "but if you make me a *shaykh*, everyone will know" (Ḥazīnī, *Cevâhiru 'l-ebrâr min emvâc-ı bihâr*, facs. ed. Cihan Okuyucu Kayseri 1995, 171-2).

Perhaps the most fruitful venue for approaching the links between doctrinal systematisations and the actual experience of the *awliyāʾ*, public or private, are hagiographical traditions intended to legitimise individual saints and the communities associated with them, especially accounts formulated before the principle of a *silsila* linked to the Prophet emerged, by the 9th/15th century, as the definitive (if never quite exclusive) mark of legitimacy. Outside the *silsila* principle, we find appeals to many other sources of legitimacy and authority: to "charismatic" sanctity as demonstrated simply through *karāmāt*; to transmitted sanctity conveyed through heredity, by receipt of a holy "legacy" or various spiritual insignia; or to "ascriptive" sanctity (claimed through attestations of status within classified hierarchies of saints, through the notion of "Uwaysī" transmission from the spirit of a deceased prophet or saint [see UWAYSIYYA], or simply through claims of divine *djadhba*). Often, of course, specific saints or their partisans appealed to different combinations of these and other legitimising principles. In any case, doctrinal defences of the legitimacy of the saints and their *karāmāt* found hagiographical adaptation in narratives evoking these various principles, typically in the context of overcoming the "rejection" (*inkār*) of a *shaykh* by his opponents, whether portrayed as formalist scholars or rival *shaykh*s.

The late 6th/12th and early 7th/13th centuries in Central Asia were especially productive of saints whose public memory has endured down to the present, above all in at least one of three major venues for ongoing "encounters" with a saint: (1) a *walī*'s spiritual descendants, in the form of a Ṣūfī order; (2) the putative natural descendants of a saint (who still form distinct social groups, despite Soviet-era efforts to dissolve such communities, throughout Central Asia); and (3) the most public aspect, the shrine. In this era lived the great Ṣūfīs adopted as the spiritual ancestors of the three major Central Asian orders: Aḥmad Yasawī (eponym of the Yasawī order, for whom the death-date customarily given, 562/1166-7, is probably a half-century too early), ʿAbd al-Khāliḳ Ghudjduwānī (spiritual ancestor of the Khʷādjagānī and later Naḳshbandī traditions, d. most probably in 617/1220), and Nadjm al-Dīn al-Kubrā (d. 618/1221, to whom is traced the Kubrawī order). In addition to the Ṣūfī communities stemming from these saints, their shrines became pilgrimage centres and benefitted from state patronage; Yasawī, and probably Ghudjduwānī, were also known as the ancestors of prominent descent groups. More locally prominent in their own time, however, were several Central Asian "patron" saints whose memory was cultivated primarily among their descendants and at their shrines; these figures, known from historical and hagiographical sources of the 8th-9th/14th-15th centuries, include Burhān al-Dīn Ḳïlïč of Uzgand in the Farghāna valley; Maṣlaḥat al-Dīn Khudjandī; Nūr al-Dīn Baṣīr of Samarḳand; Badr al-Dīn Maydānī of Bukhārā; and Zayn al-Dīn Kūy-i ʿĀrifānī of Tashkent. None of these figures was clearly fitted into any *silsila*-defined Ṣūfī community; others of this era, such as Bābā Māčīn (Tashkent), Ḥakīm Ata (Khʷārazm), Zangī Ata (Tashkent), or Shaykh Khāwand-i Ṭahūr (Tashkent) came to be implicated in spiritual or hereditary lineages linked with Yasawī or Naḳshbandī figures.

The 9th/15th century witnessed the beginnings of a flowering of hagiographical literature linked in large measure to the rise of the great *silsila*-based Ṣūfī orders. Important collective biographies of the *ʿulamāʾ* (for the regions of Samarḳand, Balkh, Khʷārazm and, probably, Kāshghar) were produced in pre-Mongol Central Asia, and hagiographical material relevant to the region appears in the basic works of al-Sulamī, Anṣārī, Hudjwīrī and ʿAṭṭār, as well as in hagiographies devoted to saints such as Abū Saʿīd b. Abi 'l-Khayr and Aḥmad-i Djām; nevertheless, individual and collective hagiographies are relatively rare in Central Asia until the 9th/15th century, which began with works devoted to Bahāʾ al-Dīn Naḳshband (especially the *Anīs al-ṭālibīn*, recently edited), saw the compilation of family-based hagiographies focused on Nūr al-Dīn Baṣīr and the Khʷādjagānī saint Amīr Kulāl, and ended with major literary compilations of saints' lives, sponsored at the Tīmūrid court in Harāt, such as Djāmī's *Nafaḥat al-uns* (and its Turkic translation by ʿAlī Shīr Nawāʾī, the *Nasāʾim al-maḥabba*) and Kamāl al-Dīn Gāzurgāhī's thematic *Madjālis al-ʿushshāḳ*. From the 10th/16th and 11th/17th centuries, a rich body of *ṭarīḳa*-based hagiographical literature may be regarded as the discursive reflection of the competitive rivalries among Ṣūfī communities; these largely unstudied works, extant in large numbers from the 10th/16th to the 19th centuries, offer important theoretical and practical perspectives on the role of the *walī* in society, by tracing the political and economic activities of Ṣūfī *shaykh*s. The 10th/16th century alone produced several works devoted to Khʷādja Aḥrār (of which the best known is the *Rashaḥāt-i ʿayn al-ḥayāt*), a series of hagiographies on the Naḳshbandī saint known as Makhdūm-i Aʿẓam and on the Djūybārī *shaykh*s, two substantial works on the Kubrawī *shaykh* Ḥusayn Khʷārazmī (the *Miftāḥ al-ṭālibīn* and the *Djāddat al-ʿāshiḳīn*), and (apparently) lost hagiographies on the Yasawī saints Khudāydād and Ḳāsim Shaykh (of which excerpts are preserved in 11th/17th-century Yasawī works).

Female saints are well represented in modern Central Asian shrine traditions (e.g. ʿAnbar Ana in Tashkent, Paraw Bibi near Gïzïl Arbat in Turkmenistan), and may be presumed to have been no less popular in the past; unfortunately, they are less often the subject of hagiographical accounts and usually appear formulaically grouped near the end of large collective hagiographies such as Djāmī's. An exception is a remarkable, though little studied, 10th/16th-century work entitled *Maẓhar al-ʿadjāʾib wa-madjmaʿ al-gharāʾib*, written by Ḥāfiẓ Baṣīr Khuzārī, on the life of a female saint called simply "Āghā-yi Buzurg", who lived near Bukhārā (see *Sobranie vostočnïkh rukopisey Akademii nauk Uzbekskoy SSR*, v [1960], no. 4137).

As suggested, the most public venue for encountering the *awliyāʾ* is the shrine. Our information on saints' shrines and pilgrimage in Central Asia from before the Mongol era is relatively sparse; we find some material on the shrines of Ḳutham b. ʿAbbās [*q.v.*] in Samarḳand, of Abū Ḥafṣ-i Kabīr in Bukhārā, and of Ḳutayba b. Muslim [*q.v.*] in the Farghāna valley, for instance, while the 6th/12th-century *Asrār al-tawḥīd* on the life of Abū Saʿīd b. Abi 'l-Khayr [*q.v.*] offers rich evidence on the public prominence of saints' shrines in northern Khurāsān; the same century also saw the "discovery" of the shrine of ʿAlī near Balkh, and the emergence (at least into our sources) of the pattern of state patronage of shrines that would become much clearer by the Tīmūrid era (e.g. in Tīmūr's own patronage of shrines in Harāt, Shahr-i Sabz, Turkistān and Tirmidh). An unexplored source from the middle of the 6th/12th century promises new insights into the veneration of saints' shrines in Central Asia and Persia; the Persian *Laṭāʾif al-adhkār li 'l-ḥuḍḍār wa 'l-suffār*, written by Burhān al-Dīn Muḥammad b. ʿUmar al-Bukhārī, offers a "defence" of the practice of *ziyāra* and describes the major shrines of several towns along an itinerary leading from Bukhārā to Mecca and Medina. The work, preserved in a single manuscript in Dushanbe (see *Katalog vostočnïkh rukopisey Akademii nauk Tadzhikskoy SSR*, i, Stalinabad 1960, no. 188), has remained unstudied, but is of interest for the study of saints and shrines in the Muslim world at large (it predates the celebrated *Kitāb al-Ziyārāt* of ʿAlī al-Harawī [*q.v.*]—see Janine Sourdel-Thomine, *Guide des lieux de pèlerinage*, Damascus 1957—by half a century).

The legitimacy of visiting saints' tombs is still defended in the 9th/15th-century *Tārīkh-i Mullāzāda*, written by a pupil of Khʷādja Muḥammad Pārsā, on the shrines of Bukhārā (in which shrines of Ṣūfīs appear alongside those of the city's jurists); the practice became such a definitive part of Central Asian religious life that later shrine guides—for Samarḳand, Balkh, Bukhārā, Khʷārazm, Sayrām and the Volga-Ural region—rarely bother to address at any length the possibility that *ziyāra* might be regarded as *bidʿa*. The veneration of saints at their shrines had by the 9th/15th century (and probably in fact much earlier) clearly become a central and accepted part of Muslim religious life, and the shrines themselves were not only the definitive features of Islamic religious geography in the region but the chief public "evidence" of the saints themselves (whether the shrine marked the grave of a pre-Islamic prophet, a member of Muḥammad's family, a martyr for the faith, an Islamiser, a communal ancestor or a Ṣūfī saint). Equivalents of the term *awliyāʾ* (with the plural used here as a singular) in modern Central Asian languages often refer simply to a shrine, whatever it is understood to signify, or to the entire cemetery typically centred upon a shrine, indicating a popular understanding of the saint's continued presence at the site. The shrines were the setting at which the *awliyāʾ*'s intercession was sought, not only for the private needs of health, fertility, success and solace but also for communal protection and solidarity; the shrine marked the continuing presence of the saint, and God's blessing, in his or her community, and the 18th-century romantic hagiography of the antinomian saint Mashrab could in effect forget the celebrated jurists buried in Bukhārā and declare that, were it not for the presence near that city of Bahāʾ al-Dīn Nakshband's shrine, Bukhārā would be an infidel town (*Dīwāna-yi-Mashrab*, tr. N.S. Likoshin, Samarḳand 1915, 194).

In more recent times, the veneration of saints' shrines was the target of intense pressure during Soviet anti-religious campaigns; many local shrines were demolished—as recently as 1986, under Gorbachev—and both pilgrims and unofficial shrine custodians were subject to prosecution. Since 1990, shrines have enjoyed a remarkable revival throughout Central Asia, with reconstruction and repair undertaken by local constituencies, though often with renewed state patronage; little work has yet been done to gauge the effects of Soviet rule on traditional conceptions and practices focused on the saints of Central Asia, or on the re-emergence and reformulation of those traditions in post-Soviet times.

Bibliography: Few specifically Central Asian hagiographical works have been edited; some relevant works include ʿAbd Allāh Anṣārī, *Ṭabaḳāt al-ṣūfiyya*, ed. Muḥammad Sarwar Mawlāʾī, Tehran 1362/1983; Farīd al-Dīn ʿAṭṭār, *Tadhkirat al-awliyāʾ*, ed. Muḥammad Istiʿlāmī, Tehran 1347/1968, repr. 1370/1991; "Muʿīn al-fuḳarāʾ", *Tārīkh-i Mullāzāda*, ed. Aḥmad Gulčīn-i Maʿānī, Tehran 1339/1960; Djāmī, *Nafaḥāt al-uns*, ed. Maḥmūd ʿĀbidī, Tehran 1370/1991; Nawāʾī, *Nasāʾim al-maḥabba*, ed. Kemal Eraslan, Istanbul 1979; Ṣalāḥ b. Mubārak Bukhārī, *Anīs al-ṭālibīn wa-ʿuddat al-sālikīn*, ed. Khalīl Ibrāhīm Ṣārī Oghlī, Tehran 1371/1992; ʿAlī b. Ḥusayn "Ṣāfī", *Rashaḥāt-i ʿayn al-ḥayāt*, ed. ʿAlī Aṣghar Muʿīnīyān, Tehran 2536/1977. A popular Turkic hagiography was published in K.G. Zaleman, *Legenda pro Khakim-Ata*, in *Izvestiya Akademii nauk*, St. Petersburg, ix/2 (1898), 105-50. See also the translation of J. O'Kane, *The secrets of God's mystical oneness or the spiritual stations of Shaikh Abu Saʿid (Asrār al-towḥid) (fi maqāmāt al-Šeyk Abi Saʿid)* [by] *Moḥammad Ebn-e Monavvar*, Costa Mesa, Calif. 1992. Useful studies of the development of Ṣūfī traditions in pre-Mongol Central Asia include F. Meier, *Abū Saʿīd-i Abū l-Ḫayr (357-440/967-1049): Wirklichkeit und Legende*, Leiden, Tehran and Liège 1976; Jacqueline Chabbi, *Remarques sur le développement historique des mouvements ascétiques et mystiques au Khurasan, IIIᵉ/IXᵉ siècle-IVᵉ/Xᵉ siècle*, in *SI*, xlvi (1977), 5-72; B. Radtke, *Al-Ḥakīm at-Tirmidhī—Ein islamischer Theosoph des 3./9. Jahrhunderts*, Freiburg 1980; idem, *Theologen und Mystiker in Ḫurāsān und Transoxanien*, in *ZDMG*, cxxxvi (1986), 536-69. For the post-Mongol era, see J. Aubin, *Un santon quhistānī de l'époque timouride*, in *REI*, xxxv (1967), 185-216; Jo-Ann Gross, *Multiple roles and perceptions of a Sufi Shaikh: symbolic statements of political and religious authority*, in *Naqshbandîs*, Istanbul and Paris 1990, 109-21; J. Paul, *Hagiographische Texte als historische Quelle*, in *Saeculum*, xli (1990), 17-43; idem, *Scheiche und Herrscher im Khanat Čaġatay*, in *Isl.*, lxvii (1990), 278-321; R.D. McChesney, *Waqf in Central Asia*, Princeton 1991; A.A. Semenov, *Unikal'nïy pamyatnik agiografičeskoy sredneaziatskoy literaturï XVI v.*, in *Izvestiya Uzbekistanskogo filiala AN SSSR* (1940), no. 12, 54-62 (1941), no. 3, 37-48; M. Hartmann, *Ein Heiligenstaat im Islam. Das Ende der Čaghataiden und die Herrschaft der Choǧas in Kašgarien*, in *Der islamische Orient*, i, Berlin 1905, nos. 6-10, 195-374; A. Frank, *Islamic shrine catalogues and communal geography in the Volga-Ural region, 1788-1917*, in *JIS*, vii (1996), 265-86. On Central Asian developments of the Uwaysī conception, see J. Baldick, *Imaginary Muslims. The Uwaysi Sufis of Central Asia*, New York and London 1993, but see also the review article of D. DeWeese, in *CAJ*, xl (1996), 87-127, and DeWeese, *An "Uvaysi" Sufi in Timurid Mawarannahr. Notes on hagiography and the taxonomy of sanctity in the religious history of Central Asia, Papers on Inner Asia*, no. 22, Bloomington Ind. 1993. For shrine traditions, see H. Einzmann, *Religiöses Volksbrauchtum in Afghanistan. Islamische Heiligenverehrung und Wallfahrtswesen im Raum Kabul*, Wiesbaden 1977; for East Turkistān, see Hamada Masami, *Islamic saints and their mausoleums*, in *Acta Asiatica*, xxxiv (1978), 79-98. No substantial studies of shrine veneration in Russian-dominated Central Asia, before or after the Soviet collapse, have yet appeared; see the survey of Maria E. Subtelny, *The cult of holy places. Religious practices among Soviet Muslims*, in *MEJ*, xliii (1989), 593-604. A list of holy sites appears in J. Castagné, *Le culte des lieux saints de l'Islam au Turkestan*, in *L'Ethnographie*, xlvi (1951), 46-124, and see I.A. Kastan'e, *Drevnosti Kirgizskoy stepi i Orenburgskago kraya*, in *Trudï Orenburgskoy Učenoy Arkhivnoy Komissii*, vïp. 22 (1910). Reflective of local traditions of saints and shrines are W. Gordlevsky, *Choğa Aḥmed Jasevi*, in *Festschrift Georg Jacob*, ed. Th. Menzel, Leipzig 1932, 57-67; V.A. Shishkin, *Mazarï v Zangi-ata, [ʿIqd al-djumān]: V.V. Bartol'du turkestanskie druz'ia, učeniki i počitateli*, Tashkent 1927, 165-70; Yu. V. Knozorov, *Mazar Shamun-Nabi (Nekotorye perežitki domusul'manskikh verovaniy u narodov Khorezmskogo oazisa)*, in *Sovetskaya étnografiya*, 1949, no. 2, 86-97; DeWeese, *Sacred history for a Central Asian town. Saints, shrines, and legends of origin in histories of Sayrām, 18th-19th centuries*, in *RMMM*, forthcoming. Soviet-era ethnographic studies include V.N. Basilov, *Kul't svyatïkh v islame*, Moscow 1970; S.M. Demidov, *Turkmenskie ovlyadï* Ashkhabad 1976; Demidov, *Sufizm v Turkmenii*, Ashkhabad 1978; G.P. Snesarev, *Khorezmskie legendï kak istočnik po istorii religioznïkh kul'tov Sredney Azii*, Moscow 1983; and, still somewhat reflective of

Soviet approaches, R.M. Mustafina, *Predstavleniya, kul'ty, obryadï u kazakhov* (*v kontekste bytovogo islama v Yuzhnom Kazakhstane v kontse XIX-XX vv.*), Alma-Ata 1992. The genre is no longer productive, but Soviet anti-religious literature remains a useful source of information (despite its obvious biases) on the veneration of saints in 20th-century Central Asia; see, for example, Yu. G. Petrash, *Sviatïe mesta obmana*, Frunze 1961; T. Säksanov, *Muqäddäs jaylär—khurafat vä bid'ät ochaghi*, Tashkent 1984; S.M. Demidov, *Legendï i pravda o "svyatïkh" mestakh*, Ashkhabad 1988.

(D. DeWeese)

6. In Muslim India.

Since 1831 orientalists like Garcin de Tassy have underlined the importance of the saints of Islam in India. They are known in Arabic as *walī* and in Persian as *pīr*, terms which apply to a living saint as much as to one who is venerated after his death.

The existence of a cult of saints and a theory of saintliness is sporadically attested in India from the beginning of the presence of Muslims there. Holy individuals not as yet attached to Ṣūfī orders were worshipped in the region of Sind [*q.v.*] in present-day Pakistan when it was under Arab domination (from the 8th to the 11th centuries), then in the Pandjab [*q.v.*] under the Ghaznawids [*q.v.*] (11th to 12th centuries).

There in Lahore Hudjwīrī (d. *ca.* 1072 [*q.v.*]), was already venerated. He left the first treatise on Ṣūfism in Persian in his *Kashf al-mahdjūb*, an ambitious theory of saintliness, which stated that "God has saints (*awliyā*) whom He has specially distinguished by His friendship and whom He has chosen to be the governors of His kingdom ... He has made the saints governors of the universe ... Through the blessing of their advent the rain falls from heaven, and through the purity of their lives the plants spring up from the earth, and through their spiritual influence the Moslems gain victories over the unbelievers" (tr. R.A. Nicholson, 212-13); furthermore, he had already described the invisible hierarchy of the saints [see ABDĀL] who govern the world (*op. cit.*, 214).

The documented history of sainthood in India begins with the founding of the sultanate of Dihlī [see DIHLĪ, SULTANATE OF] in 1210, which established Muslim supremacy on the Indian subcontinent for six centuries, and the consolidation soon afterwards of the orders of mystics [see ṬARĪḲA]. From this time onwards it is possible to outline the history of sainthood in India within the context of the Ṣūfī orders until the 16th century, throughout the unified sultanate of the 13th-14th centuries, and then the regional sultanates of the 14th-16th centuries [see HIND. iv. History]. Mystical theology was dominated by the Čishtiyya [*q.v.*] who rivalled the Suhrawardiyya [*q.v.*]; and from the 15th century onwards the Ḳādiriyya [*q.v.*] was established. The minor brotherhoods, such as the Kubrawiyya [*q.v.*] in Kashmīr, and the Firdawsiyya and then the Shaṭṭāriyya [*q.v.*] in Eastern India, had a regional importance. In contrast to the socially respectable orders, which were obedient to the *Sharīʿa*, India was also familiar with less conventional orders described as *malāmatī* [*q.v.*], and more recently by the specifically Perso-Indian expression *bī sharʿ* [*q.v.*]; these included the Ḳalandariyya [*q.v.*] and the Madāriyya [see BADĪʿ AL-DĪN SHĀH MADĀR] in the north, and the Rifāʿiyya [*q.v.*] in the west and south of the subcontinent.

The conception of sainthood which prevailed among the brotherhood was inherited from Khurāsān and Central Asia. It was first to be seen in hagiography, in which the saints close to God are seen to be endowed with supernatural powers and able to perform miracles (*karāma* [*q.v.*]). They display these gifts in an ostentatious fashion, especially in the heteropraxic orders. Then there are those who are obliged to mediate between God and man, guiding man towards Him; the distress of the faithful is consoled and their illnesses cured by their intercession (*shafāʿa* [*q.v.*]). Saints also have a cosmic role, for they may have control over the rain and the crops, like Ghāzī Miyān [*q.v.*]. But in particular, they play a political role by assuring victory for the armies of Islam, like Muʿīn al-Dīn Čishtī (d. *ca.* 1234), to whom is attributed the foundation of the sultanate of Dihlī. Saints make and unmake kings, for sainthood (*walāya* or *wilāya*) really implies "the government of a territory" (*wilāya*). Therefore it was believed that from its inception the throne of Dihlī was controlled by the great saints of the Čishtiyya, in particular Niẓām al-Dīn Awliyāʾ [*q.v.*], and it is from this that there arises conflict-ridden relations between the saints and the sultans, who found it hard to tolerate this spiritual control.

In an India where Islam was very much in the minority, Muslim saints were also competing with Hindu mystics. Saints such as ʿAbd al-Ḳuddūs Gangohī (1456-1537) and Muḥammad Ghawth Gwāliyārī (1500-62), while not hesitating to use techniques such as yoga, were intent on showing the superiority of Islam in magical contexts. Their tombs are often to be found at resanctified former Buddhist or Hindu sites. The saint within the Dihlī sultanate was most often given a highly colourful character. Alongside the sages devoted to the spiritual improvement of their disciples, like Sharaf al-Dīn Yaḥya Manērī (d. 1391), representing the Firdawsiyya, emphasis was given to the ecstatic personalities who were enamoured of music and poetry. Ḳuṭb al-Dīn Bakhtiyār Kākī died at Dihlī in 1235 after four days of ecstasy spent singing the same Persian verses. A saint could become violent in the working of miracles in order to put an end to his own adversaries.

From the middle of the 14th century onwards, saintliness became the subject of theological discussions. The influence of Ibn al-ʿArabī spread, especially through the medium of the Kubrawiyya with ʿAlī al-Hamadānī (d. 1385 [*q.v.*]), and especially with Ashraf Djahāngīr al-Simnānī (d. 1436 [*q.v.*]), who passed on to membership of the Čishtiyya.

The Mughals (16th-18th centuries [*q.v.*]) beginning with Bābur, brought a new brotherhood from Central Asia, the Naḳshbandiyya [*q.v.*]. It developed theories of sainthood by aligning itself with Ibn al-ʿArabī, especially under the influence of Aḥmad Sirhindī [*q.v.*], the founder of the *mudjaddidiyya* branch. He gave a firm emphasis to the supremacy of the *Sharīʿa* and the superiority of prophecy (*nubuwwa*) over sainthood (*wilāya*); but this did not imply, as was wrongly thought, abandoning the traditional ideas of sainthood. Sirhindī and his son placed themselves at the top of an invisible hierarchy of saints with the title of *ḳayyūm*, which like the *ḳuṭb* [*q.v.*] played the role of the *axis mundi*. Today, the Naḳshbandiyya keep alive the mediaeval conception of sainthood and align themselves with the Barelwīs (see below) in venerating saints.

The Mughals also supported other orders: Humāyūn [*q.v.*] put trust in the Shaṭṭāriyya, especially in Muḥammad Ghawth (1500-62 [*q.v.*]), a great musician and a patron of musicians; Shāh Djahān and his son Dārā Shukōh favoured the Ḳādiriyya and saints like Miyān Mīr. But since Akbar, the true organiser of the empire, who renewed links with the traditions of the Dihlī sultanate, the dynasty was placed under the protection of the Čis̲h̲tiyya. He generously donated the tomb of Muʿīn al-Dīn at Ad̲j̲mēr [*q.v.*], and he attributed the perpetuation of the dynasty to Salīm Čis̲h̲tī (d. 1571), constructing his new capital Fatḥpūr Sikrī [*q.v.*] around his tomb. In the 18th century the last Mug̲h̲als revived the cult of Ḳuṭb al-Dīn at Dihlī.

A definite cult certainly developed around thousands of saints. First, there were the great saints born outside India, especially the founders of the great brotherhoods like ʿAbd al-Ḳādir al-D̲j̲īlānī [*q.v.*]. Then there were the great historical characters of India, founders of Indian orders like Badīʿ al-Dīn, founder of the Madāriyya. There were also those who played a political or religious role in a particular region, among whom the most famous were those belonging to the Čis̲h̲tiyya, like Farīd al-Dīn (d. 1265) from Pak-Pattan, protector of the Pand̲j̲ab, Niẓām al-Dīn Awliyāʾ (d. 1325), the principal architect of the spiritual influence of the Dihlī sultanate, and Muḥammad Banda Nawāz Gēsū Darāz at Gulbarga, who consecrated the foundation of the Bahmanī sultanate in the Deccan [see BAHMANĪS]. The great saint of Bengal was the Suhrawardī D̲j̲alāl al-Dīn Tabrīzī (d. 1244). Besides these, each local branch of a brotherhood, each town and each village, even each lineage, had its local saints marking stages in religious history and covering the whole territory, and there are countless numbers of them. They fall into two groups, and they are traditionally arranged by Indian Muslims in poetry and religious manuals according to the cycle of their feasts in a double calendar: for one group (Islamic), it is the lunar calendar, and for the other group (Hindu), it is lunar and solar, for protectors of the crops, like G̲h̲āzī Miyān, must be celebrated according to the cycle of the seasons. Ethnologists have also classified the saints according to their function; thus in addition to the great all-powerful figures, there were others who specialised in curing this or that mental or physical ailment, such as G̲h̲āzī Miyān who cured leprosy, or those under the patronage of trade associations which were regrouped into castes in India [see HIND. ii. Ethnography; NEPAL], such as Ḥasan Telī, who protected the oil-pressers (*telī*), or those who were within the protected limits of a territory (villages, districts, houses).

Saints took over most of the functions of the divinities of the Hindu pantheon, and they appropriated for themselves ancient sacred sites. The cult was observed within certain buildings, which had at least to include a *mazār*, a tomb or a cenotaph of earth or stone. It could have other buildings, with varying degrees of elaboration, superimposed or surrounding it, including hospices for the servitors in charge (*k̲h̲ādim*, pl. *k̲h̲uddām*). These were generally the descendants of the saint or adherents of his mystical order, and they shared the income from the sanctuary. A large complex created in this way was called a *dargāh*, a royal palace, for the saint was treated like a sultan. The *ḳawwāls*, musicians of low status, were attached to the larger sanctuaries to perform mystic chants (*ḳawwālī*) in Persian and in Urdu.

Besides the daily devotions of the faithful, collective celebrations took place once every week (generally on a Thursday evening) or once every month. Great festivities were organised once a year on the anniversary of the death of the saint, which was called an *ʿurs*, meaning marriage (i.e. mystical marriage), the term *mawlid* not being used as in the Arab world. These festivals gave rise to pilgrimages [see ZIYĀRA].

These devotions gave rise to controversies as early as the 16th century, perhaps as a consequence of the spread of the doctrines of Ibn Taymiyya [*q.v.*], which were known (according to Ibn Baṭṭūṭa, iii, 252) as early as the reign of Muḥammad b. Tug̲h̲luḳ (1325-51). Women were forbidden to visit the tombs by Fīrūz S̲h̲āh Tug̲h̲luḳ (1351-88), and the processions in honour of G̲h̲āzī Miyān by Sikandār Lōdī (1489-1517) were banned. At the end of the 18th century S̲h̲āh Walī Allāh Dihlawī [see AL-DIHLAWĪ], and then his grandson Ismāʿīl S̲h̲ahīd [*q.v.*], a disciple of Aḥmad Brēlwī [*q.v.*] drew fresh inspiration from Ibn Taymiyya and reopened a controversy which can be traced up to the present day. Without denying the existence of saints, they denied them all powers of intercession. They condemned any devotion given to them and to their tombs. This doctrine was transmitted directly to the schools of Deoband and of the Ahl-i Ḥadīt̲h̲ [*q.vv.*], and indirectly to the modernists through the medium of Sir Sayyid Aḥmad K̲h̲ān, and to the fundamentalists who followed Abu ʾl-Aʿlā Mawdūdī [*q.vv.*]. In the face of these critics Aḥmad Riḍā K̲h̲ān of Bareilly reaffirmed the mediaeval position, reasserting the powers of the saints and justifying recourse to their intercession. His disciples formed the school of the Barelwīs. It is well organised within the framework of Pakistan but more informal elsewhere, and expresses a religiosity which remains predominant in the entire subcontinent.

Bibliography: For a general listing of works in the field and of sources, see J.A. Subhan, *Sufism, its saints and shrines: an introduction to the study of Sufism with special reference to India*, [2]New York 1970 ([1]1938); S.A.A. Rizvi, *A history of Sufism in India*, 2 vols. Delhi 1978-82; A. Schimmel, *Islam in the Indian Subcontinent*, Leiden 1980; M. Gaborieau, *Les ordres mystiques dans le sous-continent indien: un point de vue ethnologique*, in A. Popovic and G. Veinstein (eds.), *Les ordres mystiques dans l'Islam. Cheminements et situation actuelle*, Paris 1986, 105-34; C.W. Troll (ed.), *Muslim shrines in India. Their character, history and significance*, Delhi 1989.

For the saints of Arab Sind, see D.N. Maclean, *Religion and society in Arab Sind*, Leiden 1989, 110-14; Hud̲j̲wīrī, see R.A. Nicholson, *The Kashf al-Mahjúb, the oldest Persian treatise on Ṣúfism.*

On the nature of sainthood and the powers of the Indian saints according to the hagiography of the Dihlī Sultanate, see above all the synthesis of S. Digby, *Sufi Shaikh as a source of authority in Mediaeval India*, in Gaborieau (ed.), *Islam et société en Asie du Sud*, Paris 1986, 57-77; see also Digby, *ʿAbd al-Quddus Gangohi, 1456-1537. The personality and attitudes of a medieval Sufi*, in *Medieval India. A miscellany*, iii, Aligarh 1975, 1-66; idem, *Qalandars and related groups. Elements of social deviance in the religious life of the Delhi Sultanate*, in Y. Friedmann (ed.), *Islam in Asia*, i, *South Asia*, Jerusalem 1984, 60-108; idem, Shaykh *and* Sulṭān: *a conflict of claims to authority in medieval India*, in *Iran*, xxviii (1990), 71-81; idem, *To ride a tiger or a wall? Strategies of prestige in Indian Sufi legend*, in W.M. Cellewaert and R. Snell (eds.), *According to tradition. Hagiographical writing in India*, Wiesbaden 1994, 99-129; P.M. Currie, *The shrine and cult of Muin al-din Chishti of Ajmer*, Delhi 1989. See further the following translations and studies: B. Lawrence, *Notes from a distant flute. The extant literature of the pre-Mughal Indian Sufism*, Tehran 1978; idem, *Morals for the heart. Conversations of Shaykh Nizam ad-din Awliya*, New York 1992; P. Jackson, *Letters from Maneri, Sufi saint of medieval India*, New York 1980; idem, *The way of a Sufi. Sharafuddin Maneri*, Delhi 1987.

On the saints of the regional sultanates, see R.M. Eaton, *The Sufis of Bijapur, 1300-1700. Social roles of Sufis in medieval India*, Princeton 1978; idem, *The rise of Islam and the Bengal frontier, 1204-1760*, Berkeley, etc. 1993; C.W. Ernst, *Eternal garden. Mysticism, history and politics at a South Asian Sufi centre*, New York 1992.

The theological speculations about sainthood among the Naḳshbandiyya in the Mug̲h̲al and post-Mug̲h̲al periods are analysed in Friedmann, *Shaykh Aḥmad Sirhindī. An outline of his thought and a study of his image in the eyes of posterity*, Montreal 1971; J.G.J. ter Haar, *Follower and heir of the Prophet: Shaykh Ahmad Sirhindi (1564-1624) as a mystic*, Leiden 1992, 87-105; A.F. Buehler, *Sufi heirs of the Prophet. The Indian Nakshbandiyya and the rise of the mediatory Sufi Shaykh*, Columbia, S.C. 1998. On patronage of the Čis̲h̲tiyya under the Mug̲h̲als, see J.F. Richards, *The formation of imperial authority under Akbar and Jahangîr*, in idem (ed.), *Kingship and authority in South Asia*, Madison 1978, 252-89. The hagiography of the Ḳādiriyya in the Mug̲h̲al and post-Mug̲h̲al periods is studied by B. Lawrence, *Biography and the 17th century Qâdiriyya of North India*, in Anne L. Dallapicola and Stephanie Zingel-Ave Lallemant (eds.), *Islam and Indian regions*, Stuttgart 1993, i, 399-415.

For the veneration of saints, the traditional Islamic views, and the views of early orientalists, as well as the calendars, see Garcin de Tassy, *Mémoire sur les particularités de la religion musulmane en Inde*, in *JA* (1831), [2]Paris 1969, annotated Eng. tr., *Muslim festivals in India*, Delhi 1995; G.A. Herklots, *Islam in India or the Qânûn-i-Islam*, London 1832 (new annotated ed. W. Crooke, London 1921); on the calendars, see also C.W. Ernst, *An Indo-Persian guide to Sufi shrine pilgrimage*, in G.M. Smith and Ernst (eds.), *Manifestations of sainthood in Islam*, Istanbul 1993, 43-67.

For studies of ethnology and social history in general, see I. Ahmad, *Ritual and religion among Muslims in India*, Delhi 1981; Gaborieau, *The cult of saints among the Muslims of Nepal and Northern India*, in S. Wilson (ed.) *Saints and their cults. Studies in religious sociology, folklore and history*, Cambridge 1983, 291-308; Troll (ed.), *Muslim shrines in India. Their character, history and significance*, Delhi 1989.

Overviews of the veneration of saints in the different regions of the subcontinent are given by D. Matringe, *Pakistan*, Gaborieau and C. Champion, *Inde*, and Lyndell-Jones, *Bangladesh*, in H. Chambert-Loir and C. Guillot, (eds.), *Le culte des saints dans le monde musulman*, Paris 1995, 167-234; Gaborieau, *Pouvoirs et autorité des soufis dans l'Himalaya*, in V. Bouillier and G. Toffin (eds.), *Prêtrise, pouvoirs et autorité en Himalaya*, Paris 1989, 215-38; S. Bayly, *Saints, goddesses and kings. Muslims and Christians in South Indian society*, Cambridge 1989; J. Assayag, *Au confluent de deux rivières. Musulmans et Hindous au Sud de l'Inde*, Paris 1995; D.D. McGilvray, *Village Sufism in Sri Lanka*, in *Lettre d'information. La transmission du savoir dans la monde musulman périphérique* (Paris, EHESS), viii (1987), 1-12.

For detailed studies of the cult of the great saints, see e.g. P.M. Currie, *The shrine and cult of Muin al-din Chishti of Ajmer*, Delhi 1989; Eaton, *Court of Man, Court of God. Local perceptions of the shrine of Bâbâ Farîd, Pakpattan, Punjab*, in R.C. Martin (ed.), *Contributions to Asian Studies*, xxvii, *Islam in local contexts*, Leiden 1982, 44-61; Gaborieau, *Légende et culte du saint musulman Ghâzî Miyân au Népal occidental et en Inde du Nord*, in *Objets et Mondes*, xv/3-4 (1975), 289-318; idem, *Les saints, les eaux et les récoltes*, in M.A. Amir-Moezzi (ed.), *Lieux d'Islam, cultes et cultures de l'Afrique à Java*, Paris 1996, 239-54.

For the controversies around the cult of saints and the arguments of its opponents, see analyses in J.M.S. Baljon, *The religion and thought of Shâh Walî Allâh Dihlawî, 1703-1762*, Leiden 1986; idem, *Shah Wali Allah and the Dargah*, in Troll (ed.), *Muslim shrines in India*, 189-97; Gaborieau, *A nineteenth century Indian "Wahhabi" tract against the cult of Muslim saints*: al-Balāgh al-mubīn, in Troll, *op. cit.*, 198-239; idem, *Le culte des saints musulmans en tant que rituel: controversies juridiques*, in *Archives de sciences sociales des religions*, lxxxv (Jan.-March 1994), 85-97; idem, *Criticising the abuses of the Sufis: the debate in early nineteenth-century India*, in F. de Jong and B. Radtke (eds.), *Islamic mysticism contested. Thirteen centuries of controversies and polemics*, Leiden 1999. The position of the Deobandis and the Ahl-i Ḥadīth̲ is presented in B.D. Metcalf, *Islamic revival in British India. Deoband, 1860-1900*, Princeton 1982. The reaffirmation of the mediaeval doctrine by the Barelwīs is analysed in U. Sanyal, *Devotional Islam and politics in British India. Ahmad Riza Khan Barelwi and his movement, 1870-1920*, Delhi 1996, 96-165. On Mawdūdī and the saints, see S.V.R. Nasr, *Mawdūdī and the making of Islamic revivalism*, New York 1996, 122-5.

(M. Gaborieau)

7. In Southeast Asia and Indonesia.

Veneration of saints has been well established in the classical Malay and Javanese worlds of Southeast Asia since at least the 15th century. Nine legendary figures, the famous *wali sanga* ("nine saints"), are thought to have planted Islam in Java and successfully displaced the old Hindu-Javanese political and socio-religious order in the northern coastal areas. With the exception of Mawlānā Mālik Ibrāhīm, who early went to Java as a missionary from abroad and is buried in Gresik (an elaborate Gud̲j̲arātī tombstone from 822/1419 marks his grave), the saints were accorded the Javanese title *sunan* ("eminence") and most were closely associated with particular places in Central and East Java: Sunan Ampel with Surabaya, Sunan Giri with Gresik, Sunan Kalijaga with Demak, Sunan Kudus (also known as D̲j̲aʿfar al-Ṣādiḳ) with Kudus, Sunan Gunung Jati with Ceribon, Sunan Bonang with Tuban, Sunan Drajat with Demak, and Sunan Muria (a son of Sunan Kalijaga) with Pati. Sunan Kalijaga is usually considered to be the greatest of the *wali sanga*. Additional personages are also sometimes grouped with the *wali sanga*, giving rise to modern scholarly speculation that the number nine was more a symbolic than arithmetical concept. As G.W.J. Drewes suggested: "In Hindu-Javanese cosmological mythology, nine was a very important number, and it is possible that the nine saints occupy the places of the nine guardian deities who presided over the points of the compass in the old cosmological system" (*Indonesia: mysticism and activism*, in *Unity and variety in Muslim civilization*, ed. G.E. von Grunebaum, Chicago 1955, 297). Nevertheless, the listing of nine named saints continues to be widely maintained.

Although most of the sources about the *wali sanga* are hagiographical and sometimes conflicting, certain of the saints appear to have been significant religio-political leaders in their times, and they continue to enjoy a prestigious position in Javanese Muslim consciousness to the present. They may be understood to represent, among other things, the essentially harmonious and gradual transition into an increasingly Islamic worldview as the religion gradually spread inland from the coastal regions. Such cultural legacies as the shadow play, the gamelan orchestra, and the magically potent keris (wavy, double-edged dagger) are attributed to Muslim saints. Many saints since the *wali sanga* are known in Indonesia, and their cults have been extensively described in a series of articles by D.A. Rinkes in his *De heiligen van Java*, in *Tijdschrift voor indische Taal-, Land- en Volkenkunde*, lii-liii (1910-11). Annual saint festivals (*mawālīd*) in honor of the *wali sanga* and other saints are celebrated, with parades, banners, special foods, circumcisions and litanies in the graveyards, all resembling similar festivals in saint-rich countries like Egypt. People make pilgrimages [see ZIYĀRA] to Javanese saint shrines, both at the time of the *mawlid* and throughout the year. (A nuanced treatment of traditional, syncretistic Javanese—*agami jawi*—and orthodox Islamic—*agami santri*—saint-related beliefs and practices appears in Koentjaraningrat, *Javanese culture*, Singapore 1985, ch. 5.)

Not all Javanese have admired the Muslim saint tradition of their island. A controversial genre of literature developed during the later 19th century emphasising the incompatibility of Islam with traditional Javanese ideals and values. One book, the *Serat Dermagandal*, recounts the history of the last period of the Madjapahit dynasty and depicts such *walīs* as Sunan Bonang, Sunan Giri, and Sunan Kalijaga and their roles unfavourably. The book is summarised by G.W.J. Drewes, *The struggle between Javanism and Islam as illustrated by the* Sĕrat Dĕrmagandul, in *Bijdragen tot de Taal-, Land- en Volkenkunde*, cxxii (1966), 309-65.

The process of Islamisation in Java included a fair amount of accommodation with Javanese traditional religious and cultural values and symbols. It is possible that the Ḳurʾān was introduced in the interior to some degree by means of traditional Javanese song and in translation. The shrine complex of Sunan Giri in Gresik, East Java, near Surabaya, features a Madjapahit-style stone split gate with large sculpted *nagas* (Hindu serpent guardian spirits) at the entrance to the cemetery. There are also elaborately carved wooden *nagas* on either side of the entry to the *walīs* wooden tomb chamber, which is decorated with carved lotus figures. The tomb is devoid of the kinds of Arabic calligraphic designs that typically decorate saints' graves in the Middle East and South Asia. The layout of the shrine complex on a hilltop overlooking the town has a Friday mosque occupying the eastern part, with a cemetery lot beyond the *ḳibla* wall to the west (the direction of Mecca is somewhat northwest of Surabaya). Further west are several substantial tombs of venerated personages, with that of Sunan Giri occupying a pre-eminent position. The layout resembles a congregation, with the living ranged at the back of the mosque building and then the tombs of the deceased, but "living" saintly members in a higher status arrangement toward the "front", with the great saint serving, as it were, as *imām* for the prayers. A similar arrangement may be seen at the shrine complex of Sunan Kudus in the small city of that name. The *minbar* of the Sunan Giri mosque is low, with a canopy, and more than a traditional Middle Eastern *minbar*, the design resembles a traditional seat for a Hindu god. The mosque (whose actual name is *Masdjid ʿAyn al-Yaḳīn*, from another name of the *walī*) is of the early Javanese type with a three-tiered roof popularly known as the "Meru" style, after the Buddhist cosmic mountain. All of these syncretistic details designed into monumental Islamic structures bear witness to a blending of Hindu-Javanese and Islamic ideas and symbols during the period when Islamisation was taking root among the Javanese society at large, including the royalty, and not merely in the coastal market towns and ports.

Although this article has focused on sainthood in Java, the phenomenon is also found in various manifestations in the traditional Malay world. C. Snouck Hurgronje wrote of the saint veneration of a century ago in Aceh as relating principally to the fulfilment of vows by persons who visit shrines seeking favours such as healing (*The Achehnese*, Leiden 1906, ii, 292-303). Such practices were often of a popular folk character and not within the boundaries of orthodox Islam. They included bestowing gifts of food and flowers, processions with a small orchestra (*geundrang*) of a woodwind instrument and percussion, and dramatic performances, as well as recitation of the Ḳurʾān or other religious texts. In Aceh the Malay title *tuan* ("master") rather than the Ar. *walī* has been preferred (*ibid.*).

Ṣūfism has also influenced the understanding of sainthood in Southeast Asia, for example through the concept of the "Perfect Man" (*al-insān al-kāmil* [*q.v.*]) as applied to early Muslim rulers in the Straits trading-centres of Pasai and Melaka. Evidence that the concept had currency in the latter place is contained, e.g. in the 16th/17th century *Malay annals* (*Sĕjarah Mĕlayu*; see A.C. Milner, *Islam and Malay kingship*, in *JRAS*, ser. 3, i [1981], 55).

Bibliography (in addition to references given in the article): Solichin Salam, *Sekitar wali sanga* ("About the Wali Sanga"), Kudus 1960 (a popular handbook); C. Geertz, *Islam observed: religious development in Morocco and Indonesia*, New Haven 1968 (features a highly perceptive analysis of Sunan Kalijaga); M.R. Woodward, *Islam in Java: normative piety and mysticism in the sultanate of Yogyakarta*, Tucson 1989 (integrated coverage of saints, Ṣūfīs and royalty).

(F.M. DENNY)

8. In Chinese Islam.

The term *walī* does not seem to have existed in traditional Chinese Islam, whether in the form of transliteration of the Arabic into Chinese characters with a phonetic rendering distantly identical, or in translation. Moreover, when this topic is raised before a Chinese Muslim, a "Hui" in Communist China, from the milieu of strict observance, he will indignantly repudiate it as an invention of the West brought forward to harm Islam; or at most, as a Sunnī of the Ḥanafī school, he will consider it as belonging to S͟hīʿism. Nevertheless, the cult of dead saints, and to a lesser extent living ones, exists in Chinese Sunnī Islam, having strongly developed within the 19th century and the first decades of the 20th.

(i) The sacred tomb, a place of pilgrimage on a greater or lesser scale, is called in Chinese Islam *kungpei* (*gongbei* in pinyin, a term transliterated from Pers. *gunbad* = Ar. *ḳubba* [*q.v.*]). In Western China, where Muslim communities are most concentrated and the cult of tombs is at its most active, the sacred tomb generally appears as a hexagonal pavilion made of mud bricks surmounted by a dome and with an entablature curving upwards at the corners, thus giving a Chinese appearance. In the centre of Ninghsia (Ningxia, the "Autonomous Hui Region" of the PRC) [see NINGSIA], the sacred tomb has the unusual form of a lime-washed sugarloaf, in front of which is a portal lined with bricks and a hood decorated with Chinese motifs and Ḳurʾānic sūras within medallions. Inside these various structures, the tomb is roughly finished, in lime mortar, with no ornamentation, but is sometimes covered with a silken covering when the local faithful have the means for supplying this. In front of the tomb are a prayer mat, a water pot for ablutions, and—a typical Chinese custom—sticks of incense stuck into a vessel full of sand. The *kung-pei*, rebuilt or newly-built in large numbers since the religious liberalism of the 1980s, are now crowned with a crescent moon and follow a Pakistani-Middle Eastern architectural style. But this was not the case in pre-Communist times, when the faithful strove not to appear distinct from their cultural environment. In Western China, outside the brotherhoods, there is often to be found, on the edge of fields or in the heart of a Muslim cemetery, one of these tombs, whose dedicatee, often a mythical Muslim hero, has the role of being the ancestor of the local community, which pays homage to him through prayer, incense and food offerings. It does not seem that there is any adaptation of previously-existing non-Muslim cults.

(ii) The prominence of spiritual leaders is characteristic of the ensemble of popular Ṣūfism in those parts of Western China where the brotherhoods have a significant role. The *ṭuruḳ* burst forth into numerous religious, social, economic and even political small units, the *men-huan* [see TAṢAWWUF. 6. In Chinese Islam], whose pivot is, for each of them, the *kung-pei* of the founder of the line, surrounded by the *kung-pei*s of his male and female relatives. The required cult of ancestors has contributed in China, without doubt more than the influence of practices from Central Asia, to the legitimisation of hereditary transmission of the direction of the *men-huan* and to the investiture of the supreme charisma inherent in the tomb of the dead "Head of the Way" (*tao-chang* or *daozhang*, also called "Master of the Faith" *chiao-chu* or *jiaozhu*, i.e. *s̲h̲ayk̲h̲*). For the adept of the *men-huan*, the first of his obligations is to make a pilgrimage once in his life to the "Hall of the Way" (*tao-t'ang* or *daotang*, centre of the Master's *k̲h̲ānaḳāh* [*q.v.*]) and to pay homage to him by the great prostration (the *k'ou-t'ou*, whence the Western European word "kowtow"), without worrying about orientation towards Mecca, and by the offering of a "present" (*hai-ti-yeh*, i.e. *hadiyya*) of a value proportionate to his own income.

The usual ritual at these pilgrimages and the frequent mass ceremonies on the occasion of the "anniversaries" (*erh-mai-li*, i.e. *al-mawlid*) of the dead members of the sacred line, comprised the chanted recitation of the *d̲h̲ikr*, the reading of sacred texts appropriate to the *men-huan*, fumigations with incense, offerings of fruit, the presenting of "gifts" to the Master, the latter's blessing and the offering by him of a gift of a monetary value inversely proportionate to the one which he received. If the Master was an ascetic, the system of presents and presents in return functioned like a redistribution of wealth amongst the adepts; in the opposite case, it was a heavy tribute destined for the Master's treasury and that of his relatives. The Master was considered by his faithful as at least the equal of Muḥammad, if not his superior, since he had the advantage of being alive and visible. The faithful would often go so far as to say that they preferred to make a pilgrimage to a living saint rather than to a dead one, and that it was better to be wrong in the presence of the living saint than to be right against the latter's will.

(iii) An extensive religious structure in the Chinese style grew up, at least before the destructions of the Cultural Revolution, around the sacred *kung-pei* enabling the Master of the time to exercise his charisma. Thus the "Great *Kung-pei*", on a site founded in 1689 by the one who introduced the Ḳādiriyya into China, Ch'i Ching-i (1656-1719) at He-chou (the modern Lin-hsia, in the extreme west, on the borders of Kansu and Ch'inghai), extended, as it does until the present time, over *ca.* 2,700 ha, with a mosque, a Ḳur'ān school, a secular school, the administrative services of the *men-huan*, lodgings for the resident religious members and for visitors, a cemetery and, behind a low wall, the sacred mausoleum.

The importance of the sacred bodies, or at least one of their heads, in the transmission of charisma has resulted in the fact that *men-huan*s of identical *silsila* have stolen these bodies or heads from each other at the time when their power became consolidated, i.e. in the last decades of the 19th century up to the 1930s. Thus one of the *men-huan*s arising out of the D̲j̲ahriyya (a Chinese branch of the Naḳs̲h̲bandiyya), in the so-called Ling-chou line, the *men-huan* of Pan-ch'iao, held on to the headless corpse of the executed Fifth Master Ma Hua-lung (1810-71 [*q.v.*]), whilst the head was the property of the *men-huan* of Pei-shan, from the same line, at Ch'ang-chia-ch'uan (in Kansu), which further held the body of Ma Yüan-chang (1853-1920), although this last was venerated by the opposing line, of Kuan-ch'uan, which attached itself hereditarily to the D̲j̲ahriyya's founder, Ma Ming-hsin (1719-81 [*q.v.*]). Similarly, the *men-huan* of Sha-kou, at Hsi-chi (in Ninghsia), of this line of Kuan-ch'uan, after 1920 spread its domination over a mausoleum of Ma Yüan-chang, in which there was no corpse, and over the Hall of the Way of this last, as well as, by stretching its antennae over various points in Greater China, notably in Sinkiang, over the tombs of male and female ancestors of Ma Yüan-chang.

The cult of dead saints has had a revival in the 1980s in the PRC (not much is known about living saints), since, in the words of one of the faithful, addressing a saint in the hope of having one's request granted by God is like making use of the "back door" (*hou-men*), i.e. using relatives who are well placed in the Communist world in order to gain a favour.

Bibliography (in addition to references given in TAṢAWWUF. 6): J. Trippner, *Islamische Gruppen und Gräberkult in Nordwest-China*, in *WI*, N.S., vii (1961), 142-71; D. Gladney, *Muslim tombs and ethnic folklore. Charters for Hui identity*, in *Jnal. of Asian Studies*, xlvi/3 (1987), 495-517; Su Baogui (Su Pao-kuei) and Sun Junping (Sun Chün-p'ing), *Chung-kuo I-ssu-lan-chiao Che-he-jen-yeh kung-pei kai-shu*, in *Shih-chiai tsung-chiao yen-chiu*, 1993, no. 3, 112-20; F. Aubin, *Chine*, in H. Chambert-Loir and C. Guillot (eds.), *Le culte des saints dans le monde musulman*, Paris 1995, 367-88.

(FRANÇOISE AUBIN)

9. In West Africa.

While the term *walī* (and the feminine *waliyya*) is frequently applied as an epithet of holy or saintly persons in the Islamic literature of West Africa, there is little development of any "cult of saints", and tombs, although sometimes known, are generally very modest. Persons described as *walī* are generally distinguished by their being the locus of manifestations of divine grace (*karāmāt*) in the form either of thaumaturgical acts, or, more simply, by acts demonstrating extreme piety. The *Ta'rīk̲h̲ al-Sūdān* of al-Sa'dī gives brief biographies of several such persons, though none of these is among the dozen saints buried around the edges of the old city of Timbuktu who are currently considered to be the chief among its 333 guarding saints. Muḥammad al-Kābarī (mid-9th/15th century) was able to inflict leprosy on a scholar of Marrakesh who insulted him; he could also walk on water. The North African *walī* Sīdī Yaḥyā al-Tadallisī (who was also a *s̲h̲arīf*) was his contemporary and is categorised as a *ḳuṭb*. When he came to Timbuktu he used to see the Prophet nightly, but later when he engaged in business to avoid being dependent on other people, he saw him only once a week, then once a month and finally once a year. As a *sharīf*, he was not only immune to fire, but whatever he touched became similarly immune. He was reputed to be clairvoyant (*dhū mukāshafāt*), as were several others. Muḥammad ʿUryān al-raʾs (*fl.* 1009/1600), not only met with al-Khaḍir [*q.v.*], but when he exhibited signs of madness it was explained that this resulted from a vision of God. Others could relocate themselves daily to Cairo to pray in al-Azhar mosque, while the Egyptian saint Abu 'l-Makārim al-Bakrī (d. 994/1586), who had met several Timbuktu scholars when they passed through Egypt, made daily visits to Timbuktu. The only one of these saints now celebrated in any sense is Sīdī Yaḥyā al-Tadallisī, in whose name a mosque was built, and whose tomb is within the mosque enclosure. Some of the currently-existing saints' tombs in Timbuktu have keepers who receive cash offerings from the faithful who supplicate the saint, but there are no organised celebratory festivals.

The same is true for Kano. In 1406/1985 Ṣāliḥ Bābah b. Abī Bakr published in Kano a booklet entitled *Tabshīr ahl Allāh bi-dhikr man bi-Kānū min awliyāʾ Allāh*, giving brief biographies of saintly men and women buried in the city and locations of their tombs. A few of these have regular guardians, but again there is little ceremony about visitation and no large parades or gatherings. However, ʿAbd al-Ḳādir al-Djīlānī's *mawlid* was celebrated in public fashion with parades in the city and beating of *bandiri* drums during the latter part of the lifetime of Nasiru Kabara (d. 1996), the leading Ḳādirī *shaykh* of West Africa.

Only in Senegal is there the kind of annual festival and visitation that is common in Egypt and North Africa, with large boisterous crowds and a carnival atmosphere. This is the *maggal* at Touba, the burial place of the "national" saint of Senegal, Aḥmad Bamba (d. 1927 [see MURĪDIYYA]). The followers of Aḥmad Bamba, who was exiled by the French to Gabon, have developed a rich hagiography of him. The most common iconographic reminder of his miraculous powers is the picture of the saint praying upon his prayer rug cast upon the waters when the French captain of his ship to Gabon forbade him to pray on board the vessel. Angels hover above and the ship's crew looks on in disbelief. Another religious figure exiled by the French, Ḥamā Allāh (correctly Ḥamāhu 'llāh) of Nioro in Mali (d. 1943 [see ḤAMĀLIYYA]) also gained the status of *walī*; indeed, his followers saw him as the *ḳuṭb*, and in poems in praise of him proposed a status for him that was scarcely distinguishable from the divine (B. Soares and J. Hunwick, *Falkeina IV: the shaykh as the locus of divine self-disclosure: a poem in praise of Ḥamāhu 'llāh*, in *Sudanic Africa*, vii [1996], 97-112). His son Muḥammad still lives in Nioro and is the object of pious visitation and gift-giving by Muslims from a broad spectrum of Malian society. Ḥamāhu 'llāh died in exile in France, but his most devoted followers fervently believe that he did not die, and they await his return.

There were other West African saints who are said to have attained similarly exalted mystical ranks. ʿAbd Allāh al-Barnāwī (d. 1088/1677), whose mystical initiator was the angel Isrāfīl, guardian of *al-lawḥ al-maḥfūẓ* [see LAWḤ], was regarded in Bornū as a *ḳuṭb*. Another Bornū *walī* of similar name who died in 1126/1714-15, was an intimate of the well-known Moroccan saint ʿAbd al-ʿAzīz al-Dabbāgh (Aḥmad al-Mubārak al-Lamaṭī, *K. al-Ibrīz*, Cairo 1380/1961, 14). In the early 13th/19th century Muḥammad Sambo, a son of the reformer ʿUthmān b. Fūdī [*q.v.*], attained "a high rank in *walāya*, and a firm stance in divine knowledge (*maʿrifa*), and a true state in *ṣiddīqiyya*" (J.O. Hunwick, *A supplement to Infāq al-maysūr: the biographical notes of ʿAbd al-Qādir b. al-Mustafā*, in *Sudanic Africa*, vii [1996], 35-51), this latter being the station just below *ḳurba*, which is the station of *al-walāya al-kubrā* (on this see M. Chodkiewicz, *Seal of the saints: prophethood and sainthood in the doctrine of Ibn ʿArabī*, Cambridge 1993, ch. 7). According to his biographer ʿAbd al-Ḳādir b. al-Muṣṭafā "he had seen the land of the *samāsima* (*sic*) and had entered it" (*ibid.*, 15 and appendix), the *arḍ al-simsima* being "the land at the extremity of the imaginal world at the point where it adjoins the sensory world" (H. Corbin, *Terre céleste et corps de résurrection*, Paris 1961, 214).

There is not a large theoretical literature on the concept of the *walī* in West Africa. The most extensive treatment of questions relating to the *walī* is to be found in the important Tidjānī manual of *al-ḥādjdj* ʿUmar b. Saʿīd (d. 1280/1864), the *Rimāḥ ḥizb al-raḥīm* (see B. Radtke, *Studies on the sources of Kitāb Rimāḥ ḥizb al-raḥīm of al-ḥājj ʿUmar*, in *Sudanic Africa*, vi [1995], 73-114). These elaborate older concepts; the illuminated *walī* is not bound by the *madhāhib*: pledging allegiance to a perfected *walī* is like pledging allegiance to the Prophet; the Prophet is omnipresent and the *walī* has the ability to see him in a waking state. Ch. 36 deals with the seemingly innovatory claim of Aḥmad al-Tidjānī to be the "seal of the Friends of God.... and the support of the poles and the nurturers (*khātim al-awliyāʾ wa-mumidd al-aḳṭāb wa 'l-aghwāth*)", and the "ultimate link (*al-barzakh al-makhtūm*) who is the intermediary between the Prophet and the Friends of God such that none of the Friends, either of greater or lesser rank, finds an effusion [of grace] from the plane (*ḥadra*) of a prophet except through his mediation". However, the claim to be the "seal of the Friends of God" was first made by Ibn al-ʿArabī, and despite the seemingly final nature of such a phrase in its parallelism with the phrase "seal of the prophets" (*khātam al-nabiyyīn*) as applied to the Prophet Muḥammad, Chodkiewicz suggests that the term may have come to represent a rank rather than an ultimate claim (*op. cit.*, 128 ff., esp. n. 42). Whether Aḥmad al-Tidjānī saw it in this light is doubtful, in light of his claim to be the sole source of mediation of an effusion of divine grace (*fayḍa*) from the plane of a prophet; indeed, al-Tidjānī actually claims that Ibn al-ʿArabī gave up his claim to this rank in favour of him.

Bibliography (in addition to references given in the article): ʿAbd al-Raḥmān al-Saʿdī, *Taʾrīkh al-Sūdān*, ed. and tr. O. Houdas, Paris 1898-1900; H. Miner, *The primitive city of Timbuctoo*, New York 1965; Amar Samb, *Le maggal de Touba*, Dakar 1974; J.-L. Triaud, *Khalwa and the career of sainthood: an interpretive essay*, in D.B. Cruise O'Brien and C. Coulon (eds.), *Charisma and brotherhood in African Islam*, Oxford 1988, 53-66; Hamidu Bobboyi, *The ʿulamāʾ of Borno: a study of the relations between scholars and the state under the Sayfawa, 1470-1808*, Ph.D. diss., Northwestern University 1992, unpubl.; Priscilla Starratt, *Islamic influences on oral traditions in Hausa literature*, in K.W. Harrow (ed.), *The marabout and the muse*, London 1996, 159-75; G.W. McLaughlin, *Sufi, saint, sharīf. Muhammad Fāḍil wuld Māmīn: his spiritual legacy, and the political economy of the sacred in nineteenth century Mauritania*, Ph.D. diss., Northwestern University

1997, unpubl.; B.F. Soares, *The spiritual economy of Nioro du Sahel. Islamic discourses and practices in a Malian religious center*, Ph.D. diss., Northwestern University 1997, unpubl. (J.O. Hunwick)

10. In Chad and the Nilotic Sudan.

In the eastern Bilād al-Sūdān, the term *walī* overlaps in usage with *faḳīr, faḳīh*, colloq. *fakī* (which often share the pl. *fuḳarā'*), *shaykh* (pl. *mashāyikh*), *rādjil* (used in compound phrases with a place-name, e.g. *rādjil* Rayba), *mu'allim, mallam* (Hausa), and *goni* (Kanuri, strictly one who has memorised the Ḳur'ān), names which variously reflect the *walī*'s spiritual qualities and station, and social status and roles.

Awliyā' are prominent figures from the beginnings of recorded or remembered Islamic history in the region—remembered and celebrated as propagators of Islam, promoters of the *Sharī'a*, founders of lineages, clans, settlements, schools, even of dynasties. The earliest personalities are associated with (1) the flow of Islamic influences into the western end of the region along an axis extending from Tripoli southwards to Lake Chad by way of Fezzan, Tibesti and Kanem, and into the Nile valley at its eastern end from Egypt to the north and the Arabian peninsula across the Red Sea to the east; and (2) the rise of Muslim-ruled dynasties in Kanem, Sinnar, Dārfūr, Wadai, Bagirmi, Taqali and other states—dynasties that offered the holy men patronage and security in return for spiritual support, political legitimation and practical services (e.g. as scribes). Among the earliest of the *awliyā'* venerated in oral tradition and recorded in charters of immunity, genealogical treatises and biographical literature (*manāḳib*; see below) are Muḥammad b. Mānī (5th/11th century), who is associated with the conversion to Islam of the ruler of Kanem, and Ghulām Allāh b. 'Ā'id, a Yemeni who migrated to the Dongola area of Nubia and "built the mosques and taught the Ḳur'ān and religious sciences" for a people sunk in "extreme perplexity and error" (Yūsuf Faḍl Ḥasan, *The Arabs and the Sudan*, Khartoum 1973). Traditions represent the founders of kingdoms across the eastern Bilād al-Sūdān as Muslim "wise strangers", and some clearly resemble the pious charismatic figure of the *walī*, e.g. 'Abd Allāh Djammā' of the 'Abdallāb and 'Abd al-Karīm, founder of the Maba dynasty in Wadai.

The *walī*'s nearness to God endowed him (or occasionally, her) with divine blessing or grace (*baraka*), which manifested itself in extraordinary acts and capacities (*karāmāt*). The recounting of these *karāmāt* is an important genre of sacred literature and folklore, and, in the Nilotic Sudan, has been incorporated into works of *manāḳib* such as Muḥammad al-Nūr b. Ḍayf Allāh, *K. al-Ṭabaḳāt fī khuṣūṣ al-awliyā' wa 'l-ṣāliḥīn wa 'l-'ulamā' wa 'l-shu'arā' fī 'l-Sūdān*, ed. Y.F. Ḥasan, ²Khartoum 1974; Aḥmad b. Aḥmad al-Rubāṭābī, *al-Ibānat al-nūriyya fī sha'n ṣāḥib al-ṭarīḳa al-Khatmiyya*, ed. Muḥammad Ibrāhīm Abū Salīm, Beirut 1991; and 'Abd al-Maḥmūd Nūr al-Dā'im, *Azāhīr al-riyāḍ fī manāḳib al-shaykh Aḥmad al-Ṭayyib b. al-Bashīr*, Cairo 1973. The *walī* was known for the efficacy of his prayer, e.g. for rain, health and fertility, and of his curse upon the oppressor and the violator of pledges. He was distinguished by his faculty of "uncovering" the unknown (*kashf*), i.e. perceiving thoughts, distant places, the past, and the future. He personified detachment, abstinence, probity on the one hand and open-handed hospitality and generosity on the other. These attributes and capabilities fitted the *walī* to mediate in conflicts and feuds, to intercede for his followers and to provide sanctuary for the fugitive. Prominent among his regular activities were the preparation of amulets (*ḥidjāb*) and erasures (*miḥāya*, sc. verses that are washed off the writing-board and drunk by the patient), the teaching and initiation of disciples, and prolonged withdrawal into solitary meditation (*khalwa*).

The social life of the *fuḳarā'* centred on the mosque, the school and the tombs of sanctified forbears. Their instruction frequently combined Ṣūfī *dhikr* with Ḳur'ānic study, jurisprudence (following the Mālikī school), and theology (Abū 'Abd Allāh al-Sanūsī's works were popular). Significantly, the word *khalwa* (= Ṣūfī retreat, place of seclusion for prayer) is widely used in the region for Ḳur'ānic school. A substantial proportion of settlements were founded by holy men. The right of sanctuary held by the *walī*, the exemptions from taxation and other impositions by secular authorities (though the *fuḳarā'* themselves collected canonical taxes) attracted settlers and sometimes contributed to the rise of flourishing market towns. With the steady inflow of visitors and offerings, these communities became nodes of redistributive networks. There has long been a tendency for families of noted *awliyā'* to divide into "religious" and "secular" branches, with the latter handling their growing assets.

Research in recent decades has confirmed the existence, at least as early as the 17th century, of a vast network of *awliyā'*, their centres of religious instruction and devotional practice, spanning the Bilād al-Sūdān (see J. Lavers, *Diversions on a journey, or the travels of Shaykh Ahmed al-Yamani (1630-1712) from Halfaya to Fez*, in Y.F. Ḥasan and P. Doornbos (eds.), *The Central Bilād al-Sūdān. Tradition and adaptation*, Khartoum n.d. [1979]). Some holy men accompanied a diaspora of Nubian traders from the Nile (known collectively as *djallāba*) extending westward to Dārfūr and Wadai, and others a countervailing stream of Hausa merchants, Fulbe and Bornawi migrants, and pilgrims originating in the western Bilād al-Sūdān. Eastern and western influences have their counterpart in the distribution of types of Arabic script: *Maghribī* is used in Kanem and Bagirmi, *Naskhī* in Wadai and Dārfūr. Only in the Nile region did the Arabian and Egyptian style of domed tomb (*ḳubba* [*q.v.*]) become firmly implanted, during the era of Fundj rule (16th-19th centuries). School of regional importance up to the 19th century were located at Bidderi (Bagirmi), al-Dāmir (at the Nile-Atbara confluence), Arbadjī (on the Blue Nile), and Kubayh (Dārfūr). Itinerant students (*muhādjirūn*), pilgrims, traders, and *shurafā'* circulated among the schools and shrines scattered throughout the region and continually renewed linkages with the Ḥidjāz, Yemen, Egypt and the Maghrib.

The Ḳādiriyya [*q.v.*] brotherhood was pervasive and unchallenged throughout the region (except for a minor presence of Shādhiliyya [*q.v.*] along the Nile) until the 18th century when the Sammāniyya (a branch of the Khalwatiyya [see MĪRGHANIYYA]) was established in the Gezira by Aḥmad al-Ṭayyib b. al-Bashīr. The 19th century witnessed the advent of several new fraternities, notably the Khatmiyya from the Ḥidjāz, the Tidjāniyya [*q.v.*] from the Maghrib by way of Borno and Hausaland, and the Sanūsiyya [*q.v.*] from Cyrenaica. The independence, individuality, and idiosyncrasies of the *walī* were somewhat constrained within these more centralised, hierarchical and regulated brotherhoods.

During the 19th and 20th centuries, imperialism (Egyptian, British and French), social upheaval and millenarianism presented new challenges, roles and opportunities for the *awliyā'*. A number of holy men entered the arena of politics—most successfully,

Muḥammad al-Amīn al-Kānimī, who founded the Shehu dynasty of Bornu subsequent to a challenge from the Fulbe *mudjāhidūn* of the Sokoto Caliphate, and Muḥammad Aḥmad, the Mahdī, whose defeat of the Egyptian colonial government inaugurated a short-lived independent state. The subsequent Anglo-Egyptian and French colonial systems, imposed over the former Egyptian Sudan and Chad respectively, perpetuated old patterns of patronage and subsidy to control and propitiate the Ṣūfī leadership. The *ṭuruḳ* have proliferated in the 20th century, while the authority and religious culture of the *walī* has come under increasing challenge from Islamist movements in the decades since national independence.

Bibliography (in addition to references given in the text): An important biographic/bibliographic reference is J.O. Hunwick and R.S. O'Fahey (eds.), *Arabic literature of Africa*, i, *The writings of Eastern Sudanic Africa to c. 1900*, compiled by O'Fahey, Leiden 1994, ii, *The writings of Central Sudanic Africa*, compiled by Hunwick, Leiden 1995: ch. 10, "Bornu, Wadai and Adamawa" by Hamidu Bobboyi and Hunwick.

For the growing corpus of documentation relating to land grants and exemptions, see Sir Richard Palmer, *The Bornu Sahara and Sudan*, London 1936; Hamidu Bobboyi, *The Ulama of Borno. A study of the relations between scholars and the state under the Sayfawa, 1470-1808*, Ph.D. diss., Northwestern Univ. 1992; J.L. Spaulding and Muḥammad Ibrāhīm Abū Salīm (eds.), *Public documents from Sinnār*, East Lansing 1989; O'Fahey and Abū Salīm, *Land in Dār Fūr*, Cambridge 1983.

For Wadai, see Issa H. Khayar, *Tchad. Regards sur les élites ouadaïennes*, Paris 1984; Mahamat Adoum Doutoum, *L'Islam au Ouaddaï avant et après la colonisation*, in J.-P. Magnant (ed.), *L'Islam au Tchad*, Bordeaux 1992. For Dārfūr, see the works of O'Fahey, including *Saints and sultans. The role of Muslim holy men in the Keira Sultanate*, in M. Brett (ed.), *Northern Africa. Islam and modernization*, London 1973; Abdullahi Osman El Tom, *Religious men and literacy in Berti society*, Ph.D. diss., Univ. of St. Andrews 1983, and several articles. For the Nile valley: P.M. Holt, *The sons of Jābir and their kin*, in *BSOAS*, xxx (1967), 142-57; Ḥasan Muḥammad al-Fātiḥ Ḳarīb Allāh, *al-Taṣawwuf fi 'l-Sūdān ilā nihāya ʿaṣr Fundj*, Khartoum 1987; Spaulding, *The heroic age in Sinnar*, East Lansing 1985; N. McHugh, *Holymen of the Blue Nile*, Evanston 1994. For Chad as a whole, see Le Gouverneur Beyries, *L'Islam au Tchad*, CHEAM mémoire no. 2934, Paris 1957.

A number of studies focus on Ṣūfī *ṭuruḳ*: ʿAlī Ṣāliḥ Karrār, *The Sufi brotherhoods in the Sudan*, London 1992; J.O. Voll, *A history of the Khatmiyyah tariqah in the Sudan*, Ph.D. diss., Harvard Univ. 1969; Kamāl Bābikir ʿAbd al-Raḥmān, *al-Ṭarīḳa al-Sammāniyya fi 'l-Sūdān*, B.A. honours thesis, Univ. of Khartoum 1976; ʿAwaḍ al-Sīd al-Karsanī, *The Tijaniyya order in the Western Sudan [Republic]*, Ph.D. diss., Univ. of Khartoum 1985; K.S. Vikør, *Sufi and scholar on the desert edge. Muḥammad b. ʿAlī al-Sanūsī and his brotherhood*, London 1995; A. Hofheinz, *Internalising Islam. Shaykh Muḥammad Majdhūb, scriptural Islam and local context in early nineteenth-century Sudan*, Ph.D. diss., Univ. of Bergen 1996.

The study of a prominent family of *awliyā'* in the context of the political economy of the Republic of Sudan is Idrīs Sālim al-Ḥasan, *Religion in society. Nemeiri and the Turuq, 1972-1980*, Khartoum 1993. (N. McHugh)

WALĪ, Urdu poet whose pivotal significance from the viewpoint of literary history is tellingly unsupported by much reliable biographical data. Even his name is uncertain, although the best evidence suggests "Walī Muḥammad". The popular sobriquet "Walī Dakanī" indicates the general belief that he was born in the Dakan at Awrangābād, probably in 1079/1668. At the age of twenty he moved to Aḥmadābād, where he studied at the *madrasa* attached to the shrine of the Ḳādirī saint Wadjīh al-Dīn. A number of Walī's poems attest his close association with Gudjarāt, including a short *mathnawī* in praise of Sūrat. He died in Aḥmadābād, probably in 1119/1707 (rather than the now discredited suggestion of 1175/1742, although Djālibī, 537-9, argues for the early 1720s).

The later *tadhkira* writers make much of Walī's supposed meeting during a visit to Dihlī in 1112/1700 with the Naḳshbandī saint and Persian poet Shāh Saʿd Allāh Gulshan (d. 1141/1728), who advised him to write in the Urdu [*q.v.*] of Dihlī rather than the Dakhinī Urdu in which he had hitherto composed, and for the embellishment of his poetry to draw upon the full resources of Persian. Polished in the light of Gulshan's recommendations, it is said, Walī's poetry rapidly achieved a universal popularity which greatly aided the replacement of Persian by Urdu as the preferred poetic language of the courts of Dihlī and northern India. However suspect its convenient underpinning of Dihlī's cultural supremacy may be as history, the endurance of the Walī-Gulshan story as myth was ensured when Muḥammad Ḥusayn Āzād used it to initiate his immensely influential account of Urdu literature. It is this passage (*Āb-i ḥayāt*, 80), whose rhetoric neatly eliminates the entire Dakhinī phase of Urdu poetry, which generated the two clichés most commonly applied to Walī, either as the Ādam of Urdu poetry (*naẓm-i Urdū kī nasl kā Ādam*), or as its Chaucer.

Many later critics have noted the difficulty of detecting radical changes of language and aesthetic justifying any notion of consistent pre- and post-Dihlī phases in Walī's extensive *dīwān* of some four hundred *ghazals*. This is not to deny the relevance to the characterisation of Walī's poetry as transitional between older Dakhinī and later northern norms of the internal stylistic contrasts which may be partially established by suitable isolated examples (e.g. Sadiq, *History*, 64). The *dīwān* is, however, less remarkable for any internal diversity than for the general uniformity of its emphasis upon distinctly human amatory themes, often delightfully treated. While Walī's name has predictably caused the mistaken attribution to him of Ṣūfī and other religious works, little conviction attaches to attempts at mystical readings of his *dīwān* beyond the conventions of *taṣawwuf barāy-i shiʿr guftan khūb ast* "Ṣūfism is good for composing poetry".

Bibliography: *Les œuvres de Vali*, ed. Garcin de Tassy, Paris 1834; M. Āzād, *Āb-i ḥayāt*, Lahore n.d. [1910s]; *Kulliyyāt-e Walī*, ed. A.A. Mārahrawī, Awrangābād 1927; *Kulliyyāt-i Walī*, ed. Nūr al-Ḥasan Hāshimī, Delhi 1945; M. Sadiq, *Vali, his age, life and poetry*, in *Iqbal*, viii (1960), 24-43; J.A. Haywood, *Wali Dakhani and the development of Dakhhani-Urdu Sufi poetry*, in *AO*, xxviii (1964), 153-74; M.A. Khān (ed.), *Walī, taḥḳīḳī-ō tanḳīdī muṭālaʿa*, Lahore 1965; Dj. Djālibī, *Tārīkh-i adab-i urdū*, i, Lahore 1975, 529-57; M. Sadiq, *A history of Urdu literature*, ²Delhi 1984, 53-65. (C. Shackle)

WALĪ AL-ʿAHD (A.), the heir-designate to a caliph or ruler, literally "successor [by virtue of] a covenant" [see ʿAHD]. Heirs to the caliphate were more formally entitled *walī ʿahd al-muslimīn*. It is not entirely clear when the title came into use. Historians from the 3rd/9th century (e.g. Ibn Ḳutayba, 155 ff.) apply it to the Umayyad ʿAbd al-ʿAzīz b. Marwān and subsequent heir-designates of that dynasty, but this may be anachronistic. Coins from the ʿAbbāsid caliph al-Mahdī's period (158-69/775-85), proclaiming his heir Mūsā (al-Hādī) as *walī ʿahd al-muslimīn*, categorically attest to its being in use by then (al-Bās̲h̲ā, 542-3; Lane-Poole, *Cat.*, i, 54).

Designation was a standard way of transferring power, including caliphal power, throughout Islamic history. The precedent—itself based on old tribal norms—was set by the first caliph Abū Bakr, who nominated ʿUmar to succeed him; the latter in turn designated a group of leading Muslims to select the next in line from among themselves. Muʿāwiya, the first Umayyad caliph, established another precedent by naming his own son Yazīd as successor, thereby introducing a dynastic principle. A later Umayyad caliph, Marwān I, went a step further by designating not one but two of his sons, ʿAbd al-Malik and ʿAbd al-ʿAzīz, to come after him successively; but when the former of the two came to power he manoeuvred his brother out of the succession and nominated his own two sons instead. Such early practices established the pattern: succession by designation, normally of a son (not necessarily the eldest) or brother; the option of nominating more than one heir at a time; and the annulment of a designation in favour of another candidate. The majority of caliphs, and most other hereditary Islamic rulers—in the Buwayhid, Sald̲j̲ūḳ, Fāṭimid, and Mamlūk states and in Muslim Spain, among others—came to power through such procedures. The most common alternative to this practice was seizure of government by force.

Designation was effected through an *ʿahd*, a unilateral voluntary testament by the incumbent ruler. Under the Umayyads this was a relatively simple act, with the nomination sometimes made public only after the caliph's death. The ʿAbbāsids developed a more elaborate routine. A stereotypic text of the *ʿahd* was adopted, and the nomination came to be announced in a ceremony presided over by the caliph, whereupon the heir-designate was offered a *bayʿa* [*q.v.*] by the dignitaries at hand. The appointment was then publicised throughout the empire. Once designated, the *walī al-ʿahd* was accorded a black insignia, his own palace and staff and, if still a minor, a tutor. His name was mentioned in the *k̲h̲uṭba* alongside that of the caliph and inscribed on the empire's flag and coins. Upon his nomination, the *walī al-ʿahd* was given a regnal title (*laḳab* [*q.v.*]), which he later retained as caliph; al-Mahdī was the first to be so entitled, while still heir-designate, by his father al-Manṣūr. To train the candidate for his future post, he was sent as governor to a major province. Thus ʿAbbāsid heir-designates became governors of Syria, Armenia or provinces of the west; and in Ḳād̲j̲ār Persia they were customarily in charge of Ād̲h̲arbāyd̲j̲ān. The institution of *walī al-ʿahd* had its peak in the early ʿAbbāsid period, when the heir was second to none but the caliph and replaced him on the throne during the latter's absence from the capital. His status declined when caliphs came under the sway of sultans, in Bag̲h̲dād and then in Cairo, who curbed their authority and interfered in the selection of their heirs.

Based on Abū Bakr's and ʿUmar's precedents, Sunnī jurists sanctioned designation as one of two accepted modes of succession, along with election (in S̲h̲īʿī doctrine, designation carried a different sense and importance; see IMĀMA; S̲H̲ĪʿA). They saw no contradiction between these two principles: the caliph, as *imām*, was capable of selecting for the post the fittest man possessing the required mental, spiritual and physical traits, on behalf of the entire community. But his choice did not depend on the consent of the community or even a part of it; and in that sense the *bayʿa* offered to a *walī al-ʿahd* was viewed as a confirmatory measure rather than a legitimising condition. The *ʿahd* and the nomination were considered irrevocable: once an heir was designated, he could not be unilaterally deposed nor could he resign. But since in practice such appointments were repeatedly reversed or annulled, jurists justified the dissolution when both nominator and nominee agreed or when an assembly ruled that the candidate was no longer fit.

In modern times, the institution of *walī al-ʿahd* continued to exist, or was revived, in some of the dynastic Islamic states: in Persia under the Ḳād̲j̲ārs and Pahlawīs; the post-World War I kingdoms of Egypt and ʿIrāḳ; Saudi Arabia (since 1933); Jordan (since 1965), Ḳaṭar and Bahrain (since the mid-1980s).

Bibliography: Ibn Ḳutayba, *Maʿārif*, Beirut 1970, 155 ff.; Māwardī, *al-Aḥkām al-sulṭāniyya*, Cairo 1960, esp. 10-17; Ḳalḳas̲h̲andī, *Ṣubḥ al-aʿs̲h̲ā*, ix, 348 ff.; Ḥasan al-Bās̲h̲ā, *al-Alḳāb al-islāmiyya*, Cairo 1957, 542-3; A. Chejne, *Succession to the rule in Islam*, Lahore 1960; E. Tyan, *Institutions du droit publique musulman*, i, Paris 1953, 267-86, ii, Paris 1956, 60-71, 129 ff., 136-46, 251-6, 333-44, 537-42; B. Lewis, *The regnal titles of the first Abbasid caliphs*, in *Dr. Ẓakir Husain presentation volume*, New Delhi 1968, 13-22; D.J. Wasserstein, *The caliphate in the west*, Oxford 1993, *passim*; S. Henderson, *After King Fahd: succession in Saudi Arabia*, Washington 1994, esp. 1-19.

(A. AYALON)

WALĪ ALLĀH AL-DIHLAWĪ [see AL-DIHLAWĪ, S̲H̲ĀH WALĪ ALLĀH].

WĀLIBA B. AL-ḤUBĀB al-Asadī, Abū Usāma, Arab poet of the early ʿAbbāsid period, *flor.* in the later 2nd/9th century.

Wāliba was born in Kūfa where he probably spent the largest part of his life. When his cousin on his father's side, Abū Bud̲j̲ayr Yaḥyā al-Nad̲j̲ās̲h̲ī al-Asadī, was appointed governor (or landtax collector) of al-Ahwāz by al-Manṣūr, Wāliba followed him there. During his stay there he met with Abū Nuwās [*q.v.*], who was then a handsome beardless youth (*amrad*). According to some sources, this happened in al-Ahwāz, where Abū Nuwās had gone together with his employer at the time, a perfume merchant (*ʿaṭṭār*) from Baṣra, in order to offer their wares to al-Nad̲j̲ās̲h̲ī; according to others, it happened at the souk of the druggists in Baṣra, where al-Nad̲j̲ās̲h̲ī had sent his cousin to buy supplies. The ties between Abū Nuwās and Wāliba were not only of an erotic nature. Wāliba rapidly recognised the poetic talent of his *g̲h̲ulām*. He took him along to Kūfa and looked after his education; Abū Nuwās's poetry was to be decisively influenced by him.

Wāliba came to Bag̲h̲dād most likely in the time of al-Mahdī, who admired his poetry but, on account of the latter's hemistich "I am a man who sleeps with his commensals", did not want to make him one of his boon-companions. Wāliba was, however, unable to establish himself there, because he let himself be drawn into a *hid̲j̲āʾ* exchange with Abu 'l-ʿAtāhiya, in which he emerged as the loser. Abu 'l-ʿAtāhiya doubted, *inter alia*, the Arab descent of Wāliba because of the latter's light skin and blond hair. Humbled, Wāliba had to return to Kūfa. From a poem composed in alternate lines by himself and Abū Nuwās and which describes the toils of a foot march to al-Ḥīra near Kūfa, we know that he also visited that place.

Wāliba must have died before 180/796, because after Wāliba's death Abū Nuwās attached himself to Khalaf b. Ḥayyān al-Aḥmar [*q.v.*], who in turn died in 180/796. Abū Nuwās composed a *marthiya* on his teacher.

Wāliba was above all known as a poet. His inclusion in Ibn Ḥadjar's *Lisān al-Mīzān* (cf. ed. Ḥaydarābād 1331, vi, 216) probably results from the fact that, in a facetious poem, Abū Nuwās called him a transmitter of a fictitious *ḥadīth*. In Kūfa, Wāliba belonged to a circle of poets and *udabā'* who upheld a libertine lifestyle; it included also Ḥammād ʿAdjrad, Ḥammād al-Rāwiya, and Muṭīʿ b. Iyās [*q.vv.*], and, from outside Kūfa, Salm al-Khāsir, al-Ashdjaʿ b. ʿAmr al-Sulamī, and Abān al-Lāḥiḳī [*q.vv.*]. Al-Raḳīḳ al-Nadīm describes the group as follows: "Wāliba had friends (*ikhwān*) who were like him in their companionship (*futuwwa*), in their elegant and witty behaviour (*ẓarf*), and in their addiction to gluttony and entertainment (*idmān al-ḳaṣf wa 'l-lahw*). They were completely uninhibited (*khalaʿū 'l-ʿidhār*) and squandered both their acquired and their inherited wealth". In this early combination of *futuwwa* and *ẓarf* (on which see Susanne Enderwitz, *Du Fatā au Ẓarīf*, in *Arabica*, xxxvi [1989], 125-42; eadem, *Liebe als Beruf*, Beirut 1995, 31-65), a third component also played a role: indifference toward religious precepts. This won them an accusation of *zandaḳa* [*q.v.*] (cf. G. Vajda, *Les Ẓindîqs en pays d'Islam*, in *RSO*, xvii [1938], 173-229). In this respect Wāliba was probably not quite innocent, since he established the connection between *ẓarf* and *zandaḳa*, even before Abū Nuwās, by calling his friend, Yaḥyā b. Ziyād al-Ḥārithī, "wittier (*aẓraf*) than a *zindīḳ*". In this urban bohemian milieu, Arabic love poetry received a new turn: alongside the *ʿudhrī* and the *ḥidjāzī* variety of *ghazal* [*q.v.*] poetry, the *kūfī* kind now emerged (cf. Nallino, *Scritti*, vi, 143-50; G. Schoeler, in *Camb. hist. Ar. lit.*, ii, 281-2). The latter often acquired obscene traits and should in part more appropriately be called *mudjūn* [*q.v.*]. Wāliba's poems, of which hardly more than one hundred lines have been preserved, deal with pederasty on the one hand and with wine, especially the morning draught, on the other. A collection of his poetry on one hundred leaves was once known to Ibn al-Djarrāḥ [*q.v.*] (cf. Ibn al-Nadīm, tr. Dodge, i, 357).

Bibliography: 1. Sources. Abū Hiffān, *Akhbār Abī Nuwās*, ed. ʿA.A. Farrādj, Cairo 1953, 108-9; Ibn al-Muʿtazz, *Ṭabaḳāt al-shuʿarā' al-muḥdathīn*, ed. Farrādj, Cairo 1956, 87-9, 193, 208-9; Abū Nuwās, *Dīwān*, ed. E. Wagner and G. Schoeler, Cairo and Beirut 1958 ff., i, 14, 40, 70, 189, 309, ii, 79, iv, 366; for vol. v (in the press), see ms. Fâtih, fols. 12a, 88a, 136a-b, 159a; *Aghānī*[1], xvi, 148-51; *Aghānī*[3], xviii, 99-107; al-Raḳīḳ al-Nadīm, *Ḳuṭb al-surūr*, ed. A. al-Djundī, Damascus 1969, 112-13; 173; *Ta'rīkh Baghdād*, xiii, 518-20; Ibn Manẓūr, *Akhbār Abī Nuwās*, Cairo and Baghdād 1924-52, i, 7-11; Ibn Faḍl Allāh al-ʿUmarī, *Masālik*, ed. F. Sezgin, Frankfurt 1988, xiv, 265-6;

2. Studies. Ṭāhā Ḥusayn, *Ḥadīth al-arbaʿā'*, Cairo 1925, ii, 212-13; O. Rescher, *Abriss d. arab. Literaturgesch.*, Constantinople and Stuttgart 1925-35, ii, 37; Ziriklī, *Aʿlām*, ix, 123; E. Wagner, *Abū Nuwās*, Wiesbaden 1965, 24-6; Sezgin, *GAS*, ii, 468; M.M. Dziekan, *Obruchy z dywanu Wāliby Ibn al-Ḥubāba*, in *Studia arabistyczne i islamistyczne*, iii (1995), 83-97.

(E. Wagner)

al-**WALĪD**, the name of two caliphs of the Marwānid line of the Umayyads.

1. al-Walīd (I) b. ʿAbd al-Malik b. Marwān (r. 86-96/705-15).

He was probably born *ca.* 54/674 in Muʿāwiya's reign. His mother was Wallāda bt. al-ʿAbbās b. Djaz' of a well-known family of ʿAbs b. Baghīḍ of Ḳays. He was his father's nominee to inherit the caliphate and the death of his uncle ʿAbd al-ʿAzīz b. Marwān in 85/704 meant that he succeeded unopposed. After the struggles of his father's reign, al-Walīd's caliphate was generally a period of internal peace and external expansion. As caliph he never seems to have left Syria except to lead the *Ḥadjdj* in 91/710. He is said to have instituted a system of poor relief and charity in Syria. He was certainly a great patron of architecture, building the Great Mosque in Damascus in its present form and rebuilding the mosque of the Prophet in Medina. In political affairs, he continued his father's policies with little change. He attempted to keep a balance between the different groups in the Umayyad élite and control the divisions between Ḳays and Yaman. He maintained al-Ḥadjdjādj b. Yūsuf [*q.v.*] as governor of ʿIrāḳ and the East until his death in 95/714. His brother and heir, Sulaymān, was governor of Syria and, for most of the reign, his cousin, ʿUmar b. ʿAbd al-ʿAzīz, later to be caliph himself, was governor of the Ḥidjāz. Both had Yemeni sympathies and gave refuge to political opponents of al-Ḥadjdjādj.

The reign of al-Walīd saw the success of Muslim arms in many areas. In the west, Spain was invaded in 92/711 and almost completely taken by 97/716. In the East, the expansion was managed by al-Ḥadjdjādj. In Khurāsān, his governor Ḳutayba b. Muslim [*q.v.*] (86-96/705-15) launched a series of attacks on Transoxania which the Muslims had hardly penetrated before. He secured the submission of Bukhārā in 87-90/706-9, Khwārazm and Samarḳand in 91-3/711-2 and Farghāna in 94/713. From 90/708-9 Muḥammad b. al-Ḳāsim al-Thaḳafī began the Muslim conquest of Sind. Despite frequent Muslim raids, little progress was made against the Byzantines. Al-Walīd never led the campaigns himself but entrusted the frontier to his brother Maslama [*q.v.*], who built up a formidable power base in the area.

Al-Walīd died in Damascus in Djumādā II 96/late February 715. In accordance with his father's will, the caliphate was to pass to his brother Sulaymān, with whom his relations seem to have been increasingly strained. Some sources say that he was trying to secure the acceptance of his own son ʿAbd al-ʿAzīz as heir but that he died before this could be accomplished, and Sulaymān duly succeeded. His reign had been remarkably successful and represents, perhaps, the zenith of Umayyad power. It is less clear to what extent the caliph himself contributed directly to this, and perhaps his main achievement was to preserve balance and stability among the factions of the ruling family and their allies.

Bibliography: The main sources on early Islamic history all contain accounts of his reign, notably: Ṭabarī, ii, 1172-1281; Yaʿḳūbī, *Ta'rīkh*, ii, 337-51; Ibn Khayyāṭ, *Ta'rīkh*, ed. al-ʿUmarī, 299-313; Masʿūdī, *Murūdj*, iii, 365-80. See also J. Wellhausen, *The Arab kingdom and its fall*, Calcutta 1927; H.A.R. Gibb, *The Arab conquests in Central Asia*, London 1923; K.A.C. Creswell, *Early Muslim architecture*, i, Oxford 1932; M.A. Shaban, *Islamic history A.D. 600-750*, Cambridge 1971; P. Crone, *Slaves on horseback*, Cambridge 1980; G.R. Hawting, *The first dynasty of Islam*, London 1986; H. Kennedy, *The Prophet and the age of the Caliphates*, London 1986; G.M. Hinds, *The zenith of the Marwanid house* (= vol. xxiii of *The History of al-Ṭabarī*, ed. E. Yar-Shater, Albany 1990).

2. AL-WALĪD (II) b. Yazīd b. ʿAbd al-Malik (r. 125-6/743-4).

His date of birth is uncertain and estimates of his age at his accession to the caliphate vary between 37 and 45. His mother was Umm al-Ḥadjdjādj Zaynab, daughter of Muḥammad b. Yūsuf al-Thaḳafī.

His father, Yazīd II b. ʿAbd al-Malik, had nominated him to succeed his own brother Hishām. At first, Hishām seems to have regarded his young nephew with some affection but he became increasingly disillusioned by his dissolute lifestyle; he reduced his allowances and punished some of his undesirable associates. Al-Walīd in turn withdrew from court and established himself in a remote desert residence which may be the ruined site now known as Ḳaṣr al-Ṭūba in the Jordanian desert.

The exact chronology of events in al-Walīd's short reign is not clear, but he faced opposition from the time of his accession and seems to have exacerbated this by his conduct. The stories of his debauchery and wine-drinking may have been exaggerated, but they allowed his enemies to claim that it was legitimate to depose him. After taking the *bayʿa* in Damascus, he lived entirely in remote desert palaces which allowed rumour to spread and opposition to grow unchecked.

The new caliph's first actions were populist, increasing the stipends for the Syrians and other supporters and providing slaves to help the blind and crippled. However, he soon began to arouse political opposition by his reliance on members of the Ḳays-Muḍar faction and, especially, the Thaḳafī relations of his mother. The most important of these was Yūsuf b. ʿUmar Ibn Hubayra [*q.v.*], who had been appointed governor of ʿIrāḳ and the east by Hishām and was retained in office by al-Walīd. He also appointed his own maternal uncle Yūsuf b. Muḥammad b. Yūsuf al-Thaḳafī to the prestigious governorate of the Ḥidjāz. He allowed the Ḳays-Muḍar leaders to persecute their Yemeni opponents, in particular the widely-respected former governor of ʿIrāḳ, Khālid b. ʿAbd Allāh al-Ḳasrī [*q.v.*] who was effectively sold to Yūsuf b. ʿUmar and tortured to death. The caliph also took action against Hishām's sons and other members of the Umayyad family whom he suspected of opposing his accession, and the powerful Sulaymān b. Hishām was flogged and exiled to ʿAmmān. A broad coalition of interests, including many Umayyads and the family of Khālid al-Ḳasrī and other leading Yemenis emerged, and leadership of the opposition was assumed by the caliph's cousin, Yazīd b. al-Walīd. While the caliph remained in his desert retreat, the opposition was able to take over Damascus. Shortly afterwards, an expeditionary force under ʿAbd al-ʿAzīz b. al-Ḥadjdjādj b. ʿAbd al-Malik was sent to al-Walīd's palace at al-Bakhrāʾ, south of Palmyra. Here, after a short siege, the caliph was killed, according to al-Ṭabarī, on 27 Djumādā II 126/15 April 744.

Bibliography: The main sources on early Islamic history all contain accounts of his reign, notably: Ṭabarī, ii, 1740-1825; Yaʿḳūbī, *Taʾrīkh*, ii, 396-401; Ibn Khayyāṭ, *Taʾrīkh*, 362-8. See also Wellhausen, *The Arab kingdom and its fall*, Calcutta 1927; F. Gabrieli, *al-Walid b. Yazid, il califfo e il poeta*, in *RSO*, xv (1935), 1-64; Shaban, *Islamic history A.D. 600-750*; D. Derenk, *Leben und Dichtung des Omaiyadenkalifen al-Walīd ibn Yazīd*, Freiburg im Breisgau 1974; R. Hillenbrand, La Dolce vita *in early Islamic Syria*, in *Art History*, v/1 (1982), 1-35; P. Crone, *Slaves on horseback*, Cambridge 1980; G.R. Hawting, *The first dynasty of Islam*, London and Sydney 1986; H. Kennedy, *The Prophet and the age of the Caliphates*, London and New York 1986; Carol Hillenbrand, *The waning of the Umayyad Caliphate* (= vol. xxvi of *The History of al-Ṭabarī*, Albany 1989).

(H. KENNEDY)

Al-Walīd (II) as a poet.

However ill-fated as a caliph, al-Walīd gained lasting fame as one of the most original poets in Arabic literary history. He was also a gifted musician and composer, who set some of his own verses to music; this may have influenced his poetic technique. His reputation rests on his *ghazal* [*q.v.*] verses addressed to Salmā, his wife's sister, and on his wine songs [see KHAMRIYYA], which constitute an important stage in the development of the genre. Not needing to please a patron, al-Walīd was able to follow his taste and creative inspiration without restraint. His *dīwān* appears to be a genuine manifestation of his complex character, aestheticism and licentious life-style.

Al-Walīd's verses have been collected from various sources and edited with an essay by F. Gabrieli, *Al-Walīd ibn Yazīd. Il califfo e il poeta*, in *RSO*, xv [1934], 1-64, re-ed. Beirut 1967. The edition contains 102 poems and fragments, 428 verses in all, love (43 texts) and wine (14 texts) forming the main themes. Of his five elegies, two are devoted to his beloved Salmā, who died shortly after he had forced her to divorce and married her as caliph in 743 (nos. 29, 56). The remaining texts may be roughly classified as *mufākhara* and *hidjāʾ* [*q.vv.*], e.g. against his uncle Hishām, whose death he welcomed with undisguised joy (nos. 60, 84). There is also a religious *urdjūza* (no. 37) he allegedly recited as *khuṭba* at a Friday worship (*Aghānī*[1], vi, 128).

His poems are usually short (4-8 verses) and carefully structured on different linguistic levels. Metrical variation is extremely high. Al-Walīd employs 13 metres, five of them also in their shortened (*madjzūʾ*) variant, with preference, in statistical order, for *ramal madjzūʾ*, *wāfir*, *khafīf* and *ṭawīl* [see ʿARŪḌ]. Phonological and morphological repetition and syntactic parallelism are his favourite techniques (cf. R. Jacobi, *Theme and variations in Umayyad Ghazal poetry*, in *JAL*, xxiii [1992], 109-19). As a result, his verses achieve a distinctive rhythm and sound quality, a musicality, as it were, unknown in Arabic poetry before.

Al-Walīd continues the tradition of ʿUmar b. Abī Rabīʿa and Djamīl al-ʿUdhrī [*q.v.*], as he himself avows (no. 42,3). From the aspect of form, his *ghazal* was influenced by ʿUmar, but it reveals the melancholy mood and passionate devotion to one beloved of the ʿUdhrites, mixed with courtly elements and a playfulness all his own (cf. Jacobi, *Zur Gazalpoesie des Walīd ibn Yazīd*, in W. Heinrichs and G. Schoeler (eds.), *Festschrift für Ewald Wagner*, ii, Beirut 1994, 154-61). One of his most original traits is the use of nature as a lyrical medium, e.g. his dialogue with a bird (no. 74) or the image of a garden touched by autumn in his *marthiya* [*q.v.*] for Salmā (no. 56). The defiance and eroticism of his bacchic verses prepares the way for the *khamriyya* of Abū Nuwās [*q.v.*] (cf. P. Kennedy, *The wine song in Classical Arabic poetry*, Oxford 1997, 27, 100). Living in a period of transition, al-Walīd unites Umayyad lyricism and ʿAbbāsid sophistication. In his verses, if not in his life, he achieved a perfect balance, his exuberance and sensuality being controlled by poetic genius and formal discipline.

Bibliography (in addition to references in the article): *Aghānī*[1], vi, 101-41; R. Blachère, *Le prince umayyade al-Walīd [II] Ibn Yazīd et son rôle littéraire*, in *Mélanges Gaudefroy-Demombynes*, Cairo 1935, 103-23 (= idem, *Analecta*, Damascus 1975, 379-99); D. Derenk, *Leben und Dichtung des Omaijadenkalifen al-Walīd b. Yazīd*, Freiburg 1974; R.W. Hamilton, *Walid and his friends. An Umayyad tragedy*, Oxford 1988.

(RENATE JACOBI)

AL-**WALĪD** B. **HISHĀM**, Abū Rakwa, a pseudo-Umayyad pretender who led a revolt against the Fāṭimid caliph al-Ḥākim [*q.v.*]. He was an Arab, probably of Andalusian origin, who for some time had earned his living as a schoolteacher in al-Ḳayrawān and Miṣr (Old Cairo) and then went into service with the Arab Bedouin clan of Banū Ḳurra (of the Hilāl tribe) whose pasture-grounds were the hilly country of Cyrenaica south-east of Barḳa (modern al-Mardj); there he taught the boys of the clan to read and write. His nickname Abū Rakwa "the one with the waterbottle", seems to point to his Ṣūfī-like appearance. (The most detailed reports of his early career are found in al-Nuwayrī, *Nihāyat al-arab*, ed. M.M. Amīn and M.Ḥ.M. Aḥmad, xxviii, Cairo 1992, 181-4, and Ibn al-Athīr, ix, 197-8.)

When in 394/1004 a conflict broke out between the Banū Ḳurra and the caliph al-Ḥākim, the Bedouin rebelled, and young Abū Rakwa—then in his mid-twenties—took the lead in the revolt. He passed himself off for a descendant of the Umayyad caliph of Cordova ʿAbd al-Raḥmān III, and in Djumādā II 395/end of March 1005, in the village of ʿUyūn al-Naẓar in Cyrenaica he took the caliphal title of *amīr al-muʾminīn* and the royal name *al-Nāṣir li-Dīn Allāh*, the same which his alleged ancestor ʿAbd al-Raḥmān III had borne; the "caliph" posed as the champion of Sunnism against Shīʿī heresy. The Arab Banū Ḳurra under their chief Māḍī b. Muḳarrab were supported by several Berber fractions of the Zanāta, Mazāta and Luwāta tribes. Barḳa, the capital of the Cyrenaica, was evacuated by the Fāṭimid garrison in September 1005 after a siege of five months, after an Egyptian force of relief under the Turk Yināl al-Ṭawīl had been crushed by the rebels.

In 396/1006 the hordes of the rebel tribes with their tents and flocks hurled themselves against Egypt; their vanguard overran a Fāṭimid contingent near today's El Alamein. As Alexandria was too strongly fortified, Abū Rakwa led his bands to the south. Since al-Ḥākim had occupied the bridgehead of al-Djīza, the rebels were forced to march across the desert in order to gain the fertile lowlands of al-Fayyūm. Here the hordes of Abū Rakwa were engaged by the Fāṭimid main army under Faḍl b. Ṣāliḥ at Raʾs al-Birka and annihilated (3 Dhu 'l-Ḥidjdja 396/30 August 1006). Abū Rakwa fled to Nubia, where he found asylum in a Christian monastery, but he was handed over by the Nubian king at al-Ḥākim's request in exchange for a considerable ransom. He was brought to Cairo and executed there in March 1007.

The short career of Abū Rakwa was accompanied by a celestial phenomenon, a Super Nova which from May to August 1006 was observed also in Europe; in the Egyptian chronicles a parallel was drawn between its appearance and fading and the rise and fall of Abū Rakwa (Yaḥyā al-Anṭākī, 475; al-Maḳrīzī, *Ittiʿāẓ* ii, 61).

Bibliography: The main source is Idrīs ʿImād al-Dīn, *ʿUyūn al-akhbār*, vi, ed. M. Ghālib, Beirut 1984, 259-72. See also Yaḥyā al-Anṭakī, ed. I. Kratchkovsky and A. Vasiliev, in *PO*, xxiii/3, 470-80; Ibn Ẓāfir, *Akhbār al-duwal al-munkaṭiʿa*, ed. A. Ferré, Cairo 1972, 44-8; Ibn al-Athīr, ed. Beirut, ix, 197-203 (under the year 397 A.H.); Maḳrīzī, *Ittiʿāẓ al-ḥunafāʾ*, ed. M.H. Muḥ. Aḥmad, Cairo 1971, ii, 60-7; J. Aguadé, *Abū Rakwa*, in *Actas del IV Coloquio Hispano-Tunecino, Palma de Mallorca 1979*, Madrid 1983, 9-27.

(H. HALM)

AL-**WALĪD** B. AL-**MUGHĪRA** B. ʿABD ALLĀH, member of the powerful and numerous clan of Makhzūm [*q.v.*] in pre-Islamic Mecca, opponent of the Prophet Muḥammad and uncle of another opponent, Abū Djahl [*q.v.*] ʿAmr b. Hishām b. al-Mughīra, d. just after the Hidjra.

Little is known of his life, but he clearly represented the aristocratic interests of his clan and was himself prosperous, seen in the fact that he is said to have owned a garden in Ṭāʾif which he planted for pleasure only and never gathered the fruit in it (Sprenger, i, 359). According to the commentators, there are references to him in several passages of the Ḳurʾān, e.g. VI, 10, XLIII, 30, LXXIV, 11 ff. and LXXX, 1 ff., although his name is never expressly mentioned. One cannot, of course, place implicit confidence on such statements, which are sometimes based on later deductions. Muslim historians frequently mention al-Walīd among those members of Ḳuraysh who vigorously persecuted Muḥammad and endeavoured to silence him. Thus he is said to have been a member of a deputation which went to Abū Ṭālif [*q.v.*] and protested to him, but without success, at the Prophet's conduct. It is also related that Muḥammad's enemies had on one occasion, on the approach of the pilgrimage, discussed the best means to set strange visitors against Muḥammad and proposed in turn the epithets *kāhin* "sooth-sayer", *madjnūn* "possessed" and *shāʿir* "poet", but al-Walīd rejected them all until those present finally agreed to his proposal to call Muḥammad a *sāḥir* "magician", who would separate a man from his father, brother, wife and whole family, and to warn the pilgrims seriously against the alleged magician. When ʿUthmān b. Maẓʿūn [*q.v.*], a relative of al-Walīd, who had adopted Islam and taken part in the emigration to Abyssinia, but was still under al-Walīd's protection, wished to break off this relationship, the latter endeavoured to dissuade him, but in vain. After al-Walīd had therefore released himself from all obligations to his relative, ʿUthmān was severely wounded in a squabble, whereupon al-Walīd again offered him his protection but ʿUthmān rejected this kindly-meant offer.

Al-Walīd died in Mecca in the year 1, and three of his seven sons adopted Islam. In keeping with his aristocratic descent and social status, his actions were frequently characterised by magnanimity and dignity.

Bibliography: Ibn Hishām, i, 123, 167, 171, 187, 236, 238, 240, 243-4, 262, 272-3; Ṭabarī, i, see index; Ibn al-Athīr, ii, 32, 47, 53-4, 58-9, 85; Yaʿḳūbī, *Historiae*, i, 300, ii, 6, 18, 24; A. Sprenger, *Das Leben und die Lehre des Mohammad*[2], i, 90, 361, ii, 19, 21, 36, 40, 46, 48, 56-7, 70, 75, 80, 89, 109, 111-12, 161, 320, 345, 393, 405; L. Krehl, *Das Leben des Muhammed*, 41-2, 74-76, 78; F. Buhl, *Das Leben Muhammeds*, 168, 179; Caetani, *Annali dell' Islām*, i, see index with further literature in the text; W.M. Watt, *Muhammad at Mecca*, Oxford 1953, 9, 123, 134; Patricia Crone, *Meccan trade and the rise of Islam*, Oxford 1987, 120-2.

(K.V. ZETTERSTEEN*)

AL-**WALĪD** B. **ṬARĪF** al-Taghlibī al-Shaybānī al-Shārī, Khāridjite rebel in al-Djazīra in 178-9/794-5, i.e. during the reign of Hārūn al-Rashīd. The Arabic sources tell us much about al-Walīd and his outbreak, although some details are contradictory; the most explicit sources are Khalīfa b.

Khayyāṭ, the *Aghānī*, Ibn al-Athīr and Ibn Khallikān.

Starting from Naṣībīn, al-Walīd swept through Armenia and Ādharbāydjān into al-Djazīra, an old Khāridjite stronghold, defeating several caliphal armies. Hence in 179/795 Hārūn sent against him the experienced Yazīd b. Mazyad al-Shaybānī. Pressed by the caliph and accused by the Barmakīs of deliberately hanging back, Yazīd attacked al-Walīd at a place called Ghirra near Hīt [*q.v.*] on 2 Ramaḍān 179/19 November 795, defeated his army and killed the rebel. The caliph, relieved of this threat, left for the *ʿumra* and the *ḥadjdj*, performing all the prescribed ceremonies by walking.

Many of al-Walīd's own verses are cited in Arabic literature, as are also the elegies for her brother by al-Walīd's sister Fāriʿa or Laylā; contrariwise, there exist verses by Muslim b. al-Walīd [*q.v.*] praising Yazīd for his victory.

Bibliography: 1. Sources. Muslim b. al-Walīd, *Sharḥ Dīwān Ṣarīʿ al-Ghawānī*, ed. Sāmī al-Dahhān, Cairo n.d., 1-23 (see tr. in W. Heinrichs, *Muslim b. al-Walīd and Badīʿ*, in idem and G. Schoeler (eds.) *Festschrift E. Wagner*, ii, *Studien zur arabischen Dichtung*, Beirut and Stuttgart 1994, 211-45, esp. 221-42); Khalīfa, *Taʾrīkh*, ed. Zakkār, Damascus 1967-8, ii, 720-3; Yaʿḳūbī, *Taʾrīkh*, ii, 495-6; Ṭabarī, iii, 631, 638, *Aghānī*², xi, 8-11; de Goeje (ed.), *Fragmenta*, 296-7; Ibn al-Djawzī, *Muntaẓam*, ed. M. ʿAṭāʾ, Beirut 1992-3, ix, 36, 38-9; Ibn al-Athīr, vi, 141-3, 147; Ibn Khallikān, ed. ʿAbbās, vi, 31-4, 327-9; Ibn al-ʿImād, *Shadharāt*, i, 288-9.

2. Studies. Weil, *Chalifen*, ii, 147-8; L. Veccia Vaglieri, in *RSO*, xxiv (1949), 40-1; H. Kennedy, *The early Abbasid caliphate*, London 1981, 121; and see the various biographies of Hārūn al-Rashīd.

(H. EISENSTEIN)

AL-**WALĪD** B. **ʿUḲBA** B. ABĪ MUʿAYṬ, Companion of the Prophet and member of the Abū ʿAmr family of the Umayyad clan in Mecca, d. 61/680.

His father ʿUḳba fell at Badr opposing Muḥammad, but al-Walīd became a Muslim at the conquest of Mecca in 8/630. He acted as collector of the *ṣadaḳa* [*q.v.*] from the Banū Muṣṭaliḳ under the Prophet and that from the Christian Banū Taghlib [*q.v.*] in al-Djazīra under ʿUmar. Through his mother, he was a half-brother of the ʿUthmān b. ʿAffān, and when the latter became caliph he appointed al-Walīd governor of Kūfa after Saʿd b. Abī Waḳḳāṣ (29/645-6). His licentious behaviour and wine-drinking made him unpopular with the pietistic elements there, and after complaints had been made to him ʿUthmān removed him in 29/649-50. When ʿUthmān was murdered, al-Walīd fled to al-Djazīra and stayed there, standing apart from politics, dying at Raḳḳa in 61/680. He had some fame as a poet (see *Aghānī*³, v, 122-53), as did his son Abū Ḳaṭīfa ʿAmr (d. before 73/693, see Blachère, *HLA*, iii, 621, and Sezgin, *GAS*, ii, 424-5).

Bibliography: The sources are detailed in Ziriklī, *Aʿlām*, ix, 143, to which should be added Balādhurī, *Ansāb*, v, 29-35. See also G. Rotter, *Die Umayyaden und die zweite Bürgerkrieg* (680-692), Wiesbaden 1982, 111-12.

(C.E. BOSWORTH)

WĀLIDE SULṬĀN (A.), Turkish pronunciation *vālide* or *valde sulṭān*, a term meaning "mother sultana", or "queen mother". It was used in the Ottoman Empire to refer to the mother of the reigning sultan, and only for the duration of the son's reign.

The history of the position and its occupants, like a great deal of the history of the *ḥarīm* [*q.v.*] and its influence on the dynastic politics of the Ottomans, is couched in myth and exoticism, and much of its early development is completely obscured. The interference of the royal women in politics, a fact which most Ottoman chronicles of the middle period note and deplore, became intimately linked to, as well as blamed for the long decline of the empire, especially after the death of Süleymān the Magnificent in 1566. In both Turkish and Western histories, the period from the mid-10th/16th to the mid-11th/17th centuries has been known as the *ḳadînlar salṭanatî* "women's sultanate" or "the rule of the women". Abundant material is available, from both documentary and foreign observers alike, although less so in more circumspect Turkish sources, but all has to be sifted with care. Of newer work, two studies on the sovereignty and ceremonial aspects of the dynasty have placed the role of the imperial household in a more reasonable context (those of Peirce and Necipoğlu).

The source of most of the women for the imperial household was slavery [see ʿABD]. Initially, free-born daughters of rivals and allies, or captives of war, were the choice for marriage. In the middle period, women from the Caucasus and other areas, prized for their beauty, were enslaved and became part of the sultan's entourage, often as gifts. While the early sultans married in order to contract or cement alliances, once a royal palace [see TOPḲAPÎ SARĀYÎ] was constructed in Constantinople after its conquest in 1453, the private quarters of the sultan and his household altered the public role of women in the sultanate, although the *ḥarīm* remained a source of royal brides for the upper echelon of the Ottoman administration. Thereafter, the sultan himself never married, with the exceptions of Süleymān to his beloved Roxelana (d. 965/1558 [see KHURREM] and ʿOthmān II (1618-22 [*q.v.*]). Sultans had a number of favourites, usually, but not always, limited to four, called *khāṣṣekī* [*q.v.*], and those who had borne the sultan a child were called *khāṣṣekī sulṭān*.

Nothing could enhance the prestige of a *khāṣṣekī* more than to have her son become sultan. This equivalent of the dowager queens of other dynasties commanded a respect that at least partially derives from Muslim and Turkish filial piety, exemplified in the *ḥadīth* "Paradise lies at the feet of the mother". In addition, when succession was contested, the problem of a potential heir and his survival in fratricidal disputes embroiled many mothers in their sons' affairs, creating often unique, but ambivalent, bonds of affection and power. All princes of the Ottoman household after 1600 were confined to the royal precincts, given very small allowances, and prevented from producing unwanted offspring upon entering maturity. The women, especially mothers, came to assume a disproportionate influence in the safe passage of such sons to the throne. Royal mothers were paid the highest stipend [see BASHMAḲLÎḲ] in the empire (Peirce, 126). They often became considerable patrons of large building projects, and allied themselves when necessary with ambitious officials of the court, most especially, with the chief black eunuch, the guardian of the *ḥarīm*, the *Ḳîzlar Aghasî*, who in the middle period of the empire became the third most important palace official after the sultan and the Grand Vizier. As the royal women rarely appeared in public, all such political and financial arrangements were conducted from within the confines of the palace.

The *wālide sulṭān* commanded an enormous household which grew in the period 1550-1700 from under 200 to close to 1,000, in addition to the *wālide* or the *khāṣṣekī*s (Peirce, 122). The *wālide* was given special recognition on two ceremonial occasions: upon her son's accession, she too was installed in a separate ceremony, which sometimes involved a procession from the old palace (*eski sarāy*), where retired or out of favour *khāṣṣekī*s as well as royal mothers and sisters of previous sultans resided. The sultan himself greeted her at the gate of Ṭopḳapî Sarāyî. Should she die while her son was in office, the sultan bade her cortège farewell at the gate and she was treated to a royal burial. If her son died before she did, she retired to the *eski sarāy*. Palace etiquette surrounding the *wālide sulṭān* set her apart from all the other women of the *ḥarīm*, as well as from most other high dignitaries of the court.

The list of women entitled to be called *wālide sulṭān* varies according to the source, in part because the early genealogy of the dynasty is coloured with much later accretion, probably encouraged by the sultans themselves, and centring on their putative relationship to other regal bloodlines. Such is the much-embellished life of Aimée du Buc de Rivery, called the "French Sultana", a relative of Empress Josephine of France, reputedly a captive concubine in the *ḥarīm* of Selīm III (1789-1807 [*q.v.*]) and erroneously called the mother of Maḥmūd II (1807-1839 [*q.v.*]). Even the legendary mother of Ertoghrul Ghāzī, father of ʿOthmān I [*q.v.*] and Mal Khātūn (d. 726/1325-6), ʿOthmān's wife and mother to Orkhān [*q.v.*], were accorded the title of *wālide* by the 19th century. Of the eighteen *wālide*s in Alderson's list (83), a handful achieved extraordinary status: Nūr Bānū (d. 991/1583 [*q.v.*]), mother of Murād III; Ṣafiyye (d. 1014/1605 [see ṢAFIYYE WĀLIDE SULṬĀN]), mother of Meḥemmed II; Māhpaykar or Kösem (d. 1061/1651 [*q.v.*]), wife of Aḥmed, mother of sultans Murād IV and Ibrāhīm and grandmother of Meḥemmed IV; and finally, Turkhān (also Tarkhān) (d. 1094/1683), mother of Meḥemmed IV, the latter two women bitter rivals.

The most notorious mother of the dynasty, Khurrem, died before her son Selīm II (1566-74 [*q.v.*]) achieved the throne. The "rule of the women" dates from her taking up residence in Ṭopḳapî Sarāyî in 1541, necessitated by a fire in the *eski sarāy*. In each of the other four cases as well, palace intrigues and shifting coalitions characterised their exercise of political power, which was precariously attached to the well-being and accession of their sons. Notable in that regard is Turkhān's culpability in the execution of her rival Kösem, who is often blamed in Western histories for encouraging the lurid excesses of her son, the mad Ibrāhīm.

These powerful women are equally exemplary for having used their wealth and position to establish charitable foundations [see WAḲF] around mosque complexes, and financing other projects which contributed to the construction of the permanent legacy of imperial Istanbul and other cities of the empire. Ṣafiyye, for example, the fifth of the queen mothers in the palace, began the construction of the New Queen Dowager Mosque (Yeñi Wālide Djāmiʿ), known as Yeñi Djāmiʿ, at Eminönü in Istanbul, which Turkhān completed during her rule as the first truly imperial mosque of the royal women. Ṣafiyye also built a mosque in Cairo. Nūr Bānū built the Wālide-yi ʿAtīḳ mosque complex in Üsküdar, which included a school, hospital and a library, as did that of Turkhān. Nūr Bānū built numerous public baths. Kösem, who served as regent for five years before Murād IV reached maturity, exercised considerable power for close to thirty years, and is evoked in the popular imagination for her generosity and intelligence. Included among her projects was the Činili Djāmiʿ (Çinili Mosque) and its associated buildings in Üsküdar, as well as other charitable foundations. She was also the builder of a market [see KHĀN] in the centre of the city (see *EI*[1] s.v. (Deny), 1116-7, for a more complete list, and the articles in this *Encyclopaedia* on the individual *wālides*; Peirce, 200-20, discusses the role such projects played in promoting Ottoman sovereignty).

By the 18th century, when succession was more regularised, the political influence of the *wālide sulṭān* was much diminished, although the ceremonial and psychological bond between mother and son remained strong. Of *wālide*s of the 18th century, Gülnūsh (d. 1127/1715), mother of Muṣṭafā II and Aḥmed III and Naḳsh-i Dil, mother of Maḥmūd II, reputedly influenced the two great reformer sultans of the age. Alderson lists Şevkefza (i.e. Shewḳefzā), mother of Murād V, whose reign lasted 93 days in 1876, as the last designated *wālide*, but ʿAbd al-Ḥamīd II (1876-1908 [*q.v.*]) bestowed the rank on his adopted mother, Peresto Khānîm, having lost his natural mother at an early age. The mothers, like royal married sisters, were on the civil list in the 19th century and still commanded considerable salaries.

Bibliography: J. Deny, *EI*[1] art. *Wālide Sulṭān* (a complete list of primary and earlier secondary works); M. Tayyib Gökbilgin, *İA* art. *Başmaklık*, at ii, 333-4, and M. Cavid Baysun, art. *Kösem Sultan*, at vi, 915-23, listing more works in Turkish; B. Miller, *Beyond the Sublime Porte*, New Haven 1931 (still a worthy study of the palace and its residents); N. Penzer, *The Harem*, [2]London 1965 (less so); A.D. Alderson, *Structure of the Ottoman dynasty*, Oxford 1956; Gibb and Bowen, i, 71-7; Gülru Necipoğlu, *Architecture, ceremonial and power. The Topkapı Palace in the fifteenth and sixteenth centuries*, Cambridge 1991; Leslie Peirce, *The Imperial Harem*, New York 1993. The latter two have considerable bibliographies of their own. J. Freely, *Istanbul: the imperial city*, New York 1996, includes valuable information on the building projects of the *wālides*.

The literature on the harem has itself grown vast, a majority of the writers, to quote Deny, "reveal[ing] a remarkable credulity" (1118). See ḤARĪM for a fuller list. Lady Wortley-Montagu's letters of the 18th century give a clear-eyed picture of the institution in its later stages (*Selected letters*, ed. R. Halsbend, New York 1986). One of the most entertaining of the captive slave accounts is the fictionalised tale of Aimée de Buc du Rivery, in Leslie Blanch, *The wilder shores of love*, London and New York 1954. Of the autobiographies of members of the late Ottoman household, an interesting one is Ayşe Osmanoğlu's *Avec mon père le sultan Abdulhamid de son palais à sa prison*, Paris 1991, published also in English and Turkish. (VIRGINIA H. AKSAN)

WĀLIHĪ, the pen-name (*makhlaṣ*) used by several Ottoman poets of the 10th/16th century, two of whom are prominent.

1. ḲURD-ZĀDE of Edirne. After a *medrese* education, he left the *ʿIlmiyye* [*q.v.*], went to Cairo and became a *mürīd* of *seyyid* Aḥmed Khayālī, son of Ibrāhīm Gülshenī, the founder of the Gülsheniyye order. After his return to Edirne, he earned great repute as a preacher, delivering exceptionally captivating sermons (*waʿẓ*). When the Selīmiyye mosque in Edirne was completed in 982/1574, Wālihī became its first preacher, and he retained his position there until his death. However, his emotional temperament and inclination to love affairs involved him in various

incidents, one of which resulted in his temporary banishment from Edirne in 971/1563-4. He joined the Eastern expedition of Lālā Muṣṭafā Pasha [*q.v.*] and in Tbilisi, following the city's surrender to Özdemir-oghlì ʿOthmān Pasha, delivered a memorable *khuṭbe* to the army in the name of Sultan Murād III on Friday, 29 August 1578. He died in 994/1586 according to ʿAṭāʾī's calculation of the chronogram which his namesake Wālihī of Üsküb (see below) wrote on his death (or in 996/1588 according to Ḥibrī) in Edirne and was buried in the cemetery of the *sheykh* Shüdjāʿ *zāwiye* on the shore of the Tundja.

Poems by him of a lyrical (*ʿāshìkāne*) and mystical (*mutaṣawwìfāne*) character are to be found in *medjmūʿa*s and *tedhkire*s; Ḳìnalì-zāde Ḥasan Čelebi relates that he also composed pleasing chronograms (*tārīkh*). There is no mention in any of the *tedhkire*s of a *dīwān*, so that the *dīwān* attributed to him in the *ʿOthmānlì müʾellifleri* (and thereafter in other sources) must be due to a confusion with Wālihī of Üsküb, who is, in fact, the author of a *dīwān*.

Opinion is divided concerning the separate identity of a Wālihī whose particulars are very similar to those of Ḳurd-zāde Wālihī. This is Wālihī of Djisr-i Ergene or Ergene Köprüsü (Uzunköprü near Edirne), who was a pupil of Muḥashshī Sinān Efendi during the time (942-5/1535-9) when he taught at one of the Ṣaḥn-i themān [*q.v.*] *medrese*s in Istanbul. He later likewise quit the *ʿilmiyye* to join the Gülsheniyye order, becoming a *mürīd* of *sheykh* Ḥasan Ẓarīfī in Istanbul. Although Ḳìnalì-zāde Ḥasan Čelebi's *tedhkire* is the only *tedhkire* with an entry on him, the fact of Ḳìnalì-zāde's sojourn in Edirne as a contemporary of Ḳurd-zāde Wālihī, which gave him the possibility of collecting information *in situ* for his *tedhkire*, lends verisimilitude to his information. Ḳìnalì-zāde also cites a few verses by him.

2. Aḥmed of Üsküb (Skopje). The son of a *ḳāḍī*, he finished his *medrese* education in Istanbul and thereafter became a tutor (*muʿīd*) at the Sultan Bāyezīd II *medrese* in Edirne. Later, he served as *ḳāḍī*, but no details on his appointments are known. He died in Üsküb in 1008/1599-1600. Ewliyā Čelebi relates that his grave is in the *zāwiye* of *sheykh* Luṭfullāh near the fortress of Üsküb and that it has become the object of pious visits.

He enjoyed great repute as a poet and is the author of a *dīwān*. There is only one known ms. of a Wālihī *dīwān* and that is no. Diez 30 in the Staatsbibliothek Preussischer Kulturbesitz in Berlin (edition in preparation by the author). This fragmentary ms., containing about 300 *ghazel*s, is attributed to Wālihī-yi Belghradī (cf. W. Pertsch, *Die Handschriften-Verzeichnisse der Königlichen Bibliothek zu Berlin*, vi, Berlin 1889, no. 413).

A Wālihī of Belgrade is mentioned solely by Laṭīfī and is conceivably identical with Wālihī of Üsküb, for whom there is no entry in Laṭīfī's *tedhkire*. He may have been unaware of the poet's true provenance, who may have lived for a time in Belgrade in his youth, perhaps even during Laṭīfī's stay there prior to finishing his *tedhkire* in 953/1546. However, we do not know if Wālihī of Üsküb's date of birth is early enough to make this possible. Although Laṭīfī states that his given name is Meḥmed, he also remarks that he has a brother called Aḥmed, giving no further details on Wālihī's *curriculum vitae*. That Laṭīfī speaks in the most contemptuous language of Wālihī's, and his brother's, poetic capabilities should be viewed in connection with the fact that he was the butt of their satirical verses; the few verses he cites are insufficient proof for his exceedingly low opinion.

Bibliography: The *tedhkire*s of Laṭīfī, ʿAhdī, ʿĀshìḳ Čelebi, Ḳìnalì-zāde Ḥasan Čelebi, Beyānī, Riyāḍī, Ḳāf-zāde Fāʾiḍī and Riḍā; ʿAṭāʾī, *Dheyl-i Shaḳāʾiḳ*, Istanbul 1268, 364-5; Ḥādjdjī Khalīfa, i, 818; ʿAbd el-Raḥmān Ḥibrī, *Enīs el-müsāmirīn*, Istanbul Üniv. Ktp., TY 451, 77a-b; Ewliyā Čelebi, *Seyāḥat-nāme*, Istanbul 1314, v, 560, 562; Aḥmed Bādī, *Riyāḍ-ī belde-i Edirne*, Bayezid Devlet Ktp., no. 10392, 292-3, 569; Hammer-Purgstall, *Geschichte der osmanischen Dichtkunst*, ii, 554-5, iii, 48, 104-7; *Sidjill-i ʿothmānī*, iv, 601-2; Sh. Sāmī, *Ḳāmūs el-Aʿlām*, Istanbul 1316, vi, 4671; *ʿOthmānlì müʾellifleri*, ii, 476; *EI*[1], s.v. (Th. Menzel); C. Baltacı, *XV-XVI. Asırlarda osmanlı medreseleri*, Istanbul 1976, 603; *İA*, art. *Vâlihî* (Ö.F. Akün); C. Kurnaz, *Ümmî divan şairleri*, in idem, *Türküden gazele: halk ve divan şiirinin müşterekleri üzerine bir deneme*, Ankara 1997, 71-101.

(Edith G. Ambros)

WALĪLĪ, an ancient town of Morocco.

Walīlī, or Walīla as it was known to the early Muslim historians, is the arabised form of the Roman name Volubilis. Located at 27 km/16 miles north of Meknès, Walīlī occupies the ledge of the Zarhūn plateau and enjoys a privileged position in the midst of a very fertile valley. It is uncertain whether this Roman city served as capital for all of the Roman province known as *Mauritania Tingitana*, but there is no doubt that it served as the chief city of the southern part of it at least. Held for a long time to have been a Roman creation, it is clear today, on the basis of recent findings, that the agglomeration is much older than the Roman presence in this part of North Africa. It was abandoned by the Roman garrison in A.D. 285 but continued to be an important political centre for several centuries afterwards, even if it lost much of the splendour and prosperity which it had enjoyed earlier.

The Islamic history of the place started with the arrival in A.D. 788 of a Sharīfian fugitive, Idrīs b. ʿAbd Allāh, who took refuge in the far Maghrib following an unsuccessful uprising against the ʿAbbāsids of Baghdād [see idrīs i]. For a short time, Idrīs took up residence at Tangier, the other important city of Mauritania Tingitana, but he soon realised that an inland place like Walīlī would better serve his political ambitions. In fact, Walīlī happened to be well protected by the Zarhūn massif, and in the middle of rich lands belonging to the influential Awrāba Berbers. At Walīlī, Idrīs enjoyed the hospitality and support of the Awrāba chief, Isḥāḳ b. Muḥammad b. ʿAbd al-Ḥamīd. According to Ibn Khaldūn, the Awrāba were then the most powerful Berber group, something which proved to be of crucial importance in gathering the support of the other Berber tribes for the cause of Idrīs. The latter was proclaimed *amīr* by the Berbers of central and northern Morocco in a significant move to free the western Maghrib from ʿAbbāsid domination. The fact that Idrīs chose Walīlī to be the seat of his kingdom is a clear indication that, by the end of the 8th century A.D., the city was still an important urban centre, even if mediaeval sources such as Ibn Abī Zarʿ in his *Rawḍ al-ḳirṭās*, describe it as being then "a middle-sized city".

Traditional historiography has for a long time maintained that the Idrīsids contented themselves with Walīlī as capital of their kingdom until the death of Idrīs I in 187/803. It was his son Idrīs II who, according to historians such as al-Djaznāʾī or Ibn Abī Zarʿ, decided to leave Walīlī after it became too small for his growing entourage and build a new capital at Fez. However, this view has been seriously challenged, and enough historical evidence is available today to indicate that Fez could very well have been the creation of the first Idrīs rather than that of his son.

Whoever was the real founder of the new capital, it remains true that the transfer of the Idrīsid centre of government to Fez inaugurated a period of decline for Walīlī, despite the burial of Idrīs I in a place located a few kilometres only from old Volubilis, in the village which thereafter acquired the name of Mawlāy Idrīs. By the 6th/12th century, the place was no longer known under the name of Walīlī. Contemporary sources mention it under the Berber name of Tizra, which in Berber means "stones". Apparently, the place was then all in ruin and, therefore, looked more like a field full of stones. In the 8th/14th century, according to al-Djaznāʾī, it was known to the people of the far Maghrib as Ḳaṣr Firʿawn (Pharaoh's castle), a clear tendency to obliterate the memory of Roman Volubilis and to bring it within the pagan pre-Islamic heritage. This name continued to be used until the beginning of this century when, during the First World War, the French employed German prisoners to dig up a large part of the buried city. However, not far from the old Walīlī the burial place of Idrīs I grew from a village into a town-*zāwiya*, especially after the resurgence of Sharīfism during the Marīnid period (7th-9th/13th-15th centuries) and the miraculous discovery in 719/1319 of the mortal remains of Mawlāy Idrīs, in good shape and in their original shroud. Thereafter, a *zāwiya* was built to honour the founder of the Idrīsid dynasty and the town of Mawlāy Idrīs developed into the important pilgrimage centre which it remains today [see MAWLĀY IDRĪS].

Bibliography: 1. Sources. Ibn Abī Zarʿ, *K. al-Anīs al-muṭrib bi-rawḍ al-ḳirṭās*, Rabat 1972, 19-29; Ibn Khaldūn, *al-ʿIbar*, Beirut 1981, xi, 296-300; ʿAlī al-Djaznāʾī, *Djanā zahrat al-ās fī bināʾ madīnat Fās*, Rabat 1991, 12-18; Leo Africanus, *Description de l'Afrique*, tr. Epaulard, Paris 1956, i, 245-6.

2. Studies. Abdelouahed Ben Talha, *Moulay Idriss du Zerhoun, quelques aspects de la vie sociale et familiale*, Rabat 1965, 9-14; Ahmed Siraj, *L'image de la Tingitane. L'historiographie arabe médiévale et l'antiquité nord-africaine*, Rome 1995, 509-31.

(MOHAMED EL MANSOUR)

WALĪMA [see ʿURS].

WĀLISHĀN [see SIBĪ].

WALLACHIA [see EFLĀḲ].

WALLĀDA BT. MUḤAMMAD III B. ʿABD AL-RAḤMĀN, poetess and littérateuse of the Spanish Umayyad family, d. Ṣafar 480/May-June 1087 or 484/1091.

Her father was placed on the throne with the *laḳab* of al-Mustakfī, but reigned for sixteen months only 414-16/1024-5, being killed shortly afterwards. Hence Wallāda's childhood and youth coincided with the particularly troubled and confused end of the Umayyad caliphate in Spain. Aged about sixteen at this time, and the offspring of a slave mother of European origin (*djāriya*), she was able now to exercise a relatively free life and, having received a thorough education in the Islamic literary sciences, she gathered round herself at Cordova a literary salon which was "the rendezvous of the well born, frequented by writers and poets who sought out her friendship, welcoming attitude and the numerous society round her" (Ibn Bassām, *Dhakhīra*, i/1, 429). Amongst the famous persons attending her salon was Ibn Zaydūn [*q.v.*], who had an amorous relationship with Wallāda, much elaborated in the sources, e.g. al-Fatḥ b. Khāḳān, *Ḳalāʾid*, 79-93, in which she herself took the initiative, daring for her time. Wallāda composed verses on this liaison and had them embroidered on her dresses.

The relationship deteriorated, however, when Ibn ʿAbdūs [*q.v.*], the *wazīr* of Cordova under the local ruler Abu 'l-Ḥazm Ibn Djahwar [*q.v.*], succeeded in replacing Ibn Zaydūn in her heart. Ibn Zaydūn reacted furiously by trying to pin his own *al-Risāla al-hazliyya* on her, but failed to sow dissension between Wallāda and her new lover, and had to leave Cordova. Wallāda then remained Ibn ʿAbdūs's mistress until his death aged 80, never marrying, having no children and also dying aged over 80. At the time of the break with Ibn Zaydūn, Wallāda attacked her ex-lover in verses of a singular coarseness, so much so that Ibn Bassām refused to admit them to the pages of his *Dhakhīra*. The humiliated Ibn Zaydūn was nevertheless subsequently inspired to address one of the finest works of Arabic poetry to her, a *nūniyya* of over 50 verses, an unusual length in Arabic poetry for a love-poem addressed to a lady, replete with the devices of *badīʿ*. In it, Ibn Zaydūn cleverly reproached Wallāda in a gentle fashion only, mixing this with her praises and contrasting their past happiness with his present misery.

Wallāda has gradually become the type of the free woman of al-Andalus and the symbol of her emancipation. It is true that she appears as freer in her attitudes and her relaxation from certain social constraints than her oriental counterpart. But she must be regarded here as far from typical, even if the political troubles of the time and the more relaxed régimes of the Taifas allowed her a measure of freedom, and indeed, regarded as exceptional, from her father's premature death and the possible inheritance of some of the mores of the *djawārī* from her foreign mother. This exceptional status within the usual Arabo-Muslim aristocracy is probably seen also in Ibn Zaydūn's temerity in addressing to her *galant* verses and speaking freely of his liaison with her. Certainly, his poems to her have immortalised her as much as the poet himself.

Bibliography: 1. Sources. Ibn Bassām, *Dhakhīra*, i/1, 429-37; Ibn Khāḳān, *Ḳalāʾid*, 189-99; Ibn Diḥya, *Muṭrib*, 7-10; Ibn ʿIdhārī, *Bayān*, iii, 140-3; Ibn Saʿīd, *Mughrib*, i, 65-6, 143, 180; Marrākushī, *Muʿdjib*, 106-11; Maḳḳarī, *Nafḥ al-ṭīb*, iv, 205-11; Ibn Nubāta, *Sarḥ al-ʿuyūn*, 22-4.

2. Studies. A. Cour, *Un poète arabe d'Andalousie: Ibn Zaidoûn*, Constantine 1920; E. Garcia-Gómez, *Poemas arábigoandaluces*, Madrid 1930; 48-9; H. Pérès, *La poésie andalouse en arabe classique au XIe siècle*, ²Paris 1953, index; E. Dermenghem, *Les plus beaux textes arabes*, Paris 1951, 140-5; L. di Giacomo, *La littérature féminine en Espagne musulmane*, in *Hésperis*, xxxi (1944), 72; Kaḥḥāla, *Aʿlām al-nisāʾ*, Damascus 1378/1959, v, 287-90; Ben Abdesselem, *La vie littéraire dans l'Espagne musulmane sous les Mulūk al-ṭawāʾif*, Tunis forthcoming, index; W. Hoenerbach, *Zur Charakteristik Wallādas, der Geliebten Ibn Zaidūns*, in *WI*, n.s., xiii (1971), 20-25; Fedwa Malti Douglas, *Ibn Zaydūn: towards a thematic analysis*, in *Arabica*, xxiii (1976), 63-76; J.M. Nichols, *Wallāda, the Andalusian lyric and the questions of influence*, in *EW*, xxi (1977), 286-91; Teresa Garulo, *Dīwān de las poetisas de al-Andalus*, Madrid 1986 (contains Sp. trans. of her poetry); Salma K. Jayyusi (ed.), *The legacy of Muslim Spain*, Leiden 1992, index. See also the *Bibl.* to IBN ZAYDŪN.

(A. BEN ABDESSELEM)

WALWĀLĪDJ, WARWĀLĪDJ, a town of mediaeval Ṭukhāristān, in what is now northern Afghānistān, mentioned in the *Ḥudūd al-ʿālam*, tr. 72, 109, as the *ḳaṣaba* or administrative centre of the province. It lay on the road from Bal<u>kh</u> and <u>Kh</u>ulm [*q.vv.*] to Ṭālaḳān and Bada<u>kh</u><u>sh</u>ān [*q.vv.*] between the confluence of the Dō<u>sh</u>ī (Sur<u>kh</u>-āb) and Ṭālaḳān rivers, whose united stream then flowed into the Oxus. It seems to be the *A-hua* of Hiuen-tsang, attesting to its existence in pre-Islamic, Hephthalite times. E.G. Pulleyblank suggested that the element *wal-/war-* reflects the name of the Central Asian people of the Avars and that the second component reflects the Altaic word for "town", Tkish. *balïk*, Mgl. *balgasun* (*The consonantal system of Old Chinese. Part II*, in *Asia Major*, N.S. ix [1963], 258-9). The town continued to be of importance, including as a mint-centre for the early <u>Gh</u>aznawids in the 420s/1030s, until Sal<u>dj</u>ūḳ times, but thereafter seems to have been replaced by Ḳunduz (< *kuhan-diz*, perhaps the old citadel of Walwāli<u>dj</u>) [*q.v.*].

At least one literary person was connected with the place, sc. Rūḥī Walwāli<u>dj</u>ī (*sic*), mentioned by ʿAwfī (? *flor.* in the second half of the 6th/12th century; cf. Storey-de Blois, v, 509-10, 636).

Bibliography (in addition to references given in the article): Marquart, *Ērānšahr*, 68, 217, 229; Le Strange, *The lands of the Eastern caliphate*, 428; Barthold, *Turkestan down to the Mongol invasion*, 67; Zambaur, *Die Münzprägungen des Islam*, Wiesbaden 1968, i, 271. (C.E. Bosworth)

WĀMIḲ WA **ʿ<u>ADH</u>RĀʾ** "the Lover and the Virgin", the names of two exemplary lovers, often referred to in Muslim literatures together with other famous loving couples such as Laylā and Ma<u>dj</u>nūn, and Yūsuf and Zulay<u>kh</u>ā.

Although references to Wāmiḳ and ʿA<u>dh</u>rāʾ are not infrequent, no fixed and widely known story about them has been preserved. The best-known version is that of the Persian poet Abu ʾl-Ḳāsim ʿUnṣurī (d. 431/1039-40 [*q.v.*]). Of this, however, only fragments have survived, partly in isolated verses quoted in lexical works, like the *Lu<u>gh</u>at-i furs* of Asadī (d. *ca.* 473/1080), and partly in a fragmentary manuscript found as late as the 1950s (see M. Shafi, *Wāmiq-o-Adhrā of ʿUnṣurī*, Lahore 1967). These fragments show clearly that ʿUnṣurī's *ma<u>th</u>nawī* poem is based on a Greek story. For a long time the identity of this Greek romance was unclear (cf. I. Kaladze, *Epičeskoe nasledie Unsuri*, Tbilisi 1983, 39-40), but it was recently established that the Greek original is the novel of Metiochos and Parthenope (see T. Hägg, in *Symbolae Osloenses*, lix [1984], 61-91, B. Utas, in *Orientalia Suecana*, xxxiii-xxxv [1984-6], 429-41). The authorship of this Parthenope Romance, which has only been preserved in parts, is not known, but it seems to belong to the centuries around the beginning of our era (cf. H. Maehler, in *Zeitschr. für Papyrologie und Epigraphik* [1956], 1-20).

How this story reached ʿUnṣurī about a millennium later is far from clear. There is nothing to substantiate a Middle Persian intermediary, as has been deduced from an anecdote in the *Ta<u>dh</u>kirat al-<u>sh</u>uʿarāʾ* by Dawlat<u>sh</u>āh (ed. E.G. Browne, London-Leiden 1901, 30). The distortions that some of the Greek names have undergone in the ʿUnṣurī fragment speak against an intermediary in another alphabet than the Arabic, e.g. Maʿ<u>sh</u>aḳūlī as a distortion of a *Ha<u>gh</u>sifūlī for Greek Hegesipyle, the step-mother of Wāmiḳ/Metiochos. On the other hand, the *Fihrist* by Ibn al-Nadīm (ed. Flügel, 120) mentions that the director of al-Maʾmūn's <u>Kh</u>izānat al-Ḥikma, Sahl b. Hārūn al-Dastmaysānī, among his works counted a *Kitāb Wāmiḳ wa ʾl-ʿA<u>dh</u>rāʾ*, and al-Bīrūnī, in a list of his own works that is preserved in Codex Golius 133 of Leiden, maintains that he has "translated the tale (*ḳiṣṣa*) of Wāmiḳ and ʿA<u>dh</u>rāʾ". Possibly Sahl b. Hārūn had produced an Arabic version which al-Bīrūnī later translated into Persian prose, a story which easily might have been taken over and put into Persian verse by his contemporary ʿUnṣurī.

Both the fragments of the Greek novel and those of the poem by ʿUnṣurī deal mainly with the beginning of the poem (cf. Utas, *op. cit.*, 431-4). The Persian fragments first describe the wedding of ʿA<u>dh</u>rāʾ's father, Fuluḳrāṭ, i.e. Polycrates, king of the island of Samos (here written *<u>sh</u>ʾms*), and a certain *Nānī (written *yʾny*). As a result of their union, a remarkable girl is born, who because of her unequalled talents is given the name ʿA<u>dh</u>rāʾ (seemingly a translation of the Greek Parthenope "virgin"). Then the narrative turns to the hero of the story, Wāmiḳ (Ar. "ardent lover", no translation of Greek Metiochos), the son of King Mil<u>dh</u>īṭas (Greek Miltiades) of *Karūnīs (for Greek Khersonesos). Because of his evil step-mother, he is forced to flee his native land and ends up in Samos, where he happens to see ʿA<u>dh</u>rāʾ at the entrance of the (Hera) temple. The two immediately fall in love with each other. ʿA<u>dh</u>rāʾ's mother makes the king invite Wāmiḳ to a banquet in the palace, and the sage *Na<u>kh</u>minūs (i.e. the philosopher Anaximenes of Miletus) questions Wāmiḳ on the nature of Eros. This symposium scene is also preserved in the Greek version, partly in almost parallel words. After the discussion of Eros, Wāmiḳ tells a story of how Hermes (written *hrmz*) invented the musical instrument *barbaṭ* (Greek *barbiton*). After that, the available text is too fragmented to allow of a coherent interpretation.

The story of ʿA<u>dh</u>rāʾ is also found in a Persian prose version in the compilation of narratives called *Dārāb-nāma* by Abū Ṭāhir Ṭarsūsī, probably written in the 6th/12th century (ed. <u>Dh</u>. Ṣafā, Tehran 1344/1965, i, 164-5). This version, although very concise, is more complete and continues the story by telling how ʿA<u>dh</u>ra's father was executed by his enemy (in fact, the Persian Satrap Oroites, cf. Herodotos 3.124) and ʿA<u>dh</u>rāʾ herself was sold into slavery by his successor *mndʾrs* (for Greek Maiandrios). After many adventures, ʿA<u>dh</u>rāʾ is set free by a kind merchant who promises to bring her to Wāmiḳ. However, the end of the original story remains uncertain.

No less than 24 later poems about the couple Wāmiḳ and ʿA<u>dh</u>rāʾ are known, at least by name. Strangely enough the surviving versions contain stories that differ widely from each other (see Shafi, *op. cit.*, 30-129; M.J. Maḥ<u>dj</u>ūb, in *Su<u>kh</u>an*, xviii [1347], 43-52, 131-42; N. Şahinoğlu, *IA*, art. "Vâmik ve Azrâ"). The two oldest of these works, the Persian poems by Faṣīḥī <u>Dj</u>ur<u>dj</u>ānī (court poet of the Ziyārid Ḳābūs II, 5th/11th century) and Amīr Far<u>kh</u>ārī (court poet of the Sal<u>dj</u>ūḳ Kay Kāwūs in Konya, 7th/13th century) are unfortunately only known by name. After those two in time come a Persian poem by a certain Ḳatīlī Bu<u>kh</u>ārāʾī (court poet of the Uzbek <u>Sh</u>āh Yaʿḳūb, 9th/15th century) and the best-known Turkish version, that of Lāmiʿī (d. 938/1531 [*q.v.*]). The latter was made known in Europe by J. von Hammer-Purgstall (*Geschichte der osmanischen Dichtkunst*, ii, Pesth 1836-8, 45-63; cf. Utas, in *AO Hung*, xlviii [1995], 229-39). Then follows a great number of little known Turkish and Persian versions and even one poem in Kashmiri (written in 1854 by Sayf al-Dīn A<u>kh</u>und Sayf Ka<u>sh</u>mīrī, cf. ms. India Office 1733/6).

Bibliography: See also J. von Hammer, *Wamik und Asra, das ist der Glühende und die Blühende. Das älteste persische romantische Gedicht, im Fünftelsaft abgezagen*, Vienna 1833; B. Utas, *Did ʿAdhrā remain a virgin?*, in *Orientalia Suecana*, xxxiii-xxxv (1984-6), 429-41;

idem, *The ardent lover and the virgin—a Greek romance in Muslim lands*, in *AO Hung*, xlviii (1995), 229-39.

(B. Utas)

WĀN, conventionally Van, the name of a lake and of a town (lat. 38° 28' N., long. 43° 21' E.) in what is now the Kurdish region of south-eastern Turkey.

1. The lake (modern Tkish., Van Gölü). This is a large stretch of water now spanning the *ils* of Van and Bitlis. It lies at an altitude of 1,720 m/5,640 feet, with a rise in level during the summer when the snows on the surrounding mountain ranges melt. Its area is 3,737 km^2/1,443 sq. miles. Being landlocked, with no outlet, it has a high content of mineral salts, especially sodium carbonate, which makes its water undrinkable, but freshwater springs along its shores have always enabled human communities to thrive there, most notably the town of Van (see 2. below). Before the First World War and the subsequent massacres and deportations, there were many Armenians living in its towns and villages, plus some sedentary and transhumant Kurds; the population is now largely Kurdish.

In mediaeval Islamic times, Lake Van was usually known as the Lake of Ardjīsh or Akhlāṭ [*q.vv.*], from the towns on its northern shore. It was famed for its *ṭirrīkh* fish, which were adapted to its waters, and were caught and salted for export as far away as ʿIrāḳ and Khurāsān. The early 10th century Armenian church of the Holy Cross, famed for its sculptures, stands on the island of Aghthamar in Lake Van.

Bibliography: Le Strange, *The lands of the Eastern Caliphate*, 183-4; Admiralty Handbooks, *Turkey*, London 1942-3, i, 187-90; *İA*, art. *Van* (lake and region) (Süha Göney). (C.E. Bosworth)

2. The town. The name Wān is not found in the Arabic sources on the Arab conquest of Armenia (for which see armīniya), but Ibn Ḥawḳal, ed. Kramers, 348, tr. Kramers and Wiet, 342, mentions Ibn al-Dayrānī as being lord of Zawazān, Wān and Wusṭān (for these places in the Lake Van area and the principality of Vaspurakan to its east, see Marquart, *Südarmenien und die Tigrisquellen nach griechischen und arabischen Geographen*, Vienna 1930; Canard, *H'amdanides*, 183-92). In the later 3rd/9th century, the Bagratid Ashot (Ashūṭ) was recognised as king of Armenia by the ʿAbbāsid caliph, with the princes of Vaspurakan, of whom the Artsrunids were the chief, as his vassals.

Already in this century, colonies of Arabs had settled in Armenia, like the *Amīrs* of Manāzkert (Malāzgird [*q.v.*]) whom the Armenians call Kaisikkʿ (< Ḳays) and who ruled on the northern shore of Lake Wān (Apahunik), and the ʿUthmānids (in Armenian, Utʿmanikkʿ) on the northeast shore of the lake, at Bergri and Amiuk. Towards the east, Vaspurakan was exposed to the attacks of the Arab governors of Ādharbāydjān. The Sādjid Afshīn occupied Wān and Wusṭān and appointed eunuchs as governors there (cf. Thomas Artsruni, tr. Brosset, 221).

In 303/916 the Sādjid Yūsuf executed the Bagratid king Smbat in Dwin (cf. Stephen Asoḷik, *History*, iii, chs. iv-v, tr. F. Macler, 18-24). Before this catastrophe, the Artsrunid prince Gagik (through his mother, a nephew of Smbat) had enrolled himself in Yūsuf's suite and by this manœuvre was able to assert the independence of Vaspurakan against Smbat's successors (kings of Ḳars and Ani). The Artsrunid kings were overlords of the principalities of Mokkʿ (now Mukus) and Andzevatsik (cf. Markwart, *Südarmenien*, 359-82).

The Artsrunid princes are several times mentioned in Ibn Miskawayh's *Chronicle*. In 326/937, the troops of the Daylamī chief Lashkarī were defeated near ʿAḳabat al-Tinnīn by Atom b. Djurdjīn (= Gurgen), lord of Zawazān (Ibn Miskawayh, i, 402; Ibn al-Athīr, viii, 262). This Atom belonged to the elder line of the Artsrunids, which was eclipsed by that of Hadamakert. In 330/940 (*ibid.*, ii, 33), Daysam, prince of Ādharbāydjān, took refuge with Djadjīḳ b. al-Dayrānī (Gagik b. Deranik). In 342/953 (*ibid.*, ii, 151), Ibn al-Dayrānī and (?) Ibn Djadjīk (probably "Deranik b. Gagik") surrendered Daysam to the Musāfarid Marzubān.

In 1004, the Artsrunid Senekʿerim, being pressed on all sides, ceded Vaspurakan to the emperor Basil II, who gave him in exchange Sīwās, to which 40,000 Armenian families followed their king. Byzantine domination was of short duration: the battle of Malāzgird in 463/1071 lost the Byzantines the last of their possessions in Armenia.

The name of Wān is briefly mentioned among the towns of "the province of Akhlāṭ" which the Khwārazmshāh Djalāl al-Dīn besieged after the capture of Akhlāṭ in 626/1229 (Bargrī, Manāzgird, Bitlīs, Walashdjird, Wān, Wusṭān).

In the Mongol period (after Arghun Khān, 1284-91), the region of Wān was close to the summer encampments of the Mongol Il-Khānids (on the mountain of Ala-Tagh, the ancient Νιφάτμς, Tendürek, to the northeast of Lake Van), but the local authority of Wān must have been in the hands of the Kurd chiefs of Ḥakkārī (see below). Mustawfī's *Nuzhat al-ḳulūb*, 102, says that "Wān is a fortress while Wusṭān (Ostan) has been a large town but now is a medium-sized one", and "Its climate and its fruits are good, its water comes from a mountain; its taxes amount to 53,400 dīnārs (Urmiya, 74,999 dīnārs, and Ardabīl, 85,000 dīnārs)".

Towards the end of the 8th/14th century, the rule of the Ḳara Ḳoyunlu Turkomans, whose hereditary centre was at Ardjīsh, was extended over Wān, but the direct administration remained in the hands of a family of Kurdish begs. When in 789/1387 Tīmūr had plundered the Ḳara Ḳoyunlu encampments of Ala-Tagh, he ordered the destruction of the fortress, but "this building from the time of Shaddād" resisted his efforts. Tīmūr made ʿIzz al-Dīn, lord of the fortress, governor of the "*wilāyat* of Kurdistān" (*Ẓafar-nāma*, i, 421-4). The ʿIzz al-Dīn, here referred to in the *Ẓafar-nāma*, was an important figure and took part in many of the events of his time (see ʿAbd al-Razzāḳ Samarḳandī, *Maṭlaʿ al-saʿdayn*, tr. Quatremère, in *NE*, xiv, 110, 153, 180). The son of ʿIzz al-Dīn Muḥammad was well received by Shāh Rukh in 824/1421. Under Uzun Ḥasan [*q.v.*], the Aḳ Ḳoyunlu troops conquered Hakkārī and placed it under the Domboli tribe, but the local Nestorian Christians restored the power to a scion of the old family.

After the coming of the Ṣafawids, prince Zāhid b. ʿIzz al-Dīn II entertained friendly relations with Shāh Ismāʿīl. In view of the rival propaganda of the Ṣafawids, the Ottoman empire must have endeavoured to strengthen the very loose organisation given to Kurdistān by Idrīs, but the incorporation of the distant frontier district of Wān, filled with foreign elements, was full of incidents.

Thus in 940/1534, during the offensive of the grand vizier Ibrāhīm Pasha against Tabrīz, delegates from Wān gave him the keys of the fortress. But as soon as the cold weather forced Sultan Süleymān's army to withdraw, the Persians advanced to Wān and soon afterwards occupied both this town and Ardjīsh (Iskandar

Mun<u>sh</u>ī, *Tārī<u>kh</u>-i ʿĀlam-ārā*, 51; according to Ewliyā Čelebi, iv, 174, the Persians retook Wān in 953/1546). The situation during the years from 940-55/1534-48 is not very clear, but when, at the instigation of the Persian prince Alḳāṣ Mīrzā, Süleymān again marched on Tabrīz, he laid siege to Wān in Rad<u>j</u>ab 955/August 1548. The town surrendered through the mediation of Alḳāṣ Mīrzā, and the *defterdār* Čerkes Iskender Pa<u>sh</u>a was appointed governor (see von Hammer, *GOR*², ii, 209; Ewliyā Čelebi, ii, 174). From this period date the baths of Rüstem Pa<u>sh</u>a at Wān and a mosque of 975/1567-8. With the appearance of the Ottoman *mīr-i mīrān* at Wān, the Kurdish chiefs retired to their fiefs of <u>Dj</u>ūlamerk and Wusṭān.

In 1013/1604, Či<u>gh</u>āle-zāde, appointed commander-in-chief against Persia, established his headquarters at Wān (of which he had previously been *wālī* in 993/1585; see von Hammer, ii, 552). He was besieged there by the Persian troops under the command of Allāh Werdi <u>Kh</u>ān, and escaped from the fortress by boat. Very soon he undertook a new campaign against Tabrīz, but it ended in a complete débâcle in the autumn of 1014/1605; cf. Iskandar Mun<u>sh</u>ī, 474-6, and TABRĪZ; von Hammer, ii, 678, 660; Govvea, *Relation des grandes guerres*, French tr. Rouen 1649, book ii, chs. xvi-xviii, 268-86; Arakel de Tauris, *Livre d'histoires*, tr. Brosset, St. Petersburg 1874, ch. vi, 303-7.

About 1008/1600 the administrative organisation of Wān was described by Ḳod<u>j</u>a Ni<u>sh</u>ān<u>dj</u>ī (934-74/1528-67), who in his *Ṭabaḳāt*, quoted by Ḥād<u>j</u>dj<u>ī</u> <u>Kh</u>alīfa, included in this *eyālet* some places now belonging to Persia (e.g. Salmās), and by ʿAyn-i ʿAlī (cf. Tischendorf, *Das Lehnwesen in d. moslem. Staaten*, Leipzig 1872, 72) who numbers in Wān 13 *san<u>dj</u>aḳ*s and one *ḥükūmet*, including in all 1,115 large and small individual fiefs (*ḳilič*).

Ewliyā Čelebi, who in 1065/1655 accompanied his uncle Aḥmed Melek, who had been appointed *wālī* of Wān, has given us a very full description of the *eyālet* of Wān (iv, 130-90). It is curious that the text is silent about the Christian population, unless this information was suppressed from the printed text by the censorship under ʿAbd al-Ḥamīd II.

Ewliyā (iv, 176) gives 37 feudal *san<u>dj</u>aḳ*s in Wān of different dimensions and with different privileges. The most important were the *ḥükūmet* of Hakkārī (with an army of 47,000, including 10,000 with guns?), of Bidlīs, Maḥmūdī and Pinyāni<u>sh</u>.

In the autumn of 1236/1821 the heir to the Persian throne, ʿAbbās Mīrzā, took advantage of some complications with the Ottomans to invade the Turkish territory of Bāyezīd as far as Bitlīs. Diplomatic complications and more particularly the epidemic of cholera, arrested the Persian operations and the status quo was re-established (see Mīrzā Taḳī Sipihr, *Tārī<u>kh</u>-i Ḳād<u>j</u>ār*, Tehran, i, under the years 1236-7; cf. R.G. Watson, *A History of Persia . . . to 1858*, London 1866, 197-221). After the Russo-Japanese war of 1905, the Ottomans in their turn advanced claims to the "unredeemed" territories, and in July 1907 Yāwer Pa<u>sh</u>a occupied many districts of the region of Salmās [*q.v.*]. The status quo was, however, re-established after the Balkan War (Ottoman note of 12 October 1912) and given legal sanction after the delimitation of 1913-14 (on the basis of the Final Protocol of 17 November 1913).

Wān was at various points in its later mediaeval history a mint centre: under the Il-<u>Kh</u>ānids, the Tīmūrids, various Turkmen dynasties, the Ṣafawids in their brief occupation of the 10th/16th century and, on various occasions, the Ottomans (see Zambaur, *Die Münzprägungen des Islam*, Wiesbaden 1968, i, 269). It also acquired some fine buildings, especially when it came under Ottoman rule in the 10th/16th century and was administered by energetic *beylerbey*s like Iskender Pa<u>sh</u>a, Rüstem Pa<u>sh</u>a and <u>Kh</u>osrew Pa<u>sh</u>a. The citadel and walls were repaired, together with the Ulu Cami, which probably dated from the end of the 8th/14th century, and baths, a caravanserai and a covered market built (see *İA*, art. *Van. Tarih*, for details).

Towards the end of the 19th century, V. Cuinet, in his *La Turquie d'Asie*, Paris 1891-3, ii, 629-760, gave population estimates for the *wilāyet* of Wān (which then comprised the two *san<u>dj</u>aḳ*s of Wān and Hakkārī [*q.v.*] to its east: 30,000 Turks, 210,000 Kurds, 79,000 Armenians and 92,000 Nestorian or Assyrian Christians, with a total of 430,000. It was during the last decade of this century that Wān was caught up in the Armenian revolutionary activity of the time, with large-scale violence there from 3 to 11 June 1896, in which 500 Armenians and 150 Muslims were killed, and which caused much damage in the town, hardly repaired when Mark Sykes passed through Wān fifteen years later (see his *The Caliphs' last heritage*, London 1915, 419).

In the First World War, Russian troops attacked Van and held it from 20 May 1915 to 4 August 1915, and again, after a brief Turkish re-occupation, from late August until the armistice of 18 December 1917. The town had an estimated population in 1914 of 25,000 Armenians and 10,000 Muslims. Most of the Armenians left with the Russians, but many Armenian villages in the vicinity of the town were sacked and their inhabitants massacred by the Muslims. In 1918, the town was virtually derelict.

Under the Turkish Republic, the town of Van (lat. 38° 28' N., long. 43° 20' E.) gradually revived and became the chef-lieu of a *vilayet*, later *il*, replacing what in Ottoman times had been the *san<u>dj</u>aḳ* of Van. In 1970 the town had a population of 88,600 and the *il* one of 326,000; by 1997 these figures had risen to 226,965 and 762,719 respectively.

Bibliography (in addition to references in the article and the very full *Bibl.* in ARMĪNIYA): For early travellers in the region, see Ritter, *Erdkunde*, ix, Berlin 1840, 972-1009, x, 1843, 285-356; V.T. Mayevski, *Voyenno—statističeskoye opisaniye Vanskago i Bitlisskago vilayetov*, Tiflis 1904; C.F. Lehmann-Haupt, *Armenien einst und jetzt*, Berlin 1910-26, ii/1; Admiralty Handbooks, *Turkey*, London 1942-3, ii, 592-4; *İA*, art. *Van. Tarih* (Nejat Göyünç).

(V. MINORSKY-[C.E. BOSWORTH])

WANG TAI-YU (Wang Daiyu) (*Mathews' Chinese-English dictionary*, revised American ed. 1943, characters nos. 7037, 5997, 7618), Muslim author of one major work and probable author of four minor works in Chinese. His date of birth is unknown, but he called himself an "old man" in 1642; he seems to have died in 1657 or 1658. He tells us that his ancestor was an astronomer who came from Tianfang Hung-wu ("Arabia") to bring tribute during the Ming (Hongwu) era (1368-98).

Wang studied the Islamic sciences in the Islamic languages, presumably Persian and Arabic, but did not begin a serious study of Chinese until he was thirty. He became well versed in the Classics and is comfortable discussing Confucian, Taoist, and Buddhist teachings. In the introduction to his major work, he mentions colleagues who had read his book and criticised him for going too deeply into Taoist and Buddhist teachings, and he replies that without borrowing all his terminology from other traditions, he would have no way to explain Islamic teachings to those unfamiliar with the Islamic languages; it seems his intended audience was primarily well-educated, Chinese-speaking Muslims. He almost never mentions Arabic words and makes no attempt to translate Islamic ideas into Chinese in any direct fashion. His whole effort is focused on re-expressing basic Islamic perspectives in the appropriate Chinese idiom; given the time and place, this gives his writings a markedly Neo-Confucian flavour. Perhaps it needs to be pointed out that Wang and those Muslim scholars who followed him, such as Liu Chih [*q.v.*] (Liu Zhi), represent the first example in Islamic history in which Muslims discussed Islamic teachings in the language of a major intellectual tradition other than their own. He was buried in a graveyard belonging to a mosque in San-li-ho (Sanlihe) in the Western part of Peking or Pei-ching (Beijing), though neither mosque nor graveyard exists today.

Wang's longest work is *Cheng-chiao chen-ch'üan* (Zhengjiao zhenquan) ("The real commentary on the true teaching", Mathews, nos. 351, 719, 297, 1672), the earliest extant book on Islam in Chinese by a Muslim. It was first published during Wang's lifetime in 1642 in Nanking or Nan-chin (Nanjing) and several times subsequently, most recently in 1987 (existing editions also include 1657, 1801, 1873, 1904, and 1933). The editions of 1801 and onwards have a preface explaining that the text was re-engraved by the mosque of Canton. An abridged version by Ma Fu-ch'u and Ma An-li with the title *Chen-ch'üan yao-lu* (Zhenquan yaolu) was published in 1864 and has also been printed with the title *Cheng-chiao chen-ch'üan* (Zhengjiao zhenquan) (bibliographers have sometimes confused the two versions). The book is about 82,000 characters in length and consists of four sections in two books, each book with twenty chapters. Book One is devoted mainly to theological principles, such as the divine attributes, predestination, creation, and human nature. Book Two focuses more on spiritual attitudes, ethics, and various commandments of Islamic law.

A second work is *Ch'ing-chen ta-hsüeh* (Qingzhen daxue) ("The great learning of the pure and the real", nos. 1171, 297, 5943, 2780), which is about 6,000 characters in length. The word *ta-hsüeh* (daxue) or "great learning" refers to the Neo-Confucian classic of the same name, while *ch'ing-chen* (qingzhen), "The pure and the real", refers to "The pure and real teaching", i.e. Islam. The work has been published many times, but the date of its first publication is not known; existing editions include 1827, 1921, and 1931. In it Wang discusses *tawḥīd* in a much more philosophical style than is found in *Cheng-chiao* (Zhengjiao). The work's three chapters deal with topics that seem to correspond with God, the Muḥammadan Reality, and the perfect human being, although the Arabic terms are not mentioned. A third work is *Hsi-chen cheng-ta* (Xizhen zhengda) ("The true answers of the very real", nos. 2416, 297, 351, 5951), a collection of some two hundred conversations in about 25,000 characters. It was first published in 1658, apparently after Wang's death, by his disciple Wu Liang-ch'eng (Wu Liangcheng), and existing editions include those of 1827 and 1925. Some of the conversations take the form of dialogues of varying lengths, and some are single questions and answers. The questioners were Muslims, both *'ulamā'* and common people, and non-Muslims, mainly Confucians. Topics range from metaphysics to details of daily ritual. In the 1925 edition, this work includes two short treatises whose authorship has been disputed but which are apparently by Wang. One is called the "appendix" or *fu-lu* (fulu), the other the "addendum" or *sheng-yü* (shengyu). The first, in about 3,000 characters, adds thirty-six conversations in the same style as the main text; the second is a series of short questions from Buddhist monks with equally short answers in about 4,000 characters.

Bibliography: Pai Shou-i (Bai Shouyi), *Hui-tsu jen-wu-shih* (Huizu renwu shih), Ning-hsia (Ningxia) 1992, 33-7; Den Tōsen, *Chūgoko kaikyōshi*, Tokyo 1975, 137-40 (Japanese tr. of Fu Tong-hsien (Fu Tongxian), *Chung-kuo hui-chiao shi* (Zhonguo huijiao shi), Changsha 1940; Kadono Tatsudō, *Seishin daigaku kō*, in *Kaikyôken*, Tokyo 1941, 324-41, 417-26; D.D. Leslie, *Islamic literature in Chinese*, Canberra 1981, 22-4; idem, *Islam in traditional China*, Canberra 1986, 117-18; Tazaka Kōdō, *Chūgoku ni okeru kaikyô no denrai to sono gutsu*, Tokyo 1961, 1376-1431; Yu Chên-keui and Yang Huai-chung (Yu Zhengni and Yang Huaizhong), *Chang-kuo i-ssu-lan wên-hsien chu-i ti-yao* (Zhongguo yisilan wenxian zhuyi tiyao), Ning-hsia 1993, 69-73.

(Sachiko Murata)

WANGARA, a people of West Africa.

The Wangara identity appears to have been formed in the context of the long distance trade, first of imperial Ghana, and then, in the 13th century, of imperial Mali [*q.v.*]. The earliest reference to the Wangara is probably that by Abū 'Ubayd al-Bakrī of Cordova in 460/1067-8, who wrote of the black gold merchants of Yarasna, a Muslim town in lands of unbelievers somewhere in the region of the headwaters of the Niger river. Writing for Roger II of Sicily almost ninety years later, al-Idrīsī referred to the inland delta of the Niger as "the country of Wangara" and commented that "its inhabitants are rich, for they possess gold in abundance. . . ." In the 17th century the Timbuktu author of the *Ta'rīkh al-Fattāsh* essayed a definition: "The Wankara and Malinke are of one origin. Malinke is used to mean the soldier among them, whereas Wankara refers to the one who engages in trade and travels from one horizon to another."

The vast network of trade built up by the Wangara extended from the Sahelian termini of the trans-Saharan caravans and the great entrepôts of the western and central Sudan, southwards to the rich, gold-bearing forest country of the hinterland of the Guinea Coast between the Volta and Comoé rivers. Along the roads they established trading posts, most commonly adding their own quarters to existing towns and villages. Many of the communities of the Wangara diaspora were far beyond the authority of any Muslim ruler, and the settlers were obliged to live among, do business with, and rely on the protection of those whom they regarded as unbelievers.

Drawing upon writings of early Mālikī jurists, Wangara scholars rationalised their position within the *dār al-ḥarb*. Most influential of these was the late-15th to early 16th century al-Ḥādjdj Sālim Suwari who, while holding that relations with unbelievers need not be confrontational, stressed the importance of education and introduced a system of licensing, by *isnād*, teachers of the *Tafsīr al-Djalālayn* of al-Maḥallī and al-Suyūṭī, and the *Muwaṭṭa'* of Mālik. In the 19th century the "Suwarian" rejection of *djihād* as an instrument of change brought them into conflict with militant reformers. Early in the century, the Wangara of Yandoto and Kurmin Dan Ranko, in Hausaland, failed to support 'Uthmān b. Fūdī's [*q.v.*] call for *djihād*, and both towns were destroyed. In the 1880s Wa and Nasa (in present-day Ghana) were sacked by the Zabarima warlord Babatu, and in the next decade the forces of Almami Samori massacred the *'ulamā'* of Kong and

Buna (in Côte d'Ivoire or Ivory Coast). The Wangara were consequently inclined to regard the French colonial forces if not as liberators, at least as allies. The tolerant and liberal nature of the "Suwarian" ideology enabled them to adjust comfortably to French and British administrations, and to the subsequent post-independence régimes and governments.

The Wangara of the eastern diaspora have now become, other than in their own remembrance, all but totally assimilated to the culture of Hausaland. In contrast, those of the southern diaspora, extending into the modern republics of Ivory Coast, Burkina Faso and Ghana, have developed an identity of their own. They call themselves Juula (Dyula, etc.) and still, in some contexts, Wangara. They speak their own dialect of Mandekan, refer their origins to Mande Kaba in Old Mali, and continue to revere al-Ḥādjdj Sālim Suwari. They remain a highly entrepreneurial class within the modern states.

Bibliography: I. Wilks, *The transmission of Islamic learning in the Western Sudan*, in J. Goody (ed.), *Literacy traditional societies*, Cambridge 1968, 162-97; T.C. Hunter, *The development of an Islamic tradition of learning among the Jahanka of West Africa*, Ph.D. thesis, University of Chicago 1977; P.E. Lovejoy, *The role of the Wangara in the economic transformation of the central Sudan in the fifteenth and sixteenth centuries*, in *J. Afr. Hist.*, x (1978), 173-93; B.M. Perinbam, *The Julas in Western Sudanese history: long-distance traders and developers of resources*, in B.K. Swartz and R.E. Dumett (eds.), *West African culture dynamics*, The Hague 1980, 455-75; Wilks, *Wangara, Akan and Portuguese in the fifteenth and sixteenth centuries*, in *J. Afr. Hist.*, xxiii (1982), 333-49, 463-72; R. Launay, *Traders without trade. Responses to change in two Dyula communities*, Cambridge 1982; Wilks, N. Levtzion and B. Haight, *Chronicles from Gonja. A tradition of West African Muslim historiography*, Cambridge 1986; R. Law, *Central and Eastern Wangara*, in *History in Africa*, xxii (1995), 281-305; Wilks, *Consul Dupuis and Wangara: a window on Islam in early nineteenth-century Asante*, in *Sudanic Africa*, vi (1995), 55-72. (I. Wilks)

WĀNḲULĪ, Meḥmed b. Muṣṭafā al-Wānī, famous Ottoman jurist in the time of Murād III (982-1003/1574-95), who especially distinguished himself in the field of *fiḳh*, lexicography and literature.

Born in Wān [*q.v.*], he acted in a number of towns (Istanbul, Rhodes, Manisa, Salonika, Amasya, Kutāhiya, Yeñis̲h̲ehir) as *müderris*, *ḳāḍī* and *mollā*, and died in 1000/1591-2 as *mollā* of Medina, to which he had come in 998/1590 in succession to Suʿūdī. In his long period of 30 years' service, he displayed great activity in writing and translating. His principal work was the Turkish translation of the *Ṣaḥāḥ* or *Ṣiḥāḥ* of al-D̲j̲awharī [*q.v.*], more esteemed by some people than the *Ḳāmūs* of al-Fīrūzābādī. This work brought him enduring fame. It was printed in 1141/1729 by Ibrāhīm Müteferriḳa [*q.v.*], as one of the first books printed in Turkey [see maṭbaʿa. B. 2.], with a second printing, in two volumes, in 1169-70/1757-7. His translation of al-G̲h̲azālī's *Kīmiyāʾ al-saʿāda* (which according to Meḥmed Ṭāhir is also attributed by many to Nawalī) is celebrated. In addition to a few brief works like his *Tard̲j̲īḥ-i bayyināt wa-tartīb-i siyāsat*, he wrote commentaries on the *Dürer-i g̲h̲urer* entitled *Naḳd al-dürer* and on the *Ferāʾid-i seyyidī*; also one on the *Wesīle* entitled *Miftāḥ al-nad̲j̲āh*.

Bibliography: *Manāḳib-i Wānḳulī*, in the 1141/1729 *Kitāb-i lug̲h̲at-i Wānḳulī*; *S̲h̲aḳāʾiḳ-i nuʿmāniyye*, *D̲h̲eyl* of ʿAṭāʾī, 316-17; Meḥmed T̲h̲üreyyā, *Sid̲j̲ill-i ʿot̲h̲mānī*, iv, 130; Bursalı Meḥmed Ṭāhir, *ʿOt̲h̲mānlı müʾellifleri*, ii, 48; Sāmī, *Ḳāmūs al-aʿlām*, vi, 4678; von Hammer, *GOR*, ii, 575. For Wānḳulī's Turkish tr. of the *Ṣaḥāḥ*, see Brockelmann, S I, 197; Sezgin, *GAS*, viii, 223. (Th. Menzel)

WANS̲H̲ARĪS, conventionally Ouarsenis, the name of a mountain massif in the central Algerian Tell. Lying to the southwest of Algiers, Wans̲h̲arīs owes its toponomy to its central part, the Kef Sidi Amar (1,985 m/6,510 feet), whose imposing pyramidal peak dominates from 800 m/2,625 feet the nearby topography (Berber *wans̲h̲arīs* = "nothing higher"). For local people, this term only applies to the central part, but modern geographers have extended it to the whole massif.

The early history of the massif is little known, though there are numerous prehistoric sites to the west of the Oued Rhiou, such as that of Columnate, but these tend to be peripheral, and there is very little in the central and eastern parts of the massif. It seems likewise to have been avoided by the Romans, and their roads (and their *limes*) are marked out along the Chélif valley and the southern piedmont (Sersou).

The population was formerly Zanāta Berber, but the mediaeval geographers, and even Ibn K̲h̲aldūn, hardly mention them, since their itineraries could not cross this inaccessible region. C. Courtois (1955), basing himself on Procopius, suggested the hypothesis of a Wans̲h̲arīs political entity bordering on Chélif to the north and Sersou to the south. At the time of the colonial period in Algeria, Berber speech still persisted among the Beni Hindel and in the region of Théniet el Had (T̲h̲āniyat al-Ḥadd) (R. Basset, 1895), but these have totally disappeared today. This complete Arabisation of a mountain region, difficult of access, seems hard to explain when other less difficult massifs have remained Berberophone.

The local population was tribally organised and, at the time of the French conquest, local prophets, the best known being Bou Maza, tried to achieve unity there. Colonial settlements soon appeared, and were more numerous than one might expect in such an unwelcoming milieu. There were a series of zones of colonisation in the northern valleys, before the massif opens out on the Chélif (Massena, Bougainville and Lamartine), a series along the southern piedmont (Waldeck Rousseau and Liébert) and a series in the massif itself (Guillaumet, Molière, Théniet el Had and Letourneux). Today it is organised administratively as the Commune Mixte of Ouarsenis, with five component *wilāya*s, based on the piedmont towns of Ain Defla, Chélif, Relizane, Tissemsilt and Tiaret.

The Wans̲h̲arīs massif is oblong in shape, some 200 km/125 miles long and comparatively clearly delimited: in the north by the Chélif valley (100-200 m altitude), in the south by the Sersou plains and the Nahr Ouessel (900-1,000 m), to the west by the Mina valley and to the east by the course of the Chélif. The massif is made up of mountain ridges running essentially west to east, with gritstone ridges and clayey and marno-schistous formations. Deep valleys like those of the oueds Deudeur, Fodda, Rouina and Sly fall towards the great valley of the Chélif, but make communications difficult because they cut across the longitudinal lines without creating real axes for everyday life. With moderate precipitation (628 mm at Théniet el Had), there are layers of classic vegetation patterns: oleasters and lentiscus regions in the lower parts; above these, Aleppo pine forests; from 900 m/2,950 feet upwards, oak forests; and from 1,300 m/4,265 feet, a few fine cedars, which have led to the formation of national parks (Parc National de l'Ouarsenis at

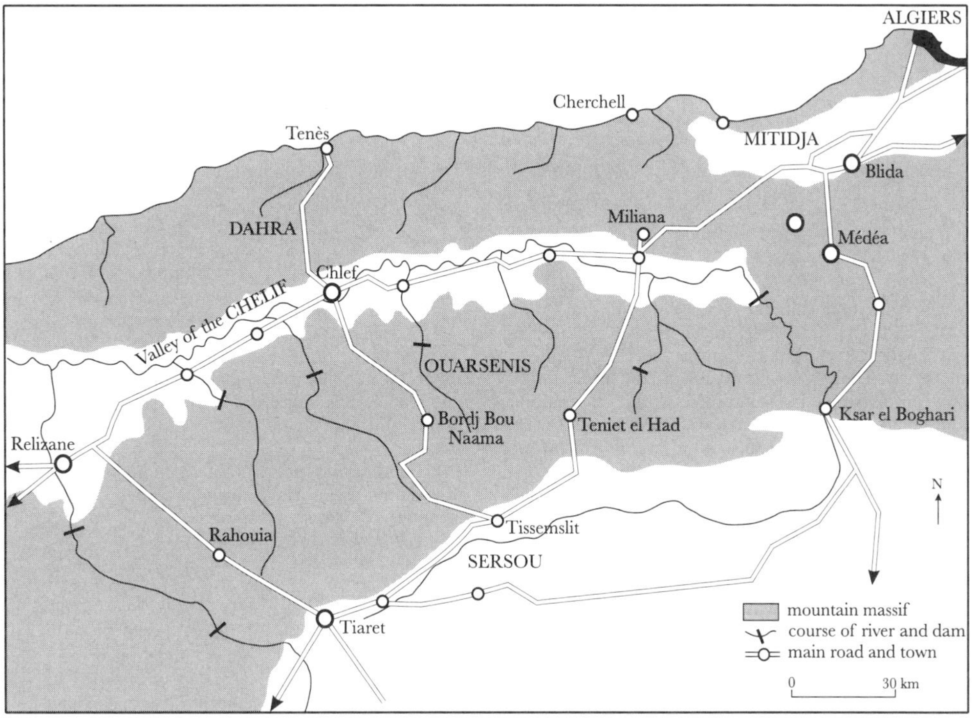

Bordj Bou Naama and the Parc Nationale des Cèdres at Théniet el Had). Until the mid-19th century, lions and panthers were numerous but they had been exterminated by the beginning of the 20th century.

A specific feature of this massif is the functioning of a mini-community, the *bocca*, whose administrative coverage often corresponds to a cleared area, with a hamlet which marks the countryside by its irrigated gardens and orchards. The people were semi-nomadic, living in tents during the hot season and in modest houses of stone during the rest of the year; they are nowadays completely sedentarised.

The tribes, comprised on average of five to twelve *bocca*s, take advantage of the complementarities of the land to compensate for the poverty of the milieu as a whole: those of the northern slopes with limits taking in the valley of the Chélif, and those of the southern slopes bordering on cereal-growing piedmont areas. One can thus understand that the century of colonisation, breaking the continuity of these administrative areas and leading to a demographic explosion, was marked by upsets to the traditional balances previously existing (Dj. Sari, 1977). Deforestation and forms of erosion are often spectacular. The population, too great for the skimpy cultivable land (average density = 60 persons per km^2), has led to the existence, for several decades, of severely disadvantaged groups.

Within the framework of independent Algeria, the installation of state enterprises, modernisation of the road system and the improvement of administrative divisions, have strongly contributed to integrating the massif into the national economy and life. Even so, the Wan<u>sh</u>arīs massif functions mainly as a reservoir for water supplies, with a dozen barrages, of varying sizes, across the north-flowing rivers and thus irrigating the Chélif valley, and as a reservoir for manpower, with a migration extending over the last four or five decades to the plains and towns around the massif. Hence the true capitals of the massif are outside it, Chélif to the north and Tiaret to the south.

Bibliography: R. Basset, *Étude sur la zenatia de l'Ouarsenis et du Maghreb central*, Paris 1895; X. Yacono, *Les bureaux arabes et l'évolution des genres de vie dans l'Ouest du Tell algérois*, Algiers 1953; C. Courtois, *Les Vandales et l'Afrique du Nord*, Paris 1955; Dj. Sari, *L'activité minière de l'Ouarsenis*, in *Annales algériennes de géographie*, vii (1969), 7-25; idem, *Les populations de l'Ouarsenis central*, in *Mediterranée*, Aix 1972, nos. 3-4, 89-117; J. Lizot, *Métidja, un village algérien de l'Ouarsenis*, Memoires du CRAPE no. 22, Algiers 1973; Sari, *L'homme et l'érosion dans l'Ouarsenis (Algérie)*, Algiers 1977. (M. Côte)

AL-**WAN<u>SH</u>ARĪSĪ**, Abu 'l-ʿAbbās Aḥmad b. Yaḥyā b. Muḥammad b. ʿAbd al-Wāḥid b. ʿAlī (834-914/1431-1508), Mālikī jurist and *muftī*, born possibly in the Ouarsenis (Algeria, Ar. Wan<u>sh</u>arīs [*q.v.*]), where he grew up and pursued his education. His family belonged to one of the numerous Berber tribes which populated these mountains. At this time, the situation was relatively unstable on the political, military and social levels, on account of the struggles for power between the Zayyānī family [see ʿABD AL-WĀDIDS], the Ḥafṣids [*q.v.*], who were intent on taking control of Tlemcen, and the local tribes who were allied with the Marīnids [*q.v.*] in opposing the kings of Tlemcen. Shortly after his birth, the family left the mountains of the Ouarsenis to settle in Tlemcen, where he was educated. The most eminent intellectual figures of Tlemcen were his teachers. These were jurists, and consequently al-Wan<u>sh</u>arīsī's education was predominantly a legal one in addition to linguistic studies.

Among the teachers whose classes he attended were: (1) Ḳāsim al-ʿUḳbānī (d. 854/1450-1), eminent jurist of Tlemcen, who travelled to the East in 830/1426-7 and was *ḳāḍī* of this city for some time before quitting his post to devote himself to teaching and the composition of *fatwās*. Al-Wan<u>sh</u>arīsī makes copious reference to him in his work (*Miʿyār*, i, 10-11, 181-6, 321-2, 428, vi, 40, 41, 42, 47-8, 504-5). (2) al-Murrī (d. 864/1460). (3) Muḥammad al-ʿUḳbānī (d. 871/1467), grandson of (1) and nephew of Ibrāhīm b. Ḳāsim al-ʿUḳbānī, cited below. He was grand *ḳāḍī* of Tlemcen, an expert in *nawāzil*; some of his *fatwās* are retained by al-Wan<u>sh</u>arīsī (*Miʿyār*, ii, 15-16, v, 107, 109-10). He composed a treatise entitled *Tuḥfat al-nāẓir wa-<u>gh</u>unyat al-<u>dh</u>ākir fī ḥifẓ al-<u>sh</u>aʿāʾir wa-ta<u>gh</u>yīr al-manākir* (Zaytūna Library, Tunis). (4) Ibn al-ʿAbbās al-ʿUbbādī (d. 871/1466), teacher of Ḳurʾānic and grammatical commentaries, jurist and *muftī*, one of the great scholars of Tlemcen and the most important of his time. He composed works on grammar and religion as well as numerous *fatwās*, some of which were retained by al-Māzūnī and al-Wan<u>sh</u>arīsī (*Miʿyār*, i, 404-7, ii, 17-18, 388-91, iv, 363-4, 449-50, 451-4, 454-7, v, 106-7, 109). (5) al-Ḳawrī al-La<u>kh</u>mī al-Miknāsī (804-72/1401-2 to 1468). Of Andalusian extraction but born in Meknès, he settled in Fās, where he was *muftī* and grand *ḳāḍī*. Among his works, an eight-volume commentary on the *Mu<u>kh</u>taṣar* of <u>Kh</u>alīl stands out. Al-Wan<u>sh</u>arīsī was to include some of his *fatwās* in his work (*Miʿyār*, ii, 396-7, vii, 187-8, 328-9). (6) Ibn al-<u>Dj</u>allāb al-Ma<u>gh</u>īlī al-Tilimsānī (d. 875/1470-1), a jurist of Tlemcen, who was capable of answering a large number of legal questions without referring to texts, relying solely on memory. He held the post of grand *ḳāḍī* of Tlemcen and was the author of *fatwās* reproduced by al-Wan<u>sh</u>arīsī (*Miʿyār*, iv, 349, 366, 454). (7) Abū Sālim al-ʿUḳbānī (808-80/1405-6 to 1475-6), *muftī* of Tlemcen and author of numerous works, who was grand *ḳāḍī* of this city following the removal of his nephew Muḥammad. His *fatwās* were collected by al-Wan<u>sh</u>arīsī (*Miʿyār*, i, 177-8, iv, 302, 326-7). (8) Ibn Ḥarzūza (d. 883/1478), preacher and expert in *uṣūl*. (9) Ibn Marzūḳ al-Kafīf (d. 901/1421), born in Tlemcen where he also died, author of a commentary on *fatwās*. (10) Ibn Zakrī al-Ma<u>gh</u>rāwī al-Mānawī al-Tilimsānī (d. 899 or 900/1493) who was *ḳāḍī* and *muftī*, and who studied the foundations and applications of the law. Author of numerous judicial works, he issued *fatwās* reproduced by al-Wan<u>sh</u>arīsī (*Miʿyār*, ii, 217-18, 228-9, ix, 312-16). (11) al-Ḳāḍī al-Miknāsī (d. 917/1511), grand *ḳāḍī* of Fās for more than thirty years, the author of a work on the judiciary.

In 885/1482, al-Wan<u>sh</u>arīsī was awarded a diploma by two Egyptian *ʿulamāʾ*, Abū ʿAmr ʿU<u>th</u>mān al-Diyyāmī and Muḥammad al-Sa<u>kh</u>āwī. When he was approaching his fortieth year, a conflict, the reasons for which are no longer known, led to a confrontation with the Zayyānī sultan Muḥammad IV (d. 910/1504). His house was ransacked and he was forced to flee and take up residence in Fās on 1 Muḥarram 874/11 July 1469.

During this second phase of his life in Fās, al-Wan<u>sh</u>arīsī was treated as a distinguished person, occupying various teaching posts, and thereby arousing hostility on the part of the *ʿulamāʾ*, leading to his dismissal from these posts. He taught in the Muʿallaḳ mosque, in the al-<u>Sh</u>arraṭīn quarter of Fās al-Ḳarawiyyīn, and occupied the *Mudawwana* chair in the Miṣbāḥiyya *madrasa*. Little is known of his personal life, but it is assumed that he married in Fās since his son ʿAbd al-Wāḥid, the only one mentioned, was born in this city *ca.* 880/1475-6.

He died on 20 Ṣafar 914/Tuesday, 20 June 1508 aged eighty, the same year that the Spanish captured Oran. He was buried in Fās, in the Kudyat al-Barāṭīl cemetery, near the tomb of Ibn ʿAbbād of Ronda (d. 792/1390). His profound knowledge of Mālikī *fiḳh* had made him the flag-bearer of the school at the end of the 9th/15th century.

As for his œuvre, the principal work of al-Wan<u>sh</u>arīsī is the *Miʿyār al-muʿrib wa 'l-<u>dj</u>āmiʿ al-mu<u>gh</u>rib ʿan fatāwī ʿulamāʾ Ifrīḳiya wa 'l-Andalus wa 'l-Ma<u>gh</u>rib*, a vast compilation of Andalusian and North African *fatwas* from the 3rd/9th to the 9th/15th centuries. He wrote some thirty books in all.

(a) Printed works.

(1) *K. al-Wilāyāt* (H. Bruno and M. Gaudefroy-Demombynes, *Le livre des magistratures d'el-Wancherisi*, Rabat 1937). This is a compendium of legal jurisdictions and public functions in relation to the judicial power, and the characteristics and functions of the *ḳāḍī*.

(2) *al-Mustaḥsan min al-bidaʿ*. Section of the *Miʿyār* on customs and social traditions, and acceptable innovations (H. Pérès, *al-Mustaḥsan min al-bidaʿ*, Algiers 1946; *Miʿyār*, ii, 461-511).

(3) *Asnā al-matā<u>dj</u>ir fī bayān aḥkām man <u>gh</u>alaba ʿalā waṭanihi al-naṣārā wa-lam yuhā<u>dj</u>ir wa-mā yatarattabu ʿalayhi min al-ʿuḳūbāt wa 'l-zawā<u>dj</u>ir*. *Fatwā* tract written in response to a question formulated by Abū ʿAbd Allāh Ibn Ḳūṭiyya on the subject of Andalusians who had emigrated to North Africa and, having failed to find a satisfactory situation, wanted to return to Spain (H. Muʾnis, *Asnā al-matā<u>dj</u>ir*. . ., in *RIEIM*, v [Madrid 1957], 129-91; *Miʿyār*, ii, 90 ff.).

(4) "Prologue" to the *Mu<u>th</u>lā* of Ibn al-<u>Kh</u>aṭīb. An epigraph written in response to the satire of the Granadan vizier attacking the notaries of his day for their corruption and incompetence.

(5) *Wafayāt*. Obituary notices honouring distinguished persons of the Ma<u>gh</u>rib from 701/1301 to 912/1507 (Ḥamzāwiyya library, ms. no. 240; al-Wan<u>sh</u>arīsī, *Wafayāt*, ed. Ḥa<u>dj</u>djī, in *Alf sana min al-wafayāt*, Rabat 1976).

(6) *Īḍāḥ al-masālik ilā ḳawāʿid al-imām Abī ʿAbd Allāh Mālik*. Compendium of judicial principles and norms for the application of the law (ed. Aḥmad Bū Ṭāhir al-<u>Kh</u>aṭṭābī, Rabat 1980, ed. al-Ṣādiḳ b. ʿAbd al-Raḥmān al-<u>Gh</u>iryānī (?), Tripoli (Libya) 1401/1991).

(7) *Naẓm al-durar al-maʾ<u>th</u>ūra wa-ḍamm al-aḳwāl al-ṣaḥīḥa* . . . Letter replying to objections and criticisms issued by a jurist of Tlemcen on the subject of a *fatwā* concerning a transaction (*Miʿyār*, vi, 574-606).

(8) *Tanbīh al-ḥā<u>dh</u>iḳ al-nadis ʿalā <u>kh</u>aṭaʾ man sawwā bayna <u>dj</u>āmiʿ al-ḳarawiyyīn wa 'l-Andalus* (*Miʿyār*, i, 251-74).

(9) *Tanbīh al-ṭālib al-darrāk ʿalā taw<u>dj</u>īh ṣiḥḥat al-ṣulḥ al-munʿaḳid bayna Ibn Saʿd wa 'l-Ḥabbāk* (*Miʿyār*, vi, 532-4).

(10) A biography of al-Maḳḳarī al-<u>Dj</u>add.

(b) Lithographed works.

(11) *al-Manha<u>dj</u> al-fāʾiḳ wa 'l-manhal al-rāʾiḳ wa 'l-maʿnā al-lāʾiḳ bi-adab al-muwa<u>thth</u>iḳ wa-aḥkām al-wa<u>th</u>āʾiḳ* (Fās 1881, 384 pp.). The central theme of this work is the composition of notary documents and the function of the notary.

(12) *<u>Gh</u>unyat al-muʿāṣir wa 'l-tālī fī <u>sh</u>arḥ fiḳh wa<u>th</u>āʾiḳ al-ḳāḍī al-Fi<u>sh</u>tālī*. This is a commentary on al-Fi<u>sh</u>tālī's work on notary documents, written in the margin of a copy of this text (Fās 1890).

(13) *Mubdī li-<u>kh</u>aṭaʾ al-Ḥumaydī*, on the marriage of people hindered by legal obstructions, such as guardianship or minority (Fās 1895).

(14) *ʿUddat al-burūḳ fī <u>dj</u>amʿ (tal<u>kh</u>īṣ) mā fi (/min) 'l-ma<u>dh</u>hab min (/fi) l-<u>dj</u>umūʿ wa 'l-furūḳ*. Large two-volume

treatise dealing with controversial questions of law (ed. Ḥamza Abū Fāris, Beirut 1990).

(15) *Īḍāʾat al-ḥalak wa ʾl-murdji ʿ bi ʾl-darak ʿalā man aftā min fuḳahāʾ Fās bi-taḍmīn al-rāʿī al-mushtarak*, the work written in Fās, responding to criticisms levelled at his judicial decisions.

(c) Works still in manuscript.

(16) *Mukhtaṣar aḥkām al-Burzulī* (Ḳarawiyyīn Library, Fās; General Library of Rabat, 1343, D. 1447; Royal Library of Rabat, 9843, 8462).

(17) *Sharḥ muṣṭalaḥāt al-Mukhtaṣar al-fiḳhī li-Ibn ʿArafa.*

(18) *K. al-adjwiba* or *Adjwiba fiḳhiyya* or *Fatāwā* (General Library of Rabat, K. 684: Tetuan Library, 654).

(19) *K. al-asʾila wa ʾl-adjwiba* (General Library of Rabat, D. 2197).

(20) *Risāla fi ʾl-masāʾil al-fiḳhiyya* (Princeton University Library, 178).

(21) *K. al-Fawāʾid al-muhimma* (General Library of Rabat, Q. 1061).

(22) *Ḳawāʿid al-madkhal* (Royal Library of Rabat, 2052).

(23) *Fahrasa* (not located).

(d) Other lost works.

(24) *K. al-wāʿī li masāʾil al-aḥkām wa ʾl-tadāʿī.*

(25) *Taʿlīḳ ʿalā Ibn al-Ḥādjib al-Farʿī.*

(26) *Ḥall al-ribḳa ʿan asīr al-ṣafḳa.*

(27) *K. al-ḳawāʿid fi ʾl-fiḳh.*

(28) *al-Durar al-ḳalāʾid wa-ghurar wa ʾl-fawāʾid.*

Bibliography: Wansharīsī, *al-Miʿyār al-muʿrib wa ʾl-djāmiʿ al-mughrib ʿan fatāwī ʿulamāʾ Ifrīḳiya wa ʾl-Andalus wa ʾl-Maghrib*, ed. Aḥmad al-Būʿazzawī, Fās 1896-7, 11 vols., repr. Beirut; ed. M. Ḥadjdjī, Rabat 1981-3, 12 vols. (references are to this ed.); F. Vidal-Castro, *Aḥmad al-Wansharīsī (m. 914/1508). Principales aspectos de su vida*, in *Al-Qantara*, xii (1991), 315-52; idem, *Las obras de Aḥmad al-Wansharīsī (m. 914/1508), Inventario analítico*, in *Anaquel de Estudios Arabes*, iii (1992), 73-111; V. Lagardère, *Histoire et société en occident musulman au Moyen Âge. Analyse du Miʿyār d'al-Wansharīsī*, Madrid 1995. (V. Lagardère)

WARAʿ (a.) in Islamic religious terminology denotes religious scrupulousness and delicacy of conscience. Neither the term itself nor its root is found in the Ḳurʾān, but it nevertheless enjoyed a great renown in relation to various spheres, their sole common point being their falling under the topic of legal status (*ḥukm*). Hence its history may perhaps be grouped under the question of the relation between the law (*sharʿ*) and the mystical perspective.

In the 3rd/9th century, in a region with a strong eremitical tradition like Egypt, one finds the conciliatory position of Dhu ʾl-Nūn al-Miṣrī [*q.v.*] for whom *waraʿ*, conceived as total abstinence, allows one to reach the extreme of asceticism (*zuhd* [*q.v.*]). However, in Baghdād at the same time, the conflict between the two attitudes became exacerbated. A *K. al-Waraʿ* attributed by tradition to Ibn Ḥanbal is actually by his immediate disciple Abū Bakr Aḥmad b. Muḥammad al-Marwazī, relating from (*ʿan*) his master. This is a collection of anecdotes concerning the uncertainty of pious Muslims that, when involved in an action apparently without consequences, they may be contaminated by its possible results, even in a long-distance fashion. This compilation is without order, but one can discern the significant frequency of verbs like *kariha* "detest"—in nineteen paragraph titles out of fifty—and *ʿadjiba* "be astonished", showing the essential motivation of the pious man as being the feeling of repulsion or at least fear of scandal. The same solicitude is found in the work of the same title by Ibn Abi ʾl-Dunyā [*q.v.*], which is more orderly, since he classifies his anecdotes by theme or by reference to famous persons. Al-Muḥāsibī [*q.v.*] in his *K. al-Makāsib wa ʾl-waraʿ wa ʾl-shubuhāt*, cites Ibn Ḥanbal four times, and explicitly places *waraʿ* below renunciation of the world (*zuhd*).

This is, furthermore, the position attributed by the texts to al-Ḥasan al-Baṣrī [*q.v.*], but one wonders whether this is not an attempt to cite an ancient authority during a polemic obviously of the 3rd/9th century. Al-Muḥāsibī's text is considered to be one written in his maturity, representing not only an elaboration of his thought but also his awareness of the various nuances in the opinions of his contemporaries. His solution was to co-ordinate them by placing them in a hierarchy. He starts from a definition of the Good as doing what God has ordained and renouncing what He has forbidden. Fear of God (*taḳwā* [*q.v.* in Suppl.]) is that which integrates purity of intention with works so that the actual work is done for God alone. The resultant *waraʿ* does not extend merely to clothing and food, as certain people think, but to the fear of God in all circumstances where there is a prohibition or an obligation. Four conditions are necessary for genuine scruple. Two are obligatory: not to do anything that God has forbidden, such as innovation or heresy, and not to take or make anything illicit that God has permitted, whilst the other two are recommended: to avoid anything ambiguous, lest it be illicit, and to avoid everything that, although licit in itself, can serve as a means for illicitness (e.g. gossip, which can lead to defamation or lying). A criterion is necessary in order to avoid becoming victim to an illusion: this consists of resisting temptation when it presents itself, intention alone not being enough. This is why renunciation is better than scrupulousness.

The various aspects of this doctrine are developed by later authorities. Al-Tirmidhī stressed the doctrine of *taḳwā*, defined by him as *wiḳāyat al-ḳalb wa ʾl-waraʿ* "guarding the heart and scrupulous abstention". But it was above all the hierarchisation of the mystical "stations", subsequently elaborated, that allowed the progressive integration of the mystical approach within the ensemble of the believer's attitudes. The following stages may be distinguished:

(1) Al-Sarrādj [*q.v.*] considers that the mystic's scrupulosity must exceed that of the ordinary believer. He places it in second place after *tawba*, repentance, but before *zuhd, faḳr*, poverty, *ṣabr*, endurance of adversity, *tawakkul*, confidence in God, and, finally, *riḍā*, submission to and agreement with the divine will.

(2) In his *Book of stages*, al-Anṣārī defines *waraʿ* as "the last stage of *zuhd* for the masses and the first one of *zuhd* for the élite", and he distinguishes three degrees of it: (a) concerning obligations; (b) "the maintaining of sanctions for what is not in itself evil, through reserve and *taḳwā*, by [desire of] elevating oneself above base things, and in order to be pure of all infringement of the legal penalties (*ḥudūd*)"; and (c) "scrupulosity towards everything which tends towards the dispersion of time and attachment for separation, and which is opposed to the state of union".

(3) Finally, al-Ghazālī [*q.v.*] in his *Iḥyāʾ*, defines four degrees: (a) simple observance of all which issues from the Islamic profession of faith, sc. abstinence from what is clearly forbidden (*ḥarām*); (b) the scrupulosity of the *ṣāliḥūn*, abstinence from everything which is dubious; (c) that of the *muttaḳūn*, sc. abstention from all that is licit in itself but which might lead to what is forbidden; and (d) that of the *ṣiddīḳūn*, which is "turning away from everything which is other than

God through fear of wasting an hour of one's life on things which do not increase one's nearness to God".

This classification was to be later completed by the idea of *tark al-waraʿ* "abandonment of scruple", to which Ibn al-ʿArabī devotes a chapter in his *Futūḥāt* after that on *waraʿ*. This concerns only gnosis. In effect, abstention from what is licit and necessary would be disobedience, and abstention from what is licit and superfluous concerns only *zuhd*. Conversely, the person who does not have his eyes fixed only on the things of this world but sees in them only the face of God cannot apprehend the signs which would guide him towards scrupulosity regarding what is doubtful.

Even so, these distinctions are not always respected by the person who makes them himself, e.g. Ibn al-ʿArabī, who in his profession of faith uses *waraʿ* and *zuhd* almost without distinction.

Bibliography: Ibn Ḥanbal, *K. al-Waraʿ*, ed. M. Zaghlūl, Beirut 1986, partial tr. G.-H. Bousquet and P. Charles-Dominique in *Hespéris*, xxxix (1952), 97-119; Muḥāsibī, *K. al-Makāsib*, ed. as *K. Makāsib al-rizḳ al-ḥalāl wa-ḥaḳīḳat al-tawakkul ʿalā ʾllāh* by M.ʿU. al-Khusht, Cairo 1403/1984; Ibn Abi 'l-Dunyā, *K. al-Waraʿ*, ed. M.ʿA.-M. al-Saʿdānī, Cairo 1993; Sarrādj, *K. al-Lumaʿ*, ed. Nicholson, Leiden-London 1914; Ghazālī, *Iḥyāʾ*, book 1, *bāb* 2, para. 8; ʿAbd al-Muʿṭī al-Lakhmī al-Iskandarānī, commentary on the *Book of stages*, ed. S. de Laugier de Beaurecueil, Cairo 1954, 51-2; Ibn al-ʿArabī, *Futūḥāt*, Būlāḳ 1329/1911, ii, 175. (D. Urvoy)

WĀRĀD [see nagyvárad].

WARADĪN (Serbian Petrovaradin, Hungarian Pétervárad, German Peterwardein), a town and centre of a *nāḥiye* in Ottoman Hungary (lat. 45° 15' N., long. 19° 55' E.), earlier a settlement on both sides of the Danube in the mediaeval Hungarian counties of Bács and Szerém; today the southern part of Novi Sad (Hungarian Újvidék) in Serbia.

The place was already inhabited in Roman times as Cusum. Of its later history nothing is known until the 13th century, when the Hungarian king Béla IV (1235-70) conveyed it to the Cistercians. After 1439 it was under the patronage of the *banus* of Macsó. The northern part of the town, which had 18 heads of families and a widow, most of them with Hungarian names and insignificant Southern Slav infiltration, was registered as Vasarus Varad in 1522. However, the inhabitants could not pay taxes since the settlement "was devastated and desolated".

Among the fortifications along the Danube, the stronghold of Waradīn was of considerable importance in the first line of the Hungarian defence system against the Ottomans. In March 1523, Bālī, the *beg* of Semendire, made an unsuccessful attempt to conquer it. During the 1526 campaign of Sultan Süleymān I, the castle was captured after a siege of two weeks.

Waradīn became the centre of a *nāḥiye* and of a *ḳaḍāʾ* within the *liwā* of Szerém/Sirem which belonged to the province of Buda [*q.v.*]. It served as a significant crossing-place during imperial and other campaigns.

In the 16th century, the population of the town was small and the yield of ordinary taxes modest. Around 1570, the majority of the inhabitants were Muslims, many of whom possessed a vineyard and a piece of arable land, and there was a strong Southern Slav minority and no Hungarians. The number of soldiers in the castle was some 300 to 400 men in peace-time. The sum to be paid from tithes and dues amounted to 3,740 *aḳčes* around 1550, 6,001 *aḳčes* in 1560, 10,001 *aḳčes* around 1570, and 12,425 in 1591. Local people failed to gain *derbenddji* status in compensation for their work at the landing-place and for the upkeep of the temporary bridges there. However, they were granted certain immunities including payment in kind. Ships owned by Muslim merchants in Waradīn appear with various goods, mainly cereals, in Buda in 1571-3.

In 1687 Waradīn, together with several strongholds in the vicinity, was taken by the forces of the Christian allies. Ottoman attempts in 1694 and 1716 at regaining it ended with failure. In the second battle for it, even the Grand Vizier died. This decisive defeat, as well as the loss of Temeshwār [*q.v.*] and Belgrade [*q.v.*] led to the 1718 peace of Požarevac [see pasarofča] when the border was drawn far below Waradīn.

Bibliography: I. Szabó, *Bács, Bodrog és Csongrád megye dézsmalajstromai 1522-böl* ("Tax-lists of Bács, Bodrog, and Csongrád counties from 1522"), Budapest 1954, 44; L. Fekete und Gy. Káldy-Nagy, *Rechnungsbücher türkischer Finanzstellen in Buda (Ofen) 1550-1580. Türkischer Text*, Budapest 1962; B. McGowan, *Sirem sancaği mufassal tahrir defteri* ("The detailed survey of the sandjaḳ of Sirem"), Ankara 1983, 158-66; G. Gömöry, *Pétervárad ostroma 1694-ben* ("The siege of Waradīn in 1694"), in *Hadtörténelmi Közlemények* (1890), 20-35; art. *Varadin* in *İA* (B. Kütükoğlu). (G. Dávid)

WARAḲA b. NAWFAL, an early Arabian monotheist and contemporary of the Prophet.

Biographical details concerning Waraḳa are few in number and legendary in character, since in one way or another they all relate to his kerygmatic role in the narrative of Muḥammad's earliest revelation. Waraḳa was the son of Nawfal b. Asad b. ʿAbd al-ʿUzzā b. Ḳuṣayy, who is said to have been killed in the last "Battle of the Sacrilege" (*yawm al-Fidjār al-ākhir*) (Ibn al-Kalbī, *Djamharat al-nasab*, Beirut 1986, 68-9), and of Hind bt. Abī Kathīr. He was thus the cousin of the Prophet's first wife Khadīdja [*q.v.*], but unlike her line (that of Khuwaylid b. Asad b. ʿAbd al-ʿUzzā), his left no descendants of note. According to Ibn Saʿd (*Ṭabaḳāt*, viii, 8; cf. al-Balādhurī, *Ansāb al-ashrāf*, i, Cairo 1959, 407), Khadīdja had been "proposed" (*dhukirat*) to Waraḳa, but the marriage did not take place; and this, at least in part, probably explains the traditionists' occasional sensitivity about their relations (Ibn Saʿd, *Ṭabaḳāt*, i/1, 130). One wonders how this account relates to another, according to which Waraḳa's sister proposed marriage to ʿAbd Allāh, Muḥammad's father.

Frequently mentioned alongside ʿUbayd Allāh b. Djaḥsh, ʿUthmān b. al-Ḥuwayrith (for whom he composed an elegy, *rithāʾ*), and Zayd b. ʿAmr (the latter sometimes called his *nadīm*, or boon companion), Waraḳa is counted among those contemporaries of Muḥammad who abandoned polytheism before his call to prophethood. Like other *ḥanīf*s, Waraḳa not infrequently appears circumambulating the Kaʿba, and for Kaʿba protocol is cited by al-Azraḳī (*Akhbār Makka*, Madrid 1979, i, 175, 182; cf. U. Rubin, Ḥanīfiyya *and Kaʿba: an inquiry into the Arabian pre-Islamic background of* dīn Ibrāhīm, in *JSAI*, xiii [1990], 97). Unlike most other *ḥanīf*s, however, Waraḳa is also said to have converted to Christianity, apparently while travelling through Syria (and elsewhere); it is presumably during these travels that he came to study under "people of the Gospel and Torah", and to learn (written) Arabic and even Hebrew. Whatever truth one attaches to these travel accounts, Waraḳa's knowledge of an Arabic Gospel is almost certainly anachronistic (see

S.H. Griffith, *The Gospel in Arabic. An inquiry into its appearance in the first Abbasid century*, in *Oriens Christianus*, lxix [1985], 144-9), even if his literacy is possible (according to al-Balādhurī, *Ansāb al-ashrāf*, i, 81, Waraḳa's sister also consulted books). Some of the poetry attributed to Waraḳa is occasionally credited to another *ḥanīf*, Umayya b. Abi 'l-Ṣalt [*q.v.*].

Although he is associated with Muḥammad very early on—Waraḳa and an unidentified Ḳurashī are said to have found the young boy, who had strayed from his suckling mother, and returned him to ʿAbd al-Muṭṭalib, an account that implicitly presumes Waraḳa's recognition of Muḥammad's prophecy at the time of his birth (thus Ibn Isḥāḳ, *al-Sīra al-nabawiyya*, i, 167)—it is in connection with accounts of the earliest *āyas* (traditionally XCVI, 1-5) that Waraḳa earned his place in early Islamic history, confirming that Muḥammad's first, tentative, revelation was indeed authentic. "There has come to him," Waraḳa says, "the greatest law (*nāmūs*) that came to Moses" (*nāmūs* being interpreted as the angel Gabriel); "surely he is the prophet of this people" (Ibn Isḥāḳ, i, 238). The exact details are very hard to pin down, however. Sometimes Khadīdja sends Muḥammad to Waraḳa; sometimes she goes alone, and reports his words to the Prophet; sometimes she is accompanied by Abū Bakr; the last of these clearly suggests that the story came to express claims about which Companion had been converted first (noted by M.J. Kister, Al-Taḥannuth. *An inquiry into the meaning of a term*, in *BSOAS*, xxxi [1968], 224 n. 13, with more sources). Aside from the question of who exactly was involved, traditionists were keenly interested in Waraḳa's response. The consensus seems to have been that, having recognised Muḥammad's prophecy, Waraḳa still retained his Christian faith. But confusion about his fate is sometimes acknowledged, some authorities counting him among the *ṣaḥāba*, indeed some even identifying him as the first (male) to convert (e.g. al-Zurḳānī, *Sharḥ ʿalā 'l-mawāhib al-laduniyya*, Būlāḳ 1278, i, 257; al-Diyārbakrī, *Taʾrīkh al-khamīs*, Cairo 1302, i, 323). According to Ibn Ḥadjar, *Iṣāba*, Cairo 1977, x, 304 ff., Waraḳa died before Muḥammad's (public) "call to the people that they convert". The account echoes others that characterise him as old and blind at the time of Muḥammad's first revelation, fits the traditional chronology of revelation, according to which the *fatra*—the suspension of revelation—followed XCVI, 5, and, finally, explains why Waraḳa is given to foretell Muḥammad's persecution at the hand of the Meccans; he himself never lived to see it.

Some say Waraḳa died in Mecca, others in Syria; the second of these occasionally forms part of a different chronology, according to which his death came after the *hidjra*. Since the Prophet is said to have forbidden insulting (the memory of) Waraḳa, and, moreover, to have had a dream of him in heaven, one surmises a lively controversy about his status in the early period. The Syrian connection is also among many features Waraḳa's story shares with the legend(s) of the monk Baḥīrā; and Nöldeke, who adduced some evidence that he was in fact a Jew (*Hatte Muḥammad christliche Lehrer?*, in *ZDMG*, xii [1858], 699 ff.), went so far as to find the origins of these legends in Waraḳa. Here he may have gone astray; but there is no question that the accounts providing monotheist collaboration for Muḥammad's prophecy frequently overlap. Needless to say, all this makes evaluating Waraḳa's significance for the birth of Islam vexing indeed. It is particularly difficult to judge what kind of influence (if any) he exerted on Muḥammad's thought; that he did has been argued in both European and Middle Eastern scholarship alike (thus Abū Mūsā al-Ḥarīrī, *Ḳāṣṣ wa-nabī* (Diyār ʿAḳl 1985).

Bibliography (in addition to the works cited in the article): Iṣfahānī, *Aghānī*[3] iii, 119 ff.; Balādhurī, *Ansāb al-ashrāf*, v, Beirut 1996, 67-8, 522; Ibn al-Athīr, *Usd*, v, 88-9; Muḥammad b. Ḥabīb, *Munammaḳ*, Ḥaydarābād 1964, 175-6, 181 ff., 531 ff.; idem *Muḥabbar*, Ḥaydarābād 1942, 171; Ibn Ḳutayba, *Maʿārif*, Cairo 1960, 59; Bukhārī, *Ṣaḥīḥ*, Leiden 1862, i, 5-6, iii, 380-1; Ḳasṭallānī, *Irshād al-sārī*, Būlāḳ 1304, i, 65 ff.; Ṭabarī, i, 1147 ff.; Yaʿḳūbī, *Taʾrīkh*, ii, 21-2; Masʿūdī, *Murūdj*, ed. Pellat, i, 81, 316, and viii, index, s.v. for more literature; Ṣafadī, *Wāfī*, Leipzig and Beirut 1931-, xxvii, 441-2; Ibn Sayyid al-Nās, *ʿUyūn al-athar fī funūn al-maghāzī wa 'l-shamāʾil wa 'l-siyar*, Cairo 1356, i, 83 ff.; Ḥalabī, *al-Sīra al-Ḥalabiyya*, Būlāḳ 1292, i, 319 ff.; Suhaylī, *al-Rawḍ al-unuf*, Cairo 1967, ii, 347, 381-2; Ibn ʿAsākir, *Taʾrīkh madīnat Dimashḳ*, Beirut 1995-, iii, 423 ff.; Baghawī, *Tafsīr*, Beirut 1987, iv, 506; Caetani, *Annali*, i, 220 ff.; H. Lammens, *L'Arabie occidentale avant l'hégire*, Beirut 1928, 33 ff.; F. Buhl, *Das Leben Muhammeds*, Leipzig 1930, 125, 134-5; T. Andrae, *Mohammed, sein Leben und sein Glaube*, Göttingen 1932, 90-1, Eng. tr. *Mohammed, the man and his faith*, London 1936, 111-2; J.W. Hirschberg, *Jüdische and christliche Lehren im vor- und frühislamischen Arabien*, Cracow 1939, 39; W.M. Watt, *Muhammad at Mecca*, Oxford 1953, 39 ff.; 50 ff., 163; U. Rubin, *The eye of the beholder. The life of Muḥammad as viewed by the early Muslims*, Princeton 1995, 103 ff.

(C.F. Robinson)

WARĀMĪN, a small town of northern Persia (lat. 35° 19' N., long. 51° 40' E.) lying in the fertile Warāmīn plain, which benefits from a good water supply from the Djādja Rūd and has been much frequented by Turkmen nomads up to modern times.

1. History.

The mediaeval Islamic geographers place it at two stages from al-Rayy (al-Muḳaddasī, 401) or at 30 *mīls* from it (Yāḳūt, *Buldān*, ed. Beirut, v, 370). Already in Būyid times it was a flourishing little town with a bazaar, but it developed especially after the Mongols sacked al-Rayy in 617/1220 and the inhabitants of the ruined city migrated to such nearby places as Warāmīn and Ṭihrān [*q.v.*]. The next two centuries were those of its greatest florescence, when it acquired some fine buildings (see 2. below) and when it was now on the highway from the Il-Khānid capital of Sulṭāniyya to the east; Ḥamd Allāh Mustawfī (740/1339-40) calls it "the administrative centre of the *tūmān* of Ray", producing corn, fruits and cotton, though characterised by a fanatically Shīʿī population (*Nuzhat al-ḳulūb*, 55, tr. 61). It was to some extent a cultural centre. Al-Samʿānī, *Ansāb*, ed. Ḥaydarābād, xiii, 306-7, mentions a well-known *muḥaddith*, ʿAttāb b. Muḥammad al-Rāzī al-Warāmīnī, d. after 310/922-3, and a certain Muḥammad b. Abī Zayd al-Ḥusaynī al-Rāzī al-Warāmīnī began writing his *Aḥsan al-kibār fī maʿrifat al-aʾimma al-aṭhār*, on the merits of the Twelve Imāms, in 739/1338-9 (Storey, i, 211, 1261; Storey-Bregel, i, 621-2). By 1405, however, when Clavijo passed through it, it was still an extensive town but lacked a wall and was showing signs of depopulation (*Embassy to Tamerlane*, tr. Le Strange, London 1928, 306), although it was still of significance in Shāh ʿAbbās I's time (Iskandar Munshī, *Tārīkh-i ʿĀlam-ārā-yi ʿabbāsī*, Tehran 1313-14/1895-7, i, 256). It then began a decline into village status until its revival in the 20th century with the general development and urbanisation of the whole Tehran region.

The present town of Warāmīn (lat. 35° 19' N., long. 51° 40' E., altitude 922 m/3,026 feet) now has significant industry, having benefited from being a station on the Tehran-Khurāsān railway, completed in the late 1930s. In *ca.* 1950 it still had a population of only 4,522, but this has by now risen considerably, Warāmīn having become part of the conurbation of Tehran.

2. Monuments.

These include several *imām-zādas*, including that of Ḥusayn Riḍā; the tomb tower of ʿAlāʾ al-Dīn, a high, brickwork cylindrical tower with a conical roof and interior dome (688/1289); and the great, square 5th/11th century citadel, the Ḳalʿa-yi Gabr. The especially fine four-*īwān* congregational mosque was built in 722-6/1322-6 during the reign of the Il-Khānid Abū Saʿīd by [Ḥasan b.] Muḥammad b. Muḥammad b. Manṣūr *al-Kūhadhī; some its inscriptions are Shīʿī in tinge although the sultan was a Sunnī. It was rebuilt in 821/1418 in the time of the Tīmūrid Shāh Rukh by the *amīr* Ghiyāth al-Dīn Yūsuf Khʷādja.

Bibliography: 1. History. Le Strange, *The lands of the Eastern Caliphate*, 216-17; Schwarz, *Iran im Mittelalter*, 793-4; Barthold, *An historical geography of Iran*, Princeton 1984, 124-6; Admiralty Handbooks, *Persia*, London 1945, 460, 539, 571; Razmārā (ed.), *Farhang-i djughrāfiyā-yi Īrān-zamīn*, i, 229; D. Krawulsky, *Īrān—das Reich der Īlḫāne. Eine topographisch-historische Studie*, Wiesbaden 1978, 323; Minorsky, *EI*[1] art. s.v.

2. Monuments. J. Dieulafoy, *La Perse, la Chaldée at la Susiane*, Paris 1887, 140-5, with illustrs.; F. Sarre, *Denkmäler persischer Baukunst*, Berlin 1901-10, i, plates, nos. xviii, liv, lv, ii, text, 58-64; V.A. Kratchovskaya, *Notice sur les inscriptions de la mosquée Djoumʿa à Véramine*, in *REI*, v (1931), 26-59; eadem, *Fragments du Miḥrāb de Varāmīn*, in *Arts Islamiques*, ii, (1943-5), 132-4; Pope, *Survey*, ii, 1050, 1093-6, 1569, 1571-2, 1679, 1683; R. Hillenbrand, *Islamic architecture. Form, function and meaning*, Edinburgh 1994, index. (C.E. Bosworth)

WARANGAL, a town of the northeastern Deccan of India (lat. 18° 00' N., long. 79° 35' E.), important in mediaeval times as the centre of a Hindu princedom in the region of Telingāṇa [*q.v.*]. It blocked the way to Muslim expansion from the central Deccan to the Bay of Bengal, hence was frequently involved in warfare during the 8th-9th/14th-15th centuries with the Dihlī Sultanate [*q.v.*] and then the local northern Deccani sultanate of the Bahmanids [*q.v.*].

Warangal lies on the eastern edge of the Deccan plateau some 130 km/70 miles to the southwest of the Godivari river. In mediaeval times, it was a strongly fortified place with two walls; traces of the outer wall remain today plus the four gateways of the inner wall. Sultan ʿAlāʾ al-Dīn Khaldjī first sent an expedition against Warangal via Bengal and Orissa in winter 702/1302-3, apparently unsuccessful; but in winter 709/1309-10 his general Malik Kāfūr [*q.v.*] marched via Devagiri or Deogir [see DAWLATĀBĀD] against Prātaparudra, the Kākatīya ruler of Telingāṇa in his capital of Warangal, and imposed on him peace and the payment of tribute. That continued payment of this tribute depended purely on Muslim coercive power was shown by the fact that in 718/1318 an army from Dihlī en route for Maʿbar [*q.v.*] had to compel the Rādjā in Warangal to resume paying tribute. However, the latter openly threw off the authority of Dihlī when the Sultanate was in 720/1320 plunged into discord with the end of the Khaldjīs and the advent of the Tughluḳids. Hence in 723/1323 Ghiyāth al-Dīn Tughluḳ's son Ulugh Khān Djawna, the future Sultan Muḥammad, had to reduce Warangal to obedience, and he may possibly have carried off the Rādjā as a prisoner to Dihlī, though a royal inscription of 1326 shows that by then he was back once more ruling in his capital. Ulugh Khān also, according to Baranī, changed the name of Warangal to Sultānpūr. It seems to have been Muḥammad b. Tughluḳ's [*q.v.*] aim, once he became sultan in 725/1325, to incorporate Telingāṇa into his kingdom rather than leave it as a tributary Hindu state, but this he was unable to secure permanently, for by *ca.* 735/1335 his commander Malik Maḳbūl was forced to relinquish Warangal to its family of local rulers under Kāpaya Nāyaka. Soon afterwards, Muslim authority in the northern Deccan passed to the Bahmanids. In 751/1350 Ḥasan Bahman Shāh led an expedition to Warangal and reimposed tribute on Kāpaya Nāyaka, but it was not until 828/1425 that Aḥmad I Shāh, provoked by an anti-Muslim alliance of the Rādjās of Telingāṇa and Vidjayanagara [*q.v.*], marched on Warangal, defeated and killed Devarāya II, and finally incorporated the city and much of Telingāṇa into the Bahmanid state, appointing the Khān-i Aʿẓam as its governor. Local Hindu rulers still remained significant in the region, and caused trouble for the later Bahmanids and their successors, but Warangal's history was henceforth largely subsumed in that of the Muslim sultanates of the Deccan and their eventual supplanters, the Mughals.

The Muslim monuments of Warangal include a palace, attributed to Shitāb Khān *ca.* 905/1500 [see MAḤALL, at vol. V, 1216b].

In British Indian times, Warangal came within the Niẓām of Ḥaydarābād's dominions. It is now in the northern part of Andhra Pradesh State of the Indian Union, and is a commercial and industrial centre with a population in 1971 of 207,000. It is also the chef-lieu of a District of the same name which extends as far as the Godivari.

Bibliography: *Imperial gazetteer of India*[2], xxiv, 355-65; R.J. Majumdar (ed.), *The history and culture of the Indian people*, vi, *The Delhi Sultanate*, Bombay 1960, 25-6, 33-4, 39, 43, 53-5, 63, 250, 258; M. Habib and K.A. Nizami (eds.), *A comprehensive history of India*, v, *The Delhi Sultanat* (*A.D. 1206-1526*), Delhi 1971, 366-7, 403-10, 972, 985, 1037; H.K. Sherwani and P.M. Joshi (eds.), *History of medieval Deccan* (*1295-1724*), Hyderabad 1973, i. (C.E. Bosworth)

WARĀWĪNĪ [see MARZBĀN-NĀMA].

WARD (A., coll., sing. *warda*), *Rosa sp., Rosaceae*, also known as *djull* or *gul* (Persian). Though *ward* can refer to any flower, it generally denotes the rose (Lane). According to Maimonides, it is known to physicians as *djull*, though the Arabs used this name only for the white rose (*Sharḥ*, no. 121); *nisrīn* was the wild rose or Chinese rose (no. 253). Ibn al-Bayṭār in his *Tafsīr* to Dioscorides explains *rūdhā* as *ward*, or as *djull*, of Persian origin; the red variety is called *ḥawdjam*, the white *watīr* (i, 101, 140).

Medicinal use. Ibn Sīnā calls it cold in the first degree, dry in the second; it quietens the yellow bile (*Adwiya mufrada*, 61). Al-Zahrāwī used rose leaves, dried rose, rose water (*māʾ al-ward*) and rose *duhn* (oil), describing the methods for making the latter (105-6) and its uses (117-18). An excellent medicine, moderately cold and astringent: internally, good for the stomach and for cases of tuberculosis; externally, soothing, and included in ointments. It was combined, in small amounts, with other ingredients. According to Ibn Waḥshiyya, the rose, its petals, leaves, rose water and rose oil, were included in several antidotes to poison. Sābūr b. Sahl in his *Aḳrābādhīn* used rose oil, rose water, dried red rose, and seeds, for a variety of ailments.

Ainslie speaks of *ward* as *Rosa centifolia* (Lin.); he considers this probably the true *gul* of Ḥāfiẓ. *R. gallica* (red rose, in P. *gul-i surkh*) was used as carminative, cephalic and tonic (*Materia Indica*, i, 345). Rose oil (*duhn*) and rose water are produced by distillation from the flowers of some types of rose (Ghaleb, ii, 364-6). Rose water today is a refreshing ingredient in lotions, has a limited medicinal use, and is used in the preparation of food, especially sweets. The dried flowers are included in some versions of the *Arbaʿīn* or "forty" substances sold by *ʿaṭṭārīn* (herbalists).

Bibliography: Ibn al-Bayṭār, *Tafsīr Kitāb Diyūskūrīdūs*, ed. Ibrahim Ben Mrad, Beirut 1990; Ibn Sīnā, *al-Adwiya al-mufrada fī kitāb al-Ḳānūn fi 'l-ṭibb*, ed. Muḥammad ʿAbd al-Amīr al-Aʿsam, Beirut 1984; Maimonides, *Sharḥ asmāʾ al-ʿuḳḳār*, ed. M. Meyerhof, Cairo 1940; S.K. Hamarneh and G. Sonnedecker, *A pharmaceutical view of Abulcasis al-Zahrawi in Moorish Spain*... (=Janus Suppl. 5), Leiden 1963; M. Levey, *Medieval Arabic toxicology. The Book on Poisons of Ibn Waḥshīya*, Philadelphia 1966; Sābūr b. Sahl, *al-Aḳrābādhīn al-Ṣaghīr*, ed. O. Kahl, Leiden 1994; W. Ainslie, *Materia Indica*, London 1826; E. Ghaleb, *Dictionnaire des sciences de la nature*, ii, Beirut 1965.

(Penelope C. Johnstone)

WARDAR, the Ottoman Turkish name for the Vardar, Grk. Axios, a river of the southern Balkans. It rises in the Šar Mountains near where Macedonia, Albania and the region of Kosovo meet, and flows northeastwards and then in a southeastern and south-south-eastern direction through the present (Slavic) Macedonian Republic [see maḳadūnyā], past Skopje or Üsküb [*q.v.*] and through Greek Macedonia to the Gulf of Salonica. Its length is 420 km/260 miles.

The lower valley of the Vardar probably passed into Ottoman Turkish hands around the time of the first Turkish capture of Salonica in 1387 [see selānīk], soon after which the Byzantine town of Pella in Macedonia was conquered and became for the Turks Wardar Yeñidjesi or Yeñidje-yi Wardar. In *ca.* 1475 there was apparently a separate *sandjaḳ* of Wardar with its chef-lieu at Ḳaraferye or Beroia, but normally, the lower part of the valley came within the *sandjaḳ* of Selānīk. The upper course of the Vardar came under Ottoman control after the defeat of the Serbians at the first battle of Kosovo or Ḳosh-owasi in 791/1389 [see ḳoṣowa, kosovo]. The Vardar valley was settled in early Ottoman times by considerable numbers of Turkmens brought in from Anatolia. It remained under Turkish rule for over five centuries until, after the Balkan War of 1912, it passed to Serbia and Greece, a position confirmed by the Treaty of London of 1913, with the middle and upper reaches of the river after 1918 coming within what was eventually called the kingdom of Yugoslavia.

Bibliography: See the *Bibls.* of the *EI*² arts. mentioned in the text, especially those of maḳadūnyā and selānīk, and also H.E. Pitcher, *An historical geography of the Ottoman Empire*, Leiden 1972, 42, 45 and Maps X, XXVI; A. Birken, *Die Provinzen des Osmanischen Reiches*, Wiesbaden 1976, 59; art. *Axios*, in *Megalē Genikē Enkyklopaideia Hydria*, ix (1980), 174-6. (Ed.)

al-**WARDJLĀNĪ** [see abū zakariyyāʾ al-wardjlānī].

al-**WARGHĪ**, Abū ʿAbd Allāh Muḥammad b. Aḥmad, Tunisian poet and *adīb*, b. *ca.* 1125/1713 at Wargha, a village near Kef, d. 1190/1776 at Tunis.

After study at a Ḳurʾān school in his native village, he went to Tunis in order to continue his studies at the Great Mosque of the Zaytūna [*q.v.*], and subsequently himself gave courses there. His wide learning and gift for writing attracted the attention of the Bey, ʿAlī I Pasha, who made him secretary in his chancery. This Ḥusaynid ruler had just dethroned his uncle al-Ḥusayn and himself assumed power in 1735, but was in turn overthrown in 1756 by his cousin Muḥammad al-Rashīd b. al-Ḥusayn. Since al-Warghī was a fervent partisan of ʿAlī I, and had been richly rewarded by him, he was after 1756 persecuted and imprisoned. Till his death, he never recovered his former privileged position, but gradually contrived to secure a pardon, regain his liberty and acquire authorisation to practise as a notary.

Al-Warghī is known above all as a poet, and especially as a eulogist of ʿAlī I, but his *Dīwān*, published at Tunis in 1975 by ʿAbd al-ʿAzīz al-Kīzānī, contains poems on many other themes, such as descriptions, love poems, petitions, verses on the hazards of fate, etc. Dominating his œuvre is a neo-classicism. He was also the author of three *maḳāmāt*, also published with his *rasāʾil* at Tunis in 1972 by al-Kīzānī, which include several of his own verses. The first, written in 1160/1747, *al-Bāhiyya*, nominally concerns the founder of the *madrasa* of that name, but reading between the lines, contains criticism of what was, according to him, misgovernment of the land by the sons of al-Ḥusayn. The second one, *al-Warghiyya* or *al-Khitāniyya*, was written for the circumcision of the son of the Bey ʿAlī II b. al-Ḥusayn in 1178/1764, and seems to indicate that, after the three years' reign of Muḥammad al-Rashīd, al-Warghī had recovered some of his former favour. A third, *al-Khamriyya*, is a eulogy of ʿAlī II who in 1183/1769 closed down a number of wine shops and taverns in the capital, but in fact contains discreet criticism of the policies of the sons of al-Ḥusayn b. ʿAlī and regrets for the passing of the reign of his old protector ʿAlī I.

Bibliography: See also M. al-Misfār, *Maḳāmāt al-Warghī wa-mā nusiba ilayhi min al-nathr*, unpubl. thesis, Fac. of Letters, Univ. of Tunis 1971; H. al-Ghuzzī, *al-Adab al-tūnisī fi 'l-ʿahd al-ḥusaynī*, Tunis 1972, 149-75; M. Maḥfūẓ, *Tarādjim al-muʾallifīn al-tūnisiyyīn*, Beirut 1986, v, 131-3; idem, *T. al-Adab al-tūnisī fi 'l-ʿahdayn al-murādī wa 'l-ḥusaynī*, Tunis 1989; and see maḳāma. (A. Ben Abdesselem)

WARGLA, conventionally Ouargla, an ancient oasis town of the Algerian Sahara (lat. 31° 58' N., long. 5° 20' E., altitude 290 m/320 feet), situated 160 km/100 miles south-south-west of Tuggurt [*q.v.*] and now the chef-lieu of a *wilāya* or province of the Algerian Republic. It occupies a depression above a sheet of underground water which is fed by the subterranean course of the Wadi Miya and which has, in the past, been tapped by wells, thus permitting vast date palm groves in the oasis (see 2. below).

1. Pre-modern history.

We have no information about Wargla before the Arab conquest. At that time, the land was occupied by Zenāta tribes. According to Ibn Khaldūn, the Banū Wargla (Berber, Urdjelan) came from the northwest along with other Berber elements (Īfran and Maghrāwa [*q.vv.*]) and founded several little towns in these regions which combined to form the town of Wargla. The people adopted Ibāḍī doctrines so thoroughly that, after the destruction of the Rustamid kingdom of Tāhart [*q.v.*] by the Fāṭimids at the beginning of the 10th century a.d., many Khāridjīs came to settle in

Wargla and founded the town of Sedrata, the ruins of which still exist buried under the sands half a day's journey to the southwest. At the same time, Abū Yazīd, the "man with the ass", who had rebelled against the Fāṭimids, recruited many followers in this region. The Ibāḍīs had nevertheless in the 6th/12th century, as a result of conflicts with the orthodox and perhaps under the pressure of Arab elements, to abandon the region of Wargla and migrate to the Tadmayt, where they finally settled and created the oases of the Mzāb [*q.v.*]. Ibāḍism, however, continued to survive at Wargla, where in the 11th/17th century it still had a few representatives.

During this period, Wargla, which according to the traveller al-ʿAyyāshī was ruled by the Banū Tūdjīn dynasty, seems to have been a prosperous city enriched by trade with the Sūdān (al-Idrīsī, tr. de Goeje, 141). The Hilālī invasion marked the beginning of a troubled era. In the course of the wars between the Ḥammādīs and the Athbādj, with whom the people of Wargla had contracted an alliance, the dynasty of the Banū Tūdjīn was overthrown and the town destroyed. Rebuilt a short distance from the original site, it suffered later in the wars between the Almohads and the Banū Ghaniyya. In the 8th/14th century, although under the suzerainty of the Banū Muznī, representatives of the Ḥafṣids in the Zāb [*q.v.*], Wargla was practically independent under the rule of sultans belonging to the family of the Banū Abī Ghabul, of the fraction of the Banū Wagguin or Uggīn (Ibn Khaldūn, *Histoire des Berbers*, tr. Slane, iii, 286). At the end of the 10th/16th century, these sultans were extremely wealthy, but according to Leo Africanus (ed. Schefer, book vi, vol. iii, 146), they had to pay heavily for the protection of the nomad Arabs. Wargla at this time still preserved the commercial importance that it owed to its situation as a "port of the desert", to use Ibn Khaldūn's phrase (*loc. cit.*). It was a market where the produce and slaves of the Sūdān were exchanged for the merchandise bought from Tunis and Constantine. Leo Africanus remarks on the beauty of the houses, the number of artisans and the wealth of the merchants. This opulence attracted the attention of the Turks of the Algerian coastlands to Wargla. In 1552 Ṣalāḥ Reʾīs, at the head of an army of Turks and Kabyles, advanced as far as Wargla, the inhabitants of which offered no resistance, and he returned after plundering the town and imposing on the sultan an annual tribute of 30 African slaves.

The expedition of Ṣalāḥ Reʾīs was followed by a new period of troubles which was ended, it seems, at the beginning of the 17th century by the proclamation of a new sultan, Allāhum, to whom local tradition attributes a Sharīfian origin; his descendants held power down to the middle of the 19th century. But the real masters of the country were the nomad Shamhaa, Banū Tūr and Sidi ʿOtba, whose continual interference in the quarrels of the two *ṣoffs* or factions [see ṢAFF. 3.] into which the settled population was divided kept up the disorder and made the authority of the sultans illusory. The latter had even to recognise the supremacy of the Banū Babia, hereditary chiefs of the oasis of Ngusa, which they did not cast off till 1841. But ten years later, a new cause of trouble arose. Muḥammad b. ʿAbd Allāh, the *sharīf* of Wargla, raised the tribes of the Sahara against the French, who entrusted the task of reducing the rebels to the *shaykh* of the Ūlād Sīdī Shaykh, Sīdī Ḥamza. The latter occupied the town in the name of France in 1853 and was given supreme command of the Sahara tribes. But the participation of the people of Wargla in the rising of the Ūlād Sīdī Shaykh in 1854 forced French columns to intervene on several occasions in the region. Another rebel, Ben Shusha, nevertheless succeeded in establishing himself in Wargla in 1871. The suppression of this rebellion resulted in the final establishment of French authority in 1872.

With the suppression of the trans-Saharan slave trade under the French rule and with a French Army fort in the oasis, Burdj Lutaud, the economic importance of Wargla declined. But it subsequently became the chef-lieu of the Territoire des Oasis Sahariennes, with the municipal status of a *commune indigène*.

Bibliography: El-Ayachi/al-ʿAyyāshī, *Voyage à la Mecque*, tr. Berbrügger, in *Explorations scientifiques de l'Algérie. Sciences historiques et géographiques*, ix, Paris 1846; L.V. Largeau, *Le pays de Rirha*, Paris 1879; O. Demaeght, *Ouargla*, in *Bull. de la Soc. de Géographie d'Oran* (1882); Goudreau, *Le pays de Ouargla*, Paris 1882; C. Bajolle, *Le Sahara de Ouargla*, Algiers-Paris 1887; Ch. Ferraud, *Ouargla dans le Sahara de Constantine*, Algiers 1887; R. Basset, *Étude sur la Zenatia du Mzab, de Ouargla et de l'Oued Rir'*, Paris 1892; Blanchet, *L'oasis et le pays de Wargla*, in *Annales de Géographie* (1900); Gognalons, *Ouargla, l'oasis et ses habitants*, in *La Géographie*, ix; idem, *Fêtes principales des sédentaires d'Ouargla (Rouagha)*, in *R. Afr.* (1909); Naval Intelligence Division. Admiralty Handbooks, *Algeria*, London 1943-4, ii, 93-4 and index; J. Lethielleux, *Ouargla, cité saharienne, des origines au début de la 20ème siècle*, Paris 1983. (G. YVER*)

2. The modern oasis and town.

Wargla owes both its historical and its present importance to its remarkable position on an isthmus of *terra firma* connecting the north and south Saharas, between the great Eastern Erg and the Great Western Erg. Its position has at all times made it of the greatest significance for trans-Saharan trade; it had relations with Gao and Timbuktu to the south, and was a transit point for the slave trade, what Ibn Khaldūn called "the gate of the Sūdān".

In the colonial period it was marginalised, with a population only one-half that of Tuggurt's, but it has today surpassed Tuggurt and Ghardaia in importance. It has benefited from the proximity of the oil field of Hassi-Messaoud (Ḥasy Masʿūd) at 80 km/50 miles to the east-south-east, and the Algerian state's decision to make Wargla a Saharan capital, with institutions serving the whole Sahara (a University, a Commission for Development and Land Reclamation, and an Institute for Saharan Agronomy). As a garrison town also, at a crossroads of modern roads, and still with important date palm groves, Wargla has today 120,000 inhabitants.

As noted above, the town lies in a north-south depression within the rims of a calcareous plateau and corresponding to the ancient course of the Wadi Miya. Situated on a low terrace above the palm groves, the town is girt with lakes and salt marshes on three sides. The ensemble has a regular concentric pattern: the *ḳṣar* in the centre, then the modern town, the palm groves, then salt flats and the rising banks of the plateau and several small ergs.

The *ḳṣar*, with its 10,000 inhabitants, is one of the most important in the Sahara. The walls and ditches which still surrounded it in the 19th century have been replaced by a ring road, and recent constructions have marred the centre; nevertheless, the tightly-knit urban structure remains, with its buildings at two levels and its associated structures coming together near the mausoleum of Sīdī al-Warglī. The three communities of the Banū Brāhīm, the Banū Uggīn

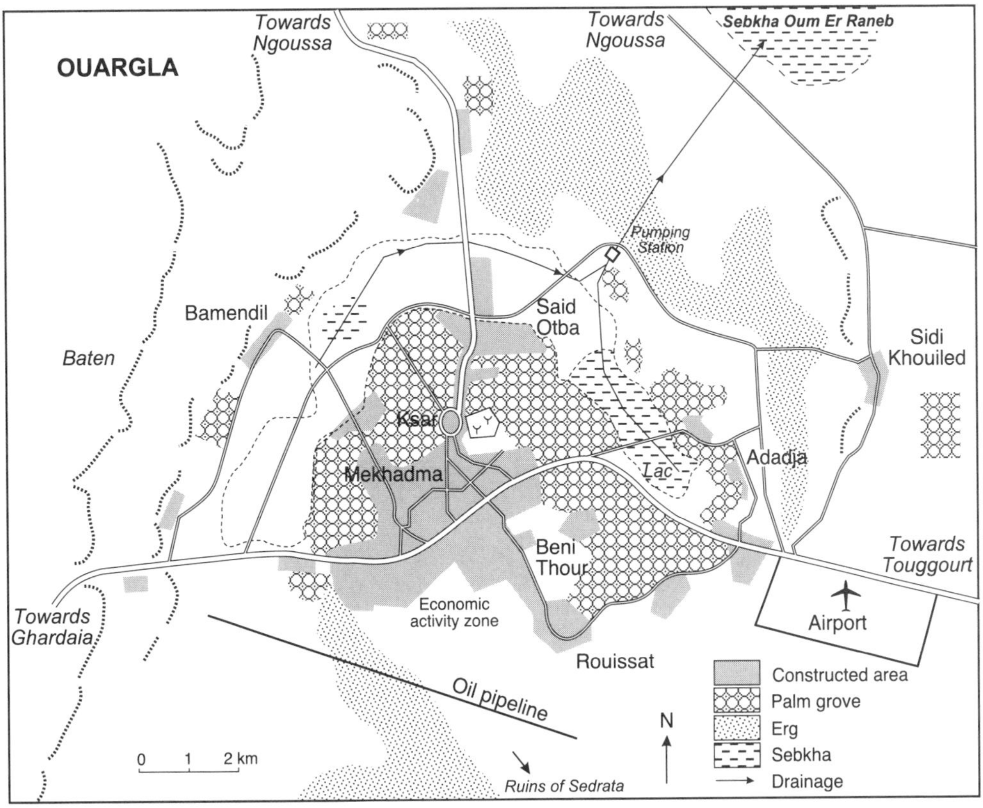

and the Banū Sissīn, Berber-speaking Zenāta, dark-skinned from the admixture there of negro blood, share the *ḳṣar* and also the palm groves, though in the urban agglomeration as a whole former Arabic-speaking nomads have become the majority. Around the *ḳṣar* the modern suburbs have developed. The "Green Triangle" of monumental buildings and greenery forms the administrative quarter laid out in the 1930s by Col. Carbillet, a disciple of Lyautey. Quarters of former nomads, now sedentarised, have sprung up in various places, and the urban sprawl has now joined up with peripheral *ḳṣūr* (Rouissat, Adjadja, Bamendil, etc.).

The palm groves, amounting to 550,000 trees, are amongst the most extensive in the Sahara. They are served by the artesian water supplies, formerly tapped by wells but now by bore holes. But the extension of lands suitable for agriculture has now reached its natural limit, stretching across lands that are becoming waterlogged through the rise of the water-table, with a veritable lake formed to the east of the town; hence it has become necessary to construct a drainage network that conveys used water to the Oum er Raneb *sabkha*. But beyond the palm groves, Wargla is becoming a centre for extensive development, thanks to its underground water levels and its alluvial soils, a sector chosen by the Algerian government for the improvement of modern Saharan agriculture; hence along the roads to Hass-Messaoud and Tuggurt stretch numerous modern developments, industrial and agricultural.

Bibliography: B. Verlet, *Touggourt et Ouargla, deux fonctions urbaines*, Travaux et Recherches de l'Inst. Saharienne, Algiers 1960, 195-8; M. Rouvillois-Brigol, *Ouargla, palmeraie irriguée et palmeraie en cuvettes*, in *Oasis du Sahara algérien*, Paris, 33-62; idem, *Le pays de Ouargla (Sahara algérien)*, Paris 1975; J. Bisson, *Les villes sahariennes*, in *Maghreb-Machreck*, Paris, (1983), 25-41. (M. Côte)

WARIḲ (A.) "silver money", distinguished from *ʿayn* "gold money", and *nuḳra*, refined silver in bars or ingots.

In the mediaeval Islamic world, as elsewhere before the introduction of central banking, gold and silver money were two separate currencies, with a fluctuating market exchange rate. The unit of silver currency was the dirham [*q.v.*], normally represented by a coin with the same name, or, more strictly speaking, by an amount of current silver money with the weight of a standard dirham; the corresponding unit of gold currency was the dīnār [*q.v.*], with its own weight standard (unminted gold in ingot form was *tibr*). To describe quantities of coins, *ʿayn* and *wariḳ* are used to designate the gold and silver portions of the sum. For example, when the caliph al-Wāthiḳ died (227/847), the treasury was inventoried and found to contain *ʿayn*, 5,000,000 dīnārs and *wariḳ*, 15,000,000 dirhams (Ḳāḍī Ibn al-Zubayr (attrib.), *K. al-Dhakhāʾir wa ʾl-tuḥaf*, 217-18, tr. Ghāda al-Qaddūmī, *Book of gifts and rarities*, Cambridge, Mass. 1996, 208). On a more humble level, a Geniza letter acknowledges receipt of "10 dīnārs, 7 in *ʿayn*, 3 in *wariḳ*" (Goitein, *A Mediterranean society*, i, 230); that is, a payment with a total value of ten dīnārs was made, of which seven dīnārs were paid in gold coin and the rest in silver coin worth three dīnārs.

In Syria and Egypt, the meanings of the pair *wariḳ/nuḳra* changed as a result of Ṣalāḥ al-Dīn's re-introduction of full-weight pure silver dirhams *ca.* 572/1176-7. Up to that time, *wariḳ* had continued to mean silver coins, in particular, the increasingly debased dirhams which were the only silver coinage of the region from the 4th/10th to 6th/12th centuries, while *nuḳra* meant pure commercial grade silver metal, or its theoretical price as calculated from the price of a silver coinage of lower fineness. When Ṣalāḥ al-Dīn introduced pure silver coins, they were called *nuḳra* dirhams, while the term *wariḳ* was reserved for the debased coins (which continued to be issued in many places). Ibn Baʿra, a 7th/13th-century writer on the Egyptian mint, describes separately the methods of production for *nuḳra* and *wariḳ* dirhams. The designation *nuḳra* stuck to the former even when, later, they too began to be debased (the term obviously had lost its specific denotation of pure silver). In 815/1412-13, we are told, the last *nuḳra* dirhams, by then containing only 10% silver, were demonetised in Egypt. The *wariḳ* dirhams that had to be distinguished from *nuḳra* had also disappeared, and *wariḳ* resumed its significance of silver coinage in general, although mainly in contexts with historical reference, such as those of *fiḳh* manuals.

Today the term *waraḳ* meaning "money", is recorded. Very probably the significance survives in part from a more common meaning of the word, "paper", but it is likely that it also continues the older usage. *Wariḳ*, with that spelling, occurs only once in the Ḳurʾān (*Sūrat al-Kahf*, XVIII, 19: when the Seven Sleepers awake, they are advised to take their money, *wariḳ*, to town to buy food). An alternative vowelling, *warḳ*, was preferred by the Ḳurʾān readers of Baṣra and Kūfa (al-Ṭabarī, *Tafsīr, ad loc.*). As early as 11/632-3, a versifier puns twice on *waraḳ/wariḳ* "leaves" or "silver money" (l. 1) (both vocalisations being prosodically possible), *waraḳ* "leaves" (l. 4) and *wariḳ* "silver money" (l. 6) (al-Ṭabarī, i, 1907-8; cf. tr. F.M. Donner, *The History of al-Ṭabarī. X. The conquest of Arabia*, Albany 1993, 83-4).

Bibliography: Given in the text.

(M.L. Bates)

al-**WARKĀʾ**, Tall, the Arabic name for what is now an archaeological site in the Nāṣiriyya *liwāʾ* or governorate of ʿIrāḳ (lat. 31° 18' N., long. 45° 40' E.). It is the Sumerian and Babylonian Uruk, Biblical Erech (Gen. x. 10), one of the leading cities and religious centres of ancient Babylonia, first surveyed by W.K. Loftus in the 1850s.

In early Islamic times it seems to have been a minor place in the district of Kaskar, with a reputation in Islamic tradition as being the birthplace of the Patriarch Ibrāhīm or Abraham (although many other places were mentioned for this) (Yāḳūt, *Buldān*, ed. Beirut, iv, 372-3). According to Sayf b. ʿUmar (in *ibid.*, iv, 373, cf. M.G. Morony, *Iraq after the Muslim conquest*, Princeton 1984, 156-7), the first encounter of probing Muslim Arabs under Harmala b. Murayṭa and Salmā b. al-Ḳayn with the Sāsānid forces took place at al-Warkāʾ.

Bibliography: See also M. Streck, *Die alte Landschaft Babyloniens nach den arabischen Geographen*, Leiden 1900, i, 32. For the older excavations, see Streck, *EI*[1] s.v., and for the more recent ones, D.N. Freedman (ed.), *The Anchor Bible dictionary*, New York 1992, ii, 571-3, and E.M. Meyers (ed.), *The Oxford encyclopedia of archaeology in the Near East*, New York 1996, v, 294-8, s.v. Uruk-Warka (R.M. Boelmer).

(C.E. Bosworth)

WARḲĀʾ b. **ʿUMAR** b. Kulayb al-S̲h̲aybānī al-Kūfī, Abū Bis̲h̲r, Ḳurʾān interpreter and traditionist who lived in al-Madāʾin and died *ca.* 160/776. He is said to have been orthodox (*ṣāḥib sunna*) as well as a Murdjiʾī. His *tafsīr* is reported to have been preferred by, amongst others, Yaḥyā b. Maʿīn and Aḥmad b. Ḥanbal [*q.vv.*], this *tafsīr* being one of the three recensions of the Ibn Abī Nadjīḥ transmission of the *tafsīr* tradition that was started by Mudjāhid b. Djabr [*q.v.*]. His recension, which is preserved in the Cairo Dār al-Kutub ms. 1075 *tafsīr*, is related to the other two but often shows a different wording and a different distribution of individual *tafsīrāt*. Al-Ṭabarī apparently set great store on the Warḳāʾ recension, but only quotes it regularly from sūra XIV onward in his *tafsīr*.

Bibliography: See biographical references in Sezgin, *GAS*, i, 37, and *Taʾrīk̲h̲ Bag̲h̲dād*, xii, 515-17. For his *tafsīr*, see mudjāhid b. djabr. The new edition by M. ʿAbd al-Salām Abu ʾl-Nīl, *Tafsīr al-imām Mudjāhid b. Djabr*, Cairo (Madīnat Naṣr) 1989, does not follow the original arrangement of the ms.

(F. Leemhuis)

WARNA, conventionally Varna, a town and seaport of northeastern Bulgaria, important in Ottoman Turkish times (lat. 43° 12' N., long. 27° 57' E.). It is situated on the Black Sea coast, on a bay of the Sea near the Devnya lake, with the region of Dobrudja [*q.v.*] to its north. At present, with 400,000 inhabitants, it is the third largest city in Bulgaria and its largest port, with road, rail and ferry connections.

1. Historical survey.

Varna has an ancient history. The Greek colony of Miletus-Odessos was founded on its site in the 6th century B.C., and on the Devnya lake there arose the Roman foundation of Marcianopolis. During the Slavic infiltration into the Balkans, Odessos was destroyed, but the name Varna appears for the region. It became part of the Byzantine empire in the late 10th century, ruled by Byzantium and Bulgaria, and from the 1340s came within the Dobrudja despotate which seceded from the Bulgarian kingdom.

Varna was conquered by the Ottomans in 1388-9, but was probably ceded to Byzantium in 1403 by Süleymān, son of Bāyezīd I. In 1444, in a valley to the west of the town, there took place the celebrated battle of Varna (to figure prominently in Ottoman historiography, with a special *G̲h̲azawāt-nāme* of Sultan Murād II devoted to it). The force of European Crusaders (Hungarians, Poles, Czechs and Vlachs) under the king of Poland and Hungary Władysław II Jagiełło/Ladislaus I and the Voivode of Transylvania Hunyády János/John Hunyadi, was defeated by Murād's Ottoman army. After the fall of Constantinople, the Ottomans seized the last independent fortresses along the Black Sea coast and confirmed their authority over Varna.

In the early 17th century, Varna suffered from Cossack raids. There were Ottoman-Russian confrontations during the 18th century, and in the war of 1828-9, the Russians captured it after a siege and held it for over two years. During the Crimean War 1853-6, it served as a base for the forces of the English, French and Piedmontese allies, with about 60,000 persons there, but was devastated by cholera and a fire. In 1878 the fortress of Varna surrendered to the Russians without a fight, and was henceforth included within the Bulgarian principality.

2. Varna under the Ottomans.

The town was a port and a fortress in the *sandjak* (from the 17th century, the *beylerbeylik*) of Silistra, and it formed one of the *nāḥiyes* of the extensive Dobrudja region. In the 17th century, Ewliyā Čelebi recorded, amongst the town's officials, a superintendent of the port customs; a commander (*muḥāfiẓ*) of the fortress; a *serdār* of the Janissaries, a *ketk̲h̲udā* of the Sipāhīs;

the *odabashï* of the Janissaries; a *muḥtesib*; and a *subashï*. In the 1840s, a *sandjak* and *kaḍā* of Varna were set up within the *eyālet* of Silistra, governed by a *müdür*, and there was a *medjlis*, consultative body (whose members included the local Orthodox metropolitan). This same structure was maintained when the region was included in the Ṭuna or Danube *wilāyet* in 1864.

In past times, the port of Varna had been difficult to use without the construction of facilities for ships. Under the Ottomans, it functioned as a transit centre for foodstuffs from Dobrudja exported to Istanbul, and it had a shipyard. Under the Treaty of Küčük Ḳaynardja [*q.v.*] of 1774, the Black Sea was opened up for foreign trade, and agreements for free navigation made with various Western powers, leading to the growth of foreign activities through the Straits and within the Black Sea. Hence by 1841 there were 14 consulates of European countries in Varna; steamships started docking there, and between 1861 and 1867 a railway linked Varna and the town of Russe on the Danube.

Varna forms part of a specific sub-region, a narrow zone along the Black Sea coast differing in demography and relief from its hinterland. The Varna region must have been Orthodox Christian on the eve of the Ottoman conquest, and there may even have been Christian Turks there in the pre-Ottoman period. Notable were the Gagauz [*q.v.*], Turkish-speaking Orthodox Christians using the so-called Karamanlidika, i.e. writing religious works in Turkish language with Greek script. In the 16th century, some 55 Yürük *odjak*s are mentioned there, and there were *sürgün* [*q.v.* in Suppl.], i.e. transplanted S̲h̲īʿīs from Eastern Anatolia. These deportations may have tipped the religious balance of the region in favour of the Muslims.

The first extant registers concerning the population of Varna date from 1526-7 and 1566-9. The *djemāʿat* of Muslims consisted of 27 households and eight bachelors, plus 29 Muslim *müsellem*s, exempt from ʿ*awāriḍ* [*q.v.*] because they served in the Varna fortress. These grew into five Muslim *maḥalle*s, totalling *ca.* 1,200-1,500 persons. Initially, the non-Muslim population formed nine *maḥalle*s, with 352 households, 128 bachelors and 60 widows as well as non-Muslim *müsellem*s and builders in the fortress. Ewliyā Čelebi speaks of 4,000 houses, and in 1659 Ph. Stanislavov mentioned 400 houses of Orthodox Christians, totalling 1,700 people, whilst the Muslims had 1,500 houses with 4,000 people. In the subsequent period, Armenian Christians are also mentioned as residents. The Russo-Turkish wars of the late 18th and early 19th centuries forced the non-Muslim population of the region either to migrate across the Danube or to move into the town of Varna, and after the 1828-9 war, when the total population of the town was about 26,000, the town lost nearly all of its non-Muslim population across the Danube or to Russia, and the Christian quarters and their churches suffered especially from the Russian bombardments. The Ottoman government took measures to facilitate the return of the emigrants. The 19th century was notable for the emancipation, and at times, confrontation, of the Greek and Bulgarian communities, with their own religious and cultural lives. They probably absorbed part of the Gagauz community. According to 19th-century observers, the Orthodox used Turkish, and church services in that language are mentioned, leading some authors to conclude that the majority of the Orthodox population were Gagauz.

Tatars settled in the region as early as the 13th century, increasing after Bāyezīd II's annexation of Bessarabia, and in the later 18th century with the population resettlement after Russia took over the K̲h̲ānate of Crimea [see Ḳi̊Ri̊M] followed by a particularly large wave *ca.* 1860-2, when a Tatar *maḥalle* emerged in Varna.

After the Crimean War, Varna's population increased rapidly. According to Kanitz, by 1855 there were *ca.* 16,000 inhabitants (8,300 Turks, 6,100 Orthodox, 1,000 Armenians, 30 Jews and 130 Greeks). The 1881 census revealed 24,561 people: 8,903 Turks, 6,721 Bulgarians, 5,367 Greeks, 837 Tatars, 541 Jews, 338 Gypsies and 186 Germans; in 1901 the total had reached 34,922 inhabitants.

The fortress that guarded the town and its port, until it was blown up in 1829 by the Russians, dated from Byzantine times; it had a double wall and towers, an *ič ḳalʿe* large enough to shelter a barracks, a Muslim *maḥalle* and a mosque, and a citadel, *bārūd-k̲h̲āne*, used as an arsenal (pulled down in 1901). The open city was around the fortress and on the ancient site of the town. The Christians remained in their pre-Ottoman settlement zones, or in parts of them, where lay their churches. By the 17th century, a relatively substantial Armenian colony, with its own church, had been established in Varna. Muslims lived relatively separately, mainly to the west or south-west. Ewliyā mentions several chief mosques (*djāmiʿ*) and 36 *mesdjid*s. Many public buildings were built by persons associated with Varna, so that there was an ʿAbd ül-Raḥmān Efendi mosque, *zāwiye* and *maḥalle*, a mosque and *medrese* of Kurd ʿAlī Efendi, a bridge and fountain of Nāʾib Aḥmed Efendi and an ʿ*imāret* of K̲h̲üsrew Ketk̲h̲udā.

Because of Cossack raids and the wars with Russia, the open town was in the 18th century fortified with an earthen rampart surrounding, on the land side, a moat with a guarded road, towers and gates. After the Russian destruction of the Ič Ḳalʿe, the Ottomans started building a new fortress, the Yeñi Ḳalʿe, largely completed in 1851, on the block fortification principle, with a central fortress and outlying forts and, in 1877, a moat. The wars with Russia and the conflagration of 1854 caused the loss of many Muslim public buildings, but many of these were replaced in the course of the 19th century. According to the *Sāl-nāme* of 1872-3, there were in the town 19 mosques, 12 schools, one *medrese* and one *tekke*. That of 1874-5 records 732 shops, 15 tanneries, 14 k̲h̲āns, 252 warehouses, three *ḥammām*s, a clock tower and a *rüs̲h̲diyye* school. There were in fact several dervish *tekke*s in the vicinity of Varna, including Bektās̲h̲ī ones in earlier times, one of the seven tombs of Sari̊ Salti̊ḳ [*q.v.*] and tombs of the s̲h̲ehīds from the battle of Varna of 1444. A collection of Ottoman inscriptions was gathered together by V. S̲h̲korpil in the Varna Archaeological Museum, inventoried with the help of local Muslims and translated. Some were carried off as trophies of war and are in the St. Petersburg Public Library, such as the inscription with an ode of 75 verses by the poet ʿAyntābī ʿAynī celebrating Maḥmūd II's visit to Varna in 1837, which decorated a fountain built by the *Mīr-Āk̲h̲ur* Ṣādi̊ḳ Ag̲h̲a when the town was reconstructed.

3. The post-1878 period.

After the declaration of Bulgaria's independence, many of the Turks of Varna emigrated, but the town remained in close connection with a Muslim-populated hinterland; a *müftülük* was still functioning in the town until the 1960s. Muslims had representatives in the state and local official bodies; and the Muslim community in Varna launched a number of important initiatives for the maintenance of the Muslim monuments that were not always positively regarded by the local authorities. Among the outstanding local scholars one should mention Osman Nuri Peremeci, the director of the Varna *rüs̲h̲diyye* in the 1920s as well as the teacher in French in the K̲h̲alīl Bey *rüs̲h̲diyye*, who made translations of inscriptions. The Varna *rüs̲h̲diyye* was founded in the 19th century by ʿĀs̲h̲ir Bey; 110 students studied in it at the beginning of the 20th century, taught by two teachers. In the 1870s there was a crafts school and a *ḳirāʾat-k̲h̲āne*; a Turkish women's society took care of orphans. There were also a printing house and a Turkish theatre company. By World War I, three Turkish newspapers were published in Varna: *Ḥuḳūḳ* ("Law"), an organ of the Young Turk Party, edited by Agop Garabedyan, banned for political reasons; *Müwāzene* ("Balance"), published by ʿAlī Fehlī, of which 377 issues came out in the period 1897-1905; *Warna Postasî*, in Bulgarian and Turkish; and, after World War II, a local organ of the Communist Party, *Halk Dâvası* ("The People's Cause").

Bibliography: 1. Sources. Registers: Istanbul BBOA, Mev. kal. 2596, 1641-1709, *avariz*: MK 2591 of 1641-2, *avariz*; Mal. müd. 4023; MMD4023, 1690-1, *cizye*; Sofia, NLCM, OAK 129/3, of 1675-7, *avariz*; Vn 31/4, of 1685, *cizye*. Texts: Ewliyā, *Seyāḥat-nāmesi*, iv, Istanbul 1985; *Sāl-nāme-yi Wilāyet-i Ṭuna*, Rus̲h̲čuk 1289, 1291.

2. Studies. A. Is̲h̲irkov, *Grad Varna*, in *Periodičesko Spisanie*, xvi (1905), no. 45; V. S̲h̲korpil, *Turskite ukrepleniya văv Varna*, in *Izvestiya na Varnedskoto arheologičesko druz̲h̲estvo*, ii; B. Abdula, *Osmanski epigrafski pametnitsi v arheologičeskiya muzey văv Varna*, in *Arheologiya* (1965), no. 4; V. Gyuzelev and A. Kuzev, *Bălgarski srednovekovni gradove i kreposti*, Sofia 1981; D. Keskioğlu, *Bulgaristan'da müsülmanlar ve Islam eserleri*, i, n.d.; E. Ayverdi, *Avrupa'da osmanlı mimari eserleri*, iv, Istanbul 1982; N. Todorov, *The Balkan town, 1400-1900*, Seattle, Wash. 1983; M. Kiel, *Art and society of Bulgaria in the Turkish period*, Maastricht 1985; S. Dimitrov, V. Tonev and N. Z̲h̲ečev, *Istoriya na Dobrudz̲h̲a*, iii, Sofia 1988. (Svetlana Ivanova)

WARRĀḲ (a.), literally, "producer or seller of leaves, *waraḳ*", in mediaeval Islam the designation for the copyist of manuscripts, paper seller, and also bookseller.

According to al-Samʿānī, *Ansāb*, ed. Ḥaydarābād, xiii, 300, the term was specifically applied to copyists of *maṣāḥif* and *ḥadīt̲h̲* compilations. The earliest material used must have been parchment and papyrus [see ḳirṭās and raḳḳ], gradually replaced largely by paper, whose production in Bag̲h̲dād began in the late 2nd/8th century and early 3rd/9th century [see kāg̲h̲ad]. From this time onwards, paper was available as a relatively cheap writing material, a factor favouring the emergence of *warrāḳūn* as a professional group. The earliest known person bearing the designation seems to be a man of Wāsiṭ called Abū ʿAbd Allāh Aṣbag̲h̲ b. Zayd (or Yazīd) al-D̲j̲uhanī al-Warrāḳ (d. 195/811) (Bahs̲h̲al = Aslam b. Sahl al-Razzāz al-Wāsiṭī, *Taʾrīk̲h̲ Wāsiṭ*, ed. G. ʿAwwād, Bag̲h̲dād 1967, 91 and n. 16; al-Samʿānī, xiii, 300-1).

Some Arabic literary sources portray a *warrāḳ*'s profession as a somewhat reprehensible craft (*ḥirfa mad̲h̲mūma*) because it did not provide the copyist an adequate income during his lifetime and he had to live in poverty, so much so that he could not afford to leave enough money to buy his shroud (*kafan*). Nevertheless, the *warrāḳ* was devoted to his craft and delighted in his work. According to al-T̲h̲aʿālibī, "a *warrāḳ* was asked, 'What is pleasure?' He replied, 'Parchment, papers, poured ink and a cleft reed pen.' " He often complained about the insecurity of his profession. On being asked about his condition, a *warrāḳ* replied that he lived a miserable life, his livelihood being narrower than the ink-pot, his body more slender than a ruler (*misṭara*); his face was darker than glue; his hand was weaker than cane, and misfortune clung to him more than gum (*al-ṣamag̲h̲*), etc. Such literary exaggerations aside, some copyists earned a good income. For instance, Abū ʿAlī al-ʿUkbarī (d. 428/1037) boasted that he used to buy paper sheets for five dirhams to make a copy of the *Dīwān* of al-Mutanabbī in three or four nights, earning thereby between 150 and 200 dirhams (cf. Ibn al-D̲j̲awzī, *Muntaẓam*, viii, 92). Another *warrāḳ* copied ten folios a day and earned 10 dirhams by selling his work thus copied (al-K̲h̲aṭīb, *Taʾrīk̲h̲ Bag̲h̲dād*, vii, 342). These cases were probably exceptional. Average copyists perhaps earned much less, yet the public regarded them highly because of their association with the literati and intellectuals in society.

It seems that a copyist of the 2nd/8th century earned a tenth of a dirham for copying a single page; but in the 3rd/9th century, a similar copyist earned a fifth of a dirham for the same amount of work. During the 4th/10th century, a *warrāḳ* earned one dirham for copying a single page for a customer. Thus the wage of a copyist for copying a page increased between the 2nd/8th and 4th/10th centuries. Some *warrāḳūn* became famous because they worked for a famous employer; such was the case with ʿAbd al-Wahhāb b. ʿĪsā al-Warrāḳ (d. 319/931), who copied the manuscripts of al-D̲j̲āḥiẓ, and similarly, Aḥmad b. Muḥammad b. al-Warrāḳ (d. 228/843), who worked for the Barmakid al-Faḍl b. Yaḥyā. It would appear from the statement of al-Yaʿḳūbī that the *warrāḳūn* as a professional group emerged during the 3rd/9th century, so much so that there were more than one hundred shops or stalls of copyists and paper sellers (*ḥānūt al-warrāḳīn*) near the site of Ḳaṣr Waḍḍāḥ in Bag̲h̲dād. Those *warrāḳūn* were also described as *aṣḥāb al-kutub* or booksellers (cf. *K. al-Buldān*, 245, tr. Wiet, 24). There were book markets in all major Islamic cities, such as Bag̲h̲dād, Baṣra, Sāmarrāʾ, Wāsiṭ and Cairo. It is recorded that a manuscript of the *History* of al-Ṭabarī was offered for the price of 100 dīnārs.

The profession of *warrāḳ* attracted men of letters of all descriptions, such as poets, theologians, commentators on the Ḳurʾān, and traditionists. Some of them had a poor reputation, but many basked in popular esteem. A *warrāḳ* such as S̲h̲ud̲j̲āʿ b. D̲j̲aʿfar b. Aḥmad al-Warrāḳ (d. 353/964) claimed an honourable genealogy from the Prophet's Companion Abū Ayyūb al-Anṣārī, and earned for himself a reputation as a preacher (*wāʿiẓ* [*q.v.*]).

ʿAllān al-Warrāḳ, who regarded himself as a man of culture, earned his living as an itinerant copyist who paid visits to his customers rather than the other way round. In some cases a large group of copyists were employed by one man who also provided them board and lodging. The degree of accuracy of knowledge and science available in the ʿAbbāsid Middle East reflected the quality of the copyists' work; a bad copyist was criticised as an embezzler of science and knowledge, as is noted by Abū Bakr al-K̲h̲ʷārazmī (*Rasāʾil*, ed. al-K̲h̲āzin, Beirut 1970, 150).

In the late mediaeval period, especially in Ṣafawid Persia, Ottoman Turkey and pre-modern and early modern Egypt, there existed guilds of various groups involved in the book trade, such as copyists, bookbinders and booksellers.

Bibliography (in addition to references given in the article): 1. Sources. Ibn al-Nadīm, *Fihrist*, Beirut 1994, 121, 136-8; Dj̲ahs̲h̲iyārī, *Lost fragments of the Kitāb al-Wuzarā' wa 'l-kuttāb*, ed. M. ʿAwwād, Beirut 1965, 49; Abū Ḥayyān al-Tawḥīdī, *Mat̲h̲ālib/Ak̲h̲lāḳ al-wazīrayn*, Damascus 1961, 142; T̲h̲aʿālibī, *Bard al-akbād*, in *K̲h̲ams rasā'il*, Constantinople 1301/1984, 112; idem, *K̲h̲āṣṣ al-k̲h̲āṣṣ*, Beirut 1966, 69; al-K̲h̲aṭīb al-Bag̲h̲dādī, vii, 342, xii, 10, 65, 94, 136, 142-3, 180, 254, 331, xiv, 281-2; Ibn al-Dj̲awzī, *Muntaẓam*, vii, 22, viii, 33-4; Ibn al-Ḳifṭī, *Ḥukamā'*, 272-3, 440; Subkī, *Muʿīd al-niʿam*, ed. D. Myhrman, London 1908, 188; Ṣafadī, *Wāfī*, xix, 558-9, xxi, 27, 372-3; Ibn K̲h̲aldūn, *Muḳaddima*, ii, 349-52, Eng. tr. Rosenthal, ii, 391-5.

2. Studies. Mez, *Renaisance of Islam*, Eng. tr. 172; G. Baer, *Egyptian guilds in modern times*, Jerusalem 1964, 38; H.J. Cohen, *The economic background and the secular occupations of Muslim jurisprudents and traditionists in the classical period of Islam*, in *JESHO*, xiii (1970), 30; M.A.J. Beg, *A contribution to the economic history of the Caliphate. A study of the cost of living and the economic status of artisans in Abbasid Iraq*, in *IQ*, xvi (1972), 163; Mehdi Keyvani, *Artisans and guild life in later Safavid period*, Berlin 1982, 84.

(M.A.J. Beg)

AL-**WARRĀḲ, ABŪ ʿĪSĀ** [see ABŪ ʿĪSĀ].

AL-**WARRĀḲ**, MAḤMŪD B. (AL-)ḤASAN al-Warrāḳ al-Nak̲h̲k̲h̲ās, poet of the early ʿAbbāsid period. He lived in Bag̲h̲dād, where he died *ca.* 230/845. As Ibn al-Muʿtazz [*q.v.*] says in his *Ṭabaḳāt al-s̲h̲uʿarā'* (ed. ʿAbd al-Sattār Aḥmad Farrādj̲, Cairo n.d., 367), "most of his poetry consists of sententious, gnomic, paraenetic and ethical sayings (*amt̲h̲āl wa-ḥikam wa-mawāʿiẓ wa-adab*), in which genres he does not fall short of Ṣāliḥ b. ʿAbd al-Ḳuddūs [*q.v.*] and Sābiḳ al-Barbarī". Specialising in epigrams on *zuhd* [*q.v.*] rarely longer than six lines, with an easy diction and almost wholly devoid of striking similes or metaphors, he was not much esteemed by literary critics. He is, however, often quoted by anthologists, notably the Cordovan writer Ibn ʿAbd al-Barr [*q.v.*], whose *Bahdj̲at al-madj̲ālis* contains more than one hundred of his epigrams. An anecdote (Ibn al-Muʿtazz, *Ṭabaḳāt*, 379-80, *Ag̲h̲ānī*[3], xiv, 197-8) presents him in a less pious and sober guise, involved in a bout of drinking and lechery in the company of the disreputable poet Abu 'l-S̲h̲ibl al-Burdj̲umī.

Bibliography: 1. Collected verse. *Dīwān Maḥmūd b. Ḥasan al-Warrāḳ*, ed. ʿAdnān Rāg̲h̲ib al-ʿUbaydī, Bag̲h̲dād 1979, ed. Muḥammad Zuhdī Yakan, Beirut 1983 (contains less than al-ʿUbaydī's edition). Short notices in al-K̲h̲aṭīb al-Bag̲h̲dādī, *Ta'rīk̲h̲ Bag̲h̲dād*, xiii, 87-9, Ibn S̲h̲ākir al-Kutubī, *Fawāt al-Wafayāt*, ed. ʿAbbās, Beirut 1974, ii, 562-4.

2. Monograph. Muḥammad ʿĀrif Maḥmūd Ḥusayn, *Dj̲awānib al-ʿiẓa wa 'l-ḥikma fī s̲h̲iʿr Maḥmūd al-Warrāḳ*, Cairo 1988. (G.J.H. van Gelder)

AL-**WARRĀḲ**, MUḤAMMAD B. YŪSUF al-Ta'rīk̲h̲ī, Abū ʿAbd Allāh (b. 292/904-5, d. 363/973-4 at Cordova), Andalusī historian and geographer. He stemmed from a family originally of Guadalajara (Wādī 'l-Ḥidj̲āra), being born either there or at Ḳayrawān (Ibn al-ʿId̲h̲ārī, tr. Fagnan, i, 188, has the latter) where, in any case, he spent his youth. "When he returned to al-Andalus (where he was born, or rather, after one of his travels ?), he became connected with al-Ḥakam (II) b. ʿAbd al-Raḥmān al-Mustanṣir (350-66/961-76 [*q.v.*]), and he wrote for him an extensive work on 'Itineraries and kingdoms' (*al-Masālik wa 'l-mamālik* [*q.v.*])" (al-Ḍabbī; Ibn al-Abbār).

Like another Spanish Muslim geographer, Abū Bakr Aḥmad b. Muḥammad al-Rāzī (d. *ca.* 344/955: Pons Boigues, no. 22; Miquel, i, p. xxix), he is called a "chronicler" (*ta'rīk̲h̲ī*). We do not know whether he was called *al-warrāḳ* because he was a copyist or a book-seller, or whether this was his father's trade, as the preface to the Arabic text of al-Bakrī might lead one to think (*Description*, 12 n. 3: Ibn al-Warrāḳ), but it is not to be excluded that he may have had the post of a librarian at the caliph al-Ḥakam's court.

Like several other scholars, he left a land occupied by the Fāṭimids and was welcomed by al-Ḥakam II, patron of scholars and littérateurs, but also glad to find in him a competent informant who could prove useful for his North African foreign policy (Brunschwig, 151; Miquel, i, 259-60).

None of his works has come down to us. Apart from his *K. Masālik Ifrīḳiya wa-mamālikihā*, he wrote works in the following field: "numerous works on the history of the rulers of Ifrīḳiya, their wars and those who rebelled against them (*kutub dj̲amma fī ak̲h̲bār mulūkihā wa-ḥurūbihim wa 'l-ḳā'imīn ʿalayhim*), as well as monographs (*tawālīf fī ak̲h̲bār*) on Tiharat (Tāhart), Wahrān, Tanas, Sidj̲ilmāsa, Nakūr and al-Baṣra (of the Mag̲h̲rib)" (al-Ḍabbī). He was equally skilled in geneaology, especially that of the Berbers (Ibn Ḥazm, 495 ff.).

He was one of the main sources for Abū ʿUbayd al-Bakrī [*q.v.*] in his *Description of North Africa*, whom he calls Muḥammad b. Yūsuf or Muḥammad (index, at 394a). It is affirmed there that his information was often first-hand, from having visited the places and following the itineraries, e.g. from Sidj̲ilmāsa to Fās (281 ff.), or else was derived from his informants. Having said this, it also happens that he gives false information (30 n. 2). Ibn Ḥayyān [*q.v.*] also combined the fragments of his work in his *History of the scholars of al-Andalus*, and Ibn al-ʿId̲h̲ārī [*q.v.*] did the same, to a lesser degree, in his *History of Africa and Spain* (i, 97, 339 ff., ii, 400 ff.).

Bibliography: 1. Sources and translations. Abū ʿUbayd al-Bakrī, *al-Mug̲h̲rib fī d̲h̲ikr bilād Ifrīḳiya wa 'l-Mag̲h̲rib*, ed. M.G. de Slane, Algiers 1857, tr. idem, *Description de l'Afrique septentrionale*, Algiers-Paris, 1911-3, both repr. Paris 1965, Frankfurt 1993; Ḍabbī, 131, no. 304, ed. I. al-Abyārī, Cairo-Beirut 1989, 182-3, no. 305; Ḥumaydī, *Dj̲ad̲h̲wat al-muḳtabis*, ed. al-Abyārī, Cairo-Beirut 1989[2] (1983[1]), i, 158, no. 160; Ibn al-Abbār, 101, no. 344 (Casiri, *Bibliotheca arabo-hispana escurialensis*, Madrid 1760-70, ii, 126), ed. ʿI. al-ʿAṭṭār al-Ḥusaynī, Cairo 1956, i, 366, no. 995; Ibn Ḥayyān, *al-Muḳtabis*, ed. M.M. Antuña, Paris 1937, tr. J. Guraieb, in *Cuadernos de historia de España*, Buenos Aires, xiii-xxx (1950-9), ed. ʿA.ʿA. al-Ḥadj̲dj̲ī, Beirut 1965, tr. E. García Gómez, *Anales palatinos del califa de Córdoba Al-Hakam II, por ʿÎsà ibn Ahmed al-Râzî*, Madrid 1967, ed. M.ʿA. Makkī, Cairo 1971, ed. P. Chalmeta *et al.*, Madrid 1979; Ibn Ḥazm, *Dj̲amharat ansāb al-ʿArab*, ed. ʿA.M. Hārūn, Cairo 1977, repr. Beirut 1983, 495 ff.; Ibn al-ʿId̲h̲ārī, *al-Bayān al-mug̲h̲rib fī ak̲h̲bār al-Andalus wa 'l-Mag̲h̲rib*, ed. R. Dozy, Leiden 1848-51, 43, 175, 451, tr. E. Fagnan, *Histoire de l'Afrique et de l'Espagne*, 2 vols. Algiers 1901-4; Maḳḳarī, *Analectes*, ii, 112-13, tr. P. de Gayangos, *The History of the Muhammadan dynasties of Spain*, London 1840-3, i, 176, ii, 171.

2. Studies. Brockelmann, S I, 233, no. 4a; R. Brunschvig, *Un aspect de la littérature historico-géographique de l'Islām*, in *Mélanges Gaudefroy-Demombynes*, Cairo 1935-45, 147-58, at 151-2; J.M. Cuoq, *Recueil des sources arabes concernant l'Afrique Occidentale du VIII*[e]

eu XVIe siècle, Paris 1975, 84; R. Dozy, see Ibn al-ʿIdhārī, introd., 43; H. Fournel, *Les Berbères, études sur la conquête de l'Afrique par les Arabes*, 2 vols., Paris 1875-81, ii, 85; Kaḥḥāla, *Muʾallifīn*, xii, 141; I.Yu. Kračkovski, *Arabskaya geografičeskaya literatura*, Leningrad 1957, 165, Ar. tr. Ṣ.ʿU. Hāshim, Cairo 1963, 169; E. Lévi-Provençal, *Documents inédits d'histoire almohade*, Paris 1928, 3 n. 1; T. Lewicki, *La répartition géographique des groupements ibāḍites dans l'Afrique du Nord au moyen-âge*, in *RO*, xxi (1957), 317, 335; A. Miquel, *La géographie du monde musulman*, i, Paris 1967, pp. xxxi-xxxii, 259-62, index s.v. Warrāq, ii, 1975, 151, index; V. Monteil, *Al-Bakrī (Cordoue, 1068), routier de l'Afrique blanche et noire du nord-ouest*, in *Bull. IFAN*, Dakar, xxx (1968), 39-116; Pons Boigues, 80-1, no. 39; W. Schwartz, *Die Anfänge der Ibaditen in Nordafrika*, Wiesbaden 1983, 84; F. Wüstenfeld, *Die Geschichtsschreiber der Araber und ihre Werke*, Göttingen 1882, 137; Ziriklī, *al-Aʿlām*, vii, 148.

(CL. GILLIOT)

WARS (A.), a yellow dye from a perennial plant cultivated in Yemen, identified usually as *Memecylon tinctorium, Melastomaceae*, or sometimes *Flemmingia rhodocarpus* BAK, *Leguminosae*.

According to Abū Ḥanīfa al-Dīnawarī's chapter on dyestuffs (165-7), it is found only in Yemen, and there only as a cultivated plant. From various sources, he describes the best *wars* as *bādira*, from a young plant, the other sort being called *ḥabashī* because of some blackness in it; however, the *ḥabashī* gives pure yellow, while *bādira* can contain some redness. Ibn Djuldjul lists it among his medicinal items "which Dioscorides did not mention": it has heads like cotton, and is used for yellow dye, like saffron (Bodleian ms. Hyde 34). Its nature is hot and costive, according to ʿAlī b. Sahl al-Ṭabarī in a chapter on spices and scents (*Firdaws*, 398). Medicinal uses seem to have been insignificant. However, Ibn Ḳayyim al-Djawziyya in *Medicine of the Prophet* gives a *ḥadīth* that the Prophet used to prescribe oil with *wars*, taken internally, for pleurisy (al-Tirmidhī, *Ṭibb*, 28; Ibn Mādja, *Ṭibb*, 17). He also mentions its use as an embrocation for freckles, itching, and some skin problems (Ar. text 444, Eng. 280).

Dyestuffs, once prepared for sale and for use, are not always so easily identified, and it may have been confused at times with *Carthamus tinctorius, Compositae*, the safflower, which also gives yellow and red dye.

Bibliography: ʿAlī b. Sahl al-Ṭabarī, *Firdaws al-ḥikma*, ed. M.Z. Siddiqi, Berlin 1928; B. Lewin (ed.), *The Book of Plants... by Abū Ḥanīfa al-Dīnawarī*, Bibl. Islamica, Wiesbaden 1974; Ibn Ḳayyim al-Djawziyya, *al-Ṭibb al-nabawī*, ed. A.A. al-Ḳalʿadjī, Cairo 1978, Eng. tr. P. Johnstone, *Medicine of the Prophet*, Cambridge 1998.

(PENELOPE C. JOHNSTONE)

WARSH, ʿUTHMĀN B. SAʿĪD b. ʿAbd Allāh al-Ḳurashī al-Miṣrī al-Ḳayrawānī, transmitter of the Ḳurʾān reading of Nāfiʿ al-Laythī [*q.v.*], born in 110/728 in Egypt where he also died in 197/812. A Copt in origin, Warsh was a student of Nāfiʿ and it was from his teacher that he is said to have received his *laḳab*; the name Warsh was given to him either because of his extreme whiteness or because of his similarity to a bird called *warashān*. Warsh taught his transmission of the Ḳurʾān to a number of his Egyptian students, and from there it spread especially through transmitters in Spain. While the Ḳurʾān reading of Ḥafṣ *ʿan* ʿĀṣim is now the most widespread in the Muslim world [see ḲIRĀʾA], the version of Warsh *ʿan* Nāfiʿ is found particularly in West and North-West Africa and has been printed in Saudi Arabia, Cairo and Tunis. The reading system of Nāfiʿ was also maintained by the Zaydiyya [*q.v.*] of the Yemen although no studies have been done to determine if this was the transmission through Ḳālūn (d. 220/835) or Warsh.

Bibliography: Sezgin, *GAS*, i, 11; Yāḳūt, *Irshād*, ed. Rifāʿī, xii, 116-21; Ibn al-Djazarī, *Ghayāt al-nihāya fī ṭabaḳāt al-ḳurrāʾ*, ed. Bergsträsser, Cairo 1932-3, no. 2090; Nöldeke *et alii*, *Gesch. des Qor.*, iii, 160-205; Labib as-Said, *The recited Koran*, tr. B. Weiss *et alii*, Princeton 1975, 127 (gives the various *ṭuruḳ* of the *riwāya* of Warsh); Kristina Nelson, *The art of reciting the Qurʾān*, Austin 1985, 133; A. Brockett, *The value of the Ḥafṣ and Warsh transmissions for the textual history of the Qurʾān*, in A. Rippin (ed.), *Approaches to the history of the interpretation of the Qurʾān*, Oxford 1988, 31-45 and references.

(A. RIPPIN)

WARWARĪ ʿALĪ PASHA, Ottoman governor and commander, d. 1058/1648.

He was a native of Warwar or Varvara (lat. 43° 49' N., long. 17° 29' E.) in Bosnia. Details of his career in state service in the first four decades of the 17th century are provided by the Pasha himself in his versified memoirs (*sar gudhasht*). Some of the high points, as he relates them, include his participation in Murād IV's campaign against Eriwan in 1045/1635 as *dümdar* (commander of the army's rear flank), in which he received a cash bonus for exceptional service of four purses (160,000 *akčes*) of silver (*Memoirs*, v. 116), and his sustaining of battle wounds during the campaign against Baghdād in 1048/1638, which led to his promotion at the end of Murād's reign to the governorship-general of Rumelia (vv. 135-40). ʿAlī Pasha regarded his appointment to the governorship of Bosnia through the intercession of the Grand Vizier Semīdh Meḥmed Pasha in 1054/1644 as the pinnacle of his career (vv. 168-9, date confirmed in Naʿīmā, *Tārīkh*, iv, 73). However, the insecurity of his position, shared by all provincial governors, is only too apparent from his record of service at the beginning of Ibrāhīm I's reign. In the first four years of that sultan's reign alone, he was appointed in rapid succession to six governorships: Mağnisa, Van, Anatolia, Adana, Diyarbekir and Bolu.

Warwarī ʿAlī Pasha is chiefly remembered for the stance which he took, bravely contradicting current government practice, in support of guaranteed conditions of service for provincial governors and for his opposing, in particular, abuses in the assessment of the appointments' gratuity customarily paid by new incumbents to higher office [see PĪSHKASH]. Uncontrolled increases in these assessments, especially during the reign of Ibrāhīm I, had left many governors in a state of chronic indebtedness. During his tenure as governor of Sivas in 1058/1648, ʿAlī Pasha's opposition took concrete form in rebellion, and during a conflict between government and provincial forces near the central Anatolian town of Čerkes in Rabīʿ II 1058/May 1648 he was captured and executed on the spot [see IPSHIR MUṢṬAFĀ PASHA]. It is ironic that, only four years later, in 1062/1052 Ipshir, clearly inspired by the example of his discredited predecessor, himself backed proposals in favour of a guaranteed three-year minimum term of service for all state appointees (Naʿīmā, v, 199, ll. 2-3). Ottoman political thinkers from the time of Ḳoči Beg [*q.v.*] to Tatardjïḳ ʿAbd Allāh Efendi [see SELĪM III] gave particular emphasis in their writings to the importance of state administrators' immunity from arbitrary dismissal (see textual refs. in *Bibl.*). Warwarī ʿAlī Pasha's sad end after long and loyal service spanning the reigns of six sultans demonstrates just how astute their observations were.

Bibliography: 1. Texts. Naʿīmā, *Tārīkh*, iv, 227-8, 244-8, 274-9; Ḳara Čelebi-zāde ʿAbd al-ʿAzīz Efendi, *Dheyl-i Rawḍat ül-ebrār*, ms. Vienna, Österr. Nationalbibliothek, H.O. 76, fols. 9b-11a; Ewliyā Čelebi, *Seyāḥat-nāme*, ms. Topkapı Sarayı, Bağdat Köskü 304, fols. 338a-366a (provides a psychological portrait of Warwarī ʿAlī Pasha lacking in other sources).

2. Biographical studies. *SʿO*, iii, 513; Hikmet Ertaylan, *Varvari Ali Paşa*, in *Türk Dili ve Edebiyatı Dergisi*, ii/3-4 (1948), 155-70; Marija Dukanović (ed.), *Rimovana autobiografija Varvari Ali-Paše*, Belgrade 1967 (gives text of his autobiographical poem in 178 rhymed couplets; her numbering of these is followed in the article above).

3. Political treatises. Ḳoči Beg's views on governorship are summarised in a supplementary *telkhīṣ* of his treatise of 1041/1631; see R. Murphey (ed.), *The Veliyuddin Telhis*, in *Belleten*, xliii, no. 171 (1979), esp. 560 (last 3 ll.) and 561 (first 3 ll.) and abbreviated Eng. tr. on 549. Tatardjïḳ ʿAbd Allāh's *lāyiḥa* of 1206/1791 has a long ch. on this theme and recommends a minimum term of office of four to five years; see Sherīf Meḥmed (ed.), *Sulṭān Selīm-i Thālith dewrinde niẓām-i dewlet ḥakkïnda muṭālaʿāt*, part 3, in *TOEM*, viii, no. 43 (1333/1917), 15-20, esp. 18 (ll. 13-23). (R. Murphey)

al-**WĀSĀNĪ**, Abu 'l-Ḳāsim al-Ḥusayn b. al-Ḥasan (or al-Ḥusayn) b. Wāsān (or Wāsāna), minor poet of invective and satirical verse. He lived in Damascus in the 4th/10th century and died in 394/1003-4. Very little is known of his life; he or his family may have come originally from Aleppo. Al-Thaʿālibī (*Yatīmat al-dahr*, Cairo 1947, i, 335) calls him the Ibn al-Rūmī [*q.v.*] of his time, on account of his invective verse [see hidjāʾ]. It is said that he once lost his job, some kind of official position, as a result of his scurrilous attacks on a certain Manashshā (Manasseh) b. Ibrāhīm al-Ḳazzāz. Most of the verse that is preserved (*ca.* 450 lines, including two very long poems, quoted in *Yatīma*, i, 325-55, and Yāḳūt's *Muʿdjam al-udabāʾ*, Cairo 1936-8, ix, 233-65) is invective of the obscene kind. His longest and best poem is a lively and entertaining description, in a *nūniyya* of 196 lines in *khafīf* metre, of a banquet given by him that got out of hand through the guests' misbehaviour; a shortened version (137 lines) is quoted by Yāḳūt.

Bibliography: Given in the article, and see (ʿAbd al-Ḳādir) al-Maghribī, *Walīmat Ibn Wāsāna*, in *RAAD*, x (1930), 641-51, 705-19 (gives only 123 lines of the banquet poem). (G.J.H. van Gelder)

WAṢF (a.), lit. "description".

I. In poetry

1. *Description*

This literary genre, through its dimensions, its significative function and its evolution, has played a role of the greatest importance in the long process of the development of Arabic poetry. By its etymology, the term signifies embellishment (al-Djawharī, *al-Ṣiḥāḥ*, Beirut 1404/1984, iv, 1438-9; *Tahdhīb al-lugha*, xii, 248a; al-Zamakhsharī, *Asās al-balāgha*, 1024a-1025a; *LA*, s.v. *w-ṣ-f*, *waṣafa al-shayʾa ḥallāhu* "he described a thing, meaning that he embellished it"). This sense has been retained by the Ḳurʾān (XVI, 62); it is attested to a quite unexpected degree in poetry throughout the classical period (*al-ʿIḳd al-thamīn*, 186, Ṭarafa; ʿĀmir b. al-Ṭufayl, *Dīwān*, 159, l. 13; Ibn Hishām, *Sīra*, 121, l. 15; *LA*, xix, 134, l. 5; under the Umayyads, *al-Aghānī*, i, 99, l. 13, al-Dārimī; *ibid.*, xi, 373, l. 5, Ismāʿīl b. ʿAmmār al-Asadī; Ibn Ḳutayba, *al-Shiʿr wa 'l-shuʿarāʾ*, 510-11, Abū Nuwās; Khālid al-Kātib, §§ 284, 297; Ibn al-Rūmī, ii, 688, *idhā mā waṣafta mraʾ^{an} li-mriʾ^{in} fa-lā taghlu fī waṣfihi wa 'ḳṣidi* "when you praise one man to another, do not exaggerate his eulogy; do it with moderation"). In this connection, a verse of the Umayyad poet Waḍḍāḥ al-Yaman establishes an equivalence between *waṣf* and *tashbīb* which come to be equated (*al-Aghānī*, vi, 235, l. 2); in fact, the latter refers predominantly to the eulogy addressed to the woman in the context of love poetry.

Under the Umayyads, *waṣf* with the meaning of description gains ground in the texts, although the primary sense is not eclipsed. It is therefore appropriate to stress that it is flattering description that is involved here, the embellishment of reality. *Waṣf* embellishment constitutes the fundamental approach of one of the great descriptive poets of Arabic literature, Ibn Khafādja: because description, he writes in the introduction to his *Dīwān*, is a style of composition which purports to express a representation based on imagery, it follows that the poet is not to be denounced for having lied (i.e. for embellishing reality), nor can he be forced to confine himself to the real (*Dīwān*, 11). All of this runs counter to the assertions of Ḳudāma b. Djaʿfar (*Naḳd*, 23) and of Ibn Rashīḳ al-Ḳayrawānī and of certain supporters of the theory of *ʿamūd al-shiʿr*; in their view, the best description is that which adheres to the real, that which transforms words into directly comprehensible images (*al-ʿUmda*, ii, 294; see also 295).

2. *The poetics of* waṣf

A large number of mediaeval theorists have studied two essential tools of the descriptive art, *al-tashbīh* (simile) and *al-istiʿāra* (metaphor), which are reckoned to show mutual resemblance. Thus it is that Ibn Abī ʿAwn, in composing the *K. al-Tashbīhāt*, and to a lesser degree al-Djāḥiẓ in *al-Bayān*, devoted most of their attention to cataloguing the system of imagery adopted by poetry; this manner of proceeding exempted them from having to examine the entity known as *waṣf*. At the end of the 3rd/9th and during the 4th/10th centuries, this habit is seen to be perpetuated, with the systematic treatises of Ibn al-Muʿtazz and of Abū Hilāl al-ʿAskarī on the one hand, and the works on *maʿānī*, giving an account of these tropes, on the other. Only a minority of original theorists addressed this art in the context of broad categories, sc. of literary genres. Ḳudāma b. Djaʿfar, 23, considers *waṣf* one of the six genres most frequently employed by poets. Some of his views on the question have an utterly modern resonance. For him, prefiguring those contemporary theorists for whom all description is narration, description consists in relating a thing on the basis of its various aspects and its successive states. Thus the most gifted descriptive writer is the one who succeeds in combining the greatest number of *maʿānī* and in emphasising those that best characterise the object in question. The most successful description will be that which imitates (*yaḥkī*) the object and renders it perceptible (*yumaththil*) to the senses (*ibid.*, 62-3). Ibn Rashīḳ (d. 456/1063) considers this art a frame broad enough to contain almost the entirety of Arabic poetry; it differs from comparison despite evident analogies, the former being concerned with reality, the latter with an imaged (*tamthīl*) and a figurative (*madjāz*) representation (*al-ʿUmda*, ii, 294-6).

Ḥāzim al-Ḳarṭādjannī (d. 684/1285) likewise asserts

that *waṣf* is predominant in rhymed discourse. This being the case, he distinguishes between four poetic genres: description, comparison, wisdom and history. To excel, the poet must be a good observer. He will thereby be capable of grasping the features of resemblance and the similitudes which exist between the afore-mentioned genres; and he will also need to be aware of the attributes (*nuʿūt*) of the notions, events and objects which he will be setting himself to describe. On the level of the treatment of themes and not of forms, al-Ḳarṭādjannī partially revives the division established by Ḳudāma, beginning with *waṣf* and *tashbīh*; the latter performs an integration between the sentiments of the poet, the diverse reflections of his nature, of his soul and of the sensibility of the object perceived. In the third place, he cites sapiential themes, including the meditations and the ideas of the poet, the fruit of his experience and of his awareness. The fourth category of poetry, designated by the term *taʾrīkh*, concerns the role of memorialist, devolved to the poet (Muḥammad Zaghlūl Sallām, ii, 195-6). In the 8th/14th century, Ibn Khaldūn (d. 784/1382), defines poetry as "discourse founded on metaphor and descriptions". Everything in the *ḳaṣīda*, he writes, belongs to description, including the *nasīb*, the camel-section and the *ḳaṣd*.

3. *Description in poetry: between theory and practice*

A. Archaic poetry

The pre-Islamic Bedouin poet was a great creator of images. He painted with words numerous details of his life and of his environment, and devoted a major portion of his discourse to serenading the lady whom he loved, and singing the praises of nature and of the animals among which he lived. This characteristic has always drawn the attention of theorists. For Ibn Khaldūn, description and the archaic *ḳaṣīda* are inseparable. He declares this in a passage devoted to the evocation of major themes in the poem: *wa-yastaṭridu min waṣfi 'l-baydāʾi wa 'l-ṭulūli ilā waṣfi 'l-rikābi awi 'l-khayli awi 'l-ṭayfi wa-min waṣfi 'l-mamdūḥi ilā waṣfi ḳawmihi wa-ʿasākirihi* "through well-arranged transitions, he moves from the description of the desert, of traces and of encampments to that of his caravan or of his horses, or that of the image of the loved one who appears to him in a dream: praise of his patron leads on to that of his people and of his troops" (Ibn Khaldūn, *Muḳaddima*, iii, 328, tr. De Slane, iii, 366, tr. Rosenthal, iii, 373-4).

Rather than setting out a catalogue of *djāhilī* descriptions, it will be more worthwhile to identify the major features.

Major descriptive themes

The bestiary, a multidimensional one, predominates. At the time of the *raḥīl*, the nocturnal journey, the poet confronts a space sown with dangers. In this section, it was accepted that the artist could, if he wished and did not deny himself the opportunity, proceed to descriptive developments. He evoked here the running of his camel, the desert, the darkness, wild animals, maleficent spirits and excesses of the elements (storms and torrential rains: numerous descriptions in ʿAbīd b. al-Abraṣ, *Dīwān*, Cairo 1957, 36-7, 43-4, 75-6 (the storm replacing the *nasīb*), 89-90 (fragment of seven verses in *kāmil muraffal* devoted to this theme), 128-9). In praising his camel, he did not hesitate to compare it to an antelope, or an onager, or both simultaneously, or to an ostrich. He could close this section by returning to his camel. It is worth noting that a certain functional division must have played a part; the description of the camel alone is attested in poems of personal or tribal boasting and in the poetry of war as in the work of ʿAntara, Ṭarafa, al-Muthaḳḳab al-ʿAbdī, Imruʾ al-Ḳays, ʿĀmir b. al-Ṭufayl, Bishr b. Abī Khāzim al-Asadī and others. However, it is the multidimensional pattern which prevails. The descriptive deployments attested are as follows: camel–antelope–onager–war-horse–camel, with all possible combinations thereof. Numerous variants and additions are attested. The ostrich can replace the onager or the antelope (for references, see Arazi, *La réalité et la fiction*, 114-18, 130-3, 142-6, 152-3). As for additions, desert and storm seem to have been especially favoured by poets.

Birds, especially birds of prey, and the ibex, etc., are less often present and are retained for their symbolic value: the *ʿuḳāb* or *liḳwa* "eagle" in the works of Imruʾ al-Ḳays (*Dīwān*, Cairo, 1984, 142, vv. 44-5; 226-7, vv. 8-11), but especially in the works of ʿAbīd al-Abraṣ, where it is the poet's sworn enemy (*Dīwān*, 18-20, vv. 39-50, famous description), representing the destiny which swoops and brings death (al-Aʿshā, xvii, vv. 3 ff.; al-Afwah al-Awdī, *Dīwān, al-Ṭarāʾif al-adabiyya*, Cairo 1937, 20; al-Balādhurī, *Ansāb*, v, Jerusalem 1936, 241; al-Bakrī, *Simṭ al-laʾālī*, Cairo 1936, ii, 965); the ibex means to express the vanity of any creature's attempts to find an impregnable refuge as protection from his destiny.

Tendencies and significations

The audience of the time must have felt overwhelmed by this incessant whirlwind of successive images: barely installed in the world of the camel, the listener finds himself introduced, without warning, to that of the antelope, where he is confronted by a squall of unparallelled violence and forced to take shelter from lightning and from torrential rain; being given no more time, he is made to share the life of an onager, before returning to the point of departure. On more than one occasion, the poet leaves him in suspense, since the loop is not closed and there is no returning to the camel which set this process in motion. Rather than seeing this as punishment which is deserved on account of the poet's obsession with excess, this multiplicity should be regarded as an attempt on the part of the artist to endow his poem with a rapid rhythm and thus gain the approval of the public.

This approval was forthcoming because of the tendency of ancient *waṣf* towards idealisation. The poet aspired to transfigure everything that he had written with the aim of transcending the circumscribed reality of daily life in the desert. The public, clearly, had only to summon a precise portrait of a camel or a horse—emaciated, hungry, thirsty, covered with dust as these creatures generally were—and then call upon the poet to perform a process of sublimation on its behalf. The exemplary case is provided by the portrait of the lady in these texts. The *mīmiyya* of Ḥātim al-Ṭāʾī includes a *nasīb* of eleven verses, six of which evoke an unnamed woman laden with jewellery; her body is of perfect beauty (vv. 6-8) and her teeth "light up my dark tent to the furthest corner, when at night she shows a smile" (*Dīwān*, Cairo 1411/1990, 221). This notion of sparkling teeth shedding light may seem exaggerated, but it does not lack human resonances: by means of poetry, the woman is idealised. The ageing wife, worn out by hard work and frequent confinements, appears in the description as a creature richly endowed, all beauty and grace, thus erasing all the difficulties and compromises of a decidedly monotonous daily life. This tendency was required to respond to the expectation of the public; the best testimony is supplied by the contest in which Imruʾ al-Ḳays confronted ʿAlḳama, the arbiter being Umm Ḏjundub; both were required to describe a horse. The latter won the day on account of his success in having infused his verse with a perfect exemplar of equine power, according to the judgment of the arbiter. The erstwhile prince of the poets was deposed on account of a fatal error, that of having sinned by excess of realism.

The descriptive register manifests great stability. In other words, it is subject to rigid conventions imposed by the public and fully accepted by the poet on the level of the sign and the signified. Themes, their deployments and tropes of comparison move within clearly defined limits. Thus conceived, this register is distinct from realism, since every convention signifies negation of realism. Of course, this is not a case of make-believe, but rather of a mimetic description. Nevertheless, a willingness is sensed on the part of the describer to restructure and interpret the real. The she-camel of Ṭarafa, given as a model of the genre, has no hump; her udders comprise four teats, but biologically, she can possess only two. Imruʾ al-Ḳays commits the same infraction. The traits retained by Musayyab b. ʿAlas, drawing a sketch of his camel, seem so contrary to reality that Ṭarafa is supposed to have exclaimed *istanwaḳa ʾl-ḏjamalu* "the camel has changed into a she-camel". The intensive use of comparative tropes, also of substantive adjectives, has made it possible to avoid calling animals, feminine anatomy and topographical details, by their names, thus conferring a certain opacity on descriptive passages. The use of metaphor, more frequent than is generally thought, endows these verses with a fine artistic element. The *ḏjāhilī* poet Bishr b. Abī Khāzim, evoking the hills in summer time has recourse to a fine metaphor, "the hills clad in shining jewellery (*lawāmiʿ*)" of which the contextual, not the linguistic meaning, is mirage (Bishr, *Dīwān*, Beirut-Aleppo 1995, 209). However, these codes experience a certain exhaustion on account of the uninterrupted repetition of the same tropes, substantive adjectives and allusive procedures in a fixed context.

Archaic poetry possesses an ambivalent character, being both description and narration. For the *nasīb* [*q.v.*] what is necessary has been said. For the bestiary, the sections dealing with the antelope and the onager are veritable dramas in miniature; the poet steps forward here as a first-rate narrator (examples and bibl. in Arazi, *La réalité*, 160-3).

This poetry, whether it describes nature, encampment remains or the bestiary, has an optimistic flavour. Life, but also the imprint of man, triumphs over all. The desert is traversed by roads and paths, human incisions in the body of this vast expanse of sand. In fact, the route, which is *muʿabbad* (worn down by traffic) *apud* Kaʿb b. Zuhayr, or *lāḥib* (clearly marked) with *ʿulūb* (imprints) that are ineradicable on account of the compression exerted by travellers *apud* ʿAlḳama (al-*ʿIḳd al-thamīn*, 106, vv. 17-9), crosses the desert from one end to the other. Here, the archaic poet uses the term *fakkara* "to pierce deeply" to show the extent to which the imprint of man and his agents (beasts of burden) is here ineradicable. Kaʿb b. Zuhayr compares these paths to plaits woven by industrious women (*Dīwān*, Krakow 1950, 21-3, vv. 23-7; 28-31, vv. 14-26, the poet gets the better of the desert; he is accompanied by a wolf and a raven; 51, vv. 12-13; 52-3, vv. 17-8). By virtue of his knowledge, man can pit himself on equal terms with this immensity. In the bestiary, the antelope, the onager and their pregnant partners, bearers of new life, escape death, despite the snares set by hunters, despite hunting dogs and sharpened arrows.

In the archaic period, the existence is noted of two descriptive approaches: dynamic description and static description. Poets of the school of Aws b. Ḥadjar (Zuhayr and his heir al-Ḥuṭayʾa) are particularly distinctive in the first instance. Here, description has the rhythm of a beating drum. Very brief poetic phrases lay out propositions where prominence is given to verbs expressive of movement. There is recourse to an alternation of decelerated or accelerated movements, all in accordance with the requirements of the motif. This has enabled the poet to tackle, on a strongly structured basis, the essence of the *ḳaṣīda*, eulogy, *fakhr*, or *hidjāʾ*. A second descriptive approach is based on the static mode, more precisely on the freezing of movement, prolonged interminably, to the extent of enfolding the entire verse. Was it the poet's intention to contrast movement that is frenetic and thus of limited duration with the stability that is synonymous with durability?

B. Post-*ḏjāhilī* description

With the triumph of Islam, a new dimension is perceptible in *waṣf*: the cosmic dimension. The Ḳurʾān is slow off the mark in evoking the skies, stars, land and rivers as evidence of the power of the Creator and the submission of nature to His will. Naturally, the surviving poets of the Ḏjāhiliyya, the *mukhaḍramūn* [*q.v.*], do not follow the movement, but with their disappearance, a period of transition begins. Over several decades, the mental revolution inspired by Islam becomes ripe in the popular mentality; movements of population with the mass exodus of the Bedouin of Arabia and the establishment of a new landscape, the urban landscape, deal a heavy blow to ancient descriptive art. Certainly, Bedouinising poets and the conservatism inherent in all poetic language perpetuate the images of yesteryear, but this is merely a case of imitation imposed by a traditionalist attitude. The umbilical cord which used to link the public, the poet and descriptive thought together is henceforward severed, except with the *nasīb* and its descriptive extensions. The major victim seems to be the range of animals and birds, and, to a lesser degree, the desert and its thematic developments. The urban poets of Kūfa, al-Uḳayshir, Ḥunayn al-Ḥīrī, ʿAbd Allāh b. al-Zabīr al-Asadī, Ismāʿīl b. ʿAmmār al-Asadī and ʿAmmār Dhū Kināz, introduce images from the hybrid world of the taverns and courtesans of al-Ḥīra. The Ḥidjāzī school offers us a full-blown introduction to the domain of women of high society. On the other hand, poets of the renewal of the 2nd/8th century continued to express the sentiment in their presentations. Muṭīʿ b. Iyās, with the two palm-trees of Ḥilwān, was to blaze a trail that is still being followed by the Arabic poetry of the present day. The 3rd/9th century was to channel this activity and guide it towards a new descriptive art that would be brought to its zenith in the two succeeding centuries. However, attention should be given to the descriptive activity of the Umayyad *ṣaʿālīk* poets [see ṢUʿLŪK].

These highway bandits, members of tribes which maintained their Bedouin character, crowded the Pilgrimage routes. The poets among them, of whom there were many, advanced towards a three-fold description of the desert which they considered a *waṭan* or homeland, a refuge and a place of terror. They were full of nostalgia for their land. They never ceased painting the landscapes of their youth, with their infinite spaces, their caressing winds, and the breeze of early morning; but these are also the places where tents are buffeted by tempestuous and icy winds in the winter (al-Ḳattāl al-Kilābī, *Dīwān*, Baghdād 1968, 19-27, 33, 41, 45, 51, 68; al-Mubarrad, *al-Kāmil*, ed. Wright, i, 290; ʿAbd al-ʿAzīz al-Ḥalafī, *Udabāʾ al-sudjūn*, Beirut 1963, 42-4, 78-80, 92-3, 96-7, 99-102; ʿAbd al-Muʿīn al-Mallūḥī, *Ashʿār al-luṣūṣ wa-akhbāruhum*, Damascus 1988, 20, 73). Other *ṣaʿālīk* placed emphasis in their verse on the solitude of these places and the wild animals which inhabit them: some portraits in this bestiary rank as genuine bravura pieces (as in ʿUbayd b. Ayyūb al-ʿAnbarī, see Ḥusayn ʿAṭwān, *al-Shuʿarāʾ al-ṣaʿālīk fi ʾl-ʿaṣr al-islāmī*, Beirut 1987, 151-9). Another category of poets, rather more placid and respectful of the law, also sang of the desert landscapes and the loves of youth, in a poetry impregnated with melancholy. There are both poets (al-Ṣimma al-Ḳushayrī, *al-Aghānī*[3], vi, 1-8; Ibn Ḳutayba, *Shiʿr*, 185-6; Abū Tammām, *al-Ḥamāsa*, index) and poetesses (Maysūn bt. Baḥdal, Hind bt. Aʿlam al-Sadūsiyya, Wadjīha bt. Aws al-Ḍabbiyya) producing treatises of *ḥanīn ilā ʾl-awṭān*. Nevertheless, these artists were regarded as marginal and seem to have played only a very limited role in the evolution of descriptive poetry in their time.

New frameworks

Under the ʿAbbāsids, the courtly poet fulfilled certain functions in addition to his role as eulogist. He was obliged to entertain his patron's guests and to commemorate mundane events with a few improvised verses. Patrons seem to have particularly appreciated brief fragments describing a youth, a pool, a villa, a garden, a still-life or whatever might present itself. The artist was required to excel in this area or to risk losing prestige and career. Few poets succeeded in evading this obligation. Biographical notices contain a large number of examples of such descriptions, commissioned and performed forthwith. The results were ambivalent: descriptive poetry was boosted to a certain extent, becoming an integral and essential part of literary activity. These well-crafted and elegantly-delivered improvisations paved the way for the appearance of the great descriptive writers from the second half of the 3rd/9th century onward. Furthermore, it must have encouraged descriptive bouts between poets: in their encounters, there was a fusion of rhymed repartee, in which pleasures were abundantly evoked, with particular insistence on the framework of enchantment expected of them, and with the aim of being capable of inviting everyone to a bacchanalian session. However, it is appropriate to note, with J. Bencheikh, how baneful improvisation proved to be for poetry; the rapidity of the repartee and the spiritual quality of these few rhymed phrases fail to conceal the absence of any personal involvement on the part of their authors. Formal elegance and the interminable repetition of the same hackneyed effects tended to stifle any exercise of considered creation, the one thing capable of creating new combinations and hence original *maʿānī* (Bencheikh, *Poétique*, 68-79). This process, in fact, played a fundamental role with regard to the least gifted poets. Thanks to all this activity, to the dominant mood in favour of this literary genre and contribution of bacchic poetry with the Bohemia of Kūfa, but also thanks to Abū Nuwās, to al-Ḥusayn b. al-Ḍaḥḥāk and to Muslim b. al-Walīd [*q.vv.*], the descriptive act removed at this time one of the most solidly based and most respected bastions of the poetic heritage of the desert, the opening with a *nasīb*; it was replaced in the 3rd/9th century by a *rawḍiyya*, as has been shown by G. Schoeler in a set-piece *ḳaṣīda* of Abū Tammām (Schoeler, 182; Bencheikh, *Poétique*, 143-6).

Abū Tammām's disciple, al-Buḥturī, took a further step on the way of renovation; he devoted an entire *ḳaṣīda* to *waṣf*, the well-known *īwāniyya*; the very detailed description of the palace of Kisrā is conceived as an illustration of universal destruction. The collapse of the poet's ambitions and the destruction of this monument constitute the two faces of a single reality; he concludes with an assertion of impotence: everything in this world is subject to a determinism of annihilation. This experiment combines two levels of description, that of the ruins at the time of the poet's visit, and that of the imagination: a mural sculpture sets in motion a return to the past, as the sculpted scene comes to life and unfolds before our eyes a living and sumptuous spectacle (*Dīwān*, ed. al-Ṣayrafī, Cairo 1963, ii, 1152-62, 58 vv.).

At the same time, Ibn al-Rūmī was gathering together all these novelties and transforming them into systematically-employed poetic procedures. Furthermore, he is credited with two important transformations regarding the fragments and the role of the *waṣf* genre in *ḳaṣīdas*. The former were made to serve in the role of brief portraits, a few features thrown quickly together to give an impression, almost a sketch, of curious people (Ibn al-Rūmī, 608, a fool; 641, the miser who breathes through only one nostril; 682, a glutton in the process of eating; cf. also 747, 762, 815). On the other hand, he replaces the *djāhilī* range of animals and birds with descriptions of nature. In numerous instances, an opening eulogy leads to a long descriptive development on the basis of an analogy established between the patron and nature, in the space formerly reserved for the *raḥīl* (*ibid.*, 489, vv. 31-9; 542-8, vv. 6-9; 604-7, vv. 4-11).

During the 4th/10th century, two eminent descriptive poets, Kushādjim and al-Sarī al-Raffāʾ [*q.vv.*], introduced *radjaz* [*q.v.*] into poems of the genre. The way in which this metre was used by them differed from its use in cynegetic poetry. The latter had imitated in this respect the Umayyad poets al-Kumayt, al-Ṭirimmāḥ, al-ʿAdjdjādj and Ruʾba b. al-ʿAdjdjādj; it opted for the *urdjūza* [see RADJAZ], on account of its aptitude to accommodate rare words and phonemes of equally rare morphological construction (*al-gharīb*). In the work of these two descriptive poets, the *urdjūza*, resuming its role as attested in the improvised fragments (verses preceding contests and lullabies), aspires, by virtue of the facility of terms and the variety of feet (*tafʿīlāt*), to have recourse to a supple and comfortable poetic phrase; they could thus enjoy a liberty without hindrance or resistance; they could then make their verses flow, preoccupied only with the sense. Whatever the case, in the works of Kushādjim there are to be found no fewer than 38 poems and fragments in *radjaz* and in the work of al-Sarī, 19. Some poets produced the finest novelties in this domain.

Themes

The hymn to nature: The poet of this era showed a pronounced inclination towards nature domesticated by man—gardens full of colours, where greenery predominates, flowers and water enclosed in a lake or flowing freely. From the second half of the Umayyad period onward, this was the backdrop for libations evoked in bacchic poems. On the other hand, *ikhwāniyyāt* (poetry singing of friendship), poetical missives often containing an invitation to a bacchic meeting, gave great prominence to the above-mentioned themes. Finally, celebrations of the *nayrūz* [see NAWRŪZ] and *mihradjān* [*q.v.*] festivals, hymns dedicated to the glories of nature implanted in the customs of the time, and for centuries to come, not only a vivid attachment to nature but also an obligation to integrate this love in verse. In these poems, the visual element plays the primary role: to the magic of colours and their blending, *apud* the poets of the 3rd/9th and 4th/10th centuries, are added olfactory and aural elements. In this connection, a fragment of al-Sarī al-Raffā' supplies a fine illustration of the use of motifs relating to the integration of these three elements: the quatrain (*Dīwān*, Bag͟hdād 1981, ii, 666) includes an invitation addressed to the *sāḳī* to serve wine to the poet who is seated in a vineyard (*karm*[in] *muʿarrash*[in]), soothed by the cooing of doves (*tug͟hannīka wurḳu 'l-ḥamā'imi*), under a sky of branches (shade) which hides the sun and prevents it from appearing, except in the form of scattered dirhams (*samā'u g͟huṣūn*[in] *taḥd͟jubu 'l-s͟hamsa an turā ʿalā 'l-arḍi illā mit͟hla 'l-darāhimi*); the last image constitutes a combination of three elements all relating to the visual: the branches filtering the light, the scattered dirhams, and the reflection of the sun through the foliage and the white colour of the silver. It is an image evocative of dreams; it is not lacking in beauty, and indicates a lively attention and an affectionate interest in all things relating to nature (similar cases in *ibid.*, 50-2, 667, 721-2, 762-3, 775). The Andalusian poet Ibn K͟hafād͟ja seems to have been particularly distinguished in this domain (*Dīwān*, 42-3, vv. 1-20; 116, vv. 5-14; 144, vv. 21-36; 184, vv. 1-4; 250, vv. 1-5; 254, vv. 1-14; 281, vv. 1-7). Ibn K͟haldūn informs us in this context that his masters expressed deep reservations regarding the poet on account of this tendency towards excess of *maʿānī* in a single verse, since this is liable to result in a certain obscurity (Ibn K͟haldūn, iii, 328-9, tr. Rosenthal, iii, 373-5).

In parallel, these same poets endow nature with a soul, such that it takes on life of its own. Its birth is seen in spring; it is, by turns, impetuous or dormant. Thus for Ibn Rūmī, a garden, at the time of sunset, is an invalid in pain: at twilight, the sun is languid and feeble (*rannaḳa*), it sprinkles (*naffaḍa*, verb of motion) the horizon with yellow; thus it bids farewell to the world below, it is in the process of dying (*wa-wad-daʿati 'l-dunyā li-taḳḍiya naḥbahā*); the flowers, suffering on account of the malady that has smitten them, lay their cheeks on the ground, in utter submission; they set themselves to weeping hot tears and staring dejectedly at the sun; green plants cover themselves with a cadaverous yellow colour (*Dīwān*, iv, 1475-6, vv. 23-34; iii, 1418). This has nothing to do with parody. This aspect led Von Grunebaum and Schoeler to detect a tendency towards animism among poets of nature at this time [see ZAHRIYYĀT].

Discovery of the world of objects: People in mediaeval times considered objects of the mundane world as faithful and useful companions. Thus Kus͟hād͟jim evokes his sadness on the loss of his cup, having carelessly broken it; he describes the débris and evokes the magnificence of the cup at the time when it was intact; it is clearly felt that he valued the object highly (*Dīwān*, 130-2). In the same sphere of ideas, he expresses his deep emotion at the sight of a broken *ʿūd*; it should be noted in this context that the title of the poem speaks of a *mart͟hiya* (*ibid.*, 465-6). Poets have described in independent fragments, setting out from an assiduously-pursued artistic project, a *harīsa* (a dish of meat and of wheat, Ibn al-Rūmī, iii, 1141, § 904), bread (*ibid.*, 1110, § 860), a dīnār (*ibid.*, 1241, § 1018), a pen (*ibid.*, 1659, § 1289), a sealed letter (*ibid.*, 978, § 726), a noria (*ibid.*, 1150, § 926-7), a scarf (Kus͟hād͟jim, 86-8), a musical instrument (*ibid.*, 73), an ink-pot (*ibid.*, 65-7, 368-9, 433), a Ḳur'ān (*ibid.*, 23-5), a calculating tablet (*ibid.*, 41), an astrolabe (*ibid.*, 127-9), a candle (in a large number of fragments, *ibid.*, 235, 350), an hour-glass (*binkām*, *ibid.*, 143-4), a jug (al-Sarī al-Raffā', ii, 293, 366-7), a cooking pot (*ibid.*, 654-5, excellent specimen) and numerous other objects. Moreover, the whole of this inanimate world may be found in the work of numerous poets. Nothing, it may be said, escapes this voracity for description. Beyond the documentary value of this corpus, it is appropriate to see here the point of departure of the literary project: the mundane possesses a poetic aspect; it is sufficient to glance at it in a new light, to discover it and regard it with love. With this form of description, Arabic poetry, a discourse formerly reserved for the extraordinary, seems to undergo a change of direction, with this willingness to take into account the poetic value of the so-called prosaic world. The "thing" deserves mention. The process of poetisation consists in applying to the object a double, narrative and imaginative, approach, as in the case of al-Sarī al-Raffā', or narrative and emotional in the case of the majority of descriptive writers. For the former, the description of the brazier possesses an exemplary value: the point of departure recounts the story of a group of friends who arrive, one winter night, in an orchard in the outskirts of Mawṣil intending to drink and to enjoy themselves: a tempest springs up, rapidly evoked; the poet resorts to imagining how good it would be to be warmed by a *kānūn* full of glowing embers; then he describes it with economy of space utilised: the whole is recounted in ten verses (al-Sarī al-Raffā', ii, 510).

This poetic interest could arise from rather more prosaic, even mercenary causes: the poet, having received a gift from his patron, sent him a note in which gratitude was blended with a description of the object received. This was a form of eulogy; in effect, the finer and more precious the gift, the more effusive the praise of the one who gave it.

The clear and the hermetic: Von Grunebaum and Schoeler, the two specialists who have left their mark on the study of *wasf*, speak of a baroque aspect of this poetry under the ʿAbbāsids. A large proportion of this corpus could be described as baroque, if by this is meant a text which bows beneath the weight of excess of ornamentation, stylistic hypertrophy and immoderate use of metaphor; this is also the case in the extent to which it extols artifice and mannerism as styles of creation. *Badīʿ* [*q.v.*] also played a considerable role since it involved a quest, knowingly pursued, for the unforeseeable image. *Badīʿ* advocated recourse to an original usage of the tropes of comparison and denied the necessity for the existence of a logical link between the compared and the comparing. To use an expression coined by W. Heinrichs, the poets opted in their descriptions for an imagery utterly divorced from nature; this led to the creation of constructions based on the imaginary, i.e. fantastic creations. Heinrichs gives as an example a description by al-Ṣanawbarī comparing red anemones stirred by the wind to banners made of cut rubies on a background of chrysolites (*Literary theory*, 26). All the describers of this period borrowed this method. Ibn al-Rūmī, for example, describes a bunch of white grapes of the al-Rāziḳī variety as balls of congealed light, transformed into balls of crystal and rose-water on account of their perfume: then, through another mutation, they be-come cloves of musk (iii, 987-9). Other poets acted no differently and their images verge on the surreal (in Kus͟hād͟jim, 73, the *ʿūd* becomes a hybrid creature equipped with an eloquent tongue; he is adored by beautiful women who never cease to embrace him; when his pulse is taken, he awakes: 76-7, 78, 235, 254-5, 356). This verbal imagery leads to a hermetic description. This is tolerable so long as the title supplies keys of the code used; otherwise, it remains incomprehensible (al-Sarī al-Raffāʾ, ii, 585, the editor not having seen that it refers to a passive pederast) as is the general case with later poets, the poets of the *Kharīda* of al-ʿImād al-Iṣfahānī. Description thus leads quite naturally to another genre, *uḥdjiyya* or *lughz*, enigma, as J. Sadan writes. The only difference is that, with the *aḥādjī*, the solution is given to us in an epilogue appended by the poet, while, for description, it figures in the title supplied by the transmitter.

Descriptive poetry continued its headlong progress under the Mamlūks: numerous poets of *waṣf* are attested here [see SHIʿR. 1. In Arabic (a), V (1), in Vol. IX, 460].

Bibliography: 1. Sources. ʿĀmir b. al-Ṭufayl, *Dīwān*, Leiden 1913; al-Aʿshā, *Dīwān*, ed. Geyer, London 1928; Ibn Hishām, *Sīrat Rasūl Allāh*, Göttingen 1858, i, 121 ff.; Abū Tammām, *Dīwān*, Cairo 1965, iv, 55 ff. (*Bāb al-awṣāf*); Ḳudāma b. Djaʿfar, *Naḳd al-shiʿr*, Leiden 1966, 23, 62-4, 117; Khālid b. Yazīd al-Kātib, *Dīwān*, Paris 1990, 115, § 274; 117, § 278; 119, § 282; 120, §§ 284-5; 121, § 287; 125, § 297; Ibn al-Rūmī, *Dīwān*, Cairo 1976-9; Abu 'l-Faradj al-Iṣfahānī, *Aghānī*[3]; al-Sarī al-Raffāʾ, *al-Muḥibb wa 'l-mahbūb*, Damascus 1407/1986, i, iii; Muḥammad b. Ṭabāṭabā, *ʿIyār al-shiʿr*, Cairo 1956, 18, 111; Ibn Rashīḳ, *ʿUmda*, ed. Abu 'l-Faḍl Ibrāhīm, Beirut 1972, *Bāb al-waṣf*, ii, 294-5; Ibn Khafādja, *Dīwān*, Cairo 1960; Nawādjī, *Ḥalbat al-kumayt*, Cairo 1357/1938, 145-65, 204-14, 226-322, 350-377.

2. Studies. W. Ahlwardt, *Über Poesie und Poetik der Araber*, Gotha 1856, 29-60; J.M. Sloane, *The poet Labīd, his life, time and fragmentary writings*, Leipzig 1877, 6-15; Ch. Lyall, *Pictorial aspects of ancient Arabian poetry*, in *JRAS* (1912), 133-52; G.E. von Grünebaum, *Die Wirklichkeitweite der früharabischen Dichtung. Eine literaturwissenschaftliche Untersuchung*, Vienna 1937, 106, 126, 132-4, 142-3, 146, 160-1, 173, 256; idem, *The response to nature in Arabic poetry*, in *JNES*, iv (1945), 137-50; L. Massignon, *Les méthodes de réalisation artistique des peuples de l'Islam*, in *Syria*, ii (1921), 47-53, 149-60; H. Pérès, *La poésie andalouse en arabe classique au XIe siècle*, Paris 1953, 116-21, 128-32, 140-2, 158-201; R. Blachère, *HLA*, ii, 440-53; J.Ch. Bürgel, *Die ekphrastischen Epigramme des Abū Ṭālib al-Maʾmūnī*, in *Nachrichten der Akad. der Wiss. in Göttingen*, phil.-hist. Kl., Jg. 1965 [1966], Nr. 14; G. Schoeler, *Arabische Naturdichtung. Die Zahrīyāt, Rabīʿīyāt und Rauḍīyāt*, Beirut 1974; W. Heinrichs, *Literary theory. The problem of its efficiency*, in *Arabic poetry, theory and development*, Wiesbaden 1973, 23-53; idem, *Paired metaphors in Muḥdath poetry*, in *Occasional Papers of the School of Abbasid Studies*, i, St. Andrews 1986, 1-22; J. Bencheikh, *Poétique arabe*, Paris 1975, 136-46; Alma Giese, *Waṣf bei Kušāǧim*, Berlin 1981; J. Stetkevych, *Name and epithet. The philology and semiotics of animal nomenclature in early Arabic poetry*, in *JNES*, xlv (1986), 89-124; *Camb. hist. Arabic lit.*, i, *Arabic literature to the end of the Umayyads*, 39, 93-104, ii, *ʿAbbāsid belles-lettres*, 164-6, 184, 411, 435-6; A. Arazi, *La réalité et la fiction dans la poésie arabe ancienne*, Paris 1989, 107-72; idem, *al-Ḥanīn ilā al-awṭān entre la Djāhiliyya et l'Islam. Le Bédouin et le citadin reconciliés*, in *ZDMG*, cxliii (1993), 287-327; S. Sperl, *Mannerism in Arabic poetry*, Cambridge 1989, 1-7, 155-80; Th. Bauer, *Altarabische Dichtkunst. Eine Untersuchung ihrer Struktur und Entwicklung am Beispiele der Onagerepisode*, 2 vols., Wiesbaden 1992; W. Fischer, *Der altarabische Dichter als Maler*, in W. Heinrichs and G. Schoeler (eds.), *Festschrift Ewald Wagner zum 65. Geburtstag*, ii, *Studien zur arabischen Dichtung*, Beirut 1994, 3-17; Muḥammad Zaghlūl Salām, *Taʾrīkh al-naḳd al-ʿarabī*, ii, *Min al-ḳarn al-khāmis ilā l-ʿāshir al-hidjrī*, Cairo 1964 [?], 36, 82, 133, 150-1, 195-6, 294-5, 301; ʿAbd al-ʿAẓīm al-Ḳanāwī, *al-Waṣf fi 'l-shiʿr al-ʿarabī. Al-Waṣf fi 'l-shiʿr al-djāhilī*, Cairo 1949; Djawdat al-Rikābī, *al-Ṭabīʿa fi 'l-shiʿr al-andalusī*, Damascus 1378/1959; al-Sibāʿī al-Bayyūmī, *Taʾrīkh al-adab al-ʿarabī*, i, Cairo 1959, 125-30; Fuʾād Ḥannā Tarazī, *Muslim b. al-Walīd Ṣarīʿ al-Ghawānī*, Beirut 1961, 189-98; Nūrī Ḥammūdī al-Ḳaysī, *al-Ṭabīʿa fi 'l-shiʿr al-djāhilī*, Beirut 1390/1970; Īliyā al-Ḥāwī, *Fann al-waṣf*, Beirut 1980; Yūsuf al-Yūsuf, *Maḳālāt fi 'l-shiʿr al-djāhilī*, Algiers 1980, 128-36; Sāsīn ʿAssāf, *al-Ṣūra al-shiʿriyya wa-namādhidjuhā fi ibdāʿ Abī Nuwās*, 1982, 43-76, 95-144; Shawḳī Ḍayf, *Taʾrīkh al-adab al-ʿarabī*, vi, *ʿAṣr al-duwal wa 'l-imārāt*, Cairo 1984, 322-42 (descriptive writers of Egypt), 741-55 (those of Syria); Maḥmūd Rizḳ Salīm, *ʿAṣr salāṭīn al-mamālīk wa-nitādjuhu al-ʿilmī wa 'l-adabī*, Cairo 1962-5, 347-440 (good documentation on the period).

(A. Arazi)

II. In law

Here *waṣf* means form, external aspects, or incident, each one of these three as opposed to substance (*aṣl*). This Aristotelian dichotomy between form and substance appears frequently in Islamic law in providing solutions to legal problems. Thus a slave, after being sold to a new owner but before his delivery to this new master, injures a limb. Will the delivery of the slave with his injured limb be valid? Al-Sarakhsī [*q.v.*] answers this question in the affirmative: the delivery will be valid because the injury of the limb affects only the *waṣf*, meaning here the incident, not the substance (*aṣl*) of the slave, while "the price [of the slave] is for the substance (*aṣl*), not for the incident (*waṣf*)" (*Mabsūṭ*, Cairo 1916, xiii, 171, ll. 20-5). However, the same dichotomy is also, and perhaps mainly, used in obfuscating solutions to legal problems. The vitiated (*fāsid* [*q.v.*]) contract is a good example. This contract is non-existent between the parties to it, but quite valid with regard to third parties (Chafik Chehata, *Le système de nullités en droit musulman hanéfite et en droit comparé*, in *Rapports généraux au VIème Congrès international de droit comparé, Hambourg 30 juillet-4 août 1962*, ed. J. Lempens, Brussels 1964, 191-203, at 195). For al-Sarakhsī, the vitiated contract is valid in its substance but invalid in its incident (*ibid.*, xiii, 24, ll. 8-10), leaving it unexplained and unclear what are the effects of the contract that belong to the substance (*aṣl*), hence are valid, and what are the effects of the contract that belong to its incident, external aspect or form (*waṣf*). Remarkably, this obfuscated definition of the vitiated contract was adopted by the *Medjelle*, the Ottoman re-statement of Islamic law, published during the third quarter of the 19th century [see MADJALLA] (section 109) and later by the 1976 Jordanian Civil Code (section 170) and the 1986 Civil Code of the United Arab Emirates (section 121). The 1951 Iraqi Civil Code, which ignores the vitiated contract, although it is one of the original features of the Islamic law of contract, maintains nevertheless the dichotomy between form and substance in its definitions of the non-existent or invalid (*bāṭil* [*q.v.*]) contract (section 137) and of the valid (*ṣaḥīḥ*) contract (section 133, though the substance there is called *dhāt*, the very term used previously by section 109 of the *Medjelle*, where both *aṣl* and *dhāt* appear).

Moreover, even where Islamic law does indicate the effects of the contract belonging to its *waṣf*, one may wonder whether they do not actually belong to the *aṣl*. A person buys a book by a certain author, but sees that the book bought is by another author. The sale of the book is valid because the identity of the author is purely incidental, not substantial (*al-Fatāwā al-hindiyya*, Cairo, ed. Maymūniyya, iii, 140-1, as cited by Nayla Comair-Obeid, *Les contrats en droit musulman des affaires*, Paris 1995, 112).

The widespread use of form and substance in Islamic law shows that, in its elements, this law is no different than any other modern system of law. Its specific character, like that of any other system of law, lies in its rearrangement of those elements.

Bibliography (in addition to the references in the text): Y. Meron, *Forme et substance en droit musulman*, in *ILS*, v (1998), 22-34. (Y. Meron)

WAṢFĪ al-TALL (1919-71), Jordanian politician and three times prime minister.

He was born in the Kurdish village of Arapkir in modern Turkey. Son of the Jordanian nationalist poet Muṣṭafā Wahbī al-Tall and a Kurdish mother, Waṣfī was raised in his father's native town of Irbid in northern Jordan. He received his secondary education in the town of al-Salṭ, and, upon graduation in 1938, went on to study at the American University of Beirut. He graduated in 1941 in the sciences. Al-Tall joined the British army in Palestine in 1942 and later served in the Arab League sponsored *Djaysh al-Inḳādh* or "Salvation Army" to fight against the partition of Palestine in 1948.

In 1951, al-Tall married Saʿdiyya Djabrī, a native of Aleppo formerly married to Palestinian nationalist Mūsā al-ʿĀlamī. He entered the Jordanian civil service, and became politically engaged. Outspoken in his opposition to Egyptian president Djamāl ʿAbd al-Nāṣir, al-Tall caught the attention of King Ḥusayn's government. In 1959 he was made Director of Broadcasting, where he used the radio effectively to counter ʿAbd al-Nāṣir's propaganda campaign against the Hashemite monarchy.

Al-Tall's first ministerial appointment was as Prime Minister (1962-3). His policies placed a premium on Jordanian sovereignty at a time of Nasserism, Arab nationalism, and Palestinian militancy. King Ḥusayn called upon al-Tall to lead governments to stave off challenges from Egypt and the Palestine Liberation Organisation in 1965-7, and again in October 1970. Accused of master-minding the Jordanian war against Palestinian commando units and their ultimate eviction from Jordanian territory, al-Tall was assassinated in Cairo on 28 November 1971 by members of the Black September organisation, a wing of the Fatah/*Fatḥ* (Palestine Liberation Movement).

Bibliography: A. Susser, *On both banks of the Jordan. A political biography of Wasfi al-Tall*, London 1994; Sulaymān Mūsā, *Aʿlām min al-Urdunn: safaḥāt min taʾrīkh al-ʿArab al-ḥadīth*, ʿAmmān 1986; Waṣfī al-Tall, *Kitābāt fī ʾl-ḳaḍāyā al-ʿarabiyya*, ʿAmmān 1980. (E. Rogan)

WASHḲA (occasionally, Washka), Roman Osca and modern Huesca (capital of the province of the same name), a town of northern Spain. It is located on a hill amidst its *huerta*, irrigated by the Isuela River (Ar., Bansha) and lies among the foothills of the Pyrenees some 50 km/30 miles west of Barbastro (Barbashturu [*q.v.*]) and 70 km/43 miles almost due north of Saragossa (Saraḳusta [*q.v.*]).

The date of Washḳa's conquest cannot be stated with precision, but it appears to have been undertaken by 95/714. According to al-ʿUdhrī's account, after a seven-year siege the defenders were granted *amān* under the condition that they pay the *djizya*. Once conquered, Washḳa became the capital of an *ʿamal* of the *thaghr al-aʿlā* [see al-thughūr. 2.]. Although it was ruled by an appointee of the court at Cordova, its isolated frontier location and a high proportion of indigenous converts ensured that it remained independent in spirit and orientation. Only a short distance separated the outer hamlets and *ḥuṣūn* of Washḳa from the settlements of its Christian neighbours, with the mountains forming a natural frontier. Cross-border raiding was frequent. Up to the 4th/10th century, various governors of Washḳa rebelled and hatched anti-Cordovan alliances with their Christian neighbours. By the early 3rd/9th century the governorship had become essentially hereditary.

Washḳa is said by geographers to have been a centre of manufacturing and trade, producing copperware and weapons. Bananas and sugar-cane were reportedly raised in the densely populated and irrigated *huerta*, and there is evidence of considerable wheat production and viticulture. The strongly-walled town had several gates and was laid out in typical Islamic style; its sizeable extramural suburbs were eventually enclosed by an outer earthen wall. Few Arabs and fewer Berbers settled in Washḳa and, if it was something of a cultural backwater with few notable figures associated with it, the persistence of the Arabic language after the Christian conquest attests to the area's deep Islamisation and Arabisation.

After the dissolution of the Umayyad caliphate and a brief independence, Washḳa came [see hūdids] under the domination of the Banū Hūd, *ṭāʾifa* rulers of Saragossa. On the death of Sulaymān b. Hūd in 438/1046, his son Lubb took control of the city, but Ramiro I of Aragón became a player in the rivalries of the Banū Hūd and helped Aḥmād al-Muḳtadir bi ʾllāh of Saragossa take the city from his brother. Under Sancho Ramírez, the Aragonese began to menace Washḳa, attacking various neighbouring territories during the 470s/1080s. In 487/1094 the king laid siege to the city, but this was abandoned following his fatal wounding during a skirmish. The task of conquest fell to his son Pedro I who, on 16 Djumādā I 489/12 May 1096, laid a second siege to the city, now considerably weakened by raids. Responding to its call for help, al-Mustaʿīn of Saragossa sent troops under his command and that of his Christian vassals. On 1 Dhu ʾl-Ḥidjdja 489/19 November 1096 the opponents met on the field of Alcoraz just outside the city and the forces of al-Mustaʿīn were routed; three days later the inhabitants sued for peace. With Washḳa fallen, the lands of the upper Ebro lay open to the Aragonese. The conquest of the city did not, however, spell the end of the Islamic presence here, for many of the Andalusī inhabitants remained in the area, a Muslim population surviving in some form until the final expulsion of the Aragonese *mudéjares* [*q.v.*] was undertaken in 1018/1609.

Bibliography: 1. Sources. Yaʿḳūbī, *Buldān*, tr. Wiet, *Les pays*, 220; Ibn Ḥayyan, *Muktabas*, v, ed. P. Chalmeta *et alii*, Madrid 1979, 146, 394, 400, 403, 452-3, 468-9, 480-2; Idrīsī, *Geografía de España*, facs. ed. A. Ubieto Arteta, Valencia 1974, 132, tr. 146; Ibn al-Athīr, tr. Fagnan, *Annales du Maghreb et de l'Espagne*, 141, 234-45; Ibn ʿIdharī, *al-Bayān al-mughrib*, iii, ed. Lévi-Provençal, 12, 222-5; Ibn al-Khaṭīb, *Aʿmāl al-aʿlām*, ed. Lévi-Provençal, Beirut

1956, 171-2, 179, 337; Ḥimyarī, *al-Rawḍ al-miʿṭār*, ed. I. ʿAbbās, Beirut 1975, 612; ʿUdhrī, *Fragmentos geográficos-históricos de al-Masālik ilā gamīʿ al-mamālik*, ed. ʿA.ʿA. al-Ahwānī, Madrid 1965, 24, 25, 30-40, 55-73; Zuhrī, *K. al-Djaʿrāfiyya*, ed. M. Hadj-Sadok, Damascus 1968, 225; Carmen Orcastegui Gros, *Crónica de San Juan de la Peña* (*Versión aragonesa*), Saragossa 1986, 36-41; A. Ubieto Arteta, *Crónica de San Juan de la Peña*, Textos Medievales 4, Valencia 1961, 55, 57-62, 63-4.

2. Studies. Afif Turk, *El reino de Zaragoza en el siglo XI de Cristo* (*V de la Hégira*), Madrid 1978; Maria Blanca Basañez Villaluenga, *La aljama sarracena de Huesca en el siglo XIV*, Barcelona 1989; C. Esco and Ph. Sénac, *Le peuplement musulman dans le district de Huesca* (*VIIIe-XIIe siècles*), in *La marche supérieure d'al-Andalus et l'Occident chrétien*, Madrid 1991, 51-66; eidem, *Musulmans et Chrétiens dans le haut moyen âge: aux origines de la Reconquête aragonaise*, Paris 1991.

(B. Catlos)

al-**WASHM** (a.), tattooing.

1. In older Arab society [see Suppl.].

2. In the recent Arab world.

Tattooing has been a long-established practice among women in the countryside and desert regions of the Arab Middle East, noted by many Western travellers from d'Arvieux in 1665 to the present. Its purpose is to enhance feminine beauty; poems quoted in Musil (190-1, 196, 251) comment favourably on tattoos on women's breasts, cheeks and arms. It was the young girls and young married women who sought tattoos.

Tattoos may be decorative in themselves or imitate precious stones, rings, bracelets or belts. Decorative tattoos on the face, neck, chest, stomach, legs and arms are usually in patterns of dots, lines and crosses, although flower motifs and crescent moons are locally common. Motifs used on the back of hands include gazelles, palm trees, swords and twisted braids.

Specialist female practitioners, gypsies or Ṣulayb [*q.v.*] did the best and most elaborate tattoos. The operator has a repertoire of patterns and motifs from which the client chooses, and decides the position of the tattoo. The practitioner pricks out the desired pattern in the skin with a needle. She then dips the needle in dye obtained by burning indigo-dyed material, and goes over the pattern. The area is bandaged or covered with grease, removed after seven days when the skin is washed. If the pricking with the indigo dye is too deep, the pattern fades. In central Jordan, some gypsy women specialists used small wooden blocks to tattoo short words, like the girl's name. Women tattoo each other with simple dots and patterns, using a needle and soot from the baking sheet mixed with butter; the scar is covered with butter mixed with turmeric.

The number of tattoos, their position and favoured motifs are affected by fashion, the availability of practitioners and the ability to pay in cash or to give gifts of wool or butter. Tattooing has become less elaborate and less common since the early to mid-20th century. It has virtually disappeared in villages, and in the *bādiya*, girls have only a line joining the eyebrows, a line down the lower lip and chin, and perhaps a flower on the cheek.

Dickson (164) says that, in the 1920s, every ʿIrāḳī tribe had special tattooing patterns that denoted women's tribal membership. Women from Jordanian and northern Saudi tribes in the 1970s said only that different groups preferred different patterns, but this reflected the repertoire of tattooists as well as fashion.

Authorities describe tattooing as varying between groups. Dickson (164), for ʿIrāḳī says the practice was less common among Bedouin women than among tribal women, but it is not clear how he distinguishes between these two groups. Bedouin tribeswomen in the north—Syria, Jordan, Palestine and Sinai—were generally tattooed. Further south, tattooing remained common, although those under Wahhābī influence tattooed less. Wellsted, travelling in ʿUmān in 1834-5, records tattooing as common among women (1,352). At present, light tattooing is frequent among tribeswomen in the southwestern reaches of the Empty Quarter (Mauger, 89, 97, 99, 109).

Dickson says (164) that men never had tattoos, while Burckhardt (51) records that Syrian tribesmen did. In the northern *bādiya*, men consider tattooing as strengthening body parts after an injury.

Bibliography: J.L. Burckhardt, *Notes on the Bedouins and Wahabys of Arabia*, London 1831; Chevalier d'Arvieux, *Mémoires*, 3 vols., Paris 1735; H.R.P. Dickson, *The Arab of the desert*, London 1949; T. Mauger, *The Bedouins of Arabia*, Paris 1988; A. Musil, *Manners and customs of the Rwala Bedouins*, New York 1928.

(W. and Fidelity Lancaster)

WASHMGĪR b. **ZIYĀR** [see wushmgīr b. ziyār].

al-**WASHSHĀʾ**, Abu 'l-Ṭayyib Muḥammad b. Aḥmad b. Isḥāḳ al-Aʿrābī, in short al-Washshāʾ or Ibn al-Washshāʾ (born *ca.* 255/869 or earlier in Baghdād, died there in 325/937), Arab man of letters, well-versed in grammar and lexicography, widely-read and an authority on good manners.

As a grammarian he was an eclectic, studying with both Thaʿlab and al-Mubarrad [*q.vv.*]. Abū ʿAṣīda, a teacher whom he often quotes (Sezgin, *GAS*, ix, 139), was a private tutor of princes. According to some sources, al-Washshāʾ also taught at the caliphal court. Others call him a schoolteacher, but this humble profession alone cannot account for his familiarity with high life. Besides, the only pupil of his that we know by name was a certain Munya al-Kātiba, a female slave of the caliph al-Muʿtamid.

Lists of his works are mentioned in Sezgin, *GAS*, ix, 165. Apart from a treatise on a question of orthography (*K. al-Mamdūd wa 'l-maḳṣūr*, ed. R. ʿAbd al-Tawwāb, Cairo 1979), three books on *adab* have been preserved.

K. al-Fāḍil fī ṣifat al-adab al-kāmil (10 mss., the oldest of which is Vienna, Nationalbibliothek 2014; uncritical ed. Y.Y. Maskūnī, Baghdād 1970-7) is on rhetorics and eloquence. A discussion of the relevant concepts in the first chapter is followed by a collection of anecdotes (*akhbār*), with sermons and speeches, wise dicta, quick-witted repartees and eloquent improvisations both in prose and poetry, all of which are to serve as guidelines for saying the right thing in every situation.

The *K. al-Muwashshā* (ed. from the unique Leiden ms. Or. 1440 by R.E. Brünnow, Leiden 1886; German tr. D. Bellmann, *Ibn al-Waššāʾ, Das Buch des buntbestickten Kleides*, Bremen 1984), is a handbook of the particular attitudes, manners and tastes which are cultivated by refined (*ẓarīf*) people. It deals with the concepts and expressions of civility (*adab*), manliness (*muruwwa*) and refinement (*ẓarf*), which involve such things as eloquence, politeness, seriousness, chivalry, loyalty, piety and discretion. Special emphasis is laid on chaste love, as there is a natural connection between *ẓarf* and unfulfilled passion (text, 47). There is also ample attention for the outward aspects of a refined lifestyle: clothes and perfumes, food and drink, toothpicks, bathing manners, suitable presents, flowers, fruits and correspondence (including love letters written on apples; cf. A. Schippers, in *JSS*, xxxiii [1988], 221-3).

The author was in direct contact with prominent *ẓurafāʾ*, such as Nifṭawayh [*q.v.*], whom he frequently quotes, and Ibn Dāwūd al-Iṣbahānī [*q.v.*], from whose *K. al-Zahra* he took over clusters of poetry without acknowledging it, including pieces by the author himself. Some of the maxims used by Ibn Dāwūd as chapter headings appear in *Muw.*, 164, as signet ring inscriptions of the refined. They are reminiscent of the ring inscriptions ascribed to ancient philosophers by Ḥunayn b. Isḥāḳ (*Ādāb al-falāsifa*, ed. A.R. Badawī, Kuwait 1985, 45-7; cf. W. Raven, *Ibn Dāwūd al-Iṣbahānī and his K. al-Zahra*, diss. Leiden 1989, 28-30, 90).

Tafrīdj al-muhadj wa-sabab al-wuṣūl ilā al-faradj (ms. Berlin 8638; ed. Cairo 1900 not seen) is a letter writer for *ẓarīf* lovers, and therefore an important source of knowledge of refined lifestyle. After a description of exquisite writing materials, it offers examples of letter openings which express confessions and complaints of love, requests and reproaches, answers as well as requests for a reply. The larger part of the text contains poetry to be quoted in letters. No names of authors or poets are mentioned.

Bibliography: Sezgin, *GAS*, viii, 175, ix, 164-5; Brockelmann I, 129, S I, 189.

Works by al-Washshāʾ: see text.

On the mss. of *al-Fāḍil*: R. Sellheim, *Materialien zur arabischen Literaturgeschichte*, i, Wiesbaden 1976, no. 89; idem, *Eine alte Handschrift des* Kitāb al-Fāḍil *von Ibn al-Waššāʾ*, in M. Forstner (ed.), *Festgabe für Hans-Rudolf Singer*, Frankfurt etc. 1991, 751-6.

On *al-Muwashshā*: E. García Gómez, *Un precedente y una consecuencia del "Collar de la paloma"*, in *al-And.*, xvi (1951), 309-30; M.F. Ghazi, *Un groupe social: "Les raffinés" (ẓurafāʾ)*, in *SI*, xi (1959), 39-71; D. Bellmann, *Das Anstandbuch des Ibn al-Waššāʾ. Ein Beitrag zur Kulturgeschichte Bagdads im 3./9. Jahrhundert*, diss. Halle 1966; J.-C. Vadet, *L'esprit courtois en Orient dans les cinq premiers siècles de l'Hégire*, Paris 1968, 317-51; Lois A. Giffen, *Theory of profane love among the Arabs: the development of the genre*, New York-London 1971; S. Enderwitz, *Du fatā au* ẓarīf, *ou comment on se distingue?*, in *Arabica*, xxxvi (1989), 125-42.

(W. RAVEN)

WAṢĪ (A., pls. *awṣiyāʾ*, *waṣiyyūn*), a theological term in Shīʿism variously rendered as legatee, executor, successor or inheritor.

It was first used to designate ʿAlī as the inheritor of Muḥammad's worldly possessions (such as his books and weapons) and of his political and spiritual authority. According to Imāmī doctrine, this inheritance passed on to al-Ḥasan and the other *imāms*, all of whom are *awṣiyāʾ*. The Imāmiyya hold that legatees existed from the beginning of human history. Their function was to uphold the law laid down by Adam and the five legislator prophets (*ulū 'l-ʿazm*): Noah, Abraham, Moses, Jesus and Muḥammad. The first *waṣī* is sometimes identified with Hābīl (Abel), but more often with Shīth (Seth) [*q.vv.*]. Lists of legatees are given in a number of 4th/10th-century sources, e.g. the *Ithbāt al-waṣiyya* attributed to al-Masʿūdī and the *Ikmāl/Kamāl al-dīn* of Ibn Bābawayh. The names of the legatees are for the most part drawn from the Judaeo-Christian tradition, though there are also lists largely made up of names of Muḥammad's Arab ancestors. The total number of legatees is given as 124,000, the same as the total number of prophets. The 8th/14th-century scholar Ḥaydar-i Āmulī [*q.v.* in Suppl.] recognised a special category of legatees: according to his system, Adam and each of the legislator prophets were followed by 12 legatees responsible for explicating the inner aspects (*taʾwīl*) of the law revealed by those prophets. These *awṣiyāʾ* (72 in all) hold a higher position than the other legatees.

The identity of the 12 legatees who were to succeed Muḥammad was communicated to the Prophet by various means, for instance, by a tablet inscribed with their names and found in Fāṭima's house. According to a widespread account, the Prophet was informed during the *miʿrādj* [*q.v.*] that ʿAlī was his *waṣī*. Another version is connected with Ḳurʾān, XXVI, 214 ("And warn your clan, your nearest kin"): after this verse was revealed, Muḥammad summoned the Banū Hāshim and asked who would like to be his *waṣī*; only ʿAlī, the youngest person present, replied in the affirmative. The Prophet spat in his mouth and between his shoulders and his breast, filling him with wisdom and knowledge. Muḥammad proclaimed ʿAlī as his legatee on various occasions, notably at Ghadīr Khumm [*q.v.*]. He also referred to him as his *wārith* (a term that means much the same as *waṣī*), as his guardian (*walī*), brother and helper (or minister, *wazīr*). In Imāmī tradition, ʿAlī is called *sayyid al-awṣiyāʾ*, *khayr al-awṣiyāʾ* and *waṣī al-awṣiyāʾ* (or *al-waṣiyyīn*). The latter appellation was also used by Djābir al-Djuʿfī [*q.v.* in Suppl.] when addressing Muḥammad al-Bāḳir [*q.v.*]. The title *khātam al-waṣiyyīn* (seal of the legatees) normally refers to the Twelfth Imām, but is also found as an epithet of ʿAlī, presumably recalling his position as successor to Muḥammad, the *khātam al-anbiyāʾ*.

The doctrine propagated by the early Ismāʿīliyya held that each of the seven historical eras was inaugurated by a speaking prophet (*nāṭiḳ*), and that each of the first six *nuṭaḳāʾ* was succeeded by a legatee (or *ṣāmit* "a silent one"). These legatees were, successively, Shīth, Sām (Shem), Ismāʿīl (Ishmael), Hārūn (Aaron) or Yūshaʿ (Joshua), Shamʿūn al-Ṣafāʾ (Simon Peter) and ʿAlī. The *nāṭiḳ* brought the scripture in its generally accepted meaning (*tanzīl*), while the *waṣī* introduced a systematic interpretation of its inner, esoteric aspects (*taʾwīl*, *ḥaḳīḳa*) and initiated a series of *imāms*, of whom the last became the *nāṭiḳ* of the following era. The *waṣī* is therefore called a founder (*asās*). At times he is described as being himself the first *imām*, while elsewhere the first *imām* is said to follow him. The *imāms* are known as *atimmāʾ* (sing. *mutimm* "completer"), since they complete the mission of the founder. It is the duty of the believer to show loyalty (*walāya*) to a *waṣī* and to dissociate himself (*barāʾa*) from a *mutawaṣṣī* (one who falsely claims to be a *waṣī*).

The term *waṣiyya* (literally "inheritance") also denotes the utterance by which a *waṣī* is appointed and, more generally, an instruction of a legal or moral nature [see WAṢIYYA].

Bibliography: al-Ṣaffār al-Ḳummī, *Baṣāʾir al-daradjāt*, ed. Muḥsin Kūčabāghī al-Tabrīzī, Ḳumm 1404, 98-103, 106, 193-4, 281, 294, 372, 445-50, 469-74, 497-9; Ibn Bābawayh, *al-Imāma wa 'l-tabṣira min al-ḥayra*, Ḳumm 1404, 21-4; Kulīnī, *Kāfī*, Tehran 1375-7, i, 189, 193, 207-9, 217, 220, 224, 228, 250-4, 272, 275, 277-85, 290-8, 378-80, 419, 445, 450; Masʿūdī, *Ithbāt al-waṣiyya*, Nadjaf 1374/1955; Khaṣībī, *al-Hidāya al-kubrā*, Beirut 1406/1986, 119, 355, 357; Abū Yaʿḳūb al-Sidjistānī, *Iftikhār*, ed. Muṣṭafā Ghālib, Beirut 1980, 65-73; idem, *Ithbāt al-nubuwwāt*, ed. ʿĀrif Tāmir, Beirut 1982, 187-90; al-Ḳāḍī al-Nuʿmān, *Daʿāʾim al-islām*, ed. A.A.A. Fyzee, Cairo 1383/1963, i, 22, 25, 43, 47, 63; idem, *Taʾwīl al-daʿāʾim*, ed. Muḥammad Ḥasan al-Aʿẓamī, Cairo n.d. [1967-9], i, 61, 203, 215, 361, 365; Ibn Bābawayh, *Ikmāl/Kamāl al-dīn*, Nadjaf 1389/1970, 24-7, 205-43, 615-27; idem, *Iʿtiḳādāt*,

Tehran 1317, 94, 102, tr. A.A.A. Fyzee, *A Shīʿite creed*, Oxford etc. 1942, 74-5, 92-3; idem, *Khiṣāl*, Nadjaf 1391/1971, 604; Ṭūsī, *al-Iḳtiṣād fīmā yataʿallaḳu bi 'l-iʿtiḳād*, Beirut 1406/1986, 349; Shahrastānī, *Livre des religions et des sectes*, i, tr. D. Gimaret and G. Monnot, Louvain 1986, index; Ibn Shahrāshūb, *Manāḳib āl Abī Ṭālib*, Beirut 1405/1985, i, 218, 251, 280, ii, 201, iii, 46-52; Ibn Ṭāwūs, *al-Yaḳīn fī imrat amīr al-muʾminīn*, Beirut 1410/1989; Ḥaydar Āmulī, *Djāmiʿ al-asrār wa-manbaʿ al-anwār*, ed. H. Corbin and O. Yahya, Tehran and Paris 1969, 239-42, 427; Radjab al-Bursī, *Mashāriḳ anwār al-yaḳīn*, Beirut n.d., 58, 61, 161, 163, 179; Madjlisī, *Biḥār al-anwār*, Tehran 1376-94/1956-74, xxiii, 57-65, xxxviii, 1-26; Corbin, *Histoire de la philosophie islamique*, Paris 1964, 130-1; idem, *En Islam iranien*, Paris 1971-2, i, 63-4, 257, iv, 356; U. Rubin, *Prophets and progenitors in the early Shīʿa tradition*, in *JSAI*, i (1979), 41-65; E. Kohlberg, *Some Shīʿī views of the antediluvian world*, in *SI*, lii (1980), 41-66; H. Halm, *Die Schia*, Darmstadt 1988, 202-3, Eng. tr. *Shiism*, Edinburgh 1991, 168-9; F. Daftary, *The Ismāʿīlīs. Their history and doctrines*, Cambridge 1990, index; P.E. Walker, *Early philosophical Shiism*, Cambridge 1993, index; Mohammad Ali Amir-Moezzi, *The divine guide in early Shiʿism*, tr. D. Streight, Albany 1994, index.

(E. Kohlberg)

WĀSIʿ ʿALĪSI (modern Tkish. Vâsi Alîsi), a member of the Ottoman *ʿulamāʾ* and outstanding representative of the *münshī* [see INSHĀʾ] tradition in the period of Süleymān Ḳanūnī [*q.v.*]. He is also referred to as ʿAlī Wāsiʿ, ʿAlī Čelebi, ʿAbd al-Wāsiʿ ʿAlīsi (or Čelebi), Mawlā (or ʿAlāʾ al-Dīn) ʿAlī b. Ṣāliḥ-zāde al-Rūmī (or just Ṣāliḥ-zāde al-Rūmī). Apparently born in Philipoppolis or Filibe (see art. *Vâsiʾ Alîsi*, in *Yeni Türk Ansiklopedisi*, Istanbul 1985), he died at an advanced age in Bursa in 950/1543-4.

Receiving a basic classical Ottoman education, including the study of calligraphy, he then studied under and served as assistant to ʿAbd al-Wāsiʿ b. Khayr al-Dīn Khiḍr. Under him he reached *mülāzim* [*q.v.*] rank and came to be known as Wāsiʿ ʿAlīsi. He is reported to have had a connection with Prince Ḳorkud [see ḲORḲŪD B. BĀYAZĪD] and to have been in the retinue travelling to Egypt with him. He taught in various well-known mosques in Bursa, Edirne and Istanbul.

Wāsiʿ's fame rests mainly on his *Humāyūn-nāme*, an Ottoman rhymed prose translation (with interspersed verses) of the Persian Ḥusayn b. ʿAlī al-Wāʿiẓ Kāshifī's [*q.v.*] well-known *Anwār-i Suhaylī* ("Lights of Suhayli"), itself a version of the Arabic *Kalīla wa-Dimna* [*q.v.*]. Dedicating his work to Sultan Süleymān or, as Menzel describes in his *EI*[1] article, to the Grand Vizier Luṭfī Pasha, Wāsiʿ was rewarded by appointment as *ḳāḍī* of Bursa, only to die shortly afterwards.

There are few extant illustrated mss. of Wāsiʿ's work, a fact leading to the suggestion that it had narrow appeal (Esin Atıl, *Kalila wa Dimna. Fables from a fourteenth-century Arabic manuscript*, Washington, D.C. 1981). Indeed, its ultra-elegant style limited the number of those understanding it. Ottoman biographers, however, recognised Wāsiʿ's achievement (see Menzel's listing of the *tedhkere* writers).

A number of Ottoman summaries were produced, and it has been widely translated. The earliest printing was in 1835 at Būlāḳ.

Bibliography: In addition to works given in the article, see E.J. Grube, *Some observations concerning the Ottoman illustrated manuscripts of the Kalilah wa Dimnah: Ali Çelebi's Humayun-name*, in *9th International Congress of Turkish Art. Summary of Contributions*, Ankara 1995, 195-9; idem, *Paralegomena for a corpus publication of illustrated Kalila wa Dimnah manuscripts*, in *Islamic Art*, iv (1990-1), 301-481; Günay Tümer, *Yeni bir Hümâyun-nâme nüshası*, in *Ankara Üniversitesi İlâhiyat Fakültesi Dergisi*, xix, (1973), 253-6.

(Kathleen R.F. Burrill)

WĀṢIF (?-1221/1806), Ottoman historian and diplomat.

Aḥmed Wāṣif was born in Baghdād, probably in the early 1730s, was educated there and first earned a living as a professional copyist. Entering the service of Gül-zāde Aḥmed Pasha-zāde ʿAlī Pasha (d. 1769) as librarian, Wāṣif accompanied ʿAlī Pasha on the Russian campaign of 1769 and on the latter's death became *mektūbdju*, secretary, to Abāẓa Meḥmed Pasha [*q.v.*] on the Hotin campaign. Captured by the Russians at the siege of Yeñi Ḳalʿe in 1185/1771, Wāṣif was a prisoner of war in St. Petersburg for nine months. Released in order to carry letters of negotiation from Catherine II, which resulted in an initial truce signed at Yergögü in 1186/1772, he was subsequently employed by both the grand vizier Muḥsin-zāde Meḥmed Pasha [*q.v.*] and the *reʾīs ül-küttāb* [*q.v.*] ʿAbd al-Rezzāḳ Efendi as diplomatic envoy in the negotiations leading to the treaty of Küčük Kaynardja [*q.v.*] (1188/1774), and in discussions which continued until 1779 over the status of the Crimean Tatars.

In 1197/1783 Wāṣif was appointed to succeed Enwerī [*q.v.*] as *waḳʿa-nüwīs* [*q.v.*] or official historian. Relinquishing this post during his embassy to Spain to secure an anti-Russian naval agreement (1201-2/1787-8), he was re-appointed *waḳʿa-nüwīs* on the accession of Selīm III [*q.v.*] in 1203/1789. Relieved of the post in 1206/1791 when appointed to the negotiations leading to the treaty of Zishtowa (Sistova) with Austria, he was re-appointed in 1207/1793 for a third tenure. Dismissed again in 1209/1794, as a result of rivalry with the *reʾīs ül-küttāb* Meḥmed Rāshid Efendi, and exiled to Midilli, he was pardoned shortly thereafter, and appointed *waḳʿa-nüwīs* a fourth time in 1213/1799 (until 1219/1805). During his career, Wāṣif also held various administrative posts in the Ottoman central bureaucracy both in between and concurrently with his periods of office as *waḳʿa-nüwīs*, culminating in his promotion to *reʾīs ül-küttāb* in 1219/1805. Wāṣif died in Shaʿbān 1221/December 1806. (For detailed biography and references, see Mücteba İlgürel, art. *Vasif*, in *IA*, xiii, 214-17; also Virginia H. Aksan, *An Ottoman statesman in war and peace: Ahmed Resmi Efendi 1700-1783*, Leiden 1995, 111-14 and *passim*.)

Wāṣif's principal work as *waḳʿa-nüwīs*, prepared during his final tenure of the post, is *Meḥāsin ül-āthār we ḥaḳāʾiḳ ül-akhbār*, a detailed chronicle of events from Muḥarrem 1166/January 1752 to Redjeb 1188/September 1774 (published Istanbul 1219/1804, Būlāḳ 1243/1827 and 1246/1831). This work incorporated the unpublished histories, much reworked, of Wāṣif's predecessors Meḥmed Ḥākim, Česmī-zāde [*q.vv.*], Mūsā-zāde, Behdjetī and, particularly, Enwerī, with additional material of his own for the period of the Ottoman-Russian war 1768-74. Although commissioned by Selīm III to maintain the history up to 1217/1802, coverage of the period after 1774 is apparently incomplete and the textual history confusing. There exists an unpublished continuation covering the five years to 1193/1779 (Topkapı Sarayı ms. Hazine 1406); a published history of events during Wāṣif's first period as *waḳʿa-nüwīs*, 1197/1783-1201/1787 (ed. İlgürel, Istanbul 1978, also under the title *Meḥāsin ül-āthār*); several manuscripts and notes for subsequent years (see İlgürel, *op. cit.*, pp. xl-xlii). Wāṣif was considered a good critical historian whose work went beyond detailed chronological narrative; his manuscripts were a principal source for Aḥmed Djewdet Pasha [*q.v.*]. He also compiled an account of his embassy to Spain, *Ispanya sefāretnamesi*, French tr. Barbier de Meynard, *Ambassade de l'historien turc Vasif Efendi en Espagne, 1787-1788*, in *JA*, ser. 5, vol. xix [1862], 507-23.

Bibliography: See that in the *İA* art., and in the edition of İlgürel, *Mehâsinü 'l-âsâr ve hak'âikü 'l-ahbâr*, see also Babinger, *GOW*, 335-7; B. Kütükoğlu, art. *Vekâyinüvis*, in *IA*, xiii, 278-80.

(CHRISTINE WOODHEAD)

WĀṢIF ENDERŪNĪ, ʿOTHMĀN, Ottoman poet, born at an unknown date, d. in 1824.

As his name implies, he was educated in the *Enderūn* or Palace School, his mother being a niece of the commander of the Bostāndjīs [*q.v.*], Khalīl Pasha, who became Grand Vizier to Aḥmed III. His life was spent filling various court offices, including for Selīm III, to whom various of his poems are dedicated. At the accession of Muṣṭafā IV in 1807, he was promoted to the service of the Royal Chamber. In 1818 he retired from palace service and became administrator of the *wakf* of Süleymān Pasha at Bolayir, dying at Istanbul; his fellow-poet ʿIzzet Mollā [*q.v.*] wrote the epitaph on his gravestone.

Wāṣif seems to have been a bon viveur, with an amusing, jolly character. He was one of the pre-*Tanẓīmāt* [*q.v.*] poets who endeavoured to break away from the rigid rules and conventions of classical Ottoman poetry, writing instead in a simpler and more natural manner, successfully incorporating elements of colloquial language and dialect into his poems. His *sharkis* [*q.v.*] form the most important section of his poetic work, being written in short metres and on his favourite subjects of love and beauty, but he also wrote *ghazels*, *kaṣīdes* and chronograms. His poetry was criticised by more traditional scholars of classical Ottoman poetry, *inter alia* for its technical failings and shallowness, but his work could be original, and it provides glimpses of daily life in Istanbul, where he often refers to the military exercises and sports of the Janissaries. Two unique poems in his *dīwān* set forth a dialogue between a mother and daughter in the Istanbul colloquial of what are apparently lower middle-class women. His poetry, set to music by his brother Saʿd Allāh Efendi and by Zekāʾī Dede, both distinguished musicians, is still sung.

Wāṣif left behind a single *dīwān*, and rumour had it that he burnt the more racy of his poems before he died. There are two mss. of the *dīwān* in Istanbul University Library, one of them (TY 9865) complete, with over 5,000 lines. The *dīwān* was printed at Būlāḳ (*Dīwān-gülshen-i afkār-i Wāṣif-i Enderūnī*, 1257/1841) and subsequently at Istanbul (1285/1868-9).

Bibliography: Gibb, *HOP*, iv; İbnülemin Mahmud Kemal İnal, *Son asır türk şairleri*, vii, Istanbul 1970; Seyit Kemâl Karaalioğlu, *Türk edebiyat tarihi*, ii, Istanbul 1978, 114-18; Muallim Naci, *Osmanlı şairleri*, Ankara 1986; Haluk Ipekten, *Enderunlu Vasıf*, Ankara 1989; art. s.v., in Türk Diyanet Vakfi, *Islam Ansiklopedisi*, xi, Istanbul 1995; W.G. Andrews, N. Black and M. Kalpaklı, *Ottoman lyric poetry*, Austin, Texas 1997, 261-2.

(ÇIĞDEM BALIM)

AL-**WAṢĪFĪ**, IBRĀHĪM B. WAṢĪF SHĀH or Ibn Waṣīf al-Ṣābiʾ, an authority much quoted by Arab historians from about 330/941-2 onward for a host of otherwise unknown materials on the history of ancient Egypt from its first settlements up to the time of Moses' Pharaoh. From among the few quotations relating to Islamic Egypt, the latest concern the period of time between 355/965 and 358/969 (*apud* Ibn Iyās, d. *ca.* 930/1524 [*q.v.*]).

As already made known by D. Chwolson, from a St. Petersburg manuscript dated 607/1211, an Ibrāhīm b. Waṣīf Shāh was the author of a *Kitāb al-ʿAdjāʾib al-kabīr . . . fī ʿadjāʾib al-arḍ wa 'l-biḥār*, the second part of which contains material about the history of Egypt up to the time of Exodus. On the basis of further Paris manuscripts, sometimes attributed to al-Masʿūdī (d. 345/956 [*q.v.*]), Carra de Vaux produced his translation *L'Abrégé des merveilles* (with introd. and index, Paris 1898; repr. Frankfurt 1994; new ed. without index, Paris 1984, with preface by A. Miquel). ʿAbd Allāh al-Ṣāwī did an Arabic edition with the title *Akhbār al-zamān* (Cairo 1938, several reprints), which is mostly quoted as "Pseudo-al-Masʿūdī", because the authorship and identity of Ibrāhīm b. Waṣīf Shāh remained open to debate. While this form of his name can be found *inter alia* in al-Maḳrīzī's (d. 845/1442 [*q.v.*]) *Khiṭaṭ* and *Ighāthat al-umma*, and in Ibn Iyās' *Badāʾiʿ*, the form al-Waṣīfī is found in Ṣāʿid al-Andalusī's (d. 462/1070 [*q.v.*]) *Ṭabaḳāt al-umam* and Muḥammad b. al-Ḳāsim al-Nuwayrī's (d. 8th/14th century [*q.v.*]) *K. al-Ilmām*.

Opinions on the value of the book and the identification of its author have diverged widely in recent years. By some it is thought to be a "Hermetic history" rather than the national history of the Copts in early Islamic Egypt and the "picturesque 'Ibrāhīm b. Waṣīf Shāh'" is suspected to be "in fact a fanciful improvement of the more prosaic 'Waṣīfī'" (cf. M. Cook, *Pharaonic history in medieval Egypt*, in *SI*, lvii [1983], 67-103; G. Schoeler, *Verzeichnis der orientalischen Handschriften in Deutschland*, Band XVII, Reihe B. *Arabische Handschriften*, Teil II, Stuttgart 1990, 364-70). Even the very historicity of Ibn Waṣīf Shāh/al-Waṣīfī is debated (cf. U. Haarmann, *Das Pyramidenbuch des Abū Ǧaʿfar al-Idrīsī*, Beirut 1991, preface, p. vii) and the *Akhbār al-zamān* are considered to be a mystification of Spanish provenance, consciously created around the year 1000 (cf. idem, *Das pharaonische Ägypten bei islamischen Autoren des Mittelalters*, in *Orbis Biblicus et Orientalis*, xlv [1990], 48).

As for the name, the *ism* Ibrāhīm may derive from Ibrāhīm b. al-Ḳāsim al-Kātib (d. after 418/1027-8 [see IBN AL-RAḲĪḲ]), who made a *mukhtaṣar* of the *K. al-ʿAdjāʾib al-kabīr* of one Ibrāhīm b. Waṣīf Shāh, mentioned in al-Nuwayrī's (d. 733/1333 [*q.v.*]) *Nihāyat al-arab*, with ample quotations from the book. "Shāh" [*q.v.*] may indicate high esteem for a person thought to hail from the northern parts of the caliphate. The true name of our author would thus be "Ibn Waṣīf", which is corroborated by the *nisba* "al-Waṣīfī". On this person Abū ʿUbayd al-Bakrī's (d. 487/1094 [*q.v.*]) *al-Masālik wa 'l-mamālik* (ed. A.P. van Leeuwen and A. Ferré, Tunis 1992) gives somewhat more detailed information; he is quoted in direct speech on his visits to Egypt, where he tested the magical efficacy of images and statues in temples and interviewed the locals (§§ 895, 905-6, 908-13). The same is indicated by Abū Djaʿfar al-Idrīsī (d. 649/1251 [see AL-IDRĪSĪ]), when he says that al-Waṣīfī was an outstanding natural philosopher and an historian who had investigated the secrets of the temples and the knowledge of the ancient Egyptian natural philosophers (cf. Haarmann, *Pyramidenbuch*, 99 [Arabic], 82 [German]). Ibn Waṣīf's excerpt from a *K. al-Maṭālāṭis* of a certain Kīnās al-Ḥakīm (cf. Sezgin, *GAS*, vii, 66) deals with talismans.

A Ṣābian origin is likely for a scholar with such interests, since for them Egypt continued to have a religious meaning even in Islamic times (cf. D. Chwolson, *Die Ssabier und der Ssabismus*, St. Petersburg 1856, repr.

Amsterdam 1965, index). Given the likely lifetime of our author, he might reasonably be identified with the Baghdād ophthalmologist (Aḥmad?) Ibn Waṣīf al-Ṣābiʾ, who was active beyond the middle of the 4th century of the Hidjra (A.D. 970 at the latest) (cf. Ibn Djuldjul [*q.v.*], *Ṭabaḳāt al-aṭibbāʾ*, Cairo 1955, 81-2; composed in 377/987). Between 330/941-2 and 340/951-2 he taught students of Ḥarrānian descent hailing from Spain. For this reason, he became well known in Spain early on, as a physician named Ibn Waṣīf, and as an authority on ancient Egypt, quoted as al-Waṣīfī. He is quoted without attribution by the author of the *Picatrix* (composed between 443/1051-2 and 448/1056, cf. Sezgin, *GAS*, iv, 295, and AL-MADJRĪṬĪ).

Ibn Waṣīf's books have not been preserved independently and their precise titles are unknown. The relevant manuscripts represent (a) a longer version, which has been shown to be two parts of [*K. Akhbār al-zamān wa-huwa*] *al-Kitāb al-Awsaṭ* (composed before 332/943) by al-Masʿūdī, who lifted large sections dealing with ancient Egypt from Ibn Waṣīf, and (b) a shorter version (*mukhtaṣar*) also attributable to al-Masʿūdī, entitled *K. al-ʿAdjāʾib*, which is the version edited by al-Ṣāwī. Carra de Vaux' translation contains sections from both versions (cf. Ursula Sezgin, *Al-Masʿūdī, Ibrāhīm b. Waṣīfšāh und das Kitāb al-ʿAǧāʾib*, in *ZGAIW*, viii [1993], 1-70; eadem, *Pharaonische Wunderwerke bei Ibn Waṣīf aṣ-Ṣābiʾ und al-Masʿūdī, I*, in *ZGAIW*, ix [1994], 229-43).

Although the Egyptologist G. Maspéro, on the basis of Carra de Vaux' translation as well, had written in 1899 that the text contained memories of all stages of Egyptian history after the downfall of its indigenous dynasties, the study of its contents and its place within the intellectual history of its time is still at its beginning.

In 1899 M. Berthelot, on the basis of Carra de Vaux' translation, had shown that several of the *ʿadjāʾib*, apparently magical objects, mentioned were traceable to the work of Alexandrian scholars. With the help of sources and studies in the history of technology (sometimes by assuming a Syriac intermediary source) and furthermore with pictorial representations and archaeological finds, it was possible to garner detailed evidence that these wondrous and miraculous objects were trick vessels, waterclocks and the like. They form a link in a tradition that straddles different linguistic and cultural areas, and they live on in mediaeval Western literature and, as display-pieces, in the cabinets of curiosities of pre-modern princes. In the al-Waṣīfī corpus, however, they were meant to serve the posthumous glory of Egyptian rulers; in this context traditions of Greek and Coptic provenance can be discerned (cf. U. Sezgin, *Pharaonische Wunderwerke, I* [and] *II*, in *ZGAIW*, ix [1994], 229-91, xi [1997] 189-249; *III* and *Addenda*, in preparation).

Judging by the detailed and scarcely exploited quotations in Abū ʿUbayd al-Bakrī, with all their clearly gnostic elements of Coptic provenance, one can guess how severe the loss of Ibn Waṣīf's extensive writings is for the intellectual and religious history of Egypt in the last centuries before and the first centuries after the rise of Islam. They enjoyed wider distribution and availability obviously only as excerpts and quotations in the works of other historians.

Bibliography (in addition to references given in the article): G. Wiet, *Introduction* to Vattier's *L'Egypte de Murtadi*, Paris 1953, 1-114. (URSULA SEZGIN)

WĀṢIL B. **ʿAṬĀʾ**, early theologian and ascetic who died in 131/748-9, shortly before the final success of the ʿAbbāsid revolution, probably as a victim of the plague which raged at Baṣra during the same year.

Further information about him is scarce and not always beyond suspicion. In a polemical letter of unknown origin addressed to ʿAmr b. ʿUbayd [*q.v.*], Wāṣil is supposed to have been present, as a rather prominent disciple, at one of the courses given by al-Ḥasan al-Baṣrī [*q.v.*] during a visit to Medina some time before 110/728. Whether at that moment he lived in the Ḥidjāz or had instead accompanied al-Ḥasan from Baṣra is not clear. He entertained relations with the ʿAlids who lived in Medina, and he may even have attended the meeting at Abwāʾ [*q.v.*] where, shortly after the assassination of al-Walīd II in 126/744, the Hāshimites tried to decide who should lead the Islamic community after the expected collapse of the Umayyad régime. Yet at approximately the same time, we also find him in ʿIrāḳ, as the member of a Baṣran delegation that had come to Wāsiṭ in order to welcome ʿAbd Allāh b. ʿUmar b. ʿAbd al-ʿAzīz [*q.v.*] who had been nominated as the new governor by al-Walīd II's opponent and successor Yazīd III. Wāṣil was probably not the most prominent among the notables who had come; he was only a *mawlā*, and the speeches were given by two professional *khaṭīb*s who were of Arabian stock. But the governor, quite unexpectedly, asked him to say a few words, and he responded with an improvised allocution of pietist character. The event seems to presuppose that the governor was interested in Wāṣil as the spokesman of a specific element of the Baṣran population on which he wanted to rely: sc. the Ḳadariyya [*q.v.*], which had come to power in Syria with the caliphate of Yazīd III. Wāṣil's performance was praised by poets such as Bashshār b. Burd and, later on, Ṣafwān al-Anṣārī [*q.vv.*]; they were particularly impressed by the fact that Wāṣil had mastered the challenge in spite of a speech defect which prevented him from pronouncing the letter *rāʾ* correctly. But he also attracted their attention by asking the governor, after having refused the usual gift offered to the orator, to promote a public undertaking in the town, probably the canal (*nahr*) named after him.

Wāṣil was a middle-class person; he earned his living by manufacturing yarn for the Baṣran cloth industry. Doctrinally speaking, Ḳadarī ideas were not his main concern; he dealt rather in grass-root politics. He tried to take up, in a new spirit, the enterprise started by al-Ḥasan b. Muḥammad b. al-Ḥanafiyya [*q.v.*] one generation before: finding a way between the conflicting factions of the first civil war, i.e. those who were afterwards to be called Sunnīs and Shīʿīs. But whereas Ibn al-Ḥanafiyya had talked about *irdjāʾ*, "postponing one's judgement", Wāṣil spoke of *iʿtizāl*, using a term that had been brought up by those who had kept aloof from the tensions of the first civil war and that was now revivified during the chaos of the third *fitna* after 126/744 [see MUʿTAZILA]. And whereas the former had acted on private initiative, Wāṣil created an organisation; he sent out propagandists (*duʿāt*) to different areas of the Islamic world, including the Ḥidjāz. His analysis of the situation was much more radical than al-Ḥasan's; though agreeing that, in a way, the community had to postpone its judgement, he left no doubt about one of the two factions having sinned, i.e. committed a crime. His conclusion was that, wherever both of them offered an opinion against each other (which seems to mean: wherever they argued against each other by means of *ḥadīth*), their testimony could not be accepted. In his opinion, the situation was to be compared to the procedure of *liʿān* [*q.v.*]: when both litigants appear together, the culprit not being known, their *ʿadāla* is suspended.

In promoting these ideas, Wāṣil seems to have used the Baṣran Ḳadariyya as a power-base. He achieved this purpose by winning over ʿAmr b. ʿUbayd, who acted as the successor of al-Ḥasan al-Baṣrī after the death of Ḳatāda b. Diʿāma (*ca.* 117/735 [*q.v.*]). But he had to persuade ʿAmr to accept another one of his basic tenets: the *manzila bayn al-manzilatayn* [*q.v.*]. ʿAmr originally followed the tradition of al-Ḥasan al-Baṣrī, who had said that the grave sinner is a *munāfiḳ* [*q.v.*] who, in spite of having accepted Islam, will end up in Hell. By means of a disputation, Wāṣil managed to demonstrate to him that this word, which had been used all the time in the earlier theological discussions, was now worn out and should be replaced by a new term, namely, *fāsiḳ*, which could equally be found in the Ḳurʾān but allowed much more easily for the conclusion that the grave sinner, even when a Muslim, would be punished in Hell eternally. The opponents of this doctrine suspected that Wāṣil had learned this rigour from the Kh̲āridjites, but it was simply a consequence of his asceticism (which he had in common with ʿAmr b. ʿUbayd and al-Ḥasan al-Baṣrī). His main innovation pertained rather to the level of what was called later on *al-asmāʾ wa ʾl-aḥkām*, sc. the introduction of a third category between believer and unbeliever. The afore-mentioned political attitude, though also representing a "middle-course", has to be clearly differentiated from this.

None of Wāṣil's writings has been preserved, not even in fragments. But several titles are mentioned, though some of them are attributed to his disciples rather than to himself. There was a report about his disputation with ʿAmr b. ʿUbayd, but he is also said to have written separately about his concept of *al-manzila bayn al-manzilatayn*. His *kh̲uṭba* in front of the governor "without the letter *rāʾ*" was obviously circulated already by al-Madāʾinī [*q.v.*], but we now have two completely different versions of it. In a treatise "on penitence" (*fī ʾl-tawba*) Wāṣil may have expounded his idea that repentance has always to be universal in order to be valid. His epistemological criteria are enumerated in two closely-related doxographical summaries; if these ideas really do go back to him, we are dealing with the earliest testimony for the agenda of *uṣūl al-fiḳh*.

Wāṣil's propaganda movement was stopped before it could mature. His untimely death prevents us from knowing whether he intended it as a merely pietistic undertaking of "inner mission" or whether he followed a political programme as did the Ibāḍiyya [*q.v.*] or, at a later period, the Ismāʿīliyya [*q.v.*]. That his expectations would not have been satisfied by the ʿAbbāsid revolution is borne out by the fact that, one decade later, a considerable portion of the Baṣran Muʿtazila supported al-Nafs al-Zakiyya [*q.v.*] who had been foreseen at Abwāʾ as the Mahdī to come. When the rebellion failed, those who survived fled to the Magh̲rib, where their successors continued to be known as al-Wāṣiliyya.

Bibliography: W. Madelung, *Der Imam al-Qāsim ibn Ibrāhīm und die Glaubenslehre der Zaiditen*, Berlin 1965, 7-38; W.M. Watt, *Was Wāṣil a Kh̲ārijite?*, in *Islamwissenschaftliche Abhandlungen Fritz Meier zum sechzigsten Geburtstag*, Wiesbaden 1974, 306 ff.; Abu ʾl-Wafāʾ al-Taftazānī, *Wāṣil b. ʿAṭāʾ. Ḥayātuhū wa-muṣannafātuhū*, in *Dirāsāt falsafiyya muhdāt ilā Ibrāhīm Madkūr*, Cairo 1979, 39 ff.; S. Stroumsa, *The beginnings of the Muʿtazila reconsidered*, in *JSAI*, xiii (1990), 265 ff.; H. Daiber, *Wāṣil ibn ʿAṭāʾ als Prediger und Theologe. Ein neuer Text aus dem 8. Jahrhundert n. Chr.*, Leiden 1988; Sulaymān al-Sh̲awāyish̲ī, *Wāṣil b. ʿAṭāʾ wa-ārāʾuhū al-kalāmiyya*, al-Dār al-ʿArabiyya li ʾl-Kitāb (Libya) 1993; J. van Ess, *Theologie und Gesellschaft im 2. und 3. Jahrhundert Hidschra*, ii (1992), 234-80, 310-21, iv (1997), 259-64, 780, v (1993), 136-64 (where the most important sources are translated).

(J. van Ess)

WĀSIṬ, a city in central ʿIrāḳ during the mediaeval period, the existence of which is attested from the later years of the 1st century/closing years of the 7th century or opening years of the 8th century, until the beginning of the 12th century/turn of the 17th-18th centuries (according to M. Djawād, *Kh̲arāb Wāsiṭ*, in *Lugh̲at al-ʿArab*, x (1931), 617 until ca. 1107/1695-6). From its foundation by the Umayyad governor of ʿIrāḳ, al-Ḥadjdjādj (75-95/694-713 [*q.v.*]), the city was the administrative and political capital of that province under the first Marwānids (65-95 or 65-105/684-713 or 684-723). The Arabs continued their policy of urban experience there which they had begun by founding the two large fortified camps, *amṣār* [see miṣr. B.], of the Sawād, Baṣra and Kūfa [*q.vv.*], which predated it and were its political rivals. On the other hand, its appearance symbolised the desire of the Umayyad power to display its munificence, and thus it served as a prelude in its architectural form to the founding of Bagh̲dād [*q.v.*] by al-Manṣūr in 145-6/762-3 (J. Lassner, *The shaping of the Abbasid rule*, Princeton 1980, 180-1).

1. Situation and site.

Locating the town on the mediaeval course of the Tigris in the ancient Sāsānid province of Sūristān, which was situated in the centre of Lower Mesopotamia or the Sawād, poses one of the most difficult problems of the historical geography of mediaeval Babylonia (M. Streck, *EI*[1] art. *Wāsiṭ*). Indeed, from the middle or the end of the 9th/15th century the branch of the Tigris which crosses Wāsiṭ began gradually to change its course, veering towards its present easterly direction during the 10th/16th and 11th/17th centuries passing through al-Kūt, and then through the town of al-Ḳurna, where it rejoins the waters of the Euphrates to form the estuary of the Sh̲aṭṭ al-ʿArab [*q.v.*]. The location of Wāsiṭ has now been definitively established following an exact geographical position fixed at lat. 32° 11' N. and long. 46° 18' E., partly thanks to the descriptions of the site by European travellers of the 19th-early 20th centuries, and partly to the various archaeological excavations which were carried out from 1936-42 (F. Safar, *Wāsiṭ, the sixth season's excavations*, Cairo 1945, 8-11). The ruins of historic Wāsiṭ are situated today 25 km/15 miles north-east of the town of al-Ḥayy, and about 70 km/45 miles south-east of the town of al-Kūt, where the Tigris branches off to its present-day easterly course. These ruins are known as al-Manāra, referring to a building from the 7th/13th century, of which all that remains is a monumental entrance gate flanked by two minarets on the north-east side of the site (Safar, *op. cit.*, 6). They extend for an area of three km^2 to the east and to the west of the dry bed of the Dudjayla, the principal branch of the mediaeval Tigris, 200 m wide today. Between 1936 and 1942 the Iraq Department of Antiquities conducted six archaeological excavations (K.A.C. Creswell, *Early Muslim architecture*, Oxford 1969, i/2, 132-3), the last of which was directed by F. Safar (*op. cit.*, 33-4) in 1942 and led to the discovery on the west of the site of the mosque of al-Ḥadjdjādj. It was built onto the south wall of the palace or Dār al-Imāra, constructed in 83/702, and brought confirmation of the existence of three other mosques superimposed on the first; one was probably constructed between 400/1009 and 550/1155 (Mosque II); another around 550/1155 (Mosque III), and a third in the Il-k͟hānid [*q.v.*] period, 656-736/1258-1335 (Mosque IV). The reconstruction and restoration work of the archaeological remains of Wāsiṭ took place from 1937 to 1965, with a view in particular to exploiting tourist interest in this historical site.

Where the city is situated also has semantic significance. The name Wāsiṭ, which is found in mediaeval sources with about twenty other variants (including Wāsiṭ al-Ḥad͟jd͟jād͟j, Wāsiṭ al-ʿUẓmā (Great Wāsiṭ) and Wāsiṭ al-ʿIrāḳ) would have been used to denote the approximate relative position of the town "in the middle" or "centrally" between al-Kūfa, Baṣra, al-Madāʾin (Ctesiphon [*q.v.*]) and al-Ahwāz, the capital of K͟hūzistān [*q.v.*].

Wāsiṭ was established after the division of the two towns by the Tigris (see below, 2). The site of the town founded by al-Ḥad͟jd͟jād͟j on the west bank was a plain (*sahl*) to the north of the Baṭīḥa [*q.v.*], the marshes where the soil was said to be saline (*arḍ sābik͟ha*) and the land was easily subject to flooding, composed of alternating steppes and reed-beds (*ḳaṣab*, from which was derived another name, Wāsiṭ al-Ḳaṣab). To the west, *al-g͟harb*, the site opened out broadly on to an arid zone, half steppe and half desert, known in 6th-century A.D. sources as the desert of Kaskar, qualified by *barriyya* or *faḍāʾ*. This situation perhaps justified the description of the climate of Wāsiṭ as healthy, *ṣaḥīḥ*, as the town was at some distance from the Baṭīḥa, which was humid and hot and infested with mosquitoes. The climate of Wāsiṭ was also described as being like that of Baṣra, capricious and changeable, *munḳalib*, as the site lay in the path of the burning winds, *samūm*, coming from the Persian Gulf to the south, and those from the north which tempered the effect.

2. Foundation.

The date of the foundation of Wāsiṭ is a matter of some debate among scholars because of the disparate traditions. The oldest of these, cited by Baḥs͟hal (d. between 288-92/901-4 [*q.v.*]) in his *Taʾrīk͟h Wāsiṭ* (Bag͟hdād 1387/1967, 43) goes back to Sulaymān b. al-Ḥakam b. ʿAwāna al-Kalbī (2nd/8th century) and is revived by Ibn al-D͟jawzī, al-D͟hahabī and Ibn Tag͟hrībirdī. This places the foundation of Wāsiṭ between 75/694 and 78/697, but does not tally with the course of events during the governorship of al-Ḥad͟jd͟jād͟j in ʿIrāḳ. The chronological details available on Wāsiṭ place the beginning of the building of the principal monuments of the town (the palace-mosque complex, the town's battlements) in 83/702 or 84/703, after the revolt by Ibn al-As͟hʿat͟h (82-3/701-2 [*q.v.*]) had been quelled, and the completion of the *tamṣīr* in 86/705. On the other hand, Wāsiṭ had been established right from its foundation as a double city. The new town, al-Madīna al-G͟harbiyya, created by al-Ḥad͟jd͟jād͟j on the west bank of the Tigris, was juxtaposed to a pre-existing town on the east bank, al-Madīna al-S͟harḳiyya, called Kaskar or Kas͟hkar [*q.v.*]. The two towns, connected as they were from the outset by a bridge of boats (*d͟jisr*), finished by forming two parts of the same city, where the new Wāsiṭ progressively absorbed the ancient Kaskar and gave it its name.

3. Wāsiṭ through the centuries.

Up to the death of al-Ḥad͟jd͟jād͟j in 95/713, Wāsiṭ remained the seat of Umayyad government in ʿIrāḳ, but from 97/715 onwards the town ceased to be the residence of the governor of this province, who was obliged to transfer to K͟hurāsān [*q.v.*], incorporated by the caliph Sulaymān (96-9/715-17) into ʿIrāḳ. ʿUmar II (99-101/717-20) divided this vast territory into three governorates, Kūfa, Baṣra and K͟hurāsān, all with separate governors; and at the same time he demilitarised Wāsiṭ, which was emptied of its Syrian occupation forces (M.A. Shaban, *Islamic history. A new interpretation*, Cambridge 1971, i, 132-3). This was returned to Wāsiṭ during the short reign of Yazīd II (101-5/719-23) under the governorships of Maslama b. ʿAbd al-Malik (102/720), and then of ʿUmar b. Hubayra (103-5/721-3). From the rule of the latter to that of Yazīd b. ʿUmar b. Hubayra (129-32/746-50), Wāsiṭ was no longer the exclusive seat of government or residence of the Umayyad governors of ʿIrāḳ, who moved between Wāsiṭ, Kūfa and al-Ḥīra [*q.v.*] (H. Djaït, *Al-Kūfa, naissance de la ville islamique*, Paris 1986, 271), in particular under Yūsuf b. ʿUmar (120-6/737-43), and from the creation of autonomous power for the Mas͟hriḳ (K͟hurāsān) by the caliph His͟hām (105-25/724-43). The town survived the revolt stirred up by Yazīd b. al-Muhallab, the governor of ʿIrāḳ after al-Ḥad͟jd͟jād͟j, in 102/721, and played a political role in the S͟hīʿī revolt of Zayd b. ʿAlī (122/739), who found partisans there. The troubles that marked the end of the Umayyad period in ʿIrāḳ, on account of the struggles between the governors to assert their power as well as the unrest among the K͟hārid͟jite S͟hurāt, took place principally at Wāsiṭ. The town was exhausted and numbed and the last Umayyad governor of ʿIrāḳ, Yazīd b. ʿUmar b. Hubayra, reconquered it in 129/746 at the expense of ʿAbd Allāh b. ʿUmar II, the *ʿāmil* of the K͟hārid͟jites. Soon afterwards, in 132/750, it had to suffer the trials of a siege by the ʿAbbāsids. The governorship of K͟hālid al-Ḳasrī (105-20/723-37) marked an upsurge in the economy and an expansion in the agriculture of the Sawād to what it had been in the time of al-Ḥad͟jd͟jād͟j. This change came about in Wāsiṭ by a modification in urban fabric. The territory of Wāsiṭ, corresponding to the *kūra* [*q.v.*] (district) of Kaskar in the administrative division of Lower ʿIrāḳ, kept its autonomy from earliest times throughout the Umayyad period in regard to the Sawād of Kūfa and of Baṣra (Kuwar Did͟jla and Kūrat Maysān), from the time of its foundation by al-Ḥad͟jd͟jād͟j. From then to the end of Umayyad power, Wāsiṭ also remained one of the most important centres for issuing the coinage of the empire, as witnessed by the collections preserved by numerous museums across the world (U.S.L. Welin, *Wāsiṭ the mint town*, in *Bulletin de la Société Royale des Lettres de Lund* [1954-5], 127-69, and 4. below).

At the time of the conquest of ʿIrāḳ by the ʿAbbāsids in 132/750, Wāsiṭ was besieged by them. It symbolised the last pocket of resistance of ʿIrāḳ to the new power. In a final convulsion, it supported the Ḥasanid revolt of 145/762. The establishment of the ʿAbbāsid régime and the founding of Bag͟hdād reduced Baṣra, Kūfa and Wāsiṭ to an inferior rank. Wāsiṭ, which was demilitarised, became nothing more than a local administrative centre.

The new dynasty inherited Umayyad landed property in Wāsiṭ and the surrounding region, and, particularly under al-Manṣūr (136-58/754-75) and al-Mahdī (158-69/775-85), attracted much agricultural development, as happened also around Baṣra, Bag͟hdād and Anbār. The *k͟harād͟j* [*q.v.*] of the *kūra* of Kaskar, already specified in the first fiscal inventory available to us referring to the year 172/788, reveals the prosperity of the region of Wāsiṭ during the reign of al-Ras͟hīd

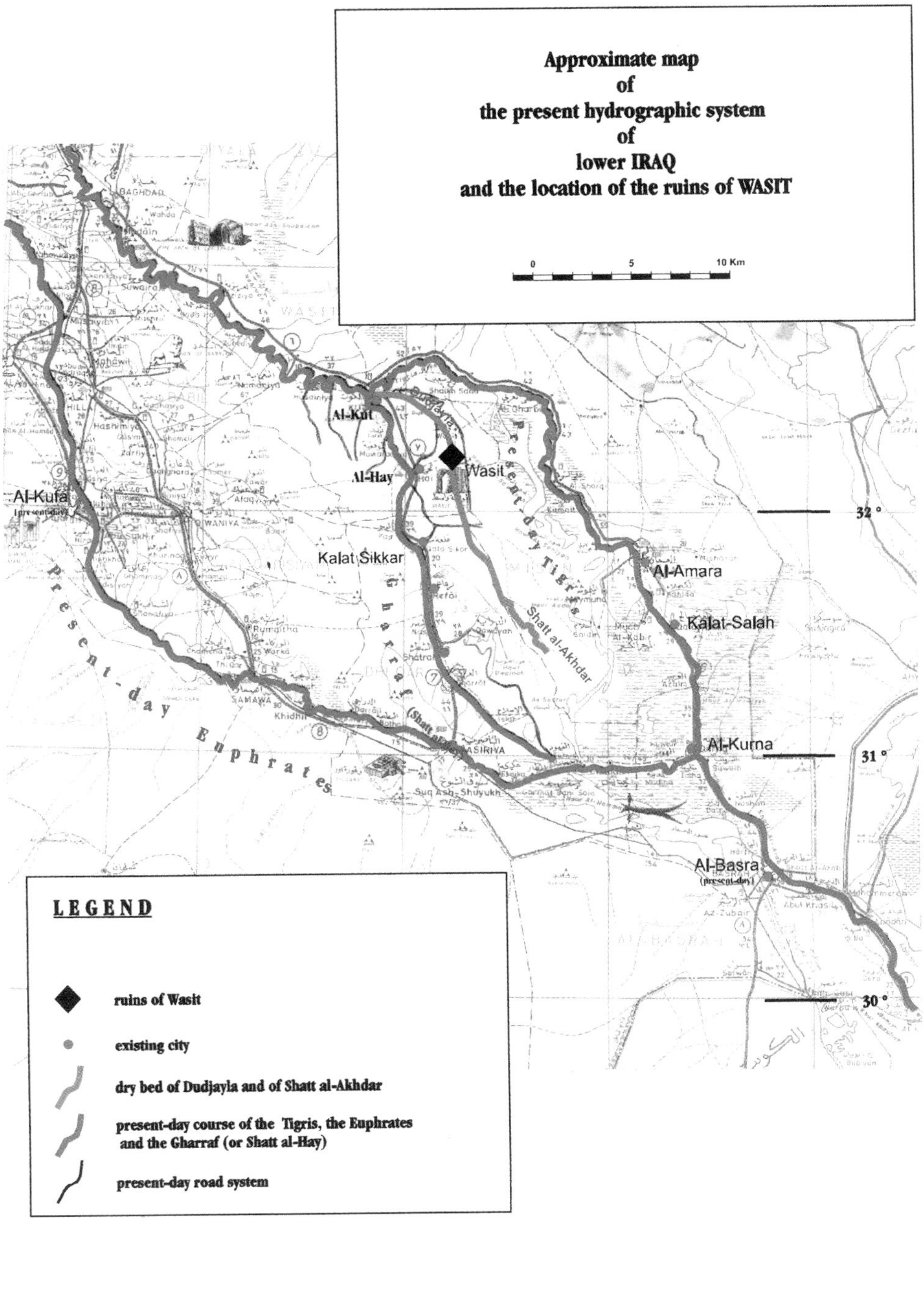
Approximate map
of
the present hydrographic system
of
lower IRAQ
and the location of the ruins of WASIT
0
5
10 Km
Al-Kut
Al-Hay
Wasit
Al-Kufa
(present-day)
Kalat Sikkar
Gharraf
(Shatt al-Hay)
Present-day Euphrates
Present-day Tigris
Shatt al-Akhdar
Dudjayla
Al-Amara
Kalat-Salah
Al-Kurna
Al-Basra
(present-day)
32 °
31 °
30 °
LEGEND
ruins of Wasit
existing city
dry bed of Dudjayla and of Shatt al-Akhdar
present-day course of the Tigris, the Euphrates and the Gharraf (or Shatt al-Hay)
present-day road system

(170-93/786-808), which was characterised by a favourable combination of circumstances, due in part to demographic growth from the middle of the 2nd/8th century onwards.

The progressive disintegration of the ʿAbbāsid state in the course of the second half of the 3rd/9th and in the 4th/10th centuries was marked by the weakening of agricultural production in ʿIrāḳ, the central province of the empire, and also by a diminution of the fiscal returns and an increase in the power of military elements after the reign of al-Maʾmūn (198-218/813-33). Consequently, because of its resources and tax income, Wāsiṭ and its surrounding region acquired particular importance for the power of Bag̲h̲dād, which explains the appearance under al-Muʿtaṣim (218-27/833-42) in the district of Kaskar of the *iḳṭāʿ* [*q.v.*], which assigned to the army generals the levying of fiscal rights of the state on the land. However, the region of Wāsiṭ suffered pillaging by the Zuṭṭ [*q.v.*] from the Sind who revolted in 219/834 against the ʿAbbāsids. After the revolt of the Zand̲j̲ slaves [*q.v.*] in the vast domains of southern ʿIrāḳ (255-70/869-83) these acts of destruction recommenced. Wāsiṭ had already been decimated by an epidemic in 258/871, when in 264/877 it suffered the destruction carried out by the Zand̲j̲, especially on its eastern side. This situation did not prevent the growth of tax-farming, *ḍamān*, and the extension of the *iḳṭāʿ* in the region of Wāsiṭ/Kaskar during the reigns of al-Muʿtaḍid (279-89/892-902) and of al-Muḳtadir (295-320/908-32). From that time onwards, the rich region of Wāsiṭ played a decisive role in supplying food to Bag̲h̲dād, despite serious flooding in the town in 292/904, which caused severe destruction of its monuments. In 310/922 there followed even more serious floods. It was therefore because of this dependence by the rulers of Bag̲h̲dād on resources coming from Wāsiṭ, among other regions, that al-Rāḍī (322-9/934-40) in 324/936 promoted the governor of Wāsiṭ, Ibn Rāʾiḳ [*q.v.*], to the office of *amīr al-umarāʾ* [*q.v.*], and he became in practice the holder of sovereignty.

In the course of the decade 324-34/936-46, which ended with the arrival of the Buwayhids (334-447/945-1055 [*q.v.*]), Wāsiṭ was coveted, because of its farming and resources, by the Bārīdīs, governors of al-Ahwāz (K̲h̲ūzistān), the various *amīr al-umarāʾ*, and the Būyids, who sought power in Bag̲h̲dād.

From 338/949 until 361/971 the town served for the *amīr*s Muʿizz al-Dawla and his successor Bak̲h̲tiyār as a base for military operations against ʿImrān b. S̲h̲āhīn [*q.v.*], the lord of the Baṭīḥa, who rebelled in the south of ʿIrāḳ, threatening the authority of the Būyids. While economic decline and depopulation were on the increase in ʿIrāḳ, Wāsiṭ continued to be a source of food supplies for Bag̲h̲dād.

When al-Muḳaddasī visited Wāsiṭ in 375/985 it was again demonstrating some resilience, as compared to Baṣra, Kūfa, Sāmarrāʾ, Anbār, Bag̲h̲dād and even to the villages in its own territory, which were in a state of dilapidation. The political unrest at the end of the Būyid period aroused the ambitions of the Mazyadids of Ḥilla regarding Wāsiṭ. They had gained power in the region, as had al-Basāsīrī [*q.v.*], who was acting on behalf of the Fāṭimids of Egypt. When their propaganda had won over many of the *amīr*s from ʿIrāḳ and the D̲j̲azīra, the governor of Wāsiṭ, Ibn Fasānd̲j̲is, in 448/1056 declared the *k̲h̲uṭba* there in the name of the Fāṭimid al-Mustanṣir. At the same time he had the principal mosque painted white, the symbolic colour of the S̲h̲īʿīs of Egypt. The Sald̲j̲ūḳs [*q.v.*] had attacked ʿIrāḳ in December 447/1055. They established their authority over Wāsiṭ, crushing Ibn Fasānd̲j̲is in 449/1057 after an exhausting siege. In 451/1059, the year of the great drought and deadly famine, the adventures of al-Basāsīrī, who had briefly recaptured the town, came to an end.

The period of instability and of the weakening of the authority of the Sald̲j̲ūḳs following the death of Malik S̲h̲āh (465-85/1063-92) was characterised by economic and social depression, a decline in the towns of ʿIrāḳ and its depopulation. The tax-farming of Wāsiṭ and the *iḳṭāʿ* of the whole region became the subject of fratricidal quarrels among the princes of the Sald̲j̲ūḳ family on the one hand, and aroused the jealousy of the Mazyadid princes of Ḥilla on the other. The town continued until 501/1107 to be a permanent *iḳṭāʿ* of these last, granted by the sultan Muḥammad (498-511/1105-18).

During the period of the renaissance of the caliphate, which was inaugurated by al-Mustars̲h̲id (512-29/1118-35) in order to throw off the tutelage of the Sald̲j̲ūḳs, Wāsiṭ underwent numerous sieges in the struggles between the caliphs and the Sald̲j̲ūḳs, whose control over ʿIrāḳ at that time hardly extended beyond the central and southern regions because of the power of the Mazyadids of Ḥilla.

The attempts by the caliphs al-Rās̲h̲id (529-30/1135-6) and al-Muḳtafī (530-55/1136-60) [*q.vv.*] to extend their power over Wāsiṭ by defying the weakened authority of the sultans brought on the town much pillaging and destruction (535/1140, 549/1154, 551/1156 and 553/1158). From that time onwards, Lower ʿIrāḳ became the caliphs' domain and their firm territorial base. Wāsiṭ seems to have enjoyed relative peace and to have preserved the traces of its former prosperity when Yāḳūt visited it (622/1225). The period after the Sald̲j̲ūḳs, which extended from the reign of al-Nāṣir (575-622/1180-1225) to that of the last caliph al-Mustʿaṣim (640-56/1242-58), was a time of new and rapid expansion in Wāsiṭ. Nearly a century of peace had restored life to the town, and al-Mustaʿṣim made an excursion there (*nuzha*) in 646/1248, a decade before the Mongol invasion.

Hūlākū (Hülegü) appeared outside Wāsiṭ on 17 Ṣafar, after his entry into Bag̲h̲dād on 4 Ṣafar 656/10 February 1058. The town put up some resistance, as seen in the loss of about 40,000 inhabitants (probably an overestimate) and by the destruction suffered. This was the beginning of the power of the Il-K̲h̲ānids (656-736/1258-1335), who annexed Wāsiṭ to Bag̲h̲dād, which was governed by ʿAṭāʾ Malik al-D̲j̲uwaynī (657-81/1258-82). He was represented locally by the *Ṣadr* Mad̲j̲d al-Dīn Ṣalāḥ. Under the Il-K̲h̲ānids, the town had relative prosperity and was partly reconstructed. Its urban framework underwent modifications, including the total ruin or disappearance of the eastern side as a result of the Mongol raids.

Under the D̲j̲alāyirids (740-813/1339-1410 [*q.v.*]), Wāsiṭ continued to figure among the centres where coins were minted. Its strategic importance was evident in the campaigns of Tīmūr, who placed a powerful garrison there in 787/1385 and 808/1405. Wāsiṭ began its slow agony under the Turcoman Ḳara Ḳoyunlu (813-72/1410-67 [*q.v.*]), especially because of the blows struck by the S̲h̲īʿī movement of the Mus̲h̲aʿs̲h̲aʿ [*q.v.*]. The founder of this movement, Sayyid Muḥammad b. Falāḥ, attacked the town after 842/1438, and again in 844/1440 and 846/1442.

The attack led by his son and successor ʿAlī in 857/1453 or 858/1454 completed the ruin of the town, when it was abandoned by its inhabitants. The death of ʿAlī al-Mus̲h̲aʿs̲h̲aʿ in 861/1456 allowed the fugitives from Wāsiṭ to go back to their decimated town. Some of them probably settled in the hamlet (the second Wāsiṭ) which they founded not far from the historic city. This latter city did not disappear, for its existence on the banks of the Tigris, which still ran through it, is attested in 941/1534, the year it was taken by the Ottomans, and even as late as 961/1553. Wāsiṭ was described in the middle of the 11th/17th century by Ḥādjdjī Khalīfa as being situated on a dry river bed (the Dudjayla) in the middle of the desert. The Tigris had just abandoned its mediaeval course for the present one, which is situated further east. The town of al-Ḥadjdjādj had disappeared.

Bibliography: See the references given in the article. There is no special monograph on Wāsiṭ nor any interest on the part of the *akhbāriyyūn*. The material for its history remains very scattered and heterogeneous.

1. The historical and topographical introd. of the *Ta'rīkh Wāsiṭ* of Aslam b. Sahl al-Razzāz al-Wāsiṭī, called Baḥshal, ed. Kūrkīs 'Awwād, Baghdād 1387/1967, cited in the article, remains basic. The sources which flesh out this work, cited by the editor (introd., 11-12) are all lost: Ibn al-Maghāzilī al-Djullābī (d. 483/1090), *al-Dhayl 'alā Ta'rīkh Wāsiṭ*; al-Dubaythī (d. 637/1239), *Ta'rīkh Wāsiṭ*; al-Dja'farī, (beginning of 10th/16th century or even before), *Ta'rīkh Wāsiṭ*; and Ibn al-Muhadhdhab, *'Adjā'ib Wāsiṭ*.

2. The standard histories include Khalīfa b. Khayyāṭ, *Ta'rīkh*; Balādhurī, *Futūḥ and Ansāb al-ashrāf*, ed. S. Zakkār, Beirut 1996 (errors); Dīnawarī, *al-Akhbār al-ṭiwāl*; Ya'ḳūbī, *Ta'rīkh* and *Buldān*; Ṭabarī, *Ta'rīkh*; Ibn A'tham al-Kūfī, *Futūḥ*, Beirut 1986, 4 vols.; Ṣūlī, *Akhbār al-Rāḍī wa 'l-Muttaḳī bi 'llāh*, Cairo 1935, tr. Canard, Algiers 1946-50; Mas'ūdī, *Murūdj* and *Tanbīh*; anon., *al-'Uyūn wa 'l-ḥadā'iḳ*, iii, ed. de Goeje and P. de Jong, Leiden 1869, iv/1, Nadjaf 1972, iv/2, Baghdād 1973; Ibn al-Djawzī, *al-Muntaẓam*, Ḥaydarābād 1357-9/1938-40, 6 vols. (useful for the period 257-574/871-1179); Sibṭ Ibn al-Djawzī, *Mir'āt al-zamān* (useful but limited to the years 495-653/1101-1255); Ibn al-Fuwaṭī, *al-Ḥawādith al-djāmi'a*, Baghdād 1932/1351 (useful for the period 626-700/1228-1301); Ibn Kathīr, *al-Bidāya wa 'l-nihāya*. Biographical and hagiographical sources. Ibn al-Kalbī, *Djamharat al-nasab*, 3 vols. Damascus 1982; idem, *Nasab Ma'add wa 'l-Yaman*, 3 vols. Damascus 1988; Ibn Sa'd, *Ṭabaḳāt*, Beirut (vol. vii for Wāsiṭ); Khalīfa b. Khayyāṭ, *Ṭabaḳāt*; Ibn Ḥibbān, *Mashāhīr 'ulamā' al-amṣār*, Wiesbaden 1959; Ibn Ḥazm, *Djamhara*; al-Ḥāfiẓ al-Silafī, *Su'ālāt*, Damascus 1983; Ibn al-Djawzī, *Ṣifat al-Ṣafwa*, ii, Ḥaydarābād 1356/758.

3. Geographical sources, *riḥalāt, ziyārāt*. These include the classic works, plus Ibn al-Faḳīh, *Buldān* (new ed. announced by Yūsuf al-Hādī, incorporating the Mashhad ms., in which Wāsiṭ figures); Shābushtī, *Diyārāt*, Baghdād 1951; Mustawfī, *Nuzha*, ed. and tr. G. Lestrange, London 1919.

4. *Adab* works. These are very useful: Djāḥiẓ, *Ḥayawān*; Ibn Ḳutayba, *Ma'ārif*; idem, *'Uyūn al-akhbār*; Ibn 'Abd Rabbih, *'Iḳd*, Tanūkhī, *Nishwār al-muḥāḍara*; idem, *al-Faradj ba'd al-shidda*; Iṣfahānī, *Aghānī*; idem, *Maḳātil al-Ṭālibiyyīn*, Beirut n.d. (hagiographical); 'Imād al-Dīn al-Iṣfahānī, *Kharīdat al-ḳaṣr wa-djarīdat al-'aṣr* (vol. iv/2, Baghdād 1973, important for Wāsiṭ).

5. *Fiḳh* works, and those on fiscal and administrative history. These include Abū Yūsuf, *K. al-Kharādj*; Abū 'Ubayd b. Sallām, *K. al-Amwāl*; Ḳudāma b. Dja'far, *K. al-Kharādj*.

6. Studies. M.G. Morony, *Iraq after the Muslim conquest*, Princeton 1982. Further, M. Streck, *Die alte Landschaft Babylonien nach den arabischen Geographen*, Leiden 1900-01, ii, 318-38 (material on important sources for Wāsiṭ, but without any interpretation); J. Périer, *Vie d'al-Ḥadjdjādj Ibn Yousof*, Paris 1904, still useful; Le Strange, *Lands of the Eastern caliphate*, Cambridge 1905; H.H. Schaeder, *Ḥasan al-Baṣrī. Studien zur Frühgeschichte des Islam*, in *Isl.*, xiv (1925), 1-75; B. Faransīs, *al-Maẓāhir al-fanniyya fī 'awāṣim al-'Irāḳ al-islāmiyya 'alā ḍaw' al-iktishāfāt al-ḥadītha: al-Kūfa, Wāsiṭ, Baghdād, Sāmarrā'*, in *Sumer*, iv (1948), 103-12; A. Sūsa, *Madīnat Wāsiṭ, rayy Sāmarrā' fī 'ahd al-Khilāfa al-'abbāsiyya*, ii, Baghdād 1949, 341-4; Y. Maskūnī, *al-Ṣinā'a wa 'l-tidjāra fī Wāsiṭ*, in *Sumer*, v (1949), 297-305; Y. Sarkīs, *Madīnat al-'ilm al-'arīḳa, Wāsiṭ*, in *Mabāḥith 'irāḳiyya*, Baghdād 1955, 34-48 (new ed. of an article which appeared in 1936); A. Djamāl al-Dīn, *Mu'djam djughrāfiyat Wāsiṭ*, in *Sumer*, xiii (1957), 119-47; O. Grabar, *Al-Mushatta, Baghdād, and Wāsiṭ*, in J. Kritzeck and R.B. Winder (eds.), *The world of Islam. Studies in honor of Philip K. Hitti*, New York 1960, 99-108; M. Djawād, *Mu'djam mawāḍi' Wāsiṭ*, in *Madjallat al-Madjma' al-'Ilmī al-'Irāḳī*, Baghdād viii (1961), 114-17; N. Ma'rūf, *Madāris Wāsiṭ*, Baghdād 1955, 257-301 (repr. Baghdād 1966, 7-60); J. Fiey, *Assyrie chrétienne*, Beirut 1968, iii; 'A. al-Ḥadīthī, *al-Ṣiyāna al-athariyya fī Wāsiṭ*, in *Sumer*, xxxi (1975), 199-210; 'A.S. al-Ma'āḍīdī, *Wāsiṭ fī 'l-'aṣr al-umawī*, Baghdād 1976; idem, *Wāsiṭ fī 'l-'aṣr al-'abbāsī*, Baghdād 1983; S.A. al-'Alī, *Ma'ālim al-'Irāḳ al-'umrāniyya*, Baghdād 1989, 127-229 (important); M.O. Rousset, *L'archéologie islamique en Iraq, bilan et perspectives*, Damascus 1992, 142.

(MONDHER SAKLY)

4. The mint.

Today virtually nothing remains of the city of Wāsiṭ, but its name lives on in the abundant Umayyad reform-style dirhams bearing its name. These outnumber by far all the other dirhams struck in more than eighty other mints operated by the Umayyads. Many of them are found in museums that contain Islamic coins, and new collectors of the series find them the easiest and least expensive way to learn about the early coinage of Islam.

Their abundance is due to the work of two men: the caliph 'Abd al-Malik who, ruling in Damascus, introduced the purely epigraphic Islamic dīnār [*q.v.*] in the year 77/696-7, and the governor of 'Irāḳ, Khurāsān and Sidjistān, al-Ḥadjdjādj b. Yūsuf [*q.v.*] who introduced a similarly epigraphic dirham [*q.v.*] in the following year, 78/697-8. Al-Ḥadjdjādj's original plan was to bring a uniform, high quality silver coinage to 'Irāḳ and Persia by opening mints in a number of strategic locations throughout the area where stocks of the former Sāsānid and Arab Sāsānid coinages could be withdrawn from circulation and restruck on the new model. Chief among these mints were al-Kūfa, his seat of government, al-Baṣra, al-Rayy, Hamadhān, Shaḳḳ al-Taymara, Djayy, Sābūr and Marw. Many lesser known mints, such as Kaskar, Mihrdjanḳudhaḳ, Arḍ and 'Umān, were open only briefly and are known today by no more than one or two specimens.

The military revolt of 'Abd al-Raḥmān b. al-Ash'ath, which came to a head in 82/701 [see IBN AL-ASH'ATH] caused, among other things, his decentralised strategy of coinage production. 'Abd al-Malik had already centralised the striking of gold and silver in Damascus, and when al-Ḥadjdjādj moved his seat of government to Wāsiṭ in 83/702, he closed all the other mints under his control. Between the years 84/703 and 89/708 all the coinage in the east was confined to Wāsiṭ. The minting monopoly granted to Wāsiṭ gave al-Ḥadjdjādj control over the money supply, a valuable advantage at a time of political unrest. However, after 85/704, when al-Ḥadjdjādj became full master over Khurāsān, this monopoly and the consequent shortage of cash probably acted as a severe brake on trade and commercial activity.

In 90/709 al-Ḥadjdjādj reversed his centralisation of financial control by re-opening mints in Khūzistān, Djibāl, Fārs, Khurāsān and Sidjistān while maintaining Wāsiṭ as the main mint in ʿIrāḳ. After his death in Ramaḍān 95/June 714, there was a brief flurry of renewed minting activity in ʿIrāḳ, but this ended early in the reign of the caliph Sulaymān. During the years 98/716-17 and 99/717-18, the mints in Khūzistān, Djibāl and Fārs were closed down once again. While minting activity continued for a time in Khurāsān, this wholesale closure effectively restored Wāsiṭ's monopoly of coinage in the east.

Upon his accession as caliph in 99/717, ʿUmar II repudiated the administrative legacy of al-Ḥadjdjādj by appointing governors to both al-Kūfa and al-Baṣra, re-opening their mints and closing that of Wāsiṭ. No coinage is known to have been struck there in the year 100/718-19. After Yazīd II became caliph in 101, the Wāsiṭ mint was briefly re-opened, but it is not known to have produced any coinage in 102. From the following year, 103/721-2, until the downfall of the Umayyad dynasty in 132/750, the Wāsiṭ mint continued, year by year, to supply most of the dirham coinage for the east. Elsewhere in the Umayyad state, dirham mints were active in Spain (*al-Andalus*), North Africa (*Ifrīḳiya*), Syria (*Dimashk*), the North (*Armīniya, Ādharbāydjān* and *al-Bāb* (Darband)) and Khurāsān (*Balkh, Balkh al-Bayḍā'* and *al-Mubāraka*).

The most useful research on the Umayyad mint of Wāsiṭ was published by DeShazo and Bates in *The Umayyad Governors of al-ʿIrāq and the changing annulet patterns on their dirhams*. Here the authors point out that the annulet patterns of the dirhams change when the provincial governors change, and each pattern is, in general, characteristic for a single governor. They then provide a table listing the governors and their associated annulet patterns from 99 until 132. The significant fact which emerges from this study is that the annulet patterns are related to governors rather than to caliphs. Control of the coinage in ʿIrāḳ thus lay in the hands of its governors rather than any centralised mint administration under direct caliphal control. Presumably the annulet patterns were placed on the coins for ease of identification at a time when few could read the unpointed Kufic script with which they were inscribed. The placing of coinage under gubernatorial control was established by al-Ḥadjdjādj b. Yūsuf and continued until the end of Umayyad rule.

Marcel Jungfleisch tells a curious tale of the Wāsiṭ mint in his *Conjectures* about how Byzantine mints frequently struck coinages for one another. He states that coinages from the Constantinian and post-Constantinian eras bore mint signatures such as ALE and ANT which did not necessarily imply that they were actually struck in Alexandria or Antioch, but "pour le compte" of these mints. He then goes on to offer, as evidence for the same practice in the Muslim world, de Morgan's excavations at Wāsiṭ. When digging up the former Arab mint, de Morgan reportedly found a considerable number of newly-struck dirhams ready to be placed in circulation bearing the inscriptions *ḍuriba bi 'l-Andalus* and *ḍuriba bi-Ifrīḳiya*. Jungfleisch adds that these coins probably bore distinguishing marks proper to the mint of Wāsiṭ.

Commenting on this report, G.C. Miles stated, "I have not been able to locate de Morgan's account of this very interesting discovery, nor is the reference available in Jungfleisch". He concludes by saying, "I have often suspected that the manufacture of many Umayyad dies was centralized, but the actual striking of *al-Andalus* dirhams in southern Iraq would seem an extraordinary phenomenon". Concerning an excavation report prepared by M. Fuad Safar in 1945 in *Wāsit, the mint-town*, Ulla Linder Welin stated that "nothing is told of this previous excursion of M. de Morgan or of the supposed or excavated site of the workshop of the Wasit mint", and she provided a table listing all the dates, with references, for the coinage struck in Wāsiṭ. The present author agrees with Miles' judgement that Wāsiṭ was a likely centre for Umayyad die production, in particular after 103 when the same crisp, elegant calligraphy of the Wāsiṭ mint is encountered elsewhere, e.g. on the coinages of al-Bāb and al-Mubāraka. In conclusion, it is true to say that the Umayyad mint of Wāsiṭ was one of the most prolific the Islamic world has ever seen and its presence was felt throughout the Islamic world years after its closure.

The fall of the Umayyads brought about the immediate end of the Wāsiṭ mint and the re-opening of those of al-Kūfa in 132/750 and al-Baṣra one year later. These towns continued to be the main centres of coinage production in ʿIrāḳ until the ʿAbbāsid mints of Madīnat al-Salām and al-Muḥammadiyya became fully operational in 148/765. This division of mint production continued substantially unchanged until the struggle for power between al-Amīn and al-Ma'mūn affected the entire functioning of the ʿAbbāsid state. In the aftermath of al-Amīn's defeat in Baghdād in 198/813 and during the subsequent revolts in ʿIrāḳ, the Wāsiṭ mint was briefly re-opened for the second time in 200 with a dirham citing al-Ḥasan (b. Sahl) and Dhu 'l-Riyāsatayn, followed by a second dirham issue dated 203 citing al-ʿIrāḳ and Dhu 'l-Riyāsatayn. Both coins are notably rare, which suggests that the mint may have been reactivated in these years to make emergency payments to the caliphal army commanded by al-Ḥasan b. Sahl, the brother and deputy of al-Faḍl b. Sahl, Dhu 'l-Riyāsatayn, the vizier of al-Ma'mūn. By the time this conflict had ended, the concept of one or two pre-eminent mints had vanished, leaving a system of several regional mints in their place. The number of these mints gradually increased during the caliphates of al-Muʿtaṣim, al-Wāthiḳ and al-Mutawakkil, and during the reign of al-Muʿtazz the mint of Wāsiṭ was re-opened for the third time. It is known to have struck its first dirhams in 253/867 and dīnārs followed in 254. For the next century, the Wāsiṭ mint reflected the town's prosperity and was one of the more active in ʿIrāḳ, striking both dirhams and occasional dīnārs on standard ʿAbbāsid and Būyid patterns. After the Būyids seized control of ʿIrāḳ in 334/945, the coinage records become increasingly irregular and gradually draw to a close in the 360s and 370s with the rise in importance of the trading cities of al-Baṣra and Sūḳ al-Ahwāz. Finally, the Wāsiṭ mint ceased activity and went into a sleep which lasted for over three hundred years.

Wāsiṭ's fourth and last period of coinage activity began after Rashīd al-Dīn [*q.v.*], Ghazan's *wazīr*, brought about the reform of the Il-Khānid coinage in 698/1298-9. The Il-K̲h̲ānids re-opened several ʿIrāḳī mints, including Wāsiṭ, Ḥilla and al-Baṣra, while Bag̲h̲dād retained its traditional position as the main mint of the province. Wāsiṭ and Bag̲h̲dād, however, shared the distinction of being the only ʿIrāḳī mints to issue silver dīnārs valued at six dirhams. The dīnār was the apex of the Il-K̲h̲ānid monetary system, with 10,000 forming the tūmān [*q.v.*], the Il-K̲h̲ānid unit of account. It is possible that the elaborately decorated dies for these large coins were prepared at the instigation of Ras̲h̲īd al-Dīn, in his role as a historian, to acknowledge the importance enjoyed by both Wāsiṭ and Madīnat al-Salām/Bag̲h̲dād in the history of Islamic coinage production (see *B.M. cat.*, vi, 129).

Wāsiṭ thus became part of the extensive Il-K̲h̲ānid mint system under G̲h̲azan, Öld̲j̲eytü and Abū Saʿīd, and its position was maintained by the later Il-K̲h̲ānids and the D̲j̲alāyirids, their successors in ʿIrāḳ. The political disorders which followed Tīmūr's invasion and occupation of ʿIrāḳ *ca.* 787-808/1385-1405, probably brought an end to minting activity in Wāsiṭ, as no coins are known from that time onwards. The demise of the city itself, brought about by the shifting of the course of the Tigris during the 9th/15th century, has precluded any revival of its former importance.

Bibliography: G.C. Miles, *The coinage of the Umayyads of Spain*, New York 1950, 22 n. 1; Ulla S. Linder Welin, *Wāsit, the mint-town*, in *K. Humanistiska Vetenskapssamfundets i Lund Årsberättelse/Bull. de la Société Royale des Lettres de Lund* (1955-6), no. IV, 127-69; M. Jungfleisch, *Conjectures au sujet de certaines lettres isolées se rencontrant sur les solidi byzantins du VIIe siècle*, in *Bull., de l'Inst. d'Egypte*, xxxi (1948-9), 111 ff.; E. von Zambaur, *Die Münzprägungen des Islams*, i, Wiesbaden 1968, 268; A.S. DeShazo and M.L. Bates, *The Umayyad governors of al-ʿIrāq and the changing annulet patterns on their dirhams*, in *NC*, 7th ser., vol. xiv (1974), 112, 116; N. Lowick, ed. E. Savage, *Early Abbasid coinage. A type corpus 132-218 H./A.D. 750-833*, unpubl. ms. 1999.

(R. Darley-Doran)

WĀSIṬA (a.), a Fāṭimid administrative term. It denoted an intermediary between the Fāṭimid ruler—the Imām—and the ruling establishment and people. The title of *wāsiṭa* conferred on chief administrators implied more limited powers and lower rank than that of vizier. The terms *wāsiṭa/wasāṭa* are attested in 5th/11th-century literary and documentary sources. The first person upon whom it was bestowed was the Kutāmī chief Ibn ʿAmmār, at the time of al-Ḥākim's coronation. Several administrators during the rule of al-Ḥākim (386-411/996-1021) and al-Ẓāhir (411-27/1021-36) [*q.vv.*] were appointed as *wāsiṭas*. However, the term disappears from the historical records around the second half of the 5th/11th century, following the militarisation of Fāṭimid politics and the rise of military viziers who wielded absolute political power in the state.

Bibliography: For 5th/11th-century literary and documentary sources, see Musabbiḥī, *Ak̲h̲bār Miṣr*, ed. A.F. Sayyid and Th. Bianquis, Cairo 1978, 18; Ibn al-Ḳalānisī, *D̲h̲ayl taʾrīk̲h̲ Dimas̲h̲ḳ*, ed. Amedroz, Leiden 1908, 80-3 (who has reproduced a letter of appointment to the post of vizier, which specifies his duties as *wāsiṭa*). For 6th/12th century and later sources, see Ibn al-Ṣayrafī, *al-Is̲h̲āra ilā man nāl al-wizāra*, ed. ʿA. Mukhliṣ, Cairo 1924, 29, 33, 34, 35 (Arabic pagination); Maḳrīzī, *Ittiʿāẓ al-ḥunafāʾ*, ed. M.H.M. Aḥmad, Cairo 1971, ii, 84, 94, 110. Of studies, see art. BARD̲J̲AWĀN; also Y. Lev, *State and society in Fatimid Egypt*, Leiden 1991, 25, 27; P. Sanders, *Ritual, politics, and the city in Fatimid Cairo*, Albany 1994, 23, 142. (Y. Lev)

WAṢIYYA (a.), in Islamic law, bequest, last will and testament.

In *fiḳh*, *waṣiyya* refers to two related notions: (1) that of bequest or legacy (defined as the transfer of the corpus or the usufruct (*manfaʿa*) of a thing after one's death without a consideration); and (2) that of appointing a testamentary executor or guardian over minor children. The term *waṣiyya* is sometimes translated as last will or testament, since for both legal acts a testamentary disposition is required.

1. *Historical background*

Several Ḳurʾānic verses mention or refer to bequests. From XXXVI, 50, it appears that making a bequest was usual among the Meccan merchants. In II, 180, those who have property are ordered to make bequests to their parents and close relatives. Making a provision to widows by bequest is commanded in II, 240. Finally, V, 106, requires the presence of witnesses when making a bequest. From these verses and other sources it is clear that the *waṣiyya* was known in pre-Islamic Arabia and was used to give the spouse relict and non-agnatic relatives a part of the estate at the expense of the male agnates. II, 180 and II, 240, are traditionally seen as the beginning of the Islamic law of succession, since they command the making of bequests, without limitations, to close relatives and spouses, who would be excluded under the pre-Islamic rules of agnatic succession. However, around the year 3/625 these verses are supposed to have been abrogated by the verses of inheritance (IV, 11, 12 and 176) that assign precise fractional shares to some of these relatives and to the spouse relict, whereas at the same time the Prophetic Sunna imposed two important restrictions, namely, that bequests were limited to one-third of the estate and that they could not be made in favour of existing heirs.

Recently, D.S. Powers (*Studies*, 143-89) has proposed a new theory on the development of the *waṣiyya*. He argues that the abrogation of the bequest verses did not become the accepted doctrine until some time after Muḥammad's death. During the first stage of the development of the Islamic law of succession there was much freedom in testation. A person could designate close relatives as heirs. If the testator chose to designate affinal relatives (wife, daughter-in-law) as such, certain relatives who would have inherited in the absence of such a provision were compensated with a share in the estate. Finally, one could make bequests, but not exceeding the value of one-third of the estate. Only later, during the 1st century A.H., was the classical doctrine generally accepted. Although Powers' theory is attractive, since it offers some explanations to certain issues that are as yet unclear, it is not uncontested. His main argument is a new and controversial vocalisation and reading of Ḳurʾān, IV, 12. Further, he maintains that of the two basic restrictions on making bequests, both laid down in *ḥadīt̲h̲s*, one, the limitation to one-third of the estate, dates from the Prophet's lifetime, whereas the other, the nullity of bequests to heirs, is of much later date.

2. *Classical legal doctrine*

(a) Bequests. In Islamic law, it is only possible to designate an heir by testament in the exceptional case that one does not have other heirs. Otherwise, testaments can only be used for the transfer of property by way of bequest or legacy. There are no formal requirements for the making of a bequest: it may be done in writing, but also orally or even through intelligible signs. In both cases witnesses must be present in order to prove it. The testator, of course, must be of full legal capacity. The making of a bequest is regarded as an offer, which needs to be accepted in order to become binding and irrevocable. Since a basic principle of the law of bequests is that the testator can revoke a bequest during his lifetime, acceptance cannot take place before the testator's death. The S͟hīʿa hold that bequests can only be revoked expressly. According to the Sunnī law schools, implied revocation, for instance if the testator alienates or destroys the property bequeathed, is also valid. If after the testator's decease the legatee dies before having declared his acceptance or refusal, the right to accept passes to his heirs. After the testator's death, the ownership of the property is suspended until acceptance by the legatee. There is some difference of opinion about when exactly the ownership is transferred. According to most legal schools, the ownership is regarded to have been passed retroactively to the legatee from the moment of the testator's death. The Mālikīs and Ḥanbalīs, however, hold that the ownership is transferred at the moment of acceptance.

For a bequest to a specific person to be valid, he must be alive at the time of making the bequest and of the testator's death. The first condition, however, does not apply if the legatees are generic, e.g. the children of X. If the legatee predeceases the testator, the bequest fails. Under S͟hīʿī law, however, it is valid and devolves to the legatee's heirs. If the testator and legatee die in the same event, the rules with regard to inheritance apply. Contrary to intestate succession, difference of religion constitutes no bar for bequests, except, under Ḥanafī and S͟hīʿī law, if the legatee lives outside the *Dār al-Islām*. With regard to the case in which the legatee has killed the testator, opinions differ. The Ḥanafīs and S͟hīʿīs compare bequests with succession and, consequently, consider such killing an impediment. The other law schools regard bequests more like gifts, for which no such bar exists.

The object of a bequest can be specific or generic. Specific bequests are gifts of the corpus or the usufruct of particular items of property or the manumission of a slave. Such bequests are only valid if these items are owned by the testator at the time of his making the bequest. Generic bequests are gifts of certain quantities of fungible goods or of money, or gifts of a share of the testator's property. Regarding this type, it is not necessary that the testator should own the goods bequeathed at the time of making the bequest.

Bequests are subject to two restrictions: together they may not exceed one-third of the value of the estate and they may not be made in favour of an existing heir. Bequests made contrary to these rules are *ultra vires* and null unless they are ratified (*id͟jāza*) by the heirs, but only after the testator's death. If some heirs approve and others do not, the ratification holds good proportionally to the shares of the heirs who have approved.

With regard to the restriction to one-third of the estate, opinions differ as to when the value of the estate must be calculated. Most legal schools take the moment of the testator's death as the crucial time. The Ḥanafīs and Mālikīs, however, calculate the value of the estate at the moment the bequest becomes complete and binding, i.e. at the moment of acceptance for the Mālikīs and of actual transfer of ownership for the Ḥanafīs. This is, of course, important in cases when the value of the estate has changed after the testator's death. If a bequest exceeds the value of one-third of the estate, it is valid for the part not exceeding this limit but fails for the surplus. If there are more bequests, together taking up more than the third of the estate, the situation becomes more complicated. The Sunnī law schools apply a *pro rata* abatement, whereas the S͟hīʿīs use chronology as a yardstick: the earlier bequests have priority over the more recent ones. If there are no heirs, bequests may exceed one-third of the estate, except according to the Mālikīs, because they regard the Public Treasury as an heir whose interests are protected in the same way as the other heirs. The second restriction operating with regard to bequests is the provision that bequests may not be made in favour of an existing heir. This rule is not accepted by the S͟hīʿīs. The moment for determining who counts as an heir is, of course, the moment of the testator's death.

(b) Last illness (*maraḍ al-mawt*). Although a person is free during his or her lifetime to dispose of his or her property as he or she pleases, this freedom ends as soon as the process of dying sets in. During the last illness, or under comparable circumstances in which death seems imminent (e.g. a shipwreck, a flood or a fire) a person is put under a limited interdiction (*ḥad͟jr*) in order to protect the interests of his or her heirs: by any dispositions—liberal acts such as gifts, *waḳf*s, manumission, suretyship, or generosity in trade or hiring—such a person may not diminish the value of his or her estate for more than one-third of the property. Under these circumstances, such acts are equated with bequests. Disadvantageous dispositions exceeding the limit of one-third of the estate may therefore be nullified by the heirs after the testator's death.

The last illness, in order to be invoked by the heirs, must have effectively ended with death. Establishing whether a certain legal act was performed during one's last illness is a retrospective activity. There are three criteria for determining whether an illness or certain circumstances can count as the last illness. (1) Was the gravity of the condition or circumstances sufficiently serious for apprehending death?. (2) Was the apprehension of impending death uninterrupted? (3) Was the death the result of the illness or circumstances?

(c) Appointment of a testamentary executor or guardian. One may appoint by testament an executor (*waṣiyy*) to take care, after one's death, of the settlement and the recovery of debts, the payment of bequests and the division of the estate among the heirs or a guardian (also called *waṣiyy*) over minor children. If the deceased has failed to do so, the *ḳāḍī* must appoint an executor to administer and liquidate the estate if the value of the debts exceeds the value of the estate, or if there are minors or missing persons among the heirs.

3. *Recent developments*

For recent reforms in the law of bequests, see MĪRĀT͟H. 2.

Bibliography: Ibn Rus͟hd, *Bidāyat al-mud͟jtahid*, Cairo 1960, ii, 334-8; Ibn Ḳudāma, *al-Mug͟hnī*, Beirut n.d., vi, 1-165; Muḥammad Ḳadrī Bās͟hā, *al-Aḥkām al-s͟harʿiyya fī 'l-aḥwāl al-s͟hak͟hṣiyya ʿalā mad͟hhab al-Imām Abī Ḥanīfa al-Nuʿmān*, Cairo 1327, §§ 435-81, 530-70; A.M. Zaid, *The Islamic law of bequest*, London 1986; D.S. Powers, *Studies in Qur'an and Hadith. The formation of the Islamic law of inheritance*, Berkeley, etc. 1986; idem, *On bequests in early Islam*, in *JNES*, xlviii (1989), 185-200; I. Edge, *Coulson's Islamic law of succession*, Cambridge 1996.

(R. PETERS)

WAṢL (A.), a term of Arabic grammar broadly denoting juncture, i.e. a syntactic or phonological "connecting"; it is thus the antonym of both interruption (*ḳaṭʿ* [*q.v.*]) and pause (*waḳf* [*q.v.*]).

Its origin is probably in Ḳurʾān recitation, where the choice of proceeding to the next word without a break depends mainly on syntactic or semantic considerations, the text being marked accordingly with signs for optional, preferable or compulsory *waṣl*.

The term occurs most commonly in the phrase *alif al-waṣl*, alternatively, but less transparently, *hamzat al-waṣl*, referring to the prosthetic *alif* found before word-initial consonant clusters and creating an artificial syllable (*ʾa-, ʾi-* or *ʾu-*, according to context), whose purpose is to split the consonant cluster and thereby avoid a non-canonical syllable beginning with two consonants, hence **ḳtul* (CCVC) becomes *ʾuḳ-tul* (CVC-CVC) etc. (In foreign loan words and names, this same process leads to *hamzat al-ḳaṭʿ*, e.g. Plato > *ʾAflāṭūn*, Aram. *Klīlā* > *ʾiklīl* "crown".) Although this feature of Arabic is well known, the rationale behind the term *hamzat al-waṣl* is obscure (a mere formal contrast with *hamzat al-ḳaṭʿ* in writing?), since the true consonantal *hamza* [*q.v.*] is unaffected by *waṣl*.

The *alif al-waṣl* arose orthographically, when words were dictated slowly enough to be spelt as if in isolation, with the *alif* still having its historical value of *hamzat al-ḳaṭʿ*. In juncture this *hamza* is elided, for which situation the *waṣla* sign was later invented, viz. a small *ṣād* (from the root *waṣala*) over the *alif* indicating that it was to be ignored. Interestingly, this *alif* and the *waṣla* sign are retained after prefixes such as *wa-, fa-, bi-* (but not *li-* before the definite article, perhaps for aesthetic reasons), suggesting that in dictation the *hamzat al-ḳaṭʿ* was preserved even here, e.g. **wa ʾuḳtul* for *wa-ḳtul* (but note the exceptional phonetic spelling in such very common phrases as *bismi llāhi* etc.). The same spelling convention implies that the definite article *ʾal*, whose first letter is itself an *alif al-waṣl*, was also dictated as if in isolation before words already beginning with *alif al-waṣl*, e.g. **ʾal ʾikhtilāf*, not *ʾalikhtilāf*. The grammarians claim that *alif al-waṣl* is basically a property of verbs, though undoubtedly it is most frequently seen with the definite article. Apart from the *maṣdars* of stems VII and higher, several relatively common nouns also have it, e.g. *ism, ibn, imraʾa, ist* and *ithnān*.

By definition, the *hamzat al-waṣl* cannot be realised as a *hamzat al-ḳaṭʿ* within a word, and therefore should never be written as one, yet this is now clearly an accepted modern spelling, e.g. *al-ʾikhtilāf* (curiously, the definite article does not acquire *hamzat al-ḳaṭʿ*). In mediaeval poetry, the *hamzat al-waṣl* sometimes becomes *hamzat al-ḳaṭʿ* for metrical reasons, but it is too early to say whether the new spelling will prevail in the surviving classical metres, in which case contemporary and mediaeval prosody will become incompatible on that point.

The notion of *waṣl* in syntax is less well defined. Various forms of stems I and IV of the root *w-ṣ-l* are used by Sībawayhi [*q.v.*] to represent the connection between verbs and their objects (Troupeau, entries rendered "parvenir à"), and *waṣl* is an occasional synonym of *ṣila* [*q.v.*] (appended clause, especially relative clause). We may also include here the cognate *wuṣla*, one of a group of terms for referential and copulative elements mostly called *ʿāʾid* but also *rābiṭ(a)* and *rāḏjiʿ*. Finally, stem VIII provides a term for such widely differing phenomena as bound pronouns (*ḍamīr muttaṣil*: opposite, *ḍamīr munfaṣil* "separate, independent pronoun") and exceptive sentences of the type (*mā) ḳāma l-ḳawmu ʾillā zaydᵃⁿ (zaydᵘⁿ)* (*istithnāʾ muttaṣil*: opposite, *istithnāʾ munḳaṭiʿ*, e.g. *mā ḏjāʾani aḥadᵘⁿ illā ḥimārᵃⁿ*).

Bibliography: W. Diem, *Untersuchungen zur frühen*

Geschichte der arabischen Orthographie, in *Orientalia*, xlviii-lii (1979-83), esp. §§ 118-19, 201 ff., 220-33; H. Fleisch, *Traité de linguistique arabe*, Beirut 1961-79, i, ch. 4 (198-200), references to other Arabic and European sources; A.S. Kaye, *The* hamzat al-waṣl *in contemporary Modern Standard Arabic*, in *JAOS*, cxi (1991), 572-3; G. Troupeau, *Lexique-index du* Kitāb *de Sībawayhi*, Paris 1976. (M.G. CARTER)

WASM (A.), pl. *wusūm*, brand. Bedouins have branded their camels since ancient times (G. Jacob, *Altarabisches Beduinenleben*, Berlin 1897, 71). A Bedouin will normally be able to identify each of his camels without the aid of a brand; but the brand is helpful when camels belonging to many different owners are gathered in one place (e.g. at a water-source). Camels often stray and sometimes are stolen; a branded camel can usually be described so fully by its owner that another Bedouin will be able to identify it with assurance on the basis of the description alone (author's observations in Sinai; cf. F. Beslay, *Les Réguibats*, Paris 1984, 58).

One *wasm* is distinguished from another not only by its appearance but also by its location on the animal's body (e.g. right cheek). The signs that make up the brand have individual names, e.g. *maṭrak* "stick", *hilāl* "crescent". Such arbitrary signs are used throughout the Arab world; but in North Africa some tribes, especially maraboutic ones, instead use letters or even whole words, e.g. Muḥammad, Allāh, Makka (P. Kahle, *Die Aulād-ʿAli-Beduinen der Libyschen Wüste*, in *Isl.*, iv [1913], 367; Le Borgne, *Vocabulaire technique du chameau en Mauritanie (dialecte hassanya)*, in *BIFAO*, xv [1953], 365).

The several signs making up a brand may signify respectively the tribe, a group within the tribe, and even a sub-group of that group. Among the Rashāʾida of the Sudan, each man adds his own individual sign to the mark of the group (W.C. Young, *The Rashaayda Bedouin*, Fort Worth, Texas 1996, 86-8); much more commonly, however, a group shares a brand, though where this is the general practice men of great wealth may still have their individual *wusūm* (H.R.P. Dickson, *The Arab of the desert*, London 1951, 420-1).

Brands are sometimes placed on animals other than camels, e.g. cattle, water-buffalo, donkeys (but not horses), and even sheep (though ear-clipping is a more usual way of marking small stock). *Wusūm* also often appear on things other than animals, e.g. tombs, rocks, wells or trees. Sometimes, at least, they indicate that the object so marked is in the territory of, or is protected by, the group whose sign it bears. The Muzayna of Sinai place the *wasm* of their descent group "on hut doors for good luck and on storage boxes for identification"; and sometimes they tattoo their brand on members of the group—on the foreheads of women, and on the backs of the hands of both men and women (Smadar Lavie, *The poetics of military occupation*, Berkeley 1990, 14-15). In northern Palestine, in contrast, tribesmen used to mark a cattle thief by burning their *wasm* on his thigh (J. Sonnen, *Die Beduinen am See Genesareth*, Cologne 1952, 162).

Bibliography: The only general study is the excellent, though now rather outdated, article by A. van Gennep, *Les "wasm", ou marques de propriété des arabes*, in *Internationales Archiv für Ethnographie*, xv (1902), 85-98. Among the many other works which contain relevant information may be mentioned H.A. MacMichael, *Brands used by the chief camel-owning tribes of Kordofán*, Cambridge 1913; O. Bates, *Ethnographic notes from Marsa Matruh*, in *JRAS* (1915), 717-39; ʿĀrif al-ʿĀrif, *al-Ḳaḍāʾ bayn al-badw*, Jerusalem 1933, 157-67;

H. Field, *Camel brands and graffiti from Iraq, Syria, Jordan, Iran and Arabia, JAOS* Supplement 15, Baltimore 1952; J. Caro Baroja, *Estudios saharianos*, Madrid 1955, 88-90; I. Cunnison, *The Baggara Arabs*, Oxford 1966, 205-8. (F.H. Stewart)

WAṢṢĀF (in full, Waṣṣāf al-Ḥaḍrat "the court panegyrist"), *nom-de-plume* of S͟hihāb al-Dīn ʿAbd Allāh b. ʿIzz al-Dīn Faḍl Allāh S͟hīrāzī, chronicler and poet of Mongol Persia in the early 8th/14th century. He was the author of the *Tāriк͟h-i Waṣṣāf* (more precisely, *Tad͟jziyat al-amṣār wa-tazd͟jiyat al-aʿṣār* "The allocation of cities and the propulsion of epochs"), a history of the Il-K͟hāns [*q.v.*] from 658/1260 in five volumes, designed as a sequel to the *Tāriк͟h-i D͟jahāngus͟hā* of D͟juwaynī [*q.v.*]. The preface is dated S͟haʿbān 699/April-May 1300 (*Tāriк͟h-i Waṣṣāf*, 6). Through the instrumentality of the viziers Ras͟hīd al-Dīn Faḍl Allāh [*q.v.*] and Saʿd al-Dīn, the author and his historical work were presented at ʿĀna on 13 Rad͟jab 702/3 March 1303 to the Il-K͟hān G͟hazan [*q.v.*], who showed him great favour and allotted him a pension (*ibid.*, 405-7). Four volumes were completed by 24 Muḥarram 712/1 June 1312, when his patron Ras͟hīd al-Dīn enabled Waṣṣāf to submit them in person to G͟hazan's successor Öld͟jeytü [*q.v.*] (Ūld͟jāītū; *ibid.*, 544). The fifth volume was finished much later, the current year being variously given as 727 and 728 (see Barthold, *Turkestan*[3], 49 n. 2).

Waṣṣāf did not merely emulate D͟juwaynī's florid and bombastic style but perpetrated even greater excesses, which were in turn to provide a model for subsequent Persian historiography. Although the two viziers allegedly praised the *Tāriк͟h* and declared that no finer combination of Persian and Arabic had ever been achieved in any historical work, Öld͟jeytü was unable to understand a word of the passage which Waṣṣāf read to him (*Tāriк͟h-i Waṣṣāf*, 405). Modern historians have often shared the Il-K͟hān's incomprehension, a circumstance which is all the more regrettable in view of the valuable material contained in the *Tāriк͟h*. Its importance for Il-K͟hānid history is that it is completely independent of our other principal source, Ras͟hīd al-Dīn's encyclopaedic *D͟jāmiʿ al-tawāriк͟h*, and provides us with a quite different perspective. Waṣṣāf, who describes himself (*ibid.*, 626) as a client of the Salg͟hūrids [*q.v.*], the former ruling dynasty of Fārs, was for some years employed in the financial administration of that province, and under Öld͟jeytü's son and successor Abū Saʿīd, he was put in charge of revenue collection in the districts of Fīrūzābād, Ḳīr and Kārzīn (*ibid.*, 653; cf. also 630, 632-3; and for these localities, see Ḥamd Allāh Mustawfī, *Nuzhat al-ḳulūb*, ed. G. Le Strange, Leiden and London 1915, 118). He is therefore particularly informative on fiscal affairs and on the history of the dynasties of southern Persia that were subordinate to the Il-K͟hāns. But he also furnishes valuable data on the history of the Mongols elsewhere, notably those of China and of the Čag͟hatay k͟hānate [*q.v.*] and the Mongol state in Central Asia ruled by Ḳaydu [*q.v.*]. In addition, the *Tāriк͟h* includes two valuable notices on the Dihlī Sultanate [*q.v.*], of which the first was incorporated by Ras͟hīd al-Dīn in 702/1303 into the section on India in his own work (ed. K. Jahn, *Die Indiengeschichte des Rašīd ad-Dīn*, Vienna 1980, 9).

Bibliography: *Tāriк͟h-i Waṣṣāf*, lith. ed. Bombay 1269/1853, abridged and simplified version by ʿAbd al-Muḥammad Āyatī, *Taḥrīr-i Tāriк͟h-i Waṣṣāf*, Tehran 1346 *s͟h.*/1967, partial ed. and tr. J. von Hammer-Purgstall, *Geschichte Wassaf's*, Vienna 1856 (vol. i only); Browne, *LHP*, iii, 67-8; Storey, i, 267-70; Storey-Bregel, ii, 768-75; R.G. Kempiners, Jr., *Vaṣṣāf's* Tajziyat al-amṣār wa Tazjiyat al-aʿṣār *as a source for the history of the Chaghadayid khanate*, in *Jnal. of Asian History*, xxii (1988), 160-87; A.K.S. Lambton, *Mongol fiscal administration in Persia*, in *SI*, lxiv (1986), 79-99, lxv (1987), 97-123. (P. Jackson)

WAṬAN (a.), "homeland, fatherland", an Arabic near-equivalent of the term *patria* of the Latin Middle Ages in most of its shades. As we learn from normative lexicographical entries and actual usage in literary and historical texts alike, *waṭan* or *mawṭin* was, in the beginning, a wholly apolitical term denoting simply the place of birth or stay (*LʿA*, Beirut ed., xiii, 451a, l. 8). In al-S͟harīf al-D͟jurd͟jānī's (d. 816/1413) *Book of definitions* (*Kitāb al-taʿrīfāt*, 237, ll. 18-20) we find the meaning of *waṭan* split into "permanent residence" and "temporary and transitory sojourn (of at least a fortnight)". The Indian encyclopaedist Muḥammad b. ʿAlāʾ al-Tahānawī (18th century) differentiates between the place of origin in whose selection one does not have any influence (*al-waṭan al-aṣlī*, *al-waṭan al-ahlī*), and a chosen place of stay of a shorter or longer duration (*waṭan al-fiṭra wa ʾl-ḳarār, waṭan al-iḳāma wa ʾl-safar*) (*Kas͟hs͟hāf iṣṭilāḥāt al-funūn*, ed. A. Sprenger, ii, 1519-20). In Prophetic tradition, *waṭan* stands side-by-side—and thus in rough equivalence—with the general terms *dār* "house" and *bilād* "land". Elsewhere we find it used in the restricted sense of *mawḍiʿ* equalling *mas͟hhad* "battlefield" (*LʿA*, xiii, 451b, ll. 3 ff.), i.e. of the place where the collective self is defended against outsiders. Battles are known to have served as important focuses of national sentiment also in the mediaeval West.

Fidelity to one's *mawṭin* in the sense of home is axiomatic. Every human is imbued with it. According to al-D͟jāḥiẓ, it is the ambience, i.e. for all practical purposes what is meant by *waṭan*, that shapes man. The sentiment of longing for the homeland (*al-ḥanīn ilā ʾl-awṭān*), also the title of one of al-D͟jāḥiẓ's famous short epistles (ed. ʿAbd al-Salām Hārūn, in *Rasāʾil*, ii, Cairo 1384/1964, 383-412), encompasses also, and even with particular intensity, the itinerant nomadic tribesman who roams around in the steppes and who—in spite of or even because of his lifestyle—feels so strongly attached to his home sites. Al-D͟jāḥiẓ's treatise on the merits of the Turks (*Risāla ilā ʾl-Fatḥ b. K͟hāḳān fī manāḳib al-Turk wa-ʿāmmat d͟jund al-k͟hilāfa*, in *Rasāʾil*, i, 5-86) abundantly testifies to this philosophy. "The country of a man is his wetnurse and his house is his cradle" (*al-Ḥanīn*, 386, l. 3), "The nature of man is kneaded from love for one's homeland" (*ibid.*, 387, l. 5), and "If a bird longs for his nest, how much more is man entitled to yearn for his homeland" (*ibid.*, 386, ll. 7-8), are some of al-D͟jāḥiẓ's patent sayings on the natural attachment of man to his home. The Western equivalent to this primordial sentiment is the *amor soli naturalis* which we find invoked by the Dominican master Humbert of Romans (d. 1277) as a lamentable impediment to the Crusading spirit.

Like the Latin *dulcis patria*, *waṭan* (or *mawṭin*) has also a more abstract, figurative meaning that sheds the distinctly local connotations by signifying the place where one comes to rest. *Waṭan* shares this metonymic meaning with *al-aṭlāl* ("traces of an abandoned encampment") and *al-manāzil wa ʾl-diyār* ("camp sites and houses"). For Averroes (d. 1198), who had long enough struggled with the boring details of Mālikī law, philosophy became the *waṭan* proper of the intellect. The mystics, in particular, liked the term *waṭan* and implemented it in various meanings. For the anonymous author of the Ṣūfī manual *Adab al-mulūk* of the

4th/10th century, the "houses of God", i.e. the mosques, were the real home (ed. B. Radtke, Beirut and Stuttgart 1991, 60-1, § 22). Other Ṣūfīs gave a spiritual meaning to the term *waṭan*. The mystic al-Sarrādj (d. 378/988), in his list of difficult mystic terms (The *Kitáb al-Lumaʿ fi 'l-Taṣawwuf of Abú Naṣr ʿAbdalláh b. ʿAlí al-Sarráj al-Ṭúsí*, ed. R. Nicholson, 369, ll. 1-12), defines it as the locality "where man is led by his state and where he settles down" (*waṭan al-ʿabd ḥaythu 'ntahā bihi 'l-ḥāl wa 'staḳarra bihi 'l-ḳarār*). That is, *waṭan* is no longer a point of departure but rather a destination for man's activities and movements. An older Ṣūfī authority quoted by al-Sarrādj, Abū Sulaymān al-Dārānī (d. 215/830; on him, see R. Gramlich in *Oriens*, xxxiii [1992], 22-85), even uses the plural *waṭanāt* (here, probably the pl. of the *nomen vicis waṭna*) in the very general meaning of solid and unimpeachable foundations, and contrasts them with the *khaṭarāt* denoting furtiveness, casualness, and lack of reliability (*Lumaʿ*, 369, ll. 9-10). Finally, in the biographies of mystics collected by al-Sulamī (d. 412/1021), the notions of "silence" (*ṣamt*), i.e. of concentrating one's thoughts on God, as well as of *ṣidḳ* "truthfulness", are related to *waṭan* (*Ṭabaḳāt al-ṣūfiyya*, ed. Nūr al-Dīn Sharība, Cairo 1406/1986, 478, 747).

The Prophet Muḥammad is credited with the famous saying, "Love of the homeland is a sign of belief" (*ḥubb al-waṭan min al-īmān*), a proposition that was to have a great impact also on modern nationalist thought. This tenet predicated on the notion of *waṭan* was also adopted by the Ṣūfīs. When an adept of the 8th/14th century *shaykh* Ṣafī al-Dīn of Ardabīl, the eponym of the Ṣafawid order and state, wondered how love for a piece of land—a natural sentiment shared by many unbelievers such as the Christians of Europe—could possibly be declared proof of proper belief, the *shaykh* responded that *waṭan* did not simply mean a geographically-definable territory but rather the heavenly kingdom for which the seeker of truth is obliged to strive (Ibn-i Bazzāz, *Ṣafwat al-ṣafā*, quoted by A.K.S. Lambton, in ḳawmiyya. iii, at Vol. IV, 785b).

Bibliography: B. Lewis, *Patriotism and nationalism*, in *The Middle East and the West*, New York 1964, 75-80; U. Haarmann, *Glaubensvolk und Nation im islamischen und lateinischen Mittelalter*, in *Berlin-Brandenburgische Akademie der Wissenschaften. Berichte und Abhandlungen*, ii (1996), 161-99, esp. 165-9.

(U. Haarmann)

WAṬANIYYA (a.), nationalism, patriotism, civic pride, in all the modern applications of these terms. The word appeared at the end of the 19th century, in the context of the extension to the field of state politics of *waṭan* (pl. *awṭān*) "homeland", hitherto applied to place of birth or of residence. The noun-adjective *waṭanī* refers to the same sectors of meaning (autochthonous, national, patriotic), while the noun *muwāṭin* denotes a compatriot or fellow-citizen.

A pioneering role in the inculcation of these notions is to be credited to Rifāʿa Rāfiʿ al-Ṭahṭāwī [*q.v.*]. "Love of country" (*ḥubb al-waṭan*), in the modern sense of the term, spans his entire corpus, but he provides a more detailed analysis of the subject in a preface to *Manāhidj al-albāb al-miṣriyya fī mabāhidj al-ādāb al-ʿaṣriyya* (1869) and in a long section of *al-Murshid al-amīn li 'l-banāt wa 'l-banīn* (1873). He starts with *milla*, in the politico-administrative extensions that it acquired in the Ottoman empire [see millet], beyond its initial application to a religious community, since it also denotes territorial communities: *al-ahālī* (indigenous, autochthonous peoples), *al-raʿiyya* (subjects), *al-djins* (race, ethnic group) and *abnāʾ al-waṭan* (inhabitants, natives, compatriots). It is to these last—whether the reference is to established populations or to those who have come in search of refuge and subsequently settled in the locality—that the qualificatives *baladī/waṭanī* (compatriot/fellow-citizen) are applied. They are part of a "patriotic brotherhood", "over and above religious brotherhood", and share the same pride in common patrimony, implanted in this case in Egyptian pre-Islam. But it is the values of "civic pride" that are denoted by *waṭaniyya* when the context is the obligations required by "patriotism": contributing to anything which has the potential to promote the glory of the common homeland, guaranteeing its prosperity through the development of public utilities and accepting the laws of the country as incarnated in the person of its sovereign.

A transference of the principal connotation to that of "nationalism" [see ḳawmiyya. i] is first observed in resistance to the financial and political control exercised by the European creditors of the Egyptian debt (1876-82). Egyptian officers of established local families (*waṭaniyyūn*), opposed from the outset to the ascendancy of Turko-Circassians, sought to operate in conjunction with constitutionalist elements. A *Djamʿiyya Waṭaniyya* (later known as the National Party) represented their claims, from April 1879 onwards. Composite and unwieldy, this movement was part of the episode known as "the ʿUrābī Pasha [*q.v.*] revolution". Its defeat was sealed by the British military occupation of Egypt.

For decades to come, *waṭaniyya* was applied to the nationalist form of Egyptian patriotism, in the sense of a demand for return of Egypt to the Egyptians, a national movement for liberation from British domination. This found its expression in political platforms, the subject of competition; for example, before the First World War, the "national" Party (*al-Ḥizb al-Waṭanī*), was the rival of *Ḥizb al-Umma* ("party of the nation").

Elsewhere, in the Mashriḳ as in the Maghrib, while trade union and other organisations describe themselves as national (*waṭaniyya*), in reference to territory produced by colonial dismemberment, *waṭaniyya* denotes the conceptual and practical aspects of what was known since the 1920s as *ḥarakat al-taḥrīr al-waṭanī* ("movement of national liberation"). It is most often applied to a particular, limited territory, but sometimes enlarged to encompass the Arab world (*niḍāl al-ʿarab al-waṭanī, ḥurriyyāt al-ʿarab al-waṭaniyya*, in the context of their struggle or their freedom). But both the adjective and the substantive can denote the positive sense and the pejorative sense of the term, for example, *al-waṭaniyya al-fāshistiyya* and *al-waṭaniyya al-istiʿmāriyya* (fascist nationalism, colonialist nationalism). It is not until the eve of the Second World War that a precise distinction is drawn, in ideological terms, between *waṭaniyya* and *ḳawmiyya*. The first refers to a territory, the second to the inhabitants of the latter, to the people, with the same convergent nuance as is attested elsewhere. Thus in 1936, in reference to the national sentiment of Abyssinians confronted by the Italian conquest, the expression *shuʿūr waṭanī ḳawmī* is encountered. But it is not always a case of redundancy, or of distinguishing oneself, as in Morocco, by using a term equivalent to that retained by an adversary or competitor. After 1933, but especially from 1936 onwards, in the columns of the Libano-Syrian journal *al-Ṭalīʿa* (a platform shared by the various branches of the Eastern national movement), although less common than *waṭaniyya* and its derivatives, *ḳawmiyya* and its derivatives made their appearance and their meaning is made precise, independently of territorial, national or regional extension, by reference to the German concept of *Volkstum*; rather than the concept of territory, it is that of the people, in the ethnoracial sense, in the blood line, that holds sway.

Differences are to be noted from the 1940s onwards. Begun by Syria and Lebanon, accession to political independence without limitations imposed by treaty became the norm. The formation of the League of Arab States (1945) gave credibility to elements favouring Arab unity, the successors of those who in the 1920s had opposed the Anglo-French partition of "natural" Syria. The party of Arab rebirth, *Ḥizb al-Baʿth al-ʿArabī*, the proponents of Nasserism, then the movement of Arab nationalists (*ḥarakat al-ḳawmiyyīn al-ʿarab*) drew a clear distinction between *ḳawmiyya* (Arab nationalism, Pan-Arabism) and *waṭaniyya*, the latter being out of favour as denoting narrow, national patriotism. Baʿthist ideology developed the terms *iḳlīmiyya/ḳuṭriyya* "regionalism" as a means of denouncing these tendencies. Marxist tendencies were most often the target, at the very time when the *ḳawmiyyūn* were professing an "Arab socialism". Their reference to *umamiyya* (the equivalent here of "internationalism") is criticised as a consequence of their *waṭaniyya/ḳuṭriyya*, limited to "class" and irrespective of the Arab *umma*. Lexical and conceptual analysis of the principal charters and of the congresses of the 1960s and the 1970s of the Arab world (an exercise previously in progress, in academic studies and in seminars under the present writer's supervision) reveals, however, a preponderance in this field for derivatives of the root *w-ṭ-n* over derivatives of the root *ḳ-w-m*.

In fact, successive failures of experiments aimed at Arab unity, in whatever form, have placed the *ḳawmiyyūn* on the "territorial" plain where they criticised the *waṭaniyyūn* for their self-cantonisation, and recent debates. In particular, an inter-Arab seminar held in Damascus at the end of 1996, made it clear that, despite the need to display realism and commitment to the preservation of the democratic achievements of each country, these *waṭaniyyūn* have not neglected to adopt a position favourable to the notion of Arab unity, on the basis of shared patrimony and shared destiny.

Bibliography: See the *Bibl.* to ḲAWMIYYA. i; also J. Berque (dir.) and J. Couland (ed.), *Bibliographie de la culture arabe contemporaine*, Paris 1981, iv; W. Chaaban, *L'apparition de la terminologie socialiste dans les textes arabes au Liban et en Syrie (1871-1939)*, unpubl. doctoral thesis, Univ. of Paris I 1987; B. Lewis, *The political language of Islam*, Chicago 1988, 40-1.

(J. COULAND)

WATHANIYYA (A.), idolatry. In classical Arabic it is the phrase *ʿibādat al-aṣnām* (or *al-awthān*) that denotes idolatry, while idolaters are called *ʿabadat al-aṣnām* (or *al-awthān*). The term *wathaniyya*, still absent from the *Lisān al-ʿArab* of Ibn Manẓūr (d. 711/1311), figures in the *Kashshāf* (1516), compiled in 1158/1745 by al-Tahānawī. According to him, the term denotes: "A group of unbelievers who worship idols while asserting that God is one. They are counted among the associators because they profess the plurality of that which deserves to be worshipped, not because they profess the plurality of the Necessary Being in itself; they do not give idols the attributes of divinity, although they apply the name to them. In fact, they take them to be the statues of prophets, ascetics, angels or stars that are taken as objects of veneration, with the aim of approaching through them that which is a god in reality (*tawaṣṣul^{an} bihā ilā mā huwa ilāh^{un} ḥaḳīkat^{an}*). This is the meaning that is conveyed by the *Sharḥ al-Mawāḳif* (of al-Djurdjānī, d. 816/1413) and the gloss on it supplied by [Ḥasan] al-Čelebī in the study of *tawḥīd*."

It is appropriate to examine (1) the vocabulary of idols in the Ḳurʾān and in *ḥadīth*; (2) the various categories of idolaters known to Muslims; (3) opinions regarding the origin of idolatry; and (4) idolatry in the context of *tawḥīd* (and its refutation).

In the Ḳurʾān, idols are explicitly mentioned with the use of two words: *ṣanam* [*q.v.*], five times, always in the plural *aṣnām*, and *wathan*, three times, always in the plural *awthān*. Of these eight instances, six relate to Abraham, while VII, 138 (*aṣnām*) anticipates a passage dealing with the Golden Calf, and XXII, 30 warns against defilement by idols (*awthān*) of the pre-Islamic pilgrimage. Scholars are divided as to the difference in meaning between the two terms. Al-Ṭabarī, xiii, 228 (*ad* Ḳurʾān, XIV, 35) cites Mudjāhid, according to whom the *ṣanam* is "a fashioned similitude" (*al-timthāl al-muṣawwar*) which would distinguish it from the simple *wathan*. The same direction is followed by Ibn al-Kalbī (d. *ca.* 204/820), *al-Aṣnām*, 47d (cf. 29d): "If it is worked in wood, in gold or in silver in the likeness of man, it is a *ṣanam*." But according to one of the views conveyed by the *LA* in its two entries (and followed by al-Tahānawī, *loc. cit.*), on the contrary, it is the *wathan* which is characterised by the representation of a body (*djuththa*); in fact, in the Ḳurʾān, two instances of *awthān* refer to the idols smashed by Abraham, which are clearly statues (*tamāthīl*, according to XXI, 52). In another passage of al-Ṭabarī, vii, 244 (*ad* Ḳurʾān, VI, 74), the two words seem to be regarded as equivalents. Among many authors, they are interchangeable. This seems already to be the case in canonical *ḥadīth*s, where one or the other term is used quite regularly.

Alongside these idols, i.e. tri-dimensional representations of animate beings addressed by a cult, there were also sacred stones [see NUṢUB]. These are mentioned three times in the Ḳurʾān, in V, 3, in LXX, 43 and (in the plural *anṣāb*) in V, 90, and there are several other references in the canonical traditions.

These fundamental texts, when they are not speaking of biblical characters, attribute idolatry to the pre-Islamic Arabs. The Muslim authors who follow echo this trend, and many of them devote long articles, or entire works, to the subject. Thus Ibn al-Kalbī, not only in his well-known *al-Aṣnām*, but also in his lost book *Adyān al-ʿArab* and doubtless in *Mathālib al-ʿArab*, which survives in manuscript form. Al-Djāḥiẓ, for his part, wrote an *Adyān al-ʿArab* and an *al-Aṣnām*. Unfortunately they are lost, as is a work by ʿAlī b. al-Ḥusayn b. Fuḍayl (end of 3rd/9th century), *al-Aṣnām wa-mā kānat al-ʿArab wa 'l-ʿAdjam taʿbudu min dūni 'llāh* (according to *Fihrist*, ed. Tadjaddud, Tehran 1391 A.H./1350 A.H.S./1971, 138). Such writings give information, which can be checked and complemented by other means, regarding the traditional religion of Central Arabia and its divinities [see HUBAL; ISĀF WA-NĀʾILA; AL-LĀT].

But Islam, born in the midst of idolaters, soon encountered others in India, whose immense numbers and intense fervour intrigued writers such as al-Djāḥiẓ or Abū Zayd al-Balkhī. The Hindu cult of images could not fail to strike, and to offend, Muslims with its sumptuousness and alien nature. These "idols" were described in the *Kitāb fīhi milal al-Hind wa-adyānuhā*, composed as early as 180/800, on his return from India, by an envoy of the vizier Yaḥyā b. Khālid al-Barmakī.

The work is lost, but is said to be the basis of all subsequent works. The latter often mention the *bidada* (plural of *budd*), i.e. statues of Buddha (or of Bodhisattva). For while Buddhism had virtually disappeared from the Indian subcontinent, it had taken firm root in the eastern half of the Iranian world and was present there on the arrival of Islam [see SUMANIYYA].

On the other hand, Muslim authors drew attention to accounts available to them concerning the idols of ancient Persia before the introduction of the cult of fire (*Murūdj*, ed. Pellat, §§ 1373, 1400, 1403; al-Shahrastānī, *Milal*, ii, 1224, tr. ii, 494). They were even more interested in the intriguing "Sabians" who are mentioned three times in the Ḳur'ān, and whose name the inhabitants of Ḥarrān appropriated, in 218/993 or just before, in order to benefit from the *djizya* [see ṢĀBI'A]. These last-named followers of Hellenistic cults are persistently credited by the Muslims with a veneration of the stars that would finally be corrupted into the worship of idols. The most remarkable presentation and refutation of this real or alleged religion are to be found in the *Milal* of al-Shahrastānī. According to him, the "primitive Sabians" addressed their cult only to the Spiritual beings (*rūḥāniyyāt*) as the natural intercessors in the presence of the Lord of lords, but the need of visible intermediaries subsequently introduced the cult of stars as Dwellings (*hayākil*) of the Spiritual beings, then of idols as representations (*ashkhāṣ*) of these Dwellings.

Furthermore, African cults are occasionally mentioned by Arab geographers and historians. Fetishes first appear in the work of Ibn Ḥazm with the name *daḳḳūr*, pl. *daḳāḳira*, then in the work of others in the form *dakkūr*, pl. *dakākīr* (cf. Monnot 1986, 115).

Over and above the strangeness and the provocation inherent in the idolatrous cults, these posed a problem for the doctrine of Islam according to which monotheism is inherent in the original nature (*fiṭra* [*q.v.*]) of man, that is, in the disposition imprinted upon him by the Creator. How then did idolatry come into being? The most thorough answer is proposed by Abū Zayd al-Balkhī (d. 322/934) in *al-Radd ʿalā ʿabadat al-aṣnām*. This refutation of idolaters is lost, but fortunately a long quotation from it has been preserved by al-Rāzī in his *Tafsīr*, xxx, 143 (tr. Monnot, 1986, 215-18). As for the origins of idolatry in the world, Abū Zayd offers no fewer than seven possibilities.

According to the first, "Idolatry is nothing other than a consequence of the doctrine according to which God is a localised entity"; the *tadjsīm* of God and of His angels is responsible for it. This explanation (reproduced for example in al-Masʿūdī, *Murūdj*, § 1370) is explicitly attributed to Abū Maʿshar, as is confirmed by other authors (cf. Monnot, 1986, 226). The second interpretation is that the Sabians "introduced the cult of idols with the aim of establishing a cult for the stars" (cf. *Murūdj*, *loc. cit.*): this is the most widely held view. The third reckons to have found the origin of talismans in judicial astrology. The fourth interpretation is that idols were initially the statues of righteous individuals, venerated for having won the favour of God in their lifetimes. The fifth interpretation, closely related to the previous one, consists in what is known in the West as euhemerism: the desire to preserve the memory and a sense of presence of great ancestors degenerating into worship of their images. The five Noachic idols of Ḳur'ān, LXXI, 23-4, are thus said to have originally represented five sons of Adam (cf., in a similar sense, al-Bukhārī, *Ṣaḥīḥ*, *tafsīr*, lxxi). The sixth interpretation is that the existence of extraordinary properties in a body is explained by the inherence (*ḥulūl*) of a god in it. Finally, according to the seventh interpretation, idols are said simply to serve as a *miḥrāb* for the worship of God.

In al-Rāzī, xiii, 36 (revised and abridged by al-Tahānawī, 771), the first two general interpretations are found in reverse order, complemented by a third, this being that idols represent the angels appointed by God to govern various elements and phenomena of nature. As for the introduction of idolatry among the Arabs, the explanation currently in favour places the responsibility on ʿAmr b. Luḥayy; he allegedly brought back to Mecca from al-Balḳā', in Syria, an idol of Hubal.

Ḳur'ān, VI, 81, or XXII, 30, accuse the idolaters of giving associates to God [see SHIRK], and Muslims like al-Rāzī (ii, 112; xiii, 35) make them one of the four or five categories of associators. However, according to Abū Zayd and others following his lead, idolatry is not directly opposed to *tawḥīd*, since no-one would be stupid enough to identify the Creator with a piece of wood. But the error of the idolaters, motivated by the desire for a presence (cf. *Milal*, 129), is twofold. First, they suppose that God has a form, which enables them to make an image of Him; this amounts to assimilation (*tashbīh*; on the prohibition of images of animate beings, see ṢŪRA). Furthermore, they imagine that they can address their appeals to these objects, whether through attributing to them the role of intermediary (see *Milal*, 770-2) or at the very least through directing prayer physically towards them (see Abū Zayd, seventh interpretation; *Mughnī*, v, 158; *Milal*, 655). This is inadmissible without revealed indication (*Milal*, 1295), and the worship of intermediaries is even contrary to reason, according to ʿAbd al-Djabbār (*Mughnī*, v, 158). In any case, the fundamental argument, even when it is left implicit, is without doubt that of the Ḳur'ān (XXI, 66; cf. VI, 74; XXVI, 72), amply propounded by al-Shahrastānī in his refutation of the Sabians: idols, which neither benefit nor cause harm, are powerless and pointless.

Bibliography: 1. Principal sources. Ibn Hishām, *Sīra*, Cairo 1375/1955, i, 78-91, Eng. tr. A. Guillaume, *The life of Muhammad*, Oxford 1955, 35-9; Ibn al-Kalbī, *K. al-Aṣnām*, ed. Aḥmad Zakī Pasha, Cairo 1924, Eng. tr. N.A. Faris, *The Book of Idols*, Princeton 1952, text and Fr. tr. W. Atallah, Paris 1969; Ṭabarī, *Tafsīr*, 30 vols. Cairo 1388-96/1968-76; Masʿūdī, *Murūdj*; Ḳāḍī ʿAbd al-Djabbār, *Mughnī*, 16 vols. Cairo 1959-65, v, 155-9, Fr. tr. Monnot, Paris 1986, 232-7; Shahrastānī, *Milal*, ed. Badrān, Cairo 1370-5/1951-5, Fr. tr. D. Gimaret, J. Jolivet and G. Monnot, 2 vols. Louvain-Paris 1986-93; Fakhr al-Dīn Rāzī, *al-Tafsīr al-kabīr*, 32 vols., Cairo 1352/1933, repr. Tehran n.d.; Tahānawī, *Kashshāf iṣṭilāḥāt al-funūn*, Bibl. Indica, 2 vols. Calcutta 1862.

2. Other texts and studies. T. Fahd, *Le panthéon de l'Arabie centrale à la veille de l'Hégire*, Paris 1968; J.M. Cuoq, *Recueil des sources arabes concernant l'Afrique occidentale du VIIIe au XIVe siècle (Bilād al-Sūdān)*, Paris 1975, 2nd. corr. and enlarged ed. Paris 1985; N.Q. King, *Encounters between Islam and the African traditional religions*, in A.T. Welch and P. Cachia (eds.), *Islam: past influence and future challenge*, Edinburgh 1979, 296-311; J.F.P. Hopkins and N. Levtzion (eds.), *Corpus of early Arabic sources for West African history*, Cambridge 1981; G. Monnot, *Islam et religions*, Paris 1986; idem, *Les dieux dans le Coran*, in J. Waardenburg (ed.), *Scholarly approaches to religion. Interreligious perceptions and Islam*, Berne 1995, 245-9.

(G. MONNOT)

AL-WĀTHIḲ BI 'LLĀH, ABŪ DJAʿFAR HĀRŪN B. AL-MUʿTAṢIM, ʿAbbāsid caliph. He was given the name Hārūn after his grandfather Hārūn al-Rashīd; his mother was a Greek slave called Ḳarāṭīs.

On the day that his father al-Muʿtaṣim bi 'llāh [*q.v.*] died (18 Rabīʿ I 227/5 January 842), al-Wāthiḳ was proclaimed his successor. Before al-Muʿtaṣim's death, an alleged descendant of the Umayyads, named Abū Ḥarb, usually called al-Mubarḳaʿ [*q.v.*] "the veiled one" from the veil that he always wore, had provoked a dangerous rising in Palestine, and Radjāʾ b. Ayyūb al-Ḥiḍārī, whom al-Muʿtaṣim sent against him, could at first make no progress. Soon after the accession of al-Wāthiḳ, Damascus also became the scene of a great rising; the rebels shut the governor up in the citadel and encamped on the plain of Mardj Rāhiṭ not far east of the town, but they were very soon routed by Radjāʾ who had been recalled from Palestine to meet the danger. He next turned his attention to al-Mubarḳaʿ. After a section of the latter's followers had left him because the sowing season was approaching, Radjāʾ succeeded in defeating and capturing him.

The Bedouin around Medina also gave the caliph trouble. When the Banū Sulaym plundered the market places of the Ḥidjāz, the governor of Medina sent a large army under Ḥammād b. Djarīr al-Ṭabarī against them; but he was defeated and slain, so that al-Wāthiḳ had to turn to the tried general Bugha al-Kabīr [*q.v.*]. In Shaʿbān 230/April-May 845, Bugha entered Medina and, after defeating the Banū Sulaym and taking the prisoners back to Medina, performed the Pilgrimage to Mecca, and then turned his attention to the Banū Hilāl, who had also taken part in the uprising. The most guilty were imprisoned in Medina and the others pardoned. Bugha now marched against the Banū Murra and the Banū Fazāra, who had seized the town of Fadak [*q.v.*], but as soon as he appeared they abandoned the town and took flight (231/845-6). In the meanwhile, the prisoners escaped from Medina and killed their warders, but were cut down by the citizens of the town with the help of the many black slaves in Medina. In the following year, Bugha had also to fight against the Banū Numayr in al-Yamāma and only subdued them after much difficulty. There were also troubles among the Khāridjīs and the Kurds. The *Sīrat al-mudjāhidīn* mentions that al-Wāthiḳ, meanwhile, meditated an expedition against Constantinople [see DHU 'L-HIMMA].

Al-Wāthiḳ died on 23 Dhu 'l-Ḥidjdja 232/10 August 847 at the age of 32, or according to others, 34 or 36. He had not the gifts of a great ruler, and his brief reign was not distinguished by remarkable events. The caliph's character also was not such as to make him beloved. It is true that he was conventionally liberal to the poor in Mecca and Medina, and he also treated the ʿAlids with great benevolence and took a considerable interest in poetry and singing, being a musician and composer himself. He favoured the singer Mukhāriḳ [*q.v.*], but was disappointed when the latter altered the notes of songs. For the rest, he is described as covetous, intolerant and devoted to sensual pleasures. At his accession, he confirmed the Baṣran profligate poet al-Ḍaḥḥāk al-Bāhilī [*q.v.*], nicknamed *al-Khalīʿ* "the debauched one", as court poet. He also extorted huge sums of money from high officials. Al-Wāthiḳ was also an ardent Muʿtazilī. The well-respected Aḥmad b. Naṣr b. Mālik al-Khuzāʿī prepared a plot to dethrone the caliph and put a check on the arrogance of his Turkish commanders. By accident, the signal was given too soon (Shaʿbān 231/April 856), so that the authorities were able to uncover the conspiracy without difficulty. When brought before the caliph, Aḥmad b. Naṣr was questioned not about the plot but about the Ḳurʾān. His answers enraged the caliph to such an extent that the latter personally oversaw al-Khuzāʿī's decapitation. Later, however, al-Wāthiḳ's original enthusiasm for the Muʿtazila seems to have evaporated.

The vizier all through al-Wāthiḳ's reign was Ibn al-Zayyāt, against whom al-Wāthiḳ had sworn vengeance during his father's reign; but once acceded to power, he seems to have found him indispensable. The period of Ibn al-Zayyāt's second vizierate thus began, in which he showed himself cruel and avaricious, inventing a spiked iron cylinder (*tannūr*) for torturing his victims, in which however he was himself to die when al-Mutawakkil came to the throne in 232/847 [see IBN AL-ZAYYĀT]. Ibn al-Zayyāt had quarrelled with the Chief Ḳāḍī Aḥmad b. Abī Duʾād [*q.v.*], but had attempted to restrain the ambitions of Turkish generals like Aytākh [see AYTĀKH AL-TURKĪ, in Suppl.]. In general, one can say that the administrative and religious policies of the previous reign were continued with little change.

Interesting episodes reported from al-Wāthiḳ's reign relate to his apparent intellectual curiosity. In 225/840 the Turkish people of the Ḳirgiz [*q.v.*], who nomadised to the north of Lake Baikal, attacked the Uyghurs [*q.v.*] and drove them from the region of the Orkhon and Selenga rivers in Mongolia into eastern Turkestan (the later Chinese province of Sinkiang [*q.v.*]) (see W. Samolin, *East Turkistan to the twelfth century. A political history*, The Hague 1964, 69-70). These population movements in Inner Asia may have caused al-Wāthiḳ to "dream" that the barrier (*sadd*) of Dhu 'l-Ḳarnayn [see ISKANDAR] had been breached. Ibn Khurradādhbih, 162 ff., relates that Sallām al-Tardjumān was sent by the caliph to investigate the story of Dhu 'l-Ḳarnayn's barrier and that Sallām told him about his adventures in search of it and showed him the report which he had drawn up for the caliph [see SALLĀM AL-TARDJUMĀN, in Suppl.]. Ibn Khurradādhbih also relates (106-7) that al-Wāthiḳ sent the celebrated astronomer and mathematician Muḥammad b. Mūsā al-Khwārazmī [*q.v.*] to the land of Rūm in order to investigate the story of the "Men of al-Raḳīm", i.e. the Seven Sleepers [see AṢḤĀB AL-KAHF].

Bibliography: Ṭabarī, iii, 1329-57, Eng. tr. J.L. Kraemer, *The History of al-Ṭabarī. XXXIV. Incipient decline*, Albany 1989, 3-44; Ibn al-Athīr, vi, 372, 376, vii, 6-9, 12-26; Masʿūdī, *Murūdj*, index; Yaʿḳūbī, *Taʾrīkh*, ii, 584-90; *Aghānī*, see Guidi, *Tables alphabétiques*; Ibn al-Ṭiḳṭaḳā, *al-Fakhrī*, ed. Derenbourg, 323-5; Ibn Shākir al-Kutubī, *Fawāt al-wafayāt*, ed. ʿAbbās, iv, 228-30; G. Weil, *Geschichte der Chalifen*, ii, 337-6; Sir William Muir, *The Caliphate, its rise, decline, and fall*³, 522-5; D. Sourdel, *Le vizirat ʿabbāside*, Damascus 1959-60, i, 260-70; H. Kennedy, *The Prophet and the age of the caliphates*, London and New York 1986, 168.

(K.V. ZETTERSTÉEN-[C.E. BOSWORTH and E. VAN DONZEL])

WATHĪḲA (A.), pl. *wathāʾiḳ*, from the verb *wathuka* "to be firm, assured", hence a document that certifies the commission of a promise or legal act, such as a covenant, contract, etc., or the appointment of a person to an office. It thus becomes a general term for an official or legal document or formulary; see for these, DIPLOMATIC. i, and on the general usage of the term, Dozy, *Supplément*, ii, 780. In modern Arabic usage, *wathāʾiḳ* is often used in the sense of "official records, archives", housed in a *dār al-wathāʾiḳ*.

(ED.)

al-WĀTHIĶĪ, Abū Muḥammad ʿAbd Allāh b. ʿUthmān, poet and political claimant of the second half of the 4th/10th and the first years of the 5th/11th centuries, who claimed descent from the ʿAbbāsid caliph al-Wāthiķ [*q.v.*].

His younger contemporary al-Thaʿālibi gives specimens of his verses plus biographical information (*Yatīma*, ed. ʿAbd al-Ḥamīd, iv, 192-3). Al-Wāthiķī began his career in ʿIrāķ and al-Djazīra as a court witness and preacher, but became involved in political intrigues. He fled eastwards to the Transoxanian lands of the Ķarakhānids [see ilek-khāns], where he produced for the Khān a forged document stating that the caliph al-Ķādir [*q.v.*] had appointed him as his *walī al-ʿahd* or heir, and he subsequently expressed intentions of marching on Baghdād to claim his rights to the throne. His schemes were unsuccessful and were related to the caliph (who cannot have taken them very seriously!). Al-Wāthiķī had to flee again, and ended up at the court of Maḥmūd of Ghazna, who imprisoned him till he died.

Bibliography: The main sources are Thaʿālibī (see above) and the extant fragment of Hilāl al-Ṣābi''s history. These are used in C.E. Bosworth, *Notes on the lives of some ʿAbbāsid princes and descendants*, in *The Maghreb Review*, xix/3-4 (1994) (= *Homage à André Miquel*), 281-2 (also in *The Arabs, Byzantium and Iran. Studies in early Islamic history and culture*, Variorum, London 1996, no. V); cf. also Barthold, *Turkestan down to the Mongol invasion*³, 258.

(C.E. Bosworth)

WATHĪMA b. **MŪSĀ** b. al-Furāt al-Fārisī al-Fasawī (in addition, in the heading of his book, al-Azhar al-Ghanī), Muslim historian and trader in silk, of Persian origin and a resident of Fusṭāṭ. The date of his birth is unknown, but he hailed from a Persian town renowned for the commerce of silk (on Fasā, see Yāķūt, *Buldān*, Beirut 1374-6/1955-7, iv, 260-1). To this natal milieu, Wathīma owed his profession, which adhered to his own name in the form of a nickname: al-Washshā' or trader in embroideries. He left the town of his birth for Baṣra, then Egypt and al-Andalus, but for how long is unknown. What is certain is that he returned to Egypt, settling in Fusṭāṭ where he remained until his death on 10 Djumādā II 237/9 December 851.

Alongside his trade, Wathīma gained a reputation as a specialist in the Islamic tradition, as is attested by certain sources including Ibn al-Faraḍī, *Ta'rīkh*, ii, 36, where he writes *expressis verbis* that the author "has departed for the Maghrib or al-Andalus, having devoted himself to the transmission of *ḥadīth*". Furthermore, several sources mention two of his works:

(1) *K. fī Akhbār al-ridda* (sometimes without *fī*), of which Ibn Khallikān in particular (ed. ʿAbbās, vi, 12, cf. others such as Ibn Shākir al-Kutubī, ii, 625, and Yāķūt, *Irshād*, vii, 226) has described the contents: "He has put into writing a book telling the story of the *ridda*, with the vicissitudes of the tribes who repudiated Islam after the death of the Prophet, the campaigns conducted against them by Abū Bakr, the battles that took place between them, and the names of those who returned to Islam, as well as those who opposed the *zakāt* and other details concerning Khālid b. al-Walīd al-Makhzūmī and his struggle against Mālik b. Nuwayra al-Yarbūʿī whom he killed in 12/634, the funeral elegy of (delivered by?) the latter's brother Mutammim, and what other poets had to say on the subject." Ibn Ḥadjar al-ʿAsķalānī apparently still had the manuscript in his possession, since he often cites it in his *Iṣāba*. Hoenerbach, 39, collected these quotations, 110 passages in total, classified and translated them into German; the impression gained from his work is that Ibn Khallikān, in his aforementioned analysis, did not follow the genuine order of the book, which was most probably arranged in historical, geographical and chronological fashion, as is observed in his second book on biblical history, and perhaps also by tribes, as may be supposed on the basis of his treatment of the *ridda* of the Banū Rabīʿa. In any case, all that remain are a few fragments which do not give a comprehensive idea of the work, which was very highly regarded by the bio-bibliographers and, according to Ibn al-ʿImād, *Shadharat al-dhahāb*, ii, 89, was not only very well written but also, and most importantly, far-reaching. Other manuscripts, yet to be properly exploited, could yield further quotations, such as *al-Iktifā'* of al-Kalāʿī, see below Fariq, *A valuable historical ms.*, 164, and *Ta'rīkh al-Ridda*, 109, 116, 145, 146.

(2) *K. Bad' al-khalķ wa-ķiṣaṣ al-anbiyā'*, which is not mentioned by sources as e.g. Ibn Khallikān, *Wafayāt, loc. cit.*, and Ibn Shākir al-Kutubī, *Fawāt al-Wafayāt*, 626. However Ibn ʿAbd al-Ḥakam quotes Wathīma, as does, naturally, a specialised source like Ibn Hishām al-Ḥadjarī, 108, 110, 127, 153; but it is Ibn Ḥadjar al-ʿAsķalānī, *Lisān al-mīzān*, vi, 217, who is the closest to the historical reality, also in terms of the grandeur of the work: *Taṣnīf kabīr fī 'l-mubtada' wa-ķiṣaṣ al-anbiyā'*, in two volumes, and after him al-Sakhāwī, *al-Iʿlān*, 171. The manuscript of one of the two volumes is in fact to be found in the Vatican Library, specifically the second part, which begins with al-Khiḍr and Moses and ends with the advent of the Prophet Muḥammad; the first, covering the period between the earliest creation and this point, being lost. Wathīma refers to numerous authors, principally Wahb b. Munabbih, and others, whose material he would have found mainly in Egypt, specifically in the private library of the judge of the country, ʿAbd Allāh b. Lahīʿa. Since those involved were Egyptian informants, disciples of the judge or settlers in Egypt, they conveyed primary information to Wathīma in a very accurate fashion, and he supplemented it with other data in such a way that we have primary sources, such as those of Wahb b. Munabbih, which can be reconstructed almost entirely by these means (with successive additions being closely followed; see an edition of this text, with a monograph analysing all the strata of *isnād*s in the book, in R.G. Khoury, *Les legendes prophétiques dans l'Islam*, 158 ff.). This accuracy of the written transmission has made it possible to obtain a complete version of the damaged pages of Wahb's *Ḥadīth Dāwūd* "Story of David", of which there were only fragments, sometimes just a few lines or words, as the papyrus edition of Wahb, 34 ff., shows very clearly (see Khoury, *Les légendes prophétiques*, 164 and n. 289, and wahb b. munabbih).

Thus the *K. Bad' al-khalķ* assumes a capital importance and remains, despite some criticism directed at Wathīma the *muḥaddith*, "the best that has ever been composed in this discipline", *min aṣlaḥ mā ṣunnifa fī dhālika 'l-fann* (Ibn Ḥadjar, *Lisān al-mīzān*, vi, 217), since it dates back to the first sources and thus rescues from oblivion the most ancient versions of biblical or prophetic stories in Islam. It enlarges the primary data, such as that contained in the Heidelberg papyrus on David, but without altering the originals which it conserves very accurately. Hence its immense value for the study of the archaic literature of the three first centuries of the Hidjra.

Bibliography: 1. Sources. Ibn al-Faraḍī,

K. Taʾrīkh ʿulamāʾ al-Andalus, ed. Codera, Madrid 1891-2; Ibn Ḥadjar al-ʿAsḳalānī, *Tahdhīb al-tahdhīb*, Ḥaydarābād 1907; idem, *Lisān al-mīzān*, ²Beirut 1971; Ibn ʿAbd al-Ḥakam, *Futūḥ Miṣr wa-akhbāruhā*, ed. Torrey, New Haven 1922; W. Hoenerbach, *Waṯīma's Kitāb al-Ridda aus Ibn Ḥağar's Iṣāba*, Wiesbaden 1951; Ibn Shākir al-Kutubī, *Fawāt al-Wafayāt*, Cairo 1951; Ibn Hishām al-Hadjarī, *Ḳiṣaṣ al-anbiyāʾ*, ms. Alexandria, Balad B 1249.

2. Studies. R. Blachère, *Regards sur la littérature narrative en arabe au Ier siècle de l'Hégire*, in *Semitica*, vi (1956), 73-86; K.A. Fariq, *A valuable historical ms. of Arabic al-Iktifāʾ*, in *IC*, xxxiii (1959), 161-8; idem, *Taʾrīkh al-Ridda* (extracts from *al-Iktifāʾ*), New Delhi 1970; T. Nagel, *Die Qiṣaṣ al-anbiyāʾ. Ein Beitrag zur arab. Literaturgeschichte*, Bonn 1967; J. Pauliny, *Ein Werk "Qiṣaṣ al-anbiyāʾ" von ʿAbdallāh Ibn Saʿīd al-Hiğrī*, in *Asian and African Stud.* (Bratislava), vi (1970), 87-91; idem, *Zur Rolle der Quṣṣāṣ bei der Entstehung und Überlieferung der populären Prophetenlegenden*, in *ibid.*, x (1974), 125-41; R.G. Khoury, *Wahb b. Munabbih. Der Heidelberger Papyrus PSR Heid. Arab 23. Leben und Werk des Dichters*, Wiesbaden 1972; idem, *Die Bedeutung der Handschrift Badʾ al-ḫalq wa-qiṣaṣ al-anbiyāʾ des ʿUmāra b. Waṯīma al-Fārisī*, in *ZDMG*, Suppl. II (1974), 186-91; idem, *Les légendes prophétiques dans l'Islam depuis le Ier jusqu'au IIIe siècle H. D'après le manuscrit d'Abū Rifāʿa ʿUmāra b. Waṯīma, K. Badʾ al-ḫalq wa-qiṣaṣ al-anbiyāʾ. Avec éd. crit. du texte*, Wiesbaden 1978; idem, *ʿAbd Allāh Ibn Lahīʿa, juge et grand maître de l'École Égyptienne. Avec éd. crit. de l'unique rouleau de papyrus arabe conservé à Heidelberg*, Wiesbaden 1986; idem, *Importance de ʿAbd Allāh Ibn Lahīʿa, juge de l'Égypte, et de sa bibliothèque privée dans la codification et diffusion des livres des deux premiers siècles islamiques. Le manuscrit arabe et la codicologie*, Rabat 1994, 105-14; H. Schwarzbaum, *Biblical and extrabibl. legends in Islamic folk-literature*, Walldorf-Hessen 1982. See also the *Bibl.* to WAHB B. MUNABBIH.

(R.G. Khoury)

WATHTHĀB b. **SĀBIḲ** al-**NUMAYRĪ**, head of the section of the Banū Numayr [*q.v.*] dominating part of Diyār Muḍar and the town of Ḥarrān, d. 410/1019 (Ibn al-Athīr, ix, 312, 413, 443, x, 443). The texts give few details on his origins and most do not even give his father's name; nevertheless, his descendants can clearly be pinpointed in northern Syria and Diyār Muḍar and played an important role. It is this line which is mainly dealt with here.

Some of the Numayr are already mentioned in central Syria around Damascus at the time of the great revolt of Abu 'l-Haytham in the time of Hārūn al-Rashīd (Ibn ʿAsākir, *T. Dimashk, ʿĀṣim-ʿĀʾid*, ed. Shukrī Fayṣal, Damascus 1977, 402) At the opening of the 4th/10th century they were among the tribes accompanying the Carmathians in the attack on the *Mardj* of Damascus. In the middle of the century they were in the regions of Sindjār and Mawṣil, opposing, in company with other tribes such as the Kilāb, Ḳushayr, ʿUḳayl, Hilāl, Sulaym and Ḳays ʿAylān, the two Ḥamdānid princes [see ḤAMDĀNIDS] Nāṣir al-Dawla (attack on Mawṣil, 359/970) and Sayf al-Dawla of Aleppo. Less vigorous than the Kilāb, they were expelled from Diyār Rabīʿa towards the Syrian Desert and thence by Sayf al-Dawla north of the Euphrates into Diyār Muḍar. In 380/990, being largely Shīʿī in faith, they supported an abortive attempt to restore the Ḥamdānids in Mawṣil. In 395/1005, several thousand cavalrymen of Numayr and Kilāb, led by the ruler in Sarūdj, Waththāb b. Djaʿfar (perhaps = Waththāb b. Sābiḳ al-Numayrī) supported the *ghāzī* Aṣfar of Taghlib against the Byzantines (for details of all these, see Th. Bianquis, *Damas et la Syrie sous la domination fāṭimide*, Damascus 1987, i, 310 n. 1). At the end of the century, the Numayr of Waththāb b. Sābiḳ constituted a principality in Diyār Muḍar around Ḥarrān [*q.v.*]. Like the Kilāb in northern Syria, the Marwānids in Diyār Bakr and the ʿUḳaylids in Diyār Rabīʿa, they chose to protect and administer for their own advantage the sedentary lands and towns rather than to pillage them, as did at this time the Banu 'l-Djarrāḥ, a Transjordanian section of the Yamanī Ṭayyiʾ. Depending on events, they also held other towns of the region such as Sarūdj, al-Ruhā/Edessa, Raḳḳa and Rāfiḳa. Having gathered together "Arabs", Waththāb sought Byzantine help in order to attack the Kurd Naṣr al-Dawla Ibn Marwān [*q.v.*] in Diyār Bakr, which he raided and then pillaged.

The latter, with help from his ʿUḳaylid ally, the *amīr* of Mawṣil Ḳirwāsh b. Muḳallad, repelled him and obtained apologies from the Byzantines (H. Kennedy, *The ʿUqaylids of Mosul . . . .*, in *Actas del XII Congresso de la U.E.A.I*, Malaga n.d.). On Waththāb's death in 410/1019, his son Shabīb succeeded him, and his descendants, the Banū Waththāb, continued to hold the region. In 417-22/1026-31 there was a fresh conflict with Naṣr al-Dawla Ibn Marwān over Edessa. Each clan chief of the Numayr formed a mini-principality around a stronghold rather than in the main town, leaving this last to be governed by a deputy. There was much internecine strife amongst these clans. Thus e.g. the lord of Edessa, ʿUṭayr al-Numayrī, refused to reside there but left it to a deputy, whose assassination he eventually procured and then was in turn himself killed. The two main Arabic sources, Yaḥyā al-Anṭākī, *Dhayl*, tr. F. Micheau and G. Troupeau, in *PO*, xlviii/4, no. 212, iii [151], Tournai 1997, and Ibn al-Athīr, see index), recount these events differently, notably the actions of the *sharīfs* and *aḥdāth* of the city and the lengthy internal combats of Muslims and Christians fortified within the towers and religious buildings of Edessa (for an account, based on Byzantine sources, see AL-RUHĀ). The Numayr resorted to arbitration by the Kilāb of Aleppo, and Ṣāliḥ b. Mirdās divided the city between the two Numayrīs Ibn ʿUṭayr and Ibn Shibl, each holding a tower in the city. The Byzantines in the end seized the city, and the Emperor Romanus III is said to have bought Ibn ʿUṭayr's share and access to his tower for 20,000 dīnārs and a certain number of villages. Shibl's forces took to flight, the Muslim inhabitants were reportedly killed and the mosques razed. On the other hand, in 421/1030 a clan of the Numayr, Ḳaṭan, inflicted a terrible defeat on the Byzantines at ʿAzāz and gained a great booty in gold coinage. But after the Byzantine riposte under the eunuch Nicetas in 423/1032, the Numayr led by Shabīb rallied to the Byzantines, and both sides accepted a delineation of the frontier leaving Edessa to the Greeks and Diyār Muḍar to its south to the Numayr. These last took part, with all the princes of the region, in the general negotiations at Constantinople to define the Graeco-Muslim frontiers in northern Syria and in al-Djazīra, negotiations which went on until Romanus III's death in 425/1034, leaving a result still imprecise, since the end of Yaḥyā's manuscript has not survived. The two Numayrī chiefs Shabīb and Ibn ʿUṭayr, former ruler of Edessa, attacked the Byzantines there in 427-9/1037-9, but after some successes, they ended in abandoning the city to the Byzantines. This check is explicable by the feebleness of their ally, the Kilābī principality of

Aleppo. Shabīb's sister, the very beautiful and intelligent al-Sayyida al-ʿAlawiyya, had married the Kilābī prince there, Naṣr b. Ṣāliḥ b. Mirdās, who was killed by the Fāṭimid army of al-Dizbirī in 429/1038. This Turkish general, the Fāṭimid governor in Syria, managed to occupy Aleppo and eject Naṣr's brother Thimāl and his brother-in-law Shabīb, but could not conquer Raḳḳa and Raḥba in the eastern part of the principality. On Shabīb's death, his brother Muṭāʿin succeeded him and took over the principality except for Raḳḳa and Raḥba, left to al-Sayyida al-ʿAlawiyya. The latter, now a widow, married her dead husband's brother Thimāl. Al-Dizbirī endeavoured to make a military and matrimonial alliance with the Marwānid Naṣr al-Dawla against the Numayr-Kilāb alliance which controlled all northern Syria and much of western al-Djazīra. However, the Fāṭimid authorities in Cairo were suspicious of al-Dizbirī's too personal policy in Syria, and he was brutally dismissed and died in humiliating circumstances in the citadel of Aleppo in 433/1042. Thimāl was able to return to Aleppo with his Numayrī spouse, who was to play on various occasions an important role in the politics of the city [see MIRDĀS, BANŪ]. The Numayr now made a rapprochement with Naṣr al-Dawla Ibn Marwān, and *ca.* 439/1048 they both countered the efforts of a *ghāzī* of the same name as that of a half-century before, Aṣfar al-Taghlibī.

In 452/1061 the then master of Ḥarrān, Māniʿ b. Shabīb b. Waththāb, grandson of the founder, went to help his maternal nephew Maḥmūd b. Ṣāliḥ b. Mirdās of Aleppo, engaged in a struggle with his uncle Thimāl, who ruled over the eastern Mirdāsid lands along the Euphrates. After some fighting amongst Kilābī groups, punctuated by truces, al-Sayyida al-ʿAlawiyya brought peace by reconciling Māniʿ and Thimāl. She accompanied her husband to Aleppo, where his sovereignty was once more made firm, then left with her young son Waththāb b. Thimāl for Cairo in order to negotiate a reconciliation with the caliph al-Mustanṣir [*q.v.*]. The rapprochement between the Banū Waththāb of Numayr and the Banū Mirdās of Kilāb is seen in the number of identical *ism*s found in children on both sides, such as Waththāb, Muḳallad, Māniʿ, Shabīb and Sābiḳ, some of these also found among the ʿUḳaylids, increasing even further the historians' confusion. In 462/1070, in dramatic circumstances, the Shīʿī princess again intervened personally to deflect the Sunnī Saldjūḳ sultan Alp Arslan from his siege of Aleppo and to try to avoid the humiliation of her son there, Maḥmūd, having to kiss the sultan's carpet. But she could achieve nothing, and the overwhelming defeat of the Byzantines at Mantzikert [see MALĀZGIRD] a few months later definitively deprived the Numayr and Kilāb of Byzantine protection.

In 471/1079 a coalition of Arabs, including the Numayr, and led by the ʿUḳaylid ruler of Mawṣil, Sharaf al-Dawla Muslim b. Ḳuraysh, defeated a Turkmen force, but in the following months the Saldjūḳ prince Tutush [*q.v.*] and his Turkmens ravaged all northern Syria. Three years later, Sharaf al-Dawla had to intervene in Aleppo, where the last three Kilābī princes Sābiḳ, Waththāb and Shabīb, sons of Maḥmūd, ended up losing their power through drunkenness and political incapacity. In 476/1083 Muslim b. Ḳuraysh, now ruler of Mawṣil and Aleppo, formed a coalition of several Ḳaysī and Yamanī tribes of Syria, including the Numayr, against the Kurds of al-Djazīra and other Arab tribal groups, including other clans of Numayr and ʿUḳayl. Thanks to support from Yaḥyā b. al-Shāṭir, a retainer of Ibn ʿUṭayr who administered the town for a child, ʿAlī b. Waththāb, Sharaf al-Dawla Muslim had occupied Ḥarrān in 474/1081 and installed a governor, Djaʿfar al-ʿUḳaylī, who promoted Shīʿism there. Whilst Muslim besieged Damascus in 476, Ḥarrān was retaken by a Ḥanbalī *ḳāḍī*, Abū Djalaba, who wished to hand over the town to Yaḥyā and the former Waththābī control. The town was taken over by Yaḥyā and Ibn ʿAṭiyya al-Numayrī, but retaken in the same year by Muslim, who executed the *ḳāḍī* and his sons and over a hundred of the citizens who had received *amān* (Sibṭ Ibn al-Djawzī, cited in Ibn al-Ḳalānisī, *Dhayl*, ed. Amedroz, n. at 116; Ibn al-ʿAdīm, *Zubda*, ed. Dahhān, ii, 81-3). In 478/1085, Muslim was in turn killed by the Turkmen Sulaymān b. Ḳutulmish [*q.v.*], the new master of Antioch. The Arab powers of northern Syria and al-Djazīra successively went down before newly-arriving Turks. The Banū Numayr contrived, however, to remain in the region since, when in 512/1118 the Franks seized the fortress of al-Sinn near ʿAzāz, they killed there Māniʿ b. ʿUṭayr al-Numayrī (al-ʿAẓīmī, *Taʾrīkh Ḥalab*, ed. Ibrāhīm Zaʿrūr, Damascus 1984, 369).

Bibliography: Given in the article.

(TH. BIANQUIS)

WATID (A.), also pronounced popularly (and also in Persian) as *watad*, pl. *awtād*, literally "tent peg", an element of scansion in *ʿarūḍ* [*q.v.*] (Arabic prosody), in which each foot has one *watid* and either one or two *sabab*s [*q.v.*]. Four types occur: (1) *watid madjmūʿ*: a sequence of two vowelled letters/consonants and one vowelless letter, paradigmatically represented as *faʿal*, translatable into syllables as ⏑ —, also called *watid maḳrūn*, e.g. in *TA*, ii, 521; (2) *watid mafrūḳ*: one vowelless letter between two vowelled letters (*faʿla*, — ⏑); (3) *watid mufrad*, defined by al-Fārābī, 1078, as "a *sabab khafīf* + one vowelless letter" (as in pausal *ḳāl*). (This is called *sabab mutawāl*^{in} in al-Ḳarṭādjannī, 236, and *sabab mutawassiṭ* in Khānlarī, 94 n. 2); (4) *watid mutadāʿif*, defined by al-Ḳarṭādjannī, 236, as two vowelled + two vowelless letters (as in pausal *maḳāl*), called *watad-i kathrat* in Khānlarī, *loc. cit.* Types 3 and 4 are outside traditional *ʿarūḍ*.

In *ʿarūḍ* theory, the stability of the *watid* is contrasted with the variable quantity of the *sabab*, which is liable to the change known as *ziḥāf* [*q.v.*]. In practice, however, many supposedly variable positions are stable. According to Weil [see ʿARŪḌ], the stability of the *watid* is concomitant with a stress on its long syllable, and to him the *watid* functions as the rhythmical core of the foot. For a different view, see Stoetzer, 110-20.

For *watad* in mysticism, see AWTĀD.

Bibliography: G.W. Freytag, *Darstellung der arabischen Verskunst*, Bonn 1830, 63-5; Fārābī, *K. al-Mūsīḳā al-kabīr*, ed. Gh.ʿA. Khashaba, Cairo n.d. [1967?]; P.N. Khānlarī, *Wazn-i shiʿr-i fārsī*, ²Tehran 1345; Ḳarṭādjannī, *Minhādj al-bulaghāʾ wa-sirādj al-udabāʾ*, ed. M. al-Ḥ. Ibn al-Khōdja, ³Beirut 1986; W. Stoetzer, *Theory and practice in Arabic metrics*, Leiden 1989. See also the *Bibl.* to SABAB. 3.

(W. STOETZER)

WAṬṬĀSIDS, BANŪ WAṬṬĀS, a Moroccan dynasty which reigned in the 9th/15th and 10th/16th centuries. The Banū Waṭṭās, Zanāta Berbers, were a branch of the Banū Marīn, descendants of the Banū Wasīn [see MARĪNIDS]. Initially nomadic horsemen, the Banū Waṭṭās left the Zāb [*q.v.*] and the highlands of the central Maghrib, reaching the Maghrib al-Aḳṣā in the early years of the 5th/11th century and occupying part of the Moroccan Rīf. In 622/1293, during the reign of the Marīnid Abū Yaʿḳūb Yūsuf, their chief ʿUmar b. Yaḥyā b. al-Wazīr took temporary control of the fortress of Tazūta which belonged to the Marīnids; however, this did not prevent the Banū Waṭṭās from occupying posts and enjoying privileges in the administration of the ruling Banū Marīn. Thus it was that on the death of the Marīnid sultan Abū ʿInān in 795/1358, effective power was exercised by various members of the Banū Waṭṭās. When the sultan Abū Saʿīd ʿUthmān was assassinated in 823/1420, the Waṭṭāsid Abū Zakariyyāʾ Yaḥyā, already *ḳāʾid* of Salé, secured the throne for Abū Muḥammad ʿAbd al-Ḥaḳḳ, the son of the deceased but still a minor, and ruled the country with the title of vizier; the reign of the Banū Waṭṭās had thus begun.

Abū Zakariyyāʾ Yaḥyā I (Abū Zekrī) had to confront anarchy which had become rife throughout Morocco: the marabouts were calling for a *djihād* against the Portuguese who had occupied Ceuta [see SABTA] in 1415, in the countryside the Arabs were agitating and taking to pillage, and the Ḥafṣid sultan of Tunis even invaded, reaching as far as Fās. As a result of the efforts of the young sultan ʿAbd al-Ḥaḳḳ, the Portuguese were unable to take Tangier [see ṬANDJA] in 1437 and forced to leave the *infante* Don Fernando as a hostage in Fās against a hypothetical restitution of Ceuta, which did not in fact take place; the *infante* died in 1443, still a captive.

Abū Zakariyyāʾ was assassinated in 852/1448 by Arabs whose rebellion he had suppressed. He was succeeded in the vizierate, or rather in the regency, by one of his kinsmen, ʿAlī b. Yūsuf, who died ten years later in 863/1458-9, likewise in the process of suppressing an Arab revolt. The Marīnid sultan ʿAbd al-Ḥaḳḳ had long since attained the age of majority, and when a third Waṭṭāsid, Yaḥyā II, son of Abū Zakariyyāʾ, succeeded ʿAlī b. Yūsuf, ʿAbd al-Ḥaḳḳ had him assassinated with all the members of his family. Fās was virtually immune from the authority of the sultan, and the city was ruled by Idrīsī *Shorfāʾ* [see SHURAFĀʾ]; one of them, Abū ʿAbd Allāh Muḥammad al-Djūṭī, was proclaimed sovereign in 869/1465. He captured ʿAbd al-Ḥaḳḳ and had him killed, thereby putting an end to the Marīnid dynasty.

Two brothers of the vizier Yaḥyā II had succeeded in escaping the massacre of the Banū Waṭṭās. One of them, Muḥammad al-Shaykh, took refuge at Arzila. He was unable to prevent the Portuguese occupying the city in 1471 (a twenty-years' truce was signed), and then Tangier in the same year. In 1472, after a long siege, Fās capitulated, the Idrīsid *sharīf* al-Djūṭī fled to Tunis and Muḥammad al-Shaykh was able to enter Fās, where he was proclaimed sovereign, thus inaugurating the rule of the Banū Waṭṭās.

The reign of the new sultan lasted until 909/1502 (or 912/1505); his foreign policy was dominated by his struggle against the intrigues of the Portuguese on the Atlantic coast of Morocco. Although he was unable to prevent their installation at Safi, Azemmour and Mazagan, he succeeded in forcing them to abandon Graciosa, a fortress which they had begun to build on an island of the Loukkos; a treaty was signed at Tchemmich on 26 Djumādā I 894/27 April 1489.

Muḥammad al-Shaykh was far from being recognised as sovereign throughout Morocco: in the north, Chechaouen (Shafshāwan) and Tetouan (Tiṭṭāwīn) were virtually independent principalities, whilst in the south the Hintāta *amīrs* were masters of Marrakech (Marrākush), and at Debdou a Marīnid amīrate had been constituted. The Waṭṭāsid sultan was in fact only the "king" of Fās. The successor to Muḥammad al-Shaykh was his son Muḥammad al-Burtuḳālī (he had been sent to Portugal in 1471), who attempted to pursue his father's policy against the Portuguese. But in the south a new power had emerged, that of the Saʿdian Shorfāʾ. Al-Burtuḳālī invited to his court two of the sons of the *sharīf* Abū ʿAbd Allāh Muḥammad, but being soon recalled by their father, the two princes returned to the south, and in 1522 took control of Marrakech; a kingdom distinct from that of Fās was thus constituted.

In Shaʿbān 932/May 1526 al-Burtuḳālī was succeeded by his brother ʿAlī Abū Ḥassūn, and in September of the same year the latter was deposed by his nephew Aḥmad al-Waṭṭāsī, whose policy differed fundamentally from that of his predecessors. The enemy to be fought was not the Portuguese, but the new arrivals on the scene, the Saʿdians [see SAʿDIDS], who, for their part, sought to oppose the Christian invaders and in addition to subdue the Banū Waṭṭās of northern Morocco. And when in 952/1545, the sultan of Fās was captured near Wadi Derna by the Saʿdian *sharīf* Muḥammad al-Shaykh al-Mahdī, he was obliged to cede to him Meknès and the Gharb in order to secure his liberation two years later. In 956/1549 Fās was seized by the same *sharīf*, and Aḥmad al-Waṭṭāsī was captured for the second time. Taken to Marrakech, he was executed in 1551. His son Muḥammad al-Ḳasrī, who had held power during his father's first period of imprisonment, suffered the same fate.

The only remaining claimant to the throne of Fās was ʿAlī Abū Ḥassūn, the temporary sultan of 932/1526, who had withdrawn to Velez de la Gomera. After the capture of Fās, he made his way to Spain, where he had an audience with the Emperor Charles V and appealed for the support of the king of Portugal in his bid to return to Morocco; he even went to Algiers in the quest for military assistance from the Turkish Pasha, which in fact enabled him to take control of Fās on 9 January 1554. His second reign was as brief as his first since, in the course of his campaign against the *sharīf*, he was killed on 21 September at Musallama. His sons sought refuge in Spain. One of them, al-Nāṣir, succeeded in returning to Morocco and rallying a few partisans, but to no avail. Numerous Waṭṭāsid princes remained in Spain, their haven of refuge, some even converting to Christianity. Thus the Banū Waṭṭās came to an end in 961/1554, and the last Berber monarchy of Morocco had disappeared. With the Saʿdians, a new history began in the Maghrib al-Aḳṣā and the Shorfāʾ succeeded in an objective which had eluded the Banū Waṭṭās, sc. the ejection of the Portuguese from Morocco.

Bibliography: 1. Sources. Luis de Mármol Carvajal, *Descripción general de Affricà*, Granada 1573, ii, 39-40; Aḥmad b. Khālid al-Nāṣirī al-Salāwī, *K. al-Istiḳṣāʾ*, Casablanca 1955, iv, 92 ff.; Leo Africanus, *Description de l'Afrique*, ed. and Fr. tr. A. Epaulard, Paris 1956; *Les sources inédites de l'histoire du Maroc*, 1st series, Spain, i-ii; Portugal, i-iv.

2. Studies. A. Cour, *La dynastie marocaine des Beni Ouattas*, Constantine 1920; H. Terrasse, *Histoire du Maroc des origines à l'établissement du Protectorat français*, Casablanca 1950, ii; Ch. de La Verónne, *Politique d'Abū Hasūn, roi de Vélez après ... 1549*, in *Actes IIe Congrès internat. Mediterranée occidentale, Malta 1976*, Algiers 1978; eadem, *Lettres inédites de partisans de Mūlāy Abū Hasūn du nord-est marocain (1550)*, in *ROMM*, xxvii (1979), 157-70; Diego de Torres, *Relación del origen suceso de los Xarifes y del estado de*

los reinos de Marruecos, Fés y Tarudante, ed. Mercedes Garcia Arenal, Madrid 1980; W.F. Cook, Jr., *The Hundred Years War for Morocco*, Boulder-San Francisco-Oxford 1994, 83-133; C.E. Bosworth, *The New Islamic dynasties*, Edinburgh 1996, 48-9 no. 19.

(Chantal de La Véronne)

WAṬWĀṬ (A., pls. *waṭāwīṭ, waṭāyīṭ*), a synonym for *khuffāsh*, pl. *khafāfīsh*, denoting all cheiropters or bats, without distinction of families (sc. the rhinolophids, vespertilionids and molossids) or species. The bat is also called *ṭā'ir al-layl* "the bird of the night", *khushshāf* and *khuṭṭāf* by comparison with the swallow. The names *saḥāt, ṭurmūk, ṭumrūk* and *ʿashraf* are also found.

In general, in the Arabic lands the bat is assimilated to a bird but one without a beak or feathers. Amongst the ancient Arabic writers on zoology, virtually only al-Djāḥiẓ provided a fairly extensive chapter on the bat in his *Ḥayawān*. He states that it flies neither in the middle of the night nor in broad daylight, but requires the half-light of the dawn and evening for searching out its diet of small flying insects. It may also happen to gobble up eggs from nests, and in the nesting season, the female vulture takes care to line her eyrie with plane-tree leaves, since the bat dislikes their smell.

According to Islamic law, it is forbidden to kill bats and eat their flesh. The bat has certain qualities. Thus, to put a bat's head on one's ear prevents sleep, and if it is boiled up in a copper or iron pot with lilac oil (*duhn al-zanbak*), it yields a lotion good for painting, as a wash, or on limbs afflicted by gout, rheumatism or swelling. A bat's heart grilled in one piece can be used as a fumigation for effectively driving away all snakes and scorpions. Its gall rubbed on the sexual organs of a pregnant woman causes immediate delivery, and it is also good for stopping incontinence of urine. The blood, mixed with milk, can be spread on the skin and removes all hair. Finally, its dung used as an unguent, removes scurfy skin.

In oneiromancy, seeing a bat in a dream is an auspicious sign which drives away all fear from a pious man and facilitates, for a pregnant woman, a smooth birth.

Bibliography: Djāḥiẓ, *Ḥayawān*, Cairo 1945, s.v. *waṭwāṭ*, i, 29-30, ii, 298, iii, 333, iv, 288-9, and s.v. *khuffāsh*, i, 30, 194, ii, 298, iii, 233, 256, 336, 526-8, iv, 396, v, 353, 537, 402, vi, 33, 231, 321, vii, 24-5, 66, 126; Damīrī, *Ḥayāt al-ḥayawān al-kubrā*, Cairo 1937, i, 295, ii, 262-3; A. Malouf, *An Arabic zoological dictionary/Muʿdjam al-ḥayawān*, Cairo 1932, s.v. Bat; R. Hainard, *Mamifères sauvages d'Europe*, Paris 1948, i, 89-145 (on cheiropters); H. Eisenstein, *Einführung in die arabische Zoographie*, Berlin 1991, index s.v. Fledermaus.

(F. Viré)

WAṬWĀṬ [see rashīd al-dīn].

WĀW, the 27th letter of the Arabic alphabet (or the 26th, if *hā'* is placed after *wāw*), with the numerical value 6. It has two principal functions in Arabic orthography, standing either for the semivowel *w* or for the long vowel *ū*. Traditional Arabic grammar reduces these two functions to one by analysing *ū* as short *u* (*ḍamma*) plus *wāw*. *Wāw* also serves (like *alif* and *yā'*) as a "support" for medial or final *hamza* [*q.v.*], reflecting, according to the most commonly held view, the situation in the ancient dialect of Mecca, where ' appears to have shifted to *w* in certain positions. In the words *ulā'ika* (أولئك) and *ulū* (أولو), *wāw* stands, exceptionally, for short *u*. On the other hand, the shortening of final *-ū* before *hamzat al-waṣl* is a regular phonetic feature; at a phonological level it should still be analysed as *-ū*. This goes also for *-ā* and *-ī* in the same position.

In the orthography of the Ḳur'ān, and in general in old manuscripts, long *ā* is represented by the letter *wāw* in the words *ṣalāt, zakāt, ḥayāt, nadjāt, ghadāt* (perhaps better read as *ghudwa*, an existing *ḳirā'a*), *mishkāt* and in the name of the goddess Manāt [*q.v.*] (who occurs also in Nabataean-Aramaic inscriptions as *mnwtw*, with *-w-*). Similarly ربوا *riban*, and الربوا for the determined *al-ribā*. Sībawayh (ed. Derenbourg, ii, 452) says that the first three of these words, at least, in the dialect of Ḥidjāz were pronounced with *alif al-tafkhīm*, that is to say, a sound intermediate between *alif* and *wāw* (presumably some sort of *ō*), but some of the later grammarians express doubts as to whether these spellings really represent a phonetic, and not merely an orthographic feature. Modern scholars have noted that some of these words are borrowings, e.g. *ṣalāt* from Aramaic *ṣlōthā*, where the Arabic spelling with *wāw* might be regarded as having been influenced by Aramaic orthography, but this does not account for all of the mentioned words. It seems thus that some dialects of ancient Arabic really did have an *ō*-like allophone not only in certain loanwords, but also in some Arabic derivates of roots with *w* as their third radical.

The personal name ʿAmr is written عمرو in the nominative (ʿAmr[un]) and genitive (ʿAmr[in]), and عمرا or عمروا in the accusative (ʿAmr[an]), retaining a spelling convention of the Arabic names in Nabataean Aramaic, thus preventing confusion with the name ʿUmar عمر. For a discussion, see most recently de Blois, *Who is King Amarō?*, in *Arabian Archaeology and Epigraphy*, vi (1995), 196-8.

In Persian, *wāw* has all of these same uses in Arabic loanwords. In native words it stands (in classical Persian) for the semivowel *w*, and for two different long vowels, *ū* and *ō*, which the indigenous lexicographers distinguish as *wāw-i maʿrūf* ("the *wāw* known [in Arabic]"), and *wāw-i madjhūl* ("unknown *wāw*") respectively. Classical poets generally avoid rhymes between *ū* and *ō*, but in modern Western Persian classical *ū* and *ō* merge as [u], and classical *w* is realised as a fricative [v], except in the diphthong *aw*, which is realised as [o[u]]. The older pronunciation of these phonemes is retained, however, in many dialects of Afghānistān and Tādjīkistān. The digraph خو stands (in classical Persian) for the labialised consonant *kh*[w], which has merged with *kh* in Western Persian, but is partially retained in Afghānistān.

Wāw stands ostensibly for short *u* in *du* ("two"), *tu* ("thou") and the postclitic particle *-u* ("and"), but in early Persian they could also be pronounced as *dō, tō* and *-ū*, and it is these that are represented by the orthography.

In Urdu *wāw* stands for the consonant *v*, the vowels *ū* and *ō* and the ex-diphthong *aw* (= Sanskrit *au*, but in Urdu realised as /ɔ/). In Turkic languages it is used for the consonant variously realised as *v* or *w*, and for the vowels *o, u, ö* and *ü*.

Bibliography (for the spelling of words like *ṣalāt*): G. Bergsträßer, in *Gesch. des Qorans*, iii, 41; A. Spitaler, *Die Schreibung des Typus* صلوة *im Koran*, in *WZKM*, lvi (1960), 212-26 (misguided); H. Fleisch, *Traité de philologie arabe*, i, Beirut 1961, 216; W. Diem, *Untersuchungen zur frühen Geschichte der arabischen Orthographie. I. Die Schreibung der Vokale*, in *Orientalia*, N.S. xlviii (1979), 207-57, esp. 242-5; A. Ḳoman, *Étude de la phonologie et de la morphologie de la koinè arabe*, i, Aix en Provence 1983, 454-60. (For Persian *ū* and *ō*): P. Horn, in *Gr.I.Ph.*, i/2, 31-2, 35-7; A. Farhâdi, *Le persan parlé en Afghanistan*, Paris 1955, 9, 12; F. Meier, *Aussprachefragen des älteren neupersisch*, in

Oriens, xxvii-xxviii (1981), 70-176, repr. in *Bausteine*, 3 vols. Istanbul 1992, ii, 1057-1164.

(F.C. de Blois)

al-**WAʾWĀʾ** al-**DIMASHḲĪ**, Abu ʾl-Faradj Muḥammad b. Aḥmad (or Muḥammad) al-Ghassānī, 4th/10th century Syrian poet, d. between 370/980-1 and 390/1000. Originally a fruit-seller in the market-place at Damascus, he may have acquired there his nickname ("the Crier" or "Howler"). His reputation as a poet was established after he was "discovered" by the *sharīf* Abu ʾl-Ḳāsim al-ʿAḳīḳī, on whom he had made an ode. He addressed some panegyric poems to Sayf al-Dawla [*q.v.*], but he is better known for his short poems in the more lyric genres: love, wine and nature. In some of these (e.g. *Dīwān*, ed. Kratschkowsky, nos. 14, 220, 238) he turns the traditional opening motif of the "abandoned encampment" into a metaphor, speaking of, or addressing, the desolate abode of his love or of his suffering. His verse is mostly smooth, polished and, the longer panegyrical poems excepted, easy of diction. A certain impersonality is partly the result of the absence of personal names and of descriptions of specific incidents, but this enhances the quotability. Particularly famous and admired by critics (first by Abū Hilāl al-ʿAskarī, *al-Ṣināʿatayn*, Cairo 1971, 257) for its condensed series of metaphors, or rather comparisons according to many rhetoricians, is a line on a weeping girl (*Dīwān*, ed. Kratschkowsky, 47): "She let pearls <tears> rain from narcissi <eyes>, watered the roses <cheeks>, and bit on jujubes <henna-stained fingers> with hailstones <teeth>"; see e.g. al-Ḥarīrī's *Maḳāma Ḥulwāniyya* and ʿAbd al-Ḳāhir al-Djurdjānī, *Dalāʾil al-iʿdjāz*, Cairo 1984, 449-51, where the literary history of this motif is sketched.

Bibliography: Thaʿālibī, *Yatīma*, Cairo 1947, i, 272-82; Ḳifṭī, *al-Muḥammadūn min al-shuʿarāʾ*, Ḥaydarābād 1966-7, i, 45-7; Ibn Shākir al-Kutubī, *Fawāt al-Wafayāt*, ed. ʿAbbās, Beirut 1974, ii, 301-6; Ṣafadī, *Wāfī*, ii, Istanbul 1949, 53-7; *Dīwān* (containing 320 pieces, some 1,560 lines), ed. I. Kratschkowsky, Leiden-Petrograd 1913-14, with a Russian tr. and study (*Abū-l-Faradž al-Waʾwā Damasskii. Materialï dlya charakteristiki poetičeskago tvorčestva*), summary by W. Ebermann in *Islamica*, iii (1927), 238-41, and survey of contents by Th. Menzel in *ArO*, ii (1930), 56-63; *Dīwān*, ed. Sāmī al-Dahhān, Damascus 1950; Rafīḳ al-Djuwaydjātī, *al-Waʾwāʾ al-Dimashḳī*, in *RAAD*, lxviii/4 (1993), 594-620. More references in Sezgin, *GAS*, ii, 498-9, ix, 294.

(G.J.H. van Gelder)

WAYHIND, the form found in mediaeval Indo-Muslim sources for a town of northwestern India, in the 12th century geography of Kashmīr by Kalhaṇa called Ūdabhānda, now marked by the settlement of Hund some 9 km/15 miles north-east of Attock [see ATAK] in Pakistan.

It was the capital of the powerful Hindū-Shāhī dynasty of Indian princes who opposed Sebüktigin and his son Maḥmūd of Ghazna in the late 4th/10th and early 5th/11th centuries, until Maḥmūd finally vanquished Rādjā Djaypāl; for further details, see hindū-shāhīs.

Bibliography: See that for hindu-shāhīs, to which should be added C.E. Bosworth, *The later Ghaznavids*, index.

(Ed.)

WAẒĪFA (a.), pl. *waẓāʾif*, literally "task, charge, impose obligation" (see Dozy, *Supplément*, ii, 820-1).

1. As an administrative term.

In the early Islamic period, the form II verb *waẓẓafa* and the noun *waẓīfa* are used as administrative-fiscal terms with the sense of imposing a financial burden or tax, e.g. of paying the *kharādj*, *ʿushr* or *djizya* [*q.vv.*], cf. al-Balādhurī, *Futūḥ*, 73, 193 (the *waẓāʾif* of the provinces of al-Urdunn, Filasṭīn, Dimashḳ, Ḥimṣ, etc.) and other references given in the *Glossarium*, 108. But as well as this loose sense, *waẓīfa* had a more specific one, as set forth by al-Khᵚārazmī, *Mafātīḥ al-ʿulūm*, 62, cf. 59, that of an extra, fixed payment, made by the *ʿāmil* or tax collector, on top of the land-tax collected; Løkkegaard compared it to the Hellenistic-Roman *annona* and the *ekstraordinaria* of the Egyptian papyri (*Islamic taxation in the classic period*, Copenhagen 1950, 126-8; C.E. Bosworth, *Abū ʿAbdallāh al-Khwārazmī on the technical terms of the secretary's art*, in *JESHO*, xii [1969], 132, 139).

Waẓīfa also came subsequently to mean the "financial allowance, stipend" paid to an official or as a reward for someone who had pleased a ruler or governor, such as a panegyric poet, and, by extension, the official post or function itself (see the examples in Dozy, *op. cit.*, ii, 821), a meaning which it retains in modern Arabic (and cf. *muwaẓẓaf* "official employee").

Bibliography: Given in the article.

(C.E. Bosworth)

2. As a term of Islamic mysticism.

In this context, *waẓīfa* is a devotional text or litany recited by the members of some Ṣūfī orders as one of the elements of their assignment of daily devotions, and also as part of the liturgy of a *ḥaḍra* [*q.v.*] or communal *dhikr* ritual. A *waẓīfa* normally consists of a sequence of prayer formulas, invocations, and verses from the Ḳurʾān. Contents differ according to Ṣūfī order, and are often explained or justified in conjunction with Prophetic traditions or special events in the life of the composer of the *waẓīfa*. The recitation of a *waẓīfa* is always prescribed for specific times of the day (generally in conjunction with the *fadjr* and *maghrib* prayers), and is governed by special conditions, such as ritual purity, and facing the *ḳibla*. In some of the commentaries on *waẓāʾif*, or in the instructions for recitation in the published versions of the various *waẓāʾif*, the text is endowed with protective qualities and recommended for reading in times of danger or distress. In some orders, the term *waẓīfa* is used to denote devotional texts or phrase-patterned devotions, which are known as *ḥizb* and *wird* [*q.vv.*] in other orders. Use of these three terms as synonyms is not uncommon, and is understandable in view of the fact that the text of an order's *waẓīfa* may overlap with or be part of its *wird* and *ḥizb*, whereas *wird* and *ḥizb* are a *waẓīfa* in the literal sense of "a duty".

An example of a *waẓīfa* as a devotional text in its own right, and never part of *aḥzāb* or *awrād*, is the *Waẓīfat al-Mashīshiyya*, also known as *al-Ṣalawāt al-Mashīshiyya*, after ʿAbd al-Salām b. Mashīsh [*q.v.*]. This text, which is in fact identical with the longer version of *Ṣalawāt Ibn Mashīsh* (numerous editions; for an accurate one, see e.g. ʿAbd al-Ḳādir Zakī, *K. al-Nafḥa al-ʿaliyya fī awrād al-Shādhiliyya*, Cairo 1321, 18 ff.), is widely known and recited by the members of many of the branches of the Shādhiliyya. The fact that so many of these have the recitation of this text as part of their daily devotions may explain why it has simply become known as *al-Waẓīfa al-Shādhiliyya*. The name of its composer is not mentioned any more in some of the manuals of present-day Shādhiliyya branches, and awareness of the author's identity seems to be disappearing. Many orders prescribe their members to recite this *waẓīfa* at least once daily, and at the beginning of the *ḥaḍra*.

Another example of a *waẓīfa* as a text in its own right is the *Waẓīfat al-Zarrūḳiyya*, known after Aḥmad

b. Zarrū<u>k</u> to whom it was allegedly dictated by the Prophet when Aḥmad was sitting on Muḥammad's tomb at Medina, and widely known and recited by many branches of the <u>Sh</u>ā<u>dh</u>iliyya; for an English translation, see Ali F. Khusaim, *Zarrūq the Ṣūfī. A guide in the Way and a leader to the Truth. A biographical and critical study of a mystic from North Africa*, Tripoli (Libya) 1976, 134-8.

The *wazīfa* of the Tid<u>j</u>āniyya [*q.v.*] order is an example of a text which incorporates much of its own *wird*, combining phrase-patterned devotions with a core text, known as the *Ṣalāt al-fātiḥ*, and another devotional text of the order, the *Dj̲awharat al-kamāl* (see Jamil M. Abun-Nasr, *The Tijaniyya. A Sufi order in the modern world*, Oxford 1965, 187, and 51-2 for the Arabic text and an English tr.). The *Ṣalāt al-fātiḥ* is said to have been delivered to Aḥmad al-Tid̲j̲ānī from Heaven on a tablet of light, whilst Aḥmad claimed that the Prophet taught him the *Dj̲awharat al-kamāl* directly. Tid̲j̲ānī adherents have to recite the *wazīfa* at least once every day, either individually or communally. Conflicting opinions concerning the number of times the *Dj̲awharat al-kamāl* should be recited contributed to the emergence of the schismatic movement of the Ḥamālliyya or Ḥamāliyya [*q.v.*] in West Africa.

Bibliography: Given in the article.

(F. DE JONG)

WAZĪR (A.), vizier or chief minister.

I. IN THE ARAB WORLD

1. The 'Abbāsids.

Etymology

The term *wazīr* occurs in the Ḳur'ān (XXV, 35: "We gave Moses the book and made his brother Aaron a *wazīr* with him"), where it has the sense of "helper", a meaning well attested in early Islamic poetry (for examples, see Goitein, *The origin of the vizierate*, 170-1). Though several scholars have proposed Persian origins for the term and for the institution, there is no compelling reason to doubt the Arabic provenance of the term or an Arab-Islamic origin and evolution of the institution of the *wazīr* (cf. Goitein, *op. cit.*; Sourdel, *Vizirat*, i, 40-61). The use of the term *wazīr* in the sense of "helper" is well illustrated in the early <u>Sh</u>ī'ī revolt of al-Mu<u>kh</u>tār [*q.v.*] in Kūfa. Claiming to be acting on behalf of Muḥammad Ibn al-Ḥanafiyya [*q.v.*], a son of 'Alī Ibn Abī Ṭālib, al-Mu<u>kh</u>tār had styled himself the "helper of the family of Muḥammad" (*wazīr āl Muḥammad*) (Goitein, *op. cit., Appendix*, 194-6). The same title was later to be adopted by Abū Salama [*q.v.*], the leader of the clandestine <u>Sh</u>ī'ī movement in Kūfa at the time of the fall of the Umayyad dynasty (al-D̲j̲ah<u>sh</u>iyārī, 84-7). From its original meaning of "helper", the term *wazīr* came to acquire the sense of "representative" or "deputy", and, under the 'Abbāsids, designated the highest-ranking civil functionary of the state next to the caliph.

History of the institution

The institution of the *wazīr* seems to have its origins both in the position of the secretary (*kātib* [*q.v.*]) as well as in that of the royal counsellor, as pointed out by Goitein (*Origin*, 175 ff.). At least some of the officials of the early 'Abbāsid administration who are characterised as *wazīr*s in the Arabic historical sources are likely only to have been especially influential counsellors rather than the holders of a position with a more distinct institutional identity. Such an institutional identity may, however, have developed by the time of the caliph al-Mahdī (58-69/775-85). *Inter alia*, this development is suggested by a list of secretaries in al-Ṭabarī's *Ta'rī<u>kh</u>*, in which Ya'ḳūb b. Dāwūd,

who served under the caliph al-Mahdī, is the first to be characterised as a *wazīr* (ii, 836-43, esp. 841; cf. Goitein, *Origin*, 181-2). It is worth noting, however, that even in later years an especially close adviser to the caliph might still be called a *wazīr* without, however, necessarily holding a corresponding office (cf. al-Ṭabarī, iii, 1139, for al-Ma'mūn's reference to his erstwhile ḳāḍī of Ba<u>gh</u>dād Yaḥyā b. Ak<u>th</u>am as *wazīr*, though Yaḥyā does not appear to have held that office at any point; cf. Sourdel, i, 238-9).

The most famous family of secretaries and *wazīr*s under the early 'Abbāsids were the Barmakids, who served in the 'Abbāsid administration until their dramatic fall from favour during the reign of Hārūn al-Ra<u>sh</u>īd [see BARĀMIKA]. <u>Kh</u>ālid b. Barmak had participated in the 'Abbāsid revolution and later served the caliphs al-Saffāḥ and al-Manṣūr as adviser, secretary and governor. His son Yaḥyā served as the tutor of Hārūn and later as his *wazīr*. According to al-D̲j̲ah<u>sh</u>iyārī, Yaḥyā was the first *wazīr* to be also given the military rank of *amīr* (*al-Wuzarā' wa 'l-kuttāb*, 177). Yaḥyā's son al-Faḍl also served as Hārūn's *wazīr*, for some time apparently together with his father. The ascendancy of the Barmakids (their *dawla* and *sulṭān*, as al-Mas'ūdī puts it, *Murūd̲j̲*, ed. Pellat, iv, 252, § 2602) continued for more than seventeen years, during which time they enjoyed unprecedented power and distinguished themselves as much for their administration as for their splendour, generosity and the scale of their patronage. As the caliph asserted greater personal control over the administration in his later years, their influence seems to have begun to decline. But their downfall was dramatic: Yaḥyā's son Dj̲a'far, a close companion and confidant of the caliph was executed in 187/803 while Yaḥyā and al-Faḍl were imprisoned, and their property was confiscated. The circumstances behind this tragic end have attracted much comment from both mediaeval and modern historians, and there is little agreement on precisely what precipitated it. The caliph's perception that his power was overshadowed by that of the Barmakids may have had some role to play in bringing about their end, and, as Kennedy has suggested, the caliph may have wanted to ensure a smoother succession for his elder son Muḥammad (al-Amīn) by eliminating a family too closely tied in its interests with the other son, the future al-Ma'mūn (H. Kennedy, *The Prophet and the age of the Caliphates*, London 1986, 143-4).

*Wazīr*s played an important role during the struggle for power and the civil war between Hārūn's sons al-Amīn and al-Ma'mūn. Al-Faḍl b. Rabī' [*q.v.*], the *wazīr* of Hārūn after the fall of the Barmakids and later the *wazīr* of al-Amīn, was influential in persuading al-Amīn to contravene the terms of succession stipulated by Hārūn and to remove al-Ma'mūn as his heir-apparent. This measure precipitated the civil war between the two brothers, which culminated in the death of al-Amīn. Al-Ma'mūn, who then acceded to the caliphate, was for his part greatly assisted during the course of this struggle by his *wazīr* al-Faḍl b. Sahl [*q.v.*], who had been a protégé of the Barmakids and had converted from Zoroastrianism to Islam at the hands of al-Ma'mūn (al-D̲j̲ah<u>sh</u>iyārī, 230-1). On al-Ma'mūn's accession, al-Faḍl was given the title <u>Dh</u>u 'l-Ri'āsatayn "the person with the two headships", which appeared on coins and which signalled his control of both the civil and the military administrations under the caliph.

The extent of the power which had been wielded by the Barmakids, and later by al-Faḍl b. Sahl until his assassination in 202/818, was not enjoyed by the latter's successors. Indeed, in his last testament, in a somewhat ambiguous reference to his sometime *ḳāḍī* and adviser Yaḥyā b. Ak<u>th</u>am [*q.v.*], al-Ma'mūn instructed his successor al-Mu'taṣim to follow the advice of the chief *ḳāḍī* Aḥmad b. Abī Du'ād [*q.v.*] rather than that of any *wazīr* (al-Ṭabarī, iii, 1139; cf. Sourdel, i, 238-9). During the period of the *Miḥna* [*q.v.*], the inquisition which was instituted towards the end of al-Ma'mūn's caliphate on the doctrine of the createdness of the Ḳur'ān and which remained in effect during the reigns of his two successors, the chief *ḳāḍī* exercised unprecedented influence over the 'Abbāsid administration. The *wazīrs* of this time, in particular Muḥammad b. 'Abd al-Malik b. al-Zayyāt [see IBN AL-ZAYYĀT], were hardly inconsequential figures, though they had to share their power with that of the chief *ḳāḍī*, which often led to considerable rivalry between the two (cf. Sourdel, i, 245-70).

As the Turkish troops grew in influence during the Sāmarrā' period of 'Abbāsid history (218-47/833-61), and as the financial difficulties of the empire multiplied, there were frequent struggles between Turkish troops and 'Abbāsid *wazīrs* over the exercise of power and, especially, over the control of the revenues. On occasion, Turkish generals themselves served as *wazīrs*, though the position was more commonly held by individuals with a secretarial background and with greater expertise in matters of financial administration (for an outline of the events of this chaotic period, see Kennedy, *op. cit.*, 158-99). The financial straits of the empire led eventually to the rise of two distinguished families of secretaries and *wazīrs*, the Banu 'l-Furāt and the Banu 'l-<u>Dj</u>arrāḥ, who dominated the 'Abbāsid administration from 296/908 until the emergence of the new position of the *amīr al-umarā'* [*q.v.*] in 324/936. Unlike the preceding decades, the *wazīrs* enjoyed very considerable power and prominence during these years, a period which Sourdel calls the "grande époque" in the history of the vizierate (Sourdel, i, 375, 387 ff.).

The most famous member of the Banu 'l-Furāt was Abu 'l-Ḥasan 'Alī b. Muḥammad b. al-Furāt [see IBN AL-FURĀT], who served as *wazīr* three times during the caliphate of al-Muḳtadir (295-320/908-32). Entrusted with the task of rescuing the 'Abbāsid administration from its fiscal troubles, Ibn al-Furāt's own reputation for financial corruption, together with his failure to deal effectively with the military challenges facing the state (in particular the depredations of the Ḳarmaṭīs [see ḲARMAṬĪ]) plus an increasingly brutal and extortionate style of administration, led eventually to his execution in 312/924. The great rival of the Banu 'l-Furāt were the Banu 'l-<u>Dj</u>arrāḥ, whose most distinguished member was 'Alī b. 'Īsā [*q.v.*]. These two families had, in fact, become the symbols of two factions in the 'Abbāsid bureaucracy, and the ascendancy or fall of a *wazīr* from one family signalled the downfall of practically all the lesser secretaries associated with the faction he represented. The downfall of a faction also meant the systematic and brutal effort, on the part of the dominant faction, to extort money from members of the fallen group [see MUṢĀDARA. 2.]. Unlike Ibn al-Furāt, however, 'Alī b. 'Īsā's image in the Arabic historical tradition is a largely positive one; he is remembered as "the good vizier" (he served in this capacity on two occasions) who strove mightily, but ultimately unsuccessfully, to reduce expenditure, reform the finances and restore order in the realm.

The rivalry of the Banu 'l-Furāt and the Banu 'l-<u>Dj</u>arrāḥ was not, however, merely over the control of lucrative positions and the consequent ability to squeeze out wealth from the other faction. Notwithstanding the many shared interests of the secretarial classes (cf. R.P. Mottahedeh, *Loyalty and leadership in an early Islamic society*, Princeton 1980, 108 ff.), this rivalry was apparently also based on differences of ideology and policy. The Banu 'l-Furāt were <u>Sh</u>ī'ī while the Banu 'l-<u>Dj</u>arrāḥ were Sunnī, a fact which may also have been involved in the positive image of 'Alī b. 'Īsā. As a Sunnī, 'Alī probably had a greater stake in the effort to reform and sustain the 'Abbāsid empire. The gradual decline in agricultural revenues, the excessive expenditure on the royal household and the army and the military challenges confronting the state all imposed severe constraints on the ability of any *wazīr* effectively to overhaul the administration of the state. The situation was greatly aggravated by the notorious corruption of many officials in the administration and the extortionate practices of the rival bureaucratic factions (on the financial state of the empire at this time, see Kennedy, *op. cit.*, 186 ff.). All this led not only to the severe weakening of the 'Abbāsid state but also to the eclipse of the 'Abbāsid *wizāra* as well.

In 324/936, the caliph al-Rāḍī's appointment of Muḥammad b. Rā'iḳ [see IBN RĀ'IḲ] as the *amīr al-umarā'* or the military overlord, whose position combined the powers of the *wazīr* with those of military commander, marked the effective end of the *wazīr* as the leading official of the 'Abbāsid administration. When the Būyids entered Ba<u>gh</u>dād in 334/945, the caliph conferred the title of the *amīr al-umarā'* on Aḥmad b. Būya Mu'izz al-Dawla. Henceforward, it was the *wazīrs* of the Būyids, and later of the Sal<u>dj</u>ūḳs, who played important roles in the administration of the state. The history of these officials, among the most distinguished of whom were such Būyid *wazīrs* as Abu 'l-Faḍl b. al-'Amīd and the Ṣāḥib Ismā'īl Ibn 'Abbād, and the Sal<u>dj</u>ūḳ *wazīr* Niẓām al-Mulk [*q.vv.*], falls outside the scope of this article. The 'Abbāsids did continue to have their own *wazīrs*, and when the authority of the Sal<u>dj</u>ūḳ sultans in 'Irāḳ began to wane after Malik <u>Sh</u>āh's death, a limited but distinct revival of the caliphs' political and military authority took place, at least within the circumscribed region of 'Irāḳ and, at times, in western Persia. Concomitant with this was the rise of certain influential *wazīrs* in the course of the 6th/12th century, such as 'Awn al-Dīn Ibn Hubayra [*q.v.*], who served al-Muḳtafī and al-Mustan<u>dj</u>id in the middle decades of the century, and his son 'Izz al-Dīn, *wazīr* to the latter caliph also. Towards the end of the century, circumstances enabled the caliph al-Nāṣir (r. 575-622/1180-1225 [*q.v.*]) to achieve a prestige and authority unequalled by any caliph for some three centuries, but among his many viziers, only Nāṣir al-Dīn Nāṣir b. Mahdī al-'Alawī, who held office 592-604/1195-1207, had serious ambitions to rule and made himself an effective force in the state (see H. Mason, *Two statesmen of mediaeval Islam, Vizir Ibn Hubayra (499-560 AH/1105-1165 AD) and Caliph an-Nāṣir li Dīn Allāh (553-622 AH/1158-1125 AD)*, The Hague and Paris, 1972).

The wazīr *in constitutional theory*

Al-Aḥkām al-sulṭāniyya of the <u>Sh</u>āfi'ī jurist al-Māwardī (d. 450/1058) as well as the similarly-entitled work of the Ḥanbalī Abū Ya'lā Ibn al-Farrā' (d. 458/1065) give considerable attention to the types, qualifications and functions of the *wazīr*. Al-Māwardī also devoted a separate work, the *Adab al-wazīr*, to this institution. The *wazīr al-tafwīḍ*, one of the two kinds he delineates, is described as the holder of extensive civil and military powers delegated (*mufawwaḍ*) to him by the caliph. These powers and functions are similar to the caliph's own, except that the *wazīr* cannot remove the caliph, nor appoint a successor to the caliph, nor even remove an official appointed by the caliph (al-Māwardī, *Aḥkām*, 24). In view of the scope of his powers and the importance of his position, the qualifications for this office are said to be the same as those for the position of the caliph itself, with the exception of membership in the tribe of Ḳuraysh̲ which is required for the latter but not for the former. A *wazīr al-tafwīḍ* must be a free, male Muslim and he must be well versed in the *S̲h̲arīʿa* to the extent of being a *mud̲j̲tahid* (al-Māwardī, *Aḥkām*, 21, 26). Besides other civil and military functions, al-Māwardī assigns to the *wazīr al-tafwīḍ* the function of presiding over the *maẓālim* [*q.v.*] courts (*ibid.*, 21, 73), a function well attested by the ʿAbbāsid chronicles (cf. Tyan, *Histoire de l'organisation judiciare*, 481-2; Massignon, *Passion*, i, 386 ff.; Sourdel, ii, 640 ff.).

The functions of the *wazīr al-tanfīd̲h̲*, on the other hand, were limited only to the implementation (*tanfīd̲h̲*) of specific policies of the caliph. Unlike a *wazīr al-tafwīḍ*, a person who was neither free nor even a Muslim could be appointed a *wazīr al-tanfīd̲h̲*, though women were expressly excluded from this position (al-Māwardī, *Aḥkām*, 26). The highly delimited position of the *wazīr al-tanfīd̲h̲* seems to be a juristic rationalisation of a situation in which the *wazīrs* of the ʿAbbāsid caliphs had lost much of their power and prestige to the military overlords who controlled the realm and who, under the Būyids and later the Sald̲j̲ūḳs, had their own powerful *wazīrs* (cf. Sourdel, ii, 714-15).

The wazīr *as patron of religion and culture*

The role of the *wazīr* in the religious and cultural history of the ʿAbbāsid times is yet to be systematically studied. The secretaries, from whose ranks the *wazīrs* were usually drawn, were among the most culturally sophisticated of the ʿAbbāsid élite, combining Islamic with "secular" learning and acting as the patrons of both. The Barmakids patronised debates among scholars of different persuasions (al-Masʿūdī, *Murūd̲j̲*, iv, 236 ff., §§ 2565 ff.) and commissioned the translation of Greek as well as Indian works into Arabic (Gutas, *Greek thought, Arabic culture*, 128-9); Ibn al-Zayyāt, *wazīr* under al-Muʿtaṣim, al-Wāt̲h̲iḳ, and al-Mutawakkil, was among the patrons of the Nestorian translator Ḥunayn b. Isḥāḳ (*ibid.*, 130-1); and several members of the D̲j̲arrāḥid family of secretaries and *wazīrs*, themselves converts from Nestorian Christianity, took a strong interest in the ancient sciences (*ibid.*, 132). Under the Būyids, the patronage of such *wazīrs* as Ibn al-ʿAmīd and the Ṣāḥib Ibn ʿAbbād contributed to an extremely rich age of cultural efflorescence (see Kraemer, *Humanism*, 241-72 and *passim*).

The non-Arab origin of most *wazīrs*, and their interest in and patronage of Greek and other ancient learning, combined with political resentments and rivalries, often led to accusations of a certain lack of commitment to Islam on their part. There are echoes of such suspicions about the Barmakids (see M. Chokr, *Zandaqa et zindiqs en Islam au second siècle de l'hégire* Damascus 1993, 24-5, 85-6), as well as about their protégé al-Faḍl b. Sahl (cf. al-D̲j̲ahs̲h̲iyārī, 316). Many secretaries and *wazīrs*, but in particular the Banu 'l-Furāt, had S̲h̲īʿī leanings and may have been somewhat suspect for that reason; but even the S̲h̲āfiʿī *wazīr* ʿAlī b. ʿĪsā was accused of secret dealings with the reviled and much dreaded Ḳarāmiṭa.

Such accusations and suspicions notwithstanding (and they seem to have usually been unfounded or exaggerated, as Sourdel, ii, 565 ff. has suggested) the *wazīrs* often played important roles in shaping or carrying out the religious policies of the state; indeed, such accusations may even have prompted certain *wazīrs* to emphasise their religious commitments more emphatically. For instance, it was on al-Faḍl b. Sahl's initiative that al-Maʾmūn, while he was pitted in a struggle over the caliphate against his brother, publicly proclaimed his commitment to upholding and acting according to the stipulations of "the Ḳurʾān and the *sunna* of the Prophet" (cf. al-D̲j̲ahs̲h̲iyārī, 278-9; for al-Maʾmūn's public recognition of al-Faḍl's own services to him, see Madelung, *New documents*). *Wazīrs* not only presided over the *maẓālim* courts, as already noted, but they also contributed to shaping the legal practice of the realm by their influence on, and often sole responsibility for, the appointment of the *ḳāḍīs*. They were also among important patrons of jurists and the schools of law, and some of them were jurists in their own right. For instance, Ibn Hubayra (d. 560/1165 [*q.v.*]), who, as noted above, served as *wazīr* under al-Muḳtafī and al-Mustand̲j̲id, was himself a scholar of Ḥanbalī law, as well as the author of a multi-volume commentary on the *Ṣaḥīḥ ḥadīt̲h̲* collections of al-Buk̲h̲ārī and Muslim.

The position of the *wazīr* was one of the most important and powerful offices of the ʿAbbāsid administration. Though theoretically subservient to the caliph and only continuing in office at the latter's good pleasure, the power of the *wazīr* could, at times, rival and even surpass that of the caliph. But even when neither the ʿAbbāsid caliph nor his *wazīr* any longer enjoyed much effective political power, the caliph's *wazīr* often continued to play a considerable role as a patron of culture and of intellectual and religious life in the ʿAbbāsid realm.

Bibliography: 1. Sources. All major chronicles of the ʿAbbāsid period contain important information on individual *wazīrs*, their actions and political fortunes. Major biographical dictionaries also devote notices to prominent *wazīrs* in addition to much incidental information. A number of works specifically about the *wazīrs* were also written during the ʿAbbāsid period, but most of these are not extant (on these works, see Ibn al-Nadīm, *al-Fihrist*, ed. R. Tad̲j̲addud, Beirut 1988, 142, 143, 150, 168. Two major authors whose works on the *wizāra* have, however, come down to us are al-D̲j̲ahs̲h̲iyārī and Hilāl al-Ṣābiʾ. See al-D̲j̲ahs̲h̲iyārī, *al-Wuzarāʾ wa 'l-kuttāb*, ed. M. al-Saḳḳā *et al.*, Cairo 1938; *Nuṣūṣ ḍāʾiʿa min kitāb al-wuzarāʾ wa 'l-kuttāb li-Muḥammad b. ʿAbdūs al-D̲j̲ahs̲h̲iyārī*, ed. M. ʿAwwād, Beirut 1964; al-Ṣābiʾ, *al-Wuzarāʾ aw tuḥfat al-umarāʾ fī taʾrīk̲h̲ al-wuzarāʾ*, ed. ʿAbd al-Sattār Aḥmad Farrād̲j̲, Cairo 1958; idem, *Rusūm dār al-k̲h̲ilāfa*, ed. M. ʿAwwād, Bag̲h̲dād 1964. On the position of the *wazīr* in juridical theory, see al-Māwardī, *al-Aḥkām al-sulṭāniyya*, Cairo 1298/1881, Eng. tr. Wafaa H. Wahba, *The ordinances of government*, Reading 1996; idem, *Adab al-wazīr*, Cairo 1929; Abū Yaʿlā Muḥammad b. al-Ḥusayn al-Farrāʾ, *al-Aḥkām al-sulṭāniyya*, ed. Muḥammad Ḥāmid al-Fiḳī, Cairo 1357.

2. Studies. The most important work on the *wazīrs* of the pre-Būyid period is D. Sourdel, *Le vizirat ʿabbāside de 479 à 936 (132 à 324 de l'hégire)*, 2 vols. Damascus 1959-60. Other works which shed light on various aspects of the history of the *wazīrs* under the ʿAbbāsids include: S.D. Goitein, *The origin of the vizierate and its true character*, in idem, *Studies in Islamic history and institutions*, Leiden 1968, 168-91, and *Appendix. On the origin of the term vizier*, in *ibid.*, 194-96; R.A. Kimber, *The early Abbasid vizierate*,

in *JSS*, xxxvii (1992), 65-85; *EIr*, art. *Barmakids* (I. Abbas); W. Madelung, *New documents concerning al-Ma'mūn, al-Faḍl b. Sahl and ʿAlī al-Riḍā*, in Wadād al-Ḳāḍī (ed.), *Studia arabica et islamica*, Beirut 1981, 333-46; H. Kennedy, *The Prophet and the age of the Caliphates*, London 1986; H. Bowen, *The life and times of ʿAlí ibn ʿÍsà, "The Good Vizier"*, Cambridge 1928; L. Massignon, *The Passion of al-Hallaj*, tr. H. Mason, Princeton 1982; J.L. Kraemer, *Humanism in the renaissance of Islam. The cultural revival during the Būyid age*, Leiden 1992; D. Gutas, *Greek thought, Arabic culture*, London 1998; E. Tyan, *Histoire de l'organisation judiciaire en pays d'islam*, Leiden 1960; A.K.S. Lambton, *State and government in medieval Islam*, Oxford 1981; C.L. Klausner, *The Seljuk Vezirate. A study of civil administration, 1055-1194*, Cambridge, Mass. 1973; G. Makdisi, *Ibn ʿAqīl et la résurgence de l'Islam traditionaliste au XIe siècle*, Damascus 1973.

(Muhammad Qasim Zaman)

2. The Fāṭimid caliphate.

Here, the office was created for Yūsuf b. Killis, probably in 368/979, and apart from a few interruptions, there were holders of the office until Ṣalāḥ al-Dīn [*q.v.*], the last vizier, who ended the dynasty in 567/1171. The *wazīr* directed the civil administration directly under the caliph's authority until 466/1074; the supreme dignity continued to belong to the caliph after that date, but it was a military man, the commander-in-chief (*amīr al-d̲j̲uyūs̲h̲*), generally also bearing the title of vizier, who held the reality of political decision-making.

The events, personalities and institutions of the Fāṭimid caliphate from 297/909-10 to 567/1171 have been covered in detail in the article fāṭimids and in the individual articles on prominent persons [see the Index]. Here, only the main features of the vizier's functioning and the variations over the course of time in its responsibilities, will be treated. A large part of what has been written on the functioning of the vizierate in the eastern lands of the Islamic world, under the ʿAbbāsids, Būyids and Sald̲j̲ūḳs, is equally valid for the Fāṭimid vizierate (see D. Sourdel, *Le vizirat ʿabbāside*..., 2 vols. Damascus 1959-60; Y. Essid, *al-Tadbīr/Oikonomia, une critique des origines de la pensée économique arabo-musulmane*, Tunis 1993, Eng. tr., idem, *A critique of the origins of Islamic economic thought*, Leiden 1995). On the opposition between *ḥād̲j̲ib* and *wazīr*, see J.-Cl. Garcin *et alii*, *États, sociétés et cultures du monde musulman médiéval, X^e^-XVe siècle*, ii, Paris 2000. For the Fāṭimid vizierate, the main source remains Ibn al-Ṣayrafī, *al-Is̲h̲āra ilā man nāla al-wizāra*, ed. ʿA.A. Muk̲h̲liṣ, Cairo 1923, 49-111; of modern studies, see G. Wiet, *L'Égypte arabe. Histoire de la nation égyptienne*, iv, Paris 1937, 179-310; M.Ḥ. al-Mināwī, *al-Wizāra wa 'l-wuzarāʾ fi 'l-ʿaṣr al-fāṭimī*, Cairo 1970. For a description of the institution and a complete bibl. of the sources, see A.F. Sayyid, *al-Dawla al-fāṭimiyya fī Miṣr, tafsīr d̲j̲adīd*, Beirut 1413/1992, 250-4, 433-54. See also Garcin, *op. cit.*, i, Paris 1995, Bibl. on the Fāṭimids at pp. XCIII-L, events 81-117; *Camb. hist. of Egypt*, forthcoming. For everything concerning coinage, tax systems, customs duties and the financial organisation of agriculture, see Cl. Cahen, *Makhzūmiyyāt. Études sur l'histoire économique et financière de l'Égypte médiévale*, Leiden 1977). A list of Fāṭimid viziers is difficult to establish with precision, since some persons only held office for a few days, whilst others were appointed and re-appointed on various occasions (a useful list, despite some errors of detail, can be found in L.S. Imad, *The Fatimid vizierate, 969-1172*, Berlin 1990, 164-70).

The successive stages of the stripping of the caliphs' power

During the reigns of the dynasty's first century, from the rise to power of al-Mahdī in Ifrīḳiya in 297/910, till the disappearance of al-Ḥākim in 411/1021, the caliphs involved themselves personally in the direction of politics and administrative matters. In the succeeding century, the son and grandson of al-Ḥākim, al-Ẓāhir (d. 427/1035-6) and al-Mustanṣir (d. 487/1094 [*q.vv.*]) in the first half of his reign, still played a certain political role, albeit within a system that they no longer controlled. It was during the reign of the latter, in 466/1074, that the civilian vizierate was replaced by a military one, concentrating all political power within the hands of the *amīr al-d̲j̲uyūs̲h̲* Badr al-D̲j̲amālī. After al-Mustanṣir's death, the Fāṭimid caliphs of the 6th/12th century, with the sole exception of al-Ḥāfiẓ, all raised to the imāmate whilst still children, were only puppets manipulated by their entourages. Parallel to this decline of the *imāms*, the influence of the *amīr al-d̲j̲uyūs̲h̲* grew notably; also bearing the title of *wazīr*, when such a person existed, he himself alone exercised the reality of power.

The tradition of the vizier in Egypt

The sources as preserved seem to show that the office of vizier did not exist amongst the Fāṭimids in Ifrīḳiya before 362/973, nor in Egypt before the accession to the imāmate of the fifth caliph al-ʿAzīz, the second to have reigned in Cairo. Probably under the influence of local tradition, with viziers in effect often existing at Miṣr-Fusṭāṭ since Aḥmad b. Ṭūlūn [*q.v.*], al-ʿAzīz appointed to this office, apparently in 368/979 (on the dates, variously given in the sources, see Th. Bianquis, *Damas et la Syrie sous la domination fāṭimide*, Damascus 1987-9, i, 168), Yūsuf b. Killis [*q.v.*], al-Muʿizz's main tax-farmer since 364/974. The new vizier, following in the previous administrative tradition, which had fallen into bad ways at the time of the disorders at the end of Kāfūr's [*q.v.*] time, reorganised an agrarian tax policy and an efficient artisanate. Likewise, two centuries later, al-Ḳāḍī al-Fāḍil [*q.v.*], who had entered the Fāṭimid *dīwān al-ins̲h̲āʾ* in 544/1149 and had been secretary successively to the Fāṭimid viziers Ṭalāʾiʿ b. Ruzzīḳ, S̲h̲āwar and S̲h̲īrkūh [*q.vv.*], remained after 567/1171 in Ṣalāḥ al-Dīn's service and then in that of the Ayyūbids, for whom, after finishing his missions in Syria, he re-organised the civil administration in Egypt on the Fāṭimid model, retiring in 591/1195. The continuity in administration during a period when political life was fluid, makes medieval Egypt a special case in the Islamic East.

Public administration and private interests

The first Fāṭimid *wazīr*, Ibn Killis, of ʿIrāḳī Jewish origin, had a long career of private and public service behind him when he was appointed. After failing as a private commercial agent in Palestine, he entered the service of the master of Egypt, Kāfūr, as director of the latter's personal estates in Syria and Egypt, and then with the task of overseeing the public finances. He made a public conversion to Sunnī Islam, but his hopes of becoming vizier were at that time unrealised. After Kāfūr's death, he became an Ismāʿīlī and in Ifrīḳiya joined al-Muʿizz, who was preparing for the invasion of Egypt, and placed at the Imām's disposal his perfect knowledge of the fiscal system of that country, notably of the cadastral survey of agricultural land and of the territorial basis of the tax burden which he had to recalculate precisely on the alluvial soil left each year after the Nile waters had subsided. Having returned to Egypt with his master, he was then the main architect of fiscal and administrative continuity between the régimes of the Ikhshīdids and Kāfūr and the Fāṭimids. At the same time as dealing with the state's finances, Ibn Killis always pursued important personal financial interests, in Egypt as well as in Syria. He strengthened a method of procedure, already begun under his predecessors, which was to be perpetuated by his successors. The main *dīwāns* of the state were traditionally headed by civilian officials who were at the same time powerful private financiers, whether as tax-farmers or as high-level merchants (see A.L. Udovitch, *Merchants and amirs. Government and trade in eleventh century Egypt*, in *Asian and African Studies*, xxii [1988], 53-72; Y. Lev, *State and society in Fatimid Egypt*, Leiden 1991; Bianquis, *op. cit.*, i, 103, 156-71; idem, *Le fonctionnement financier des dīwāns centraux fāṭimides au début de V^e/XIe siècle*, in *AI*, xxvi [1992], 46-61).

The vizierate's field of action

Ibn Killis was a great statesman in the various aspects of his duties, tax policies, modernisation of the army through the purchase of Turkish *ghulāms* and prudent actions in Syria in face of the Byzantines. During his lifetime, he was an adviser to whom the caliph always listened, even if his personal greed led to his being mulcted in 373/983-4 of 100,000 or 500,000 dīnārs, arrested and dismissed, all three penalties reversed shortly afterwards. However, the caliph al-ʿAzīz, who was so attached to his vizier, abandoned his wise counsels in favour of a foreign policy in northern Syria, about which Ibn Killis complained on his deathbed. Al-Ḥākim, al-ʿAzīz's son and successor, created a gap in the vizierate, probably in 409/1018, and replaced it by the *wasāṭa*, a function which involved interposing and interceding between the Imām and the ethnic factions of the palace and the army, and by the *sifāra*, an office in which all these groups were represented, two institutions which the caliph had created at the beginning of his reign. During the reign of his son al-Ẓāhir, the vizierate was re-established in 418/1027 for the ʿIrāḳī *kātib* Abu 'l-Ḳāsim al-Djardjarāʾī [see AL-DJARDJARĀʾĪ. 4.], representing the interests of the merchant importers (Bianquis, *Damas et la Syrie*, ii, 393-7, 791, index s.v. *vizir*). The offices of the *wasāṭa* and the *sifāra* continued to be filled irregularly till the end of the dynasty by persons with a lower rank than that of the vizier, sometimes by someone who later became a vizier (Ibn Ẓāfir, *Akhbār al-duwal al-munkaṭiʿa*, ed. A. Ferré, Cairo 1972, 88). The civilian successors of Ibn Killis were often Sunnīs, Jews or Christians, converted to a more or less sincere degree of Ismāʿīlism and often from ʿIrāḳ or Syria, provinces which enjoyed, at that time, a higher cultural level than Egypt. With the exception of al-Djardjarāʾī, the best civilian vizier of the dynasty, they were generally mediocre.

The need for economy, distrust of the ambitions of commanders stationed in Damascus and the fear of getting the Fāṭimid army too deeply engaged in continental Syria, marked the actions of the civilian viziers and the ensemble of the financial *dīwāns* until the final loss of the Syrian territories in 468/1076. Conscious of the feebleness of the Fāṭimid army *vis-à-vis* the Turkmens and Saldjūḳs, it was the first military vizier, Badr al-Djamālī, who had to decide on the abandoning of the Syrian interior, whose importance had been preached in vain by most of his civilian predecessors; he retained within the province only ports, places where customs dues were levied and a coastal band of territory (Garcin, *op. cit.*, i, 94-5, 107-9; M. Yared-Riachi, *La politique extérieure de la principauté de Damas, 1075-1154*, Damascus 1997, 87-8).

Unlike the ʿAbbāsid vizier or that of the Saldjūḳs in ʿIrāḳ and Persia, the vizier in Cairo often exercised, after 440/1050, other functions in parallel. As supreme judge, *ḳāḍī al-ḳuḍāt*, he appointed judges and pronounced the law in cases of last resort, and as chief missionary for the Fāṭimid doctrine, *dāʿī al-duʿāt*, he watched over the training of the Ismāʿīlī missionaries sent all over the Islamic world, keeping up a continued correspondence with each of them. In Cairo, the Fāṭimid vizier drew his legitimacy from the divine light, *nūr Allāh*, which, since the time of Muḥammad and ʿAlī, had perpetually illuminated the Imām; arising from this fact, the distinction between the military, political, administrative, judicial and ideological domains was less obvious than in an ʿIrāḳī Sunnī context, which was under the guiding principle of the memory of the foundations, both in Holy Writ and also transmitted orally, of *fiḳh*, a guidance exercised by the *ʿulamāʾ*.

The installation of the military vizierate

The main break in the continuity of the institution comes from the time of al-Mustanṣir, son of al-Ẓāhir. In order to end the very serious crisis which had been threatening the very existence of the régime since 457/1065, the caliph in 464/1072-3 appealed to a general of Armenian origin, Badr al-Djamālī, governor of Acre in Syria. On arrival in Egypt, Badr, henceforth called *amīr al-djuyūsh* and *wazīr*, was accorded full powers, which he exercised till his death. The civilian vizierate of execution, *tanfīdh*, in which the political conduct of affairs was the responsibility of the caliph who put his decisions into action through his vizier, became transformed into a military vizierate of delegation, *tafwīḍ*, in which a great military officer, here the commander-in-chief, legitimised by a real or fictitious act of delegation from the caliph, now exercised supreme political and military authority (al-Maḳrīzī, *Ittiʿāẓ*, ed. M.Ḥ.M. Aḥmad, Cairo 1971, ii, 329-30; see in al-Imad, *op. cit.*, 61-8, the theoretical texts of al-Māwardī, describing the situation in ʿIrāḳ but applicable here also). Born on the occasion of this crisis, the system became self-perpetuating until the end of the Fāṭimid power in 1171 by the last military vizier of the dynasty, the Sunnī Kurd Ṣalāḥ al-Dīn.

A reform and a complete updating of the cadaster and the taxation system were achieved, under the stimulus of the future vizier al-Baṭāʾiḥī, by al-Afḍal, acting on behalf of his father, the *wazīr* and *amīr al-djuyūsh* Badr, thereby assuring the Fāṭimid state of revenues at a higher level at the end of the 5th/11th century and during the next than had obtained in the time of the civilian vizierate (Cahen, *op. cit.*, 165-7, 174). The personal enrichment of the military viziers was, moreover, on a greater scale than under their civilian predecessors (an extraordinary inventory of al-Afḍal's possessions, made after his death, without taking into account six million dīnārs, is given in Ibn Ẓāfir, *op. cit.*, 91-2; see also ṬALĀʾIʿ B. RUZZĪK).

During this second period of about a century, the title of *amīr al-djuyūsh* was most often placed before that of *wazīr*, which usage was even omitted on various occasions (al-Imad, *op. cit.*, 169). This military title is to be considered in parallel to those borne by the military *amīrs* of the second period of the ʿAbbāsid caliphate. The first, Ibn Rāʾiḳ [*q.v.*], was in 324/936 appointed in Baghdād by the caliph al-Rāḍī as *amīr al-umarāʾ*, a title resumed by the Būyids in 334/945 under al-Mustakfī, who had lost all personal authority, but the Būyid *amīr al-umarāʾ* was now enriched by *laḳabs* and the Arabo-Persian titles of *malik*, *shāh* or *s̲h̲āhans̲h̲āh*, which one finds as a regnal name under the Saldjūḳs. After 447/1055, when Ṭog̲h̲rïl Beg had taken the caliph al-Ḳā'im under his protection, the Saldjūḳs consolidated their pre-eminence by using the Arabic title *sulṭān* [*q.v.*]. The Arab caliph, as a civilian, retained only his moral authority, and he shrank into the background everywhere, to the profit of a military direction within the state, with supreme political authority in future held by a great commander who was a non-Arab (see al-Subkī, *Ṭabaḳāt al-s̲h̲āfiʿiyya*, v, 314-16).

In practice, the sphere of competence of the military vizier, the *amīr al-djuyūs̲h̲*, who appeared in Cairo less than twenty years after the proclamation of the Saldjūḳ sultanate in Bag̲h̲dād, was much wider than that of his civilian predecessors, notably in the domains of application of the law and the execution of justice, as well as the defence and the diffusion of Fāṭimid doctrine. Now most of Badr's successors were not Ismāʿīlīs; amongst them were several Sunnīs and Twelver S̲h̲īʿīs and even one or two Christians. It is easy to understand how, in the 6th/12th century, the Yemeni Ṭayyibī subsect and the Persian and Syrian Nizārīs [*q.vv.*] spread more successfully than the Fāṭimid Ismāʿīlism of Cairo.

With the exception of al-Afḍal [*q.v.*], Badr's son and successor, an active personality but brutal and clumsy, and involuntarily responsible for the great Nizārī schism with its bloody consequences extending over a century and a half, and of another vizier of Armenian origin, Ṭalā'iʿ b. Ruzzīḳ [*q.v.*], the *amīr al-djuyūs̲h̲* were in general mediocre and opportunist persons who were only able to uphold the régime thanks to the unbelievable agricultural and artisanal richness of the land and the income from customs duties there, to the restructuring of the cadaster and the taxation system brought about by Badr, to the quality of the navy (see Lev, *op. cit.*) and, above all, to a skilful political game played between the Frankish states in Palestine, the Sunnī Muslim régimes of the Syrian interior and the Byzantine empire.

Bibliography: Given in the article.

(TH. BIANQUIS)

3. The Ayyūbids.

In theory, the vizierate here did not differ much from that of their ʿAbbāsid, Fāṭimid and Saldjūḳ predecessors. Appointed by the ruler, the vizier headed the administration and the *dīwāns*. With the Ayyūbid confederation, the two states of Egypt and Syria each had in principle its own vizier, but the office's importance varied much, according to the region and the rulers. Ṣalāḥ al-Dīn, himself vizier to the last Fāṭimid caliph 1169-71, never had a vizier. The excessive power which certain Fāṭimid viziers had enjoyed and his own experience in the office, probably led him not to follow this way, and even his chancellor and closest adviser, al-Ḳāḍī al-Fāḍil [*q.v.*], never had the title of vizier officially.

In Egypt likewise, the Ayyūbid sultans often did without a vizier. The most important, and the only one to exercise the office of a classic vizier, was Ṣafī al-Dīn ʿAbd Allāh Ibn S̲h̲ukr (b. in the Delta 548/1153, d. in Cairo 622/1225; the most detailed biography in al-Maḳrīzī, *al-Muḳaffā*, iv, Cairo 1991, 595-602). Whilst in the service of al-ʿĀdil (596-615/1200-18 [*q.v.*]), his extortions and tyrannical methods caused numerous officials and notables to flee, including Ibn Mammātī [*q.v.*], head of the financial office, and Ibn Abi 'l-Ḥadjdjādj, head of the army office, who went to the court at Aleppo of al-Ẓāhir G̲h̲āzī [*q.v.*]. Al-ʿĀdil ended by exiling him in 608/1212-13, replacing him by his father-in-law Fak̲h̲r al-Dīn Ibn S̲h̲ukr, and the fallen vizier went off to settle at Āmid. Later, al-Kāmil (615-35/1218-38 [*q.v.*]), after assuming power in difficult circumstances, recalled Ibn S̲h̲ukr in order to refill the state's coffers. Although the latter had become blind, he took up office in Cairo in 617/1220-1 and held it till his death four years later. Al-Kāmil then decided to do without a vizier, preferring to control the administration himself; this is the situation reflected in the administrative treatise of ʿUt̲h̲mān al-Nābulusī, one of al-Kāmil's high officials, in which the name of vizier is never mentioned.

A little later, Muʿīn al-Dīn Ibn al-S̲h̲ayk̲h̲ (d. 643/1246), youngest of the Awlād al-S̲h̲ayk̲h̲ brothers [*q.v.*], entered al-Kāmil's service, becoming "deputy of the vizier" (*nā'ib al-wizāra*), and it was not till the coming of al-Ṣāliḥ Ayyūb (637-47/1240-9) that he was appointed vizier. More than just head of the administration, Muʿīn al-Dīn was an army commander, and it was he who was charged with the conquest of Damascus in 642-3/1245.

In Damascus, Ḍiyā' al-Dīn Ibn al-At̲h̲īr [*q.v.*] was al-Afḍal's vizier from 589/1193 to 592/1196. Al-Afḍal placed complete confidence in him, but very soon both of them became enemies of Ṣalāḥ al-Dīn's former supporters, who fled to Cairo or Aleppo in large numbers. Later, under al-Muʿaẓẓam (615-24/1218-27 [*q.v.*]), no vizier is mentioned by the sources. When al-As̲h̲raf (626-35/1229-37) reigned in Damascus, he had as his vizier for some time Falak al-Dīn Ibn Masīrī (d. 643/1245), a man of mediocre talent, according to al-Maḳrīzī (*op. cit.*, iv, 84-7), and he was dismissed in 634/1236-7. More important was the next figure, Djamāl al-Dīn Ibn Maṭrūḥ (d. 649/1251), who served al-Ṣāliḥ Ayyūb in Damascus 644-7/1246-9. After an earlier career in the provincial administration of Egypt, Ibn Maṭrūḥ followed al-Ṣāliḥ Ayyūb to al-Djazīra in 629/1232. At Damascus, he not only directed the administration but also shared executive power with the *amīr* S̲h̲ihāb al-Dīn Ras̲h̲īd al-Kabīr. He was replaced by the *ḳāḍī* al-Asʿad S̲h̲araf al-Dīn al-Fā'izī, who was shortly afterwards appointed vizier in Cairo to al-Muʿaẓẓam Tūrāns̲h̲āh [*q.v.*].

It was finally at Aleppo that the vizierate enjoyed the greatest continuity in the Ayyūbid period, with six viziers succeeding almost without interruption in the years 592-658/1196-1260. The most important was Djamāl al-Dīn Ibn al-Ḳifṭī [*q.v.*], appointed *ca.* 614/1217-18; a man of great culture and deep piety, he left behind the reputation of a very good administrator. Al-ʿAzīz b. al-Ẓāhir in 628/1231 replaced him by one of his intimates, whose tenure of power turned out to be disastrous, so that Ibn al-Ḳifṭī was recalled in 634/1236, serving till his death in 646/1248 and then replaced by his brother Mu'ayyid al-Dīn, who remained in post at Aleppo till the Mongol invasion of 658/1260.

The geographical origins of these viziers varied according to the regions. In Egypt, they tended to be locally recruited, but in Aleppo, the influences of the lands further east (ʿIrāḳ and Persia), which were the origin of three out of six viziers, plus that of Egypt (the Banu 'l-Ḳifṭī), stamped the administration there with a double tradition, ʿAbbāsid-Saldjūḳid and Fāṭimid. Although less important than in the past, the influence of Christian and Jewish milieux was still at times felt. Thus al-ʿĀdil, right at the beginning of his reign, appointed a Christian convert called al-Ṣanīʿa Ibn al-Naḥḥāl. Al-Amdjad Bahrāms̲h̲āh (578-627/1182-1230) at Baalbek had a Samaritan vizier whose nephew Amīn al-Dawla al-Sāmirī (d. 648/1250), converted in his youth to Islam, was subsequently vizier to al-Ṣāliḥ Ismāʿīl at Damascus 637-43/1239-45. His excessive power, his network of spies and his financial extortions earned him the hostility of the Damascenes.

There was no specific, theoretical training for the post of vizier. Family tradition was important for most official positions. There were families of officials and even of viziers, but more often, the viziers learned on the job. They began as secretaries, accountants (*mustawfī*) and inspectors of finances (*nāẓir*) in the capital or the provinces before heading the administration. Most of them had a literary and legal-theological education. D̲j̲amāl al-Dīn Ibn al-Ḳifṭī is the best example of this, but Ibn S̲h̲ukr was an authority on traditions and Mālikī law. We know little about their financial remuneration. They probably drew a salary like other officials. Some received grants of lands, and more rarely, of *iḳṭā*ʿs (Ibn Maṭrūḥ); others enriched themselves by more or less legal means, and the leading viziers thus acquired large fortunes (Ibn S̲h̲ukr, Ibn al-Ḳifṭī).

The vizier's main function was to oversee the *dīwān*s and their personnel. Sometimes, in the absence of a head of chancery or chief of the army department, he guided the secretaries directly. His financial skills were the most important ones. The vizier also supervised provincial administration, above all, the collection of taxes which was the responsibility of the provincial governors, themselves appointed by the sultan and, occasionally, as at Aleppo, by the vizier. Nevertheless, in the financial sphere, some activities remained the prerogative of the ruler, such as the application or suppression of taxes, especially non-canonical ones, *mukūs* [see MAKS].

The vizier also had an important political role, often being part of regency councils and acting as the ruler's adviser, over whom he could have a wide influence. Certain of them even tried to replace one princely heir by another, as when the vizier of Ḥamāt, Zayn al-Dīn Ibn Furayd̲j̲, invited al-Nāṣir, the younger son of al-Manṣūr [*q.v.*], to seize power at the expense of his elder brother al-Muẓaffar. Sometimes the sultan deputed the vizier to oversee personally important projects. Thus al-ʿĀdil asked Ibn S̲h̲ukr to supervise work at Damascus on the Umayyad Mosque and the *muṣallā*. Ibn S̲h̲ukr also financed on his own account the building or restoring of two important mosques in the suburbs of Damascus and founded a Mālikī *madrasa*, the Ṣāḥibiyya, at Cairo.

In practice, the prestige and power of viziers depended a lot upon their own personality and on the ruler's authority. Not all were as highly respected as D̲j̲amāl al-Dīn Ibn al-Ḳifṭī or had as much power as Ibn S̲h̲ukr. In 604/1207, the caliph al-Nāṣir li-Dīn Allāh [*q.v.*] sent a robe of honour (*k̲h̲ilʿa*) to this last as well as to the Ayyūbid princes. In Aleppo, after the sultan had in 648/1250 left to take up residence in Damascus, the vizier Muʾayyid al-Dīn Ibn al-Ḳifṭī had the *g̲h̲ās̲h̲iya* [*q.v.*], one of the insignia of royalty, carried before him. Certain viziers, on the other hand, remained obscure persons, and in any case, their power always remained subordinate to that of the sultan, who could dismiss them at any time; it was indeed rare for viziers, even the most important, not to suffer dismissal, exile or imprisonment.

Bibliography: See the chroniclers and the biographical dictionaries for this period, given in AYYŪBIDS, and the separate articles on the main personalities. Of modern studies, see H.L. Gottschalk, *Al-Malik al-Kāmil von Egypten und seine Zeit*, Wiesbaden 1958; Cl. Cahen, introd to his ed. of al-Nābulusī's *K. al-Lumaʿ*, in *BEO*, xvi (1958-60), 124; R.S. Humphreys, *From Saladin to the Mongols. The Ayyubids of Damascus, 1193-1260*, Albany 1977; A.-M. Eddé, *La principauté ayyoubide d'Alep (579/1183-658/1260)*, Stuttgart 1999.

(ANNE-MARIE EDDÉ)

4. Muslim Spain.

In al-Andalus in the Umayyad period, every sovereign surrounded himself with various numbers of *wuzarāʾ*. Their purpose was not merely to be a source of advice and information for him but also to carry out in his name military missions as well as political and diplomatic assignments. Usually, there were no more than ten *wuzarāʾ* at any one time, though the *amīr* ʿAbd Allāh b. Muḥammad [*q.v.*] once had up to thirteen, and there were possibly as many as sixteen by the time of ʿAbd al-Raḥmān III [*q.v.*]. The appointment and dismissal of *wuzarāʾ* was particularly frequent during the government of the latter, who had a total of 46 ministers, a much higher number than any of his predecessors had had. It was only in the later years of the Umayyad dynasty that the number of these dignitaries rose. In 399/1008, at the time of the ceremony for the acclamation of ʿAbd al-Raḥmān b. Abī ʿĀmir [*q.v.*] as the successor to His̲h̲ām II [*q.v.*], there were 29 *wuzarāʾ* present.

The office of *wizāra* was a paid function. ʿAbd al-Raḥmān II arranged a salary (*rizḳ*) of 300 dīnārs for his ministers. But this office did not exclude all other work; indeed, it was usual that the bearer would hold office along with other functions, such as those of *kātib, ḳāʾid, ṣāḥib al-madīna* [*q.vv.*] etc. Up to the beginning of the 5th/11th centuries, the period when Abu ʾl-ʿAbbās Ibn D̲h̲akwān [*q.v.*] and Abu ʾl-Muṭarrif Ibn Futays (d. 402/1012) held the plural offices of *ḳāḍī* and *wazīr*, it had never been the case that anyone had at one and the same time been a religious magistrate and a vizier; but from then onwards this became a frequent practice.

The office of vizier was often held by the most influential families (*buyūtāt*), united by their ties of clientage (*walāʾ*) with the Marwānids. Even after the Umayyad period these lineages were made up of long series of viziers, among whom the most conspicuous were the Banū Abī ʿAbda, the Banū S̲h̲uhayd and the Banū Futays. It was exceptional for a member of the reigning family to occupy the post of *wazīr*, but the sovereigns took good care that representation of the other aristocratic Arab families was balanced proportionally. The case cited in the period of the *amīr* ʿAbd Allāh, of four viziers who belonged to the same clan of the Banū Abī ʿAbda, was considered unusual. This was also the *amīr* who for the first time decided to seat a person who did not belong to the Arab aristocracy among his ministers, his *fatā* [*q.v.*] Badr. The viziers in al-Andalus were always Muslim up to the period of the *mulūk al-ṭawāʾif* [*q.v.*], when there were also a few Jewish viziers, the most famous of whom was Ibn al-Nag̲h̲rālla from Granada (d. 448/1056-7).

The rank of vizier was superior to any other civil servant except that of *ḥād̲j̲ib* [*q.v.*]. In principle, the appointment to the office of vizier did not entail the responsibility of a department or duty to the government of the state. However, during the amīrate of ʿAbd Allāh, a vizier is mentioned who was invested specifically to direct one of the sectors of state administration (*idārāt*); and when in 344/955 the caliph ʿAbd al-Raḥmān reorganised state administration and divided the tasks of government into at least four sections, he placed a *wazīr* at the head of each one.

After the time of ʿAbd al-Raḥmān II, the viziers

had a room for private consultation and assembly (*bayt al-wizāra*) in the palace. The position of the viziers in this room conveyed the fact that all the dignitaries did not have the same rank; it was the *amīr* Muḥammad I (d. 273/886) who decided that the *wuzarāʾ* of eastern origin, called *shāmiyyūn*, should take precedence over the others, the *baladiyyūn*, and that consequently they should sit on the highest platforms. This priority was maintained by his successors, despite the conflict which it generated with several important *baladiyyūn*.

The honorary title of *dhu ʾl-wizāratayn* appeared in al-Andalus in 327/939, during the caliphate of ʿAbd al-Raḥmān III, who copied the title which Ibn Makhlad [*q.v.*] had received from the ʿAbbāsid caliph in 269/882 (see Hilāl al-Ṣābiʾ, *Rusūm dār al-khilāfa*, ed. M. ʿAwwād, Beirut n.d., 127). The first person to bear this title in Cordova was Abū ʿUmar Ibn Shuhayd, and his rank was superior to that of the other *wuzarāʾ*, for the name of the bearer of this title appears at the top of the list of viziers and he was paid the equivalent of the salaries of two ministers.

In the reign of al-Ḥakam II [*q.v.*] this title disappeared, but then there appears the title of *wazīr al-dawla*; it was given to al-Muṣḥafī (d. 372/982) before he was called *ḥādjib* on the day following the death of the caliph. During the first caliphate of his successor, Hishām II, the title of *dhu ʾl-wizāratayn* reappeared, and subsequently it was conferred on a child, the son of the *ḥādjib* ʿAbd al-Malik b. Abī ʿĀmir al-Muẓaffar [*q.v.*], under whose government the title *wazīr al-dawla* was again used to honour Ibn al-Ḳaṭṭāʿ al-Yaḥṣubī [*q.v.*].

In the period of the *Taifas*, quite a number of sovereigns assumed the title of *ḥādjib*, for the reason that this term had acquired such prestige under the Marwānid dynasty and also as an indication that they merely considered themselves as representatives of the caliph. These *mulūk al-ṭawāʾif* generalised the high position of vizier by applying it to all the people who were frequenting the court and whom they wished to honour; and from this period onwards there were also many persons in al-Andalus who were decorated with the title of *dhu ʾl-wizāratayn*.

The institution of the *wizāra* was so characteristic of Andalusī administration that the word *alguacil* (from Arabic *al-wazīr*) was very quickly integrated into the Castilian language. But the fact that this Arabism did not only signify "minister, counsellor or lieutenant of the sovereign", but that it was used to designate other duties or offices as well, seems to indicate that the word *wazīr* was eventually applied to different categories of public office in al-Andalus.

One of the meanings of the Castilian vocable *alguacil* in the Middle Ages was that of "governor, or lord of a city or a region, who was entrusted with civil and criminal jurisdiction" (*Diccionario histórico*, s.v.). This meaning corresponds to the expression "vizier of a district" which is frequently found in Andalusī texts from the 5th/11th century onwards and which conveys the fact that, from the period of ʿAbd al-Raḥmān III, the viziers began to fill permanent positions outside Cordova, chiefly those of governor and chief of the military region. This happened to such an extent that, at the end of the Naṣrid sultanate in Granada, the one who represented authority in each of the localities of the amīrate was given the title of *wazīr*.

After the occupation of the territory of Granada, the Castilians revived this institution and knew the member of the local community responsible for civil and fiscal matters and the representative of his fellow-citizens as *alguacil*.

Bibliography: Ibn al-Ḳūṭiyya, *Iftitāḥ*, Cairo-Beirut 1989, *passim*; Ibn Ḥayyān, *Muḳtabis*, Casablanca 1990, 21, 108; idem, *Muḳtabis*, v, ed. Madrid 1979, *passim*; Ḍabbī, 277-8; Ibn al-Abbār, *al-Ḥulla al-siyarāʾ*, ed. Ḥusayn Muʾnis, Cairo 1963, i, 120-1, 241; Ibn Saʿīd al-Maghribī, *al-Mughrib fī ḥulā al-Maghrib*, ed. Shawḳī Ḍayf, Cairo 1978, i, 46, 215-6; Ibn ʿIdhārī, ii, 80, 253; Nubāhī, *al-Marḳaba al-ʿulyā*, 13, 84-9, 92; Makkarī, *Nafḥ*, Beirut 1988, i, 216-17, 337-8, 353-6; Lévi-Provençal, *Hist. Espagne musulmane*, iii, 18-22; *Diccionario histórico de la lengua española*, s.v. *alguacil*; D. Sourdel, *Wazīr et ḥāǧib en Occident*, in *Études d'orientalisme à la mémoire de Lévi-Provençal*, Paris 1962, ii, 749-55; Ma. J. Rubiera, *Ḏū l-Wizāratayn Ibn Ḥakīm de Ronda*, in *Al-And.*, xxxiv (1969), 105-21; R. Arié, *L'Espagne musulmane au temps des Naṣrides*, Paris 1973, 198-208; M. Meouak, *Notes sur le vizirat et les vizirs en al-Andalus à l'époque umayyade (milieu du IIe/VIIIe-fin du IVe/Xe siècles)*, in *Stud. Isl.*, lxxviii (1993), 181-90.

(A. Carmona)

II. In Persia

The *wazīr* was the head of the supreme *dīwān*, the *dīwān-i aʿlā* [see dīwān. iv. Iran] and as such was the head of the bureaucracy. He had under him numerous subordinates. The heads of some branches of the administration under him were also called *wazīrs*, such as the *wazīr-i lashkar* and the *wazīrs* in charge of the finances of the provinces. The term *wazīr* was also sometimes applied to the head of the personal establishment of provincial governors, important *amīrs* and royal princes and princesses. This article will be concerned with the *wazīr* as head of the supreme *dīwān*.

The *wazīr* belonged to the "men of the pen" as opposed to the "men of the sword" and was usually of Persian rather than Turkish extraction. A common feature of society was the existence of influential bureaucratic families, such as the Djayhānīs [see al-djayhānī, in Suppl.], the Balʿamīs [see balʿamī] and ʿUtbīs; [see ʿutbī]; in the Saldjūḳ period the family of Niẓām al-Mulk [*q.v.*]; and under the Īlkhāns the Djuwaynīs and the family of Rashīd al-Dīn Faḍl Allāh Hamadānī [see rashīd al-dīn ṭabīb].

Under the Īlkhāns, and sometimes in later times also, the *wazīr* had the title *ṣāḥib dīwān*. The Ṣafawid shah ʿAbbās I [*q.v.*], gave the *wazīr* the titles *Iʿtimād al-Dawla* and *Ṣadr-i Aʿẓam*, by which title he was also known in the Ḳādjār period.

The insignia of the *wazīr* was an inkpot, usually golden, which he was given on appointment together with a diploma (*manshūr*), and a robe of honour. Ṣadr al-Dīn Khālidī, when appointed *ṣāḥib dīwān* by Gaykhātū [*q.v.*] in 691/1292 was given the *laḳab* of Ṣadr-i Djahān, a gold seal, a horse-tail standard, a war trumpet and a *tūmān* [*q.v.*] of soldiers. In the late Īlkhānid period the insignia of the *wazīr* appear to have been a golden inkpot, a jewelled belt, a royal seal (*āl*), and banner (*sandjaḳ*), a standard (*ʿalam*) and the right to kettle-drums (*ṭabl*, *naḳḳāra* [*q.v.*] (Lambton, *Continuity and change in medieval Persia*, 56). Under the Ṣafawids, his insignia were a jewelled pen and inkstand. On appointment he was given robes of honour, a headdress (*tādj u hādj*) with a plume (*djiḳa*) and a *tūmār* (Muḥammad Taḳī Dānishpazhūh, *Dastūr al-mulūk-i Mīrzā Rafīʿā wa tadhkirat al-mulūk-i Mīrzā Samīʿa*, in *Madjalla-yi dānishkada-yi adabiyyāt wa ʿulūm-i insānī*, Tehran, xvi/1-2 [1968], 77).

The *wazīr* was not the servant of the state but of the ruler, by whom he was directly appointed. He was a member of the court (*dargāh*) and accompanied the ruler on military expeditions and on his perambulations around the empire. Because of the element of personal service involved, the power and influence of the *wazīr* underwent many vicissitudes with the rise and fall of successive dynasties and rulers.

Although the *wazīr* had general supervision over the administration, his fundamental and most important duty was to oversee the finances of the state. He was usually paid by assignments on the revenue; in addition, he received various fees and allowances, the number of which increased over the years, especially under the Ṣafawids. The sources of profit open to him were many and some *wazīr*s accumulated much wealth. This enabled them to gather followers but it also made them the object of the jealousy of their peers and the suspicion of the ruler, who sometimes sought to limit their potential power by the appointment of joint *wazīrs*. These dual appointments were occasionally found under the Būyids and Kh^w^ārazm Shāhs, notably under the Īlkhāns, and at least once under the Ḳādjārs [see ḲĀDJĀR at Vol. IV, 394a]. In this the Īlkhāns may have been influenced by Chinese administrative practice. Tension between the *wazīr* and the military was a perennial feature of most reigns. Although the assignments and pay of the military went, at least in theory, through the office of the *wazīr*, only the strongest *wazīr*s could hope to maintain the pre-eminence of the bureaucracy over the military.

The office of *wazīr* was a precarious one. Its holder had no security of tenure and was subject to arbitrary dismissal and was often, after his fall, mulcted, and sometimes physically punished and murdered. Of the six men who held the office of *wazīr* under Maḥmūd of Ghazna [*q.v.*], three were dismissed and died violently; a fourth suffered disgrace and prolonged imprisonment; a fifth fell from favour and was mulcted and a sixth was executed by Masʿūd b. Maḥmūd shortly after he succeeded Maḥmūd (C.E. Bosworth, *The Ghaznavids*, Edinburgh 1963, 70-1). The situation did not materially alter in later periods. Several Saldjūḳ *wazīr*s suffered violent ends (Lambton, *op. cit.*, 46-7); and Ḥamd Allāh Mustawfī states that Tādj al-Dīn ʿAlī Shāh was the only Īlkhānid *wazīr* to die a natural death (*Tārīkh-i guzīda*, ed. ʿAbd al-Ḥusayn Nawāʾī, Tehran AHS 1336-9/1958-61, 616). Dismissal followed by mulcting, imprisonment and death was a fact of frequent occurrence up to and including the 19th century.

Under the Sāmānids the *wazīr*, known as the Kh^w^ādja Buzurg, was the head of a well-developed bureaucratic system, divided into a number of separate *dīwān*s (Barthold, *Turkestan*, 229), but towards the end of the 4th/10th century, power began to pass into the hands of the military. The historian al-ʿUtbī states that the last Sāmānid *wazīr*s had no power to restore order: "Dominion passed into the hands of the Turks and the decrees of the *wazīr*s lost their force" (quoted by Barthold, *op. cit.*, 253). Meanwhile in the western provinces the *wazīr*s under Būyid rule no longer enjoyed prestige as had the Barmakids [see AL-BARĀMIKA] under the caliphs. Their function was mainly to provide money for the military forces of the ruler. Some, however, acquired considerable power, notably al-Ṣāḥib Ibn ʿAbbād [*q.v.*], *wazīr* to Fakhr al-Dawla and Muʾayyid al-Dawla, and Abū ʿAlī b. Ismāʿīl al-Muwaffaḳ, appointed *wazīr* by Bahāʾ al-Dawla in 388/998 [see BAHĀʾ AL-DAWLA, in Suppl., at 118b].

The vizierate reached its apogee under Niẓām al-Mulk [*q.v.*], *wazīr* to the Saldjūḳ sultans Alp Arslān and Malikshāh. He supervised the general conduct of affairs on behalf of the sultan. He also had general supervision of the religious institution, and as the personal representative of the sultan he conducted relations with the caliph and other rulers. He even on occasion conducted military expeditions (Lambton, *op. cit.*, 18 ff.). The rewards of office were great but its expenses heavy. The *wazīr* was expected to maintain a large household, including armed retainers. Niẓām al-Mulk, for example, had a private army of military slaves. Custom demanded that the *wazīr* should be accessible, and his court was accordingly thronged with petitioners. The distinction between his private funds and what he expended as *wazīr* on behalf of the sultan or in the general interest is not easily made. In the late Saldjūḳ period, the vizierate declined, not only because of a lack of effective controls throughout the administration but also because of the fragmentation of the Saldjūḳ empire. Under the Kh^w^ārazm Shāhs, the *wazīr* temporarily regained some of his former importance (*ibid.*, 49).

In the early years of Mongol dominion in Persia, there was an ill-defined dual system: the *wazīr*s acted mainly as finance ministers alongside the Mongol governors of the provinces, though what their relationship was to the *ulugh bitikči*s (or chief secretaries) of the Mongol governors, whose functions appear to have been primarily the keeping of tax records and the imposition and collection of taxes, is not clear. Bahāʾ al-Dīn Djuwaynī was confirmed as *ṣāḥib dīwān* to Čin-Temür, the governor of Khurāsān, by Ögedey and was later successively *ṣāḥib dīwān* to Korgüz and Arghūn, both of whom were governors of Khurāsān. On the succession of Möngke, he was confirmed as *ṣāḥib dīwān* and sent with the Mongol *amīr* Naymatay to Persian ʿIrāḳ and Yazd, but died en route to his new post. Shams al-Dīn Djuwaynī became chief minister and *ṣāḥib dīwān* to Hülegü in 661/1262-3, which post he also held under Hülegü's successor, Abāḳā, and attained a position of great personal influence. From 678/1279 Madjd al-Mulk Yazdī, the *mushrif al-mamālik*, held office beside him and signed documents on the left while Shams al-Dīn signed on the right. Saʿd al-Dawla, *ṣāḥib dīwān* to Arghūn, and Ṣadr al-Dīn Aḥmad Khālidī, appointed *ṣāḥib dīwān* by Gaykhātū in 691/1292, both exercised wide-ranging power. The most influential Īlkhānid *wazīr* was probably Rashīd al-Dīn Faḍl Allāh Hamadānī, who held office under Ghāzān and Öldjeytü. His position was not entirely secure, however, and eventually he fell from office and was mulcted and killed. In the reign of Ghāzān he had alongside him Saʿd al-Dīn Muḥammad Sāwadjī as joint *wazīr* and Tādj al-Dīn ʿAlī Shāh in the reign of Öldjeytü.

Under Tīmūr there was a decline in the position of the *wazīr*. Power was in the hands of the military. Similarly, under the Ḳara Ḳoyunlu and the Aḳ Ḳoyunlu the *wazīr*'s power was circumscribed and confined mainly to financial affairs.

In the early Ṣafawid period, the administration of the state was fairly fluid and at times the *amīr*s, especially the *amīr al-umarāʾ*, and to a lesser extent the *ṣadr* (the chief religious official), encroached upon the powers of the *wazīr*. Shah Ismāʿīl I tended to delegate power to a chief minister, known as the *wakīl*, whose functions, if not his title, had existed under the late Aḳ Ḳoyunlu rulers (J. Aubin, *L'avènement des Safavides*, in *Moyen Orient et Océan Indien*, v [1988], 112). He was in effect the *wazīr*, and this was still the official term for the chief minister of the shah. The term *wakīl* does not appear in the official titulary in archival documents so far as is known (*ibid.*, 113-14. This corrects the statement in the art. DĪWĀN at Vol. IV,

334b, which differentiates wrongly *wakīl* from *wazīr*). Political and financial affairs (*umūr-i mālī wa umūr-i mulkī*) were delegated to him but he had no authority over the religious institution, though he did sometimes intervene in the nomination of the *ṣadr* (*ibid.*, 115-66).

From the reign of ʿAbbās I (995-1038/1587-1629), an elaborate administrative system evolved, at the head of which stood the *wazīr*. He was a member of the council of state (*d̲j̲ānkī*); at court he stood at the shah's right hand, while the *wāḳiʿa-nuwīs*, the official historiographer, stood on the left and was sometimes called the *wazīr-i čap* (R.M. Savory, *The Safavid administrative system*, in *Camb. hist. of Iran*, vi, *The Timurid and Safavid periods*, Cambridge 1986, 353).

The *Dastūr al-mulūk* of Mīrzā Rafīʿā and the *Tad̲h̲kirat al-mulūk* [of Mīrzā Samīʿā] (Persian text in facs., tr. and explained by V. Minorsky, London, 1943) describe the office of the *wazīr* of the supreme *dīwān*. The former states that his office was the greatest of all offices and that he was the most important of all the pillars of the state; the collection and expenditure of the revenue were made with his knowledge, approval and signature; subordinate *wazīr*s and other officials of the *dīwān* and the agents of the *dīwān* in the provinces were appointed by him. It was his duty to restrain unlawful acts, but if the offender was a powerful governor, he was to refer the case to the shah. The *wazīr* was to come daily to the guard-house at the gate of the *dīwān* to hear the petitions of the people (ed. Dānis̲h̲-paz̲h̲ūh, 75-7). He had no wages (*mawād̲j̲ib*) but had the right to numerous dues, fees and allowances. At the New Year he had to give a present [see PĪS̲H̲KAS̲H̲] to the shah of 1,000 *as̲h̲rafī*s and twelve stallions and mares (*ibid.*, 77).

Under Fatḥ ʿAlī S̲h̲āh (1797-1834), the functions of the *wazīr* were probably not very different from the late Ṣafavid period; but in the mid-19th century, political and administrative changes began to take place [see DUSTŪR. iv; ḲĀD̲J̲ĀR]. Mīrzā Taḳī K̲h̲ān Amīr Niẓām [see ĀMĪR KABĪR in Suppl.], chief minister (*ṣadr-i aʿẓam*) to Nāṣir al-Dīn S̲h̲āh from 1848 to 1852 and Mīrzā Ḥusayn K̲h̲ān Sipahsālār Mus̲h̲īr al-Dawla, who was appointed in 1871, both attempted to introduce far-reaching reforms but with little success; both were dismissed and the former murdered. Mīrzā Āḳā K̲h̲ān Nūrī, Mīrzā Taḳī K̲h̲ān's successor, was dismissed in 1858, and for some years the shah sought to rule without a chief minister. The experiment was not successful, though the shah repeated it again in 1873. In the 1880s, chief ministers were again appointed.

Bibliography (in addition to references given in the article): Waṣṣāf, *Ak̲h̲lāḳ al-salṭana*, in idem, *Tārīk̲h̲-i Waṣṣāf*, ed. M.M. Iṣfahānī, lith. Bombay 1269/1852-3, 484-98; Nad̲j̲m al-Dīn Rāzī, *Mirṣād al-ʿibād min al-mabdaʾ ilā ʾl maʿād*, ed. Ḥusayn al-Ḥusaynī al-Niʿmatallāhī, Tehran AHS 1312/1933; Afḍal al-Dīn Abū Ḥāmid Aḥmad b. Ḥāmid Kirmānī, *ʿIḳd al-ʿulā*, ed. ʿAlī Muḥammad ʿĀmirī Nāʾīnī, Tehran AHS 1311/1932-3; K̲h̲ʷāndamīr, *Dastūr al-wuzarāʾ*, ed. Saʿīd Nafīsī, Tehran AHS 1317/1938-9; S.D. Goitein, *The origin of the vizierate*, in *IC*, xvi (1942), 255-62, also in his *Studies in Islamic history and institutions*, Leiden 1968; ʿAbd Allāh Marwārīd, *S̲h̲araf-nāma*, facs. with tr. and commentary by H. Roemer as *Staatsschreiben der Timuridenzeit*, Wiesbaden 1952; B. Spuler, *Iran in früh-islamischer Zeit*, Wiesbaden 1952; idem, *Die Mongolen in Iran*, ³Berlin 1985; ʿAbbās Iḳbāl, *Wizārat dar ʿahd-i salāṭīn-i buzurg-i sald̲j̲ūḳī*, Tehran AHS 1338/1957-8; ʿAḳīlī, *Āt̲h̲ār al-wuzarāʾ*, ed. Mīr D̲j̲alāl al-Dīn Ḥusaynī Urmawī, Tehran AHS 1337/1958-9; Kay Kāwūs b. Iskandar, *Ḳābūs-nāma*, ed. G̲h̲ulām Ḥusayn Yūsufī, Tehran AHS 1345/1967, ed. R. Levy, London 1951, tr. idem, *A mirror for princes*, London 1951; Niẓām al-Mulk, *Siyāsat-nāma*, ed. and tr. C. Schefer, Paris 1891-3, ed. H. Darke as *Siyar al-mulūk*, ²Tehran AHS 1347/1968; G̲h̲azālī, *Naṣīḥat al-mulūk*, ed. D̲j̲alāl al-Dīn Humāʾī, Tehran AHS 1351/1972-3; C.L. Klausner, *The Seljuk Vezirate*, Cambridge, Mass. 1973; Ḥasan Anwarī, *Iṣṭilāḥāt-i dīwānī-yi dawra-yi g̲h̲aznawī wa sald̲j̲ūḳī*, Tehran 1976-7; *Tārīk̲h̲-i s̲h̲āhī-i ḳarā-k̲h̲iṭāʾiyān*, ed. Muḥammad Ibrāhīm Pārīzī, Tehran 1976-7; J. van Ess, *Der Wesir und seine Gelehrten*, Wiesbaden 1981; A.K.S. Lambton, *The dilemma of government in Islamic Persia. The Siyāsat-nāma of Niẓām al-Mulk*, in *Iran JBIPS*, xxii (1984), 55-66; eadem, *Personal service and the element of concession in the theory of the vizierate in medieval Persia*, in C.E. Bosworth *et alii* (eds.), *The Islamic World from classical to modern times*, Princeton 1989.

Documents for the *wazīr* are to be found in the following collections: Bahāʾ al-Dīn Bag̲h̲dādī, *al-Tawassul ilā ʾl-tarassul*, ed. Aḥmad Bahmanyār, Tehran AHS 1315/1936-7; Muntad̲j̲ab al-Dīn Badīʿ al-Kātib al-D̲j̲uwaynī, *ʿAtabat al-kataba*, ed. ʿAbbās Iḳbāl, Tehran AHS 1329/1951; ʿAbd Allāh b. Muḥammad b. Kiyā Māzandarānī, *Die resāla-ye falakiyya*, ed. W. Hinz, Wiesbaden 1952; H. Horst, *Die Staatsverwaltung der Grosselǧūqen und Ḫōrazmšāhs*, Wiesbaden 1964; Muḥammad b. Hindūs̲h̲āh Nak̲h̲d̲j̲iwānī, *Dastūr al-kātib fī taʿyīn al-marātib*, ed. A.A. Alizade, Moscow i, 1964, i/2, 1971, ii, 1976; see also B.G. Fragner, *Repertorium persischer Herrscherurkunden*, Freiburg im Breisgau 1980. Much material on the holders of the office of *wazīr* is to be found in chronicles and historical works, some of which give lists of *wazīr*s under the reigns of individual rulers or dynasties, and in biographical dictionaries.

(ANN K.S. LAMBTON)

III. IN THE OTTOMAN EMPIRE

Here, synonyms for the *wezīr* were such varied terms as *pas̲h̲a*, *ṣāḥib*, *āṣaf*, *wekīl*, *nāẓir* and *lala*, with the Grand Vizier also known as the *ṣadr-i aʿẓam* [*q.v.*], the First *Wezīr* in the imperial *dīwān*, with the lesser *wezīr*s as his advisers.

Background and evolution of the office

During the 8th/14th century, the Ottoman rulers appear to have chosen their *wezīr*s mostly from among the *ʿulemāʾ*-bureaucrats or *ḳāḍī*s. In Ork̲h̲an's *temlīk-nāme* of Rabīʿ II 749/June 1348 (*Topkapı Sarayı arşiv kılavuzu*, i, Istanbul 1938, facsimile I) Ḥād̲j̲d̲j̲ī Pas̲h̲a, mentioned first among the witnesses, is obviously the *wezīr*. Evidently, it was because of their expert knowledge in Islamic jurisprudence and institutions, considered of vital importance in organising the new Ottoman amīrate, that *wezīr*s were chosen from the *ʿulemāʾ* class. The first identified *wezīr*s were ʿAlāʾ al-Dīn ʿAlī Pas̲h̲a (723/1323), Aḥmad b. Maḥmūd (741/1340), Ḥād̲j̲d̲j̲ī Pas̲h̲a (towards 749/1348) and Sinān al-Dīn Yūsuf (after 749/1348). ʿAlāʾ al-Dīn Pas̲h̲a, who is believed to have been the first *wezīr* in Ottoman history, was definitely of the *ʿulemāʾ* class (see Hüsameddin, 43) and not the brother of Sultan Ork̲h̲an, as claimed in Ottoman annals. Before Čandarlî K̲h̲ayr al-Dīn Ḳara K̲h̲alīl, a chief *ḳāḍī*, was made Grand Vizier with full powers in 787/1385 or a little later, six *wezīr*s have been identified by Hüsameddin (*ibid.*). In the period 1385-1453 the Čandarlî family provided the Ottoman state with *wezīr*s and Grand Viziers, all serving as *ḳāḍī* in their earlier career. Some of the members of the family served only as simple *wezīr*s or *ḳāḍī-ʿasker*s in the imperial *dīwān* (see Uzunçarşılı, *Çandarlı vezir ailesi*).

Early popular *ghāzī* tradition (see Giese, *Chroniken*) reflects ever-present rivalry between the *wezīrs* of military background and those from the *ʿulemāʾ*. The *beylerbeyis* of Rumeli and Anadolu [*q.vv.*], as well as *wezīrs* of military background, sat in the imperial *dīwān* in this early period. The most spectacular show of rivalry between the two groups occurred between Čandarli̊ Khalīl and Shihāb al-Dīn Pasha in the period 1440-53, ending with the fall of Khalīl (see Inalcık, *Fatih devri*, 1-53).

A revolutionary change occurred in 857/1453 when the over-mighty Grand Vizier Čandarli̊ Khalīl, arrested and executed by Meḥemmed II, was replaced by *wezīrs* from amongst the military men of *ḳul* [see GHULĀM. iv] origin, although bureaucrats or *ʿulemāʾ* with expertise in finance or chancery correspondence continued to be employed as *wezīrs*. One from the latter category, Nishāndji̊ Meḥmed of Ḳaramān, holding the position of Grand Vizier, was murdered by the Janissaries on the death of Meḥemmed II in 886/1481. His rival *wezīrs* Isḥāḳ and Gedik Aḥmed [*q.v.*], military men, replaced him in the government, and all *wezīrs* from *ʿulemāʾ* or from *küttāb* or secretarial origin were dismissed. The insurgent Janissaries demanded that from then onwards, the sultan should choose his *wezīrs* exclusively from among the *ḳul* element.

However, Bāyezīd II rehabilitated the Čandarli̊ family to the vizierate and, being concerned for his security on the throne against his brother Djem [*q.v.*], he often entrusted the position to the eunuch *ḳapi̊-agha* [*q.v.*] or other trusted servants of the palace.

Consequently, in the classical age (1453-1600), the *wezīrs* were mostly men of military background. Ibn Khaldūn noted the replacement of the *arbāb al-ḳalam* by the *arbāb al-sayf* under the Mamlūk Sultans in Egypt also. It was the Grand Vizier's exclusive right to recommend to the sultan the appointment or promotion of a *wezīr*. Of course, in reality people close to the sultan, such as the *ḳapi̊-agha*, the sultan's mother or the *muṣāḥib*, a favourite adviser of the sultan, often played a role in the final decision. Appointment of the *wezīrs* was to be made directly by the sultan himself with a *khaṭṭ-i̊ hümāyūn* [*q.v.*]. In choosing a *wezīr*, his expert knowledge in a special area was also taken into account. Maḥmūd Pasha was deliberately chosen for Meḥemmed II's plans for Serbia, and Ibrāhīm Pasha for Süleymān I's campaigns in Europe. *Wezīrs* of military origin multiplied in wartime.

Wezīrs coming from among the professional secretaries, as had been the rule formerly in the ʿAbbāsid, Saldjūḳid and Ilkhānid states, were mostly to be found in the Ottoman government in the second half of the 9th/15th century when a highly developed Ottoman bureaucracy evolved. Then, most of the *wezīrs* of *küttāb* origin belonged to the literati or to *ʿulemāʾ* families. Djazarī Ḳāsi̊m Pasha from Persia, who supposedly founded the Ottoman chancery or *inshāʾ* style and who was second *wezīr* and candidate for the Grand Vizierate under Bāyezīd II, was exiled under pressure from the military *wezīrs*. In any case, state secretaries specialising in such areas as finances and chancery correspondence rose in the hierarchy to become *wezīrs* and Grand Viziers.

In the chaotic conditions of the end of the 10th/16th century, the rule that the second *wezīr* would be promoted to the Grand Vizierate was often disregarded, and the third or fourth *wezīr*, or even a governor or Janissary *agha* or *silāḥdār* outside the *dīwān*, could be appointed to the position.

As for the ethnic origins of the *wezīrs*, most of them in the classical age were of slave, *ḳul*, origin. We find, for example, a comparatively great number of *wezīrs* and Grand Viziers of Albanian and Slavic origin in the period 1430-1550 because of the fact that there were frequent expeditions in Albania, and the *devshirme* [*q.v.*] was regularly practised in the poor mountainous regions of the Balkans during this period (see Jorga, *GOR*, iii, 162-89). For the same reason, towards 983/1575 *wezīrs* were mostly of Croatian, Hungarian or Austrian origin. Passing through the palace services and provincial hierarchy, the most successful of these came back as *wezīrs* to the imperial *dīwān*. At palace schools, some gifted ones such as Luṭfī Pasha [*q.v.*] gained a good Ottoman Turkish education, while most of them acquired only martial skills, but some were illiterate and hardly able to speak Turkish. They had to rely on people in their *ḳapu* [*q.v.*], including advisers and secretaries who were responsible for their correspondence.

The accession of a new sultan to the throne meant a radical change in the *dīwān*, since the personnel which had served him in the period of his governorship expected to replace the *wezīrs* and other dignitaries of the previous sultan. The rivalry and plots of the newcomers to gain full control of the government often caused serious crises in administration, as witnessed at the accessions of Meḥemmed II, Bāyezīd II, Selīm I, Selīm II and Murād III. When the practice of the princes' governorship was abandoned under Meḥemmed III [*q.v.*], palace factions mostly determined who was to become the new sultan and his *wezīrs*. Under the sultans who were minors, in the 11th/17th century *wālide sulṭāns* [*q.v.*] became responsible for choosing the *wezīrs*.

Under the long period of regency of the *Wālide* Māhpeyker [see KÖSEM WĀLIDE], who was acting in alliance with the Janissary corps, dismissals became very frequent as a result of favouritism, clientship and bribery. Contemporary critics (see ʿĀlī, *Nuzha*; Ḳoči Bey, *Risāle*) stress that it was the loss of vizierial authority that was responsible for the anarchical conditions in the period.

At an unusually critical point in 1066/1656, the palace saw that it was indispensable to restore the vizierial authority in the person of Meḥmed Köprülü [see KÖPRÜLÜ], to whom dictatorial powers were assigned. Meḥmed, his son and relatives retained power for almost half a century, often allying with the *ʿulemāʾ* to neutralise rivals.

The character of the Ottoman vizierate and the origins of the *wezīrs* again changed radically in the period following the peace of Carlowitz [see ḲARLOVČA] in 1109/1698-9. During the war of 1683-99, the Ottoman army and government collapsed, and the palace had to call upon the Djelālī [*q.v.* in Suppl.] leaders of Anatolia. One of them, Boynu-Yarali̊ Meḥmed, a Turcoman, became Grand Vizier (Naʿīmā, vi, 197; Silāḥdār, i, 410). After the war, the palace brought to power the architect of the peace treaty, the *reʾīs al-küttāb* [*q.v.*], Rāmī Meḥmed, head of the Grand Vizier's chancery responsible for foreign affairs. The Ottomans now believed that some sort of diplomatic service was becoming crucial for the existence of the empire, so that many of the *wezīrs* were now chosen from among the *reʾīs al-küttāb* class in the 18th century (Nishāndji̊ Ismāʿīl, Meḥmed Emīn, Abū Bekr, Muḥsin-zāde, Khalīl Ḥāmid). However, in the period following the 1730 revolution, meetings of the imperial *dīwān* became obsolete. The powerful black eunuch *aghas* of the imperial harem became responsible for the choice of the *wezīrs* and Grand Viziers. Later, in the second half of the century, bureaucrats, such as Rāghib Pasha [*q.v.*], succeeded in asserting vizieral power and independence, and the Grand Vizier's *kapu* [see BĀB-I ʿĀLĪ] became the centre of all governmental affairs. In this century also, Janissary *aghas* or *kapudān-i deryās* [*q.v.*] or governors were directly chosen for the Grand Vizierate, whilst most of the *wezīrs* and the Grand Viziers came from the Turkish families whose sons were clients of the high dignitaries or servants in the imperial palace. *Intisāb*, patronage and clientship thus played a major role in the choice of *wezīrs*, so that Georgian and Circassian slaves belonging to the households of dignitaries reached this exalted position during this period (Siyāwush, Kara Ibrāhīm, ʿAlī, Kodja Yūsuf, Ḥasan and Kör Yūsuf). The *ṣadr-i aʿẓam*'s assistants in his household, the *ketkhudā* and the *mektūbdju*, assumed the role of the *wezīrs*. In 1795 an attempt was made to reform the vizierate by restricting the title only to governors.

Bureaucratic control became more pronounced in the 19th century. In 1836, with the establishment of *neẓārets*, ministeries each under a *nāẓir* or *wekīl*, the title of *wezīr* and *pasha* was then kept only as a ceremonial title for *nāẓirs*.

The Grand Vizier then bore the title of *bash-wekīl*, losing much of a Grand Vizier's responsibility (see Akyıldız, 25-35). During the *Tanẓīmāt* [*q.v.*] period (1839-76), reformist bureaucrats and diplomats such as Muṣṭafā Reshīd, ʿĀlī and Fuʾād, succeeded each other in government, while they intermittently had to leave power to the generals or palace favourites. But, in general, it was the bureaucrats specialising in foreign affairs who alone had the power to attempt to disentangle the state from the complications of the so-called Eastern Question (see Findley).

Functions

In earlier Islamic states, *wezīrs*, as the heads of the separate *dīwāns* or bureaux, appear to have had a kind of autonomy. In the Ottoman state, however, all of the *erkān-i dewlet*, that is the *wezīrs* in the first place, and *defterdārs*, *nishāndjīs* and *kāḍī-ʿaskers* [*q.vv.*], assembled together in the *dīwān-i hümāyūn* [*q.v.*], the imperial council, theoretically under the sultan himself, but in practice under his *wekīl-i muṭlak*, the first *wezīr* or Grand Vizier [see ṢADR-I AʿẒAM].

Since the unity of the sultan's authority was the paramount principle of Ottoman government, state powers were to be exercised directly and exclusively by the first *wezīr*, other *wezīrs* acting mainly as his advisers. Potentially, however, each *wezīr* was considered to have the same powers as the first *wezīr*. A regulation of the vizierate (*MTM*, iii, 498-500) stipulates that when a *wezīr* was appointed as *kāʾim-maḳām*, [*q.v.*] or as *serdār*, army commander, or as a *müfettish*, general inspector, he became superior in status to other *wezīrs*. When he was appointed a *serdār* or a *kāʾim-maḳām*, he automatically acquired "exactly the same powers as the Grand Vizier, administering all sorts of *sharʿī* and *ʿurfī* affairs and the state laws and regulations, sending imperial orders in the name of the sultan (*fermān buyurmak*), making all appointments, and taking decisions in all kinds of affairs." But in fact many *kāʾim-maḳām pashas* with such sweeping powers were tempted to replace the absent Grand Vizier. Also, a *wezīr* who was appointed governor to an *eyālet* or province or a *serdār* "was authorised on the way to his destination to hold a *dīwān* of his own to hear suits and issue *buyuruldus* or vizieral orders to prevent or correct unjust acts against the sultan's subjects". A *mufettish wezīr* had the power to dismiss or appoint local office-holders as the situation required. Even when he was dismissed from the mission, he could exercise the same powers on his way back to Istanbul.

At his appointment a *wezīr* received gifts, including a *dawāt* or *diwīt*, an ink-case which was traditionally the symbol of viziership, in all Islamic states. When on campaign, a *wezīr* carried three *tughs* [*q.v.*], used a large tent of three poles, the so-called shadow-hanging or, *sāyebān*, and had a gallery lit with candles, *kandilli sokak* (for other ceremonial distinctions, see *MTM*, iii, 498-500). Viziers of this category were distinguished as *üč-tughlu wezīr* and *ṣāḥib-i ṭughrā wezīr*. In a political treatise of around 1640 (*Ḥirz al-mulūk*, fols. 5a-10b) an ideal *wezīr* is described as being pious, just and honest, not greedy, and capable of solving problems by referring to the authoritative sources in Arabic and Persian. A Grand Vizier should, in addition, always consult other *wezīrs* before taking a decision. The author also underlines that the Grand Vizier should always be on the side of the powerless *reʿāyā* [*q.v.*], careful not to take bribes, not to attempt to get possession of public lands, and not to favour his clients for public offices. A Grand Vizier should, in the *dīwān* meetings, send most of the plaintiffs to the second *wezīr* for an impartial treatment.

The meeting days of the *dīwān* were four, from Saturday to Tuesday and the *ʿarḍ*, audience days with the sultan, two, sc. Sunday and Tuesday. In the late 11th/17th century, *dīwān* days were restricted to the *ʿarḍ* days.

In the *dīwān* meetings, *wezīrs* sat on the right-hand of the Grand Vizier in order of their seniority in the office. As advisers to the Grand Vizier, they discussed state affairs with him. The Grand Vizier Ibrāhīm, executed in 1536, was accused of neglecting consultation with the *wezīrs*. They accompanied the Grand Vizier on his audience days with the sultan. In the audience, the Grand Vizier alone spoke and made a report on affairs. A *wezīr* could make a written report to the sultan only through the Grand Vizier. Complaints by people against a *wezīr* were seen and judged in a special committee composed of the Grand Vizier, the *shaykh al-islām* [*q.v.*] and two *kāḍī-ʿaskers*.

Besides the *dīwān-i hümāyūn*, the Grand Vizier held a *dīwān* in his own residence called the *ikindi dīwānī*, the afternoon *dīwān*, to take care of lesser affairs. This residence, called *Pasha-kapīsī* or *Bāb-i ʿĀlī*, became the main *dīwān* for government affairs in the second half of the 11th/17th century.

One of the privileges of a *wezīr* was to assist the Grand Vizier and the *nishāndjī* in drawing the *ṭughrā* [*q.v.*], or sultan's seal, on the *firmāns*, a privilege for which they were called *wezīr-i ṣāḥib-i ṭughrā*. Putting the *ṭughrā* meant the validation of the sultan's order, thus making *wezīrs* the authorised agents of the ruler. Before the Ottomans, the *wizāret-i ṭughrā* was one of the highest positions in a Saldjūḳid administration.

Customarily, the second *wezīr* was the prime candidate for the Grand Vizierate, although for practical reasons the sultan could choose a *wezīr* of lower rank for the post. Breach of this rule rarely caused a political crisis [see AḤMAD PASHA, KHĀʾIN].

The number of *wezīrs* sitting at the imperial *dīwān* was customarily restricted to four in the classical period, a mystical figure representing the four corners of the world, or the four Rightly-Guided Caliphs. Under certain circumstances, however, the number might be increased to more than four. For a better consultation the increased number was recommended (*Ḥirz al-mulūk*, fols. 26b-30b). In the 10th/16th century, governors of the large distant provinces, Egypt, Baghdād,

Ḥabes̲h̲ (Abyssinia), Yemen and Buda bore the title of *wezīr*, enabling them to act independently as circumstances required. Then, the number of seven became the norm. Over the course of time, two categories of *wezīrs* appeared, those sitting in the imperial *dīwān* in Istanbul, called *dāk̲h̲il*, or of the *ḳubbe*, and those of the provinces called *k̲h̲āridj̲* or of "the *eyālet*". During the long Persian campaigns from 1587 onwards, the number of the *ḳubbe wezīrs* was increased to nine, and those of the *k̲h̲āridj̲* to sixteen. The sensitive distant frontier provinces of Tabrīz, S̲h̲īrwān, Erzurūm, and Anatolia in the east, and those of Buda, Bosna and Belgrade in the west, were put under *wezīr*-governors with full authority. A *wezīr*-governor had the authority to summon the neighbouring governors under his command in an emergency.

The navy assuming a crucial importance under Süleymān I, the grand admiral or *ḳapūdān-i deryā* was chosen from among the *ḳubbe wezīrs*, or the actual head of the navy was given the title. Also in the 10th/16th century, the title of *wezīr* began to be employed for other important office-holders such as *defterdār, nis̲h̲āndj̲ï* or *ag̲h̲a* of the Janissaries. In the early 18th century, *ḳoltuḳ* or candidate *wezīrs* appeared, since the title was used for the principal palace *ag̲h̲as* such as the *silāḥdār* [*q.v.*], *rikābdār* or *čawus̲h̲-bas̲h̲ï*. At any rate, in this period the title lost its original lofty meaning, being conferred as an honorific title even on provincial magnates.

A *wezīr*'s chance for promotion depended much on the strength of his *ḳapu*, a household retinue numbering hundreds; *wezīrs* maintained large palaces comparable in their organisation to those of the sultan. *Wezīrs* were the richest members of Ottoman society. The basic salary of a *wezīr* came from his *k̲h̲āṣṣ* [see TĪMĀR] revenues in the provinces, which was doubled by other sources of revenues including substantial gifts and bribes. A *wezīr*'s annual revenue was estimated between 16,000 and 18,000 gold ducats, while the Grand Vizier's amounted to twice as much in the 10th/16th century. In 1525, the second *wezīr* Muṣṭafā's possessions included 700 *ḳuls* and 70,000 gold ducats, whilst those of the third *wezīr* Ayās included 600 *ḳuls* and 60,000 gold ducats.

In the 1580s, a retired *wezīr* received a pension called *arpalıḳ* [*q.v.*], ranging from 200,000 to 300,000 *aḳčes*, whilst a Grand Vizier received as much as half a million *aḳčes*, or about 8,300 gold ducats. The estate of a *wezīr* of *ḳul* origin without an heir belonged to the sultan's treasury.

Bibliography: 1. Sources. Luṭfī Pas̲h̲a, *Āṣaf-nāme*, ed. ʿAlī Emīrī, Istanbul 1326; anon., *Tewārīk̲h̲-i āl-i ʿot̲h̲mān*, ed. F. Giese, Breslau 1926; *Ḳānūnnāme-i āl-i ʿot̲h̲mān*, ed. ʿĀrif, in *TOEM* Suppl., Istanbul 1330; *Ḳānūn-i wüzerā'-i ʿiẓām*, in *ʿOt̲h̲mānlï ḳānūnnāmeleri*, in *MTM*, iii, 498-508; ʿĀlī, *Nuṣḥat al-selāṭīn, Muṣṭafā ʿĀlī's counsel for the sultan of 1581*, ed. A. Tietze, 2 vols. Vienna 1979-82; Ḳoči Bey, *Risāle*, ed. A.K. Aksüt, Istanbul 1939; Silāḥdār Meḥmed, *Tārīk̲h̲*, ed. Aḥmed Refīḳ, Istanbul 1928; ʿOt̲h̲mān-zāde Tā'ib, *Ḥadīḳat ül-wüzerā'*, Istanbul 1271 (biographies of *wezīrs* up to 1703; its continuation is in the *D̲h̲eyl* of other authors); *Kitāb-i Müstetāb*, chs. XI and XII, and *Hirzü 'l-mülûk*, fols. 12b-30b, in Y. Yücel, *Osmanlı devlet teşkilâtına dair kaynaklar*, Ankara 1988; *Ḳānūn-i wizāret*, in D̲j̲ewdet, *Tārīk̲h̲*, v, Istanbul 1309, 65; Meḥmed T̲h̲üreyyā, *Sid̲j̲ill-i ʿot̲h̲mānī*, Istanbul 1308-15.

2. Studies. Zinkeisen, iii, 59-116; Ḥ. Ḥüsāmeddīn, *ʿAlā' al-Dīn Pas̲h̲a*, in *TTEM*, nos. 5-9, 43; N. Jorga, *Gesch. des osman. Reiches*, Gotha 1908-13, iii, 167-89; M.K. İnal, *Osmanlı devrinde son sadrazamlar*, Istanbul 1940-7; İ.H. Uzunçarşılı, *Osmanlılarda ilk vezirlere dair mutalea*, in *Belleten*, ix, 99-106; idem, *Osmanlı devletinin merkez ve bahriye teşkilâtı*, Ankara 1948, 186-213; idem, *Çandarlı vezir ailesi*, Ankara 1970-4; H. İnalcik, *Fatih devri*, Ankara 1954; idem, *The Ottoman empire. The classical age 1300-1600*, London 1973, 89-103; Z.A. Lalor, *Promotion patterns of Ottoman bureaucratic statesmen from the Lâle Devri until the Tanzimat*, in *Güneydoğu Avrupa Araştırmaları Dergisi*, i (1972), 77-92; R. Aboul-el-Haj, *The Ottoman Vezir and Pasha households, 1683-1703*, in *JAOS*, xciv (1974), 438-47; C.V. Findley, *Bureaucratic reform in the Ottoman empire. The Sublime Porte 1789-1922*, Princeton 1980; A. Mumcu, *Divân-i Hümayun*, Ankara 1986; Findley, *Ottoman civil officialdom*, Princeton 1989; L.P. Peirce, *The Imperial harem*, Oxford and New York 1993; A. Akyıldız, *Tanzimat dönemi, osmanlı merkez teşkilâtında reform*, Istanbul 1993, 21-176. (HALIL İNALCIK)

AL-**WAZĪR** AL-**MAG̲H̲RIBĪ** [see AL-MAG̲H̲RIBĪ. 4].

AL-**WAZĪR** AL-**ṢAG̲H̲ĪR** (A.), a term of Fāṭimid administrative usage, also called the *Ṣāḥib al-Bāb*, i.e. head chamberlain. He was equal in status to the *Isfahsālār* or *Muḳaddam al-ʿAskar*, the commander-in-chief of the army, and the two of them settled all matters of military organisation. According to al-Ḳalḳas̲h̲andī, *Ṣubḥ*, iii, 483, vi, 7-8, he was second in the civilian administrative hierarchy after the *wazīr* himself and could hear *maẓālim* [*q.v.*] when the *wazīr* was pre-occupied.

Bibliography: See also W. Björkman, *Beiträge zur Geschichte der Staatskanzlei im islamischen Ägypten*, Hamburg 1928, 98. (ED.)

WAZĪRĪS and **WAZĪRISTĀN**, the name of a Pas̲h̲tūn tribe and their region, essentially in the North-West Frontier region of present-day Pakistan.

Wazīristān, the region, lies on Pakistan's western frontier between the Kuṟam river in the north, the Gūmal in the south, and the western boundaries of the administered districts of Bannū and Dēra Ismāʿīl K̲h̲ān to the east. The western boundary of Wazīristān is roughly indicated by the international frontier with Afg̲h̲ānistān (the Durand Line) but the region extends into Afg̲h̲ānistān in Birmal and at other points. The region is a tangled mass of hills, valleys and plains and it is inhabited mainly by the Pas̲h̲tūn tribesmen from whom it takes its name, that is to say, the Wazīrīs, who trace their descent to a supposed common ancestor, Wazīr. In the central part of southern Wazīristān the Maḥsūds [*q.v.*] predominate. By origin Wazīrīs, the Maḥsūds are now regarded as a separate tribe. Elsewhere in Wazīristān are the Darwēs̲h̲ K̲h̲ēl Wazīrīs, now commonly known simply as Wazīrīs. In northern Wazīristān the ʿUt̲h̲mānzay branch are the principal inhabitants and in the southern, western and northern parts of southern Wazīristān (including the large plain of Wānā) live the Aḥmadzay branch. The eastern borders of Wazīristān are inhabited by Biṭanīs and parts of the Tōčī valley by the Dawrs. The principal occupations of the Wazīrī tribes have been agriculture and pastoralism, supplemented by trade, mining, a little manufacturing and raiding.

About the early history of Wazīristān and its inhabitants little is known. There are references in the memoirs of Bābur and in 18th-century documents from the time of Aḥmad S̲h̲āh Durrānī [*q.v.*], but most information is derived from British sources, especially from 1265/1849 onwards when British power in India was extended up to the borders of Wazīristān. To the British the Wazīrīs, especially the Maḥsūds, presented a major security problem, which they sought to solve by various devices: punitive expeditions, blockades, fines, hostages, the encouragement of settlement, the garrisoning of strategic positions and the development of roads, but none of these availed and Wazīristān remained the most disturbed area of the North-West Frontier. The demarcation of the frontier with Afghānistān in 1312/1894 coincided with a new British initiative aimed at controlling the region through garrisons (notably at Wānā) and allowances to chiefs. The Dawrs of the Tōčī valley were brought under British protection and two political agencies were created: North Wazīristān (1895) and South Wazīristān (1896). These measures provoked still more vigorous resistance led by a Maḥsūd religious figure, Mullā Muḥyī al-Dīn (d. 1913), better known as the Mullā Pōwindā, and the chiefs were abandoned in favour of dealing with the generality of tribesmen and eventually with the Mullā Pōwindā himself. These efforts were unsuccessful, and during the Third Anglo-Afghān war (1919) Britain lost control over all of Wazīristān outside the Tōčī valley. There followed a major campaign in Wazīristān (1919-23) and a new plan for roads and military garrisons, notably at Razmak in North Wazīristān, but this plan involved the defence of long lines of communication and led to further fighting. From 1936 the two most prominent leaders of Wazīrī resistance were the Darwēsh Khēl *imām*, Ḥādjdjī Mīrzā ʿAlī Khān, the Faḳīr of Ipī (*ca.* 1890-1960 [*q.v.* in Suppl.]), and (from 1938) Saʿīd al-Gīlānī, the so-called Shāmī Pīr.

The creation of Pakistan witnessed the implementation of a new policy in Wazīristān: military garrisons were withdrawn leaving only the militias (in a restricted role) and *khāṣṣadārs* to support the political agents; new services were supplied including irrigation, schools and hospitals; and tribesmen were encouraged to settle and to develop economic and political links with Pakistan. Many, especially the Maḥsūds, worked as labourers, in transport and in light engineering in Pakistan. There are no reliable series of population statistics for Wazīristān but it is evident that the population grew rapidly in the second half of the 20th century and pressures were felt particularly by the Maḥsūds who encroached on the lands of the Aḥmadzay Darwēsh Khēl Wazīrīs in southern Wazīristān and even moved into northern Wazīristān around Razmak. Aḥmadzay resentment was articulated during the 1970s by Mullā Nūr Muḥammad of Wānā, who proclaimed a *djihād* against the Maḥsūds, leading to fighting and in 1976 the intervention of government forces to quell Aḥmadzay resistance.

Their proximity to the Afghān frontier and their links with Kābul have led to various Wazīrī interventions in Afghānistān since the early 19th century. In more recent times, Wazīrīs played a vital role in the conquest of Kābul by Nādir Khān in 1929, attacked Khōst in 1933, took an important part in the Kashmīrī *djihād* of 1947, and were drawn into the Afghān civil war after 1979.

Bibliography: *Central Asia, Part 1. The North West Frontier* (compiled by Lt. Col. C.M. MacGregor) 3 vols., Calcutta 1873; *Imperial Gazetteer of India. North West Frontier Province*, Calcutta 1908; Major R.T.I. Ridgeway, *Pathans*, Calcutta 1918 (repr.); Government of India, *Operations in Waziristan, 1919-1920*, Calcutta 1921; C.E. Bruce, *The tribes of Waziristan*, London 1929; idem, *Waziristan, 1936-1937*, Aldershot 1938; C.C. Davies, *The problem of the North West Frontier, 1890-1908*, Cambridge 1932; Sir Olaf Caroe, *The Pathans, 550 B.C. to A.D. 1957*, London 1958; L. Harris, *British policy on the North-West Frontier of India, 1889-1901*, Ph.D. thesis, Univ. of London 1960, unpubl.; Major General J.G. Elliott, *The Frontier 1839-1947*, London 1968; ʿAbd al-Ḥalīm Asar Afghānī, *Ẕamūg Mudjāhidīn*, 2 vols., Peshawar 1968; Miss Lal Baha, *N-W.F.P. Administration under British rule, 1901-1919*, Islamabad 1978; Akbar S. Ahmed, *Resistance and control in Pakistan*, London 1991; H. Beattie, *Tribe and state in Waziristan, 1849-1883*, Ph.D. thesis, Univ. of London 1997, unpubl. (M.E. Yapp)

WAZN (a.), lit. "the act of weighing", from *wazana* to weigh, to balance, cf. also *mīzān* [*q.v.*], a balance, scales; and for weights in general, see makāzīl and mawāzin.

1. As a term of numismatics.

Until the 20th century, when metallic currencies were supplanted by fiduciary money and other forms of monetary instruments, the Islamic world used gold and silver as their common medium of exchange and copper as a largely token currency.

The two intrinsic qualities that governed the value of these metals as coins were the purity of their alloys and the weights at which they were struck. When ʿAbd al-Malik b. Marwān carried out his monetary reform between 77 and 79/696-98, he introduced a gold coin based on the Byzantine solidus, *ca.* 4.40 gr., but somewhat lighter, *ca.* 4.25 gr., called the dīnār [*q.v.*] and a silver coin, the dirham [*q.v.*] modelled on the Sāsānid drachm, but struck at seven-tenths the latter's weight, 2.87 gr. Both coins were made from virtually pure metal and were intended to circulate by tale, i.e. prices were established and transactions concluded in a fixed number of coins of a known standard of weight and fineness. In everyday use, a fixed ratio between the prices of gold and silver could not be established and maintained because the purchasing power of both metals depended on their local supply and demand. For taxation purposes, however, provincial governments frequently fixed an exchange rate between the two which would serve their own revenue needs. Gold and silver were refined and struck at mints under caliphal control, but copper was manufactured into *fals* [*q.v.*] under the supervision of the local authorities and sold to the public in return for dīnārs and dirhams to support commerce and raise local revenues.

At the start of the ʿAbbāsid era, the weight of the dirham appears to have been raised from 2.87 to 2.97 gr., thus establishing the well-known ratio of seven coinage dīnārs or *mithḳāls* being equal in weight to ten dirhams. This move brought into being the so-called canonical dīnār and dirham which became enshrined in the *Sharīʿa* [*q.v.*] as the official weight of the coinage *mithḳāl* and dirham, regardless of the actual weight of the coins themselves. From the accession of al-Saffāḥ in 132/749 until the death of al-Mahdī in 169/785, this seven to ten ratio was occasionally observed in the more important mints under direct caliphal control. During the reign of al-Rashīd, however, the centralised coinage system began to disintegrate in the western regions of the Islamic world. Umayyad Spain, not surprisingly, made no effort to adhere to the ʿAbbāsid weight standard, with the average dirham from the al-Andalus mint weighing 3 to 4 tenths of a gramme less than its eastern cousins. Lightweight dirhams were also produced in mints from Morocco to Egypt, large numbers of which have been found in eastern hoards. This leads one to conclude that as long as the dirham was accepted by tale rather than weight, the western regions had discovered a simple and effective means of lightening their tax burdens. Lightweight Maghribī dirhams began to appear in quantity in eastern hoards at this time, and the Yemen also adopted a light dirham standard for its own coinage in the 170s/780s-790s and 180s/790s-800s. Struck at the weight of a half, or even quarter dirham, these coins were obviously intended for circulation only within the province itself.

As the dirham standard became widely flouted, the integrity of the dīnār was also compromised through clipping or paring small slivers of gold from its circumference. While the mints continued to strike dīnārs at the usual 4.25 gr., the majority of these coins, when weighed today, are no more than 3.80 and 4.10 gr., a loss of up to 10% of their value. This would have been a tempting return for those who could avoid detection and arrest. This process probably accelerated during the civil war between al-Amīn and al-Ma'mūn and continued for a few years into the first decade of al-Ma'mūn's undisputed rule.

The widespread tampering with the weight of coins may well have provided al-Ma'mūn with the economic motive for introducing his reform style coinage in 198/813. Unlike 'Abd al-Malik's reform, which was effected within a three-year period, that of al-Ma'mūn came about gradually, spreading from his residence in Marw in Khurāsān to the other mint towns which recognised 'Alī al-Riḍā as heir between 202/817-18 and 204/819-20. In the latter year the new style was adopted by the capital mint, Madīnat al-Salām, and 206/821-2 witnessed the striking of the first mintless reform-style dīnārs and mint-bearing dirhams whose inscriptions were written in a distinctive, rounded and much more legible Kūfic script. Al-Ma'mūn's reform coinage added a second, outside marginal legend (Sūra XXX, 3-4), which is thought to be a coded reference to the inevitability of al-Ma'mūn's victory over al-Amīn, and removed the names of all officials from the field legends, returning the coinage to its original Umayyad anonymity. The addition of this marginal legend may have been intended to act as a safeguard against the clipping of coins, which would have necessitated the defacement of a Ḳur'ānic legend, an act that no pious Muslim could countenance.

The new coinage could be distinguished from the old at a glance. Both dīnārs and dirhams, now identical in design, were distinguished from one another only by their metals and the word *dīnār* or *dirham* in their inner marginal legends. These words had, however, lost their original meanings because the new coinage was no longer struck to fixed weight standards and thus could pass only by weight rather than by tale. In effect they lost their status as specie, i.e. coin money, and became bullion, no more than stamped ingots whose inscriptions were a guarantee of the purity of their metal. From then onwards, the coinage of the caliphate and all the states from Egypt to Central Asia which owed the 'Abbāsids real or nominal allegiance calculated payments by weight of metal, with a premium for coins known to be of good alloy and a discount for those of rulers who debased their precious metal content.

It is interesting to note that in the Maghrib the Aghlabids chose to retain the style and weight of the traditional 'Abbāsid dīnār for their gold coinage while adopting a new silver coinage based on the half dirham weight, and their successors, the Fāṭimids, Midrārids and Almoravids, continued to use coinages that could still pass by tale because of the accuracy of their weight. This tradition continued and was strengthened under the Almohads, Ḥafṣids, Marīnids and Naṣrids, whose coinages were very carefully struck to the weight of the standard, or non-coinage *mithḳāl* of 4.68-4.72 gr. Their square *naṣrī* silver was emitted at the weight of the half dirham, *ca.* 1.40-1.50 gr.

Very little fine silver coinage was issued in the central Islamic lands between 450 and 570/1058-1174. Its place was taken by an abundant coinage in very debased billon in Afghānistān and copper in Egypt, Syria and 'Irāḳ, which had to be weighed out to determine its value against pure gold and silver for all substantial payments. Of course, every city had its own system of weights and measures, and the values of gold and silver fluctuated independently according to the local supply and demand for these metals.

The earliest fine silver coinage to appear in quantity in the third quarter of the 6th/12th century was struck by the Mahdids [*q.v.*] in the Yemen and that was followed soon after by the dirhams of the Zangid of Aleppo, al-Malik al-Ṣāliḥ Ismā'īl b. Maḥmūd. The latter were issued at the canonical weight of 2.97 gr. and provided the foundation for the silver currency in both Rūm Saldjūḳ Anatolia and Ayyūbid Syria. The dirhams of Ayyūbid and Rasūlid Yemen weighed about 2.00-2.20 gr. which was sufficiently accurate for them to pass by tale.

Ayyūbid Egypt inherited the Fāṭimid monetary system, whose principal metal was gold that, because of its irregular weight, would have passed by weight. This was supplemented by so-called black dirhams (*dirham aswad* or *dirham waraḳ*), which Balog describes as "rough, uneven, small rectangles or squares of low silver content, the weight of which depended on the haphazard way the cold chisel of the flan cutter fell". A small number of fine silver dirhams was, however, struck under both the later Fāṭimids for presentation purposes and by al-Malik al-Nāṣir Yūsuf I, in an unsuccessful attempt to bring the debased Egyptian coinage into line with the high-quality Syrian one. By 622/1225, al-Malik al-Kāmil Muḥammad [*q.v.*], apparently acting under public pressure, felt the need to reform the silver coinage. In the event, it was no more than a cosmetic move, involving a less laborious way of flan manufacture than chiselling out irregular bits of metal. The still molten and debased alloy was poured over a cone of charcoal into a vat of water, and the spattering metal yielded lumps of variable size and weight which were then struck into coin. As Balog records, "instead of being an irregular square or rectangle, it was round, oval, or with one or two protuberances at the edge." In the 620s/1220s and 630s/1230s the production of good silver dirhams in Syria spread eastwards across al-Djazīra as far as Baghdād where, starting in 632/1334, a dirham of canonical weight was struck for the first time in centuries. Before then, the need for small change was probably met by taking the contemporary broad, thin-flan 'Abbāsid dīnārs, cutting them up into small pieces of gold of varying weight and selling them at the prevailing rate for silver or copper.

In the 8th/14th century a bi-metallic gold and silver currency was accepted in tale in Spain and the Maghrib, a debased silver and copper currency of irregular weight, supplemented by stamped gold ingots, was current in Mamlūk Egypt, a lightweight silver coinage in Anatolia, analogous to the silver penny of Western Europe, a continuously depreciating silver coinage, also supplemented by stamped gold ingots, in 'Irāḳ and Persia, and in Muslim India gold and silver tankas [*q.v.*] of stable weight and alloy that could also be accepted by tale.

A decisive shift in monetary policy took place in the 9th/15th century. Burdjī Mamlūk Egypt, Ottoman Turkey, and Aḳ Ḳoyunlu and then Ṣafawid Persia adapted the weight of their gold currency to that of the Venetian sequin or ducat. This famous gold trade coin had a nominal weight of 3.50-3.55 gr. while the Islamic equivalents were, like the original Umayyad dīnār, slightly lighter in weight, usually around 3.40-3.45 gr. The silver coinage, likewise, was no longer linked to the weight of the canonical dirham and both weight and alloy could be reduced whenever economic pressures forced this expedient on governments. Details of these debasements are recorded in ʿOTHMĀNLİ. IX. Numismatics, and TŪMĀN. 2.

The more recent centuries are basically a chronicle of increasing European influence on Islamic coinages. European economic and military pressures impoverished the Muslim world. The usual response lay in depreciating the currency through enforced devaluations. European governments whose traders were inconvenienced by the resulting monetary chaos demanded an end to systematic coinage manipulation. One by one the Muslim states were forced to adopt European-style coinages which they pledged not to debase. Because the introduction of the new bi-metallic currencies was not backed up by sufficient quantities of bullion to drive European currencies out of circulation, and because Muslim governments did not possess the necessary fiscal skills and discipline to deal successfully with European bankers and financiers, it was not long before unfavourable international loan agreements led to bankruptcy and, all too often, to colonial rule. The new colonial currencies, strong at first, shared the fate of those of the European powers in the aftermath of the World Wars of the 20th century. Decolonisation established national currencies in every Muslim country, but today their value, once determined by weight and fineness of metal, is governed by the respect they enjoy within the international financial system.

Bibliography: The literature on *wazn* begins with those coin catalogues and inventories which record the weight of the individual coin described. See the catalogues of the collections of Islamic coins in the major European and Middle Eastern museums. More detailed studies are contained in works devoted to the coinages of individual dynasties, e.g. P. Balog, *The coinage of the Ayyubids*, London 1980. Metallurgical analyses are also useful, as are studies of Islamic weights, e.g. G.C. Miles, *Early Arabic glass weights and stamps*, New York 1948. For a description of individual Islamic weights, see M.H. Sauvaire, *Matériaux pour servir à l'histoire de la numismatique et de la métrologie musulmanes*, Paris 1887. For some valuable recent observations on Islamic metrology, see the introduction by L. Ilisch to *The Turath collection. Coins of the Islamic world*, Auction Leu 64, Zurich 1996.

(R.E. DARLEY-DORAN)

2. In language and literature.

Here, *wazn* "the act of weighing" means the establishing of a pattern in morphology (*taṣrīf*) or in prosody (*ʿarūḍ*) [*q.vv.*]. Prosodical weighing or scanning is also called *taḳṭīʿ* or *tafʿīl*. As a concrete noun, *wazn* (pl. *awzān*) denotes the resulting word form or metre. A morphological *wazn* is also called *bināʾ*, pl. *abniya*.

In the *wazn* of nouns and verbs, the root consonants are replaced with *fāʾ*, *ʿayn* and *lām* (and another *lām* in case of a fourth radical), whereas auxiliary consonants (*zawāʾid*, sing. *zāʾid*) and vowels remain unchanged, e.g. *fāʿil, mafʿūl, infaʿalat* and *mutafaʿlil* for *kātib, maktūb, inkatabat* and *mutafalsif*.

The *wazn* or metre of a line of verse is expressed through paradigms such as, *inter alia, faʿūlun, mafāʿīlun, mustafʿilun*, formed with letters from the series *alif, t, s, ʿ, f, l, m, n, w* and *y*, contained in the mnemonic *lamaʿat suyūfunā* ("our swords flashed"). The prosodical quantity of the paradigms equals the quantity of the corresponding segment of the line, but no distinction between radicals and auxiliary letters is made in this case. A line whose *wazn* coincides with a recognised *ʿarūḍ*-pattern is *mawzūn* "metrical". Metricality (*wazn*) is said by Ibn Ras̲h̲īḳ, i, 134, to be the main pillar (*rukn*) in the definition of poetry.

Whereas *wazn* may refer to any metrical pattern that arises in practice, Arabic theory also recognises fifteen or sixteen ideal patterns called *buḥūr*, sing. *baḥr* [see ʿARŪḌ].

Bibliography: Muḥammad b. Abī S̲h̲anab, *Tuḥfat al-adab fī mīzān as̲h̲ʿār al-ʿarab*, Algiers 1906, 18; Ibn Ras̲h̲īḳ, *Bāb fi 'l-awzān*, ch. xxi of his *al-ʿUmda fī maḥāsin al-s̲h̲iʿr wa-ādābihi wa-naḳdih*, ed. M.M. ʿAbd al-Ḥamīd, 2 vols., ²Cairo 1374/1955.

(W. STOETZER)

WAZZĀN, conventionally OUEZZANE, a town of the northwesternmost part of Morocco (lat. 34° 52' N., long. 5° 35' W., altitude 357 m/1,050 feet) and one of the holy cities of Morocco, its development being bound up with that of the Wazzānī Ṣūfī order and its *zāwiya* there [see WAZZĀNIYYA]. The history of the town involves hagiographic elements which are difficult to separate from the purely historical facts, so that the historian is confronted with mythical narratives, often handed down orally, all aimed at giving the Wazzānī *s̲h̲urafāʾ* an aura of sanctity.

Until the second quarter of the 11th/17th century, the small village at Wazzān had no special distinction, but in the 1630s the Idrīsid *s̲h̲arīf* Mawlāy ʿAbd Allāh b. Ibrāhīm chose the place as the site for his *zāwiya*. Wazzān was in a position of strategic significance, in the foothills of the D̲j̲bāla country which gives passage between the mountains to the east and the plains of the G̲h̲arb to the west and south; it lay on the borders between the open lands where *Mak̲h̲zen* authority could be enforced and mountains difficult of access, so that the town and its region were to play a role in *Mak̲h̲zen* politics; and it was a region where the tribal territories of four groups, the Massara, the Maṣmūda, the G̲h̲azāwa and the Rahūna, met.

The *zāwiya* speedily attracted adepts and visitors at its *mawsim*, hence became significant during Mawlāy ʿAbd Allāh's lifetime, but the settlement of Wazzān remained essentially a village till the time of the third Wazzānī *s̲h̲ayk̲h̲*, Mawlāy al-Ṭayyib (d. 1767), after a period of calamitous civil warfare and famine in the late 1720s and 1730s. In the conditions of insecurity of the countryside, wealthy landowners and *ḳāʾid*s established themselves in the town, and Mawlāy al-Ṭayyib now built the great mosque and its *madrasa* and set up specialised markets and *funduḳ*s. (For the religious development of the town, see WAZZĀNIYYA.) It developed further under Sīdī ʿAlī b. Aḥmad (d. 1811), who made Wazzān and its hinterland a virtual principality, boosting commercial activity by inviting Jewish merchants to settle in the holy town, although these last did not live in a *mellāḥ* [see MALLĀḤ], as in other Moroccan towns, but in *funduḳ*s, paying rent to *s̲h̲urafāʾ* owners; only at the end of the 19th century, when in 1883 the Wazzānī *s̲h̲urafāʾ* became protégés of the French, were some wealthy Jewish merchants allowed to build private houses.

Wazzān functioned at this time as a market centre for both the plains and the mountains and their products, and also attracted imports for the *s̲h̲urafāʾ* class, this import trade being mainly controlled by traders from Fās and Jewish merchants. Its main industrial activity was the processing of local commodities like olives, tobacco and wool, with the woollen industry employing both sexes and persons from all social strata, including *sh̲arīfa*s. Its coarse woollen cloth was much used for making *d̲j̲ellāba*s, the hooded cloak worn by the male population of Morocco. There was also a significant leather-working industry, now largely ended. The *sh̲urafā'*, in particular, grew rich from donations and endowments of the shrine, so that they became major landowners, especially in the rich lands of the G̲h̲arb plain but also in regions as far away as Tuwāt [*q.v.*] in Algeria; they also enjoyed favours from the state, such as tax-farming concessions.

In general, the ʿAlawī sultans sought Wazzānī support in an area where they encountered a great deal of resistance to their new régime, whilst the Wazzānī *sh̲urafā'* were content to assert their power essentially within the religious domain. Hence there existed an implicit agreement whereby the *sh̲urafā'* furthered *Mak̲h̲zen* policy in the region in return for administrative concessions, never clearly defined but at certain times, such as the later part of the 18th century, allowing considerable Wazzānī control over the G̲h̲arb and southern D̲j̲bāla. In the later 19th century, however, relations between the *Mak̲h̲zen* and the *sh̲urafā'* deteriorated as a result of the latter's pro-French attitude. Hence a dual system was imposed, with a Wazzānī *naḳīb* over the *sh̲urafā'* and a *Mak̲h̲zen ḳā'id* over the common people, and this lasted until 1920.

By this time, Wazzān was expanding westwards, and had a population estimated at 11,000. When occupied by the French army in 1920 it was made into a municipality, and under the Protectorate served as an administrative centre for the G̲h̲arb and the southern D̲j̲bāla tribes falling within the French zone. For some time, the Wazzānī *sh̲urafā'* took part in the administration of the town, but in 1937 a rural *ḳā'id* from the neighbouring Banū Massāra was appointed head of the town's urban administration, contributing to the marginalisation of the Wazzānī élite and reinforcing the rural aspect of the town within its tribal surroundings. It did not have any significant industrial growth during the Protectorate period, hence remained only a modest goal for rural emigration. This has continued to be the case after independence in 1956, and the town at best provides a stopping-place for D̲j̲bālī migrants on their way to more attractive urban centres. Wazzān's population in *ca.* 1940 had been 16,440 (14,300 Muslims, 1,670 Jews and 475 Europeans); in 1994 it was *ca.* 52,000, hardly five times the 1900 figure, whereas the urban population of Morocco as a whole jumped from an estimate of less than half a million in 1900 to over 13 million today. Administratively, Wazzān has remained a modest centre falling within the governorship successively of Kenitra (Ḳunayṭira) and then Sidi Kacem (Sīdī Ḳāsim), and both the town and the *zāwiya* have not completely thrown off the effects of discrimination resulting from the post-1883 co-operation with the French authorities.

Bibliography: B. Meakin, *The land of the Moors*, London 1901, 320-30; E. Michaux-Bellaire, *La Maison d'Ouezzane*, in *RMM*, v (1908), 23-89; Mission scientifique du Maroc, *Villes et tribus du Maroc*, iv, *Rabat et sa région: le Gharb*, Paris 1918, 221-54; Naval Intelligence Division, Admiralty Handbooks, *Morocco*, London 1942, indices and ii, 60-1; G. Drague (pseudonym of Georges Spillman), *Esquisse d'histoire religieuse du Maroc*, Paris 1951, 227-50; Lhachmi Berrady, *Les Chorfas d'Ouezzane, le Makhzen et la France, 1850-1912*, doctoral thesis, Aix-en-Provence 1971, unpubl., 51-79; Muḥammad b. al-Ṭayyib al-Ḳādirī, *Nas̲h̲r al-mat̲h̲ānī li-ahl al-ḳarn al-hādī ʿas̲h̲ar wa 'l-t̲h̲ānī*, Rabat 1977-86, iv, 253-68; Hassan El Boudrari, *Quand les saints font les villes: lecture anthropologique de la pratique sociale d'un saint marocain du VIIe siècle*, in *Annales ESC* (May-June 1985), 489-508; Mohamed El Mansour, *Sharifian Sufism. The religious and social practice of the Wazzani Zawiya*, in E.G.H. Joffé and R. Pennell (eds.), *Tribe and state. Essays in honour of David Montgomery Hart*, Wisbech, Cambs. 1991, 69-83.

(Mohamed El Mansour)

al-**WAZZĀN**, al-**ḤASAN** b. **MUḤAMMAD** [see leo africanus].

WAZZĀNIYYA, a Moroccan Ṣūfī brotherhood, founded by the Idrīsid *s̲h̲arīf* Mawlāy ʿAbd Allāh b. Ibrāhīm (d. 1678).

Born at Tazrūt, Mawlāy ʿAbd Allāh was initiated into the S̲h̲ād̲h̲ilī-D̲j̲azūlī *silsila*, the most widespread and prestigious of the Mag̲h̲ribī *ṭuruḳ* [see shād̲h̲iliyya], by Sīdī ʿAlī b. Aḥmad al-Gurfṭī. On the latter's death in 1628, ʿAbd Allāh aimed at expanding his master's spiritual influence and sought a site for a *zāwiya* of his own, lighting on Wazzān [*q.v.*]. The *zāwiya* had an immediate success in attracting adepts, with numbers estimated at 20,000 attending its *mawsim* during his own lifetime. In the mid-18th century it spread into Algeria, becoming known there as the Ṭayyibiyya. In the later 19th century, European observers estimated the *zāwiya*'s following at half or more of the total Moroccan population, though this is impossible to verify.

The S̲h̲arīfian genealogy of the Wazzānīs was much used by them at a time when S̲h̲arīfism was being consecrated as a determining principle of social and political legitimacy, and veneration of *s̲h̲arīfī* descent came to be the dominant feature of the *ṭarīḳa*, weakening its genuinely mystical content. Sīdī Muḥammad, ʿAbd Allāh's eldest son and successor, made the Wazzānī *zāwiya* into the "house of warranty" (*dār al-ḍamāna*), meaning that the *baraka* of the *s̲h̲urafā'* was sufficient to save any sinner at the Last Judgement. The relationship of the *s̲h̲urafā'* and their followers tended to become more like that of a clientèle, with the *k̲h̲uddām* replacing *murīd*s or spiritual disciples, since as these last swelled to tens of thousands, personal spiritual guidance became impossible and the Wazzānī *s̲h̲ayk̲h̲*s became largely dispensers of *baraka* at the annual *mawsim*.

Parallel to this process, the *zāwiya* developed important material interests. The third *s̲h̲ayk̲h̲*, Mawlāy al-Tuhāmī, encouraged his sons to acquire property and wealth on the grounds that wealth deterred from greed and covetousness. Soon the *zāwiya* had much property, not only in Morocco but also in other parts of the Mag̲h̲rib, and the *muḳaddam*s or deputies of the *s̲h̲ayk̲h̲*, who were supposed to look after the Ṣūfī guidance of devotees, ended up largely as intendants and managers of the *zāwiya*'s material resources.

The gap between Ṣūfī ideals and material concerns grew wider in the 19th century, especially as the French presence in Algeria, where the *ṭarīḳa* had considerable interests, imposed some kind of accommodation with the colonial authorities there. In the second half of the century, the private lifestyle of the *s̲h̲ayk̲h̲* of the *zāwiya*, al-Ḥād̲j̲d̲j̲ ʿAbd al-Salām (d. 1892), did much to lower the order's prestige, since he chose to spend much of his time in the Europeanised city of Tangier [see ṭand̲j̲a] and married an English lady there, and in 1883 placed himself and the order under French protection. Subsequent relations with the *Mak̲h̲zen* deteriorated, and, in the 20th century, Salafī nationalists [see SALAFIYYA. 1] were able to make much of the position of the Wazzāniyya in their denunciation of the collaborationist stance of the *ṭuruḳ* in general and their betrayal of authentic Islam.

Bibliography: See the *Bibls.* to SHĀDHILIYYA and WAZZĀN, and also E. Michaux-Bellaire, *Les confréries religieuses au Maroc*, Rabat 1923.

(MOHAMED EL MANSOUR)

WEDJĪHĪ, Ottoman historian and poet (1031?-1071/1620?-1661).

He was born in Baghče Sarāy [*q.v.*], capital of the khānate of the Crimea, the son of a certain ʿAbd Allāh ʿĀrif al-Rūmī. According to Ottoman sources, his given name was Ḥasan (though Ḥüseyin sometimes occurs in later European works). His date of birth is calculated as around 1031/1620, based on a statement in his poetic *dīwān* that he was entering his fortieth year in 1070/1659. In 1624-5 his family moved to Istanbul, where he received a good secretarial and literary education. Taken into the household of the *ḳapudan-i deryā* [*q.v.*] Kemānkesh Ḳara Muṣṭafā Pasha in 1046/1636 as *mühürdār* or private secretary, he accompanied the latter on the Baghdād campaign of 1638-9 and remained in his service until the Pasha's execution whilst Grand Vizier in 1053/1644. He appears subsequently to have become a *kātib* in the *dīwān-i hümāyūn*, the Ottoman central chancery, where he remained until his death from tuberculosis in 1071/1661.

Wedjīhī's principal work is a history of the Ottoman state from 1047/1637 to 1071/1661, known generally as *Taʾrīkh-i Wedjīhī*. Although his coverage of events is relatively brief, Wedjīhī was well placed to be a close observer of Ottoman politics, particularly during the reigns of Ibrāhīm (1640-8) and of Meḥemmed IV [*q.vv.*] to 1661. His account includes a significant amount of information not given by contemporaries such as Kātib Čelebi, Meḥmed Khalīfe and Ḳara-Čelebi-zāde [*q.vv.*], particularly on events relating to the Crimea, and is notable for its open criticism of the governmental system. It was an important source for later historians such as Naʿīmā and Silāḥdār [*q.vv.*], and in its coverage of the years 1070-1/1660-1 helps fill the brief gap between the histories of Naʿīmā and Rāshid [*q.v.*]. A facsimile edition of one of the several manuscripts of the *Taʾrīkh-i Wedjīhī* was published in B. Atsız, *Das Osmanische Reich um die Mitte des 17. Jahrhunderts nach den Chroniken des Vecihi (1637-1660) und des Mehmed Halifa (1633-1660)* (Munich 1977). Wedjīhī also compiled a *dīwān* (several mss. extant, unpubl.).

Bibliography: For references and detailed bibl., see Ö.F. Akün, *İA* art. *Vecîhî*, of which the above is a summary. (CHRISTINE WOODHEAD)

WEHBĪ [see SÜNBÜL-ZĀDE WEHBĪ].

WEHBĪ SAYYIDĪ, ḤUSAYN (modern Tkish., Seyit Vehbi, Hüseyin), also known as Wehbī-yi Ḳadīm or Wehbī-yi Ewwel, Ottoman Turkish poet (1085?-1149/1674?-1736). He is not to be confused with Sünbül-zāde Wehbī [*q.v.*].

He was a native of Istanbul, court poet and prose writer, and member of the Ottoman *ʿIlmiyye* [*q.v.*] during the Lāle Dewrī [*q.v.*]. In his early years Wehbī used the pen-name Ḥüsāmi, reflecting family claims to descent from the Prophet (see Gibb, *HOP*, iii, 107-8, and Hamit Dikmen, *Seyyid Vehbi ve divanının karşılaştırmalı metni*, doctoral diss., Ankara Univ. 1991, 16-19). With a *medrese* education, Wehbī won *müderris* status in 1123/1711, served as a *ḳāḍī* and reached *mewlewiyyet* [*q.v.*] rank, aided by the patronage of Aḥmed III and the Grand Vizier Ibrāhīm Pasha (Newshehirli) [*q.vv.*]. Among his best-known poems is a *ḳaṣīda* marking completion of the Aḥmed III fountain in Istanbul, inscribed in gold on the structure (see *EI*[1] art. *Wahbī*; also Dikmen, *op. cit.*, 50-1).

Among Wehbī's works are a translation of the *Ḥadīth-i erbaʿīn* ("Forty Sayings of the Prophet") of al-Nawawī, and a short *Ṣulḥiyye* (poem in praise of peace), marking the Treaty of Passarovitz (1135/1718 [see PASAROFČA]). He is credited also with completing an unfinished *Laylā ü Madjnūn*, a *mathnawī* by Ḳāf-zāde Fāʾizī (d. 1031/1621-2), but no mss. have been discovered (see Dikmen, 33). His best-known works are:

(1) An extensive *dīwān* showing the influence of Nābī, Nedīm and (especially in *ḳaṣīdas*) Nefʿī [*q.vv.*], with good imagery, some use of simple language and local colour. Well-regarded during his lifetime, he has been criticised since for weaknesses such as lack of originality of ideas and of feeling (Seyit Kemal Karaalioğlu, *Türk edebiyatı tarihi*, i, Istanbul 1973, 705).

(2) A prose *Sūr-nāme* ("Book of the Festival") with verse prologue, giving a detailed, eye-witness account of the fifteen-days' festivities celebrating the circumcision of Sultan Aḥmed's four sons (1132/1720). An excellent source on contemporary Ottoman life (see A. Bombaci, *Storia della letteratura turca*, Florence and Milan 1969, 408-12), it was vividly illustrated by the famous miniaturist Lewnī [*q.v.*] (see E. Atıl, *Surnāme-i Vehbi, an eighteenth-century Ottoman Book of Festivals*, diss. Univ. of Michigan, Ann Arbor 1969, University Microfilms 1973).

Bibliography: Given in the article; see also *İA* art. *Seyyid Vehbi*. (KATHLEEN R.F. BURRILL)

WENEDIK, the Ottoman Turkish form for the name of the Italian city of Venice, in earlier Arabic usage, however, there appears Bunduḳiya and similar forms.

1. In earlier Islamic times.

The city was known to early Arabic geographers, such as Ibn Rusta, Ibn Ḥawḳal, etc., and these geographers had a fair knowledge of the names of many of the Italian cities and towns of the Lombard and Carolingian periods; the knowledge of later writers like al-Idrīsī was *a fortiori* much profounder after some three centuries during which the Arabs had controlled Sicily [see SIḲILLIYA] and, at times, Calabria [see ḲILLAWRIYA] and other coastal regions of the southern Italian peninsula [see, in general, ĪṬALIYA].

Ibn Rusta, 128, tr. Wiet, 143, quotes the captive of the Byzantines Hārūn b. Yaḥyā for details of the itinerary Constantinople-Rome via Salonica, Venice (*B.nd.ḳīs*) and Pavia (see on this itinerary, the detailed study of Marquart in his *Streifzüge*, 237-59). It is, in fact, various forms like this one of Bunduḳiya which appear in Arabic sources dealing with the commercial relations of the Italian merchant cities with the Islamic powers in the Levant (see on these, below, section 2). Thus al-Ḳalḳashandī furnishes a description of the *mamlakat al-Banādiḳa*, with its capital Bunduḳiya and its head the *Dūk* or Doge and its currency the ducat (*dūkāt*) (*Ṣubḥ al-aʿshā*, v, 404-5; in viii, 47-8, is given the text of the reply to a letter from the *Dūdj* or *Dūk*—described as "not exactly a king"—of 767/1366).

Bibliography: Given in the article.

(C.E. BOSWORTH)

2. Venetian relations with the Mamlūks and Ottomans.

Venice's history was deeply marked by its long and complex relationship with the Muslim world. As early as the 10th century, Popes and Emperors alike condemned the Republic for selling slaves to the Infidel. It was primarily Venice's special connection with Byzantium that launched it on the path toward an enduring domination of the eastern Mediterranean, one which was subsequently to entail extensive relations with the most important Muslim Mediterranean powers, the Mamlūks and the Ottomans [*q.vv.*].

The decline of Byzantine naval power, beginning in the 10th century, allowed Venice to take over the defence, first of the Adriatic and then of points further east. As a reward for their military support, Byzantium gave the Venetians special trading privileges with the Empire. An early example of this was the Golden Bull of 1082, issued by the Emperor Alexius I, which granted an exemption from tolls, as well as extensive trading privileges, this being Venice's compensation for having helped Alexius against the Normans of southern Italy.

It was the Fourth Crusade in 1204, however, that established Venice as the pre-eminent naval and commercial power of the eastern Mediterranean, a position that it would maintain—although not without challengers—until the end of the 16th century; Frederic Lane has called it "a turning point in Venetian history". Venetian involvement began with the agreement to provide transportation to the Holy Land for a large number of French Crusaders under the command of Geoffrey de Villehardouin. As is well known, the Fourth Crusade ended up not at the gates of Jerusalem but at the walls of Constantinople. Although Venice does not seem to have been the originator of the idea, it was willing to go along with this change of plan. Byzantine-Venetian relations had soured considerably over the course of the 11th century and Venice was angered by the Empire's willingness to extend trading privileges to the Genoese and the Pisans.

Venice's considerable territorial gains in the wake of the Fourth Crusade were expressed in the new phrase added to the Doge's title: "Lord of One Quarter and One Half [of a quarter] of the Empire of Romania". In addition to the gains in Constantinople, Venice established itself directly in Crete, Negroponte and Corfu (although Corfu was subsequently lost). Venice also extended its territorial holdings to Modon and Coron at the southern tip of mainland Greece in the Peloponnesus. These last two places became known as "the two eyes of the Republic" because all vessels returning from the Levant were ordered to stop there and give news of pirates and convoys.

At around the time that Venice was establishing itself as the most formidable Christian power in the eastern Mediterranean, the Mamlūks were establishing their power in Egypt and Syria, and by the end of the 13th century Baybars and his successors had put an end to the last remaining Crusader footholds on the Levant coast. Whereas in 1204, when Venice realised the gains of the Fourth Crusade, the region was divided into a bewildering multiplicity of states, she now at the beginning of the 14th century faced a strong and united Muslim state along the southern shores of the Levant. It is this fact—plus the disintegration of the Great Mongol successor k͟hānates in the mid-14th century—which explains the importance of the Venetian-Mamlūk relationship. If Venice hoped to continue its lucrative role as an intermediary between East and West, it had to deal with the Mamlūks into whose ports the luxury goods from the East arrived. As for the Mamlūks, they relied on Venetian commercial and naval power to provide a ready market for these goods. By the end of the 14th century, the Venetian fleet was calling regularly at Alexandria as well as the Syrian ports, and Venice's two warehouse-palaces (*funduḳ*, *fondaco*) were among the handsomest structures in Alexandria.

Although the Venetians and the Mamlūk Sultans were often at loggerheads over the price of pepper, the essential commonality of their interests is shown by the fact that, when the Portuguese threatened to disrupt the spice trade in the opening years of the 16th century, the Venetians urged the Sultan to put pressure on the rulers in South India to refuse spices to the newcomers, again demonstrating Venice's sometimes uncomfortably close relationship with the Muslim world as a result of her commercial interests. The Republic's enemies in Europe accordingly accused Venice of furnishing the Mamlūks with materials and skilled shipwrights in order to fight Christians in India.

The reasonably peaceful state of affairs between Venice and the Mamlūks was not to be duplicated in its relations with the Ottoman Empire. Although their long co-existence in the eastern Mediterranean was necessarily marked by extended periods of peace, as well as a striking capacity to resolve routine problems, the two adversaries fought six major wars between the 15th and the 18th centuries. The Ottomans, unlike the Mamlūks, aimed to unite the eastern Mediterranean under their rule, and this ambition inevitably led them to challenge Venetian territorial holdings in the area. Over the course of more than three centuries the Ottomans were so successful in driving the Venetians out of the Aegean that, by 1128/1715, the republic's holdings were reduced to the Ionian islands.

In the first Ottoman-Venetian war of 868-84/1463-79, Venice lost the Negroponte, its main base in the northern Aegean region. In 906/1499, taking advantage of the difficulties caused by the French invasion of northern Italy, the Ottomans sent their fleet into the Ionian Sea. During the course of that war (906-9/1499-1503) the Sultan's troops wrested away most of Venice's holdings in Greece, including Modon [*q.v.*] and Coron [see ḲORON]. Ottoman cavalry raided so far into northern Italy that the smoke from the burning villages could be seen from the bell tower in Saint Mark's square. Venice was only able to bring that war to a conclusion by surrendering claims to many cities in Albania and Greece.

In the next two wars against the Ottomans, Venice fought as part of a Western crusading alliance led by the Spanish Hapsburgs, who saw themselves as the leaders of the Christian world, bound by duty to combat the Islamic empire at the other end of the Mediterranean. Both of these conflicts ended badly for Venice. In the war of 944-7/1537-40, the Christian fleet had to retreat in disorder and confusion at the battle of Prevese on the coast of southern Epirus (945/1538) [see PREVEZE] and, by the time the Spaniards sailed home, the Venetians had lost almost all of their holdings in the Aegean. Although the battle of Lepanto (979/1571) [see AYNABAK͟HTĪ] was a great victory for Christendom, and was celebrated as such throughout Europe, Venice had already lost Cyprus the year before as part of the preliminary Ottoman response to the formation of yet another crusading league against her.

Venetian losses in these two wars, plus the fact that on both occasions Venice felt compelled to seek a separate peace with the Ottomans in order to preserve her commerce in the East (actions for which it was roundly condemned in the West), underlines the peculiar position of Venice, squeezed as she was between East and West. Venice was not opposed to joining with the Hapsburgs and others in attacks upon the Ottomans, since she hoped by so doing to gain some advantage for herself, but she knew full well that the Spaniards, in particular, wanted to defeat the Ottomans without increasing Venetian power in the eastern Mediterranean. In the wake of Lepanto, for instance, Philip II refused to pursue the Ottoman fleet further east precisely for this reason, and similar Venetian-Hapsburg tensions characterised the 944-7/1537-40 war as well. As the front-line state, Venice had the most to gain, but also the most to lose, from the wars of the 16th century.

During the Cyprus war, French merchants largely replaced the Venetians in the Levant and the Ottomans granted the French special trading privileges in order to have them as allies against the Hapsburgs [see IMTIYĀZĀT]. This ominous development was indicative of things to come. Venice became increasingly less important to the Ottomans as they discovered that there were other Western powers—principally, but not only, France—that could lend commercial, and even, on occasion, military assistance.

A long period of peace followed the loss of Cyprus. Although the Ottomans certainly wanted to wrest Crete from the Venetians, they did not find the strength to launch another naval war against the Republic until 1054/1644, when Maltese pirates captured an Ottoman ship with many notables aboard heading for Egypt from Istanbul. The Ottomans, having recently concluded a long war with Ṣafawid Persia, decided to use this incident as reason to finally try and dislodge the Venetians from Crete. The war that followed was extraordinarily long (1055-80/1645-69) and costly, but in the end the Ottomans were triumphant. The last Venetian soldiers left the island in Rabīʿ II 1080/September 1669, and thus the Ottomans brought to an end almost half a millennium of Venetian rule on Crete [see ḲANDIYA]. In the course of a joint Western attack on the Ottomans following the second failed siege of Vienna (1095-1111/1684-99), the Venetians were able to regain the Morea but then lost it again—as well as all remaining territory east of the Ionian islands—in the last Ottoman-Venetian war (1126-30/1714-18) [see MORA].

Despite the long centuries of Ottoman-Venetian hostility, Venice remained a cosmopolitan city that was open to Muslims in a way that other European cities were not. Envoys sent by the Sultan were a common sight in the city, as were Muslim merchants, particularly in the 16th century. Venetian painting in the early modern period testifies to this unique quality: oriental figures are commonplace, whereas they are largely absent from the art of northern Europe in the same period. And of course, it was from Venice that Sultan Meḥemmed II summoned Gentile Bellini to paint his portrait.

Bibliography: W. Heyd, *Histoire du commerce du Levant au moyen-âge*, Leipzig 1885-6, ii, 313 ff., 427 ff.; J. Wansbrough, *Documents for the history of commercial relations between Egypt and Venice 1442-1512*, Ph.D. diss., London Univ. 1961, unpubl.; idem, *A Mamluk ambassador to Venice in 913/1507*, in *BSOAS*, xxvi (1963), 503-30; idem, *Venice and Florence in the Mamluk commercial privileges*, in *BSOAS*, xxviii (1965), 483-523; F. Lane, *Venice, a maritime republic*, Baltimore 1973; D.E. Pitcher, *An historical geography of the Ottoman empire*, Leiden 1972, 170, s.vv. Venedik, etc.; P. Preto, *Venezia e i Turchi*, Florence 1975; Maria Pia Pedani, *In nome del Gran Signore. Inviati ottomani a Venezia dalla caduta di Constantinopoli alla guerra di Candia*, Venice 1994; Palmira Brummett, *Ottoman seapower and Levantine diplomacy in the age of discovery*, Albany, N.Y. 1994.

(MOLLY GREENE)

WEYSĪ, the pen-name (*maḵhlaṣ*) used by Üweys b. Meḥmed, renowned Ottoman man of letters and poet (969-1037/1561 or 1562-1628).

Born in Ala<u>sh</u>ehir as the son of a *ḳāḍī* and the nephew of the poet Maḳālī (Muṣṭafā Beg; cf. the *te<u>dh</u>kire* of Riyāḍī), he finished his *medrese* education in Istanbul under the *ʿulemāʾ* Ṣāliḥ Efendi and Aḥmed Efendi, and then had a career as *ḳāḍī*. Apart from serving as army judge (*ordu-yi̊ hümāyūn ḳāḍīsi̊*) during the Hungarian campaign under the command of the Wezīr ʿAlī Pa<u>sh</u>a, he was *ḳāḍī* in various locations in the Ottoman empire (Re<u>sh</u>īd in Egypt, A<u>k</u>hiṣār, Tire, Ala<u>sh</u>ehir, Sīrōz, Rodosd<u>j</u>uḳ, Gümüld<u>j</u>ine, Tirḥala, and Üsküb) and, for a time, financial inspector (*emwāl müfetti<u>sh</u>i*) in Aydi̊n, Ṣaru<u>kh</u>ān, Ineba<u>kh</u>ti̊ and E<u>gh</u>riboz. He died in Üsküb, after he had served his seventh term there as *ḳāḍī*, on 14 <u>Dh</u>u 'l-Ḥid<u>j</u>d<u>j</u>a 1037/15 August 1628.

Weysī's prose was greatly admired in his day. As his style is heavily laden with loan-words and rhetorical devices (though not in the same degree as that of his contemporary Nergisī [*q.v.*]), he is, on the whole, not easy to understand. ʿAṭāʾī [*q.v.*] considers his prose to be superior to his poetry (*<u>Dh</u>eyl-i <u>Sh</u>aḳāʾiḳ*, i, 715) and it is true that Weysī owes his fame to his prose works rather than to his poetry.

Weysī wrote a considerable number of prose works in various fields. Best known are the following two: (1) *Dürret al-tād<u>j</u> fī sīret ṣāḥib al-miʿrād<u>j</u>*, generally referred to as *Siyer-i Weysī*; it is incomplete, containing the *Sīrat al-Nabī* up to the battle of Badr. *<u>Dh</u>eyls* to it were written by ʿAṭāʾī, Nābī [*q.v.*] (who, after an interval of about twenty years, wrote a second *<u>Dh</u>eyl*, the *<u>Dh</u>eyl-i <u>dh</u>eyl-i Nābī*), and Naẓmī-zāde Ba<u>gh</u>dādī. The *Siyer-i Weysī* was printed together with Nābī's *<u>Dh</u>eyl* in 1245 at Būlāḳ and as part of Weysī's collected works in 1286 at Istanbul. (2) *<u>Kh</u>ʷāb-nāme*, also known as *Wāḳiʿa-nāme*. It is written in somewhat simpler language than the *Siyer-i Weysī* and is a conversation between Aḥmed I and Alexander the Great, wherein the evil deeds that have occurred in the world through the ages are recounted. As it involves a comparison of the old and new orders, it represents a critique of the time. It has been printed several times (Būlāḳ 1252, Istanbul 1263, 1293 and, in the collected works, 1286). The text was also published together with a translation by H.F. von Diez, in *Fundgruben des Orients* (Vienna), iii (1811), 249-74, and separately, Berlin 1811, as *Ermahnung an Islambol oder Strafgericht des türkischen Dichters Uweissi über die Ausartung der Osmanen, übersetzt und erläutert und mit dem türkischen Text herausgegeben*, as well as ed. and tr. F.A. Salimzyanova, *Vejsi. <u>Kh</u>ab-name* ("*Kniga snovideniya*"), Moscow 1977.

His *Düstūr al-ʿamel*, also known as *<u>Sh</u>ehādet-nāme*, which treats of various religious themes in prose, was also printed (Istanbul 1283 and, as part of his collected works, Istanbul 1286), as were some of his letters, *Mün<u>sh</u>eʾāt* (in his collected works, Istanbul 1286).

The remainder of his works have not been published. The better-known among these are: his *Dīwān* (ms. in Topkapı Sarayı, Revan Kütüphanesi, no. 776), his poems being written in simpler language than his prose; *Tewbe-nāme*, a study in verse on the wise words of Zayn al-Dīn <u>Kh</u>āfī, the *pīr* of the Zayniyya order in Anatolia; *Marad<u>j</u> al-baḥrayn fī ad<u>j</u>wiba ʿalā iʿtirāḍāt al-<u>Dj</u>awharī*, in Arabic (autograph in Ragıp Paşa Kütüphanesi, no. 1239/1415); *Risāle-yi ʿAmr b. al-ʿĀṣ*, on the conquest of Egypt; *Futūḥ-i Miṣr*, incomplete, on the history of the conquests of Egypt; the commentary on Sūra CX, *<u>Gh</u>urret al-ʿaṣr fī tefsīr sūret al-Naṣr*; and *Hediyyet al-mu<u>kh</u>liṣīn we-te<u>dh</u>kiret al-muḥsinīn* on questions of morality.

Bibliography: In addition to the comprehensive bibliography given by Th. Menzel in his art. *Waisī* in *EI*[1], see the *tedhkire*s of Ḳinalī-zāde Ḥasan Čelebi, Beyānī, Ḳāf-zāde Fā'iḍī and 'Āṣim; Ḥādjdjī Khalīfa, i, 738-9, 754, 819, ii, 1653; *İA*, art. *Veysî* (M. Kanar); *Başlangıcından günümüze kadar büyük Türk klâsikleri*, v, Istanbul 1987, 90-2; 339-41; M.K. Özgül, *Türk edebiyâtında siyâsî rûyâlar*, Ankara 1989 (date of preface), 11, 13, 24; unpubl. theses: H. Deryan, *Ḥābnāme-i Veysî*, Istanbul 1961, Türkiyat Enstitüsü, no. 571; Z. Öztürk, *Siyer-i Veysî zeyli*, Istanbul 1979, Türkiyat Enstitüsü, no. 2074; Z. Toska, *Veysî divanı. Hayatı, eserleri, kişiliği*, Istanbul 1985.

(Th. Menzel-[Edith G. Ambros])

WEZĪR KÖPRÜ, modern Vezirköprü, a small town of northern Anatolia, situated 35 km/21 miles north of Merzifon [see MERZIFŪN] and 18 km/12 miles south of the lowest stretch of the Kızıl Irmak [see ḲIZĪL-ĪRMĀḲ] (lat. 41° 09' N, long. 35° 27' E). There was apparently a town there or nearby, in classical times, in what was then southern Pamphylia, and in Byzantine times, the town of Gedegara (in Kātib Čelebi's *Djihān-nümā*, Kedeghara). In high Ottoman times, from the 10th/16th century onwards, it came within the *sandjak* of Amasya in the *eyālet* of Sivas. Ewliyā Čelebi visited it in 1057/1647, and described its citadel as in ruins (*Seyāḥet-nāme*, Istanbul 1314/1896-7, ii, 400 ff.). Originally simply called Köprü, the famous 11th/17th century statesman Köprülü Meḥmed Pasha, subsequently Grand Vizier, had in his early career held an administrative post in the town, and thereafter the name acquired its *wezīr* element [see KÖPRÜLÜ, at the beginning]. In modern Turkey, Vezirköprü is the chef-lieu of an *ilce* or district in the *il* or province of Samsun [*q.v.*]; in 1975 the population of the town was 11,705 and of the *ilce* 67,468.

Bibliography: V. Cuinet, *La Turquie d'Asie*, i, Paris 1892, 762-3; Sāmī Bey Frasheri, *Ḳāmūs al-a'lām*, Istanbul 1896, v, 3905; *İA* art. *Vezirköprü* (Besim Darkot). (C.E. Bosworth)

WIDIN, conventionally Vidin, a town of northwestern Bulgaria and a port on the River Danube (lat. 44° 00' N., long. 22° 50' E.).

The low bank (30-37 m high) has been reinforced with dykes; in the past the town used to remain an island in the marshes created during the spring floods of the Danube. It emerged as the Roman fortress of Bononia on the foundations of a Thracian settlement at Kaleto, a place where the flood does not reach. In the Middle Ages, under the name of Bdin, it was the centre of a bishopric in the Bulgarian state, and from the second half of the 14th century, of an appanage principality. After 1371, it was the centre of the independent state of Tsar Ivan Sratsimir. In 1365-9 it was conquered by the Hungarians and ruled as a Banate, with *ca.* 200,000 Orthodox Christians being forced to convert to Catholicism. As Ottoman vassal, Ivan Sratsimir surrendered Vidin to the Crusaders of Sigismund III in 1396, and the Ottoman garrison was exterminated; however, Bāyezīd routed the Crusaders at Nicopolis and gained back the city.

Today this town, with about 50,000 inhabitants, has no Muslim population, but its history, its Ottoman architectural monuments, archives and manuscripts make it important for the study of Ottoman urban and cultural history in the Balkans.

The Vidin kingdom was transformed into the Vidin *sandjak* (covering territory in both the Bulgaria and Serbia of today) within the Rumeli *beylerbeylik*. A *Ḳānūn-nāme* of 1542 and a set of 19 local laws of 1586 have been preserved, regulating the administration of the *sandjak*, which consisted of 9 *nāḥiye*s and 6 fortresses. Until the mid-16th century, the *sandjak* was part of the Ottoman frontier line, the *serḥadd*, against Transylvania, the Banat, Wallachia and Hungary, and from the 17th century onwards (when it was attacked, taken and destroyed), against Austria and Serbia. During the war with the Holy League, the Austrians captured the city on 13 October 1689 and held it for 10 months. Under the peace treaty of Passarowitz in 1718 [see PASAROFČA] the Ottoman empire lost the northwestern parts of the Vidin *sandjak*, sc. the *ḳaḍā*s of Fetḥ ül-Islam and Krayna. Vidin became again part of the *serḥadd*. Towards the end of the 18th century Vidin became the seat of 'Othmān Pazwandoghlu and the centre of one of the most important secession movements and *a'yān* rule in Rumeli. In 1864, it was a *sandjak* in the Ṭuna [*q.v.*] *wilāyet* administered by a *mutaṣarrif* and a *dīwān*, divided into *ḳaḍā*s. Under the San Stefano preliminary treaty of 1878, Vidin surrendered without a fight and was included in the Bulgarian state.

The *serḥadd* in the Vidin area consisted of the fortress and garrison in Vidin, the river fleet and considerable groups of local population, including non-Muslims. Vlachs stand out among them, these being nomad Christians used by the Ottoman state as a paramilitary group paying only the *filur* tax. With the move of the *serḥadd* to the west after 1541, the state *ca.* 1560 deprived them of their paramilitary status, but the area of Vidin remained the Ottoman rear for the conquest of Central Europe, with local non-Muslims serving in the fortress. Likewise, *khāṣṣ*es, and 12 *ze'āmet*s and *tīmār*s of *sipahī*s, but mainly of the fortress guards (about 10-15 persons in Vidin in mid-15th century, and 65 in 1560), were established, while a considerable part of the Muslim *re'āyā* were registered as members of the *aḳindji* [*q.v.*] troops. The role of the *sipāhī* troops in the area was reduced at the expense of the rise of the Janissaries and the local troops, which *ca.* 1750 numbered 5,500, more than in any other Ottoman city of the Balkans.

The sultanal *khāṣṣ* in the Vidin area expanded quickly at the expense of the Vlach villages and the *tīmār* lands, and soon turned into the largest in the Balkans. As a result, by the 18th century there was no *mīrī* land with *tīmār*s and *ze'āmet*s in the region, and the process of establishment of the *gospodarlïḳ*s began (possessions of local notables and Janissaries), catalysed by the war with the Holy League and the secession of 'Othmān Pazwandoghlu. The 19th-century agrarian reforms in the Ottoman empire were not introduced in the Vidin area. Villagers were deprived of any property rights over the land and were placed in the position of tenants of the *agha*s from Vidin, who claimed that only Muslims could possess land in this border *sandjak*. This régime provoked riots and uprisings in the 1830s to 1850s which, together with the Serbian uprising (1804-13), forced the Porte to solve the problem in favour of the villagers in 1863.

From the 15th century onwards, Vidin was a *ḳaḍā* with a *ḳāḍī* and, at least from the 17th century, with a *müftī* also. At least from mid-15th century, the local fleet and ship-building were administered by a *ḳapudan* who from *ca.* 1700 was subordinate to the Danube *ḳapudan* based in Ruse.

Vidin was the main border customs post and the largest port in this part of the Danube, with an enormous income from the state monopoly on the salt imports from Wallachia and the state fisheries organised by the *emīn* of the port. The rise in the town's population by over 25% in the 18th century was directly related to its economic role.

In the Middle Ages, the lands along the Danube banks formed a region which brought together Turks, Bulgarians, Serbs, Vlachs, Hungarians and Jews. The problem of the Turkish population in the Vidin area has been discussed extensively, and its archaic dialect has been studied as an element of the Turkish Balkan dialects. Apart from settlement of military and administrative bodies in the town, the classical Ottoman type of colonisation cannot be detected here. The Muslim population was concentrated in Vidin and a few fortresses, but was entirely absent from the rural areas of the province. Muslims rose in number through the slow infiltration of Muslim population from the upper Danubian lands during the Ottoman retreat from Hungary and Serbia after the 16th century, and it was in this way that Vidin was maintained as a predominantly Muslim city. At the same time, the numbers of Janissaries within the Muslim community in Vidin rose, and it could safely be called a Janissary town. We find Janissaries in all spheres of public life, beginning with the economy and the craftsmen's guilds and ending with the professional witnesses in the courts. All this, together with the peasant uprisings in the region and the Serbian revolt, reinforced local Muslim fanaticism against the reforms in the Ottoman empire. At the beginning of the 1860s, Tatars and Circassians from Russia were settled in the region, a small part of them being in Vidin proper. Hence there was a Tatar *maḥalle* with a mosque and a school. The number of Muslims in the town cannot be established with certainty since soldiers were not included in the registers of taxpayers, according to which in the 1520-30s there were 356 Muslim households with 10 religious functionaries (*imāms* and *mü'edhdhins*); at the same time, 225 *sipāhīs* lived in the town and the *ḳaḍā* as well as 251 members of the fortress garrison. In 1571-80, these numbered 1,207, while 2,152 households altogether were registered in the town, or nearly 11,000 inhabitants. Ewliyā Čelebi speaks of 4,700 houses or over 20,000 inhabitants of Vidin. European estimates of Vidin as a predominantly Muslim town, with between 15 and 30,000 inhabitants at the beginning of the 19th century, made it one of the most significant towns in Rumeli. According to Ottoman censuses of *ca.* 1866, there were 7,664 taxpayers (more than 23,000 inhabitants), 3,954 Muslim taxpayers included. Immediately after Bulgaria gained independence, a large part of the Muslims moved out, and by the beginning of the 20th century Vidin was no longer predominantly Muslim. According to the 1893 census, there were 2,729 Turks and 1,540 Jews among the 14,500 inhabitants of the town.

The development of the fortification system of Vidin had a major role in the development of the urban architecture. According to some data, the Roman fortification (an irregular tetragon) survived as an earthen mound until the Ottoman conquest. During the 12th-14th centuries, in the northern part of the Kaleto hill, the fortified castle of Baba Vida was built. This citadel with a moat and a draw-bridge was renewed during the rule of Bāyezīd II (1481-1512) and reconstructed with regard to the use of firearms; the first mosque and the garrison, forming a *maḥalle* with about 50 inhabitants, the house of the *muḥāfiẓ* of the fortress and the seat of the *sandjaḳ bey*, were all in it. In the mid-19th century, Sāmī Pasha established a sort of a military museum in the now largely useless citadel, which was dispersed during or shortly after the Russo-Turkish War of 1877-8.

The outer part of the town spread to the south and southwest of Baba Vida on the terrain of the Kaleto hill, where in 1523-37 there were 9 Muslim *maḥalles* with 2 mosques, 8 *mesdjids*, 4 *zāwiyes*, 2 *ḥammāms*, a candle workshop and a *bozakhāne*. Ewliyā speaks of 4 Christian, one Jewish and 19 Muslim *maḥalles*, with 24 mosques having leaden or tiled roofs with 10 minarets; he mentions also 10 *mesdjids* with wooden minarets, 7 *medreses*, 11 *mektebs* and 7 *tekkes*. Religious buildings and the economic and communal infrastructure for maintaining them were built by leading functionaries of the Vidin *serḥadd*, the *sandjaḳ beys* of the 15th century, such as Mezīd Bey, ʿAlī Bey Mikhāloghlu, the *dizdār* of Florentin, Aḥmed Ḥadjdj, and the Rumeli *beylerbey* Meḥmed Ṣoḳollu [*q.v.*]. The *Negotin čarshi*, a crossroads of seven streets, was the core of the entire urban network of Kaleto, with trade and craft functions, and a mosque; the Mosluk place, with the churches of St. Petka and St. Panteleimon was nearby. There was a natural process of confessional mixing of the population in the outer town, in the Ottoman documents of the 17th century this was called the *warosh*; the term was also used to designate the Christian community in the town and the nearby *čiftliks* (see below).

The Austrian occupation caused changes in the continuity of life in Vidin. A new fortification following the Vauban system was constructed (its beginning is attributed to the Austrians) and by 1722 was finished by the Ottomans. The semicircular fortress overlooking the river consisted of two parallel walls 6 m high and a mound between them; among the seven chordes there were eight hexagonal bastions with heavy garrison artillery; four gates; a moat filled with water from the Danube; the fortress fence along the Danube with broken-line contours consisted of two parallel, double stone walls and a mound between them; there were five gates open at the river.

These fortifications guarded the town from the spring tide and are almost entirely preserved. The fortress was dismantled under the terms of the Berlin Congress peace treaty. Part of the defences and of the gates have been preserved (seven of the inscriptions are built into the walls of the Public Library in St. Petersburg; all have *taḥrīrs* with the construction date and the names of the architects or of the overseers for the period between 1721 and 1835). The inscription compiled by the poet Behdjetī in 1735 at *Stambol ḳapi*, which was built by Aḥmed Pasha and the architect Muṣṭafā Ḳulu, has been preserved in Vidin. With its 200 guns turned at the mainland and twelve ships equipped with guns on the Danube, Vidin became an important fortress. Thus the fortified *warosh* came into existence, while the new living quarters, naturally separated from each other, emerged in the place of the former *čiftliks*. Muslims and non-Muslims, gypsies and Tatars lived separately but also in mixed *maḥalles*. It is particularly in connection with the construction of the modern *ḳale* that an exclusively Vidin phenomenon emerged related to the general framework of *dhimmī* status within the Ottoman empire. In 1718 the central authorities were approached by the local Janissaries demanding on the grounds of "*ḳānūn-i serḥadd*" that Christians should leave the (newly) fortified part of the town, after selling their properties to Muslims at appropriate prices, and settle in the unfortified part, i.e. in the emerging "outer" *warosh* of Vidin. The two main religious communities in Vidin were territorially separated (Jews remained in the fortified part). The development of the two parts of the town began—the fortified one with the semicircular

Panorama view of Vidin and the river Danube. Engraving by an unknown author.

Stambul Ḳapı̊. Archival photo.

The mosque and the library of ʿO<u>th</u>mān Pazwando<u>gh</u>lu.
Present state.

The mediaeval citadel of Baba Vida with part of the fortress wall. Archival photo.

fortress or *ḳale*, and the outer *warosh* with its *maḥalle*s, mosques and *mesdjid*s. In the southern part, around the *Stambol ḳapî*, the *waḳîf* of Muṣṭafā Paṣha, *muḥāfiz* of Vidin, permitted construction activities, as did that of the vizier, *muḥāfiz* of Belgrade and *wālī* of Vidin, 'Othmān, *ḳaṣṣāb bashî* in the capital, and Yaḥyā Paṣha, with a mosque to which Rüstem Agha added a *mekteb*.

Even before the emergence of the new fortress, to the north, on the dryest and, because of this, least protected territory, a large quarter developed, populated mainly by non-Muslims. The new outer quarter was fortified, too, in the 19th century. According to Kanitz, in the 1870s there were 12 mosques and 17 *maḥalle*s (compared to the 15 *maḥalle*s and mosques in the inner fortification); according to C. Jireček, there were 32 mosques in the town. The florescence of Vidin as a centre of Islamic culture was closely related to 'Othmān Pazwandoghlu. Documents, manuscripts and architectural monuments preserved in the National Library in Sofia and in Vidin proper reveal the sources of Pazwandoghlu's wealth and his "civil policy" in the town. He tried to modernise the Vidin fortress after the European model. He built the Square barracks (today a museum); repaired the four main roads going out of Vidin and regulated the city street network; provided the town with *česhme*s or fountains, as well as a *mosluḳ* and *sebīl* with an ice-house (a *waḳîf-name* of 1807); and founded a library (see below). In accordance with the Ottoman tradition, he also built a mosque, which has an inscription of 1800-1 with a dedication (still existing today) to his father 'Ömer, and a stone tomb of the local hero of local Turkish folklore, Ṣalāḥeddīn Baba, with a Bektāshī *tekke* in the village of Sheykh Čiftlik, at the place where the *baba* perished, leading an Ottoman detachment out of the fortress against the Austrian siege in 1689. The library of 'Othmān has a construction inscription with a chronogram 1217 (1802-3) and containing the name of the poet-compiler Māhir (also author of the inscription at the mosque of 'Othmān of 1802, and most probably the poet Sherīf Ibrāhīm Māhir Efendi, who was secretary to the *wālī* of Vidin Ḥāfiẓ 'Alī Paṣha in 1812, and is known for his Turkish adaptation of *Kalīla wa-Dimna*). The library and the mosque of 'Othmān form an architectural compound (still existing), next to a now-disappeared *medrese*. According to M. Staynova, this construction activity reveals an elaborate combination of Bektāshism and the European Enlightenment and laïcism, untypical of Ottoman classicism and the baroque forms of the *Lāle dewrī* [*q.v.*].

The 18th century witnessed considerable intellectual life in Rumeli initiated by local officials. Some data confirm that there were private libraries in Vidin at this time. The Pazwandoghlu library was in fact a public library containing the Oriental books accumulated in the town. Its core was a donation by the Pazwandoghlu family; most of the books bear the seals of 'Ömer Agha and of Ruḳiyye Khātūn, the father and mother of 'Othmān. Around 1879 it was moved to Sofia; in 1887 it was checked by an international commission, including Meḥmed Nedīm, and about 2,000 volumes were ceded to the Ottoman authorities; it seems that earlier some of the most precious manuscripts were taken by the Russians as trophies of war. The criteria for the selection of the books are unknown, as likewise their fate in both Russia and Turkey. Today about 650 volumes in Arabic, Persian and Ottoman are preserved in the National Library in Sofia; a manuscript with 18 miniatures of the *Ḳiṣaṣ al-anbiyāʾ* ("Tales of the Prophets") stands out among

them, donated by Ḥāfiẓ 'Alī Paṣha. The library contained the greater part of the works on history and geography printed at the Müteferriḳa Press [see MAṬBAʿA. B.2]; at the present moment, a manuscript catalogue of the Vidin Library of 1837, kept in the Sofia National Library, is the only one to give a relatively full idea of its content.

As well as Ṣalāḥeddīn, a famous Muslim saint and hero related to Vidin is Ḳarlî Bashe, buried by the Florentin or *Ḳarlî Bashe ḳapî*. According to legend, in 1737, during the siege of the town by the Austrians, the Ottomans attacked and Ḳarlî Bashe was the first to lead the defenders out. The governor of the *sandjaḳ*, Ḥüseyn Paṣha (who later finished the fortification works on the new fortress in 1835) began administrative reforms along the lines of the Gülkhāne *khaṭṭ-î sherīf*, breaking down Janissary opposition.

Intellectual figures connected with the town include the mathematician and teacher in military schools Widinli Ḥüseyn Tewfīḳ Paṣha (d. 1894); Widinli Muṣṭafā Efendi, a well-known teacher and publisher (d. 1855); 'Alī Shukrī Efendi (*fl.* in the mid-19th century); Ḥāsib Ṣaffeti (Aytuna) Widinli, who contributed to the development of Ottoman education before and after the Russo-Turkish War of 1877-8; and Čorbadjîzāde Meḥmed, son of Ḥüseyn Efendi Widinli, who, as *müftī* in Rusčuk, wrote in 1699 his *Zeyn ül-ʿaḳāʾid* in Turkish.

In the 19th century Vidin developed as an important economic centre stimulated by navigation on the Danube; French, Austrian and Russian trading consulates were opened. According to Ottoman censuses of 1872-4 there were 1,610 *dükkān*s, 11 *debbāghkhāne*s, 14 *khān*s, 135 storehouses, 5 *ḥammām*s, one telegraph office, 6 churches and synagogues, one clocktower; one *rüshdiyye*, two *medrese*s, one *iṣlāḥ-khāne* where girls were also taught; 7 *tekke*s (in the town and suburbs), 24 mosques and two hospitals.

After the Russo-Turkish War of 1877-8, the Muslim monuments were first regulated by the *Waḳîf Board* headed by patriotic Turks who wished to preserve them; there were also cultural, educational and sports organisations in Vidin, including the Turkish gymnastic society *Tūrān*, the charitable and educational club *Tenwīr-i Efkār* and the reading room *Shefket*. Until World War I, there was a district *müftülük*.

Bibliography: 1. Sources. Ewliyā Čelebi, *Seyāḥat-nāme*, viii, Istanbul 1985; BBA TD 370; *Sāl-nāme-yi Wilāyet-i Ṭuna*, Istanbul 1289; 52 vols. of *ḳāḍī sidjill*s in the SS. Cyril and Methodius National Library, Sofia.

2. Studies. F. Kanitz, *Donau-Bulgarien und der Balkan*, Leipzig 1882; D. Ihčiev, *Dărzhavni dokumenti za Osman Pazvantoglu Vidinski*, in *Sbornik za narodni umotvoreniya i naučna knizhnina*, xxiv (Sofia 1908); P. Miyatev, *Prinos kăm srednovekovnata arheologiya na bălgarskite zemi*, in *Godishnik na narodniya muzey za 1921*, Sofia 1922; D. Tsuhlev, *Istoriya na grad Vidin i negovata oblast*, Sofia 1932; D. Dzonova, *Vidin (historische Übersicht)*, in *Antike und Mittelalter in Bulgarien*, Berlin 1960; T. Zlatev, *Bălgarskite gradove po r. Dunav prez epohata na Văzrazhdaneto*, Sofia 1962; A. Pantev, *Krepostnoto stroitelstvo văv Vidin, kraya na XVII i părvata četvărt na XVIII v.*, in *Muzei i pametnitsi na kulturata*, 1964 no. 4; J. Németh, *Die Türken von Vidin. Sprache, Folklore, Religion*, Budapest 1965; D. Boyanić-Lukać, *Vidin i Vidinskiyat sandzhak prez 15-16 vek.*, Sofia 1975; M. Berindei, M. Kalus-Martin and G. Veinstein, *Actes de Murad sur la région de Vidin et remarques sur le qanun ottoman*, in *Südost-Forschungen*, xxxv (1976), 11-68; M. Staynova, *Ottoman libraries in Vidin*, in

Etudes balkaniques, Sofia 1979, no. 2; eadem, *Za vakăfskata deynost na Osman Pazvantoglu văv Vidin i Vidinskiya kray*, in *Vekove*, 1982, no. 6; eadem, *Osmanskite biblioteki v bălgarskite zemi, XV-XIX v.*, Sofia 1982; M. Kiel, *Urban development in Bulgaria in the Turkish period. The place of Turkish architecture in the process*, in *Internat. Jnal. of Tkish. Studies*, iv/2 (1989); M. Lačev, *Kratka istoriya na hrama "Sv. Nikolay Mirlikiyski Čudotvorets" v gr. Vidin*, in *Duhovna kultura*, Sofia 1990, no. 11; M. Harbova, *Gradoustroystvo i arhitektura po bălgarskite zemi prez XV-XVIII v.*, Sofia 1991; H. Inalcık, *Tanzimat ve Bulgar meselesi. Doktora tezi'nin 50. yılı*, Eren 1992.

(SVETLANA IVANOVA)

WILĀYA (A.), a noun form from the root *w-l-y* "to be near, adjacent, contiguous to" [someone or something] and a term with a range of meaning in the political, religious and legal spheres. For the legal meaning, see 1. below. In the political and religious spheres, *wilāya* denotes "the exercise of authority", whether temporal or spiritual, or a combination of both; hence by extension, it comes to mean the government or administration of a region or province under the supreme overlordship of a caliph, sultan or *amīr* [see WĀLĪ], or the spiritual authority and charisma of a particularly spiritually-gifted person like a Ṣūfī saint or ascetic [see WALĪ]. Among the Shīʿa, however, the slightly different vocalisation *walāya* conveys a special sense of devotion for and closeness and allegiance to the *Imām*s on the part of their followers; for this sense, see 2. below.

1. In Islamic law.

Here, it indicates representation, which signifies the power of an individual to personally initiate an action. It is seen as a legal authority (*sulṭa sharʿiyya*) by which an individual can initiate contracts (*ʿuḳūd*) and actions (*taṣarrufāt*) and actuate their effects (*āthār*). When a person acts on behalf of others, *wilāya* is more often termed *niyāba*.

Wilāya and *ahliyya* [see SHAKHṢ] are the two main requirements for any proper contract, *ʿaḳd ṣaḥīḥ*. Ahliyya represents the individual qualification to undertake an action. This requires sanity (*ʿaḳl*), adulthood (*bulūgh*) and, often, in family-related matters, profession of Islam. *Wilāya*, on the contrary, is the "authorised" ability to perform an action. A contract in which one of its contractors is not able (*ghayr walī*) or unqualified (*ghayr ahl*) is considered null (*bāṭil*). A qualified person who performed a legal contract without authority is considered as intrusive (*fuḍūlī*) and the contract will only become valid if approved by the persons concerned.

Technically, *wilāya* can be either optional (*ikhtiyāriyya*), when entered into by personal choice, such as *wakāla* [*q.v.*], or compulsory (*idjbāriyya*). However, in practice *wilāya* is a term used only to describe the latter, namely, *idjbāriyya*, which is determined by legal rule or judicial order. This can be divided into the following categories: the custody of infants (*haḍānat al-ṣaghīr*) and the custody of a person (*wilāyat al-nafs*) requiring care for a child who has passed the age of infancy or for an insane person. It also includes the marriage custody of a virgin girl. Financial custody may cover all young persons, the insane, and those with proven impediments to the exercise of normal free will.

The requirement of a *walī*, in addition to being suitable (*ahl*), is to be of the same religion, of a creditable character (*ʿadl*) and honest (*amīn*). The state is expected to oversee the *walī* in all its forms. If the *walī* behaves in an inappropriate manner, then the judge can appoint another *walī* to share responsibility. The procedure for overseeing the *walī* is, like

many judicial supervisory responsibilities, not clearly defined or codified. However, some modern legal systems imply such procedures within their legislation, such as the Syrian Law of personal status which requires the permission of the judge before selling or mortgaging the property of a person under guardianship (*ḳāṣir*).

The limitation of the *walī*'s responsibility is to act as if he is acting for his own business. The example of this cited by Ibn Ḳudāma is the orphan's guardian, who may trade using the orphan's money, avoiding any loss, while all the profits will go to the orphan.

The government or its representative, such as a judge, has the final right of *wilāya* when no eligible relative is available. They also have the right of appointing an alternative *walī* if those named are proved to be corrupt.

Two forms of *wilāya*, whether personal (*ʿalā al-nafs*) or financial (*ʿalā al-māl*), were defined by the Egyptian Law nos. 118, 119/1952 to give more control to the criminal and personal status courts.

The question whether a *walī* can appoint another person in the case of a marriage is a famous case of disagreement (*khilāf*) among jurists. According to the Shāfiʿīs, this is not permitted because even a father requires the consent of his daughter for the person chosen for her. However, Ibn Ḳudāma refuted this claim on the grounds that the *wilāya* was granted by the law and has nothing to do with the woman's consent, which is purely concerned with the final choice of husband. He also states that the Prophet married two of his daughters in this way. This kind of debate is important today with the increasing numbers of cases of women asking for equal rights in Muslim society. It is relevant to add here that the woman's *wilāya* in civil contracts is completely free, unlike that of her *wilāya* in marriage contracts, possibly attributable to the sensitivity of the Islamic legal system to the issue of sexual morality.

Since *wilāya* involves a legal representation, it can, like *wakāla*, involve all aspects and forms of personalities whether real (*shakhṣiyya ḥaḳīḳiyya*) or unreal (*iʿtibāriyya*). In both cases (*nafs* and *māl*) the *wilāya* is given to the closest member of the family. In marriage, the *wilāya* lies with the father, followed by the grandfather. Ibn Ḳudāma provided a summary of the views of various scholars such as al-Shāfiʿī, who confirmed the prerogative of the grandfather in *wilāya* over the son and brother. He also cited the view of Mālik, who prefers the son to the grandfather, basing his preference on the fact that the latter is only a second degree relative while the son is a direct relative. He also cited Ibn Ḥanbal's view that the grandfather and brother are in fact equal in the right of *wilāya* because of their equality of inheritance by male relationship (*taʿṣīb*). Ibn Ḳudāma refutes these views on the grounds of three analogies. He states that the grandfather has the right of *wilāya* before the son and brother because of his birthright as well as *taʿṣīb* like the father. Moreover, he is treated like the father should he steal his granddaughter's property, for a grandfather does not have his hand amputated. Finally, in inheritance he has stronger rights than those of a son or brother.

Bibliography: *LA*, xv, 406-15; Muḥammad Abū Zahra, *al-Ahwāl al-shakhṣiyya*, Cairo 1950, 458, 462, 474; Ibn Ḳudāma, *al-Mughnī*, Beirut 1984, vi, 338; ix, 356, 361, 363; W. Zuḥaylī, *al-Fiḳh al-islāmī wa-adillatuhu*, Beirut 1985, iv, 140.

(MAWIL Y. IZZI DIEN)

2. In Shīʿism.

For the Shīʿa, *wilāya* applies also to the position

of ʿAlī b. Abī Ṭālib as the single, explicitly designated heir and successor to Muḥammad in whom all responsibility for the guidance of the Muslims was subsequently vested. Not to acknowledge ʿAlī's *wilāya* was and is tantamount to apostasy. According to the Shīʿa, the Prophet proclaimed ʿAlī's elevation to this status at Ghadīr Khumm [*q.v.*] when he uttered the famous declaration "Of whomever I am the master (*mawlā*), ʿAlī is his master". Although the Sunnīs generally admit the validity of this *ḥadīth* (especially after it was accepted by Aḥmad b. Ḥanbal), they interpret the term *mawlā* or its equivalent here, *walī*, as meaning simply "friend" and not "master" or "guardian". By contrast, for the Shīʿa, ʿAlī was, by this pronouncement, made the guardian of the community, acting on behalf of God Himself. ʿAlī had become God's divinely chosen *walī* in a way similar to the Prophet having been God's apostle, His *rasūl*.

This doctrinal creed, which is the very core and bedrock of Shīʿism, is most succinctly expressed by successively attesting to the oneness of God, the apostleship of Muḥammad, and the guardianship of ʿAlī: *lā ilāh illā Allāh, Muḥammad rasūl Allāh, ʿAlī walī Allāh*, and this is the proper *shahāda* in use by the Shīʿīs throughout Shīʿa-dominated lands. This form of the *wilāyat ʿAlī* normally appears on Shīʿī official proclamations, coinage, the *ṭirāz*, and other examples of written and inscribed materials. It appears on all Fāṭimid coinage after the year 386/996 (other Shīʿī phrases were used earlier) and on the Shīʿī coins issued by Öldjeytü, to cite two fairly early examples. But, although admitted to be a proper, even essential, expression of Shīʿī piety by all mainstream authorities, it was not allowed as a component of the *adhān* [*q.v.*] until Ṣafawid times when this popular practice was ultimately formally accepted and declared to be *sunna*. It is now a standard part of the call to prayer among the Twelver Shīʿa.

Following the reign of ʿAlī, the *wilāya* resided in the *imāms* one after the other by virtue of designation, *naṣṣ*. The previous *imām* thereby passed it unerringly to his divinely chosen successor. Each *imām*, in turn, thus held exclusive spiritual authority over all Muslims. The *imāms* are those having power of command and whose leadership must be recognised as the *ulu 'l-amr* according to Ḳur'ān IV, 59. The adherents who recognise him and accept his guidance owe him in return the obligation of *walāya*—a term often taken as the equivalent or simply an alternate vocalisation of *wilāya* but which bears, in Shīʿī usage, the specific meaning of "devotion" and denotes the loyalty and support that is due the *imām* from his followers.

Even in classical lexicography, some authorities considered *walāya* to be the verbal noun meaning, for example, *nuṣra* "support", whereas *wilāya* is the name of the office. For the Shīʿa, this distinction attained the status of doctrine, and *walāya* is regarded as one of the pillars of Islam. Al-Kulaynī in his chapter on the *daʿā'im* (pillars) in his *Kāfī* cites a number of *ḥadīths* wherein the *imāms* have enumerated these pillars—usually four, including prayer, alms, fasting, pilgrimage, plus *walāya*—and have singled out *walāya* as especially important. In the near-contemporary *Daʿā'im al-islām* by the Ismāʿīlī jurist al-Ḳāḍī al-Nuʿmān, the author put his section on *walāya* prior to those on purity (*ṭahāra*), prayer, alms, fasting, pilgrimage, and *djihād*, the other six that he included.

In recent times, in the apparent absence of the true *imām*, the term *wilāya* in its Shīʿī sense has also come to apply by a series of extensions and modifications to the *wilāyat al-faḳīh* ("the guardianship of the jurist"), which is the position of the supreme leader in modern Iran. Acting as a surrogate, he holds powers similar in many respects but not exactly equivalent to those of the *imām*.

Bibliography: Kulaynī, *al-Uṣūl min al-Kāfī*, Tehran 1388/1967; al-Ḳāḍī al-Nuʿmān, *Daʿā'im al-islām*, Cairo 1960-3; *LA*, s.v.; Abdulaziz A. Sachedina, *The Just Ruler in Shiʿite Islam*, New York 1988, index; Liyakat A. Takim, From *bidʿa* to *sunna*. The *wilāya* of ʿAlī in the Shīʿī *adhān*, in *JAOS*, cxx (forthcoming); H. Landolt, art. *Walāyah*, in *The Encyclopedia of Religion*, ed. M. Eliade, New York 1987.

(P.E. Walker)

WIRD (A., pl. *awrād*), denotes set, supererogatory personal devotions observed at specific times, usually at least once during the day and once again at night. Abū Ḥāmid al-Ghazālī (d. 505/1111 [*q.v.*]), writing shortly before the establishment of formal Ṣūfī orders, designated as *awrād* seven divisions of the day and five of the night for the performance of devotions (both obligatory and supererogatory) by any pious Muslim (*Iḥyā' ʿulūm al-dīn*, Book X, *Kitāb tartīb al-awrād wa-tafṣīl iḥyā' al-layl*, Cairo 1358/1939, i, 339-73). The term often has referred to Ṣūfī devotions, where a *wird* is an arrangement of standard litanies and repeated formulae (e.g. *takbīr, tahlīl, tasbīḥ, taṣliya*) beginning with Ḳur'ān recitation. In this sense, the term may be compared to *dhikr* and to *ḥizb*, but a distinctive aspect of *wird* is its close association with a particular spiritual guide to whom it is attributed as well as the set times for its observance. Ṣūfī *shaykhs* have sometimes claimed to have received their *wirds* from prophets or saints in spiritual encounters or in dreams.

J.S. Trimingham's examination of the term's origins and development within Ṣūfī contexts stipulates that *wird* has at least three different senses: (1) the *ṭarīḳa* itself; (2) "a special prayer or litany"; and (3) the "office" of the *ṭarīḳa*, meaning its distinctive doctrines and devotional-meditative discipline (*The Sufi orders in Islam*, Oxford 1971, 214). "Each *ṭarīḳa* and each order derivative has its own *awrād* composed by its leaders. These form the 'theme' of the order" (*ibid.*, 215). A Ṣūfī novice typically starts out with an assigned simple, secret *wird* and progressively is introduced to more demanding ones until, when fully initiated by "taking the *wird*" (*akhdh al-wird*), he or she essentially has mastered the complete system of the order.

V. Hoffman's field-based research on contemporary Ṣūfī practices in Egypt includes valuable information about *awrād* and the ways in which they are viewed by masters and disciples in various orders. She reports, for example, that it is imperative for a person to have the permission of a *shaykh* before reciting an order's *awrād*, because they are "believed to be so spiritually powerful that a person could go mad from reciting them without proper spiritual protection and preparation" (*Sufism, mystics and saints in modern Egypt*, Columbia, S.C. 1995, 132-3). The regular recitation of *awrād*, according to Hoffman's informants, leads to "visions and other forms of spiritual revelation and [the disciple] will develop the gift of spiritual discernment that borders on clairvoyance" (133). Communal *wird* is preferred over solitary observance. Hence if one performs one's *wird* by oneself in the morning, a communal *wird* is encouraged after the evening *ṣalāt* (*ibid.*).

There is much traditional wordplay concerning the term, because of the root *w-r-d*'s range of meanings and associations, e.g. "watering place", "access, arrival" at specified times for devotion to God, and "rose". (For more on this aspect, as well as numerous translated passages from traditional *awrād*, see Constance Padwick, *Muslim devotions, prayer-manuals in common use*, London 1961, 20-2, *et passim.*)

Bibliography: In addition to works cited in the text, L. Massignon's art. s.v. in *EI*[1] remains valuable, particularly its listing of collections and manuals of *awrād* since the 8th/14th century. Massignon considered "the essential work" to be ʿAbd al-Ḥayy al-Kattānī, *Fihris al-fahāris*, 2 vols. Fās 1346.

(F.M. Denny)

WĪS u RĀMĪN, a long narrative poem in Persian by Fak̲h̲r al-Dīn Asʿad Gurgānī [*q.v.*], written not long after 441/1050 and dedicated to Abū Naṣr b. Manṣūr, the governor of Iṣfahān on behalf of the Sald̲j̲ūḳids. The story, which is set in the distant and unspecified past, deals with the love affair between Wīs, the wife of King Mōbad of Marw, and Rāmīn, her husband's younger brother. It tells of how the two lovers meet, how they are eventually discovered, and how Rāmīn rises in rebellion against his brother, in the end seizing the throne and making the widowed Wīs his queen. In the opening section, Gurgānī says that he had found the story in a book in Pahlawī, which he put into Persian verse at the request of his patron. The existence of an older Iranian poetical version of the story would seem to be confirmed by a verse by the much earlier Arabic poet Abū Nuwās referring to *fird̲j̲ardāt Rāmīn wa-Wīs*, whereby, according to the commentary by Ḥamza al-Iṣfahānī, "*fird̲j̲ardāt* are like poems (*ka 'l-ḳaṣā'id*)". (For the poem by Abū Nuwās, and Ḥamza's commentary, not yet in Wagner's edition, see M. Mīnuwī, *Yak-ī az fārsiyyāt-i Abū Nuwās*, in *Mad̲j̲alla-yi Dānis̲h̲kada-yi Adabiyyāt-i Tihrān*, i/3 [1333 *s̲h̲.*/1954], 62-77). It is evidently an Arabic spelling of Middle Persian *fragard*, "chapter, section".

On the basis of the proper names, and in particular the topographical framework of Gurgānī's poem, Minorsky has argued that the origin of the story lay in Arsacid Parthia. Gurgānī has largely resisted the temptation to adapt the story to his Islamic environment and it retains a strong Zoroastrian flavour. It exerted considerable influence on the development of the Persian romantic epic, but later fell out of favour, in part, doubtless, because of its relatively simple style, but mainly because it was considered immoral, not so much on account of the fairly explicit erotic episodes (which are not exceptional by Persian standards) but because it appears to condone adultery on the part of a woman. Copies are thus rare. Gurgānī's work was translated into Georgian, apparently in the 12th century A.D. Several scholars have claimed a decisive influence of the Persian story on the Celtic tale of Tristan and Iseult, but it is difficult to see by what paths the legend might have migrated to Europe.

Bibliography (in addition to that cited under gurgānī): The older editions of the Persian text have been superseded by the critical edition by M.A. Todua and A.A. Gwakharia, Tehran 1349 *s̲h̲.*/1970; the same scholars have also re-edited the Georgian translation, Tiflis 1962. Additional translations: *Vis and Ramin*, tr. G. Morrison, New York and London 1972; *Vis i Ramin*, tr. S. Lipkin, Moscow 1963. V. Minorsky's fundamental study *Vīs u Rāmīn. A Parthian romance*, in *BSOAS*, xi (1946), 741-63, xii (1947), 20-35, xvi (1954), 91-2, xxv (1962), 275-86, was reprinted, with considerable revision, in his *Iranica, bīst maḳāla*, Tehran 1964, 151-99. For further literature, mss., etc. see de Blois, *Persian literature*, v, 161-7.

(F.C. de Blois)

WIṢĀL (a.), or less frequently *muwāṣala* "maintaining an amorous relationship, chaste or otherwise" (*LʿA*), a technical term of Ṣūfism. *Waṣl* is employed in the same sense, with the antonym *had̲j̲r* or *hid̲j̲rān* (shunning, evasion) or even *faṣl* (separation). *Wuṣla* "amorous connection" is also recorded by the *Lisān* as an equivalent of *ittiṣāl* "the act of forming an amorous relationship".

Nascent Ṣūfism borrowed these terms from romantic poetry and integrated them into its own poetic production as well as into its doctrinal literature. Even with a poet such as ʿUmar Ibn Abī Rabīʿa [*q.v.*], *wiṣāl* or *waṣl* signifies an amorous relationship which one accuses the other of not respecting rather than a union as such (cf. *Dīwān*, Cairo 1978, 77, 168, 176). In the poetry attributed to Rābiʿa al-ʿAdawiyya [*q.v.*], the opposition between *waṣl* and *had̲j̲r* is encountered: "I have shunned (*had̲j̲artu*) all creatures in the hope of a union on Your part, my greatest desire" (quoted by ʿAbd al-Raḥmān Badawī, *S̲h̲ahīdat al-ʿis̲h̲ḳ al-ilāhī*, Cairo n.d., 163). The use by the Ṣūfīs of these terms continues to bear the mark of their origin: *wiṣāl* never signifies love in itself, but a link that is always fragile, liable to be broken or outgrown. It is not found in the lists of stages of love, borrowed from works dealing with profane love (cf. C. Ernst, *The stages of love in early Persian Sufism*, in *Classical Persian Sufism from its origins to Rumi*, ed. L. Lewisohn, London-New York 1993, 435-55). No equivalent is to be found in Ṣūfism to the lyricism of Ibn Ḥazm on *waṣl*, although in his works, the inexpressible and paradisiacal nature of the union could be considered a transition between profane love and sacred love (cf. *Ṭawḳ al-ḥamāma*, Fr. tr. L. Bercher, *Le collier du pigeon*, Algiers 1949, 152-3, Eng. tr. A.J. Arberry, *The ring of the dove*, London 1953, 118).

For al-Muḥāsibī (d. 243/857 [*q.v.*]), while love cannot be described, it nonetheless leaves behind it indubitable traces on lovers "on account of the constancy of their link with their Beloved (*li-dawām ittiṣālihim bi-ḥabībihim*), since God, in manifesting His love to them, instructs them (*id̲h̲ā waṣalahum afādahum*)" (Abū Nuʿaym, *Ḥilya*, x, 79; cf. J. van Ess, *Die Gedankenwelt des Ḥārit̲ al-Muḥāsibī*, Bonn 1961, 224). Through *wiṣāl* and its equivalents, the expression of divine love has from the outset taken two directions. One of them is poetic and based on imagery, expressing intense desire for union with, or proximity to God. D̲h̲u 'l-Nūn (d. 246/861 [*q.v.*]) thus says of Muḥammad that he was the first of the prophets to arrive in "the garden of union" (*rawḍat al-wiṣāl*) (cf. Ibn al-ʿArabī, tr. R. Deladrière, *La vie merveilleuse de Dhu l-Nun l'Égyptien*, Paris 1988, 166; see also *Ḥilya*, ix, 375). The joy shown by al-Ḥallād̲j̲ [*q.v.*] immediately before his execution, emanates, he declares, "from the coquetry of His beauty, which draws the elect towards union (*wiṣāl*)" (al-Munāwī, *al-Kawākib al-durriyya*, Cairo 1994, i, 545; *Passion*, i, 635, refers in error to *Ak̲h̲bār*, no. 16). The second, more doctrinal direction seeks to determine the reality of the union. In the abridged version of his *Ḥaḳā'iḳ*, al-Sulamī quotes, with *isnād*, the interpretation by D̲j̲aʿfar al-Ṣādiḳ of Ḳur'ān, VII, 143, when Moses asks to see God "in language of humility on the carpet of union (*bisāṭ al-wiṣāl*) in the shade of Majesty" (ed. G. Böwering, *The minor Qur'ān Commentary of Sulamī*, Beirut 1995, 146). Regarding God's reply "you shall not see Me", D̲j̲aʿfar speaks further of *wuṣla* and of *muwāṣala*, impossible to realise fully with God in this world (cf. P. Nwyia, *Le tafsir mystique de Djaʿfar al-Sadiq*, in *MUSJ*, xliii [1968], 18-19). Al-Ḥakīm al-Tirmid̲h̲ī (d. between 295 and 300/905-10 [*q.v.*]) does not hesitate, however, to speak of *ittiṣāl* in regard to the saints closest to God (*Sīrat* [or *Khatm*] *al-awliyā'*, ed. B. Radtke, in idem, *Drei Schriften des Theosophen von Tirmidh*, Beirut 1992, 65-6, 181). Sahl al-Tustarī (d. 283/896 [*q.v.*]) interprets the light of the lamp in the Verse of Light (Ḳur'ān, XXIV, 35) as that of union with God (*nūr al-ittiṣāl*) (*Tafsīr*, Cairo 1329/1911, 68), but also guards against a too literal understanding of this term (cf. Böwering, *The mystical vision of existence in Classical Islam. The Qur'anic hermeneutics of Sahl al-Tustarī*, Berlin-New York 1980, 208, 218). This reservation is explained thus by Abū Bakr al-Wāsiṭī (d. after 320/932) in his commentary on the formula "God is great": "You are too mighty to be joined (*tuwāṣalu*) through prayer and separated (*tufāṣalu*) through its neglect, for separation and union are not movements, but that which has been determined from all eternity" (al-Kalābādhī, *Ta'arruf*, ed. 'Abd al-Ḥalīm Maḥmūd, Cairo 1960, 142, ch. 64). Poetry and doctrine are in no way incompatible. In the process of defining *waṣl* and *faṣl*, al-Sarrādj relates that al-Shiblī (d. 334/945) went into a state of ecstasy (*tawādjada*) when he heard this verse of al-'Abbās b. al-Aḥnaf: "Your union (*waṣl*) is shunning (*hadjr*), your friendship is ill-treatment, your proximity is distance and your peace is war" (*Luma'*, 364, 433, tr. R. Gramlich, *Schlaglichter über das Sufitum*, Stuttgart 1990, 495). Samnūn, also known as al-Muḥibb (d. *ca.* 300/912) offers one of the best examples of amorous lament addressed to God, in union as in denial (cf. al-Sulamī, *Ṭabaḳāt al-ṣūfiyya*, ed. Nūr al-Dīn Shurayba, Cairo 1969, 198; Abu Nu'aym, *Ḥilya*, x, 310-11: M. Lings, ch. *Mystical poetry*, in *Camb. hist. of Arabic lit.*, ii, *'Abbasid belles-lettres*, Cambridge 1990, 243).

The general sense of union or of love which God manifests to those who remain faithfully and amorously attached to Him often means that *waṣl* or *wiṣāl* are not found in the technical lexicon of *taṣawwuf*, except in the case of some authors (see below). 'Amr b. 'Uthmān al-Makkī (d. 297/909) appears to be such an exception. Al-Hudjwirī quotes his *K. al-Maḥabba*, where *waṣl* is placed above proximity (*ḳurb*) and intimacy (*uns*) and associated with the most intimate part of being (*sirr*) (cf. *Kashf al-maḥdjūb*, Eng. tr. R.A. Nicholson, 309, Fr. tr. Djamshid Mortazavi, *Somme spirituelle*, Paris 1988, 355). *Ittiṣāl*, on the other hand, is more problematical, being open to various interpretations. In accordance with his method in the *Manāzil al-sā'irīn*, al-Anṣārī identifies three degrees of *ittiṣāl* and likewise of its corollary *infiṣāl* "necessary condition or surpassing of union", according to its degree (ed. and Fr. tr. S. Laugier de Beaurecueil, Cairo 1962, 99-101). In the *Iḥyā'*, al-Ghazālī stands out from his predecessors in insisting on the correspondence between sexual and spiritual union (*waṣl*), as a way of underlining its delicious and ineffable character (Beirut, iv, 311-2). It would be natural to expect to find in a text such as the *'Abhar al-'āshiḳīn* of Rūzbihān al-Baḳlī (d. 606/1209 [*q.v.*]) frequent mention of the union-separation pairing, but in fact it rarely appears except in reference to the alternating states through which the soul passes in its relationship to God (*Le Jardin des fidèles d'amour*, ed. H. Corbin and M. Mo'in, Tehran-Paris 1958, 76, 127, Fr. tr. Corbin, Lagrasse 1971, 155, 244). On the other hand, this same author makes frequent reference to union in his Ḳur'ānic commentary, the *'Arā'is al-bayān* (Indian lith. 1315/1897-8). The same observation may be applied to his predecessor, al-Ḳushayrī (d. 465/1072), who interprets the verse of the *Fātiḥa* "Guide us on the straight path" as "Divert our intimate thoughts away from vision of the other, make the risings of lights shine in our hearts . . . raise us above the domains of research and demonstration, towards the esplanades of proximity and of union" (*Laṭā'if al-ishārāt*, ed. Ibrāhīm Basyūnī, Cairo n.d., 61-2). In these two commentaries, the constant evocation of *wiṣāl* suggests what the predisposition of the heart should be in order to hear and to understand the Word of the Beloved.

Towards the end of the 6th/12th and during the 7th/13th centuries, the period of the great doctrinal syntheses, poetical expression of union lost nothing of its potency, as is shown by a well-known poem of Shihāb al-Dīn Yaḥyā al-Suhrawardī of Aleppo (d. 587/1191 [*q.v.*]) still recited today (quoted by Yūsuf Zaydān in *Shu'arā' al-ṣūfiyya al-madjhūlūn*, Beirut 1996, 31-2). An author such as Nadjm al-Dīn Kubrā [*q.v.*] accentuates in particular the dynamic of union/disunion: union with Him and separation from the other are two alternate and indissoluble phases, like *fanā'* and *baḳā'*, knowledge and love (cf. *Fawā'iḥ al-djamāl wa-fawātiḥ al-djalāl*, ed. F. Meier, Wiesbaden 1957, 47). In a detailed passage, 'Umar al-Suhrawardī (d. 632/1234 [*q.v.*]) develops the idea that to each of the degrees of union (*ittiṣāl* and *muwāṣala*) corresponds a certain "arrival" in God (*wuṣūl*), a term which does not by any means signify that the journey towards God has come to an end (cf. *'Awārif al-ma'ārif*, Beirut 1966, 516-17). Others insist on the need to move beyond such a notion. For Ibn al-Fāriḍ, union is a veil which must be lifted, since reality lies beyond it (cf. *al-Tā'iyya al-kubrā*, in *Dīwān*, Cairo 1956, 52, and tr. Nicholson, in *Studies in Islamic mysticism*, Cambridge 1921, 197, v. 441). In accordance with his unitive vision of Being, Ibn al-'Arabī (d. 638/1240 [*q.v.*]) applies to man the union/separation polarity: "You claim union (*wuṣla*) and reunion, but I fear that your union is through you alone, not through Him. You declare 'I am united' (or, have arrived, *waṣaltu*), while you are in separation!" (*Tadjalliyāt*, with commentary of Ibn Sawdakīn, ed. Osman Yahya, Tehran 1988, 247-8). Taking as a starting-point the definitions of al-Sarrādj in his *Luma'*, he assigns to the terms *faṣl*, *waṣl* and *ittiṣāl* exceedingly precise senses as phases of spiritual progression (cf. *Iṣṭilāḥāt al-ṣūfiyya*, Ḥaydarābād 1943, 8, 12, 13, and *Futūḥāt*, Beirut, ii, 131-2). But he also brings union back to its divine principle; the verse LVII, 4, "And He is with you wherever you are" signifies that God remains with His creatures forever in a state of union (*ḥāl al-waṣl*) (cf. *Futūḥāt*, ii, 480, chs. 200, 201, on *waṣl* and *faṣl*). The genuine lover "makes no distinction between union and separation, occupied as he is with his Beloved, the object of his contemplation" (*Futūḥāt*, ii, 360 ch. 178 on love, Fr. tr. M. Gloton, *Traité de l'amour*, Paris 1986, 253). 'Abd al-Karīm al-Djīlī (d. 826/1423) recognises the validity of the term *wiṣāl* when it signifies the uninterrupted reception of theophanies, while drawing attention to the difficulty that it raises: the *wāṣil*, he who enters into ties of love or who arrives at God is in a veil, since according to Reality, no sooner has arrival taken place than there is separation. In effect, *wiṣāl* implies duality and, from this point of view, its opposite, *fiṣāl*, overtakes it and is superior to it (*al-Manāẓir al-ilāhiyya*, ed. Nadjāḥ al-Ghunaymī, Cairo 1987, 160-1). 'Abd al-Razzāḳ al-Ḳāshānī (d. *ca.* 735/1334) in his *Iṣṭilāḥāt al-ṣūfiyya*, ed. M. Kamāl Dja'far, Cairo 1981, 24, 51-2, and the other two lexicons of technical terms of Ṣūfism attributed to al-Ḳāshānī both continue the work of Ibn al-'Arabī and develop original definitions of *ittiṣāl*, *waṣl*, *waṣl al-faṣl* and *waṣl al-waṣl* (cf. *Rashḥ al-zulāl fī sharḥ al-alfāẓ al-mutadāwala bayna arbāb al-adhwāḳ wa 'l-aḥwāl*, ed. Saʿīd ʿAbd al-Fattāḥ, Cairo 1995, 121, and *Laṭāʾif al-iʿlām fī ishārāt ahl al-ilhām*, ed. ʿAbd al-Fattāḥ, Cairo 1996, ii, 389-91.

Other nuances in the work of later writers can also be found. The joy of union and the sadness of separation or their simultaneous acceptance have continued to inspire Ṣūfī poets throughout the Muslim world (Annemarie Schimmel gives examples in her *Mystical dimensions of Islam*, Chapel Hill 1975, index s.v. *unio mystica*, Fr. tr. *Le soufisme ou les dimensions mystiques de l'Islam*, Paris 1976, 353, 431, 433). In poems intended to enliven sessions of *samāʿ* and of *dhikr* and to raise the aspirations of disciples, teachers have continued to use these terms, *waṣl* or *wiṣāl*, to inspire in their listeners the desire for God (cf. the Algerian *shaykh* Aḥmad Ibn ʿAlīwā (d. 1934) in the first poem of his *Dīwān*, Damascus 1963, 3-4, 8, Eng. tr. M. Lings, in *A Sufi saint of the twentieth century*, Cambridge 1971, 214-20, Fr. tr., *Un saint musulman du vingtième siècle*, Paris 1973, 247-54).

Bibliography: Given in the article.

(D. Gril)

WISĀM (a., pl. *awsima*), in modern Arabic usage a decoration, order, medal or badge of honour.

The roots *w-s-m* and *w-sh-m* mean basically "to mark, brand [an animal]", an important feature of nomadic life when ownership of beasts like horses and camels had to be determinable. For this idea of branding, marking, in Arabic desert life, see wasm. In the old Turkish nomadic society, *tamgha* had a similar sense of "tribal mark or emblem". In the modern Turkish pronunciation *damga* it is used for government revenue stamps, ministerial seals for validating government documents, cancelling postage stamps, etc. [see tamgha, and on personal seals and stamps in Islamic society in general, khātam]. *Washm* was used in Bedouin and succeeding Arab societies for tattoos and other decorative marks on the faces of both sexes but especially as beauty marks on women; see for this washm. The connection of both *wasm* and *washm* with the general sense of "to mark" > "to beautify" has yielded in Classical Arabic the adjective *wasīm* "having a comely face" and the noun *wasāma* "beauty".

Wisām tends now to be the standard Arabic word for "decoration, order, etc.", but when European-type orders were first imitated in 19th century Persia and the Ottoman empire, the term used was Perso-Turkish *nishān* [*q.v.*].

(Ed.)

al-**WISYĀNĪ**, the *nisba* of a number of Wahbī (pro-Rustamid) Ibāḍī scholars and leaders of the Banū Wisyān (Wāsīn) branch of Zanāta Berbers. Several of them originated from the town of al-Ḥāmma (El Hamma) near Tawzar (Tozeur) in the Shaṭṭ al-Djarīd [*q.v.*] region of western Tunisia.

1. Abū Khazar Yaghlā b. Zaltaf, Ibāḍī *mutakallim* and military leader, d. 380/990.

Of a modest background, Abū Khazar studied with Sulaymān b. Zarḳūn al-Nafūsī at Tābidyūt, together with Abu 'l-Ḳāsim Yazīd b. Makhlad al-Wisyānī. Both students became well known for their scholarship and were members of the circle of notable scholars (*ḥalka* [*q.v.*]). The murder of Abu 'l-Ḳāsim on the order of the Fāṭimid ruler of Ḳayrawān, Abū Tamīm al-Muʿizz li-Dīn Allāh [*q.v.*], led to an Ibāḍī revolt under the leadership of Abū Khazar. The revolt, launched in 358/968-9, found support in Tripolitania, Djabal Nafūsa, and the regions of Zāb, Rīgh and Wardjlān. It was based in particular on the Mazāta Zanāta, who alone were said to muster 12,000 horsemen. However, the Ibāḍī forces were routed by the Fāṭimids at Bāghāya, west of Ḳayrawān, thus ending the last major Ibāḍī challenge to Fāṭimid rule, sixty years after the fall of Tāhart.

Abū Khazar fled to Djabal Nafūsa. With the mediation of his supporter Abū Nūḥ Saʿīd b. Zanghīl, he received an *amān* from al-Muʿizz the following year. Al-Muʿizz kept both Ibāḍī leaders under close control in Ḳayrawān, and when he moved to Egypt three years later, he ordered both to accompany him. Abū Nūḥ managed to escape, but Abū Khazar went with al-Muʿizz to Cairo and remained there for the rest of his life. He was given a pension and apparently retired to a life of scholarship, teaching several renowned students. One anecdote relates of an occasion when a Muʿtazilī scholar came to Cairo some time after al-Muʿizz's death in 364/975, and the only man in Cairo who could defeat him in debate was Abū Khazar.

He wrote *al-Radd ʿalā al-mukhālifīn* in refutation of various sects that opposed the Wahbiyya, including the Muʿtazila. A copy of this work exists on the island of Djerba, Tunisia (A.K. Ennami, *A description of new Ibāḍī manuscripts from North Africa*, in *JSS*, xv [1970], 82).

Bibliography: Abū Zakariyyāʾ Yaḥyā b. Abī Bakr al-Wardjlānī, *Chronique d'Abou Zakaria*, tr. É. Masqueray, Algiers 1878, 288-310; Aḥmad b. Saʿīd al-Dardjīnī, *K. Ṭabaḳāt al-mashāyikh bi 'l-Maghrib*, ed. Ibrāhīm Ṭallāy, Constantine 1974, 119-43, 340-1, 421; Aḥmad b. Saʿīd al-Shammākhī, *K. al-Siyar*, Cairo 1884, 346-57; T. Lewicki, *La répartition géographique des groupements ibāḍites dans l'Afrique du nord au moyen-âge*, in *RO*, xxi (1957), 350; idem, *Ibāḍitica II*, in *RO*, xxvi (1962) 102-3; U. Rebstock, *Die Ibāḍiten im Maġrib (2./8.-4./10. Jh.)*, Berlin 1983, 197, 313.

2. Abū Mūsā Hārūn b. Abī ʿImrān al-Ḥāmmī, Ibāḍī trader and scholar, native of al-Ḥammā, who travelled to Ghāna and died there in the late 4th/10th century.

Hārūn was undoubtedly inspired by his kinsman, Tamlā al-Wisyānī, who was said to have left the Djarīd as a pauper, travelling to Tādmekka on the Niger bend. Here he amassed a great fortune and annually sent home 4,000 dīnārs to be distributed among the poor, out of piety to the Ibāḍī community of his home and to its famous son, the Ibāḍī leader Abū Khazar al-Wisyānī (above, 1.). The community notable who received the gifts was Abū ʿImrān Mūsā b. Sudrīn al-Wisyānī, Hārūn's father and in his own right one of the well-known scholars of the region. Hārūn left al-Ḥāmma for Wardjlān, at the time one of the few independent strongholds of the Ibāḍī community. He became known as a scholar, and asked the head of the oasis, Abū Ṣāliḥ b. Djannūn, for permission to set up a study circle, *ḥalka*. When this was refused, he decided instead to take up the profession of merchant, and travelled across the Sahara to Ghāna. There he settled in the town of Ghiyāra, probably on the Senegal river, in a region populated by non-Muslims, where he stayed until his death.

To Hārūn are ascribed unnamed works of *tawḥīd*; some, written at the request of Abū Ṣāliḥ, remained unfinished.

Bibliography: Shammākhī, *K. al-Siyar*, 472-3; Lewicki, *Quelques extraits inédits relatifs aux voyages des commerçants et des missionaires ibāḍites nord-africaines au pays du Soudan occidental et central au moyen âge*, in *Folia Orientalia*, ii (1960), 18-27.

3. Abū Rabīʿ Sulaymān b. ʿAbd al-Salām, Ibāḍī-Wahbī scholar of the 6th/12th-century, and author

of one of their best-known biographical works, the *Kitāb al-Siyar*.

Abū Rabīʿ's family was from the Djarīd, but he spent his youth in Adjlū in the Wādī Rīgh region. We know very little of his life, but he is said to have built up his reputation through extensive travels. His main teacher was Abū Muḥammad ʿAbd Allāh b. Muḥammad al-Lawātī [*q.v.*], originally from Cyrenaica, who had come to Adjlū in 450/1058-9. Among the important authorities from whom Abū Rabīʿ learnt was another Wisyānī, Abū Muḥammad Māksan b. Khayr. Abū Rabīʿ may also have studied with Abū Zakariyyāʾ Yaḥyā b. Abī Bakr al-Wardjlānī [*q.v.*]. Upon al-Lawātī's death in 528/1133-4, Abū Rabīʿ gathered numerous students around himself. His major work is the *K. al-Siyar*, a collection of biographical notices organised geographically, centering on his own southern Tunisian region but also including anecdotes from a wider range. It was widely used by later Ibāḍī historians, such as al-Dardjīnī. It has not been printed, but copies exist in Djerba, Beni Isguen (Mzāb, Algeria), Cairo and Cracow.

Abū Rabīʿ's date of death is not known. It must have been after 528/1134, but probably before 557/1161-2, the earliest date of a work written by an anonymous student of his.

Bibliography: Dardjīnī, *Ṭabaḳāt al-mashāyikh*, 513; Shammākhī, *K. al-Siyar*, 454; Lewicki, *Notice sur la chronique ibāḍite d'ad-Dardjīnī*, in *RO*, xi (1936), 162; idem, *Quelques extraits* (see above, *Bibl.* to 2.), 7-10; idem, *Un document ibāḍite inédit sur l'emigration des Nafūsa du Ğabal dans le Sāḥil Tunisien au VIIIe/IXe siècle*, in *Folia Orientalia*, i (1960), 181-2, 190; idem, *Les historiens, biographes et traditionnistes Ibāḍites-Wahbites de l'Afrique du nord du VIIIe au XVIe siècles*, in *Folia Orientalia*, iii (1961), 68-9; Rebstock, *Die Ibāḍiten im Maġrib* (see above, *Bibl.* to 1.), pp. xi-xv; Ennami, *Description of new Ibāḍī manuscripts* (see above, 1.), 85-6; Baḥḥāz Ibrāhīm Bakīr, *al-Dawla al-Rustamiyya: 160-296 h-777-909 m*, Algiers 1985, 26-8.

(K.S. Vikør)

WITR (a.), also *watr*, a term found in *ḥadīth* and *fiḳh* in connection with performance of the *ṣalāt* or worship and concerned with the odd number of *rakʿa*s which are performed at night.

Witr does not occur in this sense in the Ḳurʾān, but frequently in *ḥadīth*, which in this case also discloses to us a part of the history of the institution in three stages, itself probably a continuation of the history of the fixing of the daily *ṣalāt*s, as the traditions on *witr* presuppose the five daily *ṣalāt*s. Some traditions even go so far as to call *witr* an additional *ṣalāt* of an obligatory nature (see also below). When Muʿādh b. Djabal, upon his arrival in Syria, perceived that the people of this country did not perform the *witr*, he spoke to Muʿāwiya on this subject. When the latter asked him: Is then this *ṣalāt* obligatory? Muʿādh answered: Yes, the Apostle of God said: My Lord has added a *ṣalāt* to those prescribed to me, namely *witr*, its time is between *ʿishāʾ* [see mīḳāt] and daybreak (Aḥmad b. Ḥanbal, *Musnad*, v, 242). In accordance with this tradition, it is reported that when *witr* had been forgotten or neglected, it had to be performed (Aḥmad b. Ḥanbal, ii, 206; Ibn Mādja, *Iḳāma*, *bāb* 122). ʿUbāda b. al-Ṣāmit, on the other hand, denied the obligatory character of *witr* on account of a different tradition (Aḥmad b. Ḥanbal, v, 315-16, 319).

The second stage in the position of *witr* is expressed in those traditions in which Muḥammad admonishes his people to perform *witr*, "for God is *witr* (viz. One), and He loves *witr*" (e.g. Aḥmad b. Ḥanbal, i, 110).

The third stage of *ḥadīth*, which was to become the point of view of all *madhhabs* with one exception, the Ḥanafī school, is represented in those traditions which call this *ṣalāt* a *sunna*. Many traditions of this kind expressly deny its obligatory character and are consequently of a polemical nature; they are frequently ascribed to ʿAlī (e.g. Aḥmad b. Ḥanbal, i, 86, 98, 100, 115, 120, 145, 148, etc.). It may be that this question, like other ceremonial points, belonged to the polemical repertory of the early Shīʿīs.

The time of *witr* is mentioned in *ḥadīth* in connection with different parts of the night. "*Witr* consists of pairs of *rakʿa*s; whosoever fears *ṣubḥ* must add a *rakʿa* in order to make the total number odd" (Aḥmad b. Ḥanbal, ii, 5, 9, 10, 75). In other traditions, three *rakʿa*s are mentioned in order to avoid the *ṣubḥ* (*fa-bādir al-ṣubḥ bi-rakʿatayn*, e.g. Aḥmad b. Ḥanbal, ii, 71). The number of thirteen *rakʿa*s occurs also (al-Tirmidhī, *Witr*, *bāb* 4), and in general, *witr* is supposed not to be allowed after *ṣalāt al-ṣubḥ* (cf. Mālik, *Muwaṭṭaʾ*, *Witr*, trads. 24-8, and al-Ṭayālisī, no. 2192: "No *witr* for him who has not performed it before *ṣubḥ*").

Witr is also frequently mentioned in connection with the first part of the night (cf. below). Abū Hurayra performed it before going to sleep, on Muḥammad's order (al-Tirmidhī, *Witr*, *bāb* 3). Muḥammad himself is said to have performed this *ṣalāt* in any part of the night (e.g. al-Tirmidhī, *Witr*, *bāb* 4). The time between *ʿishāʾ* and daybreak appears as the largest space accorded to *witr* in *ḥadīth* (Aḥmad b. Ḥanbal, v, 242). It is prohibited to perform more than one *witr-ṣalāt* in one night (Aḥmad b. Ḥanbal, iv, 23 *bis*).

Tradition frequently mentions the *rakʿa*s, prayers, invocations and formulas by which *witr* used to be followed (e.g. al-Nasāʾī, *Ḳiyām al-layl*, *bāb*s 51, 54; Aḥmad b. Ḥanbal, i, 199, 350).

The chief regulations of *witr* as fixed by the different *madhhabs* show insignificant divergencies only (see al-Shaʿrānī, 198 ff.), with the single exception that the Ḥanafīs declare it to be obligatory. As an example, one may cite the rules of the Shāfiʿī school: the number of *rakʿa*s may vary between the odd numbers from one to eleven; the *niyya* [*q.v.*] is required; after every two *rakʿa*s and after the last a *salām* or *tashahhud* is performed. The best time is immediately after *tahadjdjud* [*q.v.*] for those who do not perform this *ṣalāt* in the first third of the night. In the second half of Ramaḍān [see tarāwīḥ], *witr* is prolonged by *ḳunūt* [*q.v.*].

Bibliography: A.J. Wensinck, *A handbook of early Muh. tradition*, s.v.; Marghīnānī, *al-Hidāya wa 'l-kifāya*, Bombay 1863, i, 152 ff.; *Fatāwā ʿālamgīriyya*, Calcutta 1829, i, 155 ff.; Shāfiʿī, *Kitāb al-Umm*, Cairo 1321, i, 123 ff.; Abū Isḥāḳ al-Shīrāzī, *Tanbīh*, ed. Juynboll, 27; Ghazālī, *K. al-Wadjīz*, Cairo 1317, i, 54; idem, *Iḥyāʾ*, Cairo 1302, i, 177 ff.; Ibn Ḥadjar al-Haytamī, *Tuḥfat al-muḥtādj bi-sharḥ al-Minhādj*, Cairo 1282, i, 203-5; Abu 'l-Ḳāsim al-Muḥaḳḳiḳ, *Kitāb Sharāʾiʿ al-Islām*, Calcutta 1255 (1839), 25; Abū Ṭālib al-Makkī, *Ḳūt al-ḳulūb*, Cairo 1310, i, 31; Shaʿrānī, *K. al-Mīzān al-kubrā*, Cairo 1219, 198-9; Lane, *Manners and customs*, index s.v. Taráweeh prayers; C. Snouck Hurgronje, *Mr. L.W.C. v.d. Berg's beoefening v. h. moh. recht*, 402 ff. (*Verspreide Geschriften*, ii, 101-2); Th.W. Juynboll, *Handleiding tot de kennis der mohammedaansche wet*, Leiden 1925, 75.

(A.J. Wensinck)

WIZE, modern Vize, a small town of Eastern Thrace, now in European Turkey (lat. 41° 34' N., long. 37° 45' E.). It lies below the southwestern slopes of the Istranca Dağları on the road connecting Kırklareli [see ḲIRḲ KILISE] with Silivri and the Sea of Marmara coast.

The Byzantine town and fortress of Bizyē (Βιζύη), Byzus of the Latins, was a bishopric by 431 and a metropolitan see by the 14th century. It was apparently first taken by the Ottomans just after the middle of the 8th/14th century; the poet Aḥmedī attributes this occupation to Süleymān, eldest son of Orkhan, who is said to have died in 1357. But this must have been only a temporary event, and according to the Byzantine chronicler Ducas, it was not until March 1453, just before the fall of Constantinople, that Meḥemmed Fātiḥ's commander Ḳaradja Beg conquered Bizyē definitively, with its two churches of St. Sophia and St. Nicholas transformed into mosques. *Yürüks* [*q.v.*] were settled in this frontier region and Wize became a *sandjak* of Rūmeli. Subsequently, it came within the province of Özü or Silistra. By 1846 it was included in the province of Edirne [*q.v.*] as the *sandjak* of Tekfürdaghî or Tekirdaghî [*q.v.*], coming within the *sandjak* of Ḳirḳ Kilise in 1879. It had been briefly occupied by the Bulgarians in the spring of 1878. During the Balkan War of 1912-13 it was again occupied by the Bulgarians, and by Greek forces in 1920-2. With the Treaty of Lausanne, the town's Greek population, who had formed the majority of the town's 3,380 inhabitants, was resettled within Greece. In Republican Turkey, it is now within the *il* of Kırklareli.

Bibliography: M. Tayyib Gökbilgin, *XV.-XVI. asırlarda Edirne ve Paşa livâsı, vakıflar—mülkler—mukataalar*, Istanbul 1952, 6-9 and index; arts. *Bizyē*, in *Megalē Hellenikē Enkyklopaideia*, vii, ²Athens 1964, 264-5, and in *Megalē Genikē Enkyklopaideia*, xiv, Athens 1980, 299; A. Birken, *Die Provinzen des osmanischen Reiches*, Wiesbaden 1976, 59, 88, 100; A.P. Kazhdan *et alii* (eds.), *The Oxford dictionary of Byzantium*, Oxford-New York 1991, i, 292-3, art. *Bizyē* (T.M. Gregory), mentioning A.M. Mansel, *Trakya'nın kültür ve tarihi*, Istanbul 1938, and V. Velkov, *Die thrakische Stadt Bizye*, in *Studia in honorem V. Beševliev*, Sofia 1978, 174-81; P. Rodakes, *The Turkish conquest of Thrace. The Thracian Muslims*, Athens 1991 (in Greek); G. Voiyatzes, *The early Ottoman domination in Thrace: immediate demographic consequences*, Thessalonica 1998 (in Greek), 304 ff., 385 ff. See also RŪMELI.

(C.E. BOSWORTH and A. SAVVIDES)

WODINA, VODINA, the Ottoman Turkish name for the Greek town of Edessa on the Via Egnatia in western Macedonia, lying to the northwest of Thessalonica [see SELĀNIK] (lat. 40° 48' N., long. 22° 03' E.). The name Vodina goes back to Slavonic *voda* "water" because of the abundance of water in the vicinity of the town.

In mediaeval times it was contested by Byzantines, Bulgarians, Serbs and Normans (see J. Perluga, in *Lexikon des Mittelalters*, iii/7, Munich-Zürich 1985, cols. 1565-7; R. Browning and A. Kazhdan, in *Oxford dict. of Byzantium*, New York-Oxford 1991, 2185). In the late 14th century it was ruled by Greek-Serbian toparchs, until the town's initial conquest by the Ottoman commander Ewrenos Beg [*q.v.*], effected by the treason of the local archon Kel Petros and variously dated by Greek and Turkish sources (Neshrī, Sa'd al-Dīn, Ewliyā Čelebi) to between 774-6/1372-4, together with Beroia [see KARAFERYE], and dates in the 1380s (see C. Seybold, *Neschri's Notiz über die Eroberung von Vodena-Edessa . . . durch Bajezid I. Jildirim, 1389*, in *ZDMG*, lxxiv [1920], 291; P. Wittek, in *BSOAS*, xiv [1952], 661 n. 3; D.E. Pitcher, *An historical geography of the Ottoman empire*, Leiden 1972, map XXVI; P. Schreiner, *Byzantinischen Kleinchroniken*, ii, Vienna 1977, 358; Stalides, i, 95-125 for details).

Definitively captured *ca.* 833/1430, Vodina became part of the *sandjak* of Selānik, internally administered by local archons (*demogērontes*). Its fortifications and products were described by Kātib Čelebi (Ger. tr. J. von Hammer, *Rumeli und Bosna*, Vienna 1812, 87) and by Ewliyā Čelebi in 1668, the latter mentioning 100 houses, 30 shops, ten *khāns* and seven Orthodox churches functioning also as schools for the Greek population (see D. Demetriades, *Central and western Macedonia according to Ewliyā Čelebi* [in Greek], Thessalonica 1973, 235, 241-2). In the 19th century, it was visited by various Western travellers, e.g. W.M. Leake in 1808 (*Travels in northern Greece*, iii, London 1835, 275-6). Edessans participated in the 1770 Russian-inspired Orlov revolt and the Greek War of Independence, whilst between 1798 and 1822 the town experienced the rule of 'Alī Pasha Tepedelenli [*q.v.*] of Albania. Bulgarian claims on the area began in the 1860s, but the town's eventual annexation to the kingdom of Greece was effected on 18 October 1912, at which time the town had a population of 4,000 Greeks, 1,530 Bulgarians, 46 Turks and a few Serbs (see J. Sarres, in *Megale Hellenike Enkyklopaideia*², ix, Athens 1964, 706-7). The town's fine 15th century mosque now houses its archaeological museum.

Bibliography: See also the detailed monograph on the town, C. Stalides, *Edessa in the period of Turkish domination, 14th century to 1912* (in Greek), Edessa 1988, i; also A. Vakalopoulos, *History of Macedonia 1354-1833* (in Greek), Thessalonica 1969, repr. 1992, index, and idem, *History of modern Hellenism* (in Greek), iv-vi, Thessalonica 1973-82, index.

(A. SAVVIDES)

WOLOF [see SENEGAL].

WOLOS [see ḲULUZ, in Suppl.].

WOYNUḲ (T.), a term of Ottoman military and administrative usage which denoted a particular category of troops amongst other Balkan Christian landholding or tax-exempt groups employed by the sultans to perform specific combat and other militarily-related tasks (for other groups, see EFLĀḲ and MARTOLOS). The term stems from the Slavonic root meaning "war", "warrior", which appears also in the office of Voywoda [*q.v.*], likewise found in Ottoman usage.

The *woynuk*s were especially useful to the sultans before the Ottoman state developed a fully-centralised, multi-functional military apparatus of its own. In newly-conquered lands along the empire's expanding Albanian and northern Balkan frontiers during the late 9th/15th and early 10th/16th centuries, *woynuk*s provided an essential complement to the timariots [see TĪMĀR] whose numbers were still insufficient to perform both offensive and defensive military functions. An idea of the numerical importance of *woynuk*s can be gained when we consider that in the Vidin region during the time of Meḥemmed II Fātiḥ, for example, *woynuk*s still outnumbered timariots by a significant margin (İnalcık, *Fatih devri*, table on p. 165 showing 231 registered *woynuk*s as against 188 *tīmār* holders). By means of the *woynuk* organisation, the Ottomans were able to secure the loyalty and co-operation of members of existing local landed military élites by confirming a kind of limited title to their own hereditary lands called *bashtine*. One limit was the satisfactory performance of the military duties assigned to them by the Ottomans. Having thus neutralised them, the Ottomans could then turn to the *woynuḳ*s to give support services essential to further military advance. The *woynuḳ*s were often employed in the first period of Ottoman expansion as guardians of the frontier and as supplementary garrison forces who assumed responsibility for protecting the hinterland as the Turks advanced towards and eventually (after the fall of Belgrade in 1521) beyond the natural boundary formed by the Danube. The provincial law codes for Bosnia in the early 10th/16th century contain explicit reference to the use of *woynuḳ*s in unsettled regions of the frontier (*iḥtiyāṭlu yerler*): as guardians of the roads and passes and as defenders of minor strongholds set up in vulnerable or strategically important sectors of the frontier and its immediate hinterland (see refs. in the law codes dated 922/1516 and 937/1530 in the *Bibl.*). In time, the *woynuḳ*s of some regions, especially in the area between the Danube and the Balkan range that, after the Ottomans' permanent establishment in Hungary in 948/1541, lost its strategic importance, lost their combat functions but kept their tax-exempt status by performing auxiliary services. Pastoralist *woynuḳ*s were employed in large numbers for the breeding, grazing and general care of the horses belonging to the imperial stables [see MĪR-ĀKHŪR]. They also accompanied regular army units on campaign, with responsibility for the care and protection of the mounts belonging to the imperial herd. Such *woynuḳ*s were attached to the imperial stables and governed by their own regulations (see the law code published by Y. Ercan, *Bulgarlar ve Voynuklar*, 114-16). They managed to preserve their place as a distinct element within the complex Ottoman court and military organisational structure until the time of the Russo-Ottoman war of 1877-8 (Uzunçarşılı, *Saray teşkilâtı*, 504).

Bibliography: 1. Sources. Ö.L. Barkan (ed.), *Kanunlar*, Istanbul 1943, 265-6 (*der beyān-i Ḳānūn-nāme-yi Woynugān*, undated but attributed to *temp.* Süleymān I), 324-5 (*Ḳānūn-i Eflāḳān-i liwā-yi Semendire*, dated 934/1527, esp. § 2); B. Durdev *et alii* (eds.), *Kānūn-i Kānūn-nāme za Bosanski, Hercegovački, Zvornički, Kliški . . . Sandžak*, Sarajevo 1957, esp. 21-5 (*Ḳānūn-nāme-yi wilāyet-i Bosna*, 922/1516), 34-41 (*Ḳānūn-nāme-yi liwā-yi Bosna*, 937/1530) (the regulations for both of these dates refer to the use of *woynuḳ*s in groups of twenty to serve as border patrols and for the staffing of lesser garrisons, whilst the second regulation (ll. 10-20) notes the use of *woynuḳ*s as *derbendjis* or guardians of the passes); Y. Ercan (ed.), *Istabl-i Amire voynukları kanunnamesi*, of 929/1523, Appx. VIII, in idem, *Osmanlı imparatorluğunda Bulgarlar ve Voynuklar*, Ankara 1986, 114-16. See also G. Galabov, *Quelques anciens documents officiels turcs concernant les voinigans*, in *Annuaire de l'Univ. de Sofia, Faculté historico-philologique*, xxxiv/2 (1938), 1-69.

2. Studies. İ.H. Uzunçarşılı, *Osmanlı devletinin saray teşkilâtı*, Ankara 1945, esp. 501-5; Pakalin, iii, 595-8; Gibb and Bowen, i, 54; H. İnalcık, *Fatih devri üzerinde tetkikler ve vesiklar*, Ankara 1954, 137-84, ch. *Stefan Duşan'dan osmanlı imparatorluğuna*; Y. Ercan, *Osmanlı askerî kuruluşlarından voynuk örgütü*, in *Birinci askerî tarih semineri. Bildiriler*, Ankara 1983, ii, 109-25.

(R. MURPHEY)

WOYWODA, a term derived from the Slavic root *vojn* that signifies pertinence to the military or the sphere of war. In mediaeval Serbia it denoted a high-ranking commander and, on the eve of the Ottoman conquest, the governor of a military district (N. Radojčić, ed., *Zakonik tsara Stefana Dushana 1349 i 1354*, Belgrade 1960, 65, 67; C. Jireček, *Staat und Gesellschaft im mittelalterlichen Serbien*, Part IV, Vienna 1919, 25-6). In early Ottoman sources the term appears in reference to former Christian lords (N. Beldiceanu, *Les Actes des premiers sultans conservés dans les manuscrits turcs de la Bibl. nationale à Paris*, Paris 1964, ii, 56-7). Soon it began to designate agents in charge of revenues from domains which enjoyed full immunity (*serbest*), i.e. the imperial demesne as well as the *khāṣṣ* fiefs granted to viziers, provincial governors and other dignitaries (İ.H. Uzunçarşılı, *Osmanlı devletinin merkez ve bahriye teşkilâtı*, ²Ankara 1984, 164-5, 321; M. Akdağ, *Türkiye'nin iktisadî ve içtimaî tarihi*, ii, ²Istanbul 1974, 89, 377-8, 382-4, 455).

With the expansion of the *muḳāṭaʿa* [*q.v.*] system since the 11th/17th century, many *ḳaḍā*'s and even *sandjaḳ*s were administered by *woywoda*s (Y. Özkaya, *XVIII. yüzyılda Osmanlı kurumları ve Osmanlı toplum yaşantısı*, Ankara 1985, 21, 200-2; Y. Cezar, *Osmanlı maliyesinde bunalım ve değişim dönemi*, Istanbul 1986, 65, 144; L.T. Darling, *Revenue-raising and legitimacy. Tax collection and finance administration in the Ottoman Empire 1560-1660*, Leiden 1996, 129). Their role was further enhanced as a result of efforts to settle the nomads as peasants and the consequent revivification of deserted areas (C. Orhonlu, *Osmanlı imparatorluğunda aşiretleri iskân teşebbüsü, 1691-1696*, Istanbul 1963, 14, 18, 44).

On the whole, *woywoda*s exerted, along with economic power, considerable political authority, since they were responsible also for public order, policing the countryside accompanied by numerous armed men. Not least for this reason they were the cause of frequent complaints (H. İnalcık, *Adaletnameler*, in *Belgeler*, ii/3-4 [1965], 49-165). The central government was hard pressed to find suitable persons for this job, i.e. persons who were acceptable also to regional interests. More often than not, local notables succeeded in controlling the *woywoda* posts in their province until the institution was abolished during the early *Tanẓīmāt* (M. Çadırcı, *Tanzimat döneminde Anadolu kentlerinin sosyal ve ekonomik yapıları*, Ankara 1991, 29-32).

Bibliography: Given in the article.

(F. ADANIR)

WU MA "the Five Mas", the group of five Muslim warlord-governors dominating Northwest China in the Republican period (1911-49).

By the turn of the 20th century, three grand Muslim clans of Ma from Ho-chou district in Kansu, led by Ma Ch'ien-ling (1826-1910), Ma Chan-ao (1830-86) and Ma Hai-yen (1837-1900) respectively, rose up to consolidate their military power. Later their descendants came to be known as "Hsi-pei Ma-chia-chun" ("the Northwestern Muslim Warlords of the Ma clans"). The five best known of them were: Ma An-liang (1844-1918), Ma T'ing-hsiang (1889-1929) (of the Ma Chan-ao clan), Ma Fu-hsiang (1876-1932) (of the Ma Ch'ien-ling clan), Ma Ch'i (1869-1931) and Ma Lin (1873-1945) (of the Ma Hai-yen clan). They were called "Lao Wu Ma" ("The Old Five Mas") distinguished from another group of five called "Hsiao Wu Ma" ("The Young Five Mas"), comprising Ma Hung-pin (1884-1960), Ma Hung-k'ui (1892-1970) (of the Ma Ch'ian-ling clan), Ma Pu-ch'ing (1901-77), Ma Pu-fang (1902-75), and Ma Chung-ying (1909-? [*q.v.*]) (of the Ma Hai-yen clan). The old and young Mas were related to each other either by blood or marriage. According to the area of their dominance, they were also known as "Ch'ing Ma", the group that controlled mainly the Ch'ing-Hai region, and "Ning Ma", which controlled mainly the Ning-hsia [*q.v.*] region. The former were led by Ma Ch'i (*r.* 1929-31), Ma Lin (*r.* 1931-38) and Ma Pu-fang (*r.* 1938-49); the latter were led by Ma Fu-hsiang (*r.* 1913-20), Ma

Hung-pin (*r.* 1921-28 and 1931-33), and Ma Hung-k'ui (*r.* 1933-49).

Most of the Ma warlords were Old Teaching (Lao Chiao) traditionalists who were more sinicised than the New Teaching (Hsin Chiao) reformists. They always complied with the central government's Han-centric policies, so that their rule was not particulary motivated by Islam. Amongst them Ma Fu-hsiang and Ma Hon-k'ui, father and son, claimed by some authorities as neo-Confucianists, made efforts to incorporate Confucianism into Muslim school curricula. In order to echo the central government's policy of modernisation, they also introduced Western sciences into Muslim education. Ma Fu-hsiang used to urge Muslim associations to reprint Han-language Muslim classics of a Confucian-Islamic synthesis in order to stimulate Muslim integration into Han society. As a result, Islam in Northwest China underwent further assimilation, and the Salafiyya [*q.v.*] reform movement there was held back. The rule of the Ma warlords had a significant impact on the Muslim communities in Northwest China. Because of their Sino-nationalist stance, the Northwestern Han-speaking Muslims' cultural identity within the universal *umma* was superseded by an identification with the Chinese motherland. The tendency of anti-acculturation and secession from China, which had burned during the second half of the 19th century, was thus momentarily stilled.

Bibliography: T'ien Chiung-chin, *Lung-shang Ts'un-hao chi Ma-chia-chun Yuan-liu Kai-kuang* ("Origins of the military leaders and Ma warlords of Northwest China"), in *Chuan-chi Wen-hsueh*, xvii/4 (1970), 5-12; M.R. Hunsberger, *Ma Pu-fang in Chinghai province, 1931-1949*, Ph.D. thesis 1977, Temple Univ., unpubl.; J.Th. Topping, *Chinese Muslim militarist. Ma Hongkui in Ningxia, 1933-49*, Ph.D. thesis 1983, Temple Univ., unpubl.; Wen-shih Tzu-liao Yen-chiu Wei-yuan-hui (ed.), *Kan-su Wen-shih Tzu-liao Hsuan-chi* ("Historical sources of Kansu"), xvi, xxi, xxiv, xxvii, Lan-chou 1983, 1985-6; J. Lipman, *Familiar strangers: a history of Muslims in northwest China*, Seattle and London 1997, 167-227; see also the *Bibl.* of MA CHUNG-YING.

(CHANG-KUAN LIN)

WUDJŪD (A.), verbal noun from *w-dj-d* "to find".

1. In philosophy.

Here, it is one of the main words used to represent "being" in Arabic renderings of Greek ontological expressions, based on the present passive *yūdjadu*, with the past passive *wudjida*, leading to the nominal form *mawdjūd*. *Al-mawdjūd* means "what is found" or "what exists", and the *maṣdar*, *wudjūd*, is used as the abstract noun representing existence. *Wudjūd* and its related terms are frequently used to represent the copula (*al-rābiṭa*), sc. the English word "is", in addition to being used to represent existence. Many philosophers writing in Arabic and Persian spend some time discussing the repertoire of terms, technical and familiar, which might be used to represent the sorts of ontological and logical points which are made in Greek philosophy. In this context, *wudjūd* tends to be identified with terms such as *anniyya*, *huwiyya* [*q.vv.*] and the verb *kāna*, by contrast with terms representing being in the sense of essence such as *māhiyya*, *ḥaḳīḳa*, *dhāt* [*q.vv.*] and in Persian usage, *djawhar*, *dhāt*. The ambiguity between *wudjūd* as the copula and as representing existence is well noted by al-Fārābī [*q.v.*], who points out that the statement *Zayd yūdjadu ʿādilan* ("Zayd is just") can be understood purely syntactically without having any implication that Zayd actually exists. In his Commentary on the *De Interpretatione*, *Sharḥ al-ʿIbāra*, he refers to the use of *wudjūd* as though it were an attribute and used to make an existential claim. But he is generally clear that existence is not part of the essence of a thing, and it is not implied by its essence either. Existence is never anything more than an accident. When he discusses Aristotle's logical terms in the latter's *Prior analytics*, the expression *ḳiyās wudjūdī* is used to represent the Aristotelian hyparctic or assertoric syllogism.

A crucial distinction made by Ibn Sīnā [*q.v.*] is between *wudjūd* and *māhiyya*, where the former represents being and existence and the latter essence or quiddity. He spoke of God as the *wādjib al-wudjūd*, the only being whose essence is to exist, in contrast with everything else which is contingent. The realm of existence can be divided up into the *wādjib al-wudjūd bi-dhātihi*, necessary being in itself, and everything else which follows from it. The idea that there are essences or concepts that need something to bring them into existence was readily adopted by many of the *mutakallimūn*, and they discussed the particular kind of existence which is appropriate to God, a very different kind than that which is applicable to His creatures.

Ibn Rushd [*q.v.*] is more explicit on the function of *wudjūd* as indicating a truth claim. Existence may be understood as attributing a predicate to a subject, an accident being applied to the substance which serves as the subject of the statement. Arguing that existence has priority over essence, he formalised a powerful line of opposition to Ibn Sīnā's views on being, however. He accepted the logical distinction between existence and essence, but criticised its application to ontology. It is not just a matter of existence being brought to an essence that allows us to talk of the essence as being actualised, since the real existence of the essence is part of the meaning of the name, and is thus a condition of our use of the essence in the first place. If the existence of a thing depended on the addition of an accident to it, then precisely the same would be the case for existence itself, leading to an infinite regress.

Manuals of logic from the 4th/10th century regarded *wudjūd* as possessing an essence that the mind can comprehend without apprehension. This point is developed at great length by Shihāb al-Dīn al-Suhrawardī [*q.v.*], who argues that the immediacy of existence represents unmediated knowledge of reality. Al-Suhrawardī took this to show that essence is prior, since if existence were a predicate of essence, essence has to exist itself before any further question of existence can be raised. In his *ishrāḳī* [see ISHRĀḲ] approach, existence is nothing more than an idea, and one can describe reality in terms of lights with different intensities, ignoring existence altogether.

Mullā Ṣadrā Shīrāzī [*q.v.*] rejected this argument and replaced it with *aṣālat al-wudjūd*, the priority of existence. He argued that existence is accidental to essence in the sense that existence is not a part of essence. But there is no problem in understanding how existence can itself exist as more than a thought, since existence is an essential feature of actuality itself, and so no regress is involved. A development of the concept is provided by Mullā Ṣadrā, who uses the term *wudjūdiyya*. He argues that the *wudjūd* in everything is real, except for the abstract notion of being where this is an entirely mental abstraction. It provides scope for making a more abstract reference to *wudjūd*, as in the expression *mawdjūdiyyat al-wudjūd*, but he maintains the distinction between the *wudjūd* which is a mental abstraction and the *wudjūd* which is real. The former tends to be identified with the notion of universality, and when *wudjūd* is used in its widest sense Mullā Ṣadrā claims that it is used *bi 'l-tas̲h̲kīk*, not in a univocal manner. Everything which exists has something in common, since otherwise we should say that they do not exist, and what they have in common is not exactly the same attribute, but something that they share analogously. By contrast to al-Suhrawardī, what everything shares is some degree of existence rather than some degree of light. Like his predecessors, he distinguishes between the copulative use of *wud̲j̲ūd* (*al-wud̲j̲ūd al-rābiṭ*) and real being (*al-wud̲j̲ūd al-ḥaḳḳ*). In the case of the former, what is connected by *wud̲j̲ūd* are ideas in the mind, not necessarily anything real. What is it, then, that the different uses of *wud̲j̲ūd* have in common, which manages to distinguish them from claims concerning non-existence? The answer for Mullā Ṣadrā is that all uses of *wud̲j̲ūd* imply either mental or real existence.

He argues that existence is the basic notion of metaphysics, not essence. He accepts that we can think of a concept existing in reality, and only existing in our minds, but this does not show that existence is merely an attribute which is tacked on to the concept's essence in the case where it actually exists. When something exists and yet we think of it as not existing, we are thinking of the same thing; our name refers to the same object, and so existence comes first, and its precise characterisation later. Even things that only exist in our minds are existing things, and we then need to say what they are like. These arguments over the relative priority of existence and essence played a leading role in the structure of Islamic philosophy.

Bibliography: 1. Sources. Fārābī, *K. al-Ḥurūf*, ed. M. Mahdi, Beirut 1970, 112-15; idem, *Commentary and short treatise on Aristotle's* De Interpretatione, tr. F. Zimmermann, London 1981, 39, 162, 168, 191; Ibn Rushd, *The incoherence of the Incoherence*, tr. S. Van den Bergh, London, 1954, 224; idem, *Tafsīr mā ba'd al-ṭabī'a*, ed. M. Bouyges, Beirut 1938, iii, 1280; Ibn Sīnā, *K. al-Is̲h̲ārāt wa 'l-tanbīhāt*, ed. S. Dunyā, Cairo 1957-60, 285; idem, *K. al-S̲h̲ifā': al-ilāhiyyāt*, ed. M. Mūsā, S. Dunyā and S. Zāyid, Cairo 1960, i, 201, 347, 349; Mullā Ṣadrā, *al-Ḥikma al-muta'āliya fi 'l-asfār al-arba'a*, ed. R. Luṭfī *et alii*, Ḳum 1958, journey 1, i, 36, 48, 60, 62, 146, 174, 291, 293, 415; idem, *K. al-Mas̲h̲ā'ir*, ed. H. Corbin, Tehran 1964, 13; Suhrawardī, *Oeuvres philosophiques et mystiques*, ed. Corbin, Tehran 1976.

2. Studies. A.-M. Goichon, *La distinction de l'essence et de l'existence d'après Ibn Sina*, Paris 1937; F. Rahman, *Essence and existence in Avicenna*, in *Medieval and Renaissance studies*, ed. R. Hunt *et alii*, London, 1958, iv, 1-16; P. Morewedge (ed.), *Philosophies of existence ancient and medieval*, New York 1982, 290, 318, 320, 322, 324; F. Shehadi, *Metaphysics in Islamic philosophy*, New York 1982; J. Lameer, *Al-Farabi and Aristotelian syllogistics*, Leiden 1994, 56-8, 85-8, 226-32; O. Leaman, *Averroes and his philosophy*, Richmond 1997, 104-16. (O.N.H. Leaman)

2. In mysticism.

As a technical term of classical Ṣūfism, *wud̲j̲ūd* is used primarily, though by no means exclusively, as a verbal noun derived, like *wad̲j̲d* and *wid̲j̲dān*, from *wad̲j̲ada*, "to find" or "to experience". The term already occurs in several meanings in the prose writings of such prominent Bag̲h̲dādī Ṣūfīs as al-K̲h̲arrāz (d. 277/890-91 [*q.v.*]), *Rasā'il*, ed. Ḳāsim al-Sāmarrā'ī, Bag̲h̲dād 1387/1967, 26, 28, 30, 39) and al-D̲j̲unayd (d. 298/910-11 [*q.v.*]), *Rasā'il*, ed. Ali Hassan Abdel-Kader, *The life, personality and writings of al-Junayd*, GMS, N.S. xxii, London 1962, Arabic text 32-3, 35-6, 51-2, 56-7), as well as in a well-known *ḳaṣīda* generally attributed to al-Ḥallād̲j̲ (d. 309/922), *Le Dîwân d'al-Hallâj*, ed. Massignon, Paris 1955², 28-9), whereas it seems to be altogether absent from the technical vocabulary of their Eastern contemporary, the "thinker" al-Tirmid̲h̲ī *al-ḥakīm* (d. *ca.* 300/912-13 or later [*q.v.*]). Al-D̲j̲unayd's peculiar usage of the formula *wud̲j̲ūdihi lahum*, referring to God's "finding" or "realising" the spirits at the primordial Covenant (*al-mīt̲h̲āḳ* [*q.v.*]), implies a kind of "existence" prior to existence in this world. Applied to the experience of the mystic, *wud̲j̲ūd* is frequently juxtaposed with *s̲h̲uhūd* "witnessing" or "presence", and/or *wad̲j̲d*, a crucial Ṣūfī term which, though usually translated as "ecstasy", is more precisely defined as an indescribable "encounter of the unseen with the unseen" (*muṣādafat al-g̲h̲ayb bi 'l-g̲h̲ayb*; cf. *Adab al-mulūk*, ed. B. Radtke, Beirut 1991, Arabic, 68, German tr., 31) and plays a key role in discussions of the Ṣūfī practice *par excellence*, "listening to music" (*samā'* [*q.v.*]). Opinions appear to have been at variance with regard to the hierarchy, if any, of the above three values; but al-Ḳus̲h̲ayrī in his authoritative *Risāla* (written 437-8/1045-6) clearly opts for the superiority of *wud̲j̲ūd*, by which he means the realisation of divine [?] "existence" in such a way that everything else is totally "wiped out" (*istihlāk*; cf. R. Gramlich, *Das Sendschreiben al-Qušayrīs über das Sufitum*, Stuttgart-Wiesbaden 1989, 115 ff., 123, 431, and the review by Landolt in *Bull. Critique des Annales Islamologiques*, vii [1990], 39-41). In a more imaginative way, Nad̲j̲m al-Dīn al-Kubrā (d. 618/1221 [*q.v.*]) in his *Fawā'iḥ al-d̲j̲amāl wa-fawātiḥ al-d̲j̲alāl*, ed. F. Meier, Wiesbaden 1957, Arabic text nos. 18, 41, 118, 119) speaks of an "exchange of existence" (*tabdīl al-wud̲j̲ūd*) and describes this experience as a kind of ascent through the seven "categories of being" (*anwā' al-wud̲j̲ūd*) until one reaches "divine existence" (*wud̲j̲ūd al-ḥaḳḳ*). It may also be noted here that in the Ṣūfī *Tract on listening to music* traditionally attributed to Aḥmad al-G̲h̲azālī (*Bawāriḳ al-ilmā' fi 'l-radd 'alā man yuḥarrim al-samā'*, ed. J. Robson, London 1938, Arabic text 157-8, tr. 98-9), but which is more likely the work of a 13th-century Aḥmad b. Muḥammad al-Ṭūsī (cf. Aḥmad Mud̲j̲āhid, *Samā' wa futuwwat*, Tehran 1360/1981, Persian text, 9), the skin stretched over the drum is said to symbolise "absolute being" (*al-wud̲j̲ūd al-muṭlaḳ*).

Philosophical speculations about "absolute being" probably played a significant role in the development of Ṣūfī thought from the times of Ibn Sīnā at least; but the question as to whether or not *al-wud̲j̲ūd al-muṭlaḳ* should be identified with God became a serious issue only as a result of the impact of the "new" doctrine of Ibn al-'Arabī (d. 638/1240 [*q.v.*]), who became famous with followers and opponents alike as the greatest spokesman for the "unity of being" (*waḥdat al-wud̲j̲ūd*). It should be noted, however, that the latter expression has not been traced to the writings of Ibn al-'Arabī himself, whereas the 13th-century Persian thinker 'Azīz-i Nasafī already distinguishes systematically between two different kinds of *waḥdat-i wud̲j̲ūd* without attributing any of them directly to Ibn al-'Arabī [see waḥdat al-s̲h̲uhūd]. According to 'Alā' al-Dawla al-Simnānī (d. 736/1336), an influential Ṣūfī critic of Ibn al-'Arabī, *al-wud̲j̲ūd al-muṭlaḳ* is applicable not to God's own existence, but only to his creative "act of bringing-into-existence (*fi'l al-īd̲j̲ād*), even though al-Simnānī himself accepts the validity of ontological *tawḥīd* in the formula "there is nothing in Being but God" (*laysa-fi 'l-wud̲j̲ūd siwā 'llāh*), which he ascribes to the classical Ṣūfī al-D̲j̲unayd. Partly based on al-Simnānī's critique, but also as a means to assert their own identity as Muslims against a certain Indo-Muslim syncretism of their own times, later Ṣūfīs such as Gīsūdīrāz (d. 825/1422) and especially the celebrated Aḥmad Sirhindī (d. 1034/1624 [*q.v.*]) laid claim to an even higher form of mystical experience than the one associated with Ibn al-ʿArabī. Their doctrine, as distinct from *waḥdat al-wudjūd*, is generally referred to as *waḥdat al-shuhūd*. On the other hand, the doctrine of *waḥdat al-wudjūd* as elaborated by Ibn al-ʿArabī's immediate followers such as Ṣadr al-Dīn al-Ḳūnawī (d. 673/1274) was vigorously defended by Nūr al-Dīn ʿAbd al-Raḥmān al-Djāmī (d. 898/1492), particularly in his scholastic treatise, *al-Durra al-fākhira fī taḥḳīḳ madhhab al-ṣūfiyya wa 'l-mutakallimīn wa 'l-ḥukamāʾ al-mutaḳaddimīn* (ed. N. Heer, Tehran 1358/1980, idem, *The Precious Pearl*, Albany 1979); and this intellectual Ṣūfī tradition in turn exercised a strong influence on the formation of a new philosophy of the "primacy of existence" (*aṣālat al-wudjūd*), as opposed to the more traditional philosophy of the "primacy of quiddity" (*aṣālat al-māhiyya*), with Ṣadr al-Dīn al-Shīrāzī (d. 1050/1640).

Bibliography (in addition to references in the article): W.C. Chittick, *Ibn al-ʿArabi's Metaphysics of imagination: the Sufi path of knowledge*, Albany 1989 (with extensive bibl.); idem, Rūmī and *waḥdat al-wujūd*, in *The heritage of Rūmī*, ed. A. Banani *et alii*, Cambridge 1994, 70-111; H. Corbin (ed., tr. and introd.), *Mollâ Sadra Shirazi. Le Livre des Pénétrations métaphysiques* (*Kitâb al-Mashâʿir*), Tehran-Paris 1964; J.J. Elias, *The Throne Carrier of God. The life and thought of ʿAlāʾ ad-dawla as-Simnānī*, Albany 1995; J.G.J. ter Haar, *Follower and heir of the Prophet. Shaykh Aḥmad Sirhindī (1564-1624) as mystic*, Leiden 1992; S.S.K. Hussaini, *Sayyid Muḥammad al-Ḥusaynī-i Gīsūdirāz (721/1321-825/1422). On Sufism*, Delhi 1983; T. Izutsu, *The concept and reality of existence*, Tokyo 1971; H. Landolt, *Der Briefwechsell zwischen Kāšānī und Simnānī über Waḥdat al-Wuğūd*, in *Isl.*, (1973), 29-81; idem, *Le paradoxe de la "face de Dieu": Azîz-e Nasafî (VIIᵉ/XIIIᵉ siècle) et le "monisme ésotérique" de l'Islam*, in *SI*, xxv (1996), 163-92; M. Molé, *Les mystiques musulmans*, Paris 1965; G. Schubert, *Annäherungen. Der mystisch-philosophische Briefwechsel zwischen Ṣadr ud-Dīn-i Qōnawī und Naṣīr ud-Dīn-i Ṭūsī*, Beirut 1995. (H. Landolt)

WUḌŪʾ (A.), lit. "cleansing", the minor ablution, purification from a minor source of impurity (*ḥadath*), obligatorily required for the performing of certain acts of the Islamic religion, including worship [see ṣalāt]. For the major ablution, see ghusl.

Together with worship, almsgiving, fasting and pilgrimage, purification (*ṭahāra*), or the fact of putting oneself in a state of purity (*ṭuhr*), is one of the five cultic acts (*ʿibādāt*) that make up, according to the religious lawyers, the bases (*uṣūl*) of Islam (see Abū Muḥammad al-Djuwaynī, *Tabṣira*, Beirut 1994, 20). The enormous mass of Prophetic traditions concerning purity, the lengthy developments of the topic in the *fiḳh* treatises and the interminable legal controversies that it generated concerning the tiniest details, bear witness to its importance for the Muslim mind.

The obligation to purify oneself before embarking on the worship, already present in Jewish ritual, is clearly set out, in a fairly detailed way, in Ḳurʾān, V, 6: ". . . when you get ready for the worship, wash your faces and hands up to the elbows . . ."), this being considered a Medinan verse (as likewise IV, 43). A consensus was thus established that a performance of the worship without being in a state of purity was invalid (see Ibn al-Mundhir, *Idjmāʿ*, Beirut 1986, 17). Furthermore, the questions of detail concerning purification gave rise to numerous controversies, on one side, between Sunnī and Shīʿī legists, and on the other, between members of the different legal schools within Sunnism (in particular, between Ḥanafīs and Shāfiʿīs).

Minor ablutions are necessary when a person's state of impurity comes from a "minor impurity" (*al-ḥadath al-aṣghar*) and when there is available a liquid considered as suitable for purification at hand for this (if not, dry ablutions, *tayammum* [*q.v.*] are permissible). The state of minor impurity has as its main effect, universally recognised, to render invalid performance of the worship. The prohibition of touching or handling a copy of the Ḳurʾān (following LVI, 77-9) or of making the *ṭawāf* [*q.v.*] in the course of the Pilgrimage are, however, subjects of controversy.

Minor impurities invalidating the state of ritual impurity are equally the subjects of controversy. According to the Shāfiʿīs, there are five causes of this state: 1. "Everything which comes forth from the two natural orifices" (except the urine of suckling infants); 2. sleep (there is discussion about a light amount of this); 3. loss of reason; 4. touching a person of the other sex with or without "passionate" intention; and 5. touching the genitalia or anus in certain conditions (see al-Shīrāzī, *Muhadhdhab*, Damascus-Beirut 1992, i, 95-100). The Ḥanbalīs add to this list apostasy and consuming camel's meat, and consider that physical contact with a member of the opposite sex must have a carnal intention to bring about impurity (see *Le précis de droit d'Ibn Qudāma*, tr. H. Laoust, Beirut 1950, 6). The Ḥanafīs retain only nos. 4 and 5, but they consider that a bout of uncontrollable mirth (*ḳahḳaha*) during the worship invalidates the state of purity, necessitating fresh ablutions and beginning the act of worship in question once more (see al-Ḳaffāl al-Shāshī, *Ḥilyat al-ʿulamāʾ*, Beirut-ʿAmmān 1980, i, 143-55; for the Mālikī doctrine, Ibn Abī Zayd al-Ḳayrawānī, *La Risâla*, tr. L. Bercher, Algiers 1975, 28-31).

Rainwater, based on Ḳurʾān, V, 11 and XXV, 48, is the purifying element (*al-waḍūʾ*) par excellence. Even on this point, there were numerous discussions: What quality of water purifies? How does one distinguish pure from impure water? What other liquids can be assimilated here to water? (see al-Ṣaymarī, *Talkhīṣ al-khilāf*, Ḳum 1987, i, 21-3).

Regarding the ways of accomplishing *wuḍūʾ*, the question of preliminary intention (*niyya* [*q.v.*]) of purifying oneself has always been a subject of debate amongst the jurists of the Ḥanafī and those of other schools. For the latter, express intention is vital, if the ablutions in question are not to be rendered invalid, following the Prophet's famous saying, "Actions are only valid according to the intention". The Ḥanafīs, however, hold that, for purifications in general, only those made with a solid substance (such as in *tayammum*) necessitate it. At the heart of Sunnism, the question has assumed such importance that it clearly constitutes one of the signs of adhesion to one or another legal school.

The acts making up *wuḍūʾ*, known from Ḳurʾān, V, 6, and numerous Prophetic traditions (sometimes contradictory), are traditionally divided into "obligatory" and "recommended". In their details, the doctrines here are so divergent that it does not seem worth going into detail. One may merely observe that the divergences are most often engendered by different interpretations of the vocabulary of purifications, e.g. regarding "rubbing the head" (*masḥ al-raʾs*), what is meant by "rubbing" and how to define "the head"? On such questions, the jurists use linguistic argumentation *ad lib.* Thus the Shāfiʿī Abū Ḥāmid al-Ghazālī considers that six acts are necessary for simple ablutions: 1. expression of intention; 2. washing the face (*ghusl al-wadjh*); 3. washing the two hands (*ghusl al-yadayn*); 4. rubbing the head; 5. washing the two feet (*ghusl al-ridjlayn*); and 6. respecting the order of performing these procedures (*al-tartīb*). He then mentions 18 elements simply "recommended", such as rinsing the mouth, washing the ears, etc. (*al-Wadjīz*, Beirut 1994, 10-13).

Cleaning the teeth with an *arāk* stick (*siwāk* [*q.v.*]) is treated separately in the legal treatises, probably because it was the particular object of a saying by the Prophet ("Were it not for my desire not to burden my community, I would have ordered them to clean the teeth before every act of worship"). Following this saying, the jurists consider this to be strongly recommended but not obligatory.

A topic which divides Sunnīs from Shīʿīs is that of "rubbing one's shoes": Is it permissible to replace washing one's feet by rubbing one's footwear, opposed categorically by the latter but accepted by the Sunnīs under certain conditions. See al-Ḳaffāl al-Shāshī, *op. cit.*, i, 130-42, and AL-MASḤ ʿALĀ ʾL-KHUFFAYN.

The principle according to which a doubt (*shakk*) cannot damage a certainty (*yaḳīn*) is often invoked as a criterion for a person to determine his own state and thus know whether he should proceed to make his ablutions. A person who is doubtful in knowing whether he has been exposed to an impurity can legitimately consider himself in a state of purity; if, however, it is his state of purity which is the subject of doubt, he can be considered as a *muḥdith* (a person in a state of impurity) and should accomplish the *wuḍūʾ* (see al-Shīrāzī, *op. cit.*, i, 102-3).

Bibliography: Given in the article; see also G.-H. Bousquet, *La pureté rituelle en Islam (Étude de fiqh et de sociologie religieuse)*, in *RHR*, cxxxviii (1956), 53-71; A.K. Reinhart, *Impurity/no danger*, in *History of Religions*, xxx (1990), 1-24; and ṬAHĀRA.

(E. CHAUMONT)

WUFŪD (A., sing. *wafd*) delegations.

1. In the time of the Prophet.

In the biography of the Prophet Muḥammad [see SĪRA] this term designates the mainly tribal deputations which came to him in Medina, mainly during the ninth year of the Islamic era known as "the Year of Delegations". They started arriving during Shawwāl 8 A.H., after the abortive siege of al-Ṭāʾif [*q.v.*] or, according to another version, after Muḥammad's return from Tabūk [*q.v.*] (Shaʿbān or Ramaḍān 9 A.H.). Earlier visits to the Prophet are also reported. Some tribesmen are said to have come to him when he was still in Mecca. The Djuhayna delegation [see ḲUḌĀʿA, at Vol. V, 315b-316a] is supposed to have arrived at Medina shortly after the Hidjra [*q.v.*], while the Muzayna [*q.v.*] are said to have come in 5 A.H. The last delegation was that of the Nakhaʿ, which came in mid-Muḥarram 11 A.H.

The abundant source material about the delegations often reveals typical features of the visitors, such as hairstyles, clothes and tribal dialects. Strange and uncommon words that an eloquent leader included in his ceremonial address sometimes account for the preserving of the whole report (cf. Madjd al-Dīn Ibn al-Athīr, *Manāl al-ṭālib fī sharḥ ṭiwāl al-gharāʾib*, ed. M.M. al-Ṭanāḥī, Mecca [1399/1979], *passim*). Most if not all of the source material was transmitted in the early days of Islamic historiography by descendants of the Prophet's Companions (or alleged Companions) wishing to secure for their ancestors a place in the sacred history of the Prophet. Indeed, in many reports about visitors—it is often difficult to tell a visitor who came on his own initiative from a tribal delegation—one finds the fingerprints of the party concerned. For example, the leader of the ʿAbd al-Ḳays [*q.v.*] delegation puts—in first person—his own praise in the Prophet's mouth; and one of the reports on the Kinda [*q.v.*, at Vol. V, 119b] delegation is specifically said to go back to al-Ashʿath [*q.v.*] b. Ḳays. In one version of Ibn Isḥāḳ's biography of Muḥammad there is a long account on al-Ṭufayl b. ʿAmr al-Dawsī with an *isnād* or chain of authorities going back to al-Ṭufayl himself. (In the other versions of the same biography the report appears without an *isnād.*)

Elders (*mashyakha, ashyākh*) also figure prominently as transmitters of reports on tribal delegations. There is evidence of written records in the "pre-historiographical" phase. Al-Wāḳidī quotes (through one intermediary) an informant of the ʿUdhra [*q.v.*] who, with regard to his tribe's delegation, quotes "the book of his ancestors" (*kitāb ābāʾī*).

Sometimes accounts on a delegation exist both as "general history" and as family history. Ibn Isḥāḳ's report on the Hawāzin [*q.v.*] delegation, the protagonist of which is Zuhayr b. Ṣurad al-Djushamī of the Hawāzin, has an *isnād* going back to ʿAbd Allāh b. ʿAmr b. al-ʿĀṣ. However, a similar (though not identical) report on this delegation exists with a family *isnād* going back to Zuhayr himself. The family account persisted well into the 3rd/9th century, and in 274/887-8 it was transmitted to the fourteen-year old al-Ṭabarānī [*q.v.*].

Monographs on the delegations were compiled by al-Wāḳidī [*q.v.*], Ibn al-Kalbī [see AL-KALBĪ, section II], al-Madāʾinī [*q.v.*] and al-Haytham b. ʿAdī [*q.v.*]. Al-Madāʾinī's monograph is said to have included the delegations of the Yaman, the Muḍar and the Rabīʿa [see RABĪʿA AND MUḌAR], which no doubt reflects its internal division. The lost monographs only comprised part of the large source material about delegations scattered throughout the Islamic literature.

In addition to tribal delegations, there was one of Ethiopians, another of Persian Abnāʾ [*q.v.*, no. II] and yet another of *Ahl al-Kitāb* [*q.v.*] (who in this case were the Jews). The Nadjrān [*q.v.*] delegation was made up of Christians and that of the Taghlib [*q.v.*] comprised both Christians and Muslims. The Nadjrānīs and the Christian Taghlibīs did not convert to Islam, unlike the Christian members in the delegations of the ʿAbd al-Ḳays, the Nakhaʿ, the Ḥanīfa [see ḤANĪFA B. LUDJAYM] and the Ṭayyiʾ. Also the *djinn* [*q.v.*] and predatory beasts reportedly sent delegations to the Prophet.

The arrival of the Thaḳīf [*q.v.*] delegation, which was a turning point in Muḥammad's career, was brought about by military pressure applied by the Hawāzin leader, Mālik b. ʿAwf [*q.v.*]. Muḥammad managed to lure him out of al-Ṭāʾif, depriving the Thaḳīf of their main Bedouin ally. Mālik's harassment of his former allies pushed them to the inevitable negotiations in Medina in which Muḥammad adopted a fairly flexible attitude (M.J. Kister, *Some reports concerning al-Ṭāʾif*, in *JSAI*, i [1979], 1-18). Similar tactics were used with regard to the South Arabian town of Djurash. Having visited Muḥammad in 10 A.H., the Azd [*q.v.*] leader Ṣurad b. ʿAbd Allāh besieged Djurash, compelling its inhabitants to dispatch a delegation to Medina. In both cases Muḥammad employed the nomads to subdue the settled.

In the short term, Muḥammad's tribal tactics were divisive. Farwa b. Musayk al-Murādī was given control over fellow tribesmen who followed him, and was instructed to fight other tribesmen who turned away from him. A combination of diplomacy and military pressure is also evident elsewhere. An imminent Muslim attack brought to Medina the Ṣudā' delegation, and the Numayr came under similar circumstances. The taking of Tamīmī captives was behind the arrival of the Tamīm [*q.v.*] delegation (E. Landau-Tasseron, *Process of redaction: the case of the Tamīmite delegation to the Prophet Muḥammad*, in *BSOAS*, xlix [1986], 253-70).

While most tribal visitors came to declare their loyalty to the new religion and its founder, some of them considered succumbing to Muḥammad's authority (which in their view was a form of Ḳurashī expansionism) as a relinquishment of their own political ambitions. ʿĀmir b. al-Ṭufayl [*q.v.*], who led the ʿĀmir b. Ṣaʿṣaʿa [*q.v.*] delegation, suggested that power be divided between him and Muḥammad, or that he become the latter's heir. Also, Musaylima [*q.v.*] reportedly demanded to succeed the Prophet.

The Prophet's recognition of tribal rights to land and water resources appears in many of the letters given to the delegations. Ownership of these resources was often disputed, and some visitors made claims to land which was not theirs (on al-Dahnā' [*q.v.*], see Kister, *Land property and Jihād*, in *JESHO*, xxxiv [1991], 270-311, at 305; cf. M. Lecker, *The Banū Sulaym*, Jerusalem 1989, 174-5).

Bibliography (in addition to references given in the article): The relevant entries in the dictionaries of the Companions; Ibn Saʿd, i/2, 38-86; J. Wellhausen, *Skizzen und Vorarbeiten*, iv, *Medina vor dem Islam*, Berlin 1889, 87-194; Ibn Shabba, *Taʾrīkh al-Madīna al-munawwara*, ed. F.M. Shaltūt [Mecca 1399/1979], ii, 499-602; al-Zurḳānī, *Sharḥ ʿalā 'l-mawāhib al-laduniyya*, Beirut 1417/1996, v, 113-238; al-Ṣāliḥī al-Shāmī, *Subul al-hudā wa 'l-rashād*, vi, ed. ʿA. al-ʿA.ʿA. al-Ḥ. Ḥilmī, Cairo 1411/1990, 395-681; M. Ḥamīdullāh, *Madjmūʿat al-wathāʾiḳ al-siyāsiyya*, [5]Beirut 1405/1985. (M. LECKER)

2. In the early caliphate.

During the time of the Rightly-Guided Caliphs, delegations continued to arrive at the caliphal court, usually headed by leaders and chiefs from outlying districts; to be sent as a member of such a mission, as a *wāfid* or *muwaffad*, was regarded as prestigious and a reward for great eloquence. Thus Ibn ʿAbd Rabbihi, in his section on delegations, the *kitāb al-djumāna fi 'l-wufūd*, ed. Aḥmad Amīn *et alii*, Cairo 1940-53, ii, 3-121, lists delegations from such groups as the people of al-Yamāma to Abū Bakr, and from Djabala b. Ayham, al-Aḥnaf b. Ḳays [*q.vv.*] and ʿAmr b. Maʿdīkarib to ʿUmar b. al-Khaṭṭāb. But the institution is particularly well documented in regard to the Umayyads, with the Sufyānid Muʿāwiya I [*q.v.*], as much in his role as *sayyid*, supreme tribal leader of the Arabs, as that of Islamic caliph, on various occasions inviting *wufūd* of powerful tribal chiefs who upheld the Umayyad cause in Syria and elsewhere but also of potential rivals and opponents, in order to consult and seek agreement on certain contentious issues (see below).

Provincial governors and local leaders would send delegations to the caliph in order to affirm their loyalty, normally receiving in return subsidies or allocations of taxation, as ʿAmr b. al-ʿĀṣ [*q.v.*] received the *kharādj* of Egypt for his loyalty to Muʿāwiya. Poets would come as *wuffād* seeking largesse from the caliph, in return for which support would be expected in their verses for the ruler and his policies (cf. *ʿIḳd*, ii, 82 ff.: Djarīr to ʿAbd al-Malik, al-Aḥwaṣ to ʿUmar b. ʿAbd al-ʿAzīz, etc.).

Some of the *wufūd* invited by Muʿāwiya dealt with highly important and delicate issues. This was clearly the case when, towards the end of his reign, in the later 670s, the caliph wished to secure the succession of his son Yazīd after his own death, a novelty in Arab ruling practice, since ʿAlī had failed to secure a lasting succession for his son al-Ḥasan. Delegations were summoned to Damascus both from the loyal Syrian chiefs and commanders and also from potentially hostile groups like the army in ʿIrāḳ and the Anṣār, although neither al-Ḥusayn b. ʿAlī nor ʿAbd Allāh b. al-Zubayr [*q.vv.*], both of whom regarded themselves as having strong claims to succeed, was present. In an opening speech, Muʿāwiya expatiated on the qualities of Yazīd for the succession, and the leader of the Ḳays in northern Syria and the Djazīra, al-Ḍaḥḥāk b. Ḳays al-Fihrī [*q.v.*], proposed Yazīd's candidature, supported by others of Muʿāwiya's partisans like ʿAbd al-Raḥmān b. ʿUthmān al-Thaḳafī, combatting arguments of the opposition. The leader of the ʿIrāḳī Arabs, al-Aḥnaf b. Ḳays [*q.v.*], was eventually won over by a substantial monetary payment (see al-Masʿūdī, *Murūdj*, v, 69-73 = §§ 1827-30, and cf. Wellhausen, *The Arab kingdom and its fall*, Eng. tr. Calcutta 1927, 141-3).

Bibliography (in addition to references given in the article): H. Lammens, *Etudes sur le règne du calife omaiyade Moʿâwia Ier*, Paris 1908, 61-2; idem, *Le califat de Yazîd Ier*, Beirut 1921, 103-6.

(C.E. BOSWORTH)

AL-WUḲŪF (A.), lit. place of standing, station, for prayer and thanksgiving on the plain of ʿArafa [*q.v.*] or ʿArafāt, some 20 km/12 miles to the east of Mecca, the culminating rite of the Meccan Pilgrimage [see HADJDJ].

A rite of *wuḳūf* existed there in pre-Islamic times and seems to have constituted a main element of the pagan *ḥadjdj*, independent moreover of that in the *ḥaram* of Mecca. The pilgrims arrived in their tribes at Dhu 'l-Madjāz, assumed a state of sacralisation and accomplished there various devotions before going down again by running towards Muzdalifa. Wellhausen suggested that it may have involved an autumn ritual linked with the trials of the end of summer and the expectation of rains, but it is impossible for us now to reconstitute with any certainty the details and the meaning of this rite for the pagan Arabs. Whatever the case, Muḥammad knew how to confer on it an eminently monotheistic dimension. He showed to the faithful the details of the ritual, henceforth Muslim, at the time of the Farewell Pilgrimage of 10/632. The pilgrims perform it on 9 Dhu 'l-Ḥidjdja. For preference, they pass the night of the 8th-9th at Minā, 6 km/4 miles from Mecca, but it is allowable to come to ʿArafāt on the evening of the 8th. The *sunna* requires a person to be there just after midday. Slightly outside the sacred area, a brief sermon is given, following the Prophet's example, and the *ẓuhr* and *ʿaṣr* worships are performed conjointly and in an abridged form. The rite proper then begins, according to modalities reduced to the most abbreviated form. ʿArafāt appears as an immense desert plain fringed with rocky hills, with no building on it except for the mosque of al-Namira; tents are merely erected to protect the pilgrims from the sun. These last perform very modest rites. No special gesture is required; the pilgrims can be seated, standing, mounted on an animal or, at the present time, in a vehicle. They turn in the direction of the *ḳibla*, and may draw near, as did the Prophet, to the hill called the hill of mercy (*djabal al-raḥma*), if possible standing without stopping in prayer to God. The text of these prayers is in one part fixed by tradition. First of all, the *talbiya* [*q.v.*] is pronounced ("Here I am, O Lord...") and various supplications, often attributed to the Prophet; but it is equally allowable to make personal prayers, for oneself or for absent ones. To ask pardon for one's sins is prescribed, for everyone will be pardoned on that particular day: "The gravest of sins for the pilgrim at ʿArafāt is to believe that God will not pardon him" (al-Ghazālī, *Iḥyāʾ*, i.7, 3). Finally, after sunset, the pilgrims go down en masse in the direction of Muzdalifa, where they spend the night. The pre-Islamic tradition of going forward precipitatedly and making as much noise as possible (an act of sympathetic magic to induce storms and rain?) was denounced by the Prophet, but it persisted, curiously, during mediaeval times and till today.

One should note that a second *wuḳūf* takes place at Muzdalifa in the morning of 10 Dhu 'l-Ḥidjdja, just after the dawn worship, an attenuated memory of the corresponding pre-Islamic ceremony dedicated to the god of thunder Ḳuzaḥ, whose mountain overhangs the place. This second standing session is not obligatory, and the crowd movements of recent decades caused by increased numbers of pilgrims make it in practice almost impossible to realise collectively. In differentiation from the rites at Mecca and Minā, those of the *wuḳūf* have not acquired an "Abrahamic" sense, perhaps because of their clearly observable religious significance.

The spiritual significance of the *wuḳūf* is immense. It forms the very heart of the *ḥadjdj*. To stand at ʿArafāt is obligatory, if only for a short instant, between the afternoon and dawn of 10 Dhu 'l-Ḥidjdja. Without it, the whole of the Pilgrimage is invalid and cannot be compensated by other sacrifices, as is the case with the omission of certain other rites. The *wuḳūf* constitutes, as attest those who have given an account of their own Pilgrimage, the most concentrated and most emotional moment of the *ḥadjdj*. In it, the Islamic community discerns its unity and its immediate, direct contact with God. This gathering together is often viewed as prefiguring the eschatological one of the Resurrection, each believer being dressed in his *iḥrām* garment as in a shroud. It is in any case the most specifically monotheistic ritual manifestation that the Muslim ritual set up or retained from pre-Islamic practice.

Bibliography: For the general significance of the rite within the Pilgrimage, see ḤADJDJ. The pre-Islamic rites evoked by Azraḳī, *Akhbār Makka*, Ibn al-Kalbī, *K. al-Aṣnām*, Ibn Saʿd, *Ṭabaḳāt*, and Ṭabarī, *Taʾrīkh*, have been gathered together and analysed by C. Snouck Hurgronje, *Het Mekkaansche feest*, Leiden 1880; J. Wellhausen, *Reste arabischen Heidentums*, ²Berlin 1897; and M. Gaudefroy-Demombynes, *Le pèlerinage à la Mecque*, Paris 1923. The details of the ritual are given in the *ḥadīth* collections under the sections called *kitāb al-ḥadjdj*. Information on mediaeval practice comes from the great travellers, e.g. Ibn Djubayr and Ibn Baṭṭūṭa. Recent practice for the *wuḳūf* is evoked in 19th and 20th century travellers' accounts, *inter alia*, those of Sir Richard Burton, *Personal narrative of a pilgrimage to el-Medinah and Meccah*, London 1859; Snouck Hurgronje, *op. cit.*; T.F. Keane, *Six months in Meccah*, London 1881; M.L. al-Batanūnī, *al-Riḥla al-ḥidjāziyya*, Cairo 1911; E. Dinet and S. Baâmer, *Le Pèlerinage à la maison sacrée d'Allah*, Paris 1930; A. Kamal, *The sacred journey, being Pilgrimage to Mecca*, New York 1961; A.M. Turki and H.R. Souami, *Récits de pèlerinage à la Mekke*, Paris 1979. For a statement on the actual contemporary organisation, D. Long, *The Hajj today. A survey of contemporary Makka Pilgrimage*, Albany 1979.

(P. LORY)

WUSHMGĪR B. **ZIYĀR**, ẒAHĪR AL-DAWLA, the second ruler of the Daylamī dynasty of the Ziyārids [*q.v.*] of northern Persia, *r.* 323-56/935-67. *Wushmgīr* is said to have meant "quail-catcher", according to al-Masʿūdī, *Murūdj*, ix, 30 = § 3603, cf. Justi, *Iranisches Namenbuch*, 359.

Wushmgīr was the lieutenant of his brother Mardāwīdj [*q.v.*], and after his death was hailed at Rayy as his successor by the Daylamī troops. Until *ca.* 328/940 he held on to his brother's conquests in northern Persia, but thereafter was drawn into warfare, in alliance with another Daylamī soldier of fortune, Mākān b. Kākī [*q.v.*], with the Sāmānids, who had ambitions in northern Persia. Wushmgīr lost Iṣfahān and Rayy to the Būyid brothers ʿAlī and Ḥasan (sc. ʿImād al-Dawla and Rukn al-Dawla [*q.vv.*]), and retrenched himself in the Caspian provinces of Gurgān and Ṭabaristān. Very soon he became willy-nilly a client of the Sāmānids, receiving support from Sāmānid armies on various occasions when the Būyids drove him out of Ṭabaristān (333/945, 335/947, etc.) and twice when he vainly attempted to regain and hold Rayy (331/943, 347/958). In 356/967 the Sāmānid general Muḥammad b. Ibrāhīm Sīmdjūrī [see SĪMDJŪRIDS] and Wushmgīr came together in Gurgān in order to launch an attack on Rukn al-Dawla, but this was aborted by Wushmgīr's death whilst hunting on 1 Muḥarram 357/7 December 967 (thus in Miskawayh, *Tadjārib*, ii, 233, tr. v, 247).

He was succeeded as ruler of the Ziyārid amīrate by his son Bīsutūn, whose rule was, however, challenged by another son, Ḳābūs [*q.v.*], who eventually secured the throne for himself. The Ziyārids were able to survive for more than a century further, but only as a local Caspian power.

Bibliography: 1. Sources. Miskawayh, i, 317, ii, 119-20, 138, 154-5, 158, 246-7, tr. iv, 358, v, 124, 144, 164-6, 169, 232-3; Gardīzī, ed. Nazim, 31, 38, 40, 44-5; Ibn Isfandiyār, tr. Browne, 217-25; Ibn al-Athīr, viii.

2. Studies. See the general one on the Ziyārids given in the *Bibls.* to MARDĀWĪDJ and ḲĀBŪS B. WUSHMAGĪR, and also W. Madelung, in *Camb. hist. Iran*, iv, 213-14, and C.E. Bosworth, *The New Islamic dynasties*, no. 81. For coins of Wushmgīr, see S.M. Stern, *The coins of Āmul*, in *NC*, 7th ser., vol. vi (1967), 220 ff.

(C.E. BOSWORTH)

WUTHŪḲ AL-**DAWLA**, Mīrzā Ḥasan Khān, Persian statesman, belle-lettrist, several times cabinet member and twice prime minister, b. in Tehran April 1875, to a prominent landowning family, and d. there February 1951. His paternal grandfather, Mīrzā Muḥammad Ḳawām al-Dawla held, among other positions, the governorship of Khurāsān in 1855 and Iṣfahān in 1872, and his maternal uncle was the reformist-minded constitutionalist Mīrzā ʿAlī Khān Amīn al-Dawla (1844-1904), chief minister to Muẓaffar al-Dīn Shāh Ḳādjār [*q.v.*]. Wuthūḳ al-Dawla's younger brother Ḳawām al-Salṭana (1876-1954) was several times prime minister, and proved instrumental in arranging for the withdrawal of Soviet troops from Ādharbāydjān in the aftermath of the Second World War; his cousin Muḥammad Muṣaddiḳ al-Salṭana [*q.v.*] was prime minister during the tumultuous years of the nationalisation of Persian oil in the early 1950s.

Mīrzā Ḥasan Khān held his first official appointment at the age of twenty as governor of Ādharbāydjān, conferred upon him, along with the title of Wuthūḳ al-Dawla, by Nāṣir al-Dīn Shāh [*q.v.*], who was impressed by his exceptional aptitude and capability. With the rise of the constitutionalist movement [see DUSTŪR. iv] in Persia in the first decade of the 20th century, Wuthūḳ al-Dawla, a strong advocate of limited monarchism, entered the first parliament in 1906 as representative of the merchant's guild. After a series of key cabinet posts in critical times, Wuthūḳ al-Dawla held the premiership for a couple of months in 1916-17, a tenure paralysed by political chaos and internal rebellion. In that brief period he collaborated with his brother-in-law, then minister of education, to establish a dozen girls' schools in the capital.

Persia withstood several partition plans in the first two decades of the twentieth century, and when Wuthūḳ al-Dawla was made prime minister again in 1918, separatist pro-Bolshevik groups, including the well-known Djangalī movement (1915-21 [*q.v.*]) led by Mīrzā Kūčik Khān, sought to establish autonomous republics along the northern borders of Persia. The first year of Wuthūḳ's second premiership then was spent in quelling riots and restoring the rule of law and order, with British help, taking advantage of an over-arching British sentiment to thwart the Bolshevik threat in the region. In 1919, in an attempt to centralise civil administration and the army, and to ensure a complete modernisation of the bureaucratic and financial sectors along western lines, he signed the provisional Anglo-Persian Agreement of 1919 with Sir Percy Cox, the British minister in Persia. The agreement which intended—in lieu of placing Persian financial and military administration under British control—to replicate western-style civil institutions in Persia, was met with opposition from the parliament and other members of the Persian court and aristocracy, as well as the Russian, French and American legations in Tehran. The controversial agreement, which did little more than recognise *de facto* British control over Persian affairs, led to Wuthūḳ al-Dawla's dismissal in 1920, and was subsequently annulled by the fourth Persian parliament. The prime minister was not only accused of forfeiting Persia's sovereignty but also of taking a bribe from the British government. In that same year, he was made a Knight of the Grand Order of Bath (Overseas List) by the British crown.

Although Wuthūḳ al-Dawla resumed limited political activity after spending a few years abroad, as minister of finance and then justice in 1926, and member of parliament in 1930, the rest of his political career was diminished both as a result of the highly unpopular agreement as well as the change of dynasty in 1925.

A poet of considerable renown, translator of Kant and Rousseau, and essayist, Wuthūḳ al-Dawla earned the respect of leading Persian intellectuals of his period. Particularly noteworthy in this regard are his *Dīwān*, with an introduction by the laureate Malik al-Shuʿarāʾ Bahār [*q.v.*], and an early lucid, and surprisingly modernist essay on the emancipation of women, written after Riḍā Shāh Pahlavī's [*q.v.*] unpopular policy of forbidding Persian women to appear veiled in public. After his retirement from political affairs, Wuthūḳ al-Dawla directed the newly-established Language Academy, the *Farhangistān-i Īrān*, for three years from 1936.

Bibliography: Malik al-Shuʿarāʾ Bahār, *Tārīkh-i mukhtaṣar-i aḥzāb-i siyāsī*, Tehran 1944, 30-45; Wuthūḳ al-Dawla, *Dīwān*, Tehran 1957, also with introd. by Īradj Afshār and facs. ed. Tehran 1994; *Documents on British foreign policy, 1919-1939*, ed. R. Butler and J.P.T. Bury, 1st ser., vol. xiii, London 1963; ʿAlī Wuthūḳ (ed.), *Āthār-i Wuthūḳ*, introd. by Malik al-Shuʿarāʾ Bahār, Tehran 1964; Djamshīd Amīr Bakhtiyārī, *Marwārīd-hā wa khazaf-hā*, Tehran 1964; Mihdī Bāmdād, *Sharḥ-i ḥāl-i ridjāl-i Īrān*, i, Tehran 1968, 348-52; J. Olson, *The genesis of the Anglo-Persian Agreement of 1919*, in *Towards a modern Iran*, ed. E. Kedourie and Sylvia G. Haim, London 1980, 185-216; Olson, *Anglo-Iranian relations during World War I*, London 1984, 153-249; N.S. Fatemi, art. *Anglo-Persian Agreement of 1919*, in *EIr*, ii, 59-61; Manūchihr Farmānfarmāiyān, *Dastān-i rushwa-gīrī-yi Wuthūḳ al-Dawla, Nuṣrat al-Dawla wa Ṣārim al-Dawla*, in *Rahavard*, xxvi (1990), 270-4; ʿAlī Wuthūḳ (ed.), *Chahār faṣl*, Tehran 1992; Ibrāhīm Ṣafāʾī, *Wuthūḳ al-Dawla*, Tehran 1995.

(NEGUIN YAVARI)

Y

YĀʾ, the 28th letter of the Arabic alphabet, with the numerical value 10. It stands for the semivowel *y* and for the long vowel *ī*, which the grammarians analyse as short *i* (*kasra*) plus *yāʾ*. For the shortening of final *-ī* before *hamzat al-waṣl*, see WĀW. *Yāʾ* is also used, like *alif* and *wāw*, as a "support" for medial or final *hamza* [*q.v.*], reflecting presumably the ancient Ḥidjāzī dialect loss of *hamza* in certain positions with concomitant glides.

In word-final position, *alif maḳṣūra* (that is to say: long *ā* not followed by *hamza*) is written sometimes with *alif* and sometimes with *yāʾ*. In the latter case, it can be transliterated as *à*; in manuscripts it is often noted as *yāʾ* with a small superscript *alif*. The rules for the distribution of the two spellings are complicated and there is much fluctuation in manuscripts; in general, the spelling with *à* is preferred in words with third radical *y* (e.g. *banà*), but also in words with third radical *w* if other forms of the same stem have *yāʾ* (e.g. *tadāʿà*, by analogy to the second person *tadāʿayta*). The position is similar regarding the particles *ilà*, *ʿalà* and *ladà*, because of forms with suffixes like *ilayhi*. In Ḳurʾānic orthography, the spelling with *yāʾ* is retained before pronominal suffixes, but the modern convention is to replace it by *alif* in non-final positions. Otherwise, non-final *ā* is written with *yāʾ* only in the loan word *tawrāt* (تورية, alongside the regular توراة), which was perhaps not borrowed directly from Hebrew *tōrāh* but from some Aramaic form with *-y-*. For a classic formulation of these rules see, for example, Ibn Ḳutayba, *Adab al-kātib*, ed. Grünert, 278-84. There is good reason to think that originally these spellings had a phonetic rationale, namely, that *yāʾ* was used to represent a final *ā* affected by "inclination" (*imāla* [*q.v.*]), that is to say, pronounced as [ē] or [ǣ]. Bergsträsser noted that in the Ḳurʾān *à* does not normally rhyme with *ā*. However, the distribution of the "inclining" and "non-inclining" allophones of *ā* must have altered after the time when the orthography of the Ḳur'ān was established. In many cases, the Kūfan school of Ḳur'ān readers still prescribed the "inclining" pronunciation in words written with *à*, and the "non-inclining" one in those with final *alif*, but the Baṣran school regarded *imāla* to be independent of the orthography and conditional on the phonetic environment.

Modern books printed in Egypt generally omit the two dots of the final form of *yā'* when it stands for *y* or *ī*, but set them if it stands for *à*, but printers in Syria and Lebanon follow exactly the opposite convention. Mediaeval pointed manuscripts either always omit the dots, or always set them, or use both pointings indiscriminately; a case can be made for always omitting them. Moreover, manuscripts often retain the points of the medial *yā'* that stands for *hamza* (adding, or not adding, the *hamza* sign above the letter), but the modern convention is to write this *yā'* without dots.

Classical Persian generally follows the Arabic conventions for writing Arabic loanwords, apart from the fact that Persian sometimes uses *yā'* also for non-final "inclining" *ā*, e.g. in ليكن, in Arabic *lākin*, for which the older Persian pronunciation was *lēkin*. In native words *yā'* stands for the semivowel *y* and for the long vowels *ī* and *ē* (called *yā'-i ma'rūf* and *yā'-i madjhūl* respectively; cf. WĀW). In good poets, Persian *ē* does not rhyme with Persian or Arabic *ī*, but it can rhyme with Arabic "inclining" *ā*. E.g. Persian *sēb* "apple" can rhyme with the loanword *rikēb* (Arabic *rikāb*), but not with *'adjīb*. In modern Western Persian, old *ī* and *ē* merge as [i], and *ay* is pronounced [e^{i}], but the old pronunciations are retained in most dialects of Afghānistān and Tādjīkistān and in the traditional Persian pronunciation in India. Thus Afghānīs still distinguish between *shīr* "milk" and *shēr* "lion", but Persians now pronounce both words as *shīr*.

Urdū generally follows the scribal conventions of classical Persian, but distinguishes in final position between undotted ی for *y* or *ī* and ے for *ē*. Turkic languages can use *yā'* for *y, i, e* or *i̇*.

Bibliography: For *alif maḳṣūra*: G. Bergsträsser, in *Gesch. des Qor.*, iii, 36-41; H. Fleisch, *Traité de philologie arabe*, i, Beirut 1961, 69-70, 315-9 (with further literature and discussion); W. Diem, *Untersuchungen zur frühen Geschichte der arabischen Orthographie. I. Die Schreibung der Vokale*, in *Orientalia*, N.S. xlviii (1979), 207-57. For Persian *ī* and *ē*: P. Horn, in *Gr. I. Ph.*, i/2, 31-2, 35-7; A. Farhâdi, *Le persan parlé en Afghanistan*, Paris 1955, 8, 11; F. Meier, *Aussprachefragen des älteren Neupersich*, in *Oriens*, xxvii-xxviii (1981), 70-176, repr. in idem, *Bausteine*, 3 vols. Istanbul 1992, iii, 1057-1164. (F.C. DE BLOIS)

AL-**YĀBĀNĪ**, the modern Arabic term for a person of Japanese descent.

1. Islam in Modern Japan. The Japanese began to receive information about the Islamic world through Chinese sources beginning in the 8th century. However, it was not until the early 18th century that a substantial introduction to the Middle East and Islam was written in Japanese by a Confucian intellectual and politician, Arai Hakuseki (1657-1725), mainly based on questions asked of the Italian Jesuit missionary Giovanni Battista Sidotti. From the Meiji Restoration (1868) and the emergence of modern Japan onwards, Japanese were allowed to travel and emigrate abroad, and some found their way to the Middle East and South Asia as travellers and immigrant workers. Japanese converts to Islam began to appear among them after the turn of the century. Also around that time, Tatar refugees fleeing to Japan from oppression in Imperial Russia and then the Soviet Union were influential in attracting Japanese to Islam. The Japanese Muslims, some of whom made pilgrimages to Mecca and wrote about their travels, constructed three mosques during the 1930s in the cities of Tokyo, Nagoya and Kobe. At the same time, both Muslim and non-Muslim scholars in Japan began to form various research associations and institutions to study Islamic civilisation; and under the then government's imperialist policies they were mobilised by the military in gaining the support of Asian Muslims in Japan's expansionist activities during World War II (H. Kobayashi, *Nihon Isurāmu-shi*). Today, there are about 2,000 Japanese Muslims practising in Japan, while Muslim immigrants from such countries as Iran, Pakistan, Bangladesh, Indonesia and Malaysia number roughly 75,000. Scholarly interest in Islam has gradually broadened from the pre-war concern with current affairs to a deeper analysis of the historical foundations of Muslim society and culture. On Japanese translations of the Ḳur'ān, see AL-ḲUR'ĀN. 9. Translations, 4.

2. Japan in early Arab geographers. It was after the 18th century that the Arabs began to call the Japanese *al-Yābānī* on the basis of European sources. Before that time, 3rd/9th and 4th/10th century Arab geographers may have been aware of the existence of Japan through Chinese sources. There was confusion with regard to a place called Wāḳwāḳ [*q.v.*]: "To the east of China lies Wāḳwāḳ, where gold is abundant to the extent that people use gold chains and collars for their dogs and monkeys" (Ibn Khurradādhbih, 69); "behind China lives a nation called Wāḳwāḳ" (Ibn al-Faḳīh, 3); "Kankdiz is the remotest town in the east, situated at the extremity of China and of Wāḳwāḳ" (al-Kh^{w}ārazmī, *Mafātīḥ al-'ulūm*, 217); "the sea of Fārs is a gulf of *al-Baḥr al-Muḥīṭ* stretching to the border of China and Wāḳwāḳ" (al-Iṣṭakhrī, 122; Ibn Ḥawḳal, 276). The "Wāḳwāḳ of China" is clearly different from the "Wāḳwāḳ of Yemen" (Ibn al-Faḳīh, 7) which may be identified with the Wāḳwāḳ cited by other Arab geographers (al-Ya'ḳūbī, i, 207; Mas'ūdī, *Murūdj*, i, 233, iii, 6-7; al-Idrīsī, *Nuzhat al-mushtāḳ* = *Opus geographicum*, 9, 87, 91-2). Later, non-Arab scholars debated the actual location of Wāḳwāḳ, both arguing that it was actually Japan, which was called *Wākwak* ("kingdom of Wa") by the Chinese (de Goeje) and tracing it as far as Sumatra (Ferrand). In Japan, J. Kuwabara upheld De Goeje's opinion with confidence in 1935, while in the post-war period, H. Sugita, after attempting to separate fact from fantasy, has more cautiously attested to the possibility. (For all the complexities of the problem, see WĀḲWĀḲ.1(b).) Some Turkish scholars regard Djābarḳā as Japan, based on Maḥmūd al-Kāshgharī's description in the 5th/11th century: "The language of Djābarḳā is unknown, due to its remoteness and its separation from China by the Great Sea" (*Dīwān lughāt al-turk*, facs. fol. 12b). However, the scientific basis for such an opinion is yet unclear.

Bibliography (in addition to references given in the article): M.T. de Goeje, *Le Japon connu des Arabes*, in P.A. van der Lith and L.M. Devic (eds.), *Le livre des merveilles de l'Inde*, Leiden 1883-6, 295-307; G. Ferrand, *Le Wāḳwāḳ est-il le Japon?*, in *JA* (1932), 193-243; J. Kuwabara, *Hojukō-no Jiseki*, Tokyo 1935, 31; M.Ş. Ülkütaşır, *Kâşgarlı Mahmut*, Istanbul 1946, 74; H. Kobayashi, *Nihon Isurāmu-shi*, Tokyo 1988; H. Sugita, *Nihonjin-no Chuto Hakken*, Tokyo 1995, 34-5. (T. SATO)

YABG̲H̲U (t.) (perhaps also Yavg̲h̲u, the Old Turkish so-called "runic" alphabet not differentiating *b* and *v*), an ancient Turkish title, found in the Ork̲h̲on [*q.v.*] inscriptions to denote an office or rank in the administrative hierarchy below the Kag̲h̲an.

The latter normally conferred it on his close relatives, with the duty of administering part of his dominions. It was thus analogous to the title S̲h̲ad̲h̲, whom the Yabg̲h̲u preceded in the early Türk empire [see turks. I. History. 1. The pre-Islamic period]. It seems to have lost some importance after this time (8th century), since Maḥmūd al-Kās̲h̲g̲h̲arī, reflecting the position in Ḳarak̲h̲ānid times, says that the Yabg̲h̲u ranks below the Yug̲h̲rus̲h̲ or vizier, who himself came after the Kag̲h̲an and the Tigin [*q.v.*] (*Dīwān lug̲h̲āt al-turk*, Tkish. tr. Atalay, iii, 32: *yafg̲h̲u* for *yaßg̲h̲u*) (the S̲h̲ad̲h̲ seems to have by now dropped out here).

In the period of the decline of the Hephthalites in northern Afg̲h̲ānistān and the extension of Arab control into the region (early 2nd/8th century), the title was borne by Turkish princes of the upper Oxus principalities such as Ṭuk̲h̲āristān and K̲h̲uttal(ān) [*q.vv.*]. It appears on Hephthalite coins as *Iapgu* in the local Hephthalite version of the Greek alphabet, and in the Arabic historical sources in an Arabo-Persian form as *d̲j̲abbūya, d̲j̲abg̲h̲ūya*, e.g. in al-Ṭabarī, ii, 1204, 1224, 1547, 1604, 1612, etc. Al-Kās̲h̲g̲h̲arī correctly connected the title also with the Ḳarluḳ and the Og̲h̲uz. The caliph al-Mahdī received the submission of the Yabg̲h̲u of the Ḳarluḳ amongst several other Transoxanian and steppe potentates (al-Yaʿḳūbī, *Taʾrīk̲h̲*, ii, 479; cf. Barthold, *Turkestan down to the Mongol invasion*[3], 202). At the opening of the 5th/11th century, Yabg̲h̲u was the title of the Og̲h̲uz ruler on the lower Syr Darya with his capital at D̲j̲and [*q.v.* in Suppl.]; the holder of the title in the 1030s and early 1040s, S̲h̲āh Malik, was at odds with the Sald̲j̲ūḳ family [see saldjūḳids. II.]. Yabg̲h̲u nevertheless occurs within the Sald̲j̲ūḳ family also, though exactly what functions, if any, Mūsā Yabg̲h̲u, son of Sald̲j̲ūḳ b. Duḳāḳ, exercised is unknown (see *ibid.*). The title still had significance in later Sald̲j̲ūḳ times, since, according to Gordlevskiy, in the military organisation of the Rūm Sald̲j̲ūḳs of Konya, the Yabg̲h̲u as representative of the K̲h̲ān/Sultan commanded the left wing of the army (cited by Doerfer, iv, 127); but after this time seems to fall out of use.

The origins and etymology of the term have excited much speculation. It seems certain that it is not a native Turkish term. It may appear in pre-Islamic, pre-Türk empire times amongst such peoples of Inner Asia as the Huns and the (?) Indo-European Wusun of eastern Turkestan, and there exist Chinese transcriptions of it. It may well be ultimately an Indo-European word, either "Tokharian" or Iranian. See the extensive discussions in G. Doerfer, *Türkische und mongolische elemente im Neupersischen*, iv, Wiesbaden 1975, 124-36 n. 1825; Sir Gerard Clauson, *An etymological dictionary of pre-thirteenth century Turkish*, Oxford 1972, 873.

Bibliography: See also C.E. Bosworth and Clauson, *Al-Xwārazmī on the peoples of Central Asia*, in *JRAS* (1975), 9-10. (C.E. Bosworth)

YĀBISA, the mediaeval Arabic name for Ibiza (Catalan, Eivissa), an island in the western Mediterranean, part of *al-D̲j̲azāʾir al-s̲h̲arḳiyya* "the Eastern islands" [of al-Andalus], sc. the Balearics [see mayūrḳa; minūrḳa and their *Bibls.*], and also the name of its chief town and port. Ibiza is the smallest of the trio (area 572 km^2), and lies 85 km to the southwest of Mallorca halfway to the Spanish coast (at Cabo de la Nao, with Denia nearby). It is flanked by the still smaller island of Formentera 4 km to its south, and the name Pityusic Islands, applied to these two in Antiquity is still used today, implying a certain distinctiveness to them within the Balearic group. The name Ibiza (Greek form Ebousos) is believed to derive from Phoenician [ʾ]*ybšm*, either *ʾī brōšīm* "island of pines" or *ʾī bōšem* "island of fragrance" (cf. A. Dietrich, *Phönizische Ortsnamen in Spanien*, Abh. für die Kunde des Morgenlandes, xxi/2, Leipzig 1936, 29-30), with the Greek translation Pityousai. The explanation of Yāḳūt, in his *Buldān*, Beirut, v, 424, "the dry island", is clearly folk etymology. Ibiza lies close to the shipping lanes connecting the eastern Mediterranean with the Iberian and Mag̲h̲ribī Mediterranean coastlands, and this position has made it a favourite way station from Phoenician times onwards. The chief town and port, acquired by colonists from Cadiz in 653 B.C., has an excellent navigational and strategic location on the southeastern coast of the island. It came under Carthaginian control a century later, and eventually had a Punic or Phoenicised population, perhaps of considerable size (some 4,000 tombs have been found in the cemetery of Puig des Molins).

The Arab conquest of Spain reached Ibiza in the course of the 2nd/8th century. There followed over four centuries of Islamic rule; after recognising the authority of the Umayyad governors and then of the caliphs of Cordova, Ibiza had close ties with the Taifa of Denia [see dāniya; mud̲j̲āhid] until the Reconquista in 1235. Arab authors refer to Ibiza as "the daughter" (*bint*) of Mallorca, and define its location at one day's sailing from Denia to the west and an equal distance from Mallorca to the northeast. The island was noted both as a port of call (with the port city itself, there were ten harbours, *marāsī*) and for its ship-building activity, benefiting from fine stands of pine trees, which were also a source of wood for charcoal burning. They praise Ibiza's fruits, vineyards, grapes and raisins, as well as the "inexhaustible" salt of its salt pans (al-Ḥimyarī, *Rawḍ al-miʿṭār*, text 198, tr. 240; al-Ḳazwīnī, *Āt̲h̲ār al-bilād*, Beirut 1960, 282). Peaceful pursuits and commerce precluded neither piracy on both sides nor attacks by Christian powers (a Pisano-Catalan expedition, 1116). This motivated the construction of still stronger fortification walls, which have recently been the object of excavations and publications (A. Costa Ramon, *La triple murada de l'Eivissa àrab*, (Ibiza 1985). Meanwhile, Arab culture on Ibiza flourished, as witnessed by the mention of two of its poets in Yāḳūt's description of the island.

Ibiza's economic and maritime role continued after 1235, and relations with the Mag̲h̲rib remained lively. The island's conqueror and subsequent feudal lord, the archbishop of Tarragona, strove to carry on the crusading spirit in the form of naval raids, but commerce asserted itself, especially as the exportation of the prized salt of Ibiza included North African ports among its destinations. Its salt flats, already praised by the Arabs (and still active today), gained primacy at this period, and between the 13th and 17th centuries they made the island one of the principal sources of salt in the Mediterranean. Thus Pīrī Reʾīs states in his *Kitāb-i baḥriyye* (932/1526; ed. Ankara 1935, 542) that as many as 50-60 *barčas* dock annually at the *iskele* of the island's *tuzla* to load salt, and that the largest number of Arab and Turkish captives held in the kingdom of Catalonia work on these salt pans (see also J.-Cl. Hocquet, *Voiliers et commerce en Méditerranée, 1200-1650* = vol. ii of his *Le sel et la fortune de Venise*, 1978-9; idem, *Ibiza, carrefour du commerce maritime et témoin d'une conjoncture méditerranéenne, 1250-1650*, in *Studi in memoria di Federigo Melis*, Naples 1978, i, 493-526). Fear of Ottoman Turkish assault appears to have motivated the construction (1554-85) of impressive new fortification walls, still standing today, around the city of Ibiza.

Bibliography: Given in the article; see also F. Retamero, *Moneda i monedes àrabs a l'illa d'Eivissa*, Ibiza 1995; B. Joan i Marí, *Historia d'Eivissa*, Ibiza 1997.

(S. Soucek)

YABRĪN, a sandy region of Eastern Arabia belonging to Banū Saʿd. It is situated within the area of al-Baḥrayn [*q.v.*], three stages from al-Falad̲j̲ and two stages from al-Aḥsāʾ [*q.v.*] and Ḥad̲j̲r (Yāḳūt, *Buldān*, ed. Beirut, v, 427). The editors of al-Ḥasan b. ʿAbd Allāh al-Iṣfahānī, *Bilād al-ʿarab*, Riyāḍ 1968, 276 n. 3, sc. Ḥamad al-D̲j̲āsir and Ṣāliḥ al-ʿAlī, state that Yabrīn is still known as an area in the west of al-Aḥsāʾ and the name is corrupted (or more probably, hypercorrected, since *d̲j̲* > *y* in the speech of that area) in modern works to D̲j̲abrīn. It does not, however, appear on modern maps. It is mentioned incidentally in the early Islamic histories such as al-Wāḳidī's *K. al-Mag̲h̲āzī* (ed. Marsden Jones, iii, London 1966, 974) and al-Ṭabarī, iii, 1163, in the latter and in Yāḳūt, v, 427, disparagingly in a poem of the Umayyad poet D̲j̲arīr [*q.v.*], "How far is Yabrīn from the gate of Paradise (*min bāb al-farādīs*)!" Al-Hamdānī, *Ṣifa*, 137, describes Yabrīn as a palm-grove, a collection of fortress houses (*ḥuṣūn*), springs—some flowing, others not—and salt marshes (*sibāk̲h̲*). He also places the area on the ʿUmān pilgrimage route (149). This statement is repeated at 145, and he adds the following details. It is situated in the east of al-Yamāma [*q.v.*]. Between Yabrīn and Ḥaḍramawt [*q.v.*] lies an extensive area called al-ʿId̲j̲am which is impassable. Between Yabrīn and the sea lie sands. It has a road leading into al-Yamāma and al-Baḥrayn. It is an area cut off among the sands with palm-groves and a little cultivation. The original Arab inhabitants were expelled by the Banū Ḳus̲h̲ayr, who were in their turn expelled by the Ḳarāmiṭa [*q.v.*]. Yāḳūt, v, 427, also mentions a Yabrīn in Syria, "one of the villages of Aleppo". There is further a Yabrīn/D̲j̲abrīn near Bahlā in ʿUmān, built by the Yaʿrubids [*q.v.*].

Bibliography: Given in the text.

(G.R. Smith)

YABRŪḤ (a.), Mandragora, the Mandrake, *Mandragora officinarum, Solanaceae*; also called *Atropa mandragora L.* and *M. officinarum Mill* (Moldenke); Hebr., *dūdāʾīm* or *yabrūaḥ*.

A perennial herbaceous plant common in the Mediterranean region, its dark green leaves, about one foot long, spread out at ground level; the flowers are purplish or whiteish-green, and the fruit are small globular berries, orange to red in colour. Its root is often forked, and is the part known as *yabrūḥ*, while the plant itself is generally called *luffāḥ*.

Ibn al-Bayṭār explains *mandrāg̲h̲ūras* of Dioscorides as *yabrūḥ*, also known as *sābīzak*, *s̲h̲ābīzad̲j̲*, *tuffāḥ al-d̲j̲inn*, or in *Laṭīnī* as *ard̲j̲ubalīṭa* (*Tafsīr*, iv, 69, 298). Ibn Samad̲j̲ūn gives the same names; Maimonides says the *ʿad̲j̲amiyyat al-Andalus* name is *ablīṭa*, presumably meaning *ard̲j̲balīṭa* (*S̲h̲arḥ*, no. 179).

Its nature was considered very cold and dry. It was used with caution, externally for skin complaints; it was known to be able to cause weakness and deafness. Ibn Waḥs̲h̲iyya calls it poisonous, causing death through its extreme cold quality (88), while D̲j̲ābir says that it causes sleep and death, working in the same way as opium (*Gifte*, 106, 187). Al-Rāzī, quoted by Ibn Samad̲j̲ūn, observed women who had used it suffering from redness and swelling of the face and body. More important than emetic or purgative properties, which it shared with other plants, was its use as a soporific and anaesthetic. It was administered, generally in a drink, before surgery or cautery (Ibn Samad̲j̲ūn and Ibn al-Bayṭār, quoting Dioscorides).

The root was often thought to resemble the human form, which gave rise to legends and superstitions, already in ancient times and in the Middle Ages. The Biblical account concerning Rachel and Leah (Gen. xxx. 14-15) presumably refers to the plant's supposed fertility-inducing qualities. Such beliefs were dismissed by Gerard in his *Herbal* of 1597 (cf. Moldenke), and are not mentioned by Culpeper (1616-54). The mandrake is still known in Arabic as *tuffāḥ al-d̲j̲inn*. In one Palestinian village in the 1970s the berries were called *tuffāḥ ind̲j̲ān*, and said to encourage broodiness in chickens. The plant is today an object of interest rather than fear.

Bibliography: 1. Sources. Ibn al-Bayṭār, *al-D̲j̲āmiʿ li-mufradāt al-adwiya wa 'l-ag̲h̲d̲h̲iya*, Cairo 1874; idem, *Tafsīr Kitāb Diyūsḳūrīdūs*, ed. I. Ben Mrad, Beirut 1990; *Das Buch der Gifte des Ǧābir ibn Ḥayyān*, tr. A. Siggel, Wiesbaden 1958; M. Levey, *Medieval Arabic toxicology. The book on poisons of Ibn Waḥs̲h̲īya*, Philadelphia 1966; Maimonides, *S̲h̲arḥ asmāʾ al-ʿuḳḳār*, ed. M. Meyerhof, Cairo 1940; P. Kahle, *Ibn Samaǧun und sein Drogenbuch. Ein Kapitel aus den Anfängen der arabischen Medizin*, in *Documenta islamica inedita*, Berlin 1952.

2. Studies. *Culpeper's Complete herbal*, frequently publ. London; J.G. Frazer, *Folk-lore in the Old Testament*, ii, London 1918; I. Löw, *Die Flora der Juden*, Vienna-Leipzig 1924-34, iii; H.N. and A.L. Moldenke, *Plants of the Bible*, Waltham, Mass. 1952; *Encyclopaedia Judaica*, Jerusalem 1971, s.v.

(Penelope C. Johnstone)

YĀBURA, the Arabic name of the modern town of Evora in southern Portugal.

The Liberalitas Julia of the Roman period had become Elbora or Erbora in the time of the Visigoths, a name revived unchanged, in the form of Yābura, by Arab authors. The history of the Arab town poses numerous enigmas.

Very little is known of its history from the time of the Arab conquest to the beginning of the 10th century. Ibn al-Faraḍī makes it the seat of a *ḳāḍī*, and the city was located in the district of Beja, capital of a *d̲j̲und* and seat of a governor since the conquest. Al-Rāzī alludes to its importance in the 4th/10th century, noting the existence of several cantons dependent on the town. However, it seems to have remained a locality of secondary importance during this period, which accounts for the fact that a writer such as Ibn Ḥawḳal makes no mention of it. The first known documentary reference confirms this secondary status: Ibn Ḥayyān and the anonymous chronicle of al-Nāṣir, quoted by the Christian chronicle known as *Crónica Leónesa y Nájarense*, record the attack led by the future sovereign Ordoño II in 301/913 and draw attention to the dilapidated state of the perimeter wall and of the defences which enabled the Christians to take possession of the town. On this occasion, the population figure given is approximately 5,000 inhabitants. Subsequently, the town was caught up in the turmoil of struggles between "local lords" during the *fitna* of the early 4th/10th century. The town, depopulated by the Christians, was besieged by allies of the ruler of Badajoz, ʿAbd Allāh Ibn Marwān al-D̲j̲illīḳī, and, with the aid of another Muwallad leader, Masʿūd al-

Surunbākī, repopulated to prevent the Berbers of the region from settling there.

The town enjoyed more tangible prosperity in the 5th/11th century, becoming the second city of the amīrate of the Afṭasids [*q.v.*] of Badajoz; the governors appointed were second-ranking officers of the amīrate such as ʿUbayd Allāh al-Djarrāz, cousin of al-Muẓaffar, killed fighting the ʿAbbādids in 442/1051; al-Mutawakkil, the last Afṭasid sovereign, served his apprenticeship as a governor there while his brother ruled in Badajoz. This information is supplied by al-Idrīsī who, in his two surviving works, evokes the prosperity of the region, on the road from Badajoz to Alcácer do Sal (Ḳaṣr Abī Dānis), the principal port of the amīrate.

Evora prospered until the capture of the city by the Portuguese warlord Giraldo Sempavor in 556/1161, as is proved by the presence of prestigious Muslim families like the Banū Wazīr who played an important part in the *fitna* which accompanied the decline of the Almoravids. Arab biographical authors and the geographer Yāḳūt underline the intellectual dynamism of the city during the 5th/11th and 6th/12th centuries; Ibn ʿAbdūn al-Yāburī (d. 528/1134) was one of its most distinguished representatives.

The perimeter wall, privileged witness of this Arab history, poses problems of dating. García y Bellido has detected, on the line of the Roman wall, an "ancient" installation and construction of the wall. A double-sided inscription, discovered outside the site, evokes two phases of construction: that of the 4th/10th century, following the sacking of the city by the Galicians, and that of the restoration of the wall by Sidray b. Wazīr between 541/1147 and 546/1151. The discovery of an elaborate installation, at the base of the curtain, in tile and brick, traversing a Roman villa of the *rua* of Burgos, as well as the general arrangement of the wall, seem to confirm construction in the Umayyad period and subsequent revival and restoration. The restoration of the 7th/13th century also corresponds to the last phase of the Islamic history of Evora, associated with a new period of autonomy under the government of Sidray b. Wazīr who minted coins in 540-1/1146.

Bibliography: 1. Sources. Idrīsī, *Nuzhat al-mushtāḳ fī 'khtirāḳ al-āfāḳ*, ed. as *Al-Idrīsī opus geographicum*, Naples-Rome 1975, and *Uns al-muhadj wa-rawḍ al-furadj*, ed. and tr. M.J. Mizal, *Los Caminos de al-Andalus en el siglo XII*, Madrid 1989, tr. R. Dozy et M. de Goeje, *Description de l'Afrique et de l'Espagne*, repr. Leiden 1968; Ibn Ḥayyān, *al-Muḳtabas min anbāʾ ahl al-Andalus*, ii, ed. Makkī, Beirut 1973, iii, ed. M. Antuña, Paris, 1937, v, ed. P. Chalmeta, Madrid 1979, tr. Vigueira-Corriente, Madrid 1981; Rāzī, *La description de l'Espagne d'Aḥmad al-Rāzī, tr. à partir de textes en Castillan et en Portugais*, ed. E. Lévi-Provençal, in *And.*, viii (1953); *Crónica del moro Rasis*, ed. D. Catalan and S. De Andres, Madrid 1975.

2. Studies. Borges Coelho, *Portugal na Espanha Arabe*, 2 vols. [2]Lisbon 1989; A. García y Bellido, *A recinto mural romano de Evora—Liberalitas Julia*, in *Conimbriga*, x (1971), 85-92; A. Goulart, *Duas inscrições árabes inéditas ne Museu de Evora*, in *A cidade de Evora*, lxviii-lxxix (1987), 3-13; B. Pavón Maldonado, *Ciudades y fortalezas lusomusulmanas. Crónicas de vigies por el sul de Portugal*, in *Cuadernos de Arte y Arqueologia*, v; A. Sidarus, *Um texto árabe do século X relativo à nova fundação de Evora e aos movimentos muladi e berbere no ocidente andaluz*, Evora 1994; C. Torres, *O Garb al-Andaluz*, in J. Mattoso, *História de Portugal*, Lisbon 1992, i, 362-437; Ch. Picard, *Le Portugal musulman. L'Occident d'al-Andalus sous domination islamique*, Paris 2000.

(Ch. Picard)

YADA TASH (t.), lit. rain stone, in Arabic texts appearing as *ḥadjar al-maṭar*, this being a magical stone by means of which rain, snow, fog, etc., could be conjured up by its holder(s). In particular, knowledge and use of such stones has been widespread until very recent times in Inner Asia.

Belief in the existence of stones and other means of controlling the weather has been widespread throughout both the Old and New Worlds (see Sir J.G. Frazer, *The golden bough, a study in magic and religion*, abridged ed., London 1922, 75-8). Belief in a stone seems to have been general amongst the early mediaeval Altaic peoples of Inner Asia, or at least, it is imputed to them by early Chinese sources and by Muslim writers on the early Turks; it may, accordingly, have been part of the Turks' ancient shamanistic beliefs. Several Islamic writers on the Turks mention it from the early 3rd/9th century onwards. The early traveller in Central Asia Tamīm b. Baḥr [*q.v.*] gives it as one of the wonders of the Turks, the stone being held by the king of the Toghuzghuz [*q.v.*] and no-one else (cited in Ibn al-Faḳīh, 329, Fr. tr. Massé, 388-9; also in V. Minorsky, *Tamīm ibn Baḥr's journey to the Uyghurs*, in *BSOAS*, xii [1947-8], 285). A certain Abu 'l-ʿAbbās ʿĪsā b. Muḥammad al-Marwazī related from the Sāmānid *amīr* Ismāʿīl b. Aḥmad [*q.v.*] that infidel Turks used the rain stone to bring down darkness and hailstones against the Sāmānid army (cited in Yāḳūt, *Buldān*, ed. Beirut, ii, 24-6, s.v. *Turkistān*). Abū Dulaf in his *First Risāla* attributes to the Kimäk [*q.v.*] a stone which attracts water (Ger. tr. A. von Rohr-Sauer, *Des Abû Dulaf Bericht über seine Reise nach Turkestân, China und Indien neu übersetzt und untersucht*, Bonn 1939, 21, 50). Gardīzī retails the story that the stone went back to Japhet, son of Noah, and was subsequently inherited by Turkish peoples like the Oghuz, Ḳarluḳ and Khazar (*Zayn al-akhbār*, ed. Ḥabībī, Tehran 1347/1968, 256). Maḥmūd Kāshgharī says that he witnessed its use as part of a magical ceremony (*kahāna*) amongst the Yaghma [*q.v.*] in Semirečʾe (*Dīwān lughāt al-turk*, Tkish. tr. Atalay, iii, 3, 159, s.v. *yat*).

Belief in the rain stone's powers apparently passed from the early Turks to the Mongols (with the original *yat/yad* appearing in Mongolian as *djada*). Its use appears, e.g. in the story of Čingiz's rise to power, when the son of Čingiz's then ally Wang Khān used it for bringing down snow on their Nayman enemies (*Secret history of the Mongols*, Ger. tr. E. Haenisch, *Die Geheime Geschichte der Mongolen*, [2]Leipzig 1948, 43), and Čingiz's son Toluy employed the services of a shaman from the Turkish tribe of the Ḳanghlï [*q.v.*] to conjure up snow and icy weather against the Tungusic Djürčen in northern China some thirty years later (Rashīd al-Dīn, tr. J.A. Boyle, *The successors of Genghis Khan*, New York 1971, 36-7). Such practices have lasted amongst Mongol peoples almost to modern times, being attested amongst *inter alios* the Kalmucks, the Buryats and, in the early 20th century, the Khalkha of the Ordos in Inner Mongolia (Mostaert). Information about beliefs of this kind seems to have reached Marco Polo, where in his travel narrative he mentions the "devilish enchantments" of the Turco-Mongol Ḳaraʾunas/Caraonas in bringing down darkness upon their enemies, and the magical powers of Kashmīrī and Tibetan shamans in the circle of the Great Khān Ḳubilay at his palace of Shan-tu in northern China (Yule-Cordier, *The Book of Ser Marco Polo*, [3]London 1902, i, 98, 105, 166, 168, 301, 309-11; and cf. also *The mission of Friar William of Rubruck*, Eng. tr. P. Jackson, London 1990, 244). The use of the bezoar (see below) as a rainstone had, in fact, been known also to the Chinese since T'ang times (see B. Laufer, *Sino-Iranica. Chinese contributions to the history of civilization in ancient Iran*, repr. Taipei 1967, 525-8).

The rain stone was identified by such 19th century writers as Grigoriev and Tomaschek with nephrite, found in the valleys of the rivers running down from the Kun-lun Mountains to the Tarim basin and in the region of Lake Baikal (cf. Marquart, *Streifzüge*, 79), but it seems more likely that the original rain stone was the bezoar (Pers. *pād-zahr*), which is a calculus or concretion formed in the alimentary tract of certain animals, mainly ruminants (see Laufer, *loc. cit.*). The origin of the Turkish word *yada* is unclear, but it is improbable that it has any connection with the precious mineral jade (Ar. *yas̲h̲m* [*q.v.*]) or—at least directly—with Pers. *d̲j̲ādū* "magic". W.B. Henning cited a Sogdian word *čdy* with a possible meaning "rain stone", and the origin of *yada* may well be ultimately Iranian. See the extensive discussions in G. Doerfer, *Türkische und mongolische Elemente im Neupersischen*, Wiesbaden 1963-75, i, 286-9 no. 157, iv, 123 no. 1822; Sir Gerard Clauson, *An etymological dictionary of pre-thirteenth century Turkish*, 881a; Molnár, *Weather magic in Inner Asia*, 104-16.

Beliefs in the rain stone have been attested amongst Turkic and Mongolian peoples of the Volga basin, Central Asia, Siberia and Mongolia by travellers in these regions during the 19th and early 20th centuries; see the material brought together by Molnár, *op. cit.*, 70-101.

Finally, one might note a curious mention, in Ibn al-ʿAdīm's account of al-Mutanabbī's [*q.v.*] alleged youthful claim to prophethood, of a "rain bead" (*ṣadḥat al-maṭar*), utilised by Arab tribes accounted of South Arabian or Yemeni genealogy, which could direct rain away from a particular spot, i.e. prevent rain from falling rather than attracting it (see W.P. Heinrichs, *The meaning of* Mutanabbī, in J.L. Kugel (ed.), *Poetry and prophecy*, Ithaca and London 1990, 137-9).

Bibliography: In addition to references given in the article, see J.A. Boyle, *Turkish and Mongol shamanism in the Middle Ages*, in *Folklore*, lxxxiii (1972), 184-93 (repr. in *The Mongol world empire, 1206-1370*, Variorum, London 1977, no. XXII), and the recent comprehensive work on the rain stone, A. Molnár, *Weather magic in Inner Asia*, Bloomington, Ind. 1994.

(C.E. Bosworth)

AL-**YADĀLĪ** (1096-1166/1685-1753), the cognomen of Muḥammad b. al-Mukh̲tār b. Muḥammad (Maḥamm) Saʿīd b. al-Mukh̲tār b. ʿUmar b. ʿAlī b. Yaḥyā b. Yiddād̲j̲ Igd̲h̲aburg̲h̲a b. Yad̲h̲rinan Tagsh̲umt (Aḥsanuhum Bas̲h̲arat[an]), Mauritanian scholar. His *nisba* shows his ethnic affiliation to one of the Zawāyā tribes forming the pentarchical alliance of the Tas̲h̲ums̲h̲a: the group of the Īdāw-dāy (eponymous founder Yiddād̲j̲ = D̲j̲addu ʿAlī).

He was born and died at Tandagsammi, in the heart of the Gibla (south-eastern Mauritania) in the region of Iguidi; his tomb is situated near the wells of Intawfokt (D̲h̲āt al-S̲h̲ams).

Renowned as he was as a polygraph in the fields of exegesis, mysticism, history and poetry, very little information is available concerning his youth and his education. At the most, the names of some of his teachers are known: these included the Alfag̲h̲a Minnaḥna b. Mūdī Mālik (d. 1151/1738), with whom he was closely associated, as well as the Alfag̲h̲a ʿAbd Allāh b. Aʿmar Agdawḳob, who initiated him into *tad̲j̲wīd*. In the sphere of *taṣawwuf*, the *wird* of the S̲h̲ād̲h̲iliyya brotherhood (Nāṣiriyya branch of Tamgrūt) is said to have been transmitted to him by his paternal cousin Nekhtāro b. al-Muṣṭafā b. Maḥamm-Saʿīd al-Yadālī, who in turn was said to have received it from Aḥmad al-Ḥabīb al-Sid̲j̲ilmāsī. As for travels, only two journeys are attributed to him: a tour of the north, in the region of Agādīr-Dūm (the Banks of Arguin), and the other, shorter one (*s̲h̲ayfara*), to a section of the Īdāybusāt, whose pastures were adjacent to his own region.

Besides the *Dīwān* of his numerous poems (essentially on themes of *zuhd, madīḥ, tahniʾa* and *rit̲h̲āʾ*), al-Yadālī is the author of some thirty works, of which only three are reckoned to be irrevocably lost. Legal writings were predominant in the Sahelian region at the time, and al-Yadālī produced four responses (*nuḳal*) to questions of *fiḳh: Risāla fī Masālik al-ʿilla* (invalidity of marriage due to *nus̲h̲ūz*, i.e. recalcitrance by the wife or ill-treatment by the husband); *Risālat al-Lafʿa* (branding of animals with red-hot irons, *mīsām*) an issue on which he differed from his master Muḥammad b. Alfag̲h̲a Minnaḥna; *Nuḳla fī ḍamān mā akalathu al-mawās̲h̲ī min al-ḥirāt̲h̲a* (compensation for damage caused by animal herds grazing over cultivated fields); and *Nuḳla fī tasrīḥ al-ṣibyān ayyām ʿuṭalihim* (responsibility in regard to a child not yet socially mature).

Regarding the history of the region, it is principally by virtue of two accounts by al-Yadālī that the story is known of the war of S̲h̲urbubba (1664-77), sc. his *S̲h̲iyam al-zawāyā* and *Amr al-walī Nāṣir al-Dīn*, now published in one volume. This is essentially a frank apology for the "Messianic" cause (*mahdawiyya*) of Nāṣir al-Dīn, the loser in this war. Besides information of a geographical and chronological nature, it offers the reader a kind of martyrology, commemorating the blood spilled by the Zawāyā, especially those of the Daymānī faction of the Ahl Ōwbak, who were slaughtered at the battle of Tirtillās (1673).

In doctrine, al-Yadālī first composed a very condensed *ʿaḳīda: Ḳawāʿid al-ʿaḳāʾid* (verse abridgement by al-Mukh̲tār Wuld D̲j̲engī, d. 1321/1903-4). He subsequently developed it into a voluminous commentary, *Farāʾid al-fawāʾid fī s̲h̲arḥ ḳawāʿid al-ʿaḳāʾid* (ms., 273 fols.). The subjects tackled here go beyond the normal themes of a doctrinal treatise, and include e.g. the problem of validation of saints in Islam, Aristotelian notions of astrology, esoteric passages regarding al-Būnī's science of letters, the fundamental differences between rival bodies of philosophers and *mutakallima*, an apparent gloss on the *ʿAḳīda al-sanūsiyya al-ṣug̲h̲rā* by ʿĪsā b. ʿAbd al-Raḥmān al-Suktānī, etc. This varied compilation has the merit of enshrining the names of writers who would otherwise be virtually unknown, such as the Moroccan exegete ʿAbd al-Raḥmān al-Figīgī (d. 1514).

In the field of *taṣawwuf*, al-Yadālī proceeded in the same manner. A relatively short letter (19 lines), *K̲h̲ātimat al-taṣawwuf*, is the object of a lengthy commentary in the *S̲h̲arḥ al-K̲h̲ātima*. These two texts, together, are reputed to have served, in the lands north of the Senegal River, as a source of inspiration for the *Masālik al-d̲j̲inān* of Aḥmadu Bamba, the founder of the *murīdiyya* [*q.v.*]. The general tone of the work recalls the *Ḳawāʿid al-taṣawwuf* of Zarrūḳ al-Barnuṣī, in that it associates a strictly initiatory content with a permanent re-evaluation of the discourse in terms of Sunnī orthodoxy.

The most voluminous work left by al-Yadālī to posterity is his complete exegesis of the Ḳurʾān (ms., 1558 fols): *al-D̲h̲ahab al-ibrīz fī tafsīr Kitāb Allāh al-ʿazīz*.

This work also presents, for essentially didactic reasons, a very composite structure. All the modes of exegesis are deployed here (*ma'thūr, i'djāz, aḥkām* and *ishāra*), but without any element of disorder. The sequence and the thread of the text are rapidly apparent to the reader in the systematic correlation which the author establishes between the exoteric and esoteric planes. Extensive contributions from the sources of mystical exegesis are then exacted: al-Ḳushayrī here comes close to Ibn al-ʿArabī (through the influence of al-Shaʿrānī) and Ibn ʿAṭāʾ Allāh (whose *ḥikam* are subjected here to commentary by the Egyptian scholar al-Munawī [*q.v.*]). The *Dhahab* is also accompanied by literary digressions such as would not primarily be expected in a work of *tafsīr*, such as those from al-Ṣafadī and al-Maḳḳarī for *adab*, al-Damīrī for zoology (theriomorphic psychology), al-Taftazānī for logic, and Ibn Khallikān and al-Ghubrīnī for biographical notices.

Bibliography: The mss. of the works of al-Yadālī cited in the article are all preserved at Nouakchott, in the private libraries of Rādjil Wuld Aḥmad Sālim and Muḥammad Sālim Wuld Maḥbūbī. See also the resources of the IMRS for partial copies of the *Dhahab* (nos. 149, 2176, 2791, 2836). For his poetical *Dīwān*, see the critical edition by A. Wuld Ākkāh, *Dīwān shiʿr Muḥammad al-Yadālī*, DES, Rabat 1989. On the author's life and the intellectual history of the Bilād Shinḳīṭ in the 18th century, see, in addition to the art. MŪRĪTĀNIYĀ: Aḥmad b. al-Amīn al-Shinkīṭī, *al-Wasīṭ fī tarādjim udabāʾ Shinkīṭ*, Cairo 1989; M. Wuld Babbāh, *al-Shaykh Muḥammad al-Yadālī*, three original texts concerning the history of Mauritania, Carthage 1990; M. Wuld Ḥāmidūn, *Ḥayāt Mūrītāniyā*, ii, *al-Thaḳāfa*, Tunis 1990; idem, *Ḥayāt Mūrītāniyā. al-Djughrāfiyā*, Rabat 1994; D. Wuld ʿAbd Allāh, *al-Ḥaraka al-fikriyya fī bilād Shinḳīṭ*, DES, Rabat 1992-3; al-Nābigha b. Aʿmar al-Ghallāwī, *al-Nadjm al-thāḳib fī baʿd mā li 'l-Yadālī min manāḳib*, ed. M. Wuld Babbāh, Nouakchott 1995; F. Leconte, *Une exégèse mystique du Coran au XVIIIe siècle dans le sud-ouest de la Mauritanie (al-Gibla)*, Aix-en-Provence 1995. (F. LECONTE)

YĀDGĀR (P.), lit. "a souvenir, a keepsake" and, by extension, in numismatics any special issue of coins struck for a variety of non-currency purposes. In Islamic history the striking of coins was a special responsibility and prerogative of the ruler [see SIKKA] together with having his name mentioned in the Friday bidding prayer [see KHUṬBA].

In general, coinage serves two major purposes. Primarily it is a medium of exchange between a government and its people, i.e. to facilitate taxation payments or to support internal and international commerce. Governments therefore generally try to provide coinages of consistent design and quality that will be familiar to their users and thus readily acceptable as legal tender.

Coinage has also traditionally been used for a variety of secondary purposes. Through their very nature coins are precious objects identified with the authority that issued them. Because of its intrinsic metallic value and officially guaranteed prestige, coinage is ideally suited as an outward and tangible sign of royal favour, its distribution being seen as a useful and eagerly-awaited feature of ceremonies of all kinds, both official and private. For a description of when coins might be used on special occasions, see MARĀSIM (official court ceremonies); MAWĀKIB (processions); NITHĀR.

One of the features of *marāsim* were the regular donative payments made to the army, civil service and court officials [see also INʿĀM]. These could take the form of bags of coins given to the troops to recognise their services and ensure their loyalty. Since these were expected to be spent by their recipients, it would be normal for the mint to strike currency coins for this purpose. Donations were regularly provided on the accession of a new sovereign when fresh coins would be issued bearing his name and titles. Moving up in the social hierarchy, however, the emphasis on the receipt of crude cash payments gives way to the desire for donations of a more ceremonial and symbolic nature, which usually involved the striking of specially designed coins. These pieces could take several forms. Some would be larger and heavier than normal, either struck as gold or silver medals of special design and iconography, with arbitrary weights bearing no relation to the standard currency, or as multiple weight dīnārs and dirhams [*q.vv.*] which, more often than not, would bear conventional legends to demonstrate their affinity with the regular coinage. Others would be of normal size and weight, but with special designs and legends which might indicate the purpose for which they were struck. Thirdly, fractional denominations of lighter weight and special design could be issued to display the riches and generosity of the donor to his subjects. The smaller size of these pieces would permit the striking of more coins from a given weight of metal and have the incidental advantage of being less likely to cause injury to those over whom they were thrown or tossed.

As a general rule, far more "souvenir" issues were produced during periods of peace and prosperity than in times of war and economic dislocation. For obvious reasons, relatively few of these special issues have survived from the time in which they were struck. Currency coins were issued in large quantities and held by a great variety of people: soldiers, merchants, townspeople and travellers. Those that have survived were concealed in hoards, either buried in the ground or hidden in the walls of buildings. Those that remained in circulation, however, would, when they became obsolete, be returned to the mint and melted down for conversion into new coin or, as today, sold to scrap metal merchants for conversion into tableware and jewellery. Special coins, *yādgār, danānīr al-ṣila*, i.e. presentation issues, were struck in much smaller quantities and were nearly always saved, but mounted for suspension and converted into jewellery. When they became worn or a better use was found for their metal, they could either be exchanged for current coin, returned to the mint for restriking or sold to a scrap metal dealer.

Thus while numismatists have a clear picture of the history of currency coins in Islam they have only a fragmentary knowledge of presentation issues. Historians mention that coins were given away or scattered on ceremonial occasions, but only rarely make any record of what these pieces actually looked like. As a result, the rôle played by the few survivors in the daily life of the states that struck them can only be guessed at. This is particularly true of issues from the earlier centuries of Islam. Later, when European travellers started to publish their memoirs of the Ottoman, Ṣafawid and Mughal courts, a much clearer pattern emerges. Our understanding of the subject is further enhanced by surviving local histories and court records. Beginning in the 11th/17th century, states began to issue regular ornamental coinages which could be classified as stamped fixed weight ingots. These have largely been employed as an adjunct to domestic saving, an important function that has certainly contributed to the continued striking of gold and silver coins at a time when precious metals have entirely lost their monetary rôle. Thus while court ceremonial has largely disappeared from the Islamic world, commemorative coins and medals continue to play a popular part in daily life. This article cannot accommodate a detailed history of Islamic donative and largesse coinages, but a summary of some of the more interesting issues known from individual dynasties will give a flavour of the subject.

There is little evidence of donative or largesse issues during the Umayyad period. The design of the standard dīnārs and dirhams was invariable and was only very rarely modified. The only variations known have the additional mint name *Maʿdin Amīr al-Muʾminīn* ("Mine of the Commander of the Faithful"), from the years 89, 90 and 91, and *Maʿdin Amīr al-Muʾminīn bi 'l-Ḥidjāz* struck in 105. There has been a good deal of conjecture about these coins, because the extant writings of Islamic historians provide no clues as to their actual place of origin or to their distinctive purpose. It is thought that the metal from which they were struck probably came from the caliphal mines in the Ḥidjāz and that they may have been minted at the site. Michael Bates of the American Numismatic Society has established a die linkage between the 105 A.H. issue and a contemporary coinage struck, presumably, in Dimashk. It is possible that the metal was presented at a special ceremony as tribute to the caliph, who may then have shared the dīnārs among his courtiers.

The first period ʿAbbāsid coinage, struck *ca.* 132-218/750-833, was of largely standard design until the accession of the caliph Hārūn al-Rashīd [*q.v.*] in 170/786. During his reign the earliest special issues began to appear, but all are extremely rare, being known from only one or two examples. They appear to have been associated with events in the caliphal family and may have been used in court ceremonies to mark those events. It was said that gold coins bearing verses and weighing 101 *mithkāls* (*ca.* 429 gr) were struck for Hārūn's *wazīr* Djaʿfar al-Barmakī [see AL-BARĀMIKA], and that 4,000 of them were found in his palace at the time of his downfall. Arab historians have mentioned *danānīr al-ṣila* weighing as much as 1,000 *mithkāls*, but as yet the largest piece actually known is no more than 10 *mithkāls*. It is likely that if these gigantic coins ever did exist they were cast as ingots rather than struck as coins, because the technology of the time did not permit the use of dies large or strong enough for the purpose.

Coinage certainly played a significant rôle in the rivalry between al-Amīn and al-Maʾmūn, and the political messages contained in the legends on the reverse of the dirhams were an important item in the propaganda war between the contending parties. Through his coinage reform in 206/821-2, however, al-Maʾmūn largely put an end to this propaganda activity by ordering the mints to strip all political information from the coin legends.

The second period ʿAbbāsid coinage (*ca.* 218-334/833-946) saw, however, the introduction of a true system of donative coinage which took several forms. The first were standard silver dirhams and gold dīnārs of careful manufacture, whose dies took up the entire face of the blank. The caliph al-Mutawakkil then introduced broad, thin-flan coins, usually struck at his court in Sāmarrāʾ/Surra man raʾā. These bore standard legends, executed in superior calligraphy, struck in the centre of the flans, but leaving a broad empty outer margin. They were probably distributed as special donative payments to troops and civil servants. While their broad outer margins made them easy to convert into jewellery without defacing the legends, their thin flans made them particularly vulnerable to wear and damage. This special medallion style of coinage was widely copied by other dynasties and is frequently found in today's collections.

The next category could be termed the court coinage on which the names and titles of the caliph became the main focus of the legends, with the *kalima*, denomination and date relegated to the single outer margins. The name of the mint usually did not appear, an absence which is not readily explicable. These coins were issued in both gold and silver and were distinguished by calligraphy of the highest quality. The blanks were prepared in a variety of sizes and weights—small and thick, broad and thick or broad and thin—and their weights often varied widely within the same year. It is assumed that these pieces were distributed at important ceremonies in the caliphal court and that they were not intended for circulation.

The third type of donative is the rarest of all. This author knows of only two examples, both of which are more in the nature of family medallions than donative coins. The first is a dirham of al-Mutawakkil with a portrait of a facing male figure on the obverse and the caliph's name in the margin, and on the reverse a camel being led by its driver with the name of the caliph's heir al-Muʿtazz and the date 241. The second is an unpublished type with a man on horseback on the obverse and the name of the caliph al-Muʿtamid in the margin; on the reverse is an elephant with the name of the caliph's son Djaʿfar al-Mufawwaḍ and the date 258 in the margin. These two unique examples cannot conjure up an entire world of private figural medallic coinage struck for the pleasure of the caliphal house, but if further examples come to light a clearer picture of these family commemorative issues should emerge.

A number of exceptional pieces bearing the name of al-Muktadir are known, the most frequently encountered being copies of Hindūshāhī [see HINDŪ-SHĀHĪS] issues. On these, one side shows to the right a horseman riding with the inscription *li 'llāh Djaʿfar* (the caliph's personal name) and on the other a Brahmin bull to the left with *al-Muktadir bi 'llāh* above. Another issue depicts a rabbit within an octagram on both faces. Al-Rāḍī also had a magnificent five-dirham weight silver piece with a handsome cloud-like pattern in the centre of the reverse field.

Very few special issues are known from Spain and North Africa. A magnificent 10-*mithkāl*'s weight dīnār of the Almohad ruler Abū Ḥafṣ ʿUmar was published by Brèthes, a photograph of which appears on the cover of his catalogue, and multiple dīnārs are also known from the time of the Saʿdian Sharīfs. The high standard of coinage design and careful manufacture maintained by the North African dynasties may well have made the regular preparation of medallic issues unnecessary. The Fāṭimids are known to have struck very few special issues, although the quarter dīnārs and one-sixteenth dirhams would have been an ideal size to use as largesse coins.

In the east, the successors to the ʿAbbāsids prepared a series of marvellous gold medals showing figures of men, as well as lions attacking antelopes or birds of prey attacking animals on both obverse and reverse. These were clearly not intended for circulation. This author, however, once saw a 10-*mithkāl*'s weight dīnār of ʿAḍud al-Dawla which was probably used at the time of his coronation in Madīnat al-Salām in 367/977. Many other such pieces may have been struck for court ceremonies, but their identity will be forever hidden because they were probably melted down for other uses in times of financial stringency. Some of the survivors appear to have been strongly influenced by the Būyids' interest in their supposed Sāsānid heritage and depict the ruler in the guise of a Sāsānid monarch. The Būyids Fakhr al-Dawla of Rayy and his successor Madjd al-Dawla also struck handsome epigraphic multiple dirhams on broad thin flans with extended legends in al-Muḥammadiyya (i.e. Rayy) which were probably used as donatives for their troops.

The Great Saldjūḳs Alp Arslan, Malik Shāh and later rulers also struck a number of dīnārs with extended Ḳur'ānic legends inscribed in tiny calligraphy on both faces, probably used as amulets by the pious as they are usually found mounted for suspension. The Istanbul Archaeological Museum possesses a multiple-weight presentation dīnār weighing 30 *mithḳāls* struck by the Rūm Saldjūḳ Kaykhusraw II in Dār al-Mulk Ḳūnya in 635 A.H. The Il-Khānid rulers Maḥmūd Ghazan, Öldjeytü and Abū Sa'īd, issued a variety of multiple-weight gold and silver coins bearing extended legends which could have been used as impressive ornaments. Elsewhere in the east, many other medallic pieces of varying quality bearing symbols of people and/or animals were manufactured for a similar purpose. While the official issues were usually struck, many were cast and still others were light-weight sandwiches of thin uniface flans stuck together to make a showy but inexpensive amulet.

In addition, these dynasties all struck tiny coins, fractions of both the dirham and dīnār, which were used for showering guests at important audiences, or brides at wedding ceremonies, or for presenting to newly-circumcised boys, or for throwing into the crowds of excited spectators watching public audiences or ceremonial processions. In more recent times, the tiny silver *aḳče* [*q.v.*] of the Ottomans was ideally suited for scattering in this way because of its small size and light weight. Specially struck Ottoman presentation coins made a relatively late appearance in the late 11th/17th century when the standard gold coin, the *sulṭānī*, began to be struck on broad thin flans for use as jewellery. Multiple examples of the standard Ottoman gold of the time, but at a slightly lighter weight, were regularly issued by all the later rulers beginning with Süleymān II. Aside from their use as donatives, they were also available for sale to the public in return for the heavier, normal weight coins for conversion into jewellery. This custom became institutionalised during the reign of 'Abd al-Ḥamīd II [*q.v.*], when the imperial mint in Istanbul manufactured the so-called *zīnet altun*. The proceeds from their sale were applied to support the state pension fund, and these ornamented broad-flan coins are still manufactured by the Turkish Republic. In Ottoman Egypt, under the Khedive Ismā'īl Pasha [*q.v.*] the government issued small quantities of 500-piastre presentation gold and regular issues of tiny 10 and 5 *ḳurūsh*/piastre largesse gold and similar 20 and 10 *para* largesse silver coins. These were specifically used to enhance wedding celebrations.

In Ṣafawid and post-Ṣafawid Persia, the distribution of multiple weight gold *tūmāns* [*q.v.*] and silver *shāhīs* [*q.v.*] was a feature of court ceremonies such as the Nawrūz [*q.v.*] celebrations, and they are usually found pierced or mounted for use as jewellery. A very rare insight into the functioning of the Persian treasury came about when Fatḥ 'Alī Shāh Ḳādjār was compelled, under the terms of the Treaty of Türkmen Čay [*q.v.*], to ship an enormous treasure to St. Petersburg. It is said that the Emperor Nicholas I was so interested in the beautiful designs on the coin ingots that made up the shipment that he spared a few sets from re-melting to donate to the Imperial Museums and members of his family. Several examples of these subsequently passed into the public domain. It is clear that the Ḳādjārs, like many other treasuries, would have found it more convenient to retain their bullion in the form of thousands of large coins rather than millions of small ones.

This is particularly borne out when we turn to India, which was famous for the magnificence of its coinage. The Ghūrid conqueror Mu'izz al-Dīn Muḥammad b. Sām, is known to have struck the 10-*mithḳāl* presentation coins in the year 598. His successors in the Sub-continent, the Dihlī Sulṭāns and their contemporaries, also struck the occasional multiple-weight gold and silver tankas. However, it was the Mughals who really transformed their coinage into works of art. The treasury regularly stored its precious metal in the form of gigantic coins, most of which have now perished. Their exotic nature and extreme rarity was emphasised when the largest coin in the world, a giant 1000-tola weight piece which was probably valued at 10,000 silver rupiya, together with the second largest, a 100 mohur, were offered for auction in Geneva in November 1987. (These appeared subsequent to the article MOHUR.) The first was struck by the Emperor Djahāngīr in Āgrā in 1022 A.H. in his eighth regnal year, weighing 11,935.8 gr with a diameter of 210 mm. The second was struck by Shāh Djahān I in Lāhawr in 1048 in his twelfth regnal year weighing 1,094.5 gr with a diameter of 96 mm. The intent behind the striking of this is clearly expressed in its legends: "When Shāh Djahān became ruler of the world in generosity he gave away treasures in a single moment. So that he could bestow one hundred mohurs instead of one, he commanded one hundred mohurs to be made into one mohur." Aside from their use as treasury reserves, they were occasionally brought out to be presented as gifts to members of the royal family, high-ranking courtiers, ambassadors or important visitors from foreign countries. It is likely that financial need on the part of the recipients made them return these coins to the mint to be exchanged for their equivalent value in currency mohurs or rupiya as the need arose. In his first regnal year, the Emperor Djahāngīr defied Islamic convention by striking a mohur bearing a sensitive portrait of his father Akbar in old age, and in his sixth to ninth regnal years he distributed a series of his own portrait mohurs as a special mark of favour to his boon companions. All of these extraordinary coins are described in Hodivala's *Historical studies in Mughal numismatics*. For the use of the specially struck *nithārs* in Mughal India, see NITHĀR. Beginning in the reign of Shāh Djahān I, it became usual to manufacture blanks that were of full weight and standard alloy but smaller than the dies with which they were struck, so that frequently a third or more of the legends were "off flan". The resulting coins did not do justice to the die-sinker's work, but on occasion special efforts were made to cut blanks to their correct size so that they could receive the full impression of the dies. These were known as *nazarāna* mohurs or rupiya. As the Mughal state became poorer, *nazarāna* coins were produced with greater regularity because gigantic coins were no longer given away, and thus the need for low-value donatives increased.

Today the use of coins as regal largesse has virtually died out. The last state to employ them was the Sultanate of ʿUmān, whose rulers, Saʿīd b. Taymūr and Ḳābūs b. Saʿīd regularly had offstrikes of their currency coins struck in gold for distribution to members of their courts. ʿUmān and nearly all other Muslim countries now follow the modern custom of striking a bewildering variety of bullion commemorative coins in both gold and silver. These have largely lost any ceremonial purpose and are sold by their governments as a way of satisfying the ever-present need for modern collector issues. The tradition of private largesse at weddings and other family occasions, however, lives on today in the custom of scattering small coin-like objects over the heads of brides at weddings, pinning bank notes to their dresses, giving gold pieces for engagements and circumcisions and, particularly in Persia, giving presents to children at Nawrūz.

Bibliography: There is no general comprehensive study of donative and largesse coins. For the early period see L. Ilisch's series of four articles on donative coins *Münzgeschenke und Geschenkmünzen in der mittelalterlichen islamischen Welt*, in *Münstersche numismatische Zeitung*, June 1984 (which includes an extensive bibl.), September 1984, December 1984 and April 1985; for North Africa, J.D. Brèthes, *Contribution à l'histoire du Maroc par les recherches numismatiques*, Casablanca 1939; for the Ottomans, N. Pere, *Osmanlılarda madeni paralar*, Istanbul 1968; for the Ṣafawids, H.L. Rabino di Borgomale, ed. M. Mochiri, *Album of coins, medals and seals of the Shahs of Iran (1500-1948)*, Tehran 1974; for the Mughals, S.H. Hodivala, *Historical studies in Mughal numismatics*, Calcutta 1923; for the two large Mughal coins, see Habsburg Feldman S.A., *Sale of two giant gold mohur coins*, Geneva 1987. There are scattered publications that occasionally illustrate presentation coins amongst the great museum catalogues. See S. Lane Poole, *Catalogue of oriental coins in the British Museum*, 10 vols., London 1875-90; H. Lavoix, *Catalogue des monnaies musulmanes de la Bibliothèque Nationale*, 3 vols, reprs. of 1887-96 edition, Bologna 1977, and G. Hennequin, iv, Paris 1985; İ. and C. Artuk, *İstanbul Arkeoloji Müzeleri teşhirdeki islamî sikkeler kataloğu*, 2 vols., Istanbul 1971; N.D. Nicol, R. el-Nabaraway and J.L. Bacharach, *Catalogue of the Islamic coins, glass weights, dies and medals in the Egyptian National Library*, Cairo 1982; M.F. al-ʿUsh, *Arab Islamic coins preserved in the National Museum of Qatar*, i, Doha 1984, and Ibrāhīm Djābir, ii, 1992. For the many recent discoveries, the reader is directed to the coin auction catalogues of Baldwin (London and Dubai), Hess (Lucerne), Bank Leu (Zurich), Münzen und Medaillen (Basel), Peus (Frankfurt), Sotheby's (London) and Spink (London and Zurich). (R.E. DARLEY-DORAN)

YĀDJŪDJ WA-**MĀDJŪDJ**, sc. Gog and Magog, the names of apocalyptic peoples known from biblical (Ezekiel xxxviii, xxxix, Apocalypse, xx. 7-10) and Ḳurʾānic eschatology. Ḳurʾān, XVIII, 93-8, refers to Dhu 'l-Ḳarnayn erecting a barrier/rampart (*sadd/radm*) against them, which, at the end of time, God Himself will raze. Ḳurʾān, XXI, 96, is an apocalyptic metaphor: "Till, when Gog and Magog are unloosed, and they slide down (*yansilūna*) out of every slope" (tr. A.J. Arberry).

Names. The reading *Yādjūdj wa-Mādjūdj* (without *hamza*) was preferred by most of the Ḥidjāzī and ʿIrāḳī *ḳurrāʾ*, while ʿĀṣim [*q.v.*] and al-Aʿradj read *Yaʾdjūdj wa-Maʾdjūdj* (al-Ṭabarī, *Tafsīr*, viii, 279; Ibn Ḥadjar, xvi, 221). The reading *Ādjūdj wa-Mādjūdj* (or *Maʾdjūdj*) is also recorded (al-Zamakhsharī, 498, 584; Fakhr al-Dīn al-Rāzī, iv, 349; Ibn Ḥadjar, *loc. cit.*). This reading bears great resemblance to the Syriac *Agog wa Magog* as found in the Song of Alexander, which in turn renders Hebrew equivalents of *Gog* and *Magog*. Arabic etymology explains the names as *yafʿūl* and *mafʿūl* forms of *adjdja*, lit. "to blaze fiercely", "to be intensive", and also "to make a rustling noise by running", because Yādjūdj and Mādjūdj move so swiftly or powerfully, see e.g. Fakhr al-Dīn al-Rāzī, iv, 349, who gives other explanations as well (Lane, *Lexicon*, s.v. *adjdja*). Others see them as *fāʿūl* forms of *yadjdja* and *madjdja*, with the second component derived from *mādja* "to be agitated with waves" following Ḳurʾān, XVIII, 99: "On that day We shall leave them surging (*yamūdju*) against each other". Still others hold that the names are of non-Arabic (*aʿdjamī*) origin (cf. Jeffery, *Foreign vocabulary*, 288-9). The two names form an onomastic rhymed pair, like Hārūt and Mārūt, Hābīl and Ḳābīl [*q.vv.*] (see also below, and cf. Miquel, *Géographie*, ii, 508).

Origin, number and appearance. The traditions around Yādjūdj and Mādjūdj, as found in the Islamic sources, are very heterogeneous. Sometimes they are considered as children of Adam but not of Eve, for they are said to originate from Adam's nocturnal emission of semen mixed with earth (Kaʿb al-Aḥbār, quoted by Ibn Ḥadjar, xvi, 221). The *Sīrat al-Iskandar* holds that only Yādjūdj descends from Adam, whereas Mādjūdj is an offspring of Eve's menstrual blood (ms. Aya Sofya 4004, fol. 152a). According to Wahb b. Munabbih, they are neither *ins* (human) nor *djinn* (al-Ṭabarī, *Tafsīr*, viii, 280), but other traditions say that they are the offspring of Yaphet (*ibid.*, ix, 83; cf. Gen. x. 2).

Yādjūdj and Mādjūdj are many peoples, each of them counting 400,000 (al-Ṭabarī, *loc. cit.*, ix, 83), or they are nine times as numerous as human beings (*ibid.*, ix, 85), while al-Ḳazwīnī says that only God can count them (*ʿAdjāʾib*, 448). According to Ibn ʿAbbās, five of the six parts (*adjzāʾ*) of the world belong to Yādjūdj and Mādjūdj and only one part to the other beings (*al-khalaf*) (Ibn al-Faḳīh, 300).

Al-Ṭabarī reports that Yādjūdj and Mādjūdj exist in three kinds: the first are as tall as a cedar, the second as broad as they are tall, the third can cover their body with one ear and lie down on the other (*Tafsīr*, viii, 283; cf. al-Ḳazwīnī, *ʿAdjāʾib*, 448). For al-Zamakhsharī there are only two kinds: one extremely tall, the other extremely short, while for al-Ḳazwīnī (*loc. cit.*) they have the stature of a middle-sized man (*radjul marbūʿ*). Al-Ṭabarī also reports that Dhu 'l-Ḳarnayn explored their country and saw that their length is half that of an average man but that males and females are equally tall. Instead of fingernails they have claws, their teeth are like those of predators, their gums are strong as a camel's and they grind their teeth when chewing. They foresee their own death; no male will die before having fathered one thousand children, and no female before having given birth to the same number; they mate like animals. Their food consists of the *tinnīn* [*q.v.*] which in spring falls down from Heaven. If they do not get it, they become barren (al-Ṭabarī, *Tafsīr*, viii, 281 f.; cf. al-Masʿūdī, *Murūdj*, ed. Pellat, i, 144). According to other traditions, they are cannibals (al-Ṭabarī, *Tafsīr*, viii, 279). (For further details on their physique, see Miquel, *Géographie*, ii, 509.) However, Yādjūdj and Mādjūdj are not always represented as fabulous creatures (see below).

Eschatological role. In Islam, their eschatological role is directly connected with the barrier which Dhu 'l-Ḳarnayn/al-Iskandar (Alexander the Great [see AL-KHAḌIR]) erected against them. According to the Ḳur'ān, Yādjūdj and Mādjūdj will be held back by the barrier until the end of time. Their coming is one of the "signs of the Hour" (*āyāt al-sāʿa*, see SĀʿA. 3; for a classification of these signs, esp. that of al-Barzandjī (d. 1103/1691; Brockelmann, S II, 529), see Attema, 164-6; cf. Kaptein, 58, 60). Yādjūdj and Mādjūdj, before Dhu 'l-Ḳarnayn built the barrier, used to come out every spring in order to eat all that is green and to carry away all that is dry (cf. al-Zamakhsharī, 498 ff.). Al-Ṭabarī describes the eschatological scenario as follows: every day Yādjūdj and Mādjūdj scrape the barrier until they can almost see the sun shining through it or, as Kaʿb al-Aḥbār relates, until the sound of their axes can be heard by their neighbours on the other side. When they are about to break through, their foreman tells them to go back and finish the work on the next day. But every night, after they have left, God restores the barrier so that it becomes stronger than it was before. Only when their foreman adds *in shā' allāh*, are they able to dig their way through. In a tradition recorded in Dienné [*q.v.*], *Inshallāh* is a young man who, when his name is pronounced by his father, will eat away what remains of Madjūdjū's barrier (Mommersteeg, *In de stad van de Marabouts*, 87-8). After that, Yādjūdj and Mādjūdj spread over the earth. When on the march, their vanguard is in Syria and their rear in ʿIrāḳ. They cover the earth, eat everything they can find and drink the waters of the Euphrates, the Tigris and the Lake of Tiberias. According to Abū Saʿīd, they also kill human beings. Man and beast take refuge in fortresses. Having reached Jerusalem, they think they have exterminated life on earth. They then shoot arrows against the sky and when these fall back stained with blood, they believe they have destroyed Heaven as well. Then God, at the intercession of Jesus, sends down worms (*naghaf*) which penetrate their noses and ears, come out at their necks and kill them. Their corpses are eaten by the beasts or, according to other traditions, are carried away to the sea by rain which purifies the earth (al-Ṭabarī, *Tafsīr*, viii, 283, 289, ix, 83-5). But according to al-Zamakhsharī, 500, they cannot reach Mecca, Medina and Jerusalem. Al-Ḳazwīnī, *ʿAdjā'ib*, 488, on the other hand, describes "living creatures" (*ḥayawānāt*) who apparently have nothing human about them, who dwell on some mountains near the barrier of al-Iskandar and are short-sized (five spans high), broad-faced, and black skinned with white spots, who climb trees and do not associate with human beings.

The traditions regarding Yādjūdj and Mādjūdj, as found in the canonical *ḥadīth* works, were collected by Attema, 134 ff. He distinguishes three groups: traditions according to which people thought that the Hour was imminent and that Yādjūdj and Mādjūdj had already begun to make a breach in the barrier during the lifetime of the Prophet (al-Bukhārī, 61.25, trad. 27; Muslim, 52.1, 3; al-Tirmidhī, 31.23; Ibn Mādja, 36.9, trad. 3; Abū Dāwūd, 34.1; Aḥmad b. Ḥanbal, ii, 341, 529, vi, 428, 429); traditions which say that Yādjūdj and Mādjūdj were met when the Muslim armies, during the conquests in the east, had come in contact with peoples "with broad faces, small eyes, gray mops, running down from every hill (cf. Ḳur'ān, XXI, 96), their faces like shields covered with leather" (Aḥmad b. Ḥanbal, v, 271; see also below); and traditions according to which Yādjūdj and Mādjūdj are continuously trying to break through the barrier in the way described above (Ibn Mādja, 36.33, trad. 10; Aḥmad b. Ḥanbal, iii, 77).

The eschatological role of Yādjūdj and Mādjūdj in Islam has parallels in Jewish and Christian traditions, cf. Lust in *Bibl.* The Biblical data on Gog and Magog were popular themes in the sermons of the Syrian Christian Church (e.g. Ephrem Syrus, *Hymni*, iii, 194-213). Ps.-Methodios, *Apokalypse*, 14-5, gives a vivid description of these impure and deformed descendants of Yaphet.

Location and identification. The barrier built by Dhu 'l-Ḳarnayn against Yādjūdj and Mādjūdj fills the gap between two mountains (cf. Ḳur'ān, XVIII, 93: *al-saddān*, XVIII, 96: *al-ṣadafān*). Ḳur'ān commentators think that these mountains are those of Armenia and Ādharbāydjān (al-Ṭabarī, *Tafsīr*, viii, 278; al-Bayḍāwī, 573), that they lie between these two regions, or that they are situated in the furthest north (Fakhr al-Dīn al-Rāzī, 348; al-Bayḍāwī, 573) or in the most eastern part of the land of the Turks (al-Ṭabarī, viii, 281). Thus the barrier was located in the Caucasus, in the north in general or in the east. Geographers writing after Ibn Khurradādhbih (see below) concentrate on the far east. Ibn al-Faḳīh, 298, 300, writing in the 3rd/9th century, says that the distance between the land of the Khazar and the place of the barrier is two months, and that Dhu 'l-Ḳarnayn measured the width of the gorge between the two mountains, this being the dividing line between the land of the Turks and the regions to the east of them. According to Ibn Ḥawḳal, 482, Rūs and Khʷārazmian merchants used to import silk and skins from the regions (*nawāḥī*) of Yādjūdj and Mādjūdj (cf. Miquel, *Géographie*, ii, 507). In the traditional division of the world into seven climes [see IḲLĪM], the lands of Yādjūdj and Mādjūdj are located, with variations, between the fifth and seventh climes. In al-Yaʿḳūbī's (d. 284/897) chronicle, they are located in the sixth clime (*Ta'rīkh*, 93). Al-Iṣṭakhrī (d. 339/950), who gives a larger number of climes, says (9) that they are found in a northern direction if one traverses the land between the Saḳāliba [*q.v.*] and the Kīmākiyya [see KIMÄK]. Al-Idrīsī (d. 565/1120) divides the climes into ten parts, the tenth lying in the extreme east of each clime. He charts Dhu 'l-Ḳarnayn's barrier in the ninth part of the sixth clime (*Opus Geographicum*, 934, 938; Idrīsī-Jaubert, 416, 420). It also comprises the land of the Khifshākh [see ḲIPČAḲ] and that of the Türgesh, which has much rain and snow. To the south, according to some geographers, the lands of Yādjūdj and Mādjūdj are adjacent to China [see AL-ṢĪN]. For the differences in view between Ibn Rusta (d. *ca.* 300/ 912-3) and al-Masʿūdī (d. 345/956) on the location of Yādjūdj and Mādjūdj, see *ibid.*, cols. 618b-619a. In the neighbourhood of Yādjūdj and Mādjūdj other peoples are found who are mentioned in the Bible as offspring of Yaphet (Gen. x. 2), namely, Tārīs, Mansak (Manshak, Mashak) and Kumāra (Kumārā) (cf. al-Dīnawarī, *al-Akhbār al-ṭiwāl*, 2; cf. al-Ḳazwīnī, *ʿAdjā'ib*, 448, who mentions only the Mansak).

By an often-used play of words based on Arabic *taraka* "to leave, leave out", the Turks are said to belong to the peoples of Yādjūdj and Mādjūdj. Originally, the latter were twenty-four peoples. When Dhu 'l-Ḳarnayn locked them up behind the barrier, one people were absent and thus were left out (*turika*), either because they were away on a raid (Ibn al-Faḳīh, 299), or because they believed in God (cf. Ibn Hishām, *K. al-Tidjān*, ed. in Lidzbarski, 302). In a tradition transmitted by al-Bukhārī (*K. al-manāḳib*,

61.25), the Turks are explicitly connected with the end of the world: "The Hour will not come before you have fought a people whose footwear is made of hair, and who fought the Turks who have small eyes, a ruddy face (*ḥumr al-wudjūh*), a small and finely chiselled nose (*dhulf al-unūf*), whereas their faces are rough and broad (*ka-anna wudjūhahum al-madjānn*[u] *al-muṭraḳa*; cf. Lane, *Lexicon*, s.v. *ṭrḳ*, 1850, and above). Another frequently reported tradition says that Yādjūdj are Turks and Mādjūdj are Djīl and Daylam (Ibn Ḥadjar, xvi, 221).

The 20th century Indian politician and theologian Abu 'l-Kalām Āzād [see ĀZĀD, in Suppl.] argues that Yādjūdj and Mādjūdj are identical, first, with the Scythians, then with the Huns, and then with the Mongols (*wa-yas'alūnaka ʿan Dhi 'l-Ḳarnayn*, 162-81). This view is elaborated by al-Shāfiʿ al-Māḥī Aḥmad in his recent *Ya'djūdj wa-Ma'djūdj*. Throughout history, the raids of the above-mentioned peoples are recorded as seven "burstings-out" (*khurūdj*) of Yādjūdj and Mādjūdj, perhaps to be followed in the future by an eighth and/or ninth *khurūdj* before their final *khurūdj* at the end of time. At present, Aḥmad maintains, the Chinese part of Mongolia forms the last refuge of Yādjūdj and Mādjūdj. Saʿfān, *al-Sāʿa*, identifies Yādjūdj and Mādjūdj with the Khazar [*q.v.*] who were converted to Judaism, with the Ashkenazi Jews in Eastern Europe and then in Israel, and with the Freemasons [see FARMĀSŪNIYYA, in Suppl.].

Yādjūdj and Mādjūdj in Arabic literature. Arabic poetry and *adab* literature use Yādjūdj and Mādjūdj as a metaphor for great numbers, e.g. "hungry soldiers as numerous as Yādjūdj and Mādjūdj" (al-Farazdaḳ (d. *ca.* 110/728), *Dīwān*, 396, quoted frequently), or for destructive power, e.g. "as if, in wickedness (*fasād*), they were Yādjūdj" (Sibṭ Ibn al-Taʿāwīdhī (d. 584/1188 [*q.v.*]), *Dīwān*, 75). The barrier serves as a metaphor for impenetrability: "If I were to give you a single dirham, I would open a door to my possessions which neither mountains nor sands could dam, even if I were able to build before them a barrier like the barrier of Yādjūdj and Mādjūdj" (al-Djāḥiẓ, *K. al-Bukhalā'*, 208); "O, if only the barrier of Yādjūdj were between you and me" (Abu 'l-ʿAtāhiya (d. 210/825 [*q.v.*]), *Dīwān*, Appx. no. 216, 4). Their lands are the farthermost imaginable place on earth: "Send me to Ḳāf [*q.v.*], and behind the rampart (*radm*), and to the barrier (*sadd*), and to Yādjūdj and Mādjūdj, to a place even Dhu 'l-Ḳarnayn did not reach and al-Khaḍir never knew about" (Abū Ḥayyān al-Tawḥīdī (d. 414/1023 [*q.v.*]), *Baṣā'ir*, iv, 158). The paired names of Yādjūdj and Mādjūdj are the subject of several anecdotes. At a funeral, a stupid person confuses their names with those of Munkar and Nakīr [*q.v.*] (Abū Saʿīd Manṣūr al-Ābī (d. 421/1030: Brockelmann, I, 351), *K. Nathr al-durar*, iv, 284; Abū Isḥāḳ Ibrāhīm al-Ḥuṣrī (d. 413/1022 [*q.v.*]), *Djamʿ al-djawāhir*, 250), or with those of Hārūt and Mārūt (cf. Marzolph, *Arabia ridens*, ii, no. 510). Another confused person insists that "Munkar is better than Nakīr, that Yādjūdj is better than Mādjūdj, and that Hārūt is better than Mārūt" (Abū Ḥayyān al-Tawḥīdī, *op. cit.*, iii, 133). Al-Ḥuṣrī, *Djamʿ al-djawāhir*, 338, reports that a tall man, who was beaten by a short soldier, exclaimed: "I wish you were shorter than Yādjūdj and Mādjūdj". This anecdote refers to a tradition, ascribed to Ibn ʿAbbās, according to which Yādjūdj and Mādjūdj are three spans (*thalāthat ashbār* = 27 inches) tall (Ibn Ḥadjar al-ʿAsḳalānī, *Fatḥ al-bārī*, xvi, 222 l. 19).

Yādjūdj and Mādjūdj play a more prominent role in two early poems, one by Ḥassān b. Thābit (d. 40/659 [*q.v.*]) (ed. ʿArafat, 471-3, tr. Nicholson, 18), and the other by ʿAlḳama b. Dhī Djadan (2nd/8th century) (see on him al-Hamdānī, *Iklīl*, ii, 300-1; Löfgren, *ʿAlqama b. ḏi Ǧadan*). Both describe how al-Iskandar built the barrier (Von Kremer, *Über die südarabische Sage*, 71 ff.; idem, *Altarabische Gedichte*, 16). Yādjūdj and Mādjūdj are also mentioned in an eschatological *urdjūza* [see RADJAZ] by ʿAbd Allāh b. Ru'ba al-ʿAdjdjādj (d. 97/715) (ed. Beirut, 345-6), as well as in several *radjaz* verses by ʿAbd Allāh's son Ru'ba (d. 145/762 [*q.v.*]) (ed. Ahlwardt, nos. 19, 33, 55), in which the coming of Yādjūdj and Mādjūdj is mentioned as an apocalyptical phenomenon, also connected with the peoples of ʿĀd and Tubbaʿ [*q.vv.*].

In the legendary literature on al-Iskandar [see AL-KHAḌIR; ISKANDAR-NĀMA; *Sīrat Iskandar*, in SĪRA SHAʿBIYYA], Yādjūdj and Mādjūdj are in general described along the same lines as in *tafsīr* and *ḥadīth* (see above). A remarkable exception is ms. Aya Sofya 4004, in which Yādjūdj and Mādjūdj appear more humanlike. The storyteller is aware of the fact that the frequent contacts between the "Muslims" and individual "Yādjūdjīs", and the diplomatic exchanges between al-Iskandar and Yādjūdj and Mādjūdj took place during the *millat Ibrāhīm* period, i.e. in pre-Islamic times. The language of Yādjūdj and Mādjūdj, described as "the inaccessible language of the Turks, which is incomprehensible" (*lughat al-Turk al-mughlaḳa wa-hiya lā tufham; ibid.*, fol. 154 l. 2), is translated into Arabic by al-Khaḍir. In this manuscript, the king of Yādjūdj and Mādjūdj is called Ḳānūn, their religion qualified as worship of sun and moon, and their dwelling-place is said to consist of seven *wādī*s. Twice a year they make raids on the neighbouring town of Asāṭīn (fol. 151 l. 3), whose king Watīd Ḳanāṭīr asks al-Iskandar to erect a barrier against them. He only starts doing this after Gabriel has revealed to al-Khaḍir God's eschatological plan concerning Yādjūdj and Mādjūdj.

Bibliography: 1. Primary sources. ʿAbd Allāh b. Ru'ba al-ʿAdjdjādj, *Dīwān, riwāyat ʿAbd al-Malik b. Ḳurayb al-Aṣmaʿī wa-sharḥuhu*, Beirut 1416/1995, 345-6; Ābī, *Nathr al-durr*, ed. M.ʿA. Ḳurna, Cairo 1980-90; Abu 'l-ʿAtāhiya, *Dīwān*, ed. Sh. Fayṣal, Damascus 1965, Appx. no. 216; Barzandji, *al-Ishā'a li-ashrāṭ al-sāʿa* (see Attema, *Voorteekenen*, 3); Bayḍāwī, *Anwār al-tanzīl*, ed. Fleischer, Leipzig 1846-8, ii, 583 ff., 624; Dīnawarī, *al-Akhbār al-ṭiwāl*, Cairo 1960; Djāḥiẓ, *K. al-Bukhalā'*, ed. Ṭ. al-Ḥadjirī, Cairo 1958, 208, 226; idem, *Ḥayawān*, ed. ʿA.M. Hārūn, Cairo 1938-69, i, 189; Ephrem Syrus, *Sancti Ephrem Syri hymni et sermones*, ed. Lamy, ii, 343-426, iii, 133-87, 194-213; Fakhr al-Dīn al-Rāzī, *Mafātīḥ al-ghayb*, Būlāḳ 1279-89/1862-72, iv, 348 ff., 537; Farazdaḳ, *Dīwān*, ed. ʿA.I. al-Ṣāwī, Cairo 1936, 396; Ḥassān b. Thābit, *Dīwān*, ed. Walid N. ʿArafat, London 1971 (cf. Nicholson, *A literary history of the Arabs*, London 1907, 18); *Ḥudūd al-ʿālam*, tr. Minorsky; Ḥuṣrī, *K. Djamʿ al-djawāhir fi 'l-mulaḥ wa 'l-nawādir*, ed. ʿA.M. al-Bidjāwī, Cairo 1953, 80, 240, 250, 338; Ibn al-Djawzī, *Tanwīr al-ghabash fī faḍl al-sūdān wa 'l-ḥabash*. ms. Gotha (*Cat. Pertsch*, iii, no. 1692) fols. 24a-26a; idem, *Akhbār al-ḥamḳā wa 'l-mughaffalīn*, Beirut n.d., 91, 168; Ibn al-Faḳīh, 298-301; Ibn Ḥadjar al-ʿAsḳalānī, *Fatḥ al-bārī*, Cairo 1379-83/1959-63; Ibn Hishām, *K. al-Tīdjān* (see M. Lidzbarski, *De propheticis, quae dicuntur, legendis arabicis*, Leipzig 1893); T. Nagel, *Alexander der Grosse in der frühislamischen Volksliteratur*, Walldorf-Hessen 1978; Ibn Ḳutayba, *ʿUyūn al-akhbār*, Cairo 1925-30, iii, 240; Ḳazwīnī, *K. ʿAdjā'ib al-makhlūḳāt*, ed. Wüstenfeld,

Göttingen 1849; A. von Kremer, *Altarabische Gedichte ueber die Volkssage von Jemen als Textbelege zur Abhandlung "Ueber die südarabische Sage"*, Leipzig 1867; Mas'ūdī, *Murūdj*, ed. Pellat, i, 144; Ps.-Methodius, *Die Apokalypse des Pseudo-Methodios*, ed. A. Lolos, Meisenheim am Glan 1976 (Beiträge zur klassischen Philologie, 83); Muḳaddasī, 362-5; Nuwayrī, *Nihāyat al-arab*, Cairo 1347/1928-9, i, 374, iv, 17; Ru'ba b. al-'Adjdjādj, ed. W. Ahlwardt, Berlin 1903, nos. 19, 33, 51; Sibṭ Ibn al-Ta'āwīdhī, *Dīwān*, ed. D.S. Margoliouth, Cairo 1903, 75; Ṭabarī, *Tafsīr*, Beirut 1412/1992; Tawḥīdī, *K. al-Baṣā'ir wa 'l-dhakhā'ir*, ed. W. al-Ḳāḍī, Beirut 1408/1988, iii, 133, iv, 158, vii, 112; Ya'ḳūbī; Zamakhsharī, *Kashshāf*, ed. Nassau Lees, Calcutta 1856.

2. Secondary sources. Abu 'l-Kalām Āzād, *Wa-yas'alūnaka 'an Dhi 'l-Karnayn*, Cairo n.d. [1972], 162-81; al-Shāfi' al-Māḥī Aḥmad, *Ya'djūdj wa-Ma'djūdj: fitnat al-māḍī wa 'l-ḥāḍir wa 'l-mustaḳbal*, Beirut 1416/1996; D.S. Attema, *De Mohammedaansche opvattingen omtrent het tijdstip van den jongsten dag en zijn voorteekenen*, Amsterdam 1942; A. Jeffery, *The foreign vocabulary of the Quran*, Baroda 1938, 288-9; L. Kaptein, *Eindtijd en Antichrist (ad-Dağğāl) in de Islam. Eschatologie bij Ahmed Bīcān (ca. 1466)*, Leiden 1997; von Kremer, *Über die südarabische Sage*, Leipzig 1866; Lidzbarski, *Zu den arabischen Alexandergeschichten*, in *ZA*, viii (1893), 263-78; O. Löfgren, *'Alqama Ibn dī Ğazan und seine Dichtung nach der Iklīl-Auswahl in der Bibliotheca Ambrosiana*, in *al-Hudhud, Festschrift Maria Höfner*, ed. Roswitha G. Stiegner, Graz 1981, 199-209; J. Lust, *Gog, Magog*, in *Dictionary of Deities and Demons in the Bible*, Leiden 1995; U. Marzolph, *Arabia ridens*, Frankfurt/Main 1992; G. Mommersteeg, *In de stad van de Marabouts*, Amsterdam 1998; Th. Nöldeke, *Beiträge zur Geschichte des Alexanderromans*, in *Denkschriften der Kaiserl. Akad der Wiss. zu Wien*, Phil.-hist. Kl., Abh. V, 38 (1890), 1-56; Kāmil Sa'fān, *al-Sā'a al-khāmisa wa 'l-ishrūn: al-Masīḥ, al-Dadjdjāl, Ya'djūdj wa-Ma'djūdj, al-Mahdī al-muntaẓar*, Cairo 1415/1995; 'Ukāsha 'Abd al-Mannān al-Ṭībī, *Ya'djūdj wa-Ma'djūdj: ṣifatuhum wa-'adaduhum wa-makānuhum wa-ḳiṣṣat Dhi 'l-Karnayn ma'ahum*, Cairo 1410/1989-90; A.J. Wensinck, *Ya'djūdj wa-Ma'djūdj* in *EI*[1]; idem, *Handbook*, s.v. Yādjūdj and Mādjūdj. We wish to thank Kathrin Müller, Munich, for references provided, and Faustina Doufikar-Aerts, Hilversum/Leiden, who generously put at our disposal copies of manuscripts of the *Sīrat Iskandar*, to appear as part of her Ph.D. thesis.

(E. VAN DONZEL and CLAUDIA OTT)

YĀFĀ, YĀFA, conventionally Jaffa, older Joppa, a port on the Palestinian seaboard, in pre-modern times the port of entry for Jerusalem, since 1950 part of the municipality of Tel Aviv-Yafo in the State of Israel (lat. 32° 05' N., long. 34° 46' E.).

Situated on a 30 m/100 feet-high promontory on the otherwise straight coastline of central Palestine, Jaffa is a very ancient town. Thutmosis III's forces seized the Canaanite town of *Y-pw* in the 15th century B.C. and it became a provincial capital during the Egyptian New Kingdom; since the 1950s, archaeological excavations have revealed the monumental gateway of the Egyptian citadel. It passed to the Philistines, and appears in Phoenician texts as *Y.p.y.* Jaffa was the port of entry for the timber floated down from Tyre by king Aḥiram for Solomon to use for the Temple in Jerusalem (II Chron. ii. 16). The Apostle Peter stayed at Jaffa in the house of Simon the Tanner (Acts ix. 42), but in Roman times its value as a port declined in favour of Caesarea. In Byzantine times, Ἰόπη or Ἰόππη was the seat of a bishopric.

In the year 15/636 'Amr b. al-'Āṣī (according to others, Mu'āwiya) took the town (al-Balādhurī, *Futūḥ*, 138). The importance of the old port for Jerusalem further increased when the Umayyad Sulaymān b. 'Abd al-Malik founded the new capital of *Djund Filasṭīn*, al-Ramla [*q.v.*], some 14 miles south-east of Yāfā. Yāfā, with the rest of Filasṭīn, passed in 264/878 into the hands of Aḥmad b. Ṭūlūn [*q.v.*] and remained under the rule of the Ṭūlūnids of Egypt until in 292/905 it passed to the 'Abbāsid caliph al-Muktafī. After Dja'far b. Fallāḥ had conquered Syria for the Fāṭimid al-Mu'izz [*q.v.*] in 359/969, the Ḳarmaṭians penetrated in 360/971 under Ḥasan al-A'ṣam as far as Yāfā, inside which the troops (11,000 men) sent to Syria by Djawhar b. 'Abd Allāh were blockaded. After the Ḳarmaṭians had been driven out of Egypt in 362, Yāfā was relieved and the garrison brought back to Egypt. The Turkish *amīr* Atsiz b. Abaḳ took al-Ramla in 463/1071, but Yāfā and 'Asḳalān did not come into his power.

The possession of the town was hotly disputed during the Crusades. The Franks, who made it a vassal duchy of the kingdom of Jerusalem, were able to hold it until the Third Crusade (1099-1187). The Fāṭimid vizier al-Afḍal sought in vain to take it from them in 1101, 1105, 1113 and 1115. After his murder, the caliph al-Āmir besieged the town in 1122 but was driven back, and again in 1123 as a result of the destruction of his fleet by the Venetians. After the battle of Ḥaṭṭīn (583/1187 [see ḤIṬṬĪN]) most of the coast towns surrendered to Ṣalāḥ al-Dīn, and Yāfā to his brother al-Malik al-'Ādil. Richard Coeur-de-Lion recaptured it for the Crusaders in 587/1191. Ṣalāḥ al-Dīn besieged it in 1192 and regained it for the Saracens; he could not, however, take the citadel, and Richard, who hurried to the help of its garrison, drove the Ayyūbid troops out of the town and refortified it. At the truce of al-Ramla, the Christians were confirmed in possession of Yāfā.

By 593/1197, however, al-Malik al-'Ādil had again taken Yāfā, destroying the fortifications and, it is said, killing 20,000 Christians in the fighting. In the following year, Saxon and Brabantine troops temporarily occupied the town, but abandoned it again in 595/1199, whereupon al-'Ādil regained it by a coup-de-main. After the Fourth Crusade (1204), the town was again in the hands of the Franks. The Emperor Frederick II restored the fortifications in 1228, as did Louis IX in 1250 after his release.

In the Mamlūk period, Yāfā belonged to the district of al-Ramla, one of the four districts of the coast, which were part of the *mamlaka* of Dimashḳ; for a time, however (under Ṣalāḥ al-Dīn's successors), it was under that of Ghazza (al-Dimashḳī, ed. Mehren, 230).

The Mamlūk sultan Baybars attacked the town unexpectedly on 20 Djumādā II 666/8 March 1268, and took it and its citadel in one or two days (inscription on the White Mosque at Ramla, ed. van Berchem, *Inscriptions Arabes de Syrie*, Cairo 1897, 57-64). He destroyed the town with all its houses, walls and the citadel. A certain *amīr* Djamāl al-Dīn ... b. Isḥāḳ, according to an inscription preserved in Yāfā, built there in 736/1335 the sanctuary of Ḳubbat Shaykh Murād which is still in existence (Clermont-Ganneau, *Matériaux inédits pour servir à l'histoire des Croisades*, Paris 1876; idem, *Archæological researches in Palestine during the years 1873-1894*, ii, London 1896, 154). When the kings of England and France were planning a new crusade in 1336, al-Nāṣir had the harbour of Yāfā destroyed to make it impossible for the Franks to land there. For the same reason, the town as well as the harbour, was destroyed in 746/1345 (Tolkowsky, in *Journ. Pal. Orient. Soc.*, v [1925], 82-4).

The Arab geographers describe Yāfā as a small, strongly fortified coast town which, as the port of Jerusalem and al-Ramla, enjoyed thriving trade and busy markets in times of peace. In times of war it was greatly exposed to enemy raids, in the first centuries of Islam, for example, to attacks by the Byzantine fleet, the Mardaites and the Cibyrraiotes. To protect the coast against these raids, watch-towers (*ribāṭ* [*q.v.*]) were built, like those of Byzantium from Lu'lu'a to Constantinople, from which was signalled, by smoke or fire to the capital al-Ramla, the approach of Byzantine ships, which also used to visit the ports from G̲h̲azza to Arsūf to ransom prisoners (al-Muḳaddasī, 177).

After the battle of Mard̲j̲ Dābiḳ [*q.v.*] in 922/1516, the whole of Syria passed to the Ottomans. Yāfā, which was in ruins, only began to revive gradually in the second half of the 17th century, especially after its quays were built. From 1770 onwards, the Pas̲h̲a of Dimas̲h̲ḳ fought for several years with ʿAlī Bey and his followers for the town, in which the Mamlūks perpetrated a frightful massacre on 19 May 1776. The French behaved even worse after the capture of the town by Napoleon (6 March 1799); 4,000 prisoners were shot on the shore. Immediately after the entry of the garrison, plague broke out in the French army which suffered heavily. Ibrāhīm Pas̲h̲a, son of Meḥemmed ʿAlī, occupied Yāfā in 1831, which reverted to the Turks in 1840. An earthquake in 1838 destroyed many houses and a portion of the defences.

Jaffa was always the port of entry for Christian pilgrims to Jerusalem, and it had many hospices to accommodate the new arrivals. In the late 19th century, two colonies of the Protestant German Tempelgesellschaft from Württemburg were founded at Wilhelma and Sarona to the north of Jaffa (1870-1), whilst there were Jewish agricultural colonies to its south. Under a concession from the Ottomans, in 1890-2 a metre-gauge railway was constructed by a French company from Jaffa to Lydda and Jerusalem (widened to standard-gauge by the British authorities after the occupation of 1917 and after). In 1909 the Jewish garden suburb of Tel Aviv ("Hill of Spring") was founded adjacent to Jaffa. During the First World War, the Ottomans deported the whole population of Jaffa-Tel Aviv out of fear that they would help advancing Allied troops; but the British forces of General Allenby entered Jaffa unopposed on 16 November 1917, and the population gradually returned thereafter. Anti-Jewish riots broke out at Jaffa in May 1921, the most serious of these in the early years of the British Mandate of Palestine [see MANDATES], and soon afterwards, Tel Aviv was separated from Jaffa with its own municipal status.

In the inter-war period, the port of Jaffa was adversely affected by the development of that of Haifa [see ḤAYFĀ] (1933) and further declined after the Arab political strike of 1936 closed it for almost a year, during which goods for Tel Aviv began to be landed by lighter. The better-off Jewish population began to move into Tel Aviv, leaving Jaffa with a poorer, predominantly Arab population. After 1948, almost the entire Arab element, which in 1941 had numbered 62,000, fled, and the largely deserted town was two years later incorporated into the municipality of Tel Aviv-Yafo in Israel. The decayed and inadequate port of Jaffa was shut down in 1965, superseded by the modern port of Ashdod further south. Tel Aviv-Yafo now has a population (1994 estimate) of 355,200.

Bibliography: 1. The older period. *PW*, ix, cols. 1901-2 (Beer); F. Buhl, *Die alter Geographie Palästinas*, Grundriss der theol. Wissenschaften, Reihe 2, Bd. 4, Freiburg-Leipzig 1896; Sir George Adam Smith, *The historical geography of the Holy Land*, [20]London n.d. (orig. publ. 1894), 136-8, 141-2; P. Thomsen, *Loca sancta*, Halle 1907, i, 73.

2. The Islamic and modern periods. For the information of the Arabic geographers, see Le Strange, *Palestine under the Moslems*, London 1890, 28-9, 39, 41, 551, and A.-S. Marmardji, *Textes géographiques arabes sur la Palestine*, Paris 1951, 7, 103, 106, 160, 206-7, to which should be added K̲h̲ʷārazmī, *K. Ṣūrat al-arḍ*, ed. H. von Mzik, in *Bibl. arab. Historikern und Geographen*, iii, Leipzig 1926, 19 no. 251, and Suhrāb/Ibn Serapion, in *ibid.*, v, Leipzig 1930, 27 no. 221. See also R. Hartmann, *Palästina unter den Arabern*, Leipzig 1915; M. Gaudefroy-Demombynes, *La Syrie à l'époque des Mamelouks*, Paris 1923, p. CV, 10 n. 1, 29, 56-7; L. Tolkowsky, *The gateway of Palestine, a history of Jaffa*, London 1924; idem, in *Jnal. Palestine Oriental Soc.*, v (1925), 82-4; H.C. Luke and E. Keith-Roach, *The handbook of Palestine and Trans-Jordan*, London 1930, 38, 114-15, 281-2, 285-7; Naval Intelligence Division. Admiralty Handbooks, *Palestine and Transjordan*, London 1943, 307-11, 341-2, 346, 357-8 and index; Moshe Gil, *A history of Palestine*, Cambridge 1992, index.

(F. BUHL-[C.E. BOSWORTH])

YĀFIʿ, an ancient and important collection of tribes of the Yemen who established themselves in the lofty mountain ranges in Sarw Ḥimyar to the north and north-east of Aden [see ʿADAN], about 120 km/75 miles distant.

Yāfiʿ is divided into the Upper and Lower Sultanates (see map of Serjeant, in *Yāfiʿ*, 84), with al-Maḥd̲j̲aba the capital of the former and al-Ḳāra, the old capital of the sultans of the Banū Ḳāsid, that of the latter. The former has five tribes: Kaladī, Saʿdī, Yazīdī, Yaharī and Nāk̲h̲ibī. The latter also has five: Muflaḥī, Mawsaṭī, Ẓabī, Buʿsī and Ḥaḍramī.

They were certainly pre-Islamic in origin and the Old South Arabian inscription *RES* 4613 contains the form *yfʿm*. The Yāfiʿ, who were agriculturalists and figure prominently as mercenaries, are mentioned also in the 4th/10th-century *Ṣifat D̲j̲azīrat al-ʿArab* of al-Hamdānī (ed. Müller, 89, 95, 98). Inhabiting such inaccessible country, the Yāfiʿ were seldom completely controlled by any central authority. They served the Rasūlids [*q.v.*] as mercenaries, though they did not pay them taxes (Serjeant, *Yāfiʿ*, 83). They travelled in numbers to Ḥaḍramawt [*q.v.*] in the 11th-12th/17th-18th centuries, originally as mercenaries, although they eventually wielded some independent power there. Indeed, in the early 12th/18th century rival contestants for the Kat̲h̲īrī sultanate in Ḥaḍramawt called in Yāfiʿ tribesmen to assist them. Many were employed in the same way in India also, notably in Ḥaydarābād. In 1903, the British Government of India entered into a series of treaties with various sections of the Yāfiʿ in exchange for stipends (*Arab tribes*, 205-15), although it was reported in 1909 (*ibid.*, 63) that the Aden Residency had little contact with Upper Yāfiʿ. It was only after the Second World War that the government in Aden was able to develop their relations with the Yāfiʿ, and then almost exclusively with the Lower Yāfiʿ, some of whose territory was in the fertile cotton-growing area of Abyan [*q.v.*] and whose sultanate later became a member state of the Federation of South Arabia.

Bibliography: See also Government of Bombay, *An account of the Arab tribes in the vicinity of Aden*, Bombay 1909, 63-73, 205-15; R.B. Serjeant, *Yāfiʿ, Zaydīs, Āl Bū Bakr b. Sālim and others: tribes and sayyids*, in *On both sides of al-Mandab. Ethiopian, South-Arabic and Islamic studies presented to Oscar Löfgren on his ninetieth birthday 13 May 1988 by colleagues and friends*, Stockholm 1989, 83-105 (contains full references).

(G.R. Smith)

al-**YĀFIʿĪ**, Abū ʿAbd Allāh b. Asʿad, Abu 'l-Saʿāda ʿAfīf al-Dīn (b. in Yemen *ca.* 698/1298, d. at Mecca 768/1367), scholar and Ṣūfī. His father, impressed by his son's intellectual and spiritual precociousness, sent him to study at Aden. After his first Pilgrimage in 712/1313, he returned to Yemen, taking up life as an ascetic and anchorite and becoming a disciple of the Ṣūfī master ʿAlī al-Ṭawās͟hī, to whom he remained close until the latter's death. In 718/1319 he moved to Mecca and completed his education in the Islamic sciences with the judge there, Raḍī al-Dīn al-Ṭabarī. Renouncing a marriage he had made, he went to live as an ascetic by the two *ḥarams* of Mecca and Medina. In 734/1335 he travelled to Palestine and Egypt, meeting there famed local Ṣūfīs.

He himself was mainly affiliated to the Ḳādiriyya [*q.v.*], of which he founded a branch, the Yāfiʿiyya, still existing in Yemen today (J.S. Trimingham, *The Sufi orders*, Oxford 1971, 273). He also received initiation into the Adhamiyya (al-Zabīdī, *Itḥāf al-aṣfiyāʾ*, ms. from 1329/1911, private coll., fol. 5; Massignon, *La passion de Ḥallâj*, ²Paris 1975, i, 85), but his relations with the S͟hādhiliyya are problematical (A. ʿAmmār, *Abu 'l-Ḥasan al-S͟hādhilī*, Cairo 1952, ii, 185-7).

When he was travelling in the Near East, his fame was already great since the sources indicate that he tried to keep himself incognito in Egypt. He acquired great prestige at Mecca, where he settled on his return and remarried. He was sought out for his knowledge but above all for his spiritual direction; among his many disciples were S͟hāh Niʿmat Allāh (d. 834/1431) (see T. Graham, *S͟hāh Niʿmatullāh Walī, founder of the Niʿmatullāhī Sufi order*, in L. Lewisohn (ed.), *The legacy of mediaeval Persian Sufism*, London-New York 1992, 173-4; and niʿmat-allāhiyya). Although he lived in penury, his *baraka* was sought, and he seems to have acted as an arbiter in Mecca on several occasions. He made only one brief further trip to Yemen in 738/1337 to see his master al-Ṭawās͟hī, and died at Mecca on 20 D̲j̲umādā II 768/22 February 1367. His aura of sanctity was such that his modest clothes were sold as relics (al-Isnawī, *Ṭabaḳāt al-s͟hāfiʿiyya*, Bag͟hdād 1391/1971, ii, 582).

As an *ʿālim*, al-Yāfiʿī above all taught *ḥadīt͟h*. As a fervent As͟hʿarī, he combatted both Muʿtazilī rationalism and Ibn Taymiyya's anthropomorphism (his main polemical and apologetic work was *Marham al-ʿilal al-muʿḍila fi 'l-radd ʿalā aʾimmat al-muʿtazila*, Calcutta 1910). He well embodied the ideal of the scholar-Ṣūfī, so prized in mediaeval Islam, and was described by al-S͟hard̲j̲ī as "master of the two ways" (sc. exoteric and esoteric). Like al-Suyūṭī, who often cited him, al-Yāfiʿī used his fame for mounting a defence of Ṣūfism, seen in his best-known works: *Nas͟hr al-maḥāsin al-g͟hāliya fī faḍl al-mas͟hāyik͟h al-ṣūfiyya* (Cairo 1961), and above all, his *Rawḍ al-rayāḥīn fī ḥikāyāt al-ṣāliḥīn* (many eds., inc. Cairo 1989, and Cyprus n.d.), which give edifying stories of the saints whilst including the doctrinal elements belonging to Ṣūfism. The *Rawḍ* was much used by later authors writing on stories of the saints. In the field of hagiography, he wrote an *Asnā al-mafāk͟hir fī manāḳib al-s͟hayk͟h ʿAbd al-Ḳādir [al-D̲j̲īlānī]*. He also courageously upheld the sanctity of al-Ḥallād̲j̲ and Ibn al-ʿArabī (al-Suyūṭī, *Taʾyīd*, 71; Massignon, *op. cit.*, ii, 41, 46, 309-10), and it was not surprising that his disciple S͟hāh Niʿmat Allāh should translate into Persian and write commentaries on the works of Ibn al-ʿArabī.

It would be an abuse of language to call al-Yāfiʿī an historian, since his *Mirʾāt al-d̲j̲anān wa-ʿibrat al-yaḳẓān* (Ḥaydarābād 1339/1920) is mainly a compilation drawn from Ibn al-At͟hīr, Ibn K͟hallikān and al-D͟hahabī. He wrote many mystical poems (especially on the Prophet, whom he claimed often to see in dreams or in night vigils), but very few of these have been published.

Bibliography: The work of al-Isnawī (d. 772/1370) cited above is the essential source on al-Yāfiʿī's life; all later authors draw on it. There are, however, original items in Taḳī al-Dīn al-Fāsī, *al-ʿIḳd al-t͟hamīn*, Cairo 1966, v, 104-15 and Ibn Ḥad̲j̲ar, *al-Durar al-kāmina*, Beirut n.d., ii, 247-9. Al-S͟hard̲j̲ī's notice of him, in *Ṭabaḳāt al-k͟hawāṣṣ*, Cairo 1321/1903, 67, is hagiographical. See also Subkī, *Ṭabaḳāt al-s͟hāfiʿiyya al-kubrā*, Cairo 1964, x, 33; Ibn al-Mulaḳḳin, *Ṭabaḳāt al-awliyāʾ*, Beirut 1986, 555-6; Brockelmann, ²II, 226-8, S II, 227-8.

(E. Geoffroy)

YĀFIT͟H, the Japheth of the Bible.

He is not mentioned by name in the Ḳurʾān (although he is alluded to in VII, 64, X, 73, XI, 40, XXIII, 27 and XXVI, 119), but the exegetes are familiar with all the sons of Noah [see nūḥ]: Ḥām, Sām [*q.vv.*] and Yāfit͟h (the pronunciation Yāfit is mentioned as possible in al-Ṭabarī, i, 222). The Biblical story (Gen. ix. 20-7) of Ḥām's sin and punishment and the blessing given to Sām and Yāfit͟h is known in Muslim legend, but it is silent about Noah's planting the vine and becoming intoxicated. Al-Kisāʾī totally transforms the story: in the Ark, Noah could not sleep from anxiety, so when he came out of the boat, he fell asleep on Sām's chest. The wind revealed his nakedness, Sām and Yāfit͟h covered him up and Ḥām laughed so loudly that Nūḥ was awakened. As a result, he uttered the following curse: prophets shall be born descendants of Sām, kings and heroes of Yāfit͟h and black slaves of Ḥām. However, Ḥām's descendants intermarried with Yāfit͟h's family such that the Abyssinians, Hind and Sind were born to Kūs͟h b. Ḥām, and the Copts were the descendants of a union between Ḳūt b. Ḥām and a descendant of Yāfit͟h.

Yāfit͟h's descendants are variously given, sometimes according to the biblical tradition (al-Ṭabarī, i, 217), sometimes with variations (al-Kisāʾī, i, 101). He is usually regarded as the ancestor of Yād̲j̲ūd̲j̲ and Mād̲j̲ūd̲j̲ [*q.v.*] often of the Turks and the K͟hazars, more rarely of the Slavs [see ṣaḳāliba]. Persia and Rūm are sometimes traced to Sām but sometimes to Yāfit͟h. To Yāfit͟h is also attributed Cyrus, who killed Belshazzar, son of Evilmerodach, son of Nebuchadnezzar, and Yazdagird. In sum, Sām is the father of the Arabs, Yāfit͟h of Rūm, and Ḥām of the Sūdān. Of the three, the Semitic tradition naturally prefers Sām. Yāfit͟h is only rarely spoken of unfavourably, as he is in the case of al-Ṭabarī, i, 223, where we are told nothing good comes from Yāfit͟h and his descendants are deformed. On the other hand, the 72 languages of the world are divided as follows: 18 to Sām, 18 to Ḥām and 36 to Yāfit͟h. He is the blessed son of Noah.

Bibliography: Ṭabarī, i, 211-25, Eng. tr. W.M. Brinner, *The History of al-Ṭabarī. Prophets and patriarchs*, Albany 1987, 10-22; T͟haʿlabī, *Ḳiṣaṣ al-anbiyāʾ*, Cairo 1325, 38; Kisāʾī, *Ḳiṣaṣ al-anbiyāʾ*, ed. Eisenberg,

Leiden 1922, i, 98-102, Eng. tr. W.M. Thackston, Jr., *The Tales of the Prophets of al-Kisaʾi*, Boston 1978, 105-8. (B. Heller-[A. Rippin])

YAʿFURIDS [see yuʿfirids].

YĀGHISTĀN (p.), lit. "the land of the rebels", (*yāghī* "rebel", *istān* "region") referred to different sanctuaries used by Mudjāhidūn [see mudjāhid] against the British authorities in the 19th and early 20th centuries, in the various independent tribal areas, mainly inhabited by the Pakhtūns, in the hinterland of what became the North-West Frontier Province (NWFP) of British India such as the Mohmand Agency, Bunēr, Dīr, Swāt, Kohistān, Hazāra and Čamarkand (extending into the Kunār province of Afghānistān and Badjawr in NWFP). A popular term rather than a formally recognised one, the name was in use long before the British colonial period, historically referred to as Yāghistān al-ķadīm, and sometimes as Riyāsat-hāʾi-Yāghistān.

Though Yāghistān comprised mainly mountainous terrain, the Mudjāhidūn carefully selected their centres around fertile valleys, lakes and rivers in order to be self-reliant as regards agricultural products and to find hideouts to support their guerilla warfare. With the rise of Muslim resistance, first to Sikh rule in Pandjāb and Kashmīr and then to the gradual British colonial expansion in South Asia, the Mudjāhidūn from different regions started gathering in Yāghistān. In spite of their initial success under the charismatic leadership of Sayyid Aḥmad Brēlwī [*q.v.*], the movement suffered a setback at Bālākōt on 6 May 1831 in which Aḥmad Brēlwī and most of his companions were killed by the Sikhs. During the first Afghan-British war (1839-42), the Mudjāhidūn leader Mawlawī Naṣīr al-Dīn sided with Dūst Muḥammad [*q.v.*] by sending a contingent of fighters from Yāghistān to Kābul and Ghazna. After him, the leadership of the Mudjāhidūn gradually passed first to Mawlānā Wilāyat ʿAlī (d. 1852) and then to his younger brother Mawlānā ʿInāyat ʿAlī (1858). Through an effective network of devotees, which extended as far as Bengal, the Mudjāhidūn regularly received fresh recruits, money and moral support in their frequently-changing centres in Yāghistān, such as Sitāna, Mulka and Ambīla. The Yāghistānī Mudjāhidūn always kept in close contact with their supporters, and at times used secret messages in code. Though most of the *djihād* centres in Yāghistān were attacked and destroyed by British Indian forces during the second half of the 19th century, the resistance of the Mudjāhidūn continued under such leaders as Nadjm al-Dīn Hadda Mullā (d. 1902) and Saʿd Allah Khān Mullā Mastān (branded as the Mad Mulla by his opponents; d. 1916).

In 1902, the Mudjāhidūn leader ʿAbd al-Karīm b. Wilāyat ʿAlī chose Asmast in Bunēr near Swāt valley as his headquarters. During the First World War, a rival centre slowly grew up and prospered in the Afghān part of Čamarkand, where leaders such as Mawlāna Muḥammad ʿAlī Ķaṣūrī (see his *Mushāhidāt-i-Kābul wa Yāghistān*, Lahore 1986), Mawlawī ʿAbd al-Karīm Ķannawdjī (d. 1922), Mawlawī Muḥammad Bashīr (d. 1934), Ḥādjdjī Tarangzaʾī (d. 1937) and Mawlawī Faḍl Ilāhī Wazīrābādī (d. 1951; see his *Kawāʾif-i Yāghistān*, Gujranwala 1981) led a number of skirmishes against the imperial army in Shabķadar, Čakda, Mohmand Agency and many other places in NWFP. At times, the Yāghistānī Mudjāhidūn also developed alliances with a number of other anti-colonial movements such as Ḥizb Allāh, Djunūd Rabbāniyya, Ḥukūmat-i Muwaķķata-yi Hind and Djamʿiyyat al-Anṣār.

With the independence of Pakistan in 1947, Yāghistān gradually became part of the historical past. The original Djihād movement also lost its impetus, although the independent character of certain Pakhtūn tribes (e.g. the Afrīdīs) and their systems (e.g. the *djirga* [*q.v.*, in Suppl.]) in these areas is still recognised by Pakistan. Many tribal Mudjāhidūn and the activists of the Djihād movement took part in the struggle of the Kashmīrī Muslims against India in 1948 and thereafter, and subsequently in the popular Afghān uprising against the Soviet Russian-supported communist régime in Kābul in the 1980s.

Bibliography: Col. J. Adye, *Sitana: a mountain campaign on the borders of Afghanistan*, London 1867; Muin-ud-Din Ahmad Khan, Sayyid Muḥammad ʿAlī, *Makhzan-i Aḥmadī*, Agra 1881; *Selections from Bengal Government records on Wahhabi trials (1863-1870)*, Dacca 1961; Mawlānā ʿUbayd Allāh Sindhī, *Sargudhasht-i Kābul*, Islamabad 1980; Muḥammad Khawāṣṣ Khān, *Rūʾīdād-i Mudjāhidīn-i Hind*, Lahore 1983; Qeyamuddin Ahmad, *The Wahhabi movement in India*, New Delhi 1994; Asadullah Al-Ghalib, *Ahl al-Ḥadīth Andolon*, Rajshahi 1996.

(Mohammad Yusuf Siddiq)

YAGHMA, in Arabic orthography Yaghmā, a Turkish tribe of Central Asia mentioned in accounts of the early Turks and their component tribal groups. P. Pelliot thought that the Chinese *Yang-mo* presupposed a nasalised form **Yangma* (*Notes sur le "Turkestan" de M.W. Barthold*, in *T'oung-Pao*, xxvii [1930], 17).

There are sections on the Yaghma in *Ḥudūd al-ʿālam*, tr. 95-6 § 13, cf. comm. 277-81, and Gardīzī, *Zayn al-akhbār*, ed. Ḥabībī, Tehran 1347/1968, 260. Abū Dulaf does not mention them by name in his *First Risāla*, but Marquart thought that his Bughrādj tribe referred to the Yaghma and that his mention of the place al-Khargāh (lit. "tent" = Ordu-kand "army camp") referred to their centre of Kāshghar (cf. A. von Rohr-Sauer, *Des Abû Dulaf Bericht über seine Reise nach Turkestân, China und Indien neu übersetzt und untersucht*, Bonn 1939, 18, 19-20). Gardīzī makes Yaghma originally a chief of the Toghuzghuz [*q.v.*], hence the Yaghma would appear to have been associated, at some early date, with the latter tribe. The *Ḥudūd al-ʿālam* states that the ruler of the Yaghma was indeed from the princely line of the Toghuzghuz, and has information on the two locations of the Yaghma, this division being perhaps the result of a tribal split. The first, most important location, spanned the central and western T'ien-Shan range, from the Naryn river in eastern Farghāna across the mountains to Kāshghar [*q.v.*] in eastern Turkestan, possession of which town was at some point disputed by both the Yaghma and Ķarluķ. The second location was in Semirečʾe [see yeti su], in the Ili valley and around the Issïķ Kol, where Maḥmūd al-Kāshgharī, *Dīwān lughāt al-turk*, Tkish. tr. Atalay, i, 92, places them alongside the Čigil and Tukhsï (cf. also Barthold, *Zwölf Vorlesungen über die Geschichte der Türken Mittelasiens*, Berlin 1935, 75-6, on these locations).

The anonymous *Mudjmal al-tawārīkh*, ed. Bahār, Tehran 1318/1939, 421, calls the ruler of the Yaghma Bughra Khān (cf. the Bughrādj of Abū Dulaf), and the appearance of this *onghun* or totemistic title amongst the early Ķarakhānids [see ilek-khāns] has led to suggestions that the latter dynasty arose from the Yaghma, especially as early centres of the Ķarakhānids were at Kāshghar and Özkend [*q.v.*] in eastern Farghāna. O. Pritsak, in a series of studies, has averred that the Ķarakhānids stemmed from the ruling clan of the Ķarluķ, with the Yaghma and Čigil as the two most important tribal elements of the Ḳarluḳ confederation; see the discussion of these views by P.B. Golden, in D. Sinor (ed.), *The Cambridge history of early Inner Asia*, Cambridge 1990, 355-7, see also Golden, *An introduction to the history of the Turkic peoples. Ethnogenesis and state-formation in medieval and early modern Eurasia and the Middle East*, Wiesbaden 1992, 201. The Yag͟hma would have still remained a distinct body within the Ḳarluḳ Ḳag͟hanate, although Golden notes that it is somewhat strange that al-Kās͟hg͟harī, himself writing under the Ḳarak͟hānids (and frequently mentioning the Yag͟hma in other connections) nowhere links the rulers of the Ḳarak͟hānids specifically with the Yag͟hma or Ḳarluḳ.

After the Ḳarak͟hānid and Sald͟jūḳ periods, the Yag͟hma seem to drop out of historical mention.

Bibliography: In addition to references given in the article, see J. Marquart, *Über das Volkstum der Komanen*, in *Abh. Akad. der Wiss. in Göttingen*, philos.-hist. Kl., N.F. xiii, no. 1, Berlin 1914, 93-5.

(C.E. Bosworth)

YAG͟HMĀ D͟JANDAḲĪ, the *tak͟hallus̤* or pen-name of the Persian poet Mīrzā Abu 'l-Ḥasan Raḥīm (*ca.* 1196-1276/*ca.* 1782-1859), often called by his fellow-poets *Ḳaḥba-zan* "whore" from the expression repeated monotonously in his obscene verse.

He was born at K͟hūr in the D͟jandaḳ oasis in the central desert of the Das͟ht-i Kawīr, roughly half-way between Yazd and Simnān. He began his life as a camel-herd but by the age of seven his natural gifts had been noticed by the owner of the oasis, Ismāʿīl K͟hān ʿArab-i ʿĀmirī, whose secretary (*muns͟hī-bās͟hī*) he ultimately became. His first nom-de-plume was Mad͟jnūn. In 1216/1802 Ismāʿīl K͟hān, after a rising against the government, had to flee to K͟hurāsān, while D͟jandaḳ was occupied by D͟hu 'l-Fiḳār K͟hān, representative of the governor of Simnān and Dāmg͟hān. Yag͟hmā was forcibly conscripted as an ordinary soldier but at Simnān his gifts obtained him the post of secretary to the governor. In 1223/1808 as a result of a false charge, the poet received the bastinado and his property was handed over as plunder (*yag͟hmā*) by the soldiery. The poet's innocence was proved and he regained his freedom but the act of injustice had embittered him. He then assumed the pen-name of Yag͟hmā and composed a scurrilous satire, *Sardāriyya*, on D͟hu 'l-Fiḳār K͟hān. Exiled, he wandered in Persia and via Bag͟hdād and Yazd reached Tehran, where fortune shone upon him again and he gained the good graces of Ḥād͟jd͟jī Mīrzā Aḳāsī, the first minister of Muḥammad S͟hāh Ḳād͟jār. Yag͟hmā was appointed *wazīr* to the governor of Kās͟hān, but a new satire (*K͟hulās̤at al-iftid̤āḥ*) against a family of Kās͟hān notables caused him to be ostracised again and he was denounced as a *kāfir* from the pulpit of the mosque. His wandering life was resumed. We know that he accompanied Muḥammad S͟hāh to Harāt. He only returned to his native land as an octogenarian to die at K͟hūr on 16 Rabīʿ II 1276/16 Nov. 1859 and was buried near the tomb of Sayyid Dāwūd.

Yag͟hmā's works in prose and verse were collected in his *Kulliyyāt* and published at Tehran (?) in 1283/1866 with a preface by Ḥād͟jd͟jī Muḥammad Ismāʿīl (389 fol. pp.).

Yag͟hmā practised all varieties of verse, and his poems (*g͟hazal, rit͟hāʾ, ḳitʿa, tard͟jīʿ-band*) show a great mastery of language and form. The most original part perhaps of his work is in the field of funeral chants (*nawḥa-yi sīna-zanī*) which he invented. They were obviously intended for the public lamentations in Muḥarram [see TAʿZIYA]. They are in the form of a *mustazād* in which each line is prolonged by a refrain which the audience is intended to murmur as a spontaneous echo. These *nawḥa*s are composed in simple and unaffected language. E.G. Browne, *LHP*, iv, 340, mentions the popularity of this genre among the poems of the constitutional period (1905-11).

Probably not well acquainted with Arabic as a result of his defective education, Yag͟hmā employed in his prose letters a simple Persian style (*fārsī-nigārī*) with a minimum of Arabic loan words; he is thus a precursor of 20th-century attempts, especially under the Pahlawīs, at evolving a Persian purged of extraneous elements. He also extensively annotated his personal copy of the *Burhān-i ḳāṭiʿ* dictionary, the ms. of which was handed down to his family. Yag͟hmā's most characteristic work however, was his satirical, slanderous and obscene poetry, his *hazliyyāt*. They have been viewed as denunciations of contemporary society, but other critics have merely seen them as expressions of personal grievances. In his mixture of ribaldry and simple piety, as expressed in his *nawḥa*s, Browne suggested Verlaine as a modern European parallel. Yag͟hmā also wrote verses in his native dialect of K͟hūr.

Bibliography: 1. Works. In addition to the *editio princeps* of 1283/1866, repr. Tehran 1339/1960, the *G͟hazaliyyāt* and *Sardāriyya* were ed. Muḥ. Ḥusayn Ṭabarī, Tehran 1337/1958.

2. Studies. Riḍā Ḳulī K͟hān, *Mad͟jmaʿ al-fuṣaḥāʾ*, ii, 580; Ḥabīb Yag͟hmāʾī (grandson), *S͟harḥ-i ḥāl-i Yag͟hmā*, Tehran n.d. (*ca.* 1927?) (originally publ. in the journal *Armag͟hān*, v); Browne, *LHP*, iv, 337-44; Rypka *et alii*, *History of Iranian literatures*, Dordrecht 1968, 333-4.

(V. Minorsky*)

YAG͟HMĀʾĪ, Ḥabīb (b. K͟hūr, 17 December 1898, d. Tehran, 14 May 1984), Persian poet and literary editor.

A descendant of the early Ḳād͟jār poet Yag͟hmā D͟jandaḳī [*q.v.*], Ḥabīb Yag͟hmāʾī was born in the small town of K͟hūr near D͟jandaḳ and Bīyābānak in the central desert of Persia. He first studied with his father, Ḥād͟jd͟j Asad Allāh Muntak͟hab al-Sādāt K͟hūrī, and subsequently left K͟hūr in 1916-17 for the nearby towns of Dāmg͟hān and S͟hāhrūd in order to pursue his education. In Dāmg͟hān he studied at the Nāẓimiyya school founded by ʿAbd Allāh Yāsāʾī in 1917. In 1921 he went to Tehran and enrolled first in the Alliance school and, a year later, in the Teachers' Training College (Dār al-Muʿallimīn-i ʿĀlī). This period is further marked by Yag͟hmāʾī's entry into Tehran literary circles. In 1923 he joined the Literary Society of Iran (*And͟juman-i Adabī-yi Īrān*) and in the following year he began his collaborations with the literary section of the radical paper *Ṭūfān* published in Tehran by Muḥammad Farruk͟hī Yazdī [*q.v.*]. In 1927-28 Yag͟hmāʾī studied at the School of Law and Political Science (later a Faculty of Tehran University). He returned to K͟hūr in 1928 as the head of the Birth Registry Office there; in the same year he took charge of the Office of Education and Endowments (*Awḳāf*) of Simnān. In 1930 Yag͟hmāʾī began teaching Persian literature at different high schools in Tehran, including the Dār al-Funūn. In 1934 he joined the Publication Department of the Ministry of Education. From 1943 to 1946 he was the editor of *Nāma-yi Farhangistān*, the organ of the Iranian Academy, and in 1944 he became an editor (for volumes 14, 15, and 23) of *Āmūzis͟h wa Parwaris͟h*, a cultural and educational journal. In 1948 he launched his own literary and historical journal, *Yag͟hmā*, which was published regularly for thirty years (1948-79). In the same year he also served for a few months as the head of the local office of the Ministry of Education in the city of Kirmān. In 1949 he returned to Tehran as an Inspector of the Ministry of Education, and he also acted as head of the Publication Department of the Ministry of Culture in 1952. In 1962-3 Yag̲h̲mā'ī taught at the Teachers' Training College and at the College of Foreign Languages and Literatures, receiving in 1976 an Honorary Doctorate of Literature and Humanities from Tehran University.

Yag̲h̲mā'ī belonged to a generation of Persian literary scholars who, though conservative in their preference for literary style and diction, contributed significantly to the development of Persian literary education and scholarship in the 20th century. In its entire thirty-year period, the journal *Yag̲h̲mā* served as a forum for literary and historical studies. In addition to his own writings, such as an earlier historical romance (*Dak̲h̲ma-yi Arg̲h̲ūn*) (Tehran 1933, ²1957) and a collection of poems (*Sarniwis̲h̲t*, Tehran 1972), Yag̲h̲mā'ī compiled several historical and literary surveys and also edited a number of texts, including the *Gars̲h̲āsb-nāma* of Asadī Ṭūsī (Tehran 1936, ²1975) and the Persian translation of the *Tafsīr* of al-Ṭabarī (Tehran 1960-65, 7 vols.).

Bibliography: For a full chronology and bibliography, see Īrad̲j̲ Afs̲h̲ār, *Zandagī-nāma wa Fihrist-nāma-yi āt̲h̲ār-i Ḥabīb Yag̲h̲mā'ī*, in *Āyanda*, x/4-5 (1984), 280-4; based on an earlier version which appeared in Īrad̲j̲ Afs̲h̲ār, Muḥammad Ibrāhīm Bāstānī-Pārīzī and G̲h̲ulām-Ḥusayn Yūsufī, *Yādgār-nāma-yi Ḥabīb Yag̲h̲mā'ī*, Tehran 1977, pp. ix-xvi. For further information on Yag̲h̲mā'ī's life, see Afs̲h̲ār, *Čihil sāl bā Ḥabīb Yag̲h̲mā'ī*, in *Āyanda*, x/4-5 (1984), 251-9; Sayyīd 'Alī Āl-i Dāwūd, *Yād-hā-yi dīgar az Ḥabīb Yag̲h̲mā'ī*, in *Āyanda*, x/10-11 (1984-5), 740-8; Aḥmad Mahdawī Dāmg̲h̲ānī, *Yādī az Ḥabīb Yag̲h̲mā'ī*, in *Kilk*, nos. 61-4 (1995), 486-94.

(Ali Gheissari)

YAG̲H̲MURĀSAN b. Zayyān b. T̲h̲ābit, Abū Yaḥyā, *s̲h̲ayk̲h̲* of the Banū 'Abd al-Wād, a branch of the Zanāta [*q.v.*] Berbers, who lived in the region of Tlemcen [see tilimsān] under the suzerainty of the Almohad sultans of Morocco, and who was the founder of the independent dynasty of the Zayyānids or 'Abd al-Wādids [*q.v.*] of Tlemcen, d. 681/1283. Born in 603/1206-7 or 605/1208-9, he succeeded his brother Abū 'Uzza Zaydān as head of the 'Abd al-Wādids in 633/1236, but not till 637/1239-40 was he formally invested by the Almohad sultan 'Abd al-Wāḥid al-Ras̲h̲īd. The power of the Moroccan sultans became so weakened that the 'Abd al-Wādids assumed their own independence.

Yag̲h̲murāsan thus became ruler in Tlemcen, and had first of all to fight against the Ḥafṣid *amīr* of Tunis Abū Zakariyyā', who in 640/1242 or five years later, managed to penetrate into the town of Tlemcen. Yag̲h̲murāsan, who had fled to the Banū Urnīd, was summoned by Abū Zakariyyā' to govern the town. The two *amīr*s made an alliance against the Almohad sultan Sa'īd, who in turn attacked Tlemcen, and then Tamazdig̲h̲t, where Yag̲h̲murāsan had taken refuge; in the battle which followed, Sa'īd was killed (646/1248). A large part of his reign was now taken up with fighting against various Arab tribes of the Sahara, against the Tūd̲j̲īn and Mag̲h̲rāwa, etc., and above all, against the Marīnids [*q.v.*] of Fās; Yag̲h̲murāsan even allied with Alfonso X of Castile to prevent the Marīnids making incursions into Spain. In 656/1257 the Zayyānid *amīr* besieged Sid̲j̲ilmāsa, but did not capture it until 662/1264. He remained on good terms with the Ḥafṣids, and it was whilst going forth to meet a princess of Tunis as bride for his son 'Ut̲h̲mān that he died near Miliana in 681/1283. Yag̲h̲murāsan left behind the reputation of a prudent and brave prince, the patron of scholars and littérateurs, and he built the minarets of the great mosques of Agādir (at Tlemcen) and Tāgrārt. Between the Marīnids to his west, and the Ḥafṣids to his east, he was able to preserve his own kingdom's independence.

Bibliography: Abū Zakariyyā' Yaḥyā Ibn K̲h̲aldūn, *Bug̲h̲yat al-ruwwād fī d̲h̲ikr al-mulūk min Banī 'Abd al-Wād*, ed. 'A.H. Ḥad̲j̲iyāt, Algiers 1400/1980, Fr. tr. A. Bel, *Hist. des Beni Abd el-Wad, rois de Tlemcen*, Algiers 1904; 'Abd al-Raḥmān Ibn K̲h̲aldūn, *'Ibar*, Būlāḳ 1284/1867, Fr. tr. de Slane and P. Casanova, iii, 340-68; Muḥammad b. 'Abd Allāh al-Tanasī, *Ta'rīk̲h̲ Banī Zayyān, mulūk Tilimsān*, extract from the *Naẓm al-durr wa 'l-'iḳyān fī bayān s̲h̲araf Banī Zayyān*, ed. Mahmud Bouayed, Algiers 1405/1985, 115-28, Fr. tr. J.J.L. Bargès, *Hist. des Beni Zaiyan, rois de Tlemcen*, Paris 1852; Ibn al-Aḥmar, *Rawḍat al-nisrīn fī dawlat Banī Marīn*, ed. and Fr. tr. G. Bouali and G. Marçais, Paris 1917, ed. 'Abd al-Wahhāb b. Manṣūr, Rabat 1962, Span. tr. M.A. Manzano, Madrid 1989, 92-101; Abbé Bargès, *Complément à l'hist. des Beni Zeiyan*, Paris 1887; Sid-Ahmed Bouali, *Les deux grands sièges de Tlemcen dans l'histoire et la légende*, Algiers 1984. See also 'abd al-wādids.

(Chantal de La Veronne)

YAHŪD, the common collective (sing. *Yahūdī*) in Arabic for "Jews". A less common plural *Hūd* is also used (e.g. Ḳur'ān, II, 111, 135, 140). The word is borrowed from Aram. *Yahūd*, and ultimately from late bibl. Heb. *yehūdīm*, "Judaeans", the latter itself derived from members of the tribe of Judah). The Ḳur'ān also uses a stative verb *hāda*, "to be Jewish" or "to practice Judaism".

1. In the D̲j̲āhiliyya.

Jews had lived in various parts of the Arabian Peninsula since Antiquity, and the numbers of those living in northwestern Arabia must have been swelled by refugees from Judaea when the great rebellions against Rome were suppressed in A.D. 70 and 135. By the late D̲j̲āhilī period, the Jews of the peninsula spoke Arabic, were organised into clans and tribes, and were generally highly assimilated into Arab society. Their numbers probably also included a greater or lesser number of indigenous Arabs who accepted Judaism. However, in spite of their overall acculturation, they were nonetheless viewed as a separate group with their own peculiar customs. Jews and some of their distinctive practices are occasionally mentioned in pre-Islamic Arabic poetry (for examples, see D.S. Margoliouth, *The relations between Arabs and Israelites prior to the rise of Islam*, London 1924, 73; I. Lichtenstädter, *Some references to Jews in pre-Islamic Arabic literature*, in *PAAJR*, x [1940], 185-94; J. Horovitz, *Koranische Untersuchungen*, Berlin and Leipzig 1926, 144 ff. and 153 ff.; and Hirschberg, *Yisrā'ēl ba-'Arav*, 112-16).

Not only were the pre-Islamic Arabs familiar with Jews and Jewish religious practices, Jewish religious ideas, ethical concepts and homiletic lore, but even some Aramaic and Hebrew terms were absorbed among those Arabs who came into close contact with Jews, just as Christian ideas and elements of vocabulary were also subconsciously assimilated (see e.g. S. Fraenkel, *Die aramäischen Fremdwörter im Arabischen*, Leiden 1886; and A. Jeffery, *The foreign vocabulary of the Qur'ān*, Baroda 1938). Because of the admixture of Aramaic and Hebrew in the everyday language of the Arabian Jews, the pagan Arabs perceived it to be a distinct Jewish dialect which they referred to as *al-yahūdiyya* (see Ibn Saʿd, ii/2, 66; al-Wāḳidī, *Kitāb al-Maghāzī*, ed. M. Jones, London 1966, i, 392; and G.D. Newby, *Observations about an early Judaeo-Arabic?*, in *JQR*, N.S., xli [1970], 212-21). Thus, there was a considerable degree of awareness of Jews and Judaism, as there was of Christians and Christianity, in the society into which the Prophet Muḥammad was born.

2. In the Ḳurʾān.

Despite the general Arabian familiarity with Jews and Judaism and despite the traditions that Muḥammad himself had met Jews prior to his theophany, there is no specific mention of *Yahūd* (or *Naṣārā*, Christians, or any other non-pagan religious group for that matter) in the revelations from the Meccan period. Only the term *Banū Isrāʾīl* [*q.v.*] (the Children of Israel), which is not found in what can be identified as genuine pre-Islamic poetry (Horovitz, *Koranische Untersuchungen*, 91), appears in the Meccan sūras. Most of these references are to the biblical Israelites, although a few clearly are to contemporary Jews (e.g. XXVI, 197; XVII, 101). In some Meccan and Medinan sūras (e.g. XLIII, 59; LXI, 14), *Banū Isrāʾīl* refers to both Jews and Christians of the time of Jesus, with allusions perhaps to some remnants of Judaeo-Christians, such as the Ebionites or the Elchasaites, who may still have existed in Muḥammad's own days (concerning the latter, cf. P. Crone, *Islam, Judeo-Christianity and Byzantine iconoclasm*, in *JSAI*, ii, [1980], 59-95, and J. Danielou, *Christianity as a Jewish sect*, in *The crucible of Christianity*, ed. A. Toynbee, London 1969, 282).

As noted above, the words *Yahūd, Yahūdī*, and *Hūd* first appear in the Medinan sūras—albeit a total of fifteen times, compared with the forty-three specific mentions of the *Banū Isrāʾīl* throughout the entire Ḳurʾān (the verbal form [*alladhīna*] *hādū*—"those who are Jewish"—appears ten times.) During this fateful time, fraught with tension after the Hidjra, when Muḥammad encountered contradiction, ridicule and rejection from the Jewish scholars in Medina, he came to adopt a radically more negative view of the people of the Book who had received earlier scriptures. This attitude was already evolving in the third Meccan period as the Prophet became more aware of the antipathy between Jews and Christians and the disagreements and strife amongst members of the same religion. The Ḳurʾān at this time claims that it will "relate [correctly] to the Children of Israel most of that about which they differ" (XXVII, 76).

Whereas the term *Banū Isrāʾīl* appears in the Ḳurʾān in both positive and negative contexts, the term *Yahūd* is most frequently negative. The *Yahūd* are associated with interconfessional strife and rivalry (II, 113). They believe that they alone are beloved of God (V, 18), and only they will achieve salvation (II, 111). They blasphemously claim that Ezra is the son of God, as Christians claim Jesus is (IX, 30) and that God's hand is fettered (V, 64). Together with the polytheists, Jews are "the most vehement of men in enmity to those who believe" (V, 82). Some of those who are Jews (*min alladhīna hādū*) "pervert words from their meanings" (IV, 44), have committed wrongdoing, for which God has "forbidden some good things that were previously permitted them" (IV, 160), they listen for the sake of mendacity (V, 41), and some of them have taken usury and will receive "a painful doom" (IV, 161).

3. In the *Ḥadīth* and early traditional literature.

The Jews are mentioned frequently in the canonical traditions, the *Sīra*, and the early literature about the Prophet's struggles (*maghāzī*) and the lives of his companions (*ṭabaḳāt al-ṣaḥāba*), as well as in Ḳurʾānic exegesis (*tafsīr*).

As in the Ḳurʾān, both the terms *Banū Isrāʾīl* and *Yahūd* continue to be used in the traditional literature, with the former having the broader meanings of both ancient Israelites and contemporary Jews (and again, even sometimes Jews and Christians, i.e. *ahl al-kitāb*). However, the designation *Yahūd* now becomes very common, and frequently the term *Yahūd* appears in contexts that are most frequently negative, as in Muḥammad's encounters with the Jewish tribes in Medina (the Banū Ḳaynuḳāʿ, al-Naḍīr and Ḳurayẓa [*q.vv.*]) and with the inhabitants of the oasis of Khaybar, all of which are related in the greatest of detail in the *Sīra* and the *Maghāzī*. For example, the rabbis of the Jews in Medina are singled out as "men whose malice and enmity was aimed at the Apostle of God" (Ibn Hishām, *Sīra*, Cairo, 1955, i, 516; *hāʾulāʾi aḥbār al-Yahūd, ahl al-shurūr wa 'l-ʿadāwa li-Rasūl Allāh*). The *Yahūd* in this literature appear not only as malicious, but also deceitful (e.g. al-Wāḳidi, *Maghāzī*, i, 363 ff.), cowardly (Ibn Hishām, ii, 57) and totally lacking resolve (*ibid.*, 236). However, they have none of the demonic qualities attributed to them in mediaeval Christian literature, neither is there anything comparable to the overwhelming preoccupation with Jews and Judaism (except perhaps in the narratives on Muḥammad's encounters with Medinan Jewry) in Muslim traditional literature. Except for a few notable exceptions, such as Ḥuyayy b. Akhṭab, a leader of the Banu 'l-Naḍīr, and the Ḳuraẓī chieftain Kaʿb al-Asad, the Jews in the *Sīra* and the *Maghāzī* are even heroic villains. Their ignominy stands in marked contrast to Muslim heroism, and in general, conforms to the Ḳurʾānic image of "wretchedness and baseness stamped upon them" (II, 61).

In the *Ḥadīth*, the *Yahūd* are mentioned most often in traditions that emphasise the differences between Muslims and non-Muslims, as for example with regard to sexual mores, purity laws, and various customs and practices (cf. Abū Dāwūd, *Sunan*, *k. al-nikāḥ, bāb* xlviii; Muslim, *Ṣaḥīḥ, k. al-ḥayḍ, bāb* xvi; and especially al-Bukhārī, *Ṣaḥīḥ, k. al-anbiyāʾ, bāb* 1, 2-10) and that express disapproval of non-Muslim practices (cf. *ibid., k. al-ṣalāt, bāb* xlviii). In traditions, dealing with the proper ways of interacting with non-Muslim monotheists—as for example in the case of how to salute members of the *ahl al-dhimma*—the Jews are specifically mentioned because of their malicious punning on the *taslīm* with *al-sām ʿalayk* instead of *al-salām ʿalayk*, to which a Muslim should respond *wa-ʿalayk* or *wa-ʿalaykum* (cf. e.g. al-Bukhārī, *k. al-istiʾdhān, bāb* xxii). By contrast, when the tradition allows for a more positive, or at least neutral, identification with Jews (and perhaps Jews and Christians generally), the term *Banū Isrāʾīl* is more likely to be used, as in the well-known *ḥadīth* that it is not a transgression to relate traditions on the authority of the Children of Israel (al-Bukhārī, *k. al-anbiyāʾ, bāb* 1, 9: *ḥaddithū ʿan Banī Isrāʾīl wa-lā ḥaradja*).

4. In mediaeval Islamic law, literature and society.

Because of the decidedly more negative connotations of the term *Yahūd*, as opposed to *Banū Isrāʾīl*, the latter increasingly became the polite usage in Arabic when referring to Jews (in a semantic parallel to early modern French usages *juif* versus *israélite*). *Al-Isrāʾīlī* was the usual *nisba* for distinguished Jews, such as Mūsā b. Maymūn al-Isrāʾīlī al-Andalusī (Ibn al-Ḳifṭī, *Ḥukamāʾ*, ed. Lippert, 317) as well as for Jewish converts to Islam, such as the poet Abū Isḥāḳ

b. Sahl al-Isrāʾīlī [*q.v.*]. This use of the term *Banū Isrāʾīl* as more euphemistic than *Yahūd* was merely a tendency, particularly in religious literature and was by no means consistent in any case. Mediaeval Arab historians and geographers on the whole referred to Jews as such without either a negative or positive connotation. Thus for example, Ibn Khurradādhbih refers to Radhanite Jewish merchants as *tudjdjār al-yahūd al-rādhāniyya* (*Masālik*, 153), while al-Masʿūdī refers to the Jews of ʿIrāḳ as *Banū Isrāʾīl* and as *Yahūd* (*Tanbīh*, 79 and 113). Naturally, *Yahūd* is invariably used when authors make a distinction from Christians or specify them alongside Christians, as does, for example, al-Muḳaddasī when describing the population of Jerusalem (167).

The perception of Jews in the Middle Ages was on the whole even more condescending than that of Christians. In fact, the great 3rd/9th century essayist al-Djāḥiẓ notes that the Muslim masses perceived the Christians as being "more sincere than the Jews, closer in affection, less treacherous, less unbelieving, and deserving of a lighter punishment [on Judgment Day]". He goes on to analyse the historical and sociological reasons for this popular preference, namely, that the Jews had opposed the Prophet in Medina and generally belonged to a lower socio-economic stratum of society than either the Christians or Zoroastrians (*K. al-Radd ʿalā ʾl-Naṣārā*, ed. J. Finkel, Cairo 1926, 13-14; see also Wasserstrom, *Between Muslim and Jew*, 19-46).

Despite what may have been the greater social prejudice in early Islam towards the *Yahūd*, Islamic law made no distinction between Jews and other tolerated non-Muslims. Administrative decrees meant to interpret, amplify, and execute the *Sharīʿa* rules of *ghiyār* [*q.v.* and see also LIBĀS] sometimes made differentiation as to the badge or garment colour for members of each of the various *dhimmī* communities. But from a strictly constitutional point of view, all were subsumed under the same legal category of *ahl al-dhimma* [*q.v.*], or protégés of the *umma*. The fact that the Jews shared their *dhimmī* status with the far more numerous and conspicuous Christians and Zoroastrians mitigated and diffused any specifically anti-Jewish sentiments into a broader prejudice against the *ahl al-dhimma*. Furthermore, Jews did not have to bear the onus of suspicion that was harboured toward some of the Christian communities and that grew from the period of the Crusades onward, that they were friendly toward the European powers and a potential fifth column.

Only when a Jew was perceived to have egregiously transgressed the bounds of proper conduct as stipulated in the theoretical contract of protection (*dhimma* or *amān*) with the Islamic state by rising too high in the bureaucracy and not conducting himself in an appropriately humble manner, could specifically anti-Jewish sentiments be stirred up and given voice in satires aimed at the Jews. Such satires about the *Yahūd* circulated when the Tustarīs were at the height of their power and influence in Fāṭimid Egypt, the Ibn Naghrelas held the vizierate in Zīrid Granada, and Saʿd al-Dawla was vizier to the Il-Khānid ruler of ʿIrāḳ and Persia (Ibn Muyassar, *Taʾrīkh Miṣr*, ed. H. Massé, Cairo 1919; Dozy, *Recherches*[3], pp. lxii-lxvii; al-Waṣṣāf, *Taʾrīkh-i Waṣṣāf*, BL ms. Add. 23517, fol. 202a, cited in Fischel, *Jews*, 111; see also Stillman, *Jews of Arab lands*, 51, 59, 214-16). In these and similar cases, as for example the rioting that followed the downfall of the Jewish vizier Hārūn b. Baṭash in Marīnid Fās (ʿAbd al-Bāsiṭ b. Khalīl, *al-Rawḍ al-bāsim*, ed. R. Brunschvig, Paris 1936, 49-55, tr. in Stillman, *Jews of Arab lands*, 281-6), popular animus could overflow into violence not only against the individual Jewish official, but against the entire Jewish community as well. However, such specifically anti-Jewish manifestations were exceptional. The Geniza documents show that mediaeval Jews were aware of hostility towards their community specifically as Jews and referred to it by the Judaeo-Arabic word *sinʾūth* (Goitein, *Med. soc.* ii, 278).

Mediaeval Muslim theologians devoted only a very small part of their polemics against other religions and doctrines to Judaism. There is nothing in Islam comparable in quantity and rarely in sheer vitriol to the *Adversus Judaeos* literature of the Church. With the exception of Ibn Ḥazm's *Risāla fi ʾl-radd ʿalā Ibn al-Naghrīla al-Yahūdī* (*Rasāʾil Ibn Ḥazm*, ed. I. ʿAbbās, Beirut 1981, 41-70), which is prompted more by the sentiments stirred up by Jews holding high office than by specific theological questions, there are relatively few independent exposés of the falseness of Judaism. Most of the latter seem to have been written by Jewish converts to Islam anxious to prove their neophyte zeal by exposing the errors of their former faith. Among the best-known of such works are al-Samawʾal al-Maghribī's *Ifḥām al-Yahūd* (ed. and tr. M. Perlmann, New York 1964 [= *PAAJR*, xxxii]), Saʿīd b. Ḥasan's *Kitāb Masālik al-naẓar* (ed. and tr. S.A. Weston, in *JAOS*, xxiii [1904], 312-83), and ʿAbd al-Ḥaḳḳ al-Islāmī's *al-Sayf al-mamdūd fi ʾl-radd ʿalā aḥbār al-Yahūd* (ed. and tr. E. Alfonso, Madrid 1998). All three of these treatises are rather late, dating from the 6th-8th/12th-14th centuries. Earlier anti-Jewish treatises did exist, but none prior to Ibn Ḥazm's from the 5th/11th century has survived. In marked contrast to these militant polemics are the admirably academic and dispassionate descriptions of Jews and Judaism in the histories and compendia of religions and beliefs, such as al-Bīrūnī's *al-Āthār al-bāḳiya ʿan al-ḳurūn al-khāliya* (ed. E. Sachau, Leipzig 1878) and especially al-Shahrastānī's *al-Milal wa ʾl-niḥal* (ed. W. Cureton, London 1842-46 and numerous other editions).

5. In folklore.

Jews are occasionally depicted in Arabic folktales or mentioned in popular proverbs, but once again, neither quantitatively nor qualitatively comparable to their place in the folklore of western Christendom. The *Alf layla wa-layla* contains, in addition to pious tales belonging to the *isrāʾīliyyāt* [*q.v.*] genre in which the principal characters are called Israelites (see the examples cited in M. Gerhardt, *The art of story-telling*, Leiden 1963, 365-69), some isolated Jewish individuals who are identified as Jews simply to provide colour and spice to an ethnic mosaic of characters, such as the Jewish doctor in the Hunchback cycle of tales (ed. M. Mahdi, i, Leiden 1984, 280-379).

Overall, Jews are mentioned only peripherally in later Arabic folklore, although perhaps somewhat more in the Maghrib than in the Levant, since no indigenous Christians remained in North Africa after the Almohad period. Proverbs and folktales stereotypically portray the *Yahūdī* as sly, untrustworthy and occasionally malevolent (E. Westermarck, *Wit and wisdom in Morocco*, London 1930, 130-1, nos. 468-73). However, there are also examples of more positive images in which the Jews are depicted as useful and even better than a vile Muslim (*ibid.*, 131, nos. 474-6).

6. In the modern era.

Increased European commercial, missionary and imperialist activities within the Muslim world during the 19th and 20th centuries introduced anti-Semitic ideas and literature into the region. At first these prejudices only found a reception among Arabic-speaking Christian protégés of the Europeans in Syria, Lebanon and Egypt and were too new and too palpably foreign for any widespread acceptance among Muslims. However, with the ever-increasing conflict between Arabs and Jews in Palestine during the period of the British Mandate, the language and imagery of European anti-Semitism began to appear in political polemics both in the nationalist press and in books (Stillman, *New attitudes toward the Jew in the Arab world*, in *Jewish Social Studies*, xxxvii [1975], 197-204; idem, *Antisemitism in the contemporary Arab world*, in *Antisemitism in the contemporary world*, ed. M. Curtis, Boulder and London 1986, 70-85). For more than two decades following 1948, this trend increased greatly, but peaked by the 1970s, and declined somewhat as the slow process of rapprochement between the Arab world and the state of Israel evolved in the 1980s and 1990s; it remains to be seen how the tensions arising in 2000 will affect the trend.

Bibliography (in addition to works given in the text): C. Adang, *Muslim writers on Judaism and the Hebrew Bible from Ibn Rabban to Ibn Ḥazm*, Leiden 1996; W.J. Fischel, *Jews in the economic and political life of mediaeval Islam*, rev. ed. New York 1969; S.D. Goitein, *Jews and Arabs: their contacts through the ages*, rev. ed. New York 1974; idem, *A Mediterranean society*, Berkeley and Los Angeles, 1967-93; B. Lewis, *The Jews of Islam*, Princeton 1984; M. Perlmann, *The medieval polemics between Islam and Judaism*, in *Religion in a religious age*, ed. S.D. Goitein, Cambridge, Mass. 1974, 103-38; N.A. Stillman, *The Jews of Arab lands: a history and source book* Philadelphia 1979; idem, *The Jews of Arab lands in modern times*, Philadelphia 1991; idem, *Muslims and Jews in Morocco: perceptions, images, stereotypes*, in *Proceedings of the seminar on Muslim-Jewish Relations in North Africa*, New York 1975, 13-27; S. Wasserstrom, *Between Muslim and Jew: the problem of symbiosis under early Islam*, Princeton 1995. See also, on the legal and constitutional position of Jews in Islamic society, DHIMMA. (N.A. STILLMAN)

YAḤYĀ B. **ʿABD ALLĀH** B. AL-ḤASAN B. AL-ḤASAN b. ʿAlī, Medinan ʿAlid leader of a revolt in Daylam and Zaydī *imām*. His mother was Ḳurayba bt. Rukayḥ b. Abī ʿUbayda b. ʿAbd Allāh b. Zamʿa b. al-Aswad, niece of the mother of his paternal brothers Muḥammad al-Nafs al-Zakiyya [*q.v.*] and Ibrāhīm, leaders of the Ḥasanid revolt against the caliph al-Manṣūr in 145/762. As a much younger brother, born perhaps around 128/745-6, he did not participate in that revolt. He was partly brought up and taught by the Imāmī S͟hīʿī *imām* D̲jaʿfar al-Ṣādiḳ [*q.v.*], presumably after the imprisonment of his father in 140/758, and D̲jaʿfar (d. 148/765) made him one of his legatees. Yaḥyā seems to have revered him. He followed him in his ritual practice and transmitted legal doctrine mainly from him. He appears in Imāmī books as a transmitter from D̲jaʿfar.

Yaḥyā took a prominent part in the revolt of the Ḥasanid al-Ḥusayn b. ʿAlī Ṣāḥib Fak̲h̲k̲h̲ [*q.v.*] in Medina in 169/786. After the collapse of the revolt he, his brother Idrīs [see IDRĪS I], and some others found shelter with a tribesman of K̲h̲uzāʿa who aided them to escape by boat to Abyssinia. There they stayed some time with the king. After returning to Arabia, the two brothers met with a group of loyal supporters at S̲h̲iʿb al-Ḥaḍārima near Mecca. They agreed that Ibrāhīm should seek support in the Mag̲h̲rib, while Yaḥyā first went to Yemen. The sources give different accounts about his peregrinations during the following years. According to the best one, he went from Yemen to Upper Mesopotamia, Armenia, and then to Bag̲h̲dād. Having been discovered, he fled again to Yemen and stayed for eight months in Ṣanʿāʾ with a man of the Abnāʾ. It was at this time, perhaps in 174/790-1, that al-S̲h̲āfiʿī [*q.v.*] studied with him and became one of his supporters. He then went on to K̲h̲urāsān and wrote, probably just after the murder by poison of his brother Idrīs by an agent of the caliph Hārūn al-Ras̲h̲īd, to S̲h̲arwīn b. Surk̲h̲āb, the Bāwandid ruler of Firīm in the mountains of Ṭabaristān, requesting asylum for three years. S̲h̲arwīn responded positively but guided him to D̲justān, king of Daylam, who would be in a better position to protect him. That he, in accordance with another account, also travelled to D̲jūzd̲jān, Balk̲h̲, Transoxania and stayed with an unidentified "K̲h̲āḳān of the Turks" (perhaps the Afs̲h̲īn of Us̲h̲rūsana), is more doubtful. It is to be noted, however, that al-Faḍl b. Yaḥyā al-Barmakī, when sent to capture him, first defeated the K̲h̲āḳān, who had intruded deeply into the territory of Islam. This is confirmed by two lines of contemporary poetry by Abū T̲h̲umāma al-K̲h̲aṭīb.

Yaḥyā arrived in Daylam in 175/791-2 and was soon joined by a substantial number of supporters. In 176/792 he proclaimed his rising against the caliph. Al-Ras̲h̲īd was deeply alarmed and sent al-Faḍl b. Yaḥyā as governor of D̲jibāl, Rayy, D̲jurd̲jān, Ṭabaristān, Ḳūmis, Dunbāwand and Rūyān with an army of 50,000 and much money to meet the challenge. Al-Faḍl took al-Ṭālaḳān, and set himself up nearby at As̲h̲hab in the Elburz mountains from where he sent letters to Yaḥyā and D̲justān offering pardon to the former and a million dirhams to the king. A report that al-Faḍl had earlier advised and helped Yaḥyā to seek refuge in Daylam and that al-Ras̲h̲īd, informed of his treason, sent him against the ʿAlid in order to test him, is hardly credible. Yaḥyā eventually accepted an ironclad letter of amnesty and safety for himself and seventy followers, formulated by himself and handwritten by the caliph and endorsed by legal scholars, judges, and prominent ʿAbbāsids, together with lavish gifts. He obtained a further letter of safety from al-Faḍl and then surrendered. Later, he explained that he surrendered because the wife of the king of Daylam pressed the latter to accept al-Faḍl's offers out of greed and because there was discord between himself and some of his Kūfan followers who would not heed his S̲h̲īʿī prohibition of *masḥ ʿalā ʾl-k̲h̲uffayn* [*q.v.*] and drinking of date wine. The son of the Kūfan Batrī leader al-Ḥasan b. Ṣāliḥ b. Ḥayy on one occasion led the prayer of his followers without waiting for Yaḥyā, who then performed his prayer separately, knowing that al-Ḥasan's son practiced *masḥ*. The latter remarked to his companions, Why should they allow themselves to be killed for a man who did not consider prayer with them licit?

Yaḥyā was received by the caliph in Bag̲h̲dād with great honours, and the event was celebrated as signifying a reconciliation between ʿAbbāsids and ʿAlids. He is said to have received gifts of 200,000 or 400,000 dīnārs from both al-Ras̲h̲īd and al-Faḍl. The caliph, however, sought to keep him under supervision in Bag̲h̲dād, against the letter of pardon which guaranteed him the right of free movement anywhere. Yaḥyā participated in a pilgrimage to Mecca and then was allowed by al-Faḍl, without the caliph's knowledge, to move to his family estate At̲h̲yab outside Suwayḳa near Medina. The caliph asked al-Faḍl to bring him back, but the latter evidently insisted on keeping the terms of the pardon. Yaḥyā now used the money he had been given to pay the debts of the Ṣāḥib Fak̲h̲k̲h̲ and support needy ʿAlids. There is no evidence that he had any seditious designs, but the caliph remained deeply suspicious. He appointed two members of the fiercely anti-ʿAlid family of al-Zubayr as governors of Medina, first ʿAbd Allāh b. Muṣʿab b. Thābit (180/796-7) and then his son Bakkār (181-93/797-809). Soon after his accession, Bakkār complained to al-Rashīd that Yaḥyā was behaving like a second caliph and was venerated by the people, who visited him from everywhere. He insinuated that the ʿAlid was engaged in treason and advised the caliph to recall him in order to forestall a major rebellion. Al-Rashīd ordered Yaḥyā to be sent back to Baghdād.

There are numerous reports, partly of a legendary character and contradictory, about the vicious treatment of Yaḥyā by the caliph after his recall. It is clear that Yaḥyā was confined, rather than kept in prison, for part of the time. One well-informed account speaks of three occasions on which he was imprisoned (al-Ṭabarī, iii, 624). In 184/800 ʿAbd Allāh b. Muṣʿab, now at the caliphal court, told al-Rashīd that he had received a call (*daʿwa*) from Yaḥyā to back his seditious aspirations. He suggested that, given the enmity between Zubayrids and ʿAlids, Yaḥyā must have already received the backing of everybody at court for his designs and that the caliph thus could not trust anyone of his wives, servants, and army leaders. Al-Rashīd confronted him with Yaḥyā, who denied the accusation and demanded that the truth be established by an oath of *mubāhala* [*q.v.*] between himself and his opponent. This was done, and ʿAbd Allāh b. Muṣʿab, according to the account, died on the same day. His death (27 Rabīʿ I 184/29 March 800) was, in any case, accepted by the caliph as a vindication of Yaḥyā.

Al-Rashīd felt, however, increasingly frustrated by his letter of pardon. He was particularly infuriated by Yaḥyā's refusal to identify his seventy supporters protected by the pardon and accused him of protecting all his Shīʿī followers by claiming, whenever one of them was caught, that he belonged to those granted amnesty. He convened a group of legal scholars, among them the Ḥanafī Muḥammad b. al-Ḥasan al-Shaybānī, and prominent men to have the letter declared invalid. When al-Shaybānī categorically stated that the letter was valid and inviolable, al-Rashīd in his anger hit his head with an inkstand. Abu 'l-Bakhtarī Wahb b. Wahb then declared the letter invalid and cut it up with a knife. According to one account, al-Rashīd on that occasion set up Yaḥyā b. Khālid al-Barmakī to testify that Yaḥyā b. ʿAbd Allāh had secretly sent his propagandists who had obtained the pledge of allegiance of the common people of Baghdād for him and that a man had been apprehended on the way to Balkh with letters summoning the people of Khurāsān to rebellion. Such a role of Yaḥyā b. Khālid is not implausible since he had in 183/799 undertaken to have the Shīʿī Imām Mūsā al-Kāẓim [*q.v.*] murdered in order to protect his son al-Faḍl, who had aroused the caliph's anger by failing to carry out his order to kill him.

Al-Rashīd, however, still had scruples to execute Yaḥyā in public. He handed him over to the Barmakid Djaʿfar b. Yaḥyā, indicating to him that he wanted him dead. Djaʿfar is said to have been ready to carry out the caliph's wishes, but then was persuaded by Yaḥyā to let him escape on a commitment that he would immediately leave for Byzantine territory and stay there as long as al-Rashīd was alive. Yaḥyā was apprehended at Maṣṣīṣa and was brought before Muḥammad b. Khālid b. Barmak, governor of the border towns, who recognised him. Realising that the fate of the Barmakids would be sealed if the caliph learned of Yaḥyā's liberation by Djaʿfar, Muḥammad hastened to inform the caliph secretly during his pilgrimage to Mecca in 186/802. Al-Rashīd concealed the matter until his return from the pilgrimage, when he ordered the execution of Djaʿfar and the arrest of the other Barmakids and confiscation of their property with the exception of Muḥammad b. Khālid. That Djaʿfar's brutal execution was caused by his release of Yaḥyā is categorically affirmed in another account by Abū Muḥammad al-Yazīdī, who, according to al-Ṭabarī, was said to have had the most intimate knowledge of the affairs of the Barmakids.

Yaḥyā was now handed over to al-Sindī b. Shāhak, police prefect of Baghdād, who had three years before brought about the death of Mūsā al-Kāẓim in prison. Yaḥyā also died in his prison, most likely in 187/803. According to his grandson Idrīs b. Muḥammad, he was killed in prison by starvation and thirst. Reports that he was either buried alive in a village near Rayy during al-Rashīd's campaign there in 189/805 or escaped are unreliable.

Yaḥyā's revolt paved the way for the spread of Zaydī Shīʿism among the Daylamīs and in Ṭabaristān and Gīlān. A number of Daylamīs were converted by him to Islam and are said to have built his house and mosque in their country. They later used to call themselves "helpers of the Mahdī (*anṣār al-mahdī*)".

Bibliography: Zubayrī, *Nasab Ḳuraysh*, ed. E. Lévi-Provençal, Cairo 1953, 54: Yaʿḳūbī, 492-3; Wakīʿ, *Akhbār al-ḳuḍāt*, ed. al-Marāghī, Cairo 1947-50, i, 248-9; Ṭabarī, iii, 552-64, 612-24, 669-72, tr. C.E. Bosworth, *The ʿAbbāsid caliphate in equilibrium*, Albany 1989, 16-34, 113-31, 205-8; Aḥmad b. Sahl al-Rāzī, *Akhbār Fakhkh wa-khabar Yaḥyā b. ʿAbd Allāh*, ed. Maher Jarrar, Beirut 1995; Abu 'l-Faradj al-Iṣfahānī, *Maḳātil al-Ṭālibiyyīn*, ed. A. Ṣaḳr, Cairo 1949, 463-86 and index; *Arabic texts concerning the history of the Zaydī Imāms*, ed. W. Madelung, Beirut 1987, esp. 55-70, 79-84, 173-208; *Taʾrīkh Baghdād*, xiv, 110-12; C. van Arendonk, *Les débuts de l'imāmat Zaidite au Yemen*, tr. J. Ryckmans, Leiden 1960, 65-70, 317-19; D. Sourdel, *Le vizirat ʿabbāside*, Damascus 1959-60, index; Jarrar, introd. to al-Rāzī, *Akhbār Fakhkh*, esp. 53-8, 68-88.

(W. MADELUNG)

YAḤYĀ B. ĀDAM b. Sulaymān, Abū Zakariyyāʾ al-Kūfī, Ḳurʾān, *ḥadīth* and *fiḳh* scholar, d. 203/818. He had the *nisba*s al-Ḳurashī and al-Umawī because, through his father Ādam who was probably of Persian origin, he was a client (*mawlā*) of a certain Khālid b. Khālid b. ʿUmāra b. al-Walīd b. ʿUḳba b. Abī Muʿayṭ al-Umawī, also al-Makhzūmī (e.g. in al-Nawawī, but according to Schacht in *EI*[1], this is a mistake), and the *laḳab* is al-Aḥwal (Sezgin, i, 520; Shākir, 8). His biography as transmitted is very sparse.

Born after 130/747-8, probably *ca.* 140/757-8, he grew up and for the most part lived in al-Kūfa, as the *nisba* al-Kūfī seems to indicate. He possibly lost his father, also a traditionist, before he was born (al-Dhahabī, *Siyar*, 1982). Almost nothing is known about his life. It is said that he visited the caliph Hārūn al-Rashīd in al-Ḥīra, together with his teacher Abū Bakr b. ʿAyyāsh (d. 193/809) (Sezgin, i, 520, after Yāḳūt, *Irshād*), but it is not clear whether such information permits us to conclude that he was a "distinguished" man. His good reputation, if not his renown, is supported by the fact that the Persian secretary, ʿIrāḳī governor and father-in-law of al-Maʾmūn, al-Ḥasan b. Sahl [*q.v.*], prayed over Yaḥyā when he died around the middle of Rabīʿ I 203/21 September 818 at Fam al-Ṣilḥ, not far from Wāsiṭ. Al-Ḥasan, shocked by the murder, perpetrated in 202/818 near Sarakhs [*q.v.*], of his famous brother, the pro-Iranian vizier and former Barmakid pupil al-Faḍl b. Sahl [*q.v.*], performed this ceremony at the place where he possessed an estate and where he later had his refuge (Ibn Ḳutayba, *Maʿārif*).

In spite of this, the deceased was apparently considered as a foreigner at this place; perhaps he had fled there from the restlessness of al-Kūfa in those days, unless al-Ḥasan had ordered him to come, alone or together with others, on his own behalf or in the name of the ruler, in order to benefit from his spiritual and moral authority. Yaḥyā's life span comprised six caliphates, apparently without him having entered the services of any caliph or having held public posts in the juridical, political or administrative fields (as did his colleagues Abū Yūsuf and Abū ʿUbayd [*q.vv.*]). It is as if he lived only for the acquisition and transmission of learning; he never became dependent and kept out of everyday disputes on religion and politics while sharing this abstention from politics with other conscientious men of his time (Shākir, 11-12). From the spirit of his way of working and the reports about him, it seems that he grew up in the austere style of early Islam, that he was marked by a profound study of the *Sīra* and Sunna of the Prophet and the *salaf* [*q.v.*], by piety, honesty and a conciliatory character, and that he was led by well-grounded principles of religious law which he intended to transmit faithfully; he thus probably aimed at an ideal harmonising of the so-called *ʿibādāt* and *muʿāmalāt* [*q.vv.*] on the basis of Ḳurʾān, Sunna and *fiḳh*. In doing this he found himself in a relatively independent and uncommitted legal position within a juridical system that, moreover, had not yet solidified. His contemporaries and the authors of *ridjāl* [*q.v.*] works considered him, among other things, as a leader in Ḳurʾānic, *ḥadīth* and legal disciplines, highly trustworthy and reliable, an outstanding figure in his fields of knowledge, and one of the *imāms* and highlights of Islamic scholarship and traditionalism, as if the accumulated knowledge of preceding great men had come together in his esteemed personality, described as almost perfect (al-Dhahabī, *Siyar*, 1982, 522-9; idem, *Tadhkirat al-ḥuffāẓ*, 327-8; Ibn al-ʿImād, *Shadharāt*, 8; al-Dāraḳuṭnī, 405; Ibn Ḥadjar, *Tahdhīb*, 175; al-Nawawī, *Tahdhīb*, 150).

Among his teachers one finds such illustrious names as al-Ḥasan b. Ṣāliḥ b. ʿAyyāsh and his brother Abū Bakr b. ʿAyyāsh, Sufyān al-Thawrī, Sufyān b. ʿUyayna, Sharīk b. ʿAbd Allāh al-Nakhaʿī, Ibn al-Mubārak, Wakīʿ and Ḥammād b. Salama; among his students were Aḥmad b. Ḥanbal, Ibn Abī Shayba and Yaḥyā b. Maʿīn (lists in al-Dhahabī, *Siyar*, ix, 523; idem, *Tadhkirat al-ḥuffāẓ*, 327-8; Ibn al-ʿImād, ii, 8; Ibn Ḥadjar, xi, 175; al-Nawawī, *Tadhkirat al-asmāʾ wa 'l-lughāt*, ii, 150).

Ḳurʾānic studies were apparently an important part of his activity. The author of the *Fihrist* ascribes two works to him: a *K. al-Ḳirāʾāt* and a *K. Mudjarrad aḥkām al-Ḳurʾān* (35, 38). The latter, however, belongs rather to *fiḳh*. As a Ḳurʾān teacher with his own pupils, Yaḥyā stands less in the Kūfan tradition of al-Kisāʾī [*q.v.*] than in that of ʿĀṣim (d. 127-8/745), whose *tadjwīd* and *ḥurūf* he took over through the *rāwī* Abū Bakr b. ʿAyyāsh and whose lectures he wrote down "letter by letter" in a note-book which he carried with him for decades (al-Dhahabī, *Siyar*, ix, 527). On the other hand, it is said that Yaḥyā did not meet Shuʿba (b. ʿAyyāsh), the other *rāwī* of ʿĀṣim (*ibid.*, ix, 523). If it is correct that he also transmitted readings of al-Kisāʾī; even if only a few, this would indicate a certain independence in the field of *ḳirāʾāt*.

Three other works which the *Fihrist* ascribes to Yaḥyā point to his scholarship as that of a traditional jurist: a *K. al-Farāʾiḍ*, a *K. al-Zawāl*, and *K. al-Kharādj*, a work on the land tax that so far has survived in only one manuscript. This last has been judged variously. Schacht was of the opinion that it was a refutation of a book of the same name by Abū Yūsuf, but this seems unlikely. In Yaḥyā's work there is no trace of any feeling against Abū Yūsuf, rather, it is complementary to the latter's transmission of materials (*Taxation*, 17). A refutation would contain something polemical, and would hold one's own better judgement against the opponents. Of this, however, nothing can be detected. Brockelmann's judgement (I, 192), that Yaḥyā was a scholar of *ḥadīth*, mainly occupied with juridical questions without following one particular school, is certainly close to the truth. Ben Shemesh keeps Yaḥyā out of the "controversies and disputes of his time", and does not classify him in any juridical current of opinion (*Taxation*, 2). He traces his neutral position here to the fact that the differences between the schools were not yet distinctly marked, and that his peaceful mind "prevented him from attacking higher-placed persons" (*Taxation*, 3; cf. Ibn Ḥadjar, *Tahdhīb*, xi, 176). He could, as it were, take from everybody without being a follower. He was certainly quite close to his most important teacher and informant, the pious Kūfan *faḳīh*, Zaydī theologian and co-founder of the Ṣāliḥiyya, al-Ḥasan b. Ṣāliḥ b. Ḥayy (d. 167/784 [*q.v.*]), but without being a full-fledged adherent of his way of thinking, nor was he a real Zaydī (*pace* Van Ess, *Theologie*, i, 246-7). It is not surprising that his *Kitāb al-Kharādj* "was above all passed on in Ḥanbalī circles" (Van Ess, *ibid.*); his neutral stance and in, particular, his orthodox traditionalism must have appealed to the Ḥanbalīs, as is clear from the listeners' certificates in the manuscript studied by Ben Shemesh. The *Kitāb al-Kharādj* is mainly a compilation of traditions (probably collected for his students in the first place) referring to the usual procedures regarding the land tax and its various types as practised by Muslims and *Dhimmīs*. According to Ben Shemesh, the work adds few explanations by Yaḥyā himself, and offers a rigid model which, because of its lack of variability and creativity, can hardly be harmonised with the actual circumstances as they were developing in landed property and land matters, and with the administration of the estates and fixed property of the *futūḥ* in general (*Taxation*, 6-7). It would seem that many of Yaḥyā's explanations for the statements of the traditions, strung together according to topoi, are of a remarkably realistic and pragmatic nature, competent, clever, displaying his experience, but always somewhat old-fashioned; moreover, the work deals in particular with the Sawād [*q.v.*] (of Kūfa), with Western Persia and with the Arabian Peninsula. The weakness of the work affects more or less all *kharādj* books, in particular those focussing on traditions, such as the *K. al-Amwāl* of Abū ʿUbayd.

Wherever possible, the book is based on the Ḳurʾānic model and the earliest juridical practice, (allegedly) used during the *maghāzī* and the *futūḥ* by the Prophet, the *ṣaḥāba* (in particular the "Rightly-Guided Caliphs") and the Successors, or by individual persons such as ʿUmar b. ʿAbd al-ʿAzīz. The work also preserves older types of (Arab and to a lesser extent, Sāsānid) landed property, poll tax, taxes on land and property in their dependence on the status of the land, on conquest vs. capitulation, on the various kinds of yield, income and also irrigation [see KHARĀDJ, DJIZYA, ʿUSHR, ZAKĀT], of modalities of purchase and lease, etc. The book puts a high value on authentic tradition whose timeless model character it upholds, but does not go much into the practical applicability in real-life land taxation. None of the *kutub al-kharādj* was likely to be satisfactory in real life. But Yaḥyā also left some "lee-way": adaptations to new situations, should they become necessary, could always be done by caliphal fiat.

Bibliography: 1. Sources. Ibn Saʿd, vi, 281; Ibn Ḳutayba, *Maʿārif*, ed. Wüstenfeld, 258; Ibn al-Nadīm, *Fihrist*, 227; Nawawī, *Tahdhīb al-asmāʾ*, Cairo 1927, ii, 150; Ibn Ḥadjar, *Tahdhīb al-Tahdhīb*, Ḥaydarābād 1327, xi, 175-6; Dhahabī, *Ḥuffāẓ*, i, 327-8; idem, *Siyar aʿlām al-nubalāʾ*, Beirut 1982, ix, 522-9 no. 204; Ibn al-ʿImād, *Shadharāt*, ii, 8; Dāraḳuṭnī, *Dhikr asmāʾ al-tābiʿīn wa-man baʿdahum*, Beirut 1985, i, 405; Yaḥyā b. Adam, ed. Th.W. Juynboll, *Le livre de l'impôt foncier*, Leiden 1896, repr. with introd., notes and indices by A.M. Shākir, Cairo 1347, 1384. For an illustration of the first page of the unique Paris ms. (written 489/1096) and four *samāʿ*s from the beginning of the 7th century A.H., see G. Vajda, *Album de paléographie arabe*, Paris 1958, pl. 20.

2. Studies. F. Pfaff, *Historisch-kritische Untersuchungen zu dem Grundsteuerbuch des Jahjâ ibn Âdam*, diss. Erlangen 1917; A. Ben Shemesh, *Taxation in Islam*, i, *Yaḥyā ben Ādam's Kitāb al-Kharāj*, Leiden 1967; J. Schacht, *EI*[1] s.v.; Brockelmann, I[2], 192-3, S I, 308; Sezgin, *GAS*, i, 520. (W. SCHMUCKER)

YAḤYĀ B. ʿADĪ, Christian Arab philosopher and theologian, translator and commentator of the works of Aristotle. Coming from the Christian town of Takrīt on the Tigris (but given a Persian genealogy in some of the manuscripts), he spent his active life in Baghdād, where he earned his living as a copyist and bookseller (*warrāḳ*); this activity is recorded by his contemporary Ibn al-Nadīm (d. 380/990 [*q.v.*]), who drew extensively on Yaḥyā's library for information on the Greek philosophers and their Arabic transmitters (*Fihrist*, 264, cf. 246, 250-3). There he died on 21 Dhu 'l-Ḳaʿda 363/13 August 974 at the age of 81 years.

Ibn ʿAdī was recognised by his contemporaries as master of the *falāsifa* in his time. He took the teaching of Aristotelian philosophy from the Nestorian translator Abū Bishr Mattā b. Yūnus (d. 328/940 [*q.v.*]) and from the latter's most eminent Muslim student, Abū Naṣr al-Fārābī (d. 339/950 [*q.v.*]). Following Mattā's tradition, he translated (from the Syriac) and annotated parts of the *Organon* of logic and of Aristotle's physical and metaphysical work. Al-Fārābī's concept of philosophy as demonstrative science, where absolute knowledge is based on the principles established in Aristotle's *Analytica posteriora* (the *K. al-Burhān*) is upheld by Ibn ʿAdī as the universal foundation of sound thinking and righteous action.

The greater part of his extant philosophical work is devoted to logic and epistemology. The parts of Aristotle's *Organon* of logic, translated or re-translated by Isḥāḳ b. Ḥunayn, Abū ʿUthmān al-Dimashḳī and Mattā b. Yūnus [*q.vv.*], and his own version of the *Sophistici elenchi* (combined with two alternative versions), compiled and annotated by himself and his school, were copied from his holograph by his students and successors, ʿĪsā b. Zurʿa (d. 398/1008) and al-Ḥasan b. Suwār (d. after 407/1017), in the Paris manuscript, B.N. ar. 2346—an impressive document of the extent and standard of Aristotle reading in his school (cf. H. Hugonnard-Roche, *Une ancienne «édition» arabe de l'Organon d'Aristote: problèmes de traduction et de transmission*, in *Les problèmes posés par l'édition critique des textes anciens et médiévaux*, Louvain-la-Neuve 1992, 139-57). Apart from that on logic, he translated other works of Aristotle and his ancient commentators (e.g. parts of the *Physics* and *Metaphysics*; only his translation of Themistius' paraphrase of Aristotle's *De caelo* has survived in a Hebrew version). His own contributions are devoted to the traditional topics of introduction to the study of logic and philosophical method: a commentary of the book *Alpha minor* of Aristotle's *Metaphysics*, and numerous *quaestiones* and lecture notes on the elements of epistemology, the categories and the syllogism, and theoretical physics. A popular compendium of ethics, called *Tahdhīb al-akhlāḳ* "The refinement of character" (like that of his contemporary, Miskawayh [*q.v.*]), is founded on the Platonic tripartition of the soul (appetitive, spiritual, rational); after giving a catalogue of the virtues and vices of each part, the author shows the way to perfection under the rule of reason (see Khalil Samir, in *Arabica*, xxi [1974], 111-38, xxvi [1979], 158-78; the latest of several editions by Djād Ḥātim, Beirut 1985).

Most significant as a philosophic statement in the context of Muslim Arab society are his treatises on topics discussed in Islamic theology, not in a theological discourse, but by applying the tools of demonstrative logic to various concepts of *kalām*. Such diatribes are devoted to (1) the meaning of *tawḥīd*, the unicity of God (ed. Khalīl Samīr, *Maḳālat al-tawḥīd*, Jounieh 1980); (2) the establishment of contingent being (ed. C.-R. Ehrig-Eggert, *Die Abhandlung über den Nachweis der Natur des Möglichen von Yaḥyā ibn ʿAdī*, Frankfurt am Main 1990, Ar. text ed. by idem, in *ZGAIW*, v [1989], [Arabic part] 63-97); (3) the refutation of atomism (ed. G. Endress, in *ZGAIW*, i [1984], 155-79); (4) the concept of "acquisition" (*iktisāb*) by man of the acts created by God, current in contemporary Ashʿarism (ed. and tr. S. Pines and M. Schwarz, *Yaḥyā ibn ʿAdī's refutation of the doctrine of acquisition*, in *Studia Orientalia memoriae D.H. Baneth dedicata*, Jerusalem 1979); and in the same vein, (5) he established, against the claims of the Arab grammarians, philosophical logic as the universal tool to control correct reasoning (defending the position taken by Abū Bishr Mattā, "On the difference between the arts of philosophical logic and Arabic grammar", ed. Endress, in *Jnal. for the Hist. of Arab Science*, ii [Aleppo 1978], 38-50, 156; Ger. tr. and comm. by idem, *Grammatik und Logik: arabische Philologie und griechische Philosophie im Widerstreit*, in B. Mojsisch (ed.), *Sprachphilosophie in Antike und Mittelalter*, Amsterdam 1986, 163-299).

As a Christian theologian, Yaḥyā b. ʿAdī defended the Monophysite concept of the Incarnation against Nestorianism, and made use of the same theological-philosophical model for his apology for the Christian faith, notably the dogma of the Triune God, against Muslim polemical arguments. God is one in substance, but constituted of three essential attributes (*ṣifāt*) called *personae* (hypostases, *aḳānīm*): goodness (*djūd*), wisdom (*ḥikma*), and might (*ḳudra*). This interpretation of the Trinity reflects the primary divine triad of Neoplatonic theology (Christianised by Ps.-Dionysius Areopagita), and in the philosophical model of Ibn ʿAdī, is considered equivalent to the three aspects of the divine intellect thinking itself: absolute intellect (*ʿaḳl*), intelligence (*ʿāḳil*, thinking its own essence), and intelligible (*maʿḳūl*, being its own primary object of knowledge). These essences—the Father, the Son, and the Spirit, in the language of religion—are perceived separately, but are inseparable from the divine substance. Incarnation is the conjunction of the divine *logos*—which is one substance—with a human nature, of which the Virgin Mary is the material cause.

Both in philosophy and theology, his teaching was continued by his Christian disciples, among whom ʿĪsā b. Zurʿa was the most prominent. But his influence went well beyond this circle, and through Muslim philosophers and intellectuals like Abū Sulaymān al-Sidjistānī and Abū Ḥayyān al-Tawḥīdī [*q.vv.*], over the following generations he reached a wide readership of courtiers, scientists, and even *mutakallimūn*.

Bibliography: Texts. A. Périer, *Petits traités apologétiques de Yahyâ ben ʿAdî*, Paris 1920; E. Platti (ed. and tr.), *La grande polémique anti-nestorienne de Yaḥyā b. ʿAdī, I-II*, 4 vols. Louvain 1981-2 (= CSCO, 427-8, 437-8); idem (ed. and tr.), *Abū ʿĪsā al-Warrāq, Yaḥyā b. ʿAdī, De l'Incarnation*, 2 vols. Louvain 1987 (= CSCO, 490-1); Saḥbān Khulayfāt (Khalīfāt), *Maḳālāt Yaḥyā b. ʿAdī*, ʿAmmān 1988.

2. Studies. A. Périer, *Yaḥyâ ben ʿAdî, un philosophe arabe chrétien du Xe siècle*, Paris 1920; M. Meyerhof, *Von Alexandrien nach Bagdad*, Berlin 1930, 31; Graf, *GCAL*, ii, 233-49; R. Walzer, *Greek into Arabic*, Oxford 1962, 66 ff.; G. Endress, *The works of Yaḥyā ibn ʿAdī: an analytical inventory*, Wiesbaden 1977; Platti, *Yaḥyā ibn ʿAdī, théologien chrétien et philosophe arabe: sa théologie de l'Incarnation*, Leuven 1983 (Orientalia Lovanensisa Analecta, 14); E. Giannikis, *Yaḥyā ibn ʿAdī against John Philoponus on place and void*, in *ZGAIW*, xii (1998), 245-302. (G. ENDRESS)

YAḤYĀ B. **AKTHAM**, ABŪ MUḤAMMAD al-Marwazī al-Tamīmī, *faḳīh* who had been a pupil of al-Shāfiʿī, judge and counsellor of ʿAbbāsid caliphs, d. 242/857.

A native of Marw, he became Grand Judge (*ḳāḍī 'l-ḳuḍāt*) of Baghdād after having been being appointed judge in Baṣra by al-Ḥasan b. Sahl [*q.v.*] in 202/817-18. He soon became a member of al-Maʾmūn's court circle as an adviser and boon-companion, thus exemplifying a trend under this caliph to take legal scholars rather than administrators as political counsellors. He accompanied al-Maʾmūn to Syria and Egypt and on the campaign against Byzantium of 216/831 (al-Ṭabarī, iii, 1104). There were persistent accusations against him of pederasty, and on al-Maʾmūn's death he fell from power. Re-appointed Grand Judge under al-Mutawakkil during the years 237-40/851-5, he again fell into disgrace, departed for the Pilgrimage but died at al-Rabadha near Medina at an advanced age on 15 Dhu 'l-Ḥidjdja 242/14 April 857. He is said to have been the author of various works on *fiḳh*, none of which has survived.

Bibliography: See D. Sourdel, *Le vizirat ʿabbāside*, i, 238-9, and Pellat's ed. of Masʿūdī, *Murūdj*, index, vii, 763-4, detailing the primary sources for Yaḥyā's life, and also Ziriklī, *Aʿlām*, ix, 167. Al-Khaṭīb al-Baghdādī, *Taʾrīkh Baghdād*, xiv, 191-204 no. 7489, and Ibn Khallikān, ed. ʿAbbās, vi, 147-65, tr. de Slane, iv, 33-51, have substantial biographical entries on him. (C.E. BOSWORTH)

YAḤYĀ B. **ʿALĪ** [see MUNADJDJIM, BANU 'L-. 4].

YAḤYĀ (or YUḤANNĀ) B. AL-**BIṬRĪḲ**, Abū Zakariyyāʾ, scholar, who was probably a Mālikī, famed for his translations from Greek into Arabic, *fl.* in the first part of the 3rd/9th century.

Although the Arabic biographers (Ibn al-Nadim, Ibn Djuldjul, Ibn al-Ḳifṭī and Ibn Abī Uṣaybiʿa) devote to him short notices, his life is almost wholly unknown. His father al-Biṭrīḳ was himself a translator in the time of al-Manṣūr (136-58/754-75 [*q.v.*]). The author of the *Fihrist* states that he was part of the entourage of the vizier al-Ḥasan b. Sahl [*q.v.*] and that he was part of a delegation sent by the caliph to the Byzantine lands in order to collect manuscripts. Ibn Djudjul, repeated by Ibn al-Ḳifṭī, calls him Yuḥannā and makes him a *mawlā* of al-Maʾmūn (198-218/813-33 [*q.v.*]), adding that he was a faithful translator but with a faulty knowledge of Arabic, and that he was more philosopher than physician. Ibn Abī Uṣaybiʿa writes, rather curiously, that he knew Arabic and Greek badly, since, being a Latin (*latīnī*), he knew the language and literature of the Rūm of his time.

According to the Arabic biographers and to mentions in the introductions of manuscripts, a dozen or so works are attributable to him: Of Plato, the Timaeus (*K. Ṭimāʾus*). Of Aristotle, his Meteorology (*al-Āthār al-ʿulwiyya*, ed. Badawī, Cairo 1961, ed. Petraits, Beirut 1967; On the heavens and the earth (*K. al-Samāʾ wa 'l-ʿālam*; Book of animals (*K. al-Ḥayawān*, ed. Brugman and Drossaart Lulofs, Leiden 1971, ed. Badawī, Kuwait 1977-8); *First analytics* and a compendium of the *De anima* (*Djawāmiʿ kitāb al-nafs*). Of Galen, the Theriac of Piso (*K. al-Tiryāḳ ilā Bīsan*). Of Alexander of Tralles, a treatise on pleurisy (*K. al-Birsām*). Finally, attributed to Hippocrates is a *K. fi 'l-buthūr* or *Fi 'l-mawt*. The *Fihrist* further attributes to him two original works on pharmacology, the one on poisons, *K. al-Sumūmāt* (partly extant), and the other on insects, *K. Adjnās al-ḥasharāt*.

Yaḥyā b. al-Biṭrīḳ is also given as the translator of the *Secretum secretorum* (*Sirr al-asrār* or *K. al-Siyāsa fī tadbīr al-riyāsa*), the famous pseudo-Aristotelian treatise, which had a great renown in the Islamic world as also in the Christian West. The attribution of the Arabic version to Yaḥyā is based on the preface (cited by Ibn Djuldjul), in which the translator relates how he allegedly procured the work and then transposed it from the Greek into *rūmī* and Arabic. Nevertheless, it seems now established that this treatise is an Arabic apocryphal work written towards the middle of the 4th/10th century, and that the preface belongs to the realm of literary fiction (M. Grignaschi, *L'origine et les métamorphoses du* Sirr al-ʾasrār (*Secretum secretorum*), in *Archives d'Histoire Doctrinale et Littéraire du Moyen Age* [1976], 7-112).

Bibliography: 1. Sources. Ibn al-Nadīm, *Fihrist*, ed. Flügel, 243-4, 246, 250-1, 293, 317; Ibn Djuldjul, ed. Fuʾād Sayyid, 67; Ibn al-Ḳifṭī, ed. Lippert, 41, 55, 131, 379; Ibn Abī Uṣaybiʿa, ed. Müller, i, 205, ed. Beirut 1965, 282.

2. Studies and reference works. D.M. Dunlop, *The translations of al-Biṭrīq and Yaḥyā (Yuḥannā) b. al-Biṭrīq*, in *JRAS* (1959), 140-50; L. Cheïkho, *ʿUlamāʾ al-naṣrāniyya fi 'l-islām*, ed. C. Hechaïme, Jounieh-Rome 1983, 51-2; J. Nasrallah, *Histoire du mouvement littéraire dans l'Église melchite*, Beirut 1988, ii/2, 82-6; Brockelmann, I^2, 221-2, S I, 364; Graf, *GCAL*, ii, 32, 112-13; Sezgin, *GAS*, iii, 225 and index. (FRANÇOISE MICHEAU)

YAḤYĀ B. **ḤAMZA** AL-**ʿALAWĪ**, rhetorician, Zaydī scholar and *imām* (669-745/1270-1344; a death date of 749/1348 is also mentioned).

Yaḥyā b. Ḥamza b. ʿAlī b. Ibrāhīm al-Ḥusaynī al-ʿAlawī al-Ṭālibī, a versatile and prolific Yemeni scholar, was descended from ʿAlī b. Abī Ṭālib and the *imām* ʿAlī al-Riḍā [*q.vv.*]. He was born in Ṣanʿāʾ and played a role in politics, for after the death of al-Mahdī Muḥammad b. al-Muṭahhar in 729/1329 he ruled over part of Yemen as Zaydī *imām* under the name al-Muʾayyad bi 'llāh until his death. It is said that the number of quires (*karārīs*) written by him equalled the number of days in his life, together forming some hundred volumes. He wrote works on Zaydī theology and law, such as *al-Shāmil* and *al-ʿUmda* (on law, in six volumes), *al-Ḥāwī* (on *uṣūl al-fiḳh*, in three volumes), *Ṭawḳ al-ḥamāma* (on the imāmate), *al-Intiṣār ʿalā ʿulamāʾ al-amṣār* (18 volumes), *Mishkāt al-anwār* (against the Bāṭiniyya) and *al-Risāla al-Wāziʿa li ʾl-umma ʿan al-iʿtirāḍ ʿalā ʾl-aʾimma* (ed. Gīza 1409/1989, with an extensive commentary warning against its Shīʿī and Muʿtazilī elements by Muḳbil b. Hādī al-Wādiʿī). Whereas most Zaydīs based themselves on the Muʿtazilī theology according to ʿAbd al-Djabbār [*q.v.*], he preferred that of Abu ʾl-Ḥusayn al-Baṣrī [*q.v.* in Suppl.]. Works on grammar are *al-Ḥāṣir* (a commentary on the *Muḳaddima* of Ibn Bābashādh) and *al-Muḥaṣṣal* (commentary on *al-Mufaṣṣal* by al-Zamakhsharī [*q.v.*]). His three-volume *al-Ṭirāz al-mutaḍammin li-asrār al-balāgha wa-ʿulūm ḥaḳāʾiḳ al-iʿdjāz* (ed. Cairo 1332/1914) is an interesting, intricately subdivided and voluminous work (more than 1,300 printed pages) on rhetoric, the third of whose three main sections (*funūn*) is devoted to *iʿdjāz al-Ḳurʾān* [*q.v.*] (for an evaluation and brief discussion of its sources, see AL-MAʿĀNĪ WA ʾL-BAYĀN. 1. In Arabic). The inspiration for the book, as the author says (i, 5) was reading al-Zamakhsharī's commentary on the Ḳurʾān, *al-Kashshāf*. He sees himself as writing in the tradition of ʿAbd al-Ḳāhir al-Djurdjānī [*q.v.* in Suppl.], even though he knew the latter's two seminal works *Dalāʾil al-iʿdjāz* and *Asrār al-balāgha* only from quotations.

Bibliography: Shawkānī, *al-Badr al-ṭāliʿ*, Cairo 1348, ii, 331-3; ʿAbd al-Wāsiʿ b. Yaḥyā al-Wāsiʿī, *Furdjat al-humūm* (*Taʾrīkh al-Yaman*), Cairo 1346, 35-7; Ḥusayn b. Aḥmad al-ʿArshī, *Bulūgh al-marām*, Cairo 1939, 51; Ziriklī, *Aʿlām*, s.v.; Kaḥḥāla, *Muʿdjam al-muʾallifīn*, s.v.; Muḥ. Zaghlūl Sallām, *Taʾrīkh al-naḳd al-ʿarabī*, ii, Cairo n.d., 277-89; Aḥmad Maṭlūb, *al-Balāgha ʿinda ʾl-Sakkākī*, Baghdād 1964, 357-68 and see index; idem, *al-Ḳazwīnī wa-shurūḥ al-Talkhīṣ*, Baghdād 1967, 509-16 and see index.

(G.J.H. VAN GELDER)

YAḤYĀ B. **KHĀLID** [see AL-BARĀMIKA].

YAḤYĀ B. **MAʿĪN** b. ʿAwn al-Murrī al-Ghaṭafānī al-Baghdādī, ABŪ ZAKARIYYĀʾ, traditionist, b. 158/775 near al-Anbār, d. 233/847 on pilgrimage in Medina. A client (*mawlā*) of al-Djunayd b. ʿAbd al-Raḥmān al-Murrī, he inherited considerable wealth from his father and is reported to have spent it all on the acquisition of *ḥadīth*. Among his teachers were Sufyān b. ʿUyayna and Ibn al-Mubārak [*q.vv.*]. Authorities like Aḥmad b. Ḥanbal, al-Bukhārī and Ibn Saʿd are reported to have been among his pupils. Together with Ibn Saʿd and five others, he was ordered in 218/833 by al-Maʾmūn to profess the createdness of the Ḳurʾān. Threatened with death, they complied and the event was well publicised (al-Ṭabarī, iii, 1116). Ibn Ḥanbal never spoke to them subsequently. He reputedly exposed many traditions as false and is regarded as one of the most critical early experts on *ridjāl* [*q.v.*]. He reportedly left behind a huge library. Some of his works have been recently published.

Bibliography: See references in Sezgin, *GAS*, i, 107. Printed works. *Maʿrifat al-ridjāl*, ed. M. Kāmil al-Ḳassār, M. Muṭīʿ al-Ḥāfiẓ and Ghazwa Budayr, 2 vols. Damascus 1985; *Suʾālāt Ibn al-Djunayd*, ed. Aḥmad M. Nūr Sayf, Medina 1988, and further editions of *ridjāl* works by Nūr Sayf, Damascus-Beirut 1980; W.M. Patton, *Aḥmed ibn Ḥanbal and the Miḥna*, Leiden 1897, index. (F. LEEMHUIS)

YAḤYĀ B. **MUḤAMMAD**, al-Manṣūr al-Mutawakkil, of the Ḥamīd al-Dīn family, from the Ḳāsimī branch, Zaydī Imām and first ruler of the Mutawakkilī Kingdom of Yemen, b. *ca.* 1869, d. 1948.

On the death in June 1904 of his father Muḥammad b. Yaḥyā Ḥamīd al-Dīn, who had in 1891 rebelled against the Ottomans, Yaḥyā obtained the *bayʿa* of most of the tribes and *sayyid* clans of Yemen and assumed the *laḳab* of al-Mutawakkil ʿalā ʾllāh. Rejecting, like his predecessors, the authority of the Porte, he rose against the Turks and in April 1905 captured the capital Ṣanʿāʾ and several other towns. Ottoman reinforcements allowed Aḥmed Feyḍī to drive him out, but faced with guerilla warfare, the Turks came to an understanding with Yaḥyā, conceding *inter alia* the application of *Sharīʿa* law. Yaḥyā raised a further revolt in 1911, in concert with the *Amīr* of ʿAsīr, Muḥammad b. ʿAlī al-Idrīsī, whilst the Turks were preoccupied with events in the Balkans and Libya, besieging Ṣanʿāʾ and attacking other towns. The commander Aḥmed ʿIzzet Pasha relieved the capital but, wishing to have his hands free to deal with ʿAsīr, came to a treaty agreement with Yaḥyā in October 1911 at Daʿʿān. Yaḥyā accepted the suzerainty of the Porte in exchange for Ottoman recognition of his authority over the Zaydī parts of Yemen, and this was confirmed by an imperial *fermān* of 22 September 1913; the modern Yemeni state was thus born.

Yaḥyā remained loyal to the Turks until the end of the War in 1918, but after the Mudros armistice he took control of Ṣanʿāʾ and the whole country; some Turkish officials and soldiers remained in his service, including the last Ottoman *wālī*, Maḥmūd Nedīm Pasha. Thus what might be considered as a first "Arab revolt" left Yemen as the first independent Arab state. He now tried to build up his state as a sovereign one, with its "historic frontiers", creating a militia and an army, enforcing the *Sharīʿa* in its Zaydī interpretation, and in 1920 changing the Zaydī Imāmate into the "Mutawakkilī Kingdom of Yemen". Nevertheless, wishing to remain accessible to all Yemenis, he delegated none of his power, governing from his palace, which housed the administration, with a modest life-style. Hostile to all *bidaʿ*, he honestly believed that all progress was inimical to his people, hence he isolated the country from foreign influences as much as possible, so that his rule inevitably became tyrannical and obscurantist.

The first difficulties that he had were with the tribes, hostile to all state control and avid for subsidies. In 1922-3 his armies campaigned in the Djawf and in 1929 warfare was carried on by the Crown Prince Aḥmad against the Shāfiʿī Zarāniḳ of the Tihāma. After this, Yaḥyā took numerous hostages from leading families to ensure their fidelity. With dreams of establishing a "Greater Yemen" that would include the ancient kingdom of Ḥimyar, from ʿAsīr to ʿUmān, Yaḥyā stirred up strife against the British along the eastern frontiers of his land, but with less success than against the Turks; reprisals led to the bombing of Taʿizz in 1928. A third enemy also appeared for Yaḥyā in the shape of the Suʿūdī family, who had conquered ʿAsīr in 1920 and were now pressing southwards towards the Nadjrān oasis [*q.v.*]. Despite British attempts to restrain the Suʿūdīs, the latter occupied Nadjrān by 1934; but the question remained unsettled legally and remains a cause of discord to the present day.

Yaḥyā's policy of isolation was incompatible with his aims of independence and expansionism, which required a modern army and arms, necessitating recourse to outside powers. In 1931 he established links with ʿIrāḳ, which became fully independent the following year, and sent persons for military education there, an experiment speedily terminated when these last became infected with modernist ideas. But this was too late. Opposition grew from such modernists; from certain tribes, especially the S̲h̲āfiʿī, anti-Zaydī ones chafing at commercial restrictions imposed on them; from émigrés and refugees in Aden; and even from *sayyids* and *ʿulamāʾ* hostile to Yaḥyā's requirement of *bayʿa* in 1938-9 to his son Sayf al-Islām Aḥmad's eventual succession. A Movement of Free Yemenis (*al-Aḥrār al-Yamaniyyūn*) became active in Yemen in the mid-1940s. Yaḥyā sent Aḥmad to Aden in 1946 in an attempt at conciliation, promising some reforms and measures to open up the country. He had already joined the Arab League in 1945 and secured the admission of Yemen to the United Nations in September 1947.

However, an opposition plot had already taken shape, under the inspiration of an Algerian nationalist, al-Fāḍil al-Warṭilānī, a disciple of Ibn Bādīs with close links with the Muslim Brotherhood, and led by an ʿIrāḳī officer in Yemen, D̲j̲amāl D̲j̲amīl. ʿAbd Allāh b. Aḥmad al-Wazīr was designated as future *Imām*. A first attack on Yaḥyā in January 1948 failed, but before he could call up help from his son Aḥmad, governor of Taʿizz, a second assassination attempt succeeded on 17 February. The plot to seize power nevertheless failed through Aḥmad's success in rallying loyal tribes, but after his death in September 1962, his son and successor Muḥammad al-Badr was overthrown within a few days by Nasserist officers under Col. ʿAbd Allāh al-Sallāl. A "Yemeni Arab Republic" eventually emerged, which in May 1990 achieved Yaḥyā's dream of an enlarged, united Yemen.

Bibliography: B. Harris, *A journey through the Yemen*, Edinburgh 1893; W. Bury, *Arabia Infelix*, London 1915; ʿAbd al-Wāsiʿ al-Wāsiʿī, *Taʾrīk̲h̲ al-Yaman*, [2]Cairo 1947; E. Macro, *Bibliography of the Arabian Peninsula and notes on Mocha*, Miami 1960; W.H. Ingrams, *The Yemen. Imams, rulers and revolutions*, London 1963; M.W. Wenner, *Modern Yemen*, Baltimore 1967; Macro, *Yemen and the Western world since 1571*, New York 1968; R.W. Stookey, *Yemen*, Boulder, Colo. 1978; J. Baldry, *Imām Yaḥyā and the Yamanī uprising of 1904-1907*, in *Abr-Nahrain*, xviii (1980), 33-73; A. Rouaud, *Al-Mutawakkil ʿalā Allāh Yaḥyā, fondateur du Yémen moderne*, in *L'Afrique et l'Asie modernes*, cxli (1984), 56-73; J. Chelhod, *Bibliographie sélective du Yémen axée sur les sciences sociales*, in idem, *L'Arabie du Sud*, iii, Paris 1985, 359-415; F. Mermier, *Livres arabes. Yémen. Trente années d'édition sur le Yémen contemporain*, in *Cahiers bibliographiques* (Cairo), nos. 6-7 (winter 1989-90). (A. Rouaud)

YAḤYĀ b. PĪR ʿALĪ [see new'ī].

YAḤYĀ b. SAʿDŪN [see al-ḳurṭubī].

YAḤYĀ b. YAḤYĀ al-LAYTH̲Ī (d. 234/848), Cordovan *faḳīh*, descendant of a Berber (Maṣmūda) soldier who entered the Peninsula at the time of the conquest. His family, known as the Banū Abī ʿĪsā, was always closely connected to the Umayyad family whom they served with the pen and the sword. Yaḥyā b. Yaḥyā was the first member of the family to devote himself to religious knowledge (*ʿilm*). He took part in movements of opposition against the Umayyad *amīr* al-Ḥakam I, being mentioned among the participants in the famous Revolt of the Arrabal (al-Rabaḍ). He had to flee Cordova, unsuccessfully looking for refuge among his fellow tribesmen, but receiving it in Toledo. Once he obtained the pardon of the *amīr*, Yaḥyā exercised great influence in religious and intellectual life during the reign of ʿAbd al-Raḥmān II. According to the sources, this *amīr* did not appoint any judge without consulting Yaḥyā, and their relationship is described as the ideal that should exist between the ruler and the scholar: the latter teaches the former, advises him and legitimises his rule before the people, whilst the ruler solicits the scholar's advice. For example, ʿAbd al-Raḥmān II is said to have accepted a heavy expiation dictated by Yaḥyā for having broken his fast during Ramaḍān.

The figure of Yaḥyā b. Yaḥyā is of great relevance for the study of a crucial phase in the formation of al-Andalus, the phase of the reception of the Mālikī school of law and of the appearance and consolidation of the scholars as a group.

As regards the first aspect, Yaḥyā is considered to have introduced Mālik's *Muwaṭṭaʾ* in al-Andalus. His transmission of this work became canonical in the Islamic West and was also widely diffused in the East. This role of introducer of the *Muwaṭṭaʾ* has been challenged by N. Calder, whose conclusions, however, cannot be accepted. It is true that there is ground to doubt that a direct relationship between Yaḥyā b. Yaḥyā and Mālik b. Anas existed, but the Cordovan was undoubtedly the pupil of Mālik's pupils such as the Egyptians Ibn Wahb (d. 197/812) and Ibn al-Ḳāsim (d. 191/806) [*q.vv.*]. It is also without doubt that Yaḥyā transmitted Mālik's *Muwaṭṭaʾ*, as well as al-Layt̲h̲ b. Saʿd's *ḥadīt̲h̲*. He also transmitted *masāʾil* from Ibn al-Ḳāsim that were compiled into ten books known as *ʿAs̲h̲arat Yaḥyā*; its diffusion can be attested until the 6th/12th century. Yaḥyā had a decisive role in the Andalusī preference for Ibn al-Ḳāsim's opinions over those of other pupils of Mālik. He was also the introducer of customs and doctrines that took root in al-Andalus, such as abandoning the Ḳurʾānic precept of two arbiters sent to the house of a husband and wife to solve their marital problems, and substituting for it the practice of sending the couple to the house of a trusted man (*dār amīn*).

As regards the second aspect, Ibn Ḥazm stated that there were two legal schools that became established thanks to *riyāsa* and *sulṭa*: Abū Ḥanīfa's school, and that of Mālik b. Anas in al-Andalus. Yaḥyā b. Yaḥyā was consulted by the *amīr* on the nomination of judges, and he indicated only the names of his own companions and of those who followed his *mad̲h̲hab*. Not every judge appointed by ʿAbd al-Raḥmān II, however, was a protégé of Yaḥyā, as there were other rival factions, the most important being that of ʿAbd al-Malik b. Ḥabīb [*q.v.*]. Yaḥyā himself is said to have refused to be appointed judge, arguing that the *amīr* would be unable to find someone with greater authority than his to deal with complaints against the judges. He represents in fact a phase in which political power needed a new type of expert for the administration of justice, not only for technical reasons (given the development of *fiḳh*), but also for reasons of religious legitimacy. His fame is directly related to the large number of his pupils, a number due to the influence he had with the *amīr*, and also to his longevity. Yaḥyā b. Yaḥyā's influence can be explained, apart from his training, also by his family connections and his intellectual abilities. He had an acute intelligence (he was known as *ʿāḳil al-Andalus*), great discerning power, ability for textual interpretation, a sense of opportunity and a realist understanding common to men far from religious extremism. He strove and succeeded in establishing in al-Andalus the model of scholarly behaviour that he had witnessed in the East, in order that scholars should be treated with the same respect, awe and reverence that his Eastern teachers enjoyed.

Bibliography: M. Fierro, *El alfaquí beréber Yaḥyà b. Yaḥyà, "el inteligente de al-Andalus"*, in *Estudios onomástico-biográficos de al-Andalus. VIII*, ed. M.L. Avila and M. Marín, Madrid 1997, 269-344.

(MARIBEL FIERRO)

YAḤYĀ B. **ZAKARIYYĀʾ**, the New Testament John the Baptist, mentioned by name five times in the Ḳurʾān. The spelling of the name is evidenced from pre-Islamic times and is probably derived from Christian Arabic usage (see J. Horovitz, *Koranische Untersuchungen*, Berlin 1926, 151-2; A. Jeffery, *Foreign vocabulary of the Quran*, Baroda 1938, 290-1); Muslim exegetes frequently trace the name from a root sense of "to quicken" or "to make alive" in reference to John's mother's barrenness and his people's absence of faith. In Ḳurʾān, III, 39, John is spoken of as noble, chaste and a prophet who will "witness the truth of a word from God", that is, Jesus. VI, 85 speaks of John along with Zechariah, Jesus and Elias as being of the "righteous". XIX, 7 gives the announcement of the forthcoming birth of John to Zechariah with the note that this name was used for the first time (or that this was the first prophet by that name; cf. Luke, i. 59-63 for the likely background to this verse. Also see Ibn Kat̲h̲īr, *Tafsīr*, Cairo (Ḥalabī) n.d., iii, 112 and Muḳātil b. Sulaymān, *Tafsīr*, Cairo 1983, ii, 621: this is the first time a child had been named Yaḥyā, and that he had the name because he was the first child ever born to an aged father and a barren mother). XIX, 12, conveys the command to John to be a prophet with a book (usually taken by Muslim exegetes to mean that John confirms the Torah, not that he brought a new scripture); and in XXI, 90, John's birth is explained as a response to Zechariah's request, his wife's barrenness being cured for the occasion.

The details of the story of John in the Ḳurʾān are few, but even those slight references have given rise to a number of extended discussions throughout Muslim history. For example, the idea that John was "chaste" (*ḥaṣūr*) provoked a good deal of debate. In their discussions of Ḳurʾān, III, 39, some exegetes, such as al-Ṭabarī, considered this word to be intended in its sexual sense of being incapable of coitus ("he had a penis no bigger than this piece of straw", al-Ṭabarī, *Tafsīr*, vi, 377, a prophetic *ḥadīt̲h̲* on the authority of Saʿīd b. al-Musayyab) or of being abstentious; others, such as Ibn Kat̲h̲īr, *Tafsīr*, ii, 35-6, rejected that view, for it would suggest some sort of imperfection on the part of the prophet if he were unable to have sexual intercourse, and they argued that the word means that John was free from impure actions and thoughts, and that, as such, it does not preclude John having been married and having children. (The material on this word is usefully brought together in M.M. Ayoub, *The Qurʾān and its interpreters. II. The House of ʿImrān*, Albany 1992, 109-12; see also E. Beck, *Das christliche Mönchtum im Koran*, Helsinki 1946, 27.)

The Muslim rendering of the birth, life and death of John have, in some versions, been elaborated on the basis of the Christian accounts. John, it is said, was born six months prior to Jesus (al-Ṭabarī, i, 711); John and Jesus met in the Jordan River when Jesus was 30; and John was killed before Jesus' ascension. The mother of Mary (Hanna) and the mother of John (Elizabeth) were sisters (see MARYAM, at VI, 630a, for tables presenting the Muslim understanding of the genealogical relationships). John became a prophet, travelled to Palestine, met and baptised Jesus and departed with 12 disciples to teach the people (al-Ṭabarī, i, 712). He was put to death by Herod at the instigation of Salome (*ibid.*, i, 719).

However, many of the accounts have become quite confused because of the idea that John lived in the era of Nebuchadnezzar [see BUK̲H̲T-NAṢ[Ṣ]AR]. It is in the stories of John's death (not mentioned in the Ḳurʾān) that the extent of the confusion about him becomes evident. The Israelite king Josiah, it is said, killed John, the son of Zechariah, and Nebuchadnezzar attacked Israel as a result (al-Ṭabarī, i, 657). The cause of this was the king's desire to marry his niece, something of which John disapproved. The conspiracy of the girl's mother then led to the death of John (cf. the story of Salome, Matt., xiv. 1-11, Mark, vi. 16-29). Nebuchadnezzar invaded in order to solve problems that arose as a result of John's death (or God simply inspired him to do so). The source of the confusion here is likely the name Zechariah, a name that had already created mix-ups within the biblical tradition (cf. Matt., xxiii. 35, for the (mis-)identification of the author of the Biblical book of Zechariah with the Zechariah of Isa., vii). The prophet Zechariah of II Chron., xxiv. 22, was killed by King Joash. The Talmud (*Giṭṭin*, 57b) speaks of his "blood bubbling up warm" after his death. Nebuzaradan, Nebuchadnezzar's commander, noticed this and he was told by the inhabitants of Jerusalem that "there was a prophet among us who used to reprove us for our irreligion, and we rose up against him and killed him, and for many years his blood has not rested." Nebuzaradan then said to them, "I will appease him", and proceeded to slaughter many people. It would appear that this legend has become associated in the Muslim tradition with the death of John through the common element of the name Zechariah (see D. Sidersky, *Les origines des légendes musulmanes dans le Coran et dans les vies des prophètes*, Paris 1933, 139-40). Al-Ṭabarī, i, 713, reports that a drop of John's blood fell to the ground when he was killed and kept boiling until Nebuchadnezzar came to destroy Jerusalem; in a slightly different version (al-Ṭabarī, i, 715), John's blood boiled in the pan in which his severed head (which could still talk) had been placed. Al-Ṭabarī, i, 718, also indicates that he is well aware that many hold this story to be not true and to be a historical error, there being 461 years between the lives of Nebuchadnezzar and John the Baptist.

Bibliography (in addition to sources mentioned in the article): J.C.L. Gibson, *John the Baptist in Muslim writings*, in *MW*, xlv (1955), 334-45; G. Parrinder, *Jesus in the Qurʾan*, London 1965, ch. 5; H. Schützinger, *Die arabische Legende von Nebukadnezar und Johannes dem Täufer*, in *Isl.*, xl (1965), 113-41; R. Tottoli, *Le* Qiṣaṣ al-anbiyāʾ *di Ṭarafī*, Ph.D. diss., Naples Univ. 1996, unpubl., 487-8 (notes to paragraphs 426-31), which includes an extensive list of Arabic sources parallel to al-Ṭabarī.

(A. RIPPIN)

YAḤYĀ B. **ZAYD** B. ʿALĪ B. AL-ḤUSAYN, ʿAlid fugitive and rebel killed late in 125/summer-autumn 743. His mother was Rayṭa, daughter of Abū Hās̲h̲im [*q.v.*] b. Muḥammad b. al-Ḥanafiyya.

As the eldest son of Zayd b. ʿAlī, he participated in Zayd's revolt in Kūfa in Muḥarram 122/end of 739. After his father's death, he escaped, relentlessly sought by Yūsuf b. ʿUmar al-T̲h̲aḳafī, governor of ʿIrāḳ [*q.v.*] Yaḥyā went first to Nīnawā near Karbalāʾ. He was then given protection by the Umayyad ʿAbd al-Malik b. Bis̲h̲r b. Marwān, who concealed him in a village owned by him that later became Ḳaṣr Ibn Hubayra [*q.v.*]. After a while, he set out for K̲h̲urāsān, stopping first in al-Madāʾin. Yūsuf b. ʿUmar, learning of his whereabouts, sent a detachment after him, but he escaped to al-Rayy. From there he moved on via Naysābūr to Sarak͟hs. There he stayed for six months with Yazīd b. ʿUmar al-Taymī, a S͟hīʿī and brother of an army leader under Abū Muslim al-K͟hurāsānī, and began to seek support for armed revolt. A group of K͟hāridjīs offered their backing, but his host warned him against accepting it. Together with Yazīd he went on to Balk͟h, where al-Ḥarīs͟h b. ʿAbd al-Raḥmān al-S͟haybānī sheltered him. Yaḥyā sent an appeal in poetry to the Banū Hās͟him in Medina, challenging them to avenge his father. The leader of the Hās͟himiyya movement in K͟hurāsān, Bukayr b. Māhān, however, instructed his followers not to rise in support of Yaḥyā since the Imām, Ibrāhīm b. Muḥammad, had predicted Yaḥyā's death.

In 125/743 Yūsuf b. ʿUmar was informed of Yaḥyā's hiding place and asked Naṣr b. Sayyār, governor of K͟hurāsān, to press al-Ḥarīs͟h to surrender him. When Naṣr's deputy in Balk͟h, ʿAḳīl b. Maʿḳil al-Layt͟hī, tortured al-Ḥarīs͟h, the latter's son betrayed Yaḥyā in order to save his father's life. Yaḥyā and his companions were delivered as captives to Naṣr in Marw, but when Yūsuf b. ʿUmar informed the caliph al-Walīd b. Yazīd, he gave orders to release them. Naṣr provided Yaḥyā with money and two mules, ordering him to proceed to the caliph's court and instructing his district prefects in Sarak͟hs, Ṭūs, and Naysābūr to make him move on without lingering. When Yaḥyā reached the border of K͟hurāsān at Bayhaḳ, he decided to turn back, afraid of entering the territory of Yūsuf b. ʿUmar. Joined by seventy supporters, he defeated the superior forces moving against him from Naysābūr, Ṭūs, and Sarak͟hs at Bus͟htaniḳān (see Yāḳūt, i, 630), killing the governor of Naysābūr, ʿAmr b. Zurāra al-Ḳus͟hayrī. With the booty, Yaḥyā moved via Harāt to Djūzdjān, where the number of his men swelled to 150. Naṣr now sent a strong army under Salm b. Aḥwaz al-Māzinī in pursuit of him. After three days of fighting at a village called Arg͟hūy(a), Yaḥyā was struck by an arrow in his forehead and died, at the age of 28. Most of his men were also killed. His head was sent to Damascus where the caliph al-Walīd exhibited it in the palace and his body was crucified at the gate of Anbēr (Anbār), the capital of Djūzdjān.

The violent death of Yaḥyā made a deep impression among the S͟hīʿa in K͟hurāsān, and revenge for him became a major motive in the ʿAbbāsid revolutionary movement, which had failed to back him before. Among the first measures of Abū Muslim after the rising was to have his body properly buried and to seek out and execute all those involved in his death. Yaḥyā's tomb at or near Anbēr was visited for centuries. The Zaydī S͟hīʿa count him as one of their *imāms*.

Bibliography: Balād͟hurī, *Ansāb*, ii, ed. Maḥmūd al-Fardūs al-ʿAẓm, Damascus 1996, esp. 542-7; *Ak͟hbār al-dawla al-ʿAbbāsiyya*, ed. ʿAbd al-ʿAzīz al-Dūrī and ʿAbd al-Djabbār al-Muṭṭalibī, Beirut 1971, 242-4 and index; Ṭabarī, ii, 1709-10, 1713-14, 1770-4, tr. Carole Hillenbrand, *The waning of the Umayyad caliphate*, Albany 1989, 47-8, 51-2, 120-5; Abu 'l-Faradj al-Iṣfahānī, *Maḳātil al-Ṭālibiyyīn*, ed. A. Ṣaḳr, Cairo 1949, 142-3, 152-8; Ibn Aʿt͟ham, *Futūḥ*, Ḥaydarābād 1968-75, viii, 126-36 (partly legendary); Abū Ṭālib al-Nāṭiḳ bi 'l-Ḥaḳḳ, *al-Ifāda*, ed. Muḥ. Sālim ʿIzzān, Ṣanʿāʾ 1996, 68-72; J. Wellhausen, *Die religiös-politischen Oppositionsparteien*, Berlin 1901, 97-8; C. van Arendonk, *Les débuts de l'imamat Zaidite au Yemen*, tr. J. Ryckmans, Leiden 1960, 33-5; E. Daniel, *The political and social history of Khurasan under Abbasid rule 747-820*, Minneapolis and Chicago 1979, index.

(W. Madelung)

YAḤYĀ al-ANṬĀḲĪ [see al-anṭāḳī].

YAḤYĀ BEY (Beg) [see tas͟hlîdjalî yaḥyā].

YAḤYĀ ḤAḲḲĪ, a major figure in the development of modern Egyptian fiction, and also a diplomat, critic, and journalist (1905-92).

He was born into a distinguished Egyptian family in 1905; his uncle was Maḥmūd Ṭāhir Ḥaḳḳī, author of one of the very first experiments in novel writing in Egypt, *ʿAd͟hrāʾ Dins͟hawāy* (1906). Like many of his literary contemporaries (for example, Muḥammad Ḥusayn Haykal and Tawfīḳ al-Ḥakīm [*q.vv.*]) Ḥaḳḳī's field of study at university was the law, and he graduated in 1925. For a short period he served the legal system in Manfalūṭ, Upper Egypt, as a *muʿāwin* (adjutant). In 1929, however, he began a diplomatic career and saw service in a number of countries, including Turkey, France and Libya. Later in life, he became editor of the renowned Cairo literary journal, *al-Madjalla*, and in 1969 he was awarded the State Prize for Literature. He retired from public life in 1970 and died in December 1992.

Ḥaḳḳī was not a prolific writer, but his published works of fiction reveal the craft of an early master of its shorter genres. His most famous contribution is, without doubt, *Ḳindīl Umm Hās͟him* (1944; Eng. tr., *The saint's lamp*, 1973), a novella that marks a distinct advance over its predecessors in the fictional treatment of the themes of cultural conflict and modernisation. The story concerns a young Egyptian student, Ismāʿīl, who travels to England to obtain a degree in ophthalmology. When the training he has received fails to cure the eye disease of his own fiancée, the ensuing crisis engenders a highly symbolic (and not entirely convincing) conflict between the power of modern science and the more traditional rituals of faith. As with all classic novellas, these large themes—with their many and varied ramifications—are encapsulated in a narrative of great economy and artistry. Here and in other works of fiction, Ḥaḳḳī's skillfully crafted prose possesses an allusive quality that manages to capture the atmosphere of a scene or an entire community by the judicious choice of a word and image. These stylistic traits also contribute, needless to say, to the artistry of Ḥaḳḳī's short stories, of which he produced three collections: *Dimāʾ wa-ṭīn* (1945?), *Umm al-ʿawādjiz* (1955), and *ʿAntar wa-Djuliyāṭ* (1961?). In many of these stories, Ḥaḳḳī goes back to his experiences in the provinces of Egypt: two of the more famous examples are *al-Bustagī* ("The postman") and *Ḳiṣṣat sidjn* ("Prison story"). Those set in urban environments are more variegated in their subject-matter and explore contrasting patterns of wealth and life-style: *Kunnā t͟halāthat aytām* ("We were three orphans"), for example, about marriage prospects for a brother and two sisters who have lost their parents, and *ʿAntar wa-Djuliyāṭ*, an engaging story named after two dogs, the life-style of whose owners reflects the glaring contrasts between rich and poor.

Ḥaḳḳī was also a distinguished literary critic, and, with his *Fadjr al-ḳiṣṣa al-miṣriyya* ("Dawn of the Egyptian short story", 1960), the invaluable historian of the school of pioneer Egyptian short-story writers in the 1920s known as the *Djamāʿat al-madrasa al-ḥadīt͟ha* "New School Group", of which he himself was a part. Through this and other works of criticism, such as *K͟huṭuwwāt fi 'l-naḳd* (1961) and *ʿIṭr al-aḥbab* (1971), Ḥaḳḳī contributed his own brand of methodical opinion to the assessment of modern movements in Egyptian literature, his diplomatic tours abroad permitting him to remain above the fray during some of the more contentious periods and to preserve the quieter, more detached approach to critical reasoning that he clearly cherished.

Bibliography: 1. Works by Ḥaḳḳī. *Ḳindīl Umm Hās̲h̲im*, Cairo 1944; *Dimā' wa-ṭīn*, Cairo 1945?; *Umm al-'awādjiz*, Cairo 1955; *Fad̲j̲r al-ḳiṣṣa al-miṣriyya*, Cairo 1960; *'Antar wa-D̲j̲uliyāṭ*, Cairo 1961?; *Ḵẖutuwwāt fi 'l-naḳd*, Cairo 1961; *'Iṭr al-aḥbāb*, Cairo 1971.

2. Translations. "The brass four-poster" and "An empty bed," in *Arabic writing today. The short story*, ed. Mahmoud Manzalaoui, Cairo 1968, 76-107; *The saint's lamp and other stories*, tr. M.M. Badawi, Leiden 1973: "Antar and Juliette", tr. P. Cachia, in *JAL*, iv (1973), 146-56; "Mother of the destitute", in *Modern Arabic short stories*, tr. D. Johnson-Davies, London 1967, 97-105; "A story from prison", in *Egyptian short stories*, tr. Johnson-Davies, London 1978, 118-32; *Good morning, and other stories by Yaḥyā Ḥaḳḳī*, tr. Miriam Cooke, Washington 1987.

3. Studies. 'Abbās Ḵẖidr, *al-Ḳiṣṣa al-ḳaṣīra fī Miṣr*, Cairo 1966, 252-5; Sayyid Ḥāmid al-Nassād̲j̲, *Taṭawwur fann al-ḳiṣṣa al-ḳaṣīra fī Miṣr*, Cairo 1968, 280-92; Na'īm 'Aṭiyya, *Yaḥyā Ḥaḳḳī wa-'ālamuhu al-ḳaṣaṣī*, Cairo 1978, Miriam Cooke, *The anatomy of an Egyptian intellectual: Yaḥyā Ḥaḳḳī*, Washington 1984; J. Brugman, *An introduction to the history of modern Arabic literature in Egypt*, Leiden 1984, 263-86; Sabry Hafez, *The genesis of Arabic narrative discourse*, London 1993. (R.M.A. ALLEN)

YAḤYĀ KEMĀL (with the surname adopted in Republican times of BEYATLI), highly renowned Turkish poet and essayist, b. 2 December 1884, d. 1 November 1958.

His given name was Aḥmed Āgāh, and his earliest published poems bear the name Āgāh Kemāl. He was born in Üsküb as the son of Ibrāhīm Nād̲j̲ī Beg, who was mayor of this town, and Naḳiyye Ḵẖānim, the niece of the poet Leṣḳofčali G̲h̲ālib Beg (1828 or 29-1867). He was educated successively in Üsküb, Selānīk, Istanbul and Paris (École Libre des Sciences Politiques), and during his stay of nine years in Paris he frequented literary and political circles there. After his return to Istanbul in 1912, he taught history and literature in several institutions (Dār el-Shafaḳa Mektebi, Medreset el-Wā'iẓīn, Heybeliada Baḥriyye Mektebi, Dār el-Fünūn Edebiyyāt S̲h̲u'besi). From 1923 onwards he held various public offices, serving as a member of parliament for Urfa, Yozgat, Tekirdağ and Istanbul, and as ambassador in Warsaw, Madrid, Lisbon and Karachi. He retired in 1949 to Istanbul; his grave is in the Rumelihisarı cemetery in Istanbul.

Yaḥyā Kemāl was of the opinion that poetry is a kind of music; he developed a personal style in which the prosodic rules of *'arūḍ* [q.v.] are applied to the educated colloquial Turkish of Istanbul. A further characteristic of his style is that his poems, as well as his essays, reflect his attachment to Ottoman culture and heritage, his interest in history and his love of Istanbul; the main themes of his poetry are indeed love, patriotism, death and Istanbul.

During his lifetime, Yaḥyā Kemāl published his work only in periodicals and newspapers. Starting in 1961, the Yahya Kemal Enstitüsü (founded in the same year) published the collected works (*Yahya Kemal külliyatı*) that comprise four volumes of poetry, namely, *Kendi gök kubbemiz* (1961), *Eski şiirin rüzgârıyle* (1962), *Rubâîler ve Hayyam rubâîlerini Türkçe söyleyiş* (1963) and *Bitmemiş şiirler* (1976); and eight volumes of essays, short stories, recollections and letters, namely, *Aziz İstanbul* (1964), *Eğil dağlar* (1966), *Siyasî hikâyeler* (1968), *Siyasî ve edebî portreler* (1968), *Edebiyata dair* (1971),

Çocukluğum, gençliğim, siyasî ve edebî hâtıralarım (1973), *Târih musâhabeleri* (1975), and *Mektuplar-Makaleler* (1977).

Bibliography: See the comprehensive bibl. in *Türkiye Diyanet Vakfı İslâm ansiklopedisi*, vi, Istanbul 1992, art. *Beyatlı, Yahya Kemal* (M.O. Okay); *Dünden bugüne İstanbul ansiklopedisi*, ii, Istanbul 1994, art. *Beyatlı, Yahya Kemal* (E. Canberk); Ş. Elçin, M. Tevfikoğlu and S.K. Tural (eds.), *Ölümünün yirmibeşinci yılında Yahya Kemâl Beyatlı*, Ankara 1983; M. Demirci, *Yahya Kemal ve Mehmed Akif 'te tasavvuf*, Izmir 1993.

(EDITH G. AMBROS)

YAḤYĀ AL-MAKKĪ, Abū 'Ut̲h̲mān Yaḥyā b. Marzūḳ, an honoured court musician in early 'Abbāsid times and head of a family of court singers.

He was born in Mecca as a *mawlā* of the Banū Umayya, but went to Bag̲h̲dād at the beginning of the reign of al-Mahdī (158/775), and still performed under al-Ma'mūn (198-218/813-33). It is said that he died at the age of 120. He was considered an excellent composer and an expert in the Ḥid̲j̲āzī style of music. Ibn D̲j̲āmi' [q.v.], and both Ibrāhīm and Isḥāḳ al-Mawṣilī [q.v.] were among his disciples. He also composed a "book of songs" (*Kitāb al-Ag̲h̲ānī*), a collection of "classical" compositions, which he dedicated to 'Abd Allāh b. Ṭāhir [q.v.]. The book was criticised, however, for its incorrect attributions (*manḥūlāt*). It was corrected under the title of *Taṣḥīḥ Kitāb al-Ag̲h̲ānī* by his son Abū D̲j̲a'far Aḥmad b. Yaḥyā, who followed his father as a court musician from the time of al-Ma'mūn until the beginning of the reign of al-Musta'īn (248/862). Yaḥyā's son, Aḥmad b. al-Makkī, dedicated his father's corrected song book, as well as his own voluminous *Kitāb al-Ag̲h̲ānī*, to Muḥammad b. 'Abd Allāh b. Ṭāhir. Both books are quoted in the *Kitāb al-Ag̲h̲ānī al-kabīr* by Abu 'l-Farad̲j̲ al-Iṣbahānī. In his own compositions, Aḥmad b. al-Makkī favoured verses of his friend, the poet Di'bil [q.v.]. Aḥmad's son Muḥammad, i.e. Yaḥyā's grandson, sang at the court of al-Mu'tamid (256-79/870-92). He was a *murtad̲j̲il* singer who accompanied himself by using the traditional wand (*ḳaḍīb*). Muḥammad's transmission of the *ak̲h̲bār* of the al-Makkī family was used as a biographical source by Abu 'l-Farad̲j̲.

Bibliography: *Ag̲h̲ānī*[3], vi, 173-89, xvi, 311-6 and indices; Nuwayrī, *Nihāyat al-arab*, Cairo 1923 ff., vi, 320-3; Ibn Faḍl Allāh al-'Umarī, *Masālik al-abṣār*, facs. ed. Frankfurt 1988, x, 136-41, 144-5; S̲h̲ābus̲h̲tī, *Diyārāt*, Bag̲h̲dād 1951, 98; Ṣafadī, *Wāfī*, xiii, 249; H.G. Farmer, *A history of Arabian music*, London 1929, 113-5, 160 and *passim*; idem, *The sources of Arabian music*, Leiden 1965, nos. 9, 37, 38; E. Neubauer, *Musiker am Hof der frühen 'Abbāsiden*, Frankfurt 1965, 140-1, 167-8, 207-8; Ziriklī, *A'lām*, ix, 217; Kaḥḥāla, *Mu'd̲j̲am al-mu'allifīn*, xiii, 231. (E. NEUBAUER)

YAḤYĀ AL-NAḤWĪ, the name in Arabic sources for Johannes Grammaticus (*ca.* A.D. 490-575), the Alexandrian philologist, commentator on Aristotle, and Jacobite Christian theologian, also known in Greek as Philoponos, lit. "Lover of toil" or "Diligent", referring to a group of Alexandrian Monophysitic lay Christians—the *philoponoi*—active in debating pagan professors of philosophy. In Alexandria, John Philoponus began his career teaching philology and then studied philosophy with Ammonius son of Hermeias, the head of the Neoplatonic school there. Most of Philoponus' commentaries on Aristotle were written early in his career and are based on his master's lectures. In 529 Philoponus published his polemical *Against Proclus on the eternity of the world* (*Contra Proclum*), in which he defended creation *ex nihilo* against Proclus' famous eighteen arguments. He later directed his fire against

Aristotle's notions of infinity in his *Against Aristotle on the eternity of the world* (*Contra Aristotelem*), after which he probably revised his previously written commentary on the *Physics*, arguing now against the eternity of motion.

For these attacks on Proclus and Aristotle, Philoponus was vilified by another student of Ammonius, the pagan Neoplatonist Simplicius (*fl. ca.* A.D. 530), who, by referring to Philoponus as *grammatikos*, i.e. professor of philology (e.g. *in Cael.*, *CAG*, vii, 119,7; *in Phys.*, *CAG*, x, 1129,29), implied that Philoponus had not yet advanced to the stage of *philosophos* (professor of philosophy), and that his attacks on Proclus and Aristotle were therefore precocious and baseless.

The snideness of Simplicius' use of *grammatikos* was lost when the epithet was translated into Arabic as *al-naḥwī*. The bio-bibliographers, citing ʿUbayd Allāh b. D̲j̲ibrāʾīl b. Bak̲h̲tīs̲h̲ūʿ, simply list Philoponus' strength in philology alongside his expertise in philosophy and medicine: Ibn al-Ḳifṭī, *Taʾrīk̲h̲ al-ḥukamāʾ*, ed. Lippert, 354,15-16, and Ibn Abī Uṣaybiʿa, *ʿUyūn al-anbāʾ*, ed. Müller, 154,12-13.25.

Accounts of Yaḥyā al-Naḥwī's life, including apocryphal events such as a meeting with ʿAmr b. al-ʿĀṣ, are found in Ibn al-Nadīm, *Fihrist*, 254,19-255,5 (= Ḳ 354,3-357,13, and aU 154,3-155,32). The bio-bibliographers list Arabic translations of the following works: *On Aristotle's Categories*: N 248,21 (= Ḳ 35,3, and aU 155,15-16); *On Aristotle's De interpretatione*: N 249,2 (= Ḳ 35,18); *On Aristotle's Prior Analytics* (partial): N 249,9 (= Ḳ 36,8-9, and aU 155,16-17); *On Aristotle's Posterior Analytics*: N 249,13 (= Ḳ 36,14-15, and aU 155,17); *On Aristotle's Topics*: aU 155,17-18; *On Aristotle's Physics*: N 250,18 (= Ḳ 39,14; 245,5, and aU 155,18); *On Aristotle's De generatione et corruptione*: N 251,7 (= Ḳ 40,21, and aU 155,18-19); *On Porphyry's Isagoge*: aU 155,31-32; *Refutation of Proclus on the eternity of the world*: N 252,14 (= Ḳ 89,4-6, 356,5, and aU 155,28); *That the force* (reading *ḳuwwatuhu* with N and aU rather than Ḳ's *mawtuhu*) *of every finite body is finite*: N 254,25-26 (= Ḳ 356,5-6, and aU 155,28-29); *Refutation of Aristotle*: N 254,26 (= Ḳ 356,6-7, and aU 155,29); *Tafsīr mā bāla li-Arisṭūṭālīs*: N 254,26-27 (= Ḳ 356,7, and aU 155,19) (on the identity of this work, as well as two other unidentified treatises, see Steinschneider, 161-3); *Refutation of Nestorius*: N 254,27 (= Ḳ 356,8, and aU 155,28-29).

A number of medical treatises, including a history of medicine (cited by N 286,17; 287,13.22.24; 289,8; 293,7 [= Ḳ. 92,21; 93,1.6-7.14.19; 126,3; 127,17; 183,18-19, and aU 17,21; 22,4-5; 23,11; 33,19; 71,16-17; 76,1]) as well as commentaries on Galen's works (e.g. in *De usu partium*; N 264,26 = Ḳ 246,3, and aU 155,29), are also attributed to Yaḥyā; for a full list and a summary of Meyerhof's objections to their authenticity, see Sezgin, *GAS*, iii, 157-60.

Despite the fact that Philoponus' commentaries on Aristotle were both astute and plentiful, the *falāsifa* mention Philoponus rarely as an authority, at least compared to Alexander of Aphrodisias. Although Averroes does cite Philoponus' infinite force argument in his commentary on *Metaph.*, xii (*Tafsīr mā baʿd al-ṭabīʿa*, ed. M. Bouyges, iii, 1628,10-15), Philoponus received no credit from the *falāsifa* for his theory of impetus, perhaps his most important contribution to later thought. According to Philoponus (e.g. *in Phys.*, *CAG*, xvii, 641,13-642,20) someone who throws an object imparts a force to it that causes its continued motion. This is in contrast to the theory of Aristotle who, wedded to the notion that a moving object requires an external mover, explained projectile motion as resulting from the push given to the object by the following air. In his final discussion of impetus, Philoponus extends the theory to the moving heavens, to which God imparts a kind of dynamic inclination (*De opificio mundi*, ed. W. Reichardt, 29,2-3). Whether Avicenna's apparently similar notion of an inclining force (cf. *K. al-s̲h̲ifāʾ: Ilāhiyyāt*, ed. G. Anawati *et al.*, 383,4-13; *Fi ʾl-samāʾ wa ʾl-ʿālam*, 3,18, and *Fi ʾl-kawn wa ʾl-fasād*, 193,2-194,16, both ed. M. Ḳāsim) resulted from or developed independently of Philoponus' own impetus theory, is a question complicated by Avicenna's lack of attribution. The philosophers' ambivalence about Philoponus may well have arisen from their perception that Philoponus betrayed Aristotle in the *Contra Aristotelem* (see al-Fārābī's counter-refutation, ed. and tr. Mahdi). This betrayal cast Philoponus into the camp of the theologians: Ibn al-Ḳifṭī (306,1-2) mentions Philoponus' dialectical style of argumentation, and Averroes groups Philoponus with the Muslim *mutakallimūn* (*Tafsīr mā baʿd al-ṭabīʿa*, iii, 1498,1-7).

On the other hand, Philoponus' well-known involvement in christological and trinitarian debates—the bio-bibliographers even claim (incorrectly) that he was a Bishop (*uskuf* = *episkopos*): N 254,20 (= Ḳ 354,5, and aU 154,5)—may have also inhibited the *mutakallimūn* from openly citing his celebrated arguments (e.g. *in Phys.*, *CAG*, xvi, 428,19-429,20) against Aristotle's notion of infinity. For example, the Muʿtazilī al-K̲h̲ayyāṭ (*K. al-Intiṣār*, ed. H. Nyberg, 35,4-36,3) as well as the As̲h̲ʿarīs al-G̲h̲azālī (*Tahāfut al-falāsifa*, ed. Bouyges, 31,10-32,12) and al-S̲h̲ahrastānī (*Nihāyat al-iḳdām*, ed. A. Guillaume, 29,1-11) all appear to use, without attribution, one of Philoponus' arguments against the world's eternity (Philoponus ap. Simplicium, *In Phys.*, *CAG*, x, 1179,15-27). For whatever reason, the fact remains that Philoponus' influence on mediaeval Muslim intellectuals, while profound, tended to be hidden.

Bibliography: The most complete recent bibliographies are in R. Sorabji (ed.), *Philoponus and the rejection of Aristotelian science*, London 1987; C. Scholten (ed. and tr.), *Johannes Philoponus: De opificio mundi*, Freiburg 1997; and F. de Haas, *John Philoponus' new definition of prime matter*, Leiden 1997. For three different views on his life and career, see É. Évrard, *Les convictions religieuses de Jean Philopon et la date de son Commentaire aux* Méteorologiques, in *Bulletin de l'Academie royale de Belgique, Classes des Lettres et des Sciences Morales et Politiques*, v/39 (1953), 299-357; K. Verrycken, *The development of Philoponus' thought and its chronology*, in R. Sorabji (ed.), *Aristotle transformed*, London 1990, 233-74; and L. MacCoull, *A new look at the career of John Philoponos*, in *Journal of Early Christian Studies*, iii/1 (1995), 47-60. On the *philoponoi*, see F. Trombley, *Hellenic religion and Christianization c. 370-529*, Leiden 1994, ii, 1-51. On Simplicius' hostility to Philoponus, see P. Hoffman, *Simplicius' polemics*, in Sorabji, *Philoponus*, 57-83. On the epithet *grammatikos*, see M. Wolff, *Geschichte der Impetustheorie*, Frankfurt 1978, 108; and L. Westerink, *The Alexandrian commentators and the introductions to their commentaries*, in Sorabji, *Aristotle transformed*, 328.

Philoponus Arabus is covered comprehensively by M. Steinschneider, *Johannes Philoponus bei den Arabern*, in *Mémoires de l'Académie Impériale de St.-Petersbourg, VII*, xiii/4 (1869), 152-76, and partially by L. S̲h̲ayk̲h̲ū, *Yaḥyā al-Naḥwī: man huwa wa-matā kāna*, in *al-Mas̲h̲riḳ*, xvi (1913), 47-57; M. Meyerhof, *Von Alexandrien nach Baghdad*, in *Sb. Pr. Ak. W., Phil-hist. Kl.*, xxiii (1930), 389-429; idem, *Johannes Grammatikos (Philoponos) von Alexandrien und die arabische Medizin*, in *Mitteilungen des deutschen Institutes für ägyptische Altertumskundė in Kairo*, ii/1 (1931), 1-21; S. Pines, *Les précurseurs musulmans de la théorie de l'impetus*, in *Archeion*, xxi (1938), 298-306; F. Rosenthal, *Isḥāq b. Ḥunayn's Ta'rīkh al-aṭibbā'*, in *Oriens*, vii (1954), 55-80; A. Abel, *La légende de Jean Philopon chez les arabes*, in *Correspondance d'Orient*, x (*Acta Orientalia Belgica*) (1963-4), 251-80; J. Kraemer, *A lost passage from Philoponus'* contra Aristotelem *in Arabic translation*, in *JAOS*, lxxxv (1965), 318-27; M. Mahdi, *Alfarabi against Philoponus*, in *JNES*, xxvi (1967), 233-60; H. Davidson, *John Philoponus as a source of medieval Islamic and Jewish proofs of creation*, in *JAOS*, lxxxix (1969), 357-91; Mahdi, *The Arabic text of Alfarabi's* Against John the Grammarian, in S. Hanna (ed.), *Medieval and middle eastern studies in honor of Aziz Suryal Atiya*, Leiden 1972, 268-84; Pines, *An Arabic summary of a lost work of John Philoponus*, in *IOS*, ii (1972), 320-52; Davidson, *The principle that a finite body can contain only a finite power*, in S. Stein and R. Loewe (eds.), *Studies in Jewish religious and intellectual history presented to Alexander Altmann*, Alabama 1979, 75-92; G. Troupeau, *Un épitomé arabe du* De contingentia mundi *de Jean Philopon*, in E. Lucchesi and H. Saffrey (eds.), *Mémorial A.-J. Festugière. Antiquité païenne et chrétienne*, Geneva 1984, 77-88; D. Gutas, *Philoponos and Avicenna on the separability of the intellect: a case of orthodox Christian-Muslim agreement*, in *Greek Orthodox Theological Review*, xxxi (1986), 121-9; F. Zimmermann, *Philoponus' impetus theory in the Arabic tradition*, in Sorabji, *Philoponus*, 121-9; E. Giannakis, *Philoponus in the Arabic tradition of Aristotle's* Physics, unpubl. doct. diss., Oxford 1992; P. Lettinck, *Aristotle's* Physics *and its reception in the Arabic world*, Leiden 1994; idem, *Philoponus: on Aristotle, Physics 5-8*, London 1994; A. Hasnawi, *Alexandre d'Aphrodise* vs *Jean Philopon. Notes sur quelques traités d'Alexandre "perdus" en Greque, conservés en arabe*, in *Arabic Sciences and Philosophy*, iv/1 (1994), 53-109. (R. Wisnovsky)

YAKAN, ʿADLĪ, Egyptian politician (b. Cairo 1864, d. Paris 1933). His father, Khalīl b. Ibrāhīm Yakan, was a grandson of Muḥammad ʿAlī's sister. The child of a wealthy landed family and educated in part in European and Ottoman schools, ʿAdlī was a member of the Turko-Egyptian aristocracy that had emerged in 19th-century Egypt.

He was a leading figure in Egyptian politics from World War I to the early 1930s. He served as Minister of Education in the Cabinets of Ḥusayn Rushdī during the War. In late 1918–early 1919 he engaged, along with Rushdī, in an unsuccessful attempt to form a delegation to go to London to negotiate Egypt's post-war status. As Foreign Minister in 1920, he did proceed to London to discuss the Egyptian question with Lord Milner. Appointed Prime Minister for the first time in March 1921, ʿAdlī again went to London to re-negotiate Egypt's status with Lord Curzon. Excluded from the negotiations and suspicious of ʿAdlī's more accommodating position, Saʿd Zaghlūl [*q.v.*] and the Wafd denounced the ʿAdlī-Curzon negotiations. Faced with Wafdist opposition, the ʿAdlī ministry resigned in December 1921 without concluding an agreement.

ʿAdlī was a founding member of the Liberal Constitutionalist Party in October 1922, serving as the party's president until 1924. He again became Premier in June 1926, in a coalition government with the Wafd. Criticism of his moderate policies by the Wafdist parliamentary majority led to his ministry's resignation in April 1927. In October-December 1929 he led a caretaker ministry charged with supervising parliamentary elections. President of the Senate in 1930, he resigned the post in October 1930 in protest against Ismāʿīl Ṣidḳī's abrogation of the Constitution of 1923. Aristocratic and aloof but a man of personal dignity and integrity, ʿAdlī ended his political career as a respected elder statesman, dying in 1933.

Bibliography: Ziriklī, *Aʿlām*[2], v, 6; ʿAbd al-Raḥmān al-Rāfiʿī, *Thawrat sanat 1919*, 2 vols. Cairo 1955; idem, *Fī aʿḳāb al-thawra al-Miṣriyya*, 3 vols. Cairo 1959; Afaf Lutfi al-Sayyid Marsot, *Egypt's liberal experiment, 1922-1936*, Berkeley, etc. 1977; Marius Deeb, *Party politics in Egypt*, London 1979. (J. Jankowski)

YAKAN, MUḤAMMAD WALĪ AL-DĪN, Ottoman-Egyptian liberal spokesman and neoclassicist poet (1873-1921). The son of Ḥasan Sirrī and the grandson of Ibrāhīm Pasha Yakan, a cousin of Muḥammad ʿAlī, Walī al-Dīn Yakan was born in Istanbul on 2 March 1873. He was brought to Egypt by his family as a child. Orphaned at six, Walī al-Dīn was raised by his uncle ʿAlī Ḥaydar, a high official of the Khedivial establishment, and attended the Princes' School (*Madrasat al-Andjāl*) where children of the dynasty were educated. After graduating, Walī al-Dīn worked briefly in the Public Prosecutor's Office and for Khedive ʿAbbās Ḥilmī II [*q.v.*]. After a visit to Istanbul in 1895, he became a vehement critic of the Ottoman régime of ʿAbd al-Ḥamīd II [*q.v.*]. His short-lived periodical *al-Iʿtimād* was eventually banned by the Ottoman government. Returning to Istanbul, Walī al-Dīn worked in the Customs Service and was eventually made a member of the Supreme Council for Public Instruction. Continued criticism of the Ḥamīdian régime let to his banishment to Sīwās from 1902 until the Young Turk Revolution in 1908. Walī al-Dīn returned to Egypt shortly after the Young Turk Revolution. He worked in the Justice Ministry until 1914, when Sultan Ḥusayn Kāmil [*q.v.*] made him his Arabic Secretary. Afflicted with asthma, in 1919 Walī al-Dīn retired to Helwan in 1919, and died there on 6 March 1921.

Walī al-Dīn Yakan is best known as a neoclassicist Arabic poet and a champion of liberalism and toleration within the late Ottoman empire. His autobiographical *al-Maʿlūm wa 'l-madjhūl* (1909, 1911) was largely an exposé of Ḥamīdian despotism. Although originally a supporter of the Young Turk movement, his other pre-World War I works *al-Ṣaḥā'if al-sūd* (1910) and *al-Tadjārib* (1913) contained criticisms of the ethnic inclinations of the Unionist régime which succeeded ʿAbd al-Ḥamīd II. More an Ottoman patriot than an Egyptian nationalist, Walī al-Dīn also took a relatively sympathetic view of the British occupation and the British impact upon Egypt. He once described himself as a liberal Ottoman who had become a literary Arab.

Bibliography: Walī al-Dīn Yakan's *Dīwān* was published posthumously, Cairo 1924. Two biographies are Sāmī al-Kayyālī, *Walī al-Dīn Yakan*, Cairo 1960, and ʿAlā' al-Dīn Waḥīd, *ʿĀshiḳ al-ḥurriya, Walī al-Dīn Yakan*, Cairo 1987. Evaluations of his place within modern Egyptian literature may be found in Mounah A. Khouri, *Poetry and the making of modern Egypt, 1882-1922*, Leiden 1971, 111-13, and J. Brugman, *An introduction to the history of modern Arabic literature in Egypt*, Leiden 1984, 54-6. Brief biographical sketches are available in Khayr al-Dīn al-Ziriklī, *al-Aʿlām*, [5]Beirut 1980, viii, 118, and A. Goldschmidt, Jr., *Biographical dictionary of modern Egypt*, Boulder 2000, 229-30. (J. Jankowski)

YAKHSHI FAḲĪH, Ottoman historian, d. after 816/1413.

Yakhshi Faḳīh is the earliest known compiler of *menāḳib* [see MANĀḲIB] or exemplary tales of the Ottoman dynasty in Ottoman Turkish. However, his compilation has not survived as an independent work, and the only reference to it is that made by ʿĀs̲h̲ïḳpas̲h̲azāde [*q.v.*]. The latter records that in 816/1413, while accompanying Meḥemmed I's army on campaign, he fell ill and "remained behind at Geyve, in the house of Yak̲h̲s̲h̲i Faqīh, the son of Ork̲h̲ān Beg's *imām* . . . it is on the authority of the son of the *imām* that I relate the *menāqib* of the Ottoman House as far as [Bāyezīd I]" (V.L. Ménage, *The menāqib of Yak̲h̲s̲h̲i Faḳīh*, in *BSOAS*, xxvi [1963], 50; ʿĀs̲h̲ïḳpas̲h̲azāde, *Taʾrīk̲h̲*, ed. ʿĀlī, Istanbul 1332/1914, 84). Ménage suggests that, contrary to previous assumptions, it is not the material that ʿĀs̲h̲ïḳpas̲h̲azāde and the Anonymous Chronicles have in common which derives from Yak̲h̲s̲h̲i Faḳīh but, rather, certain information that is unique to ʿĀs̲h̲ïḳpas̲h̲azāde. According to a variant reading in one manuscript of ʿĀs̲h̲ïḳpas̲h̲azāde's history, Yak̲h̲s̲h̲i Faḳīh had a written (rather than an oral) version of the *menāḳib* that was seen by the younger historian.

Aside from ʿĀs̲h̲ïḳpas̲h̲azāde's statement that Yak̲h̲s̲h̲i Faḳīh was the son of Isḥāḳ Faḳīh, *imām* to sultan Ork̲h̲ān [*q.v.*], no other biographical details are known.

Bibliography: For additional references, see Ménage, *art. cit.*, in *BSOAS*, xxvi (1963), 50-4.

(Christine Woodhead)

YAʿḲŪB, the Arabic name for the Old Testament Patriarch Jacob, son of Isaac, son of Abraham.

Yaʿḳūb is mentioned by name in the Ḳurʾān 16 times in ten sūras. The nature of his appearance tends to be formulaic in that he often appears in reference to other prophets and personages familiar also from the Bible. In what have traditionally been deemed earlier sūras, he appears in the following formula: "We gave [Ibrāhīm] Isḥāḳ and Yaʿḳūb . . ." (VI, 84; XIX, 49; XXI, 72; XXIX, 27). This has been thought by some scholars to demonstrate that in the early revelations Jacob was considered to be a son of Abraham and not his grandson. This notion might have been corrected in XI, 71, where the divine narrator informs Abraham's unnamed wife: "So We gave her the good news of Isaac, and after Isaac Jacob." Certainly in II, 133, when Jacob on his death bed queries his sons whether they will remain believers, they reply: "We will worship your God, the God of your fathers Abraham, Ishmael and Isaac" (see also XII, 6). In other late sūras (II, 136, 140; III, 84; IV, 163), he appears in a different sequence: "Ibrāhīm, Ismāʿīl, Isḥāḳ, Yaʿḳūb, and the tribes", which seems to correspond more fully with biblical representations. In all of these references, Jacob is portrayed as an ancient and pious biblical prophet, but his character is not developed.

In XIX, 6, Jacob is mentioned in the context of the divine promise to Zakariyyā of the impending birth of Yaḥyā (cf. Luke i. 5-64). Here, the name Jacob carries that of the biblical Israelites as a whole, still without any character development.

We learn slightly more about Jacob in the Joseph sequence of sūra 12. Although mentioned by name only three times, he is referred to indirectly another twenty-five times. Jacob does not trust his sons (XII, 11, 18, 83) and they do not respect their father (XII, 8, 16-17, 95). Jacob's prophetic nature is evident from his knowledge of Joseph's future greatness (XII, 6), his foreboding of and response to the supposed death of Joseph (XII, 13, 18), and in his response to the sons' plight in Egypt (XII, 83, 86-7, 96).

Post-Ḳurʾānic literature, which clarifies the Ḳurʾānic genealogical ambiguity by bringing it in line with that of the Bible, greatly expands the role and character of Jacob, often in parallel with the biblical narrative and Jewish aggadic extensions. Jacob's honorific *laḳab* is *al-ṣafiyy* "the pure". He was to emerge from his mother's womb before his twin, Esau, but after the latter threatened to block his mother's womb and kill her, Jacob gave way. Esau resisted or disobeyed (*ʿaṣā*), so was called ʿAyṣ or ʿAyṣā, while Jacob was born grasping the heel (*ʿaḳib*) of his brother. Jacob is called Isrāʾīl because he is noble in the eyes of God (*sariyy Allāh*) or because he travelled at night (*yasīr fī 'l-layl* or *yasrī bi 'l-layl*) to escape the wrath of Esau. Some exegesis has Jacob marry Leah's sister Rachel only after Leah's death (cf. IV, 23). He knew the truth that the entire family would bow down to Joseph all along (cf. XII, 86).

Jacob is cited in the Ḥadīt̲h̲ as an example of one who is patient and trusting in God in the face of suffering (cf. XII, 18), and suggestions are offered in the exegetical literature as to why he suffered; e.g. he does not insist that his sons feed a poor boy who has come to their door, but years later insists on exceptional behaviour for them because they are a community of prophets.

Bibliography: Buk̲h̲ārī, *Ṣaḥīḥ, anbiyāʾ*, 16; Ibn Ḳutayba, *Maʿārif*, ed. ʿUkās̲h̲a, 38-42; Ṭabarī, i, 294, 354-60, 404-5; T̲h̲aʿlabī, *Ḳiṣaṣ al-anbiyāʾ*, Beirut n.d., 89, 94-125; Kisāʾī, *Ḳiṣaṣ al-anbiyāʾ*, ed. Eisenberg, 154-6, 170, tr. W.M. Thackston, *The tales of the prophets of al-Kisaʾi*, Boston 1978, 163-6, 180-1; Ibn Ḥad̲j̲ar, *al-Fatḥ al-bārī*, Cairo 1398/1978, xiii, 166; T.P. Hughes, *A dictionary of Islām*, 223; L. Ginzberg, *The legends of the Jews*, Philadelphia 1909-36, i, 317-424, v, 270-323; J. Walker, *Biblical characters in the Koran*, Glasgow 1930; *EI*[1] s.v. (R. Paret); H. Speyer, *Die biblische Erzählungen im Quran*, Gräfenhainichen 1931, 213-14, 217-18, 220.

(R. Firestone)

YAʿḲŪB b. **ʿALĪ S̲H̲ĪR** [see germiyān-og̲h̲ullarï].

YAʿḲŪB b. **DĀʾŪD** [see abū ʿabd allāh yaʿḳūb].

YAʿḲŪB b. **KILLIS** [see ibn killis].

YAʿḲŪB b. al-**LAYT̲H̲** al-Ṣaffār ("the coppersmith"), Abū Yūsuf, adventurer in Sīstān and founder of the dynasty there of Ṣaffārids [*q.v.*], functioned as *amīr* in Sīstān from 247/861 and then as ruler of an extensive military empire in the eastern Islamic lands until his death in 265/879, in practice independent of the ʿAbbāsid caliphs.

The origins of Yaʿḳūb's family in Sīstān were clearly humble, despite attempts of later historians to elevate his father al-Layt̲h̲ to the status of head of the guild of coppersmiths in the province. He was one of four brothers who were members of local bands of *ʿayyārs* [*q.v.*], in the Sīstān context something between anti-K̲h̲ārid̲j̲ite vigilantes, also called in the sources *muṭṭawwiʿa* "volunteer fighters for the faith", and bands of brigands and rowdies. However, little in Yaʿḳūb's later career shows him as a fervent warrior for the cause of Sunnī orthodoxy, and once in supreme power in Sīstān, he did not hesitate to come to an agreement with the local K̲h̲ārid̲j̲ites and to incorporate many of them in his own army.

Abandoning the trade of coppersmith, Yaʿḳūb rose to power in the capital Zarang [*q.v.*] by first serving under but then setting aside the *ʿayyār* leaders Ṣāliḥ b. al-Naḍr and Dirham b. Naṣr, and was recognised as *amīr* in Sīstān in Muḥarram 247/April 861. He had first to dispose of the threat from the dispossessed Ṣāliḥ, who had fled eastwards to Bust and had sought help from the Zunbīl [*q.v.*], the local ruler in southeastern Afg̲h̲ānistān, the regions of Zamīndāwar and Zābulistān [*q.vv.*]. Ṣāliḥ was captured and killed by the end of 250/early 865, and the Zunbīl defeated and killed in battle in the region of al-Rukhkhadj [*q.v.*], that of the later Ḳandahār (251/865). A major campaign in 256/869-70 took Yaʿḳūb as far as Kābul, Bāmiyān and Pandjhīr, having marched through Zābulistān via Ghazna, in pursuit of the son of the former Zunbīl. A further campaign into Zābulistān first secured the capture of the Zunbīl's son at the fortress of Nāy Lāmān (nothing more is heard of his fate) and then pushed on northwards to Balkh, where Yaʿḳūb captured the city from its ruler, Dāwūd b. Abī Dāwūd [see bānīdjūrids, in Suppl.]. These conquests also gave Yaʿḳūb temporary control of the silver mines of Pandjhīr and Badakhshān [*q.vv.*], and coins of his were minted there from 259/872-3 to 261/874-5. These Ṣaffārid activities in eastern Afghānistān spelt the end of the dynasty of Zunbīls who had blocked expansion of the Arabs there for some two centuries, and the Islamisation of that region, including the Kābul valley (but not the lands to its north, Kāfiristān [*q.v.*]) now presumably took shape.

Yaʿḳūb was now ready to attack the Ṭāhirids [*q.v.*], nominal suzerains over Sīstān as governors of the East for the ʿAbbāsids, although they had not in fact exercised any control over Sīstān since 239/854. There were clashes in the frontier zone of western Afghānistān where the spheres of Ṣaffārid and Ṭāhirid authority met, possibly over taxation, and in 253/867 Yaʿḳūb attacked Harāt and Pūshang, capturing various of the *Ṭāhiriyya* (members of the family or their partisans?). Negotiations over their release brought Yaʿḳūb into direct contact with the ʿAbbāsid caliphs for the first time, and al-Muʿtazz was compelled to award Yaʿḳūb the governorship of Fārs if he could secure it, explicit recognition for the first time of Yaʿḳūb's rising power in the East. In 259/873, however, Yaʿḳūb was ready for a final onslaught on the Ṭāhirids' capital, Nīshāpūr, at a moment when Ṭāhirid authority was already being weakened in Khurāsān by pressure from the Zaydī Shīʿīs of Ṭabaristān and their Daylamī allies. Yaʿḳūb entered the city in Shawwāl 259/August 873 without striking a blow, captured Muḥammad b. Ṭāhir II b. ʿAbd Allāh [*q.v.*], and advanced into the Caspian coastlands, pursuing the Zaydī Imām al-Ḥasan b. Zayd [*q.v.*]. The ʿAbbāsid caliph protested mildly in that same year at Yaʿḳūb's annexation of Khurāsān, and more vigorously in 261/874, when ʿUbayd Allāh b. ʿAbd Allāh b. Ṭāhir I assembled the pilgrims from northern and eastern Persia at Baghdād, denounced Yaʿḳūb's actions as being without caliphal authority and absolving them from allegiance to him.

Yaʿḳūb's considered response was to spend the next two years consolidating his position in Kirmān, Fārs and Khūzistān in southern Persia, having temporarily taken over Fārs in 255/869 though unable to hold it whilst he was involved with the affairs of Khurāsān and the Caspian provinces. But in 261/875 Yaʿḳūb re-appeared in Fārs, defeated the local chief Muḥammad b. Wāṣil, and moved westwards to Rāmhurmuz and Khūzistān, thereby threatening Lower ʿIrāḳ and making feasible a junction with the Zandj [*q.v.*] rebels there against the caliphate (in practice, Yaʿḳūb rejected overtures from the Zandj leader ʿAlī b. Muḥammad, but the appearance of the Ṣaffārid armies undoubtedly bolstered the Zandj cause indirectly). The panic-stricken caliph al-Muʿtamid offered Yaʿḳūb a vast array of governorships if he would halt his advance, but the latter refused and advanced into ʿIrāḳ. However, in a battle near Dayr al-ʿĀḳūl [*q.v.*] on the Tigris (9 Radjab 262/8 April 876), Yaʿḳūb's army was decisively defeated, abandoning his baggage and allowing various of his captives, including Muḥammad b. Ṭāhir, to escape. The threat to Baghdād was thus lifted. Yaʿḳūb spent the last three years of his life in Khūzistān and Fārs, still spurning an alliance with the Zandj, and died of an abdominal malady in Shawwāl 275/June 879. He was succeeded as ruler over the Ṣaffārid empire by his brother ʿAmr b. al-Layth [*q.v.*].

Yaʿḳūb's meteoric rise and the great empire of military conquest which he assembled mark the first breach in the fabric of the united ʿAbbāsid caliphate, for Yaʿḳūb dismissed the "caliphal fiction" where by all local rulers, however much autonomy they enjoyed in practice, acknowledged their authority as arising from an act of caliphal delegation. The provincial Persian Yaʿḳūb, on the other hand, rejoiced in his plebeian origins, denounced the ʿAbbāsids as usurpers, and regarded both the caliphs and such governors from aristocratic Arab families as the Ṭāhirids with contempt. Frugal in his mode of life and a fearless military commander, Yaʿḳūb was sceptical in questions of inherited power and social prestige, and was an exponent of *Realpolitik*. He cannot have taken seriously the attempts of the eulogists, who inevitably gathered in his entourage, to link the obscure Layth family with the Sāsānid emperors and the mythical first kings of Persia, nor is it at all certain whether we should regard the scraps of verse in New Persian emanating from his circle as showing Sīstān as a cradle of the New Persian literary revival [see muḥammad b. waṣīf].

Bibliography: 1. Sources. The main ones are Yaʿḳūbī, *Taʾrīkh*; Ṭabarī; Ibn (Abī) al-Azhar (in Ibn Khallikān's extensive biography of Yaʿḳūb, ed. ʿAbbās, vi, 402 ff., tr. de Slane, iv, 301 ff.); Masʿūdī, *Murūdj*; Gardīzī and Ibn al-Athīr (both using the lost history of the governors of Khurāsān by Muḥammad al-Sallām [*q.v.*]); Djūzdjānī and, above all, the anonymous local history, the *Tārīkh-i Sīstān*.

2. Studies. The pioneering study was that of Th. Nöldeke, *Yakúb der Kupferschmied und seine Dynastie*, in his *Orientalische Skizzen*, Berlin 1892, 187-217, Eng. tr. *Sketches from oriental history*, London and Edinburgh 1892, 172-206. The early career of Yaʿḳūb is treated in detail by C.E. Bosworth in *Sīstān under the Arabs, from the Islamic conquest to the rise of the Ṣaffārids (30-250/651-864)*, Rome 1968, 109-21, and his career of conquest in idem, *The history of the Saffarids of Sistan and the Maliks of Nimruz (247/861 to 949/1542-3)*, Costa Mesa and New York 1994, 67-180. See also idem, in *Camb. hist. Iran*, iv, 106-16; *The New Islamic dynasties*, Edinburgh 1996, 172-3 no. 84; and ṣaffārids.

(C.E. Bosworth)

YAʿḲŪB BEG, Muḥammad, ruler of Kāshghar 1282-94/1865-77.

He was born in 1820, or rather 1826-7, in Pishkend near Tāshkend. His father was Pīr Muḥammad Mīrzā (or Muḥammad Laṭīf), who claimed descent from Tīmūr. Originally from Ḳaratigīn [*q.v.*], he became *ḳāḍī* of Kurama and moved on to Pishkend in 1234/1818. Yaʿḳūb Beg's mother was the sister of the influential Shaykh Niẓām al-Dīn, who tutored Yaʿḳūb Beg in his youth. Traditionally, he should have become a *mullā*, but instead through his brother-in-law, Nūr Muḥammad Khān, governor of Tāshkend, he joined the Khoḳand army, and in 1261-2/1845, with the rank of *ḳosh-begi* [*q.v.*] was entrusted with the defence of Aḳ-Masdjid. Here he married a Ḳïpčaḳ woman from Juelik, who bore him his first son, Beg Ḳulī Beg, in 1265/1848. In 1270/1853 he had to abandon

Aḳ-Masdjid to the Russians. When he defended Čimkend in 1281/1864, he again had to retire to Tās̲h̲kend, where he joined ʿĀlim Ḳul, *de facto* ruler of K̲h̲oḳand. In the same year, to remove a possible rival, he was sent by ʿĀlim Ḳul with 66 followers to support Buzurg K̲h̲ān's claims as head of the K̲h̲ʷādja family in Kās̲h̲g̲h̲ar [*q.v.*]. He had been recalled by the usurper Ṣiddīḳ Beg to legitimise his rule. Ṣiddīḳ Beg was killed after a bloody feud, and Buzurg K̲h̲ān recognised the ruler of K̲h̲oḳand as his suzerain and appointed Yaʿḳūb Beg *kos̲h̲-begi.* In 1284/1867 Yaʿḳūb Beg ousted Buzurg K̲h̲ān. After he was joined by K̲h̲oḳand refugees in 1282/1865, Yaʿḳūb Beg managed to lift the Chinese siege of the new town of Kās̲h̲g̲h̲ar. In 1283-4/1866-7 he consolidated his rule over the southern part of Eastern Turkistan [see SINKIANG], and the Amīr of Buk̲h̲ārā conferred upon him the title of *Atalïḳ g̲h̲āzī.*

In 1287/1870 Yaʿḳūb defeated the Dungans [see AL-ṢĪN], when he drove them from Urumči. After that, he controlled almost all of Eastern Turkistan except for the Ili valley, occupied by the Russians the same year. In 1293-4/1876-7 the Chinese under Zuo Zongtang reconquered Sinkiang or Xinjiang.

Yaʿḳūb Beg died probably on 16 Djumādā I 1294/29 May 1877 from unknown causes. His son Beg Ḳulī Beg after a short civil war became his legitimate successor, but fled to K̲h̲oḳand in Ṣafar 1295/February 1878, from where he tried to enter Kās̲h̲g̲h̲ar again until 1299/1881.

His contemporaries were fascinated by Yaʿḳūb Beg's personality and success in state-building. Attributing to him a rather reckless youth, he became in the eyes of his contemporaries the founder of the first quasi-modern state in Central Asia with a seemingly efficient army and a civilian administration based strictly on the *S̲h̲arīʿā*. The members of the Forsyth mission in 1289-90/1872-3 found a well-functioning administration, while the Chinese reports from 1294/1877 onwards—from a war-stricken country—paint a different picture. In the Chinese sources, Yaʿḳūb Beg is normally called an adventurer coming from outside Sinkiang and imposing an Islamic rule on a multi-ethnic and multi-religious population [see MASRAḤ]. Buğra, himself from Sinkiang, condemns him for imposing foreign Andidjānī rule on the Muslims in Sinkiang. While Russians and Britains regarded him as a possible and not negligible pawn in the "Great Game", Sāyrāmī and Ottoman sources describe him as a proponent of Muslim unity.

Yaʿḳūb Beg built up his power by trusting almost exclusively his K̲h̲oḳandī kin, exceptions being Ḥakīm K̲h̲ān, descendant of the K̲h̲ʷādjas, and Niyāz Beg of K̲h̲otan. Both of these deserted the toppling Kās̲h̲g̲h̲arī state in the final crisis to become rivals for power. He resorted also to diplomatic means to achieve recognition. Mainly through his most important agent and nephew, Sayyid Muḥammad Yaʿḳūb K̲h̲ān, he concluded treaties of trade with Russia in 1872 and Britain in 1873, and gained the recognition of the Ottoman empire as Amīr of Kās̲h̲g̲h̲ar, receiving a modest amount of military help.

Bibliography: 1. Sources. Mehmed ʿĀtif, *Kās̲h̲g̲h̲ar tārīk̲h̲i. Bāʿit̲h̲-i ḥayret āḥwāl-i g̲h̲arībesi*, Istanbul 1300; Mūsā Sāyrāmī, *Tārīk̲h̲-i Ḥāmidī* (Chin.: *Imidi shi*), Beijing 1986; A.N. Kuropatkin, *Kashgarija. Historical and geographical sketch of the country: its military strength, industries and trade*, tr. W.E. Gowan, Calcutta 1882; T.D. Forsyth, *Report of a mission to Yarkand in 1873, with historical and geographical information regarding the possessions of the Ameer of Yarkand*, Calcutta 1875; R.B. Shaw, *Visits to High Tartary, Yarkand, and Kashghar (formerly Chinese Tartary), and return journey over the Karakoram Pass*, London 1871; Y. Halaçoğlu, *Binbaşı Ismail Hakkı Bey'in Kaşgar'a dair eseri*, in *Tarih Enstitüsü Dergisi*, Istanbul xiii (1987), 527-49.

2. Studies. D.Ch. Boulger, *The Life of Yakoob Beg, Athalik Ghazi, and Badaulet, Ameer of Kashgar*, London 1878; idem, *The late Yakoob Beg of Kashgar*, in *Central Asian questions. Essays on Afghanistan, China, and Central Asia*, London 1885, 360-95; M. Saray, *Rus işgali devrinde Osmanlı devleti ile Türkestan hanlıkları arasındaki siyasi münasebetler (1775-1875)*, new ed. Ankara 1994; M.E. Buğra, *S̲h̲arḳi Turkistān tārīk̲h̲i*, Srinagar 1940; Kim Ho-dong, *The Muslim rebellion and the Kashgar emirate in Chinese Central Asia 1864-1877*, Ph.D. diss. Harvard Univ. 1986, unpubl.; R. von Mende-Altayli, *Die Beziehungen des osmanischen Reiches zu Kashghar und seinem Herrscher Yaʿqub Beg, 1873-1877*, Bloomington, Ind. 1999.

(RANA VON MENDE-ALTAYLI)

YAʿḲŪB BEY [see GERMIYĀN-OG̲H̲ULLARĪ].

YAʿḲŪB ČELEBI [see GERMIYĀN-OG̲H̲ULLARĪ].

YAʿḲŪB ḲADRĪ, ḲARA-ʿOT̲H̲MĀNOG̲H̲LU, in modern Turkish orthography, Yakub Kadri Karaosmanoğlu, Turkish author, journalist, politician and diplomat (1889-1974).

In 1909, he was a charter member of the literary movement *Fedjr-i Ātī* ("The Dawn of the Future") [*q.v.*], which embraced the motto "Art for art's sake". After becoming conscious of the deleterious effects for Turkey of the Balkan War of 1912, his philosophy of art changed; he now argued that art was first and foremost the expression of a society, of a nation, and of a historical period. Hence all of his nine novels depict a specific period in modern Turkish history. In order of their publication in book form, these novels are: *Kirālïḳ ḳonaḳ* ("Mansion to let", 1922), *Nūr Baba* (1922), *Ḥüküm gedjesi* ("The night of judgement", 1927), *Ṣodom we Gomōre* ("Sodom and Gomorrah", 1928), *Yaban* ("The stranger", 1932), *Ankara* (1934), *Bir sürgün* ("An exile", 1937), *Panorama* (1953-4), *Hep o şarkı* ("Forever that song", 1956) [see ḲIṢṢA. 3(b)]. The most controversial of these novels were *Nūr Baba* and *Yaban*. *Nūr Baba* was attacked for revealing Bektās̲h̲ī secrets and presenting a dervish lodge in a negative light. *Yaban* dramatised the alienation of the intellectual from the masses for whom he purported to speak. All of his novels demonstrate his deft use of irony.

He was elected to the Grand National Assembly in 1923, and served as a representative till 1934. In 1932, he started to publish a journal called *Kadro* ("The staff"). Critical reaction from within his party to the journal's ideas led him to be appointed ambassador in 1934. He served as an ambassador in various posts till his retirement in 1955. He recounts his years as a diplomat in his memoir *Zoraki diplomat* ("Forced diplomat", 1955). His other memoirs are: *Anamın kitabı* ("My mother's book", 1957), *Vatan yolunda* ("On the road to and for the nation", 1958), *Politikada 45 yıl* ("Forty-five years in politics", 1958), *Gençlik ve edebiyat hatıraları* ("Memories about youth and literature", 1969).

In 1912, he contracted tuberculosis, from which he suffered all his life. Perhaps because of his frail health, he was of a pessimistic bent, but nevertheless he always remained an idealist. He was a fervent admirer of Atatürk and his ideals, believing that Kemalism was the first humanist reaction to imperialism and as such had a universal dimension. He presents his ideas on Mustafa Kemal in his monograph *Atatürk* (1946).

Bibliography: Hasan Ali Yücel, *Edebiyat tari-*

himizden ("From our literary history"), Ankara 1957; Niyazi Akı, *Yakup Kadri Karaosmanoğlu*, Istanbul 1960; Selim İleri, *Çağdaşlık sorunları* ("Problems of modernisation"), Istanbul 1978, 71-118; Berna Moran, *Türk romanına eleştirisel bir bakış* ("A critical look at the Turkish novel"), Istanbul 1983, i, 136-67; Sibel Erol, *The image of the intellectual in Yakup Kadri Karaosmanoğlu's works*, in *The Turkish Studies Association Bulletin*, xvi 1 (April 1992), 1-21. (Sibel Erol)

YAʿḲŪB al-MANṢŪR [see abū yūsuf yaʿḳūb al-manṣūr].

YAʿḲŪB PASHA, physician and official for the Ottoman sultan Meḥemmed the Conqueror.

Ottoman, Jewish and Venetian sources provide information about him, called Jacopo or Giacomo in Italian sources, yet due to the possibility that other personalities named Yaʿḳūb or even anonymous ones may have been intended by some of the surviving texts, much of his life remains obscure. He was born around 829-34/1425-30 and came from the Italian town of Gaeta. Of a Jewish family, he remained a Jew through most of his career, but became a Muslim late in life, along with several of his sons, although it is likely that some of his descendants retained their original religion. The date of his conversion is not known, but it must have occurred before Muḥarram 888/ February 1483, when a document establishing a pious foundation of his was witnessed by many high-level courtiers, the future Grand Vizier Mesīḥ Pasha among them. No mention of his name later than this date has apparently been located. Thus an older assumption, namely, that Yaʿḳūb Pasha was killed during the disturbances following the demise of Meḥemmed II in 863/1481 cannot be correct. An Istanbul town quarter was apparently named after Yaʿḳūb Pasha's foundation, but by the middle of the 10th/16th century, both these had disappeared.

We do not know where Yaʿḳūb/Giacomo received his medical training, but he appears in the entourage of the young Sultan Meḥemmed II, whom he served not only as a physician but also in administrative capacities, among other things as a *defterdār*. Without stating his sources, Meḥmed Thüreyyā in his *Sidjill-i ʿothmānī* (Istanbul 1308-after 1316/1888-99) claims that he also achieved the titles of *wezīr* and *muṣāḥib* and was highly respected, placing his subject's death in 889/1484. Yaʿḳūb Pasha's descendants may well have received a diploma exempting them from various taxes, the poll-tax (here called *bash kharādjī*) and the *ʿawāriḍ* among them. However, as the relevant diploma is only extant in a rather free translation into Hebrew, which moreover leaves out the name of the beneficiary, it is possible that it was granted not to Yaʿḳūb/ Giacomo but to some other, less well-known Jewish medical man of Meḥemmed's.

Writing before 965/1558, Ṭashköprüzāde praises Yaʿḳūb/Giacomo's medical skills and records several anecdotes describing them. These seem to have earned him the sultan's trust throughout the latter's reign; however, during Meḥemmed's last illness, it was not he who treated the ruler but the Persian physician Lārī. Already in 861-2/1457, Giacomo had received a gift of fine red velvet from the Venetian Senate, so that he must have been regarded as an influential figure at court. In 875-6/1471 the Venetian Senate contacted him through intermediaries after an offer on the physician's part to have the sultan murdered, an overture to which the Senate responded positively. However, there is no evidence that Giacomo of Gaeta ever followed up on his promises, nor was he at the Ottoman court ever accused of plotting with Venetians or others. He may in actual fact have been an Ottoman secret agent, exploring Venetian intentions on behalf of the sultan.

Bibliography: *Eš-šaqāʾiq en-noʿmānijje von Ṭašköprüzāde*, tr. and annotated O. Rescher, Istanbul 1927, 143; F. Babinger, *Jaʿqûb-Pascha, ein Leibarzt Mehmed's II. Leben und Schicksale des Maestro Jacopo aus Gaeta*, in *RSO*, xxvi (1951), 87-113; idem, *Mehmed, der Eroberer, und Italien*, in *Byzantion*, xxi (1951), 127-70; B. Lewis, *The privilege granted by Mehmed II to his physician*, in *BSOAS*, xiv (1952), 550-63; E. Birnbaum, *Hekim Yaʿqub, Physician to Sultan Mehemmed the Conqueror*, in *The Hebrew Medical Journal*, i (1961), 222-50; M.A. Epstein, *The Ottoman Jewish communities and their role in the fifteenth and sixteenth centuries*, Freiburg 1980, 79-83, final lines of *wakfiyye* on p. 290.

(Suraiya Faroqhi)

al-YAʿḲŪBĪ, early Arab historian and geographer, *fl.* in the second half of the 3rd/9th century.

Life. Abu 'l-Abbās Aḥmad b. Abī Yaʿḳūb b. Djaʿfar b. Wahb b. Wāḍiḥ was born in Baghdād in the 3rd/9th century. Trained as a member of the secretarial class, he went to Armenia as a young man and later served under the Ṭāhirids [*q.v.*] in Khurāsān. After the fall of the Ṭāhirids there in 259/872-3, he settled in Egypt, and died there in the early 4th/10th century, but apparently not before 292/905.

Works. Three of al-Yaʿḳūbī's works have come down to us. The first in importance is the *Taʾrīkh* which, as he himself describes it, is a "concise" account of the origins and history of the world (ii, 2). Published in two volumes, the first part begins with Adam and his descendants (the section dealing with the creation of the world is lost) and includes accounts, *inter alia*, of the Israelites, Assyrians, Babylonians, Indians, Greeks, Romans, Persians, Chinese, Egyptians, Yemenis and Syrians. In his discussion of the Israelites, he frequently quotes from the Hebrew Bible, to which he probably had access in Arabic via versions in Greek and Syriac (Adang, 120), and he cites the New Testament in describing the life of Jesus. Biblical materials are often seamlessly combined in al-Yaʿḳūbī's narrative with *midrashim* and apocrypha, reflecting no doubt the way such materials reached him and other mediaeval Muslim historians (Adang, 117-20 and *passim*). His emphasis throughout is on highlighting the cultural achievements of the peoples he describes, and it is on this same note, with an account of the religious and cultural life in pre-Islamic Arabia, that his first volume ends.

A substantial part of the second volume is devoted to the life of Muḥammad, following which the history of Islam is organised by the reigns of individual caliphs. His history is in fact one of the earliest surviving works to follow this mode of organisation (Noth, 46). The *ayyām* of Abū Bakr, ʿUmar and ʿUthmān are described in sequence before "the caliphate of the commander of the faithful ʿAlī b. Abī Ṭālib" (ii, 206) and of his son al-Ḥasan; the account then proceeds with the *ayyām* of Muʿāwiya b. Abī Sufyān and his Umayyad successors, followed by the ʿAbbāsids, the last of whom to be described is the caliph al-Muʿtamid (d. 279/892 [*q.v.*]). Al-Yaʿḳūbī also gives considerable attention to the Imāmiyya and the travails of their *imāms*, which has led scholars to debate (inconclusively) whether he ought to be considered as a Shīʿī, and if so in what sense. Petersen, *ʿAlī and Muʿāwiya*, 173, sees al-Yaʿḳūbī as trying "to find a compromise between the conflicting views" on the first *fitna*; but al-Yaʿḳūbī's hostile account of the caliphate of ʿUt̲h̲mān (ii, 186-206) seems to leave little room for any such compromise. While his hostility towards the Umayyads stands out clearly, as does his proclivity for ʿAlī, the precise character of al-Yaʿḳūbī's religious orientation remains uncertain. His attitude towards the ʿAbbāsids seems, in general, to have been favourable though there are discordant notes. His characterisation of ʿAbbāsid rule as mere *ayyām* rather than as *k̲h̲ilāfa* might suggest some ambivalence in his attitude towards the régime, for instance; and his account of the death of Mūsā al-Kāẓim [*q.v.*], the seventh *imām* in the reckoning of the Twelver S̲h̲īʿa, while in custody of Hārūn al-Ras̲h̲īd (ii, 499-500) is not complimentary to the ʿAbbāsids, even though the caliph is not explicitly blamed for the death. Though al-Yaʿḳūbī does not give *isnāds* for his accounts, some of his information comes from ʿAbbāsid family sources (he himself was a *mawlā* of the ʿAbbāsid family); but it also comes from the ʿAlids (in particular, through D̲j̲aʿfar b. Muḥammad [*q.v.*], the sixth *imām*) (ii, 3; cf. also Duri, 67).

Owing perhaps to his secretarial background but, equally, in the interest of narrative embellishment, al-Yaʿḳūbī offers a generous sampling of letters which purport to have been written by some of the individuals who figure prominently in his accounts. He also shows considerable interest in the *awāʾil* [*q.v.*]. Other literary forms such as speeches and lists are common as well in his narratives. One noteworthy instance of the latter is the listing of scholars (usually characterised here as *fuḳahāʾ*) appended to the reigns of individual caliphs. Such lists seem intended to suggest the early origin of religious scholars recognisable as a determinate group—from the time of the Rightly-Guided Caliphs [see AL-K̲H̲ULAFĀʾ AL-RĀS̲H̲IDŪN, in Suppl.] onwards—as well as the continuity of this institution in later generations. Yet it is odd that there are no such lists for the reign of al-Maʾmūn—precisely the caliph who, with the *miḥna* [*q.v.*], inaugurated a strenuous conflict with many of the *ʿulamāʾ*—or, for that matter, for any of his successors. This example may, however, indicate no more than the selective, anthology-like character of al-Yaʿḳūbī's work which belongs, in this as in other respects, firmly to the genre of *adab* [*q.v.*].

Al-Yaʿḳūbī's other major work is the *Kitāb al-Buldān*, which he completed in Egypt in 278/891, and which is an administrative geography of the lands of Islam, of the Turks and of the Nubians; portions describing Byzantium, India and China are no longer extant. Based on al-Yaʿḳūbī's travels in Armenia, Ād̲h̲arbāyd̲j̲ān, India and North Africa, and, no doubt on his experience in the caliphal administration, this book provides much historical, topographical and statistical information on the regions it describes. Like the *Taʾrīk̲h̲*, the *Buldān* is also a work of *adab*. In their interest in the influence of climate on human life and culture (a theme already investigated by al-D̲j̲āḥiẓ [*q.v.*]), their celebration of Bag̲h̲dād as the unique and blessed meeting place of the peoples and cultures of the world (*Buldān*, 233 ff.; Miquel, iv, 225 ff.), and, in general, their concern to provide an abridgement (*muk̲h̲taṣar*) of such knowledge which "one cannot afford to ignore" (233), the *Buldān* and the *Taʾrīk̲h̲* evince features common to many a work of the *adab* genre.

Al-Yaʿḳūbī is also the author of a short treatise entitled *Mus̲h̲ākalat al-nās li-zamānihim* in which he shows, in a highly schematic and impressionistic fashion, some of the ways in which the life and tastes of people are modelled on those of the caliphs under whose reign they live (the caliphs are described in chronological sequence, from Abū Bakr to the ʿAbbāsid al-Muʿtaḍid, d. 289/902 [*q.v.*]). In its attention to the supposed origin of particular practices and those who instituted them, as Millward has observed, this work is of interest as an early example of the *awāʾil* genre. More important, however, is this work's testimony to al-Yaʿḳūbī's search for patterns in history, a concern which is occasionally also in evidence in both his *Taʾrīk̲h̲* and *Buldān* (cf. Khalidi, *Arabic historical thought*, 124 ff.).

In general, the principal importance of al-Yaʿḳūbī's historical work is threefold. One of the earliest surviving examples of "universal" history in Islam, it is especially noteworthy for its attention to the cultural peculiarities and diversity of the ancient, pre-Islamic nations and cultures it surveys. Also significant in this regard is his unusually extensive use of non-Islamic sources, e.g. biblical, midrashic and apocryphal materials, to provide a detailed account of the beliefs and practices of the peoples he describes (cf. Adang, 38, 71 ff., 117 ff.). Second, though the character of al-Yaʿḳūbī's S̲h̲īʿī proclivities remains uncertain and, in any case, almost all classical works of history preserve traditions with many different tendencies (cf. Noth, 9-10 and *passim*), the *Taʾrīk̲h̲*, like the work of al-Masʿūdī [*q.v.*], does provide much insight and information on early S̲h̲īʿī attitudes and, in so doing, supplements works with a decidedly Sunnī perspective on what we know about the formation of religious identities in the first centuries of Islam. Finally, al-Yaʿḳūbī's work represents, even as it contributed to, the growth of *adab*-historiography, an increasingly ascendant trend which even the massive *Taʾrīk̲h̲* of al-Ṭabarī [*q.v.*], based on the methodology of *ḥadīt̲h̲*-scholarship, could do little to displace.

Bibliography: 1. Editions. *Taʾrīk̲h̲*, ed. M.Th. Houtsma, *Historiae*, 2 vols. Leiden 1883; *K. al-Buldān*, ed. M.J. de Goeje, Leiden 1892, French tr. G. Wiet, *Les pays*, Cairo 1937; *Mus̲h̲ākalat al-nās li-zamānihim*, ed. W.G. Millward, Beirut 1972, Eng. tr. idem, *The adaptation of men to their times. An historical essay by al-Yaʿqūbī*, in *JAOS*, lxxxiv (1964), 329-44.

2. Studies. Brockelmann, I², 258-60; E.L. Petersen, *ʿAlī and Muʿāwiya in early Arabic tradition*, Copenhagen 1964, 169-74; F. Rosenthal, *A history of Muslim historiography*, ²Leiden 1968, 133-4; A. Miquel, *La géographie humaine du monde musulman*, Paris 1967-88, i, 102-4, 285-92; W.G. Millward, *Al-Yaʿqūbī's sources and the question of Shīʿa partiality*, in *Abr-Nahrain*, xii (1971-2), 47-74; Y. Marquet, *Le Šīʿisme au IXᵉ siècle à travers l'histoire de Yaʿqūbī*, in *Arabica*, xix (1972), 1-45, 101-38; T. Khalidi, *Islamic historiography. The histories of Masʿūdī*, Albany 1975, index; *Dict. of the Middle Ages*, New York 1982-9, xii, 718-19, art. *al-Yaʿqūbī* (L.I. Conrad); A.A. Duri, tr. Conrad, *The rise of historical writing among the Arabs*, Princeton 1983, 64-7, 150, 158-9; B. Radtke, *Weltgeschichte und Weltbeschreibung im mittelalterlichen Islam*, Beirut 1992, 11-15 and index; Khalidi, *Arabic historical thought in the classical period*, Cambridge 1994, 115-18, 120-1 and index; C. Adang, *Muslim writers on Judaism and the Hebrew Bible, from Ibn Rabban to Ibn Ḥazm*, Leiden 1996, 36-9, 71-6, 117-21, 226-7, 231-2, 250-3.

(MUHAMMAD QASIM ZAMAN)

YAʿḲŪBIYYŪN, YAʿĀḲIBA, YAʿḲŪBIYYA, pls. of Yaʿḳūbī, the Arabic term for the Jacobite Christians.

"Jacobites" is the designation for members of the Syrian Orthodox Church, whose dogmatical position (Christ's divinity and humanity coming together into one nature), known as monophysitism, was thought to be at variance with the moderate dyophysite christology formulated by the Fourth Ecumenical Council of Chalcedon (451; one divine and one human nature united into one person and hypostasis). Consequently, the "Monophysites" were considered as heretics by the leaders of the Imperial Church. In the aftermath of the Council, the situation in the Patriarchate of Antioch was much confused, with some members of the clergy and the laity professing a monophysite christology, and others, nicknamed *Malkāyē* (Melkites), i.e. followers of the Emperor (*malkā*), supporting the resolutions of Chalcedon. Allegiances, however, could change, and periods of fierce persecution by the imperial authority alternated with attempts at reaching a compromise. A complex mixture of cultural (a certain, but not absolute, opposition Greek-Syriac), nationalistic (erosion of the unitarian ideology of the Roman Empire), socio-economic (recession in Syria connected with social unrest; repression) and theological factors contributed to promoting feelings of a distinct "monophysite" identity. The activity of Jacob Burdʿānā (Arabic: Bardāʿī, also Bardānī, d. A.D. 578), who ordained several bishops and appointed a monophysite Patriarch for the see of Antioch, brought about the result that, along with the Imperial Church, an independent monophysite Church came into being in the Patriarchate of Antioch. Its members were mainly Syriac-speaking, but also included some Arab tribes (Ghassān, Taghlib [*q.vv.*]) who belonged to the monophysite community and even had their own bishops. Before Jacob's lifetime, the Monophysites had already crossed the classical boundaries of the Antiochian Patriarchate and settled in Sāsānid territory, sc. in ʿIrāḳ, mainly in the region around Takrīt. The name of the Jacobite Church is to be traced back to Jacob Burdʿānā, but the Jacobites consider the christianisation of Edessa [see AL-RUHĀ] as the true beginning of their Church.

Though in the course of history, the term "Jacobites" was currently used by the Jacobites to designate themselves and was also known to Muslim heresiographers, in modern times the name "Syrian Orthodox" or "West Syrian" (the opposite of "East Syrian", i.e. "Nestorians" [see NASṬŪRIYYŪN] and "Chaldaeans") is preferred, with "Syrian Orthodox" as the correct self-designation. In a more general sense, "Jacobites" was also used as synonym for all monophysite Christians, including the Copts (e.g. al-Masʿūdī, *Tanbīh*, 151).

1. The Islamic period.

On account of a lack of contemporary Jacobite sources, it is a matter of discussion whether the advance of the first Islamic troops and their conquest of important centres of Jacobite Christians such as Edessa (16/637) and neighbouring cities in Mesopotamia and Syria were welcomed as a liberation from the persecutions by the Greeks. Echos of this assumption can be found in the writings of later West Syrian historiographers such as the Patriarch Dionysius of Tell Maḥrē (d. 845), the Patriarch Michael the Syrian (d. 1199) or the bishop and scholar Gregory Barhebraeus (d. 1286 [see IBN AL-ʿIBRĪ]). In Persia, the West Syrian Metropolitan of Takrīt, Mārūtā, took the side of the Muslims and opened the gates of the citadel to them (Barhebraeus, *Chron. ecclesiasticum*, ed. J. Abbeloos and Th. Lamy, Louvain 1877, iii, 123-5). On the other hand, the same sources frequently stress the cruelty of the Muslim invaders and seem to consider the consequences of their attacks as a just punishment by God for the sins committed by the Jacobite community.

During the reign of the first Umayyad caliphs, Christians had many opportunities ("as scribes, managers and administrators" according to Dionysius of Tell Maḥrē) to contribute to the development of the new society in Syria. Incidentally, we also know the names of West Syrians holding public functions. One of the best known was al-Akhṭal [*q.v.*], a member of the Banū Taghlib and court poet under ʿAbd al-Malik b. Marwān. The latter also summoned the rich Edessan merchant Athanasius b. Gummāyē to his court and appointed him secretary to his brother ʿAbd al-ʿAzīz, governor of Egypt (Dionysius of Tell Maḥrē, in *Chronique de Michel le Syrien*, ed. J.-B. Chabot, Paris 1899-1910, iv, 447, ii, 474). During the reign of the same caliph, however, the Jacobite Church was also confronted with the problem of apostasy, mainly due to mixed marriages, as we may infer from some ecclesiastical canons issued by bishop Jacob of Edessa (d. 708), but also the first discriminatory measures aimed at Christians played a role here. Patriarch John II (d. 754) was the first to obtain official recognition of his dignity from the caliph himself (Marwān II).

In the ʿAbbāsid period, with the transfer of the seat of government to ʿIrāḳ, most areas populated by Jacobite Christians were situated relatively far from the capital, partly even outside Muslim territory. This situation laid Jacobite church leaders open to the accusation of being on the side of the Byzantines (Fiey, *Abbassides*, 183). This did not prevent Patriarchs regularly undertaking the journey to Baghdād to obtain their investiture diploma, or even to appeal to the caliph against rival candidates or simply to settle matters of church discipline. The institution of the maphrianate (see below) appeared to be a practical solution for the problem of the contacts of the Jacobites with the authorities in Baghdād. In 301/913, a patent delivered by al-Muḳtadir to the East Syrian Catholicos Abraham Abrāzā (d. 937) regulates the official relationship between the Nestorian, Jacobite and Melkite hierarchies and the Muslim authorities, to the advantage of the Nestorians, who became the preferred interlocutors of the court (Fiey, *Abbassides*, 130). Only the Nestorian Catholicos was entitled to have his official residence in the capital. The creation of Crusader states in areas important for the Jacobite community, such as Edessa and Antioch (491/1098) and Jerusalem (492/1099), allowed the West Syrians to develop a cautious openness to the Church of Rome in theological and church political matters, without wishing, however, to submit to papal authority, as this openness was readily interpreted by the Latin clergy in Jerusalem and Antioch.

By the end of the 5th/11th century, much of the power of the ʿAbbāsids was taken over by the Saldjūḳ Turks, who settled in the traditional homelands of the Jacobites, including those territories which had so far remained outside Muslim rule. According to Michael the Syrian, the relations between Saldjūḳ and Jacobite leaders were, on the whole, relatively good. He praised their tolerant attitude in matters of faith, and he maintained good relations with the Rūm Saldjūḳ Kilīdj Arslan II. An entire chapter of his chronicle is devoted to the origin of these "Turkāyē" or "Turḳāyē" (*Chron. Michel Syr.*, iv, 149 ff., 566 ff.).

In the later ʿAbbāsid period, important parts of the Christian population had embraced Islam on account of the growing number of discriminatory measures. The Jacobite church was nevertheless able to maintain an extensive network of metropolitan sees and important monasteries, which, in the 13th century, extended from Acre on the Mediterranean coast to Tabrīz in Ādharbāydjān. After the destruction of Baghdād by the Mongols (656/1258), the centre of gravity of power again moved eastward. The first Mongol leaders were initially well disposed towards the Christians, mainly East

Syrians, but the Jacobites also took advantage of this situation. Their Maphrian, Gregory Barhebraeus, frequently stayed in the Il-K̲h̲ānid capitals of Tabrīz and especially at Marāg̲h̲a, where he was able to study contemporary Persian accounts of the Mongol invasions such as the *Tārīk̲h̲-i D̲j̲ahān-gus̲h̲āy* by D̲j̲uwaynī. By the end of the 13th century, however, the Mongols proclaimed Islam as the official religion of their empire. The 14th century was a period of decline, not only on account of the changed religious policy of the Mongol leaders, but also due to inner dissensions (see below). The Turco-Mongol incursions by Tīmūr Lang at the turn of the 14th and 15th centuries accelerated this process and brought about the destruction of important Jacobite centres in Āmid (Diyārbakir), Mārdīn and the Ṭūr ʿAbdīn. Thereafter, the West Syrians became almost everywhere a minority, living on the margin of society. Only some isolated villages in the Ṭūr ʿAbdīn [*q.v.*] and northern Mesopotamia remained entirely Jacobite. Their immediate neighbours were mostly Kurdish tribes, whose feudal structure they shared, at least in some regions. In the Ṭūr ʿAbdīn they also kept their own Aramaic language, surviving to the present day [see ṬŪR ʿABDĪN. 4.].

This situation continued during much of the Ottoman period. The position of the Jacobites was still further weakened by the creation of a Uniate Syrian Catholic Church (1662 and, on a permanent basis, from 1783 onwards), to which many important members of the Jacobite community felt attracted. Since the end of the 18th century the Armenian Patriarch in Istanbul had become the sole representative of all monophysite Christians of the empire, a tangible proof of the marginal position of the West Syrians. Only in 1882 was the Jacobite church recognised as an independent *millet* [*q.v.*]. Due to their close ties with the Armenian community, the West Syrians became involved in the Turco-Armenian conflict. During the massacres of 1895-6, the West Syrians succeeded in conveying to the Turks that their community was different from that of the Armenians, hence they generally escaped unharmed; but this distinction from the Armenians (and the Assyrian Christians) was not made in 1915-16, when about one-third of the population of the Ṭūr ʿAbdīn fell victim to the violence of the Ottoman soldiers and their Kurdish allies, amongst many other massacred Christians.

Though in 1923 the Patriarch had been compelled to leave Dayr al-Zaʿfarān, the age-old see of the Patriarchate (see below), the first years of the new Turkey of Muṣṭafā Kemāl were relatively calm due to its non-religious, nationalist orientation. After his death in 1938, the West Syrians had to pay for the fact that the Treaty of Lausanne (1923) only speaks of the religious and cultural rights of non-specified, "non-Islamic minorities". According to the current interpretation by the Turkish authorities, only the Jewish, Greek and Armenian communities are recognised as such, and not the West Syrians.

From the 1960s onwards, many West Syrians from Turkey and the Middle Eastern countries emigrated to Western Europe and North America initially as economic migrants, but since the 1980s also as applicants for political asylum (see further on this emigration; ṬŪR ʿABDĪN. 2).

2. Ecclesiastical structure.

The head of the Syrian Orthodox Church is the Patriarch "of Antioch and all the East", "all the East" referring to a classical Roman administrative division in the region east of Antioch. In the pre-Islamic as well as in the Islamic periods, the Patriarch had no fixed residence, but mainly stayed in important monasteries outside Antioch, and in the Crusader period, also in Antioch itself.

From the 11th century till 1293 he used to reside in the monastery of Mār Barṣawmā near Malaṭya. In 1293 the seat of the Patriarchate was transferred to Dayr al-Zaʿfarān, near Mārdīn, which the Patriarch left only in 1923 for Ḥimṣ (Syria). Since 1959 his residence has been in Damascus, with a recently-erected clerical training school in Maʿarrat-Ṣaydnāyā. Official texts are published in *al-Mad̲j̲alla al-Baṭriyarkiyya.* The Metropolitan of Takrīt, since the 11th century called *Maphreyānā* or Maphrian, was the official representative of the Patriarch for the eastern dioceses of the West Syrian Church. He had far-reaching powers, such as the right to convene synods and the ordination of metropolitans. Since 1152 his actual place of residence was in Mawṣil or its neighbourhood (monastery of Mār Mattay). In the ʿAbbāsid period, he had to intervene frequently at the court on behalf of his coreligionists. The function was abolished in 1859, but re-established in 1974 for the ancient community of Syrian Orthodox in India. A schismatic patriarchate and maphrianate existed in Ṭūr ʿAbdīn between 1364 and 1495.

3. The Church within the Islamic religious and cultural milieu.

(a) *Apologetic and polemical literature.* It does not seem that in the context of literary contracts with Islam (both in Syriac and Arabic), the Jacobites developed special themes absent from the writings of authors belonging to different Christian communities such as the Melkites or, especially, the Nestorians. Only in the field of christology had the Jacobites to be aware that their emphasis on the unity of the divine and human aspect in Christ was difficult to accept by Muslim thinkers, some of whom felt more sympathy for a "Nestorian" christology, which, by its presumed emphasis on the separation between Christ's divinity and humanity, seemed less to jeopardise God's transcendence. Thus the caliph al-Mahdī agreed with the East Syrian Catholicos Timothy I that the christological position of the West Syrians virtually amounted to theopaschitism. Yaḥyā b. ʿAdī [*q.v.*] took it upon himself to defend the traditional Jacobite christological position against an (otherwise unknown) Muslim thinker, Aḥmad Abu 'l-Ḥusayn al-Miṣrī, who partly supported the Nestorian point of view (E. Platti, *La grande polémique anti-nestorienne de Yahya b. ʿAdi*, CSCO, 427-8, 437-8, Louvain 1981-2).

The oldest example of West Syrian apologetics is the record (in Syriac) of a dispute between Patriarch John I d-Sedraw(hy) (d. 768) and a Muslim *amīr.* Though the dispute itself may have been a historical event which took place as early as 24/644, the record is a literary fiction composed in a much later period (the end of the 7th or beginning of the 8th centuries A.D., see G. Reinink, *The beginnings of Syriac apologetic literature in response to Islam*, in *Oriens Christianus*, lxxvii [1993], 165-87): It deals with issues such as the doctrine of the godhead of Christ, the Trinity, the superiority of Christianity and the presence of legislative texts in Christian scriptures. The language of this dispute is simple and straightforward, and lacks the philosophical terminology, which became characteristic of later West Syrian apologists. Thus the archdeacon Nonnus of Nisibis (middle of the 9th century) defended the Jacobite creed with arguments based on Scripture, but, especially, on discursive reasoning. His work (in Syriac) was mainly directed against Jews and Muslims, but the author clearly expressed his preference for Islam which he considers to be more akin to Christianity than all other outside religions, including Judaism. To substantiate this claim, he adduced what became in later times the classical argument of the Ḳurʾān's recognition of Christ as being born from a Virgin and Christ and as being "the Word and Spirit of God" (A. Van Roey, *Nonnus de Nisibe. Traité apologétique*, Louvain 1948). Nonnus' teacher Ḥabīb b. Khidma Abū Rāʾiṭa (first half of the 9th century) was the author of several apologetic treatises, all composed in Arabic. His intention was to present a Christian readership with a solid apologetic argumentation that could help them to formulate adequate answers to Muslim objections and questions. To explain the dogma of the Trinity, he made use of the classical, Islamic method of reasoning by analogy (*ḳiyās*). His efforts to be understandable to Muslims by employing the philosophical and lexical terminology of contemporary Muslim *mutakallimūn* are especially noteworthy. In order to discourage conversion to Islam he analyses the different motives that caused Christians to give up their religion (S. Griffith, *Habib ibn Hidmah Abu Raʾitah, a Christian mutakallim of the first Abbasid century*, in *Oriens Christianus*, lxiv [1980], 160-200). The problem of free will and predestination was treated by Moses b. Kēphā (d. 903). Chapter six of his treatise on this subject (in Syriac) is directed against the Mhaggrāyē (= *muhādjirūn* or Sons of Hagar), whose *mutakallimūn* are depicted, without any nuance, as defending a strict determinist position (Griffith, *Free will in Christian kalam. Moshe b. Kepha against the teachings of the Muslims*, in *Le Muséon*, c [1987] 143-59). Like Abū Rāʾiṭa, Yaḥyā b. ʿAdī, the capable student of Abū Naṣr al-Fārābī [*q.v.*], and the Nestorian philosopher Abū Bishr Mattā b. Yūnus [*q.v.*], tried to defend the Christian dogmas of the Trinity and the Incarnation with the help of a common, Muslim-Christian philosophical language, refuting one by one all single elements of the objections of his adversaries with great logical consistency. Due to the fact that he gives lengthy quotations of his Muslim interlocutors, some otherwise lost works have been preserved, e.g. of Abū Yūsuf al-Kindī or Abū ʿĪsā al-Warrāḳ (D. Thomas, *Anti-Christian polemic in early Islam. Abu ʿIsa al-Warraq's "Against the Trinity"*, Cambridge 1992). Abū ʿAlī Ibn Zurʿa and Muḥyī al-Dīn al-Iṣfahānī, authors respectively of a treatise on God's Unicity and Trinity (ed. M. Allard and G. Troupeau, Beirut 1962) and of a refutation of Islam, were to continue the tradition of West Syrian apologetics in Arabic. The last important West Syrian polemicist writing in Syriac was Dionysius bar Ṣalībī, Metropolitan of Āmid (d. 1171). His tract against the Muslims contains a section that describes the different groups into which the Muslims were divided, and it offers Syriac translations for Islamic technical terms, as well as quotations in Syriac from the Ḳurʾān (Griffith, *Dionysius b. Salibi on the Muslims*, in H. Drijvers *et alii* (eds.), *IVth Symposium Syriacum 1984*, Orient. Christ. Analecta 229, Rome 1987, 353-6).

Apologetic elements can also be found in works not primarily composed to serve apologetic purposes. Several works of historiography contain passages on different aspects of Islam. An example is the secular chronicle of Barhebraeus devoting much attention to the biography of Muḥammad, to *kalām*, etc. The same holds true for some theological writings composed primarily for the community itself, such as the *Kitāb al-Murshid*, a general theological, ethical and liturgical handbook by Yaḥyā b. Djarīr (end of the 11th century). In many passages, the author takes great care to make certain aspects of the Christian doctrine intelligible to Muslim readers by using a specific Muslim terminology such as *imām*, *sharīʿa*, *sunna*, *nāsikh-mansūkh* (to explain the relation between the New and Old Testaments), etc. Other examples of such works are the (not yet edited) theological summa of Jacob bar Shakkō (d. 1241) known as the "Book of Treasures" (in Syriac) with a passage on the *Ṭayyāyē* "Arabs, Muslims". The theological summa of Barhebraeus, the "Candelabra of the sanctuary" contains passages refuting the Muslim accusation of *taḥrīf* [*q.v.*] (*Candélabre du sanctuaire. IV. De l'Incarnation*, ed. J. Khoury, in *PO*, xxxi, Paris 1964, 110).

(b) *Canonical decisions.* The growing influence of Islam can also be gathered from a number of canonical decisions dealing with different aspects of the relations with the Islamic world. The Jacobite canonists were mostly worried about the apparently growing number of Christian women marrying Muslims. Jacob of Edessa allows these women to continue to receive Holy Communion lest they apostasise. The Patriarch Athanasius II of Balad (d. 686) denounces the participation of Christians in Muslim festivals. The Patriarch Giwargis (d. 785) states that Christians are not allowed to marry their daughters to Muslims. Those who do, as well as the women concerned, are not allowed to receive Holy Communion. The Synod of the Monastery of Shilā (846) excommunicates all Christians who "marry Ḥanpē (lit. "pagans", but in this context to be interpreted as Muslims), Jews and Magi". Also, Dionysius bar Ṣalībī, in his penitential canons, devotes some attention to women entering into relations with "Arabs and Turks". Another important issue was the problem of Christians converted to Islam but desiring to return to their old faith. Instances of how this problem was dealt with can also be found in historiographical works, e.g. the case of the apostate Maphrian Ignatius b. Kīkī (*Chron. Michel Syr.*, iii, 127 iv, 554); Jacob of Edessa stipulates that rebaptism is not necessary, but a time of penitence has to be imposed. An allusion to mixed marriages is possibly to be found in a canon of bishop John of Mārdīn (d. 1165), stipulating that children of *Mashlemānē* are only entitled to receive the baptism of John for the remission of sins, to be distinguished from the baptism administered to Christian children (*The Synodicon in the West-Syrian Tradition. II*, ed. A. Vööbus, Louvain 1976, 246).

(c) *Cultural interaction.* Though to a lesser degree than the East Syrians, West Syrians also participated in the transmission of Greek philosophy and science to the Arab world, thus contributing to the achievements of the first ʿAbbāsid period. Important translators into Arabic were ʿAbd al-Masīḥ b. Nāʿima al-Ḥimṣī, Yaḥyā b. ʿAdī and Ibn Zurʿa, all mentioned in Ibn al-Nadīm's *Fihrist*. Yaḥyā b. ʿAdī was at that time still the teacher of a number of Muslim students. In a later period, however, this situation was reversed. Barhebraeus states "we from whom (the Arabs) have acquired wisdom through translators who were all Syrians, are now in the necessity of asking for wisdom from them" (*Civil chron.*, ed. St. Ephrem the Syrian Monastery-Glanerbrug 1987, 90b). Authors like Jacob bar Shakkō, John bar Maʿdanī and, especially, Barhebraeus were influenced by Islamic thinkers, the latter not only in his scientific, medical and philosophical writings (especially from Ibn Sīnā and Naṣīr al-Dīn al-Ṭūsī) and in his chronicles, but also in his ecclesiastical treatises (the second part of his nomocanon, a work of canon law, is strongly influenced by *fiḳh*) and, surprisingly, in his works on spirituality: both the *Ethicon* and the *Book of the Dove* show influences from al-Ghazālī's *Iḥyāʾ ʿulūm al-dīn* (H. Teule, *Barhebraeus' Ethicon, al-Ghazali and Ibn Sina*, in *Islamochristiana*, xviii [1992], 73-85).

Bibliography: Partly given in the article; see also NAṢĀRĀ, with many bibliographical references.

1. General. Ephrem I Barṣawm, *Kitāb al-Luʾluʾ al-manthūr fī taʾrīkh al-ʿulūm wa ʾl-ādāb al-suryāniyya*, St. Ephrem the Syrian Monastery, Glanerbrug 1974; A. Baumstark, *Geschichte der syrischen Literatur*, Bonn 1922; P. Khoury and R. Caspar, *Bibliographie du dialogue islamo-chrétien. Auteurs chrétiens de langue arabe*, in *Islamochristiana*, i (1975), 152-69; Samir Khalil, in ii (1976), 201-42; L. Sako, *Auteurs chrétiens de langue syriaque*, in x (1984), 273-92; H. Suermann, in xv (1989), 169-74; G. Graf, *GCAL*, ii, 220-93, iv, 3-93; Cl. Sélis, *Les syriens orthodoxes et catholiques. Fils d'Abraham*, Turnhout 1988 (with extensive bibl.); B. Spuler, *Die westsyrische (monophysitische/jakobitische) Kirche*, HdO, I, 8, Leiden 1961, 170-216.

2. Specific themes and periods. H. Anschütz, *Die syrischen Christen vom Tur ʿAbdin. Eine altchristliche Bevölkerungsgruppe zwischen Beharrung, Stagnation und Auflösung*, Würzburg 1985; Th. Benner, *Die syrisch-jakobitische Kirche unter byzantinischer Herrschaft im 10. und 11. Jahrhundert*, Marburg 1989; S. Brock, *Syriac views of emergent Islam*, in G. Juynboll (ed.), *Studies on the first century of Islamic society*, Carbondale Ill. 1982 (repr. in Brock, *Syriac perspectives on Late Antiquity*, London 1984, art. VIII); H. Dryvers, *Jacob of Edessa's response to Islam*, in *Aram*, vi/1-2 (1994), 104-14; J.M. Fiey, *Chrétiens syriaques sous les Abbassides*, CSCO 420, Louvain 1980; idem, *Chrétiens syriaques sous les Mongols*, CSCO 362, Louvain 1975; S. Griffith, *Disputes with the Muslims in Syriac Christian texts. From Patr. John (d. 648) to Bar Hebraeus (d. 1286)*, in *Religionsgespräche im Mittelalter. Procs. of the 25th Wolfenbültel symposium (June 1989)*, ed. B. Lewis and F. Miewöhner, Wiesbaden 1992, 251-73; W. Hage, *Die syrisch-orthodoxe Kirche in frühislamischer Zeit*, Wiesbaden 1966; R.G. Hoyland, *Seeing Islam as others saw it. A survey and evaluation of Christian, Jewish and Zoroastrian writings on early Islam*, Princeton 1997; R. Jabre Mouawad, *The Kurds and their Christian neighbours. The case of the Orthodox Syriacs*, in *Parole de l'Orient* (Kaslik) (1992), 127-41; J. Joseph, *Muslim-Christian relations and inter-Christian rivalries in the Middle East. The case of the Jacobites in an age of transition*, Albany 1983; P. Kawerau, *Die Jakobitische Kirche im Zeitalter der syrischen Renaissance. Idee und Wirklichkeit*, Berlin 1955; A. Palmer, S. Brock and R. Hoyland, *The seventh century in the West-Syrian chronicles*, Translated Texts for Historians 15, Liverpool 1993; J.J. Roldanus, *De Syrisch Orthodoxen in Istanbul*, Kampen n.d. [1985]; H. Teule, *Istanbul, de (as)syrische kerken en de mogelijkheden van een binnenlands vluchtalternatief*, in *Het Christelijk Oosten* (1995), 3-5, 235-45; idem, *"It is not right to call ourselves orthodox and the others heretics". Ecumenical attitudes in the Jacobite Church in the time of the Crusaders*, in K. Ciggaar, A. Davids and H. Teule (eds.), *East and West in the Crusader States II*, Orient. Lovan. Analecta, Louvain 1999; A. Vööbus, *Syrische Kanonessammlungen. I. West-syrische Originalurkunden*, CSCO 307, 317, Louvain 1970. (H.G.B. TEULE)

YĀḲŪT (A.), corundum, one of the outstanding gems according to early and later Islamic writers, the others being *zumurrud* (emerald) and *luʾluʾ* (pearl) (al-Bīrūnī, *Djamāhir*, 81; *Nawādir*, 73 [from a manuscript dated 390/1000]). *Yāḳūt* (ruby) is considered by al-Bīrūnī to be the first-rated, most valuable and most expensive of all gems (*ibid.*, 32).

Etymology. Al-Djawharī opines that the word *yāḳūt* is an arabicised Persian word (*Ṣiḥāḥ*, ed. A.ʿA. ʿAṭṭār, Cairo n.d. [*ca.* 1372/1956], i, 271). Ḥamza al-Iṣfahānī, as quoted by al-Bīrūnī, derives *yāḳūt* from the Persian *yākand*. However, the term is most probably derived from the Greek *hyakinthos* via the Syriac *yakkundā* or *yakkuntā* (there are further variants, see C. Brockelmann, *Lexicon Syriacum*, Hildesheim 1966, 307a); the Greek may also be the origin of the Persian term.

In the Ḳurʾān, *yāḳūt* is referred to only once to describe the young pure virgins in Paradise as resembling it (LV, 58); al-Bīrūnī says that *yāḳūt aḥmar* (ruby) is intended here, rather than any other variety of the stone (*ibid.*, 33).

Definition. A discussion of *yāḳūt* ought to begin with clarifying the common but erroneous modern use of the word as an equivalent to ruby. In mediaeval Arabic literary and scientific textual sources, *yāḳūt* is equivalent to all varieties of the mineral corundum that we know today. Corundum is a crystallised form of alumina (Al_20_3) which occurs in many colours, among which *yāḳūt aḥmar* ("red corundum" or "ruby") is the finest. The second best, according to al-Tīfāshī [*q.v.*], is the *yāḳūt asfar*, known in English as "yellow sapphire" or "oriental topaz" (Cipriani, *Macdonald Encyclopedia of Precious stones*, 106). The third in rank is the *yāḳūt akhab* or *azraḳ* ("blue sapphire"), and the last is *yāḳūt abyaḍ* ("leuco-sapphire"). Al-Bīrūnī wondered how transparent stones like *yāḳūt* crystallised and obtained their various colours, and thought that knowing this was beyond man's comprehension. We know now that the different colours of the various types of *yāḳūt* are due to traces of a metallic oxide present in the stone as an impurity (Webster, *Gems*, 60; Bauer, *Precious stones*, 261).

Each of the four main types has gradation in colour. The *yāḳūt aḥmar*, for instance, being the most valuable, has seven shades of red, ranging from deep red, *bahramānī* (Rubicelle, Escarboucle) or *rummānī* (defined at the present time as "carmine" or "pigeon's blood"), to the pale rose-pink *wardī*. The colours of the *yāḳūt asfar* range from the deeply saturated (*djullanārī*) to the palest or straw-coloured (*tibnī*). The *yāḳūt akhab* or *azraḳ* ranges from the dark *kuḥlī* (ink blue) down to the lighter *samāwī* or *asmāndjūnī* (sky blue). The *yāḳūt abyaḍ* has two shades, the more prized of which is the *mahawī* or *billawrī* (rock crystal-like).

These four types, classified according to colour and value by a number of mediaeval Islamic writers such as Ibn Māsawayh, al-Bīrūnī quoting al-Kindī, al-Tīfāshī, Ibn al-Akfānī [*q.vv.*] and others, represent essentially varieties of the same mineral with the same degree of hardness and density.

Provenance. The mines of *yāḳūt* are in the Mogok region in Burma, in Thailand, Cambodia, Sri Lanka and other places. Al-Ḳazwīnī in *ʿAdjāʾib*, 277, locates its mines in the countries around the equator. The rough *yāḳūt* is obtained from deposits eroded from the mother-rock, and thus is normally found among sand, gravel and clay brought down the mountains by torrents and wind (Ibn Māsawayh, *Djawāhir*, 41-3; al-Bīrūnī, *Djamāhir*, 44; al-Tīfāshī, *Azhār*, 64; Bauer, 287). The best *yāḳūt* is that washed down by torrents, according to the first two of these authors.

Physical properties. *Yāḳūt* is brittle, though it is the hardest of all minerals after the diamond (*Djamāhir*, 48; *Azhār*, 70; *Nukhab*, 8), having number 9 in Mohs' scale of hardness (Bauer, 263; Webster, 74). It is also the densest of all precious stones, according to al-Bīrūnī, and it has a very high specific gravity of *ca.* 4 with insignificant variations (sapphire's specific gravity is 4.08, slightly higher than that of ruby which ranges between 3.99 and 4.06 (Bauer, 282). Al-Bīrūnī (*Djamāhir*, 77) states that, if the weight of a sapphire is 100, that of a ruby of the same size is 97⅛, the ratio in integers being 800 to 777.

Yāḳūt is described in Muslim sources as resistant to fire; it neither melts nor calcifies as other precious stones like emerald do. When *yāḳūt* is exposed to high temperature, the red variety is neither changed nor destroyed, this being a test for simulants or fakes. Al-Tīfās̲h̲ī mentions that in the *K. al-Aḥd̲j̲ār*, ascribed to Aristotle, it is said that when *yāḳūt aḥmar* is exposed to the blowpipe, it is infusible, but its beauty enhances (*Azhār*, 72). However, while the colour of the ruby remains unaltered, that of the sapphire under similar conditions will disappear; blue and yellow *yāḳūt* turn white. Sapphire can be decolourised but it does not melt in fire. Resistance to heat without loss of colour is strictly a property of *yāḳūt aḥmar*.

The same authorities state that the immediate visible characteristics and distinctive features of *yāḳūt* are its vitreous lustre and its *s̲h̲uʿāʿ* (double refraction). Transparency is expressed by "abundance of water" (*wafrat al-māʾ*), by *mas̲h̲affa*, i.e. *s̲h̲affāfiyya* "translucency," or by *ṣafāʾ* "clarity". Uniform, intense and deeply saturated colour, *is̲h̲bāʿ* or *kat̲h̲rat al-ṣibg̲h̲*, is, in addition to glittering brightness, *rawnaḳ*, one of the good features that raise its value.

Defects or impurities appear in the form of "cleavage", *s̲h̲ibh al-tas̲h̲kīk*, *tas̲h̲ʿīr*, or *s̲h̲aʿra*; "freckles" or "inclusions", *namas̲h̲*; "cavities", *k̲h̲urūḳ* (sg. *k̲h̲arḳ*), like *sūs* in wood, either filled with air, *rīḥ*, or water, *māʾ*, or mud, *raym*, or sometimes worms, *dūd*. All of these could be removed from the stone by a drill; if left within, the stone will crack. Another defect is the uneven distribution of colour which gives an appearance of "piebaldness", *bulḳa*. While the ruby is usually coloured uniformly throughout, the distribution of colour in the sapphire is often very irregular. Moreover, if the colour of the ruby is not uniform, it will become uniformly coloured through gradual heating (Bauer, 265, 282).

Cloudiness, *g̲h̲aym*, is one of the flaws mentioned by al-Kindī and Ibn al-Akfānī, who call it *g̲h̲amāma bayḍāʾ ṣadafiyya* (i.e. milky and nacreous cloud), which sticks to the surface, and if not deep, disappears through rubbing. One of the flaws enumerated by al-Kindī is the *namas̲h̲* or "freckles", which appear as patches different from the original colour; if abundant and if deep and spreading, they will be difficult to remove (cited in al-Bīrūnī, *D̲j̲amāhir*, 38).

Medical and magical uses. Apart from the physical properties of *yāḳūt*, medicinal, psychological, and talismanic qualities were also attached to it. Ibn al-Akfānī quotes Aristotle, Ibn Sīnā, Ibn Zuhr and al-G̲h̲āfiḳī as saying that, if worn as a pendant or ring, *yāḳūt* repels pestilence vapours and poison, prevents attacks of epilepsy, and cures haemorrhage (*Nuk̲h̲ab*, 11). As for its psychological effect, Ibn Sīnā is quoted as saying that it is efficacious in strengthening the heart and boosting one's mood. The talismanic property is characterised as attracting divine favour and thus fulfilling the wearer's needs. The lucky wearer would also be assured of reverence among people and high regard by kings.

Prices and values. Besides size, high prices depend on the fulfillment of a set of quality conditions, namely, intensity of colour, *s̲h̲ibaʿ*; full "éclat" or transparency, *māʾ*; clarity, *ṣafāʾ*; splendour, *rawnaḳ*; and freedom from flaws (al-Bīrūnī, *D̲j̲amāhir*, 50). This same author, depending on information he read in a manuscript on precious stones written in al-S̲h̲ām, says that during the reign of the Umayyad ʿAbd al-Malik [*q.v.*], *yāḳūt aḥmar* and excellent *luʾluʾ* "pearls" were equal in value and price (*loc. cit.*). In the early ʿAbbāsid period, al-Manṣūr [*q.v.*] paid 100,000 dīnārs for the two-*mit̲h̲ḳāl* ruby called *al-d̲j̲abal* (see below). Al-D̲j̲āḥiẓ [*q.v.*] stated that the price of half a *mit̲h̲ḳāl* of *bahramānī* ruby was 5,000 dīnārs (*Tabaṣṣur*, 18-19). During al-Maʾmūn's reign, the price of one *mit̲h̲ḳāl* of *bahramānī* was 800 dīnārs, and centuries later, in Ibn al-Akfānī's time (8th/14th century), the prices of *yāḳūt* and other gems increased tremendously (*Nuk̲h̲ab*, 8-9).

Historical records of the ruby. The Rightly-Guided Caliphs abstained from collecting gems, and distributed those obtained through booty among the Muslims. Only a few of the Umayyads filled their treasuries with gems, and these were later seized by the ʿAbbāsids, most of whom had a passion for collecting and increasing their assets, according to al-Bīrūnī. In particular, Hārūn al-Ras̲h̲īd [*q.v.*] was known for his ardent passion for gems (*D̲j̲amāhir*, 57-8, 62-3).

Unset rubies were used by rulers either as a sign of power or out of a belief in their talismanic, medicinal, or magical powers. As described in the texts, and especially in the *K. al-Hadāyā wa 'l-tuḥaf* erroneously ascribed to the *ḳāḍī* Ibn al-Zubayr, a few known pieces were, when held in one hand, so large as to stick out from both ends of the fist. One was confiscated by the Umayyad His̲h̲ām from his governor in Baṣra. Of two others, which both looked like a handle of a mirror, one belonged to the G̲h̲aznawid Masʿūd I b. Maḥmūd [*q.v.*], the other to a king of Ceylon. A fourth, which was carved in the form of a lion, belonged to the G̲h̲aznawid Maḥmūd of G̲h̲azna [*q.v.*]. Still another piece, sculpted in the form of a phoenix head, was found by the Buwayhid Abū Kālīd̲j̲ār [*q.v.*] in the citadel of Iṣṭak̲h̲r. Corundum stones were carved in the form of small bowls, spoons, goblets, bottles and knife handles. During the Umayyad period, Yazīd I sent a ruby bottle as a gift to the Kaʿba (*D̲j̲amāhir*, 67). A scent pomade container of ruby belonged to ʿAbda, daughter of the Fāṭimid caliph al-Muʿizz [*q.v.*]. Ruby cabuchons were set in rings, the most famous cabuchons being known as *al-d̲j̲abal* ("mountain"), most probably due to their huge size. One was bought by the ʿAbbāsid caliph al-Mahdī [*q.v.*] (*D̲j̲amāhir*, 61), and another by al-Mutawakkil [*q.v.*] (*D̲j̲amāhir*, 56, 61; *Hadāyā*, 183). Hārūn's wife Zubayda had a *subḥa* or rosary made of *rummānī* ruby beads, each the size of a hazelnut and grooved like watermelon slices (*D̲j̲amāhir*, 58).

Bibliography: 1. Sources. Ibn Māsawayh, *K. al-D̲j̲awāhir wa-ṣifātihā*, ed. ʿImād ʿAbd al-Salām Raʾūf, Cairo 1976; D̲j̲āḥiẓ, *al-Tabaṣṣur bi 'l-tid̲j̲āra*, ed. Ḥasan Ḥusnī ʿAbd al-Wahhāb, Cairo 1966; Masʿūdī, *Murūd̲j̲*; Bīrūnī, *Kitāb al-D̲j̲amāhir fī maʿrifat al-D̲j̲awāhir*, Beirut n.d.; Ḳazwīnī, *ʿAd̲j̲āʾib al-mak̲h̲lūḳāt*, ed. Fārūḳ Saʿd, [3]Beirut 1978; Tīfās̲h̲ī, *K. Azhār al-afkār fī d̲j̲awāhir al-aḥd̲j̲ār*, ed. Muḥammad Yūsuf Ḥasan and Maḥmūd Basyūnī K̲h̲afād̲j̲ī, Cairo 1977; Ibn al-Akfānī, *Nuk̲h̲ab al-d̲h̲ak̲h̲āʾir fī aḥwāl al-d̲j̲awāhir*, Cairo n.d.; Ibn al-Wardī, *K̲h̲arīdat al-ʿad̲j̲āʾib wa-farīdat al-g̲h̲arāʾib*, ed. Maḥmūd Fāk̲h̲ūrī, Beirut and Aleppo n.d.; Ḳāḍī Ibn al-Zubayr [ascr.], *K. al-Hadāyā wa 'l-tuḥaf*, tr. and ann. Ghāda al-Ḥijjāwī al-Qaddūmī, *Book of gifts and rarities*, Cambridge, Mass. 1997.

2. General reference works. M. Bauer, *Precious stones*, ii, London and New York 1968; C. Cipriani, *The Macdonald encyclopedia of precious stones*, London 1986; R. Webster, *Gems: their sources, descriptions and identification*, London and Boston n.d.

(Ghada al-Hijjawi al-Qaddumi)

YĀḲŪT al-**MUSTAʿṢIMĪ**, D̲j̲amāl al-Dīn Abu 'l-Durr b. ʿAbd Allāh, famed Arabic calligrapher (*ca.* 618-98/*ca.* 1221-98), who derived his *nisba* from his master, the last ʿAbbāsid caliph in Bag̲h̲dād, al-Mustaʿṣim [*q.v.*], who brought him up and had him educated.

Although Ḳāḍī Aḥmad states that he was a native of Abyssinia, another tradition identifies him as a Greek from Amasia, later an important centre of calligraphers. A eunuch, Yāḳūt had a school at Bag̲h̲dād and his six most outstanding students were permitted to sign his name to their calligraphies, making the task of identifying authentic works by Yāḳūt extremely difficult. Yāḳūt himself was the continuer of the master of the six cursive scripts, ʿAlī b. Hilāl, known as Ibn al-Bawwāb (d. 413/1022 [*q.v.*]), who had refined the scripts codified and regularised in the 4th/10th century by Ibn Muḳla [*q.v.*]. His ability to imitate Ibn al-Bawwāb is illustrated by an anecdote in which he fooled his patron al-Mustaʿṣim into believing that an example of his own work was actually that of Ibn al-Bawwāb. However, his reputation rests on his calligraphic innovations rather than solely his skill in duplicating the work of his predecessor.

By cutting the nib of the *ḳalam*, or reed pen, at an angle and maintaining a long point, Yāḳūt produced a more elegant, rhythmic script than that of Ibn al-Bawwāb while still adhering to the rules of proportion established by Ibn Muḳla for the six scripts, *t̲h̲ulut̲h̲, rayḥān, muḥaḳḳaḳ, nask̲h̲, tawḳīʿ* and *riḳʿa*. Called the *ḳiblat al-kuttāb*, or model of calligraphers, Yāḳūt copied two *d̲j̲uzʾ* [*q.v.*], of the Ḳurʾān every day and completed two Ḳurʾāns every month. He is reputed to have produced 1,001 Ḳurʾāns in his lifetime and to have given away 70 samples of his writing every day. In addition to being a demanding teacher, Yāḳūt himself was an incessant worker. When the Mongols took Bag̲h̲dād in 656/1258, Yāḳūt took refuge in a minaret. He brought a pen and ink with him, but, lacking paper, he wrote on a linen towel, which in the 10th/16th century was preserved in the collection of Bahrām Mīrzā, the brother of the Ṣafawid S̲h̲āh Ṭahmāsp I. Although an album was compiled for Bahrām Mīrzā (TKS, H.2154), it does not contain Yāḳūt's writing on linen.

Yāḳūt spent his whole life in Bag̲h̲dād, where he died reportedly at the age of eighty. Under the ʿAbbāsids, Yāḳūt had worked as librarian of the Mustanṣiriyya *madrasa* in Bag̲h̲dād, and after the Mongol conquest he became the protégé of the historian D̲j̲uwaynī; amongst his own compositions, a collection of *nawādir* by him is extant in several mss., see Sezgin, *GAS*, ii, 89. The limited number of extant works convincingly attributed to his pen reveal the elegant, clear cursive scripts for which he is renowned.

Although a thorough stylistic study of works attributed to Yāḳūt has not been achieved, the following attributions are plausible: Ḳurʾān, dated 681/1282-3, parts 2 and 12, Topkapı Saray Library, Istanbul, EH227, EH226; part 8, Chester Beatty Library, Dublin, ms. 1452; part 15, Nasser D. Khalili Collection, London; Ḳurʾān, dated 688/1289, B.N., Paris, ms. arab. 6716; and possibly Ḳurʾān, dated 693/1294, Topkapı Saray Library, Istanbul, EH74 and Āstān-i Ḳuds Library, Mas̲h̲had, Faḍāʾilī, p. 202. Of non-Ḳurʾānic literature, he copied the *Dīwāns* of several Arabic poets, and copies from his pen are extant of the *Dīwāns* of the pre-Islamic poets al-Mut̲h̲aḳḳib al-ʿAbdī and Ḳuṭba al-Ḥādira, of the *Dīwān* of the *muk̲h̲aḍram* poet Abū Miḥd̲j̲an al-T̲h̲aḳafī, and of a selection (*muk̲h̲tār*) from the poems of al-Mutanabbī (see Sezgin, ii, 89, 189, 214, 301, 497).

Bibliography: Ziriklī, *Aʿlām*², ix, 157-8, with references to Arabic biographical sources; Brockelmann, I², 432-3, S I, 598; Cl. Huart, *Les calligraphes et les miniaturistes de l'Orient musulman*, Paris 1908, repr. Osnabrück 1972, 84-6; Ḳāḍī Aḥmad, tr. V. Minorsky, *Calligraphers and painters*, Washington 1959, 57-60; Ḥ. Faḍāʾilī, *Aṭlas-i k̲h̲aṭṭ*, Tehran 1350/1971, 202; P.P. Soucek, *The arts of calligraphy*, in B. Gray, *The arts of the book in Central Asia*, London 1979, 10-12; D. James, *The master scribes. The Nasser D. Khalili Collection of Islamic art*, ii, London 1992, 58-67.

(Sheila R. Canby)

YĀḲŪT al-**RŪMĪ**, or, according to the genealogy that he adopted in order to conceal his slave's name, S̲h̲ihāb al-Dīn Abū ʿAbd Allāh Yaʿḳūb b. ʿAbd Allāh al-Ḥamawī, celebrated traveller and scholar. He was born in 574 or 575/1179, and died on Sunday, 20 Ramaḍān 626/12 August 1229 at Aleppo.

1. His life.

His life can be divided into two parts: (a) from 574 or 575 to 606; and (b) from 606 to his death.

Life in the service of ʿAskar al-Ḥamawī. Yāḳūt was born in Byzantine territory of non-Arab parents, reduced to slavery while still a very young child, and taken to Bag̲h̲dād at the age of five or six. There he was bought by an almost illiterate merchant, ʿAskar b. al-Naṣr al-Ḥamawī (d. 606/1209; Ibn K̲h̲allikān, vi, 127; Sellheim, 95), who gave him a Ḳurʾānic education, so that he could be useful to him in his business (al-Ḳifṭī, iv, 80-1). In fact, Yāḳūt made numerous journeys on behalf of his master to the island of Kīs̲h̲ (Ḳays [*q.v.*]) and to al-S̲h̲ām. Later, however, following a disagreement between the two men, he was emancipated and dismissed by his master (596/1199-1200), who afterwards re-engaged him. However, he had already become a copyist and a transcriber (*warrāḳ*), which was how, in the period of his dismissal between 596 and 603, he was able to copy 300 *mud̲j̲allads* (ʿAbbās, vi, 2887) to earn his living.

The scholar. His training began quite early, thanks to the education that ʿAskar had granted him, though also because of his intellectual curiosity, which he put to good use chiefly during his business travels. He perfected this throughout his life, through numerous profitable encounters and extended visits to libraries like that of Ibn al-Ḳifṭī in Aleppo, and to those of Marw al-S̲h̲āhid̲j̲ān [*q.v.*], where he said he stayed for three years (see below, 2., *f-h*); also to the libraries of the al-Samʿānī, S̲h̲araf al-Malik al-Mustawfī, Niẓām al-Malik Muḥammad b. Isḥāḳ, al-Wazīr Mad̲j̲d al-Malik, al-ʿAmīdiyya, al-ʿAzīziyya, al-K̲h̲ātūniyya, al-Kamāliyya and al-Ḍamriyya families (*Muʿd̲j̲am al-buldān*, iv, 509-10/v², 114).

It is worth noting that, among his teachers, he included the following (ʿAbbās, vii, 2907-9): Abu 'l-Murad̲j̲d̲j̲ā al-Bag̲h̲dādī for Arabic and metrics (Sālim b. Aḥmad, *Udabāʾ*³, no. 513); al-Wad̲j̲īh al-Mubārak b. al-Mubārak al-Ḍarīr, who taught grammar for many years at the Niẓāmiyya of Bag̲h̲dād and of whom it was said that he knew Armenian, Greek, Ethiopian and "Indian" (*Udabāʾ*³, no. 932); Abu 'l-Baḳāʾ al-ʿUkbarī al-Bag̲h̲dādī [*q.v.*], the scholar of grammar, lexicography, exegesis, law, *kalām* and Ḳurʾānic studies (*Udabāʾ*³, no. 645); the grammarian Abu 'l-Yumn al-Kindī (Zayd b. al-Ḥasan; *Udabāʾ*³, no. 504), whom he knew in Damascus; the historiographer Ibn al-Dubayt̲h̲ī [*q.v.*]; Abu 'l-Muẓaffar al-Samʿānī (ʿAbd al-Raḥīm; D̲h̲ahabī, *Siyar*, xxii, 107-9), the son of Abū Saʿd al-Samʿānī [*q.v.*], who allowed him to visit the two rich libraries owned by his family at Marw; Ibn Yaʿīs̲h̲ [*q.v.*] (*Udabāʾ*, iii, 77/ii³, 841, 869; Sellheim,

107) by whom he was taught either in Aleppo or Baalbek. He had no other teacher specifically for geography or astronomy, and none of his pupils is known. As can be seen from the long citations that he makes from the history of Kh^w^ārazm by Maḥmūd al-Kh^w^ārazmī, in which the latter attacks al-Shahrastānī [*q.v.*], he had but little appreciation of philosophy (*Muʿdjam al-buldān*, iii, 343/iii², 388).

He also had contact with learned friends and with his patrons. Among these were al-Ḳāḍī al-Akram, *wazīr* of Aleppo, Ibn al-Ḳifṭī [*q.v.*], whom he met in 609/1212 (Sellheim, 96) and to whom he wrote a letter from Mawṣil in 617/1220 or 618, expressing his distress at the Mongol advance (al-Ḳifṭī, iv, 86-7, with the answer on 87 ff.; Sellheim, 101-2). His profession as a copyist in Baghdād led him to share his love of books with his friend Abū Saʿd Ibn Ḥamdūn (al-Ḥasan b. Muḥammad; *Udabāʾ*³, no. 353; ʿAbbās, vii, 2887), the son of Abu 'l-Maʿālī Ibn Ḥamdūn [*q.v.*]), all of whom were great bibliophiles. He also formed a firm friendship at Mawṣil with the brother of Ibn al-Shaʿʿār al-Mawṣilī (al-Mubārak b. al-Bakr, d. 654/1256), which allowed him to have frequent contact with the latter, a great connoisseur of poetry and the poets (Ibn al-Shaʿʿār, *Ḳalāʾid al-djumān*, ix, 341; ʿAbbās, vii, 2955). His encounters with Andalusian scholars also motivated him to gather documentary evidence on the geography and culture of their region. This was also the case in Baghdād with Muḥammad b. Aḥmad b. Sulaymān al-Zuhrī, whom he claimed as a friend (*Udabāʾ*³, no. 991; al-Ṣafadī, *Wāfī*, ii, 104-5), and likewise in Aleppo with Ibn al-Muwaffaḳ (al-Ḳāsim b. Aḥmad al-Mursī al-Lūrḳī, d. 661/1263), who taught him the Spanish philological tradition, though he was probably also one of his sources for the geography of that region (Sellheim 104, no. 21, 108, 111; *Udabāʾ*, vi, 152-3/v³, no. 900).

2. His travels.

These not only gave him the opportunity of seeing many of the places to which he had devoted an entry in his geographical dictionary, with the exception of the toponyms of the Muslim West, where he never went; they also enabled him to collect scholarly and literary information from the libraries and sometimes from other sources for his dictionaries of scholars and poets.

The following survey of his travels is based on Sellheim's map (see foldout, and cf. Wüstenfeld, *Jâcût's Reisen*; ʿAbbās, vii, 2881 ff.).

a. Baghdād-Kīsh-Baghdād, *ca.* 586/1190 and 606/1209.

b. Baghdād-Āmid-Syria-Baghdād, 593-4/1197-8.

c. Baghdād-Syria-Tabrīz-Baghdād, 607-10/1210-13.

d. Baghdād-Aleppo, 611/1214.

e. Aleppo-Egypt-Damascus (the first Aleppo journey) 611-12/1214-15 (or 613/1216).

f. Aleppo-Khurāsān (particularly Nīshāpūr and Marw), 613-14/1216-17.

g. Travelling around Khurāsān (Balkh, Marw al-Rudh, Harāt, etc.), 616/1219.

h. Marw-Kh^w^ārazm (Djurdjāniyya), 616/1219.

i. Khurāsān to Mawṣil, then to Aleppo, 617/1220 (618).

j. Aleppo-Egypt-Damascus (the second Aleppo journey), 624/1227.

In addition to the pitfalls which were commonplace for travellers in that remote period, he met with particular difficulties. On one occasion he had to flee from Damascus where he had expressed certain anti-ʿAlid ideas, which may have caused him to be considered a proponent of the Khāridjites; he was almost lynched, took refuge for a few months in Aleppo (al-Ḳifṭī, iv, 82; Sellheim, 97), and continued his flight in the direction of Khurāsān (journeys *e-f*).

But a test, this time of a sentimental nature, awaited him at Nīshāpūr (Shādhiyākh), where he bought a very beautiful Turkish slave of whom he was enamoured, but from whom, to his great despair, he soon separated (*Muʿdjam al-buldān*, iii, 330/iii², 306-7; Sellheim, 97). The greatest peril, however, and the greatest disaster for him consisted of the advance of the troops of Čingiz Khān [*q.v.*] and it is known that Bukhārā [*q.v.*] among others surrendered to them in 615/1220 (travels *h-i*; Maʿrūf, *al-Ghazw*).

3. His works.

Dictionaries and historical works.

a. *Muʿdjam al-buldān*: the idea came to him at Marw in 615/1218-19, during a course with his teacher Abu 'l-Muẓaffar al-Samʿānī. The first draft was finished not at Mawṣil, as is often thought, but at Aleppo, on 20 Ṣafar 621/13 March 1224 (Sellheim, 103-4). He began what was to be the final version that same year and continued to revise it afterwards. He undertook the definitive edition on 21 Muḥarram 625/1 January 1228. This was for the library of his patron Ibn al-Ḳifṭī, but in this last revision he did not reach the article "Ruṣāfat Baghdād" (Sellheim, 108-9, no. 26; ʿAbbās, vii, 2916). This great work not only comprises geographical and toponymic information but also literary and poetic subjects and biographical details of prominent figures originating from the toponyms presented. Certain cities or regions are treated in more detail, such as Aleppo and district, and also Marw, etc., such places as Yāḳūt had stayed in for a long time. For the sources for this dictionary, see Herr and also Barbier de Meynard. The abridged version that ʿAbd al-Muʾmin b. ʿAbd al-Ḥaḳḳ (d. 735/1339) made is limited to the *materia geographica: Marāṣid al-iṭṭilāʿ ʿalā asmāʾ al-amkina wa 'l-biḳāʿ*, i-iv, ed. A.W.T. Juynboll, Leiden 1851-64, i-iii, ed. ʿA. al-Bidjāwī, Cairo 1954.

b. *al-Mushtarik waḍʿ^an^ wa 'l-muftariḳ ṣuḳʿ^an^* is a register of toponyms with identical orthography but designating different places. He composed it in 623/1226, then reworked it until his death. Ibn al-Shaʿʿār regards it as a sort of abridged form of the previous work.

c. *Muʿdjam/Akhbār al-shuʿarāʾ* (Mustawfī, 320) is a dictionary that has not survived to the present day. He began to assemble the material and perhaps even to draft it before his *Udabāʾ* (*Udabāʾ*³, i, 8). One of his principal sources was the *K. al-Aghānī*, and also the works of Ibn Sallām, Ibn Ḳutayba, al-Marzubānī, Ibn al-Muʿtazz, etc. The interest of this dictionary lay chiefly in the later poets whom he knew personally and from whom he received poetic pieces. It is perhaps even possible that some of the accounts found in the *Muʿdjam al-udabāʾ* in the state that we know them may have been included by Yāḳūt in his *Dictionary of poets* (ʿAbbās, vii, 2920). He himself wrote poems and fragments of his poetry have been collected (*Udabāʾ*³, vii, 2928-39).

d. *Muʿdjam al-udabāʾ/Irshād al-arīb ilā maʿrifat al-adīb/Irshād al-alibbāʾ ilā maʿrifat al-udabāʾ*. The idea of writing a dictionary apparently came to Yāḳūt in his twentieth year, when he met the poet and lexicographer Shumaym al-Ḥillī (ʿAlī b. al-Ḥasan b. ʿAntar; *Udabāʾ*³, no. 742) at Āmid (594/1198). He continued enriching the contents at will from his reading and from the people he met until the end of his life (ʿAbbās, vii, 2923). Unfortunately this monumental work has not completely survived to the present day even though in his recent edition I. ʿAbbās was able to restore 32 accounts that were not in that of Margoliouth. He did this by recourse to the part that was recovered from the abridged version of ʿAlī b. ʿAbd al-Sallām al-Takrītī (?), entitled *Bug̲h̲yat al-alibbāʾ min Muʿd̲j̲am al-udabāʾ*, and to a part of the addenda of Muṣṭafā D̲j̲awād (ʿAbbās, i, introd.). Furthermore, as stated earlier, the editors or copyists included in this may have been part of the original of his *Muʿd̲j̲am al-s̲h̲uʿarāʾ*.

Apart from the classical sources already indicated for this work (see G. Bergsträsser, in *ZDMG*, lxv, 797 ff.; *ZS*, ii, 184-218), attention should be given to the following histories: of Iṣfahān, by Ḥamza al-Iṣfahānī [*q.v.*]; of Bayhaḳ, by Abu ʾl-Ḥasan al-Bayhaḳī [*q.v.*]; of K̲h̲ʷārazm [*q.v.*], by Maḥmūd al-K̲h̲ʷārazmī, or by al-Bīrūnī; of Marw, by Abū Saʿd al-Samʿānī [*q.v.*]; of Harāt, by ʿAbd al-Raḥmān b. ʿAbd al-D̲j̲abbār al-Fāmī (d. 546/1151); and of Hamad̲h̲ān, by S̲h̲īruwayh Abū S̲h̲ud̲j̲āʿ (d. 509/1115) (ʿAbbās, vii, 2924-5); a great number of other works, among them the *Muʿd̲j̲am al-safar* of Abū Ṭāhir al-Silafī [*q.v.*], could also be mentioned.

e. Lost works: *al-Mabdaʾ wa ʾl-maʾāl fi ʾl-taʾrīk̲h̲*, perhaps identical to *Taʾrīk̲h̲ ʿalā ʾl-sinīn*, mentioned by Ibn al-Nad̲j̲d̲j̲ār; *K. al-Duwal* (ʿAbbās, vii, 2911-12).

The following titles are of works which have also been lost.

Grammatical works.

Mad̲j̲mūʿ kalām Abī ʿAlī al-Fārisī; K. al-Abniya; Awzān al-asmāʾ wa ʾl-afʿāl al-ḥāṣira li-kalām al-ʿArab; al-Radd ʿalā Ibn D̲j̲innī (*ʿinda kalāmihi fi ʾl-hamza wa ʾl-alif min Sirr al-ṣināʿa*).

Miscellaneous works.

ʿUnwān (or *ʿUyūn*) *K. al-Ag̲h̲ānī* (abridged); *al-Muḳtaḍab fi ʾl-nasab*, or *K. fi ʾl-Nasab*, or *K. al-Ansāb*, abridged as *al-D̲j̲amhara* by al-Kalbī [*q.v.*]; *Ḍarūrat al-s̲h̲iʿr*. With regard to the *Ak̲h̲bār al-Mutanabbī*, they were most definitely a part of his *Muʿd̲j̲am al-s̲h̲uʿarāʾ* (ʿAbbās, vii, 2913).

Bibliography: 1. Sources on Yāḳūt. D̲h̲ahabī, *Siyar aʿlām al-nubalāʾ*, ed. S̲h̲. al-Arnaʾūṭ *et al.*, Beirut 1981-8, xxii, 312-3; idem, *Taʾrīk̲h̲ al-islām*, 63rd class, *ann.* 621-30, ed. B.ʿA. Maʿrūf *et al.*, Beirut 1988, 244-8, no. 380; Ibn al-ʿImād, *S̲h̲ad̲h̲arāt*, v, 121-2; Ibn K̲h̲allikān, ed. I. ʿAbbās, Beirut 1968-72, vi, 127-39, no. 790; Ibn al-Nad̲j̲d̲j̲ār, *D̲h̲ayl Taʾrīk̲h̲ Bag̲h̲dād* [*al-Mustafād min*..., by Ibn al-Dimyāṭī], ed. Ḳ Abū Farad̲j̲, Ḥaydarābād 1988, 253-4, ed. M.ʿA. ʿAṭāʾ, Beirut 1997, 252-3, no. 196, ed. M.M. K̲h̲alaf, Beirut 1986, 428-8, no. 196; Ibn al-S̲h̲aʿʿār al-Mawṣilī, *Ḳalāʾid al-d̲j̲umān fi s̲h̲uʿarāʾ al-zamān*, facs. ed., Frankfurt 1995, ix, 339-49; (Ibn) al-Ḳifṭī, *Inbāh al-ruwāt*, ed. M. Abu ʾl-Faḍl Ibrāhīm, Cairo-Beirut 1986, iv, 80-98, no. 840 (1950-73[1], iv, 74-92); Mund̲h̲irī, *al-Takmila li-wafayāt al-naḳala*, ed. B.ʿA. Maʿrūf, Beirut 1981, iii, 249-50, no. 2256; Mustawfī al-Irbilī, *Taʾrīk̲h̲ Irbil*, ed. S. al-Ṣaḳḳār, Bag̲h̲dād 1980, 319-24, no. 223; Yāfiʿī, *Mirʾāt al-d̲j̲inān*, Ḥaydarābād 1918-20, iv, 59-63.

2. Published works by Yāḳūt. (i) *Muʿd̲j̲am al-buldān* [*Jacut's Geographisches Wörterbuch*], i-vi, ed. F. Wüstenfeld, Leipzig 1866-73/1924[2], repr. Tehran 1965 and Frankfurt 1994, i-v, Beirut 1955-7; (ii) *al-Mus̲h̲tarik waḍʿ^an wa ʾl-muftariḳ ṣuḳʿ^an* [*Lexicon geographischer Homonyme*], ed. Wüstenfeld, Göttingen 1846, repr. Bag̲h̲dād 1963, Frankfurt 1994; (iii) *Irs̲h̲ād al-arīb ilā maʿrifat al-adīb* [*Muʿd̲j̲am al-udabāʾ*], i-vii, ed. D.S. Margoliouth, Leiden-London 1907-27, i-vi, 1923-31, repr. [2]Bag̲h̲dād 1964, i-xx, ed. A.F. al-Rifāʿī, Cairo 1936-8 (very defective copy of the preceding), i-vii, ed. I. ʿAbbās, Beirut 1993 (indicated above as *Udabāʾ*[3]). For the older editions of (i) and (iii), see Blachère, Brockelmann and Sarkīs.

3. Studies. R. Blachère, art. *Yāḳūt al-Rūmī*, in *EI*[1]; Brockelmann, I[2], 630-2, S I, 880; ʿU.R. Kaḥḥāla, *Muʿd̲j̲am al-muʾallifīn*, xiii, 178-80; Sarkīs, ii, 1941-3; F. Wüstenfeld, *Die Geschichtsschreiber der Araber und ihre Werke*, Göttingen 1882, 310; Ziriklī, *Aʿlām*, vii, 131; ʿAbbās = his two introductions to his ed. of the *Muʿd̲j̲am al-udabāʾ*; K.M. Abdur Rahman, *Sources of Yāqūt's Geographical Dictionary*, in *Dacca Univ. St.*, ii (1938), 70-104 [Sezgin, *Islamic geography* (see below) = IG, 224]; A.J. Arberry, *A volume in the autograph of Yāqūt the geographer*..., London 1951; C. Barbier de Meynard, *Dictionnaire géographique, historique et littéraire de la Perse et des contrées adjacentes. Extraits du Moʿdjem el-Bouldan de Yaqout, et complété*..., i-ii, Paris 1861, Frankfurt 1994; M. D̲j̲awād, *al-Ḍāʾiʿ min Muʿd̲j̲am al-udabāʾ*, Bag̲h̲dād 1995 [originally in *MMʿIʿI*, vi (1959)]; F.J. Herr, *Die historischen und geographischem Quellen in Jāqūt's Geographischem Wörterbuch*, Straßburg 1898 [IG, 224]; IG, see Sezgin; W. Jwaideh (annotated tr.), *The introductory chapters of Yāqūt's Muʿjam al-buldān*, Leiden 1959; J.J. Kratchkovsky, *Arabskaya geografičeskaya literatura*, Leningrad 1957, 330-42, Ar. tr. Ṣ.ʿU. Hās̲h̲im, Cairo 1963, 335-44, [2]Beirut 1987, 359-71; A. von Kremer, *Ueber zwei arabische geographische Werke*..., in *SBAk. Wien* (1850), 72-84 [IG, 224]; B.ʿA. Maʿrūf, *al-G̲h̲azw al-mug̲h̲ūlī kamā ṣawwarahu Yāḳūt al-Ḥamawī*, in *al-Aḳlām* (Bag̲h̲dād), i/12, 48-65; ʿA. al-Maymanī, *Ṭurar ʿalā Muʿd̲j̲am al-udabāʾ*, in *RAAD*, xl (1965), 644-59, 860-63 and *passim*; A. Miquel, *La géographie du monde musulman*, i-iv, 1967-88; J.-T. Reinaud, *Notice sur les dictionnaires géographiques arabes*, in *JA*, 5e série, xvi (1860), 65-106 [IG, 223]; O. Rescher, *Sachindex zu Wüstenfeld's Ausgabe von Jâqût's "muʿǧam al-buldân"*, Stuttgart 1928 [IG, 224]; ʿA.F. al-Saʿdī, *Yāḳūt al-Ḥamawī. Dirāsa fi ʾl-turāt̲h̲ al-d̲j̲ug̲h̲rāfī al-ʿarabī*..., Beirut 1992; R. Sellheim, *Neue Materialien zur Biographie des Yāqūt*, in W. Voigt (ed.) *Forschungen und Fortschritte der Katalogisierung der or. Hss. in Deutschland*, Wiesbaden 1966, 87-118 + 35 Tafeln (bibl. 90-1 n. 2); F. Sezgin (ed.), *Studies on Yāqūt al-Ḥamawī*, i-ii (= Islamic Geography, 223 and 224), Frankfurt 1994; Abu ʾl-Futūḥ M. al-Tawānisī, *Yāḳūt al-Ḥamawī*..., Cairo 1971; F. Wüstenfeld, *Jâcût's Reisen, aus seinem geographischen Wörterbuche beschrieben*, in *ZDMG*, xviii (1864), 397-493 [IG, 223]; idem, *Der reisende Jâcût als Schriftsteller und Gelehrter*, in *NGW Gött.*, 1865, 233-43 [IG, 223]. (CL. GILLIOT)

YALAVAČ [see MAḤMŪD YALAWAČ].

YALİ, YALU (T.), in modern Turkish, *yalı*, literally, "bank, shore", but coming to mean in Ottoman Turkish "residence, villa on the shore", cf. Redhouse, *A Turkish-English dictionary*, 2192: "a waterside residence".

1. Etymology.

The Turkish word stems from the Greek: Homeric Grk. αἰγιαλός, Modern Grk. γιαλός. It must have appeared in Ottoman Turkish early, since it is found in ʿĀs̲h̲ıḳ-pas̲h̲a-zāde and Nes̲h̲rī (end of the 9th/15th century). It entered into place-names, e.g. Yalıkavak, Yalıköy, Küçükyalı, etc.), and spread into the Balkans in one direction (Serbo-Croat *ìgolo*) and into Persia in the opposite direction (Pers. *yālū* "seashore, river bank").

Bibliography: R. Kahane and A. Tietze, *The lingua franca in the Levant. Turkish nautical terms of Greek origin*, Urban, Ill. 1958, 499-501 no. 929; G. Doerfer, *Türkische und mongolische Elemente im Neupersischen*, iv, 109-10 no. 1810. (ED.)

2. Architecture.

There are less than 40 *yalī*s now left along the Bosphorus shores, and some of these have been altered by the use of concrete behind the original woodwork. Formerly, fire was prevented in some *yalī*s by having a layer of sand between the ceiling and the floor above. There might also be layers of charcoal with which to absorb the damp. The quays of the houses have always been vulnerable to the fast current of the Straits, and now to the wash from tankers and large freighters. The ideal *yalī* was built with as many windows as possible from which to enjoy the view. These windows were made to standard sizes so that they could be replaced quickly after a storm.

By the end of the 17th century there were many kiosks with large gardens, but it is accepted that the first true *yalī* was built in 1698 by the Grand Vizier Amūdja-zāde Ḥüseyn Köprülü Pasha [see ḤUSAYN PASHA, AMŪDJA-ZĀDE], and it still stands, projecting dramatically over the water at Kanlıca. The great salon, although in need of restoration, was never surpassed. It is almost independent of the mansion behind. In the centre of the salon is a magnificent fountain under a shallow dome, and three-sided sofa areas form intimate retreats like those of the Baghdād Kiosk at Topkapı Sarayı; they have splendid views of the sea and boats and the wooded hills opposite. Faded, but still impressive, the formal paintwork turns this room into a paradaisical garden. Plans of *yalī*s vary, but central to the tradition is the landing on the first floor reached by a fine staircase. There are fine rooms at each corner which project over the quays or the gardens. There is concealed access to the harem wing from the central landing, but the harem, like the *ḥammām* [*q.v.*], could also be set quite separately from the *yalī* itself. Surviving, or partly surviving examples of various types of *yalı* include the remains of the Aptullah Yalı at Emirgân; the Hasıp Paşa Yalı at Beylerbey; the Köçeoğlu Yalı and the Yılanlı Yalı at Bebek; and the former Osterog Yalı at Kandilli.

Turkish love of the open air and picnics required terraced gardens that were filled with ornate fountains (*çeşme, sebil, selsebil*) and formal pools where trees and flowers rambled and intermixed. If there were guests in the evening, lanterns hung from tree to tree. Judas and magnolia blossom transformed the shores of the Bosphorus in the spring. The Pasha's garden was divided from the harem garden by high walls, a few of which can still be seen. Up the hillside beyond the formal terraces there were parks, such as that at the Kıbrızlı Yalı at Anadolu Hısar.

Bibliography: A.I. Melling, *Voyage pittoresque de Constantinople et des rives du Bosphore*, Paris 1819; Emel Esin, *An eighteenth-century Yalı*, in *Procs. Second Internat. Congress of Turkish Art*, Naples 1965; G. Goodwin, *A history of Ottoman architecture*, London 1971, index s.v. yalıs; S.H. Eldem, *Boğazıcı anıları*, Istanbul 1979.

(G. GOODWIN)

YALOWA, modern Turkish YALOVA, a town and district of Turkey situated on the southern coast of the Sea of Marmara (the town in lat. 40° 40' N., long. 29° 17' E.).

The district occupies the northern edge of the Armutlu peninsula which runs between the Gulf of Izmit to the north and the Gulf of Gemlik to the south, and ends in the Boz Burun cape, in the south-east of the Sea of Marmara. In Antiquity, it was the region of Pitiya, incorporated after 280 B.C. within the kingdom of Bithynia, and like the latter, conquered by Rome in 74 B.C. The settlements of Pitipolis and Drapenon were created there, as well as thermal baths established under the protection of Hercules and a shrine to Aesculapius. The Emperor Constantine the Great erected Drapenon into a town called Helenapolis, after his mother's name, she having reconstructed the baths there. The town grew in importance because of its position on the road from Constantinople to Nicaea, and, amongst other visitors, received the Empress Theodora with a suite of 4,000 persons. At the time of the First Crusade, the retreat to Helenapolis of the people's army led by Peter the Hermit and Gauthier Sans Avoir, in face of the Saldjūḳ Turks, witnessed the death of 25,000 Crusaders. In 1307 the town passed into the hands of Yalwačoghlu, one of ʿOthmān's [*q.v.*] lieutenants, and it now took the name of Yalaḳābād, later replaced by that of Yalowa.

In the 19th century, up to 1867, Yalowa was a *ḳaḍā* of the central *sandjaḳ* of the *wilāyet* of Khudāwendigār [*q.v.*] or Bursa. It was then attached to the *wilāyet* of Istanbul, together with the whole of the *sandjaḳ* of Izmid, then in 1888 made into a *mutaṣarrifliḳ* directly attached to the Ministry of the Interior. Yalowa was at that time the chef-lieu of a *nāḥiye* dependent on the *ḳaḍā* of Ḳara Mürsel, with 27 villages and 2,426 houses. The town had *ca.* 1,025 inhabitants, 500 of them Muslim Turks, 250 Greek Orthodox and 275 Gregorian Armenians.

In 1930, under the Republic, Yalova was attached, at Atatürk's prompting, to the *il* of Istanbul as an *ilçe* of 496 km^2 with 36 villages. It had 22,235 inhabitants in 1950, 3,833 in the town and 18,422 in the villages. The town grew rapidly, thanks to its baths and hot springs being much frequented by people from Istanbul, it being a stage on the Istanbul-Bursa route, the place of boarding boats coming from Kabataş on the European shore of the Bosphorus or from Kartal, on the Asiatic shore of the Sea of Marmara, and on the route for road passenger transport connecting with Bursa via Orhangazi and Gemlik. According to the 1990 census, it had 65,823 persons. The rural population, 47,594 in 1990, is engaged in growing cereals, fruit trees (apples and peaches) and vegetables under glass. The towns of Çınarcık to Yalova's west and Çiftlikköy to its east have also developed bathing facilities and now have municipalities. The *ilçe* of Yalova, with territories added to it totalling 817 km^2, in 1995 became an *il*, the population of which reached 163,916 (78,210 in the town of Yalova and 85,706 in the smaller towns and villages) in 1997. Yalova and adjacent coastal resorts were severely damaged by the earthquake of 17 August 1999, which killed over 2,500 people in the *il* of Yalova.

Bibliography: V. Cuinet, *La Turquie d'Asie*, iv, Paris 1894, 318-20, 369-72; art. *Istanbul*, in *Yurt Ansiklopedisi*, Istanbul vi, 3889 ff. (M. BAZIN)

YĀM, the Persian and Arabic transcription of the Mongol term *jam (djam)*, originally denoting "road, route, direction". In the 13th century, at the time of the creation of the Mongol empire, the term *yām* also signifies in general the postal service of the Mongol Khāns and sometimes a postal relay. Information regarding this state institution of the Mongols is available from Chinese, Persian, Arabic, Armenian and Western sources (see bibl. in Gazagnadou). The postal relay of the Mongol authorities seems to have been borrowed from the Chinese postal system (*yi*), dating from the time of Čingiz Khān (Waley, 50, 75); it was progressively diffused throughout the empire in tandem with conquests (Gazagnadou, ch. II). The very bureaucratic organisation of the post of the Mongols of China is quite well known (Olbricht). On the other hand, a great deal less information is available on its functioning in the rest of the empire. But the topographical, technical, military and political constraints that the Mongol authorities were obliged to surmount in organising the rapid circulation of postal couriers (*yāmči, ulači, ilči*), make it possible to deduce the major principles of the organisation of the Mongol postal service.

The material and administrative organisation seems to have been as follows: relays were established every 18 to 30 km or thereabouts (Rashīd al-Dīn, i, 671), depending on the topography and on the type of animals used. There were two types of relay: either substantial buildings comprising accommodation, stabling, etc. (Djuwaynī, i, 24), or simple relay stations where the courier changed mounts (*ulagh*). The network of routes marked out by postal relays probably covered several tens of thousands of kilometres linking hundreds of relays. Horses were used predominantly, but sometimes camels, dromedaries and mules were used, and even, in Russia, sleigh-dogs, if Marco Polo is to be believed (tr. Yule-Cordier, ii, 480, Fr. tr. *Le devisement du monde*, ii, 528). The number of horses or other mounts maintained at each relay varied between one and several dozens. For the whole of the Mongol empire, Marco Polo gives the figure of 200,000 post horses (Yule-Cordier, i, 433-5, *Le devisement du monde*, i, 252-3). Each relay was supervised by a functionary (also *yāmči*, but here in the sense of the one responsible for the postal relay) who was required to oversee its efficient running and to report to the central authorities regarding the state and the requirements of his relay, especially in terms of mounts. This supervisor was in charge of employees, including ostlers (also *ulači*, but here in the sense of the one responsible for the welfare of the post horses). According to J.A. Boyle, it seems that a postal service involving the use of chariots also existed (62 n. 270). Relays were usually entrusted to the charge of the nearest town or village. According to the importance of the information being conveyed, there was recourse to either express couriers or normal couriers. Mongol couriers, riding day and night and changing horses at regular intervals, could carry messages over hundreds of kilometres in record time. They were supplied with an imperial tablet (*pāiza*) and a decree (*yarlīgh*) marked with a seal (*tamghā*), these giving them absolute powers of requisition. Couriers of the *yām* only conveyed official correspondence of the Khāns and of Mongol officials, never that of individuals, except by special imperial decree or in cases of corruption. The co-ordination of the Mongol postal service with the army seems to have been quite strong; postal couriers maintained constant liaison between the military units themselves, and between the latter and the residence of the Khān. Furthermore, the couriers conveyed information of fiscal and political nature concerning each *tumen*, an administrative and military zone comprising, besides the resident population, ten thousand combatants (Lambton, 1988). The Mongols offered opportunities, in exceptional cases, to merchants and certain others, to utilise the *yām*. Special imperial instructions were then given, and these merchants or distinguished invitees were issued with a *pāiza*, and a *yarlīgh* bearing the *ṭamghā* of the Khān, these enabling them to travel in security over postal routes, and to use the horses and other facilities of the institution. Overseeing the smooth operation of the *yām* was a responsibility devolved to a representative of the Mongol authorities (*darughači*) in charge of regional administration (*ibid.*, 51).

The decline of the Mongol empire did not result in the immediate disapearance of this postal system. On the contrary, each khānate attempted to retain it for as long as possible. The Ming dynasty, on expelling the Mongols from China, revived the strong and ancient Chinese postal tradition, which was maintained until the end of the 19th century. Among the Mongols of Persia and ʿIrāḳ, as in the Golden Horde of Southern Russia and in Central Asia, the system of the *yām* was retained for better or worse until the end of the khānates. Their disintegration prevented the maintenance of this institution, based as it was on a stable network and on postal relays. The Mongol postal service influenced the regions in which it was installed so strongly that, in the 15th century, the term *yām* was still being used in the Persian world to denote the last postal relays (see, for example, Ḥāfiẓ-i Abrū, *Zubdat al-tawārīkh*). In Russia, the postal relay service introduced by the Mongols continued for centuries. The efficacy of the *yām* so impressed travellers and enemies of the Mongols that it was borrowed by the Mamlūks of Egypt during the sultanate of Baybars al-Bunduḳdārī. The Mongol *yām* may also have influenced the postal systems of the West in the late Middle Ages (Gazagnadou). The definitive dissolution of the Mongol powers (14th-15th centuries) led to the disappearance of one of the most remarkable systems for the transmission of news of the premodern era.

Bibliography: 1. Sources. Djuwaynī, *Tārīkh-i Djahān-gushā*, ed. Ḳazwīnī, Leiden 1912; Rashīd al-Dīn, *Djāmiʿ al-tawārīkh*, 4 vols. Tehran 1373/1994; idem, tr. J.A. Boyle, *The successors of Genghiz Khan*, London 1971; Ibn Faḍl Allāh al-ʿUmarī, *al-Taʿrīf bi 'l-muṣṭalaḥ al-sharīf*, Beirut 1988; Ḥāfiẓ-i Abrū, *Zubdat al-tawārīkh*, Tehran 1372/1993, ii, 817-65; Marco Polo, *The Book of Ser Marco Polo*, 2nd ed. tr. Yule-Cordier, London 1902; idem, *Le devisement du monde*, 2 vols. Paris 1982; Dihkhudā, *Lughat-nāma*, art. *yām*.

2. Studies. C. Yuanyuan, *A study of the postal system in the Tang dynasty*, in *Yenching Annual of Historical Studies*, i/5 (1933); J. Sauvaget, *La poste aux chevaux dans l'empire des Mamelouks*, Paris 1941; W. Kotwicz, *Contribution aux études altaïques. Les termes concernant le service des relais de postes*, in *RO*, xvi (1950); P. Olbricht, *Das Postwesen in China unter der Mongolherrschaft*, Wiesbaden 1954; A. Waley, *The travels of an alchemist. The journey of the Taoist Ch'ang-chung from China to the Hindu Kush at the summons of Chingiz Khan*, London 1963; D. Morgan, *The Mongols*, London 1986; S. Pasquet, *L'évolution du système postal. La province chinoise de Yunnan à l'époque Qing*, Paris 1986; A.K.S. Lambton, *Mongol fiscal administration in Persia*, in *SI*, lxiv (1986); eadem, *Continuity and change in medieval Persia*, London 1988; D. Gazagnadou, *La poste à relais. La diffusion d'une technique de pouvoir à travers l'Eurasie, Chine-Islam-Europe*, Paris 1994.

(D. Gazagnadou)

YĀM, an Ismāʿīlī tribe now inhabiting the area of Nadjrān in southern Saudi Arabia, although at the time of the Ayyūbid conquest of the Yemen in 569/1173 [see AYYŪBIDS; TŪRĀNSHĀH B. AYYŪB] they also held Ṣanʿāʾ [*q.v.*] and territory to the north and north-east of the city in the Djawf area, which was overlooked by Djabal Yām and where they may have originated (see Ibrāhīm Aḥmad al-Maḳhafī, *Muʿdjam al-buldān wa 'l-ḳabāʾil al-yamaniyya*, 706). Al-Hamdānī, 115, describes *Balad Yām* in some detail, giving their main *waṭan* as Nadjrān and other territories as far north as the borders of the Ḥidjāz.

Yām are of Ḥās͟hid and one of the fifteen *baṭn*s of Hamdān (ʿUmar b. Yūsuf Ibn Rasūl, *Ṭurfat al-aṣḥāb fī maʿrifat al-ansāb*, ed. K.W. Zetterstéen, Damascus 1949, 7). Al-Mak͟hafī gives a genealogy: Yām b. Aṣbā b. Dāfiʿ b. Mālik b. D̲j̲us͟ham b. Ḥās͟hid, etc., right back to Saba' (see also Ibn al-Kalbī-Caskel, *Ǧamharat an-nasab*, i, Leiden 1966, 229, and Muḥammad b. Aḥmad al-Ḥad̲j̲arī, *Mad̲j̲muʿ buldān al-Yaman wa-ḳabā'ilihā*, iv, Ṣanʿā' 1984, 774). ʿUmar Riḍā Kaḥḥāla's two entries *Yām* and *Yām b. Aṣbā* (*Muʿd̲j̲am ḳabā'il al-ʿArab*, iii, Beirut 1982, 1259) should therefore rather be one single entry. Ibn al-Kalbī-Caskel, ii, 272, and Ibn Rasūl, *Ṭurfa*, 9, also mention a Yām which was a *baṭn* of ʿAns of Mad͟hḥid̲j̲ [*q.v.*].

Yām came to historical prominence from about 533/1138 when a family, the Banū Ḥātim (II), the third of three Hamdān families, Banū Ḥātim (I), Banu 'l-Ḳubayb and Banū Ḥātim (II), took control of Ṣanʿā'. They contested authority over the city and the territory to the north with the Zaydīs, and after 569/1173, with the Ayyūbids after their conquest of the southern highlands and Tihāma (see ṢANʿĀ' and G.R. Smith, *The Ayyūbids and early Rasūlids in the Yemen*, London 1974-8, ii, 68, 70-5). The Banū Ḥātim (II) were certainly of Yām and continued as a political force until about 590/1193. One or two of their *amīr*s, despite their following forms of Ismāʿīlī Islam and their masters' staunch orthodoxy, found favour and high position with the Rasūlid administration in the north of the Yemen, particularly under the second Rasūlid sultan, al-Malik al-Muẓaffar Yūsuf (647-94/1249-95 [see RASŪLIDS]).

When the Ottoman sultan Selīm I's forces invaded Yemen, the Yām assisted the Turks and were rewarded by a grant of the right to levy tribute on the tribes forcibly subdued by the Turks. Nevertheless, they supported the Ḳāsimid Imām in *ca.* 1640 in driving out the Turks. From *ca.* 1760 the office of the *Dāʿī* of the Yām became hereditary in the Makramī family. In 1834 the then *Dāʿī* renewed relations with the Ottomans, and the tribe supported Turkish power in Yemen up to its end in 1918.

Bibliography: For older references, see A. Grohmann's *EI*[1] art. The major mediaeval historical sources are given in the text. Smith, *The Ayyūbids*, ii, 68-75, provides references to the original Yemeni works, both Sunnī and Zaydī, which throw light on the Yām in the history of Yemen. See also F. Daftary, *The Ismāʿīlīs, their history and doctrines*, Cambridge 1990, index s.v. Yām.

(G.R. SMITH)

AL-**YAMĀMA**, at the present time a town in the Kingdom of Saudi Arabia about 70 km/45 miles south-east of the capital al-Riyāḍ [*q.v.*] and situated in the region of al-K͟hard̲j̲ within the al-Riyāḍ emirate, close to Maḥaṭṭat al-K͟hard̲j̲ on the al-Riyāḍ to al-Ẓahrān (Dhahran) railway (Hussein Hamza Bindagji, *Atlas of Saudi Arabia*, Oxford 1980, 49; Zaki M.A. Farsi, *National guide and atlas of the Kingdom of Saudi Arabia*, 1989, 71). The town is now relatively small and has a population of less than 50,000 (Bindagji, 3). The origin of the name may be *yamāma*, singular of the collective *yamām*, meaning wild pigeons, as opposed to *ḥamām*, meaning domesticated ones (see Yāḳūt, *Muʿd̲j̲am al-buldān*, v, Beirut 1979, 441-2, for other less likely etymologies).

In early Islamic times al-Yamāma was a region of Nad̲j̲d [*q.v.*] with its centre Ḥad̲j̲r (Yāḳūt, v, 442). During his lifetime, the Prophet was visited in Medina by a deputation of the Banū Ḥanīfa from al-Yamāma, including Musaylima b. Ḥabīb al-Ḥanafī [*q.v.*], later called al-Kad͟hd͟hāb "the Great Liar" by Muslim writers. When the delegation arrived back in al-Yamāma, he renounced Islam and declared himself to be a prophet. The tribe were permitted to drink wine and dispense with prayer (Ibn His͟hām, *al-Sīra al-nabawiyya*, ed. Muṣṭafā al-Saḳḳā *et alii*, ii, Cairo 1955, 576-7). The long struggle to bring Musaylima to book carried out by the famous Muslim warrior K͟hālid b. al-Walīd [*q.v.*] is chronicled by al-Ṭabarī (i, 1929-50; see also *The History of al-Ṭabarī*, x, tr. F.M. Donner, Albany 1993, 105-26) and Ibn al-Athīr, ii, Beirut 1965, 360-5). Musaylima was killed by the Muslims in al-Yamāma in the year 11/632 (Yāḳūt, 442, has the year 12).

Ibn K͟hurradād͟hbih [*q.v.*] (193) calls al-K͟hard̲j̲ a *manzil* or relay station of al-Yamāma, while the 4th/10th-century al-Hamdānī (139) states that al-K͟hard̲j̲ was a village of Yamāma. There were scattered fortresses, al-Hamdānī continues, palm groves and gardens (*riyāḍ*). He also mentions silver and gold mines there (153-4). He calls Ḥad̲j̲r the chief town (*miṣr*) and centre of al-Yamāma, the seat of its *amīr*s. He mentions that there is an ancient market there (180).

Al-Yamāma was visited in the 5th/11th century by the Persian traveller Nāṣir-i K͟husraw, who has some very interesting observations on the area (*Safar-nāma* ed. M. Dabīr-Siyāḳī, Tehran 1335/1956, 107-8, Eng. tr. W.M. Thackston, New York 1986, 85-6). He mentions a large and ancient fortress and a market in which all manner of crafts can be found, and a beautiful mosque. The *amīr*s of the region are ʿAlawīs, Nāṣir-i K͟husraw goes on, and have been for a very long time. No one is able to seize al-Yamāma from them, so powerful are they, with their 300-400 cavalry. They belong to the Zaydī *mad͟hhab* [see ZAYDIYYA], he declares, and the words of their *iḳāma* (i.e. the second call to prayer [*q.v.*]) are *Muḥammad*[un] *wa-ʿAliyy*[un] *k͟hayru 'l-bas͟har; wa-ḥayya ʿalā k͟hayri 'l-ʿamal*. Nāṣir-i K͟husraw goes on to mention the palm groves of al-Yamāma and says that, when dates are plentiful, a thousand *mann* (one *mann* = approximately two pounds; see W. Hinz, *Islamische Masse und Gewichte*, Leiden 1970, 16-23) cost only one dīnār. He ends by informing his reader that the route to al-Ḥasā [*q.v.*] from al-Yamāma is 40 parasangs, although the journey can only be undertaken during the winter when water is available.

By the 19th century, al-Yamāma had already become a town of the region of al-K͟hard̲j̲, and a population figure of 6,000 is quoted by R. Bayly Winder from a report of 1865 by Col. Lewis Pelly (*Saudi Arabia in the nineteenth century*, London etc. 1965, 212).

Bibliography: Apart from the references found in the text, see the 3rd/9th century author al-Ḥasan b. ʿAbd Allāh al-Iṣfahānī, *Bilād al-ʿArab*, ed. Ḥamad al-D̲j̲āsir and Ṣāliḥ al-ʿAlī, Riyāḍ 1968, *passim*, and Hamdānī, *passim*, for routes to and from al-Yamāma, mountains, water, wadis and villages, etc. in the area; L. Pelly, *Report on a journey to the Wahabee capital of Riyadh in Central Arabia*, Bombay 1866 (not seen).

(G.R. SMITH)

AL-**YAMAN**, YEMEN, the southwestern part of the Arabian peninsula, now coming substantially within the unified Republic of Yemen (which also includes as its eastern region the former People's Democratic Republic of South Yemen, the pre-1967 Aden Protectorate, essentially the historic Ḥaḍramawt [*q.v.* in Vol. III and also in Suppl.; see also SUḲUṬRA]).

1. Definition and general introduction
2. Geography

3. History
   (a) From pre-Islamic times to 1962
   (b) From 1962 to the present day
4. Ethnology and social structure of the Yemeni highlands
5. The Arabic dialects of al-Yaman

1. Definition and general introduction. The name is variously explained in the Arabic sources; some say it was given because al-Yaman lies to the right of the Kaʿba or to the right of the sun (al-Bakrī, ii, 856), others because Yuḳṭan b. ʿĀbir and his companions turned right on separating from the other Arabs (Ibn al-Faḳīh, 33, tr. Massé, 37-8; Yāḳūt, iv, 1034), while others again derive the name from the eponymous hero Yaman b. Ḳaḥṭān (cf. al-Wāsiʿī, *Taʾrīkh al-Yaman*, Cairo 1346/1927-8, 281). Sprenger thought that the Greeks and Romans translated Teman and Yaman by *Eudaemon* and *Felix* and included under Arabia Felix all the land south of al-Shām. This coincides roughly with the delimitation of al-Yaman attributed to Muḥammad, who is said to have climbed a mound at Tabūk and, pointing to the north, said "All this is al-Shām" and turning to the south, "All this is al-Yaman" (Sprenger, *Die alte Geographie Arabiens*, Berne 1875, 9). The greatest extension of al-Yaman to the north actually corresponds very well with the boundary of Arabia Felix which, according to Ptolemy, vi. 7, 2, 27, began about 6 miles south of al-ʿAḳaba, with its northern frontier running from there northeastwards to the foot of the Sharāʾ range and then, turning east, crossing the northern edge of the desert of the Nafūd [*q.v.*], ending at al-Nadjaf. Al-Wāsiʿī (282) also represents al-Yaman as bounded in the east by the Persian Gulf, in the south by the Arabian Sea, in the west by the Red Sea and in the north by the Gulf of Ḳulzum, the Syrian desert and ʿIrāḳ. The frontiers given by the Arab geographers are considerably narrower. According to Ibn Khurradādhbih (135, 137, 189), and al-Idrīsī (143-4), the northern frontier of al-Yaman ended at the tree called Ṭalḥat al-Malik between al-Muhdjira and Sarūm Rāḥ, south of Mecca. According to others, it began below Tathlīth, while al-Aṣmaʿī (in Yāḳūt, iv, 1035) made the northern boundary run from ʿUmān through Nadjrān; al-Hamdānī (*Ṣifa*, 51; Yāḳūt, iv, 1035) more accurately traced it through Yabrīn, south of al-Yamāma, via al-Hudjayra, Tathlīth, Djurash and Kutna to the coast towards Kudummul near Ḥamiḍa (lat. 17° 52'). Ibn Ḥawḳal (18), who included two-thirds of the Diyār al-ʿArab in al-Yaman, put the northern limit at al-Sirrayn, Yalamlam and al-Ṭāʾif, and made it run through the highlands to the Persian Gulf; this makes it intelligible why some geographers even include Mecca in the Tihāma of Yemen. Towards the east, al-Yaman extends over Ḥaḍramawt, al-Shiḥr (Mahra) and Ẓafār (Ḍofār); even ʿUmān is sometimes included in al-Yaman when it is not (as e.g. in al-Muḳaddasī, 68) made a separate province. The whole of this extensive territory, which al-Dimashḳī (*Nukbat al-dahr*, 216) divided into 24 administrative districts (*mikhlāf* [*q.v.*]), was in the early days of Islam divided into three: Ṣanʿāʾ, al-Djanad and Ḥaḍramawt (or Ẓafār), under separate governors. The taxes under the ʿAbbāsids yielded 600,000 dīnārs (Ibn Khurradādhbih, 144, 249, 251). After al-Yaman broke off from the ʿAbbāsid empire, its area diminished considerably and its administrative divisions varied substantially; sometimes the Sunnī Tihāma, with its capital Zabīd [*q.v.*], was actually independent of the Zaydī Shīʿī highlands with Ṣanʿāʾ as capital. When Carsten Niebuhr travelled in al-Yaman, he ascertained that the following districts were independent:

1. al-Yaman in the narrower sense, with Ṣanʿāʾ; 2. Aden, with its hinterland; 3. Kawkabān; 4. Ḥāshid and Bakīl; 5. Abū ʿArīsh; 6. the lands lying between this and the Ḥidjāz; 7. Khawlān; 8. Sahān with Ṣaʿda; 9. Nadjrān; 10. Ḳaḥṭān; 11. al-Djawf, with Mārib; 12. Nihm; 13. Khawlān, to the south-east of Ṣanʿāʾ; 14. Yāfiʿ.

The geographical definition of al-Yaman becomes still narrower under Ottoman Turkish rule. The *wilāyet* according to the provincial law of 19 Rabīʿ II 1331/28 March 1913 comprised the *sandjak* of Ṣanʿāʾ, with the *ḳaḍās* of Ḥarāz, Kawkabān, Anis, Ḥadja, Dhamār, Yarīm, Radāʿ and ʿAmrān; the *sandjak* of al-Ḥudayda, with the *ḳaḍās* of Zabīd, Luḥayya, Zaydiyya, Djabal Rīma, Ḥadjūr, Bayt al-Faḳīh and Bādjil; and the *sandjak* of Taʿizz, with the *ḳaḍās* of Ibb, ʿUdayn, Ḳaʿṭaba, Ḥudjariyya, Mukhā and Ḳamāʿira. In the north it was adjoined towards lat. 18° N. by the independent districts of Abū ʿArīsh, Ḳaḥṭān, Wādaʿa and Bilād Yām (Nadjrān); in the east by the Balad Kitāf, Baraṭ, the oasis of Khabb, al-Djawf with Arḥab and Nihm, and also Mārib, Khawlān, Ḥarīb, Bayḥān and Yāfiʿ, as well as the Faḍlī region; and in the south by the hinterland of Aden, which had been under a British protectorate since the later 19th century.

Bibliography: For the Arabic geographers and the European travellers in al-Yaman, see the *Bibl.* to *EI*[1] art. s.v. (A. GROHMANN)

2. Geography. The highlands of Yemen form the southern end of the mountain chain that runs down the west coast of Arabia from the Ḥidjāz [see AL-SARĀT] and through ʿAsīr [*q.v.*] and that becomes more lofty as it goes southwards. The chain is an uplifted block, falling away along lines of faulting on its eastern edge to the desert interior; the ʿAsīr-Yemen highlands are in fact part of a single uplifted block that also comprises the Ethiopian highlands, cut in two by the rift valleys of the Red Sea and Gulf of Aden. In Yemen, a core of granite and schists is overlain with sandstone and limestone, in turn covered by a layer of volcanic basalt some 100 m/330 feet thick. This is the highest part of the Arabian peninsula, with Djabal Ḥāḍir Nabī Shuʿayb to the west-south-west of Ṣanʿāʾ rising to 3,760 m/12,336 feet; even the mountains in slightly lower ʿAsīr reach 2,820 m/9,250 feet in Djabal Suda. There is a steep western escarpment overlooking the Tihāma [*q.v.*] or coastal plain, but a less steep eastern one that slopes down to the sandy basin of the Ramlat al-Sabʿatayn. In the southeastern part of Yemen, the highland plateau is connected with the almost equally high crystalline ridges of the Kawr mountains, which in turn join the much-dissected limestone plateau of the Djōl or Djawl, which rises to 2,112 m/6,927 feet. The broad depression of the Djawf Mulays and Djawf Khudayf, which contain the sand dunes of Ramlat al-Sabʿatayn as their core, probably once, in a pluvial period after the Ice Age, contained a lake, but now its underground water drains to the east, through a narrow exit, to irrigate the oases of the Wādī Ḥaḍramawt. This wadi continues eastwards, sometimes with surface water, for some 320 km/200 miles before turning southwards to the Gulf of Aden through the precipitous Wādī al-Masīla [see further, ʿARAB, DJAZĪRAT AL-. ii-iii; ḤAḌRAMAWT. 3., in Suppl.].

In regard to climate, Yemen and the other lands of southern Arabia, Ḥaḍramawt and Ẓafār [*q.v.*], benefit from lying within the sphere of the South-West

Monsoon which brings appreciable rain to the highlands between June and September. The Tihāma of Yemen, about 80 km/50 miles wide, is very barren, as the monsoon rains fall on the higher mountain slopes, but these rains supply streams of water flowing down from the hills, often perennially, to irrigate the typically African crops of the "beehive" villages: millet, cotton, indigo (*nīl* [*q.v.*]), *wars* [*q.v.*], madder, safflower, henna and other dye-producing plants and shrubs and bananas. Above the Tihāma, the lower mountain slopes are semi-desert, with acacia and tamarisk scrub. But beyond 1,500 m/4800 feet, the monsoon winds bring rainfall amounting to more than 75 cm/30 inches per annum in e.g. the southwestern corner of the plateau, to the north and north-east of Taʿizz, and in midsummer the hillsides are cloaked in cloud and mist, and there are heavy dews. These conditions are ideal for coffee trees [see ḲAHWA], and the carefully-maintained multiple terraces also support plantations of fruits, nuts and the mildly narcotic qat or chat, *Cathula edulis* Forsk. [see ḲĀT]. The bulk of the rains and clouds fail, however, to mount the western crests, so that the high plateau to the east is in a rain-shadow, with a drier climate, and the fields of fertile wind-blown soil (loess) rely heavily on streams from the peripheral mountains for irrigating the staple cereal, millet, and the orchards of vines (cultivated since ancient times; the early Arabic geographers mention vineyards in Sarūm Rāḥ, K͟haywān, At͟hāfir and the Wādī Ḍahr) and oranges. Unusually for Arabia, cattle are kept as draught animals. Temperatures may vary widely up here, with cold winter nights and frosty spells; ice is observed at Ṣanʿāʾ on winter mornings more frequently than the occurrence of frost would appear to warrant, an anomaly due to the low atmospheric pressure at over 2,200 m/7,200 feet combined with low humidity, which results in such rapid evaporation of water that its temperature can drop to freezing-point when the air temperature is several degrees above it. On the eastern edges of the highlands at the mouths of valleys there are perennial streams and springs, and such oases as Mārib have extensive date groves. Irrigation systems here have always been complex; it was in this region that ancient South Arabian kingdoms like Sabaʾ and Maʿin [*q.vv.*] arose, and the Dam of Mārib achieved fame in both pre-Islamic South Arabia and in post-Islamic lore and legend.

The Red Sea coastland of Yemen runs for about 450 km/280 miles down to the Bāb al-Mandab with a trend slightly east of south. There are sandy, mangrove-fringed beaches sloping gently up to the coastal plain of the Tihāma. The most significant ports of this coastland, which have historically served for the commerce of the more productive highland zone, are Luḥayya, al-Ḥudayda, Muk͟hā [*q.vv.*] or Mocha, and Perim [see MAYYŪN]. Along the Gulf of Aden lies, of course, the fine double port of Aden in a drowned volcano. The southern coastal plain from the Bāb al-Mandab eastwards through Aden is less continuous than that of the Tihāma of Yemen. Its widest part is the irrigated delta of Laḥid͟j [*q.v.* in Suppl.], which produces dates, coconuts, rice and cotton.

Yemen, together with Ḥaḍramawt and Ẓafār, formed the *Arabia Odorifera* of classical times, and in Yemen, in particular, such aromatics as myrrh were grown; but Yemen's ancient role as an entrepôt for the wares and products of India has long departed.

Bibliography: Naval Intelligence Division, Admiralty Handbooks, *Western Arabia and the Red Sea*, London 1946, 51-3, 59 ff., 134-41, 156 ff., 201-5, 475 ff.; W.C. Brice, *A systematic regional geography. VIII. South-West Asia*, London 1966, 249-52, 389; W.B. Fisher, *The geography of the Middle East*, 7London 1978, 471-9. See also section 1., above.

(W.C. BRICE)

3. History.

(a) From pre-Islamic times to 1962.

Pre-Islamic Yemen. For the history of the four major pre-Islamic states of Yemen, the reader is referred to SABAʾ, ḲATABĀN, MAʿĪN and ḤAḌRAMAWT. Perhaps the history of the country would best be surveyed briefly here from the 1st century A.D. From beginnings in this century in the southern highlands, to a time towards the end of the 3rd century, a large tribal confederation, called Ḥimyar [*q.v.*] (D͟hū Raydān in the pre-Islamic inscriptions) with its capital in Ẓafār [*q.v.*] near modern-day Yarīm, had annexed the territories of Sabaʾ, conquered Ḥaḍramawt and driven the Abyssinian colonialists from the land. In the late 4th century, the paganism of Ḥimyar had been replaced by Judaism, and this newly-found religious fervour had carried out the notorious massacre of the Christian community of Nad͟jrān [*q.v.*]. This act brought the Christian Abyssinians back into Yemen under Abraha [*q.v.*] who, after dealing with Ḥimyar, had become the virtual king of the country. Abraha's fame is mainly based on his building of a cathedral in Ṣanʿāʾ [*q.v.*] (al-Ḳalīs), his instigating what were to be the final repairs made to the already crumbling structure of the Mārib [*q.v.*] dam and, above all, his attempts at conquering Mecca [see MAKKA], allegedly, but impossibly, in the renowned "Year of the Elephant", A.D. 570, given in many traditions as the year of the birth of the Prophet Muḥammad. The task of ridding Yemen of the Abyssinian conquerors had been left to a leader from the Ḥimyarites, Abū Murra Sayf b. D͟hī Yazan, although, by bringing in military assistance from the Persians, he had merely substituted one colonial power for another. The Persians thus ruled Yemen from Ṣanʿāʾ and continued even after the advent of Islam as governors there [see BĀD͟HĀM, in Suppl.].

If we were to believe without careful thought the Muslim writers who touch on the Islamisation of Yemen, we would accept that in 8/628 the governor in Ṣanʿāʾ, a Persian by the name of Bād͟hān, embraced Islam and the whole of the country immediately followed suit. In fact, we have information from Nestorian Christian sources implying the continued existence of Christianity, for example, at Ṣanʿāʾ and Nad͟jrān till *ca.* 900.

The pre-dynasty Islamic history. One of the greatest frustrations that the historian of early Islamic and mediaeval Yemen must face is the plain fact that there is so little information available concerning what can be termed the pre-dynasty history of the country. The Yuʿfirids [*q.v.*] (see below), centred on S͟hibām Kawkabān, and rulers on occasion over Ṣanʿāʾ itself, established the first local dynasty in Islamic Yemen in 232/847, and the period prior to their period, from the advent of Islam in A.D. 622, is what is more precisely meant by this term "pre-dynasty Islamic". The fact of the matter is that we have no contemporary literary sources extant and are compelled to rely on either later non-Arabian sources (e.g. al-Ṭabarī, Ibn al-At͟hīr, al-Balād͟hurī [*q.vv.*], etc.), or on even later Yemeni sources (e.g. al-D͟janadī, al-K͟hazrad͟jī [*q.v.*], Ibn al-Daybaʿ, etc.). All are equally disappointing, uninformative on the question of whence their data come, and in any case lacking in any detailed historical information.

Certainly under the Rightly-Guided Caliphs, when

the Islamic conquests got under way, thousands of Yemenis must have joined the Muslim armies, and indeed, Yemen provided the vast majority of the man-power for these military endeavours of such historical importance (see ʿAbd al-Muhsin Madʿaj M. al-Madʿaj, *The Yemen in early Islam 9-233/630-847, a political history*, London 1988, 64-101; also Radhi Daghfous, *Le Yaman islamique des origines jusqu'à l'avenement des dynasties autonomes* (Ier-IIIème *s./* VIIème-IXème *s.*), Tunis 1995, i, 506).

The sources mention also any number of "representatives" despatched to Yemen by Muḥammad, but such accounts are full of confusion and contradiction. They become no more reliable for the later days of the Rightly-Guided, the Umayyad and the ʿAbbāsid caliphates. Surprisingly, the picture is not made any clearer after reference to the not inconsiderable numismatic evidence available to us (see e.g. in particular Ramzi J. Bikhazi, *Coins of al-Yaman 132-569 A.H.*, in *al-Abḥāth*, xxiii [1970], 3-127). Such representatives are usually described as governors (sing. *wālī*), though there were also on occasion *ḳāḍī*s and teachers, as well as alms collectors (sing. *dj̲āmiʿ al-ṣadaḳa*). Some of those appointed, however, never reached Yemen for one reason or another and this further complicates the issue. The senior governor was the one appointed to Ṣanʿāʾ, although others were sometimes sent to al-D̲j̲anad, nowadays a suburb of Taʿizz [*q.v.*], and to Ḥaḍramawt, where they were on occasion to all intents and purposes independent and on other occasions evidently subordinate to Ṣanʿāʾ (see G.R. Smith, *The early and medieval history of Ṣanʿāʾ*, in R.B. Serjeant and R. Lewcock (eds.), *Ṣanʿāʾ, an Arabian Islamic city*, 53-4, and al-Madʿaj, *Yemen*, table 1, 13-14, table 4, 148-49, table 6, 169-70, table 8, 190-92 and table 11, 220-22, for attempts at listing these representatives).

The interesting question is, of course, what precisely were the duties of these officials? Initially they probably controlled little or nothing outside the walls of the town. They appear to have had a force under arms for the day-to-day policing of the urban area, though it is clear from our sources that they could not impose their will by tyrannical means on the local population; a number tried to do this, and complaints to the caliph, though perhaps slow to receive attention, eventually brought justice either in the form of a reprimand or in the actual dismissal of the governor and his replacement by another. Perhaps more importantly, they would have been charged with the task of promoting Islam and teaching the tenets of the new religion and the Islamic way of life.

As noted above, it is impossible to accept the naive assertion that with Bād̲h̲ān's acceptance of Islam the whole population immediately followed. It is imperative that we now view the Islamisation of Yemen as a gradual process, taking place over at least three centuries. It is probably in this context, too, that we should see the appointments of governors to al-D̲j̲anad and Ḥaḍramawt. Ṣanʿāʾ, one assumes, still operated as a commercial and trading centre under some kind of special sanctity derived from the pre-Islamic *maḥram* institution. Al-D̲j̲anad and Ḥaḍramawt may also have operated in a similar fashion, and trade as much as anything else would have played the major role in the dissemination of Islam in Yemen over the years.

The Islamic history of Yemen down to the first Turkish invasion, 3rd-6th/9th-12th centuries. For the most part the history of the dynasties that held power in Yemen at this time can be seen in some detail in the entries devoted to them, and therefore only very brief notes are given below. The Ziyādids (203-409?/818-1018? [*q.v.*]) take their name, the Banū Ziyād, from Muḥammad b. Ziyād, a protégé of the ʿAbbāsid minister al-Faḍl b. Sahl [*q.v.*]. He was sent by the caliph al-Maʾmūn to quell tribal unrest in Tihāma [*q.v.*] and arrived there in 203/818. As commanded, Muḥammad founded and built a new capital of Tihāma, Zabīd [*q.v.*], and the dynasty appears to have held territory in the Yemeni highlands and along the Indian Ocean coast, as well as in Tihāma.

The Yuʿfirids (232-387/847-997 [*q.v.*]) were the first local Yemeni dynasty to emerge in Islamic times. The dynasty owes its name, the Banū Yuʿfir, to one Yuʿfir b. ʿAbd al-Raḥmān of D̲h̲ū Ḥiwāl of S̲h̲ibām Kawkabān [*q.v.*], north-west of Ṣanʿāʾ. Their territory extended from Ṣaʿda [*q.v.*] in the northern to al-D̲j̲anad in the southern highlands. It was during this period that the Ḥasanī *s̲h̲arīf*, Yaḥyā b. al-Ḥusayn, settled in the northern highlands and created a Zaydī imāmate that was to endure right down to the year 1962 [see ZAYDIYYA].

The Nad̲j̲āḥids, the Banū Nad̲j̲āḥ (412-551/1021-1156 [*q.v.*]), were named after a black Abyssinan slave, Nad̲j̲āḥ, and ruled over Tihāma from Zabīd, for the most part vying with the Ṣulayḥids [*q.v.*] (see below) for control there.

The Ṣulayḥids, the Banu ʾl-Ṣulayḥī (439-532/1047-1138 [*q.v.*]), were a S̲h̲īʿī dynasty acknowledging the Fāṭimids and named after ʿAlī b. Muḥammad al-Ṣulayḥī, who had been brought up within orthodox Islam in the Ḥarāz area, south-west of Ṣanʿāʾ, and who was later converted by a Fāṭimid *dāʿī* operating in Yemen. They ruled firstly from Ṣanʿāʾ (439-*ca.* 480/1047-*ca.* 1087), but later from D̲h̲ū D̲j̲ibla (*ca.* 480-532/*ca.* 1087-1138) and fought with the Nad̲j̲āḥids over Tihāma, controlling much of the country south of Ṣanʿāʾ.

The Sulaymānids were Ḥasanī *s̲h̲arīf*s, originally from Mecca, who controlled northern Tihāma from Ḥaraḍ between the years *ca.* 462-569/*ca.* 1069-1173. They were firstly embroiled with the Nad̲j̲āḥids and later with the Mahdids), and it is suggested in some sources that they wrote to the Ayyūbids [*q.v.*] in Egypt and were instrumental in urging upon them their conquest of Yemen in 569/1173 (see below).

The Zurayʿids, the Banū Zurayʿ (473-569/1080-1173 [*q.v.*]), were named after Zurayʿ b. al-ʿAbbās, the son of a Ṣulayḥid protégé, and the family was of Yām [*q.v.*]. They were a S̲h̲īʿī dynasty, acknowledging the Fāṭimids like their masters, and they ruled over Aden and its surrounding area.

During the period 492-569/1099-1173, three separate dynasties of Hamdān dominated Ṣanʿāʾ and the territory north: the Banū Ḥātim (I), the Banu ʾl-Ḳubayb and the Banū Ḥātim (II). The first two were in all probability of Fāṭimid allegiance, and the Banū Ḥātim (II), who claimed descent from the Yām, were certainly openly so. They vied with the Ayyūbids, particularly over Ṣanʿāʾ, and were not completely overwhelmed by them; indeed, we find them later in the service of the Rasūlids after they had taken over control in the southern highlands and Tihāma from the Ayyūbids.

The Mahdids [*q.v.*], the Banū Mahdī (554-69/1159-73), were founded by ʿAlī b. Mahdī, who had earlier in the 6th/12th century preached a religious message in Tihāma, where their power lay. The Mahdid dynasty had Zabīd as its capital and was finally crushed by the invading Ayyūbid army from Egypt which, under the command of Tūrāns̲h̲āh b. Ayyūb [*q.v.*], the brother of Ṣalāḥ al-Dīn Yūsuf b. Ayyūb [*q.v.*], the Saladin of Western writers, in 569/1173 conquered much of southern Yemen and Tihāma.

The reasons for this conquest are several and complex, and cannot be dealt with here (see G.R. Smith, *The Ayyūbids and early Rasūlids in the Yemen*, ii, London 1978, 31-49) but the outcome is clear. The advancing Ayyūbid army wiped the Zuray'ids in Aden and the Mahdids in Tihāma off the historical map, and less dramatically brought an end to the Sulaymānids of northern Tihāma. Their solid military achievements during the years 569-628/1173-1230 paved the way for the political, administrative and cultural brilliance of their successors, the Rasūlids.

The Rasūlids [*q.v.*], who controlled vast areas of the southern highlands, Tihāma, and, at their zenith, as far east as Ẓafār, in what is at present the southern part of the Sultanate of Oman, and Ḥaḍramawt, brought unprecedented political stability to Yemen. Their period of power was between the years 626-858/1228-1454, and among their rulers were several who made their name as much for their literary and scientific efforts as for their political and administrative acumen [see RASŪLIDS. 3, 5].

Even the mighty and brilliant Rasūlids could not withstand the internal squabbles of the house, the revolts of the *mamlūk* troops and fickle tribes, and the ravages of the plague. Their rule in the southern highlands and Tihāma gave way in 858/1454 to a local Yemeni dynasty of *mas͟hāyik͟h* from the area south of Radā', the Ṭāhirids [*q.v.*] or Banū Ṭāhir, a rule that was to last until 923/1517. The Ṭāhirids were defeated by an Ottoman force in 922/1516 near Zabīd, the main reason for this defeat apparently being the presence among the Ottoman troops of firearms, the first recorded evidence of their use in Yemen.

Ever fearful of the infidel Portuguese presence in the Red Sea and Indian Ocean, the Ottoman Turks launched a massive naval expedition into the area and arrived off the Red Sea island of Kamarān [*q.v.*] in 945/1538. The Zaydī *imāms*, who had taken much of the country after the downfall of the Ṭāhirids, were about to be much reduced in authority as a period of almost one hundred years of Turkish rule began.

The first Turkish occupation of the Yemen, 945-1045/1538-1636. After their naval victory, the Turks began to expand inland. They were besieging Ta'izz by the year 946/1539, were marching on Ṣan'ā' by 951/1544, and the city was in Turkish hands by about 954/1547 after a hard siege. The capital of Turkish Yemen was thus established, and the *ḳaṣr* in the east of Ṣan'ā' became the official residence of the governor-general (*beylerbeyi*), the first being Özdemir Pas͟ha [*q.v.*].

The Turkish invasion of Yemen sent the Zaydīs in the north reeling for some time, and it was a while before they recovered. The recovery of their fortunes is first apparent in the person of the Zaydī *imām* al-Muṭahhar, son of Imām S͟haraf al-Dīn Yaḥyā, who had died in 965/1557. Al-Muṭahhar had actually advanced on Ṣan'ā' in 974/1566, and the Turkish garrison was compelled to surrender to him. The imperial *dīwān* in Istanbul, greatly disturbed at this turn of events, appointed Sinān Pas͟ha [see SINĀN PAS͟HA, K͟HODJA. 2.] as commander-in chief of Yemen, and al-Muṭahhar was himself obliged to abandon Ṣan'ā' after a fierce counter-action against the Zaydīs led by Sinān.

Intermittent resistance on the part of the Zaydīs against the occupying Turks continued. Their struggle to recapture Yemen is associated with the *imām* al-Ḳāsim b. Muḥammad, generally known as al-Ḳāsim al-Kabīr. Before his death in 1029/1620, al-Ḳāsim had struggled at first against Sinān Pas͟ha al-Kayk͟hiyā, albeit somewhat unsuccessfully, and later against the forces of D͟ja'fer Pas͟ha. With al-Ḳāsim's death in 1029/1620, and since the Ottomans remained in parts of the country, it was left to his son, al-Mu'ayyad, to expel them. Sinān's successor Meḥmed Pas͟ha, and in turn his successor, Ḥaydar Pas͟ha, were relentlessly pushed back by al-Mu'ayyad. In 1038/1629, Ṣan'ā' fell to the Zaydīs, as did Ta'izz in the same year. Whilst the Turks remained a danger, particularly in Tihāma, their surrender to the Zaydīs in 1045/1636 brought an end to their first occupation of Yemen. Their commanders had on the whole been harsh with the Yemenis, and had imposed heavy taxes on them; the majority of governors, if not all of them, left Yemen having made their own personal fortunes.

The Zaydī imāmate up to the second Turkish invasion, 1045-1251/1636-1835. The major force throughout the country during this period of almost two centuries was the Zaydī imāmate. It would be wrong to assume, however, that the political situation was a consistent one, for the imāmate, as indeed had always been the case, was at times strong morally and physically, in which case the country was relatively stable and united and life more peaceful. Too often, however, a weak *imām* meant internal squabbles among the Zaydīs themselves, other claimants to the imāmate and tribal anarchy almost anywhere in the country. A few highlights of this period may be mentioned here, but the reader is referred to a more detailed history of the Zaydī *imāms* in the article ZAYDIYYA.

Al-Mutawakkil 'alā Allāh Ismā'īl (1054-87/1644-76 [*q.v.*]) presided over the imāmate for 33 years, during which the most brilliant era of Zaydī imāmic rule can be seen; the period also marks the furthest extent of their territory in Yemen. In particular, Ḥaḍramawt was conquered by the Zaydīs and that in its turn brought them into contact with the maritime power of 'Umān. Internally, al-Mutawakkil concerned himself with law and order and economic affairs, in particular, trying to regulate taxes. Security brought in merchants from other countries to trade in Yemen. Prosperity followed, and the *imām* was able to establish relations with India, with the Ḥid͟jāz and even with Istanbul.

Al-Mahdī Muḥammad (1098-1130/1687-1718), called Ṣāḥib al-Mawāhib, the latter place being where he resided near D͟hamār, south of Ṣan'ā', may be briefly mentioned. He undid much of the great good which al-Mutawakkil had done, extracting unjust taxes and spending profligately.

Al-Mahdī 'Abbās (1161-89/1748-75) was well known for his scholarship as well as for his strength of character and effectiveness in authority. He did away with many oppressive practices that existed in the country, and would appear to have been the nearest to the Zaydī ideal of warrior-king, a follower of the *s͟harī'a* and a generous benefactor. There followed less able *imāms*, involving periods of internal anarchy, confusion and misery with Turco-Egyptian and Ottoman interference externally.

The second Turkish occupation of Yemen, 1289/1872-1918. The opening of the Suez Canal in 1286/1869 allowed the Ottomans ready access to maritime Arabia via the Red Sea, and during the latter half of the 13th/19th century they had gained a foothold on the Red Sea coast at al-Ḥudayda [*q.v.*] Aḥmed Muk͟htār Pas͟ha settled the affairs of 'Asīr [*q.v.*] and returned to al-Ḥudayda, whence he was invited by the people of Ṣan'ā', weary of the chaos caused by disaffected tribes, to enter their city. The Ottoman general entered Ṣan'ā' in 1289/1872, when there appeared to be no recognised *imām* and thus began a second Turkish involvement in Yemen which was to last until the end of the First World War.

After an administrative overhaul that resulted in the appointment of Turks into the administration and the removal of Yemeni officials, the Ottomans opened up a military campaign in the north that had certain successes, notably the capture of the stronghold of Kawkabān, rarely taken in all the history of Yemen. In 1296/1879, a new Zaydī *imām*, al-Hādī Sharaf al-Dīn, proclaimed himself ruler, and for the decade of his reign he fought with some courage against the Turks.

After Imām Sharaf al-Dīn's death in 1307/1890, the Zaydīs turned for their *imām* to the Ḥamīd al-Dīn family, wherein the imāmate was to reside until its abolition in 1962. Al-Manṣūr bi'llāh Muḥammad b. Yaḥyā Ḥamīd al-Dīn was recognised as *imām*. Al-Manṣūr proved completely uncompromising in his struggle against the Turks, and in the words of one Yemeni historian, his wars against the Turks "would fill several books (*dafātir*)" (ʿAbd al-Wāsiʿ b. Yaḥyā al-Wāsiʿī, *Taʾrīkh al-Yaman*, Cairo 1346, 134). When the Turks sent an emissary to al-Manṣūr in 1309/1891, the latter gave a reply implying that the Yemenis were quite capable of providing a government themselves, one that, moreover, ruled in accordance with the laws of Islam. He accused the Turks of all manner of un-Islamic practices and forwarded complaints about their abuses to Istanbul, the Turkish officials being charged with serious corruption.

On al-Manṣūr's death in 1322/1904, his son Yaḥyā was elected *imām* with the title al-Mutawakkil ʿalā Allāh [see YAḤYĀ B. MUḤAMMAD, AL-MUTAWAKKIL]. Yaḥyā continued the policy of all-out opposition to the Turks, giving instructions that Turkish-held towns were to be attacked and besieged. The anti-Turkish cause was helped by failure of the rains and the ensuing famine. In addition, it is clear that the long arrears of pay of the Turkish occupying troops led to much discontent. There are reports, for example, of a serious mutiny in Ṣanʿāʾ in 1324/1906. The Porte's attempts to make peace with Yaḥyā failed. Although a Turkish force with Arab volunteers left Ṣanʿāʾ during the First World War to attack the British in Aden and actually defeated a small British force at Laḥdj [*q.v.*] a few miles to the north of the port, they were forced to surrender in Aden when the armistice was declared.

The years 1918-62: the Imāms Yaḥyā, Aḥmad and Muḥammad al-Badr. Imām Yaḥyā was above all renowned for his extreme stinginess. He also followed a strict policy of almost complete isolation from the outside world. He was assassinated in 1948 by order of the dissident contender for the imāmate, ʿAbd Allāh al-Wazīr, as he drove near the village of Ḥizyaz just south of Ṣanʿāʾ. The conspiracy was put down after a short while, and the ringleaders executed. Yaḥyā's son Aḥmad was elected *imām*, but lacking support in Ṣanʿāʾ after the city's sacking during the revolt, he moved to Taʿizz where he ruled until his death from natural causes in September 1962. He will always be remembered for his ruthless behaviour in the face of any trace of opposition, although he was undoubtedly both a brave and learned ruler. The economic problems of the country had grown and grown, and Arab nationalism and a succession of military coups in the Arab world, as well as interference from the then USSR, all helped destabilise Yemen under Imām Aḥmad.

His son, Muḥammad al-Badr, who had played a high profile role in affairs of state in the late 1950s, was proclaimed *imām*. Only a week later, his residence was attacked by army officers and he and his guards fled. ʿAbd Allāh al-Sallāl then became the first president of the Yemen Arab Republic.

Bibliography (in addition to references given in the article): 1. Pre-Islamic Yemen. Several chapters as follows from W. Daum (ed.), *Yemen. 3000 years of art and civilisation in Arabia Felix*, Innsbruck and Frankfurt/Main n.d. [1988]: W.W. Müller, *Outline of the history of ancient southern Arabia*, 49-55; and R. Audouin, J.-F. Breton and Chr. Robin, *Towns and temples—the emergence of South Arabian civilization*, 63-78; see also the excellent work, Robin (ed.), *L'Arabie antique de Karibʾîl à Mahomet*, Aix-en-Provence 1991, *passim*, but in particular, the ch. of Robin, *Quelques épisodes marquants de l'histoire sudarabique*, 55-71.

2. Islamic history down to the first Turkish invasion. G.R. Smith, *The political history of the Islamic Yemen down to the first Turkish invasion*, 129-40 in Daum, *Yemen*, with full references.

3. Islamic history after the first Turkish invasion. R.B. Serjeant, *The post-medieval and modern history of Ṣanʿāʾ and the Yemen*, in Serjeant and Lewcock, *Ṣanʿāʾ*, 68-108, with full references; Husayn b. ʿAbdullah al-ʿAmri, *The Yemen in the 18th and 19th centuries, a political and intellectual history*, London 1985; Ḥusayn b. ʿAbd Allāh al-ʿAmrī, *Miʾat ʿām min taʾrīkh al-Yaman al-ḥadīth* (*1161-1264/1748-1848*), Damascus 1984, an excellent survey with full bibl.; R.D. Burrowes, *Historical dictionary of Yemen*, Lanham and London 1995, an extremely competent dictionary of modern and contemporary Yemen.

(G.R. SMITH)

(b) From 1962 to the present day.

The Republic of Yemen (ROY) was created on 22 May 1990 out of the peaceful unification of North Yemen and South Yemen, officially the Yemen Arab Republic (YAR) and the People's Democratic Republic of Yemen (PDRY), respectively. About two-and-a-half years earlier, in 1987, the YAR had celebrated its twenty-fifth anniversary and the PDRY its twentieth. Throughout this political generation, the question of Yemeni unification had been confounded by contradictory political legacies: the millennia-old idea of one Yemen and one Yemeni people, on the one hand, and two distinct modern national political struggles and resultant territorial states, on the other.

i. *The YAR.*

The YAR was preceded immediately in North Yemen by the imāmate state led and revived over the first six decades of the 20th century by the two great *imāms* of the Ḥamīd al-Dīn family, Yaḥyā and his son Aḥmad [see YAḤYĀ B. MUḤAMMAD, AL-MUTAWAKKIL; and the last section of 3(a) above]. They both revitalised the traditional Yemeni cultural and socio-political system and further insulated and isolated North Yemen from the outside, modern world. In retrospect, the history of the YAR can best be divided into three periods: (a) the al-Sallāl era (1962-7), the wrenching first five years under President ʿAbd Allāh al-Sallāl, marked by the 26 September Revolution that overthrew the imāmate, the long civil war and Egyptian-Saudi intervention that quickly followed, and, above all, the rapid and irreversible opening of the country to the modern world; (b) a 10-year transition period (1967-77), distinguished by the end of both the Egyptian military presence and the civil war, the Republican-Royalist national reconciliation under President ʿAbd al-Raḥmān al-Iryānī, and the attempt by the young President Ibrāhīm al-Ḥamdī to strengthen the state and restructure politics; and (c) the Ṣāliḥ era (1978-90), a 12-year period identified with both the long tenure of President ʿAlī ʿAbd Allāh Ṣāliḥ and the change from political weakness and economic uncertainty at the outset, to political stability, the discovery of oil, and the prospect of oil-based development and prosperity in more recent years. This last period of YAR history ended with the unification of the two Yemens and the creation of the ROY, with President Ṣāliḥ at its head.

Of the many important political and socio-economic changes that took place in the YAR since its birth in 1962, most of the positive ones were compressed into the years since the republic's fifteenth anniversary in 1977. Nevertheless, the decade from the late 1960s to the late 1970s was also important, a transitional period in which much needed time was bought by a few modest but pivotal acts of state-building and, most important, by economic good fortune. Above all, global and regional economic events over which the YAR had no control facilitated a huge flow of funds into the country in the form of both foreign aid and remittances from Yemenis working abroad. This period of transition was much needed, because the changes that had buffeted Yemen in the five years following the 1962 revolution had left it both unable to retreat into the past and ill-equipped to go forward. The ability to advance rapidly in the 1980s was very much the result of the possibility afforded for a breather in the 1970s.

ii. *The PDRY.*

The path taken by, or, more correctly, imposed upon, South Yemen after the British occupation of Aden in 1839 was quite different. Of critical importance was Britain's preoccupation with the port of Aden and its neglect of the dozen or so statelets in the hinterland with which it signed treaties of protection only in the last quarter of the 19th century. As a consequence, no single political system embraced even most of what was to become an independent South Yemen in late 1967. Instead, what existed was the 75-square-mile Aden Colony—a city-state, a partly modern urban enclave and major world port—and a vast, mostly distant, politically-fragmented hinterland that was, for the most part, based on subsistence agriculture and traditional socio-cultural institutions.

At independence in 1967, the infrastructure barely holding together the major settlement areas consisted of dirt tracks, unpaved roads, a number of airstrips, and the telegraph. The country consisted of many micro-economies, most of them agriculturally based and largely self-sufficient. The isolated Wādī Ḥaḍramawt was an odd case, dependent as it was upon emigration to and remittances from Southeast Asia, East Africa, Saudi Arabia and the rest of the Gulf. What little market economy existed centred on the port of Aden and its environs, and this in turn was plugged less into its hinterland than into the international economic system via its sea lanes. This fragile modern sector was dealt devastating blows near the time of independence, when the blocking of the Suez Canal during the Six-Day War nearly brought port activities to a halt and Britain's rapid withdrawal ended both subsidies from London and the significant economic activity tied to the large British presence.

The history of South Yemen since independence is distinguished by three major periods: (a) the period of political takeover and consolidation (1967-9), the initial phase during which the National Liberation Front established control in Aden and over the hinterland at the same time that the balance of power within the party passed from the nationalists led by Ḳaḥṭān al-S̲h̲ābbī to the party's left wing; (b) the period of uneasy leftist co-leadership of Salīm Rubayy ʿAlī and ʿAbd al-Fattāḥ Ismāʿīl (1969-78), distinguished by the efforts of these two bitter rivals both to organise the country in terms of their competing versions of Marxist "scientific socialism" and to align the country with the socialist camp and the national liberation movements around the world; and (c) the era of ʿAlī Nāṣir Muḥammad (1980-5), the period in which the consolidation of power in a single leader was paralleled by increasing moderation in both domestic affairs and external relations, especially with the YAR.

The period of co-leadership, which ended in 1978 in armed conflict between the two rival factions within the ruling party and the execution of Salīm Rubayy ʿAlī, was followed by two years during which ʿAbd al-Fattāḥ Ismāʿīl ruled alone. The era of ʿAlī Nāṣir Muḥammad, which began with the exile of Ismāʿīl in 1980, ended in January 1986 with the intra-party bloodbath and ʿAlī Nāṣir's ejection and flight into exile, and was followed by the nearly four years of troubled domestic and external politics that led up to unification with the YAR. Despite this pattern of bitter and sometimes lethal intra-party conflict, the PDRY régime over more than two decades did maintain its rule and order throughout the country, made progress in bridging the gap between Aden and the rest of the country, pursued with some success certain admirable social goals, and made good use of extremely limited resources in efforts to develop a very poor country, e.g. in the fields of education, health, and equality of the sexes.

iii. *The unification process and the ROY.*

In 1989, the renewed drive for Yemeni unification came suddenly and at the initiative of a newly self-confident YAR. The PDRY régime, weakened by the intra-party bloodbath and the sharp decline in political and economic support from the Soviet Union and the Socialist bloc, was unable to resist the proposal. In its final form, the unification plan called for: (a) formal unification in May 1990; (b) a two-and-a-half year transition period during which power would be shared equally by the two ruling parties of the former YAR and the PDRY; and (c), in late 1992, national elections throughout unified Yemen.

Unification was embraced enthusiastically by most Yemenis and proceeded apace, enjoying a year's honeymoon. However, the increasing dominance of President Ṣāliḥ and his allies and the collapse of the economy—the latter caused largely by a drastic drop in external aid and workers' remittance, the result of the ROY failure to join the U.S. and Saudi-led coalition against ʿIrāḳ during the Gulf War, soon led to protracted political conflict between Ṣāliḥ's faction and most of the top southern leaders. Despite the holding of relatively free and fair elections in April 1993, and many efforts at mediation, the political crisis worsened, leading in early 1994 to fighting between the yet-unmerged armies of the two parts of Yemen and to a bloody two-months civil war in mid-1994. The forces loyal to President Ṣāliḥ won a decisive victory over the Saudi-supported secessionist forces, and Yemen remained united.

The fighting over, the ROY was faced with the virtually complete collapse of the economy and political isolation in the region. Regarding the latter problem, relations with the Arab Gulf states and other Arab states improved considerably during the period 1995-7. However, relations with Kuwait and Saudi Arabia remained problematical—most notably, the serious Yemeni-Saudi border dispute resisted solution. With the assistance of the International Monetary

Fund, the World Bank, and various European donors, the ROY in early 1995 addressed the former problem by adopting and then implementing a largely successful three-year package of economic reforms; this demanding and painful process was facilitated in part by the continued discovery and development of modest oil and gas reserves. President Ṣāliḥ and his allies strengthened the political system and—to a degree at least—Yemeni political life was reorganised during this period. Despite the economic hardships of recent years, the régime was able to hold relatively free and fair national elections in April 1997, elections that produced a clear-cut victory for President Ṣāliḥ and his party. Mid-1998 marked the end of Ṣāliḥ's twentieth year as president of the YAR and the ROY.

Bibliography: M.W. Wenner, *Modern Yemen, 1918-1966*, Baltimore 1967; D.A. Schmidt, *Yemen. The unknown war*, New York 1968; E. O'Ballance, *The war in Yemen*, London 1971; R.W. Stookey, *Social structure and politics in the Yemen Arab Republic*, in *MEJ*, xxviii/3 (Summer 1974), 248-60, xxviii/4 (Autumn 1974), 409-18; F. Halliday, *Arabia without sultans. A study of political instability in the Arab world*, London 1975; Stookey, *Yemen. The politics of the Yemen Arab Republic*, Boulder, Colo. 1978; idem, *South Yemen. A Marxist republic in Arabia*, Boulder 1982; J.E. Peterson, *Yemen. The search for a modern state*, Baltimore 1982; R. Bidwell, *The two Yemens*, Boulder 1983; B.R. Pridham (ed.), *Contemporary Yemen. Politics and historical background*, London 1984; Helen Lackner, *P.D.R. Yemen, outpost of socialist development in Arabia*, London 1985; S. Page, *The Soviet Union and the Yemens. Influence in assymetrical relationships*, New York 1985; S.A. Badeeb, *The Saudi-Egyptian conflict over North Yemen, 1962-1970*, Boulder 1986; Tarik Y. and Jacqueline Ismael, *The PDRY. Politics, economics and society. The politics of socialist transformation*, Boulder 1986; Jamal S. al-Suwaida, *The Yemen Arab Republic. The geopolitics of development, 1962-1986*, Boulder 1987; R.D. Burrowes, *Oil strike and leadership struggle in South Yemen. 1986 and beyond*, in *MEJ*, xl/3 (Summer 1989), 437-54; P.K. Dresch, *Tribes, government and history in Yemen*, Oxford 1989; F.G. Gause, III, *Saudi-Yemeni relations. Domestic structures and foreign influences*, New York 1990; Halliday, *Revolution and foreign policy. The case of South Yemen, 1967-1987*, Cambridge 1990; Burrowes, *Prelude to unification. The Yemen Arab Republic, 1962-1990*, in *IJMES*, xxiii (1991), 483-506; Sheila Carapico, *From ballot box to battlefield. The war of the two ʿAlis*, in *M.E. Report*, xxiv/5, no. 190 (Sept.-Oct. 1994), 24-7; Burrowes, *Historical dictionary of Yemen*, Lanham, Md. 1995; idem, *The Yemeni civil war of 1994. Impact on the Arab Gulf states*, in al-Suwaida (ed.), *The Yemeni war of 1994. Causes and consequences*, London 1995, 71-80; A.N. Almadhagi, *Yemen and the USA. A superpower and a small-state relationship, 1962-1992*, London 1996; J. Kostiner, *Yemen. The tortuous quest for unity, 1900-94*, London 1996; Burrowes, *It's the economy, stupid. The political economy of Yemen and the 1997 elections*, in G. Joffe and E. Watkins (eds.), *Yemen today. Crisis and solutions*, London 1997; idem, *The Republic of Yemen. The politics of unification and civil war, 1989-1995*, in M.C. Hudson (ed.), *Regional integration in the Arab world. Problems of political and economic fragmentation*, New York 1998; Carapico, *Imagine an Arab democracy. Civil society and the Yemeni state*, New York 1998. (R.D. BURROWES)

4. Ethnology and social structure of the Yemeni highlands.

The population of the high plateaux of Yemen is chiefly Zaydī by persuasion [see ZAYDIYYA]. However, a strong S̲h̲āfiʿī Sunnī presence [see S̲H̲ĀFIʿIYYA] has been making its mark on the capital city of Ṣanʿāʾ [*q.v.*] since the 1970s (where at the last census in 1994 there were 954,448 inhabitants), as also in the massif of Ḥarāz [*q.v.*], which is shared between the Zaydīs and the S̲h̲āfiʿīs. The Ismāʿīlī [see ISMĀʿĪLIYYA] community of Yemen is concentrated in the latter region around Manāk̲h̲a [*q.v.*]. In addition there are several hundred Jews living in the regions around Ṣaʿda and Rayda [*q.vv.*].

With the exception of Ṣanʿāʾ, the territory of which belongs to no single tribe (*ḳabīla*) in its own right, towns such as Ṣaʿda (K̲h̲awlān b. ʿAmr), K̲h̲amir (Banū Ṣuraym), Ḥūt̲h̲ (ʿUsaymāt), D̲h̲amār [*q.v.*] (ʿAns) or ʿAmrān are all contained within the territory of single tribes. Part or all of their non-tribal population is composed of "market people" (*ahl al-sūḳ*) and religious men (*sayyids* and *ḳāḍīs*). The *hid̲j̲ra* sites such as Ḥūt̲h̲ are generally inhabited by the latter, and the market as well as the tribal assembly places, called *misrāk̲h̲*, were subject to tribal protection. The inviolable nature of the *hid̲j̲ras*, the "sanctuaries" of knowledge and religious law, was in fact only recognised by the tribes that were linked to them, often by a formal ageement, and who used them as neutral territory. The principal confederation of tribes of the highlands of Yemen are those of the Ḥās̲h̲id and the Bakīl [*q.vv.*]; the Mad̲h̲ḥid̲j̲ (D̲h̲amār, Radāʿ, Ḥarīb [*q.v.*] and Mārib [*q.v.*]) do not actually exist, as the number of its tribes was incorporated in the course of time among the Bakīl, whereas the tribes of the Murād (Ḥarīb) and the ʿAbīda (Mārib), who were supposed to belong there, have no confederal ties. On the other hand, the tribe of K̲h̲awlān b. ʿAmr (Ṣaʿda) has no links with any other. However, it would be an exaggeration to place any real importance on the idea of a confederation apart from that of the Ḥās̲h̲id, which is numerically less important than that of the Bakīl; it has greater cohesion though relatively so, stemming largely from the role in national politics played by the supreme *s̲h̲ayk̲h̲* (*s̲h̲ayk̲h̲ al-mas̲h̲āyik̲h̲*), ʿAbd Allāh b. Ḥusayn al-Aḥmar.

The morphology and tribal subdivisions vary just as their degree of mobility. Membership of a tribe is based on real or supposed family relationships, but tribal unity is above all based on territory, and the majority of tribesmen are sedentary farmers. The different sections of the tribe are thought to be descended from a common ancestor (*d̲j̲idd*) and to be bound by fraternal ties, although this genealogical fiction does not imply a detailed acquaintance or the existence of actual family relationships between its members. The practice of customary law (*ʿurf* [*q.v.*]), with regard to the role of guarantor of the honour of the group and of intra- and inter-tribal arbitrator, makes the function of the *s̲h̲ayk̲h̲* an important factor of the social life of the highlands, and even at the national level for those who combine economic success and political stature. Recognition by the state of the representative function of the *s̲h̲ayk̲h̲s*, who from the early years of the Republic onwards have been paid by the Ministry of Tribal Affairs, has given their traditional role of mediator an official status.

However, the social structure of the highlands is not limited to the tribal system. It overlaps with a system of social ranks to which the tribal system is pivotal. The traditional social hierarchy is indeed composed of status groups graded in the hierarchical system according to certain criteria, the most important of which are those of ancestry (*aṣl*) and professional activity. Up to the founding of the Republic in 1962 the descendants of the Prophet (*sayyid*, pl. *sāda*) including the Zaydī Imāms, took their place at the top of the hierarchical order. Because of their prestigious genealogy and the primacy granted to them in religious matters and spiritual direction, they played the role of arbitrator among the tribes, though this position could also be filled by the "religious judges" of tribal origin (*ḳāḍī*, pl. *ḳuḍāt*).

The other status groups were the tribesmen (*ḳabīlī*, pl. *ḳabāʾil*), city dwellers of tribal origin (*ʿarabī*), and at the bottom of the social order those who had menial occupations without tribal origin. They were designated by the generic noun *banu 'l-khums* or *ahl al-ṭaraf*, literally, "sons of the fifth", i.e. potential recipients of public charity or "people of the extremity". Menial jobs (market gardeners, butchers, workers at the public bath, cess-pit cleaners, barber-circumcisers, blood-letters, tanners, shoemakers, potters and the *dawshān*, a sort of tribal herald) were considered as such in relation to a system of tribal values in which the idea of honour played a dominant role, and which would forbid members of the tribe being put into the position of servant or middle-man. In this predominantly agrarian society, commercial activity was regarded as menial, whereas agriculture, the traditional occupation of tribesmen, was not considered in any way discreditable. In certain cities, and particularly in Ṣanʿāʾ, the city dwellers felt that they belonged to a more distinctive sort of community, and their cultural model was distinguished from the tribal one by reason of the greater significance it attached to religious values. Besides, in contrast to the *sūḳs* in the tribal territories, the market of Ṣanʿāʾ was distinguished by its great social diversity and was frequented by representatives of all the status groups of the city. To belong to these status groups was a matter of heredity and very often was no longer connected with the original "occupation".

The rules for matrimonial alliance have constituted and still do constitute one of the essential ways of reproducing status groups. The main principles governing marriage in Yemeni society are those of *aṣl* (origin) and *kafāʾa* [*q.v.*], a term denoting the idea of parity, sc. the equality of status of the two partners. These principles allow society to maintain the hierarchical system, since they relate to descent, the patrilinear nature of which authorises a man to marry a woman of equivalent or inferior status. The woman herself may not marry a man of inferior status as the children will inherit their father's status. This traditional social order was indicated by the distinctive dress of the wearer. The most important sign was the dagger, which was worn differently according to the status group. However, this traditional social order has been considerably weakened by a number of factors: the founding of a Republican régime; the appearance of intense social mobility (promoted by the years of emigration); the existence of new economic opportunities; and finally, strong urban growth, facilitating a degree of social anonymity and the influence of state institutions through school, public office and army.

Bibliography: There are so many sources for the ethnology of the highlands of Yemen that here only a selected number of titles is given, viz. J. Chelhod *et alii, L'Arabie du Sud. Histoire et civilisation. iii. Culture et institutions du Yémen*, Paris 1985; P. Dresch, *Tribes, government and history in Yemen*, Oxford 1989; F. Mermier, *Le Cheikh de la nuit. Sanaa, organisation des souks et société citadine*, Arles 1997; R. Leveau, Mermier and U. Steinbach (eds.), *Le Yémen contemporain*, Paris 1999; Martha Mundy, *Domestic government. Kinship, community and polity in North Yemen*, London-New-York 1995; B. Messick, *The calligraphic state. Textual domination and history in a Muslim society*, Berkeley, etc. 1993; T. Gerholm, *Market, mosque and mafraj. Social inequality in a Yemeni town*, Stockholm 1977; R.B. Serjeant, *Société et gouvernement en Arabie du Sud*, in *Arabica*, xiv/3 (1967), 284-97; idem, *South Arabia*, in C.A.O. van Nieuwenhuijze (ed.), *Commoners, climbers and notables. A sampler of studies on social ranking in the Middle East*, Leiden 1977 226-47; Shelagh Weir, *Qât in Yemen. Consumption and social change*, London 1985; P. Bonnenfant (ed.), *Sanaa. Architecture domestique et société*, Paris 1995; S.C. Caton, *"Peaks of Yemen I summon". Poetry as cultural practice in a North Yemeni tribe*, Berkeley, etc. 1990; Faḍl Abū Ghānim, *al-Bunyat al-ḳabaliyya fi 'l-Yaman bayn al-istimrār wa 'l-taghyīr*, Damascus 1985; Ismāʿīl b. ʿAlī al-Akwaʿ, *Hidjar al-ʿilm wa-maʿāḳiluhu fi 'l-Yaman*, 5 vols., Damascus 1995; W.F. Madelung, *The origins of the Yemenite Hijra*, in A. Jones (ed.), *Arabicus Felix, Luminosus Britannicus. Essays in honour of A.F.L. Beeston on his eightieth birthday*, Oxford 1991, 25-4; W. Dostal, *Egalität und Klassengesellschaft in Südarabien. Anthropologische Untersuchungen zur sozialen Evolution*, Horn 1985; A. Gingrich *et al.* (eds.), *Studies in oriental culture and history. Festschrift for Walter Dostal*, Frankfurt 1993; Suzan Dorsky, *Women of ʿAmran. A Middle Eastern ethnographic study*, Salt Lake City 1986; T.B. Stevenson, *Social change in a Yemeni highlands town*, Salt Lake City 1985; Najwa Adra, *The tribal concept in the central highlands of the Yemen Arab Republic*, in Saad Eddin Ibrahim and N.S. Hopkins (eds.), *Arab society. Social science perspectives*, Cairo 1985, 275-85; Gabriele Vom Bruck, *Enacting tradition: the legitimation of marriage practices amongst Yemeni sadah*, in *Cambridge Anthropology*, xvi/2 (1992-3), 54-68.

(F. MERMIER)

5. The Arabic dialects of al-Yaman.

The main dialect areas partly correspond to the physical nature of the country: One block is the western coast, Tihāma [*q.v.*]. A transitional zone are the Tihāma foothills. In the western mountain range from the outermost north down to the south-east (Yāfiʿ [*q.v.*]) extremely archaic dialects, the so-called *k*-dialects, are spoken. This originally coherent area is now interrupted in the south by the Ḥudjariyya dialects. In the border zone to Saudi Arabia, dialects are quite remote from other Modern Arabic dialects. From Ṣaʿda down south to Djuban, in the highlands, but also in Aden, dialects less deviating from other modern Arabic dialects are spoken. The dialects of the Djawf and the Mārib area are little known. They are related to Bedouin dialects of the north and the south-east of the peninsula. In the former People's Democratic Republic of Yemen (PDRY), the regions of Aden, Ḥaḍramawt, Dathīna, Laḥdj and the Yāfiʿ area are more or less explored dialectologically, but little is known from the southern coast. The actual distribution of dialects still reflects the characterisation of Yamanī dialects given by al-Hamdānī, and regions of which he classifies the language as "bad Arabic", "unintelligible" or "Ḥimyaritic" still have the most deviating dialects. A mere sketch, however, cannot do justice to the dialectological diversity of Yemen.

i. *Phonology*.

Hamza, in most modern Arabic dialects a marginal phoneme, has maintained its status in many dialects; in the Taʿizz area we can even notice the opposite of what normally happens, i.e. a shift of verbs with final *y* to hamzated verbs: **ramā* > *ramaʾ*, **ramat* > *ramaʾat*. In some fifty items, *b* corresponds to *m* in

CA, e.g. *ṣarab* "to harvest" vs. *ṣarama* "to cut", *banā* "to intend" vs. *tamannā* "to wish". In the Tihāma *d* may be realised as a flap, *d* and *t* in the Yāfiʿ region are "soft apicals" and not dentals, according to Vanhove. Interdentals are preserved, except in Aden and al-Ḥudayda. Both **d* and **z* have merged into *ʾdh*, except in Dat͟hīna: **d* > *ḷ* vs. **z* > *ʾdh*; in D͟jabal Yazīdī (former PDRY), **d* is *ḍ*, but **z* = *ʾdh*; also in the north (Bani ʿAbādil, Saʿda area), *ḍād* and *z̧āʾ* are separate phonemes *ʾdh* and *ʾth*. In Minabbih (Saʿda area) the merger is *ʾth*. In D͟jabal Rāziḥ, in some fifty words the reflex of **d* is a slightly retroflex *č* (**ḍabaṭa* > *čabaṭ*). In the same area (Minabbih) the reflex of **ṣ* is *st: stadīgin* "a friend", reflecting a former **ts* or **tsʾ*. There are several lexemes indicating a merging of **ṣ* (**tsʾ*) and **z* (**ʾth*) in historical dialects of Yaman as attested in Sabaic, e.g. *liṣī* "to kindle", CA *laziya* "to burn brightly". In Minabbih **s͟h* is a slightly retroflex medio-palatal fricative close to the German "ch" in "Buch" (neither [x] nor [ç]). As for **s*, there are lexical relics hinting at sound shifts like those in Modern South Arabian, e.g. **sākah* > *hākah* "tail-pole" in the southern Tihāma. In the central highlands *ṭ* is realised as [d] in pre- and intervocalic position, hence *ḍallab* "to beg". The reflexes of **g* vary between *g* (southern Tihāma, Ḥud͟jariyya down to Aden, Yāfiʿ), a palatal stop *j* (e.g. central Tihāma), the affricate *d͟j* (especially in the central highlands) and *y* in Ḥaḍramawt. In the central Tihāma **ʿ*, and often in a parallel fashion **g͟h*, have merged into *ʾ*: *ʿaynun* > *ʾēnu* "eye", *g͟hanamun* > *ʾanamu* "sheep", only **g͟h* > *ʾ* is found in the southwestern mountains: *g͟hanam* > *ʾanam*. In Dat͟hīna, Upper ʿAwlaḳī and D͟jabal Yazīdī: *g͟h* > *ʿ*: *ʿanam*, and partly *ʾ*: *ʾanam*. North of Ṣanʿāʾ, in parts of the east, in the Saʿda area, and also in the Wādī Bannā *g͟h* is an affricated [k͟x] or *ḳ*: *ḳanam*; in Yāfiʿ *ḳ* and *g͟h* are free variants: *ḳanam ~ g͟hanam*. The main reflexes of **ḳ* are *ḳ* and *g*, the former characteristic of most of Tihāma and the southern mountains from the Taʿizz area down to Aden. In Tihāma, **ḳ* has been shifted to *g* or *j* in roots containing *d*: *ḳaʿādah* > *jaʾādah* "bed". Still in Tihāma, a voiced uvular *ḳ* is to be heard. In central *k*-dialects the allophones of *kāf* are in complementary distribution: *k* (initial, geminated)—*g͟h* (intervocalic)—*k͟h* (final). In Minabbih, **k* is shifted to *č* and varies with *k* in lexical distribution. Emphatic *ḷ* is frequent in the dialects of the D͟jawf and Mārib: *gāḷ* "he said". Emphatic *ṛ* is rare.

Diphthongs are preserved in the majority of dialects. The short vowels *a, i, u* are preserved in all dialects. Apart from the D͟jawf and Mārib area (**ḥimārah* > *ḥmārah*) the syllable structure is extremely conservative, e.g. *libisat* "she has dressed", *yisāfirū* "they travel". Long vowels in final syllables are also preserved. In southern Tihāma and Ḥud͟jariyya, however, they are short and not lengthened in the case of suffixation: *ʾdharabu + ik → ʾdharabuyk* "they beat you", *ʾdharabna + ak → ʾdharabnak* "we beat you", *ʾdharabna + uh → ʾdharabnuh* "we beat him". Elisions often are due to the fluctuation of accent: *yiḥtárig* "it gets burnt" vs. *yiktsír* "it gets broken". The fluctuation of accent (*máwd͟jūd* vs. *mawd͟jûd*, *al-ḥimār* vs. *al-ḥimâr*) is still one of the mysteries of Yamani dialects (for explanations, see Diem, 10-12, and Naïm-Sanbar).

Other remarkable phonotactic phenomena are pausal glottalisation in the highlands: *kat͟hīr → kat͟hīʾr #*, pausal nasalisation in Tihāma and parts of the northern and southern mountain ranges: *ani → aniŋ #* and devoicing of geminates in the central highlands: *ḥaggī → ḥakkī*.

ii. *Morphology.*

a. V e r b s.

All verbal endings of CA (except the dual) can be found in Yamani dialects. In Minabbih, **-a* of the 3rd m. perfect appears in the case of suffixation: *baytūh #* "his house", but *g͟hasal + u → g͟hasálaw* "he washed him", *ṣawwar + ča → ṣawwaráča* "he took a picture of you". In the northern Tihāma, the forms of the 1st and 2nd f. sg. still have the classical endings: *katabtu-katabt-katabti*. Elsewhere, mainly in Ḥud͟jariyya, only the 1st person has preserved *-u: katabtu*-2nd m. *katabt*. In the extreme north and the Yarīm area, the opposite is found: 1st *katabt*-2nd m. *katabta*. Feminine forms in the plural are preserved except in Tihāma, the Saʿda region and Aden. The endings of 2nd pl. *-tum, -tinna* and 3rd pl. *-ū, -na* are typical of the highlands north and west of ʿAmrān and the extreme north (there even *-tum, -tunna*). South Semitic perfect endings (*-ka, -ki, -ku* vs. *-ta, -ti, -tu*) are preserved in the western mountain range from the outermost north down to Ḥud͟jariyya and in the Yāfiʿ area. Rare are *k*-perfects with the old vocalic endings (D͟jabal Yazīdī, former PDRY: *waṣalku*) but in some dialects the inner vowel is assimilated to them: *katabku > katubk, katabka > katabk, katabki > katibk* (Taʿizz area). Elsewhere, the *-k* of the 1st person is labialised. Central and northern *k*-dialects, but also Yāfiʿ, also have *kashkasha*-forms for the 2nd f. sg.: *katabč, katabs͟h(i)*. Major innovations are the generalisation of *-aw* (*-ō*) for the 3rd pl. m. *ramaw → katabaw* in the central Tihāma and in the east (Mārib, D͟jawf), and for the f. pl. the extension of *-ayn* (CA *ramayna*) to all verb classes and the 2nd pl.: *ramayn → katabayn → katabtayn* (central highlands down to the south-east). In some places in Tihāma, the ending of the 2nd sg. f. has been assimilated to that of the imperfect: *tiktubin → katabtin*. In Tihāma and the Saʿda area, before the merging of f. and m. in the plural, the 3rd sg. f. perfect (**-at*) was adapted to the 3rd pl. f. (**-na*): **katabat > kataban*. In D͟jabal Rāziḥ, Ḥud͟jariyya and Yāfiʿ, the 3rd sg. f. perfect follows the noun: *katabah* corresponds to *baḳarah*, with suffixes: *katabtuh* corresponds to *baḳartuh*. In the imperfect, the *ya*-prefix is to be found in the extreme north and most parts of Tihāma. Landberg reported the Maghribī forms for the 1st sg. and pl. *niktub-niktubu* for the Bedouins of Ḥud͟jariyya. Long forms have been preserved in central and northern Tihāma, sporadically in the east, and in a compact area in the former PDRY (Ḥaḍramawt, Yāfiʿ): *tiktubīn* "you (f.) write", *tiktubūn, yiktubūn*. When suffixed in Tihāma, the *-ī-* is shortened and the *-n* geminated: *tiktubinnuh*. This has led to re-analysis in some dialects in central Tihāma: *kataban-katabannuh, tiktubīn-tiktubinnuh → tiktubin-tiktubinnuh*. Internal passives are attested everywhere: *s͟huwik, yis͟hwak* "to be stung by a thorn"; they are frequent in the east: *dhbiḥ/yidhbaḥ* "to be killed", *s͟hill, yis͟hall* "to be taken away".

As in other modern Arabic dialects, there are preverbs for the present continuous or habitual, e.g. 1st. p. *bayn-*, the rest of the paradigm *bi-* in Ṣanʿāʾ, and for the future: e.g. *s͟hā* (south, Tihāma) *s͟hā-/ʿa-* (Ṣanʿāʾ), *bā-* (east and south). Reflexes of **kad* are used as an auxiliary: *giduh s͟hug͟hayyiru* "he is young". In many dialects, *kān* is not conjugated: *ams kānnī bu Ṣaʿda* "yesterday I was in Ṣ".

Hamzated verbs are common in the southern mountains: *yaʾkul* "he eats", *siʾir* "it remained", *karaʾ* "he read". Characteristic of the east are imperfect forms with *ō: yōkul* "he eats".

There are cases of class change for verbs with initial *w*: **wat͟haba > t͟hāb* "to sit" (Minabbih), **wakaba > **wabaka > bāk* "to go" (Tihāma).

Geminate verbs have been assimilated to verbs with final *y* in northern Tihāma: *madda, yimidda*, in Ḥudjariyya: *maddī, yimidd* (Ḍāliʿ *madda, yimidd*), and in Djabal Rāziḥ: *maddē, yimidd.*

The two perfect types of hollow verbs are preserved in most regions, a third has been added mainly in the *k*-dialects: *ḳalku* "I said", in others the distribution of *a, i* and *u* is conditioned by the persons: 1st. *surk*-2nd m. *sark*-2nd f. *sirk* (Taʿizz area), *surk-sirk-sirki* (north of Taʿizz) or, in Djabal Rāziḥ, *suruk-sirik-siric*. In some places only one type is attested: *giltu*, respectively *ḳilk* or *ḳaltu*. In the participle, *hamza* is preserved, especially in the southern mountains: *ghāʾib* "being absent", elsewhere *ghāyib*, also with reduction of *-āyi-> ey, ē: ghēb* (northern Tihāma, the East).

Verbs with final *y*: in the highlands from Khamir down to Ḥudjariyya only one type is left: *ramā-nasā, ramī-nasī* or *rimī-nisī*. Elsewhere *a-* and *i*-type are preserved with partial levelling, e.g. *ramu-nisyu, ramaw-nisiyaw*. In the *k*-dialects, the suffix vowel has influenced the different forms: 1st sg. **ramayku* > **ramawku* > *ramawk/ramōk*-2nd sg. m. **ramayka* > *ramayk*. Especially in the southern *k*-dialects and in Ḥudjariyya, the vowel of the perfect of form II follows the imperfect: *ghaddī/yighaddī* "to give a lunch", accordingly V: *atghaddī-yitghaddī* "to have lunch".

The verb "to come" behaves like verbs with final *y* with the usual assimilations in the *k*-dialects: 1st sg. *guʾk*-2nd sg. m. *gaʾk*-2nd f. *giʾk* or *ʾatawk-ʾatayk-ʾatayk* and similar forms. In Ḥudjariyya, hybrid forms of **djāʾa*-*ʾ*atā* are attested: *ʾagā*. In parts of Tihāma, the imperfect is irregular: *yiʾēt*. For the imperative *taʿāla* is rare; the respective roots are used: *djiʾ*! *ʾati*! Other forms are *hālak*! (southern Tihāma) or *duwēnak*! (the east).

Verbal forms: IX has been replaced by II: *ḥammar* "to become red". IV is still used. VII is used mainly in the east, the passive-reflexive function being normally expressed by VIII or the internal passive: *summiyat* "she was called", *yiḥtarig* "it gets burnt".

b. Nouns.

Tanwīn is preserved in Minabbih: *stayfin* "a guest", in northern Tihāma: *shtarētu djamalun* "I bought a camel", and as *-u* in the rest of Tihāma: *banātu* "girls", *juhdu* "boy". The normal feminine endings are *-ah, -eh* (*-ih*), in many dialects conditioned by the preceding vowel: *bagara-tisʿe*. In Djabal Rāziḥ the ending is *-it* whenever the noun is definite: *bagarah* "a cow", but *ib-bagarit* "the cow". Gender distinction has been given up in several dialects with adjectives of the type *faʿil* and participles: *hiyya ksil* "she is lazy", *anī dārī* "I (f.) know", *is-sayyārit mujannab* "the car is parked". As for the syntax of the numerals, all Yamanī dialects follow the model of CA: *khams banātin* "five girls", *khamsah ridjālah* "five men". Characteristic nominal forms are those with an *-ī*-suffix: participles like *nāzilī* "going down", also of the true Ethiopian type *faʿālī: falāḥī* "fox" (Djabal Rāziḥ), nouns like *shugrī* "chicken", *buhmī* "donkey", *buḳrī* "cow", *kitlī* "tea-pot", *mushgurī* "small bouquet". Other typical forms are plurals like *ṭirwag* "ways", sg. *ṭarīg, shirwaṭ* "tapes", sg. *sharīt, binwat* "girls" and the infinitives of II: *tafʿūl, fiʿʿāl*.

The genitive marker is *ḥagg*. The definite article is *(a)m* all over Tihāma. In the north-east, in the east from Mārib down to the Wādī Ḥaḍramawt, *im-* is frequent, *b-* is attested in northern Tihāma. The Ṣaʿda area is rich in forms with *al-, il-, im-, in-, an-, hā-*. The predominant form is *al-* whilst *il-* is characteristic of some eastern dialects. The *-l* of the article is assimilated to all letters mainly in the southern mountains: *ab-baḳarah*. The relative pronoun in the central mountains is a gender-indifferent *alladhī*, a compact area in the south-east has the Ḥimyaritic *dhī*, southern Tihāma *allī*, and there are other shorter forms like *lī, dī, alī*.

c. Pronouns.

The 1st sg. has been differentiated on the model of the 2nd sg. (*anta-anti*): *anā* m.-*anī* f. in Tihāma and parts of the central and southern highlands down to Aden. Consequently, the suffixes of the 1st persons: *-nī, -nā* were re-analysed: m. *anā*, suffix *-nā* (*bētnā* "my house"), f. *anī*, suffix *-nī* (*bētnī*); *-nā* not being available any more for the plural, the independent pronoun equally serves as a suffix: *baytiḥnā* "our house" (Tihāma), *shāfniḥna* "he saw us" (Aden). Among the 2nd forms, those of Djabal Rāziḥ are remarkable: m. *ak*, f. *ać*, identical with the suffixes. In southern Tihāma in one spot, *-ak* has been added to the pronoun: *antak*, whilst the feminine form has been assimilated to the verb: *antīn*. Such analogous formations are mainly attested for Tihāma (*ʾantīna, ʾantīn, ʾantin*). For the 3rd persons short and long forms are attested: *hū, hī, huwwa-hiyya*, in the south forms with a prefix copying the radical vowel: *uhu-ihi*. Most remarkable is the fusion of m. and f. in the dialect of Minabbih: *ahā* "he, she". Forms of the 1st pl. are less aberrant, the most frequent one being *iḥna* or *ḥna*, whilst *niḥna* is attested for the east and the south, for this last even *naḥnu*; in Djabal Rāziḥ: *anḥā*. For the 2nd persons, we have *antum-antunna, antum-antinna* in the extreme north and *antu-antinna* in the northern highlands. The western mountain range has *antum-antin* (*antun, antan*), the east mainly *antu-antan* (*intu-intan*); the central highland dialects, parts of the east and the southern mountains have feminine forms remodelled on the verb: *antum katabtum-antayn katabtayn*. Tihāma has forms with *-n* for both genders: *(a)ntun, ʾantūn*. Extremely deviating again is Djabal Rāziḥ: *akkum-akkun*. The most common forms of the 3rd pl. are *hum-hin*. Longer forms are attested only for the feminine: *hunnah, hinnah*. Tihāma mainly has *hun*, sporadically with a prefix: *uhun*. Comparable forms are to be found in Minabbih: *ihim-ihinna*.

d. Pronominal suffixes.

For 1st persons see above. The 2nd m. is predominantly *-ak*, only in the southeast is it *-uk*, sporadically *-ik*, Minabbih: *-ča*. For the feminine, *kashkasha* forms are dominant, namely *-iš* (north, centre, east, south-east), in northern and central *k*-dialects *-ič, -ić* and in the Djabal al-Ẓāmir area even *-it: baytit* "your house", elsewhere *-ik*, Minabbih: *-či*. With nouns ending in *-u*, in Tihāma no distinction is made between m. and f.: *abūk* "your father", while in some dialects north of Ṣanʿāʾ, an allomorph *-ki* is used for the f.; in southern dialects: *abu* + *ik* → *abuyk*, or with umlaut: *abīk* (m. *abūk*). The suffix of the 3rd sg. m. is *-ih* all over the north, centre and south-east, *-uh* is the form of Tihāma and the southern mountains and also Aden, *-ah* is attested mainly in central Tihāma and the south-east. Djabal Rāziḥ has *-ō*. The f. form is predominantly *-hā*, in the south-eastern mountains *-i* or *-ē* (*baḳarti, baḳartē*), in Djabal Rāziḥ *-ā*. For the 1st pl., see above. The suffixes of the 2nd and 3rd persons follow the respective pronouns (*-kum-kin, -kum-kinna, kum-kan, -kun*), in Djabal Rāziḥ: *-ām, -ōn* for the 3rd pl.

e. Demonstrative pronouns and adverbs.

A central strip from the highlands down to Aden has forms nearer to CA, whereas Tihāma and the extreme north, but also partly the east, have all kinds of short forms: *dhā-tā, dhī-tī, dhā-dhī, dhih-tih, dhāk-tāk, ʾdhāk-tāk*, and there are also forms with a deictic element *dhn* (as in Sabaic): *dhīnek* (remote deixis pl.)

<u>dh</u>innek, <u>dh</u>innāk, mainly in Ḥudjariyya. Most dialects have a series of diminutive or deprecative demonstratives like dhayya-tayya, but used deictically as well (medium range). The demonstrative adverb "now" is <u>dh</u>alḥīn all over the country with slight variations. Short forms for "here" are to be found mainly in the east, Tihāma and in the south, the central highlands down to Ḥudjariyya have long forms like hāna and hawna. For "there" the most common forms are hunāk and hināk, in southern Tihāma we have forms like halah.

f. Interrogatives.

As for "what" the main forms comprise mā all over the Tihāma, the central highlands and the north-east (maw, mō, mū in the southern mountains, mī in some central k-dialects, mād<u>h</u>ī in <u>Dj</u>abal Rāziḥ). From the north-east down to the south ay<u>sh</u> and similar forms are normal. There is more variation in the case of "why": lay<u>sh</u>, limā, lilma, lilmeh, lamū, ninma, liyyeh, lēh, even way'. "Where" has the more "classical" forms in the central highlands: ayn; Tihāma has forms like fiyān; and forms with w- are attested in the east. Also for "when", the centre again has a new formation: ayyiḥīn, and Tihāma has variations of it: yaḥin etc. In the north and the east, we find reflexes of *matā or *matay: matē (<u>Dj</u>abal Rāziḥ).

iii. Lexicon.

There is a good deal of the South Semitic lexicon: da and similar forms, dimm(ī) "cat", <u>dh</u>aḥal "rust", girbah "field". There are also words from the Semitic lexicon not attested in CA, like <u>th</u>āb, ya<u>th</u>ūb "to sit", lammad "to train the ox for ploughing". There is much of the Classical lexicon not to be found in, say, Mediterranean dialects, like ʿafw "young donkey", (h)āyab "to return". The lexicon of Tihāma is highly aberrant: ḥād "to see", 'amm "to drink", bāk "to go", juhdeh "girl". An important part of its modern vocabulary has been furnished by English, mainly via the south, like rayfal "rifle", kitlī "tea pot," recte kettle, kili<u>sh</u> "clutch".

Bibliography: C. de Landberg, Etudes sur les dialectes d'Arabie méridionale. I. Ḥaḍramoût, II. Datînah, Leiden 1901, 1905-13; W. Diem, Skizzen jemenitischer Dialekte, Beirut 1973; J. Greenman, A sketch of the Arabic dialect of the central Yamani Tihāmah, in ZAL, iii (1979), 47-61; P. Behnstedt, Die nordjemenitischen Dialekt. I. Atlas, Wiesbaden 1985; idem, Die Dialekte der Gegend von Saʿdah, Wiesbaden 1987; M. Piamenta, A dictionary of post-classical Yemeni Arabic, 2 vols. Leiden 1990-1; M. Vanhove, Note sur le dialecte qəltu de Dhalaʿ (province de Lahej, Yémen), in MAS-GELLAS, nouvelle série v (1993), 175-99; Janet C.E. Watson, A syntax of Ṣanʿānī Arabic, Wiesbaden 1993; S. Naïm-Sanbar, Contribution à l'étude de l'accent yéménite. Le parler des femmes de l'ancienne génération, in ZAL, xxvii (1994), 67-89; Vanhove, Notes on the Arabic dialectal area of Yāfiʿ, in Procs. of the Seminar for Arabian Studies, xxv (1995), 142-52.   (P. BEHNSTEDT)

YAMĪN (A.), pls. aymān, aymun, literally, "the right hand", but often used in Arabic with the transferred sense of "oath".

In human life and activity, the right hand often symbolises power and the ability to initiate actions. The Arabic word yamīn has such connotations as fortune and prosperity, whilst the wider term yad "hand in general" covers a vast semantic range: power, help, strength, sufficiency, ability to act, etc. The right hand can have a cultic significance, as with the bronze hand, probably from the vicinity of Ṣanʿāʾ and now in the British Museum, with a South Arabian ex voto inscription (illustrated and discussed by Ch. Robin, in

idem (ed.), L'Arabie antique de Karib'îl à Mahomet = RMMM, no. 61 [1991-3], 143-4).

Because oaths were often, in early societies such as the Arab one, taken by the two parties to a contract or agreement clasping their right hands together and pledging a solemn oath to fulfil the undertaking, yamīn came to be a general word for "oath". It has in fact tended, in Arabic usage, to become the most general term for "oath", in company with the verb ḥalafa "to swear", but other terms exist such as ḳasam, ḥalaf and aliyya/alwa/ilwa. See further, ḲASAM and also ḤILF, this last term denoting originally "a covenant, agreement" but often coming to mean "oath", and see the Bibls. there, to which should be added N. Calder, Hinth, birr, tabarrur, taḥannuth: an enquiry into the Arabic vocabulary of vows, in BSOAS, li (1988), 214-39.   (ED.)

YAMŪT B. AL-**MUZARRAʿ** AL-ʿABDĪ, Abū Bakr, multifaceted scholar of the second half of the 3rd/9th century, d. ca. 303-4/915-16. He belonged to the tribe of ʿAbd al-Ḳays [q.v.], and was al-<u>Dj</u>āḥiẓ's nephew on his mother's side; the latter was the source of several anecdotes transmitted by Yamūt.

Because of the ominous meaning of his name, "he dies", Yamūt tried to replace it with Muḥammad, which was, however, not generally accepted. Nonetheless, al-<u>Kh</u>aṭīb al-Ba<u>gh</u>dādī decided to enter him into his Ta'rī<u>kh</u> Ba<u>gh</u>dād under both names. The bad omen of his name also caused Yamūt to have himself announced simply as Ibn al-Muzarraʿ when he visited the sick.

Yamūt came from Baṣra. After the death of his uncle al-<u>Dj</u>āḥiẓ in 255/868-9, Yamūt went to Syria and settled in Tiberias, where his son Muhalhil was born. Only at an advanced age did he visit, in 301/913, Ba<u>gh</u>dād, where he appeared as a transmitter, from inter alios the philologists Abū Ḥātim al-Sidjistānī (d. 255/869 [q.v.]) and Abū ʿU<u>th</u>mān al-Māzinī (d. ca. 248/862 [q.v.]). Several times he travelled to Egypt, the last time in 303/915, dying according to some at Tiberias in 303/915, according to others at Damascus in 304/916.

Yamūt was a Ḳur'ān reader, grammarian, poet, and above all an historian (a<u>kh</u>bārī). In this last capacity he restricted himself to the transmission of historical anecdotes (mulaḥ wa-nawādir). Thus he is cited amongst others by al-Marzubānī in his Muwa<u>sh</u><u>sh</u>aḥ, by Abu 'l-Faradj al-Iṣbahānī, and by al-Mubarrad in his Kāmil. Al-Masʿūdī counts Yamūt moreover among the ahl al-ʿilm wa 'l-naẓar wa-'l-maʿrifa wa 'l-djadal. Yamūt, according to al-<u>Dh</u>ahabī, wrote several books the titles of which are not mentioned at all. Al-<u>Dh</u>ahabī himself did not mention any title, too. A Damascene manuscript of Ibn Durayd's Fawā'id al-a<u>kh</u>bār, however, has a small supplement of four pages entitled A<u>kh</u>bār Yamūt b. al-Muzarraʿ. It contains eleven poems and anecdotes transmitted by Yamūt. It was published by Ibrāhīm Ṣāliḥ together with a much more comprehensive collection of Yamūt's traditions taken from the secondary literature. As a poet, Yamūt praised <u>Dh</u>akā' al-Aʿwar, who was governor of Egypt from 303/915 until 307/919. In addition, he addressed several poems to his son Muhalhil, who was his consolation in times of distress and to whom he sent waṣiyya-like admonitions.

Muhalhil became famous as a wine and love poet. His Dīwān, no longer extant, was put together by Ibrāhīm b. Aḥmad Tūzūn. Preserved is Muhalhil's Risāla on the plagiarisms of Abū Nuwās, which Ḥamza al-Iṣfahānī included as ch. 13 in his Dīwān of Abū Nuwās. A counter-treatise (naḳīḍa) on the strengths of Abū Nuwās's poetry (maḥāsin <u>sh</u>iʿr Abī Nuwās), mentioned by Ḥamza and by Muhalhil himself in his preface to the Risāla, was finished too late for Ḥamza to include it in the *Dīwān* of Abū Nuwās. It is not preserved. Muhalhil must have died after the year 334/946, since he composed an elegy (*mart̲h̲iya*) on the Ik̲h̲s̲h̲īdid Muḥammad b. Ṭug̲h̲dj [*q.v.*], who died in that year.

Bibliography: Masʿūdī, *Murūdj*, §§ 3148-51; Ḥamza al-Iṣfahānī, *Dīwān Abī Nuwās*, ms. Fâtih 3775, fols. 122b-124b (to appear in vol. v of *Dīwān Abī Nuwās*, ed. E. Wagner, in the press); Zubaydī, *Ṭabaḳāt al-naḥwiyyīn*, ed. M. Abu 'l-Faḍl Ibrāhīm, Cairo 1954, 235-6; Marzubānī, *Muʿdjam al-s̲h̲uʿarāʾ*, ed. ʿA.A. Farrādj, Cairo 1960, 505-6; *Taʾrīk̲h̲ Bag̲h̲dād*, iii, 308 (Muḥammad), xiv, 358-60 (Yamūt), xiii, 273 (Muhalhil); Ibn al-Anbārī, *Nuzha*², 144-5; Ibn al-Djawzī, *Muntaẓam*, Beirut 1992-3, xiii, 172-3; Yāḳūt, *Udabāʾ*, vii, 305-6; Ibn K̲h̲allikān, ed. ʿAbbās, vii, 53-61, tr. de Slane, iv, 385-93; D̲h̲ahabī, *Siyar aʿlām al-nukalāʾ*, Beirut 1987-9, xiv, 247-8; Yāfiʿī, *Mirʾāt al-djanān*, Ḥaydarābād 1337-39, ii, 241-5; Ibn Kat̲h̲īr, *Bidāya*, Cairo 1348-51, xi, 127; Ibn al-Djazarī, *G̲h̲āyat al-nihāya fī ṭabaḳāt al-ḳurrāʾ*, ed. G. Bergsträsser and O. Pretzl, Cairo 1932-5, ii, 392; Suyūṭī, *Bug̲h̲ya*, ed. Ibrāhīm, Cairo 1964, ii, 353; Ibn al-ʿImād, *S̲h̲ad̲h̲arāt*, year 304; Ziriklī, *Aʿlām*, ix, 277. The most extensive modern biographies of Yamūt may be found in the introductions to M.M. Haddāra's ed. of Muhalhil's *Sariḳāt Abī Nuwās*, Cairo 1957, 14-28 (including his son Muhalhil), and to Ibrāhīm Ṣāliḥ's ed. of Yamūt's *Ak̲h̲bār* in his *Nawādir al-rasāʾil*, 2nd printing Beirut 1986, 41-122 (45-57: introd.; 63-70: *Ak̲h̲bār*; 73-122: collection of traditions from the secondary literature.

(E. WAGNER)

YANBUʿ, conventionally Yanbo or Yambo, the name of a port on the Red Sea coast of the Ḥidjāz, now a flourishing town of Suʿūdī Arabia (lat. 24° 05' N., long. 38° 03' E.), also formerly called *Yanbuʿ al-baḥr* ("Y. of the sea") or *S̲h̲arm Y.* ("the inlet of Y."), and also of an inland town, known as *Yanbuʿ al-nak̲h̲l* ("Y. of the date-palms"). The name is said to derive from Ar. *yanbūʿ* "well", because of the many wells at the foot of the escarpments of the nearby Raḍwā [*q.v.*] (Yāḳūt, *Buldān*, i, 1038). Ibn Djubayr indeed writes *Yanbūʿ*. Yanbuʿ seems to be identical with Ptolemy's *Iambia Kōmē*.

In pre-Islamic times, Yanbuʿ al-Nak̲h̲l was a centre of worship of the god Suwāʿ [*q.v.*]. It is mentioned several times in the *g̲h̲azawāt* (see AL-MAG̲H̲ĀZĪ and al-Ṭabarī, i, 1269, 1271; Yāḳūt, *Buldān*, i, 1038) and, according to al-Bakrī, ed. Wüstenfeld, *Muʿdjam*, i, 425 ff., it was conquered by the Prophet, who is said to have conducted the *ṣalāt* in its mosque. Town and region were then inhabited by the Banū Djuhayna [see ḲUḌĀʿA]. The Arab geographers describe the town as large, well populated and defended by a strong castle. Life was easy because of the many date groves (*The History of al-Ṭabarī*, xxx, tr. C.E. Bosworth, Albany 1989, 321-2). Al-Muḳaddasī, 101, adds that there were gold-mines between Yanbuʿ and al-Marwa (this last can hardly be the mountain near Mecca; possibly D̲h̲u 'l-Marwa in the Wādī 'l-Ḳurā is meant); he also mentions enmities and fighting (*ʿadāwāt wa-ḥurūb*) in the town between Sunnīs and S̲h̲īʿīs. It gradually came to replace al-Djār [*q.v.*] as port of Medina.

Ḳatāda b. Idrīs [*q.v.*], the ancestor of the S̲h̲arīfs of Mecca, was born in Yanbuʿ in 540/1145-6. He rebuilt the fortress, which was in the hands of his family, and used the town as the basis for his conquest of Mecca in 596/1202. In 1503 there was an *amīr* in Yanbuʿ, and in 1583 the Ottomans restored the fortress again (Faroqhi, *Mekka*, 105, 134). In 1819, G. Forster Sadleir, *Diary*, 110, described the port as miserable, surrounded by a recently-made tottering wall, with the old walls and one gate still standing; several waste spots were appropriated for dunghills, burial grounds and receptacles for dead horses and camels; the supply of water was very precarious. The population lived mainly by the trade of Medina with Suways (Suez), Ḳuṣayr and Ḳunā [*q.vv.*] (cf. Wellsted, *Travels*, ii, 207 ff.). In 1816 Ibrāhīm Pas̲h̲a [*q.v.*] landed at Yanbuʿ where he started his campaign against al-Dirʿiyya [*q.v.*], the capital of the Wahhābīs. In the early 20th century the port was described as standing on a bay, protected by a small sandy island, the entry to the inlet being between reefs. Outside, the water was deep, but in the entrance the depth decreases rapidly. The port was divided by an arm of the sea into two parts. On the landside, there was still a wall with towers and two gates. Formerly the port had 4,000 to 5,000 inhabitants, but their number had dwindled to about 1,500 since the opening of the Ḥidjāz railway [*q.v.*], swelling temporarily during the Pilgrimage (Hogarth, *Hejaz*, 25-6).

Until recently, Yanbuʿ's economy was based on the Pilgrimage and on the export of agricultural products, mainly dates. In 1975 King K̲h̲ālid signed a decree charging a Royal Commission with overseeing the creation of Yanbuʿ Industrial City (*Madīnat Yanbuʿ al-ṣināʿiyya*) together with its twin on the Gulf coast, Djubayl. This creation *ex nihilo* has made Yanbuʿ one of the most important industrial areas in the Kingdom, especially for the petrochemical industry; two pipelines connect it with the oilfields in the Gulf, one for crude oil and one for natural gas. Port facilities and the airport have been expanded. In 1993 the population was estimated at 40,000.

Bibliography: Ibn Djubayr, *Riḥla*, ed. Wright and de Goeje, Leiden and London 1907, 145; Suraiya Faroqhi, *Herrscher über Mekka. Die Geschichte der Pilgerfahrt*, Munich-Zürich 1990; G. Forster Sadleir, *Diary of a journey across Arabia*, ed. F.M. Edwards, New York 1977; D.G. Hogarth, *Hejaz before World War I*, ed. R.L. Bidwell, New York 1978; J.R. Wellsted, *Travels in Arabia*, ed. F. Scholz, 2 vols. Graz 1978; British Admiralty, *Western Arabia and the Red Sea*, London 1930; A. Grohmann, *EI*¹ *s.v.*; ʿAbdullah al-Wohaibi, *The Northern Hijaz in the writings of the Arab geographers*, Beirut 1973; see also the *Bibl.* to AL-LUḤAYYA, and H.-J. Philipp, *Saudi Arabia. Bibliography on society-politics-economics*, Munich-New York 1984, 361 *s.v.* Port descriptions; E. O'Sullivan, *Saudi Arabia. A MEED practical guide*, London 1993, 151-2.

(E. VAN DONZEL)

YANINA [see YANYA].

YĀNIS, al-Amīr ABU 'L-FATḤ NĀṢIR (or Amīr, Ibn Tag̲h̲rībirdī, *Nudjūm*, v, Cairo 1913-17, 240) al-Djuyūs̲h̲ Sayf al-Islām S̲h̲araf al-Islām, al-Rūmī al-Armanī al-Ḥāfiẓī (d. 16 D̲h̲u 'l-Ḥidjdja 526/1132), the fourth of six Muslim Armenian viziers of the Fāṭimids (over the period 1074-1163).

A former *mamlūk* of al-Afḍal, in 516/1122-3, Yānis was appointed chief of the *ṣibyān* and head of the treasury by al-Āmir's vizier Maʾmūn al-Baṭāʾiḥī (al-Maḳrīzī, *K̲h̲iṭaṭ*, ed. al-Malīgī, iv, 268). Rising to the posts of chamberlain and commander-in-chief, the political career of Yānis developed through his involvement in the events following the assassination of al-Āmir: the regency of the caliph's cousin Abu 'l-Maymūn ʿAbd al-Madjīd for the heir al-Ṭayyib, the overthrow of the Fāṭimid Imāmate by the Imāmī Kutayfāt and the liquidation of the latter by the *ṣibyān al-k̲h̲āṣṣ al-Āmirī* (led by him). As a reward for his role in reinstating the Ismāʿīlī state, Yānis was proclaimed vizier (see the *sidjill* for this of al-Ḥāfiẓ, in al-Ḳalḳashandī, *Ṣubḥ*, ix, 297). A tough disciplinarian and man of *hayba*, Yānis took the initiative in punishing anarchic elements within the *ṣibyān*, and eliminated about 300 of them; he also imprisoned prominent figures in the administration and promoted a private regiment of military slaves known as the *Yānisiyya* (*Khiṭaṭ*, iii, 26-7; *Ittiʿāẓ*, ed. M. Aḥmad, Cairo 1919, iii, 144; Ibn Muyassar, *Akhbār*, 75; F. Daftary, *The Ismāʿīlīs*, Cambridge 1992, 268). Fearful of the vizier's growing power during the nine months in office, al-Ḥāfiẓ arranged his murder by poisoning his ablutions water (*Khiṭaṭ*, *loc. cit.*; *Akhbār*, ii, 75-6). Yānis built two mosques, the *Masdjid al-Fatḥ* and the *Masdjid Yānis*, completed posthumously by his two sons (*Khiṭaṭ*, ii, 268-9, 324), whom al-Ḥāfiẓ had taken under his protection.

Bibliography: H. Sufian, *Armenian princes and Mamlūks in the Fāṭimid period* (in Arm.), Cairo 1928; G. Messerlian, *Prominent Armenians in Egypt* (in Arm.), Cairo 1947; S.M. Stern, *The succession to the Fāṭimid Imām al-Āmir*, in *Oriens*, iv (1951), 193-255; N. Ter Mikaelian, *The Armenian community in Egypt* (in Arm.), Beirut 1980; Y. Lev, *State and society in Fatimid Egypt*, Leiden 1991; S.B. Dadoyan, *The Fatimid Armenians*, Leiden 1997. (SETA B. DADOYAN)

YANYA, the Ottoman form for YANINA, a town of the Epirus region of northwestern Greece, situated on the west bank of lake Pamvotis at an altitude of 520 m/1,700 feet and dominated by the Pindus mountains.

The date of its foundation is unknown, and though certain historians maintain that it is mentioned in a document concerning the Council of Naupactus (673), it is only mentioned for certain in a decree of the Emperor Basil II in 1020. It must have already existed for some centuries and is said to have originated from a monastery of St. John the Baptist, around which grew a settlement called Agioanneia or Agioannina. Walls were built in the 10th century, and Anna Comnena records in her *Alexiad* that these were in very good condition at the time of the Norman conquest of the town in spring 1082. Important repairs to the enceinte were not made until the end of the 18th century by ʿAlī Pasha Tepedelenli [*q.v.*], with the work going on till 1815 and being accompanied by the building of a second citadel on the acropolis; within this interior fortress (*ič ḳalʿe*) was ʿAlī Pasha's great palace and the magazine tower (*bārūd-khāne*).

The town's history has been full of incident. After the Latin conquest of Constantinople in 1204, Michael Angelus Comnenus founded the despotate of Epirus with the intention of using it as a base for the re-establishment of the Byzantine empire. After this last was restored by the Palaeologi of Nicaea in 1261, the despots of Epirus retained their independence till 1319, when Yanina and its district came briefly under Byzantine control, till in 1346 the Serbian king Stephen IX annexed it. The Florentine Esau de Buondelmonti held it from 1385-1411, then followed two decades under the Counts of Cephalonia Charles I and II Tokkos, till the Ottoman conquest by Murād II on 9 October 1430. The town remained in Turkish hands till February 1913.

Under the Turks, Yanina, as the centre of one of the three *pashaliḳs* in Epirus, enjoyed a period of relative stability, with various Islamic monuments constructed, some of which still exist. According to Ewliyā Čelebi, in the later 11th/17th century it had some 30 mosques and oratories, seven *medreses*, as many *tekkes*, an *ʿimāret-khāne*, several schools, three caravanserais, two *ḥammāms* and 1,900 shops. The region continued nevertheless to be disturbed, especially with the rising of 1611 organised by the metropolitan of Larissa, Dionysius, which was fiercely repressed, with withdrawal of the privileges granted at the time of the town's conquest, expulsion of the Christian population to outside the walls, and the confiscation of *tīmārs* [*q.v.*] from those who held them. This Ottoman repression led to many conversions to Islam. At the end of the 18th century, Yanina was transformed by ʿAlī Pasha of Tepedelen (1744-1822), appointed governor of Epirus in 1787, who governed what was in effect a quasi-autonomous state that included, as well as the *pashaliḳ* of Yanina, part of modern Albania, Thessaly, and northern Euboea and Peloponnesus. For some thirty years, Yanina enjoyed an unprecedented prosperity until the fall and death of ʿAlī Pasha in 1822.

Despite the conversions of the 17th century, the population of Ottoman Yanina remained till the end in majority Christian. The first fiscal register known to survive, from 1564, mentions 50 Muslim hearths and 1,250 Christian ones, whilst a register from 1579 also mentions Jews. When Ewliyā was there *ca.* 1670, he counted 37 quarters, almost half of these (18) being Muslim and the rest comprising 14 Christian ones, 4 Jewish ones and one of gypsies, with an estimated 4,000 hearths for the whole town. At the beginning of the 19th century, F. Pouqueville counted 3,200 hearths (2,000 of Christians, 1,000 of Muslims and 200 of Jews). In the later 19th century, this disparity continued. According to the Ottoman census of 1881-93, the central *ḳaḍā* of the province of Yanina had 4,759 Muslims, 77,258 Greek Orthodox (covering also Christian Albanian speakers), 3,334 Jews and 207 "foreigners".

If the Muslims were less numerous than the Christians, they were nevertheless very prominent in the town. Yanina was of military importance since the conquest, with a garrison of troops from all over the empire, before 1837 lodged among the population, after then in barracks and other buildings prominent in the urban landscape. These soldiers were, together with the Ottoman civilian officials, substantially the only Turkish speakers there, since the autochthonous Muslims used Albanian and, above all, Greek. These Greek speakers, known as "Turcoyaniots", were probably descended from Christian *sipāhīs* converted towards the mid-11th/17th century.

Greek was not only a demotic language but might be used by the Ottoman authorities in public acts. Thus in the last decades of the 19th century, the meetings of the municipal council were held in Greek, and the newspaper *Wilāyet*, published from 1868 onwards, was bilingual in Greek and Turkish. This preponderance of Greek was further reflected in the sphere of education. If there were several turcophone schools in the last days of Ottoman domination, the local élites continued to prefer Greek institutions, in particular the renowned Zosimaia school.

In 1913, as part of the Treaty of Bucharest ending the Balkan Wars, Yanina and southern Epirus passed to the Kingdom of Greece, and ten years later, as part of the exchanges of populations between Greece and the Turkish Republic, the Turcoyaniots left. During the Second World War, it was the turn of the small Jewish community to disappear into the Nazi extermination camps. Despite these two happenings, Yanina and its region continues to have a certain ethnic mixture; as well as Greeks, there are Albanian speakers and small groups of Vlachs.

Bibliography: Ewliyā Čelebi, *Seyāḥat-nāme*, viii, 646-59; R.A. Davenport, *The life of Ali Pasha of Tepeleni, vizier of Epirus*, London 1837; P. Aravantinos, *Perigraphē tēs Epeirou*, 3 vols., Ioannina 1866, repr. 1984; *Sālnāme-i wilāyet-i Yanya*, years 1871, 1875, 1876, 1877, 1889, 1890, 1894, 1901; Sh. Sāmī, *Ḳāmūs al-aʿlām*, vi, 4788 ff.; V. Pyrsinellas, *Hē idrusis tōn Iōanninōn kai hē onomasia autōn*, Ioannina 1956; İsmail Hakkı Okdaş, *Yanya'dan Ankara'ya*, Istanbul 1975, 41-145; Melik Delilbaşi, *The establishment of Ottoman sovereignty in Thessaloniki and Ioannina*, in *Belleten*, li, no. 199 (1987), 75-106; R. Delven, *The Jews of Ioannina*, Athens 1990; J. Strauss, *Das Vilayet Janina 1881-1912. Wirtschaft und Gesellschaft in einer "geretteten Provinz"*, in H.G. Majer and R. Motika (eds.), *Türkische Wirtschafts- und Sozialgeschichte von 1071 bis 1920*, Wiesbaden 1995, 297-319; I. Kourmantzis, *The Jewish community of Ioannina. History, spatial distribution and social structure*, in I.K. Hassiotis (ed.), *The Jewish communities of southeastern Europe from the fifteenth century to the end of World War II*, Thessaloniki 1997; *İA*, art. *Yanya* (Nazif Hoca). See also the *Bibl.* to ʿALĪ PASHA TEPEDELENLI.

(MEROPI ANASTASSIADOU)

YAO, a Bantu people and language (Chi-Yao), whose earliest recorded habitat lay east of the Ruvuma River in present Mozambique. At latest from the end of the 16th century, they were engaged in petty trade with Kilwa [*q.v.*] and the east coast of Africa, peddling tobacco, iron hoes and animal skins in exchange for cloth (for the well-to-do only), brassware, swords, salt and beads. Slowly an export trade in ivory developed, together with captives who had been enslaved to carry it to the coast.

This trade greatly advanced in the 18th century and reached its apogee in the 19th. By mid-19th century a series of Yao towns followed the trail from the east side of Lake Nyasa (Marawi, Malawi), in close association with Arab traders from Zanzibar, financed by Indians with Indian Ocean connections. The Arabs were few in number, and the Yao were able to acquire firearms for protection as well as for slave-catching. By 1860 it was noted that better-to-do men affected Arab dress, a sign already of acculturisation towards Islam. Only *ca.* 1880 did any substantial conversion to Islam become noticed. By then there were Yao populations in what was to become Masasi District, and separately round Songea (in present Tanzania) east of the lake. The number of adhesions to Islam greatly enhanced in the First World War, when German Benedictine missionaries working in the area were interned, leaving Christian converts leaderless, so that these last found a ready response from Islamic fraternities in both areas.

Bibliography: Chapters by R.A. Oliver, J.M. Gray and A. Smith in *Oxford hist. of East Africa*, i, Oxford 1962; E.A. Alpers, *Ivory and trade in East Central Africa*, London 1975; J.C. Russell and N.C. Pollock, *News from Masasi*, Beiträge zur Afrikanistik, Band 45, no. 62, Inst. für Afrikanistik und Aegyptologie der Universität Wien, 1993; and personal knowledge of both areas.

(G.S.P. FREEMAN-GRENVILLE)

YARBŪʿ (A.), the jerboa, jumping mouse or jumping hare (*Jaculus*) of the class of rodents and family of dipodids (*Dipus*).

The name jerboa is itself derived from *yarbūʿ*, which may come from Aramaic, as also the name gerbil. *Dipus* is the "two-legged rat". It holds itself up on long backlegs like the kangaroo, whilst the front legs are very short and are used to grasp prey and scrape out its burrows. In Pliny, the jerboa is often confused with the "white rat" (*Mus albus*). The Dipodid family comprises a dozen species, typified by the "Arrow-bolt jerboa" (*Dipus sagitta*). The Arabic authorities on zoology mention three kinds of jerboa: (a) *al-shufārī* "big and elongated"; (b) *al-tadmurī* "that of Palmyra"; and (c) *dhu 'l-rumayḥ* "bearing a short lance", because of its long, upright tail terminated by a brush of hair. There is a certain terminology for the jerboa. Thus its young is called *dirṣ*, pl. *adrāṣ*, *durūṣ*; its burrow with its several exits is called *nāfiḳāʾ* (pl. *nawāfiḳ*), *ḳuṣʿa*, *ḳuṣāʿa*, *ḳāṣiʿāʾ*, *ḳuṣaʿāʾ*, *ḳuṣayʿa* (pl. *ḳawāṣiʿ*), whence the verbs *naffaḳa* and *ḳaṣṣaʿa*, further, *damm*, *dumma*, *dumamāʾ* is found. The spoils from an excavated burrow are piled into a heap called *dammāʾ*, *dummāʾ*, *dāmmāʾ*, *rāhiṭāʾ*, *ruhaṭāʾ*, *ruhaṭa*. All this vocabulary of rodents, rats, mice and jerboas, is given by al-Djāḥiẓ, who devoted several chapters to the jerboa (see *Bibl.*). He mentions there that certain of the Bedouin happily eat jerboas, whilst others avoid it, considering it one of the djinns' mounts. Islamic law has varying views about the lawfulness of eating jerboa flesh, since the Prophet is said to have forbidden the killing of this little rodent.

The jerboa's name is found in several proverbial sayings of comparison: *aḍall min walad al-yarbūʿ* "more astray than the jerboa's young", and *ka 'l-mushtarī al-ḳāṣiʿāʾ bi 'l-yarbūʿ* "like someone who buys the burrow in exchange for the jerboa", meaning someone who turns away from the substance and follows (its) effect and prefers the transient to the permanent" (al-Maydānī, *Madjmaʿ al-amthāl*, ed. M.M. ʿAbd al-Ḥamīd, Cairo 1379/1959, ii, 155b, no. 3099). The jerboa's blood is said to be good as an ointment for hairiness of the eyelids, making these hairs fall out and not grow again.

Finally, in oneiromancy, seeing a jerboa in a dream reveals a person who is a voluble liar, ready to quarrel; the reasoning behind this interpretation remains enigmatic.

Bibliography: Djāḥiẓ, *Ḥayawān*, Cairo 1947, iv, 260, v, 276, vi, 46; Damīrī, *K. al-Ḥayawān al-kubrā*, Cairo 1937, ii, 408-9; Ḳazwīnī, *ʿAdjāʾib*, on margins of Damīrī, i, 371 (the sole mention of *dhu 'l-rumayḥ*); Dr. Chenu, *Encyclopédie d'histoire naturelle*, vol. *Les rongeurs et pachydermes*, Paris 1967, 164-8; A. Malouf, *An Arabic zoological dictionary/Muʿdjam al-ḥayawān*, Cairo 1932, s.v. Jerboa; H.R.P. Dickson, *The Arab of the desert*, London 1949, 465, 590-2; L. Guyot and P. Gibassier, *Les noms des animaux terrestres*, Coll. Que sais-je?, Paris 1967, 111-12; H. Eisenstein, *Einführung in der arabische Zoographie*, Berlin 1990, index s.v. Springmaus.

(F. VIRÉ)

YARBŪʿ, an important group of the tribe of Tamīm [*q.v.*] with the genealogy Yarbūʿ b. Ḥanẓala b. Mālik b. Zayd Manāt b. Tamīm (see Caskel-Strenziok, in *Bibl.*). The same name is borne by other ethnic groups not only Tamīmī (e.g. Yarbūʿ b. Mālik b. Ḥanẓala, cf. *Mufaḍḍaliyyāt*, ed. Lyall, 122, l. 18 and parallel passages) and also Yarbūʿ b. Tamīm in Caskel-Strenziok), but also of other tribes, of the south (Kalb, Saʿd Hudhayn, Djuhayna) and of the north (Ghaṭafān, Thaḳīf, Ghanī, Sulaym, Ḥanīfa, ʿĀmir b. Ṣaʿṣaʿa; we also find among the Ḳuraysh a Yarbūʿ b. ʿAnkatha b. ʿĀmir b. Makhzūm).

Yarbūʿ being the name of a rodent widely found in Arabia, the jerboa (see previous article), its application to the tribe has been taken as an example of totemism (W. Robertson Smith, *Kinship and marriage in early Arabia*[2], 235), a theory that is, however, now abandoned. Mythological legend, which has survived to a greater extent in this connection than elsewhere among the traditions of the Tamīm, dwells on the mother of Yarbūʿ, Dj̲andala bt. Fihr, of the Kināna, who is said to have been violated one stormy night by Mālik b. ʿAmr b. Tamīm and later married to him (Ibn al-Kalbī, *Dj̲amhara*, B.L. ms. fol. 62a; *Naḳāʾiḍ*, ed. Bevan, 225, n. 1; this is perhaps an etiological myth, formed to explain certain connections between neighbouring clans). Compared with the other groups descended from Ḥanẓala, reunited under the name of al-Barādj̲im, the Yarbūʿ appear isolated, probably because they were powerful enough to do without a federative alliance. Indeed we find that even some of the sub-groups of the Yarbūʿ enjoy a certain autonomy, like the Riyāḥ, the Kulayb, the Salīṭ, the T̲h̲aʿlaba and the G̲h̲udāna. They are divided into two sections, the exact nature of which we do not know: al-Aḥmāl (T̲h̲aʿlaba, ʿAmr, Subayra and al-Ḥārit̲h̲) and al-Uḳad (Kulayb, G̲h̲udāna and al-ʿAnbar). Their territory was very extensive, for we find them practically throughout the whole extent of the territory of the Tamīm, from Yamāma to below the Euphrates; but their centre was the valley of al-Hazn, of remarkable fertility (cf. Yāḳūt, *Muʿdj̲am*, ii, 261, iii, 870; the name of one of their oases was Firdaws al-Iyād). Although tradition mentions "towns" belonging to them (Wüstenfeld, *Register*, 254) they led a nomadic life, like most of the Tamīm.

The history of the Yarbūʿ during the Dj̲āhiliyya is closely connected with that of the rest of the Tamīm, and on several occasions they took command in the wars of the latter. Sometimes, however, we find them engaged by themselves in war with one or another of the neighbouring tribes; thus they fought several battles alone with the Banū S̲h̲aybān, the best known being those of D̲h̲ū Ṭulūk (*Naḳāʾiḍ*, 45-59, 73) and of al-Iyād (*ibid.*, 580-7, also known by other names), in which they took prisoner the famous S̲h̲aybānī leader Bisṭām b. Ḳays (cf. E. Bräunlich, *Bistam ibn Qais, ein vorislamischer Beduinenfürst und Held*, Leipzig 1923, *passim*) in spite of the support given to the latter by the Persian governor of ʿAyn Tamr.

At the beginning of Islam, the attitude of the Yarbūʿ was that of hostile reserve. They did not dare declare openly against the powerful prophet of Medina, but on his death they were the first to rebel. The prophetess Sadj̲āḥ [*q.v.*] was one of them (the tradition that makes her belong to the Tag̲h̲lib seems to have little authority). To the Yarbūʾ also belonged the two brothers Mālik and Mutammim b. Nuwayra [*q.v.*], whose relations with K̲h̲ālid b. al-Walīd made such a stir. After the suppression of the *ridda*, however, the Yarbūʿ like the rest of the Tamīm proved faithful to Islam and took an active part in the conquests; but their turbulent and rebellious nature was revealed in the considerable support they gave to the K̲h̲āridj̲īs. In the *Ag̲h̲ānī*[1], vi, 4, it is noted that at the battle of Dawlab, in 65/684-5, where the forces of the Azraḳīs were crushed, the leaders of the two parties, ʿUbayd Allāh b. Bas̲h̲īr al-Salīṭī and al-Rabīʿ b. ʿAmr al-G̲h̲udānī, were both of Yarbūʿ.

The many details that we possess of the deeds of the Yarbūʿ during the wars of the Dj̲āhiliyya, and even of those of the tribal wars of the Islamic period, have survived mainly because these wars are mentioned in the verses of Dj̲arīr (who belonged to the clan of the Kulayb b. Yarbūʿ) and because his commentators discuss them fully.

The Yarbūʿ, moreover, gave to the poetry of the pre-Islamic period and of the 1st/7th century quite a number of remarkable poets; in addition to the well-known poets, one may mention Suḥaym b. Wat̲h̲īl al-Riyāḥī [*q.v.*] (cf. especially, *Aṣmaʿiyyāt*, ed. Ahlwardt, 76), Ḥārit̲h̲a b. Badr al-G̲h̲udānī and al-S̲h̲armardal b. S̲h̲arīḳ [*q.v.*], of the Banū T̲h̲aʿlaba b. Yarbūʿ.

Bibliography: See that to TAMĪM, and also Caskel-Strenziok, *Ǧamharat an-nasab*, i, Table 330, ii, 591.

(G. LEVI DELLA VIDA)

YARG̲H̲U (T.), trial, interrogation, the Mongolian tribunal or court of justice (Doerfer, iv, 58 ff. n. 1784), hence *yarg̲h̲uči*, a judge.

Čing̲h̲iz K̲h̲ān's adopted brother (or according to Ras̲h̲īd al-Dīn, adopted son, *Dj̲āmiʿ al-tawārīk̲h̲*, i/1, ed. A. Romaskevič, L. K̲h̲etagurov and A.A. Alizade, Moscow 1965, 178; *ibid.*, ed. B. Karīmī, Tehran 1970, i, 414) S̲h̲igi-Ḳutuku was made *yarg̲h̲uči* at the *ḳuriltay* held in 1206 (D.O. Morgan, *The Mongols*, Oxford 1986, 97). He was to judge certain criminal cases on an *ad hoc* basis and to supervise the distribution of subject peoples and to record what was done in a "blue book" (*kökö debter*) (idem, *The "Great Yāsā of Chingiz K̲h̲ān" and Mongol law in the Īlk̲h̲ānate*, in *BSOAS*, xlix [1986], 164; L. Ligeti (ed.), *Histoire secrète des Mongols*, Budapest 1971, 173-4; F.W. Cleaves, *The secret history of the Mongols*, Cambridge, Mass. 1982, 143-4). Ras̲h̲īd al-Dīn states that S̲h̲igi-Ḳutuku "conducted courts of enquiry justly (*yarg̲h̲uhā bi-rāstī pursīdī*), and he was solicitous and helpful to many criminals and caused his words to be repeated, lest (they) should confess out of terror and fear; and he said, 'Do not be afraid, but speak the truth'. And in the discussions of the *yarg̲h̲uči*s it became well known from that time to this, in the country (*wilāyat*) of Mug̲h̲ulistān and those regions, that the foundations of the *yarg̲h̲u*s are laid on the regulations (*ḳawāʿid*) that he established and followed" (*Dj̲āmiʿ al-tawārīk̲h̲*, i/1, ed. Romaskevič *et alii*, 180, quoted by Morgan, *op. cit.*, 174-5). It would seem, therefore, that a kind of case law grew up on the foundations laid down by S̲h̲igi-Ḳutuku. This is borne out by the account of the *Dastūr al-kātib* (see below). The *yarg̲h̲u*, held at the court of the Great K̲h̲ān was called the Great Yarg̲h̲u, according to Dj̲uwaynī, ed. Ḳazwīnī, i, 50.

Courts of interrogation were also held by Mongol *amīr*s and provincial governors. Major cases were referred by them to the Great Yarg̲h̲u. The rulers of the various Mongol k̲h̲ānates, including the Īlk̲h̲ānate in Persia, had their own *yarg̲h̲u*s. From Ibn Baṭṭūṭa's description of the practice prevailing under Ḳutlug̲h̲ Temür, the governor of K̲h̲ʷārazm in or about 734/1334, it seems that the procedure of the *yarg̲h̲u* had by this time become somewhat similar to that of the *maẓālim* [*q.v.*, and see also MAḤKAMA]. Ibn Baṭṭūṭa states, "It is one of the regular practices of this *amīr* that the *ḳāḍī* comes daily to his audience hall and sits in the place assigned to him, accompanied by the jurists and his clerks. Opposite him sits one of the great *amīr*s, accompanied by eight of the great *amīr*s and *s̲h̲ayk̲h̲*s of the Turks, who are called *arg̲h̲udj̲ī*s [i.e. *yarg̲h̲uči*s]. The people bring their disputes to them for decision; those that come within the jurisdiction of the religious law are decided by the *ḳāḍī*, and all others are decided by these *amīr*s" (*Riḥla*, tr. Gibb, iii, 545).

In the early years of the Īlk̲h̲ānate, the cases heard in the *yarg̲h̲u*, such as are mentioned in the sources, were mainly to do with Mongol state affairs, cases between Mongols or between Mongols and Persians, and concerned with sedition and irregularities over taxation.

S̲h̲arʿī courts continued to exist and their autonomy and nature were not fundamentally altered. The relation of the *yarg̲h̲u* to the *maẓālim* and *ʿurfī* courts is less clear. With the conversion of G̲h̲azan K̲h̲ān [*q.v.*] to Islam there may have been a revival in the importance of the *maẓālim* jurisdiction (Lambton, *Continuity and change in medieval Persia*, London 1988, 93 ff.). Naṣīr al-Dīn Ṭūsī includes the *yarghuči* among the "men of the pen" (*Madjmūʿa-i rasāʾil az taʾlīfāt-i Khwādja Naṣīr al-Dīn Ṭūsī*, ed. M. Riḍawī, Tehran 1957, 29. See also V. Minorsky and Mojtaba Minovi, *Naṣīr al-Dīn Ṭūsī on finance*, in *BSOS*, x, [1940-2], 758 and revised version by Minorsky in *Iranica, bīst maḳāla*, Tehran 1964, 68). In doing so he was, perhaps, influenced by the tradition relating to Shigi-Ḳutuku. In practice, *yarghuči*s were probably also concerned with the apprehension of those summoned to the *yarghu* and possibly with the execution of the sentences of the court also (cf. *Tārīkh-i shāhī-i Ḳara Khitāʾiyān*, ed. M.I. Bāstānī Pārīzī, Tehran 1976-7, 156).

No one was immune from interrogation in the *yarghu*, whether a member of the royal house, an *amīr* or a high official. Ābish Khātūn, who was married to Tash Möngke, one of Hülegü's sons, was summoned to the *ordu* to answer in the *yarghu* accusations of alleged misdemeanours in Fārs (see Lambton, *op. cit.*, 273-5. See also Rashīd al-Dīn, *Djāmiʿ al-tawārīkh*, ed. Karīmī, ii, 811). Shams al-Dīn Djuwaynī [*q.v.*] was interrogated in the *yarghu* and bastinadoed before he was put to death in 683/1284 (Abū Bakr al-Ḳutbī al-Āharī, *Tārīkh-i Shaykh Uways*, ed. J.B. van Loon, The Hague 1954, 138-9). Another notorious case was that of Rashīd al-Dīn [*q.v.*], who was tried in the *yarghu* for an alleged attempt to poison Öldjeytü and was killed together with his son Khwādja Ibrāhīm on the orders of Öldjeytü in 718/1318 (Ḥāfiẓ Abrū, *Dhayl-i Djāmiʿ al-tawārīkh-i rashīdī*, ed. Khān Bābā Bayānī, ²Tehran AHS 1350/1971, 128).

From the documents in the *Dastūr al-kātib* of Muḥammad b. Hindūshāh Nakhdjawānī, who lived into the Djalāʾirid period, it seems that Mongol *amīr*s and soldiers were still subject to the *yarghu* down to the end of the Īlkhānate and perhaps longer. He gives the text of a document for the office of *amīr yarghu* issued in favour of a certain Amīr Bayān, who "more than any of the *amīr*s of the day was endowed with experience and knowledge of the customs and regulations (*rusūm wa ḳawāʿid*) of the Mongol sultans and *amīr*s and their *yasaḳhā* and *turahā*". He was to oversee the affairs of the *yarghu*, to enquire diligently into the cases of the Mongols and to act in accordance with the *ḳutatghu bilik* of Čingiz Khān and the (precedents) laid down by the great *yarghuči*s. He was not to transgress by one jot the rule of justice and equity and was to decide cases in accordance with the Čingiz-khānid *yāsāḳ*. When the rightness of one of the disputants was apparent, he was to be given a *yarghu-nāma* as a record to produce should his opponent(s) trouble him again. He and his followers (*nawkarān*) and the scribe who wrote the *yarghu-nāma* were to receive the usual fee on the termination of the case (ed. Alizade, ii, Moscow 1976, 29-35).

Few details concerning the rules of procedure of the *yarghu* are available. The infliction of torture and beating by bastinado to induce confession appear to have been common. Djuwaynī describes the referral of an alleged conspiracy by a number of Uyghur leaders to massacre the Muslim population in Besh Balīgh to the Great Yarghu at Möngke Ḳaʾan's court. Written declarations of their innocence and an attestation from the *amīr* who had revealed the alleged conspiracy were taken in Besh Balīgh but no settlement was reached and so they went to Möngke's court. After confessions were extracted from the conspirators by torture, Möngke Ḳaʾan gave the order for them to be sent back to Besh Balīgh and executed (i, 35 ff.).

One of the earliest cases recorded in the Persian sources of the application of the *yarghu* to Mongols in Persia is that of Körgüz, who had been sent to Khurāsān and Māzandarān, where he had carried out a new census and reassessed the taxes. His predecessor, Edgü-Temür, and others accused him of malpractices and he eventually went to Ögedey's court to answer the accusations made against him. A *yarghu* was held, but although it sat for several months, it failed to bring about a reconciliation between the two parties. Finally, Ögedey himself sat in judgement. Edgü-Temür and his supporters were found guilty; some were beaten and others handed over to Körgüz to be put in the cangue (Djuwaynī, ii, 230 ff.). Then in 637/1239 Körgüz returned to Khurāsān. Intrigues against him continued and he again set out, probably in 639/1241-2 for Ḳaraḳorum, presumably to defend himself. However, passing through the territories of Čaghatay (who had recently died) he had an altercation with an official during which he made a remark which offended Čaghatay's widow. Fearful of the consequences he hurried back to Khurāsān. The wives and sons of Čaghatay sent after him to arrest him and bring him to Čaghatay's *ordu* at Ulugh-Ef. There the *amīr*s held a *yarghu*. Its proceedings were inconclusive, hence it was decided to send Körgüz to Ḳaraḳorum to Töregene, Ögedey's widow, who had become the regent of the empire. There it was decided that, since his alleged crime had been committed in Čaghatay territory, he should be sent back to Ulugh-Ef. Körgüz, as apparently was his wont, spoke roughly to those in charge and was killed on the spot (*ibid.*, 240 ff.). The *amīr* Arghun, who succeeded Körgüz, was also subjected to calumny and intrigue by his subordinates. He was examined by the *yarghu* at the *ordu* in 647/1249 and again in 651/1253 and cleared on both occasions. On the second, those who had accused him were handed over to him. Some were executed at the *ordu* and others he took back with him to Ṭūs, where he killed them (*ibid.*, 259-60). Three points emerge from Djuwaynī's account: first, that the *yarghu* was concerned with reconciliation as well as judgement; second, that the various Mongol kingdoms exercised a degree of independence in the administration of justice; and third, that those found guilty by a *yarghu* might be handed over to the other party for punishment. These features are also to be observed in the operation of the *yarghu* in the Īl-khānate (see further, Lambton, *op. cit.*, 83 ff.).

An early case submitted to the *yarghu* in the Īl-khānate was that of Madjd al-Dīn Ibn al-Athīr, a *nāʾib* of ʿAṭāʾ Malik Djuwaynī. Yesü-Buḳa, governor of Baghdād, reported to Abaḳa that Madjd al-Dīn had been heard to speak of the power and greatness of the Mamlūk army. This, Yesü-Buḳa alleged, showed that Madjd al-Dīn and the Djuwaynī brothers were in league with the Mamlūks. Abaḳa ordered Madjd al-Dīn to be seized. Although he was interrogated in the *yarghu* and given one hundred strokes of the bastinado, his guilt was not established and he was handed over to Shams al-Dīn Djuwaynī, who sent him to Sīwās as governor (Rashīd al-Dīn, *Djāmiʿ al-tawārīkh*, iii, 156-7. See also for a slightly different account Djuwaynī, tr. Boyle, i, pp. xxii-xxiii). Another case of alleged sedition, also during the reign of Abaḳa, is that of Angyanu. He had been sent to Fārs as governor in 667/1268-9. The vigour of his administration and his success in collecting taxes aroused opposition and alienated the Mongol *amīr*s in the province. A number of them fled the province and went to Abaḳa's court, where they accused Angyanu of planning rebellion and committing peculation. He was summoned to the *ordu*, tried by *yarghu* and found guilty. He succeeded in exonerating himself but lost his government (Waṣṣāf, *Tārīkh*, ed. M.M. Iṣfahānī, lith. Bombay 1269/1852-3, 193, 195. See further Lambton, *Mongol fiscal administration in Persia*, in *SI*, lxv, 104-5).

There are various cases of a *yarghu* being held to look into failure in military operations. Tekelle, the Atabeg of Greater Luristān, who had joined Hülegü on his march against Baghdād, decamped with his followers (who had no experience of siege operations) when Ket-Buḳa remonstrated with him for his lack of effort in prosecuting the siege of Baghdād. After the fall of Baghdād, Ket-Buḳa was sent in pursuit of him. Eventually he was brought to Tabrīz, subjected to interrogation in the *yarghu* and executed (Muʿīn al-Dīn Natanzī, *Muntakhab-i tawārīkh-i muʿīnī*, ed. J. Aubin, Tehran AHS 1336/1957, 43). *Yarghus* held by Ghazan and Öldjeytü to investigate military failures are also recorded. The former held a *yarghu* at Ūdjān on 12 Dhu 'l-Ḳaʿda 702/28 June 1303 after the battle of Mardj al-Ṣuffar [*q.v.*] to try the *amīrs* who had been responsible for the defeat of the Īl-Khānid army. Initially, it appears that the trial was carried out by persons other than Ghazan. Rashīd al-Dīn states, "Although they (sc. the *amīrs*) had been closely interrogated, when the *yarghu-nāma* was presented to Ghazan he made a few pertinent remarks. They were then interrogated again, the points made by Ghazan being taken into consideration. Finally, on the first day of Dhu 'l-Ḥidjdja (17 July) the interrogations (*yarghuhā*) were completed and Aghutay Tarkhān, the son of Haybak Tarkhān, and Toghan-Temür of the Mangit were executed and whatever was in accordance with the Great Yāsā was carried out in every respect" (*Tārīkh-i mubārak-i ghāzānī*, ed. K. Jahn, London 1940, 149-50). According to al-Maḳrīzī's account, the Īl-Khān was with difficulty restrained from putting the commander of the force, Ḳutlugh-Shāh, to death, and the onlookers are said to have rushed at the prisoner and spat in his face. Al-Maḳrīzī adds that Ḳutlugh-Shāh was banished to Gīlān (*Hist. des sultans mamlouks de l'Egypte*, tr. Quatremère, Paris 1837-45, ii, 204-5, quoted by Boyle, in *Camb. hist. Iran*, v, 395). There was a similar case during the reign of Öldjeytü when the Mongol army was put to flight during a campaign in Gīlān in 706/1306-7. A *yarghu* was held, and some of those found guilty were executed and others bastinadoed (Ḥāfiẓ Abrū, *Dhayl-i djāmiʿ al-tawārīkh-i rashīdī*, 76).

One of the best-documented cases of a *yarghu* held to investigate alleged peculation is that of the Shaykh al-Islām Djamāl al-Dīn Ibrāhīm b. Muḥammad al-Ṭībī, the Malik al-Islām, a rich merchant, who held an extensive *muḳāṭaʿa* [*q.v.*] for Fars during the reign of Ghazan (see Lambton, *Continuity and change in Medieval Persia*, 88-9, 335 ff.).

It was not only cases directly concerning Mongol affairs that were heard in the *yarghu*. Ḳuṭb al-Dīn, the Ḳutlugh-khānid ruler of Kirmān (632-55/1235-57), appealed to Möngke for help against his cousin Rukn al-Dīn Khwādja Djuḳ b. Baraḳ Ḥādjib, who had turned him out of Kirmān. The case was referred to the *yarghu*. After examination, Möngke handed Rukn al-Dīn over to Ḳuṭb al-Dīn, who killed him and re-established himself in Kirmān [see further KIRMĀN, at vol. V, 161-2]. After Ḳutlugh Terken succeeded her husband Ḳuṭb al-Dīn as ruler of Kirmān, some dissatisfied persons complained against her to Arghun, the governor of Khurāsān. He realised that their reports were lies, and on his instructions Ḳutlugh Terken referred the matter to the *baskaḳs* and *yarghučis* of the province. Those who had complained were tied up naked outside Kirmān for several days and, "as was the custom of the Mongols", interrogated until they confessed and signed statements of their guilt. Some were executed and others sent to the *ordu* (*Tārīkh-i shāhī-i Ḳarā Khiṭāʾiyān*, 156. See further Lambton, *op. cit.*, 86). Another case concerning local rulers is that of Ḥusām al-Dīn ʿUmar. He had overthrown and killed Ṣamṣām al-Dīn Maḥmūd and his son and seized Lesser Luristān. He was summoned to the *ordu* after the grandson of Shaykh Zayn al-Milla wa 'l-Dīn Kāmūʾī, the brother of Ṣamṣām al-Dīn's widow, had appealed to the *ordu* for blood-wit. He was interrogated in the *yarghu* by Ghazan and killed in retaliation for the murder of Ṣamṣām al-Dīn and his son (Muʿīn al-Dīn Natanzī, 62).

A rather unusual case is that of a *yarghu* which was held to decide the possession of Sīrdjān [*q.v.*], which was disputed between Ḳutlugh Terken, the ruler of Kirmān, and the *maliks* of Shabānkāra [*q.v.*]. The matter had been discussed at Hülegü's *ordu* but not settled. However, in 663/1264-5 Abaḳa, who had succeeded Hülegü, sent two officials to Sīrdjān to hold a land court (*yarghu-yi amlāk*) and to examine the documents and title deeds of the two parties (*Tārīkh-i shāhī-i Ḳara Khiṭāʾiyān*, 192, 275-6. See further Lambton, *op. cit.*, 86-7).

After the fall of the Īl-khānate, the term *yarghu* seems gradually to have fallen out of use. There are a few references to it under the Tīmūrids in the sense of both a court of interrogation and the process of interrogation (e.g. Niẓām al-Dīn Shāmī, *Ẓafar-nāma*, ed. F. Tauer, ii, 31, 89, and Khwāndamīr, *Rawḍat al-ṣafā*, Tehran AHS 1338-51/1957-72, vi 70, 86). Niẓām al-Dīn Shāmī mentions a *yarghu-yi djangī* held by Tīmūr in Samarḳand (ii, 66); and most of the cases recorded appear to have concerned the interrogation of *amirs*. It seems that the procedures of the *yarghu* were gradually modified and transferred to the *dīwān-i buzurg* (cf. B.F. Manz, *The rise and rule of Tamerlane*, Cambridge 1989, 169).

Bibliography: Given in the article.

(ANN K.S. LAMBTON)

YĀRKAND, a town of the Tarim basin, Eastern Turkestan, now coming within the Sinkiang/Xinjiang Autonomous Region of the People's republic of China and having in Chinese the (revived) name of So-ch'e/Shache (lat. 38° 27' N., long. 77° 16' E., altitude 1,190 m/3,900 feet).

Yārkand lies on the river of the same name, which rises in the northern part of the Karakoram mountains near the imperfectly delineated border between Kashmīr and China and then flows eastwards to join the Tarim river; with its perennial flow, it is the main source stream of the Tarim. The town was also situated on the southern branch of the historic Silk Route which skirted the southern edge of the Tarim basin and the Takla Makan desert, being about 220 km/138 miles from Kāshghar [*q.v.*] and 320 km/182 miles from Khotan [*q.v.*], in the computation of mediaeval Islamic travellers, four days' and then ten days' march respectively (cf. Minorsky (ed. and tr.), *Sharaf al-Dīn Ṭāhir Marwazī on China, the Turks and India*, tr. London 1940, 18). Since caravan routes from the upper Oxus region and the Pamirs joined the southern Tarim basin route at Yārkand, it was always a significant trading centre (the Portuguese missionary Benedict de Goës, en route from India to China in 1603, noted that the caravan from Kābul terminated at what he calls *Hiarcàn* and a fresh caravan was put together for the journey onwards to China: see Yule-Cordier, *Cathay and the way thither*, London 1914-15, iv, 215-22). Also, the fertile, well-irrigated oasis surrounding the town has always supported a considerable agricultural population; the present one is estimated at 60,000. See Sir Aurel Stein, *Ancient Khotan*, Oxford 1907, i, 87-9.

Little is known of the pre-Islamic history of Yārkand. Like Kāshghar, Khotan and other towns of the region, it was probably a foundation of the Indo-European Sakas, and a *Saka-rādja* is mentioned who may have been the ruler of Saka, the older name of Yārkand, cf. the Sha-ch'a of the Chinese annals of the 1st century B.C. (the Chinese forms for what appears to be the town of Yārkand are discussed in detail by P. Pelliot, *Notes on Marco Polo*, Paris 1959-73, ii, 880-2). The language of the people of Yārkand, as also those of Kāshghar, would thus have been, at this time, an Indo-European one similar to the Iranian tongues of Khotan, Tumshuḳ, etc. In this 1st century B.C., the king of Sha-ch'a paid tribute to the Hsiung-nu of the northern and western fringes of China, and in the 1st century A.D. the king Hsien (*r.* 33-61) for a brief period extended his power across the "Western Region" as far as Farghāna and Ḳuča, whilst the later Han were distracted by internal problems and the Hsiung-nu were in a weakened condition (see W. Samolin, *East Turkestan to the twelfth century, a brief political survey*, The Hague 1964, 28-30; R. Grousset, *The empire of the steppes. A history of Central Asia*, New Brunswick, N.J. 1970, 37, 39-41, 43; D. Sinor (ed.), *The Cambridge hist. of early Inner Asia*, Cambridge 1990, 128, 146, 173). From about this time, Mahayana Buddhism began to spread in the Yārkand oasis, as elsewhere in Eastern Turkestan, amongst other things bringing Sanskrit as an hieratic language; the early 7th century pilgrim Hüan-tsang/Xuan-zang, returning from India to China, found many Buddhist monasteries at *Che-ku-ka* = Yārkand, though several were in ruins (T. Watters, *On Yuan Chwang's travels in India*, London 1904-5, ii, 293-5). The later 7th century and the later 8th century saw periods of domination by the Tibetans over much of the southern Tarim basin (see C.I. Beckwith, *The Tibetan empire in Central Asia. A history of the struggle for great power among Tibetans, Turks, Arabs, and Chinese during the early Middle Ages*, Princeton 1987, 28 ff., 34 ff., 42, 102-3, 152-7), but the Iranian-speaking, Buddhist city-state of Yārkand continued under its own rulers, like those in neighbouring Khotan, at first subject to the T'ang emperors of China, but with an infiltration of Turkish ethnic elements. A Uyghur state was established in the northern part of the Tarim basin after 843, and in the 10th century the Ḳarluḳ Ḳarakhānids [see ILEK-KHĀNS] moved across the T'ien-shan into the western Tarim basin. Khotan became Muslim in 396/1006, so the establishment of the new faith at Yārkand must have taken place at some previous date with the advent of the Ḳarakhānids. Certainly, the Buddhist religion, and the local Iranian and "Tokharian" languages, began to disappear as part of the eventual Islamisation and Turkicisation of the whole of the Tarim basin. See in general on this period, Samolin, *East Turkestan to the twelfth century*, esp. 61-3, 69-70, 80-2; *EIr*, art. *Chinese Turkestan. II. In pre-Islamic times* (V. Mair and P.O. Skjaervø).

The actual name Yārkand is first attested for certain in Maḥmūd al-Kāshgharī's *Dīwān lughāt al-turk* (later 5th/11th century) (tr. Atalay, i, 484, cf. Brockelmann, *Mitteltürkischer Wortschatz*, Budapest 1928, 244). Pelliot, *Notes on Marco Polo*, index, iii, 295, propounded a Turco-Iranian etymology for this toponym, Tk. *yār* "cliff" (but more precisely, it would seem, "eroded, vertical bank or gorge of a river", see Clauson, *An etymological dictionary of pre-thirteenth century Turkish*, 953-4) + Ir. *kand/kend* "town". We possess coins from the Ḳarakhānid Eastern Khānate, which was based on Kāshghar, minted at Yārkand (thus spelt on the coins) in 404/1013-14 by Nāṣir al-Dawla Malik al-Mashriḳ Ḳadir Khān Yūsuf b. Bughra Khān Hārūn or Ḥasan (d. 423/1032) and by his son Sulaymān Arslān Khān (d. 449/1057-8) (see Barthold, *Turkestan down to the Mongol invasion*, 281; E. von Zambaur, *Die Münzprägungen des Islams zeitlich und örtlich geordnet*, Wiesbaden 1968, i, 272; T. Mayer, *Sylloge numorum arabicorum Tübingen. Nord- und Ostzentralasien. XV b Mittelasien II*, Tübingen-Berlin 1998, 72-3). It is strange that the *Ḥudūd al-ʿālam* (372/982-3) mentions Kāshghar, Khotan and possibly some minor places along the southern Tarim basin route but not Yārkand (cf. map iv in Minorsky's tr. at 261). We possess some information reflecting social and cultural conditions in the Yārkand oasis under the Ḳarakhānids in the later 5th/11th and early 6th/12th centuries from a collection of legal documents that were found in a garden there in 1911 and preserved by Sir George Macartney, the then British Consul-General at Kāshghar. They are in Arabic and in Turkish, the latter written in both the Uyghur and Arabic scripts, and cover the years 473-529/1080-1135. They give the name *Yār.k.n.d.h* (thus spelt) mostly to the district or *kūra*, but also to the town or *balda* itself, and through their use of standard Islamic legal formulae and phraseology show that Islamic faith and culture had well penetrated life in the Yārkand oasis by the end of the 11th century. One document, from Dhu 'l-Ḥidjdja 474 or 494/May 1082 or September-October 1101 mentions the then ruler in Kāshghar as Abū ʿAlī al-Ḥasan Tafghač Bughra Ḳara Khāḳān b. Sulaymān Arslan Ḳara Khāḳān, i.e. the ruler of the Eastern Khānate 467-96/1075-1103 and dedicatee of Yūsuf Khāṣṣ Ḥādjib's *Ḳutadghu bilig* [*q.v.*, and see ILEK-KHĀNS at Vol. III, 1114a]. See, on this collection of documents, much commented upon but with the originals now disappeared, Monika Gronke, *The Arabic Yārkand documents*, in *BSOAS*, xlix (1986), 454-507, with detailed bibl. of previous work on the collection at 506-7. Towards the middle of the 6th/12th century, the Ḳarakhānids fell under the general suzerainty of the Western Liao or Ḳara Khitay [*q.v.*]. Chinese sources state that in 1123 the Gür Khān Ye-liu Ta-shi invaded the Tarim basin from the region northwest of Shensi in China and captured Kāshghar, Yārkand and Khotan; but the Arab historian Ibn al-Athīr records a victory in 522/1128 by the ruler of the Eastern Khānate, Arslan Khān Aḥmad or Hārūn b. Ḥasan over the Ḳara Khitay (ed. Beirut, xi, 83).

In the 7th/13th century, again according to Chinese histories such as the *Yüan-shi*, after his killing of the Nayman chief Küčlüg, Čingiz Khān sent an expedition into Eastern Turkestan, and Kāshghar, Yārkand and Khotan surrendered to the Mongols; subsequently, the Great Khān ordered 13 water-stations to be set up between Yārkand and Khotan (E. Bretschneider, *Mediaeval researches from East Asiatic sources*, London 1910, i, 234, ii, 47-8; river communication between the two towns seems to be implied). When Marco Polo passed through Yārkand (his *Yarcan*) in *ca.* 1274 en route for China, he noted the presence there of Nestorian and Jacobite Christians as well as the majority Muslims, and observed that the population there suffered much from goitre (a fact later confirmed by European travellers such as Sven Hedin); the town belonged to a nephew of the Great Khān, i.e. of Ḳubilay [*q.v.*], whilst Kāshghar and the lands beyond belonged to "Great Turkey", the empire of Ḳubilay's rival Ḳaydu [*q.v.*] (Yule-Cordier, *The Book of Ser Marco Polo*, ³London 1902, i, 187-8; Barthold, *Zwölf Vorlesungen über die Geschichte der Türken Mittelasiens*, Berlin 1935, 187).

Eastern Turkestan now came within the dominions of the Čaghatayids, with Yārkand as one of the *Altï Shahr* or "Six Cities" (with Aḳsu, Uč Turfan, Ḳuča, Kāshghar and Khotan). The Čaghatayids' rival Tīmūr sent an expedition into Kāshgharia led by his grandson Iskandar Mīrzā b. ʿUmar Shaykh in 802/1399-1400, which captured Kāshghar, Yārkand and Aḳsu. Nevertheless, for over two-and-a-half more centuries the region continued to form part of the Čaghatayid Khānate, but with members of the powerful Turco-Mongol Dughlāt family, influential in the region since the later 8th/14th century, as actual rulers. In 920/1514 Mīrzā Muḥammad Ḥaydar Dughlāt ejected a usurper from Kāshgharia and restored Čaghatayid suzerainty there, making Yārkand his capital, having irrigation canals dug in the oasis and building a citadel in the town with six gateways and an inner *arg* (Mīrzā Muḥammad, *Tārīkh-i Rashīdī*, ed. and tr. N. Elias and E. Denison Ross, *A history of the Moghuls of Central Asia*, London 1895, Introd. 11, 122, tr. 296-8; see also DŪGHLĀT). Towards the end of the 10th/16th century, the *ordo* or centre of power of the Čaghatayid ʿAbd al-Karīm Khān b. ʿAbd al-Rashīd was usually at Yārkand, where his brother Muḥammad had succeeded him when Benedict de Goës passed through in 1603. But from this same time onwards, the power of the Naḳshbandī religious line of the *sayyid* Khodjas [*q.v.* in Suppl.] grew in Kāshgharia, with the Āfāḳiyya or Aḳtaghlïḳ, "People of the White Mountains", lineage exercising real power at Yārkand. The Čaghatayids lingered on till the second half of the 11th/17th century, when they were extinguished (1089/1678) and Kāshgharia united under the theocratic rule of the Khodjas as protégés of the Mongol Oyrats or Kalmuks [*q.v.*] centred on the Ili basin and Dzungaria. Thus the charismatic Khodja, Ḥaḍrat Āfāḳ/Apak Hidāyat Allāh, was installed at Yārkand and Kāshghar in 1091/1680, Yārkand now becoming for the remainder of this century and for over half of the next one the capital of the Khodjas. In the 1750s, the Khodja Ḳïlïč Burhān al-Dīn led a Muslim crusade against the infidel domination of the Kalmuks, but this brought down in 1758 a Chinese army which, after annexing Dzungaria three years previously, turned on the Khodjas and captured Yārkand; Kāshgharia was now annexed to the Ch'ing/Qing empire. See Grousset, *The empire of the steppes*, 425-6, 459, 485, 500-1, 527-8; *EIr*, art. *Chinese Turkestan. v. Under the Khojas* (Īsenbike Togan).

The Chinese maintained Yārkand rather than Kāshghar as their capital for the new province. But Ch'ing authority in Central Asia declined over the next decades, and from 1820 onwards, when the Khodja pretender Djahāngīr returned from Khokand and launched a rebellion in the Altï Shahr, there were a series of revolts by the Turkish Muslims of the province, culminating in the outbreak at Yārkand in August 1863 which signalled the great rebellion of the Khoḳandī Muḥammad Yaʿḳūb Beg [see YAʿḲŪB BEG], who proclaimed himself Khān of Eastern Turkestan at Kāshghar (1867-77). We owe knowledge of Yārkand at this time to the published accounts resulting from British missions at this time to Yaʿḳūb Beg, that of the merchant R.S. Shaw in 1868 and those of the Government of India envoy Sir Thomas D. Forsyth in 1870 and 1873. After the suppression of Yaʿḳūb Beg's movement, the three regions of "Uyghuristān", Altï Shahr and Dzungaria were formed into the new imperial province of Sinkiang "New Territory" (1884). The Chinese *Tao-t'ai* or Circuit Commissioner made his residence at Kāshghar rather than Yārkand, and it was at this former town that Russian and British consulates were now established.

In the 20th century, Yārkand was involved in several "Turco-Islamic" secessionist movements of the Uyghur Turks in the southern Tarim basin during the 1930s and 1940s, the era of the warlords in China, since southern Sinkiang was a stronghold of conservative Islamic religious sentiment. In March-May 1933 both Old Yārkand (= the traditional Muslim town) and New Yārkand (= the Chinese and other non-Turkish town) fell to troops of the secessionist "Khotan Islamic Government" under the *amīr* ʿAbd Allāh Khān, with a total collapse of Han authority in southern Sinkiang. This last was restored by the warlord Sheng Shih-ts'ai, with considerable Soviet Russian backing, but a further revolt, the so-called "Sabīl Allāh" one, involved the occupation of Yārkand from April to September 1937 by anti-Sheng, anti-Communist Turkish rebels, and it was likewise involved in the 1945-6 anti-Chinese and anti-Russian revolt against Kuomintang misrule in Sinkiang. Similar outbreaks are reported to have occurred in southern Sinkiang in the 1950s and possibly later, but massive Han Chinese immigration after the imposition of Communist rule in 1949 has meant that secessionist movements have had less and less chance of success. See A.D.W. Forbes, *Warlords and Muslims in Chinese Central Asia. A political history of Republican Sinkiang 1911-1949*, Cambridge 1990, 68, 77-9, 140 ff., 204-6.

Bibliography: In addition to references given in the article, see also M. Hartmann, *Chinesisch-Turkestan. Geschichte, Verwaltung, Geistesleben und Wirtschaft*, Halle 1908. For the Turkish language of the Yārkand region, part of the southern dialect of Neo-Uyghur Turkish, see G. Raquette, *A contribution to ... the eastern-Turkestan dialect ... in the districts of Yarkand and Kashghar*, in *Jnal. de la Soc. Finno-Ugrienne*, xxvi/5 (1909), 1-53; K. Schriefl, *Bemerkungen zur Sprache von Kašgar und Jarkend*, in *Keleti Szemle*, xiv (1913-14), 178-89, xv (1914-15), 277-303; E. Rossi, *Nota sul turco di Yarkand (Turkestan Orientale)*, in *RSO*, xvii (1938), 283-5; G. Jarring, *Material to the knowledge of Eastern Turki. Tales, poetry, proverbs, riddles, ethnological and historical texts from the southern parts of Eastern Turkestan*, i, *Texts from Khotan and Yarkend*, Lund 1946; and O. Pritsak, in *PTF*, i, 525 ff., with further bibl. at 535.

(C.E. BOSWORTH)

YARLÏGH, YARLÏḲ, a term of Inner Asian Turkish origin, employed in the chanceries of the Mongol empire and in those of certain of its successor states both before and after their Islamisation, in its original (i.e. pre-Mongol and pre-Islamic) meaning of "[Imperial] decree, edict, command". In general, in Islamic chancery practice, *yarlïghs* are contextually equivalent to the more specific documentary forms of *firmān*, *ḥukm* or *barāt* [*q.vv.*; and see DIPLOMATIC. iii]; cf. Clauson, *Dictionary*, 966: "a command from a superior to an inferior, sometimes with some connotation of a grant of favour"; *Drevnetyurskii slovar'*, 242, s.v. *jarlïγ*: "prikaz, predpisanie, ukaz".

In Old Turkish, *yarlïgh* is a typical Uyghur word: it is not attested in the (Oghuzian) runic (Orkhon) inscriptions, and is expressly denoted by al-Kāshgharī as a non-Oghuz word, employed by the Čigil to denote an imperial writing or command (*yarligh huwa kitābu 'l-sulṭān wa-amruhu bi 'l-lughati čigil wa-lā taʿrifuhu 'l-ghuzziya*). Conversely, the term appears in the Uyghur runic mss. In Ottoman usage (where it is chiefly used to refer to the edicts of the Crimean *khāns*) it is, the above usage apart, an exotic loan-word known in only a few texts (*TTS*, i, 789, ii, 1006) and documents (see below). In Arabic (Mamlūk) usage, one encounters the broken plural form *yarāligh/yarālīgh* (also *yārlīghāt*, cf. al-Ḳalḳashāndī, *Ṣubḥ*, vii, 229, 230; Björkman, *Beiträge*, 47, 128: *bārlighāt* [sic] "Reisepass", with reference to Ilkhānid usage).

The Turkish word *yarlîgh* is a second-period (sc. 8th-13th centuries) loan-word in Mongol (*jarliγ*) as a technical administrative term for a government edict (Clauson, *loc. cit.*; N. Poppe, *The Turkic loan words in middle Mongolian*, in *CAJ*, i [1955], 38). (The once widespread view, put forward by e.g. Spuler, *Goldene Horde*[1], 306, n. 2, and previously by Russian scholars from the mid-19th century onwards, such as V.V. Grigor'ev, that "Džarlyḫ" [*sic*] is a Mongol word, cannot now be substantiated.) As a loan-word, it was specifically employed in imperial (i.e. Khāḳānic) decrees (*qaan jarliγ manu*, "unser kaiserlicher Erlaß", A.P. Grigor'ev, *Mongol'skaya diplomatika XIII-XV vv.*, Leningrad 1978; cf. E. Haenisch, *Zu den Briefen der mongolischen Il-khane Argun und Öljeitu an den König Philipp den Schönen von Frankreich (1289 u. 1305)*, in *Oriens*, ii [1949], 222) and in, e.g., the *Secret History*, whereas documents emanating from subordinate members of the Čingizid dynasty utilised the phrase *üge manu* "our word (sc. decree)". For the use of the Turkish term *sözüm*[*iz*] "my/our word" (calqued from the Mongol *üge manu*) as a validating formula or associated with the *tughrā* [*q.v.*] in later *yarlîghs* and other documents; see the discussion in Fekete, *Arbeiten der grusinischen Orientalistik*, 13 ff. (Fekete's misreadings of Crimean Tatar documents in this context are corrected by Mary Ivanics, *Formal and linguistic peculiarities*, 215 n. 15).

The route of transmission of the term from pre-Islamic Uyghur to Islamic usage must have been via the use of Uyghur scribes in Mongol service producing chancery documents in Mongolian and Turkish (see, for a detailed discussion and analysis, A.P. Grigor'ev, *op. cit.*). From the prestige and widespreadness of the term in Čingizid usage stems not only its reborrowing into e.g. south-western Turkish but also its presence from the Mongol period with the same meaning in Russian (*yarlïk*: first occurrence 1267; Vasmer, *Russisches etym. Wörterbuch*, Heidelberg 1958, iv, 493) and in many other languages of Eurasia, including 7th/13th century Oghuz (A.M. Shčerbak, *Oguz-nāme*, 11, 21). It was also still current at this time with its old (sc. Uyghur/Buddhist) secondary meaning of "Divine command" amongst the Nestorian Christians of Central Asia (C. Džumagulov, *Yazîk siro-tyurskikh pamyatnikov Kirgizii*, 91 ff.); for further borrowings see Doerfer, *Elemente*, iv, 153-8, no. 1849. The word survives at the present day in Russian with the meaning "label, tag".

Čingizid *yarlîghs* were written in Chinese (cf. E. Chavannes, *Inscriptions et pièces de chancellerie chinoises de l'époque mongole*, in *T'oung-pao*, sér. 2, v [1904], 357-447, vi [1905], 1-42, ix [1908], 297-428, *passim*); in Mongol, in both Uyghur and quadratic scripts; and in Ḳîpčaḳ Turkish. The language used in the earliest *yarlîghs* of the Golden Horde remains a matter of dispute. The earliest documents still extant as originals date from the later 8th/14th century and are written in Ḳîpčaḳ Turkish, in Uyghur characters. It has been suggested by A.P. Grigor'ev, on the basis of his reconstruction of early texts surviving only in Russian translation, that the earliest Golden Horde edicts were also written in Mongolian (cf. also the exhaustive study by M.A. Usmanov, *Žalovannye aktî Džučieva ulusa, XIV-XVI vv.*, Kazan 1979). The most important surviving document written in Turkish is the *yarlîgh* of Toḳtamîsh Khān [*q.v.*] for Jogaila Algirdaitis (Jagiello), Grand Duke of Lithuania and king (as Władysław II) of Poland (1386-1434), which was issued "in camp on the river Don" "in the Year of the Fowl, 8 Radjab 795 [/20 May 1393]" (reproduction of the first 13 lines of the document in Reychman and Zajączkowski, *Zarys*, 103 = *Handbook*, 155; transcription-text in Kurat, *Yarlık ve bitikler*, 147). This document lacks almost all evidence of Islamic influence over the original Mongol form, possessing no *invocatio* and only the most basic form of *intitulatio* and *inscriptio* (*Toḳtamîsh sözim/Yagaylaga*); yet the year of issue is given in both its Twelve-animal cycle and *Hidjrī* forms; the month and day of issue follow the Muslim calendar. (The use of the Twelve-animal cycle in conjunction with *Hidjrī* dating lasted in Crimean and Ottoman usage until the mid-to-later 9th/15th century.) Under the Il-khāns [*q.v.*], the texts of *yarlîghs* were also engraved in stone. Cf. W. Barthold, *Die persische Inschrift an der Mauer der Manūčehr-Moschee zu Ani*, in *ZDMG*, ci [1951], 241-69 (Russian original in his *Sočineniya* iv, Moscow 1966, 313-38); P. Wittek, *Ankara'da bir Ilhani kitabesi*, in *Türk Hukuk ve Iktisat Tarihi Mecmuası*, i (1931), 161-4; cf. idem, *Zur Geschichte Angoras im Mittelalter*, in T. Menzel (ed.), *Festschrift Georg Jacob*, Leipzig 1932 (= idem, *La formation de l'empire ottoman*, ed. V.L. Ménage, London 1982, no. III), 347-8.

Mongol, pre-Islamic concepts thus lingered in the forms and usages employed in post-Čingizid *yarlîghs* long after the formal Islamisation of the rulers who issued them. The designation *yarlîgh* (e.g., as in the combination *ḥukm-i yarlîgh*) remained current in Persia until the end of the 9th/15th century [see DIPLOMATIC. iii] and in the successor states of the Golden Horde for much longer. The well-known *yarlîgh* of the first khān of the Crimea, Ḥādjdjī Girey I, dated 857/1453 (see below), combines, after the *basmala* (serving, as noted, as *invocatio*) the following assertions of divine authority, set out in three equally prominent lines: (1) [Arabic-Islamic] *bi 'l-ḳuwwati 'l-Aḥadiyya wa 'l-muʿdjizāti 'l-Muḥammadiyya* ("through the strength of the One and the miracles of Muḥammad"); (2) [Turkish-Mongol/Islamic]: *Mängü-Täñri küčinde Muḥammad Resūlü'llāh wilāyetinde* ("in the strength of the Great God [and] in the protection of Muḥammad the Prophet of God"); and (3) [Turkish]: *Ḥādjdjī Girey sözim* ("Ḥādjdjī Girey—my decree"). (For a discussion of the adoption (in 932/1525) of this "Mongol-Crimean assertion of the source of authority" into Ottoman chancery practice, see V.L. Ménage, *On the constituent elements*, 300 ff.) *Yarlîghs* of the later khāns of the Crimea conform much more closely in both form and language to contemporary Ottoman usage (A. Bennigsen *et alii*, *Le Khanat de Crimée dans les archives du musée du palais de Topkapı*, Paris-The Hague 1978; but cf. the useful corrections and amplifications by V. Ostapchuk, in *Harvard Ukrainian Studies*, vi/4 [1982]), 500-28, and *Turcica*, xix [1987], 247-76; there is a valuable discussion and analysis of *yarlîghs* in Crimean chancery practice in Ivanics, *Formal and linguistic peculiarities*, *passim*; cf. also Fekete, *Einführung in die osmanische Diplomatik*, Budapest 1926, pp. lxi-lxii; J. Matuz, *Krimtatarische Urkunden im Reichsarchiv zu Kopenhagen*, Freiburg 1976).

As mentioned above, *yarlîghs* also served the same

function as the *barāt* [*q.v.*; and see SOYŪRGHĀL], i.e. as a diploma of investiture and a grant of immunities. The khāns of the Golden Horde and its successor dynasties not only issued diplomas of investiture to e.g. the subject princes of Rus', and the Metropolitans of All Rus', employing their issue and the ever-present threat of their summary withdrawal as a powerful means of political control over their tributary principalities, but also large numbers of so-called *tarkhanlîk yarlîghs*, or grants of privilege/immunity from taxes and services in kind, to their own subjects (specimen text in Kurat, *Yarlık ve bitikler*, no. 4, 62-80, a document of Ḥādjdjī Girey 857/1453. Cf. also the studies by Halasi-Kun, Grigor'ev, and Muhamedyarov and Vásáry as detailed in *Bibl.* below, all with useful discussion and analyses. Comparable documents were issued by the Il-khānid rulers of Persia and their political successors (cf. Minorsky, *A soyūrghāl of Qāsim b. Jahāngir Aq-Qoyunlu (903/1498)*); in Ottoman usage, exemption documents of a similar nature are known as *muʿāfiyet-nāme*).

Yarlîghs issued down to the early 9th/16th century were validated by the *khān*'s *al-tamgha*. This was a quadrilateral seal impressed, usually in vermilion, sometimes in black, blue or gold, either towards the head or at the foot of the document, and over the pasted joins of individual sheets making up the roll. Later *yarlîghs* of the Golden Horde largely followed Ottoman practice, making use of a *penče* [*q.v.*]-type *ṭughra* for documents issued by the *khān* or the immediately subordinate members of the dynasty (*ḳalgha, nūreddīn*) plus the formula *sözümiz* at the head of the document (see ṬUGHRA, and cf. Matuz, *Krimtatarische Urkunden*, 77-80 and facsimiles).

Bibliography (in addition to references in the text): *Drevnetyurskiĭ slovar'*, Leningrad 1969, s.vv. jarlïγ, ʒarlïγ; Sir Gerard Clauson, *A dictionary of pre-thirteenth-century Turkish*, Oxford 1972, 966-8; Doerfer, *Türkische und Mongolische Elemente im Neupersischen*, s.v.; M. Vasmer, *Russisches etym. Wörterbuch*, Heidelberg 1958; A.M. Shčerbak, *Oguz-nāme*, Moscow 1959; C. Džumagulov, *Yazîk siro-tyurskikh pamyatnikov Kirgizii*, Frunze 1971; *Tanıklariyle tarama sözlüğu*, i, Istanbul 1943, 789; Ḳalḳashandī, *Ṣubḥ al-aʿshā*, iv, 423, 428, vii, 229, 230; W. Björkman, *Beiträge zur Geschichte der Staatskanzlei im islamischen Ägypten*, Hamburg 1928, 47, 128; A.N. Kurat, *Topkapı sarayı müzesi arşivindeki Altın Ordu, Kırım ve Türkistan hanlarına ait yarlık ve bitikler*, Istanbul 1940; A.P. Grigor'ev, *Mongol'skaya diplomatika, XIII-XV vv.*, Leningrad 1978; M.A. Usmanov, *Žalovannye aktî Džučieva ulusa, XIV-XVI vv.*, Kazan 1979, both with very full bibls., cf. also Grigor'ev, *Grants of privileges in the edicts of Toktamiš and Timur-Qutluġ*, in G. Kara (ed.), *Between the Danube and the Caucasus. Oriental sources on the history of the peoples of Central and Southeastern Europe*, Budapest 1987, 85-104, and Shamil Muhamedyarov and I. Vásáry, *Two Kazan Tatar edicts (Ibrahim's and Sahib Girey's yarlıks)*, in *ibid.*, 181-216, with extensive discussions; T. Halasi-Kun, *Monuments de la langue tatare de Kazan*, in *Analecta Orientalia memoriae A. Csoma de Körös dicata*, Budapest 1947, 138-55; idem, *Kazan turkçesine ait dil yadigârları*, in *AÜDTCFD*, vii (1949), 603-44. Equally full bibliographical references to earlier, mainly Russian, studies and publications exist in J. Reychman and A. Zajączkowski, *Zarys dyplomatyki osmańsko-tureckiej*, Warsaw 1955, 103 ff. (= *Handbook of Ottoman-Turkish diplomatics*, The Hague-Paris 1968, 95 ff.). For short but valuable discussions of elements of the Mongol *yarlîgh* in the context of Islamic chancery practice, see S.M. Stern, *Fāṭimid decrees*, London 1964, 160 ff., with further bibl.; V.L. Ménage, *On the constituent elements of certain sixteenth-century Ottoman documents*, in *BSOAS*, xlviii (1985), 283-304, *passim*; and L. Fekete, *Arbeiten der grusinischen Orientalistik auf dem Gebiete der türkischen und persischen Paläographie und die Frage der Formel Sözümüz*, in *AO Hung.*, vii/1 (1957), 1-20. See also Mary Ivanics, *Formal and linguistic peculiarities of 17th century Crimean Tatar letters addressed to princes of Transylvania*, in *ibid.*, xxix/2 (1975), 213-24, and V. Minorsky, *A soyūrghāl of Qāsim b. Jahāngir Aq-Qoyunlu (903-1498)*, in *BSOS*, ix (1937-8), 927-60. For a 17th-century Muscovite fabrication of a putative *yarlîgh* of the Golden Horde ruler Aḥmed Khān, see E.L. Keenan, *The* jarlyk *of Axmed-Xan to Ivan III: a new reading*, in *Internat. Jnal. of Slavic Linguistics and Poetics*, xi (1967), 33-47. (C.J. HEYWOOD)

YARMŪK, the main left bank affluent of the Jordan river [see AL-URDUNN. 1], famed in history as the site of a historic battle between the Arabs and Byzantines.

1. Geography.

The Yarmūk flows into the Jordan some 9 km/5 miles to the south of Lake Tiberias, with headwaters on the southwestern slopes of the Ḥawrān [*q.v.*] in southern Syria. It follows a deeply-incised valley which nevertheless provides the main access through the eastern wall of the Jordan rift valley, the Ghawr or Ghōr, to the north-south routes along the western fringes of the Syrian Desert. As such, it was followed, with difficulty, by the narrow-gauge railway from Ḥayfā via Samākh to Darāʿa/Deraa, where it connected with the Ḥidjāz railway [*q.v.*]. In Antiquity, it was called by Pliny the Elder, *Natural history*, v. 74, the Hieromix or Hieromices. Part of the river's lower course today forms the political boundary between Syria and Jordan. The waters of the Yarmūk could irrigate the Jordan valley if its lowermost course were to be diverted to Lake Tiberias as a reservoir for its waters; but this would entail the improbable co-operation of Syria, Jordan and Israel.

Bibliography: Yāḳūt, *Buldān*, ed. Beirut, v, 434; Le Strange, *Palestine under the Moslems*, London 1890, 53-5; Naval Intelligence Division, Admiralty Handbooks, *Palestine and Jordan*, London 1943, 29, 247, 403-4, 406-7, 506; W.C. Brice, *A systematic regional geography. VIII. South-west Asia*, London 1966, 217, 223-5, 339, 369-72. (C.E. BOSWORTH)

2. The battle.

This was fought near the confluence of the Yarmūk River and the Wādī 'l-Ruḳḳād, which today marks part of the border between Jordan and Syria, and it determined the fate of Byzantine Syria. The Byzantine Emperor Heraclius, who was not personally present, in early 636 collected a very substantial Byzantine and Christian Arab force in order to reverse recent Muslim victories in Syria, Transjordania and Palestine, and to drive the Muslims out of Syria and Palestine. The site strategically included high ground, water supplies, pasture and domination of important routes between Damascus and Galilee (see 1. above). It was an important sedentary base and crucial pasture-grounds of the Ghassān [*q.v.*], and lay near the intersection of four Byzantine provincial boundaries. A major battle had previously taken place near it in 614, at which the Persian general Shahrbarāz had inflicted a resounding defeat on the Byzantines, opening the way into Palestine for the Persians. The terrain's strategic significance was apparent to both sides and in theory was familiar to them. On the eve of the battle, the Byzantines had not succeeded in developing any effective new tactics or strategy for checking the Muslims.

The battle of the Yarmūk or D̲j̲ābiya lasted more than a month if one includes the preliminary manoeuvrings. It began in the vicinity of al-D̲j̲ābiya [q.v.], the traditional base of the G̲h̲assān, with these manoeuvrings, and terminated on 12 Rad̲j̲ab 15/20 August 636. Byzantine forces had come from Ḥimṣ (Emesa) under the general Vahān, who was probably the *Magister Militum per Orientem*, and Theodore Trithurios, the *Sakellarios* (Treasurer). D̲j̲abala b. al-Ayham [q.v.], king of the G̲h̲assān, led G̲h̲assānid forces. Other Christian Arabs, whom Heraclius had recruited in upper Mesopotamia and elsewhere, participated. There are contradictory reports concerning whether Theodore, the brother of Heraclius, was present. Although he participated in planning some of the campaign, Theodore had probably been recalled to Constantinople in disgrace before the final stages of the battle. Muslim forces under Abū ʿUbayda b. al-D̲j̲arrāḥ [q.v.] withdrew from Ḥimṣ and Damascus in the face of the approach from the north of stronger Byzantine armies. They retired to a line between Dayr Ayyūb and Ad̲h̲riʿāt [q.v.], where they waited for more than a month, in a topographically strong position, to deter any Byzantine move further south. On 13 D̲j̲umādā II 15/23 July 636 the Muslims won an initial clash near al-D̲j̲ābiya. The Byzantines attempted to use the waiting period to familiarise their forces with the Muslims and, unsuccessfully, to encourage desertion and dissension within Muslim ranks. Both sides received reinforcements, but the decisive clash took place when the Muslims were continuing to gain more reinforcements. The Byzantines, together with their Christian Arab allies, probably enjoyed numerical superiority, having troops that totaled up to 15,000 to 20,000 men, possibly even more.

By a feigned retreat, the Muslims lured the Byzantines into attacking Muslims and their camp near Dayr Ayyūb. The Muslims penetrated the exposed Byzantine left flank, and then exploited gaps that yawned between Byzantine foot and cavalry. Byzantine infantrymen apparently attempted to lock shields and to engage in intricate and complicated and risky exercises (the so-called "mixed formation") that involved opening the ranks of foot for horsemen to pass through and then relocking shields. Poor Byzantine coordination allowed the Muslims to exploit the gap and to slay many exposed Byzantine infantry. Byzantine forces withdrew into territory that lay between the Wādī 'l-Ruḳḳād and Wādī 'l-ʿAllān, both west of the Wādī 'l-Ḥarīr, to what they believed to be a secure encampment that received protection from the high bluffs of the wadis. But in a night raid, the Muslims under K̲h̲ālid b. al-Walīd [q.v.] seized the critical bridge over the Wādī 'l-Ruḳḳād, which offered the only viable retreat route for the encircled men and animals of the Byzantine army. The Byzantines found themselves blocked and could not retreat in formation, or fight their way out, or negotiate a reasonable settlement. The Byzantines panicked, having learned that they were cut off. The Muslims stormed their camps between the wadis as well as at the village of Yāḳūsa, on the edge of the D̲j̲awlān [q.v.]. The Byzantines lost cohesion and most were slaughtered, although a few may have managed to flee down the steep walls of the wadis. The Muslims took few or no prisoners. Some Christian Arabs allegedly wavered in their loyalty to the Byzantine cause and managed to flee, which aided the Muslims. One Muslim tradition reports that some dejected and defeated Byzantine troops, having perceived the hopelessness of their situation, fatalistically awaited their slaughter.

The battle destroyed the only viable Byzantine army in Syria and its commanders, and it ceased to exist as a fighting force. A rout ensued. For the Muslims, the victory eliminated the possibility of any Byzantine penetration further south, reconfirmed Muslim control of Palestine and Transjordania, and opened the way for the Muslim conquest of the Biḳāʿ [q.v.] valley, Damascus and beyond it, all of Syria. The Muslims consolidated their victory by a rapid and far-stretching and ruthless pursuit of retreating Byzantines, giving them no respite. The battle had great psychological as well as material effects: it broke the will of the Byzantines to give more open battle. The Byzantines henceforth avoided open battle with the Muslims in Syria and upper Mesopotamia, and ended their efforts to recover or hold Syria. Together with Heraclius, who was staying first at Ḥimṣ and then at Antioch, they evacuated northern Syria and withdrew into Anatolia, where the emperor attempted to improvise new defences.

The Byzantines had suffered logistical problems on the eve of the battle. They lacked experience in handling and supplying large numbers of troops in the regions of these operations, and this inexperience may have contributed to their logistical problems and to tensions with local civilians. Byzantine leaders found it difficult to procure adequate supplies from local inhabitants on the eve of the engagements. Manṣūr son of Sergius, the local fiscal official at Damascus, refused to provide supplies to the unprecedentedly large Byzantine forces. These last included heterogeneous ethnic elements, many of whom had no experience in operating or fighting in the region. There was probably mistrust, misunderstandings and friction between Greeks, Armenians and Christian Arabs within the Byzantine forces. There is no indication that the local inhabitants participated in fighting on either side. The Byzantines were already suffering psychological shock from a series of recent defeats at the hands of the Muslims. Muslim losses were considerable, but far smaller than the human and material ones of the Byzantines. But all statistics for the battle, both numbers of combatants and numbers of casualties, should be regarded with suspicion.

The account that Ibn ʿAsākir preserved in his *Ta'rīk̲h̲ Madīnat Dimas̲h̲ḳ* is probably the best. No documentary records or eyewitness accounts survive. Memory of the actual facts of the battle soon faded and quickly became embellished with legends. The magnitude of the Muslim victory received instant recognition and continued to resound later in the 7th century. The military manual entitled the *Strategikon* of Maurice, although written *ca.* A.D. 600, provides some reliable insight into actual contemporary Byzantine fighting techniques and logistics that were probably utilised in the battle. The reigning Byzantine Heraclian dynasty appears to have attempted to shift the responsibility for the disaster from itself to others: to an alleged abortive rebellion of the Armenian Byzantine general Vahān or to the failure to follow Emperor Heraclius' injunctions to watch out for Arab ambushes, or to the adverse climate. There is no evidence that Christian religious dissension affected the outcome. Muslim writers later celebrated the role of Islamic religious zeal, but superior Muslim leadership as well as superior morale, including confidence that derived from their recent pattern of successes, were important factors in their victory.

Bibliography: 1. Sources. Eutychius, *Annales*, ed. and tr. M. Breydy, CSCO, Leuven 1985, text 136-8, tr. 114-16; Sebeos, *Histoire d'Héraclius*, tr.

F. Macler, Paris 1904, 97; *Maurice's Strategikon*, tr. G. Dennis, Philadelphia 1984; Theophanes, *Chronographia*, tr. C. Mango and R. Scott, Oxford 1997, 469-71; Fredegarius, *Chronicon*, ed. B. Krusch, Monumenta Germania Historica, Scriptores Rerum Merovingicarum, ii, Hanover 1888, 153-4; Balā<u>dh</u>urī, *Futūḥ*, 135-8; Ibn Aʿ<u>th</u>am al-Kūfī, ed. ʿAbd al-Muʿīd <u>Kh</u>ān, Ḥaydarābād 1968, i, 230-71; Yaʿḳūbī, *Taʾrī<u>kh</u>*, ii, 160-1; Ṭabarī, i, 2081-2113, 2347-9, 2393-4, tr. Kh.Y. Blankinship, *The challenge to the empires*, Albany 1993, 77-114, tr. Y. Friedmann, *The battle of al-Ḳādisiyyah and the conquest of Syria and Palestine*, Albany 1992, 132-5, 178-80; Ibn ʿAsākir, i, ed. Muna<u>dj</u><u>dj</u>id, 131-2, 159-76; Azdī, *Taʾrī<u>kh</u> Futūḥ al-<u>Sh</u>ām*, ed. M. ʿĀmir, Cairo 1970, 217-45.

2. Studies. M.J. de Goeje, *Mémoire sur la conquête de la Syrie*, Leiden 1900, 103-6; F.McG. Donner, *The early Islamic conquests*, Princeton 1981, 130-46; A. Palmer (ed.), *The seventh century in the West-Syrian chronicles*, Liverpool 1993; W.E. Kaegi, *Byzantium and the early Islamic conquests*, Cambridge 1995, 112-45.

(W.E. Kaegi)

YAʿRUBIDS (a., pl. Yaʿāriba, sing. Yaʿrubī), a dynasty of ʿUmān [*q.v.*] who ruled the country, mostly from al-Rustāḳ but also from <u>Dj</u>abrīn [*q.vv.*] and al-Ḥazm, *ca.* 1024-1164/1615-1749. There are a number of different versions of the date on which the first *imām* of the dynasty, Nāṣir b. Mur<u>sh</u>id, was given the oath of allegiance: al-Sālimī (ii, 4) suggests it was 1024/1615, whereas Nāṣir's biographer, ʿAbd Allāh b. <u>Kh</u>alfān b. Ḳayṣar (13), and the author of *Ka<u>sh</u>f al-<u>gh</u>umma*, Sirḥān b. Saʿīd b. Sirḥān (Ross, *Annals*, 46), give 1034/1624. The origins of the dynasty are not entirely clear. Wilkinson (*Imamate*, 219) supposes them to be of the Nabāhina, but he quotes another tradition which has them of al-Azd.

The 11/17th century saw ʿUmān free of external forces and united, with the rulers free to pursue an active naval policy against the Portuguese and one of expansion overseas, particularly in East Africa. In fact, their struggles against the Portuguese were so successful that ʿUmān became the major maritime power in the Indian Ocean, taking over the Portuguese previous position. Maritime power meant that commercial prosperity and profits were put back into trading interests and also into the building of palace fortresses at home. Nāṣir's successor, Sulṭān b. Sayf I (1059-91/1649-80) began the process by building the massive round fort of Nizwā [*q.v.*]. His son and successor Balʿarab (1091-1104/1680-92) built the magnificently-decorated fort of <u>Dj</u>abrīn and redeveloped the agricultural lands in the area. Balʿarab's brother and successor, Sayf b. Sulṭān I (1104-23/1692-1711) presided over the zenith of ʿUmānī sea power and Mombasa, Kilwa and Pemba were captured by the ʿUmānīs as they waged war on the Portuguese with their greatly expanded navy, and they compelled the Persians to grant them right of entry into the Gulf. Internally, Sayf repaired water channels (sing. *fala<u>dj</u>*) seventeen major ones in all, developed land and planted extensive date and coconut palm groves.

Sayf's son, Sulṭān II (1123-33/1711-19), extended ʿUmānī overseas power yet further with the conquest of al-Baḥrayn [*q.v.*]. He also built the fine fortress of al-Ḥazm which became his residence. But the great wealth brought with it problems. The Yaʿrubī state had become a society of rich merchants and landlords exploiting a class of peasants and slaves. At his death in 1133/1719, Sulṭān left only a minor as his successor, Sayf II. The *ʿulamāʾ* stepped in, unable to support the Yaʿrubī policy of dynastic succession any longer, and put forward their own contender for the imāmate. A confused period of civil war followed, with Sayf returning to the imāmate in 1141/1728. His later intrigues with the Persians, allowing them to enter internal ʿUmānī politics and the struggle for the imāmate, further exacerbated the situation. Sayf died in 1156/1743. Power eventually passed to one Aḥmad b. Saʿīd, who had been appointed Sayf's *wālī* in Ṣuḥār, and who had finally expelled the Persians from ʿUmān. Aḥmad belonged to the Āl Bū Saʿīd [*q.v.*] who have ruled ʿUmān to this day.

Bibliography: The best ʿUmānī sources for this period are ʿAbd Allāh b. <u>Kh</u>alfān b. Ḳayṣar, *Sīrat al-Imām Nāṣir b. Mur<u>sh</u>id*, ed. ʿAbd al-Ma<u>dj</u>īd Ḥasīb al-Ḳaysī, Muscat 1977, the biography of the first Yaʿrubī *imām*; Sirḥān b. Saʿīd b. Sirḥān, *Ka<u>sh</u>f al-<u>gh</u>umma*, tr. E.C. Ross in *Annals of Oman*, Calcutta 1874, repr. Cambridge 1984, 44-57 (up to the year 1728 only); and ʿAbd Allāh b. Ḥamīd al-Sālimī, *Tuḥfat al-aʿyān bi-sīrat ahl ʿUmān*, ii, 3-150. Of modern sources, J.C. Wilkinson, *The Imamate tradition of Oman*, Cambridge 1987, is excellent, with a comprehensive family tree of the Yaʿrubī *imāms* with dates at 13 and an historical summary of the period at 217-25. Wilkinson's *Water and tribal settlement in south-east Arabia*, Oxford 1977, also has some useful remarks on the dynasty, as does his *A short history of Oman from earliest times*, Muscat 1972, 5-8.

(G.R. Smith)

YĀS, Banū, a conglomeration of tribes which in the 18th century ranged in the interior of al-Ẓafra [*q.v.*; see also al-djiwāʾ; dubayy], the region in the United Arab Emirates [see al-imārāt al-ʿarabiyya al-muttaḥida, in Suppl.] extending southward from the Gulf. The island of Ṣīr Banī Yās [*q.v.*] is mentioned by the Venetian traveller Gasparo Balbi in 1580, who thus implies that the Banū Yās were already in the area at that time (Slot, *The Arabs*, 39-40, 143). They are also mentioned in the early 17th century (Slot, *op. et loc. cit.*) and by Niebuhr in the 18th century (*Beschreibung*, 342). The town of Abū Ẓabī [*q.v.*] is said to have been founded by them at about 1174/1760-1. In 1209/1794-5 <u>Sh</u>a<u>kh</u>būṭ b. <u>Dh</u>iyāb of the Āl Bū Falāḥ, the ruling family of Abū Ẓabī settled in the town. The Banū Yās resisted the Wahhābī invasions of 1800-14 [see wahhābiyya], which earned them friendly relations with Saʿīd b. Sulṭān of the Āl Bū Saʿīd [*q.v.*]. In the early 1820s, the Banū Yās, led by a certain Suwaydān b. Zaʾal, who appears to have been head of the Mahāriba section of the Banū Yās, made maritime depredations from al-Dawḥa [*q.v.*, and see also Lorimer, *Gazetteer*, i, pt. III] (Doha) in Ḳaṭar, bringing Abū Ẓabī close to war with Baḥrayn. The raiding ceased when Suwaydān returned to Abū Ẓabī in 1828. The economic interests of the Banū Yās lay mainly in the date groves of al-<u>Dj</u>iwāʾ (Līwā) and in the pearl fisheries around Dalmā Island. Unlike the al-Ḳawāsim [*q.v.*], they thus were far from the navigation channels of the Gulf and therefore had no conflict with the British at sea. In 1835, however, severely depressed by prolonged warfare with the al-Ḳawāsim and by the loss of the annual pearl fishery for several years running, they made a wholesale attempt upon the trade of the Gulf in order to redress their revenues. Outfought and scattered by the British [see kurṣān. iii], they had to pay fines for piracy and many emigrated to al-ʿUdayd, an inlet (*<u>kh</u>awr*) in southern Ḳaṭar, causing much friction between Ḳaṭar and Abū Ẓabī. They left al-ʿUdayd in 1878 and returned to Abū Ẓabī in 1880.

In the modern Gulf States, the Mazrūʿī [*q.v.*] are

regarded as an Abū Ẓabī section of the Banū Yās.

Bibliography: Muhammad Morsy Abdullah, *The United Arab Emirates*, London-New York 1978; G. Rentz, *'Oman and the southern coast of the Gulf*, Aramco 1952; B.J. Slot, *The Arabs of the Gulf, 1602-1784*, Leidschendam 1993; J.G. Lorimer, *Gazetteer of the Persian Gulf, 'Oman and Central Arabia*, Calcutta 1908-15, repr. Farnborough 1970, 2 parts in 6 vols., i, 763-72 and enclosure; C. Niebuhr, *Beschreibung von Arabien*, Copenhagen 1772; see also the *Bibls.* to the articles referenced in the text.

(E. van Donzel)

YĀSĀ (thus the usual orthography in Arabic script, Mongolian *jasaq, jasaγ*, see Doerfer, *Türkische und mongolische Elemente im Neupersischen*, iv, 71-82 no. 1789 s.v. *yāsāq*) may be translated variously, according to context, as "law" or, virtually synonymous with *yarlīgh* [*q.v.*], as "decree" or "order". Hence the sources for the Mongol period speak of what is generally called "the Great *Yāsā* of Čingiz Khān", in the sense of a comprehensive legal code laid down by the founder of the Mongol empire; but in many if not most instances of the use of the term, a specific decree is what is meant. In some cases it is far from certain which sense was in the mind of the writer.

1. Amongst the Mongols.

The traditional view of the Great *Yāsā* is that it was laid down by Čingiz as a written legal code, probably at the *ḳuriltay* [see ḲŪRĪLTĀY] of 1206 which affirmed and proclaimed his supremacy over the tribes of Mongolia and which preceded the Mongol campaigns of conquest in China and Central Asia. There are serious difficulties in accepting this view: these are discussed in MONGOLS. 3. The evidence does not support the notion of a written legal code dating from 1206, and indeed it is very difficult to demonstrate with any degree of certainty that a written code ever existed. D. Ayalon showed that most of what we known about the contents of the Great *Yāsā* derives from al-Djuwaynī's account of it (*The Great* Yāsa *of Chingiz Khān: a reexamination. A*, in *SI*, xxxiii [1971], 97-140, repr. in his *Outsiders in the lands of Islam: Mamluks, Mongols and eunuchs*, London 1988). Al-Djuwaynī (i, 16-25; Djuwaynī-Boyle, 23-34) certainly tells us that certain of Čingiz's decrees had been written down in a Great Book of *Yāsās* (*yāsā-nāma-i buzurg*), and that this book was taken out, consulted and its precepts followed by the Mongol élite whenever appropriate. But the matters with which these *yāsā*s were concerned were more administrative than technically legal (the organisation of the hunt, the army and the postal courier system).

Nevertheless, there is no doubt that a Great *Yāsā* was believed to exist, and that it was regarded as embodying the founder of the dynasty's unalterable decrees on all manner of state and legal matters. It has been suggested, on the basis of Chinese evidence, that a written version may have been first promulgated in 1229, two years after Čingiz's death, at the *ḳurilitay* that proclaimed the accession of his son Ögedey [*q.v.*] as Great Khān (I. de Rachewiltz, *Some reflections on Cinggis Qan's* Jasaγ, in *East Asian History*, vi [1993], 91-104). However, the view presented in MONGOLS. 3., that there may never have been a written version, and that as an oral body of laws and precepts, remembered as having been laid down by Čingiz, it continued to be augmented by Mongol rulers after his time, appears still to be a likely interpretation of the scanty evidence. If there was more to it than that, the evidence would in all probability be much less scanty than it is. The Great *Yāsā* remained of great symbolical importance, not least in the Islamic world, as an entity conceived as being in opposition to the *Sharī'a* (see 2. below).

Bibliography: In addition to the references in the article, see the studies cited in MONGOLS. 3. (particularly, for the interpretation of the evidence advanced here, D.O. Morgan in *BSOAS*, xlix/1 (1986), 163-76). P. Ratchnevsky's biography of Čingiz Khān, listed there, has been skilfully translated into English by T.N. Haining as *Genghis Khan. His life and legacy*, Oxford 1991 (see especially, for the *Yāsā*, 187-96).

(D.O. Morgan)

2. Amongst the Mamlūks.

The constituting of the Mongol empire in Western Asia had a great impact on the Mamlūks. The two great powers were enemies for some three-quarters of a century, but relations were necessarily close, and the two groups of Mongols and Mamlūks felt themselves as ethnically close, sharing a common *djinsiyya* (cf. D. Ayalon, in *SI*, xxxvi [1972], 117 ff., xxxviii [1973], 148-52). The Mamlūks [*q.v.*] drew their military slave manpower from lands under Mongol control, in particular from South Russia and the Dasht-i Ḳïpčaḳ [*q.v.* in Suppl.], and soldiers coming to Egypt and Syria from the lands of the Golden Horde Khāns included, as well as Ḳïpčaḳ and other Turks, Turkicised Mongols and some pure Mongols. Other, free Mongols arrived in Egypt as an element of the *Wāfidiyya*, amongst whom the Oyrat were notable in the last four decades of the 7th/13th century and especially in the reigns of Baybars I [*q.v.*] and Kitbughā, the latter himself from the Oyrat [see WĀFIDIYYA].

Whether the Mamlūks had access to a text of the Great *Yāsa* attributed to Čingiz Khān [see above, 1.] is problematical, even though a source like Ibn Taghrībirdī attributes its introduction to Baybars I, an admirer of the Mongols. There is no evidence that there existed a copy of this within the Mamlūk Sultanate. Few Mamlūk *amīrs* can have been expert in Mongolian, and even fewer in the Uyghur script which must have preceded the apparent adoption of the Arabic script for diplomatic documents between the Mongols and Mamlūks in the 8th/14th century (al-Ḳalḳashandī, *Ṣubḥ al-a'shā*, i, 167, states that the correspondence of the Golden Horde Khāns with the Mamlūks was *bi 'l-lugha al-mughuliyya bi 'l-khaṭṭ al-'arabī*).

The veracity of a passage in al-Maḳrīzī's *Khiṭaṭ*, ed. Būlāḳ, ii, 220, stating that his source, one Abū Hāshim Aḥmad b. al-Burhān, had seen a copy of the Great *Yāsa* in the Mustanṣiriyya library in Baghdād, was questioned also by Ayalon. He believed that al-Maḳrīzī introduced this passage, with its description of the alleged contents of the *Yāsa* (in fact, derived from Ibn Faḍl Allāh al-'Umarī and, ultimately, from al-Djuwaynī), because the *ḥādjib*s or chamberlains, acting as judges, and especially of the Mamlūks, were applying administrative law, *siyāsa* and the practice of *al-naẓar fī 'l-maẓālim*, as complements to the *Sharī'a* and were, in the historian's view, encroaching upon the *ḳāḍī*'s sphere. To combat this tendency, al-Maḳrīzī asserted that the *siyāsa* of the *ḥādjib*s was nothing but the *Yāsa*, whch was the antithesis of the *Sharī'a*. He even claimed (perhaps with his tongue in his cheek) that the word *siyāsa* derived etymologically from *Yāsa* (see *Khiṭaṭ*, ii, 220-1; and see SIYĀSA. 1, at Vol. IX, 694a, and 3., at 696a).

The earliest reference to the Mongol *Yāsa* amongst the Mamlūks found by the late D. Ayalon was in al-Ṣafadī, *A'yān al-'aṣr* (cited in *SI*, xxxviii [1973], 134-5), in which an *amīr* and confidant of Sultan al-Nāṣir

Muḥammad b. Ḳalāwūn [*q.v.*] in the first half of the 8th/14th century, Aytamish al-Muḥammadī, is said to have mastered the Mongolian language for diplomatic purposes, to have studied closely the *sīra* of Čingiz Khān and to have judged the élite members of the *khāṣṣakiyya* [*q.v.*], the royal bodyguard, according to the *Yāsa* of Čingiz. Another of the sultan's *amīrs*, Ariḳtāy, is also said to have been knowledgeable about the *Yāsa*. Ayalon's conclusion (*pace* the assertions of A.N. Poliak, in *REI*, ix [1935], 213-48, and *BSOS*, x [1940-2], 862-76, that Mongol influence in the Mamlūk state was pervasive and lasted until the dynasty's end) was that, even if the *Yāsa* had played some rôle in early Mamlūk society, this cannot have been long sustained, given the fact that the *Yāsa* and other Mongol customs must have been losing ground within the territories directly ruled by the Mongols, a process accentuated by the conversion to Islam of most of the Western Asian Mongols during the first decades of the 8th/14th century.

Bibliography: In addition to references in the text, see the thoroughgoing study of D. Ayalon, *The Great* Yāsa *of Chingiz Khān, a re-examination*, in *SI*, xxxiii (1971), 97-140, xxxiv (1971), 151-80, xxxvi (1972), 113-58, xxxviii (1973), 107-56, repr. in his *Outsiders in the land of Islam: Mamluks, Mongols and eunuchs*, Variorum, London 1988, no. IV; R. Amitai-Preiss, *Ghazan, Islam and Mongol tradition. A view from the Mamluk Sultanate*, in *BSOAS*, lix (1996), 1-10.

(C.E. Bosworth)

YASAḲNĀME [see ḳanūnnāme].

YĀSAMĪN, Yāsimīn, Yāsamūn (a.), a masc. noun denoting the jasmine shrub, of the Oleaceae tribe, family of jasmines (Jasminaceae).

It was cultivated for its yellow or white or purple flowers and for the oil obtained from it by distillation. In the poets, the abbreviated forms *yāsam*, *yāsim*, are found. Several sub-species of jasmine are found in the Arabic-speaking lands, sc. (a) *Jasminum floribundum*, called *habb al-zalīm* "male ostrich seeds"; (b) *J. fructicans*, called *yāsamīn al-barr* "country jasmine"; (c) *J. grandiflorum*; (d) J. *grasissimum*, called *ḳayyān* "flourishing, blooming", and *suwayd* "blackish", proper to Yemen; (e) *J. officinale*, called *ḳīn*, *sidjillāṭ*; and (f) *J. sambac* or *Nyctanthes sambac* or *Mogorium sambac*, called *full*, the Arabian jasmine cited by al-Ḳazwīnī for certain of its properties and effects. According to Ibn Sīnā, jasmine used in a lotion, either dried or fresh, gets rid of freckles. Too much inhaling of its odour yellows the face and causes migraine, whilst its oil, *duhn al-yāsamīn*, taken in a potion cuts off catarrhal mucus.

Bibliography: Ḳazwīnī, *ʿAdjāʾib al-makhlūḳāt* (in margin of Damīrī), Cairo 1937, ii, 42; Dr. Chenu, *Encyclopédie d'histoire naturelle*. ii, *Botanique*, Paris 1876, 337; G. Bonnier and G. de Layens, *Flore de France, Suisse et Belgique*, Paris 1974, 211; A. Issa, *Dictionnaire des noms des plantes/Muʿdjam asmāʾ al-nabāt*, Cairo 1981, 101.

(F. Viré)

YASAWĪ [see aḥmad yasawī].

YASAWIYYA, a Ṣūfī brotherhood present in Transoxania, in Khʷārazm, in the Kazakh steppe and in the Tatar world in Eastern Turkestān, in Turkey, in China and even in India.

Its eponymous founder was Aḥmad Yasawī (d. 562/1166-7 [*q.v.*]). It had as its centre the town of Yasi (or Ḥadrat), modern Turkistān [*q.v.*] in present-day Ḳazakhstān [*q.v.* in Suppl.], where the mausoleum of the founder described as "the Kaʿba of Turkistān" (cf. Bernardini) is situated. Concerning the spiritual filiation of the Yasawiyya, the Naḳshbandī sources (e.g. Fakhr al-Dīn ʿAlī b. Ḥusayn Wāʿiẓ Kāshifī, *Rashaḥāt ʿayn al-ḥayāt*, ed. ʿAlī Aṣghar Muʿīniyān, Tehran 1977, 17) maintain that Aḥmad Yasawī was a disciple of Abū Yūsuf Hamadānī (d. 534/1140), the inspiring force behind the *ṭarīḳa-i khʷādjagān*, but this is erroneous. Recent work shows on the contrary that the Yasawiyya belong to the movement of the Mubayyiḍiyya ("those dressed in white"), a Shīʿī sect which brought together the supporters of Abū Muslim [*q.v.*] after his death, and which integrated certain Manichaean and Zoroastrian beliefs (cf A. Muminov, *Mübeyyidiyye-Yaseviyye alâkası hakkında*, in *Bir*, i [Istanbul 1994], 115-23). The Mubayyiḍiyya stemmed from the Kaysāniyya [*q.v.*], one of the most radical Shīʿī groups, who recognised the imāmate of Muḥammad b. al-Ḥanafiyya (d. 81/700 [*q.v.*]) and awaited his return. They were protected by the Turkish dynasty of the Ḳarakhānids at the beginning of its period of power. In one of the oldest genealogies of Aḥmad Yasawī, translated from Arabic into Eastern Turkish in 590/1291 (Mawlāna Ṣafī al-Dīn Orunk Kūlāḳī, *Nasab-nāma*, ed. A. Muminov and Z. Žandarbekov, Turkistān, Ḳazakhstān 1992, Turkish tr. K. Eraslan, *Mevlānā Safiyyüʾd-dīn, Neseb-nāme tercümesi*, Istanbul 1996), there is mention of a certain Isḥāḳ Bāb, who certainly seems to have been, according to Muminov, Isḥāḳ al-Turk (cited in al-Nadīm, *Fihrist*), a supporter of Abū Muslim, who had come from Damascus to Central Asia in 150/767-8 to propagate Islam in Farghānā and in Eastern Turkistān, and to convert the Zoroastrians (*mūgh*) and the Christians (*tarsā*). According to al-Nadīm, *loc. cit.*, Isḥāḳ Bāb professed to be the successor to Zoroaster and the rites of the Mubayyiḍiyya, according to al-Maḳdisī, resemble those of the "dualists" (*zindīḳ*) (Barthold, *Turkestan*, 199-200). According to the *Nasab-nāma* cited above, Aḥmad Yasawī was descended from ʿAlī Murtaḍā (ʿAlī b. Abī Ṭālib) and from Muḥammad b. al-Ḥanafiyya. His spiritual master, Arslan Bāb, was the leader of the Mubayyiḍiyya in Utrār [*q.v.*], and it was as a representative of this movement that Aḥmad Yasawī was sent to Yasi. The Ṣūfī schools of Baghdād and of Khurāsān did not form an essential part of the development of the Yasawiyya, even though several of their mystical themes are subsequently to be found in the Yasawī texts. To establish what were the primitive practices of the order it is not possible to follow blindly the poetry (*ḥikmat*) attributed to Aḥmad Yasawī, for it is known that it was largely the work of later Yasawīs. It should be noted that in the *Nasab-nāma*, Aḥmad Yasawī and his disciples followed an orthodox Islam (construction of mosques, mausoleums and Ṣūfī hospices, *khānaḳāhs*) and that their Ṣūfism was essentially based on a privileged relationship with the Prophet Khiḍr and the practice of retreat (*khalwa*).

The representatives (*khalīfa*) of Aḥmad Yasawī, such as Ḥakīm Atā (d. 582/1183) or Saʿīd Atā (d. 615/1218), and the disciples of their disciples, such as Zangī Atā, Uzūn Ḥasan Atā, Sayyid Atā, Ismāʿīl Atā, Isḥāḳ Atā, Ṣadr Atā, etc., preached Islam in the region of the Volga, of Khʷārazm, in eastern Turkey, and as far as India (*Rashaḥāt ʿayn al-ḥayāt*, 17-30; ʿAlī Shīr Nawāʾī, *Nesāyim ül-maḥabbe min shemāyim il-fütüvve*, ed. Eraslan, Istanbul 1979, 385). Then, according to the *Shadjarat al-Atrāk* (written in the 16th century), Sayyid Atā, at the beginning of the 16th century, is supposed to have converted Uzbek Khān, the leader of the Golden Horde, to Islam. They also assisted the emergence in Khʷārazm of an influential Yasawī line of descent, the Atāʾiyya (i.e. of Sayyid Atā, 14th century; cf. D. DeWeese).

From the 13th century onwards, fleeing from the

Mongols, the Yasawī *shaykh*s arrived in Anatolia and became involved with an order of *ḳalandar*s called Ḥaydariyya, founded by Ḳuṭb al-Dīn Ḥaydar al-Zāwa'ī (d. 1221, cf. Ahmet Yaşar Ocak), who has been stated to be a disciple of Aḥmad Yasawī (*Nesāyim ül-maḥabbe*, 383-4; Ḥādjdjī Bektāsh Welī, *Wilāyet-nāme. Manakıb-ı Hünkār Hacı Bektāsh-ı Veli*, ed. A. Gölpınarlı, Istanbul 1958, 9-11). The Anatolian mystical movements issuing from the Ḥaydariyya, such as the Bektāshiyya, called upon the patronage of Aḥmad Yasawī who thus appeared to be a heterodox Ṣūfī, which he was not in Central Asia. The same phenomenon of the absorption of the Yasawiyya by the Ḳalandariyya or the association of the Yasawiyya with the heterodox Ṣūfī orders, was recorded in other regions of the Muslim world: in the north of India where an alleged descendant (?) of Aḥmad Yasawī, Sharaf al-Dīn Turk Pānīpānī (d. 1349-50), was found leading a branch of the Čishtī *ṭarīḳa* (cf. Th. Zarcone); in Eastern Turkestan (cf. the *Dīwān* of Muḥammad Ṣādiḳ Zalīlī, 18th century, ed. Imīn Tursun, Peking 1985); and in certain regions of Mā warā' al-nahr (e.g. Khʷādja Ḳalandar in the 18th century, who was thought to be a descendant of Aḥmad Yasawī, according to Riḍā Fakhr al-Dīn, in *Athar*, i/2 (Orenburg 1901), 44).

In the 14th to 15th centuries the Yasawiyya were in competition with the Naḳshbandiyya, who criticised various aspects of their doctrines and practices, such as the principle of the hereditary succession for the position of *shaykh*, the 'Alid origins of the order, the practice of repetitive oral prayer (*dhikr djahrī*) called "*dhikr* of the saw (*arra*)" (in Arabic, *dhikr al-minshār*) (cf. H. Algar; J. Fletcher) which gave the Yasawiyya the name of *Djahriyya*. Over against this prayer, the Naḳshbandīs set the silent repetitive prayer (*dhikr khafī*) and, finally, the Naḳshbandīs criticised the dance (*samā'*) of the Yasawiyya. These two brotherhoods competed with each other, for the Yasawiyya did not proselytise exclusively among the nomads of the steppe, but equally among the sedentary inhabitants of Transoxania, where they played both a political and a social role. There was not, however, an equal sharing of influence between the Yasawiyya and the Khʷādjagān-Naḳshbandiyya according to ethnic linguistic, economic or regional criteria, as is made clear by DeWeese, *The Mashā'ikh-i Turk and the Khojagān: rethinking the links between the Yasavī and Naqshbandī Sufi traditions*, in *Jnal. of Islamic Studies*, vii/2 [1996], 180-207). At the beginning of the 16th century an influential branch of the Yasawiyya (the offshoot of a spiritual line of descent from Zangī Atā and Ṣadr Atā) known as 'Azīziyya and remaining true to the customs and practices of the order (preserving the *dhikr* of the saw, the *khalwa* and the dance) was established in the region of Samarḳand by Kamāl al-Dīn 'Azīzān (d. 912/1507), who was called "the second Aḥmad Yasawī". It spread out as far as Harāt in Afghānistān. The principal figures of this branch were 'Azīzān Shaykh Khādim (d. 1573), then 'Azīzān Shaykh Djamāl al-Dīn (d. 1505) and Khudāydād 'Azīzān (d. 1532). In the same period, several practices of the Yasawiyya were adopted by important Naḳshbandī *shaykh*s: Muḥammad Ḳāḍī, who was the first to adopt the retreat (*khalwa*), and Mawlānā Khʷādjagī Kāsānī Dakhbidī (Makhdūm-i A'ẓam), who demonstrated that dance (*samā'*) and the *dhikr* of the saw were not contrary to the *Sharī'a* (for the *shaykh*s of the 'Azīziyya and their practices, see Muḥammad 'Ālim al-Ṣiddīḳī al-'Alawī, *Lamaḥāt min nafaḥāt al-Ḳuds*, Tashkent 1909, written in 1034/1625). The *shaykh*s who came from Central Asia and belonged to this movement could be found in other parts of the Muslim world, such as Turkey, India and Syria. They declared themselves to be members of the Naḳshbandiyya, sometimes from the Yasawiyya or even quite frequently they belonged to both orders at the same time (cf. Zarcone; Hazini, *Cevāhiru 'l-ebrār min emvāc-ı bihār*, ed. Cihan Okuyucu, Kayseri 1995, an ed. of ms. no. 3893 from the Istanbul University Library, dated 1002/1593-4).

In the 16th and 17th centuries the Yasawiyya finally disappeared in favour of the Naḳshbandiyya, but in the 18th and 19th centuries references were still made to Yasawī *shaykh*s, who were apparently isolated and who numbered among their ranks some who declared themselves to be descendants of Aḥmad Yasawī (cf. Riḍā Fakhr al-Dīn, in *Athar*, i/2 (Orenburg 1901), 44, and i/5 (1903), 228). However, the Yasawiyya acquired an important popular dimension, particularly among the nomads. Consequently, the successors of the Yasawī *shaykh*s centralised their activities around the mausoleums of the *bāb* of the Mubayyiḍiyya and those of the Yasawī saints. They abandoned the role of the *shaykh* of the brotherhood in favour of that of intercessor with the saints on behalf of pilgrims. It was in this form that the Yasawiyya have survived the Soviet period and lasted right up to the present day, despite the continued attacks of Marxist propaganda which denounced its "reactionary, feudal and clerical" aspects (cf. A. Bennigsen; Ch. Lemercier-Quelquejay; K. Çağatay; Zarcone).

It is possible today to determine the genealogical lines of the families that represented it, thanks to the genealogical documents (*shadjarat idjāza*) bequeathed to their families by their ancestors. These families are chiefly located in the south of Ḳazakhstān (Dasht-i Ḳipčak, Turkistān, Čimkent), where they are known as *khʷādja* (with the family names Aḳḳorghan, Khurāsān, Duāna, Ḳïlïshti, Sabïlt, etc.), and in Turkmenistān among the *Awlād* tribes (the tribes of Atā, Khʷādja) (cf. S.M. Demidov, Muminov and K. Tayžanov). The Yasawiyya have disappeared from the other regions of the Muslim world except for Xinjiang (People's Republic of China), where they were still attested at the beginning of the 20th century, mingled with the Ḳalandariyya (cf. G. Jarring).

Three types of writings have been ascribed to Aḥmad Yasawī and to the Yasawiyya. The principal type is the *Dīwān-i ḥikmat*, of which a great number of manuscripts and several editions exist, which essentially can be classified as poetry (*Divân-hikmet'ten seçmeler*, ed. Eraslan, Istanbul 1983; and the *Divan-ı hikmet*, ed. Yusuf Azmun, Istanbul 1994). Secondly, there is the *Faḳr-nāma*, a short text in prose, which probably was used to introduce the first group (Eraslan, *Yesevī'nin Fakr-nâmesi*, in *Türk Dili ve Edebiyat Dergisi*, xviii, Istanbul 1977, 45-120). The third group, called the *Risāla*, largely ressembles the previous one. The *Dīwān-i ḥikmat*, a collection of poetry in Eastern Turkish, has been so enriched over the centuries that no one any longer knows whether certain poems were really written by the founder of the order (cf. Borovkov). This poetry, which was printed for the first time at Kazan in 1887, has as its themes divine love, unity with God, love of the Prophet, loyalty to the (Sunnī) tradition of the Prophet, encouragement of the practice of religion, privation and asceticism, and love of humanity. These poems were sung during ceremonies and are still sung today (Raziya Sultanova, *Poyushčee slovo uzbekskikh obryadov* (*Opït liričeskogo issledovaniya*), Tashkent 1994). Other poets and Ṣūfīs subscribe to this literary and mystical tradition inaugurated by Aḥmad Yasawī which has permeated all Central Asian literature: Turcoman;

Transoxanian, with Īshān Iḳānī (the *laḳab* of Kamāl al-Dīn ʿAzīzān), Ḳul ʿUbaydī (perhaps the pseudonym of the *khān* Özbeg ʿUbayd Allāh himself) and ʿAẓīm Khʷādja Īshān (cf. ʿAẓīm Khʷādja Īshān, *Ḥikmat*, Tashkent 1894-5, repr. 1993; ʿAbd al-Raʾūf Fiṭrat, *Aḥmad Yasawī*, in *Maʿārif wa oḳituwčī*, Tashkent 1927, 6, 7, 8; and Begali Kasimov); also Tatar literature, especially where this has given rise to a school of literature where the chief important names, after Aḥmad Yasawī and his disciple Sulaymān Bāḳirghānī (Ḥakīm Atā), in the 18th and 19th centuries were Bashīr b. ʿAbd Allāh, ʿAbdī and ʿAbd al-Salām (cf. ʿÄziz ʿÄli Rähim, *Tatar ädäbiyati tarikhi*, Kazan 1923, 84-119; and E. Sibgatullina). After its publication had been forbidden in the Soviet period, the *Dīwān-i ḥikmat* has been reprinted in Uzbekistān and in Ḳazakhstān with other works concerning the Yasawiyya and their representatives.

Bibliography: As well as the books and articles mentioned in the text of this article, further reference may be made to the following: H. Algar, *Silent and vocal dhikr in the Naqshbandi order*, in *Akten des VII. Kongresses für Arabistik und Islamwissenschaft, Göttingen, 15. bis 22. August 1974*, 39-46; Erhan Aydın, *Ahmed Yesevî üzerinde bibliografya denemesi*, in *Bir* (Istanbul) (1995/3), 7-32; Bakhtiyor Babadjanov, *Yasaviya i Nakshbandiya v Maverannakhre: iz istorii vzaimootnosheniy (ser. XV-XVI vv.)*, in *Yasaui taghïlïmï*, Turkestan (Kazakhstan) 1996, 75-96; V.N. Basilov, *Proiskhoždenii Turkmen-Ata (prostonarodnïe formï srednеaziatskogo sufizma)*, in *Domusul'manskie verovaniya i obryadï ve Sredney Azii*, Moscow 1975, 138-68; A. Bennigsen and Chantal Lemercier-Quelquejay, *Le Soufi et le commissaire. Les confréries musulmanes en URSS*, Paris 1986; M. Bernardini, *A propos de Fazlallah b. Ruzbehan Khonji Esfahani et du mausolée d'Ahmad Yasavi*, in *L'Héritage timouride. Iran-Asie centrale-Inde XVe-XVIIIe siècles*, Cahiers d'Asie centrale, 3-4, Aix-en-Provence 1997, 281-96; A.J.E. Bodrogligeti, *Yasavî ideology in Muhammad Shâybânî Khân's vision of an Uzbek Islamic empire*, in *Jnal. of Turkish Studies (Annemarie Schimmel Festschrift)*, xviii (1994), 41-57; A.K. Borovkov, *Očerki po istorii uzbekskogo yazïka (opredelenie yazïka Khikmatov Akhmada Yasevi)*, in *Sovetskoe vostokovedenie*, Moscow and Leningrad 1948, 230-50; K. Çağatay, *Bağımsızlıktan önce Türkistan cumhuriyetlerinde Ahmed Yesevî*, in *Türk Kültürü*, xxxi/no. 366, 599-607; S.M. Demidov, *Turkmenskiy ovlyady*, Ashkhābād 1976; D. DeWeese, *Yasavian legends on the Islamization of Turkistan*, in D. Sinor (ed.), *Aspects of Altaic civilization. III. Proceedings of the thirtieth meeting of the Permanent International Altaistic Conference, Indiana University, Bloomington, Indiana, June 19-25, 1987*, Bloomington 1990, 1-19; idem, *A neglected source on Central Asian history: the 17th-century Yasavî hagiography Manâqib al-Akhyâr*, in B.A. Nazarov and D. Sinor (eds.), *Essays on Uzbek history, culture, and language*, Bloomington 1993, 38-50; idem, *An "Uvaysî" Sufi in Timurid Mawarannahr. Notes on hagiography and the taxonomy of sanctity in the religious history of Central Asia*, Bloomington 1993; idem, *Islamization and native religion in the Golden Horde. Baba Tükles and conversion to Islam in historical and epic tradition*, University Park, PA 1994; idem, art. *Atâʾîya order*, in *EIr*, ii, 904-5; idem, *The descendants of Sayyid Ata and the rank of naqîb in Central Asia*, in *JAOS*, cxv (1995), 612-34; J. Fletcher, *The Naqshbandiyya and the Dhikr-i Arra*, in *Jnal. of Turkish Studies*, i (1977), 113-19; G. Jarring, *Dervish and Qalandar. Texts from Kashghar*, Stockholm 1985-6; *Khazrat bashir tarikhi*, ed. A. Čoriev, Tashkent 1994; Ahmet T. Karamustafa, *Early Sufism in eastern Anatolia*, in L. Lewisohn (ed.), *Classical Persian Sufism: from its origins to Rumi*, London 1993, 175-98; Begali Kasimov, *Keyingi davr özbek adabiyatida yassaviy anʾanalari*, in *Milletlerarası Hoca Ahmed Yesevî semposyumu bildirileri*, 213-17; Fuat Köprülü, *Türk edebiyatında ilk mutasavvıflar*, repr. Ankara 1966; L. Yu. Man'kovskaya, *Towards the study of forms in Central Asian architecture at the end of the fourteenth century: the mausoleum of Khwaja Ahmad Yasavî*, in *Iran*, xxiii (1985), 109-27; Irène Mélikoff, *Les origines centrasiatiques du soufisme anatolien*, in *Turcica*, xx (1988), 7-18; eadem, *Sur les traces du soufisme turc. Recherches sur l'islam populaire en Anatolie*, Istanbul 1992, 151-61; eadem, *Ahmed Yesevi et la mystique populaire turque*, in *ibid.*, 139-150; *Milletlerarası Ahmed Yesevî semposyumu bildirileri (26-27 Eylül 1991, Ankara)*, Ankara 1992; *Milletlerarası Hoca Ahmed Yesevî semposyumu bildirleri (26-29 Mayis 1993)*, Kayseri 1993; Ashirbeg Muminov, *Novïe napravleniya v izučenii istorii bratstva yasaviya obshčestvennïe nauki v Uzbekistane*, Tashkent 1993, 11-12, 34-8; idem, *O Proiskhoždenii bratstva yasaviya*, in *Islam i problemi mežtsivilizatsionnikh vzaimodestvyu*, Moscow 1994, 219-31; idem, *Veneration of holy sites of the mid-Sïrdarʾya Valley: continuity and transformation*, in M. Kemper *et al.* (eds.), *Muslim culture in Russia and Central Asia from the 18th to the early 20th centuries*, Berlin 1996, 355-67; Muminov and Z. Žandarbekov, *Yassaviya taʾlimoti vužudga kelgan mukhit khakkida yangi mukhim manba*, in *Sharkshunoslik* (Tashkent), *Fanlar Akademiyasi*, 5 (1994), 82-8; Ahmed Yaşar Ocak, *Un cheik yesevî et babaî dans la première moitié du XIIIe siècle en Anatolie: Emîrci Sultân*, in *Turcica*, xii (1980), 114-24; idem, *Anadolu sufiliğinde Ahmet-i Yesevî ve yesevîlik'in yerine dair*, in idem, *Türk sufiliğinde bakışlar*, Istanbul 1996, 64-73; Mambetaliev Satïbaldï, *Perežitki nekotorïkh musul'manskikh tečeniy v Kirgizii i ikh istoriya*, Frunze 1969; Elfine Sibgatullina, *Hoca Ahmet Yesevî'nin Kazan-Tatar edebiyatına tesiri*, in *Milletlerarası Ahmed Yesevî semposyumu bildirileri* 89-97; K. Tayžanov and Kh. Ismailov, *Osobennosti doislamskikh verovaniy u uzbekov-karamurtov*, in *Drevnie obryadï verovaniya i kul'tï narodov sredney Azii*, Moscow 1986, 110-38; Zeki Velidi Togan, *Yeseviliğe dair bazı malûmat*, in *Fuad Köprülü armağanı*, Istanbul 1953, 523-9; *Yasaui taghïlïmï*, Turkestan (Kazakhstan) 1996; K.G. Zaleman', *Legenda pro Hakim-Ata*, in *ZVOIAR*, ix/2 (1898); Th. Zarcone, *Histoire et croyances des derviches turkestanais et indiens à Istanbul*, in *Anatolia moderna*, ii (Paris 1991), 137-200; idem, *Turkish Sufism in India: the case of the Yasaviyya*, in F. Delvoye (ed.), *Confluence of culture. French contribution to Indo-Persian studies*, New Delhi 1994; idem, *Some remarks on the influence of Central Asia on the early development of an Indian Sufi order (the Chishtiyya), 14th-16th centuries*, in M. Alam *et al.* (eds.), *The making of the Indo-Persian culture, Indian and French studies*, New Delhi 2000; idem, *Ahmad Yasawî. Héros des nouvelles républiques centrasiatiques*, in *Héros mythiques et légendes du monde musulman*, in *REMMM*, forthcoming. (Th. Zarcone)

YASH [see Suppl.].

YASHM (p.), the Persian term for the mineral generally termed jade. This is made up of one or the other hard, fine-grained translucent stones jadeite or nephrite, the first a silicate of sodium and aluminum and the second a silicate of calcium and magnesium. Both may be white or colourless, but are often found in a variety of other colours, such as green, brown, yellow, etc., because of the presence of traces of other elements such as iron, chromium and manganese.

1. In Islamic history.

Nephrite was known to Eastern Turkic peoples as

kash (see Clauson, *An etymological dictionary of pre-thirteenth century Turkish*, 669-70), to the Mongols as *khas* and to the Chinese, who much prized it for artistic purposes, as *yü*. The Persian word has passed into Arabic usage. The English, French and German words "jade" have no connection, as was earlier suggested, with the name of the ancient Turks' so-called "rain stone" (*yada tash* [*q.v.*]) (see Yule and Burnell, *Hobson-Jobson, a glossary of Anglo-Indian words and phrases*, ²London 1903, 444-5).

The prime source for the nephrite used in the Islamic world, as in China, was the region of Khotan [*q.v.*] in the southern part of the Tarim basin [*q.v.*] of eastern Turkestan, where recovery of jade from local rivers is mentioned in Chinese sources as far back as the early 7th century A.D. Already in Maḥmūd al-Kāshgharī's time (11th century), two rivers flowing by Khotan were known as the Ürüñ Kash and the Ḳara Kash "White Jade" and "Black Jade", from the varieties of jade recovered from them respectively (*Dīwān lughāt al-turk*, tr. Atalay, iii, 152, tr. Dankoff and Kelly, ii, 226). On his journey from Kāshghar of 1895, Sven Hedin found jade on sale in Khotan and visited the site to the north-east of the town where jade was obtained from the bed of the Ürüñ Kash (*Through Asia*, London 1898, ii, 748, 754). Islamic geographers had known of its origin there from the 10th century, at a time when Khotan was not yet Muslim; the author of the *Ḥudūd al-ʿālam* (372/982) states that "jade stone" (*sang-i yashm*) came from the rivers of Khotan (tr. Minorsky, 85-6, § 9.18, comm. 234).

Bibliography: See also Yule-Cordier, *The Book of Ser Marco Polo*, London 1902, i, 191, 193; eidem, *Cathay and the way thither*, London 1915, ii, 221, iv, 218-19. (C.E. Bosworth)

2. In Islamic art.

Jade, or more properly nephrite, is mentioned in texts as early as the 2nd/8th century, but the first surviving objects of jade carved in the Islamic lands date only from the 9th/15th century, after 828/1424-5, when the Tīmūrid prince Ulugh Beg (796-853/1394-1449), grandson of Tīmūr and governor of Samarḳand, defeated the ruler of Mogholistān [*q.v.*] and gained access to the jade mines there. There is no evidence that earlier lapidaries worked the stone, but fine jade objects were produced for the next five centuries, mainly for princes and courts in the eastern Islamic lands, where jade vessels were commonly believed to counter the effects of poison.

The first and largest jade object produced in the Islamic lands is the cenotaph of dark green jade over Tīmūr's grave in the Gūr-i Mīr in Samarḳand. Measuring 1.92 × .36 × .30 m, the block is engraved on the upper face with a niche and an inscription about Tīmūr's ancestry, as well as the history of the particular stone, which was seized as booty along with another block and dragged back to Samarḳand. As the carving is that of a skilled mason rather than of a lapidary, the cenotaph must have been carved in the Tīmūrid capital where there was no indigenous jade-working tradition.

A group of drinking vessels, probably intended for wine, is also associated with Ulugh Beg and likewise attributed to Samarḳand. These include four cups with handles carved in the shape of a dragon's head. One made of olive-green jade in the British Museum, London (OA 1959.11-20.1(36)) is inscribed on the bottom with Ulugh Beg's name and the title *gūragān*, implying that it was made before he acceded to the sultanate in 850/1447. An oval cup of green jade in Varanasi (Banares Hindu University, Bharat Kala Bhavan, 3/8860) is also inscribed with Ulugh Beg's name. A similar but anepigraphic cup of almost black jade, showing green only in strong light, also in the British Museum (1961.2-13,1) and another cup that the Ṣafawid Shāh ʿAbbās I (*r.* 995-1038/1587-1629) gave to the dynastic shrine at Ardabīl and is now in the National Museum of Iran, Tehran, can be associated with the two inscribed cups. These cups owe their form to the type of Chinese water reservoir called a *cheng*. Such cups with dragon-handles were prized by the Mongol rulers of Persia and Central Asia, and silver and gold examples were excavated at New Saray, the Golden Horde capital on the Volga. The awkward carving of some pieces, such as the handle on the inscribed piece in London, leaves no doubt that these jade cups were carved in Islamic Central Asia.

Other drinking vessels made for the Tīmūrids take the form of a globular jug with a short cylindrical neck and an S-shaped dragon handle, secured by rivets. The most impressive is a white jade example in the Gulbenkian Foundation, Lisbon (328). Inscribed around the neck with Ulugh Beg's name and regnal titles, the jug can be attributed to 851-3/1447-9 and may have been made to commemorate his accession to the sultanate. Based on the shape, other jugs can also be assigned to this group and dated to the second half of the 9th/15th century. They include an undecorated drinking pot of green jade in the Sackler Gallery, Smithsonian Institution, Washington, D.C., and one in the Museum of Natural History in Paris once belonging to Louis XIV. A pear-shaped example in a private collection (see Pinder-Wilson, fig. 5), like the Paris jug, has a small projection at the back of the neck pierced with a tiny hole by which a lid was once attached. Another pot of very dark green jade in the British Museum (1945-10-17-257) has lost its handle.

A third shape of jade drinking vessel associated with the Tīmūrids is a bowl. A dark green example in the Louvre (MR199) is bell-shaped, like Chinese porcelains, and carved with chinoiserie decoration of lotus blossoms on a gracefully curving scroll. The poem inscribed in cartouches on the exterior links it to a hemispheric bowl of striped agate in the Art and History Trust Collection (on loan to the Sackler Gallery, Smithsonian Institution, Washington, D.C.), which was made in 876/1471-2 for the Tīmūrid ruler Sulṭān Ḥusayn Bayḳara and was similarly inscribed with a poem in cartouches.

Several other jade objects are inscribed with the names of members of the Tīmūrid family. A tiny cylindrical container of white jade in the Asian Art Museum, San Francisco, bears a dedicatory inscription in the name of Ulugh Beg's nephew, ʿAlāʾ al-Dawla (820-64/1417-60), and a jade seal in the Hermitage, St. Petersburg (SA-13650) is inscribed with the name of Ulugh Beg's mother Gawharshād. By their function, other jade objects may be associated with royal patronage. A small object with dragons' heads in the Metropolitan Museum of Art (02.18.765) may have been the quillon (blade-guard) for a dagger. A small circular pendant or belt-buckle of dark green jade in the Chester Beatty Library, Dublin (no. 29), decorated with chinoiserie blossoms and inscribed with apotropaic verses, undoubtedly served as a talisman.

The Tīmūrid tradition of jade working was continued in the early Ṣafawid period, for a black jade jug decorated with delicate spiral arabesques inlaid in gold in the Topkapı Palace Museum is inscribed on the neck with the name of the first Ṣafawid Shāh

Ismāʿīl I (*r.* 907-30/1501-24). It is unclear whether this object represents a new Ṣafawid creation or a plain Tīmūrid object decorated in the early Ṣafawid period, for undecorated Tīmūrid objects such as the handleless jug in the British Museum were decorated at the Mug̲h̲al court, to which many Tīmūrid jades passed. The Mug̲h̲al emperors D̲j̲ahāngīr (*r.* 1014-37/1605-27) and S̲h̲āh D̲j̲ahān (*r.* 1037-68/1628-57) were avid collectors of Tīmūrid jades, no doubt because they traced their ancestry to the Tīmūrid dynasty, and their names were inscribed or inlaid in gold or silver on several objects, including the Varanasi cup and the white jug.

Jade continued to be used at the Ottoman court in Istanbul, where objects were made of and decorated with jade, itself often inlaid with gold arabesques and encrusted with precious stones. Some jade objects may have been captured in 920/1514 when the Ottomans defeated the Ṣafawids at the battle of Čāldirān [*q.v.*]. A two-handled cup of dark green jade inlaid with gold arabesques and encrusted with rubies in collar mounts in the Topkapı Palace Museum (3815) has inlay similar to that on the jug of Ismāʿīl I, although the encrusted rubies set in collar mounts are typical Ottoman work. A comparable jade dish in the National Collection, Kraków, was given in 1699 by Sultan Muṣṭafā II (*r.* 1106-15/1695-1703) to Stanislas Malachowski, voivode of Poznań, on the occasion of the treaty of Carlowitz [see KARLOFČA], although the dish may have been in the Ottoman treasury for centuries. More typically Ottoman is a covered tankard of milky-green jade encrusted with cabuchon rubies and emeralds in collar mounts set in a tracery of inlaid gold scrolls (Topkapı Palace Museum 3832). It can be attributed to the late 10th/16th or 11th/17th century on the basis of its shape, first attested in ceramic from *ca.* 1560. A covered ewer (Topkapı Palace Museum 3800), with a shape known from 11th/17th-century Ottoman metalwork, has sides of jade plaques and a neck of jade held together and encrusted with gold and jewels. Also attributable to this period are two mirrors with solid jade handles and gold backs set with plaques of gold and jade encrusted with rubies and emeralds (Topkapı Palace Museum 1795 and Hermitage, NV2 720).

Jade was also used in Ottoman times for military and ceremonial objects, many preserved in the Topkapı Palace Museum. The most famous is a gold canteen with a dragon-headed spout and set with jade plaques, themselves encrusted with rubies and emeralds on gold tracery (3825). This type of flask, used to hold the sultan's drinking water, is depicted carried by the Master of the Wardrobe in illustrations to chronicles of the period 973-98/1566-90, and this object may have been made late in the reign of Süleymān II (*r.* 926-74/1520-66). An 11th/17th-century quiver is decorated with jade plaques, and an 11th/17th or 12th/18th-century mace has a jade head (126 and 724, respectively). Imported jade objects encrusted at Istanbul in the Ottoman taste include a Mug̲h̲al condiment dish of dark green jade in the form of a palmate leaf (3822), Indian cups, jugs, boxes, and Chinese cups.

Luxury objects produced for the Ḳād̲j̲ār court of Persia also combined jade with other precious materials. A jewelled jade dish in the Kunsthistorische Museum, Vienna (Plastikensammlung no. 3223) presented by the Persian ambassador Abu 'l-Ḥasan K̲h̲ān to the Austrian Emperor Francis I (*r.* 1792-1835) has a central gold plaque enamelled by the painter ʿAlī, who also painted an oval mirror with a carved jade handle now in the Crown Jewels Collection, Tehran.

Bibliography: R. Skelton, *The relations between the Chinese and Indian jade carving traditions*, in W. Watson (ed.), *The westward influence of the Chinese arts from the 14th to the 18th century = Colloquies on Art and Archaeology in Asia, Percival David Foundation of Chinese Art*, 3, London 1972, 98-110; E.J. Grube, *Notes on the decorative arts of the Timurid period*, in A. Forte *et alii* (eds.), *Gururajamañjarika. Studi in onore di Giuseppe Tucci*, Naples 1974, 233-79; C. Köseoğlu, *Topkapı Sarayı Müzesi*, Tokyo 1980, tr., ed. and expanded by J.M. Rogers as *Topkapi Saray Museum. The Treasury*, Boston 1987; Grube, *Notes on the decorative arts of the Timurid period II*, in *Islamic Arts*, iii (1988-89), 175-208; T.W. Lentz and G.D. Lowry, *Timur and the princely vision. Persian art and culture in the fifteenth century*, Los Angeles 1989, nos. 50-2 and 120, 123-4, 126-9 and fig. 46; S. Markel, *Fit for an Emperor. Inscribed works of decorative art acquired by the Great Mughals*, in *Orientation*, xxi (August 1990), 22-36; R. Pinder-Wilson, *Jades from the Islamic world*, in *Marg*, xliv/2 (1992), 35-48; A. Soudavar, *Art of the Persian courts. Selections from the Art and History Trust Collection*, New York 1992; Skelton, art. *Islamic art. § VIII.8. Jade*, in Jane Turner (ed.), *The dictionary of art*, London 1996, xvi, 527-9.

(SHEILA S. BLAIR AND J.M. BLOOM)

YAS̲H̲RUṬIYYA, a Ṣūfī order of the S̲h̲ād̲h̲iliyya [*q.v.*], founded by ʿAlī Nūr al-Dīn b. Muḥammad b. Nūr al-Dīn Aḥmad al-Mag̲h̲ribī al-Yas̲h̲ruṭī al-S̲h̲ād̲h̲ilī al-Tars̲h̲iḥī (*ca.* 1218-1309/*ca.* 1804-91) from Banzart [*q.v.*] in Tunisia.

After having been initiated into the *ṭarīḳa* [*q.v.*] of the S̲h̲ād̲h̲iliyya-Madaniyya [*q.v.*] in Miṣrāta [*q.v.*] by Muḥammad b. Ḥamza Ẓāfir al-Madanī (d. 1263/1847), ʿAlī Nūr al-Dīn travelled extensively. In 1266/1850 he settled in ʿAkkā on the Palestinian coast where he married the wealthy widow K̲h̲adīd̲j̲a Tūsīz. In 1297/1862-3 he opened his first *zāwiya* [*q.v.*] in Tars̲h̲iḥa. The order quickly spread among the notables, the *ʿulamāʾ* [*q.v.*] and the female members of their households to Ṣafad, Jerusalem, Beirut, the Biḳāʿ valley, Saida, Aleppo, Damascus, Jaffa and Istanbul. Each *zāwiya* had a local administrator, its *muḳaddam* [*q.v.*]. S̲h̲ayk̲h̲ ʿAlī Nūr al-Dīn's daughter Fāṭima vividly describes the daily life and the dogmatic foundations in her *Riḥla ilā 'l-ḥaḳḳ*, Beirut 1373/1954, 4th rev. ed. by Aḥmad Yas̲h̲ruṭī, 1417-18/1997; *Nafaḥāt al-ḥaḳḳ*, Beirut 1382/1963, 3rd rev. ed. by idem, 1418-19/1998; *Mawāhib al-ḥaḳḳ*, Beirut 1385/1966, 3rd rev. ed. by idem, 1417-18/1997, and *Masīratī fī ṭarīḳ al-ḥaḳḳ*, Beirut, 3rd rev. ed. by idem, 1417-18/1997. After her father's death the *mas̲h̲yak̲h̲a* was handed down to his eldest son Ibrāhīm al-Yas̲h̲ruṭī and after his death in 1927 to Muḥammad al-Hādī al-Yas̲h̲ruṭī. Due to political instability, the order frequently shifted its main centre of activities, first from Palestine to Lebanon and then, under Aḥmad al-Yas̲h̲ruṭī, to ʿAmmān. Since the end of the Civil War in Lebanon, the Yas̲h̲ruṭiyya has opened a *zāwiya* in K̲h̲alde, south of Beirut, and one in Kāmid al-Lawz in the Biḳāʿ valley. It has a predominantly Palestinian following in Lebanon, Jordan, Syria, Israel, Brazil and Canada. Male and female members recite a number of individual and congregational prayers and litanies, the *awrād* (sing. *wird* [*q.v.*]) and *waẓīfa* [*q.v.*]. Once a week a *ḥadra* [*q.v.*] is held in the local *zāwiya*, and an occasional *mud̲h̲ākara*, a lesson on the Ḳurʾān and the *ṭarīḳa*.

Bibliography (in addition to the sources mentioned in the text): F. de Jong, *Les confréries mystiques musulmanes au Machreq arabe*, in A. Popovic and

G. Veinstein (eds.), *Les ordres mystiques dans l'Islam. Cheminements et situation actuelle*, Paris 1986, 217-20; Muṣṭafā b. Muḥyī al-Dīn Nadjā al-Shādhilī al-Yashruṭī, *Kashf al-asrār li-tanwīr afkār al-ṭarīka wa-sharḥ al-waẓīfa al-shādhiliyya al-yashruṭiyya*, 6th ed. Beirut 1418/1997; Muṣṭafā Abū Rīsha al-Ḳādirī, *al-Nafaḥāt al-ḳudsiyya al-ʿaliyya bi-sharḥ al-waẓīfa al-shādhiliyya al-yashruṭiyya*, 5th ed. Beirut 1418/1997; Wafāʾ Aḥmad Sawāfaṭa, *Unmūdhadj ʿan al-wudjūd al-ṣūfī fī 'l-mashrik al-ʿarabī: al-shaykh ʿAlī Nūr al-Dīn al-Yashruṭī wa 'l-ṭarīka al-shādhiliyya al-yashruṭiyya*, Ph.D. diss., Lebanese University 1420/1999, unpubl. (not seen); J. van Ess, *Die Yašruṭīya*, in *WI*, xvi (1975), 1-103. (Annabelle Böttcher)

YATHRIB [see al-Madīna].

YATĪM (a.) denotes a child, below the age of puberty, who has lost his father.

1. In the Ḳurʾān and classical Islamic law.

According to the lexicographers, this term, which occurs in the Ḳurʾān, denotes in the human realm a fatherless child, whilst in the animal world, it denotes a young one that has lost its mother (in both cases, it is a question of the loss of the one regarded as its nourisher). A child who has lost its mother is called *munḳaṭiʿ*, and a child who has lost both father and mother, i.e. an orphan, is called *laṭīm*. But at the age of puberty, the fatherless child is no longer called *yatīm*, unless in a derived sense (hence Muḥammad, though an adult, was still called *yatīm*). *Yutm* is the abstract noun denoting the state of being fatherless. In classical Islamic doctrine and law, the cases of the *yatīm* and *laṭīm* are regarded as radically different from that of the *laḳīṭ* [*q.v.*], the foundling, one "picked up", whose family background is unknown.

The theme of the *yatīm* whose property cannot be despoiled but whom one must, on the contrary, assist, is common all through Muḥammad's preaching. One of the characteristic traits of "him who accounts false the Last Judgement", i.e. who refuses to recognise the new revelation brought by Muḥammad, is that of "repelling orphans" (Ḳurʾān, CVII, 1-2). It is difficult not to view this theme except in relationship to the Prophet's situation, who, as noted in XCIII, 6 ("Did He not find you an orphan and give you a refuge?"), was himself a *yatīm* from birth. Thus the Ḳurʾānic descriptions of the unenviable lot of orphans probably convey the bitter memories that Muḥammad had of his early years in pre-Islamic Meccan society. The case of orphan girls whose guardians try to despoil their property by refusing to let them marry (or by marrying them themselves) is exposed in IV, 126/127.

As well as verses reproving in a general manner, sometimes very harshly (cf. IV, 11/10), those who oppress orphans, the Ḳurʾān stipulates more precise provisions for them. (1) A part of the fifth of booty (*ghanīma* [*q.v.*]) taken is to be reserved for orphans (VIII, 42/41). (2) A part, not precisely laid down, of the *fayʾ* [*q.v.*] (goods and property taken from the enemy without fighting) should likewise be allotted to them (LIX, 7/6). (3) When orphans are present at the dividing-up of an inheritance, they should be given something (IV, 9/8). Furthermore, as well as the prohibition against despoiling orphans' goods and property directed against evil-minded guardians, the Ḳurʾān lays down, in rather vague terms, that the moment when guardianship over orphans' property ceases is when the *yatīm*, by now having reached puberty and capable of marriage, is considered mature enough to look after his or her own fortune (IV, 5/6; VI, 153/152; XVII, 36/34). A saying of the Prophet transmitted by Abū Dāwūd (*K. al-waṣāyā, bāb matā yanḳaṭiʿ al-yutm*) confirms that "the status of orphan ends with puberty" (*lā yutm baʿd al-ḥulum*).

The lawyers define variously the precise moment when guardianship over the *yatīm*'s goods ceases (see al-Djaṣṣāṣ, *Aḥkām al-Ḳurʾān*, [Cairo] n.d., ii, 63). The quality of *rushd*, which the *yatīm* must have to be able freely to dispose of his goods, is likewise defined in various ways; against Abū Ḥanīfa, al-Shāfiʿī holds that religious uprightness should be taken into account. Moreover, the Ḥanafīs hold that a *yatīm* who has not yet reached puberty but who is clearly of rational judgement, may, if his guardian so authorises him, enter into commercial transactions, whilst the other legal schools do not authorise this till puberty is reached. If, after being judged capable of looking after his own goods, the *yatīm* turns out to be a spendthrift (*safīh*), the control of his goods can, according to al-Shāfiʿī, be taken back from him (see al-Rāzī, *al-Tafsīr al-kabīr, ad* IV, 5/6, and, concerning guardianship, see wilāya).

Following the Ḳurʾānic recommendations, classical Islamic legal doctrine discusses the case of the *yatīm* in relation to, on the one hand, bequests (*waṣiyya*), and on the other, to the division of plunder and of *fayʾ*. Bequeathing something to fatherless children is a meritorious act, but the jurists differ on the definition of a *yatīm* in this context; according to some, a *yatīm* who is rich has no part in this distribution, and the same question is posed in regard to the allocation of a share (*sahm*) in plunder and *fayʾ* (see al-Shīrāzī, *Muhadhdhab*, Beirut-Damascus 1996, iii, 728, v, 302).

In the conditions of poverty and of social and family disruption prevailing today in many Islamic lands, the status of the *yatīm* is often parlous, above all in the towns and cities. They are little regarded, and form a reservoir of cheap manual labour, vulnerable to merciless exploitation and oppression (in certain countries there are organised networks for exploiting this cheap labour); in order to escape this status, they frequently choose to live on the streets (see the chapters by A. al-Azhari Sonbol, *Adoption in Islamic society. A historical survey*, and A.B. Rugh, *Orphanages in Egypt. Contradiction or affirmation in a family-oriented society*, in E.A. Fernea (ed.), *Children in the Muslim Middle East*, Cairo 1996, 45-67 and 124-41, respectively).

Bibliography: Given in the article, but see also T.P. Hughes, *A dictionary of Islām*, London 1885, 448-9; Fazlur Rahman, *Major themes of the Qurʾān*, Minneapolis and Chicago 1980, 47.

(E. Chaumont)

2. In modern legislation.

i. *The status of the orphan as an heir.*

Islamic law defines an orphan (*yatīm*) as a minor whose father has died. Under the basic *sharʿī* rule that "the nearer in degree excludes the more remote", orphaned grandchildren are excluded from any share in their grandparent's estate if that grandparent is survived by a son. This denial of the orphan's inheritance right was mitigated within the extended agnatic family, as the deceased's responsibilities towards his lineal descendants were fulfilled by passing the inheritance *en bloc* to the first degree of his issue. With the growing breakdown of extended family ties in contemporary society, however, the *sharʿī* rule is no longer readily supportable.

Protection of orphaned grandchildren within the immediate family has traditionally been undertaken by grandparents by means of voluntary gifts *inter vivos*, bequests and *waḳf*s [*q.v.*]. The grandparent often allocates his orphaned grandchild a share equivalent to the share that the orphan's father would have been entitled to had he survived his father (the orphan's grandfather), thereby introducing the principle of representation, not recognised under the *Sharīʿa*.

Several Islamic countries have resorted to legislative means. The 1913 Ottoman Inheritance Law (based on a German model), introducing the principle of representation, enabled the orphaned grandchild to take the part of his deceased father in his grandfather's legacy of *mīrī* property.

Egyptian reformers, adopting the system of "obligatory bequests", decreed (1946 Law of Wills: Articles 76-9) that a grandparent with orphaned grandchildren is presumed to bequeath in their favour what their deceased parent would have taken had he or she survived, provided that this does not exceed the "bequeathable third", and that the grandparent has not made a gift of the same value to the orphaned grandchildren *inter vivos*. If he has made them a lesser gift *inter vivos*, the obligatory bequest is reduced by this amount. If he has made other bequests instead, the obligatory bequests receive priority (1946 Law of Waḳf: Article 29 permits, but does not oblige, the grandparent, as a founder of a *waḳf*, to provide for his orphaned grandchildren in the same manner).

These provisions, justified by the reformers on the basis of Ḳurʾān, II, 180, were substantially adopted in Syria (1953), Tunisia (1956), Morocco (1958), Kuwait (1971), Jordan (1976), Iraq (1979), Algeria (1984) and Israel (1996). Contrary to the Egyptian version, the Syrian, Moroccan, Jordanian and Algerian reforms concern only grandchildren orphaned by a predeceased son, and make no provision for grandchildren orphaned by a predeceased daughter. Also contrary to the Egyptian version, the Tunisian, Kuwaiti, Iraqi and Israeli reforms do not provide for orphaned great-grandchildren.

The Pakistani 1961 Muslim Family Laws Ordinance prescribes (section four) that if any son or daughter of the propositus predeceases the propositus, the children of the predeceased son or daughter shall receive *per strips* the amount their parent would have received had he or she outlived the propositus. This reform represents the alternative system of "inheritance by right" and is based on the principle of representation.

Similarly to the Egyptian reform, the Pakistani one treats the predeceased daughter's children identically to the predeceased son's children. Contrary to the Egyptian reform, the Pakistani one does not provide for orphaned great-grandchildren. The main difference between the Pakistani reform and those of other Middle Eastern countries is that the Pakistani one places no maximum limit on the share that may be taken by orphaned grandchildren.

Both the Egyptian and the Pakistani reforms led to contradictory interpretations, some of which disrupted Ḳurʾānic-based rules of intestate succession. The Islamisation of laws currently taking place in Pakistan endangers the survival of this reform.

ii. *The management of an orphan's property*.

The *sharʿī* motivation is to prevent abuse of an orphan's property by relatives or by strangers. In the absence of a guardian, an orphan's property is deposited in the *Sharīʿa* court (it was called *tābūt*, or *mūdaʿ al-ḳuḍāt*, or *bayt māl al-ḳuḍāt*), its management supervised by a *ḳāḍī*.

Modern legislation obliges the guardian of a minor to obtain a *Sharīʿa* court's approval before concluding transactions affecting his ward's property (1858 Ottoman Land Code: Article 52). Moreover, the *Medjelle* (Articles 356, 441, 459) invalidates the guardian's sale or rent of his orphan ward's property if the price obtained was lower than the proper one.

iii. *Orphanages, foster care and adoption*.

The modern period has witnessed the establishment of orphanages (Egypt, in the last decade of the 19th century), mainly supported by public *waḳfs*. Modern governments provide pensions and aid in case of the parents' death or incapacity. They supervise and support institutions providing occupational training and general education for orphans, and continue to support them after they leave the institution upon reaching the legal age of majority. Modern governments have also established a system of orphan foster care.

Adoption is not recognised under the *Sharīʿa*. So far, statutory adoption has been introduced only in Turkey (1926), Tunisia (1958) and Somalia (1975). In India, the Adoption of Children Bill (1972) was opposed by Indian orthodox Muslims and consequently shelved. Modern states such as Egypt and India have created forms of *de facto* adoption, however.

Bibliography: J.N.D. Anderson, *Law reform in the Muslim world*, London 1976; Adel Azer, *Rights of the child in Egypt*, in *Columbia Human Rights Law Review*, xiii (1981), 315-45; Lucy Carroll, *Definition and interpretation of Muslim law in South Asia. The case of gifts to minors*, in *ILS*, i (1994), 83-115; eadem, *Orphaned grandchildren in Islamic law of succession. Reform and Islamization in Pakistan*, in *ILS*, v (1998), 409-47; N.J. Coulson, *Succession in the Muslim family*, Cambridge 1971; Kemal Faruki, *Orphaned grandchildren in Islamic succession law. A comparison of modern Muslim solutions*, in *Islamic Studies*, iv (1965), 253-74; A. Layish, *The Mālikī family* waqf *according to wills and Waqfiyyāt*, in *BSOAS*, xlvi (1983), 1-32; idem, *Bequests as an instrument for accommodating inheritance rules: Israel as a case study*, in *ILS*, ii (1995), 282-319; idem, *The family waqf and the sharʿī law of succession in modern times*, in *ILS*, iv (1997), 352-88; Tahir Mahmood, *Muslim personal law. Role of the state in the Subcontinent*, New Delhi 1977; D.S. Powers, *The Maliki family endowment. Legal norms and social practices*, in *IJMES*, xxv (1993), 379-406; Y. Reiter, *Family Waqf entitlements in British Palestine (1917-1948)*, in *ILS*, ii (1995), 174-93; S.A.H. Rizvi *et alii*, *The concept of adoption. Islamic socio-legal view point*, in *Islamic & Comparative Law Quarterly*, ii (1982), 118-26; Andrea B. Rugh, *Family in contemporary Egypt*, Syracuse 1984; R. Shaham, *Family and the courts in modern Egypt. A study based on decisions by the Sharīʿa Courts 1900-1955*, Leiden 1997; E. Tyan, *Histoire de L'organisation judiciaire en pays d'Islam*, Leiden 1960. (R. Shaham)

YAWM (A., pl. *ayyām*), "day" (a Common Semitic word, e.g. Akkad. *ūmum*, Hebr. *yōm*, Aram. *yawmā*, ESA *ywm*), denoting the whole 24-hour cycle making up a day, whereas *nahār* means "the daylight period", i.e. from sunrise to sunset. See further on this, AL-LAYL WA 'L-NAHĀR.

Yawm occurs as an isolated term in various specialised uses, in particular, in pre- and early Islamic times in the meaning of "day of battle"; for this, see AYYĀM AL-ʿARAB. The pl. *ayyām* can also occur, especially in early Arabic poetry, in a similar sense to its apparent antonym *layālī* "nights", referring to the passage of time = "destiny, fate"; see H. Ringgren, *Studies in Arabian fatalism*, Uppsala 1955, 38-9, and also DAHR.

In the compound *yawm al-dīn* we have a technical Islamic eschatological sense, the "day of judgement, retribution" [see DĪN and SĀʿA. 3]. For other compound expressions of a religious nature, see T.P. Hughes, *A dictionary of Islām*, 694-5.

For the divisions of the day, used by the ancient

Arabs in the absence of chronometers of any kind and subsequently applied in several cases to the times for the Muslim *ṣalāt* or worship, see ʿAṢR; ʿATAMA; ḌUḤĀ; ṢALĀT. III.

Bibliography: Given in the article. (ED.)

YAYA (T.), lit. "pedestrian", denoted, in Ottoman military usage of the 8th-10th/14th-16th centuries, infantryman.

Originally forming part of the *khāṣṣa* army serving directly under the ruler, in the 10th/16th century the *yaya* were considered part of the provincial forces. According to Meḥmed Neshrī [*q.v.*], under Sultan Orkhān peasant taxpayers were offered the opportunity of joining the army as *yaya*, and large numbers of people applied. Under Murād II, the *yaya* were supposedly given the nickname *enik* (puppy) as a form of derision (Neshrī, *Kitâb-ı Cihân-nümâ*, ed. Faik Resat Unat and Mehmed A. Köymen, Ankara 1949, i, 155-7); this may have been linked to their making a living from agriculture. Like the *müsellems*, who performed military service on horseback under analogous conditions, the *yaya* were gradually demilitarised in the 10th/16th century, serving on building projects such as the restoration of the Aya Ṣofya. However, while many former *müsellems* succeeded in becoming *tīmār* holders, the *yaya*, when their corps was abolished in the last quarter of the 10th/16th century, were declared ordinary peasants.

Organised in units known as *odjaḳ*, the *yaya* took turns serving in the field, with those staying home (*yamak*) supplying those who went to war. An *odjaḳ* before the rule of Selīm I generally consisted of 2-4 men; by the end of the 10th/16th century, this had increased to 4-15 persons. The *yaya* were granted lands consigned to special registers, which were inalienable and could not be divided among heirs, such holdings being especially numerous in the *sandjaḳs* of Sulṭānönü and Ḥamīd. In spite of their peasant lifestyle, the *yaya* were considered servitors of the sultan (*ʿaskerī*); as dues, they only paid the bride tax and monetary penalties in case of crimes or misdemeanours. Non-attendance at campaigns was deemed a serious crime, with mutilation a possible punishment. This rule was only rescinded shortly before the abolition of the *odjaḳ*, in part because the depredations of the Djelālī rebels had made it impossible for many *yayas* to support themselves.

Bibliography: Pakalın, iii, 608-11; Zeki Arıkan, *XV-XVI. yüzyıllarda Hamit sancağı*, Izmir 1988, 90-9; Halime Doğru, *Osmanlı imparatorluğunda Yaya-Müsellem-Taycı teşkilatı (XV. ve XVI. yüzyılda Sultanönü sancağı)*, Istanbul 1990; eadem, *XVI. yüzyılda Eskişehir ve Sultanönü sancağı* Istanbul 1992, 107-16.

(SURAIYA FAROQHI)

YAYÏḲ, the name in mediaeval Turkish usage for the Ural River, whence Russian Yaika. The river rises in the Ural Mountains separating modern European from Asiatic Russia and flows past the recent cities of Orenburg [see ÖRENḲALʿE, in Suppl.] and Kral'sk into the northern end of the Caspian Sea east of the Volga estuary, having a total course of 2,430 km/1,510 miles.

The Greek sources record it as *Daix* (Ptolemy, 2nd century A.D.), *Daikh* (Menander Protector, 6th century) and *Gēekh* (Constantine Porphyrogenitus, 10th century). The name was perhaps originally a Sarmatian one, the Sarmatians being masters of the lower Ural region in Ptolemy's time. In the surmise of Sir Gerard Clauson, the change from the Greek name to Yayïḳ in Turkish (i.e. a change in the initial consonant *dh* > *y*) probably took place later, when the region had become ethnically Turkish, the Turkish people in question being unable to pronounce the voiced dental fricative. See Gy. Moravcsik, *Byzantinoturcica*, Berlin 1958, ii, 116; Clauson, *Turkish and Mongolian studies*, London 1962, 124-5.

The river is almost certainly mentioned by the 4th/10th century geographer and historian al-Masʿūdī in his *Tanbīh* and in the anonymous *Ḥudūd al-ʿālam*, but under varying names. Thus the latter source, § 6.42, tr. Minorsky 75, wrongly calls it the Artush (a confusion with the İrtïsh [*q.v.*]?) and has it empty into the lower Volga. The traveller Ibn Faḍlān [*q.v.*] must have crossed the Emba and Ural rivers on his way from Khwārazm to Bulghār; his *Riḥla* mentions many rivers but does not clearly name the Emba and Ural. Exactly when the Turkish name of the river came into general usage is uncertain, although Maḥmūd al-Kāshgharī (later 5th/11th century) does not mention it as such.

The steppes north of the Caspian and Aral Seas were in early Islamic times roamed over by such Turkish peoples as the Oghuz [see GHUZZ], Kimäk [*q.v.*] and, somewhat later, the Ḳïpčaḳ [*q.v.*], the whole region becoming known in Mongol times as the Dasht-i Ḳïpčaḳ [*q.v.* in Suppl.].

Bibliography: *Ḥudūd al-ʿālam*, comm. 213-16, 309-10, 213-14; J. Marquart, *Über das Volkstum der Komanen*, in *Abh. Akad. Wiss. Göttingen*, phil.-hist. Kl., N.F. xiii/1, Berlin 1914, 101-2.

(C.E. BOSWORTH)

YAYLAḲ (T., originally *yaylagh*), "summer quarters", applied to the summer residences of the old Turkish *kaghans* or the summer pastures of nomadic or transhumant tribes of Inner Asia, its antonym being *ḳïshlaḳ* [*q.v.*] "winter quarters".

The origin of the word is from *yay* "summer" (but this originally meant "spring", cf. Kāshgharī, *Dīwān lughāt al-turk*, Tkish. tr. Atalay, iii, 160-1, though already in the Orkhon inscriptions it means "summer", and it comes to mean this in most Turkic languages, with *yaylamaḳ* "to spend the summer", cf. Sir Gerard Clauson, *An etymological dictionary of pre-thirteenth century Turkish*, 980, 981).

In Islamic times, the Turco-Mongol rulers and leaders who, from the 5th/11th century onwards came into the "northern tier" of the Middle East as far west as Anatolia with their pastoralist hordes, long kept up the pattern of alternate winter and summer residences, the latter usually in cooler and greener upland regions. The Il-Khānids favoured pasture grounds in eastern Anatolia, such as the Alatagh, and in Ādharbāydjān and Ḳarabāgh (see B. Spuler, *Die Mongolen in Iran*, [1]Leipzig 1939, 334-5, 404). These, and then later, those of the Ṣafawids, are described by European travellers such as Kaempfer and, especially, Chardin; see the latter's *Voyages*, ed. Langlès, Paris 1811, ii, 285-6: the *yelac*. See, in general, Doerfer, *Türkische und mongolische Elemente im Neupersischen*, iv, 252-4 no. 1941. A somewhat curious usage amongst the Mongols and Turco-Mongols of the 7th/13th century was Yaylaḳ as a personal name for nobles, both male and female; see Rashīd al-Dīn, tr. J.A. Boyle, *The successors of Genghis Khan*, New York and London 1971, 105, 126-7, 129. A later Ottoman form, with a pseudo-Arabic ending, was *yaylaḳiyya* "rent paid for summer pastures or lodgings", see W. Radloff, *Versuch eines Wörterbuches der Türk-Dialecte*, iii/2, 11.

The Arabic equivalent *maṣīf* is found in the 4th/10th century geographers and is the word normally adduced to define *yaylaḳ* in the Turkish-Arabic vocabularies of the Mamlūk period, though Kāshgharī, iii, 47, has *yaylagh* = *muṣṭāf*. In Persian, an approximate synonym was *sardsīr* "cool region". See further on these Arabic and Persian usages, ḳi̊shlaḳ.

Bibliography: Given in the article.

(C.E. Bosworth)

YAZAN, an influential clan in pre-Islamic Ḥaḍramawt, first attested about the middle of the 5th century A.D. by inscriptions (with the spelling *Yz'n*) in the Wādī ʿAmāḳīn, in the Ḥabbān area. A little later they emerge as closely allied with the important Sabaean clan *Gdn*, and by the early 6th century they were probably the most powerful family in the Ḥimyarite kingdom [see ḥimyar; tubbaʿ], claiming "lordship" (signified by the prefix Dhū) over virtually the whole of what had been, up to around 300 A.D., the ancient kingdom of Ḥaḍramawt, together with the Dhofar coast around modern Ṣalāla, and the island of Suḳuṭra [*q.vv.*]. In the early 6th century, their members furnished the principal military commanders serving kings Maʿdikarib and Yūsuf As'ar (= Dhū Nuwās [*q.v.*]). Tradition (without epigraphic support) assigns to later in that century a legendary hero Sayf b. Dhī Yazan [*q.v.*], who is also the centre of a cycle of folk tales.

Bibliography: M.A. Bafaqih, *New light on the Yazanite dynasty*, in *Procs. Seminar for Arabian Studies*, ix, London 1979, 5-9. (A.F.L. Beeston)

YAZD, a city of central Persia, and capital of the province of the same name. It is situated on the Persian plateau at lat. 31° 54' N. and long. 54° 24' E. (at an elevation of 1,230m/4,240 feet), in an elongated interior basin stretching from near Kāshān to Bāfḳ and bordered by the Dasht-i Kawīr. It was known in early times as Katha (Le Strange, *Lands*, 285; *Ḥudūd al-ʿālam*, tr. Minorsky, London 1937, 128, 380), after a fortress and prison alleged to have been founded by Alexander (Aḥmad b. Ḥusayn b. al-Kātib, *Tārīkh-i djadīd-i Yazd*, ed. Īradj Afshār, Tehran AHS 1345/1966, 16). According to legend, later foundations grew up on this site (Muḥammad Mufīd Bāfḳī, *Djāmiʿ-i mufīdī*, ed. Afshār, Tehran AHS 1340-2/1961-3, i, 14 ff.). Yazd became known as *dār-al-ʿibāda*, when Ṭoghrïl Beg assigned it to the Kākūyid Abū Manṣūr Farāmurz ʿAlā' al-Dawla, in 443/1051 (see below). The modern city has a population, according to the 1996 census, of 326,976.

1. Geography, topography and social structure.

Ibn Ḥawḳal describes Yazd in the 4th/10th century as a well-built fortified city with two iron gates (Le Strange, *Lands*, 285). Ḥamd Allāh Mustawfī Ḳazwīnī states that it was built of sun-dried bricks which lasted as long as burnt bricks elsewhere because there was hardly ever any rain, though water was plentiful, being brought in by channels from the hills and each house had its own storage tank (*ibid.*). Wind towers [see bādgīr, in Suppl.] were (and are) a distinguishing feature of the architecture of the city, so constructed as to convey any breeze available in the upper air into the *sardābs* (semi-underground chambers) of the houses or other buildings (see Īradj Afshār, *Yazd-nāma*, Tehran AHS 1371/1992-3, i, 337-57). Aḥmad b. Ḥusayn al-Kātib mentions *bādgīrs* constructed in the Muẓaffarid and Tīmūrid periods (*Tārīkh-i djadīd-i Yazd*, 86, 92, 94). The domed roofs of the *āb-anbārs* or *miṣnaʿas* (water storage cisterns) are another distinguishing feature of the city, and also its fine mosques (see Afshār for a comprehensive account of monuments, religious and secular, of Yazd, the inscriptions to be found in them and also on tombstones, *Yazd-nāma*, and *Yādigārhā-yi Yazd*, 3 vols., Tehran AHS 1348-54/1970-5).

According to Aḥmad b. Ḥusayn al-Kātib, Abū Manṣūr Farāmurz ordered the city wall (*ḥiṣār*) to be built with towers and four iron gates (*op. cit.*, 61. See also Afshār, *Yādigārhā-yi Yazd*, ii, 671-2). Part of the wall was destroyed by floods in 673/1275 (73). It was restored by the Atabeg Yūsuf Shāh b. Tughān (685-714/1286-7 to 1314-15) (74). Mubāriz al-Dīn Muḥammad Muẓaffar (713-59/1313-14 to 1358) built an outer wall with seven gates enclosing various districts within the city (83). Shāh Yaḥyā, who took possession of the city in 779/1367-8, made further additions, including a ditch, towers and gate (87; Djaʿfar b. Muḥammad b. Ḥasan Djaʿfarī, *Tārīkh-i Yazd*, ed. Afshār, Tehran AHS 1338/1960, 36, and see also Muḥammad Mufīd, iii, 738). The latter author states that Pīr Muḥammad b. ʿUmar Shaykh, after putting down a rebellion against the Tīmūrids, built a fort for the residence of governors on the orders of Tīmūr and in 808/1405-6 a wall and a deep ditch in the south of the city (iii, 740; Aḥmad b. Ḥusayn al-Kātib, 91-2). The fort was partly destroyed by Shāh ʿAbbās (Afshār, *Yādigārhā-yi Yazd*, ii, 697). In 1821 Muḥammad Walī Mīrzā, when governor of Yazd, repaired the city wall and the ditch (Ḥusayn Nā'īnī, *Djāmiʿ-i Djaʿfarī*, ed. Afshār, Tehran AHS 1353/1974-5, 715-16. See also Afshār, *Yādigārhā-yi Yazd*, ii, 674-5 and *Survey of Persian art*, iii, 1242-4).

In the 19th century, the city of Yazd was still enclosed by a ditch and a double wall with numerous detached towers in it, all in tolerable repair. Its circumference was about 2½ miles. The inner city was surrounded by gardens and habitations. It had 24 *maḥallas*, 8 of which were within the walls, 31 mosques and 11 *madrasas*. The bazaar contained some 100 shops, and 34 caravanserais (A. Amanat, *Cities and trade. Consul Abbott on the economy and society of Iran 1847-1866*, London 1983, 131-2, referred to below as Abbott). Major Oliver St. John states that Yazd had 50 mosques, 65 baths and 8 *madrasas* in 1872 (*Narrative of a journey through Baluchistan and southern Persia, 1872*, in F.J. Goldsmid, *Eastern Persia, an account of the journeys of the Persian Boundary Commission, 1870-1-2*, London 1876, 175). Curzon, who visited Persia in 1889-90, states that the fort, which was partly ruined and partly built into or over, still retained a double wall with a broad deep ditch before the outer rampart, while the citadel inside the fort, where the governor resided, was separately walled to a height of 30 or 40 feet (*Persia and the Persian question*, London 1892, ii, 240, and see ḥiṣn. ii, at Vol. III, 502).

In the early centuries of the ʿAbbāsid caliphate, Yazd was included in the district of Iṣṭakhr of the province of Fārs under the name of Katha. After the Mongol invasions it became part of the Djibāl and, later, part of Kirmān province [see kirmān, at Vol. V, 147b]. In the Ṣafawid period it was one of the districts under the direct administration of the central government (*Tadhkirat al-mulūk*, tr. and comm. Minorsky, London 1943, 42). In the 19th century, when the Ẓill al-Sulṭān was at the height of his power, it formed part of the Iṣfahān province. On the Ẓill al-Sulṭān's disgrace in 1888 it became again an independent government but was returned to the Ẓill al-Sulṭān in 1890 (Curzon, *op. cit.*, ii, 243). For a time during the 19th century, Kūhbanān and Shahr-i Bābak, belonging to Kirmān, were attached to Yazd as also were some of the villages of Fārs (Abbott, 144-5). At the present day the province covers an area of over 76,156 km² and consists of seven *shahristāns*, Yazd, Ardakān, Bāfḳ, Taft, Abarḳūh [*q.v.*], Mihrīz and Maybud (*Yazd nigīn-i kawīr*, a tourist guide and information brochure published by the Society of Yazd Public Libraries, 1375/1996-7, 29-30).

The province is bordered on the north and west by the province of Iṣfahān, on the north-east by Khurāsān, on the south-west by Fārs and in the south-east by the province of Kirmān. The Shīr Kūh massif, rising to 4,075 m/13,366 feet, lies in the south and west of the province. In the centre of the province to the north of the city of Yazd is the Kharānik massif, the highest point of which is 3,158 m/10,358 ft. In the east there are lesser mountains in the districts of Khūr, Biyābānak, Djandāḳ and Ribāṭ-i Pusht-i Bādām. There are small deposits of iron ore, lead, zinc and copper in the province, Ibn Ḥawḳal mentions that a lead mine near Yazd was productively worked (Le Strange, *Lands*, 285); and old workings of lead ore survive near Bāfḳ (Abbott, 134, 135). Marble is found in the Tūrān-pusht mine in the Pīsh-Kūh district to the south and south-west of the city of Yazd.

Large areas of the province are occupied by sterile, or almost sterile, hammadas due either to their low rainfall or to an excess of salt in the soil or both (M. Zohary, *On the geo-botanical structure of Iran*, in *Bull. of the Research Council of Israel. Section D. Botany, Suppl.*, vol. xi D Suppl. [March 1963], 182). Violent dust storms are frequent and moving sands encroach upon the city of Yazd, upon Ashkidhar, Bāfḳ and elsewhere. Ḥusayn b. Muḥammad b. Abi 'l-Riḍā Āwī in his translation of Māfarrūkhī's *Maḥāsin Iṣfahān*, made in 729/1328-9, mentions the planting of tamarisk (*gaz*) to stabilise moving sands by the people of Yazd (*Tardjuma-yi maḥāsin Iṣfahān*, ed. ʿAbbās Iḳbāl, Tehran AHS 1328/1950-1, 43). The climate of the province is described as temperate (*muʿtadil*) (Ḥamd Allāh Mustawfī Ḳazwīnī, *Nuzha*, ed. Le Strange, London 1915, Persian text, 74). Ibn Balkhī adds that since it is situated on the edge of the desert the climate is inclined to be warm (*mayl bi-garmī; Fārs-nāma*, ed. Le Strange, London 1921, 122). The summers in the city of Yazd are, in fact, extremely hot.

The province lies in the rain shadow of the Alborz in the north and of the Zagros in the west. The average annual rainfall, which occurs in winter and spring, varies from 20 mm in Shīr Kūh to 60 mm in the lower parts of the province; in the city of Yazd it is only 55.4 mm. Ground water is provided by *ḳanāts* (*q.v.* and see Lambton, *The qanāts of Yazd*, in *JRAS*, 3rd series, vol. 2, pt. 1 [April 1992], 21-35). From the 1960s onwards a large number of deep and semi-deep wells have been sunk, which has led to a lowering of the water-table. Of the 3,331 *ḳanāts* alleged to exist in the province, only 2,615 were said to be in operation in 1997. Some are over 50 km/31 miles long and 100 m deep (Afshār, *Yazd-nāma*, 413-14). Ground cover in most of the province is sparse owing to lack of rainfall, fluctuations in temperature and the destruction of plants over the centuries for charcoal burning and other purposes. Failure of rain has frequently resulted in shortages and sometimes famine. In 850/1446-7 a period of drought was accompanied by famine and plague (*wabā*) (Aḥmad b. Ḥusayn al-Kātib, 10). In 858/1454 the rains failed again and famine and plague ensued with heavy loss of life (276). Sudden or unusually heavy rains have also occasioned damage. In 673/1275 five days of consecutive rain in Urdī Bihisht/April-May resulted in floods and much damage to the city of Yazd (73-4). In 860/1456 there was again severe flooding in the city of Yazd as a result of heavy rain in Farwardīn/March-April (276). Muḥammad Mufīd records that there were heavy snowfalls in 1057/1647-8 and that snow lay in the streets of Yazd for nearly three months (*Djāmiʿ-i mufīdī*, i, 133).

Despite unfavourable climatic conditions, the city of Yazd and the towns and villages of the province are surrounded by cultivated fields (*kishtkhʷān*), orchards and gardens. The mountain districts are carefully terraced. Water rights and land in many parts of the province are separately owned and highly sub-divided [see MĀʾ, at Vol. V, 871a-b]. Absentee landownership does not appear to have been common. Local landowners predominated, some of whom enjoyed considerable wealth. Peasant proprietorship also existed. *Awḳāf*, especially in the form of shares in *ḳanāts*, were widespread (Lambton, *Awḳāf in Persia: 6th-8th/12th-14th centuries*, in *ILS*, iv/3, 298-318; ʿAbd al-Wahhāb Ṭarāz, *Kitābča-yi mawḳūfāt-i Yazd*, ed. Afshār, in *FIZ* [1962-3], 3-123). Lands assigned as *iḳṭāʿ*s or *tiyūl*s [*q.vv.*] and crown lands (*khāliṣadjāt*) appear to have been rare, though Ṭoghrïl Beg assigned Yazd, as stated above, and Abarḳūh to Abū Manṣūr Farāmurz in 443/1051 and Abū Saʿīd, the Il-khān, gave Maybud as an *iḳṭāʿ* to Muḥammad b. Muẓaffar (Aḥmad b. Ḥusayn al-Kātib, 82), allotted wages (*marsūm*) to him and appointed 200 men to be in his service, and there were cases of land being assigned as *tiyūl* under the Ṣafawids (e.g. Muḥammad Mufīd, iii, 276). There are frequent references to crown lands in the Ṣafawid period but few details (*ibid.*, iii, 366 and *passim*). A *farmān* of Nādir Shāh, dated 1155/1742-3, appointing Mīrzā Ḥusayn (formerly *ḍābiṭ* of Naṭanz) governor of Yazd, ordered him, *inter alia*, to exert himself in increasing *khāliṣa* property (Afshār, *Si farmān wa yak ḥukm marbūṭ bi Yazd*, in *FIZ*, xxv [AHS 1361/1982], 396). In the Ḳādjār period there was also some *khāliṣa* property in Yazd. Several *ḳanāts* were wholly, or in part, *khāliṣa* (cf. Muḥammad Djaʿfar, 310, 460, 591, 593, 594).

Grain was grown in the province but not in sufficient quantity for its needs (cf. Mustawfī, *Nuzha*, 74). In the 19th century it sufficed for only two to three months, the deficit being met from Iṣfahān and elsewhere. Fruit was grown abundantly, including mulberries, pomegranates (those of Maybud being especially good: Ibn al-Balkhī, 122), apples, pears, cherries, apricots, plums and grapes; and a variety of vegetables; cotton was grown, and silk manufactured and used in Yazd's flourishing textile industry. Rashīd al-Dīn Faḍl Allāh Hamadānī [see RASHĪD AL-DĪN ṬABĪB] includes much information on the crops and agricultural methods of Yazd in his book *Āthār wa aḥyāʾ* (ed. Afshār and M. Sutūda, AHS Tehran 1368/1989-90. See also Lambton, The Āthār wa aḥyāʾ *of Rashīd al-Dīn Faḍl Allāh Hamadānī and Rashīd al-Dīn's contribution as an agronomist, arboriculturist and horticulturalist*, in R. Amitai-Preiss and D.O. Morgan (eds.), *The Mongol Empire and its legacy*, Leiden 1999). He draws attention to the skill and thrift shown by Yazdīs in agricultural development and states that the return they got from the land was seldom equalled in other places. He also mentions that the production of silk was higher than elsewhere. In the 19th century, much silk was still produced but of inferior quality. It was not enough to supply local workshops, and raw silk was imported from Gīlān and Khurāsān. In the second half of the century the production of silk declined and was largely displaced by opium and cotton (G.G. Gilbar, *Persian agriculture in the late Qājār period 1860-1906: some economic and social aspects*, in *Asian and African Studies*, xii/3 [1978], 350, and see Abbott, 105). Among other crops grown in the 19th century Abbott mentions Indian corn, millet, lentils, pulse, beans, madder, asafoetida, fruits, nuts and vegetables (134).

From early times Yazd had a thriving trade. Its

manufactures of silk and cotton were famous and exported to other parts of the Islamic world and India. Al-Iṣṭak͟hrī and Ibn Ḥawḳal mention cotton garments made in Yazd. Ibn al-Balk͟hī, writing at the beginning of the 6th/12th century, states that "in the districts round [Yazd], silk is produced, for the mulberry tree is here abundant. Further, they (sc. the Yazdīs) manufacture excellent cloths in brocade also, of the kind named *mus͟htī, farak͟h*, and the like, for in Yazd they rear goats only, no sheep, and the hair from these is very strong" (20, quoted by R.B. Serjeant, *Islamic textiles*, Beirut 1972, 55-6). Al-Ḳazwīnī found in Yazd makers of silk (*ḥarīr*) of *sundus* (a kind of green brocade), extremely beautiful and close-woven which is taken from there to all countries (*Kosmographie*, ed. Wüstenfeld, ii, 187, quoted in Serjeant, *op. cit.*, 56). Al-Maḳrīzī mentions the import of Yazdī textiles into Egypt in the 8th/14th century (*ibid.*, 115). Marco Polo noted that Yazd "is a good and noble city, and it has a great amount of trade. They weave there quantities of a certain silk tissue known as Yesdi, which merchants carry into many quarters to dispose of" (H. Yule, *The Book of Ser Marco Polo, the Venetian*, London 1871, i, 89, quoted in Serjeant, 56). Pedro Teixeira mentions that the richest and finest carpets came from Yazd "from which place I saw some, each of which, on account of its workmanship and perfection, was valued at more than a thousand ducats", while the fabric known as *al-ḳaṭīfa* was "the best, the finest and the most perfect" (quoted in Serjeant, *loc. cit.*). Friar Odoricus (in 1325) and Josafa Barbaro (in 1474) state that Yazd was a great silk mart and Raphael de Mans describes how gold thread was made there (*Estat de la Perse en 1660*, ed. C. Schefer, Paris 1890, 195, quoted in Serjeant, 85).

At the beginning of the 19th century Yazd was a large and populous city, celebrated among merchants for its security. Commerce in silk, carpets, felts, shawls and coarse cotton cloth flourished (Malcolm, *Melville papers*, quoted by C. Issawi, *The economic history of Iran 1800-1914*, Chicago and London, 1971, 262). Capt. Christie, who passed through Yazd in 1810, states that it was "a great mart between Hindoostan, Khorasan, Baghdad and Persia" and was said to be a place of greater trade than any other place in the latter empire (*Abstract from Captain Christie's Journal after his separation from Lieut. Pottinger, at Nooshky June (1810)*, in H. Pottinger, *Travels in Beloochistan and Sinde*, London 1816, 421). He mentions that there were over 50,000 camels in the city (421-2), which is an indication of the extent of the trade. J.B. Fraser, who was in Yazd in the early years of the 19th century, states that Yazd was one of the most prosperous towns of Persia and one of the great entrepôts between East and West. Caravans from Kābul, Kas͟hmīr, Buk͟hārā, Harāt, Mas͟hhad and Kirmān were met in Yazd by merchants from Iṣfahān, S͟hīrāz, Kās͟hān and Tehran and a great interchange of commodities took place. Its manufactures of silk and other stuffs, felts, sugar-candy and sweetmeats commanded a ready market everywhere in Persia (*An historical and descriptive account of Persia*, ²Edinburgh 1834, 64). E. Scott Waring also mentions that Yazd was an emporium for all the trade of Persia. Coarse perpets were sent there and sold to the Uzbegs and the people of K͟hurāsān, the merchant taking on his return journey silks, carpets, felts and Kas͟hmīrī shawls (*A tour of Sheeraz*, London 1807, 76). By the middle of the century there had been a decline in the manufacture of textiles (Abbott, 79). Despite an attempt by Muḥammad K͟hān, who was governor of Yazd 1863-70, to encourage the silk trade, the decline continued and by the end of the 19th century, or the beginning of the 20th, there were only some 800 workshops and 2,000 cotton looms (Issawi, 268), whereas in 1870 Major Euan Smith had reported that there were 18,000 silk workshops in Yazd, employing probably 9,000 hands and that the silk was considered by some to be the best in Persia (*The Perso-Baluchistan Frontier Mission 1870, 1871*, in Goldsmid, *Eastern Persia*, i, 175). Nevertheless E. Stack, who visited Yazd in 1881, wrote that prosperity was "a notable feature of Yazd. Hardly a beggar was to be seen and the busy bazaars and well-kept houses, as well as the dress of the people, and the number of merchants, were signs of a city supported by brisk trade" (*Six months in Persia*, London 1882, i, 267).

Meanwhile, although the silk trade had declined, the opium trade had increased in importance (see further, Gilbar, *op. cit.*, 314 and *passim*). Rabino noted that towards the end of the century the opium crop absorbed all the floating capital of the province and that the money went to the villages (*Banking in Persia*, in *Jnal. of the Institute of Bankers*, xiii [1892], 35, quoted by Issawi, *op. cit.*, 352). Other exports from Yazd included coarse loaf sugar, made from raw sugar imported from India, Java and Siam, which was sent to all parts of Persia (Abbott, 104), cotton, carpets, felts, madder roots, and nuts. The principal imports were cotton fabrics, copper, tin, lead, iron, drugs and spices and tea from India, and oil, candles, sugar, furs, crockery and piece goods from Russia (see further Curzon, ii, 241-2. See also Lambton, *Persian trade under the early Qajars*, in D.S. Richards (ed.), *Islam and the trade of Asia*, Oxford 1970, 118-19). Henna was also brought to Yazd for processing and in 1907-8 there were some 60 enterprises engaged in this (Issawi, 299). In spite of the changes in production and manufacture, Yazd nevertheless remained a major distribution centre in the early years of the 20th century (G. Jones, *Banking and Empire in Iran*, Cambridge 1986, i, 99).

The local histories are rich in details of the lives of officials, landowners, *ʿulamāʾ*, merchants and others, but these are beyond the scope of this article. Many of them held land and shares in *ḳanāt*s; some were very rich. The extent to which they expended their wealth on buildings, religious and secular, in the city and throughout the province, and on *ḳanāt*s and agricultural development, is notable. Some of the Muslim merchants, as well as the Zoroastrian ones, had links with India, at least from the Ṣafawid period if not before.

The *sayyid*s were a numerous and influential group. D͟jaʿfar b. Muḥammad states that there were nearly 1,000 descendants of the Imām D͟jaʿfar al-Ṣādiḳ [*q.v.*] in Yazd when he was writing, i.e. in the 9th/15th century (108). Prominent among the Ḥusaynī *sayyids*, descended from D͟jaʿfar al-Ṣādiḳ, were Rukn al-Dīn Muḥammad b. Ḳawām al-Dīn b. Niẓām (d. 732/1331-2) and his son S͟hams al-Dīn Abū ʿAbd Allāh Muḥammad (d. 733/1332-3), both of whom disposed of a great deal of property in shares in *ḳanāt*s, land and real estate, much if not all of which they constituted into *waḳf* (Lambton, *Continuity and change in medieval Persia*, New York, 1988, 156. See also J. Aubin, *Le patronage culturel en Iran sous les Ilkhans: une grande famille de Yazd*, in *Le monde iranien et l'Islam*, iii, [1975], 107-18). Among Sayyid Rukn al-Dīn's many benefactions was the complex consisting of a *madrasa*, mosque, observatory (*raṣad*) and pharmacy (*bayt al-adwiya*) in the *Waḳt wa sāʿat* quarter of the city, which took its name from the observatory (D͟jaʿfar b. Muḥammad, 81-3; Aḥmad b. Ḥusayn al-Kātib, 122-5; Afs͟hār, *Yādigārhā-*

yi Yazd, ii, 711; and see Parwiz Mohebbi, *Technique et resources au Iran du 7e au 19e siècle*, Institut français de recherches en Iran, Tehran 1996, 199).

In the 7th-9th/13th-15th centuries there appears to have been an increase in the number of Ṣūfīs in the province (Afs̲h̲ār, *Yazd-nāma*, i, 30). One of the most famous was S̲h̲ayk̲h̲ Taḳī al-Dīn Muḥammad Dādā (d. 700/1300-1), who migrated from Iṣfahān to Yazd and built *k̲h̲ānaḳāh*s at Bundarābād, As̲h̲kid̲h̲ar, Maybud, and in various other locations (D̲j̲aʿfar b. Muḥammad, 112; Afs̲h̲ār, *Yādigārhā-yi Yazd*, i, 126-8).

Physicians were another influential group in the city. Ras̲h̲īd al-Dīn's early connection with Yazd appears to have been through two physicians, S̲h̲araf al-Dīn ʿAlī and S̲h̲ams al-Dīn Raḍī (Lambton, *Continuity and change in medieval Persia*, 308. See also Afs̲h̲ār, *Ras̲h̲īd al-Dīn wa Yazd*, in *Īrān-s̲h̲ināsī*, ii/1 [1970], 23-33).

The local histories also mention poets, painters and calligraphers who lived in Yazd. A marked feature of the population was the existence of skilled craftsmen, builders, weavers, potters, *muḳannī*s (also known as *čāhk̲h̲ūyān*, who were highly rated for their skill and often employed outside Yazd), and a thrifty peasantry, many of whom worked not only on the land but also as craftsmen and weavers. Among the peasants there was probably a higher proportion of peasant proprietors than in most other districts of Persia. Al-Kās̲h̲ānī states that Ras̲h̲īd al-Dīn took some 300 draft oxen with their *gāw-band*s (those who worked them) from Yazd to Tabrīz. The purpose of this, he alleges, was that the oxen should be used to transport night soil from the city to Fatḥābād and other properties that Ras̲h̲īd al-Dīn was developing (*Tārīk̲h̲-i Ūld̲j̲āytū*, ed. Mahin Hambly, Tehran AHS 1348/1969, 116). This seems unlikely to be the only reason, or even the real reason. More likely Ras̲h̲īd al-Dīn brought the *gāw-band*s with their oxen to Tabrīz in order to make use of their agricultural skill.

Ibn al-Balk̲h̲ī states that the Yazdīs were Sunnīs, very pious and of right religion (*Fārs-nāma*, 122). Aḥmad b. Ḥusayn al-Kātib remarks that the people of the Yaʿḳūbī quarter of Yazd had a sense of solidarity (*ṣāḥib ittifāḳ*), were fanatical (*taʿaṣṣub-dār*) and somewhat parochial in their attitude (*wa ḥukm-i du dānga dārand*); they were continually occupied in earning their living (*kasb*) and worship (*ṭāʿat*), and most of them were well-to-do (*muraffah al-ḥāl*) (61). There is no information in the local histories of when or how the Yazdīs were converted to S̲h̲īʿism. It would seem that their piety and devotion were carried over from Sunnism to S̲h̲īʿism.

A further feature of the population was the existence of a Zoroastrian community [see MAD̲J̲ŪS], between which and India there was constant intercourse. According to Abbott, there were some 200 Zoroastrian families in the town and 640 in eight villages round about (137). As *d̲h̲immī*s [*q.v.*] they were forced to wear special clothing and subject to other restrictions (138; see also Napier Malcolm, *Five years in a Persian town (Yazd)*, London 1905). Euan Smith states that the number of Zoroastrians under the government of Yazd was estimated at 3,800 (175). Towards the end of the century their numbers rose. E.G. Browne, who was in Persia in 1887-8, states that there were 7,000-10,000 Zoroastrians in Yazd and its dependencies (*A year among the Persians*, Cambridge 1927, 404).

There was a small Jewish community, numbering about 1,000 in Yazd in 1867-8 (Issawi, 32), but Euan Smith put it at only 800 in 1870 (175). Bābīs [*q.v.*] were to be found in Yazd in the middle of the 19th century and took part in the Bābī rising of 1848 (Browne, 67). The Bahāʾīs in Yazd were given the right to trade in 1860 and to open schools in 1870, but as a result of anti-Bahāʾī riots in 1903, they were virtually exterminated in Yazd (F. Bémont, *Les villes de l'Iran*, Paris 1969, 205-6). In the 19th century there were also a few Hindu merchants from Sind resident in Yazd. They enjoyed British protection and were engaged in trade with India (Abbott, 132; Euan Smith, 173).

2. History.

Details of the pre-Islamic history of Yazd are sparse. Whether in fact Yazdagird III spent two months in Yazd after his defeat at Nihāwand in 21/642 before he set out for Marw, where he arrived in 31/651, seems doubtful. The story related in the *Tārīk̲h̲-i d̲j̲adīd-i Yazd* by Aḥmad b. Ḥusayn al-Kātib that he buried his treasure in three wells in the Yazd district, and that the first of these was later found by the Atabeg ʿIzz al-Dīn Langar (599-604/1194 to 1207-8), the second by Mubāriz al-Dīn Muḥammad b. Muẓaffar (713-59/1314-58) and the third by the people of Yazd in the time of Iskandar b. ʿUmar S̲h̲ayk̲h̲, who became governor of Yazd in 808/1405-6 (46-8), is almost certainly legendary.

There is mention of the appointment of ʿUmar b. Mug̲h̲īra as governor of Yazd during the caliphate of ʿUt̲h̲mān and some settlement of Arabs of the Banū Tamīm is alleged (Aḥmad b. Ḥusayn al-Kātib, 53; D̲j̲aʿfar b. Muḥammad, 16). Conversion to Islam is said by Aḥmad b. Ḥusayn al-Kātib to have taken place during this same caliphate (53). In fact, it is likely that conversion was more gradual. Those who retained their Zoroastrian faith were subject to the *d̲j̲izya* [*q.v.*]. It seems probable that Yazd formed part of Fārs during the Umayyad caliphate. With the rise of Abū Muslim, his supporters appear to have defeated Abu 'l-ʿAlāʾ al-Tawḳī, the Umayyad governor. Little, however, is known of the history of Yazd under the early ʿAbbāsids; it is not until the Sald̲j̲ūḳ period that more detail is available, and even then the information in the local histories of Yazd (which are of much later dates) is confused and chronologically unreliable.

When Ṭog̲h̲ril Beg took Iṣfahān from the Kākūyid Abū Manṣūr Farāmurz [see KĀKŪYIDS] in 443/1051 and made Iṣfahān his capital, he assigned to Abū Manṣūr as an *iḳṭāʿ* Abarḳūh and Yazd, both of which had been controlled by the Kākūyids. There is a *dirham* struck in Yazd in 421/1030 by the Kākūyid *amīr* ʿAlāʾ al-Dawla Muḥammad acknowledging the caliph al-Ḳādir as suzerain (C.E. Bosworth, *Dailamis in Central Iran: the Kakuyids of Jibal and Yazd*, in *Iran*, viii [1970], 77). Bosworth has meticulously examined the evidence for Kākūyid rule in Yazd and found it impossible to elucidate the exact chronology of the Kākūyid governors of Yazd (*op. cit.*, 84-5).

Both Abū Manṣūr Farāmurz and his son Muʾayyid al-Dawla ʿAḍud al-Dīn ʿAlī appear to have been treated with favour by the Sald̲j̲ūḳs. The former accompanied Ṭog̲h̲ril Beg when he went to Bag̲h̲dād in 455/1063 to meet his bride, the caliph's daughter. The latter married in 469/1076-7 Arslān K̲h̲ātūn bt. Čag̲h̲rī Beg, whose first husband, the caliph al-Ḳāʾim, had died in 467/1075. Yazd appears to have prospered under the Kākūyids. Abū Manṣūr Farāmurz built a palace, a Friday mosque, and (as stated above) a wall round the city of Yazd. His successors continued for some years as local rulers of Yazd. New villages and *ḳanāt*s were made in the vicinity of the city. The last Kākūyid ruler, Gars̲h̲āsp b. ʿAlī b. Farāmurz, was with Sultan Sand̲j̲ar [*q.v.*] at the battle of the Ḳaṭwān steppe (536/1141) and was killed in the battle. During the reign of Arslān b. Ṭoghrïl (556-71/1161-76) Garshāsp's two daughters ruled Yazd. Rukn al-Dīn Sām b. Langar was appointed atabeg to them and married to one of them. He was apparently incompetent and replaced by his brother ʿIzz al-Dīn (Djaʿfar b. Muḥammad, 23), who was the real founder of the dynasty known as the Atabegs of Yazd. The benefactions of Garshāsp's daughters in Yazd are spoken of in the local histories and seem to have been considerable; and under the Atabegs prosperity and development continued.

ʿIzz al-Dīn Langar was succeeded by his son Wardānzūr, who had an uneventful rule of twelve years. He was succeeded by Ḳuṭb al-Dīn, during whose rule further building and development was carried out (Aḥmad b. Ḥusayn al-Kātib, 69-70). Ḳuṭb al-Dīn died in 626/1228-9. He was succeeded successively by his son Maḥmūd Shāh and the latter's son Salghur Shāh, who sent an offer of submission to Hülegü and received in return a diploma for Yazd. He was succeeded by his son Taḳī Shāh, who ruled for some twenty years and died in 670/1271-2 (72-3). During the reign of his son and successor ʿAlāʾ al-Dawla (ʿAlāʾ al-Dīn), the great flood of 673/1274-5 occurred. Aḥmad b. Ḥusayn al-Kātib relates that ʿAlāʾ al-Dawla was so shaken by the flood that he died within a month (74). His brother Yūsuf Shāh succeeded him.

Towards the end of the 7th/13th century Yazd became increasingly subject to interference from the Mongols. According to Mustawfī, the *tamgha* dues of Yazd and the province amounted to 251,000 dīnārs (*Nuzha*, 74). Rashīd al-Dīn states that in 694/1294-5 Baydu gave a draft for 1,000 dīnārs on the taxes of Yazd to Nawrūz and the government of Yazd to Nawrūz's son Sulṭān Shāh, whose mother was, he states, Sulṭān Nasab Khātūn, the daughter of ʿAlāʾ al-Dīn, the son of the Atabeg Maḥmūd Shāh (*Tārīkh-i mubārak-i ghāzānī*, ed. K. Jahn, London 1940, 75). If Aḥmad b. Ḥusayn al-Kātib's account of the genealogy of the Atabegs is correct, she must have been the great-great-granddaughter and not the granddaughter of Maḥmūd Shāh. There is, however, no record of Sulṭān Shāh taking up his government.

According to Rashīd al-Dīn, Yazd like many other places suffered from the depredations of the Mongol tax-collectors. He gives a lurid account of their extortion in the villages of Yazd (*op. cit.*, 249) and of a particular occasion when they descended on the village of Fīrūzābād (259). The owner of this village has been identified by Aubin as the Sayyid Niẓām al-Dīn ʿAlī b. Maḥmūd b. Maḥfūẓ b. Raʾīs Yazdī, a friend and contemporary of Rashīd al-Dīn (*Une grande famille de Yazd*, 111). That extortion took place is very probable, but at the same time the foundations of Shams al-Dīn Djuwaynī and his agent in Yazd, Shams al-Dīn Muḥammad Tāzīkū (Tadjīk-i Kūčik) of Rashīd al-Dīn himself, and more particularly, of Sayyid Rukn al-Dīn and Sayyid Shams al-Dīn are witness to wealth and prosperity in Yazd at the close of the 7th/13th and the early years of the 8th/14th century (Lambton, *Awqāf in Persia*, 313-5; eadem, *Continuity and change in medieval Persia*, 65-6). After Ghāzān became established in Tabrīz, the Atabegs apparently sent an annual *pīshkash* [*q.v.*] to the *ordu*. Yūsuf Shāh withheld this. Ghāzān sent Yesüder (or Toghāy b. Yesüder) to Yazd with instructions to confirm Yūsuf Shāh in his government if he paid the tribute. When Yesüder drew near to Yazd, Yūsuf Shāh fortified himself in the city and sent his mother to Yesüder with presents to intercede for him. Yesüder treated her with gross disrespect and refused the presents that she had brought. She returned to Yazd and told Yūsuf Shāh what had happened. He was furious, made a night sortie from the city, killed Yesüder and took his women prisoner. When Ghāzān heard of this, he sent the governor of Iṣfahān Muḥammad Īdādjī with 3,000 cavalry to overthrow Yūsuf Shāh. The latter, realising that resistance was impossible, fled with his women, army and the prisoners whom he had taken from Yesüder to Sīstān. The people of Yazd submitted to Īdādjī, who, having appointed an *amīr* as *dārūgha* [*q.v.*], returned to Iṣfahān (Djaʿfar b. Muḥammad, 26-8; Aḥmad b. Ḥusayn al-Kātib, 74-6). Muḥammad b. ʿAlī b. Muḥammad Shabānkāraʾī adds the information that Yūsuf Shāh was captured in Khurāsān, taken to the *ordu* and executed (*Madjmaʿ al-ansāb*, ed. Mīr Hāshim Muḥaddith, Tehran AHS 1363/1984-5, 210-14). Rashīd al-Dīn does not refer in detail to these events; he merely mentions that Toghāy b. Yesüder was dismissed (i.e. turned out) from the office of *shiḥna* of Yazd (*op. cit.*, 357).

Yūsuf Shāh was the last of the Atabegs of Yazd to exercise effective rule: his son Ḥādjdjī Shāh was finally overthrown by a combination of Muẓaffarids and Īndjūʾids [*q.vv.*] in 718/1318-19. In 719/1319-20 Mubāriz al-Dīn Muḥammad b. Muẓaffar was recognised as governor of Yazd by Abū Saʿīd, the last Il-khān. In the disorders that occurred after the death in 736/1335 of Abū Saʿīd, Yazd was subject to the constant movement of troops (though the numbers were probably small). In 751/1350-1 the Īndjūʾid Abū Isḥāḳ besieged Mubāriz al-Dīn in Yazd but failed to take the city, and as he retired, he laid waste the countryside and closed the roads. Snow and rain also impeded movement. No grain reached the city and severe famine ensued (Muʿīn al-Dīn b. Djalāl al-Dīn Muḥammad Muʿallim Yazdī, *Mawāhib-i ilāhī*, ed. Saʿīd Nafīsī, Tehran AHS 1326/1947, 217 ff.) However, by 754/1353 Mubāriz al-Dīn had established his supremacy over a wide area, including Yazd. Before long, internecine strife broke out among the Muẓaffarids which led to Mubāriz al-Dīn's deposition in 759/1358. Internecine strife continued under his successors.

In spite of the prevailing turbulence and the internal warfare of the Muẓaffarids, the city apparently prospered under them and was extended. New villages and *ḳanāt*s were made (Mufīd, i, 121-2 and *passim*), *madrasa*s and libraries built. Yaḥyā b. Shāh Muẓaffar, who took possession of Yazd after Tīmūr's withdrawal after his first invasion of Persia in 789/1381, and others of his family made a number of buildings in the city and its vicinity, including the Sulṭān Ibrāhīm bazaar built by Shāh Yaḥyā's sister's son, and the Khātūn bazaar beside the Friday mosque, consisting of 60 shops with *ḥudjra*s above them, built by Shāh Yaḥyā's mother; Shāh Yaḥyā's *wazīr* Rukn al-Dīn also built the Dallālān bazaar (Djaʿfar b. Muḥammad, 36-7; Aḥmad b. Ḥusayn al-Kātib, 86-7; and see further R. Pinder-Wilson, *Timurid architecture*, in *Camb. hist. of Iran*, vi, 730 ff.).

In 795/1392 Shāh Manṣūr b. Muẓaffar was defeated and killed by Tīmūr [*q.v.*] who had left Transoxiana in 794/1392 to begin his second campaign against Persia. The remaining Muẓaffarid princes submitted to Tīmūr and were executed, apart from two of Shāh Shudjāʿ's sons (who had earlier been blinded, one by Shāh Shudjāʿ and the other by Shāh Manṣūr; Mufīd, i, 160). Tīmūr's eldest son, ʿUmar Shaykh, became governor of Fārs, including Yazd. He died in 796/1394 and was succeeded by his son Pīr Muḥammad. Disorders meanwhile broke out in Yazd and the neighbourhood and Pīr Muḥammad set out for Yazd and successfully besieged the city in 797/1394-5. Aḥmad b. Ḥusayn al-Kātib says that there was severe famine in the city and that nearly 30,000 died, but his account is somewhat confused (89-91). As a result of these events, new fortifications were constructed in the city by the Tīmūrids (as stated above) and completed in 799/1396-7. In 808/1405-6 Iskandar b. ʿUmar Shaykh came to Yazd and made further additions to the fort and the wall and added a moat (Aḥmad b. Ḥusayn al-Kātib, 92).

In due course Shāh Rukh [*q.v.*] became Tīmūr's successor. Governors were appointed over Yazd. The most notable of them was the *amīr* Djalāl al-Dīn Čaḳmāḳ, who held office from *ca.* 831/1427-8 until 850/1446-7 and gave Yazd a period of peace. He and his wife Bībī Fāṭima and son Amīr Shams al-Dīn Muḥammad Mīrak erected many buildings, religious and secular, in Yazd and the neighbourhood and constituted many *awḳāf* for them. Among them was the new Friday mosque in the Lower Dahūk quarter, which was richly endowed by Amīr Čaḳmāḳ. It was begun in 840/1436-7 and completed by Bībī Fāṭima in the following year. In the neighbourhood of the mosque a *khānaḳāh*, a caravanserai, a *ḥammām*, a cistern, a *ḳannādkhāna* (confectioner's shop) and a bazaar were built and a well dug (Djaʿfar b. Muḥammad, 79-80; Aḥmad b. Ḥusayn al-Kātib, 97, 99; Mufīd, i, 170 ff. The *waḳf-nāma* of the New Friday Mosque, dated 849/1445, is printed as an annex to the *Djāmiʿ-i mufīdī*, iii, 871-84). Bībī Fāṭima, among her other benefactions, made a mill outside Yazd in the Sar Āb-i Naw quarter near Dihābād. It was, so Aḥmad b. Ḥusayn al-Kātib states, continually in operation and the nearest mill to the city (98). Encouraged no doubt by the stability provided by the government of Amīr Čaḳmāḳ, a number of buildings were also made by the inhabitants of Yazd in the city and the neighbourhood.

By 857/1453 control over most of Persia, including Yazd, had passed to the Ḳara Ḳoyunlu [*q.v.*], who were succeeded by the Aḳ Ḳoyunlu [*q.v.*]. In 858/1454 there was, according to Muḥammad Mufīd, severe famine in Yazd, heavy loss of life and an outbreak of plague owing to the movement of troops and the dispersal of the population (i, 204-6). The severe floods of 860/1456 caused further damage. Troop movements and struggles between the contending parties for supremacy continued in Yazd and the neighbourhood as elsewhere in Persia throughout the second half of the 9th/15th century. This does not appear to have caused major disruption in the economic life of Yazd, for the Venetians in the late 9th/15th century recognised Yazd as an important manufacturing centre (Josafa Barbaro and Ambrogio Contarini, *Travels to Tana and Persia*, Hakluyt Soc., first series, no. 49, London 1873, 60, 72-4, 127). Trade with India, which was to become important in the Ṣafawid period, was also probably increasing at this time.

In 907/1501 Ismāʿīl Ṣafawī [see ISMĀʿĪL] was crowned in Tabrīz, but Yazd was not taken until 909/1504. Thereafter, Yazd became a province of the empire, with governors and officials appointed over it and taxation levied by the central government. For most of the Ṣafawid period, Yazd was under the *khāṣṣa* administration, i.e. directly administered by the central government under a *wazīr* sent by the central government to the province (K.M. Röhrborn, *Provinzen und Zentralgewalt Persiens im 16. und 17. Jahrhundert*, Berlin 1966, 122-6). Few of these were local men, though there were exceptions, for example Mīrzā Khalīl Allāh, whose family came from Bihābād, one of the villages of Bāfḳ, and who became *wazīr* of Yazd in 1034/1624-5 (Mufīd, iii, 190 ff.). Officials who came from outside did not, on the whole, spend their wealth in Yazd on local development nor did they arouse the confidence or loyalty of the local population. Trade flourished and local patriotism continued, but in the absence of strong local government it did not express itself in local development to the extent that had been the case under the Kākūyids, the Atabegs of Yazd, the Muẓaffarids and Amīr Čaḳmāḳ.

During the reign of Shāh Sulṭān Ḥusayn there was a weakening of royal authority and a decline in security. In 1110/1698-9 Baluch tribesmen ravaged Kirmān and almost reached Yazd (L. Lockhart, *The fall of the Safavī dynasty*, Cambridge 1958, 46). Revolts broke out in various parts of the empire. Finally, Maḥmūd b. Mīr Ways set out from Ḳandahār to attack the Ṣafawids. After an abortive siege of Kirmān, he advanced on Yazd, the outskirts of which he reached in February 1722. The population shut the gates of the city and prepared for a siege. The Afghāns were driven back with some loss of life and so Maḥmūd abandoned the siege and marched on Iṣfahān (*ibid.*, 131-2) and in 1134/1722 the Persian forces were defeated at Gulnābād. During the brief period of Afghān domination Yazd was besieged several times.

With the defeat of Ashraf by Nādir Ḳulī Khān (later Nādir Shāh Afshār [*q.v.*]) in 1142/1729, ʿĪsā Khān, the Afghān governor of Yazd, fled. Nādir was now in control of a wide area including Yazd (Mīrzā Mihdī Astarābādī, *Djahāngushā-yi nādirī*, ed. Sayyid ʿAbd Allāh Anwar, Tehran AHS 1341/1962, 118). In due course, Afshārid governors were appointed over Yazd (Muḥammad Djaʿfar, 282 ff.). It may be that Yazd benefited from Nādir Shāh's exemption of taxation, which he granted to Persia after his successful Indian campaign in 1151-2/1738-9 (as Muḥammad Djaʿfar alleges), but the remission was soon to be rescinded and exactions were renewed; 4,000 *tūmāns* were demanded from Yazd (284). This provoked an uprising. Meanwhile, news of the assassination of Nādir in 1160/1747 arrived. The Afshārid governor of Yazd fled (285-6). ʿĀdil Shāh, Nādir's nephew, then sent ʿAlam Khān to Yazd as governor. His extortionate conduct provoked a rebellion (289), and in 1161/1748 Muḥammad Taḳī Khān Bāfḳī set out from Bāfḳ for Yazd with 70 riflemen (302). After a siege of three or four days, ʿAlam Khān escaped from the fortress and fled to Khurāsān (304-5). Muḥammad Taḳī Khān, having made himself master of Yazd, received a *raḳam* from Shāh Ḳulī Mīrzā, Nādir's grandson, who had succeeded Nādir's nephews, ʿĀdil Shāh and Ibrāhīm (307). He held office for 52 years, first under the Afshārs, then under the Zands and finally under the Ḳādjārs. He was succeeded by his sons ʿAlī Naḳī, who held office for seven years, and ʿAbd al-Raḥīm Khān, who was dismissed and succeeded by a series of Ḳādjār governors. During Muḥammad Taḳī Khān's government Yazd experienced a new period of development and prosperity, an increase of population, and the bringing into operation of new *ḳanāts*, the creation of gardens and charitable buildings and the institution of *awḳāf* for their upkeep (308 ff., 326, 340-83, 463). His son ʿAlī Naḳī also made many benefactions in Yazd and the neighbourhood (493 ff.). However, during these years Yazd was not entirely immune from military expeditions by the contending parties and their demands for revenue. The precise course of events is, however, somewhat confused and the sources vary in their accounts. After Karīm Khān had made himself master of most of Persia by 1179/1765, his officials came to Yazd to collect taxes (415). His successors attacked Yazd several times and demanded revenue.

The Ḳādjārs, like the Ṣafawids, sent governors to Yazd. Many of them were Ḳādjār princes. The appointment of a local man to the government was the exception. The most notable of the prince governors was Muḥammad Walī Mīrzā, who held office from 1821 to 1828. He constructed a number of *ḳanāts* and repaired others (Muḥammad Dja'far, 705 ff.), and founded charitable buildings (606, 620 ff.). During his governorate, trade prospered (680). Of Nāṣir al-Dīn Shāh's twenty-four governors, Muḥammad Khān Walī, who held office twice (1863-70 and 1876-80), was the most outstanding.

During the Russo-Persian war of 1826-8 disorder spread throughout the country. In Yazd 'Abd al-Riḍā Khān b. Muḥammad Taḳī Khān Bāfḳī headed a revolt during the absence of the governor Muḥammad Walī Mīrzā in Tehran, and turned out the latter's family and entourage from Yazd. Ḥusayn 'Alī Mīrzā Shudjā' al-Salṭana was appointed governor of Kirmān, which had also revolted, and of Yazd, and was sent to restore order. He laid siege to Yazd but failed to reduce it and set out for Kirmān. In 1830 he renewed operations against Yazd without permission from Tehran. 'Abbās Mīrzā [*q.v.*] was accordingly sent from Tehran to restore order. He succeeded and proceeded to Kirmān. After he was summoned back to Tehran, 'Abd al-Riḍā Khān and Shafī' Khān of Rāwar (who had been in rebellion in Kirmān) joined forces and renewed their rebellion but were defeated and captured by government forces. 'Abd al-Riḍā Khān was taken to Tehran, and was handed over to Muḥammad Walī Mīrzā and killed in revenge for his action in turning out Muḥammad Walī Mīrzā's family and entourage from Yazd ('Abd al-Ghafūr Ṭāhirī, *Tārīkh-i Yazd*, included in his *Tadhkira-yi Djalālī*, in Afshār, *Yazd-nāma*, i, 177-237, at 206 ff.).

On the death of Muḥammad Shāh in 1834, there was renewed rioting in Yazd, but it subsided after Nāṣir al-Dīn established himself on the throne in Tehran. In 1840 Āḳā Khān Maḥallātī [see AGHĀ KHĀN] mounted a rebellion in Kirmān and Yazd. In 1848, there was a Bābī uprising. Riots took place against the Tobacco Régie in 1890, against the Belgian customs administration set up in 1899, and against new tariff charges in 1903. In the latter part of the 19th century, modernisation began. There was an increase in the number of schools and of the local press. In the 20th century there was strong support for the Constitutional Movement and the formation of *andjumans* in its support [see DUSTŪR. iv; DJAM'IYYA. iii]. Under the Electoral Law, Yazd had the right to send two deputies to the National Assembly. Some of those elected played an outstanding part in the deliberations of the Assembly.

Yazd, throughout the Islamic period, maintained its distinctive character. Strong local patriotism was a marked feature. It is to be ascribed, in part at least, to the remoteness of Yazd and its situation on the edge of the Central Desert of Persia, and the fact that it did not lie in the path of invaders. More than any other city in Persia, it owed its development and growth to *ḳanāts*. Without them it could not have existed, still less have sustained a civilisation that, from time to time, attained a high degree of excellence. It shared the religion, language and literary heritage of its neighbours, but "because of its utter dependence upon *ḳanāts* it developed a strong personality of its own, different from that of other cities; and its people acquired a stability and firmness of character, self-confidence and assurance which distinguished them from the inhabitants of other cities. They had a special sense of identity with the soil. They tended it with love and care and made it flourish with the water of its *qanāts*, which they brought out with skill and toil from the depths of the earth" (Lambton, *The qanats of Yazd*, 35). Until the development of modern communications, the spasmodic nature of the control exercised by the successive governments that ruled in Persia enabled local culture to flourish, and the fact that Yazd was situated on one of the trade routes from the Persian Gulf to the interior of Persia and Central Asia undergirded its economic development.

Bibliography (in addition to references given in the article): Īradj Afshār, *Awḳāf-i rashīdī dar Yazd*, in *FIZ*, xvi-xvii, AHS 1349/1970-1; idem, *Yazd-nāma*, vol. ii, forthcoming; 'Abd al-Ḥusayn Āyatī, *Ātishkada-yi yazdān yā tārīkh-i Yazd*, AHS 1317/1938-9; H.W. Bailey, *Yazd*, in *BSOS*, viii (1936), 335-61 (also in idem, *Opera minora*, ed. M. Nawābī, Shīrāz 1981, i, 309-36); M.E. Bonine, *From qanāt to kort: traditional irrigation terminology*, in *Iran*, xx (1982), 145-59; idem, *Yazd, and its hinterland: a central place system of dominance in the Central Iranian plateau*, Marburg/Lahn 1980; Mary Boyce, *Some aspects of local farming in a Zoroastrian village of Yazd*, in *Persica*, iv (1969), 121-40; eadem, *The Zoroastrian houses of Yazd*, in C.E. Bosworth (ed.), *Iran and Islam*, Edinburgh 1971, 125-48; D.M. Centlivres, *Une communauté des poitiers en Iran. Le centre de Maybod (Yazd)*, Wiesbaden 1971; Captain Christie, *Abstract of Captain Christie's Journal*, in H. Pottinger, *Travels in Beloochistan and Sinde*, London 1816, 403-23; Muḥammad Taḳī Dānish-pazhūh and Afshār (eds.), *Djāmi' al-khayrāt*, in *FIZ*, ix (AHS 1345/1966-7), revised ed. in Afshār, *Yādigārhā-yi Yazd*, ii, Tehran AHS 1354/1975-6, 391-557; E. Ehlers, *Iran. Grundzüge einer geographischen Landeskunde*, Darmstadt 1980; E. Ehlers and M. Momeni, *Religiöse Stiftungen und Stadtentwicklung: das Beispiel Taft/Zentraliran*, in *Erdkunde*, xliii (1989), 16-26; *Government of India. Gazetteer of Persia*, ii, Simla 1905, under *Yezd*; *Historical gazetteer of Iran*, ed. L.W. Adamec, i, Graz 1976, 688-96; Renata Holod, *The monuments of Yazd 1300-1450*, unpublished diss. Harvard Univ. 1972; A.K.S. Lambton, *Landlord and peasant in Persia*, repr. Oxford 1969; eadem, *The Persian land reform 1962-1966*, Oxford 1969; L. Lockhart, *Persian cities*, London 1960; Aṣghar Mahdavī *et alii*, *Preliminary report on the handweavers of Yazd*, Univ. of Tehran, Murdād 1342/1962; Isabel Miller, *Local history in ninth/fifteenth century Yazd: the Tārīkh-i Jadīd-i Yazd*, in *Iran*, xxvii (1989), 75-80; Mu'īn al-Dīn Naṭanzī, *Muntakhab al-tawārīkh*, ed. J. Aubin, Tehran AHS 1336/1957; Akbar Ḳalamsiyāh, *Tārīkh-i sālshumārī-i Yazd*, Tehran AHS 1370/1981-2; idem, *Yazd dar safar-nāmahā*, Yazd AHS 1373/1994-5; Rashīd al-Dīn Faḍl Allāh Hamadānī, *Wakf-nāma-yi rab'-i rashīdī*, ed. M. Mīnuwī and Afshār, Tehran 1977-8; R.B. Serjeant, *Islamic textiles, material for a history up to the Mongol conquest*, Beirut 1972; M. Siroux, *Le Masdjid-é Djum'a de Yezd-i Khast*, in *BIFAO*, Cairo, xliv (1947), 119-76; I. Stchoukine, *Une Khamseh de Nizami illustrée à Yazd entre 1142 et 1144*, in *Arts asiatiques*, xii (1965), 3-20; idem, *La peinture à Yazd au milieu du XVe siècle*, in *Syria*, xl (1963), 139-45; idem, *La peinture à Yazd au début du XVe siècle*, in *Syria*, xliii (1966), 99-104; Tādj al-Dīn Ḥasan b. Shihāb Yazdī, *Djāmi' al-tawārīkh-i ḥasanī*, ed. M. Hosein Modarresi Tabātabā' and Iradj Afshar, Karachi 1987. Afshār in *Yazd-nāma*, i, 49-140, gives a detailed description of Persian sources for the history of

Yazd, some, but not all of which, are mentioned and utilised in the article.

(ANN K.S. LAMBTON)

YAZDADJIRD III, in Persian, Yazdagird, son of Shahriyār, son of Khusraw Aparwīz, the last Sāsānid emperor (reigned from the end of 632 or beginning of 633 till his murder at Marw in 31/651). It was in the early years of his reign that the Arabs started raiding into ʿIrāḳ, defeating the Sāsānid army at al-Ḳādisiyya [*q.v.*] and in other battles, capturing the capital Ctesiphon-al-Madāʾin in March 637, and gradually extending across the Iranian plateau to occupy the whole of Persia. For further details, see SĀSĀNIDS, at Vol. IX, 80.

YAZDĪ, MĪRZĀ MUḤAMMAD (Farrukhī) (1889-1939), Persian poet, journalist, and one-time *Madjlis* deputy in the post-Constitutional and early Pahlawī periods. Born of modest origins in Yazd, he spent a few years in the traditional *maktab*s and briefly attended a school founded in Yazd by English missionaries. The Constitutional movement (1905-9) attracted him to politics, and his "patriotic *musammaṭ*" poem of 1909 so enraged Ḍirgham al-Dawla Ḳashḳāʾī, the governor of Yazd, that he ordered the sewing together of his lips, an event which provoked protests in Yazd and Tehran. In late 1910 Farrukhī left Yazd for the capital, where he published his poems in the radical press such as *Āzādī* ("Liberty"). When Ḍirgham al-Dawla fell from office, the new governor of Yazd, Ḥādjdj Fakhr al-Mulk, made some compensation to Farrukhī.

During the First World War, Farrukhī was among those journalists who, in November 1915, left Tehran for Ḳum and the *Kumīta-yi Difāʿ-i Millī* ("Committee of National Defence"), which later moved to Kirmānshāh where it founded the *Dawlat-i Muwaḳḳat-i Millī* ("Provisional National Government") under the premiership of Niẓām al-Salṭana Māfī. When the Russians took over western Persia and suppressed the Provisional Government, Farrukhī went to ʿIrāḳ where he was detained by the British army. He escaped from Baghdād and eventually returned to Persia, where he was briefly taken into Russian custody on suspicion of being a British agent.

In 1919 Farrukhī opposed the premier Wuthūḳ al-Dawla's [*q.v.*] ill-fated agreement with the British, and again in 1921 he opposed the coup d'état of Riḍā Khān (the future Riḍā Shāh Pahlawī). Subsequently he founded his newspaper *Ṭūfān* ("Storm"), of which the first issue appeared on 26 August 1921. Publication of *Ṭūfān* was often interrupted, and during the eight years of its life, the paper was suppressed more than fifteen times; yet each time it was banned, Farrukhī would publish in other periodicals such as *Sitāra-yi Shark* ("Star of the East"), *Paykār* ("Battle"), *Ḳiyām* ("Uprising"), and *Talīʿa-yi Āʾīna-yi Afkār* ("The Primal Mirror of Ideas").

In 8 March 1922 Farrukhī and a group of opposition journalists took refuge in the Soviet embassy in Tehran, but were persuaded to leave by Riḍā Khān, then the Minister of War. When, on 28 October 1923, Riḍā Khān became Prime Minister, Farrukhī expressed his opposition, but in the same period favoured Riḍā Khān's short-lived inclination towards forming a republic in Persia. In 1927, as the editor of *Ṭūfān*, and in view of his political sympathies, Farrukhī was invited to Moscow to attend the tenth anniversary of the Russian Revolution. In 1928 he was elected as a deputy from Yazd to the seventh *Madjlis*, where he joined the *frāksīyun-i aḳalliyyat* ("minority faction"), traditionally a coalition of socialists. In the seventh session, however, that lobby consisted only of Farrukhī and Maḥmūd-Riḍā Ṭulūʿ, a deputy and fellow-journalist from Lāhīdjān. From March 1928 Farrukhī also published a weekly edition of *Ṭūfān* with a historical and literary orientation.

At the end of the seventh *Madjlis* (October 1930), and with no more parliamentary privilege to rely on, Farrukhī left Tehran for Moscow and then for Berlin. There he wrote against the political situation in Persia in the periodical *Paykār* ("Battle") founded in 1930 by Persian activists in Berlin, and then in his own *Nihḍat* ("Movement"), until both were suppressed and Farrukhī was ordered to leave Germany. Meanwhile, ʿAbd al-Ḥusayn Taymurtāsh, minister of the royal court, met with Farrukhī in Berlin and assured him of his safety if he returned to Persia. Farrukhī agreed, and in 1932 returned, but after a year of indigence in Tehran, he was arrested on a civil charge for debts owed to the paper supplier of *Ṭūfān*.

Although the initial charges were of a civil nature, his political agitation inside the prison, expressed at times in passionate poems, soon turned him into a political prisoner and led to his constant transfer from one gaol to another: his term was extended first to 27 months, then to 30 months, and finally to three years. In the end he was transferred from Ḳaṣr prison to the infamous "clinic" at the police headquarters in Tehran, where on 18 October 1939 he was murdered by the prison's notorious medical practitioner, *Pizishk* ("physician") Aḥmad Aḥmadī, by air injection.

Although in poetical style Farrukhī observed the traditional patterns of prosody (*ʿarūḍ*), the content of his poems focussed on contemporary social and political topics. Major themes of the Constitutional period, such as patriotism and the quest for civil liberties and social justice, were expressed in his verse, hence his contribution to the composition of political *ghazal* is noteworthy. In Persian poetry, he can be placed in the long tradition of the poetry of protest against arbitrary rule.

Bibliography: For a fuller biography, see Ali Gheissari, *Poetry and politics of Farrokhi Yazdi*, in *Iranian Studies*, xxvi/1-2 (1993), 33-50. For Farrukhī's poems and biography, see *Dīwān-i Farrukhī Yazdī*, ed. with introd. by Ḥusayn Makkī, 7Tehran 1984. For his career in journalism, see Muḥammad Ṣadr Hāshimī, *Tārīkh-i Djarāʾid wa madjallāt-i Īrān*, Iṣfahān 1950-3, ii, 87-91, iii, 168-86; and for his period in prison, Dj. Djawān, *Muḥammad Farrukhī Yazdī (1267-1318)*, repr. in Muḥammad Gulbun and Yūsuf Sharīfī (eds.), *Muḥākima-yi muḥākimagarān (ʿĀmilān-i kushtār-i Sayyīd Ḥasan Mudarris, Farrukhī Yazdī, Taḳī Arrānī, Sardār Asʿad Bakhtiyārī)*, Tehran 1984, 157-83.

(ALI GHEISSARI)

YAZĪD (I) B. **MUʿĀWIYA**, the second Umayyad caliph (*r.* 60-4/680-3). He was named as his successor by his father [see MUʿĀWIYA I]. His mother was Maysūn, a sister of the Kalbī leader Ibn Baḥdal [see ḤASSĀN B. MĀLIK]. The Banū Kalb [see KALB B. WABARA] were strong in the southern regions of Syria, and Muʿāwiya appointed Yazīd as his successor in preference to an older half-brother, ʿAbd Allāh, born of a Ḳurashī mother. Yazīd's *kunya*, Abū Khālid, refers to one of his own younger sons [see KHĀLID B. YAZĪD]. During his father's caliphate, Yazīd commanded expeditions (*ṣawāʾif*, see ṢĀʾIFA. 1.) against the Byzantines and participated in an attack upon Constantinople (in 49/669 or 50/670) that is mentioned in both Muslim and non-Muslim sources. He is also named as having led the *ḥādjdj* in various years. Reports make him less than 40 at the time of his death at Ḥuwwārīn [*q.v.*] in Rabīʿ I 64/November

683, variant dates and other details being given about his birth. He had apparently nominated his eldest son Muʿāwiya [see MUʿĀWIYA B. YAZĪD] as his succcessor, but the latter received only limited acceptance as caliph and died within months.

Yazīd's caliphate marked the beginning of the crisis, commonly referred to as *fitna* [*q.v.*], during which the Umayyads came close to losing the caliphate. Eventually they re-established their hold on the institution but in the person of Marwān I b. al-Ḥakam [*q.v.*] and his descendants rather than a representative of the Sufyānid branch of the family, to which Yazīd belonged. Following his father's death in Radjab 60/April 680, Yazīd was faced with the continuing refusal of ʿAbd Allāh b. al-Zubayr and al-Ḥusayn b. ʿAlī b. Abī Ṭālib [*q.vv.*], both then in Medina, to give him allegiance. Most of the reports about his caliphate concern his attempts to overcome their opposition and that of others. Al-Ḥusayn's attempt to make good his own claim to the caliphate ended in his death at the hands of a force sent by Yazīd's governor of ʿIrāḳ, ʿUbayd Allāh b. Ziyād [*q.v.*] at Karbalāʾ in Muḥarram 61/October 680. Ibn al-Zubayr's opposition led, in 64/683-4, to the siege of Mecca, where he had taken refuge, and to the bombardment of the town with catapults (*madjānīḳ*) by an army sent by Yazīd. During the siege, the Kaʿba was damaged by fire, but there are variant accounts of how exactly that happened and who was responsible for it. Yazīd's army, initially commanded by Muslim b. ʿUḳba al-Murrī [*q.v.*], had been raised in 63/683 primarily in response to the actions of the people of Medina, who had thrown off their allegiance to Yazīd, expelled those Umayyads living there and, according to some accounts, established contacts with Ibn al-Zubayr. After defeating the Medinans at the battle on the Ḥarra [*q.v.*], Muslim entered (and, it is said, sacked) the town, and compelled a number of its prominent men to return to their allegiance to Yazīd. He then set off for Mecca, intending to force Ibn al-Zubayr, who had received the support of others of Yazīd's opponents, including several Khāridjites [*q.v.*], to submit. On the way, Muslim died and his position as leader of the Syrian army was assumed by al-Ḥuṣayn b. Numayr al-Sakūnī [*q.v.*]. He it was who commanded the siege of Mecca. News of Yazīd's death in Syria reached him while the siege was in progress, and after fruitless negotiations with Ibn al-Zubayr he withdrew the army back to Syria.

In broad terms, Yazīd seems to have continued the form of rule developed by his father which depended on the relationship between the caliph, his governors and the tribal notables (*ashrāf*) in the provinces. His governor of ʿIrāḳ, ʿUbayd Allāh, was the son of Muʿāwiya's governor there, Ziyād. A Christian, Sardjūn, who had been prominent in the administration of Muʿāwiya, continued to be influential under Yazīd. (Robert Hoyland has questioned whether this Sardjūn, sometimes called "the *mawlā* of Muʿāwiya", sometimes "of Yazīd", and variously described as Yazīd's drinking companion or as *ṣāḥib amrihi*, was the father of John of Damascus, as Lammens and others have assumed.) The custom of receiving delegations (*wufūd* [*q.v.*]) from the provinces at the court to win them over with gifts and flattery, institutionalised by his father, was less successful when Yazīd attempted to use it to head off the opposition of the Medinans. The image of Muʿāwiya as operating more like a tribal *shaykh* than a traditional Middle Eastern despot, perhaps embodied in the well-known description of him by Theophanes as a "chief governor" (*protosymboulos*), also seems applicable to Yazīd and may be behind the eulogy of him in the *Byzantine-Arab chronicle of 741*: "he never... sought glory for himself by virtue of his royal rank but lived as a citizen along with all the common people" (*nullam unquam... sibi regalis fastigii causa gloriam appetivit, sed communis cum omnibus civiliter vixit*; tr. Hoyland). The breakdown, beginning under Yazīd, of the system of government used more successfully by Muʿāwiya, may be ascribed partly to difficulties associated with the succession to the caliphate but more fundamentally to the changes taking place in the structure of the conquest society, analysed by Patricia Crone in her *Slaves on horses*.

Yazīd is often credited with the creation of the new *djund* of Ḳinnasrīn [*q.v.*]. For an extensive discussion of that and other incidental information about him and his caliphate (his reduction of the tribute to be paid by the Christians from Nadjrān [*q.v.*], his suppression of privileges enjoyed by the Samaritans, his involvement in irrigation work, etc.), see Henri Lammens, *Le Califat de Yazîd Ier*. For a Sāsānid type coin dated "year 1 of Yazīd", see the article by Mochiri cited in the *Bibl.*

As the caliph under whom the Prophet's grandson al-Ḥusayn was killed, the two holy cities of Arabia attacked, and the Kaʿba set on fire, and as the one who benefited from an appointment presented in Muslim tradition as a crucial stage in the corruption of the caliphate into a kingship, it is not surprising that the tradition generally is hostile to Yazīd. There are frequent mentions of his penchant for drinking, singing girls, sexual licentiousness, hunting, playing with his tame monkey, and other such things which show him as a frivolous libertine. As James Lindsay has illustrated, however, some of the traditional material emphasises Yazīd's closeness to the generation of the Prophet and his role in the transmission of Muslim tradition, and there are different versions of an apocalyptic tradition ascribed to ʿAbd Allāh b. ʿAmr b. al-ʿĀṣ [*q.v.*] which includes "the King of the Holy Land (*malik al-arḍ al-muḳaddasa*)", Muʿāwiya, and his son in a line of righteous *khalīfas*. Even Ibn ʿAbbās is said to have given Yazīd the *bayʿa* and to have spoken favourably of him and his father.

The glowing account of Yazīd in the *Byzantine-Arab chronicle* was cited by both Wellhausen and Lammens, who presented him, at least after his accession to the caliphate, as an able and worthy ruler traduced by opponents who hypocritically appealed to religion. More recently, Lindsay has argued that Ibn ʿAsākir's biography of Yazīd, although unable to ignore entirely the unfavourable traditional material, seeks to present as sympathetic an image as possible in order to convey a moral and religious message of its own. If that interpretation is valid, it is nevertheless true that the Damascene scholar was able to draw on some favourable material already existing in the tradition. It is probably impossible on the basis of the evidence available to make a judgement about Yazīd's ability or his character. Any attempt to do so, however, must seek to understand both the historical situation in which he ruled (insofar as that can be recreated) and the nature of the Muslim historical tradition which crystallised after the Umayyads had been overthrown.

Bibliography: 1. Sources. Ṭabarī, index (ii, 216-429 for his caliphate, Eng. tr. I.K.A. Howard, *The History of al-Ṭabarī*, xix, *The caliphate of Yazīd b. Muʿawiyah*, Albany 1990); Balādhurī, *Ansāb al-ashrāf*, ivb, 1-74; idem, *Futūḥ*, index; Yaʿḳūbī, ii, 281-302; Masʿūdī, *Murūdj*, v, 126-68, ed. Pellat, iii, 247-70; *Aghānī, Tables*, Index I, s.v.; Ibn ʿAsākir, *Taʾrīkh Madīnat Dimashk*, ed. al-ʿAmrī, 65 vols., Beirut 1998, lxv, 394-412; Dhahabī, *Taʾrīkh al-Islām*, ed. Tadmurī, Beirut 1990, s.a. 60-3 (the notice on Yazīd in the necrology of the 7th *ṭabaka*, 269-75, has a useful bibl. provided by the editor).

2. Studies. J. Wellhausen, *Das arabische Reich und sein Sturz*, Berlin 1902, 88-105, Eng. tr. *The Arab kingdom and its fall*, Calcutta 1927, 140-69; H. Lammens, *Études sur le règne du calife omaiyade Moʿâwia Ier*, Paris 1908, index (extracted from *MFOB*, i-iii); idem, *Le califat de Yazîd Ier*, in *MFOB*, iv (1910), 233-312, v (1911), 79-267, v/2 (1912), 589-724, vi (1913), 401-92, vii (1921), 211-44; P. Crone, *Slaves on horses*, Cambridge 1980, esp. 29-36; eadem and M. Hinds, *God's Caliph*, Cambridge 1986, 7, 130; M.I. Mochiri, *A Sasanian-style coin of Yazīd b. Muʿāwiya*, in *JRAS* (1982), 137-41; J.E. Lindsay, *Caliphal and moral exemplar? ʿAlī Ibn ʿAsākir's portrait of Yazīd b. Muʿāwiya*, in *Isl.*, lxxiv (1997), 250-78; R. Hoyland, *Seeing Islam as others saw it*, Princeton 1997, index.

(G.R. Hawting)

YAZĪD (II) b. **ʿABD** al-**MALIK**, the ninth Umayyad caliph, *r.* 101-5/720-4. He was born in Damascus *ca.* 71/690-1. His mother was ʿĀtika bt. Yazīd b. Muʿāwiya, and he was named after his Sufyānī grandfather, the caliph Yazīd I. Thus Yazīd II joined in his person the Marwānid and the Sufyānid branches of the Umayyad family, making him a natural candidate for the succession. Like most other Umayyad princes, he appears to have travelled outside of Syria only to the Ḥidjāz. Also, he seems to have received neither administrative nor military preparation for ruling, although Sulaymān b. ʿAbd al-Malik designated him his second successor in 99/717. Thus he was crown prince under ʿUmar II and then became caliph on ʿUmar's death on 21 Radjab 101/9 February 720. He probably spent most of his reign at Damascus or on his estates in the *djund* of al-Urdunn [*q.v.*], where he died at Irbid on 24 Shaʿbān 105/26 January 724.

At the beginning of his reign, Yazīd II faced a serious if short-lived revolt in ʿIrāḳ led by Yazīd b. al-Muhallab al-Azdī (101-2/720). This rebellion expressed the continuing dissatisfaction of the Yamanī elements in ʿIrāḳ with Umayyad rule and elicited from the Umayyads a harsh reaction against the Yamanīs there. In order to strengthen the Umayyad position in ʿIrāḳ, Yazīd II reintroduced Syrian troops and tended to rely on the Muḍar tribal elements against the Yamanīs, as shown by his appointment of his Djazīran-domiciled brother Maslama b. ʿAbd al-Malik (102-3/720-1 [*q.v.*]) and the latter's protégé, the Muḍarī Djazīran ʿUmar b. Hubayra al-Fazārī (103-6/721-5 [see ibn hubayra]), to be governors of the East.

His apparent tilt toward the Muḍar has caused Yazīd II often to be portrayed as a pro-Muḍar and anti-Yaman extremist, but such a judgement is unfair, as he actually tried to balance the conflicting groups, just as other Umayyad rulers did. Certainly, Yazīd retained the confidence of the Syrian Yamanīs, for he gave them the governorships of the other two great provinces, the West and also al-Djazīra, including Ādharbāydjān and Armenia. Before joining it to the province of the East, he even appointed a Syrian Yamanī general as governor of Khurāsān.

On the other hand, relations between the Syrians and others, especially the Kūfans, remained poor. Also, Yazīd II alienated the non-Arab Muslims or *mawālī* by seeking to annul the reforms of ʿUmar II that favoured them. Thus in Sind, Khurāsān, North Africa and Spain, attempts were made to reimpose the *djizya* that had recently been removed from the *mawālī*. These attempts seem not to have been very successful. In Khurāsān, the new policy, applied under Saʿīd b. ʿAmr al-Harashī (103-4/721-2), contributed to revolts and wars that continued for twenty years and played a considerable rôle in the Umayyads' later downfall. In North Africa, Yazīd II's governor Yazīd b. Abī Muslim was assassinated almost immediately for trying to implement such a policy (102/720), leading to a loss of caliphal authority and prestige and presaging the great North African revolt under Hishām (from 122/740).

On the frontiers, Yazīd II resumed the traditional Umayyad policy of military expansion after its brief suspension by ʿUmar II. During Yazīd's short reign, campaigns were carried out against the Franks in France and Sardinia, the Byzantines in Sicily and Anatolia, the Khazars in the Caucasus and the Turks in Transoxania. Furthermore, ideological struggle against other religions intensified, especially against Christian icon worship, with Yazīd II's issuance of an iconoclastic decree commanding the destruction of all images of humans and animals throughout the caliphate (103-4/721-3), a step that preceded and anticipated the Byzantine emperor Leo III's iconoclasm.

Despite the momentous events of his reign, both mediaeval sources and modern scholars often portray Yazīd II as a frivolous slave to passion, especially to his singing girls Ḥabāba and Sallāma. While there is no doubt that he cultivated poetry, like the other Umayyads, and had a refined artistic taste, the picture of his lack of seriousness and of Ḥabāba's influence has been much exaggerated.

Bibliography: 1. Sources. Khalīfa b. Khayyāṭ, *Taʾrīkh*, ed. al-ʿUmarī, Beirut 1397/1977, 321-36; Balādhurī, *Ansāb al-ashrāf*, ms. Reisülküttap, no. 598, 179-229; Yaʿḳūbī, *Taʾrīkh*, Beirut 1379/1960, ii, 310-5; Ṭabarī, ii, 1372-1466, Eng. tr. D.S. Powers, *The History of al-Ṭabarī*, xxiv, *The empire in transition*, Albany 1989, 105-96; *Aghānī*[1], viii, 6-15, xiii, 154-66 = *Aghānī*[3], viii, 339-51, xv, 122-45; *al-ʿUyūn wa 'l-hadāʾiḳ*, iii, ed. de Goeje and de Jong, Leiden 1869, 64-81.

2. Studies. J. Wellhausen, *The Arab kingdom and its fall*, Calcutta 1927, 312-25; M.A. Shaban, *Islamic history. A new interpretation, A.D. 600-750 (A.H. 132)*, Cambridge 1971, 130-7; Ḥusayn ʿAṭwān, *Sīrat al-Walīd b. Yazīd*, Cairo 1980, 14-47 = *al-Walīd b. Yazīd, ʿarḍ wa-naḳd*, Beirut 1401/1981, 15-60 (but missing a passage); G.R. Hawting, *The first dynasty of Islam. The Umayyad caliphate A.D. 661-750*, London and Sydney 1986, index; K. Blankinship, *The end of the Jihād state*, Albany 1994, index.

(H. Lammens-[Kh.Y. Blankinship])

YAZĪD (III) b. al-**WALĪD** (I) b. ʿAbd al-Malik b. Marwān I, Umayyad caliph for approximately six months in 126/744. He is known in tradition as al-Nāḳiṣ (the Depriver, or the Deficient; various explanations are given). He is said to have boasted that through his mother, one of Yazdagird III's granddaughters captured in Transoxania, he had inherited both Sāsānid and Byzantine blood. He has a reputation for asceticism and piety, and was accepted as a righteous Imām not only by his immediate supporters but by some later theorists too (al-Ḳāḍī ʿAbd al-Djabbār, *Mughnī*, Cairo n.d., xx/2, 150).

Yazīd obtained the caliphate by overthrowing his cousin and predecessor, al-Walīd II b. Yazīd II [*q.v.*], an act which initiated the third "civil war" in Islam [see fitna]. The main support for Yazīd came from the Kalbīs of the region around Damascus, and his short rule promoted Kalbī and Yamanī interests at the expense of Ḳays and Muḍar. He sent the Kalbī Manṣūr b. Djumhūr to ʿIrāḳ to depose the pro-Ḳaysī governor Yūsuf b. ʿUmar al-Thaḳafī [see al-Thaḳafī], but subsequently he made ʿAbd Allāh b. ʿUmar II his governor there.

He is frequently described as a Ḳadarī [see Ḳadariyya] and as supported by the Ghaylāniyya [see Ghaylān al-Dimashḳī]. The conception of the caliphal office put forward in his accession *khuṭba* and in a letter he sent to the ʿIrāḳīs, both of which have been accepted as largely authentic in spite of the variant versions transmitted, was certainly unusual among the Umayyads. As well as promising to right certain abuses with which his Umayyad predecessors had been charged, he appealed to the Book of God and the Sunna of His Prophet, put forward the view that the caliph should be chosen as a result of consultation (*al-amr shūrā*), and offered to stand down if found to fall short himself, so long as he was given the chance to repent. If another could be found who was considered preferable, he would be the first to give him the oath of allegiance.

Yazīd seems to have died of natural causes—according to one report he was a victim of the plague (*al-ṭāʿūn*)—in Dhu 'l-Ḥidjdja 126/September 744, and was succeeded by the equally ephemeral Ibrāhīm b. al-Walīd (I) [*q.v.*].

Bibliography: Ṭabarī, ii, 1825-75, Eng. tr., Carole Hillenbrand, *The History of al-Ṭabarī*, xxvi, *The waning of the Umayyad caliphate*, Albany 1989, 183-244; Balādhurī, *Ansāb al-ashrāf*, 13 vols. ed. Zakkār and Ziriklī, Beirut 1996, ix, 189-97; M.J. de Goeje and P. de Jong (eds.), *Fragmenta historicorum arabicorum*, Leiden 1869-71, i, *al-ʿUyūn wa 'l-ḥadāʾiḳ*, 148-53, and index; Khalīfat b. Khayyāṭ, *Taʾrīkh*, ed. Fawwāz, Beirut 1995, 240-2; Ibn ʿAbd Rabbihi, *ʿIḳd*, ed. Raḥīnī, Beirut 1983, v, 205-9 and index; Dhahabī, *Taʾrīkh al-islām*, ed. Tadmurī, Beirut 1991, vol. covering A.H. 121-40, 14-15, 311-13 (there is no entry for Yazīd III in Ibn ʿAsākir's *Taʾrīkh Dimashk*); J. Wellhausen, *Das arabische Reich und sein Sturz*, Berlin 1902, 226-30, Eng. tr. *The Arab kingdom and its fall*, Calcutta 1927, 366-9; J. van Ess, *Les Qadarites et la Gailānīya de Yazīd III*, in *SI*, xxxi (1970), 269-86; P. Crone, *Slaves on horses*, Cambridge 1980, 46-8; eadem and M. Hinds, *God's caliph*, Cambridge 1986, index; G.R. Hawting, *The first dynasty of Islam*, ²London 2000, 94-6.

(G.R. Hawting)

YAZĪD b. **ABĪ MUSLIM** (Dīnār), Abu 'l-ʿAlāʾ, secretary and governor under the Umayyads. He was a *mawlā*, not by manumission (presumably by conversion), of Thaḳīf [*q.v.*], and foster-brother and secretary, but not *mawlā*, of al-Ḥadjdjādj [*q.v.*] (thus al-Djahshiyārī and al-Djāḥiẓ). He ran the *dīwān al-rasāʾil* for al-Ḥadjdjādj and took charge of the taxes of ʿIrāḳ when the latter died in 95/714, but was dismissed and jailed on Sulaymān's accession in 96/715. His cruelty was so notorious that ʿUmar II reputedly left him in jail, or alternatively sent him home when he joined a summer campaign as a member of the *dīwān*. His pay as secretary was 300 dirhams a month. As a member of the *dīwān* [*al-muḳātila*] he received 2,000 (a year, i.e. *sharaf al-ʿaṭāʾ*), which ʿUmar allegedly reduced to 30 (*sic*, Ibn al-Djawzī, *Sīrat ʿUmar b. ʿAbd al-ʿAzīz*, 88-9, 90; al-Fasawī, *al-Maʿrifa wa 'l-taʾrīkh*, i, 606-7). Yazīd II appointed him to North Africa where he was killed in 102, either for branding his Berber bodyguards with the word *ḥarasī* in alleged imitation of Byzantine practice or for continuing the policy adopted in ʿIrāḳ of repatriating and reimposing the taxes on *dhimmīs* who left their land as converts to Islam. He was rumoured to be a Khāridjite.

Bibliography: Djahshiyārī, *Wuzarāʾ*, ed. al-Saḳḳā, 42-3, 56-5; Djāḥiẓ (attrib.), *al-Burṣān wa 'l-ʿurdjān*, ed. al-Khūlī, 100; Ṭabarī, ii, 1112, 1268, 1282, 1435, iii, 24, 435; Mubarrad, *Kāmil*, ed. Shākir, 546-7, 949, 968; Ibn ʿAbd Rabbih, *ʿIḳd*, ed. Amīn *et alii*, iv, 427; Balādhurī, *Futūḥ*, 231; Ibn ʿIdhārī, i, 48; Khalīfa b. Khayyāṭ, *Taʾrīkh*, ed. Zakkār, 411, 471-2, 485; Ibn Khallikān, ed. ʿAbbās, vi, 309-12 (no. 817).

(Patricia Crone)

YAZĪD b. **ABĪ SUFYĀN** b. Ḥarb b. Umayya, Arab commander of the conquests period, son of the Meccan leader Abū Sufyān [*q.v.*] by his wife Zaynab bt. Nawfal and half-brother of the subsequent caliph Muʿāwiya I [*q.v.*], d. 18/639 without progeny (Ibn Ḳutayba, *Maʿārif*, ed. ʿUkāsha, 344-5).

With his father and brother, he became a Muslim at the conquest of Mecca in 8/630, took part in the ensuing battle of Ḥunayn [*q.v.*] and was one of "those whose hearts are won over", receiving from the Prophet a gift of 100 camels and 40 ounces of silver (Ibn Saʿd, ii/1, 110, vii/2, 127; al-Wāḳidī, iii, 944-5; and see al-Muʾallafa ḳulūbuhum). In Abū Bakr's caliphate, he operated in Palestine with Shuraḥbīl b. Ḥasana and ʿAmr b. al-ʿĀṣ [*q.vv.*], and after the Byzantines were defeated at al-Adjnādayn [*q.v.*] and Damascus fell, he campaigned in the Balḳāʾ [*q.v.*] and captured the citadel at ʿAmmān (14/635). When ʿAmr left Palestine for Egypt, he appointed Yazīd in charge of Syria, but Yazīd died there, in company with many other Arab commanders such as Abū ʿUbayda and Muʿādh b. Djabal, in the notorious "Plague of Emmaus" [see ʿAmwās] in 18/639.

Yazīd is called in later sources "Yazīd al-Khayr", with a good image because of his part in the conquests and the manner of his death, accounted by some authorities as that of a *shahīd* [*q.v.*]

Bibliography: In addition to references given in the article, see Khalīfa b. Khayyāṭ, *Taʾrīkh*, ed. Zakkār, Damascus 1387-8/1967-8, i, 103, 130, 157; Ṭabarī, i, 1827, 2079, 2390, 2397, 2402, 2512, 2516, 25-26; Zubayrī, *Nasab Ḳuraysh*, ed. Lévi-Provençal, 124, 125-6; Ibn Ḥadjar, *Iṣāba*, Cairo 1328/1910, iii, 656-7; Ibn al-Athīr, *Usd*, v, 112-13; F.McG. Donner, *The early Islamic conquests*, Princeton 1981, 114 ff. and index.

(C.E. Bosworth)

YAZĪD b. **DĪNĀR** [see Yazīd b. Abī Muslim].

YAZĪD b. **ḤĀTIM** al-**MUHALLAB** [see Muhallabids. (iv)].

YAZĪD b. Miḳsam **IBN ḌABBA** al-Thaḳafī (*fl.* first half of the 2nd/8th century). Arab poet, member of the circle around the caliph al-Walīd b. Yazīd [*q.v.*].

He was a *mawlā* of the tribe of Thaḳīf in al-Ṭāʾif; according to the philologist al-Aṣmaʿī [*q.v.*], who knew him, his Arabic was nonetheless pure (*Aghānī*, vii, 103). Since his father died when he was still young, he became known as Ibn Ḍabba after his mother, who as the dry nurse of the children of al-Mughīra b. Shuʿba [*q.v.*] and of his son ʿUrwa was a woman of some standing. He seems to have befriended al-Walīd early on, since on account of this friendship he was snubbed by the caliph Hishām (who disliked his nephew) at the latter's enthronisation in 105/724, whereupon he retired to al-Ṭāʾif, there to live on funds provided by al-Walīd. He returned to Damascus at al-Walīd's accession in 125/743 and apparently stayed in his entourage. He may have returned to al-Ṭāʾif after al-Walīd's death, since al-Aṣmaʿī (b. possibly in 123/741) met him there.

Of his allegedly voluminous poetic output ("one thousand *ḳaṣīdas*", according to the local patriotism of the Ṭā'ifites, *Aghānī*³, vii, 103), besides a few fragments only three longish poems have been preserved: a complaint about Hishām's behaviour, a congratulatory panegyric to al-Walīd on becoming caliph and an impromptu description of al-Walīd's horse, at the latter's behest, on the occasion of a successful hunt (all of them included in the *Aghānī* article on him). The narrative connected with the descriptive poem (mentioned in Hamilton, *Walid*, 128, but without Yazīd's name) gives us a fascinating glimpse into the "handling" of poetry: after applauding Yazīd's feat, al-Walīd asks him to add an amatory prelude (*tashbīb*) to his poem—which would turn it into a complete *ḳaṣīda*—and give it (the prelude, not the entire poem) to two well-known singers to set to music. Which he does.

The complaint poem against Hishām is composed in the more traditional metre *wāfir musaddas*, whereas the ode to al-Walīd is in the short and more "modern" metre *hazadj murabbaʿ*, probably more to the taste of the addressee. The Hishām poem displays a strange rhyme: *-Cnā*, where *-nā* is the pronominal ending "we" of the perfect, and *-C-* is represented 20 times by the consonant /d/ and three times by another consonant. So we have to consider it a *nūniyya* with a strong tendency for *luzūm mā lā yalzam* [*q.v.*]. Al-Aṣmaʿī remarks (*loc. cit.*) that he sought out difficult rhymes (*ḳawāfī muʿtāṣa*).

Most of the material gathered on the *Aghānī* is traced back by *isnād* to Yazīd's grandson, ʿAbd al-ʿAẓīm b. ʿAbd Allāh.

Bibliography: Abū Ḥātim al-Sidjistānī, *Suʾālāt Abī Ḥātim al-Sidjistānī li 'l-Aṣmaʿī wa-radduhu ʿalayhi Fuḥūlat al-shuʿarāʾ*, ed. Muḥ. ʿAwda Salāma Abū Djarī [?], Cairo 1414/1994, 58; *Aghānī*³, vii, 95-103; Sezgin, *GAS*, ii, 432; R.W. Hamilton, *Walid and his friends. An Umayyad tragedy*, Oxford 1988.

(W.P. Heinrichs)

YAZĪD b. al-**MUHALLAB** [see muhallabids. (i)].

YAZĪD b. **ZURAYʿ**, Abū Muʿāwiya al-Baṣrī, traditionist of Baṣra, b. 101/720 and d. in Baṣra Shawwāl 182/Nov.-Dec. 798. His father had been governor of al-Ubulla [*q.v.*], presumably under the later Umayyads. He is described as the outstanding *muḥaddith* of Baṣra in his time, a *thiḳa* and *ḥudjdja*, and was the teacher of the historian and biographer Khalīfa b. Khayyāṭ [see ibn khayyāṭ]. Ibn Saʿd says that Yazīd was a supporter of the ʿUthmāniyya [*q.v.*].

Bibliography: Ibn Saʿd, vii/2, 44; Ibn Ḥadjar, *Tahdhīb*, xi, 325-8; Ziriklī, *Aʿlām*², ix, 235.

(Ed.)

YAZĪDĪ, Yazīdiyya, the name of a mainly Kurdish-speaking group whose communal identity is defined by their distinctive religious tradition.

Appellations and definitions. The Kurdish appellation generally used by the community itself is *Ēzdī*, with a variant *Ēzīdī*. Most Western scholars now hold that the word derives from the name of Yazīd b. Muʿāwiya [*q.v.*]; a derivation from Old Iranian *yazata*, Middle Persian *yazad* "divine being", was once widely accepted and is still preferred by many Yazīdīs. Popular etymologies include a derivation of the term from *ez dā*, which is understood to mean "I (i.e. God) created". In the Yazīdī hymns (*ḳawl*, see below), some of whose terminology goes back to the early stages of the history of Yazīdism, the community is occasionally referred to as "the Sunna" (*Sinnat*). Other appellations are *Ṣuḥbatiyya* "those who claim discipleship", "those who belong to the circle of disciples [of Shaykh ʿAdī]" and *Dāsinī* or *Dāsin*, originally perhaps the name of an influential Yazīdī tribe. The Yazīdīs are sometimes referred to by outsiders as "devil-worshippers". Their worship of the Peacock Angel (*Ṭāʾūs-ē Malak* or *Malak Ṭāʾūs*), whom some non-Yazīdīs associate with the devil, and their extreme veneration for ʿAdī b. Musāfir [*q.v.*], were contributory factors in a process that caused the Yazīdīs to become alienated from the Islamic community. Most modern Yazīdīs emphatically reject any connection between their religion and Islam.

Numbers and territories. No reliable data are available as to the size of the various Yazīdī communities. Estimates of the total number of Yazīdīs vary from 200,000 or less, to over a million; a conservative estimate would seem to be around 240,000. The largest group of Yazīdīs (perhaps 120,000) now live in ʿIrāḳ. There is one community in the Shaykhān region northeast of Mawṣil; this area comprises the valley of Lālish, the religious centre of Yazīdism, Bāʿadhrā, the seat of its leader (Mīr, see below), and the traditional centre of Yazīdī learning, the twin villages of Baʿshīḳa and Baḥzānē. The second Yazīdī community in ʿIrāḳ is found in the area of Djabal Sindjār [*q.v.*] to the west of Mawṣil. The number of Yazīdīs in Transcaucasia is estimated at 60,000; most of these live in the Republic of Armenia, with a smaller group in Georgia. In Syria there are some 15,000 Yazīdīs, with communities in the Kurd Dāgh region and in the Syrian Djazīra. In Turkey, small remnants of the once large Yazīdī community still live in the south-east [see ṭūr ʿabdīn. 4. Languages]. In the 1980s most Yazīdīs from Turkey found refuge from religious persecution in Western Europe, notably Germany, where the number of Yazīdīs is estimated at 20,000 to 40,000. Persistent reports about the existence of a Yazīdī community in western Iran have not so far been corroborated.

Language and origins. All known Yazīdī communities speak a form of Northern Kurdish [see kurds, kurdistān. v.]; the first language of the inhabitants of Baʿshīḳa and Baḥzānē is Arabic, but they use Kurdish as the language of their religious tradition. Many Yazīdīs regard themselves as Kurds but others, especially in Armenia and in the European diaspora, insist on being considered as a separate ethnic group.

Aspects of Yazīdī culture. Pre-modern Yazīdī society was largely organised along tribal lines. This is still the case in some communities, but elsewhere the importance of tribal institutions is much reduced. Traditionally, it was forbidden for most Yazīdīs to learn to read and write, and until recently most of Yazīdī culture was transmitted orally. Another characteristic of Yazīdī society is its division into hereditary endogamous classes or "castes".

Early history. A movement known as the Yazīdiyya, which sympathised retrospectively with the Umayyad caliphs and in particular with Yazīd b. Muʿāwiya, was active in the Kurdish mountains before Shaykh ʿAdī b. Musāfir, who was of Umayyad descent, settled there some time before 505/1111. At the same time, some Kurdish tribes in these areas still adhered to a faith which is described as "Magian" and was presumably of Iranian origin. Shaykh ʿAdī founded a Ṣūfī order, the ʿAdawiyya, whose centre in the Kurdish areas was the valley of Lālish, where his tomb later continued to be venerated by his followers. The ʿAdawiyya had a following outside Kurdistān, but by the time of Shaykh ʿAdī's successor Ḥasan b. ʿAdī [see ʿadī b. musāfir], the Kurdish group appears to have acquired some characteristics which distinguished them from other ʿAdawīs. The group's peculiar beliefs and observances increasingly alienated it from the

surrounding Muslim population; the first major conflict, which widened the rift, took place in 817/1414.
The appellation "Yazīdī", which was already known
locally, presumably came to be associated with the
group on account of <u>Shaykh</u> 'Adī's Umayyad origins.

Powerful Kurdish tribes joined the followers of
<u>Shaykh</u> 'Adī, and during the first centuries after his
death these played a prominent role in local politics.
This power later decreased and from the 16th century onwards a long succession of persecutions characterised the community's history. In the 19th century
some Yazīdī tribes sought refuge in Christian Armenia
and Georgia. The latter half of the 20th century saw
large group of Yazīdīs from Turkey seeking sanctuary in Western Europe, followed by Yazīdī immigrants from 'Irāḳ.

The community's own account of its early history
comprises legends explaining its origin and exceptional
ontological status (the Yazīdīs are said to have been
engendered by Adam alone, without Eve), and tales
about <u>Shaykh</u> 'Adī's arrival among the Kurds, his
miraculous deeds and his associations with some of
his contemporaries; the latter accounts are held to
explain the origin of the various lineages of <u>Shaykh</u>s
and Pīrs (see below).

Religion. Although most modern Yazīdīs deny any
links with Islam, their religious textual tradition reflects
the syncretistic origins of their faith. Theology and
mythology, particularly the cosmogony, show traces of
a non-Islamic tradition which may be of ancient
Iranian origin. Religious vocabulary and imagery, on
the other hand, largely derive from Ṣūfism. While
Yazīdīs have some characteristic beliefs, mythology,
religious observance and acceptance of the obligations
arising from a complex social system play at least as
important a role in their religious life.

(a) *Beliefs.* Yazīdīs believe in one God, who created
the world but is held to have entrusted it to seven
archangels, the "Seven Mysteries" (*Haft surr*), whose
leader is the Peacock Angel. Yazīdīs themselves do
not admit the objective existence of good and evil,
but whatever befalls the world—including what others
might call evil—is attributed in Yazīdism to *Ṭāʾūs-ē
Malak*. While Yazīdīs reject claims that their greatest
Archangel is identical with the devil (<u>Shayṭān</u>), the strict
taboo on the use of words associated with the latter
suggests an awareness of some connection between
the two. Some Yazīdīs say that Iblīs [q.v.] has been
forgiven and is once more close to God.

Besides God and the Seven, Yazīdīs venerate a
large number of "holy figures" (<u>khā</u>ṣṣ or *mēr*), some
of whose names correspond to those of early Ṣūfī
saints, whereas others may originally have been local
heroes or early community leaders. Most <u>khā</u>ṣṣ have
special links with a lineage of <u>Shaykh</u>s or Pīrs; they
can be worshipped by means of visits to shrines dedicated to them and by gifts to members of the lineage representing them. Some <u>khā</u>ṣṣ are thought to
have special curative powers; otherwise their individual character and functions are in most cases not
clearly defined.

Both reincarnation (*donādon*, also *kirās gihorrīn* "changing one's shirt") and the existence of heaven and hell
are referred to in Yazīdī texts, and to some extent
in community discourse; some traditions exist which
seek to reconcile these beliefs.

(b) *Myths and legends.* The Yazīdīs have a rich mythology, in which ancient Iranian, Christian and Judaeo-
Islamic elements can be distinguished, and which also
comprises tales that have their origin in community
history or serve to explain Yazīdī observance. Only

a relatively small part of the corpus of Yazīdī myths
and legends has so far been described in Western
sources.

The myth of creation describes how God fashioned
an embryonic form of the universe in the shape of
a pearl, upon which he evoked the Seven Mysteries
and made a Covenant with them, entrusting them
with the control of the world. The Yazīdī cosmogony
has a direct parallel in the tradition of the Ahl-i Ḥaḳḳ
[q.v.], with which Yazīdism has several features in
common, and shows some similarities to the Zoroastrian cosmogony. It has been suggested that the
myth goes back to an ancient western Iranian tradition which was not deeply Zoroastrianised. The theme
of a Flood also figures prominently in Yazīdī accounts
of the origin of the world.

The textual tradition. As literacy was traditionally forbidden to all but a few Yazīdīs, most of their textual tradition has long been transmitted by word of
mouth. This has influenced its character: the style is
rarely abstract, and anecdotes, myths and legends predominate. These can be told in the form of "stories"
(*čīrok*), and they are frequently alluded to in the sacred
hymns (*ḳawl*).

(a) *The Ḳawls.* The Hymns, a large corpus of texts
which is still imperfectly known in the West, represent the Yazīdī counterpart to both the sacred and
the learned traditions of other cultures. Until the
beginning of the 20th century this knowledge is said
to have been taught in a "school" (*maktab*) for Ḳawwāls
in the twin villages of Baʿshīḳa and Baḥzānē.

(b) *The "Sacred Books".* The texts known in the West
as the Yazīdī "Sacred Books", the *Maṣḥaf-ā Ra<u>sh</u>* and
the *Kitēb-ī D̲j̲ilwa*, were probably written down by
non-Yazīdīs on the basis of information deriving from
the teachings of the *Ḳawwāl* school. A series of manuscripts containing these texts, first in Arabic and later
also in Kurdish, came to light in the late 19th and
early 20th centuries, and were sold to Western
researchers and institutions. A long academic debate
concerning the status of these texts has resulted in a
virtual consensus that the written texts do not represent an ancient tradition. The evidence of the *Ḳawls*
suggests, however, that the contents of the texts (though
not the manuscripts) represent a genuine Yazīdī
tradition.

Observance. Prayer in Yazīdism is felt to be a private, individual matter; communal prayer is unknown.
Individual praying habits vary, as do prayer texts.
Tying the "sacred girdle", and on some occasions kissing the neckline of the "sacred shirt" (on both garments, see below), form part of traditional praying
routine. Paying homage to the rising sun by bowing
to it, or kissing the spot where its first rays fall, are
traditional non-verbal acts of worship. Pilgrimages to
the shrines of holy figures and regular visits to one's
<u>Shaykh</u> and Pīr are also important parts of Yazīdī
observance.

Some Yazīdī "taboos" (*mamnūʿāt*) should be observed
by the community as a whole (e.g. the ban on using
words connected with Satan or cursing, wearing blue
clothes, eating certain foods, and polluting earth, air,
water or fire by certain acts), while others concern
only <u>Shaykh</u>s of a certain lineage and their followers.
Observance of taboos is now generally less strict than
in the past.

(a) *Holy places and objects.* Yazīdī villages normally
have a local shrine, which is dedicated to a holy figure and functions as a religious centre. Further shrines,
usually also associated with a <u>khā</u>ṣṣ, are found all over
the territories where Yazīdīs live. The most impor-

tant and holy centre of Yazīdī religious life is the area referred to as "Shaykh ʿAdī" or "Lālish". This sacred part of the Lālish valley, entry to which is marked on one side by a small bridge known as the "Ṣirāṭ Bridge" (*pirra Silāt*), contains shrines dedicated to most of the important holy figures of Yazīdism. Chief among these is the central sanctuary dedicated to Shaykh ʿAdī. Holy places in the area further include a subterranean cave under Shaykh ʿAdī's sanctuary where the water of the "Zamzam" spring bursts from the rock, and a second sacred spring, the *Kāni-yā Sipī* ("White Spring"). One of the mountains surrounding the valley is known as "Mt. ʿArafāt", another as Mishēt (cf. Djabal Mushayṭ, near Medina).

Barāt, little balls of dust from Lālish made with water from the Zamzam spring or the *Ḳāni-yā Sipī*, have great religious significance, and most Yazīdīs carry some of these with them at all times. The *Sandjaḳ*, sacred effigies of the Peacock Angel, traditionally play an important role in Yazīdī observance (see below). There were originally seven of these images, two of which are still known to exist. Garments with religious significance include the *khirḳa*s [*q.v.*] of contemporary Faḳīrs (see below) and of ancient holy figures, the "sacred girdle" (*shutik*), and "sacred shirt" (*kirās*, whose neckline is called *girīvān*), both of which were worn until recently by many religious Yazīdīs. A "sacred cord" (*ristik*) is worn by a few religious dignitaries. A sacred shirt (*sadra*, which has a pocket called *girebān*) and a sacred girdle or cord (*kustī*, which is untied and retied before prayer, cf. above) are also known in Zoroastrianism.

(b) *Rites of passage*. Baptism (*mor kirin*) with holy water from Lālish and male circumcision are practised by most Yazīdīs. Weddings and funerary ceremonies require the services of a Shaykh, a Pīr, and a "Brother (or Sister) of the Hereafter" (see below).

(c) *Festivals*. Yazīdī festivals can be divided into local and general observances. Some of the latter have a counterpart in Islam and follow the lunar calendar, while others follow the "Eastern" calendar (which, in the 20th century, is 13 days behind the Gregorian one).

In the Shaykhān area, the principal local religious feasts are the *ṭawāf* and the arrival of the *Sandjaḳ*. Most villages hold an annual festival (*ṭawāf*) in the name of the *khāṣṣ* to whom their shrine is dedicated. Formerly, groups of Ḳawwāls (see below) and other religious dignitaries toured all the Yazīdī lands at least once a year to display the *Sandjaḳ*, chant *Ḳawls* to the accompaniment of the "sacred" tambourine (*daf*) and flute (*shabāb*), preach a sermon (*mushābat*), distribute holy water, and collect taxes. Such tours, known as *Ṭāʾūs gērran* ("taking the Peacock around"), still take place in Shaykhān and Sindjār.

The Čēlkān tribe, whose ancestral territories are in the Ṭūr ʿAbdīn area [*q.v.*] in Turkey and in the border regions between Turkey and Syria, celebrate a seven-day festival in mid-winter known as *Bātizmiya*, which seems to be associated with the Christian New Year.

Among the movable feasts, some Yazīdīs observe counterparts to two ceremonies of the Muslim Ḥadjdj [*q.v.*], sc. on the sojourn at ʿArafa (which is celebrated on Mt. ʿArafāt at Lālish) and the *ʿĪd al-Aḍḥā* [*q.v.*], and to the *ʿĪd al-Fiṭr* [*q.v.*]. An equivalent to the Islamic *Laylat al-Barāʾa* [see BARĀʾA] is observed at the Sanctuary of Shaykh ʿAdī.

The immovable feasts of Yazīdism include a spring New Year (*Sar-ē Sāl*), and forty-day fasts (*čilla*) around mid-summer and mid-winter, which are kept by some religious leaders. More widely observed is a three-day winter fast, ending with a feast which is associated with the birth of Ēzīd (one of the great holy figures). The most important occasion in the Yazīdī religious year is the seven-day autumn festival known as "Feast of the Assembly" (*Djažn-ā Djamāʿiyya*), for which all those who are able must gather at Lālish. Important elements of the *Djamāʿiyya* celebrations are the *samāʿ* (sessions which include a solemn procession by the chief dignitaries of the faith, and the chanting of *Ḳawls* to the accompaniment of music), the ritual sacrifice of a bull at the shrine of Shaykh Shams (one of the Seven), and a ceremony in which an object known as the "bier of Shaykh ʿAdī" is brought out from the Shrine, solemnly washed, and returned.

Social organisation. The most fundamental division of Yazīdī society is that into three hereditary, endogamous classes or castes: Shaykhs, Pīrs and *murīds* (laymen). The Shaykhs are subdivided into three endogamous branches (Shamsānī, Ādānī and Qātānī), each with several sub-branches. There are forty lineages of Pīrs, most of which may intermarry. The lineages of Shaykhs and Pīrs essentially represent the Seven Mysteries and other holy figures of the Yazīdī tradition.

Every Yazīdī, including Shaykhs and Pīrs, must have a Shaykh and a Pīr. A *murīd*'s relationship with his Shaykh and Pīr is hereditary, and members of each tribe can be affiliated to Shaykhs and Pīrs from certain lineages only. This creates a complex web of social relations and obligations that is made even more intricate by the obligation on each individual to have a "Brother (or Sister) of the Hereafter" (*birā-yē ākhiratē*, *khushk-ā ākhiratē*, usually from a lineage of Shaykhs), a *murabbī* or preceptor (this is now observed only in Northern ʿIrāḳ) and, in the case of males, a *karīf*, an unrelated male on whose knees one has been circumcised and with whom a life-long bond exists.

Membership of three other social groups, the Ḳawwāls, Faḳīrs and Kočaks, is also largely hereditary. The Ḳawwāls are the repositories of Yazīdī learning, who have been trained to recite the *Ḳawls* or to play the sacred instruments. They live at Baʿshīḳa and Baḥzānē, and belong to either of two tribes (Hakkārī or Dumilī). The Faḳīrs, who wear a black *khirḳa* and must lead pious and abstemious lives, now form a more or less closed group; the organisation of the group shows similarities to that of some Ṣūfī *ṭarīḳa*s, however, and membership may originally have been more open. The Kočaks ("little ones"), wear white clothes and are known for their piety. Kočak families come from all three castes; male members of these families often act as "servants" at Lālish, but the term *kočak* is properly used for visionaries, diviners and miracle-workers who are thought to communicate with the "World of the Unseen" (*ʿālam al-ghayb*) [see AL-GHAYB] by means of dreams and trances.

The temporal and spiritual leader of the community is known as the *Mīr* (Prince) of Shaykhān. The *Mīr* and other dignitaries representing the groups described above have a seat on the Yazīdī Religious Council (*Madjlis-a Rūḥānī*), which has considerable powers.

Bibliography: A.H. Layard, *Nineveh and its remains*, London 1849; W.F. Ainsworth, *On the Izedis, or Devil Worshippers*, in *Transactions of the Syro-Egyptian Society* (1855), 1-4; N. Siouffi, *Notice sur le Chéikh 'Adi et la secte des Yézidis*, in *JA*, v (1885), 78-100; J. Menant, *Les Yézidiz, épisodes de l'histoire des adorateurs du diable*, Paris 1892; R. Frank, *Scheich ʿAdî, der grosse Heilige der Jezîdîs*, Berlin 1911; P. Anastase Marie, *La découverte récente des deux livres sacrés des Yézîdis*, in *Anthropos*, vi (1911), 1-39; M. Bittner, *Die Heiligen Bücher der Jeziden oder Teufelsanbeter (Kurdisch und Arabisch)*, Vienna 1913; F. Nau and J. Tfinkdji, *Receuil de textes et de documents sur les Yézidis*, in *ROC*, xx (1915-17), 142-200, 225-75; A. Mingana, *Devil-worshippers; their beliefs and their sacred books*, in *JRAS* (1916), 505-26; idem, *Sacred books of the Yezidis*, in *ibid.* (1921), 117-19; R.H.W. Empson, *The cult of the Peacock Angel*, London 1928; G. Furlani, *Testi religiosi dei Yezidi*, Bologna 1930; M. Guidi, *Origine dei Yazidi e storia religiosa dell'Islam e del dualismo*, in *RSO*, xii (1932), 266-300; R. Lescot, *Enquête sur les Yezidis de Syrie et du Djebel Sinjār*, Beirut 1938; E.S. Drower, *Peacock Angel*, London 1941; Ṣ. al-Dāmlūdjī, *al-Yazīdiyya*, Mawṣil 1949; C.J. Edmonds, *A pilgrimage to Lalish*, London 1967; R.Y. Ebied and M.J.L. Young, *An account of the history and rituals of the Yazīdīs of Mosul*, in *Le Muséon*, lxxxv (1972), 481-522; J. Guest, *Survival among the Kurds. A history of the Yezidis*, London and New York 1993; P.G. Kreyenbroek, *Yezidism. Its background, observances and textual tradition*, Lewiston, etc. 1995; Kh. Djindī, *Nahwa ma'rifat ḥaḳīḳat al-diyāna al-Yazīdiyya*, Uppsala 1998.

(P.G. Kreyenbroek)

al-**YAZĪDĪ**, Abū Muḥammad Yaḥyā b. al-Mubārak b. al-Mughīra al-ʿAdawī al-Baṣrī al-Baghdādī, with the *laḳab* or *shuhra* of al-Yazīdī (so named after Yazīd b. Manṣūr al-Ḥimyarī, d. 165/781, maternal uncle of the caliph al-Mahdī), Ḳurʾān teacher, grammarian, lexicographer, poet and man of letters, d. 202/817-18.

1. Al-Yazīdī, the father.

Born around 128/745-6 in Baṣra (?) as a client of the Banū ʿAdī b. ʿAbd Manāt, he frequented the local philologists, particularly Abū ʿAmr b. al-ʿAlāʾ, Yūnus b. Ḥabīb and al-Khalīl b. Aḥmad [*q.vv.*]. He became the main transmitter of the seven canonical readings or *ḳirāʾāt* [see ḲIRĀʾA and also AL-DIMYĀṬĪ AL-BANNĀʾ] of his teacher Abū ʿAmr and the main antagonist of his "Kūfan" colleague al-Kisāʾī [*q.v.*]. Appointed educator of the sons of his sponsor, Yazīd, whose historical role was as governor of Baṣra, Yemen and Kūfa, al-Yazīdī came into close contact with the court. Hārūn al-Rashīd appointed him teacher of his son al-Maʾmūn, who in turn entrusted his own sons to him. For them, he is said to have composed a *K. al-Mukhtaṣar fi 'l-naḥw*; previously, he had apparently dedicated a *K. fi 'l-lugha* to the Barmakī Djaʿfar b. Yaḥyā [*q.v.*]. Of the works attributed to him starting with the list contained in the *Fihrist*, 50-1, which is probably based on al-Marzubānī [*q.v.*], only "quotations" have been preserved, as commonly happens with this early generation of scholars. Also "lecture notes" [see MUḤAMMAD B. AL-ḤASAN B. DĪNĀR], written down after the session (*ḥalḳa, madjlis*; cf. below I.3), existed and were transmitted further [see MATHAL. iii]. At the age of seventy-four, al-Yazīdī died in 202/817-18 in Khurāsān, probably in Marw, the then residence of al-Maʾmūn. He is said to have been, like some of his descendants, a follower of the Muʿtazila. He is the forefather of the first extended family of scholars in Islam.

Bibliography (on al-Yazīdī and his descendants): 1. Sources. Ibn Ḳutayba, *Maʿārif*, Cairo 1960, 544, 597; Ibn al-Muʿtazz, *Ṭabaḳāt al-shuʿarāʾ*, Cairo 1375/1956, 273-5; Ibn al-Djarrāḥ, *al-Waraḳa*, Cairo 1953, 27-9; Zadjdjādjī, *Madjālis al-ʿulamāʾ*, Kuwait 1962, *passim*; idem, *Amāli 'l-Zadjdjādjī*, Cairo 1382/1962, *passim*; Abu 'l-Ṭayyib al-Lughawī, *Marātib al-naḥwiyyīn*, Cairo 1375/1955, 67, 98; *Aghānī*[3], xx, 215-62; Marzubānī, *al-Muḳtabas* (*Nūr al-ḳabas*), Wiesbaden-Beirut 1964, 80-94 (frequently quoted in G. Makdisi, *The rise of humanism in Classical Islam and the Christian West*, Edinburgh 1990); idem, *Muʿdjam al-shuʿarāʾ*, Cairo 1379/1960, 487-8; *Fihrist*, 50-1, tr. Dodge, 109-11; Sīrāfī, *Akhbār al-naḥwiyyīn al-baṣriyyīn*, Paris-Beirut 1936, *passim*; Azharī, *Tahdhīb al-lugha* (introd.), in *MO*, xiv (1920), 16-17; Zubaydī, *Ṭabaḳāt al-naḥwiyyīn wa 'l-lughawiyyīn*, Cairo 1373/1954, *passim*, [2]Cairo 1393/1973; Tanūkhī, *Taʾrīkh al-ʿUlamāʾ al-naḥwiyyīn*, Riyāḍ 1401/1981, 113-20; al-Khaṭīb al-Baghdādī, *Taʾrīkh Baghdād*, xiv, 146-8; Samʿānī, ed. Ḥaydarābād 1402/1982, xiii, 499-504; Ibn Khayr, *Fahrasa*, Saragossa 1894-5/Baghdād 1382/1963, 67; Ibn al-Anbārī, *Nuzhat al-alibbāʾ*, Cairo 1386/1967, 81-4; Yāḳūt, *Udabāʾ*, vii, 289-90; Ibn al-Athīr, ed. Beirut, vi, 350; idem, *al-Lubāb*, Cairo 1369/1949, iii, 308; Ibn al-Ḳifṭī, *Inbāh al-ruwāt*, Cairo 1393/1973, iv, 25-33; Ibn Khallikān, s.n.; Dhahabī, *al-ʿIbar*, Kuwait 1960, i, 338; idem, *Duwal al-Islām*, [2]Ḥaydarābād 1364/1945, i, 91; idem, *Siyar aʿlām al-nubalāʾ*, Beirut 1402/1982, ix, 562-4; Yāfiʿī, *Mirʾāt al-djanān*, Ḥaydarābād 1338/1919, ii, 3; Ibn al-Djazarī, *Ghāyat al-nihāya fī ṭabaḳāt al-ḳurrāʾ*, Leipzig-Cairo 1352/1933, ii, 375-7; Ibn Taghrībirdī, *al-Nudjūm al-zāhira*, Cairo 1349/1930, ii, 173; Suyūṭī, *Bughya*, 414-15, [2]Cairo 1384/1964, ii, 340; idem, *al-Muzhir*, [4]Cairo 1378/1958, i-ii, index; Ṭāshköprüzāde, *Miftāḥ al-saʿāda*, Cairo n.d. [*ca.* 1968], i-iv, index; Ibn al-ʿImād, *Shadharāt*, ii, 4; Baghdādī, *Khizānat al-adab*, i-iv, Būlāḳ 1299/1881, repr. Beirut 1968, iv, 26-7; Khwānsārī, *Rawḍāt al-djannāt*, Tehran 1367/1948, 743-4; Ismāʿīl Pasha, *Īḍāḥ al-maknūn*, ii, 336; idem, *Hadiyyat al-ʿārifīn*, ii, 513-14.

2. Studies. Brockelmann, I[2], 110-11, S I, 169-70; Sezgin, i, 6, 9, 17, ii, 610-1, viii, 196, 205, ix, 63-4, *Gesamtindices* s.nn. -Yazīdī; R. Sellheim, *Materialien zur arabischen Literaturgeschichte*, i-ii, Wiesbaden-Stuttgart 1976-87, i, 33, 38-9; G. Flügel, *Die grammatischen Schulen der Araber*, Leipzig 1862, 89-92, with genealogy; O. Rescher, *Abriss*, ii, 135-7; M. Fleischhammer, *Die Familie Yazīdī, ihre literarische Wirksamkeit und ihre Stellung am Abbasidenhof*, in *ZDMG*, cxii (1962), 299-308, with genealogy; Sellheim, *al-ʿIlm wa 'l-ʿulamāʾ fī ʿuṣūr al-khulafāʾ*, Beirut 1392/1972, *passim*; idem, *Gelehrtenfamilien im islamischen Mittelalter*, in *Festschrift der Wissenschaftlichen Gesellschaft an der J.W. Goethe-Universität Frankfurt am Main*, Wiesbaden 1981, 431-46; idem, *"Familiennamen" im islamischen Mittelalter-Eine Skizze*, in *Orientalia Suecana*, xxxiii-xxxv (1984-6), 375-84; Kaḥḥāla, *Muʾallifīn*, xiii, 220-1; Ziriklī, *al-Aʿlām*, Beirut 1979, viii, 163; M.ʿA. Mudarris, *Rayḥānat al-adab*, [2]Tabrīz n.d. [*ca.* 1347/1969], vi, 393-5; Dihkhudā, *Lughat-nāma*, s.nn. Yazīdī.

2. The descendants.

From among al-Yazīdī's sons (I) there are six, among his grandsons (II), fifteen, and among his great-grandsons (III), seven, who excelled as philologists, Ḳurʾān readers, traditionists or poets. Their extant verse has been collected, albeit incompletely, and edited by Muḥsin Ghayyāḍ, *Shiʿr al-Yazīdiyyīn*, Nadjaf 1973. Among those who acquired a scholarly reputation, the following four sons should be mentioned: Abū ʿAbd Allāh (I.1) Muḥammad (d. shortly after 214/829 in Egypt; Ghayyāḍ, 93-4); Abū Isḥāḳ (I.2) Ibrāhīm (d. 225/840 in Baghdād; Kaḥḥāla, i, 126-7); Abū ʿAlī (I.3) Ismāʿīl (d. after 275/888-9; Kaḥḥāla, ii, 300); and Abū ʿAbd al-Raḥmān (I.4) ʿAbd Allāh, known as Ibn al-Yazīdī (alive before 207/822; Kaḥḥāla, vi, 139-40).

Like their father, they all stood in a relationship of trust with al-Maʾmūn, some of them even with the rank of privileged companion (*nadīm* [*q.v.*]). Ibrāhīm, together with his nephew Aḥmad (see below II.1), accompanied the caliph on his travels and military campaigns against the Byzantines. None of their numerous works has come down to us as such, except for a fragment of Ibrāhīm's dictionary of homonyms, *Mā 'ttafaḳa lafẓuhu wa 'khtalafa maʿnāhu*; this work once consisted of 700 folios and kept the author busy, according to his own testimony, from the seventeenth year of his life to the sixtieth (Yāḳūt, *Udabā'*, i, 360; al-Ziriklī, *Aʿlām*, Beirut 1979, i, 79; Sezgin, ix, 74). Of Ismāʿīl, we have a *riwāya* of a small *amthāl* book by his teacher Abū Fayd Mu'arridj al-Sadūsī, which was obviously transmitted to him orally. In 263/876 he transmitted it by dictation in the house of the vizier Sulaymān b. Wahb [see WAHB, BANŪ, and MATHAL. iii (1b)]. His elegy on the death, in 275/888-9, of ʿAlī b. Yaḥyā al-Munadjdjim [*q.v.*] yields a *terminus a quo* for his death.

From among al-Yazīdī's grandsons, two sons of (I.1) Muḥammad should be listed: his second son, just mentioned, i.e. Abū Djaʿfar (II.1) Aḥmad (d. shortly before 260/873-4; Yāḳūt, *Udabā'*, ii, 34-5), and his seventh son Abu 'l-ʿAbbās (II.2) Faḍl (d. 278/891; see AL-MUBARRAD). Both are frequently-quoted authorities in the transmission of texts ranging from *ḳirā'a* to *adab*.

This is especially true of the great-grandson Abū ʿAbd Allāh (III.1) Muḥammad b. al-ʿAbbās, the oldest son of (I.1) Muḥammad. He was born in 228/843 or 230/845 and died on 17 Djumādā II 310/12 Oct. 922 (al-Ziriklī, *Aʿlām*, vi, 182). Among his teachers, al-Riyāshī and Thaʿlab have pride of place, the former as a member of the so-called Baṣran, the latter as the head of the so-called Kūfan school. The lost (?) *Ṭabaḳāt al-shuʿarā'* of his great-uncle (I.2) Ismāʿīl (Sezgin, ii, 96; viii, 165-6) and the *Naḳā'iḍ* [*q.v.*] *Djarīr wa 'l-Farazdaḳ*, with the text according to Abū ʿUbayda > Ibn Ḥabīb > al-Sukkarī, are owed to his recension (*riwāya*). His collection of poems (*dīwān*) of al-Ḥādira [*q.v.*] was published in 1858 in Leiden (with a Latin tr.), then again in Rampur 1939 and Cairo 1969 (Sezgin, ii, 213-14). His collection of elegies (*marāthī*) from pre-Islamic and Islamic times, based on the texts of Ibn Ḥabīb and his uncle (II.2) Faḍl, was published at Ḥaydarābād in 1367/1948 under the title *K. al-Amālī* (H. Ritter, in *Oriens*, v [1952], 196, vi [1953], 189n; Sezgin, ii, 84, x, 261). This *K. al-Marāthī*, under this title, was newly published in Damascus and at the same time in Rabat 1991 (diploma thesis of 1985, cf. *Akhbār al-turāth al-ʿarabī*, xxviii [1407/1986], 20). A *riwāya* of the *K. al-Madjālis* of his teacher Thaʿlab can also be traced back to him (*Fihrist*, 74). The *K. Gharīb al-Ḳur'ān wa-tafsīruhu* (Sezgin, viii, 173) of his great-uncle (I.4) ʿAbd Allāh b. Yaḥyā in his *riwāya* was published in Beirut in 1407/1987. His *K. Manāḳib Bani 'l-ʿAbbās* seems not to be extant; neither, unfortunately, is his *K. Akhbār al-Yazīdiyyīn*, the history of his family, which was accessible to the author of the *Aghānī*, Abu 'l-Faradj al-Iṣbahānī (d. after 362/973), al-Marzubānī (d. 384/994) and Ibn al-Nadīm (d. 380/990). Towards the end of his life, the caliph al-Muḳtadir entrusted him with the education of his sons.

Bibliography: Given in the article, and see the *Bibl.* to 1. above. (R. SELLHEIM)

YAZIDJI (T.), lit. "writer, secretary" < Tkish. *yaz-* "write", hence the Turkish equivalent of *kātib*, *dabīr* and *munshī*.

The term was used in Ottoman times for the clerks in the various government departments, such as the treasury, with a *bash yazidji* at their head. It could also be used for the secretaries of high court and military officials, e.g. of the Ḳizlar Aghasi "Chief Eunuch of the Women", who was also, in the 10th/16th century, in charge of the *ewḳāf* for the Ḥaramayn, Mecca and Medina, and other great mosques of the empire [see ḤARAMAYN, at Vol. III, 175b].

Bibliography: Gibb and Bowen, *Islamic society and the West*, i/1, London 1950, 334; Doerfer, *Türkische und mongolische Elemente im Neupersischen*, iv, 67-71 no. 1788. (ED.)

AL-**YĀZIDJĪ**, the name of a famous Lebanese Maronite family from Kafr Shīmā eminent in the Arab literary renaissance (*Nahḍa* [*q.v.*]) of the 19th and early 20th centuries.

1. al-Shaykh Nāṣīf b. ʿAbd Allāh (1800-71), the son of a physician and founder of the family's fame, who although he received no formal education, became a teacher, revered philologist and poet. During the first half of his life he held secretarial positions such as that to the Greek Catholic Patriarch (1816-18). He worked closely with American missionaries whom he assisted in a translation of the Bible, as well as becoming a key member of a society established by them entitled *al-Djamʿiyya al-sūriyya* [see DJAMʿIYYA. i.], a literary and scientific circle set up in 1847 in Beirut to raise cultural awareness. He wrote books, mainly popular school texts, on *bayān* [*q.v.*], syntax and morphology (of which one of the best known is *Djawf al-farā*, a work on syntax written in a verse of approximately 1,000 lines that was probably modeled on Ibn Mālik's [*q.v.*] famous *Alfiyya*). Nāṣīf also wrote on logic and medicine. However, he is probably best known for his poetry and his famous collection of prose *Maḳāmāt* [*q.v.*]. Nāṣīf was essentially a follower of the classical tradition. In his poetry he was influenced by al-Mutanabbī, on whom he prepared his well-known commentary entitled *al-ʿArf al-ṭayyib fī dīwān Abi-'l-Ṭayyib*, edited and published by his son Ibrāhīm in 1882. His predilection for classical works and language might have contributed to the animated dispute between Ibrāhīm and the progressive al-Shidyāḳ [*q.v.*], which appears to have begun when al-Shidyāḳ took offence at one of Nāṣīf's poems. Nāṣīf's apparent reluctance to learn foreign languages is another illustration of his traditional outlook. He wrote three *dīwāns* of poetry and a collection of letters in poetic forms containing correspondence with Arab literary figures, the *Kitāb Fākihat al-nudarā' fī murāsalat al-udabā'* (Beirut 1889). Some of his poetry was religious, as evidenced in the collection of *dīniyyāt* in F. al-Bustānī's *al-Shaykh Nāṣīf al-Yāzidjī: muntakhabāt shiʿriyya* (Beirut 1950), in which he sets out to prove the divinity of Christ. Despite this, his interest in the Arabic language, particularly as a symbol of Arab identity, is an important indication that language rather than religion was the main unifying factor in the Arab world at that time. Nāṣīf's prose writing is best exemplified in his famous collection of *Maḳāmāt*, the *Madjmaʿ al-baḥrayn* (Beirut 1856). By his own admission, he strove in this work to produce something comparable to that of the mediaeval al-Ḥarīrī [*q.v.*] in both form and content. These *maḳāmas* were initially well received in the Arab world and Europe, and were translated into several languages. Although lacking in real originality, this collection re-established the roots of Classical Arabic prose after centuries of stagnation and helped the Arabic language in Lebanon (and elsewhere) to become "a medium of culture and self-expression on an artistic level" (S. Jayyusi, *Trends and movements*, i, 20). Although he was not a moderniser,

he nonetheless played an invaluable role in awakening the national consciousness of the Arabs, as well as being a key figure in the 19th century Arab literary revival.

2. Ibrāhīm (1847-1906) was the second eldest son of Nāṣīf, from whom he received his early education. He became one of the most eminent scholars of his day, spending the first part of his life in Lebanon but then moving to Egypt where he lived until his death. Ibrāhīm was principally a philologist, stylist and lexicographer, but also wrote essays and articles on a wide range of subjects such as astronomy, chemistry, physics and medicine. As a journalist he established and edited three major journals and literary periodicals that, aside from their intellectual value, formed part of his major contribution to the development of printing in the Arab world. As a poet he produced a *dīwān* to express his patriotic fervour, using poetry as a vehicle to arouse nationalistic sentiments in the Arabs and to call them to seek independence from Ottoman rule. He also wrote a number of letters in poetic form to learned friends and literary figures dealing with mainly linguistic themes collected together in his *Rasāʾil al-Yāzidjī* (Cairo 1920). He was a reformer who played a major role in the revival of the Arab linguistic heritage that had laboured under centuries of foreign rule. It was initially through his own journals such as *al-Bayān* (1897-8) and *al-Ḍiyāʾ* (1898-1906) that he was able to convey his strong reformist views on language. It was also in these journals and in those owned by his friend Buṭrus al-Bustānī [see AL-BUSTĀNĪ, in Suppl.] (*al-Djinān*) and his main rival al-Shidyāḳ (*al-Djawāʾib*) that many acrimonious intellectual and personal battles were fought. His serialised articles attacking the standards of Arabic employed by his fellow journalists were published in one of his most famous books, *Lughat al-djarāʾid* (Cairo 1901). In this work, he tried to show the decline in Classical Arabic in the wake of the Ottoman empire. Although he never argued against the need for the Arabic language to adapt to the requirements of the modern age, his reformist ideas were always based on classical, normative principles, often with an intent to "purify". His lexical innovations for foreign concepts were based on Arabic forms, such as the introduction of *minṭād* for "balloon". Moreover, such was his passion for Classical Arabic that he wrote critiques on the *Lisān al-ʿarab*, and al-Bustānī's *al-Muḥīṭ*, two of the most famous Arabic dictionaries. His own dictionary, *al-Farāʾid al-ḥisān min ḳalāʾid al-lisān*, was left unfinished. Ibrāhīm had his critics, of whom the most vociferous were al-Shidyāḳ, Anastās al-Karmalī and Rashīd al-Shartūnī. However, he also had many supporters, especially amongst the al-Bustānī family, who helped to bring him the prestige he acquired. It is also said that he greatly influenced the Lebanese poet Khalīl Muṭrān [*q.v.*] in his mastery of the language. Notable amongst his other scholarly achievements are that he completed, edited and wrote commentaries on some of his father's works, and that he was instrumental in a revised Roman Catholic translation of the Old Testament, which included the Vulgate, into Arabic.

3. Khalīl (1858-89), youngest son of Nāṣīf, produced a varied but limited literary output owing mainly to his early death. His play in verse entitled *al-Murūʾa wa 'l-wafāʾ* (Cairo 1884, 1902), was one of the first original tragedies in Arabic. His anthology of poetry called *Nasamāt al-awrāḳ* (Cairo 1888, 1908) was described by Djurdjī Zaydān as one of the finest *dīwāns* ever written. He also wrote on stylistics, as evidenced in an unpublished work on epistolary style, and contributed to the debate on the status of Classical Arabic *vis-à-vis* colloquial Arabic through his unpublished dictionary on the spoken language, *al-Ṣāliḥ bayn al-ʿāmmī wa 'l-faṣīḥ*. He also subscribed in journals to the common view that the success of the Arab world was dependent on a clear and uniform linguistic strategy. He spent some time in Egypt, where he established a short-lived journal called *Mirʾāt al-sharḳ* before returning to his native Lebanon to teach.

4. Warda (1838-1924), daughter of Nāṣīf, produced mainly poetry which was published in a *dīwān* of about 100 pages (Beirut 1867, 1881; Cairo 1913) entitled *Ḥadīḳat al-ward*. Her poetry consisted principally of elegies (*marāthī*) which reflected the classical tradition more than the contemporary scene (as did the works of her father and brothers). Of more significance, perhaps, is that she was one of the early women writers in Arabic of the 19th century. The esteem in which she was held as a key representative of women in society at that time can be seen in the tribute paid to her by Mayy Ziyāda [*q.v.*] in a lecture published in the journal *al-Muḳtaṭaf* in 1924, in which she acknowledged her as one of a group of geniuses that manifests "the cognitions and emotions of its society", and as a "blessed daughter" of the Arabs (*Opening the gates. A century of Arab feminist writing*, ed. M. Badran and M. Cooke, London 1990, 241; tr. by M. Cooke). A portrait of Warda was donated by the women of Beirut and hung next to those of the great men in the city's public library. She died in Egypt, where she in fact spent most of her life.

5. Ḥabīb (1833-70), eldest son of Nāṣīf, was intellectually active in Beirut literary circles and learned several languages. However, his only recorded work of substance was an unpublished commentary on one of his father's books on prosody and rhyme. He also translated literary works into Arabic.

Bibliography: 1. Nāṣīf. Kaḥḥāla, *Muʿdjam al-muʾallifīn*, Damascus 1961, xiii, 73-4; A. al-Maḳdisī, *al-Funūn al-adabiyya wa-aʿlāmuhā fi 'l-nahḍa al-ʿarabiyya al-ḥaditha*, [5]Beirut 1990, 55-65, 67-107; I.M. Saba, *al-Shaykh Nāṣīf al-Yāzidjī*, [3]Cairo n.d.; P. Sadgrove, art., *al-Yāzidjī*, in *Encyclopedia of Arabic literature*, ed. J.S. Meisami and P. Starkey, ii, London 1998, 812-13; A. Gully, *Arabic linguistic issues and controversies of the late nineteenth and early twentieth centuries*, in *JSS*, xlii (1997), 75-120; S.K. Jayyusi, *Trends and movements in modern Arabic poetry*, ii, Leiden 1977, 19-20; M. Moosa, *The origins of modern Arabic fiction*, [2]Colorado and London 1997, 124-5; M. Sawaie, *Nâṣîf ibn ʿAbdullâh al-Yâzijî*, in *Lexicon grammaticorum: Who's who in the history of world linguistics*, ed. H. Stammerjohann *et al.*, Tübingen 1996, 1035; K. al-Yāzidjī, *Ruwwād al-nahḍa al-adabiyya fī Lubnān al-ḥadīth 1800-1900*, Beirut 1962; Brockelmann, II, 646, S II, 765-6; L. Cheikho, *al-Adab al-ʿarabī fi 'l-karn al-tāsiʿ ʿashar*, [2]Beirut 1924-6, repr. of 1924 ed., ii, 27-35; I. Kratschkowsky, art., *al-Yāzidjī*, in *EI*[1]; Dj. Zaydān, *Tarādjim mashāhīr al-sharḳ*, [3]Beirut 1970, 16; idem, *Taʾrīkh ādāb al-lugha al-ʿarabiyya*, Beirut 1983, repr. of 1910-13 Cairo ed., ii, 598-99; Y.A. Dāghir, *Maṣādir al-dirāsāt al-adabiyya: al-fikr al-ʿarabī al-ḥadīth fī siyar aʿlāmihi*, Beirut 1955, ii, 752-58, Beirut 1972, iii/2, 1411-13; P.D. Ṭarāzī, *Taʾrīkh al-ṣiḥāfa al-ʿarabiyya*, i, Beirut 1913, 82-9; A. Shalaḳ, *al-Nathr al-ʿarabī fī namādhidjihi wa-taṭawwurihi li-ʿaṣray al-nahḍa wa 'l-ḥadīth*, [2]Beirut 1974, 84-5; R. al-Ḳāsim, *Ittidjāhāt al-baḥth al-lughawī al-ḥadīth fi 'l-ʿālam al-ʿarabī*, i, Beirut 1982, 334-5; Ziriklī, *al-Aʿlām*, [3]Beirut 1969, viii, 314.

2. Ibrahim. Shalaḳ, *op. cit.*, 85-6; P. Soueid, *Ibrahim al-Yaziji: l'homme et son oeuvre*, Beirut 1969; Kaḥḥāla, i, 120-21; Ṭarāzī, ii, 88-98; al-Maḳdisī, *op. cit.*, 65; Dj. Zaydān, *Tarādjim*, ii, 144-65; idem, *Ta'rīkh*, ii, 603-4; Sadgrove, in *op. cit.*, ii, 812; A.T. Ḥasanayn. *Dawr al-shāmiyyīn al-muhādjirīn ilā Miṣr fi 'l-nahḍa al-adabiyya al-ḥadītha*, Damascus 1983; I.M. Saba, *al-Shaykh Ibrāhīm al-Yāzidjī (1847-1906)*, Cairo n.d.; Gully, *op. cit., passim*; Brockelmann, II, 646, S II, 766-7; Dāghir, *op. cit.*, ii, 759-63; Kratschkowsky, *loc. cit.*; Cheikho, *op. cit.*, ii, 38-43; Ḳāsim, *op. cit.*, i, 247-56, 286-300; ii, 62; A. al-Shiblī, *al-Shidyāḳ wa 'l-Yāzidjī*, Beirut 1950; Ziriklī, i, 72.

3. Khalīl. al-Maḳdisī, *op. cit.*, 65; Kratschkowsky, *op. cit.*, 1171; Brockelmann, S II, 767; Zaydān, *Ta'rīkh*, ii, 582; idem, *Tarādjim*, ii, 352-60; Ziriklī, ii, 370; Sadgrove, in *op. cit.*, ii, 812-13; Gully, *op. cit.*, 84-5; Cheikho, *op. cit.*, ii, 36-8; Kaḥḥāla, iv, 128-9; Dāghir, *op. cit.*, iii/2, 1411-13.

4. Warda. Dāghir, *op. cit.*, iii/2, 1414-16; al-Maḳdisī, *op. cit.*, 66; Kratschkowsky, *loc. cit.*; Brockelmann, *loc. cit.*; Cheikho, *op. cit.*, ii, 44; Ziriklī, ix, 130; Kaḥḥāla, xiii, 164; J.T. Zeidan, *Arab women novelists. The formative years and beyond*, New York 1995, 56-7; M. Booth, art. *Warda al-Yāzijī*, in Meisami and Starkey (eds.), *op. cit.*, ii, 813.

5. Ḥabīb. Brockelmann, *loc. cit.*, Cheikho, *op. cit.*, ii, 35-36; Kratschkowsky, *loc. cit.*, Dāghir, *op. cit.*, iii/2, 1408-10; Kaḥḥāla, iii, 186. (A.J. Gully)

YAZÎDJÎ-OGHLU, Aḥmed [see bīdjān].

YAZÎDJÎ-OGHLU, or Yazîdjî-zāde, Meḥmed, a venerated religious figure and poet of the first half of the 9th/15th century. He was the son of Yazîdjî (i.e. scribe) Ṣāliḥ b. Süleymān [*q.v.* in Suppl.], who wrote a Turkish *methnewī* on astrology called the *Shemsiyye*. The date of his birth is unknown and its place is uncertain, but may have been Ḳāḍī Köy in the Thracian district of Malḳara [*q.v.*]. After he had gone to Persia and Transoxania to complete his studies, he settled in Gallipoli (Gelibolu). He met Ḥādjdjī Bayrām [*q.v.*], probably whilst the latter was passing through Gelibolu, and became his novice (*murīd*). He spent the period of religious retirement and privation (*čile*) in two small cells hewn into a large rock on the Ḥamza Köyü shore in the Namāzgāh district of Gelibolu. He died in 855/1451 and his grave is outside Gelibolu on the road to Istanbul, with the grave of his brother Aḥmed Bīdjān [*q.v.*] close by it. He enjoyed great veneration through the centuries and his grave became an object of pilgrimage. The former presence of a Yazîdjî-oghlu *tekiyye* [see tekke] in Gelibolu leads to the supposition that he was a (presumably Bayrāmiyye) *sheykh* and had dervish followers, but there is no documentation for this.

He first wrote a prose work in Arabic called *Maghārib al-zamān*. This he later translated into Turkish in verse form, whilst his brother Aḥmed Bīdjān translated it into Turkish prose (his *Enwār el-ʿāshiḳīn*). Yazîdjî-oghlu Meḥmed gave his work the name *el-Risāle el-Muḥammediyye* ("The Muhammedan treatise"), but it is generally known simply as the *Muḥammediyye*. He completed it in late Djumādā II 853/August 1449.

The *Muḥammediyye* is a voluminous didactic religious poem of 9,008 verses. Throughout the work, the monorhyme scheme (in the form of *ḳaṣīdes*, *ghazels*, *terdjīʿ-i bends*, *terkīb-i bends*, *ḳiṭʿas* and *müstezāds*) alternates with the *methnewī* "double rhyme" scheme. About half-a-dozen *ʿarūḍ* [*q.v.*] metres are used, the most frequent being *hazadj* and *ramal*. Although Ṣūfī elements are to be found in this work, its overall approach is quite orthodox. It treats, in accordance with the Ḳur'ān and the *ḥadīth*, of the Creation, the Prophets, the lives of the Prophet Muḥammad and of the caliphs Abū Bakr, ʿUmar, ʿUthmān and ʿAlī, of the Judgement Day and the Resurrection, of Heaven and Hell, but its primary theme is the life and prophethood of Muḥammad. The style is mixed; plain Turkish dominates in the passages composed in shorter metres, whilst more ponderous language is to be found in the passages written in longer metres. The *Muḥammediyye* enjoyed immense popularity through the centuries, as the remarkable number of manuscripts attest (an autograph is to be found under no. 431/a in the Vakıflar Genel Müdürlüğü, Arşiv ve Neşriyat Müdürlüğü Kütüphanesi), and it was printed repeatedly (cf. F. Babinger, in *EI*[1], art. *Yazîdjî-oghlu*).

Of the several commentaries on the *Muḥammediyye*, that by Ismāʿīl Ḥaḳḳî [*q.v.*], *Faraḥ al-rūḥ*, is greatly renowned (first printed Būlāḳ 1252), an earlier *sharḥ* being that by Esīrī (Meḥmed Yūsuf Efendi, d. 1000/1591), which is a prose version in simple language. Several imitative works (*naẓīres*) were also written, for example by Yūsuf-î Bīčāre under the same title (11,690 verses, completed in 913/1507-8; ms. in İstanbul Üniversitesi Kütüphanesi, no. TY 4051). As in the case of the *Wesīlet el-nedjāt* (better known as *Mewlid*) of Süleymān Čelebi [*q.v.*], parts of it were publicly recited, besides being read in private circles in Turkish homes.

The fame of the *Muḥammediyye* extended farther than that of Süleymān Čelebi's *Mewlid*, beyond the boundaries of Anatolia to the Crimea, Kazan, the Bashkirs and to Persia. However, it is not as popular as the *Mewlid* in Turkey today.

Yazîdjî-oghlu Meḥmed also wrote a succinct Arabic *sharḥ* on Muḥyī al-Dīn Ibn al-ʿArabī's [*q.v.*] *Fuṣūṣ al-ḥikam*. Other works attributed to him, such as the *Saltuḳ-nāme* reported by Ewliyā Čelebi [*q.v.*], *Seyāḥat-name*, iii, 366, are no longer extant.

Bibliography: The *tedhkire* of ʿĀshîḳ Čelebi; ʿĀlī, *Künh al-akhbār*, Medjdī, *Terdjeme-yi Shaḳā'iḳ-i nuʿmāniyye*, Istanbul 1269, 127-8; Kātib Čelebi, *Keshf el-ẓunūn*, Istanbul 1270, ii, 1746; Saʿd el-Dīn Efendi, *Tādj el-tewārīkh*, Istanbul 1279, i, 40; *ʿOthmānlî mü'ellifleri*, i, 194-5; Hammer-Purgstall, *GOR*, i, 497, 601; idem, *Geschichte der osmanischen Dichtkunst*, i, 127 ff.; Gibb, *HOP*, i, 389-410; F. Babinger, art. in *EI*[1], s.v.; *IA*, art. s.v., Â. Çelebioğlu and K. Eraslan (with further bibl.); *Yazıcıoğlu Mehmed, "Kitab-ı Muhammediyye"*, ed. Âmil Çelebioğlu, 4 vols. Istanbul [1975] (basically the editor's unpubl. Ph.D. diss., Atatürk Üniversitesi, Erzurum 1971: *Yazıcı-oğlu Mehmed ve Muhammediye'si*); *Başlangıcından günümüze kadar büyük Türk klâsikleri*, ii, Istanbul 1985, 153-5; Atilla Batur, *Yazıcı Salih ve Şemsiyyesi: inceleme, metin*, unpubl. diss., Erciyas Üniversitesi, 1998. (Edith G. Ambros)

al-**YĀZURĪ**, Abū Muḥammad al-Ḥasan (or al-Ḥusayn) b. ʿAlī b. ʿAbd al-Raḥmān, vizier to the Fāṭimids in Egypt 440-50/1050-8 (al-Maḳrīzī, *Ittiʿāẓ*, ii, 203-40; list of his *laḳabs* in L.S. al-Imad, *The Fatimid vizierate, 969-1172*, Berlin 1990, 166; A.F. al-Sayyid, *al-Dawla al-fāṭimiyya, tafsīr djadīd*, Cairo 1996, index at 461).

He was born at Yāzur in Palestine, where his father was *ḳāḍī*, in a Ḥanafī Sunnī family who were the owners of a landed estate. After a Pilgrimage, a piece of the Prophet's Mosque at Medina fell on his shoulder, the presage of a splendid future (Ibn Ẓāfir, *Akhbār al-duwal al-munkaṭiʿa*, ed. Ferré, Cairo 1972, 79-80, with a very detailed biography). He became *ḳāḍī* of Yāzur, then of al-Ramla, from where, after falling out with the governor, he had to flee to Cairo. He entered the service of the great eunuch Rizḳ and became *nāẓir* of the personal *dīwān* of the princess-mother of the caliph al-Mustanṣir [*q.v.*] and then grand *ḳāḍī* of Egypt before succeeding, thanks to Rizḳ's support, Ṣadaḳa b. Yūsuf al-Falāḥī, who had been put to death. (On al-Yāzurī's relations with the rival parties of al-Tustarī and al-Falāḥī, both of Jewish origin, see M. Gil, *A history of Palestine, 634-1099*, Cambridge 1992, 403-4 and index.) Although of Sunnī origin, al-Yāzurī was the first person in Egypt to exercise simultaneously the three supreme offices of the régime, *wazīr, ḳāḍī al-ḳuḍāt* and *dāʿī al-duʿāt*.

Under his vizierate in 448/1056-7, the body of the great Fāṭimid general Anūs̲h̲takīn al-Dizbarī [see *EI²* Index of Proper Names, s.v. Anūs̲h̲tigin al-Duzbarī] was brought from Aleppo, where he had been buried unceremoniously in 433/1042 after his dismissal by Ibn al-D̲j̲ard̲j̲arāʾī [*q.v.*], to Jerusalem, his corpse to lie in glory at the side of former Ṭūlūnid and Ik̲h̲s̲h̲īdid [*q.vv.*] masters of Egypt. It is likely that al-Yāzurī was responsible for this exceptional posthumous act of homage to a great figure in the Fāṭimid state, devoted completely to Syria and unjustly persecuted by a vizier of ʿIrāḳī origin (Th. Bianquis, *Damas et la Syrie sous la domination fāṭimide*, Damascus 1989, ii, 521-3).

The vizier's irascible character and his pretensions led him to pursue an aggressive foreign policy. In 443/1052, al-Yāzurī reproached the Zīrid of Ifrīḳiya al-Muʿizz b. Bādis [*q.v.*] for having placed before his own name, at the end of an official letter to Cairo, the expression *ṣanīʿatuhu* "his creature" and not the time-honoured formula *ʿabduhu* "his slave", thus showing a lack of consideration on the part of this prince towards the vizier. Ibn al-At̲h̲īr, ix, 556, who tells this anecdote, sees nothing wrong in al-Yāzurī's reaction here but considers it that of a parvenu peasant. It was in order to punish the Zīrid that al-Yāzurī is said to have unleashed the Banū Riyāḥ and the Zug̲h̲ba, two components of the Hilāl [*q.v.*], against North Africa, who pillaged Egypt and Tripolitania and who were to became notorious, together with the Banū Sulaym [*q.v.*], in Ifrīḳiya. In fact, the Byzantines had warned Cairo that the Zīrid state had thrown off S̲h̲īʿism and Fāṭimid obedience in favour of a return to Mālikī Sunnism and the k̲h̲uṭba for the ʿAbbāsid caliph in Bag̲h̲dād. The impolite letter was merely the pretext for a rupture announced by the Zīrid coinage issued from 441/1050 onwards.

The end in 449/1057 of the truce between Egypt and Constantinople is partly explicable by the difficulties that all the countries of the eastern Mediterranean littoral were at that time experiencing in securing grain supplies. An agreement provided for an exchange of grain, in time of famine, between Byzantium and Egypt, in favour of the country that was most affected. This arrangement had normally functioned in Egypt's favour at the time of the 447/1055-6 famine, but in 449/1057, the export of cereals was forbidden by the new Byzantine emperor, provoking in reprisal a renewal of Fāṭimid operations in northern Syria (see Bianquis, *op. cit.*, ii, 506 ff.), against Lād̲h̲aḳiyya and then Aleppo. This action was to end in 452/1060, after al-Yāzurī's death, in the definitive loss by the Fāṭimids of northern Syria and in a rapprochement between Byzantium and the new power of the Sald̲j̲ūḳs [*q.v.*], protectors of the ʿAbbāsids.

Finally, breaking Cairo's tradition since the death of the Būyid ʿAḍud al-Dawla [*q.v.*] in 383/972 of Fāṭimid non-intervention to the south and east of al-Raḥba on the middle Euphrates, in order to avoid

conflict with the ʿAbbāsids, al-Yāzurī organised, in concert with the *dāʿī* al-Muʾayyad fi 'l-Dīn, the ill-fated expedition of al-Basāsīrī [*q.v.*] against Bag̲h̲dād, a venture which, after initial success, ended miserably in 451/1060 after al-Yāzurī's death. For Ibn Muyassar (*Ak̲h̲bār Miṣr*, ed. A.F. Sayyid, Cairo 1981, 16, 20-1), the invasion of Fāṭimid Syria by the Turkish G̲h̲uzz [*q.v.*], which followed shortly after the vizier's death, was the direct result of the anti-Sald̲j̲ūḳ provocation by al-Basāsīrī and the permanent depletion of the Fāṭimid treasury after this very costly expedition.

Even in Egypt itself, where he treated the Christians badly, Upper Egypt [see AL-ṢAʿĪD] seems to have slipped partly from his control (J.Cl. Garcin, *Un centre musulman de Haute Égypte médiévale, Ḳūṣ*, Cairo 1976, 91, n. 3).

The arrest of al-Yāzurī, with eight of his accomplices, and then his execution in the *dār al-wizāra* of Tinnīs, is said to have been motivated by several accusations against him. He was allegedly guilty of high treason: whilst supporting al-Basāsīrī, he was at the same time reportedly corresponding with Ṭog̲h̲ril Beg [*q.v.*] and with Ibrāhīm Inal, the latter's brother and enemy, inciting the Sald̲j̲ūḳs to occupy first Syria and then Egypt in order to put an end to the Fāṭimid régime. He was said to have been equally guilty of misappropriation. The riches of his table during the famine of 447/1055-6 are said to have drawn al-Mustanṣir's attention. At a later date, he is said to have sent gold, hidden in coffins, to Palestine, notably for his son K̲h̲aṭīr al-Mulk or for Wafī al-Mulk, his associate in the vizierate and the supreme judicature, at that moment in post at Jerusalem. At the time of al-Yāzurī's arrest, three million dīnārs are said to have been confiscated from him, and his mounts sold for one thousand dīnārs. Al-Nuwayrī, *Nihāyat al-arab*, ms. Dār al-kutub al-miṣriyya, *ʿāmma* 546, vol. xxvi, fol. 19, records that his son K̲h̲aṭīr al-Mulk, having later fallen into penury, earned his bread mending clothes in the mosque of Fuwwa in Upper Egypt.

It is from al-Yāzurī's vizierate that one can date the end of the Fāṭimid empire outside Egypt and the fall of the civil administration which, after the crisis of 457-64/1065-72, became a military régime in which the caliph was placed under the thumb of the commander-in-chief, the *amīr al-d̲j̲uyūs̲h̲* [see WAZĪR. 1(b)].

Bibliography: Given in the article.

(Th. Bianquis)

YEĞANA, ʿALĪ MÜNĪF (1874-1950), Ottoman administrator, deputy, and minister during the constitutional period (1908-18), deputy during the republic, was born in Adana. He graduated from the *Mekteb-i Mülkiyye*, the civil service school in Istanbul where he learned Arabic and Persian, in 1896. There he joined the secret opposition to ʿAbd ül-Hamīd II [*q.v.*] and promised to support the constitutional movement wherever he was posted. ʿAlī Münīf was sent to Gallipoli (1896) and to towns in the Balkans. While he was *ḳāʾim-maḳām* of Köprülü, he permitted the secret Committee of Union and Progress (CUP) (*Ittiḥād ve Teraḳḳī D̲j̲emʿiyyeti* [*q.v.*]) to operate in relative freedom. He met and became friendly with Meḥmed Talʿat [*q.v.*], one of the most important leaders in the CUP.

ʿAlī Münīf supported the constitutional movement when it broke out in Macedonia in June 1908. When elections were held in November, he was elected deputy for Adana and put in charge of the CUP's parliamentary party. But after the failure of the counter-revolution of April 1909, the Committee decided to strengthen its position in the provinces, and such able administrators as ʿAlī Münīf were sent there. He was appointed governor (*wālī*) of Ankara in November 1910, and then of Manāstir in July 1911 where the CUP had its roots. However, in July 1912 the liberal opposition seized power through a military coup d'état. ʿAlī Münīf was dismissed along with other Unionist officials and was forced to work within the CUP. He was elected to the Central Committee, the *Merkez-i ʿUmūmī*, which played a critical role while in opposition. It organised popular meetings during the Balkan War favouring belligerency, and ʿAlī Münīf says that he addressed one such meeting on 21 September 1912.

The CUP recaptured power with the coup d'état of 23 January 1913. ʿAlī Münīf was sent as *wālī* of Aleppo and instructed to appease the nationalists in Syria with concessions recognising the use of Arabic in local education and administration.

When Ṭalʿat became Interior Minister, he appointed ʿAlī Münīf his under secretary. But in September 1915 he was sent to Syria, partly to curb Djemāl Pasha's [*q.v.*] authority and partly to assert Ottoman sovereignty as governor of Mount Lebanon. He replaced Ohannes Kuyumjiyan, a Catholic Armenian, and remained in office until May 1916. On his recall, local notables, both Christian and Muslim, protested to Istanbul, describing ʿAlī Münīf as "just and neutral", and his administration as "honourable and beneficial". But Ṭalʿat wanted ʿAlī Münīf by his side, appointing him Minister of Public Works when he became Grand Vizier in February 1917. He was elected deputy for Aleppo in the by-election of December 1917, and in the same year the CUP arranged his marriage to Sabīḥa Hānim, the granddaughter of Aḥmed Rātib Pasha, a creature of the old régime.

ʿAlī Münīf resigned in October 1918, with the rest of the Ṭalʿat Pasha cabinet, under British pressure, and he was arrested in January 1919 by the sultan's government as a former Unionist. He was imprisoned, tried, and exiled to Malta, returning to Istanbul in April 1921. He joined the nationalist movement, but was suspect as someone with close ties to Ṭalʿat Pasha. Muṣṭafā Kemāl wanted to send him as the Nationalists' representative to Afghānistān, a form of exile. ʿAlī Münīf chose to return to Adana, where he had political roots. He organised resistance to the French occupation of the Čukorova and after the French left, he was elected mayor of Adana. He played an important role in the town's rehabilitation from the ravages of war and in the development of agriculture and irrigation in the Čukorova.

The Republic was founded in October 1923, and ʿAlī Münīf was elected deputy for Mersin and later Seyḥān on the Republican People's Party (RPP) ticket. He kept a low political profile during these years, and this saved him from arrest and trial for involvement in the Izmir conspiracy of former Unionists in 1926. His friend from the *Mülkiyye*, Meḥmed Djāwīd, was hanged. Though he supported the formation of the Free Party led by his friend ʿAlī Fetḥī [Okyar] [*q.v.*], he took care not to join it. In the election that followed he was omitted from the RPP list but was elected as an Independent; he refused to accept election unless he was rehabilitated. He was taken back into the RPP and continued to be elected on its ticket until the first multi-party election of 1946, when he became the oldest member of the new assembly. ʿAlī Münif, who had adopted the surname Yeğana in 1934, died on 3 March 1950, two months before the May election when the RPP lost to the Democrat Party.

Bibliography: Taha Toros, *Ali Münif Bey'in hatiralari*, Istanbul 1996; Mücellitoğlu Ali Çankaya, *Mülkiye tarihi ve mulkiyeliler* ii-iii, n.p. n.d. 317-8; Alaettin Gövsa, *Türk meşhurları ansiklopedisi*, n.p. n.d. [1945], 403. For the political background to ʿAlī Münīf's career before 1908, see E.E. Ramsaur, *The Young Turks*, Princeton 1957; for his relationship with Ṭalʿat Pasha, see Mahmud Kemal İnal, *Osmanlı devrinde son sadri-azamlar*, 14 pts., Istanbul 1940-53, 1909-2040, and Tevfik Cavdar, *Talat Paşa*, Ankara 1984. Information about ʿAlī Münīf's activities in Aleppo and Beirut provided by Professor Hasan Kayalı in personal communications; see his *Arabs and Young Turks. Ottomanism, Arabism, and Islamism in the Ottoman Empire, 1908-1918*, Berkeley 1997; Cemal Kutay, *Siyasi mahkumlar: Malta*, Istanbul 1963; Bilal Şimşir, *Malta surgünleri*, Istanbul 1976.

(Feroz Ahmad)

YEGEN MEḤMED PASHA [see meḥmed pasha, yegen].

YEGEN ʿOTHMĀN PASHA [see ʿothmān pasha, yegen].

YEGEN, WALĪ al-DĪN [see yakan, muḥammad walī al-dīn].

YEMISHDJI ḤASAN PASHA (d. 1012/1603), one of twelve Grand Viziers under Meḥemmed III (1003-12/1595-1603 [*q.v.*]) during the Long War (1593-1606) with the Holy Roman Empire. Albanian in origin, he was raised in the palace system, began service in the Janissaries in 1580, was appointed as Yeñi Čeri Aghasi on the Hungarian battlefields in Shawwāl 1002/June 1594, and became Grand Vizier on 21 Muḥarram 1010/12 July 1601 on the death of his predecessor Dāmād Ibrāhīm Pasha [*q.v.*]. His period as Grand Vizier was punctuated with battlefield service, especially at the restoration of Istolnī Belgrad in 1602, and intrigue, when a rumoured palace coup made him dash to Istanbul in that same year, where his life was spared by the intercession of his protectress Wālide Ṣulṭān Ṣafiyye [*q.v.*]. In a period of chaos and disorder, he is especially noteworthy for greedy ambition, maliciousness and abuse of friend and foe alike, and was one of three of Meḥemmed III's Grand Viziers to be executed, shortly after his dismissal on 27 Rabīʿ II 1012/24 September 1603. He was married to Ibrāhīm Pasha's widow, ʿĀʾishe Sulṭān.

Bibliography: See Orhan F. Köprülü, *İA* art. *Hasan Paşa Yemişçi*, for a detailed account of his career and an extensive bibl.

(Virginia H. Aksan)

YEÑI BĀZĀR, in Turkish "new market", in Serbo-Croat Novi Pazar, denotes both a region, the former "Sandjak of Yeñi Bāzār/Sandžak of Novi Pazar", and a town, now in Yugoslavia, on the Raška river (lat. 43° 09', long. 20° 29' E.).

1. The region. This and Zeta constitute the original heartland of mediaeval Serbia, corresponding largely to the ancient Rascia, and was in mediaeval times very important, as the remains of imposing churches, monasteries and baths there show. The Sandjak (in the Ottoman *wilāyet* of Kosovo till 1912) was an upland region situated between Serbia, Bosnia and Montenegro, of great strategic and military importance, since it assured communications between Bosnia and Rumelia, and prevented a direct link of Serbia with Montenegro and the Adriatic coast. It was part of the Ottoman empire for four centuries (mid-15th century to 1878), then with its western part, the "region of Lim", garrisoned, according to the provisions of the Congress of Berlin, by Austro-Hungarian

troops till it was restored to the Ottomans in 1908. Entered by Serbian and Montenegrin troops in 1912, it was divided amongst these two powers, occupied again by Austria-Hungary in 1915-18, and then became part of Yugoslavia (except during 1941-4 when it was attached to "Greater Albania" under a Fascist Italian protectorate).

2. The town. This was founded *ca.* 1460 by the governor of Sarajevo G̲h̲āzī ʿĪsā Beg [see BOSNA, at Vol. I, 1263a] after the Ottoman conquest of the region *ca.* 1456, and called "New" to distinguish it from the settlement of Pazarište or Trgovište, called in Turkish Eski Bāzār. Thanks to its favourable situation on a plain at the crossroads of important routes between Bosnia and Macedonia, connecting towns like Sarajevo, Ragusa/Dubrovnik, Niš and Istanbul, the town developed rapidly, with a colony of Ragusan merchants apparently attested in 1461 and iron mines in the vicinity; it also served as a concentration-point for military conquests further west and northwest. It was visited and described by many Western travellers [see *EI*[1] art. *Novibazar*, with references to their works], with its apogee in the later 17th century, when Ewliyā Čelebi visited it (1660); he mentions, with some exaggeration, 40-50 *maḥalles*, 23 mosques, 11 *mesd̲j̲ids*, 5 *medreses*, 2 *tekkes*, etc. But this prosperity was ended by the Turco-Austrian wars, with the town devastated by Austrian troops and Serb insurgents in 1689 and again in 1737. A period of anarchy under semi-independent beys, such as the Ferhadagić or Ferhādog̲h̲ullarï followed, aggravated by plague outbreaks. Commerce and agriculture declined, and Novi Pazar became in the 18th century, and even more so in the 19th century, a place of little importance. In such a climate, relations between Muslims and non-Muslims in both the town and the region remained difficult, with the landowning *beys* residing in the towns, to which also came influxes of Muslim *muhād̲j̲irs* [*q.v.*] from Montenegro and Serbia; after 1912, more or less massive emigrations of Muslims back to Turkey took place. The town is said to have had 7,000 inhabitants in 1836, 13,433 in 1913 and 23,000 in 1968. The situation of the remaining Muslims in the town and region has been complicated. Part of these Muslims have settled in adjacent regions, such as Macedonia and Bosnia-Hercegovina, and notably in Sarajevo, where they have recently played an active role in the *Savez Demokratske Akcije* ("Union of Democratic Action") of M. Alija Izetbegović. This has made the identity problems of the Muslims in the Sandžak even more complex, with groups at various times and in various circumstances calling themselves "Muslim Serb", "Musulman", "Sandžaklije" or "Bošnjak".

Bibliography: See, above all, the art. *Novibazar* by Babinger in *EI*[1]; V. Radovanović, *Novi Pazar*, in *Narodna Enciklopedija*, Zagreb 1928, iii, 114-15; and M. Lutovac, *Novi Pazar*, in *Enciklopedija Jugoslavije*, vi, Zagreb 1965, 309-10; as well as the detailed monograph of M. Maletić (ed.), *Novi Pazar i okolina*, Belgrade 1969. Also Th. Ippen, *Novibazar und Kossovo (Das alte Rascien)*, Vienna 1892; E.J. Cvetić, *Novopazarski Sandžak*, Jagodina 1909, [2]1912; I. Kosančić, *Novo-Pazarski Sandžak i njegov etnički problem*, Belgrade 1912; I. Tomitch, *Les Albanais en Vieille-Serbie et dans le Sandjak de Novi-Bazar*, Paris 1913; G. Gravier, *Le Sandžak de Novi Pazar*, in *Ann. de Géogr.*, xxii/121 (1913), 41-67; K. Isović, *Austro-ugarsko zaposedanje Novopazarskog Sandžaka 1879 godine*, in *Godišnjak Društva Istoričara Bosne i Hercegovine*, ix (Sarajevo 1958), 109-37; V. Šalipurović, *Kulturno-prosvetne i političke organizacije u Raškoj 1903-1912*, Belgrade 1972, Dj. Pejović, *Politika Austro-Ugarske, Italije i Srbije u Novopazarskom Sandžaku 1878-1912, i uvodjenje reformi u Turskoj*, in *Tokovi Revolucije*, iii/1-2 (Belgrade 1973), 1-38; S. Bandžović, *Iseljavanje Muslimana iz Sandžaka*, Sarajevo 1991.

(A. Popovic)

YEÑI ČERI (T.), lit. "new troop", a body of professional infantrymen of the Ottoman empire in its heyday.

1. Origins.

The "new troop", so-called not so much because of the novelty of the idea as because at the time of its introduction by the vizier K̲h̲ayr al-Dīn Pas̲h̲a [see D̲J̲ANDARLÏ] in the 760s/1360s it opposed then-prevailing military traditions cherished by the frontier warriors. The predecessors of Murād I [*q.v.*], rather than maintaining a standing army funded by the central fisc, had relied almost exclusively on the military services provided, on a voluntary basis, by Turkmen horsemen and border raiders (*aḳïnd̲j̲ï*), who served under semi-independent commanders of the frontier districts (*ud̲j̲ beyleri*). Although the recruitment of cash-paid soldiers had plenty of precedents, from the Rūm Seld̲j̲ūḳ *d̲j̲īra-k̲h̲ʷārs* (Bombaci, 345) to the *yaya* [*q.v.*] troops introduced by Sultan Ork̲h̲ān [*q.v.*] after the fall of Iznik in 734/1331 (Kemāl Pas̲h̲a-zāde, *II. Defter*, 47-55), those with a vested interest in the preservation of the old military order saw the "new troop" as a threat. Ottoman sources closest to the events, such as the anonymous chronicles, reflect the considerable unease which the creation of the *yaya* and later the *yeñi-čeri* caused among the frontier forces. Apart from its importance as a means of confronting the military might of neighbouring states, Ottoman sultans increasingly came to regard the possession of a personal army of permanent salaried troops (*k̲h̲āṣṣa ordusu*) as an essential tool in combating centrifugal tendencies among the Turkmen beys. For ceremonial purposes, too, a court-based imperial bodyguard, called by the Ottomans *ḳapu ḳullarï* but closely modelled on the Seld̲j̲ūḳid *g̲h̲ulām-i dargāh* (Bombaci, 349), gained an increased importance from the time of Ork̲h̲ān onwards as the Ottomans sought to set themselves apart from neighbouring Muslim states in Anatolia, whom they regarded as belonging to the petty dynasts or *mulūk al-ṭawāʾif*. It was, however, only after the Ottomans' acquisition of Edirne and the opening up of a new sphere for imperial expansion in Europe after the mid-760s/1360s that the need for a dependable, centralised military organisation began to assert itself more convincingly.

The initial source of recruitment for the corps was the *pend̲j̲ik resmi* or one-fifth treasury tax on war captives whose introduction by the Ottomans is dated in sources of a later period to 764/1363-4 (*Osmanlı kanunnameleri*, in *MTM*, i/2, 325). This practice, despite the outcries by traditionalists and supporters of the early Ottoman status quo, who regarded it as a hateful innovation [see BIDʿA], actually rested on long-standing Islamic precedent [see FAYʾ]. The "newness" of the *yeñi čeri* can also be questioned on the grounds of the duties and functions performed by it in the period immediately after its establishment. Apart from the parallel institution of the *yaya*, another group, the *ʿazab* [*q.v.*], played a very similar battle role to the Janissaries and outnumbered them in the first period by a very considerable margin (Inalcik, *Military expenditure*, 93). The collective presence of the Janissaries in the army of Murād I was limited to no more than 2,000 (Ferīdūn, *Müns̲h̲eʾāt*, i, 114) and it seems that his great-grandson Murād II, who died in 855/1451, was still only capable of mustering a Janissary force of about 3,000 men (Inalcik, *Fatih devri*, 118). Ottoman military practice was not revolutionised by the introduction of the Janissaries, whose only distinction in comparison to the *ʿazab*s was their permanent salaried status. In this early period, as later, the Janissaries' coveted position as *khünkār ḳulu* was a source of jealousy not just among the *akindji* border raiders (see above), but also a source of grievance to the irregular infantry forces whose conditions of service, armaments and fitness for battle were indistinguishable from the Janissaries. The Janissaries' continued use of the cross-bow and related technologies in the late 8th/14th century is attested in a variety of Ottoman sources (see, for example, the *Ḳawānīn-i Yeñičeriyān*, fol. 110b). Because of their limited numbers, sufficient in practical terms for little more than vanguard and imperial escort services, Janissaries did not assume a crucial offensive role in the Ottoman army until they came into their own after the mid-9th/15th century in a more specialised role as troops trained for the assault of fortified places.

The still undeveloped state of Ottoman siege techniques in the early period is apparent from contemporary accounts describing the failed sieges of Kruje in 854/1450 [see AḲ-ḤIṢĀR. 4] and Belgrade in 860/1456. Contemporary sources on the Belgrade campaign concur in their view that, while Ottoman artillery achieved its purpose in penetrating enemy defences, the assault troops failed to capitalise on the opportunity which their success had offered (Mihailović, 107-10, and Tursun Bey, 38-40). By contrast a detailed account of Ottoman success in the Belgrade siege of 927/1521 attributed a leading role to the Janissaries who, by advancing ahead of the artillery, cleared a path for the best placing of the siege guns thereby ensuring the success of the final assault (see events of 1 Ramaḍān/4 August; Tauer, *Histoire de la campagne*, Persian text, fol. 95b [pp. 78-9], French tr., 53). Despite the early textual evidence referring to Janissaries and other Ottoman troops armed with arquebuses (see Petrović, in Parry and Yapp (eds.), *War and society*, 193-4), the most authoritative sources on the state of Ottoman warfare in the mid-9th/15th century, such as the anonymous account of the battle of Varna, give an equal prominence to the continuing use in battle of more "primitive" weapons such as axes, picks and maces (see the index of Inalcik and Oguz (eds.), *Gazavatname, s.v. balta, külünk, topuz*) in addition to the still ubiquitous bow and arrow. Firearms did not assume a dominant place at the centre of Ottoman military provision until the early years of the 10th/16th century (see Inalcik's remarks on the "modernisation" of the Ottoman military order under Sultan Süleymān I (1520-66), in Parry and Yapp, *op. cit.*, 198).

While we do not have enough detailed knowledge of the actual state of Janissary tactics and training during the first century of the corps' existence to reach any conclusive assessments, from the standpoint of its institutional continuity there can be little doubt that the period of the interregnum which followed the Ottomans' defeat by Tīmūr at the battle of Ankara in 804/1402 brought serious disruption to evolving Janissary service traditions. It is thus only from the reign of Meḥemmed II onwards (see below) that we can confidently trace the evolutionary phases through which the corps passed.

2. The evolution of the Janissary corps (1450-1700).

Institutional growth and development

The size of the corps inherited by Meḥemmed II at the time of his second accession in 855/1451 was still modest. Two years later, as a natural consequence of the transfer of his capital to Istanbul and the creation of an extended administrative apparatus, the membership of his standing military corps increased.

From Meḥemmed's time, it became necessary to distinguish Janissary regiments according to the time and circumstances of their creation in three principal subdivisions: the *djemāʿat* or *piyādegān* (later expanded to 101 regiments) for those created before Meḥemmed's reign; the *segbān* [*q.v.* in Suppl.] (*sekbān*), a small corps of keepers of the palace hounds absorbed into the ranks of the Janissaries by Meḥemmed in 855/1451 (later expanded to 34 regiments); and the *bölük* or *agha bölükleri* (numbering 61 regiments), created in a further expansion undertaken early in the reign of Bāyezīd II [*q.v.*]. Hence by the 1480s, when the Janissary institution had already assumed its final structural profile, the "imperial bodyguard" of the early 15th century had grown to 196 infantry regiments each referred to by the generic term *orta* (i.e. "common", "shared" [*q.v.*]), which meant that each had its separate mess arrangements and a chief officer called (in the case of the *agha bölükleri*) the *čorbadji* (i.e. dispenser of the soup [*q.v.*]). These smaller units within the three divisions formed the actual focus of loyalty and identification for the majority of Janissaries, who in a further allusion to the communal nature of their joint enterprise were also referred to as hearthmates (*odjak-eri*; see ODJAḲ). Some Janissary regiments had specialised functions which served to accentuate their sense of distinctiveness and separation. Consequently, when speaking of general institutional developments, it is important to be wary of the obvious but dangerous assumption that the Janissaries always functioned as a monolithic and cohesive whole and remain conscious of the degree to which regimental pride and loyalty motivated Janissary behaviour (see section 4, below).

The expansion of the Janissaries during the reign of Meḥemmed II from about 5,000 to perhaps 10,000 by the end of his reign (Inalcik, *Fatih devri*, 118) reflects the needs of an expanding empire, and if we accept that each of the 61 new regiments introduced by his successor Bāyezīd had, at first, 50 members (*Ḳawānīn-i Yeñičeriyān*, fol. 84a), its increase to roughly 13,000 over less than half a century was formidable. Meḥemmed's decision to try to meet the empire's growing military needs by converting *wakf* and *mülk* lands to *mīrī* ownership and redistributing them as *tīmār* to the growing ranks of the provincial cavalry had met with fierce resistance from established Muslim families in Anatolia. Bāyezīd's alternative plan of expanding the Janissaries had the double advantage of appeasing public opinion while at the same time providing the empire with a professional soldiery on a scale unmatched in either Europe or Asia at the time. Neither the fiscal nor the political implications of Bāyezīd's military policies seems to have attracted much critical notice or caused any of the furore associated with a later phase of the Janissaries' expansion in the closing decades of the 10th/16th century (see below).

During the reign of Sultan Süleymān I [*q.v.*], the corps experienced a period of relative stability, maintaining its size and proportional share of treasury allocations with consistency. While it retained its nominal strength of between 12-13,000 members, in battle deployments the usual figure was more like half that number, as the record of a salary distribution in the field while on campaign in Hungary demonstrates (Topkapı Sarayı Müzesi Arşivi, D. 9619 dated 948/1541, showing the presence in Süleymān's army of

6,362 Janissaries). Ottoman military provision, including levels of Janissary enrolment, was closely linked to realistic assessment of the empire's actual strategic requirements. In the aftermath of the drastic devaluation of the silver *aḳče* [*q.v.*] in 994/1586, the spiralling cost of maintaining the Janissaries caused widespread concern, but the realities of the Ottomans' new initiatives in the Caucasus and their intermittent two-front war with the Habsburgs and Ṣafawids between 1000/1591 and 1015/1606 made a further expansion inevitable. The steepest increase seems to be associated not with remobilisation for war in Hungary after 1000/1591 but earlier, in connection with the twelve-year struggle between 986/1578 and 998/1590 focused on control of Ādharbāydjān and prompted, at least in part, by the Ṣafawids' development of a musket-bearing infantry corps of their own [see ʿABBĀS I; GHULĀM. ii]. By the death of Murād III in 1003/1595, the Janissaries already numbered 25,000 (Muṣṭafā ʿĀlī, *Künh ül-akhbār*, fol. 92b). Throughout the 11th/17th century the Ottomans were intermittently engaged on both the eastern and western fronts, and exceptional mobilisations for major new undertakings such as the Cretan offensive in particular years periodically pushed Janissary enrolments near to the 40,000 mark (Murphey, *Ottoman warfare*, 45, table 3.5). The gist of Ottoman advice literature of the early 11th/17th century in which the *leitmotif* of Janissary "corruption" caused by recruitment irregularities is repeatedly emphasised (see below), does not adequately reflect the Ottomans' real manpower needs and strategic requirements in an epoch dominated by siege warfare. The new military realities had rendered both the ideals and the social structure which had supported the landed timariot class of the past increasingly obsolete.

By the early 11th/17th century, the Janissaries had evolved beyond their former role as an élite troop with principal responsibility for escorting and guarding the imperial presence to a position (together with the also proliferating *djebedji* and *topdju* artillerymen) as the indispensable operational core of the Ottoman army. An indication of the important part played by Janissaries in general military provision is given by the fact that, despite the conclusion of their war with the Habsburgs by treaty in 1015/1606, and despite their having entered into a phase of retrenchment in the east, which was shortly to lead to the abandonment of many of the forward positions occupied during the first phase of their conflict with the Ṣafawids, when ʿAyn-i ʿAlī surveyed the Ottomans' military position in 1018/1609 he found 9,046 *ʿadjemi oghlanlarï* still in the pipeline, most of them destined for induction into one of the 196 standing regiments of the Janissaries (ʿAyn-i ʿAlī, *Ḳawānīn*, 89).

3. The role of the Janissaries in Ottoman politics.

According to Ottoman protocol, the *agha* of the Janissaries' position as the top-ranking officer of the select palace guard called the "officers of the stirrup" [see RIKĀB] required that he remain close to the sultan. Although he maintained a residence of his own called the *agha ḳapusu*, a sprawling complex built on a site overlooking the Golden Horn adjacent to the Süleymāniyye mosque (see Plate IV), by making use of his unrestricted right of private audience with the sultan (*Tewḳīʿī ʿAbd al-Raḥmān Pasha ḳānūnnāmesi*, 524-5), he maintained an exceptionally close personal relationship with the sovereign and served as one of his inner group of advisers both in peacetime and war. The *agha* of the Janissaries also bore a heavy responsibility (along with the Grand Vizier [see ṢADR-I AʿẒAM]) for the maintenance of law and order in the capital. Given the nature of his position as a close aide and confidant of the sultan, the commander of the Janissaries exerted a powerful influence on the government. There is a tendency, apparent in the Ottoman court chronicles, to ascribe a negative role to the Janissaries and to highlight their participation in mutinies and their commission of other acts of intransigence associated especially with the regencies necessitated by the accession of minor sultans in the 11th/17th century [see KÖSEM WĀLIDE] and the obvious breakdown of Janissary discipline in the 18th century (see below). However, it bears remembering that even the most powerful, determined and militarily active sultans such as Meḥemmed II, Selīm II and Süleymān I experienced considerable difficulties in dictating terms to their *ḳullar*.

The role of the Janissaries as caretakers and guardians of the sovereign authority during regencies and interregna is attested in all periods of Ottoman history. One striking example is the role played by the Janissaries in securing the pseudo-succession of Ḳorḳud which lasted for seventeen days until the safe arrival of his father Bāyezīd from Amasya in 886/1481 [see ḲORḲUD B. BĀYEZĪD; and Tursun Bey, 64]. The sponsorship of the Janissaries was essential to sultans in securing their succession to the throne. This was particularly true of the period of Ottoman history up to the accession of Meḥemmed III in 1003/1595 since, until that time, all candidates for the succession resided not in the capital but in their princely governorates in Anatolia. The Janissaries' intervention in politics was, however, by no means limited to succession struggles and dethronements. An illustration of the delicate relationship of mutual dependence between sovereign (*khünkār*) and servitor (*ḳul*) is provided in a much-quoted passage in a letter of the Habsburg envoy Busbecq written in 1560, where he reflects on the causes of Sultan Süleymān's anxiety and notes the Janissaries' ability to "transfer their loyalty to whomever they will" (Busbecq, *Letters*, 159). Busbecq's remarks serve as the strongest possible reminder that, long after the distribution of the obligatory accession gratuity [see BAKHSHĪSH] as one of their first acts in office, sultans were still engaged in ongoing negotiations with the Janissaries to gain their cooperation.

Under normal conditions, the loyalty and obedience of the Janissaries to their protector and benefactor (*welī niʿmet*) was unquestioning, but maintaining the relationship of mutual trust required constant effort and vigilance on both sides. The one-sided ascription of blame for periodic breakdowns in the relationship to the natural disposition of the Janissaries to rebelliousness and sedition (*fitna*) misses the essential point that nurturing the bonds of filial duty placed an equal burden of responsibility on the sultan to provide for the basic needs of his troops, which included not just prompt and full payment of their basic wages (*ʿulūfe*) but also, when merited, bonuses for exceptional service distributed as *teraḳḳī* (salary increases) and other forms of sultanic largesse [see INʿĀM]. The classic case of the gradual unravelling of this relationship based on mutual trust is collapsed into a short but dramatic period of Ottoman history during the rule of ʿOthmān II (1027-31/1618-22). Janissary fears over the sultan's intention to replace them in an ill-conceived plan concocted by the chief of the Harem, the Dār ul-Saʿāde Aghasï Süleymān Agha, compounded by the general spirit of mutual recrimination following the failed Polish campaign of the previous year [see KHOTIN] led to a serious crisis of confidence culminating in the

Janissary vanguard observes the crossing of the Drava en route to Sigetwār in 1566. Miniature from the supplement (*tatimma*) to the *Süleymān-nāme* of Luḳmān b. Sayyid Ḥusayn [*q.v.*] covering the years 968-74/1561-66. Chester Beatty Library, MS T 413, folio 60b; reproduced by kind permission of the Trustees of the Chester Beatty Library, Dublin.

Detail from the 1559 Istanbul panorama of Melchior Lorichs showing the *agha kapusu* or headquarters and chief residence of the Janissary commander located behind the Süleymāniyye mosque. Courtesy of Leiden University Library (BPL 1758, Tafel X).

Janissaries' rejection and refusal of the sultan's patronage by the overturning of their soup cauldrons. Aside from such moments of exceptional and irresolvable bitterness, however, the Janissaries took their responsibility for protecting the honour, reputation and personal safety of the sultan as a sacred trust. The historian ʿĀshiḳ Pasha-zāde [*q.v.*], while holding some reservations about the legal basis as well as usefulness of the corps in the early days of its existence (see above), still gave recognition to this protective aspect of the Janissaries' responsibilities in his account when he noted: "the sovereign needs the household troops at his [right]/that they might watch over him [day and night]" (*gereklüdür Yeñičeri ḳapuda/ki Khānī gözleyeler her ṭapuda*) (*Tārīkh*, 50; on the multiple senses of *ṭapu* as used in this verse, see the *Bibl.* under this author).

4. Janissary self-governance: the traditions of jurisdictional autonomy and judicial immunity as sources of regimental cohesion.

Although they performed key fixed roles in court ceremonial and battle field deployment, the Janissaries were keenly aware and jealously protective of their independence and sense of regimental pride. While heedful of the superior position of the sultan as the ultimate source of patronage, they staunchly defended their jurisdictional autonomy. One sign of each regiment's status as a closed corporation was that each maintained a separate communal welfare chest (*orta ṣandïghï*), from which Janissaries could draw in retirement and which also provided for widows and orphans of deceased Janissaries. Each regiment also had an officer called the *wekīl-i khardj* (paymaster-general), who oversaw the distribution of funds held in trust for use by those in special need as well as the collection of contributions for each regiment's independent campaign provisions fund (*ḳumanya*). All these special funds were administered at the regimental level (*Ḳawānīn-i Yeñičeriyān*, fol. 39a). From the standpoint of fiscal autonomy and responsibility for the discipline of and imposing of punishments on its own members, each regiment within the 196 was run as a separate entity with a principled objection to outside interference in its members' welfare. This organisational structure fostered a strong sense of regimental pride and loyalty, a source of Janissary strength that neither the sultan nor the *agha* of the Janissaries himself was disposed to tamper with. Rules for the punishment of lapses in Janissary discipline were precise and allowed maximum scope for the carrying out of the required punishments (usually flogging) in the relative privacy of the offending soldier's regimental barracks (*Ḳawānīn-i Yeñičeriyān*, fols. 41b-42a). In the final analysis, the Janissaries' élite status derived not so much from their material condition, since (barring income from another source) their maximum entitlement when they reached the top of the pay scale after more than a decade of active service was no more, in the early 10th/17th century, than 12 *aḳčes* per day [see ʿULŪFE], but rather from their visible separation from the common rank of society conveyed by the privilege of wearing a regimental uniform and the immunity from public prosecution which it symbolised. The very strong impression is left in one of the few genuinely contemporary accounts surviving of the deposition and murder of ʿOthmān II in 1031/1622 that it was the sultan's persistent disregard for the time-honoured tradition of the Janissaries' judicial immunity that so provoked their anger (Tughī, *ʿIbretnümā*, 493, 504). The communal ethos binding Janissaries together was felt most forcefully at the regimental level among smaller cohorts of men who were both recruited and trained under very similar conditions and who, after completion of their training, served together in a succession of campaigns as comrades at arms (*yol-dash*). The protection of each unit's administrative autonomy thus had considerable importance for the maintaining of general morale within the corps.

The General Commander of the Janissaries reserved promotion to some of the regimental commands for those who had served at his side as one of the personal aides and as attendants who made up his obligatory suite on special ceremonial occasions (see the section on the *agha gediklileri* in the *Ḳawānīn-i Yeñičeriyān*, fols. 75a-76b). By this means, he had knowledge of and was able to exert some control over the mood of his troops at the regimental level. However, in combat situations especially, the higher level of authority represented by the *agha* of the Janissaries had little direct influence over the soldiers' performance.

Recommendations for promotion and commendation for deeds of valour on the battlefield were admittedly processed by means of the commander's *ʿarḍ* (petition) to the sultan, but this list of candidates for reward was itself generated within the regiments. With very few exceptions, moreover, (see the list in *SʿO*, iv, 771-8) the average term of office for *aghas* of the Janissaries was relatively brief. Because of their overriding concern with institutional aspects of the corps' history, even the seemingly most comprehensive works on the Janissaries have left a perhaps exaggerated impression that Janissaries belonged to a monolithic entity governed by clear lines of authority and possessing a distinct chain of command which emanated from the centre.

5. Recruitment, training, promotion and battle performance of Janissaries.

The effectiveness of the Janissaries as a key element of Ottoman military provision in the era of the *Pax Ottomanica* in the 10th/16th and 11th/17th centuries is generally recognised. Opinion is, however, divided on the question of whether their recognised superiority derived from selectivity in recruitment, thoroughness in training or the exceptional quality of the *esprit de corps* generated in individual Janissary units whose fighting strength represented, in round figures, about 100 men. While the subject is too large to treat in any detail here, a review of some of the basic elements of the system may help to clarify some controversial aspects. From what we know of Ottoman recruitment practices it seems that they gave preference in selection to boys who had already entered early manhood. This is reflected in the rates of the *pendjik*, which in several examples dating from the pre-Süleymānid era (texts transcribed in Uzunçarşılı, *Kapukulu ocakları*, 87-90) indicate that the ages between 12 and 19 were considered optimal for the purpose of military training. Such theoretical guidelines were apparently also followed in the actual practice of the *devshirme* [*q.v.*], since we know from a published example relating to Bosnia that the actual age span found in one group of recruits ranged from 13 to 19 (see the study by Meriç cited in DEVSHIRME). Other texts of the early 10th/17th century (see the example in Refik, *Devşirme usulu*, 4-5, dated 1031/1621) suggest the consistent adherence to an age at first recruitment between 15 and 20, which may indicate a bias towards a slightly shorter period in training but otherwise conforms closely to earlier practice. If we accept that most Janissaries began their training at the age of 14 or 15 and completed a course of basic training lasting a minimum of four to five years, they were ready to enter active service at the age of 19 or 20 at the peak of their physical development and endurance potential. References in the advice literature to an optimum period of 15-20 years in basic training before admission to active Janissary units seem not just highly unlikely but wholly impractical (see, for example, Ḳoči Bey's *risāle* of 1041/1631-2, Aksüt, 71: *on-besh yigirmi čuhalu olmayindja* . . ., and the anonymous *Kitāb-i Müsteṭāb* of *ca.* 1029/1620, Yücel, 7, which recommends that cadets should serve terms of 6-7 years as *ʿadjemī oghlān*, then 5-10 years as *bostandji* [*q.v.*] before being inscribed in the Janissary rolls). At all events, Janissary vacancies (*maḥlūl*) created by the retirement or death of veterans had be filled on a semi-continuous basis by those most fit for service between the ages of 18 and 23 without regard to the regular intervals prescribed for the general exodus in which candidates destined for the scribal services also took part.

Irrespective of its duration, the emphasis during the initial training period was placed on fitness, physical endurance, self-discipline and deference, as well as obedience to those with greater seniority and rank. The probationary period actually continued even after a cadet's induction into a permanent Janissary regiment, termed "going up to the gate" (*kapuya čiḳmak, be-dergāh olmaḳ*), as recent inductees were initially assigned menial chores such as floor sweeping and mess duties in the Istanbul barracks. Although target practice and other drill was routinely carried out during the off-season between campaigns, it would not be too far from the truth if we were to suppose that formal training in the arts of war began with exposure to actual conditions of battle at the front. The emphasis on recruitment and peace-time training of Janissaries which follows in its main lines the views expressed in the Ottoman advice literature [see NAṢĪḤAT AL-MULŪK] misses the essential point that battle experience was the most crucial element in a soldier's training. One of the chief deficiencies of the Janissary corps in the 12th/18th century was not inadequate training, but the lack of recent combat experience as the inevitable consequence of the prolonged period of peace between the signing of the Treaty of Belgrade in 1152/1739 and the empire's remobilisation for war with Russia in 1182/1768.

Idealised perceptions of the quality of the corps before the introduction of new recruitment categories beginning from *ca.* 990/1582 (see below) have given a distorted weight to selection criteria which, despite their undoubted importance, must be considered as only one of the relevant variables affecting Janissary performance. Allowances for campaign equipment and provisions (*yay aḳčesi, sefer filorisi*), and bonuses and rewards for exceptional deeds of bravery, distributed both on the battlefield to encourage the troops and as part of generalised celebrations held to mark significant Ottoman victories [see DONANMA. 2], also played a very significant role in motivating the Janissaries to achieve the maximum performance levels which their training, fitness and expertise permitted.

6. Attitudes towards the Janissaries in Ottoman political writing of the late 10th/16th and early 11th/17th centuries.

Although the expense of maintaining an expanded Janissary corps had already begun to attract notice in Ottoman political writing as early as Luṭfī Pasha's [*q.v.*] treatise dating from the mid-950s/1560s (*Āṣafnāme*, ed. Kütükoğlu, 35), the topic acquired increased urgency from about 1580 onwards. A series of authors beginning with the prolific ʿĀlī saw the problems besetting the Janissary corps in their time as chiefly due to irregularities in the method of their recruitment and the resultant insinuation of non-*devshirme* recruits, referred to in the texts as *edjnebī* (outsiders) or *saplama* (intruders) spoiling the purity of the corps. ʿĀlī's remarks in a work written towards the end of his life in 1007/latter part of 1598-early 1599 fixed on the circumstances connected with Murād III's precedent-setting grant of fast-track promotion to the Janissary corps to a group of what he called "city boys" as part of the celebrations to mark the circumcision feast held for prince Meḥemmed (later Meḥemmed III [*q.v.*]) in 990/1582 (see the *Fuṣūl-i ḥall*, Nuruosmaniye ms. 3399, fol. 132a: *sūr-i hümāyūnda "Istanbul dewshirmesine" rukhṣat verildi, ol ṭarīḳ mukhtall oldu*). In the aftermath of ʿĀlī's retrospection regarding the significance of the events of 1582, which he regarded as the defining moment in the Janissaries' general slide towards mediocrity, a group of later writers took up the theme of the corruption of the Janissaries reproducing and immortalising ʿĀlī's brief remarks in close paraphrase. Among them Ḳoči Bey, writing in 1041/1631-2, more than thirty years after the penning of ʿĀlī's treatise, repeated the reference to the *sūr-i hümāyūn* of 990/1582 as the source of all later corruption (*First risāle*, ed. Aksüt, 44). Tracts written in the intermediate years also insisted on the seriousness of admitting city boys (*shehir oghlanlari*, a code term for recruits among whom Turks and other Muslims had insinuated themselves) to Janissary membership without explaining the unsuitability of Turks for military service except by the repetition (or unexpressed assumption) of standard ethnic stereotypes which held them to be "unruly". It is clear that the views of such "traditionalists" were seriously out of touch with the military realities facing the empire, as their texts contain no reference to the empire's pressing need for recruits to man the dozens of new garrisons which were being erected, renovated and expanded to guard the Ottomans' advancing frontier in the east during the 990s/1580s and beyond [see ʿOTHMĀN PASHA (ÖZDEMIR-OGHLĪ)].

Whatever its basis in fact, the theme of the corruption of the Janissaries gained general acceptance in the popular consciousness and achieved a particular popularity in the aftermath of ʿOthmān II's dethronement and murder in which the Janissaries were implicated. Anti-Janissary sentiments reached a kind of climax during the term in office of the reformist Grand Vizier Kemānkesh Ḳara Muṣṭafā Pasha between Shaʿbān 1048/December 1638 and Dhu 'l-Ḳaʿda 1053/January 1644, but the kind of dramatic spending cuts he was advocating, while desirable in the abstract, were hardly practicable, since the empire was on the eve of gearing up for a renewed phase of its centuries-long confrontation with Venice which would involve a significant military build-up in both Dalmatia and Crete [see IḲRĪTISH]. Kātib Čelebi [*q.v.*] was one of the few Ottoman thinkers of the mid-11th/17th century to see the desirability of maintaining steady Janissary enrolments, both because of their obvious military value and also as a means of avoiding the political turmoil associated with sudden or dramatic changes to their status. In his view, a slight oversupply of military capacity in peacetime was preferable to last-minute attempts to supplement the regular soldiery by recruiting inexperienced *lewends* [*q.v.*] and other irregulars on the eve of battle. As the son of a soldier himself, with considerable first-hand exposure to conditions at the front, where he had served in a variety of scribal capacities, Kātib Čelebi was better equipped than most to draw sound conclusions. Unswayed by the anti-Janissary sentiments afflicting many of his contemporaries, he fully realised that Ottoman reliance on forced conscription of peasants to man fortresses in remote areas of the frontier represented the worse of two evils (see ch. 2 of the *Düstūr al-ʿamel*, 129-32).

It is noteworthy that later theorists such as Ṣarî Meḥmed Pas̲h̲a [*q.v.*], writing *ca.* 1120/1708 at a time when the Janissary numbers had mounted to 53,200, including pensioners (*oturaḳ*), thus representing a huge burden on the treasury, tended to follow in Kātib Čelebi's footsteps in advocating a gradual diminishing of the Janissary ranks as the best policy (Wright, *Ottoman statecraft*, 114: "slowly and deliberately accomplished").

7. Peacetime and non-combatant duties of the Janissaries.

Apart from their duties associated with the waging of war, the Janissaries played a very considerable role in state ceremonial and ritual [see MARĀSIM. 4]. The regular pay distributions to the sultan's household troops were themselves organised as ceremonial occasions called *ʿulūfe dīwānî* or *g̲h̲alebe dīwānî* [see DĪWĀN-Î HÜMĀYŪN], often timed to coincide with the presence in the capital of foreign diplomatic missions. On these occasions, the presence of the Janissary regiments in full strength made a powerful impression on Western envoys, who were in any case already in awe of the Ottomans because of the scale of their permanent standing armed forces, which dwarfed those of contemporary European states. The four *ṣolaḳ* regiments (the 60th to 63rd *d̲j̲emāʿats*) created in the time of Bāyezīd I with a nominal membership of 20 each (*Ḳawānīn-i Yeñičeriyān*, fol. 102b) but later expanded to 100 each [see ṢOLAḲ] were reduced to an exclusively ceremonial function under sultans who, as became increasingly common after the reign of Meḥemmed III [*q.v.*], declined to accompany the army on campaign. The laws of protocol also dictated that the *ag̲h̲a* of the Janissaries should personally escort the sultan to and from the palace on the occasion of his obligatory Friday visits to one of the capital's principal mosques [see SELĀMLÎḲ]. In addition to these fixed duties, Janissary units assumed general responsibility for essential functions of municipal governance from fire fighting (*Ḳawānīn-i Yeñičeriyān*, fol. 48a-b) to night sentry duties and the preservation of law and order, both in the capital (*kol dolas̲h̲maḳ*, see *ibid.*, fols. 49a-50b) and the provinces (*yasaḳd̲j̲îlîḳ*, see *ibid.*, fols. 50b-52b). The latter assignments were typically for periods of either three or nine months, depending on the town's proximity to the capital. The nine-month term for provincial inspectorate and guard duty was reserved for assignments to the remoter parts of the empire (*tas̲h̲ra*). Janissaries accustomed to a privileged life at the centre of the empire's political, cultural and economic life regarded these stints in the provinces as hardship postings, and anxiously awaited their rotation back to the capital.

Janissaries assigned to provincial garrison duty were intended only to supplement locally recruited forces (*yerlü ḳul*) but, if war-time circumstances required, their times could be extended. References found in normative sources of the 11th/17th century (see the *Second risāle* of Ḳoči Bey, ed. Aksüt, 92, and *Ḳara Kemānkes̲h̲ Pas̲h̲a lāyiḥasî*, ed. Unat, 450) suggest that Janissaries posted as *ḳalʿe nöbetd̲j̲ileri* served a term lasting three years, but there was quite a wide variation in actual practice. The essential point is that, at any given time, a very substantial proportion of the corps was employed in this manner as part of the empire's frontier defences. This proportion might rise in the context of a prolonged conflict in a particular sector of the frontier to as much as one-third of the total membership. For example, figures provided by Ḥüseyn Hezārfenn [*q.v.*] for the year 1080/1669-70 show 14,379 out of a total of 53,849 Janissaries, or 26.7%, were employed in provincial garrison duty, but ten years earlier in 1070/1660 the proportion had been 39.5% or 21,428 out of a total membership of 54,222 (see Murphey, *Ottoman warfare*, 45). The fact that Janissaries were counted as absent (*nā-mewd̲j̲ūd*), when roll calls were carried out in the trenches during wartime, is a reflection not of Janissary truancy but rather of the actual pattern of use to which Janissaries were put. To a very considerable degree, these legitimately included responsibilities for defence and other non-combatant duties. It was the permanent responsibility of the 34 *sekbān* regiments to function as the home guard, and it was the *ag̲h̲a* of the *sekbān*s who, as the corps' second-ranking officer, deputised for the *ag̲h̲a* of the Janissaries and fulfilled his superior's ceremonial and administrative duties when his chief was absent on campaign. While their numbers in all but the key strategic fortresses like Buda and Bag̲h̲dād were counted not in thousands but hundreds, Janissaries formed an integral part of the social fabric in the provinces as much as the capital. By restricting ourselves to an assessment of the narrow range of their activities when Janissaries were being used as commandos and assault troops, we gain a distorted picture of their role, which was in its essence and by design multi-functional.

8. The economic position of the Janissaries.

The most impressive presence of the Janissaries was in Istanbul, since in addition to two barracks of their own, the *eski* and the *yeñi odalarî*, and the residence of the Janissary *ag̲h̲a* himself called the *ag̲h̲a ḳapusu* (see above), there were also thousands of Janissary cadets domiciled in the palace gardens scattered all round the imperial capital. The presence of tens of thousands of Janissaries and Janissary trainees in the city meant that the interpenetration of military and civilian life was an inescapable part of the urban experience in Ottoman Istanbul. The involvement of Janissaries during peacetime as artisans and tradesmen is noted in Ottoman sources as early as the reign of Meḥemmed II soon after the city's capture [see ISTANBUL, at Vol. IV, 242b], and this dimension of the Janissaries' activities cannot be regarded as an aberrant behaviour associated with the decline of the Janissary corps as a fighting force in the 18th century (see 9., below). As for the impact of the smaller Janissary presence on life in the provinces, and the social position and administrative role of the lesser Janissary commanders, who were called, at the *ḳaḍā* level, *yeñičeri serdārî*, we have little direct evidence apart from what is provided in subjective accounts by Christian travellers to the Balkans or equally unsympathetic diatribes by indigenous clerics, both of which groups were only able to tell half, and perhaps not the most interesting half, of the story (see Georgieva, in *Bibl.*) The periodic excesses of Janissaries tempted to take advantage of their extra-judicial status during secondments to the provinces, when they were removed from the supervisory control of their superior officers, cannot be ruled out as a destabilising influence on provincial society in certain periods and places; but to suppose that the net effect of Janissary presence in a locality was always the terrorisation of the local populace seriously overstates the case.

The Janissaries were wage earners, a relative rarity, especially in provincial society. Whatever cash surpluses they could accumulate represented a welcome source of stimulus for the local economy, which was heavily based on production of goods for immediate household consumption. As official institutions, too, the Janissary garrisons were purchasers on a grandiose scale of basic supplies from local markets. Moreover, when the Janissaries' basic policing function was properly carried out, the protection they offered provincial populations from the depredations of brigands and other sowers of provincial anarchy provided the necessary environment of safety and security favouring trade and sustained economic growth.

An indication of the general economic position of Janissaries, although biased towards the higher-ranking and most prosperous group among them, is provided in data compiled from the probate records of 11th/17th-century Istanbul. Table I is a summary of this information which, although it is silent on the crucial subject of the sources from which Janissary wealth was accumulated, nonetheless gives a valuable impression of the high social standing and economic position of the Janissaries at the peak of their power and influence in the 11th/17th century.

9. The retirement of the Janissaries from active service after 1700, their elimination in 1826 and its after-effects.

The common association of the Janissaries with growing political instability of the Ottoman empire in the 12th/18th century needs careful reassessment. Recent research has cast some considerable doubt on the once prevalent notion of the endemic predisposition of the Janissaries to revolt and rebellion. This research (see refs. in *Bibl.* under Janissary-*eṣnāf* relations) goes a long way towards refuting or at least muting the constant harping on the theme of Janissary waywardness as found in the Ottoman court chronicle tradition and repeated by modern proponents of the "conspiracy theory" of 18th-century Ottoman politics. From the strictly military point of view, however, there can be no doubt that the 18th century brought major changes both in public perceptions concerning the Janissaries and the new position assigned to them in the altered deployment patterns of the period. In the new environment, partly determined by the Ottomans' consistently non-interventionist stance in Europe after 1739, the size and expense of the corps became increasingly difficult to justify. In military terms, the Janissaries had already begun to outlive their usefulness when, driven by fiscal pressures, Maḥmūd I [*q.v.*] decided in 1153/1740 to legalise the selling of Janissary pay-certificates (*esāme*) (Aḥmed Djewād, *Tārīkh-i ʿaskerī*, iii, 52-3, and Aksan, *Whatever happened*, 26-7). The timing of this decision from the standpoint of the Janissaries' regimental cohesion could not have been more unfortunate, as the inauguration of a prolonged period of peace, lasting until 1182/1768, meant that no new Janissaries were being recruited or trained. At the same time, the corps' existing members either retired or lapsed into varying degrees of inactivity. Thirty years after the introduction of Maḥmūd's fiscal measures the empire was not noticeably better off, while the effect on its military preparedness was catastrophic. When it went to war with Russia in the late 1760s it did so with inexperienced, demoralised and sadly ineffective troops, which included large numbers of superannuated Janissaries brought back from retirement to face Russia's recently-modernised army. The Ottomans' desperate attempts during the 1767-74 war to pick up where they had left off three decades earlier placed intolerable strains on Ottoman resources, and policy makers' attention was necessarily divided between demands from competing services. In the aftermath of the disastrous defeat at Česhme [*q.v.*] in 1184/1770, it was natural that naval concerns should gain a certain predominance in their thinking. Significantly, in the post-war period, too, when the Ottomans undertook a broad-based renovation of all the empire's defence capabilities, the naval sphere was again assigned priority. The Ottomans' first imperially-sponsored technical school founded in 1187/1773 and called the *mühendis-khāne-yi baḥr-i hümāyūn* was, as the name suggests, intended to give priority to the naval sphere. The founding of its counterpart institution, the *mühendis-khāne-yi berr-i hümāyūn*, devoted to the scientific and technical aspects of land wars, was deferred until 1208/1793. Worries about Ottoman naval preparedness continued during the reign of the military moderniser *par excellence* Selīm III [*q.v.*] and while some of his advisers such as Tatārdjïk ʿAbdullāh Efendi advocated undertaking a serious (and well-funded) effort to improve the condition of the Janissaries (see his *Lāyiḥa*, pt. ii, 259-70), the demands for a modern navy were given equal priority (*Lāyiḥa*, pt. i, 330-9) and in the end other options for upgrading the Ottomans' land forces were pursued [see NIẒĀM-I DJEDĪD].

Between 1770-2, when the Ottomans were still at war with Russia, experimentation with alternatives to the Janissaries had in any case already begun. The very existence of the *süratdjïs* (rapid-fire artillerymen) being trained by the Baron de Tott in the capital, although ostensibly a replacement for the *ṭopdjus* rather than the Janissaries proper, was enough in itself to engender real fears among the Janissaries at the front about their collective future. The fact that the experiment was essentially a failure and that the prototype unit ordered to the front never actually reached its destination (Aksan, "*Wretched Fanaticks*") did little to allay these fears, and the truth is that already in the 1770s, their days were numbered. Finding a viable replacement for the Janissaries was, however, a complicated problem, and the last half-century of the corps' existence saw a series of phased reforms and policy reversals. There were valid reasons for this gradualism, and it is wrong to attribute the slowness of reform principally to Janissary obstinacy, resistance and conservatism, as is sometimes implied.

Even the "abolition" of the corps by Maḥmūd II's imperial fiat in 1242/1826, dubbed in the sources the "auspicious event" (*waḳʿa-yi khayriyye*), was not so absolute or final as the name would suggest. The transition to local recruitment models was, in some areas, painfully slow and, especially in border areas such as Bosnia, it met with fierce resistance from the local Muslim notables. In Bosnia, for example, it took seven years for the sultan's "abolition" of the corps to take full effect and be replaced with a reliable local militia (O. Moreau, *Recruitment*, 264). It was in the provinces closest to Istanbul and least vulnerable to attack that the transition to a regionally recruited land army was quickest and most successful [see RADĪF. 3]. In the short to medium term, it cannot be said that the removal of the Janissaries brought any real solution to the empire's military difficulties. The empire was militarily unprepared in both the 1828-9 Russo-Ottoman war and the first phase of its conflict with Muḥammad ʿAlī [*q.v.*] in 1832-3 and the diplomatic interventions needed to bring these disastrous episodes to a close, established a new pattern of Ottoman dependency on foreign aid which lasted to the era of the Crimean War and beyond. The 1830s heralded not so much a new era of promise for accelerated military modernisation by the Ottomans as the inau-

Table I

Value of estates left by retired and active members of the Janissary* corps between 1005/1594 and 1078/1668 (based on Öztürk, *Istanbul tereke defterleri*, 438-93)

name of deceased	P. no. in Öztürk	inventory no. in Öztürk	date of death (*hid͟jrī*)	place of death	value of estate (in *aḳčes*)
Meḥmed Čāwūs͟h	438	15	1005	sefer-i sulṭānī	127,676
Muṣṭafā Ag͟ha	444	68	1027		529,378
Ṣāliḥ Čāwūs͟h	448	137	1037	s͟harḳ seferi	380,819
Mataraḏjî Meḥmed Ag͟ha	450	24	1046	sefer-i hümāyūn	260,000
Red͟jeb b. Ḥaydar	450	26	1046	sefer-i s͟harḳ	273,750
el-Ḥād͟jd͟j Yaḥyā (ṣolaḳ)	452	56	1048	s͟harḳ seferi	862,150
Derwīs͟h Ag͟ha (turnad͟jî-bas͟hî)	452	73	1048	Ordu-i hümāyūn'da	1,021,146
Ḥasan Ag͟ha	452	78	1048		201,486
Ibrāhīm (su-bas͟hî)	454	83	1048	sefer-i s͟harḳ	134,418
ʿAbdī Ag͟ha	454	117	1055		849,435
Ḥamza Bes͟he	456	125	1055		123,975
Muṣṭafā Ag͟ha	458	26	1058	Muḥārebe-i Sandira	127,243
Muṣṭafā Bes͟he	460	68	1059		100,887
ʿAlī Ag͟ha	462	84	1059	Girid	187,003
Aḥmed (čorbad͟jî)	462	101	1060		398,880
Oruč Ag͟ha	462	107	1060		118,415
Murād (su-bas͟hî)	462	109	1060		631,751
Meḥmed (oda-bas͟hî)	466	37	1070		129,017
ʿĀbidīn (oda-bas͟hî)	476	213	1079	Girid	81,440
Aḥmed Bes͟he (bayraḳtār, 47th bölük)	476	226	1079		247,623
ʿAlī Bes͟he	478	256	1079	Ḳandiye ḳalʿesi	266,857
S͟haʿbān (oda-bas͟hî)	480	2	1077		238,352
ʿAbd al-Raḥmān b. S͟haʿbān (ṣolaḳ)	480	21	1078		206,830
Meḥmed Ag͟ha	480	36	1077	Girid	1,728,902
Meḥmed Ag͟ha (yeñičeri ketk͟hudā-yeri)	482	55	1078	Girid	2,447,921
Meḥmed Bes͟he	482	59	1078	Girid	225,070
K͟halīfe b. Muṣṭafā (yeñičeri, 9th d͟jemāʿat)	482	78	1078	Rumeli	145,840**
Muṣṭafā Ag͟ha (zirihd͟ji)	484	90	1078	Bag͟hdād	1,378,634
Muṣṭafā K͟halīfe (yeñičeri)	484	108	1078	Girid	9,659,838***
Ḥasan Ag͟ha	484	110	1078	Girid	89,344
Meḥmed Ag͟ha (čorbad͟jî)	486	135	1078	Girid	145,634
Meḥmed Ag͟ha (donanma ag͟hasî)	486	148	1078	Ḳandiye	662,537
Ḳāsim Ag͟ha	488	163	1078	Girid	105,032
ʿAlī Čāwūs͟h	488	177	1078	Girid	473,162
Aḥmed Ag͟ha (muḥḍir)	488	185	1078	Girid	644,153
ʿAlī Ag͟ha (mehter-bas͟hî)	490	197	1078	Girid	141,450
Süleymān Ag͟ha	490	204	1078	Girid	471,434

* Some titles (e.g. *čāwūs͟h*) are ambiguous and could refer to military or non-military officials other than Janissaries. In a few cases, however, additional, functionally specific, information is given (e.g. *ṣolaḳ, turnad͟jî-bas͟hî, oda-bas͟hî, matarad͟jî*, etc.) confirming the individual's status as a member of the Janissary corps. When the place of death is given as "on campaign" (e.g. *sefer-i s͟harḳ, sefer-i sulṭānī*), this increases the likelihood that individuals bearing ambiguous titles were in fact Janissaries.

** This estate was also composed mostly (145,300 *aḳčes*' worth) of cash. Many Janissaries lived in barracks as bachelors and thus had no private homes to dispose of at the time of death.

*** This estate was composed almost entirely of cash in the amount of 9,054,530 *aḳčes*, with a further 32,368.5 *aḳčes* owed to the estate by creditors.

guration of the "Eastern Question" in western politics.

Bibliography: 1. Primary Ottoman historical sources. Anon., *Gazavat-i Sultan Murad b. Mehemmed Han*, ed. H. Inalcık and M. Oğuz, Ankara 1978; Kemāl Pas̲h̲a-zāde, *Tevārīk̲h̲-i āl-i ʿOt̲h̲mān, VII. Defter*, ed. Ş. Turan, Ankara 1954, *II. Defter*, ed. idem, Ankara 1983; Tewḳīʿī ʿAbd ul-Raḥmān Pas̲h̲a, *Ḳānūnnāme [1087/1676]*, ed. A. Şeref, in *MTM*, i/3 (1331/1916), 497-544; Tartārd̲j̲îḳ ʿAbdullāh Efendi, *Lāyiḥa [1206/1791]*, ed. Ş. Mehmed, *Sulṭān Selīm-i t̲h̲ālit̲h̲ dewrinde dewlet ḥaḳḳînda muṭālaʿāt*, pt. 1, in *TOEM*, vii/41 (1332/1917), 321-46, pt. 2, vii/42 (1332/1917), 257-84, pt. 3, viii/43 (1333/1918), 15-34 (remarks on the Ottoman navy in pt. 1, 330-9; remarks on land forces, primarily Janissaries, pt. 2, 259-70); ʿĀs̲h̲îḳ-Pas̲h̲a-zāde, *Tārīk̲h̲*, ed. F. Giese, Leipzig 1928 (in the passage from p. 50 of the Giese ed., the word *tapu* carries a variety of connotations. Its primary meaning is "presence" or "vicinity" (see *Tarama sözlüğu*, v, 3748-51) implying the obligation of the Janissaries never to abandon the sultan whether in his sleeping or his wakeful state, while a collateral meaning of the term refers more to active "service" (*ibid.*, v, 3754-5) with the obvious reference in the case of Janissaries to military service); Tursun Bey, facs. of text and summary, English tr. Inalcik and R. Murphey, *The History of Mehmed the Conqueror by Tursun Bey*, Minneapolis and Chicago 1978; Ḥüseyn Tug̲h̲ī, *ʿIbretnümā*, text in Roman transcription by M. Sertoğlu, in *Belleten*, xi/43 (1947), 489-514; Muṣṭafā ʿĀlī, *Künh ül-ak̲h̲bār*, Istanbul Univ. Lib. ms. T.Y. 5959; C. Römer (ed. and Ger. tr.), *Die Osmanische Belagerung Bagdads 1034-35/1625-26. Ein Augenzeugenbericht*, in *Isl.*, lxvi (1989), 119-36 (text of a private letter from a Janissary officer at the front); L. Fekete (ed. and German tr.), *Türkische Schriften aus dem Archive des Palatin Nikolaus Esterhazy, 1606-1645*, Budapest 1932 (nos. 51-77 (pp. 149-203) are private letters; see in particular the letters exchanged between Janissary officers garrisoned in Hungary (Buda and Eğri/Eger), nos. 60-1 (pp. 172-7)). On the abolition of the Janissaries, see Meḥmed Esʿad, *Üss-i ẓafer*, 2Istanbul 1293/1876.

2. Ottoman advice texts (listed chronologically in order of composition). Luṭfī Pas̲h̲a, *Āṣaf-nāma* (*ca.* 960/1553), ed. M. Kütükoğlu, *Lutfi Paşa Asafnamesi*, Istanbul 1991; ʿĀlī, *Nuṣḥat al-salāṭīn* (989/1581), ed. and Eng. tr. A. Tietze, *Mustafa Ali's counsel for sultans of 1581*, 2 pts. Vienna 1979-82 (pt. 1, *Denkschriften der Österreichischen Akad. Wiss.*, phil.-hist. Kl., cxxxvii; pt. 2, *ibid.*, clviii); anon., *Ḳawānīn-i Yeñičeriyān* (1015/1606), fasc. ed. and Russian tr. Y.E. Petrosiyan, *Mebde-i kanun-i yeniçeri ocag̲h̲i tarik̲h̲i*, Moscow 1987; anon., *Kitāb-i Müsteṭāb* (*ca.* 1029/1620), ed. Y. Yücel, Ankara 1974; ʿĀlī, *Fuṣūl-i ḥall* (1007/1598-9), Nuruosmaniye Lib. ms. 3399; ʿAyn-i ʿAlī, *Risāle* (1018/1609), Istanbul 1280/1863; Ḳoči Bey, *First risāle* (1041/1631-2), text in Roman transcription, ed. A. Aksüt, in *Koçi Bey Risalesi*, Istanbul 1939, 18-75; idem, *Second risāle* (*ca.* 1050/1640), text in Roman transcription in *ibid.*, 77-127; anon. (attrib. to Kemānkes̲h̲ Ḳara Muṣṭafā Pas̲h̲a), *Lāyiḥa* (*ca.* 1050/1640), text in Roman transcription, ed. F.R. Unat, *Sadrazam Kemankeş Kara Mustafa Paşa layihasi*, in *Tarih Vesikalari*, i/6 (1942), 443-50; Kātib Čelebi, *Düstūr al-ʿamel fī iṣlāḥ al-k̲h̲alel* (1063/1653), Istanbul 1280/1863; Ṣarī Meḥmed Pas̲h̲a (Defterdār), *Naṣāʾiḥ ul-wüzerā* (*ca.* 1132/1720), ed. and Eng. tr. W.L. Wright, *Ottoman statecraft. The Book of Counsel for Veziers and Governors*, Princeton 1935.

3. Studies on advice texts. T. Gökbilgin, *XVII. asırda Osmanlı devletinde islahat ihtiyac ve temayülleri ve Katib Çelebi*, in S. Ünver *et al.* (eds.), *Katib Çelebi. Hayatı ve eserleri hakkında incelemeler*, Ankara 1957, 197-218; K. Röhrborn, *Untersuchungen zur osmanischen Verwaltungsgeschichte*, Berlin 1973, esp. 6-11; P. Fodor, *Bir nasihat-name olarak "kavanin-i yeniçeriyan"*, in *Beşinci milletlerarası Türkoloji kongresi, Bildiriler*, pt. III, *Türk tarihi*, i, Istanbul 1985, 217-24; G. Kaldy-Nagy, "*The Strangers*" (ecnebiler) *in the 16th century Ottoman military organization*, in G. Kara (ed.), *Between the Danube and the Caucasus*, Budapest 1987, 165-9.

4. Primary accounts in Western languages. Konstantin Mihailović, *Memoirs of a Janissary*, Eng. tr. B. Stolz, Ann Arbor 1975; O.G. de Busbecq, Eng. tr. E.S. Forster, *The Turkish letters of Ogier Ghiselin de Busbecq, Imperial ambassador at Constantinople, 1554-1562*, Oxford 1927; Paul Rycaut, *The present state of the Ottoman Empire containing the maxims of the Turkish politie*, London 1668.

5. Studies on the Janissaries, 1360-1700. (a) General. H. Inalcik, *Expenditure for the Ottoman army*, in Inalcik and D. Quataert (eds.), *An economic and social history of the Ottoman Empire*, Cambridge 1994, 88-93; idem, *Fatih devri üzerinde tetkikler ve vesikalar*, Ankara 1954; A. Bombaci, *The army of the Saljuqs of Rum*, in *AIUON*, N.S. xxxviii/4 (1978), 343-69; G. Kaldy-Nagy, *The first centuries of the Ottoman military organization*, in *AO Hung.*, xxxi (1977), 147-83; S. Eyice, art. *Ağa kapısı*, in *Dünden bügüne Istanbul ansiklopedisi*, i, Istanbul 1984, 78-80; A. Refik, *Devşirme usulu. Acemi oğlanlar*, in *Dar al-Funûn, Edebiyat Fakültesi Mecmuası*, v (1926), 1-14.

(b) Social and economic aspects. H. Sahillioğlu, *Yeniçeri çuhası ve II. Bayezid'in son yıllarında yeniçeri çuha muhasebesi*, in *Güney-Doğu Avrupa Araştırmaları Dergisi*, ii-iii (1973-4), 415-66; S. Öztürk, *Askeri kassamına ait onyedinci asır Istanbul tereke defterleri (sosyo-ekonomik tahlil)*, Istanbul 1995; Y. Ercan, *Osmanlı şehirlerinde askerlerin ekonomik durununa ilişkin bazı bilgiler*, in *Birinci Askeri Tarih Semineri*, 4 vols., Ankara 1983, ii, 169-78; D. Bojanič-Lukač, *Sırp-Hırvat halk destanlarından üç yeniçeri destanı*, in J.-L. Bacqué-Grammont and B. Flemming (eds.), *Türkische Miszellen. Robert Anhegger Festschrift*, Istanbul 1987, 63-8; C. Georgieva, *Yenicarte v bulgarskite zemi*, Sofia 1988 (French summary of contents in *Études Balkaniques*, xxv [1989], 132-6); C. Georgieva, *Le role des Janissaires dans la politique ottomane en les terres bulgares (XVIe-milieu du XVIIe siècle)*, in *Études Historiques*, Sofia, viii (1978), 179-90; C. Kafadar, *On the purity and corruption of the Janissaries*, in *Turkish Studies Association Bulletin*, xv (1991), 273-9; M. Ilgürel, *XVII. yüzyıl Balikesir şer'iyye sicillerine göre subaşılık*, in *Sekizinci Türk Tarih Kongresi. Bildiriler*, ii, Ankara 1981, 1275-81; J.-P. Pascual, *The Janissaries and the Damascus countryside at the beginning of the seventeenth century according to the archives of the city's military tribunal*, in T. Khalidi (ed.), *Land tenure and social transformation in the Middle East*, Beirut 1984, 357-69.

(c) Weapons and equipment. In addition to the studies on Ottoman gun-casting by Lefroy (1870) and Foulkes (1930) cited by V.J. Parry, in art. BARUD. iv, see V. Schmidtchen, *Riesengeschütze des 15. Jahrhunderts. Technische Höchstleistungen ihrer Zeit*, in *Technikgeschichte*, xliv (1977), 153-73, 213-37; J. Plaskowski, *The technology of gun-casting in the army of Muhammad II*, in *Birinici Uluslararası Türk-Islam Bilim ve Teknoloji Kongresi, Bildiriler*, 4 vols. Istanbul 1981, iii, 163-70; Inalcik, *The socio-political effects of the diffusion of fire arms in the Middle East*, in V.J. Parry and M.E.

Yapp (eds.), *War, technology and society in the Middle East*, London 1975, 164-94; D. Petrovic, *Fire-arms in the Balkans on the eve of and after the Ottoman conquests of the fourteenth and fifteenth centuries*, in *ibid.*, 195-217; P. Jaeckel, *Ausrüstung und Bewaffnung der türkischen Heere*, in H. Glassner (ed.), *Kurfürst Max Emmanuel. Bayern und Europa um 1700*, Munich 1976, i, 373-456; idem, *Wehr und Waffen der Türken*, in B. Kellner-Heinkele and D. Rohwedder (eds.), *Türkische Kunst und Kultur aus osmanischer Zeit*, 2nd ed. in 2 vols., Recklinghausen 1985, ii, 343-72; idem, *Vom Türkischen Heerwesen und Heerlager*, in M. Kretschmar, W. Raunig *et al.* (eds.), *Osmanisch-Türkisches Kunsthandwerk aus Süddeutschen Sammlungen. Katalog zur Ausstellung im Bayerischen Armeemuseum*, Munich 1979, 24-45; G. Düriegl *et al.*, *Die Waffen der Osmanen*, in R. Waissenberger (ed.), *Die Türken vor Wien. Europa und die Entscheidung an der Donau*, [2]Vienna 1983, 181-212; Z. Zygulski, *Turkish militaria in the light of the exhibitions of 1983*, in *Waffen- und Kostümkunde*, xxvi (1984), 139-45; C.J. Heywood, *Activities of the state cannon-foundry (tophane-i ʿamire) at Istanbul in the early sixteenth century according to an unpublished Turkish source*, in *Prilozi za Orientalnu Filologiju*, xxx (1980), 209-17; G. Agoston, *Ottoman artillery and European military technology in the fifteenth and seventeenth centuries*, in *AO Hung*, xlvii (1994), 15-48; A.Z. Hertz, *Armament and supply of Ottoman Ada Kale*, in *Archivum Ottomanicum*, iv (1972 [1974]), 95-171.

6. Studies on the Janissaries, 1700-1830s. A.C. Eren, *Mahmud II zamanında Bosna-Hersek*, Istanbul 1965; O. Moreau, *The recruitment of Bosnian soldiers during the 19th century (1826-1876)*, in *Islamic Studies*, xxxvi (1997), 263-79; Y. Özkaya, *Anadolu'daki yeniçerilerin düzensizliği ile ilgili belgeler ve Izmir'de yeniçeriliğin kaldırılması hakkında bir belge*, in *AÜDTCFD*, xxiii (1965), 75-90; Y. Özkaya, *Orta Anadolu'da Nizam-i Cedid'in kuruluşu ve kaldırılışı*, in *Dil Tarih-Coğrafya Fakültesi. Atatürk'ün 100. doğum yılına armağan dergisi*, Ankara 1982, 509-35; D.R. Sadat, *Ayan and ağa. The transformation of the Bektashi corps in the 18th century*, in *MW*, lxiii (1973), 206-19; H. Reed, *Ottoman reform and the Janissaries: the eşkinci layihasi of 1826*, in H. Inalcik and O. Okyar (eds.), *Social and economic history of Turkey, 1071-1920*, Ankara 1980, 193-8; Reed, *The destruction of the Janissaries by Mahmud II in June 1826*, unpubl. Ph.D. diss. Princeton University 1951; S.J. Shaw, *Between old and new. The Ottoman Empire under Sultan Selim III, 1789-1897*, Cambridge, Mass. 1971; V.H. Aksan, *Whatever happened to the Janissaries? Mobilization for the 1768-1774 Russo-Ottoman War*, in *War in History*, v (1998), 23-36; eadem, *Baron de Tott's "Wretched Fanaticks" and Ottoman military reform in the late eighteenth century*, unpublished paper (cited by gracious permission of author); M. Cezar, *Osmanlı tarihinde levendler*, Istanbul 1965; Meḥmed Esʿad, *Mir'āt-i mühendis-k͟hāne-i berr-i hümāyūn*, Istanbul 1312/1894; M.S. Kütükoğlu, *Sultan II. Mahmud devri yedek ordusu redif-i ʿasakir-i mansure*, in *Tarih Enstitüsü Dergisi*, xii (1981-2), 127-58; M. Çadırcı, *Renovations in the Ottoman army (1792-1869)*, in *Revue Internationale d'Histoire Militaire*, lxvii (1988), 87-102; E.Z. Karal, *Selim II.'ün hatti hümayunları. Nizam-i cedid (1789-1807)*, Ankara 1946 (see esp. 43 ff. for Selīm's military reforms, and 63-71 on naval reforms); T.J. Hope, *The early life and career of Admiral Sir William Sidney Smith in the Balkans and the Near East. The missing years, 1782-83*, in *Bull. de l'Association Internationale d'Études du Sud-Est Européen*, xii (1974), 221-39; M. Kaçar, *Osmanlı imparatorluğunda askeri teknik eğitimde modernleşme çalışmaları ve mühendishanelerin kuruluşu (1808'e kadar)*, in F. Günergun (ed.), *Osmanlı bilimi araştırmaları*, ii, Istanbul 1998, 69-137 (see in particular his remarks on the experiment with the *sürat ṭopd͟julari* in the early 1770s, 79-81); R. Çamuroğlu, *Yeniçerilerin Bektaşiliği ve vaka'i şeriyye*, Istanbul 1991; G. Öz, *Yeniçeri-Bektaşi ilişkileri ve II. Mahmud*, Istanbul 1997; A. Raymond, *Le Caire des Janissaires. L'apogée de la ville ottomane sous Abd al-Rahman Kathuda*, Paris 1995 (concerns the reorientation of Janissaries in a provincial setting to the spheres of local commerce and politics during the lull in fighting on the European front between 1739 and 1768); S. Mutlu, *Yeniçeri ocağının kaldırılışı ve II. Mahmud'un Edirne seyahatı-Mehmed Danış Bey ve eserleri*, Istanbul 1994 (contains the texts in Roman letters of some eye-witness accounts which describe the abolishing of the Janissary corps in 1826).

7. Studies on Janissary-*eṣnāf* relations. R.W. Olson, *Jews, Janissaries and the revolt of 1740 in Istanbul. Social upheaval and political realignment in the Ottoman Empire*, in *JESHO*, xx (1977), 185-207; Aksan, *Mutiny and the eighteenth-century Ottoman army*, in *Turkish Studies Association Bulletin*, xxii (1998), 116-25; C. Kafadar, *Yeniçeri-esnaf relations. Solidarity and conflict*, unpubl. M.A. thesis, McGill University, Montreal 1981 (see esp. ch. 5, "The Revolts", 86-119).

8. General works. (a) Academic studies. N. Weissman, *Les Janissaires. Étude de l'organisation militaire des ottomans*, Paris 1964 (focuses mostly on the connection between the Bektās͟hī order and the Janissary corps); Uzunçarşılı, *Osmanlı devleti teşkilâtından kapu kulu ocakları*, 2 vols. Ankara 1943-4; R. Murphey, *Ottoman warfare, 1500-1700*, London 1999; Muṣṭafā Nūrī, *Netā'id͟j al-wuḳūʿāt*, 2nd printing, 4 vols. Istanbul 1327/1911; Aḥmed D͟jewād, *Tārīk͟h-i ʿaskerī-yi ʿot͟hmānī, kitāb-î ewwel: yeñičeriler*, Istanbul-Paris 1299/1882; Maḥmūd S͟hewket, *ʿOt͟hmānlî tes͟hkīlāt we kiyāfet-i ʿaskeriyyesi*, 2 vols. Istanbul 1325/1909; Pakalın; Meḥmed T͟hüreyyā, *SʿO*, iv (list of names and dates of appointment of Janissary commanders at 771-8, to be compared with a similar list found in a *med͟jmūʿa* preserved in the Süleymaniye Library, Esad Efendi 3622/4); D.E. Pitcher, *An historical geography of the Ottoman Empire*, Leiden 1972.

(b) "Popular" works. G. Schweizer, *Die Janitscharen. Geheime Macht des Türken-Reichs*, Salzburg 1979, repr. Vienna-Munich 1991; G. Goodwin, *The Janissaries*, London 1994; D. Nicolle, *The Janissaries*, London 1995; A. Bakshian, *The Janissaries*, in *The Quarterly Journal of Military History*, iv (1992), 32-43.

(R. Murphey)

YEÑI ḲALʿE, in Turkish, "the New Fortress", a fortress in the southeastern Crimea.

It was founded by the Ottoman sultan Muṣṭafā II [*q.v.*] in 1114/1702 to protect the nearby port of Kerč [*q.v.*] and provide a counterweight to Azov, which had been conquered by Peter the Great in 1696 (and held by Russia for 17 years) [see azaḳ]. When Catherine the Great's armies marched into the Crimea in 1771, Yeñi Ḳalʿe and Kerč fell into Russian hands without resistance and in the Treaty of Küčük Ḳaynard͟ja [*q.v.*] of 1774, the Porte ceded its rights to them, thus giving Russia control of the northern Black Sea shores.

Bibliography: See that to ḳirim. (Ed.)

YEÑI ʿOT͟HMĀNLÎLAR, the Young Ottomans, a political grouping which strove for the establishment of a constitutional régime in the Ottoman empire.

The group was formed in 1865 by a group of six young civil servants who had been trained in the new government offices created under the *Tanẓīmāt*, and specifically in the Translation Bureau of the Porte. Some of the leading members of the group, such as Namïḳ Kemāl [*q.v.*], also pioneered modern journalism in the empire. The Young Ottomans opposed the leading statesmen of their day, Meḥmed Amīn ʿAlī Pasha and Fuʾād Pasha [*q.vv.*], accusing them of establishing a tyrannical régime, of giving in to foreign pressure and betraying the Ottoman interests in the Balkans and on Crete, and of neglecting the Islamic heritage of the empire.

The group formed in 1865 originally called itself the *Ittifāḳ-ï Ḥamiyyet* (Patriotic Alliance). It was loosely modelled after similar movements in Europe, notably the Carbonari in Italy. From 1867 onwards, the group received powerful support from Muṣṭafā Fāḍil Pasha [see FĀḌIL PASHA], a brother of the Egyptian Khedive Ismāʿīl, who had been a high Ottoman bureaucrat, but had fallen out of favour with Fuʾād Pasha. Muṣṭafā Fāḍil Pasha bore Fuʾād an even stronger grudge when the succession to the khedivate was changed in 1866 and he lost his position of heir-apparent to Ismāʿīl. In February 1867, Muṣṭafā Fāḍil, who had been living in Paris since 1866, declared himself the head of the "Party of Young Turkey" to the French press. This apparently denoted a vaguer group of Ottoman reformists than the Patriotic Alliance, which did not recognise him as its head.

At the same time, the Young Ottomans in the empire came under increasing pressure because of their criticism of the régime and their support for Muṣṭafā Fāḍil. Leading members of the group were banned from the capital. Fāḍil Pasha reacted by inviting them to Paris, whither they escaped with the help of the French embassy. For the next three years, the Young Ottomans waged a war of words on the government of Fuʾād and ʿAlī Pasha in Istanbul by way of numerous newspapers that they published in London, Paris and Geneva. Muṣṭafā Fāḍil Pasha made his peace with Sultan ʿAbd al-ʿAzīz during the latter's visit to Paris in August 1867 and returned to Istanbul, but he continued to subsidise some of the Young Ottoman publications. Other powerful politicians, among them Khedive Ismāʿīl, also tried to use the Young Ottomans to put pressure on the government in Istanbul.

The Young Ottomans were a loose grouping of individuals with very different ideological standpoints. Under their general and vague constitutionalism, some came close to European liberalism (Namïḳ Kemāl), while others were more conservative and monarchist (Ḍiyā Bey, later Pasha) or Islamist (ʿAlī Suʿāwī [see SUʿĀWĪ]). The most accomplished political thinker in the group, Namïḳ Kemāl, tried to show that "European" ideas like liberalism, constitutionalism and parliamentarianism were not alien to Ottoman tradition, but could be found in early Islam as well. The effort to explain European liberalism to an Ottoman audience necessitated the development of a new vocabulary as well. Modern political terms such as *millet* ("nation"), *waṭan* ("patrie") or *ḥürriyyet* ("liberté") were coined by the Young Ottomans.

After the deaths of Fuʾād Pasha (1869) and ʿAlī Pasha (1871), almost all Young Ottomans returned to Istanbul. Their hopes of gaining political influence were soon dashed, however. Their newspaper publications again brought them into conflict with the authorities. In 1873 Namïḳ Kemāl used another novel medium—European-style theatre—to convey his message in a patriotic play called *Waṭan yākhūd Silistre* ("The Fatherland, or Silistria"). This brought about an outburst of public support but also led to most of the Young Ottomans being sent into internal exile. When an Ottoman constitution was finally proclaimed in December 1876, this was the work of a number of very senior statesmen and soldiers who were not directly influenced by the Young Ottomans. Although the movement soon lost whatever strength it had had, it remained extremely important as an example to later generations of reformists. The Young Turks, who brought about the constitutional revolution of 1908, took much of their ideals from the Young Ottomans. As important as the strictly political role of the Young Ottomans was their role in the development of journalism (and therefore of "public opinion") in the Ottoman empire [see DJARĪDA. iii].

For the course of events involving the Young Ottomans and Young Turks from 1875 onwards, see DUSTŪR. ii. and ʿOTHMĀNLİ. I. 5; and for the reformist and intellectual currents of the time, see IṢLĀḤ. iii. and PAN-TURKISM.

Bibliography: The definitive work on the Young Ottomans is Şerif Mardin, *The genesis of Young Ottoman thought. A study in the modernization of Turkish political ideas*, Princeton 1962. Niyazi Berkes, *The development of secularism in Turkey*, Montreal 1964, and B. Lewis, *The emergence of modern Turkey*, Oxford 1961 also have valuable sections on the Young Ottomans. Among the older sources, Ebüzziya Tevfik's *Yeñi ʿOthmānlïlar taʾrīkhi* (originally published in instalments in 1909, mod. Tkish. ed. Istanbul 1973, 3 vols.), is still very interesting since Tevfik was a member of the group himself.

(E.J. ZÜRCHER)

YEÑI SHEHIR, modern Turkish Yenişehir, a town of northwestern Anatolia, in what was the classical Bithynia. It lies in lat. 40° 17' N. and long. 29° 38' E. at an altitude of 245 m/800 feet in a long depression running from Inegöl in a northeasterly direction, where this narrows; this plain is drained by the Gök Su, whose waters are used here for irrigation purposes and which flows past Yeñi Shehir into the Sakarya river [*q.v.*].

Yeñi Shehir played an important role in early Ottoman history. It was the first town of significance to be taken at some point in the early 8th/14th century by ʿOthmān I [*q.v.*], who made this town and Sögüd [*q.v.*] his headquarters, using Yeñi Shehir as a base for expansion westwards to the Sea of Marmara, thus cutting the communications of Bursa [*q.v.*], the last independent Byzantine city in the region, with Constantinople, so that ʿOthmān's son Orkhan [*q.v.*] was able to capture Bursa in Djumādā I 716/April 1326. This northwestern region eventually became the *eyālet* or province of Khudāwendigār [*q.v.*]. After Tīmūr had defeated Bāyezīd I at Ankara in Dhu 'l-Ḥidjdja/July 1402, the Tīmūrid army ravaged first Bursa and then Yeñi Shehir and Iznik. Two decisive battles subsequently took place at Yeñi Shehir. On 22 Rabīʿ II 886/20 June 1481 the Ottoman prince Djem [*q.v.*], who had made Bursa his capital in his bid for his father Meḥemmed II Fātiḥ's succession, was defeated by his elder brother Bāyezīd (II) and the commander Gedik Aḥmed Pasha, and fled with his family and the last Ḳaramānid prince Ḳāsim b. Ibrāhīm to the Mamlūk court in Cairo. On 27 Muḥarram 919/15 April 1513 a further battle took place at Yeñi Shehir when Selīm I [*q.v.*], exactly one year after his accession, defeated his elder brother and rival for power, Aḥmed, and executed him.

Thereafter, Yeñi Shehir played only a reduced role in Ottoman history, although it was the home town of Yeñishehirli ʿAbd Allāh Efendi, *Sheykh al-Islām* 1130-42/1718-30 under Aḥmed III. The European guide books of the late 19th century describe it as a modest place, the centre of a *ḳaḍā* in the *sandjak* of Ertoghrul in Khudāwendigār province (actually erected in 1885 out of the former *sandjak* of Biledjik), with around 2,500 inhabitants, all Muslims, several mosques, including the mosque and *ʿimāret* of Sinān Pasha, a *khān*, baths and the *türbe* of a certain Baba Sulṭān (see *Murray's Handbook for Constantinople, Brûsa, and the Troad*, London 1898, 129; a population figure of less than 5,000 is given in *Baedekers Konstantinopel, Balkanstaaten, Kleinasien, Archipel, Cypern*, Leipzig 1914, 265). Yenişehir is now, in the Turkish Republic, the chef-lieu of an *ilce* in the *il* or province of Bursa.

Bibliography: See the indices of the standard histories of early Ottoman times, e.g. C. Imber, *The Ottoman empire 1300-1481*, Istanbul 1990, and R. Mantran (ed.), *Hist. de l'empire ottoman*, Paris 1989. Also Sāmī Bey, *Ḳāmūs al-aʿlām*, s.v.; V. Cuinet, *La Turquie d'Asie*, iv, Paris 1894. (C.E. Bosworth)

YEÑI SHEHIR, the Ottoman name (Yeñi-Shehir i-Fenārī, since 1423) of Larissa (i.e. "citadel"), the chief central Greek city of Thessaly [see TESALYA], lying near the river Peneios and on the highway connecting Athens with Thessalonica [see SELĀNIK]. It is now the seat of Larissa prefecture (*nomos*) (1981 pop. 102,426). Founded in Antiquity, it was fortified by Justinian (6th century), became one of the administrative and military seats of the Byzantine theme of Hellas (9th-10th centuries) and was attacked and temporarily captured by the Bulgarians (985-6), the Latin Crusaders (1204) and the Serbs (1348), withstanding a Norman siege in 1082-3 (see refs. in J. Koder-F. Hild, *Hellas und Thessalia*, Vienna 1976, 198-9; further bibl. in A. Savvides, *Splintered medieval Hellenism: the semi-autonomous state of Thessaly, A.D. 1213/22-1454/70*, in *Byzantion*, lxviii [1998]).

There were in fact three Ottoman conquests of Larissa: in 1386-7 by Evrenos Beg [*q.v.*] and Khayr ul-Dīn Pasha; between 1392-3 and 1396-7 by sultan Bāyezīd I [*q.v.*]; and definitively in 1423 (not A.H. 848, i.e. 1444, according to Ewliyā Čelebi) by the renegade Turakhān Beg [*q.v.*] (refs. in Savvides, *Problems of the Ottoman conquest and the spread of the conquerors in the Thessalian area* [in Greek], in *Thessaliko Hemerológio*, xxviii [1995], 33-64, esp. 36-9, 49-50). From 1423 Larissa-Yeñi Shehir developed into a characteristic Turkish city with a large Muslim population throughout the long period of Ottoman domination (see Helen Angelomate-Tsougarake, *A contribution to the history of economic, social and educational life of Larissa during the Tourkokratia* [in Greek], in *Mesaionika kai Nea Hellenika*, iii [1990], 255-332, esp. 255, 259, citing the *taḥrīr defters* of 1454-5 for Thessaly), remaining steadily an Ottoman base (since 1770 as the seat of Thessaly's central administration, numbering about 40,000 inhabitants; see N. Kladas, art. *Larissa*, in *Megale Hellenike Enkyklopaideia*, xv, ²1964, 802C), despite isolated cases of rebellion, like that of 1600-1 headed by the city's bishop Dionysius. Turakhān Beg himself became Thessaly's first governor and was succeeded by his son ʿÖmer Beg (1456), who also established his headquarters in Yeñi Shehir, where his mosque survived during the time of Ewliyā Čelebi's visit in 1668 (see Th. Palioungas, *The mosque of Omer bey in Larissa. A topographical note* [in Greek], in *Thess. Hemerol.*, xii [1987], 185-92 and idem, *Larissa in the travel accounts of Ewliya Čelebi* [Greek tr.], in *Thess. Hemerol.*, xxvi [1994], 81-104). The town's local fair developed in the 17th-18th centuries, and the sultan Meḥemmed IV [*q.v.*] himself visited it, also in 1668, to find there his future sultana (see C. Spanos, in *Makedoniko Hemerologio* [1972], 349-52; İ.H. Uzunçarşılı, *Osmanlı tarihi*, iii/1, ³Ankara 1983, 415-16).

Although the city's crucial location did not enable it to participate in the Greek War of Liberation (1821-30), still it suffered devastations by the Ottoman generals Meḥmed Reshīd Pasha and Maḥmūd Pasha [see TESALYA]. The Turks held it until 1881, when Thessaly was annexed to the Kingdom of Greece, though Larissa was briefly recaptured by the Ottomans in the course of the Graeco-Turkish war of 1897 (see Kladas, *op. cit.*, 802C-803A; B. Kodaman (ed.), *1897 Türk-Yunan savaşı. Tesalya tarihi*, Ankara 1993, 92 ff.; I. Aktsoglou, in *Thess. Hemerol.*, xxxi [1997], 17-26, with Greek tr. of a Turkish telegram and two poems mentioning the event). In any case, the exodus of the city's Muslim residents was completed by the 1920s.

Bibliography: General manuals (in Greek): E. Pharmakides, *Larissa . . . until its annexation to Greece, 1881. Topographical and historical study*, Volos 1926; Th. Palioungas, *Larissa during the Tourkokratia, 1423-1881*, i, Larissa 1996. See also Y. Halaçoğlu, *Teselya Yenişehiri ve Türk eserleri hakkında bir araştırma*, in *Güney Doğu Avrupa Araştırmaları Dergisi*, ii-iii (1974-9), 89-100; M. Kiel, *Das Türkische Thessalien. Etabliertes Geschichtsbild versus Osmanische Quellen. Ein Beitrag zur Entmythologisierung der Geschichte Griechenlands*, Göttingen 1996; A. Risos, *Wirtschaft, Siedlung und Gesellschaft in Thessalien im Übergang von der byzantinisch-fränkischen zum osmanischen Epoche*, Amsterdam 1996; Savvides, *A conspectus on Ottoman-dominated Thessaly and pertinent research issues* [in Greek], in *Thessaliko Hemerologio*, xxxiii (1998), 149-59; and *Bibl.* to TESALYA.

(A. Savvides)

YERLIYYA, colloquial Turkish-Arabic term derived from the Turkish *yerlü* "local". It was used by the Damascene sources for the local Janissary corps (Turkish *Yerlü Čeri*) to distinguish it from the Ḳapï Ḳullarï Janissary corps (slaves of the Gate or Imperial Janissaries) referred to by the same sources as *Ḳābiḳūl*.

A *fermān* dated 4 Djumādā I 985/20 July 1577 commanded the governor of Damascus to give the places that fell vacant in the Janissary corps to men from Rūm (Anatolia and Rumelia) and not to rich and wealthy natives (*yerlü*) and non-Turkish subjects (*tāt*) (U. Heyd, *Ottoman documents on Palestine, 1522-1615*, Oxford 1960, 61). The *fermān* was not heeded, and natives and foreigners continued to join the corps, which numbered 1,000 in the 1570s. One of the duties of the Janissary corps was to assist the *Defterdārs* of Damascus and Aleppo in collecting taxes (Heyd, 73 n. 3; al-Muḥibbī, *Khulāṣat*, ii, 129, iii, 156, 299, 417-18, 427-8, iv, 449-50; al-Murādī, *Silk*, i, 166, ii, 63; al-Ghazzī, *Nahr al-dhahab*, iii, 266, 279; al-Ṭabbākh, *Iʿlām*, iii, 129). Suffering from the devaluation of the Ottoman silver currency (*aḳče*) with which they were paid, the Janissaries of Damascus imposed extra taxes on the peasants. When the government took disciplinary action against them, they rose in revolt. Between roughly the last quarter of the 16th century, when these events first occurred, and 1069/1658-9, when the Ḳapï Ḳullarï were established in Damascus, the government—and especially under Sultan Murād IV (1032-49/1623-40)—killed at intervals several of the mutinous Janissary chiefs of Damascus, among whom figured Rūmī and non-Turkish individuals. This opened the way to influential Damascenes, mostly grain merchants from the Mīdān quarter, to enroll in the corps. In 1069/1658-9, the Janissary corps in Damascus supported the revolt of the governor of Aleppo, Ḥasan Pasha. But Ḳapï Ḳullarï Janissary troops loyal to the Sultan put down the revolt, punished the rebellious Janissary chiefs and established themselves in Damascus to counter its Janissary corps that was becoming dominated by Damascenes and known accordingly as Yerliyya or "locals". Thus two Janissary corps came to exist in Damascus. The Ḳapi̊ Ḳullari̊ Janissaries took control of the citadel, the walls and the gates of the city. The Yerliyya Janissaries were entrusted with garrisoning the fortresses along the Pilgrimage route to the Ḥidjāz, but most of them stayed in Damascus to serve their own personal interests. The Yerliyya Janissaries were known in Damascus as *Dawlat Dimashk* ("masters of Damascus") and the Ḳapi̊ Ḳullari̊ Janissaries as *Dawlat al-Ḳalʿa* ("masters of the citadel"). The strongholds of the Yerliyya were in the Mīdān and in Sūḳ Sārūdja that was close to the citadel. The Ḳapi̊ Ḳullari̊ were rotated at intervals and reinforced by fresh troops periodically to keep them immune to infiltration by local people. Many of them, however, lived in the city quarters and joined the guilds, which further caused economic rivalry between them and the Yerliyya (Abdul-Karim Rafeq, *al-ʿArab wa 'l-ʿUthmāniyyūn, 1516-1916*, ²Damascus 1993, 142-7, 193-7; idem, *The province of Damascus, 1723-1783*, ²Beirut 1970, 26-35; idem, *The local forces in Syria in the seventeenth and eighteenth centuries*, in V.J. Parry and M.E. Yapp (eds.), *War, technology and society in the Middle East*, London 1975, 277-81.

In 1740, the Yerliyya, in concert with other Damascene power groups and with the approval of the sultan, expelled the Ḳapi̊ Ḳullari̊ from Damascus. The prestige of the Yerliyya soared as they controlled the citadel, the walls and the gates of the city. A group of them, known locally by the Turkish term *zorab* or *zorbāwāt* (sing. *zorba*, meaning "insolent one" or "rebel"), went out of control (Redhouse, *Turkish dictionary*, 589; Dozy, *Supplément*, i, 584; Aḥmad al-Budayrī al-Ḥallāḳ, *Ḥawādith Dimashk al-yawmiyya, 1154-1175/1762-1741*, ed. Aḥmad ʿIzzat ʿAbd al-Karīm, Cairo 1959, 62 ff.). Challenged by the *zorab*, the governor Asʿad Pasha al-ʿAẓm (1743-57) used his private troops, the Dalātiyya, in 1746 to discipline them. Many of them were killed and their houses destroyed (al-Budayrī, 66-70; Rafeq, *al-ʿArab*, 258-61). To guard against the resurgence of Yerliyya power, Asʿad Pasha reinstated the Ḳapi̊ Ḳullari̊ Janissaries in Damascus. Further clashes between the two corps weakened the Yerliyya, who sought help from the local Ashrāf (al-Budayrī, 214-16; Rafeq, *Province*, 171-5, 223-6). The animosity between the two Janissary corps, each representing special interests, continued until 1826 when the Janissary corps was altogether abolished in the Ottoman empire and replaced by the new European-style army known as Niẓām-i̊ Djedīd [*q.v.*].

Bibliography: Given in the article.

(Abdul-Karim Rafeq)

YESHIL IRMAK, modern Tkish. Yeşil Irmak ("the Green River"), a river of northern Anatolia, the classical Iris in the province of Pontus (see *PW*, ix/2, col. 2045).

The upper course of the river, called the Tozanlı Su, rises in the Köse Dağ to the northeast of Sivas and flows westwards by Tokat [*q.v.*] and Turhal. Here there is a fertile plain, the Kazova or "Goose Plain", which is now irrigated by waters from the Almus dam on the river's course above it, completed in 1966, and a canal running off and parallel to the river, enabling cereals, sugar-beet and vines to grow there (for a description of the Kazova as it was over a century ago, see H. Van Lennep, *Travels in little-known parts of Asia Minor*, London 1870, ii, 86-7). The river turns northwards by Amasya [*q.v.*] and another fertile region and then eastwards, taking in the Kelkit as an important right-bank affluent, then northwards through a narrow valley with defiles to emerge at the Black Sea coast in a delta built up by silt carried down from the mountains of the interior. The delta is partly wooded and partly used for agriculture, but with marshes, in the past malarial, towards the sea. The small town of Çarşamba, 32 km/20 miles to the east of Samsun [*q.v.*], is situated here on the Yeşil Irmak's left bank. A road runs along the east-west trough of the upper and middle sections of Yeşil Irmak's course, with a short stretch of the valley between Turhal and Amasya carrying the railway from Kalın near Sivas to Samsun, but the river has never been navigable.

Bibliography: Naval Intelligence Division, Admiralty Handbooks. *Turkey*, London 1943, i, 167-8, ii, 152-3, 254, 312-13 and indices; *İA*, art. *Yeşilırmak* (Metin Tuncel).

(C.E. Bosworth)

YESHILKÖY, a town of what is now the urban agglomeration of Istanbul, on the shores of the Sea of Marmara 15 km/9 miles from the city centre; before 1924 it was known as Agios Stephanios in Greek and Ayastefanos in Turkish.

The place is not mentioned in Byzantine sources, but appears in Villehardouin when he describes the arrival of the Crusader fleet in 1203 and mentions "an abbey at St. Stephen three leagues from Constantinople" (ed. Paris 1961, 127). After the Ottoman conquest, Meḥemmed II deported large numbers of persons during his Serbian campaign of 1454 and installed them there (Ducas, xlii, 11; *Anonymus Giese*, 111; Kritovoulos, B22 (2)). It was probably from these that the Ottoman village of Ayastefanos arose; in 1498 the inhabitants comprised 20 hearths of share-cropping slaves (*ortakdji̊ ḳullar*) with Slav forenames and 24 hearths of free *reʿāyā*, with Slav and Greek forenames, and a few Muslims, a total of *ca.* 170 persons (BBA, Tapu tahrir 1086, ff. 64b-66a).

By an act of *waḳf* in October 1505, Bāyezīd II attached the village to the mosque that he built in the capital, and *ca.* 1525 the *Defterdār* Ibrāhīm Čelebi rented out to the *waḳf* a stretch of ground at the modern village of Bakırköy as a pleasure garden, which was taken into the *waḳf* after his execution in 1534. Ewliyā Čelebi probably exaggerated when he counted 500 hearths at Ayastefanos in the mid-17th century, but mentions a *tekke*, a small bazaar and two churches. Parallel to agricultural acivities there (the requirement of milk delivery to the capital for a yoghurt factory there, *yoghurtdju kārkhānesi*, is mentioned for March 1762: *Istanbul külliyâtı*, vii, 119-20), the village early acquired a residential character. The Wallachian prince Constantine Brancovan retired to a house there after his deposition in 1713. The place prospered above all thanks to the Armenian Dadian family, who in 1796 founded a gunpowder factory in the adjacent village of Āzādli̊. Ohannes Dadyan (d. 1869) built in 1826 an Armenian church of St. Stephen, and the Greek church, of the same dedication, was renovated in 1845 by his nephew Boghos Dadyan. A Greek primary school was opened in 1862, a Roman Catholic church was added in 1865 and the first mosque built in 1905 (cf. Pars Tuğlacı, *The role of the Dadian family in Ottoman social, economic and political life*, Istanbul 1993).

At the time of the Russo-Turkish War of 1877-8, the Russian army reached Ayastefanos, and it was there that the Treaty of San Stefano was signed setting up an (in fact, ephemeral) Greater Bulgaria (3 March 1878). The village was connected to the capital by steamer in 1852 and by a suburban railway line, utilising the

Orient railway line, in the 1880s. In 1887, lands of the Dadian family between the railway line and the sea were granted out for development, permitting a considerable expansion of the village, which had 160 families in 1905. During the counter-revolution of 1909, the deputies of the new Ottoman parliament retired to Ayastefanos, to which there also arrived the first battalion of the relieving Army of Salonica ('Abd ül-Raḥmān Sheref Efendi, *Tārīkh*, Ankara 1998, 20-1, 34-5). The Greek population of the village was not included in the population exchanges of the post-war period. It now in 1924 took on the name of Yeshilköy. The original military airport of 1911 gradually became the main airport for Istanbul. In 1990 Yeşilköy had 22,674 inhabitants.

Bibliography: Given in the article.

(S. Yerasimos)

YETI SU, in mediaeval Turkish "[the land of] the seven rivers", rendered in recent times by Russian scholars as Semirečʾe, a region of Central Asia.

It comprised essentially the lands north of Transoxania [see mā warāʾ al-nahr] which stretched from the basin of the Issïk-Kol [*q.v.*] lake northwards to Lake Balkhash [*q.v.*], and it derived its name from the numerous rivers draining it, such as the Ču [*q.v.*], which peters out in the desert to the northeast of the middle Sïr Daryā [*q.v.*], and several rivers flowing into Lake Balkhash such as the Ili [*q.v.*], which rises in Dzungaria and flows through Ḳuldja [*q.v.*] into Semirečʾe, and the Ḳaratal, Aḳsu and various others rising in the northern slopes of the Tien Shan and in the Alatau mountains further north. What was the mediaeval Semirečʾe is now comprised in the northern part of the new republic of Kirghizia and the southeastern part of that of Kazakhstan.

Although the lower reaches of the Ču and the rivers entering Lake Balkhash run through arid, desert lands, in their upper courses, along the foothills of the mountain massifs, and in the lands around the Issïk-Kol, the terrain has always been attractive for human settlement, with at times towns and agriculture and with pastures suitable for nomads and their herds. This has given Semirečʾe a geographical and cultural identity of its own, and at several periods it has played a significant role in Inner Asian history. In particular, the generally east-west-running rivers provide routes through the Tien Shan into eastern Turkistan (the Chinese Sinkiang [*q.v.*]), with the Ili, further north, forming a particularly important strategic corridor via Ḳuldja into Dzungaria, with the possibility of passing by Urumči and Ḳomul [*q.v.* in Suppl.] through the Kansu [*q.v.*] corridor into the western part of China proper. Hence these routes have always been important, *inter alia*, for commercial exchanges between Western Asia and China.

In pre-Islamic times, Chinese annals of the 2nd century A.D. mention Semirečʾe as being in the hands of a nomadic people, the Wu-sun, with the Hsiung-nu or Huns controlling the upper Irtish river [*q.v.*] lands to the north of it and Dzungaria. In the 4th century, the Zhuan-zhuan confederacy, which had arisen out of the disintegration of the Huns, incorporated Semirečʾe in their territories. In the early 7th century, the Buddhist pilgrim Huien-Tsang (Xuan-zang) found many towns there, with flourishing agriculture and a commerce dominated by Sogdian colonists, and with the Manichaean faith widespread amongst the people. There must also have been already Nestorian Christians, whose graves have been found in Semirečʾe with dates indicating their presence there well into Mongol times (see in general, Barthold, *Zur Geschichte des Christentums in Mittel-Asien bis zur mongolischen Eroberung*, Tübingen and Leipzig 1901, and, more specifically, below). By this time, the Western Turks were dominant in the region, but their empire collapsed in the mid-8th century and the resultant confusion facilitated the Arabs' penetration of Transoxania at this time, although Talas [see ṭarāz] for long marked the limit of the Muslim advance northwards into the steppes. Turkish tribes meanwhile consolidated their hold on Semirečʾe, with the Ḳarluḳ [*q.v.*] in 766 occupying the former Türgesh capital of Suyab to the north of the Ču (probably to be situated to the northeast of Pishpek) (see O. Pritsak, *Von den Karluk zu den Karachaniden*, in *ZDMG*, ci [1951], 277-8). Islamic geographers of the 4th/10th century mention not only the Ḳarluḳ, amongst whom Islam had begun gradually to spread, but other Turkish tribes like the Toghuzghuz [*q.v.*], Čigil and Tukhsï (see *Ḥudūd al-ʿālam*, tr. Minorsky, maps v and vi) who resisted Islam for much longer. Towns, clearly of some importance, now begin to be noted, such as Barskhān on the shores of the Issïk-Kol and Balāsāghūn [*q.v.*] situated somewhere in the Ču valley, whose seizure, being by then a Muslim town, by pagan Turks in *ca.* 940 is recorded in Islamic sources (see Barthold, *Zwölf Vorlesungen über die Geschichte der Türken Mittelasiens*, Berlin 1935, 77-8). These infidel Turks must have been the early Ḳarakhānids [see ilek-khāns] before their conversion to Islam. Within a generation or so, these last had become Muslim, and they used Semirečʾe as a base for their take-over of Transoxania from the Sāmānids. In the early 5th/11th century, Aḥmad Ṭoghan Khān, brother of the Ilig Naṣr, ruled Semirečʾe and Kāshgharia, but lost the latter to his second cousin and rival Yūsuf Ḳadïr Khān. From the middle of this century onwards, Semirečʾe, being with Eastern Turkistan the original Ḳarakhānid dominions, constituted the Eastern Khānate of the dynasty.

Over the next century and a half, Semirečʾe was fought over by various rival Ḳarakhānid princes. It was in this time that much of the region became Islamised, but a new power came on the scene in the 1130s, the people of the Kitan or Khiṭay, Buddhist in faith and possibly of proto-Mongol or (less likely) Tungusic ethnic origin, the Western Liao of Chinese historians [see ḳara khiṭay, and now D.C. Twichett, in *Camb. hist. of China*, vi, *Alien regimes and border states 907-1368*, Cambridge 1994, 45-6]. According to one source, the Khiṭay had infiltrated into northern Semirečʾe a century earlier in 433/1041-2. After *ca.* 1140, the army camp of the Gurkhān or ruler of the Ḳara Khiṭay, called *khosun ordo* "strong encampment", was situated on the banks of the Ču, and the Gurkhāns' basically hostile attitude to Islam imposed on Muslims there. After *ca.* 1209, their position was disputed by the Nayman Mongol adventurer Küčlüg, who speedily ended the power of the Ḳara Khiṭay and took over both Semirečʾe and Eastern Turkistan, using Semirečʾe and the eastern Sïr Daryā region as his base against the Khʷārazm Shāh ʿAlāʾ al-Dīn Muḥammad [see khʷārazm-shāhs]. But a Čingizid Mongol force under Ḳubilay Noyon had already reached northern Semirečʾe in 1211, disputing with Küčlüg for control there, and in 1218 Čingiz's commander Djebe Noyon defeated Küčlüg and entered Balāsāghūn without a fight, the Muslim inhabitants there being thankful to shake off Küčlüg's tyranny. Semirečʾe thus escaped devastation by the Mongols, and travellers through the region in the 13th and early 14th centuries, both Chinese and Western ones, describe there a flourishing agricultural and commercial economy, with populous towns such as Almalïgh [*q.v.*] in the upper Ili valley.

The rule of the Mongol Čag̲h̲atayids [see ČAG̲H̲ATAY K̲H̲ĀN; ČAG̲H̲ATAY K̲H̲ĀNATE] was favourable to the adherents of non-Muslim faiths, for the Čag̲h̲atayid K̲h̲āns themselves resisted conversion to Islam until the mid-14th century. The Nestorian Christian cemeteries at Ṭokmaḳ and Pis̲h̲pek, discovered by Russian amateur archaeologists at the end of the 19th century, have yielded nearly 600 gravestones inscribed in Syriac script, most of them in Syriac language but some in eastern Turkish; their dates range from 1186 to 1345. In the reign of the K̲h̲ān Čangs̲h̲i (1334-8) Roman Catholic missionaries built a fine church near Almalïg̲h̲, and in this same century there existed an Armenian monastery on the shores of the Ïssïk-Kol (Barthold, *Zwölf Vorlesungen*, 206; T.W. Thacker, *A Nestorian gravestone from Central Asia in the Gulbenkian Museum, Durham University*, in *Durham University Jnal.*, N.S., xxviii [1966-7], 94-17). But the definitive conversion to Islam of the Čag̲h̲atayids in the mid-14th century led to persecution of the Christians of Semireč'e, and thereafter, mention of their faith fades away. Semireč'e was in any case much disturbed from this time onwards by internecine warfare amongst Mongol claimants to power, and in 776/1335 Tīmūr [*q.v.*] invaded Mog̲h̲olistān [*q.v.*], as the whole region north of Transoxania was now generally known, the first of several expeditions against the local Turco-Mongol ruler of Semireč'e, Ḳamar al-Dīn, who was eventually driven out and fled to the Altai mountains region. Soon afterwards began incursions into Semireč'e by the Buddhist Mongol Oyrats, called by the Muslims Ḳalmuḳs [see KALMUKS], who now became an enduring factor in the history of the region and who raided as far as the Sïr Daryā province. As a result of all this unrest, Chinese sources of the 15th century no longer speak of flourishing towns and villages in Semireč'e but of a land exclusively inhabited by nomads who dwelt in tents.

At the beginning of the 16th century, pagan tribesmen of the Turkish tribe of the Ḳirg̲h̲iz [*q.v.*], who had traditionally lived in the upper Yenisei region, moved southwards into Semireč'e, this being the first attestation of this people in the neighbourhood of what has become their modern home, the new republic of Kirghizia. Threats by both the Ḳalmuḳs and the Ḳirg̲h̲iz against Transoxania led to attacks on them by the Turco-Mongol *amīrs* of Transoxania, including Mīrzā Muḥammad Ḥaydar Dug̲h̲lāt [*q.v.*], in whose *Tārīk̲h̲-i Ras̲h̲īdī* these invading peoples from the northern steppes, what subsequently became known as the Kazakh Steppe, and their territory of Mog̲h̲olistān, are designated the D̲j̲ätä, with a pejorative implication that this means "marauders, robbers" (cf. Ottoman *čete* "band, group", with a neutral meaning, however: Radloff, *Versuch eines Wörterbuches der Türk-Dialecte*, iii, 1983, and see also Mīrzā Muḥammad Ḥaydar, tr. N. Elias and E.D. Ross, *A history of the Moghuls of Central Asia*, London 1895, introd., 75-6; Barthold, in *Four studies on the history of Central Asia*, i, 54, 139). Nevertheless, Ḳalmuḳ domination of Semireč'e lasted until the mid-18th century, when in 1755-8 Chinese armies came westwards and overthrew the Ḳalmuḳs. The Ḳirg̲h̲iz and Kazakhs were now left virtually independent in Semireč'e until the armies of Imperial Russia advanced through the Kazakh Steppe. The Russian occupation of Semireč'e brought them up to the frontier with China, and in 1864 a treaty between the two empires defined this frontier, thus enabling Russian forces to secure their flank for an assault on the K̲h̲ānate of K̲h̲oḳand [*q.v.*], and in 1865 Russia put an end to K̲h̲oḳand's independence. Semireč'e was henceforth part of the Russian governorate-general of Turkestan, and in 1899 formally became one of its five component districts (*oblast*). Alma Ata or Almaty (now the capital of the Kazakhstan Republic) was developed as the administrative centre of Semireč'e under the name of Vernyi ("the loyal [city]"). After the Russian Revolution and the civil wars in Russia, the region was divided between the Kazakh and the Kirghiz SSRs, and the name Semireč'e became obsolete.

Bibliography: The only monograph specifically devoted to the region is Barthold's early work *Očerkʿ istorii Semireč'ya*, Vernyi [Alma Ata] 1898, repr. in *Sočineniya*, ii/1, Moscow 1963, 21-106, Eng. tr. V. and T. Minorsky, *History of the Semirechyé*, in *Four studies on the history of Central Asia*, i, Leiden 1956, 73-171. In addition to references given in the article, there are further ones in Barthold, *Turkestan down to the Mongol invasion*[3], index, and other general works on the history of Central Asia such as Grousset, *L'empire des steppes*; Sinor (ed.), *The Cambridge history of early Inner Asia*; etc. (C.E. BOSWORTH)

YILDIZ [see TĀD̲J̲ AL-DĪN YILDIZ].

YÏLDÏZ KÖS̲H̲KÜ [see YÏLDÏZ SARĀYÏ].

YÏLDÏZ SARĀYÏ, the most recent of the Imperial Ottoman palaces, situated on the heights above the European Bosphorus shore and above the quarter of Beşiktaş. The whole complex of buildings, set in a large park, covers almost 50 ha.

Like other Imperial residences along the Bosphorus, it had its origin in a garden and a hunting ground. Mentions of pre-19th century buildings are confused. The first trace is of a fountain with an inscription from 1219 [/1804] which apparently went with a pavilion built by Selīm III for his mother Mihris̲h̲āh Sulṭān. It was probably this building which for the first time bore the name Yïldïz "star" since it is not mentioned by the meticulous chronicler of Selīm's movements, Aḥmed Efendi, in his *Rūznāme*, but first appears in the *Ta'rīk̲h̲-i Enderūn* of K̲h̲iḍr Ilyās Ag̲h̲a (Istanbul 1987, 63) in connection with a visit of Maḥmūd II (1808-39 [*q.v.*]) on 3 August 1812; it is also mentioned at the same period by Andreossy. In 1834-5 Maḥmūd built a small pavilion surrounded by a garden. It was demolished in 1842 and replaced by ʿAbd ül-Med̲j̲īd (1839-61 [*q.v.*]) with a building for his mother, called the Ḳaṣr-i Dilküs̲h̲ā, and he also undertook the laying out of amenities to the west of a vast park surrounding this structure. Following a first plan done by the German Stefel, other German landscape architects, Schlerf in 1860 and Vienhild in 1862, also worked there.

The Čirag̲h̲ān palace completed in 1871 on the Bosphorus shores by ʿAbd ül-ʿAzīz (1861-76 [*q.v.*]) was linked by a bridge over the road with the Yïldïz park, making the latter a pleasure ground for the new palace. The Malta and Tent Kiosks were then built there by the Balian brothers, Sarkis and Hagop. At the same time, the sultan embarked on a series of buildings on the higher part of the park destined to function for public audiences and the reception of ambassadors and dignitaries, the Büyük Mābeyn Kös̲h̲kü and the Indian Lady Pavilion. Round this nucleus, ʿAbd ül-Ḥamīd II (1876-1909 [*q.v.*]), fearing that being too near the coast would make him vulnerable, built his own residence and made Yïldïz a symbol of his absolute power. A new team of landscape specialists, German, Italian and French, laid out gardens in the English style, whilst the architectural construction was undertaken by Sarkis Balian and then Raimondo d'Aronco.

Access to the palace was by a rise, to the right of which was built in 1885-6 the Ḥamīdiyye mosque, convenient for the sultan to attend the Friday worship, with the nearby Terrace Pavilion built for the congregation. The rise ended in the Harem Gate, the main one of the palace, giving on to a court blocked by a long building, that of the sultan's aides-de-camp and servants (*yāwerān we bendegān dā'iresi*). To the left of the court was situated on the west the Great Chancery, and on the north the Indian Lady Pavilion. To the right of the Harem Gate was a long range comprising the kitchens, cellars, armoury and coachmen's quarters with those of the Albanian guards on the floor above. Facing this, the prolongation of the aides-de-camp's building housed the library and a cabinet of curiosities.

A door in the angle between the Indian Lady Pavilion and the aides-de-camp's building gave access to the private apartments. Within was the Small Chancery, Küčük Mābeyn, with the sultan's office and a building containing the private apartments, of great simplicity, of ʿAbd ül-Ḥamīd, a theatre (these structures being the work of the Italian architect Raimondo d'Aronco, 1857-1932) and a building with the quarters of the chief eunuchs, governesses and the less favoured odalisques. Behind this last was the interior garden, arranged round an artificial water scheme with an island in it on which was a miniature farm. At the south end of the garden was the Belvedere Kiosk, Dji̲hānnümā Kös̲h̲kü, and at the north end the apartments of the wives and the odalisques; the whole ensemble of the private apartments and garden was surrounded by a high wall. To the west of the ensemble were the service buildings and further out, and isolated, the apartments of the royal princes. At the extreme north was a grand pavilion for the reception of guests, the Chalet, S̲h̲ale Kös̲h̲kü, which connected with both the private apartments and the great park situated to the east. The building was built in three phases, corresponding to the rhythm of royal visits, including the German Kaiser Wilhelm II's two visits of 1889 and 1898, the first two phases being the work of Balian and the third that of d'Aronco. In the park there were also workshops for carpentry and ceramics, the latter making the porcelain known as Yildiz, functioning from 1895-1909, 1911-20 and now from 1962 onwards.

ʿAbd ül-Ḥamīd's deposition in 1909 meant that the palace fell into disfavour and was even partially pillaged. Nevertheless, Meḥemmed VI (1918-22 [*q.v.*]) spent the greater part of his reign at Yildiz. In the 1930s the Yildiz estate was divided into three, with the greater part used by the Military Academy, Harp Akademisi; the Chalet and other service buildings designated for the use of the President of the National Assembly; and the other palace buildings, along with the Malta and Tent Kiosks, given to the municipality of Istanbul and opened to the public in 1940. With the move of the Military Academy to Ankara in 1968, new arrangements were made: the main buildings were transferred to the Ministry of Culture for use as museums and the service buildings to the west were taken over by the Yıldız Technical University. In 1999 the Ministry of Culture's section houses the Yıldız Museum and the Museum of the City of Istanbul, a research institute for Islamic history, art and culture, etc.

Bibliography: 1. Works on the history of the complex under ʿAbd ül-Ḥamīd. P. de Régla, *La Turquie officielle*, Paris 1889, 41-59; G. Dorys, *Abdul-Hamid intime*, [7]Paris 1907, 101-41; ʿO̲t̲h̲mān Nūrī, *ʿAbd ül-Ḥamīd-i t̲h̲ānī we dewr-i salṭanatī*, Istanbul 1327/1909; Tahsin Paşa, *Abdülhamid ve Yıldız hatırları*, Istanbul 1931; Ziya Şakir, *II. Sultan Hamit, şahsiyeti ve hususiyetleri*, Istanbul 1943; İ.H. Uzunçarşılı, *II. Sultan Abdülhamid'in hal'i ve ölümüne dâir bâzı vesikalar*, in *Belleten*, x (1946), 705-48; S. Ünüvar, *Saray hatıralarım*, Istanbul 1964; Bekir Sıtkı Baykal, *Ibretnüma. Mâbeynci Fahri Bey'in hatıraları ve ilgili bazı belgeler*, Ankara 1968; Aïché Osmanoglou, *Avec mon père, le Sultan Abdulhamid de son palais à son prison*, Paris 1991.

2. Works on the history and architecture of the complex. *İA*, art. *Yıldız Köşkü*; Çelik Gülersoy, *Yıldız parki ve Malta Köşkü*, Istanbul 1979; Metin And, *Saraya bağlı tiyatrolar ve II. Abdülhamid'in Yıldız Sarayı tiyatrosu*, Istanbul 1987; Önder Küçükerman, *Dünya sarayların prestij teknolojisi. Porselen sanatı ve Yıldız çini fabrikası*, Istanbul 1987; Pars Tuğlaci, *The role of the Balian family in Ottoman architecture*, Istanbul 1990, 289, 497-506, 546-656; Metin Sözen, *Devletin evi saray*, Istanbul 1990, 196-213; Mustafa Cezar, *XIX. yüzyıl Beyoğlu*, Istanbul 1991, 333-48; arts. on the palace, its park and its various buildings, in *Günden bügüne İstanbul ansiklopedisi*, 8 vols. Istanbul 1993-5; Diana Barillari and Ezio Godoli, *Istanbul 1900*, Istanbul 1997, 67-77.

(S. Yerasimos)

YIRMISEKIZ MEḤMED [see meḥmed yirmisekiz].

YOG̲H̲URT (t.), from older Turkish *yug̲h̲ur-*, Ottoman *yog̲h̲urmaḳ/yoğurmak* "to knead [dough, etc.], yoghourt, a preparation of soured milk made in the pastoralist, more temperate northern tier of the Middle East, Central Asia and the Balkans, appearing as *yog̲h̲urt/yog̲h̲rut* in Maḥmūd al-Kās̲h̲g̲h̲arī (*Dīwān lug̲h̲āt al-turk*, tr. Atalay, i, 182, ii, 189, iii, 164, 190; Brockelmann, *Mitteltürkischer Wortschatz*, 92. Cf. also Radloff, *Versuch eines Worterbuch der Türk-Dialecte*, iii/1, 412-13; Doerfer, *Türkische und mongolische Elemente im Neupersichen*, iv, 173-5 no. 1866; Clauson, *An etymological dictionary of pre-thirteenth century Turkish*, 906-7). It seems to have been used for therapeutic purposes by the pre-Islamic Uyg̲h̲ur Turks (G.R. Rachmat [Arat], *Zur Heilkunde der Uiguren. I*, in *SPWAW Berlin*, phil.-hist. Kl., xxiv [1930], 6, 12, *Pt. II*, in *ibid.*, xxv [1932], 8).

Partially skimmed milk is reduced over a slow heat, and after cooling, a quantity of a previous fermentation is introduced and then the whole left slowly to cool and become more solid. The product is called *māst* in Persia; *laban* in Syrian and Palestinian Arabic; *zabādī* in Egyptian Arabic; *liban* in ʿIrāḳī Arabic; *rā'ib, laban, labne*, etc. in the Arabian peninsula. A cool, refreshing drink is also made from yoghourt and water (*ayran* in Turkish; *dūg̲h̲* in Persian; *lassi* in India). Yoghourt figures extensively in Middle Eastern eating practices, both in cooked dishes (see e.g. D. Waines, *In a caliph's kitchen. Mediaeval Arabic cooking for the modern gourmet*, London 1989, 64-5, 78-9) and mixed with vegetables such as cucumber (the *māst-k̲h̲iyār* of Persian cuisine, cf. E.G. Browne, *A year amongst the Persians*, [2]Cambridge 1926, 190-3).

Bibliography: See also *İA*, art. *Yoğurt* (Kâzim Yetiş); *Larousse gastronomique*, s.v. *yoghourt, yagourt.*

(C.E. Bosworth)

YORGAN LADIK [see lād̲h̲iḳ. 2].

YORUBA, a people of West Africa. The present article deals with the role of Islam among the Yoruba.

The earliest attested presence of Islam among this people of what is now Nigeria would seem to date back to the Old Ọyọ empire in the 16th century. The role of Songhay-speaking Muslim traders in the early spread of Islam is reflected in a number of Songhay loanwords in Yoruba. The earliest term for the Muslims, *imalé* "People from Mali", probably refers to this group. Islam apparently first took root among traders, craftsmen (especially weavers) and warriors (especially horsemen) in Ọyọ towns. Muslim slaves from the north were also absorbed into the royal and aristocratic households. All these groups became involved in the overthrow of the empire (*ca.* 1797-1837) and in the establishment of new warrior city states. The heterogenous Muslim groups of Ilọrin overthrew their Ọyọ warlord in 1824 and founded an Islamic amīrate under Sokoto [*q.v.*] authority. The *amīrs*, descendants of a Fulani preacher who had forged the Islamic community, were elected and controlled by a council of the leading warlords. The cosmopolitan but increasingly Yorubanised town became famous for its Islamic schools and its scholars and saints.

Ibadan, the second warrior state and Ilọrin's most formidable antagonist, also developed a Muslim majority. Ilọrin, Ibadan and their dependent Yoruba towns became crucial for the spread of Islam as an element of urban culture and associational life, especially among the Yoruba marketwomen. The same happened in Lagos, a British colony since 1861 with sizeable groups of Muslim slave returnees from Sierra Leone and Brazil. Yoruba Muslim slaves and freedmen had already played a leading role in the *Malé* revolt of 1835 in Bahia.

Islamic communities expanded markedly during the colonial period (1895-1960). Widely propagated by preachers and local associations and increasingly entrenched in the communal structures, Islam grew along with Christianity in Yorubaland. As Christian missionary education came to dominate the educational institutions in Western Nigeria the Muslims tried to meet the challenge. The spread of the Aḥmadiyya [*q.v.*] since 1916 was followed by the foundation of the *Young Ansar-Ud-Deen Society* (Lagos 1923) and other societies which established "Western" Schools for Muslims and became models of reform for Yoruba Islamic communities. Local Islamic learning was adapted to Arab educational models, mainly by young Islamic scholars and preachers from Ilọrin, like Kamāl al-Dīn (b. 1906) and Ādam al-Ilūrī (1916-92) who also became one of the most prolific Arabic writers in West Africa. Contacts with Arab countries and with al-Azhar and other Islamic universities strongly increased after independence. Since the 1970s, Arabic schools expanded tremendously. The *Muslim Students' Society (MSS)*, founded in Lagos in 1954, was instrumental in bringing together Muslim students of different educational and regional backgrounds; it became the first national Islamic organisation, mobilising and transforming the younger Muslim élite of the south. The highly educated, well-organised and sometimes very wealthy Yoruba Muslims, both men and women, became politically important. They were often able to mediate between North and South and between Muslims and Christians within Nigeria. Chief Moshood Abiọla, the presidential candidate who died in detention in 1998, owed much of his nationwide electoral success in 1993 to his skills in this field. The Yoruba remain one of the rare peoples with an almost equal share of Islam and Christianity.

Bibliography: H.J. Fisher, *Aḥmadiyya. A study in contemporary Islam on the West African coast*, London 1963; E.D. Adelọwọ, *Islam in Ọyọ and its districts in the nineteenth century*, Ph.D. thesis, Univ. of Ibadan 1978; T.G.O. Gbadamosi, *The growth of Islam among the Yoruba 1841-1908*, London 1978; A. Shitu-Agbẹtọla, *Islam in Ondo State of Nigeria, 1850-1960*, Ph.D. thesis, Univ. of Ibadan 1983; I.A.A. Seriki, *Islam among the Ẹgba and Ijẹbu peoples (1841-1982)*, Ph.D. thesis, Univ. of Ibadan 1986; Ādam al-Ilūrī, *Nasīm al-ṣabā fī akhbār al-islām wa-ʿulamāʾ bilād Yūrubā*, Cairo 1987; S. Reichmuth and R.D. Abubakre, in J.O. Hunwick (ed.), *Arabic literature in Africa*, ii, Leiden 1995: *Ilorin and Nupe in the nineteenth and twentieth centuries*, 439-92, *Ibadan, Lagos and other areas of Southern Nigeria*, 493-549; Reichmuth, *Education and the growth of religious associations among Yoruba Muslims. The Ansar-Ud-Deen Society of Nigeria*, in *Journal of Religion in Africa*, xxvi (1996), 365-405; idem, *Islamische Bildung und soziale Integration in Ilorin (Nigeria) seit ca. 1800*, Münster 1998. See also ỌYỌ and its *Bibl.*

(S. Reichmuth)

YÖRÜK, Yürük, a term applied to pastoral nomadic groups in the Ottoman empire.

Three main meanings are attested in the literature: (1) in the Ottoman empire, primarily a special term with legal, administrative and fiscal implications denoting a particular class of nomads obliged to serve in the Ottoman army; (2) in modern ethnological and anthropological literature, a term for, and also a self-designation of, nomadic pastoralists, including elements in various stages of sedentarisation, used in an ethnic sense as opposed to Türkmen [*q.v.*], Kurdish [see kurds, kurdistan] or other pastoralist tribal groups of Anatolia; and (3) in Ottoman and modern times, a general, and therefore less appropriate, term for nomadic pastoralist Turkish tribal groups.

Etymology and significations.

The term Yörük/Yürük is usually derived from the old Turkic verb "to walk, to march" *yorï-* (references in Sir Gerard Clauson, *An etymological dictionary of pre-thirteenth-century Turkish*, Oxford 1972, 957). Middle Turkic forms range from *yori* "to walk, to travel" (see e.g. Maḥmūd al-Kāshgharī, *Dīwān lughāt al-turk*, ed. and tr. R. Dankoff and J. Kelly, *Compendium of the Turkic dialects*, iii, Cambridge, Mass. 1985, index 231) to *yüri-* and *yürü-* in texts from the 13th to 15th centuries (Clauson, *ibid.*). In most modern Turkic languages the stem is found with high rounded front vowels, e.g. Ttü. *yürü-* "to move, to march, to go". In Anatolia, also, the forms *yüri-* and *yürü-* "to march" are attested in vocalised texts from the 14th century, e.g. in the *Kitāb-i Ghunya* in Old Anatolian Turkish (ed. Muzaffer Akkuş, Ankara 1995, index); for further examples for the 15th to 17th centuries, see *Tarama sözlüğü*, vi, Ankara 1972, 4775-7. The noun *yörük/yürük* (with deverbal nominal-forming suffix *-k*) "walking, going briskly, running, fast (horse)" appears only in Čaghatay, Crimean Tatar and Ottoman Turkish (W. Radloff, *Versuch eines Wörterbuches der Türk-Dialecte*, iii, St. Petersburg 1905, col. 604). In Ottoman historical texts, mainly of the 15th and 16th centuries, the term *yörük/yürük* has a specific administrative or fiscal meaning (see below). European lexicographers tend to render only the general meaning, probably because by their time, the word had to a certain extent lost its particular meaning; see e.g. F. Meninski (1623-98), who has for *yürük* "vagabond, person of no fixed abode" (*Lexicon Arabico-Persico-Turcicum*, Vienna 1780, iv, col. 5617); J.Th. Zenker lists *yörük/yürük* as meaning "someone who walks, runs, a vagabond", while *Yürükler* is for him the name of a nomadic tribe and a village in Asia Minor (*Türkisch-arabisch-persisches Handwörterbuch*, Leipzig 1866, ii, 971), reflecting the ethnic connotation of the term prevalent from the 19th century onwards. J.W. Redhouse goes a step further and lists for *yürük*, 1. "active, that goes fast, fleet", 2. "nomadic, especially (with pl. *yürügān*) a nomadic, pastoral Turkman settled in Asia Minor" (*A Turkish and English lexicon*, Constantinople 1890, 2214); K. Steuerwald, however, has *yürük*, 1. "going briskly, marching", 2. "fast (horse)", 3. hist. "infantry connected to the Janissaries" and the ethnonym *Yörük* "Türkmen (*sic*) nomads in Anatolia" (*Türkisch-Deutsches Wörterbuch*, Wiesbaden 1972, 1040, 1034). In regional forms of modern Turkish, the verbal stem *yörü-* "to march" and similar meanings, is attested as well as *yörük* "göcebe" (nomad), *yörük* "dağlı, kaba kişi" (mountain-dweller, rough person), while *yürük* is connected with *yüğrük* "güçlü, çevik, çalışkan, eline ayağına çabuk" (strong, quick, diligent, nimble) (*Türkiye'de halk ağzından derleme sözlüğü*, xi, Ankara 1979, 4310, 4333, 4325).

History.

The phenomenon of the Yörük should be set within the context of the immigration of Türkmen tribal groups into Anatolia beginning with the 11th century. In pre-Mongol times and in connection with the Mongol conquests (13th century) and Mongol claims over large areas of Asia Minor up to the mid-14th century, unknown numbers of Türkmen took hold of grazing grounds for seasonal migration. To date, no source antedating the mid-15th century has been found that spells out the name Yörük (Cl. Cahen, *La Turquie pré-ottomane*, Istanbul 1988, 107, as opposed to Çabuk, in *İA* (1986), 430-1). When from the second part of the 14th century onwards, Türkmen nomadic groups, along with the colonising dervishes, began to take possession of the Balkan peninsula in an organised way, they contributed eventually to its Turkicisation and Islamisation. Some of the tribesmen might have been the ancestors of those people who were to become known under the name of Yörük two generations later.

In a brief separate section, the code of laws (*ḳānūn-nāme* [*q.v.*]) for the taxpaying subjects (*reʿāyā*, sing. *raʿiyya* [*q.v.*]) of Meḥemmed II the Conqueror (*r.* 1451-81) specifies the organisation, military equipment and obligations of the Yörük who, as auxiliary troops, were considered as belonging to the *ʿaskerī* class and therefore were exempt (*müsellem*) from all but military service (ed. and tr. F. Kraelitz-Greifenhorst, *Ḳānūnnāme Sultan Meḥmeds des Eroberers*, in *MOG*, i [1921-2], 28, 43; Akgündüz 1990, i, 354-5). It specifies that a unit (*odjaḳ*) should consist of 24 men serving in rotation, one of them as soldier (*eshkindji*), three as his aides (*čatal*) and the remaining 20 (*yamaḳ*) paying for the four fighters' expenses and shouldering their duties back home. Under Süleymān Ḳānūnī, the number of men in a unit was raised to 30 (Akgündüz 1992, iv, 548). General, provincial and district *ḳānūnnāmes* as well as those specially issued for the Yörük dating from the reigns of Bāyezīd II, Selīm I and Süleymān regulate with increasing detail the functions of the Yörük and the legal and fiscal framework they had to comply with (Akgündüz, ii-v, index). A *ḳānūnnāme* of the mid-15th century specifies that the Yörük may migrate along their traditional routes, but should they cause damage to the fields or harvest, the fine they would have to pay would be assessed in regular court proceedings (Fr. tr. N. Beldiceanu, *Les actes des premiers sultans conservés dans les manuscrits turcs de la Bibliothèque Nationale à Paris. I. Actes de Mehmed II et de Bayezid II du ms. fonds turc ancien 39*, Paris-The Hague 1960, 123; Ott. text in Akgündüz 1990, i, 463). The damage caused by the pastoralists might have been one of the reasons for the Ottoman state's perennial policy of forced settlement and deportation. Extreme examples are that of Yörük deportations to Cyprus after the conquest of this island (1571) or, in the early 18th century, from western Anatolia to northern Syria. The main reason, however, was their independent way of life, which was considered incompatible with the basic system of the centralised Ottoman administration.

Tax registers from the time of Süleymān Ḳānūnī (1520-66) permit us to assess globally the nomadic population in western Anatolia alone at 80,000 households (*khāne*) for 1520-35 (İnalcık 1994, 34-5), with the greatest nomadic concentrations in the districts (*sandjaḳ* [*q.v.*]), of Anḳara, Kütāhiya, Menteshe, Aydi̊n, Ṣarukhān, Teke and Ḥamīd [*q.vv.*], or, in other words, areas where the Türkmen principalities of the 14th and 15th centuries had flourished. By 1570-80, their number had increased to around 120,000. Unfortunately, the registers do not permit a systematic distinction between Türkmen and Yörük tribes. However, the term Türkmen tended to be more closely associated with those Anatolian tribes that showed a preference for Shīʿism (İnalcık 1986, 40-2). On the European side, Yörük tribes pursued their life of seasonal transhumance, with a growing tendency toward sedentarisation, in Thrace, eastern Bulgaria, the Dobrudja, in the Rhodope and Balkan mountains adjoining the Maritsa and Vardar river valleys, and north of Thessaloniki (İnalcık 1994, 36). The most comprehensive study, based on archival materials, of the names, locations, numbers and functions of the Rumelian Yörüks from the 15th to 19th centuries is Gökbiligin 1957, summarised in Çabuk 1986. Based on tax registers, Ö.L. Barkan suggests for the early 16th century a total number of almost 38,000 Yörük households, or one-fifth of the total population of the European provinces (*Essai sur les données statistiques des registres de recensement dans l'empire ottoman aux XV*e *et XVI*e *siècles*, in *JESHO*, i [1957], 32-3). From the early 17th century onward, the number of households registered as Yörük was in steep decline (Gökbilgin 1957, 56-92). On the economic plane, Yörüks engaged primarily in animal husbandry, producing wool and hides as well as carpets for an international market, while their small-scale agricultural activities were concentrated on cash-crops such as wheat, cotton and rice (İnalcık 1994, 37-9; for taxes on the Yörük in the 17th century, see *Regional structure in the Ottoman economy. A Sultanic memorandum of 1636 A.D.*, ed. R. Murphy, Wiesbaden 1987, index). In war and peace, they also played an important role in long-distance transportation.

Different from the Eastern Anatolian Türkmen and Kurdish tribal federations, the Yörük were organised in military conscriptions within the Ottoman administration, serving mostly as provincial auxiliary forces, as guards of roads and mountain passes, as falconers, and horse raisers, in military transport, road construction and maintenance, ship building and mining. Their leaders were indifferently called *beg/bey* (A. Birken, *Die Provinzen des Osmanischen Reiches*, Wiesbaden 1976, 60, based on Ewliyā Čelebi), a title that was abolished under Sultan ʿAbd ül-Ḥamīd II (1876-1909) (Tsakyroglous 1891, 344) or *Yörük pashasi̊/Ewlād-i̊ fātiḥān ḍābiṭi* (Defterdār Ṣāri̊ Meḥmed Pasha, *Zübde-i vekayiât, 1066-1116/1656-1704*, ed. Abdülkadir Özcan, Ankara 1995, *passim*).

During the 17th century, owing to large-scale sedentarisation, the number of Yörüks registered in Rumelia decreased considerably. In 1102/1690-1, during the protracted war with Austria, the tribal Yörük were reorganised as more tightly disciplined auxiliary forces under the name *Sons of the Conquerors* (*Ewlād-i̊ fātiḥān*). This system was modified only in 1243/1827-8, when Maḥmūd II (1808-39), in another attempt to reform the army, incorporated Yörük forces in the new *ʿAsākir-i manṣūre*. From 1261/1845-6, the Yörük were subject to taxes and military service like the rest of the population (Gökbilgin 1957, 255-342, with texts of twelve relevant tax (*taḥrīr*) registers and list of 26 additional documents up to 1846).

During the *Tanẓīmāt* [*q.v.*] period, from *ca.* 1860 onwards, in order to strengthen central state control, the Ottoman government again made every effort to settle the volatile nomadic tribes (Tsakyroglous 1891, 342; Wenzel 1937, 83-7). In his *Teḏẖākir*, Aḥmed Ḏjewdet Pas̲h̲a [*q.v.*] gives a general idea of how the pacification and reform in the Kozan and Çukurova regions of southeastern Anatolia were put into effect (ed. Cavid Baysun, Ankara 1986, *tezkires* 26-9).

Ethnography.

The earliest European ethnographic information dates from the end of the 19th century. Tsakyroglous (1891), who *ca.* 1880 became acquainted with Yörük groups with winter quarters in Borlu and summer camps near Gördes, and Bent (1891), who seems to have visited Yörüks of southwestern and southern Anatolia, contradict each other in the description of the physical appearance of the Yörük. Otherwise, they describe in some detail their economy, transhumance, tribal structure and beliefs. Both sources mention strictly pastoralist Yörüks migrating from winter (*ḳis̲h̲la/ ḳis̲h̲lak* [*q.v.*]) to summer (*yayla/yaylaḳ* [*q.v.*]) encampments, and half-settled Yörüks cultivating modest fields.

The Ottoman policy of controlling the nomadic pastoralists by encouraging and enforcing settlement was continued under the Turkish Republic, because nomadism was now considered retrograde. Since the 1950s, the policy of large-scale agricultural development through irrigation in the coastal plains of western and southern Anatolia, as well as in the Çukurova plain, has left a majority of tribes without grazing land and has brought about their impoverishment and social break-up. With his novel *Binboğalar efsanesi* (1971), the Turkish author Yaşar Kemal set up a literary monument to the decline of Yörük tribal life. In contrast, some groups who happened to become landowners in the newly-irrigated areas became wealthy by growing fruit-trees and cotton, some of them eventually giving up most of their cattle-raising activities or even becoming fully sedentarised (Roux 1961 for the case of the Antalya region).

In modern and contemporary research, the Yörük are mainly studied as keepers of the traditional ways of life of nomadic and semi-nomadic pastoralists in the Anatolian part of the Republic of Turkey. The patterns and conditions of their migrations, their economy and adaptation to new forms of economic demands, their social organisation and handicrafts have attracted field-researchers from Turkey and abroad. The question whether the popular designation of all Turkish-speaking nomads as Yörük/Yürük is an improper generalisation, and in which way the term reflects an historical, ethnic and social reality, seems to have been settled by ethnologists to the extent that there is indeed a distinction to be made between Türkmen, Yörük, Tahtacı and Çepni. The Tahtacı [see TAḴẖTAḎJĪ] are set apart by their religious affiliation—they are Alevîs—and by their exclusive occupation as wood-cutters; the Çepni, also Alevî, claim descent from the Og̲h̲uz [see G̲H̲UZZ]. An historical relationship between Türkmen and Yörük is assumed by most scholars, although exact details remain somewhat elusive. The Türkmen and the Yörük themselves acknowledge this relationship insofar as a Türkmen might not consider himself a Yörük, whereas a Yörük might think of himself also as Türkmen (A. Gökalp, *Têtes rouges et bouches noires*, Paris 1980, 32-3). According to research conducted since the 1950s, a majority of the Yörük tend to call themselves Yörük, whilst a minority prefer their tribal name, which is often a personal or a place name, no common ancestor, mythical or historical, being claimed. Among Sunnī Yörüks, group identity is maintained through patrilineal descent. They are organised in tribes (*aşiret*), lineages (*kabile, sülâle*) and families (*aile*), with marked endogamy, but without paramount chiefs (Andrews 1989, 59-60).

The present number of Yörük is not known, since they speak Turkish and are therefore not separately listed in the official census. A recent study estimates their number at *ca.* one million, *ca.* 10,000 of these being fully nomadic, while the rest are part-time nomads or are settled (Kunze 1994, 71, 77). Today they are distributed primarily along the Taurus mountain range from western Anatolia (Izmir, Söke) all the way along the southern coast via the gulf of Antalya to Adana and its hinterland up the Ceyhun river. The winter quarters are in the coastal river plains, while the summer ones are beyond the Taurus in the high plateaus of inner Anatolia (Denizli, Afyon Karahısar, Konya, Kayseri, Bolu, Sivas, Maraş). Settled Yörük are recorded for the same region and also in the areas of Manisa, Balıkesir, Kütahya and Eskişehir (cf. Andrews 1989, 59; Kunze 1994, *passim* and map at p. 73; *Tübinger Atlas des Vorderen Orients* (*TAVO*), map A VII 14, Wiesbaden 1987). Probably very few Yörük remain in the Balkan peninsula. In the 1980s, Svanberg came across *ca.* 200 Yörük who led a traditional life in some isolated hamlets in the mountains of Macedonia. According to him, they belonged to the Bektās̲h̲ī religious community (I. Svanberg, *Gagavouzika and Juručki. Urgent tasks for Turkologists*, in *CAJ*, xxxii [1988], esp. 114-16). Most Yörüks are said to belong to the Ḥanafī school of Sunnī Islam, but there are also Alevî Yörük, about whom not much is known (Andrews 1989, 59, 62). Folklore studies and recent research on Yörük textiles refer to the preservation of pre-Islamic or shamanistic beliefs (Brüggemann 1993).

The Yörük dialects still await study in more detail. A recent study on the Anatolian dialects states that they show minor variations in vocabulary, phonetics and morphology in comparison with the dialects of settled Turks (Demir 1996).

The characteristic traits of the Yürük "black tent" (*kara çadır*), made from goat hair, as well as the textile arts of the Yörük, embroidered clothing, saddlebags (*heybe*), sacks (*çuval*) and, in particular, kelims and brocaded flatweaves, have now been quite well studied. The most comprehensive study of their flatweaves is by Brüggemann (1993), who, however, deals also with Türkmen ones, since he postulates that Turkish nomadic tribes shared over the course of time a common language of patterns, motives and techniques. Yörük folklore, customs, music and dances have been studied more systematically since the 1950s, but increased sedentarisation and interior and exterior migration have caused these traditional arts to fade away.

Bibliography: A bibl. with 190 items is I. Svanberg, *A bibliography of the Turkish-speaking tribal Yörüks*, in *Materialia Turcica*, v (1979) [1981], 25-40; the subsequent publications are listed s.v. *Yürüken* in *Turkologischer Anzeiger/Turkology Annual*, i ff., Vienna 1975 ff. Almost every volume of the journal *Türk Folklor Araştırmaları* (i ff., 1949-50 ff.) contains an article on Yörük customs and material culture. In addition to references in the article, see Ahmed Akgündüz, *Osmanlı kanunnâmeleri ve hukukî tahlilleri*, i-v, Istanbul 1990-2; *Ethnic groups in the Republic of Turkey*, comp.

and ed. P.A. Andrews with the assistance of R. Benninghaus, Wiesbaden 1989, 58-62, 265 and map 1; F. Bajraktarević, in *EI*[1] art. *Yürük*; D.G. Bates, *Differential access to pasture in a nomadic society. The Yörük of southeastern Turkey*, in *Perspectives on nomadism*, ed. W. Irons and N. Dyson-Hudson, Leiden 1972, 48-59; idem, *Nomads and farmers. A study of the Yörük of Southeastern Turkey*. Ann Arbor 1973; Th. Bent, *The Yourouks of Asia Minor*, in *J. of the Anthropological Institute of Great Britain and Ireland*, xx/3 (1891), 269-76; P.N. Boratav, *Textes de la tradition orale des Yörük et des Tahtacı*, in *Mélanges offerts à Louis Bazin*, ed. J.-L. Bacqué-Grammont and R. Dor, Paris 1992, 129-35; W. Brüggemann, *Yayla. Form und Farbe und türkischer Textilkunst*, Frankfurt a. M. and Berlin 1993; V. Çabuk, *İA*, art. *Yörükler*; N. Demir, *Einige Merkmale yörükischer Dialekte*, in *Symbolae turcologicae*, ed. A. Berta, B. Brendemoen and C. Schönig, Uppsala 1996, 61-70 with a bibl. of earlier linguistic field-work; M. Tayyib Gökbilgin, *Rumeli'de Yürükler, Tatarlar ve Evlâd-ı Fâtihân*, Istanbul 1957; Kemal Güngör, *Anadolu yörüklerin etno-antropolojik tetkiki*, Ankara 1941; H. İnalcık, *Osmanlılar'da raiyyet rüsûmu*, in *Belleten*, xxii (1959), 575-610; idem, *The Yürüks. Their origins, expansion and economic role*, in *Oriental carpet and textile studies*, i, ed. R. Pinner and W. Denny, London 1986, 39-65; idem, *The Ottoman state. Economy and society, 1300-1600*, in *An economic and social history of the Ottoman Empire, 1300-1914*, ed. H. İnalcık and D. Quataert, Cambridge 1994, 9-409, esp. 34-43; *Yörük. Nomadenleben in der Türkei*, ed. A. Kunze, Munich 1994; J.-P. Roux, *La sédentarisation des nomades Yürük du vilayet d'Antalya*, in *L'Ethnographie*, N.S. lv (1961), 64-78; M.-H. Sauner-Nebioglu, *Evolution des pratiques alimentaires en Turquie. Analyse comparative*, Berlin 1995 (Yörük cuisine from Denizli); M. Tsakyroglous, *Die Jürüken*, in *Das Ausland*, lxiv/18 (1891), 341-4, lxiv/19 (1891), 366-71; H. Wenzel, *Forschungen in Inneranatolien. II. Die Steppe als Lebensraum*, Kiel 1937. (Barbara Kellner-Heinkele)

YOUNG TURKS [see yeñi ʿothmānlılar].

YOZGAT, a town of north central Anatolia, lying some 160 km/100 miles east of Ankara on both sides of a tributary of the Delice Irmak (lat. 39° 50' N., long. 34° 48' E., altitude 1,320 m/4,330 feet).

It was founded by members of the Djebbārzāde/Čapanoghlu family (supposedly *yoz* means "pasture, herd", while *gat* is a dialectal word for "town"). On record since 1116/1704, this dynasty, possibly of Mamalu-Türkmen background, constituted one of the major *aʿyān* lines of central Anatolia, controlling a territory far beyond its original power-base in the *sandjak* of Bozok (*wilāyet* of Rūm, see Özcan Mert, *XVIII. ve XIX. yüzyıllarda Çapanoğulları*, Ankara 1980). Very few towns existed in this region when the Djebbārzāde came to live in Yozgat sometime in the mid-12th/18th century. The settlement grew as the Čapanoghullari encouraged immigration, part of it non-Muslim (V. Cuinet, *La Turquie d'Asie*, Paris 1892, i, 297; this author stresses the modern, well-built aspect of the town, which at that time possessed 15,000 inhabitants). Such urban development conformed to a pattern not rarely encountered in the 12th/18th century, when the Ottoman state encouraged its appointees to revive trade and communications; slightly earlier, Newshehir [*q.v.*] had been established, located only about 150 km/95 miles to the south. Muṣṭafā Pasha built the new town's principal mosque, along with a mausoleum for the founder's family (1192/1778). It was enlarged by his son Süleymān Beg in 1210/1795, who created a unique ensemble by transforming the *son djemāʿat yeri* of the older mosque into a link between the two structures (G. Goodwin, *A history of Ottoman architecture*, London 1971, 400-2).

The next major event in the history of Yozgat pertains to the Turkish War of Independence, when in 1920 members of the Čapanoghlu family, still powerful in the area, in the name of Sultan Meḥemmed VI Waḥīd al-Dīn rebelled against the Nationalist forces led by Muṣṭafā Kemāl (Atatürk). The uprising was quelled by the Yeshil Ordu troops of Čerkes Edhem [*q.v.*]; however, the latter's demand that a governor deemed responsible for the incident be handed over to him for punishment was refused by Muṣṭafā Kemāl. These events are often regarded as the beginning of the rift between Atatürk and Cerkes Edhem (see art. *Yozgat*, in *Yurt ansiklopedisi, Türkiye il il, dünü, bugünü, yarını*, x, Istanbul 1982-4, 7646-7; contains extensive bibl.). They may also have caused the Turkish language to acquire the expression *bu işin altından bir çapanoğlu çıktı* to denote a troublesome situation. Present-day Yozgat is an *il* or provincial capital (over 36,000 inhabitants in the 1980s) and the centre of a largely rural area. A lack of industrial employment opportunities, and the fragmentation of village holdings, have led to large-scale emigration from this area.

Bibliography: See also Naval Intelligence Division, Admiralty Handbooks, *Turkey*, London 1943, ii, 594-5 and index. (Suraiya Faroqhi)

YÜCEL, ḤASAN ʿALĪ (1897-1961), Turkish statesman, educator and author.

He was born, the son of a post and telegraph inspector ʿAlī Riḍā and Neyyire, the daughter of an army colonel, in Istanbul on 17 December 1897. Ḥasan ʿAlī attended the *Wefāʾ Iʿdādīsi* between 1911-5, and then, after military service during the First World War, graduated from Istanbul University in 1921. Until 1927, he worked as a teacher in several lycées in Izmir (Erkek Muallim Mektebi) and Istanbul (Kuleli, Istanbul Erkek, Galatasaray) where he lectured on philosophy, literature and Turkish language. He continued his career at various posts in the Ministry of Education, and was sent to Paris to study the French educational system. In 1935 he was elected to Parliament as the representative for Izmir of the Halk Partisi, and in 1938 was appointed the Minister of Education, playing a leading role in the Turkish modernisation process by initiating various reforms within the educational and cultural spheres. The translation of various world classics and encyclopaedias, the establishment of the Ankara State School of Music, studies on the Turkification of language and the realisation of the Village Institutes project [see khalḳevi] were among his major initiatives. After resigning from office in 1946 and from the party in 1950, he served as the consultant to İş Bankası Cultural Publications between 1956-60. During 1960, he worked on the Commission for the Preparation of the National Education Plan. He died in Istanbul, on 26 February 1961.

Throughout his life, Ḥasan ʿAlī wrote many books and articles for various newspapers and magazines, including *Akşam*, *Ulus*, *Cumhuriyet*, *Öncü* and *Dünya*. The most often recurring themes of his works were culture, education and philosophy; in them, he expressed his faith in modernisation harmonised with traditional values. He also wrote poetry and collected his works in several volumes.

Bibliography: 1. Selected works. *Goethe, bir dehanın romanı*, Istanbul 1932; *Türk edebiyatına toplu bir bakış*, Istanbul 1932; *Dönen ses*, Istanbul 1933; *Fransada kültür işleri*, Istanbul 1936; *Pazartesi konuşmaları*, Istanbul 1937; *Türkiyede orta öğretim*, Istanbul

1938; *İyi vatandaş iyi insan*, Ankara 1956; *Hürriyet gene hürriyet*, i, Ankara 1960, ii, Ankara 1966; *Kültür üzerine düşünceler*, Ankara 1974; *Geçtiğim günlerden*, Istanbul 1990; *Öğretmen-öğrenci köşesi*, Ankara 1995.

2. Studies. H.Z. Ülken, *Türkiye'de çağdaş düşünce tarihi*, [3]Istanbul 1992, 468-9; S. Akşin, *Düşünce tarihi (1945 sonrası)*, in idem (ed.), *Türkiye tarihi*, v, Istanbul 1995, 229-30; M. Çıkar, *Hasan-Ali Yücel ve Türk kültür reformu*, [2]Ankara 1998. (Aylin Özman)

YUʿFIRIDS, the first local dynasty to emerge in the Yemen in the Islamic period (232-387/847-997). The name is often erroneously vocalised "Yaʿfurids", but the 4th/10th century Yemeni scholar al-Hamdānī, who was a contemporary of the Yuʿfirids, makes it clear that Yuʿfirids is the correct spelling (*al-Iklīl, Südarabisches Muštabih*, ed. O. Löfgren, Uppsala etc. 1953, 36, and *al-Iklīl*, ii, ed. Löfgren, Uppsala 1965, 71).

The family was of Dhū Ḥiwāl, a tribe from Shibām-Kawkabān some 40 km/25 miles north-west of Ṣanʿāʾ [*q.v.*]. The founder of the dynasty, Yuʿfir b. ʿAbd al-Raḥmān al-Ḥiwālī, had been waiting in the wings watching the increasing impotence of the ʿAbbāsid governors in Ṣanʿāʾ. In 232/837, after some skirmishes with, and a failed attack upon, the ʿAbbāsid forces in the Yemen, the Yuʿfirid army defeated the ʿAbbāsid governor, Ḥimyar b. al-Ḥārith.

We hear little of the rule of Yuʿfir b. ʿAbd al-Raḥmān, other than that the dynasty held vast areas of the Yemen from Ṣaʿda [*q.v.*] in the north to al-Djanad near Taʿizz [*q.v.*] in the south, and for some time the Yuʿfirids maintained their outward allegiance to the ʿAbbāsids in Baghdād. In 258/872, the old and infirm Yuʿfir handed over the reins of power to his son, Muḥammad.

In 262/876 Muḥammad left the Yemen to perform the pilgrimage, leaving his son Ibrāhīm in authority. In 269/882, Yuʿfir, presumably to deny them a role in the government of the house, conspired with Ibrāhīm to have both Muḥammad and his brother, Aḥmad, murdered in the minaret of the mosque in Shibām. Such an appalling crime brought widespread chaos to the Yemen with many tribes in revolt against the perpetrator Ibrāhīm, who withdrew to Shibām. The ʿAbbāsid caliph al-Muʿtamid despatched as governor to the Yemen ʿAlī b. al-Ḥusayn in a move to attempt to strengthen the hand of the Yuʿfirids, but he was unable to reach the country until 282/895. The new governor did manage to pacify the area around Ṣanʿāʾ.

At this particular juncture, our historical sources turn their attention elsewhere. With much of the north of the Yemen in complete chaos, Yaḥyā b. al-Ḥusayn, the future first Zaydī *imām*, al-Hādī ilā ʾl-Ḥakk, entered Ṣaʿda in 284/897 and over the next few years a Zaydī imāmate was established there [see zaydiyya]. The only historical information which we have on the Yuʿfirids at this time is that of their struggles against the Zaydī forces. In the south of the country, too, another dangerous enemy lurked. Two Fāṭimid-Ismāʿīlī propagandists, Manṣūr al-Yaman [*q.v.*] and ʿAlī b. al-Faḍl, were building up a strong force and threatening to move northwards on Ṣanʿāʾ. The history of the period is now a confused account of tripartite power struggles in the whole of the country, involving Yuʿfirids, Zaydīs and Ismāʿīlīs.

Al-Hādī died in 298/911 and the two Fāṭimids in 302/915. This at last left the Yuʿfirids without serious threat. Asʿad b. Ibrāhīm, the leader of the dynasty, was able to establish peace in Ṣanʿāʾ and throughout much of the country, although we cannot be sure how far north his authority extended. When Asʿad died in 344/955, leaving no clear instructions for his succession, serious family squabbles broke out. Ṣanʿāʾ was lost and the last Yuʿfirid ruler, ʿAbd Allāh b. Ḳaḥṭān b. ʿAbd Allāh died in Ibb in 387/997, after a tour of Tihāma [*q.v.*] and the south, and this date marks the end of the Yuʿfirid house.

The Yuʿfirid mosque in Shibām stands to this day, although the minaret in which the 269/882 murders took place was replaced at a later date (see R. Lewcock and G.R. Smith, *Two early mosques in the Yemen: a preliminary report*, in *AARP*, iv [1973]). The tomb, set at right angles to the western outer wall of the mosque, mentioned a Yuʿfir, perhaps Yuʿfir b. ʿAbd al-Raḥmān himself, and local tradition has it that it is his tomb. A visit to the mosque in 1997, however, revealed that the tomb is now in ruins and no inscription immediately visible.

Bibliography: Detailed treatment of the Yuʿfirids is given in G.R. Smith, *The early and medieval history of Ṣanʿāʾ*, in R.B. Serjeant and R. Lewcock (eds.), *Ṣanʿāʾ, an Arabian Islamic city*, London 1983, 55-7, and in Smith, *The political history of the Islamic Yemen down to the first Turkish invasion (1-945/622-1538)* in W. Daum, *Yemen, 3000 years of art and civilisation in Arabia Felix*, Innsbruck and Frankfurt [1988], 130-1, both relying on primary and early sources including ʿImād al-Dīn Idrīs, *Kanz al-akhyār fī maʿrifat al-akhbār*, B.L. ms. Or. 4581, now ed. ʿAbd al-Muḥsin al-Madʿadj, Kuwait 1992, and ʿAlī b. Muḥammad al-ʿAbbāsī al-ʿAlawī, *Sīrat al-Hādī ilā ʾl-Ḥakk*, ed. Suhayl Zakkār, Damascus 1972. Mention should also be made of the excellent, though still unpublished, Ph.D. thesis of C. Geddes, *The Yuʿfirid dynasty of Ṣanʿāʾ*, University of London 1959. (G.R. Smith)

YUGOSLAVIA "land of the South Slavs", a Balkan state which came into being through the peace treaties consequent on the end of the First World War, 1919-20 (St-Germain, Neuilly, Trianon), as the Kingdom of the Serbs, Croats and Slovenes under the ruling house of its largest component, Serbia. According to the constitution which came into effect on 1 January 1921, this was to be a unitary state, but this was never fully achieved, and arrangements in August 1939 envisaged a federal structure. Such developments were cut short by the German invasion of April 1941, after which the territories of Yugoslavia fell under Axis (German, Italian, Bulgarian) occupation till 1944-5. After the Second World War, Yugoslavia came under Communist control, with the January 1946 constitution abolishing the monarchy and setting up a Socialist Federal Republic of Yugoslavia that lasted until the break-up of the federation in the early 1990s.

Such regions of what became Yugoslavia as Macedonia, South Serbia ("Old Serbia") and above all Bosnia and Hercegovina had substantial Muslim populations, comprising ethnic Turkish incomers and converted indigenous Slav peoples. Many of the former element returned to Turkey after 1919 [see muhādjir. 2], but substantial numbers of Muslims have remained in Bosnia, and in recent decades, the numbers of Muslims in the Kosovo region of South Serbia [see ḳoṣowa, kosovo] have grown through the immigration thither of Albanians [see arnawutluḳ]. In the census of 1953, the last one which noted religious affiliation, 12% of the population of Yugoslavia was returned as Muslim.

See for the history in Islamic times of the various regions of Yugoslavia, bosna; ḳaradagh; ḳoṣowa; māḳadūnyā; ṣirb; dalmatia, in Suppl.; also muslimūn. 1, and the *Bibls.* there, especially A. Popovic, *L'Islam balkanique*, Berlin-Wiesbaden 1986. (Ed.)

YŪḤANNĀ B. SARĀBIYŪN, a Christian (Nestorian) physician of the 3rd/9th century. He wrote in Syriac a medical compendium (*kunnās̲h̲*) in two different forms, one with seven, the other with twelve *maḳālāt.*

The second, called the large compendium (*al-kunnās̲h̲ al-kabīr*), was corrected by the Ṣābian Abu 'l-Ḥasan T̲h̲ābit b. Ibrāhīm b. Zahrūn (d. 369/980). An extract was made by Yaḥyā b. D̲j̲amāl al-Dīn al-Ḥīrī al-Mutaṭabbib al-Ḥalabī (who was still alive in 1198/1783). The complete work has been preserved in the Istanbul ms. Ayasofya 3716.

According to Ibn Abī Uṣaybiʿa, the first compendium, called the small one (*al-kunnās̲h̲ al-ṣag̲h̲īr*), was translated into Arabic by the secretary Mūsā b. Ibrāhīm al-Ḥadīt̲h̲ī on behalf of the physician Abu 'l-Ḥasan b. Nafīs. This translation is said to have been superior, stylistically speaking, to that of Abū Bis̲h̲r Mattā b. Yūnus al-Ḳunnāʾī (d. 328/940) and to that of the well-known annotator Ḥasan b. Bahlūl al-Awānī. This *kunnās̲h̲* was translated by Gerhard of Cremona under the title *Practica Joannis Serapionis aliter breviarium nuncupata*; in later times this translation was often reprinted. The Latin translation led to a Hebrew one by Mōshē b. Mazliaḥ (Steinschneider, *Hebräische Übersetzungen*, no. 474). In this way, the structure and the contents of the work became known rather early. The seven treatises deal with: 1) diseases of body and nerves; 2) diseases of eye, mouth, lungs, breast and heart; 3) diseases of stomach, intestines, and those caused by worms; 4) diseases of liver, spleen, kidneys, bladder, gout; 5) skin-diseases, wounds caused by a bite, gynaecological diseases; 6) fever; 7) composite medicines (*aḳrābād̲h̲īn*).

Most of the quotations from Yūḥannā are found in al-Rāzī, the others in the *D̲h̲ak̲h̲īra* of (Ps.) T̲h̲ābit, in the *D̲j̲āmiʿ* of Ibn al-Bayṭār, in the *Minhād̲j̲* of Kūhīn, in the *Aḳrābād̲h̲īn* of Ḳalānisī and others (enumerated in M. Ullmann, *Die Medizin im Islam*, 102-3). According to the critical al-Mad̲j̲ūsī who, in the preface to his main work, the *Kāmil al-ṣināʿa al-ṭibbiyya*, reviews the achievements of his predecessors, not many positive elements are to be found in Yūḥannā's work: e.g., he finds fault with the latter for limiting therapy to medicaments and diets, while disregarding "manual treatment" (surgery); furthermore, there are allegedly many complaints about omissions, deficiencies and inaccuracies (see Ullmann, *Medizin*, 142-3).

From a quotation in Abū Sahl Bis̲h̲r b. Yaʿḳūb al-Sid̲j̲zī's *al-Rasāʾil al-ṭibbiyya*, it might perhaps be concluded that Yūḥannā also wrote a *Kitāb fī ʿAs̲h̲r maḳālāt li-D̲j̲ālīnūs*, see Dietrich, *Medicinalia Arabica*, Göttingen 1966, 67 l. 18.

Bibliography: Ibn al-Nadīm, *Fihrist*, 296; Ibn al-Ḳifṭī, *Ḥukamāʾ*, 380; Ibn Abī Uṣaybiʿa, i, 109, ll. 17-22; L. Leclerc, *Histoire de la médecine arabe*, i, 105-11; M. Ullmann, *Die Medizin im Islam*, Leiden 1970, 102-3; idem, *Yūḥannā ibn Sarābiyūn. Untersuchungen zur Überlieferungsgeschichte seiner Werke*, in *Medizinhistorisches Journal*, vi (1971), 278-96. For the tradition in Syriac, see A. Baumstark, *Geschichte der syrischen Literatur*, 231, with the addendum on 353; G. Graf, *GCAL*, ii, 131; R. Degen, in *Medizinhist. Journal*, vii (1972), 122 n. 49.

(A. Dietrich)

YULBĀRS K̲H̲ĀN, the Uyg̲h̲ur Turkish leader of a Muslim rebellion at Ḳomul [*q.v.* in Suppl.] in Eastern Turkistan or Sinkiang [*q.v.*] during the 1930s, b. 1888, d. ? in the mid-1970s.

In 1928 the second Republican Chinese governor of Sinkiang, Chin Shu-jen, overthrew the last autonomous k̲h̲ānate of Central Asia, that of Ḳomul in the extreme eastern end of the province, adjacent to the frontiers with Mongolia and Kansu. His anti-Muslim policies provoked a rebellion there in April 1931 of the Uyg̲h̲urs, and possibly some of the Tungans [*q.v.*], under the joint leadership of Yulbārs K̲h̲ān, who had been an adviser and official of the last two K̲h̲āns of Ḳomul, and the less effective K̲h̲od̲j̲a Niyāz Ḥād̲j̲d̲j̲ī. Yulbārs appealed to the Han Muslim warlord of northwestern Kansu, Ma Chung-yin [*q.v.*], and the latter's intervention enabled local Turkish elements to take over most of southern Sinkiang and set up in September 1932 an "Eastern Turkestan Republic" based on Kās̲h̲g̲h̲ar [*q.v.*], which in November 1933 became the "Turkish-Islamic Republic of East Turkestan". Yulbārs and K̲h̲od̲j̲a Niyāz, however, represented conservative Ḳomulī sentiment, seeking limited autonomy for Ḳomul rather than secession from China, and they were suspicious of local Muslim leaders who were prepared to call in Soviet Communist support. Yulbārs was a fluent Chinese speaker, and he was later to choose exile in Taiwan rather than Turkey.

It soon became clear that Ma Chung-yin was following his own interests rather than those of the Turkish peoples of Sinkiang, and in early 1934 his forces destroyed the Kās̲h̲g̲h̲ar republic, although further rebel activity was to continue there. Yulbārs fled to Nanking in 1937, but returned to Ḳomul in 1946 as an adherent of the Kuo Min-tang. He fought against the increasing power of the Chinese Communist in Sinkiang, but in the winter of 1950-1 had to flee to Tibet and thence to Taiwan, where he retained the post of governor of Sinkiang in exile, eventually dying there.

Bibliography: A.D.W. Forbes, *Warlords and Muslims in Chinese Central Asia. A political history of Republican Sinkiang 1911-1949*, Cambridge 1986, see index s.v. and esp. the biography at 254 (photograph at 50).

(C.E. Bosworth)

YŪNĀN refers to the ancient Greeks, reflecting the name "Ionians". *Yūnānī* means Greek (noun and adjective) and *al-yūnāniyya* or, less commonly, *al-yūnānī* (with or without *lug̲h̲a* or *lisān*), the ancient Greek language. The vocalisation *yūnānī*, instead of *yawnānī* favoured by some (cf. al-Tawḥīdī, *Baṣāʾir*, ed. W. al-Ḳāḍī, Beirut 1408/1988, viii, 11), is stated to be the generally accepted form by al-Samʿānī, *Ansāb*, ed. Ḥaydarābād, xiii, 536, and may have been favoured by the Arabic word formation *fuʿlān*. The ancient Near Eastern designation of the "Greeks" as Ionians had continued being used through the ages in the Near East and eventually became common, apparently through some Aramaic form, in Muslim civilisation as a kind of cultural artifact. Authors such as al-Yaʿḳūbī, i, 161, 164 (referring to Ptolemy, *Ḳānūn*); al-Masʿūdī, *Tanbīh*, 115; al-Samʿānī, *loc. cit.*, quoting His̲h̲ām Ibn al-Kalbī; *Kitāb al-D̲j̲aʿrāfiyya*, ed. Mahammad Hadj-Sadok, Damascus 1968, § 161, had no doubt that *yūnānī* was derived from the name of the biblical Yūnān b. Yāfit̲h̲ (Javan, the son of Japheth: Gen. x. 2, 4), although in the genealogy offered in al-Ṭabarī, i, 218, the form of the name is the traditional *Yawān*. In fact, the form *Yūnān* for Javan is not attested elsewhere in older times, at least as is known so far (Syriac *Yawnān* < Greek accus. *Iōnan*, for Jonah/Yūnus, is not applicable here). Although biblical names underwent as yet unexplained changes on their way into Arabic, in this case it seems likely that the noun/adjective *yūnānī*, derived on the model of Aram. *yawnāy* (Ar. *āʾī* > *-ānī*), was primary and led to a reconstructed form *Yūnān* for *Yawān*. In translations from the Greek, *yūnāniyyūn* is the ordinary rendering of *Hellēnes*, but occasionally also occurs for synonyms like *Achaioi*, cf. *WKAS*, Letter L, 1629a, citing Artemidorus, whose Arabic translator also used an additional *yūnāniyyūn* to clarify Greek *palaioi* "ancients" (cf. E. Schmitt, *Lexikalische Untersuchungen zur arabischen Übersetzung von Artemidors Traumbuch*, Wiesbaden 1970, 386a). Plenty of information on everything Greek seeped, of course, from the Graeco-Arabic translation literature [see TARDJAMA. 2.] into wider learned circles, but only a few general points can be made here.

The internal Muslim geographic/cartographic tradition had no precise notion on where to locate the Yūnān, except for some vague generalities such as Athens being the capital of the ancient Greek philosophers or Macedonia being the country of Alexander the Great. Their status as the predecessor nation and dynasty to the contemporary Rūm [*q.v.*] was known but not widely understood among mediaeval Muslims, except some favourably placed scholars. Historical tradition and speculation preferably assumed an original habitat for the Yūnān in Asia Minor or Syria. There were other, highly speculative theories, as, for instance, one credited by Ḥamza al-Iṣfahānī, *Ta'rīkh*, book IV beg., to a 3rd/9th-century Christian source about an era dating from the departure of a legendary Yūnān from Babel and lasting until the merger of the Yūnān into the Rūm and their eventual disappearance. Following earlier interpretations of Gen. x. 2 and 4, Rome occasionally appears as a foundation of Javan and his descendants (*Dja'rāfiyya*, § 187). Even al-Andalus could be said to have had them as its first rulers (Ibn Khallikān, ed. 'Abbās, v, 323, 326, in the article on the conqueror of Spain Mūsā b. Nuṣayr [*q.v.*]).

The relationship of the ancient Greek language to the language of the (eastern) Rūm, which moreover involved the distinction between pagans and Christians, was widely acknowledged but again not known in detail, cf. the discussion by N. Serikoff, *Rūmī and Yūnānī*, in *Orientalia Lovaniensia Analecta*, clxxv [1996], 169-94). The excellent knowledge of ancient Greek possessed by certain scholars in the Muslim world in early 'Abbāsid times faded rapidly in the 4th/10th century. A few technical terms, book titles, names and the like continued to be widely recognised as ancient Greek and in some cases acquired the status of cultural icons, especially names such as Sukrāṭ, Aflāṭūn, Arisṭūṭālīs (Arisṭū), Buḳrāṭ and Djālīnūs. In general, however, even concerned Muslims like al-Kindī, al-Fārābī or al-Bīrūnī knew little, if anything at all, of the language. In some regions, learned Christian scholars retained some knowledge of Greek sufficient for translating minor texts into Arabic. In Western Islam, *ighrīkī*, *ighrīkiyya*, is occasionally mentioned as the correct designation of the ancient Greek language (Ṣā'id al-Andalusī, tr. R. Blachère, 58, 77; *IAU*, ii, 47, cf. F. Rosenthal, *The Classical heritage in Islam*, London 1975, 39, 195).

Notwithstanding all this natural lack of information about long past and forgotten historical reality, the fundamental importance of the ancient Greeks and their intellectual achievements for the formation of Islamic civilisation was fully realised among Muslims. It became, and has remained to this day, the subject of a never-ending and often passionate discussion between supporters and opponents, Muslims and non-Muslims alike. Graeco-Arabic relations indeed occupy a central position in Islamic studies today; however, the meaning of the ancient Greek heritage for every and all individuals in Muslim intellectual life still needs comprehensive investigation. During the early centuries, a statement like that of the historian al-Ya'ḳūbī, i, 106-7, characterised the ancient Greeks as "philos-

ophising sages" who cultivated medicine, the "essential verities" (i. e. metaphysics), arithmetic, geometry, astronomy/astrology, agriculture, alchemy and elixirs as well as talismans and (magical) apparatus. This view would have found general concurrence at the time. In a way, it has remained the popular view throughout. At the same time, sophisticated learned schemes of organising all human knowledge began to evolve. They classified all the sciences, (scientific) medicine, logic and philosophy as the realm of the "non-Arabs", that is, predominantly, the ancient Greeks, as against the "Arab" disciplines concerned with matters of religion and language, literature and philology. In various forms, these classifications became standard throughout mediaeval Islam.

A vehement opposition to all learning connected to the ancient Greeks began at a very early date and intensified in the course of the centuries. The reasons were manifold, such as its evidently foreign and non-Muslim origin and its introduction into Arabic by mostly non-Muslim translators. Above all, it threatened a most severe conflict on the religious level in that it introduced ideas and methods contradicting traditional Muslim beliefs and raised the eternal problem of faith versus reason much more explicitly than had been the case before in the Near Eastern environment. This provoked an attitude of distance and hostility to the very term *yūnānī* and often the rejection of everything considered "Greek", as, for instance, the rejection of "philosophy" as heresy, pointedly expressed in the proverbial *man tafalsafa tazandaḳa* "he who philosophises commits heresy" [see ZINDĪḲ].

The struggle between defenders and opponents is exemplified, for instance, by the witty parody of a narrow-minded official who is represented as being shocked by the sacrilegious implications of Euclidean geometry (cf. Abū Ḥayyān al-Tawḥīdī, *Akhlāḳ al-wazīrayn*, Damascus 1385/1965, 235-47, see also AL-SARAKHSĪ), or is seriously pictured in the debate about (Arabic) grammar and (Greek) logic led by al-Sīrāfī [*q.v.*], reported by the same al-Tawḥīdī in another work and most recently discussed by G. Endress, *Grammatik und Logik*, Amsterdam 1986, 163-299 (*Bochumer Studien zur Philosophie* 3 = B. Mojsisch (ed.), *Sprachphilosophie in Antike und Mittelalter*). By far the most detailed and instructive discussion of the subject remains I. Goldziher, *Stellung der alten islamischen Orthodoxie zu den antiken Wissenschaften*, in *Abh. Pr. Ak. Wiss.* (1916), no. 8. In the end, a kind of compromise came about. While Greek logic and metaphysics as such were mostly, but not always, vilified and rejected, they played an often unacknowledged vital role in Muslim theological and juridical discussion. On the other hand, the Greek heritage in the sciences was accepted as indispensable, often with apologies and accompanied by efforts to prove the usefulness of those sciences for religious purposes, as in the case of mathematics and astronomy. And medicine continued to rely almost exclusively and without apology on the ancient Greek authorities and their writings [see ṬIBB].

Bibliography: For the history of Graeco-Arabic relations, cf. the fundamental study by D. Gutas, *Greek thought, Arabic culture*, London and New York 1998. The subject touches practically all spheres and levels of Muslim intellectual activity and thus much of the modern scholarly literature. The small selection of references given in this article may most conveniently be supplemented by the numerous articles in the *EI* devoted to Greek authors and sciences, see, for instance, FALSAFA and FALĀSIFA or the entries on pharmacology, medicine, agriculture, astronomy, astrology, or alchemy as listed in P.J. Bearman, *Index of subjects*, [4]Leiden 1998. (F. ROSENTHAL)

AL-**YŪNĪNĪ**, KUṬB AL-DĪN ABU 'L-FATḤ MŪSĀ b. Muḥammad b. Aḥmad b. ʿAbd Allāh, Syrian historian and Ḥanbalī *shaykh*, b. Damascus in 640/1242, d. Baʿlabakk in 726/1326, best known as the author of the *Dhayl Mirʾāt al-zamān*, a continuation of the *Mirʾāt al-zamān* of Sibṭ Ibn al-Djawzī (d. 654/1256 [*q.v.*]). Al-Yūnīnī belonged to a scholarly family originally from Yūnīn, a small town in the region of Baʿlabakk; his family claimed descent from Djaʿfar al-Ṣādik [*q.v.*] and in some sources, bore the *nisba* al-Ḥusaynī. Following the death of his father, then that of his elder brother, he inherited the role of leader of the Ḥanbalīs of Baʿlabakk, an important centre of Syrian Ḥanbalism at the time. He conformed to the family tradition in his capacity of scholar and *shaykh*, in maintaining stable relations with the dynasty in power, and in his sympathetic attitude towards the Ṣūfīs.

His father Muḥammad Taḳī al-Dīn Abū ʿAbd Allāh (572-658/1176-1260) was linked to the Ḥanbalī Ṣūfī *shaykh* ʿAbd Allāh al-Yūnīnī (534-617/1139-1220), whose daughter he married and whom he succeeded. His biographers present him as a Ḳādirī mystic who, like his father-in-law ʿAbd Allāh, claimed kinship with the *shaykh* ʿAbd al-Ḳādir al-Djīlānī [*q.v.*]. His mother, Zayn al-ʿArab bt. Naṣr Allāh b. Ṣanīʿ al-Dawla al-Ḥasan b. Yaḥyā, who died in 693/1294, came from a scholarly Syrian family. His half-brother Sharaf al-Dīn Abu 'l-Ḥusayn ʿAlī (621-701/1223-1302), a scholar known primarily as the transmitter of the *Ṣaḥīḥ* of al-Bukhārī, provided a list of al-Yūnīnī's masters, which has survived; cf. G. Vajda, *La mašyaḫa de ʿAbd al-Qādir al-Yūnīnī*, in *JA*, cclix [1971], 223-46. Finally, the marriage of his daughter to Aybak al-Iskandarī al-Ṣāliḥī, a Mamlūk thirty years her senior who died in 674/1276, consolidated the family's links with the Baḥrī Mamlūks.

Al-Yūnīnī first attended classes in Baʿlabakk and Damascus, where he was taught by the eminent masters of the various *madhhabs*. In 659/1260, the year following the death of his father, his elder brother ʿAlī, who had taken responsibility for his education, sent him to Egypt. He subsequently visited Egypt twice, in 675-6/1276-7 and then in 688/1289, taking the opportunity to pursue his research into *ḥadīth* and visit sages and Ṣūfīs; he also received *idjāza*s from scholars such as the Mālikī Yaḥyā b. ʿAlī al-ʿAṭṭār and the Shāfiʿī ʿIzz al-Dīn ʿAbd al-ʿAzīz Ibn ʿAbd al-Salām [see AL-SULAMĪ]. His principal activity was the collection of testimonies and data concerning his contemporaries, original material that he later incorporated into his work. In 673/1275, he made the Pilgrimage to Mecca. When in 680/1281, al-Malik al-Manṣūr Ḳalāwūn was fighting the Mongols, he made his way to Ḥimṣ and participated in the campaign; he was subsequently to devote a biographical notice to a scholarly friend who accompanied him and who died in battle. After his third visit to Egypt, he spent most of his time in Baʿlabakk and in Damascus where he continued his compilation of information. It was on the death of his brother ʿAlī, assassinated in 701/1302 in his library, that he became *shaykh* of the Ḥanbalīs of Baʿlabakk and dedicated himself to this function, to the dissemination of knowledge and to the editing of his own works.

Al-Yūnīnī first chose to summarise a universal history which he admired, the *Mirʾāt al-zamān* by Sibṭ Ibn al-Djawzī, in a *Mukhtaṣar* of four vols. Then, around 680/1281, he decided to compose a supplement, with a chronicle of events starting from the year 654, the date of the death of the Sibṭ (and continuing until the year 711, judging from the manuscripts which have survived) which he entitled *Dhayl Mirʾāt al-zamān*. Al-Yūnīnī thus placed his *Dhayl* within a family of works: *al-Muntaẓam* by Ibn al-Djawzī [*q.v.*], the *Mirʾāt al-zamān* by Ṣibṭ Ibn al-Djawzī and the *Ḥawādith al-zamān* of al-Djazarī [*q.v.*], with the pattern of chronological presentation comprising, for each year, a list of sovereigns and princes followed by an account of events (*ḥawādith*) and then obituaries (*wafayāt*). In spite of its title, *dhayl*, which identifies it as a "continuation" or "supplement", the originality of al-Yūnīnī's work was recognised by Western scholars as soon as the first volumes were published, on the initiative of Fritz Krenkow. Subsequently, Cl. Cahen described several manuscripts of the *Dhayl*, of which there exist two versions of unequal length. He made efforts to uncover the sources of the work and to identify reciprocal borrowings between the author and his contemporaries, while stressing the originality of the work. Ulrich Haarmann, and then Li Guo, have pursued this project, comparing al-Yūnīnī's work in particular with that of al-Djazarī. They have also analysed the role of al-Birzālī [*q.v.*] in the transmission of the works of the two authors. In his study devoted to al-Yūnīnī, *Early Mamluk Syrian historiography*, Li Guo has laid emphasis, largely in accordance with a formal analysis of the classification of obituaries, on the differences between the two versions of the text: one, more developed and with obituaries arranged in alphabetical order, contains personal testimonies, accounts and anecdotes that are not found elsewhere and that give information concerning the history of Baʿlabakk, of Damascus and of al-Shām in general; while in the second text, which is shorter, obituaries are arranged in chronological order and the other type of material is lacking.

The sources used by al-Yūnīnī are of various natures: chronicles and biographical dictionaries found in the library of learned Syrians of the time, such as Ibn Khallikān, Abū Shāma, Ibn Ḥammawayh al-Djuwaynī, Ibn Shaddād, Ibn ʿAbd al-Ẓāhir and Ibn Wāṣil in particular, certain of these owing a great deal to Sibṭ Ibn al-Djawzī, not to mention works relating more specifically to each region: the *Taʾrīkh Irbil* by Ibn al-Mustawfī, the *Dhayl Taʾrīkh Baghdād* by Ibn al-Nadjdjār or even the *Taʾrīkh Ḥalab* by Ibn al-ʿAdīm. To these may be added the official documents, judicial registers and correspondence to which al-Yūnīnī had access by virtue of his good relations with the Mamlūk officials, or indeed Ṣūfī works of the *manāḳib* [*q.v.*] genre which were familiar to him.

Currently, the state of edition of the *Dhayl* is as follows: years 654-86 were edited by Krenkow and Muḥammad Munīr al-Shādhilī; years 687-90 by Antranig Melkonian (unpublished diss.); and years 697-701 by Li Guo (thus the years 687 to 696 and 702 to 711 are not yet published). Continuing Cahen's work, Li Guo has also reconstructed families of manuscripts, of the *Mukhtaṣar Mirʾāt al-zamān* of the *Dhayl*, for which he has listed 23 manuscripts. What may be added here in this context concerns the identification of the "mysterious Istanbul manuscript" which has served as a basis for the edition of part of the text published in Ḥaydarābād (four volumes covering the years 654/1256 to 686/1287). In fact, while the years 654 to 672 (vols. i and ii and the first part of vol. iii) were edited on the basis of known manuscripts (those of Istanbul, Aya Sofya 3146, 3199 and of Oxford, Bodleian, Pococke 132), the section concerning the years 673 to 686 (beginning at p. 111 of vol. iii and including the whole of vol. iv) is based on a manuscript which is imprecisely identified on the title pages. It is in fact a manuscript preserved in the B.L. London under the classification India Office Isl. 3452, but not featuring in the printed catalogue. The manuscript was copied by Krenkow in 1945-6 and served as the basis for the edition made by a group of Indian scholars under the direction of Muḥammad Munīr al-Shādhilī (cf. J. Sublet, *Un manuscrit égaré*).

Furthermore, a work of *manāḳib* has been attributed to al-Yūnīnī, but its authenticity is problematical. Li Guo relies on Ḥādjdjī Khalīfa, vi, 155 no. 13042 (Kātib Čelebi 1834-44) and on Bağdatlı İsmail Paşa, *Hadiyyat al-ʿārifīn*, ii, 479, in saying that al-Yūnīnī, finding that Sibṭ Ibn al-Djawzī had devoted to al-Djīlānī only a very short notice, is said to have written a work intitled *Manāḳib ʿAbd al-Ḳādir al-Djīlānī*. Some additional information may be supplied in this context. The Arabic manuscript of the Bibliothèque Nationale de France contains a copy dating from 961/1554 of which the first (corrupt) folio bears the title *Bahdjat al-asrār*. G. Vajda (in his unpublished notes on the manuscripts of the BnF) identified the text as *Manāḳib ʿAbd al-Ḳādir al-Djīlānī wa-ʿAbd Allāh b. ʿUthmān al-Yūnīnī*. This is thus a case of apologetic biographies of both al-Djīlānī and of ʿAbd Allāh al-Yūnīnī, our author's father-in-law. Vajda considered the text identical to that of Berlin (Wetzstein 1855) which is, according to Ahlwardt's catalogue (no. 10097), the work of ʿAlī b. Muḥammad al-Yūnīnī, who died in 701/1301, our author's brother. It may be deduced from this that numerous members of the Yūnīnī family composed *Manāḳib ʿAbd al-Ḳādir al-Djīlānī*, thus rendering homage to the Ṣūfī *shaykh* whose memory they all revered, and as a result confusion was created between members of this family. Li Guo also poses the question of the identification of a *Taʾrīkh Baghdād* that was allegedly composed by al-Yūnīnī but of which the text has not been found.

The cordial relations that al-Yūnīnī maintained with scholars and historians ensured that numerous biographical notices would be dedicated to him, although in his own time he enjoyed only a modest reputation. Thus al-Dhahabī [*q.v.*], who attended his transmission sessions in Damascus and in Baʿlabakk, paid him restrained homage.

Works such as the *Dhayl* contain an impressive store of materials for the history of Syria in the second half of the 7th/13th century and in the early 8th/14th century. The Syrian authors of the time may be considered as constituting a school, and analysis of their works entails a redefinition of the historiography of the region in the period of the first Mamlūks.

Bibliography: 1. Sources. Yāfiʿī, *Mirʾāt al-djanān*, Ḥaydarābād 1920-1, iv, 276; Baghdādī/Bağdatlı (Ismail Paşa), *Hadiyyat al-ʿārifīn*, Istanbul 1951-5, ii, 479; Ibn Radjab, *Dhayl ʿalā Ṭabaḳāt al-ḥanābila*, Cairo 1953, 379, no. 489; Ṣalāḥ al-Dīn al-Munadjdjid, in *Madjallat maʿhad al-makhṭūṭāt al-ʿarabiyya*, ii, 100; idem, *Muʿdjam al-muʾarrikhīn al-dimashḳiyyīn*, Beirut 1978, 130-1, 447; Ibn Taghrībirdī, *al-Dalīl al-shāfī ʿalā al-Manhal al-ṣāfī*, Mecca 1978, ii, 752; Dhahabī, *Min dhuyūl al-ʿIbar*, Beirut 1985, iv, 76-7; Ṣafadī, *Wāfī*, ms. Istanbul, Topkapı Saray Ahmet III 2920/26, fol. 144b; Ibn Kathīr, *Bidāya*, xiv, 126; Ibn Ḥadjar al-ʿAsḳalānī, *Durar*, iv, 382 no. 4900; Ibn al-ʿImād, *Shadharāt*, vi, 73-4; Ḥādjdjī Khalīfa, vi, 155 no. 13042; Kaḥḥāla, *Muʿdjam al-muʾallifīn*, xiii, 45-6.

2. Studies. The principal work of reference is Li Guo, *Early Mamluk Syrian historiography. Al-Yūnīnī's* Dhayl Mirʾāt al-zamān, 2 vols. Leiden 1998, incl. ed. of the years 697-701. See also Brockelmann, S I, 338; Cl. Cahen, *Les chroniques arabes . . . dans les bibliothèques d'Istanbul*, in *REI*, x (1936), 344-5; F. Krenkow, *Quṭb al-Dīn al-Baʿlabakkī*, in *IC*, xx/4 (1946), 341-4; idem [Sālim al-Krankawī], *Dhayl mirʾāt al-zamān*, in *MMIA*, xxi (1946), 378-80; H. Laoust, *Le hanbalisme sous les Mamlouks Bahrides*, in *REI*, xxviii (1960), 1-72; F. Rosenthal, *A history of Muslim historiography*, Leiden 1968, 44 ff.; A. Melkonian, *Die Jahre 1287-1291 in die Chronik al-Yūnīnīs*, diss. Freiburg 1975; J. Sublet, *Un manuscrit égaré: les années 673-686 du Dayl Mirʾāt al-zamān de Yūnīnī*, in *Arabica*, xlvi/2 (April 1999), 259-61.

(JACQUELINE SUBLET)

YUNNAN (YÜN-NAN), a province in the southwest of China, bounded in the east by the provinces of Kuei-chou, Kuang-hsi and in the north by the province of Ssū-ch'uan, and in the south to west by Vietnam, Laos and Burma.

1. History.

The province, first established under the Mongol Great Khān Ḳubilay in A.D. 1253, received its name from that of ancient Yunnan county, which is identified with Hsian-yun Prefecture, Yunnan province. Yunnan Province is a highland country; the climate is generally mild, but agricultural products are not always plentiful. According to the statistics of the government of the People's Republic of China, the Hui (Muslim) population of Yunnan is given as 522,046 (1.36% of the total population of Yunnan province in 1990). They are mostly distributed in the eastern part of the province, mainly near rivers and roads. They live alongside Han Chinese and native non-Chinese minorities.

Under the T'ang dynasty, in the middle of the 8th century, a native tribe of Yunnan called *U-man* ("Black Barbarian"), which is identified with the Qaradjan belonging to the Thai race, rose to power in 937 and founded the Nanchao kingdom (with its capital at Tali). In the Sung period, the Nanchao kingdom was succeeded by the Tali one, which survived for about 150 years in the same territory up to the mid-13th century. Then came the Mongol domination over Yunnan province. In the historical sources for the T'ang dynasty, it is reported that Taji (i.e. Tādjīk, that is, Arab) soldiers who had come to help the dynasty as reinforcements, migrated to Yunnan province in the early 9th century, settling there and becoming the first Muslims in Yunnan; but this tale is uncorroborated elsewhere.

The origin of the Yunnan Muslims should probably be traced back to the early Yüan dynasty, when the Mongol Royal Prince (later Great Khān) Ḳubilay [*q.v.*], who marched into China proper, conquered the above-mentionned Tali kingdom. Many soldiers and merchants from West Asia, and Central Asian Uyghurs who were members of Ḳubilay's army, settled in the province, many of them being Muslims. A Muslim general, Sayyid-i Adjall Shams al-Dīn ʿUmar (1211?-79), who was reported to be of Bukhāran origin, is said to have surrendered to Čingiz Khān in Transoxiana in 1219, to have become Čingiz's vassal, and then to have participated in the expedition to China, subsequently being appointed civil governor of Yunnan in 1273. He is further said to have pacified local tribes and to have spread the Islamic religion there. The town of K'un-ming, situated in eastern Yunnan, now became the administrative capital, and was later also called Yunnan-fu (see further on this implantation of Islam in Yunnan, AL-ṢĪN. 4.). Under the administration of Sayyid-i Adjall Shams al-Dīn and his descendants, Muslims in Yunnan, Ssŭ-ch'uan and Shen-hsi prospered in the later 13th century and were gradually absorbed into local society as time went on. After the collapse of the Yüan, the first Ming Emperor Ch'u Yüang-ch'uang in 1381 ordered that Han and Muslim generals should proceed to Yunnan to get rid of any Mongol remnants, and they established Ming rule there. In general, the Yunnan Muslims, like those of other provinces, were gradually Sinicised under the Ming; also, many Muslims immigrated from surrounding provinces into Yunnan.

Under the Ch'ing dynasty that took over from the Ming in the early 17th century, a policy began of colonising native peoples of Yunnan with the power of both Han Chinese and Hui armies. Chinese and Muslims gradually spread further into the province: the Muslim population of the province is reported to have reached at this time *ca.* 800,000, making it the second densely-populated province of Muslims in China next to Kansu [*q.v.*]. As the Ch'ing policy of colonisation and absorption of the native Yunnan population continued in the early 19th century, Chinese pressure increased, with friction between Muslims and Han Chinese, especially in the western region with its centre at Yung-ch'êng fu (Pao-an). Revolts of the Yunnan Muslims against the Ch'ing authorities now began to occur. Quarrels between Muslims and Han Chinese at Ch'u-hsiung fu in 1854 marked the opening of the Great Rebellion which continued and raged for eighteen years all over the province; for details, see PANTHAY and TU WEN-HSIU. After a period of subsequent repression, there was comparative calm, or at least an uneasy peace, for the Yunnan Muslim community. But with the triumph of the Communist régime in 1950 and its pursuit of a militantly anti-religious policy, the position of the Yunnan Hui, and their perceived "differentness" in a state which was pathologically suspicious of all non-Han religious and ethnic identities, worsened. In such a closed state, details of discrimination and persecution are largely lacking, but the lowest point of Hui fortunes under Communism was clearly reached during the Cultural Revolution, epitomised in the "Shadian Incident". Shadian is a village in southwestern Yunnan adjacent to the Vietnam border and has been famed since Ming times as a centre of Muslim piety and learning. After requests by the Hui of Shadian for the re-opening of their mosques had been refused by the local Communist Party authorities, in July-August 1975 units of the People's Liberation Army moved in, razed Shadian to the ground and massacred over 1,600 Hui of the district, with 866 killed from Shadian village alone. Not until 1979, after the Fall of the Gang of Four, were apologies given and reparations made; but Yunnan Muslims understandably remain suspicious of PRC government attitudes and policies. For details of the Incident, see Gladney, *Muslim Chinese*, 137-40.

2. The community.

Yunnan Muslims have been and are still engaged in farming, handicraft, retail trade (especially with Burma), salt manufacturing (salt mining), eating-houses, inns, transportation, pottery-making, etc. They were also engaged in the mining of silver, copper and tin in the employment of local Ch'ing authorities. The Yunnan Muslims are not dissimilar from those Muslims of other provinces of China. They are Chinese-speaking Muslims calling themselves either *Hui* (Muslim), *Hui-min* (Muslim people) or *ch'ing-ch'êng (pure-true) Hui-hui*, and now, under the People's Republic of China, they are called *Hui-tsŭ* (Muslim people). Each Muslim community is located around their own *ch'ing-ch'êng ssŭ* (mosque). There are now reportedly about 600 mosques in the region. As religious leaders, they usually have an *akhon* (leader of the worship), a *khalīfa* (student, apprentice), and sometimes an *imām* (hereditary leader of the worship), just as in other provinces. They observe the Two Great *ʿĪds*, the *mawlūd al-nabī* (Muḥammad's birthday), *ʿāshūrāʾ*, the *miʿrādj*, *barāʾat*, *shab-i ḳadar*, etc.

Most Yunnan Muslims follow the *ḳadīmī* or "old", "traditional" or "orthodox" form of Chinese Islam, basically that of Ḥanafism, as observed by 90% of all the Chinese Muslims. There are also the *Djahriyya* order and the *Ikhwān* movement among Yunnan Muslims. The *Djahriyya* originally appeared in Kansu province in the early 18th century. It had its own centres at Sining, Ning-hsia and also at Peking, and must have been propagated in Yunnan. For Djahrī practices, see KANSU and TAṢAWWUF. 8. In Chinese Islam. The *Djahriyya* was specifically called *Hsin-chao* or New Religion, i.e. new as opposed to the *Ḳadīmīs*. The Ikhwān maintain strict observance of the *Sharīʿa* and spurn membership of the *mêng-huan* or the *ṭarīḳa* institutions [see TAṢAWWUF. 8.]. In Yunnan the Ikhwān make up *ca.* 10% of all Muslims.

Bibliography: E. Rocher, *La province chinoise de Yünnan*, 2 vols. Paris 1879-80; M. Broomhall, *Islam in China: a neglected problem*, London 1910; D'Ollone, *Recherches sur les musulmans chinois. Etudes de A. Vissière, notes de E. Blochet et de divers savants*, Paris 1911; *Hui-min ch'i-i* ("Chinese source on Muslim rebellions under the Ch'ing dynasty"), ed. Pai Shou-i, 4 vols., Peking 1953, vols. i-ii "Rebellions in Yunnan province"; T. Tazaka, *Chūgoku ni okeru kaikyō no den-rai to sono gutsū* ("Islam in China, its introduction and development"), 2 vols. Tokyo 1964; Y. Nakada, *Kai-kai minzoku no shomondai* ("Problems of the *Hui-hui* people in China"), Tokyo 1971; R. Israeli, *Muslims in China. A study in cultural confrontation*, London and Malmö 1980; D.D. Leslie, *Islam in traditional China*, Canberra 1986; Hu Chên-hua (ed.), *Chung-kuo hui-tsu* ("General survey of Chinese Muslims"), Ying-ch'uan, Ning-hsia 1993; Wu Chien-wei (ed.), *Chung-kuo ch'ing-ch'êng ssŭ tsung-lan* ("General survey of Muslim mosques of China"), Ying-ch'uan, Ning-hsia 1995; D.C. Gladney, *Muslim Chinese, Ethnic nationalism in the People's Republic*, [2]Cambridge, Mass. 1991; Jianping Wang, *Concord and conflict. The Hui communities of Yunnan society in historical perspective*, Stockholm 1996; Jacqueline M. Armijo-Hussein, *Sayyid 'Ajall Shams al-Din: a Muslim from Central Asia serving the Mongols in China and bringing "civilization" to Yunnan*, diss. Harvard 1996, unpubl.

(T. SAGUCHI)

YŪNUS B. MATTĀ, the prophet Jonah, son of Amittai (II Kings xiv. 25). The name entered Arabic ultimately from the Greek Septuagint rendering of the Hebrew, most likely transmitted through Christian Palestinian.

The Ḳurʾān mentions Jonah four times as Yūnus, without giving his father's name, once as Dhu 'l-Nūn (XXI, 87) and once (LXVIII, 48) as *ṣāḥib al-ḥūt* "the Man of the Whale". Yūnus is the only one of the major and minor biblical prophets who is mentioned by name in the Ḳurʾān; a prophet who is swallowed by a whale naturally figured significantly in the popular imagination. Yūnus is numbered among the apostles of God (IV, 163; VI, 86). Sūra X is named after Yūnus, and tells of a town which came to believe in the one

God and therefore its fate of "chastisement and degradation in the present life" was averted (X, 98). A paraphrastic rendering of the story of Jonah appears in XXXVII, 139-48 (cf. also XXI, 87-8): Yūnus, an apostle of God, fled on a ship which was overloaded. He was condemned by lot and a fish swallowed him. He was worthy of blame. If he had not praised God, he would have remained in the fish's belly until the resurrection. However, he was thrown sick upon a barren shore, and a gourd was caused to grow up over him. He was then sent to rule over a hundred thousand people who became believers and God gave them respite for a further period.

Al-Bukhārī and al-Nawawī quote a *ḥadīth ḳudsī* which says "No one can say he is better than Yūnus b. Mattā, even if his genealogy goes back to his father" (see Nöldeke, *Gesch. des Qor.*, i, 257; W. Graham, *Divine word and prophetic word in early Islam*, The Hague 1977, saying 44); al-Thaʿlabī, *Ḳiṣaṣ*, 366, quotes this simply as a statement of Muḥammad and provides the understanding that Mattā was Yūnus's mother's name and that the characteristic of being a prophet and carrying the name of one's mother was distinctive with ʿĪsā and Yūnus alone.

Muslim legend further develops the material. Yūnus served God in Nineveh at the time that he became enraged. The puzzle of why he became angry is answered in at least two ways:

(1) He became angry because his mission to warn the people of Nineveh of their need to repent in order to avoid their forthcoming destruction was so urgent that the angel Gabriel did not allow him time to mount a steed or put on a shoe before leaving.

(2) He was angry because the calamity that he had prophesied would befall Nineveh was delayed at the last minute, thus making him appear to be a liar worthy of death. Yūnus prophesied that the punishment would come after 40 days; on the 37th day the colour of the sinners changed. They repented, restored all that they had unjustly acquired, even the objects immured in their houses (cf. the principle enunciated in BT, *Gittin*, 55a); men, women, children and animals clothed themselves in sackcloth; suckling offspring, of both women and animals, were separated from their nurses. But on the day of ʿĀshūrāʾ, God granted forgiveness.

Urged by Satan, Yūnus embarked on the ship. The overloaded ship could not go backward or forward, a sign that a runaway slave was on board. Jonah confessed his guilt, but the sailors would not throw him into the sea; three times they cast lots and then threw down an arrow oracle (al-Thaʿlabī). Finally, Yūnus threw himself into the jaws of the whale (Ibn al-Athīr), which, it is said, had come from India on account of Yūnus (al-Kisāʾī). God commanded the whale, saying, "Whale, O whale! We shall not make Jonah into your sustenance! Rather We make you a retreat for him, a sanctuary" (al-Ṭabarī, i, 783). The threefold darkness (see Ḳurʾān, XXI, 87) of the inside of the fish, depth of the sea and the darkness of the night enveloped Yūnus. The fish was swallowed by another fish and then that one by still another (al-Ṭabarī, *Tafsīr*, *ad* Ḳurʾān, XXI, 87, as a second opinion on the meaning of the "darkness"). God made the fish transparent so that Yūnus could see the wonders of the deep. He heard the songs of praise of the sea monsters just as the angels heard his prayers from the inside of the fish. It is disputed whether Yūnus remained 3, 7, 20 or 40 days in the fish. Hurled out upon the shore, he was given shade by a gourd tree, and was suckled by a goat (Ibn al-Athīr) or an antelope (al-Thaʿlabī) or a gazelle (al-Kisāʾī). Yūnus found shade under a gourd tree which then withered, causing him to lament. God then reproached him for not having lamented the 100,000 people whose death he sought. This admonition was impressed upon him by other means also: by fruit trees torn up, by the example of a potter who is anxious about his pots, and a sower who is anxious about his seeds. Then Yūnus had a shepherd announce his approach: the earth, a tree, and an animal of his herd, all miraculously bore witness to the truth of the message. These motifs reflect the apparent connection between Jonah and nature and especially the animal kingdom. The king ceded his throne to the shepherd, and himself went to live with Yūnus as an ascetic. Notably absent here are any of the messianic aspects of the story developed in the New Testament (Matt. xxii. 39, Luke xi. 29) and in the Midrash (L. Ginzberg, *The legends of the Jews*, Philadelphia 1909-38, iv, 253, vi, 351 n. 38).

The feature that God forgives the sinful town on the day of ʿĀshūrāʾ suggests a Jewish basis for these developments in the legend; the Book of Jonah is recited in Jewish worship in the afternoon of the Day of Atonement, which was connected in early Islam to the fast of ʿĀshūrāʾ [*q.v.*]. According to al-Kisāʾī, Yūnus was conceived on ʿĀshūrāʾ (see W.M. Thackston, *The Tales of the Prophets of al-Kisaʾi*, Boston 1978, 350 n. 90, for a list of other events in the lives of the prophets which happened on this day).

A legend, mentioned by al-Yāfiʿī [*q.v.*] in his *Rawḍ al-rayāḥīn*, probably originated at a later date and indicates the extent of the active development of legendary material throughout the centuries, even down to contemporary times (see e.g. P. Bachmann, *Das Skandalon des Propheten Yūnus und eine neue arabische Jona-Geschichte*: Yūnus fī baṭn al-ḥūt, *von ʿAbd al-Ġaffār Mikkāwī*, in J.M. Barral (ed.), *Orientalia Hispanica, sive studia F.M. Pareja octogenario dicata*, Leiden 1974, i, 55-76). Yūnus asked the angel Gabriel to show him the most pious person in the world. The angel showed him a man who lost his feet, hands and eyes one after another and, notwithstanding, put his confidence in God and gave himself up to Him (cited in R. Basset, *Mille et un contes, récits et légendes arabes*, Paris 1927, ii, 122, no. 77).

Al-Kisāʾī extended the miraculous elements to the earlier history of the prophet. His father was 70 when Yūnus was born. His mother, who became a widow soon after, had nothing left but a wooden spoon, which proved to be a cornucopia. As a result of a miraculous dream, he married the daughter of Zakariyyāʾ b. Yaḥyā (see ZAKARIYYĀʾ; here reflecting the chronological confusion surrounding this person). He loses his wife, both his sons and his property. He therefore will not pray with the others on the ship. In the end, everything is miraculously restored to him.

Bibliography: Ṭabarī, i, 782-9, tr. M. Perlmann, *The History of al-Ṭabarī. iv. The ancient kingdoms*, Albany 1987, 160-6; Ṭabarī, *Tafsīr*, on X, 98, XXI, 87-8, LXVIII, 48; Ibn al-Athīr, *Kāmil*, Būlāḳ 1290, i, 143-5; Thaʿlabī, *Ḳiṣaṣ al-anbiyāʾ*, Cairo n.d., 366-70; Kisāʾī, *Ḳiṣaṣ al-anbiyāʾ*, ed. Eisenberg, Leiden 1922-3, 296-311; Abū Rifāʿa al-Fārisī, *Badʾ al-khalḳ wa-ḳiṣaṣ al-anbiyāʾ*, in R.G. Khoury (ed.), *Les légendes prophétiques dans l'Islam*, Wiesbaden 1978, 223-37; A. Geiger, *Was hat Mohammed aus dem Judenthume aufgenommen?*, Leipzig 1902, 188-9; J. Horovitz, *Jewish proper names and their derivatives in the Koran*, in *Hebrew Union College Annual*, ii (1925), 170-1; idem *Koranische Untersuchungen*, Berlin-Leipzig 1926, 154-5; A. Jeffery, *Foreign vocabulary of the Quran*, Baroda 1938, 295-6; H. Speyer, *Die biblischen Erzählungen im Qoran*, Gräfenhainichen 1931, 407-10; D. Sidersky, *Les origines de légendes musul-*

manes dans le Coran et dans les vies des prophètes, Paris 1933, 129-31; C.C. Castillo, *Jonas en leyenda musulmana*, in *al-Qanṭara*, iv (1983), 89-100.

(B. Heller-[A. Rippin])

YŪNUS b. ḤABĪB, prominent Baṣran grammarian and philologist (*ca.* 90-182/708-98).

In the early sources, his important position as a grammarian is indicated by the 230 occurrences of his name in both syntactic and morphological parts of Sībawayhi's *Kitāb*. He is mentioned as a direct source of information in Abū ʿUbayda's *Madjāz al-Ḳurʾān* (transmitting Abū ʿAmr b. al-ʿAlāʾ's teaching), and the books of al-Farrāʾ and al-Akhfash. In al-Djumaḥī's *Ṭabaḳāt*, Yūnus describes personally the development of grammatical studies from the early days of ʿAbd Allāh b. Abī Isḥāḳ (d. 117/728 [*q.v.*]). His fabulous readiness to share knowledge is mentioned by the early short biographical treatise of Abū Ḥāmid. The many details added by the later sources include a grandfather's name and *kunya* (both of these being ʿAbd al-Raḥmān), dates of life and origin. He is presented as a *mawlā* of several Arab tribes. A Persian origin was mentioned by a Shuʿūbī author (Talmon, *Arabic grammar*, 7 n. 35). A recurring anecdote seems to suggest attribution by some biographers of pro-ʿAlid sentiments to this scholar. The list of Yūnus's teachers and students seems to draw mainly on the meagre information extracted from the early sources referred to above. Ibn al-Nadīm mentions five books written by this scholar, of lexical and philological, not grammatical, character. These include *Maʿānī al-Ḳurʾān*, *K. al-Lughāt*, *K. al-Nawādir* (*al-kabīr* and *al-ṣaghīr*) and *K. al-Amthāl*, cf. Sezgin, viii, 57-8, for possible traces of these books in later works. Yūnus's grammatical views presented in the *Kitāb* indicate a sophisticated systematic analogical reasoning, not much inferior to Sībawayhi's and al-Khalīl's.

Bibliography: Flügel, *Die grammatischen Schulen der Araber*, Leipzig 1862; H. Ṭaʿʿān, *Makhṭūṭ farīd nafīs fī marātib al-naḥwiyyīn*, in *al-Mawrid*, iii (1974), 137-44; ʿA. Djabbūrī, *Yūnus b. Ḥabīb, ḥayātuhu wa-ārāʾuhu fī ʾl-ʿarabiyya*, in *Madjallat Ādāb al-Mustanṣiriyya* (1975-6), 97-136; G. Troupeau, *Lexique-index du Kitāb de Sībawayhi*, Paris 1976; R. Talmon, *Naḥwiyyūn in Sībawaihi's* Kitāb, in *ZAL* (1982), 12-38 (esp. the appendix); Sezgin, *GAS*, viii, 57-8, 266 (including a detailed list of mediaeval sources), ix, 49-51; Talmon, *Arabic grammar in its formative age*, Leiden 1997.

(R. Talmon)

YŪNUS EMRE, an immensely popular Anatolian Turkish mystic poet of the second half of the 13th and the first quarter of the 14th century. The information on Yūnus Emre's life is fragmentary and inconclusive in many respects, being partly of a legendary character (see the hagiological writings especially of the Bektāshiyye) or dependent on the interpretation of some passages in his *Dīwān*.

Yūnus Emre's birthplace is uncertain; the likeliest site seems to be a village in the environs of either Sivrihisar (Eskişehir) or Bolu. There are indications that Yūnus Emre married and had one or more children and that he travelled quite extensively, not only in Anatolia but farther east to Damascus, Tabrīz, etc. There is no proof that Yūnus Emre studied at a *medrese*. On the other hand, he was certainly not illiterate (the allusions to illiteracy in his *Dīwān* should be seen in the light of the concept of being *ummī* [*q.v.*], which does not necessarily imply factual illiteracy). His considerable learning probably derives primarily from his *tekke* [*q.v.*] education and ambience.

It is not certain to which Islamic mystical order (*ṭarīḳa* [*q.v.*]) Yūnus Emre belonged. The main assertions are that he was affiliated to the Bektāshiyye or the Mewlewiyye, but it has also been alleged that he was a member of the Khalwetiyye, the Ḳādiriyye, etc. On the evidence of passages in his *Dīwān*, Yūnus Emre's spiritual director and initiator (*murshid* [*q.v.*]) was Ṭapduḳ Emre, who, according to Bektāshī hagiology, was admitted to the order by Ḥādjdjī Bektāsh [see bektāshiyya]. On the other hand, Yūnus Emre's mention of Djalāl al-Dīn Rūmī [*q.v.*] in a few verses reflects a spiritual bond between him and the Mewlewiyye. His poetry documents him as deeply religious in conformance with the teachings of the Ḳurʾān and the *sīra* [*q.v.*], with an understanding of Islamic mysticism (*taṣawwuf* [*q.v.*]) in the tradition of Ibn al-ʿArabī [*q.v.*]. Yūnus Emre's religious philosophy aims at "the unity of existence" (*waḥdat al-wudjūd*). This pantheistic view is complemented by the doctrine of "the perfect human being" (*al-insān al-kāmil* [*q.v.*]).

It is generally accepted that Yūnus Emre died in 720/1320-1, as documented by the entry on fol. 38b of the ms. *Mecmua* no. 7912 at the Beyazıd Umumî Kütüphanesi, Istanbul. The site of Yūnus Emre's grave is not certain. The fact that about a dozen graves (or *maḳāms*) situated all over Anatolia are attributed to him attests to his immense popularity. Of these, the grave in Bursa is almost certainly that of ʿĀshïḳ Yūnus (d. 843/1439-40), a mystic who wrote poetry in the manner of Yūnus Emre. For the rest, the grave that has found most credibility is that in the village of Sarıköy in the vicinity of Sivrihisar (Eskişehir), and in 1970 the mortal remains in this grave were transferred to the memorial grave built for the poet in Sarıköy.

Yūnus Emre is known to be the author of two works: a *Dīwān* and the *methnewī* called *Risālet el-nuṣhiyye*.

1. The *Dīwān*. There are a great number of mss. of this work. *Medjmūʿa*s (collections of literary works) also contain many poems by Yūnus Emre. The mss. show great discrepancies with regard to the number of poems, number and sequence of verses, etc. Yūnus Emre used the pen-name (*makhlaṣ* [see takhalluṣ]) *Yūnus*, occasionally in the form *Yūnus Emre(m)* or with attributes such as *Miskīn*, *Bī-čāre*, *ʿĀshïḳ*, and once each as *Ṭapduḳ Yūnus*, *Ṭapduḳlu Yūnus*. A considerable number of poems by poets using the pen-name *Yūnus*, or even an altogether different pen-name, have erroneously been attributed to him and included in mss. of his *Dīwān*. In fact, one of the most popular *ilāhīs* [*q.v.*] today, namely that starting *Shol djennetüñ ïrmaḳlarï * Aḳar Allāh deyü deyü*, "Those streams of Paradise * Flow, calling Allah Allah", is generally attributed to Yūnus Emre, although it is actually by the poet ʿĀshïḳ Yūnus mentioned above.

The latest critical edition of the *Dīwān* (by M. Tatcı) contains 417 poems. Yūnus Emre composed a considerable number of poems according to the rules of the Arabo-Persian metrical system (*ʿarūḍ* [*q.v.*]), albeit with frequent faults. Nevertheless, the greater part of his *Dīwān* is composed according to the original Turkic method of versification, wherein the verses are not based on quantity as in *ʿarūḍ* but on the number of the syllables and the stress positions (*parmaḳ ḥisābï* or *hedje wezni*). A third group of poems shows only traces of composition in conformance with *ʿarūḍ*, so that these poems must be regarded (at least until further mss. supply metrically more correct versions) as composed according to *parmaḳ ḥisābï*. Yūnus Emre's application of *parmaḳ ḥisābï* is very successful. On the other hand, the frequent *ʿarūḍ* mistakes are understandable as Yūnus Emre lived at a time when the application of the Arabo-Persian metres to the Turkish language was in its initial phase. Furthermore, oral transmission of the poems through the centuries is certain to be responsible for a considerable number of the *ʿarūḍ* faults found in the mss.

The *ʿarūḍ* metre Yūnus Emre used by far most frequently is *aṣlī redjez* (*mustafʿilun-mustafʿilun-mustafʿilun-mustafʿilun*). Of the syllabic lengths of *parmaḳ ḥisābī*, he used almost all, including such rare lengths as 10 and 12 syllables. He used aural rhyme, without regard for total accord (Turkish *geč* rhyming with Arabic *muḥtādj*, for example). Apart from one short *methnewī* of 28 verses, all the poems in the *Dīwān* have the rhyme scheme of the *ghazel* [see TURKS. 4.]. The lengths of these poems also corresponds to the usual lengths of the *ghazel* (only a few poems have more than 15 verses and one has 45). A considerable number of these are totally or partially *musammaṭ*, that is, have "inner rhyme" (the rhyme scheme *aa, xa, xa*, etc. thereby becoming *xaxa* [the first verse is usually without "inner rhyme"], *bbba, ccca*, etc.). The *musammaṭ* poems are mostly in the above *aṣlī redjez* metre consisting of 16 syllables and are often metrically faulty; such a faulty verse is practically indistinguishable from a quatrain with lines of 8 syllables composed according to *parmaḳ ḥisābī*. The genres of poetry found in the *Dīwān* are predominantly the *ilāhī* (respectively the *nefes* [*q.v.*]) and the *nuṭuḳ* (didactic mystical poem). However, there are a few examples of other genres such as the *münādjāt* (supplication addressed to God), the *naʿt* (eulogy, especially of Muḥammad), the *miʿrādj-nāme* [see MIʿRĀDJ], the *shaṭḥiyye* [see SHAṬḤ], etc.

Yūnus Emre's poems are in Old Anatolian Turkish. He expresses himself simply and directly, in the idiom of the common people, using similes, metaphors, expressions, sayings, etc. that are familiar to them. His use of Arabic and Persian words is restricted enough not to have hindered the (at least superficial) comprehension of the bulk of his *Dīwān*. Frequently, an Arabic or Persian word is used in close proximity to its Turkish synonym. Yūnus Emre contributed to the forming of a Turkish mystical vocabulary based on the classic Ṣūfī terms. The *Dīwān* contains quotations from the Ḳurʾān, the *ḥadīth* [*q.v.*], the sayings of Ṣūfīs and allusions to Indo-Persian and Greek mythology and to folk tales.

The most recurrent theme in Yūnus Emre's *Dīwān* is mystic love. Yet he is no recluse and the conditions of everyday life are reflected in his poems. His mostly easily understandable religious and moral advice is couched in lyrical language of heartfelt sincerity and often great intensity of feeling. His poetry was of central importance in the dissemination of Ṣūfī teachings in Anatolia, influenced the *tekke* poetry of the following centuries, and played an initiative role in the application of the *ʿarūḍ* metric system to Turkish. The intense religious and humane feeling in his poetry has not lost its appeal today. It is not therefore surprising that his *ilāhī*s continue to be sung at events of a religious nature or that in 1946 Adnan Saygun composed his *Yunus Emre oratoryosu* using some of Yūnus Emre's poems as its libretto.

2. The *Risālet el-nuṣḥiyye*, a Turkish *methnewī* of 600 verses with a moralising didactic message, was composed in 707/1307-8. After an introductory section of thirteen verses in the metre *ramal* (*fāʿilātun-fāʿilātun-fāʿilun*), there is a short section in prose followed by the main text composed in the metre *hazadj* (*mafāʿīlun-mafāʿīlun-faʿūlun*). This *methnewī* shows a mastery of the rhetoric device of *teshkhīṣ* (anthropomorphism), but it does not possess the lyrical quality of the poems in the *Dīwān*.

Bibliography: For a comprehensive bibliography, see M. Tatcı, *Yunus Emre bibliyografyası*, Ankara 1988; A. Gölpınarlı, *Yunus Emre Divanı* (*metinler, sözlük, açılama*), Istanbul 1943; idem, *Yunus Emre ve tasavvuf*, Istanbul 1961; idem, *Yunus Emre: Risâlat al-Nushiya ve Dîvân*, Istanbul 1965; idem, *Yunus Emre (hayatı ve bütün şiirleri)*, Istanbul 1971; M.F. Köprülü, *Türk edebiyatı'nda ilk mutasavvıflar*, [2]Ankara 1966; F.K. Timurtaş, *Yûnus Emre dîvânı*, Istanbul 1972 (2nd enlarged ed. 1980); A.S. Erzi, *Türkiye kütüphanelerinden notlar ve vesikalar. I. Yûnus Emre'nin hayatı hakkında bir vesika*, in *Belleten*, xiv/53 (1950), 85-9; T.S. Halman (ed.), *Yunus Emre and his mystical poetry*, Bloomington 1981; J.C. Bürgel, *Grösse und Grenzen gewaltlosen Handelns. Aktualisierung islamischer Mystik in einem modernen türkischen Drama* [namely, Recep Bilginer's play "Yunus Emre"], in *WI*, N.S., xxiii-xxiv (1984), 1-25; N. Pekolcay and E. Sevim, *Yunus Emre'nin şahsiyeti ve Yunus Emre şerhleri. Yunus Emre'nin bir eseriyle ilgili şerhlerin yazmaları*, Ankara 1991; C. Kosal (ed.), *Yunus ilâhîleri güldestesi*, Ankara 1991; M. Bozdemir (ed.), *Yunus Emre, Message universel* (*Actes du Colloque*, Paris 1991), Paris 1992; A. Schimmel, *Yunus Emre*, in *Turkish Review*, vii/32 (1993), 67-90; *Uluslararası Yunus Emre. Sempozyumu bildirileri*, Ankara 1995; A. Özgüven, *Two mystic poets: Yunus Emre and William Blake*, in *Journal of Turkish Studies/Türklük Bilgisi Araştırmaları*, xx (1996) (= *In memoriam Abdülbaki Gölpınarlı*, ii), 234-47; Tatcı, *Yûnus Emre Dîvânı*, 2nd revised ed., i (*inceleme*); ii (*tenkitli metin*); iii (*Risâlet'ün-Nushiyye: tenkitli metin*); iv (*Âşık Yûnus*, actually a collective edition of poems by ʿĀshiḳ Yūnus and other poets with the pen-name *Yûnus* without specification of the respective authorship), Istanbul 1997. (EDITH G. AMBROS)

YŪNUS AL-KĀTIB AL-MUGHANNĪ, Abū Sulaymān Yūnus b. Sulaymān b. Kurd b. Shahriyār, well-known musician and writer on music in the first half of the 2nd/8th century.

He was the son of a jurist (*faḳīh*) of Persian origin and a *mawlā* of the family of al-Zubayr b. al-ʿAwwām (Ḳuraysh). Yūnus was born and grew up in Medina. He entered the local *dīwān* as a scribe, hence his surname al-Kātib. Early in life, however, he was attracted by music, and he is said to have taken lessons mainly from Maʿbad [*q.v.*], but also from Ibn Suraydj, Ibn Muḥriz, al-Gharīḍ [*q.vv.*], and Muḥammad b. ʿAbbād al-Kātib. He was also a gifted poet. Whilst on a visit to Syria during the reign of Hishām (105-25/724-43) his fame in music brought him the patronage of the *amīr* al-Walīd b. Yazīd. This event forms the basis of a highly-coloured story in the 684th and 685th nights of the *Alf layla wa-layla*. Returning to Medina, Yūnus provoked a scandal by composing his *Zayānib*, a cycle of seven songs extolling Zaynab, a niece of the Successor (*Tābiʿī*) ʿAbd al-Raḥmān b. al-Ḥārith al-Makhzūmī. On the accession of al-Walīd b. Yazīd in 125/743, Yūnus was summoned to the Damascus court where he was treated with "high honour and munificence". He was still alive under the early ʿAbbāsids. Having lost his voice he gave singing lessons by using chironomic signs. His best-known pupil was Siyāṭ (d. 169/785), a teacher of Ibrāhīm al-Mawṣilī [*q.v.*]. Hence a musical tradition and, at the same time, a literary *isnād* connects the masters Maʿbad, Yūnus al-Kātib, Siyāṭ, Ibrāhīm al-Mawṣilī, and Isḥāḳ al-Mawṣilī [*q.v.*]. Yūnus died, around 147/765, at over eighty and possibly in Baghdād.

As a composer, Yūnus has a place among the great musicians of the classical era, as we know from the high esteem accorded his songs. They were even imitated by later musicians, in a so-called "Zayānib style" (*ghinā' zayānibī*). As a singer, he seems to have been one of the *murtadjil* singers who used to accompany themselves by beating the musical metre (*īkā'*) with a wand (*kaḍīb*). Yūnus left several books on music and musicians. Among them was a record of the tonal system of the Medinan music school, called *K. al-Nagham*. From this book, a quotation on the division of the octave seems to have survived. He also composed a book on the renowned female singers (*K. al-Ḳiyān*), a collection of his own song texts (*K. Mudjarrad Yūnus*), and an extensive systematic collection (*tadwīn*) of song texts (*K. fi 'l-Aghānī*), also called *Dīwān Yūnus*. The latter contained, in the redaction known to Ibn Khurradādhbih [*q.v.*], 825 song texts by 35 male and female singers of the first two "classes" (*ṭabaḳāt*) in Islam. In a redaction described by Ibn al-Ṭaḥḥān (d. after 449/1057 in Cairo), the number of song texts is said to have increased to 6,300. They were in alphabetical order, followed by complete musical indications, and by the names of the poet and the composer. Abu 'l-Faradj al-Iṣfahānī [*q.v.*] quoted the book frequently in his *K. al-Aghānī al-kabīr*. He made use of this "fundamental source" (*aṣl*) in a redaction by al-Hishāmī (3rd/9th century) who had supplied the musical indications (*adjnās, ṭarā'iḳ*) omitted by Yūnus. The advanced and extensive literary production of Yūnus al-Kātib proves in itself that he cannot have been "the first" to write on music in Islam, as was often stated.

Bibliography: Ibn Khurradādhbih, *Mukhtār min K. al-Lahw wa 'l-malāhī*, Beirut 1961, 40-43 and *passim*; *Aghānī³*, i, 42-3, 251, ii, 231-3, iv, 398-404, v, 230, vi, 152, 171, viii, 220-1, xii, 126, xvii, 223, xix, 133, and indices; Ibn al-Nādim, *Fihrist*, 145; Ibn al-Ṭaḥḥān, *Hāwī al-funūn wa-salwat at-maḥzūn*, facs. ed. Frankfurt 1990, 37-8; Nuwayrī, *Nihāyat al-arab*, Cairo 1923 ff., iv, 292-3; Ibn Faḍl Allāh al-ʿUmarī, *Masālik al-abṣār*, facs. ed. Frankfurt 1988, x, 132-3; Ṣafadī, xxix, 390-2; A. Caussin de Perceval, *Notices anecdotiques sur les principaux musiciens arabes*, in *JA*, série 7, vol. ii, 399-592, esp. 507-10; H.G. Farmer, *A history of Arabian music*, London 1929, 83-4, and index; idem, *The minstrelsy of "The Arabian Nights"*, Bearsden, Glasgow 1945, 18-19; idem, *The sources of Arabian music*, Leiden 1965, nos. 1-4; Sezgin, *GAS*, i, 368-9; E. Neubauer, *Zur Bedeutung der Begriffe Komponist und Komposition in der Musikgeschichte der islamischen Welt*, in *ZGAIW*, xi (1997), 307-63, esp. 311-12, 318; idem, *Arabische Musiktheorie von den Anfängen bis zum 6./12. Jahrhundert*, Frankfurt 1998, index.   (H.G. FARMER-[E. NEUBAUER])

YURT [see KHAYMA. iv].

YÜRÜK [see YÖRÜK].

YŪSHAʿ B. NŪN, the Joshua of the Bible. The Ḳurʾān does not mention him by name but alludes to him. When Moses wished to lead his people into the holy land and Israel was afraid to fight with the giants, they were encouraged by two God-fearing men (V, 20-6) who may be recognised as Joshua and Caleb. Neither can it be doubted that the young man (*fatā* = *naʿar*, Exod. xxxiii. 11) who accompanies Moses on a journey to al-Khaḍir [*q.v.*] (not named) in XVIII, 60-64, is any other than Joshua (see al-Ṭabarī, i, 428).

Al-Ṭabarī was certainly well informed of the features of the biblical tradition concerning Joshua: the crossing of the Jordan with the ark, the spies, the fall of Jericho, the dishonesty of Achan, the artifice of the Gibeonites, the solstice, Bezek. However, Muslim legend has also supplied the figure of Yūshaʿ with features not found in the Bible, most of which parallel the material in the Haggada. Yūshaʿ was given the task of summoning the Children of Israel to the true faith

(al-Ṭabarī, i 503-4). To enable Moses to depart this life without anxiety, Yūshaʿ was installed as a prophet in his lifetime (see L. Ginzberg, *The legends of the Jews*, Philadelphia 1909-38, iii, 436-9). He was present at Moses's death and Moses's garments remained in Yūshaʿ's hands when Moses died. Yūshaʿ was suspected of having killed Moses but all the Israelites had a dream in which Moses refuted the suspicion to calm the affair. Yūshaʿ conquered the giants in Jericho, but the traditions vary as to whether the victory was won in the time of Moses or not until after his death. Balaam [see BALʿAM] supported the battle against the Israelites. In Ibn al-Athīr, the story is embellished; Balaam's wife was bribed to incite him to evil (see H. Schützinger, *Die arabische Baleam-Erzählung*, in *Isl.*, lix [1982], 195-221). Ḳurʾān, VII, 175-7 is also connected to Balaam. Yūshaʿ could not cross the Jordan for 40 days. He then prayed and the two hills on the banks became a bridge across which people could pass (al-Kisāʾī). Jericho was besieged for six months, and in the seventh the walls fell down at the blowing of the trumpets. The miracle in which Yūshaʿ makes the sun stand still is mentioned sometimes in connection with the conquest of Jericho and sometimes in the war against the united kings. In both cases, the story is told that Friday evening was close to arriving. If the sabbath began, the fighting could not be continued and the victory would be incomplete. Yūshaʿ wished to stop the sun; at first it refused, saying it was fulfilling divine orders just as Yūshaʿ was; finally, the sun agreed. After the victory, Yūshaʿ collected the booty and desired to offer it as a sacrifice but no flame came down from heaven to consume it (cf. Lev. ix. 24; I Kings xviii. 23-4; I Chr. xxi. 26; II Chr. vii. 1). There must have been some dishonesty. The lot pointed to Achan as the sinner. According to another tradition, Yūshaʿ summoned the heads of the tribes. The hand of the sinner stuck to the hand of Yūshaʿ. Al-Kisāʾī records another divine judgment; each tribe had a mark on Aaron's robe and the mark of the guilty tribe became distorted. A bull's head studded with pearls and jewels was found in the sinner's possession and was added to the booty. Flames then consumed the booty, including the bull's head, along with the sinner.

Yūshaʿ rooted out the inhabitants of Canaan, but a fraction of them migrated under the leadership of Ifrīḳīs to Africa; their king Djirdjir (i.e. Gregory) was killed; from the others, the North African Berbers are descended.

In al-Ṭabarī, i, 558, the isolated tradition is found that the dead man conjured up by Ṭālūt (Saul) was Yūshaʿ rather than Samuel (cf. I Sam. xxviii. 11-19). The tomb of Yūshaʿ is a pilgrimage site, probably dating from pre-Islamic times, in Maʿarrat al-Nuʿmān [*q.v.*, at Vol. V, 926b].

Bibliography: Ṭabarī, i, 414-29 (on al-Khaḍir), 498-9, 503-16, tr. W. Brinner, *The History of al-Ṭabarī, iii, The Children of Israel*, Albany 1991, 1-18, 80-2, 86-98; Ibn al-Athīr, *Kāmil*, Būlāḳ 1290, i, 78-9; Thaʿlabī, *Ḳiṣaṣ al-anbiyāʾ*, Cairo n.d., 191-4, 199-203; Kisāʾī, *Ḳiṣaṣ al-anbiyāʾ*, ed. Eisenberg, Leiden 1922-3, 240-2; Abū Rifāʿa al-Fārisī, *Badʾ al-khalḳ wa-ḳiṣaṣ al-anbiyāʾ*, in R.G. Khoury (ed.), *Les légendes prophétiques dans l'Islam*, Wiesbaden 1978, 51-9; J. Horovitz, *Jewish proper names and their derivatives in the Koran*, in *Hebrew Union College Annual*, ii (1925), 179, on the use of the name Yūshaʿ in al-Wāḳidī.
                                              (B. HELLER-[A. RIPPIN])

AL-YŪSĪ, ABŪ ʿALĪ AL-ḤASAN b. Masʿūd, Moroccan man of letters (1040-1102/1631-91).

Of the Berber tribe of Aït Yūsī, he was born in

Fāzāz [*q.v.*] in the upper Malwiya region of Morocco. His travels first led him southwards to Marrakesh and then to Tāmgrūt, where he studied under the *shaykh* Muḥammad b. Nāṣir. He then went to the *zāwiya* of al-Dilā' [*q.v.* in Suppl.], where he enjoyed a long period of stability in his life until the destruction of this marabout principality by the ʿAlawī sultan Mawlāy al-Rashīd in 1079/1688. Al-Yūsī was compelled to follow the sultan back to Fās, where he gave courses that enjoyed much popularity at the Ḳarawiyyīn [*q.v.*]. But rivalries and frictions with colleagues, as well as a nomadic temperament, prevented him from adapting to life in a large city. He gave up teaching and finally left Fās in 1084/1673 for further travels. He visited various shrines before spending a good while in Marrakesh, where he taught in the mosque of the Shorfa. Towards the end of his life he made the Pilgrimage, and died in Fās soon after his return. He is buried near the town of Sefrou, his mausoleum being the centre of a cult [see ṢUFRŪ].

Al-Yūsī's oeuvre covers several areas of scholarship. His *Ḳānūn fī ibtidā' al-ʿulūm* is an attempt to define and classify the different sciences. The breadth of his interests can also be seen in his epistles (*Rasā'il Abī ʿAlī al-Ḥasan b. Masʿūd al-Yūsī*, ed. Fāṭima Khalīl al-Kablī, 2 vols. Casablanca 1981), which touch on points of theology, law and mysticism. The most famous are those reproaching the ruler, as in the case of the epistle called *barā'at al-Yūsī* in which, not without boldness, he reproaches Mawlāy Ismāʿīl for having disarmed the whole group of Moroccan tribes. In another one, known as the *djawāb al-kitāb* and composed in reply to a letter (now lost) from the same sultan, al-Yūsī dilates at length on the topic of scholars' relations with the sovereign power.

His *Dīwān* includes a *dāliyya* in honour of his master Ibn Nāṣir and a *rā'iyya* in which he evokes memories of the *zāwiya* of al-Dilā'. His verses have a mystical tone, and the most remarkable ones have a nostalgic feeling for his native land. He also compiled a collection of proverbs, *Zahr al-akam fī 'l-amthāl wa 'l-ḥikam* (ed. M. Ḥadjdjī and M. al-Akhḍar, 3 vols. Casablanca 1981). His *Muḥāḍarāt*, written in 1095/1684 (ed. Ḥadjdjī and Aḥmad Sharḳāwī, 2 vols. Beirut 1982) are conversations, of the *adab* genre: anecdotes, poetic quotations (including some in *malḥūn* [*q.v.*]), autobiographical confidences, travel narratives, and reflections upon such varied topics as sainthood, Mahdism, food customs in the *zāwiya*s, couscous and the story-tellers of the Djāmaʿ al-Fnā. Despite the discrete nature of its subjects, this work remains an irreplaceable document on the ruling classes, scholars, saints and the common people of the time.

Bibliography: Muḥ. b. al-Ṭayyib al-Ḳādirī, *Nashr al-mathānī*, ed. Ḥadjdjī and Aḥmad Tawfīḳ, Rabat 1077-86, iii, 25-49; Lévi-Provençal, *Shorfa*, 269-72; J. Berque, *Al-Yousi, problèmes de la culture marocaine au XVIIe siècle*, Paris and The Hague 1958; C. Geertz, *Islam observed*, New Haven 1968; Abdelfattah Killito, *Speaking to princes: al-Yusi and Mawlay Ismaʿil*, in Rahma Bouqia and Susan G. Miller (eds.), *In the shadow of the sultan*, Cambridge, Mass. 1999, 30-46. There is a full bibl. of al-Yūsī in ʿAbbās al-Djirārī, *ʿAbḳariyyat al-Yūsī*, Casablanca 1981.

(ABDELFATTAH KILLITO)

YŪSUF B. YAʿḲŪB, in the Ḳur'ān and later Islamic literature parallels, the Joseph of the Hebrew Bible and Jewish and Christian tradition. The character of Yūsuf is popular in Islamic pietistic and devotional literature, in prose and in poetry from the earliest commentaries until the present day.

1. In the Ḳur'ān.

Outside of sūra XII, Yūsuf is mentioned only twice. In VI, 84, he is merely listed among other biblical prophets, and in the following order: Ibrāhīm (VI, 83), Iṣḥāḳ and Yaʿḳūb, Nūḥ "[whom] We guided previously, and from his progeny, Dāwūd, Sulaymān, Ayyūb, Yūsuf, Mūsā and Hārūn". XL, 34 is included in a longer section treating the story of Moses, where it is stated that Yūsuf came before Moses with clear divine messages that were nevertheless doubted by his people, and that these same people thought that God would not send another prophet after him.

All other Ḳur'ānic references to Yūsuf occur in sūra XII, a complete telling of the Joseph story, the longest Ḳur'ānic narrative and the only lengthy chapter of the Ḳur'ān representing a single and complete literary unit. The Ḳur'ānic Joseph story not only exhibits a close intertextual relationship with the versions represented in the Hebrew Bible and post-biblical Jewish and Christian narrative exegesis, but also finds important parallels with the tale of Bellerophon of the *Iliad* and the pre-biblical Egyptian "Tale of two brothers". One of the central themes of sūra XII, that of al-ʿAzīz's wife making vain overtures of Yūsuf and then accusing him of attempting to force her, represents a common motif of folk literatures throughout the world (motif K 2111 in S. Thompson's *Motif index of folk literature*, v). Questions of "influence" and "borrowing" become extremely complex in light of such a complicated intertextuality. However, it is clear from a diachronic perspective that "biblicist" material—that is, deriving from the Bible and its exegesis—impacted the emergence of sūra XII, while Ḳur'ānic and post-Ḳur'ānic Islamic material in turn impacted later renderings of the tale in Jewish and Christian circles.

The Ḳur'ānic Yūsuf embodies the chief qualities of a prophet: knowledge, trust and uprightness. In contrast to the biblical rendering and biblical narrative in general, the Ḳur'ān depicts Yūsuf as protected from error through its portrayal of the positive moral attributes of patience, trust, veracity, judgment and discernment and absolute faith epitomised not only by the prophet Yūsuf but also by his father, the prophet Yaʿḳūb. This, among many other differences between the biblical and Ḳur'ānic renderings of the tale, reflects the different eras, cultures and contextual world views that the two versions reflect. Whereas the biblical version typifies the "heroic tale" portraying a sacred history of progenitors and patriarchs, the Ḳur'ānic version serves far more as a didactic tale in which positive and negative behaviours are clearly depicted and assessed through the conduct of the tale's actors. The Ḳur'ānic rendering thus reflects the realm of pietism which, in turn, parallels post-biblical Jewish and Christian exegetical reflections of the tale that serve largely as teaching parables about chastity, temptation, faith and uprightness in the face of adversity.

Recently, synchronic approaches to the narrative have been taken by Johns, Stern and Mir. Johns stresses the unique oral nature of the Ḳur'ānic telling and the use of repetition and "replays", while Stern has shown how the story may be seen as an allegorical rendering of the traditional biography of Muḥammad. Both Yūsuf and Muḥammad were accused by their detractors (brothers or tribal kin) of seeking superiority over others for their own personal ends, but their very critics could not understand until the end that the two prophets were asserting themselves only because God had thrust a special role on them for the purpose of bringing about their people's own salvation. Mir has demonstrated the chiastic structure of the narrative by showing not only how the tensions built up in the first half of the story (1-44) are resolved in reverse order in the second half (45-100) but also how certain motifs recur antithetically and heighten the story's drama.

The didactic and moralistic nature of the Ḳurʾānic rendering leaves the main protagonists' characters largely flat and undeveloped, and fails even to provide names for those actors in the drama that do not personify right behaviour. This, along with the exceptional length and narrativity of the sūra, encouraged a great deal of thinking and discussion which resulted in voluminous exegesis on *Sūrat Yūsuf.*

2. In post-Ḳurʾānic literature.

Yūsuf is largely absent from the *Ḥadīth*. Direct and indirect exegesis of *Sūrat Yūsuf* may be found in the *Tafsīr* literature, the universal histories of al-Ṭabarī, Ibn Kathīr, etc., hagiographic literature (*ḳiṣaṣ al-anbiyāʾ* [*q.v.*]), and in the poetry and pietistic literatures of virtually all religious, ethnic and linguistic sub-groups in the vast Islamic world from Spain to China and from Russia to South Africa. These literatures fill in the obvious lacunae of the Ḳurʾānic telling, resolve and respond to conflicts and parallels with biblicist literatures, and capitalise on the nature and authority of the scriptural tale in order to promote various independent or creative ideas or perspectives on the religious, moral, spiritual or creative life. At the most basic level, names and narrative depth are provided for secondary characters in the Ḳurʾānic telling, including certain of Yūsuf's brothers, the trader(s) who purchase Yūsuf from his brothers, the Egyptian to whom he is sold, his wife, the king of Egypt, his servants who know Yūsuf in jail, etc. The Egyptian is known variously as Ḳiṭfīr, Iṭfīr, Ḳūṭifar, Ḳiṭṭin, etc., all deriving from the biblical name Potiphar. His wife is named Rāʾīl, a development from the common Arabising pattern of Hebrew names (Ḳābīl and Hābīl, Sāmwīl, Rāḥīl, etc.), and, later, Zulaykhā (Zālīka, Zulayka). Some biblicist material not found in the Ḳurʾānic rendering sometimes appears in the exegetical literature. In a Malay telling, for example, al-ʿAzīz is referred to as Potiphar, and his wife is called Asnath rather than Rāʾīl or Zulaykhā. So also do local *realia* appear in re-tellings of the tale, such as the brothers telling Yaʿḳūb in the Malay version that Yūsuf has been killed by a tiger rather than a wolf.

Reasons are provided in the secondary literature for difficult aspects of the Ḳurʾānic story. Yaʿḳūb's intense suffering over the purported loss of his son is a result of his slaughtering a calf before the eyes of its mother, because he did not share his meal with the hungry, or because he separated a young slave-girl from her parents. Yūsuf suffers initially because of his vanity or because he relies on human help before trusting totally in God.

Because Yūsuf's story of suffering has resonated with the Shīʿī tradition of redemptive suffering and endurance, his and his father's tribulations find a place in the Shīʿī *taʿziya* [*q.v.*] plays commemorating the suffering and martyrdom of al-Ḥusayn. These expand and heighten the torment and suffering depicted in the Ḳurʾānic rendering and associate them with the future suffering of al-Ḥusayn and his family. Yūsuf and Yaʿḳūb represent the best of human suffering until the rise of Islam and the extraordinary suffering of al-Ḥusayn, which exceeds that of the early prophets and therefore receives greater redemptive merit for his Shīʿī followers.

Yūsuf serves as a model of virtue and wisdom in pietistic literature. He is extolled in Ṣūfī manuals such as that of Abū Naṣr al-Sarrādj's *K. al-Lumaʿ* as a paragon of forgiveness, based on XII, 92. He also epitomises the chastity that is based on complete trust in God, for it was his absolute piety that prompted God to personally intervene to prevent him from the transgression of succumbing to sexual temptation (XII, 24). So, too, does he exemplify deep wisdom by, for example, knowing to instruct his brothers to throw his shirt over Jacob's face rather than simply giving it to him, because Yaʿḳub's joy in learning of his son's survival would make him forget to rub the shirt over his eyes and restore his eyesight (see XII, 93, 96).

The most frequent reference to Yūsuf's attributes in post-Ḳurʾānic literature is to his extraordinary beauty. His beauty was so exceptional that the behaviour of the wife of al-ʿAzīz is forgiven, or at least mitigated, because of the unavoidably uncontrollable love and passion that his countenance would rouse in her. Such portrayals are found in many genres of Islamic literatures, but are most famous in Nūr al-Dīn ʿAbd al-Raḥmān Djāmī's [*q.v.*] *Yūsuf wa Zulaykhā*, which incorporates many of the motifs and attributes associated with his beauty in earlier works.

Certainly by the 7th/13th century, and up to the 10th/16th in Persian areas at the very least, Yūsuf was looked to by artists and rulers alike as a patron of the arts. The Ṣūfī Nadjm al-Dīn Rāzī Dāya (d. 1256) dedicates his *Mirṣād al-ʿibād* to the Saldjūḳ sultan of Rūm Kayḳubād, likening him to Yūsuf in hopes of receiving his patronage, and a famous Ṣafawid illustrated manuscript of Djāmī's *Yūsuf wa Zulaykhā* has the name of the Tīmūrid sultan and patron, Ibrāhīm Mīrzā (d. 1476) inscribed over a portrait of Yūsuf on the eve of his wedding to Zulaykhā. On the other hand, Yūsuf's role as temporal ruler rendered him suspect among some pietists, for the pollution of wordly kingship rendered even Yūsuf a delay in being accepted into the Garden.

Like the other earlier prophets, Yūsuf possesses special insights, often mystical and certainly exceptional, that may be emulated by spiritual adepts and other religious seekers. But the exceptional motifs and symbols found in *Sūrat Yūsuf* give his persona an even higher status than most in Islamic religious literature and civilisation. Renard has aptly noted the broad impact of Yūsuf and his story on this culture. "The well and prison into which Joseph is thrown refer to all forms of adversity through which one must live in patience and trust. Allusions to Joseph's shirt have come to mean any experience that restores the blinded seeker's sight. The expression 'to cut one's hand', an allusion to the guests at Zulayka's dinner party, has become a coded reference to the seeker's experience of stark bewilderment in the presence of the Beloved. And Joseph's necessary separation from, and eventual reunion with, his father offers a perfect pattern to console the lover of God who seems to experience God's absence. Most of all, Joseph's beauty keeps the poets enthralled as the most apt image for the deepest of all experiences, the ever-present yearning for the source of all life and being. As Rumi writes of his own experience of longing for the Beloved, 'Like Jacob I am crying alas, alas; the fair visage of Joseph of Canaan is my desire'."

The very fact that the tale of Yūsuf represents the one complete literary narrative structured as such in the Ḳurʾān rendered it special significance in Islamic literary and cultural tradition. Wahb b. Munabbih [*q.v.*] is quoted in al-Kisāʾī's *Ḳiṣaṣ al-Anbiyāʾ* as saying, "God would never send any prophet without telling him the story of Yūsuf, just as He told it to our prophet Muḥammad".

Bibliography: 1. Sources. Ṭabarī, i, 371-414, Eng. tr. W.M. Brinner, *The History of al-Ṭabarī*, ii, *Prophets and patriarchs*, Albany 1987, 148-85; T̲h̲aʿlabī, *ʿArāʾis al-madj̲ālis fī ḳiṣaṣ al-anbiyāʾ*, Beirut n.d., 94-125; Kisāʾī, *Ḳiṣaṣ al-anbiyāʾ*, ed. Eisenberg, 156-79; Ibn al-At̲h̲īr, i, 54-61; A.F.L. Beeston, *Baiḍāwī's commentary on Surah 12 of Qurʾān*, Oxford 1963; Ibn Kat̲h̲īr, *Ḳiṣaṣ al-anbiyāʾ*, Beirut 1982/1402, i, 317-66; Dj̲āmī, *Yusuf and Zulaykha*, tr. D. Pendelbury, London 1980.

2. Studies. B. Heller, *Die Sage von Sarge Yusufs*..., in *MGWF* (1926), 271-6; J. Macdonald, *Joseph in the Qurʾān and Muslim commentary. A comparative study*, in *MW*, xlvi (1956), 113-31, 207-24; J. Knappert, *Four Swahili epics*, Leiden 1964, 9-58; J.D. Yohanan (ed.), *Joseph and Potiphar's wife in world literature. An anthology of the story of the chaste youth and the lustful stepmother*, New York 1968; R.Y. Ebied and M.J.L. Young (eds.), *The story of Joseph in Arabic verse (the Leeds Arabic manuscript 347)* = Supplement 3 to Annual of Leeds University Oriental Society, Leiden 1975; Angelika Neuwirth, *Zur Struktur der Yūsuf-Sure*, in W. Diem and S. Wild (eds.), *Studien aus Arabistik und Semitistik, Anton Spitaler zum siebzigsten Geburtstag*, Wiesbaden 1980, 123-52; A.H. Johns, *Joseph in the Qurʾān. Dramatic dialogue, human emotion, and prophetic wisdom*, in *Islamochristiana*, vii (1981), 29-51; M.S. Stern, *Muhammad and Joseph. A study of Koranic narrative*, in *JNES*, xliv (1985), 193-204; Mustansir Mir, *The Qurʾanic story of Joseph. Plot, themes and characters*, in *MW*, lxxvi (1986), 1-15; G. Rendsburg, *Literary structures in the Qurʾānic and biblical stories of Joseph*, in *MW*, lxxviii (1988), 118-20; A.-L. de Prémare, *Joseph et Muhammad. Le chapitre 12 du Coran*, Aix-en-Provence 1989; M.A.S. Abdel Haleem, *The story of Joseph in the Qurʾān and the Old Testament*, in *Islam and Christian-Muslim Relations*, i (1990), 171-91; Susan T. Hollis, *The Ancient Egyptian "Tale of two brothers"*, Norman, Okla. 1990; Fedwa Malti-Douglas, *Woman's body, woman's world. Gender and discourse in Arabo-Islamic writing*, Princeton 1991; Annemarie Schimmel, *Yusuf in Mawlana Rumi's poetry*, in L. Lewisohn (ed.), *The legacy of medieval Persian Sufism*, London 1992, 45-60; J. Morris, *Dramatizing the Sura of Joseph. An introduction to the Islamic humanities*, in M.E. Subtelny (ed.), *Annemarie Schimmel Festschrift* = *Jnal. of Turkish Studies*, xviii (1994), 201-24; Shalom Goldman, *The wiles of women, the wiles of men. Joseph and Potiphar's wife in Ancient Near Eastern, Jewish, and Islamic folklore*, Albany 1995; J. Renard, *Seven doors to Islam*, Berkeley, etc. 1996, 259-72; M. McGaha, *Coat of many cultures. The story of Joseph in Spanish literature 1200-1492*, Philadelphia 1997; M. Bernstein, *Stories of Joseph. Intertextuality in Judaism and Islam*, Detroit, forthcoming. (R. FIRESTONE)

YŪSUF B. **ʿABD** AL-**HĀDĪ**, in fuller form Dj̲amāl al-Dīn Abu 'l-Maḥāsin Yūsuf b. Ḥasan b. Aḥmad... b. ʿAbd al-Hādī, also known as Ibn al-Mibrad, Ḥanbalī scholar and author, advocate of a revival of the *ḥadīt̲h̲* studies which had once flourished at Damascus, b. end of 840/June 1437 or in the next year, d. 16 Muḥarram 909/14 September 1503.

He stemmed from a branch of the Ibn Ḳudāma [*q.v.*] line of the Ḥanbalī Maḳdisī families who had come in the 6th/12th century and founded the Damascus suburb of al-Ṣāliḥiyya [*q.v.*], but is not to be confused with another famous Ibn ʿAbd al-Hādī from the same family, S̲h̲ams al-Dīn Muḥammad b. Aḥmad (d. 744/1344), see Marwān ʿAṭiyya, in *Madj̲allat Madj̲maʿ al-Lug̲h̲a al-ʿArabiyya al-Urdunnī*, xlix [1995], 91-166). Little is known of Yūsuf's professional life except that he lectured at the ʿUmariyya *madrasa* in al-Ṣāliḥiyya, and led a life of teaching and scholarship. A large number of Damascus manuscripts contain notes from his own hand certifying the audition of himself or of his pupils and family. Most of his own work consists of small booklets (*adj̲zāʾ*), unstructured and *isnād*-based, like the reading copies of *ḥadīt̲h̲* which he used for study and teaching. His works, and the certificates related to them as well, are almost exclusively preserved in his own handwriting; it is thus obvious that his energetic activity did not meet with much response in his time. His personal library, of which he listed 600 titles, he gave to the ʿUmariyya, although his pupil Ibn Ṭūlūn [*q.v.*] bought some works from Yūsuf's children, and much of the ʿUmariyya *waḳf* library was subsequently dispersed, with its remaining remnants incorporated into the Ẓāhiriyya library.

Yūsuf b. ʿAbd al-Hādī is praised as both a *muḥaddit̲h̲* and a *faḳīh* by his biographers, although his Ḥanbalī learning was more in the field of historical studies than legal ones. However, his works, only partly printed, go far beyond these fields to include theology, biography, *sīra*, *adab*, medicine, etc. He was especially interested in the topography of Damascus and its buildings, cf. his *Rasāʾil dimas̲h̲ḳiyya*, Damascus 1988, and *T̲h̲imār al-maḳāṣid fī d̲h̲ikr al-masādj̲id*, Damascus 1975; he wrote a history of al-Ṣāliḥiyya, partly preserved in quotations by Ibn Ṭūlūn in his *Ḳalāʾid* and in the abridgement of Ibn Kanān, *al-Murūdj̲ al-sundusiyya al-fatḥiyya fī talk̲h̲īṣ Taʾrīk̲h̲ al-Ṣāliḥiyya*, Damascus 1947. He also wrote brief treatises on aspects of everyday life, e.g. a *K. al-Ṭibāk̲h̲a* and a *K. al-Ḥisba*, ed. Ḥabīb Zayyāt, in *Machriq*, xxxv [1937], 370-6, 384-400). With the increased interest in him during recent decades, several of his specifically religious and legal works have been edited and published, e.g. in *fiḳh* and biography, his *K. Ḳawāʿid al-kulliyya fi 'l-ḍawābiṭ al-fiḳhiyya*, Beirut 1994; *al-Durr al-naḳī*, Dj̲udda 1991; *Muʿdj̲am al-kutub* (mostly Ḥanbalī titles), Riyāḍ 1989; *al-Dj̲awhar al-munaḍḍad fī ṭabaḳāt mutaʾak̲h̲k̲h̲irī aṣḥāb Aḥmad*, Cairo 1987; *Ak̲h̲bār al-nisāʾ*, Ḥims 1993. On dogmatics and piety: *al-Tamhīd fi 'l-kalām ʿalā 'l-tawḥīd*, Riyāḍ 1997; *Baḥr al-damm fī man takallam fi 'l-Imām Aḥmad*, Beirut 1992; *Faḍl lā ḥawl wa-lā ḳuwwa illā bi 'llāh*, Damascus 1995; *al-Istiʿāna bi 'l-Fātiḥa*, Damascus n.d. On *Sīra: al-S̲h̲adj̲ara al-nabawiyya*, Damascus 1994; *Iḳtibās al-iḳtibās bi-ḥall mus̲h̲kil Sīrat Ibn Sayyid al-Nās*, Cairo 1937. In *adab: Itḥāf al-nubalāʾ bi-ak̲h̲bār al-kuramāʾ wa 'l-buk̲h̲alāʾ*, Cairo 1989; and ed. Yusrā ʿA. ʿAbd Allāh, Beirut 1410/1990. See also for his life and lists of his works, Brockelmann, II^2, 130-1, S II, 130; Kaḥḥāla, xiii, 289; Fedwa Malti-Douglas, *Yūsuf ibn ʿAbd al-Hādī and his autograph of the* Wuqūʿ al-Balāʾ bil-Bukhl wa-l-Bukhalāʾ, in *BEO*, xxxi (1979), 17-50. A survey of his work is given by Ṣalāḥ Muḥammad al-K̲h̲iyamī, in *MMMA*, xxvi/2 (1982), 775-809.

Bibliography: In addition to references in the article, see Kattānī, *Fihris al-fahāris*, ed. ʿAbbās, [2]Beirut 1982; G̲h̲azzī, *al-Naʿt al-akmal bi-aṣḥāb al-Imām Aḥmad b. Ḥanbal*, Damascus 1982; Ibn Ṭūlūn, *al-Ḳalāʾid al-dj̲awhariyya fī 'l-taʾrīk̲h̲ al-Ṣāliḥiyya*, Damascus 1981-2; Nuʿaymī, *al-Dāris fī taʾrīk̲h̲ al-madāris*, Damascus 1988. For the role of the Maḳdisī families in Damascus, see S. Leder, *Charismatic scripturalism. The Ḥanbalī Maqdisīs at Damascus*, in *Isl.*, lxxiv (1997), 279-304. (S. LEDER)

YŪSUF B. **ʿABD** AL-**RAḤMĀN** b. Abī ʿUbayda AL-**FIHRĪ** (*ca.* 72-142/691-759), last governor of al-Andalus before the accession to power of the Umayyad ʿAbd al-Raḥmān I.

Great grandson of the conqueror of the Mag̲h̲rib,

ʿUḳba b. Nāfiʿ [*q.v.*], he also belonged to one of the most prestigious Arab families to have settled in the Muslim West, renowned on account of its aristocratic Ḳura̲sh̲ī lineage and the participation of several of its members in the conquest of both shores of the Strait. Two brothers, Ḥabīb and ʿAbd al-Raḥmān, sons of Abū ʿUbayda ʿUḳba b. Nāfiʿ, accompanied the troops of Mūsā b. Nuṣayr [*q.v.*] at the time of the first crossing in the direction of al-Andalus. The former of the two remained in the Iberian Peninsula as lieutenant of ʿAbd al-ʿAzīz, son and successor of Mūsā, who was later assassinated. Subsequently, both brothers returned to Ifrīḳiya.

Yūsuf, born in Ḳayrawān, remained in Ifrīḳiya; after the return of his father, quarrels between the two of them induced him to leave for al-Andalus, governed at the time by Bi̲sh̲r b. Ṣafwān (103-9/721-7). He became governor of al-Andalus in 129/746 and was able to rely, initially at least, on the general support of the various factions dividing the Arabs of the Iberian Peninsula. But this unanimity was short-lived and the governor of al-Andalus, portrayed by the sources as a man totally manipulated by his lieutenant al-Ṣumayl b. Ḥātim [*q.v.*], was obliged throughout the term of his mandate to confront rebellions and revolts. With more or less ease he succeeded in suppressing the unrest; he even dared to rid himself of the tutelage of al-Ṣumayl, sending him away to govern the Upper March [see al-t̲h̲ug̲h̲ūr. 2.], a most difficult assignment. The latter came close to losing all prestige here, Yūsuf being unable—or unwilling—to come to his aid. Finally, rescued by members of his *d̲j̲und*, al-Ṣumayl returned to his post in the service of Yūsuf without, apparently, bearing any grudge against the latter regarding the perils to which he had exposed him. Furthermore, when in 138/755 the Umayyad pretender ʿAbd al-Raḥmān b. Muʿāwiya, the future ʿAbd al-Raḥmān [*q.v.*], arrived in al-Andalus, al-Ṣumayl remained loyal to his superior even though the Umayyad agents approached him in the first instance, recognising his power and his influence.

All attempts to reach a peaceful accord having failed, the confrontation between the Umayyad and al-Fihrī took place: the latter was defeated at the battle of al-Muṣāra near Cordova, in D̲h̲u'l-Ḥid̲j̲d̲j̲a 138/May 756. Yūsuf fled to Toledo, where he mustered a large army with the intention of resisting ʿAbd al-Raḥmān b. Muʿāwiya, but subsequently, in negotiations near Granada, Yūsuf agreed to surrender to the sovereignty of the Umayyad, retaining in exchange his life and his possessions (Ṣafar 139/July 756). Having established himself in Cordova, he was unable to resist for long the advice of those who incited him to attempt the recovery of his power; he escaped from the city and made his way to Merida, recruiting a significant contingent of troops before advancing on Cordova. But before reaching this city, he took the field against the governor of Seville, ʿAbd al-Malik b. ʿUmar b. Marwān, suffering a bloody defeat at his hands. Once more, and for the last time, Yūsuf was forced to take flight. He was assassinated near Toledo in 142/759. According to some sources, his murderers were two of his slaves; according to others the perpetrators were the inhabitants of a hamlet which he was passing through, people who wanted to put an end to the war and knew that this would only be achieved through the death of one of the two adversaries, the loser.

Bibliography. 1. Sources. In addition to all the chronicles concerning this period, prominent among which are the *A̲k̲h̲bār mad̲j̲mūʿa*, ed. and tr. Lafuente y Alcantara, 56-100, reference may be made to the biography of Yūsuf al-Fihrī in Ibn al-Abbār, *al-Ḥulla al-siyarā'*, ed. H. Mu'nis, ii, 347-50; Ibn al-K̲h̲aṭīb, *Iḥāṭa*, iv, 339-40; Maḳḳarī, *Nafḥ al-ṭīb*, ed. I. ʿAbbās, iii, 25-6.

2. Studies. See those listed in the *Bibl.* to al-ṣumayl b. ḥatim.

(L. Molina)

YŪSUF b. ABI 'l-SĀD̲J̲ DĪWDĀD, Abu 'l-Ḳāsim, commander of Transoxanian Iranian origin who acted as governor of Ād̲h̲arbāyd̲j̲ān, Arrān and Armenia for the ʿAbbāsid caliphs 288-315/901-28 as part of the short-lived line of Sād̲j̲id governors there established by his brother Muḥammad in 276/189-90. He was killed in battle near Kūfa by the Ḳarāmiṭa or Carmathians [see ḳarmaṭī] in D̲h̲u 'l-Ḥid̲j̲d̲j̲a 315/February 928, the last effective governor of his line in northwestern Persia. For details of his career, see sād̲j̲ids.

Bibliography: See that for sād̲j̲ids, and add C.E. Bosworth, *The New Islamic dynasties*, Edinburgh 1996, 147 no. 70.

(Ed.)

YŪSUF b. ʿĀBID al-IDRĪSĪ, Moroccan mystic (*ṣūfī*) claiming Idrīsid descent, born *ca.* 966/1559, died 992/1584. After studying for six years at the *madrasas* of Fās and in the meantime visiting leading Moroccan Ṣūfīs, he proceeded in 990/1582 to Egypt to meet the leader of the Bakriyya order, S̲h̲ayk̲h̲ Muḥammad b. al-Ḥasan al-Bakrī. Eventually Yūsuf arrived in Ḥaḍramawt and, in 1036/1627, at the age of seventy, he dictated there his *Multaḳaṭ al-riḥla*, an account of his journey from Morocco to Ḥaḍramawt, in which he gave the reasons for his departure to the East and his decision to settle in Ḥaḍramawt.

Nearly three-quarters of the ms. (120 folios, found in the Great Mosque of Tarīm in Ḥaḍramawt) deal with social and cultural life in Morocco during the reign of the Saʿdid sultan Aḥmad al-Manṣūr. Yūsuf describes, at some length, the curricula at the various *madrasas* in Fās as well as the numerous Ṣūfī orders (*ṭarīkas*) in Morocco. He also briefly describes the defence measures taken on Morocco's Atlantic coast to ward off Portuguese attacks.

In Cairo, Yūsuf b. ʿĀbid attended lectures on *tawḥīd* (dogmatic theology) at al-Azhar delivered by S̲h̲ayk̲h̲ Mak̲h̲lūf al-Magh̲ribī who informed him that Abū Bakr b. Sālim, Ḥaḍramawt's leading Ṣūfī, was expecting a young *s̲h̲arīf* from Fās. "If you are a *s̲h̲arīf*," S̲h̲ayk̲h̲ Mak̲h̲lūf said to Yūsuf, "go to him, for he is your man." Yūsuf thereupon visited S̲h̲ayk̲h̲ Abū Bakr b. Sālim in ʿAynāt near Tarīm in Ḥaḍramawt, where the *s̲h̲ayk̲h̲* gave him a warm welcome and named him a teaching *s̲h̲ayk̲h̲*.

When Abū Bakr died eight months later (992/1584), Yūsuf thought of returning to Morocco, but he changed his mind as S̲h̲ayk̲h̲ Abū Bakr had urged his disciples to learn *ʿilm al-tawḥīd* at his hands, since Ḥaḍramawt was devoid of this *ʿilm*. At Say'ūn mosque, Yūsuf lectured on al-Sanūsī's *al-ʿAḳīda al-ṣug̲h̲rā* and became famous throughout Ḥaḍramawt for his lectures on *ʿilm al-tawḥīd*.

The picture depicted of Yūsuf b. ʿĀbid in the ms. is that of a Ṣūfī with a great thirst for knowledge and a fervent desire to meet prominent Ṣūfī leaders in Morocco and the East. The impression that comes across in the ms., however, is that of a second-rate writer who lacks style and originality.

Bibliography: Yūsuf b. ʿAbīd al-Idrīsī, *Multaḳaṭ al-riḥla*, ed. and annotated, with full introduction and bibliography, by Amīn T. Ṭībī, Casablanca 1988.

(Amin Tibi)

YŪSUF b. TĀS̲H̲UFĪN or Tās̲h̲fīn, Abū Yaʿḳūb, the real founder of the Almoravid dynasty [see AL-MURĀBIṬŪN] in North Africa (*r.* 453-500/1061-1106). According to tradition, he was born in 400/1009-10, but nothing at all is known of him until 453/1061 when his cousin Abū Bakr b. ʿUmar made him his lieutenant before himself returning to the Sahara to suppress a revolt. Yūsuf was a Berber from the Banū Turgut (Turguit) of the Ṣanhād̲j̲a [*q.v.*]. He married the beautiful and redoubtable Zaynab al-Nafzawiyya, and on her advice, cleverly got rid of his cousin and completed the conquest of Morocco before passing across the Straits of Gibraltar into Spain to achieve his victory at Zallāḳa [*q.v.*].

Yūsuf's history is bound up with that of the Almoravids, and, enjoying the favour of the chroniclers, he is often placed in parallel with the Reyes de Taifas [see MULŪK AL-ṬAWĀʾIF] whom he sent into exile, and the story of his relations with the poet-prince al-Muʿtamid Ibn ʿAbbād [*q.v.*], exiled under surveillance to Ag̲h̲māt [*q.v.*], continue to inspire authors. Yūsuf laid down the foundations for a kingdom spanning North Africa and Spain, and introduced an innovation by adopting the title *Amīr al-Muslimīn* preceded by that of the fictitious caliph ʿAbd Allāh (see E. Lévi-Provençal, *Le titre souverain des Almoravides*, in *Arabica*, ii [1955], 266-8). He appeared as a model Islamic prince, virtuous, even-tempered and sober. The historians' near-unanimity in his favour is explicable both by his personal qualities and also by a documentary aspect: virtually all information on him stems from the lost work by the official historiographer of the Almoravid dynasty, Abū Bakr Yaḥyā b. Muḥammad, Ibn al-Ṣayrafī, his *al-Anwār al-d̲j̲aliyya fī ak̲h̲bār al-dawla al-murābiṭiyya*.

Yūsuf is said to have had a dark brown complexion (*asmar* can also mean a distinctly black colouring), and he may have been incapable of expressing himself in Arabic. With his ascetic and frugal habits, he remained faithful to his way of life and his desert costume; living off barley meal, milk products and camel meat, he seems to be the antithesis of the indolent and ostentatious princes of al-Andalus. He was pious, level-headed and generous towards the *fuḳahāʾ*, whom he never failed to consult, and avoided acts of cruelty. A great strategist, he put together a formidable army comprising Sudanese contingents, Christian mercenaries (*ʿUlūd̲j̲*) and the Saharan tribes of the Gudāla, Lamtūna [*q.vv.*] and Masūfa. This remarkable fighting instrument enabled him to secure the conquest of Morocco and much of the Iberian peninsula. He never hesitated in negotiations and entrusted great powers to his commanders. Enriched by the Saharan trade, he minted coins which became, for several centuries to come, the basis of the gold standard for the Mediterranean lands. His personal skills were shown in his bloodless removal of his cousin Abū Bakr and his attachment to his own side of his cousin's Saharan vassals. He is said to have used ruses to rid himself of uncertain allies like the ruler of the mountain Gzoula. The foundation of Marrakesh is attributed to him, although the city's bases were laid by Abū Bakr (cf. Lévi-Provençal, *La fondation de Marrakech (462/1070)*, in *Mélanges d'histoire et d'archéologie de l'Occident musulman*, ii, Algiers 1957, 117-20), but Yūsuf enlarged and embellished the capital, just as he did other major urban works in places like Sabta, Fās/Fez and Tilimsān/Tlemcen.

He died in Muḥarram 500/September 1106 and was buried in Marrakesh; he was succeeded by his equally long-reigning son ʿAlī.

Bibliography: 1. Sources. Anon., *K. al-Ḥulal al-maws̲h̲iya fī 'l-ak̲h̲bār al-marrākus̲h̲iyya*, Casablanca 1979; Ibn al-Kattān, *Naẓm al-d̲j̲umān*, ed. M.ʿA. Makkī, Beirut 1990; Ibn Ibrāhīm al-Marrākus̲h̲ī, *al-Iʿlām bi-man ḥalla Marrākus̲h̲*..., Rabat 1974-7; Ibn K̲h̲allikān, *Wafayāt*, ed. ʿAbbās, vii, 3-19; Ibn al-K̲h̲aṭīb, *al-Iḥāṭa*, Cairo 1973-7; idem, *Aʿmāl al-aʿlām*, ed. Lévi-Provençal, Rabat 1934, ed. ʿAbbādī and Kattānī, Casablanca 1964; ʿAbd Allāh b. Buluggīn, *al-Tibyān*, ed. Amin Tibi, Rabat 1995, Eng. tr. Tibi, *The Tibyān, Memoirs*..., Leiden 1986; Ibn ʿId̲h̲ārī, *al-Bayan al-mug̲h̲rib*, Beirut 1967, iv, 21; Ibn Abī Zarʿ, *al-Rawḍ al-ḳirṭās*, Rabat 1972; M. Yaʿlā (ed.) *Tres textos arabes sobre berbères en el Occidente islamica*, Madrid 1996; Ibn al-At̲h̲īr, ed. Beirut, x, 178-9; Ibn Faḍl Allāh al-ʿUmarī, *Masālik al-abṣār*, introd. and tr. M. Gaudefroy-Demombynes, Paris 1927; Maḳḳarī, *Azhār al-riyāḍ*, Rabat 1978-80; idem, *Nafḥ al-ṭīb*, ed. ʿAbbās, Beirut 1968; Marrākus̲h̲ī, *K. al-Muʿd̲j̲ib fī talk̲h̲īṣ ak̲h̲bār al-mag̲h̲rib*, Cairo 1944; Nāṣirī, *K. al-Istiḳṣāʾ*, Casablanca 1967, Fr. tr. in *AM*, xxxi-xxxiii, Rabat 1925, 1927, 1934.

2. Studies. G. Deverdun, *Marrakech des origines à 1912*, Rabat 1949; R.A. Messier, *The Almoravids, West African gold and the gold currency of the Mediterranean basin*, in *JESHO*, vii (1974); S. Aʿrāb, *Maʿ al-ḳāḍī Abī Bakr Ibn al-ʿArabī*, Beirut 1987; ʿIṣmat A. Dandas̲h̲, *Dawr al-murābiṭīn fī nas̲h̲r al-Islām fī g̲h̲arb Ifrīḳiya, 430/515 H.-1038/1121 M.*, Beirut 1988; H. Ferhat, *Sabta des origines au XIVe siècle*, Rabat 1993; V. Lagardère, *Les Almoravides*, Paris 1994; H.A. Norris and P. Chalmeta, *EI*² art. *al-Murābiṭūn* (fundamental).

(HALIMA FERHAT)

YŪSUF B. **ʿUMAR** AL-**T̲H̲AḲAFĪ** [see AL-T̲H̲AḲAFĪ].

YŪSUF AḲČURA (Akčurin, Akçuraoğlu) (1876-1935), Tatar nationalist and Pan-Turkist intellectual.

Born at Simbirsk, on the Volga, he began his education at military schools in Istanbul, continuing it in Paris (1900-3), at the Ecole des Sciences Politiques. Active within Young Turk circles in the Ottoman Empire and Western Europe, his intellectual make-up shows influences from the reform-minded Tatar revival in Kazan and the increasing interest in past Turkish culture in Istanbul. Thus equipped, he returned to Russia in 1904, teaching, writing in the Tatar press and entering politics, trying in this way to recruit Muslims for concerted action in the 1905 First Duma. He subsequently promoted the political and cultural organisation of such Muslims in a Pan-Turk perspective. Following the Young Turk Revolution of 1908, he emigrated to Istanbul. In order to preach his own cultural-nationalist and Pan-Turkist views [see PAN-TURKISM], in 1911 he founded *Türk Yurdu*, editing and contributing to what soon became a first-class intellectual journal. In the Republic of Turkey, he participated in the Kemalist resistance, joined the People's Party, and was elected to the Grand National Assembly. In addition, he taught, lectured and published historical studies, which led to his election as first president of the *Türk Tarih Kurumu* [see MAD̲J̲MAʿ ʿILMĪ. iii].

In *Üč ṭarz-ï siyāset* ("Three systems of politics"), he analysed the main lines of government policies in recent Turkish history: (a) Ottomanism, intended to unite all nationalities into one Ottoman nation; (b) Pan-Islamism [*q.v.*], aiming at basing Ottoman power on Islamic solidarity; and (c) Pan-Turkism [*q.v.*], whose goal was to establish "a political Turkish nationality based on race". A realist in his approach, Aḳčura examined each of the three for usefulness and feasibility, favouring Pan-Turkism, the main obstacle to whose achievement being internal, hence manageable. A student of politics, he held that Pan-Turkism was the best panacea for the empire, by providing it with the cohesion of ethnic solidarity, internal and external, needed to save it from dismemberment or to rebuild it after a possible loss of territory. In the Kemalist Republic, whose founder had clearly rejected Pan-Turkism, Aḳčura still managed to defend the concept when writing its history in 1928 in *Türk yılı*. However, then and later he advocated Turkism (i.e. Turkish national solidarity), rather than Pan-Turkism, on the cultural level, with due respect to social and economic factors.

Bibliography: Yūsuf Aḳčura's two main works are *Üč ṭarz-i siyāset*, in *Türk* (Cairo), nos. 24, 25, 27 (April-May 1904), repr. in book-form, Cairo 1907 and repeatedly afterwards; and *Türk yılı*, Istanbul 1928, which he edited and in which he wrote his *Türkčülügün taʾrīkhi we gelishimi*, 287-455, later repr. in bookform. Among his numerous pamphlets and articles are *Midhat-Pacha, la constitution ottomane et l'Europe*, Paris 1903; *ʿUlūm we taʾrīkh*, Kazan 1906; *Mewḳūfiyyet khāṭiralari*, Kazan 1906, 2nd ed., Istanbul 1330/1912; *Eski shūrā-yi ümmet'de čiḳan maḳālelerimden*, Istanbul 1329/1911; *Türk, Djermān we Islāwlarin münāsebāt-i taʾrīkhiyyeleri*, Istanbul 1330/1912; *L'Etat actuel des aspirations des Turco-Tatares musulmans de Russie*, Lausanne 1916; *Rūsyā üserā muraḳhkhaṣi Yūsuf Aḳčūrā Bey'in rāpōrū*, Istanbul 1919; *Taʾrīkh-i siyāsī nōtlari: shark mesʾelesine dāʾir*, Istanbul 1920; *Muʿāṣir Avrūpāʾda siyāsī we idjtimāʿī fikirler we fikrī djereyānlar*, Istanbul 1339; *Siyāset we iḳtiṣād ḥaḳḳinda khiṭābe we maḳāle*, Istanbul 1924; *Osmanlı devletinin dağılma devri (XIII. ve XIX. asırlarda)*, Istanbul 1940. See also M.F. Togay. *Yusuf Akçura hayatı ve eserleri*, Istanbul 1944; S.M. Arsal, *Dostum Yusuf Akçura*, in *Türk Kültürü*, no. 174 (April 1977), 346-54; H.Z. Koşay, *Yusuf Akçura*, in *Belleten*, xli/162 (April 1977), 389-400; Th. David, *Yusuf Akçura and the intellectual origins of the Üč ṭarz-ı siyāset*, in *Journal of Turkish Studies*, ii (1978), 127-40; A. Temir, *Yusuf Akçura*, Ankara 1987, 2nd ed. Ankara 1997; *Ölümünün ellinci yılında Yusuf Akçura sempozyumu 11-12 mart 1985*, Ankara 1987; J.M. Landau, *Pan-Turkism. From irredentism to cooperation*, Bloomington, Ind., 1995; F. Georgeon, *Aux origines du nationalisme turc. Yusuf Akçura, 1876-1935*, Paris 1980, also in Turkish 1996.

(J.M. Landau)

YŪSUF, ʿALĪ (1863-1913), successful Egyptian journalist and editor of the influential newspaper daily *al-Muʾayyad*, which dominated the Muslim press from 1889-1913.

Shaykh ʿAlī Yūsuf was born in the remote village of Balṣafūra in Upper Egypt, to poor parents. His father died a year after his birth, forcing his mother to move with him back to her own village of Banī ʿAdī, where he was given a traditional religious education, memorising the Ḳurʾān by the age of 12. In 1881, at the age of 18, he left for Cairo, where he enrolled in al-Azhar. It seems that he quit his studies prematurely; the Khedive ʿAbbās Ḥilmī II [*q.v.*] suggests in his *Mudhakkirāt* (published in *al-Miṣrī*, April-July 1951) that Yūsuf frequented the Teachers' School (*madrasat al-muʿallimīn*), but there is nothing to show that he received a diploma or even completed his studies there (Ṣāliḥ, 19).

Yūsuf's early ambitions were in the realm of poetry, and in 1885 he published a *dīwān* entitled *Nasamāt al-saḥar* ("Whiffs of dawn", Ṣāliḥ, 20-1; Kaḥḥāla, vii, 10 gives *Nasīm* or *Nasama*, cf. Brockelmann, S III, 84); it encountered little success, whereupon he quickly turned to writing prose of a more journalistic nature. From submission of articles, he moved to actual employment, learning the trade of newspaper editing first at Aḥmad Fāris al-Shidyāḳ's [see fāris al-shidyāḳ] daily *al-Ḳāhira*, and from there at *Mirʾāt al-Shark* sometime after 1884. After suspension of this latter daily in March 1886, he founded in 1887 his own weekly literary newspaper *al-Ādāb*, with the financial support of an al-Azhar crony, Shaykh Aḥmad Māḍī, who two years later would again come to his aid financially with the establishment of the Egyptian nationalist daily *al-Muʾayyad* that would set ʿAlī Yūsuf on the political map.

The first newspaper to be published by an Egyptian, *al-Muʾayyad* appeared on the streets a few months after publication of the pro-British *al-Mukaṭṭam*, and quickly began serving as a forum for nationalist and reformist circles, backed by the Egyptian Prime Minister Muṣṭafā Riyāḍ Pasha, who had seriously fallen out with Lord Cromer, the British Consul-General. The paper soon gained a large following, publishing columns by such leading nationalists as Muṣṭafā Kāmil, Muḥammad Farīd and Saʿd Zaghlūl [*q.vv.*], and reformists such as Rashīd Riḍā, Muḥammad ʿAbduh, Ḳāsim Amīn (whose treatise on the emancipation of women, *Taḥrīr al-marʾa*, was serialised), and al-Kawākibī [*q.vv.*]. Throughout its existence, *al-Muʾayyad* enjoyed the support of the Khedive ʿAbbās Ḥilmī, who had formed close personal ties with ʿAlī Yūsuf. When in 1898 the Khedive moderated his anti-British stance, after the Fāshōda [*q.v.*] incident between the British and the French, ʿAlī Yūsuf and *al-Muʾayyad* followed suit. This move would constitute a break with the more vehement anti-British nationalists and result *inter alia* in Muṣṭafā Kāmil and Aḥmad Luṭfī al-Sayyid [*q.v.*] founding rival newspapers, weakening the position of *al-Muʾayyad* as organ for the nationalist movement. The interdependency of khedival patronage, on the one hand, and unequivocal khedival policy support, on the other, effectively meant the dissolution of both the newspaper and its mirror political organisation, the Constititutional Reform Party (*Ḥizb al-Iṣlāḥ al-Dustūrī* [see ḥizb, at Vol. III, 515b])—formed by ʿAlī Yūsuf in 1907 in support of the Khedive and with his continued backing—upon ʿAlī Yūsuf's death in 1913.

Although history might judge his role as ephemeral, ʿAlī Yūsuf and his newspaper were a catalyst for some major reforms in the Egyptian state, in particular in the field of educational reform. One of two scandals that rocked Egyptian society, with ʿAlī Yūsuf in the middle, revolved around his refusing in 1896 to divulge the source of information he had published in defiance of British censorship; the case, which became known as "the telegraph incident", stands as a fine case of two press principles unrecognised at the time: freedom of expression and the confidentiality of sources. ʿAlī Yūsuf was acquitted, and he became a hero to the populace who applauded his standing up to their oppressors. The second scandal, in 1904 when he eloped with a daughter of one of the country's most venerated families against her father's wishes, introduced him to the seamier side of celebrity. His humble beginnings and unworthy trade—the press was not considered a particularly noble institution, despite his earlier successes—were not deemed suitable to a woman of his bride's background, and the marriage was annulled by court ruling, with a large part of the same populace now decrying his audacity. The Khedive and other powerful friends of ʿAlī Yūsuf intervened, however, and the father Shaykh ʿAbd al-Khāliḳ al-Sādāt later did allow his daughter's marriage.

In 1912 ʿAlī Yūsuf resigned from *al-Muʾayyad* to succeed his brother-in-law ʿAbd al-Ḥamīd al-Bakrī as head of the Ṣūfī order al-Wafāʾiyya (de Jong, 187 n.), only to die a year later, on 25 October 1913, of heart failure.

Bibliography: A comprehensive biography of ʿAlī Yūsuf and his influential newspaper is Sulaymān Ṣāliḥ, *al-Shaykh ʿAlī Yūsuf wa-djarīdat al-Muʾayyad. Taʾrīkh al-ḥaraka al-waṭaniyya fī rubʿ ḳarn*, 2 vols., Cairo 1990. An English study is the unpubl. Ph.D. thesis of Abbas Kelidar, *Shaykh Ali Yusuf, political journalist and Islamic nationalist. A study of Egyptian politics, 1889-1913*, Univ. of London 1967 (unseen); and idem, *Shaykh ʿAli Yusuf, Egyptian journalist and Islamic nationalist*, in Marwan R. Buheiry (ed.), *Intellectual life in the Arab East, 1890-1939*, Beirut 1981, 10-20. For a contemporary view, in particular of the marriage scandal, see A. Goldschmidt, Jr. (tr.), *The memoirs and diaries of Muhammad Farid, an Egyptian nationalist leader (1868-1919)*, San Francisco 1992, 112-14; see also Aḥmad Bahāʾ al-Dīn, *Ayyām lahā taʾrīkh*, 3Cairo 1967, 63-85; Salāma Mūsā, *al-Ṣiḥāfa, ḥirfa wa-risāla*, Cairo 1963, 22. An excellent recent work on journalism and the press is A. Ayalon, *The press in the Arab Middle East, a history*, New York 1995. For the Ṣūfī orders in Egypt, F. de Jong, *Ṭuruq and ṭuruq-linked institutions in nineteenth century Egypt*, Leiden 1978.

(Peri Bearman)

YŪSUF AL-BARM, sc. Yūsuf b. Ibrāhīm, a *mawlā* of Thaḳīf, rebel against ʿAbbāsid rule in eastern Khurāsān during the caliphate of al-Mahdī, d. 160/777 or shortly afterwards.

Yūsuf's rising was only one of a series of revolts by both Arabs and local Iranians in Transoxania and eastern Khurāsān during the early ʿAbbāsid period. Whilst the sources impute certain religious motives to Yūsuf, including use of the traditional slogan summoning to *al-amr bi ʾl-maʿrūf wa ʾl-nahy ʿan al-munkar*, it seems that the revolt was basically political and directed against the arbitrary power of the caliph and his governors. From Gardīzī's account, it appears that its epicentre was northern Afghānistān, the regions of Bādghīs, Marw al-Rūdh, Gūzgān and Ṭālakān [*q.vv.*]. It was suppressed, largely by al-Mahdī's general Yazīd b. Mazyad, with Yūsuf being captured and then crucified at Baghdād. A further revolt in Khurāsān, by a grandson of Yūsuf's, is mentioned during al-Maʾmūn's caliphate.

Bibliography: The main sources are Yaʿḳūbī, *Taʾrīkh*, ii, 478-9; Ṭabarī, iii, 470-1; and Gardīzī, *Zayn al-akhbār*, ed. ʿA.Ḥ. Ḥabībī, Tehran 1347/1968, 126-7. Of studies, see Barthold, *Turkestan down to the Mongol invasion*², 198, 201, 208; E.L. Daniel, *The political and social history of Khurasan under Abbasid rule 747-820*, Minneapolis and Chicago 1979, 166-7.

(C.E. Bosworth)

YŪSUF KĀNDHALAWĪ DIHLAWĪ, Mawlānā Muḥammad, the son of Muḥammad Ilyās (1885-1944), the founder of the Tablīghī Djamāʿat [*q.v.*], whom he succeeded in the leadership of this movement (d. 1965).

He was born in his ancestral village of Kāndhala in 1917. He studied exoteric religion with his father at Nizamuddin (Dihlī), and then later at the seminary of Sahāranpūr, which is associated with Deoband [*q.v.*], where his maternal uncle, Muḥammad Zakariyyā Kāndhalawī (d. 1982), also taught. The latter was his teacher of *ḥadīth*, whose two daughters he married. He devoted himself firstly to studying *ḥadīth* and wrote the *Īmānī al-Akhbār*, an unfinished commentary on the *Sharḥ maʿānī al-athār* commentary on the *ḥadīth* of Imām al-Ṭaḥāwī.

He was initiated into the Ṣābiriyya Čishtiyya brotherhood by his father, who from 1938 onwards forced him, despite his reticence, to take part in the missionary journeys of the Tablīghī Djamāʿat, where he showed his talents as an orator. On the death of his father in 1944 he was elected *amīr* of the movement and lived in its headquarters at Nizamuddin. He made five pilgrimages to Mecca (1938, 1955, 1959, 1961 and 1964), firstly with his father and then with hundreds of Tablīghīs. He died at Lahore (Pakistan) on 12 April 1965, and his body was interred at Nizamuddin.

The name of Muḥammad Yūsuf remains connected with the worldwide expansion of the Tablīghī Djamāʿat [*q.v.*, where further details are given]. He systematically, applied ideas which his father had tried to put into practice at the time of the pilgrimage in 1938. He firstly consolidated the enterprise of the movement in the subcontinent by creating secondary centres in Western Pakistan and then Eastern Pakistan (now Bangladesh). He then established it worldwide by sending missions to the Arab countries from 1946 onwards, to Western countries from 1950 onwards, and to Afro-Asian countries from 1956 onwards. The essential structure of his worldwide network was in place at the time of his death in 1965, however little this was recognised in that period.

Bibliography: Muḥammad Thānī Ḥasanī, *Sawāniḥ-i Ḥaḍrat Mawlānā Muḥammad Yūsuf Kāndhalawī*, Lucknow 1967; ʿAzīz al-Raḥmān Bidjnawrī, *Tadhkira-yi Mawlānā Muḥammad Yūsuf Ṣāḥib, amīr-i tablīgh*, Bhera (Sargodha, Pakistan) 1980; M. Gaborieau, *Muḥammad Yūsuf Kāndhalawī Dihlawī*, in M. Gaborieau, N. Grandin, P. Labrousse and A. Popovic (eds.), *Dictionnaire biographique des savants et grandes figures du monde musulman périphérique, du XIXe siècle jusqu'à nos jours*, i, Paris 1992, 19-20; idem, *The transformation of Tablīghī Jamāʿat into a transnational movement under the leadership of Muḥammad Yūsuf, 1944-1965*, in M.K. Masud (ed.), *Travellers in faith. Studies of Tablīghī Jamāʿat as a transnational movement for faith renewal*, Leiden 2000.

(M. Gaborieau)

YŪSUF KARAM (1823-89), Maronite *shaykh* and notable from the village of Ihdin (northern Lebanon), who during the socio-religious hostilities in 1860 emerged as one of the most prominent leaders of the Christians—the other, very different one being Ṭanyūs Shāhīn [*q.v.*]—without, however, providing effective military support to his coreligionists fighting against the Druzes in central and southern Mount Lebanon.

Impelled by far-reaching political aims, Karam initially managed to be (alternately) on good terms with French, British, and Ottoman representatives in Lebanon. These relations rapidly deteriorated, when in 1861, and after the establishment of a new administrative order which was to be permanently headed by a governor (*mutaṣarrif*) of non-Lebanese origin, Karam's own hopes of appointment as governor over all Mount Lebanon came to nothing. Though the first *mutaṣarrif*, Dāwūd Pasha [*q.v.*], tried hard to win Karam's cooperation, the latter finally refused and started a rebellion from his northern home, thereby expressing a wide-spread discontent among the Maronite Christians who had hoped for greater political influence in the new system. After three years in exile, Karam returned, only to start a new revolt against the Ottomans who, on their part, avoided open fighting as much as possible. When, therefore, Karam's actions gradually petered out, the Ottomans declared an amnesty and in 1867 sent Karam into a second exile, this time permanently, in Algiers and Europe. He died in Italy after many vain requests for permission to return to Lebanon. For ten years he was paid by Istanbul a considerable monthly stipend, which only stopped because of his ongoing polemical publications against the régime in Mount Lebanon and his contacts with various political groups and states.

In spite of Karam's total failure to change the *status quo* in Lebanon, dissatisfaction among the Maronites continued. Karam was held up by them, as well as by certain circles in France, as the supreme example of the Lebanese national hero. Biographers and local historians clearly testify to such a view of "Lebanese Christian nationalism". On the other hand, one must consider Karam's contacts with the Algerian *amīr* ʿAbd al-Ḳādir regarding an Arab confederation (i.e. a certain autonomy for Arabs within the Ottoman Empire), first still under Muslim leadership, but in the long run, on a non-confessional, secular and national basis. In this vein, the role and the success of freemasonry [see FARMĀSŪNIYYA], in general rather influential among intellectuals and politicians in these times, was obviously very crucial: an issue which, however, still needs further research.

Bibliography: K.S. Salibi, *The modern history of Lebanon*, London 1965, 68, 102-3, 112-14; F. Steppat, *Eine Bewegung unter den Notabeln Syriens 1877-78*, in *ZDMG*, Suppl. I (1969), 631-49; T. Touma, *Paysans et institutions féodales chez les Druses et les Maronites du Liban du XVIIe siècle à 1914*, Beirut 1971-2, 294-312, 315-33; J.P. Spagnolo, *France and Ottoman Lebanon 1861-1914*, London 1977, 58-65, 100-10 and *passim*; E.D. Akarlı, *The long peace. Ottoman Lebanon, 1861-1920*, Berkeley etc., 1993, 37-8; ʿAbd al-Raʾūf Sinnū, *al-Nazaʿāt al-kiyāniyya al-islāmiyya fi 'l-dawla al-ʿuthmāniyya, 1877-1881*, Beirut 1998, 48-52. For other modern works and sources in Arabic, cf. the bibls. in the studies listed.

(A. HAVEMANN)

YŪSUF KHĀN RIḌWĪ, Mīrzā, Mughal commander and governor, d. 1010/1601-2.

The son of Mīrzā Aḥmad Riḍwī, he was appointed by the Emperor Akbar *ṣūbadār* or governor of Kashmīr in 995/1586-7. He imposed Mughal authority in the Kashmīr valley and secured the submission of the Čak [*q.v.* in Suppl.] chiefs. Yūsuf Khān himself rebelled against the Mughals in 1001/1592-3, but came back into favour and in 1003/1594-5 was *dārūgha* or superintendent of the Ṭop-khāna or arsenal.

Bibliography: Mohibbul Hasan, *Kashmir under the sultans*, Calcutta 1959, index; A.R. Khan, *Chieftains of the Mughal empire during the reign of Akbar*, Simla 1977, 18-19, 52; M. Athar Ali, *The apparatus of empire. Award of ranks, offices and titles to the Mughal nobility 1574-1658*, Delhi 1985, index for Akbar's reign. See also KASHMĪR. I.

(ED.)

YŪSUF KHĀṢṢ ḤĀDJIB, Turkish poet of the 5th/11th century whose work, the *Ḳutadghu bilig* [*q.v.*] ("Wisdom of Royal Glory"), completed in 462/1069-70, is the oldest monument of Islamic Turkish literature. He is not mentioned in any other source, so we must deduce what we know about him from the three surviving mss. of his work. (For the interrelation of the mss., see R. Dankoff, *Textual problems in* Kutadgu Bilig, in *Jnal. of Turkish Studies*, iii [1979], 89-99.) Two of these contain a verse prologue, written perhaps a century after the work was completed, and all three contain a shorter prose prologue which appears to be a summary of the verse prologue. These prologues provide the information that the author was originally from Balāsāghūn [*q.v.*]; that he completed the work in Kāshghar, where he presented it to the king, Tavghač Bughra Khān; and that he was awarded the office of *khāṣṣ ḥādjib* or privy chamberlain. His patron has been identified as the Khān Ḥasan b. Sulaymān, ruler of the eastern branch of the Ḳarakhānids or Ilek-Khānids [*q.v.*]. Yūsuf himself names him near the beginning of the work, in a section entitled "Ode to spring and praise of Ulugh Bughra Khān".

The prologues also, trying to assimilate the work to known genres, somewhat contradictorily label it both as a "Mirror for Princes" (*Adab al-mulūk*, etc.) and a "Book of Kings" (*Shāh-nāma*). The only similarity it has to the *Shāh-nāma* of Firdawsī [*q.v.*] is the use of the *mutaḳārib* metre. To be sure, Yūsuf does, in an introductory passage (ll. 276-80), identify the legendary hero of the Turks, Tonga Alp Er, with Afrāsiyāb, the ruler of Tūrān in the Persian epic, thus following a tradition also found in the work of his contemporary, Maḥmūd al-Kāshgharī [*q.v.*]. But in the body of the work, Tonga Alp Er appears only once (l. 5861) as the authority for one of the sententious sayings of political wisdom (*bilig*) attributed elsewhere to various anonymous Khāns and Begs. Still, one can say that Yūsuf, in attempting to assimilate the Inner Asian traditions of royalty and wisdom to the Irano-Islamic ideals of statecraft in a Turkish dress, was following the model of Firdawsī, who had consolidated the Iranian traditions of kingship within the framework of Islamic culture in a Persian dress (see Dankoff, *Qarakhanid literature and the beginnings of Turco-Islamic culture*, in *Central Asian monuments*, ed. Hasan B. Paksoy, Istanbul, 1992, 73-80; H. Inalcik, *Turkish and Iranian political theories and traditions in Kutadgu Bilig*, in *The Middle East and the Balkans under the Ottoman Empire*, Bloomington 1993, 1-18).

"Mirror for Princes" is a more accurate generic label. The *ḳut* ("glory, fortune") referred to in the title is the Turkish equivalent of Persian *farr*, designating the ruler's charisma, and *Ḳutadghu bilig* literally means "The wisdom that conduces to royal glory or fortune". The first half of the work is largely concerned with traditional matters of statecraft: the virtues of the king and his obligations to his subjects; the qualities and duties of the various courtiers; and the establishment of justice. The second half, however, introduces a new theme: the conflict between the political goals of the state and the religious conscience of the individual. Here Yūsuf incorporates Ṣūfī asceticism as an opposing, and ultimately complementary, ideal to the prevailing community and statecraft ethics; in this regard he may be considered a precursor of al-Ghazālī [*q.v.*].

Another original contribution of Yūsuf to the Mirror for Princes genre is to dramatise the issues in the form of dialogues, within a frame story, among characters with significant allegorical names. The king, Kün Toghdi ("the sun has risen"), who represents justice, longs for a good vizier, and his trusty chamberlain presents to him Ay Toldi ("the moon is full"), who represents fortune. Ay Toldi suffers a fatal illness, but before he dies he commends his son Ögdülmish ("praised"), who represents intellect, to the king's care. The king discovers the young man's virtues and appoints him as chief counselor. Ögdülmish advises the king well on worldly matters, and then informs him of a kinsman named Odhghurmish ("awakened"), who represents otherworldly concerns. The king summons Odhghurmish to court, and the latter, after refusing several times to abandon his life of ascetic withdrawal and religious contemplation, eventually visits the king and gives him counsel of a moral and spiritual nature, before he too dies. The allegory, then, can be interpreted as follows: Justice, to be exercised properly, requires Fortune, Intellect, and Religion; but Fortune cannot be depended on, and worldly and otherworldly concerns are not easily reconcilable; thus Justice and Intellect are left to administer the realm.

Appended to the text in one of the mss. are two odes in which the author complains of old age and expresses disillusion with the world and the times. As a high court official, with leanings toward the solitary life (ll. 6570-1), Yūsuf apparently suffered within himself the conflicts which he portrayed in his work. In the course of writing a Mirror for Princes, he broke the traditional boundaries of that genre. Especially in the second part of the work, in the confrontation and reconciliation of the wise courtier and the Ṣūfī ascetic, Yūsuf achieved a dramatic portrayal quite unique in Islamic literature.

Bibliography: In addition to the references given above and the older literature in the *Bibl.* of KUTADGHU BILIG, see the Introd. to Yūsuf Khāṣṣ Ḥādjib, *Wisdom of royal glory (Kutadgu bilig). A Turko-Islamic Mirror for Princes*, tr. with an introd. and notes, by R. Dankoff, Chicago 1983, where older interpretations are weighed and criticised. The standard edition of the text is by R.R. Arat, *Kutadgu bilig. I. Metin*, Istanbul 1947. Arat also published the three mss. in facsimile, *Kutadgu bilig tıpkıbasım*, 3 vols. Istanbul 1942-3, and a modern Turkish tr. *Kutadgu bilig. II. Tercüme*, Ankara 1959, repr. 1974. For the English tr. by Dankoff, see above. There is also a Russian tr., Yūsuf Balasaguni, *Blagodatnoe znanie*, redaktsionnaya kollegiya Yu.A. Andreev . . . *et al.*, perevod S.N. Ivanova, vstupitel'naya stat'ya M.S. Fomkina, primečaniya A.N. Malekhovoi, Leningrad 1990. (R. DANKOFF)

YŪSUF AND ZULAYKHĀ, a popular story in mediaeval Islamic literature.

1. In Persian literature.

The Biblical story of Joseph and Potiphar's wife, who later received the name of Zulaykhā, entered into Persian literature mainly through Arabic sources, consisting first of Sūrat Yūsuf (XII) of the Ḳur'ān, and then of commentaries on this "most beautiful of stories" and traditions on the lives of ancient Prophets (*ḳiṣaṣ al-anbiyā'* [*q.v.*]). The many additions to the story as it was told in the holy scriptures were derived from the Hebrew Midrash and Christian works in Syriac (cf. the studies by M. Grünbaum), which were further elaborated in the post-Ḳur'ānic Muslim sources. An immediate influence of the former on Persian versions is unlikely, except in the case of Judaeo-Persian literature.

The Persian versions include full narratives, but also episodic anecdotes and incidental references which occur in prose works, didactic and lyrical poetry and even in drama. The motif was particularly suited to be used by Ṣūfī writers and poets as one of the most important models of the relationship between the manifestation of Divine beauty in the world and the loving soul of the mystic.

Persian commentaries on sūra XII often provide a mystical reading of the story, for instance in the 6th/12th-century *tafsīr* of Maybudī [*q.v.*]. An earlier commentary focussing on this Ḳur'ānic story is *Anīs al-murīdīn wa-rawḍat al-muḥibbīn* by Abu 'l-Ḳāsim Maḥmūd b. Ḥasan Djayhānī, which was wrongly attributed to the Ṣūfī *shaykh* al-Anṣārī al-Harawī [*q.v.*] (see R. Levy, in *JRAS* [1929], 103-6). In 475/1082-3, the text was incorporated into Abū Naṣr Bukhārī's *Tādj al-ḳiṣaṣ*, a collection of prophetic legends (cf. Storey, i, 159, 1208, 1251; Lazard, *La langue des plus anciens monuments de la prose persane*, Paris 1963, 96). Many similar works are extant, the most notable among them being *Djāmi' laṭā'if al-basātīn*, or *al-Sittīn al-djāmi'*, by Tādj al-Dīn al-Ṭūsī (Storey, i, 29, 1195; Storey-Bregel', i, 185; ed. M. Rawshan, Tehran 1345 *sh.*/1966, repr. Tehran 2526 *Shāhanshāhī*/1977); *Ḥadā'iḳ al-ḥaḳā'iḳ* (known also by other titles) by Mullā Mu'īn al-Dīn Farāhī Miskīn (d. 907/1501-2; see Storey-Bregel', i, 125-6, iii, 1337; ed. Sayyid Dj. Sadjdjādī, Tehran 1346/1967-8); and *Kashf al-arwāḥ* or *Yūsuf-nāma*, by Pīr Djamāl Ardistānī (d. 879/1474-5; Munzawī, i, 55). As far as their contents are concerned, they do not differ much from the collections of edifying tales which also include both general and specialised writings (listed in Storey, i, 168-72; supplemented in Storey-Bregel', i, 529-36, iii, 1409-13).

To the Ṣūfīs, the Yūsuf story became a rich source of motifs to be used as examples for key concepts of their discourse. 'Ayn al-Ḳuḍāt al-Hamadhānī [*q.v.*] saw the Sūra from the beginning to end as a parable of "God's way" (*rāh-i Khudā*), which the mystic should travel (*Nāmahā*, ed. 'Alī-Naḳī Munzawī and 'Afīf 'Usayrān, Tehran 1348-50 *sh.*/1969-71, i, 366-8), more specifically of "the way of love": to understand the meaning of this story one should have the nature of a Zulaykhā and the nickname of a Madjnūn [*q.v.*] (*ibid.*, ii, 130). According to Rūzbihān Baḳlī [*q.v.*], it contains emblems of two different kinds of love: the passion of a lover as well as the devotion of a father to his lost son (*'Abhar al-'āshiḳīn*, ed. H. Corbin and M. Mu'īn, Tehran-Paris 1958, 9; see also al-Hudjwīrī [*q.v.*], *Kashf al-maḥdjūb*, tr. R.A. Nicholson, London 1911, 310). In his allegory of mystical love, Shihāb al-Dīn Yaḥyā al-Suhrawardī [*q.v.*] introduced Yūsuf as the personification of eternal beauty as it is manifested in the created world (*Mu'nis al-aḥrār*, in al-Suhrawardī, *Oeuvres philosophiques et mystiques*, ii, ed. S.Ḥ. Naṣr and H. Corbin, Tehran-Paris 1970, 267-91).

As far as we at present know, the story was first treated in narrative poetry by Abu 'l-Mu'ayyad Balkhī (*fl.* 4th/10th century) and Bakhtiyārī, a poet who cannot now be identified. Their works have perished, but they are both mentioned as predecessors by the still unidentified writer of a *mathnawī* entitled *Yūsuf u Zulaykhā*, probably dating from the 5th/11th century. It is extant now in at least two different redactions, the number of its distichs varying between 6,500 and 9,000 (cf. Rieu, ii, 545-6). The manuscripts show considerable discrepancies in the introductory parts of the poem, and these seriously aggravate the problem of the true authorship of this poem. It was composed in the *mutaḳārib* metre, also used in the *Shāh-nāma*. For long it has indeed been regarded as a work by Firdawsī [*q.v.*], an attribution which can be found already in the prose introduction to the redaction of the *Shāh-nāma* made in 829/1425-6 for the Tīmūrid prince Bāysunghur [*q.v.*]. According to some copies, the poet is said to have turned away from the writing of poems about ancient Iranian heroes to devote himself to a more pious subject. There are also passages indicating an origin in western Persia, but they do not match other facts known about Firdawsī's life. His authorship was accepted, among others, by the translator O. Schlechta-Wssehrd and the editors H. Ethé and Ḥ.M. Ṣiddīḳ, but has been challenged in recent scholarship. As an alternative, Sa'īd Nafīsī proposed the name of Amānī, an otherwise unknown poet who seemed to mention himself in a line of the poem which can, however, also be read differently. The most reliable clue for the dating is a dedication, found in one manuscript, to Shams al-Dawla Ṭughānshāh, the son of Alp Arslān, who in the second half of the 5th/11th century acquired a reputation as a patron of the poets at his court in Harāt [see SALḎJŪḲIDS. VII. 1. Literature]. The poem still awaits a critical edition and a systematic investigation of its textual history (for a recent *status quaestionis*, see F. de Blois, in Storey-de Blois, v/2, 576-84).

In the "Firdawsī" version, the story is framed by the life of Yūsuf's father, the prophet Yaʿḳūb, and is told on the lines of traditional prophetic legend. Wahb b. Munabbih and his "son" Kaʿb al-Aḥbār, famous transmitters of the *Isrāʾīliyyāt* [*q.v.*], are mentioned as spokesmen. The religious significance of the subject is emphasised, but no mystical meanings are implied. There are several miraculous traits and emotional episodes are elaborated in particular. The poem is an interesting specimen of the romantic *mathnawī* before the time of Niẓāmī [*q.v.*].

In spite of its relative obscurity in the history of Persian literature, the impact of this poem is noticeable in later works, the oldest among which is the Judaeo-Persian version by Shāhīn-i Shīrāzī [*q.v.*]. It is as a part of his *mathnawī* on the Book of Genesis, now known as the *Bereshit-nāma*, written *ca.* 1358 in the metre *hazaḏj-i musaddas-i maḥḏhūf*. Although Shāhīn was familiar with Hebrew sources, he based his work mainly on the Persian Muslim tradition, in particular the "Firdawsī" version (cf. Bacher, 117-24).

The most celebrated version in Persian was undoubtedly written by Mullā ʿAbd al-Raḥmān Ḏjāmī [*q.v.*] in 888/1483 as one of the parts of his *Khamsa* [*q.v.*]. The subject takes the place of Niẓāmī's *Khusraw wa Shīrīn*, with which this poem shares some features, including the metre, which happens to be the same as that used by Shāhīn. Ḏjāmī turned the story into a mystical allegory explaining in numerous asides the spiritual teachings implied. The love story is placed in the foreground so that Zulaykhā's role becomes equal to that of Yūsuf. As a pair they personify the epiphany of eternal beauty and the responses to it on the part of the loving human soul.

Ḏjāmī had many imitators, most of whom met with little success (see Munzawī, iv, 3331-46). The only exception is the *Yūsuf wa Zulaykhā* by Mullā Farrukh Ḥusayn Nāẓim [*q.v.*], a poet of the 11th/17th century at the court of the Beglerbeg ʿAbbās Ḳulī Khān at Harāt. Although he mainly followed Ḏjāmī's poem, he also refers to Firdawsī as a predecessor. Nāẓim's poem gained some popularity, especially in Central Asia. It was printed at Lucknow 1286/1869-70, and Tashkent 1322/1904-5; fragments were quoted by Hermann Ethé in the notes to his edition of the "Firdawsī" version.

The story of Yūsuf offered a very rich store of motifs to poets of lyrical *ghazals* which were not exclusively used in a religious context. In love poetry, Yūsuf appears as the supreme example of male beauty. To call a beloved person "another Yūsuf" or "the Yūsuf of the age" constituted a strong hyperbole. In nature scenes, the rose is a said to be a Yūsuf, reigning over the Egypt of the meadow. The story of his career provided the contrast between suffering and glory. This is often succinctly expressed by a pun on the words *čāh* ("the pit") and *ḏjāh* ("honour"). The dimple in the beloved's chin is compared to the pit. Other elements of the story frequently used by *ghazal* poets are Yaʿḳūb's weeping over the separation from his son, his retirement to the "house of sorrows" (*bayt al-aḥzān*), his blindness and the recognition of Yūsuf's shirt by the smell, Zulaykhā being drawn from behind

her chaste veil by her passion, and the Egyptian ladies who cut their hands instead of the oranges (for examples in *ghazals*, see Daniel Meneghini Correale and Riccardo Zipoli, *The collected Lirica persica*, i, Venice 1998). In the didactical *mathnawī*s of Sanāʾī, ʿAṭṭār, Ḏjalāl al-Dīn Rūmī, Saʿdī [*q.vv.*] and others, the story is represented both through anecdotes and incidental references.

The aspect of suffering inherent in Yūsuf as a narrative character provided an obvious parallel to the martyrdom of al-Ḥusayn b. ʿAlī [*q.v.*]. In the *mathnawī* ascribed to Firdawsī, God's wish to comfort Muḥammad for the future suffering of his grandson is said to have been the reason for the revelation of Sūra XII. In *Yūsufiyya*, an outspokenly Shīʿī work written by Muḥammad Hādī Nāyīnī between 1243-50/1827-34, the stories of Yūsuf and al-Ḥusayn are brought together (Storey, i, 172; Storey-Bregel', i, 527). The cruel handling of Yūsuf by his brothers was also adopted in the repertoire of passion plays [see TAʿZIYA]. Popular prints of Yūsuf's story are still being sold in Iran (cf. U. Marzolph, *Dāstān-e Šīrīn*, Stuttgart 1994, 69-70).

Bibliography: 1. Editions and translations. (a) The "Firdawsī" version. Ed. H. Ethé, i, Oxford 1908 (not continued); ed. Ḥusayn Muḥammad-zāda Ṣiddīḳ, Tehran 1368 *sh.*/1990 (reproduces the ms. no. 5063/1 of the Kitābkhāna-yi Markazī, Tehran; a critical edition is announced); tr. O. Schlechta-Wssehrd. *Jussuf und Suleicha. Romantisches Heldengedicht von Firdussi*, Vienna 1889 (parts of this translation were also publ. in *ZDMG*, xli [1887], 577-99, and in *Verhandlungen des VII. Internationalen Orientalisten-Congresses... Semitische Section*, Vienna 1888, 47-72). (b) Shāhīn. Ed. Simon Khakam, in *Sefer sharḥ-i Shāhīn-i Torah*, i, B, Jerusalem 5662/1902 (in Hebrew characters); by Amnon Netzer, *Muntakhab-i ashʿār-i fārsī az āthār-i yahūdiyyān-i Īrān*, Tehran 1352 *sh.*/1973, 58-106 (transcribed into Arabic script). (c). Ḏjāmī. Ed. and German tr. V. von Rosenzweig, Vienna 1824; ed. Murtaḍā Mudarris-i Gīlānī, in *Mathnawī-yi Haft awrang*, Tehran 1337 *sh.*/1958, 578-748; English tr. R.T.H. Griffith, London 1882, and D. Pendlebury, London 1980 (abridged); French tr. A. Bricteux, Paris 1927.

2. Studies. Ch. Rieu, *Catalogue of the Persian manuscripts in the British Museum*, ii, London 1881; H. Ethé, *Firdausi's Yûsuf und Zalîkhâ*, in *Verhandlungen des VII. Internationalen Orientalisten-Congresses... Semitische Section*, Vienna 1888, 19-45, and *Neupersische Literatur*, in *GIPh*, ii, 229-31; M. Grünbaum, *Zu "Jussuf und Sulecha"*, in *ZDMG*, xliii (1889), 1-29, and *Zu Schlechta-Wssehrd's Ausgabe des "Jussuf und Suleicha"*, in *ZDMG*, xliv (1890), 445-77 (both articles repr. in F. Perles (ed.), *Gesammelte Aufsätze zur Sprach- und Sagenkunde von Max Grünbaum*, Berlin 1901, 515-93); W. Bacher, *Zwei jüdisch-persische Dichter, Schahin und Imrani*, Strassburg 1908, 35-9, 117-24; S. Nafīsī, *Le "Yūsuf et Zalīkhā" attribué à Firdowsy*, in *ArO*, xviii/1-2 (1950), 351-3; H. Ritter, *Das Meer der Seele*, Leiden 1955, *Analytischer Index*, 721; E. Hilscher, *Der biblische Joseph in orientalischen Literaturwerken*, in *Mitteilungen des Instituts für Orientforschung*, iv, Berlin 1956, 81-108; Dh. Ṣafā, *Tārīkh-i adabiyyāt dar Īrān*, i, ⁴Tehran 1342 *sh.*/1963, 489-92, and *Ḥamāsa-sarāʾī dar Īrān*, ³Tehran 1352 *sh.*/1973, 175; A. Munzawī, *Fihrist-i nuskhahā-yi khaṭṭī-yi fārsī*, i, Tehran 1348 *sh.*/1969, iv, Tehran 1351 *sh.*/1972; C.A. Storey-Yu.E. Bregel, *Persidskaya literatura*, 3 vols., Moscow 1972; Storey-F. de Blois, *Persian literature*, v, London 1992-7; Ḏjalāl Sattārī, *Dard-i ʿishḳ-i Zulaykhā*, Tehran 1373 *sh.*/1995.

(J.T.P. DE BRUIJN)

2. In Turkish literature.
The revealed story of the prophet Yūsuf, amplified by authenticated commentaries, occupies a central place in al-Rabghūzī's [*q.v.*] prose stories of the Prophets in Khwārazmian Turkish, with interspersed poetry, completed in 710/1310. The author gives the arguments for its being the best of stories. Yūsuf, the dreamer of dreams, favourite of his father, cast into a well by his brothers, rescued and sold to the master of a caravan, led into Egypt, encounters the female protagonist, Zulaykhā, the wife of the mighty one of Egypt, ʿAzīz Miṣr [*q.v.*] named Ḳiṭfīr [*q.v.*]. Her beauty is second only to that of Yūsuf. She wishes to commit adultery with him; Yūsuf is acquitted but goes to prison, where he interprets dreams. Zulaykhā's love is eventually rewarded when as an aged, blind and poor widow, she is brought before Yūsuf. She recovers her youth, her beauty, and her sight, and Djibrīl performs their marriage (cf. that of Fāṭima [*q.v.*]). Zulaykhā is a virgin, Ḳiṭfīr having been an eunuch. They live together for eighteen years and have seven children.

The story provided enough realistic detail and drama to make it part of the "romantic" *mathnawī* [*q.v.*] tradition. The divinely-attested inclination of Yūsuf toward Zulaykhā (Ḳurʾān, XII, 24) could be invoked subliminally in every rendering of Zulaykhā's hopeless illicit love; a love that eventually mutated into contemplation of the divine beauty personified in Yūsuf.

Ḥamdī [*q.v.*] completed his Ottoman Turkish version soon after Djāmī [*q.v.*] in 897/1492. His *mathnawī*, written in the *khafīf* metre interspersed with *ghazals*, is considered the best Turkish poem on the theme. Putting some emphasis on Yūsuf and his envious brothers, Ḥamdī devotes much space to Zulaykhā, the daughter of King Taymūs, who marries Ḳiṭfīr by mistake, having fallen in love with Yūsuf in a dream; her attempts to obtain her desire by entreaty and by craft, and Yūsuf's almost faltering resolution, flight, and imprisonment; his appointment as *ʿazīz* of Egypt, followed by the death of Zulaykhā's husband, are described.

She ages through grief and is reduced to poverty and blindness, but turns in penitence to God and finds favour in His eyes. Yūsuf marries Zulaykhā, whose beauty and sight are restored to her; her love, however, has passed from love for Yūsuf to the love of the divine beauty, so that she flees from him and they are equal in their love. Reunited with his father and brothers, Yūsuf dies. Zulaykhā dies on his grave (*HOP*, ii, 151-72).

More research is needed into the old Turkish versions mentioned in ḲIṢṢA. 3 (a), including that by Shayyād Ḥamza [*q.v.*]; a Mamlūk version in Anatolian Turkish was composed by Ḍarīr [*q.v.*]; and a Čaghatay rendering was completed in 874/1469 by Ḥāmidī. For Kemālpashazāde's and Yaḥyā Beg's [*q.vv.*] versions, see MATHNAWĪ. Fuḍūlī's [*q.v.*] often-illustrated *Ḥadīḳat al-suʿadāʾ*, recounting stories and legends of prophets and saints, contains scenes from the life of the prophet Yūsuf and of Zulaykhā's love for him.

Bibliography: See ḲIṢṢA. 3 (a); MATHNAWĪ. 3. In Turkish; *HOP*, ii, 149; İsmail Ünver, *Mesnevî*, in *Türk Dili* (1986); Erika Glassen, *Die Josephsgeschichte im Koran und in der persischen und türkischen Literatur*, in F. Link (ed.), *Paradeigmata. Literarische Typologie des Alten Testaments*, i, Berlin 1989, 161-79; *Al-Rabghūzī. The Stories of the Prophets. Qiṣaṣ al-Anbiyāʾ. An Eastern Turkish version*, crit. ed. by H.E. Boeschoten, M. Vandamme and S. Tezcan, with the assistance of H. Braam and B. Radtke, vol. ii, tr. by Boeschoten, J. O'Kane and Vandamme, Leiden 1995. For iconography, see Norah M. Titley, *Miniatures from Turkish manuscripts*, London 1981.

(BARBARA FLEMMING)

YŪSUFĪ, the *takhalluṣ* or pen-name of Yūsuf b. Muḥammad b. Yūsuf Khurāsānī, native of Khwāf and émigré to India, where he became physician to the Mughal emperors Bābur and Humāyūn [*q.vv.*] and a prolific writer on medical topics. It is also very probably the same Yūsufī who is the author of an *inshāʾ* collection (see below).

Several of his Persian medical works are extant, including a *Dalāʾil al-bawl* on diagnosis through examination of the urine; a *Dalāʾil al-nabḍ* on interpretation of the pulse; various *ḳaṣīdas* and *ḳiṭʿas* on medical topics; *rubāʿiyyāt*, on which he himself wrote a commentary, the *Djāmiʿ al-fawāʾid*, with notes on the various diseases of the body; and a metrical treatise on food, *Makʾūl u mashrūb* (most of these have been printed in India).

The *munshī* Mawlānā Yūsufī also worked for the Mughals, and in 940/1533-4 composed for his son Rafīʿ al-Dīn Ḥusayn and other students a collection of model letters, the *Badāʾiʿ al-inshāʾ*, which was very popular in Muslim India. The book begins with a *muḳaddima* on the different kinds of modes of address which must be regulated by the relation of the correspondents to one another in rank; Yūsufī then divides the different kinds of correspondence (*muḥāwarāt*) into three parts: letters to persons of higher rank (*murāḳaʿāt*), of the same rank (*murāsalāt*) and to those of lower rank (*riḳāʿ*). Then comes a series of forms of letters which are divided into sections, such as sultans to sultans of higher, equal or lower rank, princes to sultans and princes, princesses to princesses, *amīrs*, grand-viziers, viziers, officials of the *Dīwān*, secretaries (*munshīʾ*), sayyids (*sādāt*), *shaykhs*, judges, poets and astronomers. Then come what one might call private letters: to relations and friends on various occasions, e.g. if a reply has not been received, when on a journey, on grief at separation, longing for home, on returning soon, faithlessness, reconciliation, excuses, congratulations, condolences etc. A *khātima* gives examples of addresses (*ʿunwān*).

Bibliography: For the manuscript catalogues, see *EI*[1] art. s.v. See now C.L. Elgood, *A medical history of Persia and the Eastern Caliphate*, Cambridge 1951; Storey-de Blois, ii, 235-40, iii, 270; Rypka *et alii*, *History of Iranian literature*, 434, 476.

(E. BERTHELS-[C.E. BOSWORTH])

YŪSUFZAY, the name of a Pakhtū-speaking tribal confederation inhabiting the North West Frontier Province of Pākistān and divided into two broad groups: the Mandans (Mandaṅrs) who (together with the Baīzay Yūsufzays) inhabit the so-called Yūsufzay plain (mainly falling into Mardān district and divided into the *taḥṣīls* of Sawābī and Mardān); and (confusingly) the Yūsufzays of the valleys of Swāt, Pandjkōra, Dīr and Bunēr and of the region to the east of the river Indus lying on the western slopes of the Black Mountain. These two main groups are in turn subdivided into many smaller divisions. In terms of political organisation, the Yūsufzays may be described as an acephalous segmentary society in which considerable power was exercised by *khāns* and *maliks* and at various times by the numerous class of people with claims to religious sanctity (*sayyids*, *pīrs*, *faḳīrs*, *mullās*, etc.). In Swāt [*q.v.*], the descendants of one religious leader, the Ākhūnd of Swāt, created a state which endured from 1917 to 1969. In Dīr [*q.v.*], uniquely, *khāns* ruled continuously for over two hundred years.

The Yūsufzays moved into the region which they now occupy in the late 15th and early 16th centuries, expelled the Dardic-speaking Dilazāk population and took up agricultural life, apportioning the conquered land between the various lineage groups. A peculiar feature of the land settlement was the institution of *wēsh*, or periodic redistribution of the holdings, a practice which continued well into the 20th century. Under Mughal rule, the Yūsufzays alternately resisted and submitted, but from the end of the 17th century were more or less wholly independent, a status which they strove to maintain under Sikh rule. However, after 1849 the Mandans of the Yūsufzay plain were gradually brought under British administrative control (although there were frequent expeditions, chiefly against the Baīzays) and their country developed through irrigation, becoming a centre for the production of sugar cane and tobacco. The Mandans enlisted in the British Indian army in considerable numbers.

The Yūsufzays beyond the mountains, however, long retained their independence. During the 19th century, there was constant fighting among the *khān*s of Swāt, Pandjkōra, Dīr and Bunēr, and Yūsufzays from these regions clashed with British forces at Ambēla in 1863 and during the 1897 tribal uprising. Despite frequent raids from Swāt into British-administered territory, no British troops entered the Swāt valley until the Čitrāl Relief Expedition of 1895 [see ČITRĀL]. British authority also came into conflict with the Yūsufzays of the Black Mountain and several expeditions were launched against them, notably in 1888, 1891 and 1892. Dīr and Swāt were included in the Mālākand Political Agency in 1895; Bunēr and the Black Mountain Yūsufzays were dealt with separately. Under Pākistān, this system was at first continued but eventually Dīr, Swāt and Bunēr were incorporated as districts in the Mālākand division and designated as Provincially Administered Tribal Areas. It is difficult to estimate the number of Yūsufzays, but on the basis of the 1981 census for Mardān district and estimates for the mountainous valleys, the total was likely then to have been somewhere between 3 and 4 million.

Bibliography: *Imperial Gazetteer of India*², xix, 148-70; *Gazetteer of the Hazara District*, 1907, London 1908; C.M. Macgregor, *Central Asia. Part I. The North West Frontier*, 3 vols., Calcutta 1873; C.U. Aitchison (comp.), *Treaties, engagements and sanads*, xi, Calcutta 1909; Mountstuart Elphinstone, *An account of the Kingdom of Caubul*, ³London 1839; H.W. Bellew, *A general report on the Yusufzay*, Lahore 1864; Captain A.H. McMahon and Lt. A.D.G. Ramsay, *Report on the tribes of Dir, Swat and Bajour, etc.* Calcutta 1901, repr. Peshawar 1981; *A dictionary of the Pathan tribes on the North-West Frontier of India*, Calcutta 1899; Major R.T.I. Ridgway, *Pathans*, Calcutta 1918; Sir Olaf Caroe, *The Pathans*, London 1958; H.C. Wylly, *From the Black Mountain to Waziristan*, London 1912; J.W. Spain, *The Pathan borderland*, The Hague 1963, 43-4; *The story of Swat as told by the founder Miangul Abdul Wadud Badshah Sahib*, Peshawar 1983; *The last Wali of Swat. An autobiography as told to Fredrik Barth*, Oslo 1985; F. Barth, *Political leadership among Swat Pathans*, London 1959; Akbar S. Ahmad, *Millenarianism and charisma among Pathans*, London 1976; *1981 District Census Report of Mardan*, June 1983, Islamabad.

(M.E. YAPP)

YÜZELLİLİKLER, T., literally, "the 150 [undesirables]".

During the peace negotiations between the Allies and Turkey at Lausanne in 1923, Great Britain demanded that a general amnesty in Turkey should form part of the final settlement. The British were concerned that, otherwise, those inhabitants of Turkey who had been opposed to Muṣṭafā Kemāl and his nationalist movement in Anatolia would be persecuted. The Turkish delegation would not agree to an amnesty without exceptions, but it did not have at its disposal a list of persons whom it wanted excepted. Hence in the end, the Turkish representatives on the subcommission on minorities, led by Dr. Riḍā Nūr [*q.v.*], accepted a general amnesty but reserved the Turkish government's right to ban up to 150 (unnamed) Muslims from the country.

Drawing up the list of these 150 undesirables proved difficult. The Lausanne treaty was ratified without it and when the law on the general amnesty was passed on 16 April 1924, it was still not ready. Finally, on 23 April, a list was produced with only 149 names on it. After some discussion, one more person was added and on 1 June 1924 the list was accepted by Parliament. Those banned were all people who had opposed the nationalists in 1919-22. They fell into the following categories: persons from Sultan Meḥemmed VI's personal and political entourage; from his counter-insurgency forces (the *Ḳuwā-yi Inḍibāṭiyye*); members of the bureaucracy, the armed forces and the police; the renegade nationalist commander Čerkes Edhem's [*q.v.*] family and supporters; and journalists.

Bibliography: Cemal Kutay, *Yüzellilikler faciası*, Istanbul n.d.; İlhami Soysal, *Yüzellilikler*, Istanbul 1985.

(E.J. ZÜRCHER)

Z

ZĀʾ [see ZĀY].

ẒĀʾ, the seventeenth letter of the Arabic alphabet, numerical value: 900. The transliteration /ẓ/ reflects an urban/sedentary pronunciation as "emphatic" (pharyngealised) /z/. Sībawayh (d. 177/793 [*q.v.*]), however, describes the sound as an "emphatic" voiced interdental, thus /ḏ̣/ (iv, 436), and this is the way it is pronounced in those dialects, mainly Bedouin, that have preserved the interdentals. There is, however, an additional complication: with very few exceptions (in Northern Yemen, see Behnstedt, 5), all modern dialects of Arabic have coalesced the sounds represented by <ẓ> and <ḍ> into one sound, which is *grosso modo* pronounced /ḏ̣/ in the Bedouin dialects and /ḍ/ in the sedentary ones. In loans from the *fuṣḥā*, sedentary dialects, which do not have interdentals, imitate these sounds by using the corresponding sibilants, thus /ḏ̣/ > /ẓ/. Compare *muḏ̣āhara* > *muẓāhara* "demonstration" vs. the correct dialect correspondence in *ḏ̣uhr* > *ḍuhr* "noon". The two resulting pronunciations were secondarily used to distinguish between *ẓāʾ* and *ḍād*, and this became the pronunciation in urban Standard Arabic which was also received into Western transliteration. In what follows the original /ḏ̣/ will be used instead of /ẓ/.

The phoneme /ḏ̣/ forms the "emphatic" unit of the interdental triad. For the articulation of the interdentals, see THĀʾ. Minimal pairs would be: *ḏ̣alla* "he remained" vs. *thalla* "he tore down", *dhalla* "he became humble", and also *ḍalla* "he went astray" (the /ḍ/ being, according to Sībawayh's description, a voiced "emphatic" lateral [see ḌĀD]).

The Arabic /ḏ̣/ appears in cognates as /ṭ/ in Aramaic, /ṣ/ in Akkadian, Hebrew and Ethiopic. The fact that this phoneme is represented mainly by voiceless realisations has prompted its Proto-Semitic reconstruction as */ṯ̣/. The voiced representative in Arabic may have something to do with the shift of "emphasis" from glottalisation to pharyngealisation. But apart from that, it is phonemically immaterial whether the "emphatic" unit in a triad is voiced or voiceless; it is simply marked by "emphaticness". As a matter of fact, a voiceless /ṯ̣/ is attested in some Northern Yemeni dialects of Arabic (see Behnstedt, 5-6, 183-4), and a voiceless /ṯ̣/ occurs in North African sedentary dialects (see Cantineau, 45).

For assimilations, especially in sandhi, see Cantineau, 42-3, and Fleisch, 86-7. In the conjugation of verbs, the following assimilations are noteworthy: *ḥafiḏ̣tu* > *ḥafiḏ̣ḏ̣u* "I preserved", some grammarians even note *ḥafiṭṭu* (see Fleisch, 92). For the VIIIth form the most common assimilation of the infixed /t/ in **iḏ̣talama* is *iḏ̣ḏ̣alama* "he was wronged", but *iḏ̣ṭalama* and *iṭṭalama* are also mentioned (Fleisch, 95-6).

As already mentioned, most Bedouin dialects preserve the interdentals and thus /ḏ̣/. The same is true for a fair number of rural sedentary dialects. Otherwise, the sedentary dialects (urban as well as some rural dialects) shift the interdentals to dentals, thus /ḏ̣/ > /ḍ/. Unusual shifts of interdentals to sibilants (Kozluk-Sason group and some other dialects of Anatolian Arabic, Uzbekistan-Arabic) with /ḏ̣/ > /ẓ/, and to labiodentals (Siirt group and some other dialects of Anatolian Arabic) with /ḏ̣/ > /v/ have also been noted (Jastrow, 34-9).

The grapheme <ẓ> is identical with that of <ṭ>, and distinguished from it by a superscript dot. The reason for this is the "cognate" principle in Nabataean spelling: the Nabataeans realised that Nabataean /ṭ/ corresponded to both /ṭ/ and /ḏ̣/ in Arabic. They, therefore, used the grapheme <ṭ> to render both Arabic sounds, thus e.g. the name *Ḥanḏ̣al*[un] appears as *ḥnṭlw* in Nabataean inscriptions. The diacritical mark was added later; it is first attested in a papyrus by Ḳurra b. Sharīk [*q.v.*], dated Rabīʿ I, 91 = February 710 (Gruendler, 74b). Gruendler, 72-5, gives a description and tables for the development of the shape of *ṭāʾ/ẓāʾ* from Nabataean to Arabic.

In Persian and Persian-influenced languages, the sound /ḏ̣/ in Arabic words is pronounced /z/.

Bibliography: Sībawayh, ed. Hārūn, Cairo 1395/1975; P. Behnstedt, *Die Dialekte der gegend von Ṣaʿda (Nord-Jemen)*, Wiesbaden 1987; J. Cantineau, *Cours de phonétique arabe*, Paris 1960; H. Fleisch, *Traité de philologie arabe*, i, Beirut 1961; W. Fischer and O. Jastrow, *Handbuch der arabischen Dialekte*, Wiesbaden 1980; Jastrow, *Die mesopotamisch-arabischen Qeltu-Dialekte*. Band I: *Phonologie und Morphologie*, Wiesbaden 1978; Beatrice Gruendler, *The development of the Arabic scripts*, Atlanta 1993. (W.P. HEINRICHS)

ZĀB, with its pl. ZĪBĀN, the name of a region of the Algerian Sahara around Biskra [*q.v.*], extending over an area of *ca.* 150 km/100 miles from west to east and 40 km/25 miles from north to south.

1. Geography.

The Zībān form part of the great Saharan piedmont which stretches from Agadir to Gabès. Within this, they have a special dual role, the first role derived from their position at the narrowest part of the Maghribī mountain rim and at the opening of the great southern axis of communication of eastern Algeria (Skikda-Constantine-Batna-Biskra); and second, from the agricultural potential of the region, found hardly anywhere else in this piedmont, arising from suitable soils and important water resources. It is therefore not surprising that oases and important towns (e.g. Biskra) are to be found there and that the region has been attractive to the ruling powers of the Maghrib from Roman times onwards.

The Zībān comprise a depressed and short sloping surface, which starts off at 100 m/328 feet altitude on the southern slopes of the Atlas and ends in the salt flats of the Shaṭṭ Melhrir at 40 m/130 feet below sea level. From its piedmont nature, it has scattered soils of a muddy and fertile nature. From its contact with the Saharan Atlas, it has rich water supplies, including what were previously 80 rich springs, now tapped through bore holes. From its low-lying position and very dry atmosphere come the quality of its dates, the most famed being the Deglet Nour (Daglat al-nūr) variety. The Zāb Gharbī, in the west, has plentiful water and rich palm groves; the Zāb Sharḳī, in the east, has fewer deep water supplies but benefits from its position up against the Aurès (Awrās) Mountains and from flood waters, so that it is now a region of market-gardening irrigated by diesel pumps.

Thus the Zībān at present form a prosperous agricultural region, with 1.8 million palm trees spread over 20,000 ha and 16,000 ha of market gardens. With 22,000 workers engaged in agriculture, the Zībān are the leading agricultural region of the Algerian Sahara, ahead of the Wād Ghīr. This prosperity has been encouraged by legislation (1983) on land ownership, by a good network of local roads and by the founding of a certain number of agrarian centres. The total population is *ca.* 500,000, with its urban centre, Biskra, having over 150,000. This last has a central position within the region, is a great commercial centre for dates (with 100,000 palm trees there), as well as being the administrative centre of a *wilāya* and a gateway to the Sahara, commanding the Skikda-Tuggurt communications axis (a *route nationale* and railway). It now has a university, an airport and an industrial zone. It has no medina, but a centre laid out by the Europeans; thanks to its rapid expansion, the town has spread across the Wād Biskra (*ca.* 500 m/1,630 feet wide) to the left bank, so that three main bridges now link the two halves. See further, BISKRA.

2. History.

Little is known of the early history of the Zībān, but date cultivation goes back over two millennia. The name Zāb may be connected with Zabi, a Roman town in the vicinity of Hodna [see ḤUḌNA]. The Romans established some control over the region by constructing fortified places (Gemellae, Tolga, Vescera, Thouda and Badia), and the research of J. Baradez (in his *Fossatum Africae, recherches aériennes sur l'organisation des confins sahariens à l'époque romaine*, Paris 1949) has thrown light on the *limes* in this part of the Maghrib. The Sāḳiyat Bint al-Rās, a long trough running for 60 km/37 miles to the south of the Wād Djadī, marked along its length by mounds some 12 m/

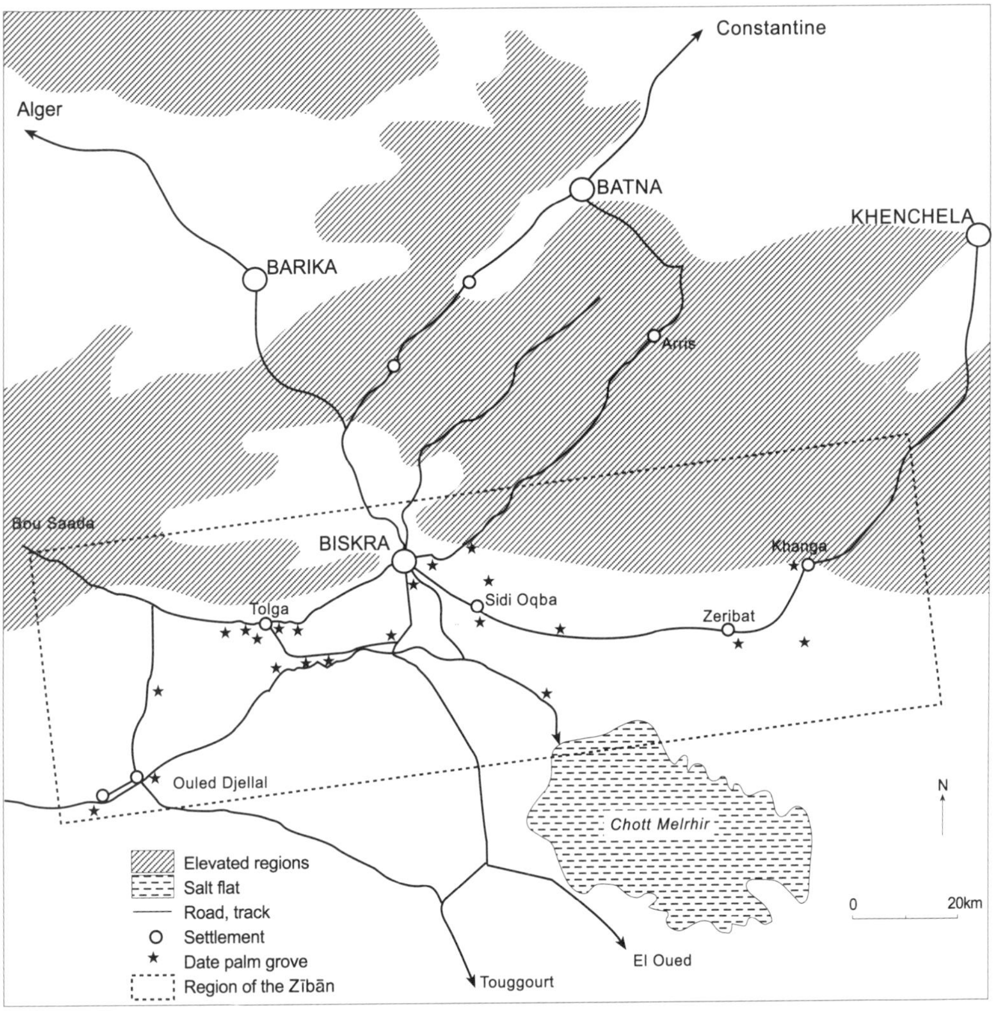

Constantine
Alger
BATNA
KHENCHELA
BARIKA
Arris
Bou Saada
BISKRA
Khanga
Sidi Oqba
Tolga
Zeribat
Ouled Djellal
N
Chott Melrhir
0
20km
Elevated regions
Salt flat
Road, track
Settlement
Date palm grove
Region of the Zībān
El Oued
Touggourt

40 feet in diameter, constituted an advance barrier of this *limes* against the nomads. From the 5th to the 7th centuries, Biskra was an episcopal see, and one bishop, Opta, was canonised as a saint.

It was in this region that in 63/683 the Arab commander ʿUḳba b. Nāfiʿ [*q.v.*] was killed, near an oasis with a village that subsequently bore his name, Sīdī ʿUḳba. Under the Aghlabids, the Zībān enjoyed a period of prosperity. Biskra was surrounded by a rampart and ditch, suburbs grew up *extra muros*, and forts built for the Arab *djund*. In the 17th century, the Turks placed a garrison in Biskra. After an outbreak of plague there in 1740, the town, then on an elevation in the heart of the palm groves, spread into seven village centres scattered through the groves, which remain to the present day. During the entire Turkish period, and then the early French one, the Zībān were dominated by two great families, the Bū ʿAzzāz and the Ben Gana, who each struggled for sole control (for details, see BISKRA).

The *amīr* ʿAbd al-Ḳādir [*q.v.*] intervened there, contributing to the local anarchy, until in 1844 the Duc d'Aumale occupied Biskra; but after the massacre of the French garrison later that year, a new fort and a new town were constructed outside the palm groves, 2 km north of the old town. In 1849, the region of Zaʿatča in the western Zībān broke out in revolt under Bū Ziyān, involving also the Aurès and members of the Raḥmāniyya Ṣūfī brotherhood, but Bū Ziyān was unable to rally the rest of the country. Besieged in Zaʿatča by the French army for 52 days, Bū Ziyān's followers preferred to kill themselves rather than surrender; 10,000 palms were cut down, and the region substantially pacified.

Bibliography: See also L.C. Feraud, *Le Sahara de Constantine, notes et souvenirs*, Algiers 1887; [collective work] *Les Ziban, essai de mise en point*, in *Revue Rhumel*, Constantine, no. 1 (1982), 7-13; P.L. Cambuzat, *L'évolution des cités du Tell en Ifrikiya du 7ème au 11ème siècle*, Algiers 1986; M. Côte, *Formes de mise en valeur nouvelles sur une vieille frange saharienne, les Ziban*, in *Les oasis au Maghreb*, Tunis 1995, 173-92; P. Morizot, *Archéologie aérienne de l'Aurès*, Paris 1997; S. Ouatmani, *L'insurrection de Zaatcha en 1849. Résistance et solidarité dans les Ziban*, diss. Univ. of Aix-en-Provence, 1998, unpubl. (M. CÔTE)

AL-ZĀB, the name of two left-bank tributaries of the Tigris [see DIDJLA] in northern ʿIrāḳ, both of them rising in the Zagros mountain chain in Kurdistān.

1. The Great or Upper Zāb (*al-Zāb al-akbar* or *al-aʿlā*) was already known to the Assyrians, as *Zabu ēlū* "the upper Zāb", and appears in classical Greek as Λύκος (cf. *PW*, xiii, cols. 2391-2), Byzantine Greek as ὁ μέγας Ζάβας, in Syriac as *Zābā* and in later Armenian as *Zav*. In Kurdish it is known today as the *Zē'-i Bādinān* and in Turkish as *Zap*. J. Markwart discussed possible etymologies and suggested a link with older Aramaic *dēbā*, also in Syriac, "wolf", older Armenian *gail* "wolf", a basic meaning which would account for the Classical Greek calque Λύκος (see his *Südarmenien und die Tigrisquellen nach griechischen und armenischen Geographen*, Vienna 1930, 429-30).

It rises in the modern Turkish *il* of Van near the frontier with Persian Ādharbāydjān, flows southwards through Hakkâri into the Kurdish region of north-eastern ʿIrāḳ, where its waters are utilised by the Bakhma dam, and then flows southwestwards to its confluence with the Tigris 47 km/30 miles south of Mawṣil, having received as a right-bank affluent the Khāzir [*q.v.*].

2. The Lesser or Lower Zāb (*al-Zāb al-asghar* or *al-asfal*) was called *Zabū šupalū* "the lower Zāb" by the Assyrians, in Classical Greek Κάπρος (see *PW*, x, col. 1921) and in Byzantine Greek ὁ μικρὸς Ζάβας or ὁ ἕτερος Ζάβας. In Kurdish it is known today as *Zē'i Koya*. It is formed from the confluence of several streams, but the main stream rises just over the border from ʿIrāḳ in Mukrī Kurdistān. Within ʿIrāḳ, it flows southwards after the Dukān dam past the town of Altun Köprü [see ALTÎN KÖPRÜ] and meets the Tigris 80 km/50 miles above Takrīt [*q.v.*].

In the period before Islam, the region between the two Zābs formed the Eastern Christian Church's ancient diocese of Adiabene, with its centre at Erbil, the later Irbil (see J.M. Fiey, *Assyrie chrétienne. Contribution à l'étude de l'histoire et de la géographie ecclésiastiques et monastiques du nord de l'Iraq*, Beirut 1965-8, i, 37 ff.), whilst the region to the north of the Upper Zāb formed the diocese of Marga (see *ibid.*, i, 225 ff.). In early Islamic times, these regions continued to be strongly Christian, with many monasteries spread through them.

The mediaeval Islamic geographers describe the two rivers (in *Ḥudūd al-ʿālam*, tr. Minorsky, 76, **al-Zābayn*) and the very fertile plains (the granary of ancient Assyria) along their lower reaches, and called them both *al-Madjnūn* "the demoniacally-possessed" from their impetuous courses as torrents coming down from the mountains. The Arab geographers state that the Great Zāb flowed from a district known as *Mushangar and Bābghish (Syriac, Bēt Barghash) and joined the Tigris at the monastery of ʿUmr Bārḳānā near the "new town" of al-Ḥadītha [*q.v.*]/Ḥadīthat al-Mawṣil. The Lesser Zāb joined the Tigris near the town of al-Sinn "the Tooth", known more specifically as al-Sinn of Bārimmā (see Le Strange, *The lands of the Eastern Caliphate*, 90-1; Schwarz, *Iran im Mittelalter*, 695).

The Great Zāb has played a considerable role in history, being several times mentioned in the campaigns of the Emperors Maurice and Heraclius against the Persians, e.g. in Heraclius's Assyrian campaign of later 617 when he led his army down the eastern bank of the Tigris, across the two Zābs, against the Sāsānid palace at Dastgird to the north of Ctesiphon (see J.B. Bury, *A history of the later Roman Empire from Arcadius to Irene (395 A.D. to 900 A.D.)*, London 1889, ii, 242). According to Theophylactus Simocatta, the lower course of the Great Zāb was navigable (ναυσίπορος), and it may be that inflated rafts or *keleks* [*q.v.*] were used for travelling downstream as they have been used up to modern times. A fierce battle was fought on its tributary the Khāzir between the Umayyad governor of ʿIrāḳ ʿUbayd Allāh b. Ziyād and the rebel Ibrāhīm al-Ashtar (67/686) [see AL-KHĀZIR]; above all, it was on the banks of the Great Zāb that the last Umayyad caliph Marwān II b. Muḥammad [*q.v.*] was decisively defeated by the advancing revolutionary forces of the ʿAbbāsids led by ʿAbd Allāh b. ʿAlī b. ʿAbd Allāh b. al-ʿAbbās in 132/750 (cf. M. Sharon, *Black banners from the East. The establishment of the ʿAbbāsid state—incubation of a revolt*, Jerusalem 1983, 13-14).

In modern ʿIrāḳ, attempts have been made to control the great volume of water and silt brought down each spring by snows melting in the Zagros Mountains, and to store water for irrigation purposes during the hot and dry summer, by the construction of dams at Dukān on the Little Zāb and Bakhma on the Great Zāb.

Bibliography: In addition to references given in the article, see Naval Intelligence Division, Admiralty Handbooks, *Iraq and the Persian Gulf*, London 1944, 102 ff. (C.E. BOSWORTH)

ZABADĀNĪ, the name currently given to a town of Syria, and also to an administrative region (*minṭaḳa idāriyya*), to a smaller administrative unit (*nāḥiya*) composed of eight villages and six farms (*mazraʿa*), and to a river which flows from the north through the town. Various fanciful etymologies have been suggested from *zabad*, some of them alluding to its fertility. Whatever the case, Zabadānī was and still is known for the abundance of its apple trees.

Under the Byzantines, the town of Zabadānī was attached to the bishopric of the town of Abilla in Sūḳ Wādī Baradā, but after the Arab-Islamic conquest of Syria, the bishopric was moved to Zabadānī. A pottery oil-holder (*maṭra*), used by Christian pilgrims to hold sacred oil and dating back to the 6th century A.D., has been found in Zabadānī; it bears pictures of the Virgin Mary, the Angel and the Star, and has a Greek inscription saluting Mary.

Located on the northern edge of the Zabadānī plain in the Anti-Lebanon, at an elevation of about 1,200 m/3,940 feet above sea level, the town of Zabadānī counted in the early 1990s about 17,000 inhabitants. In the mid-1950s, one-fourth of its population were Christians. It then had six mosques, a Greek Orthodox church and a Greek Catholic church. The town is about 47 km/30 miles to the north-west of Damascus and is attached administratively to the Rural Area of the Governorate of Damascus (*Muḥāfaẓat Rīf Dimashk*). It is bounded on the north by Sirghāyā; on the east by Blūdān and Baḳḳīn; and on the south by Maḍāyā and the valley of the Baradā river. All these locations are major summer resorts for Damascenes and other Syrians.

Bibliography: Yāḳūt, *Muʿdjam al-buldān*, ed. Beirut, iii, 130; Abu 'l-Fidā', *Taḳwīm al-buldān*, ed. Fuat Sezgin *et alii*, Frankfurt 1992, xxiii, 255; Zakariyyā, *al-Rīf al-Sūrī. Muḥāfaẓat Dimashk*, Damascus 1374-6/1955-7, ii, 268-93; *al-Muʿdjam al-djughrāfī*, 5 vols. Damascus 1990-3, iii, 539-41; (Father) Mitrī Hādjī Athanasiyū, *Sūriyya al-Masīḥiyya fi 'l-alf al-awwal al-mīlādī*, in *Mawsūʿat Baṭriyarkiyyat Anṭākiya al-taʾrīkhiyya*, 5 vols. to date, Damascus 1997, v, 220-1.

(ABDUL-KARIM RAFEQ)

ZĀBADJ, ZĀBIDJ, ZĀBAG, the name of an island placed in the northeastern part of the Indian Ocean by the Arabic geographical writers. It appears as early as the *Akhbār al-Ṣīn wa 'l-Hind* of Sulaymān al-Tādjir and in the *K. al-Masālik wa 'l-mamālik* of Ibn Khurradādhbih (3rd/9th century) and then in almost all subsequent texts, and the title of its ruler, the Mahārādj[ā], is also regularly used from an early date.

The location of Zābadj in Southeast Asia is certain. The Arabic authors describe it as a trading empire, and place it in relation to known places, such as India, Ḳimār [*q.v.*] (Khmer = Cambodia) and Kalāh. From this there emerges that we have a country on the route between India and China, but further south than these; al-Bīrūnī, *K. al-Tafhīm*, ed. R.R. Wright, London 1934, 16, actually places it on the equator. The authors state that the ruler of the country of Zābadj ruled from a capital of the same name over the islands of the "Eastern Sea", and amongst a considerable number of these islands are listed Djāwa, Kalāh and Wākwāk [*q.vv.*]. The Mahārādjā appears as main king in the land, but with subordinate governors (*maliks*) owing allegiance to him, and with a powerful army and navy. Abū Zayd, in G. Ferrand, *Relations de voyages et textes relatifs à l'Extrême Orient*, Paris 1913-14, ii, 95-7, has a long account of his attack on Cambodia, the only historical fact mentioned. One source describes people from dependent islands, and also from Cambodia, turning their faces towards Zābadj and prostrating themselves as a sign of their allegiance.

The capital Zābadj was a flourishing commercial centre and a rendezvous for foreign ships, those of the Arabs, the Indians and Chinese. The Zābadjīs are said to have traded as far as Africa and to have brought iron from there to sell on the Asian mainland (al-Idrīsī, tr. A. Jaubert, Paris 1836-40, 58). Foreign traders provided the state with much revenue. Local customs mentioned are ordeal by fire and the ceremony of *bersila* (i.e. sitting cross-legged out of politeness: the actual Malay word is used in the Arabic texts) before the Mahārādjā (*ʿAdjāʾib al-Hind*, ed. Van der Lith, 154, tr. Freeman-Grenville, 90).

The exact identification of Zābadj from the Arabic sources is virtually impossible, although it is almost certainly somewhere in the Western Indonesian archipelago. Early European scholars preferred Java, because of a similarity in names (Skr. *yava*, Gk. *iabadiou*) and the fact that extensive ruins there showed the previous existence of a large empire, but a strong case can also be made from these sources for Sumatra (since its products gold and camphor are described as coming from Zābadj) and a defensible case for Borneo. Ferrand produced the Indian term Djāwaka as the equivalent of Zābadj and of Chinese She-p'o-t'i = Sumatra. See further on this, W. Mahdī, *Wie hiessen die Malaien, bevor sie "Malaien" hiessen?*, in *Südostasien und Wir: Grundsatzdiskussionen und Fachbeiträge. Tagung des Arbeitskreises Südostasien und Ozeanien Hamburg 1993, Austronesiana*, ed. A. Bormann *et al.*, Munster 1993, 162-76.

Modern scholars have linked the Mahārādjā with the Buddhist Sailendra rulers of Southeast Asia, who seem to have been the only rulers to call themselves by this title before the 10th century; it is therefore probable that, when Arabic writers speak of the Mahārādjā, they are referring to that dynasty. Around this we must build all our hypotheses. The present theory with regard to the history of the Sailendras is that they first appeared in Java, and became the dominant dynasty there, soon after the reign of the Hindu Sanjaya about A.D. 760. By about 860, a younger branch of the family established itself on the throne of Śrīvijaya centred at Palembang and perhaps in later times at Malayu (Jambi), a throne which they held for over three centuries, or at least, the title of Mahārādjā remained with this kingdom until its dissolution. The Sailendra dynasty in Java had lost its control of Java by the beginning of the 10th century, hence all references originating after this time would apparently refer to the Sumatran kingdom. Similarly, all references before 860 would refer to Java. Any Arabic writer therefore who uses sources before 860 referring to the kingdom of the Mahārādjā would be dealing with the Sailendras in Java, and any Arabic writer using sources originating from the 10th century onwards would be talking about Sumatra. Thus the references of Ibn Khurradādhbih and possibly those of the other early geographers would refer to Java and not to Sumatra.

A major problem is identifying the place which Ibn Khurradādhbih, 46 (quoted by al-Idrīsī and in other texts), calls Djāba, near Salāhit, Harang (*H.z.l.dj* in al-Idrīsī, *Opus geographicum*, i, 81) and Māʾit, fifteen days' journey from the Spice Islands, with a king apparently a Buddhist, and producing coconuts, bananas and sugar-cane. From this text alone, it would appear that Djāba and the three neighbouring places were near the southern tip of the Malay peninsula, since they fall on the route to China between the ports of Kalāh and Ḳimār. But there is a complication in that in both places where the *Akhbār al-Ṣīn wa 'l-Hind* mentions Zābadj, Ibn Khurradādhbih, 17, mentions Djāba; thus the former states that Kalāh is a kingdom of Zābadj and the latter that it belongs to the kingdom of Djāba al-Hindī. Also, Ibn Khurradādhbih mentions Buddhism as the religion of Djāba, but the expression Djāba al-Hindī could be expected to refer to a Hindu king there; possibly there were two Djābas, one Buddhist and one Hindu in faith. In fact, the name Djāba occurs in no other original text except in Ibn Khurradādhbih/al-Idrīsī, and if Djāba was in Sumatra, as the evidence suggests, it cannot be the same as Zābadj if this last, at this early stage, was located solely in Java. In any case, no more is subsequently heard of the name Djāba, unless its name is echoed in the later name of Djāwa. This is complicated by the fact that Java and Sumatra were frequently confused with one another and sometimes thought of as one island.

The next two relevant Arabic texts, those of Abū Zayd and al-Mas'ūdī, stem from the mid-10th century, i.e. the time when the Sailendras ruled from Śrīvijaya (in Arabic, Sirbuza) only, but seem to show a mixture of earlier and later material. Thus mention of Sirbuza as an island in the empire of the Mahārādjā could stem from the period when the seat of the Mahārādjā was still in Java but the kingdom of Śrīvijaya was under his sway. Abū Zayd's account of the attack on Cambodia obviously comes from the Java period. Cambodia was subject to attacks like this from Java in the later 8th century (767-87), but after 802, the accession date of Jayavarman, threw off all relics of allegiance to Java. Also, Abū Zayd's account does not stress the importance of maritime trade, as one would expect with Śrīvijaya, but rather, of agricultural prosperity, which one would connect with Java. Al-Mas'ūdī's information sounds more up-to-date and deals with a Zābadj which could quite easily be Sumatra. He stresses the importance of sea trade and that sailors from the Persian Gulf continually voyaged to Kalāh and Zābadj, all this connecting easily with Śrīvijaya, the later seat of the Sailendra Mahārādjā.

Thus the texts seem to suggest that Zābadj was formerly a toponym attached to the island of Java, and then the Arabic sources attached it to the Sailendra Mahārādjās as a kind of title, i.e. the king of Zābadj, and then to the empire which he controlled. After the fall of the Sailendras in Java *ca.* 907, the main court of the dynasty was transferred to Śrīvijaya but Zābadj still remained as a loose term for the Sailendra empire in general. Almost contemporary with this transfer of the name to the Sumatran empire, the Arabic sources begin to mention Śrīvijaya in the geographical and travel accounts as Sirbuza (with various readings). The position of this last is fairly obvious from the texts. The *'Adjā'ib al-Hind*, ed. Van der Lith, 176, tr. Freeman-Grenville, 104, places it at the extremity of the island of Lamūrī and on a bay which penetrates 50 farsakhs into the island. Apart from the exaggerated distance, the description could well apply to Palembang in southeast Sumatra. The local crocodiles are frequently mentioned. Arab sailors would apply the name of the town to the whole island.

Thus it appears that, from the time of al-Mas'ūdī in particular, the Arabic authors had two names for the same thing, sc. Sirbuza and Zābadj. Insensible to or unaware of political conditions, they are interested primarily in Sirbuza for its trade, and regarded it as merely a province of the Mahārādjā's empire with its own governor or petty king, who levied dues on ships bound for China (*'Adjā'ib*, 111). The description of the place and its products is just what one would expect of the port of Palembang at this time. The term Zābadj, on the other hand, remained connected with the Mahārādjā and became more the name of an empire and less that of a place, so that even Sirbuza became "an island of Zābadj". The capital of the empire is unnamed, but is obviously a Sumatran town on an estuary. It is in fact only through studying non-Arabic sources that the Arabic Sirbuza can be shown as the capital of the Mahārādjā's empire. On Arabic evidence alone, one might think that the capital was further north and nearer the Malacca Straits, although it is possible that there were periods in the history of the empire when the capital was in fact further north, so that these sources may have in them an element of truth.

A further development in the history of Zābadj can be seen in Yāḳūt's mention (early 6th/12th century) of Djāwa (thus spelt with *wāw*, not the earlier *bā'*), which, he says, is the first part of China and is on the sea coast; merchants do not go to China, but only to Djāwa. This is likely to be Sumatra, since direct trade with China had been cut off and Arabic ships only went as far as Kalāh and Sirbuza at this time. The new Djāwa was an important trading centre, and this new reference tallies with the information of Marco Polo and other European authors that the island we know as Sumatra was called Java [the Less] (see Yule-Cordier, *The Book of Ser Marco Polo*, London 1903, ii, 284, 286 n. 1). Authors like the historian Rashīd al-Dīn and the traveller Ibn Baṭṭūṭa (cf. *Riḥla*, iv, 224, 228 ff., tr. Beckingham, iv, 873, 876 ff.) show that Djāwa meant for them Sumatra. Also, contemporary information in Ibn Sa'īd (d. 672/1274) provides a full description of the island, although placed to the south of the islands of the Mahārādjā; he gives a town of Djāwa in the centre of the island, but has no mention here of Sirbuza. The Chinese annals mention no embassies to China from San-fo-ch'i between 1178 and 1370, although the Ming annals say that this place continued to send embassies until the end of the Sung dynasty, and it is possible that, during the 13th century, Śrīvijaya lost its importance in Southeast Asian trade, the state of Malayu on the Jambi river possibly taking its place, especially as other sources than the Arab ones do not mention Śrīvijaya at this time. The popular Filipino belief that Zābadj and "Sanfotsi" (San-fo-ch'i) are in fact to be located in the Philippines is based on uncritical readings of the terms in the sources (e.g. the 13th-century *Chu fan-chi*, 75 ff.) and would appear rather to be the product of nationalist zeal.

Bibliography: In addition to the *Bibl.* in G. Ferrand, *EI*[1] art. *Zābag*, and to references given in the article, see Buzurg b. Shahriyār, *Kitāb 'Adjā'ib al-Hind. Livre des merveilles de l'Inde*, ed. P.A. van der Lith, Fr. tr. L.M. Devic, Leiden 1883-6, ed. Y. al-Shārūnī, London 1990, Eng. tr. G.S.P. Freeman-Grenville, *Captain Buzurg ibn Shahriyar of Ram Hurmuz. The book of the wonders of India, mainland, sea and islands*, London-The Hague 1980; H. Yule and A.C. Burnell, *Hobson-Jobson. A glossary of Anglo-Indian colloquial words and phrases*, [2]London 1903, 454-6; G. Gerini, *Researches on Ptolemy's geography of Eastern Asia*, London 1909; J.L. Moens, *Srivijaya, Yava en Kataha*, in *Tijdschr. voor Indische Taal-, Land- en Volkenkunde, Batavia*, lxxvii (1937); G. Coedès, *Les états hin-*

douisés d'Indochine et d'Indonésie, Paris 1948, Eng. tr.
W.F. Vella, Honolulu 1968; S. Maqbul Ahmad,
EI[2] art. ḎJUGHRĀFIYĀ'; Chau Ju-Kua, *Chu fan-chi*,
ed. and tr. Fr. Hirth and W.W. Rockhill, Amsterdam 1966; O.W. Wolters, *Early Indonesian commerce.
A study of the origins of Sri Vijaya*, Ithaca, N.Y. 1967;
idem, *The fall of Sri Vijaya in Malay history*, London
1970; F. Viré, *L'Océan indien d'après le géographe . . .
AL-IDRISI . . . Extraits traduits et annotés du «Livre de
Roger»*, in P. Ottino (ed.), *Etudes sur l'Océan indien*,
St. Denis de la Réunion 1979; G.R. Tibbetts, *A
study of Arabic texts containing material on South-East
Asia*, London 1979, 104 and n. 14; A. Abeydeera,
Taprobane, Ceylan ou Sumatra? Une confusion féconde, in
Archipel, xlix (1994), 87-124.

(G.R. TIBBETTS and SHAWKAT M. TOORAWA)

AL-ZABĀNIYYA (A.), a word found in Ḳurʾān,
XCVI, 18, usually interpreted by the commentators
as the guardians of Hell or else the angels
who carry off the souls at death [see MALĀʾIKA.
1]. A. Jeffery, The *foreign vocabulary of the Qurʾān*, Baroda
1938, 148, thought that an origin from Syriac *zabūrā*,
the *ductores* who, says Ephraim Syrus, lead the departed
souls for judgment was likely; but W. Eilers, *Iranisches
Lehngut im arabischen*, in *Indo-Iranian Jnal.*, v (1962), 220,
favoured an Iranian etymology, from MP *zen(dān)bān*
"warder, keeper of a prison", NP *zindānbān*.

Bibliography: Given in the article.   (ED.)

AL-ZABBĀ', the more common of the two Arabic
names given in the Islamic sources to the famous
Queen of Tadmur/Palmyra, the other being
Nāʾila, undoubtedly identifiable with the Greek and
Aramaic forms of her name, Zenobia and Bath-Zabbay, both attested epigraphically. Al-Zabbāʾ "the
hairy (?)" was possibly her surname while Nāʾila was
her given name.

In spite of embroideries and accretions that have
accumulated around her in the Islamic sources, these
are valuable as they document the Arab profile of
the history of al-Zabbāʾ, on which the Classical sources
are silent, just as the Arabo-Islamic sources are silent
on the Roman profile. The two sets of sources thus
complement each other and the task of scholarship is
to disentangle fact from fiction in the Islamic sources,
and so reach the kernel of historical truth which they
undoubtedly have.

Al-Zabbāʾ appears in these sources as the daughter
of one ʿAmr b. al-Ẓarib, the ruler of Ḏjazīra (Mesopotamia) and part of al-Shām. A military encounter
between him and the Tanūkhid king of al-Ḥīra, Ḏjadhīma [*q.v.*], left him dead, and al-Zabbāʾ's subsequent history became a story of revenge. She offered
Ḏjadhīma her hand in marriage, pretending that this
would unite and strengthen their respective realms,
and invited him to come to her in Palmyra. His counsellor, Ḳaṣīr, warned him of the ruse, but Ḏjadhīma
did not listen and proceeded from his castle on the
Euphrates, Baḳḳa, to Palmyra, where he was trapped
and where he died a dolorous death after al-Zabbāʾ
asked her maid to open the veins in his arm. As
a result, she became herself the object of revenge.
Ḳaṣīr returned to al-Ḥīra, where he asked ʿAmr b.
ʿAdī, Ḏjadhīma's nephew and adopted son (who
became the first Lakhmid king), to avenge the death
of his uncle. This ʿAmr finally did by a ruse reminiscent of that of the Trojan Horse, which enabled
him to enter Palmyra and overpower its garrison. Al-Zabbāʾ, however, fled and died by her own hand
after she sucked her poisoned seal-ring, thus avoiding
being killed by ʿAmr.

The sources also speak of her construction of two

castles on both banks of the Euphrates, one for herself
and another for her sister Zabība, and of her campaign in north Arabia against Dūma and Taymāʾ and
their two fortresses Mārid and al-Ablaḳ. This campaign and the episode involving Ḏjadhīma and ʿAmr
gave rise to many attractive Arabic proverbs.

The kernels of truth in these Islamic accounts may
be presented as follows: (i) On chronological and other
grounds, the encounter with Ḏjadhīma is perfectly credible and it is just possible that Ḏjadhīma did indeed
meet his death at al-Zabbāʾ's hands. As for her own
death, its Arabic account has to be wholeheartedly
rejected since the incontestable Greek and Latin sources
testify to her defeat by the Roman emperor Aurelian
in A.D. 272, whose triumph in Rome she later graced.
But Lakhmid participation in Aurelian's campaign
against her is probably historical.

(ii) Her campaign against Dūma and Taymāʾ is also
possible to accept, as is her construction of a castle
on the Euphrates. Palmyra was a great caravan city,
and it was natural that al-Zabbāʾ should have wanted
to annex these important trade stations controlling the
routes to Arabia and Mesopotamia. Her foundation
on the Euphrates is attested in the Greek sources and
is known as Zenobia, present-day Halabiyya.

The extraordinary career of al-Zabbāʾ impressed
the pre-Islamic poets of 6th-century Arabia, fragments
of whose poetry on her have survived. The most complete of these is the one by the Ḥīran poet ʿAdī b.
Zayd [*q.v.*].

Bibliography: *Dīwān ʿAdī b. Zayd*, ed. M. al-Muʿaybid, Baghdād 1965, 181-4; Ṭabarī, i, 756-68;
Masʿūdī, *Murūḏj*, ed. Pellat, ii, 217-23; Ibn al-Athīr,
ed. Beirut, i, 345-50; D.R. Hillers and Eleanore
Cussini, *Palmyrene Aramaic texts*, Baltimore and London
1996; M. Piotrovsky, *The Arabic version of Queen Zenobia's (al-Zabbāʾ) story*, in *Palestinskii Sbornik*, lxxxiv
(1970), 170-84; G.W. Bowersock, *Roman Arabia*,
Cambridge, Mass. 1983, 136-7.

(IRFAN SHAHĪD)

ZABĪB (A.), dried grapes, raisins, or currants. In the mediaeval Islamic culinary tradition,
raisins were deemed indispensable for meat dishes of
chicken or mutton with a sweet-sour character, such
as those of Persian origin called *zirbāḏj* or *sikbāḏj* [*q.v.*],
in which the sweetness of the dried grapes (sometimes
combined with another dried fruit like apricot or additional sugar) is balanced by the acidity of vinegar. In
another kind of preparation, the meat is initially cooked
in a vinegar and raisin stock. A dish called *zabībiyya*,
probably of Egyptian provenance, was prepared from
fresh fish with a sweet and sour spiced sauce poured
over it. In the recipes for substantial main dishes, two
kinds of raisin, *zabīb aḥmar* and *zabīb aswad* are mentioned. The best kind of raisin was large with a lot
of flesh and small seeds.

Raisins occurred also in a variety of other domestic preparations. For example, a kind of "mustard
sauce" to accompany fowl was made from raisin extract
(*māʾ zabīb*) and pomegranate seeds (presumably the
acidic variety) in which dried spices, crushed almonds
and salt were "dissolved". Raisins were also used in
the preparation of a beverage called *fuḳḳāʿ*, a sparkling,
fermented beer-like liquor. Certain home-made remedies, like the electuary (*maʿḏjūn*), called for a large
quantity of raisins, the seeds of which had to be removed before cooking; the preparation was used to
avoid stomach disorders after eating greasy, fatty foods.

In the mediaeval medical literature devoted to dietetics, raisins are described as moderately hot and moist
in character and as having a fattening quality. Abū

Marwān ʿAbd al-Malik b. Zuhr (d. 557/1162) was of the opinion that wine made from raisins was weaker than that produced from grape juice.

In the Prophetic medicine (*al-ṭibb al-nabawī*) tradition, raisins are also very positively judged for their many benefits. Ibn Ḳayyim al-Djawziyya (d. 751/1350 [*q.v.*]) provides two traditions, albeit unsound ones, in which raisins are described by the Prophet as excellent food which sweeten the breath and remove phlegm and fatigue; they were also said to strengthen the nerves, calm anger and contribute to a clear complexion. In a similar work attributed to al-Suyūṭī (d. 911/1505), Tamīm al-Dārī [*q.v.*] is reported to have given the Prophet some raisins, which he then shared among his Companions; the Prophet also had *zabīb* soaked in water which he would drink the following day. To the Prophet's attitude to raisins there is added Ibn ʿAbbās's caution that, while the flesh contained a healing property, the seeds were harmful and should be spat out. Nonetheless, according to the traditionist al-Zuhrī, their value in the religious life was that anyone who wished to memorise *ḥadīth* should eat raisins.

Bibliography: C. Elgood, *Tibb-ul-Nabi or medicine of the Prophet*, in *Osiris*, xiv (1962), 33-192; anon., *Kanz al-fawāʾid fī tanwīʿ al-mawāʾid*, ed. M. Marín and D. Waines, Beirut-Stuttgart 1993; Ibn Sayyār al-Warrāḳ, *K. al-Ṭabīkh*, ed. K. Öhrnberg and S. Mroueh, Helsinki 1987; Irmeli Perho, *The prophet's medicine*, Helsinki 1995. (D. Waines)

ZABĪD, a town in the Tihāma [*q.v.*] coastal plain of Yemen, at about 25 km/15 miles from the Red Sea, in a region of fertile agricultural lands irrigated by two major *wādīs*, Zabīd to the south and Rimaʿ to the north. It is the centre of an administrative district, a *mudīriyya*, with the same name, which falls under the jurisdiction of the governorate of al-Ḥudayda [*q.v.*].

1. History.

Originally known as al-Ḥuṣayb, a village of the Ashāʿir tribe, Zabīd took on the name of the *wādī*, to which it owed its prosperity, when it was founded in Shaʿbān 204/January 820 by Muḥammad b. ʿAbd Allāh b. Ziyād [see ziyādids], who was sent by the ʿAbbāsid caliph al-Maʾmūn to quell the rebellion of the Ashāʿir and ʿAkk tribes. During his rule and that of his descendants (until 407/1016), Zabīd became the seat of government. Its location on the important commercial and pilgrimage route Aden-Mecca brought it substantial material and cultural wealth, and many important scholars from different parts of the Islamic world stopped in Zabīd and contributed to its growing reputation as the main centre for Sunnī religious learning in Yemen. Both the Ashāʿir and the Great Mosques, built by the prolific Ziyādid patron al-Ḥusayn b. Salāma (*r.* 373-402/983-1012), became focal points for scholars. Zabīd continued to be the political capital for successive dynasties: the Nadjāḥids (412-553/1022-1158 [*q.v.*]), and the Mahdids (553-69/1158-74 [*q.v.*]). This period is characterised by a number of Ḳarmaṭī and Ṣulayḥid [*q.vv.*] incursions into the Tihāma, during which Zabīd suffered intermittent assaults as well as capture by the Ṣulayḥids during the latter part of the 5th/11th century.

The Ayyūbid conquest of Yemen in 569/1174 confirmed Zabīd as the administrative and economic capital of the region, even though several of their rulers preferred to settle elsewhere. However, Zabīd enjoyed its heyday under the Rasūlids (626-858/1229-1454 [*q.v.*]). Although they made Taʿizz their capital, the sultans continued to favour Zabīd by spending their winters there. They also established numerous religious foundations which attracted many prestigious scholars, such as al-Fīrūzābādī [*q.v.*], whose tomb in Zabīd is still known as that of *Ṣāḥib al-Ḳāmūs*. The number of quarters, palaces, gardens, markets, and religious monuments was higher in Zabīd during the Rasūlid period than in any other town of Yemen, including their official capital Taʿizz. Al-Khazradjī reported that a survey of the mosques and *madrasas* of Zabīd, ordered by Sultan al-Ashraf Ismāʿīl in 795/1392, put their number at between 230 and 240 buildings. The Rasūlids also constructed several palaces and pavilions in the lush Wādī Zabīd, amongst the date plantations, which they used as retreats during the hunting season, and for the date-gathering festival, known as *subūt al-nakhīl*. Ibn al-Daybaʿ describes how blessed Zabīd was with water, where each house had its own well, while underground channels fed the orchards in the town and its environs: His list of fruits, as well as references to date palms, sugar cane and rice attest to the richness of local agriculture. The cultivation of cotton and indigo also helped to develop an indigenous textile industry. As late as 1936, Zabīd had 150 textile workshops.

Although the Ṭāhirids (858-923/1454-1517 [*q.v.*]) followed the Rasūlids' habit of using Zabīd as a winter residence, and continued the upkeep of religious buildings, the town began a steady decline in the late 9th/15th century. Reports of floods, fires, earthquakes and other natural disasters, point to its shrinking size. The demise of the Ṭāhirids at the hands of the Mamlūks, and the subsequent control of the Tihāma and Zabīd by their mercenaries, the Lewend [*q.v.*], between 927/1521 and 943/1536, accelerated this decline. During their first occupation of Yemen (945-1045/1538-1635), the Ottomans' use of Zabīd as one of their main bases led to repeated devastating Zaydī [see zaydiyya] attacks. The latter's victory and the consolidation of their power over the whole of Yemen meant the loss of Zabīd's role as a focus for Sunnī autonomy in the Tihāma. Furthermore, Yemen's period of economic boom in the 17th and 18th centuries resulting from the coffee trade, completely bypassed Zabīd, which was supplanted by al-Mukhā and Bayt al-Faḳīh [*q.vv.*] as the principal centres of mercantile activities. When Carsten Niebuhr visited Zabīd in the 1760s, he found that its buildings occupied only about one-half of the ancient area of the town. The emergence of al-Ḥudayda as the administrative centre of the Tihāma during the 19th and 20th centuries, and notably during the second Ottoman occupation (1872-1918) further overshadowed Zabīd, which also suffered from internal social unrest between 1902 and 1917.

2. Structure of the town.

According to al-Muḳaddasī, Zabīd was known as the Baghdād of Yemen owing to its circular shape, a characteristic that sets it apart from other Yemeni towns, and this seems to have remained unchanged throughout its history. A fortified mud wall with four gates was already in place in the 3rd/9th century, even though the first wall was attributed to al-Ḥusayn b. Salāma by several later historians. A second wall was built by the Nadjāḥid Abū Manṣūr Mann Allāh al-Fātikī sometime between 520/1126 and 524/1130, a third wall was erected by al-Mahdī b. ʿAlī or his brother ʿAbd al-Nabī between 554-69/1159-73, and a fourth one by Ṭughtakīn b. Ayyūb in 589/1193. Ibn al-Mudjāwir's drawing of the plan of Zabīd shows the walls as concentric rings. Ibn al-Daybaʿ noted the Ayyūbid wall as still standing in his day, although it had been restored many times, and its mud bricks had been replaced by baked bricks during the Rasūlid period. Most reports mention the existence of four main gates: Bāb al-Shabāriḳ in the east, Bāb Ghulayfiḳa in the west, Bāb Sihām in the north and Bāb Ḳurṭub in the south, although al-Khazradjī refers to the restoration of eight gates during the reign of sultan al-Mudjāhid ʿAlī (*r.* 721-64/1322-63), which suggests the existence of a double wall. The four gates which still stand in Zabīd have kept the same names, with the exception of Bāb Ghulayfiḳa, which became known, as early as the 8th/14th century, as Bāb al-Nakhīl. Zabīd's wall was torn down in 1045/1635-6 on the orders of the Imām al-Muʾayyad bi 'llāh b. al-Manṣūr following his victory against the Ottomans. It seems that Zabīd remained without a wall until it came under the control of Sharīf Ḥammūd of Abū ʿArīsh (*r.* 1798-1810). The wall was finally dismantled in the 1960s in order to sell its bricks. What remains of the walls is a trench which encircles the town.

Zabīd has 21,000 inhabitants according to the 1994 census, and is divided into four quarters: al-ʿAliyy, al-Djāmiʿ, al-Mudjanbadh and al-Djizʿ. It has a central covered market, which is rivalled by a new food market built in the mid-1980s on the northern side of town. The once important crafts of weaving and indigo dyeing have completely disappeared from Zabīd as a result of the influx of imported textiles and changes in fashion. Zabīd has lost its importance as a centre of Islamic learning, although its eighty-five surviving mosques and *madrasas* attest to its former glory.

The historical and aesthetic importance of Zabīd's distinctive religious and domestic brick architecture led to its being placed on UNESCO's list of historic towns in December 1993.

Bibliography: 1. Sources. Muḳaddasī, 84-5; Hamdānī, *Ṣifat Djazīrat al-ʿArab*, ed. Muḥammad al-Akwaʿ, Ṣanʿāʾ 1982, 73, 258; Khazradjī, *al-ʿUḳūd al-luʾluʾiyya*, ed. al-Akwaʿ, 2 vols. Ṣanʿāʾ 1983, ii, 181, 203; idem, *al-Kifāya wa 'l-iʿlām fī-man waliya al-Yaman*, Leiden ms. 805, 77-82; ʿAbd al-Raḥmān b. ʿAlī Ibn al-Daybaʿ, *al-Faḍl al-mazīd ʿalā Bughyat al-mustafīd fī akhbār madīnat Zabīd*, ed. J. Chelhod, Ṣanʿāʾ 1983, 47-50; Ibn al-Mudjāwir, *T. al-Mustabṣir*, ed. O. Löfgren, Leiden 1951-4, 63-90; ʿUmāra b. ʿAlī, *al-Mufīd fī akhbār Ṣanʿāʾ wa-Zabīd*, Ar. text and Eng. tr. in H.C. Kay, *Yaman: its early mediaeval history*, London 1892.

2. Studies. Carsten Niebuhr, *Travels through Arabia and other countries in the East*, tr. R. Heron, 2 vols. repr. Reading 1994, i, 281-4; Zāhir Riyāḍ, *Dawla ḥabashiyya fī 'l-Yaman*, in *al-Madjalla al-Taʾrīkhiyya al-Miṣriyya*, viii (1959), 101-30; Ṭāhir Muẓaffar al-ʿAmīd, *Bināʾ madīnat Zabīd fī 'l-Yaman*, in *Madjallat Kulliyyat al-Ādāb, Djāmiʿat Baghdād*, xiii (1970), 340-60; J. Chelhod, *Introduction à l'histoire sociale et urbaine de Zabîd*, in *Arabica*, xxv (1978), 48-88; Rāḍī Daghfūs, *Min maṣādir taʾrīkh al-Yaman fī 'l-ʿahd al-Islāmī: al-maṣādir al-taʾrīkhiyya li-dirāsat taʾrīkh madīnat Zabīd al-Yamaniyya fī 'l-fatra al-Islāmiyya al-wasīṭa*, in *CT*, nos. 109-10 (1980), 201-27; E.J. Keall, *The dynamics of Zabid and its hinterland: the survey of a town on the Tihamah plain of North Yemen*, in *World Archaeology*, xiv (1983), 378-92; ʿAbd al-Raḥmān al-Ḥaḍramī, *Djāmiʿat al-Ashāʿir, Zabīd*, Beirut 1985; Keall, *A few facts about Zabid*, in *Procs. Seminar for Arabian Studies*, xix (1989), 61-9; al-Ḥaḍramī, *Aswār Zabīd al-thalātha*, in *al-Iklīl*, xxii (1992), 137-43; Daghfūs, *La dynastie des Ziyādides à Zabīd (204-407/819-1016)*, in *CT*, nos. 162-3 (1992-3), 33-69; P. Bonnenfant, *Zabîd, anti-développement et potentialités*, in *Peuples Méditerranéens*, nos. 72-73 (juillet-déc. 1995), 219-42; Anne Meneley, *Tournaments of value. Sociability and hierarchy in a Yemeni town*, Toronto 1996; N. Sadek, *The mosques of Zabīd, Yemen. A preliminary report*, in *Procs. Seminar for Arabian Studies*, xxviii (1998), 239-45. (Noha Sadek)

al-**ZABĪDĪ, MUḤAMMAD MURTAḌĀ** [see muḥammad murtaḍā].

ZĀBUL, ZĀBULISTĀN, the name found in early Islamic times for a region of what is now eastern Afghānistān, roughly covering the modern Afghān provinces of Ghaznī and Zābul.

The early geographers describe what was a remote region on the far eastern frontiers of the *Dār al-Islām* in understandably vague terms as an extensive province with Ghazna [*q.v.*] as its centre. It thus emerges that it lay between Kābul and the Kābul river valley on the north and the territories around the confluence of the Helmand river and Arghandāb known as Zamīndāwar and al-Rukhkhadj [*q.vv.*], but the boundaries here were clearly very imprecise. The name appears in the 7th century Armenian geography as *Zaplastan* < MP *Zāpulistān* (Marquart, *Ērānšahr*, 39-40). Only one or two of the Arabic geographers mention it, e.g. al-Muḳaddasī, 299, who has *Djāwulistān*, but historians like al-Balādhurī and al-Ṭabarī were familiar with the name because of raids into it by the Muslims during the first three centuries or so of Islam. For long, Arab expansion here was checked by a line of powerful rulers with the title of Zunbīl (the resemblance between Zābul and Zunbīl must, however, be fortuitous), who were probably epigoni of the Southern Hephthalites [see hayāṭila]; the upland regions of Zābulistān seem to have been their summer quarters. Arab commanders had only occasional successes against these Zunbīls, such as when al-Manṣūr's commander Maʿn b. Zāʾida [*q.v.*] pursued this local ruler into Zābulistān (third quarter of the 8th century), and it was only the Ṣaffārid Yaʿḳūb b. al-Layth [*q.v.*] who in 256/870 penetrated through Zābulistān to Ghazna and Gardīz as far as Kābul (see C.E. Bosworth, *Sīstān under the Arabs from the Islamic conquest to the rise of the Ṣaffārids (30-250/651-864)*, Rome 1968, 82-3, 120; idem, *The history of the Saffārids of Sistan and the Maliks of Nimruz (247-861 to 949/1542-3)*, Costa Mesa and New York 1994, 99-103).

Marquart devoted a detailed and complex study to the region, its rulers and its religious cult, approximating its name to the Buddhist pilgrim Hüan Tsang's *Tsau-kiu-čʾa* (see *Bibl.*). The region was probably Islamised in the course of the 4th/10th century. Whether there was any connection between the older Zunbīls and the local family, the *Lawīks, who controlled Ghazna in the mid-century just before Alptigin [*q.v.*] and others of the Sāmānids' Turkish slave commanders took over there (cf. Bosworth, *Notes on the pre-Ghaznavid history of eastern Afghanistan*, in *IQ*, ix [1965], 16 ff.), is unknown. Sebüktigin's son Maḥmūd of Ghazna [see maḥmūd b. sebüktigin] married a wife from a family of chiefs in Zābulistān, and is accordingly sometimes referred to as Maḥmūd-i Zāwulī. From the 5th/11th century onwards, the name fades from usage, but Zābul has been revived since the 1964 administrative reform in Afghānistān for the name of a modern province (see above).

Bibliography (in addition to references given in the article): *Ḥudūd al-ʿālam*, tr. Minorsky, 112, comm. 345-6; Marquart, *Ērānšahr*, 37, 39-40, 247-8, 253-4, 292 ff.; Le Strange, *The lands of the Eastern Caliphate*, 334, 349; Marquart and J.J.M. de Groot, *Das Reich Zābul und der Gott Žūn vom 6.-9. Jahrhundert*, in G. Weil (ed.), *Festschrift Eduard Sachau*, Berlin 1915, 248-92. (C.E. Bosworth)

ZABŪR (A.), a term found in pre-Islamic poetry referring to a written text, and in the Ḳur'ān referring to divine scripture, in some contexts specifically to a scripture of David [see DĀWŪD], probably the Psalms.

The Arabic root *z-b-r* is associated with "stone" (*ḥidjāra*), and verbal forms from it convey such meanings as stoning, lining a well with stones or setting stones in walls according to an overlapping pattern (an unrelated word is *zubra*, said to designate a piece of iron). A further range of meanings associated with the root conveys the sense of reciting or writing a text. Here perhaps a dialect variation renders either *zabartu 'l-kitāb* or *dhabartu 'l-kitāb* as *ḳara'tuhu* "I recited/read it". Western scholarship has tended to view the first range of meaning as the root's original sense and the second range a result of Biblical traditions. However, with the recent discovery of South Arabian cursive writing on palm ribs and wooden sticks it has become evident that *zabara* and *zabūr* refer to this particular way of writing; see W.W. Müller, *L'écriture* zabūr *du Yémen pré-islamique dans la tradition arabe*, in J. Ryckmans, Müller and Yusuf M. Abdallah, *Textes du Yémen antique inscrits sur bois*, Louvain-la-Neuve 1994, 35-9. This is reflected in Imru' al-Ḳays referring to the remains of an abandoned camp *ka-khaṭṭ^i zabūr^in fī ʿasībiyy^in yamānī* "like the lines of a text written on Yemeni palm branches" and, in another context, *ka-khaṭṭ^i zabūr^in fī maṣāḥif^i ruhbānī* "like the lines of a text in the books of monks".

Western scholars have tended to understand *zabūr* as related to Hebrew *mizmōr*, with support from Arab grammarians who say that *faʿūl* may have a passive meaning, the equivalent of *mafʿūl*. The root meaning of Hebrew *z-m-r* is "to make music", with the noun form *mizmōr* found in the Hebrew Bible for a poetic hymn or psalm in praise of God, and with cognates in Syriac *mazmōrā* and Ethiopic *mazmūr*. One may also note the similarity between *zabūr* and Biblical Hebrew *zāmīr* "song". The exchange of *b* with *m* may, however, be considered problematical. It is also possible that the Hebrew/Aramaic/Syriac *dibbūr, dibbūrā/dʿvīrā*, meaning "speech" or "utterance" and often referring to revelation, represents a Semitic parallel. It may have influenced the meaning of the Arabic *zabara/dhabara* as referring to a written text in pre-Islamic Arabia, thereby conveying the meaning of sacred or revealed text, although this becomes less likely now that we know that *z-b-r* refers to South Arabia (see above). Pre-Ḳur'ānic rabbinic Hebrew *dibbūr* does refer to revelation (Gen. Rab. 44:6, Lev. Rabb. 1:4, Song Rabb. 1:2:2, Yeb. 5b, San. 99b), and even revelation to gentile prophets (Gen. Rab. 74:7). The poetic and linguistic evidence therefore suggest that *zabūr* referred to text and perhaps even sacred text among some pre-Islamic Arabian communities, whether Jewish, Christian, or practitioners of indigenous Arabian religious traditions. By the time of the Ḳur'ānic revelations, the term was already known to refer to, among other things, a written text of scripture.

The root *z-b-r* occurs in the Ḳur'ān thirteen times. In some contexts it occurs as a plural, *zubur*, in parallel with *bayyināt* ("proofs" III, 184, XVI, 43, XXXV, 25), *al-kitāb al-munīr* ("enlightening scripture" III, 184, XXXV, 25), *dhikr* ("the reminder" XVI, 43), and *tanzīl* ("revelation" or "bringing down" XXVI, 192-6), thereby referring in general to revealed books. The reference to *zubur* in XXIII, 53 seems to denote different scriptures over which certain groups are divided and which contrasts with the undivided community of Islam (*umma wāḥida*) religiously obedient to God. In sūra LIV, al-Ḳamar, the plural *zubur* refers to heavenly books in which are recorded human deeds (vv. 43, 52-3), probably referring to a divine ledger in which human behaviour is recorded (*mustaṭar*) as a basis for final judgment (cf. vv. 48, 54). In contrast, XVIII, 96, refers to pieces of iron (*zubar al-ḥadīd*) by which Dhu 'l-Ḳarnayn separates a people from the terror of Gog and Magog.

The singular *zabūr* occurs three times in the Ḳur'ān. Twice it refers specifically to a certain revelation given to David that is mentioned either within the context of prophethood in general (XVII, 54) or in a context referring to revelations given to Muḥammad and other prophets (IV, 163). In both places David is singled out as the recipient of a divinely given *zabūr* (*wa-ātaynā Dāwūd^a zabūr^an*). In XXI, 105, God is referred to as citing from what the context suggests is a recognised work: "We have written in the *zabūr* after the reminder (*min baʿd al-dhikr*) that My righteous servants shall inherit the earth (*anna 'l-arḍ yarithuhā ʿibādī al-ṣāliḥūn*)". This verse represents a close and rare linguistic parallel with the Hebrew Bible and, more pointedly, with Ps. xxxvii ascribed specifically to David (see vv. 9, 11, 29 which refer to the meek, the righteous or "those who wait upon the Lord" as they who shall inherit the earth (*yirshū 'āreṣ*); cf. K. Ahrens, *Christliches im Qoran*, in *ZDMG*, lxxxiv (1930), 29). It should be noted also in relation to Ḳur'ān, IV, 163, and XVII, 54, that the entire Biblical collection of Psalms is ascribed to David according to Jewish and Christian tradition.

Al-Ṭabarī collects the comments of early Ḳur'ānic exegetes in his *Tafsīr*, including definitions of terms such as *zabūr*, which vary depending on the verse. On XXI, 105, he records the meaning of *zubur* as "all the books of the prophets that God brought down to them" (Saʿīd b. Djubayr, Ibn Zayd), "the books revealed to the prophets after Moses" (Ibn ʿAbbās, al-Ḍaḥḥāk), and "a specific book revealed to David" (ʿĀmir, al-Shaʿbī). Al-Ṭabarī also defines the term in relation to its context. In his commentary on III, 184, it is a generic term for a book based on pre-Islamic poetic evidence. On IV, 163, he writes, "It is the name of the book that was revealed to David, just as He named the book that was revealed to Moses as the Torah and that which was revealed to Jesus as the Gospel and that which was revealed to Muḥammad as the Furḳān, because that is the name by which what was revealed to David was known. The Arabs say *zabūr Dāwūd*, and because of that the rest of the peoples know his book."

Apart from the question of the term *zabūr*, many passages in the Ḳur'ān that remind us of the Bible are reminiscent of the Psalms. It is likely that some form or forms of a Psalter circulated in pre-Islamic Arabia immediately prior to the rise of Islam. A fragment of a translation of the Psalms, dated on palaeographical grounds to the 2nd/8th century, the oldest known specimen of Christian-Arabic literature, was identified in Damascus by B. Violet. It contains an Arabic translation of Ps. lxxviii. 20-31, 51-61, in Greek majuscule writing. Al-Kindī, in his *Risāla* (composed *ca.* 204/819), and Ibn Ḳutayba, as cited in Ibn al-Djawzī's *Wafā'*, quote verses from the Psalms in literal translation. ʿAlī b. Rabban al-Ṭabarī [*q.v.*] devotes a chapter of his "Book of Religion and Empire" (*ca.* 240/854) to the Psalms, and al-Masʿūdī (*Tanbīh*, 112) mentions Arabic translations of the Bible which include the Psalms. Recensions of the Arabic translation-commentary by Saʿd b. Yūsuf al-Fayyūmī, i.e. Saʿadyā Gā'ōn (d. 330/942 [see SAʿADYĀ BEN YŌSĒF) of the Hebrew Bible, including the Psalms, exists to this day.

Bibliography: See also Ṭabarī, *Tafsīr*, Beirut 1405/1984, iv, 198, vi, 27-8, xvii, 102-5; I. Goldziher, *Ueber muhammedanische Polemik gegen Ahl al-kitâb*, in *ZDMG*, xxxii (1878) (= *Gesammelte Schriften*, ii, 1-47), 351-2, 371, 377; T.P. Hughes, *A dictionary of Islam*, London 1885, 698; B. Violet, *Ein zweisprachiges Psalmfragment aus Damaskus*, in *OLZ*, Berlin, iv (1901), 384-403, 425-41, 475-88; L. Cheikho, *Quelques légendes islamiques apocryphes*, in *MFOB*, iv (1910), 40 ff., 47 ff.; J. Horovitz, *Koranische Untersuchungen*, Berlin 1926, 69 ff.; A. Jeffery, *The foreign vocabulary of the Qur'ān*, Baroda 1938, 148-9.

(J. Horovitz-[R. Firestone])

ZADJAL (a.), the name of a genre of vernacular strophic poetry that acquired literary status around 500/1100 in al-Andalus. It was cultivated by numerous Andalusian poets (the most famous being Ibn Ḳuzmān [*q.v.*]), later also spreading to the Maghrib and the Arabic-speaking East. Since the 7th/13th century its strophic structure is also encountered in the poetry of several Romance languages. In present-day Arabic the term *zadjal* may denote various types of dialect poems, even those with monorhyme. The non-technical meaning of *zadjal* is "a voice, sound or cry, or the uttering of the voice, etc.; a trilling, or quavering of the voice; or a prolonging of the voice, and modulating it sweetly, also a play, sport" (cf. Lane, *s.v.*). This etymology makes it probable that *zadjal* originally referred to sung poetry, songs (cf. also below, *The performance of the* zadjal).

1. In mediaeval Islam.

The language

The language of the Andalusian *zadjal* is only rarely the pure and regular Andalusian dialect. Since the poems were hardly ever really popular products, but mostly works of educated poets who, to be sure, endeavoured to speak like the people but also tried hard to bestow literary quality on their poems, and since the poets were accustomed to write in the Classical language, and were subject to the strictures of metre, rhyme, and length of line, one finds time and again influences and intrusions from the "higher register" of the Classical language and bastardisations in both directions (cf. F. Corriente, *Poesía dialectal*, 39). Some scholars go even further and speak of a "hybrid language drawn from both the spoken language and the literary" (T.J. Gorton, in *JAL*, ix [1978], 34; similarly A. Jones in *JSS*, xxvii [1982], 129, and Abu Haidar, *A study*). In the poems of al-Shushtarī (d. 668/1269 [*q.v.*]), consisting of *zadjals* as well as *muwashshahs* (sometimes difficult to distinguish), one encounters great linguistic multiformity. The gamut runs from poems entirely composed in Classical Arabic (mostly *muwashshahs*) via various intermediate stages (dialect poems with Classical "intrusions", e.g. nouns with *iʿrāb*, and, on the other side, high-register poems with dialectal insertions) down to *zadjals* composed entirely in Andalusian Arabic (cf. F. Corriente, *Poesía . . . aš-Šuštarī*, 19). In addition, one finds in al-Shushtarī also poems in Maghribī or Maghribī-influenced language; even poems in Eastern dialects, or approximations of such, and in mixtures of dialects seem to occur. The language of the older Eastern—Egyptian, Syrian, and ʿIrāḳī—*zadjdjālūn*, such as ʿAlī b. Muḳātil, al-Amshāṭī, Ṣafī al-Dīn al-Ḥillī *et al.* has not been much studied. Apparently these poets, whose models were Ibn Ḳuzmān and the other Andalusian *zadjdjālūn*, tried to imitate the Andalusian dialect in their *zadjals*, but did not have complete command of it (cf. the examples in al-Ḥillī, *ʿĀṭil*, 99 ff.; Ibn Ḥidjdja, 104 ff.; cf. Corriente, in *JAL*, xxviii [1997], 134-5).

Strophic structure

The basic form of the Andalusian *zadjal* ("*zadjal* proper") has the following rhyme scheme: *aa bbb a, ccc a, ddd a*, etc. If we call rhymes that change from stanza to stanza separate rhymes, and rhymes that keep re-occurring throughout the poem common rhymes, we may describe the present strophic structure as follows. The poem starts with two common rhyme lines (*maṭlaʿ*). The following first stanza consists of three lines with separate rhyme and one line with common rhyme (acting as "stanza closure"). The remaining stanzas all have the same rhyme scheme as the first. The rhyme of the last line in each stanza is thus the same throughout the poem and echos the rhyme of the initial *maṭlaʿ*. It is important to note that the rhyme scheme of the stanza closures (common rhyme lines) in the "*zadjal* proper" constitutes one-half of the rhyme scheme of the introductory lines (*maṭlaʿ*). This is true also for the less common variant with the rhyme scheme *abab ccc ab, ddd ab*, etc. *Zadjals* proper without *maṭlaʿ*, i.e. with the rhyme scheme *bbb a, ccc a*, etc., are rare in the early period; a few examples can, however, be found in the *Dīwān* of al-Shushtarī (e.g. nos. 40, 42). Ibn Ḳuzmān uses in the large majority of cases the structure of the *zadjal* proper (about two-thirds of the extant poems). The remaining poems have a different structure: The stanza closures here consist of at least two lines and always reflect exactly the introductory lines (if any), thus e.g. *aa bbb aa, ccc aa*, etc.; or *ab ccc ab, ddd ab*, etc.; or (without *maṭlaʿ*) *dedede abcb, fgfgfg abcb, hihihi abcb*, etc. Since this structure corresponds exactly to that of the *muwashshah* [*q.v.*]—some of the poems are known to be contrafacts (*muʿāraḍāt*) of famous *muwashshahs* (cf. Stern, 171 ff.)—and since these poems mostly also display the other peculiarity of the *muwashshah*, i.e. the *khardja*, they are called "*muwashshah*-like *zadjals*".

In length the *zadjals* vary greatly. While the *muwashshah*-like type, like the *muwashshah* itself, mostly consists of five or six (and occasionally up to eleven) stanzas, the *zadjal* proper may be much longer. The longest poem of Ibn Ḳuzmān is no. 9; it consists of 42 stanzas.

Terminology

Ṣafī al-Dīn al-Ḥillī, the most important theorist of the genre, calls *muzannam* those *zadjals* in which, contrary to rule, the Classical language (*iʿrāb*) is preponderant. To denote jocular or obscene *zadjals* he uses the term *bullayḳ*, those that contain lampoons he terms *ḳarḳī*, and for those containing admonitions and wisdom he uses *mukaffir* (*ʿĀṭil*, 10). The terminology for the stanza and its parts is not uniform with the theorists. In al-Ḥillī, the entire stanza is called *bayt*, the introductory lines *maṭlaʿ*, and all the lines with common rhyme—not only those in the last stanza (!)—*khardja*. He applies the terms *ḳufl* and, more rarely, *ghuṣn* indifferently to single lines, irrespective of whether they have common or separate rhyme (cf. Hoenerbach, *ʿĀṭil*, German part, 20). The terminology of Ibn Saʿīd/Ibn Khaldūn is the clearest and most frequently used today; according to it, *bayt* = "stanza", *ḳufl* = "line with separate rhyme", and *simṭ* = "line with common rhyme" (cf. muwashshah).

The performance of the zadjal—zadjal *as poetry set to music*

We may assume as certain that the *zadjal* originally was sung; this assumption is suggested already by the etymology (cf. above). This, however, in no way means that a tune was composed right away to each *zadjal*. The poems of Ibn Ḳuzmān were in all likelihood recited as a rule, and not sung. This is not true of the *zadjals* of al-Shushtarī; they were conceived as songs or at least imitate the structure of songs. In al-Shushtarī's *Dīwān*, one encounters numerous *zadjals* and *muwashshaḥs* in which the refrain line(s) are written out. This allows us to address the question of *zadjal* "performance". That the refrain line(s) were meant for a chorus can not only be deduced from internal evidence but is also attested in parallels in Hebrew poetry (cf. Stern, 16-17). In al-Shushtarī, there are *inter alia* poems with genuine refrain (e.g. nos. 14, 68, 84), and poems with so-called internal refrain (e.g. nos. 44-8, 50, 82, 83). The former are characterised in their basic form by the following scheme: *(aa) AA bbb a AA, ccc a AA, ddd a AA*, etc.; the latter, in contrast, have the following scheme: *a A bbb a A, ccc a A, ddd a A*, etc. (where A represents the refrain line in which the rhyme of the *maṭlaʿ*, i.e. the common rhyme, is taken up again). Thus, while in the first, the entire *maṭlaʿ* is repeated by the chorus as a refrain after each stanza (according to the Hebrew testimonies, the *maṭlaʿ*, too, sung first by the soloist will be repeated immediately by the chorus), in the second only the second line of the *maṭlaʿ* will be repeated by the chorus. Exact parallels to this performance technique exist not only in Hebrew-Andalusian poetry but also in the more or less contemporaneous Romance *zadjal* (thus in numerous *Cantigas de Santa María*).

Metrics and rhyme

The metrics of the Andalusian *zadjal*, like that of the *muwashshaḥ*, were controversial for a long time. However, in recent years a consensus has to a large extent been reached among Arabists. Most agree that practically all *zadjal* (and *muwashshaḥ*) metres can be scanned quantitatively, which means that the poets must have intended quantitative metres; they agree also that, apart from regular Khalīlian metres (*ramal, khafīf* and *basīṭ*), they also used numerous non-Khalīlian quantitative metres and feet ("extended, or expanded, Khalīlian system", according to Gorton, Jones and Latham). The question how occasional irregularities are to be explained is still controversial. While Corriente brings in his hypothesis of an "Andalusian accentual adaptation of *ʿarūḍ*" (cf. MUWASHSHAḤ), according to which e.g. unstressed long syllables may be counted as short, other scholars point to similar metrical licences that occasionally already occur in Classical Arabic poetry, especially in *radjaz* (cf. Ullmann, *Rağazpoesie*, 69 ff.), thus shortening (*idjtizāʾ*) and lengthening (*ishbāʿ*) of vowels (Gorton, in *JAL*, vi [1975], 24 ff.; Schoeler, in *BO*, xl [1983], 311-22; idem, in M. Forstner (ed.), *Festgabe für H.-R. Singer*, ii, 887-909). All sides also agree today that, in rare cases, one has to reckon with foot substitution (a procedure first noted by Corriente).

The rules for the rhyme in *zadjal* are stricter than they are in *ḳaṣīd*. The most important difference is that words with /ū/ or /ī/ before the rhyme consonant (*īK*/*ūK*) do not rhyme.

Themes

On the themes treated in Ibn Ḳuzmān's *zadjals*, see IBN ḲUZMĀN. However, a particular theme deserves to be pointed out here, one that is sometimes subsumed under the category of *madīḥ*, although the relevant poems differ greatly from the other praise poems. They are request or begging poems in which the poet, due to his impecuniousness and in a melancholy mood, requests a lamb from a sponsor for the *ʿĪd al-Aḍḥā* (nos. 8, 48, 82, 85, 118). Since the same theme is also treated in one of the extant *zadjals* of Ibn Ḳuzmān's predecessor Ibn Rāshid (cf. below), but never occurs in a *muwashshaḥ* or a *ḳaṣīda*, one has to assume that this style belongs to the genre of *zadjal* in general. The original *zadjal* was possibly a popular or minstrel request song, introduced into élite literature by Ibn Rāshid and Ibn Ḳuzmān. In support of this one might adduce that also in the Romance *zadjal*, which is also originally a minstrel genre, request poems are typical (Juan Ruiz, *Libro de buen amor*, stanzas 1650 ff., 1656 ff.; Alfonso Alvarez de Villasandino, *El Cancionero de Baena*, nos. 196, 219). The *zadjals* (and *muwashshaḥs*) of al-Shushtarī, the other great *zadjdjāl* of whom a *Dīwān* is extant, are all of mystical content. It is again worth noting that the Romance *zadjal* was also adopted into the service of religion (*Cantigas de Santa María* of Alfonso el Sabio, Juan Ruiz, Villasandino; *Laude* of Jacopone da Todi).

The earliest poets

Some information on this point is provided by Ibn Ḳuzmān; further indications can be gleaned from the admittedly late and non-Andalusian poetics of the genre written by al-Ḥillī (*ʿĀṭil*, 66) as well as in Ibn Saʿīd/Ibn Khaldūn (*Muḳaddima*, iii, 404). Ibn Ḳuzmān names two predecessors: in the introduction to his extant *Dīwān*, 18-19, he refers to a certain (al-)Akhṭal b. Numāra, from whom he quotes a few fragments. In the poems themselves he mentions Yakhlaf b. Rāshid (no. 134/10/2; no. 186/1/1). Ibn Rāshid appears to have been a slightly older contemporary of Ibn Ḳuzmān; two fragments of his have been preserved (*Muḳaddima*, iii, 407; Stern, 185, 193 ff.). Al-Ḥillī, *ʿĀṭil*, 16-17, answers the question as to the first *zadjdjāl* by giving a list of names in two groups. Among these only the already-mentioned Yakhlaf b. Rāshid can be considered a precursor of Ibn Ḳuzmān.

The genesis of the zadjal

About the genesis of the *zadjal* genre the indigenous tradition is much more reticent than about that of the *muwashshaḥ*. The term *zadjal* for a popular poem or song is indeed attested early (in Aḥmad b. ʿAbd Allāh b. ʿAbd al-Raʾūf's treatise on *ḥisba*, possibly from the first half of the 4th/10th century, and in the *K. ʿAbd al-Malik al-usḳuf* from the middle of the 5th/11th century; cf. most recently J.T. Monroe, in *Oral Tradition*, iv [1989], 45 ff.). It is, however, very unlikely that the songs mentioned are *zadjals* in the later technical sense. A vernacular distich from the 4th/10th century has been identified as a kind of "proto-*zadjal*"; the lines rhyme according to the Arabic, not the Romance, system: *laban ummuh fī fummuh—rās ban Ḥafṣūn fī ḥukmuh* (Ibn Ḥayyān, *Muḳtabas*, v, 64). This distich might probably be considered a parallel to the vernacular *khardjas* attested much later (cf. MUWASHSHAḤ) (thus Corriente, *Poesía dialectal*, 79-80).

The often-raised question concerning the derivation of the strophic structure and the rhyme scheme of the genuine *zadjal* (*aa bbb a, ccc a*, etc.) can be answered today with certainty: this structure has been taken from the *musammaṭ* [*q.v.*]. A special form of the *musammaṭ*, attested in the East at the latest since the 4th/10th century, displays this very structure. So far, three specimens of this type have become known: (Ps.?-)Ḥammād al-Rāwiya, in *Aghānī*, v, 27-8; Abū Nuwās, *Dīwān*, ed. Wagner, iii, 332-3 (no. 287 in the recension of Ḥamza al-Iṣfahānī); and (Ps.-)Imruʾ al-Ḳays, in Ibn Rashīḳ, *ʿUmda*, i, 179; to these should be added a Persian imitation by Amīr Muʿizzī (d. *ca.* 520/1126) (*Dīwān*, 597 ff.; for these *musammaṭs*, see Schoeler, in *AS*, li [1997], 618 ff.). Three of these poems can be read either as a *musammaṭ* or as a *ḳaṣīda* with regularly applied internal rhyme. This is impossible with the *musammaṭ* of (Ps.-)Imruʾ al-Ḳays, since here all lines have the same length; this poem thus exactly follows the structure of the *zadjal* in every respect.

Since Judaeo-Spanish poets (e.g. Ibn Gabirol) use this rhyme scheme already in the 5th/11th century in Hebrew liturgical poems (cf. Monroe, *op. cit.*, 44), this might be considered evidence that Arabic *zadjals* (in the technical sense) already existed at the time, to be imitated by the Hebrew poets. (The hypothetical Arabic models may have been popular or minstrel songs that had not yet ascended to élite literature.) However, this assumption is far from certain: the Hebrew poets may also have used as their models Arabic *musammaṭs* of the above-mentioned structure. The derivation of the structure of the *muwashshaḥ*-like *zadjal* poses no difficulties: it is simply an imitation of the *muwashshaḥ* in the vernacular.

The trend to compose poetry in the colloquial soon also affected the *ḳaṣīd*: Mudghalīs (or Madghalīs), a younger contemporary of Ibn Ḳuzmān, composed so-called *ḳaṣāʾid zadjaliyya*, of which numerous examples have been preserved (ed. W. Hoenerbach and H. Ritter, in *Oriens*, v [1952], 269-30). Summing up, the following can be said about the genesis of the *zadjal*: (1) Lines of poetry in the vernacular are attested in al-Andalus already in the 4th/10th century. (2) At a certain point in time (most likely in the 5th/11th century) this poetry, under the influence of a specific type of *musammaṭ*, acquired the rhyme structure *aa bbb a, ccc a*, etc. (3) Finally, probably shortly before the time of Ibn Ḳuzmān (around 500/*ca.* 1100), poems of this type attained to literary status. Deriving the *zadjal* from hypothetical Romance models, as most recently tried again by Monroe (*op. cit.*), is speculative and seems to overlook the existing Arabic models.

Spread of the zadjal

Born in al-Andalus, the *zadjal* soon spread to the East. Outside Spain *zadjals* are first encountered in the Maghrib (cf. Stern, 200 ff.). There the genre was cultivated down to the middle of the 10th/16th century in the Andalusian vernacular, which had become the "classical" language of the *zadjal*. (The *malḥūn* [*q.v.*], written in the Maghribī dialect since the 10th/16th century, although also called *zadjal* and *ḳaṣīda zadjaliyya*, is entirely different from the "classical" *zadjal*.) In the first half of the 8th/14th century, imitations of literary *zadjals* in the manner of Ibn Ḳuzmān became very popular with court poets in the Mamlūk and Mongol spheres of influence, i.e. Egypt, Syria, and ʿIrāḳ (cf. W. Hoenerbach, in *Homenaje a Millás Vallicrosa*, i, Barcelona 1954, 725). In the 11th/17th century at the latest, minstrel *zadjals* in Egyptian, or would-be Egyptian, vernacular are attested in the written record (on these cf. Schoeler, in *Festgabe für H.R. Singer*, ii 902 ff., and M. Voegeli, *Manṣūbāt Ṣafā l-ʿAiš*, Lizentiatsarbeit, Basel 1994 unpubl.). Starting in the 19th century, scholars, initially all European, have collected and published folksongs from the Near East; these are called *zadjal*, especially in Lebanon (the terminology is, however, confused), and they often, but not always, display an identical or similar structure to that of its Andalusian counterpart (cf. Jargy, *La poésie*, with bibl., 321 ff.).

From the 13th century onwards, several Romance literatures have produced poems that have the exact same structure of the *zadjal* (in Galician: the majority of the *Cantigas de Santa María* of Alfonso X [1221-84]; in Castilian: *estribotes* and *villancicos*, some poems in the *Libro de Buen Amor* of Juan Ruiz [1283-1351]; in Provençal: *dansas* and *baladas*; in French: *virelais* and *ballades*; and in Italian: *ballate, frottole, laude* of Jacopone da Todi [1236-1306]). Since one has here complete identity of the forms (predominantly poems of the rhyme structure *aa bbb a, ccc a*, etc., thus "*zadjals* proper"), and since in the performance there is evidence also for identical ways of presentation (use of the introductory lines as refrains—thus in many *Cantigas* of Alfonso X—as well as internal refrain), an assumption of a direct dependence of the Romance "*zadjal*" on the Arabic would seem difficult to counter (cf. Schoeler, *Muwaššaḥ und Zağal*, 456-8).

Collections of Andalusian zadjals *and works on poetics*

The only two extant *dīwān*s are the *Iṣābat al-aghrāḍ fī dhikr al-aʿrāḍ* of Ibn Ḳuzmān (presumably only a selection from his poems, and even that not complete in the only extant manuscript) and the *Dīwān* of al-Shushtarī. The first and most important poetics of the *zadjal* (and other vernacular genres) is the *K. al-ʿĀṭil* of Ṣafī al-Dīn al-Ḥillī (d. *ca.* 749/1348 [*q.v.*]). The work contains numerous poems, from the Andalusian "classics" (among them poems by Ibn Ḳuzmān not contained in the *Iṣāba*) as well as from the author himself and other Eastern poets. Strongly dependent on this work is the *Bulūgh al-amal fī fann al-zadjal* by Ibn Ḥidjdja al-Ḥamawī (d. 837/1434). In contrast, the anonymous author of *Dafʿ al-shakk wa 'l-mayn fī taḥrīr al-fannayn* (9th/15th century) develops his own ideas. The *Safīna* of ʿAlī b. Mubārakshāh is also an important source for otherwise lost *zadjals*, even for some by Ibn Ḳuzmān (cf. Hoenerbach, in al-Ḥillī, *ʿĀṭil*, German part, 8 ff.).

Bibliography: 1. Sources. Ibn Ḳuzmān al-Ḳurṭubī, *Dīwān. Iṣābat al-aghrāḍ fī dhikr al-aʿrāḍ*, ed. F. Corriente, Cairo 1415/1995 (the best among the existing editions, in Arabic script; supersedes all earlier editions, including E. García Gómez, *Todo Ben Quzmān*, i-iii, Madrid 1972, which, due to its many manipulations in the text, can only be used with the utmost caution); Abu 'l-Ḥasan al-Shushtarī, *Dīwān*, ed. ʿA.S. al-Nashshār, Alexandria 1960; Šuštarī, *Poesía estrófica . . . atribuida al-místico granadino*, ed. and tr. F. Corriente, Madrid 1988 (ed. in transliteration); W. Hoenerbach and H. Ritter, *Neue Materialien zum Zacal. I. Ibn Quzmān*, in *Oriens*, iii (1950), 266-315, *II. Mudġalīs*, in *ibid.*, v (1952), 269-301; F. Corriente, *Textos andalusíes de cejeles no quzmanianos en Alḥillī, Ibn Saʿīd Almaġribī, Ibn Xaldūn y en la Geniza*, in *Foro Hispanico*, vii (1994), 61-104; *Ṣafīyaddin Ḥillī. Die Vulgärarabische Poetik al-Kitāb al-ʿĀṭil al-ḥālī wal-muraḫḫaṣ al-ġālī*, ed. Hoenerbach, Wiesbaden 1956; Ibn Ḥidjdja al-Ḥamawī, *Bulūgh al-amal fī fann al-zadjal*, ed. R.M. al-Ḳurayshī, Damascus 1974; Shams al-Dīn Muḥammad Nawādjī, *ʿUḳūd al-laʾāl fi 'l-muwashshaḥāt wa 'l-azdjāl*, ed. ʿA. al-Shihābī, Baghdād 1982.

2. Studies (only monographs and comprehensive studies in articles; see also the *Bibl.* to MUWASHSHAḤ, and H. Heijkoop and O. Zwartjes, *A supplementary bibliography of Andalusī strophic poetry*, in *BiOr*, lv (1998), 642-726). S.M. Stern, *Studies on Ibn Quzmān*, in *Hispano-Arabic strophic poetry*, selected and ed. L.P. Harvey, Oxford 1974, 166-203; ʿA. al-Ahwānī, *al-Zadjal fī 'l-Andalus*, Cairo 1957; I. ʿAbbās, *Taʾrīkh al-adab al-andalusī*, ii, [5]Beirut 1978, 252-79; J. Abu Haidar, *A study of certain linguistic, metrical, and literary aspects of the Dīwān of Ibn Quzmān*, Ph.D. diss., London 1975, unpubl.; O. Zwartjes, *Love-songs from al-Andalus. History, structure and meaning of the* Kharja, Leiden 1997 (with comprehensive bibl.); F. Corriente, *Poesía dialectal árabe y romance en Alandalús*, Madrid 1997 (with comprehensive bibl.); G. Schoeler, *Muwaššaḥ und Zağal. Einfluss auf die Troubadour-Dichtung?*, in *Neues Handbuch der Literaturwissenschaft*, Bd. 5, *Orientalisches*

Mittelalter, ed. W. Heinrichs, Wiesbaden 1990, 440-64; J.T. Monroe, *Zajal and muwashshaha*, in S.K. Jayyusi (ed.), *The legacy of Muslim Spain*, Leiden etc. 1992, 398-419; S. Jargy, *La poésie populaire traditionelle chantée au proche-orient arabe*, Paris-The Hague 1970 (with comprehensive bibl.); P. Le Gentil, *Le Virelai et le villancico. Le problème des origines arabes*, Paris 1954; M. Frenk Alatorre, *Estudios sobre lírica antigua*, Madrid 1978, 309-26.

On the metrical debate. T.J. Gorton, *The metre of Ibn Quzmān: a "classical" approach*, in *JAL*, vi (1975), 1-29; idem, *Zajal and Muwaššaḥ: the continuing metrical debate*, in *JAL*, ix (1978), 32-40; Schoeler, *Ibn Quzmāns Metrik*, in *BiOr*, xl (1983), 311-32; F. Corriente, *Again on the metrical system of muwaššaḥ and zajal*, in *JAL*, xvii (1986), 34-49; Schoeler, *Über die Metrik andalusischer und nicht-andalusischer Zaǧals*, in M. Forstner (ed.), *Festgabe für H.-R. Singer*, Frankfurt 1991, ii, 887-909; Corriente, *Further remarks on the modified ʿarūḍ*, in *JAL*, xxviii (1997), 123-40. (G. Schoeler)

2. In modern times.

Zadjal is used nowadays as a term for a poem in vernacular Arabic, often one meant to be sung, or sung directly when improvised. The term is also used for vernacular poetry in general. The *zadjal* poet is called *zadjdjāl* as well as—in the context of improvisation—*ḳawwāl* [see SHĀʿIR. 1. E].

In a restricted sense, *zadjal* may refer specifically to a non-classical strophic poem of the *murabbaʿ* type [see MUSAMMAṬ], with four-line stanzas and an optional prelude (*maṭlaʿ* or *lāzima*), rhyming *aa bbba ccca* . . . (thus corresponding with the prevalent form of its Andalusian namesake, see above under 1.), or some other related pattern. In informal parlance, the term may include altogether different types of poems.

In its broadest sense, *zadjal* covers a wide range of subjects and a great variety of forms with a correspondingly large arsenal of technical terms not always clearly defined in the literature. Sometimes it comes close to being the equivalent of the general expressions *shiʿr ʿāmmī* ("colloquial poetry"), *shiʿr shaʿbī* (literally "popular", but often synonymous with "non-classical poetry") and *shiʿr ghayr muʿrab* ("poetry without *iʿrāb*", i.e. with non-classical grammar), and of such regional expressions as *malḥūn* [*q.v.*] (used in Morocco, Algeria, Yemen), *shiʿr ḳawmī* (Sudan, Lebanon), *ḥumaynī* (Yemen), and *shiʿr nabaṭī* [*q.v.*] (Arabia). But *zadjal* does not seem to embrace all vernacular poetry: it does not refer, as *shiʿr shaʿbī* may, to the truly popular poetry of folk literature. *Zadjal* may be couched in the "popular" language, but it is often practised by the educated and enjoyed by them as much as by the illiterate. For their part, the members of the modern Egyptian school of colloquial poetry, for whom the term *zadjal* has become associated with a traditionalism that is out of touch with modern ideas, stress the fact that they write poems rather than unsophisticated *zadjal*s.

Elsewhere, no such negative associations are involved, as when al-Djirārī (50-61) argues for the adoption of the term *zadjal*—rather than *malḥūn* or ten other names—as the appropriate designation for any poem in Moroccan Arabic, or in Lebanon where *zadjal* features at festivals with poetic duelling between *zadjal* poets and their accompanying troupes (*djawḳāt*, sg. *djawḳa*) and enjoys a huge popularity with wide sections of the public (Haydar, 202-10) as well as with the government (cf. the conference that it sponsored where a resolution was passed calling for the teaching of colloquial poetry in schools and universities: *al-Muʾtamar al-awwal li 'l-shiʿr al-ʿāmmī al-lubnānī 1995*, [Beirut] 1995-6, 202). The media, for their part, focus regularly on the *zadjal* (e.g. six pages on "500 years of colloquial poetry" in *al-Nahār* newspaper of 6 March 1999).

Lecerf (234-5), writing in 1932, divides the Lebanese forms of *zadjal* into the sung genres of *mawwāl* [see MAWĀLIYĀ], *ʿatāba* [*q.v.*], *mīdjānā*, *dalʿōna* and *shurūḳī* (*ab ab ab ab*); and the recited genres of *ḳaṣīd* (*ab ab ab ab*), *maṭlaʿ* or *muʿannā* (predominant type *aaba bbba ccca*), *ḳarrādī* (heptasyllabic) and *djannāz*. He notes a preference for *shurūḳī* and *ḳaṣīd* in Djabal ʿĀmil as against *muʿannā* and *ḳarrādī* in the Lebanese mountains (221). The subject matter of Lebanese *zadjal* is varied: the topics of Khalīl's thematic anthology are nature, beauty, love, songs, customs, wisdom, the fatherland, society, and politics.

The related Palestinian improvised poetry (*shiʿr murtadjal* [see IRTIDJĀL]) is divided by Sbait (214) into the genres of *ʿatāba*, *ḥidā*, *farʿāwī*, *mḥōraba*, *mʿannā*, *ḳarrādī* and *ḳaṣīda*.

In common with the vernacular poetry of other regions, ʿIrāḳī poetry has forms that show many characteristics of Lebanese, Syrian and Palestinian *zadjal*, but which are not normally designated as such. *Zadjal* is said to be extinct in ʿIrāḳ (Mādjid Shubbar, *al-Adab al-shaʿbī al-ʿirāḳī*, London 1995, 164-5), but it may be noted that the ʿIrāḳī poet ʿAbbūd al-Karkhī (1861-1946) is referred to as a *zadjal* poet (*shāʿir zadjalī*) in the introduction to the second edition of vol. i of his *Dīwān al-Karkhī* (Baghdād 1956).

As a literary form between the "high" *fuṣḥā* literature in standard Arabic and the literature in the colloquial, *zadjal* employs an intermediate language with characteristics originating from both. The metre appears to be quantitative and akin to those of the classical Arabic system [see ʿARŪḌ], but extended with non-classical patterns and rules. According to D. Semah (*Modern Arabic zajal*, 82-3), "No evidence has ever been given to support the often-repeated claim that Arabic *zajal* is not composed according to the quantitative Khalilian metres, but is cast in syllabic metres, in which rhythmic regularity depends only on an equal number of syllables, irrespective of their length", but he qualifies this statement by adding that, with its seven syllables of random quantity, the Lebanese *ḳarrādī* is an exception. Nor does he include the prosody of Maghribī vernacular poetry where the issue appears to be not so clear-cut [see MALḤŪN].

In 19th-century Egypt, *zadjal* widened its scope; it had entertained the élite as a literary pastime, and, in the case of the religious *zadjal*, expressed the devotion of pious Ṣūfīs, but it subsequently found a new function in the broader socio-political context of populist patriotism, especially in the wake of the ʿUrābī [*q.v.*] revolt. This development was furthered by the growing importance of the press and the rise of many specialised satirical magazines such as those under the editorship of Yaʿḳūb Ṣannūʿ (1839-1912 [see ABŪ NAḌḌĀRA]) and ʿAbd Allāh al-Nadīm (1845-96 [*q.v.*]). For his part, Muḥammad ʿUthmān Djalāl (1828-98 [*q.v.*]) not only wrote *zadjal*s but translated Western drama and other literary forms into vernacular poetry, thereby heralding the heightened literary status that the spoken idiom was to gain in a later era.

In the 20th century, *zadjal* continued to be a voice for political and social criticism. Satirical periodicals were launched by *zadjdjāl*s such as Bayram al-Tūnisī (1893-1961 [*q.v.*]), Ḥusayn Shafīḳ al-Miṣrī (1882-1948), Maḥmūd Ramzī Naẓīm (1887-1959) and Badīʿ Khayrī in Egypt, and ʿAbbūd al-Karkhī in ʿIrāḳ. In the same period, the Lebanese poet Rashīd Nakhla (1873-1939), who in 1932 received the title of *amīr al-zadjal*, is said to have combined a political career with the writing of 18,000 lines in vernacular Arabic, mostly in the sphere of traditional love poetry but with a new vitality that contributed, as did the poetry of al-Tūnisī and al-Karkhī in their countries, to the rise of the new trends in vernacular poetry. The transition to this new stage is particularly visible in the work of Mīshāl Ṭrād (1912-98) in Lebanon, Fu'ād Ḥaddād (1927-85) and Ṣalāḥ Djāhīn (1930-86) in Egypt, and Muẓaffar al-Nawwāb (b. 1934 in ʿIrāḳ). Their poetry moves from local to universal issues, from the concerns of the collectivity to those of the individual, from traditional forms towards a colloquial "free verse" or *shiʿr ḥurr* [see SHIʿR], and is couched in a new language with sophisticated imagery. There is a notable shift, for instance, from Djāhīn's early nationalistic *zadjals* to his volumes *Rubāʿiyyāt* ("Quatrains") and *Ḳaṣāḳīṣ waraḳ* ("Confetti"). This trend is continued by Sayyid Ḥidjāb in his *Ṣayyād wi-djinniyya* and is present in the work of a poet like ʿAbd al-Raḥmān al-Abnūdī (b. 1938). There is now a growing awareness with a wider public that the vernacular is as suitable a vehicle for the highest literary creation as any other language, as long as it is used poetically. It has even been suggested that the new colloquial poetry stands some chance of becoming the true successor of an obsolete and exhausted traditional *fuṣḥā* poetry (Semah, *op. cit.*, 91).

The appreciation of modern *fuṣḥā* and modern colloquial verse as equal partners had already surfaced with Luwīs ʿAwaḍ (1914-90) in his *Plutoland* (*Pulūtūlānd wa-ḳaṣā'id ukhrā*, Cairo 1947), and in the work of Saʿīd ʿAḳl (b. 1912) who, by using his adapted Latin script for the vernacular poems in his collection *Yāra* (1961), has distanced himself from tradition more than anyone before him.

The new perception of the role of the vernacular has not, however, put an end to the more traditional Egyptian *zadjal*, for the cultivation of which organisations such as the *Rābiṭat al-zadjdjālīn*, founded in Cairo in 1932 by Muḥammad ʿAbd al-Munʿim Abū Buthayna (1905-80), and the *Djamʿiyyat udabā' al-shaʿb* of Alexandria have continued to provide a framework with conferences and collective publications, notably of a nationalistic strain. The Egyptian crossing of the Suez canal into occupied Sinai in 1973, for example, produced a collection of seventy poems and *zadjals* under the title *Malḥamat al-ʿubūr* "the epic crossing" (ed. ʿAbd al-Fattāḥ Shalabī, Cairo 1975).

Political and social events all over the Arab world have sparked off the writing of *zadjals* throughout the modern period, written to a limited degree by workers (their short-lived poetic-social movement is discussed by Beinin), but more often by leftist intellectuals. The most popular and explicitly political representative in the second half of 20th-century Egypt is Aḥmad Fu'ād Nadjm (conventionally: Nigm) (b. 1929), who became famous for his partnership with the blind singer al-Shaykh Imām (1918-95). His poems are an indictment of the policies of the Nasser and Sādāt régimes.

Zadjal has a long-standing relationship with the popular song and the operetta (*masraḥ ghinā'ī*), with famous poets writing for famous singers: Badīʿ Khayrī for Sayyid Darwīsh (1892-1923), Aḥmad Rāmī (1892-1981) and Bayram al-Tūnisī for Umm Kulthūm [*q.v.*], and the Raḥbānī brothers and Saʿīd ʿAḳl for Fayrūz (b. 1936).

Zadjal has also provided all sorts of humoristic entertainment (early examples in F. Kern, *Neuere ägyptische Humoristen und Satiriker*, in *MSOS As.*, ix [1906], 47-9); special forms are the *fazzūra* or riddle (a favourite item during Ramaḍān) and *al-shiʿr al-ḥalamantīshī*, burlesque poems in a mixture of standard and vernacular Arabic parodying famous classical examples (W. Stoetzer, *Classical poetry parodied: the case of Ḥusayn Šafīq al-Miṣrī (1882-1948)*, in *The Arabist* (Budapest Studies in Arabic), xv-xvi [1995], 229-38).

See also MALḤŪN, NABAṬĪ and the passage on "Writing dialects; dialectal literature" in AL-SHĀM, 3., at Vol. IX, 280.

Bibliography (in addition to references given in the article): An extensive list of texts and secondary sources, not repeated here, is in M. Booth, *Poetry in the vernacular*, in M.M. Badawi (ed.), *The Cambridge history of Arabic literature. Modern Arabic literature*, Cambridge 1992, 463-82, 546-50; scholarship in German until 1986 on non-classical poetry in F. Sezgin (ed.), *Bibliographie der deutschsprachigen Arabistik und Islamkunde*, iv (1991), 119-33; recent writings on *malḥūn* in A.A. Dellai, *Guide bibliographique du melhoun: Maghreb 1834-1996*, Paris 1996. Other references: J. Lecerf, *Littérature dialectale et renaissance arabe moderne*, in *B.Ét.Or.*, ii (1932), 179-258, iii (1933), 44-173; ʿAbbās b. ʿAbd Allāh al-Djirārī, *al-Zadjal fī 'l-maghrib: al-ḳaṣīda*, Rabat 1970; Khalīl Aḥmad Khalīl, *al-Shiʿr al-shaʿbī al-lubnānī*, Beirut 1974; Suʿūd al-Asadī, *Aghānī min al-Djalīl: ashʿār zadjaliyya*, Nazareth 1976; Muḥammad al-ʿAyyāshī, *al-Īḳāʿ al-shiʿrī fī ghinā' Umm Kulthūm*, n.p. [Tunis?] 1987; K. Abdel-Malek, *The khawāga then and now: images of the West in modern Egyptian zajal*, in *JAL*, xix (1988), 162-78; idem, *A study of the vernacular poetry of Aḥmad Fu'ād Nigm*, Leiden 1990; idem, *Muḥammad in the modern Egyptian popular ballad*, Leiden 1995; P. Cachia, *Popular narrative ballads of modern Egypt*, Oxford 1989; A. Haydar, *The development of Lebanese zajal: genre, meter, and verbal duel*, in *Oral Tradition*, iv/1-2 (1989), 189-212; D.Ḥ. Sbait, *Palestinian improvised-sung poetry: the genres of ḥidā and qarrādī: performance and transmission*, in *ibid.*, 213-35; J.-F. Belleface, *ʿAtābā des villes ou ʿatābā des champs*, in *B.Ét.Or.*, xli-xlii (1989-90), 161-70; Mādjid Yūsuf, *Mulāḥaẓāt ḥawla shiʿr al-ʿāmmiyya al-miṣriyya fī 'l-sabʿīnāt*, in *Alif*, xi (1991), 148-57; K. Eksell, *Three strophic patterns in Palestinian and some other Semitic poetry*, in *Orientalia Suecana*, xli-xlii (1992-3), 82-95; J. Beinin, *Writing class: workers and modern Egyptian colloquial poetry* (zajal), in *Poetics Today*, xv/2 (1994), 191-215; D. Semah, *Modern Arabic zajal and the quest for freedom*, in *JAL*, xxvi (1995), 80-92 (with further references); idem, *Karmiliyyat. Studies on forms and metrics in Arabic poetry*, Nazareth 1995 (in Arabic); Ḥasan Maḥmūd Abū ʿUlaywī, *al-Ashʿār wa 'l-aghānī al-shaʿbiyya*, Beirut 1996; Amīn al-Ḳārī, *Rawā'iʿ al-zadjal*, Tripoli, Lebanon 1998; R. Snir, *Synchronic and diachronic dynamics in modern Arabicliterature*, in S. Ballas and R. Snir (eds.), *Studies in canonical and popular Arabic literature*, Toronto 1998, 87-121. (W. STOETZER)

AL-**ZADJDJĀDJ**, ABŪ ISḤĀḲ IBRĀHĪM B. AL-SARĪ, Arabic grammarian who worked most of his life in Baghdād; he was born *ca.* 230/844 and died in 311/923. He was the main teacher of al-Zadjdjādjī [*q.v.*], who took his *nisba* from him. Among his other pupils are al-Fārisī, Ibn Wallād and al-Rummānī [*q.vv.*]. Al-Zadjdjādj himself had learnt grammar from both Thaʿlab and al-Mubarrad [*q.vv.*], combining in his own teachings what he had learnt from these representatives of both the Baṣran and the Kūfan schools. He may be regarded as the link between the old generations of Kūfan and Baṣran grammarians and the new grammar that was developed in Baghdād in the 4th/10th century under the influence of Greek logic.

Among his writings are a number of lexicographical treatises (e.g. his treatises on the *khalḳ al-insān* and his book on the differences between *faʿaltu* and *afʿaltu*), and an important treatise on diptote and triptote nouns (*K. mā yanṣarif wa-mā lā yanṣarif*, ed. by H.M. Ḳarāʿa, Cairo 1971), which was the first to present a comprehensive theory of the phenomenon of incomplete declinability. His main work dealt with Ḳurʾānic philology, the *Maʿānī 'l-Ḳurʾān* (preserved in several manuscripts; the edition by I. al-Abyārī, 3 vols., Beirut 1986 of a work *Iʿrab al-Ḳurʾān* attributed to al-Zadjdjādj probably contains another, later book; cf. Sezgin, *GAS*, viii, 100, and al-Abyārī's conclusions in his edition, iii, 1095-1100).

Al-Zadjdjādj remained an authority in the history of the Arabic grammatical tradition. His opinions are quoted for instance frequently by al-Rāzī in his Ḳurʾān commentary (more than 500 times, cf. Lagarde's index *s.v.*, Leiden 1996, 82-3); rather surprisingly, his favourite pupil al-Zadjdjādjī does mention him as his teacher, but when he quotes his opinion on complete and incomplete declinability from the *K. mā yanṣarif wa-mā lā yanṣarif* he does so without mentioning his name (cf. Versteegh, 1995, 164, 172, 174).

Bibliography: Brockelmann, I², 111-12, S I, 170; Sezgin, *GAS*, viii, 99-101, ix, 81-2; Ibn al-Anbārī, *Nuzha*, ed. Amer, Stockholm 1963, 147; Suyūṭī, *Bughya*, i, 411; Sīrāfī, *Akhbār*, 108; Zubaydī, *Ṭabaḳāt al-naḥwiyyīn wa 'l-lughawiyyīn*, ed. M.A. Ibrāhīm, Cairo 1984, 111-12; Flügel, *Die grammatischen Schulen der Araber*, Leipzig 1862, 98; Shawḳī Ḍayf, *al-Madāris al-naḥwiyya*, Cairo 1968, 135; C. Versteegh, *The explanation of linguistic causes. Az-Zaǧǧāǧī's theory of grammar, introduction, translation, commentary*, Amsterdam 1995. (C.H.M. VERSTEEGH)

AL-**ZADJDJĀDJĪ**, ABU 'L-ḲĀSIM ʿABD AL-RAḤMĀN b. Isḥāḳ, famed Arabic grammarian. He was born in Nihāwand in western Persia in the second half of the 3rd century A.H. (i.e. around 860-70), received his training as a grammarian in Baghdād, and was active in Damascus and Aleppo. He probably died in Ṭabariyya (Tiberias), either in 337/948 or 339-40/949-50. Almost nothing is known about his life except for a few anecdotes. It is clear from his grammatical writings that he was a Muʿtazilī (he mentions with approval such typically Muʿtazilī tenets as *al-kalām fi 'l al-mutakallim* and the non-identity of *ism* and *musammā*; cf. Versteegh, 1995, 36 n. 20, 37 n. 21) and there is one report that mentions his Shīʿī leanings (al-Dhahabī, *Siyar*, xv, 476 ll. 7-8).

Al-Zadjdjādjī's teachers are well known, since he himself gives a list of them in his *Īḍāḥ* (78-9); among them are not only grammarians belonging to the Baṣran school such as al-Zadjdjādj, al-Akhfash al-Ṣaghīr, and Ibn al-Sarrādj, but also those belonging to the Kūfan school, such as Ibn Kaysān, Ibn Shuḳayr and Abū Bakr Ibn al-Anbārī [*q.vv.*]. As a matter of fact, al-Zadjdjādjī is proud to present himself as an intermediator between the two schools of grammar, stating that he reformulated the arguments of the Kūfan grammarians in Baṣran terms. His main teacher was al-Zadjdjādj [*q.v.*], from whom he received his *nisba* because of his long association with him. Among his own students are a few grammarians known as such from other sources (e.g. Aḥmad b. Muḥammad b. Salama Ibn Sarrām, cf. al-Suyūṭī, *Bughya*, i, 357, and al-Ḥasan b. ʿAlī al-Ṣiḳillī, cf. *ibid.*, i, 515).

Al-Zadjdjādjī's chief fame rests on his *K. al-Djumal* "Book of summaries" (rather than "sentences", the usual meaning of this term in grammar), a didactic introduction to Arabic grammar (ed. M. Ben Cheneb, Paris 1957) of the kind that became popular in the 3rd-4th centuries; similar books were written by Ibn al-Sarrādj, al-Fārisī and Ibn Djinnī. In the *K. al-Djumal*, he simply lists the rules of Arabic grammar without going into explanations or controversies. This book became one of the most popular textbooks in the Arab world, especially in North Africa, where at one time more than 120 commentaries were current (Ibn al-ʿImād, *Shadharāt*, ii, 357); 49 commentaries are preserved in manuscripts, some of which have been published, among them those of al-Baṭalyawsī (d. 521/1127), ed. H.ʿA. al-Nashratī, al-Riyāḍ 1979, and Ibn ʿUṣfūr (d. 669/1270), ed. S.Dj. Abū Djanāḥ, 2 vols., Baghdād 1980-2 (cf. Sezgin, *GAS*, ix, 89-94).

More interesting from a theoretical point of view is his *K. al-Īḍāḥ fī ʿilal al-naḥw* "Book of the explanation of grammatical causes" (ed. M. al-Mubārak, Cairo 1959), which deals with the *ʿilal* "causes" [see ʿILLA] of the discipline of linguistics. The term *ʿilla* in the title is essential for the understanding of al-Zadjdjādjī's theoretical principles, and at the same time difficult to understand. In the fifth chapter (*Īḍāḥ*, 64-6) he states that there are three kinds of linguistic causes: the *ʿilal taʿlīmiyya*, the *ʿilal ḳiyāsiyya* and the *ʿilal naẓariyya wa-djadaliyya*. These represent the levels of explanation grammarians provide for linguistic phenomena: the first category are the simple rules (such as those presented in the *K. al-Djumal*), and the second category the explanations of these rules in terms of resemblance and relative force of linguistic elements, but the third category contains extra-linguistic or logical explanations that justify the explanations of the second level. Al-Zadjdjādjī claimed that he was the first to write such a book; this assertion may be exaggerated, but nevertheless, his distinction of epistemological levels in linguistic explanations must be regarded as a unique contribution to the Arabic tradition, even though there are connections with other texts, e.g. al-Sīrāfī's commentary on the *Kitāb Sībawayhi*. Unlike the *K. al-Djumal* and perhaps because of its uniqueness, the *Īḍāḥ* does not seem to have had much impact on Arabic grammatical literature. There is only one manuscript and the book is rarely cited by later grammarians, although there are lengthy quotations in later compilations such as al-Suyūṭī's *Muzhir*.

Among the other books that have been preserved from his writings are a treatise on particles containing an *l* (*K. al-Lāmāt*, ed. M. al-Mubārak, Damascus 1969), a book on the functions of particles (*K. Maʿānī 'l-ḥurūf*, ed. Farhūd, 1982), a treatise on the etymology of the names of God (*K. Ishtiḳāḳ asmāʾ Allāh*, ed. al-Daḳḳāḳ, Damascus 1975), as well as several collections of notes and comments, the most important of which is the *K. al-Madjālis*, one of the most important sources on debates between grammarians (ed. ʿA.M. Hārūn, Kuwait 1962). Other books are mentioned by title in the sources, but have not been preserved in manuscript form, e.g. his *Risāla*, a commentary on the introductory chapters of the *Kitāb Sībawayhi*, which he himself mentions in the *Īḍāḥ* (41; cf. Versteegh, 1995, 32 n. 8). For a complete list see Sezgin (*GAS*, ix, 88-95) and Versteegh (1995, 3-6).

It is not easy to assess al-Zadjdjādjī's value and impact: as *ṣāḥib al-Djumal*, he was celebrated, but the original ideas in his *Īḍāḥ* are largely forgotten. This means that his special blend of grammar on a logically epistemological basis never caught on. In fact, later grammarians were more concerned with the semantics and pragmatics of the Arabic language—apart from the traditional preoccupation with morphological and syntactic analysis—so that they had no time for the methodological points which al-Zadjdjādjī attempted to make. This applies in particular to such typical topics treated by him as the relative priority of noun, verb, and particle, or the explanation of the fact that the verb does not have a genitive, and that the noun does not have a jussive. Even with regard to the definition of the parts of speech, later grammarians tended to mention just a few definitions, whereas he analyses them in detail (*Īḍāḥ*, 48-55).

In general, what is characteristic of his work as a grammarian is his relentless quest for the "cause" or explanation of linguistic phenomena. Mention should also be made of his special style, a personal approach to polemics that is absent from most other grammarians. A comparison between al-Sīrāfī's and his own treatment of the same problem (that of the status of the weak consonants in the declension of the dual and the plural, cf. *Īḍāḥ*, 121-9, with al-Sīrāfī, *Sharḥ*, i, 214-23; cf. Versteegh, 1995, 224-5) makes clear that there is a large difference in style: al-Sīrāfī's presentation is dry and concise, whereas al-Zadjdjādjī makes an attempt to present the discussion as an actual debate.

Bibliography: 1. Sources. Brockelmann, S I, 170-1; Sezgin, *GAS*, vii, 354, viii, 105-6, ix, 88-95; Flügel, *Die grammatischen Schulen der Araber*, Leipzig 1862, 99; Shawḳī Ḍayf, *al-Madāris al-naḥwiyya*, Cairo 1968, 252-5; Dhahabī, *Siyar aʿlām al-nubalāʾ*, ed. Sh. al-Arnāʾūṭ and I. al-Zaybak, Beirut n.d.; Ibn al-Anbārī, *Nuzha*, ed. Amer, Stockholm 1963, 183; Ibn al-ʿImād, *Shadharāt*, ²Beirut 1979; Suyūṭī, *Bughya*, ii, 77; Ibn Khallikān, *Wafayāt*, ed. ʿAbbās, iii, 136; Zubaydī, *Ṭabaḳāt al-naḥwiyyīn wa 'l-lughawiyyīn*, ed. M.A. Ibrāhīm, Cairo 1984, 119; Ḳifṭī, *Inbāh*, ed. Ibrāhīm, Cairo 1950-73, ii, 160-1; Ṣafadī, *Wāfī*, xviii, 112-13; Sīrāfī, *Sharḥ Kitāb Sībawayhi*, ed. R.ʿA. ʿAbd al-Tawwāb and M.F. Ḥidjāzī, i, Cairo 1986.

2. Studies. J.-P. Guillaume, *La "cause" des grammairiens. Etude sur la notion de* ʿilla *dans la tradition grammaticale arabe (fin IIIᵉ/IXᵉ-milieu du IVᵉ/Xᵉ s.)*, thèse de 3ème cycle, Univ. Paris III; H. Hamzé, *Les théories grammaticales d'az-Zaǧǧâǧî*, thèse d'état, Université de Lyon II, 1987; M. al-Mubārak, *al-Zadjdjādjī, ḥayātuhu wa-āthāruhu wa-madhhabuhu al-naḥwī min khilāl kitābihi al-Īḍāḥ*, Damascus 1960; J. Owens, *The syntactic basis of Arabic word classification*, in *Arabica*, xxxvi (1989), 211-34; M.Y. Suleiman, *Sībawaihi's "parts of speech" according to Zajjājī. A new interpretation*, in *JSS*, xxxv (1990), 245-63; idem, *The notion* ʿilla *in Arabic linguistic thinking*, in *Procs. BRISMES Annual Conference*, Leeds 1988, 20-31; C. Versteegh, *The definition of philosophy in a 10th century grammarian*, in *JSAI*, xii (1989), 66-93; idem, *The notion of "underlying levels" in the Arabic grammatical tradition*, in *Historiographia Linguistica*, xxi (1994), 271-96; idem, *The explanation of linguistic causes. Az-Zaǧǧāǧī's theory of grammar, introduction, translation, commentary*, Amsterdam 1995.

(C.H.M. Versteegh)

ZADJR [see ʿIYĀFA].

ẒAFĀR, i.e. Ẓafārⁱ, the name of the ancient capital of the South Arabian kingdom of Ḥimyar. The present small village of the same name on the ruins of the ancient town is located approximately 8 km/5 miles to the south of the town of Yarīm; the geographical co-ordinates of Ẓafār are lat. 14° 13' N. and long. 44° 24' E.

The identity of the site has been known in Yemen since Antiquity and is confirmed by Late Sabaic inscriptions found at this place. The site of Ẓafār is located at the foot of a hilltop with the ruins of an ancient castle, and remains of foundations and walls can be found at some points. Many fragmentary architectural elements, inscriptions and sculptures as well as items decorated with geometric designs, plant motifs, animal motifs, and various other motifs, like griffons, sphinxes, mythical creatures and signs of the zodiac, bear testimony to a strong influence of orientalised Hellenism in the 4th and 5th centuries. Ẓafār was already in existence in the middle of the 1st century A.D. Pliny (*Natural History*, vi, 104) mentions in the inland of Arabia Felix a town called Sapphar, which is the residence of the king, and the unknown author of the *Periplus of the Erythraean Sea* (§ 22) writes that nine days' further inland from the Red Sea is Saphar, the capital, residence of Charibael, the legitimate king of the two nations, namely, of the Homerite and of the Sabaean; also Ptolemy (*Geography*, vi, 7, 41) calls Sapphar a metropolis. The earliest inscriptional evidence of Ẓafār occurs in the title "king of Saba' and Dhū-Raydān", since the name Raydān in this title is that of the castle on the hill above the town of Ẓafār which is still known locally by the name of Raydān and which was the seat of the Himyarite kings. The town of Ẓafār is explicitly mentioned in a dozen Sabaic inscriptions, mainly in votive texts from the temple Awām in the oasis of Mārib [*q.v.*]. According to an inscription (Jamme 631) from the time of king Shaʿirum Awtar in the first quarter of the 3rd century A.D., the town had to be defended from an Abyssinian army which had marched to Ẓafār. The text Iryānī 14 from *ca.* 270 reports that the two kings Yāsirum Yuhanʿim and his son Shammar Yuharʿish went from the castle of Raydān in the town of Ẓafār to the palace of Salḥīn [*q.v.*] in the town of Mārib, and from the inscription Iryānī 32 we learn that *ca.* 315, after a successful campaign against Ḥaḍramawt, the Himyarite army returned with rich booty into the town of Ẓafār.

Ca. 342 the Byzantine emperor Constantius II sent ambassadors under the leadership of a certain Theophilus to the ruler of the Himyarites, and as a result of the mission three churches were built, one of them in the capital Tapharon (Philostorgius, *Ecclesiastical history*, iii, 4). The first testimonies to Himyarite monotheism are to be found in two inscriptions from Ẓafār (Glaser 389 and Bayt al-Ashwal 2) dated to 378, in which king Malikkarib Yuhaʾmin and two of his sons record the building of the palaces Shawḥaṭān and Kallānum in their capital "through the power of their Lord, the Lord of Heaven". Ẓafār's further embellishment is documented by an inscription (Ẓafār Museum 1), which says that king Shuraḥbi'il Yaʿfur erected a magnificent palace named Hargab in the capital in 457. The Abyssinian presence and influence are to be seen in an inscription (Ẓafār Museum 579) dated to 504, according to which the dedicators, whose names are clearly Ethiopian, refer to themselves as envoys and claim to have built a house in Ẓafār. When King Yūsuf As'ar Yathʾar, who professed the Jewish faith, came to power, he launched military operations against the Abyssinians in Southern Arabia along with their allies the Christians. According to the testimony of the Sabaic rock-inscriptions Ryckmans 508, Jamme 1028 and Ryckmans 507, in 518 the Himyarite king killed the Abyssinians in Ẓafār, three hundred in number, and burnt the church there. An account of the persecution of the Abyssinians and Christians and of the burning of the church in the town of Ẓafār (*ṭpr*, *ṭypr*) and the massacre of all who were in it, is also found in two Syriac hagiographic works (*The Book of the Himyarites*, ed. A. Moberg, Lund 1924, 7; the letter contained in *The Martyrs of Najrân, new documents*, ed. I. Shahîd, Brussels 1971, II A). The martyrdom of the Himyarite Christians prompted a military intervention and an invasion of an Abyssinian army under the Christian king Caleb Ella Aṣbeḥā, who conquered Yemen in 525. A vivid report on the capture of the royal city of Taphar by the Abyssinians is given in the *Acts* of Saint Arethas and his companions (chs. 35-7). The *Vita* of Gregentius (ch. 63), who later was installed as bishop in Ẓafār, lists three churches built by Caleb in Tephar. With the fall of the Himyarite kingdom, however, Ẓafār lost its imperial status, power and influence, and went into an irrevocable decline; it was already in mediaeval times a ruined site and became the small village it is still today.

The most detailed description of the ancient site of Ẓafār is given by the 4th/10th-century scholar al-Hamdānī [*q.v.*] in the eighth volume of his *Iklīl*, which deals with the antiquities of Yemen (*Iklīl*, viii, ed. M. al-Akwaʿ al-Ḥiwālī, Damascus 1979, 65-74). He says that, in addition to Raydān, which was the royal palace, there were two other castles in Ẓafār, named Shawḥaṭān and Kawkabān. The town had nine gates which are all enumerated by name. At these gates stood attendants (*awhāz*) who served as guards and without whose permission no-one was allowed to enter the town. Attached to the gate were bells (*maʿāhira*) which could be heard from a distance whenever the gate was opened or closed. Many verses of various poets are quoted by al-Hamdānī, in which Ẓafār is praised as a wealthy city of castles and in which the brightness and uniqueness of the royal palace Raydān is celebrated.

Bibliography (in addition to the references given in the article): H. von Wissmann, *Ḥimyar, ancient history*, in *Le Muséon*, lxxvii (1964), 429-97; W. Radt, *Bericht über eine Forschungsreise in die Arabische Republik Jemen*, in *Archäologischer Anzeiger*, 1971/2, 253-93; P. Costa, *Antiquities from Ẓafar (Yemen)*, in *AION*, xxxiii (1973), 185-206, pls. i-xxvi; Part II, in *ibid.*, xxxvi (1976), 445-56, pls. i-xxx; I. Shahîd, *Byzantium in South Arabia*, in *Dumbarton Oaks Papers*, xxxiii (1979), 25-94; R.D. Tindel, *Ẓafar. Archaeology in the land of frankincense and myrrh*, in *Archaeology*, xxxvii/2 (1984), 40-5; W.W. Müller, art. *Himyar*, in *Reallexikon für Antike und Christentum*, xv (1989), 303-31.

(W.W. Müller)

ẒAFĀR, a former settlement on the Indian Ocean coast and modern name of the Southern Region of the Sultanate of Oman. In early, mediaeval and late mediaeval times it was never actually a port, and is now a ruined site called al-Balīd, a few miles to the east of the chief town of the southern region, Ṣalāla [*q.v.*].

In modern times, the name came to be used for the whole of the Southern Region of the Sultanate of Oman [see ʿUMĀN] and was officially Anglicised as Dhofar. There can be no longer any doubt about the correct vocalisation of the Arabic name, for both lexicographers (e.g. Ibn Manẓūr, *LA*, Beirut 1955, v, 519-20) and geographers (e.g. Yāḳūt, *Muʿdjam al-buldān*, Beirut 1979, iv, 60) are agreed that the name is of the pattern *faʿāli*, i.e. undeclinable and ending in *kasra*.

Despite local tradition that Ẓafār was a pre-Islamic settlement in origin, there is nothing to substantiate this. The idea may stem from the fact that the whole area was an incense growing one, though we know that the pre-Islamic incense port was SMHRM/SMRM, present-day Khawr Rawrī, east of al-Balīd (Jacqueline Pirenne, *The incense port of Moscha (Khor Rori) in Dhofar*, in *Jnal. Oman Studies*, i [1975], 81-96). Furthermore, its pre-Rasūlid [*q.v.*] history cannot be recounted in any great detail and it would be wise to commence with the Mandjū/Mandjawiyyūn who arrived in the area after the decline of Sīrāf [*q.v.*] in the 5th/11th century, according to Ibn al-Mudjāwir (*fl.* early 7th/13th century) (*T. al-Mustabṣir*, ed. O. Löfgren, Leiden 1951-4, 270). According to Abū Makhrama (d. 947/1540), Sultan Muḥammad b. Aḥmad al-Mandjawī, nicknamed al-Akḥal, was from a people known as Bulukh and he died in 600/1203-4, upon which the dynasty came to an end (*T. Thaghr ʿAdan*, in Löfgren (ed.), *Arabische Texte zur Kenntnis der Stadt Aden im Mittelatter*, Leiden 1936, 194-5). The historian of Ḥaḍramawt, Muḥammad al-Kindī (d. 1310/1892-3) (*T. Ḥadramawt*, ed. ʿAbd Allāh Muḥammad al-Ḥibshī, i, Ṣanʿāʾ 1991, 97), generally following Abū Makhrama closely, tells us, however, that Bulukh (the text has Bulḥ) belong to the Yemeni tribe of Madhḥidj [*q.v.*], but he gives no evidence for his statement. It was these settlers who built the nearby port of Mirbāṭ [*q.v.*], continues Ibn al-Mudjāwir, thus called because it was initially where they tethered their horses.

Early in the 7th/13th century (our sources differ on the question of dates and even names), Ẓafār was taken over by a Ḥaḍramī family from Ḥabūḍa (Ḥabūẓa?) near Shibām, the Ḥabūḍids. The account of the destruction and rebuilding of the settlement in the early 7th/13th century is found in some detail in Ibn al-Mudjāwir's *Taʾrīkh* and, since he was a contemporary of these events, he can be paraphrased here. About 618/1221, the leader of the Ḥabūḍī family, Aḥmad, destroyed Ẓafār, fearing its capture by the Ayyūbids [*q.v.*] from Yemen. He then built a new town on the site, called al-Manṣūra, also al-Ḳāhira, although the name Ẓafār continued to be used. The town was well fortified with four gates; the air was good, the water sweet, and sugar cane and bananas grew well in the area. All the inhabitants were Ḥaḍramīs, perhaps, though Ibn al-Mudjāwir does not mention this, brought by Aḥmad to populate his new town (265-6; G.R. Smith and Venetia Porter, *The Rasulids in Dhofar in the VIIth-VIIIth/XIIIth-XIVth centuries*, in *JRAS*, 1988/1, 28).

Space does not permit a detailed account of the remarkable Rasūlid conquest of Ẓafār in 677/1278. The reasons for the conquest and the three-pronged attack from Aden by a naval force, a second detachment travelling along the coastal route and a third which marched from the Yemen to Ẓafār via Wādī Ḥaḍramawt, no doubt to wave the flag there, are dealt with in Smith and Porter, *op. cit.*, 29-31, with full references. All this military effort proved unnecessary, for, after the rendezvous of the Rasūlid troops at Raysūt, the port of Ẓafār, the Ḥabūḍids capitulated when their leader, Sālim, was killed early on in the fray. The local inhabitants of the town were granted an amnesty by the Rasūlids, whose accompanying merchants soon began to open up trade in the area.

Thereafter, until the late 8th/14th century, there would seem to have been a Rasūlid presence in Ẓafār, on occasions an independent ruler of the house, on others a ruler dependent on the Rasūlid government centred in Taʿizz [*q.v.*] in Yemen (al-Khazradjī, *al-ʿUḳūd al-luʾluʾiyya fī taʾrīkh al-dawla al-Rasūliyya*, GMS III, v, Leiden and London 1918, 134, 276, 277-8, 285). Apart from these few references, there is nothing of the history of Ẓafār to report until mention of the rise of the Kat͟hīrīs [*q.v.*], a tribal group from the area, in the late 9th/15th century. In 867/1462-3, they took al-S͟hiḥr [*q.v.*], then the port of Ḥaḍramawt, and their subsequent history played out in the area of greater Ḥaḍramawt, in which we can, for convenience, include Ẓafār.

As for the site of Ẓafār, now called al-Balīd, and situated about 5 km/3 miles from Ṣalāla, the chief town of the Southern Region, it has been examined and studied in some depth by P.M. Costa (*The study of the city of Ẓafar (al-Balīd)*, in *Jnal. of Oman Studies*, v [1979], 111-50). Drawings, maps and photographs of the site are many, and what excavations have been carried out there are described in some detail. Perhaps the most remarkable feature of the site is the Great Mosque (Costa's plan, fig. 25, fold-out opposite p. 133). The site which stretches along the sea shore is over one km/1,000 yards in length and it is perhaps worthy of mention that it is larger than the area of the Rasūlid capital, Taʿizz [*q.v.*].

The modern area of Ẓafār, the Southern Region of the Sultanate of Oman and one of its governorates (sing. *wilāya*), covers an area of about 120,000 km^2/ 75,000 sq. miles, a third of the total area of the country. The population was estimated at about 160,000 (Oman Ministry of Information, *Sultanate of Oman, the promise and the fulfilment*, Muscat n.d., 30) in the 1980s, and the large majority are Sunnī S͟hāfiʿīs, unlike those of the Bāṭina coast and al-D͟jabal al-Ak͟hḍar region of the north of Oman who follow Ibāḍī Islam [see ʿUMĀN]. The main towns and villages of the Ẓafār region are: Ṣalāla, Mirbāṭ [*q.vv.*], Ṭāḳa and Raysūt. Geographically, the region of Ẓafār can be divided into three: the coast with its fishing and agricultural settlements; the mountains which enjoy plentiful monsoon rainfall and are the home of cattle rearers; and the Nad͟jd, a desert area extending north from the foothills to al-Rubʿ al-K͟hālī [*q.v.*]. For the languages spoken in Ẓafār, see ʿUMĀN, heading (the modern South Arabian languages), and 4. The modern Arabic dialects.

Bibliography: Apart from the sources mentioned above, the following may also be mentioned as the best source by far of the Rasūlid conquest of Ẓafār: Muḥammad Ibn Ḥātim, *K. al-Simṭ al-g͟hālī al-t͟haman fī taʾrīk͟h al-mulūk min al-G͟huzz bi 'l-Yaman*, in G.R. Smith (ed.), *The Ayyūbids and early Rasūlids in the Yemen*, GMS, N.S. XXVI, i, London 1974, 505-29.

(G.R. SMITH)

ZAʿFARĀN (A.) saffron, *Crocus sativus* L. or *Crocus officinalis* Pers., one of some eighty species of low-growing perennial plants of the family Iridaceae, found throughout the Mediterranean area, mid-Europe and Central Asia. A product, used in antiquity as an important source of yellow orange dye, was obtained from the stigma (*s͟haʿr, s͟huʿayra*) of the sterile cultigen *C. sativus*.

1. Domestic uses.

Saffron was, and remains, also widely used in Middle Eastern culinary traditions. In the extant Arabic culinary manuals of the mediaeval period (4th/10th to 8th/14th centuries), ranging in provenance from ʿIrāḳ to the Iberian peninsula, saffron appears frequently in a wide variety of domestic preparations. A representative selection of recipes may be found in the anonymous *Kanz al-fawāʾid*, probably of Mamlūk Egyptian origin.

In substantial dishes containing meat, often together with one or more vegetables, saffron was used to lend colour, a purpose sometimes explicitly stated in the recipe. For example, in a sweet-sour dish of Persian origin, *zirbād͟j*, chicken is tinted with saffron before vinegar is added to the cooking pot. However, in other cases, saffron is used to add flavour. One of the stages of preparation for *ṭabāhid͟ja* calls for a combination of saffron with honey, nuts, corn starch, pepper and various spices mixed together and added to the pot. The complement of the distinctive aroma of saffron was likely intended when, in a meatless recipe, it was sprinkled with sugar and rosewater on top of the finished dish; indeed, saffron is often found in combination with aromatic rose water [see MĀʾ AL-WARD, in Suppl.]. A mustard sauce, *k͟hardal*, containing saffron and other dried spices, was mixed with brown vinegar, the preparation being used to prevent the "transformation" of fish.

Other, less known, domestic uses for saffron were its frequent appearance, among many other ingredients, in preparations for "home remedies" such as stomachics (*d͟jawāris͟h*), one such being said to sweeten the breath and prevent snoring. Finally, *māʾ zaʿfarān*, a clear liquid distilled from saffron, was used to scent clothing without leaving a trace of its colour.

Bibliography: Anon., *Kanz al-fawāʾid fī tanwīʿ al-mawāʾid*, ed. M. Marín and D. Waines, Beirut-Stuttgart 1993, index s.v.; Ibn Sayyār al-Warrāḳ, *K. al-Ṭabīk͟h*, ed. K. Ohrnberg and S. Mroueh, Helsinki 1987.

(D. WAINES)

2. As a medicament.

As well as being used in food preparation, saffron is one of the simple medicaments, abundantly cited in Arabic medical treatises. At the present time, it is used in traditional medicine of the Arab-Muslim domain (*ṭibb ʿarabī, ṭibb yūnānī*). It has been used since Antiquity (cited in the *Iliad*, xiv. 348) as an aromatic, colourant and simple medicinal herb. In mediaeval Islamic literature it appears under various names: *zaʿfarān* (the most common), *rayhaḳān, d͟jādī, d͟jād͟hī* and *d͟jisān*. Dāwūd al-Anṭākī [*q.v.*] thought that the Syriac name of this herb was *kurkum*, but this term in fact denotes the curcuma, often mixed up with saffron on account of the similarity in colour. Saffron was cultivated in many parts of the Islamic world, but was also imported. Ibn al-ʿAwwām [see FILĀḤA. ii] gives a precise description of the plant's cultivation in al-Andalus, near to Seville (*K. al-Filāḥa*, i, 116-18). There were various varieties known in the classical period: the Mag͟hribī and the Edessan (*ruhāwī*), but also the Frankish or Genoese (*ifrand͟jī, d͟janawī*). Al-Bīrūnī mentions Persian varieties (*iṣbahānī, rāzī* and *k͟hurāsānī*) and Syrian (*s͟hāmī*) ones. The products of the Sūs [*q.v.*], in southern Morocco, were especially appreciated, as stated by al-Anṭākī and the anonymous *Tuḥfat al-albāb*; contemporary Moroccan herbalists further mention the *zaʿfarān zebbūdī* (cultivated by the Zebbūd of the Sūs).

Saffron was considered to be a stimulant for the nervous system, but also an aphrodisiac, a tonic for the heart and a cordial (*mufarrid͟j*). It was used in the composition of collyria, as indicated by Ibn Sīnā [*q.v.*] (*Ḳānūn*, i, 306-7) and al-Anṭākī (*Tad͟hkira*, 178-9), since the powers of dissolving white specks in the eye and strengthening the eyesight were attributed to it. Finally, it was used as an emmenagogic, a diuretic and a lithotriptic, but also, on the fringes of magic, in amulets for helping with labour in parturition. At the present time, folk medicine uses the "ink" of saffron in the making of amulets bearing cabbalistic inscriptions aimed at combatting the evil eye. Another usage, fairly current in the medical treatises, is as a calming remedy for pains and inflammations of the ear. Since saffron was a precious and expensive product, fraudulent substitutes of all kinds were current, to the degree that Kōhēn al-ʿAṭṭār [*q.v.*] devotes a section of his treatise to describing the techniques for verifying the authenticity of this simple (*imtiḥān al-zaʿfarān*) (*Minhādj*, 159). Most of the falsifications were done by using the curcuma rhizome (sc. that of *Curcuma longa* L., *kurkum*) or the bastard saffron (*Carthamus tinctorius* L., *ʿuṣfur*), because of their close resemblance to genuine or medicinal saffron.

Bibliography: 1. Sources. Ibn Sīnā, *al-Ḳānūn fi 'l-ṭibb*, Cairo 1877, 159; Bīrūnī, *K. al-Ṣaydana*, Tehran 1950, 311-13; *Tuḥfat al-albāb. Glossaire de la matière médicale marocaine*, ed. H.P.J. Renaud and G.S. Colin, Paris 1934, 69-70; Maimonides, *Sharḥ asmāʾ al-ʿuḳḳār (L'explication des noms de drogues), un glossaire de matière médicale*, ed. and tr. M. Meyerhof, Cairo 1939, 66; Ibn al-ʿAwwām, *K. al-Filāḥa*, tr. J.-J. Clément-Mullet, *Livre de l'agriculture*, Paris 1864-7, i, 116-18; Kōhēn al-ʿAṭṭār, *Minhādj al-dukkān wa-dustūr al-aʿyān*, Cairo 1870, 159; Nuwayrī, *Nihāyat al-arab*, xii, Cairo 1937, 125-6; Dāwūd al-Anṭākī, *Tadhkirat ulī 'l-albāb*, Cairo 1864, repr. Beirut n.d., 178-9.

2. Studies. A. Issa Bey, *Dictionnaire des noms de plantes*, Cairo 1930, 60; E. Ghaleb, *al-Mawsūʿa fī ʿulūm al-ṭabīʿa*, Beirut 1965, i, 490; N.H. Henein and Th. Bianquis, *La magie par les Psaumes*, Cairo 1975, 121-2; Ahmad, G. Honda and W. Miki, *Herb drugs and herbalists in the Middle East*, in *Studia Culturae Islamicae*, v, Tokyo 1979; F. Sanagustin, *Contribution à l'étude de la matière médicale traditionelle chez les herboristes d'Alep*, in *BEO*, xxxv (1983), 84.

(F. Sanagustin)

AL-**ZAFAYĀN**, ʿAṬĀʾ B. USAYD (or Asīd) Abu 'l-Mirḳāl al-ʿUwāfī al-Saʿdī, Umayyad *radjaz* poet, *fl. ca.* 80/700. His *Dīwān*, collected by Muḥammad b. Ḥabīb, has been only incompletely preserved (ten fragmentary poems, 230 verses) and published by W. Ahlwardt (*Sammlungen alter arabischer Dichter*, ii, 1903, lx-lxv, 91-100; with four additional fragments, 30 verses). The *Dīwān* was in better condition when used by al-Ṣaghānī in the 7th/13th century.

Further fragments (41 verses), with corrections to the edition of Ahlwardt, have been collected in J. Hämeen-Anttila, *az-Zafayān and his place in literary history*, forthcoming in *Asiatische Studien*, where the history of al-Zafayān's *Dīwān* is discussed in detail.

Al-Zafayān is rarely quoted in philological literature and almost nothing is known of his life. One of his poems (no. 8) refers to the defeat of Abū Fudayk in 73/693 and another (no. 6) is dedicated to a Marwānid caliph with typical Marwānid propagandistic themes such as are also found in poems by Djarīr [*q.v.*]. The poems of al-Zafayān resemble those of his contemporary, al-ʿAdjdjādj [*q.v.*], and show the development towards polythematic *urdjūza*s [see RADJAZ]. Some of his poems exhibit the lexicographical orientation of the Baṣran *radjaz* poets, whereas in others al-Zafayān uses a simple and straightforward language.

There seems to have been another *radjaz* poet of the same name, al-Zafayān b. Mālik b. ʿAwāna, living in Baṣra a century later (Yāḳūt, *Udabāʾ*; ii, 130-1), but almost nothing is known of his works.

Bibliography: In addition to references given in the article, see Sezgin, *GAS*, ii, 370.

(J. Hämeen-Anttila)

AL-**ẒĀFIR BI-AʿDĀʾ ALLĀH**, ABŪ MANṢŪR ISMĀʿĪL, twelfth Fāṭimid caliph and the ninth to reign in Egypt (born mid-Rabīʿ II 527/February 1133, *r.* 544-9/1149-54).

His four older brothers having predeceased their father, ʿAbd al-Madjīd al-Ḥāfiẓ, the latter appointed him, in writing, as heir to the caliphate. Al-Ẓāfir, at sixteen years of age, received the *bayʿa* on Sunday, 4 Djumādā II 544/10 October 1149, the day following the night of his father's death, at a time when Cairo was the scene of confrontation between Turkish cavalry and black military slaves. To pacify the troops, he distributed cash payments to them and promised to ensure their welfare. As soon as his vizier, Nadjm al-Dīn Abu 'l-Fatḥ Salīm b. Muḥammad Ibn Maṣāl al-Lukkī al-Afḍal or al-Mufaḍḍal [see IBN MAṢĀL], a native of Barḳa, had eliminated the instigators of unrest in Shaʿbān/November, al-Ẓāfir, a young man of exceptional beauty, was free to devote his time to recreation in the company of his concubines. There then erupted the rebellion of the governor of Alexandria, Sayf al-Dīn ʿAlī b. al-Sallār (or Salār), who overthrew Ibn Maṣāl and had himself recognised by the Palace as vizier with the *laḳab* of al-ʿĀdil [see AL-ʿĀDIL B. AL-SALĀR]. He then sent his stepson, ʿAbbās b. Abi 'l-Futūḥ [*q.v.*] Yaḥyā b. Tamīm b. al-Muʿizz b. Bādis al-Zīrī, accompanied by Ṭalāʾiʿ b. Ruzzīk [*q.v.*] to execute (on 19 Shawwāl 544/11 February 1150, at Ibn Maṣāl's refuge at Dillas) the deposed vizier and his ally, Badr b. Rafīʿ, who had been unable to protect the Arab tribes of the Delta.

A month earlier, in Ramaḍān 544/January 1150, Ibn Sallār had gathered together all the "cadets" of Cairo, *ṣibyān al-khāṣṣ*, sons of dignitaries and officers receiving military training. Hearing of a conspiracy amongst them against him, he executed the majority of them and sent the others to garrison the frontiers.

In Radjab 545/October-November 1150, a Frankish contingent attacked al-Faramā, which was sacked and burned. Less than a year later, Rabīʿ I 546/July-August 1151, al-ʿĀdil retaliated by sending a fleet to raid the Frankish coast, causing severe damage to Yāfā, ʿAkkā, Ṣaydā, Beirut and Tripoli and slaughtering a large number of Christian pilgrims. The expedition cost the Fāṭimid treasury 300,000 dīnārs, and in Cairo it was necessary to suspend the free distribution by the *dīwān*s of clothing and various other items. Nūr al-Dīn b. Zangī [*q.v.*], then the prince of Aleppo, was tempted to support the efforts of the Egyptian fleet with a land attack on the Frankish positions, but concern about his relations with Abak, prince of Damascus led him to decide against it (M. Yared-Riachi, *La politique extérieure de la principauté de Damas 468-549 h./1076-1154*, Damascus 1997, 229-30).

In Muḥarram 548/April 1153, concerned at the pressure being exerted by the Franks, Ibn Sallār appointed ʿAbbās to conduct on his behalf the relief of the Egyptian garrison of ʿAsḳalān [*q.v.*] in Palestine, a relief which took place every six months. While ʿAbbās and his companions, including the renowned Usāma Ibn Munḳidh [see MUNḲIDH, BANŪ], were on the way, they became disenchanted with the idea of going and isolating themselves so far from Cairo in a fortress to which the Franks were laying siege. Arriving in Bilbays, they appealed to Naṣr, the son of ʿAbbās and a very close friend of al-Ẓāfir, to go and persuade the latter to appoint his father vizier in place of Ibn Sallār. The young man obtained the agreement of al-Ẓāfir, who refused him nothing, then went to the house where his grandmother was cohabiting with Ibn Sallār, beheaded him with a single sword blow and alerted his father by carrier-pigeon (Ibn Ẓāfir, *Akhbār al-duwal al-munḳaṭiʿa*, ed. A. Ferré, Cairo 1972, 102-3). The next day, 12 Muḥarram 548/9 April 1152, ʿAbbās arrived in Cairo. He negotiated with al-Ẓāfir's courtiers and the latter appeared in the *manẓara* above the Bāb al-Dhahab (see A.F. Sayyid, *La capitale de l'Égypte jusqu'à l'époque fāṭimide. Al-Qāhira et Fusṭāṭ, essai de reconstitution topographique*, Beirut

1998, index at 727-32) brandishing the head of Ibn Sallār for all the people assembled at the gate to see, then had it exhibited in the *khizānat al-ruʾūs* of the Palace. ʿAbbās was generally congratu-lated for his action, all the more so since Ibn Sallār, a man of no discernible qualities whatsoever, was detested for his greed and his cruelty. Both Ibn Ẓāfir and Ibn Muyassar give detailed accounts of the brutal and vindictive crimes perpetrated by him in the wake of his seizure of power. On the other hand, when the *faḳīh* Aḥmad b. Muḥammad al-Salafī al-Iṣfahānī arrived in Egypt, Ibn Sallār had a *madrasa* built for him in Alexandria, known as al-ʿĀdiliyya (completed in 546/1151-2), where Sunnī *fiḳh* was taught. He may also have been responsible for the appointment of a Shāfiʿī Sunnī, Abu 'l-Maʿālī b. Djumayʿ al-Arsūfī, to the post of grand *ḳāḍī* of Egypt. After his assassination, the vizier's Sunnī supporters appealed to the caliph al-Ẓāfir to punish the one responsible, in their view, for instigating the murder, Muʾayyad al-Dawla Ibn Munḳidh, whom they presented, rather curiously for non-Ismāʿīlīs, as a stranger to the Egyptian tradition, agent of a Syrian power hostile to the Fāṭimids and a person capable of actions detrimental to the reigning caliph. Ibn Munḳidh, informed of their threats and fearing for his life, shared with his friend ʿAbbās the unsavoury rumour that was circulating in the palace concerning the dubious relationship between al-Ẓāfir and Naṣr b. ʿAbbās. Ibn Munḳidh urged the furious ʿAbbās to have al-Ẓāfir killed and replaced by another caliph. ʿAbbās then put pressure on Naṣr to kill the caliph. Al-Ẓāfir was invited by the latter to come, with a small escort, to spend a night at Dār al-Maʾmūn (or al-Maʾmūniyya, see Sayyid, *op. cit.*, 507-8, extensive bibl. on the episode in question), the vizier's residence, close to the palace. In the entrance hall, the members of the escort were slaughtered and the caliph himself, then twenty-one years old, was executed. The bodies were thrown into a nearby pit and then hidden under fragments of blue marble (early Muḥarram 549/later March 1154).

The following morning, alerted to the murder by his son, the vizier ʿAbbās presented himself openly at the Palace, on horseback, demanding to see the caliph on urgent business. He was sought everywhere, in vain. However, a minor slave in al-Ẓāfir's escort had witnessed the murder of the caliph, having hidden in an embrasure, and in the morning he informed the Palace. The women took to mourning while a guard was sent to tell ʿAbbās that the caliph had left the Palace the previous evening to visit his son and had not returned. ʿAbbās dismounted from his horse and with his escort forced his way into the Palace. Having installed himself in the great hall of the fountains, *ḳāʿat al-baḥr* (Sayyid, *op. cit.*, 466, perhaps known under a different term), where the caliph was accustomed to holding solemn receptions, he ordered that the two younger brothers of al-Ẓāfir, Djibrīl and Yūsuf, be brought to him. They told the vizier that his son should be asked what had become of their brother. ʿAbbās ordered his men to kill the two princes, then went out to announce publicly that they had confessed to the murder of al-Ẓāfir. The vizier had al-Ẓāfir's son ʿĪsā, a child of five years old, brought to the same room, perched him on his shoulder, and before the assembled dignitaries of the Palace, introduced him as al-Fāʾiz bi-Naṣr Allāh, successor to his father whom his two uncles had assassinated. The officers of the court declared with one loud voice that they had heard and would obey. The newly appointed child-caliph, shocked by the sight of the blood-stained bodies of his uncles and intimidated by the vehemence of the cry of unanimous support, was permanently traumatised, and was never to regain his health or his sanity.

From this tragic reign of a declining dynasty, one salient feature to be noted is the Sunnī upsurge which marginalised the official Ismāʿīlism of the Fāṭimids at the same time as there developed a strong sense of Egyptian identity in confrontation with the Muslim powers of Syria, a sense which was the power-base of successive viziers, often accorded the title of *sulṭān* by the chroniclers. Also to be noted is the effectiveness of the Egyptian battle fleet, at a time when the army was incapable of defending ʿAsḳalān, which fell to the Franks in Radjab 549/August 1153.

Bibliography: The most complete account is in Ibn Muyassar, *al-Muntaḳī min akhbār Miṣr*, ed. A.F. Sayyid, Cairo 1981, 141-4 and bibl. at 185-90; the list of sources, abundant for this period and all already exploited, may be found in Ibn Ẓāfir, *Akhbār al-duwal*, notes and 21-7; Y. Lev, *State and society in Fatimid Egypt*, Leiden 1991, 61-3, 199-210; Sayyid, *al-Dawla al-fāṭimiyya, tafsīr djadid*, Cairo 1413/1992, 207-11, 433-55; J.Cl. Garcin (ed.), *États, sociétés et cultures du monde musulman médiéval, Xᵉ-XVᵉ siècle*, i, Paris 1995, pp. xlii-l, 113; C. Petry (ed.), *The Cambridge history of Egypt*, i, Cambridge 1998, 154, 168, 560-71; J. Prawer, *Histoire du Royaume latin de Jérusalem*, Paris 1969, i, 394-415 (analyses in detail the contribution of Christian sources for the period).

(TH. BIANQUIS)

ẒĀFIR AL-ḤADDĀD, ABŪ MANṢŪR (Abū Naṣr in al-Dānī, Abu 'l-Ḳāsim in al-Maḳrīzī, see *Bibl.*) b. al-Ḳāsim al-Barḳī, Fāṭimid poet from Alexandria. His father was from Djudhām and his mother from Lakhm, tribes which had migrated to Egypt in early Islamic times. His date of birth is unknown. He died in Dhu 'l-Ḥidjdja 528/Sept.-Oct. 1134 or Muḥarram 529/Oct.-Nov. 1134.

At first he worked as a blacksmith like his father, but was drawn to literature and frequented meetings of poets until they acknowledged him as one of their own. He wrote panegyrics on governors and judges in Alexandria and al-Fusṭāṭ, having settled down in al-Fusṭāṭ after 508/1114-15. There he praised the Fāṭimid caliphs al-Āmir and al-Ḥāfiẓ and the viziers al-Afḍal al-Maʾmūn, al-Baṭāʾiḥī, al-Akmal and others. In addition to panegyrics, the main themes of his poetry were love-poetry and descriptive poetry, excelling in descriptions of nature, both in Alexandria and in al-Fusṭāṭ; his descriptions of Alexandria evince nostalgic memories of his youth there.

Critics admired his poetry, lauding his tender and musical language and his knack for apt similes, and the critic M. Kāmil Ḥusayn (see *Bibl.*) has ranked him among the greatest poets of his age. ʿImād al-Dīn al-Iṣfahānī accused him of committing many linguistic mistakes, and other critics accused him of plagiarism. He was perhaps the first to compose *muwashshaḥāt* [see MUWASHSHAḤ] in Egypt and also wrote a *maḳāma* addressed to al-Dānī in the ornate style of his day.

Bibliography: 1. Sources. ʿImād al-Dīn al-Iṣfahānī, *Kharīdat al-ḳaṣr. Ḳism shuʿarāʾ Miṣr*, ed. A. Amīn, Sh. Ḍayf and I. ʿAbbās, Cairo 1952, ii, 1-17; Yāḳūt, *Irshād*, ed. Rifāʿī, Cairo 1355 ff./1936 ff., xii, 27-33; Ibn Khallikān, *Wafayāt*, ed. ʿAbbās, ii, 540-3; Ṣafadī, *Wāfī*, xvi, ed. Wadād al-Ḳāḍī, Beirut 1411/1991, 521-8; Maḳrīzī, *al-Muḳaffā al-kabīr*, ed. M. al-Yaʿlāwī, Beirut 1411/1991, iv, 39-41; Abu 'l-Ṣalt Umayya b. ʿAbd al-ʿAzīz al-Dānī, *al-Risāla al-miṣriyya*, ed. ʿA. Hārūn, in *Nawādir al-makhṭūṭāt*, i, Cairo 1951, 53-4; Ibn Taghrībirdī, *Nudjūm*, Cairo n.d., v, 376-8.

2. Edition. *Dīwān*, ed. Ḥ. Naṣṣār, Cairo 1969.

3. Studies. Naṣṣār, *Ẓāfir al-Ḥaddād*, Cairo 1975; M. Zaghlūl Salām, *al-Adab fi 'l-ʿaṣr al-fāṭimī*, Alexandria 1994, 161-95; Sh. Ḍayf, *Taʾrīkh al-adab al-ʿarabī*, vi, *ʿAṣr al-duwal wa 'l-imārāt*, Cairo 1980, 176, 251-6; M. Kāmil Ḥusayn, *Fī adab Miṣr al-fāṭimiyya*, ²Cairo 1963; A. al-Nadjdjār, *al-Intādj al-adabī fī madīnat al-Iskandariyya fi 'l-ʿaṣrayn al-fāṭimī wa 'l-ayyūbī*, Cairo 1383/1964, 105-9, 149-55, 158-9, 164, 175-7, 181, 183-5, 202-3, 207-9, 234-5; ʿAbd al-ʿAlīm al-Ḳabbānī, *Maʿa 'l-shuʿarāʾ aṣḥāb al-ḥiraf*, Cairo 1967, 9-32. (Ḥusayn Nassar)

AL-ẒAFRA, conventionally Dhafarah, the interior region of the shaykhdom of Abū Ẓaby [*q.v.*], now a constituent of the United Arab Emirates [see AL-IMĀRĀT AL-ʿARABIYYA AL-MUTTAḤIDA, in Suppl.], the undefined southern frontier of which marches with the easternmost part of Saudi Arabia. Al-Ẓafra forms the traditional territory of the Banū Yās [*q.v.*] and the Banu 'l-Manāṣīr [*q.v.*].

Bibliography: J.G. Lorimer, *Gazeteer of the Persian Gulf, 'Oman and Central Arabia*, Calcutta 1908-15, ii.A, 412-26. (Ed.)

ZAGHANOS PASHA (Greek forms Záganos, etc., cf. Moravcsik, *Byzantinoturcica*², ii, Berlin 1958, 128-9), Ottoman official and general of the 9th/15th century, Grand Vizier 1444-52 and commander-in-chief of the army 1452-64, in which last year he probably died. He was an ex-Christian of the *dewshirme* [*q.v.*], possibly of Greek or Albanian origin, and was both the son-in-law of sultan Murād II and father-in-law of Meḥemmed II [*q.vv.*].

He was tutor and chief counsellor of the latter, together with the second vizier, Shihāb al-Dīn Pasha. The two of them exercised considerable influence over Meḥemmed in persuading him in 1453 to pursue the siege of Constantinople when the Grand Vizier Khalīl Pasha Djandarlî [*q.v.*] had temporarily considered lifting the siege for fear of possible Western intervention. After the conquest of the city and the execution of Khalīl, Zaghanos replaced him in his office, with a new tradition "whereby the most important positions in the central government were filled by the slaves of the sultans" (S.J. and Ezel K. Shaw, *History of the Ottoman Empire and modern Turkey*, Cambridge 1976-7, i, 58; cf. Uzunçarşılı, *Osmanlı tarihi*, ⁵Ankara 1988, i, 430-1, 439-40, 479, 499, ii, 9-10; C.H. Imber, *The Ottoman Empire 1300-1481*, Istanbul 1990, 153, 156). In the preparations for the final assault on Constantinople, Zaghanos had played an important role in preparing pontoons and siege engines, and he also shared in the construction of Rūmeli Ḥiṣārî on the European shore of the Bosphorus (see S. Runciman, *The fall of Constantinople*, Cambridge 1965, 110-11, 118-19, 162-3; A. Savvides, *Constantinople in a vice. Some notes on Anadolu Hisarı (1395/6) and Rumeli Hisarı (1452)*, in *Acta Patristica et Byzantina*, viii [Pretoria 1997], 144-9; Imber, *op. cit.*, 146, 155 ff.). Both he and Shihāb al-Dīn were summarily dismissed in 1456, and Zaghanos was exiled to Anatolia. But this exile was only brief, for he soon appears as governor of Gallipoli [see GELIBOLU], of Thessaly [see TESALYA] and of the Morea [see MORA] between 1457 and 1463 (see Savvides, *Problems of the Ottoman conquest and the spread of the conqueror in the Thessalian area* [in Greek], in *From Byzantium to the Turkish domination...*, Athens 1997, 296).

In October 1459 he succeeded Ismāʿīl Pasha as *ḳapudan-i deryā* and with his fleet attacked the Latin garrisons in Samothrace [see SEMEDIREK] and Thasos [see TASHÖZ], and from spring 1460 he was involved in the conquest of most of the Byzantine despotate of the Morea as well as of eastern Attica and Boeotia. His atrocities in the Morean campaign led to his eventual replacement in the governorship there, according to Chalcocondyles (see K.M. Setton, *The Papacy and the Levant*, Philadelphia 1976-8, ii, 220-2; Uzunçarşılı, ii, 25; Savvides, *Morea and Islam, 8th-15th centuries: a survey*, in *From Byzantium to the Turkish domination*, 319 n. 173). He then completed the annexation of the Florentine duchy of Athens (1460), executing at Thebes its last ruler (see Savvides, *The Ottoman conquest of Thebes and Levadeia* [in Greek], Athens 1993, 36, 58-9). In 1463 he became commander-in-chief of the army and possibly governor of Macedonia, and it was at this time that he took into his harem Anna, daughter of the last Byzantine emperor of Trebizond [see ṬARABZUN], eventually forcing her to adopt Islam. He died soon afterwards, probably in 1464.

Bibliography (in addition to references in the article): A. Nimet, *Die türkische Prosopographie bei Laonikos Chalcocandyles* [*sic*], Hamburg 1933, 42-4; F. Babinger, *Mehmed the Conqueror and his time (1432-1481)*, Princeton 1978, index; Uzunçarşılı, i-ii, index; Setton, *op. cit.*, index; E. Trapp *et alii*, *Prosopographisches Lexikon der Palaiologenzeit*, fasc. iii, Vienna 1978, no. 6.415; Savvides, *Notes on Zaghanos Pasha's career*, in *Jnal. of Oriental and African Studies* [Athens], x (1999); and see the *Bibl.* to MEḤEMMED II. (A. Savvides)

ZAGHARDJÎ BASHÎ (T.), the title of one of the three commanders who formed the *dīwān* or administrative focus of the Janissary corps of the Ottoman army (the other two being the Shamsundjî Bashî and the Turnadjî Bashî). Since *zaghar* means "hound" and *zaghardjî* "keeper of the hounds", the *orta* or company of the *zaghardjî*s (no. 64 in the Janissary corps) was probably in origin part of the hunting force of the early Ottoman sultans (cf. also the Segbāns [*q.v.* in Suppl.]).

Bibliography: İ.H. Uzunçarşılı, *Osmanlı devleti teşkilâtından kapı kulu ocaklar*, Ankara 1943-4, i, 199 ff.; Pakalın, iii, 645-6; Gibb and Bowen, i, 315; and see YEÑI ČERI. (Ed.)

ZAGHĀWA, the name given to a part Saharan, part-Sahelian tribe or people, who inhabit parts of the Republics of the Sūdān and Chad. They appear in the mediaeval Arabic sources and in more recent travel and anthropological literature in three distinct contexts:

(a) A pagan, albeit superficially Islamised, divine monarchy, which held sway within the existing territories of Wadai (Wādāy) and Kanem. E.W. Bovill, in his *Caravans of the Old Sahara*, Oxford and London 1933, remarked (264) that "Probably no event in the history of the Western Sudan had more far-reaching consequences than the Zaghawa invasion. Unfortunately we know nothing of its circumstances—how it came about, or the manner of its achievement", but H.A. MacMichael in his *The tribes of Central and North Kordofan*, 105-10, found it hard to quote solid historical evidence to justify this claim. Islamic sources are silent about such an "invasion". The Zaghāwa are described, in some detail, by several Arab geographers, notably al-Yaʿḳūbī (d. 259/872-3); al-Muhallabī (d. 380/990), quoted by Yāḳūt in his *Muʿdjam al-buldān*; and al-Idrīsī (d. 548/1154) in his *Kitāb Rudjdjār*. The Zaghāwa were, in part, Berber-speaking (the Ṣadrāta) and were semi-sedentary. They possessed a capital that was located in the region of Borkou (Burkū).

According to Lewicki, the Zag͟hāwa included four peoples that were later to form a part of the Tubu of Tibesti [*q.vv.*], sc. the Teda, Daza, Bideyat and a group which have retained the name of the Zag͟hāwa. According to Isḥāḳ b. Ḥusayn al-Munadjdjim (d. *ca.* 340/950-1), they had a town in the area of the Baḥr al-G͟hazāl and others which are now hard to locate, Mānān and Tarāzkī, Sag͟hwa (which also denoted camel-breeding nomads) and S͟hāma. The Zag͟hāwa also controlled Bilma, Kawar and parts of Aïr (Ayar). These towns developed trading links with Egypt via Nubia, and with the Mag͟hrib via the oasis of Ouargla (Wardjalān) in Algeria. The chief items of exchange were wheat, sorghum, cowpeas and slaves. The Zag͟hāwa facilitated the diffusion of Nubian culture into the Central Sudan, especially in crafts associated with leather and metals.

One of the last of the Zag͟hāwa kings was the reputedly nominally Muslim Arkū b. Būlū (*r. ca.* 414-59/1023-67), who established slave colonies in Kawar and at Zaylā in the Fezzan [see FAZZĀN].

(b) The Zag͟hāwa were represented amongst the slave population in lower ʿIrāḳ during the ʿAbbāsid age. Seven Zag͟hāwa slave girls are mentioned by Abu 'l-ʿAlāʾ al-Maʿarrī in his verse. A *g͟hulām*, whose name is mentioned by al-Ṭabarī and by Yāḳūt as Sālim al-Zag͟hāwī, played an active role in the great Zandj revolt (see J. Wansbrough, *Africa and the Arab geographers*, in *Language and history in Africa*, ed. D. Dalby, London 1970, 98-9, and M.A. Shaban, *Islamic history, a new interpretation*, ii, *A.D. 750-1055* (*A.H. 132-448*), Cambridge 1976, 110-13; and ZANDJ. 2.).

(c) Today, the term Zag͟hāwa denotes a partially Islamised, linguistically distinct, mixed Negro and Hamitic tribal group, who are akin to the Tubu and who are to be found in the Eastern Sahara between Lake Chad and Dārfūr province in the Sudan Republic. They are associated with the Dādjū Sultanate of Sila. According to Henri Berre, citing A.J. Arkell, (8-12) the Dādjū (or Kabdja) claim to be related to the Zag͟hāwa and to have emigrated from the east. Some lay claim to an Arab genealogy which attaches them either to the Banū K͟huzām (var. K͟hazzām, according to Arkell, but possibly to be read as Djud͟hām), or to the Banū Djuhayna (see MacMichael, *op. cit.*, 111).

Bibliography: G. Nachtigall, tr. A.G.B. and H.J. Fisher, *Sahara and Sudan*, London 1971-4, ii, *Kawar, Bornu, Kanem, Borkou and Ennedi*, 453-80; H. Carbou, *La région du Tchad et du Ouadaï*, i, *Etudes ethnographiques, dialect toubou*, Paris 1912, 1-48; W. Cline, *The Teda of Tibesti, Borko and Kawar in the Eastern Sahara*, Menasha, Wisc. 1950, 11-22; H.G. Balfour Paul, *A prehistoric cult still practised in Muslim Darfur* (*by the Zaghawa*), in *Jnal. Royal Anthrop. Institute*, lxxxvi (Jan.-June. 1956), 77-86; M.J. Tubiana, *Un rite de vie: le sacrifice d'une bête pleine chez les Zaghawa Kobé du Ouaddai*, in *Jnal. de psychologie normale et pathologique* (1960), 291-310; J.S. Trimingham, *A history of Islam in West Africa*, Oxford 1962, 104-8; A.J. Arkell, *The influence of Christian Nubia in the Chad area between AD 800-1200*, in *Kush*, ii (1963), 315-19; R. Capot-Rey, *Le nomadisme des Toubous*, in *Nomades et nomadisme au Sahara*, Recherches sur le zone aride, XIX, Paris 1963, 81-92; Tubiana, *Survivances préislamiques en pays Zaghawa*, Paris 1964; H.A. MacMichael, *The tribes of northern and central Kordofan*, London 1967, 105-14; J.M. Cuoq, *Receuil des sources arabes concernant l'Afrique occidentale du VIIIe au XVIe siècle* (*Bilād al-Sūdān*), Paris 1975, 78; T. Lewicki, *Notes magrébines et soudanaises*, i, Warsaw 1976 60-2; J.C. Zeltner, *Pages d'histoire du Kanem, pays tchadien*, Paris 1980, 11, 27-38; J.F.P. Hopkins and N. Levtzion, *Corpus of early Arabic sources for West African history*, Cambridge 1981, 21-2, 119-20; H. Berre, *Sultans Dadjo du Sila* (*Tchad*), Paris 1985, 8-13; *The Chad region as a crossroads*, in I. Hrbek (ed.), *UNESCO General history of Africa, abridged edition*, iii, *Africa from the seventh to the eleventh century*, Berkeley, etc. 1988-92, 216-22.

(H.T. NORRIS)

ZAGROS, a mountain chain of western and southwestern Persia; the geographers of Classical times identified the Zagros Mountains as the range that separated the empires of Assyria (Mesopotamia) and Media (Central Persia).

This is one of the great Tertiary fold ranges of the Middle East, which begins in the high knot of volcanic mountains, Ararat, Nemrut and others, around Lake Van, and sweeps south-south-east to the eastern edge of the Persian Gulf. At the Straits of Oman the ranges turn eastwards through Fārs and Makrān, beyond where they bend sharply to the north to form the border ramparts between Baluchistan and Sind. The mountains of Muscat and Oman are the exposed section of a flooded pendent offshoot of these same ranges.

The name Zagros is nowadays applied to that part of this mountain system lying between Kurdistān to the north and Fārs to the south, approximately between the latitudes of 29° and 35° N. or the cities of Hamadān and S͟hīrāz.

The entire range imposes a very effective physical barrier to movement, because of its great width of some 250 km/155 miles, its structure of many parallel folds which rise to 4,000 m/13,100 feet, and the narrow and precipitous nature of the few valleys that cut through them. The Zagros therefore constituted the western defensive wall of Parthian and Sāsānid Persia against assaults from Imperial Rome and Byzantium. Subsequently, the same ranges for long formed the border zone between Ottoman and Ṣafawid territory, and along their western foothills runs the present political frontier between ʿIrāḳ and Iran.

At their northern extremity, the only way over the Zagros is an old caravan route along the Great Zāb river from Irbīl, through Ruwandiz, to Miyānduʾāb, and thence to Tabrīz. By widening, between 1928 and 1932, critical parts of the gorges at Ruwandiz and Berserini, this way was made fit for motor traffic. The high pastures in this region are occupied in summer by Kurdish tribes. Lower down, the oak forests have suffered severely from uncontrolled cutting. The foothills, with an annual rainfall of some 60 mm and with the aid of terracing and irrigation, can support vines, maize and rice. The population includes both Assyrian Christians and a substantial Turkish element that was moved here in Ottoman times. There was formerly a Jewish population of some significance, speaking either Arabic or Neo-Aramaic dialects; this group has now emigrated to Israel. Further south, between the rivers Diyālā and Dez, the Zagros ranges are at their widest and highest, and are made up of regular folds, of mainly limestone rocks, of a height of some 4,000 m/13,100 feet, with few outstanding peaks. These mountains receive an appreciable precipitation, of 100 mm/40 inches or more, from the winter cyclones. This falls mainly in the form of snow, which melts through the summer to supply the extensive pastures of the high valleys and plateaux between the ranges. Summer storms here provide a further water-supply.

These wide grasslands are in effect the preserve of the main mobile tribesfolk of Iran, the Lurs (including the great Bak͟htiyārī confederacy) and the Ḳas͟hḳāʾī [*q.vv.*, and see also ILĀT]. Their population was estimated in Pahlawī times at between four and five millions, about a quarter of that of all Persia, and they could sometimes mount a threat to the central government, as in 1906. In winter these high plateaux are snow-bound, and the tribes have then to descend to the foothills and Mesopotamian plains.

This pattern of movement, with two migrations during the year, one up, one down, along established wide paths, is strictly speaking transhumant rather than nomadic. The tribes are at their most vulnerable during these movements, and it was then that, especially in the reign of Riḍā S̲h̲āh Pahlawī [*q.v.*], the army would waylay them and attempt to restrain them throughout the year in their winter camps. This enforced sedentarisation was a virtual death-sentence for both herds and herders.

The rivers of the high Zagros are active and powerful, and have in many cases captured the headwaters of their streams as far back as the main plateau. The watercourses pass through successions of isolated valleys separated by steep and narrow gorges or *tangs* which are practically impassable. In consequence, streams above and below these constrictions are often called by different names. Thus the river which begins as the Gamasiyāb is thereafter known as the Saidmarreh, and reaches the lowlands of K̲h̲ūzistān as the Karkheh [see KARK̲H̲A].

It follows that these river plains are very isolated, and only accessible by *tāḳs* or *kotals*, passes over the ranges. These very rarely link to make a continuous route across the whole mountain system. Much the most important through route is the Ṭāḳ-i Girra, the ancient *Portae Zagriacae* or *Medicae*, the Zagros or Median Gates. This road climbs from Bag̲h̲dād up the Diyālā river [*q.v.*], which occupies a natural rift opening a way through the outer ranges. The railway to K̲h̲āniḳīn takes advantage of this gap. From there the well-used road passes by Ḳaṣr-i S̲h̲īrīn and Karand, crosses the Paylak Pass to Bāk̲h̲tarān (Kirmāns̲h̲āh) in the valley of the Ḳara Sū, and then goes by way of the Ṭāḳ-i Bustān past the rock of Behistun (*Mons Bagistanus*) with its sculptures and trilingual inscriptions celebrating the conquests of Darius. Thence there is an easy approach over the plain of Čamčamāl to Hamadān, which under the name of Ecbatana was the capital of ancient Media.

Further to the east, there is another possible crossing of the heart of the Zagros, from the town of Dizfūl, along the lower Saidmarreh river and its tributary the Kashgan to K̲h̲urramābād, and thence to the fringe of the central plateau at Burūd̲j̲ird. This, however, was never an important trade route, and is essentially a highway of seasonal movement for the Bak̲h̲tiyārī tribesfolk between their winter and summer quarters. At a slight distance to the east, the Trans-Persian Railway pioneered in 1935 the very difficult route up the Diz river valley from Dizfūl to Arāk.

The foothill ranges of the Pus̲h̲t-i Kūh, about 2,000 m/6,560 feet high, separate the main Zagros from the plains of K̲h̲ūzistān. Their gypsum rocks make poor saline soils, and support only a thin cover of scrub oak. The main oil fields of Iran are trapped in these hills, between Masd̲j̲id-i Sulaymān and Gačsarān. The tribes had to pass across this area on their seasonal migrations, and it was here that they were often ambushed.

Eastwards again, the high Zagros grades into the somewhat lower ranges of the province of Fārs, about 3,000 m/9,840 feet above sea-level at their highest. Rainfall here is appreciably less, the rivers less continuous and powerful, and the high plains often contain not streams of fresh water but salty lakes at the centre of systems of inland drainage, as in the Nirīz basin and the Daryā-i Mahārlū in the high plain of S̲h̲īrāz. Seasonal transhumance is much less common here than in the central Zagros, and most of the population relies on the scattered oases irrigated by cisterns and *ḳanāts*.

The mountains are here crossed by two well-established caravan routes, from the port of Bushire (Būs̲h̲īr) up the Shāhpūr valley to Kāzarūn and S̲h̲īrāz (improved by British troops in 1918-19); and from Bandar ʿAbbās by the Tang-i Zindān to Sīrd̲j̲ān and Kirmān.

Bibliography: J.V. Harrison, *The Bakhtiari country, South-West Persia*, in *GJ*, lxxx (1932), 193-210; Naval Intelligence Division, Admiralty Handbooks, *Persia*, London 1945, esp. chs. II, XI; V. Cronin, *The last migration*, London 1952; W.C. Brice, *South-west Asia*, London 1966, esp. ch. 9.

(W.C. BRICE)

AL-ZAHĀWĪ, D̲J̲AMĪL ṢIDḲĪ (b. 18 June 1863 in Bag̲h̲dād, d. 23 February 1936), neo-classical poet and eminent representative of the *Nahḍa* [*q.v.*] in ʿIrāḳ.

A son of the Kurdish élite family of al-Bābān from Sulaymāniyya [*q.v.*]—his father Muḥammad Fayḍī was *Muftī* of Bag̲h̲dād and his mother of Kurdish upper-class origin also—he spent his childhood with his mother, who lived separately from his father. At about 7 years old he became his father's pupil in traditional Arabic learning at a time when modern-type Arabic schools did not exist in ʿIrāḳ. The father encouraged his son's poetic attempts in Arabic and Persian, but D̲j̲amīl later confessed that his real interests were the "modern sciences", in which he acquired some knowledge self-taught from translations into the languages he knew: Arabic, Persian and Turkish (Kurdish was not yet a literary language). After teaching at the Sulaymāniyya School in Bag̲h̲dād, he was appointed a member in the *Mad̲j̲lis al-maʿārif* in Bag̲h̲dād, later becoming director of the government printing house and responsible for the Arabic part of the official newspaper *al-Zawrāʾ* and also a member of the appellate court. In *ca.* 1903, having been summoned to the Porte in Istanbul, he visited Cairo and met with progressive Egyptian intellectuals. The Sultan ʿAbd al-Ḥamīd II, aware of al-Zahāwī's enmity towards the government, sent him as *wāʿiẓ ʿāmm* with a deputation to Yemen. After his return 11 months later, he was given a military rank and a medal, but his Young Turkish sympathies and a critical poem which he wrote on Ḥamīdian policies earned him two weeks' imprisonment and a return to Bag̲h̲dād under guard but with a monthly salary. When the Constitution was restored, he became professor of Islamic philosophy at the *D̲j̲emʿiyye-i mülkiyye* and of Arabic literature at the *Dār ul-Fünūn* in Istanbul. Health problems caused him to return to Bag̲h̲dād, where he taught the *Med̲j̲elle* [*q.v.*], later translated by him into Arabic, at the *Madrasat al-ḥuḳūḳ*.

His first books deal with varied topics: philosophy (1894, lectures in Turkish, 1906); horses and horse racing (1896); physical and philosophical questions of the universe (1897); chess (n.d.); a disputation concerning the condemnation of folk belief in miracles and saints, evidently meant to support ʿAbd al-Ḥamīd II's policy towards the Wahhābiyya [*q.v.*] (1905 or 1907); and gravity (1910). In October 1896 he proposed in the Egyptian journal *al-Muḳtaṭaf* a reform of

Arabic script (ed. al-Rashūdī, pp. 186-7). Only at the age of 40 did he return to poetry. He criticised the Arabic poetic tradition, characterising mono-rhyme and mono-metre as a straight-jacket. In 1905 he composed the first Arabic poem in *shiʿr mursal* (*Dīwān*, 149). All his later poetry is in mono-rhyme and, mostly, mono-metre. Already his first *dīwān*, *al-Kalim al-manẓūm* (Beirut 1907), voices his religious scepticism and his role as a social and cultural critic and an advocate of progress in ʿIrāḳ, foreshadowing his later anthologies *Dīwān al-Zahāwī* (Beirut 1924), *al-Lubāb* (Baghdād 1928), *al-Awshāl* (Baghdād 1934), *al-Thumāla* and *al-Ziyādāt* (publ. posthumously Baghdād 1939). The translation of ʿUmar al-Khayyām's *Rubāʿiyyāt* (Beirut 1924) inspired him to his own *Rubāʿiyyāt* (Baghdād 1928), which criticise in short and pugnacious verses social injustice (especially as regards the position of Muslim women), and the contrast between ʿIrāḳ's former glory and its present educational situation. He praises technical progress and supports the then highly-contested Darwinism. His audacious article *al-Marʾa wa 'l-difāʿ ʿanhā* in the Egyptian newspaper *al-Muʾayyad* (1910, publ. Nādjī, 255-8) scandalised orthodox circles. After a short (reading) drama *Layla wa-Sumayr* (in *Lughat al-ʿArab*, v [1927], 578-608) he published his brilliant *Thawra fi 'l-djaḥīm*, an epic poem of 433 verses in the *khafīf* metre. Inspired by al-Maʿarrī's [*q.v.*] *Risālat al-Ghufrān*, and, probably, by Asín Palacios' *La escatologia musulmana en la "Divina comedia"* (1924), its main idea is that heaven's inhabitants were faint conformists, always submissive to the ruling élite and traditions, while hell's inhabitants, of whom he names eminent historical authorities from East and West, were intellectually independent, courageous, creative, and therefore dangerous. Finally, in an overwhelming fight they conquer heaven, the place that they deserve (ed. in *al-Awshāl*, German tr. Widmer, in *WI*, xvii [1935], 1-79). Al-Zahāwī himself considered his *Dīwān al-Nazaghāt* as the most provocative. After a several months' stay in Cairo in 1924, where his expectations for more tolerance were soon deeply disappointed, he delivered it to Salāma Mūsā [*q.v.*]. Published only by Hilal Nādjī, Cairo 1963, it openly and ironically, but with ambiguities, voices the poet's scepticism in nearly every religious principle of Islam. The complete work of al-Zahāwī still awaits publication.

Bibliography: 1 Works. Kūrkīs ʿAwwād, *Muʿdjam al-muʾallifīn al-ʿirāḳiyyīn*, Baghdād 1969, i, 273-5; Muḥammad Y. Nadjm, *Dīwān al-Zahāwī*, Cairo 1955; ʿAbd al-Ḥamīd al-Rashūdī, *al-Zahāwī, dirāsāt wa-nuṣūṣ*, Beirut 1966; Hilāl Nādjī, *al-Zahāwī wa-dīwānuhu al-mafḳūd*, Cairo 1963.

2. Studies. M.M. Badawi, *A critical introduction to modern Arabic poetry*, Cambridge 1975, 47-75; Salma K. Jayyusi, *Trends and movements in modern Arabic poetry*, Leiden 1977, 184-93; ʿAbd al-Razzāḳ al-Hilālī, *al-Zahāwī fī maʿārikihi al-adabiyya wa 'l-fikriyya*. Baghdād 1982; W. Walther, *Ǧamīl Ṣidqī az-Zahāwī, ein irakischer Zindīq*, in *Oriens*, xxxiv (1994), 430-50; Julie S. Meisami and P. Starkey (eds.), *Encyclopedia of Arabic literature*, London and New York 1998, ii, 818; Brockelmann, S III, 483-8.

(WIEBKE WALTHER)

ZĀHID [see ZUHD].

ZĀHIDĀN, a city of southeastern modern Iran (lat. 29° 32' N., long. 60° 54' E.), this being the new name, adopted in the time of Riḍā Shāh Pahlawī [*q.v.*], for the older settlement of Duzdāb.

Duzdāb/Zāhidān lies on the north-south highway connecting Čābahār on the Persian coast of the Gulf of Oman through Birdjand to Khurāsān (now of special importance as a supply link to the newly-independent central Asian republics), at some 40 km/25 miles south of the point where the borders of Iran, Afghānistān and Pakistani Balūčistān meet. Though situated in a harsh desert environment (average rainfall p.a., 75 mm/3 inches), the place has had a considerable commercial and strategic significance over the last century or so, and during the First World War it became the western terminus of the railway extended from Quetta [see KWAṬṬA] through the northern part of what was then British Balūčistān. There were plans in the 1930s to connect the railhead of Zāhidān with the Trans-Iranian railway constructed by Riḍā Shāh (see Naval Intelligence Division, Admiralty Handbooks, *Persia*, London 1945, 550, 563); but it was not till the second half of the century that the railway was extended from Ḳum to Yazd and Kirmān city and beyond the latter for mineral traffic, although the passenger traffic line has not yet reached Zāhidān (see *The Middle East and North Africa*, 47th ed. London 2001, 560).

The present city of Zāhidān is almost wholly a modern one. In *ca.* 1950 it had a population of some 10,000, a mixture of Persians and Balūč (Razmārā (ed.), *Farhang-i djughrāfiyā-yi Īrān-zamīn*, viii, 218-19), which by the census of 1996 had grown to 419,518. It is the administrative centre for the province of Balūčistān and Sīstān, and has such amenities as an airport and a university.

Bibliography: Given in the article.

(C.E. BOSWORTH)

ẒAHĪR (A.), conventional form *dahir*, an administrative term of the Muslim West.

Here *ẓahīr*, meaning "help, support", came to mean a royal decree issued by the sovereign and conferring an administrative prerogative, such as nomination to a political or religious post, or granting a privilege, either moral or material, upon the beneficiary. In the case of conferred privileges, the beneficiary could share them with his relatives or even pass them on to his descendants if the sovereign was generous enough to include such a favour in the document.

The early dynasties

The term first appeared under the Almohad dynasty (524-668/1130-1269), replacing another term, *ṣakk*, used earlier by the Almoravids (454-541/1062-1147) and the Andalusian *ṭāʾifa* kingdoms to refer to the same type of royal or princely decree. As such, the use of the term *ẓahīr* was especially associated with the royal administrative tradition in the Maghrib and Islamic Spain. The *ẓahīr* was, in the first place, a document the ruler delivered to a state official upon his appointment. In the case of a governor, it would define the administrative prerogatives and the territorial limits within which he would exercise his powers. Along with the royal decree, the governor would also receive a seal and a garment. A copy of the document was usually addressed to the subjects of the appointee in order to introduce the new official and reiterate the duty of obeying those representing the princely authority. The content of the *ẓahīr* was made known in a public reading, usually at the main mosque following the Friday prayer. An ambassador on mission to a foreign court was also supposed to carry a *ẓahīr* introducing him to the authorities of that country. In this case, the document was no different from an official letter of accreditation. In fact, in common usage, *ẓahīr* became synonymous with "royal letter", but *ẓahīr* in its strict sense refers to a document endowed with a legal binding power, which a letter does not necessarily have.

Another use of the document consisted in bestowing privileges upon merchants, dignitaries, religious figures or former state servants as a reward for their past services or in recognition of their loyalty to the sovereign. These privileges could be symbolic, in the form of "distinction and respect" (*at-tawḳīr wa 'l-iḥtirām*), or they could be material in the form of a regular allowance, land grant (*tanfīdha*), the right to farm taxes within a defined territory, or a trade monopoly. *Ẓahīrs* were also delivered to the *shaykhs* of the Ṣūfī lodges and to members of Sharīfian families to confirm their distinguished status or to corroborate their claim to a holy lineage, on the basis of which they would be entitled to a number of privileges, such as exemption from non-religious taxation, arbitrary impositions, *corvée* obligations and military service. They also involved respect (*tawḳīr*) and special treatment by the local authorities, thereby demonstrating the state's consideration for those whose descent or social distinction placed them above the common people.

The bestowal of such privileges by a Muslim sovereign by means of *ẓahīr* was not limited to his Muslim subjects. Christian or Jewish subjects were also among the beneficiaries. The Almohad ruler Abū Ya'ḳūb Yūsuf II (1213-23) even wrote a *ẓahīr* in favour of a Christian monastery located beyond the northern Andalusian border, giving the monks the right to drive their cattle south to the more favourable grazing lands of the Almohad domains. The most famous Almohad ruler, Ya'ḳūb al-Manṣūr (1184-99 [see ABŪ YŪSUF YA'ḲŪB AL-MANṢŪR]), also wrote *ẓahīrs* in favour of his Jewish subjects. The practice of extending *ẓahīr* privileges to Jews became even more common during the modern period with the growing role of Jewish merchants in domestic and international trade.

Under the Sa'dids and 'Alawīs

Under the Sharīfian rule of the Sa'dī and 'Alawī dynasties (916/1510-present day), the issuing of *ẓahīrs* became more frequent as a result of the special privileges acquired by the *sharīfs* and because of the proliferation of saintly lineages. The growing weakness of the central government and its inability to extend its effective rule to the whole country also meant that sultans were more disposed to grant privileges for those local religious and political figures who would return the favour and support the state's policies at the regional level. Under these two Sharīfian dynasties, the most common form of *ẓahīr* became the *ẓahīr al-tawḳīr wa 'l-iḥtirām* delivered to Sharīfian families, maraboutic figures, *shaykhs* of the Ṣūfī orders and faithful servants.

This form of *ẓahīr* usually conferred upon the holder and his relatives the two kinds of privileges mentioned above, moral and material. Every *ẓahīr* of this category was by definition a title of distinction conferred by the highest political and religious authority of the land. The mere fact of possessing such a document was enough to guarantee its holder special treatment by the local authorities and to free him from the exactions and abuses usually suffered by the common people. The royal decree could also involve material benefits, such as exemption from non-religious taxes, or even more, the authorisation to pay the legal religious taxes, normally due to the state treasury (*bayt al-māl*), to the poor among the grantee's relatives. In the case of *zāwiyas*, such a favour amounted to a practical exemption from religious taxation, since it was up to the *shaykh* of the *zāwiya* to decide how he would spend the proceeds of the *zakāt* and *'ushr* [*q.vv.*]. In the case of an influential *zāwiya*, the sultan could also make concessions in the form of land grants, the right to collect taxes from tribes or villages for the benefit of the *zāwiya*, and even the right to nominate judges or other officials within the territory that fell within the *zāwiya*'s sphere of influence. The *ẓahīr* of respect could also turn the residence or the domain of the beneficiary into a sanctuary (*ḥaram*, *ḥurm* in Moroccan usage) where people and property would be immune from state prosecution or intervention.

By the end of the 19th century, the number of subjects holding *ẓahīrs* of distinction freeing them from state obligations had reached unbearable proportions. This inflation of *ẓahīrs*, in addition to the harmful effects of European consular protection, led to the deterioration of state finances. However, reforms by which *ẓahīr* privileges would be abolished, or at least limited, were doomed to failure since traditional groups benefitting from state-bestowed privileges vigorously opposed any attempt at reform which would harm their interests. Under the French protectorate régime, which ruled the country after 1912, and after Moroccan independence in 1956, the *ẓahīr* as a title of exemption from state obligations was *de facto* abolished, even if Moroccan sultans (after 1956, kings) continued to deliver *ẓahīrs* to reconfirm the Sharīfian status of those who held similar documents issued by their predecessors. The significance of such documents became purely honorific. Nowadays, usage of the term *ẓahīr* is strictly limited to legislation bearing the royal seal or to appointments to a high state position.

Bibliography: 'Abd al-Raḥmān Ibn Zaydān, *al-'Izz wa 'l-ṣawla fī ma'ālim nuẓum al-dawla*, 2 vols. Rabat 1961-2; Ahmed Azzaoui, *Nouvelles lettres almohades*, Publs. Fac. des Lettres et des Sciences Humaines, Kenitra 1995, i.

(MOHAMED EL MANSOUR)

ẒĀHIR (A., pl. *ẓawāhir*), lit. the outward meaning of a word, language or event, a term of *uṣūl al-fiḳh* [*q.v.*]. It is the meaning first comprehended by the mind upon hearing a particular term or expression that potentially has two or more meanings. Deriving from a root suggesting a notion of strength, *ẓāhir* is applied to that meaning which in effect takes over the term, thus imparting it before it does the other meanings carried therein. That particular meaning is made prominent by virtue of conventional (*'urfī*) or technical (*ṣinā'ī*) usage. Cast in opposition to *naṣṣ*, which designates a univocal term, *ẓāhir* is epistemologically probabilistic (*muḥtamal*). Yet *ẓāhir* is also contrasted with *khafī*, this being a term carrying an unclear meaning that is established or deduced only after a hermeneutical effort has been made. This interpretive activity is said to result in the *bāṭin* meaning of the term. Accordingly, the term *ẓāhir* stands somewhere in the middle of a spectrum whose two extreme ends are the *naṣṣ* and the *khafī*.

The term is also applicable to events, states or situations in so far as they are analysable in terms of discourse. If a Muslim is caught carrying wine, claiming that it is either not his or that he intends to ferment it into vinegar, then he would not be held liable if it can be shown that he is pious and of good character. In such an instance, it is said that the *ẓāhir* of his overall situation and character is an argument in his own vindication. It is in this sense that the jurists held the view that legal construction must, as a rule, be based on the *ẓāhir* (*al-binā' 'alā al-ẓāhir wādjib*).

In the Ḥanafī school of law, the *ẓāhir al-riwāya* or alternatively *ẓāhir al-madhhab* is the most authoritative doctrine, that which is transmitted from Abū Ḥanīfa, Abū Yūsuf and al-Shaybānī through a large number of channels by trustworthy and highly qualified jurists.

Bibliography: Bādjī, *K. al-Ḥudūd fi 'l-uṣūl*, ed. Nazīh Ḥammād, Beirut 1973, 43, 48; Aḥmadnagarī, *Djāmiʿ al-ʿulūm*, 4 vols., Ḥaydarābād 1911-12, ii, 286; Ibn ʿĀbidīn, *Nashr al-ʿurf*, in *Madjmūʿat rasāʾil Ibn ʿĀbidīn*, 2 vols., n.p. 1970, ii, 128; Ps. al-Djuwaynī, *al-Kāfiya fi 'l-djadal*, Cairo 1979, 49; al-Sharīf al-Djurdjānī, *al-Taʿrīfāt*, Cairo 1938, 124.

(Wael Hallaq)

AL-**ẒĀHIR** WA 'L-**BĀṬIN** (A.), two terms of Arabic theological and philosophical discourse, the first, *ẓāhir*, meaning "outward, external, exoteric sense", hence "apparent, manifest sense", and the second, *bāṭin*, its antonym, meaning "hidden, inner, esoteric sense". This pair of words occurs together four times in the Ḳurʾān: in VI, 120, to describe the outwardness and the inwardness of a sin; in XXXI, 20, as adjectives to describe God's blessings, both manifest and hidden; in LVII, 3, as names of God to mean that He is the Outward and the Inward [reality], and in LVII, 13, as opposites portraying both the inside as well as the outside of a thing (*Muʿdjam alfāẓ al-Ḳurʾān al-karīm*, Cairo 1409/1988, i, 141, ii, 732, 733; Lane, i, 219-22, ii, 1926-30).

The Shīʿa, both the Imāmīs and the Ismāʿīlīs, maintain that the Ḳurʾān has both an outer (*ẓahr*) as well as an inner dimension (*baṭn*). To support their contention they report a tradition wherein the Prophet is stated to have said, "Not a verse of the Ḳurʾān has come down [to me] but it has a *ẓahr* (a literal expression or an apparent meaning) and a *baṭn* (an interpretation or an inner meaning)" (al-Ḳāḍī al-Nuʿmān, *Asās al-taʾwīl*, ed. A. Tāmir, Beirut 1960, 30; Abū Djaʿfar al-Ṭūsī, *al-Tibyān fī tafsīr al-Ḳurʾān*, ed. Aḥmad al-ʿĀmilī, Beirut, n.d., i, 9; see also Muḥyī al-Dīn Ibn al-ʿArabī [attrib.], *al-Tafsīr*, ed. M. al-Ghamrāwī, Cairo n.d., i, 2; al-Suyūṭī, *al-Itḳān fī ʿulūm al-Ḳurʾān*, ed. Abu 'l-Faḍl, Beirut 1988, iv, 196-8; *LʿA* and *TʿA*, s.v. *ẓ-h-r*). The aforementioned Shīʿī tradition further states that the inner dimension has yet another dimension; in fact, it states, there are up to seven or seventy inner dimensions (al-Sayyid Muḥammad Ḥusayn al-Ṭabāṭabāʾī, *al-Mīzān fī tafsīr al-Ḳurʾān*, Ḳumm n.d., i, 7). Referring to the inner meaning or the interpretation (*bāṭin*) of the Ḳurʾān, the Imām Djaʿfar al-Ṣādiḳ is reported to have said, "We can speak about a word in seven ways." One of the followers in the audience, expressing his surprise, asked, "Seven, O son of the Messenger of God?" The Imām replied, "Yes, [not only seven], but seventy" (*Asās al-taʾwīl*, 27). ʿAlī b. Abī Ṭālib is reported to have said, "The apparent meaning (*ẓāhir*) of the Ḳurʾān is elegant, and its inner meaning (*bāṭin*) is profound; the marvels [of the Ḳurʾān] cannot be fathomed and its wonders cannot be exhausted" (al-Faḍl b. al-Ḥasan al-Ṭabrisī, *Madjmaʿ al-bayān fī tafsīr al-Ḳurʾān*, ed. Hāshim al-Rasūlī and F. al-Ṭabāṭabāʾī, [Tehran] 1379/1959-60, ii, 9; see also *al-Mīzān*, *op. cit.*, i, 12). In his *al-Uṣūl min al-kāfī*, ed. ʿAlī Akbar al-Ghaffārī, Tehran 1388/1968, i, 228, Abū Djaʿfar Muḥammad b. Yaʿḳūb al-Kulīnī states, "No-one except the *awṣiyāʾ* [i.e. the Imāms] can claim that they possess the whole of the Ḳurʾān, both its *ẓāhir* and its *bāṭin*."

The Prophet Muḥammad was the recipient of God's revelation, its transmitter and its interpreter. The Shīʿa, both the Imāmīs and the Ismāʿīlīs, maintain that God revealed both the Ḳurʾān (often called *tanzīl*, because it was sent down or revealed) and its exegesis (*taʾwīl* [*q.v.*]) to the Prophet. The Prophet, in turn, transmitted the revelation but reserved the transmission of its *taʾwīl* for the Imāms. The latter therefore have a unique relationship to the Ḳurʾān. In a well-known tradition, related by both Shīʿī and Sunnī traditionists (with some variations in the wording), the Ḳurʾān is presented as "the greater weight" (*al-thaḳal al-akbar*) and the Imāms as the "lesser weight" (*al-thaḳal al-aṣghar*). The Prophet, according to this tradition, is said to have told the Muslims, "I am leaving among you two things of great weight (*al-thaḳalayn*), the Book of God and my kindred (*ʿitratī*), the people of my House (*ahl baytī*, i.e. the Imāms), and these two shall never be separated until they return to me at the Pool (*ḥawḍ*) just like these two." Then the Prophet put together the index fingers of his two hands, coupling them and equalising them in all respects. He added "And not like this," and extended the middle and index fingers of his right hand, "because one reaches out beyond the other. Indeed, the likeness of these [two things of great weight], is Noah's ark. He who boarded it was saved, and he who left it was drowned" (al-Ḳāḍī al-Nuʿmān, *Daʿāʾim al-islām*, ed. Fyzee, Cairo 1963, i, 28, Eng. tr. Fyzee, revised and annotated by I. Poonawala, forthcoming; *al-Kāfī*, i, 294; *Madjmaʿ al-bayān fī tafsīr al-Ḳurʾān*, i, 9; Walī al-Dīn Muḥammad al-Tabrīzī, *Mishkāt al-maṣābīḥ*, ed. Muḥammad al-Albānī, Damascus 1961, iii, 255, 258, Eng. tr. J. Robson, Lahore 1975, ii, 1350, 1353; Wensinck, *Concordance*, s.v. *th-ḳ-l*; transmitted by Ibn Ḥanbal, Muslim, al-Tirmidhī and al-Dārimī).

Thus it is apparent from the foregoing discussion that the *ẓāhir* (or *ẓahr*) and *bāṭin* (or *baṭn*) of the Ḳurʾān have been identified by the Shīʿa with the principles of *tanzīl* and *taʾwīl*. The former refers to the revealed text of the Ḳurʾān and the latter to its inner, esoteric meaning. Al-Kulīnī's *kitāb al-ḥudjdja*, in his *al-Uṣūl min al-kāfī*, and al-Ḳāḍī al-Nuʿmān's *kitāb al-walāya*, in his *Daʿāʾim al-islām*, are eloquent testimonies and detailed accounts of their respective views on the subject. It should be noted, however, that in comparison with the Ismāʿīlīs' use of it, the principle of the *ẓāhir* and *bāṭin* is used by the Imāmīs somewhat moderately. The Ismāʿīlīs, in contrast, assert that every exoteric meaning has an esoteric counterpart; therefore, all aspects of religion are divided into *ẓāhir* and *bāṭin*. The former consists of exterior aspects, such as knowing the apparent meaning of the Ḳurʾān and performing the obligatory acts as laid down in the *Sharīʿa* [*q.v.*]. The latter, on the other hand, is comprised of knowing the hidden, inner, true meaning of the Ḳurʾān and the *Sharīʿa*. The *ẓāhir*, which represents the body, can be perceived by the senses, while the *bāṭin*, which represents the spirit, is derived by special knowledge called *taʾwīl*. The apparent meaning of the Ḳurʾān, the Ismāʿīlīs state, perishes in the opacity and servitude of legalist religion. It is necessary to bring out the transparency of its depth, the esoteric meaning. Attaining comprehension of *bāṭin*/*taʾwīl* is like a spiritual birth that enables the person to enter a new world, to accede to a higher plane of being. They further contend that the *ẓāhir* was the miracle of the Prophet while the *bāṭin* is the miracle of the Imāms (*Asās al-taʾwīl*, 31; Abū Yaʿḳūb al-Sidjistānī, *K. al-Iftikhār*, ed. Poonawala, forthcoming, ch. xii). Al-Ḳāḍī al-Nuʿmān's *Taʾwīl al-daʿāʾim*, ed. M. Aʿẓamī, Cairo n.d. and al-Sidjistānī's *K. al-Iftikhār* are good examples of Ismāʿīlī *bāṭin*/*taʾwīl* doctrine. The conviction that to everything apparent, literal, exoteric there corresponds something hidden, spiritual, esoteric, is the fundamental principle at the very foundation of Ismāʿīlī doctrine. *Bāṭin* is the central postulate of esoterism and of esoteric *taʾwīl* (hermeneutics). Because of their insistence on this principle, the Ismāʿīlīs are very often called *al-Bāṭiniyya* by their opponents, and they are classified as extremist Shīʿa by the Muslim heresiographers (see ʿAbd al-Ḳāhir al-Baghdādī, *al-Farḳ bayn al-firaḳ*, ed. M. Muḥyī al-Dīn, Cairo n.d., 281 ff.; al-Shahrastānī, *al-Milal wa 'l-niḥal*, ed. ʿAbd al-ʿAzīz al-Wakīl, Cairo 1968, i, 192; al-Ghazālī, *Faḍāʾiḥ al-bāṭiniyya*, ed. ʿAbd al-Raḥmān Badawī, Cairo 1964; I. Goldziher, *Streitschrift des Gazālī gegen die Bāṭinijja-Sekte*, Leiden 1916; Abū Muḥammad al-Yamanī, *ʿAḳāʾid al-thalāth wa-sabʿīna firḳa*, ed. Muḥammad al-Ghāmidī, Medina 1414/1993, ii, 477). The Zaydīs are opposed to *Bāṭinī taʾwīl* as practiced by Ismāʿīlīs and Imāmīs. Druzes [see DURŪZ], on the other hand, affirm that the Bible, the Ḳurʾān and their own scriptures have esoteric as well as exoteric meanings. They further maintain that in addition to these two levels of meaning there is yet another level, called "the esoteric of the esoteric" (Samy Swayd, *The Druzes. An annotated bibliography*, Kirkland, Wash. 1998, 36).

The Ṣūfīs also maintain this principle of *ẓāhir* and *bāṭin* with regard to the Ḳurʾān. The *tafsīr* of Sahl al-Tustarī (d. 283/896 [*q.v.*]), one of the oldest extant works representing mystical interpretation of the Ḳurʾān, is a good case in point. At the basic level of interpretation al-Tustarī's division is twofold: *ẓāhir* (exoteric) and *bāṭin* (esoteric). The former aspect comprises mostly traditions (*aḥādīth*) explaining religious law, occasions of revelations, and other obvious matters, while the latter aspect comprises mystical explanations. Referring to the Ḳurʾān, at the beginning of the *tafsīr*, al-Tustarī states, "Its apparent meaning (*ẓāhir*) is beautiful and its inner meaning (*bāṭin*) is profound, and no mind is capable of comprehending it" (*Tafsīr al-Ḳurʾān al-ʿaẓīm*, Cairo 1326/1908, 2; G. Böwering, *The mystical vision of existence in classical Islam. The Qurʾānic hermeneutics of the Ṣūfī Sahl al-Tustarī*, New York 1980, 139). Further explaining the meaning of the Ḳurʾānic verses, he states, "Each verse has four levels of signification: a *ẓāhir*, a *bāṭin*, a *ḥadd* and a *maṭlaʿ* (or *muṭṭalaʿ*). The *ẓāhir* is the recitation of that verse, the *bāṭin* is its [proper] understanding, the *ḥadd* defines what is lawful and what is unlawful, and the *maṭlaʿ* (the point of transcendency) or the *muṭṭalaʿ* (anagogical meaning) is the spectacle of the heart and its meaning intended by God" (see also al-Sulamī, *Ḥaḳāʾiḳ al-tafsīr*, in Böwering, *The mystical vision*, 140; this fourfold division is attributed by al-Sulamī to ʿAlī b. Abī Ṭālib in *Itḳān*).

Abū ʿAbd al-Raḥmān al-Sulamī's (d. 412/1021) *Ḥaḳāʾiḳ al-tafsīr*, which holds a unique place in the history of Ṣūfī *tafsīr*, also uses the distinction of *ẓāhir* and *bāṭin* (Böwering, *The Qurʾān commentary of Sulamī*, in *Islamic studies presented to Charles Adams*, ed. W. Hallaq and D.P. Little, Leiden 1991, 41-56; al-Sulamī, *Ziyādāt ḥaḳāʾiḳ al-tafsīr*, ed. Böwering, Beirut 1995, 1, 24, 38, 42, 43, 101, 106.) This trend of Ṣūfī esoteric interpretation of the Ḳurʾān was continued by Rūzbihān al-Baḳlī (d. 606/1209), Ibn al-ʿArabī (d. 638/1240), and others.

Bibliography (in addition to the references listed in the article): ʿUmar b. al-Fāriḍ, *Dīwān*, Cairo n.d., esp. *al-Tāʾiyya al-kubrā*; Goldziher, *Die Richtungen der islamischen Koranauslegung*, ²Leiden 1974 (although now dated in important respects, still a comprehensive work), Arabic tr. M. ʿAbd al-Ḥalīm al-Nadjdjār, *Madhāhib al-tafsīr al-islāmī*, Cairo 1965; L. Massignon, *Essai sur les origines du lexique technique de la mystique musulmane*, ²Paris 1968; P. Nwyia, *Le Tafsīr mystique attribué à Jaʿfar al-Ṣādiq*, in *MUSJ*, xliii (1968), 181-230; idem, *Exégèse coranique et langage mystique*, Beirut 1970; idem, *Trois oeuvres inédites des mystiques musulmans*, Beirut 1973; Kāmil M. al-Shaybī, *al-Ṣila bayn al-taṣawwuf wa 'l-tashayyuʿ*, ²Cairo 1969, 407-25; H. Corbin, *L'imagination créatrice dans le Soufisme d'Ibn ʿArabî*, Paris 1958, Eng. tr. R. Manheim, *Creative imagination in the Ṣūfism of Ibn ʿArabī*, Princeton 1969; Sezgin, *GAS*, i, 19-49; Hanna Kassis, *A concordance of the Qurʾan*, Berkeley 1983, 345-6, 1338; Mahmoud Ayoub, *The Speaking Qurʾān and the Silent Qurʾān. A study of the principles and development of Imāmī Shīʿī* tafsīr, in *Approaches to the history of the interpretation of the Qurʾān*, ed. A. Rippin, Oxford 1988, 177-98; Ismail Poonawala, *Ismāʿīlī* Taʾwīl *of the Qurʾān*, in *ibid.*, 199-222; Naṣr Ḥāmid Abū Zayd, *Falsafat al-taʾwīl. Dirāsa fī taʾwīl al-Ḳurʾān ʿinda Muḥyī al-Dīn b. ʿArabī*, Cairo 1983; Muḥammad Ḥusayn al-Dhahabī, *al-Tafsīr wa 'l-mufassirūn*, Cairo 1995, esp. vols. ii and iii (his views on the Shīʿa and the Ṣūfīs reflect the standpoint of a modern orthodox Sunnī); Muḥammad Kāmil Ḥusayn, *Ṭāʾifat al-Durūz, taʾrīkhuhā wa-ʿaḳāʾiduhā*, Cairo 1962; Nejla Abu-Izzeddin, *The Druzes. A new study of their history, faith and society*, Leiden 1993. (I. POONAWALA)

AL-ẒĀHIR [see BARḲŪḲ; BAYBARS I].

AL-ẒĀHIR BI-AMR ALLĀH, ABŪ NAṢR MUḤAMMAD b. al-Nāṣir, 35th ʿAbbāsid caliph, *r.* 622-3/1225-6. In 585/1189 he was designated by al-Nāṣir [*q.v.*], as his father's elder son, to succeed him, but in 601/1205, probably under the influence of the Shīʿī vizier Ibn Mahdī, the caliph changed his mind and made his heir his younger son ʿAlī, more favourable towards Shīʿism than the elder one, who was very attached to Sunnī orthodoxy. To explain and justify this decision, a letter was produced, signed by two witnesses, in which the prince Abū Naṣr Muḥammad asked his father to relieve him of the function of *walī al-ʿahd*, which he felt incapable of assuming. However, ʿAlī died in 612/1215-16, and since the caliph had no other heir, Abū Naṣr was restored to his former status but kept under close surveillance until 615/1218-19 or 618/1221-2.

On his father's death, he was hailed as caliph at the end of Ramaḍān 622/beginning of October 1225 when he was more than 50 years old, and chose the regnal *laḳab* of al-Ẓāhir. His reign was only 9 months and 14 days, since he himself died on 14 Radjab 623/11 July 1226; but he is unanimously praised by the historians as a just, generous and pious ruler who gave extensive alms, freed unjustly-confined prisoners and restored to their owners lands confiscated by his father.

In the political and religious fields, he had hardly any time to accomplish any major work. The influence of the Ḥanbalīs increased in Baghdād, whilst as his external policy, the caliph tried to end the fratricidal strife of the Ayyūbid princes in Syria and Egypt, hoping to make them his own vassals. To this end he despatched Muḥyī al-Dīn Yūsuf Ibn al-Djawzī, son of the famous Ḥanbalī theologian [see IBN AL-DJAWZĪ] with robes of honour and investiture diplomas. In the economic and fiscal spheres, he undertook a series of important measures, at the risk of diminishing the state revenues, by forbidding uncanonical taxes (*mukūs*), abolishing the increases in land tax made by his father and attacking the frauds that were rife within the public treasury. He further combatted the excessive price rises of staple foods, especially at the time of the great famine which affected all of Upper Mesopotamia during the year of his reign. Within Baghdād, he had constructed a second bridge of boats across the Tigris and abolished the espionage and intelligence service set up in every quarter of the city by his father, to the great relief of the population.

Bibliography: 1. Sources. Ibn al-Athīr, ed. Beirut, xii, 441-4, 456-7; Sibṭ Ibn al-Djawzī, *Mirʾāt al-zamān*, ed. Ḥaydarābād, viii, 522-3, 592, 636; Abū Shāma, *Dhayl*, Cairo 1947, 50-1, 145, 149; Bar Hebraeus, *Chronography*, tr. Budge, London 1932, i, 389; al-Makīn Ibn al-ʿAmīd, in *BEO*, xv (1958), 135-6; Ibn Wāṣil, *Mufarridj al-kurūb*, iv, ed. Ḥasanayn Rabīʿ and Saʿīd ʿĀshūr, Cairo 1972, 191-6; Ibn al-Tiḳṭaḳā, *Fakhrī*, ed. Dérenbourg. 443-4, Eng. tr. Whitting, 316-17; Suyūṭī, *T. al-Khulafāʾ*, Aleppo 1991, 412-14.

2. Studies. H.L. Gottschalk, *al-Malik al-Kāmil von Egypten und seine Zeit*, Wiesbaden 1958, 130-2; Angelika Hartmann, *An-Nāsir li-dīn Allāh (1180-1225). Politik, Religion, Kultur in der späten ʿAbbāsidenzeit*, Berlin and New York 1975, index.

(ANNE-MARIE EDDÉ)

AL-ẒĀHIR LI-IʿZĀZ DĪN ALLĀH, Abu 'l-Ḥasan (or Abū Hāshim) ʿAlī b. al-Ḥākim bi-amr Allāh, seventh Fāṭimid caliph and the fourth to reign at Cairo in Egypt.

After the death of al-Ḥākim on 27 Shawwāl 411/14 February 1021, Sitt al-Mulk [*q.v.*], the latter's half-sister, refused to recognise the rights of the heir presumptive, Abu 'l-Ḳāsim ʿAbd al-Raḥīm (or ʿAbd al-Raḥmān) b. Ilyās, al-Ḥākim's cousin, designated *walī al-ʿahd* by the latter in 404/1014-5 and at the time governor of Damascus (A.F. Sayyid, *al-Dawla al-fāṭimiyya, tafsīr djadīd*, Cairo 1413/1992, 108-9, 117-18). Recalled to Cairo, he allegedly committed suicide some months later. Sitt al-Mulk, the favourite daughter of the caliph al-ʿAzīz, who had been constantly humiliated by the Palace since her father's death, secured the succession for her nephew, born in Ramaḍān 395/1005, who received the public *bayʿa* at sixteen years of age on 10 Dhu 'l-Ḥidjdja 411/28 March 1021. The princess, who retained her Christian faith, was a true stateswoman, negotiating a treaty with Byzantium. She exercised the reality of power in the state until her death, which took place in Dhu 'l-Ḳaʿda 413/February 1023. After the death of the princess, al-Ẓāhir was notorious until the end of his life for his political incompetence. Unlike his father, tormented to the point of insanity by his political, moral and religious responsibilities, al-Ẓāhir seems to have been a hedonist, enjoying the wine and the black slaves supplied to him by a Jewish merchant, the future *wazīr* Abū Saʿd Ibrāhīm b. Sahl al-Tustarī (Ibn Muyassar, *Akhbār Miṣr*, ed. Sayyid, Cairo 1981, 2-5). Al-Ẓāhir never showed any interest in the wielding of real power, and was the first Fāṭimid caliph to shift the responsibility for any important decision on to his entourage, inaugurating a tradition of personal impotence on the part of the Imām which was to persist until the end of the dynasty. His contemporary, al-Musabbiḥī [*q.v.*] wrote a chronicle of which a few months have been preserved, from 414-5/1024-5 (*La chronique d'Égypte*, ed. Sayyid and Th. Bianquis, Cairo 1978), recounting in detail on the one hand, the public life of the caliph, the reception of the military, administrative and religious hierarchy in the great hall, and solemn processions around Cairo and its neighbourhood (P. Sanders, *Rituals, politics and the city in Fatimid Cairo*, New York 1994, index at 231), and on the other, the secret and ruthless struggles erupting between the various nexuses of power at the heart of the palace, dominated by a faction of three civilians and a military eunuch who joined forces to deprive the caliph of all executive power (Bianquis, *Damas et la Syrie sous la domination fāṭimide*, ii, Damascus 1989, 391-8; idem, *Le fonctionnement financier des dīwāns centraux fāṭimides au début du Vᵉ/XIᵉ siècle*, in *AI*, xxvi [1992], 46-61).

The powerlessness of the state was evident when in 415/1024-5 Egypt experienced a serious famine, followed by an epidemic and rural and urban disorder, and the Fāṭimid presence in Syria was threatened by attacks on the part of three major tribes: Ṭayyiʾ Djarrāhids from Transjordan against Ramla, Kalb ʿAdawīs from Palmyra or Tadmur against Damascus and Kilāb Mirdāsids [*q.vv.*] from northern Syria against Aleppo (see Bianquis, *Une crise frumentaire dans l'Égypte fāṭimide*, in *JESHO*, xxiii [1978], 67-101; idem, *Damas et la Syrie*, ii, 399-511; Sayyid, *al-Dawla al-fāṭimiyya*, 119-23 and index). However, the public teaching of the Ismāʿīlī doctrine with the aid of works written by the *ḳāḍīs* al-Nuʿmān and Ibn Killis continued in Egypt (see H. Halm, *The Fatimids and their traditions of learning*, London 1997). Propagandists sent secretly to the East enjoyed some success in southern ʿIrāḳ but failed in the Ghaznawid state, resolutely Sunnī and loyal to the ʿAbbāsids.

However, thanks to the efforts of two exceptional individuals, the most serious problems were resolved. In Cairo, in Rabīʿ I 418/ April-May 1027, the ʿIrāḳī *kātib* Abu 'l-Ḳāsim ʿAlī b. Aḥmad al-Djardjarāʾī, former steward of Sitt al-Mulk and a force in the palace since 415/1025, was appointed *wazīr*, an office that had been suppressed by al-Ḥākim and replaced by the *wisāṭa* and the *sifara*. In southern and central Syria, Fāṭimid domination was restored by the able Turkish general Anushtakīn al-Dizbarī [*q.v.*] who, despite the hostility of the *dīwāns* of Cairo, won a decisive victory over the Bedouin coalition at al-Ukhuwāna, to the east of Lake Tiberias (Rabīʿ II or Djumādā I 420/May 1029).

In 413/1023, a treaty between Byzantines and Fāṭimids, putting an end to the unfavourable relations existing between al-Ḥākim and the Emperor Basil II, was to have been concluded, but the death of Sitt al-Mulk led to its cancellation. In 418/1027, a provisional agreement guaranteed that, in the mosque at Constantinople, the invocation would be made in the name of the Fāṭimid Imām, and that the Basileus had the right to rebuild the Church of the Holy Sepulchre in Jerusalem, burned on the orders of al-Ḥākim, as well as all the churches in Egypt which had been destroyed and not transformed into mosques. In 423/1032, in an exceptional episode in the history of relations between Constantinople and the Muslim powers, a combined Fāṭimid-Byzantine expedition attacked the Druzes in the Djabal Summaḳ, driving them into caves and slaughtering them (see *Histoire de Yahya ibn Said d'Antioche*, ed. I. Kratchkovsky, Fr. tr. Françoise Micheau and G. Troupeau, in *PO*, vol. xlvii, fasc. 4, no. 212, Tournai 1997, 152-3). It was not until 425/1034, after protracted negotiations brought together representatives of all the principalities of the Middle East, of which Yaḥyā al-Anṭāḳī gives a detailed account, that the definitive version of the treaty came into existence. It included a clause stipulating that in the event of famine, corn would be transferred from the better-off state to the needy one.

Al-Ẓāhir died on the eve of his thirty-second birthday, in mid-Shaʿbān 427/1036, and was succeeded by his son, Abū Tamīm Maʿadd al-Mustanṣir [*q.v.*].

Bibliography: In addition to Musabbiḥī, *op. cit.*, Ibn Ẓāfir, *Akhbār al-duwal al-munḳaṭiʿa*, ed. A. Ferré, Cairo 1972, 66 ff. is the most informative regarding this caliphate, giving the list of administrators and *ḳāḍīs*; see the numerous other traditional sources of Fāṭimid history, in particular Ibn al-Dawādārī, *Kanz al-durar*, vi, ed. Ṣ. al-Munadjdjid, Cairo 1380/1961, 313-41; Maḳrīzī, *Ittiʿāẓ al-ḥunafāʾ*, ed. M.Ḥ.M. Aḥmad, ii, Cairo 1971, 124-83; see also the detailed or annotated bibliographies in Th. Bianquis, *Damas et la Syrie*, ii, 705-40; L.S. al-Imad, *The Fatimid vizierate, 969-1172*, Berlin 1990, 197-224; Y. Lev, *State and society in Fatimid Egypt*, Leiden 1991, 199-210; M. Gil, *A history of Palestine, 634-1099*, Cambridge 1992, 862-911; A.F. Sayyid, *al-Dawla al-fāṭimiyya*, 433-55; J.Cl. Garcin (ed.), *États, sociétés et cultures du monde musulman médiéval, X^{e}-XVe siècle*, i, Paris 1995, pp. xlii-l; C. Petry (ed.), *The Cambridge history of Egypt*, i, Cambridge 1998, 560-71; for an overview of the general topography of Cairo and the disposition of the caliphal palaces, consult A.F. Sayyid, *La capitale de l'Égypte jusqu'à l'époque fāṭimide: al-Qāhira et Fusṭāṭ, essai de reconstitution topographique*, Beirut 1998, 209-326.

(TH. BIANQUIS)

AL-MALIK AL-**ẒĀHIR GHĀZĪ**, GHIYĀTH AL-DĪN, Ayyūbid [*q.v.*] ruler of Aleppo, third son of Ṣalāḥ al-Dīn, b. mid-Ramaḍān 568/end of April 1173, d. 20 Djumādā II 613/4 October 1216.

In Rabīʿ II 579/July-August 1183, after the conquest of Aleppo, Ṣalāḥ al-Dīn made al-Ẓāhir nominal regent of the city under the tutelage of an *amīr*. Soon afterwards, in Shaʿbān-Ramaḍān 579/November-December 1183, he restructured his realm and gave Aleppo to his brother al-ʿĀdil [*q.v.*]. Al-Ẓāhir returned to the court of his father. The next restructuring occurred three years later after submission of the Djazīra [see ZANGIDS], when Ṣalāḥ al-Dīn bestowed Aleppo on al-Ẓāhir, in Djumādā II 582/August-September 1186. During his father's campaigns against the Crusaders in 584/1188, al-Ẓāhir distinguished himself as a vigorous and able warrior.

At the death of Ṣalāḥ al-Dīn in 589/1193, al-Ẓāhir held sway over the principality of Aleppo, from the Euphrates in the east, the borders of Armenian Cilicia in the north, the Crusader principality of Antioch in the west and the Ayyūbid principality of Ḥamāt [*q.v.*] in the south. In 589/1193 he reinforced al-ʿĀdil, who had to suppress the rebellion of the dependent principalities in the Djazīra. In the ensuing struggles for supremacy within the Ayyūbid house, al-Ẓāhir first sided with the coalition of the designated heir al-Afḍal [*q.v.*] and al-ʿĀdil against his ambitious brother al-ʿAzīz ʿUthmān of Egypt. In Radjab 591/June 1195, when al-Afḍal's incapacity became apparent, al-Ẓāhir supported al-ʿAzīz, but the coalition of al-Afḍal and al-ʿĀdil proved stronger. A reconciliation mainly on the basis of the status quo was reached. During the final stages of the power struggle, al-Ẓāhir sided with al-Afḍal again, now against a coalition of al-ʿAzīz and al-ʿĀdil, who had become al-ʿAzīz's main supporter. As a result, al-ʿAzīz was acknowledged as supreme sultan in Egypt and al-ʿĀdil got Damascus. Al-Ẓāhir was confirmed in his possessions in 592/1196.

More struggles followed the death of al-ʿAzīz in Muḥarram 595/November 1198, extending over the next three years. Al-Ẓāhir favoured al-Afḍal again, now as regent for al-ʿAzīz's son, al-Manṣūr Muḥammad, in Egypt. Al-ʿĀdil, at that time besieging Mārdīn, was forced to withdraw in order to secure Damascus, besieged by al-Afḍal. In Shaʿbān 595/June 1199, al-Ẓāhir set out to join al-Afḍal. Finally, the coalition broke up, and they lifted the siege of Damascus soon afterwards. The first phase ended in 596/1200 when al-ʿĀdil took Cairo and deposed al-Manṣūr in order to become supreme sultan himself. However, al-Afḍal now became recognised as supreme sultan by his main supporter al-Ẓāhir and his northern Mesopotamian allies. Meanwhile, al-Ẓāhir consolidated his position in northern Syria by conquering various towns and an attack on Ḥamāt. In Dhu 'l-Ḳaʿda 597/August 1201, al-Ẓāhir and al-Afḍal besieged Damascus again for over a month, but without success. Finally, in Djumādā II 598/March 1202 al-Ẓāhir agreed to acknowledge al-ʿĀdil's suzerainty. He remained outwardly loyal but lived with the persistent threat that his uncle might seize his principality. When in 606/1209 al-ʿĀdil tried to conquer the Zangid principalities, al-Ẓāhir tried to maintain the balance of power in northern Mesopotamia and supported diplomatically the besieged lord of Sindjār [see ZANGIDS]. The marriage with al-ʿĀdil's daughter Ḍayfa Khātūn in 609/1212 and the designation of her son al-ʿAzīz Muḥammad, born in 610/1213, as heir, lowered the tension here.

After al-Ẓāhir came to terms with his uncle, he turned his attention mainly to the development of the principality of Aleppo. He launched major building projects on fortifications, on religious institutions and on the water supplies (*ḳanawāt*). He promoted commerce and trade, notably with the Venetians, who in 604/1207-8 were given privileged access to the mint of Aleppo for imported European silver (Pozza, Bates). From Egypt, important scholars and able officials fled to his court, namely, Ibn al-Ḳifṭī and Ibn Mammātī [*q.vv.*]. The historian Ibn al-ʿAdīm [*q.v.*] dedicated a treatise to al-Ẓāhir on the occasion of the birth of al-ʿAzīz Muḥammad (Brockelmann, I^{2}, 405).

At the end of al-Ẓāhir's reign, the ambitious Armenian king Leon II threatened his realm in the north. Al-Ẓāhir found a natural ally in Bohemund IV, Count of Tripoli and lord of Antioch. The conquest of the latter city by Leon II in 612/1216 finally brought al-Ẓāhir in closer contact with the Rūm Saldjūḳs.

Al-Ẓāhir died in 613/1216 after a severe illness. His three-year-old son al-ʿAzīz Muḥammad succeeded him under the tutelage of the *mamlūk* Shihāb al-Dīn Ṭoghrïl, whilst Ḍayfa Khātūn became in 634/1236 an influential regent of Aleppo for her grandson al-Nāṣir Yūsuf II [*q.v.*].

Bibliography: 1. Sources. Abū Shāma, *Dhayl*, ed. ʿI. al-ʿAṭṭār, Cairo 1947; Ibn al-ʿAdīm, *Zubda*, ed. S. al-Dahhān, iii, Damascus 1954; Ibn al-Athīr, xi, xii; Ibn Naẓīf, *al-Taʾrīkh al-Manṣūrī*, ed. A. Dūdū, Damascus 1981; Ibn Shaddād, *al-Aʿlāḳ al-khaṭīra*, ed. D. Sourdel, *La description d'Alep*, Damascus 1953; Ibn Wāṣil, *Mufarridj al-kurūb*, ed. Dj. al-Shayyāl, i-iii, Cairo 1957-60; Ibn Khallikān, ed. ʿAbbās, iv, 6-10; Dhahabī, *Taʾrīkh al-Islām*, ed. ʿU.ʿA. Tadmurī, Beirut 1988-, xli, 158-62; M. Pozza, *I trattati con Aleppo*, Venice 1990.

2. Studies. F.-J. Dahlmanns, *al-Malik al-ʿĀdil*, diss. Giessen 1975; R.S. Humphreys, *From Saladin to the Mongols*, Albany 1977; P. Balog, *The coinage of the Ayyūbids*, London 1980; M. Bates, *Crusader coinage*, in *A history of the Crusaders*, vi, ed. H.W. Hazard and N.P. Zacour, Madison and London 1989, 421-39; A.-M. Eddé, *La principauté ayyoubide d'Alep (579/1183-658/1260)*, Stuttgart 1999.

(S. HEIDEMANN)

AL-**ẒĀHIR ČAḲMAḲ** [see ČAḲMAḲ].

ẒAHĪR-I FĀRYĀBĪ, or ẒAHĪR AL-DĪN ABU 'L-FAḌL ṬĀHIR b. Muḥammad AL-FĀRYĀBĪ, Persian poet of the 6th/12th century, born at Fāryāb (modern Dawlatābād) near Balkh about 550/1156, d. 598/1201. As a court poet he served patrons in various parts of Persia; the earliest known to us was ʿAḍud al-Dīn Ṭughānshāh, a local ruler of Nīshāpūr. In 582/1186-7 he went to Iṣfahān and three years later from there to Māzandarān, where he was attached to the *ispahbād* Ḥusām al-Dīn Ardashīr b. Ḥasan of the Bāwandids [*q.v.*]. Still later he settled down at the court of the Eldigüzids or Ildeñizids [*q.v.*], writing panegyrics to the Atābegs Muẓaffar al-Dīn Ḳizil Arslān ʿUthmān (581-7/1186-91) and Nuṣrat al-Dīn Abū Bakr b. Pahlawān (591-607/1195-1210). One of the *ḳaṣīdas* preserved in Ẓahīr's *Dīwān* is adressed to the Saldjūḳ Sultan Ṭoghril III (d. 590/1194). Towards the end of his life, he retired from the world and led a life of devotion in Tabrīz. In Rabīʿ I 598/December 1201 he died in that city and was buried at Surkhāb in the cemetery of the poets (Mustawfī, *Guzīda*, 737-8).

The *Dīwān* of Ẓahīr was collected shortly after his death by Shams-i Sudjāsī (d. 602/1205-6), who is probably also the author of a prose introduction handed down in some manuscripts (Storey-de Blois, v/2, 536). The best preserved part of his work are the *ḳaṣīdas* and the *muḳaṭṭaʿāt*. These poems were composed in the same learned style which marks the panegyrics of Anwarī and Khāḳānī [*q.vv.*]. In the 7th/13th century, the critical comparison between Anwarī and Ẓahīr became a topic of literary discussion in which the poets Madjd-i Hamgar and Imāmī participated (cf. the introduction to *Dīwān-i Anwarī*, i, 108-10). Saʿdī [*q.v.*] objected to Ẓahīr's extravagant use of hyperbole (*Būstān*, 40). His style as a court poet has been characterised as polished and graceful, but somewhat insipid (Browne, *LHP*, ii, 414). Of his *ghazals*, few seem now to be extant; most of the *ghazals* attributed to him in printed versions of the *Dīwān* were really composed by another Ẓahīr, a Shīʿī poet of the 10th/16th century. Some *ḳaṣīdas* by his contemporary Shams-i Ṭabasī have also been mistaken for works of Ẓahīr (see further de Blois, v/2, 558).

Bibliography: Anwarī, *Dīwān*, ed. M.T. Mudarris-i Raḍawī, i, Tehran 1347 *sh.*/1968; ʿAwfī, *Lubāb*, ii, 298-307; Dawlatshāh, 109-14; Saʿdī, *Būstān*, ed. Gh.Ḥ. Yūsufī, Tehran 1359 *sh.*/1980; Dh. Ṣafā, *Taʾrīkh-i adabiyyāt dar Īrān*, ii, [3]Tehran 1339 *sh.*/1960, 750-64; J. Rypka, *History of Iranian literature*, Dordrecht 1968, 209; idem, in *Cambridge hist. Iran*, v, Cambridge 1968, 577; A. Munzawī, *Fihrist-i nuskhahā-yi khaṭṭī-yi fārsī*, iii, Tehran 1350 *sh.*/1971, 2421-5; further references in Storey-de Blois, *Persian literature*, v/2, London 1994, 557-61, and *EIr*, s.v. Fāryābī.

(CL. HUART-[J.T.P. DE BRUIJN])

ẒĀHIR AL-ʿUMAR AL-ZAYDĀNĪ, local ruler in northern Palestine in the 18th century (*ca.* 1690-1775).

His father and grandfather had already been *multazims* of Tiberias, and as a young man, Ẓāhir al-ʿUmar struck an alliance with the al-Ṣaḳr tribe of eastern Galilee and made Tiberias his first power base. The 1730s were filled with efforts to expand his realm and consolidate his rule. In 1738 he conquered the fortress of Djiddīn, which controlled the region of Tarshīḥa, Wabar and Abū Sinān, and Ṣafad surrendered to him shortly after. Ẓāhir's growing power between Tiberias and Ṣafad now straddled the trade route and communications between Damascus and Nablus and, by extension, those with Egypt. Repeated attempts by the governors of Damascus to dislodge him from Tiberias were defeated and ended in 1743 in a stalemate. Ẓāhir now turned his full attention westwards, aiming to control western Galilee, Acre and the lucrative cotton trade. By 1746 the French cotton merchants called him *gouverneur* of Acre. In 1751 he had walls built around the city and resided in it permanently. In 1768 he was given by the Ottoman government the title of "Shaykh of Acre, Amīr of Nazareth, Tiberias, Ṣafad, and Shaykh of all Galilee". By then he had forged a close alliance with his neighbours to the north, the Mutawālīs [*q.v.*]. At the zenith of his power now, but not strong enough against a determined Ottoman attack, Ẓāhir turned for support to ʿAlī Bey al-Kabīr of Egypt. Between November 1770 and June 1771 Egyptian troops conquered all of Palestine and Damascus only to return abruptly to Egypt when their commander, Abu 'l-Dhahab, refused to carry on an open war against the sultan. Though deserted by his ally, Ẓāhir was able to consolidate and even expand his power, holding now the whole coast from Sidon to Jaffa and sending troops into the Ḥawrān.

The Ottoman government seemingly acquiesced in his growing power, but once peace with Russia was concluded in 1774, it turned against the rebel. Abu 'l-Dhahab was encouraged to move against him, but he suddenly died. The reprieve for Ẓāhir was, however, brief because the Ottoman government now sent a naval force under the *Ḳapūdān Pasha* Ḥasan. In August 1774 Acre was conquered and Ẓāhir was killed fleeing on 21 August 1775.

Ẓāhir al-ʿUmar was unique among his contemporaries in recognising that political power was not only based on troops but on a sound economy. He also was unusual in that he realised that excessive exploitation of the peasantry was detrimental to the increase of revenues in the long run. Greater productivity had to be encouraged through investment and not extortion. With his keen interest in the local economy and commerce, he is comparable to Muḥammad ʿAlī [*q.v.*] of Egypt two generations later. It was Ẓāhir's recognition of the potential and the profitability of the cotton trade from Galilee via Acre to France for increasing his own revenues, which gave his political ambitions content and direction. He further realised that the profits could be all his if he exerted exclusive control over the cultivation and the trade of cotton, and this motivated his conquest of Western Galilee, the fortress of Acre and expansion along the coast. His policy of state economic monopoly was new to the region and was driven by the enormous profits to be made from cotton exports to France. The prosperity thus created brought a veritable boom to Acre, making it the most important city on the Syrian coast.

Ẓāhir al-ʿUmar's rise to power was part of a general contemporary trend towards greater provincial autonomy. A severely weakened Ottoman empire was unable to prevent the ascendancy of the al-ʿAẓm family in Damascus, the defiance of the Mamlūks in Egypt and the consolidation of a completely new power centre in Acre and northern Palestine. Ẓāhir was—at least for a time—more successful than his contemporaries because he was able to finance his political aspirations by innovative economic policies and by linking up with European markets.

Bibliography: ʿA. al-Ṣabbāgh, *al-Rawḍ al-ẓāhir fī taʾrīkh al-Ẓāhir*, B.N. Paris, ms. arabe no. 4610; M. al-Ṣabbāgh, *Taʾrīkh al-shaykh Ẓāhir al-ʿUmar al-Ẓaydānī*, Ḥarīṣā 1935; Uriel Heyd, *Ẓāhir al-ʿUmar, shalīṭ ha-Galīl*, Jerusalem 1942; A. Cohen, *Palestine in the 18th century*, Jerusalem 1973; T. Philipp, *Acre, the rise and fall of a Palestinian city, 1730-1831. World markets and local politics*, forthcoming.

(T. PHILIPP)

ẒAHĪR AL-DĪN MARʿASHĪ b. Nāṣir al-Dīn, Sayyid, Persian commander, diplomat and historian of the Caspian region, b. *ca.* 815/1412, d. after 894/1489. He was a scion of the important family of Marʿashī Sayyids who dominated Māzandarān from the later 8th/14th century until the province's incorporation into the Ṣafawid empire by Shāh ʿAbbās I in 1005/1596 [see MARʿASHĪS].

Ẓahīr al-Dīn stemmed from the main branch of the Marʿas̲h̲īs, that of Kamāl al-Dīn b. Ḳiwām al-Dīn (d. 801/1379). He owned estates at Bāzargāh in Gīlān, and was employed by Sultan Muḥammad II of the Kār Kiyā line in Gīlān and then by his son and successor Mīrzā ʿAlī (*r.* 881 or 883/1476-8 to 909 or 910/1503-5). He was sent to resolve militarily a succession dispute in adjacent Rustamdār and he led other expeditions, including an unsuccessful siege of Nūr in 868/1463. It was for Mīrzā ʿAlī that Ẓahīr al-Dīn wrote his *Tārīk̲h̲-i Tabaristān u Rūyān u Māzandarān*, extending from the origins of the local dynasties up to 881/1476 (ed. B. Dorn, St. Petersburg 1850; ed. ʿAbbās S̲h̲āyān, Tehran 1333/1954-5), and his *Tārīk̲h̲-i Gīlān u Daylamistān*, carried up to 894/1489 (ed. H.L. Rabino, Rasht 1330/1912), both valuable for the intricate history of the petty principalities of the Caspian region. Another work of his that is mentioned, but not apparently extant, is a *Tārīk̲h̲-i Gurgān u Rayy*, and he wrote verse, probably under the pen-name of Ẓahīr, which are quoted by him in his histories.

Bibliography: Dorn, *Sehir-eddin's Geschichte von Tabaristan, Rujan und Masanderan*, St. Petersburg 1850, 13-22; Rabino, *Mázandarán and Astarábád*, GMS, London 1928, p. xxiii (résumé of the *Tārīk̲h̲-i Gīlān*); Storey, i, 361-2; Storey-Bregel, ii, 1073-4, 1076.

(C.E. BOSWORTH)

AL-**ẒĀHIRA**, "the rearwards region", conventionally Dhahirah, the name given to the interior, landwards part of ʿUmān, that lying behind the D̲j̲abal Ak̲h̲ḍar range and merging into the desert fringes of the Empty Quarter [see AL-RUBʿ AL-K̲H̲ĀLĪ]. The term al-Ẓāhira contrasts with that of al-Bāṭina, the coastlands of ʿUmān. The religious and political history of this "inner ʿUmān", and its social and cultural development, with local Ibāḍī elements mingled with Sunnīs, have frequently diverged from that of the Sultanate of Muscat and Oman established for over two centuries in the coastal region [see BŪ SAʿĪD].

Bibliography: J.G. Lorimer, *Gazeteer of the Persian Gulf, 'Oman and Central Arabia*, Calcutta 1908-15, ii.A, 427-30; and see ʿUMĀN. (ED.)

AL-**ẒĀHIRĪ, K̲H̲ALĪL** B. **S̲H̲ĀHĪN** [see IBN S̲H̲ĀHĪN].

AL-**ẒĀHIRIYYA**, a theologico-juridical school in mediaeval Islam which may be situated, among *mad̲h̲hab*s as a whole, "at the furthest limit of orthodoxy" (R. Brunschvig, *Polémiques médiévales autour du rite de Mālik*, in *Études d'Islamologie*, ii [1976], 83). It is, furthermore, the only school that owes its existence and its name to a principle of law, Ẓāhirī in this case. Thus it relies exclusively on the literal (*ẓāhir*) sense of the Ḳurʾān and of Tradition, rejecting *raʾy*, but also *ḳiyās* [*q.vv.*], although the latter is retained by al-S̲h̲āfiʿī (d. 204/820 [*q.v.*]) who is regularly cited as the point of departure of Ẓāhirī methodology (J. Schacht, *An introduction to Islamic law*, Oxford 1964, 63-4, Fr. tr. Paris 1983, 59). In other words, and to quote R. Arnaldez in *Grammaire et théologie chez Ibn Ḥazm de Cordoue*, Paris 1956, 199, Ẓāhirism "accepts only the facts clearly revealed by sensible, rational and linguistic intuitions, controlled and corroborated by Ḳurʾānic revelation".

Sources. As the best means of reconstructing Ẓāhirī thought, recourse should be had to the writings of its founder, the traditionist Dāwūd b. K̲h̲alaf (d. 270/884 [*q.v.*]). But it has long been known that nothing of his work has survived into the present day (I. Goldziher, *Die Ẓâhiriten*, Leipzig 1884, Eng. tr., Leiden 1971, 26-30). We must therefore be content with the works of authors who quote him, in particular al-Nawawī (d. 676/1277 [*q.v.*]), al-S̲h̲aʿrānī (d. 973/1565 [*q.v.*]) and, most of all, the earlier authority Ibn Ḥazm (d. 456/1063 [*q.v.*] (Goldziher, *op. cit.*, 30-157). Following the lead of the Hungarian scholar, it has become customary to refer primarily to this Cordovan thinker who "illuminated, almost single-handedly in the Mālikī milieu, the literalist or Ẓāhirī school" (R. Brunschvig, *Pour ou contre la logique grecque chez les théologiens-juristes de l'Islam: Ibn Ḥazm, al-G̲h̲azālī, Ibn Taymiyya*, in *Études d'Islamologie*, i, 304-5).

For the constantly-burgeoning interest witnessed over more than a century in Ḥazmian studies, especially from the angle of Ẓāhirism, see A.-M. Turki, *Notes sur l'évolution du ẓāhirisme d'Ibn Ḥazm de Cordoue, du Taqrīb à l'Iḥkām*, in *SI*, lix (1984), 175-7. As to the credibility of recourse to Ibn Ḥazm, in view of this rehabilitation, see also, by the same author, *Polémiques entre Ibn Ḥazm et Bād̲j̲ī sur les principes de la loi musulmane*, Algiers 1976, Ar. tr. ²Beirut 1994; see especially the index of this edition, 551; here are to be found 16 references to Dāwūd, 14 in which Ibn Ḥazm is in agreement with his master, the two others showing rather a convergence with the son of Dāwūd, known to be a Ẓāhirī himself. This is useful for the *uṣūl al-fiḳh* [*q.v.*] which are the subject at issue here, but it will be seen that this is also the case for the applied *fiḳh* [*q.v.*] where Ibn Ḥazm notes a scarce point of disagreement with the master.

Theological aspects. Here our exclusive source is Ibn Ḥazm in his *Faṣl fi 'l-milal wa 'l-ahwāʾ wa 'l-niḥal*, 2 vols., Cairo 1317-21/1899-1903 (Sp. tr. M. Asín Palacios, *Abenházam de Córdoba y su historia crítica de las ideas religiosas*, 5 vols. Madrid 1927-32). In *Die Ẓâhiriten*, Goldziher drew substantially from the *Faṣl*, at that time still in manuscript. He stressed negation of the attributes (*ṣifāt*) except those mentioned in the Ḳurʾān; to underline Ibn Ḥazm's original contribution, he recalled that the Ẓāhiriyya were never called anything other than a *mad̲h̲hab fiḳhī* and that it therefore does not figure among the *mad̲h̲āhib kalāmiyya* (*op. cit.*, 123-56). Goldziher also dealt with this subject in his *Le livre de Moh. Ibn Toumert, Mahdi des Almohades*, introd. and Fr. tr., Algiers 1903, where he stated that the history of Muslim theology shows that Ẓāhirī *fiḳh* was in accordance with the most diverse dogmatic tendencies, and he insisted once more on the exclusive contribution of Ibn Ḥazm in creating a synthesis of Ẓāhirī *fiḳh* and of dogmatic Ẓāhirism.

M. Abū Zahra will serve as a guide for a considerable portion of this article; in his work on *Ibn Ḥazm, ḥayātuh wa-ʿaṣruh, ārāʾuh wa-fiḳhuh*, ²Cairo 1393/1954, he analyses the various aspects of Ḥazmian thought, while underlining its originality by means of a brief but informative comparative study. He refers to the *Faṣl*, naturally, but also to the *Iḥkām fi uṣūl al-aḥkām*, 8 vols. in 2, Cairo 1345-7/1927-9; as well as to the *Muḥallā fi 'l-fiḳh al-ẓāhirī*, 11 vols. in 8, Cairo 1347-52/1929-33. The principal and characteristic aspects of the Ḥazmian, and thus Ẓāhirī, credo are as follows. First of all, to exalt the oneness of God, while acknowledging the exclusive privilege enjoyed by His Prophets and Messengers in terms of the manifestation of miracles, the sign of sanctity and of keeping God free from anthropomorphism (*tanzīh*); and then to declare that God is one by means of His essence, while stressing the worth of His names, to the detriment of that of His attributes. In short, Ibn Ḥazm seeks to strip his credo of any trace of anthropomorphism (*tas̲h̲bīh*). God, he further maintains, is unique in His creative action (*k̲h̲alḳ wa-takwīn*). Also, the power of man over his actions is affirmed not only in his continually active reality but also in his gradually surmountable limitations (*op. cit.*, 207-36).

On the fate reserved for the perpetrator of great sins (*murtakib al-kabīra*), Ẓāhirism oscillates between, on the one hand, clemency and divine pardon, and on the other, the Last Judgment (*ḥisāb*) and punishment, all those notions being explicitly supported by the sacred texts (*op. cit.*, 337-40). A.M. Turki, *L'engagement politique et la théorie du califat d'Ibn Ḥazm de Cordoue*, in *Théologiens* (1982), 70, n. 10, following the lead of Abū Zahra, states that, while placing himself in a position of perfect continuity with regard to juridical classicism, Ibn Ḥazm sets forth instances which only the politico-social situation of his country could explain: legitimising the designation of a successor by the caliph already in place; and where no successor is named, occupation of the throne by the first claimant provided he is considered worthy, if only by one other person of equal worth. Notable here is the insignificant role played by the oath of allegiance (*bayʿa*) in this theory; also worth recording is the particular concern to show the political superiority of Muʿāwiya over ʿAlī [*q.vv.*]. Reverting to Abū Zahra's work, this author reviews the very detailed arguments presented by Ibn Ḥazm, still in the *Faṣl*, regarding the pre-eminence (*mufāḍala*) of the Companions. Ibn Ḥazm affirms categorically only the superiority of the wives of Muḥammad, and those of Abū Bakr and of ʿUmar. The concept of anteriority in time is also taken into account, in such a fashion that those who fought at the battle of Badr [*q.v.*] are superior to those who fought at the battle of Uḥud [*q.v.*], and so on throughout history (*op. cit.*, 253-9; cf. Turki, *L'idée de justice dans la pensée politique musulmane. L'interprétation d'Ibn Ḥazm de Cordoue*, in *SI*, lxviii [1988], 5-28). Furthermore, and still in the context of this credo founded on absolute certitude, see *La réfutation du scepticisme et la théorie de la connaissance dans les Fiṣal*, in *Théologiens*, 159-98. The point at issue is the refutation of the principle of the absolute equality of proofs (*takāfuʾ al-adilla*) all of which is related to doubt; this leads the Ẓāhirī thinker to exalt his ardent faith, which is founded on the primary evidence of the senses and of reason (*op. cit.*, 196).

Legal aspects

(a) *Principles of law* (*uṣūl al-fiḳh*). The Ẓāhiriyya above all adopted a methodology which sought to rid *fiḳh*, as far as is possible, of any trace of subjectivity, confining it within the narrow limits of the evident meaning of the sacred text. Opposing the free use of opinion (*raʾy* [*q.v.* in Suppl.]), and hence the imitation of those who practised it (*taḳlīd* [*q.v.*]), it called for an effort of search (*id̲j̲tihād* [*q.v.*]) which, far from being identified with Ḥanafī *raʾy* or with S̲h̲āfiʿī reasoning by analogy (*ḳiyās* [*q.v.*]), could only be involved with the search for a text. This current of thought has always been perceived as a continuation of S̲h̲āfiʿism. In fact, al-S̲h̲āfiʿī had recourse to *ḳiyās* in order to curb the free use of *raʾy* and to rebut *istiḥsān* [*q.v.*]. He rejected the consensus (*id̲j̲māʿ* [*q.v.*]) of the ancient juridical schools to replace it with that of the unanimous Muslim community, for the good reason that it could only be realised on the basis of a body of Tradition which could not be overlooked by everybody. However, Dāwūd, a disciple of al-S̲h̲āfiʿī albeit an indirect one, systematised the methodological critique still further; thus he rejected *ḳiyās* on account of its recourse to the deductive principle of the motivation (*taʿlīl* [see ʿILLA]) founding the analogy; in parallel, he only admitted the validity of the consensus of the Companions. See details in Goldziher, *Die Ẓāhiriten*, 18-36, but also Schacht, *op. cit.*, 55-60. The latter has shown that the Ẓāhiriyya were themselves unable to do without deductions and conclusions on the basis of the fundamental texts, but they attempted to present these conclusions as implied by these very texts (*op. cit.*, 59). In summary, everything happens as if through a process of syllogism, reliable according to Ibn Ḥazm's terms, because here the conclusion is included in the premises. This is the famous *dalīl* [*q.v.*] which will be observed at a later stage.

Here again, reference is to be made to the works of *uṣūl al-fiḳh* of Ibn Ḥazm. Although they cannot all be cited here (see Turki, *Polémiques*, 458), mention should be made of the *Iḥkām* and of *Marātib al-id̲j̲māʿ fi ʾl-ʿibādāt wa ʾl-muʿāmalāt wa ʾl-iʿtiḳādāt*, Cairo 1357; another expressive title amongst these works is to be noted, sc. that of the *Mulak̲h̲k̲h̲aṣ ibṭāl al-ḳiyās wa ʾl-raʾy wa ʾl-istiḥsān wa ʾl-taḳlīd wa ʾl-taʿlīl*, Damascus 1379/1960. But within the limited scope of this article, Abū Zahra and *Polémiques* will continue to be the major points of reference.

Ibn Ḥazm does not object categorically to *taḳlīd* as practised by mankind in general (*ʿāmmī*), but he prescribes an attitude of prudence and of vigilance, even a critical disposition if the individual is capable of this (Abū Zahra, 278-81). It has already been seen that the sacred text is defined as the Ḳurʾān, Tradition and the consensus of the Companions, or the *dalīl* drawn from one of these, and this has nothing in common with the *ḳiyās* of the jurists. The presumption of continuity (*istiṣḥāb* [*q.v.*]) is accepted, but not the pretexts (*d̲h̲arāʾiʿ*) invoked to legitimise a judgement (*ḥukm* [*q.v.*]). The abrogation (*nask̲h̲* [*q.v.*]) of the Ḳurʾān is possible through the *sunna* [*q.v.*], which, in turn, may be abrogated by the Ḳurʾān. Ibn Ḥazm goes so far as to accept the abrogation of the Ḳurʾān through the *k̲h̲abar al-āḥād* [see K̲H̲ABAR AL-WĀḤID], a tradition owing its transmission to a single authority. *Taḳlīd* is always rejected, even if is practised with reference to a Companion (*op. cit.*, 282-340, 364-81, 429-39).

For an illustration of these fundamental principles, see *Polémiques*, where there is detailed study of the original points of view of Ibn Ḥazm, with references to the *Iḥkām* in particular. Virtually all of the aspects of the *uṣūl al-fiḳh* are tackled, from a comparative angle. The overall scheme is as follows: problems of interpretation (81-93): formulation of the order; general sense; and particular sense of two contradictory traditions; problems of transmission of traditions (99-130); *k̲h̲abar al-āḥād/sunna* and *ḥadīt̲h̲/k̲h̲abar mursal*; normative value of the practice (*ʿamal* [*q.v.*]) of the people of Medina; and licence for transmission of *ḥadīt̲h̲* sc. *id̲j̲āza* [*q.v.*]. There follow the problems raised by the concept of consensus, as well as acceptance or rebuttal of reasoning by analogy (133-268, 271-393).

(b) *Application of the law* (*furūʿ*) [see FIḲH; UṢŪL]: here, reference will be made in particular to Ibn Ḥazm's *Muḥallā*, the study of which has been facilitated since the appearance of an index of topics, *Mawsūʿa taḳrīb fiḳh Ibn Ḥazm* ([1]Cairo 1412/1992). It is possible to follow Goldziher, *op. cit.*, 30-53, and R. Strothmann, *EI*[1] art. *al-Ẓāhirīya*, in referring to the *Mīzān* of al-S̲h̲aʿrānī, who has preserved "a large number of decisions of the historical Ẓāhirīya" (Strothmann). A few typical examples picked out from the *Mīzān* by Strothmann are as follows. A point at issue is the prohibition imposed on vessels of gold and of silver and intended only for drinking; eating from them is permitted, since no prohibition is mentioned by the ḥadīth. Cleaning the teeth with a tooth-pick in the course of ablutions is a necessity; knowingly neglecting to do this would render the prayer invalid. Wine, although forbidden, is not impure. There follows a host of examples concerning purification (*ṭahāra* [*q.v.*]); the minor (*wuḍū'* [*q.v.*]) and major (*ghusl* [*q.v.*]), as well as dry ablutions (*tayammum* [*q.v.*]): touching a copy of the Ḳur'ān in a state of impurity (*ḥadath* [*q.v.*]) is permitted. In *wuḍū'*, invoking the name of God is obligatory. Reciting the Ḳur'ān in a state of major impurity (*djanāba* [*q.v.*]) is permitted.

Schacht referred to the Ḥanbalī Muḥammad al-Shaṭṭī (d. 1305/1887-8), author of a *K. fī masā'il al-Imām Dāwūd al-Ẓāhirī*, in which he assembles a large number of Dāwūd's decisions, compared with corresponding Hanbalite doctrines. Nevertheless the essential source remains Ibn Ḥazm. Goldziher made use of his *Ibṭāl al-ḳiyās*, but on a small scale (42-67). But Abū Zahra devotes lengthy chapters to the topic of these decisions, almost all of them drawing on the *Muḥallā*. The following are the most interesting points. On marriage, Ibn Ḥazm maintains that it is a legal obligation but one that is only incumbent on the man, and dependent on his eligibility for it; this follows from the Ẓāhirī notion that Ḳur'ānic solicitation (*ṭalab*) constitutes a necessity (*luzūm*). Ibn Ḥazm asserts the equality of the slave and the free man in contracting marriage with four wives and in taking a concubine, all of these simultaneously. He declares as forbidden, marriage with a daughter-in-law and with one raised in the bosom (*fī ḥidjrih*) of a father-in-law, according to the Ḳur'ānic position; this, naturally, after dissolution of the alliance contracted with the mother. He acknowledges the right of the *ḳāḍī* to dissolve a marriage, but for a number of lesser reasons which he takes to be ordinary; thus no account is taken of the so-called latent vices of the husband, neither his prolonged absence, nor poverty preventing him from supplying the needs of his wife. In this last case it is she who is supposed to support her husband (441-63). See also Turki, *Femmes privilégiées et privilèges féminins dans le système théologique et juridique d'Ibn Ḥazm*, in *Théologiens*, 101-58.

The following are a few more original positions regarding legacies and wills. Any decision involving patrimony taken by a man suffering from a mortal sickness is declared valid, one's state of health having no legal status (Abū Zahra, 464-80). Ibn Ḥazm maintains that making a will is a duty subject to neither restriction nor condition of any kind whatsoever. It is certainly to the advantage of close relatives (*ḳarāba*) having no hereditary rights, as is stipulated by a Ḳur'ānic verse which was never abrogated; in this last case it belongs to the one holding the authority to substitute himself for the *de cuius*, a testator who has defaulted in his lifetime.

Ibn Ḥazm also considers (in Abū Zahra, 497-8) the case of the grandmother whose hereditary capacity should amount to one-third of the patrimony if she is alone in her degree of kinship and in the absence of descendants and collaterals, brothers and sisters in this instance: he considers her as equivalent to a mother, in the latter's absence, which leads him to grant her a portion double that of her son—an unexpected solution, but drawn from the sacred text, Ibn Ḥazm asserts. See Turki, *Femmes*..., 147-9, for this specific case.

Still in the context of family law, Ibn Ḥazm rejects proportional reductions of hereditary portions (*ʿawl*) in cases where the total of these parts exceeds the unitary whole; here he adopts the viewpoint of the Companion Ibn ʿAbbās, giving certain privileged shares to the detriment of others (in Abū Zahra, 498-504). Furthermore, gifts must be given to close relatives (*aḳārib*), orphans and paupers who are present at the time when the patrimony is being distributed; doing this is incumbent upon each heir but left to his discretion. In case of refusal, it belongs to the one holding the authority to act as executor in his place. This is, Ibn Ḥazm asserts, a position dictated by the Ḳur'ānic text, which should be taken literally, so long as no *dalīl* is opposed to it (504-6), and which assumes the implementation of the principle of *istiṣḥāb*.

Various cases of transactions (*muʿāmalāt* [*q.v.*]) follow. At the time of the conclusion of a deed of sale, performance of the witnessing required by law is an obligation which can be dispensed with only if there are no witnesses available. Otherwise, an offence has been committed, but the deed remains valid. If payment is to be made in advance, putting the deed into writing is obligatory. Otherwise, an offence has been committed, but the deed is not nullified. However, the obligation lapses in the absence of a scribe. This is what Ibn Ḥazm, on the basis of the Ḳur'ānic verse, takes to be a *farḍ* [*q.v.*], imposing a duty, which others consider to be simple guidance (*irshād*, 507-10). The option (*khiyār al-sharṭ* [see KHIYĀR]) stipulated by the contracting parties to the agreement at the time of the conclusion of the deed of sale, is refuted by Ibn Ḥazm, on pain of nullification of the deed whatever the duration of the option (510-1).

A last example gives Ibn Ḥazm the opportunity to express his individualism, this time in relation to Dāwūd, as he chooses to cite him. The issue is the prohibition on hiring out land for agricultural purposes (*al-arḍ al-mazrūʿa*); whatever the formula, the contract concluded can only be nullified. The only possibility envisaged by Ibn Ḥazm is a partnership, either for sowing (*muzāraʿa* [*q.v.*]), yielding an agreed proportion of the produce of the land, or for a leasehold agreement (*mughārasa* [*q.v.*]). If a building is placed on the land in question it alone can be the object of the hire, from which the ground is excluded. For the details of this issue, see Ziaul Haque, *Landlord and peasant in early Islam*, Islamabad 1977, 80-9, 337-43.

History of the school. For the masters of Ibn Ḥazm, see Goldziher in *Die Ẓâhiriten*, who traced the roots of the school indirectly back to al-Shāfiʿī and, directly, to Dāwūd (19-106). This may be supplemented by Abū Zahra, 85, 268-72, and by S. Yafūt, 45-52, who supplies a list of 38 masters of Ibn Ḥazm.

For the followers of the Ẓāhirī school of Cordova, see Goldziher, *op. cit.*, 156-86, where there is a panorama of the most important representatives of the Ẓāhiriyya from the 5th/11th to the 9th/15th century. See also Abū Zahra, 516-23 and Camilla Adang, *Beginnings of the Ẓāhirī madhhab in al-Andalus*, in P. Bearman, R. Peters and F.E. Vogel, *The Islamic school of law. Evolution, devolution and progress*, forthcoming. A problem that merits mention is that of the Ḥazmian influence which might possibly have affected Ibn Tūmart (d. 520/1130 [*q.v.*]). Goldziher affirmed this, not on the level of dogma, on account of the Ashʿarism of the Mahdī, but on that of the *uṣūl al-fiḳh*. See the two studies by R. Brunschvig, with references to Goldziher, *Sur la doctrine du Mahdī Ibn Tūmart*, and *Encore sur la doctrine du Mahdī Ibn Tūmart*, in *Études d'Islamologie*, i, 281-93, 295-302.

Bibliography: Given in the article, to be supplemented by the bibls. of S. Yafūt, *op. cit.*, 84-7 (Notes) and A.M. Turki, *Polémiques* and *Notes*.

(ABDEL-MAGID TURKI)

(AL-)**ẒAHRĀN**, conventionally Dhahran, a town of Saudi Arabia (lat. 26° 18' N., long. 50° 05' E.) in the eastern province (*al-minṭaḳa al-sharḳiyya*), situated in the Dammām oilfield just south of the Gulf port of al-Dammām. Near the site of the original discovery of oil in Saudi Arabia in 1938, the town did not really develop until after 1945 with the exploitation of oil by the Aramco company, one of whose main centres it still remains today. Situated on a hill in the town, the government-sponsored College, now University, of Petroleum and Minerals was established in 1964 and has an international reputation. Dhahran has a modern international airport and is now part of a vast urban and oil-producing ensemble stretching for some 40 km/25 miles from north to south along the Gulf, including the towns of al-Ḳaṭīf, al-Dammām and al-Khubar [*q.vv.*], the point where the bridge linking Saudi Arabia with Bahrain Island leaves the mainland. Dhahran now (2000) has a population of 130,000.

Less than 20 km/13 miles to the north al-Ḳaṭīf remains famed for its palm groves, its date production and its gardens. It is this proximity which permits one to envisage the ancient history of Dhahran (even in the shape of a settlement of unknown name), confirmed by archaeology. The natural environment is relatively favourable: although located in a zone of *sabkha* [*q.v.*] (a coastal zone with high salinity), the region has abundant springs and artesian wells, the basis of an active and long-established agriculture despite the arid climate. This last is confirmed by recent archaeological work in the immediate surroundings of Dhahran (P.B. Cornwall, 1940-1; H.R.P. and Violet Dickson, 1942; T.G. Bibby, 1962-5; and R. Stiehl 1964-6), which has produced large numbers of artefacts showing that the local hillocks were settled as soon as the waters of the Gulf receded (after 10,000 B.C.). Ceramic fragments of the Ubaid period (4th millennium B.C.) shows trade contacts with Mesopotamia, and the hundreds of burial tumuli have yielded objects indicating that the region of Dhahran formed part of the kingdom of Dilmun at the turn of the 3rd-2nd millennia B.C. (see on the archaeology of the region, D.T. Potts, *The Arabian Gulf in Antiquity*, Oxford 1990).

The actual name al-Ẓahrān does not appear in the Arabic historians and geographers, who call the region al-Baḥrayn or Yamāma [*q.vv.*]; they attest its richness, also known from the time of the Carmathian state there (8th-11th centuries [see KARMAṬĪ]), with the town of al-Ḳaṭīf often mentioned. Western travellers of recent centuries do not mention al-Ẓahrān either, although in the 1760s Carsten Niebuhr stressed the agricultural richness of the region, then under the control of the Banū Khālid; in 1863 W.G. Palgrave halted in the small port of al-Ḳaṭīf, guarded to the south by the imposing fort of al-Dammām, but does not name al-Ẓahrān among the villages there. However, in the early 1870s, the Ottoman governor of ʿIrāḳ, Midḥat Pasha [*q.v.*], invaded the province of Ḥasā and introduced various projects for improving the agriculture of the al-Dammām–al-Ẓahrān region, and the latter name now starts to appear in Ottoman documents.

Bibliography: See the *Bibls.* to AL-ḲAṬĪF and NAFṬ. 3, to which should be added A.J. Cottrell (ed.), *The Persian Gulf states, a general survey*, Baltimore and London 1980, Part 2. (J.-F. SALLES)

AL-**ZAHRĀWĪ**, ʿABD AL-ḤAMĪD, Syrian Arab politician and journalist, author of numerous writings advocating political, social and religious reform [see IṢLĀḤ. i.]. The date of his birth in Ḥimṣ is not certain; in Arabic sources, it ranges from 1855 to 1863 or even 1871 (see Tarabein, 118 n. 1, and ʿAllūsh, *Madkhal*, 12). He was born into a Sunnī family claiming descent from al-Ḥusayn b. ʿAlī and Fāṭima [*q.vv.*], and from the latter's honorific title, *al-Zahrāʾ*, the family derived its *nisba*. Over several generations, it had held the position of *naḳīb al-ashrāf* [*q.v.*] in Ḥimṣ.

ʿAbd al-Ḥamīd received his formal education at a *kuttāb* [*q.v.*] and at a *rüshdiyye* [see MAʿĀRIF. I. i.]. Later on, he studied privately with a number of local scholars who directed his interest, *inter alia*, to the writings of Ibn Taymiyya, Ibn Ḳayyim al-Djawziyya and Ibn Khaldūn [*q.vv.*].

In 1890 or slightly later he was in Istanbul and then Cairo, and in this last place came into contact with a number of Arab and Turkish intellectuals critical of the régime of Sultan ʿAbd ül-Ḥamīd II [*q.v.*]. He was in Istanbul for about four years from 1895 onwards, contributing articles to the Arabic section of the Turkish newspaper *Maʿlūmāt*. Regarded with suspicion by the Ottoman authorities, he was back in Damascus in 1899, at this time associating with Syrian Salafī circles [see SALAFIYYA], but escaped to Cairo in 1902 or afterwards, where he wrote for a number of newspapers and journals such as *al-Muʾayyad, al-Djarīda* and *al-Manār* [*q.v.*].

After the restoration of the Ottoman constitution in 1908, al-Zahrāwī returned to Ḥimṣ. Soon afterwards he was elected deputy, for the provincial district of Ḥamāt, in the lower chamber of the Ottoman parliament. In the following years, as member of parliament and also as editor of an Arab newspaper that he had founded in Istanbul, *al-Ḥaḍāra* (1910-12), he made himself known as a defender of Arab rights. At the same time, however, he called on all subjects of the Ottoman empire to support this state against the encroachments of European imperialism (his articles published in *al-Ḥaḍāra* are reprinted in *al-Aʿmāl al-kāmila*, iii, see *Bibl.*).

After the dissolution of the parliament in 1912, the military coup of January 1913 and the subsequent repression of all Arab reform committees, al-Zahrāwī began openly supporting Arab nationalism. He was elected president of the first Arab Congress held in Paris in June 1913. In October of the same year, however, he travelled to Istanbul in order to establish new contacts with the C.U.P. [see ITTIḤĀD WE TERAḲḲĪ DJEMʿIYYETI] government.

In January 1914 he was nominated member of the Ottoman senate. While his acceptance of this post was regarded as a betrayal by some, al-Zahrāwī defended his step by stating that the government had finally confessed its past mistakes towards the Arabs and intended not to repeat them. Rather, it would implement the reforms demanded by the Paris congress. As a member of the senate, he showed considerable moderation—at least in public—over Arab rights. However, when in December 1914 Djemāl Pasha [*q.v.*], the commander of the Ottoman Fourth Army and military governor, arrived in Damascus, he had already been informed about the contents of French diplomatic documents implicating a number of Arabs, including al-Zahrāwī, in secret dealings with the Allies. Together with several others, al-Zahrāwī was publicly hanged in Damascus on 6 May 1916 (list of those executed in Tauber, *Arab movements*, 55).

Al-Zahrāwī's execution has made him a martyr of the Arab national movement, although some earlier and modern authors have viewed certain aspects of his career rather critically. As for the development of his religious and political ideas, the publication of his *Aʿmāl kāmila* (see *Bibl.*) may finally allow a thorough analysis.

Bibliography: 1. Works in Arabic. Adham al-Djundī, *Aʿlām al-adab wa 'l-fann*, i, Damascus 1954, 11-12; idem, *Shuhadāʾ al-ḥarb al-ʿālamiyya al-kubrā*, Damascus 1960, 97-9 (see also 239-40); Yūsuf Asʿad Dāghir, *Maṣādir al-dirāsa al-adabiyya*, ii/1, Beirut 1956, 427-8; Ziriklī, *Aʿlām*, [7]Beirut 1986, iii, 288; Djawdat al-Rikābī and Djamīl Sulṭān, *al-Irth al-fikrī li 'l-muṣliḥ al-idjtimāʿī ʿAbd al-Ḥamīd al-Zahrāwī*, Damascus 1963 (repr. as vol. iii of *al-Aʿmāl al-kāmila*, see below); Muḥammad Rātib al-Ḥallāḳ, *ʿAbd al-Ḥamīd al-Zahrāwī, dirāsa fī fikrih*..., Damascus 1995; Nādjī ʿAllūsh, *Madkhal ilā ḳirāʾat ʿAbd al-Ḥamīd al-Zahrāwī*, Damascus 1995; Zahrāwī, *al-Aʿmāl al-kāmila*, 5 vols.: i-ii, ed. ʿAbd al-Ilāh Nabhān; iii, ed. Dj. al-Rikābī and Dj. Sulṭān; iv-v, ed. Nādjī ʿAllūsh, Damascus, 1995-7.

2. Works in Western languages. *La verité sur la question syrienne. Publié par le commandement de la 4ème Armée*, Istanbul 1916; D.D. Commins, *Politics and social change in late Ottoman Syria*, New York and Oxford 1990; Ahmed Tarabein, *ʿAbd al-Hamid al-Zahrawi. The career and thought of an Arab nationalist*, in Rashid Khalidi *et alii* (eds.), *The origins of Arab nationalism*, New York 1991, 97-119; Sabine Prätor, *Der arabische Faktor in der jungtürkischen Politik*, Berlin 1993; E. Tauber, *The emergence of the Arab movements*, London 1993; idem, *The Arab movements in World War I*, London 1993; Hasan Kayalı, *Arabs and Young Turks*, Berkeley, etc., 1997. (W. Ende)

AL-**ZAHRĀWĪ**, Abu 'l-Ḳāsim Khalaf b. al-ʿAbbās, important Andalusian physician. Virtually nothing is known of his life or education, though it is assumed from his *nisba* that he came from or resided in Madīnat al-Zahrāʾ [*q.v.*], near Cordova, where a royal residence and governmental centre was established in 325/936 by ʿAbd al-Raḥmān III al-Nāṣir [see ʿAbd al-Raḥmān. 3]. His residence there is confirmed by references within his writings to patients being "amongst us in al-Zahrāʾ" (*ʿindanā bi 'l-Zahrāʾ*). His direct connection with the court is a matter of speculation, though later (16th-20th-century) scholars assert his service to either ʿAbd al-Raḥmān III, his son al-Ḥakam II al-Mustanṣir [*q.v.*] or al-Manṣūr bi 'l-lāh [*q.v.*], the *de facto* ruler of al-Andalus from 368/978 to 392/1002.

Given his subsequent influence, the biographical sources are surprisingly limited. According to al-Ḥumaydī (d. 488/1095 [*q.v.*]), he died in al-Andalus after 400/1009. Al-Ḥumaydī added that al-Zahrāwī was a person of distinction, religion, and learning, and that in the field in which he excelled, medicine, he wrote a large and famous book of great usefulness. After providing the title of al-Zahrāwī's treatise, al-Ḥumaydī quoted the fulsome praise of the work given by Ibn Ḥazm [*q.v.*]: "If indeed we were to say that no one in medicine has written a better summary with respect to expression (*ḳawl*) and practice (*ʿamal*), then we would speak the truth." No other details are provided. Ibn Bashkuwāl (d. 578/1183 [*q.v.*]) repeats verbatim the account given by al-Ḥumaydī, adding only that al-Zahrāwī was mentioned amongst the teachers of one Ibn Sumayḳ. This latter fact was omitted by al-Ḍabbī (d. 599/1203 [*q.v.*]), who repeated (without credit) the account given by al-Ḥumaydī.

At what time and to what extent al-Zahrāwī's writings were known to Arabic writers outside of Spain has yet to be determined. Ibn Abī Uṣaybiʿa (d. 668/1270 [*q.v.*]), writing in Syria, said that al-Zahrāwī was "experienced (*khabīr*) with simple and compound remedies and outstanding in therapy (*djayyid al-ʿilādj*)." The short entry is of significance since no mention of al-Zahrāwī is to be found in the biographical sources on which Ibn Abī Uṣaybiʿa is known to have relied. It differs from Andalusian sources in that no dates are given and it states that he produced several treatises, one of which was known as *al-Zahrāwī* and one was entitled *al-Taṣrīf*, the latter being the largest, most famous, and the culmination of his thought.

Later historians add very little. Al-Maḳḳarī (d. 1041/1632 [*q.v.*]), giving al-Zahrāwī's name as Khalaf b. ʿAyyāsh al-Zahrāwī, quotes in full the *risāla* on the state of literature in al-Andalus by Ibn Ḥazm which praised al-Zahrāwī. Al-Maḳḳarī also gives the addenda to Ibn Ḥazm's *risāla* by Ibn Saʿīd al-Maghribī (d. 685/1286 [*q.v.*]), in which it is said that al-Zahrāwī's treatise served as one of the sources for the *materia medica* of Ibn al-Bayṭār (d. 646/1248 [*q.v.*]). Kātib Čelebī (d. 1067/1657 [*q.v.*]) listed the *K. al-Taṣrīf* by al-Zahrāwī, stating that it consisted of 30 *maḳālāt*, most of which were on compound remedies arranged like *kunnāshāt* (a term often used for early Arabic, Greek, and Syriac therapeutic manuals).

The precise date of his death has been the subject of much speculation. According to the earliest sources, he died in al-Andalus after 400/1009. In the *De viris quibusdam illustribus apud Arabes*, completed in 1527 and attributed to Leo Africanus [*q.v.*], it is said that al-Zahrāwī was physician to al-Manṣūr [bi 'llāh], "*consiliarius*" of Cordova, and died in 404/1013 at the age of 101. Al-Maḳḳarī, in quoting Ibn Ḥazm's praise of al-Zahrāwī's book, inserted a phrase stating that he [Ibn Ḥazm] had encountered him and seen him himself (*wa-ḳad adraknāhu wa-shāhadnāhu*); this statement was subsequently interpreted as meaning that Ibn Ḥazm (d. 456/1064) had met al-Zahrāwī (see Gayangos, 464-5 n. 134; Brockelmann, I[2], 276; Hamarneh and Sonnedecker, 19). Others suggested that he died in 500/1106-7 (see Casiri, ii, 136; Hamarneh and Sonnedecker, 20 n. 2).

His only preserved treatise is an enormous manual usually entitled *K. al-Taṣrīf li-man ʿadjiza ʿan al-taʾlīf* ("The arrangement [of medical knowledge] for one who is unable to compile [a manual for himself]"). The form and meaning of the title has generated considerable discussion, with the final word sometimes read as *al-taʾālīf* and interpreted as for one "who cannot cope with compilations" (Spink and Lewis, viii). Occasionally the last term is written as *taṣnīf* (see Sezgin, *GAS*, iii, 324). The titles *K. al-Zahrāwī* or *K. al-Zahrāwī al-kabīr* also occur in some manuscript copies.

The *Taṣrīf* is made up of 30 books (*maḳālāt*), of which the first (on general principles), the second and largest (on the symptoms and treatments of 325 diseases discussed in sequence from head to foot), and the thirtieth (on surgery) form almost half the volume. The rest are rather short and concerned with various aspects of pharmacology, including compound remedies, substitute drugs, and the preparation of medicaments.

While al-Zahrāwī relied extensively on earlier sources (especially Paulus of Aegina, Ibn Māsawayh, Sābūr b. Sahl, Isḥāḳ b. ʿImrān, Ḳusṭā b. Lūḳā, al-Rāzī, and Ibn al-Djazzār), he also included his own experiences and case-histories, thus providing an important source for our knowledge of a practicing physician. Many claims have been made for his originality, though most have not sufficiently examined his sources. He certainly contributed a number of technological innovations, including a concealed knife for opening abcesses in a manner that would not alarm the nervous patient, a variety of obstetrical forceps (though not for use in live births), new variations in specula or dilators, and a scissor-like instrument for use in tonsillectomies. The final book, on surgery, appears to be the first to have been illustrated with diagrams of instruments, for there is no evidence that Greek surgical writings were illustrated, except for a tenth-century Byzantine treatise on bonesetting.

In 870/1465-6 the surgical book was translated into Turkish by S̲h̲araf al-Dīn Ṣābūndj̲ī-og̲h̲lu for Meḥemmed II [q.v.]. The illustrator of this Turkish version, concerned with producing an entertaining manuscript for a royal patron, inserted a large number of colourful miniatures showing physicians at work, though these illustrations added nothing to the understanding of the surgical procedures or instrumentation (and had no subsequent influence in surgical literature).

In Europe the Taṣrīf may have had greater influence than in the Islamic world. The 30th book, on surgery, was translated into Latin by Gerard of Cremona (d. 1187) and widely influenced European surgical writing, especially that of Guy de Chauliac (d. ca. 1370) and through him the subsequent writing for several centuries. In the mid-13th century the first two books were translated into Hebrew and then into Latin and printed in Augsburg in 1519 as *Liber theoricae nec non practicae Alsaharavii*. At the end of the 13th century the 28th book, on the manufacture and preparation of medicaments from plants, minerals, and animals, was translated as *Liber servitoris* by Simon of Genoa and Abraham Judaeus of Tortosa and printed at Venice in 1471, with numerous subsequent printings. In Latin the author was known as Albucasis (with many variants) and as Alsaharavius (also with many variants), with the result that many early-modern European scholars thought they were two separate authors.

Bibliography: 1. Sources and bio-bibliographical works. Ḥumaydī, *D̲j̲ad̲h̲wat al-muḳtabis*, ed. Muḥammad ibn Tāwīt al-Ṭand̲j̲ī, Cairo 1953, 195 no. 421; Ibn Bas̲h̲kuwāl, 166 no. 308; Ḍabbī, 271-2 no. 715; Ibn Abī Uṣaybiʿa, ʿUyūn al-anbāʾ, ed. A. Müller, 2 vols., Cairo 1882-4, ii, 52; Maḳḳarī, *Analectes*, ii, 119, 125; P. de Gayangos, *The history of the Mohammedan dynasties in Spain*, 2 vols., London 1840-3, i, 187, 198, ii, 149; Kātib Čelebi, i.e. Ḥadjdjī K̲h̲alīfa, ii, 302-3 no. 3034; J.H. Hottinger, *Bibliothecarius quadripartitus*, Zurich 1664, 256; M. Casiri, *Bibliotheca arabico-hispana Escurialensis*, 2 vols., Madrid 1770, ii, 136-7; Brockelmann, I², 276-7, S I, 425; Sezgin, *GAS*, iii, 323-5, 414; M. Ullmann, *Die Medizin im Islam* (Handbuch der Orientalistik, I, vi, 1), Leiden 1970, 149-51, 271; C. Peña, A. Díaz et alii, *Corpus medicorum arabico-hispanorum*, in *Awrāq*, iv (1981) 82-5 no. 12.

2. Studies and editions. (a) *General*. There has been no printed text or translation of the entire *Taṣrīf*. A facsimile of Istanbul, Süleymaniye Beşir Ağa ms. 502, containing the entire treatise, was issued in 1986 at Frankfurt a.M. (Series C, xxxi/1-2). For the contents of the 30 books, see S.K. Hamarneh and G. Sonnedecker, *A pharmaceutical view of Abulcasis al-Zahrāwī in Moorish Spain* (Janus, suppl. v), Leiden 1963 (cf. revs. by M. Plessner, in *ZDMG*, cxvii [1967], 412-7; O. Spies, in *WI*, x [1965-7], 102-4; R. Sellheim, in *Sudhoffs Archiv*, xlix [1965], 209-11; G. Strohmaier, in *OLZ*, lxii [1967], 482-5); E. Martini-Böltau, *Die Urologie in der "Chirurgie" des Abū ul-Qāsim*, diss. Düsseldorf 1967; many studies

of al-Zahrāwī have been repr. in *Abu 'l-Qāsim al-Zahrāwī. Texte und Studien*, ed. F. Sezgin, 2 vols., Frankfurt a.M. 1996; Usamah Demeisi, *Zur Geschichte der Erforschung von Leben und Werk des Abu 'l-Qāsim az-Zahrāwī (um 936-um 1013) unter besonderer Berücksichtigung der Zahnheilkunde*, diss. Berlin 1999.

(b) *Surgical (30th) book*. J. Channing, *Albucasis De chirurgia, arabice et latine*, 2 vols. Oxford 1778; L. Leclerc, *La chirurgie d'Albulcasis*, Paris 1861, repr. Frankfurt a.M. 1996; P. Huard and M.D. Grmek, *Le premier manuscrit chirurgical turc rédigé par Charaf ed Din (1465)*, Paris 1960; M.S. Spink and G.L. Lewis, *Albucasis on surgery and instruments. A definitive edition of the Arabic text with English translation and commentary*, Berkeley 1973; E. Savage-Smith, *Some sources and procedures for editing a medieval Arabic surgical tract*, in *History of Science*, xiv (1976), 245-64; J. Grimaud, *La chirurgie d'Albucasis (ou Albucasim), texte occitan du XIVᵉ siècle*, Montpellier 1985; Savage-Smith, *John Channing, eighteenth-century apothecary and arabist*, in *Pharmacy in History*, xxx (1988), 63-60; Şerefeddin Sabuncuoğlu, *Cerrāhiyyetü 'l-ḫāniyye*, ed. İlter Uzel, 2 vols. Ankara 1992; Guigonis de Caulhiaco (Guy de Chauliac), *Inventarium sive Chirurgia Magna*, ed. and comm. M.R. McVaugh and M.S. Ogden, 2 vols. Leiden 1997.

(c) *Pharmacological books*. H. Sauvaire, *Traité sur les poids et mesures par Ez-Zahrâwy*, in *JRAS*, xvi (1884), 495-524 (= partial tr. of 29th book); Hamarneh and Sonnedecker, *A pharmaceutical view of Abulcasis* (= ed. and tr. of the 25th book); Hamarneh, *The first known independent treatise on cosmetology in Spain*, in *Bull. of the History of Medicine*, xxxix (1965), 309-25 (study of 19th book); M. Engeser, *Der "Liber servitoris" des Abulcasis (936-1013). Übersetzung, Kommentar und Nachdruck der Textfassung von 1471*, Stuttgart 1986; L.M. Arvide Cambra, *Un tratado de polvos medicinales en Al-Zahrāwī*, Almería 1994 (= ed. and tr. of 16th book); C. Gil Gangutia, *La maqāla XVIII del Kitāb al-taṣrīf de Al-Zahrāwī*, diss. Almería 1995, unpubl. (= ed. and tr. of 18th book); Arvide Cambra, *Tratado de pastillas medicinales según Abulcasis*, Almería 1996 (= ed. and tr. of the 17th book); E. Llavero Ruiz, *Estudio farmacológico de la Maqāla XXI del Kitāb al-Taṣrīf de Al-Zahrāwī*, in *Ciencias de la naturaleza en Al-Andalus: textos y estudios IV*, ed. C. Álvarez de Morales, Granada 1996, 235-55.

(EMILIE SAVAGE-SMITH)

ZAHRIYYĀT (A.), sing. *zahriyya*, from *zahr* "flower, blossom" (or, more precisely, "yellow flower, yellow blossom"), like *nawriyyāt* [q.v.], designates poetry dedicated to the description of flowers. The term is attested in the list of chapters of the *Dīwān* of Ṣafī al-Dīn al-Ḥillī [q.v.].

1. In Arabic.

Descriptions of meadows (*rawḍ, riyāḍ*) and flowers are encountered sporadically already in d̲j̲āhilī poetry. In the *nasīb* [q.v.], the comparison of the scent of the beloved with the fragrance of a blooming meadow could result in a detailed description of the meadow (in the framework of a so-called extended simile). A famous example occurs in ʿAntara's *muʿallaḳa* (ll. 15 ff.); another in al-Aʿs̲h̲ā's *Waddiʿ Hurayrata* (ll. 14 ff.). In the context of his meadow description, al-Aʿs̲h̲ā presents one of the flowers in greater detail; its blossom he depicts with the (subsequently very frequent) metaphor "star".

Also in d̲j̲āhilī poetry, in the description of the abandoned campsites of the beloved contained in the *ḳaṣīda* prologue, the depiction of its vegetation sprouting after rainfall could be included (e.g. in Labīd's *muʿallaḳa*, l. 6). In the tradition of this motif one finds for the first time the comparison of flowering meadows with a variety of garments, mats, and similar objects—a comparison that later became part of the stock imagery of the genre. Garden flowers (partly with Persian names) are first mentioned by poets who were in contact with the court of al-Ḥīra [*q.v.*], impregnated as it was with a Persian life-style. Al-Aʿs͟hā in particular, in the wine scenes of his *ḳaṣīda*s, names and describes numerous flowers that are used to adorn the wine tavern, especially roses and narcissuses. These descriptions mirror without doubt Persian mores and lifestyle; however, they cannot be used to prove the influence, on Arabic wine and flower poetry, of a hypothetical Middle Persian bacchic poetry.

The depictions of garden flowers in wine scenes lead in a direct line to the later *zahriyyāt* and subsequently develop further, mainly in the context of wine poetry (*k͟hamriyyāt* [*q.v.*]). Abū Nuwās (d. *ca.* 200/815) stimulated this development considerably; many of his wine poems contain detailed flower descriptions and garden and spring descriptions, since in his time carousals could be held outdoors. Some of his *k͟hamriyyāt* contain more lines describing flowers than those dealing with the wine and the party (e.g. *Dīwān*, iii, ed. E. Wagner, Stuttgart 1988, nos. 138, 293). Best known is the following much-quoted and imitated description of narcissuses: "[a wine] next to freshly-gathered narcissuses as if they were eyes, when we turn our eyes to them" (*ibid.*, no. 267, l. 12). The comparison of the narcissus with eyes (or the corresponding metaphor) is one of the most frequently used images in Arabic (and Persian) flower poetry [see NARD͟JIS].

Abū Tammām (d. *ca.* 231/845) resumed the tradition of depicting nature in the prologue of the *ḳaṣīda* and reached a new high point. In a famous panegyric for the caliph al-Muʿtaṣim (*Dīwān*, ed. M.ʿA. ʿAzzām, ii, ²Cairo 1969, no. 71), he entirely replaces the *nasīb* by a long depiction of spring that also contains descriptions of the rain and of flowers of various colours. The spring description is at the same time connected with the praise in an ingenious way (spring as an imperfect image of the caliph). This innovation of Abū Tammām's acquired a model character in a singular way: numerous later Arabic poets (al-Buḥturī, Ibn al-Rūmī, al-Ṣanawbarī *et alii*), but also Persian, Hebrew, and Ottoman poets, started their *ḳaṣīda*s with spring descriptions.

In al-Buḥturī's (d. 284/897 [*q.v.*]) nature descriptions, the inventory of nature described becomes richer; in addition to flowers, he also pays attention to the wind and clouds, the song of birds, trees and rivers, and other elements of the landscape (e.g. the lands in bloom around al-Raḳḳa, in *Dīwān*, ed. Ḥ.K. al-Ṣayrafī, Cairo 1963 ff., iv, no. 903, ll. 12 ff.; the Tigris and the D͟jazīra, *ibid.*, no. 818, ll. 16 ff.). Within the *madīḥ* of his *ḳaṣīda*s, al-Buḥturī describes the garden of the *mamdūḥ*, at times together with his palace (*Dīwān*, iii, no. 641, ll. 25-6; cf. below). In a famous *ḳaṣīda* he develops out of the praise one of the most beautiful descriptions of the spring in Arabic poetry, the connecting thought being "Unto you came the merry spring" (*Dīwān*, iv, no. 791 ll. 25-30).

Probably the most important nature poet of the Arab East is al-Buḥturī's contemporary, Ibn al-Rūmī (d. 283/896 [*q.v.*]). In addition to prologues to *ḳaṣīda*s that often contained very detailed spring and flower descriptions (a meadow with many flowers in *Dīwān*, ed. Ḥ. Naṣṣār, Cairo 1973 ff., iii, no. 956; narcissuses in ii, no. 413; spring and red anemones in vi, no. 1223, ll. 14 ff.), he composed the first substantial independent flower poems. The most famous one is a poem of fourteen lines, in which the narcissus is given precedence over the rose (a pre-*munāẓara* [*q.v.*]) (*Dīwān*, ii, no. 470). This *zahriyya* was imitated or "refuted" countless times. Equally remarkable are a number of *rawḍiyyāt* that are unusual for the empathy for nature they express (see below, and also NAWRIYYA).

Ibn al-Muʿtazz (d. 296/908 [*q.v.*]) draws above all "epigrammatic sketches" and "poetic snapshots" (G.E. von Grunebaum) of flowers. His main techniques are the bilateral simile and the metaphor. These poems, consisting mostly of only a few lines, can be found, together with other "ecphrastic epigrams" (J.Ch. Bürgel) in the chapter *Awṣāf* "Descriptions" of his *Dīwān*. However, Ibn al-Muʿtazz also resumes the tradition of garden descriptions in wine poetry. His well-known *muzdawid͟ja* "On criticising the morning draught" (*fī d͟hamm al-ṣabūḥ*) (*Dīwān*, ed. B. Lewin, Istanbul 1945-50, iv, no. 99) starts with a long flower and garden description; as with Abū Nuwās, the garden serves as the backdrop for the drinking party.

In al-Ṣanawbarī (d. 334/945-6 [*q.v.*]), the *zahriyyāt, rawḍiyyāt*, etc., form a separate genre. In addition to numerous short poems in the vein of Ibn al-Muʿtazz, he also composed many long "*ḳaṣīda*s" whose main or sole theme is a garden or spring or a field in bloom. Alongside a literary debate (a full-fledged *munāẓara*) (*Dīwān*, ed. I. ʿAbbās, Beirut 1970, *takmila*, no. 123), in which, in reaction to Ibn al-Rūmī, he gives precedence to the rose over the narcissus, he also composed a "war of the flowers" (*Dīwān*, no. 77). Nature description can form a prologue to the panegyric *ḳaṣīda* with al-Ṣanawbarī also; moreover, it penetrates almost all other genres cultivated by him (see further, NAWRIYYA).

The perception of nature in later Arabic literature is predominantly optical, aiming at the decorative (G.E. von Grunebaum). In addition to the visual, acoustic (bird song) and olfactory impressions (flower scent) are expressed, though less frequently. The main means of description are simile and metaphor which serve to visualise mostly the form and colour of the flowers; the image donors are most frequently precious stones and metals ("roses like rubies") and parts of the human body ("roses like cheeks", "narcissuses like eyes"). The natural objects are often personified (Ibn al-Muʿtazz: "riders of drops of flowers on horses urged on in the morning by the whips of wind", *Dīwān*, iv, no. 111); the animation is often combined with a fantastic reinterpretation of real qualities (*tak͟hyīl* [*q.v.*], *ḥusn al-taʿlīl*) (Ibn al-Rūmī: "The cheeks of the roses glowed with shame"). In *zahriyyāt* like these, many of the motifs, images, rhetorical figures, and conceits can be found that are also characteristic for the poetry of European mannerism (cf. Bürgel, *Epigramme*, and Schoeler, *Naturdichtung*, 100 ff., 260-1).

Only rarely does one find something like a "romantic" feeling for nature, by which real human feelings are projected on to (personified) nature. This is the case e.g. in al-Buḥturī's famous spring depiction already mentioned: "There came to you serene Spring, strutting his stuff, laughing with beauty, so that he nearly talked; and Nawrūz, in the darkness before daybreak, has awakened the first roses which yesterday were still asleep . . ." (*Dīwān*, iv, no. 791, ll. 25 ff.).

Quite outside the customary is a small group of nature poems by Ibn al-Rūmī (cf. Schoeler, *Naturdichtung*, 219 ff.). The poet describes in these a nature that lives its own life; a nature which through its splendour uplifts man and forces him to praise God; which animates man through the scent of its flowers and diverts him through its birdsong; and which through its cool breeze removes the sorrow of the sorrowful: "A northwind with a cool breeze which heals the heat of the fever of thirsting hearts: when it arises in the early morning in the clouded east, it removes the sorrow of the sorrowful . . . as if it came from the Garden of Bliss" (*Dīwān*, vi, no. 1179).

In the longer poems of al-Ṣanawbarī, one often notices a lyrical-hymnic tone; such passages sometimes replace or supplant the pure description: "Do you not rejoice at the olive trees of Biṭyās and at al-Ṣāliḥiyya with its cypresses and myrtles? . . ." (*Dīwān*, no. 180). At one point al-Ṣanawbarī regards the gardens almost as a sanctuary: "If I had for once the power to preserve the gardens, no base man would step on their grounds" (*Dīwān, takmila*, no. 13).

In al-Andalus flower and garden descriptions are among the favourite themes of the poets. One of the oldest Arabic anthologies from Spain, that of Abu 'l-Walīd al-Ḥimyarī (d. *ca.* 440/1048), bears the title *al-Badīʿ fī waṣf al-rabīʿ* (ed. H. Pérès, Rabat 1940) and contains exclusively spring and flower poems; likewise, in the even older work on *tas̲h̲bīhāt* by Ibn al-Kattānī (d. *ca.* 420/1029), the *K. Tas̲h̲bīhāt as̲h̲ʿār ahl al-Andalus* (ed. I. ʿAbbās, Beirut 1966), the flower theme takes up much space.

In the 4th/10th century, under the ʿĀmirids, a new variety of *zahriyyāt* appears sporadically in al-Andalus: the short, improvised flower poem with panegyrical closure or secondary theme. Its most important representative is Ibn Darrād̲j̲ al-Ḳasṭallī (d. 421/1030 [*q.v.*]) (cf. e.g. *Dīwān*, ed. M.ʿA. Makkī, Damascus 1961, nos. 16-22, 149), who also composed a long panegyrical *ḳaṣīda* addressed to al-Muẓaffar, to which is prefixed as a prologue a famous description of a drinking party, a garden, and lilies (*Dīwān*, no. 15). The theme of the prologue is artfully connected with the main theme by *metaphora continuata* (drinking party = military campaign; the lily = fort, etc.).

For the 5th/11th century, Ibn Zaydūn (d. 463/1070-1 [*q.v.*]) should be singled out, although he is not a nature poet proper. In a poem addressed to his beloved Wallāda [*q.v.*] (*Dīwān*, ed. ʿA. ʿAbd al-ʿAẓīm, Cairo 1957, 139), objects of nature participate in his longing, the relationship between man and nature being established by fantastic reinterpretations (*ḥusn al-taʿlīl*) ("the breeze . . . is feeble, *as if affected by pity for me*", "*it is as if the eyes of the flowers*, when they see my sleeplessness, *were weeping about that* [pain] which is in me [since they are covered with dew] . . .").

The most important nature poet of al-Andalus is Ibn K̲h̲afād̲j̲a (d. 533/1139 [*q.v.*]). In his *Dīwān*, descriptions of nature take up much, if not most, of the space. More commonly than with other poets, in Ibn K̲h̲afād̲j̲a the description of flowers and gardens is combined with other objects of nature, such as trees, rivers, dew, clouds and hills, all of these sometimes artfully intertwined, being treated in one single poem. The scenes of nature, very often combined with love and/or drinking scenes, can be lavishly appointed. An example is *Dīwān* (ed. M. G̲h̲āzī, Alexandria 1960), no. 113, in which the following themes are taken up: the dream image of the beloved, the night drawing to a close, daybreak, and the flowers on a hill and alongside a watercourse; this description of nature is framed by a love scene. Ibn K̲h̲afād̲j̲a's attitude toward nature is characterised by the fact that nature is almost constantly personified and/or seen in a relationship with man: "[a cloud] that has coined white dirhams of blossoms which fingertips of boughs have tendered *to you*" (no. 184, l. 4). Through his use of metaphors he frequently projects phenomena of the macrocosm on to the microcosm of horticulture ("An *arāk* tree that has erected over us a dewy sky, while the stars of the wine cups have been set into circular motion" (no. 221 m, p. 351).

In the foregoing, only eminent Andalusian poetic personalities who developed their own styles have been focused on; it must be stressed, however, that the average Andalusian flower poem, as found e.g. in anthologies, does not significantly diverge from the Eastern Arabic one. It may be noted, though, that in al-Andalus the theme of flowers and gardens is also taken up in strophic poems (*muwas̲h̲s̲h̲aḥ, zad̲j̲al* [*q.vv.*]).

2. In Persian.

In Persian poetry, poetic spring and flower descriptions are already found in the great lyrical poets of the 4th/10th century: Rūdakī, Daḳīḳī and Kisāʾī [*q.vv.*]. Rūdakī, in clear continuation of the Arabic tradition of Abū Tammām and al-Buḥturī (he mentions Abū Tammām in one of his poems by name, see S. Nafīsī, *Aḥwāl-u as̲h̲ʿār-i . . . Rūdakī . . .* iii, Tehran 1319/1940, 1016), opens one of his panegyric *ḳaṣīda*s with a detailed spring description which leads to a short bacchic description at the end (*ibid.*, iii, 968-70). In the 5th/11th century (in such poets as ʿUnṣurī, Farruk̲h̲ī, Manūčihrī and Ḳaṭrān), the spring description, often combined with a drinking party description, becomes a favourite, if not the most favourite, theme of the prologue of the *ḳaṣīda*. This may be explained by the fact that the Persian panegyrical *ḳaṣīda* was composed as a rule for a celebration, especially the spring celebration (*nawrūz*). Since also at the autumn celebration (*mihrd̲j̲ān*), poems were dedicated and recited to the *mamdūḥ*, we find, besides spring descriptions, many autumn descriptions (cf. Fouchécour, *Description*, 13 ff.). Apart from the *ḳaṣīda* prologue, nature descriptions can also be inserted in the *madīḥ* section, e.g. in the context of the description of the *mamdūḥ*'s palace (as in al-Buḥturī) (cf. *ibid.*, 5). Finally, the theme may also be treated in the framework of a *ḳiṭʿa*, either in a bacchic context or completely independently. This happened already in the 4th/10th century: among the collected fragments of Kisāʾī (ed. M.A. Riyāḥī, Tehran 1347/1968) one finds a few poems with the themes of spring (77, 84), the narcissus (78) and the water lily (85).

In most of the Persian spring descriptions in *ḳaṣīda*s, the focus is not on a garden as a whole, under which the details are subsumed; rather, the poet treats a whole series of nature objects and phenomena as objects in their own right (cf. Reinert, *Probleme*, 74). The effect of spring on man is often included in the description. Rūdakī treats the following in his already-mentioned *ḳaṣīda* prologue: spring (its colours, its fragrance, the rejuvenating effect it has on man), the sky with clouds, lightning, thunder, rain; the sun, the thawing of the snow, the brook, tulip, nightingale, starling and dove. One hundred years later, in a comparable nature scene in ʿUnṣurī (d. 431/1039-40), we have wind, tree, garden, lily, earth, sun, cloud, night, stars, mountain and snow (the last present, but not mentioned) (*Dīwān*, ed. Y. Ḳarīb, Tehran 1341/1962, 45). Again, almost one hundred years later, in Amīr Muʿizzī (d. *ca.* 520/1126), we find season, earth, garden, mountain, tree, meadow, cypress, rose bough, dove, nightingale, cloud, tulip, stars and snow (again, the last not mentioned) (*Dīwān*, ed. ʿA. Iḳbāl, Tehran

1318/1939, 122-3). Finally, after another hundred years, Khāḳānī (d. 595/1199 [*q.v.*]) has the following: wind, branches with blossoms, sun, night, day, blossoms, moon, earth, cloud, pond, violet, brook, narcissus, rose bush, fragrant flowers, leaves, water, meadow, lily, cypress, tulip, jasmine, rosebud, mallow, dew, Judas tree, plane tree, ringdove, poppy, rose and nightingale (*Dīwān*, ed. M. ʿAbbāsī, Tehran 1336/1957, 177). The Persian nature scenes are, accordingly, as a rule richer than their Arabic counterparts. In the realm of imagery, metaphorical expression (which supersedes the bilateral simile for the most part or uses it only in a subordinate function) plays from the beginning a much greater role than it does in Arabic poetry (where the simile remains an important means of imagery, especially in Ibn al-Muʿtazz but also in al-Ṣanawbarī). Characteristic for Persian nature depictions are the numerous personifications (thus already in Rūdakī, "the tulip is *laughing* from afar in the field"; "see that thunder that is *moaning* like a sad lover") (cf. Reinert, *Probleme*, 74). In later poetry, personification is very often combined with fantastic etiology (*ḥusn-i taʿlīl*): the juxtaposition of two nature objects is thus reinterpreted as a cause-effect relationship; the choice of images is harmonically adjusted (*murāʿāt-i naẓīr*, cf. Ritter, *Bildersprache*, 7 ff.): "From greenness the water donned verdigris-coloured chainmail; when the lily saw this, it created a chainmail-piercing lance" (fantastic reinterpretation of the shape of the pistil of the lily) (from the aforementioned *ḳaṣīda* prologue of Khāḳānī).

Added to the images customarily used in Arabic nature descriptions for natural objects and phenomena there are a number of new images in Persian, e.g. those taken from the religious sphere (the earth in spring is a paradise [full of houris]; spring brings to life like Jesus; the garden because of its colours is a temple of idols or a picture gallery of Mani; the tulip kindles the fire of Nimrod).

After the *ghazal* had superseded the *ḳaṣīda* as the most important lyrical genre, nature descriptions also increasingly penetrated the *ghazal*. Saʿdī (d. 691/1292 [*q.v.*]) begins some of his *ghazaliyyāt* with garden and spring descriptions and then, with a phrase like "then I thought of you—and forgot the gardens", switches to the *maʿshūḳ* (*Kulliyyāt*, ed. M.ʿA. Furūghī, Tehran 1337/1958, *Ṭayyibāt*, 525, similarly 532). With Ḥāfiẓ (d. 792/1390 [*q.v.*]), the garden and spring depictions can occupy the larger part of the *ghazal*. They are often connected with a call to drinking wine and to *carpe diem*; thus e.g. in the poem beginning "Now that in the meadow the rose has stepped from non-being into being, the violet has laid its head at [the rose's] feet in prostration" (*Dīwān*, ed. M. Ḳazwīnī and Ḳ. Ghanī, Tehran [1320/1941], no. 219). However, the garden description may also be the almost exclusive topic of a Ḥāfiẓian *ghazal*, as in poem no. 295: "In the early morning I went to the scent of the rosebed in the garden, in order to heal [my] sorrow like the sad/loving nightingale" (note that a consolatory effect is here attributed to nature).

Finally, in epic poetry [see ḤAMĀSA] the description of nature is frequently used as a frame into which the poet puts his protagonist. Such descriptions can be found already in Firdawsī's *Shāh-nāma* (a spring description occurs e.g. at the beginning of Isfandiyār's fourth adventure). It is handled in virtuoso style by Niẓāmī (d. 605/1209 [*q.v.*]) (cf. Ritter, *Bildersprache*, 41 ff.). Very frequently, Niẓāmī depicts a landscape, often a spring landscape with many flowers, before he puts his hero on the stage. Niẓāmī uses nature as a staging area and as a décor of the epic action; however, he often establishes a relationship between nature and human affects; the former may be consonant or dissonant with a psychological condition (*ibid.*, 43). Thus in *Laylī-u Madjnūn* the story of Laylī's death is introduced by an autumn description, in which the images are chosen in such a way that they exactly conform to the psychological content of the subsequent narrative: "the cheek of the garden becomes pale . . ., the rose takes up the book of grief in its hand" (ed. W. Dastgirdī, 248; cf. Ritter, *ibid.*, 45).

Bibliography: 1. Anthologies (in addition to those mentioned in the article). al-Sarī b. Aḥmad al-Raffāʾ, *K. al-Muḥibb wa 'l-maḥbūb wa 'l-mashmūm wa 'l-mashrūb*, pts. 1-4, ed. M.Ḥ. al-Dhahabī, Damascus 1985-6 (pt. 3 = *al-Mashmūm*); Djunayd b. Maḥmūd al-ʿUmarī, *Ḥadāʾiḳ al-anwār wa-badāʾiʿ al-ashʿār*, ed. H. Nādjī, Beirut 1995.

2. Studies. Of fundamental importance are those by H. Ritter, *Über die Bildersprache Niẓāmīs*, Berlin and Leipzig 1927; G.E. von Grunebaum, *The response to nature in Arabic poetry*, in *JNES*, iv (1945), 137-51; J.Ch. Bürgel, *Die ekphrastischen Epigramme des Abū Ṭālib al-Maʾmūnī*, Göttingen 1965 (on *waṣf*, but not specifically on descriptions of nature); and G. Schoeler, *Arabische Naturdichtung*, Beirut 1972. See also A. Hamori, *On the art of medieval Arabic literature*, Princeton 1974, 78-98. On Andalusian-Arabic poetry and specifically the flower and garden poetry, see H. Pérès, *La poésie andalouse en arabe classique au XIe siècle*, ²Paris 1953; M. Raḥīm, *al-Nawriyyāt fī 'l-shiʿr al-andalusī*, Beirut 1986; Salma Kh. Jayyusi, *Andalusī poetry. The Golden Age* [and] *nature poetry in al-Andalus and the rise of Ibn Khafādja*, in *The legacy of Muslim Spain*, ed. eadem, Leiden 1992, 317-97; Schoeler, *Ibn al-Kattānīs* Kitāb al-Tašbīhāt *und das Problem des Hispanismus der andalusisch-arabischen Dichtung*, in *ZDMG*, cxxix (1979), 43-97; Magda M. al-Nowaihi, *The poetry of Ibn Khafāja. A literary analysis*, Leiden 1993; Bürgel, *Man, nature and cosmos as intertwining elements in the poetry of Ibn Khafādja*, in *JAL*, xiv (1983), 31-45. Fundamental for Persian nature poetry of the 5th/11th century is Ch.H. Fouchécour, *La description de la nature dans la poésie lyrique persane du XIe siècle*, Paris 1969. On Persian poetry and nature poetry, see B. Reinert, *Probleme der vormongolischen arabisch-persischen Poesiegemeinschaft und ihr Reflex in der Poetik*, in *Arabic Poetry. Theory and development*, Wiesbaden 1973, 71-105; idem, *Die persische Qaṣīde*, in *Neues Handbuch der Literaturwissenschaft*, Band 5, *Orientalisches Mittelalter*, ed. W. Heinrichs, Wiesbaden 1990, 242-57; J.S. Meisami, *Medieval Persian court poetry*, Princeton 1987; M. Glünz, *Die panegyrische Qaṣīda bei Kamāl ud-Dīn Ismāʿīl aus Isfahan*, Beirut 1993.

(G. SCHOELER)

ZAʿĪM (A., pl. *zuʿamāʾ*), "chief", "leader". Etymologically, *zaʿīm* denotes the spokesman of a group of individuals such as a tribe, or, metaphorically, claimant to the name of this group; but *zaʿīm* has long been used, according to different periods of history, in a political or military sense.

Of the seventeen occurrences of the term in the Ḳurʾān, in two cases (LXVIII, 40: *sal-hum ayyahum bi-dhālika zaʿīm^un*; and XII, 72: *wa-anā bihi zaʿīm^un*) it appears in the sense of "guarantor", "trustee", a meaning which recurs in numerous treatises of Islamic law. Al-Ḳalkashandī (*Ṣubḥ al-aʿshā*) notes for the Mamlūk state the meanings of "chiefs of the non-Muslim community" (in the expression *zuʿamāʾ ahl al-dhimma* applied to the patriarchs of Christian communities, iv, 194) and of "military chief" (in Egypt, vi, 51), while the honorific title of *al-zaʿīm al-aʿẓam* may be applied to the caliph himself (v, 444, 448).

The *zeʿāmet* (Turkish pronunciation of *ziʿāma*) is a form of *tīmār*, military fief, an institution of the Ottoman patrimonial system borrowed from the Saldjūḳids [see TĪMĀR; ZEʿĀMET] and probably retained from the previous Byzantine institution. Attested since the beginning of the Ottoman period (Barkey, 36-7), it corresponded to a particularly extensive donation of land, allocated as a prebend to the chieftains of the Ottoman cavalry who controlled the provinces of the empire. In return for service in times of war and maintaining security in the province, the *zaʿīm* collected taxes on the sultan's behalf. This revenue linked to a title marks the correspondence between social power and the functions of individuals bearing certain titles, to the point where the *zeʿāmet* tended to become hereditary, and intense competition between *zuʿamāʾ* incited them to military confrontation.

The term *zaʿīm* has retained its military dimension, attested by the name of Zaʿīm-oghlu, the Egyptian general who led Muḥammad ʿAlī's expedition to the Ḥidjāz, at a time when the *iḳṭāʿ* [*q.v.*] had fallen into disuse. In modern Egyptian usage, it is applied to the leaders of political parties, for example Saʿd Zaghlūl (1860-1927 [*q.v.*]), leader of the *Wafd* in the 1920s, and especially Djamāl ʿAbd al-Nāṣir (1918-70 [see ʿABD AL-NĀṢIR, in Suppl.]). As the *Zaʿīm al-ʿarab*, the latter was the archetype of the *zuʿamāʾ*, authoritarian and charismatic leaders of the independent states of the Arab East in the second half of the 20th century, another example being the ʿIrāḳī ʿAbd al-Karīm Ḳāsim (1914-63 [*q.v.*]), *al-zaʿīm al-awḥad* "the unique leader".

In contemporary Lebanon, the organic institution of *zaʿāma* has gradually taken the place of the quasi-feudal relationship of the *iḳṭāʿ*, the latter having been abolished in the Ottoman reforms of 1858. Officially deprived of his military function, and having exchanged his status as tax-farmer (*multazim*) for the position of a landowner or a state official, the *zaʿīm* is a political entrepreneur whose function is to serve as intermediary between his community and the state—Ottoman empire, French mandatory power or Lebanese state—and to keep the inter-community game in balance. He is a central figure of the cliental system whereby a political leader, most often a parliamentary deputy, assures himself of the loyalty of a local community in exchange for economic redistribution (A. Hottinger, 104). The *zuʿāmāʾ* of Lebanon have succeeded in perpetuating a system of balanced community élites by making their status hereditary (S. Khalaf, *Lebanon's predicament*, New York 1987, 125-43). Combining manipulation with coercion, they constructed sophisticated electoral machines which enabled them to maintain control of their clientele during the crisis of 1958 (M. Johnson, *Class and client in Beirut*, London 1986, 105-11) under the patronage of the "patron" *par excellence*, the President of the Republic. The civil war of 1975-90 signalled a revival of the institution of *zaʿāma*. Certain *zuʿamāʾ* had to surrender their prestige in rural areas (the Asʿad in southern Lebanon) or in urban ones (the Salām in Beirut) to new leaders enriched or made powerful by the war (E. Picard, *Les habits neufs du communautarisme*, in *Cultures et Conflits*, xv-xvi [1994], 49-70). But the key institution of the Lebanese social and political system retains its vitality.

Bibliography: Lane, *Lexicon*, 1233-4. On the Ottoman institution, the article of reference remains that of J. Deny, *Zeʿāmet*, in *EI*[1], iv, 1221-2, which may be supplemented now by the article in *EI*[2] (s.n., S. Faroqhi) and by K. Barkey, *Bandits and bureaucrats. The Ottoman route to state centralization*, Ithaca and London 1994; see also the art. TĪMĀR. On usage of the term in the contemporary Arab East, see A. Hottinger, *Zuʿamāʾ in historical perspective*, in L. Binder (ed.), *Politics in Lebanon*, New York and London 1966, 85-105; B. Lewis, *The political language of Islam*, Chicago and Ithaca 1988, 59-60, 139-40; Y. Besson, *Identités et conflits au Proche-Orient*, Paris 1991, 131-40.

(ÉLIZABETH PICARD)

AL-**ZAʿĪM**, ḤUSNĪ (1889-1949), the first head of state in the Syrian Republic to arise out of a military coup.

An officer in the Ottoman Army and then in the Special Forces of the French mandate [see MANDATES and AL-SHĀM. 2 (b)], Ḥusnī al-Zaʿīm was born in Aleppo into a Kurdish family of Hamāt. He was imprisoned in 1944-5 for complicity with the Vichy army, but at independence, the colonel al-Zaʿīm was made inspector-general of the police. Wishing to put an end to the corruption (to which he himself was no stranger), on 30 March 1949 he overthrew the government of the President Shukrī al-Ḳuwatlī. He proclaimed himself Prime Minister, and on 25 June, Marshal and head of state with special powers, by a vote of 88.9% out of 816,321 electors. Inspired by the secularist, egalitarian and developmental ideas of Kemal Atatürk [*q.v.*], he imposed a new constitution which suppressed confessional representation, gave the right to vote to educated women, made a start on agrarian reform and abolished private *waḳfs*. Externally, fearing Hashemite ambitions, he moved closer to Egypt, Saudi Arabia and, above all, the Western powers, who had welcomed his seizure of power: France, ratifying on 16 April a financial agreement concluded on 7 February by Khālid al-ʿAẓm; and the United States, ratifying on 16 May an agreement with Aramco guaranteeing the free flow of the oil pipe line within Syria. On 12 April, he proposed to Israel, with which he had had secret negotiations since the end of 1948, to install 250,000 Palestinian refugees in the Djazīra [*q.v.*] in return for economic aid from the Truman government of the United States; these negotiations came to nothing through David Ben Gurion's refusal.

More concerned with personal glory than the national interest, and corrupted by the exercise of power, Ḥusnī al-Zaʿīm installed a police-controlled dictatorship in Syria, surrounding himself with a Kurdish praetorian guard, hounding his political opponents, from the Communists to the Muslim Brotherhood, and handling over Anṭūn Saʿāda, head of the Parti Populaire Syrien (PPS), for whose plot he had provided arms, to the Lebanese authorities on 8 July. He was overthrown on 13 July by a coalition of his former allies led by Colonel Sāmī al-Ḥinnāwī, and killed the next day by officers of the PPS.

Bibliography: F.M. Ṣiḳāl, *Min dhikrayyāt ḥukūmat al-zaʿīm Ḥusnī al-Zaʿīm*, Cairo 1951; Khālid al-ʿAẓm, *Mudhakkirāt*, Beirut 1973, ii, 179-208; N. Fansa, *Ayyām Ḥusnī Zaʿīm*, Beirut 1982 (reference work); A. Shlaim, *Ḥusnī al-Zaʿīm and the plan to resettle Palestinian refugees in Syria*, in *Jnal. of Palestine Studies*, xv/4 (1986). For general works on the history of Syria at this time, see the *Bibl.* to AL-SHĀM. 2 (c).

(ÉLIZABETH PICARD)

ZAʿĪM, MEḤMED [see MEḤMED ZAʿĪM].

ZAINUDDIN [see MAPPILA].

ZĀ'IRDJA (A.) or ZĀ'IRADJA, a divinatory technique which, in the same manner as geomancy [see KHAṬṬ] and ḏjafr [q.v.], and under various outside influences, had a wide diffusion in the mediaeval Islamic lands. It involved a mechanical means of calculating portents, strongly imbued with magic and astrology, in which were strongly mingled the talismanic sciences, based on the ʿilm al-khawāṣṣ "knowledge of secret properties", the ʿilm al-awfāk "knowledge of conjunctions", ʿilm al-ṭilasmāt "knowledge of talismans" and ʿilm al-ḥurūf "knowledge of letters" [see ḤURŪF]. Ḏjafr and ḥurūf led to the zā'irḏja.

1. Origins and use in mediaeval Islam.

This mechanical technique (ṣināʿiyya) functioned with the aid of a series of concentric circles, like the Ars magna of Raymond Lull, combining the letters of the alphabet, geomancy and astrology. From Khaldūn, Muḳaddima, i, 213-20, iii, 146-79, cf. Fahd, Divination, 243-4, there emerges that the table on which these calculations were made represented the image of the celestial sphere. It was formed from seven concentric circles, the largest of which had the names of the signs of the zodiac, while the fourth contained twelve circles in which were written numbers and letters. Four other circles occupied the four corners of the square in which was a circular table. The answer to a question posed to the device was implicitly contained in the question itself, whose consonantal elements were groups, differently combined, replaced by their numerical values and set out on the tablet. After having taken into account the degree of the ecliptic which rose at the horizon at the moment of operation, one proceeded to complex calculations from which there resulted a series of numbers. When these were converted into letters, they yielded a phrase giving the answer to the question posed.

There were several methods of using letters of the alphabet for divinatory aims, as set forth in a work attributed to Ibn al-ʿArabī (d. 638/1240 [q.v.]), the K. Uṣūl al-ʿukūl fi 'l-zā'irḏja (ms. Köprülü, Fâzil Paşa 163, fols. 1-75; Bursa, Ulucami 3544, fols. 141b-194b). Two works on geomancy speak of zā'irḏja ramliyya (ʿUmar al-Khiṭā'ī), al-Ḏjadāwil al-zuhariyya fī īḍāḥ ʿilm al-raml wa 'l-zā'irḏja al-ramliyya, ms. Gotha 1317, Land. Br. 476; and Aḥmad b. ʿAbd al-Salām al-Tūnisī (9th/15th century), Kanz al-asrār al-khafiyya fī aḥkām al-zā'irḏja al-ramliyya, Bankipore, xxii, 126, 2457.

This description is to be compared with the table described by E. Savage-Smith and M.B. Smith in Islamic geomancy and a thirteenth century divinatory device, Malibu 1980, which gives a precise idea of the workings of the features combined from geomancy and astrology. It concerns a metallic contrivance in the British Museum, of remarkable workmanship and signed by a certain Muḥammad Khuṭlukh al-Mawṣilī and dated 634/1241-2. It is composed of four main figures (ummahāt), from which were derived twelve secondary figures (banāt), thus a total of sixteen, placed in correspondence with the lunar mansions (cf. 32 ff.), starting from the principle of the action of the heavenly bodies on the various parts of the human body and the influence of the constellations on the various countries of the world. In the eyes of the astrologers and geomancers, this allowed them to foretell the fate of humans and to predict revolutions and wars (see the review by Fahd, in BiOr, xxxviii/5-6 [1987], cols. 773-6).

The use of tables is also attested for horoscopes, the best-known work on this topic being the K. al-Zā'irḏjāt fi 'l-hilāḏj wa 'l-kadkhudāh of the famous mathematician and astrologer Abū Saʿīd al-Sidjzī (fl. second

half of the 4th/10th century, cf. Sezgin, GAS, vii, 177), who organises his subject-matter into five tables, referring to Greek sources (see Sezgin, GAS, vii, 177-82).

Regarding the origin of this technique, the first mention of the term zā'irḏja goes back to Ṭumṭum al-Hindī (see Goldziher, in OLZ, xiii [1910], 59-61), who is reported to have himself commented upon one of his own works called Zā'irḏja (Sezgin, iv, 119, 4). As we have just seen, it was used by al-Sidjzī, as also by Abū Maʿshar (ibid., iv, 151) and Māshā'allāh (iv, 106). But the invention of the circular table and the mode of its use are generally attributed to Shams al-Dīn Abu 'l-ʿAbbās al-Sabtī (d. 698/1298?), author of al-Risāla al-sabtiyya fi 'l-zā'irḏja (ms. Paris ar. 2694) and of the R. al-Shuḥrūr fi 'l-zā'irḏja (ms. Bursa, Ulucami 3544, fols. 195b-199b).

Bibliography: See Ibn Khaldūn, Muḳaddima, i, 213-20, Fr. tr. de Slane, i, 245-53, and iii, 146-79, pages not tr. by de Slane, who give instead a long note and a description of the procedure (iii, 200-6). But Rosenthal, in his Eng. tr. i, 238-45, iii, 182-214, gives two reproductions after p. 204 of this table, and at the end of vol. iii, in a pocket, there is a transliteration and tr. of the constituent elements of this table. A contemporary of Ibn Khaldūn attests the veracity of the experience in question in iii, 163 ff., 201 ff., Eng. tr. iii, 199 ff. Cf. on this subject, H.P. Reinaud, Divination et histoire nord-africaine du temps d'Ibn Khaldūn, in Hespéris, xxx (1943), 213-21. Cf. an expansion of this art. in Fahd, La divination arabe, Leiden 1966, repr. Paris 1987, 243-5.   (T. FAHD)

2. In mysticism and philosophy, and later survivals.

Texts of Ṣūfī inspiration hold zā'irḏja to be a path of awareness of the highest degree, allowing direct access to divine secrets, some of which, such as knowledge in the correct order of the Ninety-Nine Names of God [see AL-ASMĀ' AL-ḤUSNĀ], guarantee entry to Paradise. Also found here are cosmological developments which insist on the correspondence (rabṭ) existing between heaven and earth and which could constitute the substructure on which the concentration of the diagram is based (Ibn al-ʿArabī (attrib.), K. Uṣūl al-ʿukūl, cf. O. Yahia, Histoire et classification de l'oeuvre d'Ibn ʿArabī, Damascus 1964, ii, 519 n. 808, and Fahd, La divination arabe, 244-5 no. 6; among others, B.N. ms. arabe 2684, fols. 91a, 98a, or ms. 2694, fols. 2a, 12b; and the anonymous K. Ṭuruḳ al-sālikīn wa-kunūz asrār al-ʿārifīn, B.N. 2684, fols. 31-52, later than al-Sabtī (see 1. above) cited on fol. 39b, cf. especially the opening and fol. 391-b).

The zā'irḏja has attracted the attention of "Lullian" studies and of scholars researching into the history of numbers. D. Urvoy has established Lull's debt, in his Ars magna, to zā'irḏja, especially when purged of its esoteric and divinatory elements; see his Penser l'Islam. Les présupposés islamiques de "l'Art" de Lull, Paris 1980, 23, 89-90, iii, 162-4. It was thus that the philosopher Leibnitz came into direct contact with al-Sabtī's system.

As regards the practice of zā'irḏja, there are indications of its persistence in the 14th, 16th, 17th and even 19th centuries in North Africa (modern Morocco, Algeria and Tunisia) (Dozy, Supplément, i, 577; Leo Africanus, tr. A. Épaulard, Description de l'Afrique, Paris 1956, i, 219). The region of Ceuta in northern Morocco was probably the scene of important activity in the 6th/12th century; but E. Doutté did not mention having observed it at the beginning of the 20th century (Magie et religion dans l'Afrique du Nord,

Algiers 1908, repr. Paris 1994, 381-3). E.W. Lane encountered a simplified version of it in early 19th-century Cairo, see his *Manners and customs of the modern Egyptians*, ch. xi "Superstitions-*continued*," with an illustration of a table. Today, it is still practiced in Yemen by an adept of great regional renown, the *shaykh* Mahdī Amīn (cf. *al-Natīdja*, containing his annual predictions, where *z.y.r.dj.h* is noted on the fourth part of the cover). Furthermore, the treatise of ʿAbd al-Fattāḥ al-Ṭūkhī, *al-Zā'irdja al-handasiyya fī kashf al-asrār al-khafiyya*, Cairo 1367/1948, 1-61, as also his *Zā'irdjat al-Ṭūkhī al-falakī wa-hiya khulāṣat djāmiʿ al-zayāridj*, Cairo n.d., 139-87, also Beirut 1411/1991, seeks to perpetuate the practice.

Bibliography: See also L. Massignon, *Inventaire de la littérature hermétique arabe*, in A.-J. Festugière (ed.), *La révélation d'Hermès Trismégiste*, i, *L'astrologie et les sciences occultes*, Paris 1950, repr. 1989, appx. iii, 399; R.B. Serjeant, ch. *Islam*, in M. Loewe and Carmen Blacker (eds.), *Oracles and divination*, Boulder, Colo. 1981, 239-41, repr. in Serjeant, *Society and tradition in South Arabia*, Variorum, Aldershot 1996, no. XIV. (Anne Regourd)

ZĀKĀNĪ, ʿUBAYD [see ʿubayd-i zākānī].

ZAKARAWAYH b. **MIHRAWAYH**, one of the earliest Ismāʿīlī missionaries in ʿIrāḳ. In modern literature, the name, a Persian diminutive of Zakariyyā' (originally Zakarōye), is often misread as Zikrawayh.

Zakarawayh came from the village of al-Maysāniyya near Kūfa and was the son of one of ʿAbdān's [*q.v.*] first missionaries; he propagated the Ismāʿīlī doctrine among the Bedouin of the tribe of Kulayb on the fringes of the desert west of Kūfa. When in 286/899 a schism split the Ismāʿīlī community, he was instrumental in doing away with his master ʿAbdān who had apostatised from the Ismāʿīlī doctrine and fallen away from the headquarters of the movement at Salamiyya [see ismāʿīliyya at Vol. IV, 198a-b]. Out of fear of blood vengeance, Zakarawayh had to go into hiding; in 287/900 he reappeared and was again active in missionary work among the tribes of the Syrian desert, Asad, Ṭayyi' and Tamīm [*q.vv.*]; his hiding-place and headquarters was the village of al-Ṣaw'ar, 7 km/4 miles west of al-Ḳādisiyya. In 288/901 he sent two of his sons as missionaries to the Kalb in Palmyrene; it was these men, Yaḥyā, the "Man with the She-camel" (*ṣāḥib al-nāḳa*) and al-Ḥusayn, the "Man with the Birthmark" (*ṣāḥib al-shāma*), who in 289/902 won the support of several clans of this tribe for an armed rebellion against the ʿAbbāsid régime. They plundered the town of Ruṣāfa near the Middle Euphrates and besieged Damascus from December 902 until July 903 without success. This evidently pro-Fāṭimid rebellion seems to have been a premature undertaking on the part of Zakarawayh and his sons, unauthorised by the leaders of the Ismāʿīlī movement. It caused al-Mahdī ʿUbayd Allāh's [*q.v.*] flight from Salamiyya, and after the rebellion had been put down by an ʿAbbāsid army in 291/903, the whole enterprise was disavowed by the Fāṭimids; in later Fāṭimid sources, Zakarawayh and his sons are the subject of a *damnatio memoriae*.

After this catastrophe, Zakarawayh renewed his subversive activities in 293/906. His hordes of Kalb Bedouin plundered Buṣrā and Ṭabariyya (Tiberias) in Syria and Hīt on the Euphrates; on the day of the Feast of the Sacrifice 293/2 October 906 they made a sudden attack on Kūfa. After having defeated caliphal troops who tried to destroy his headquarters at al-Ṣaw'ar, Zakarawayh in November 906 attacked the second of the three caravans of ʿIrāḳī pilgrims at al-ʿAḳaba (today a border post between ʿIrāḳ and Saudi Arabia) and captured an immense booty. But on 10 January 907/22 Rabīʿ I 294, his partisans were attacked by ʿAbbāsid troops under the command of the general Waṣīf near the so-called ruins of Iram in Wādī Dhī Ḳār (*ca.* 160 km/100 miles west of Baṣra); in a two-day battle, the Bedouin suffered a crushing defeat, and Zakarawayh himself was mortally wounded. From the interrogation of his brother-in-law, the authorities in Baghdād got the detailed information concerning Zakarawayh's whereabouts which al-Ṭabarī made use of in his chronicle.

Bibliography: The main sources are Ṭabarī, iii, 2127, 2130, 2217-50, 2255-78; ʿArīb, *Ṣila*, 9-18, 36; Ibn al-Dawādārī, *Kanz al-durar*, ed. al-Munadjdjid, vi, Cairo 1961, 47-83; Maḳrīzī, *Ittiʿāẓ al-ḥunafā'*, ed. al-Shayyāl, i, Cairo 1967, 155, 168-73. Of studies, see H. Halm, *Die Sohne Zikrawaihs und das erste fatimidische Kalifat (290/903)*, in *WO*, viii (1975), 30-53; idem, *The empire of the Mahdi*, Leiden 1996, 62-88, 183-90. (H. Halm)

ZAKARIYYĀ', also Zakariyyā, the father of John the Baptist, reckoned in the Ḳur'ān (VI, 85) along with John, Jesus, and Elias as among the righteous. The name most likely entered Arabic via its Syriac rendering. The Ḳur'ān gives the substance of Luke i. 5-25, as follows: Zakariyyā' guards the Virgin Mary [see maryam, at Vol. VI, 630] in the niche (*miḥrāb*) and always finds fresh fruits there. He prays to God; angels announce to him that a son will be born to him, Yaḥyā, a name not previously given to anyone, a pious man, a prophet, Jacob's heir, pleasing to God. Zakariyyā' thinks he is too old. As a sign, he is struck dumb for three days (Ḳur'ān, III, 37-41, XIX, 1-11, XXI, 89-90).

Later legend expands the Gospel story and says that Gabriel was the announcer (Luke i. 19) and that Zakariyyā' was struck dumb as a punishment for his doubts (Luke i. 20). It elaborates the details as follows: nineteen people anxious to take charge of Maryam wrote their names each on a reed; these were thrown into the pool of Siloam, and the reed with Zakariyyā''s name came to the top. Zakariyyā' grew old and resigned his office of custodian, which a reed oracle gave to Joseph, the carpenter. In Mary's niche there was winter fruit in summer and summer fruit in winter; this encouraged Zakariyyā' to pray that his aged body also might be fruitful out of season.

Muslim legend has Zakariyyā' the prophet die a death of a martyr. After Yaḥyā's death, he escaped into a tree which opened for him. But the hem of his cloak remained outside the tree. Iblīs betrayed him, the tree was felled and with it Zakariyyā' (al-Thaʿlabī, 341-2; Ibn al-Athīr, Būlāḳ 1290, i, 120). This is modeled on the Haggada and the martyrdom of Isaiah [see shaʿyā, and references cited there].

Muslim legend amalgamates the Zakariyyā' of the Gospel with the prophet Zechariah, of whom the Haggada records that, after his martyrdom, his blood boiled until Nebuchadnezzar's general Nebuzaradan came. The latter sought to calm the spirit with the blood of Israel but in vain. Only his final threat to kill all of Israel calmed it. Muslim legend tells this of Yaḥyā b. Zakariyyā' [*q.v.*, and references cited there]. Zechariah, son of the High Priest Jehoiada, who was martyred by King Joash (II Chr. xxiv. 22), is identified with Zechariah, the father of John the Baptist, not only in Muslim legend but also in Christian apocryphal texts (*Protoevangelium Jacobi*, xxiv; this text provides the parallel for a number of other elements in the story also).

Bibliography: Ṭabarī, i, 733-4, tr. M. Perlmann, *The History of al-Ṭabarī*, iv, *The ancient kingdoms*, Albany N.Y. 1987, 119-20; Thaʿlabī, *Ḳiṣaṣ al-anbiyāʾ*, Cairo n.d., 333-42; Kisāʾī, *Ḳiṣaṣ al-anbiyāʾ*, ed. Eisenberg, Leiden 1922-3, 301-3; Abū Rifāʿa al-Fārisī, *Badʾ al-khalḳ wa-ḳiṣaṣ al-anbiyāʾ*, in R.G. Khoury (ed.), *Les légendes prophétiques dans l'Islam*, Wiesbaden 1978, 297-321; L. Baeck, *Secharya ben Berechja*, in *MGWJ*, lxxvi (1932), 233-319; D. Sidersky, *Les origines des légendes musulmanes dans le Coran et dans les vies des prophètes*, Paris 1933, 139-40; C.C. Torrey, *The Jewish foundation of Islam*, New York 1933, 58, 67, 80; M. Gaster and B. Heller, *Der Prophet Jesajah und der Baum*, in *MGWJ*, lxxx (1936), 35-52, 127-8.

(B. Heller-[A. Rippin])

ZAKARIYYĀʾ al-**ANṢĀRĪ**, Abū Yaḥyā b. Muḥammad b. Zakariyyā, Zayn al-Dīn al-Sunaykī, Egyptian scholar and Ṣūfī, born *ca.* 823/1420.

After growing up in a humble milieu in the Sharḳiyya, he had the opportunity of making his way to Cairo to study Islamic sciences; he was the pupil of Ibn Ḥadjar al-ʿAsḳalānī [*q.v.*]. At the same time, he frequented Ṣūfī circles and became associated with numerous initiatory "paths" (*ṭuruḳ* [see ṭarīḳa]). In his role as scholar (*ʿālim*), he excelled in particular in Shāfiʿī law, for which he composed commentaries which soon became part of the courses in the *madrasas* (such as the *Sharḥ Rawḍ al-ṭālib*, Cairo 1313, 4 vols.). A renowned teacher, in the course of his long career he educated three generations of Shāfiʿī scholars from all parts of the Near East. On numerous occasions he refused the post of Shāfiʿī Grand Ḳāḍī (*ḳāḍī al-ḳuḍāt*), but ultimately he was persuaded by the Mamlūk sultan Ḳāyitbāy to take on this function, which he exercised for a period of twenty years, from 886/1481 to 906/1500. When he received the honorific title of *shaykh al-Islām* [*q.v.*], he was even hailed by some as the "renovator" (*mudjaddid* [*q.v.*]) of the 9th century of the *hidjra*.

This renown acquired in the exoteric sciences enabled him to protect his spiritual life from any external scrutiny and to hide the social influence of his holiness (*walāya*): this amounted to the status of an authentic *malāmatī* [*q.v.*]. He succeeded in his enterprise, to the extent that posterity remembers him primarily as a great jurist. The pages dedicated to him by al-ʿAydarūsī, for example, present only the exoteric side of his personality (*Taʾrīkh al-nūr al-sāfir*, Baghdād 1934, 120-4). Only his closest pupils, such as al-Shaʿrānī [*q.v.*], who revered him, and certain Ṣūfī masters of Cairo, were aware of his spiritual dimension and were prepared to declare themselves on this subject (cf. al-Shaʿrānī, *al-Ṭabaḳāt al-kubrā*, Cairo 1954, ii, 122-4; *al-Ṭabaḳāt al-ṣughrā*, Cairo 1970, 37-45). Al-Anṣārī did, however, write in the domain of Ṣūfism (*al-Futūḥāt al-ilāhiyya fī nafʿ arwāḥ al-dhawāt al-insāniyya*, ed. in *Ḥaḳīḳat al-taṣawwuf al-islāmī*, Cairo 1992, 5-25; a commentary on the *Risāla* of al-Ḳushayrī, Cairo 1957; and a commentary on the *Risāla fī 'l-tawḥīd* of Shaykh Arslān, in *Shurūḥ risālat al-shaykh Arslān*, Damascus 1969, 181-99). The great influence wielded by al-Anṣārī in Cairo at the end of the Mamlūk period is clearly reflected in late compilations of initiatory lineages (*asānīd*): M. al-Sanūsī, *al-Salsabīl al-maʿīn fī 'l-ṭarāʾiḳ al-arbaʿīn*, Beirut 1968; M. al-Zabīdī, *Itḥāf al-asfiyāʾ bi-rafʿ salāsil al-awliyāʾ*, and *ʿIḳd al-djumān al-thamīn fī 'l-dhikr wa-ṭuruḳ al-ilbās wa 'l-talḳīn*, ms. dating from 1339/1920-1, private collection).

Zakariyyāʾ al-Anṣārī incarnates in fact the model of the Ṣūfī scholar, equally at home in the exoteric and the esoteric sciences; such a profile is often encountered at the end of the mediaeval period. Al-Anṣārī died aged 101, in 926/1520, and was buried in Cairo in the sanctuary of the Imam al-Shāfiʿī.

Bibliography: Sakhāwī, *al-Ḍawʾ al-lāmiʿ*, Beirut n.d., iii, 234-8; Ghazzī, *al-Kawākib al-sāʾira*, Beirut 1945, 196-206; E. Geoffroy, *Le soufisme en Egypte et en Syrie sous les derniers Mamelouks et les premiers Ottomans*, IFEAD, Damascus 1995, 553 (index), 517-18 (suppl.); idem, *Le voile des apparences, ou la double vie du grand cadi Zakariyyā al-Anṣārī*, in *JA*, cclxxxii/2, 271-80.

(E. Geoffroy)

ZAKARIYYĀ KĀNDHALAWĪ SAHĀRANPŪRĪ, Shaykh al-Ḥadīth Mawlānā Muḥammad, an Indian traditionist and influential member and ideologist of the Tablīghī Djamāʿat [*q.v.*], d. 1982. He was related by birth to the leaders of this movement and closely linked with them.

Born in his ancestral village of Kāndhala in what was then the United Provinces (now Uttar Pradesh), he was educated in esoteric religious studies at the seminary in Sahāranpūr [*q.v.*], which was affiliated to the school of Deoband [*q.v.*], under the direction of his father. He also had Khalīl Aḥmad Ambathawī as his teacher of *ḥadīth* and as spiritual guide. In 1915 he was initiated, and in 1925 he was authorised to initiate other disciples into the major brotherhoods (Čishtiyya, Suhrawardiyya, Ḳādiriyya and Naḳshbandiyya [*q.vv.*]). From 1916 to 1969 he taught tradition at the seminary in Sahāranpūr, and he became director there in 1954. He published commentaries on two collections of *ḥadīth* (the *Muwaṭṭaʾ* of Mālik, and the *Ṣaḥīḥ* of al-Bukhārī). He made the pilgrimage to Mecca four times (1920, 1925, 1964 and 1967), but in 1969 he had to stop teaching because he was suffering from cataracts. He went to live in Medina in 1973, and there he died and was buried in 1982.

He is famous for his prominent role in the development of the Tablīghī Djamāʿat. Between 1924 and 1964 he published in Urdu a series of treatises on the merits (*faḍāʾil*) of the fundamental practices of Islam. These are known under the collective title of *Tablīghī niṣāb*, and they have been translated into several major languages (Arabic, English and French). To this day they form the basic manuals for the movement. Muḥammad Zakariyyā was a very influential counsellor to the successive leaders of the Tablīghī Djamāʿat, and he did much to extend the movement in Arabia, in England (he travelled there twice, in 1979 and 1981), and in locations around the Indian Ocean, such as Réunion, South Africa and East Africa (where he went, also in 1981).

Bibliography: The only work of his widely available is the *Tablīghī niṣāb*, Dihlī n.d., Eng. tr. *The teachings of Islam*, Dihlī n.d., Fr. tr. *Les enseignements de l'islam*, Dihlī-Saint-Denis de la Réunion n.d.). Concerning the contents of this volume and the use that can be made of it, see B.D. Metcalf, *Living Ḥadīth in the Tablīghī Jamāʿat*, in *The Journal of Asian Studies*, lii/3 (1993), 584-608. For the biography of Muḥammad Zakariyyā, see Abu 'l-Ḥasan ʿAlī Nadwī, *Ḥaḍrat Shaykh al-Ḥadīth Mawlānā Muḥammad Zakariyyāʾ Ṣāḥib*, Lucknow 1982; M. Gaborieau, *Muḥammad Zakariyyā Kāndhalawī Sahāranpūrī*, in Gaborieau *et al.* (eds.), *Dictionnaire biographique des savants et grandes figures du monde musulman périphérique, du XIXe siècle jusqu'à nos jours*, i, Paris 1992, 20.

(M. Gaborieau)

ZAKĀT (a.), the obligatory payment by Muslims of a determinate portion of specified categories of their lawful property for the benefit of the poor and other enumerated classes or, as generally in Ḳurʾānic usage, the portion of property so paid.

1. Introduction
2. *Zakāt* in the Ḳurʾān
3. *Zakāt* in the *Ḥadīth*
4. *Zakāt* in Islamic history
5. *Zakāt* in Islamic law
   i. *Zakāt* on livestock
   ii. *Zakāt* on crops
   iii. *Zakāt* on gold and silver
   iv. *Zakāt* on mines (*maʿdin*) and treasures (*rikāz*)
   v. *Zakāt* on merchandise (*tid̲j̲āra, ʿurūḍ*)
   vi. Holding period (*ḥawl*)
   vii. Persons subject to *zakāt*
   viii. Ownership
   ix. Debts
   x. Estimation
   xi. Recipients
   xii. Collection and payment
   xiii. Intention (*niyya*)
   xiv. *Zakāt* avoidance and non-payment
6. *Zakāt al-fiṭr*
7. *Zakāt* in Ṣūfism
8. *Zakāt* in the modern period

1. Introduction.

There is disagreement as to when the obligation of *zakāt* was imposed: according to a common opinion, this occurred in the month of S̲h̲awwāl of the year 2/624 after the introduction of *zakāt al-fiṭr* in S̲h̲aʿbān of the same year, or, according to others, at the same time as *zakāt al-fiṭr*. Others place its introduction in the year 1/622-3 or 4/625-6 or even as late as 9/630-1 (al-Ṭabarī, iv, 1722, cf. Ibn Ḥad̲j̲ar al-ʿAsḳalānī, *Fatḥ al-bārī*, Cairo 1378/1959, iv, 8-9)). Another popular opinion is that *zakāt* was introduced in general terms before the *hid̲j̲ra* and then in detailed fashion in Medina. *Zakāt* is one of the "pillars" (*arkān, daʿāʾim*) of Islam (cf. al-Buk̲h̲ārī, *al-Ṣaḥīḥ*, Cairo 1418/1998, i, 19), and to deny its obligatoriness amounts to unbelief (*kufr*). Failure to pay *zakāt* when due is a grave sin (*kabīra*) (al-D̲h̲ahabī, *Kitāb al-Kabāʾir*, Cairo 1356, 32-7). Acceptance of *zakāt* on the part of those qualified to receive it is a collective obligation (*farḍ kifāya*) (Abu 'l-Hudā al-Ṣayyādī, *Ḍawʾ al-s̲h̲ams*, 1394/1974, ii, 5-7).

Muslim scholars almost universally regard the term *zakāt* as Arabic in origin and derive it form the verb *zakā*, which has among its meanings "to increase" and "to be pure". *Zakāt*, on this view, takes its name from its functions of increasing, i.e. blessing, the property from which it is taken and purifying from sin those who give it or their property (Lane, iii, 1241). Modern scholarship has regarded the term as a borrowing, almost certainly from the Judaeo-Aramaic *zāk̲h̲ūt̲h̲ā* or righteousness, as evidenced by its orthography in the Ḳurʾān (A. Spitaler, *Die Schreibung des Typus ṣlwt im Koran*, in *WZKM*, lvi [1960], 217), and it has been suggested that *zakāt* was formed to rhyme with *ṣalāt*, another borrowing from Aramaic (C. Brockelmann, *Semitische Reimwortbildungen*, in *ZS*, v [1927], 14). While the use of the noun *zāk̲h̲ūt̲h̲ā*, unlike the related verb *zʿkā* for alms, is not attested in Rabbinic writings (M. Sokoloff, *Dictionary of Jewish Palestinian Aramaic of the Byzantine period*, Ramat-Gan 1990, 177, cf. J. Horovitz, *Zakāt*, in *Isl.*, viii [1918], 137-8), in targumic literature *zāk̲h̲ūt̲h̲ā* functioned as the Aramaic equivalent for the Hebrew *ṣʿdāḳā*, which had from its original sense of righteousness come to serve as the ordinary term for alms and was borrowed with this sense into Arabic as *ṣadaḳa* [*q.v.*]. Although some of the *zakāt* rates have obvious parallels outside of Islam, e.g. one-tenth or one-fortieth (Mis̲h̲na, Tʿrūmōt̲h̲. iv, 3), there is no reason to doubt that the classical system of *zakāt* is unique to Islam.

Ṣadaḳa, in common use for voluntary alms, is also frequently used for *zakāt*, especially *zakāt* on livestock and crops. The use of *zakāt* in the sense of voluntary alms, if known at all, is rare (cf. al-Ḳurṭubī, *al-D̲j̲āmiʿ li-aḥkām al-Ḳurʾān*, Beirut 1965, vi, 222 on Ḳurʾān V, 55). The forms of *zakāt*, including *zakāt al-fiṭr*, considered here, are in turn classified under the larger heading of *ṣadaḳa*, in a further, expanded sense that includes obligatory and voluntary alms as well, *kaffāra* [*q.v.*] (al-Suyūrī, *Kanz al-ʿirfān*, Tehran 1384, i, 318). *Zakāt* is sometimes used in a figurative sense, for any offering, even one that is intangible: thus praying for other believers is said to be the *zakāt* of one without property. *Zakāt* was used in mediaeval times for various taxes without a basis in Islamic teaching [see MAKS]. The choice of the term *zakāt* for these was likely prompted by its positive religious associations and its use for a compulsory payment, as opposed to voluntary *ṣadaḳa* (cf. H. Rabie, *The financial system of Egypt A.H. 564-741/A.D. 1169-1341*, London 1972, 86, 96; P. Jackson and L. Lockhart (eds.), *Camb. hist. Iran*, Cambridge 1986, vi, 134, 541).

2. *Zakāt* in the Ḳurʾān.

The word *zakāt* occurs thirty-two times in the Ḳurʾān, always in the singular, and, according to some, only in Medinan passages (A. Jeffery, *The foreign vocabulary of the Qurʾan*, Baroda 1938, 153). In at least two such occurrences (XVIII, 81; XIX, 13) it bears the sense of righteousness. The command for Muslims to give *zakāt* is so often joined with the command to offer prayer (*ṣalāt*) that *zakāt* was later termed the "companion" (*ḳarīna*) of prayer. The same pairing occurs in connection with earlier prophets. Abraham, Isaac and Jacob were instructed to pray and give *zakāt* (XXI, 73), as were the Israelites (II, 83, cf. VII, 156) and later Jesus (XIX, 31), and Ishmael so instructed his household (XIX, 55). Muslim exegetes, however, sometimes questioned whether the *zakāt* known before Islam was identical with *zakāt* as they knew it. Only in XXIII, 4 is "doing" or "practicing" (*fāʿilūn*) *zakāt* found in place of "giving", where *zakāt*, if it refers to alms, may bear the meaning of the practice of giving, rather than as elsewhere the portion of property to be given (cf. ʿĪsā, *al-Muṣḥaf al-muyassar*, Cairo 1385, 445; R. Bell, *The Qurʾān*, Edinburgh 1937, i, 327; F. Rosenthal, *Sedaka, charity*, in *HUCA*, xxiii/1 [1950-1], 422 n. 39). The command to give *zakāt* is addressed to Muḥammad's followers in II, 110; XXII, 78; XXIV, 56; LVIII, 13; and LXXIII, 20, and specifically to Muḥammad's wives in XXXIII, 33. It is addressed to the Jews of Medina in II, 43. On the use of *ṣadaḳa* in the Ḳurʾān for *zakāt*, see ṢADAḲA. *Zakāt* may also be intended in some of the frequent references to spending (e.g. VIII, 3). *Māʿūn* in CVII, 7 has also been interpreted as *zakāt* (al-Bayhaḳī, *Maʿrifat al-sunan wa 'l-āt̲h̲ār*, ed. al-Ḳalʿad̲j̲ī, Cairo 1411/1991, vi, 9).

Those entitled to receive *zakāt* are listed in IX, 60 (*āyat al-ṣadaḳa*), said to have been revealed after the battle of Ḥunayn (8/630 [*q.v.*]) in response to criticism by hypocrites [see AL-MUNĀFIḲŪN] of the equity of Muḥammad's distribution of *zakāt* (IX, 58-9), which until then had been left to his personal judgement (al-Māwardī, *al-Aḥkām al-sulṭāniyya*, Cairo 1386/1966, 122). Institutionalisation of *zakāt* within Muḥammad's lifetime is evidenced by the mention of agents for its collection in IX, 60, reportedly first sent out in the year 9/630-1, and by the requirement of the pagan Arabs that they practice prayer and give *zakāt* for their lives to be spared (IX, 5) and for them to become "brethren in religion" (IX, 11, cf. IX, 18; and cf. al-Bukhārī, iii, 7). In LVIII, 13 the obligation of giving of *zakāt* is opposed to the voluntary *ṣadaḳa* for an audience with the Prophet.

Muslim interpreters have found in the Ḳur'ān references to *zakāt* on crops (II, 267; VI, 141), gold and silver (IX, 34), merchandise (II, 267; LI, 19; LXX, 24), and mines (II, 267). A reference to the intention (*niyya*, see 5.xiii below) required for the validity of *zakāt* has been found in XXX, 39. Ḳur'ān IX, 103, sometimes said to have been revealed to provide a means of atonement (*kaffāra*) for specific individuals who repented of their misconduct (al-Ḳurṭubī, viii, 242-5), is nonetheless among the most cited verses in connection with *zakāt*. Ḳur'ān XXX, 39 contrasts the intended increase of wealth in usury (*ribā* [*q.v.* in Suppl.]), which is vain in the estimation of God, with the genuine increase gained by those who give *zakāt*. The polytheists (*mushrikūn*) do not give *zakāt* (XLI, 7). The *munāfiḳ* will wish after he dies for another opportunity to obey the injunction to give *zakāt* (LXIII, 10: *fa-aṣṣadaḳa*).

Muslim jurists disagreed on the extent to which the Ḳur'ān provided adequate information for implementing the obligation of giving *zakāt*. A minority found a basis in the Ḳur'ān (IX, 103) for imposing *zakāt* on all property (*amwāl*) unless there was evidence to the contrary (e.g. the Zaydī *imām* al-Hādī, *K. al-Aḥkām*, 1990, i, 180), a position sometimes attributed to Abū Ḥanīfa. Others regarded the Ḳur'ānic provisions as insufficiently detailed (*mudjmal*) and in need of clarification from the Prophet, a position commonly ascribed to al-Shāfi'ī, who did in fact regard the clarification of the Ḳur'ānic provisions on *zakāt* provided by the *sunna* as paradigmatic of the relation between these sources of law (*al-Umm*, ed. Cairo, ii, 3).

There is disagreement whether the obligation of *zakāt* abrogated other Ḳur'ānic provisions for obligatory giving (e.g. II, 219) and more generally whether there are any Islamic obligations on property beyond *zakāt* (*fī 'l-māl ḥaḳḳ siwā al-zakāt*) (al-Ghazālī, *Iḥyā' 'ulūm al-dīn*, on the margin of al-Zabīdī, *Itḥāf al-sāda al-muttaḳīn*, ed. Beirut, iv, 105-6; Ibn al-'Arabī, *K. al-Ḳabas*, ed. Walad Karīm, Beirut 1992, ii, 461-2).

3. *Zakāt* in the *Ḥadīth*.

Apart from the Ḳur'ānic list of beneficiaries, the other major elements of the law of *zakāt* are based on *ḥadīth*: the kinds of property subject to *zakāt*, the minimum quantity (*niṣāb*) in each case, the rate of *zakāt*, and the rule of a one-year holding period (*ḥawl*) (Ibn Mādja, *al-Sunan*, Cairo, i, 547). The best-known traditions regulating the *zakāt* due on camels and sheep are reports of written instructions for their collection (*kitāb*, *ṣaḥīfa*, *'ahd*) that came to be preserved as family heirlooms. These are the instructions of the Prophet to 'Amr b. Ḥazm whom he sent to Yemen (cf. al-Nasā'ī, *al-Sunan*, ed. 'Abd al-Wārith 'Alī, Beirut 1416/1995, viii, 41-2), the instructions that the Prophet is said to have prepared but was unable to issue before his death, and which were then implemented by Abū Bakr and 'Umar, and later by 'Umar b. 'Abd al-'Azīz (Mālik, *al-Muwaṭṭa'*, ed. 'Abd al-Bāḳī, Cairo, 175-6; Abū Dāwūd, *al-Sunan*, ed. al-Khālidī, Beirut 1416/1996, i, 458-9), and the instructions of Abū Bakr to Anas b. Mālik, whom he sent to collect *zakāt* in Baḥrayn (al-Bukhārī, iii, 39-41) (on these traditions, see 'Iyāḍ b. Mūsā, *Ikmāl al-mu'lim bi-fawā'id Muslim*, ed. Ismā'īl, al-Manṣūra 1419/1998, iii, 489-90). The *zakāt* due on cattle appears in the Prophet's instructions to Mu'ādh b. Djabal, whom he sent to Yemen (Abū Dāwūd, i, 462), known, unlike the rest of Arabia, for its cattle-raising (al-Zarkashī, *Sharḥ al-Zarkashī 'alā mukhtaṣar al-Khiraḳī*, ed. al-Djibrīn, ii, 392-3, cf. al-Hamdānī, i, 201). In some formulations one can detect a mnemonic intent: "No *ṣadaḳa* is payable on less than *five* camel-loads of dates, on less than *five* ounces of silver, and on fewer than *five* camels" (al-Bukhārī, iii, 10). Similar details are found in the Shī'ī *ḥadīth* transmitted from 'Alī and the other *imāms*.

Both those who pay *zakāt* and those who collect are cautioned: the former to make sure that the collector leaves them well pleased, the latter not to exact more than is due, which is as bad as refusing to pay (al-Tirmidhī, *al-Sunan*, ed. 'Abd al-Bāḳī, Beirut, iii, 38). Owners of livestock need not pay with their most valuable animals, unless they freely choose to do so (al-Bukhārī, iii, 43). The collector who acts according to law is likened by the Prophet to the warrior in God's cause (*ghāzī*, *mudjāhid*) (al-Tirmidhī, iii, 37). While the instructions of Abū Bakr to Anas are preceded by the statement that those of whom more *zakāt* is demanded than is due are not to pay it, other traditions urge the *zakāt* payer to comply with exorbitant demands, for which the collectors will be held responsible (cf. al-Shawkānī, *Nayl al-awṭār*, ed. al-Ṣabābiṭī, Cairo 1413/1993, iv, 147). There are also warnings to those who accept *zakāt* to which they are not entitled that what they acquire is only an ache in their heads and a burning in their innards.

Failure to pay *zakāt* is a sign of hypocrisy, and the prayers of those who do not pay *zakāt* will not be accepted. No poor person would ever go hungry, lack clothing or be hard-pressed if the wealthy paid their *zakāt*, but it is admitted that there is no obligation more demanding than the payment of *zakāt*. *Zakāt* serves as a purification (*ṭuhra*, *ṭuhūr*) of those who pay. It safeguards their other property, whereas giving voluntary alms (*ṣadaḳa*) heals the sick. No property at land or sea is ever lost except on account of the withholding of *zakāt*. *Zakāt* is never left commingled with other property without bringing about its ruin. Failure to pay *zakāt* brings on drought and loss of livestock, while the payment of *zakāt* ensures rain. Property on which *zakāt* has been paid is not the treasured-up gold and silver condemned in the Ḳur'ān (IX, 34), even when it is buried deep in the earth. On the Day of Resurrection (*ḳiyāma* [*q.v.*]), equivalent to fifty thousand years in this world, those who have not paid *zakāt* will be confronted by the *zakāt* they have withheld (cf. Ḳur'ān IX, 35): their gold and silver treasure (*kanz*) will pursue them in the form of a large fearsome serpent (cf. Ḳur'ān III, 180), with the cry: "I am your treasure," and those who have withheld *zakāt* from livestock will be trampled and gored by the animals they have not paid, now grown large and fat.

4. *Zakāt* in Islamic history.

According to the Islamic sources, the collection of *zakāt* was already in full force during the lifetime of the Prophet Muḥammad. He is said to have dispatched "innumerable" collectors of *zakāt*, some of them among the most famous of his Companions, such as 'Umar and 'Alī (al-Khuzā'ī, *K. Takhrīdj al-dalāla al-shar'iyya*, ed. Abū Salāma, Cairo 1401/1981, 544; Ibn Sa'd, ii/1, 115). On the other hand, the *ḥadīth* indicates that the Prophet died before the definitive guidelines for the collection of camels and sheep were issued. The system of *zakāt* collection was gravely threatened during the caliphate of Abū Bakr, when some of the Arabian tribes refused to acknowledge that the Prophet's authority to collect *zakāt* had passed to his successor. This movement in resistance to the collection of *zakāt* is associated with the apostasy of the *ridda* [*q.v.* in Suppl.] wars, but it became widely accepted among Muslim scholars that only some of those who withheld *zakāt* were true apostates, the others being more properly classified as rebels (*bug̲h̲āt*) and not to be judged by the same standard as later Muslims who reject the obligation of *zakāt* (al-K̲h̲aṭṭābī, *Maʿālim al-sunan*, ed. al-Ṭabbāk̲h̲, Aleppo 1352/1933, ii, 2-10, *locus classicus*).

Of the succeeding Rightly-Guided Caliphs, ʿUmar is reported to have had the greatest interest in the details of *zakāt* and its collection. To ʿUmar is attributed the institution of collectors posted on roads to collect *zakāt* from Muslim merchants (at the rate of 2.5%) as well as imposts on the merchandise of non-Muslim traders, both indigenous (*d̲h̲immī*) and foreign (*ḥarbī*). From the rate applied to alien non-Muslim merchants of 10% (*ʿus̲h̲r*), these collectors became known as *ʿus̲h̲s̲h̲ār* (sing. *ʿās̲h̲ir*). In the course of time, these collectors on bridges and in ports came to exceed the limits imposed by the law and acquired an exceedingly unsavory reputation for venality. ʿUmar is said to have been the first to take merit, and not merely need, into consideration in the distribution of *zakāt* (Muslim b. Abī Karīma, *Risālat Abī Karīma fi ʾl-zakāt*, ʿUmān 1982, 10). It was ʿUmar, too, according to some, who definitively declared that Islam had achieved such a state of security as to no longer need the services of "those whose hearts are to be won over," one of the Ḳurʾānic classes of recipients of *zakāt* (on these, see Ibn al-ʿArabī, *Aḥkām al-Ḳurʾān*, ed. al-Bid̲j̲āwī, Cairo 1387/1967, ii, 951-4, and AL-MUʾALLAFA ḲULŪBUHUM). But the most significant change in the practice of *zakāt* collection is attributed to ʿUt̲h̲mān. This is the rule that the official collectors of *zakāt* have authority to demand payment on "apparent" (*ẓāhir, nāṭiḳ*) property only, i.e. livestock and crops, leaving owners the choice of paying *zakāt* on "unapparent" (*bāṭin, ṣāmit*) property, i.e. gold, silver and merchandise, either to the collectors or directly to the recipients of *zakāt*. It is said that ʿUt̲h̲mān was concerned that rapacious collectors would enrich themselves with the property of the Muslims, and in fact allegations of corruption in the collection of *zakāt* were already made against ʿUt̲h̲mān's collectors. Some, however, held that the Prophet himself never demanded payment of *zakāt* on *bāṭin* property (Ibn Ḳudāma, *al-Kāfī*, ed. al-S̲h̲āwīs̲h̲, i, 328), and others have rejected the distinction entirely: the Zaydī *imām* al-Hādī insisted that it was a contrivance of jurists aimed at checking over-reaching collectors (*K. al-Aḥkām*, i, 192-3).

During the Umayyad period, zeal in the collection of *zakāt* grew. Muʿāwiya, for example, is said to have been the first to deduct *zakāt* from state stipends (J. Schacht, *The origins of Muhammadan jurisprudence*, Oxford 1950, 199-200). But the increasing lack of confidence in the integrity of administration of the *zakāt* system is reflected in the reported disagreement among early jurists whether it was still appropriate to pay *zakāt* to the official collectors. The position of Ibn ʿUmar (d. 73/692) that such payment would discharge one's obligation proved to be the most influential (cf. Madelung, *ʿAbd Allāh b. ʿAbbās and Shīʿite law*, in *Law, Christianity and modernism in Islamic society*, ed. Vermeulen and Van Reeth, Louvain 1998, 21-3). A review of existing practice in the collection of *zakāt* formed part of the reform of fiscal matters under ʿUmar b. ʿAbd al-ʿAzīz (d. 101/720 [*q.v.*]), and his rulings on questions of *zakāt* are widely, sometimes inconsistently, reported in later writings, along with references to his efforts to procure copies of instructions to collectors from the Prophet's day. A prominent feature of his rule was an effort to bring the *ʿus̲h̲s̲h̲ār* into conformity with Islamic law. The establishment of a special government office, *dīwān al-ṣadaḳa*, for the receipt of *zakāt* occurred under the caliph His̲h̲ām (d. 125/743).

From the *Kitāb al-K̲h̲arād̲j̲* of the *ḳāḍī* Abū Yūsuf (d. 182/798 [*q.v.*]), written in the form of counsel to the ʿAbbāsid caliph Hārūn al-Ras̲h̲īd, it emerges that the system for the collection of *zakāt* in his day was both corrupt and inefficient. Collection of *zakāt* was in the hands of the collectors of *k̲h̲arād̲j̲* [*q.v.*], who did not keep the proceeds distinct as required by law, while *zakāt* on merchandise collected by the *ʿus̲h̲s̲h̲ār* was administered separately from the other forms of *zakāt* (*K. al-K̲h̲arād̲j̲*, with the commentary of al-Raḥbī, *Fiḳh al-mulūk wa-miftāḥ al-ritād̲j̲*, Bag̲h̲dād 1975, i, 536-7). The joint administration of *zakāt* and the income of caliphal *awḳāf* (*dīwān al-birr wa ʾl-ṣadaḳāt*) introduced in 315/927 (Miskawayh, i, 152), suggests a decline in *zakāt* revenue.

Virtually nothing is known about the details of the official collection of *zakāt* throughout most of its history. References in the historical sources are scattered and meagre in detail, and the evidence of the Arabic papyri is limited (G. Khan, *Arabic papyri: select material from the Khalili Collection*, London 1992, 53). By contrast, the legal sources occasionally provide vivid details about such practices as the counting of livestock (al-S̲h̲āfiʿī, *Umm*, ii, 51, describing the procedure for collection for livestock of his uncle, a *zakāt* collector). Al-S̲h̲āfiʿī reports that collectors of *zakāt* on livestock were sent out in Muḥarram (ii, 14), while Mālik states that the practice was for them to go out in May (Saḥnūn, *al-Mudawwana*, ed. Muḥammad, Beirut 1419/1999, ii, 446, cf. *al-K̲h̲irs̲h̲ī ʿalā muk̲h̲taṣar K̲h̲alīl*, ed. Beirut, ii, 161-2). The animals collected as *zakāt* were specially branded (with the words "for God", according to al-S̲h̲āfiʿī: see al-Muzanī, *al-Muk̲h̲taṣar*, on margin of *al-Umm*, iii, 244; others state that the brand was "*zakāt*" or "*ṣadaḳa*"), although some jurists disapproved of this practice. The Ḥanafī al-Sarak̲h̲sī tells us that it was the custom of collectors to give receipts (*barāʾa*) (*al-Mabsūṭ*, ed. Beirut, ii, 161, 202), although their legal force was disputed, and this practice is corroborated by the papyri (Grohmann, *Arabic papyri in the Egyptian Library*, Cairo 1938, iii, 178-9, from 148/765-6) and historical sources (Ibn Yaʿḳūb, *Sīrat al-Imām al-Manṣūr bi ʾllāh*, ed. al-Ḥibs̲h̲ī, Ṣanʿāʾ 1417/1996, 29).

Little, too, is known about how governments distributed the proceeds of *zakāt* or the extent of corruption involved. Administrative costs, which in the worst case could run so high as to consume the entire *zakāt* collected, appear to have been high (cf. Abū Yūsuf, *K. al-K̲h̲arād̲j̲*, i, 536), and there is some evidence of *zakāt* farming (Khan, *Arabic legal and administrative documents in the Cambridge Genizah collections*, Cambridge 1993, 283-5, from 480/1088, cf. Khalid Abou El Fadl, *Tax farming in Islamic law (qibālah and ḍamān of kharāj): a search for a concept*, in *Islamic Studies*, xxxi/i [1992], 5-32). The local distribution encouraged by Islamic law would tend to facilitate the use of *zakāt* to reward favourites and cultivate clients. In any case, the example of the Imām al-Hādī (d. 298/911) in Yemen suggests the political obstacles that could face even a ruler of impeccable learning and religious conviction in his efforts to impose a system of *zakāt* in accordance with the law (Madelung, *Land ownership and land tax in Northern Yemen and Najrān: 3rd-4th/9th-10th century*, in T. Khalidi (ed.), *Land tenure and social transformation in the Middle East*, Beirut 1984, 89-193).

The collectors of *zakāt* in some cases exercised further roles. In the time of the Prophet they were charged with teaching the elements of Islam (cf. al-Bukhārī, iii, 3-4), as were later the collectors sent out by the Imām al-Hādī (al-ʿAlawī, *Sīrat al-Hādī*, ed. Zakkār, Beirut 1401/1981, 45). Mālikī sources indicate that collectors of livestock possessed a limited judicial authority (*al-Khirshī ʿalā mukhtaṣar Khalīl*, ii, 149).

According to the Fāṭimid jurist al-Ḳāḍī al-Nuʿmān (d. 363/974 [*q.v.*]), *zakāt* among the Sunnīs of his day was largely limited to private distributions to the poor, despite the approval by leading Sunnī jurists of payment to the state, and those who did pay *zakāt* in any form were a distinct minority (*Daʿāʾim al-Islām*, ed. Fayḍī, Cairo 1383/1963, i, 257-8, 261-2). By about the year 493/1100, governmental collection of *zakāt* across the Muslim world had become largely a thing of the past and has remained so ever since for the great majority of Muslims. The Andalusian Mālikī Ibn ʿAbd al-Barr (d. 463/1071 [*q.v.*]) noted that the scholars of his day no longer made the coming of the *zakāt* collectors a condition for the obligation to pay, as had Mālik, in whose time they did regularly come (*K. al-Kāfī*, ed. al-Mūritānī, Riyāḍ 1398/1978, i, 311). Similarly, the Shāfiʿī Fakhr al-Dīn al-Rāzī (d. 606/1210 [*q.v.*]) in the East writes of the collectors as a class of *zakāt* recipients that no longer exists (*al-Tafsīr al-kabīr*, Cairo 1357/1938, xvi, 115), as does the ʿIrāḳī Mālikī Ibn ʿAskar (d. 732/1332) a century later (*Irshād al-sālik*, ed. Sūsa, 1989, 38). The Egyptian al-Ḳalḳashandī (d. 821/1418 [*q.v.*]) reports that, in his day, the collection of *zakāt* was confined to the activity of the *ʿushshār* in the ports and to some limited collection of livestock (*Ṣubḥ al-aʿshā*, iii, 457-8).

Rulers with a reformist mission would, as might be expected, favour a revival of *zakāt* collection: the Almohads, Ṣalāḥ al-Dīn (Rabie, 96), the Sokoto Caliphate, the Arabian Wahhābīs and the Sudanese Mahdists. In some cases, local dynasties were able to maintain a more or less traditional form of *zakāt* collection, but often alongside non-Islamic sources of revenue, into the modern period, for example, the ʿAlawīs of Morocco until 1901 and the Zaydīs of Yemen until the revolution of 1962. In Kuwayt, *zakāt* was collected on livestock, crops and fish until the increase in wealth brought about by the discovery of petroleum in the 1920s.

The general disappearance of official *zakāt* collectors did not in itself leave the distribution of *zakāt* to individual property owners, since there were intermediaries ready to fill the gap, ranging from local village *imāms* as in pre-colonial Malaysia to powerful Ṣūfī orders in Africa and elsewhere. Such intermediaries functioned as both recipients and collectors for further distribution. Sectarian groups typically developed their own channels for collection and distribution: The Shīʿī *imāms* were succeeded in this role by the leading jurists among the Twelver Shīʿīs, and by the *dāʿī muṭlaḳ* among the Indian Bohras (F. Daftary, *The Ismāʿīlīs: their history and doctrine*, Cambridge 1990, 317; and see BOHORĀS). Among these groups, as among the Ibāḍīs, *zakāt* was largely confined to the community of fellow adherents.

5. *Zakāt* in Islamic law.

The law of *zakāt* is a hybrid between the elements of ritual and revenue-raising, elements that have historically competed for primacy and continue to do so today. Insofar as paying *zakāt* is a ritual act of purification, the focus is on the payer; as a system of revenue-raising, the centre of concern is the recipients, particularly the poor. The hybrid quality of the law of *zakāt* is most strikingly evident in the distinction sometimes made by Ḥanafīs between *zakāt* proper, which is said to be a pure act of worship, and the tithe (*ʿushr*) on crops, which is a form of revenue (*muʾna*, literally impost) with an element of worship (e.g. Shaykhzāda, *Madjmaʿ al-anhur*, ed. Istanbul, i, 214), but it is also apparent in the treatment in many Shāfiʿī legal texts, following al-Muzanī's (d. 264/878 [*q.v.*]) *al-Mukhtaṣar*, of the basic rules of *zakāt* in the section on ritual (*ʿibādāt*) and the rules for its distribution (*ḳasm*) separately in a section on revenues of the state. The dimension of *zakāt* as a source of revenue is, of course, especially prominent in its treatment in the relatively small but significant legal literature on governance (*aḥkām sulṭāniyya*) and public finance (*amwāl, kharādj*).

Zakāt is commonly classified as a tax on property rather than income, but this is only approximately correct, since, for example, *zakāt* is due on crops only once, when they are harvested, without the requirement of a holding period. In any event, the theory developed by the classical jurists to explain why *zakāt* is payable only on certain kinds of property appeals to the notion of "growth" (*namāʾ*): *zakāt* is due on property that represents growth or is devoted to growth, actually or virtually (*taḳdīr^an*). Thus grazing livestock and trade goods represent property actually devoted to growth, and gold and silver, by their very nature as media of exchange, property virtually devoted to growth, while crops and mined minerals represent growth itself. The requirement of a holding period of one year (*ḥawl*), where applicable, is understood to provide an opportunity for such growth, and the fact that *zakāt* is paid out of growth encourages compliance (Muḥammad b. ʿAbd al-Raḥmān al-Bukhārī, *Maḥāsin al-islām*, Cairo 1357, 17). This theory gained near-universal acceptance, to the extent that it was even invoked as an explanation of the term *zakāt* (Ibn Rushd, *al-Muḳaddimāt*, ed. Ḥadjdjī, Beirut 1408/1988, i, 271), and it remains popular today. The element of growth is even more obvious in the view of a minority of early jurists who are said to have imposed *zakāt* generally on property as soon as it was acquired (see below, 5.vi). One of the few opponents of the theory of growth was the Ẓāhirī Ibn Ḥazm (d. 456/1064 [*q.v.*]) (cf. *al-Muḥallā*, ed. al-Bindārī, iv, 45, 146, 149, 187).

There is disagreement as to whether *zakāt* is an obligation *in rem* (*fī ʾl-māl, fī ʿayn al-māl*) or *in personam* (*fī ʾl-dhimma*). The former view, itself subject to several interpretations, is that commonly defended, but if fully pressed would, among other unacceptable consequences, make the recipients of *zakāt* co-owners of the *zakāt* payer's property (al-Zarkashī, ii, 460-2; cf. Walī al-Dīn al-Baṣīr, *al-Nihāya*, ed. ʿUmayrāt, Beirut 1416/1995, 113, where they are co-owners). A more limited, commonly cited implication of the dispute arises in the case of the owner of forty sheep who fails to pay *zakāt* for two consecutive holding periods. On the *in personam* analysis, his *zakāt* liability at the end of the two years is two sheep; on the *in rem* analysis only one sheep, since with one sheep from the flock now encumbered by *zakāt* there is no longer a *niṣāb* (minimum number of forty, see below) during the second holding period (Ibn Hubayra, *al-Ifṣāḥ*, ed. al-Dabbās, Aleppo 1366/1947, i, 141). In fact, the law of *zakāt* is a product of the application to one degree or another of both views (cf. Ibn Radjab, *al-Ḳawāʾid*, ed. Saʿd, Cairo 1392/1972, 207). There is, in any case, universal agreement that qualified recipients of *zakāt* cannot exercise self-help in taking their share but must await distribution by the government or the individual *zakāt* payer.

The theme of fairness is central to the classical theory of *zakāt*. It is considered only just that, as a charitable sharing of wealth (*muwāsāt*), *zakāt* should be in the first instance payable from the very property on which it is imposed and only from property of average quality. It is also commonly held that the rate of *zakāt* is inversely related to the effort expended in producing the growth from which *zakāt* is due, as is particularly evident in the differential rate of *zakāt* for crops according to the method of irrigation used in their production (see below) (al-Sayyāghī, *al-Rawḍ al-naḍīr*, ed. Beirut, ii, 389-90, but see al-Sarakhsī, *al-Mabsūṭ*, iii, 4, according to whom, the rationale for the different rates of *zakāt* is not knowable). Concern with fairness also appears in the balancing of interests between the payers of *zakāt* and its recipients that is attributed to the Lawgiver and that arises frequently in the discussions of the jurists.

Muslim jurists sometimes speculated as to the underlying reasonableness of the apparently arbitrary quantities that abound in the laws of *zakāt*. The Shāfiʿī al-Ḳaffāl al-Shāshī (d. 365/976) suggested that the *ṣāʿ* of grain paid as *zakāt al-fiṭr* could produce enough bread to feed a poor person for the day of the feast and the customary three-day celebration that followed, when no work would be available (al-Bādjūrī, *Ḥāshiyat al-Bādjūrī ʿalā Ibn al-Ḳāsim*, ed. Cairo, i, 280). Shāh Walī Allāh al-Dihlawī (d. 1175/1762 [see AL-DIHLAWĪ]) proposed that the minimum amounts of agricultural produce and silver subject to *zakāt* were each enough to sustain for one year a family consisting of a husband, wife and one dependent, and were thus a reasonable measure of wealth (*Ḥudjdjat Allāh al-bāligha*, ed. Ḍamīriyya, Riyāḍ 1420/1999, ii, 727-8, tr. M.K. Hermansen, *The conclusive argument from God*, Leiden 1996, 297-8). Along similar lines, it was even suggested that the apparently complex rate of *zakāt* on camels was in fact the familiar 2.5% for gold and silver and merchandise (al-Sarakhsī, ii, 150). Such speculations have re-emerged in modern discussions of *zakāt* as contemporary theorists attempt to formulate a rationalised version of the traditional law.

Muslim jurists have often rested the authority of the government to demand the payment of *zakāt* on the protection (*ḥimāya*) it provides to property, an analysis most fully developed by the Ḥanafī jurists, who use it to justify the collection of *zakāt* on merchandise, a form of *bāṭin* property, by the *ʿushshār*. The *ʿushshār* acquire the authority to demand *zakāt* on such property when the owner takes it on to the public roads and brings it into the government's sphere of protection (Ibn al-Humām, *Fatḥ al-ḳadīr*, Cairo 1389/1970, ii, 224). This analysis the Ḥanafīs extend to the imposts demanded by *ʿushshār* on the property of non-Muslims (*ibid.*, ii, 227). A similar principle is reported to have been given practical application by the Ibāḍīs of ʿUmān *ca.* 1000, who would not collect *zakāt* from foreign Muslim merchants until a year of residency had passed, which established the requisite protection (al-Bisyawī, *Djāmiʿ Abi ʾl-Ḥasan al-Bisyawī*, ʿUmān 1404/1984, ii, 190). Likewise, an Ibāḍī *imām* taking office after a break in the imāmate must wait one year before collecting *zakāt* (Muḥammad b. Yūsuf Aṭṭafayyish, *Sharḥ al-nīl*, Beirut 1392/1972, iii, 286).

Niṣāb. *Zakāt* is due on property only if a minimum quantity (*niṣāb*, pl. *nuṣub*, *anṣiba*, literally "base", less commonly *daradja*) is held, e.g. five camels (on the introduction of *niṣāb* as a legal term of art, see Abū ʿUbayd al-Ḳāsim b. Sallām, *K. al-Amwāl*, ed. Ḥarrās, Cairo 1388/1968, 560-1, cf. Mālik, *al-Muwaṭṭaʾ*, 177). The *zakāt* payable increases with the amount of property held, and where, as in the case of livestock, such increases in the property subject to *zakāt* are not pro-rata (*bi ʾl-ḥisāb*), but set at discrete increments, each of these increments represents a further *niṣāb*, with eleven such *nuṣub* in the most complex case, that of camels. The amount of property below the first *niṣāb* and between each subsequent *niṣāb* is termed *waḳṣ*/*waḳaṣ* (also *shanaḳ*) (cf. al-Nawawī, *Tahdhīb al-asmāʾ wa ʾl-lughāt*, Cairo n.d., i, 193-4). It is generally held that no *zakāt* is due on the *waḳṣ* between the *nuṣub*, hence the further term *ʿafw* for the *waḳṣ*. Thus the one sheep or goat due on nine camels (the second *niṣāb* being ten) is in fact due on only five, the four additional camels being *waḳṣ*, and should four of the nine perish after *zakāt* is due, there will be no proportionate reduction in the amount of *zakāt* to be paid.

As in other areas of Islamic law, there is considerable disagreement among Muslim jurists over the details of the law of *zakāt*. The discussion here focuses on the doctrine of the Shāfiʿī school with some notice of the most salient points of disagreement between the schools. Twelver Shīʿī law alone recognises cases where *zakāt* is recommended (*mustaḥabb*) but not obligatory (cf. al-Ḥalīmī, *K. al-Minhādj fī shuʿab al-īmān*, ed. Fawda, Beirut 1979, ii, 343), a categorisation that serves to reconcile conflicting evidence for and against the imposition of *zakāt*.

i. *Zakāt* on livestock (*ḥayawān*, *māshiya*, *naʿam*). *Zakāt* is imposed on camels (*ibil*), cattle (*baḳar*), and sheep and goats (*ghanam*) according to the number of animals owned. According to the great majority of jurists, for the calculation of the number of animals in the herd, male and female animals, young and old, healthy and diseased count equally. The Ẓāhirīs alone do not count animals under one year of age (*al-Muḥallā*, iv, 82). Animals of different breeds (*anwāʿ*), such as Bactrian and Arabian camels, cattle and water buffalo, are counted together, as are sheep (*ḍaʾn*) and goats (*maʿz*). *Zakāt* is normally due in the form of adult (over one year), female, healthy, and defect-free animals. The assumption throughout is that greater age and feminine gender increase the value of the animal. Except for the Ḥanafīs, who accept male and female cattle and sheep indifferently, male animals are acceptable only where indicated below or if all the animals in the herd are male. Where the entire herd consists of under-age or unhealthy animals or those suffering from defects, these are accepted as *zakāt*, except by the Mālikīs, who even in these cases require that *zakāt* be paid with healthy, defect-free, adult animals. Where the herd consists of animals of different breeds or of both sheep and goats, the *zakāt* is to be paid in the form of animals that reflect the relative values of the different breeds in the make-up of the herd. Thus for a herd consisting of thirty female goats and ten female sheep, the one sheep or goat due as *zakāt* for forty animals must be worth as much as three-fourths of a female goat and one-fourth of a female sheep. Apart from adjustments (*djubrān*) in the form of cash or sheep, admitted by some jurists in the case of camels alone, the *zakāt* payer who cannot supply the required animals from his herd is required to acquire them in order to make payment. The Ḥanafīs accept in all cases payment of their value (*ḳīma*), even in the form of fewer but fatter animals (see below, 5.xii).

Pasturage. According to the great majority of jurists, a condition for the imposition of *zakāt* on livestock is that the animals be put out to pasture (*sawm*) for breeding or milk. Animals that subsist on fodder (*ʿalaf*) are not subject to *zakāt*, nor are animals that live on pasturage but are put to work by the owner or hired out for work. The Mālikīs impose *zakāt* on livestock without regard to whether the animals subsist on pasturage or fodder and, in the case of camels and cattle, whether or not they are put to work, a rule also followed by some Ẓāhirīs including Ibn Ḥazm (*al-Muḥallā*, iv, 144).

Camels. There is general agreement among the Muslim jurists as to the rate of *zakāt* on camels up to one hundred twenty as follows:

number of camels	*zakāt* due
5-9 camels	1 sheep or goat
10-14 camels	2 sheep or goats
15-19 camels	3 sheep or goats
20-24 camels	4 sheep or goats
25-35 camels	1 female camel in its second year (*bint makhāḍ*)
36-45 camels	1 female camel in its third year (*bint labūn*)
46-60 camels	1 female camel in its fourth year (*ḥiḳḳa*)
61-75 camels	1 female camel in its fifth year (*djadhaʿa*)
76-90 camels	2 female camels in their third year
91-120 camels	2 female camels in their fourth year

Twelver S͟hīʿīs assess five sheep or goats for 25 camels and a *bint makhāḍ* for 26-35 camels. This variation, based on a tradition from ʿAlī, was also accepted by Zayd b. ʿAlī (d. 122/740 [*q.v.*]) (*Corpus juris*, ed. Griffini, Milan 1919, 90), but not by later Zaydīs (cf. Muḥammad b. Sulaymān al-Kūfī, *K. al-Muntak͟hab*, Ṣanʿāʾ 1414/1993, 75) nor by the Ismāʿīlī al-Ḳāḍī al-Nuʿmān (*Daʿāʾim al-Islām*, i, 253). From 121 camels onwards, there is disagreement among the jurists: for the majority, the rate thereafter is one *bint labūn* per 40 head and one *ḥiḳḳa* per 50. The exceptional circumstance of *zakāt* on camels being payable in the form of another species is explained as arising out of a desire to avoid the hardship to both *zakāt* payers and *zakāt* recipients of fractional shares (*tas͟hḳīṣ*) of camels.

Cattle and sheep. The *niṣāb* for cattle is thirty. The rate of *zakāt* is one cow or bull in its second year (*tabīʿ*) for every thirty head and one cow in its third year (*musinna, t͟haniyya*) for every forty. The Mālikīs understand the animals required to be in their third and fourth years respectively. The S͟hāfiʿīs, Mālikīs and Ḥanbalīs impose this rate on multiples of thirty and forty, and according to them one *tabīʿ* is due for from 40 to 59 head of cattle. The Ḥanafīs impose *zakāt* at the rate of one-fortieth of the value of a *musinna* for each additional head from 40 to 59. For Ibāḍīs, the *zakāt* for cattle emulates that for camels, and they impose one sheep or goat for each five head of cattle to twenty-four and thereafter for each *niṣāb* substitute cattle of the required age for the corresponding camels (ʿAmr K. Ennāmī, *Studies in Ibāḍism*, [Libya] 1972, 108-9). The historian and jurist al-

Ṭabarī (d. 310/923) imposed *zakāt* on cattle at the rate of one head per fifty (al-Sayyāg͟hī, ii, 397), as did Ibn Ḥazm before he came to accept the view of the majority (*al-Muḥallā*, iv, 106).

The *niṣāb* for sheep and goats is forty. For forty sheep or goats, the *zakāt* due according to the S͟hāfiʿīs and Ḥanbalīs is one female sheep in its second year (*djadhaʿa*) or one female goat in its third year (*t͟haniyya*), while Mālikīs accept a goat in its second year. Abū Yūsuf and al-S͟haybānī, but not Abū Ḥanīfa, accept animals under one year of age. For 121 animals, the *zakāt* due is two such sheep or goats, for 201, three, for 400, four, and thereafter the rate is one per hundred. The Twelver S͟hīʿīs impose four sheep or goats on 301 to 399, the rate thereafter being one animal per hundred.

Horses. Abū Ḥanīfa, opposed on this point by his disciples Abū Yūsuf and al-S͟haybānī, imposed *zakāt* on horses, either females alone or a mixed herd of males and females. There is no *niṣāb*, so that *zakāt* is due even on a single horse, at the rate of either one dīnār per animal or, at the option of the owner, of five dirhams per 200 dirhams of the horse's value (2.5%). This rate is reported to have been applied to horses by the caliph ʿUmar. Although many Ḥanafī jurists preferred the view that horses were not subject to *zakāt*, Abū Ḥanīfa's opinion was approved by important authorities within his *mad͟hhab* (Ibn ʿĀbidīn, *Ḥās͟hiyat radd al-muḥtar*, Cairo 1386/1966, ii, 282). Unlike the *zakāt* on other livestock, that on horses is not collected by the state (Ibn al-Humām, ii, 183). For Twelver S͟hīʿīs, *zakāt* on female horses is recommended, at the rate of two dīnārs per pure-bred animal (*ʿatīḳ*) and one dīnār per work horse (*birdhawn*) (al-ʿAllāma al-Ḥillī, *Nihāyat al-aḥkām*, ed. al-Radjāʾī, Beirut 1406/1986, ii, 376-7).

ii. *Zakāt on crops* (*ḥart͟h, ḥubūb wa-t͟himār, nābit, k͟hāridj min al-arḍ, muʿas͟hs͟harāt*). There is considerable disagreement among the jurists as to what crops are subject to *zakāt*, ranging from the Twelver S͟hīʿīs, who impose *zakāt* only on wheat, barley, dates and raisins, to the Ḥanafīs and Zaydīs, who impose it on virtually all products of the soil. In the middle are the S͟hāfiʿīs and Mālikīs, according to whom *zakāt* is due on dates and grapes and on crops of the sort cultivated and stored by humans as a staple foodstuff (*ḳūt muddak͟har*), to the exclusion of those products like vegetables that are not stored and those that are not staples like spices and condiments; the crops thus subject to *zakāt* include wheat, barley, rice, chickpeas and lentils, and for the Mālikīs, olives, on which *zakāt* is taken as oil. The Ḥanbalīs, somewhat more broadly, assess *zakāt* on crops that are measured by volume and stored, thus including almonds and pistachios, but continuing to exclude vegetables and most fruits. In addition to the four crops on which *zakāt* is obligatory, Twelver S͟hīʿīs recommend paying *zakāt* on crops that are measured by weight, but not on vegetables or fruits. Some jurists, including the Ḥanafīs and Ḥanbalīs, impose *zakāt* on honey.

Apart from the opinion of Abū Ḥanīfa that there is no *niṣāb* for crops, the universal *niṣāb* for crops is five *awsuḳ* (sing. *wasaḳ*), a measure of volume, which, like other legally significant measures of volume, is determined by the practice of Medina, and is reportedly equivalent to three hundred *ṣāʿ* according to the *ṣāʿ* of the Prophet. Legal texts commonly give approximate equivalents to this *niṣāb* in measures of weight, e.g. 609.84 kg. These approximations are intended as rough guides, it being understood that the *niṣāb* must be exactly satisfied (*taḥdīd*) before *zakāt* is due. The *niṣāb* is applied to dates and grapes once they have been dried and to other crops once chaff and other foreign matter have been removed. The costs of preparing the harvest for measurement are borne by the *zakāt* payer. According to the S̲h̲āfiʿīs, for crops such as rice which are stored in but not eaten with their husks, the husks are deemed to constitute one-half of the harvest, and the *niṣāb* is fixed at ten *awsuḳ*. In the case of dates and grapes alone, the harvest, while still unpicked, is subject to a process on the part of the collecting authorities that estimates its yield as dry fruit (see below).

Varieties of a single species are combined for the purpose of determining whether the *niṣāb* exists; the Mālikīs go further and treat as single species wheat and barley, and so also all legumes (*ḳaṭānī*). The entire yield of a single species for a period of twelve lunar months is considered as a unit with respect to *zakāt*, without regard to different rates of ripening due to climate or other circumstances. The entire future yield becomes liable to *zakāt* once any dates or grapes ripen or other crops harden, and the owner of the crop at the time such ripening commences is liable for its *zakāt*. In the case of land leased for cultivation, Abū Ḥanīfa alone imposed *zakāt* on the owner of the land, not the lessee.

The rate of *zakāt* on crops depends on the mode of irrigation employed in their cultivation. Where the crop has been irrigated without expenditure on water or the employment of human or animal labour in conveying the water to the plants, the rate is 10% (one-tenth, *ʿus̲h̲r*). This rate applies to crops watered by natural sources such as rain and surface (*sayḥ*) and underground water (*baʿl* land), as well as canals (*ʿat̲h̲arī* land). The rate for crops that have been irrigated by water purchased for this purpose or with animal- or water-driven wheels is 5% (one-half of one-tenth, *niṣf al-ʿus̲h̲r*). Twelver S̲h̲īʿīs in principle allow for a deduction of expenses incurred in the growing and harvesting of the crop, but jurists commonly counsel that this deduction not be taken (al-K̲h̲umaynī, *Zubdat al-aḥkām*, Tehran 1404, 119-20).

iii. *Zakāt* on gold and silver (*at̲h̲mān, ʿayn, naḳd, nāḍḍ*). *Zakāt* is due on gold and silver, whether in the form of raw metal, coins or manufactured objects, but, except for the Zaydīs, on no other metals or precious stones. Twelver S̲h̲īʿīs impose *zakāt* only on gold and silver coinage, whether or not it is in actual use. The *niṣāb* for gold is twenty dīnārs (*mit̲h̲ḳāls*) (*ca.* 84.7 gr), present value *ca.* \$800 US, and for silver 200 dirhams (five *ūḳiyya*) (*ca.* 592.9 gr), present value *ca.* \$90 US. The equivalences given for these in grams by Twelver S̲h̲īʿīs are 19% lower. Like other legally significant measures of weight, these are determined by the practice of Mecca. The weight of the dirham, previously variable, was reportedly fixed under ʿUmar I or ʿAbd al-Malik b. Marwān, and subsequently ratified by consensus, at ten dirhams to each seven *mit̲h̲ḳāls*, the *mit̲h̲ḳāl* having remaining unchanged from pre-Islamic to Islamic times (cf. M. Morony, *Iraq after the Muslim conquest*, Princeton 1984, 50). The majority of jurists, but not the S̲h̲āfiʿīs, Ẓāhirīs and Twelver S̲h̲īʿīs, combine gold and silver (*ḍamm, ḥaml*) in determining whether a *niṣāb* exists and in assessing *zakāt*. The calculation proceeds according to "units" (*adj̲zāʾ*), that is, according to the legal exchange rate of ten dirhams per dīnār, except for the Zaydīs and Ibāḍīs, who combine the metals according to actual market value (*taḳwīm*). The Mālikīs alone allow some slight leeway in the calculation of the *niṣāb* in the case of underweight coins that are accepted commercially.

The rate of *zakāt* on each metal is 2.5% (one-fourth of one-tenth, *rubʿ al-ʿus̲h̲r*), which is applied pro-rata for any amount above the *niṣāb*, except by the Ḥanafīs, Twelver S̲h̲īʿīs and Ibāḍīs, who apply it only to increments of forty dirhams or four dīnārs. There is some support in the Ḥanafī school for subjecting the value of coins made of base metal (*fulūs*) to the rule for gold and silver. Others treat such coins as merchandise.

Gold and silver in the form of decorative articles for wearing (*ḥaly*) are exempted from *zakāt* except by the Ḥanafīs, Zaydīs, Ibāḍīs and Ẓāhirīs. The exemption, however, is not absolute, and the S̲h̲āfiʿīs will, for example, impose *zakāt* when the owner intends some prohibited (*muḥarram*) or disapproved (*makrūh*) use or a permitted use in an exorbitant fashion (*isrāf*) or is holding the piece as a form of wealth (*kanz*).

iv. *Zakāt* on mines (*maʿdin*) and treasures (*rikāz*). According to the Sunnī schools, except for the Ḥanafīs, *zakāt* is due on gold and silver upon extraction from a mine. The *niṣāb* is that for gold and silver as above, and *zakāt* is assessed at the same rate (2.5%). The *niṣāb* is applied to the entire yield of a mine that has been continuously worked without justified interruption. The yield becomes subject to *zakāt* once in the possession of the *zakāt* payer, but the *niṣāb* is assessed and *zakāt* paid on the metals only after the removal of dirt and other extraneous matter, the cost of which is borne by the *zakāt* payer. The Ḥanbalīs extend *zakāt* to other metals and minerals, including petroleum, extracted by mining. According to the S̲h̲āfiʿīs, gold and silver in the form of buried treasure (*rikāz*) is subject upon discovery to the same *niṣāb* as gold and silver extracted by mining, but *zakāt* is assessed at the rate of 20% (one-fifth, *k̲h̲ums*). The treasure subject to *zakāt* is that which bears the marks of pre-Islamic times. Other jurists treat this fifth from buried treasures as *fayʾ* [*q.v.*].

v. *Zakāt* on merchandise (*tid̲j̲āra, ʿurūḍ*). This, potentially the broadest category of property subject to *zakāt*, is recognised by all except ʿIbn ʿAbbās, the Ẓāhirīs and, among later jurists, the Yemeni al-S̲h̲awkānī (d. 1250/1834 [*q.v.*]). It is among the recommended forms of *zakāt* according to the Twelver S̲h̲īʿīs. Apart from its support in *ḥadīt̲h̲*, the imposition of *zakāt* on merchandise rested on the obvious ground of public interest (*maṣlaḥa ʿāmma*) (Ibn al-ʿArabī, *K. al-Ḳabas*, ii, 470), which made it unthinkable to exempt so large a source of wealth. *Zakāt* is due on all objects, including land and slaves, acquired for a consideration (*muʿāwaḍa*) for the purpose of sale for a profit. The *zakāt* is applied not to such objects directly but to their monetary value (*ḳīma*) as determined by a sale or by a valuation for *zakāt* purposes. The consideration need not be monetary, so that property acquired by a wife as her dower (*mahr*), if she intends it for trade, is subject to *zakāt*. The Ḥanbalīs require an affirmative act of acquisition but do not require that it be for a consideration. The Zaydī *imām* al-Hādī went further and imposed *zakāt* also on the value of objects acquired for their rental income (*mustag̲h̲allāt*) (Ibn Miftāḥ, *al-Muntazaʿ al-muk̲h̲tār*, Cairo 1332, repr. Ṣanʿāʾ, i, 450-1).

The *niṣāb* for merchandise is the same as that for gold and silver, and *zakāt* is assessed at the same rate (2.5%). For the purpose of determining the existence of a *niṣāb*, the value of the merchandise is combined with the value of the gold and silver of the *zakāt* payer. The S̲h̲āfiʿīs, who assess gold and silver separately, apply one or the other of these precious metals as the standard of valuation: the appropriate metal to be used is that with which the object was acquired, if gold or silver was in fact the consideration. Where the consideration was some other object or was not monetary in nature, the appropriate metal is that which prevails as the measure of exchange in the community (*ghālib naḳd al-balad*) at the time of acquisition.

The Mālikīs alone distinguish between active traders (*mudīr*) and investors (*muḥtakir*, *muddakhir*), who look to long-term gain. The former need assess the value of their stock, combined with their holdings of gold and silver, once a year. The latter owe no *zakāt* until they sell their investments and then never for more than one holding period. An active trader can assume the status of an investor by a change of intention, but the change from investor to trader requires a change in intention coupled with a transaction.

Double zakāt: In light of a tradition (*lā thinā fi 'l-ṣadaḳa*) understood to prohibit a double application of *zakāt* to the same property for the same period, the jurists had to determine which category of *zakāt* was to be given priority when more than one applied, as in the case of grazing animals held for sale. In such cases, the Shāfiʿīs and Mālikīs give preference to the imposition of *zakāt* under the heading of livestock, the Ḥanafīs and Ḥanbalīs under that of merchandise. The Ḥanafīs extend the principle of avoiding a double incidence of *zakāt* to *zakāt al-fiṭr* and do not require that it be paid on behalf of slaves held for trade.

vi. Holding period (*ḥawl*). Except for the *zakāt* due on crops, mined gold and silver, and buried treasure, *zakāt* is imposed only if the property has been held for a period of one lunar year. There is almost universal agreement on the requirement of a holding period; the Companions Ibn Masʿūd and Ibn ʿAbbās are among the few reported to have held otherwise. Twelver Shīʿīs, following a tradition from Djaʿfar al-Ṣādiḳ, consider the holding period to end with the sighting of the new moon of the twelfth month, although the next holding period begins only at the end of the twelfth month (al-Ḥillī, *Nihāyat al-aḥkām*, ii, 312).

In principle the majority of jurists require that a *niṣāb* of property subject to *zakāt* already be owned in order for the calculation of a *ḥawl* to commence and require that the *niṣāb* be maintained throughout the *ḥawl*, as opposed to the Ḥanafīs who allow a drop below the *niṣāb* during the *ḥawl*. There are, however, important exceptions made for growth, in the form of offspring or profits, from an original stock. The Mālikīs, for example, treat the offspring of livestock as sharing the *ḥawl* of their mothers, even when the latter begin the *ḥawl* below the *niṣāb*. Thus when a herd of four camels has been held for eleven months, the birth of a camel in the last month, or even on the last day, before the end of the *ḥawl* will suffice to reach the *niṣāb* of five camels and subject the herd to the *zakāt* of one sheep or goat. The Shāfiʿīs and Mālikīs make a similar exception for trade goods, the value of which must meet the *niṣāb* only at the end of the *ḥawl*, provided that the increase is derived solely from a rise in value of the original stock of merchandise or from profit earned in trading with it. Because they do not combine gold and silver, the Shāfiʿīs further require that in order for this increase to share the *ḥawl* of the original stock it must be "unrealised", that is, not reduced to the precious metal designated for the valuation of the original stock. Again in principle, the majority of jurists, as opposed to the Ḥanafīs, do not attribute the *ḥawl* of the original *niṣāb* to additions acquired other than by growth (*fāʾida*, *māl mustafād*). Here, too, however, the Mālikīs make an exception for livestock and impute the *ḥawl* of an original *niṣāb* to animals of the same species acquired from outside the herd. Thus the owner of five camels owes two sheep for those five and for an additional five inherited on the last day of the original holding period. This rule has been explained as a concession to the convenience of the *zakāt* collector (al-Dardīr, *al-Sharḥ al-ṣaghīr*, ed. Waṣfī, Cairo 1972, i, 593).

vii. Persons subject to *zakāt*. *Zakāt* applies almost exclusively to the property of private individuals. The property of the government, including the assets of the public treasury (*bayt māl* [*q.v.*]) is not subject to *zakāt* except according to some Zaydīs (Ibn Miftāḥ, i, 450, cf. C. Imber, *Ebu's-suʿud: the Islamic legal tradition*, Stanford 1997, 82-3; J.R.I. Cole, *Roots of North Indian Shīʿism in Iran and Iraq*, Berkeley 1988, 201). According to the Shāfiʿīs and Ḥanbalīs, property constituted as the corpus of a *waḳf* [*q.v.*] is not subject to *zakāt*, nor is the income (*ghalla*), when the beneficiaries are a general class such as the poor or the incumbents of an office such as *imām* of a mosque. When the beneficiaries of the *waḳf* are specified individuals, however, the income of the *waḳf* property is subject to *zakāt*. Thus *zakāt* is due on fruits or crops when the *niṣāb* is satisfied by the entire yield, without regard to the individual shares of the beneficiaries, according to the Shāfiʿīs (see below on co-ownership), while the Ḥanbalīs require that the share of each beneficiary amount to a *niṣāb* (cf. al-Mardāwī, *al-Inṣāf*, ed. al-Fiḳī, Cairo 1400/1980, iii, 14-15). The Mālikīs collect *zakāt* from the founder of the trust, whether the beneficiaries are specified individuals or a class. The Ḥanafīs require no *zakāt* from *awḳāf* except for the *zakāt* on crops, which they regard as an impost on the land itself.

According to the majority of jurists, the property of minors and those with an incapacity, like the mentally ill, is subject to *zakāt*, which is payable by their guardians. The Ḥanafīs do not impose *zakāt* on the property of the incapacitated with the exception of the *zakāt* for fruit and crops (cf. Schacht, *Origins*, 216-17) and *zakāt al-fiṭr*. The Twelver Shīʿīs regard the payment of *zakāt* on the property of minors, except livestock, as recommended. Except according to the Ẓāhirīs, slaves do not pay *zakāt* on property in their control. All Sunnī schools but the Mālikīs impose *zakāt* for such property on the slave-owner.

viii. Ownership. According to the Shāfiʿīs, where the property to which *zakāt* applies is subject to joint undivided co-ownership (*khulṭat shuyūʿ*, *ishtirāk*, *aʿyān*), the applicable *niṣāb* is assessed against the entire property so owned without regard to the size of the individual shares. Thus one sheep or goat is due on forty sheep or goats jointly owned by two individuals. Where the shares of the joint owners are unequal, the partner with the smaller share will have recourse against his co-owner for the amount of *zakāt* paid that exceeds his pro-rata liability, and each co-owner is authorised by law to pay *zakāt* on the entire property.

Where the property is individually owned but jointly managed (*khulṭat al-djiwār*, *al-awṣāf*), *zakāt* is assessed against the entire property so managed without regard to the size of the individual holdings. In the case of livestock, the test for determining whether joint management exists is the existence of common places for the watering of the animals, assembly prior to grazing (*masraḥ*), grazing (*marʿā*), and for keeping during the night, as well as the use of a common male for impregnation (*faḥl*) and common herdsmen. For fruit and crops, joint management will be found where common watchmen are used for guarding and where the places for drying the fruit or winnowing the grain are common. Joint management of merchandise depends on a common shop (*dukkān*), and common guards and places of safekeeping as well as common appurtenances such as scales. Thus two individuals, each owning twenty sheep or goats, will be liable for the *zakāt* due on forty sheep or goats when they jointly manage their animals. The effect of joint management in this case is to create a liability to *zakāt* that would not otherwise exist, since neither individual's holding amounts to a *niṣāb*. In other cases involving livestock, joint management may have the effect of increasing an existing liability to *zakāt* or of diminishing it. Where some of the herd of a *zakāt* payer is co-owned or jointly managed while the rest is held independently, the favoured solution is to extend the effect of co-ownership or joint management to all his property (*k͟hulṭat milk*), rather than limit it to that portion actually co-owned or jointly managed (*k͟hulṭat ʿayn*) (al-Nawawī, *Rawḍat al-ṭālibīn*, ii, 180).

The Mālikīs and Ḥanbalīs recognise co-ownership and joint management as legally significant only in the case of livestock, with the Mālikīs requiring that the share of each owner amount to a *niṣāb*. Like the S͟hāfiʿīs, they require that the co-owners and joint managers all be subject to the law of *zakāt*, i.e. be Muslims. The Ḥanafīs, Twelver S͟hīʿīs and Ẓāhirīs give no recognition to co-ownership or joint management and look only to the property of each owner.

Possession. Although liability for *zakāt* is predicated on ownership, the law in some cases takes into account the separation of ownership from possession. Where the owner has no access to his property (*māl ḍimār*), as when it has been misappropriated or lost, the Ḥanafīs assess no *zakāt* on such property should it eventually be recovered years later, and the Mālikīs require the payment of *zakāt* for no more than one year. The S͟hāfiʿīs require that *zakāt* be paid for the actual time that possession was lost.

ix. Debts. Debts figure in the calculation of *zakāt* in two ways. To the extent that the *zakāt* payer is a creditor, there is the question of the payment of *zakāt* for the debts he is owed but has not collected. To the extent that the *zakāt* payer is a debtor, there is the question of what effect his debts are to be given in assessing the *zakāt* he owes.

The S͟hāfiʿīs include in the property subject to *zakāt* collectible currently due debts (*dayn ḥall ʿalā malī*), including a wife's claim for unpaid dower (*ṣadāḳ*), but not debts payable in livestock, inasmuch as the requisite grazing cannot occur. The Mālikīs apply *zakāt* to collectible currently due commercial debts of active traders. Debts uncollectible either because a case cannot be made against the debtor or the debtor is insolvent are treated according to the rules for misappropriated property. The Ḥanafīs and Ḥanbalīs require no payment of *zakāt* that has accrued on debts until they are collected.

The Ḥanafīs deduct debts owed by the *zakāt* payer from the value of the property on which *zakāt* is payable, provided that such debts are subject to collection, in which category they include debts for unpaid *zakāt*. The value of such debts is applied in the first instance against the gold and silver and trade goods owned by the *zakāt* payer, any remaining debts being deductible from the value of livestock and crops. The Mālikīs and Ḥanbalīs allow the deduction of debts from *zakāt* on gold and silver and trade goods only. The S͟hāfiʿīs make no allowance for the deduction of debts.

x. Estimation. In the case of dates and grapes, it is recommended that the ruler dispatch officials to estimate (*k͟harṣ, tak͟hrīṣ*) the eventual yield of the crop as dried fruit as a step in determining the *zakāt* due and ensuring that it be paid. According to the S͟hāfiʿīs, the estimator, who must be a reliable (*ʿadl*), free, male Muslim, can act singly and is authorised upon completing his estimation to offer the owner the option of eating or otherwise transacting in the raw fruit on the condition that the owner become personally liable (*taḍmīn*) for the *zakāt* due on the estimated yield. If the owner chooses not to accept this offer, he is not permitted to make any use of the crop until the *zakāt* has been paid. The practice of estimation is traced back to the Prophet, who employed a number of such estimators (al-Māwardī, *al-Ḥāwī*, ed. Matrad͟jī, Beirut 1414/1994, iv, 205). In the absence of an official estimator, the owner can avail himself of the advantages of the practice by resorting to two reliable men capable of performing the estimation (al-Ramlī, *Nihāyat al-muḥtād͟j*, Cairo 1386/1967, iii, 82). Some opposed the practice of estimation as unduly speculative, and al-S͟haʿbī (d. 103/721 [*q.v.*]) is reported to have denounced it as an "unwarranted innovation" (*bidʿa* [*q.v.*]). The Ḥanafīs do not recognise the practice at all. Only the Ḥanbalīs require that the estimator exempt one-third or one-fourth of the crop for the personal use of the owner.

xi. Recipients. Those entitled (*mustaḥiḳḳūn, maṣārif, ahl al-suhmān, ahl al-zakāt*) to receive *zakāt* fall into eight classes, enumerated in Ḳurʾān IX, 60, an enumeration understood to be exhaustive and exclusive. There is a dispute as to which of the first two classes, (1) the poor (*fuḳarāʾ*) and (2) the indigent (*masākīn*), is more disadvantaged, but the dispute is extraneous to the law of *zakāt*, and some even regarded these as a single class. In both *ḥadīt͟h* and legal literature the needy, as the most numerous and best-known recipients of *zakāt*, stand in for the other classes. The collecting agents (*ʿāmilūn alayhā*) constitute class (3). These include the official sent by the government (*sāʿī, muzakkī, muṣaddiḳ, ḳābiḍ, wālī al-ṣadaḳa*) and his assistants. From the rule that *zakāt* on livestock was to be collected where the animals were watered, the agent for their collection was sometimes termed *wālī al-māʾ*. The most controversial of the classes are (4) "those whose hearts are won over" (*al-muʾallafa ḳulūbuhum* [*q.v.*]). These, according to the S͟hāfiʿīs, include converts to Islam whose enthusiasm is in doubt and prominent converts who, it is hoped, will be able to win over others, as well as converts enlisted to deal with hostile non-Muslims or Muslims who refuse to pay *zakāt*. Some jurists, including the Ḥanafīs and Mālikīs, regarded this class as having lapsed. Class (5) are the "slaves" (*riḳāb*), an expression commonly interpreted to refer to slaves who have contracted to purchase their freedom (*mukātabūn*) but are unable to make their scheduled payments. The Mālikīs, however, prefer that *zakāt* designated for this class be used to purchase the freedom of full slaves (*ḳinn*). The patronage (*walāʾ*) of such freedmen, according to the Mālikīs, inheres in the Muslim community as a whole, and not in the *zakāt* payer, a rule that removes any taint of self-interest from the payment. Class (6) are the debtors (*g͟hārimūn*) who lack the means to satisfy their debts. The S͟hāfiʿīs give preference in this class to those who have incurred indebtedness to avert possible violence among Muslims; these need not lack the means to pay their debt to qualify for *zakāt*. Those "in the path of God" (*fī sabīl Allāh*) constitute class (7). The most common interpretation is that these are the volunteers engaged in *djihād* [*q.v.*]. They are to be given *zakāt* to meet their living expenses and the expenses of their military service (animals, weapons). The Twelvers came to adopt a broader interpretation that encompasses a range of public services, including the repair of mosques and bridges (H.M. Tabātabā'ī, *Kharāj in Islamic law*, London 1983, 25-6). The Ḥanafīs, among others, rejected the use of *zakāt* for such purposes on the ground that the valid payment of *zakāt* requires a transfer of ownership from one person to another (*tamlīk*). Finally, class (8) comprises the travellers (*ibn al-sabīl*) who in the course of their journey, or according to the Shāfiʿīs, even upon setting out, find themselves without immediately available assets to meet their expenses.

Given the nature of *zakāt* as a religious obligation, the law imposes a minimal burden of proof as to entitlement. Thus those who present themselves as poor will not need to establish their status by oath (cf. ʿAbd al-Razzāḳ al-Ṣanʿānī, *al-Muṣannaf*, ed. al-Aʿẓamī, Beirut 1983, iv, 149-50) or by witnesses, unless some doubt arises. The prevention of unqualified claimants from taking *zakāt* is within the authority of the *muḥtasib*.

The Shāfiʿīs are the most demanding with respect to the allocation of *zakāt* to these classes. When distribution of *zakāt* is in the hands of the ruler, all existing classes are to be allotted equal shares, and to the extent that the collected *zakāt* permits, all those entitled under each class are to be given what they require. When the *zakāt* is distributed by the *zakāt* payer he, too, to the extent possible, is obligated to give *zakāt* to each qualifying recipient in his vicinity from the existing classes, but not necessarily in equal shares. At the very least, the private *zakāt* payer must give *zakāt* to three individuals from each class to discharge his obligation. By contrast, the Ḥanafīs permit distribution to a single individual from any class. Some later Shāfiʿī jurists accepted the validity of following (*taklīd* [*q.v.*]) the more lenient Ḥanafī rule.

Disqualifications. Disqualified from receipt of *zakāt* under classes (1) and (2), and according to the Ḥanafīs, all other extant classes except (3) and (8), are the wealthy (*ghanī*). There is disagreement on the test to be applied for determining wealth. The Shāfiʿīs, among others, apply a means test, i.e. one is wealthy if he can meet the expenses of the lifestyle, including food, clothing and shelter, to which he and his dependents are accustomed from his lawful property, distributed over an average lifetime (said to be sixty-two years), or from his lawful earnings. Such a person is said to possess a "sufficiency" (*kifāya*). Since the test is relative, ownership of a dwelling place, fine clothing or slaves does not in itself mean that a sufficiency exists. Opportunity to earn a sufficiency is significant only if the occupation is appropriate to one's station and will not interfere with the pursuit of religious knowledge if one has an aptitude for learning. The Ḥanbalīs, Mālikīs and Twelver Shīʿīs also apply a means test but look to sufficiency for one year; the Mālikīs, however, do not take into consideration the possibility of gainful employment, even when appropriate work is available. The Ḥanafīs apply a property test to determine wealth. For them wealth is ownership of the value of a *niṣāb* of property, whether or not subject to *zakāt*, above one's basic needs, without regard to one's possible earnings. The Shāfiʿī standard allows for the same individual to be both a payer and a recipient of *zakāt*, a possibility excluded by the Ḥanafīs (although for them not every "wealthy" person will owe *zakāt*). The difference in the tests used to determine wealth is indicative of fundamentally different notions of the function of *zakāt* as an instrument to transfer wealth. Consistently with their understanding of *zakāt*, the Shāfiʿīs provide that those of the poor with trades are to be given enough to set them up in their trade for life. Those without trades are to be given enough to purchase land from the income of which they can live without future dependence on *zakāt*. By contrast, the Ḥanafīs recommend that a poor person receive enough *zakāt* to relieve him of the need to beg for one day, while they disapprove of giving to a poor person property of the value of a *niṣāb*.

A further disqualification from receipt of *zakāt* is unbelief (*kufr*), although the early jurists al-Zuhrī (d. 124/742) and Ibn Shubruma (d. 144/776) [*q.vv.*] are reported to have permitted giving *zakāt* to poor *dhimmīs* (cf. al-Ṭabarī, *Djāmiʿ al-bayān*, Cairo 1388/1968, ix, 959). Many, but not the Shāfiʿīs, recognise an exception to this disqualification for class (4) and for menial tasks under class (3). Slavery is a disqualification except for entitlement under class (5), and the payer's own slave is always disqualified from receiving his *zakāt*. The majority of jurists hold that one cannot validly pay *zakāt* to one's direct ascendants or descendants, and husbands cannot pay *zakāt* to their wives, a rule which some extend to the payment of *zakāt* by wives to their husbands. A further disqualification, according to the majority of jurists, is descent from or a client relationship with the Family of the Prophet, for these are not to be demeaned by receiving *zakāt*, which has become soiled in the process of cleansing the property of its payers (*awsākh al-nās*). They are, however, permitted to receive *zakāt* from one another. There is disagreement whether the disqualification of the Prophet's relatives remains in effect when they fail to receive their allotted portion of revenue (*khums al-khums*), but there is a discernible tendency among later Ḥanafī, Mālikī and Twelver Shīʿī jurists to permit them to receive *zakāt*, although strictly within their needs. The question has remained a topic of lively debate among the Yemeni Zaydīs (ʿAlī b. Muḥammad al-ʿAdjrī, *K. al-Makāṣid al-ṣāliḥa*, Ṣanʿāʾ 1411/1991, 220-42, cf. al-Ḥasan b. Aḥmad al-Djalāl, *Ḍawʾ al-nahār*, Ṣanʿāʾ 1405/1985, ii, 333-40). Women, according to the Shāfiʿīs, are disqualified from receiving *zakāt* under classes (3) and (7). Strict piety is not a requirement for eligibility to receive *zakāt*, although it may be a ground for preference among competing claimants. Sectarian differences are potentially more significant. Twelver Shīʿīs go so far as to require that *zakāt* be paid only to Twelvers, and a Muslim who adopts Twelver Shīʿism must pay *zakāt* a second time for past years unless the recipients were Twelver Shīʿīs.

xii. Collection and payment. It is an obligation on Muslim rulers, following the example of the Prophet and the early caliphs, to send out officials to collect *zakāt* to assist property owners in fulfilling their obligation of *zakāt*. The ruler and his *zakāt* collectors are understood to represent the recipients of *zakāt*, whose best interests they are duty bound to safeguard. While this much is agreed upon, there is considerable disagreement among the jurists as to the scope for individual distribution when the state is fulfilling its obligation of collecting *zakāt*, for the distinction between *ẓāhir* and *bāṭin* property does not in itself preclude the payment of all *zakāt* to the state (al-Māwardī, *al-Aḥkām al-sulṭāniyya*, 113). The Zaydīs, for example, insist that all *zakāt*, whether the property is *ẓāhir* or *bāṭin*, must be paid to the official collectors representing the legitimate government of the Zaydī *imām*. Any other form of payment will not discharge the obligation of giving *zakāt*. While the majority of Sunnīs, following Ibn ʿUmar, recognise payment of *zakāt* to even a corrupt (*dj̲āʾir*) ruler as discharging the obligation of *zakāt*, the Ḥanbalīs prefer that the payer, where possible, personally undertake its distribution, even on *ẓāhir* property (Ibn Ḳudāma, *al-S̲h̲arḥ al-kabīr*, ed. Medina, ii, 673-5). In this they represent an attenuated version of a legal tradition that was unwilling to put *zakāt* into the hands of the rulers, who could be expected to ignore the rules for its distribution. Thus Sufyān al-T̲h̲awrī (d. 161/778 [*q.v.*]) reportedly urged that one should even go so far as to swear falsely to the collectors to avoid paying them *zakāt* (*ibid.*, ii, 673). Among the Sunnī schools, the Mālikīs go furthest in their deference to the official collectors: they make the coming of the collector (*madj̲īʾ al-sāʿī*) a condition for the obligation of *zakāt* on livestock in addition to the passing of the *ḥawl*, so that payment before his coming is invalid. The S̲h̲āfiʿīs stand in the middle, preferring that *zakāt* on *ẓāhir* property be paid to the ruler, unless he is corrupt.

For the S̲h̲āfiʿīs and Mālikīs, liability (*ḍamān*) for *zakāt* requires, in addition to the passing of the *ḥawl*, actual possibility of payment (*tamakkun al-adāʾ*), which e.g. includes access to the property from which *zakāt* will be paid and the availability of qualified recipients. For the Ḥanbalīs, loss of all or part of the property after the *ḥawl* does not affect the *zakāt* due, while according to the Ḥanafīs, a loss, whether before or after possibility of payment, proportionately reduces it.

The majority of jurists require that *zakāt*, except for trade goods, be paid in kind, while the Ḥanafīs and Twelver S̲h̲īʿīs permit the payment of the value (*ḳīma*) of the *zakāt* in all cases. The Zaydīs permit payment of value when payment in kind is not possible (Ibn Miftāḥ, 1, 500; but see al-ʿAdj̲rī, *al-Maḳāṣid al-ṣāliḥa*, 218-9). The Mālikīs go only so far as to allow *zakāt* due in gold to be paid in its market value in silver and vice-versa. The requirement of payment in kind, even when strongly upheld, did not obviate constant recourse to valuation in the assessment of *zakāt*. The inconvenience of the rule against payment in cash led later S̲h̲āfiʿīs and Mālikīs to favour the Ḥanafī rule, which very likely reflected common practice.

There is disagreement as to whether it is better to pay *zakāt* privately or in the open (cf. Ḳurʾān II, 271), the majority of jurists favouring the latter view. The Mālikīs, however, prefer that one pay *zakāt* through an agent to preserve the piety of the act from self-aggrandisement. The religious quality of the act of giving is enhanced by a recommended prayer to be uttered by the payer and by a blessing uttered by the *imām* or collector (Ibn Ḳudāma, *al-S̲h̲arḥ al-kabīr*, ii, 678-9), the latter harking back to Ḳurʾān IX, 103 (cf. Ibn Saʿd, vii/1, 88, blessing by ʿUmar). Favoured months for the giving of *zakāt* are Muḥarram, Ramaḍān, D̲h̲u ʾl-Ḥidj̲dja (al-G̲h̲azālī, *Iḥyāʾ ʿulūm al-dīn*, iv, 109-11), and Radj̲ab. Ibāḍī jurists go so far as to suggest a collusive transfer and re-transfer of one's property to permit timing one's giving in a favoured month (al-D̲j̲annāwunī, *K. al-Waḍʿ*, ed. Aṭṭafayyis̲h̲, ed. ʿUmān, 175-6).

According to the S̲h̲āfiʿīs, the ruler, but not a private *zakāt* payer, is free to remove (*naḳl*) *zakāt* from the location of the property from which it has been collected. The *zakāt* payer is authorised to do so only in the event that the *zakāt* exceeds the needs of the local classes of recipients, in which case he may remove the *zakāt* for distribution in the nearest locality with qualified recipients. *Zakāt* for which no qualified recipients are found is retained for eventual future distribution. The Mālikīs prohibit removal and invalidate the payment of *zakāt*, unless it is removed to recipients as needy as those of the original location; the Ḥanbalīs prohibit removal but do not invalidate the *zakāt* so removed. The Ḥanafīs disapprove of removing *zakāt* unless it is for the purpose of distributing it to needy relatives or those in greater need than the local qualified recipients.

Finally, the death of the owner prior to the payment of the *zakāt* due does not terminate the obligation, according to the S̲h̲āfiʿīs and Ḥanbalīs. According to the Ḥanafīs, it always does except for *zakāt* on crops, and according to the Mālikīs, if the unpaid *zakāt* was one or more years overdue. In those cases where the obligation of *zakāt* lapses on account of death, it may still be collectible, if only in part, if the decedent has so provided by will.

Pre-payment. Provided that a *niṣāb* exists, payment of *zakāt* may be made before the end of the *ḥawl*. The Ḥanafīs permit such pre-payment (*taʿdj̲īl*) for any number of years ahead, the Ḥanbalīs for up to two years, and the S̲h̲āfiʿīs for one. The Mālikīs permit pre-payment one month in advance, except for crops.

xiii. Intention (*niyya* [*q.v.*]). The validity of the payment of *zakāt* as an act of worship (*ʿibāda*) depends on the requisite intention, which must make reference to the payment of *zakāt* or obligatory *ṣadaḳa*, but need not specify the property on which *zakāt* is being paid. The necessity of such an intention was agreed upon by all except the Syrian jurist al-Awzāʿī (d. 157/774 [*q.v.*]). There was, however, no agreement as to the role, if any, of an intention when the *zakāt* was collected by force from a recalcitrant property owner. There is evidence among later jurists of an attenuation of the requirement of an intention when one family member paid *zakāt* on behalf of another (ʿUlays̲h̲, *Fatḥ al-ʿalī al-mālik*, ed. Beirut, i, 163). There is no requirement that the payer must state to the recipient that the payment represents the giving of *zakāt*, and some jurists preferred that this not be done in order to spare the recipient embarrassment. When the *zakāt* is pre-paid, however, the failure to inform the recipient of the nature of the gift can prejudice the possibility of its recovery in the event of a change of circumstances rendering it invalid as *zakāt*.

xiv. *Zakāt* avoidance and non-payment. It is relatively simple to avoid the incidence of *zakāt*. The requirement of a holding period, especially, provided property owners with an easy means to do so. A collusive interfamilial transfer, for example, would terminate the *ḥawl*. This and other devices (*ḥiyal* [*q.v.*]) were a matter of controversy. The Mālikīs and Ḥanbalīs treat them as void, the property remaining subject to *zakāt*; the S̲h̲āfiʿīs and Ḥanafīs disapprove of such transactions but regard them as valid and assess no *zakāt*. Such transfers are, in fact, reported of some wealthy Ḥanafī scholars, but their validity did not necessarily mean that they were not subject to criticism (M.L.R. Choudhury, *The Din-i-ilahi or religion of Akbar*, Calcutta 1952, 46). Further devices were employed to recover *zakāt* paid, and disqualified recipients similarly resorted to stratagems to circumvent the law (Ibn Miftāḥ, *al-Muntazaʿ al-muk̲h̲tār*, i, 539-42).

The great majority of jurists refused to follow a tradition authorising the imposition of a fine for non-payment of *zakāt* (Abū Dāwūd, i, 462; al-K̲h̲aṭṭābī, *Maʿālim al-sunan*, ii, 33-4). Failure to pay *zakāt*, however, may subject the property owner to corrective discretionary punishment (*taʿzīr*) either on the part of the collector or the *muḥtasib*, in addition to seizure of the *zakāt* on *ẓāhir* property. It is generally held that delay in paying *zakāt* when due results in loss of testimonial capacity.

6. *Zakāt al-fiṭr*.

Zakāt (ṣadaḳat) al-fiṭr (also *zakāt al-fiṭra* (a later term), *zakāt Ramaḍān, zakāt al-ṣawm*) is a payment due on behalf of all Muslims, male and female, minor or adult, slave or free, in connection with the termination of the fast (*fiṭr*) of Ramaḍān. For the Ḥanafīs and Twelver Shīʿīs, it is also due on behalf of non-Muslim dependents of Muslims. As a *zakāt* for persons, not property, it is also termed *zakāt al-badan* and *zakāt al-raʾs*. The amount paid (*fiṭra*) purifies the one who gives it from his unseemly conduct and other shortcomings during the fast of Ramaḍān and at the same time relieves the poor from having to beg for food on the *ʿīd al-fiṭr* [*q.v.*] (Abū Dāwūd, i, 473). The practice of giving *zakāt al-fiṭr* is based on *ḥadīth*, although Ḳurʾānic verses are sometimes cited in support (e.g. LXXXVII, 14; cf. Ibn Abī Zayd al-Ḳayrawānī, *al-Nawādir wa ʾl-ziyādāt*, ed. al-Ḥulw, Beirut 1999, ii, 301). The opinion that it was abrogated by the *zakāt* for property was almost universally rejected, and *zakāt al-fiṭr* is, according to the great majority of Muslim jurists, an obligation, but its denial does not amount to unbelief. The Ḥanafīs label it compulsory (*wāḏjib*), in accordance with their terminology for obligations that are not entirely beyond doubt. There is disagreement as to its classification as *ẓāhir* or *bāṭin*. According to al-Māwardī, the Shāfiʿīs of his day considered it to be *ẓāhir*, but, as he notes, there was a long-standing practice of distributing it personally (*Ḥāwī*, iv, 432), and it is thus commonly classified as *bāṭin*, but not by the Zaydīs (al-ʿAnsī, *al-Tāḏj al-muḏhhab*, Ṣanʿāʾ 1380/1961, i, 222). One need not have fasted during Ramaḍān or even be subject to the fast for *zakāt al-fiṭr* to be due (cf. al-Kāsānī, *Badāʾiʿ al-ṣanāʾiʿ*, ed. Cairo, repr. Beirut 1406/1986, ii, 70).

According to the Shāfiʿīs, those obligated to make the *zakāt al-fiṭr* payment are, with some exceptions, Muslims or non-Muslims, who are under a legal obligation to provide support (*nafaḳa*) for those persons on whose behalf it is due, and who also have the means to pay it (*yasār*). The means to pay *zakāt al-fiṭr* is defined as sufficient wealth to defray the cost of the payment beyond the needs of oneself and one's dependents (*maʾmūn*) for the day of the festival, such needs including food, clothing, shelter and the household services of slaves. The Ḥanafīs and Twelver Shīʿīs measure ability to pay *zakāt al-fiṭr* by wealth as for *zakāt* on property (see above).

It is agreed that *zakāt al-fiṭr* is payable in the form of wheat, barley, dates and raisins, to which list may be added other basic foodstuffs. The Shāfiʿīs, for example, add several milk products including dried curd (*aḳiṭ*), yogurt (*laban*) and cheese (*ḏjubn*). The amount due is one *ṣāʿ* (*ca.* 2.03 litres) [*q.v.*], except that according to the Ḥanafīs, when payment is made with wheat, the amount due is one-half *ṣāʿ*, a rule traced back to both ʿUmar and Muʿāwiya. The Ḥanafīs also differ as to the size of a *ṣāʿ*, which they take to be the equivalent of eight Baghdādī *raṭl*s, not five and one-third *raṭl*s as the other schools have it. The Ḥanafīs and Twelver Shīʿīs admit payment of the value of the *zakāt al-fiṭr* due, and payment in cash is now in any case widespread (*ca.* $7 per person in the U.S.).

Although preferable that it be paid on the day of the feast prior to the festival prayer (in the absence of a valid excuse, it must be paid before sunset of the day of the feast), the Shāfiʿīs admit payment of *zakāt al-fiṭr* from the beginning of Ramaḍān, the

Ḥanbalīs and Mālikīs two days prior to the festival, and the Ḥanafīs prior to Ramaḍān.

7. *Zakāt* in Ṣūfism.

Classical Ṣūfī sources portray the Ṣūfī as standing outside the system of *zakāt*. Owning no property, the true Ṣūfī pays no *zakāt*, and despite his poverty, the Ṣūfī's spiritual wealth disqualifies him as a recipient. The Ṣūfī writers, however, find ample scope for the giving of *zakāt* in a wider sense that encompasses acknowledgment of all the benefits bestowed by God. Abū Naṣr al-Sarrāḏj (d. 378/988 [*q.v.*]) records an opposing position among Ṣūfīs in favour of accepting *zakāt*, refusal to do so being regarded as prideful, and popular works like the *Ḳūt al-ḳulūb* of Abū Ṭālib al-Makkī (d. 386/996) and the *Iḥyāʾ ʿulūm al-dīn* of al-Ghazālī (d. 505/1111) [*q.vv.*] urged that preference in paying *zakāt* be given to the poor among the Ṣūfīs. The popularity of Ṣūfīs as favoured recipients of *zakāt* was noted by the Syrian Shāfiʿī jurist Taḳī al-Dīn al-Ḥiṣnī (d. 829/1426), himself a Ṣūfī, who warned against giving *zakāt* to heterodox or superficially pious groups whose Ṣūfī affiliation he called into question (*Kifāyat al-akhyār*, Beirut n.d., 121-2).

8. *Zakāt* in the modern period.

The period since approximately the Second World War has witnessed a re-examination of *zakāt* unprecedented since the formative period of Islamic law. During this time there has also been renewed interest in the implementation of the law of *zakāt*, both in the form of increased individual compliance and governmentally sponsored or mandated efforts at collection. Academic discussion of *zakāt* has taken place within the two camps of jurists and economists. Although Muslim jurists affiliated with the schools of law continue to develop the law of *zakāt*, more influential have been the writings of scholars with an independent point of view who have undertaken critically to survey the law of the classical period with a view to developing a law of *zakāt* appropriate for modern conditions. Efforts toward a revival of the institution of *zakāt* have led to the convening of frequent conferences, the publication of numerous manuals and pamphlets instructing Muslims how to fulfill their obligation of *zakāt*, and the formation of various private organisations that aim at assisting in this compliance. There have also been notable instances of governmental involvement in the collection and distribution of *zakāt*, and legislation has been enacted that mandates the payment of at least some forms of *zakāt*.

Even before this period, Muslim reformers had begun broadening the traditional purposes to which *zakāt* had been put. In his interpretation of Ḳurʾān IX, 60, Rashīd Riḍā [*q.v.*] had urged that the class of "slaves" might now include not only individuals but societies "enslaved" by colonialism and that the *zakāt* for the "path of God" should go, not to a *ḏjihād* waged with arms, but to one waged with the weapons of argument and persuasion in the interest of a restoration of Islam. Some interest in directing *zakāt* to wider social purposes than recognised by the traditional law was not new (cf. Ibn ʿĀbidīn, *Ḥāshiyat radd al-muḥtār*, ii, 345-6, *ḥīla* to use *zakāt* for building a mosque); new was the willingness of the part of the reformers to resort to direct reinterpretation of the Ḳurʾān to attain their goals. One can already see in the reformers the shift from regarding *zakāt* primarily as an act of piety (an atttitude that, of course, still persists in some circles) to the emphasis on *zakāt* as the foundation of the Islamic social and economic system that dominates its modern revival.

Essential to the implementation of this vision of

zakāt is the insistence that Muslim governments must once again assume the duty of collecting *zakāt* and not leave its payment and distribution to the conscience of individuals. There is widespread agreement among the modernists that the classical distinction between *ẓāhir* and *bāṭin*, according to which the government had authority to collect only the former, is no longer tenable, either because the distinction itself was not necessarily intended to be eternally binding or because under modern conditions of saving and investing very little property is truly *bāṭin*. They have also called for an expansion of the property base (*wiʿāʾ*) on which *zakāt* is to be assessed. The modernists have no inclination, as did some jurists of the past, to blur the distinction between *zakāt* and secular taxes (cf. Ibn Ha̲d̲jar al-Haytamī, *Fatāwā al-kubrā al-fiḳhiyya*, ed. Cairo, ii, 48; Ibn ʿĀbidīn, *op. cit.*, ii, 288-90), for *zakāt* is now seen as an entirely viable alternative to the latter.

It is now generally accepted that the generic *niṣāb* applicable to new cases is that for gold, which unlike silver has historically maintained its value. The rules for gold and silver are now widely applied to paper money, and the formerly held view that paper money be potentially treated as merchandise (ʿUlays̲h̲, *Fatḥ al-ʿalī al-mālik*, i, 164-5) is no longer much in evidence, although it continues in the treatment of stocks and bonds. It has thus been urged that *zakāt* at the rate of 2.5% should be payable on horses and any other grazing animals with the value of the *niṣāb* for gold. Similarly, the *zakāt* for crops should encompass all produce from the soil, with the *niṣāb* for gold applicable to those crops not measured by volume. Furthermore, it is often argued, fairness dictates that the expenses incurred in the growing and harvesting of the crop be deducted in the calculation of the *niṣāb*. Similar arguments have been put forth to extend *zakāt* to all minerals derived from mining and to all products derived from the ocean, including fish. Rental income from buildings, factories, taxis, buses and ships has also been drawn into the scope of *zakāt*, at the rate for trade goods according to some, or the rate for crops according to others. Salaries from professions and trades should also be subject to *zakāt* as earned, once the *niṣāb* has been met, and the view dispensing with a holding period, formerly merely a legal curiosity, is now very much alive. A minority has gone so far as to call for an updating of the classical *nuṣub*.

Modernist writers have, like their reformist predecessors, insisted that the proceeds from the collection of *zakāt* be available for a wider range of purposes than the classical law generally allowed. They have also been concerned with the mechanisms of *zakāt* collection, and have argued that *zakāt* must be payable in cash to spare government agencies the costs of caring for livestock or storing foodstuffs. In general, however, discussions of the specifics of the administration of *zakāt* collection are less developed than those concerned with the property base and the rate of *zakāt*. Modernists are optimistic that under ordinary circumstances *zakāt* will generate sufficient revenues to fund "all the activities of a state" (Fazlur Rahman, *Major themes of the Qurʾān*, [2]Minneapolis 1994, 41). They do, however, tend to acknowledge the possibility that states may, under one circumstance or another, need to find other sources of revenue. In the interests of equity, it is often held that non-Muslim citizens of Muslim states should be subjected to a tax that mirrors *zakāt*.

At the present time payment of one form or another of *zakāt* is enforceable by law in six Muslim nations: Saudi Arabia, Libya, Yemen, Malaysia, Pakistan and Sudan. Reference to the responsibility of the state for the implementation of *zakāt* appears in the Constitutions of Yemen (Art. 21), Pakistan (Art. 31) and Sudan (Art. 10).

Collection of *zakāt* in the Kingdom of Saudi Arabia is governed by Royal Decree no. 17/2/28/8634 dated 29 D̲j̲umādā II 1370/7 April 1951 which imposed *zakāt* on both individuals and companies with Saudi nationality. *Zakāt* on livestock and crops is under the jurisdiction of the General Bureau of Public Revenues of the Ministry of Finance aind National Economy, that on other items under the Zakāt and Income Tax Department of the Ministry. Special committees composed of both government officials and private citizens assess the *zakāt* due on livestock and crops, which the owners then pay directly to those whom local committees have determined to be entitled. *Zakāt* is also collected on the merchandise, cash and other liquid assets, but not the fixed assets, of businesses, and on the income of self-employed professionals, the latter at the rate of 1.25%, the law authorising individuals to personally distribute to the needy one-half of the *zakāt* otherwise due. The entire cost of collection is borne by the public treasury. The law imposes no penalties or fines for failure to pay *zakāt*, but administrative pressures have been brought to bear against companies that have failed to make their payments and in egregious cases there is the possibility of detention by the police.

The *Zakat Law* of Libya (Law 89 of 1971) applies to all property, including paper money and company shares, but provides for the compulsory collection of *zakāt* on only *ẓāhir* property. While drawing on Mālikī law for some details, it departs from it in its broader coverage of grains and fruits and its allowance of a deduction from the crop of the expenses of harvesting as well as in applying debts against livestock, and in admitting for the payment of *zakāt al-fiṭr* in cash. In the case of non-payment, the law imposes a penalty not to exceed double the *zakāt* due. Libyan law earmarks 50% of the proceeds of *zakāt* for distribution to the poor.

Compulsory collection of *zakāt* in the Yemen Arab Republic goes back to 1975. Its collection, including that of *zakāt al-fiṭr*, which is deducted from the salary of public employees in Ramaḍān, is under the Department of Duties (*maṣlaḥat al-wād̲j̲ibāt*) of the Ministry of Finance. As in Saudi Arabia, collection of *zakāt* on livestock and crops depends on local assessment. The proceeds from *zakāt* collection are deposited in the Central Bank and disbursed by the Ministry of Finance as an integral part of the state budget. The costs of collection run as high as 25%. Individuals are authorised to distribute personally 25% of their *zakāt*.

The collection of *zakāt* in Malaysia is separately administered in each state by the Religious Affairs Councils. The property from which *zakāt* is taken varies from state to state, but the greatest sources of *zakāt* revenues are rice (*padi*) and *zakāt al-fiṭr*. Non-compliance is widespread, except for *zakāt al-fiṭr* (*ca.* $1 US per person), explainable in part by the preference, going back to colonial times, on the part of some growers to distribute *zakāt* personally (*zakat peribadi*) rather than pay it to the government (*zakat raja*). The law provides for fines and imprisonment for non-payment, but enforcement is reportedly lax.

The Pakistani and Sudanese laws have attracted the greatest interest inasmuch as they formed part of larger programmes of Islamisation of the law. The Pakistani *Zakat and Ushr Ordinance of 1980* was enacted during the régime of General Zia ul-Haq [see ZIYĀ AL-ḤAḲḲ] and introduced by him as a fulfilment of what was considered by him as the centuries' long aspirations of the Muslims of the region. It departs from the classical law in imposing *zakāt* on various forms of what would traditionally have been classified as *bāṭin* property, including savings bank accounts, a measure justified by an appeal to Ḥanafī doctrine (cf. Tanzil-ur-Rahman, *Introduction of Zakat in Pakistan*, Islamabad [1981],15-21). The law differs from Ḥanafī teaching in imposing *zakāt* on the property of minors (*ibid.*, 24-5). Most of the traditional classes of property subject to *zakāt*, including gold and silver, trade goods and animals are left to self-assessment. The greater part of the Ordinance deals with the collection and administration of *zakāt* and provides for three levels of Zakat Funds, headed by the Central Zakat Fund, which receives the *zakāt* from savings accounts and other proceeds deducted at source, by far the greatest source of revenue under the Ordinance. The proceeds from the collection of *ʿus͟hr* go to the numerous Local Zakat Funds. Resistance by Pakistani S͟hīʿīs immediately led to an amendment providing for an exemption from the law for those Muslims following a recognised system of *fiḳh* who file a declaration that their faith and *fiḳh* do not oblige them to comply in whole or in part with the Ordinance.

Implementation of the Ordinance has been beset by substantial evasion through the transfer of savings accounts to current accounts before the annual valuation date of the first of Ramaḍān and even, it has been reported, by some conversions to S͟hīʿism by wealthy families. There have also been persistent complaints of corruption in collection and distribution. Low proceeds from the collection of *ʿus͟hr* led to the transfer in 1993 of its collection and administration from the Local Zakat Committees to the provincial revenue departments in the hope that that latter will be more successful in dealing with powerful landowners. One study of the operation of the Ordinance for the years 1987-8, while admitting some success in the goal of wealth redistribution, nonetheless concluded that the less wealthy were paying a disproportionate share of the *zakāt* and that in Sind the recipients were wealthier than the payers (G.A. Jehle, *Zakat and inequality: some evidence from Pakistan*, in *Review of Income and Wealth*, ii [1994], 205-16).

The Sudanese *Zakat and Taxation Act of 1984* (*Ḳānūn al-zakāt wa 'l-ḍarāʾib*), introduced as part of the Islamising movement during the régime of al-Numayrī (d. 1985), took the radical step of substituting *zakāt* for a wide range of taxes within the existing revenue system, a decision that precipitated a disastrous deficit in both the central and regional budgets. The *Zakat Law of 1986* remedied this situation and removed the administration of *zakāt* from the Ministry of Finance to the Ministry of Social Welfare and created a new Zakat Bureau (*dīwān*) separate from the existing tax system. Further changes were made under the *Zakat Law of 1990*. The reach of the Sudanese law is quite extensive, and it covers all the traditional classes of property subject to *zakāt* as well as the salaries of civil servants and professionals, and income from dairies, poultry farms and fisheries. *Zakāt* on crops has come to be collected in cash since practical problems arose in its collection in kind. *Zakāt* on livestock is also collected in cash, but implementation in this area has been hesitant. The law provides for payers to distribute personally 20% of their *zakāt*. A penalty not to exceed the *zakāt* due is imposed for non-payment.

The majority of Muslims continue to pay *zakāt* outside of a compulsory legal scheme for its collections and distribution. There has, however, been a movement across the Muslim world to create new intermediaries to receive voluntary payments of *zakāt*. Prominent among these are quasi-governmental agencies such as the Jordanian (1978) and Baḥraynī (1979) Zakat Funds (*ṣundūḳ al-zakāt*) and the more autonomous Kuwaytī Zakat House (*bayt al-zakāt*) (1982) and Egyptian Nasser Social Bank (1977). *Zakāt* paid to such agencies, like *zakāt* paid under the compulsory schemes, typically enjoys the advantage of being deductible from the national income tax. Some see in these voluntary schemes a stage on the way to compulsory collection, as in the case of Sudan, where the Zakat Fund (1980) preceded the Zakat Law. Only in Jordan did the Zakat Fund replace a scheme, albeit of limited scope, for compulsory *zakāt* collection (Law No. 35 of 1944). The activities of these intermediaries now often include the making of interest-free loans (*ḳarḍ ḥasan*), a form of assistance not provided for by the classical law of *zakāt*.

More informally-organised intermediaries continue to function throughout the Muslim world and among minority Muslim populations, both in competition with each other and sometimes in competition with legislated compulsory and voluntary schemes. Such organisations are increasingly taking advantage of modern technology such as the Internet to reach potential *zakāt* payers, and provision for payment by credit card is by no means uncommon. While insisting that *zakāt* has nothing to do with taxation, these new intermediaries have readily adopted the vocabulary (e.g. "zakatable") and trappings of modern systems of taxation, including more or less elaborate tables for calculation, and a variety of forms for "*zakāt* returns". Much, however, remains to be done in the effort toward greater compliance. For while virtually all Muslims are aware that there is an obligation of *zakāt*, accurate information about its implementation is far rarer and compliance is still very limited. A recent study of *zakāt* in rural Egypt indicated that, while 96% of the farmers knew that *zakāt* was an obligation, only 20% paid it on their crops, as compared with 76% who paid *zakāt al-fiṭr*, a relatively small obligation and one intimately associated with Ramaḍān (A.T. Abū Kurays͟ha, *al-Zakāt wa 'l-tanmiya*, Cairo 1999).

Bibliography: In addition to references in the text and in ṢADAḲA, see the following titles, grouped according to the numerical headings above:

1. Juynboll, *Handbuch*, 94-112; C. Snouck Hurgronje, *Selected works*, ed. G.-H. Bousquet and J. Schacht, Leiden 1957, 150-70.

2. Muḳātil b. Sulaymān, *Kitāb Tafsīr al-k͟hams miʾa āya*, ed. I. Goldfeld, Shfaram 1980, 45-62; W.M. Watt, *Muhammad at Medina*, Oxford 1956, ii, 369-72 (*zakāt* in the Ḳurʾān associated with the Jews); J.B. Simonsen, *Studies in the genesis and early development of the caliphal taxation system*, Copenhagen 1988, 26-39 (distinguishes *ṣadaḳa* and *zakāt* in the Ḳurʾān); S. Bashear, *On the origins and meaning of zakāt in early Islam*, in *Arabica*, xl/1 (1993), 84-113 (philology and early Ḳurʾānic exegesis).

3. Bag͟hawī, *S͟harḥ al-sunna*, ed. Muʿawwaḍ and ʿAbd al-Mawd͟jūd, Beirut 1412/1992, iii, 307-444; Ibn S͟haddād, *Dalāʾil al-aḥkām*, ed. S͟hayk͟hānī and al-Ayyūbī, Damascus 1413/1992, ii, 555-649; al-Muttaḳī al-Hindī, *Kanz al-ʿummāl*, ed. al-Dimyāṭī, Beirut 1419/1998, vi, 126-271; ʿAlī al-Ḳārī, *Mirḳāt*

al-mafātīḥ, ed. al-ʿAṭṭār, Beirut 1412/1992, iv, 258-346; al-Ḥurr al-ʿĀmilī, *Wasāʾil al-shīʿa*, ed. al-Rabbānī, Tehran 1378, iv, 2-255, ʿAbd al-Ḥayy al-Kattānī, *al-Tarātīb al-idāriyya*, ed. Beirut, i, 396-400 (collectors and estimators in time of Prophet); M. Ḥamīd Allāh, *Madjmūʿat al-wathāʾiḳ al-siyāsiyya li ʾl-ʿahd al-nabawī wa ʾl-khilāfa al-rāshida*, Beirut 1389/1969, 169-77 (instructions to collectors).

4. Balādhurī, *Futūḥ*, 230 (collection in course of Islamic conquest); ʿAbd al-ʿAzīz al-Dūrī, *al-Nuẓum al-islāmiyya*, Baghdād 1950; Aḥmad al-Mazīnī, *al-Zakāt wa ʾl-ḍarāʾib fi ʾl-Kuwayt ḳadīm^{an} wa-ḥadīth^{an}*, Kuwayt 1404/1984, 64-72; Muḥammad Saʿīd al-Ḳaddāl, *al-Siyāsa al-iḳtiṣādiyya li ʾl-dawla al-mahdiyya*, Khartūm 1986, 146-57; Muḥammad al-Ḥabīb al-Tadjkānī, *al-Iḥsān al-ilzāmī fi ʾl-islām wa-taṭbīḳātuhu fi ʾl-Maghrib*, Muḥammadiyya 1410/1990, 566-645; S. Lane Poole, *Catalogue of oriental coins in the British Museum*, London 1880, v, 102, 107 (Ḳurʾān IX, 34 on ʿAlawid coinage); J.N. Hollister, *The Shīʿa of India*, London 1953 (index); J.F.P. Hopkins, *Medieval Muslim government in Barbary until the sixth century of the hijra*, London 1958 (index); D. Sourdel, *Le vizirat ʿabbāside de 749 à 936*, Damascus 1960, ii, 593 (misappropriation of *zakāt*), H.J. Fisher, *Ahmadiyyah: a study in contemporary Islām on the West African coast*, Oxford 1963 (index); E. Shoufani, *al-Riddah and the Muslim conquest of Arabia*, Toronto 1973 (index); M.A.S. Siddiqi, *Early development of zakat law and ijtihad*, Karachi 1403/1983; Abdul Aziz bin Muhammad, *Zakat and rural development in Malaysia*, Kuala Lumpur 1993, 105-30; A.I. Abu Shouk and A. Bjørkelo, *The public treasury of the Muslims: monthly budgets of the Mahdist state in the Sudan, 1897*, Leiden 1996, pp. xxvii-xxviii; H. Weiss, *A tentative note on Islamic welfare: zakāt in theory and practice in the Sokoto caliphate*, in *Hemispheres*, xiii (1998), 63-77.

5. Public finance and governance. Ibn Zandjawayh, *Kitāb al-Amwāl*, ed. Fayyāḍ, 3 vols. Riyāḍ 1986; Najib Abdul Wahhab al-Fili, *A critical edition of Kitāb al-Amwāl by Abū Jaʿfar Aḥmad b. Naṣr al-Dāwūdī (d. 401/H)*, Ph.D. diss., Exeter University, 1989, unpubl.; Abū Yaʿlā Ibn al-Farrāʾ, *al-Aḥkām al-sulṭāniyya*, ed. al-Fiḳī, Cairo 1386/1966, 115-35; A. Ben Shemesh, *Taxation in Islam*, 3 vols. Leiden 1967-9. Shāfiʿī law. Rāfiʿī, *al-ʿAzīz, sharḥ al-Wadjīz*, ed. Muʿawwaḍ and ʿAbd al-Mawdjūd, Beirut 1417/1997, ii, iii, vii; Nawawī, *al-Madjmūʿ*, ed. Yūsuf, Cairo, v-vi; Ibn al-Naḳīb al-Miṣrī, *Reliance of the traveller*, tr. N.H.M. Keller, Evanston, Ill. 1991, 244-76; Muḥammad b. ʿUmar Nawawī, *Nihāyat al-zayn*, ed. Cairo, 167-83; Muḥammad ʿAbd Allāh al-Djurdānī, *Fatḥ al-ʿallām*, ed. al-Hadjdjār, ed. Aleppo, iii, 1-199; al-Kūhadjī, *Zād al-muḥtādj*, ed. al-Anṣārī, Beirut 1982, i, 425-99. Ḥanafī law. Shaybānī, *Kitāb al-Aṣl*, ed. al-Afghānī, Ḥaydarābād 1388/1969, ii, 1-185; M. Brandel-Syrier (tr.), *The religious duties of Islam as taught and explained by Abu Bakr Effendi*, Leiden 1960, 117-36. Mālikī law. Ibn al-Djallāb, *al-Tafrīʿ*, ed. al-Dahmānī, Beirut 1408/1987, i, 273-99; Ibn Shās, *ʿIḳd al-djawāhir al-thamīna*, ed. Abu ʾl-Adjfān and Manṣūr, Beirut 1415/1995, i, 277-353; ʿAbd al-Raḥmān al-Mundjara, *al-Fatḥ al-mubīn fī bayān al-zakāt wa-bayt māl al-muslimīn*, ed. al-Tadjkānī, Rabāṭ 1993; Muḥammad ʿArafa al-Dasūḳī, *Ḥāshiya ʿalā al-sharḥ al-kabīr*, ed. Cairo, i, 430-509. Ḥanbalī law. Ibn Ḳudāma, *al-Muḳniʿ*, ed. Cairo, i, 289-355; Buhūtī, *Kashshāf al-ḳināʿ*, ed. Hilāl, ed. Riyāḍ, ii, 165-295; Muḥammad b. Ṣāliḥ al-ʿUthaymīn, *al-Sharḥ al-mumtiʿ ʿalā zād al-mustaḳniʿ*, Riyāḍ 1416/1996, vi, 7-307 (modern presentation). Twelver Shīʿī law. Nadjafī, *Djawāhir al-kalām*, ed. Beirut, xv; Taḳī al-Tabātabāʾī al-Ḳummī, *Mabāni minhādj al-ṣāliḥīn*, Beirut 1418/1997, vi, 318-571; Muḥammad Amīn Zayn al-Dīn, *Kalimat al-taḳwā*, Ḳumm 1414/1993, ii, 147-240. Zaydī law. al-Nāṭiḳ bi ʾl-Ḥaḳḳ, *K. al-Taḥrīr*, ed. ʿIzzān, Sanʿāʾ 1418/1997, 132-65. Ibāḍī law. Muḥammad b. Ibrāhīm al-Kindī, *Bayān al-sharʿ*, ed. ʿUman, xvii-xix (extensive citations from *al-Ishrāf* of Ibn al-Mundhir (d. 319/931); al-Djayṭālī, *Ḳanāṭir al-khayrāt*, ʿUmān 1403/1983, ii, 2-38 (based on Ghazālī, *Iḥyāʾ*). Ḥiyal. Khaṣṣāf, *K. al-Ḥiyal wa ʾl-makhāridj*, ed. Schacht, Hanover 1923, 103; Ḳazwīnī, *K. al-Ḥiyal*, ed. Schacht, Hanover 1924, 4-5. Ḥisba. Ibn al-Ukhuwwa, *Maʿālim al-ḳurba*, ed. Shaʿbān and al-Muṭīʿī, Cairo 1976. Ikhtilāf. Baghdādī, *al-Ishrāf ʿalā nukat masāʾil al-khilāf*, ed. Ṭāhir, Beirut 1420/1999, i, 369-422; Ṭūsī, *al-Khilāf*, i, 270-336; Ibn Rushd, *Bidāyat al-mudjtahid*, ed. Cairo, i, 207-39, tr. I.A.K. Nyazee, *The Distinguished jurist's primer*, London 1994, 283-329; al-ʿAllāma al-Ḥillī, *Tadhkirat al-fuḳahāʾ*, Ḳumm 1414, vi, 7-405; Dimashḳī, *Raḥmat al-umma fi ikhtilāf al-aʾimma*, on margin of Shaʿrānī, *al-Mīzān al-kubrā*, ed. Cairo, i, 91-113; Ibn al-Murtaḍā, *al-Baḥr al-zakhkhār*, Beirut 1394/1975, iii, 137-203; ʿA. al-Djazīrī, *Kitāb al-Fiḳh ʿalā al-madhāhib al-arbaʿa*, Cairo [1950-57], i, 471-511; Maghniyya, *The five schools of Islamic law*, Ḳumm 1416/1995, 148-63 (tr. of his *al-Fiḳh ʿalā al-madhāhib al-khamsa*); *al-Mawsūʿa al-fiḳhiyya*, Kuwayt 1412/1992, xxiii, 226-345.

Studies. N.P. Aghnides, *Mohammedan theories of finance*, New York 1916, 199-347, 439-64 (detailed comparative account); N. Calder, *Zakāt in Imāmī Shīʿī jurisprudence from the tenth to the sixteenth century A.D.*, in *BSOAS*, xliv (1981), 469-80; Ersilia Francesca, *L'elemosina rituale secondo gli Ibāḍiti*, in *Studi magrebini*, xix (1987), 1-64; Calder, *Exploring God's law: Muḥammad ibn Aḥmad ibn Abī Sahl al-Sarakhsī on zakāt*, in C. Toll and J. Skovgaard-Petersen (eds.), *Law and the Islamic world past and present*, Copenhagen 1995, 57-73; B. Johansen, *Contingency in a sacred law: legal and ethical norms in the Muslim fiqh*, Leiden 1999, 129-52 (*zakāt al-fiṭr* and *ẓāhir/bāṭin* distinction, sociological approach, cf. G.-S. Colin, in *Hesperis*, xxxi [1947], 74).

6. ʿAbd al-Raḥīm b. al-Ḥusayn al-ʿIrāḳī, *Kitāb Ṭarḥ al-tathrīb fī sharḥ al-taḳrīb*, ed. Aleppo, iv, 43-66; Ibn Nubāta, *Dīwān khuṭab minbariyya*, ed. Bombay, 85-6 (sermon on *zakāt al-fiṭr*).

7. Ibn al-ʿArabī, *al-Futūḥāt al-makkiyya*, ed. Y. ʿUthmān, Cairo 1403-5/1983-5, viii, ix (symbolic interpretation of *zakāt*, cf. al-Ḳāḍī al-Nuʿmān, *Taʾwīl al-daʿāʾim*, ed. al-Aʿẓamī, ed. Cairo, ii, 85-133); Ibn ʿAṭāʾ Allāh, *al-Tanwīr fī isḳāṭ al-tadbīr*, Cairo 1971, 375 (prophets not subject to *zakāt*).

8. Aḥmad al-Ḥusaynī, *Bahdjat al-mushtāḳ fī bayān ḥukm zakāt amwāl al-awrāḳ*, Cairo 1329 (assimilates paper money to gold and silver); Ḳaraḍāwī, *Fiḳh al-zakāt*, Beirut 1389/1969, 2 vols. (standard work), tr. London 1999; al-ʿAzbāwī, *al-Mawārid al-māliyya al-islāmiyya wa ʾl-ḍarāʾib al-muʿāṣira maʿa aḥkām wa-taṭbīḳāt al-zakāt wa ʾl-ḍarāʾib bi ʾl-mamlaka al-ʿarabiyya al-suʿūdiyya*, Cairo 1396/1976, 81-140; Muḥammad ʿUḳla Ibrāhīm, *al-Taṭbīḳāt al-taʾrīkhiyya wa ʾl-muʿāṣira li-farīḍat al-zakāt*, ʿAmmān 1406/1985, 153-91 (surveys major modern developments and literature in Arabic); Maḥmūd Shaltūt, *Fatāwā*, Cairo 1411/1991, 114-129 (*zakāt* for an Islamic socialism); Muḥammad Bashīr ʿAbd al-Ḳādir, *Niẓām al-zakāt fi ʾl-Sūdān*, Umm Durmān 1993; Ḳaraḍāwī,

Li-kay tandjaḥ mu'assasat al-zakāt fī 'l-taṭbīḳ al-mu'āṣir, Beirut 1414/1994; Mu'assasat ahl al-bayt, *al-Zakāt wa 'l-takāful al-idjtimā'ī fi 'l-Islām*, 'Ammān 1415/1994 (papers and selection of legislative materials); M.S. al-Ashkār *et al.*, *al-Buhūth al-fiḳhiyya fī ḳaḍāya al-zakāt al-mu'āṣira*, 'Ammān 1418/1998, ii, 865-907 (collects conference recommendations); Bū al-Shinḳīṭī, *al-Ḳawl al-musaddad fī ḥukm zakāt al-awrāḳ wa-shurūṭ al-fatwā wa 'l-idjtihād al-muṭlaḳ wa 'l-muḳayyad*, n.p. 1420/1999 (attacks the assimilation of paper money to gold and silver); *Ladjnat zakāt wa-ṣadaḳāt al-Khalīl, fa''āliyyat al-ladjna wa-indjizātuhā*, Khalīl [1999] (use of *zakāt* funds); Farishta G. de Zayas, *The law and philosophy of zakat (The Islamic social welfare system)*, Damascus 1960 (detailed modernist re-examination); M. Khurshid Chowdhry *et al.*, *A study of attitudes of people toward zakat in village Gharibabad*, Peshawar 1961 (small-scale survey), M.A. Sabzwari, *A study of zakat and ushr with special reference to Pakistan*, Karachi 1979; Monzer Kahf, *The calculation of zakah for Muslims in North America*, Plainfield, Ind. 1980; Ziauddin Ahmad, *Niṣāb of zakāt*, in *Islamic Studies*, xx/3 (1981), 239-59; M. Raquibuz Zaman (ed.), *Some aspects of the economics of zakah*, Plainfield, Ind. 1981 (modern conference proceedings); Mahmoud Abu-Saud, *Contemporary zakat*, Cincinnati 1988 (tr. of his *Fiḳh al-zakāt al-mu'āṣir*, critical of classical law); Ann E. Mayer, *Islamization and taxation in Pakistan*, in A.M. Weiss, *Islamic reassertion in Pakistan*, Syracuse 1986, 59-77; G. Clark, *Pakistan's zakat and 'ushr as a welfare system*, in *ibid.*, 79-95; J.C. Scott, *Resistance without protest and without organization. Peasant opposition to the Islamic zakat and the Christian tithe*, in *Comparative Studies in Society and History*, xxix/3 (1987), 417-52, esp. 424-37 (avoidance of official *zakāt* in Malaysia); S. Ben-Nefissa, *Zakât officielle et zakât non officielle aujourd'hui en Égypte*, in *Égypte/Monde Arabe*, vii (1991), 105-20; Muhammad Farooq-i-Azam Malik, *Al-Zakah: the Islamic financial responsibility*, Houston 1993; Abu al-Hasan Sadeq, *A survey of the institution of zakah: issues, theories and administration*, Jidda 1415/1994; A.A. El-Ashker and M. Sirajul Haq, *Institutional framework of zakah: dimensions and implications*, Jidda 1416/1995 (surveys implementation in several nations), J.A. Khan, *Islamic economics and finance: a bibliography*, London 1995, 118-23; Nasim Shah Shirazi, *System of zakāt in Pakistan: an appraisal*, Islamabad 1417/1996; Marghoob Ahmed Quraishi, *Annual zakat computation guide*, Palo Alto 1997. (A. Zysow)

AL-**ZAḲĀZĪḲ**, conventionally Zagazig, a town in the east of the Nile delta of Egypt, 90 km/55 miles to the northeast of Cairo. It is now the chef-lieu of the Sharḳiyya province, and in 1998 had almost 270,000 inhabitants.

The town was founded in the first third of the 19th century on the *baḥr* Muwīs, a canal following the ancient course of the Tanaitic branch of the Nile. The Egyptian ruler Muḥammad 'Alī Pasha [*q.v.*] entrusted to a specialist hydraulic engineer, Aḥmad al-Bārūdī, the construction of six dams on this canal and its branches, in order to irrigate the Sharḳiyya province as a whole. The original site of al-Zaḳāzīḳ corresponds to the dockside huts of mud and reeds built for the workers on the main dam, called Ḳanāṭir al-Tis'a, at the bifurcation of the *baḥr* Muwīs and the *baḥr* Mashtūt. The only remarkable feature of this site was the archaeological tell of the ancient Bubastis (modern Tell Basta) at some kilometres to the south-east, at that time exploited by the *sabbākhūn*, and nearby, an ancient dam whose existence was going to be decisive for choosing the site of the new dam and for fixing the settlement. Work on the dams took from 1827 to 1832, and when they were completed, a permanent settlement, with more durable buildings, grew up on the site.

The name of the town, whose origin is controversial, is said to have come from a member of the family of a certain Aḥmad Zaḳzūḳ, which settled at the end of the 18th century half-a-kilometre to the north of the future dockyard, in a village which is said to have taken its name from the newly-arrived family/clan: Kafr al-Zaḳāzīḳ. Naturally, in the late 1820s, in order to complete the new dams, recourse would have been made to local manpower, and especially to the workers of Kafr al-Zaḳāzīḳ, including some of the descendants of Aḥmad Zaḳzūḳ, who are said to have called their dockside settlement Nazlat al-Zaḳāzīḳ. This patronymic would also be kept in the engineer Aḥmad al-Bārūdī's administrative documents and was definitively confirmed by Muḥammad 'Alī when he visited the site shortly after its completion. However, other etymologies persisted more strongly in folk memory in the later 19th and early 20th centuries. Its origin was attributed to a species of fish like the carp, the *zaḳzūḳ*, pl. *zaḳāzīḳ*, caught in large quantities in the *baḥr* of Muwīs; at the present time, the preferred derivation is from the root *zaḳzaḳa*, denoting the twittering of the large numbers of birds in the trees along the main road of the town alongside the canal.

The town rapidly developed after its foundation, thanks to the transfer at an early date of the irrigation offices of the Sharḳiyya from Bilbays to al-Zaḳāzīḳ, followed a year later by the town's elevation to the rank of capital of the province (*mudīriyya*, now *muḥāfaẓa*) of the Sharḳiyya, all at the expense of Bilbays. Muḥammad 'Alī considered al-Zaḳāzīḳ as having a more central site. The arrival of numerous officials was followed by that of merchants and the development of infrastructures, notably the arrival of the railway, making the town definitively the main centre of the Delta, so that it had 40,000 inhabitants in 1911. This population came from diverse origins, seen e.g. in the town's Coptic community; the family of Salāma Mūsā (1887-1958 [*q.v.*]), originally from Asyūṭ, settled in al-Zaḳāzīḳ in the years after its foundation.

The two first mosques there were built early, one by Muḥammad 'Alī on the eastern bank of the canal and the other on the western bank by a government dignitary, the *amīr* Yūsuf, the so-called "Little Mosque". The third mosque, from the second half of the 19th century, well reflects the development and modernisation of the town, being built, with steel columns, by a local rich merchant, Sulaymān al-Sharbīnī. Today, however, most important in the town is the Mosque of the Conquest financed by the singer 'Abd al-Ḥalīm Ḥāfiẓ, originally from the district. The town's Muslim community has further acquired, in less than two centuries, two tutelary saints, Abū Khalīl and Abū 'Āmir, whose *mawlid* is celebrated by Muslims and Copts equally.

The town's prosperity derives nevertheless from economic and commercial activities. In the later 19th century, al-Zaḳāzīḳ became one of the main Egyptian centres for the corn trade, and above all for the preparation and marketing of cotton. Several dozen European merchants (English, French, Greek) invested capital in the cotton industry and installed factories for cotton ginning and spinning. This foreign presence, increasingly visible through the development of land and the building of churches and of colonial villas surrounded by gardens, led, in the 1870s, to conflicts in the town between the locals and the newcomers; hence Aḥmad ʿUrābī [see ʿURĀBĪ PAS̲H̲A], originally from this region, was to find strong support from the citizens of the town at the time of his revolt in 1881.

Bibliography: ʿAlī Bās̲h̲ā Mubārak, *al-K̲h̲iṭaṭ al-tawfīḳiyya*, xi, Būlāḳ 1887, 93-4; S. Mūsā, *The education of Salāma Mūsā*, Leiden 1961; S. Māhir, *Muḥāfaẓāt al-D̲j̲umhūriyya al-ʿarabiyya al-muttaḥida wa-āt̲h̲āruhā al-bāḳiya fī ʾl-ʿaṣr ʾl-islāmī*, Cairo 1966, 126-8; Muḥammad Ramzī, *al-Ḳāmūs al-d̲j̲ug̲h̲rāfī liʾl-bilād al-miṣriyya*, repr. Cairo 1993, ii/1, 89-92.

(J.-M. MOUTON)

ZĀK̲H̲IR, ʿABD ALLĀH, polemicist, copyist, translator, printer and painter, born in Aleppo 1680, died at the Monastery of Mār Yuḥannā, al-S̲h̲uwayr, Lebanon, 30 August 1748. The son of a Greek Orthodox goldsmith, Zāk̲h̲ir learned his father's trade before studying with Christian scholars and the Muslim *s̲h̲ayk̲h̲* Sulaymān al-Naḥwī. He worked as a copyist for the Catholic missionaries in Aleppo amongst others, especially for the Jesuits, whose translations of works of theology and spirituality he also rendered into acceptable Arabic. After the Greek Orthodox former patriarch At̲h̲anāsiyūs Dabbās returned from Wallachia, having had two Arabic liturgical books printed there [see MAṬBAʿA. 1.B.1], Zāk̲h̲ir cooperated with him in setting up the first Arabic press in the Near East, using equipment, and with financial support, from Romania. Between 1706 and 1711, when it ceased working, this Aleppo press published 10 titles.

Zāk̲h̲ir's polemical writings date from 1722 onwards, when the break between Greek Orthodox and Greek Catholics became open. Accepting Papal claims to supremacy, he refuted the Orthodox teaching on the issues that separated the two traditions. The target of Orthodox hostility, he left Aleppo for Lebanon, where he eventually settled at the monastery at al-S̲h̲uwayr. The press he set up there in 1733 was to function with interruptions until 1899; the first book it produced, in 1734, was *Mīzān al-zamān*, a translation of an ascetic work by the Jesuit J.E. Nieremberg.

In his original writings and correspondance, Zāk̲h̲ir demonstrates not only command of the *ʿarabiyya* (he was a contemporary of D̲j̲armānūs Farḥāt [*q.v.*]) but also a well-developed rhetorical sense and capacity for argument; he was understandably feared as a polemicist. Though never ordained or a monk, he lived a life of asceticism and service to others, which earned him the title of *s̲h̲ammās* (lit. "deacon"). He is perhaps the first Arab painter to have left us a self-portrait, together with portraits of some of his contemporaries.

Bibliography: Zāk̲h̲ir's biography by a disciple in *Masarra*, iv/6 (August 1913), repr. in *Masarra*, xxxiv/7 (1948) (special issue on the bicentenary of Zāk̲h̲ir's death), 386-96; J. Nasrallah, *Histoire du mouvement littéraire dans l'Église Melchite du Ve au XXe siècle*, iv/2, *Époque ottomane 1724-1800*, Louvain-Paris 1989, 111-37, with the bibl. given there, to which may be added Usāma ʿĀnūtī, *al-Ḥaraka al-adabiyya fī bilād al-S̲h̲ām fī ʾl-ḳarn al-t̲h̲āmin ʿas̲h̲ar*, Beirut 1985, index; B. Heyberger, *Les chrétiens du Proche-Orient au temps de la réforme catholique*, Rome 1994, index.

(HILARY KILPATRICK)

ZAK̲H̲RAFA (A.), in Islamic art, "ornament, ornamentation". The word is connected with the noun *zuk̲h̲ruf* "gold" > "ornamental work" used in Ḳurʾān, XVII, 95/93, *bayt min zuk̲h̲ruf*, and there is an adjective *muzak̲h̲raf* "ornamented"; the origin of *zuk̲h̲ruf* seems to be in a deformation, via Syriac, of Grk. *zōgrapheō* "to paint", see Jeffery, *The foreign vocabulary of the Qurʾān*, Baroda 1938, 150.

Islamic ornament possesses certain qualities that, even if not exclusive to this art, are sufficiently distinct to be recognisable. One is that it is independent from the underlying structure, be it a building or an object of art. It therefore can easily be transferred from one material to the other, and from one technique to another. As in other civilisations, the ornament can be classified either by the elements of which it is composed or by the method by which it is organised. In addition, it can be interpreted symbolically, can communicate ideas or can have metaphoric qualities.

The most common elements are vegetal, geometric, epigraphic and figural. In order to create order and harmony—one of the most characteristic functions of Islamic ornament—it is organised by two principles: geometry and symmetry. To achieve this aim, the Islamic artist used a number of methods, the most typical being framing and linking. Plants may completely grow into each other and form an infinite pattern generally termed "arabesque" [*q.v.*].

The predominance of vegetal motifs in Islamic ornament hardly needs to be reiterated. Its development can broadly be divided into three main periods: the formative, roughly between the 7th and 10th centuries A.D.; the ornamental integration, from about the 10th to the later 13th centuries, and the final phases, from about the 14th to the 17th centuries. The first centuries are characterised by an enormous variety of motifs adopted from pre-Islamic civilisations. In the course of time, acanthus and vine leaves, palmettes, half-palmettes, lotus blossoms and grapes, to mention only the most common vegetal designs, were flattened out, became two-dimensional, and made into space for additional small ornamentation. Composed without background, divided only by bevelled lines, these ornaments create abstract designs that give the impression of uniform patterns, though their floral and vegetal origin is still recognisable. The best examples attesting to the transformation and integration of these elements into ornamental patterns stem from late 8th-century Syria and 9th-century Sāmarrā, from where they spread to Egypt and other parts of the Islamic world (Plate V, Figs. 1 and 2). Only Spain was less affected by these tendencies. Depending on Umayyad tradition, such as the mosaics of the Dome of the Rock [see ḲUBBAT AL-ṢAK̲H̲RA] or the eastern façade of Ms̲h̲attā [*q.v.*], deeply carved and feathery leaves are folded over, so that the design becomes three-dimensional instead of being flattened out.

In the following centuries, the changes within plant ornaments occur primarily in the central Islamic lands. Of particular importance is the development of the arabesque. While its preliminary stages may already date from the 11th century, it reached its full scope only in the following two centuries, culminating in Asia Minor, where full use of the potential qualities of the arabesque is attested from works made in Ḳonya (Plate V, Fig. 3). Because of the Mongol invasions, Central Asian motifs—lotus blossoms, peonies, composite flowers and the like—enrich the vegetal repertoire and remain a constant feature from the second half of the 13th century onwards. The earliest Chinese-inspired floral motifs seem to occur on ceramics, but were immediately adopted also in other media such as metal, wood, glass, textiles and manuscript illuminations. Assimilated to the Islamic tradition and taste, they became favourite motifs in Persian and Central Asian architecture, and by the second half of the 14th century, intricate and organically-growing floral patterns, transformed into flat, coloured faience mosaics, become a common decoration on religious and secular buildings alike. Thanks to trade relations and wandering workshops, this vocabulary reached also Syria, Egypt and Turkey and brought about a new taste, which preferred a more exotic and less traditional floral répertoire. In the course of the 16th and 17th centuries, Ottoman Turkey in particular excelled in combining a multitude of stalks, buds and flowers from different origins, which in colour and composition remain unique (cf. the wares of Iznīḳ [*q.v.*]).

Although not used as ornaments on religious buildings or objects produced for religious purposes, animals and birds were part of the decorative répertoire from its very beginning. At first they reflect the same artistic traditions as the vegetal ornaments. Yet by the 9th century, first in Mesopotamia, and almost instantaneously in Egypt and Persia also, these animals become less realistic. Their bodies lose plasticity, details such as hair, felt or feathers are replaced by ornaments unrelated to their indigenous shape, and the whole figure is often adapted to the shape of the object it decorates. Or, following the bevelled style of Sāmarrā, the shape of a bird is transformed into an abstract pattern, composed of fully merged three-petalled lotus blossoms, half-palmettes and undulating stems (Plate VI, Fig. 4). In eastern Persia, this abstract style continued for some time, while in Egypt the animal figure become again more realistic. The number of species increases, and on portable objects of art fabulous, occasionally even grotesque creatures figure in the centre of an object as its major decoration. The fascination with imaginary animals, including Far Eastern dragons, unicorns, qilins and the like that appear after the Mongol invasion, culminates between the 12th and 14th centuries. In the following periods, realistic animal figures become less frequent, while Far Eastern creatures continue to appear in Persian and Turkish manuscripts (Plate VI, Fig. 5) and on tiles, textiles, rugs, etc.

As with the vegetal and figural motifs, so do squares, lozenges, circles, polygons and star patterns go back to much earlier civilisations. It was, however, the preoccupation with geometric forms and their development into virtuoso intricacies which, together with symmetry, became a dominating feature in Islamic ornament. Rectilinear patterns constructed of squares divided either diagonally or inscribed within each other were employed by Islamic artisans since early Islamic times. Pattern of lozenges, polygons and stars formed by either raised or recessed bricks feature on 10th to 12th-century Persian brick buildings, and transferred to stone appear in Anatolian stone carvings and on 13th to early 14th-century Persian faience mosaics. By using glazed and unglazed bricks, terracotta tiles and faience mosaics, Persian artisans differentiated between the various forms and highlighted the stellar elements. A good example of tile and faience decoration is the ornamentation of the Madrasa G͟hiyā-t͟hiyya at K͟hargird (846-8/1442-5) (Plate VI, Fig. 6), where dark blue and light brown faience mosaics accentuate the centre of the stars, while strips of light blue glazed brick or terracotta and white glazed cut tiles form the overall stellar grid. Similar ornaments were used for the decoration of Ḳur'ān frontispieces, Egyptian 15th and early 16th-century *minbar*s, or a wooden Turkish Ḳur'ān box from the mausoleum of Sultan Selīm II. Another decoration generated by geometric forms are stalactites or *muḳarnas* [*q.v.*]. In contrast to the patterns mentioned above, they are three-dimensional, and became one of the most conspicuous architectural ornaments created in the Islamic world. Finally, signatures, foundation inscriptions, quotations from the Ḳur'ān, proverbs and the like, often became the main and only decoration of buildings or objects of art. The latter, documented since the 8th century on ceramic, glass and metal objects, even precede inscriptions on architecture. In the course of the centuries, Islamic calligraphers invented a variety of styles, and the inscriptions became integrated into the rest of the decoration [see K͟HAṬṬ]. Limited in time and material is a script in which either the whole letter or part of it assumes a human or animal form. Except for the ornithomorphic script, which appears for the first time on 10th-century eastern Persian ceramics, it is limited to metalwork, produced between the mid-12th and late-13th centuries. Beginning with the early 14th century, inscriptions, written in either *nask͟hī* or *t͟hulut͟h* styles, became a dominant feature in architecture as well as in minor arts. Mamlūk dignitaries favoured a radiating arrangement of the script which, set in roundels or polylobed medallions, was meant to glorify their names and titles. Perhaps the first sultan who used this device was al-Nāṣir Muḥammad b. Ḳalāwūn [*q.v.*] in the early 14th century (Plate VII, Fig. 7). These epigraphic roundels were equally favoured by high officers and other members of his dynasty. By the 15th century, only a few Mamlūk rulers continued to write their names and honorary titles in a radiant composition. They re-appear, however, in Ottoman epigraphic roundels of a religious content. The ornamental qualities of the script were fully exploited in epigraphic panels in which the words, made up of unadorned Kūfic letters, form a regular geometric design. This script was exclusively used for religious inscriptions, repeating the name of the Prophet, the names of the Imāms and various saints, or else the Muslim creed or *s͟hahāda* [*q.v.*]. After the mid-13th century, these decorative panels enjoyed considerable popularity in Anatolian, Egyptian and Persian architecture, wood carvings and manuscript illuminations, and this popularity has continued up to the present day.

The most common means of creating an overall pattern was by means of frames and borders, which outlined the primary motifs and set them into medallions, panels, cartouches and arches, giving the pattern an inner cohesion. Due to the survival of antique elements in Syrian, Egyptian and Coptic art, niches and arcades remained a relatively frequent feature until the end of the Mamlūk period. In other instances, round enclosures or arches were provided with lobed outlines, a feature that entered Islam from China long before the Mongol invasion. They often formed continuous bands, decorating objects of art and architectural monuments alike. In patterns where the decorative elements completely eliminated the background, the basic design was repeated in a reciprocating fashion, applicable to larger surfaces as well as to closed panels and frames. Carved with slanting outlines or painted on flat surfaces, they remained in vogue up to about the 14th century, often differentiated by their colour (Plate VIII, Fig. 8). Other methods of creating coherent overall designs involved placing different geometric forms next to each other; determining the structure of a pattern by continuously crossing and overlapping bands, or creating a three-dimensional design by arranging up to four decorative schemes one on top of the other.

Ornaments, however, also communicated—either explicitly or implicitly—certain ideas. Their interpretation remains equivocal. Yet it would seem that, aside from being aesthetically attractive, some of these orna-

Fig. 1. Vine plant in plaster in audience chamber (*dīwān*), Khirbat al-Mafdjar, *ca.* 725-30.

Fig. 2. Overall patterns of palmettes, lotus buds and trefoils aligned vertically. From house at Sāmarrā, *ca.* mid-3rd/9th century.

Fig. 3. Ḳurʾān stand elaborately carved with arabesques, *ca.* 1278-9, Ḳonya.

Fig. 4. Bird carved in wood. Egypt, Ṭūlūnid period. Paris, Musée de Louvre, Inv. MAO 459.

Fig. 5. Coloured drawing of dragons on foliage. Ottoman, mid-10th/16th century. The Cleveland Museum of Art 44.492.

Fig. 6. Tile and faience decoration from the Madrasa G͟hiyāt͟hiyya, 846-8/ 1442-5.

Fig. 7. Radiating inscription. Incense burner of Muḥammad b. Ḳalāwūn. Egypt or Syria, 693-741/1294-1340.
The Nuhad es-Said Collection.

Fig. 8. Border pattern with reciprocating motif. Sulṭān Khān, begun 629/1231.

Fig. 9. Fish pond ornament at bottom of early 14th-century Persian brass bowl. Naples, Museo Nazionale, Inv. H.3253.

ments evoked additional connotations. Among these one may suggest that fruit-bearing trees were recharged with ancient connotations of fertility, conveyed blessings to the deceased in the afterlife and had associations with Paradise. Flowers seem to have conveyed notions of well-being, while arches and arcades, because of their formal resemblance to the *miḥrāb* [*q.v.*], were occasionally charged with religious symbolism. As in the domes of Late Antiquity, which were decorated with whorls and stars, domes were now given cosmological symbolism, transforming a cupola or ceramic bowl into the vault of heaven. This is further enforced by Persian poems, in which the vault of heaven is called *ṭās-i nigūn* lit. "upturned bowl", i.e. "heaven", or *ṭās-i sipihr* "bowl of heaven". Other ornaments with metaphoric qualities are fish and water creatures (Plate VIII, Fig. 9), imitations of jewellery, or animal wheels. It has, however, to be reiterated that our quest for understanding the meaning of ornaments is still at its beginning and awaits future studies in depth.

Bibliography: E. Baer, *Islamic ornament*, Edinburgh 1998. Cf. G. Necipoğlu, *The Topkapi scroll. Geometry and ornament in Islamic architecture. With an essay on the geometry of the muqarnas by Moḥammad al-Asad*, The Getty Center for the History of Art and the Humanities, Santa Monica 1995. (EVA BAER)

ZĀKHŪ, local pronunciation Zāk͟hō, a Kurdish town on the Lesser K͟hābūr river [*q.v.*] in northern ʿIrāḳ, situated about 8 km/5 miles from the Turkish border and 20 km/12 miles from the Syrian border (lat. 37° 2' N., long 42° 8' E.). It became world-famous after the Gulf War (1990) when thousands of Kurdish refugees, fearing retaliation by the ʿIrāḳī army, tried to escape to Turkey but eventually were resettled in Zāk͟hū or near it; as a result, by 1992 Zāk͟hū's population rose to about 350,000 (?), compared to only about 30,000 (?) in 1950.

In addition to the largely Kurdish Muslim population, Zāk͟hū had also a Christian community (Nestorians and Chaldaeans, Armenians, etc. totalling *ca.* 5,000 persons in 1992), and a Jewish community (about 350 families before their emigration en masse to Israel in the early 1950s). However, according to the table in M. Chevalier, *Les montagnards chrétiens du Hakkari*, 285, the estimates of various travellers vary widely. Each community lived usually in a separate quarter, close to its house of worship (4 churches, 2 synagogues, and a few mosques). The Kurds spoke the Kurmānd͟jī dialect of Kurdish [see KURDS, KURDISTĀN. v.], whereas the Christians and the Jews spoke Neo-Aramaic, each community having its own dialect. Zāk͟hū's commercial and communal life centred around the river, which was, before the advent of motorised vehicles, the main route for the transport of materials from central Kurdistān to the Tigris plains, so that Zāk͟hū was an important shipping centre. About seventy Jewish families in the town were loggers and raftsmen who transported goods and wood to Mawṣil and beyond on large rafts made of logs tied together alone or over inflated sheepskins [see KELEK]. Other typical occupations included peddlers, butchers, weavers (mostly Christians), dyers (Jewish), shop owners (mixed), carpenters, farmers (mostly Kurds), teachers and government officials (mostly Christians). Zāk͟hū may be an old town, and probably identical with the *bēṯ zāk͟hū* ("House of Victory") mentioned in an 11th-century Syriac manuscript (Budge, 183; cf. Fiey, 261, 880: "B[ēt]Zāḫō"). Zāk͟hū has three modern bridges, but a fourth one, made of huge stones and associated with a legend, is popularly assumed to be from the ʿAbbāsid period. The oldest synagogue there had an inscription dated 5568 (= 1798). Social and commercial relations between the communities were generally good, with the Jews feeling secure under the protection of the local S͟hemdīn *ag͟has*.

Bibliography: E.A. Wallis Budge, *The histories of Rabban Hōrmīzd the Persian and Rabban Bar-ʿIdtā*, London 1902, 183; D.N. MacKenzie, *Kurdish dialect studies*, London 1962, ii, 347-67 (Kurdish texts and legends about Zāk͟hū); J.M. Fiey, *Assyrie chrétienne*, Beirut 1965-8, see index, 880; Y. Sabar, *The folk literature of the Kurdistani Jews. An anthology*, New Haven 1982 (introd. includes details of Jewish life in Zāk͟hū); M. Chevalier, *Les montagnards chrétiens du Hakkari*, Paris 1985; Sabar, *The Christian Neo-Aramaic dialects of Zakho and Dihok*, in *JAOS*, cxv (1995), 33-51 (includes report of visit after the Gulf War).
(Y. SABAR)

AL-**ZAḲḲĀḲ**, ʿALĪ B. AL-ḲĀSIM b. Muḥammad al-Tud͟jībī al-Fāsī, Abu 'l-Ḥasan (d. 912/1507), famous Mālikī jurist, whose *laḳab* is explained in the sources as being unconnected with the trade of making skin vessels for holding wine. He studied K͟halīl's *Muk͟htaṣar* with Muḥammad b. Ḳāsim al-Ḳawrī al-Miknāsī al-Fāsī (d. 872/1468) and al-Mawwāḳ al-G͟harnāṭī (d. 897/1492), whose *al-Tād͟j wa 'l-iklīl* he also transmitted. Al-Zaḳḳāḳ is the author of an *urd͟jūza* [see RAD͟JAZ] in which he explained the basic principles of the Mālikī legal school, entitled *al-Manhad͟j al-muntak͟hab ilā uṣūl al-mad͟hhab* (ms. National Library of Madrid); a commentary was written by Mayyāra (d. 1072/1662). He also wrote a famous *Lāmiyya*, known as *al-Zaḳḳāḳiyya*, of which many mss. are preserved. It was edited by Merad ben Ali, *La Lamiya ou Zaqqaqiya du jurisconsulte maroccain Zaqqaq, manuel maroccain de jurisprudence musulmane*, Casablanca 1927; a commentary was written by Aḥmad al-Mand͟jūr (d. 995/1587). The *Lāmiyya* shows the existence of solutions in which the *ʿamal fāsī* was adopted. In the last years of his life, al-Zaḳḳāḳ was *k͟haṭīb* in the mosque of al-Andalus at Fās. Some of his descendants were also famous scholars.

Bibliography: Ibn al-Ḳāḍī, *D͟jad͟hwat al-iḳtibās*, ii, 476-7, no. 532, and *Durrat al-ḥid͟jāl*, iii, 252; Aḥmad al-Mand͟jūr, *Fihris*, Rabat 1976, 57; Aḥmad Bāba, *Nayl*, 211; Ben Cheneb, *Étude*, 123-4, no. 70; Brockelmann, II, 264; S II, 376; Ziriklī, iv, 320; Kaḥḥāla, vii, 169; J. Berque, *Ville et université. Aperçu sur l'histoire de l'école de Fès*, in *Revue Historique du Droit Français et Étranger*, lxiv, no. 116 (1949), 90; M. Hajji, *L'activité intellectuelle au Maroc à l'époque Saʿdide*, 2 vols. Rabat 1976-7, i, 171; F. Rodríguez Mediano, *Familias de Fez (siglos XV-XVII)*, Madrid 1995, 62, 199, 225, 260-1. (MARIBEL FIERRO)

ZAḲḲŪM (A.), a tree that figures in Islamic eschatology as growing in Hell, with bitter fruit which the damned are condemned to eat. It is mentioned in the Ḳurʾān three times (XXXVII, 60/62; XLIV, 43; LVI, 52).

The lexicographers explain it as an evil-smelling tree that grows in the Tihāma, but also as a medically beneficial one that grows in the Jordan valley around Jericho; and as a foodstuff of the Arabs, composed of fresh butter with dates (see Lane, 1239a-b). Richard Bell, *The Qurʾān translated*, ii, 556 n. 1, cited as a parallel the same word in Syriac meaning "the hogbean"; Bell must have taken from Payne Smith, *Thesaurus Syriacus*, col. 1148, *zḳwmʾ/zāḳōmā*, citing the agricultural treatise *Geoponika*, 115 l. 20, in which *zḳwmʾ* are something dried in front of a fire before eating, and where the word is probably a corruption of *ḳwmʾ*

and its Greek equivalent κύσμοι "lentils". In any case, it seems a long way from a tree with bitter fruit.

Bibliography: Given in the article.

(C.E. Bosworth)

ZAKLISE, the Ottoman Turkish name for the Greek island of Zakynthos, Ital. Zacinto, Fr. and Eng. Zante, the southernmost of the Ionian islands, lying off the westernmost tip of the Peloponnese [see MORA].

Lost to Byzantium in 1185, it passed under the control of various Western powers until 1328 when it was seized by the Italian Tocco family, whose Ionian Islands dominions were to prosper till the later 15th century, receiving large numbers of refugees from the Greek mainland. Zakynthos, together with Cephalonia and Levkas/Aya Mavra [see LEVKAS], was briefly captured in late 1479 by Aḥmed Pas̲h̲a Gedik [*q.v.*], but recovered in the next year by Count Leonardo III Tocco. In 1483, however, the Toccos were driven out by Venice, who secured possession of it and Cephalonia by an annual tribute to the Ottoman sultan, maintained until 1699 (see D. Pitcher, *The historical geography of the Ottoman empire*, Leiden 1972, 65, 86-7, 132 and Map XVI; P. Soustal and J. Koder, *Nikopolis und Kephallonia*, Vienna 1981, 77 ff., 278-9; arts. *Ionian Sea*, *Zakynthos* and *Tocco*, in *The Oxford dict. of Byzantium*, New York-Oxford 1991).

In the long Venetian period, Zakynthos suffered numerous Ottoman naval attacks and raids, in the 16th century commanded by K̲h̲ayr al-Dīn Pas̲h̲a, Ṭorg̲h̲ud Reʾīs and ʿUlūdj ʿAlī [*q.vv.*] (see W. Miller, *The Latins in the Levant*, London 1908, 483 ff.; idem, *The Ionian Islands under Venetian rule*, in *EHR*, xliii [1928], 209-39; A. Krantonelle, *History of piracy in the Tourkokratia*, 2 vols. Athens 1985-91, in Greek). Zakynthians participated in the battle of Lepanto in 1571, in the Russian-incited insurrection of 1770 and in the Greek War of Independence, when the island became a base for insurgents. It had been ceded by the Venetians to the French by the Treaty of Campo Formio (1797); there was a brief Russo-Turkish occupation (1799-1807); a French re-occupation (1807-14); and finally, it became a British protectorate until 1864, when the Ionian Islands were ceded to the kingdom of Greece.

Bibliography: In addition to references in the article, see the following sources in Greek: art. *Zakynthos*, in *Megalē Hellenikē Enkyklopaideia*², xi, Athens 1964, 897-9; L. Zoes, *History of Zakynthos*, Athens 1957; D. Konomos, *Zakynthian chronicles, 1485-1953*, Athens 1970; idem, *Zakynthos, 500 years (1478-1978)*, 3 vols. Athens 1979-81; A. Vakalopoulos, *History of modern Hellenism* (in Grk.), Thessalonica 1968-88, index.

(A. Savvides)

ZALĪDJ (A., pl. *zalāʾidj*, also *zallīdj*, a word somehow related to Perso-Arabic *lādjward/lāzward* "lapis lazuli" (see Dozy, *Supplément*, i, 598; idem and W.H. Engelmann, *Glossaire des mots espagnols et portugais dérivés de l'arabe*, ²Leiden 1869, 229), a mosaic composed of fragments of pottery squares with a coloured enamelled surface. The technique involved is more one of marquetry than mosaic, since the pieces are cut into shape according to the place they will occupy in the motif as a whole (G. Audisio, *La marquetterie de terre émaillée (mosaïque de faïence) dans l'art musulman d'Occident*, Algiers 1926, 8). Also attested for this technique is the Spanish term *alicatado* (see Dozy and Engelmann, *op. cit.*, 140). The usage of the term is essentially a Hispano-Mag̲h̲ribī one; the Moroccan traveller Ibn Baṭṭūṭa [*q.v.*] compared *ḳās̲h̲ānī* tiles on the buildings of Nadjaf in ʿIrāḳ with the *zalīdj* of his own country (*Riḥla*, i, 415, tr. Gibb, i, 256).

The technique is first attested in ancient Persia and Mesopotamia, e.g. on the palace of Sargon (Seton Lloyd, *The art of the ancient Near East*, London 1963), and then used by the Romans and Byzantines. The use of pieces of marble of different colours runs through the centuries, to appear in a rather clumsy fashion in the Great Mosque of Cordova and in certain pavements at al-Madīna al-Zahrāʾ [*q.v.*]. For *zalīdj stricto sensu*, the main attestation is at the Ḳalʿat Banī Ḥammād [see ḤAMMĀDIDS] (5th/11th century), where one finds enamelled bricks and genuine marquetry (G. Marçais, *Poteries et faïences de la Kalaa des Beni-Hammad*, Constantine 1913). After this, there is the minaret of the Kutubiyya in Marrakesh (586/1190), then the Great Mosque at Tlemcen/Tilimsān (679/1280), where Saldjūḳ influence from Konya is discernible, culminating in the Alhambra at Granada. The Western Islamic lands acquired the appropriate technology and seem to have been culturally propitious for a widening use—perhaps delayed by Almohad austerity—of the art of *zalīdj*, seen in its spread within the dynastic art of the Marīnids and Naṣrids [*q.vv.*].

At first, this use of enamelled marquetry work, resistant to weather, appears on exteriors, and especially on minarets and door surrounds (Chella near Rabat, and Tlemcen) and on the retaining walls of patios. But in the 8th/14th century it was interior use, within rooms that were lived in (especially at Seville and Granada and, to a lesser extent, at Fās), that provide the finest aesthetic usage of *zalīdj*: on pavements, niches, walls and columns, though only exceptionally in *miḥrāb*s and prayer halls. Artists preferred flat surfaces, with symmetrical and repeating designs, usually on the lower parts of surfaces. Animal and human motifs are not found; the few epigraphic examples of these are to be found at Tlemcen and, above all, in the Alhambra (Tower of the Captive, Hall of the Two Sisters). The difficulty of cutting fragments with curved edges explains the rarity of floral decorations, although delicate curvilinear designs are to be found at the Alhambra (the above examples and the Hall of Ambassadors). Likewise rare, apart from a few Egyptian examples, are epigraphic motifs, difficult to execute. Use of the Kūfic script would have allowed the formation of curves and reverse curves, but was no longer fashionable in the 8th/14th century in the Muslim West, where arrangements and geometrical patterns reigned supreme. Rectilinear elements, combined with infinitely repetitive geometrical patterns, characterised Marīnid and Naṣrid decoration, which was inspired by Berber traditions but was adapted to Islamic taste.

Bibliography (in addition to references in the article): W. and G. Marçais, *Les monuments arabes de Tlemcen*, Paris 1903, i, 79; J. Hoedgecoe and S. Samur, *Zillīg. L'art de la céramique marocaine*, Damlugi 1993; J. Zozaya, *Alicatados y azulejos hispano-musulmanes: los origenes*, in *La céramique médiévale en Méditerranée. Actes du VIᵉ Congrès de l'AIECMM*, Aix-en-Provence 1997, 601-13.

(A. Bazzana)

AL-**ZALLĀḲA**, a decisive battle which took place in Muslim Spain near Badajoz (479/1086) and was won by the Almoravids [see AL-MURĀBIṬŪN] in their first encounter with Alfonso VI of Castile.

Alfonso's capture of Toledo (478/1085) posed a great threat to the *Ṭāʾifa* princes of al-Andalus, driving them to seek the help of the Almoravid sovereign of Morocco, Yūsuf b. Tās̲h̲ufīn [*q.v.*], who responded to their appeal and called on the Andalusī *amīr*s to join his campaign. On learning of the advance of the Muslim troops, Alfonso raised his siege of Saragossa and sought help from Sancho Ramírez of Aragon and from other Christians beyond the Pyrenees. The ensuing encounter thus assumed the character of a holy war, just one decade before the first Crusade in the East.

The battle of al-Zallāḳa (Span. Sagrajas) took place on the plain of the latter name on the banks of the Guerrero, some 8 km/5 miles north-east of Badajoz, on Friday 12 Radjab 479/23 October 1086; hence the reference to the battle in Arabic sources as *Yawm (al-)ʿarūba* ("Friday encounter").

It is quite clear from the eyewitness account of ʿAbd Allāh b. Buluggīn, the Zīrid *amīr* of Granada, that, in contrast to Alfonso's eagerness to engage in battle, Yūsuf b. Tās̲h̲ufīn was extremely reluctant to do so and even hoped that Alfonso would give up and withdraw.

The Andalusī contingents were led by al-Muʿtamid b. ʿAbbād [*q.v.*], king of Seville, while the Almoravid troops were deployed in such a way as to enable them to join battle as required. When the latter failed to arrive, however, some of the Andalusīs sought refuge within the city walls of Badajoz. The Almoravid sovereign, in the meantime, despatched a force to set fire to Alfonso's encampment, while he himself joined the fray with his big drums resounding like thunder in the hills and wreaking havoc on Alfonso's troops and horses. According to Ibn Abī Zarʿ, it was the Almoravid himself who set fire to Alfonso's encampment and then launched an attack on the Christian troops from the rear, annihilating most of them. Alfonso is said to have escaped with barely 500 survivors.

Details in Arabic sources about the battle have reached us primarily through the exaggerated accounts of later Muslim chroniclers such as al-Ḥimyarī, Ibn Abī Zarʿ and the anonymous author of the *Ḥulal.* It is surprising that the Zīrid *amīr* of Granada, himself a participant in the battle, has little to say about it. He simply refers to the encounter as the battle of Badajoz, and he does not give the day or date on which it took place, nor does he mention his role or that of other Andalusīs in the battle. All that he says is that Alfonso mounted a surprise attack, that Muslim troops were outnumbered, and that the Almoravid sovereign returned to Seville "safe and victorious" (*ʿalā ḥāli salāmat^in^ wa-naṣr*). Could it be that the Zīrid's brief and somewhat casual account is due to the fact that he and other Andalusīs did not distinguish themselves?

His defeat at al-Zallāḳa cost Alfonso the loss of a large number of his seasoned troops, checked the progress of the Reconquista, stopped the payment of tributes to Alfonso by the *Ṭāʾifa amīr*s and, above all, revived the hopes and raised the morale of the Andalusīs. The Almoravid sovereign's popularity with the Andalusī masses and, of course, with the *fuḳahāʾ*, was greatly enhanced. Although the Almoravids did not attempt to recover Toledo, their intervention helped to prolong Muslim presence in al-Andalus, which, to quote al-Marrākus̲h̲ī, had been on the verge of being handed over to the Christians.

Bibliography: 1. Sources. Anon, *al-Ḥulal al-maws̲h̲iyya*, ed. I.S. Allouche, Rabat 1936, 36-56; Ibn Abī Zarʿ, *al-Anīs al-muṭrib bi-rawḍ al-ḳirṭās*, ed. C.J. Tornberg, Uppsala 1846, 93-8 (Sp. tr. Huici Miranda, i, Valencia 1964, 281-93); ʿAbd Allāh b. Buluggīn, *Tibyān*, ed. A. Ṭībī, Rabat 1995, 121-5, Eng. tr., Leiden 1986, 113-17; Ḥimyarī, *al-Rawḍ al-miʿṭār*, ed. I. ʿAbbās, Beirut 1975, 287-92, Fr. tr. Lévi-Provençal, *La Péninsule Iberique*... Leiden 1938, 103-16; Marrākus̲h̲ī, *Muʿdjib*, ed. ʿAryān and ʿAlamī, Cairo 1949, 132-5; Maḳḳarī, *Nafḥ*, iv, ed. ʿAbbās, Beirut 1968, 354-70; R. Dozy, *Scriptorum ar. loci de Abbadidis*, ii, Leiden 1852.

2. Studies. A. Huici Miranda, *Los Almorávides y la batalla de Zallaca*, in *Hesp.*, xl (1953), 17-76; idem, *Las Grandes Batallas de la reconquista*..., Madrid 1956, 19-82; E. Lévi-Provençal *et al.*, *Novedades sobre la batalla llamada de al-Zallaqa (1086)*, in *And.*, xv (1950), 111-55; R. Menéndez Pidal, *La España del Cid*, i, Madrid 1969, 330-9; Dozy, *Histoire des musulmans d'Espagne*, new ed. Paris 1932, 126-30; A. Ṭībī, *Waḳʿat al-Zallāḳa*, in *Dirāsāt wa-buḥūt̲h̲ fī taʾrīk̲h̲ al-Mag̲h̲rib wa 'l-Andalus*, Tripoli-Tunis 1984, 156-71.

(AMIN TIBI)

ZALZAL, Manṣūr b. Djaʿfar al-Ḍārib, famous lute-player at the early ʿAbbāsid court. He was a dark-skinned *muwallad* of humble, possibly "Nabatean" origin from Kūfa [see BARṢAWMA, in Suppl.]. Under the tuition of Ibrāhīm al-Mawṣilī [*q.v.*], his future brother-in-law who gave him an education in "Arab music" (*al-g̲h̲ināʾ al-ʿarabī*), he became one of the rare musicians to be proverbially known as an instrumentalist without being a singer (*aṭrab min ʿūd Zalzal*). He seems first to have appeared at court under the caliph al-Mahdī (*r.* 158-69/775-85). Under Hārūn al-Ras̲h̲īd (*r.* 170-93/786-809) he reached the highest class (*ṭabaḳa*) of court musicians. His best known pupil in lute playing was Isḥāḳ al-Mawṣilī [*q.v.*]. During his lifetime, Zalzal had a well dug in the southern suburbs of Bag̲h̲dād, and thus for centuries the place and the neighbouring quarter were known as Birkat Zalzal.

After having been imprisoned by Hārūn al-Ras̲h̲īd, he is said to have died in 174/790. This date, mentioned by Ibn Tag̲h̲rībirdī (who describes Zalzal as a lute player *and* a singer, and a *mawlā* of ʿĪsā b. Djaʿfar b. al-Manṣūr), can be questioned. Isḥāḳ al-Mawṣilī states that Zalzal's imprisonment under Hārūn al-Ras̲h̲īd lasted for "about ten years", hence, when he was released "his hair and his beard had whitened". Accordingly, he may have died between *ca.* 185/801 and 193/809. In a *k̲h̲abar* related in *Ag̲h̲ānī*[3], v, 280-2, Zalzal is still the hero of a contest with the lute player Mulāḥiẓ in the presence of the caliph al-Wāt̲h̲iḳ (*r.* 227-32/842-7). This text, however, seems to suffer from inconsistency and anachronism. Zalzal's famous name may have slipped into the story to replace that of the less well-known lute player Rabrab, who was a contemporary of Mulāḥiẓ (*ibid.*, xi, 337).

In the history of music, Zalzal finds a place as the inventor of a lute called *ʿūd al-s̲h̲abbūṭ* on account of its shape resembling the round and flat fish of that name. His name is also connected with the introduction of the middle, or neutral, third among the frets (*dasātīn*) of the lute. The interval was called *wusṭā Zalzal* and first described by al-Fārābī [*q.v.*]. It is the characteristic interval of the main mode of Arab music called *rāst* (see MAḲĀM). Al-Fārābī placed it at the ratio of 27:22 between the nut and the bridge of the lute (355 Cents above the pitch of the open string). This corresponds to the modern note *sīkāh* as given by 19th and 20th-century theoreticians from Syria and Egypt (Collangettes; Amīn al-Dīk). Ibn Sīnā defined the *wusṭā Zalzal* differently by giving it the ratio of 39:32 (342 Cents). His value reappeared also in the 19th century, namely, in the scale of Mīk̲h̲āʾīl Mus̲h̲āḳa [*q.v.*].

Bibliography: 1. Sources. *Ag̲h̲ānī*[3], v, 197, 201-2, 211, 227, 241, 271-2, 275, vi, 298, 304, x, 194, xix, 294, xx, 358-9; (Ps.-)Djāḥiẓ, *al-Tādj fī ak̲h̲lāḳ al-mulūk*, Cairo 1914, 38-41, *passim*, tr. Ch. Pellat, *Le livre de la couronne*, Paris 1954, 65, 67-8; Ibn ʿAbd Rabbih, *al-ʿIḳd al-farīd*, Cairo 1949, vi, 31, 37, tr.

H.G. Farmer, *The minstrels of the golden age of Islam*, in *IC*, xvii (1943), 271-81, xviii (1944), 53-61, esp. 53, 58; Wa<u>sh</u><u>sh</u>āʾ, *Muwa<u>sh</u><u>sh</u>ā*, Beirut 1965, 257; Fārābī, *K. al-Mūsīḳī al-kabīr*, Cairo 1967, 127-8, tr. R. d'Erlanger, *La musique arabe*, Paris 1930-59, i, 47-8; <u>Kh</u>ʷārazmī, *Mafātīḥ al-ʿulūm*, Leiden 1895, 239; Ibn al-Ḳifṭī, *Inbāh al-ruwāt*, Cairo 1950-4, ii, 272-3; Yāḳūt, *Buldān*, i, 592-3; Ibn Ta<u>gh</u>rībirdī, *Nu<u>dj</u>ūm*, Cairo ii, 78, 139, 281.

2. Studies. G. Le Strange, *Baghdād during the ʿAbbāsid caliphate*, Oxford 1900, 61-2; M. Collangettes, *Étude sur la musique arabe*, in *JA*, 10ᵉ série, iv (1904), 365-422, esp. 403-5; H.G. Farmer, *A history of Arabian music*, London 1929, 118-19 and index; idem, *Studies in Oriental music*, Frankfurt 1997, ii, 107-8, 185-7; M.A. al-Ḥifnī, *al-Mūsīḳā al-ʿarabiyya wa-aʿlāmuhā min al-<u>dj</u>āhiliyya ilā 'l-Andalus*, Cairo 1951, 170-4; L. Zolondek, *Diʿbil b. ʿAlī*, Lexington 1961, 62 (poem no. CL), cf. ʿA. al-A<u>sh</u>tar, *<u>Sh</u>iʿr Diʿbil b. ʿAlī*, Damascus 1983, 197-8, 517; A. Taymūr, *al-Mūsīḳā wa 'l-<u>gh</u>ināʾ ʿind al-ʿarab*, Cairo 1963, 80, 98-9; L. Manik, *Das arabische Tonsystem im Mittelalter*, Leiden 1969, 42, 48, 124, 126, 130 and index; E. Neubauer, *Der Bau der Laute und ihre Besaitung nach arabischen, persischen und türkischen Quellen des 9. bis 15. Jahrhunderts*, in *ZGAIW*, viii (1993), 279-378, esp. 298-9, 331.

(H.G. Farmer-[E. Neubauer])

ZALZALA (a.), also Zilzāl, pl. *zalāzil*, earthquake, a fact of life in many parts of the Islamic world, from Morocco to Southeast Asia, a zone that coincides in large part with the great Alpide belt stretching from the Azores to the Indonesian archipelago. Along this zone of collision between the Eurasian plate to the north and various smaller tectonic plates to the south, the main areas of activity within the Islamic heartlands are the Anatolian fault zone, the Dead Sea-Jordan transform fault system, the Red Sea and Gulf of Aden, the Alburz and Zagros ranges in Iran and the Chaman fault in Afghanistan (see Fisher, 11-23; Blake *et al.*, 26-7; Balland, 636-9; Gupta, 61-71; Barazangi; Jackson and McKenzie). (See Fig. 1.)

Earthquakes in Islamic belief, cosmology and science

The earliest surviving study of earthquakes in the Muslim world was written by <u>Dj</u>alāl al-Dīn al-Suyūṭī, the Egyptian polymath (d. 911/1505 [*q.v.*]). His *Ka<u>sh</u>f al-ṣalṣala ʿan waṣf al-zalzala* lists some 130 earthquakes that occurred in the area from Spain to Transoxania, and was inspired by reading a report of the large earthquake of 702/1303 that was strongly felt in Egypt (al-Suyūṭī, 54-5; Ambraseys, Melville and Adams, 44). It is based on a thorough survey of the work of Muslim traditionists and Arabic chroniclers and is the fundamental source for understanding the mediaeval Islamic perception and knowledge of earthquakes (see, especially, Clément).

The name *Sūrat al-zalzala* is given to one of the early chapters of the Ḳurʾān (sūra XLIX), and the imagery of this verse, particularly the phrase *a<u>kh</u>ra<u>dj</u>at al-arḍ a<u>th</u>ḳālahā* "The earth brought forth its burdens", is often used to convey the terror of earthquakes, regarded as one of the forerunners of the Day of Judgement (*yawm al-ḳiyāma* [see ḳiyāma]; cf. Ḳurʾān, XVII, 58-9). Another Ḳurʾānic phrase "We turned their uppermost nethermost" (XI, 84; XV, 74) is also frequently found as a descriptive formula. There is disagreement over whether sūra XLIX is a late Meccan or early Medinan revelation. The experience of earthquakes that possibly lies behind it is recorded in the earliest Islamic traditions (*ḥadī<u>th</u>*), involving the Prophet and his Companions. Following an ancient chronological practice of naming years after a universally significant (and memorable) occurrence, the 5th year of the *hi<u>dj</u>ra* (626-7) was called the "Year of the Earthquake", according to al-Bīrūnī (*al-Ā<u>th</u>ār al-bāḳiya*, 31), apparently with reference to an event in Medina. The very birth of Muḥammad is said to have been heralded by an earthquake that shook the idols in the Kaʿba and damaged the palace of the <u>Kh</u>usraws at Ctesiphon (al-Yaʿḳūbī, i, 5; al-Suyūṭī, 21), clearly a literary fiction. Several stories concerning Muḥammad and the first caliphs give an anthropomorphic portrayal of the earth, which does not know what it is doing and needs correction; ʿUmar b. al-<u>Kh</u>aṭṭāb is particularly violent in lashing the earth with his whip to restore it to order (see e.g. al-Suyūṭī, 22; cf. Clément, 265).

Al-Bīrūnī [*q.v.*] is conspicuous among mediaeval authors for his scientific discussion of geological processes, touching on the effects of earthquakes (e.g. in his *Taḥdīd*, 20-3), and citing Ibn al-ʿAmīd's lost work on the construction of cities, which seems to have taken a practical approach to earthquake hazard. On the whole, Classical theories that attributed earthquakes to subterranean winds or escaping gasses, formulated particularly by Aristotle (*Meteorologica*, 2.7-8, and developed by Seneca, *Naturales quaestiones*, 6.16-17, 20) and probably adopted by Muslim authors such as al-Kindī (see his lost work listed in Ibn al-Nadīm's *Fihrist*, 261; cf. Taher, *Traité*, 133), did not enjoy much currency. In so far as a physical or mechanical cause was envisaged, earthquakes were explained as the movement of the bull on whose horns the world rests, or of the fish which in turn supports the bull, though logically any such movement would shake the whole world rather than a specific region. Similar, but more precise, was the explanation that each territory was underlain by a root that went back to the mountain of Ḳāf [*q.v.*] which encircles the earth; when God wished to punish a people, he ordered the angel in charge to animate the appropriate root (al-Suyūṭī, 1, 3). Al-Muṭahhar al-Maḳdisī (*al-Badʾ wa 'l-taʾrī<u>kh</u>*, ed. Huart, ii, 37, tr. ii, 35), would only accept this tradition on the doubtful authority of the *Ahl al-Kitāb*, and says its purpose was to popularise the idea that God was the prime mover, rather than an independent natural cause. Other early Arabic geographers and historians also had a reasonably "philosophical" view of earthquakes, though note al-Muḳaddasī's response to the destruction of Sīrāf on the Persian Gulf (cited in Miquel, iii, 105), similar to Abu 'l-Dardāʾ's sermon following an earthquake in Damascus in the mid-7th century (al-Maḳdisī, *loc. cit.*).

After the 10th-11th centuries, Muslim theory more generally eschewed even such pseudo-physical explanations and regarded earthquakes simply as the signs of God's will, being sent either to assist, or to warn, or, more usually, to terrify and punish the people, each type of sin meriting a particular correction. However, in view of the numerous contradictions in the writings of the theologians and traditionists, al-Suyūṭī preferred to view earthquakes rather as a sign of God's majesty and power (Clément, 272, 275-8). A later author, Ibn al-<u>Dj</u>azzār, writing in the aftermath of the earthquake of 984/1576, considers even the level of detail given by al-Suyūṭī to be redundant and in bad taste (cf. Taher, *Traité*, 133).

Nevertheless, in common with their European counterparts, Middle Eastern chroniclers were interested in recording earthquakes along with other natural phenomena. Some, such as Ibn al-<u>Dj</u>awzī [*q.v.*], evidently believed that it was among their primary concerns and functions (cf. Rosenthal, 144-5 [on Ibn al-<u>Dj</u>awzī],

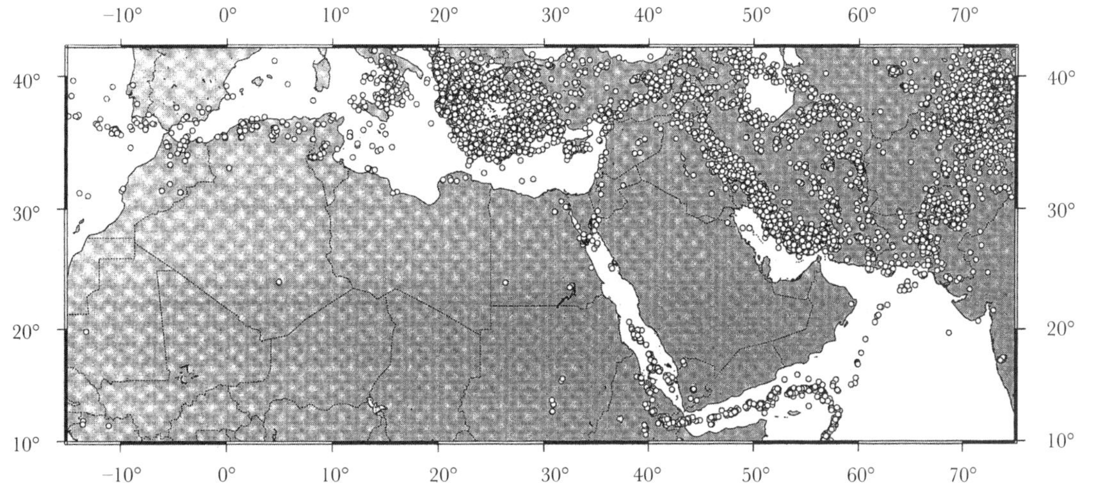

Fig. 1. Earthquakes from 1964 to 1997 (International Seismological Centre).

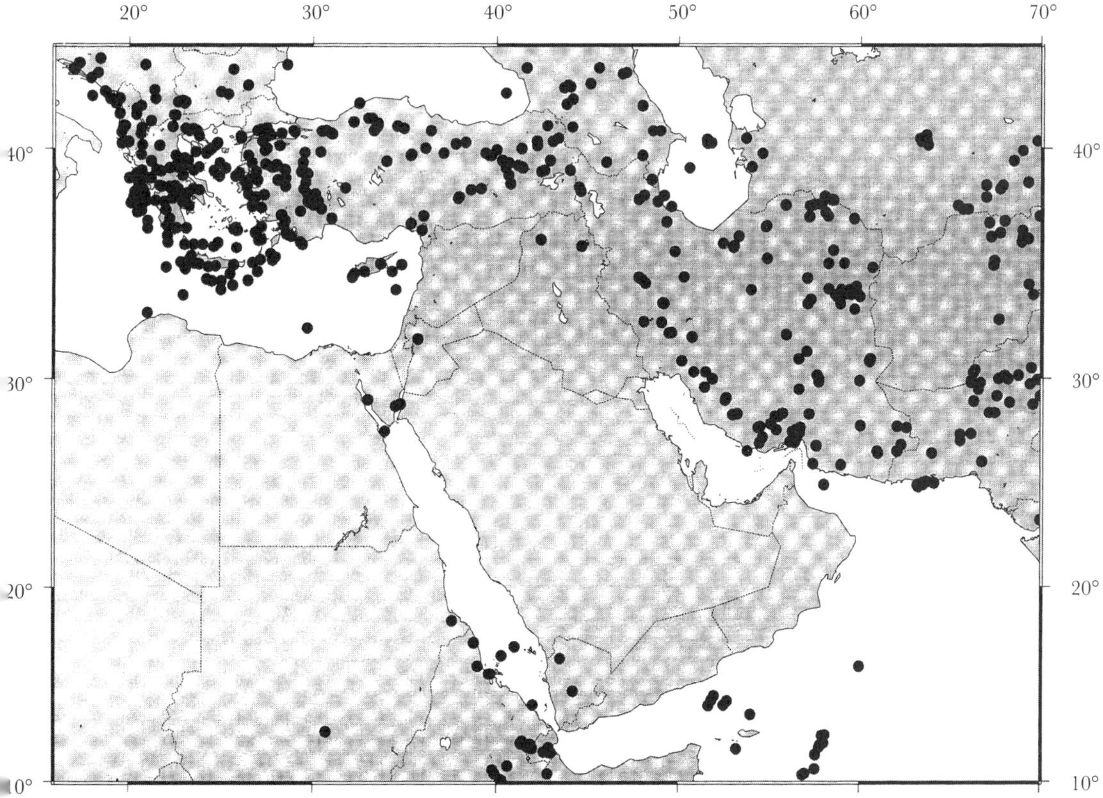

Fig. 2. Earthquakes of magnitude 6 and greater, 1900-98 (J.A. Jackson, *pers. comm.*).

252, 488). News of earthquakes and the destruction they might have caused was, of course, a matter of practical concern, and large events could be reported with a certain amount of detail, including (most usefully for the purpose of modern assessments of seismic activity) the names of the places affected. One outstanding example of this is the report of an earthquake round Ibb in Yemen in 549/1154 (Ambraseys, Melville and Adams, 34-7; al-Maneefi, esp. 151-62), evidently based on a detailed field investigation by al-ʿArash̲ānī. Nevertheless, the title of his (lost) work, *al-Mawāʿiẓ wa 'l-ʿibar*, indicates that here as elsewhere, if any gloss was put on the report of an earthquake by historians, it was normally that the event was a portent of some political or social upheaval (see Ambraseys, Melville and Adams, 7, for some examples), or, as with the theologians, understood as a punishment from God, which encouraged people to repent of their sins (*ibid.*, see index). Al-ʿArash̲ānī also composed another work called *al-Zalāzil wa 'l-ash̲rāṭ* (Taher, *Traité*, 134), probably with the same orientation. Despite such views, in general the chroniclers do provide a full and often quite factual account of the seismicity of the region and of the largest events that have occurred.

Survey of regional seismicity

Apart from the work of al-Suyūṭī, no reliable integrated catalogue of Middle Eastern seismicity exists. Early works by Tholozan (1879) and Sieberg (1932) were inaccurate and incomplete; the derivative list by Ben-Menahem (1979) for the Levantine Middle East, and the work of Poirier and Taher (1980) for the historical period, based on primary sources (see Taher, *Corpus*), are the most comprehensive in their scope. For the best part of 40 years, the work of N.N. Ambraseys has dominated the field and inspired numerous studies of different regions and periods, the most substantial being on Persia, Egypt and Turkey (Ambraseys, *A reappraisal*). A significant contribution has also been made by researchers taking the Mediterranean world as their focus (e.g. Bousquet *et al.*; Guidoboni *et al.*). This modern, long-term research, which has concentrated on retrieving archaeological and historical evidence of earthquakes in the region as well as early seismological data, though still in progress, has greatly expanded the information available about the seismicity of the Middle East and adjacent areas.

Fig. 2 shows the pattern of the largest earthquakes in the central part of the region since 1900 (magnitude greater than 6.0). As can be seen, many parts of the Islamic lands do not show up strongly on such modern maps of world seismicity, although a few recent events indicate that the risk can be serious, particularly in view of increasing population and poor building techniques. Thus the Agadir (Morocco) earthquake of 29 February 1960, though of moderate size (magnitude 5.9) was responsible for 12,000 deaths. The town was previously destroyed by an earthquake in 1731. In Algeria, the total destruction of El Asnam (Orléansville) on 10 October 1980 by a magnitude 7.3 earthquake was foreshadowed by a smaller but equally disastrous event on 9 September 1954 (M = 6.8), and earlier destructive earthquakes in central Algeria in 1716 and Oran in 1790. The recent seismicity of Tunisia and Libya is low, though an earthquake of magnitude 5.4 caused damage and around 300 casualties at Barce in Cyrenaica on 21 February 1963. Historical evidence is also rather sparse for North Africa, partly due to a dearth of sources and low population density in most of the region. For further details and references, see Adams and Barazangi, 1012-13; Ambraseys and Vogt; Vogt and Ambraseys; Ambraseys, *Libya*; Ambraseys, Melville and Adams.

Similarly, there is no evidence of earthquakes in the Sudan before the mid-19th century (Ambraseys and Adams), despite the occurrence of a large event in southern Sudan on 20 May 1990 (M = 7.2). To the north, however, Egypt has a long history of recorded earthquakes, though few were sufficient to cause significant damage (see Tucker). Most of the stronger shocks experienced originated outside Egyptian territory, in the Hellenic Arc (such as the 702/1303 earthquake) to the north or in the Gulf of Suez–Gulf of Aqaba to the east (e.g. the events of 1212, 996/1588 and 1969). In Egypt itself, the earthquake of 12 October 1992 (M = 5.2), with an epicentre about 10 km south of Old Cairo, caused heavy damage to over 9,000 buildings, killed over 500 people and injured 6,500, a reflection largely of the high vulnerability of the ageing building stock. A previous earthquake on 7 August 1847 was probably a similar event and caused widespread damage and loss of life between Cairo and Beni Suef (Ambraseys, Melville and Adams).

The Arabian Peninsula is one of the most stable areas of the world and it is only in Yemen, in the southwest corner, that significant events have occurred (Ambraseys and Melville, *Yemen*), most recently the D̲h̲amār earthquake of 13 December 1982 (M = 6.1), which killed about 2,500 people. Seismicity in this region occurs mainly offshore along the zone of seafloor spreading in the Red Sea and Gulf of Aden. In northern Ḥid̲j̲āz, however, several large earthquakes have been reported in historical times that have not recurred in the instrumental period, notably in 259/873 (al-Yaʿḳūbī, ii, 624), 460/1068 (Ibn al-Bannā', 250-1, 256; Ibn al-D̲j̲awzī, viii, 256), and 996/1588 (al-S̲h̲ād̲h̲ilī, 64; al-Isḥāḳī, 154), all apparently affecting the area round Taymā' and Tabūk on the Pilgrimage route (Ambraseys and Melville, *Evidence*; Ambraseys, Melville and Adams, 27, 36-2, 56-7). These events are to be associated with the southern end of the Dead Sea fault system at the northwest boundary of the Arabian plate.

It is particularly in this area that the past century of instrumental observation is not representative of the longer-term seismicity. The Dead Sea zone has been extremely active in historical times, in clusters of activity within a few decades, alternating with long periods of seismic quiescence (Ambraseys and Barazangi). The earliest periods are covered by Russell, partly on the basis of archaeological data (see also Guidoboni *et al.*). In the 12th century, Crusader and Arabic sources report major earthquakes on 12 August 1157, 29 June 1170 and 20 May 1202 (Poirier *et al.*; Ambraseys and Melville, *An analysis*), the second of which interrupted campaigning with a temporary truce (Lyons and Jackson, 39). In the early 15th century, a series of destructive shocks culminated in a severe earthquake on 29 December 1408 round Antioch (Ambraseys and Melville, *Faulting*) and again in the 18th century, a disastrous earthquake in the Biḳāʿ (Bekaa) Valley on 25 November 1759 killed between 10 and 40,000 people according to contemporary estimates (Taher, *Textes*; Ambraseys and Barazangi, 4011). The visual evidence for the damage in Baalbek has been investigated by Lewis. All these events were associated with surface faulting and, together with a series of similar events to the northeast during the 19th century, help to delimit an East Anatolian Fault zone that does not show up on the basis of instrumental data (Ambraseys, *Temporary quiescence*). Details of other, smaller shocks in Syria and Palestine during the Ottoman period are presented by al-Ḥāfiẓ. One of the most severe earthquakes of this century, on 11 July 1927, caused widespread damage and about 500 casualties in the region north of the Dead Sea (Kallner-Amiran, 234-6), but was only of moderate magnitude (M = 6.2).

In Turkey, the North Anatolian Fault zone, delineated by a series of surface ruptures during the present century, has been more or less continuously active throughout recorded history. The largest earthquakes this century (M > 7.0) include those of 9 August 1912 (Saros-Marmara), 26 December 1939 (Erzincan, with more than 30,000 deaths), 18 March 1953 (Yenice Valley), 28 March 1970 (Gediz) and 24 November 1976 (Çaldıran), all causing heavy loss of life (Ambraseys and Finkel, *The Saros-Marmara earthquake*; Ambraseys, *Engineering seismology*, 17-70). The largest historical event along this fault zone was the earthquake of 17 August 1668, felt throughout northern Anatolia, with an estimated magnitude between 7.8 and 8.0 (Ambraseys and Finkel, *The Anatolian earthquake*; eidem, *The seismicity of Turkey*). For earlier centuries, see Guidoboni *et al.*; Ambraseys and White; and for an assessment of risk in Turkey, Kolars).

The Alpide belt continuing east through northern Persia has been the focus of persistent heavy seismicity in both historical and modern times (Ambraseys and Melville, *Persian earthquakes*; de Planhol; Berberian, *Historical record*; idem, *Natural hazards*; Taher, *Grandes zones*). As in the case of Turkey, most of the largest events have also been associated with faulting, and have caused heavy casualties. Among the most significant, from both viewpoints, are the earthquakes of 23 January 1909 (Sīlākhūr), 1 May 1929 (Kopet Dāgh), 6 May 1930 (Salmās), 1 September 1962 (Buyīn Zahrā), 31 August 1968 (Dasht-i Bayāḍ), 16 September 1978 (Ṭabas-i Gulshan) and the recent disaster of 20 June 1990, which killed around 40,000 people in the Rūdbār-Mandjīl area of Gīlān. Given the vulnerability of traditional Persian adobe brick dwellings, even relatively small earthquakes can cause devastation in rural areas.

Among historical events of particular importance are the Ḳūmis (Dāmghān) earthquake of 242/856, a series of destructive shocks in Ādharbāydjān that have ruined the historical monuments of Tabrīz, particularly in 1721 and 1780 (Melville, *Tabriz*; Dhukā'; Berberian, *Natural hazards*, 172-98), and a series of earthquakes in Nīshāpūr that destroyed the mediaeval city (Melville, *Nishapur*). Among the other important cities of Persia, Kāshān was severely damaged by two earthquakes in the 18th century (in 1755 and 1778) (Rota) and Shīrāz suffered a series of damaging events in the 19th century (1812, 1824, 1853 and 1862). Iṣfahān, on the other hand, has seldom been affected by earthquakes, one of the reasons for the survival there of many historical structures, particularly minarets (cf. Mihdī, 86). In contrast with northern and eastern Persia (for which see also the recent study of the 1549 earthquake by Szuppe), the Zagros belt, though clearly delineated by the instrumental record of earthquakes, has generated relatively few large events, much of the deformation occurring along this zone being taken up aseismically. Most of the moderate to large events in ʿIrāḳ are associated with the Zagros folded belt; the pattern of historical seismicity (Alsinawi and Ghalib) is distorted by the influence of the chief cities, Mawṣil and Baghdād, on the survival of reported felt data.

Further east, significant activity has been observed on the west-east Herat fault and its extension into Badakhshān, and the north-south Chaman fault zones, the latter associated at its northern end, in historical times, with a violent earthquake north of Kabul on 6 July 1505, felt as far as Agra (Bābur, 247-8; Badā'ūnī, i, 421-2) and at its southern extremity with a magnitude 7.6 event that destroyed Quetta on 30 May 1935 (for further details and references, see Quittmeyer and Jacob; Balland; Gupta, 67-71; and KWAṬṬA). In the same general region, on the modern Indian-Pakistan border and not far from a massive earthquake off the Makrān coast in 1945 (M = 8.0), a major event on 16 June 1819 in the Rann of Cutch caused the formation of the "Allah Bund" along a fault escarpment, with a total vertical displacement of 7-9 metres. The land level changes associated with this event, extensively discussed by Lyell and later supported by Charles Darwin's observations in Chile, were fundamental to the birth of the science of geology. Eight hundred years earlier, al-Bīrūnī had taken for granted the uplift of land from the sea (e.g. *Taḥdīd*, 17-18, 20-1), though it is true he was considering long-term processes rather than extreme catastrophic events.

Bibliography: 1. Sources. Bābur, *Bābur-nāma*, tr. A.S. Beveridge, *Memoirs of Babur*, London 1921; Badā'ūnī, *Muntakhab al-tawārīkh*, tr. G.S. Ranking, Calcutta 1898; al-Muṭahhar al-Maḳdisī, *al-Badʾ wa 'l-taʾrīkh*, ed. and tr. Cl. Huart, *Le livre de la création et de l'histoire*, 3 vols., Paris 1899-1903; Bīrūnī, *al-Āthār al-bāḳiya*, ed. C.E. Sachau, Leipzig 1878; idem, *Taḥdīd nihāyat al-amākin*, tr. Jamal Ali, Beirut 1967; Ibn al-Nadīm, *Fihrist*; Ibn al-Bannā', tr. G. Makdisi, *Autograph diary of an eleventh-century historian of Baghdad, part II*, in *BSOAS*, xviii (1956), 239-60; Ibn al-Djawzī, *al-Muntaẓam*; Ibn al-Djazzār, *Taḥṣīn al-manāzil min hawl al-zalāzil*, see M.A. Taher, *Traité*; Iṣḥāḳī, *Laṭāʾif al-akhbār*, ed. Cairo 1310/1892; Muḥammad Mihdī, *Nisf-i djahān fī taʿrīf-i Isfahān*, ed. M. Sutūda, Tehran 1340/1961; Shādhilī, continuator of Suyūṭī, *Kashf al-ṣalṣala*, 62-4; Suyūṭī, *Kashf al-ṣalṣala ʿan waṣf al-zalzala*, ed. A. Saʿdānī, Fez 1971, Fr. tr. S. Nejjar, Rabat 1974; Yaʿḳūbī, *Taʾrīkh*.

2. Studies. R.D. Adams and M. Barazangi, *Seismotectonics and seismology in the Arab region: a brief summary and future plans*, in *Bull. Seism. Soc. Amer.* [= *BSSA*], lxxiv/3 (1984), 1011-30; S. Alsinawi and H. Ghalib, *Historical seismicity of Iraq*, in *ibid.*, lxv (1975), 541-7; N.N. Ambraseys, *Middle East—a reappraisal of the seismicity*, in *Qtly. Jnl. Engng. Geol.*, xi (1978), 19-32; idem, *Temporary seismic quiescence: SE Turkey*, in *Geophys. J.*, xcvi (1989), 311-31; idem, *Material for the investigation of the seismicity of Libya*, in *Libyan Studies*, xxv (1994), 7-22; idem, *Engineering seismology*, in *Earthq. Eng. and Struct. Dyn.*, xvii (1998), 1-105; Ambraseys and R.D. Adams, *Seismicity of the Sudan*, in *BSSA*, lxxvi/2 (1986), 483-93; Ambraseys and M. Barazangi, *The 1759 earthquake in the Bekaa Valley. Implications for earthquake hazard assessment in the eastern Mediterranean region*, in *J. Geophys. Res.* xliv, no. B4 (1989), 4007-13; Ambraseys and C.F. Finkel, *The Saros-Marmara earthquake of 9 August 1912*, in *Earthq. Eng. and Struct. Dyn.*, xv (1987), 189-211; eidem, *The Anatolian earthquake of 17 August 1668*, in W. Lee (ed.), *Historical seismograms and earthquakes of the world*, San Diego 1988, 173-80; eidem, *The seismicity of Turkey and adjacent areas. A historical review, 1500-1800*, Istanbul 1995; Ambraseys and J.A. Jackson, *Faulting associated with historical and recent earth-*

quakes in the Eastern Mediterranean region, in *Geophys. J. Int.*, cxxxiii (1998), 390-406; Ambraseys and C.P. Melville, *A history of Persian earthquakes*, Cambridge 1982; eidem, *Seismicity of Yemen*, in *Nature*, ccciii (1983), 321-3; eidem, *An analysis of the eastern Mediterranean earthquake of 20 May 1202*, in Lee (ed.) *Historical seismograms and earthquakes of the world*, 181-200; eidem, *Evidence for intraplate earthquakes in northwestern Arabia*, in *BSSA*, lxxix (1989), 1279-81; eidem, *Historical evidence of faulting in eastern Anatolia and northern Syria*, in *Annali di Geofisica*, xxxviii (1995), 337-43; Ambraseys, Melville and Adams, *The seismicity of Egypt, Arabia and the Red Sea. A historical review*, Cambridge 1994; Ambraseys and J. Vogt, *Materials for the investigation of the seismicity of the region of Algiers*, in *European Earthquake Engineering*, iii (1988), 16-29; Ambraseys and D. White, *The seismicity of the eastern Mediterranean region 550-1 BC: a re-appraisal*, in *J. Earthq. Eng.*, i (1997), 603-32; D. Balland, *Earthquakes. i. In Afghanistan*, in *EIr*, vii, 626-9; Barazangi, *A summary of the seismotectonics of the Arab region*, in K. Cidlinsky and B.M. Rouhban (eds.) *Assessment and mitigation of earthquake risk in the Arab region*, UNESCO 1983, 43-58; A. Ben-Menahem, *Earthquake catalogue for the Middle East 92 BC–1980 A.D.*, in *Boll. Geofis. Teor. i Applic.*, xxi (1979), 245-313; M. Berberian, *Natural hazards and the first earthquake catalogue of Iran. i. Historical hazards in Iran prior to 1900*, UNESCO 1994; idem, *Earthquakes. iv. The historical record of earthquakes in Persia*, in *EIr*, vii, 635-40; G. Blake, J. Dewdney and J. Mitchell (eds.), *The Cambridge atlas of the Middle East and North Africa*, Cambridge 1987; B. Bousquet, J.-J. Dufaure and P.-Y. Péchoux, *Connaître les séismes en Méditerranée: de la vision antique à la vision actuelle*, in *Tremblements de terre, histoire et archéologie*, Valbonne 1984, 23-37; J.-F. Clément, *Jalal al-Din al-Suyuti, séismosophe*, in *ibid.*, 253-87; X. de Planhol, *Earthquakes. iii. In Persia*, in *EIr*, vii, 633-5; Yaḥya D͟hukā', *Zamīnlarza-hā-yi Tabrīz*, Tehran 1368/1989; W.B. Fisher, *The Middle East*, [7]London 1978; E. Guidoboni, A. Comastri and G. Traini, *Catalogue of ancient earthquakes in the Mediterranian area up to the 10th century*, Publ. Istituto Nazion. di Geofisica, Rome 1994; H.K. Gupta, *Seismic hazard assessment in the Alpide belt from Iran to Burma*, in *Annali di Geofisica*, xxxvi/3-4 (1993), 61-82; M.M. al-Ḥāfiẓ, *Nuṣūṣ g͟hayr mans͟hūra ʿan al-zalāzil*, in *BEO*, xxxii-iii (1982), 256-64; J.A. Jackson and D. McKenzie, *Active tectonics of the Alpine-Himalayan belt between western Turkey and Pakistan*, in *Geophys. J.R. Astr. Soc.*, lxxvii (1984), 185-264; D.H. Kallner-Amiran, *A revised earthquake-catalogue of Palestine*, in *Israel Exploration J.*, i/4 (1950-1), 223-46, ii/1 (1952), 48-65; J. Kolars, *Earthquake-vulnerable populations in modern Turkey*, in *Geog. Review*, lxxii/1 (1982), 20-35; N.N. Lewis, *Baalbek before and after the earthquake of 1759: the drawings of James Bruce*, in *Levant*, xxxi (1999), 241-53; M.C. Lyons and D.E.P. Jackson, *Saladin. The politics of the Holy War*, Cambridge 1982; A.A.A. al-Maneefi, *Earthquake hazard and vulnerability in Yemen*, unpubl. PhD thesis, Imperial College, London 1995; C. Melville, *Earthquakes in the history of Nishapur*, in *Iran*, xviii (1980), 103-22; idem, *Historical monuments and earthquakes in Tabriz*, in *ibid.*, xix (1981), 159-71; A. Miquel, *La géographie humaine du monde musulman jusqu'au milieu du 11e siècle*, iii, Paris 1980; J.P. Poirier and M.A. Taher, *Historical seismicity in the Near and Midde East, North Africa, and Spain from Arabic documents (VIIth-XVIIIth century)*, in *BSSA*, lxx/6 (1980), 2185-2201; Poirier, B.A. Romanowicz and Taher, *Large, historical earthquakes and seismic risk in Northwest Syria*, in *Nature*, cclxxxv (1980), 21-20; R.C. Quittmeyer and K.H. Jacob, *Historical and modern seismicity of Pakistan, Afghanistan, northwestern India, and southeastern Iran*, in *BSSA*, lxix/3 (1979), 773-823; F. Rosenthal, *Muslim historiography*, Leiden 1968; G. Rota, *Some descriptions of earthquakes in XVII-XIX century Persian historical sources*, in *Annali di Ca' Foscari*, xxxvi/3 (1997), 459-69; K.W. Russell, *The earthquake chronology of Palestine and Northwest Arabia from the 2nd through the mid-8th century A.D.*, in *BASOR*, cclx (1985), 37-59; A. Sieberg, *Erdbeben und Bruchschollenbau im Östlichen Mittelmeergebiet*, in *Denk. d. Medizin.-Naturwiss. Ges. zu Jena*, xviii/2 (Jena 1932); M. Szuppe, *Un tremblement de terre dans le Qohestân, 956/1549*, in *St. Ir.* xviii/1 (1989), 59-75; Taher, *Traité de la fortification des demeures contre l'horreur des séismes*, in *AI*, xii (1974), 131-59; idem, *Textes d'histoires damascènes sur les tremblements de terre du XIIe siècle de l'hégire (XVII-XVIIIe s.)*, in *BEO*, xxvii (1975), 51-109; idem, *Corpus des textes arabes relatifs aux tremblements de terre et aux catastrophes naturelles de la conquête arabe au XII H./XVIII J.C.*, thèse de Doctorat d'Etat, Univ. of Paris I, 1979; idem, *Les grandes zones sismiques du monde musulman à travers l'histoire. I. L'Orient musulman*, in *AI*, xxx (1996), 89-104; J. Tholozan, *Sur les tremblements de terre qui ont eu lieu en Orient*, in *Comptes Rendues Acad. Sci.*, lxxxviii (1879), 1063-6; W.F. Tucker, *Natural disasters and the peasantry in Mamluk Egypt*, in *JESHO*, xxiv/2 (1981), 215-24; Vogt and Ambraseys, *Matériaux relatifs à la sismicité de l'Algérie occidentale au cours de la deuxième moitié du XIXe et au début du XXe siècle*, in *Méditerranée*, iv (1991), 39-45.

(C. Melville)

ZAMAKHSHAR, a small town of mediaeval Islamic K͟hʷārazm [*q.v.*].

It lay between the small town of Nūzwār and Gurgand͟j [*q.v.*], the later mediaeval capital of the province. In the 8th/14th century Ibn Baṭṭūṭa placed it as a village four miles from the "city of K͟hʷārazm", i.e. New Urgenč [*q.v.*], the city which had grown up after the Mongols had in 618/1221 devastated Old Urgenč (= the later Kunya/Kuhna "Old" Urgenč) (*Riḥla*, iii, 6, tr. Gibb and Beckingham, iii, 543). It never seems to have been of more than modest size. Al-Muḳaddasī, 289, mentions that in the later 4th/10th century it had a citadel, prison, congregational mosque, walls with iron gates and a protective ditch with bridges that were drawn up at night. Its subsequent fame came from its having been the birthplace in 467/1075 of the philologist and Ḳur'ān commentator Abu 'l-Ḳāsim Maḥmūd al-Zamak͟hs͟harī [*q.v.*]. Al-Samʿānī, *Ansāb*, ed. Ḥaydarābād, vi, 315-16, described it as "a large village like a small town". Whether it was sacked by the Mongols is unrecorded. Ibn Baṭṭūṭa implies that it was still in existence when he visited the great scholar's tomb (*kubba*) there in the first half of the 8th/14th century, but thereafter it fades from recorded history; Barthold, *Turkestan down to the Mongol invasion*[2], 148-9, thought that the modern ruins of Zmukhshir almost certainly mark the site of mediaeval Zamak͟hs͟har.

Bibliography: See also Le Strange, *The lands of the Eastern Caliphate*, 454, 456.

(C.E. Bosworth)

AL-**ZAMAK͟HS͟HARĪ**, Abu 'l-Ḳāsim Maḥmūd b. ʿUmar, called D͟jār Allāh, one of the outstanding scholars of later mediaeval Islamic times who made important contributions, first, in the fields of the linguistic sciences of grammar, philology, lexicography and the collecting of proverbs, in which sciences he was, despite his own Iranian descent, a strong proponent of the Arab cause *vis-à-vis* the Persophile partisans of the Shuʿūbiyya [*q.v.*]; and second, in the fields of theology and Ḳurʾān exegesis, his approach to these being that of the Muʿtazila [*q.v.*], of whom he may be considered as one of their last significant representatives. He was born at Zamakhshar [*q.v.*] in Khʷārazm on 27 Radjab 467/18 March 1075 and died at Djurdjāniyya in Khʷārazm on 10 Dhu 'l-Ḥidjdja 538/14 June 1144, where Ibn Baṭṭūṭa, *Riḥla*, iii, 6, tr. Gibb, iii, 543, was still able to view his tomb.

Al-Zamakhsharī travelled extensively and stayed at least twice in Mecca to study grammar, theology and Ḳurʾānic exegesis, which gained him his *laḳab*. Among his teachers were Abu 'l-Ḥasan ʿAlī b. al-Muẓaffar al-Naysābūrī and Abū Muḍar Maḥmūd b. Djarīr al-Iṣbahānī (d. after 507/1113-14; al-Suyūṭī, *Bughya*, ii, 276); the latter was held responsible for the introduction into Khʷārazm of Muʿtazilism, of which al-Zamakhsharī became an ardent follower. We do not have much information about his students; among them were the Persian *mufassir* Abu 'l-Futūḥ al-Rāzī and Abu 'l-Faḍl Muḥammad b. Abu 'l-Ḳāsim b. Bāʾidjuk al-Baḳḳāl al-Khʷārazmī (d. 562/1167; Brockelmann, S I, 513); a female student of his, Zaynab bt. al-Shaʿrī, is mentioned by Ibn Khallikān (*Wafayāt*, v, 171 l. 22); his favourite student seems to have been Diyāʾ al-Dīn al-Makkī (Brockelmann, S I, 513; d. *ca.* 550/1155).

Al-Zamakhsharī rejected the aims of the Shuʿūbiyya (*Mufaṣṣal*, 2); for him, Arabic is the language that has been selected by God for the revelation. Those who support the Shuʿūbiyya do not understand that Arabic grammar is the source for all the sciences, whose issues ultimately depend on the comprehension of the Arabic language and its grammar (*Mufaṣṣal*, 3 ll. 8-13). Not only that, but it is also the language that is used as the administrative language by the rulers of the Islamic empires, as shown by the fact that it is the language used on their coins.

Al-Zamakhsharī's most important grammatical work is the *K. al-Mufaṣṣal fi 'l-naḥw* (ed. J.P. Broch, Christiania 1859, rev. ed. 1879; in the introd., 4 ll. 5-6, he calls it the *K. al-Mufaṣṣal fī ṣanʿat al-iʿrāb*), which is a compendium on Arabic grammar. The most obvious difference between this highly popular work and other grammatical writings, starting with the *Kitāb Sībawayhi*, is the arrangement of the material. Instead of the classic arrangement in syntax, morphology and phonology, al-Zamakhsharī chose to divide the treatment according to the three parts of speech (nouns, verbs and particles, with a fourth section about *mushtarak*, i.e. (morpho-)phonological topics that concern two or three parts of speech, such as *imāla*, *iddighām* and the treatment of the weak consonants). Within the sections on the noun and the verb, he first deals with constructions involving the nominative, then those involving the accusative and, finally, those involving the genitive or the apocopate. Morphological questions such as the diminutive in the nouns or the quadriliteral in the verbs are dealt with after the syntactic questions.

For all topics in the *Mufaṣṣal*, the treatment is similar: each chapter begins with a general definition and a general rule; this is followed by a number of *fuṣūl*, in which exceptions to the rule and special problems are dealt with, supported by quotations from poetry or the Ḳurʾān and including divergent opinions of other grammarians (Kūfan grammarians, for instance, are quoted 18 times). The grammarian quoted most frequently is Sībawayhi [*q.v.*] (73 times); the only other grammarians quoted with any frequency are al-Akhfash al-Awsaṭ (25 times), al-Khalīl (24 times) and al-Mubarrad (13 times) [*q.vv.*]. Al-Zamakhsharī does not very often express a personal opinion, at least not in the *Mufaṣṣal*; nevertheless, some of his divergent views are quoted by later grammarians (cf. Ḍayf 1968, 286-7). In the often-discussed matter of the regent of the predicate in a nominal sentence, he held that it is the *isnād* which governs both the topic and the predicate (*Mufaṣṣal*, 12-13). With regard to declension, he held that the nominal cases represent grammatical functions or meanings (*maʿānī*, whereas the verbal cases do not (*ibid.*, 109; cf. Sāmarrāʾī 1970, 334-9; Ermers 1999, 174-5). His view that the second and the fourth verbal measure differed in meaning in that both are causative, but the former is iterative as well (Ibn Hishām, *Mughnī*, 578), is connected with his general idea that meaning should be reflected in sound and *vice-versa* (cf. Sāmarrāʾī 1970, 285-94; Leemhuis 1977, 9).

With regard to the *shawāhid* used by al-Zamakhsharī, it may be noted that he accepted verses from modern poets (*muḥdathūn, muwalladūn*), such as Bashshār b. Burd and Abū Nuwās (e.g. in *Mufaṣṣal*, 103), as testimony of the language of the Arabs. This is noted explicitly by al-Baghdādī (*Khizānat al-adab*, ed. ʿAbd al-Salām Muḥammad Hārūn, Cairo 1979-86, i, 6-7).

The *Mufaṣṣal* was a popular work; the list in Brockelmann, I 344, S I, 507, contains a total of 24 commentaries, of which the best-known is that by Ibn Yaʿīsh [*q.v.*]. In spite of its elementary nature, the *Mufaṣṣal* has also exercised considerable influence on Western grammars of Arabic. It formed the basis for Caspari's grammar (1848) and, through its English translation by Wright, for all subsequent grammars of Arabic.

Al-Zamakhsharī occupied himself intensively with the *Kitāb Sībawayhi*. He wrote a commentary on its poetical *shawāhid* (Sezgin, *GAS*, ix, 60, quoted by al-Suyūṭī, *Bughya*, 388) and he played an important role in the reception of the *Kitāb*. Humbert (1995, 93-115) has shown that the Çorum manuscript of the *Kitāb* designated as Umumi Usul 2562-5 (completed in 647/1250) is a copy of al-Zamakhsharī's recension of the *Kitāb* (one of the later copies of this manuscript served as a basis for Derenbourg's edition under the siglum A). In this recension, al-Zamakhsharī collated several versions of the *Kitāb*, among them an Andalusī one, and added a large number of glosses from other grammarians, which are still unedited.

Among his other grammatical works (for a complete list with editions and manuscripts, see Brockelmann, I, 345-50, and *EI*[1] art. s.v. [Brockelmann]) are:

1. an excerpt from the *Mufaṣṣal* (*al-Unmūdhadj fi 'l-naḥw*; Fr. tr. of part of this treatise with commentary by Muḥammad b. ʿAbd al-Ghānī al-Ardabīlī (d. 1036/1626) in de Sacy, *Anthologie grammaticale arabe*, [2]Paris 1829, repr. Osnabrück 1973, 240-80; Ar. text, 99-118);
2. a work on syntax (*K. al-Mufrad wa 'l-muʾallaf fi 'l-naḥw*);
3. a work on grammatical controversies (*al-Aḥādjī 'l-naḥwiyya*; ed. M. al-Ḥaḍarī, Ḥamā 1969);
4. a commentary on Ibn Durayd's [*q.v.*] *Maḳṣūra*;
5. a collection of 3,500 Arabic proverbs (*al-Mustaḳṣā fi amthāl al-ʿArab*; 2 vols. Ḥaydarābād 1381/1962; cf. Sellheim 1954, 145-51);
6. a commentary on al-Shanfarā's [*q.v.*] *Lāmiyyat al-ʿArab* entitled *Aʿdjab al-ʿadjab* (Damascus 1408/1987).

He also wrote a series of *maḳāmāt* containing moral exhortations to himself, on which he himself wrote a commentary.

In lexicography, al-Zamakhsharī wrote a thesaurus of the Arabic language, *Asās al-balāgha* (Cairo 1299/

1882, 1341/1922-3), and a bilingual Arabic-Persian dictionary, *Muḳaddimat al-adab* (ed. J.G. Wetzstein, Leipzig 1843-50); the manuscript of the latter work contains numerous glosses with information about Khʷārazmian, the Iranian language of al-Zamakhsharī's country of birth [see IRĀN. iii. Languages (c), in Suppl.]. He also compiled a list of expressions used in *ḥadīth* (*al-Fāʾiḳ fī gharīb al-ḥadīth*, ed. ʿA. Muḥammad al-Bidjāwī and Muḥammad Abu 'l-Faḍl Ibrāhīm, Cairo 1971), and a geographical lexicon (*Kitāb al-amkina*, ed. M. Salverda de Grave, Leiden 1856).

Bibliography (in addition to references given in the article): 1. Sources. Ibn al-Anbārī, *Nuzha*, ed. A. Amer, Stockholm 1963, 231-2; Suyūṭī, *Bughya*, ii, 269-70; Ibn Khallikān, *Wafayāt*, ed. ʿAbbās, v, 168-74; Yāḳūt, *Irshād*, ed. Margoliouth, vii, 147-51.

2. Studies. J.A. Haywood, *Arabic lexicography*, [2]Leiden 1965, 104, 118; Shawḳī Ḍayf, *al-Madāris al-naḥwiyya*, Cairo 1968, 283-7; J. Benzing, *Das chwaresmische Sprachmaterial einer Handschrift der* Muqaddimat al-adab des *Zamaxšarī*, Wiesbaden 1968; R. Ermers, *Arabic grammars of Turkic*, Leiden 1999; G. Humbert, *Les voies de la transmission du* Kitāb *de Sībawayhi*, Leiden 1995; F. Leemhuis, *The* D *and* H *stems in Koranic Arabic*, Leiden 1977; N. Poppe, *Eine viersprachige Zamaxšarī-Handschrift*, in *ZDMG*, ci (1951), 301-32; F.S. al-Sāmarrāʾī, *al-Dirāsāt al-naḥwiyya wa 'l-lughawiyya ʿind al-Zamakhsharī*, Baghdād 1971; R. Sellheim, *Die klassisch-arabischen Sprichwörtersammlungen*, The Hague 1954; E. Trumpp, *Beiträge zur Erklärung des Mufaṣṣal*, in *SBBayer. Ak.* (1878), 197-316; idem, *Beiträge zur Übersetzung und Erklärung des Mufaṣṣal*, in *SBBayer. Ak.* (1884), 621-850.

(C.H.M. VERSTEEGH)

For al-Zamakhsharī's contribution in the fields of theology, Ḳurʾānic exegesis, and *adab*, see Suppl.

ZAMĀN (A.), time.

1. In philosophy

Time, for those who recognised the authority of the Greeks, sc. the *falāsifa* [*q.v.*], had numerous meanings: it denoted the near millennium and a half that separated them from the "first master", and it signified that of which Aristotle (Arisṭūṭālīs [*q.v.*]) had propounded the theory in the 4th and 8th books of the *Physics*, a work which, ancient though it was, seemed to them as if written only yesterday; see *al-Ṭabīʿa*, ed. ʿAbd al-Raḥmān Badawī, Cairo 1964-65, 2 vols., tr. of the *Physics* by Isḥāḳ b. Ḥunayn [*q.v.*], accompanied by commentaries of Abū ʿAlī b. Samḥ (d. 1207), of Yaḥyā b. ʿAdī (d. *ca.* 364/973-4), of Mattā b. Yūnus (d. 328/940 [*q.v.*]), of Abu 'l-Faradj b. al-Ṭayyib (d. 435/1043) and of a certain "Yaḥyā", under which name John Philoponus is currently recognised (sc. Yaḥyā al-Naḥwī [*q.v.*]); see also P. Lettinck, *Aristotle's "Physics" and his reception in the Arabic world, with an edition of the unpublished parts of Ibn Bājja's "Commentary of the Physics"*, Leiden 1994. This latter work adds to the analysis and paraphrase of the text and glosses appended to Isḥāḳ's translation, the commentaries of Ibn Rushd and Ibn Bādjdja [*q.vv.*] and gives, on the basis of the latter, the text of the ms. of Berlin, lost after the Second World War and recently rediscovered in Cracow). And time furthermore signified that "mobile image of eternity" which the demiurge of the *Timaeus* (37d), having become "Creator", had wanted to add to his work. Definitely, nothing of that with which the *falāsifa* nourished their thoughts was alien to time, to its essence, to its "cause" and to its duration, beginning with themselves and with the combination of distance and proximity which linked them to the Greeks. With the initial developments of *Physics*, iv, 10, setting forth *aporias* on the existence of time, the Arabic encyclopaedic tradition associates the definitions of it given by the *mutakallimūn*: for them, it is something imagined (*mawhūm*) and could indeed not exist (see below).

The *falāsifa*, for their part, were considerably less inclined to doubt its existence and conceived themselves to be its heirs. It was their duty to continue, to make fruitful, or at least to safeguard, that which the Greeks had bequeathed to them. The work demanded, as a condition of feasibility, a "history", a time appropriate to movements, to transfers of knowledge. In different ways, all assumed the representation of a cumulative and threatened science, of a durable culture whose fragile continuity enabled them to learn from their masters and to teach their disciples. All appealed equally for recognition of their right to be instructed by distant nations from which they were separated by history, geography, language and religion. See on this point, for al-Kindī [*q.v.*], the introduction to the *Livre sur la philosophie première*, in R. Rashed and J. Jolivet, *Œuvres philosophiques et scientifiques d'al-Kindī*, ii, *Métaphysique et cosmologie*, Leiden 1998; Arabic text and Fr. tr., 10-14, and in the *Risāla fī kammiyyāt kutub Arisṭūṭālīs* (*Rasāʾil al-Kindī*, ed. Abū Rīda, Cairo 1950, i, 362-84) the distinction between a human science and a divine science, 372-3; for al-Fārābī, *Taḥṣīl al-saʿāda*, ed. Āl Yāsīn, in *Al-Fārābī, al-aʿmāl al-falsafiyya*, i, Beirut 1992, 181-2, Eng. tr. M. Mahdi, *Alfarabi's philosophy of Plato and Aristotle*, [2]New York 1969, 43; see also how the *Kitāb al-Ḥurūf*, 2nd part, ed. M. Mahdi, Beirut 1970, gives an account of the "historical" development that has taken place since the invention of language, culminating in the perfecting of logic and philosophy, by way of the creation of religions and the caprices of their transmission. See also the account that Ibn Abī Uṣaybiʿa attributes to al-Fārābī (*ʿUyūn al-akhbār fī ṭabaḳāt al-aṭibbāʾ*, ed. Müller, Cairo 1882, ii, 134-5, repr. Frankfurt 1995) of the transference from Alexandria to Baghdād of the teaching of philosophy (cf. the recent treatment of this subject by D. Gutas, *The "Alexandria to Baghdad" complex of narratives. A contribution to the study of philosophical and medical historiography among the Arabs*, in *Documenti e studi sulla tradizione filosofica medievale*, x [1999], 155-93); for Abū Bakr b. Zakariyyāʾ al-Rāzī [*q.v.*], see Abu Ḥātim al-Rāzī, *K. Aʿlām al-nubuwwa*, passim, fragments reproduced in P. Kraus, *Alchemie, Ketzerei, Apokryphen im frühen Islam*, Hildesheim-Zurich-New York 1994, 256 ff., text ed. Ṣalāḥ al-Ṣāwī, Tehran 1397/1977; for Ibn Sīnā [*q.v.*], see D. Gutas, *Avicenna and the Aristotelian tradition*, Leiden 1988, 199-218; for Ibn Rushd, see e.g. *Faṣl al-maḳāl*, ed. G.F. Hourani, Leiden 1959, 9-11.

It is not easy to unravel in the representations of time permeating those of their works which have survived, how much derives from physics, from metaphysics and from cosmogony, from theology, ethics or political philosophy. Al-Kindī and Ibn Rushd devote to the question all or part of several of their works, the former bound to the eastern beginnings of this scholastic tradition, and the latter to his Andalusian upbringing. Several of al-Kindī's letters (see below) devote important considerations to it, while his dialectical monument, the *Tahāfut al-tahāfut*, reserves for it the most vivid, in scale and extent, of its controversies. Between the two, all the *falāsifa*, from al-Fārābī to Ibn Ṭufayl [*q.v.*] by way of Ibn Sīnā [*q.v.*] and Ibn Bādjdja, have reflected aspects of their doctrines in a concept putting them into contact with the *mutakallimūn*, since this concept engaged, among other motifs of controversy, the question of eternity (*ḳidam* [*q.v.*]) or of the creation (*ḥudūth*) of the world, but also of the Ḳur'ān, and with it, that of particular providence of causality furthermore; it was necessary for the time of the philosophers to be determined in relation to that which separated, for Islam, the creation of the world from its end and which was punctuated by the revival of prophecies, the so-called "scandal" of miracles and the rhythm of prayers (see L. Massignon, *Le temps dans la pensée islamique*, in *Opera minora*, ii, Beirut 1963, 606-12, R. Brunschvig, *Le culte et le temps dans l'Islam classique*, repr. in *Etudes d'Islamologie*, Paris 1976, i, 167-77).

Encyclopaedic Arabic surveys devote to *zamān* composite and similar treatments; see e.g. Ṣadr al-Dīn al-Shīrāzī (i.e. Mullā Ṣadrā [*q.v.*]), *al-Ḥikma al-mutaʿāliya fi 'l-asfār al-ʿaḳliyya al-arbaʿa*, first *safar*, 3rd part, Tehran 1383 A.H., iii, 115-16; al-Īdjī, *al-Mawāḳif, sharḥ al-Djurdjānī wa-ākharīn*, Istanbul 1286, iii, 49-70 (*al-maḳṣad al-sābiʿ* and *al-maḳṣad al-thāmin*); Fakhr al-Dīn al-Rāzī (d. 606/1204 [*q.v.*]), *al-Mabāḥith al-mashriḳiyya*, Beirut 1990, i, 755-6 (the article by P. Kraus, *Les controverses de Fakhr al-dīn Rāzī*, repr. in his *Alchemie, Ketzerei*..., 190-218); Abu 'l-Baḳā', *al-Kulliyyāt*, Beirut 1993, 486-7; special mention should be made of the originality of the *Faṣl fī māhiyyat al-zamān min aḳāwīl al-ʿulamā'*, in *al-Risāla al-ūlā fi bayān al-hayūlā wa 'l-ṣūra* of the Ikhwān al-Ṣafā' [*q.v.*], i, 13 ff., ed. al-Ziriklī, Cairo 1347/1928.

Al-Tahānawī, *Kashshāf iṣṭilāḥāt al-funūn*, opens the article that he devotes to time with the mention of the doctrine of "some ancient philosophers" (*ḳudamā' al-falāsifa*). He cites by name only Plato (Aflāṭūn [*q.v.*]) and Aristotle and begins by presenting definitions of time corresponding, with the exception of the first, to those evoked by Aristotle in the doxographical survey of *Physics*, iv, 10, 218a 32-b 18 (*al-Ṭabīʿa*, 411-13): "Some declare that it is a substance separated from matter to which no body is attached, and which, by essence, does not accept that it is not (*lā yaḳbal al-ʿadam li-dhātihi*) and which is thus necessary through itself [...]. Some sages assert that it is the uppermost sphere [...]. Similarly, it is claimed that it is the movement of the uppermost sphere." The order and the sequence of the text testify to the dominance of the *Physics* since these remarks are followed immediately by the definition given by Aristotle himself: "He says: 'It is the measure of the movement of the uppermost sphere." Instead and in place of the first of the definitions mentioned (time is a substance), *Physics*, iv, 10, reveals *aporias* concerning the existence of time. In fact, al-Tahānawī kills two birds with one stone: the substantiality of time makes it possible to refer allusively to the traditions of Arab Neoplatonism (see below) and, turning the first definition into a *petitio principi*—if time existed as a substance, it could certainly not do other than exist, but... does it really exist?—to link the beginning of the Aristotelian treatise to the positions of the *mutakallimūn*: for them, time does not exist. It is valid only in the changing appreciation of discontinuous events, of "new events" (*mutadjaddidāt*) and recurrencies with no connection between them other than the entirely imaginary one where judgement gathers them together as a convenient way of dating them. Al-Tahānawī recalls the definition given it by the Ashʿarīs (see also al-Īdjī, *op. cit.*, 69 and al-Djurdjānī, *K. al-Taʿrīfāt*, s.v.): "It is a well-known new event whereby an unknown new event is measured as a means of dispelling obscurity" (*mutadjaddid maʿlūm yuḳaddaru bihi mutadjaddid mubham li-izālat ibhāmihi*); thus in "I shall come to see you at sunrise!", it is well known that sunrise will occur and the ignorance of the moment of the visit is dispelled by its imagined association with the expectation of the dawn. The unreality of time results from its wholly exterior determination (*lā yataʿayyan*), since two persons will date two events by reference to each other, interchangeably; thus it may be said "Zayd came when ʿAmr came" and "ʿAmr came when Zayd came". The definition retains only atomic facts, insular occurrences between which judgement builds imaginary bridges. It accords with that constellation, that "Milky Way of instants" in which L. Massignon recognised the Muslim vision of time and on which the theologians based their occasionalism (see for a critique of this position, J. Berque, *L'idée de temps dans le Coran*, in *Homenaje al Professor Jacinto Bosch Vilà*, Granada 1991, i, 1155-64; the position of al-Ghazālī, as reported and discussed by Ibn Rushd in the *Tahāfut al-tahāfut*, ed. Bouyges, Beirut 1930, 517 ff., illustrates occasionalism).

On the identity of those who saw in time a substance and did not, as Aristotle, see in it an accident, Abu 'l-Baḳā' gives an indication when, in compiling the *Kulliyyāt*, he mentions Plato, attributing to him the opinion that there exists, in the world of commandment (*ʿālam al-amr*), a substance which has never begun to be, which modifies itself, changes, renews itself and wears itself out in accordance with things which change and not only with truth and essence. This substance, with regard to the relationship of its essence with fixed things, is called "eternal" (*sarmadī*); it is called "perpetuity" (*dahr*) when it is anterior to things and "time" when it is concurrent with them. It is only superficially paradoxical to attribute to Plato, of whom Aristotle says (*Physics*, viii, 251b, 11; *al-Ṭabīʿa*, 810-11) that he is precisely the one never to have subscribed to it, the doctrine which holds that time, in its essence, is intemporal: the essence of time is indeed eternity, if in itself it is no more than "mobile image".

The identity mentioned by al-Tahānawī between time and the movement of the celestial sphere, or between time and the sphere itself can also claim the support of the *Timaeus*, which has the heavens and time born together with the setting in order of "that which was not in repose but moved itself without harmony and without order" (30a, tr. Robin; see de Boer, *EI*[1], art. *Zamān*: the Ancients attributed one and the other thesis, respectively, to Plato and to Pythagoras). Abū Bakr b. Zakariyyā' al-Rāzī avers very explicitly his Platonist allegiance: "That which Plato affirms on the subject of time is not in any way opposed to what I think" (in Abū Ḥātim al-Rāzī, *K. Aʿlām al-nubuwwa*, in P. Kraus, *Alchemie, Ketzerei*..., 269). He does not believe that he is at odds with the *Timaeus* when he affirms the existence of two quite distinct times: *al-zamān al-lābith* (*lābith* for "delay"), a number of movement of bodies, is concomitant with them, but it has, like the life of a man or the duration of a reign, a beginning and an end, i.e. it is *maḥṣūr*. It takes place in a limitless flux of "now" which, for its part, never stops, an "absolute time" which is extension and perpetuity, and has never begun: *zamān muṭlaḳ... huwa al-mudda wa 'l-dahr wa-huwa al-ḳadīm wa-huwa mutaḥarrik ghayr lābith* (*op. cit.*, 268; see for a synthetic presentation of the five principles of al-Rāzī, M. Mahdi, *Remarks on al-Rāzī's principles*, in *BEO*, xlviii [1996], 145-53).

It is in the same tradition of the *Timaeus*, but subject to monotheistic modifications and taken in terms of an entirely different inspiration, that the Neo-Platonist speculations of pseudo-Aristotle belong (see the recent study by G. Endress, *L'Aristote arabe. Réception, autorité et transformation du Premier Maître*, in *Médioevo*, xxiii [1997], 1-42; C. D'Ancona Costa, *Recherches sur le Liber de Causis*, Paris 1995, and the art. of Maroun Aouad on the *Theology*, in R. Goulet (ed.), *Dictionnaire des philosophes antiques*, i, Paris 1989, 541-90). The *Theology* (ed. ʿAbd al-Raḥmān Badawī, in *Aflāṭūn ʿind al-ʿarab*, ²Kuwait 1977) and the *De Causis* (*K. al-Īḍāḥ fi 'l-khayr al-maḥḍ*, ed. idem in *al-Aflāṭūniyya al-muḥdatha ʿind al-ʿarab*, Kuwait 1977) develop an emanatist cosmogony which sets out the first principle as "the cause of time" (*ʿillat al-zamān*). The former of these apocrypha opens with the following declaration: the intention of the treatise is "to discuss sovereignty, to make appear that which is, what is the first cause, and show that perpetuity and time are subordinate to it..." (ed. Badawī, 6). The fifth *mīmar*, devoted to creation (*ibdāʿ*) denies to the "Creator" any form of temporality: whether they are temporal or not, things are accomplished in Him, complete and perpetual. It is only when they are expressed outside Him that those among them which are temporal "are extended" and "unfold" (*imtaddat wa-nbasaṭat*), that they admit the before and the after and become, to one another, causes of generation (*ibid.*, 67). In his commentary on the treatise, Ibn Sīnā distinguishes between the "domains" which keep the first principle away from generation and corruption: "The superior world is in the domain (*ḥayyiz*) of eternity (*sarmad*) and of perpetuity (*dahr*); it is a fixed world. It is not an innovating (*mutadjaddid*) world like that in which deliberation and remembrance supervene (*al-fikr wa 'l-dhikr*). The world of innovation (*ʿalam al-tadjaddud*) is the world of movement and of time" (*Arisṭū ʿind al-ʿarab*, ed. Badawī, Cairo 1947, 46; see also *al-Khayr al-maḥḍ*, 4-5; the first cause is "superior to perpetuity and is anterior to it" (*aʿlā min al-dahr wa-ḳablahu*), the Intellect is with perpetuity and the Soul is in the inferior domain of perpetuity and above time).

The heritage of the *Timaeus* placed in the first rank of philosophical preoccupations the question of eternity or of the creation of the world and of time. The work supported both interpretations, since according to Plotin, Proclus [see BURUḲLUS] and John Philoponus could equally lay claim to it. According to the former, if Plato is entitled to describe the world as a "benevolent god" (*Timaeus*, 34b, 8-9) it is because all reality, sensible or intelligible, emanates eternally from its author: it is a part of him. As for the demiurge, he is himself only an emanated hypostasis; for Philoponus, on the other hand, the demiurge becomes the God, henceforward the sole God, Who one day took the free decision to create the world (see K. Verrycken, *Philoponus' interpretation of Plato's cosmogony*, in *Documenti e studi sulla tradizione filosofica medievale*, viii [1997], 269-318). From Proclus, Ḥunayn b. Isḥāḳ had translated the proofs favouring the eternity of the world (see G. Endress, *Proclus Arabus. Zwanzig Abschnitte aus der Institutio Theologica in arabischer Übersetzung*, Beirut 1973); the *De Aeternitate Mundi contra Proclum* by Philoponus was also translated into Arabic but only a few fragments of this translation have been preserved. The hazards of the transmission of the Greek heritage to the Arabs gave rise to bizarre attributions: Proclus finds himself credited with propositions deriving from Philoponus, which is also the case for Alexander of Aphrodisias (see R. Goulet and M. Aouad, art. *Alexandros d'Aphrodisias*, in *Dictionnaire des philosophes antiques*, 125-39 and Aḥmad Ḥasnāwī, *Alexandre d'Aphrodise vs. Jean Philopon. Notes sur quelques traités d'Alexandre "perdus" en grec, conservés en arabe*, in *Arabic Science and Philosophy*, iv/1 [1994], 53-109). Alexander himself is reputed to be the author of texts that are in fact based on the *Elements of Theology* of Proclus (see F. Zimmerman, *Proclus Arabus rides again*, in *ibid.*, 9-51).

Against Philoponus, Abū Naṣr al-Fārābī aimed a riposte: *al-Radd ʿalā Yaḥyā al-Naḥwī* (ed. M. Mahdi, *The Arabic text of Alfarabi's work against John the Grammarian*, in *Medieval and Middle Eastern studies in honor of Aziz S. Atiyya*, Leiden 1972, 264-84, analysis and Eng. tr. by Mahdi, *Alfarabi against Philoponus*, in *JNES*, xxvi [1967], 233-60). Following Muhsin Mahdi (*ibid.*, 236), it is possible to identify succinctly two camps in this dialectical morass of arguments and attributions. On the side of Philoponus, to varying degrees, were: al-Kindī, Abū Bakr b. Zakariyyāʾ al-Rāzī, the school of Christian philosophers of Baghdād in the 4th/10th and 5th/11th centuries, al-Ghāzālī and Abu 'l-Barakāt al-Baghdādī; confronting them in the opposing camp were al-Fārābī, Ibn Sīnā, Ibn Bādjdja and Ibn Rushd. Shlomo Pinès has expressed some reservations regarding this division (*An Arabic summary of a lost work of John Philoponus*, in *IOS*, ii [1972], 320-52, repr. in *The collected works of Shlomo Pinès*, ii, Jerusalem-Leiden 1986, 294-326, 312-13 n. 266). Certainly, real affinities exist between the arguments of al-Ghāzālī (*Tahāfut al-falāsifa*) and those of Philoponus, but al-Bayhaḳī is perhaps exaggerating when he suggests that "the majority of points evoked by al-Ghazālī (...) are a re-affirmation of the arguments of Yaḥyā al-Naḥwī" (*Tatimmat Ṣiwān al-ḥikma*, ed. Shāfīʿ, Lahore 1953, 24, cited in Pinès, *ibid.*, 339). In any case, the belief of Abū Bakr al-Rāzī in a creation of the world and his critique of Aristotle are surely inspired by the religious motifs which al-Kindī and al-Ghazālī direct towards comparable themes.

Abu 'l-Barakāt al-Baghdādī [*q.v.*], called *Awḥad al-Zamān*, himself occupies a singular place. His *K. al-Muʿtabar fi 'l-ḥikma*, Ḥaydarābād 1356, reviews in two instances, in pages marked by the seal of his throwing off all authority, the question of time (2nd part, 69-70 and 3rd part, 35-6). Instructive in this regard is the critique that he delivers of the distinctions between *sarmad, dahr* and *zamān* which Avicenna, glossing Plotinian texts, insists should insulate the All-Powerful from change. "We have explained that the being in every being (*wudjūd kulli mawdjūd*) is in an extension (*mudda*) which is time; that it is impossible for a being that is not in time to be represented. Those who, seeking to rescue the being of their Creator from time, affirm that He is in 'perpetuity' and in 'eternity' (*al-dahr wa 'l-sarmad*), even that His very being is perpetuity and eternity, may indeed have changed the names of time, but not its meaning" (*op. cit.*, 3rd part, 41). Abu 'l-Barakāt has recourse to the first certitude: the soul seizes time at the same time that it seizes itself and seizes being, before any other thing. It is a primary notion co-extensive with being: "It would be much better to say that it is the measure of being (*miḳdār al-wudjūd*) than declare that it is the measure of movement" (*ibid.*, 39). It follows that the Creator is, just as we are, in time.

Finally, if Ibn Ṭufayl is absent from this roll-call of the opposing camps, it is no doubt because Ḥayy b. Yaḳẓān [*q.v.*], the protagonist of his narration, expounds both theses as a spectator but declines to take sides. The author furthermore professes externally equal allegiance to al-Ghazālī and to Ibn Sīnā (*Hayy ben Yaqdhân, roman philosophique d'Ibn Thofail*, Arabic text and Fr. tr. L. Gauthier, ²Beirut 1936, 61-5 of the tr., 80-6 of the text) and, according to the deductions of Ḥayy, the two positions lead to the same consequences. Al-Tahānawī speaks as the echo of equivalence: "Know, according to what we have mentioned, that it is the same whether we say 'the world has been created by a temporal creation' (*ḥādith bi 'l-ḥudūth al-zamānī*) as is the opinion of the *mutakallimūn*, or by an 'essential creation' (*bi 'l-ḥudūth al-dhātī*), as is the opinion of the sages."

Al-Kindī often returns to the question of time (see *Oeuvres philosophiques et scientifiques d'al-Kindī*, ch. 2, *Philosophie première*, 26-38; on *L'unicité de Dieu et la finitude du corps du monde*, 135-47; on *La quiddité de ce qui ne peut être infini et que l'on appelle infini*, 149-55; *Pour expliquer la finitude du corps du monde*, 157-65, texts to which should be added the *Sermo de tempore* from the *Liber de quinque essentiis* [Latin text and Arabic tr. by Abū Rīda], in the second volume of this same scholar's edition of the *Rasā'il al-Kindī*, Cairo 1953, 33-5). For the sake of simplicity, his position reverts to the extension to time of the Aristotelian considerations of the *Physics*, iii, 5, 204a, 8-206a, 9, on the finitude of place. Furthermore, the Arabic translation of this last text is matched by a commentary of Philiponus which purports to prove by a mathematical argument the impossibility of an infinite in action and, in particular, that of an infinite time. For Philiponus as for al-Kindī, time must have a beginning and an end (see P. Lettinck, *Aristotle's "Physics"*..., 235-6). Doubtless the arguments of Philiponus would have inspired al-Kindī, who developed some very similar concepts. This heritage takes in his thinking the form of a definition of time which favours the transference to it of the finitude of the body; time is an interval, an extension, an extent measured by movement, *mudda taʿudduhā al-ḥaraka, ghayr thābitat al-adjzā'* (*Risāla fī ḥudūd al-ashyā'*, ed. Abū Rīda, *Rasā'il*..., i, 167). The letter of the definition is not Aristotelian, but its spirit is not so far removed from that continuous quantity which, according to Aristotle, renders time interchangeable with movement in terms of measure (*Physics*, iv, 220b, 14-32). There appears, in any case, a genuine ambiguity in the writings of Aristotle, in the definition of the "now" (is it a simple mathematical limit or *plenum*, totality? See on this subject, V. Goldschmidt, *Temps physique et temps tragique chez Aristote*, Paris 1982, 147-8). This alternative definition is also to be found in a letter attributed to Alexander (*Maḳāla li-Iskandar al-Afrūdīsī fi 'l-zamān*, ed. Badawī, in *Commentaires sur Aristote perdus en grec et autres épîtres*, Beirut 1971, 19-24; see in this regard the article by Aouad in *Dictionnaire des philosophes antiques*, 135). Its stated object is to disclose "the opinion of Aristotle on the nature of time and the demonstration of its quiddity, of its essence [...], without contradicting it in any respect. It is the number of the movement of the uppermost sphere [...], according to another definition, it is an extension numbered by movement".

When al-Kindī specifies the sense that he gives to *mudda*, sc. "extension is that in which there is existence (*mā huwa fīhi huwiyya*), meaning that in which a being is what it is" (*Philosophie première*, tr. Jolivet, 34-5), he transfers to time the limit of space: "The existence of the body of the universe is necessarily finite; it is thus impossible that the body of the universe be eternal" (*ibid.*). For al-Kindī, the world began and it will have an ending (see J. Jolivet, *Al-Kindī, vues sur le temps*, in *Arabic Sciences and Philosophy*, iii [1993], 55-75: "We have shown that body, movement and time did not precede one another in existence; therefore neither body nor movement nor time is eternal, but there is an eternal essence at the beginning of existence" (*Philosophie première*, tr. Jolivet, art. cit., 66).

The position evidently contradicts the Aristotelian deduction of an infinite time and of an eternal movement (see *Physics*, iii, 203b, 13-7; viii, 1, 250b, 11-252b, 7, see respectively *al-Ṭabīʿa*, 212-4 and 801-2; Lettinck, *op. cit.*, 217-18 and 563-4, and the arguments of Yaḥyā and of Abu 'l-Faradj). What may be retained from this "demonstration" is the formulation attributed to Alexander in the letter cited above: "The demonstrative proof (*burhān*) that time has neither generation nor beginning nor end is that generation supervenes only in time. We do not say 'he was', 'he shall be', 'he is', 'he was not' except in terms of time, and the same applies when we say 'before', 'after', 'when', etc. If somebody declares: 'previously, this time was not, but it is now' or 'it is now but afterwards it will not be', it follows necessarily that there is a time before time, and a time after the end of time. If the 'before' and the 'after', the 'was' and the 'will not be' did not require time, then the hour, the day and the month would not require it either. In itself, time is one. It does not multiply itself except according to our imagination. In itself it is one, permanent (*dā'im*), continuous (*muttaṣil*), in a single state (*ʿalā ḥāl wāḥida*)" (*op. cit.*, 24; cf. the *Maḳāla* attributed to Alexander, *fī mabādi' al-kull bi-ḥasab ra'y Arisṭūṭālīs al-faylasūf*, in Badawī, *Arisṭū*..., 264, l. 8: time is exempt from generation and corruption; on this treatise, cf. Aouad's art. in *Dictionnaire des philosophes antiques*..., 135-6). The rest may be presented as the dialectical avatars of this simple argument in favour of the infinitude of time. Reduced to itself and invariably taken up by the encyclopaedias (e.g. Fakhr al-Dīn al-Rāzī, *Mabāḥith*, i, 772-3), it amounts to this paradox: saying that time has an origin or an end amounts to denying that it has an end or an origin.

In the judgement of al-Fārābī, it could be in order to avoid the fate of Socrates (*ḥattā lā yanālahu* [...] *mā nāla Suḳrāṭ*) and to reassure his co-religionists as to his orthodoxy that Philoponus undertook to contradict Aristotle on this point (*al-Radd ʿalā Yaḥyā al-Naḥwī*, *"The Arabic text"*, 277, Eng. tr. in *Alfarabi against Philoponus*, 256-7). But in doing this, he would have chosen to take inspiration from opinions institutionalised in religions, however remote they might be from the nature of things. To obtain a similar outcome without sacrificing the *Physics* of Aristotle, could have been the objective pursued by al-Fārābī himself in the treatment of time in his treatise on *L'harmonie entre les opinions de Platon et d'Aristote* (Arabic text and Fr. tr. Fawzi Mitri Nadjdjar and D. Mallet, Damascus 1999, 128-9; of al-Fārābī's commentary on the *Physics*, only the extracts quoted by Ibn Bādjdja and Ibn Rushd have been preserved): "Time results from the movement of the sphere and it is thus impossible that the creation of the latter should have a beginning in time. It thus becomes certain that [the sphere] results from a creation *ex nihilo* on the part of the Creator on a single occasion without duration in time and that, from its movement, time results." Al-Fārābī would thus preserve the Aristotelian analyses, sc. that, taken as a whole, the world has neither beginning nor end, and render them reconcilable with a Creator-God Who would be, of the world and of time, simultaneously the final and efficient cause (Mahdi, *Alfarabi against Philoponus*, 236; Pines, *An Arabic summary, loc. cit.*). Whatever reservations the Neo-Platonist texts of al-Fārābī may have inspired in him (see e.g. *Tahāfut al-tahāfut*, 179), Ibn Rushd rallies to this position in the *Faṣl al-maḳāl* (ed. Hourani, 19-20; see also *Tahāfut al-tahāfut*, 124, Eng. tr. S. Van Den Bergh, *Averroes' Tahafut al-Tahafut*, London 1954, i, 73) when he accepts that there exist three classes of beings. The first comprises that which is apprehended by the senses, brought into being by an efficient cause and preceded by time; the second comprises that which is apprehended by demonstration, which derives from nothing and which time does not precede (God); the third comprises the world taken as a whole (*al-ʿālam bi-asrihi*) which no time precedes but which derives from an efficient cause. It does no violence to the text to draw the conclusion that, according to Ibn Rus͟hd, there is strictly speaking no connection between the "creation" of the world which philosophy conceives and the "creation" which the theologians, among whom Abū Ḥāmid al-G͟hazālī stands out, imagine on the basis of a *ḳiyās al-g͟hāʾib ʿalā 'l-s͟hāhid*. The reproach addressed to the former, of not giving credence to the erroneous results of their own analogies with generation, turns to the advantage of philosophy. It is in the same fashion that Ibn Rus͟hd repels another of the three principal indictments issued by al-G͟hazālī, that of not believing in the divine science of the particulars. As with the preceding question, here time is clearly the nexus of the dispute. Al-Tahānawī alludes to it by saying, if Abu 'l-Barakāt is wrong and "if the Creator, the Most High, is not in time, there will not be in relation to Him past nor present nor future and therefore from His awareness of things which change there will ensue no change in His awareness".

Ibn Rus͟hd reviews the question. It forms the subject of the *Ḍamīma*, of several lines of the *Faṣl al-maḳāl* (ed. Hourani, 18) and of the thirteenth dispute of the *Tahāfut al-tahāfut* (see on this subject Mahdi, *Averroes on divine law and human wisdom*, in *Ancients and Moderns. Essays on the tradition of political philosophy in honor of Strauss*, ed. J. Cropsey, New York-London 1964, 114-31). The solution of Ibn Rus͟hd is in form very similar to that posited for the preceding question: in terms of knowledge man and God are solely homonyms (*ism al-ʿilm al-maḳūl ʿalayhimā bi-is͟htirāk al-ism*). "To know" is said of one and of the other as *ṣārim* is said of the dawn and of the black night, and *d͟jalāl* of a trifle and of enormity (*Faṣl, loc. cit.*). In God, knowledge (as with the other "attributes") added to Himself makes only one. His intellect is His essence; a pure act, it derives its intelligence from knowledge which is inclusive, since it causes all things which are. The *Tahāfut* concludes this point with several lines borrowed from a mystical feeling, the codification of which is associated, perhaps, in the spirit of their author, with the evocation of his senior Ibn Ṭufayl: "Such is clearly what is meant by the opinion of the Ancients when they affirm that God is Himself all the beings, with which He provides us in His munificence (*al-munʿim bihā*) and of which He is the author (*al-fāʿil*). This is why the mystical masters (*ruʾasāʾ al-ṣūfiyya*) say: 'He is that which He is' (*lā huwa illā huwa*). But only those who are rooted in knowledge know this. It does not need to be written, nor should all be required to make of it an article of faith. This is surely why the Law does not teach it. He who reveals it to those who should be ignorant of it commits a fault, as does he who hides it from those who should know it" (*Tahafut al-tahafut*, 463).

Bibliography: To the references cited in the article may be added Ḥusām al-Alūsī, *al-Zamān fi 'l-fikr al-dīnī wa 'l-falsafi 'l-ḳadīm*, Beirut 1980, 55-66, which provides a useful synthesis, and H.A. Davidson, *Proofs for eternity and the existence of God in medieval Islamic and Jewish philosophy*, New York-Oxford 1987. See also ABAD; DAHRIYYA; ḤARAKA; K͟HALḲ; ḲIDAM.

(D. MALLET)

2. In the sense of timekeeping. See the entry Time in the *Index of subjects*.

ZAMĪNDĀR (P., lit. "land-holder"), a term used in Muslim India for landowners, possessors of estates.

It seems to be a term of exclusively Indian origin; it does not appear in pre-modern lexicons compiled in Persia, while, on the other hand, it occurs in fairly early Persian texts and in lexicons compiled in India. It is defined in an 8th/14th-century dictionary, the *Farhang-i Ḳawwās* as "controller of a territory". The historians Ḍiyāʾ Baranī (d. 758/1357 [*q.v.*]) and S͟hams Sirād͟j ʿAfīf (d. *ca.* 802/1400 [see S͟HAMS AL-DĪN. I. SIRĀD͟J ʿAFĪF]) employ it generally for Hindu chiefs outside, as well as within, the limits of the Dihlī Sultanate. But by the second half of the 8th/14th century, the sense was extended to cover all holders of superior rights over land: in 754/1353, in a royal proclamation, village headmen (*muḳaddams*), land holders appointed by the administration (*mafrūḍiyān*) and landowners (*mālikān*), are all put under the general designation of *zamīndārs*. Yet until the reign of the Mug͟hal emperor Akbar (*r.* 964-1013/1556-1605 [*q.v.*]), the term does not seem to have obtained wide currency. It does not, for example, appear in Bābur's *Memoirs*.

The term seems to spring into wider use in texts written after 988/1580. The *Āʾīn-i Akbarī*, the great official manual and statistical record compiled by Abu 'l-Faḍl ʿAllāmī (in 1003/1595 [*q.v.*]), adopted it (together with what was deemed to be its synonym, a freshly-coined term, *būmī*) as a blanket term for all rural superior holders of rights over land, in whatever varied ways the right might have originated, whether by its holder being the descendant of earlier chieftains, or having risen to local eminence through subordinating peasants to himself, or obtaining the land or any kind of right over it by purchase. Generally, however, the *zamīndār* was not part of the state apparatus, and his rights or jurisdiction did not derive from the Emperor's own nomination. But from Awrangzīb's reign (1068-1119/1659-1707), grants or even temporary assignments of *zamīndārī* rights begin to appear.

Moreland's assumption that the term was exclusively used for chieftains and that *zamīndārs* were not present in directly-administered areas of the Mug͟hal empire, no longer holds when considered in the light of the tabulation of *zamīndār* castes in the *Āʾīn-i Akbarī* and the extensive documentation from the 11th/17th century that is now available.

The universalisation of the term *zamīndār* in Mug͟hal administrative use was brought about by its replacing various local terms for corresponding agrarian rights, such as *satārahī* and *biswī/bīsī* in Awadh, *bhaum* in Rad͟jasthān, *bānth/vanth* in Gud͟jarāt and *vartana* in Mahārās͟htrā (whence the *waṭan* of 12th/18th-century Mahārās͟htrā). The actual features of the right became subject to some general imperial regulations. It was held to be a proprietary right (*ḥaḳḳ-i milkiyyat*) and as such could be freely sold and purchased (except in case of chieftaincies), and was inheritable according to Hindu and Muslim laws. Women could also accordingly be *zamīndārs*. It entitled the holder to certain customary claims over the peasant's land (a particular charge or fee on harvest) together with levies on jungle and water produce. He was also paid an allowance (*nānkār*) out of the land-revenue (*māl/k͟harād͟j*), it being expected that he would collect the land revenue due from peasants within his jurisdiction. Should he fail to do so, he could be removed from a role in tax-collection, but then an allowance known as *mālikāna* ("proprietor's allowance" [see MĀLIKĀNE]) was still held to be due to him; this amounted generally to a tenth of the land revenue, except for Gudjarāt, where it amounted to a quarter.

There is some evidence that the *zamīndār* was entitled to allot uncultivated land to peasants and the *ḳāḍī* Muḥammed Aʿlā (early 12th/18th century) would even allow him the right to evict peasants, though in conditions of land abundance the right was not of much consequence.

The *zamīndārs*' territories were paralleled by those known as *raʿiyyatī* or purely peasant-held, which theoretically had no *zamīndārs*. Such villages might by sale or even by imposition of *zamīndārs* by the state, get converted into *zamīndārī* villages; conversely, *zamīndārī* villages might become *raʿiyyatī* by the decline or dispersal of the original *zamīndārs*.

The *zamīndārs* were of use to Mughal administration primarily as revenue-payers and revenue-gatherers. *Zamīndārs* who paid revenue not only on their own jurisdictions but also on those of other *zamīndārs*, began to be called *taʿallukdārs*, from the late 11th/17th century onwards. Inevitably, in many cases, the *zamīndārs* came to be treated almost on a par with other revenue officials, as in Awrangzīb's *farmān* to Rasikdās (1075/1666).

An essential attribute of *zamīndārī* was the maintenance of armed retainers by the *zamīndār*, a right fully recognised by the Mughal administration, as is evident from the testimony of the *Āʾīn-i Akbarī*, which gives the number of *zamīndārs*' retainers in the entire empire as exceeding 4.4 million and then goes on to give a detailed break-down of these figures by localities. These retainers were mainly foot soldiers (4,277,000) but also included 385,000 cavalry; *zamīndārs* in some localities are also shown as possessing elephants, guns and boats. The larger *zamīndārs* could also maintain their castles (*ḳilaʿčas* and *gaṛhīs*). The maintenance of an armed force was an essential means for enforcing their rights; and however much the Mughal authorities felt irritated by this presumption and possible potential for sedition, they themselves often needed the *zamīndārs*' assistance to collect the revenue.

The British in the beginning tended to treat the *zamīndārs* in the same manner as their Mughal predecessors. But the East India Company's drive for maximum revenue led to a financial crisis in Bengal, for which the system of Permanent Settlement was proposed as a solution. Proclaimed in 1203/1789 and confirmed in 1206/1792, this decreed the *zamīndārs* to be proprietors of the land but fixed a perpetual tax on them, which was theoretically set at $^{10}/_{11}$ of the rental, thus leaving only one-eleventh for the *zamīndārs*. It took time for *zamīndārs* to grow into landowners, helped partly by a slow expansion of cultivation and the 13th/19th-century inflation. A modified, short-term (and harsh) settlement was made with *zamīndārs* in upper Gangetic areas (1237/1822) and a very liberal one with the Pandjāb *zamīndārs* later in the century. On the other hand, settlements in the Madras and Bombay Presidencies (1230s/1820s) were termed "ryotwari" (*raʿiyyatwārī*), the revenue being fixed on the fields, and theoretically (though not so much in practice) excluding the *zamīndārs*. Here, too, commercialisation often led to the growth of landlordism which, in popular eyes, was seen to be a new form of *zamīndārī*.

In independent India, agrarian reform has especially been directed against the growth of landlordism; and the U.P. Zamindari Abolition Act of 1951 was the first important measure in this direction, followed by other laws of various degrees of radicalism in other states of the Indian Union.

Bibliography: 1. Sources. Fakhr al-Dīn Mubārak Ḳawwās, *Farhang-i Ḳawwās* (written *ca.* 743/1342-3), ed. Nāẓir Aḥmad, Tehran 1974; Ḍiyāʾ al-Dīn Baranī, *Tārīkh-i Fīrūzshāhī*, ed. Sayyid Aḥmad Khān, W. Nassau Lees and Kabīr al-Dīn, Bibl. Indica, Calcutta 1862; Shams al-Dīn Sirādj ʿAfīf, *Tārīkh-i Fīrūzshāhī*, ed. Wilāyat Ḥusayn, Bibl. Indica, Calcutta 1891; Abu 'l-Faḍl, *Āʾīn-i Akbarī*, ed. H. Blochmann, Bibl. Indica, Calcutta 1867-77 (but the statistical tables under "Twelve *Ṣūbas*" have to be corrected by reference to columnar tabulation followed in the mss., e.g., BL. Add. 7652 and Add. 6552); Awrangzīb's *farmān* to Rasikdās, tr. S. Moosvi, in *Medieval India, 1*, Delhi 1992, 198-208; Ḳāḍī Muḥammad Aʿlā, *Risālat Aḥkām al-arāḍī*, Aligarh, M.A. Lib. ms. ʿAbd al-Salām, ʿArabiyya (4) 331.

2. Studies. W.H. Moreland, *The agrarian system of Moslem India*, Cambridge 1929; Irfan Habib, *Agrarian system of Mughal India (1556-1707)*, Bombay 1963, 2nd. revised ed. Delhi 1999; T. Raychaudhuri and Irfan Habib (eds.), *Cambridge economic history of India*, i, Cambridge 1982; Shireen Moosvi, *The economy of the Mughal Empire, c. 1595. A statistical study*, Delhi 1987. (SHIREEN MOOSVI)

ZAMĪNDĀWAR, the name found in pre-modern usage for a region of what is now eastern Afghānistān, also appearing in mediaeval Arabic usage as its Arabic equivalent Bilād al-Dāwar. The region straddled the courses of the upper Helmand river and the Arghandāb to the north of their confluence at Bust, hence it was bounded on the north by Zābulistān and al-Rukhkhadj [*q.vv.*] on the south and southeast, but the boundaries of all these regions were indeterminate, and Zamīndāwar, in particular, seems often to have been confused in the sources with that of Zābulistān.

The early Arabic geographers and historians mention it, usually as Bilād al-Dāwar, in connection with Arab raids from Sīstān and Bust into the region [see the references for these given in AL-RUKHKHADJ and ZĀBULISTĀN]. When the Arabs raided from Sīstān and Bust towards the end of the 7th century, Bilād al-Dāwar is mentioned as having its own *marzbān* (al-Balādhurī, *Futūḥ*, 394). The celebrated shrine of the local deity Zūn or Zhūn [*q.v.*], cult centre of the local rulers, the Zunbīls, was located in Zamīndāwar. J. Marquart and J.J.M. de Groot, *Das Reich Zābul and der Gott Zūn, vom 6.-9. Jahrhundert*, in G. Weil (ed.), *Festschrift Eduard Sachau*, Berlin 1915, 280-1, 287, saw the title Zunbīl as a theophoric one going back to an MP original, **Zūn-dātbar* "Zūn the justice-giver" or **Zūn-dādh* "given by Zūn"; in the first case, the geographical name Zamīndāwar would also reflect this, from **Zamīn-i Dātbar* "land of the justice-giver".

In the 4th/10th century the *Ḥudūd al-ʿālam*, tr. Minorsky, 111, comm. 345, mentions as amongst its towns Till or Dartall and Darghash, situated on the right bank of the Helmand, which were frontier posts (*thughūr* [*q.v.*]) against the pagan region of Ghūr [*q.v.*]; other towns mentioned by the geographers include Baghnīn and Sarwar. The Ghaznawid historian Bayhaḳī states that peacocks were bred in Zamīndāwar; that Maḥmūd of Ghazna regarded it as blessed because it was the first place his father Sebüktigin gave him to govern; and that on two or three occasions Maḥmūd used it as the base for attempts to raid into Ghūr (*Tārīkh-ī Masʿūdī*, ed. Ghanī and Fayyāḍ, Tehran 1324/1945, 111, 113, 120). The name of the province continued in use long after the Ghaznawid period.

Djūzdjānī mentions it several times. Bābur campaigned there in *ca.* 928/1522 against the Arghuns (*Bābur-nāma*, tr. A.S. Beveridge, London 1922, 27, 337-9; cf. also Mīrzā Muḥammad Ḥaydar Dughlāt, *Tārīkh-i Rashīdī*, tr. Elias and Ross, London 1895, 202); but in recent times the name seems to have dropped out of use.

Bibliography (in addition to references given in the article): Marquart, *Ērānšahr*, 37 and index s.v. Dāwar; Le Strange, *The lands of the Eastern Caliphate*, 339, 345-6. (C.E. Bosworth)

ZAMM, a town on the left bank of the Oxus river [see ĀMŪ DARYĀ] in mediaeval Islamic Central Asia.

It lay some 190 km/120 miles upstream from Āmul-i Shaṭṭ [see ĀMUL. 2.] in the direction of Tirmidh [*q.v.*], hence this Āmul was sometimes called "the Āmul of Zamm", from Zamm's being the next crossing-place along the river (see e.g. al-Balādhurī, *Futūḥ*, 410). Zamm was significant as a crossing-place connecting Khurāsān with Mā warā' al-nahr [*q.vv.*]. It figures in historical accounts of the early Arab invasions of Transoxania as an entry-point for armies aiming at Paykand, Bukhārā, etc. (e.g. *ibid.*, 420; al-Ṭabarī, ii, 1145-6, 1186, 1189, 1198, 1548, 1584-5). In the account of al-Ḥadjdjādj's operations against the rebel Ibn al-Ash'ath [*q.v.*] there is mentioned in Yazīd b. al-Muhallab's forces the *ṣāḥib* of Zamm, Ghazwān b. Iskāf, who had converted to Islam at al-Muhallab's hand (*ibid.*, ii, 1078). The 4th/10th century geographers often group Zamm administratively with Akhsīsak on the opposite bank of the river and say that it was the same size as Āmul; according to al-Muḳaddasī, Zamm was a considerable town with a covered market and a congregational mosque. Al-Sam'ānī, *Ansāb*, ed. Ḥaydarābād, vi, 321-2, and Yāḳūt, *Buldān*, ed. Beirut, iii, 151, mention various *'ulamā'* from the town.

Ancient Zamm is marked by the modern town of Kerki (lat. 37° 53' N., long. 65° 10' E.), now within the Turkmenistan Republic.

Bibliography: See also Le Strange, *The lands of the Eastern Caliphate*, 403-4; Barthold, *Turkestan down to the Mongol invasion*³, 80-1; idem, *An historical geography of Iran*, Princeton 1984, 19. (C.E. Bosworth)

ZAMZAM (A.), the sacred well located at the perimeter of the sacred complex of Mecca. It is situated to the east of the Ka'ba [*q.v.*] alongside the wall where the "Black Stone", *al-ḥadjar al-aswad*, is enshrined, a little further from the centre than the *maḳām Ibrāhīm* [*q.v.*], the "station of Abraham". The well is currently a subterranean arrangement, also opening towards the east. The sacred water is distributed through taps (on earlier architectural features since the beginning of the 'Abbāsid era, see M. Gaudefroy-Demombynes, *Pèlerinage*, 77-80, where is found information concerning the *ḳubba* [*q.v.*], the basin for ablutions and the circular basin around the curb-stone of the well where water for drinking was collected in buckets and lifted with the aid of a system of pulleys, to be subsequently transferred to pitchers or earthenware casks).

The noun *zamzam* is of onomatopoeic type. It is apparently to be associated with the qualificatives *zamzam* or *zumāzim* which denote, according to mediaeval Arabic dictionaries, an "abundant supply of water", *mā' zumāzim* = *kathīr* or, reverting to a regular sense of *mā'* in ancient contexts, a "water-point" regarded as "never drying up".

In the Islamic textual sources of the 'Abbāsid period, the Meccan well is integrated into a mythic discourse on the past which goes far beyond what seems to be authorised by the Ḳur'ānic text, which does not refer directly to the well. This mythic discourse can no longer be regarded as relating historical facts. A brief list of the numerous versions of accounts relating to the sacred well is to be found in Yāḳūt, *Mu'djam al-buldān*, which reviews earlier data (s.v. *Zamzam*). The modern survey which, in the most thorough fashion, provides traditional information as well as references from the classical era to the administration of the well and the rituals associated with it, is that of M. Gaudefroy-Demombynes in *Le pèlerinage à la Mekke*, Paris 1923, 71-101; for the caliphal period, he relies especially on accounts relayed by Abu 'l-Walīd al-Azraḳī (d. 249/858) in his *Akhbār Makka*, ii, 39-61; he also quotes important visual evidence which the Andalusian pilgrim of the second half of the 6th/12th century, Ibn Djubayr, conveys in his *Riḥla* on the administration of the well and the veneration with which it was treated, a text expertly annotated by Demombynes in *Ibn Jobair. Voyages*, Paris 1949, introd. 15, tr. 103-4, 154, 162-6.

Explanations given in these mythic accounts are mostly constructed according to the sense—also of onomatopoeic type—which associates the qualificatives *zamzam* and *zumāzim* with a dull sound. This sound can apply equally well to a distant roll of thunder presaging rain, or to any guttural sound with closed mouth emitted by an animal (camel or horse, etc.) or by a man. In the last-mentioned case, it refers to a murmuring perceived as unintelligible and therefore ultimately as the vehicle for sacrality and for mystery. The abundant water of the water source could also be associated with this basic notion of sound.

The mediaeval Arabic sources generally attribute the murmuring of the *zamzama* to the sayings or to the prayer of the Zoroastrians [see AL-MADJŪS; ZAMZAMA]. Their association with the well of Zamzam is described in the following fashion: they made regular pilgrimages to Mecca on account of "their kinship with Abraham" (*sic*), and are said to have prayed, according to their own custom, over the sacred well. This account is relayed by the polygraph al-Mas'ūdī (whom Yāḳūt quotes by name; a passage effectively attested in the *Murūdj*, in the chapter *dhikr ansāb fāris*). In another version relayed by Yāḳūt (who is content to pass on successive explanations without expressing a preference for any of them), it is the angel Gabriel, Djibrīl, himself who is said to have murmured thus over the well, bearing in mind the fact that, in the sacred but non-Ḳur'ānic accounts relating the legend of Hagar and her son Ismā'īl, brought by Abraham to Mecca, it is the angel who makes an inexhaustible supply of water spring up for the woman and the child who are on the verge of dying of thirst (Ibn Hishām, *al-Sīra al-nabawiyya*, i, *dhikr ḥafr zamzam*). Another account that is definitely later is even further from any context of origin. It is relayed by al-'Aynī, the annotator of al-Bukhārī (quoted by Gaudefroy-Demombynes, 73) in his *'Umdat al-ḳāri'*. This account, which does not feature in the work of Yāḳūt, loses all etymological association with the word. According to al-'Aynī, the noun *zamzam* is to be understood as deriving from *zamāzima*, the precious "bridles" that the eponymous ancestor of the Sāsānids is supposed to have donated to the well.

However, it is apparent that not all of these accounts are of the same period or of the same provenance or purpose. An attempt to establish a chronology would be a worthwhile project. Thus the accounts relayed by Ibn Hishām and, in part, those of al-

Azraḳī, seem to belong to a more ancient stratum than those of al-Masʿūdī. The account of the pilgrimage of the Zoroastrians is not mentioned before the latter. On the other hand, there is very early reference to the story of Hagar and the discovery of the source of water (which was to be embellished and amplified in the later versions such as that of Yāḳūt) as well as the rediscovery of the source, accompanied by miraculous signs, attributed to ʿAbd al-Muṭṭalib, the grandfather of Muḥammad. In the latter case, it is a typical revival story. This is taken to justify the function of giving water to pilgrims, *siḳāya*, which was to remain in the lineage of al-ʿAbbās, one of the sons of ʿAbd al-Muṭṭalib, uncle of Muḥammad and ancestors of the ʿAbbāsid dynasty (on the *siḳāya* and the composition of the beverage known as *sharāb*, *nabīdh* or *sawīḳ*, prepared by macerating raisins and subsequently dates—ingredients which could be pressed by hand, yielding a fermented liquor which was rapidly transformed by the heat into vinegar—doubtless to improve the taste of the water, see Gaudefroy-Demombynes, *Pèlerinage*, 90-4).

Before its revival by the family of Muḥammad, the water source which had sprung up "in the time of Hagar" was dried up by God on account of the misconduct of the Djurhum [*q.v.*]. This tribe, supposedly of Yemeni origin, is associated with Ismāʿīl, who is said to have married into the tribe once he had settled in Meccan territory. Various accounts tell of this alliance, which is said to have been blessed by Abraham himself in the course of his visits to Mecca with the intention of finding his son.

The grandfather of Muḥammad is supposed to have found in the well that he had just rediscovered offerings consisting primarily of gazelles cast in gold and precious swords. Al-Masʿūdī sees this as proof of the coming of "Persians" to Mecca since, according to him, the local tribes would have been incapable of contributing such luxuries (*Murūdj*, ed. Pellat, Paris 1962, i, 215, 216; tr. and commentary on numerous accounts relating to Zamzam and to this episode, J. Chabbi, *Le Seigneur des tribus*, Paris 1997, 163-9, and 34-5 on Ḳurʾān, XIV, 35, 37). The last representative of the "Magians" is said to have been Sāsān, ancestor of the dynasty of the same name. The Sāsānids (destined to be vanquished by the Muslims) would subsequently turn away from this cult. According to this vision, which could be described as opportunist, converted Iranians are said thus to have rediscovered, through Islam, the lost religion of their forebears, making a form of return to sources. Wellhausen, *Reste arabischen Heidentums*, ²Berlin 1897, reckoned that, if offerings were brought to the Meccan site (without commenting on their nature, since the precious objects evoked is more than problematical), they would have been destined for the dry well located in the sacred enclosure of the Kaʿba rather than for the well of Zamzam with its plentiful water, even if it is the latter which seems to monopolise the accounts. The former, adjacent to the functioning well and situated in a place infused with sacrality, could have played the role of a simulacrum in a ritual of donation.

However, it does not appear that any of these accounts is associated with a Ḳurʾānic theme. On the contrary, in the vulgate, Abraham leads his family to Mecca for their safety (XIV, 35, 37). All of these narratives seem to derive from the exegetical imagination emanating from various milieux of the early ʿAbbāsid period. The models then constructed were clearly directed towards the quest for foundation stories, intended to establish a new Muslim identity which would become common to populations of different origin and traditions. The Persianisation of the account, as presented by al-Masʿūdī, is utterly foreign to the Ḳurʾān. It therefore appears, in this respect, particularly significant.

Even if these sacral accounts attributing a supernatural origin to the discovery of the water are left aside, it appears that the presence, and probably the consecration, of the well must have been considerably anterior to the Muslim period. In the absence of archaeological elements which have long been inaccessible, a hypothesis of historical topography should be proposed. It could be thought that the presence of this probably perennial water (Wellhausen describes it as a *Quelle*, a spring which is said to have been the only Meccan water, *Reste*, 76, n. 2; Gaudefroy-Demombynes relays the information given by mediaeval Arab geographers, according to which the well was allegedly supplied by three springs, *Pèlerinage*, 81; given the orientation of these springs, "towards the Black Stone", for example, it might be thought that myth is already beginning to dictate the narrative), in a place which is the confluence of numerous dry valleys in the lowest part (vulnerable to occasional flooding by pluvial streams; dates of devastating floods of the Muslim era are supplied by Gaudefroy-Demombynes, *op. cit.*, 39-41) of the Meccan site, called *al-Baṭḥāʾ*, the "hollow" or *baṭn Makka* "the belly of Mecca" (in the sense of cavity or basin for the retention of water).

It is on the basis of this singularity of terrain that the installation came about of the betylic complex which probably constituted the original perimeter of the Kaʿba and its adjacent sacred stones (al-Ṣafā and al-Marwa). This sacred complex would have taken precedence over the water-point, relegating it to second place in ritual and in representation.

Wellhausen had already proposed the hypothesis of the origin of the site on the basis of the water-point in his *Reste*, 76-7. The complex would then have pursued what was most likely to be a local development (there is no case, in fact, for adhering to the notion, all too evocative of an Islamic ideal, of the sacred Meccan site radiating its influence over the whole of Arabia), culminating in the "visit", *ʿumra*, to the sacred places of the city. The *ʿumra* [*q.v.*], often known as "Lesser Pilgrimage", probably attracted other citizens of western Arabia, Yathribīs and people of the neighbouring city of al-Ṭāʾif, but certainly not the prosperous Bedouin herdsmen of Nadjd. The Meccan visitation was apparently characterised by circumambulations (*ṭawāf* [*q.v.*]), still practised today, but also by sacrifices on various sacred rocks. That of al-Marwa is said to have been named, significantly, the "feeder of vultures", *muṭʿim al-ṭayr*. Such sacrifices are well attested before Islam (Wellhausen, *Reste*, 78) and even in ancient Muslim tradition (Chabbi, *Seigneur*, 322-4, 327-9). But this *intra-muros* sacrifice was subsequently to disappear, as did all the other Meccan sacrifices, to the benefit of the exterior site of Minā. The specifically Meccan pilgrimage of the *ʿumra* was thus to be distinguished from the unified pilgrimage with departure from the site towards ʿArafāt which was to become the Muslim pilgrimage (a combination of a pilgrimage of herdsmen, the *ḥadjdj*, with that of the *ʿumra* specific to Mecca). The instituting of the larger pilgrimage should thus be placed at the extreme end of the Medinan period with the "pilgrimage of farewell", *ḥadjdjat al-wadāʿ*, in the tenth year of the Hidjra, shortly before the death of Muḥammad.

Gaudefroy-Demombynes (*Pèlerinage*, 81) writes with

justification that "the cult of Zemzem... has not taken its place (in the pilgrimage) in the form of an obligatory rite"; he also draws attention (74-5) to doubts regarding "the sovereignty of Zemzem" under the Umayyads, who are said to have confiscated a spring on Mount T̲h̲abīr and to have used it to improve the supply of water to the lower city of Mecca. This aroused the hostility of the inhabitants, even though the water thus provided was more pure and more pleasant to drink than that of the sacred well.

Despite this downgrading of this cult at Mecca, the fervent faith of pilgrims, from early Islamic times to this day, has not ceased to lend outstanding qualities to the water of the well of Zamzam, which is perceived as bearer of *baraka* and as a "curative source" (*ibid.*, 81-2). It is stressed that Muḥammad drank this water and used it regularly for various purposes (prophetic traditions are to be found in Wensinck, *Concordance*, index of places, viii. In his article on Zamzam, Yākūt attributes to Mud̲j̲āhid, taken to be a habitual transmitter of Ibn ʿAbbās, the following words: "If you drink at Zamzam in the hope of a cure, God will cure you; if you are thirsty, God will quench your thirst; if you are hungry, God will satisfy you!" This fervour has led to modes of conduct which can be described as being of a magical type (e.g. linen dipped in the holy water to serve later as a shroud, calculated to avert the anger of certain jurists, Gaudefroy-Demombynes, *Pèlerinage*, 85; the question of ablutions, and which parts of the body may be sprinkled with the water of Zamzam is also posed, *ibid.*, 86). *Zamzamiyyāt*, small phials (of clay or metal) sealed and sold as containing water from the sacred well, are still today highly-prized by pilgrims and taken back by them to their own countries (on the role of accredited and licensed drawers of water, the *zamāzim*, pl. of *zamzamī*, since mediaeval times, see *ibid.*, 87, 88).

There are also popular traditions that other holy wells, e.g. the one in the Great Mosque at al-Ḳayrawān, are subterraneously connected with Zamzam.

Bibliography (in addition to references in the text): see the geographers for the elements concerning the well of Zamzam in the description given by each author of the Meccan stage of the Pilgrimage: Iṣṭak̲h̲rī, i, 15, 16; Ibn Ḥawḳal, ii, 28; Muḳaddasī, iii, 72; Ibn Rusta, vii, 40-2 (the most detailed account); Ibn al-Faḳīh al-Hamadānī, v, 18, 19, supplies a description strewn with mythical allusions (he mentions the curative properties of the water of Zamzam). Yaʿḳūbī, curiously, does not mention the well of Zamzam, but notes that the Meccans are watered by a system of canals supplied by wells dug on the order of a princess, daughter of the caliph al-Manṣūr, vii, 316. Nor is there any mention in the works of caliphal functionaries such as Ibn K̲h̲urradād̲h̲bih, vi, 132, or Ḳudāma b. D̲j̲aʿfar, vi, 187. See also Ibn Ḥabīb (d. 245/860), *al-Munammaḳ fi ak̲h̲bār Ḳuraysh̲*, 133 (the part played by Zamzam in a conversion), 333, 334 (the rediscovery of the well by ʿAbd al-Muṭṭalib and the exclusive right of *sikāya* awarded to him: all other members of the tribe fall ill). T. Fahd, *Le panthéon de l'Arabie centrale*, Paris 1968, 208-12, presents pan-Semitic speculations regarding the sacred Meccan site and the well of Zamzam which appear difficult to sustain. See also on the development of the cult of Zamzam, G.R. Hawting, *The disappearance and rediscovery of Zamzam and the "well of Mecca"*, in *BSOAS*, xliii (1980), 44-54.

(Jacqueline Chabbi)

ZAMZAMA (A.), in early Arabic "the confused noise of distant thunder" (Lane, 1249b), but widely used in the sources for early Islamic history for the priests of the Magians reciting and intoning the Zoroastrian prayers and scriptures, producing (to the Arabs' ears) an indistinct, droning sound. Thus in al-Ṭabarī, i, 1042, we have the *zamzama* of the Herbadhs, in 2874 the *muzamzim* or adherent of Zoroastrianism, and in 2880 *zamzama* for the Zoroastrian rites and *zamāzima* for the Magians in general.

The term may have passed into Christian Sogdian texts, probably in the early Islamic period, as *zmzmʾ*, see M. Dresden, in *Camb. hist. Iran*, iii/2, 1225.

Bibliography: Given in the article.   (Ed.)

ZANĀNA (P.), conventionally Zenana, lit. "female, womanly", whence the particular use of the term especially in Muslim India for the private quarters of the womenfolk in a house, the equivalent of Arabic *ḥarīm* [*q.v.*], *ḥaram* and Turkish *ḥaramlïk*. See Yule and Burnell, *Hobson-Jobson, a glossary of Anglo-Indian words and phrases*, [2]London 1903, 980; and ḤARĪM.

ZANĀTA, the name in Arabic sources of one of the major groups of the Berber population which dominated the greater part of the Mag̲h̲rib in the 4th/10th and then in the 7th-9th/13th-15th centuries.

Al-Masʿūdī was one of the first to compile an inventory of the nomads (*bawādīn*) of his time, including a list of the names of Berber groups, twenty-seven in number, among which he located, in second place, the Zanāta. A century later, al-Bakrī supplies information regarding the geo-political characteristics of the group, with particular reference to the situation existing at the end of the 4th/10th century: the Zanāta were the masters of the central Mag̲h̲rib; the seat of their political power was located at Tlemcen; they were most numerous between Tahart and Tlemcen, but they were encountered as far away as Constantine and beyond, and to the south they held Sid̲j̲ilmāsa from 366/976-7 onward; and they were firmly established at Awdag̲h̲ost at the end of the trans-Saharan route.

Transhumant stock-breeders (*ḳawm raḥḥāla*) as they certainly were, the Zanāta were also cultivators, and sedentary (*mutaḥaddirūn*), al-Idrīsī was to say, describing their major rural settlement of Ibn Mud̲j̲abbir. They were also beyond any doubt traders, as is shown by their long-range activity on the western trans-Saharan route or indeed by the foundation, by one of their members, an Ifrānī, of the old market of Fakkān. Finally, as a politico-military power, the Zanāta asserted themselves by means of their cavalry (*akt̲h̲ar Zanāta fursān*, according to al-Idrīsī).

In the 4th/10th century, their confederation effectively came to dominate a shifting Mag̲h̲ribī political landscape, benefiting from the diplomatic support, the politico-religious legitimacy and the state wealth of the Umayyad caliphs of Cordova from the reign of ʿAbd al-Raḥmān III onwards. At this time, the Mag̲h̲rāwa [*q.v.*] imposed their leadership over the Zanāta as a whole, with their tribal chieftains Muḥammad b. K̲h̲azar or Zīrī b. ʿAṭiyya superseded by the chieftain of the Banū Ifran, among whom was Abū Yazīd [*q.v.*] "the man on the donkey", instigator of a revolt against the Ṣanhād̲j̲a Fāṭimids of Ifrīḳiya. Restoring their relations with al-Andalus, many of the Zanāta came to settle there and were recruited, especially under al-Manṣūr, in the caliphal armies. In the 5th/11th century they played their own game amid the struggles for power in Cordova and contributed considerably, with the Ṣanhādja of the eastern regions, to the hastening of the end of the Umayyad caliphal régime.

Subsequently, as domination passed into the hands of two other major Berber groups, the Sanhādja Almoravids (422-541/1050-1147) and the Maṣmūda Almohads (525-667/1130-1269), the Zanāta were dispersed and, as minority groups, concluded alliances sometimes with the Almoravids, constituting, for example, an entire corps of the army of ʿAlī b. Yūsuf, and at others with the Almohads, to whom they contributed administrative personnel (in the case of ʿAbd Allāh al-Zanātī or of the Zanāta of Tifsart) and military elements (the squadrons of Abū Ḥafṣ, according to al-Baydhaḳ, "are composed of Almohads as well as of Zanāta"). The Kūmiya, the tribe of ʿAbd al-Muʾmin himself, was also an offshoot of the Zanāta.

The collapse of the Almohads gave the Zanāta of the Banū Wasīn branch the opportunity to regain the political initiative and to assume power in the central and the western Maghrib with the dynasty of the ʿAbd al-Wādids at Tilimsān/Tlemcen (646-962/1248-1554) and that of the Banū Marīn at Fās (633-861/1235-1465 [see MARĪNIDS]). Although genealogically close, the two dynasties opposed each other in a cyclical fashion, and with the decline of the Marīnids, a third grouping appeared on the scene, the Banū Waṭṭās [see WAṬṬĀSIDS], who were to mark the final phase of the political power of the Zanāta in the Maghrib.

The second wave of the Zanāta was differentiated from the first by the development of alliances which had become inevitable with the Arab tribal chiefdoms which with their powerful contingents dominated the regions outside the city states. Arabisation became definitive under the reign of the Zanāta. This is clearly seen in the debate on the subject of their origins. It was not only authors such as al-Idrīsī who insisted on endowing them with a Muḍarī Arab ancestry ("Djana, the father of the Zanāta of the Maghrib is the son of Luwā, son of Barr, son of Ḳays, son of Yās, son of Muḍar"), but there is also the fact that all reasoning depended on the framework of Arab genealogical science, based on patrilineal descent, incompatible with the social and political organisation of Berber kinships. Ibn Khaldūn, the leading informant on the subject of the Zanāta, contributed extensively to an Arab reading of their history. At one point, however, he revives the question, when he credits them with "a language of their own among the Berbers, with a specific nature that is recognised as such and is distinct from other Berber dialects" (*ʿIbar*, vii/2). In another domain, al-Idrīsī holds that the Zanāta of his time are specialists in "the science of the omoplate", i.e. a form of divination, and following him Ibn Khaldūn adds (*Muḳaddima*, Fr. tr. Monteil, Eng. tr. Rosenthal, i, 229) that "among the people who have practised geomancy . . . and have written books on the principles of this art is Abū ʿAbd Allāh al-Zanātī". The writings of this author deserve scrutiny, since they have for some time constituted the obligatory reference for everything involving geomancy in Muslim Africa.

Bibliography: Idrīsī, *Description de l'Afrique et de l'Espagne*, ed. Dozy and de Goeje, Leiden 1866; Masʿūdī, iii, 240-1= § 1104; Ibn Khaldūn-de Slane, *Histoire des Berbères*, Paris 1925, i, 168-85, iii, 178-495, and iv; E. Lévi-Provençal, *Documents inédits d'histoire almohade*, Paris 1928, 3rd part: the memoirs of al-Baydhaḳ); idem, *Hist. Esp. mus.*, Paris 1950-67, ii, 78-110, 259-72, 304-41, iii, 167ff.; Ch.A. Julien, *Histoire de l'Afrique du nord*, Paris 1952-75, ii, 41-75, 132-203; Bakrī-de Slane, *Description de l'Afrique septentrionale*, repr. Paris 1965; Ibn Khaldūn, *Muḳaddima*, Fr. tr. V. Monteil, Paris 1967-8, Eng. tr. F. Rosenthal, New York 1958; idem, *ʿIbar*, Beirut 1391/1971, vi, vii; B. Kassibo, *La géomancie ouest-africaine. Formes endogènes et emprunts extérieurs*, in *Cahiers d'Études africaines*, cxxviii (1992); Dj. Souidi, *Généalogie et pouvoir au Maghreb, du IIe au VIIe/VIIIe au XIIIe siècle*, doctoral thesis, Paris 1966, unpubl., 134-58, 269-301.

(C. HAMÈS)

ZAND, an Iranian pastoral tribe of the eastern central Zagros, from which sprang a dynasty that ruled western Persia 1164-1209/1751-94.

The Zand belonged to the Lakk group of Lurs [see ĪLĀT], centred on the villages of Parī and Kamāzān near Malāyir. In 1144/1732 Nādir Shāh [*q.v.*] launched punitive raids on several Zagros tribes and deported thousands of Bakhtiyārī and a number of Zand families to northern Khurāsān. After Nādir's assassination in 1160/1747, they made their way home, the Bakhtiyārī under ʿAlī Mardān Khān and the Zand under Muḥammad Karīm Beg (also called Tūshmāl Karīm, and later Karīm Khān [*q.v.*]). When Nādir's successors were unable to reassert Afshārid hegemony over Iṣfahān, these two chieftains in alliance occupied the former Ṣafawid capital in 1163/1750 in the name of a Ṣafawid princeling, whom they styled Ismāʿīl III. ʿAlī Mardān made an unsuccessful bid for sole power, but was defeated in battle and later (1167/1764) assassinated. Karīm Khān adopted his title of *wakīl al-dawla* or regent. Having defeated three other contestants for power by 1176/1762, he pacified most of western Iran from the Caspian littoral and Ādharbāydjān to Kirmān and Lār, and took up residence in Shīrāz from 2 Ṣafar 1179/21 July 1765 until his death on 13 Ṣafar 1193/1 March 1779.

Karīm Khān did not assume the title of *shāh*, being content with that of *wakīl*; this, moreover, he reinterpreted as *wakīl al-raʿāyā* "representative of the subjects", the designation of a local official appointed by the Shāh to investigate crimes and complaints of administrative abuse (Perry, *Justice for the underprivileged*). "Ismāʿīl III" predeceased him in 1187/1773, and the fiction of a Ṣafawid revival was finally dropped. Karīm Khān did not attempt to recover Khurāsān, which fell intermittently into the orbit of the Afghān monarch Aḥmad Shāh Durrānī [*q.v.*], but devoted his efforts to reviving trade and agriculture in Fārs and western Persia. He remodelled Shīrāz, adding a covered bazaar and other fine buildings that are still standing. He concluded commercial agreements with the East India Company at Būshahr (Bushire), the natural port of Shīrāz. His control over the outlying provinces (where he generally appointed local leaders as governors) was enhanced by marriage alliances and hostages kept at court, though these were never subjected to reprisals. One of them, Āghā Muḥammad Khān Ḳādjār, escaped from Shīrāz on Karīm Khān's death and began to consolidate Ḳādjār power at Astarābād.

The *wakīl* had neglected to make provision for his succession, and his four incompetent sons immediately became pawns in a power struggle between his brothers and cousins. Zakī Khān slaughtered most of his rivals even before the funeral, and ruled in Shīrāz in the name of Muḥammad ʿAlī; ʿAlī Murād Khān, of the Hazāra branch of the Zand, seized Iṣfahān in the name of Abu 'l-Fatḥ. When Zakī marched on Iṣfahān, his own men, outraged by the atrocities which he committed in the village of Īzadkhʷāst, mutinied and killed him. ʿAlī Murād was distracted by a Ḳādjār threat, enabling Karīm's brother Ṣādiḳ Khān to seize

Simplified Genealogical Table of the Zand Dynasty

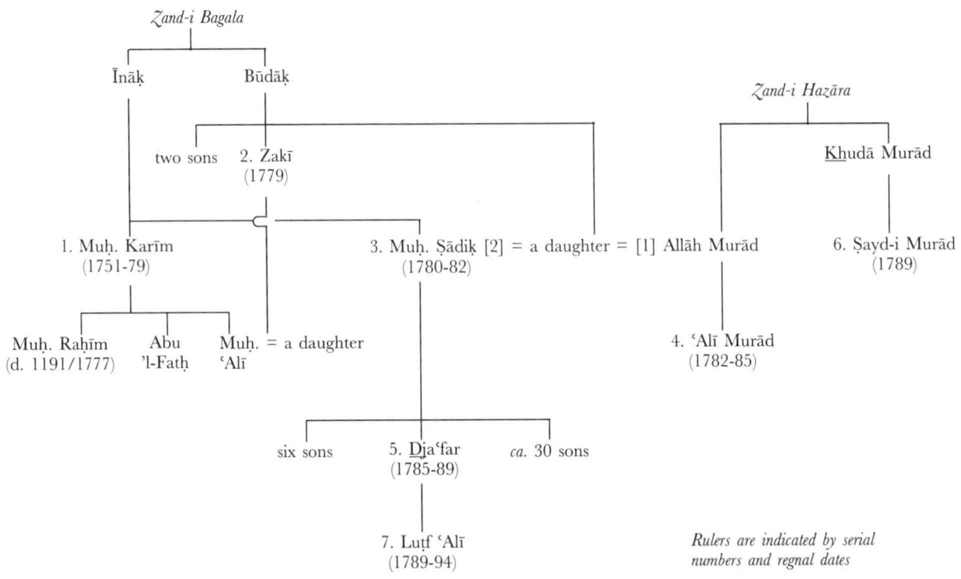

Shīrāz as effective ruler in 1195/1780. ʿAlī Murād captured Shīrāz the following year, killing Ṣādiḳ and all his sons, but was again forced to march north against the Ḳādjārs. His half-brother (and Ṣādiḳ's son) Djaʿfar Khān marched on Iṣfahān, and ʿAlī Murād died on his way back to defend the city in Rabīʿ II 1199/February 1785. From this time forth, Zand control of northern Persia was relinquished to the Ḳādjārs. Djaʿfar was twice driven from Iṣfahān to Shīrāz by the forces of Āghā Muḥammad Khān Ḳādjār, and was poisoned and beheaded in 1203/1789 in a palace coup led by Ṣayd-i Murād Khān. Djaʿfar's eldest son, Luṭf ʿAlī Khān [*q.v.*], then at Kirmān, sought refuge and reinforcements from Shaykh Nāṣir of Būshahr and, aided from within Shīrāz by the *kalāntar* (mayor), Ḥādjdjī Ibrāhīm, secured the Zand capital.

Luṭf ʿAlī's youth and courage appeared to have won him the support of the populace. He held Shīrāz against a Ḳādjār assault, recaptured Kirmān and in 1205/1791 marched on Iṣfahān. Suspicious of Ḥādjdjī Ibrāhīm's loyalty, he took the *kalāntar*'s son with him as a hostage; the *kalāntar* thereupon seized control of Shīrāz and, through his brother, fomented a mutiny in Luṭf ʿAlī's field army. From this time forth, Luṭf ʿAlī, with the gates of the Zand capital closed against him, fruitlessly sought support and refuge on the Gulf coast and in Kirmān, pursued by the Ḳādjār army. In 1207/1792 Āghā Muḥammad entered Shīrāz in triumph. Luṭf ʿAlī was driven from refuge in Kirmān, where the Ḳādjārs in reprisal killed or blinded the adult male population, and fled to Bam. Handed over by the governor, he was tortured and executed at Tehran in Rabīʿ II 1209/November 1794.

The dynasty's reputation rests on its founder Karīm Khān, who was able to weld together an army from the Iranian pastoral tribes of the Zagros and also to build a measure of trust and some lasting alliances with the bureaucrats and magnates of the major cities of western Persia (Iṣfahān, Shīrāz, Tabrīz and Kirmān). He endorsed the majority Twelver Shīʿa, without seeking the support of the *ʿulamāʾ*. Bandar ʿAbbās and other Gulf ports often withheld revenue, and the Turkmen Ḳādjārs at Astarābād were never completely subdued. The *wakīl* took advantage of Ottoman weakness to occupy the rich port of Baṣra in 1190/1776, but his subsequent death forced a withdrawal and negated any commercial advantage. His shrewd economic policies and notable humanity (by the standards of the time) are recorded in many popular anecdotes. His successors, none of whom aspired to the title of *wakīl*, devoted their energies to internecine warfare; they were unable to inspire confidence in the urban establishment, as typified by Ḥādjdjī Ibrāhīm, and so forfeited the Zand mandate to the Ḳādjārs.

Bibliography: Abu 'l-Ḥasan Ghaffārī, *Gulshan-i murād*, ed. Gh. Ṭabāṭabāʾī-Madjd, Tehran 1369 (up to 1199/1785); Abu 'l-Ḥasan Gulistāna, *Mudjmil al-tawārīkh*, ed. M. Raḍawī, Tehran 1344 (with supplement by Kūhmarraʾī, up to 1203/1789); *Rūznāma-yi Mīrzā Muḥammad-i Kalāntar-i Fārs*, ed. ʿA. Iḳbāl, Tehran 1325; Ṣādiḳ-i Nāmī, *Tārīkh-i Gītī-gushā*, ed. S. Nafīsī, Tehran 1317; Muḥammad Hāshim Āṣaf, *Rustam al-tawārīkh*, ed. M. Mushīrī, Tehran 1348, index (some fanciful anecdotes); Birgitt Hoffmann, *Persische Geschichte 1694-1835 erlebt, erinnert und erfunden. Das Rustam at-tawārīḫ in deutscher Bearbeitung*, 2 vols., Bamberg 1986; Ḥasan Fasāʾī, *Fārsnāma-yi Nāṣirī*, lith. Tehran 1313, i, 205-40; Riḍā Ḳulī Khān Hidāyat, *Rawḍat al-ṣafā-yi Nāṣirī*, Tehran 1339, ix, index; A.A. Amin, *British interests in the Persian Gulf 1747-1780*, Leiden 1967; Aḥmad Farāmarzī, *Karīm Khān-i Zand wa Khalīdj-i Fārs*, Tehran 1343; Hādī Hidāyatī, *Tārīkh-i Zandiyya*, vol. i only, Tehran 1334; J.R. Perry, *Karim Khan Zand, a history of Iran 1747-1779*, Chicago 1979 (most complete bibl.); idem, *Justice for the underprivileged. The Ombudsman tradition of Iran*, in *JNES*, xxxvii/3 (1978), esp. 209-12; Parwīz Radjabī, *Karīm Khān-i Zand wa zamān-i ū*, Tehran 1352; *Camb. hist. of Iran*, vii, Cambridge 1991, 63-126, 964-8, Pls. 1-3 (illustrations and extensive bibl.).

See also ḲĀDJĀR; KARĪM KHĀN ZAND; LUṬF ʿALI KHĀN.

(J.R. Perry)

ZANDAḲA [see ZINDĪḲ].

AL-**ZANDJ** (A.), a term found in Arabic literature,

but apparently of non-Arabic origin, denoting the peoples of Black Africa, and especially those with whom the Arabs came into contact through their voyages and trade in the western part of the Indian Ocean and living in the eastern parts of Africa. For the territories in question, the term *bilād al-Zandj* was used.

1. As a territorial term.

Here, it forms the second of al-Idrīsī's four divisions of the eastern coast of Africa. The term first occurs in Strabo (A.D. 6), who uses a Greek form *Azania*; in Latin, Pliny (A.D. 79) writes of *Azania* as north of Adulis on the Ethiopian coast, and of a people whom he calls Zangenae, of uncertain location. In agreement with al-Idrīsī 1,100 years later, the anonymous Alexandrine *Periplus of the Erythraean Sea* (*ca.* A.D. 50) describes Azania as the area of the coast from Ras Hafun in modern Somalia as far as Rhapta, a trading station of greatly disputed location. Claudius Ptolemy, whose present text on eastern Africa represents a revision probably edited *ca.* 400, places "Rhapta metropolis" on a river, possibly the Rufiji. Cosmas Indicopleustes, an Alexandrine merchant who travelled down the Red Sea in 524, and wrote his account in a monastery in 547, writes of an area called *Zingion* and of a Cape *Zingion*. All of these terms seem transitional to the form used by the Arab authors and in Swahili.

The *Bilād al-Zandj*, peopled by the Zunūdj, is an area whose name is cognate with the Swahili Unguja, still used in current speech for Zanzibar and for the ancient, deserted site of the former capital, Unguja Kuu. It is first attested by the poet Djarīr (d. 110/728-9), and by al-Djāḥiẓ. Buzurg b. Shahriyār of Rāmhurmuz (d. 342/953) speaks of trading visits to Zandj; the traveller al-Masʿūdī visited Zandj in 303/916, and gives an account of its government and its trade. It was known to the geographers Ibn Ḥawḳal (4th/10th century) and al-Idrīsī (549/1154), and to Yāḳūt al-Ḥamawī, whose geographical encyclopaedia was completed in 625/1228. Marco Polo did not visit Zandj; his description seems rather to have derived from ill-informed gossip in India *ca.* 1295. His statement that Zanzibar is an island 2,000 miles round suggests confusion in his mind between the mainland area described by the Arab authors and the island of Zanzibar. The pharmacological writer Ibn al-Bayṭar says that black rhubarb is called *zandj* from its colour and not from its provenance, but *zandj* and *zunūdj* mostly mean "black people" in Arabic literature, see 2. below. Likewise, the use of "Azania" by some southern African political movements is anomalous. In 1964, when the former Tanganyika united with the Republic of Zanzibar, it was thought necessary to find a new name for the political union. After discussion, the name Tanzania (< Tan[ganyika] + Zan[zibar] + ia) was decided upon, thus approximately recalling a history of the term already some 2,000 years old.

Before the colonial period there were no unitary states in the modern political sense but rather a series of coastal merchant states, self-governing as separate entities. For these individual states, see the articles listed below in the *Bibl.*, including those concerning trading relations.

The history of Islam in the region has not yet been written. The earliest reference is in al-Djāḥiẓ, and the second one to conversion to Islam of a mainland indigenous sovereign in Buzurg b. Shahriyar. So far only one ancient mosque, occupied for worship until the 9th/15th century, has been fully excavated. At Shanga, in the Lamu Archipelago, it was the ninth successive mosque on the same site, each successor mosque becoming slightly more elaborate than its predecessor: the most ancient of all has been ascribed by M.C. Horton on ceramic grounds to the mid-2nd/8th century, that is, to the period of Djarīr. The earliest mosque was a simple enclosure of reeds orientated towards Mecca, its successors constructed first in mud and wattle and finally, as the community became more prosperous, in stone, with a carved *miḥrāb*. There is no literary history of the mosques of the region, and inscriptions recording dates of foundation hardly occur before the 10th/16th century. The earliest such inscription, however, is that of the Friday Mosque at Kizimkazi, Zanzibar, 500[/1106-7].

Bibliography: B. Krumm, *Words of oriental origin in Swahili*, London 1940; [A.]G. Mathew, *The Coast, c. A.D. 100-1489*, in *The Oxford history of East Africa*, Oxford 1963; H.N. Chittick and R.I. Rotberg (eds.), *East Africa and the Orient*, New York 1965 (arts. by J.S. Trimingham with very detailed references to the Zandj); G.S.P. Freeman-Greenville (ed. and tr.), *The book of the wonders of India. Buzurg ibn Shariyar of Ramhormuz*, London 1981; idem, *Tanzania, problems of a toponym*, in *Geographical Notes and Queries* (cyclostyled), repr. in idem, *The Swahili coast, second to nineteenth centuries*, Variorum, London 1988; L. Casson, *The Periplus Maris Erythraei*, Princeton 1989. See also KILWA; KIZIMKAZI; LAMU; MAFIA ISLANDS; MAḲDISHŪ; MALINDI; MANDA ISLAND; MERCA; MKWAJA; MOMBASA; MTAMBWE MKUU; MOZAMBIQUE; PATE; PEMBA; SOFĀLA; WĀḲWĀḲ. 1; ZANDJIBĀR.

(G.S.P. FREEMAN-GRENVILLE)

2. The Zandj revolts in ʿIrāḳ.

The Zandj, like many other black slaves originally from the East African coastlands (whether obtained by capture, purchased or received as tribute from tributary powers), were imported into ʿAbbāsid ʿIrāḳ in large numbers from an undetermined date onwards. Their living conditions must have been extremely harsh, since they rebelled three times within a space of two centuries.

(a) The first rising was in 70/689-90 during the time of Khālid b. ʿAbd Allāh, the successor to Muṣʿab b. al-Zubayr. It seems to have been of small significance, since it apparently involved small bands of rebels engaged in pillaging, which were dispersed without great effort by the caliphal forces. The prisoners were beheaded and their corpses gibbeted (see references in Popovic, *La révolte des esclaves en Iraq au IIIe/VIIIe siècle*, 63).

(b) The second revolt took place five years later, in 75/694. It seems to have been more important and, above all, better prepared. The Zandj had a leader, one Rabāḥ (or Riyāḥ ?), called *Shīr Zandjī* "The Lion of the Zandj", and the authorities had to march against him twice in order to crush the rebels. The character of this revolt seems to have been more complex, but our information about it is scanty: "The information we possess on this movement does not allow us to uncover its true character; but one has to believe that it did not break out spontaneously and that the Zandj had been worked upon by a certain amount of propaganda" (Ch. Pellat, *Le milieu baṣrien et la formation de Ǧāḥiẓ*, Paris 1953, 41-2).

(c) The third revolt of the Zandj is best known, for it caused a violent disturbance over fifteen years (255-70/869-83) in Lower ʿIrāḳ and Khūzistān, causing innumerable material losses and tens of thousands of lives lost. It was the work of a remarkable person, apparently without scruples, ʿAlī b. Muḥammad, called *Ṣāḥib al-Zandj* [see ʿALĪ B. MUḤAMMAD AL-ZANDJĪ]. A revolutionary character, of obscure origins—but one able to approach the highest levels of power, such as court circles of his period—he was a talented poet, educated, well-versed in the occult sciences, follower of various doctrines and instigator of several previous risings (notably in Baḥrayn and at Baṣra), and he succeeded in stirring up the greatest servile insurrection in the history of the Islamic world.

Four reasons underlie his success and the long duration of his revolt. These were, first, the extreme misery of these bands of slaves. The rebels were employed, according to our main source, al-Ṭabarī, iii, 1742-87, 1835-2103, Eng. tr. D. Waines, *The History of al-Ṭabarī. An annotated translation. XXXVI. The revolt of the Ẓanj*, Albany 1992, 29-67, 108-207, tr. P.M. Field, *XXXVII. The ʿAbbāsid recovery*, Albany 1987, 1-43, as workers on the soil, *kassāḥīn*, cultivating the earth of Lower Mesopotamia, removing the nitrous topsoil (*sibākh*) and putting it into small piles in order to render cultivable the ground of the Shaṭṭ al-ʿArab [*q.v.*] region; in the words of Massignon, *EI*[1] art. *Ẓandj*, "they were penned up in working gangs of 500 to 5,000 men, and dumped there permanently with only a few handfuls of meal, semolina and dates". Second, the region was suitable for guerilla warfare [see AL-BAṬĪḤA]. Third, there was the precarious nature of the central authority in Baghdād at this time (anarchy in the central lands, and severe problems in more distant provinces). Fourth, there were the personal qualities—as organiser, warrior and politician—of ʿAlī b. Muḥammad.

Two periods of the revolt can be clearly distinguished. The first (255-66/869-79) was one of expansion and success for the rebels; the central power was unable, for internal and external reasons, to combat them efficaciously. The rebels organised themselves, procured arms and fortified themselves within camps in inaccessible places, from where they launched their raids. After many ambushes and battles that went in their favour (for the "army" of the rebels was continually being strengthened by freed slaves), they seized temporary control of the main cities of Lower ʿIrāḳ and Khūzistān (al-Ubulla, ʿAbbādān, Baṣra, Wāsiṭ, Djubbā, Ahwāz, etc.). The ʿAbbāsid forces reoccupied, without great difficulty, the towns that the Zandj had taken, sacked and abandoned, but were unable to extinguish the outbreak or to inflict a decisive defeat on an enemy everywhere and nowhere. Also, since the government in Baghdād had other more urgent problems to solve, for several years the rebellion of the Zandj was relegated to the second rank of importance. During this time, the "Master of the Zandj" was solidly installed in the canal region, where he had his "capital" [see AL-MUKHTĀRA], minting his own coins, organising his "state" and attempting, with varying degrees of success, to establish links with other anti-caliphal movements of the time (e.g. those of Ḥamdān Ḳarmaṭ [see ḲARMAṬĪ] and of Yaʿḳūb b. al-Layth [*q.v.*]).

The second period (266-70/879-83) was just a drawn-out agony before the final crushing of the movement. The suppression of the Zandj now became the prime consideration for the caliphate, which moved methodically, cleansing the territories before it and driving the Zandj to take refuge in the canal region, where they were subjected to a methodical siege directed by the regent al-Muwaffaḳ [*q.v.*] and his son Abu 'l-ʿAbbās (the future caliph al-Muʿtaḍid [*q.v.*]). Finally, ʿAlī b. Muḥammad was killed and his close companions and commanders taken as prisoners to Baghdād, where they were beheaded two years later, whilst some members of his family ended their days in prison.

One may conclude by saying that the Zandj revolt was both a political one, in its aim at securing power, and also a social one, aiming at relieving the harsh living conditions of one class of the population; but several important points involved in this remarkable episode merit an extended consideration (the personality of the revolt's leader, his alleged genealogy, his credo and ideology, the political and social organisation of the new "state", and its relations with the various classes of the population and with other movements of the time) which cannot be gone into here. One may nevertheless stress one essential aspect, sc. that if the movement has a unique place amongst various insurrections in the history of mediaeval Islam, it is because it put paid to a unique attempt, in the Islamic world, at transforming domestic slavery into a colonial-type slavery.

Bibliography (in addition to references given in the article): Th. Nöldeke, *A servile war in the East*, in *Sketches from eastern history*, London and Edinburgh 1892, 146-75; ʿAbd al-ʿAzīz al-Dūrī, *Dirāsāt fi 'l-ʿuṣūr al-ʿabbāsiyya al-mutaʾakhkhira*, Baghdād 1945, 75-106; Fayṣal al-Sāmir, *Thawrat al-Ẓandj*, Baghdād [1]1954, [2]1971; Aḥmad S. Olabi, *Thawrat al-Ẓandj*, Beirut 1961; H. Halm, *Die Traditionen über den Aufstand ʿAlī Ibn Muhammads, des "Herrn der Zanǧ", eine quellenkritische Untersuchung*, diss. Bonn 1967; A. Popovic, *La révolte des esclaves en Iraq au III*[e]*/IX*[e] *siècle*, Paris 1976, Eng. tr. *The revolt of African slaves in Iraq in the 3rd/9th century*, Princeton 1998, with detailed and updated bibl.

(A. POPOVIC)

ZANDJĀN, a town of northwestern Persia, situated on the Zandjān Rūd, a right-bank affluent of the Safīd Rūd [*q.v.*]. It lies on the highway from Tehran and Ḳazwīn to Tabrīz at a distance of 314 km/195 miles from Tehran and 302 km/188 miles from Tabrīz, and at an altitude of 1,625 m/5,330 feet (lat. 36° 40' N., long. 48° 30' E.).

The mediaeval geographers mostly placed Zandjān in Djibāl province, usually linking it with Abhar [*q.v.*] or Awhar some 80 km/50 miles to its south-east, but they usually stated that it was on the frontier with Ādharbāydjān, and some authorities attributed it to Daylam or to Rayy. According to legend, it had been founded, as Shahīn, by the first Sāsānid Ardashīr b. Pāpakān (Mustawfī, *Nuzha*, 61, tr. 67). It was conquered *ʿanwat*[an] in 24/645 by Arabs led by al-Barrāʾ b. ʿĀzib after Abhar and Ḳazwīn, and al-Balādhurī further narrates that, in the late 2nd/early 9th century, the people of Zandjān, weary of the depredations of bandits (*ṣaʿālīk* [see ṢUʿLŪK] and the oppression of local governors, placed themselves under the protection of the governor of northern Persia, Hārūn al-Rashīd's son al-Ḳāsim so that Zandjān and its region became part of the caliphal estates (*al-ḍiyāʿ al-khāṣṣa*) (*Futūḥ*, 322-3). In the 4th/10th century, it came within the sphere of local Daylamī dynasties like the Musāfirids [*q.v.*]. The Arab traveller Abū Dulaf [*q.v.*] visited it, noting mines of iron sulphate, borax and alum in the adjacent mountains; the manuscript of his *Second Risāla* records the name as spelt with initial *zh*, sc. Zhandjān (*Abū-Dulaf Misʿar ibn Muhalhil's travels in Iran* (*circa A.D. 750*), ed. and tr. Minorsky, Cairo 1955, § 11, tr. 34, comm. 71).

In the early 7th/13th century, Zandjān was held by the Khʷārazm-Shāh's son Djalāl al-Dīn (Djuwaynī-Boyle, ii, 702), but then devastated by the Mongols and its extensive walls demolished. For the Mongols, the upland pastures between the region of Zandjān and Tabrīz were favoured grazing grounds, and the name of the district Ūryād preserves the name of the Oyrat Mongols. Not far south of Zandjān was the Il-Khānid capital Sulṭāniyya [*q.v.*], and the Il-Khān

Arg͟hun was buried at nearby Sud͟jās (the *koruk-i Arg͟hūn*, Mustawfī, 64, tr. 69). Zand͟jān shared in the general prosperity of northwestern Persia at this time, and Mustawfī fixed its revenues at 12,000 dīnārs plus another 8,000 from the hundred or so villages around it, and also stated that the inhabitants spoke "pure Pahlawī", i.e. a Median or northern form of Persian (*Nuzha*, 61-2, tr. 67).

In later times, fighting between the Ottomans and the Ṣafawids and their successors extended as far as Zand͟jān, but the town became best known in the 19th century as a centre of the Bābīs [*q.v.*], being the birthplace of one of the Bāb's leading supporters, Mullā Muḥammad ʿAlī Ḥud͟jd͟jat al-Islām Zand͟jānī. The Zand͟jān rising of 1266/1850 by the Bābīs of the town, numbering only a few hundreds, caused a crisis for the Ḳād͟jār state, since government troops were for several months unable to quell the rebels, and the resistance of Zand͟jān may have influenced the decision to execute the Bāb himself in S͟haʿbān 1266/July 1850 (see E.G. Browne, *Personal reminiscences of the Bábí insurrection at Zanján in 1850...*, in *JRAS* [1897], 761-827; Abbas Amanat, *Resurrection and renewal. The making of the Babi movement in Iran, 1844-1850*, Ithaca and London 1989, 101-2, 397 and index; J. Walbridge, *The Babi rising in Zanjan: causes and issues*, in *Iranian Studies*, xxix/3-4 [1996], 339-62). Despite the bloody suppression of the outbreak, Zand͟jān continued to produce some of the leading Bābī and Bahāʾī figures (see Browne, *Materials for the study of the Bábí religion*, Cambridge 1918, 36).

Zand͟jān was formerly the chef-lieu of a *s͟hahrastān* of the same name in the province of Gīlān, but is now the *markaz* of an independent province of Zand͟jān. In the late 1930s it became a station on the Tehran-Tabrīz railway. Its population in *ca.* 1950 was 48,000, which had risen by the 1996 census to 286,295. Although somewhat detached geographically from the main Azeri speech area, the population of Zand͟jān is ethnically Turkish and essentially Turkish-speaking.

Bibliography: See also the older bibl. in Minorsky, *EI*[1] art. s.v.; Le Strange, *The lands of the Eastern Caliphate*, 221-2; Schwarz, *Iran im Mittelalter*, 729-31; Razmārā (ed.), *Farhang-i d͟jug͟hrāfiyā-yi Īrān-zamīn*, ii, 140-1; Sayyid Mūsawī Zand͟jānī, *Tārīk͟h-i Zand͟jān*, Tehran 1351/1972; L.W. Adamec (ed.), *Historical gazetteer of Iran*. i. *Tehran and northwestern Iran*, Graz 1976, 709-10; D. Krawulsky, *Īrān—das Reich der Īlk͟hāne. Eine topographisch-historische Studie*, Wiesbaden 1978, 325-6. (C.E. Bosworth)

al-**ZAND͟JĀNĪ** [see Suppl.].

ZAND͟JIBĀR (or al-zand͟jabār), officially spelt Zanzibar, is an island in lat. 6° S., with a capital of the same name. It is about 53 miles in length and 24 miles at its broadest. The area is about 640 sq miles. A channel about 20 miles wide separates it from the Tanzanian mainland. Its history and economy are bound up with the prevailing winds, the south-west and north-east monsoons, which set in with clockwork regularity. The south-west monsoon begins in March, bringing the *Masika*, or Long Rains, which last with decreasing vigour for about three months. The *Mvuli*, or Short Rains, fall in October and November. Until the coming of the steamship, the whole economy of eastern Africa depended on these monsoons.

Although linked with the mainland United Republic of Tanzania, Zanzibar is a self-governing territory, together with the island of Pemba [*q.v.*] and some small islands of trifling importance. Except for Tumbatu [*q.v.*], they are uninhabited, and visited only by fishermen and tourists.

1. The island and town of Zanzibar up to 1890.

(a) *In Antiquity and prehistoric times*

Before the coming of Islam to eastern Africa, certainly up to the 8th century A.D., there are only some scattered and casual allusions in Greek and Roman writers, for which see zand͟j. One major source, *The Periplus of the Erythraean Sea*, refers to it in *ca.* A.D. 50. It is an account of trading voyages down the eastern African coasts, along southern Arabia and as far as India, if not to China. It has links with Egypt and the western Indian Ocean. Scholars have disputed endlessly whether its reference to a single island, Menuthias, off the eastern African coast, is to Pemba or to Zanzibar or to Mafia. Ptolemy even thought the island to be Madagascar. Menuthias is said to have numerous rivers: Zanzibar has one only; Pemba has some streams, but also numerous deep inlets which, seen from the sea, resemble estuaries. It is low and wooded. Pemba reaches a maximum of 150 m above sea level, Zanzibar 100 m. Again, Pemba's deep inlets with hilly sides give the impression of a hilly island when seen from the sea, whereas Zanzibar is more uniformly level. Both islands are wooded. The inhabitants are said to be fishermen who employ fish traps, dug-outs and also "sewn boats", that is, with their timbers sewn together with coconut coir. The "sewn boats" are no longer constructed but the other practices survive. The balance of probability could swing either way.

Two of the sites so far excavated have pre-Islamic occupation levels, Fukuchani in the north and Unguja Ukuu in the south of the island. From these are imported sherds from the Persian Gulf and from Roman North Africa, at occupation levels dating probably from the 5th to 8th centuries A.D. The most recent excavations at Unguja Ukuu (1999) show that it was a major exporter of ivory to Egypt, whence to Constantinople and through the Mediterranean, via Pelusium. The evidence is based on the existence of sherds of Byzantine pottery and on carbon dating. In Unguja Ukuu there are found in middens of the same period bones of *rattus rattus*, the black rat, which is not indigenous of Africa but whose fleas are the vectors of bubonic plague. The first recorded outbreak of the Great Plague of 541-7, in which more than a quarter of a million people died in Constantinople alone, was at Pelusium, which makes it logical to ascribe the source to Zanzibar. Local pottery suggests that the inhabitants belonged to the Early Iron Age communities of East Africa, whose working of shells and iron formed part of the economy of the time.

(b) *Before the Portuguese*

Pending further investigation it can be said that the claims of W.H. Ingrams (*Zanzibar*, London 1931) and others, of the existence of a "Heliolithic Culture", or of the presence of Sumerians, Assyrians, Akkadians, Chaldaeans, Medes, Persians, Ancient Egyptians or Phoenicians, rest on no historical or archaeological foundation. There are Palaeolithic remains at Kilwa [*q.v.*] and of the Early Iron Age in Mafia [*q.v.*].

The Swahili *History of Pate* [see pate] whose redaction in its present state cannot be dated before 1810, claims that the fifth Umayyad caliph, ʿAbd al-Malik b. Marwān (695-705), heard of East Africa "and that his soul desired to found a new kingdom". He sent Syrians, who founded "the cities of Pate, Malindi, Zanzibar, Mombasa, Lamu and Kilwa". Other towns are mentioned in oral traditions, from Mogadishu as far as the Comoros.

Next, Hārūn al-Ras͟hīd (*r.* 786-801 [*q.v.*]) is alleged to have founded many coastal towns, but not in Pemba or Zanzibar. He is said to have sent Persians. There is no evidence to support these claims; they could well be 19th-century embroidery upon what could be known from 10th-century sources, such as al-Masʿūdī and Buzurg b. S̲h̲ahriyār. Neither of these refer to Zanzibar, but mention Ḳanbalū, most likely Ras Mkumbuu in Pemba. There, recent excavation has disclosed a mosque capable of accommodating seventy worshippers; it rested upon the remains of two earlier mosques, one of stone and the other of timber. The topmost building is possibly 10th century, the substrata from the 9th and 8th centuries, the earliest Islamic structures yet found in sub-Saharan Africa. It seems clear that Pemba, and particularly Ras Mkumbuu, had an importance that Zanzibar lacked.

Nevertheless, history is not entirely mute. The Arabic *History of Kilwa*, redacted as we have it perhaps *ca.* 1550, claims that Zanzibar gave refuge to a deposed sultan of Kilwa in *ca.* 1035, and then reinstated him on the throne. Not long afterwards, a mosque was built at Kizimkazi in Zanzibar, of which original sections still survive; it has an elaborate *miḥrāb*, with a carved foundation inscription dated 500/1107. This last is in a Kūfic script similar to a number of inscriptions excavated in Sīrāf. The stone, however, is of Zanzibar coral and so could only have been carved on Zanzibar. Local traditions assert that there was a local sultanate based on Kizimkazi, where a number of (later) stone buildings survive.

João de Barros preserves a second *History of Kilwa*, originally written in Arabic, in a Portuguese translation. It was redacted perhaps in 1505. It asserts that Sulaymān b. al-Ḥasan of Kilwa (*r.* 1170-89) made himself "lord of the commerce of Sofāla" [*q.v.*], and of the islands of Pemba, Mafia and Zanzibar, and a great part of the mainland shore". In 1224 Yāḳūt's *Muʿd̲j̲am al-buldān* reports that Languja was the residence of the King of the *Zunūd̲j̲*. Languja is a corruption of al-Unguja, still the ordinary Swahili name for Zanzibar. If not independent, he may have been a subject of Kilwa.

In 1865 a hoard of dīnārs was "discovered" in a mound in the centre of Unguja Ukuu, which was turned over in the hope of finding further treasure. One piece survived, dated to A.D. 797. There are now no visible standing walls earlier than the 19th century. A mosque was noted in 1920; its well is still in use. There are local traditions of a Portuguese *feitoria* ("factory" or trading agency) but nothing survives. Recent excavations conducted by the Zanzibar Director of Antiquities have disclosed buildings believed to date to the 10th century, with quantities of imported pottery, chiefly from the Persian Gulf, of the 8th to 10th centuries. Some sherds from there of African Red Slip pottery have been dated by radiocarbon dating to the 6th century. Occupation ceased in the 10th/11th century, with some reoccupation in the 16th. This site would certainly appear to be the Languja of al-D̲j̲āḥiẓ. Its abandonment may be linked to a decline in the market for *zand̲j̲ī* slaves following the Zand̲j̲ revolt. So far, it can be said that very many pieces of what is a jig-saw puzzle have been found; how to fit them together is another question.

Of possible relevance is the limited excavation that has taken place at Mkokotoni, in the northwest of the island and opposite Tumbatu. The first phase covers the 8th-10th centuries but is much eroded by the sea. Its stone buildings have been entirely robbed but cover an area extending 500 m along a low cliff. There is a hiatus until the 14th century, which is very rich in deposits. Particularly striking are the bead finds, in huge quantities that suggest either a huge store or their manufacture. Locals searching for beads have also found quantities of coins, both Chinese and Indian, but none of any local currency. It was here that a major coin hoard was found in 1984 and smuggled out of the country. It may have included three gold coins of al-Ḥasan b. Sulaymān of Kilwa III (*r.* 1310-33), which were brought to London and of which casts were made in the British Museum. They were reported to have been "found at Tumbatu".

Returning to the historical record, the *History of Pate* already quoted asserts that the Pate ruler ʿUmar b. Muḥammad (*r.* 1332-48) gained possession of all the Swahili towns from Pate as far as the Kerimba Islands but failed to take Zanzibar. There is no evidence elsewhere for this alleged event, which perhaps was no more than a raid.

In 1442, when there was a dispute about the succession to the throne in Kilwa, the *Amīr* of Zanzibar is said to have intervened but was bought off by a bribe of 100 gold *mit̲h̲ḳāls*. At this time, Zanzibar had its own copper currency.

There are many minor traditions and legends associated with smaller sites. There are numerous traditions of people known in Swahili as Wa-debuli and Wa-diba (*wa-* being a prefix denoting the class). They had no fixed settlements but moved from place to place; the Wa-debuli could well have been itinerant Indian traders from the port of Daybul [*q.v.*] and the Wa-diba from the Maldive Islands, which the Arab geographers term Diba.

Midden excavations at Unguja Ukuu and Fukuchani have shown evidence of the diet of the people in the form of bone remains. Cattle, goat and sheep are not unexpected. Pig also are included. Chicken and pigeon, too, were eaten; the nearby ocean abounded, as it still does, in fish. Bone remains also included the Zanzibar Pouched Rat (*cricetomys gambianus* Cosensi) known locally as *buku*. They are reported to be nearly three feet long from snout to the end of the tail. It is unknown today for them to be eaten in Zanzibar but some non-Islamic groups on the mainland like them. Monkeys were also eaten in some quantity.

As to religion, al-Masʿūdī reports (*ca.* 920) that the kings of the Zunūd̲j̲ and their subjects were pagan. By the time of al-Idrīsī (1154), the inhabitants of Unguja, Swahili speakers, although mixed, were mostly Muslims. The excavated evidence from mosques suggests that al-Masʿūdī was not well informed. Certainly, Islam was not the official religion of the kings whom he describes, but the process of Islamisation would have been a slow one, which, it may safely be assumed, had begun by the 8th century A.D. This is not to say that ancient beliefs did not linger on, as they still do today, notably in the Nairozi ceremonies [see NAWRŪZ. 2.] and those connected with *rites de passage*.

(c) *Under Portuguese hegemony 1505-1698*

For the Portuguese period local sources are silent, and we are dependent upon Portuguese historians and writers. Local traditions allege two fortified houses or farms to have belonged to the Portuguese, at Mvuleni and at Fukuchani, the latter built over an earlier pre-Islamic site.

In 1499 Vasco da Gama, returning from India, anchored off Zanzibar to take on provisions and water. It was for one night only; he and his men were eager to return home. Next, in 1503, a single vessel commanded by Rui Lourenço Ravasco arrived and cruised off the island, blockading it and capturing twenty local vessels laden with provisions. These, says Damião de Goes, he ransomed for money. It is alleged that the locals opened hostilities with "many guns and arrows", to which Ravasco replied with a bombardment. Both sides accused the other, and subsequently Ravasco was censured in Lisbon. Nevertheless, Zanzibar paid a tribute of 130 gold *mit̲h̲ḳāls*—a sum compared with 1,000 paid at Kilwa and 100 at Pate.

In 1528 Nuno da Cunha's fleet lost its bearings and was driven up a creek in southwestern Zanzibar. A captive pilot conducted them to a safe anchorage. Two hundred sick men were left ashore, but it is not apparent whether a permanent *feitoria* was set up.

If, indeed, it was set up, it was not of stone. By 1571 Fr Monclaro S.J. reported that the ancient capital, "once as large as Kilwa.... is now destroyed and in ruins". Perhaps this was the result of Ravasco's bombardment, but "there were Kaffir rebels from the mainland, who kept the country in confusion". The people were in fear; the Portuguese fought the rebels, with the result that the King of Zanzibar made a gift of the island to Portugal "with great solemnities". Some Portuguese resided on the island and had their own chapel and chaplain. They were traders in cloth, beads, iron, ivory and some ambergris. The island was very fertile. There is no mention of a *feitoria*.

The first positive evidence of a *feitoria* comes from Edmund Barker of Ipswich, the Lieutenant of the *Bonaventure*, under Sir James Lancaster, who wintered there in 1591-2. He was told of the mean and spiteful dealings of the Portuguese by a Christian Moor, but with no details. Gaspar de São Bernardino O.P. reports that a cargo of slaves was carried from Zanzibar to Mombasa in 1606, but there is no reason to suppose that it was a regular item of trade. The King of Zanzibar is reported to have been friendly. João dos Santos O.P. speaks of the rough and high-handed conduct of the Portuguese. He had converted to Christianity a nephew of the king, whom he sent to Goa to be educated.

A report of 1606 speaks of Augustinian "vicars" at Lamu, Pate and Faza on the mainland, in addition to their convent at Mombasa, but not at Zanzibar. An Augustinian stationed in Zanzibar with a chapel is not mentioned until a Papal Bull of 1612. The two dates would seem to bracket the foundation of the chapel, as being an adjunct of the *feitoria*. Recent excavations in the centre of what eventually was reconstructed as an ʿUmānī fort suggest that it was on the site of a 12th-century fishing and trading village. Sgraffiato, Chinese celadon and monochrome porcelain, as well as local red wares have been found. The foreign connection was not just casual. A large hoard of copper coins, locally minted, has been found, and ascribed to the 14th or the 15th century.

Parts of the church still exist. It was cruciform. In 1710 the ʿUmānīs fortified it, rebuilding it completely in 1760. Nevertheless, in a strange way it has kept its name. In Swahili the fort is spoken of as *gereza*, a corruption of Portuguese *igreja* "church". In the 19th century, when the ʿUmānīs had ceased to use the fort as a residence, it was made into a prison. The name Gereza remained, to become the name for a prison wherever Swahili is spoken. In the 1920s it had a new twist of fortune. It was partly demolished to provide a railway station for the seven-mile line from the town to the plantations at Bububu. By 1946 it was derelict, and restored for use as a purdah Ladies' Club. In the 1990s it became an open-air theatre.

There is little trace today of the Portuguese period. The principal cultural legacy was of the slightest, some 120 words which passed from Portuguese into Swahili. It is intelligible that a quarter of them concern the sea and shipping. A second large group are of useful fruit, trees and vegetables, some of which—cashew, cucumber, lime, pawpaw, avocado and guava, potatoes, cassava (manioc), tobacco, and most usefully, *mboleo* "manure"—have taken permanent root. There is a small domestic vocabulary, and one for the games of dice and picquet. The Swahili word for a tavern or brothel, *dangelo*, derives from *danceador*. These are only a few examples. In the Torre do Tombo National Archives in Lisbon, and in the National Library, there is evidence of another kind, of Portuguese written in Arabic script, and of Swahili also. It would seem that for a time Portuguese was a *lingua franca* in the Indian Ocean until it was superseded by English.

The expulsion of the Portuguese from Fort Jesus, Mombasa, in 1698, does not seem to have had any immediate repercussions in Zanzibar. No appointment was made as successor to Fr. Manoel de Conceiçao O.S.A. as Vicar of Zanzibar, who had been murdered by tribesmen in 1694. A queen of Zanzibar, Fatuma or Fatima, gained peaceful possession, only to be subject to new overlords. The site of her palace is pointed out near the Gereza.

(d) *Under the ʿUmānī Arabs* ca. *1700-1890*

Now for more than a century history is almost silent. In 1712 a spy employed by the Portuguese Viceroy of Goa reported that the "Arabs" had constructed "a ridiculous fort" out of the *feitoria* and a stone house built by João Nunes at the end of the 17th century. The Swahili royalty remained in office, but control was in the hands of the Mazrūʿī [*q.v.*] rulers of Mombasa until their final eviction by Sultan Sayyid Saʿīd [*q.v.*] in 1837.

A. Sheriff's *History and conservation of Zanzibar Stone Town* gives valuable details of its expansion. The Portuguese *feitoria* and church may have had no more than palm-thatched huts around them. They lay on a peninsula connected to the mainland by a narrow isthmus. Two maps published by him, of 1846 and 1896, provide an instructive summary for the period. The peninsular buildings are almost exclusively from the 19th and 20th centuries; a creek separates the Stone Town from the mainland, on which, in 1846, very few constructions, all apparently huts, were to be found. The town thus consists, as now, of two parts, the Stone Town, the older part; and the opposite side of the creek known in Swahili as *Ngambo*, meaning "the other side". The creek, when kept clean, provided a sheltered harbour for Portuguese vessels; the shallow draught of the almost flat-bottomed Swahili vessels and boats meant that they were generally drawn up on shelving beaches, any larger vessels being propped up on stilts at low tide. By 1896 Ngambo had grown to four times the size of the Stone Town, a clear indication of mercantile prosperity.

Inscriptions and other evidence for the foundation dates of mosques are likewise instructive. The earliest mosque in the Stone Town is dated 1766; one other was built in the 18th century. Sayyid Saʿīd first visited Zanzibar in 1828, removing his court to Zanzibar only in 1842. Three mosques were erected in 1830 and one more in 1840. From 1850 to 1890, no less than twenty-seven mosques were erected, with five more in the present century. Scholarship was not deficient, and Sir Richard Burton, never slow to criticise, particularly admired the eminent knowledge of S̲h̲ayk̲h̲ Muḥyī al-Dīn b. S̲h̲ayk̲h̲ b. ʿAbd Allāh al-K̲h̲aytānī, *ḳāḍī* of Zanzibar from 1841 to 1870. He wrote works of history and *fiḳh*, and was a poet. The greater number of mosques reflects population growth and the flourishing economy, of which C.S. Nicholls has given a portrait in depth up to Sayyid Saʿīd's death in 1856. It is carried forward by M.R. Bhacker up to the proclamation of the British Protectorate in 1890. Traders were attracted from all quarters, Arabs from ʿUmān and Ḥaḍramawt, Indians (the majority), and American, British, French, German and Portuguese entrepreneurs. Sayyid Saʿīd said modestly "I am only a merchant", but truly he made Zanzibar a "metropolis of the Indian Ocean".

European immigrants and officials formed a more or less homogeneous society, the easterners deeply divided by race and sects. The Arabs and Swahili were of the S̲h̲āfiʿī legal school, save for the ʿUmānī rulers who were of the Ibāḍī branch of the K̲h̲āridjites. They had few differences with the S̲h̲āfiʿīs and were tolerant. Among Indians, Hindus were wholly apart, as were Parsis; among Indian Muslims were Sunnīs, Twelver S̲h̲īʿa and K̲h̲ōdja Ismāʿīlīs, who predominated over the Dāʾūdī Bohorās and smaller sects. In addition, there were Sikhs and Baluch, these last providing the Sultanic guard. Few of them mixed with the local population. Whereas in former times Africans had brought their products to the coast, under Sayyid Saʿīd Indian-financed caravans now journeyed into the African interior as far as Uganda and Kinshasa. Islamic religious brotherhoods had members among them and set up pockets of their adherents along the trade routes. By the 20th century, substantial areas were Islamised. The Swahili, both in the town and countryside, still reflect syncretistic practices as part of their local traditions.

Sayyid Saʿīd had sixty or seventy concubines, in accordance with the regal dignity of the age. A number of palaces survive, of which many are mentioned in Princess Salme's (Emily Saʿid Ruete) memoirs (*An Arabian princess between two worlds*, tr. E. van Donzel, Leiden 1993, originally published as *Memoirs of an Arabian princess*, New York 1888). They provided homes for his numerous surviving children. His principal residence was at Mtoni, enlarged with Persian baths, a more spacious *ḥarīm* and stores as well as reception rooms, from a former private house. A short way away was a private mosque, a square *muṣallā*, the roof supported by a single column, and the *miḥrāb* set in the thickness of the wall in the Ibāḍī fashion. There was a separate palace at Dunga for the Mwinyi Mkuu, the last of the indigenous rulers, with a room for the royal *siwa* (horn) and drums.

Bibliography: See that to ZANDJ. 1. and those of the other articles cited there. Also Sir R. Coupland, *East Africa and its invaders*, Oxford 1939; J.M. Gray, *History of Zanzibar from the Middle Ages to 1856*, Oxford 1962; C.S. Nicholls, *The Swahili coast 1798-1856*, London 1971; J.S. Trimingham, *The Arab geographers and the East African coast*, in H.N. Chittick and R.I. Rotberg (eds.), *East Africa and the Orient*, New York 1975; B.G. Martin, *Muslim brotherhoods in nineteenth century Africa*, Cambridge 1976; J. Middleton, *The world of the Swahili*, New Haven 1992; M.R. Bhacker, *Trade and empire in Zanzibar*, London 1992; A. Sheriff, *The history and conservation of Zanzibar Stone Town*, London 1995; al-Amīn b. ʿAlī al-Mazrūʿī, *The history of the Mazrui dynasty of Mombasa*, ed. and tr. J. McL. Ritchie, London 1995; A.M. Juma, *The Swahili and Mediterranean worlds. Pottery of the Late Roman period from Zanzibar*, in *Antiquity*, lxx (1996), 148-54; M.C. Horton, *Zanzibar and Pemba. Archaeological investigations of an Indian Ocean archipelago*, London 1999; idem, in *University of Bristol Newsletter*, iii/15 (3.6.1999). (G.S.P. Freeman-Grenville)

2. Since 1964.

The Zanzibar revolution in January 1964 brought a sudden end to the newly-independent sultanate. The revolution was organised by John Okello (b. 1937), a Ugandan worker who came to Zanzibar in 1959 and who believed that he had a God-given mission to lead a revolution of African liberation (J. Okello, *Revolution in Zanzibar*, Nairobi 1967, 72-3). Okello named established opposition figures as leaders of the new régime, with Abeid Karume (1905?-1972), head of the Afro-Shirazi Party (ASP), as president. Karume soon consolidated his position by securing the exclusion of Okello from Zanzibar in March 1964, and, in April, led Zanzibar into union with Tanganyika.

Karume established a radical, one-party régime similar to many in the Africa of the 1960s. During the revolution, Zanzibarians of Asian and Arab origin, who had been part of the old political and economic élite, were harassed and many were killed or fled. Karume continued these policies, with the result that the traditional Muslim scholarly and devotional leadership was weakened. Established lines of transmission of both Ṣūfī piety and Islamic studies were disrupted (Allyson Purpura, *Knowledge and agency: The social relations of Islamic expertise in Zanzibar Town*, Ph.D. diss., City University of New York 1997, unpubl., 136-9). During Karume's rule, the activities of Islamic organisations like the Ṣūfī orders were severely limited and Islamic scholarship restricted.

Karume was murdered in 1972, but the ASP one-party régime continued under his successor Aboud Jumbe (b. 1920). However, Jumbe moved away from the authoritarianism of Karume, reduced the commitment to leftist economic policies, and relaxed restrictions on Islamic organisations. In an attempt to gain religious support, he established BAMITA (*Baraza la Misikiti wa Tanzania*, Council of Tanzanian Mosques). In the early 1980s, support for Zanzibari separatism grew, and in 1984 Jumbe was forced to resign because he was unable to control these tendencies. His successor as president of Zanzibar (and Vice-President of Tanzania) was Ali Hassan Mwinyi, a close associate of Julius Nyerere, who succeeded Nyerere as national president when the latter retired in 1985. The next presidents of Zanzibar were Idris Abdul Wakil (1985-90) and Salmin Amour who won the last one-party elections in 1990 and also, by a bare 50.2% of the votes, the first multiparty election in 1995.

During the final two decades of the 20th century, Islamic activist sentiments have increased in Zanzibar. With the end of the authoritarianism of Karume, Muslim teachers and scholars began to reassert their position as intellectual and devotional leaders. Older Ṣūfī *ṭarīḳas* had survived the times of suppression, and new groups of scholars inspired by Islamist movements in other parts of the Muslim world became more visible. By the 1990s, strict purist teachers such as Shaykh Khamisi Jafar were popular among the students and younger professionals, advocating a style of Islamic interpretation similar to that articulated by the Muslim Brotherhood in the Middle East.

Two incidents illustrate the revival of Muslim activism. In 1988, Sophia Kawawa, the wife of the then secretary-general of the Tanzanian ruling party, made disparaging remarks about the situation of women under Islamic law. This sparked major demonstrations in Zanzibar, reflecting both resentment against mainland control of island affairs and Islamic sensitivities. In 1993, it was announced that Zanzibar had joined the Organization of the Islamic Conference (OIC). While this was popular in Zanzibar, a parliamentary commission declared the association to be unconstitutional and Zanzibar withdrew. It was clear by the late 1990s that Muslim sentiments in Zanzibar had been significantly influenced by the global resurgence of Islam. This was expressed locally by increased demands for Zanzibar separatism and by more visible expressions of Islamist sentiments similar to those in other parts of the Muslim world.

Bibliography (in addition to the works cited in the text): E.B. Martin, *Zanzibar, tradition and revolution*, London 1978; A. Clayton, *The Zanzibar revolution and its aftermath*, Hamden, Conn. 1981; R.L. Pouwells, *Horn and crescent. Cultural change and traditional Islam on the East African coast*, Cambridge 1987; Abdin N. Chande, *Islam, Ulamaa and community development in Tanzania*, San Francisco 1998, 247-61.

(J.O. Voll)

ZANGĪ, Abu 'l-Muẓaffar ʿImād al-Dīn b. Ḳasīm al-Dawla Aḳsunḳur b. Il-Turghān, Turkmen commander, governor of ʿIrāḳ, later ruler of al-Mawṣil and Aleppo (521-41/1127-46) and founder of the Zangid dynasty, d. 541/1146.

Early youth. Born in Aleppo in 480/1087-8, he was the last surviving son of the Saldjūḳ commander Aḳsunḳur [*q.v.*], who became governor of Aleppo 480-7/1087-94. After his father's death in 487/1094, Zangī was raised at the court of the governors of al-Mawṣil [*q.v.*] and distinguished himself in the internal warfare of rival Saldjūḳ princes and the wars against the Crusaders.

Governor in ʿIrāḳ 516-21/1122-7. In 516/1122-3 Zangī led a successful expedition against the Mazyadid *amīr* Dubays b. Ṣadaḳa [see mazyad, banū] in southern ʿIrāḳ. On behalf of Aḳsunḳur al-Bursuḳī [*q.v.*], governor of ʿIrāḳ and Zangī's protector, he was given his first appointment as governor of Wāsiṭ and al-Baṣra. In 519/1125 he crushed an army of the caliph al-Mustarshid [*q.v.*], who was trying to conquer southern ʿIrāḳ and expel the Saldjūḳs. On 18 Dhu 'l-Ḥidjdja 519/4 January 1126 sultan Maḥmūd b. Malik Shāh [*q.v.*] appeared on the outskirts of Baghdād attacking the caliph. Reinforcing Maḥmūd, Zangī moved with a powerful army with surprising rapidity up the Tigris valley and decided the battle in favour of the sultan, who in Rabīʿ I 520/April 1126 appointed him governor (*shiḥna* [*q.v.*]) of Baghdād and ʿIrāḳ.

Establishing the amīrate 521-2/1127-8. Later in that year, Aḳsunḳur al-Bursuḳī, then governor of al-Mawṣil, Diyār Rabīʿa, Diyār Muḍar, parts of the Diyār Bakr and Aleppo, was assassinated. Maḥmūd finally made Zangī governor of al-Bursuḳī's provinces in exchange for his ʿIrāḳī ones. He placed two sons, Alp Arslān and Farrukhānshāh (Elisséeff, ii, 381, argued that they were the same person) under Zangī's tutelage and bestowed on him the title of Atabeg. Zangī made his formal entrance into al-Mawṣil in Ramaḍān 521/September-October 1127, and then took Djazīrat Ibn ʿUmar, Naṣībīn, Sindjār, the Khābūr valley and Ḥarrān [*q.vv.*], some of them having been previously annexed by the Artuḳids. Under the constant pressure from the Crusaders, Aleppo had fallen into internal strife and anarchy. Zangī sent a force to restore order on entering the city in Djumādā II 522/June 1128, and was much welcomed in memory of the days of his father.

Consolidation of an autonomous amīrate within the Saldjūḳ empire 522-30/1122-36. Meanwhile in al-Rayy, the supreme sultan Sandjar [*q.v.*] had ordered Maḥmūd to take al-Mawṣil from Zangī and to bestow it upon Dubays. However, the caliph opposed Maḥmūd. After a meeting with Zangī in 523/1129, Maḥmūd finally confirmed him as king of the west (*malik al-gharb*). In the same year Zangī took Ḥamāt from the Būrids [*q.v.*] and in the next year the Crusader stronghold of Athārib near Antioch. In 525/1131 Zangī and the caliph al-Mustarshid became estranged over the issue of Dubays. After the death of sultan Maḥmūd in 525/1131, Zangī was drawn into the wars of succession amongst the Saldjūḳs. In retaliation for an attack on Baghdād by Zangī and Dubays in the previous year, the caliph besieged al-Mawṣil for three months in 527/1133, during which the Būrid of Damascus, Shams al-Mulūk Ismāʿīl, took the opportunity to regain Ḥamāt. In 528/1133-4 Zangī consolidated his power by occupying the strongholds in the vicinity of al-Mawṣil and in Diyār Bakr at the expense of the Artuḳids and the Kurds, who had supported the caliph previously. After the murder of al-Mustarshid in Dhu 'l-Ḳaʿda 529/August-September 1135, Zangī allied himself with the new caliph al-Rāshid [*q.v.*] and the Saldjūḳ pretender Dāwūd in order to fight sultan Masʿūd. In 530/1135-6 Masʿūd conquered ʿIrāḳ and Baghdād, with Zangī and al-Rāshid fleeing to al-Mawṣil. Masʿūd in turn set up a new caliph al-Muḳtafī [*q.v.*], who was acknowledged throughout the empire except by Zangī; only later that year did he acknowledge Masʿūd, Sandjar and al-Muḳtafī as his overlords, receiving in return the territories he already possessed.

Period of expansion 529-38/1135-44. The only possibility of further expansion, without the risk of conflicts with the Saldjūḳs in ʿIrāḳ, lay in campaigns in the west, in Syria and northern Mesopotamia, at the expense of the Būrids, the Crusaders and the Artuḳids. In Djumādā I 529/February 1135, he laid siege to Būrid Damascus. Unexpectedly, the city was well defended, and Zangī only achieved recognition as overlord in Damascus. On his way back to Aleppo he regained Ḥamāt, then attacked outposts of the principality of Antioch, but at the end of the year, after an unsuccessful attack on Ḥimṣ, had to return to al-Mawṣil for affairs in ʿIrāḳ. However, in 531/1137 he resumed his military campaigns in Syria, and gained the strategic Crusader castle of Baʿrīn (Monsferrandus) between Tripoli and Ḥamāt.

In 531-2/1136-8 the Byzantine emperor John II invaded Cilicia and northern Syria. After allying himself with Raymond of Antioch, he attacked Aleppo, but unable to take the city by force, he besieged Shayzar [*q.v.*] instead; after accepting ransom money he returned to Antioch in Ramaḍān 532/May-June 1138. Later that year, Zangī obtained Ḥimṣ by diplomacy as a dowry from the Būrids, and re-occupied the lost strongholds between Antioch and Aleppo.

In 533-4/1139-40 Zangī made his last attempt to reach his ultimate strategic goal, Damascus, in order to complete his supremacy over the western parts of the Saldjūḳ empire. In 533/1139 he took Baʿlabakk [*q.v.*] by force and went on to besiege Damascus in Rabīʿ II 534/December 1139. He had to lift the siege five months later in order to fight the Crusaders, who had overrun the Ḥawrān, but returned for a sudden attack on Damascus on 7 Dhu 'l-Ḳaʿda/22 June, only to withdraw in the end to al-Mawṣil. He had achieved two aims, the capture of the strategic fortress of Baʿlabakk dominating the fertile Biḳāʿ valley [*q.v.*] and suzerainty over Damascus. In the following years, Zangī had to check numerous raids by the northern Crusader states Antioch and Edessa as well as by the Artuḳids and the Kurds.

At the zenith of his power; the fall of Edessa. In 538/1143-4 sultan Masʿūd tried again to remove the overmighty Zangī, whom he held responsible for the continous unrest within his realm, but Zangī came to an agreement with the sultan and promised an indemnity. He turned his attention to the Artuḳid Diyār

Bakr, and utilised the absence of Joscelin II from his capital to seize Edessa after a 28 days' siege, on Saturday 26 Djumādā II 539/23 December 1144. This was the first Muslim reconquest of a major capital of the Crusaders. The victory led western Christianity to undertake the Second Crusade and earned Zangī an outstanding reputation as hero of *djihād* among the Muslims.

Zangī's death. In the following years Zangī faced many troubles and setbacks. After an unsuccessful siege of al-Bīra [*q.v.*], at the strategic crossing of the Euphrates, the Crusaders abandoned it to the Artuḳid ruler Ḥusām al-Dīn Timurtāsh, a vigorous opponent of Zangī. In Dhu 'l-Ḳa'da 539/May 1145 the Saldjūḳ prince Alp Arslān (Ibn al-Athīr) or Farrukhānshāh (Ibn al-Ḳalānisī and Ibn al-ʿAdīm) (see above) made an unsuccessful rebellion in al-Mawṣil. In 541/1146 Zangī set out to attack the ʿUḳaylid stronghold of Ḳalʿat Djaʿbar [*q.v.*], but some of his own *mamlūks* murdered him in the night of Sunday, 6 Rabīʿ II 541/14-15 September 1146. He was succeeded by his sons Sayf al-Dīn Ghāzī in al-Mawṣil and Nūr al-Dīn Maḥmūd in Aleppo.

The historians, in particular Ibn al-Athīr, have bestowed the highest praise on Zangī for his political and military qualities and his achievements, especially with regard to the war against the Crusaders; nevertheless, they were aware of his unscrupulousness. Zangī was the first Muslim ruler who fought the Crusader states effectively; however, he never fought them with the same vigour as he did in the case of the strategically much more important Damascus. Ibn al-Athīr also praises him for the return of prosperity to al-Mawṣil and all his lands after the period of Bedouin domination and of continuous warfare amongst the Saldjūḳs, his main political aim to carve out an autonomous amīrate within the framework of the Saldjūḳ empire.

Bibliography: 1. Sources. Bundārī; Ibn al-Athīr, *Kāmil*, x, xi; idem, *al-Ta'rīkh al-bāhir fi 'l-dawla al-atābakiyya*, ed. ʿA.A. Ṭulaymat, Cairo and Baghdād 1963; Ibn al-ʿAdīm, *Zubda*, ed. S. al-Dahhān, ii, Damascus 1954; idem, *Bughya*, ed. S. Zakkār, viii, Damascus 1988, 3845-57; Ibn al-Djawzī, *Muntaẓam*, Beirut 1992, xvii-xviii; Ibn al-Ḳalānisī, *Dhayl ta'rīkh Dimashḳ*, ed. Zakkār, Damascus 1403/1983, tr. H.A.R. Gibb, *The Damascus chronicle of the Crusades*, London 1932; Ibn Khallikān, ed. ʿAbbās, 327-9, tr. de Slane, i, 539-41; Bar Hebraeus, *Chronography*, ed. and tr. E.A. Wallis Budge, London 1932; Michael the Syrian, *Chronicle*, ed. and tr. J.-B. Chabot, Paris 1903.

2. Studies. Gibb, *Zengi and the fall of Edessa*, in *A history of the Crusades*, i, ed. K.M. Setton, Philadelphia 1962, 449-62; N. Elisséeff, *Nūr ad-Dīn*, ii, Damascus 1967, 293-338; ʿI. Khalīl, *ʿImād al-Dīn Zangī*, Beirut 1971; C. Alptekin, *The reign of Zangi (521-541/1127-1146)*, Erzurum 1978; D. Patton, *A history of the Atabegs of al-Mawṣil and their relations with the Ulema*, diss. New York 1982, 81-115.

(S. Heidemann)

ZANGĪ ĀTĀ or Zangī Bābā, Ṣūfī saint of Central Asia, d. 657/1259.

He was a shepherd from Tashkent, with swarthy colouring from his Arab origins, whence his name (*zangī* "black"). His father Tāsh Ātā was a descendant of Arslān Bāb, the master of the great saint of Central Asia, Aḥmad Yasawī [*q.v.*]. Zangī Ātā was first of all initiated by his own father into the mystical way, and then, after his father's death he became the disciple of Ḥakīm Ātā, Aḥmad Yasawī's famous *khalīfa*. At Ḥakīm Ātā's death, he went on pilgrimage to his tomb in Khʷārazm, and married Anbar Bībī, the saint's widow. The Naḳshbandī ʿUbayd Allāh Aḥrār [see Aḥrār, in Suppl.] held Zangī Ātā in high regard, and claimed to have heard God's voice when he was at the saint's tomb in Tashkent. Zangī Ātā also cultivated the practice of "*dhikr* of the saw" (*dhikr-i arra*).

Amongst his four main *khalīfas*—Uzun Ḥasan Ātā, Sayyid Ātā, Ṣadr Ātā and Badr Ātā—the second of these was sent into the Dasht-i Ḳipčaḳ to spread Islam and to convert the ruler Özbeg Khān to that faith. In the 19th century, oral tradition attached Zangī Ātā to the Ḳādirī *ṭarīḳa* ("Khodrié", see Schuyler), which was, in reality, simply the Naḳshbandiyya-Djahriyya. Built on Tīmūr's orders, the ensemble around his mausoleum (16 km/10 miles from Tashkent) is one of the finest architectural works in Central Asia and one of the oldest pilgrimage places in the region. It comprises the saint's tomb, a *madrasa* dating from the 18th-19th centuries, a hostel for pilgrims, a mosque (1870), a minaret (1914-15) and a monumental portal. There is a great basin stretching out in front of the ensemble and a vast cemetery on one of its sides. Nearby is the tomb of his wife, Anbar Bībī. Each year, at the beginning of September, there was a religious festival in Zangī Ātā's honour, he having become the patron saint of Tashkent. The festival lasted two or three days, gathering together the whole population of Tashkent in prayers, communal meals and festivities. It was described in the second half of the 19th century by the American traveller Eugene Schuyler (*Turkistan. Notes of a journey in Russian Turkistan, Khokand, Bukhara, and Kuldja*, London 1876, i, 138-40), and several traditions linked with the saint's mausoleum were collected by J. Castagné in his study of the saints of Central *Asia* (*Le culte des saints de l'Islam au Turkestan*, in *L'Ethnographie*, Paris 1951, 53-4). Since the break-up of the USSR, the pilgrimage has taken on a new life, and practices linked with popular Islam (healing sessions by *bakhshīs* [*q.v.*], amongst others) have taken place at the approaches to the funerary complex of Zangī Ātā. The saint's name further appeared in incantations put together by *bakhshīs* in the last century (see the text of a Ḳazaḳ *bakhshī* collected by Castagné).

Bibliography (in addition to references mentioned in the article): 1. Texts. ʿAlī b. Ḥusayn Wāʿiẓ Kāshifī, *Rashaḥāt ʿayn al-ḥayāt*, ed. ʿAlī Aṣghar Mi'niyān, Tehran n.d., 21-3; Khʷādja Bahā' al-Dīn Ḥasan Nithārī Bukhārī (10th/16th century), *Mudhakkir al-aḥbāb*, Ḥaydarābād 1969, 493-4; Muḥammad ʿĀlim al-Ṣiddīḳī al-ʿAlawī (11th/18th century), *Lamaḥāt min nafaḥāt al-ḳuds*, Tashkent 1909, 70-2.

2. Studies. *Tashkent entsiklopediya*, Tashkent 1992, 120-1; D. DeWeese, *Islamization and native religion in the Golden Horde. Baba Tükles and conversion to Islam in historical and epic tradition*, University Park, Pa. 1994, 371-5; idem, *The Yasavî order and Persian hagiography in seventeenth-century Central Asia*, in L. Lewisohn and D.O. Morgan (eds.), *The heritage of Sufism. III. Late classical Persianate Sufism (1501-1750)*, Oxford 1999.

(Th. Zarcone)

ZANGIDS, a Turkmen dynasty which reigned over Syria, Diyār Muḍar and Diyār Rabīʿa [*q.vv.*] from 521-2/1127-8 onwards, in the tradition of Turkmen-Saldjūḳ collective familial sovereignty: in Aleppo until 579/1183, in al-Mawṣil until 631/1233, and with minor branches in Sindjār, Djazīrat Ibn ʿUmar and in Shahrazūr.

The progenitor Aḳsunḳur [*q.v.*], a Turkish *mamlūk* commander in the service of the Saldjūḳ sultan Malik Shāh, was appointed governor of Aleppo in 480/1087-8. During the wars of succession following the sultan's assassination, Aḳsunḳur was executed in 487/1094.

His eldest son and eponym of the dynasty, Zangī [*q.v.*], was raised and trained at the court of the governors of al-Mawṣil. In Rabīʿ II 520/April 1126 the sultan entrusted him with the military governorship of Baghdād and ʿIrāḳ. After the assassination of his protector Aḳsunḳur al-Bursuḳī [*q.v.*], the sultan gave Zangī the former possessions of al-Bursuḳī, al-Mawṣil, Aleppo and parts of the Djazīra. He placed one or two of his sons [see ZANGĪ] under Zangī's tutelage and bestowed on him the title of an *atābak* [*q.v.*], which became almost synonymous for the rulers of al-Mawṣil. During 521-2/1127-8 Zangī took possession of his realm, which had been rent by internal strife and had been annexed partially by the Artuḳids.

Zangī's policy encompassed four main directions. First, he consolidated his amīrate within the Saldjūḳ empire and made it almost autonomous. He took part in the continuous power struggles of the Saldjūḳ sultans, pretenders and the caliphs. In 523/1129 he achieved acknowledgement as king of the west (*malik al-gharb*) by sultan Maḥmūd [*q.v.*]. In the wars of succession after the murder of the caliph al-Mustarshid [*q.v.*] in 530/1136, Zangī sided with the short-reigning caliph al-Rāshid [*q.v.*], but was forced to acknowledge the new caliph al-Muḳtafī and the sultans Masʿūd and Sandjar as overlords.

The persisting political instability in Masʿūd's realm allowed Zangī to turn his attention to matters in Syria, the second direction. He launched four campaigns into the autonomous realm of the Būrids [*q.v.*] with the ultimate goal of conquering Damascus between 523/1129 and 533-4/1139-40. He never succeeded in this, though he gained Ḥamāt and Ḥimṣ [*q.vv.*], and eventually had to be content with the nominal overlordship.

The third direction of expansion was towards the Artuḳid and Kurdish principalities in Diyār Bakr. In various campaigns, raids and intrigues with the Artuḳid houses of Mārdīn and Ḥiṣn Kayfā he gained several strongholds there.

The fourth direction was towards the Crusader principalities. He seized fortresses mainly in the region between Antioch and Aleppo, and at the zenith of his power in 539/1144 conquered al-Ruhā [*q.v.*], the capital of the Crusader County of Edessa. This caused the Second Crusade and earned Zangī his outstanding reputation among Muslim historians as a hero of the *djihād*.

The succession of Zangī after his death in 541/1146 was disputed between his sons, but it resulted in practice in a division of territories between two of them, Sayf al-Dīn Ghāzī in al-Mawṣil with the territories in Djazīra, and Nūr al-Dīn Maḥmūd [*q.v.*] in Syria and al-Ruhā. Sayf al-Dīn Ghāzī first became the head of the family, and then later Nūr al-Dīn.

The principality of Aleppo. After the murder of his father, Nūr al-Dīn Maḥmūd achieved control in Aleppo. He spent the first year of his reign in consolidating his territory, threatened by an unsuccessful attempt of Joscelin of Edessa to retake his capital with the help of the resident Armenians. He reached a conciliation with his brother Sayf al-Dīn Ghāzī, acknowledging the latter's suzerainty. In the south, Muʿīn al-Dīn Unur of Damascus, together with the Crusaders of Jerusalem, tried to regain territory and independence.

The first eight years were occupied with the unification of Syria under his rule. In July 1148 the leaders of the Second Crusade in Jerusalem made the ill-fated decision to attack Damascus, although the Būrids had been the allies of Jerusalem for years against Zangīd ambitions. Unur of Damascus had to call in Nūr al-Dīn. On his advance, the Crusaders lifted the siege. The year 544/1149-50 saw four major events favourable for Nūr al-Dīn. In Ṣafar 544/June 1149 he won a decisive battle against the Crusaders near Inab, where Raymond of Antioch was killed. He then took Afāmiya, Ḳalʿat Mudīḳ and Ḥārim. In Rabīʿ II 544/August 1149 his opponent Unur of Damascus died. In Djumādā II 544/November 1149 his brother in al-Mawṣil died and was succeeded by his third and younger brother Ḳuṭb al-Dīn Mawdūd. The supremacy within the family confederation was disputed, but eventually it was agreed that Nūr al-Dīn should get the rich family treasure, which had been deposited in Sindjār, for financing the *djihād*, as well as the major cities in Diyār Muḍar and also Ḥimṣ. In Dhu 'l-Ḥidjdja 544/April 1150 Joscelin of Edessa was captured by Turkmens, which provided an opportunity for Nūr al-Dīn to seize the remaining strongholds of the former county of Edessa. In Ṣafar 549/April 1154 he finally conquered Damascus and extended his realm as far as Buṣrā and Ṣalkhad.

A power struggle in the already-weakened Fāṭimid caliphate in 558/1163 resulted in a competition between Amalric of Jerusalem and Nūr al-Dīn over political and military domination of Egypt as the key to hegemony in the region. Three times between 559/1164 and 564/1168, their armies both penetrated into Egypt. Finally, in Rabīʿ II 564/January 1169 Shīrkūh, the commander of Nūr al-Dīn's army, became master of Egypt as *wazīr* of the Fāṭimid caliph. After the death of the last Fāṭimid, al-ʿĀḍid, on 10 Muḥarram 567/12-13 September 1171, Ṣalāḥ al-Dīn [*q.v.*], who had succeeded his uncle Shīrkūh as *wazīr*, changed the *khuṭba* and *sikka* in favour of Nūr al-Dīn Maḥmūd and the ʿAbbāsid caliph, thus re-establishing Sunnī supremacy in Egypt.

Two years before, Ḳuṭb al-Dīn Mawdūd had died in Dhu 'l-Ḥidjdja 565/September 1170. Sayf al-Dīn Ghāzī II, the leader of a faction hostile to Nūr al-Dīn, became the lord of al-Mawṣil. The question of supremacy within the Zangīd family was raised again. In 566/1170-1 Nūr al-Dīn conquered the Djazīra in order to restructure the Zangīd realm. Ghāzī II remained in al-Mawṣil but acknowledged Nūr al-Dīn's suzerainty. Nūr al-Dīn's candidate for al-Mawṣil, ʿImād al-Dīn Zangī II, the younger son of Mawdūd, was compensated with Sindjār, but had to acknowledge the suzerainty of his brother in al-Mawṣil. With a united Syria, Diyār Muḍar and the rich province of Egypt, as well as the overlordship of al-Mawṣil and Diyār Rabīʿa, Nūr al-Dīn was at the zenith of his power in order to fight the Crusaders. In the following years, he tried to gain the Crusader castles Karak and Shawbak [*q.vv.*], but Ṣalāḥ al-Dīn's increasing tendency to build up Egypt as his independent power base hindered these ambitions. Nūr al-Dīn Maḥmūd died on 11 Shawwāl 569/15 May 1174. He founded several urban institutions, *madrasas* and hospitals and restored the fortifications of the cities and citadels in Aleppo, Damascus and al-Mawṣil. He was the patron of Sunnī orthodoxy, to the detriment of the Shīʿī population and institutions.

He was succeeded by his son al-Ṣāliḥ Ismāʿīl, an eleven-year-old boy. His uncle Sayf al-Dīn of al-Mawṣil immediately challenged his position and in 569/1174 reconquered the Zangīd Djazīra for al-Mawṣil. In the south, Ṣalāḥ al-Dīn advanced from Egypt, taking Damascus and Ḥamāt in 570/1174. After a victory over the combined Zangīd forces in Shawwāl 571/ April 1176, he revoked the fiction of al-Ṣāliḥ Ismāʿīl's overlordship, thus creating a formally independent principality. When al-Ṣāliḥ died in Radjab 577/1181 he left a principality threatened by Ṣalāḥ al-Dīn and bequeathed to ʿIzz al-Dīn Masʿūd of al-Mawṣil. However, instead of fighting Ṣalāḥ al-Dīn, in Shawwāl 577/February 1182 Masʿūd exchanged Aleppo for Sindjār in order to expel Zangī II from the immediate neighbourhood of al-Mawṣil. During his first Djazīra campaign in Ṣafar 579/June 1183, Ṣalāḥ al-Dīn took Aleppo from Zangī II in exchange for Sindjār.

The principality of al-Mawṣil. After the death of Zangī, Sayf al-Dīn Ghāzī became head of the family. The politics of the Mawṣil branch were intent on maintaining a balance of power and concentrated on the economic and cultural development of the principality. Ghāzī, his successors and the élite of al-Mawṣil became patrons of architecture and art, benefactors of religious institutions and scholars. When Ghāzī died in 544/1149, the *amīrs* of al-Mawṣil transferred the government to his younger brother Ḳuṭb al-Dīn Mawdūd. An intervention by Nūr al-Dīn reduced the principality considerably (see above). Al-Mawṣil at that time was run by the powerful regent al-Djawād and the *amīr* ʿAlī Küčük [see BEGTEGĪNIDS]. Only in 554/ 1159 did al-Mawṣil once again enter the persistent Saldjūḳ power struggles, when ʿAlī Küčük briefly supported the Saldjūḳ pretender Sulaymān Shāh, who had been detained in al-Mawṣil for several years. The death of Mawdūd in 565/1170 resulted in a succession crisis, in which Nūr al-Dīn intervened. The realm of the successor Sayf al-Dīn Ghāzī II became rather diminished and divided (see above). However, as soon as Nūr al-Dīn died, Ghāzī extended his realm at the expense of his nephew al-Ṣāliḥ Ismāʿīl (see above). The weakness of the Syrian régime drove Ghāzī into war with Ṣalāḥ al-Dīn in 570-1/1175-6. A treaty concluded in Muḥarram 572/July 1176 confirmed the status quo. Back in al-Mawṣil, Ghāzī II installed Mudjāhid al-Dīn Ḳaymaz as *wazīr*, who directed the affairs with only one interruption up to 595/1198. In 576/1180 Ḳaymaz administered the succession of the deceased *atābak* in favour of the brother ʿIzz al-Dīn Masʿūd. The sons of Ghāzī II received only an *iḳṭāʿ*, Djazīrat Ibn ʿUmar and al-ʿAḳr al-Ḥumaydiyya, both of which formed the nucleus of later Zangīd principalities.

Ṣalāḥ al-Dīn made two expeditions into the Djazīra, in 578-9/1182-3 and in 581/1185-6, in order to subdue the Zangīds and to direct the resources of the Djazīra to battlefields in Syria and Palestine. After his first campaign, the principality of al-Mawṣil became reduced to al-Mawṣil itself and Djazīrat Ibn ʿUmar and some territories east of the Tigris. Due to an intrigue, the powerful regent of al-Mawṣil Ḳaymaz was forced to step down in Djumādā I 579/August-September 1183. Sandjar Shāh of Djazīrat Ibn ʿUmar and Yūsuf b. ʿAlī Küčük of Irbil saw the opportunity to secede from al-Mawṣil, and acknowledged the suzerainty of Ṣalāḥ al-Dīn. After ten months, Masʿūd re-installed Ḳaymaz. His immediate attempts to regain Irbil were the cause for Ṣalāḥ al-Dīn's second campaign. Both campaigns fragmented the Zangīd realm into five separate principalities, all of them acknowledging Ayyūbid suzerainty in the *khuṭba* and *sikka*: two Begtigīnid principalities (Ḥarrān/al-Ruhā and Irbil) and three Zangīd principalities (al-Mawṣil, Djazīrat Ibn ʿUmar and Sindjār/Naṣībīn). On 27 Ṣafar 589/4 March 1193 Ṣalāḥ al-Dīn died, and Masʿūd, Zangī II of Sindjār and other lords of the Djazīra tried vainly to break away. Ṣalāḥ al-Dīn's brother al-ʿĀdil [*q.v.*], the Ayyūbid lord of Mesopotamia, secured the Ayyūbid supremacy. In the aftermath of these campaigns, Masʿūd died on 29 Shaʿbān 589/30 August 1193, and Ḳaymaz directed the succession of Nūr al-Dīn Arslān Shāh. In 594/ 1198, after the death of Zangī II of Sindjār, a clash over the possession of Naṣībīn resulted in a weakening of both principalities and the death of Ḳaymaz in Rabīʿ I 595/January 1199. The death of the formal head of the Ayyūbid house, al-ʿAzīz ʿUthmān, in 595/1198 provided the opportunity for the three Zangīd principalities to rebel against al-ʿĀdil in favour of al-Afḍal ʿAlī b. ʿUthmān and his supporter al-Ẓāhir Ghāzī of Aleppo [*q.v.*]. Al-ʿĀdil succeeded in subjugating the Zangīd principalities. At the beginning of 601/September 1204, a treaty was arranged on the basis of the *status quo ante*. In 606/1209 al-ʿĀdil attempted to annex the Zangīd states, beginning with Naṣībīn, but Kökbürī of Irbil and Arslān Shāh joined forces in order to thwart al-ʿĀdil's ambitions. A reconciliation was achieved, but Naṣībīn and the Khābūr valley remained in the hands of al-ʿĀdil, and the Zangīds had to send provisions for his campaigns. In Radjab 607/January 1211 ʿIzz al-Dīn Masʿūd II succeeded his father. Arslān Shāh had chosen his *mamlūk* Badr al-Dīn Lu'lu' [*q.v.*] as regent of al-Mawṣil. Lu'lu''s power grew to such an extent that in 631/1233 he was able to depose the Zangīds from being *atābaks* of al-Mawṣil. Arslān Shāh's second son ʿImād al-Dīn Zangī III was compensated with the fortresses of al-ʿAḳr al-Ḥumaydiyya and al-Shūsh as *iḳṭāʿ*s. In Rabīʿ II 615/July 1218 Lu'lu' secured the smooth succession for Nūr al-Dīn Arslān Shāh II in al-Mawṣil. The death of al-ʿĀdil in Djumādā II 615/August 1218 encouraged rulers in the Djazīra to revolt and expand their territory. Zangī III took the fortresses of al-ʿImādiyya that were dependent on al-Mawṣil, which remained loyal to the Ayyūbids. He became master of the Kurdish mountain region north and northeast of the city, supported by Kökbürī of Irbil. Lu'lu' sought help from al-Ashraf Mūsā, the successor of al-ʿĀdil in the Djazīra. Lu'lu' in turn served al-Ashraf Mūsā as check on Ayyūbid enemies in the east. The caliph mediated a peace agreement. Soon afterwards, in 616/1219, Arslān Shāh II died and Lu'lu' secured the succession of the three-year-old al-Nāṣir al-Dīn Maḥmūd b. Masʿūd II, but Zangī III and Kökbürī challenged Lu'lu' in Kurdistān. From 620/1223 to 624/1227 an internal war broke out in the Ayyūbid realm, which strengthened Lu'lu''s power as ally of al-Ashraf Mūsā. When in 630/1233 Kökbürī died, he had bequeathed his territory to the caliph in Baghdād. He had been the last powerful advocate of the Zangid cause, and Lu'lu', now at the zenith of his power, could get rid of the last Zangīd of the al-Mawṣil line. In Rabīʿ I 631/December 1233 he received an investiture diploma for al-Mawṣil and the honorific of *al-Malik al-Raḥīm* as official recognition from the caliph.

The principality of Sindjār. This was set up by Nūr al-Dīn in 566/1170-1 for his nephew ʿImād al-Dīn Zangī II, who had to acknowledge his brother Sayf al-Dīn Ghāzī of al-Mawṣil as immediate overlord. The relation between the branches in Sindjār and al-Mawṣil remained tense and frequently hostile. In 577/1182 Zangī II exchanged Sindjār with Masʿūd for Aleppo. Ṣalāḥ al-Dīn conquered Sindjār as early as Ramaḍān 578/December 1182 and gave it in the next year, together with Naṣībīn, the Khābūr valley, al-Raḳḳa and Sarūdj, to Zangī II in exchange for Aleppo (see above). The possession of Naṣībīn remained strongly disputed between Sindjār and al-Mawṣil. In Muḥarram 594/November 1197 Ḳuṭb al-Dīn Muḥammad succeeded his father; in 595/1199 he joined the coalition against al-ʿĀdil, but was the first to recognise him as overlord again in 600/1204. In 606/1209 al-ʿĀdil captured the Khābūr valley and Naṣībīn and unsuccessfully besieged Sindjār. Ḳuṭb al-Dīn had a good reputation as a just ruler and a supporter of commerce. When he died in Ṣafar 616/April 1219, a violent dynastic crisis arose and within a year his two sons fought and succeeded each other. Then in Djumādā I 1617/July 1220 the last Zangīd ruler of Sindjār transferred his principality to al-Ashraf Mūsā.

The principality of Djazīrat Ibn ʿUmar. After the death of Ghāzī II in 576/1180, his son Muʿizz al-Dīn Sandjar Shāh obtained Djazīrat Ibn ʿUmar as *iḳṭāʿ* within the realm of al-Mawṣil. It can be regarded as autonomous principality from 579/1183, when he acknowledged the overlordship of Ṣalāḥ al-Dīn after the deposition of Ḳaymaz. Following the death of the Ayyūbid al-ʿAzīz ʿUthmān, Sandjar Shāh took part in the rebellion against al-ʿĀdil, but in 600/1204 changed sides, now fighting Arslān Shāh in al-Mawṣil. Sandjar Shāh was murdered in 605/1208-9 and his son, al-Muʿaẓẓam Maḥmūd, succeeded him. Like his father, the latter is described as tyrannical, but he managed to rule for over forty years by keeping good relations with the Ayyūbids as well as with Luʾluʾ in al-Mawṣil. When he died in 648/1251, he was succeeded by his son al-Malik al-Masʿūd Shāhānshāh, but Luʾluʾ absorbed this principality, too. With an investiture diploma from the Ayyūbid al-Nāṣir Yūsuf II, he conquered the city in 649/1251. The last ruling Zangīd was drowned in captivity on the way to al-Mawṣil.

The principality of Shahrazūr [*q.v.*]. This was the final result of the succession regulations in 607/1211. ʿImād al-Dīn Zangī III received the fortresses of al-ʿAḳr al-Ḥumaydiyya and al-Shūsh as *iḳṭāʿ*s. In 615/1218, when Luʾluʾ placed Arslān Shāh II on the throne of al-Mawṣil, Zangī III felt deprived of his claim and vainly attempted to displace Luʾluʾ with the support of Kökbürī. When al-ʿĀdil died in the same year, Zangī III tried to extend his power into the northern region of al-Mawṣil. In 617/1220 he lost his fortresses and all his territorial gain to Luʾluʾ and fled to Ādharbāydjān, in 619/1222 attempting anew to regain his possessions but was compelled to abandon them in exchange for the distant Shahrazūr, acknowledging the overlordship of Kökburī. In Ramaḍān 633/May 1236 he was succeeded by his son Nūr al-Dīn Arslān Shāh III. After his death in 14 Shaʿbān 642/15 January 1245, Shahrazūr was given to an *amīr* of the caliph, and four months later it was conquered by the Mongols.

After one-and-a-half centuries of Bedouin domination and urban decline in Syria and northern Mesopotamia, the Zangīds, following the Saldjūḳ conquest, brought back an urban-based political structure to the region. They rebuilt the devastated cities, and founded numerous urban and religious institutions. They promoted Sunnī Islam where Shīʿism had earlier prevailed. They cared for scholarship, commerce and the development of an indigenous currency. Together with the Artuḳids, they created at their courts a distinctive style of classical revival, and it may be said that the Zangīds laid the institutional foundation on which the Ayyūbids and Mamlūks could build.

Bibliography: 1. Sources. Abū Shāma, *K. al-Rawḍatayn*, Cairo 1287-88/1870-1, ed. M. Aḥmad, M. Ḥilmī and M.M. Ziyāda i/1-2, Cairo 1956-62; Ibn al-Athīr, x-xii; idem, *al-Taʾrīkh al-bāhir fi ʾl-dawla al-atābakiyya*, ed. ʿA.A. Ṭulaymāt, Cairo-Baghdād 1963; Ibn al-ʿAdīm, *Zubda*, ed. S. al-Dahhān, ii-iii, Damascus 1954; Ibn al-Fuwaṭī, *al-Ḥawādith al-djāmiʿa*, ed. M.R. al-Shabībī and M. Djawād, Baghdād 1932; Ibn al-Ḳalānisī, *Dhayl taʾrīkh Dimashḳ*, ed. S. Zakkār, Damascus 1983, tr. H.A.R. Gibb, *The Damascus chronicle of the Crusades*, London 1932; al-Kātib al-Iṣfahānī, *al-Fatḥ al-ḳussī fi ʾl-fatḥ al-ḳudsī*, ed. C. Landberg, Leiden 1888, tr. H. Massé, *Conquête de la Syrie et de la Palestine par Saladin*, Paris 1972; Ibn Wāṣil, *Mufarridj al-kurūb fi akhbār banī Ayyūb*, ed. Dj. al-Shayyāl, Ḥ.M. Rabīʿ and S.ʿA. ʿĀshūr, 5 vols., Cairo 1957-72.

2. Historical studies. M. Hilmy and M. Ahmad, *Some notes on Arabic historiography during the Zengid and Ayyubid periods (521/1127-648/1250)*, in *Historians of the Middle East*, ed. B. Lewis and P.M. Holt, London 1962, 79-97; K.M. Setton (ed.), *A history of the Crusades*, i, Philadelphia 1962, 449-62, 513-27; N. Elisséeff, *Nūr ad-Dīn*, 3 vols. Damascus 1967; C. Alptekin, *The reign of Zangi (521-541/1127-1146)*, Erzurum 1978; D. Patton, *A history of the Atabegs of Mawṣil and their relations with the Ulema*, diss. New York 1982; idem, *Ibn al-Sāʿī's account of the last of the Zangids*, in *ZDMG*, cxxxviii (1988) 148-58; idem, *Badr al-Dīn Luʾluʾ*, Seattle 1991; C.E. Bosworth, *The New Islamic dynasties*, Edinburgh 1996, 190-2 no. 93.

3. Architecture and art. T. Allen, *A classical revival in Islamic architecture*, Wiesbaden 1986; M.B. al-Ḥusaynī, *al-ʿUmla al-islāmiyya fi ʾl-ʿahd al-atābakī*, Baghdād 1966; S. al-Daywahdjī, *al-Mawṣil fi ʾl-ʿahd al-atābakī*, Baghdād 1958; W.F. Spengler and W.G. Sayles, *Turkoman figural bronze coins and their iconography*, ii, *The Zengids*, Lodi, Wisc. 1996.

(S. Heidemann)

ZĀR, the name for a popular cult of spirits found in northeastern Africa and such adjacent regions as the Arabian peninsula.

1. In the Horn of Africa and the Arabian peninsula.

The *zār* ritual or practice seems to have originated in the Horn of Africa and, especially, in Ethiopia. According to E. Cerulli, the word (Ar. *zār*, Amharic *zar*, Somali *saar*, etc.), may be said to derive from "the name of the supreme god of the pagan Cushitic peoples, the Sky-God called in Agaw (Bilen) *djār*, and in the Sidamo languages (Kaffa) *yarō* and (Buoro) *darō*". The Italian scholar further thought that, in the context of Ethiopian Christianity, this god must have been reduced to the role of an evil spirit, one which has been likewise retained among the Muslims and, probably, among the Falasha. These propositions do not provide answers to all the questions involved, but are still of value in so far as they have not been replaced by more information. Etymologies deriving *zār* from the Arabic verb *zāra* "to visit" seem fantastic, although current in Arab milieux.

An important Cushitic people, the Oromo, who entered Ethiopia from the 16th century onwards, could have played an important role in the formation of the ritual and its diffusion. Nevertheless, it spread (sometimes with changes of name and assimilating local practices and beliefs) throughout northeastern Africa, the Maghrib and the Arabian peninsula, above all in the 19th century. Slaves carried off from the Horn of Africa contributed to this expansion and, in more recent times, the Ethiopian, Eritrean and Somali diasporas. Links with other similar rituals in West Africa and the Arab world are clear but remain to be clarified.

In Ethiopia itself the *zar* ritual assumes many forms, but it is possible to discern a basic structure. It is devoted to spirits capable of sparking off illnesses and all sorts of accidents of life among those possessed by them. The *zar* can fasten on any person, but in order to make that person openly ill, spontaneously invoke a trance or provoke an accident, the person in question must have "a star easily gripped", receive a *zar* through heredity or find him or herself in one of the circumstances or the places favourable to and attractive for the *zar* (seasons, places, odours, the victim's failure to fulfil various usages or his or her faults towards the *zar*, etc.).

In practice, the *zar* ritual is only found in urban centres. Those who are possessed—comprising mainly women—form a sort of fraternity or sorority under the power of a healing man or woman (Amhar. *baläzar*) "superior possessed person", whom the very important *zars* allow to release sufferers from the less important *zars* who afflict them. The sick or possessed persons group themselves round the *baläzar* during the sessions (*wädadja*), during which spirits are evoked by clapping the hands or beating drums or by singing. The healer then proceeds to bring about peace between the *zar* and the possessed person. He makes the *zar* give his name and makes him "come down to" the sufferer, who then goes into a trance (*gurri*), and afterwards negotiates with him. The *zar* has to promise, after an exchange of sacrifices or presents (jewels, necklaces, etc., at the cost of the possessed person and which will be borne by him or her because he/she has become the incarnation of his or her *zar* or "mount"), not to trouble the sufferer any longer. In addition to propitiatory sacrifices of chickens, sheep, cows, etc., there are rites of expulsion (the sufferer is rubbed with the corpse of a slaughtered animal, into which the illness passes), ablutions in vegetable decoctions, the spitting out of quids of *ḳāt* [*q.v.*] chewed by the *baläzar* over the patient, unctions of coffee grounds, etc.

The *zar* are not demons (they have a white face, whilst demons have black ones), nor *budas*, nor *ḳolles*, nor *djinn*, but sometimes they have complex relations with these other spirits. The invisible world of these spirits is the image of Ethiopian society and its members. The *zar* wear clothes, eat, have their own special character (they are delicate and sensitive), temperaments, origins and histories. They include both males and females, they marry, and can even become crossed with demons and *djinn*, producing a class of métis or halfbreeds. Hence they have their own genealogies, and all social groups are represented.

Islamic elements are present within the ritual as a whole (proper names given to the *zar*, the vocabulary of the rituals, use of *ḳāt* which, in Ethiopia, is a "Muslim" plant, etc.), which leads one to think of a large involvement of the Ethiopian Muslim peoples—Oromo, Argobba, etc.—and a prominent role of the great Muslim centre of Harar [*q.v.*] in the diffusion of the cult into Somaliland on the one hand, and to Aden and the Yemen on the other. The Somalis themselves have been able to relay or strengthen this diffusion from their centres of emigration within the Arabian peninsula, such as Aden and Sūr in ʿUmān. At the present time, the *zar* ritual is widespread in the Persian Gulf region, not only on the Arab coasts but also on the Persian ones, in ʿUmān and in Yemen, especially at Aden and in the Tihāma. In this last region, introduction of the ritual is attributed to the Akhdām, a people of African origin who have to endure a special status and who have made music and dancing their specialities. The importance of the *zar* ritual in Saudi Arabia, where it has long been attested, is difficult to estimate.

The *zar* ritual displays not only medico-magical aspects but also has religious, sexual, familial and societal, legal and moral, economic, aesthetic and artistic aspects which cannot be gone into here. It has been attacked (and its adepts sometimes persecuted) by religious authorities, Christian and Muslim, by the British colonial power, by the Marxists of the former P.D.S.Y., and now by Islamic fundamentalists. It is often recognised within Islamic countries that the *zar* is a mental affliction and a means for women to create a space of freedom for themselves.

Bibliography: This has over the years become especially abundant for the Sudan and Egypt (see 2. below), whereas the Arabian peninsula has had little treatment by scholars, probably because research on such subjects is frowned upon by the authorites. The bibls. given in the works below should be consulted, and in the work of Makris and Nakvig given below, there is reference to bibls. and analyses of 106 articles and books.

C. Snouck Hurgronje, *Mecca in the latter part of the nineteenth century*, Leiden 1931; M. Leiris, *La possession et ses aspects théatraux chez les Ethiopiens de Gondar*, Paris 1958, repr. 1980; D.J. Marsden, *Spirit possession on the Persian Gulf*, in *Jnal. Durham Anthropological Soc.*, ii (1972); Sheekh Cali Myriam, *Somali literature on Zar*, Somali National University 1984; Muʿammar ʿAbd Allāh, *Djalīsāt al-zār fī Tihāma*, in *al-Yaman al-Djadīd*, vii, 42-75; R. Natvig, *Oromos, slaves, and the Zar spirits. A contribution to the history of the Zar cult*, in *Internat. Jnal. of African Historical Studies*, xx/1 (1987), 669-89; E. Pelizzari, *Le Mingis en Somalie. Analyse d'une version du culte de possession «saar»*, Centre d'Etudes Africaines, Paris 1991; J. Tubiana, Zar *and* Buda *in northern Ethiopia*, in I.M. Lewis *et alii* (eds.), *Women's medicine. The* Zar-Bori *cult in Africa and beyond*, Edinburgh 1991, 19-33; Zubaydah Ashkanani, *Zar in a changing world: Kuwait*, in *ibid.*, 219-29; P. Makris and Natvig, *The* Zar, Tumbura *and* Bori *cults. A select annotated bibliography*, in *ibid.*, 233-82; L. Kapteijns and J. Spaulding, *Women of the zār and middle-class sensibilities in colonial Aden, 1923-1932*, in *Sudanic Africa*, v (1994), 7-38; N. Grisaru and E. Witztum, *The Zār phenomenon among Ethiopian emigrants in Israel. Cultural and clinical aspects*, in *Sihot*, ix (June 1995) (in Hebrew); T. Battain, *Osservationi sul rito zār di possessione degli spiriti in Yemen*, in A. Regourd (ed.), *Divinisation, magie, pouvoirs au Yémen*, in *Quaderni di Studi Arabi*, xiii (1995), 117-30; J. Mercier, *Les métaphores nuptiale et royale du zar*, in *Northeast African Studies*, iii/2 (1996), 127-48; Pelizzari, *Possession et thérapie dans la Corne de l'Afrique*, Paris 1997.

(A. Rouaud)

2. In Egypt.

The existence of the *zār* ritual has been recorded on the shores of the Red Sea from 1860 onward, then in the remainder of the country, especially in Upper Egypt, in Alexandria and in Cairo. Its introduction into the harems of Egyptian and Turkish *pashas* is attributed to Sudanese and Ethiopian slaves and concubines.

The ritual structure of the *zār* is very flexible, facilitating its adaptation to different social, cultural and religious circles. The adepts are mostly women—of any age, civil or socio-economic status and education—and Muslim. Christians and men, primarily homosexuals, participate sporadically in the rites.

The *zār* in Egypt has developed and enriched the ancient belief in possession by *djunūn*: these spirits, living in an invisible world and capable of anger and even of infatuation with a woman, enter her body and provoke a state of trance, a physical or mental illness, or various other problems. The spirits of the *zār*, called "masters" (*asyād*), often grouped into families (of e.g. African, Egyptian, Turkish, European, Indian origin, etc.), are identified by name, sex, status or occupation (king, queen, soldier, physician, lawyer, schoolgirl, etc.), land of origin, place of residence (mountain, river, cemetery, mosque, the threshold of a house, etc.), religion (Muslim, Christian, Jewish, polytheist), clothing and ornamentation, colour, incense, an emotion or sentiment, and, finally, by songs and dances, foodstuffs and specific sacrificial animals (pigeon, chicken, sheep, calf, camel, etc.). These elements characterise and distinguish the spirits from one another and constitute the liturgy of the *zār*.

Once possessed, the victim organises ceremonies for as long as she lives and in different places, with the aim of being reconciled with the spirits. The possessed person, called "bride" (*ʿarūsa*), under the guidance of the chief celebrant, known as *kūdiya* (a term of unknown origin) or *shaykha*, concludes a pact of alliance with her "masters", one after the other. The rite takes on the appearance of a marriage ceremony between the spirit and the adept, with the celebrant introducing at different times divination by dreams, called "discovery of traces" (*kashf al-āthār*), the music and dance called "beating" (*dakka*) which accompany the trance, ablutions and fumigation with incense, the use of different ritual objects, the sacrifice of edible animals, and offerings of foodstuffs and ritual meals. Currently, the groupings of ritual music are "the Egyptian", "the Sudanese" and a third which belongs to the Ṣūfī brotherhood of the master Abu 'l-Ghayth. The first is constituted by women who play drums and tambourines. The second is a mixed group that also includes dancers with a belt made from sheep-skin shoes (*mandjūr*), and a leader who plays the lyre (*tambūra*), a sacred instrument, considered the dwelling-place of African spirits. Finally, the Ṣūfī one is constituted by dancers with little castanets, long hair and the *tannūra*, a large swirling woman's dress, and players of tambourines and flutes, who sing the praises of the Muslim saints.

The ritual structure reproduces the fundamental stages of a woman's life such as marriage, maternity and birth. These are staged according to a process of transformation: the novice, starting as the spouse of the spirit, subsequently becomes a mother and then a newborn child: the animal changes from its position as substitute for the spirit to that of substitute for the novice; it is slaughtered and the different parts distributed between the novice, the celebrant and the persons invited (the blood is poured over the novice, the meat and the entrails are cooked and eaten). Furthermore, there are ceremonies which are part of an initiatory process whereby the adept can become a celebrant, by passing through various ritual stages which permit her to progress and which are underlined by the adoption of different titles.

The Egyptian *zār* is not simply a therapeutic ritual; it is considered a religious ritual, and its celebrants and disciples are recognised as good Muslims. However, the spirituality of the *zār* transcends religions, whether they be Muslim, Christian or Jewish, while recognising them and embracing them in its ritual. It is thus considered a ritual of actualisation and of manifestation of the "grace" (*baraka*) of Allāh. The *kūdiya* becomes the vehicle of God's blessing, and assists the other possessed persons in their processes of transformation, by virtue of her special relationship with the spirits and her mastery of possession, which implies having the authority, knowledge and power necessary to perform the rites effectively. She is also called "she who knows the way" (*ʿārifat al-sikka*). Thus *zār*, while presenting the syncretic elements of the recognised religions, is thus revealed to be a specific and uniquely feminine-orientated religious form. Hence, while popular and widely diffused among various countries, *zār* is all too often misunderstood and opposed by men of religion, both orthodox and mystics, as well as by governments.

The religiosity of *zār* is expressed in the form of the union, "of love", between the "spouse of the *zār*" (whether she be possessed or celebrant) and the spirits. This marital relationship is confined to the rites in the case of possessed, but becomes permanent in the case of celebrants. Renewal of the alliance pact takes place through the constant performance of the rites. Each one of the ensemble of rites comprises variations of the model ceremony according to the intervention of a different spirit linked to a specific place and demanding the sacrifice of a particular animal. This initiatory process is the catalyst for the actualisation and organisation of the hierarchical universe of spirits and a particular cosmology, since *zār* appeals not only to natural or zoomorphic spirits but also to other categories, including the Christian saints Jesus and Mary, the family of the Prophet, and Muslim saints or mystics.

The Egyptian *zār* displays a complex structure combining a series of repetitive ceremonies. The celebrant is the pivot of the system around which the ritual unfolds and without her the rites could not take place while, at the same time, as a former possessed initiate herself, she is the culmination of the ritual system.

The rite of possession as thus defined shows that these ceremonies are only the links in a chain of initiation that leads from suffering to religious mastery. And this initiation is specifically feminine because any woman can, by successfully completing the ritual phases, become a *kūdiya*. The *zār* is thus differentiated from other initiatory rites, such as the rites of Ṣūfī brotherhoods, where ascent to the highest ranks of the religious hierarchy is achieved by way of a hereditary, essentially masculine path.

Bibliography: C.B. Klunzinger, *Upper Egypt*, London 1878; Niyya Salima, *Harems et musulmanes d'Égypte*, Paris 1902; P. Kahle, *Zār-Beschwörungen in Ägypten*, in *Isl.*, iii (1912), 1-41; E. Littman, *Arabische Geisterbeschwörungen aus Ägypten*, Leipzig 1950; R. Kriss and H. Kriss-Heinrich, *Volksglaube in Bereich des Islam*, Wiesbaden 1962; al-Fāṭima Ḥusayn Miṣrī, *al-Zār. Dirāsa nafsiyya taḥlīliyya anthrūbūlūdjiyya*, Cairo 1975; G. Viaud, *Magie et coutumes populaires chez les Coptes d'Égypte*, Paris 1978; I.M. Lewis, Ahmed al-Safi and Sayyid Hurreiz, *Women's medicine. The* Zar-Bori *cult in Africa and beyond*, Edinburgh 1991; T. Battain, *Le rituel du zār en Égypte. De la souffrance à l'accomplissement*, unpubl. doctoral thesis, Paris, EHESS, 1997.

(Tiziana Battain)

ZARĀDUSHTIYYA [see madjūs].

ZARĀFA (a.), pls. *zarāfāt, zarāfī, zarāʾif, zurāfa*, the giraffe (in Persian, *ushtur-gāw-palang* "camel-cow-leopard"), a large African mammiferous animal, one of the two representatives of the Giraffid family and well known through its western type *Giraffa camelopardalis* or cameleopard. In Antiquity, and according to all the ancient writers on natural history, the giraffe was considered as a hybrid coming from crossings of wild species of camelids, bovines and felines, male or female, and because of its long front legs and short back ones, as involving a limping and jerky gait.

It is astonishing that al-Damīrī makes no mention of the giraffe in his *Ḥayāt al-ḥayawān al-kubrā*, nor does al-Ḳazwīnī in his *ʿAd̲j̲āʾib al-makhlūḳāt*; only al-D̲j̲āḥiẓ speaks of it, refuting and criticising all the beliefs asserting that this large, long-necked beast was a hybrid (*Ḥayawān*, Cairo 1947, i, 38, 241-3). In short, one may say that the Arabs hardly knew the giraffe and were uninterested in it; for them, its only asset was the beauty of its spotted coat, since they regarded it as stupid, and only localised it in Nubia.

In astronomy, the Giraffe is the name given to a secondary boreal constellation situated between that of the Waggoner (*Mumsik al-aʿinna*, D̲h̲u ʾl-ʿinān*) and that of the Little Bear (*al-Dubb al-aṣg̲h̲ar*).

> *Bibliography*: Dr Chenu, *Encyclopédie des sciences naturelles*, vol. *Ruminants*, Paris 1874, 89-102; L. Lavauden, *Les vertébrés du Sahara*, Tunis 1926, s.v.; A. Maʿlūf/Maalouf, *Muʿd̲j̲am al-ḥayawān/An Arabic zoological dictionary*, Cairo 1932, s.v. Giraffe; H. Eisenstein, *Einführung in die arabische Zoographie*, Berlin 1990, index s.v. Giraffe.　　　　(F. VIRÉ)

ZARAFS̲H̲ĀN, conventionally ZERAFSHAN, a landlocked river of Central Asia, now coming within Tajikistan and Uzbekistan.

In early Islamic times, it was known as "the river of Sogdia", Nahr Sug̲h̲d [see ṢUG̲H̲D] or "the river of Buk̲h̲ārā" (see al-Yaʿḳūbī, *Buldān*, 293-4, tr. Wiet, 110-11; al-Iṣṭak̲h̲rī, 319-21; Ibn Ḥawḳal, ed. Kramers, ii, 495-7, tr. Kramers and Wiet, ii, 475-7; *Ḥudūd al-ʿālam*, tr. Minorsky, 55, 73, comm. 198, 211). It flowed westwards from sources in what the geographers called the Buttamān mountains, in fact, between what are now the east-west-lying ranges of the Turkistan mountains, separating the Zarafs̲h̲ān from the upper Sı̊r Daryā [q.v.] valley, and the Hissar mountains separating it from the rivers running southwards through Čag̲h̲āniyān [q.v.] to the upper Oxus. Its waters served a series of towns, from Pand̲j̲ikath to Samarḳand and Buk̲h̲ārā, and their agricultural areas, with a complex irrigation system for the Samarḳand district beginning at the village of Warag̲h̲sar "head of the dam"; al-Yaʿḳūbī says that the river was as important as the Euphrates. Ultimately, it petered out in marshes in the desert before it could reach the middle Oxus towards K̲h̲wārazm.

The name Zarafs̲h̲ān "gold spreader" (the mountains around its headwaters being famed as auriferous and bearing many useful other metals in early Islamic times) only appears from the 18th century onwards. An earlier name corruptly given in the text of al-Yaʿḳūbī, 293, tr. 111, was interpreted by Barthold, *Turkestan down to the Mongol invasion²*, 82, and then Marquart, *Wehrot und Arang*, 30, as *Nāmik, to be compared with the Chinese rendering *Na-mi*, and Marquart went on to suggest an etymology from Iranian *nāmik* "famed", citing the name for the river in Greek sources πολυτίμητος "highly honoured"; but all this remains speculation.

The mountain valleys where the Zarafs̲h̲ān rises have provided a refuge area for the Middle Iranian language, Yaghnobi [see ĪRĀN. iii. Languages, in Suppl.].

> *Bibliography* (in addition to references in the article): Le Strange, *The lands of the Eastern Caliph-*ate, 460; Marquart, *Ērānšahr*, 150; Barthold, *K istorii oros̲h̲eniya Turkestana*, St. Petersburg 1914, 103-25, repr. in *Soč̲ineniya*, iii, Moscow 1965, 185-204; Marquart, *Wehrot und Arang*, index.　　　　(C.E. BOSWORTH)

ZARAND̲J̲ [see ZARANG].

ZARANG, Arabised as Zarand̲j̲, the main town of the early Islamic province of Sīstān. Its ruins lie a few miles north of what was in the late 19th and early 20th centuries the administrative centre of Persian Sīstān, Nuṣratābād or Nāṣirābād, modern Zābul. Its remaining traces are visible within the vast ruined site known as Nād-i ʿAlī, to the east of the present course of the Hilmand river [q.v.] before it peters out in the Hāmūn depression [see ZIRIH] just inside Afg̲h̲ān Sīstān; the site has, however, been much depleted by periodic flooding and the re-use of its materials for local building. In recent years, a "New" Zarang has been founded as a minor administrative centre just inside the Afg̲h̲ān border.

Zarang is an ancient name. The province Zarangianē (< Drangiana) appears in the Greek text of Isidore of Charax (? *flor.* 1st century A.D.), and had already figured in the Behistun inscription of Darius I and the Persepolis one of Xerxes as Z̲ara(n)ka or Z̲ra(n)ka, Akkadian *za-ra-an-ga* (cf. W. Tomaschek, in *PW*, new ed. iv/2, cols. 1665-7, s.v. *Drungai*). In Sāsānid times, coins were minted at *Sakastān (*SK*) from the time of S̲h̲āpūr II (309-79) onwards, and specifically at Zarang (*ZR, ZN, ZRNG*) from the first reign of Kawad̲h̲ I (488-97). Sīstān (i.e. Zarang) figures as the seat of a Nestorian bishopric in the acts of councils of 430 and 577; Christians are still mentioned there at the beginning of the 11th century.

In the first century of Islam, the Arabs first appeared before Zarang in 31/651-2 when ʿAbd Allāh b. ʿĀmir [q.v.] sent al-Rabīʿ b. Ziyād al-Ḥārit̲h̲ī against Sīstān. After a battle with the incomers, the *dihḳān* of Zarang decided to make a peace agreement and promised to pay an annual tribute of money and slaves, an arrangement confirmed by the Marzbān or Ispahbad̲h̲ of Sīstān. Coins of Arabo-Sāsānid type were minted in Sīstān, presumably at Zarang (which appears on such coins as *ZR*) from the years 31 and 32 (cf. E. von Zambaur, *Die Münzprägungen des Islams*, i, Wiesbaden 1968, 132, 139). When in 33/653-4 ʿAbd Allāh b. ʿĀmir appointed a new governor, ʿAbd al-Raḥmān b. Samura, Zarang revolted and had to be pacified, this time with a heavier tribute; it was ʿAbd al-Raḥmān's twelve-year governorship which now made Arab rule firm in Sīstān. Zarang now became a base for Arab raids further eastwards, to Bust and against the local rulers in eastern Afg̲h̲ānistān, the Zunbīls [q.v.], and beyond them, the Kābul-S̲h̲āhs. It remained the bastion of Arabic rule in Sīstān, even when, up to the 3rd/9th century, much of the surrounding countryside was controlled by anti-caliphal, K̲h̲ārid̲j̲ite bands.

The uncertain political situation in K̲h̲urāsān caused by Abū Muslim's revolt plunged Zarang into disorder, with various Arab tribal factions disputing power there; it was not until 138/755 that the caliph al-Manṣūr's authority was established. At the end of the 8th century, Sīstān and much of eastern K̲h̲urāsān was shaken by the thirty years' K̲h̲ārid̲j̲ite revolt of Ḥamza b. Ād̲h̲arak. Although Zarang remained faithful to the ʿAbbāsid connection, its governors had little control over the countryside outside the city, and the forwarding of revenue from the province was cut off. In 206/821 the governor of K̲h̲urāsān, Ṭāhir b. al-Ḥusayn D̲h̲u ʾl-Yamīnayn [q.v.], was able to appoint a governor for Sīstān, and taxation started flowing once more from the province to Nīs̲h̲āpūr and, ultimately, to Baghdād. But this period was short-lived, for the last Ṭāhirid governor in Sīstān, Ibrāhīm b. al-Ḥuḍayn al-Ḳūsī, had to abandon Zarang in 239/854 to local *ʿayyār* leaders, out of whom there emerged as *amīr* in Zarang Yaʿḳūb b. al-Layth al-Ṣaffār [*q.v.*].

For the next 150 years, till the Ghaznawid occupation of 393/1002, Zarang was the capital of the Ṣaffārids [*q.v.*], for the first part of this, of a vast empire in the Eastern Islamic world. In these years, Zarang reached a peak of prosperity. We have detailed descriptions of it from such 4th/10th century geographers as al-Iṣṭakhrī, Ibn Ḥawḳal and al-Muḳaddasī, when the city was flourishing under the *amīrs* Abū Djaʿfar Aḥmad and his son Khalaf. André Miquel has used these to put together a picture of Zarang as a typical Islamic *miṣr* or provincial capital, having the institutions of government and commerce and being integrated with the agrarian economy of its hinterland; he estimates that the whole urban area may have been 10 km/6 miles across (*La géographie humaine du monde musulman jusqu'au milieu du 11e siècle*, iii, *Le milieu naturel*, Paris-The Hague 1980, 211-15). It appears to have been basically a concentric-patterned city on the Baghdād model, with the three-fold division of a *rabaḍ*, suburb; a *madīna* or *shahristān*, town proper; and a *ḳalʿa* or *arg*, citadel. There were walls protecting both the *rabaḍ* and the *madīna*, the latter one with five iron gates. The *rabaḍ* had palaces built by Yaʿḳūb and ʿAmr b. al-Layth respectively, and the *madīna* contained the citadel built by ʿAmr, housing his treasury, and also the Friday mosque and the government building or *dār al-imāra*. In a woodless and stoneless environment, the standard building material was sun-dried brick. There was a plentiful water supply brought by canals from the Hilmand when that river had an adequate flow, and when its flow was high, it was possible to sail in a boat along the final stretch, the Sanārūdh canal, up to the city itself. The surrounding agricultural area was rich, but the drawbacks were the scorching heat and the notorious "wind of 120 days" in spring and summer, which swept along the sand dunes so that barriers of brushwood, shrubs, etc., were necessary to protect the city's buildings.

The city suffered considerably in the rising of 393-4/1003-4 aimed at the Ghaznawid conquerors of Sīstān, with the Friday mosque plundered by the Ghaznawid troops and many people slaughtered; but it revived to become the capital of the Naṣrid *maliks* (421-622/1030-1225) and then of the Mihrabānid ones (from 633/1236 onwards). The actual name Zarang drops out of usage on coins and in literature around the mid-5th/11th century, to be replaced by locutions like *madīnat Sidjistān* and *shahr-i Sīstān*. It is assumed that the ancient Zarang, whatever its current name, continued on the same site until Tīmūr's sack of the Sīstān capital at the end of the 8th/14th century (see below). The Mongols had swept into Sīstān and reached Zarang in Dhu 'l-Ḳaʿda 619/December 1222, killing there the Naṣrid *malik* Nuṣrat al-Dīn b. Yamīn al-Dīn Bahrām Shāh, but it was Tīmūr's devastations, in Shawwāl 785/November-December 1383, which finally finished Zarang/Shahr-i Sīstān; hence in 826/1422 the Mihrabānid *malik* Shams al-Dīn began the construction of a new capital, Shahr-i Sīstān, on a fresh site called ?B.r.k or Mirak "well away from the sands and by the banks of the Hilmand", in the words of the local historian of Sīstān Malik Shāh Ḥusayn.

Bibliography: See for the geographers, Marquart, *Ērānšahr*, 37-9; Le Strange, *The lands of the Eastern Caliphate*, 335-8, and *Ḥudūd al-ʿālam*, tr. Minorsky, 110. For the general history of the city in both pre- and post-Islamic times, see C.E. Bosworth, *Sīstān under the Arabs, from the Islamic conquest to the rise of the Saffārids (30-250/651-864)*, Rome 1968, and idem, *The history of the Saffarids of Sistan and the Maliks of Nimruz (247/861 to 949/1542-3)*. Costa Mesa and New York 1994, indices, with full references; especially notable are Miquel, *op. cit.*, and G.P. Tate, *Seistan, a memoir on the history, topography, ruins and people of the country*, 4 parts, Calcutta 1910-12.

(C.E. Bosworth)

ẒARF (A., pl. *ẓurūf*), lit. "vessel, container", in grammar denotes a subset of nouns of place or time in the dependent (*naṣb*, *vulgo* "accusative") form indicating when or where the event occurs, e.g. *djalastu yawm-a-n warāʾ-a-hu* "I sat one day behind him". Because of their dependent form, the Arab grammarians classify them as objects of the verb, specifically as the "object of location", *mafʿūl fīhi*, lit. "thing in which something is done". Neither of the western terms "adverb" or "preposition" can properly be applied to these elements, whose noun status is confirmed by, amongst other things, the existence of diminutives such as *ḳubayla* and *buʿayda* "a little before", "a little after". The Greek origin of the term proposed by Merx in 1889 (*angeion* "vessel", cf. Versteegh and Elamrani-Jamal) is interesting but unverifiable. Whether *ẓarf* in the technical sense can really be traced back to al-Khalīl b. Aḥmad (d. *ca.* 175/791 [*q.v.*]) likewise cannot be proved (cf. Talmon), though at least we can be certain that it was fully current by the time of Sībawayhi (d. *ca.* 180/796 [*q.v.*]).

There are two general limitations: (a) not all *ẓurūf* have the full range of nominal functions, e.g. *ʿinda* "at", *thamma* "there", *maʿa* "with" (but note the indefinite form *maʿan* "together"), which makes them appear misleadingly similar to our adverbs and prepositions, and (b) nouns denoting a particular place (whether proper names or defined by the article) cannot normally function as *ẓurūf*: *dakhaltu 'l-bayta* "I went [into] the house" or *dhahabtu 'l-Shāma* "I went [to] Syria" are tolerated only as extensions of standard usage (*saʿat al-kalām*). This second limitation is probably universal, arising from the essential difference between what Sībawayhi calls a "point" in time (*waḳt fī 'l-azmina*) and a "point" in space (*waḳt fī 'l-amkina*) in his discussion of this topic (*Kitāb*, ed. Derenbourg, i, 12, ed. Būlāḳ, 16). There was also considerable debate among the grammarians as to whether locative phrases can be predicates in verbless sentences, the consensus being that sentences of the type *zaydun ʿindaka* "Zayd is with you" presuppose an elided verb or participle such as *yastaḳirru*/*mustaḳirrun* "is situated".

Bibliography: Sībawayhi, *Kitāb*, ed. H. Derenbourg, Paris 1881-9, repr. Hildesheim, 1970, ed. Būlāḳ 1898-1900, repr. Baghdād [1965]; R. Talmon, *Arabic grammar in its formative age. Kitāb al-ʿAyn and its attribution to Ḫalīl b. Aḥmad*, Leiden 1997, 46-7. For Merx, see C.H.M. Versteegh, *Greek elements in Arabic linguistic thinking*, Leiden 1977, 8-9, and A. Elamrani-Jamal, *Logique aristotélicienne et grammaire arabe*, Paris 1983, 33-4. General sources. M.G. Carter, *Arab linguistics, an introductory classical text with translation and notes*, Amsterdam 1981, §18.0 (with further references); J. Owens, *Early Arabic grammatical theory, heterogeneity and standardization*, Amsterdam and Philadelphia 1990, index s.v. *ḏarf*; H. Reckendorf, *Arabische Syntax*, Heidelberg 1921, 92 ff., 132; W. Wright, *A grammar of the Arabic language* ii, 109-12, 270.

(M.G. Carter)

ẒARĪF (A.), pl. *ẓurafāʾ*, denotes in mediaeval Islamic social and literary life a person endowed with *ẓarf* "elegance", "refinement", also translatable as "man of the world", "dandy", or, in the plural, "refined people".

The *ẓarīf* (or *mutaẓarrif*) is generally considered as a type of *adīb*, indeed *taẓarruf* is viewed as an intensification of certain features, intellectual, literary, social, and personal, that are held to characterise the man of *adab* [*q.v.*]. Interestingly, *ẓarf* was not deemed gender-specific: Ibn al-Washshāʾ (d. 325/936-7) refers to *baʿḍ mutaẓarrifāt al-ḳuṣūr* (*K. al-Muwashshā*, ed. Brünnow, 42). The first exponent of *ẓarf* as an individual who combined the literary and social dictates of refinement is held to be al-ʿAbbās b. al-Aḥnaf (d. in the first decade of the 9th century A.D. [*q.v.*]), although attempts to read his *dīwān* as a summa of *taẓarruf* are inconclusive and unconvincing, as are attempts to identify an emergent concept of *ẓarf* in the early Islamic period. Ibn al-Washshāʾ (*op. cit.*, 50), for example, presents al-ʿAbbās in a negative and foolish light, which is not what one would expect from a supposedly anachronistic codification of a defunct socio-ethical ideal based on the character of al-ʿAbbās as paradigmatic of that ideal.

Ibn al-Washshāʾ's work is to be viewed as part of the current that culminated in the Aristotelian ethics of the *Tahdhīb al-akhlāḳ* of Miskawayh (*ca.* 320-421/ *ca.* 932-1030 [*q.v.*]), an attempt to harmonise an ʿAbbāsid vision of pre-Islamic *muruwwa* [*q.v.*], *adab* and *ẓarf* within an encompassing Islamic context; as such it is distinct from an exclusively and rigorously *ḥadīth-sunna*-based ethic, such as that promoted, for example, by al-Bukhārī. The *K. al-Ẓahra* of Ibn Dāwūd endeavours to strike a balance between the two visions of an Islamic ethic. It is controversial to attempt to extrapolate theories of social stratification, class mobility, humanism or individuality from such texts, as they argue for and present visions of an Islamic order which are often in competition, but which were also often received in combination (see e.g. Bauer, *Raffinement und Frömmigkeit*).

Bibliography: 1. Sources. Ibn al-Washshāʾ, *K. al-Muwashshāʾ*, ed. R. Brünnow, Leiden 1886, also ed. Beirut 1965, German tr. D. Bellmann, *Das Buch des buntbestickten Kleides*, Leipzig-Weimar 1984, Span. tr. T. Garulo, *El libro del brocado*, Madrid 1990; Ibn Dāwūd al-Iṣfahānī, *K. al-Ẓahra*, ed. A.R. Nykl and I. Tuqan, Chicago 1932.

2. Studies. G.E. von Grunebaum, *Medieval Islam*, Chicago 1953, 221-58; M.F. Ghazi, *Un groupe sociale: les "raffinées" (Ẓurafāʾ)*, in *SI*, xi (1959), 39-71; J.-C. Vadet, *L'esprit courtois en Orient dans les cinq premiers siècles de l'Hégire*, Paris 1968, 267-351 and *passim*; Lois Giffen, *The theory of profane love among the Arabs*, New York 1971, *passim*; W. Raven, *Ibn Dâwûd al-Iṣbahânî and his* Kitâb al-Zahra, Amsterdam 1989; S. Enderwitz, *Du* fatā *au* ẓarīf, *ou comment on se distingue?*, in *Arabica*, xxxvi (1989), 125-42; S. Bonebakker, Adab *and the concept of* belles-lettres, in J. Ashtiany *et alii* (eds.), *The Cambridge history of Arabic literature. ʿAbbasid belles-lettres*, Cambridge 1990, 16-30, esp. 19-24; A. Hamori, *Love poetry* (Ghazal), in *ibid.*, 202-18, esp. 208-15; J.L. Kraemer, *Humanism in the renaissance of Islam. The cultural revival during the Buyid age*, Leiden 1992; Enderwitz, *Liebe als Beruf*, Beirut 1995, 31-65; T. Bauer, *Raffinement und Frömmigkeit. Säkulare Poesie islamischer Religionsgelehrter der späten Abbasidenzeit*, in *Asiatische Studien*, 1 (1996), 275-95; idem, *Liebe und Liebesdichtung in der arabischen Welt des 9. und 10. Jahrhunderts*, Wiesbaden 1998, 56-92; idem, *al-ʿAbbās ibn al-Aḥnaf. Ein literaturgeschichtlicher Sonderfall und seine Rezeption*, in *WZKM*, lxxxviii (1998), 65-107; Giffen, art. *Ẓarf*, in J.S. Meisami and P. Starkey (eds.), *Encyclopedia of Arabic literature*, London 1998, ii, 821-2.

(J.E. MONTGOMERY)

AL-**ZARḲĀʾ**, conventionally Zarka or Zerka, a city of modern Jordan, situated 23 km/15 miles to the northeast of the capital ʿAmmān (lat. 32° 04' N., long. 36° 06' E., altitude 619 m/2,030 feet). It lies on a plateau bordering the desert and intersected by various small valleys which, in the winter, pour water into the Zarḳāʾ river, the main east-bank tributary of the Jordan after the Yarmūk river. The site is also known for its underground water and springs, recognised by mediaeval geographers and travellers, and Pilgrimage caravans used to halt there to replenish their water supplies.

There does not seem to have been any settlement there in the Mamlūk and early Ottoman periods, although a Ḳaṣr Shabīb al-Tubbaʿī (a person about whom nothing is known) is mentioned there, and this *ḳaṣr* was restored and fortified by the Ottoman authorities in 1899 and garrisoned by their troops as protection against Bedouin marauders. In 1903, some 66 Čečen families, refugees from the Caucasus, were settled there, and subsequently, some Circassians. The small community was surrounded by a wall against Bedouin of the Ḥasan, Ṣakhr, Ruwala and Sharārāt tribes. In 1910 nomads of the region took part in the rebellion against the Ottomans [see AL-URDUNN. 2. History (b)]. The Ḥidjāz Railway passed through al-Zarḳāʾ, with a station there. During the First World War, it was a communications and supply centre for the Ottoman army, but was occupied by the British in 1917. During 1918-20 it came within the Sharīf Fayṣal b. al-Ḥusayn's amīrate based on Damascus, and from 1921 came within the new state of Transjordan under his elder brother Amīr, later King, ʿAbd Allāh.

The new administration in 1926 chose al-Zarḳāʾ to be the headquarters of the border force, so that security was established in the region. Military and administrative personnel began to move there, together with people from outside the country, including some arriving after the 1925 Druze revolt against the French mandatary power in Syria, and in the wake of the discovery of phosphates in the region. Christian immigration included Armenians, and in 1949 there also arrived 800 Palestinians, so that al-Zarḳāʾ became a town of significance. It has continued to expand, with a population in 1996 of 585,000 and with several industries, including an oil refinery.

Bibliography: Admiralty Handbooks, Naval Intelligence Division, *Palestine and Transjordan*, London 1943, 408-10, 469, 475, 483, 510; Kamal Salibi, *The modern history of Jordan*, London and New York 1993, index. (M.A. AL-BAKHIT)

ZARḲĀʾ AL-**YAMĀMA**, lit. "the blue-eyed woman of Yamāma", a semi-legendary figure of early Arabic lore. She was endowed with such piercing eyesight that she could descry an object some thirty miles away, hence the proverb *abṣaru min Zarḳāʾ al-Yamāma*.

She belonged to the tribe of Ṭasm [*q.v.*], but was married to a member of the sister tribe Djadīs. After the massacre of the former by the latter, a survivor, her brother, invoked the aid of the South Arabian king Ḥassān, who marched against Djadīs in Yamāma. Although Ḥassān's army was camouflaged with leafy branches (cf. the march of Birnam Wood in Shakespeare's *Macbeth*), Zarḳāʾ caught sight of it and warned Djadīs, but they did not believe her, whereupon Ḥassān fell upon them unawares and massacred them. He captured Zarḳāʾ, gouged out her eyes, and found the veins of her eyes treated with antimony. He then crucified her on the gate of Djaww al-Yamāma. The kernel of truth in the account is discernible, supported by echoes in the genuine verses of three of the poets of the *Muʿallaḳāt*, al-Nābigha, al-Aʿshā and al-Ḥārith.

Yellow journalism in early Islamic times accused her of lesbianism [see SIḤĀḲ], involving the Lakhmid princess of al-Ḥīra, Hind bt. al-Nuʿmān (early 7th century). Ṭasm and Djadīs were "archaic" tribes that belonged to the category of *al-ʿArab al-bāʾida* "the extinct Arabs"; hence the three centuries or so that separate Hind from Zarḳāʾ invalidate the slanderous charge, already rejected totally by the sober ʿAbd al-Ḳādir al-Baghdādī in his *Khizāna*.

Bibliography: Ṭabarī, i, 771-4; Masʿūdī, *Murūdj*, ed. Pellat, ii, 263-72; Ibn al-Athīr, ed. Beirut, i, 351-4; Yāḳūt, *Buldān*, s.v. al-Yamāma; *Aghānī*, Beirut 1971, ii, 110; ʿAbd al-Ḳādir al-Baghdādī, *Khizānat al-adab*, ed. ʿAbd al-Salām Hārūn, Cairo 1977, vi, 70-1. See also the *Bibl.* to ṬASM.

(IRFAN SHAHÎD)

AL-**ZARḲĀLĪ**, ABŪ ISḤĀḲ IBRĀHĪM b. Yaḥyā al-Naḳḳāsh al-Tudjībī, known as WALAD AL-ZARḲIYĀL (Ṣāʿid al-Andalusī, *Ṭabaḳāt al-umam*, Beirut 1985, 179-81, tr. Blachère, 138-9; Ibn al-Ḳifṭī, 57), Spanish Muslim writer on practical and theoretical astronomy, d. 493/1100. Although al-Zarḳālī is the conventional form of his name, in Ibn al-Abbār, *Takmila*, Algiers 1920, 169-70, we have al-Zarḳālluh. It therefore seems likely that al-Zarḳālluh or al-Zarḳiyāl are the correct forms, and that al-Zarḳālī/Zarḳānī and al-Zarḳāla are classicised Eastern forms undocumented in Andalusī sources.

Life.

According to Isaac Israeli's *Liber Jesod ʿolam seu Fundamentum mundi* (1310), ed. Goldberg and Rosenkrantz, Berlin 1846-8, bk. IV, ch. vii, he worked as an instrument maker in Toledo for Ṣāʿid al-Andalusī [*q.v.*] and the Dhu 'l-Nūnid prince al-Maʾmūn amongst others. His patrons lent him the necessary books for teaching himself astronomy, so that he assumed a leading position in the group around Ṣāʿid, mentioned in the *Ṭabaḳāt* as belonging to the younger Toledan generation (*al-aḥdāth*), though he was active from at least 440/1048-9 onwards and must have begun his solar observations by the early 1050s at the latest. An anonymous Toledan contemporary states that he used a large-size instrument. Al-Zuhrī in his *K. al-Djaʿrāfiyya*, ed. Hadj-Sadok, 223-4, describes a water-clock that marked the date of the lunar month and that was built at Toledo by a certain Abu 'l-Ḳāsim b. ʿAbd al-Raḥmān, known as al-Zarḳāl, but it is doubtful whether he is referring to the same person.

Ibn al-Zarḳālluh (as he will be henceforth termed here) left Toledo for Cordova either at the beginning of the reign of Yaḥyā II al-Ḳādir or when Alfonso VI conquered Toledo. In Cordova, he was patronised by the ʿAbbādid al-Muʿtamid [*q.v.*], to whom he had already dedicated a work on the use of the instrument called *al-ṣafīḥa al-ʿabbādiyya* in 440/1048-9, when the future ruler al-Muʿtamid was only eight or nine years old, and he continued his observations there until at least 480/1087-8, dying in Cordova on 8 Dhu 'l-Ḥidjdja 493/15 October 1100 (Ibn al-Abbār).

Works.

1. *Astronomical instruments.*

(a) A treatise on the construction of the armillary sphere, extant in an Alfonsine Castilian translation; see M. Rico, *Libros del saber de astronomía*, 5 vols. Madrid 1863-7, ii, 1-24.

(b) Two treatises on two variants of the same universal astrolabe, which he calls *al-ṣafīḥa al-mushtaraka li-djamīʿ al-ʿurūḍ* ("the common plate for all latitudes") [see SHAKKĀZIYYA]. This instrument, also called *ṣafīḥa zarḳāliyya*, had, on its face, a double grid of equatorial and ecliptical coordinates and a ruler-horizon, and, on the back, a zodiacal scale, and orthographic projection of the celestial sphere, a sine quadrant and a diagram (circle of the moon) which, combined with a most elaborate alidade (transversal ruler), allowed the computation of the geocentric distance of the moon for a given time (R. Puig, *Los tratados de construcción y uso de la azafea de Azarquiel*, Madrid 1987; idem, *Al-Zarqālluh's graphical method for finding lunar distances*, in *Centaurus*, xxxii [1989], 294-309; J. Samsó, *Islamic astronomy and medieval Spain*, Variorum, Aldershot 1994, no. XV). At a later date, he seems to have dedicated a new account of his instrument to the same al-Muʿtamid, usually called *al-shakkāziyya*, divided into 60 chapters. The instrument is apparently a simplified version of the *ʿabbādiyya* type, with only one complete grid of equatorial coordinates and an ecliptical grid limited to the great circles of longitude for the beginnings of the zodiacal signs on its face, while its back resembles that of a standard astrolabe (Puig, *Concerning the ṣafīḥa šakkāziyya*, in *ZGAIW*, ii [1985], 123-39; idem, *Al-Šakkāziyya. Ibn al-Naqqāš al-Zarqālluh*, Barcelona 1986).

(c) Two treatises on the construction of the equatorium which he calls *al-ṣafīḥa al-zīdjiyya* (M. Comes, *Ecuatorios andalusíes*, Barcelona 1991, 189-236). The oldest reference to this instrument, a collection of Ptolemaic planetary models made to scale and used to solve graphically the problem of the determination of planetary longitudes, appears in the *Zīdj al-ṣafāʾiḥ* of Abū Djaʿfar al-Khāzin (d. *ca.* 350-60/961-71 [*q.v.*]) and, in al-Andalus, an earlier equatorium was designed by Ibn al-Samḥ [*q.v.*] *ca.* 416/1025-6. The latter instrument consisted of a series of plates kept within the mother of an astrolabe, but Ibn al-Zarḳālluh's equatorium is totally independent and represents all the planetary deferents and related circles on both sides of a single plate, while a second plate bears all the epicycles. The complexity of the Ptolemaic Mercury model led him to represent Mercury's deferent not as a circle but as an ellipse, which he identified as such: this is the first known instance of the use of conic sections in astronomy (Samsó and H. Mielgo, *Ibn al-Zarqālluh on Mercury*, in *Jnal. Hist. Astronomy*, xxv [1994], 289-96).

(d) Al-Marrākushī's *Djāmiʿ* attributes to Ibn al-Zarḳālluh a sine quadrant with movable cursor (*madjarra*) in the line of the *quadrans vetustissimus* (J.M. Millás, *La introducción del cuadrante con cursor en Europa*, in *Isis*, xvii [1932], 218-58; repr. in idem, *Estudios sobre historia de la ciencia española*, Barcelona 1949, 65-110), although Ibn al-Zarḳālluh's cursor is only a graphic scale of solar declinations in which the argument used is the solar longitude and not, as in the *quadrans vetustissimus*, the date of the Julian year.

2. *Astronomical tables.*

(e) The *Toledan Tables* are known through a Latin translation; they seem to be the result of an adaptation of the best available astronomical material (al-Khʷārazmī, al-Battānī) to the coordinates of Toledo made by a team led by Ṣāʿid and in which Ibn al-Zarḳālluh seems to have had an outstanding position (G.J. Toomer, *A survey of the Toledan Tables*, in *Osiris*, xv [1968], 5-174; L. Richter-Bernburg, *Ṣāʿid, the Toledan*

Tables, and Andalusī science, in D.A. King and G. Saliba (eds.), *From deferent to equant*, New York 1987, 373-401; R. Mercier, *Astronomical tables in the twelfth century*, in C. Burnett (ed.), *Adelard of Bath. An English scientist and Arabist of the early twelfth century*, London 1987, 104-12). In them, the mean motion tables are original and the result of observations, the parameter for the solar mean motion was not altered in Ibn al-Zarḳālluh's later works and it reappeared in the Andalusī-Maghribī school of *zīdj*s which begins with Ibn Isḥāḳ [see ZĪDJ]. Ṣā'id does not mention these tables, although they had been completed before the writing of the *Ṭabaḳāt* (460/1068); Abū Marwān al-Istidjdjī quotes repeatedly "our corrected *zīdj* (*zīdjunā al-muṣaḥḥaḥ*)" in his *Risāla fi 'l-tasyīrāt wa-maṭāriḥ al-shu'ā'āt* (ms. Escorial 939) dedicated to Ṣā'id from Cuenca.

(f) The *Almanac*, which has been preserved in Arabic, Latin and in an Alfonsine translation (Millás, *Estudios sobre Azarquiel*, Madrid-Granada 1943-50, 72-237; M. Boutelle, *The Almanac of Azarquiel*, in *Centaurus*, xii [1967], 12-19, repr. in E.S. Kennedy *et al.*, *Studies in the Islamic exact sciences*, Beirut 1983, 502-10), is based on a Greek work computed by a certain Awmātiyūs in the 3rd or 4th century A.D., although the solar tables seem to be the result of the Toledan observations, and its purpose is to simplify the computation of planetary longitudes; for that purpose, Babylonian planetary cycles ("goal years") are used. After the completion of one of these cycles, the longitudes of a given planet will be the same on the same dates of the year as at the beginning of the cycle. Perpetual almanacs seem to be characteristic of Andalusian astronomy, and they were also used in the Maghrib and in mediaeval Spain.

3. *Astronomical theory.*

(g) A lost work in which he summarises his twenty-five years of solar observations and which was probably written between 467-72/1075-80. Its title was either *Fī sanat al-shams* ("On the solar year") or *al-Risāla al-djāmi'a fi 'l-shams* ("Comprehensive epistle on the Sun"). Its contents are known through secondary sources, both Arabic and Latin (Toomer, *The solar theory of az-Zarqāl. A history of errors*, in *Centaurus*, xiv [1969], 306-36; idem, *The solar theory of az-Zarqāl. An Epilogue*, in King and Saliba (eds.), *From deferent to equant*, 513-19; Samsó, *Isl. astr.*, no. X). In it, Ibn al-Zarḳālluh established that the solar apogee had its own motion of about 1° in 279 Julian years, and he designed a solar model with variable eccentricity which became extremely influential both in the Maghrib and in Latin Europe until the time of Copernicus [see SHAMS].

(h) A treatise on the motion of the fixed stars, written *ca.* 476/1084-5 and extant in a Hebrew translation (Millás, *Azarquiel*, 247-343; B.R. Goldstein, *On the theory of trepidation according to Thābit b. Qurra and al-Zarqalluh and its implications for homocentric planetary theory*, in *Centaurus*, x [1964], 232-47; Samsó, *Isl. astr.*, nos. VIII, IX). It contains a study of three different trepidation models, in the third of which variable precession becomes independent of the oscillation of the obliquity of the ecliptic. Trepidation had already attracted the attention of Ṣā'id and his team; the trepidation table extant in the *Toledan Tables*, which also appears in some manuscripts of pseudo-Thābit's *Liber de motu octaue sphere*, is probably due to the Toledan group and, according to Ibn al-Hā'im, Abū Marwān al-Istidjdjī wrote a *Risālat al-Iḳbāl wa 'l-idbār* ("Epistle on accession and recession").

(i) We have indirect references to two other lost theoretical works: one is a *Maḳāla fī ibṭāl al-ṭarīḳ allatī salakahā Baṭlīmūs fī istikhrādj al-bu'd al-ab'ad li-'Uṭārid* ("On the invalidation of Ptolemy's method to obtain the apogee of Mercury") mentioned by Ibn Bādjdja [*q.v.*]. On the other hand, Ibn al-Hā'im had read in Ibn al-Zarḳālluh's own writing (*bi-khaṭṭ yadihi*) a description of a modified lunar Ptolemaic model; the centre of the Moon's mean motion in longitude was not the centre of the Earth but was placed on a straight line linking the centre of the Earth with the solar apogee. The maximum correction in the lunar mean longitude amounted to 24'. This correction appears in Andalusī (Ibn al-Kammād) and Maghribī (Ibn Isḥāḳ, Ibn al-Bannā') *zīdj*s as well as in the Spanish canons of the first version of the *Alfonsine Tables*.

4. *Magic.*

Mss. Vienna 1421, B.L. 977 (Add. 9599), Cairo National Library Taymūr *Madjāmi'* 424 and *Ḥurūf wa-awfāḳ* 124 contain the only known magical work by Ibn al-Zarḳālluh, *Risāla fī ḥarakāt al-kawākib al-sayyāra wa-tadbīrihā* ("On the motions and influences of planets") (Millás, *Azarquiel*, 480-3; King, *A survey of the scientific manuscripts in the Egyptian National Library*, Winona Lake, Ind. 1986, B87, 50). These mss. contain, at least, two very different recensions of the text, and a third one appears in a summarised Latin translation in ms. Vienna lat. 5239 (J. Sesiano, *Un traité médiéval sur les carrés magiques. De l'arrangement harmonieux des nombres*, Lausane 1996, 10, 34). It is a treatise on talismanic magic which uses magic squares for the making of talismans.

Bibliography: Given in the text. The essential general survey is still Millás, *Azarquiel*; an updated revision is in J. Samsó, *Las ciencias de los antiguos en al-Andalus*, Madrid 1992, 147-52, 166-240.

(J. SAMSÓ)

AL-**ZARḲĀLLUH** [see AL-ZARḲĀLĪ].

AL-**ZARNŪDJĪ**, BURHĀN AL-DĪN, Muslim scholar and traditionist, probably from eastern Persia, who in the late 6th/12th or early 7th/13th century composed a popular treatise on educational etiquette and ethics.

Very little is certain about him; not even his *ism* is known, and his period can only be approximately stated. W. Ahlwardt in the Berlin Catalogue under no. 111 estimated that he flourished about 620/1223, but the correct date may be slightly earlier. The various authorities cited in his treatise *Ta'līm al-muta'allim* suggest that al-Zarnūdjī lived and wrote at the end of the 6th/12th or the beginning of the 7th/13th century. For example, he several times identifies Burhān al-Dīn 'Alī b. Abī Bakr al-Farghānī al-Marghīnānī [*q.v.*], author of the *Hidāya*, an important Ḥanafī textbook, as his teacher; his comments make it clear that he was writing after al-Marghīnānī's death in 593/1197. He also names as his teacher Fakhr al-Islām al-Ḥasan b. Manṣūr al-Farghānī Ḳāḍīkhān [*q.v.*], who died in 592/1196. In another passage he records that the Shaykh Ẓahīr al-Dīn al-Ḥasan b. 'Alī al-Marghīnānī [*q.v.*] recited verses before him; al-Ḥasan had himself been the teacher of both Burhān al-Dīn al-Marghīnānī and Ḳāḍīkhān. He further tells us that he heard a story from Shaykh Fakhr al-Dīn al-Kāshānī; the reference is almost certainly to Abū Bakr Mas'ūd b. Aḥmad (d. 597/1191; see Brockelmann, *GAL*, I², 465). Finally, he tells us that Rukn al-Dīn Muḥammad b. Abī Bakr, known as Imām Khʷāharzāda, recited something to him; this probably refers to a *muftī* of Bukhārā who died in 573/1177-8 (see von Grunebaum and Abel, 60). If we take all these data together, we come to the conclusion that al-Zarnūdjī may have flourished a little earlier than Ahlwardt thought, but his work was certainly composed after 593/1197.

Al-Zarnūdjī's only known work, *Taʿlīm al-mutaʿallim ṭarīḳ al-taʿallum* "Teaching the learner the method/way of learning", was one of the most popular examples of a common genre of mediaeval Islamic literature, sc. treatises outlining the proper manner of behaviour for individuals involved in the study of the religious sciences. As such, it parallels works by Badr al-Dīn Muḥammad Ibn Djamāʿa (d. 733/1333) and Abū Yaḥyā Zakariyyāʾ al-Anṣārī (d. 916/1511), as well as portions of Abū Ḥamid al-Ghazālī's (d. 505/1111) famous *Iḥyāʾ ʿulūm al-dīn*. Al-Zarnūdjī has much to say concerning the physical and mental conditions necessary for successful study, the manner of instruction, attitudes to the written and spoken word, and especially the ideal character of the teacher-student relationship.

There were a number of late mediaeval commentaries on the *Taʿlīm al-mutaʿallim*; on them, see Brockelmann, *GAL*, I², 606, S I, 837. The text itself was printed in Leipzig in 1838, in Cairo in 1311/1893-4, and in several modern editions. It was translated into English by G.E. von Grunebaum and Theodora M. Abel, *Instruction of the student: the method of learning*, New York 1947, and into Spanish by Olga Kattan, *Instruccion del estudiante: el metodo de aprender*, Madrid 1991.

Bibliography: In addition to the editions cited in the text, see M.A. Khan, *The Muslim theories of education during the Middle Ages*, in *IC*, xviii (1944), 418-33; J. Berkey, *The transmission of knowledge in medieval Cairo. A social history of Islamic education*, Princeton 1992. (M. Plessner-[J.P. Berkey])

ZARWĀNIYYA [see madjūs].

ZĀTĪ [see dhātī].

ZĀTĪ (SULAYMĀN) [see sulaymān dhātī, in Suppl.].

ZĀWA, a district and town of Khurāsān. The town (modern Turbat-i Ḥaydarī or Ḥaydariyya, see below) is some 140 km/88 miles south of Mashhad on the road to Gunābād and lies at an altitude of approximately 1,280/4,200 feet (lat. 35° 16' N., long. 59° 08' E.).

Al-Muḳaddasī, 319 n. *a*, describes it as being just a rural district with no town, but Yāḳūt, *Buldān*, ed. Beirut, iii, 128, names its *ḳaṣaba* as Rukhkh or Rīkh. In Il-Khānid times, the town of Zāwa seems to have flourished, with 50 villages dependent on it, producing silk and fruits (Mustawfī, *Nuzha*, ed. Le Strange, 154, tr. 152; Ḥāfiẓ-i Abrū, ed. D. Krawulsky, *Ḫorāsān zur Timuridenzeit*, Wiesbaden 1982, text 41). Its rise must have been at least in part connected with the *baraka* and the shrine of a local *shaykh*, Ḳuṭb al-Dīn Ḥaydar (d. 630/1232), founder of the Ḥaydariyya dervish order. Ibn Baṭṭūṭa visited Zāwa and noted the ascetic practices of the Ḥaydariyya, including loading their limbs with iron rings and infibulation of the penis (*Riḥla*, iii, 79-80, tr. Gibb, iii, 583; cf. J.S. Trimingham, *The Sufi orders in Islam*, Oxford 1971, 39). Presumably after this time dates the transformation of the town's name to its contemporary one, Turbat-i Ḥaydarī, the shrine there—a brick-built mausoleum of the saint—being still venerated. In *ca*. 1950 it had a population of 2,354, which had risen by 1991 to 81,781.

Bibliography: See also Sir F.J. Goldsmid, *Eastern Persia, an account of the journey of the Persian Boundary Commission 1870-1872*, London 1876, i, 353; Curzon, *Persia and the Persian question*, i, 203, ii, 517; Le Strange, *The lands of the Eastern Caliphate*, 356; Razmārā (ed.), *Farhang-i djughrāfiyā-yi Īrān-zamīn*, ix, 196; Krawulsky, *Īrān—das Reich der Īlḫāne. Eine topographisch-historische Studie*, Wiesbaden 1978, 325-6; L. Adamec (ed.), *Historical gazetteer of Iran. II. Meshed and northeastern Iran*, Graz 1981, 650-5; M.R. Khusrawī, *Djughrāfiya-yi tārīkhi-yi wilāyat-i Zāwa*, Mashhad 1366/1988. (C.E. Bosworth)

ZAWĀḲĪL (a.), a shadowy group of Arab brigands and mercenaries active in al-Shām and al-Djazīra [*q.vv.*] during the ʿAbbāsid period (the etymology of the designation is unclear: the Arabic verb *zawḳala* means "to let the two ends of a turban hang down from one's shoulders").

Although most of the *zawāḳīl* known by name hail from Ḳaysī tribes (as noted by D. Ayalon, *The military reforms of Caliph al-Muʿtaṣim* . . ., 16-18, in *Islam and the Abode of War*, London 1994), they appear to have been a group of tribal outcasts, like many such brigand groups [see ṣuʿlūk and liṣṣ]. ʿAmr b. ʿAbd al-ʿAzīz al-Sulamī, for example, is mentioned with the famous Naṣr b. Shabath [*q.v.*] as one of the leaders of the *zawāḳīl* during the Fourth Civil War between al-Amīn and al-Maʾmūn (al-Ṭabarī, iii, 845). He began his career as an escaped convict—as a soldier he had murdered his commander—and then took to brigandage in southern al-Shām (Michael the Syrian, 491/iii, 21). The ʿAbbāsid authorities certainly saw the *zawāḳīl* as social flotsam: al-Maʾmūn's letter to Naṣr derides the latter's followers as coming "from the near and distant corners of the lands, with their scum and worst elements, those thieves and robbers who have rallied to your side and those whom their land has spewed forth, or whose tribe has expelled because of their bad reputation within it" (al-Ṭabarī, iii, 1070-1, tr. C.E. Bosworth, *The History of al-Ṭabarī*, xxxii, *The reunification of the ʿAbbāsid caliphate*, Albany 1987, 141-2).

The *zawāḳīl* are first mentioned in connection with the revolt of the Ḳaysī notable Abu ʾl-Haydhām al-Murrī in and around Damascus in 176-7/792-3. In the Ḳays-Yaman factionalism preceding the revolt, a group of Ḳaysī tribesmen enlisted the aid of the *zawāḳīl* and "a group of *mawālī* of Ḳuraysh" to exact revenge for a slain kinsman. During the revolt itself, these *zawāḳīl* fought on the side of the Ḳaysiyya against the Yamanīs and the ʿAbbāsid authorities (Ibn ʿAsākir, *Taʾrīkh madīnat Dimashḳ*, ed. ʿAmrāwī, Beirut 1995, xxvi, 66). One of their leaders was a Duʿāma b. ʿAbd Allāh, who had been one of a triumvirate of bandit leaders in southern al-Shām (*ibid.*, vii, 162). Shortly after the revolt, *zawāḳīl* are mentioned in 180/796-7 as participants in another explosion of tribal factionalism in al-Shām, which was summarily supressed by Djaʿfar b. Yaḥyā al-Barmakī (al-Ṭabarī, iii, 639).

As might be expected, the collapse of central authority in al-Shām and the west with the death of al-Rashīd and the accession of al-Amīn in 193/809 provided an ideal context in which the *zawāḳīl* could achieve a degree of local autonomy or could otherwise derive profit. In the early years of al-Amīn's reign, the *zawāḳīl* leaders Naṣr b. Shabath and al-ʿAbbās b. Zufar terrorised the region around Ḳurus/Cyrrhus and co-operated against mutual rivals. One of the latter was the Ḳaysī ʿUthmān b. Thumāma from the region of Ḳinnasrīn, who later joined Naṣr. At Aleppo, the descendants of the ʿAbbāsid noble Ṣāliḥ b. ʿAlī called upon Naṣr, al-ʿAbbās and their followers to put down a rebellion of Yamanī tribesmen of Tanūkh (al-Yaʿḳūbī, ii, 541; al-Balādhurī, *Futūḥ*, 145-6; Michael the Syrian, 497/iii, 31).

Groups of *zawāḳīl* (under ʿAmr b. ʿAbd al-ʿAzīz al-Sulamī) turn up as mercenaries yet again in 195/811 during the revolt of the Umayyad pretender Abu ʾl-ʿUmayṭir al-Sufyānī against the local governor in

Damascus (Michael the Syrian, 491/iii, 21-2; Ibn Manẓūr, *Mukhtaṣar ta'rīkh Dimashk*, ed. A. Murād, Damascus 1984-, xviii, 111-12). In this conflict, the *zawāḳīl* supplied mercenaries to Abu 'l-ʿUmayṭir's predominantly Yamanī following and to the Ḳaysī counter-rebellion as well. Ibn ʿAsākir's account of the revolt has the Yamanīs scorn their foes as "these [mere] *zawāḳīl*" (*hādhihi al-zawāḳīl*), while later sending for contingents of their own (*baʿathū ilā zawāḳīlihim*).

Not long afterward, ʿAmr b. ʿAbd al-ʿAzīz and his followers left these events in Damascus and headed for al-Raḳḳa [*q.v.*], where they joined Naṣr b. Shabath, al-ʿAbbās b. Zufar, and a host of other *zawāḳīl al-Shām*, all responding to al-Amīn's call for irregular troops to assist him in his conflict against his brother al-Ma'mūn. It was here that a conflict broke out between, on the one hand, the *zawāḳīl* and the other Syro-Djazīran troops, and, on the other, al-Amīn's loyal troops from the *Abnā'* [*q.v.*] and the *ahl Khurāsān*. According to the account of al-Ṭabarī, the fighting broke out because one of the *Abnā'* had been among the ʿAbbāsid troops defeated during Abu 'l-ʿUmayṭir's revolt in Damascus, and he recognised his horse among those of the *zawāḳīl* assembled in al-Raḳḳa. In the ensuing mêlée, the *zawāḳīl* and their Syrian companions were routed; many fled back to their homes (al-Ṭabarī, iii, 842-5).

After the accession of al-Ma'mūn, the fate of the *zawāḳīl* becomes more obscure, compounded by the tendency of some authors to use the name as a term for brigands and mercenaries in general. After the débâcle at al-Raḳḳa, some of the *zawāḳīl* stayed on with Naṣr b. Shabath in his stronghold of Kaysūm in the Djazīra, from which he fended off the approaching armies of al-Ma'mūn. It seems, though, that the *zawāḳīl* were soon co-opted by the state, finding a niche in the ʿAbbāsid military. Indeed, Naṣr's defeated followers were absorbed into the army of the victorious general ʿAbd Allāh b. Ṭāhir and accompanied him to Khurāsān, where they were decimated in battle in 213/828 (al-ʿAẓīmī, *Ta'rīkh Ḥalab*, ed. I. Zaʿrūr, Damascus 1984, 247). Some may also have joined later; al-Mutawakkil had a contingent of *zawāḳīl* in his army (al-Ṭabarī, iii, 1463; al-Masʿūdī, *Tanbīh*, 362).

The final fate of the Syro-Djazīran brigand group or groups known as the *zawāḳīl* is unknown. Ibn al-ʿAdīm, writing in Aleppo *ca.* 640/1242, discusses the long-standing enmity between two local tribes, the Ḥabbāliyyūn of Asad and the Ḳaysī Zawāḳila of Kilāb (*Bughyat al-ṭalab min ta'rīkh Ḥalab*, ed. S. Zakkār, Damascus 1988, i, 536-7), but the relationship of the latter to the *zawāḳīl* is only presumed. It may be that, over time, the *zawāḳīl* came to identify themselves as a separate tribe despite the diverse origins of their early members [cf. ḤILF].

Bibliography: In addition to the references given in the article, see I. ʿAbbās, *Ta'rīkh bilād al-Shām fi 'l-ʿaṣr al-ʿabbāsī*, ʿAmmān 1993; P.M. Cobb, *White banners. Contention in ʿAbbāsid Syria, 750-880*, Albany 2001, index at 221. (P.M. COBB)

ZAWĀRA, a small town in Persia lying some 15 km/9 miles to the northeast of Ardistān, on the southwestern edge of the central desert of the Dasht-i Kawīr (long. 52° 25' E., lat. 33° 30' N.). It falls administratively within the *ustān* or province of Iṣfahān and is the chef-lieu of a canton or *dihistān*. In *ca.* 1951 it had a population of 5,400; and according to the census of 1375/1996-7, one at that time of 7,710, representing 1,911 households.

This small and isolated place has played no role in wider Persian history, but is of significance for its surviving architecture. It clearly enjoyed prosperity and a local importance in Saldjūḳ and Il-Khānid times, attested by two monuments there. The Masdjid-i Pā Minār was restored, and a minaret built for it, according to an inscription on the latter from 461/1068-9, the time of Alp Arslan, by a local patron. The Friday mosque, from 530/1135, i.e. the reign of Masʿūd b. Muḥammad, provides the first dated example of a mosque with a central courtyard and four *īwāns* [*q.v.*].

Bibliography: A. Godard, *Ardistān et Zawārè*, in *Athār-e Īrān*, i (1936), 285-309, ii, 351; Razmārā (ed.), *Farhang-i djughrāfiyā-yi Īrān-zamīn*, x, 104; Sylvia A. Matheson, *Persia, an archaeological guide*, [2]London 1976, 173-4; S.R. Peterson, *The Masjid-i Pa Minar at Zavareh. A restating and an analysis of early Islamic Iranian sources*, in *Artibus Asiae*, xxxix (1977), 60-90; Sheila S. Blair, *The monumental inscriptions from early Islamic Iran and Transoxiana*, Leiden 1992, 137-9 no. 51, and pls. 90-3; R.M. Hillenbrand, *Islamic architecture, function and meaning*, Edinburgh 1994, 156, 487. (C.E. BOSWORTH)

AL-**ZAWĀWĪ** [see IBN MUʿṬĪ].

ZAWDJ (A., pl. *azwādj*), basically "two draught animals yoked together", from which, in both literary and dialectal Arabic usage, a number of senses have developed, including "piece of land which a yoked pair of beasts can plough in a determined time", "two things", "pair, couple", from which verbal forms have also developed. At the side of "one part of a pair", "half of a couple" (especially "spouse", and often with the fem. ending *-at* "wife"), the signification "couple, pair", though rejected by the purists, is attested from mediaeval Islamic times onwards, and the co-existence of the two concepts is frequent in most varieties of Arabic.

1. Etymology and early usage.

Although the classical philologists and lexicographers were convinced that it was a pure Arabic word, no Semitic parallel forms exist, and there is no doubt that *zawdj* stems from Grk. *zeugos* "yoke", probably via Aramaic; from this last, the word passed also into Rabbinical Hebrew, Ethiopic and Syriac. The word is thus distantly cognate with Skr. *jugám*, Lat. *iugum*, Ger. *Joch*, Eng. *yoke*, Fr. *joug*, etc. It must have been an early entrant into Arabic, since it appears in pre-Islamic poetry, e.g. in ʿAntara, and is frequent in the Ḳur'ān in various nominal and verbal forms (II, 23/25, 33/35, 96/102, 234, etc.). In the Ḳur'ān, the dominant usage of *zawdj* is in the sense of "spouse" = "wife, woman", but there are also several instances (e.g. XI, 42/40; XIII, 3; XXIII, 27; XLI, 49; LIII, 46/47; LXXV, 39) where the dual *zawdjayn* means "pairs, groups of two", which may be further specified as ". . . of man and woman". The later form *zawdja* "wife" nowhere appears in the sacred text. The differentiation of sex *zawdj*/*zawdja* is clearly a later development, but seems to have taken place by the end of the first century A.H., since *zawdja* "wife" is found in the poetry of al-Farazdaḳ and Dhu 'l-Rumma.

Bibliography: S. Fraenkel, *Die aramäischen Fremdwörter im Arabischen*, Leiden 1886, 106-7; A. Jeffery, *The foreign vocabulary of the Qur'ān*, Baroda 1938, 154-5; J.W. Fück, *ʿArabīya. Untersuchungen zur arabischen Sprach- und Stilgeschichte*, in *Abh. Sächs. Akad. Wiss. zu Leipzig*, xlv/1, Berlin 1950, 25, 120, Fr. tr. *ʿArabīya. Recherches sur l'histoire de la langue et du style arabe*, Paris 1955, 38, 184. (C.E. BOSWORTH)

2. Usage in the dialects of the Muslim West.

Whilst in numerous Eastern dialects, the metathesised form *djawz* (hence a homonym of the loan from

Persian *djawz* "nut") is used for "spouse" and "pair," in the Maghrib the form is without metathesis but often has assimilation of the voiced post-alveolar fricative and the voiced alveolar fricative, which may be regressive: *djūdj* and variants (esp. in the west: Morocco), or progressive (*zūz* and variants (esp. in the east: Tunisia, Libya). In numerous dialects, especially the urban ones of Algeria and Morocco, and for a long time back (as attested in mediaeval Maghribī, Andalusī and Sicilian Arabic, and also in Maltese), this form serves as a cardinal numeral "two". But in none of these has it completely eliminated the old **ithnayn*, the only word used when enumerating the cardinal numbers ("one, two, three . . .") and also the word appearing almost always in the composed numeral forms (a form like *jūj u khamsīn* "52" is rare, if not indeed exceptional). **Zawdj* "two" (sometimes in the diminutive, *zwayyidj*) is attested, either alone or at the side of **ithnayn* in dialects which have kept alive usage of the dual (and where its use often therefore serves to reinforce the dual), and alone in those which have only a "pseudo-dual"; it seems that there is a linkage between the disappearance of the dual and the replacement of **ithnayn* by **zawdj*.

The syntagm associating the noun of the object counted with the cardinal number has two constructions (which may be mutually exclusive or co-exist, according to different dialects): (a) *zawdj* + pl. noun, and (b) *zawdj* + particle (*d*, *dyāl*, etc.) + def. article + pl. noun (each of these constructions has a variant where the noun is in the sing., for certain types of collectives, or for certain units of measure, of money, etc.). In Maltese, there is a third construction in which the cardinal number assumes a special form when standing in the construct state (*zewdjt-*). In all the dialects concerned, the sense of "pair" remains in general for **zawdj*; it is sometimes distinguished from that of "two" by a special form in *-a* or by the diminutive *zwīdja*, but the plural remains in that case that of **zawdj*. The choice between collective or pl. in the noun of the object counted, or the use of the dual or pl. of **zawdj*, in some cases allows one to get round the ambiguities of "two", "pair", "element of a pair". Thus at La Chebba, Tunisia, one finds *zūz klāṣt* or *zūzēn klāṣt* "a pair of socks". Finally, one should note that some dialects (mainly Algerian, it seems) have made an ordinal number out of **zawdj*, sc. *jāwej* (La Saoura), *zāwadj* "second".

Bibliography: For the forms, usages and constructions of **zawdj* "two", this article has used the well-documented monograph of K. Mörth, *Die Kardinalzahlwörter von eins bis zehn in den neuarabischen Dialekten*, Vienna 1997, 25, 33-5, 138-49, 212-13 and map 6, and 302 sections *h* and *i*. For older attestations, see J. Blau, *The emergence and linguistic background of Judaeo-Arabic*, ²Jerusalem 1981, 117; F. Corriente, *A grammatical sketch of the Spanish Arabic dialect bundle*, Madrid 1977, 88. (J. LENTIN)

3. Usage in the dialects of the Muslim East [see Suppl.].

ZĀWĪ B. **ZĪRĪ** b. Manād al-Ṣanhādjī, the Berber founder of an independent taifa (*ṭāʾifa* [see MULŪK AL-ṬAWĀʾIF. 2]) or principality in Granada at the time of the dismemberment of the Umayyad caliphate of Cordova and its first ruler (403-10/1013-19).

The Zīrids, who belonged to the Talkāta, the most important tribe of the Ṣanhādja [*q.v.*], had settled in the area between Ifrīḳiya and the central Maghrib. Zāwī and his followers, including the two sons of his brother Māksan, were among the prominent Berbers in North Africa who were invited by the ʿĀmirid *ḥādjib* of Cordova, ʿAbd al-Malik al-Muẓaffar [*q.v.*], to join him in his perennial campaigns against the Christians of northern Spain. Al-Muẓaffar's father al-Manṣūr, however, had his own misgivings about Zāwī, who was reputed to be cunning, shrewd and troublesome.

After the fall of the ʿĀmirids and the outbreak of civil strife in al-Andalus, Zāwī is said to have contemplated returning to North Africa but changed his mind when the people of Elvira sought his protection. In fact, the Zīrids played a decisive role in the course of events, and it was largely thanks to Zāwī that the Umayyad Sulaymān al-Mustaʿīn was proclaimed caliph (Rabīʿ I 400/November 1008). If Zāwī had really intended to leave al-Andalus, one may well ask why he had stayed behind for eight years and taken such an active part (Ibn Ḥayyān describes Zāwī as "the spark that kindled the civil war after the ʿĀmirid dynasty") in events which secured for his people the rich province of Elvira.

It was the Berbers who had forced Sulaymān to divide between them the southern districts of al-Andalus and, consequently, the province of Elvira fell to Zāwī and his kinsmen. It is most unlikely that Zāwī's arrival in Elvira was, as claimed by the last Zīrid *amīr* of Granada (*Tibyān*, 59, tr. 45), in response to an invitation from the Elvirans, who had recently suffered so much at his hands. The Elvirans probably had no say in the matter. It is more likely that, prior to Sulaymān's re-entry into Cordova (403/1013), Zāwī had already established himself in Elvira and Sulaymān had to accept that as a *fait accompli*.

Aware of the bitter hostility of the Andalusians to the Berbers, Zāwī suggested that the people of Elvira move to the nearby and more defensible mountain fortress of Granada. Soon after, the Andalusians, led by the newly-proclaimed Umayyad caliph al-Murtaḍā, launched an assault but were routed just outside Granada, almost six years after Zāwī had settled there. The Zīrids' victory was swift and decisive, thanks mainly to the defection from al-Murtaḍā's ranks of the ʿĀmirid Khayrān of Almeria and of al-Mundhir b. Yaḥyā of Saragossa.

Shortly after his victory, however, Zāwī surprisingly decided to return to Ifrīḳiya, prompted no doubt by his keen awareness of the Andalusians' hostility and their numerical superiority. Moreover, he aspired to the throne of Ḳayrawān, whose occupant at the time was an eight-year-old Zīrid, al-Muʿizz b. Bādīs [*q.v.*], a great grandson of Zāwī's brother Buluggīn. Ibn Ḥayyān also mentions Zāwī's obsessive fear that the Zanāta Berbers, traditional foes of the Ṣanhādja, might join forces with the Andalusians against the Zīrids, hence Zāwī's description of the Zanāta as "the real enemies" (Ibn Bassām, *Dhakhīra*, i/1, 402; Ibn al-Khaṭīb, *Aʿmāl*, 131).

Zāwī, who was born and brought up in North Africa, must have felt isolated and insecure throughout his 18-year sojourn in al-Andalus, and it is not surprising that his thoughts should turn to his native land. Furthermore, the situation in North Africa had completely changed since his arrival in al-Andalus in 392/1002; the Fāṭimid caliphs had moved from Ifrīḳiya to Egypt; the Zanāta ruler of Fās, Zīrī b. ʿAṭiyya, could no longer count on Umayyad support; and the internecine struggle, raging since 409/1014 between the Zīrids of Ifrīḳiya [*q.v.*] and their kinsmen the Ḥammādids of al-Ḳalʿa [*q.v.*], had exhausted both sides.

Zāwī left Almuñecar (al-Munakkab) for Ifrīḳiya some

time in 410/1019-20, with the consent of al-Muʿizz who is said to have come out in person to greet him. At least initially, Zāwī's kinsmen in Ḳayrawān seemed to welcome his return, since they badly needed someone of his age and calibre to head the Zīrid house and fill the vacuum left by the death of al-Muʿizz's father. There were those amongst al-Muʿizz's *wazīrs*, however, who regarded "the accession of the child al-Muʿizz. . . ., over whom they had control, preferable to surrendering power to a shrewd character like Zāwī, over whom they had not a scrap of authority. Someone was therefore hired to administer poison to Zāwī, who died in that country" (*Tibyān*, 64, tr. 51).

Ibn Ḥayyān says that Zāwī died in Ḳayrawān of the plague but does not give the date of his death; nor does *amīr* ʿAbd Allāh in the *Tibyān*.

Bibliography: 1. Sources. ʿAbd Allāh b. Buluggīn, *Tibyān*, ed. and annotated A.T. Tibi, Rabat 1995, 57-64, Eng. tr. Leiden 1986, 44-51; anon., *Mafāk͟hir al-Barbar*, ed. E. Lévi-Provençal, Rabat 1934; Ibn Bassām al-S͟hantarīnī, *D͟hak͟hīra*, ed. I. ʿAbbas, i, iv/1 Beirut 1975-9; Ibn ʿId͟hārī, *Bayān*, ed. Colin and Lévi-Provençal, i, iii, Beirut 1980; Ibn K͟haldūn, *ʿIbar*, iv, vi, Būlāḳ 1867; Ibn al-K͟haṭīb, *Aʿmāl*, ed. Lévi-Provençal, Beirut 1956, 227-9; idem, *Iḥāṭa*, ed. M.A. Inān, i, Cairo 1973, 513-17.

2. Studies. Lévi-Provençal, *Hist. Esp. mus.*, ii; H.R. Idrīs, *La Berbérie orientale sous les Zīrīdes*, i, Paris 1959; idem, *Les Zīrīdes d'Espagne*, in *And.*, xxix (1964), 39-137; A. Handler, *The Zīrids of Granada*, Miami 1974; C.E. Bosworth, *The New Islamic dynasties*, Edinburgh 1996, 17, no. 6. (AMIN TIBI)

ZAWĪLA, the mediaeval Islamic capital of the Fazzān [*q.v.*], today south-western Libya (lat. 26° 11' N., long. 15° 06' E.).

Zawīla (Zuwayla) was established probably in the early 2nd/8th century. It did not yet exist in 46/666-7 when the Arab conqueror ʿUḳba b. Nāfiʿ [*q.v.*] passed by the site, but had a century later become the centre of the region. It was then dominated by Hawwāra Berbers, predominantly Ibāḍīs.

After he had crushed the first Ibāḍī state in Tripolitania, the ʿAbbāsid general Muḥammad b. al-As͟hʿat͟h al-K͟huzāʿī sent a force to Zawīla. It fell in 145/762-3 and its leader ʿAbd Allāh b. Ḥayyān al-Ibāḍī was killed. However, Zawīla remained an Ibāḍī centre. During the Rustamid period, it was partly under the control of Tāhart, but on the periphery of their influence. Thus both the Wahbī and other Ibāḍī currents (in particular the K͟halafiyya [*q.v.*]) co-existed in the town. In 306/918-19, after the fall of Tāhart [*q.v.*], the Banū K͟haṭṭāb established an independent Ibāḍī dynasty that lasted until the 6th/12th century. During at least part of the mediaeval period, the Fazzān was divided into two. The western region was then a separate polity dominated by the older capital D͟jarma (Garama), while the eastern and probably the richest part had Zawīla as its capital. Both followed the Ibāḍiyya [*q.v.*].

Zawīla was a prosperous town, with ample irrigation producing dates and vegetables. It had in the 3rd/9th century inhabitants from K͟hurāsān, Baṣra and other remote regions, and a lively Ibāḍī scholarship. The basis of its economy was the trans-Saharan trade through Kawar to the Lake Chad region, in particular to Kanem. The main trade item was slaves, but also other goods contributed to its prosperity. Zawīla also produced a special leather called *zawīla*. Besides the Berber majority, there was a smaller free population of Sudanic origin, either Teda [see TUBU] or (proto-)Kanuri speakers. The Fāṭimids recruited a corps of *zawīla* soldiers from this group (hence the Bāb Zuwayla in their capital al-Mahdiyya and later in Cairo).

From the 5th/11th century, raiders from the Sudanic state of Kanem [*q.v.*] started to appear. The Banū K͟haṭṭāb dynasty was ended in 572/1176-7, when an Armenian *mamlūk*, S͟haraf al-Dīn Ḳarāḳūs͟h [*q.v.*] came from Egypt and conquered Zawīla and the Fazzān, passing on to Tripolitania. In the chaotic period that followed, Kanem increased its hold, and had by the end of the century taken effective control of the Fazzān. The rulers of Kanem established their own capital in Trāg͟han a few miles west of Zawīla.

Kanem retained control thoughout the 7th/13th century, but later their governors broke free and established an independent dynasty, the Banū Nasūr. In the early 9th/15th century, the province came under the (perhaps fluctuating) domination of the Ḥafṣids of Tripoli, and the capital was probably returned to Zawīla. At the same time, troubles in Kanem led to a reduction of the trans-Saharan trade that the town lived on. When trade later started to pick up, Zawīla had lost its rank of capital and trade centre. In the first half of the 10th/16th century, the Awlād Muḥammad dynasty took political power in Fazzan. They built a new capital at Murzuḳ [*q.v.*], slightly west of Zawīla. Trade now went there, and Zawīla soon thereafter declined into obscurity.

Bibliography: Ibn ʿAbd al-Ḥakam, *Futūḥ Miṣr wa 'l-Mag͟hrib*, ed. and tr. A. Gateau, Algiers 1942, 64; Ibn ʿId͟hārī, i, 73; Abū ʿUbayd al-Bakrī, *K. al-Masālik wa 'l-mamālik*, ed. and tr. de Slane, Paris 1911-13, 10; Yaʿḳūbī, *Buldān*, 345; Idrīsī, *Nuzhat al-mus͟htāḳ fī ik͟htirāḳ al-āfāḳ*, ed. A. Bombaci *et alii*, Naples-Rome 1970, 115-16, 313; T. Lewicki, *La répartition géographique des groupements ibāḍites dans l'Afrique du nord au moyen-âge*, in *RO*, xxi (1957), 301-43; E. Rossi, *Storia di Tripoli e della Tripolitania. Dalla conquista araba al 1911*, Rome 1968.

(K.S. VIKØR)

ZĀWIYA (A., pl. *zawāyā*), lit. "corner, nook [of a building]", originally the cell of a Christian monk and then, in the Islamic context, a small mosque, oratory or prayer room. In late mediaeval times, particularly in North Africa (see 2. below), the term came to designate a building designed to house and feed travellers and members of a local Ṣūfī brotherhood.

1. Architecture.

In plan, these buildings often comprised cells arranged around a courtyard. Both form and decoration resemble those used in other communal institutions such as the *madrasa*, and without epigraphic or textual evidence, it can be difficult to distinguish a *zāwiya* from another type of building. For example, a ruined building discovered at ʿAyn Ḳarwash in Morocco was first thought to be a house but then identified as either a *madrasa* or *zāwiya*.

*Zāwiya*s were often constructed around the tomb of the founder. As the number of disciples increased, the units were incorporated into larger complexes that not only provided space for teaching and accommodation for the devotees but also served as centres of pilgrimage, gathering, and retreat for the community at large. By nature agglomerative, these popular shrines were often restored and rebuilt.

*Zāwiya*s were introduced to Morocco under the Marīnids (614-869/1217-1465 [*q.v.*]). The sultan Abu 'l-Ḥasan ʿAlī (*r.* 731-49/1331-48) ordered a *zāwiya* in

Zāwiya for the ʿAdawiyya shaykh Zayn al-Dīn Yūsuf (d. 697/1298) in the southern cemetery of Cairo, as seen from the east. Photo: Jonathan M. Bloom, April 1978.

Zāwiya built by the Marīnid sultan Abu ʾl-Ḥasan ʿAlī in the family necropolis Shālla outside Rabāṭ, as seen from the south. Photo: Jonathan M. Bloom, July 1978.

the family necropolis known as Chella (Ar. Sh̲ālla), south of Rabāṭ on the site of the Roman outpost of Sala Colonia. Now ruined, the complex was a rectangular block (44 × 29 m) comprising a mosque, minaret, and several tombs, as well as the *zāwiya* proper in the northern third. Reached down a flight of steps, the two-story *zāwiya* was set around a large pool with fountains. Galleries on the long sides gave access to cells. On the east, or *ḳibla* end, was a sanctuary; facing it on the west was another hall and a small tiled minaret. Although the building is commonly identified as a *zāwiya*, the term is not used epigraphically. Abu 'l-Ḥasan's son and successor Abū ʿInān Fāris (*r.* 749-59/1348-58) built the *zāwiyat al-nussāk* outside Salé. Excavations have revealed an unusually spacious plan, but all that remains is a door.

*Zāwiya*s became more common and more elaborate in Morocco under the patronage of the Saʿdid (916-1069/1510-1659) and ʿAlawid (1041-/1631-) *sharīf*s, descendants of the Prophet who often allied themselves with local religious fraternities. The largest and finest *zāwiya*s were those endowed by rulers, such as the complex built in Marrakesh in the mid-10th/16th century for the *shaykh* al-Djazūlī (d. 869/1465 [*q.v.*]). His followers had been instrumental in bringing the Saʿdids to power, and al-Djazūlī became one of the seven patron saints (*sabʿatu rid̲jāl* [*q.v.*]) of the city. His *zāwiya* is a large, irregularly-shaped complex set around a court (Blair and Bloom, fig. 323). It includes a mosque, the saint's tomb, a cemetery for his followers, a school with a fountain, a residence for the superintendent who also served as leader of the order, a hospice for pilgrims and members of the order, ablution facilities and a bath across the street. These shrines were often recipients of lavish fittings and devotional objects including silken tomb covers and pilgrimage banners and illustrated prayer books (*ibid.*, figs. 331, 332).

*Zāwiya*s appeared in Tunisia during the period of Ḥafṣid rule (627-982/1229-1574). The oldest are thought to be in Ḳayrawān. The *zāwiya* of Sīdī Ṣāḥib (also known as the Mosque of the Barber), for example, was founded in the 8th/14th century around the grave of the Prophet's companion Abu 'l-Balawī but reconstructed in the 11th/17th century (*ibid.*, fig. 317), and the *zāwiya* of Sīdī ʿAbīd al-Gh̲aryānī was begun by a Ḥafṣid prince before 724/1324 but only completed in 804/1402 when the present tomb was associated with it. The most celebrated in Tunis are those of Sīdī Ben ʿArūs (895/1490) and Sīdī Ḳāsim al-Djalīzī (*ca.* 901/1496). The latter is elaborately decorated with tilework reflecting the occupation of the founder, a maker of tiles (*zallīd̲j* [*q.v.*]) who had emigrated from Andalusia to Tunis, where his spiritual merits brought him to the attention of the Ḥafṣid princes.

*Zāwiya*s were also established in Mamlūk Egypt as institutions for popular Ṣūfism, distinct from the more formal *kh̲ānḳāh* [*q.v.*], and often built for foreign *shaykh*s. Many are mentioned in texts (al-Maḳrīzī, for example, lists 26 in Cairo), but the only building epigraphically designated a *zāwiya* is the one for Zayn al-Dīn Yūsuf (d. 697/1298) in the southern cemetery of Cairo. Begun in 697/1297-8 as subsidiary rooms around the *shaykh*'s domed tomb (*ḳubba* [*q.v.*]), the stone complex was enlarged to a cruciform plan in 725/1325-6. Later in 736/1335-6 a large portal was added on the street side of the complex, now called a *zāwiya* in the foundation inscription. No patrons are mentioned, though the fine construction and lavish decoration bespeak significant funding. Texts suggest

that there were many *zāwiya*s in 9th/15th-century Egypt, but the lack of surviving examples makes it difficult to say anything about their architectural form.

Turkish scholars also use the term *zâviyeli* to refer to a type of "Convent Mosque" with a domed or vaulted central hall flanked by side rooms or *īwān*s [*q.v.*]. This distinctive T-plan was common in the complexes built by the Ottoman sultans at Bursa, beginning with the one founded by Orkh̲ān Gh̲āzī *ca.* 739/1339 (Blair and Bloom, fig. 171). The side rooms are thought to have been hostels for travelling dervishes and the religious brotherhoods who provided much of the support for Ottoman expansion. The term *zāwiya*, however, is not used in the foundation inscriptions for these constructions, which are called mosque (*masd̲jid*) or noble and blessed building (*ʿimāra sharīfa mubāraka*).

Bibliography: H. Basset and E. Lévi-Provençal, *Chella, une nécropole mérinide*, in *Hespéris*, ii (1922), 1-92, 255-316, 385-425, repr. as *Chella, une nécropole mérinide*, Paris 1923; G. Marçais, *L'architecture musulmane d'occident*, Paris 1954; Aptullah Kuran, *The mosque in early Ottoman architecture*, Chicago 1968; Layla ʿAlī Ibrahim, *The Zāwiya of Šaiḥ Zain al-dīn Yūsuf in Cairo*, in *Mitteilungen des Deutschen Archäologischen Instituts. Abteilung Kairo*, xxxiv (1978), 79-110; Sheila S. Blair, *Sufi saints and shrines. Architecture in the early fourteenth century*, in *Muqarnas*, vii (1990), 35-49; eadem and J.M. Bloom, *The art and architecture of Islam, 1250-1800*, London and New Haven 1994.

(SHEILA S. BLAIR)

2. In North Africa.

The term in North Africa denotes a social institution with a wide range of forms and functions. Sometimes rendered as "lodge" in English and "monastère" in French, the *zāwiya* is primarily a meeting place for spiritual pursuits and religious instruction. In this sense it is the Maghribī counterpart of the *kh̲ānaḳāh* or the *tekke* [*q.vv.*]. In the eastern Islamic world, the term *zāwiya* was often specifically applied to a smaller mosque or Ṣūfī meeting place (D.B. Little, *The nature of* khānḳāhs, ribāṭs, and zāwiyas *under the Mamluks*, in *Islamic studies presented to Charles P. Adams*, Leiden 1991, 91-105). In the Maghrib, a *zāwiya* is typically associated with a religious lineage. Frequently housing a *walī*'s *ḳubba* or tomb and surrounded by a cemetery, it may be a shrine and a place of pilgrimage.

Beyond serving as the residence of the *shaykh* [*q.v.*] or head of the *zāwiya*, as well as his family and retainers, some rural *zāwiya*s also provide lodging for pilgrims (*funduḳ*) and contain libraries, schools, mosques, workshops and granaries stockpiled for local relief in times of famine. In addition, a *zāwiya* may function as an intellectual centre, a sanctuary offering asylum, and a political focus. In the past, *zāwiya*s often played an important commercial role by protecting trade routes and creating networks of exchange among its members. In contrast, a *zāwiya* in an urban setting is often not much more than a room where local members of a wide-ranging or regional *ṭarīḳa* [*q.v.*] meet to perform *ḥaḍra* or *d̲hikr* recitation. Finally, beyond referring to an actual building, the word *zāwiya* in the Maghrib is also used to denote the *ṭarīḳa* itself and is synonymous for the *ṭarīḳa*'s collective membership.

Historically, the *zāwiya*'s financial support derived from *ḥubūs* [see WAḲF] lands and the gifts of pilgrims or its members' dues in the case of a *ṭarīḳa*; both sources of revenue are known as *ziyāra* or pilgrimage offerings. In theory, all revenues are charity and are thus considered divine gifts. Colonial governments confiscated the *wakf* lands of *zāwiyas* in the late 19th and early 20th centuries in an effort to reduce their political power. Some *zāwiyas* continue to receive governmental stipends for their maintenance and preservation as part of the national patrimony. Over the past century *zāwiyas*, which were also opposed by reformist Salafī Muslims [see SALAFIYYA], have suffered a reduction in prestige and a limitation in their social role.

The *zāwiya* as an institution antedates the establishment of the Ṣūfī *ṭarīḳas* in North Africa. It finds its sources in the *ḳubba* shrine as well as the *rābiṭa*, a hermitage to which a holy man retired and was surrounded by his followers, and the *ribāṭ* [*q.v.*], in the Maghrib an institution that had served *inter alia* as a centre for waging *djihād* [*q.v.*]. The *zāwiya*'s administrative organisation is, however, fundamentally that of the *ṭarīḳa*. The *shaykh* of the *zāwiya* acts primarily as a spiritual guide to the *zāwiya*'s members, but in some instances he is the descendant of the holy personage buried in the *zāwiya*'s shrine and thus an inheritor of his *baraka* [*q.v.*] or charisma. This distinction between *zāwiyas* affiliated with Ṣūfī orders and *zāwiyas* primarily associated either with a sharīfian descent or a holy lineage led colonial-era French commentators to make a distinction between "confrérie" or "brotherhood" *zāwiyas* and "maraboutic" *zāwiyas*.

Below the *shaykh* in the administrative hierarchy of the *zāwiya* is his *khalīfa* or deputy, sometimes also referred to as a *nā'ib* or *naḳīb*. The *khalīfa* himself or an officer known in some instances as a *wakīl* has responsibility for the day-to-day operation of the *zāwiya* and oversees servants known as *khuddām* or *shuwwāsh*. Administering individual local *zāwiyas* is a delegate of the *shaykh* known as a *muḳaddam* [*q.v.*], who initiates, instructs and supervises members. A *muḳaddam* receives no official remuneration for his role. In some *ṭarīḳas*, couriers known as *rukkāb* also served to link the local *zāwiyas* with the "mother" *zāwiya*.

Members of North African *zāwiya* can go by a variety of names: *aṣḥāb* "companions", *khuddām* "servants", *fuḳarā'* "poor men" and *ikhwān* "brothers". An individual seeking guidance from a *shaykh* is a *murīd* or aspirant. Female members are known as *khwatāt* "sisters" and are placed under the supervision of a female deputy of the *shaykh* known as a *muḳaddama*. While *muḳaddams* and *muḳaddamas* are appointed by the *shaykh*, they are named with the agreement of the majority of the members of a *zāwiya*. Factors in their nomination include length of time in the *ṭarīḳa*, knowledge or ritual, moral character and personal qualities, piety, and an ability to maintain harmony among the *zāwiya*'s members. A family tie to the *shaykh* may be a positive factor but is not a requirement for being appointed a *muḳaddam*.

Dhikr recitation sessions known as *ḥaḍra* provide regular, most often weekly, occasions for *zāwiya* members to gather. Presided over by the *shaykh*, the recitation is led by the *shaykh al-ḥaḍra*. In urban areas the character of the membership in the various *zāwiyas* typically reflects the social stratification of the community. Certain professions or one social stratum predominate in one *zāwiya*, with other professions predominating in another. On the occasion of anniversary celebrations of a *walī*, known as *mawāsim* [see MAWSIM], thousands of pilgrims may attend festivities at a *zāwiya*.

In rural areas, *zāwiya* heads often mediate in local tribal factional disputes or between the tribes and the central government. With the Sanūsiyya [*q.v.*] *ṭarīḳa* in Libya and the eastern Sahara in the 19th century, the creation of scores of *zāwiyas* led to the identification of a tribe with its *zāwiya*. In periods of weak authority by the Moroccan *makhzan* or central government, such as the 10th-11th/16th-17th centuries, some *zāwiyas*, like the Nāṣiriyya *zāwiya* in Tamgrūt [*q.v.*], were regional centres of power and operated almost as autonomous principalities. Other *zāwiyas* contested and occasionally sought to supplant the central government. At other times, for example, under the Ḥafṣids and under the Ḥusaynid Beys in 19th-century Tunisia, *zāwiyas* received governmental support and patronage.

In the 19th century, *zāwiya* membership was widespread; in 1880 Rinn estimated there to be over 355 *zāwiyas* in Algeria, with a membership of 167,019 out of an Algerian Muslim population of slightly less than three million (*Marabouts et khouan*). Estimates for Morocco put members in 1939 at between 5% and 10% of the population. While some *zāwiyas* and *ṭarīḳas* took an active role in organising opposition to colonial rule, others have been condemned as collaborationist. Although the *zāwiyas* have generally been opposed by nationalists in North Africa, significantly the organisational model of the *zāwiya* was employed in Morocco by the Istiḳlāl or Independence Party [see ḤIZB. i, at Vol. III, 525]. Its leader ʿAllāl al-Fāsī [*q.v.* in Suppl.] was referred to as the *shaykh*, and party members, self-styled *ikhwān*, called themselves ʿAllāliyya and ʿAllāliyyūn, organised local chapters known as *ṭā'ifas*, and levied dues known as *ziyāra*.

Bibliography: 1. General. L. Rinn, *Marabouts et khouan. Étude sur l'Islam en Algérie*, Algiers 1880; O. Depont and X. Coppolani, *Les confréries religieuses musulmanes*, Algiers 1897; E. Lévi-Provençal, art. *Zāwiya* in *EI*[1]; B.G. Hoffman, *The structure of traditional Moroccan rural society*, The Hague 1967, 120-6; S. Andezian, *L'Algérie, le Maroc, la Tunisie*, in A. Popovic and G. Veinstein (eds.), *Les voies d'Allah. Les ordres mystiques dans l'Islam des origines à aujourd'hui*, Paris 1996, 389-408.

2. Studies on modern North African *zāwiyas*. E. Gellner, *Saints of the Atlas*, Chicago 1969; D.E. Eickelman, *Moroccan Islam. Tradition and society in a pilgrimage center*, Austin 1976; A. Hammoudi, *Sainteté, pouvoir et société. Tamgrout aux XVIIe et XVIIIe siècles*, in *Annales ESC*, xxxv (1980), 615-41; F. Colonna, *The transformation of a saintly lineage in the northwest Aurès mountains (Algeria): nineteenth and twentieth centuries*, in E. Burke III and I.M. Lapidus (eds.), *Islam, politics and social movements*, Berkeley 1988, 91-6; A. Būkārī, *al-Zāwiya al-sharḳāwiyya: zāwiya Abi 'l-Djaʿd, ishʿāʿuhā al-dīnī wa 'l-ʿilmī*, Marrakech 1985; M. Mansour, *Sharifian Sūfism: the religion and social practice of the Wazzani zāwiya*, in E.G.H. Joffé and C.R. Pennell (eds.), *Tribe and state. Essays in honour of David Montgomery Hart*, Wisbech 1991, 69-83; G. Joffé, *The zāwiya of Wazzan: relations between the shurafa and tribe up to 1860*, in *ibid.*, 84-118; J.A. Miller and D.L. Bowen, *The Nasiriyya brotherhood in southern Morocco*, in Bowen and E.A. Early (eds.), *Everyday life in the Muslim Middle East*, Bloomington 1993, 146-56; J. Clancy-Smith, *Rebel and saint, Muslim notables, populist protest, colonial encounters (Algeria and Tunisa 1800-1904)*, Berkeley 1994; K.S. Vikør, *Ṣūfī scholar on the desert edge. Muḥammad b. ʿAlī al-Sanūsī and his brotherhood*, Evanston 1995. (J.G. KATZ)

3. In sub-Saharan Africa.

The institution of the *zāwiya* is linked, in Islamised black Africa, to the development of the network of Islamic brotherhoods (*ṭuruḳ*) and is consequently a late phenomenon (12th-13th/18th-19th centuries). Saharan staging-posts played a capital role, as models for the functioning of *zāwiya*s and as instruments of diffusion.

Such was the case with the *zāwiya* of Shaykh Sīdī Mukhtār al-Kuntī (d. 1226/1811) in the region of the Azawad (Mali). It was through his teachings, writings and disciples, but also through the commercial network of his tribe, the Kunta [*q.v.*], that settlements of the Ḳādiriyya came into being in western Africa. Some Kunta *zāwiya*s were established at Timbuktu by one of the sons of the founder, Sīd Aḥmad al-Bakkāy (d. 1281/1865), and at Talaya, in the Adrār of the Ifoghas, in Tuareg circles, by one of the grandsons, Sīdī Bay (*ca.* 1281-1348/1865-1929). To them is owed the adherence to the Ḳādiriyya of the Djihādist ʿUthmān Dan Fodio (Sokoto) and of Shaykhū Aḥmadū (Māsina).

A second Saharan staging-post was provided by the *zāwiya* of Būtilimit of the Ahl Shaykh Sīdiyya, the founder of which, Shaykh Sīdiyya al-Kabīr (1195-1286/1780-1869) was raised among the Kunta. From this *zāwiya* was to emerge the Senegalese brotherhood of the Murīd of Aḥmadu Bamba Mbacké (1270-1346/1853-1927), whose *zāwiya*s covered the Wolof land and monopolised the cultivation of the groundnut [see MURĪDIYYA].

Shaykh Muḥammad Fāḍil (1176-1286/1780-1869) and his numerous descendants constituted a third staging-post of the Ḳādiriyya in the direction of black Africa. Located in the Mauritanian Ḥawḍ, his *zāwiya* extended his influence beyond the river Senegal into Gambia and Guinea. His son, Shaykh Saʿd Būh (d. 1336/1917), based at his *zāwiya* of Nimdjat (Mauritanian Trārza), educated numerous *talāmīdh*, including two leading Senegalese scholars, Shaykh Mūsā Kamara, the author of *Zuhūr al-basātīn* (1344/1925) and Siré-Abbas Sūh, the author of *Chroniques du Fouta sénégalais* (1331/1913).

All the *zāwiya*s of Ḳādiriyya allegiance are part of a pastoral Saharan society where activities take place either in the tent (*khayma*) or, sometimes, on the move, with herds and families. Occasionally, the *zāwiya* constitutes the origin of a fixed settlement, as in the case of the Sīdiyya at Būtilimit. Income is derived from stockbreeding but also from the gifts or *hadāyā* of pupils and the fruits of visits to shrines (*ziyāra*) performed by the *shaykh*. General and mystical instruction remains their principal function.

The Tidjāniyya [*q.v.*] have also evolved through Saharan intermediaries, in the person of Muḥammad al-Ḥāfiẓ (d. 1246/1830) and his tribe of the Idawali. However, the centres of this brotherhood developed directly in black Africa. The best known of these *zāwiya*s, on account of its colonial history and its network of subsidiaries, has been that of Shaykh Ḥamāllāh (1301-63/1883-1943 [see ḤAMĀLIYYA]) at Nioro-du-Sahel (Mali). Some of its characteristics may be applied to the totality of African *zāwiya*s. Thus the family of the *shaykh*, teachers, disciples, students, and domestic staff, all live, eat and sleep in the *zāwiya*, perform the canonical prayers there (rather than in the mosque) and carry out the rituals of the *dhikr*. It is often a place of independence and economic wealth. Among the offshoots of the Ḥamāliyya of Nioro, the twelve current *zāwiya*s of Ouagadougou (Burkina Faso) should be included. That of the Ḥamdallāhiyya quarter, built in 1378/1958 by Shaykh Doukouré has, for some time, been the rival of the *zāwiya* of the Kamsonghin quarter, founded in 1374/1954 by al-Ḥādjdj Būbakar Maiga. In the decade commencing 1348/1930, these two *shaykh*s had, respectively, been responsible for the creation of the *zāwiya*s of Djibo and Ramatoullaye, in the north of the country. Thus the transfer of centres of brotherhoods from rural zones towards the cities, and especially towards the capitals, appears to be a gradual but radical evolution since *zāwiya*s have been often transformed into institutions subject to national legislation and have lost some of their independence. The Ḥamāliyya have also reached the Ivory Coast with the establishment, from 1357/1938 onwards, of the *zāwiya* of Yaʿḳūba Sylla (d. 1408/1988), at Gagnoa, characterised as much by its commercial as by its religious activity. Also to be noted are branches in Niger (the *zāwiya* of Shaykh ʿAlī Gaty at Niamey-Karadjé, since 1366/1946), in Senegal, Mauritania, Nigeria and France.

The network of the Ḥamāliyya, broadly decentralised, has nonetheless retained a certain degree of coordination, both in regard to individuals and also in connection with religious considerations. This is much less the case with other centres of the Tidjāniyya, especially those in Senegal. Here, each *zāwiya* represents an independent unit and tends to be concentrated around a religious dynastic line. Such is the case of the *zāwiya* of Sy (al-Ḥādjdj Mālik Sy, 1272-1341/1855-1922), founded at Tivaouane in 1326/1906; and it is still the case of the closed community that resided at Madina-Gounasse from 1355/1936 onwards, on a utopian model, under the leadership of the Peul Mamadu Saydu Ba, and only became open to the outside world in 1397/1977, when the founder was succeeded by his heir. The history of the branch of Shaykh Ibrāhīma Nyās (1320-95/1902-75) whose *zāwiya* is at Kaolack, shows a break with the preceding model since from 1371/1951 onwards, it has been spreading in the north of Nigeria (Kano). Senegalese *zāwiya*s, without exception, practise annual gatherings which attract considerable crowds, e.g. the *Magal* of the Murīds at Touba, in honour of their founder, and the *Gamu* of Tivaoune, marking the anniversary of the birth of the Prophet.

These festivities have their equivalent in eastern Africa, with the celebration of the *mawlid* [*q.v.*] of the Prophet, which gives the *zāwiya*s the opportunity to exercise, at large gatherings, their mystical rituals. This part of Africa was affected at a later date and in a less dense fashion by the Ṣūfī brotherhoods, which often emanated from Somalia (cf. the role of Shaykh ʿUways, 1263-1327/1847-1909, of Brava). Worth mentioning among the *zāwiya*s of the Ḳādiriyya are that of Shaykh Ramiyya at Bagamayo (Tanzania, 14th/late 19th-early 20th centuries), that of Shaykh Mtumwa at Nkhota-kota (Malawi, 14th/early 20th century) and the *zāwiya* of the Ḥusayniyya at Isiolo (Kenya).

Attempts by the Sanūsiyya [*q.v.*] to migrate from Libya towards black Africa saw the creation of *zāwiya*s in Niger (Chemidour, 1279/1862) and especially in Chad (since 1318/1900: Bir Alali, Gouro, Ayn Galakka, etc.). These *zāwiya*s, political institutions in spite of themselves, were administered by Arabic-speaking foreigners and depended directly on the leading *zāwiya*.

The same centralism has persisted in the Sudan, with the Mīrghaniyya [*q.v.*] (or Khatmiyya) maintained by the descendants of the founder (al-Ḥasan al-Mīrghanī, 1235-86/1819-69, *zāwiya* of the Khatmiyya, in the Sudan; Sayyid Hāshim, 1265-1319/1849-1901, *zāwiya* of Massala, in Eritrea). Conversely, the Ḳādiriyya generated independent branches, such as the Madjdhūbiyya (12th/18th century), with its commercial *zāwiya* of al-Damīr, or indeed the Mikashfiyya (early 14th/late 19th century) and its village-*zāwiya* of Shikaynayba.

While the African movement of the Ṣūfī brotherhoods of the late 14th/20th century has adopted the path of urbanisation, of concentration in capitals and of emigration out of Africa, past history indicates that the model of the *zāwiya* was rural and extremely diversified in its modes of organisation, its functions and material arrangements.

Bibliography: P. Marty, *Les Kounta de l'est*, in *RMM*, xxxvii (1918-19); Cheikh Tidjane Sy, *La confrérie sénégalaise des Mourides*, Paris 1969; C.C. Stewart, *Islam and social order in Mauritania: a case study from the nineteenth century*, Oxford 1973; C. Hamès, *Cheikh Hamallah ou qu'est-ce qu'une confrérie islamique (tarîqa)?*, in *Archives des Sciences Sociales des Religions*, lv/1 (1983); idem, *Pour une histoire de Boutilimit (Sahel mauritanien)*, in *Journal des Africanistes*, lv (1985); M.W. Daly (ed.), *Al-Majdhubiyya and al-Mikashfiyya. Two Sufi tariqas in the Soudan*, Khartoum 1985; F. Constantin (ed.), *Les voies de l'islam en Afrique orientale*, Paris 1987; J.L. Triaud, *La légende noire de la Sanûsiyya. Une confrérie musulmane saharienne sous le regard français (1840-1930)*, 2 vols., Paris 1995; S. Bousbina, *Analyse et commentaire de la littérature de la confrérie Tijâniyya à travers les oeuvres d'al-Hâjj 'Umar, 'Ubayda ben Anbûja, Yirkoy Talfi and al-Hâjj Malik Sy*, doctoral thesis, Paris I 1996, unpubl.; B. Savadogo, *La Tijâniyya Hamâwiyya en Afrique occidentale (Burkina Faso, Côte d'Ivoire, Mali, Niger): 1909-1965*, doctoral thesis, 2 vols., Aix-Marseille I 1998, unpubl.; R. Boubrik, *Saints et société en islam. La confrérie ouest-saharienne Fâdiliyya*, Paris 1999; A. Popovic and G. Veinstein (eds), *Les voies d'Allah. Les ordres mystiques dans le monde musulman, des origines à aujourd'hui* (ch. 14, Mauritania; ch. 15, Western and Central Africa; ch. 16, North-Eastern and East Africa; ch. 17, Contemporary Western Europe).

(C. Hamès)

ZAWZAN (in local Persian pronunciation, Zūzan), a town of mediaeval Islamic Khurāsān, now only a village in the *shahrastān* of Khʷāf in the province of Khurāsān (lat. 59° 52' N., long. 34° 21' E.). It lies 35 km/22 miles to the southeast of Khʷāf [*q.v.*] and 60 km/37 miles from the present Afghān frontier on a plain called the Djulga-i Zawzan.

The latest archaeological investigations on the site (2000) tend to show that colonisation of the then arid plain of Zawzan must have occurred after the introduction of *ḳanāt*s [*q.v.*] to bring water for irrigation; Polybius, *History*, x. 26, mentions these for the Seleucid period in the neighbouring province of Ḳūmis. The oldest archaeological layer at Zawzan itself seems to be Sāsānid, found beneath the ruins of the *ḳibla īwān* of the imposing mosque of Zawzan. An ancient tradition attributed the foundation of Zawzan to the establishment there of a fire temple (Yāḳūt, ii, 958), and the prophet and Zoroastrian reformer Bih'āfrīd [*q.v.*], executed in 131/749 by Abū Muslim at the behest of the Zoroastrian priests, is said to have been a native Zawzanī (al-Bīrūnī, *al-Āthār al-bāḳiya*, 210; Gardīzī, *Zayn al-akhbār*, ed. Ḥabībī, Tehran 1347/1968, 119). The date of the Arab conquest of Zawzan is unknown, but may have occurred *ca.* 31/651-2 when 'Abd Allāh b. 'Āmir [*q.v.*] marched on Nīshāpūr (al-Ṭabarī, i, 2884-5; al-Balādhurī, *Futūḥ*, 404).

In the first centuries of Islam, Zawzan was governed by local potentates with the title *ra'īs*, sufficiently independent and sometimes powerful enough to lead rebellions, e.g. in 444/1052 (Nāṣir-i Khusraw, *Safar-nāma*, ed. Dabīr-Siyāḳī, Tehran 1356/1977, 172, tr. W.M. Thackston, Albany 1986, 102). The countryside there was flourishing, and produced cotton cloth (*karbās*), felt and possibly also silk and madder (al-Muḳaddasī, 321; *Ḥudūd al-ʿālam*, tr. 103; Mustawfī, *Nuzhat al-ḳulūb*, ed. Le Strange, 154, tr. 152).

Remains of round or polylobed columns of fired brick of the first mosque there, the *djāmiʿ*, bear witness to the town's significance already in the 3rd/9th century, called by al-Muḳaddasī in the next century a *miṣr* (47, 50, 321; see map and the monumental epigraphic remains in Adle, *Masdjid wa madrasa-i Zawzan*, in *Āthār*, xv-xvi [1367/1989], 231-48, at 245). However, this *djāmiʿ* and its *īwān* became inadequate and were enlarged in the 5th-6th/11th-12th centuries. One of the finest *mihrāb*s of Persian mosques, made by one Abū Saʿd at the behest of the *ra'īs* Abū Muḥammad towards the end of the 5th/11th century, has been recovered almost intact from its surroundings. The town was important at this time for its artisans and its scholars, hence was known as "little Baṣra" (al-Samʿānī, *Ansāb*, ed. Ḥaydarābād, vi, 342; Yāḳūt, ii, 958-9). In the early Ghaznawid period it had produced the official and littérateur Abū Sahl Zawzanī, who served Sultan Masʿūd I but who was regarded by the historian Bayhaḳī as that ruler's evil genius (see Bosworth, *The Ghaznavids, their empire in Afghanistan and eastern Iran 994-1040*, Edinburgh 1963, 60-1); and slightly later, the *adīb* al-Ḥusayn b. Aḥmad al-Zawzanī (d. 486/1093), who composed a well-known commentary on the *Muʿallaḳāt*, much used by early Western scholars writing on these poems, and on the famed *bā'iyya* ode of Dhu 'l-Rumma (see Sezgin, *GAS*, ii, 51, 397, ix, 256).

But it was on the eve of the Mongol invasions that Zawzan reached its apogee, when the *malik-i muʿazzam* of Zawzan, Abū Bakr b. ʿAlī al-Zawzanī, controlled a principality stretching eastwards towards Kābul and westwards to the frontiers of Fārs, and from near Nīshāpur to Hormuz and the shores of the Gulf of Oman; yet he never coined his own money, and acknowledged ʿAlā' al-Dīn Muḥammad Khʷārazm Shāh as his suzerain (see Adle, *Une contrée redécouverte: le pays de Zuzan à la veille de l'invasion mongole*, in Denise Aigle (ed.), *L'Iran face à l'invasion mongole*, Tehran 1997, 23-36). His residence, the *ḳalʿa-i ḳāhira*, situated in the citadel (*kuhandiz*) to the east of the town, is described as imposing by contemporary historians, and the remains of its 15 m high walls still dominate the hidden town. The town at that time had a quasi-rectangular plan, but thinking its second mosque inadequate, its lord began to raze it and to start on a third, yet more magnificent one. This was left unfinished because of his assassination in Shawwāl 614/January 1218, followed by the arrival of the Mongols three years later. The mosque (or *madrasa*, according to Sheila S. Blair, *The madrasa at Zuzan. Islamic architecture in eastern Iran on the eve of the Mongol invasion*, in *Muqarnas*, iii [1985], 75-9) comprised at that time an *īwān* to the east and another towards the conventional *ḳibla*, sc. to the west, vast and with a height of 30 m. It is dated Rabīʿ I 615/June 1218 on the façade, and inside has a great epigraphic frieze in *kashī* [*q.v.*] in the name of Abū Ḥanīfa and dated 616/1219. Terrified by the Mongols, the people of Zawzan prevented the last Khʷārazm Shāh Djalāl al-Dīn from taking refuge in the *ḳalʿa-i ḳāhira* (Adle, *op. cit.*, 35). Hence the town was spared but it was destroyed later by a violent earthquake that struck the region in 737/1336. The vault of the great *īwān* disintegrated and the palace of the lord of Zawzan, Ghiyāth al-Dīn Fīrūz, was destroyed, its owner being crushed to death in it; 30,000 to 40,000 people are said to have died in the region (Khʷāfī, *Rawḍa-i khuld*, ed. M. Farrukh, Tehran 1346/1948, 117; Faṣīḥī, *Mudjmal*, ed. Farrukh, 3 vols. Tehran 1339-40/1960-1, iii, 52-3; N.N. Ambraseys and C. Melville, *A history of Persian earthquakes*, Cambridge 1982, 44-5 and Fig. 3.7).

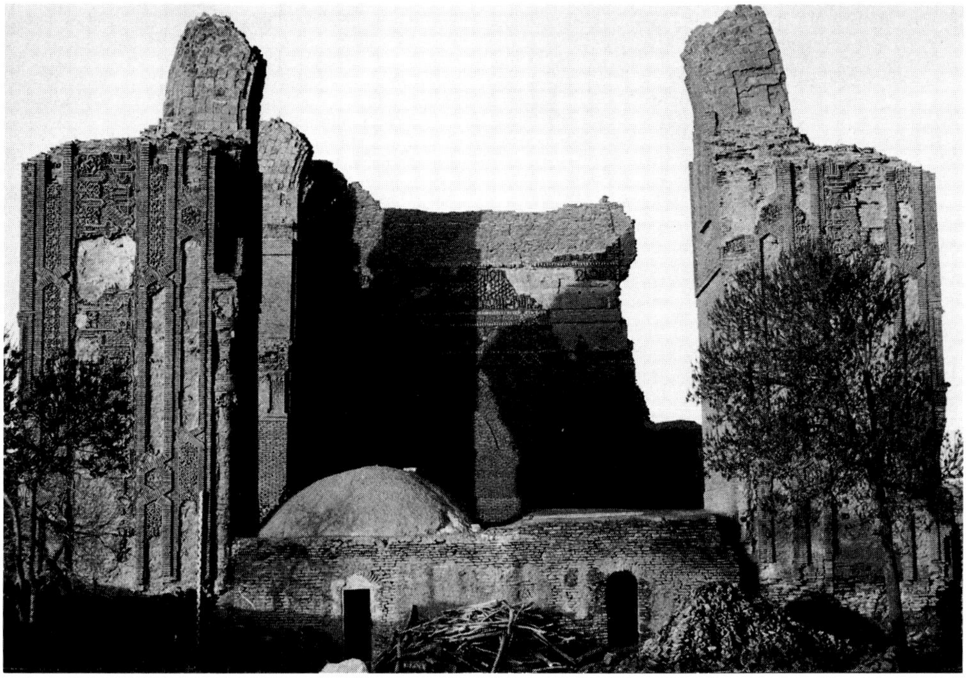

The mosque at Zawzan. Façade of the main *īwān* just before the beginning of the restoration works in 1988.

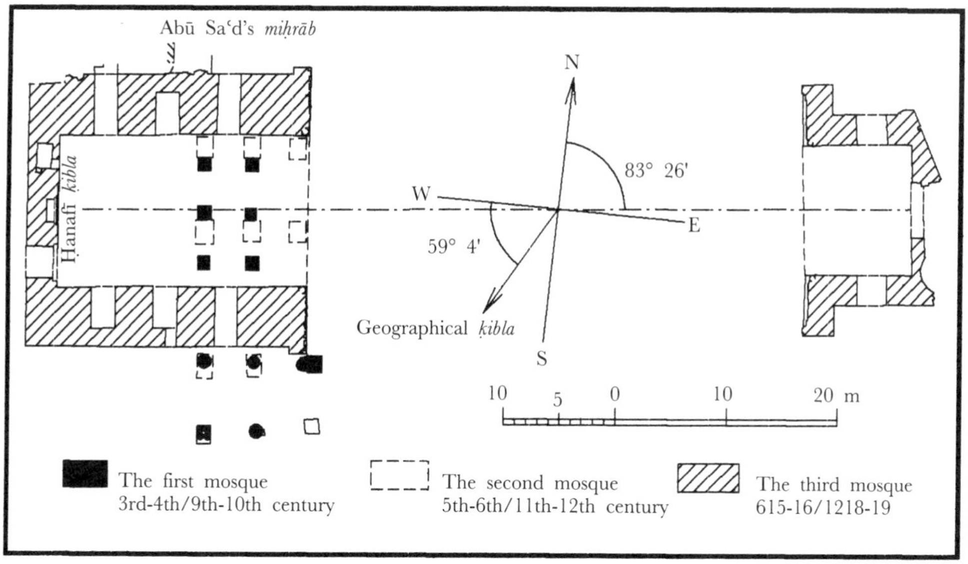

The monumental mosque at Zawzan.

Zawzan never recovered. Its present inhabitants are not indigenous to the region, but according to the accounts of elders, were largely brought from south-western Persia—perhaps in the 18th century—in order to repopulate the cultivable land. Present family names there, e.g. the Arabic tribal name Khuzāʿī, may reflect this. The population of Zawzan was only 680 in the late 1940s (*Farhang-i djughrāfiyā-Īrān-zamīn*, ix, 201) and 786 in 1966 (*Farhang-i ābādīhā-i kishwar*, iv, *Ustān-i Khurāsān*, Tehran 1347/1969, 16), but by the 1991 census it had reached 2,087 with the demographic explosion since the Islamic Revolution of 1969. Contrary to the people of the numerous neighbouring villages who are Ḥanafīs, the population of Zawzan has been since its repopulation wholly Shīʿī.

Bibliography (in addition to references given in the article): A. Godard, *Khorāsān*, in *Athār-è Īrān*, iv/1 (1949), 113-25; Ḥāfiẓ-i Abrū, ed. Dorothea Krawulsky, *Ḫorāsān zur Timuridenzeit nach dem Tārīḫ-e Ḥāfeẓ-e Abrū (verf. 817-823). I. Edition und Einleitung*, Wiesbaden 1982, 37; C. Adle, *Archéologie et arts du monde iranien, de l'Inde musulmane et du Caucase d'après quelques recherches récentes du terrain, 1984-1995*, in *Comptes-rendus de l'Académie d'Inscriptions et de Belles-Lettres* (Jan.-March 1996), 321-9, cf. 375-6; idem, *Nigāhī ba-Zawzan wa Bisṭām*, in *Āthār*, xxix-xxx (1377/1998), 90-108; R. Hillenbrand, *Islamic architecture. Form, function, meaning*, Edinburgh 1994, 181-3. For a good general view of the regions of Zāwa (the present Turbat-i Ḥaydariyya) and Kh^{w}āf, see M.R. Khusrawī, *Djughrāfiyā-yi tārikhī-yi wilāyat-i Zāwa*, Mashhad 1366/1988.

(C. Adle)

ZĀY, also, more rarely, **ZĀʾ**, the eleventh letter of the Arabic alphabet, numerical value 8. The former variant of the letter name retains the /y/ of the original letter name (as in Hebrew *zayin*), while the latter has the innovative ending *-āʾ*, which occurred legitimately with *fāʾ* (Hebr. *pē*) and *hāʾ* (Hebr. *hē*) and then spread to *bāʾ* (Hebr. *bēt*), *tāʾ*/*thāʾ* (Hebr. *tāw*), *ḥāʾ*/*khāʾ* (Hebr. *ḥēt*), *rāʾ* (Hebr. *rēsh*), *ṭā*/*ẓāʾ* (Hebr. *ṭēt*), and *yāʾ* (Hebr. *yōd*), with loss of the final consonant of the original letter name.

The letter is transliterated /z/ and represents a voiced sibilant (*ḥarf al-ṣafīr*), which forms a triad with the unvoiced /s/ and the "emphatic" (pharyngealised) unvoiced /ṣ/. A neighbouring sound is the voiced interdental /dh/. Minimal pairs are: *zāda* "he increased" vs. *sāda* "he ruled", *ṣāda* "he hunted", and *dhāda* "he drove [s.o.] away".

For the "emphatic" variant /ẓ/, see ẒĀʾ.

Arabic /z/ appears as /z/ everywhere else in Semitic. However, Egyptian transliterations of North-west Semitic words show that the sibilants were earlier on pronounced as dental affricates (/t^s/, /d^z/, /ṭ^s/ [or, more likely, an ejective /$t^{s'}$/]), and this is usually posited for Proto-Semitic.

A number of roots in Arabic (and in other Semitic languages) show a variation between /z/ and /ṣ/, more rarely also between /z/ and /s/: *zaʿaqa* vs. *ṣaʿaqa* "he screamed", *bazaḳa* vs. *baṣaḳa* and *basaḳa* "he spat").

For assimilations that either produce or replace a /z/, both word-internally and in sandhi, see Cantineau, 47-8; Fleisch, 86-7. In the VIIIth form the infixed /t/ becomes /d/ after /z/: **iztāna* > *izdāna* "it became adorned", but the grammarians allow also total assimilation: *izzāna* (cf. Fleisch, 97).

In loanwords and transliterations from Greek, /z/ represents /ζ/, but a Syriac intermediary is likely in most cases: Ζευς > *Zāwush* (and variants, see P. Kunitzsch, *Zeus in Bagdad*, in W. Diem and S. Wild (eds.), *Studien aus Arabistik und Semitistik Anton Spitaler zum siebzigsten Geburtstag*, Wiesbaden 1980, 99-113), and ζευγος > Syr. *zawgā* > *zawdj* "one of a pair, spouse", Pahlavi /z/ is retained in Arabic: *nāzag* "lance" > *nayzak* "lance, meteorite". Several *nisbas* referring to Persian places have an intrusive *-z-* borrowed from Persian, as in *Rāzī* (from *al-Rayy*), *Marwazī* (from *Marw*), *Sidjzī* (from *Sidjistān*; used alongside *Sidjistānī*).

The dialects of Arabic have mostly preserved /z/.

In some Jewish dialects in North Africa, /z/ and /ž/ (< /dj/) coalesce and are pronounced either /z/ or /ž/, depending on the environment (cf. Fischer and Jastrow, 253). In some dialects the interdentals have been shifted to sibilants (Kozluk-Sason group and some other dialects of Anatolian Arabic and Uzbekistan Arabic), thus /dh/ > /z/ (Jastrow, 34-9; Fischer and Jastrow, 50). The same shift is also typical for loans from the standard language into sedentary dialects that have not preserved the interdentals; speakers try to imitate /dh/ by using /z/ (rather than the dialect equivalent /d/), compare the *fuṣḥā* loan *dhahāb* > *zahāb* "going" with the true dialect form *dhahab* > *dahab* "gold". A special case of de-emphatisation and assimilation is the frequent word *zghīr* < *ṣaghīr* "small" (also in the diminutive *zghayyir*).

The grapheme <z> has become identical in shape with <r> and is distinguished from it by a diacritical dot on top (already in the oldest Arabic papyrus, dated 22/643, see Gruendler, 22a). In carefully written manuscripts, the <r> may be additionally marked by a v-shaped sign on top (*ʿalāmat al-ihmāl*). One of the reasons for *zāy* and *rāʾ* acquiring the same shape is the fact that neither can be connected to the left in Nabataean cursive writing, a fact that is continued in the Arabic script (for the historical development of the shape, see Gruendler, 60-3).

In Persian, <z> is used to render /z/ in Persian words (and, of course, those Arabic words that have it). The phoneme /z/ may, however, be written <z>, <ẓ>, <dh>, or <ḍ>, depending on the Arabic etymology. The grapheme <z> is also used to create a grapheme for /ž/, by adding three triangularly arranged superscript dots. For Pashto, a special sign for retroflex /z/ has been developed which looks like a *rāʾ* with two dots diagonally across its middle, and in Kashmiri the Persian grapheme <ž> is used to write /ts/.

Bibliography: J. Cantineau, *Cours de phonétique arabe*, Paris 1960; H. Fleisch, *Traité de philologie arabe*, i, Beirut 1961; W. Fischer and O. Jastrow, *Handbuch der arabischen Dialekte*, Wiesbaden 1980; O. Jastrow, *Die mesopotamisch-arabischen Qeltu-Dialekte*. Band I. *Phonologie und Morphologie*, Wiesbaden 1978; Beatrice Gruendler, *The development of the Arabic scripts*, Atlanta 1993. (W.P. Heinrichs)

ZĀYANDA-RŪD, lit. "river which increases", a river of the central basin of Persia which flows past Iṣfahān. It is so called because it was believed that springs along its course increased the volume of its water (Ibrāhīm Khān Taḥwīldār, *Djughrāfiyā-yi Iṣfahān*, ed. M. Sotoodeh, Tehran AHS 1342/1963-4, 37). Early authors called it Zinda-Rūd. In the *Bundahishn* it is mentioned as Zendeh Rud (A. Houtum-Schindler, *Eastern Persian Irak*, London 1898, 17). Abū Ḥusayn b. Muḥammad b. Abi 'l-Riḍā Āwī states that it was also known as Zarīn-Rūd, the "Golden River", because of the abundance and wealth which its waters bestowed on the land that it irrigated (*Tardjuma-i Maḥāsin Iṣfahān*, ed. ʿAbbās Iḳbāl, Tehran AHS 1328/1949-50, 47-8).

The principal source of the river is the Čashma-i Djanān on the eastern slope of the Zarda Kūh [see iṣfahān, at Vol. IV, 98). After a run of about 18 km/11 miles it receives the waters of the Čihil Čashma and is then called Djanāna-Rūd. Further on it receives the Khursang River from Firaydan on the north and the Zarīna-Rūd from Čahār Maḥall on the south and is then known as the Zinda-Rūd. Flowing south-east, it enters the Āydughmish district of Lindjān and continues through Lindjānāt and Mārbīn to Iṣfahān, receiving from the left the overflow drainage from Tīrān and Karwan. Passing through Iṣfahān, it flows through Djay, Barzarūd, Karāridj, Barāʾān and Rūydasht into the Gāwkhānī marsh. A total of 105 major canals (*mādīs*) are led off from it between its entrance into Lindjān and its end in the Gāwkhānī (Houtum-Schindler, 17-18; Taḥwīldār, 37; Ḥusayn ʿĀbidī states that there are 150 canals (*Iṣfahān*, Iṣfahān AHS 1334/1955-6, 76), but this is presumably a printer's error. All other authorities give 105). Writing at the end of the 19th century, Houtum-Schindler stated that in summer the Gāwkhānī had very little water, a few inches in depth covering about 15 square miles, but that in spring it formed a lake 35 miles in length and 8-10 miles in breadth and was in parts 15-18 feet deep (126). During the spring when the snows are melting, the river carries a considerable flow, part of which was formerly lost in flood water. In 1809 there was much damage done by flood water in Iṣfahān and the neighbourhood (Morier, *A Journey through Persia, Armenia, and Asia Minor to Constantinople in the years 1808 and 1809*, London 1812, 213). In recent years, the Gāwkhānī has virtually dried up owing to the drawing off of water for irrigation higher up the river.

Fourteen bridges span the river. The first was a temporary wooden bridge a few miles above Lindjān, erected only in the spring season, and the fourteenth is near Warzāna in Rūydasht (Houtum-Schindler, 17-18; ʿĀbidī, 70-1 gives only thirteen). Five of these bridges are in the city of Iṣfahān: the Mārnān Bridge between Djulfā and Iṣfahān; the Allāhwardī Khān Bridge, called after ʿAbbās I's general of that name, also known as the Sī u Sih Čashma Bridge, connecting Iṣfahān with the eastern part of Djulfā [see ʿabbās i]; the Djūy Bridge and the Khādjū Bridge, built by ʿAbbās II [*q.v.*] on the ruins of an older bridge, and the Shahristān Bridge. During the reign of Muḥammad Riḍā Shāh Pahlawī, an iron bridge was also built over the river (ʿAlī Djawāhir Kalām, *Zinda-Rūd*, ²Tehran AHS 1348/1969-70, 47). Below the Warzāna Bridge there were three dykes for the purpose of raising the water to the lands on both sides of the river: the Band-i Marwān in Rūydasht; the Band-i Allāh Ḳulī Khān, built in the reign of Nādir Shāh [*q.v.*]; and the Band-i Shānzdah Dih built in the reign of Shāh Sulaymān (Houtum-Schindler, 19). Orders were apparently given for this last dam in 1100/1688-9 (Luṭf Allāh Hunarfar, *Gandjīna-i āthār-i tārīkhī-i Iṣfahān*, Iṣfahān AHS 1344/1966-7, 637).

In the reign of Ṭahmāsp I (930-84/1524-76 [*q.v.*]) an abortive attempt was made to divert water from the source of the Kārūn River into the Zāyanda-Rūd. When Iṣfahān became the capital of the empire under ʿAbbās I, the need to increase cultivation to feed the growing population and the fact that the land round Iṣfahān (the Maḥāll), which was watered by the Zāyanda-Rūd, belonged to the royal *dīwān*, made the availability of the water of the Zāyanda-Rūd and its regulation of special interest to the state. In 1027/1618 Shāh ʿAbbās sent Muḥibb ʿAlī Beg Lāla, the *sarāy-dār-bāshī* of the royal buildings, to Kūhrang to report on the possibility of diverting the water of the Kārūn (see R.D. McChesney, *Four sources on Shah ʿAbbās's building of Isfahan*, in *Maqarnas*, v [1988], 122) and subsequently Imām Ḳulī Khān Beglarbegi of Fārs, Ḥusayn Khān, governor of Luristān, and Djahāngīr Khān Bakhtiyārī were ordered to start operations. This attempt also proved abortive. In 1030/1620-1 Shāh ʿAbbās himself set out for the source of the Zāyanda-Rūd. New operations to cut through the mountain were begun but remained unfinished (Iskandar Mun<u>sh</u>ī, *Tārī<u>kh</u>-i ʿĀlamārā-yi ʿabbāsī*, Tehran AHS 1334/1956, ii, 949-50, 959). Work was renewed under ʿAbbās II, but again proved abortive as also were later projects. It was not until after the Second World War that the problem of feeding a growing population again brought the plan to divert the headwaters of the Kārūn into the Zāyanda-Rūd to the fore; it was accorded high priority in successive development plans. The diversion was finally accomplished in the 1950s and 1960s by means of a tunnel driven through the mountain ridge which forms the watershed between the Kārūn River and the Zāyanda-Rūd. Various plans were also put forward for the construction of storage reservoirs on the upper reaches of the river. Under the Third Development Plan (1962-8), a dam called the <u>Sh</u>āh ʿAbbās Great Dam, was constructed, having a height of 95 m and a storage capacity of 450 million m^3, enabling (officially) 100,000 ha. to be irrigated in the Iṣfahān area and permitting the generation of 60,000 kw of electricity. By the time the Fourth Development Plan began, the dam was well established and the area it fed was gradually extended.

The basis of the division of the waters of the Zāyanda-Rūd is probably of great antiquity. The distribution in force in the mid-20th century went back at least to Ṣafawid times. The details are contained in a document known as <u>Sh</u>ay<u>kh</u> Bahāʾī's *tūmār*, which is (or was) held in the Department of Finance, Iṣfahān. Ibrāhīm Bāstānī Pārīzī mentions an edition published by the Department of Agriculture, Iṣfahān (*Siyāsat wa iḳtiṣād-i ʿaṣr-i Ṣafawī*, Tehran AHS 1348/1969-70, 89). The present writer has not been able to obtain a copy of this. The authorship and date of the *tūmār* are uncertain. The document contains the words "Written in the sealing office of the late <u>Sh</u>āh Ṭahmāsp in 923/1517". This is clearly an anomaly. <u>Sh</u>āh Ṭahmāsp did not ascend the throne until 930/1524; and <u>Sh</u>ay<u>kh</u> Bahāʾī, to whom the document is attributed, was not born until 953/1546-7. He became *ṣadr* of Iṣfahān under <u>Sh</u>āh ʿAbbās I and may have been responsible for a revision of the traditional regulation of the river water. Among other anomalies in the document there is mention of various *mādī*s which had no share assigned to them in the original distribution. According to the *tūmār*, the water of the river was regulated in detail from the Kalla Bridge in Āydu<u>gh</u>mi<u>sh</u> to Warzāna in Rūyda<u>sh</u>t, having regard to the cropping needs of each *bulūk* or district [see MĀʾ. 6. Irrigation in Iran, at Vol. V, 873-4].

The present writer was told by an official in the Department of Agriculture, Iṣfahān, in 1938 that the regulation of the river water as laid down in <u>Sh</u>ay<u>kh</u> Bahāʾī's *tūmār* had some years previously fallen into disuse but that in 1928-9 local people had requested that it be re-activated and, in due course, the system, with some modifications, was again brought into force. She was also told that a *mīrāb* was not invariably appointed and was not necessarily from among the *kad<u>kh</u>udā*s of <u>D</u>jay as <u>Sh</u>ay<u>kh</u> Bahāʾī's *tūmār* had laid down; if he was appointed, his wages were fixed on a daily basis and paid locally. If no *mīrāb* was appointed, each *bulūk* sent a representative to oversee the division of the water within that *bulūk* when its turn came. Ibrāhīm Taḥwīldār states that this was the case in 1877 (*<u>Dj</u>u<u>gh</u>rāfiyā-yi Iṣfahān*, 128). The *mādī-sālār*s (those in charge of the major canals leading off from the river) were appointed locally and paid (in most cases) by the landowners. In recent years, with the increased flow of water after the construction of storage dams in the upper reaches of the river, major modifications have been made in the distribution of water.

Bibliography: Given in the article, and see A.K.S. Lambton, *The regulation of the waters of the Ẓāyanda Rūd*, in *BSOS*, ix (1939), 663-73.

(ANN K.S. LAMBTON)

ZAYD B. ʿALĪ B. AL-ḤUSAYN, great-grandson of ʿAlī b. Abī Ṭālib and Fāṭima and leader of the revolt that gave rise to the Zaydiyya [*q.v.*] branch of the <u>Sh</u>īʿa.

He was born in Medina in 75/694-5 according to his son al-Ḥusayn. This date seems more reliable than the year 79/698 or 80/699 usually mentioned by the Sunnī sources. He was thus at least 18 years younger than his brother Muḥammad al-Bāḳir, who became the head of the Ḥusaynids after the death of their father ʿAlī Zayn al-ʿĀbidīn in 94/712-13 and was widely recognised as the *imām* by the <u>Sh</u>īʿa. Zayd's mother was a woman of slave origin from Sind named <u>D</u>jaydā, who is said to have been presented to his father by the <u>Sh</u>īʿī rebel leader al-Mu<u>kh</u>tār or was bought by the father. Zayd acquired a high standing in religious learning in his family and in Medina and is known to have transmitted from his father, his brother Muḥammad, Abān b. ʿU<u>th</u>mān, ʿUrwa b. al-Zubayr and ʿUbayd Allāh b. Abī Rāfiʿ.

As head of the Ḥusaynids, his brother Muḥammad entrusted him with the litigation on their behalf in the long-standing dispute between the families of al-Ḥasan and al-Ḥusayn over the control of the endowments (*ṣadaḳāt*) of ʿAlī b. Abī Ṭālib. The case was pursued before the Umayyad governors of Medina Ibrāhīm b. Hi<u>sh</u>ām (106-14/724-32) and <u>Kh</u>ālid b. ʿAbd al-Malik (114-17/732-5). The Ḥasanids were at first represented by <u>D</u>jaʿfar b. al-Ḥasan b. al-Ḥasan and then by his brother ʿAbd Allāh b. al-Ḥasan, who was in fact in control of the endowments after the death of his father. The case evidently involved the leadership of the descendants of Muḥammad through Fāṭima and thence their potential claim on the caliphate. ʿAbd Allāh b. al-Ḥasan, who harboured ambitions, at first for himself and later for his son Muḥammad al-Nafs al-Zakiyya [see MUḤAMMAD B. ʿABD ALLĀH], is reported to have accused Zayd before the governor of aspiring to the caliphate although he, as the son of a non-Arab slave woman, was not qualified for it. When Zayd complained to his aunt Fāṭima bt. al-Ḥusayn, the mother of ʿAbd Allāh b. al-Ḥasan, about the insult to his mother, she encouraged him to answer by insulting herself. Zayd then took revenge by casting aspersions on his aunt's undignified conduct toward an earlier governor. As it became evident, however, that the governor <u>Kh</u>ālid b. ʿAbd al-Malik was using the dispute to discredit the Family of the Prophet in front of the public of Medina, Zayd broke off the litigation, assuring ʿAbd Allāh b. al-Ḥasan that he would never again raise the case before the governor. Reports that the dispute was further pursued before the caliph Hi<u>sh</u>ām do not seem to be reliable. According to another report, Zayd vainly tried to raise it before the caliph, who refused to receive him. A letter of Hi<u>sh</u>ām to the governor Yūsuf b. ʿUmar confirms, however, that Zayd was engaged in litigation against ʿUmar b. al-Walīd, son of the caliph al-Walīd b. ʿAbd al-Malik, before Hi<u>sh</u>ām (al-Ṭabarī, ii, 682). No details are known about the case.

When <u>Kh</u>ālid al-Ḳasrī was replaced as governor of ʿIrāḳ by Yūsuf b. ʿUmar in <u>D</u>jumādā I 120/May 738, he claimed, under torture by his successor, that Zayd and several other men of Ḳuray<u>sh</u> were in possession of deposits of his. According to some accounts, it was Khālid's son Yazīd or his *ghulām* Ṭāriḳ who made the claim, but it must, in any case, have concerned deposits belonging to the deposed governor. Yūsuf b. ʿUmar informed the caliph Hishām, who sent for the Ḳurashīs. That Zayd was already present at the caliph's court, as some reports state, is unlikely. All of the accused denied the claims against them. Hishām cleared them of suspicion but insisted on sending them to Yūsuf b. ʿUmar in al-Ḥīra in order to confront them with their accuser. Zayd's son ʿĪsā was born in al-Ḥīra. As their accuser withdrew his charges, they were freed. While most of the Ḳurashīs returned to Ḥidjāz, Zayd stayed in Kūfa together with the ʿAbbāsid Dāwūd b. ʿAlī. The caliph now sent a letter to Yūsuf b. ʿUmar instructing him to send Zayd forthwith to Ḥidjāz and not to let him tarry. He had, so he wrote, observed Zayd in his dispute with ʿUmar b. al-Walīd to be argumentative, loquacious, apt to forge and to distort in his discourse, and to beguile men by the sweetness of his tongue. If he were allowed to stay among the Kūfans, who believed in the superior religious status of his family, he would incite them to rebellion, thus splitting the Muslim community.

Yūsuf ordered his deputy in Kūfa, al-Ḥakam b. al-Ṣalt, to press Zayd to leave, but the latter, offering various excuses, remained four or five months in the town. When he left and reached al-Ḳādisiyya or al-Thaʿlabiyya, Kūfan Shīʿīs caught up with him and urged him to return, promising him massive support. They said they hoped he would become the Manṣūr who would overthrow the Umayyad régime. Dāwūd b. ʿAlī warned him of the fickleness of the Kūfans and continued on to Ḥidjāz, but Zayd decided to return. He stayed secretly, moving from tribe to tribe, for over ten months, interrupted by a two months' visit to Baṣra. He married two women of the tribes of Sulaym and al-Azd in order to strengthen his ties with them. His summons to the people called for *djihād* against the wrongdoers, redress of grievances and support of the Family of the Prophet in general against their enemies. Twelve or fifteen thousand men are said to have pledged allegiance to him in Kūfa. He also sent his summons abroad and gained followers in the Sawād, in al-Madāʾin, Baṣra, Wāsiṭ, Mawṣil, Upper Mesopotamia, Rayy and Djurdjān. Support for him was nevertheless patchy. Some *ʿulamāʾ* actively backed him, but others, while offering sympathy, expressed doubts that the Kūfans would stand up for him. Abū Ḥanīfa is said to have sent him money but to have excused himself from fighting. The Banū Hāshim, ʿAlids and ʿAbbāsids, also failed to show solidarity, in part probably because of ambitions of others among them. ʿAbd Allāh b. al-Ḥasan is reported to have warned him in a letter of the well-known treachery of the Kūfans. Muḥammad al-Bāḳir's son Djaʿfar al-Ṣādiḳ is said to have advised his followers to pledge allegiance to Zayd. Most of them withdrew their backing, however, when Zayd refused to condemn the conduct of the early caliphs Abū Bakr and ʿUmar. The sources stress this incident, describing it as the cause of the schism between the radical Imāmiyya and the moderate Zaydiyya.

As Zayd's presence in Kūfa was betrayed to Yūsuf b. ʿUmar, he was forced to call the revolt before the date originally set. On Yūsuf's order, al-Ḥakam b. al-Ṣalt had summoned the Kūfan leaders and warriors to the great mosque and detained them under a guard of Syrian soldiers. Thus less than three hundred men followed Zayd's call to revolt, though the number then swelled to around a thousand. They were fought mainly by a force of Syrians whom Yūsuf had brought to Kūfa. On the third day, Zayd was hit in the evening by an arrow penetrating his brain. He died when a physician or a cupper extracted it. Various dates are mentioned for his death. The most likely is Thursday, 2 Ṣafar 122/7 March 740. His followers sought to hide his body by burying him at night in a spot that they drenched with water. The location, however, was betrayed the next day, and his body was exhumed. His head was sent to Hishām in Damascus, who exhibited it and then sent it to Medina. His body was crucified on the Kunāsa in Kūfa and left there until after the death of Hishām some three years later, when his successor al-Walīd b. Yazīd ordered Yūsuf to burn it and scatter the ashes in the Euphrates. Revenge for Zayd became one of the slogans of the ʿAbbāsid revolution and, after its success, Hishām's remains were unearthed in Damascus, crucified and burned.

Zayd's activity as a scholar and his religious opinions are largely obscure. He was given the honorary title *ḥalīf al-Ḳurʾān* and numerous readings of his Ḳurʾān codex are cited in the Sunnī works on *ḳirāʾāt*. They do not reflect a notable Shīʿī tendency (see A. Jeffery, *The Qurʾān readings of Zaid b. ʿAlī*, in *RSO*, xvi [1936], 249-89, and *Further Qurʾān readings of Zaid b. ʿAlī*, in *ibid.*, xviii [1940], 218-36). Zaydī tradition has preserved various theological treatises ascribed to him. These are too disparate in style and doctrinal positions to be the work of a single author and may mostly be seen to represent currents in the early Kūfan Zaydiyya. A compendium of religious law attributed to him was collected by the Zaydī Ibrāhīm b. al-Zibriḳān (d. 183/799) on the basis of the transmission of the Kūfan Abū Khālid al-Wāsiṭī who claimed to have heard it from Zayd while visiting Medina as a pilgrim in five years. The work, first published by E. Griffini as *Corpus Iuris di Zaid b. ʿAlī* (Milan 1919), reflects Kūfan legal tradition and it is unlikely that Zayd had any significant part in it. Abū Khālid also transmitted a commentary on the difficult (*gharīb*) words of the Ḳurʾān (ed. Ḥ.M. al-Taḳī al-Ḥakīm, Beirut 1992). In these texts, Zayd appears as an anti-Ḳadarī supporter of predestination and as upholding a moderately anti-anthropomorphist concept of God. This agrees with the views of the early Kūfan Zaydiyya. Late Zaydī tradition describes him as agreeing with Muʿtazilī teaching.

Bibliography: Ibn Saʿd, v, 239-40; Balādhurī, *Ansāb*, ii, ed. M. al-Fardūs al-ʿAẓm, Beirut 1996, 520-41; Yaʿḳūbī, 390-1; Ṭabarī, ii, 1667-88, 1698-1716; Masʿūdī, *Murūdj*, ed. Pellat, §§ 2220-25; Abu 'l-Faradj al-Iṣfahānī, *Maḳātil al-Ṭālibiyyīn*, ed. A. Ṣaḳr, Cairo 1949, 127-51; Abū Ṭālib al-Nāṭiḳ bi 'l-Ḥaḳḳ, *al-Ifāda*, ed. M.Y.S. ʿIzzān, Ṣanʿāʾ 1996, 61-7; C. van Arendonk, *Les débuts de l'imāmat Zaidite au Yemen*, Leiden 1960, 28-33, 307-12; R. Strothmann, *Das Problem der literarischen Persönlichkeit Zaid b. ʿAlī*, in *Isl.*, xiii (1923), 1-52; W. Madelung, *Der Imam al-Qāsim ibn Ibrāhīm*, Berlin 1965, esp. 53-61; Sezgin, *GAS*, i, 552-60.

(W. Madelung)

ZAYD b. ʿAMR b. Nufayl, a so-called *ḥanīf* [*q.v.*] and "seeker after true religion", who lived in Mecca before Muḥammad's mission (though some pronounced him a Companion of the Prophet). In a major battle before Islam Zayd reportedly led the Ḳuraysh [*q.v.*] clan to which he belonged, the ʿAdī b. Kaʿb. The cycle of reports about him in Islamic historiography all but presents him as Muḥammad's precursor. Some scholars even went as far as declaring him a prophet who received revelations, and a messenger sent to mankind. Precisely like Muḥammad before his call, Zayd is said to have practiced *taḥannuth* [*q.v.*] on Mt. Ḥirāʾ [*q.v.*]. Other rites attributed to him, such as prostration in the direction of the Kaʿba, are consonant with Islamic practice.

In a widespread account, Zayd appears as an old man leaning against the Kaʿba and claiming to be the only Ḳurashī holding on to the *dīn Ibrāhīm*. His claim to exclusivity smacks of competition with other Ḳurashīs who repudiated idol worship. Far more problematic, however, are reports involving Muḥammad in which Zayd is given a spiritual advantage over the future prophet. One account reportedly going back to his son Saʿīd b. Zayd [*q.v.*] (through his son and grandson), is a typical itinerary of a *ḥanīf* in quest of true religion. Zayd was travelling with Waraḳa b. Nawfal [*q.v.*], who soon became Christian, abandoning the search. Continuing his journey, Zayd learned from a monk that the religion he was looking for was about to be initiated in his own land. Having returned to Arabia, Zayd was offered by Muḥammad, but declined, the meat of an animal slaughtered in association with idol worship. Following Zayd's example, Muḥammad abstained from such meat and, what is more, abandoned idol worship.

At least some of these unorthodox statements originated with Zayd's offspring and other members of the ʿAdī b. Kaʿb. They were not discarded because they included an element of *dalāʾil al-nubuwwa* "proofs of prophethood". Instead, they gave rise to various forms of apologetics, since they contradicted the more comprehensive form of *ʿiṣma* [*q.v.*] or infallibility, which developed over the period preceding Muḥammad's mission.

Bibliography: The relevant entries in the Companion dictionaries; Ibn ʿAsākir, *Taʾrīkh madīnat Dimashk*, ed. ʿU.Gh. al-ʿAmrawī, Beirut 1415-/1995-, xix, 493-516; Dhahabī, *Siyar aʿlām al-nubalāʾ*, ed. Sh. al-Arnāwūṭ *et al.*, Beirut 1401-9/1981-8, i, 124-43; Balādhurī, *Ansāb al-ashrāf*, v, ed. I. ʿAbbās, Beirut 1417/1996, 520-4; Baghdādī, *Khizānat al-adab*, ed. Hārūn, Cairo 1387-1406/1967-86, index; M.J. Kister, *'A bag of meat': a study of an early* ḥadīth, in *BSOAS*, xxxiii (1970), 267-75, repr. in idem, *Studies in Jāhiliyya and early Islam*, Variorum, London 1980, no. VI; U. Rubin, *Ḥanīfiyya and Kaʿba: an inquiry into the Arabian pre-Islamic background of* dīn Ibrāhīm, in *JSAI*, xiii (1990), 85-112, at 99-103; idem, *The eye of the beholder*, Princeton 1995, index.

(M. Lecker)

ZAYD b. ḤĀRITHA al-Kalbī, or Zayd *al-ḥibb* "the beloved", a slave, and later a *mawlā* [*q.v.*] and adoptive son of the Prophet Muḥammad. The details of his early biography are disputed. One account has it that he was sold into slavery in Mecca by members of his own tribe.

However, according to al-Wāḳidī's [*q.v.*] account, Zayd's father died amidst his wife's tribe, the Ṭayyiʾ [*q.v.*], bequeathing to his son an unspecified number of camels. Certain Bedouin who hired the camels from the stripling, treacherously sold him at the market of ʿUkāẓ. The buyer was Ḥakīm b. Ḥizām who was trading on behalf of his paternal aunt Khadīdja [*q.v.*].

According to al-Kalbī's account, Zayd and his mother, while on a visit to her tribe, were attacked by horsemen of al-Ḳayn [*q.v.*] b. Djasr. The attackers sold Zayd at ʿUkāẓ to Ḥakīm b. Ḥizām who purchased him for Khadīdja. After her marriage to Muḥammad, Khadīdja gave him Zayd. In al-Kalbī's version, Zayd's father (who was still alive) vowed to look for his son. Having been discovered in Mecca by fellow tribesmen, Zayd chose to remain Muḥammad's slave, and in due course became Muḥammad's adoptive son.

Zayd's offspring transmitted—at least to the 4th/10th century—a different account. Zayd grew up in his mother's family and when she died, he remained with his grandfather. Then he was carried off by horsemen of the Fazāra [*q.v.*] who sold him at ʿUkāẓ to Khadīdja's paternal cousin, Waraḳa b. Nawfal [*q.v.*]. Zayd was recognised by a fellow tribesman, but chose to stay with Muḥammad. In this account Zayd's father (and, after a while, also his brother, Djabala) embraced Islam. As attested by the Companion dictionaries, the family managed to secure Companion status for both of them.

Zayd's earliest marriage link, with Muḥammad's dry nurse and *mawlāt* Umm Ayman (Baraka), took place in Mecca, probably not long after Muḥammad's call. She gave birth to Usāma [*q.v.*] eight or ten years before the Hidjra. Although Usāma was dark-skinned while Zayd was fair, a physiognomist [see ḲIYĀFA] reportedly removed all doubts regarding Zayd's parentage.

Zayd's other marriages took place in Medina after the Hidjra. He married Muḥammad's cousin, Zaynab bt. Djaḥsh [*q.v.*] (whose mother was Muḥammad's paternal aunt). Zaynab's marriage to Muḥammad shortly afterwards gave rise to claims by the so-called Hypocrites, that Muḥammad was acting against his own ruling which prohibited marriage to the former wife of one's son. Consequently, a verse (Ḳurʾān, XXXIII, 5) was revealed terminating the state of adoption and returning Zayd to his Kalbī affiliation. With regard to the same situation, Zayd is the only Companion of Muḥammad whose name appears in the Ḳurʾān (XXXIII, 37). Several years later Zayd married successively three women of Ḳuraysh, one of whom was yet another cousin of Muḥammad (the daughter of his paternal uncle, Abū Lahab [*q.v.*]). At some stage Zayd was married to a woman of the Medinan Khazradj [*q.v.*]).

Zayd, a fine archer who led several military expeditions, was killed in the battle of Muʾta [*q.v.*] of 8/629, aged fifty or fifty-five.

Bibliography: The entries on Zayd, his father Ḥāritha, and his brother Djabala, in the Companion dictionaries; Ibn ʿAsākir, *Taʾrīkh madīnat Dimashk*, ed. ʿU.Gh. al-ʿAmrawī, Beirut 1415-/1995-, xix, 342-74; Ibn Manẓūr, *Mukhtaṣar taʾrīkh Dimashk li-Ibn ʿAsākir*, ix, ed. N. Nashshāwī, Damascus 1405/1985, 122-31; Dhahabī, *Siyar aʿlām al-nubalāʾ*, ed. Sh. al-Arnāwūṭ *et al.*, Beirut 1401-9/1981-8, i, 220-30; Balādhurī, *Ansāb*, i, ed. Ḥamīd Allāh, Cairo 1959, 467-76; Muḳātil b. Sulaymān, *Tafsīr*, ms. Topkapı Sarayı, Ahmet III 74, ii, fols. 86b-87a, 91b-93a.

(M. Lecker)

ZAYD b. al-ḤUSAYN b. ʿALĪ (1898-1970 or 1972), fourth son of the Grand Sharīf of Mecca, al-Ḥusayn b. ʿAlī [*q.v.*] by a Circassian wife. His involvement in Hāshimī activities and politics was limited. He participated as a leader in the early stages of the Arab Revolt in Ḥidjāz in 1916. He was his father's representative in 1924 at a British-sponsored conference in Kuwayt which tried to resolve Hāshimī-Suʿūdī border differences. In 1947 he was a minister in London for ʿIrāḳ after Britain decided to refer the Palestine problem to the United Nations.

Bibliography: R. Baker, *King Husain and the kingdom of Hejaz*, Cambridge 1979, 3; Mary Wilson, *King Abdullah, Britain and the making of Jordan*, Cambridge 1987, 14, 45, 80; Avi Shlaim, *The politics of partition*, Oxford 1990, 19, 22, 78; Kamal Salibi, *The modern history of Jordan*, London 1993, 68. See also ḤĀSHIMIDS.   (HUSSEIN SIRRIYEH)

ZAYD B. THĀBIT, an Anṣārī [see ANṢĀR] Companion of the Prophet Muḥammad credited with a crucial role in the collection of the Ḳurʾān [*q.v.* at Vol. V, 404b-405b]. He belonged to the Banu 'l-Nadjdjār of the Khazradj, or more precisely, to the ʿAbd ʿAwf b. Ghanm b. Mālik b. al-Nadjdjār. His mother, al-Nawār bt. Mālik, was of the ʿAdī b. al-Nadjdjār. Much of the rather detailed biographical information about Zayd was preserved by *ḥadīth* transmitters from among his offspring who were intensely interested in the life and work of their great ancestor.

Zayd's father was killed in the battle of Buʿāth [*q.v.*], when Zayd was six years old; at the time of the Hidjra [*q.v.*], Zayd was eleven. His education between these events was of major importance for his career. Already before the Hidjra he acquired Arabic literacy at the *midrās* or *kuttāb* [*q.v.*] of a Jewish group called Māsika; his knowledge of the Hebrew or Syriac script presumably goes back to the same period.

Zayd's first-born son was probably Saʿīd, hence Saʿīd's mother, Umm Djamīl bt. al-Mudjallil of the Ḳuraysh [*q.v.*], must have been Zayd's first wife. Widowed in Ethiopia, she arrived at Medina after the conquest of Khaybar [*q.v.*] in 7 A.H. with two small children. Neither of the children was called Djamīl, and it follows that she could have been married twice before marrying young Zayd.

As one of the Prophet's scribes, Zayd wrote down Ḳurʾān verses as well as letters to "the kings". Some said that Zayd was the scribe of Abū Bakr and ʿUmar, and he was also said to have officiated as *ḳāḍī* under ʿUmar and ʿUthmān.

Zayd's literacy was accompanied by a knowledge of arithmetic: he was a famous expert on the division of inheritances [see FARĀʾIḌ] and was considered an authority on calendrical calculations. Abū Bakr instructed him to calculate the *khums* of the Kinda [*q.v.*] captives brought to Medina from al-Nudjayr (in Ḥaḍramawt), and Zayd later collected their ransom. After the Battle of the Yarmūk, Zayd divided the spoils, having done the same for the Prophet at Khaybar and Ḥunayn [*q.v.*]. When food supplies sent by ʿUmar's governor in Egypt were to be distributed, Zayd prepared written orders for the transfer of subsistence (*sikāk*) which were made of papyrus [see ḲIRṬĀS] and stamped at the bottom; he was the first Muslim to prepare such orders. ʿUthmān appointed him over the treasury (*bayt al-māl* [*q.v.*]) after Zayd's predecessors had resigned because of ʿUthmān's illegal use of state money. In due course, ʿUthmān allowed Zayd to appropriate a surplus of more than 100,000 dirhams. However, a pro-ʿUthmānī source denies all this: the former officials grew old and were too weak to function; the surplus was of 1,000 dirhams only, and Zayd spent it on construction works in the Prophet's mosque.

When ʿUthmān was later besieged in his court, Zayd protected him in defiance of his fellow Anṣār, most of whom supported ʿAlī. Abū Ayyūb al-Anṣārī [*q.v.*] accused Zayd of being motivated by the many palm trees which he received from ʿUthmān. It should be borne in mind that at the *saḳīfa* [*q.v.*], immediately after the Prophet's death, Zayd—whose first wife was probably the Ḳuraysh—eloquently supported the political supremacy of the *muhādjirūn* [*q.v.*] over the Anṣār.

Zayd was one of the few Anṣār who did not pledge their allegiance to ʿAlī; a pro-Shīʿī source explained that ʿUthmān appointed him over both the *dīwān*

[*q.v.*] and the treasury. Obviously, Zayd was not a member of ʿAlī's administration, but at the beginning of Muʿāwiya I's [*q.v.*] reign we again find him in charge of the *dīwān* of Medina. Zayd advised Muʿāwiya and his governor in Medina, Marwān b. al-Ḥakam [*q.v.*], on various legal matters.

The dates given for Zayd's death range from 42/662-3 to 56/675-6. The large amount of gold and silver that he bequeathed had to be cut with a broad iron instrument called *mifrāṣ*; in addition, he left orchards and estates valued at 100,000 dīnārs, or, alternatively, at 150,000 dīnārs and 700,000 dirhams. Considering Zayd's humble starting-point, his career during the first half-century of Islam was phenomenal.

There is much controversy over the collection of the Ḳurʾān. One thing is, however, certain: when ʿUthmān looked for a qualified scholar to oversee the preparation of its official edition, Zayd's total commitment to the Ḳurashī cause was taken into consideration.

Bibliography: 1. Sources. Dhahabī, *Siyar aʿlām al-nubalāʾ*, ed. al-Arnāwūṭ *et al.*, Beirut 1401/1981 ff., ii, 426-41; Ibn ʿAsākir, *Taʾrīkh madīnat Dimashḳ*, ed. al-ʿAmrawī, Beirut 1415/1995 ff., xix, 295-341; Ibn Manẓūr, *Mukhtaṣar taʾrīkh Dimashḳ li-Ibn ʿAsākir*, ed. R. al-Naḥḥās *et al.*, Damascus 1404/1984 ff., ix, 114-22; Ṭabarānī, *al-Muʿdjam al-kabīr*, ed. al-Salafī, ²Cairo 1400/1980 ff., v, 106-63; the relevant entries in the Companion dictionaries; Ibn Ḳudāma al-Maḳdisī, *al-Istibṣār fī nasab al-ṣaḥāba min al-anṣār*, ed. Nuwayhiḍ, Beirut 1392/1972, 69, 71-3; Ibn Ḥubaysh, *al-Ghazawāt al-ḍāmina*, ed. Zakkār, Beirut 1412/1992, i, 139-40; Yaʿḳūbī, *Taʾrīkh*, ii, 177; Diyārbakrī, *Taʾrīkh al-khamīs*, Cairo 1283/1866, ii, 267-8; Ibn Ḳutayba, *al-Maʿārif*, ed. ʿUkāsha, Cairo 1969, 355; Masʿūdī, *Murūdj*, ed. Pellat, iii, 77; Aḥmad b. ʿAbd Allāh al-Rāzī, *Taʾrīkh madīnat Ṣanʿāʾ*, ed. al-ʿAmrī, ²Ṣanʿāʾ 1401/1981, 66-7.

2. Studies. *Gesch. des Qor.*, ii, *passim*, esp. 54, 56; J. Burton, *The collection of the Qurʾān*, Cambridge 1977, index; A. Neuwirth, *Koran*, in *Grundriß der arabischen Philologie*, ii, *Literaturwissenschaft*, ed. H. Gätje, Wiesbaden 1987, 96-135, at 101-4; M. Lecker, *Zayd b. Thābit, "a Jew with two sidelocks": Judaism and literacy in pre-Islamic Medina (Yathrib)*, in *JNES*, lvi (1997), 259-73.   (M. LECKER)

ZAYDĀN, DJURDJĪ (b. 14 December 1861 in Beirut, d. 21 July 1914 in Cairo), outstanding representative of the *Nahḍa* [*q.v.*] or Arabic cultural and literary renaissance of the 19th and early 20th centuries.

Son of an illiterate Greek Orthodox cook who considered education, except for some reading and writing skills, unnecessary, Zaydān was more than any other Arab intellectual of his time a self-made man. His autobiography (Eng. tr. Th. Philipp, 1979, 1990) gives information on his amazing intellectual development, from being a waiter and cook in his father's small restaurant at the age of 11, to apprenticeship in a workshop for European-style shoes, to bookkeeping for his father, until his enrolment for studying medicine in the Syrian Protestant College in September 1881. He soon became top of his class, but left with some friends after an incident caused by one of the American teachers' lecturing on Darwinism, which the students ardently supported, claiming a right of free speech in this regard. Supported financially by a friend, he went to Cairo in 1883 to continue his studies, but the Armenian owner of the newspaper *al-Zamān* offered him its editorship, which he undertook till 1884. Then he joined Wolseley's expedition to relieve Gordon in Kharṭūm as a dragoman and guide, and after its failure, returned to Beirut in 1885 to study Hebrew and Syriac. In the summer of 1886 he travelled to London, where he became acquainted with the works of European orientalists. Health troubles led him to return to Cairo, where he henceforth resided permanently. He was offered the job of administrative manager and assistant editor of the journal *al-Muḳtaṭaf* [see DJARĪDA i. A], which he took over for 15 months. After quitting this post, he produced his first books. In *al-Alfāẓ al-ʿarabiyya wa 'l-falsafa al-lughawiyya* (1886, republ. 1904, 1964), which gained him membership of the Royal Asiatic Society of Italy, he applied evolutionary theory to languages. A historical study of Freemasonry—which highly attracted Arab intellectuals at that time [see FARMĀSŪNIYYA, in Suppl.]—and a book on the modern history of Egypt, used in schools, appeared in 1889. Probably for financial reasons, he became head teacher for Arabic at a Greek Orthodox School. In 1890 he published a small *General history*, intended as a textbook. Together with a friend, he founded in 1891 a small printing house which, however, closed down in 1892. Zaydān re-opened it alone in 1893 and renamed it in 1896 as the *Maṭbaʿat al-Hilāl*. In 1891 he published his first historical novel *al-Mamlūk al-shārid* (German tr. M. Thilo, 1917), whose success encouraged him to leave his teaching job. Up to his death, Zaydān published 22 novels, which were most recently republished with commentaries in 1984 and are still widely read. They have been translated into other oriental languages, such as Persian, Ottoman Turkish, Hindi and Uzbek Turkic. His goal was to awaken in the Arab public a historical consciousness and a pride in the great days of Arabo-Islamic history. Only *Djihād al-muḥibbīn* (1893) is a love story, probably based on his love for the Syrian Christian immigrant Maryam Maṭar, his wife since 1891. Enthusiastic in his youth about folk romances told in old Beirut, he wrote in a plain style mixing historical facts, events and personalities, such as famous persons like *al-Ḥadjdjādj ibn Yūsuf* (1902), *Abū Muslim al-Khurāsānī* (1905) *al-Amīn wa 'l-Maʾmūn* (1907), *Ṣalāḥ al-Dīn al-Ayyūbī* (1913) and *Shadjar al-Durr* (1914), with fictitious love stories, intrigues and adventures. This and his rather openly anti-Umayyad standpoint annoyed Arab nationalists and fundamentalists. Showing narrative skill, Zaydān produces tension and excitement, although his heroes are mainly either good or evil and remain static. Except where the historical facts stand in the way, he closes with a happy ending or a tragic death. He is incontestably the pioneer of the historical novel as a literary genre in Arabic.

Still of value today amongst his many scholarly works, with which he aimed to popularise Western knowledge and methods of work and thought, are *Tarādjīm mashāhīr al-shark fi 'l-karn al-tāsiʿ ʿashar* (1907, republ. 1960 as *Buhāt al-nahḍa al-ʿarabiyya*) and volume iv of his *Taʾrīkh Ādāb al-lugha al-ʿarabiyya* (1910-13) since they provide information on contemporaries. The fourth volume of his *Taʾrīkh al-tamaddun al-islāmī* (i-v, 1901-6) was translated by D.S. Margoliouth into English (GMS IV, Leiden and London 1907) because amongst Zaydān's sources used for it were unpublished manuscripts. In his *al-ʿArab ḳabl al-Islām* (1907-8, republ. 1958) and other works he was certainly the first Arab intellectual to trace Arab history back to Hammurabi and the Pharaohs, thus creating a new Arab identity at a time of the emergence of Arab nationalism and an Arab bourgeoisie as a social class. In other publications, he characterised the Arabic language, one based on the Ḳurʾān but regarded as a living and developing organism, as the unifying link for all Arabs and the basis of their culture. In 1892 Zaydān founded *al-Hilāl*, a journal still existing today. In 22 volumes, he gave information on scientific developments and cultural events, and on European and Arab publications, later including (for female readers) information on health, hygiene and family problems; and he serialised his novels and longer essays. Deeply convinced of the civilising value of education and learning, he abstained, however (like other prominent Arab Christians of the *Nahḍa*), from political statements, except for espousing the cause of the Young Turks in 1908 and after, but he provided background information to political events and personalities. In 1910 he was offered a professorship of Islamic history at the Egyptian University, but this was withdrawn after heated debates occasioned by his Christian origin.

Bibliography: Th. Philipp, *Ǧurǧī Zaydān, his life and thought*, Beirut 1979, with bibl. and discussion of secondary sources; Shawkī Abū Khalīl, *Djurdjī Zaydān fi 'l-mīzān*, ²Damascus 1981 (fundamentalist critique of his historical novels); J.A. Crabbs, *The writing of history in ninetenth-century Egypt*, Detroit 1984, 191-8; Aḥmad Ḥusayn al-Ṭamāwī, *Djurdjī Zaydān*, Cairo 1992 (Zaydān as literary critic); Julie S. Meisami and P. Starkey, *Encyclopedia of Arabic literature*, London and New York 1998, ii, 823; for older literature, see Brockelmann, S III, 186-90.

(WIEBKE WALTHER)

ZAYDĀN, MAWLĀY [see SAʿDIDS].

ZAYDIYYA, a branch of the Shīʿa [*q.v.*] arising out of the abortive revolt of Zayd b. ʿAlī b. al-Ḥusayn [*q.v.*] in Kūfa in 122/740. During the preparations for the revolt, a part of the Kūfan Shīʿa withdrew their support from Zayd in protest against his refusal to condemn unconditionally the early caliphs preceding ʿAlī and backed Zayd's nephew Djaʿfar al-Ṣādiḳ as their *imām*. This schism led to a lasting division of the Shīʿa into a radical and a moderate wing in terms of their religious break with the Sunnī Muslim community. The Zaydiyya, as the moderates, did not classify the Sunnī Muslims generally as infidels. In political terms, however, they were, in contrast to the radical but quietist Imāmiyya, militant, espousing revolt against the illegitimate Sunnī rule as a religious duty.

1. The early Kūfan phase.

The Zaydiyya was initially formed by the merger of two currents in Kūfan Shīʿism, the Djārūdiyya [*q.v.*] and the Batriyya [*q.v.* in Suppl.]. The Djārūdiyya were named after Abu 'l-Djārūd Ziyād b. al-Mundhir, a former companion of Zayd's brother Muḥammad al-Bāḳir, who backed Zayd's revolt when he was deserted by most of al-Bāḳir's followers. They brought some of the radical elements of al-Bāḳir's teaching into the Zaydiyya. Thus they rejected the imāmate of the three caliphs preceding ʿAlī, holding that ʿAlī had been appointed by the Prophet as his legatee (*waṣī*) and implicitly as his successor. Condemning the majority of the Companions and the Muslim community for their desertion of the rightful *imām*, they repudiated the legal tradition transmitted by the Sunnī traditionists and upheld the transmission of the religious law by the Family of the Prophet as solely legitimate. In contrast to the Imāmiyya, however, they did not confine legal teaching authority to their *imāms* but accepted in principle the teaching of any member of the *ahl al-bayt* qualified by religious learning. The Batriyya were at first a group of moderate Shīʿīs who were critical of some of al-Bāḳir's teaching and failed to accept him as their *imām*. While considering

ʿAlī as the most excellent of Muslims after the Prophet, they generally admitted the imāmate of his predecessors since he had pledged allegiance to them. They did not concede any superior knowledge to the Family of the Prophet, but recognised the religious knowledge handed down in the Muslim community as valid and allowed the use of individual reasoning (*idjtihād, ḳiyās*) in establishing the law. The Batriyya were part of the general Kūfan traditionalist movement. As Kūfan traditionalism became absorbed by Sunnism during the 3rd/9th century, the views of the Djārūdiyya came to prevail among the Zaydiyya.

The legitimate imāmate was at first not confined to the descendants of ʿAlī. Before the fall of the Umayyad caliphate, Kūfan Zaydīs backed ʿAbd Allāh b. Muʿāwiya [*q.v.*], a descendant of ʿAlī's brother Djaʿfar. In the 4th/10th century there was still a group of Zaydīs known as Ṭālibiyya who recognised all descendants of ʿAlī's father Abū Ṭālib as eligible for the imāmate. The majority, however, considered only descendants of al-Ḥasan and al-Ḥusayn as legitimate claimants. According to common Zaydī doctrine, the first three *imāms*, ʿAlī, al-Ḥasan and al-Ḥusayn, were *imāms* by designation (*naṣṣ*) of the Prophet. After al-Ḥusayn, the imāmate became legally established through armed rising (*khurūdj*) and a formal summons (*daʿwa*) to allegiance by a qualified candidate. Among the qualifications, religious knowledge was emphasised. Many Zaydī *imāms* throughout the centuries have been highly educated religious scholars and authors. They were, however, generally not considered as immune from error and sin (*maʿṣūm*), although some late Zaydīs conceded such immunity to the first three *imāms*.

In theology, the Kūfan Zaydiyya were determinist, strongly opposed to the Ḳadariyya and Muʿtazila, though also admitting some responsibility of man for his acts. They were anti-anthropomorphist, but upheld the reality of the attributes of God against their reduction to descriptions of the divine essence by the Muʿtazila. They rejected the doctrine of the created nature of the Ḳurʾān, but did not insist on belief in its coeternity with God. Against Murdjiʾī doctrine, they taught that works were part of faith (*īmān*). Like the Ibāḍiyya, they classed the grave offender (*fāsiḳ*) as an unbeliever by ingratitude (*kāfir niʿma*), not by polytheism (*shirk*) or by denial of God (*djuḥūd*). Land under Sunnī domination was an abode of unbelief by ingratitude (*dār kufr niʿma*). As for the Ibāḍiyya [*q.v.*], this justified their revolt against the established order while also allowing them to associate peacefully with other Muslims.

In religious law, the Zaydiyya relied at first on the teaching of various ʿAlid authorities, among them Muḥammad al-Bāḳir, Djaʿfar al-Ṣādiḳ, Zayd b. ʿAlī and Muḥammad al-Nafs al-Zakiyya, and sometimes on the claim of a consensus of the Family of the Prophet. In the 3rd/9th century four legal schools emerged on the basis of the teaching of Aḥmad b. ʿĪsā b. Zayd [*q.v.* in Suppl.], al-Ḳāsim b. Ibrāhīm al-Rassī [*q.v.*], al-Ḥasan b. Yaḥyā b. al-Ḥusayn b. Zayd and Muḥammad b. Manṣūr al-Murādī. They are described by Abū ʿAbd Allāh al-ʿAlawī (d. 445/1053) in his *Kitāb al-Djāmiʿ al-kāfī* as authoritative among the Kūfan Zaydiyya in his time.

Among the abortive revolts supported by Kūfan Zaydīs were those of Muḥammad al-Nafs al-Zakiyya and his brother Ibrāhīm in 145/762-3, al-Ḥusayn b. ʿAlī Ṣāḥib Fakhkh in 169/786, Yaḥyā b. ʿAbd Allāh in 176/792, Muḥammad b. Ibrāhīm Ṭabāṭabā in 199/814, Muḥammad b. al-Ḳāsim Ṣāḥib al-Ṭālaḳān in 219/834, and Yaḥyā b. ʿUmar b. Yaḥyā in 250/864. Thereafter, Zaydī activity successfully shifted to remote mountain regions south of the Caspian Sea and in Yemen, which tended to elude the control of the central government.

2. The Caspian Zaydiyya.

Zaydī Islam was first preached on a limited scale among the non-Muslim Daylamīs by the ʿAlid rebel leader Yaḥyā b. ʿAbd Allāh [*q.v.*] and his Kūfan supporters in 175/791-2. Much more effective was the missionary activity of some local followers of al-Ḳāsim b. Ibrāhīm (d. 246/860) in western Ṭabaristān, the region of Rūyān, Kalār and Shālūs. Al-Ḳāsim's teaching in theology represented a shift from early Kūfan Zaydī doctrine to more anti-determinist and radically anti-anthropomorphist positions, dissociating God from evil acts and stressing the absolute dissimilarity of God to all creation. While distinct from contemporary Muʿtazilī doctrine, it paved the way for the adoption of Muʿtazilī theology among his later followers. His teaching in the religious law represented a Medinan moderate Shīʿī tradition relatively independent of Kūfan Zaydī school doctrine. In 250/864 the people of Rūyān revolted and invited the Ḥasanid al-Ḥasan b. Zayd from al-Rayy to lead them. Al-Ḥasan established the first Zaydī state, with the capital in Āmul. He officially supported Shīʿī ritual and law and Muʿtazilī theology, and is known to have written books on law and the imāmate. However, neither he nor his brother Muḥammad, who succeeded him and ruled until 287/900, was recognised as *imāms* by the later Zaydīs, and his teaching was ignored by the school tradition.

After the overthrow of Muḥammad b. Zayd, the Ḥusaynid al-Ḥasan b. ʿAlī al-Uṭrūsh al-Nāṣir li 'l-Ḥaḳḳ was active in Gīlākdjān and Hawsam [*q.v.* in Suppl.], converting the Daylamīs north of the mountain range and the Gīlīs east of the Safīd Rūd. In 301/914 he conquered Āmul and restored Zaydī rule in Ṭabaristān, reigning until his death in 304/917. Al-Nāṣir left numerous writings on law and theology and was generally recognised as an *imām*. His teaching differed to some extent from that of al-Ḳāsim b. Ibrāhīm. In its basic theses his theology was similar to al-Ḳāsim's, but also polemically anti-Muʿtazilī. In ritual and law he was closer than al-Ḳāsim to the Kūfan Zaydī tradition and often to Imāmī Shīʿī doctrine. Thus he adopted the Imāmī law of inheritance, repudiating the privileged position accorded to the agnates in Sunnī law, and the Imāmī prohibition of the irrevocable triple repudiation of the wife (*ṭalāḳ al-bidʿa*).

The Caspian Zaydiyya was thereafter divided into two rival schools and communities, the Ḳāsimiyya prevailing in western Ṭabaristān, Rūyān and the adjoining Daylam, and the Nāṣiriyya among the eastern Gīl and the interior Daylam. The Ḳāsimiyya maintained close ties with the family of al-Ḳāsim. His grandson Yaḥyā b. al-Ḥusayn al-Hādī ilā 'l-Ḥaḳḳ [*q.v.* in Suppl.] came to Āmul during the reign of Muḥammad b. Zayd, but aroused the suspicion of the latter by being addressed by some of his followers as *imām* and had to leave quickly. After he established Zaydī rule in Yemen, he was joined by groups of Zaydī volunteers from Ṭabaristān and Kalār. Al-Hādī's works on religious law were immediately adopted by the Ḳāsimiyya and commented upon by Caspian ʿAlid scholars. The close relationship between the Ḳāsimiyya and the Yemeni Zaydiyya was to continue for a long time. The Nāṣiriyya tended to look to the descendants of al-Nāṣir li 'l-Ḥaḳḳ for leadership. All of these were given the *laḳab* al-Nāṣir, and al-Nāṣir li 'l-Ḥaḳḳ's tomb in Āmul remained for centuries a place of pilgrimage for the Nāṣiriyya. However, only one of his descendants, al-Ḥusayn b. Dja'far al-Nāṣir ruling in Hawsam (432-72/1040-80), gained recognition as a Zaydī *imām.* The antagonism between the two schools was initially intense until the Imām Abū ʿAbd Allāh b. al-Dāʿī al-Mahdī li-Dīn Allāh (d. 360/970) actively promoted the thesis that both school doctrines were equally valid.

Conditions among the Caspian Zaydiyya, where often ʿAlids without the full qualifications for the imāmate came to reign, or two or more ʿAlids contemporaneously gained local support, required recognition of a rank of legitimate ruler below that of *imām.* These were commonly called *dāʿīs* "summoners", and themselves frequently adopted titles composed with this term. Al-Ḥasan b. Zayd, his brother Muḥammad, and al-Ḥasan b. al-Ḳāsim, who succeeded al-Nāṣir li 'l-Ḥaḳḳ, all took the title al-Dāʿī li 'l-Ḥaḳḳ, while others claimed the title al-Dāʿī ilā 'l-Riḍā, *al-riḍā* referring to the expected *imām* of the Family of the Prophet. Other Zaydī ʿAlid rulers merely adopted the title *amīr.*

In spite of their mutual recognition, the two Caspian Zaydī communities often backed different rulers. After the final fall of the Zaydī rule in Āmul, Hawsam became the centre of learning of the Nāṣiriyya and the seat of an ʿAlid dynasty founded by Djaʿfar b. Muḥammad al-Thāʾir fi 'llāh [*q.v.*], grandson of a brother of al-Nāṣir li 'l-Ḥaḳḳ. Although their reign in Hawsam was often disputed by descendants of al-Nāṣir and others, they regularly regained control of the town. When Hawsam was replaced by Lāhīdjān [*q.v.*] as the chief town of eastern Gīlān in the 6th/12th century, descendants of al-Thāʾir came to rule there. Among the Ḳāsimiyya, Langā, located between Hawsam and Shālūs, became the seat of several *imāms* during the later 4th/10th and the 5th/11th centuries. Later, as much of the Zaydī territories in Rūyān and Daylamān came under the control of the Nizārī Ismāʿīlīs, some Ḳāsimiyya *imāms* were active in eastern Gīlān.

Religious scholarship among the Ḳāsimiyya reached a peak in the *imāms* Aḥmad b. al-Ḥusayn al-Muʾayyad bi 'llāh (d. 411/1020), and his brother Abū Ṭālib al-Nāṭiḳ bi 'l-Ḥaḳḳ (d. *ca.* 424/1033). Born in Āmul, both studied for some time in Baghdād and then belonged to the circle of the Būyid vizier al-Ṣāḥib Ibn ʿAbbād, an active promoter of Muʿtazilī theology and Shīʿism, and of the Muʿtazilī chief *ḳāḍī* ʿAbd al-Djabbār in al-Rayy. Both wrote major legal works and commentaries in the Ḳāsimiyya school tradition, though al-Muʾayyad is sometimes considered the founder of a new school, the Muʾayyadiyya. In theology they fully adopted the Baṣran Muʿtazilī school doctrine represented by ʿAbd al-Djabbār. The close ties between Zaydiyya and Muʿtazila at this time were reflected in the increasingly pro-ʿAlid tendency in the Muʿtazilī doctrine on the imāmate. Two Muʿtazilī scholars and authors of the school of ʿAbd al-Djabbār, Abu 'l-Ḳāsim al-Bustī and al-Muḥsin b. Karāma al-Ḥākim al-Djushamī (d. 484/1101 [*q.v.* in Suppl.]), became active Zaydīs. The numerous works of the latter, in particular, became prestigious among the Zaydiyya. Al-Muʾayyad also wrote a treatise on Ṣūfī devotion, *Risālat Siyāsat al-murīdīn,* which remained influential in defining the Zaydī attitude to Ṣūfism. It praises the early Ṣūfīs from Fuḍayl b. ʿIyāḍ to al-Djunayd, endorsing the ascetic, penitential and devotional aspects of their practice, but denounces the delusions of the Ṣūfīs that induce them to engage in practices contrary to the religious law, such as listening to chants and dancing.

In the course of the 6th/12th century, the Caspian Zaydiyya declined substantially, partly because of the expansion of Ismāʿīlism which confined it to eastern Gīlān and partly because of quarrels between ʿAlid pretenders backed by different factions. Little is known about developments in the following century and a half. In 769/1367-8 Sayyid ʿAlī Kiyā b. Amīr Kiyā, backed by Zaydī penitents (*tāʾibān*), set out to conquer eastern Gīlān. He gained recognition as *imām* by the Zaydī scholars of Rānikūh and Lāhīdjān. His descendants ruled in Lāhīdjān on the basis of dynastic succession as Zaydīs until 933/1526-7, when Sulṭān Aḥmad Khān, with most of his Zaydī subjects, converted to Imāmī Shīʿism. The survival of a tradition of Zaydī learning in eastern Gīlān until that date is attested by a number of manuscripts of Zaydī texts written there in the last phase before the conversion.

3. The Zaydiyya in Yemen.

The Zaydī imāmate in Yemen was founded in 284/897 by al-Ḳāsim b. Ibrāhīm's grandson al-Hādī ilā 'l-Ḥaḳḳ, who had been invited by local tribes in the hope that he would settle their feuds. Although Shīʿī sentiments had been manifest in parts of Yemen since the rise of Islam, there is little evidence of specifically Zaydī activity before his arrival. Al-Hādī established his capital in Ṣaʿda [*q.v.*]. He and his sons Muḥammad al-Murtaḍā (d. 310/922) and Aḥmad al-Nāṣir li-Dīn Allāh (d. 322/934), both of whom were consecutively recognised as *imāms,* were buried in the congregational mosque there, and Ṣaʿda has ever remained the stronghold of Zaydī faith and learning in Yemen. Al-Hādī's teaching in the religious law, laid down in his *Kitāb al-Aḥkām* and *Kitāb al-Muntakhab,* was based on that of his grandfather al-Ḳāsim, but adopted more Shīʿī positions, for instance in prescribing the *ḥayʿala,* the Shīʿī formula of the call to prayer. It has remained basic for the Hādawiyya legal school, the only one authoritative among the Zaydiyya in Yemen. In theology, his doctrine was close to the contemporary Baghdād school of the Muʿtazila, but he did not expressly state his agreement with it. Regarding the imāmate, he upheld the Djārūdī position, unambiguously condemning Abū Bakr and ʿUmar as usurpers.

After Aḥmad al-Nāṣir, the descendants of al-Hādī quarrelled among themselves and none gained recognition as *imām.* The imāmate was restored by al-Manṣūr bi 'llāh al-Ḳāsim al-ʿIyānī (388-93/999-1003 [*q.v.*]), a descendant of al-Hādī's uncle Muḥammad b. al-Ḳāsim. Al-Manṣūr's son al-Ḥusayn al-Mahdī li-Dīn Allāh (401-4/1010-13) was also recognised as *imām.* His qualification of religious knowledge, however, was soon questioned. He defended himself, making extravagant claims that he equalled the Prophet in rank and that he was the Expected Mahdī. When he was killed in battle, his followers and his family asserted that he had not died and would return. Thus a sect arose, called the Ḥusayniyya. Led by descendants of al-Mahdī's brother Djaʿfar, the Ḥusayniyya, having acquired and fortified the impregnable mountain stronghold of Shahāra, became the main force of opposition to the Ismāʿīlī rule of the Ṣulayḥids [*q.v.*] in northern Yemen during the 5th/11th century.

In the same period another Zaydī sect arose, the Muṭarrifiyya [*q.v.*], founded by Muṭarrif b. Shihāb (d. after 459/1067). Muṭarrif explicitly based his religious teaching on the works of al-Ḳāsim b. Ibrāhīm, al-Hādī, and the early Yemeni *imāms,* as well as on some statements ascribed to ʿAlī. He interpreted them, however, in an arbitrary manner, developing a theology and cosmology that deviated substantially from Muʿtazilī doctrine. This brought him in conflict with the Baṣran Muʿtazilī teaching espoused by the Caspian Ḳāsimiyya *imāms.* The Muṭarrifiyya also manifested distinct ascetic and pietist tendencies. On the basis of the doctrine of *hidjra*, the obligation to emigrate from the land of injustice, that had been taught by al-Ḳāsim b. Ibrāhīm and other Zaydī authorities, they founded "abodes of emigration" where they congregated to engage in worship, ritual purification, ascetic practices and teaching. These *hidjras*, usually forming a protected enclave in tribal territory, became the prototype of the protected teaching centres called *hidjras* common among the later Yemeni Zaydiyya in general.

At first, during the Ṣulayḥid age, the Muṭarrifiyya could spread without strong opposition from the mainstream Zaydiyya. After the restoration of the imāmate by Aḥmad b. Sulaymān al-Mutawakkil ʿalā ʾllāh (532-66/1137-70), they came under increasing pressure. Al-Mutawwakkil favoured the unity of the Zaydiyya in and outside Yemen, equally recognising the Caspian and Yemeni *imāms*. He acknowledged the pro-Shīʿī wing of the Muʿtazila as close allies, asserting that the founder of the Muʿtazila, Wāṣil b. ʿAṭāʾ [*q.v.*], had received his doctrine from the Family of the Prophet. He furthered the teaching of Caspian Zaydī scholars and of Yemeni scholars who had studied with Zaydī scholars in the Caspian region, Rayy and Kūfa, and encouraged a massive transfer of Caspian Zaydī religious literature to Yemen. A leading part in this transfer and in spreading Caspian Zaydī and Muʿtazilī teaching was played by the *ḳāḍī* Djaʿfar b. Abī Yaḥyā Shams al-Dīn [*q.v.* in Suppl.]. Al-Mutawakkil severely criticised the Muṭarrifiyya and the Ḥusayniyya for splitting the unity of the Zaydiyya. The Imām al-Manṣūr bi ʾllāh ʿAbd Allāh b. Ḥamza (593-614/1197-1217), a strong supporter of Muʿtazilī theology, declared the Muṭarrifiyya dangerous heretics, persecuted them, and destroyed their *hidjras*. Both Ḥusayniyya and Muṭarrifiyya vanished during the 9th/15th century.

The domination of Muʿtazilī theology, as espoused by the school of *ḳāḍī* Djaʿfar, did not, however, remain unchallenged. The Sayyid Ḥumaydān b. Yaḥyā (early 17th/13th century) demonstrated in several of his treatises that the early Zaydī authorities, in particular al-Ḳāsim b. Ibrāhīm and al-Nāṣir li ʾl-Ḥaḳḳ, had differed on many points with the Muʿtazila, while accusing the latter of heretical innovations in numerous details of their teaching. He ignored the Caspian Ḳāsimiyya *imāms* and claimed, with tenuous arguments, that even al-Manṣūr ʿAbd Allāh b. Ḥamza in reality did not support Muʿtazilī theology.

The teaching of the Imām al-Muʾayyad bi ʾllāh Yaḥyā b. Ḥamza (719-47/1328-46), a prolific author, reflected a lack of sectarian zeal and openness to Sunnī learning. He praised Abū Bakr, ʿUmar and ʿUthmān as early Companions of Muḥammad on a par with ʿAlī. He adopted the Muʿtazilī theology of the school of Abu ʾl-Ḥusayn al-Baṣrī which, in contrast to the school of *ḳāḍī* ʿAbd al-Djabbār, previously prevalent, recognised the reality of *karāmāt*, the miracles of Ṣūfī saints. His book on religious ethics *Taṣfiyat al-ḳulūb min daran al-awzār wa ʾl-dhunūb* was patterned on al-Ghazālī's *Iḥyāʾ ʿulūm al-dīn* and quoted widely from the sayings of the early Ṣūfīs. He sharply criticised al-Ghazālī, however, for his approval of *samāʿ*, listening to music and singing by the Ṣūfīs.

The spread of Ṣūfī orders in the Sunnī lowlands of Yemen during this period put pressure on the Zaydiyya to re-examine their attitude to Ṣūfism. The militant anti-Shīʿī stand of these orders made it difficult to come to terms with them. A Zaydī school of Ṣūfism was founded, however, by ʿAlī b. ʿAbd Allāh b. Abi ʾl-Khayr, an initiate of the Kurdish Ṣūfī *shaykh* al-Kūranī [*q.v.*], and his disciple Ibrāhīm al-Kaynaʿī (d. 793/1391). Al-Kaynaʿī was closely associated with the Imām al-Nāṣir Ṣalāḥ al-Dīn Muḥammad (783-93/1371-91), and was able to found Ṣūfī communities and *hidjras* throughout northern Yemen. The majority of the *imāms* thereafter, however, were opposed to Ṣūfism and denounced the Ṣūfīs for their unlawful practices and fanciful claims of inspiration.

The stigmatising of Ṣūfism as heretical reached a peak under the Imam al-Manṣūr al-Ḳāsim b. Muḥammad (1006-29/1598-1620 [see AL-MANṢŪR BI ʾLLĀH]), the founder of the Ḳāsimi dynasty of *imāms*. Al-Manṣūr's anti-Ṣūfī polemics were partly provoked by the strong support of the Ṣūfī orders for the Ottoman Turkish occupiers of Yemen, against whom he fought a relentless war. He likened the Ṣūfīs to the Ismāʿīlīs, who had long been the arch-enemies of the Zaydiyya, describing them as Bāṭiniyya whose basic thought was derived from Zoroastrianism and Mazdakism, and he singled out Ibn al-ʿArabī for particular condemnation, calling him the chief of the Ṣūfī incarnationists (*ḥulūliyya*).

Al-Manṣūr generally upheld the Shīʿī foundation of the Zaydiyya by re-affirming the Djārūdī position on the imāmate. Inspired by Ḥumaydān's views, he stressed the differences between the teaching of the Zaydiyya and the Muʿtazila. While admitting that they agreed in their basic theological theses, he maintained that the early *imāms* had confined their teaching to what could be safely established by reason, the unambiguous text of the Ḳurʾān and the generally-accepted Sunna. They had not followed the Muʿtazila in their abstruse speculation and absurd fantasies.

Descendants of al-Manṣūr reigned Yemen until the fall of the imāmate in 1382/1962. Whereas some of his early successors were learned men in the Zaydī tradition, the later *imāms*, while still claiming the title of *imām*, in fact ruled on the basis of dynastic succession. As the Zaydī *imāms* gained control of the more populous and prosperous lowlands of Yemen, they found it increasingly expedient to accommodate the religious views and sentiments of the majority of their subjects. Thus they came to favour the neo-Sunnī school that first arose out of the teaching of the *sayyid* Muḥammad b. Ibrāhīm al-Wazīr (d. 840/1436). Ibn al-Wazīr, member of an ʿAlid family of distinguished Zaydī scholars, had accepted the Sunnī canonical collections of *ḥadīth* as unconditionally authoritative in religion. On this basis, he had systematically defended Sunnī school doctrine and criticised the opposing Zaydī teaching in his voluminous *al-ʿAwāṣim wa ʾl-ḳawāṣim fi ʾl-dhabb ʿan sunnat Abi ʾl-Ḳāsim*. He insisted, however, that he was not joining any Sunnī school and was simply employing sound, independent *idjtihād*. Major scholars and authors of his school were Ṣāliḥ b. Mahdī al-Maḳbalī (d. 1108/1696-7), Muḥammad b. Ismāʿīl al-Amīr (d. 1182/1768-9) and Muḥammad b. ʿAlī al-Shawkānī (d. 1250/1834 [*q.v.*]). The latter, *muftī* and chief judge under several *imāms*, vigorously attacked traditional Zaydīs in his writings and, in his official position, persecuted some of their intransigent leaders. He gained wide recognition in the Sunnī world and is considered one of the founders of Islamic modernism. In the Republic of Yemen, Zaydī (Hādawī) law, as expounded in the *Kitāb al-Azhār fī fiḳh al-aʾimma al-aṭhār* and its *Sharḥ* by Muḥammad b. Yaḥyā b. al-Murtaḍā (d. 840/1437), is officially recognised as valid next to Shāfiʿī law. Official ideology, however, favours the neo-Sunnī school and is putting the traditional Zaydiyya on the defensive.

Bibliography: R. Strothmann, *Das Staatsrecht der Zaiditen*, Strassburg 1912; idem, *Kultus der Zaiditen*, Strassburg 1912; C. van Arendonk, *De opkomst van het Zaidietische Imamaat in Yemen*, Leiden 1919, tr. J. Ryckmans, *Les débuts de l'Imamat Zaidite au Yemen*, Leiden 1960; W. Madelung, *Der Imam al-Qāsim ibn Ibrāhīm und die Glaubenslehre der Zaiditen*, Berlin 1965; idem, *Zaydī attitudes to Sufism*, forthcoming; Aḥmad al-Ḥusaynī, *Muʾallafāt al-Zaydiyya*, Ḳumm 1413/[1992-3]. (W. MADELUNG)

ZĀYIRDJA [see ZĀʾIRDJA].

ZAYLAʿ, a port on the Gulf of Aden [see ʿADAN] and on the African coast, situated in lat. 11° 21' N., long. 43° 30' E. (Ar. Zaylaʿ, Somali Seylac, Audal; Fr., Ital., Eng. Zeila, Zeyla, etc.). In the colonial period it came within British Somaliland (1884-1960), and then in the Republic of Somalia, inaugurated in July 1960 by the union of the former British Somaliland and the Italian colony of Somalia [see SOMALI. 3. History]. The falling-apart of the Republic of Somalia, since 1991, has placed it once more in the newly-independent Somaliland, which has become independent *de facto* but has not as yet (2000) been recognised internationally.

The town is over 200 km/125 miles west of the capital Berbera [*q.v.*], but only some 40 km/25 miles from the frontier separating Somaliland from the Republic of Djibouti/Djibūtī [*q.v.*]. Opposite the town, which offers a secure anchorage, protected on the east by a peninsula, are the isles of Saʿd al-Dīn and, somewhat larger, of Aybat. The population of the hinterland is today made up of ʿIssas/ʿIse Somalis.

Zaylaʿ has through the centuries been one of the points of contact between the Horn of Africa and the outside world via the Red Sea and the Indian Ocean. Its port was in lively relationship with all the other ports of the region, with Tadjūrra, but above all with al-Mukhā [*q.v.*]/Mocha and the other ports of Western and Southern Arabia. It was also the point of arrival and departure for caravans connecting the coastlands with the southern part of the Ethiopian highlands. Certain of these started from the well of Tocoshah for Shoa and Christian Ethiopia [see ḤABASH, ḤABASHA], others from the well of Warambot for Gildessa. At Gildessa, the road bifurcated, one way going towards Erer and Ankober in Shoa, and the other to Harar [*q.v.*], where caravans entered by the Bāb al-Futūḥ. This last destination was the most important, to the point that Zaylaʿ could be called "the port of Harar". Other tracks then led towards the Arusi country, the southwest and the region of the East African lakes. Coffee, hides, gum, resin, fats, ostrich plumes, cattle, slaves, ivory, etc. were exported from Zaylaʿ; imports comprised rice, salt, tobacco, textiles, manufactured objects, etc. Hence it was via Zaylaʿ that Arab merchants penetrated into the southern part of the Horn of Africa, as also slave dealers, and with them, Islam and various outside influences.

The oldest mention of Zaylaʿ under that name is in al-Yaʿḳūbī (late 3rd/9th century), and most of the Arab travellers who crossed the region mention the town; however, it existed before this, at the time of the *Periplus of the Erythraean Sea*. It always played in the south the role that Maṣawwaʿ [*q.v.*]/Massawa played in the north, sc. that of a privileged access into Ethiopia. In the 7th/13th century, Zaylaʿ belonged to the sultanate of Ifat/Awfat [*q.v.*], from where the first attacks on Christian Ethiopia were launched in the 8th/14th century. Ethiopia at first successfully resisted. The Negus Yeshāḳ defeated the ruler of Ifat, Saʿd al-Dīn [see ADAL] in 1415, but soon had to appeal to the Portuguese for assistance. Pedro de Covilham, sent by João II in 1487 to organise a Portuguese-Ethiopian alliance, arrived in the land via Zaylaʿ. After the permanent defeat of Islam and the incorporation of the Red Sea region into the Ottoman empire *ca.* 1540, the town received a governor who was dependent, according to various periods, on the Yemeni towns of al-Mukhā and al-Ḥudayda.

Some centuries later, it was also from Zaylaʿ that the second great Islamic attack on Ethiopia—this time by the Egyptians—was launched. In August 1875, Raʾūf/Rawf Pasha seized control of Zaylaʿ and its hinterland in the name of the Khedive Ismāʿīl Pasha [*q.v.*]. The Egyptians, however, were only nominally in control, and in order to protect caravans, they had to seek the help of the *ugās* of the ʿIssas and of Abū Bakr, the former "Sultan" of Zaylaʿ. From their base on the coast, the Egyptians seized Harar, occupying it for ten years and thus controlling the Zaylaʿ-Harar axis. At Zaylaʿ, they demolished the walls and four of the five gates, and prohibited the slave trade. On their departure, Major Hunter landed at Zaylaʿ in February 1884, inaugurating the period of British rule which lasted till 1960. At the same time, Ethiopia lost its outlet to the sea, which gradually became Eritrea Italiana. At various times, the British had the idea of ceding Zaylaʿ to Addis Ababa, which sought an outlet to the sea, in exchange for various advantages, mainly territorial, but the cession of Eritrea to Ethiopia in 1952 ended this possibility for the British.

The decline of Zaylaʿ, which had begun with the silting-up of its port, was largely accomplished by the mid-19th century. The creation of Djibouti (1896), the construction of the railway linking this new port with Addis Ababa (1897-1917), and the growing importance of Berbera (which had in its favour a location well to the south of Aden) brought about the definitive ruin of Zaylaʿ, whilst the relegation in importance of Harar, overshadowed by Diredawa, the new stopping-place on the railway, finalised the disappearance of the Zaylaʿ-Harar route. Today the town is reduced to a dilapidated village with a few hundred inhabitants, held by a small garrison of the army of Somaliland, although it has a radio mast for the service of the fishing industry.

Bibliography: Since there is no monograph on Zaylaʿ, the sparse items of information must be sought in the Arab and European travellers' accounts and in works about Ethiopia and Somaliland, their Islamisation and on the history of Egyptian expansion in the Red Sea region. See the various works of I.M. Lewis, esp. his *Modern history of Somalia. Nation and state in the Horn of Africa*, ²London 1988 (¹1965), and, for the references in them; J. Doresse, *Histoire sommaire de la Corne orientale de l'Afrique*, Paris 1971; R. Pankhurst, *History of Ethiopian towns*, 2 vols. Wiesbaden 1982-5. Alfred Bardey, the employer of Rimbaud, has left a precious report of his first caravan journey, *Barr-Adjam. Souvenirs d'Afrique orientale, 1880-1887*, to which is prefixed J. Tubiana, *Le patron de Rimbaud*, Paris 1981. (A. ROUAUD)

ZAYN AL-ʿĀBIDĪN ("Ornament of the Worshippers") ʿALĪ B. AL-ḤUSAYN B. ʿALĪ B. ABĪ ṬĀLIB, the fourth Imām of the Twelver Shīʿa. His *kunya* is variously given as Abū ʿAbd Allāh, Abū Bakr, etc. According to many sources he was born (in Medina) in 38/658-9, though the years 33, 36 and 37 are also given. If accounts that he had not reached puberty at the time of the Karbalāʾ massacre (61/680) are to be trusted, this would put his birthdate forward to the 40s/660s; these accounts are, however, rejected by al-Wāḳidī and other authorities.

His mother's name is variously given as Barra, Ghazāla, Djaydā, etc.; some say that she was an *umm walad* [*q.v.*] from Sind (or Sidjistān), while Shīʿī tradition has it that she was a daughter of the last Sāsānid emperor Yazdagird III and that her Persian name was Djihānshāh, Shahrbānū(ya) or Shāhzanān. Some say she threw herself into the Euphrates after the battle, but others maintain that she was among the survivors of Karbalāʾ. Shīʿīs refer to ʿAlī as *ibn al-khiyaratayn* "the son of the two elect" since, according to a tradition of the Prophet, the Ḳuraysh are the elect of the Arabs and the Persians are the elect of the non-Arabs.

Zayn al-ʿĀbidīn was not the only son of al-Ḥusayn called ʿAlī; another was killed at Karbalāʾ and is known as ʿAlī al-Shahīd. Some historians, including Ibn Saʿd, Ibn Ḳutayba, al-Balādhurī and al-Ṭabarī, refer to him as ʿAlī al-Akbar and to Zayn al-ʿĀbidīn as ʿAlī al-Aṣghar. Others (e.g. al-Ḳāḍī al-Nuʿmān) maintain that Zayn al-ʿĀbidīn was the older of the two, and accordingly refer to him as ʿAlī al-Akbar and to his martyred brother as ʿAlī al-Aṣghar. For many Twelver authors, the title ʿAlī al-Aṣghar refers to an infant brother who was also killed at Karbalāʾ; some of these authors maintain that Zayn al-ʿĀbidīn was the middle brother (hence ʿAlī al-Awsaṭ), while the eldest was ʿAlī al-Shahīd; others reverse the position of the two older brothers.

At Karbalāʾ, Zayn al-ʿĀbidīn is said to have been too ill to join in the fighting; after the battle Shamir b. Dhi 'l-Djawshan found him lying on a mat in the women's tent and ordered him to be killed but was overruled by ʿUmar b. Saʿd, the commander of the Syrian army. When ʿAlī was brought before ʿUbayd Allāh b. Ziyād in Kūfa, the governor ordered his execution, but relented after pleas by al-Ḥusayn's sister Zaynab. ʿAlī and the other survivors were taken to Yazīd in Damascus, and he sent them back to Medina. The *mashhad ʿAlī*, forming part of the great mosque in Damascus, is said to have been built at the place of Zayn al-ʿĀbidīn's incarceration (cf. L. Pouzet, *Damas au VIIe/XIIIe siècle*, Beirut 1988, 352).

In Medina ʿAlī led a pious life which earned him the honorifics Zayn al-ʿĀbidīn, al-Sadjdjād ("he who constantly prostrates himself"), al-Zakī ("the pure") and Dhu 'l-Thafināt (referring to the calluses on his skin in the places touching the ground in prostration). Whenever the time of prayer drew near, he would tremble and go pale, and his devotional practices caused fears for his health. He was counted among the *bakkāʾūn* [*q.v.*], since for years he would weep for his father and the other martyrs of Karbalāʾ. He used to go out at night with his face covered in order to distribute charity (*ṣadaḳat al-sirr*), and it was only after his death that people discovered the identity of their benefactor. When his body was washed, marks were found on his shoulders, the result of his carrying heavy loads of food at night for the poor.

ʿAlī studiously avoided any involvement with the authorities and adopted a quiescent attitude towards the Umayyads and the Zubayrid anti-caliphate. After the battle of the Ḥarra (63/683), Muslim b. ʿUḳba [*q.v.*], acting on orders from Yazīd, treated him with respect and did not try to exact from him an oath of allegiance to the caliph. The reasons for this special treatment were that ʿAlī had been unwilling to be associated with the Medinan rebels and had sheltered the entourage of Marwān b. al-Ḥakam, including Marwān's wife ʿĀʾisha bt. ʿUthmān, at his estate at Yanbuʿ. Non-Shīʿī sources describe a friendly relationship between ʿAlī and the caliphs Marwān and ʿAbd al-Malik: the former lent him money to purchase concubines and, before his death, decreed that his heirs should not demand that it be repaid; the latter consulted him about a message he had received from the Byzantine emperor. Shīʿī authors, in contrast, maintain that ʿAlī's dealings with the authorities were based on *taḳiyya*. ʿAlī proved magnanimous even when wronged: Hishām b. Ismāʿīl used to insult him during his four years as governor of Medina, yet after Hishām's dismissal by al-Walīd (7 Rabīʿ I 87/26 February 706) ʿAlī forbade his family and friends to speak ill of him. A famous story has it that when the future caliph Hishām b. ʿAbd al-Malik came to Mecca on pilgrimage, he was unable to approach the Kaʿba because of the crowds; for ʿAlī, however, the crowds parted, allowing him unhindered access. On that occasion, al-Farazdaḳ [*q.v.*] is said to have improvised a poem in praise of ʿAlī, thereby arousing Hishām's ire; but the eulogy, which exists in various versions, has been judged to be mostly or entirely unauthentic (J. Hell, *Al-Farazdaḳs Loblied auf ʿAlī ibn al-Ḥusain* (*Zain al-ʿĀbidīn*), in *Festschrift Eduard Sachau*, ed. G. Weil, Berlin 1915, 368-74; J. Weiss, in *Isl.*, vii [1917], 126-7). ʿAlī did not pledge allegiance to ʿAbd Allāh b. al-Zubayr, but he did escort his sister Sukayna bt. al-Ḥusayn [*q.v.*] to ʿIrāḳ for her marriage with ʿAbd Allāh's brother Muṣʿab b. al-Zubayr [*q.v.*], from whom he received a gift of 40,000 dīnārs.

Among the Shīʿa, ʿAlī at first enjoyed little support; most Shīʿīs turned to Muḥammad b. al-Ḥanafiyya, whose imāmate was promoted by al-Mukhtār [*q.v.*]. In their polemical writings, Twelver authors attempt to show that Ibn al-Ḥanafiyya acknowledged ʿAlī's leadership; an oft-repeated story has it that the two agreed to abide by the ruling of the Black Stone in the Kaʿba; the stone miraculously spoke, upholding ʿAlī's rights. Abū Khālid al-Kābulī, who had originally adhered to Ibn al-Ḥanafiyya, is said consequently to have switched his allegiance to ʿAlī. In the view of some Ismāʿīlīs, Ibn al-Ḥanafiyya had been appointed by al-Ḥusayn as a veil (*sitr*) in order to protect ʿAlī's identity as the true *imām*; he was a temporary *imām* (*mustawdaʿ*, lit. "trustee"), while ʿAlī was the permanent *imām* (*mustaḳarr*). Following Ibn al-Ḥanafiyya's death, a subgroup of the Kaysāniyya [*q.v.*] reportedly recognised ʿAlī as *imām*; in contrast, due to ʿAlī's quietism most (but not all) Zaydīs did not regard him as an *imām* (cf. R. Strothmann, *Das Staatsrecht der Zaiditen*, Strassburg 1912, 107; W. Madelung, *Der Imam al-Qāsim ibn Ibrāhīm und die Glaubenslehre der Zaiditen*, Berlin 1965, 172).

The relationship between ʿAlī and al-Mukhtār was an uneasy one: when al-Mukhtār sent ʿAlī a gift of 100,000 dirhams, ʿAlī did not wish to accept it but dared not send it back; after al-Mukhtār's death he offered the sum to ʿAbd al-Malik, who told him to keep it. Various stories told about the two reflect the ambivalent attitude of Twelver authors to al-Mukhtār. Among these are the claim that al-Mukhtār was anxious to gain ʿAlī's support and only turned to Ibn al-Ḥanafiyya after being rejected; and the report that ʿAlī publicly cursed al-Mukhtār; or the account that al-Mukhtār gained ʿAlī's gratitude by sending him ʿUbayd Allāh b. Ziyād's head after the latter's death in the battle on the river Khāzir (67/686).

In Sunnī *ḥadīth* collections ʿAlī appears as a transmitter from ʿAbd Allāh b. ʿAbbās, from his father, his uncle al-Ḥasan and others. Among those who transmitted from him were some of his sons, as well as Abū Isḥāḳ al-Sabīʿī, al-Ḥakam b. ʿUtayba, ʿAmr b. Dīnār and al-Zuhrī. According to al-Zuhrī (who held ʿAlī in high esteem), he transmitted little (*kāna ḳalīl al-ḥadīth*).

ʿAlī is said to have died in 94/712 or 95/713; other dates mentioned are 92, 93, 99 and 100. He was buried in al-Baḳīʿ cemetery. Sh̲ī̲ʿī authors maintain that he was poisoned on the orders of the reigning caliph al-Walīd or his brother Hishām. He is said to have had between eight and fifteen offspring, of whom four were sons from his wife Umm ʿAbd Allāh bt. al-Ḥasan b. ʿAlī, the rest being from concubines.

A number of short texts are ascribed to ʿAlī, including a certain al-Ṣaḥīfa fī ʾl-zuhd (Kulīnī, Kāfī, viii, 14-7). He is also credited with a Risālat al-Ḥuḳūḳ, preserved (in two versions) in two 4th/10th century works: Ibn Bābawayh's K. al-Kh̲iṣāl (Nadjaf 1391/1971, 529-36) and Ibn Sh̲uʿba's Tuḥaf al-ʿuḳūl (Beirut 1394/1974, 184-95). ʿAlī's collection of prayers known as al-Ṣaḥīfa al-kāmila or al-Ṣaḥīfa [al-kāmila] al-sad̲j̲d̲j̲ādiyya gained wide popularity; there are numerous redactions and over twenty commentaries, and it was translated into Persian in the Ṣafawid period. Fifteen "whispered prayers" (munād̲j̲āt) ascribed to ʿAlī have been added to several modern editions of the Ṣaḥīfa; an English translation of the entire work is now available (Imām Zayn al-ʿĀbidīn ʿAlī b. al-Ḥusayn, The Psalms of Islam: al-Ṣaḥīfat al-kāmilat al-sajjādiyya, tr. with an introd. and annotation by W.C. Chittick, London 1988).

Bibliography: Ibn Saʿd, Ṭabaḳāt, Beirut 1380-8/1960-8, v, 211-22; Ps.-Nās̲h̲iʾ (D̲j̲aʿfar b. Ḥarb), Uṣūl al-niḥal, ed. J. van Ess as Masāʾil al-imāma, in Frühe muʿtazilitische Häresiographie, Beirut 1971, 25 (Arabic), 29-31 (German); Zubayrī, Nasab, 48, 58-9; Ibn Ḳutayba, Maʿārif, Cairo 1353/1934, 94; Balād̲h̲urī, Ansāb, iii, ed. Muḥammad Bāḳir al-Maḥmūdī, Beirut 1397/1977, 73, 101-2, 146-7, 206-8, 214, 217, 220, 273, iv/2, ed. M. Schloessinger, Jerusalem 1938, 34, 39, v, ed. Iḥsān ʿAbbās, Beirut 1417/1996, 94, 121, 162, 300, 303, 500; Dīnawarī, al-Akh̲bār al-ṭiwāl, index; Mubarrad, al-Kāmil, index; Muḥammad Aḥmad al-Dālī, Beirut 1406/1986, index; Yaʿḳūbī, Taʾrīkh̲, Nadjaf 1358, ii, 45-8; Nawbakh̲tī, Firaḳ al-shīʿa, Nadjaf 1379/1959, index; Ṭabarī, index; Kulīnī, Kāfī, Tehran 1377-81, i, 303-4, 348, 466-8; Ibn al-Haytham, K. al-Munāẓarāt, ed. and tr. W. Madelung and P.E. Walker, The advent of the Fatimids, London 2000, Ar. text 3-2, 37-8, Eng. tr. 87-8, 92-3; Masʿūdī, Murūd̲j̲, ed. Pellat, iii, §§ 1925, 1927, 1936-7, 2120; Ibn Ḥibbān al-Bustī, Mashāhīr ʿulamāʾ al-amṣār, ed. M. Fleischham... Cairo and Wiesbaden 1379/1959, 63 no. 423; Abu ʾl-Farad̲j̲ al-Iṣfahānī, Maḳātil al-ṭālibiyyīn, ed. Aḥmad Ṣaḳr, Cairo 1368/1949, 112-3, 120-1, 131; Ag̲h̲ānī, Tables, 496; Maḳdisī, al-Badʾ wa ʾl-taʾrīkh̲, i, 74, vi, 11; al-Sh̲ayk̲h̲ al-Mufīd, K. al-Irs̲h̲ād, Beirut 1399/1979, 253-61, tr. I.K.A. Howard, London 1981, 380-92 and index; Abū Nuʿaym al-Iṣfahānī, Ḥilyat al-awliyāʾ, Cairo 1351-7/1932-8, iii, 133-45; Shahrastānī, Livre des religions et des sectes, i, tr. with introd. and notes D. Gimaret and G. Monnot, Louvain 1986, index; Ṭabrisī, Iʿlām al-warā, Nadjaf 1390/1970, 256-64; Ibn ʿAsākir, xli, ed. al-ʿAmrawī, Beirut 1417/1996, 360-416; Ibn Sh̲ahrāsh̲ūb, Manāḳib āl Abī Ṭālib, Beirut 1405/1985, iv, 129-78; Ibn al-D̲j̲awzī, Ṣifat al-ṣafwa, Ḥaydarābād 1355-7, ii, 52-7; Ibn Ḳudāma, al-Tabyīn fī ansāb al-ḳurashiyyīn, ed. Muḥammad Nāyif al-Dulaymī, Baghdād 1402/1982, 108-10; Ibn Kh̲allikān, ed. ʿAbbās, iii, 266-9; Irbīlī, Kas̲h̲f al-g̲h̲umma, Beirut 1405/1985, ii, 285-328; Mizzī, Tahd̲h̲īb al-kamāl, ed, Bash̲s̲h̲ār ʿAwwād Maʿrūf, Beirut 1413/1992, xx, 382-404, no. 4050; D̲h̲ahabī, Siyar aʿlām al-nubalāʾ, ed. Sh̲uʿayb al-Arnaʾūṭ and Maʾmūn al-Ṣāg̲h̲irdj̲ī, Beirut 1405/1985, iv, 386-401; Ibn Kat̲h̲īr, Bidāya, ix, 103-15;

Ibn ʿInaba, ʿUmdat al-ṭālib, Beirut 1390, 159-60; Ibn Ḥad̲j̲ar al-ʿAsḳalānī, Tahd̲h̲īb, Ḥaydarābād 1325-7, vii, 304-7; Idrīs al-Ḳuras̲h̲ī, ʿUyūn al-ak̲h̲bār, iv, ed. Muṣṭafā G̲h̲ālib, Beirut 1406/1986, 142-79 and index; Mad̲j̲lisī, Biḥār al-anwār, Tehran 1956-74, xlvi, 2-209; Sezgin, GAS, i, 526-8, 632; Muḥsin al-Amīn, Aʿyān al-s̲h̲īʿa, iv/1, Beirut 1367/1948, 313, 321-3, 325-6, 328, 331-2, 337-48, 405-565; E. Kohlberg, Some Imāmī Sh̲īʿī interpretations of Umayyad history, in Studies on the first century of Islamic society, ed. G.H.A. Juynboll, Carbondale 1982, 145-59, 249-54, repr. in E. Kohlberg, Belief and law in Imāmī Sh̲īʿism, Variorum, Aldershot 1991, no. XII; M. Ayoub, Redemptive suffering in Islām, The Hague 1978, index; S.H.M. Jafri, The origins and early development of Shiʿa Islam, London 1979, index; M. Momen, An introduction to Shīʿi Islam, New Haven 1985, index; L. Capezzone, Abiura dalla Kaysāniyya e conversione all'Imāmiyya: il caso di Abū Ḥālid al-Kābulī, in RSO, lxvi (1992), 1-13; W. Madelung, art. ʿAlī b. al-Hosayn, in EIr, i, 849-50; idem, The succession to Muḥammad, Cambridge 1997, index.

(E. Kohlberg)

ZAYN AL-ʿĀBIDĪN, the regnal name of the Kas̲h̲mīr Sulṭan Sh̲āhī Kh̲ān b. Iskandar, greatest of the line of Sh̲āh Mīr Swātī, hence called Bud Sh̲āh "Great King", r. 823-75/1420-70.

It was his merit to put an end to the persecutions of his father Sikandar But-Sh̲ikan [q.v.], who had forcibly converted Hindus and destroyed their temples. Zayn al-ʿĀbidīn now in effect abolished the d̲j̲izya, allowed the rebuilding of temples, etc. The realm was secured by strong military policies, and internal prosperity secured by such measures as the digging of canals and the founding of new towns. He encouraged arts and crafts, and paper-making and book-binding were introduced from Samarḳand. Himself a poet in Persian, he patronised learning, and under him, the Mahābhārata and Kalhaṇa's metrical chronicle the Rājataraṅginī were translated into Persian. His reign was very much a Golden Age for Kas̲h̲mīr, but much of his work was undone by his weaker successors.

Bibliography: Mohibbul Hasan, Kashmir under the Sultans, Calcutta 1959; R.K. Parmu, A history of Muslim rule in Kashmir, Delhi 1969; Habib and Nizami (eds.), A comprehensive history of India. V. The Delhi Sultanat (A.D. 1206-1526), Delhi 1970, 751-9; C.E. Bosworth, The New Islamic dynasties, Edinburgh 1996, 310-11 no. 162. See also kashmīr. i.

(C.E. Bosworth)

ZAYN AL-ʿĀBIDĪN MARĀGHAʾĪ, Persian merchant and writer (1255-1328/1839-1910).

From a Kurdish family which had recently become Sh̲īʿī, Marāghaʾī from the age of sixteen engaged in the family trading activity. After failing at Ardabīl, he sought his fortune in the Caucasian region and became Persian consul-general at Tiflis in Georgia, where he again took up commerce but ruined himself helping indigent Persians. Fleeing to Russian territory, he surfaced in the Crimea and in Istanbul. Before the Russo-Turkish War of 1877 he was a cloth merchant at Yalta; he supplied the Imperial family with goods and assumed Russian citizenship, with his three children learning only Russian.

Ca. 1890, in search of his religious and national identity, he sold his trading business and went to Istanbul, moving amongst the Persian reformist milieux, and in 1904 abandoned his Russian nationality and re-assumed his Persian one. In Istanbul, he contributed to the reformist newspaper Ak̲h̲tar and published anonymously, at Cairo, the first volume of his

Siyāḥat-nāma-i Ibrāhīm Beyg, to which he later added two more volumes, only revealing his name at the end of the third one. In the style of James Morier's *Hajji Baba of Ispahan*, he tells of the travels in Persia of a young Persian patriot, of liberal views, born in Egypt, in which he discovers the moral and political decadence of his land. Referring to Islam, citing Ṭālibūf [*q.v.*]/Talibov and influenced by Malkom Khān [*q.v.*], he displays the bad conscience of an idealistic patriot who only knows his country through travellers' accounts. His convincing ardour in denouncing despotism was to assure him a great, immediate success (reprints in Istanbul, India and even at Tehran in 1323/1905). As a good representative of the preconstitutionalist Ādharī milieu, linked with the Caucasus region, which spread within Persia the democratic ideal, Marāghaʾī was to inspire not only the revolutionaries of 1906 but also several succeeding reformers up to the present time, such as Aḥmad Kasrawī [see KASRAWĪ TABRĪZĪ].

Bibliography: *Siyāḥat-nāma-i Ibrāhīm Beyg yā balā-yi taʿaṣṣub-i ū*, [1]Cairo n.d. [1896?], vol. iii, Istanbul 1327/1909, modern abridged ed. B. Muʾminī, Tehran 2537/1978, complete text ed. Muḥammad-ʿAlī Sipānlū, Tehran 1364/1985, Ger. tr. W. Schulz, *Zustände im heutigen Persien. Wie sie das Reisebuch Ibrahim Begs enthüllt aus dem Persischem übersetzt und bearbeitet*, Leipzig 1903. See also Dihkhudā, *Lughat-nāma*, new ed. Tehran 1373/1994, viii, 11,550, s.n. *Zayn al-ʿĀbidīn Marāghaʾī*; Ch. Balay, *La genèse du roman persan moderne*, Tehran-Louvain 1998, 247-77 (detailed literary analysis of the story). (Y. RICHARD)

ZAYN al-**ʿĀBIDĪN SHĪRWĀNĪ**, called "Mast-ʿAlī Shāh", with the pen-name "Tamkīn", Persian scholar and mystic (1193-1253/1779-1837). He was born into a Shīʿī family of Shīrwān, accompanied his father Mullā Iskandar to Karbalā at five years of age and studied there for twelve years. Having made the acquaintance of the Niʿmatallāhī Ṣūfī masters Maʿṣūm ʿAlī Shāh Dakanī and Nūr-ʿAlī Shāh Iṣfahānī (both d. 1212/1797), he made his way to Baghdād and thence embarked on a life of travel, punctuated by encounters with mystical masters or political leaders, whom he evokes in his major encyclopaedic works (for example, *Riyāḍ al-siyāḥa*, ed. Rabbānī, 129-30). Having crossed the Iranian plateau, he reached Kābul where he spent four years in the company of the master Ḥusayn-ʿAlī Iṣfahānī (d. 1216/1801-2). After the death of the latter, he travelled around India for eight years, then returned to Persia via Kābul and Khurāsān. From the Persian Gulf, he made his way to the Ḥidjāz and traversed the entire Arabian Peninsula from north to south. After the Pilgrimage and a stay in Mecca, he travelled to Egypt and then to Damascus and Istanbul, stopping for months at a time at each stage of the journey. On his return to Persia in 1229/1814, having enjoyed honorific receptions everywhere, he tried to establish his domicile in various places, finally settling in Shīrāz where he trained his disciple Zayn al-ʿĀbidīn Raḥmat-ʿAlī Shāh (d. 1278/1861). Harassed by the Shīʿī clergy, he moved his residence to the vicinity of Iṣfahān. Once again the victim of a wave of anti-Ṣūfī intolerance, he tried to flee from Persia but in the process only narrowly escaped death and lost all his goods and his writings. After some time in Kāshān, he returned to Shīrāz (1241/1825-6), where he remained until a final Pilgrimage to Mecca, in the course of which he died. Since the accession of Muḥammad Shāh (1249/1834), protector of the Ṣūfīs, he had enjoyed a quiet life and the revenues of an estate given to him by the ruler.

In those of his works that have survived, Shīrwānī tells of the various places that he visited and expands upon the teaching of Ṣūfism and upon his personal philosophy. The Persian historian A. Hairi has shown that, fascinated by the Britons encountered in India, Zayn al-ʿĀbidīn lost all critical sense (*Nakhustīn rūyā-rūʾī-hā*, 436-7). Rather than a mystical work, it is a mine of information on Niʿmatallāhī Ṣūfism and on the daily and cultural life of the early 19th century. Riḍā-Ḳulī Hidāyat was among the direct disciples of Shīrwānī.

Bibliography: 1. Works. *Bustān al-siyāḥa* (written 1248/1833), lith. Tehran 1315/1897, repr. 1378/1958; *Riyāḍ al-siyāḥa* (written 1237/1821-2), lith. Iṣfahān 1339/1921, ed. Aṣghar Ḥāmid Rabbānī, Tehran 1339/1960.

2. Studies. E.G. Browne, *LHP*, iv, 450-2; R. Gramlich, *Die schiitischen Derwischorden Persiens*, 3 vols. Wiesbaden 1965, 1976, 1981, i, 50-1; Y. Āryanpūr, *Az Ṣabā tā Nīmā. Tārīkh-i 150 sāl-i adab-i fārsī. I. Bāz-gasht*, [4]Tehran 1354/1975, 199-200; N. Pourjavady and P.L. Wilson, *Kings of love. The poetry and history of the Niʿmatullahi Sufi order*, Tehran, Boulder and London 1978, 147-51 (with trs. of poems); ʿAbd al-Hādī Ḥāʾirī, *Nakhustīn rūyārūʾī-hā-yi andīshagarān-ī Īrān bā du rūya-yi tamaddun-ī burzhūāzi-i gharb*, Tehran 1367 *sh*./1988. (Y. RICHARD)

ZAYN al-**DĪN** b. **ʿALĪ** [see AL-SHAHĪD AL-THĀNĪ].

ZAYN al-**DĪN, SHAYKH AḤMAD** [see MAPPILA].

ZAYNAB [see AL-MURĀBIṬŪN].

ZAYNAB bt. **ʿABD ALLĀH** al-**MAḤḌ** b. al-Ḥasan al-Muthannā, Umm al-Ḥusayn, the mother of the Ḥasanid ʿAlid martyr al-Ḥusayn b. ʿAlī, Ṣāḥib Fakhkh [*q.v.*], who led a revolt in Medina in 169/786 during the caliphate of Mūsā al-Hādī. According to Abu 'l-Faradj al-Iṣfahānī, *Maḳātil al-ṭālibiyyīn*, Nadjaf 1385/1965, 285-6, she and her husband were so famed for their religious devotion that they were known as "the pious couple", *al-zawdj al-ṣāliḥ*.

Bibliography: See also Muḥsin al-Amīn al-ʿĀmilī, *Aʿyān al-Shīʿa*, Damascus-Beirut 1356-74/1938-55, xxxiii, 169 no. 6825; and for her paternal ancestors, K. Öhrnberg, *The offspring of Fāṭima. Dispersal and ramification*, Helsinki 1983, Tables 16, 27. (ED.)

ZAYNAB bt. **DJAḤSH** b. Riʾāb al-Asadiyya, one of the Prophet's wives, whom he married after her divorce from Muḥammad's freedman and adopted son Zayd b. Ḥāritha [*q.v.*].

Zaynab's mother was a maternal aunt of the Prophet, Umayma bt. ʿAbd al-Muṭṭalib, and her father, from the tribe of Asad, a client of the clan of ʿAbd Shams. One of the first emigrants to Medina, she was a virgin (according to some traditions, a widow) when Muḥammad gave her in marriage to Zayd. In the year 4/626 Muḥammad saw Zaynab alone in her house, was taken with her and had Zayd divorce her so that he himself might marry her, she being at that time about 35 years old. Zayd's scruples were set aside by the Ḳurʾānic revelation XXXIII, 37-8, and she received a dowry of 400 dirhams. Zaynab is reported as being proud of the circumstances of her marriage, and as saying that her marriage to the Prophet was superior to the other ones because it had the confirmation of divine revelation. The "verse of veiling", *āyat al-ḥidjāb* (XXXIII, 53), is said to have been revealed at the time of her wedding feast, and some traditions also connect LXVI, 1, with Zaynab and with the other wives' envy of her.

Zaynab was friendly with ʿĀʾis̲h̲a [*q.v.*], and supportive of her during the so-called "affair of the lie" (*ḥadīt̲h̲ al-ifk*). Her charity was famed, as "the longest-handed" of the Prophet's wives; ʿUmar allotted to her a large stipend, but when she died (according to Ibn Saʿd, in 20/641), she was penniless, having given it all to the poor.

In medieval Christendom, the episode of Muḥammad's infatuation with Zaynab and his compelling Zayd b. Ḥārit̲h̲a to divorce her, was made much of by anti-Muslim propagandists (cf. L. Marracci, *Prodromus ad refutationem Alcorani*, Padua 1691, 562; N. Daniel, *Islam and the West, the making of an image*, Edinburgh 1960, 31, 97-100, 292). Reacting to this, modern Muslim apologists and biographers of the Prophet have endeavoured to place it in a more favourable light (cf. Muḥammad Ḥusayn Haykal, *Ḥayāt Muḥammad*, Cairo 1936, 307 ff.; M. Lings, *Muhammad, his life based on the earliest sources*, London 1983, 212-14).

Bibliography: Ibn His̲h̲ām, 734, tr. Guillaume, 495-6; Ibn Saʿd, viii, 71-82, Balād̲h̲urī, *Ansāb al-as̲h̲rāf*, i, ed. M. Hamidullah, Cairo 1959, 433-7; Ibn Ḳutayba, *Maʿārif*, ed. ʿUkkās̲h̲a, 215, 457, 555; Ṭabarī, i, 1772-3, tr. I.K. Poonawala, *The History of al-Ṭabarī. IX. The last years of the Prophet*, Albany 1990, 134; Ibn Ḥad̲j̲ar, *Iṣāba*, vii, 667-70; F. Buhl, *Das Leben Muhammeds*, Leipzig 1930, 282, 361; Nabia Abbott, *Ayesha, the beloved of Mohammed*, Chicago 1942, 16-21, 46-7, 98-9; W.M. Watt, *Muhammad at Medina*, Oxford 1956, 396; ʿUmar Riḍā Kaḥḥāla, *Aʿlām al-nisāʾ*, Damascus 1379/1959, ii, 59-63; M. Gaudefroy-Demombynes, *Mahomet*, Paris 1969, 225-7. (C.E. BOSWORTH)

ZAYNAB BT. **K̲H̲UZAYMA** b. al-Ḥārit̲h̲ al-Hilāliyya, from the tribe of ʿĀmir b. Ṣaʿṣaʿa [*q.v.*], one of the Prophet's wives, already known in the *D̲j̲āhiliyya* as Umm al-Masākīn "Mother of the destitute" from her charitable activities. Her first husband divorced her, and her second one, ʿUbayda b. al-Ḥārit̲h̲, was killed fighting at Badr [*q.v.*]. Muḥammad then married her in either 4/626 or the preceding year when she was about 30 years old, and gave her a dowry of 400 dirhams; but according to al-Balād̲h̲urī, she died eight months later at the end of Rabīʿ II 4/early October 625. She was buried in the cemetery of Baḳīʿ al-G̲h̲arḳad [*q.v.*].

Bibliography: Ibn Saʿd, viii, 82; Balād̲h̲urī, *Ansāb al-as̲h̲rāf*, i, ed. Hamidullah, 429; Ibn Ḳutayba, *Maʿārif*, ed. ʿUkkās̲h̲a, 87, 135, 158; Ṭabarī, i, 1775-6, tr. Poonawala, 138; Ibn al-At̲h̲īr, *Usd al-g̲h̲āba*, v, 466-7; Nabia Abbott, *Ayesha, the beloved of Mohammed*, 12; W.M. Watt, *Muhammad at Medina*, Oxford 1956, 396; Kaḥḥāla, *Aʿlām al-nisāʾ*, ii, 65. (C.E. BOSWORTH)

ZAYNAB BT. **MUḤAMMAD**, daughter of the Prophet by his first wife K̲h̲adīd̲j̲a [*q.v.*], and said to have been his eldest one. Before Muḥammad began his public ministry, she married a rich man of Ḳuray̲s̲h̲ from the clan of ʿAbd S̲h̲ams, her maternal cousin Abu 'l-ʿĀṣ Laḳīṭ b. al-Rabīʿ.

She was in al-Ṭāʾif at the time of Muḥammad's *hid̲j̲ra*, and did not follow him to Medina. Her husband, still a non-Muslim, was captured at Badr. Zaynab sent a necklace that had belonged to her mother K̲h̲adīd̲j̲a to ransom him, and the Prophet freed him on condition that Zaynab should come to Medina. On the way thither she was maltreated by al-Habbār b. al-Aswad and had a fall which caused her to miscarry; al-Habbār only escaped subsequent punishment for this by a timely conversion to Islam. Zaynab's husband was taken prisoner a second time in 6/627 during the expedition of al-ʿĪṣ, and freed by his wife's intercession. He became a Muslim in 7/628 and was re-united with his wife by a second marriage.

Zaynab died in Medina in 8/629. She had two children, ʿAlī, who died in infancy, and Umāma, who married ʿAlī b. Abī Ṭālib after Fāṭima's death.

Bibliography: Ibn His̲h̲ām, 464-8, tr. Guillaume, 313-16; Ibn Saʿd, viii, 20-4; Ibn Ḳutayba, *Maʿārif*, ed. ʿUkkās̲h̲a, 72, 127, 141-2; Balād̲h̲urī, *Ansāb al-as̲h̲rāf*, i, ed. Hamidullah, 357-8, 397-401; Ṭabarī, i, 1767, tr. Poonawala, 127; H. Lammens, *Fâtima et les filles de Mahomet. Notes critiques pour l'étude de la Sîra*, Rome 1912, index; F. Buhl, *Das Leben Muhammeds*, 120; W.M. Watt, *Muhammad at Mecca*, Oxford 1953, 38-9; idem, *Muhammad at Medina*, Oxford 1956, 45, 322; Kaḥḥāla, *Aʿlām al-nisāʾ*, ii, 107-10; M. Gaudefroy-Demombynes, *Mahomet*, 67, 124-5, 233-4, 582. (V. VACCA*)

AL-**ZAYNABĪ**, ʿALĪ B. ṬIRĀD (or ṬARRĀD) b. Muḥammad, Abu 'l-Ḳāsim S̲h̲araf al-Dīn, vizier to the two ʿAbbāsid caliphs al-Mustars̲h̲id and al-Muḳtafī [*q.vv.*] in the first half of the 6th/12th century, b. 462/1069-70, d. 538/1144.

The *nisba* refers to descent from Zaynab bt. Sulaymān b. ʿAlī b. ʿAbd Allāh b. al-ʿAbbās, and this ʿAbbāsid descent doubtless helped al-Zaynabī's father Ṭirād or Ṭarrād, called D̲h̲u 'l-S̲h̲arafayn, to secure in 453/1061 the office of *naḳīb* [see NAḲĪB AL-AS̲H̲RĀF] of the Hās̲h̲imī *s̲h̲arīf*s and also to pursue a career in diplomacy on behalf of the caliphs. ʿAlī inherited this office after his father's death in 491/1098 and in 517/1123 combined it with the *niḳāba* of the ʿAlids also. He eventually acquired the *laḳab* of Niẓām al-Ḥaḍratayn from his liaison work between the two courts of the ʿAbbāsids and the Sald̲j̲ūḳ sultans in Bag̲h̲dād.

He had already functioned as vizier to the caliph in fact if not in name, when in Rabīʿ II 523/March-April 1129 he formally became vizier to al-Mustars̲h̲id until succeeded by his bitter rival Anūs̲h̲irwān b. K̲h̲ālid [*q.v.*] in 526/1132. Al-Mustars̲h̲id was murdered and his son al-Rās̲h̲id [*q.v.*] succeeded him in 529/1135, but the new caliph was deposed after a year by a *fatwā* of the *ʿulamāʾ* and *fuḳahāʾ* at the instigation of al-Zaynabī; on the intervention of the Sald̲j̲ūḳ sultan Masʿūd b. Muḥammad [*q.v.*], al-Muḳtafī was made caliph with al-Zaynabī as his vizier (530/1136). The two men soon quarrelled, however; al-Zaynabī sought the protection of the sultan but was dismissed in 534/1139-40. He was soon afterwards reconciled to al-Muḳtafī and was able to return to Bag̲h̲dād. He died there in straitened circumstances on 1 Ramaḍān 538/8 March 1144, but, says al-Ṣafadī, he had nevertheless continued to pay allowances he had customarily made (*idrār*) to all his dependents and protégés.

Al-Zaynabī is conventionally praised in the sources for his piety and good works, and was the *mamdūḥ* of such poets of the time as Ḥayṣa Bayṣa [*q.v.*].

Bibliography: Ibn al-D̲j̲awzī, *Muntaẓam*, ix-x (death notice at x, 109); Samʿānī, *Ansāb*, ed. Ḥaydarābād, vii, 372; Ibn al-At̲h̲īr, x-xi, years 491, 501, 512, 516-17, 522-3, 526, 529-32, 534, 536, 538; Ibn K̲h̲allikān, ed. ʿAbbās, iv, 454, tr. de Slane, iii, 151, cf. 154; Ṣafadī, *Wāfī*, xxi, ed. Muḥammad al-Ḥuğairī, Wiesbaden 1988, 155-6, with other biographical sources indicated at 155 n. 105; Ibn al-Tiḳṭaḳā, *Fak̲h̲rī*, ed. Derenbourg, 411-18, Eng. tr. Whitting, 295-9. (C.E. BOSWORTH)

ZAYT (A.), in the classical lexicon, the oil or expressed juice of the olive (*zaytūn* [*q.v.*], botanical name *Olea europaea* L.), although it could apply today to any oil. Here only the use of olive oil will be discussed. In his Book on Dietetics (*K. al-Aghdhiya*), al-Isrāʾīlī (d. *ca.* 935) adds that oil extracted from any plant other than the olive was called *duhn.*

Cultivated throughout the Mediterranean basin since about 3,000 B.C., the fruit of the olive tree was used for cooking, as food, as a cosmetic and for lamp oils. It is in this last usage that *zayt* occurs in the famous Ḳurʾānic "Verse of Light" (XXIV, 35). This reference gave rise to Traditions from the Prophet who approved its use because it came from "a blessed tree". Graded according to the acidic content, the very best "virgin" oil would contain 1% of oleic acid, while poor oil with acidity too high for eating would be used as lamp oil. The term *zayt maghsūl* ("washed oil" or alternatively *zayt al-māʾ*) might refer either to the Roman technique of removing a bitter glucoside from the fruit by first soaking it in a solution of lye followed by a thorough washing, or by crushing the olives and then purifying the liquid by floating it on water. Al-Isrāʾīlī again notes that both the previously-mentioned terms refer to oil extracted (after crushing?) by means of hot water. On the other hand, in the dietetic treatise of the Andalusī author Abū Marwān ʿAbd al-Malik b. Zuhr (d. 557/1162), he says that the very best olive oil is taken from ripe olives that have not been mixed with salt or other substance, as this adulterates the fruit's moist elements and unbalances its nature; this may reflect a traditional Iberian taste for the more acidic grades of the oil.

Ibn Ḥabīb's (d. 238/853) small medical compendium preserves a couple of sayings attributed to the Prophet Muḥammad indicating the several uses of olive oil and its magical property of protecting from Satan for forty days anyone who is anointed with it. The composition of olive oil was described as hot and moist in the first degree. In the mediaeval Arab culinary tradition, represented by the anonymous *Kanz al-fawāʾid* (see index s.v.), olive oil was employed in a variety of preparations. As a frying agent, it was also occasionally replaced by sesame oil (*shīradj*), as in the preparation of fish; in egg preparations, the two oils were often used together. Oil sprinkled over a prepared condiment lent its flavour to the dish. A mixture of salt, water and oil was used to clean chicken before cooking it, and oil was used in a herbal-based mixture in which to marinate fish.

Bibliography: Abū Marwān b. Zuhr, *K. al-Aghdhiya*, ed. and tr. E. García Sánchez, Madrid 1992; *Kanz al-fawāʾid fī tanwīʿ al-mawāʾid*, ed. M. Marín and D. Waines, Beirut-Stuttgart 1993; Isḥāḳ b. Sulaymān al-Isrāʾīlī, *K. al-Aghdhiya*, ed. F. Sezgin, Frankfurt 1986; Ibn Ḥabīb, *Mukhtaṣar fi 'l-ṭibb*, ed. C. Alvarez de Morales and F. Giron Irueste, Madrid 1992; T. Stobart, *The cook's encyclopaedia*, London 1980.

(D. Waines)

ZAYTŪN (a.), the olive and olive tree (*Olea europaea* L., the cultivated olive; *O. oleaster*, the wild one).

1. In materia medica and folklore.

Olives and their oil (*zayt* [*q.v.*]) have been used as a food and medicine since ancient times. In the Ḳurʾān, Sūrat al-Tīn, XCV, 1, we have an introductory oath "By the fig and the olive . . .".

According to Dioscorides, leaves of wild and cultivated olive are beneficial for the eyes, skin conditions, pains and inflammations (i, 137-140). Al-Zahrāwī describes the extraction and use of oils (*adhān*) notably various types of olive oil. Green unripe olives give *infāḳ* (*omphakion*: cf Dioscorides, i, 29); according to him, oil washed in water is *rikābī*, a "vehicle" for other ingredients (but see 2. below for another, more widespread explanation of the term). Olive oil is mentioned as useful in ointments (*marāhim*) which need astringent properties; his *maḳāla* 24 on ointments lists 86 prescriptions, of which 47 contain oil. He quotes Dioscorides that oil warms and softens the skin and protects from the cold (Albucasis 81, 90, 98-100, 114-15, cf. Dioscorides, i, 30) Ibn Sīnā recommends it for many internal and external ailments (*Ḳānūn*, i, 309-10). Al-Kindī uses oil for burns (nos. 120, 135) and abscesses (nos. 129, 131), whilst Galen recommends it for headache (310-12).

Olive oil has long featured in folk medicine, continuing up to the present time. It has the authority of the Prophet, for it is "from a blessed tree", and is recommended in particular for erysipelas, itch, ulcers, and skin eruptions (*Medicine of the Prophet*, tr. Johnstone, 227). In Persia of the 1930s, it was "much used in magical rites". Gabriel was said to have told Adam to plant an olive tree and from the fruit to extract an oil which could be used for any pain; thus it was said to cure "every illness except that one from which a person is destined to die" (Donaldson, *The wild rue*, 141, 144). Earlier, in Palestine, it is mentioned as being used for wounds (Canaan, *Aberglaube*, 69). In this region in the 1970s, it was recommended, in villages or by the local herbalist (*ʿaṭṭār*), for earache, sprains, as a massage on the throat for the tonsils, and on the joints for cases of acute influenza; with ghee (*samna*) and sesame oil (*shīradj*) it was used for ulcers on the leg. It could also be used with soap and egg white as a "plaster" for fractures, and was drunk in small quantities for kidney stone.

Modern Western use is mainly culinary, but also as eardrops and in compound oils.

Bibliography: Ibn al-Bayṭār, *al-Djāmiʿ li-mufradāt al-adwiya wa 'l-aghdhiya*, Cairo 1874; Ibn Sīnā, *al-Ḳānūn fi 'l-ṭibb*, Būlāḳ 1294/1877, repr. Beirut n.d.; T. Canaan, *Aberglaube und Volksmedizin im Lande der Bibel*, Hamburg 1914; *The Greek Herbal of Dioscorides . . . [translated by] John Goodyer 1655*, ed. R.T. Gunther, Oxford 1934; B.A. Donaldson, *The wild rue. A study of Muhammadan magic and folklore in Iran*, London 1938, repr. New York 1973; C.E. Dubler and E. Terés, *La Materia Médica de Dioscórides*, ii, Tetuan 1952; S.K. Hamarneh and G. Sonnedecker, *A pharmaceutical view of Albucasis . . .* (*Janus*, Suppl. 5), Leiden 1963; M. Levey, *The Medical Formulary or Aqrabādhīn of al-Kindī*, Madison 1966; *Kitāb Djālīnūs ilā Ghaluḳūn . . .* (Ḥunayn b. Isḥāḳ), Cairo 1982; Ibn Ḳayyim al-Djawziyya, *Medicine of the Prophet*, tr. P. Johnstone, Cambridge 1999.

(Penelope C. Johnstone)

2. Olive cultivation.

The domesticated olive tree was an important food plant in the Mediterranean region and Asia Minor during the Islamic era. The primary centre of cultivation was Syria and Palestine, but substantial groves were also found in Spain. In Egypt there was limited production of olives in the Delta, especially near Alexandria, according to al-Muḳaddasī and al-Ḳalḳashandī. Olives were cultivated in the Fayyūm and the Sīwa oasis since the Hellenistic period. Ethnographic descriptions of olive planting and the folklore surrounding olives focus on Syria and Palestine (see Crowfoot and Baldensperger, and Dalman), especially in reference to biblical studies (see Moldenke).

Information is available in the major mediaeval agricultural treatises about the cultivation of olives and their use in the form of olive oil (*zayt*), although much of this is copied from earlier classical texts. The most extensive source on olive cultivation comes from the widely-quoted *al-Filāḥa al-Nabaṭiyya* attributed to Ibn Waḥshiyya [*q.v.*] and reflecting much older practices in the region of ʿIrāḳ and Syria. According to this source, the best time for planting olive trees is when the sun is at the midpoint of the zodiacal house of Pisces until it reaches the middle of Taurus, during February and March; this general time frame is frequently reported in the mediaeval almanacs. In most cases, the young shoots should be irrigated, especially right after the planting, and manure is recommended. Classical sources quoted by Arab authors indicate that human dung is not suitable for fertilising olive trees. Much of the technical advice is mixed with magical claims for pomoting growth, protecting from pests and treating diseases, changing the taste or colour of the olives, and preparation of olive oil. For example, planting is said to be more propitious if the moon is waxing and is in the one of the two houses of Saturn.

A variety of methods are recorded for planting olive trees from shoots around the base of an existing tree. These are sometimes grafted with stock from wild varieties. The sources note that trees planted from seed, which usually occurs in late autumn, do poorly under domestication. The sources suggest planting in fine and pliable soil in locations protected from hot winds. Olives do not grow well in saline soils. Cultivation is preferable in the mountains because of the cool air.

Olive production occurs after the tree reaches maturity, generally in about 15 years. It is difficult to kill an olive tree by cutting it down, since new shoots will be sent up from the roots. In Palestine, excessive dew and heavy moisture can damage the pollen when the olive tree is flowering. The best olives come from trees which are 40-60 years old. Olives were traditionally harvested in November in Palestine and Syria, either by men climbing the trees and throwing the olives down or by beating the trees with sticks. Al-Aṣmaʿī quotes ʿAbd al-Mālik b. Ṣāliḥ b. ʿAlī that olives trees can survive up to 3,000 years (!).

One of the best varieties of olives was the Syrian *rikābī*, so-called because it was exported from Syria on camelback. Al-Thaʿālibī noted that this variety was especially regarded for the purity and clarity of its oil. *Rikābī* olives and their oil were exported widely in the Islamic world, including Yemen and Mecca, where olives were not grown.

Bibliography: Ibn al-ʿAwwām, *Libro de agricultura* (*Kitāb al-Filāḥa*), Madrid 1802, i, 225-45; Ibn Waḥshiyya, *al-Filāḥa al-Nabaṭiyya*, ed. T. Fahd, *L'agriculture nabatéenne*, Damascus 1993, i, 12-53; Thaʿālibī, *Laṭāʾif al-maʿārif*, tr. C.E. Bosworth, *The book of curious and entertaining information*, Edinburgh 1968, 118; G.M. Crowfoot and L. Baldensperger, *From cedar to hyssop*, London 1931; G. Dalman, *Arbeit und Sitte in Palästina*, Gütersloh 1935, iv, 153-290; H.N. and A.L. Moldenke, *Plants of the Bible*, New York 1952, 156-60; M. Ṣāliḥiyya and I. al-ʿAmd (eds.), *Miftāḥ al-rāḥa li-ahl al-filāḥa*, Kuwait 1984, 191-3.

(D.M. Varisco)

ZAYTŪN, or more probably Zītūn, the name given in the later Arabic geographers (Ibn Saʿīd al-Maghribī [*q.v.*], who flourished in the 7th/13th century, being apparently the first to mention it) and in Muslim travellers like Ibn Baṭṭūṭa [*q.v.*] (who landed there after his Chinese voyage of *ca.* 1346-7) to a great commercial port of China. It is usually identified as Ch'üan-chou or Quanzhou in the modern Fukien or Fujian province, facing the Formosa strait (lat. 24° 53' N., long. 118° 36' E.) or possibly as the nearby Chang-chou or Zhangzhou near Amoy in this same province (lat. 24° 31' N., long. 117° 40' E.). In Sung and Yüan times (12th-14th centuries) it had a flourishing colony of Arab and Persian Muslim merchants, who lived in a separate urban area of their own with all necessary buildings for the practice of their cult and for the meeting together of Ṣūfīs, whilst the Christian community had its own suffragan bishopric there under the Roman Catholic archdiocese of Khānbalīḳ or Peking (one incumbent of Zaytūn is mentioned as Andrew of Perugia) and Franciscan convents.

Bibliography: Sir Henry Yule and H. Cordier, *Cathay and the way thither, being a collection of mediaeval notices of China*, 4 vols. London 1914, i, 169 ff., iv, 117 ff. (Ibn Baṭṭūṭa's account) and index; P. Pelliot, *Notes on Marco Polo*, 3 vols. Paris 1959-73, s.v. *Çaiton*; A. Herrmann, *An historical atlas of China*, Edinburgh 1966, maps at 35, 37, 39, 41, 43, 44 etc.; and see mīnāʾ. 9; al-ṣīn at Vol. IX, 620-1, with further references.

(C.E. Bosworth)

ZAYTŪN, in Ottoman usage Zeytūn, a town of southeastern Anatolia, now called Süleymanlı. The town (lat. 37° 53' N., long. 36° 50' E., altitude 940 m/3,080 feet) lies in the basin of the upper reaches of the Djayhān [*q.v.*]/Ceyhan river, and the old part of it rises in terraces on the slopes of a steep hill crowned by a Turkish-period fortress.

Its former Armenian inhabitants called it Zetʿun or Ulnia, or simply Kegʿ "village". An Aplgharip (? ʿAbd al-Ḳarīb) of Fornos, to the southwest of Zaytūn, is mentioned at the beginning of the reign of Leon I of Little Armenia (1129-37) (*Rec. hist. Crois., Doc. arm.*, i, 636, iii, 636). On the other hand, the town of Zaytūn is first mentioned after the capture of the last Rupenid King of Little Armenia (1375). According to local tradition, the inhabitants came from the fortress of Ani or Anē-dzor, which probably lay in the Cilician plain. The earliest mention of the town which Alishan could find is in 1526 (Bishop Narses of Zethun, *Sissouan*, 199, 201). Paul of Aleppo calls Zaytūn in 1699 "the well-known town of the Armenians". The inhabitants were for long (till about 1864) able to maintain a certain independence. A rising broke out in 1819 as a protest against the heavy taxes imposed by the Porte. The people of Zaytūn resisted Ibrāhīm Pasha from Egypt on behalf of the Turks. The troubles of 1862 lasted till 1872 and broke out again in 1878 and 1884. In the summer of 1876 the residence of the governor was burned down; it was rebuilt in 1877. The conflagrations of 22 September 1884 and 26 July 1887 were much worse, and almost the whole of the town was destroyed. New unrest was caused by the outbreak of smallpox, from which 400 children in Zaytūn died in 1890. The worst was the uprising of 1895-6 following the general persecution of Armenians in Turkey. The governor of Marʿash besieged the little town in which 15,000 fugitives from the surrounding country had taken refuge; completely exhausted by bombardments, epidemics and lack of munitions, the defenders were only able to secure peace and an amnesty from the Porte through the intervention of the European Powers, notably France; they had to surrender their arms and were granted government by a Christian *ḳāʾim-maḳām*. The massacres during the First World War and shortly afterwards led to the migration of the surviving Armenians to Syria and beyond, and Zaytūn has since been a Turkish town.

In *ca.* 1880, the population of Zaytūn and its

surrounding district was estimated at nearly 36,000, including 27,500 Armenians and 8,300 Turks. It was the seat of an Armenian bishopric. The men of the town had been engaged in the iron mines of the Berit Dağı to the north of Zaytūn, and silkworms had also been reared in the region, as well as cultivation of the olive tree which gave the place its name.

In late Ottoman times, Zaytūn was the chef-lieu of a *ḳaḍā* in the *wilāyet*, formerly *sandjak*, of Marʿash [*q.v.*]. In modern Turkey, it comes within the *il* or province of Kahramanmaraş.

Bibliography: Recueil des hist. orient. des Croisades, Docum. armén., i, 636, iii, 471 n., 636, 720 n. 3; Paul of Aleppo, *The travels of Macarius, Patriarch of Antioch*, tr. F.C. Belfour, London 1836, ii, 451; Léon Paul, *Journal de voyage. Italie, Egypte, Judée...*, Paris 1865; J.J. Allahwerdian, *Ulnia or Zethun, a mountain town in Cilicia*, Istanbul 1884 (in Armen.); Cuinet, *La Turquie d'Asie*, ii, 246-7; L. Alishan, *Sissouan ou l'Arméno-Cilicie* (in Armen. 1885), Venice 1899, 186-209; P. Dashian, *Das Hochland Ulnia oder Zeitun*, in *Mitt. Geogr. Ges. Wien*, xxxiii (1890), 424-58; *Murray's guide, Asia Minor, Transcaucasia, Persia, etc.*, London 1895, 262-3; Aghassi, *Zeïtoun depuis les origines jusqu'à l'insurrection de 1895*, tr. Archag Tchobanian, Paris 1897; Anatolio Latino (i.e. Consul-General Vitto in Beirut), *Gli Armeni e Zeitun*, Florence 1897, ii, 137 ff.; Earl Percy, *Highlands of Asiatic Turkey*, London 1901, 95-9; Sir Mark Sykes, *Dār al-Islām*, London 1904, 71-2; Vannutelli, *Anatolia meridionale e Mesopotamia*, Rome 1911, 278-83; H. Grothe, *Meine Vorderasien-expedition*, ii, Leipzig 1912, index, 314, s.v. *Seïtūn* M. Sēmērčean, *Zetʿuni ancʿealēn eu nerkayēn*, in *Zaytūn in the past and present* (in Armen.), Istanbul 1909; W.J. Childs, *Across Asia Minor on foot*, ²Edinburgh and London 1917, 397-403. (E. Honigmann*)

ZAYTŪNA, Djāmiʿ al-, the celebrated mosque-university in the city of Tunis.

1. Archaeological survey and construction of the mosque.

Foundation. ʿAbd Allāh al-Bakrī (5th/11th century) gives two facts: the building by ʿUbayd Allāh b. Ḥabḥāb [*q.v.*] in 114/732-3 of a Friday mosque, *djāmiʿ*, and the building of a *masdjid* by Ḥassān b. al-Nuʿmān [*q.v.*] at the time of his capture of Tunis *ca.* 79/698-9 (*K. fī dhikr al-bilād Ifrīḳiya wa 'l-Maghrib*, Algiers 1911, 37). This account has given rise to two theses, taken up by modern historians. Most of these trace the creation of the Zaytūna mosque to the end of the 7th century A.D., assuming that Ibn Ḥabḥāb rebuilt it. Lucien Golvin, on the other hand, considered that Ibn Ḥabḥāb built the original Zaytūna mosque but places the date in 116/734, the year in which he became governor of Ifrīḳiya (*Essai sur l'architecture religieuse musulmane*, Paris 1974, iii, 152). In fact, there is nothing to confirm the thesis of a continuity between the two buildings, which al-Bakrī seems to describe as two separate buildings.

Do we have here a creation *ex nihilo*? Historians raise the question of the reconstruction of a former Byzantine church dedicated to St. Olive. Restoration work from 1969-70 allows one to affirm that the mosque was built on stone pillars which ran from west to east, being survivals of an ancient building covering a cemetery (conclusion of Ḥāmid al-Adjābī, director of the restoration work, in *Ifriqiyyata. Revue de l'Institut national des antiquités et des arts*, Tunis n.d., vii-viii, 15-24). Putting forward a new thesis, Muḥammad al-Bādjī Ibn Māmī believes that there may be here an ancient Byzantine defensive construction, with the Arab conquerors building their mosque within the ramparts of a fort (*Djāmiʿ al-Zaytūna*, in *al-Muʾarrikh al-ʿarabī*, Baghdād [Dec. 2000]).

The building and its history. The architectural history of the mosque and a description of it have been delineated by Golvin, *op. cit.*, iii, 159-62, and restated by Muḥammad al-ʿAzīz Ibn ʿĀshūr, *Djāmiʿ al-Zaytūna, al-maʿlim wa-ridjāluhu*, Tunis 1991, and ʿAbd al-ʿAzīz al-Dawlātlī, *al-Zaytūna, ʿashra ḳurūn min al-fann al-miʿmārī al-tūnisī*, Tunis 1996. The mosque was built under the Aghlabids. Inscriptions bearing the date 250/864 testify that the prayer hall, if not the entire mosque, were reconstructed and enlarged, probably reaching their present area. During a second building spell, 380-5/990-5, under the Zīrids, were built the galleries of the court (*mudjannabāt*), the crypt (*dāmūs*) and the dome (*ḳubba*) of the Bāb al-Bahw. The Ḥafṣids completed the construction of the mosque: a *siḳāya* or basin in 648/1250, restoration and decorative works in 676/1277, rebuilding of the wall of the prayer hall in 716/1316, construction of *maḳṣūras* or antechambers in 751/1351 and 822/1419, etc. Significantly, the Ḥafṣids provided the great mosque of al-Zaytūna with a minaret *ca.* 842/1438-9 on the site of the modern minaret. The absence of a minaret, from the mosque's foundation till the mid-9th/15th century, seems to strengthen the hyposthesis of an original fort in which watch towers replaced minarets for making the call to worship.

The actual building of the great mosque is the Aghlabid one restored and enlarged by the Ḥafṣids. The present prayer hall, a rectangle 56 m × 24 m, covering 1344 m², is much less spacious than ʿUḳba b. Nāfiʿ's mosque at al-Ḳayrawān [*q.v.*]. It has fifteen naves, on average three metres wide, except for the centre and extreme ones which are wider (4.50 m). It has some common features with the mosque at al-Ḳayrawān: its T-shape, a dome before the *miḥrāb* and perpendicular naves on the base wall (A. Lézine, *Deux villes d'Ifrīqiya. Études d'archéologie, d'urbanisme et de démographie: Sousse, Tunis*, Paris 1971, 159). The pillars, mainly of marble, came from Roman or Byzantine buildings, probably at Carthage. The gallery-narthex, made up of a single east-west passage, is ornamented at its central part by the famous dome of Bāb al-Bahw, which gives on to a court 1,810 m². The present minaret, rebuilt in 1312/1894, is 40 m high and belongs to the Maghribī-Andalusī style.

Bibliography: See also Aḥmad Fikrī, *Masdjid al-Zaytūna, al-djāmiʿ fī Tūnis*, Cairo 1953; G. Marçais, *L'architecture musulmane d'Occident*, Paris 1954; Lézine, *Architecture de l'Ifriqiya, recherches sur les monuments aghlabides*, Paris 1966; idem, *Note sur les coupoles de la Grande Mosquée al-Zaytuna de Tunis*, in *ROMM*, ii (1966), 95-105; Naïdé Ferchiou, *Rinceaux antiques remployés dans la grande mosquée de Tunis: parenté de leur style avec celui de certains monuments de Carthage*, in *Antiquités africaines*, xvii (1981), 143-63. For the study of the different historical versions, see Ḥ.Ḥ. ʿAbd al-Wahhāb, *Waraḳāt*, Tunis 1965, i, 115-16; Golvin, *op. cit.*, 150-2. For the inscriptions dating the monument, see Slimane-Mostafa Zbiss, *Corpus des inscriptions arabes de Tunisie*, Tunis 1955, 27 ff.

2. Instruction in the mediaeval period.

Can one state, as a historically-attested fact, that the Zaytūna mosque was a centre for scholarship and instruction right from its foundation? Ḥ.Ḥ. ʿAbd al-Wahhāb seems to have asserted this when he said "this is the oldest centre for instruction in the Arab world" (*Waraḳāt*, i, 31). Celebrated *ʿulamāʾ* were probably educated in its precincts, but explicit references to the Zaytūna are late. There were probably some

Dj̲āmiʿ al-Zaytūna.

D̲j̲āmiʿ al-Zaytūna.

courses of instruction in the religious sciences and related spheres, given voluntarily by *ʿulamāʾ*, but nothing like organised teaching (Mahmoud Abdel Moula, *L'université zaytounienne et la société tunisienne*, Tunis 1971, 31).

As an analysis of the biographies of scholars attests, the Zaytūna only succeeded in overtaking in prestige the mosque of ʿUḳba b. Nāfiʿ at al-Ḳayrawān at the beginning of the Ḥafṣid period, when the latter place declined and Tunis flourished as the capital of Ifrīḳiya (Muḥammad Ḥassān, *al-Madīna wa 'l-bādiya fi 'l-ʿahd al-ḥafṣī*, Tunis 1999, ii, 706). Nevertheless, higher education was by no means centralised on Tunis, nor, *a fortiori*, monopolised by right or in practice by the Zaytūna, even at the time of its apogee; the biographies of scholars show a multiplicity of centres of instruction in Ifrīḳiya, above all at al-Ḳayrawān, which was able to support some highly celebrated great masters, and in urban centres which were centres for more modest education. At Tunis, a certain number of well-known *ʿulamāʾ* were often summoned by the ruler to teach in the madrasas (al-Zarkas̲h̲ī, *Taʾrīk̲h̲ al-Dawlatayn, al-muwaḥḥidiyya wa 'l-ḥafṣiyya*, Tunis 1289/1872-3, 41, 58).

The system of teaching, in its organisational principles, methods used and subjects of courses, was similar to that of other Islamic *d̲j̲āmiʿ*s [see MADRASA. I. 6]. Attendance was voluntary and students followed the courses of the monasters of their own choice. The rhythm of teaching was rather relaxed, with weekly holidays on Thursdays and Fridays, periods of leave, the Muslim festivals and, probably, no courses in the summer. There were no examinations, but certificates of *id̲j̲āza* [*q.v.*] attesting the following of a course and authorisation to teach it in turn. We have little information on the teaching at the Zaytūna before the 8th/14th century, when signs of the decline of Arab-Islamic culture began to appear (see IBN K̲H̲ALDŪN, in Vol. III, 828a). Placing foremost the teaching of Islamic knowledge and the juridical-theological disciplines (Ḳurʾānic exegesis, *ḥadīt̲h̲*, *fiḳh*, Arabic grammar, division of inheritances, etc.), the instructor used manuals, résumés, explanations and commentaries on the works of the Golden Age masters (Muḥammad Ḥassān, *op. cit.*, ii, 709). Even so, these methods did not prevent the emergence of great scholars and outstanding personalities such as Muḥammad b. ʿArafa and Ibn K̲h̲aldūn. Increased affluence in the 8th/14th century meant that over 70 circles in mosques could be counted then.

The occupation of La Goletta on 14 July 1534 by the Spanish, their entry into Tunis, their breaking into the Zaytūna and the dispersion of its library, inevitably brought with them great traumas.

Bibliography (in addition to references given): Ibn K̲h̲aldūn, *Muḳaddima*; Brunschvig, *Ḥafṣides*; Muḥammad al-Bād̲j̲ī Ibn Māmī, *Madāris madīnat Tunis min al-ʿahd al-ḥafṣi ilā 'l-ʿahd al-murādī*, diss. in Études arabes, Fac. of Letters and Human Sciences of Tunis 1981, 2 vols., unpubl.

3. Instruction in the modern and contemporary periods.

A widespread judgement is that teaching declined in the period of the transition of power from the Ḥafṣids to the Ottomans. This crisis, however, seems to have been rapidly surmounted, with teaching at the Zaytūna speedily recovering its audience. Introducing new norms for evaluating the *ʿulamāʾ*, sc. *al-riwāya* (transmission of knowledge) and *al-dirāya* (discernment), Ibn Abī Dīnār [*q.v.*] thought that all his contemporaries, some of whom had acquired great fame, were limited to *riwāya*, whilst Muḥammad Tād̲j̲ al-ʿĀrifīn al-Bikrī and his son Abū Bakr were at a much higher level through their mastery of both *riwāya* and *dirāya* (*al-Muʾnis fī ak̲h̲bār Ifrīḳiya wa-Tūnis*, Tunis 1387/1967-8, 314-19). The editing of the *D̲h̲ayl* of Ḥusayn K̲h̲od̲j̲a now allows a better knowledge of the disciplines taught and the manuals used, these being essentially late commentaries, *ḥās̲h̲iya*s and glosses (*D̲h̲ayl bas̲h̲āʾir al-īmān bi-futūḥāt āl ʿUt̲h̲mān*, Tunis 1975, 197-8, 201). Certain scholars, such as Muḥammad al-Ḥad̲j̲d̲j̲ī (d. 1109/1696-7) became famed for editing a large number of abridgements.

In the 18th century, the Zaytūna benefited by a renewed wave of interest. Until then financially based essentially upon its *waḳf*s, the financing of courses was assisted by the Ḥusaynid Beys who used to pay salaries for the teachers out of the yield of the capitation tax (see for the measures taken by ʿAlī b. Ḥusayn Bey in 1183/1769-70, Ḥammūda b. ʿAbd al-ʿAzīz, *al-Kitāb al-bas̲h̲ī*, Tunis 1970, 204, 296). However, the Zaytūna continued to use the same methods of instruction, and one may further note that there was a serious regression in the teaching of the profane sciences.

In defining the evolution of teaching during the 19th century, a severe verdict must be pronounced, and Tunisian historians have often spoken of "a schlerotic system of instruction" (e.g. Ahmed Abdesselem, *Les historiens tunisiens des XVIIe, XVIIIe et XIXe siècles, essai d'histoire culturelle*, Tunis 1973, 81) and of a fixed, crabbed system of knowledge. Bonaparte's Egyptian expedition in Egypt (1798-1801) and the occupation of Algiers in 1830 revealed a European superiority, of which the military aspect was only a beginning. But the "establishment" of the Zaytūna opted for passive resistance to change, avoiding all idea of reform and upgrading. It was, however, from graduates of the Zaytūna that the reforming Tunisian élite was recruited, such as Maḥmūd Ḳābādū (1812-71), Aḥmad Ibn Abī Ḍiyāf (1804-74 [*q.v.*]), Bayram V (1840-99), etc., strengthened by the adherence to their ideas of the minister K̲h̲ayr al-Dīn (1822-90 [*q.v.*]). The latter's master work, *Aḳwam al-masālik fī maʿrifat aḥwāl al-mamālik*, published in 1867, affirmed the backwardness of the Muslim lands and called for an enlargement of the spheres of the sciences and knowledge as a *sine qua non* for the development of civilisation (89, 93, 122-8). Reform of the Zaytūna system of teaching became the order of the day from now onwards. As a supreme act of defiance against the *ʿulamāʾ*, Ibn Abī Ḍiyāf announced that "*id̲j̲tihād* had continued uninterruptedly" (Ṭayyib al-ʿAnnābī, *Wat̲h̲āʾiḳ tūnisiyya*, in *Ḥawliyyāt al-D̲j̲āmiʿa al-Tūnisiyya* [1967], no. 4, 153-9).

Minded to abolish a fact of discrimination, on 24 February 1840 Aḥmad Bey gave to the Mālikī *ʿulamāʾ* the same treatment as their Ḥanafī colleagues. In practice, the Mālikī Zaytūna had had to integrate Ḥanafī teaching with their own since the establishment of the Ottomans, who favoured the scholars of that school. On 27 Ramaḍān 1258/1 December 1842 Aḥmad Bey reformed the organisation of the Zaytūna's functioning. Each *mudarris* had to give two courses a day in the different disciplines. Periods of holiday were henceforth fixed: two days per week, the two festivals of the *ʿĪd*s and the month of Ramaḍān. The institution was placed under the control of *ḳāḍī*s of the two law schools and of the two *s̲h̲ayk̲h̲ al-islām*s. Within the framework of this reform, the Bey nominated 30 *mudarrisūn*, following the pattern of parity between the two schools established by him and reserved for financing this the revenues of the *bayt al-māl* (Aḥmad Ibn Abī Ḍiyāf, *Itḥāf*, iv, 35, 65-7). During his time as

Grand Vizier (1873-7), Khayr al-Dīn had to take in hand, in parallel with the creation of the modern al-Ṣādiḳī college [see AL-ṢĀDIḲIYYA], the reform of teaching at the Zaytūna. His *manshūr* or circular of 28 Dhu 'l-Ḳa'da 1292/26 December 1875, completed a month later, contained proposals for reorganising teaching at the Zaytūna, but an examination of the material (dominated by teaching of the religious sciences) and of the list of books used for teaching purposes shows that a certain sluggishness stifled the will to reform. A far-reaching innovation was that the internal reform envisaged instituting an academic handbook and regulated such topics as application to work and discipline (Mongi Smida, *Khereddine, ministre réformateur*, Tunis 1970, 320-7).

After the establishment of the French Protectorate (1881), the Zaytūna inevitably became a centre of dispute. Probably influenced by the development of modern education, its students organised to demand reform of teaching methods and programmes. The history of the Zaytūna, from 1910 to 1952, was marked by cycles of student unrest (1910-12, 1920, 1928-30, 1935-7, 1947-50) and desires for reform, studied by special commissions for this, but the results were below expectation. But, apart from the threefold system of primary (*ahliyya*), secondary (*taḥṣīl*) and higher education (*'ālimiyya*), the commissions were unable to envisage reforms or to introduce the teaching of the sciences (see Mukhtār al-'Ayyāshī, *al-Bī'a al-zaytūniyya 1910-1945*, Tunis 1990, 21-82, 143-75). Remarkably, this traditional system of education was to see developing within its midst, as a reaction, an avant-garde cultural movement, seen in the great poet Abu 'l-Ḳāsim al-Shābbī (1909-40 [*q.v.*]) and the reformer Ṭāhir al-Ḥaddād, who shook the Zaytūna establishment by publishing at Tunis in 1930 a book-manifesto advocating the freedom of women and abolition of polygamy, *Imra'atunā fi 'l-sharī'a wa 'l-mudjtama'*. The growing number of students at the Zaytūna (600 in 1881, 9,818 in 1927 and almost 20,000 in 1956), in the two annexes of Tunis and the sections created in the provinces (eight of these from 1949), showed the development of its recruitment.

After independence, primary and secondary education were undertaken by modern schools and colleges for public instruction. The Zaytūna was made into a faculty and then into a university specialising in the religious sciences and installed in modern premises; its rich library was integrated within the National Libraries of Tunis.

Bibliography (in addition to references given in the article): Muḥammad b. Makhlūf, *Shadjarat al-nūr al-zakiyya fī ṭabaḳāt al-mālikiyya*, Cairo 1349/1930-1 and suppl. 1350/1931-2; Muḥammad b. 'Uthmān al-Ḥashā'ishī, *T. Djāmi' al-Zaytūna*, Tunis 1974; Muḥammad b. 'Uthmān al-Sanūsī, *Musāmarāt al-ẓarīf bi-ḥusn al-ta'līf*, Tunis 1983; Muḥammad b. Khūdja, *T. Ma'ālim al-tawḥīd fi 'l-ḳadīm wa 'l-djadīd*, Beirut 1985; Mhamed Ferid Ghazi, *Le milieu zitounien de 1920 à 1933 et la formation de Abū al-Ḳāsim al-Shābbī*, in *CT*, 1959/4, 437-74.

On the Zaytūna library, see Muḥammad b. Khūdja, in *al-Madjalla al-Zaytūniyya*, i/1 (Radjab 1355/September 1936), 71-6, i/3 (Ramaḍān 1355/November 1936), 136-9; idem, *T. Ma'ālim al-tawḥīd*, 97-9; Ḥashā'ishī, *op. cit.*, 53-61.

(KHALIFA CHATER)

AL-**ZAYYĀNĪ**, ABU 'L-ḲĀSIM B. AḤMAD b. 'Alī b. Ibrāhīm, Moroccan statesman and historian of the 18th century.

Al-Zayyānī, a member of the great Berber tribe of the Zayyān in central Morocco, was born in Fās in 1147/1734-5. He received his education in this city. At the age of 23, he accompanied his parents on the Pilgrimage to Mecca and after an exciting journey, coming as well as going, which lasted over two years, he returned to Fās, where he obtained a position as secretary to the *makhzan* [*q.v.*] of sultan Muḥammad III b. 'Abd Allāh. His ability, his knowledge of Berber dialects and the course of events rapidly brought him to the fore; having played an active part in the suppression of a rising against the tribe of the Ayt Amālū, he gained the confidence of his ruler and was entrusted with negotiations with the various un-subdued Berber elements of the empire. He now travelled up and down Morocco incessantly and made several journeys to distant Tāfīlālt. In 1200/1786 al-Zayyānī was charged by the sultan with a mission to the Ottoman ruler 'Abd al-Ḥamīd I [*q.v.*]. He reached the Ottoman capital after many vicissitudes, and spent over three months there, which enabled him to write on his return a very full description of it. On his return, after carrying out several confidential missions, he was appointed governor of Sidjilmāsa [*q.v.*], where he remained till the death of Muḥammad III b. 'Abd Allāh in 1204/1790.

The sultan's successor, his son Yazīd, put an end to the political career of al-Zayyānī, whom he hated. It was only by a miracle that the latter escaped death when Yazīd in 1206/1792 himself succumbed to a wound received in a fight against the pretender Hishām. Al-Zayyānī, at the time a prisoner in Rabāṭ, was set free and immediately took an active part in the proclamation at Meknès of another son of Muḥammad b. 'Abd Allāh as sultan, Mawlāy Sulaymān (Slīmān). The latter gave him the office of governor (*'āmil*) of the district of the town of Udjda [see WADJDA], but on taking up his post, al-Zayyānī was attacked and defeated by the people he had been sent to govern. This misfortune gave him a distaste for public life, and he retired to Tlemcen, where he spent 18 months in studious seclusion, which only ended when he decided to undertake once again the journey to Istanbul, this time in a private capacity and to perform the pilgrimage for a second time. On his return in 1210/9175-6), he was summoned by Mawlāy Sulaymān and returned to Fās. In spite of his great age, he was now employed on a number of important missions and received the title of *dhu 'l-wizāratayn*, as the head of the sovereign's *makhzan*. He remained in office for several years, then was dismissed and died at Fās in 1249/1833 at the age of 99. He was buried in the *zāwiya* of the Ṣūfī brotherhood of the Nāṣiriyya in the Siyādj quarter.

Famous in Morocco as a statesman, al-Zayyānī was no less celebrated as a writer. In the course of his stirring life, he found time to write some fifteen books, almost all on history and geography. The first in date of these works was a general history of Islam entitled *al-Turdjumān al-mughrib 'an duwal al-Mashriḳ wa 'l-Maghrib*, in which he focussed on the Sharīfian dynasties of Morocco and which he later continued, keeping pace with events down to the year 1228/1813. The part of the *Turdjumān* relating to the 'Alids of Morocco was published and translated into French in 1886 by O. Houdas as *Le Maroc de 1631 à 1812* (*PELOV*, 2nd ser., vol. xviii). It is a narrative, in parts a résumé, of events in Morocco from the foundation of the 'Alid dynasty to the early years of the 19th century. A more detailed version of this part of the *Turdjumān*, in which he dealt specially with events in which he had himself played a part, or of which he had been a witness, was later prepared by al-Zayyānī, and he gave it two different titles: *al-Bustān al-ẓarīf fī dawlat awlād Mawlāya ʿAlī al-S̲h̲arīf*, and *al-Rawḍa al-sulaymāniyya fī d̲h̲ikr mulūk al-dawla al-ismāʿīliyya*. Another important work of his was a very full account of his various journeys, to which he added all kinds of digressions, literary, historical and biographical; he called it *al-Turd̲j̲umāna al-kubrā allatī d̲j̲amaʿat ak̲h̲bār mudun al-ʿālam barr*^{an} *wa-baḥrā*. This book, which is both *riḥla* and *fahrasa*, is also a very curious geographical treatise, with maps (e.g. a map of the seas, reproduced in Lévi-Provençal, *Historiens des Chorfa*, between pp. 188 and 189). All these works of al-Zayyānī are to be found in manuscript in Morocco in various private libraries. A complete list is given in *ibid.*, 167-8.

Al-Zayyānī's work is the principal source we possess, with the more recent *K. al-Istiḳṣā* of al-Nāṣirī al-Salāwī [see AḤMAD AL-NĀṢIRĪ AL-SALĀWĪ], for the history of the ʿAlid dynasty of Morocco. It is full of valuable details and deserves serious study. It gives throughout an impression of accuracy and precision in historical as well as topographical matters. Information is given about innovations and social reforms and about the monumental history of the towns of Morocco. Al-Zayyānī also shows a remarkable acquaintance with events in Europe. Finally, all that he tells us about what he saw on his journeys to Istanbul is worth publishing in full.

Bibliography: al-Nāṣirī al-Salāwī, *K. al-Istiḳṣā*, Cairo 1312/1894, iv, 33, 108-9, 116-18, 132; Kattānī, *Salwat al-anfās*, Fās 1313/1895, i, 263; O. Houdas, introd. to *Maroc de 1631 à 1812*, Paris 1886; Budgett Meakin, *The Moorish empire*, London 1899, 518; G. Salmon, *Un voyageur marocain à la fin du XVIII*^{ème} *siècle, la Rihla d'az-Zyâny*, in *AM*, ii, Paris 1905, 330-40; A. Graulle, *Le Boustan adh-dharif d'Az-Ziyânî*, in *RMM*, xxiv, 311-17; Coufourier, *Une description géographique du Maroc d'az-Zyâny*, in *AM*, vi, Paris 1906, 436-56, cf. also *ibid.*, 457-60; Brockelmann, *GAL*, S II, 878-80; Huart, *Littérature arabe*, 423; E. Lévi-Provençal, *Les historiens des Chorfa. Essai sur la littérature historique et biographique au Maroc du XVI*^{ème} *au XX*^{ème} *siècle*, Paris 1922, 142-99.

(E. LÉVI-PROVENÇAL)

ZAYYĀNIDS [see ʿABD AL-WĀDIDS].

ZĀZĀ, an ethnonym designating the speakers of Zāzākī, an Iranian language spoken in southeastern Anatolia, to the northwest of the Kurdish-speaking regions. Its centre of dissemination is the triangle between the towns of Siverek, Erzincan and Varto. There are no reliable statistics about its number of speakers; in southeastern Anatolia they may number between 1.5 and 2 millions. About the same number of Zāzā have emigrated to the urban centres of Western Anatolia, and to Western Europe, during the last 40 years. These numbers include all "ethnic" Zāzā, however, a large number of whom may have become assimilated to Turkish or Kurdish in the meantime, with no longer an active command of their mother tongue.

The people. In religion, all Zāzā are Muslims, but in their home country they are divided into one northern and one southern group (of about the same size), the first of which follows the ʿAlawī S̲h̲īʿī religious confession, and the second which follows one of the Sunnī *mad̲h̲āhib* (mostly the S̲h̲āfiʿī one). Their common religious confession connects the Sunnī Zāzā closely with the neighbouring (to the southeast) Sunnī Kurds. Therefore, the question whether all the Zāzā constitute one people has to be separated from the question (to be answered in the affirmative) whether Zāzākī is a language in its own right. As very little was known about the Zāzā and their language up to the early 1980s, it was always taken for granted that they are Kurds speaking a dialect of Kurdish. Only recently has Zāzākī been increasingly written (starting in the European diaspora), and parallel to this a growing number of Zāzā (mainly ʿAlawīs) have become aware of their own language, culture, and distinct identity. But to this day, many Zāzā still feel that their common cultural and political ties to the Kurds weigh more heavily and do not insist on a separate Zāzā ethnic identity.

The name "Zāzā" seems to have been a pejorative label originally, possibly suggesting incomprehensible speech (like English "bla bla"). Although as such it was not the self-denomination of the majority of Zāzā (many Sunnī Zāzā call their language *Dimlī*, some ʿAlawī Zāzā call it *Kirmānd̲j̲kī* or simply *zōnē mā* "our language"), it seems to have gained the widest acceptance today. The name *Dimlī* can be understood as pointing to the geographical origins of the Zāzā, if it is to be connected to the historical region of Daylam south to the Caspian Sea (there are no other sources relative to the Zāzā's earlier history).

The language. Zāzākī was not written or studied before the mid-19th century. It is a NW Iranian language; other NW Iranian languages that are most closely related to it include Gūrānī (spoken in southern Kurdistan) and the Iranian Ād̲h̲arī dialects (e.g. Harzandī). Although Zāzākī has been heavily influenced by neighbouring (Kurmānd̲j̲ī) Kurdish for a long time (especially in lexicon, phraseology and syntax), it is genealogically not a very close relative of Kurdish (as compared to Gūrānī and Ād̲h̲arī). Zāzākī has undergone most of the sound changes that characterise NW Iranian, e.g. IE (Indo-European) **k̑/*g̑* > Zāz. *s/z*, $*g(^{u})(h)^{pal}$ > *-ǰ-*, **tr* > *(hī)r*, **d(h)w* > *b*, **rd/*rz* > *r̄/rz*, **sw* > *w* (e.g. Zāz. *zān-*, *ǰinī*, *hīre*, *ber*, *ser̄i*, *wen-* "to know, woman, three, door, year, to eat"; Kurdish has undergone only the first two of these, cf. *zān-*, *žin*, but shows SW development in: *sē*, *der*, *sāl*, *xō*).

Zāzākī noun morphology shows a system of two cases (rectus and obliquus), two numbers (sg., pl.), and two grammatical genders (m., f.). In addition, it can distinguish definiteness and animacy. In some dialects, a suffix *-(e)r* originating from the IE relationship suffix *-tér-* has been generalised as a feminine oblique ending. Attributive adjectives and nouns in genitive relation that qualify a (head) noun follow it immediately and are connected to it with an enclitic particle, the *iḍāfa*. Together with the inflectional endings that can precede them, the forms of the *iḍāfa* constitute a system of four cases, where a particle *-d-* (apparently borrowed from NW Semitic) is an important oblique marker (e.g. *lāžē mi* "my son", but *lāždē mi* "[to, of, etc.] my son").

The Zāzākī verbs distinguish three persons and two numbers, and, in the 2nd/3rd persons sg. of indicative verbs, also grammatical gender. The verbal system includes the following tenses: present (formed with the suffix *-(e)n*, not as in Persian and Kurdish with a prefix), analytical future, preterite, imperfect, perfect I/II and pluperfect. The present is formed from the present stem, and all past tenses from the preterite stem. The present subjunctive is formed from a third stem, the subjunctive one (from which can also be derived, with the suffix *-(i)y-*, passive forms).

Syntactically, Zāzākī is a SOV language and shows morphological split ergativity (only with verbal forms derived from the past stem). In noun phrases (see above) the modifier always follows the head; there is a complex system of adpositions in which postpositions predominate, but in which there are also various pre- and circumpositions.

Bibliography: O. Mann, *Mundarten der Zâzâ, hauptsächlich aus Siwerek und Kor. (Kurdisch-Persische Forschungen, Abt. III, Bd. IV)*, ed. K. Hadank, Berlin 1932; T.L. Todd, *A Grammar of Dimilī (also known as Zaza)*, Ann Arbor (UMI) 1985; Malmisanij, *Zazaca-türkçe sözlük/Ferhengê dımılki-tırki*, Uppsala 1987; P.A. Andrews, *Ethnic groups in the Republic of Turkey*, Wiesbaden 1989, index; L. Paul, *Zazaki. Grammatik und Versuch einer Dialektologie*, Wiesbaden 1998; idem, *Zazaki—Dialekt, Sprache, Nation?* in B. Köhler (ed.), *Religion und Wahrheit. Religionsgeschichtliche Studien. Festschrift für Gernot Wießner zum 65. Geburtstag*, Wiesbaden 1998, 385-99; idem, *The position of Zazaki among West Iranian Languages*, in N. Sims-Williams (ed.), *Procs. of the 3rd European Conference of Iranian Studies (held in Cambridge, 11th to 15th September 1995). Part I, Old and Middle Iranian Studies*, Wiesbaden 1998, 163-76; Zülfü Selcan, *Grammatik der Zaza-Sprache, Nord-Dialekt*, Berlin 1998. (L. Paul)

ZEKĀʾĪ DEDE (1824-97), one of the most important 19th-century Turkish composers, often considered the last great master of the classical style. Born at Istanbul in Eyyūb, he became an expert calligrapher under his father's guidance, while his musical talent brought him to the attention of Ḥammāmī-zāde Ismāʿīl Dede, who accepted him as a pupil. In 1845 he entered the service of Muṣṭafā Fāḍil Pas͟ha [*q.v.*], and spent the greater part of the following 13 years with him in Cairo, returning definitively to Istanbul in 1858, when Muṣṭafā Fāḍil was appointed vizier.

Unfortunately, very little is known about his musical contacts and activities in Egypt, although he did compose a number of hymns to Arabic texts (*s͟hug͟hl*). In 1864 he entered the Mewlewī [see MAWLAWIYYA] order, and in 1884 became *ḳudümzenbas͟hi̊* at the Bahāriyye *mewlewī-k͟hāne*. He composed five vocal cycles (*āyīn*) for the Mewlewī ceremony, and a large number of hymns (*ilāhī*) and pieces in other religious genres, but his extensive output was by no means confined to these: it also included songs in the large-scale *kār* and *beste* forms as well as lighter *s͟harḳ*is [*q.v.*]. In addition he was an active and successful teacher who maintained traditional methods of oral tuition and transmission, thereby helping to ensure the survival of the repertoire he himself had been taught. Among his many pupils were a number of major composers and scholars, including Raʾūf Yektā Bey, Ṣubḥī Ezgi, and his own son Aḥmed Irsoy, thanks to whose efforts much (although by no means all) of his work has been preserved.

Bibliography: Raʾūf Yektā Bey, *K͟hod͟ja Zekāʾī Dede Efendi* (*Esātīd͟h-i elḥān*, i), Istanbul 1318/1902; *Türk musikisi klasiklerinden. Mevlevi ayinleri*, Istanbul 1934-9; *ibid.*, *Hâfız Mehmed Zekâi Dede Efendi külliyatı*, 3 vols. Istanbul 1940-3; Y. Öztuna, *Türk musikisi ansiklopedisi*, ii/2, Istanbul 1976; C. Behar, *Aşk olmayınca meşk olmaz*, Istanbul 1998. (O. Wright)

ZENOBIA [see AL-ZABBĀʾ].

ZENTA (Serbian Senta), a town on the right bank of the Tisza in the ancient Hungarian county of Bács-Bodrog, today in northern Serbia. A decisive battle was fought in its vicinity on 24 Ṣafar 1109/11 September 1697 between the forces of Sultan Muṣṭafā II [*q.v.*] and Prince Eugene of Savoy.

Ottoman rule in Hungary collapsed relatively rapidly after Buda was recaptured in 1686. Resistance to the allied Christian armies was sparse and took place along the Drava-Danube line only. Following a serious defeat at Szalánkemén (Stari Slankamen) in 1102/1691, where the Grand Vizier Köprülü Muṣṭafā [*q.v.*] also lost his life, and an abortive attempt to regain Waradīn [*q.v.*] in 1694, the next great Ottoman offensive started in 1697. This campaign, unprecedented since the siege of Eger [*q.v.*] and the battle of Mezőkeresztes [*q.v.*] in 1596, was led by the sultan in person. A successful assault on Titel encouraged the Ottomans to cross the Tisza. First, they simulated a march against Waradīn, but were in reality intent on reconquering Szeged, the key fortress blocking their route along the Maros to Transylvania, and they soon turned northwards. Misled by this stratagem, the allied troops left their post near Zenta and arrived at the Danube on 6 September. They had to return by a forced march to their original place, where a circumvallation was being constructed by the Turks. The fight between the two armies, numbering some 50-70,000 warriors on both sides (the Ottomans slightly outnumbering their enemy), started shortly before nightfall and quickly ended in a great Christian triumph. The Ottomans lost the Grand Vizier Elmās Muṣṭafā, the *ag͟ha* of the Janissaries, and several *sand͟jaḳ-begis*, as well as some 20,000 warriors.

The defeat at Zenta led to the Peace of Ḳarlofča [*q.v.*] (Karlowitz) in 1699, which put an end to a long period of wars and to Ottoman rule in most of the former Hungarian territories.

Bibliography: *Feldzüge des Prinzen Eugen von Savoyen*, Nach den Feld-Acten und anderen authentischen Quellen hrsg. von der Abtheilung für Kriegsgeschichte des k. k. Kriegs-Archivs, Serie 1, Band ii, *Feldzüge gegen die Türken 1697-1698 und der Karlowitzer Friede 1699*, ed. M. Edlen von Angeli, Vienna 1876; Gy. Dudás, *A zentai csata* ("The battle of Zenta"), Szeged 1886; L. Szita and G. Seewann, *A legnagyobb győzelem* ("The greatest victory"), Pécs-Szigetvár 1997 (introd. to and collection of European documents). (G. Dávid)

ZERBADIS, Zerbadees, a term, of unknown origin, denoting a Muslim community in Burma [*q.v.*].

It was formerly used in a slighting or even contemptuous way to describe the offspring of Indian Muslim males and Burmese females—the latter usually being converts to Islam. Burma has always been and remains an overwhelming Buddhist country, and the Muslim minority was never more than 4% of the total population at any time. The latest complete figures are from the 1931 census and give a total of just under six millions. This includes (a) the Arakan [*q.v.*] Muslims, (b) Indian immigrant Muslims from British India, and (c) the Zerbadis, also known as "Burmese (or Burma) Muslims". The Zerbadis have been estimated as comprising just about a half of the total Muslim community. The 1931 census was the last complete count done (the returns for 1941 were destroyed in the Second World War) though partial returns for 1953 and 1954 suggest a Muslim presence of about the same percentage. However, as against this it should be remembered that many Indian Muslims left India in 1962-4 when severe restrictions were placed on those who were not "Burmese citizens". There are no data from 1964, when the imposition of military rule effectively closed down the institutions of civil society. The Zerbadis are culturally Burmese in all things except religion, but this was enough for the rather chauvinist Burmese to lump them together with the Indian immigrant Muslims. Like the latter, they were targets in the severe anti-Muslim riots of 1938, though they had little in common with the Indian Muslims. But the fact of being Muslims militates against a full acceptance, despite the fact that they usually attend Burmese schools, speak Burmese and generally know no other language, except that some can recite by rote parts of the Ḳur'ān. The Zerbadi insistence on Burmese language was a major issue of contention between them and the Indian Muslims, who insisted on Arabic and, for the majority, Urdu. The result was an increasingly severe split between the communities, with the Zerbadis emphasising their identity as Burmese and having also their own separate associations. In politics, the Zerbadis were supporters of the Burmese National Movement, whilst the Indian Muslims looked towards India and the Muslim League. The former envisage a national integration for themselves in independent Burma, and object to pan-Islamism. For the majority Burmese population, this is not really enough; for them, one is only truly Burmese if one is Buddhist. Adherence to a "foreign" religion diminishes one's national identity.

This is nowhere more clearly illustrated then in matters of law. A prevalent question was to what extent the Burmese "Buddhist" (i.e. customary) law applied to Zerbadi matters? The issue arose because the female party to a marriage was ethnically Burmese and was related to Burmese Buddhists, as were her children. In certain matters, especially inheritance and wills, the rules of Burmese Buddhist law were more advantageous to the wife and female children than were those of the Sharīʿa. They should, therefore, apply on the twin grounds of ethnicity and kinship. The question was debated for the half century from the 1890s to the 1950s, the argument being that Burmese Buddhist law was a "customary law" and thus would be an exception to the rule that Islamic law applied in the affairs of Muslims. The result turned on the provisions of the Burma Laws Act of 1898 (section 13), which provided that each religious and racial group in British Burma had its own law: Burmese Buddhist law for Burmese, (Anglo-)Hindu law for Hindus, and (Anglo-)Muhammadan law for Muslims. The decisions given in the courts were consistent: Burmese Buddhist law could not apply as a customary exception. Islamic law had a clear and exclusive jurisdiction in Muslim matters. On a strictly technical reading of the legislation, this is an acceptable result. However, it is difficult not to suppose that judicial policy also played a part, i.e. the courts were most reluctant to create internal conflict by mingling the two different laws. Needless to say, this approach satisfied nobody, and in 1939 (in the wake of the 1938 riots) Buddhist women were protected by special legislation. But what was a "Buddhist" woman when married to a Muslim? This raises the vexed questions of conversion and apostasy which troubled the courts in British Burma from the 1860s onwards and were, of course, centred on the Zerbadis. It appears that conversion was for the purposes of marriage only, and quite often, conversion was merely "simulated". In such cases, "apostasy" was not allowed to end a marriage as the classical Sharīʿa would direct. Religion was not permitted to be used in such a way, and a conversion, once made, was binding in respect of divorce and succession.

The fate of the Zerbadis in post-1964 Burma is not clear. Assimilation to the Buddhist majority must be a possibility, given the sometimes minimal adherence to the religion of Islam.

The history of the Zerbadis is instructive as illustrating yet again the impossibility of maintaining a law that has no cultural roots in a foreign state. It can never be more than artificial and, given the Burmese identity of the Zerbadis and their wish to be identified with the majority Burmese, the future for Islam would seem problematical. But this may perhaps be too pessimistic a view.

Bibliography: Khin Khin U, *Marriage in the Burmese Muslim community*, in *Jnal. of the Burma Research Society*, xxxvi (1954), 25-33; N.R. Chakravarti, *The Indian minority in Burma*, London 1971; M. Yegar, *The Muslims of Burma*, Wiesbaden 1972; M.B. Hooker, *Islamic law in South East Asia*, Kuala Lumpur 1984.
(M.B. Hooker)

ZEYBEK, a generic name for the Turkish mountaineers in Western Anatolia, especially in the regions of Izmir, Aydın, and Manisa.

Various etymologies have been proposed for Zeybek, none completely satisfactory. Thus M.R. Gazimihal claimed that it derived from a place name among the Ḳirghiz in Central Asia (*Zeybek sözü*, in *Fikir*, no. 2 [1947], 20-3); H.H. Bayındır asserted that it came from *sağbek*, meaning a wise, trustworthy man (*Tarihte zeğbeklik ve musiki*, Aydın 1964, 17); and S. Türkoğlu suggested that it originated from either *su/sü bek*, meaning a military leader, or *zeyl-i beğ* (i.e. *dheyl-i beg*) meaning a kind of assistant to a *beg* (*Tarih içinde Zeybek kıyafeti*, in *III. Milletlerarası Türk folklor kongresi bildirileri*, Ankara 1987, v, 418).

The origin of the Zeybek as fiercely independent, swashbuckling mountaineers is unclear. Their roots may go back to the settlement of Türkmen or Yürüks [*q.vv.*] in Western Anatolia in the 13th century (Mehmet Eröz, ch. 7, *Zeybeklik ve Zeybekler*, in his *Millî kültürümüz ve meselelerimiz*, Istanbul 1983, 85-6), but they were not, as F. Babinger states (*EI*[1], art. *Zeibek*), a tribe. On the basis of close similarities in costume, it has been proposed that the Zeybek were the successors of the Levends (İ.H. Uzunçarşılı, *İA*, art. *Levend*), freebooters who overran parts of Western Anatolia between the 16th and 18th centuries (İ. Özboyacı, *Ege'de Zeybek giyimi ve kışlık olarak kullanılan "aba"*, in *III. Milletlerarası Türk folklor kongresi bildirileri*, v, 292).

The Zeybek do not appear in official Ottoman documents until the first half of the 19th century (Özboyacı, *ibid.*, 298). We do not know when they first appeared in folklore, but it was no doubt somewhat earlier. Ewliyā Čelebi (d. *ca.* 1684/1095) does not mention them except perhaps indirectly (cf. M.R. Gazimihal, *Sarı Zeybek*, in *Fikirler*, no. 6 [1947], 24). The first European traveller to describe the Zeybek was the Hon. George Keppel (*Narrative of a journey across the Balcan . . .*, London 1831, esp. i, 124-26, 339), followed by F.V.J. Arundell (*Discoveries in Asia Minor*, London 1834, ii, 212-14; for additional references to travellers' accounts, see W. Heffening, *Türkische Volkslieder*, in *Isl.*, xiii [1923], 251 n. 1).

The chiefs of the Zeybek communities were called *efe* and their assistants were called *kızan*. The *efe*'s word was law, even the decision whether or not a young man should marry or abduct a girl (on their character traits, see E.B. Şapolyo, *Efe, Zeybek, kızan . . . yaşayışları ve âdetleri*, in *Türk yurdu*, i [1954], 43-55, with early photographs).

The Zeybek apparently constituted a kind of militia for local notables at the end of the 18th century and beginning of the 19th century. According to Keppel (*op. cit.*, ii, 124), the Zeybek were a band of mercenary mountaineers who were employed as body guards to the pashas. They also formed a kind of guard in the coffee-houses and could levy a tax on travellers for their protection. Throughout the 19th century, they participated as volunteer units in the Ottoman Army (T. Baykara, *Zeybekler* [*Zeybek elbisesi giyme yasağı*], in *Belgelerle Türk tarihi dergisi*, no. 22 [July 1969], 59). They joined the Turkish Nationalists in 1920-2.

Today the term Zeybek applies not so much to the mountaineers of Western Anatolia but to their folk costume and dance (including music and song). The distinctive male dress of the Zeybek, which was noted by 19th-century travellers (the earliest illustration being the frontispiece in Keppel, i) and raised the ire of the Ottoman authorities, was as follows: on the head, a red fez around which was wrapped a headkerchief printed with flowers and with needle embroidered flowers along the edge; on the back, a striped quilted jacket with stiff collar, over it a double-breasted waistcoat of violet broadcloth embroidered with black braids, over it another waist coat called a *cepken* or *sallama* with eyehooks on the sleeves; from the waistcoats to the knees, baggy trousers (*şalvars*) made out of two metres of silk cloth and with black braids embroidered around the leg openings and on the borders of the pockets; at the waist, between the groin and the chest, a knitted sash over which was wound a shawl, over which was a weapons' belt made of black or red leather and attached with three rows of straps, and covering the torso up to the breasts; tucked into the front of the weapons' belt was a handkerchief embroidered with silver; on the feet, wool socks, light shoes called *yemeni* and gaiters from ankle to knee (M. Özbek, *İA* art. *Zeybek*).

In the 19th century, various Ottoman officials regarded the Zeybek's short baggy trousers in particular as offensive to the Muslim sense of propriety. A government attempt to forbid their dress in 1838 resulted in an uprising that could only be suppressed with much loss of life. Nevertheless, the Zeybek continued to wear their traditional costume. Attempts to suppress it in 1894 and 1905 were equally ineffective (see Baykara, *op. cit.*, 59-61).

As for the Zeybek dances, they are no longer confined to Western Anatolia. Indeed, variations on them have spread throughout much of Central Anatolia and even to the Western Black Sea region. Zeybek dances can be performed by one or more persons, men, women, or men and women together. The archetypical Zeybek dance, expressing bravery and heroism, is performed by one or two men, but always in solo character. This dance is preceded by a slow introductory part in which the dancer takes leisurely steps. This is done with the arms at the side, then at shoulder level, and finally outstretched with elbows as high as the shoulders and fingers snapping. Meanwhile, the dancer keeps one leg in half-bent position between hops, and from time to time drops to his knees (M. And, *Turkish dancing*, Ankara 1976, 159, illustrations in pl. 81). The main centres of Zeybek dances are still in the west: Izmir, Balıkesir, Muğla, Aydın and Denizli.

Bibliography: For additional references to those in the text, see Özbek, *İA* art. *Zeybek*, in which the emphasis is on dress and dance; A. Haydar Avcı, *Zeybeklik ve Zeybekler*, Hückelhoven (Germany) 2001.

(G. Leiser)

ZHŌB, a river of what is now the northeasternmost part of Pakistani Balūčistān, and also an administrative District of that province, with its centre in the town of Zhōb (the former Fort Sandeman, at lat. 31° 25' N., long. 69° 20' E.). In British Indian times, Zhōb was an administrative division of British Baluchistan. The river rises in the northern end of the Sulaiman range and flows in a southwesterly direction into the Gomal river. The present District comprised in 1981 27,129 km^2, with a recorded population of 361,647. The region is important for its position to the southwest of the Gomal Pass [see gūmāl, in Suppl.], one of the age-old conduits for peoples, commodities and ideas passing between highland Afghānistān and the Indus valley.

Ethnically, Pashtūns are most numerous in Zhōb, with the Kākaṙ [*q.v.* in Suppl.] as the main permanent residents of the Zhōb river valley. In the continuum of Pashto pronunciation, these Zhōb Pashtūn speakers fall within the middle of the conventional (but rather too hard-and-fast) division between speakers of "hard" and "soft" varieties of the language [see afghān. (ii)]. Sulaymān Khēl [*q.v.* in Suppl.] of the Ghalzay Pashtūns predominate among the more transient and commercially active Afghān nomads (variously called *kūčīs*, *lōhānīs* and *pōwindas*).

Little is known of the region's early history. Pashtūn genealogies and histories from the Mughal period give the Sulaiman range in eastern Zhōb as the destination of migrations from Ghūr [*q.v.*] by the immediate descendants of Ḳays ʿAbd al-Rashīd, progenitor of all the Pashtūns. On a firmer historical basis, Pashtūn tribal and Hindu merchant elements were to be found there by Mughal times, along with a development of agriculture by *kārīz* irrigation [see ḳanāt] and "tribal transit trade" via the frontier market towns of Ḳandahār and Dēra Ismāʿīl Khān [*q.vv.*]. The Zhōb district came within the Durrānī dominions shortly after Aḥmād Shāh Durrānī [*q.v.*] began to constitute his empire in 1747, but in the early 19th century was once more autonomous. British encroachment began in the 1830s but subsided after the First Afghan War (1839-42). In the 1870s and 1880s renewed British interest in Balūčistān and the Gomal Pass region, under the impetus of Sir Robert Sandeman, who founded the military centre of Fort Sandeman at the former Apozay, drew Zhōb into the British Indian orbit, and in 1890 the region was formally ceded by the Afghān government to British India.

Since then, Zhōb has come under various administrative arrangements. Its internal and external economic relations were transformed by the establishment of Fort Sandeman and the related establishment of the Hindūbagh (now Muslimbagh) and Ḳalʿa-i Sayfallāh *ḳaṣabas*. The most notable change of the period of Pakistani rule has been the almost complete replacement of mainly Hindu (principally Shikārpūrī) banking and trading communities by non-Pashtūn Muslim groups, such as Balūčī, Hindkō, Siraikī, Pandjābī and Urdū speakers, and these minority ethnic groups remain vital components of Zhōb's society and economy.

Bibliography: Niʿmat Allāh Harawī, *Makhzan-i afghānī*, tr. B. Dorn, *History of the Afghans*, London 1829-36, pt. II, 52-3, 63, 65; Mountstuart Elphinstone, *An account of the Kingdom of Caubul*, London 1815, 451-3; S.M. Ḥayāt Khān, *Ḥayāt-i afghānī* (1865), ed. and tr. H. Priestly, *Afghanistan and its inhabitants*, Lahore 1874, 55, 148-53, 162-76; H.G. Raverty, *Notes on Afghanistan and parts of Baluchistan*, London 1881-3, ii, 521-7; S.M.K. Gandapūr, *Tawārīkh-i Khurshīd-i djahān*, Lahore 1894; Government of India, *Baluchistan District Gazeteers series*, i, *Zhob*, Bombay 1907; Sir Olaf Caroe, *The Pathans, 550 BC-AD 1957*, London 1958, index s.v.; Government of Pakistan, *1981 District census report of Zhob*, Islamabad 1983.

(Shah Mahmoud Hanifi)

ZIʿĀMET (T. < A. *ziʿāma*), a term of Ottoman Turkish military and land tenure organisation.

The *ziʿāmet* was in fact a larger size *timār* [*q.v.*], which in the 10th/16th century was worth between 20,000 and 100,000 *aḳčes*; in earlier periods, the limits were less clearly defined. In early 10th/16th century *idjmāls*, we sometimes encounter the heading "*timārhā-i zuʿamā ve erbāb-i timār*" which indicates that the expression *timār* was used generically, to encompass *ziʿāmet* as well (*387 numaralı muhâsebe-i vilâyet-i Karaman ve Rûm defteri* (*937/1530*), Ankara, T.C. Başbakanlık Devlet Arşivleri Genel Müdürlüğü (from now on DAGM), 1997, ii, 44, and elsewhere). The holder is known as a *zaʿīm*. Similarly to *timār*-holders, most *zaʿīms* served in the Ottoman army when called upon. *Zaʿīms* assigned to seaboard provinces also commanded detachments which were carried in ships of the navy (*12 numaralı mühimme defteri, 978-979/1570-72, özet, transkripsiyon ve indeks*, Ankara, DAGM 1996, ii, 37).

While at home, *ziʿāmet* holders might be ordered to pursue robbers after consultation with the local *ḳāḍī* (*3 numaralı mühimme defteri 966-968/1558-1560, özet ve transkripsiyon*, Ankara, DAGM 1993, 132). A *zaʿīm* with a reputation for local knowledge concerning the remote province of Menteshe might be charged with police duties in lieu of military service (*5 numaralı mühimme defteri (973/1565-66), özet ve indeks*, Ankara, DAGM 1994, 224, no. 1386). In other instances, we find *zaʿīms* along with other soldiers occupied as tax collectors (*ibid.*, ii, 118-19). Often *ziʿāmets* were granted to middle-level commanders such as those known as *ṣubashi*, who were responsible for urban citadels (Metin Kunt, *The Sultan's servants. The transformation of Ottoman provincial government, 1550-1650*, New York 1983, 12). The *idjmāl* register covering the *wilāyets* of Diyār-i Bekr, ʿArab and Dhu 'l-Ḳadriyye of 937/1530 records the issuance of *ziʿāmets* to the *mīr-alay* and *ser* [or *mīr-i*] *ʿasker* (*998 numaralı muhâsebe-i vilâyet-i Diyar-i Bekr, ʿArab ve Zü'l-Kadiriyye defteri* (*937/1530*), Ankara, DAGM 1998, i, 122, of the facsimile).

In areas bordering the Syrian desert, *ziʿāmets* might be granted to tribal dignitaries (*3 numaralı mühimme defteri*, 27). Such dignitaries also were assigned *ziʿāmet* as *odjaḳ*. This implied that they had to finance the soldiers to be drafted from their province; thus the *ziʿāmet*-holders of the eastern Anatolian *ḳaḍā* of Pertek, who belonged to the *djemāʿat-i millī*, in 979/1571-2 were required to contribute to the upkeep of the *piyāde* soldiers serving in the armies conquering Cyprus (*12 numaralı mühimme defteri*, Ankara, DAGM 1996, ii, 60). In border territory, special services might be rewarded by a *ziʿāmet*; thus in 973/1565-6, a Caucasian soldier who was to bring a Persian woman to Erzurum was to be awarded a *ziʿāmet* if he fulfilled his promise (*5 numaralı mühimme defteri, özet ve indeks*, 206, no. 1269). A fortress commander delegated to oversee the procurement of saltpetre also received a *ziʿāmet* (*12 numaralı mühimme defteri*, i, 110, no. 135).

Non-military dignitaries were occasionally awarded *ziʿāmet* as well. Thus a register from the reign of Bāyezīd II mentions an Ottoman princess possessing this source of revenue (N. Beldiceanu, *Le timar dans l'État ottoman, début XIVe-début XVIe siècle*, Wiesbaden 1980, 46). In 973/1565-6, a *reʾīs ül-kuttāb* enjoyed this privilege as well (*5 numaralı mühimme defteri* (*973/1565-66*), 151, no. 889). During the conquest of Cyprus, financial officials such as the *defter emīni* might receive a *ziʿāmet* (*12 numaralı mühimme defteri*, i, 329, no. 519).

The *ziʿāmet* normally fell into the category of *serbest* tax assignments. This implies that certain dues, the amount and type of which varied from one province to the next, could be retained by the *zaʿīm* himself; in non-*serbest timārs*, these were collected by the holder of a nearby *serbest timār*, such as the provincial governor (*sandjaḳbegi*) (Beldiceanu, *Timar*, 36-7). In exceptional cases when the collection of revenues was particularly difficult, a *zaʿīm* might receive permission to farm out his revenues, but the administration in the 10th/16th century was concerned that this practice might lead to the exploitation of the taxpayers (*6 numaralı mühimme defteri* (*972/1564-65*), Ankara, DAGM, 1995, ii, 57).

Similarly to *timārs*, the extent of *ziʿāmets* was, in principle, determined in the course of preparing the *taḥrīr* [*q.v.*]. Governors in outlying provinces occasionally asked for permission to make rearrangements, but this permission was often refused. Thus the *beglerbegi* of Dhu 'l-Ḳadriyye was warned that it was not permitted to divide the holding of a deceased *zaʿīm* as a fresh (*ḳilič*) *timār* among his sons (*5 numaralı mühimme defteri*, 146, no 850). Equally, the *beglerbegi* of Baghdād was not allowed to join an existing *ziʿāmet* to the *khāṣṣ* already enjoyed by a local governor (*12 numaralı mühimme defteri*, i, 94, no. 98). However, the situation might be different if a *ziʿāmet* was reported to be worth more than 200,000 *aḳčes*, in which case it might be taken from the holder and added to the *khawāṣṣ-i hümāyūn* in order to determine its veritable yield (*5 numaralı mühimme defteri*, 23-4, no. 121).

Bibliography: Given in the article. See also Halil Sahillioğlu, art. *Zeʿāmet*, in *IA*.

(SURAIYA FAROQHI)

ZĪB AL-NISĀʾ BEGUM [see MAKHFĪ].

ZIʾBAḲ (A.), mercury, a heavy silver-white metallic element which is liquid at atmospheric temperature and also called quicksilver (*argentum vivum*, ἄργυρος χυτός, ὑδράργυρος = Hg). It was first mentioned by Aristotle [see ARISṬŪṬĀLĪS] in his *De Anima*. Variant forms of the Arabic term include *zaybaḳ*, *zība/iḳ*, and *zāwuḳ* (< Persian *zhīwa* < Sanskrit ?). From ancient times, quicksilver was associated with the Graeco-Egyptian god Hermes-Thoth and his Roman counterpart Mercury; it is therefore ascribed to Hermes Trismegistos [see HIRMIS], the alleged founder of occult science, and represented by the sign of the planet mercury ☿ [see ʿUṬĀRID]. In the Islamic Middle Ages, quicksilver came mainly from mines in Spain and Central Asia [cf. MAʿDIN].

In alchemy [see KĪMIYĀʾ], quicksilver was considered a "spirit" (*rūḥ*), i.e. one of the ultimate elements or principles of which all material substances were supposed to be compounded, and a means of converting one metal into another. Thus it played a crucial role in the struggle of the alchemists to synthesise gold. Next to the theory of the elixir [see IKSĪR], the so-called quicksilver-sulphur method seemed to be the most promising approach to imitate nature, namely, by determining the exact ratio of these two baser substances as contained in gold, and by recreating the latter on the basis of this ratio. The alloys of quicksilver or amalgams were well known and employed for various procedures, as was cinnabar, its red crystalline sulphide and principal ore (HgS); quicksilver was further used in the construction of mechanical devices and clocks and in jewellery. Finally, and in consequence of the alchemists' concern to keep the making of gold a secret, quicksilver occurs in the relevant literature under more than 140 cryptonyms (*rumūz*).

In medicine [see ṬIBB], quicksilver was considered a "kind of silver" (*min d̲j̲ins al-fiḍḍa*), and Muslim physicians generally shared the attitude of their ancient fellow-medical men who hardly ever used it because of its toxicity. Warnings are frequent, particularly against the noxious properties of its "vapour" (*duk̲h̲ān*), which was said to cause hemiplegia, tremors, fainting, loss of hearing and sight, madness, etc. However, an unguent prepared from the "dust" (*turāb*) of the sublimate, with either vinegar or rose oil, was supposed to cure itching and scabies when applied to the skin; this powder was also used as a pesticide to kill lice and mice and to drive out snakes, scorpions and other vermin.

Bibliography: A. Siggel, *Decknamen in der arabischen alchemistischen Literatur*, Berlin 1951, 11-12, 33-54; C.W. Wood and A.K. Holliday, *Inorganic chemistry*, ²London 1963, 388-90; W. Schmucker, *Die pflanzliche und mineralische Materia Medica im Firdaus al-Ḥikma des Ṭabari*, Bonn 1969, 224; M. Ullmann, *Die Natur- und Geheimwissenschaften im Islam*, Leiden 1972, 260-1, 266-7; Yūsuf b. ʿUmar al-G̲h̲assānī, *al-Muʿtamad fi ʾl-adwiya al-mufrada*, ³Beirut 1395/1975, 212-13. (O. KAHL)

AL-**ZIBRIḲĀN** B. **BADR**, tribal leader and poet of the Tamīm [*q.v.*] who was a Companion of the Prophet Muḥammad. His real name was al-Ḥusayn, but he was nicknamed al-Zibriḳān "the moon" because of his beauty: he used to enter Mecca (at the time of pilgrimage) wearing a turban so as not to seduce the womenfolk; or he was given this nickname because in battle he wore a yellow turban (*yuzabriku ʿimāmatahu*, i.e. in order to make himself visible to the enemy).

He belonged to the Bahdala b. ʿAwf b. Kaʿb b. Saʿd b. Zayd Manāt b. Tamīm (see chart at Vol. X, 174); or more precisely, to the K̲h̲alaf b. Bahdala, K̲h̲alaf being al-Zibriḳān's great-grandfather. Originally, though, he was of the Yas̲h̲kur b. Bakr b. Wāʾil. He was married to al-Farazdaḳ's [*q.v.*] paternal aunt.

Al-Zibriḳān came to the Prophet Muḥammad as a participant in the Tamīm delegation [see WUFŪD], and was charged with levying taxes from part of the Saʿd b. Zayd Manāt and from the Ribāb. (It is noteworthy that al-Zibriḳān's mother was of the ʿUkl, who were a component of the Ribāb.) The rest of the Saʿd had another tax-collector, namely, Ḳays b. ʿĀṣim [*q.v.*], and it appears that the Ribāb came under al-Zibriḳān's authority so that the military balance within the Saʿd was maintained.

At the beginning of the *ridda* [*q.v.* in Suppl.], Muḥammad reportedly asked both al-Zibriḳān and Ḳays b. ʿĀṣim—through a messenger—to co-operate in order to kill Musaylima [*q.v.*]. Al-Zibriḳān is said to have remained loyal to Islam and to have brought to Abū Bakr the camels he had received as taxes. However, at some stage he must have had contacts with Musaylima and Sad̲j̲āḥ [*q.v.*]. During the conquest of ʿIrāḳ, he was K̲h̲ālid b. al-Walīd's [*q.v.*] deputy in al-Anbār [*q.v.*].

Al-Zibriḳān was also employed as tax-collector by ʿUmar b. al-K̲h̲aṭṭāb. Moreover, three of al-Zibriḳān's sons-in-law were governors under ʿUmar. By far the most important among them was the governor in Kūfa, Saʿd b. Abī Waḳḳāṣ [*q.v.*]. The other two were in charge of regions which were closer to al-Zibriḳān's tribal territory: the governor of ʿUmān and Baḥrayn, ʿUt̲h̲mān b. Abi ʾl-ʿĀṣ al-T̲h̲aḳafī, and ʿUt̲h̲mān's brother, al-Ḥakam, who was his deputy in Baḥrayn. (Al-Ḥakam's wife, Bakra bt. al-Zibriḳān, was reportedly the first Arab woman who sailed the sea; this was no doubt related to her husband's expeditions across the Persian Gulf.) However, al-Zibriḳān's goodwill was crucial not only for the state, but also for merchants traversing central Nad̲j̲d.

Al-Zibriḳān was still alive at the time of Muʿāwiya I [*q.v.*]. His descendants in the Arabian desert and in al-Andalus were numerous. In al-Andalus they settled in a village called al-Zabāriḳa (pl. of al-Zibriḳān), and later in Talavera.

Bibliography: The relevant entries in the Companion dictionaries; Balād̲h̲urī, *Ansāb*, vii/1, ed. Ramzi Baalbaki, Beirut 1997, index; D̲j̲umaḥī, *Ṭabaḳāt fuḥūl al-s̲h̲uʿarāʾ*, ed. Maḥmūd S̲h̲ākir, Cairo 1394/1974, index; Ṭabarī, index; Bag̲h̲dādī, *K̲h̲izānat al-adab*, ed. Hārūn, Cairo 1387-1406/1967-86, index; *Naḳāʾiḍ D̲j̲arīr wa ʾl-Farazdaḳ*, index; Ibn Ḥazm, *D̲j̲amharat ansāb al-ʿarab*, ed. Hārūn, Cairo 1382/1962, 219; Blachère, *HLA*, ii, 260; Sezgin, *GAS*, ii, 200-1. (M. LECKER)

ZĪD̲J̲, in Islamic science an astronomical handbook with tables, after the models of the Sāsānid Persian *Zīk-i S̲h̲ahriyār*, the Indian *Sindhind* [*q.v.*], and Ptolemy's *Almagest* and *Handy Tables* [see BAṬLAMIYŪS]. A typical *zīd̲j̲* might contain a hundred folios of text and tables, though some are substantially larger than this. Most of the relevant astronomical and astrological concepts are clearly explained in the *Tafhīm* of al-Bīrūnī [*q.v.*]. The history of Islamic *zīd̲j̲*s constitutes a major part of the history of Islamic astronomy [see ʿILM AL-HAYʾA].

i. ETYMOLOGY

Arabic *zīd̲j̲* (pl. *zīd̲j̲āt*) is best translated as "astronomical handbook"; although it normally contains tables, it is not merely a "collection of astronomical tables", but has explanatory material as well. Moreover (as Mercier has noted) Arabic authors apply this word also to Indian astronomical writings, although these do not contain tables. The Arabic word *zīd̲j̲*, which is also attested in the meaning "plumbline", was generally recognised to be a borrowing from Persian. Al-K̲h̲ʷārazmī (*Mafātīḥ al-ʿulūm*, 219) and al-Bīrūnī (*al-Ḳānūn al-Masʿūdī*, i, Ḥaydarābād 1954, 271; English tr. and commentary on the passage by de Blois, *apud* Panaino, 155-7), derive it from Persian *zih* "bowstring". In fact, it comes from Middle Persian *zīg*, attested in the meanings "rope, towline" and also (in one post-Sāsānid work) "astronomical handbook". Although *zih* and *zīg* do come from the same root, they are not identical. Al-Bīrūnī claims that astronomical books are called *zīd̲j̲āt* because astronomers need to know about "chords" (*awtār*, literally "bowstrings"); for this alleged technical use of *zih* he compares Arabic *d̲j̲īb* ("half-chord, sine"), which, as he says rightly, comes from Sanskrit *jīva* "bowstring". If Middle Persian *zīg* was really used for "chord" or "sine", one could indeed imagine that the Persians gave this name to astronomical handbooks because they contained trigonometrical tables.

The Indo-Persian dictionaries claim that *zīg* means "a weaver's warp" (*tār*), but the word is not in fact attested in this meaning in any text. Nallino, taking his cue from these lexica, thought that the *zīd̲j̲* had its name from the fact that the lines separating the columns of the tables look like the threads of a warp. Mercier has recently suggested that *zīg* is a translation of Sanskrit *tantra*, literally "warp, loom", but used in ancient India also to mean "textbook, system of learning" and applied specifically to certain astronomical treatises. Although this seems more apposite than Nallino's suggestion, it shares with it the difficulty that *zīg* ("rope") does not actually mean the same as *tantra* ("warp"). Panaino, on the other hand, linked *zīdj* with the ancient Persian notion that the planets are attached to the earth by strings.

Bibliography: C.A. Nallino, *Raccolta di scritti*, v, Rome 1944, 120; R. Mercier, art. *Zīj*, in *Encyclopaedia of the history of science, technology and medicine in non-Western cultures*, Dordrecht [1997], 1057-8; idem, *From tantra to zīj* (unpubl. typescript); A. Panaino, *Tessere il cielo*, Rome 1998 (with detailed discussion of the etymology). (F.C. de Blois)

ii. The Scope of the *zīdj* literature

1. *The number of* zīdjs *compiled in the Islamic Middle Ages.*

In the 7th/13th century, the Yemeni astronomer Muḥammad b. Abī Bakr al-Fārisī was able to cite the names of 28 *zīdj*s, and the 10th/16th-century Indian encyclopaedist Abu 'l-Faḍl al-ʿAllāmī [*q.v.*] listed in his *Āʾīn-i Akbarī* the titles of 86 works of this genre. In 1956 E.S. Kennedy presented information on some 125 *zīdj*s. We now know that over 200 *zīdj*s were compiled in the Islamic world between the 2nd/8th and 13th/19th centuries. They constitute a major source for our understanding of the development and application of mathematical astronomy in the mediaeval period. Of these works, just less than one-half are lost and known only by references to their titles or their authors, but enough survive to convey a very clear impression of the scope and variety of the activities of the Muslim astronomers in this field and to reveal some of their most outstanding contributions.

Most *zīdj*s are intended to serve a single locality, in the sense that a terrestrial longitude underlies the solar, lunar and planetary tables and a terrestrial latitude underlies the tables for spherical astronomy. Some of the more important *zīdj*s were the results of serious observational programmes [see marṣad, and also Sayılı, *The observatory in Islam*]. However, many *zīdj*s were simply rehashings of earlier ones, with minor variations, such as a change of meridian for the planetary tables, or a new set of spherical astronomical tables for a different latitude. Such modified versions can be of singular historical importance if the original works are no longer extant. Not all *zīdj*s contain the extensive explanations of the astronomical and mathematical background typical of, say, Ptolemy's *Almagest*. Furthermore, there are numerous extensive sets of related tables which are not usually found in *zīdj*s.

Already in the 19th century, extracts dealing with observation accounts from the *Zīdj* of Ibn Yūnus had been published by A.P. Caussin de Perceval, and the introduction to the *Zīdj* of Ulugh Beg had been published by L.-A. Sédillot. Before 1950 only two *zīdj*s had been published in their entirety, namely, those of al-Battānī by C.A. Nallino and of al-Khʷārazmī by H. Suter *et al.* (the latter is extant only in a form substantially different from the original). In 1952 J. Vernet published the canons of the *zīdj* of Ibn al-Bannāʾ. The *zīdj* of al-Bīrūnī was published in 1954-6, in an edition orginally prepared by M. Krause. In 1956 E.S. Kennedy published his survey of some 125 *zīdj*s and laid the foundation for serious study of this genre of literature. In 1962 O. Neugebauer published an English translation of the text of the *Zīdj* of al-Khʷārazmī in the form in which it survives for us, together with a commentary and an analysis of the tables. The year 1985 saw the publication of a Byzantine recension of the *zīdj* of al-Fahhād by D. Pingree. Most recently, in 1999, a doctoral thesis by A. Mestres presented an analysis of the *Zīdj* of Ibn Isḥāḳ. Full references to these studies are found in the *Bibl.* Many studies of parts of other *zīdj*s, of specific topics in several *zīdj*s, or of individual tables of particular interest, have been published during the past 50 years; only a few of these will be mentioned in this article, although most are found in the collected studies and festschrifts listed in the *Bibl.* Also, certain mediaeval treatises on the concepts underlying *zīdj*s, of the genre *kutub ʿilal al-zīdjāt* [see ʿilla], have attracted attention: these include the works of al-Hāshimī, Ibn al-Muthannā, Ibn Masrūr, Ibn ʿEzra and Muḥammad b. Abī Bakr al-Fārisī. Others are lost (including those by al-Farghānī, al-Sarakhsī, Thābit b. Ḳurra and al-Bīrūnī), or are currently being studied (notably that of al-Samawʾal al-Maghribī, on which see Sezgin, *GAS*, vi, 65-6).

In the 1970s, various categories of tables not found in *zīdj*s were identified, many even more extensive than a typical *zīdj*. In view of the lack of any article on tables in general, called *djadwal* in Arabic, such tables will also be briefly treated below (see *Categories of Tables*). (The article djadwal deals mainly with magical arrangements of letters and symbols.)

2. *The purpose of a* zīdj.

A *zīdj* could provide astronomers with all that they needed in the way of theory and tables for such tasks as calculating the positions (longitudes and latitudes) of the Sun, Moon and five naked-eye planets, and the time of day or night from solar or stellar altitudes. In addition, the astronomer could use a *zīdj* to determine the possibility of lunar crescent or planetary visibility. Stellar positions he could simply take from the star-catalogue. Calculations for meridians other than that underlying the tables could be modified for the longitude differences apparent from the geographical tables. The astronomer could calculate the duration of twilight and the altitude of the Sun at midday or at the time of the afternoon prayer. He could apply the mathematical procedures outlined in the *zīdj* to specific geographical data and compute the *ḳibla* [*q.v.*] of any locality. He could also determine the ascendant at a given time and the longitudes of the astrological houses, and having calculated the positions of the Sun, Moon and planets, he could set up a horoscope: it could be argued that this was the main purpose of *zīdj*s, but there is precious little historical evidence how these works were used in practice. In any case, there are a host of other useful operations one can learn from any *zīdj*. But a *zīdj* was only part of the astronomer's equipment. Other sets of tables were compiled which were not usually contained in *zīdj*s and which greatly facilitated some of the above tasks. In addition, various instruments were available, notably for solving problems relating to spherical astronomy and timekeeping [see asṭurlāb; mizwala; rubʿ; shakkāziyya].

3. *The regional schools of astronomy and their* zīdjs.

The earliest Islamic *zīdj*s from the 2nd/8th century were based on Indian and Persian models, but in the 3rd/9th century the Ptolemaic tradition was introduced and eventually predominated, if not universally. After the 4th/10th century, regional schools of astronomy developed in the Islamic world, with different authorities and different interests and specialities. They also achieved different levels of sophistication and had different fates, both with regard to their own internal development and to the nature of their encounter with the new Western science from the 16th century onwards. In the past few years, some attention has been paid to these regional schools, and the main studies are listed in the *Bibl.* In particular, each regional school had its favorite *zīdj* or *zīdj*s.

In the central lands of Islam, the *Mumtaḥan* tradition was important, together with al-Battānī and Abu 'l-Wafā' al-Būzdjānī. In Persia and Central Asia, numerous early *zīdj*s eventually gave way to the *Zīdj-i Īlkhānī* of Naṣīr al-Dīn al-Ṭūsī. In Egypt, the *Ḥākimī Zīdj* of Ibn Yūnus was never surpassed. In al-Andalus, the *zīdj*s of al-Kh̲wārazmī and al-Battānī, based respectively on the Indo-Persian and Hellenistic traditions, played a role perhaps greater than either deserved, and the contributions made by Ibn al-Zarḳālluh were highly significant. In the Maghrib, the *Zīdj* of Ibn Isḥāḳ and a mini-version thereof prepared by Ibn al-Bannā' dominated the scene. In the late period, the only *zīdj* to achieve any kind of supremacy all over the Islamic world was the *Zīdj-i Sulṭānī* of Ulugh Beg (see below for details of these).

iii. An Overview of *zīdj* production

1. *The Indo-Persian tradition.*

The first Islamic *zīdj*s were part of an Indo-Persian tradition which has a pre-Ptolemaic Greek origin. This is the case of the *Zīdj al-Arkand* written in Arabic in 117/735 probably in the Sind region, which is related to the *Khaṇḍakhādyaka*, composed in Sanskrit by Brahmagupta in 665. The same main influence appears in the *Zīk-i Shahriyār*, translated into Arabic ca. 175/790 as the *Zīdj al-Shāh*: it was used by an unidentified astrologer who, soon after A.D. 679, computed a series of horoscopes illustrating the early history of Islam. The *Zīdj al-Shāh* was also used by Māshā'allāh (see below), Nawbakht, 'Umar b. Farrukhān al-Ṭabarī and al-Fazārī to compute the horoscope for the foundation of Baghdād on 30 July 762. Although neither the Pahlavi nor the Arabic texts of the *Zīdj al-Shāh* are extant, its main features are known from indirect sources studied by E.S. Kennedy and D. Pingree, who established, for example, the parameters of the mean motion of Saturn, Jupiter and the lunar nodes using the collection of historical horoscopes compiled by the Jewish astrologer of Baṣra Māshā'allāh (d. ca. 200/815) [q.v., and also the art. in *DSB*] and computed with this *zīdj*. Both the *Zīdj al-Shāh* and the *Zīdj al-Arkand*—as well as, probably, other early *zīdj*s—were the vehicles by means of which the astrology of great conjunctions was introduced in Islam [see ḳirĀn].

The third great *zīdj* within the Indo-Persian tradition was the *Sindhind*. This text seems to derive, indirectly, from the Sanskrit *Brahmasphuṭasiddhānta* composed in 629 by Brahmagupta, through a work the title of which was probably *Mahāsiddhānta*. According to tradition, this *Mahāsiddhānta* was introduced in Baghdād in 154/771 or 156/773 by an Indian embassy sent to the court of the caliph al-Manṣūr. With the help of one of the members of this embassy, the astronomers Ya'ḳūb b. Ṭāriḳ and al-Fazārī translated the Sanskrit text of the *Sindhind* into Arabic. Both these men compiled several *zīdj*s based on the *Sindhind* system, which was used by them to compute the tables of the mean motions of the planets, although the planetary equations were taken from the *Zīdj al-Shāh*. At the same time, the extant scattered indirect quotations from these *zīdj*s bear witness to the first limited appearance of Ptolemaic elements in Islamic astronomy (see D. Pingree, *The fragments of the works of Ya'qūb Ibn Ṭāriq*, in *JNES*, xxvii [1968], 97-125; and idem, *The fragments of the works of al-Fazārī*, in *ibid.*, xxix [1970], 103-23).

The influence of the Indo-Persian tradition in future Islamic astronomy was secured by the revision of the *Sindhind* prepared by al-Kh̲wārazmī (ca. 210/825) [q.v., and also the art. in *DSB*], the first Islamic *zīdj* which is still extant, and which has been published and

translated, albeit in a form substantially different from the original. Most of al-Kh̲wārazmī's original text has not been preserved, but we do possess one complete Latin translation, made by Adelard of Bath (*fl.* 1116-42) of a revision of the *zīdj* by Andalusī astronomers. Other Kh̲wārazmian materials can be recovered from various commentaries. See further van Dalen, *Al-Khwārizmī's tables revisited*, 196-211, and also below, iv. The Contents of *zīdj*s, 4.

2. *Al-Ma'mūn and the earliest Ptolemaic* zīdj*s.*

The first translation of Ptolemy's *Almagest* was into Syriac. The date is not certain, but the Syriac translation clearly preceded the first Arabic one, prepared either by a certain al-Ḥasan b. Ḳuraysh for the caliph al-Ma'mūn (according to Ibn al-Ṣalāḥ) or somewhat earlier by other translators for Yaḥyā b. Khālid b. Barmak (d. 189/805 [see al-barāmika]), in effect the *wazīr* of Hārūn al-Rashīd (according to Ibn al-Nadīm). Neither of these translations is extant. The new translation from the Greek was achieved by al-Ḥadjdjādj b. Yūsuf b. Maṭar in 212/827-8. This survives in one complete manuscript and another fragmentary one. A related translation from the Greek is by Isḥāḳ b. Ḥunayn [q.v.], prepared for the *wazīr* Abu 'l-Ṣaḳr b. Bulbul (d. ca. 280/890). Shortly thereafter, this was revised by Thābit b. Ḳurra [q.v.], whose version survives in ten manuscripts, only two of which are complete, the version of Isḥāḳ being available only in the form of quotations (by Ibn al-Ṣalāḥ). The Isḥāḳ/Thābit version was edited by Naṣīr al-Dīn al-Ṭūsī [q.v.] in 672/1274, whose version survives in several copies. Djābir b. Aflaḥ [q.v.] used the translations of both al-Ḥadjdjādj and Isḥāḳ that were available in al-Andalus in the 6th/12th century, and this is confirmed by the Latin translation of Gerard of Cremona, also from that century.

The Muslim astronomers were concerned from the outset to test and to improve what they found in the astronomical traditions to which they were heirs. Al-Ma'mūn's reign marks a turning point in the development of Islamic astronomy. Although al-Nihāwandī (*fl. ca.* 175/790) had made observations of his own in Djundishapur [q.v.], the first systematic programme of astronomical observations took place between 213/828 and 218/833 in the Shammāsiyya quarter of Baghdād (in 213/828, led by Yaḥyā b. Abī Manṣūr) and in the monastery of Dayr Murrān in Mount Ḳāsiyūn, near Damascus (218/833, led by Khālid b. 'Abd al-Malik al-Marwarrūdhī) [see marṣad]. Al-Ma'mūn may have sponsored these observations for astrological reasons (like his predecessor al-Manṣūr, he was a keen believer in astrology), although it seems probable that the main purpose of the programme was to reach definite conclusions about the problem of contradictory parameters and geometrical models in use in early Islamic astronomy, resulting from the simultaneous application of three main known traditions: Indian, Persian and Greek. The programme seems to have concentrated mainly on solar, lunar and stellar observations but it also determined new parameters for the mean planetary motions. Several *zīdj*s were written as a result of these observations: the official one was compiled by Yaḥyā b. Abī Manṣūr and bore the title of *al-Zīdj al-mumtaḥan*. Other astronomers who were directly or indirectly associated with the observatories of Baghdād and Damascus also wrote their own *zīdj*s: among these, the *zīdj* of Ḥabash al-Ḥāsib [q.v.] is the most prominent. This is extant in two manuscripts in Istanbul and Berlin. Only the former has been properly investigated, although it has not been published. The latter is a later recension.

Although Ḥabash̲ (d. *ca.* 864-74) does not seem to have taken an active part in the Ma'mūnī observations, he used their results for the compilation of his *zīdj*. An analysis of both Ḥabash̲'s and Yaḥyā's *zīdj*s shows that they are Ptolemaic in character and that they improved certain parameters, especially the solar ones. On the other hand, both *zīdj*s preserve a certain number of elements from the Indo-Persian tradition.

After al-Ma'mūn, Islamic astronomy followed along the same lines. Observations continued almost without interruption either in small private observatories or in more or less organised institutions with official support. These resulted in the compilation of new *zīdj*s in which the old Indo-Persian tradition seems to be forgotten (except in al-Andalus—see below, 4), and the tradition of the *Almagest* and the *Handy tables* was followed. The authors accepted Ptolemy's kinematic models but used new parameters and destroyed some dogmatic beliefs of the *Almagest*, such as the invariability of the obliquity of the ecliptic, the constant character of the precession of equinoxes, the immobility of the solar apogee, and the impossibility of annular solar eclipses. Some of the changes introduced are improvements, whilst others are understandable mistakes resulting from the fact that Muslim astronomers relied excessively on the accuracy of observations made in Antiquity and in their own times. In any case, it is obvious that Ptolemaic astronomy was not always followed unquestioningly. In particular, Muslim astronomers made substantial contributions to the development of spherical trigonometry and the solution of problems in spherical astronomy by projection methods.

3. *The major Mas̲h̲riḳī* zīdjs.

It is possible to mention only a limited number of later *zīdj*s from the Mas̲h̲riḳ, arranged here more or less according to the geographical location where they were compiled.

Al-Zīdj al-Ṣābi' of al-Battānī [*q.v.*, and also the art. in *DSB*] (Raḳḳa *ca.* 300/900), is a respectable and orderly work, if lacking the originality of the *zīdj*s of Yaḥyā and Ḥabash̲. This was one of the most important works for the transmission of Ptolemaic astronomy to Europe, but it enjoyed far less influence in the Islamic world (not least because there it had more competition). The tables of a *zīdj* were engraved on the mater and plates of an astrolabe [see ASṬURLĀB] in an instrument labelled *Zīdj al-ṣafā'iḥ* by Abū Dja'far al-K̲h̲āzin (Bag̲h̲dād *ca.* 350/950 [*q.v.*]), of which an example survives in Berlin. Two *zīdj*s by Kūs̲h̲yār b. Labbān (*ca.* 400/1000) [*q.v.*, and also the art. in *DSB*] entitled *al-Zīdj al-djāmi'* and *al-Zīdj al-bālig̲h̲* are extant in several copies of varying content.

The unique manuscript of a *zīdj* entitled *al-Madjisṭī* by Abu 'l-Wafā' al-Būzdjānī (*ca.* 370/970) [*q.v.*, and also the art. in *DSB*] alas lacks the tables; nevertheless, the sections on trigonometry and spherical astronomy are extensive and systematic and of considerable historical interest. The later, anonymous *zīdj* entitled *al-Zīdj al-s̲h̲āmil*, was based on that of Abu 'l-Wafā', and was clearly of some influence, with some spherical astronomical tables for the latitude of Mardin.

Al-Ḳānūn al-Mas'ūdī by al-Bīrūnī (421/1030), dedicated to the newly-acceded Sulṭān Mas'ūd I [*q.v.*] of G̲h̲azna, is much more than an ordinary *zīdj*, being a great astronomical handbook, full of good sense, containing substantial information about the author's personal astronomical research as well as about the development of astronomy in Islamic regions until the author's time. The *Ḳānūn* was not as influential as it should have been (the same is true of al-Bīrūnī's other productions); some of the trigonometric tables were taken over in the *Zīdj-i Īlk̲h̲ānī* (see below) and the geographical tables, albeit in a slightly modified form, as if read from a map, in the *Sandjarī Zīdj* by 'Abd al-Raḥmān al-K̲h̲āzinī (*fl. ca.* 1120, see the art. in *DSB*). No recensions or modified versions of the *Ḳānūn* have come to light. The *Sandjarī Zīdj* dedicated to the Saldjūḳ sultan Sandjar b. Malik S̲h̲āh, is another imposing work on which much more research needs to be done.

Several *zīdj*s, including one called *al-Zīdj al-'Alā'ī*, are associated with al-Fahhād (S̲h̲irwān, *ca.* 550/1150), none extant in their original form. The Yemeni astronomer Muḥammad b. Abī Bakr al-Fārisī, as well as various Byzantine astronomers, used al-Fahhād's work and preserve for us substantial portions of it. Before we discuss later developments in Iran and Central Asia, we will mention the main activity in Egypt, Yemen and Syria.

A monumental work entitled *al-Zīdj al-Ḥākimī al-kabīr*, compiled *ca.* 400/1000 for the Fāṭimid caliph al-Ḥākim by Ibn Yūnus [*q.v.*, and also the art. in *DSB*], is some four times as large as the *Zīdj*s of Yaḥyā and al-Battānī. Substantial parts of the work survive in manuscripts in Leiden, Oxford and Paris. Of particular historical interest are the accounts of observations by the author and his predecessors in 'Abbāsid Bag̲h̲dād. The *Ḥākimī Zīdj* was influential in later Egypt and also the Yemen. Thus e.g. the Geniza astrological almanacs as well as the mediaeval Yemeni ephemerides [see TAḲWĪM and also below, v. CATEGORIES OF TABLES NOT CONTAINED IN ZĪDJS, 3] are based on calculations using the mean motion and equation tables of the *Ḥākimī Zīdj*. The *Muṣṭalaḥ Zīdj* was the most popular *zīdj* in mediaeval Egypt, and relied heavily on the *Ḥākimī Zīdj*. Later Egyptian *zīdj*s include recensions of those of Ibn al-S̲h̲āṭir and Ulug̲h̲ Beg.

Altogether, some 18 *zīdj*s are known from the Yemen, starting with al-Hamdānī [*q.v.*] in the early 4th/10th century, and the latest from the 13th/19th century. Their historical importance derives not only from the fact that they attest a serious Yemeni tradition of mathematical astronomy for close to a millennium but also from the fact that they preserve for us 'Abbāsid and Fāṭimid materials which would otherwise have been lost (see King, *Astronomy in Yemen*).

Al-Zīdj al-djadīd of Ibn al-S̲h̲āṭir (Damascus *ca.* 750/1350; see the art. in *DSB*) contains equation tables based on the author's new planetary models, which represent the culmination of the Islamic activities to replace those of Ptolemy [see 'ILM AL-HAY'A]. This work merits detailed investigation. Several recensions were made for Damascus in later centuries, also one for Algiers and another for Cairo.

The major production of a group of astronomers working at Marāg̲h̲a [*q.v.*] under Naṣīr al-Dīn al-Ṭūsī and purportedly based on their observations is the *Īlk̲h̲ānī Zīdj*, still in the Ptolemaic tradition. The parameters underlying the solar, lunar and planetary tables were, however, taken from Ibn al-A'lam and Ibn Yūnus, and the trigonometric tables lifted from Ibn Yūnus and al-Bīrūnī. What is new is the calendrical material [see TA'RĪK̲H̲. 2]. There is no influence of the important modifications of the Ptolemaic planetary models conceived by the Marāg̲h̲a astronomers.

The *Zīdj-i Īlk̲h̲ānī* was revised and corrected by Djams̲h̲īd al-Kās̲h̲ī in his *Zīdj-i K̲h̲āḳānī*, a work completed towards 820/1420, before the end of the cycle of observations made by the team of astronomers at the Samarḳand observatory. These latter observations were, however, used by Ulug̲h̲ Beg (796-853/

1393-1449 [*q.v.*]) to compile his *Zīdj-i Sulṭānī* (completed between 1437 and 1448), which is the last great Ptolemaic *zīdj* of the Islamic Middle Ages. This *zīdj* is extant in numerous manuscripts, yet to be sorted. The main parts of the *zīdj*, namely, the tables, have still not received the attention they deserve. (See, most recently, E.S. Kennedy, *Ulugh Beg as scientist*, and *The heritage of Ulugh Beg*, first published in idem, *Studies*, nos. X-XI.) Recensions were prepared for Damascus, Cairo, Istanbul, Tunis and India.

Two *zīdj*s for Istanbul were compiled by Taḳī al-Dīn (*ca.* 980/1580 [*q.v.*]) and remain to be studied. Turkish recensions of the astronomical tables of Cassini (d. 1756) and Lalande (d. 1807) and other European astronomers are available (see İhsanoğlu, *Introduction of Western science to the Ottoman world*).

From India we have the *Zīdj-i Nāṣirī*, compiled by Maḥmūd b. ʿUmar *ca.* 650/1250 for the Dihlī Sultan Nāṣir al-Dīn Abu 'l-Muẓaffar Maḥmūd b. Shams al-Dīn Iltutmish [*q.v.*]. A copy of this appears to be preserved in a private library in Tabriz (Storey, *PL*, ii/1, 52) but it has never been studied. It could be a work of considerable historical interest.

Later Indian *zīdj*s are based either on Ulugh Beg or on European works (see Khan Ghori, *Development of zīj literature in India*).

4. *Andalusī and Maghribī* zīdjs.

For al-Andalus and al-Maghrib, the history of astronomy has been studied more intensively than for other regions of the Islamic world. It is thus possible to place the activity relating to the compilation of *zīdj*s in a clearer historical perspective.

The first *zīdj*s, probably based on an Indo-Persian tradition, were introduced in al-Andalus in the time of ʿAbd al-Raḥmān II (206-38/822-52); one of these was al-Khʷārazmī's *Zīdj al-Sindhind* (D. Pingree, *Indian astronomy in medieval Spain*, in *Vernet Festschrift*, i, 39-48). This *zīdj* (see below, iv. The Contents of *Zīdj*s, 1) was the object of new recensions by Maslama al-Madjrīṭī (d. 398/1007-08 [*q.v.*]) and his disciples Ibn al-Ṣaffār (d. 426/1035 [*q.v.*]) and Ibn al-Samḥ (d. 426/1035 [*q.v.*]), as well as by Ibn Ḥayy (d. 456/1064) and ʿAbd Allāh al-Sarāḳusṭī (d. 448/1056-7), who wrote a treatise on the errors of the *Sindhind* method. Of all these materials, only a disappointing fragment of Ibn al-Ṣaffār's version is extant in Arabic (M. Castells and J. Samsó, *Seven chapters of Ibn al-Ṣaffār's lost* Zīj, in *AIHS*, xlv [1995], 229-62), while Maslama's version has been preserved in the Latin translation of Adelard of Bath and in a recension by Petrus Alfonsi. Adelard's version contains materials derived from al-Khʷārazmī's original *zīdj*, Maslama's modifications and additions and, probably, other later materials, such as the table, attributed elsewhere to a certain al-Ḳallās, as yet unidentified, for determining the visibility of the new Moon for a latitude of 41;35° (Saragossa?). Maslama introduced modifications in the chronological and in the mean-motion tables (al-Khʷārazmī used the Persian calendar and the era of Yazdidjird III, while the extant tables use the Muslim calendar and the beginning of the Hidjra). He also adapted the radix positions of the lunar ascending node and of the mean oppositions and conjunctions of the Sun and the Moon to the meridian of Cordova which, in these tables as well as in a passage of Ibn al-Ṣaffār's canons, is placed at a distance of 63° west of Arīn (not 79;40° as in al-Khʷārazmī's original *Zīdj*). This correction appears in a horoscope cast in Cordova and dated 328/940, and it has the effect of reducing the length of the Mediterranean to a much more reasonable value than was implied by Ptolemy. Other Maslamian additions can be found in trigonometric (sine and cotangent) and astrological tables such as those concerned with the equalisation of the houses and the projection of rays, computed for a latitude of 38;30°, presumably Cordova, and much better than the original tables of al-Khʷārazmī, preserved in another source. (For an overview of the origin of the various tables in the Latin version see van Dalen, *Al-Khwārizmī's tables revisited*, 196-211.)

Al-Khʷārazmī's astronomical tradition was never fully abandoned in al-Andalus or in the Maghrib. It was followed by Ibn Muʿādh (d. 485/1093) in his *Tabulae Jahen* (that is, the *zīdj* of Djayyān: Jaén in al-Andalus), of which only the canons are extant in a Latin translation by Gerard of Cremona (see H. Hermelink, *Tabulae Jahen*, in *AHES*, ii [1964], 108-12). Arabic passages of these canons as well as tabular materials have been discovered in late Maghribī sources (see Samsó and H. Mielgo, *Ibn Isḥāq al-Tūnisī and Ibn Muʿādh al-Jayyānī on the Qibla*, first published in Samsó, *Studies*, no. VI; A. Mestres, in *Vernet Festschrift*, i, 402-3, 435; Samsó, *ibid.*, ii. 601-10; and idem, in *ZGAIW*, xi [1997], 91-2).

Far more successful were the *Toledan Tables*, the result of an adaptation of the available astronomical material (mainly al-Khʷārazmī and al-Battānī) to the coordinates of Toledo made by a group of Toledan astronomers led by the famous *ḳāḍī* Ṣāʿid al-Andalusī (d. 462/1070 [*q.v.*]). Even if the results achieved were not brilliant, the mean-motion tables are original and constitute the result of a programme of observations which must have begun earlier than 460/1068 and which was continued by Ibn al-Zarḳālluh (Azarquiel) (d. 493/1100 [see al-Zarḳālī]), one of the collaborators of *ḳāḍī* Ṣāʿid, until much later. (On the *Toledan Tables* and Ibn al-Zarḳālluh's *Almanac*, see G.J. Toomer, *A survey of the Toledan Tables*, in *Osiris*, xv [1968], 5-174; L. Richter-Bernburg, *Ṣāʿid, the Toledan Tables, and Andalusī science*, in *Kennedy Festschrift*, 373-401; F.S. Pedersen, *Canones Azarchelis. Some versions and a text*, in *Cahiers de l'Institut du Moyen Age Grec et Latin* (Copenhagen), liv [1987], 129-218; J.-M. Millás Vallicrosa, *Estudios sobre Azarquiel*, Madrid-Granada 1943-50, 72-237; and R. Mercier, *Astronomical tables in the twelfth century*, in *Adelard of Bath. An English scientist and arabist of the early twelfth century*, ed. C. Burnett, London 1987, 87-118, esp. 104-12. On the date of the *Toledan Tables*, see Samsó and H. Berrani, *World-astrology in eleventh century al-Andalus: the Epistle on* tasyīr *and the projection of the rays by al-Istijjī*, in *JIS*, x [1999], 293-312. An edition of the *Toledan tables* is being prepared by F.S. Pedersen.) These tables, like those of al-Khʷārazmī, presented sidereal longitudes but added trepidation tables allowing the calculation of tropical longitudes. The topic of trepidation studied by several members of Ṣāʿid's team (Ṣāʿid himself, Ibn al-Zarḳālluh and Abū Marwān al-Istidjdjī), together with other theoretical innovations developed by Ibn al-Zarḳālluh (cycles that regulate the obliquity of the ecliptic, motion of the solar apogee, solar model with variable eccentricity, corrections in the Ptolemaic lunar model), became standard in the Andalusī and Maghribī tradition. Ibn al-Zarḳālluh also adapted a perpetual *Almanac* from a Hellenistic work computed by a certain Ammonius in the 3rd or 4th century A.D., which allowed astrologers to obtain planetary longitudes without all the computation involved in the use of a *zīdj*. (This was published in Millás Vallicrosa, *op. cit.*, 72-237; preliminary analysis in M. Boutelle, *The Almanach of Azarquiel*, in *Centaurus*, xii [1967], 12-19, repr. in Kennedy *et al.*, *Studies*, 502-10; corrections by N. Swerdlow, in *Mathematical Reviews*, xli/4 [1971], no. 5149; also Samsó, *Ciencias de los Antiguos*, 166-71.) This kind of table was often used in al-Andalus, the Maghrib and mediaeval Christian Spain (see below on the tables of Zacut).

Ibn al-Kammād (active in Cordova *ca.* 510/1110) and Ibn al-Hā'im (*fl. ca.* 600/1200) wrote *zīdj*s in the Zarḳāllian tradition. The former was probably a disciple of Ibn al-Zarḳālluh and composed three such works, of which only one, *al-Muḳtabas*, is extant in a Latin translation, although materials from the other two can be recovered in Castilian translations or in Maghribī sources. Ibn al-Kammād (like Ibn al-Hā'im, Ibn Isḥāḳ, Ibn al-Raḳḳām in his *Shāmil Zīdj*, and Ibn 'Azzūz al-Ḳusanṭīnī, on whom see below) apply the Zarḳāllian motion of the solar apogee (1° in 279 Julian years) to that of the apogees of the other planets, which poses the problem of establishing whether this was Ibn al-Kammād's contribution or whether it already appeared in the lost work of Ibn al-Zarḳālluh. Apart from Zarḳāllian materials, Ibn al-Kammād also used other sources such as Ya'ḳūb b. Ṭāriḳ (*fl. ca.* 175/790) and the *Mumtaḥan Zīdj* of Yaḥyā b. Abī Manṣūr (*fl.* A.D. 830), which seems to have been known to Maslama. Ibn al-Kammād deviated from Zarḳāllian orthodoxy in several items, such as his trepidation model (in which trepidation of the equinoxes is connected to the oscillation of the obliquity of the ecliptic), and he was strongly criticised by Ibn al-Hā'im, who dedicated his *al-Zīdj al-kāmil fī 'l-ta'ālīm* to the Almohad caliph Abū 'Abd Allāh Muḥammad al-Nāṣir (595-610/1199-1213). This work is not a standard *zīdj* as it contains an extremely elaborate set of canons (173 pages in the unique ms. Oxford Bodl. Marsh 618), with careful geometrical proofs, but no numerical tables. It also contains a great amount of historical information on the work done by the Toledan school in the 5th/11th century, as well as corrections in the Zarḳāllian parameters. (On Ibn al-Kammād, see J. Chabás and B.R. Goldstein, *Andalusian astronomy*: al-Zīj al-Muqtabis [*sic*] *of Ibn al-Kammād*, in *AHES*, xlviii [1994], 1-41; idem, *Ibn al-Kammād's star list*, in *Centaurus*, xxxviii [1996], 317-34; J.L. Mancha, *On Ibn al-Kammād's table for trepidation*, in *AHES*, lii [1998], 1-11. On Ibn al-Hā'im's *Kāmil Zīdj*, see E. Calvo, *Astronomical theories related to the sun in Ibn al-Hā'im's al-Zīj al-Kāmil fī 'l-ta'ālīm*, in *ZGAIW*, xii [1998], 51-111; and two new studies, R. Puig, *The theory of the moon in the al-Zīj al-Kāmil fī-l-ta'ālīm of Ibn al-Hā'im (ca. 1205)*, in *Suhayl*, i [2000], 71-99, and M. Comes, *Ibn al-Hā'im's trepidation model*, in *ibid.*, ii [2001]. The *Muḳtabas Zīdj* seems to be the main source of the astronomical tables prepared in the 14th century for King Peter IV of Aragon (Chabás, *Astronomía andalusí en Cataluña: las Tablas de Barcelona*, in *Vernet Festschrift*, i, 477-525).

After Ibn al-Hā'im, the main development of Western *zīdj*s took place in the Maghrib. There, already at the beginning of the 5th/11th century, the famous astrologer Ibn Abi 'l-Ridjāl al-Ḳayrawānī [*q.v.*] had composed a *zīdj* entitled *Ḥall al-'aḳd wa-bayān al-raṣd*, which has not survived. No other *zīdj*s are extant until *ca.* 600/1200, when we have the set of tables prepared by Abu 'l-'Abbās Ibn Isḥāḳ al-Tamīmī al-Tūnisī (*fl.* Tunis and Marrakesh *ca.* 589-619/1193-1222), which survive, among other materials, in a unique Ḥaydarābād manuscript (copied in Ḥimṣ in 716-17/1317). According to Ibn Khaldūn [*q.v.*], Ibn Isḥāḳ's tables were based on observations made by a Sicilian Jew; this does not seem to be true and Ibn Isḥāḳ's authentic tables seem to derive directly from

the Andalusī tradition. But Ibn Isḥāḳ's *zīdj* was left unfinished; it lacked an adequate set of canons and four "editions" at least of this work were prepared, in the Maghrib, by three different astronomers of the end of the 7th/13th and beginning of the 8th/14th centuries. One of them was the compiler of the Ḥaydarābād manuscript, who, *ca.* 665-80/1266-81, added to the original *zīdj* an impressive collection of materials (both canons and numerical tables) in which the predominant influence is clearly Andalusī, but the compilation was enormous and ill-suited for practical use. (See now the publications of A. Mestres listed in the *Bibl.*)

Ibn al-Bannā' of Marrakesh (654-721/1256-1321 [*q.v.*]) wrote his *Minhādj al-ṭālib fī ta'dīl al-kawākib* with an entirely different structure, mainly a selection of Ibn Isḥāḳ's tables accompanied by a readily comprehensible collection of canons which makes the *zīdj* accessible for the computation of planetary longitudes. This is accompanied by some formal modifications intended to make calculations easier: for the first time in the western Islamic world Ibn al-Bannā' uses "displaced" equations for the Sun and the planetary equations of the centre, and he applies the Ptolemaic lunar method of calculation to the computation of the equation of anomaly of Saturn and Jupiter which, like the Moon, have small epicycles. (See J. Vernet, *Contribución al estudio de la labor astronómica de Ibn al-Bannā'*, Tetuán 1952; Samsó, *Studies*, no. X; and Samsó and E. Millás, *The computation of planetary longitudes in the Zīj of Ibn al-Bannā'*, in *ASP*, viii [1998], 259-86.)

The two other "editions" of Ibn Isḥāḳ's *zīdj* were prepared by Muḥammad b. al-Raḳḳām (*fl.* Tunis and Granada, d. 715/1315). His two *zīdj*s are entitled *al-Zīdj al-shāmil fī tahdhīb al-Kāmil* and *al-Zīdj al-kawīm fī funūn al-ta'dīl wa 'l-taḳwīm*. The former was composed in Tunis in 679/1280-1 by copying, word for word, the canons of Ibn al-Hā'im's *Kāmil Zīdj*, but omitting all the careful geometrical demonstrations. To this he added the numerical tables of Ibn Isḥāḳ. The *Kawīm Zīdj* seems to contain a simplified rewording of the canons of the *Shāmil Zīdj* but it adds a few tables adapted to the geographical coordinates of Granada—after Ibn al-Raḳḳām's arrival in this city under Muḥammad II (671-701/1273-1302)—for which the author uses a latitude of 37;10°, identical to the modern value. (See E.S. Kennedy, *The Astronomical tables of Ibn al-Raqqām, a scientist of Granada*, in *ZGAIW*, xi [1997], 35-72. A partial edition of, and commentary on the *Shāmil Zīdj* is M. 'Abd al-Raḥmān, *Ḥisāb aṭwāl al-kawākib fī 'l-Zīj al-shāmil fī tahdhīb al-Kāmil li-Ibn al-Raqqām*, diss. University of Barcelona 1996, unpubl.) A third *zīdj* by Ibn al-Raḳḳām, *al-Zīdj al-mustawfī*, is extant in Rabat and Tunis, but the relation between it and the *Zīdj* of Ibn Isḥāḳ has not yet been studied.

The Andalusī tradition was also developed by two astronomers from Constantine who were active in Fez in the 8th/14th century. One of them is Ibn 'Azzūz al-Ḳusanṭīnī (d. 755/1354), who compiled his *al-Zīdj al-muwāfiḳ* correcting the mean motion parameters in Ibn Isḥāḳ's *zīdj* on the basis of observations made in Fez *ca.* 745/1345, later corrected using a peculiar "experimental" method: the mean motions were adjusted for casting horoscopes which could fit the historical reality of well-known events of the past, such as the battle of Faḥṣ Ṭarīf (El Salado, 741/1340). Other materials in this *zīdj* also derive from Andalusī sources, mainly Ibn al-Kammād, but it also contains interesting information such as tables of planetary velocities (also attested in the Alfonsine tradition), and the oldest mention of a lunar cycle of 11,325 days which can be used for the computation of lunar longitudes using almanac techniques. (See Samsó, *Andalusian astronomy in 14th century Fez:* al-Zīj al-Muwāfiq *of Ibn ʿAzzūz al-Qusanṭīnī*, in *ZGAIW*, xi [1997], 73-110; idem, *Horoscopes and history. Ibn ʿAzzūz and his retrospective horoscopes related to the Battle of El Salado (1340)*, in *North Festschrift*, Leiden 1999, 101-24.) Ibn ʿAzzūz included in his *Zīdj* a table for planetary velocities that is also found in many Latin copies; the original compiler of this table has not been determined, but he was almost certainly Andalusī. (See Samsó, al-Zīj al-Muwāfiq, 88-9, 104-5; Goldstein, Chabás and J.L. Mancha, *Planetary and lunar velocities in the Castilian Alfonsine tables*, in *Procs. Amer. Philosophical Soc.*, cxxxviii [1994], 61-95.)

Another person of the same origin, Abu 'l-Ḥasan ʿAlī al-Ḳusanṭīnī, compiled a small *zīdj*, the canons of which were written in verse so that they could easily be learnt by heart. This work is the only known Western Islamic document extant in Arabic in which the planetary theory is Indian and not Ptolemaic. In addition to this material, ultimately due to al-Khʷārazmī, this *zīdj* also however shows the influence of Ibn Isḥāḳ and Ibn al-Bannāʾ. (See E.S. Kennedy and D.A. King, *Indian astronomy in fourteenth-century Fez: the versified* Zīj *of al-Qusunṭīnī* [*sic*], in *JHAS*, vi [1982], 3-45, repr. in King, *Studies*, A-VIII.)

The *zīdj*s derived from Ibn Isḥāḳ were used in the Maghrib until the 13th/19th century, for they allowed the computation of sidereal longitudes which were used by astrologers. We have, however, a limited amount of information about observations made in the Maghrib in the 7th/13th and 8th/14th centuries which established that precession exceeded the amounts fixed in "Andalusī" trepidation tables and that the obliquity of the ecliptic had fallen below the limits of Ibn al-Zarḳālluh's model and tables. This explains the introduction of eastern *zīdj*s in the Maghrib from the 8th/14th century onwards. In them, mean motions were tropical, trepidation was replaced by constant precession and there were no tables to compute the obliquity of the ecliptic. The *Tādj al-azyādj* of Ibn Abi 'l-Shukr al-Maghribī (d. 680/1283) and the *al-Zīdj al-djadīd* of Ibn al-Shāṭir (d. 777/1375) were known in Tunis from the late 8th/14th century onwards, while the *Zīdj-i sulṭānī* of Ulugh Beg was known in the Maghrib towards the end of the 11th/17th, and it became very popular during the next two centuries. There were at least two Tunisian recensions of this *zīdj* prepared by Muḥammad al-Sharīf, called Sandjaḳ Dār al-Tūnisī, and by ʿAbd Allāh Ḥusayn Ḳusʿa al-Tūnisī; the former was produced in the late 11th/17th century and it contains, for the first time in the Maghrib, double-argument tables which combine the equation of the centre with the equation of the anomaly. The transmission was not all one-way; e.g. the Maghribī astronomer Abū ʿAlī al-Marrākushī [*q.v.*], who was active in Cairo *ca.* 680/1280, mentioned Ibn al-Zarḳālluh and Ibn al-Kammād in his monumental book on instrumentation, *Mabādiʾ wa-ghāyāt*. Also, the unique Ḥaydarābād manuscript of the *Zīdj* of Ibn Isḥāḳ was copied in Syria, and fragments attributed to the same author are found in various Yemeni sources.

The change of mentality represented by these eastern *zīdj*s also reached the Maghrib in the 10th/16th century through a different channel. The Jewish astronomer of Salamanca, Abraham Zacut, left Portugal in 1496 and lived in Fez, Tlemcen and Tunis until at least 911/1505. In one of these cities he compiled a new set of astronomical tables (1501) and his perpetual *Almanac* was translated from the printed Castilian version of 1496 into Arabic in the Maghrib in the early 11th/17th century by Aḥmad b. Ḳāsim al-Ḥadjarī. The new Arabic tables were the object of several commentaries. The *Almanac* represented not only a renewal of the old Andalusī tradition but also the introduction in the Maghrib of Alfonsine astronomy and of the astronomical research made in Southern France by Levi ben Gerson in the 14th century. It was still used in Morocco in the 19th century. (See Goldstein, *The Hebrew astronomical tradition: new sources*, in *Isis*, lxxii [1981], 237-51; idem, *Abraham Zacut and the medieval Hebrew astronomical tradition*, in *JHA*, xxix [1998], 177-86; and now Chabás and Goldstein, *Astronomy in the Iberian Peninsula. Abraham Zacut and the transition from manuscript to print*, in *Trans. Amer. Philosophical Soc.*, Philadelphia 2000.)

iv. The Contents of *Zīdj*s

1. *Sexagesimal alphanumerical notation.*

The entries in the tables in *zīdj*s and other corpora of tables are expressed sexagesimally, that is, to base 60, although integers are invariably expressed decimally. (In the modern notation standard in the history of the exact sciences, a number expressed in the form a,b;c,d stands for a × 60 + b + c ÷ 60 + d ÷ 3600.) The entries are written in Arabic alphanumerical notation [see abdjad], with the attendant traps for the careless copyist and the trusting reader. One of the challenges to modern investigators is the restoration of original values from carelessly-copied entries. The standard errors are inevitable or careless or compound. "Inevitable" refers to those cases where the omission of a diacritical point or two in one copy of a table invites an ambiguous interpretation in the next copy (thus, 14 ↔ 54 or 38 ↔ 33 or 80 ↔ 100). "Careless" refers to situations where the sloppy rendition of one letter or ligature leads to its misinterpretation as another (thus, 0 ↔ 5, 14 ↔ 15, 40 ↔ 47, 50 ↔ 7, 20 or 21 ↔ 9, 38 ↔ 18, 44 ↔ 47, or 18 ↔ 70). "Compound" refers to a combination of the previous two (thus 14 ↔ 15 ↔ 55 or 58 ↔ 18 ↔ 13 or 150 ↔ 87). (See R.A.K. Irani, *Arabic numeral forms*, in *Centaurus*, iv [1955], 1-12, repr. in Kennedy *et al.*, *Studies*, 710-21; Kennedy and Kennedy, *Islamic geographical tables*, x; Kunitzsch, *Sternkatalog des Almagest* (cited below, 10), i, 19-21; and King, *World-maps*, 161-63.)

2. *Chronology and calendar conversion.*

All *zīdj*s begin with one or more chapters and sets of tables devoted to the definition of the various eras and calendars in use at the time and place of writing, to methods of converting dates from one calendar to another, and to the problem of determining the *madkhal*, that is, the day of the week corresponding to the first day of a given year and month in a given calendar. The most common are the lunar Hidjra calendar and various solar calendars, including the Seleucid (Alexander), the Coptic (Diocletian), and the Persian (Yazdidjird), and, in the West, the Julian (A.D. and Spanish Era). The Persian calendar, using the Egyptian year of 365 days and no intercalation, is particularly convenient for astronomical purposes. Less commonly treated calendars are the Jewish, Syrian, Mālikī, Śaka and Chinese-Uighur [see taʾrīkh. 2.]. A few *zīdj*s treat the lunar mansions and the Arab system of dividing the year according to the mansions [see manāzil and anwāʾ].

3. *Trigonometry.*

All *zīdj*s contain trigonometric tables, usually of at least the sine (*al-djayb*) and the cotangent (*al-ẓill*) functions. The sine, first used by Indian astronomers, replaced the Ptolemaic chord function (*al-watar*) amongst the Muslims. The argument of the sine was an arc (rather than an angle) θ of a circle of radius R units, where R is a base, usually 60, occasionally 1. In the Indian tradition R was usually taken as 150; in the Hellenistic tradition it was taken as 60. The mediaeval sine function is denoted by Sin θ and is related to Ptolemy's chord function and the modern function by: Sin θ = 1/2 Chd (2θ) = R sin θ. In timekeeping, the versed sine (*al-sahm*) [*q.v.*] was also used (Vers θ = R - Cos θ), and occasionally also the cosecant function (*kuṭr al-ẓill*) (Cosec θ = R^2/Cos θ = R cosec θ). The earliest sine tables, from the 3rd/9th century, gave values to three sexagesimal places for each 1° of argument. By the 9th/15th century, accurate tables were available displaying the function to five places for each minute of argument. This was achieved by first deriving a very precise value of Sin 1° and utilising a clever method of second-order interpolation. The cotangent function invariably had the solar altitude as argument, and used a base equal to the length of a gnomon, so that the function measures the length of the horizontal shadow cast by the gnomon. The units for the gnomon length used were 12 digits (*iṣbaʿ*, pl. *aṣābiʿ*), or 7 feet (*ḳadam*, pl. *aḳdām*), although other values were also used. Al-Bīrūnī has a detailed discussion in his treatise *On shadows* (*Ifrād al-maḳāl fī amr al-ẓilāl*). The cotangent function was also first tabulated in the 3rd/9th century.

Trigonometric functions were occasionally tabulated independently, that is, not in *zīdj*s. Various procedures were used for interpolation in tables [see TAʿDĪL BAYN AL-SAṬRAYN]. (See further Kennedy, *Zīj survey*, 139-40; Schoy, *Beiträge zur arabischen Trigonometrie*, in *Isis*, v [1923], 364-99, and idem, *Die Gnomonik der Araber*, Bd. I: F of E. von Bassermann-Jordan (ed.), *Die Geschichte der Zeitmessung und der Uhren*, Berlin and Leipzig 1923, both repr. in idem, *Beiträge*, ii, 448-83 and 351-447; al-Bīrūnī, *Shadows*, 71-80. See also J.L. Berggren, *Episodes in the mathematics of medieval Islam*, New York, etc. 1986, 127-56.)

4. *Spherical astronomical functions.*

The study of spherical astronomy, sc. the mathematics of the celestial sphere and of the apparent daily rotation of the sphere, was of prime concern to Muslim astronomers, not least because of the importance of astronomical time-keeping [see MĪḲĀT]. The formulae for deriving time from solar or stellar altitude were known from the 2nd/8th century onwards and are discussed in every *zīdj*. (On the basic tables for spherical astronomy, see Kennedy, *Zīj survey*, 140-1; D.A. King, *Astronomical works of Ibn Yūnus*; al-Bīrūnī, *Maḳālīd*; al-Marrākushī, *Mabādiʾ wa-ghāyāt*; Berggren, *Spherical astronomy in Kūshyār ibn Labbān's* Jāmiʿ Zīj, in *Kennedy Festschrift*, 15-33; Kennedy, *Spherical astronomy in al-Kāshī's* Khāqānī Zīj, in *ZGAIW*, ii [1990], 1-46, repr. in idem, *Studies*, no. VII.)

We can distinguish between several groups of functions that were regularly tabulated in *zīdj*s:

a. The solar declination as a function of solar longitude. Underlying such tables was a value for the obliquity of the ecliptic, a parameter which changes slowly with time [see MAYL; SHAMS; MINṬAḲA].

b. The half length of daylight for different latitudes, as a function of solar longitude, in equatorial degrees and minutes, or in hours and minutes. Sometimes the latitude-dependent tables would be presented for the climates of Antiquity [see IḲLĪM].

c. The right ascensions as a function of ecliptic longitude, defining the rising time of a given arc of the ecliptic (measured from the vernal point) over the horizon at the equator, and the oblique ascensions, defining the corresponding times for the horizons of different localities [see MAṬĀLIʿ]. Often the latter would be tabulated for a series of latitudes.

d. The solar meridian altitude, and less frequently the rising amplitude of the Sun and the solar altitude in the prime vertical, all for specific latitudes. Likewise the solar altitude in the azimuth of the *ḳibla* [*q.v.*] for specific localities, also tabulated for each degree of solar longitude.

e. Certain functions with no immediate astronomical significance were also tabulated on account of their utility in the computation of other functions. We may mention as examples such "auxiliary" functions as the tangent of the declination (labelled *fuḍūl al-maṭāliʿ li 'l-arḍ kullihā*), the sine of the right ascension (*djayb al-maṭāliʿ*), and the product of the cosines of the declination and the terrestrial latitude (*al-aṣl al-muṭlaḳ*) (see King, *SATMI*, i). The culmination of this activity was the compilation of sets of tables of a series of such functions, combinations of which could yield solutions to problems of spherical astronomy for any latitude. Of these only the auxiliary tables of Ḥabash al-Ḥāsib are found in a *zīdj*: see further below, v. CATEGORIES OF TABLES NOT CONTAINED IN *ZĪDJ*S, 7.

Numerous other minor tables are found in corpora of tables relating to astronomical time-keeping, independent of *zīdj*s; see below, *ibid.*, 8. These collections also contain some more extensive tables for time-keeping; the only variety of these occasionally found in *zīdj*s is a table displaying the time (T) since rising of the Sun or any star as a function of the meridian altitude (H) and the instantaneous altitude (h), for a specific latitude: these tables are trapezoidal in shape since h < H and are called *zīdj al-ṭaylasān*, after the name of a shawl.

5. *Planetary mean motions, equations and latitudes.*

These constitute the hard core of all *zīdj*s. Extensive tables display the epoch positions and the mean motions (*wasaṭ*, pl. *awsāṭ*) of the "planets" (*al-kawākib al-sayyāra* or *al-mutaḥayyara*), that is, the Sun, Moon and five naked-eye planets. The tables are intended for a specific terrestrial longitude, usually that of the locality where the *zīdj* was compiled; if required, they can easily be modified to the meridian of another locality. The motions for a given number of completed years, months, days and hours are be added to the epoch positions (Ar. *aṣl*, Lat. *radix*) to derive the actual mean positions. These then needed to be modified by equations (*taʿdīl* [*q.v.*], pl. *taʿādīl*) to derive the true ecliptic positions (sometimes called *al-muḥkam* or *al-muʿaddal*). The operation of finding the true positions is called *taḳwīm* [*q.v.*], an expression also used for ephemerides. In the Ptolemaic tradition, the equations are calculated by successive applications of a series of auxiliary trigonometric functions for each planet [see SHAMS, and more especially ḲAMAR and TAʿDĪL]. (See Kennedy, *Zīj survey*, 141-2; Kennedy and H. Salam, *Solar and lunar tables in early Islamic astronomy*, in *JAOS*, lxxxvii [1967], 492-7, repr. in Kennedy *et al.*, *Studies*, 108-13.) More extensive double-argument tables for the equations are sometimes found in *zīdj*s (see M.J. Tichenor, *Late medieval two-argument tables for planetary longitudes*, in *JNES*, xxvi [1967], 126-8, repr. in Kennedy *et al.*, *Studies*, 122-4; C. Jensen, *The lunar theories of al-Baghdādī*, in *AHES*, viii [1971-2], 321-8; and G. Saliba, *The double-argument lunar tables of Cyriacus*, in *JHA*, vii (1976), 41-6), and sometimes tabulated separately (see below, *Categories of Tables*, 6). The apogees (*awdj*, pl. *awdjāt*) of the planets need to be considered in such calculations, and their positions, which vary with time, were also tabulated. Occasionally, especially—but not only—in Andalusī and Maghribī *zīdj*s, we find tables relating to trepidation (*al-iḳbāl wa 'l-idbār*), the presumed oscillation of the equinoxes; see above, iii. AN OVERVIEW, 4. Additional auxiliary tables enabled the computation of the planetary latitudes (*al-ʿarḍ*). In the case of the Moon, a single table would suffice, the argument being the nodal distance, derived from the lunar longitude and the position of the ascending node, which was tabulated along with the mean motions. In the calculation of solar and lunar eclipses (see below), also the equation of time [see TAʿDĪL AL-ZAMĀN], that is, the difference between true and mean solar time, with a maximum of around 30 minutes, had to be considered; tables for this function were likewise standard *zīdj*s. (See, most recently, Kennedy, *Two medieval approaches to the equation of time*, in *Centaurus*, xxxi [1988], 1-8, repr. in idem, *Studies*, no. VIII; van Dalen, *Al-Khwārizmī's tables revisited: analysis of the equation of time*, in *Vernet Festschrift* i, 195-252.) All of the necessary instructions for using these various tables are found in the typical *zīdj*.

6. *Planetary stations and visibility.*

Additional tables enabled the investigation of the direct and retrograde motions of the planets, their stations, and their visibility, which depends on their apparent elongation from the Sun.

7. *Solar and lunar parallax and eclipses.*

In *zīdj*s we also find tables for calculating the parallax of the Sun and Moon (*ikhtilāf al-manẓar*), preparatory to the prediction of eclipses (*kusūf* for the Sun and *khusūf* for the Moon [see KUSŪF]). This would be achieved by means of tables of the times of syzygies, of true solar and lunar motions in small critical periods of time, of apparent solar and lunar radii, and others. (See Kennedy, *Zīj survey*, 143-4; idem, *Parallax theory in Islamic astronomy*, in *Isis*, xlvii [1956], 33-53, repr. in idem *et al.*, *Studies*, 164-84.)

8. *Lunar visibility.*

Particular attention was paid by Muslim astronomers to the prediction of the visibility of the lunar crescent on the first evening after a conjunction of the Sun and Moon [see RUʾYAT AL-HILĀL]. From the 3rd/9th century onwards, tables were prepared to facilitate such predictions, underlying which were limiting conditions on various functions based on the apparent positions of the Sun and Moon relative to each other and to the local horizon. Numerous such tables, of varying sophistication and complexity, are found in various *zīdj*s. (See, for example, King, *Some early Islamic tables for determining lunar crescent visibility*, in *Kennedy Festschrift*, 185-225, repr. in idem, *Studies*, C-II; and J.P. Hogendijk, *Three Islamic lunar crescent visibility tables*, in *JHA*, xix [1988], 29-44.)

9. *Geographical tables.*

Tables displaying longitudes and latitudes of numerous localities are standard in *zīdj*s. They have been published in various formats, that is, according to locality, source, increasing longitudes and increasing latitudes, by E.S. and M.H. Kennedy, who provided a valuable research tool (*Geographical coordinates of localities from Islamic sources*, Frankfurt am Main 1987) that is currently being extended by M. Comes of Barcelona. These geographical coordinates were included in *zīdj*s in order to facilitate the use of planetary tables for other meridians, for which the longitude difference has to be taken into consideration, and also for computing the *ḳibla*. A minority of tables also display the *ḳibla* for each locality.

10. *Star catalogues.*

In a typical *zīdj* we find a table displaying the ecliptic or equatorial coordinates of selected stars [see NUDJŪM]. Procedures for coordinate conversion are also described. The star catalogue in the Arabic *Almagest* has been published by P. Kunitzsch (*Claudius Ptolemäus–Der Sternkatalog des Almagest–Die arabisch-mittelalterliche Tradition*, 3 vols., Wiesbaden 1986-91; see also idem, *Studies*, as well as *Kunitzsch Festschrift*). More research is necessary to establish the relationships between individual star catalogues, not all of which are related in a trivial way to that in the *Almagest*. Thus, for example, the tables in the *Kitāb Ṣuwar al-kawākib, On constellations*, by ʿAbd al-Raḥmān al-Ṣūfī [*q.v.*], and those in the *Zīdj* of Ulugh Beg, are essentially Ptolemaic (see E.B. Knobel, *Ulughbeg's catalogue of stars*, Washington, D.C. 1917; M.Y. Shevchenko, *An analysis of the errors in the star catalogues of Ptolemy and Ulugh Beg*, in *JHA*, xxi [1990], 187-201; K. Krisciunas, *A more complete analysis of the errors in Ulugh Beg's star catalogue*, in *JHA*, xxiv [1993], 269-80). Independent star-tables are found in the *Mumtaḥan Zīdj*, the *Ḥākimī Zīdj*, the *Huihui li* (a Chinese tr. of an independent Islamic *zīdj*), etc.

11. *Tables for mathematical astrology.*

*Zīdj*s usually contain tables useful for astrological purposes [see NUDJŪM, AḤKĀM AL-] notably, for drawing up a horoscope for a certain moment or for a series of such moments, such as each year in the life of an individual. Given the horoscopus or ascendant, that is, the point of the ecliptic instantaneously rising over the horizon [see ṬĀLIʿ], one needs to determine the positions of the astrological houses and to assign the Sun, Moon and five naked-eye planets to the appropriate house, and then to investigate the supposed significance of their positions relative to each other. Some *zīdj*s contain tables displaying the ecliptic longitudes of the cusps of the houses as a function of the longitude of the horoscopus, for a fixed latitude. Occasionally we find tables displaying the longitude of the horoscopus as a function of the altitude of the Sun throughout the year or of various fixed stars, also for a fixed latitude. Various tables in *zīdj*s serve the astrological notions of the "projections of the rays" (*maṭāriḥ al-shuʿāʿāt*), the "year transfers" (*taḥāwīl al-sinīn*), the "excess of revolution" (*faḍl al-dawr*), and the duration of gestation (*makth al-mawlūd fī baṭn ummihi*) (see Kennedy and H. Krikorian-Preisler, *The astrological doctrine of projecting the rays*, in *Al-Abhāth*, xxv [1972], 3-15, repr. in Kennedy *et al.*, *Studies*, 372-84; several papers in Kennedy *et al.*, *Studies*, 311-84, and idem, *Studies*, nos. XV-XVIII; idem, *The astrological houses as defined by medieval Islamic astronomers*, in *Vernet Festschrift*, ii, 535-78, repr. in Kennedy, *Studies*, no. XIX; Hogendijk, *The mathematical structure of two Islamic astrological tables for casting the rays*, in *Centaurus*, xxxii [1989], 171-202; idem, *Mathematical astrology in the Islamic tradition* (dealing with houses, rays and progressions), in a forthcoming publication including selected papers given at a conference "New perspectives on science in medieval Islam" held at the Dibner Institute, Cambridge, Mass., 6-8 Nov. 1998; see also below, v. CATEGORIES OF TABLES NOT CONTAINED IN *ZĪDJ*S, 12.) We may also find tables of the positions of the elusive, not least because fictitious, astrological body *al-Kayd* [*q.v.*]. Of all the aspects of mediaeval Islamic astronomy, mathematical astrology is the least researched.

12. *Analysis of tables and parameters.*

Already in the early 1960s, Kennedy applied the electronic computer to facilitate the analysis of medi-

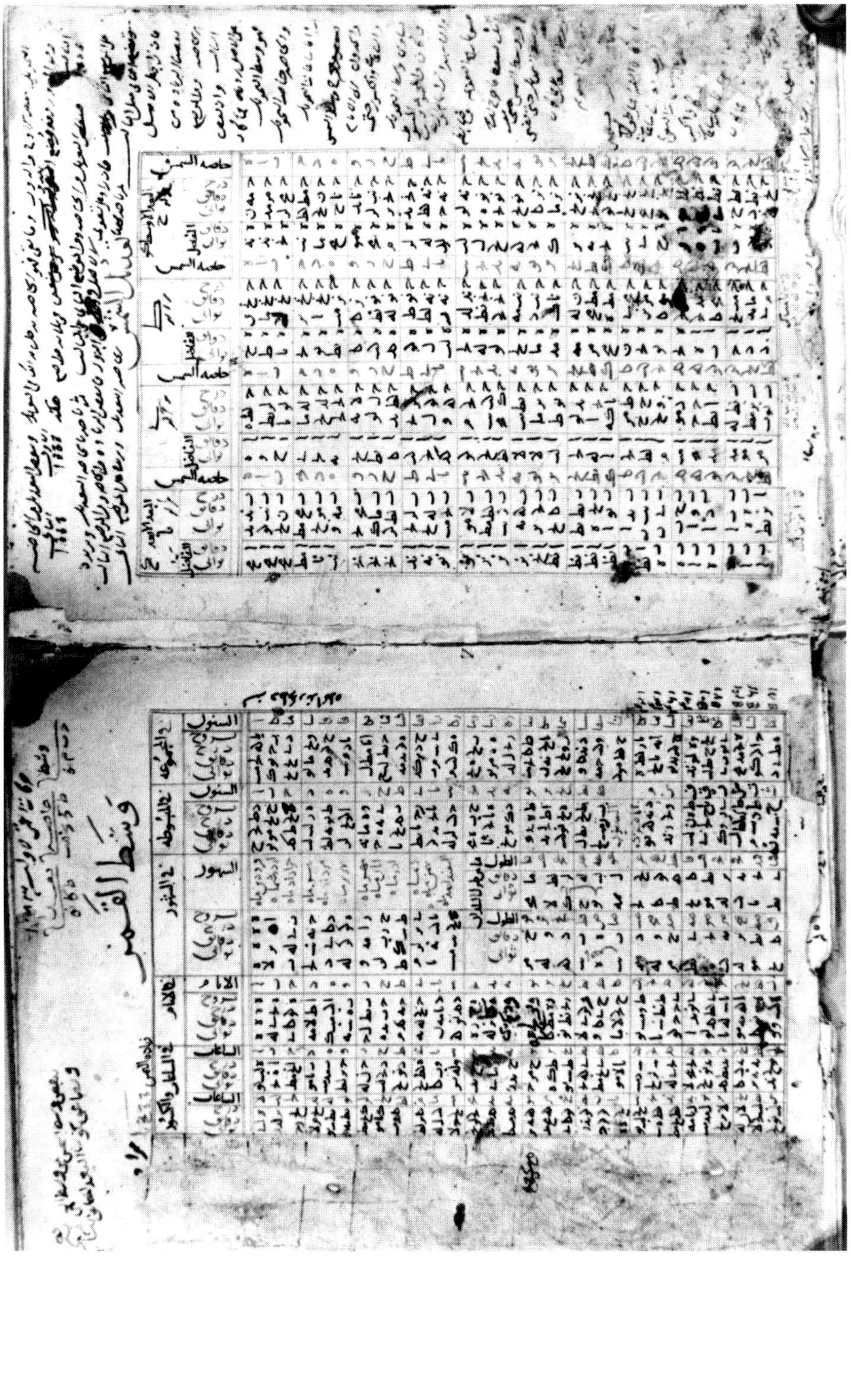

An extract from the solar and lunar tables in a Yemeni copy from *ca.* 650/1250 of the *Zīdj* of Kūshyār Ibn Labbān, compiled in Iran *ca.* 400/1000. (From ms. Cairo DM 400, courtesy of the Egyptian National Library.)

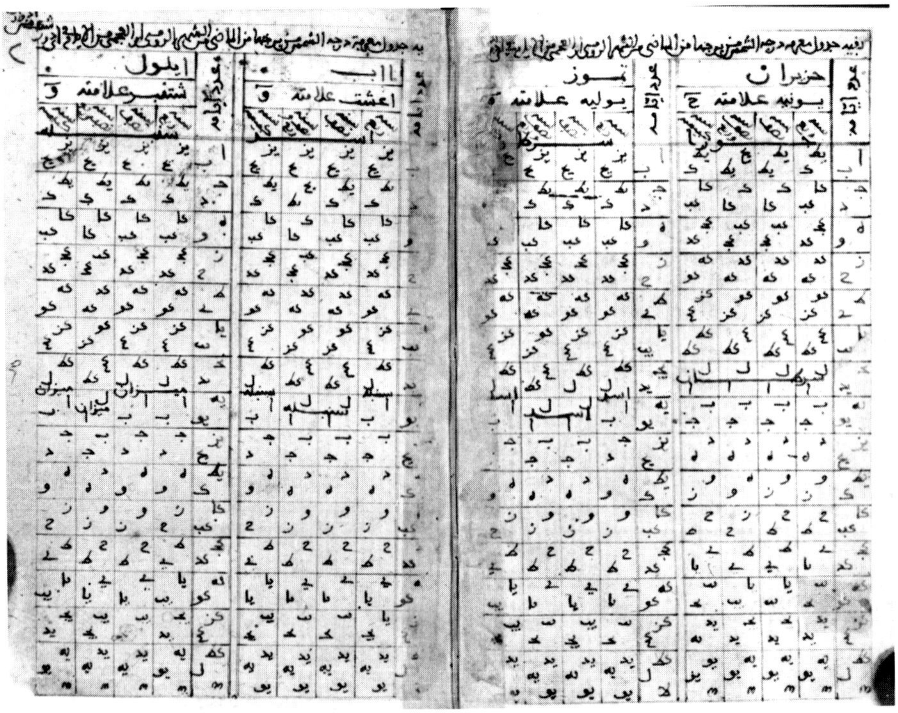

An extract from a set of Tunisian tables, copied *ca.* 1600, of the kind known in mediaeval scientific Arabic as s͟habaka, which enable the user to determine the solar longitude at any date. (From ms. Cairo DM 689, fol. 1v, courtesy of the Egyptian National Library.)

Solar tables in the astronomical handbook of the early 7th/13th-century Coptic scholar al-Asʿad b. al-ʿAssāl, copied *ca.* 1200/1800. The entries are written partly in Arabic alphanumerical notation and partly in the cumbersome Coptic numerical notation. (From ms. Cairo DM 910,1, copied *ca.* 1800, courtesy of the Egyptian National Library.)

The tables of a *zīdj* engraved on an astrolabe. This is the sole surviving example of an instrument known as *Zīdj al-ṣafāʾiḥ*, "The astronomical handbook on the plates of an astrolabe", devised by the mid-4th/10th-century Khurasānī astronomer Abū Djaʿfar al-Khāzin, and constructed by Badīʿ al-Zamān Hibat Allāh in Baghdād in 514/1120-1. (Photo provided in the 1970s by the late Alain Brieux, Paris.)

Lists of festivals in the calendars of the Magians and the Christians, as well as the dates of the heliacal risings of various bright stars and lunar mansions in the Christian (Syrian) calendar. (From ms. Berlin Ahlwardt 5751, pp. 194-5, courtesy of the Deutsche Staatsbibliothek (Preußischer Kulturbesitz).)

Part of the star-catalogue from the *Ḥākimī Zīdj* of Ibn Yūnus, giving the ecliptic coordinates (*ṭūl* and *ʿarḍ*, longitude and latitude) for some 58 stars calculated for 400 Yazdigird [= A.D. 1032]. (From ms. Cairo MM 188,2, fol. 81v, courtesy of the Egyptian National Library.)

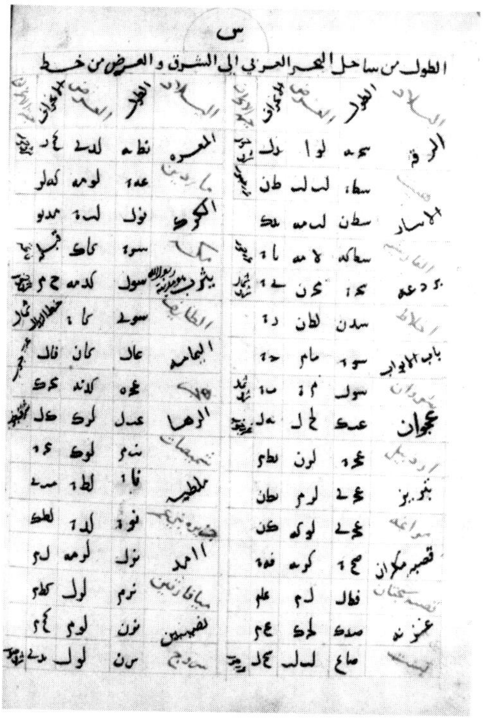

An extract from the geographical tables of the 8th/14th-century Damascus astronomer Ibn al-Shāṭir, from a copy of an Egyptian recension of his *Zīdj* for Cairo by the 9th/15th-century astronomer al-Kawm al-Rīshī. (From ms. Cairo DM 637,1, courtesy of the Egyptian National Library.)

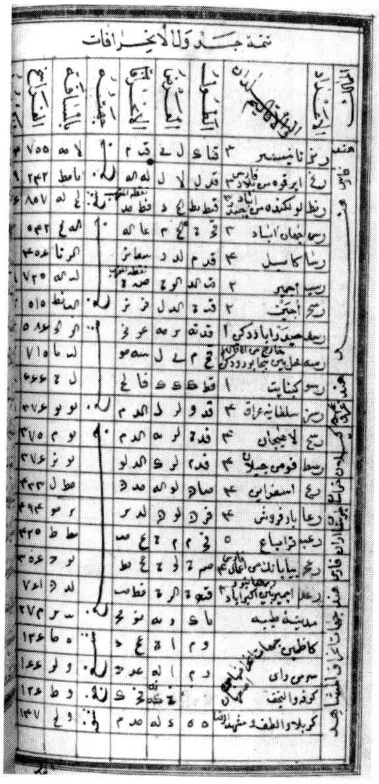

An extract from an early-12th/18th-century ʿIrāḳī recension of some anonymous 9th/15th-century geographical tables displaying longitudes, latitudes, *kibla*s and distances to Mecca of some 275 localities. (From ms. London B.L. add. 7489, fol. 58v, courtesy of The British Library.)

A table from a Mamlūk Egyptian manuscript showing a table for calculating the length of life of an individual from the longitude of the ascendant at his birth. The table was compiled by the late-2nd-century Hellenistic astrologer Vettius Valens. (From ms. Cairo DM 1108,4b, fol. 20v, courtesy of the Egyptian National Library.)

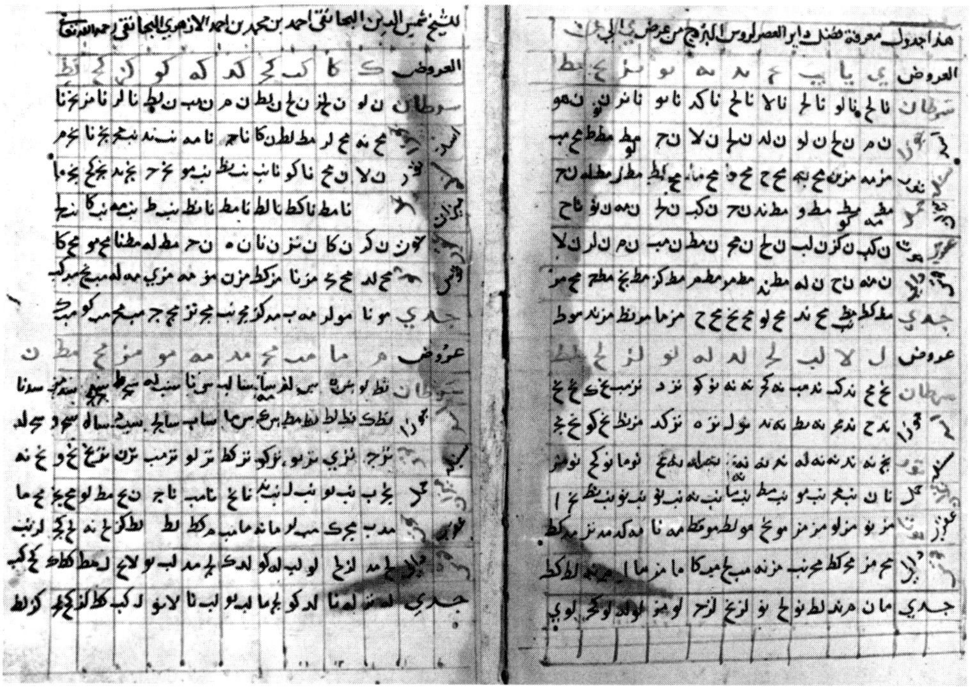

Parts of a table displaying the hour-angle at the beginning of the *ʿaṣr* prayer for each zodiacal sign of solar longitude and each degree of terrestrial latitude from 10° to 50°. (From ms. Cairo MM 33,2, fols. 6v-7r, courtesy of the Egyptian National Library.)

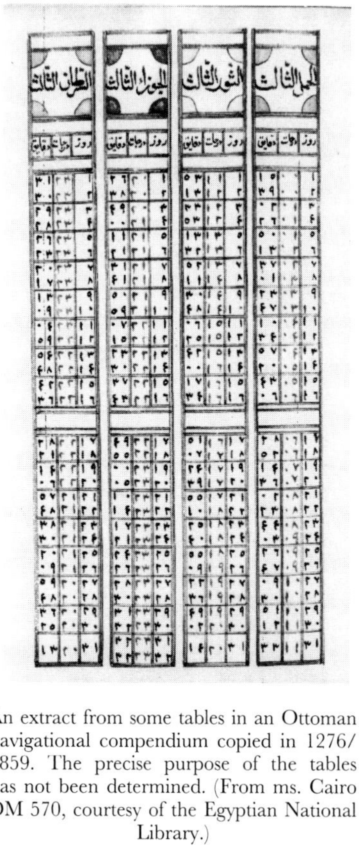

An extract from some tables in an Ottoman navigational compendium copied in 1276/1859. The precise purpose of the tables has not been determined. (From ms. Cairo DM 570, courtesy of the Egyptian National Library.)

An extract from a sexagesimal multiplication table displaying the products of the numbers m × n, where m and n are integers from 1 to 59. (From ms Cairo Zakiyya 740, fol. 1v, courtesy of the Egyptian National Library.)

An extract from a set of sine tables attributed to the late-4th/10th-century Egyptian astronomer Ibn Yūnus. (From ms. Berlin Ahlwardt 5752, fol. 13v, courtesy of the Deutsche Staatsbibliothek (Preußischer Kulturbesitz).)

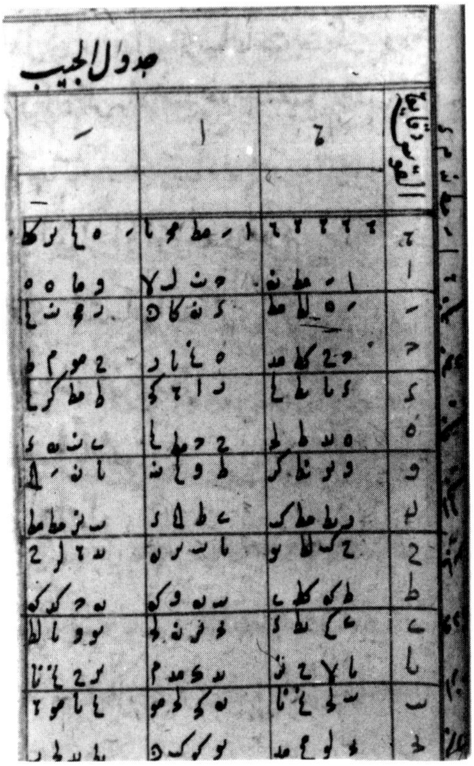

An extract from the sine tables in the *Zīdj-i Sulṭānī* of Ulugh Beg completed in 842/1438-9. (From an unidentified manuscript in Cairo, courtesy of the Egyptian National Library.)

aeval tables, an activity that was continued by some of his students and independently by R. Mercier. A third generation of younger researchers is currently active: statistical techniques have been applied to individual tables and groups of tables, notably by B. van Dalen and G. Van Brummelen. The former scholar has reactivated a file of over 2,000 parameters found in *zīdj*s which was started by Kennedy. (See Kennedy, *The digital computer and the history of the exact sciences*, in *Centaurus*, xii [1968], 107-13, repr. in idem *et al., Studies*, 385-91; van Dalen, *Ancient and mediaeval astronomical tables: mathematical structure and parameter values*, Utrecht 1992; idem, *A statistical method for recovering unknown parameters from medieval astronomical tables*, in *Centaurus*, xxxii [1989], 85-145; G. Van Brummelen, A *survey of the mathematical tables in Ptolemy's* Almagest, in A. von Gotstedter (ed.), *Ad radices...*, Stuttgart 1994, 155-70; and Mielgo, *A method of analysis for mean motion astronomical tables*, in *Vernet Festschrift*, i, 159-80.)

v. Categories of tables not contained in *zīdj*s

The varieties of tables mentioned here rarely occur in *zīdj*s, sometimes because the individual tables were even more voluminous than a typical *zīdj*, occasionally because they are more suited to inclusion in treatises on instruments, or simply because they formed part of a corpus of tables for time-keeping for a specific latitude.

1. *Sexagesimal multiplication tables.*

These are tables of sexagesimal products m × n (m, n: 1, 2, ..., 60) and they are common in the manuscript sources (*al-djadwal al-sittīnī*); they invariably contain some 3,600 entries. Less common were larger tables for m = 0;1, 0;2, ... 59;59 and n = 1, 2, ..., 60 containing some 216,000 entries (aptly called *al-djadwal al-sittīnī al-kabīr*). These were of use in working the extensive sexagesimal calculations involved in working with a *zīdj*. (See further King, *On medieval Islamic multiplication tables*, in *HistMath*, i [1974], 317-323, and idem, *Supplementary notes...*, in *ibid.*, vi [1979], 405/17, repr. in idem, *Studies*, A-XIV and XV.)

2. *Trigonometric tables.*

In Mamlūk Egypt, the sine and cotangent functions for each minute of argument were tabulated separately. Such tables, to greater accuracy, were found in the *Sulṭānī Zīdj* of Ulugh Beg (see above), and these were also copied separately.

3. *Ephemerides.*

Ephemerides displaying positions of the Sun, Moon and five planets for each day of a given year were compiled already in Baghdad in the 3rd/9th century and the production continued in various centres until the 13th/19th century. [For details, see taḳwīm.]

4. *Auxiliary tables for compiling ephemerides.*

Since the motions of the Sun, Moon and planets are cyclical, a given set of tables defining one complete cycle can be used to calculate positions by simply plugging into the table at the right place for beginning of a given year: the positions for the entire year can then be derived with facility. This was recognised already in Antiquity, and some Islamic tables reflect this, for example, the tables of Ibn al-Zarḳālluh and Zakut, which could be used to calculate individual positions. Two other sets of such auxiliary tables specifically for generating ephemerides are known, but there are surely more: an anonymous set for the Sun and Moon, compiled in Persia at the end of the 5th/11th century, and tables for the Sun and Moon compiled by Ibn al-Madjdī in Cairo in the 9th/15th century, with tables for the planets contributed by various later Egyptian astronomers (see Kennedy, *A set of medieval tables for quick calculation of solar and lunar ephemerides*, in *Oriens*, xviii-xix [1967], 327-34, repr. in idem *et al., Studies*, 114-21; and idem and King, *Ibn al-Majdī's tables for calculating ephemerides*, in *JHAS*, iv [1980], 48-68, repr. in King, *Studies*, A-VI).

5. *Tables for determining lunar crescent visibility.*

In addition to the tables in *zīdj*s, we also find occasional sets of calculations for visibility over a series of months, or lists of minimum apparent distances between the Sun and Moon to assure visibility, with values given to the nearest degree for each zodiacal sign [see ru'yat al-hilāl].

6. *Double-argument planetary equation tables.*

In the case of the extensive lunar equation tables attributed to Ibn Yūnus [*q.v.*], these are not presented in a *zīdj*, although the unique manuscript is labelled as such (see King, *A Double argument table for the lunar equation attributed to Ibn Yūnus*, in *Centaurus*, xviii [1974], 129-46, repr. in idem, *Studies*, A-V). Numerous later sets from Egypt to India were likewise copied separately.

7. *Auxiliary tables for solving spherical astronomical problems for all latitudes.*

Muslim astronomers compiled several sets of tables of trigonometric functions with no specific significance but so conceived that ordered applications of them could lead to the solution of problems of spherical astronomy (see already above, iv. The Contents of *zīdj*s, 4). Their progress in mathematical methods is well reflected in these tables, of which over a dozen sets are known (these are surveyed in King, *SATMI*, i-9). The four most significant examples are the following: the *Djadwal al-taḳwīm* of Ḥabash al-Ḥāsib (Baghdād and Sāmarrā, 3rd/9th century) with five functions and 450 entries, found in his *Dimashḳī Zīdj* and also in the *Muṣṭalaḥ Zīdj* (see Irani, *The* Jadwal al-taqwīm of *Habash al-Ḥāsib*, M.Sc. thesis, American University of Beirut 1956, unpubl.); the *Djadwal al-daḳā'iḳ* of Abū Naṣr b. ʿIrāḳ (Gurgān, *ca.* 400/1000) with five functions and 225 entries (analysed in C. Jensen, *Abū Naṣr's approach to spherical astronomy as developed in his treatise* The table of minutes, in *Centaurus*, xvi [1971], 1-19); the *Djadāwil al-dā'ir al-āfāḳī* of Nadjm al-Dīn al-Miṣrī (Cairo, *ca.* 700/1300), serving both as a table for finding the time of day or night from the altitude of the Sun or any non-circumpolar star and also as a universal auxiliary table, with a single main function for three independent arguments and a grand total of *ca.* 420,000 entries (see now F. Charette, *A monumental medieval table for solving the problems of spherical astronomy for all latitudes*, in *AIHS*, xlviii [1998], 11-64); and *al-Djadwal al-āfāḳī* of Shams al-Dīn al-Khalīlī (Damascus, *ca.* 760/1360) (see the art. on him in *DSB*, Suppl.) with three main functions and *ca.* 14,000 entries (see King, *Al-Khalīlī's auxiliary tables for solving problems of spherical astronomy*, in *JHA*, iv [1973], 99-110, repr. in idem, *Studies*, A-XI; also Van Brummelen, *The numerical structure of al-Khalīlī's auxiliary tables*, in *Physis*, xxviii [1991], 667-97). These tables are part of a tradition in Islamic astronomy of devising solutions to problems of spherical astronomy for all latitudes (see King, *Universal solutions in Islamic astronomy* (publ. 1987), and idem, *Universal solutions to problems of spherical astronomy from Mamluk Egypt and Syria* (publ. 1988), repr. in idem, *Studies*, C-VI and VII, and again in idem, *SATMI*, vi; see also idem, *World-maps*, chs. 2-4 and 9).

8. *Tables for time-keeping by the Sun and stars.*

Extensive corpora of tables of the hour-angle (*faḍl al-dā'ir*) and the time since rising (*al-dā'ir*), as well as the azimuth (*al-samt*), for specific latitudes were compiled [see mīḳāt]. All such tables are analysed in King, *SATMI*, i.

9. *Tables for regulating the times of Muslim prayer.*

The first tables for regulating the times of prayer [see MĪḲĀT; AL-SHAFAḲ] were compiled in the 3rd/9th century. All such tables are analysed in King, *SATMI*, ii.

10. *Tables for finding the* ḳibla.

Between the 3rd/9th and 8th/14th centuries, Muslim astronomers compiled various tables displaying the *ḳibla*, measured from the local meridian, as a function of longitude difference and latitude difference from Mecca [see ḲIBLA].

11. *Tables for constructing astrolabes and sundials.*

A series of Muslim astronomers addressed the problem of the calculation of the size and position of the various markings on astrolabes and sundials in trigonometric terms, as well as using the better-known methods of geometric construction [see ASṬURLĀB; MIZWALA, and also King, *Islamic astronomical tables*, 51-5].

12. *Astrological tables.*

There are all manner of astrological tables to be found in works other than *zīdj*s (Sezgin, *GAS*, vii, 22-5, lists some important sources, mainly unstudied).

vi. CONCLUDING REMARKS

The scope of the *zīdj* literature and Islamic astronomical tables in general is a clear indication of the interest of Muslim scholars in astronomy for over a millennium. It is an accident of Islamic history that a few of these *zīdj*s became known in mediaeval Europe and that this spawned an interest there too. Alone the computational accuracy of the vast majority of the tables in the *zīdj*s is a clear sign of the competence of their compilers. Their errors, if they are original and not due to copyists, can provide useful clues to the way in which the tables were calculated. But the accompanying texts also merit our attention, and sometimes the tables cannot be understood without them. The study of Islamic mathematical astronomy is progressing slowly but constantly, and the reader should understand that this brief overview is intended to encourage the reader to consult Kennedy's *Zīj survey* and the many writings it has already inspired and will continue to inspire in the future.

Bibliography: The following abbreviations are used for various journals not listed in the *Abbreviations for periodicals*, etc.: *AHES: Archive for History of Exact Science; AIHS: Archives internationales d'Histoire des Sciences; ASP: Arabic Science and Philosophy; Centaurus: Centaurus—International Magazine of the History of Mathematics, Science, and Technology; HistMath: Historia Mathematica; HistSci: Historia Scientiarum* (Brussels); *HS: History of Science* (Cambridge); *IJHS: Indian Journal for History of Science; Isis: Isis—An International Review Devoted to the History of Science and its Cultural Influences; JHA: Journal for the History of Astronomy; JHAS: Journal for the History of Arabic Science* (Aleppo); *Physis: Physis—Rivista internazionale di storia della scienza; Suhayl: Suhayl—Journal for the History of the Exact and Natural Sciences in Islamic Civilisation* (Barcelona).

References to publications on individual tables as well as specific classes of tables are given in the text. This article is condensed from a more extensive overview in *Suhayl* (see below), ii (2001). The main study of *zīdj*s is E.S. Kennedy, *A survey of Islamic astronomical tables*, in *Trans. Amer. Philosophical Soc.* N.S., xlii 2 (1956), 123-77, repr. n.d. [*ca.* 1990], with separate pagination. See also J. Samsó, *Calendarios populares y tablas astronómicas*, in *Historia de la Ciencia Arabe*, Madrid 1981, 127-62. On categories of tables not contained in *zīdj*s, see D.A. King, *On the astronomical tables of the Islamic Middle Ages*, in *Studia Copernicana*, xiii (1975), 37-56, repr. in idem, *Studies* (see below), A-I (with addenda). A work still of prime importance is A. Sayılı, *The observatory in Islam* (Publs. of the Turkish Historical Soc., Series VII, No. 38), Ankara 1960, repr. New York 1981. Much of the most recent research on Islamic mathematical astronomy and astrology is collected in the *Kennedy Festschrift* and *Vernet Festschrift* (see below). On the mediaeval astronomers there are occasionally articles in this *Encyclopaedia* or in *DSB: Dictionary of scientific biography*, 14 vols. and 2 suppl. vols., New York 1970-80.

Several of the studies listed in this article are reprinted in various volumes to which references are abbreviated as follows: Goldstein, *Studies*: B.R. Goldstein, *Theory and observation in ancient and medieval astronomy*, Variorum, London 1985; Kennedy *et al.*, *Studies*: E.S. Kennedy, Colleagues and Former Students, *Studies in the Islamic exact sciences*, ed. M.H. Kennedy and D.A. King, Beirut 1983; Kennedy, *Studies*: E.S. Kennedy, *Astronomy and astrology in the medieval Islamic world*, Ashgate-Variorum, Aldershot and Brookfield, Vt. 1998; King, *Studies*, A-C: D.A. King, *Islamic mathematical astronomy*, Variorum, London 1986, 2nd rev. ed., Variorum, Aldershot 1993 (A); *Islamic astronomical instruments*, Variorum, London 1987, repr. Variorum, Aldershot 1995 (B); and *Astronomy in the service of Islam*, Variorum, Aldershot 1993 (C); Kunitzsch, *Studies*: P. Kunitzsch, *The Arabs and the stars*, Variorum, Northampton 1989; Langermann, *Studies*: Y.T. Langermann, *The Jews and the sciences in the Middle Ages*, Variorum, Aldershot 1999; Lorch, *Studies*: R.P. Lorch, *Arabic mathematical sciences. Instruments, texts, transmission.* Variorum, Aldershot 1995; Millás Vallicrosa, *Estudios*, A-B: J.-M. Millás Vallicrosa, *Estudios*, and *Nuevos estudios sobre historia de la ciencia española* (first publ. Barcelona 1949 and 1960, respectively), repr. together in 2 vols., Madrid 1987; Nallino, *Scritti*, v: C.A. Nallino, *Raccolta di scritti editi e inediti*, v, *Astrologia—Astronomia—Geografia*, ed. M. Nallino, Rome 1944; Saliba, *Studies*: G. Saliba, *A history of Arabic astronomy. Planetary theories during the Golden Age of Islam*, New York and London 1994; Samsó, *Studies*: J. Samsó, *Islamic astronomy and medieval Spain*, Variorum, Aldershot 1994; Schoy, *Beiträge*: F. Sezgin *et al.* (eds.), *Carl Schoy. Beiträge zur arabisch-islamischen Mathematik und Astronomie*, 2 vols., Frankfurt 1988; Suter, *Beiträge*: F. Sezgin (ed.), *Heinrich Suter. Beiträge zur Geschichte der Mathematik und Astronomie im Islam*, 2 vols., Frankfurt 1986; Vernet, *Estudios*, A-B: J. Vernet, *Estudios sobre historia de la ciencia medieval*, Barcelona-Bellaterra 1979, and idem, *De ʿAbd al-Raḥmān I a Isabel II, recopilación de estudios dispersos*, Barcelona 1989; Vernet (ed.), *Estudios*, A-B: idem (ed.), *Textos y estudios sobre astronomía española en el siglo XIII*, and *Nuevos estudios sobre astronomía española en el siglo de Alfonso X*, Barcelona 1981, 1983. Also important for the study of transmission of Islamic tables to Byzantium and Europe are Tihon, *Studies*: A. Tihon, *Études d'astronomie byzantine*, Variorum, Aldershot 1994, and Poulle, *Studies*: E. Poulle, *Astronomie planétaire au Moyen Âge latin*, Variorum, Aldershot 1996. Other studies are published in collected works, such as *Kennedy Festschrift*: D.A. King and G. Saliba (eds.), *From deferent to equant. A volume of studies in the history of science in the ancient and medieval Near East in honor of E.S. Kennedy*, in *Annals of the New York Academy of Sciences*, d [= 500] (1987); *North Festschrift*: A. Vanderjagt and L.L. Nanta (eds.), *Between demonstration and imagination. Essays in the history of science and philosophy presented to John D. North*, Leiden 1999;

Kunitzsch Festschrift: M. Folkerts and R.P. Lorch (eds.), *Sic itur ad astra. Studien zur Geschichte der Mathematik und Naturwissenschaften. Festschrift für den Arabisten Paul Kunitzsch zum 70. Geburtstag*, Wiesbaden 2000; and *Vernet Festschrift*: J. Casulleras and J. Samsó (eds.), *From Baghdad to Barcelona. Studies in the Islamic exact sciences in honour of Prof. Juan Vernet*, 2 vols., Barcelona 1996.

The standard bio-bibliographical sources for the history of Islamic astronomy are (in chronological order): Suter, *MAA*: H. Suter, *Die Mathematiker und Astronomen der Araber und ihre Werke*, in *Abh. zur Geschichte der mathematischen Wissenschaften*, x (1900), and *Nachträge und Berichtigungen*, in *ibid.*, xiv (1902), 157-85, repr. Amsterdam 1982, and again in Suter, *Beiträge*, i, 1-285 and 286-314; Renaud, *Additions à Suter*: H.J.P. Renaud, *Additions et corrections à Suter, "Die Mathematiker und Astronomen der Araber"*, in *Isis*, xviii (1932), 166-83; M. Krause, *Stambuler Handschriften islamischer Mathematiker*, in *Quellen und Studien zur Geschichte der Mathematik, Astronomie und Physik*, Abt. B: Studien, Band 3, Heft 4 (1936); Storey, ii/1: *A. Mathematics. B. Weights and measures. C. Astronomy and astrology. D. Geography*, London 1958, repr. 1972: Sezgin, *GAS*, esp. v, *Mathematik*, vi, *Astronomie*, vii, *Astrologie*; Matvievskaya and Rosenfeld, *MAMS*: G.P. Matvievskaya and B.A. Rosenfeld, *Matematiki i astronomi musulmanskogo srednevekovya i ikh trudi*, 3 vols., Moscow 1983; *Cairo ENL survey*: King, *A survey of the scientific manuscripts in the Egyptian National Library* (Publications of the American Research Center in Egypt, Catalogs, 5), Winona Lake, Ind. 1986; E. İhsanoğlu (ed.), *Ottoman astronomy* and *Ottoman mathematics*: idem (ed.), *Osmanlı astronomi literatürü tarihi*, 2 vols., and *Osmanlı matematik literatürü tarihi*, 2 vols. (IRCICA Studies and Sources on the History of Science, 7-8), Istanbul 1996, 1999.

An indispensable research tool is Kennedy and Kennedy, *Islamic geographical coordinates*: E.S. and M.H. Kennedy, *Geographical coordinates of localities from Islamic sources*, Frankfurt 1987. References are also made to King, *SATMI*: King, *Studies in astronomical timekeeping in medieval Islam*, 10 pts., including i, *A survey of tables for reckoning time by the sun and stars*; ii, *A survey of tables for regulating the times of prayer*, vi, *Universal solutions in medieval Islamic astronomy*, Leiden, forthcoming; idem, *World-maps for finding the direction and distance to Mecca*, Leiden-London 1999.

Most of the underlying astronomical and astrological notions are outlined in Bīrūnī, *Tafhīm*: R.R. Wright, *The Book of instruction in the elements of the art of astrology by Abu 'l-Rayḥān ... al-Bīrūnī*, London 1934, repr. Baghdād n.d. On spherical astronomy, two indispensable works are Bīrūnī, *Maḳālīd*: M.-Th. Debarnot (ed. and tr.), *al-Bīrūnī, Kitāb Maqālīd ʿilm al-hayʾa. La trigonométrie sphérique chez les Arabes de l'est à la fin du Xe siècle*, Damascus 1985, and Marrākushī, *Mabādiʾ wa-ghāyāt*, A-B: J.-J. Sédillot, *Traité des instruments astronomiques des Arabes composé au treizième siècle par Aboul Hhassan Ali de Maroc*, 2 vols., Paris 1834-5, repr. in 1 vol., Frankfurt 1985, and L.-A. Sédillot, *Mémoire sur les instruments astronomiques des Arabes*, in *Méms. de l'Acad. Royale des Inscriptions et Belles-Lettres de l'Institut de France*, i (1844), 1-229, repr. Frankfurt 1989. The approaches to the subject are quite different in these two works, being based on spherical trigonometry and projection methods, respectively. See also Bīrūnī, *Shadows*: E.S. Kennedy, *The exhaustive treatise on shadows by Abū al-Rayḥān ... al-Bīrūnī. Translation and commentary*, Aleppo 1976.

On regional developments in Islamic astronomy, see first Sayılı, *The observatory in Islam*. On the development of the professional astronomers responsible for the regulation of the calendar and times of prayer, see King, *On the role of the muezzin and the muwaqqit in medieval Islamic society*, in F.J. Ragep and S.P. Ragep, with S.J. Livesey (eds.), *Tradition, transmission, transformation. Proceedings of two conferences on pre-modern science held at the University of Oklahoma*, Leiden, etc. 1996, 285-346. The following regional surveys are available. Early Islamic (mainly ʿIrāḳ and Persia): D. Pingree, *The Greek influence on early Islamic mathematical astronomy*, in *JAOS*, xciii (1973), 32-43; idem, *Indian influence on Sassanian and early Islamic astronomy and astrology*, in *The Journal of Oriental Research* (Madras), xxxiv-xxxv (1964-6), 118-126. ʿIrāḳ: al-ʿAzzāwī, *Taʾrīkh ʿilm al-falak fi 'l-ʿIrāḳ*, Baghdād 1958 (to be used with caution). Egypt, Syria and Yemen: King, *Aspects of Fatimid astronomy*, in M. Barrucand (ed.), *L'Égypte Fatimide: son art et son histoire. Actes du colloque organisé à Paris les 28, 29 et 30 mai 1998*, Paris 1999, 497-517; idem, *The astronomy of the Mamluks*, in *Isis*, lxxiv (1983), 531-55, repr. in idem, *Studies*, A-III; idem, *L'astronomie en Syrie à l'époque islamique*, in S. Cluzan *et al.* (eds.), *Syrie, mémoire et civilisation*, Paris 1993, 386-95, 432-43, 480; idem, *Mathematical astronomy in medieval Yemen. A biobibliographical survey*, Malibu, Ca. 1983. Al-Andalus: Millás Vallicrosa, *Estudios*, A-B; Vernet, *Estudios*, A-B; Vernet (ed.), *Estudios*, A-B; J. Samsó, *Studies*; and idem, *Las ciencas de los antiguos en al-Andalus*, Madrid 1992; numerous other publications of the Barcelona school; L. Richter-Bernburg, *Ṣāʿid, the Toledan Tables, and Andalusī science*, in *Kennedy Festschrift*, 373-401. See also G. Toomer, *A survey of the Toledan Tables*, in *Osiris*, xv (1968), 5-174. The Hebrew tradition: B.R. Goldstein, *The survival of Arabic astronomy in Hebrew*, in *JHAS*, iii (1979), 31-9, repr. in idem, *Studies*, no. XXI; idem, *Astronomy in the medieval Spanish Jewish community*, in *North Festschrift*, 225-41; and Y.T. Langermann, *Science in the Jewish communities of the Iberian Peninsula. An interim report*, in idem, *Studies*, i. The Maghrib: King, *An overview of the sources for the history of astronomy in the medieval Maghrib*, in *Actes du 2e Colloque Maghrébin de l'Histoire des Mathématiques Arabes, Tunis, 1-3 déc. 1988*, Tunis (Institut Supérieur de l'Éducation et de la Formation Continue), n.d. [*ca.* 1990], 125-57, updated as *On the history of astronomy in the medieval Maghrib*, in *Études philosophiques et sociologiques dédiées à Jamal ed-Dine Alaoui*, Fez 1998, 27-61; Samsó, *An outline of the history of Maghribī zījes from the end of the thirteenth century*, in *JHA*, xxix (1998), 93-102. Persia and Central Asia: Kennedy, *The exact sciences in Iran under the Seljuqs and Mongols*, in *Camb. hist. Iran*, v, Cambridge 1968, 659-79, and *The exact sciences in Iran under the Timurids*, in *ibid.*, vi, Cambridge 1986, 568-80; H.J.J. Winter, *Persian science in Safavid times*, in *ibid.*, 581-609; T. Heidarzadeh, *From the Maragha School to the Darolfonun. A historical review of astronomy in Iran from the 13th to the 19th century*, unpubl. paper presented at the symposium "Science and Technology in the Turkish and Islamic World", Istanbul, 3-5 June 1994; King, *World-maps*, 128-34; *EI*² art. ṢAFAWIDS. IV.III. The Byzantine tradition: A. Tihon, *Tables islamiques à Byzance*, in *Byzantion*, lx (1990), 401-25; numerous studies by D. Pingree mentioned below. Ottoman Turkey: İhsanoğlu, *Introduction of Western science to the Ottoman World. A case study of modern astronomy (1660-1860)*, in idem (ed.), *Transfer of modern science and technology* *to the Muslim world*, Istanbul (IRCICA) 1982, 67-120; idem (ed.), *Ottoman astronomy* and *Ottoman mathematics*. India: S.A. Khan Ghori, *Development of zīj literature in India*, in *IJHS*, xx (1985), 21-48, 438-41 (notes), 480-1 (bibl); S.M.R. Ansari, *On the transmission of Arabic-Islamic astronomy to medieval India*, in *AIHS*, xlv (1995), 273-97; Pingree, *Islamic astronomy in Sanskrit*, in *JHAS*, ii (1978), 315-30; idem, *Indian reception of Muslim versions of Ptolemaic astronomy*, in Ragep and Ragep (eds.), *Tradition, transmission, transformation* (cited above), 471-85.

On various individual *zīdj*s of prime importance, see the following. On the *Zīdj* of al-Kh^{w}ārazmī, see H. Suter *et al.* (eds.), *Die astronomischen Tafeln des Muhammed ibn Musa al-Khwārizmī*, in *Kgl. Danske Vidensk. Skrifter*, 7. R., *Hist. og filos. Afd.*, 3/1 (1914), providing an edition of the Latin text; O. Neugebauer, *The astronomical tables of al-Khwārizmī*, in *ibid.*, 4/2 (1962), with Eng. tr. of the text and a commentary; Goldstein, *Ibn al-Muthannā's commentary on the astronomical tables of al-Khwārizmī*, New Haven 1967. In B. van Dalen, *Al-Khwārizmī's tables revisited. Analysis of the equation of time*, in *Vernet Festschrift*, i, 195-252, the various tables are sorted according to their Baghdādī or Andalusī origin. On the *Dimashkī Zīdj* of Ḥabash, see M.Th. Debarnot, *The Zīj of Ḥabash al-Ḥāsib. A survey of MS Istanbul Yeni Cami 784/2*, in *Kennedy Festschrift*, 35-69. On the *Zīdj* of al-Battānī, see C.A. Nallino (ed., tr. and comm.), *al-Battānī sive Albatenii opus astronomicum*, 3 pts., Milan 1899-1907, repr. in one vol. Hildesheim and New York 1977, pts. I-II repr. Frankfurt 1969, pt. III (Ar. text) repr. Baghdād n.d. [*ca.* 1960]. On the *Ḥākimī Zīdj* of Ibn Yūnus, see A.P. Caussin de Perceval, *Le livre de la grande table Hakémite observée par le Sheikh . . . ebn Iounis . . .*, in *Notices et extraits des manuscrits de la Bibliothèque Nationale* 7 (An XII: 1804), 16-240 (separatum paginated 1-224); King, *The astronomical works of Ibn Yūnus*, dissertation, Yale Univ. 1972, available through University Microfilms, Ann Arbor, Mich. The *Zīdj* of Bīrūnī is available as al-Bīrūnī, *al-Ḳānūn al-Masʿūdī*, 3 vols., Ḥaydarābād 1954-6, publ. without the critical apparatus of the editor, M. Krause; see also the table of contents with commentary by Kennedy, *Al-Bīrūnī's Masudic Canon*, in *Al-Abḥāth*, xxiv (1971), 59-81, repr. in idem *et al.*, *Studies*, 573-95. A Byzantine recension of one *zīdj* of al-Fahhād is published in Pingree, *The astronomical works of Gregory Chioniades*, i, *The Zīj al-ʿAlāʾī*, Amsterdam 1985-6. On the *Zīdj* of Ibn Isḥāḳ, see A. Mestres, *Maghribi astronomy in the 13th century. A description of manuscript Hyderabad Andra Pradesh State Library 298*, in *Vernet Festschrift*, i, 383-443; idem, *Materials andalusins en el Zīj d'Ibn Isḥāq al-Tūnisī* (ed. text and tables, with introd. and comm. in Eng.), diss., University of Barcelona 2000. On the *Zīdj* of Kāshī, see various studies by Kennedy, including *Spherical astronomy in Kāshī's* Khāqānī Zīj, in *ZGAIW*, ii (1985), 1-46, repr. in idem, *Studies*, no. VII; idem, *On the contents and significance of the* Khāqānī Zīj *by Jamshīd Ghiyāth al-Dīn al-Kāshī* (*Islamic Mathematics and Astronomy*, lxxxiv), Frankfurt 1998. On the *Sulṭānī Zīdj* of Ulugh Beg, see Sédillot, *Prolégomènes des tables astronomiques d'Oloug-Beg. Traduction et commentaire*, 2 vols., Paris 1847-53, for the text and the chronological tables. (D.A. King and J. Samsó)

ZIḤĀF (a.), refers in Arabic metrics to the optional reduction of a long to a short syllable (CVC → CV; or CV̄ → CV) or of two short syllables to one (CVCV → CVC; CVCV → CV̄; or CVCV → CV).

The alternation between two short syllables in one line and one syllable in another occurs in *wāfir*, *kāmil* and *mutadārik*; in the other metres the choice is between one long and one short syllable. Per line of verse, there usually are between four to six anceps positions that allow *ziḥāf* reductions.

In indigenous Arabic metrical theory or *ʿarūḍ* [*q.v.*], *ziḥāf* is presented as a deviation from the standard foot or *djuzʾ*, and, more particularly, from that part of the foot which is designated as *sabab* [*q.v.*]. Corresponding to the two types of reduction mentioned above, two types of *sabab* are distinguished: the *sabab khafīf*, defined as a moving letter + a quiescent letter (i.e. a consonant with a short vowel followed by a vowelless consonant: CVC), the second of which is elided in the case of *ziḥāf*; and the *sabab thaḳīl* or two moving letters (CVCV), the second of which becomes vowelless or is elided. Any such change thus concerns the second letter of the *sabab*, as is stated in the definition of *ziḥāf* as "a non-obligatory change, specific to the second letters of *sabab*s" (*taghyīr mukhtaṣṣ bi-thawānī 'l-asbāb muṭlak^{an} bi-lā luzūm*, al-Damanhūrī, 40).

Ziḥāf provides Arabic verse with versatility: four anceps positions will spawn 16 metrical variants, six as many as 64. It therefore contrasts with *ʿilla* [*q.v.*], the other change phenomenon of Arabic theory, which, being obligatory in all lines of the composition, provides rigidity rather than variation and is only a change insofar as it represents a departure from the idealised circle metre or *baḥr* [see ʿarūḍ].

Arabic theory has special names for cases of *ziḥāf* where the second, fourth, fifth or seventh vowelless letter of the foot is elided (respectively *khabn*, *ṭayy*, *ḳabḍ* and *kaff*); cases where the second or fifth vowelled letter is elided (*waḳṣ* and *ʿaḳl*, respectively); and cases where the second or the fifth vowelled letter of the foot is rendered vowelless (*iḍmār* and *ʿaṣb*, respectively). E.g. in the foot *mustafʿilun* (– – ⏑ –) the variant ⏑ – ⏑ – is a case of *khabn* and – ⏑ ⏑ – a case of *ṭayy*; in *faʿūlun* (⏑ – –) the variant ⏑ – ⏑ is a case of *ḳabḍ*; in *mutafāʿilun* (⏑ ⏑ – ⏑ –) the variant – – ⏑ – is a case of *iḍmār*.

A distinction is also made between single (*mufrad*) and double (*muzdawidj*) *ziḥāf* (respectively one or two cases of *ziḥāf* per foot). The four types of double *ziḥāf* are called: *khabl* (combines *khabn* and *ṭayy*); *khazl* (*iḍmār* + *ṭayy*); *shakl* (*khabn* + *kaff*); and *naḳṣ* (*ʿaṣb* + *kaff*). E.g. the foot *fāʿilātun* (– ⏑ – –) with *shakl* becomes ⏑ ⏑ – ⏑. Many of these *ziḥāfāt* are rare in practice and some do occasionally occur in ancient, but not in later poetry.

Arabic metrical theory discusses three aesthetic categories of *ziḥāf*: good (*ḥasan*), acceptable (*ṣāliḥ*) and bad (*ḳabīḥ*). In *ṭawīl*, e.g., the reduction of the long third or tenth syllable counts as "good" (it belongs to the system and is found in any poem in this metre); the reduction of the long sixth syllable of either hemistich, which is seldom found in later poetry, counts as "acceptable". The rare case of the reduction of the seventh syllable of the second hemistich in *Mufaḍḍaliyya*, 47 l. 2 (verse by Muraḳḳish) is "bad".

In Persian prosody, where Arabic metrical concepts are forced upon an essentially different type of metre, *ziḥāf* occurs as a technical term, but its function is different: it is not an element of variation within the same poem, but is used to distinguish one metre from the other, rather like *ʿilla*.

Bibliography: G.W. Freytag, *Darstellung der arabischen Verskunst*, Bonn 1830, 77-114; M. Ben Cheneb, *Traité de métrique arabe* (= *Tuḥfat al-adab fī* *mīzān a<u>sh</u>ʿār al-ʿarab)*, [3]Paris 1954, 8-20; Muḥammad al-Damanhūri, *al-Ir<u>sh</u>ād al-<u>sh</u>āfī*, [2]Cairo 1957, 38-60; L.P. Elwell-Sutton, *The Persian metres*, Cambridge 1976 (contains a full account of all *ziḥāf* forms in Arabic and Persian); W. Stoetzer, *Theory and practice in Arabic metrics*, Leiden 1989 (contains *inter alia* a short Arabic text on the aesthetic divisions of *ziḥāf*). A list of *ziḥāfāt* described as a set of erasure rules is given in G. Bohas, J.-P. Guillaume and D.E. Kouloughli, *The Arabic linguistic tradition*, London and New York 1990, 145-8.

(W. Stoetzer)

ZIMĀM (a., pl. *azimma*), lit. "rein, halter", refers to a department of the central administration in the mediaeval caliphate and then comes to refer in Fāṭimid times to a person in control, one holding the reins of power.

The *dīwān al-azimma*, an office of control and audit, is traditionally said to have been founded by the ʿAbbāsid caliph al-Mahdī in 162/778-9 (al-Ṭabarī, iii, 522), when it seems that the task of overseeing and controlling all the *dīwān*s of the administration was too much for a single hand. H.F. Amedroz suggested that every *dīwān* came to have a *zimām* attached to it by way of control but that all the *azimma* might be held by one man, who had a general function of control over all the *dīwān*s (*Abbasid administration in decay, from the Tajarib al-Umam*, in *JRAS* [Oct. 1913], 829-32). M.G. Morony has, however, noted the existence of a department concerned with the registration of documents, headed by a *ṣāḥib al-zimām* (in the tradition of Ibn al-Muḳaffaʿ and al-Madāʾinī), in much earlier times and going back to the Sāsānids of Persia (*Iraq after the Muslim conquest*, Princeton 1984, 66-7).

Under the Fāṭimids, the term had a wide range of meanings, including director of the treasury and major domo. It appears also in military and naval contexts, meaning "officer, commander", alongside such terms as *ʿarīf, raʾīs, muḳaddam* and *mutawallī*, but it must be pointed out that the structure of command in the Fāṭimid armed forces and navy is vague.

Bibliography (in addition to references in the article): See the sources mentioned in D. Sourdel, *Le vizirat ʿabbāside*, Damascus 1959-60, i, 112-14; Paula Sanders, *Ritual, politics, and the city in Fātimid Cairo*, New York 1994, index s.v. *zimām*.

(Ed.)

ZINĀ or **ZINĀʾ** (a.), unlawful sexual intercourse, i.e. intercourse between a man and a woman who are not married to one another nor in a state of lawful concubinage based on ownership (the relationship between the owner and his female slave). The Ḳurʾān disapproved of the promiscuity prevailing at that time in Arabia and forbade e.g. the prostitution of slave girls by their masters (XXIV, 33). Several verses refer to unlawful sexual intercourse. Some of these mention that it is a sin (*fāḥi<u>sh</u>a*) and that it will be punished in the Hereafter (XVII, 32, XXV, 68-9). Most verses, however, deal with the legal aspects. Making *zinā* a punishable offence was a means to enforce the uniform system of marriage introduced by Muḥammad. IV, 15-16 lay down that both parties to it must be punished and required four witnesses for proving the offence. The punishment mentioned in IV, 15 for women committing *zinā*, viz. detention in their homes, is commonly regarded as abrogated by XXIV, 2, which verse stipulates that fornicators must be punished with one hundred lashes. XXIV, 3 ("The male fornicator (*zānī*) shall only marry a female fornicator or a polytheist and the female fornicator (*zāniya*) shall only be married to a male fornicator or polytheist") was regarded as problematical by later commentators. They generally hold that the verse has been abrogated by later verses.

The Ḳurʾān does not mention the punishment of stoning for *zinā*. The enforcement of this penalty is based on the *sunna*. Nearly all *ḥadī<u>th</u>* collections include three *ḥadī<u>th</u>*s that are central in the legal arguments about the punishment for *zinā*: one to the effect that the Prophet has enforced this punishment in a case of unlawful intercourse among Jews on the basis of the Torah (cf. V, 43-4); a second one, transmitted by Abū Hurayra and Zayd b. <u>Kh</u>ālid al-<u>D</u>juhanī relating that the Prophet, in a case of intercourse between a young man and a married woman, sentenced the woman to stoning and the young man to flogging and banishment for a year; and a third one in which ʿUmar b. al-<u>Kh</u>aṭṭāb asserts that there was a revelation (*āyat al-ra<u>dj</u>m*) to the effect that those who are *muḥṣan* [*q.v.*] and have unlawful intercourse are to be punished with stoning, but that this verse was left out in the final version of the Ḳurʾānic text, cf. Ibn Ḥa<u>dj</u>ar, *Bulū<u>gh</u> al-marām*, nos. 1230, 1232, 1236. The *ḥadī<u>th</u>* related by Abū Hurayra and Zayd b. <u>Kh</u>ālid al-<u>D</u>juhanī has been the basis of the *fiḳh* doctrine, as we shall see. The jurists have argued that this *ḥadī<u>th</u>* has specified the meaning of XXIV, 2 (or, according to some, even abrogated it). J. Burton has plausibly argued that the story about the verse of stoning was put into circulation by <u>Sh</u>āfiʿī scholars who did not accept that a *sunna* can abrogate a Ḳurʾānic revelation and were forced to find a source with higher authority for the lawfulness of stoning for fornication (Burton, *Origin*).

All Sunnī schools of jurisprudence agree that *zinā* is to be punished with stoning if the offender is *muḥṣan*, i.e. adult, free, Muslim (except in <u>Sh</u>āfiʿī law, where a *<u>dh</u>immī* can also be *muḥṣan*) and having previously enjoyed legitimate sexual relations in matrimony (regardless of whether the marriage still exists). The Ḥanafīs and Ḥanbalīs require that both partners in the act be *muḥṣan* for stoning to be applied. Persons who are not *muḥṣan* are punished with one hundred lashes if they are free and with fifty lashes if they are slaves (cf. IV, 25), followed, according to all schools except the Ḥanafīs, with banishment for the period of one year (six months for slaves). The offenders must have acted out of their free will; a woman who has been raped (*mustakraha*) cannot be punished with the *ḥadd* penalty.

About homosexual intercourse, *liwāṭ* [*q.v.*], there is difference of opinion. The <u>Sh</u>āfiʿīs and Ḥanbalīs regard it as *zinā*. If the act has been testified to by four male eyewitnesses, the active partner, if he is *muḥṣan*, is to be punished with stoning, the passive partner with flogging and banishment. The Mālikīs do not require *iḥṣān* for the imposition of stoning. According to the Ḥanafīs, homosexual intercourse can only be punished on the strength of *taʿzīr* [*q.v.*].

<u>Sh</u>īʿī doctrine on *zinā* is somewhat different. Here *zinā*, in addition to heterosexual intercourse, includes a great variety of sexual behaviour: buggery, both with men and women, lesbian intercourse and petting. Furthermore, <u>Sh</u>īʿī legal doctrine defines *muḥṣan* as an adult, free Muslim who is in a position lawfully to have sexual intercourse and whose partner is actually available and not e.g. imprisoned or absent on a journey. The punishments are the same as in Sunnī Islam. However, a non-*muḥṣan* can be sentenced to death if there are aggravating circumstances such as incest (intercourse between close relatives), rape or intercourse between a non-Muslim man with a Muslim

woman. Homosexual intercourse with penetration (*īḳāb*) is, according to the Shīʿī doctrine, to be punished with death by way of *ḥadd* punishment, whereby the *ḳāḍī* has the choice between execution with a sword, by stoning, by throwing the offender from a [high] wall or by burning him. If there has been no penetration, and in cases of sexual activity between women (*musāḥaḳa* [see SIḤĀḲ]), the *ḥadd* punishment is one hundred lashes.

Minimal proof for *zinā* is the testimony of four male eyewitnesses. The Shīʿīs, however, also admit the testimony of women, if there is at least one male witness, testifying together with six women. All witnesses must have seen the act in its most intimate details, i.e. the penetration (like "a stick disappearing in a kohl container (*mukḥula*)," as the *fiḳh* books specify). If their testimonies do not satisfy the requirements, they can be sentenced to eighty lashes for unfounded accusation of fornication (*ḳadhf* [*q.v.*]). If the accused admits the offence, the confession must be repeated four times according to the Ḥanafīs, the Ḥanbalīs and the Shīʿīs. Circumstantial evidence is not admitted, with one exception: under Mālikī law, pregnancy of an unmarried woman is regarded as evidence of fornication. However, even if the act has been proved, punishment can be averted by *shubha* [*q.v.*], viz. uncertainty about the unlawfulness of the proven act, due to circumstances that confer to it a semblance of legality, such as intercourse between two parties to a marriage that is null and void, between the master and a female slave of whom he is a co-owner or whom he has acquired on the strength of an invalid purchase, or between a blind man and a woman whom he takes for his wife or female slave.

In Saudi Arabia and in those countries where Islamic criminal codes have been introduced, *zinā* is a criminal offence to be punished according to the prescriptions of the *fiḳh* (Libya, Law 70 of 1973 on the introduction of the *ḥadd* punishment for *zinā*, which actually does not impose stoning but only flogging; Pakistan, Offence of Zina (Enforcement of Hudood) Ordinance, 1979; Penal Code of Sudan, 1991, arts. 146-52; Criminal Code of Iran, 1991, arts. 63-134; Penal Code of Yemen, 1994, arts. 163-281). According to reports of human rights organisations, the punishment of stoning has recently only been enforced in Saudi Arabia and Iran.

Bibliography: Ibn Ḳudāma, *al-Mughnī*, Beirut 1993, viii, 157-212; Ibn Rushd, *Bidāyat al-mudjtahid wa-nihāyat al-muḳtaṣid*, Cairo 1960, ii, 433-40; Ibn Ḥadjar al-ʿAsḳalānī, *Bulūgh al-marām fī adillat al-aḥkām*, ²Riyāḍ 1997; ʿAbd al-Raḥmān al-Djazīrī, *Kitāb al-Fiḳh ʿalā 'l-madhāhib al-arbaʿa*, v, *al-ʿUḳūbāt al-sharʿiyya*, Cairo n.d., 41-138; A. Bouhdiba, *La sexualité en islam*, Paris 1975; J. Burton, *The origin of the Islamic penalty for adultery*, in *Trans. Glasgow University Oriental Society*, xxvi (1978), 16-26; U. Rubin, "*Al-walad li-l-firāsh*". *On the Islamic campaign against zinā*, in *SI*, viii (1993), 5-26; R. Peters, *The Islamization of criminal law. A comparative analysis*, in *WI*, xxxiv (1994), 246-74. (R. PETERS)

ZINDĪḲ.

1. *The word.*

Zindīḳ, pl. *zanādiḳa*, abstract/collective noun *zandaḳa*, is an Arabic word borrowed (at least in the first instance) from Persian, and used in the narrow and precise meaning "Manichaean" (synonym: *Mānawī*, or the quasi-Aramaic *Manānī*), but also loosely for "heretic, renegade, unbeliever", in effect as a synonym for *mulḥid, murtadd* or *kāfir*. The earliest attestation of the word, in any language, is in the Middle Persian inscription of the Zoroastrian high priest Kirdīr on the so-called Kaʿba-yi Zardusht, from the end of the 3rd century A.D. (precisely at the time when the Sāsānid state was busy combating Manichaeism), which boasts of the author's success in suppressing various foreign religions and their followers, among them Jews, Buddhists, Brahmanists, Christians and *zndyky* (see Ph. Gignoux, *Les quatre inscriptions du mage Kirdīr*, Paris 1991, 60). Then, in the 5th century, the Armenian Christian author Eznik, in his polemics against Manichaeism, uses the word *zandik* to designate the followers of that religion, and it is applied in the same way by the Armenian historian Elishe (whose date is the subject of controversy). Similarly, in Zoroastrian religious books in Middle Persian there are a fair number of passages where *zandīk* is used unambiguously in the sense "Manichaean" (collected in de Menasce). But also in Arabic, *zindīḳ* is quite commonly used for "Manichaean", that is, as the name for the follower of a specific religion; the usage as a vague term for Muslim or non-Muslim "heretics" is clearly secondary, though widespread. Muslim law denies Manichaeans the status of *ahl al-dhimma*, putting them in the same legal position as renegades from Islam, and it is evidently for this reason that the words *zindīḳ* and *mulḥid* became interchangeable. A parallel for this semantic development is the German word *Ketzer*, originally a deformation of the self-designation of the dualist Christian sect of the *Cathari* (i.e. καθαροι "pure ones") but then applied indiscriminately to all religious dissenters, finally becoming the usual German word for "heretic".

Al-Masʿūdī (*Murūdj*, ii, 167-8 = § 594) says that the name *zindīḳ* first appeared at the time of Mānī, and for the following reason: Zoroaster had once brought to the Persians a book called the Avesta (*bastāh*), together with a commentary called the *zand*, which was a clarification of the allegorical interpretation (*taʾwīl*) of the Avesta. Thus whenever anyone "introduced into their religion anything that was at variance with the revelation, namely the Avesta, and turned towards the allegorical interpretation, namely the *zand*, the Persians called him a *zandī*". The Arabs, he continues, changed this to *zindīḳ*. "The dualists (*thanawiyya*) are *zanādiḳa*, but with these are grouped together anyone else who believes in the doctrine of pre-eternity (*ḳidam*) and denies the creation of the world." Similarly, al-Samʿānī (*Ansāb*, s.v. *zandī*) says that Mānī was called a *zindīḳ* because he claimed that his book *Shābuhragān* was the *zand*, or commentary (*tafsīr*), of Zoroaster's book; ʿAbd al-Djabbār (*Tathbīt*, i, 170) also says that Mānī produced a *tafsīr* of the Avesta, but he does not link this with the name *zindīḳ*. On the other hand, al-Khʷārazmī (*Mafātīḥ al-ʿulūm*, 37-8) says that it was Mazdak who brought forth a book which he called the *zand* and which he claimed contained the *taʾwīl* of the Avesta, and that consequently his followers took the name *zandī*. And al-Bīrūnī (*al-Āthār al-bāḳiya*, in J. Fück, *Documenta islamica inedita*, Berlin 1952, 79; missing in Sachau's edition), after saying much the same thing, goes on to claim that the name *zindīḳ* is applied to the Manichaeans only "in a figurative and metaphorical sense", as it is also to "the *bāṭiniyya* in Islam". In other words, the real *zanādiḳa* are the Mazdakites. This is naturally wrong, for, as mentioned, the word *zandīk* was used already by Kirdīr, 300 years before the time of Mazdak. But the explanation given by al-Masʿūdī is also quite untenable. The *zand*, which the Persians believed to have been revealed by their prophet, is not an "allegorical interpretation" of the Avesta, but a translation into Middle Persian (with commentary) of what the Zoroastrians of the Sāsānid period perceived to be the literal meaning of the scripture; there can consequently be no question of the Manichaeans having turned away from the Avesta to the (Zoroastrian) *zand*, as al-Masʿūdī implies (see Darmesteter). Nor is there any evidence that the Manichaeans produced a *zand* of their own (as al-Samʿānī and ʿAbd al-Djabbār claim) or that they considered their religion to be an allegorical interpretation of the Avesta (as Schaeder has argued). In fact, extant Manichaean writings make it quite clear that they did not accept the Avesta as a genuine prophetic revelation. It seems rather that the etymology offered by al-Masʿūdī and his successors results from an analogy between Manichaeism and "the *bāṭiniyya* in Islam", i.e. Ismāʿīlism, and specifically from an attempt to tarnish the latter by association with Manichaeism. But this analogy is spurious. Manichaeism was not an esotericist, but a literalist religion, one which saw truth in the literal meaning of Mānī's own writings.

From the vantage point of modern linguistic knowledge it would seem more likely that Middle Persian *zandīk* was borrowed from Aramaic *zaddīḳ* "righteous" (thus already Bevan, in Browne, *LHP*, i, 159-60). We know from Syriac authors that Manichaeans used *zaddīḳē* as a designation for their "elect", that is, the full members of the Manichaean community, just as Muslim authors (Ibn al-Nadīm, al-Bīrūnī, etc.) use the equivalent Arabic *ṣiddīḳūn* for the Manichaean "elect" and *sammāʿūn* for the lower-ranking "auditors". The so-called dissimilation of the geminated stop to nasal plus stop can be observed in other Aramaic loan words in Persian, e.g. Persian *shamba* "Saturday", versus Syriac *shabbthā*, or Persian *gund* (cf. Ar. *djund*) "army", versus Syriac *guddā*. It is naturally possible that already in Middle Persian the loan word *zandīk* was reinterpreted as **zandīg* "follower of a *zand*", but this is hardly the original meaning.

2. *The history of Manichaeism, especially in the Arab and Islamic world.*

The name of the founder of Manichaeism appears in Arabic as Mānī (Greek Μάνης, Latin Manes, Syriac and New Persian Mānē, in Persian poetry rhyming with *yāʾ-i madjhūl*). He was born in 527 Seleucid (A.D. 216-17) in Babylonia and was brought up in a community of Elchasaites, a Jewish Christian baptist sect (Ibn al-Nadīm's *mughtasila*). As a young man Mānī began to receive revelations from his supernatural "Twin", who eventually instructed him to leave the Elchasaites and propound his own gospel. He travelled extensively in the Persian empire, preaching. Early in the reign of the second Sāsānid ruler, Shābuhr (Ar. Sābūr) I, probably in 240, or shortly thereafter, Mānī attached himself to the court of the emperor. Two of Shābuhr's brothers converted to Manichaeism and the king himself was the dedicatee of Mānī's *Shābuhragān*, a systematic account of his faith. Mānī retained the favour of Shābuhr's son, Hormizd I, but fell out with his successor, Wahrām (Ar. Bahrām) I, who had the prophet thrown into prison, where he died, probably in 274 or 277. Manichaean texts, imitating Christian imagery, sometimes speak of Mānī's "crucifixion", just as those composed in the Buddhist environment of Central Asia refer to his death as an "entry into nirvāṇa"; Muslim authors, misled by the former phrasing, generally state that Mānī was actually crucified/gibbeted (*ṣuliba*).

The prophet's death was followed by a severe persecution of the Manichaeans in the Sāsānid realm, but missionaries had already put down firm roots outside of the empire, in Roman territory (especially in Egypt) and in Central Asia among the Iranian (mainly Sogdian) population. There is evidence for Manichaean missions among the Arabs as well. A Coptic text reports on how, during the reign of the Sāsānid Narseh (ruled 293-302), the Manichaeans were protected by a king called Amarō, in which we must see a Coptic spelling of the Arabic name ʿAmr. Narseh's own inscription at Paikuli mentions, in the list of his vassals, two kings of this name: "ʾ*mrw* king of the Lakhmids" (evidently the ʿAmr b. ʿAdī of Arab tradition) and "ʾ*mrw* [king] of the sons of Abgar" (perhaps an otherwise unrecorded member of the Arab dynasty at Edessa), but it is debated which of the two is intended by the Coptic text (see the relevant articles by Tardieu and de Blois, with different conclusions). A later tradition, reported by Ibn al-Kalbī, Ibn Ḳutayba and others, says that before Islam some of the Arabs were Christians, some Jews, some Zoroastrians (*madjūs*), and others *zanādiḳa*; this last religion was followed, it is claimed, by some of the Ḳuraysh, who had it from al-Ḥīra (references, and discussion of the conflicting versions of this story, in de Blois, *The Sabians*, 48-50, where it is suggested that the *ṣābiʾūn* of the Ḳurʾān [see ṢĀBIʾ and ṢĀBIʾA] might have been these Arab Manichaeans). The fact that *zanādiḳa* are mentioned alongside other specified religions would seem to indicate that the word is used here to mean "Manichaeans", and not undiscriminated "heretics", but it is naturally debatable whether the story has any historical value.

Despite harassment by the Sāsānids, a Manichaean community survived in Babylonia (ʿIrāḳ), which remained the seat of the *archegos* (Ar. *imām*), though his authority was contested by the Manichaeans in Transoxania (in Arabic called the Dīnāwariyya, from the Sogdian word for "elect"). After the Muslim conquest, Manichaeans benefited from the tolerance (or indifference) of the Umayyads. The *archegos* Mihr, who flourished at the time when Khālid b. ʿAbd Allāh al-Ḳasrī [*q.v.*] was governor of ʿIrāḳ (*ca.* 105-20/*ca.* 723-38), and who (according to his enemies) accepted luxurious gifts from the Muslim governor, made attempts to regain the allegiance of the Dīnāwariyya, but he was faced by dissent within his own community; this led to the formation of a rival faction under a certain Miḳlāṣ. ʿAbd al-Djabbār (*al-Mughnī*, v, 18-9, quoting al-Mismaʿī) gives a brief account of the doctrinal differences between the Miḳlāṣiyya and what he simply calls "the Manichaeans" (evidently meaning the followers of Mihr), from which emerges that the former upheld the (in fact orthodox Manichaean) doctrine of the eternal damnation of the souls of sinners while the latter held the (revisionist) view that all particles of light (i.e. all souls) would eventually be liberated from darkness. Ibn al-Nadīm (*Fihrist*, ed. Tadjaddud, 397-8) quotes, from a pro-Mihrī Manichaean source, what must be a wildly exaggerated account of the successes of the Mihriyya in winning over the followers of the Dīnāwariyya and the Miḳlāṣiyya, but he goes on to indicate that the Miḳlāṣiyya in fact survived at least until the time of al-Muʿtaṣim (218-27/833-42). A Sogdian Manichaean text (published by Sundermann) contains polemics against certain "Syrian" co-religionists, evidently Manichaeans from the Near East who had recently emigrated to Central Asia, and mentions the Mihrī and Miḳlāṣī factions, unfortunately in a broken context.

The only systematic Muslim persecution of Manichaeans that we know about began in 163/779 by order of the ʿAbbāsid caliph al-Mahdī and continued at least until the end of the reign of al-Hādī in

170/786. The sources do not give a clear indication
of the reason for the persecution, but it is surely no
coincidence that it occurred shortly after the conversion of the Uyg̲h̲ur rulers to Manichaeism in 762;
Manichaeism became the state religion of an important neighbouring kingdom and was evidently henceforth perceived as a threat to the security of the
caliphate. A special inquisitor, called ṣāḥib al-zanādiḳa,
ferreted out the suspects, who were confined in a particular prison (ḥabs al-zanādiḳa). Those who abjured
their beliefs were required to spit on the portrait of
Mānī and released; those who refused were beheaded.
After 170/786 we have reports only of sporadic persecution, and the Manichaeans succeeded in maintaining a limited presence in Bag̲h̲dād for another two
centuries. Al-Maʾmūn (198-218/813-33) is said to have
organised a debate between the Manichaean leader
Yazdānbuk̲h̲t and Muslim theologians and to have
given the former safe conduct and assigned guards to
protect him from the mob, but other reports speak
of the persecution of Manichaeans by the same caliph.
Ibn al-Nadīm wrote that in the days of Muʿizz
al-Dawla (334-56/945-67) he had personally been
acquainted with "about 300" Manichaeans in Bag̲h̲dād,
but that "now (i.e. in 377/987-8) there are not even
five in the capital", though they still survived in
Sogdiana, their leader residing in Samarḳand. And
about a decade later al-Bīrūnī (Āt̲h̲ār, ed. Sachau, 209)
similarly speaks of a thriving Manichaean community
in Samarḳand, where they were called ṣābiʾūn. On
the other hand, Ibn al-Nadīm's story, from a non-
Manichaean source (ed. Tad̲j̲addud, 400-1), of how
the Manichaeans migrated back and forth between
Transoxania and ʿIrāḳ and how, at the time of al-
Muḳtadir (r. 295-320/908-32), the Manichaeans in
Samarḳand were protected from their Muslim overlords through an intervention of "the king of China",
bristles with anachronisms and has little historic value.

After the 4th/10th century, there is no firm evidence for Manichaeism anywhere in the Islamic world,
but it survived in Central Asia, even after the fall of
the Uyg̲h̲ur kingdom to the Ḳi̊rg̲h̲i̊z in 840, in the
remnant Uyg̲h̲ur principality in the Turfan [q.v.] basin
(in modern Xinjiang), probably until the time of the
Mongol invasions.

3. *Muslim accounts of Manichaeism and of the so-called*
zanādiḳa *in Islam*.

The earliest substantial Muslim description of
Manichaean cosmology of which any trace survives is
by Abū ʿĪsā al-Warrāḳ [q.v.] from about the middle
of the 3rd/9th century; extensive and explicit quotations have been preserved by Ibn al-Malāḥimī and
briefer extracts (quoted at second hand, via a lost
work by al-Ḥasan b. Mūsā al-Nawbak̲h̲tī) from Abū
ʿĪsā form the main substance of the accounts by ʿAbd
al-D̲j̲abbār, al-S̲h̲ahrastānī, Ibn al-Murtaḍā and others, though both al-Nawbak̲h̲tī and those who copied
from him also had other documents at their disposal.
Abū ʿĪsā is the principal source of the picture of
Manichaeism in Muslim theological writings, a picture
which, without being exactly wrong, is excessively
schematic, overly cerebral and largely ignores the religious content of Manichaeism, namely, its ethics and
its doctrine of personal salvation.

The most extensive, and most valuable account of
Manichaeism by a Muslim author is in the *Fihrist*
of Ibn al-Nadīm. This contains a sketch of the life
of Mānī, a detailed summary of the Manichaeans'
cosmology and eschatology, a description of their ethics
and cultic practices, of the Manichaean sects after the
prophet's death and a long list of books by Mānī and

his pupils. Much of this is evidently derived from
authentic Manichaean writings in Arabic that were
not used by any other extant author, but it is interspersed with data from Muslim sources. Two uncred-
ited quotations from Abū ʿĪsā's version (*Fihrist/*
Tad̲j̲addud, 393:3-5 and 393:23-394:21; cf. Ibn al-
Malāḥimī, 562:5-9 and 563:11-565:ult., respectively)
have been inserted, confusingly, into a much better
account of the cosmological myth, and there is also
some worthless material, e.g. the absurd statement
that Mānī taught that Jesus was sent by the devil.

Al-Bīrūnī had access to translations of Mānī's own
books, from which he brings some important quotations. Otherwise, Muslim accounts are of limited value.
The verbose refutations of Manichaeism and other
forms of dualism in Muslim writers are of real interest only for the history of Islamic theology. See also
T̲H̲ANAWIYYA, where much of this is assessed differently.

After the above-mentioned account of Manichaeism,
Ibn al-Nadīm appends a list of "the theologians who
outwardly professed Islam but inwardly professed
al-zandaḳa", of poets who fell into the same category,
and of "the kings and grandees who were accused of
al-zandaḳa", lists which can be supplemented from
other sources. It is, however, impossible to confirm
that any of these people were really Manichaeans and
it is more likely that the only thing they have in common is that their enemies accused them of not being
good Muslims, and consequently "secret *zindīḳ*s". It is
clear that *zindīḳ* was used quite freely as a term of
abuse; it is consequently futile for modern historians
to attempt to construct a picture of the "*zanādiḳa* in
Islam" as a coherent intellectual movement.

For example, the previously-mentioned Abū ʿĪsā al-
Warrāḳ was himself suspected of Manichaeism evidently only because he wrote about (but also refuted)
that religion. The poet al-Maʿarrī was accused of
being a *zindīḳ* by his contemporaries mainly because
he was a vegetarian, like the Manichaean elect. Many
of the Ṣūfīs, beginning with al-Ḥallād̲j̲, were accused
of *zandaḳa*, though their whole world outlook is dia-
metrically opposed to Manichaean dualism. Even in
the case of the famous littérateur, and universally
decried *zindīḳ*, Ibn al-Muḳaffaʿ [q.v.], the evidence that
he was ever really a Manichaean is not conclusive.
Al-Mismaʿī (quoted by ʿAbd al-D̲j̲abbār, *al-Mug̲h̲nī*, v,
20; also in Ibn al-Malāḥimī, 590) reports, on the one
hand, that Ibn al-Muḳaffaʿ was a dualist who taught
that Light manipulated (*dabbara*) Darkness and introduced itself into Darkness only for its own advantage;
the idea that the mixture of Light and Darkness was
intentionally provoked by the former is indeed a
specifically Manichaean doctrine which distinguishes
it clearly from Zoroastrianism and from other forms
of dualism. But al-Mismaʿī goes on to say that "he
rejected the disgusting stories which the Manichaeans
told about the war between the two principles". The
implication is thus that Ibn al-Muḳaffaʿ was not a
member of the Manichaean church (for which the
cosmological myth was an indispensable article of
faith), though he shared some of the theoretical premises of Manichaeism.

4. *Manichaeism and Islam*.

Until the end of the 19th century, Manichaeism
was known only from reports in non-Manichaean
sources, but the subsequent spectacular discovery of
a large number of Manichaean manuscripts in Egypt
(in Coptic and Greek) and Central Asia (mainly in
Middle Iranian languages and Old Turkish) means
that it is now possible to form a very precise picture
of Manichaean doctrine and practice from original

sources. But there is much disagreement about the place of Manichaeism in the history of religion. Some scholars still regard Manichaeism as an essentially Iranian phenomenon, an off-shoot of Zoroastrianism, but the prevalent view is that its roots lie mainly in Western traditions, in Christianity or Gnosticism, and that, although Mānī was aware of Zoroastrianism (and of Buddhism), the influence of Iranian and Indian doctrines on his teaching was at best superficial.

As a dualist religion, which posited two co-eternal opposing principles of good (light) and evil (darkness), Manichaeism stands in a very stark contrast to Islam, with its implacable monotheism. Muslim theologians were quite right to insist on this difference. At the same time, the two faiths do have some points of contact. Both teach that God has instructed mankind through a series of prophets, all of whom brought essentially the same message at different times. Some Manichaean sources see Mānī as the successor of prophets from the Judaic tradition like Adam, Seth, Enosh, Shem and Enoch, others mention only the Buddha, Zoroaster and Jesus as his predecessors, yet others combine the two series. Mānī, like Muḥammad, is the "seal of the prophets" (discussed, with controversial conclusions, by Colpe and Stroumsa) and the Paraclete predicted by Jesus. The Buddha, Zoroaster and Jesus taught the pure religion, but did not commit their teachings to writing; the books that their followers now read were written after the deaths of the prophets and corrupted their teachings, but Mānī wrote down his own teachings and produced a definitive written account of the true religion (for a similar view in Islam, see TAḤRĪF). Finally, both Manichaeism and Islam deny that Jesus actually died on the cross. But it is doubtful whether any of this indicates a direct influence of Manichaeism on Islam. It is more likely that both share a common substratum in Jewish Christianity.

Bibliography: 1. Primary sources. Ibn al-Nadīm's account of Manichaeism and the *zanādiḳa* was first published, with translation and very copious notes, in G. Flügel, *Mani, seine Lehre und seine Schriften*, Leipzig 1862; text repr. in his posthumous edition of the *Fihrist*, 327-38; re-edited (from an old manuscript, sometimes, but not always, with better readings than Flügel) in ed. R. Tadjaddud, 391-402; Dodge's translation has to be used with caution. Virtually all of the then available Arabic and New Persian sources were reprinted in the immensely useful book by S.Ḥ. Taḳīzāda and A. Afshār Shīrāzī, *Mānī wa dīn-i ū*, Tehran 1335 *sh*/1956; the principal new texts are ʿAbd al-Djabbār, *al-Mughnī fī abwāb al-tawḥīd wa 'l-ʿadl*, v, ed. al-Khuḍayrī, Cairo 1965, 10-21; idem, *Tathbīt dalāʾil al-nubuwwa*, ed. ʿAbd al-Karīm ʿUthmān, Beirut [1966], i, 80, 106, 114-5, 169-71, 184, 187; Ibn al-Malāḥimī, *al-Muʿtamad fī uṣūl al-dīn*, ed. McDermott and Madelung, London 1991, 561-97.

2. Studies. J. Darmesteter, *Zendîk*, in *JA*, 8ème série, tome iii (1884), 562-5; H.H. Schaeder, *Zandik-Zindiq*, in his *Iranische Beiträge*, i (= all published), Halle 1930, 76-93; G. Vajda, *Les zindîqs en pays d'islam au début de la période abbaside*, in *RSO*, xvii (1937), 173-229; idem, *Le témoignage d'al-Māturīdī sur la doctrine des manichéens, des dayṣānites et des marcionites*, in *Arabica*, xiii (1966), 1-38, 113-28 (both articles repr. in his *Études de théologie et de philosophie arabo-islamiques à l'époche classique*, Variorum, London 1986); J. de Menasce, *Škand-gumānīk vičār*, Fribourg 1945, 228-44, 252-9; C. Colpe, *Der Manichäismus in der arabischen Überlieferung* (typescript), Göttingen 1954; idem, *Anpassung des Manichäismus an den Islam (Abū ʿĪsā al-Warrāq)* in *ZDMG*, cix (1959), 82-91; idem, *Das Siegel der Propheten*, in *Orientalia Suecana*, xxxiii-xxxv (1986), 71-83; G. Monnot, *Penseurs musulmans et religions iraniennes: ʿAbd al-Jabbār et ses devanciers*, Paris and Beirut 1974; M. Boyce, *A reader in Manichaean Middle Persian and Parthian*, Leiden 1975 (with a good sketch of Manichaean history and doctrine in the introd.); W. Sundermann, *Probleme der Interpretation manichäisch-soghdischer Briefe*, in J. Harmatta (ed.), *From Hecataeus to al-Ḫuwārizmī*, Budapest 1984, 289-316; S. Shaked, *From Iran to Islam*, in *JSAI*, iv (1984), 31-67 (esp. 50-9: "Notes on Ibn al-Muqaffaʿ's alleged Manichaeism and some related problems"); G.G. Stroumsa, "*Seal of the prophets", the nature of a Manichaean metaphor*, in *JSAI*, vii (1986), 61-74; F. de Blois, *Burzōy's voyage to India and the origin of the book of Kalīlah wa Dimnah*, London 1990, 25-33 (on Ibn al-Muḳaffaʿ); idem, *The "Sabians" (Ṣābiʾūn) in pre-Islamic Arabia*, in *AO*, lvi (1995), 39-61; idem, *Who is King Amarō?*, in *Arab. Arch. and Epigr.*, vi (1995), 196-8; J. van Ess, *Zwischen Ḥadīṯ und Theologie. Theologie und Gesellschaft im 2. und 3. Jahrhundert Hidschra*, Berlin-New York 1991-7, esp. i, 416-56, ii, 4-41 (with exhaustive bibl.); M. Tardieu, *L'arrivée des manichéens à al-Ḥīra*, in *La Syrie de Byzance à l'Islam*, ed. P. Canivet and J.-P. Rey-Coquais, Damascus 1992, 15-24; idem, *L'Arabie du nord-est d'après les documents manichéens*, in *Stud. Ir.*, xxiii (1994), 59-75; M. Chokr, *Zandaqa et zindiqs en islam au second siècle de l'hégire*, Damascus 1993.

(F.C. de Blois)

ZINDJIRLI, Modern Tkish. Zincirli, a village of southeastern Turkey, lying in the Karasu valley between the Gâvur Dağları (Amanus) and the Kurd Dağı/Djabal al-Akrād, near the small town of Islahiye. It now comes within the western part of the *il* or province of Gaziantep.

A tell there, excavated by Berlin archaeologists 1888-1902, revealed the capital *Y'dy*; the earlier vocalisation as Yaudi is now regarded as uncertain, but it is to be identified with the place known as Sam'al in the records of the Assyrian king Tiglath Pileser III. A stele of a later Assyrian king Esarhaddon (680-669 B.C.) has been found. There has been considerable interest in the official Aramaic inscriptions found at or near the site, particularly the colossal statue of the god Hadad erected by Panammu I, who styles himself *mlk y'dy* "king of Y'dy", and those erected as a result of building activity on the site by Bar-rakkab *mlk sm'l* "king of Sam'al", one in honour of his father Panammu II and another in which he swears allegiance to Tiglath Pileser, who allowed him to succeed to the throne after his father.

No trace of the name Sam'al seems to have survived into the Islamic period, and the origin of the recent Turkish name, literally "enchained, placed in a chain or series", remains obscure, unless it is a corruption of the name of the fortress Zandjtara mentioned by al-Nuwayrī (see Honigmann, in *EI*[1] s.v.).

Bibliography: In addition to the *Bibl.* of the *EI*[1] art., see Sir Charles Wilson, *Murray's Handbooks, Asia Minor, Transcaucasia, Persia etc.*, London 1895, 275-6; *Meyers Reisebücher Palästina und Syria*, [4]Leipzig and Vienna 1907, 257; *Baedeker's Palestine and Syria*, [5]Leipzig 1912, 367; J.B. Pritchard, *Ancient Near Eastern texts relating to the Old Testament*, [3]Princeton 1969, 654-5; J.C.L. Gibson, *Syrian Semitic inscriptions*, ii, Oxford 1975, 60-92. (M.E.J. Richardson)

ZĪRIDS, the name of two mediaeval Berber dynasties of the Muslim West.

1. The Zīrids (Banū Zīrī) of Ifrīḳiya

This was the first great Ṣanhād̲j̲a Berber dynasty in North Africa, originating in the central Mag̲h̲rib and established in al-Ḳayrawān in 361/972 by Buluggīn b. Zīrī [*q.v.*] on the departure of the fourth Fāṭimid caliph al-Muʿizz [*q.v.*] to Egypt. The dynasty, collateral with the Ḥammādids of Ḳalʿat Bani 'l-Ḥammād [*q.v.*] and the Zīrids of Spain (see 2. below), ruled for some 176 years (361-543/972-1148) until the last *amīr*, al-Ḥasan b. ʿAlī, lost the kingdom to the Normans of Sicily.

With the approval of the Fāṭimids, the dynasty's progenitor Zīrī b. Manād had founded a principality at As̲h̲īr [*q.v.*] in *ca.* 328/940 as a bulwark against the anti-Fāṭimid Zanāta Mag̲h̲rāwa [*q.v.*], allies of the Umayyads of Cordova. Zīrī's most signal service to the Fāṭimids was the relief of their capital al-Mahdiyya when it was about to fall into the hands of the K̲h̲ārid̲j̲ite rebel Abū Yazīd [*q.v.*] in Ṣafar 334/September 945. Before moving to Egypt, and in recognition of Zīrī's loyalty, the caliph al-Muʿizz appointed Zīrī's son Buluggīn governor of Ifrīḳiya and all the territory he could wrest from the pro-Umayyad Zanāta in the Mag̲h̲rib. On assuming power, Buluggīn campaigned vigorously in the Mag̲h̲rib and, in the course of his last campaign (368-73/979-84), he took Fās and Sid̲j̲ilmāsa, but died on the return journey (21 D̲h̲u 'l-Ḥid̲j̲d̲j̲a 373/25 May 984). Five years before Buluggīn's death, Tripolitania (but not Sicily) was ceded to him by the Fāṭimid caliph al-ʿAzīz.

Unlike his father, al-Manṣūr b. Buluggīn (373-86/984-96) began to act in every way like an independent ruler. As soon as he assumed power, al-Manṣūr declared to the notables of al-Ḳayrawān, "I am not one of those who get appointed and dismissed by a stroke of the pen, for I have inherited the kingdom from my father and my ancestors" (*Bayān*, i, 240).

Bādīs b. al-Manṣūr (386-406/996-1016 [*q.v.*]) entrusted his uncle Ḥammād b. Buluggīn with campaigning against the Zanāta and promised to let him rule any territories he conquered. Having succeeded in his campaigns against the Zanāta in the central Mag̲h̲rib, Ḥammād, who founded the Ḳalʿa in 398/1008, carved out for himself an independent entity immediately to the west of Ifrīḳiya.

The realm of al-Muʿizz b. Bādīs (406-54/1016-62) was the largest the Berbers had held in Ifrīḳiya, and his reign was the most luxurious and ostentatious (Ibn K̲h̲aldūn, vi, 158). Ifrīḳiya seems to have enjoyed economic prosperity at the start of al-Muʿizz's reign, as attested by the abundance of the wheat crop particularly in the Bād̲j̲a region, a fact which probably encouraged al-Muʿizz in 440/1049 to renounce his allegiance to the Fāṭimid caliph al-Mustanṣir and to proclaim his allegiance to the ʿAbbāsids. The Fāṭimid caliph retaliated by encouraging the Arab nomad tribes of the Banū Hilāl and the Banū Sulaym [*q.vv.*] in Upper Egypt to overrun and ravage the Zīrid kingdom, thus ridding himself of a troublesome group of people and ensuring that they would bring about the downfall of the Zīrids. Al-Muʿizz's army was routed at Ḥaydarān, between Ḳābis and al-Ḳayrawān, on 11 D̲h̲u 'l-Ḥid̲j̲d̲j̲a 443/14 April 1052, and in 449/1057 al-Muʿizz had to abandon al-Ḳayrawān and take refuge with his son Tamīm, governor of al-Mahdiyya on the coast. The Hilālīs, meanwhile, occupied large parts of the interior. Ibn K̲h̲aldūn was the first historian to stress the destructive role of the invaders, comparing them to a cloud of locusts. More recently, however, it has been argued that the invasion was not so destructive and that, prior to the arrival of the Hilālīs, the Zīrid state was disintegrating and in decline.

With most of their territory overrun and ravaged by the Hilālīs, the Zīrids turned their attention to the sea; they built a fleet and sought to interfere in Sicily's affairs. In 416/1025-6, a Zīrid fleet, on its way to Sicily, was destroyed by a storm off Pantelleria. Between 417/1026 and 426/1035 the Zīrid fleet frequently raided Byzantine territory in the Adriatic and the Aegean Seas.

Tamīm b. al-Muʿizz (454-501/1062-1108 [*q.v.*]) inherited a kingdom politically divided and economically weak. As a result of the Hilālī invasion, Tamīm's authority was confined to the coastal strip stretching from Sūsa to Ḳābis. In 480/1087, in retaliation for Zīrid maritime raids, a combined Genoese and Pisan fleet occupied and sacked al-Mahdiyya and its suburb Zawīla and, in order to get rid of the invaders, Tamīm had to pay them a sum of 100,000 dīnārs. It was also during Tamīm's reign that the Normans of southern Italy completed in 484/1091 their conquest of Muslim Sicily. After a reign of almost 50 years, Tamīm left the kingdom in a worse state than before.

Yaḥyā b. Tamīm (501-9/1108-16) built a large fleet and launched several raids aginst Genoa and Sardinia. Under ʿAlī b. Yaḥyā (509-15/1116-21) relations worsened with Roger II of Sicily after the Zīrid had sought the help of the Almoravid sovereign ʿAlī b. Yūsuf for launching joint naval operations against Sicily. In 517/1123 an Almoravid flotilla occupied and sacked Nicotera in Calabria, an operation which Roger believed was instigated by the Zīrid, and so he launched a counter-attack against the Zīrid fort of al-Dīmās; this was, however, checked, thanks largely to the resistance of the Hilālī Arabs. In 529/1135 the Normans occupied the island of D̲j̲erba [see d̲j̲arba] but, although it was nominally under Zīrid suzerainty, the Zīrid *amīr* of al-Mahdiyya failed to come to its rescue.

From the close of the 4th/10th century, the economy of Zīrid Ifrīḳiya was in steady decline due to a number of factors, namely, the transfer of the Fāṭimid caliphate to Egypt, the destructive effect of the Hilālī invasion, the Norman occupation of Sicily, the frequent hostilities with the Ḥammādids and the Normans, the disruption of trans-Saharan trade as the caravan routes shifted from Ifrīḳiya westwards to Almoravid Morocco and Ḥammādid Bid̲j̲āya (Bougie) and eastwards to Egypt, and the rise of the Italian maritime city-states and their growing control of Mediterranean trade.

Following further sea raids by the Almoravids on Norman territory, Roger II decided to seize al-Mahdiyya at a time when the Zīrid state was weakẹned by successive years of drought and famine. In the reign of al-Ḥasan b. ʿAlī (515-43/1121-48), the Zīrid capital surrendered (543/1148) to a Norman fleet under the command of George of Antioch, and thus the Zīrid dynasty came to an end. Al-Ḥasan sought refuge with his Ḥammādid cousin, Yaḥyā b. ʿAzīz, who kept al-Ḥasan under surveillance in Algiers lest he establish contacts with the Almohad caliph ʿAbd al-Muʾmin in Marrākus̲h̲. Al-Ḥasan, however, joined ʿAbd al-Muʾmin when the latter took Algiers in 547/1151. In Marrākus̲h̲, al-Ḥasan kept urging the Almohad caliph to liberate al-Mahdiyya from Norman occupation until eventually this took place on 10 Muḥarram 555/22 January 1160. An Almohad governor was installed in the city, but al-Ḥasan was allowed to reside in Zawīla, where he spent eight years. On the death of ʿAbd al-Muʾmin, al-Ḥasan was ordered by the new Almohad caliph, Yūsuf b. ʿAbd al-Muʾmin, to move to Marrākus̲h̲, but on his way to the Almohad capital, al-Ḥasan died in Tamesna (563/1167).

Bibliography: 1. Sources. Ibn al-Athīr, *Kāmil*, Beirut 1980, vi, viii; Ibn Bassām, *Dhakhīra*, iv/2, ed. I. ʿAbbās, Beirut 1979, 613-15; Ibn ʿIdhārī, *Bayān*, ed. Colin and Lévi-Provençal, Leiden 1948-51, i; Ibn Khaldūn, *ʿIbar*, vi, Būlāḳ 1867, 88-95; Ibn al-Khaṭīb, *Aʿmāl*, ed. ʿAbbādī and Kattānī, Casablanca 1964, iii, 61-83; Maḳrīzī, *Ittiʿāẓ*, i, Cairo 1967, iii, Cairo 1973; Ibn Muyassar, *Akhbār Miṣr*, ed. H. Massé, Cairo 1919, ii; Tidjānī, *Riḥla*, Tunis 1958, 328-49.

2. Studies. G. Marçais, *La Berbérie musulmane et l'Orient au Moyen Âge*, Paris 1946; H.R. Idris, *La Berbérie orientale sous les Zīrīdes*, 2 vols., Paris 1959; Ḥ.Ḥ. ʿAbd al-Wahhāb, *Khulāṣat taʾrīkh Tūnis*, Tunis 1968, 105-20; C.A. Julien, *History of North Africa*, London 1970, 62-74; R. Le Tourneau, *North Africa to the sixteenth century*, in *Cambridge history of Islam*, ii, Cambridge 1970, 218-21; A. Laroui, *The history of the Maghrib*, Princeton 1977, 136-44; R. Daghfūs, *al-ʿAwāmil al-iḳtiṣādiyya li-hidjrat Banī Hilāl*..., in *al-Muʾarrikh al-ʿarabī*, xx (Baghdād 1981), 13-46; *UNESCO General history of Africa*, abridged ed. I. Hrbek, iii, Paris 1992, 171-5; C.E. Bosworth, *The New Islamic dynasties*, Edinburgh 1996, 17 nos. 5 and 6.

2. The Zīrids of Spain

This line was established in Granada by Zāwī b. Zīrī [*q.v.*] shortly after the fall of the ʿĀmirids [*q.v.* and see al-Manṣūr] and the outbreak of civil strife in al-Andalus. The dynasty, under four successive *amīrs*, lasted for almost 80 years (403-83/1013-90) until the last *amīr*, ʿAbd Allāh b. Buluggīn [*q.v.*], was deposed by the Almoravids, who annexed Granada and Málaga to Morocco.

Following Zāwī's departure for Ifrīḳiya (410/1019), his nephew Ḥabbūs b. Māksan (410-29/1019-38) assumed power in Granada. Ḥabbūs impressed on his Ṣanhādja kinsmen the imperative need for unity since, like his paternal uncle Zāwī, he was very conscious of the Andalusians' hostility to, and numerical superiority over, the Ṣanhādja. He entrusted running the affairs of the kingdom to a Jewish vizier, Samuel Ibn al-Naghrilla (ha-Nagīd; Abū Ibrāhīm Ismāʿīl, in Arabic sources), a thing unprecedented in Muslim Spain.

Ḥabbūs was succeeded by his son Bādīs, whose long reign (429-65/1038-73) marked the zenith of Zīrid power in Spain. Initially, Bādīs had to deal with a rival to the throne, his cousin Yiddīr, as well as his neighbours who cast covetous eyes on his kingdom, hence Bādīs's suspicion throughout his reign of Andalusian and Berber elements among his subjects, and reliance even more than his father on Samuel Ibn al-Naghrilla and, later, on Samuel's son Joseph (Yūsuf) for running the affairs of his kingdom.

Bādīs managed to rid himself of Yiddīr and triumphed over Zuhayr, the *amīr* of Alméria who, on receiving news of Ḥabbūs's death, had marched against Granada in the hope of seizing it.

Bādīs grew in stature, becoming the redoubtable leader of the Berbers in opposing the aggressive and anti-Berber policy of al-Muʿtaḍid b. ʿAbbād [*q.v.*], king of Seville. Bādīs became so furious at al-Muʿtaḍid's annexation of the Berber-held principalities of Morón, Arcos and Ronda in 445/1053—thanks partly to the pro-ʿAbbādid sympathies of their Arab populations—that he is said to have seriously considered the massacre of the Arab population of Granada, had it not been for his Jewish vizier Samuel, who eventually managed to persuade Bādīs not to do so lest all Andalusians should rise against him. In 446/1054, al-Muʿtaḍid seized Algeciras and, to forestall a similar fate for Málaga, Bādīs proceeded to annex Málaga to his kingdom.

On the death of Samuel Ibn al-Naghrilla (448/1056), his son Joseph succeeded him as vizier, but, unlike his father, was detested by the Muslims of Granada because of his arrogance and the many favours he bestowed on his co-religionists. He is accused in Andalusian sources of having poisoned Buluggīn, heir presumptive to Bādīs, and of having conspired with the *amīr* of Almería, Ibn Ṣumādiḥ, to surrender Granada to him on condition that "a state for the Jews is established in Alméria with himself as prince" (*Bayān*, iii, 266). An uprising took place against the Jews of Granada on 10 Ṣafar 459/30 December 1066, as a result of which Joseph Ibn al-Naghrilla and some 3,000 Jews were massacred.

Bādīs's growing domestic troubles in the last five years of his reign whetted the appetites of his neighbours: al-Muʿtaḍid unsuccessfully tried to wrest Málaga from Bādīs (458/1066), while Ibn Ṣumādiḥ of Almería seized Guadix. Despite his advanced years and domestic troubles, Bādīs nevertheless repulsed the ʿAbbādid assault on Málaga, and recovered Guadix from Ibn Ṣumādiḥ (459/1067) and Jaén from his rebellious son Māksan.

By the end of Bādīs's reign, Granada grew into an important city surrounding the citadel on the west bank of the Darro (*Hadarro*). The Zīrids established their court in the old Alcazaba district, now part of the Albaicin. Two of the gates to the Zīrid fortress and large stretches of the wall which protected it have survived. A bridge on the Darro, still called "Puente del Cadi", was built in 447/1055 by the *ḳāḍī* of Granada ʿAlī b. Muḥammad b. Tawba and named after him *ḳanṭarat al-ḳāḍī*, as was the adjoining mosque immediately to the south of the bridge. Muʾammal, a *mawlā* of Bādīs, is credited with a number of public works in Granada, such as the public fountain at Bāb al-Fakhkhārīn and the poplar promenade along the bank of the Genil named after him (*Ḥawr Muʾammal*), which survived until the time of Ibn al-Khaṭīb three centuries later.

ʿAbd Allāh, son of Buluggīn b. Bādīs, succeeded his grandfather on the throne of Granada (465/1073), while his brother Tamīm became independent ruler of Málaga. Taking advantage of ʿAbd Allāh's youth, his neighbours (al-Muʿtamid b. ʿAbbād of Seville in particular) cast covetous eyes on ʿAbd Allāh's territory. To avoid being attacked by al-Muʿtamid, who was in alliance with Alfonso VI, King of Castile, ʿAbd Allāh concluded an agreement with Alfonso whereby he undertook to pay him an annual tribute of 10,000 dīnārs. Fortunately for ʿAbd Allāh, al-Muʿtamid became embroiled with the *amīr* of Toledo, al-Maʾmūn b. Dhi 'l-Nūn [see dhu 'l-Nūnids], who had managed to annex Cordova for a few months. A few years later, al-Muʿtamid was pre-occupied with Murcia where his favourite vizier Ibn ʿAmmār [*q.v.*] sought independence (471/1079). ʿAbd Allāh seized the opportunity to get rid of his all-powerful vizier Simādja and assumed himself full power in his kingdom. The Zīrid then mounted successful expeditions against his brother Tamīm in Málaga and Ibn Ṣumādiḥ of Almería, both of whom had been encroaching upon his territory.

To check Alfonso's growing threat after his capture of Toledo (478/1085), ʿAbd Allāh joined al-Muʿtamid in appealing to the Almoravid sovereign Yūsuf b. Tāshufīn [*q.v.*] for assistance and, subsequently, took part in the battle of al-Zallāḳa [*q.v.*]/Sagrajas (479/1086) and in the siege of Aledo castle. Growing suspicious and disillusioned, however, after the abortive siege of Aledo (481/1088), ʿAbd Allāh began to strengthen his fortresses as a precautionary measure, probably having learnt a lesson from the failure of the Almoravids to seize Aledo castle. At the same time, the Zīrid sought to win over the Ṣanhādja in Granada by enlisting more of their numbers in his service, thereby redressing the imbalance which, under Bādīs, had been tilted in favour of the Zanāta whom ʿAbd Allāh refers to as the outsiders (*al-ṣinf al-barrānī*), a step taken by him at that particular time probably in order to ingratiate himself with the Ṣanhādja Almoravids.

Time and again in his memoirs (see below), ʿAbd Allāh claims that his defamation in the eyes of the Almoravids was the work of the *faḳīh* Ibn al-Ḳulayʿī and a number of disgruntled functionaries who had defected and falsely accused him of collusion with Alfonso VI against the Almoravids.

Yūsuf b. Tās̲h̲ufīn's third crossing to al-Andalus (483/1090) had no objective other than the deposition of ʿAbd Allāh, who initially seems to have been bent on resistance but soon decided to surrender after seeing his fortresses fall one-by-one to the Almoravids without resistance. ʿAbd Allāh's Ṣanhādja troops, on the one hand, had sided with their Almoravid kinsmen, while the masses in Granada welcomed the Almoravids because they sought to be free from the payment of taxes other than alms and tithes.

Having surrendered to the Almoravids (10 Radjab 483/8 September 1090), ʿAbd Allāh was exiled to Āg̲h̲māt [*q.v.*] in southern Morocco. Soon afterwards, his brother Tamīm was removed from Málaga and banished to al-Sūs [*q.v.*], but was allowed later to settle in Marrākus̲h̲, where he died in 488/1095.

It was during his exile in Āg̲h̲māt that ʿAbd Allāh, the last Zīrid *amīr* of Granada, wrote his memoirs, the *Tibyān*, in which he chronicled the history of the Zīrids since their arrival in al-Andalus up to the author's deposition by the Almoravids. Among the salient points emphasised in the *Tibyān* are: the division of the Muslims in 5th/11th-century Spain into two distinct and hostile groups (Andalusians and Berbers); the practice of dividing property by lottery among the Berber chieftains in al-Andalus; the reasons which led Ḥabbūs b. Māksan and his son Bādīs to appoint Jews, rather than Andalusians or fellow Berbers, as viziers; and the active, and often important, role of women in Berber society.

Bibliography: 1. Sources. ʿAbd Allāh b. Buluggīn, *Tibyān*, ed. and annotated A.T. Ṭībī, Rabāt 1995, Eng. tr. Leiden 1986; Ibn Bassām, *D̲h̲akh̲īra*, ed. I. ʿAbbās, Beirut 1978-9; i, iv; Ibn ʿId̲h̲ārī, *Bayān*, iii, ed. E. Lévi-Provençal, Paris 1930, 125-9, 262-6; Ibn al-K̲h̲aṭīb, *Aʿmāl*, ed. Lévi-Provençal, Beirut 1956, 227-36; idem, *Iḥāṭa*, ed. M.A. ʿInān, Cairo 1973-5, i, iii.

2. Studies. R.P.A. Dozy, *Histoire des musulmans d'Espagne*, new ed., iii, Leiden 1932; Lévi-Provençal, *Hist. Esp. mus.*, ii, Paris-Leiden 1950; H.R. Idris, *Les Zīrides d'Espagne*, in *And.*, xxix (1964), 39-137; A. Handler, *The Zirids of Granada*, Miami 1974; A. Tibi, Amīr *ʿAbd Allāh b. Buluggīn, last Zīrid* amīr *of Granada*, in *Dirāsāt wa-buḥūt̲h̲ fī taʾrīk̲h̲ al-Mag̲h̲rib wa 'l-Andalus*, Tripoli-Tunis 1984, 200-18; C.E. Bosworth, *The New Islamic dynasties*, Edinburgh 1996, 35-6 no. 13. (Amin Tibi)

ZIRIH, Zarah, an inland lake in Sīstān [*q.v.*], now straddling the borders of Persia and Afg̲h̲ānistān and the largest stretch of inland fresh water on the Iranian plateau. The name comes from Avestan *zrayah-*, O Pers. *drayah-* "sea, lake". The lake played a role in ancient Iranian legend about a Saos̲h̲yant or Redeemer, a son of Zoroaster, who would arise from it; Islamised versions of such legends describe King Solomon as commanding his army of jinn to lower the surface of the lake so that the land masses thereby appearing could be used for agriculture (see Bosworth, *The Saffarids of Sistan*, 36).

The mediaeval Islamic geographers emphasised the variability of the Zirih's extent, fed as it was by rivers from the mountains of central and eastern Afg̲h̲ānistān: the Helmand or Hilmand [*q.v.*], and the K̲h̲ʷās̲h̲, Farāh and Hārūt Ruds, with its maximum extent in the late spring when the snows had melted. The *Ḥudūd al-ʿālam*, tr. Minorsky, 55, cf. comm. 185, describes it as 30 *farsak̲h̲s* long by 7 wide, but sometimes it expanded so much that it flooded lowlands as far as the borders of Kirmān province. In mediaeval times, the reedy, shallow waters of the lake supported fishermen, whilst a flourishing agriculture along its shores was supplied by irrigation waters from the lake and its feeders (Ibn Ḥawkal, ed. Kramers, 405-6, tr. Kramers and Wiet, 417-18).

The lake has clearly shrunk in more modern times, judging by the descriptions of late 19th-early 20th century European travellers and officials (such as P.M. Sykes, C.E. Yate, and G.P. Tate and his colleagues on the Seistan Boundary Commission of 1903-5) of the Hāmūn depression as a whole; they also mention the cattle-raising along its shores and the population element of the *ṣayyāds*, fisherfolk and wildfowlers, who navigate through the reeds in cigar-shaped rafts of reeds called *tūtins*. Modern geographers estimate that the lake covers, at its maximum extent in May, some 1,158 sq. miles. However, intense summer evaporation reduces the water to three separate, permanent sheets of water, sc. the Hāmūn-i Hilmand proper, the Hāmūn-i Ṣābarī to its north and the Hāmūn-i Puzāk to its northeast. Also, water runs out of the southern end of the Hāmūn-i Hilmand in times of flooding and flows southeastwards through the Shela channel or Rūd-i S̲h̲alaḳ into the Gawd-i Zirih depression south of the Hilmand bend and in the extreme southwestern tip of modern Afg̲h̲ānistān. Irrigation works of recent decades along the course of the Hilmand in southeastern Afg̲h̲ānistān may have reduced the flow of water into the Hāmūn basin and adversely affected the hydrography and environment of Sīstān as a whole.

Bibliography: See also Le Strange, *The lands of the Eastern Caliphate*, 334, 338-9; C.E. Yate, *Khurasan and Sistan*, Edinburgh-London 1900, 79 ff.; P.M. Sykes, *Ten thousand miles in Persia or eight years in Irán*, London 1902, 364 ff.; G.P. Tate, *Seistan, a memoir on the history, topography, ruins and people of the country*, 4 parts, Calcutta 1910-12, 108-25; J. Humlum *et alii*, *La géographie de l'Afghanistan. Etude d'un pays aride*, Copenhagen 1959, 51, 103-4; W.B. Fisher, in *Camb. hist. Iran*, i, 78-81; C.E. Bosworth, *The history of the Saffarids of Sistan and the Maliks of Nimruz (247/861 to 949/1542-3)*, Costa Mesa and New York 1994, 44 ff. (C.E. Bosworth)

ZIRYĀB, Abu 'l-Ḥasan ʿAlī b. Nāfiʿ, the greatest musician of Muslim Spain. His nickname Ziryāb (a black bird) is said to have referred to both his dark-coloured complexion and his versatile tongue.

Born, probably around 175/790, into a family of *mawālī* of the caliph al-Mahdī, Ziryāb was educated, at an early age, by Ibrāhīm al-Mawṣilī [*q.v.*]. Isḥāḳ al-Mawṣilī [*q.v.*] introduced him to Hārūn al-Ras̲h̲īd (170-93/786-809) who, as later sources tell us, was greatly impressed by the young musician. This seems to have provoked Isḥāḳ's jealousy to the extent that Ziryād was forced to quit Bag̲h̲dād. Several years later we find him in the service of the Aghlabid ruler at Ḳayrawān, Ziyādat Allāh I (201-23/817-38). After falling into disgrace he turned to the Umayyad court at Cordova, where, in the year 206/822, he was received by ʿAbd al-Raḥmān II (206-38/822-52) who treated him with the greatest consideration. Being well versed in poetry, history, astronomy and geography, Ziryāb was considered the perfect boon companion (*nadīm*). He propagated also the latest fashion in cooking, clothing and the other arts of the *ẓurafāʾ* of the eastern capital. In Cordova he founded a music school in which he taught the theory and practice of the Mawṣilī school of Baghdād. Ziryāb died in Cordova, about forty days before his patron, at the end of Ṣafar 238 or beginning of Rabīʿ I/middle of August 852.

His pupils and three of his eight sons, in particular, ʿAbd al-Raḥmān, secured the survival of his musical teachings. The philosopher and musician Ibn Bādjdja (d. 533/1139 [*q.v.*]) was still credited with a musical "enrichment" (*ziyāda*) of an "eastern composition" (*talḥīn mashriḳī*) once introduced and performed by Ziryāb. Several innovations regarding the lute and lute playing [see AL-ʿŪD. II] were ascribed to him. He is said to have added a fifth string to the four-stringed lute and to have attributed it to the soul (*nafs*), giving it the red colour of blood. Both coloured strings and the addition of a fifth string were, however, already familiar to his contemporaries in Baghdād. Another novelty attributed to Ziryāb was the use of the quill feather (*ḳādima*) of a vulture (*nasr*) instead of a wooden plectrum. He is also said to have used gut of young wolves for the production of the two lower strings of the lute, and to have propagated a different method of cleaning the silk used for the two higher lute strings. Finally, he pretended that his own lute was lighter by about one-third than other lutes. Ziryāb practised the eastern style of beginning a measured song (*basīṭ; ʿamal*) with an unmeasured recitative (*nashīd; istihlāl*), and he followed the eastern scheme of increasing lightness and tempo in text and music in a performance, thus supporting the development of the later musical form of the vocal "suite" or *nawba* [*q.v.*]. A collection of his song texts (*K. fī Aghānī Ziryāb*), described as "a very extraordinary collection" (*dīwān ʿadjīb djidd^an^*), was edited by the brother of one of his sons-in-law, the *adīb* Aslam b. Aḥmad b. Saʿīd b. Aslam b. ʿAbd al-ʿAzīz.

Bibliography: Ibn ʿAbd Rabbih, *al-ʿIḳd al-farīd*, Cairo 1949, vi, 34, tr. H.G. Farmer, *The minstrels of the golden age of Islam*, in *IC*, xvii (1943), 271-81, xviii (1944), 53-61, esp. 56; Ibn Ḥazm, *Ṭawḳ al-ḥamāma*, Cairo 1975, 153; Ibn al-Ṭaḥḥān, *Ḥāwī al-funūn wa-salwat al-funūn*, facs. ed. Frankfurt 1990, 95; Ibn Ḥayyān, *Muḳtabis*, Beirut 1973, 87; Ibn Saʿīd, *Mughrib*, Cairo 1964, i, 51; Ḍabbī, *Bughyat al-multamis*, Madrid 1884, 138-9, 192, 224-5; Maḳḳarī, *Nafḥ al-ṭīb*, Beirut 1968, i, 344, iii, 122-33 (quoting Ibn Ḥayyān), 615; Farmer, *A history of Arabian music*, London 1929, 128-30; R. d'Erlanger, *La musique arabe*, v, Paris 1949, 388-91; M.A. al-Ḥifnī, *Ziryāb mūsīḳār al-Andalus*, Cairo n.d. [1966]; M. b. T. al-Ṭandjī, *al-Ṭarāʾiḳ wa 'l-alḥān al-mūsīḳiyya fī Ifrīḳiya wa 'l-Andalus*, in *al-Abḥāth*, xxi (1968), 93-116, esp. 110; E. Neubauer, *Der Bau der Laute und ihre Besaitung nach arabischen, persischen und türkischen Quellen des 9. bis 15. Jahrhunderts*, in *ZGAIW*, viii (1993), 279-378, esp. 291-2, 306, 312, 316-7, 320, 332.

(H.G. FARMER-[E. NEUBAUER])

ZISHTOWA, the usual Ottoman Turkish rendering of the Bulgarian town Svištov. In the Ottoman registers it appears variously as Zigitewa, Zigit, Zishtovi and Zishtowa. The town is situated on the right bank of the river Danube in its lower course, in the neighbourhood of the ancient city of Nove, where a small fortress was erected probably in the 12th-13th centuries A.D.; it was conquered by the Ottomans in 1388. In 1598 it was put to fire by the Wallachians. In 1791 the separate peace treaty between Austria and the Ottoman Empire was signed in Svištov. In 1810 it was destroyed by a Russian detachment and was in fact built anew. After the Russo-Turkish War in 1877-8, the town became part of the Bulgarian state.

Under the Ottomans, the settlement was first the centre of a *nāḥiye* and from the 17th century, a *ḳaḍā* in the *sandjaḳ* of Nikopolis. In the 18th and the 19th centuries, the town rose as a trade centre. With the opening of Austrian navigation along the lower course of the Danube in the 1840s, and the construction of its port, Svištov became the most important point on the lower course of the river.

After the seizure by the Ottomans, a small garrison was stationed in Svištov, but the majority of the population were Orthodox Christians, sc. Bulgarians and Vlachs; in the 18th century Greeks settled there too. The Muslim *maḥalle* appeared only in the 17th century, including an *imām* and a *müʾedhdhin*. After the Treaty of Carlowitz [see ḲARLOFČA], many Muslim families settled in Svištov, and new Muslim *maḥalles* came into being. According to Ewliyā Čelebi, in 1651-2 there had always been a small garrison consisting of 8 soldiers and a *dizdar* in the fortress of Svištov, with barracks and a mosque. The town (the *varosh*) was situated below on the river bank and comprised 300 houses. The census of 1865 recorded 4,554 Turks, 674 Bulgarians and 6,116 Gypsies, that is, 11,915 inhabitants altogether, and in 1874-5, 8,088 Muslims and 14,856 non-Muslims; nowadays, there are about 30,400 inhabitants altogether and 3,000 Turks. The *waḳf* documentation from the middle of the 17th century shows that there was a mosque in the town, the "New mosque" in the fortress, a *mekteb* and an *ʿimāret*. In the 18th and especially in the 19th centuries, new Muslim places of worship emerged, such as the Yi̊ldi̊ri̊m Djāmiʿ (1728), the mosque at the Horse Market with a *medrese*, or all in all, according to the *sālnāme* from 1872-3, 19 mosques, 1 *medrese*, 1 *mekteb-i rüshdiyye* and 3 *mektebs*. In 1900 there was only one Turkish grammar school. A library was established by Dār ül-Saʿāde Beshīr Agha (d. 1746) at the Old mosque; some of the manuscripts are preserved in the town museum. Some of the mosques were preserved until the 1920s, but only one remains today. Under the Ottomans, a few churches were built.

There emerged around the port a significant business nucleus with *khāns* and warehouses. In the 1870s there were in Svištov 746 workshops, 170 *maghazas*, 17 *khāns*, 6 tanneries and 22 watermills. In 1765-6 a clock tower was built (today a monument of culture) as a *waḳf* of the *voyvoda* Ḥüseyn Agha b. ʿAlī. In the middle of the 19th century, Ḥādjdjī Emīn built all the *waḳf* fountains in Svištov. A two-metre column dedicated to the visit of Sultan Maḥmūd II is preserved in the town museum.

Bibliography: Istanbul, BBK MK 11, TTD 416, 718, 775; MK 2974; MK 2596; *Sālnāme-yi wilāyet-i Tuna*, n.p. 1289/1872-3; *ibid.*, Rusçuk 1291/1874-5; G. Khristov, *Svishtov v minaloto, 86-1877 g.*, Sofia 1937; T. Zlatev, *Bŭlgarskite gradove po r. Dunav prez epokhata na Văzrazhdaneto*, Sofia 1963; Keskinoğlu, *Bulgaristan'da bazi Türk abideleri ve vakıf eserleri*, in *Vakıflar Dergisi*, xviii.

(SVETLANA IVANOVNA)

ẔIYĀ GÖK ALP [see GÖKALP ẔIYĀ].

ẔIYĀʾ AL-ḤAḲḲ, Ḍiyāʾ AL-Ḥaḳḳ, conventionally Zia ul-Haq, Muḥammad (1924-88), called after his death Shahīd al-Islām, administrator of martial law and then President of the Islamic Republic of Pakistan from 1977 till his death in an accident in 1988.

Born on 12 August 1924 at Ḍjullundār into a modest family in the eastern Pandjāb, Zia ul-Haq belonged to the community of the Araʿins. He entered the then Indian Army at the end of the Second World War, and within the Pakistani Army rose rapidly through the various ranks. In 1976 the President Ḍhu ʾl-Fiḳār ʿAlī Bhutto made him Joint Services Chief of Staff. Considering his youthfulness, it was hoped that he could be easily manipulated. The rigged elections of 1977 provoked an unprecedented wave of agitation, and on 5 July, Zia ul-Haq, at the head of a group of officers, arrested and detained Bhutto, proclaiming himself administrator of martial law. He refused to pardon Bhutto, who was accused of complicity in an assassination, and Bhutto was hanged in 1979.

In his first speeches, Zia presented himself as a simple muʾmin or believer to whom God had provisionally entrusted the government of Pakistan. He quoted the Ḳurʾān profusely, and never missed an occasion to make the point that he had performed the Ḥadjdj several times and prayed five times a day. He repeated that Islam was the cornerstone of Pakistan and that the niẓām-i muṣṭafā was not on the agenda of the main political parties. To reinforce the legitimacy of his power and to make up for a lack of charisma compared with his predecessor, he met Mawdūdī [q.v.] and relied on the support of his party, the Djamāʿat-i islāmī. After the Soviet invasion of Afghānistān, Mawdūdī proclaimed djihād as legitimate.

From 1979 onwards, Zia promulgated a series of Islamic laws hailed by Mawdūdī as the first steps towards the installation of an Islamic state. The first series, known as the "Hudood Ordinances", created a category of "Islamic crimes", such as adultery, rape, theft, fornication, etc. These crimes were to be dealt with by special courts with the task of applying the Ḳurʾānic penalties. These courts were themselves placed under the authority of the Federal Sharia Court, made up of judges and ʿulamāʾ. In 1980, the second series of measures envisaged the Islamisation of the economic sector. Two islamic taxes, the zakāt and the ʿushr [q.vv.], were created. Bank loans were regulated on a basis of the Ḳurʾānic prohibition of usury, ribā [q.v.]. The law envisaged a division of the risks run by the borrower and the lender. Interest was fixed on the basis of a common agreement, and indexed according to the financial performance of the banks.

In 1985 the war in Afghānistān entered a new phase with the Soviet Russian retreat. Zia at last organised elections, which marked a decline in support for the Djamāʿat. He then decided to seek the support of the Muslim League and the ethnic parties. The break was made, and the Djamāʿat then accused Zia of using Islam for political ends. In the economic sphere, Zia introduced reforms which, aided by favourable economic circumstances, brought about a growth in the national income of 7%. On the international level, partly thanks to the Afghān War, he managed to get increased American support whilst at the same time moving closer to China. Inter-ethnic troubles persuaded him, certainly in a very gradual fashion, to move towards democracy. In 1988 he announced that new elections would take place, but on 17 August of that year he died in an aeroplane accident whose circumstances remain obscure.

Bibliography: C. Baxter (ed.), Ẕiyāʾs Pakistan. Politics and stability in the frontline state, Lahore 1985; L. Ziring, Public policy dilemmas and Pakistan's nationality problem. The legacy of Ẕiâ ul-Haq, in Asian Survey, xxviii/8 (August 1988); S.J. Burki and G. Baxter (eds.), Pakistan under the military. Eleven years of Ẕiâ ul-Haq, Boulder, Colo. 1989; A. Hyman, M. Ghayur and N. Kaushik, Pakistan and after, New Delhi 1989; S. Azzam (ed.), Muhammad Ẕiâ-ul-Haq, Shaheed-Ul-Islam, London 1990; M. Hussain, Pakistan's politics. The Ẕiyâ years, Lahore 1990.　(M. BOIVIN)

ẔIYĀ PASHA, Ḍiyā Pasha, renowned Ottoman poet and essayist of the Tanzīmāt [q.v.] era.

Ẕiyā Pasha's given name was ʿAbd ül-Ḥamīd Ẕiyāʾ ül-Dīn. He was born in Kandilli on the Bosphorus in 1829, the son of Ferīd ül-Dīn Efendi, a native of Erzurum who worked as clerk in the Galata customs, and ʿIṭir Khānim. After graduating from the School of Literary Education (Mekteb-i ʿUlūm-i̊ Edebiyye), and having learned Persian and Arabic, he worked as scribe at the Grand Vizierate (Ṣadāret-i ʿUẓmā Mektūbī Odasi̊) for nine or ten years. During this period he frequented literary circles. Through the goodwill of the Grand Vizier Reshīd Pasha [q.v.], he was engaged in 1855 as fifth scribe of the imperial palace (Mābeyn-i Hümāyūn) and promoted to fourth scribe in 1859. In this position he also learned French and started translating from this language.

In 1862 he was dismissed, and the rest of his career is characterised by his repeatedly being sent away to posts distant from Istanbul. In 1862 he was appointed governor (mutaṣarrif) of Cyprus, then member of the Supreme Council of Judicial Ordinances (Medjlis-i Wālā-yi̊ Aḥkām-i̊ ʿAdliyye), governor of Amasya in 1863 and of Canik in 1865. In 1866 he was re-appointed a member of the Supreme Council of Judicial Ordinances. When in 1867 the Grand Vizier ʿĀlī Pasha [q.v.] decided to send him away from Istanbul again as governor of Cyprus, Ẕiyā Pasha refused and on 17 May 1867 fled to Paris with Nāmiḳ Kemāl [q.v.], followed by other members of the Society of New Ottomans (Yeñi ʿOthmānlilar Djemʿiyyeti [see YEÑI ʿOTHMĀNLILAR]). After a few months he went to London and published, initially there together with Nāmiḳ Kemāl and later on alone in Geneva, the newspaper Hürriyyet "Liberty".

In 1871 he returned to Istanbul and first became chairman of the Executive Assembly of the Council of Judicial Ordinances (Dīwān-i̊ Aḥkām-i̊ ʿAdliyye Idjrā Djemʿiyyeti), the executive branch of the newly-divided Supreme Council (Medjlis-i Wālā), then member of the legislative branch of the same, the Council of State (Shūrā-yi̊ Dewlet), and lastly, under-secretary for educational affairs (maʿārif müsteshāri̊). After ʿAbd ül-Ḥamīd II's ascension to the throne in 1876, he worked together with Nāmiḳ Kemāl in the Constitution Commission (Ḳānūn-i̊ Esāsī Endjümeni). In 1877 he was again sent away from Istanbul, being appointed governor first of Syria, then of Konya and, in 1878, of Adana, where he died on 17 May 1880. His grave is in the cemetery of the Ulu Djāmiʿ in Adana.

Ẕiyā Pasha is a representative of the transition period of Ottoman literature from the Dīwān literature to western-oriented literature. More traditional and less consistent in his outlook on literature than Nāmiḳ Kemal, he was of a more political and ideological turn of mind than Shināsī Bey [q.v.] and influential through the articles he wrote in Europe on subjects such as justice, equality, individual morality, prevailing conditions, etc.

As a poet, Ẕiyā Pasha remained true to Dīwān

poetry, using (with only rare exceptions) *ʿarūḍ* [*q.v.*] and classical forms such as the *ḳaṣīde, g̲h̲azel, terd̲j̲īʿ-i bend, terkīb-i bend*, etc. The main merits of his poems are their straightforward language and, above all, the innovative use of satire.

Besides his articles in newspapers (mainly in *Muk̲h̲bir* and *Ḥürriyyet*) and his translations from French (of works by Molière, J.-J. Rousseau, Fénelon *et alii*), he published the anthology *K̲h̲arābāt* in 1874. This consists of three volumes of Turkish, Persian and Arabic poetry, and an introduction (in *met̲h̲newī* verse) which is not consistent with his previous literary opinions as published in his essay *S̲h̲iʿr we ins̲h̲ā* (*Ḥürriyyet*, no. 11, 1868). He included a considerable number of his own poems in this anthology, a fact which was severely criticised by Nāmiḳ Kemāl in his *Tak̲h̲rīb-i K̲h̲arābāt* and *Taʿḳīb*.

Żiyā Pas̲h̲a's important satirical work is *Ẓafer-nāme*, which he wrote in Paris to criticise ʿĀlī Pas̲h̲a. It consists of a *ḳaṣīde* of 66 verses, the *tak̲h̲mīs* of this *ḳaṣīde*, and a commentary on the same. In *Rüʾyā*, which resembles Weysī's [*q.v.*] *K̲h̲ʷāb-nāme*, he criticised ʿĀlī Pas̲h̲a and the Sublime Porte, and in *Werāt̲h̲et-i Salṭanat-i Seniyye*, which consists of two letters, Fuʾād Pas̲h̲a [*q.v.*].

Ziyā Pas̲h̲a's collected poems were published only posthumously (first ed. *Es̲h̲ʿār-i Ẓiyā*, Istanbul 1881).

Bibliography: Gibb, *HOP*, v, 41-111; M.K. Bilgegil, *Harâbât karşısında Namık Kemal*, Istanbul 1972; idem, *Ziyâ Paşa üzerinde bir araştırma*, ²Ankara 1979; *Başlangıcından günümüze kadar büyük Türk klâsikleri*, viii, Istanbul 1988, 341-3 (with further bibl.); H. Yorulmaz, *Terci-i bend ve terkib-i bend: Ziya Paşa*, Istanbul 1992; H. Tanyaş, *Bağdatlı Ruhi ve Ziya Paşa. Terkib-i bentler ve terci-i bent*, Ankara 1995; *Türk dili ve edebiyatı ansiklopedisi*, viii, Istanbul 1998, 666-9; H. Kolcu, *Ziya Paşa'nın Zafernâmesine reddiyye ve tekzîbiyye*, Istanbul 1998. (Edith G. Ambros)

ZIYĀD b. **ABĪHI**, Abu 'l-Mug̲h̲īra, governor of ʿIrāḳ and the eastern provinces of the Umayyad caliphate during the reign of Muʿāwiya b. Abī Sufyān [*q.v.*].

Ziyād was born out of wedlock in al-Ṭāʾif, probably some time in the first year of the *Hid̲j̲ra*, A.D. 622, or in 2/623-4, and died in al-T̲h̲awiyya (or al-T̲h̲uwayya) near al-Kūfa in Ramaḍān 53/673. His name is variously given as Ziyād b. ʿUbayd, Ziyād b. Sumayya, Ziyād b. Abī Sufyān, Ziyād b. Ummihi (Ibn Abi 'l-Ḥadīd, xvi, 179-80) and Ziyād *al-amīr* (Ibn ʿAsākir, xix, 164-5). A S̲h̲īʿī tradition relates that ʿĀʾis̲h̲a [*q.v.*] was accustomed to call him Ziyād b. Abīhi (the son of his father), since his father was not known (*Biḥār al-anwār*, xliv, 309). Lammens thought that this offending *nisba* appeared during the ʿAbbāsid era, while Ziyād himself used the *nisba* Ibn Sumayya or Ibn Abī Sufyān (Lammens, 43).

The sources diverge on the origin of Ziyād's mother, Sumayya. According to al-Balād̲h̲urī, she was a female slave of a Yas̲h̲kurī living in the suburbs of Kaskar (the place on which Wāsiṭ was built). Having been ill, he performed the *ḥad̲j̲d̲j̲* and was treated successfully in al-Ṭāʾif by the physician al-Ḥārit̲h̲ b. Kalada al-T̲h̲aḳafī [*q.v.* in Suppl.]. He gave Sumayya to al-Ḥārit̲h̲, who was the natural father of Nāfiʿ and of the Companion (*ṣaḥābī*) Nufayʿ, known as Abū Bakra [*q.v.*]. Later, al-Ḥārit̲h̲ gave Sumayya to one of his wife's slaves, ʿUbayd, who was *rūmī* (not necessarily of Byzantine origin, in many cases of Syrian origin). An allusion to this non-Arab origin appears in a version of Ziyād's reply to Muʿāwiya's letter: "He will find that I am a Persian [warrior] . . . after his adoption by Muʿāwiya, he became an Arab from the Banū ʿAbd Manāf" (*la-yad̲j̲idannī aḥmara ḍarrāb^an bi 'l-sayfi . . . fa-lammā iddaʿāhu Muʿāwiyatu ṣāra ʿarabiyy^an manāfiyy^an*, Naṣr b. Muzāḥim, *Waḳʿat Ṣiffīn*, ed. ʿAbd al-Salām Hārūn, Cairo 1981, 366-7).

Ziyād was born "on the bed of ʿUbayd" (*ʿalā firās̲h̲i ʿUbayd^in*, al-Balād̲h̲urī, *Ansāb*, ivA, 163-4). He was thus, according to *d̲j̲āhilī* usage and Muḥammad's precepts, the legal offspring of ʿUbayd, the owner of the bed (U. Rubin, *Al-walad li-l-firāsh*, 5-7). ʿAwāna al-Kalbī [*q.v.*] claimed that Sumayya was a female slave of the *dihḳān* [*q.v.*] of Zaydaward in Kaskar. She was given to al-Ḥārit̲h̲, who was invited to the region to treat the Sāsānid king (Kisrā) and later attended the *dihḳān* (Ibn ʿAsākir, 173).

Some traditions relate that Sumayya was the mother not only of Ziyād, but also of the Companion ʿAmmār b. Yāsir [*q.v.*]. Modern research proves that there were two different women named Sumayya, both connected with al-Ḥārit̲h̲ (G.R. Hawting, *The development of the biography of al-Ḥārith ibn Kalada and the relationship between medicine and Islam*, 131-2). Abū ʿUbayda [*q.v.*] reports that Ziyād (or his family) claimed that his mother was Sumayya (or Asmāʾ) bt. al-Aʿwar, from the Banū ʿAbd S̲h̲ams b. Zayd Manāt of Tamīm (al-Balād̲h̲urī, *Ansāb*, ivA, 169; *Ag̲h̲ānī*¹, xvii, 67).

Ziyād became a Muslim during the caliphate of Abū Bakr [*q.v.*]. He was one of the first Muslim settlers in the great garrison town of al-Baṣra [*q.v.*]. He arrived with his half-brothers Nāfiʿ and Abū Bakra, accompanying the son-in-law of al-Ḥārit̲h̲ b. Kalada, ʿUtba b. G̲h̲azwān al-Māzinī, the first governor of the new settlement. Ziyād was in his teens when his unusual abilities were first noticed. He began performing little jobs in the *dīwān* [*q.v.*] of Baṣra during the caliphate of ʿUmar b. al-Khaṭṭāb [*q.v.*].

Ziyād's first appearance in the public arena took place when he was very young. Al-Madāʾinī reports that Ziyād was 14 years old when ʿUtba asked him in 14/635 to be the distributor (*ḳāsim*) of the booty of al-Ubulla (Apologos), in southern ʿIrāḳ (al-Ṭabarī, i, 2388). He distinguished himself as an intelligent, open-minded secretary, who was devoted to his master and to public service. He showed an unusual aptitude for accounting and had an excellent command of epistolary art. The sources report that ʿUmar was impressed by some of Ziyād's letters and by the fact that the governor (*ʿāmil*) of Baṣra, Abū Mūsā al-As̲h̲ʿarī [*q.v.*], appointed him as his *locum tenens* when he had to leave the city to take part in the conquests. ʿUmar summoned Ziyād to Medina and subjected him to a test. The results were remarkable. The caliph granted him 1,000 dirhams which he used to manumit his father ʿUbayd (al-Balād̲h̲urī, *Ansāb*, iv/A, 164-5) or his mother Sumayya (al-Ṣafadī, xv, 12).

It seems that in the same year he was appointed secretary (*kātib* [*q.v.*]), in the service of ʿUtba. After ʿUtba's death in 15/636, Ziyād pursued his career under four of his successors: Abū Mūsā al-As̲h̲ʿarī, al-Mug̲h̲īra b. S̲h̲uʿba [*q.v.*] of T̲h̲aḳīf, both on behalf of ʿUmar, ʿAbd Allāh b. ʿĀmir on behalf of ʿUt̲h̲mān and ʿAbd Allāh b. al-ʿAbbās on behalf of ʿAlī b. Abī Ṭālib [*q.vv.*] (Ibn ʿAsākir, xix, 169).

Ziyād's reputation grew when he was invited to Medina in 17/638 to testify in the case of al-Mug̲h̲īra, who had been charged with adultery. Three witnesses, including two of Ziyād's half-brothers, Abū Bakra and S̲h̲ibl b. Maʿbad al-Bad̲j̲alī (*Tahd̲h̲īb*, iv, 305) so attested as required in Ḳurʾān, XXIV, 4, but Ziyād gave a partial testimony which meant the acquittal of al-Mug̲h̲īra and the flogging of those three. ʿUmar did not conceal his relief (Abū al-ʿArab Muḥammad b. Aḥmad al-Tamīmī, *K. al-Miḥan*, ed. Yaḥyā Wahīb al-Djabbūrī, 1983, 284-5; Ibn Abi ʾl-Ḥadīd, xii, 227-46).

In 36/656, after the battle of the Camel, ʿAlī appointed his cousin ʿAbd Allāh b. al-ʿAbbās governor of Baṣra and named Ziyād responsible for the collection of the real estate taxes and the treasury (*ʿalā ʾl-kharādj wa-bayt al-māl*). ʿAlī's appreciation of Ziyād's talents was so great that he ordered his cousin to accept Ziyād's advice. However, Ibn al-ʿAbbās soon left the city to take part in ʿAlī's preparations against Muʿāwiya; he designated Ziyād as acting governor of the province (Ibn Ḥabīb, *al-Muḥabbar*, 295; Ps.-Ibn Ḳutayba, *al-Imāma wa ʾl-siyāsa*, 105-6). At the end of the hostilities at Ṣiffīn (37/657), ʿAlī sent Sahl b. Ḥunayf as governor of Fārs, but the Muslim army there expelled him. ʿAlī then sent Ziyād, who won their confidence and was therefore able to collect the taxes (Muḥammad b. Ḥibbān al-Bustī, *al-Sīra al-nabawiyya wa-akhbār al-khulafāʾ*, ed. Sayyid ʿAzīz Bek, Beirut 1987, 545). It seems that Ziyād stayed in a fortress in Fārs for three or four years, and considered himself a representative of the legal government of ʿAlī, even after ʿAlī was murdered in 40/661. As a result of this, the fortress was called Ḳalʿat Ziyād (Ibn ʿAsākir, xix, 173) and later, Ḳalʿat Manṣūr (Ibn al-Djawzī, *al-Muntaẓam*, v, 160). Busr b. Abī Arṭāt, the emissary of Muʿāwiya, seized the offspring of Ziyād in Baṣra and threatened to kill them. Ziyād surrendered. ʿAwāna reports that Ziyād made use of the opportunity of Maṣḳala b. Hubayra being on his way to visit Muʿāwiya, and demanded that he ask the caliph if there was reason to believe the rumours claiming that Ziyād was the son of Abū Sufyān (Ibn ʿAsākir, 172-3). This seems to be the starting point of the idea of the *istilḥāḳ*, the official recognition of Ziyād as the son of Abū Sufyān.

The *istilḥāḳ* of Ziyād in 44/665 caused a strong reaction in the ranks of the Umayyad family: Muʿāwiya's son Yazīd and the Marwānids protested against this act. It was reported that ʿAbd Allāh b. ʿĀmir, Ziyād's predecessor as governor of Baṣra, threatened to procure a *ḳasāma* (50 persons who would swear in confirmation of something) attesting that Abū Sufyān never met Sumayya. The resolute intervention of Muʿāwiya silenced Ibn ʿĀmir. The Marwānids feared the results of the *istilḥāḳ*, which took place after ʿAmr b. al-ʿĀṣ [*q.v.*] joined Muʿāwiya and became governor of Egypt. Abū ʿUbayda [*q.v.*] reports that Muʿāwiya threatened to flog (*ḥadd al-ḳadhf*) some Marwānid leaders for having rejected the relationship and recognition of it, even though it was supported by witnesses, in confirmation with Ḳurʾān, XXIV, 4 (al-Zubayr b. Bakkār, *al-Akhbār al-muwaffaḳiyyāt*, ed. Sāmī Makkī al-ʿĀnī, Beirut 1996, 155-63). Muʿāwiya paid money to soften the opposition to the adoption of Ziyād (al-Ābī, *Nathr al-durr*, ii, 33 a).

It seems that Ziyād's affiliation was a catalyst in the polemic within the new Muslim society about affiliation (*istilḥāḳ*, *diʿwa*) of an illegitimate child (*walad zinā*), a custom which was usual in the *Djāhiliyya*. ʿUmar b. al-Khaṭṭāb, to whom Muslim historians ascribe the institution of many legal proceedings, initiated the rule that a *walad zinā* born in the *Djāhiliyya* could be attributed to his biological father on condition that the father paid to the mother's owner the price of the child. In this case the child was liberated and affiliated with his father's pedigree. If the intercourse and the claim of genealogy had taken place in the Islamic period, the claim was annulled and the child continued to be a slave. Later jurists opposed this opinion and this may well be the reason for their disapproval of Ziyād's affiliation by Muʿāwiya (*LA*, s.v. *s-ʿ-ā*, xiv, 387). Pro-Umayyad authors pretended that Muʿāwiya had supposed that Ziyād's affiliation was legal (Ibn al-ʿArabī, *al-ʿAwāṣim min al-ḳawāṣim*, 248-57).

A few months after the *istilḥāḳ*, in Rabīʿ II or Djumādā I 45/July 665, Ziyād was nominated as governor of Baṣra and of the provinces which depended on it, Khurāsān and Sidjistān. His inaugural speech in the mosque of Baṣra just after his nomination is considered a masterpiece of eloquence. This discourse is named *al-batrāʾ* or *al-butayrāʾ* (Ibn ʿAsākir, xix, 179), "the truncated speech", since at the beginning of his address Ziyād did not praise God and did not bless the Prophet (*li-annahu lam yaḥmidi ʾllāha fīhā wa-lam yuṣalli ʿalā ʾl-nabī*) (*LA*, s.v. *b-t-r*). In it, Ziyād defined his policies very clearly: since transgressors, libertines and thieves predominated at Baṣra, he declared that he would inflict a penalty even if a person was merely suspect, and that he was ready to kill anyone who would not be ready to turn from his wrong ways. Ziyād promised to pay the stipends regularly, not to send the warriors too far away and not to keep them in the field overlong (*tadjmīr* [*q.v.*]).

After the death of al-Mughīra b. Shuʿba in 50/670, Kūfa was added by Muʿāwiya to Ziyād's governorship. He used to spent the summer there, leaving Samura b. Djundab [*q.v.*] as substitute, and the winter in Baṣra, leaving ʿAmr b. Ḥurayth as his deputy in Kūfa. Ziyād is considered the first governor of these two towns together (*awwal man djumiʿa lahu ʾl-miṣrāni*). He had to face two hostile groups, the Khāridjites [*q.v.*] in Baṣra and the ʿAlids in Kūfa, in addition to the problems raised by the different clans. He used one group to control another. The Khāridjites transplanted their activities outside Baṣra. The ʿAlids persisted in their agitation in Kūfa under the leadership of Ḥudjr b. ʿAdī al-Kindī [*q.v.*]. Ziyād's predecessor, al-Mughīra, treated him with clemency. Ziyād forewarned Ḥudjr on several occasions and made it clear that he was ready to execute him if he continued to curse Muʿāwiya publicly (*idhā aẓhara laʿna Muʿāwiya*). Ziyād succeeded in isolating Ḥudjr and his supporters. In 51/671, Ḥudjr was arrested and sent to Damascus. He was put to death in Mardj ʿAdhrāʾ, east of Damascus, with six of his supporters. This capital punishment, the first political execution in Islam, had its expected effects (Shaban, *Islamic history*, 89-90; I. Hasson, *Recherches sur Muʿāwiya b. Abī Sufyān, sa politique tribale, militaire et agraire*, unpubl. Ph.D. thesis, The Hebrew University, Jerusalem 1982, 133-9, 157-60).

There are some reports indicating that Ziyād aspired to be elected by Muʿāwiya as heir to the throne (Ibn ʿAsākir, xix, 196-7), but the caliph acted rapidly and nominated his son Yazīd [*q.v.*] as *walī ʿahd*. Ziyād asked Muʿāwiya to add Ḥidjāz to his governorship. Al-Kalbī reports that the caliph complied with Ziyād's wish but that the appointment reached its destination only shortly before Ziyād's death (Ibn ʿAsākir, xix, 204-5).

Ziyād is known as one of the most gifted governors of the Umayyad era. He had a good understanding of his task as governor, and had a great influence on his successors concerning the conception of the duties of rulers. At the beginning of his rule, he gave several examples of severity to win the confidence of the population. He implemented important administrative reforms, first in Baṣra and later in Kūfa, aiming to put an end to the chaotic situation prevailing in these *amṣār* in consequence of the large influx of tribesmen. The system of the *ʿarīf* [*q.v.*] and *ʿirāfa* (small group of tribesmen massed together for the purpose of the distribution of the stipends, *ʿaṭāʾ* [*q.v.*]), set up in the time of ʿUmar, had became inefficient. This system was based on the nobility (*as͟hrāf*), whose status was fixed by their receiving from the government a grant of 2,000-2,500 dirhams annually (al-Balād͟hurī, *Ansāb*, v, introd., 11). Ziyād gave rise to new *ʿirāfa*s by joining related clans into larger tribal divisions. He created five groups (*k͟hums*, pl. *ak͟hmās*) in Baṣra and four groups (*rubʿ*, pl. *arbāʿ*) in Kūfa instead of the seven groups (*subʿ*, pl. *asbaʿ*), as determined by ʿUmar. This reorganisation contributed to a better control of the cities (Shaban, *Islamic history*, 86-90; M.G. Morony, *Iraq after the Muslim conquest*, 58). Ziyād updated the records of the *dīwān*, paid the *ʿaṭāʾ* regularly and succeeded in maintaining order and security not only in Baṣra and Kūfa, but in the entire eastern provinces.

In spite of his internal preoccupations in Baṣra, Ziyād used K͟hurāsān as a base to continue the conquests in the East. His lieutenants al-Ḥakam b. ʿAmr al-G͟hifārī, G͟hālib b. ʿAbd Allāh (or Fuḍāla) al-Layt͟hī and Rabīʿ b. Ziyād al-Ḥārit͟hī re-established Muslim authority in Ṭuk͟hāristān. Balk͟h and Ḳūhistān were reoccupied. It was reported that al-Ḥakam had crossed the River Oxus (al-Ṭabarī, ii, 81-2, 84, 109-11, 155-6).

Ziyād struck coins in the Sāsānid style bearing his own name in the form of "Ziyād ibn Abī Sufyān" (Morony, *op. cit.*, 46). He initiated many development schemes, such as the digging of the canal called Nahr Maʿḳil in Baṣra, wrongly attributed to Maʿḳil b. Yasār (Ibn Durayd, *al-Is͟htiḳāḳ*, ed. ʿAbd al-Salām Hārūn, Bag͟hdād 1979, 181). He transferred population from one country to another. He conveyed 50,000 Arab families from Baṣra and Kūfa to K͟hurāsān to settle with the Muslim Arab army there. They formed the nucleus of the later Ahl K͟hurāsān. His deliberate intention was to establish a permanent Arab settlement in this province (M. Sharon, *Black banners from the East*, 66 n.)

Ziyād is charged with alleged cruelty: he mutilated or crucified some ʿAlids and mistreated their corpses (*Musnad Abī Yaʿlā al-Mawṣilī*, ix, 79-80; *al-Imāma wa 'l-siyāsa*, 202-3; Ibn Aʿt͟ham, *K. al-Futūḥ*, iv, 203; al-Mad͟jlisī, *Biḥār*, xliv, 126, 213).

Some sources indicate that Ziyād transmitted utterances of the Prophet, not directly but with ʿUmar's intermediacy. He is considered a Successor (*tābiʿī* [see TĀBIʿŪN]), belonging to the first class (*ṭabaḳa*) of the Baṣrans (K͟halīfa b. K͟hayyāṭ, *K. al-Ṭabaḳāt*, ed. A.Ḍ. al-ʿUmarī, Riyāḍ 1982, 191). The pro-Umayyad author Abū Bakr Ibn al-ʿArabī (d. 543/1149) regards him as a Companion (*al-ʿAwāṣim min al-ḳawāṣim*, 250). Abū Nuʿaym al-Iṣfahānī [*q.v.*] said that he was a *zāhid*. He is regarded by some as an expert on the Ḳurʾān and its precepts, and as skilled in jurisprudence (Ibn ʿAsākir, xix, 165-7).

Ziyād was considered a first-rate orator. The question of the authenticity of his inaugural speech remains open, even though it is found in sources belonging to different genres and tendencies: *adab*, rhetoric, history and polemics (al-D͟jāḥiẓ, *al-Bayān wa 'l-tabyīn*, ii, 61-6; Ibn Ḳutayba, *ʿUyūn al-ak͟hbār*, ii, 241-3; al-Ṭabarī, ii, 73-5; Ibn ʿAbd Rabbih, *al-ʿIḳd al-farīd*, iv, 110-13; Ibn Abi 'l-Ḥadīd, *S͟harḥ Nahd͟j al-balāg͟ha*, xvi, 200-3). Fragments of Ziyād's speeches and utterances are often cited as examples of excellent oral or written expression. Ibn Abi 'l-Ḥadīd (i, 278-9) charged him with trying to imitate ʿAlī's style, considered as the highest level of Arabic after the Ḳurʾān and the sayings of the Prophet.

S͟hīʿī sources tried to discover early signs of his treachery and his dishonesty in the interval between the battle of the Camel and Ṣiffīn. Thus it is reported that ʿAlī reprimanded Ziyād for mistreating his emissary (Ibn Abi 'l-Ḥadīd, xvi, 196). The same sources attribute Ziyād's talent and ingenuity to the fact of his being an offspring of illicit intercourse, since such offspring are intelligent (*awlād al-zinā nud͟jub*[un]) (al-Mad͟jlisī, *Biḥār al-anwār*, lith. Tabrīz n.d., viii, 522).

Ziyād is supposed to be the first author of a treatise on *mat͟hālib* [*q.v.*] (*GAS*, i, 261). If this is true, then he evidently collected reports on vices, immoral practices or habits, and sexual immorality, especially prostitution among the different tribes in the *D͟jāhiliyya* and early Islamic era, with the purpose of using them against his detractors.

The interest in Ziyād's history started at a very early stage. Treatises called *Ak͟hbār Ẓiyād b. Abīh* were composed by Abū Mik͟hnaf, His͟hām b. Muḥammad al-Kalbī and ʿAbd al-ʿAzīz b. Yaḥyā al-D͟jalūdī (*GAS*, i, 262). In the literature of the *awāʾil* [*q.v.*], Ziyād occupies a noticeable place. He is often included in the category of the three or four shrewd politicians and statesmen (*dāhiya*, pl. *duhāt*) among the Arabs, the other three being Muʿāwiya, al-Mug͟hīra and ʿAmr b. al-ʿĀṣ.

Bibliography: 1. Sources. Ibn Ḳutayba, *Maʿārif*, ed. Wüstenfeld, 176, 217, 274; Ps.-Ibn Ḳutayba, *al-Imāma wa 'l-siyāsa*, ed. ʿAlī S͟hīrī, Beirut 1990, i, 105-6, 203, ii, 26-7; Balād͟hurī, *Ansāb*, iv/A, ed. Schloessinger and Kister, 163-236; idem, *Futūḥ*, index; Ibn Hilāl al-T͟haḳafī, *al-G͟hārāt aw al-istinfār wa 'l-g͟hārāt*, ed. ʿAbd al-Zahrāʾ al-Ḥusaynī al-K͟haṭīb, Beirut 1987, 265-7, 269-71, 273-6, 278-83, 445-8; Ṭabarī, index; Yaʿḳūbī, *Taʾrīk͟h*, Beirut 1960, ii, 218-22; Ibn Aʿt͟ham al-Kūfī, *K. al-Futūḥ*, ed. M.A. Muʿīd K͟hān, Ḥaydarābād 1971, iv, 169-203; *Ag͟hānī*[1], xii, 73-6, xiv, 145-7, xvi, 3-10, xvii, 54-71; ʿAskarī, *al-Awāʾil*, Beirut 1987, 167-8, 202-7, 228-9; Abū Bakr Ibn al-ʿArabī, *al-ʿAwāṣim min al-ḳawāṣim*, ed. Muḥibb al-Dīn al-K͟haṭīb, Cairo 1408, 248-57; Ibn ʿAsākir, *Taʾrīk͟h madīnat Dimas͟hḳ*, ed. Muḥibb al-Dīn ʿUmar al-ʿAmrawī, Beirut-Damascus 1995, xix, 162-209; Ibn al-D͟jawzī, *al-Muntaẓam*, ed. M. ʿAbd al-Ḳādir ʿAṭā *et alii*, Beirut 1992, v, 159-60, 195, 210, 212-3, 241-3, 261-4; Ibn al-At͟hīr, *al-Kāmil*, Beirut 1987, iii, 284, 299-302, 304-8, 317-24, 326-39, 341-2; Ibn Abi 'l-Ḥadīd, *S͟harḥ Nahd͟j al-balāg͟ha*, ed. Muḥammad Abu 'l-Faḍl Ibrāhīm, xvi, 179-204; D͟hahabī, *Taʾrīk͟h al-Islām*, ed. ʿUmar ʿAbd al-Salām Tadmurī, Beirut 1989, ch. *ʿAhd Muʿāwiya b. Abī Sufyān*, 207-10, and rich bibl. in footnotes; Ṣafadī, *Wāfī*, xv, Wiesbaden 1982, 10-3; Ibn Kat͟hīr, *al-Bidāya wa 'l-nihāya*, Beirut n.d., vii, 246, 256, 318, 321-2; viii, 45-55 and index; al-Mad͟jlisī, *Biḥār al-anwār*, Beirut 1983, index; lith. edition, Tabrīz n.d., viii, 522, 524-5.

2. Studies. Wellhausen, *The Arab kingdom and its fall*, tr. M.G. Weir, Calcutta 1927, 119-30 and index; K.A. Fariq, *A remarkable early Muslim governor, Ẓiyād b. Abīh*, in *IC*, xxvi (1952); idem, *Ẓiyād b. Abīh*, London 1966; Ziriklī, *Aʿlām*, iv, 53; Sezgin, *GAS*, i, 261-2; C.E. Bosworth, *Sīstān under the Arabs*, Rome 1968, 20-4; L. Veccia Vaglieri, *The Patriarchal and Umayyad caliphates*, in P.M. Holt *et alii* (eds.), *The Cambridge history of Islam*, Cambridge 1970, i, 57-103; M.A. Shaban, *The ʿAbbāsid revolution*, Cambridge 1970, 29-34; idem, *Islamic history, A.D. 600-750 (A.H. 132), a new interpretation*, Cambridge 1971, 86-90; S͟hawḳī Ḍayf, *Taʾrīk͟h al-adab al-ʿarabī, al-ʿaṣr al-islāmī*, Cairo 1974, 422-8; F.Mc.G. Donner, *The early Islamic conquests*, Princeton 1981, 231-50, 415; P. Crone, *Jāhilī and Jewish law: the* qasāma, in

JSAI, iv (1984), 153-201; M.G. Morony, *Iraq after the Muslim conquest*, Princeton 1984, index; E. Kohlberg, *The position of the* walad al-zinā *in Imāmī Shīʿism*, in *BSOAS*, xlviii (1985), 237-66; Crone and M. Hinds, *God's caliph. Religious authority in the first century of Islam*, Cambridge 1986; H. Kennedy, *The Prophet and the age of the caliphates*, London and New York 1986, 82-103; G.R. Hawting, *The first dynasty of Islam, the Umayyad caliphate AD 661-750*, London 1987, 40-5; idem, *The development of the biography of al-Ḥārith ibn Kalada and the relationship between medicine and Islam*, in C.E. Bosworth *et alii* (eds.), *The Islamic world from classical to modern times*, Princeton 1989, 127-40; A. Arazi, *Les enfants adultérins* [daʿīs] *dans la société arabe ancienne: l'aspect littéraire*, in *JSAI*, xvi (1993), 1-34; U. Rubin, Al-walad li-l-firāsh. *On the Islamic campaign against* zinā, in *SI*, lxxx (1994), 5-26. (I. HASSON)

ZIYĀD B. **ṢĀLIḤ** AL-**ḤĀRITHĪ** [see ZIYĀD B. ṢĀLIḤ AL-KHUZĀʿĪ].

ZIYĀD B. **ṢĀLIḤ** AL-**KHUZĀʿĪ**, Arab commander in the service of Abū Muslim at the time of the ʿAbbāsid Revolt (d. 135/752-3).

He was one of the *naḳībs* [*q.v.*] chosen by Abū Muslim from the leaders of the Arabs in Khurāsān in 1340/747-8. With the triumph of the ʿAbbāsid cause, Abū Muslim appointed Ziyād governor of Bukhārā and Sogdia, where he suppressed a rebellion of the discontented Arab garrison in Bukhārā led by Sharīk (or Shurayk) b. Shaykh al-Mahrī (133/750-1). Shortly afterwards he commanded the Arab expedition sent into the land of the Turks beyond the Syr Darya in order to combat a Chinese army which had appeared in Central Asia and had attacked Čač or Shāsh (the later Tashkent [*q.v.*]). In a great battle near Talas or Ṭarāz [*q.v.*], known mainly from the Chinese sources, Ziyād won a great victory over the Korean general Kao hsien-chih and wrought great slaughter in his army (Dhu 'l-Ḥidjdja 133/July 751); in effect, this was the end of Chinese intervention in the Western lands.

Ziyād's own downfall followed shortly after this, however. In 135/752-3 he rebelled in Sogdia against Abū Muslim, but was abandoned by his commanders. He fled to Bārkath, whose *dihḳān* handed him over to Abū Muslim for execution. It seems that Ziyād had not acted entirely of his own accord, but had been secretly promised the governorship of Khurāsān by the ʿAbbāsid caliph al-Saffāḥ if he would rise up against his over-mighty subject Abū Muslim.

Bibliography: Ṭabarī, ii, 1988, iii, 80, 81-2; Barthold, *Turkestan down to the Mongol invasion*², 194-6; Gibb, *The Arab conquests in Central Asia*, London 1923, 95-6; W. Samolin, *East Turkistan to the twelfth century, a brief political survey*, The Hague 1964, 66-7; E.L. Daniel, *The political and social history of Khurasan under Abbasid rule 747-820*, Minneapolis and Chicago 1979, 87-8, 89, 111-12.

The above is not to be confused with his homonym and contemporary Ziyād b. Ṣāliḥ al-Ḥārithī (from the Yemeni tribe of al-Ḥārith b. Kaʿb [*q.v.*] or Balḥārith), who was governor of Kūfa for the last Umayyad governor of ʿIrāḳ, Ibn Hubayra, in 132/749-50 but who soon afterwards defected to the advancing ʿAbbāsids. See Patricia Crone, *Slaves on horses. The evolution of the Islamic polity*, Cambridge 1980, 172; M. Sharon, *Black banners from the east. II. Revolt. The social and military aspects of the ʿAbbāsid revolution*, Jerusalem 1990, 218-19. (C.E. BOSWORTH)

ZIYĀD AL-**AʿDJAM**, Ibn Salmā (or Sulaym, or Sulaymān, or Djābir, see al-Bakrī, *Simṭ al-laʾālī*, *Dhayl*, ed. al-Maymanī, 8) Abū Umāma, poet of the Umayyad period. Of Persian origin, he was a *mawlā* of the ʿĀmir b. al-Ḥārith, a branch of the ʿAbd al-Ḳays [*q.v.*]. For his biography, the primary source is the *K. al-Aghānī*, most of the information being provided by ʿUmar b. Shabba and Ibn ʿĀʾisha.

According to Yāḳūt (*Irshād*, iv, 221), in 23/643 he is said to have participated with Abū Mūsā al-Ashʿarī and ʿUthmān b. al-ʿĀṣ in the conquest of Iṣṭakhr, where he is said to have subsequently lived, according to Ibn Sallām (*Ṭabaḳāt*, 693). In fact, he spent his entire life in the entourage of governors of Khurāsān and of Fārs such as ʿUmar b. ʿUbayd Allāh b. Maʿmar (*Agh.*, xiv, 104-6), ʿAbd Allāh b. al-Khashradj (*ibid.*, x, 151, 155, xiv, 105; Ibn Sallām, *Ṭabaḳāt*, 696) and ʿAbbād b. al-Ḥuṣayn (*Agh.*, xiv, 106), whose patronage he sought.

He associated himself at an early stage with the Umayyad general al-Muhallab b. Abī Ṣufra [*q.v.*], whose victory over the Khāridjites near Nahr Tustar he applauded in a *bāʾiyya*, of which five verses have been preserved by al-Dīnawarī (*al-Akhbār al-ṭiwāl*, ed. ʿĀmir, Cairo 1960, 272), and numerous episodes in his life are linked to his connection with him and his family. In particular, it seems that al-Muhallab protected him and defended his rights even at the expense of his own sons; thus when al-Muhallab's son, Ḥabīb, tore a silk robe that Ziyād wore in the Persian fashion, in revenge for a previous quarrel in which his father had also given his support to Ziyād (*Agh.*, xiv, 103-4), he composed verses declaring that it was not only his robe that had been torn but also the skin of al-Muhallab. The latter again supported him and demanded that his son pay compensation (Ibn Khallikān, *Wafayāt*, ed. ʿAbbās, biography of al-Muhallab, no. 754). Evidently al-Muhallab feared his satirical mode, of which he had had a taste in two scarcely flattering verses composed by Ziyād on the subject of the circumcision, late in life, of al-Muhallab's father Abū Ṣufra. According to Yāḳūt (*Irshād*, iv, 222), Ziyād died *ca.* 100/718 and, according to *Agh.*, xiv, 10, in Khurāsān.

Ziyād owed his nickname al-Aʿdjam to the fact that he had a strong Persian accent; according to anecdotes cited by the *Aghānī*, his mastery of spoken Arabic was not perfect, either in pronunciation or even in grammar. Al-Muhallab presented him with a well-spoken slave to recite his poems on his behalf (*Agh.*, xi, 165), provoking a hostile reaction on the part of another poet at the court of al-Muhallab, al-Mughīra b. Ḥabnāʾ. In exchanges of invective between the two, al-Mughīra b. Ḥabnāʾ never tired of reminding Ziyād of his barbarous origins; he also poked fun at the Rabīʿa who, as a tribe, had asked for a barbarian "of *aʿdjamī* tongue" to defend their honour in his poetry (*Agh.*, xi, 166-7).

But his status as a *mawlā* did not prevent Ziyād from gaining a reputation as a political satirist or from being recognised as "our *lisān*" by the Rabīʿa (*Agh.*, xi, 167). The other poet of the court of al-Muhallab with whom Ziyād exchanged invective was Kaʿb al-Ashḳarī, of the Azd, in a conflict which erupted between the latter and the ʿAbd al-Ḳays. Ziyād attacked Kaʿb, vowing that he would make "him and his people the target of every tongue" (*Agh.*, xiii, 58-9). Even al-Farazdaḳ, who intended to attack the ʿAbd al-Ḳays, abandoned his project in the face of Ziyād's riposte (*Agh.*, xiv, 107-8; Ibn Ḳutayba, *Shiʿr*, ed. Shākir, 431; verses also in Ibn Sallām, *Ṭabaḳāt*, 695-6). Ziyād also satirised the Banū Yashkur, in circumstances which vary according to the sources: Ibn

Ḳutayba (*Shiʿr*, 430) mentions the name of the Yashkurī poet Ḳatāda; Ibn Sallām quotes two of Ziyād's verses concerning this tribe, *Ṭabaḳāt*, 699; according to *Agh.*, xi, 171, cited by al-Baghdādī, *Khizāna*, ed. Hārūn, vi, 126, the Banū Yashkur approached their poet, Suwayd, asking him to reply to Ziyād, but he refused.

The acknowledged imperfections of his spoken Arabic did not prevent the recognition of his poetry, from the time of al-Aṣmaʿī onward (*Fuḥūlat al-shuʿarāʾ*, ed. Khafādjī and al-Zaynī, Cairo 1953, 31), as a *ḥudjdja* and as linguistically irreproach-able, to such an extent that his verses are cited as grammatical or lexical *loci probantes* by, among others, Sībawayh; al-Mubarrad, *Kāmil*, ed. Wright, 178, 324, 365-6, 632, although al-Mubarrad gives elsewhere a corrected version of the verse most cited as a grammatical *shāhid*; Ibn Khallikān, biography of Khālid al-Tamīmī, no. 215; Abū ʿUbayda, *Madjāz al-Ḳurʾān*, see *Khizāna*, x, 208-9, and Sezgin, *GAS*, ii, 373-4; and al-Wahhābī, *Marādjiʿ tarādjim al-udabāʾ al-ʿarab, s.v.* He is also quoted several times in the *LA*. Some of the verses attributed to him have also been attributed to al-Akhṭal or to al-Farazdaḳ (Ibn Khallikān, biography of Yazīd b. al-Muhallab, no. 816; the biographer adds here that he has seen the *dīwān* of Ziyād, as is also claimed by al-ʿAynī, *al-Maḳāṣid al-naḥwiyya fī sharḥ shurūḥ al-alfiyya*, Būlāḳ 1299, iv, 597, see Ibn Ḥadjar, *Iṣāba*, iv, 199-200).

Ziyād's best known poem, and the best preserved (in particular by al-Yazīdī, *K. al-Amālī*, and by al-Bakrī in his *dhayl* to al-Ḳālī's *Amālī*, the *Simṭ al-laʾālī*, is his *ḥāʾiyya* on the death of al-Muhallab's son Abū Firās al-Mughīra, who predeceased his father in 82/701. This elegy has been translated and published, with discussion of the sources, by F. Krenkow, *The elegy upon al-Mughīra Ibn al-Muhallab*, in *Islamica*, ii [1926-7], 344-54; the remainder of Ziyād's production survives only in fragments, recently collected by Y. Bakkār, *Shiʿr Ziyād al-Aʿdjam*, Damascus 1983. By means of a detailed analysis of the sources and the fragments, Bakkār aims at defining more clearly the biography and the personality of this poet and does not exclude the hypothesis, formed on the basis of a passage in the *LA* (s.v. *ʿudjm*), that Ziyād was in fact, despite his linguistic failings, an Arab by birth. On the subject of the *ḥāʾiyya*, al-Bakrī (*Simṭ al-laʾālī*, 7-8) recounts numerous traditions, taken up by Krenkow and Bakkār, according to which this poem would be attributable not to Ziyād but to his fellow-tribesman al-Salaṭān al-ʿAbdī (on whom see Nallino, *La letteratura araba*, 920)—further evidence of the extent to which this *mawlā* was integrated into his adoptive tribe.

It is perhaps all this that Blachère refers to when he writes (*HLA*, 512) that, while the work of Ziyād remains inaccessible to us, his biographical data "make this individual one of the most interesting figures from the point of view of our knowledge of relations between the Arab world and Iran, in poetry, at this time".

Bibliography (in addition to references given in the article): *Tahdhīb taʾrīkh Ibn ʿAsākir*, v, 401-3; *Khizāna*, x, 4-9; C.A. Nallino, *La letteratura araba*, Rome 1948, 137-8; S.M. Yusuf, *Al-Muhallab and the poets*, in *IC*, xxiv (1950), 197-99, as well as the references cited in Sezgin, *GAS*, ii, 373-4.

(LIDIA BETTINI)

ZIYĀDAT ALLĀH [see AGHLABIDS].

AL-**ZIYĀDĪ**, ABŪ ḤASSĀN AL-ḤASAN b. ʿUthmān al-Shīrāzī (this *nisba* from some apparent connection with the Persian city; see Yāḳūt, *Buldān*, ed. Beirut, iii, 381), judge, traditionist and historian of the early ʿAbbāsid period, b. 156/773 in Baghdād and died there Radjab 242/Nov.-Dec. 856 (al-Ṭabarī, iii, 1434, and al-Khaṭīb al-Baghdādī) or the following year.

A traditionalist in his views and associate of al-Shāfiʿī, he was questioned under the *Miḥna* [*q.v.*] at the end of al-Maʾmūn's reign (al-Ṭabarī, iii, 1121-5, 1128, 1132). But he came into his own under the more orthodox al-Mutawakkil and was in 240/854-5 appointed *ḳāḍī* of the Sharḳiyya quarter of Baghdād; whilst in office there, he had a certain ʿĪsā b. Djaʿfar (presumably a Shīʿī) flogged to death for insulting the Shaykhayn, i.e. Abū Bakr and ʿUmar, and ʿĀʾisha and Ḥafṣa (*ibid.*, iii, 124-6). He was regarded as trustworthy in relating traditions. He was close to the historian al-Wāḳidī [*q.v.*] and was himself the author of a history, now lost, which was an important source for Ibn Abī Ṭāhir Ṭayfūr, whence for al-Ṭabarī, on contemporary and near-contemporary history.

Bibliography: Ṭabarī, see Indices; al-Khaṭīb al-Baghdādī, vii, 356-61 no. 3877; Yāḳūt, *Irshād*, Cairo 1936-8, ix, 18-24; Ibn al-ʿImād, *Shadharāt*, ii, 100; L. Massignon, *Cadis et naqībs baghdadiens*, in *WZKM*, li (1948), 108; Sezgin, *GAS*, i, 316.

(C.E. BOSWORTH)

ZIYĀDIDS, a dynasty of southwestern Arabia centred on Tihāma [*q.v.*] between the years 203-409(?)/818-1018, but having control also in the northern highlands of the Yemen [see AL-YAMAN] and along the Indian Ocean coast. Unfortunately, our sources are late and little informed, there are discrepancies in the dates given and even the names of the later members of the family are unknown.

The dynasty is named after Muḥammad b. Ziyād, who traced his pedigree back to the Umayyad dynasty and who, during the caliphate of the ʿAbbāsid al-Maʾmūn [*q.v.*], became the protégé of his minister, al-Faḍl b. Sahl [*q.v.*]. In 202/817 a letter arrived at the ʿAbbāsid court with news of a rebellion of tribes in Tihāma. Al-Faḍl b. Sahl advised al-Maʾmūn to despatch Muḥammad b. Ziyād there in order to crush it. Ibn Ziyād was duly sent with the additional order to build a new capital in Tihāma. After performing the Pilgrimage in 203/818, he pressed on south into Yemen. There he fought many hard battles against recalcitrant tribes and succeeded in winning control over the whole of Tihāma. In 204/819, he built the new capital, as he had been instructed, and it was named Zabīd [*q.v.*]. Before his death in 245/859, he extended the territory of the dynasty far beyond Tihāma: to Ḥaḍramawt [*q.v.*], along the southern coast to al-Shiḥr [*q.v.*] and Mirbāṭ in modern ʿUmān, to Aden [see ʿADAN] and Abyan [*q.v.*] and north along the Red Sea coast to Ḥaly Ibn Yaʿḳūb.

Ibn Ziyād was followed in power by his son, Ibrāhīm (d. 283/896), he by his own son, Ziyād (d. 289/902), he by his own son, (Ibn) Ziyād (d. 299/911), who was succeeded by one Abu ʾl-Djaysh. The latter died in 371/981 and this is the last name and last firm date in the history of the family; 409/1018 is, however, mentioned specifically as the date of the demise of the dynasty.

Bibliography: The Yemeni Arabic sources are all late, the best being: ʿUmāra al-Yamanī, *Taʾrīkh al-Yaman*, in H.C. Kay, *Yaman, its early mediaeval history*, London 1892, 1-18 (Eng. tr.) and 1-14 (Ar. text); ʿAbd al-Raḥmān b. ʿAlī Ibn al-Daybaʿ, *Ḳurrat al-ʿuyūn bi-akhbār al-Yaman al-maymūn*, ed. Muḥammad b. ʿAlī al-Akwaʿ, 2 vols., Cairo 1977; see also G.R. Smith, *The political history of the Islamic Yemen down to the first Turkish invasion* (*1-945/622-1538*), in W. Daum (ed.), *Yemen: 300 years of art and civilisation in Arabia Felix*, Innsbruck and Frankfurt

1988, 130-1 (with full references); C.E. Bosworth, *The New Islamic dynasties*, Edinburgh 1996, 98 no. 41.

(G.R. Smith)

ZIYĀNIYYA, a Maghribī branch of the Ṣūfī order of the Shādhiliyya [*q.v.*].

The eponymous founder was Muḥammad b. ʿAbd al-Raḥmān Ibn Abī Ziyān (d. 1145/1733), a descendant of the Prophet (*sharīf*) originally from the Moroccan southwest (Wadi Draʿa, near Figuig). At an early age he went to Sidjilmāsa and was initiated into Ṣūfism by a *muḳaddam* of the Nāṣiriyya [*q.v.*], Sīdī Muḥammad b. ʿAzza. On the latter's death, he left for Fās in order to complete his education in the Islamic sciences, notably under Muḥammad b. ʿAbd al-Ḳādir al-Fāsī (d. 1116/1704). According to Rinn, he was allegedly expelled from Fās by Sultan Mawlāy Ismāʿīl (*Marabouts et Khouan*, Algiers 1884, 412); but the hagiographical work devoted to Ibn Abī Ziyān, the *Ṭahārat al-anfus wa 'l-arwāḥ al-djismāniyya fi 'l-ṭarīḳa al-ziyāniyya al-shādhiliyya*, mentions that it was his care for a "decent obscurity" which impelled him to return to his ancestral land (tr. of this work by A. Cour, in *RMM*, xii [1910], see 365). There at Kanādhā (or Kenadsa) he founded a *zāwiya* [*q.v.*] which became a beacon in the region. The brigands of the Sahara feared the saint, famed for his miracle-working and from now on known as "Mawlāy Būziyān"; this last extended his protection over all the caravans crossing his region (documents with the *shaykh*'s seal made these caravans inviolable, according to Depont and Coppolani, who reproduce this seal in *Les confréries religieuses musulmanes*, Algiers 1897, 497). Devotees from the *zāwiya* often escorted the caravans, and soon Ibn Abī Ziyān had his own, involving him in extensive commercial activity. In the same realm of ideas, it was said that the *shaykh* had the supernatural power of facilitating the Meccan Pilgrimage when obstacles intervened (Cour, *op. cit.*, 378-9, 571-9).

The office of *shaykh* was always transmitted hereditarily among the Ziyāniyya, usually from father to son. The order's influence spread particularly in Algeria, notably at Algiers and Oran (see the table in Depont and Coppolani, *op. cit.*, 500). The Ziyāniyya remained faithful to the Shādhilī spirit, in both their *dhikr* [*q.v.*] formulae and their stress on knowledge of the esoteric sciences, and furthermore, in the sobriety of their behaviour (see Cour, 582-3). When the fame of Shaykh Ibn Abī Ziyān had spread throughout Morocco, he enjoyed the favour of Mawlāy Ismāʿīl (*ibid.*, 579), and this positive attitude of the holders of political power towards the Ziyāniyya became generalised. Under the Protectorate, the French authorities appreciated the benevolent and pacific role of the leaders at the Kanādhā *zāwiya*, and Depont and Coppolani note that these last "gave appreciable services" to the French forces.

Bibliography: See also J.Cl. Garcin, *Assises matérielles et rôle économique des ordres soufis*, in G. Veinstein and A. Popovic (eds.), *Les Voies d'Allâh. Les ordres mystiques dans le monde musulman des origines à aujourd'hui*, Paris 1996, 221-2. J.S. Trimingham, *The Sufi orders in Islam*, Oxford 1971, 88, has only a brief mention of the Ziyāniyya as a branch of the Nāṣiriyya.

(E. Geoffroy)

ZIYĀRA (a., pl. *ziyārāt*), pious visitation, pilgrimage to a holy place, tomb or shrine.

1. In the central and eastern Arab lands during the pre-modern period
2. In the central Arab lands from 1800 to the present day
3. Amongst the Copts in Egypt
4. In the Maghrib
5. In Persia and other Shīʿī lands
6. The Turkish lands, including the Balkans and Central Asia
7. In Muslim India
8. In Indonesia
9. In Central and West Africa
10. In the Horn of Africa

1. In the central and eastern Arab lands during the pre-modern period.

Unlike the *ḥadjdj* [*q.v.*], the canonical pilgrimage to Mecca, and the lesser pilgrimage, the *ʿumra* [*q.v.*], the *ziyāra* lacked the authority of Scripture. Mediaeval Arabic and Hebrew sources frequently refer to Jews and Christians making a *ziyāra* to tombs and shrines of holy persons (cf. J.W. Meri, *Sacred journeys to sacred precincts. The cult of saints among Muslims and Jews in medieval Syria*, D. Phil. thesis, Oxford Univ. 1998), and Near Eastern Jews routinely undertook pilgrimages to holy places in the Holy Land, Bilād al-Shām, ʿIrāḳ and Persia.

The first and most fundamental sense of this word applies to visiting the graves of the dead (*ziyārat al-ḳubūr*), as is reflected in the various *Sunan* collections (see Wensinck, *Handbook*, s.v. graves), but never specifically in the context of saints and prophets. Other related expressions which appear in mediaeval sources include *safar* "journeying" and *safar ilā ziyārat al-ḳubūr* "journeying to visit graves". *Ḥadīth* traditions generally refer to the Prophet's stricture against visiting Christian places of worship, and his concern that Muslims would follow idolatrous and polytheistic practices and raise tombs above the ground [see masdjid. I. C. 4.]. The Prophet urged visiting the tombs of the deceased to pray and supplicate on their behalf. *Ziyāra* also appears in other contexts. Devotees made a *ziyāra* to mosques and other holy places, many of them associated with holy persons and their legends, e.g. springs, wells, caves, mountains, etc. *Ziyāra* was also made to dead saints (*awliyāʾ*), prophets, mystics and other holy persons [see walī]. Another type of *ziyāra* was made to such venerable objects as the Prophet's sandal (cf. al-Yūnīnī, *Dhayl mirʾāt al-zamān*, Ḥaydarābād 1954-61, ii, 45-6; Meri, *op. cit.*, 123-4). Devotees also visited living holy men (saints, Ṣūfīs) or other such individuals revered for their piety, learning, spiritual insight and *baraka* [*q.v.*]. (cf. M.M. Chamberlain, *Knowledge and social practice in medieval Damascus 1190-1350*, Cambridge 1994, 132-3; Meri, *op. cit.*, ch. 2).

One of the earliest records of Muslim theologians discussing the proper etiquette (*adab*) of visiting tombs dates from the 2nd/8th century. Al-Ḥasan al-Baṣrī (d. 110/728 [*q.v.*]) expressed concern with the manner and custom of properly conducting oneself when visiting tombs; he rebuked people for forgetting its solemn purpose and for engaging there in unacceptable behaviour, such as eating (al-Turkumānī, *K. al-Lumaʿ fi 'l-ḥawādith wa 'l-bidaʿ*, ed. S. Labīb, Cairo 1986, i, 214).

(a) *Shīʿī* ziyāra *in Arab lands*

All Shīʿīs, wherever they resided, recognised the importance of making the *ziyāra* to the tomb of the Prophet's grandson al-Ḥusayn and the other Shīʿī Imāms. Although the *ziyāra* was not in fact obligatory as the *ḥadjdj* was, a similar obligatory status, merits and recompense were nevertheless ascribed to it. The major Shīʿī *ʿatabāt* [*q.v.* in Suppl.] or pilgrimage cities were almost a "secondary *ḳibla*". The threat of divine punishment for not performing the *ziyāra* figures prominently in *ziyāra* traditions. Shīʿīs upheld the intercession of the Imāms for their followers, in contrast to the Sunnīs, among whom the orthodox scholars like al-Ghazālī and Ibn Ḳayyim al-Djawziyya denied the intercession of saints but only attributed it to the Prophet.

Ziyāra traditions arose in the context of Sunnī-Shīʿī antagonism precipitated by the massacre of al-Ḥusayn and his party at Karbalāʾ [*q.v.*]. Performing canonical prayer (*ṣalāt al-farīḍa*) was equivalent to the obligatory status of performing the *ḥadjdj* and supererogatory prayer to that of the recommended *ʿumra*. Other Shīʿī traditions mention that performing the pilgrimage to Karbalāʾ on the day of ʿArafa equals "one thousand Pilgrimages, one thousand lesser pilgrimages and one thousand military expeditions with the Prophet..." (al-Shaykh al-Mufīd, *K. al-Mazār*, Ḳum 1988, 20). Since the *ziyāra* did not represent a legal substitute or alternative to the *ḥadjdj*, the award of merits surpassing those of the *ḥadjdj* was explicit. Al-Ḥusayn's son Abū ʿAbd Allāh likened the requirements of setting out on a *ziyāra* to al-Ḥusayn to those of the *ḥadjdj*. "What is incumbent upon us (*mā yalzamunā*) is what is incumbent in the *ḥadjdj*" (Ibn Ḳūlūya, *Kāmil al-ziyārāt*, Beirut 1997, 250-1). A number of traditions further address the commendable status of *ziyāra* (cf. *ibid.*, Nadjaf 1356/1437-8, 141).

Shīʿīs placed greater emphasis on *ziyāra* ritual than did Sunnīs. In fact, no Shīʿī theologian opposed making a *ziyāra*. The institutionalisation of ritual contributed to the formation of pilgrimage centres in the towns and cities of ʿIrāḳ. Similarly, the devotional role ascribed to the Shīʿī Imāms and the Family of the Prophet in Fāṭimid Egypt continued with the successor Sunnī dynasties (C.S. Taylor, *Reevaluating the Shiʿi role in the development of monumental Islamic funerary architecture: the case of Egypt*, in *Muqarnas*, ix [1992], 3-10; C. Williams, *The cult of ʿAlid saints in the Fatimid monuments of Cairo*, in *ibid.*, i [1983], 37-52, iii [1985], 39-60).

(b) *Opposition to* ziyāra

Opposition to *ziyāra* crystallised after the founding of the Ḥanbalī school of jurisprudence in ʿIrāḳ. It was not its founder Ibn Ḥanbal (d. 241/855 [*q.v.*]), but rather subsequent generations of disciples who were concerned with Muslims engaging in *ziyāra* practices which violated the Ḳurʾān and the Sunna. However, Ibn Ḥanbal at first forbade reciting the Ḳurʾān at funerals, but immediately changed his mind afterward (cf. al-Ghazālī, *Iḥyāʾ ʿulūm al-dīn*, iv, 492). Ḥanbalīs affirmed that so long as no precedent existed in the Ḳurʾān or Sunna for the veneration of saints and for making a *ziyāra* to tombs (with the exception of reading the opening chapter of the Ḳurʾān, supplicating on behalf of the dead and contemplating death and the Hereafter, etc.), *ziyāra* was to be considered an heretical innovation (*bidʿa*) and venerating saints as polytheism (*shirk*). They also rejected the *ziyāra* on the grounds that it encouraged immoral practices, such as the intermingling of the sexes, especially at festivals and on saints' days (*mawsim*).

One of the earliest Ḥanbalī condemnations of *ziyāra* came from the Baghdādī jurisconsult and resident of Damascus Ibn ʿAḳīl (d. 513/1119 [*q.v.*]), who castigates the ignorant and wretched (i.e. the common people) for practices "which they created for themselves", namely, glorifying tombs and physically coming in contact with them. Ibn ʿAḳīl argues that proponents of the cult of saints justified pilgrimage to tombs and shrines by invoking a tradition on the authority of the Companion Djābir b. ʿAbd Allāh (d. 78/697) in which the Prophet visited the Mosque of the Aḥzāb on Monday, Tuesday and Wednesday (G. Makdisi, *Ibn ʿAqīl, religion and culture in classical Islam*, Edinburgh 1997, 209). On the basis of this tradition, he and later generations of Ḥanbalīs deliberated whether it was legal to perform *ziyāra* to saints' tombs, shrines (*mashāhid* [see MASHHAD]) and mosques with tombs in them. Devotees would engage in nights of religious devotion called *iḥyāʾ* during which they would recite the Ḳurʾān and pray. Such occasions, it was implausibly alleged, engendered immoral behaviour. Ibn ʿAḳīl refers to men and women committing immoral acts and to the expenditure of great sums of money. He further elaborates on objectionable rituals which include kindling lights, kissing tombs and covering them with perfume, addressing the dead with petitions, writing formulae on paper, taking earth from the tomb as a blessing, hanging rags on trees, etc. Such practices, he argues, were tantamount to *djāhilī* practices (Makdisi, *op. cit.*, 210).

Ibn Taymiyya (d. 728/1328 [*q.v.*]) was one of the foremost critics of the cult of saints and the author of several highly controversial legal opnions (*fatāwā*) and treatises concerning *ziyāra*, which provide insight into the rituals of saint devotion among Muslims and Christians throughout the Near East, particularly in Damascus, where he lived most of his life.

Ibn Taymiyya distinguishes between the heretical *ziyāra* (*al-ziyāra al-bidʿiyya*), which he associates with pagans, Jews and Christians, and the legal *ziyāra* (*al-ziyāra al-sharʿiyya*), which is enjoined by the Prophet. The former, tantamount to polytheism, is when "the visitor intends that his supplication be fulfilled at the tomb or that he supplicate the deceased, supplicate for rain through him and make a request of him or take an oath by God, requesting a need" (*Madjmūʿ fatāwā*, al-Riyāḍ 1991, xxvii, 31-2). However, Ibn Taymiyya does not deny the possibility that supplication can be fulfilled, going so far as to say that "if anything is granted, it should be attributed to the personal merit of the tomb's patron" (*Iḳtiḍāʾ al-ṣirāṭ al-mustaḳīm mukhālafat ahl al-djaḥīm*, Cairo 1950, 374). While some theologians acknowledged the symbiotic nature of the relationship between the living and the dead, Ibn Taymiyya argues that "in the legally permissible *ziyāra*, the living does not have need for the dead by making a request of him (*masʾala*) or seeking his intercession (*tawassul*). But rather, the dead derive benefit from the living, and God the Exalted has mercy upon the living who supplicate for the dead" (*Madjmūʿ fatāwā*, xxvii, 71).

Ibn Taymiyya's disciple Ibn Ḳayyim al-Djawziyya (d. 1275/1350 [*q.v.*]) continued his master's crusade against *ziyāra* practices which threatened orthodoxy and in a scathing polemic against them argued that mediaeval Syrians in performing *ziyāra* were observing rites (*manāsik*) similar to those of the Pilgrimage to Mecca (Ibn Ḳayyim al-Djawziyya, *Ighāthat al-lahfān min maṣāyid al-shayṭān*, Beirut 1986, i, 220-21, 304). Concerning such parallels, see Meri, *The etiquette of devotion in the Islamic cult of saints*, in *The cult of saints in Late Antiquity and the Middle Ages. Essays on the contribution of Peter Brown*, ed. J. Howard-Johnston and P.A. Hayward, Oxford 1999, 263-86; idem, *Sacred journeys*.

During the early 20th century, the puritanical Wahhābiyya [*q.v.*], adherents of the doctrines of Ibn Taymiyya, destroyed the monuments that stood over the tombs of the Companions throughout the Ḥidjāz.

(c) *Affirming the* ziyāra

Writing in defence of the *ziyāra* in his *Iḥyāʾ ʿulūm al-dīn*, Abū Ḥāmid al-Ghazālī (d. 505/1111 [*q.v.*])

took the opponents of *ziyāra* to task by affirming the existence of saints and the permissibility of making a *ziyāra* to all tombs. But he, too, qualified the true meaning of *ziyāra*, which he did not merely associate with saints. The presence of holiness made a pilgrimage site efficacious. Muslims possessed a universal sense of the holiness of the dead which manifested itself in the devotee's physical and spiritual contact with the site. Al-Ghazālī stresses the universality of the interpersonal experience of self-surrender and embracing the dead with all one's senses, a recurring theme in the pilgrimage guides (*op. cit.*, iv, 492).

Ziyāra should be conducted in accordance with the Sunna of the Prophet. For al-Ghazālī, the goals of *ziyāra* were contemplation, remembering death and obtaining blessings, a view with which even the Ḥanbalīs would agree. However, the devotee may obtain blessings only through his own contemplation and supplication and not through the dead saint. The exception is the Prophet. Al-Ghazālī cites two traditions, one of which commends *ziyāra*: "Visiting tombs is altogether recommended for remembrance (*dhikr*) and contemplation (*iʿtibār*). Visiting the tombs of the righteous is recommended for the purpose of seeking blessings [and] contemplation. The Messenger of God... forbade visiting tombs and then permitted that afterwards" (iv, 490). Al-Ghazālī then quotes a canonical Tradition related by ʿAlī in which the Prophet changed his mind about permitting Muslims to visit the dead.

Unlike the Ḥanbalīs, al-Ghazālī did not distinguish between *ziyāra* to the tombs of loved ones and those of saints. The goals were one and the same—supplicating to God on behalf of the dead. Since the Prophet visited his mother's grave, it is permissible for Muslims to visit all graves and remember the dead. However, the Prophet never kissed, lay upon or rubbed against tombs.

(d) *Pilgrimage literature*

Pilgrimage guides are collectively referred to as *kutub al-ziyārāt*. The guide was a companion for learned pilgrims to remember and invoke blessings upon the dead saint and to make a pilgrimage to his tomb or shrine. Although they reflect a variety of influences and traditions from the early Islamic period, pilgrimage guides provide a real sense of the variety of *ziyāra* ritual and thus constitute an important source for understanding the veneration of holy persons. Guides occasionally mention Jewish, Christian and common holy sites.

A number of factors contributed to the emergence of pilgrimage guides as a devotional genre. The Islamic territorial expansion from the 1st/7th to the 3rd/9th centuries led to Muslim scholars recording and commenting on the burial sites of the Prophet's Companions who had settled in the garrison towns and of those martyred in battle. Similar traditions, of varying degrees of authenticity, concerning the prophets and other scriptural figures are also frequently mentioned.

Ziyāra traditions evolved from *faḍāʾil* traditions which emphasise the Islamic nature and sanctity of a location by identifying the burial place of a prophet, martyr or hero. Such traditions extol the merits of particular cities, holy sites and saints. The systematic compilation of traditions contributed to the emergence of regional histories and pilgrimage guides for such cities as Cairo, Damascus, Aleppo, Kūfa and Nadjaf, and of other literary genres which often mention pilgrimage sites.

The only known specimen of pilgrimage literature for the entire Islamic world and parts of the Christian Mediterranean and Byzantium during the late 6th/12th and early 7th/13th centuries is the Syrian savant and ascetic ʿAlī b. Abī Bakr al-Harawī's (d. 611/1215 [see AL-HARAWĪ AL-MAWṢILĪ]) *K. al-Ishārāt ilā maʿrifat al-ziyārāt* (ed. J. Sourdel-Thomine, Damascus 1953). Almost all of our knowledge of pilgrimages to shrines in the Arabian peninsula derives from this source. The author records sites and popular traditions concerning them, based on first-hand knowledge and second-hand accounts. Al-Harawī regularly includes popular traditions, which he indicates in a number of ways: "It is said" (*ḳīla/yuḳāl*), "according to local custom" (*kamā dhakarū/yadhkurūn*), or "according to what the people of the site mentioned" (*kamā dhakara ahl al-mawḍiʿ*). He often questions these traditions by stating that "the truth is..." (*wa 'l-ṣaḥīḥ anna...*).

The *Ishārāt* provided a basis for late mediaeval pilgrimage guides and regional histories, particularly in al-Shām. Unlike other pilgrimage guides, however, there is no evidence to suggest that it was employed during a *ziyāra*. In fact, the author dedicated the work to the ʿAbbāsid caliph (Y. Rāghib, *Essai d'inventaire chronologique des guides à l'usage des pèlerins du Caire*, in *REI*, xli [1973], 272-3). Morever, it is not as explicit as Egyptian pilgrimage guides in providing directions and distances. The *Ishārāt* is akin to a travel itinerary, but it does not provide distances between places or mention the time spent in a given location. In fact, the guide is a compilation from memory, trustworthy sources, and notes which may have survived being appropriated by the Franks in 588/1192. All pilgrimage guides employ a common language to refer to pilgrimage sites, a language not merely descriptive in nature but one indicative of the rituals that devotees performed and the sacred nature of sites.

In the absence of a universal tradition of pilgrimage guides, many traditions emerged which reflected a variety of local and regional practices as attested in the diversity of guides. Pilgrimage guides throughout the Islamic world tend to be derivative in nature, often relying upon previous traditions. The earliest known pilgrimage guide is of Shīʿī provenance, the *K. al-Ziyārāt* of the Kūfan jurist al-Ḥasan b. ʿAlī b. Faḍḍāl al-Taymī al-Kūfī (d. 224/838-9). No correlation exists between the growth of Shīʿī pilgrimage guides in ʿIrāḳ and the development of pilgrimage guides in Egypt. Neither the Egyptian or later Syrian guides betray a Shīʿī origin. Authors of Sunnī and Shīʿī guides rely upon the *faḍāʾil* literature for the purpose of glorifying a location. However, the Shīʿī guides also draw upon traditions attributed to a number of the Imāms, most notably the sixth Imām Djaʿfar al-Ṣādiḳ [*q.v.*], which largely concern al-Ḥusayn, ʿAlī and other members of the Prophet's Family.

(e) *Shīʿī pilgrimage guides*

These are concerned with rites (*manāsik*) of *ziyāra* and not only with *adab* or etiquette as in the Sunnī case. *Manāsik* ordinarily and in Sunnī usage refers to the ceremonies and rites of the *ḥadjdj*. Shīʿī guides stress the importance of ritual behaviour to a greater degree than Sunnī ones. The earliest known Shīʿī guides include that of al-Kūfī (see above), Ibn Ḳūlūya's (d. 368/978-9) *Kāmil al-ziyārat*, his disciple Muḥammad b. Muḥammad al-Nuʿmān al-Ḥārithī (al-Shaykh al-Mufīd)'s (d. 413/1022) *K. al-Mazār* and Ibn Dāwūd al-Ḳummī's (d. 368/978 or 379/989) *K. al-Mazārāt al-kabīr*. Such guides describe ritual behaviour and supplications pronounced before undertaking a pilgrimage, such as the types of rituals and rites which al-Shaykh al-Mufīd refers to as *manāsik*. He and Ibn Ḳūlūya cite traditions indicating that Shīʿīs placed great emphasis on the *ziyāra* to ʿAlī's tomb in Nadjaf and that of al-Ḥusayn in Karbalāʾ. One such tradition of Abū ʿAbd Allāh b. al-Ḥusayn states that "making a *ziyāra* to al-Ḥusayn . . . is equal to and more meritorious than twenty pilgrimages to Mecca" (Ibn Ḳūlūya, ed. Nadjaf, 161). A similar tradition concerns visiting al-Ḥusayn on the day of ʿArafa.

Since prescribed ritual acts constituted a central part of Shīʿī *ziyāra* devotion, Shīʿī scholars and Imāms exercised control over its rites and urged devotees to make the *ziyāra* according to the traditions of the Imāms to the extent that not doing so was considered un-Islamic and would result in a shorter lifespan (*ibid.*, 43).

This is in contrast to the Sunnī *ziyāra*, in which little control existed. For the Shīʿī, performing the *ziyāra* had many benefits in addition to receiving the temporal benefits of performing the *hadjdj* and *ʿumra*, as well as dispelling sadness and expurgating sins. Wherever they resided, Shīʿīs observed the same rites and rituals. The formalisation and consolidation of ritual was a necessary corollary to the development of central pilgrimage centres, which did not exist for the Sunnīs.

Nor were local cults insignificant. However, local ritual practices were not preserved in pilgrimage guides, but have only survived in local histories. The Shīʿī Ḥamdānid ruler of Aleppo Sayf al-Dawla (*r.* 333-56/944-67 [*q.v.*]) was a devotee of saints who patronised and constructed shrines in Aleppo and its outlying villages.

It was incumbent upon the Shīʿī pilgrim to abstain from worldly pleasures. *Ziyāra* to the shrine of al-Ḥusayn in Karbalāʾ was a special experience which demanded the full participation of the devotee in the martyrdom of al-Ḥusayn and the expression of great sorrow, not merely the sadness one expresses over the death of relations but rather its ultimate manifestation requiring the pilgrim to experience physical and emotional debilitation.

Unlike the majority of Sunnī guides, Shīʿī ones were written by prominent theologians, such as the aforementioned Ibn Ḳūlūya and his disciple al-Shaykh al-Mufīd. The latter's *K. al-Mazār* is divided into two parts, the first of which concerns the merits (*faḍāʾil*) of Kūfa, its [congregational] mosque and the Euphrates, etc. This is followed by a description of the *ziyāra* to ʿAlī's tomb and a discussion of the necessity of visiting that of al-Ḥusayn and the merits of performing the *ziyāra* to it, especially on various holy days. So highly developed were the *ziyāra* rites that Shīʿīs pronounced formulaic expressions at every stage. Shīʿī guides could perhaps be regarded as manuals for theologians who would instruct illiterate and common pilgrims in the ways of the group activity of *ziyāra*. The second part of the guide deals primarily with *ziyāra* to the Prophet Muḥammad and his Household, who were buried in Medina, and to the Shīʿī Imāms. Al-Shaykh al-Mufīd devotes a section to abridged supplications, which suggests that they were meant primarily for instantaneous memorisation before the performance of the *ziyāra* rather than for reading or study.

Shīʿīs also prayed special *ziyāra* prayers as at the tomb of the first Imām ʿAlī, which consisted of a series of supplications and recitations of particular chapters of the Ḳurʾān, placing the right and left cheek on the ground and pronouncing imprecations against the enemies of ʿAlī and those who wronged him.

These guides do not mention places in Syria to which ʿIrāḳī Shīʿī pilgrims undertook pilgrimage, as no Imāms were buried there. However, the Shīʿīs of Syria and Lebanon performed many of the same rites and rituals mentioned in these guides at local shrines as those done at the shrines of the Imāms in ʿIrāḳ and Persia. In spite of the absence of evidence concerning Shīʿī *ziyāra* rituals in Syria, Aleppan and Damascene Shīʿī theologians would have travelled to the holy cities of ʿIrāḳ, and theologians who hailed from the east and settled in al-Shām would have disseminated the proper teachings of the Imāms and taught proper *ziyāra* rites.

The earliest surviving Egyptian pilgrimage guide, which served as a basis for later works, is the *Murshid al-zuwwār ilā ḳubūr al-abrār* of the Shāfiʿī jurisconsult and *ḥadīth* scholar ʿAbd al-Raḥmān b. ʿUthmān (d. 615/1218) (publ. Cairo 1995). Like other guides, it begins with the sacred topography of the pilgrimage centre, in this case Djabal al-Muḳaṭṭam and the Ḳarāfa cemeteries. This is followed by descriptions of mosques and their endowers, historical accounts concerning the *ziyāra* and traditions concerning the dead hearing the living, discussion of the propriety of walking in the cemetery with sandals, formulas pronounced upon entering the cemetery, pilgrimage etiquette, and various ritual acts (making sacrifice, prayer, etc.). Finally, the author lists tombs, their efficacious qualities, associated rituals and exact pilgrimage routes. The guide was not merely descriptive but also prescriptive. In fact, it is replete with instructions and directions to the pilgrim as he walked from station to station. A contemporary of Ibn ʿUthmān, Madjd al-Dīn b. Muḥammad b. ʿAbd Allāh al-Nāsikh (d. *ca.* 696/1296-97), a minor Egyptian official in the service of the vizier Ibn Ḥanna, wrote a second guide, *Miṣbāḥ al-dayādjī wa-ghawth al-rādjī wa-kahf al-lādjī*. During the 9th/15th century, the Ṣūfī mystic Shams al-Dīn Abū ʿAbd Allāh Muḥammad b. Muḥammad b. al-Zayyāt (d. 815/1412) composed *al-Kawākib al-sayyāra fī tartīb al-ziyāra fi 'l-ḳarāfatayn al-kubrā wa 'l-ṣughrā* (Cairo 1907). Another guide was composed by Nūr al-Dīn Abu 'l-Ḥasan ʿAlī b. Aḥmad b. ʿUmar b. Khalaf b. Maḥmūd al-Sakhāwī al-Ḥanafī (d. 1482/3?), entitled *Tuḥfat al-aḥbāb wa-bughyat al-ṭullāb fi 'l-khiṭaṭ wa 'l-mazārāt wa 'l-tarādjim wa 'l-biḳāʿ al-mubārakāt*. The Cairene *ziyāra* developed into an elaborate institution with learned guides known as *mashāyikh al-ziyāra* who conducted visitors (*zuwwār*) through the Ḳarāfa cemeteries on Djabal al-Muḳaṭṭam [*q.v.*].

Pilgrimage guides developed much later in al-Shām than they did in Egypt. However, most of our knowledge of mediaeval Syrian *ziyārat* derives from historical sources. In contrast to Egypt, where *ziyāra* literature was known in Fāṭimid and Mamlūk times, the earliest extant pilgrimage guide for Syria dates to the early 10th/16th century. The absence of institutionalised Sunnī control over the *ziyāra* as with the later *mashāyikh al-ziyāra*, and of an early tradition of scholarship centered around pilgrimage traditions, prompted the later appearance of guides. However, poems such as the one recited to the Damascene historian Ibn ʿAsākir (d. 572/1176 [*q.v.*]) on Mt. Ḳāsiyūn, praise the performing of the *ziyāra* to its pilgrimage sites. Muslims were accustomed to writing poetry about their holy places. Brief descriptions of pilgrimage sites are also found in geographical works like al-Dimashḳī's *Nukhbat al-dahr* and fuller accounts in travel itineraries like the *Riḥla*s of Ibn Djubayr and Ibn Baṭṭūṭa, who routinely mention the pilgrimage sites in a given locality. Khalīl b. Shāhīn al-Ẓāhirī (d. 873/1468) in his *Zubdat kashf al-mamālik*, ed. and tr. E.F.C. Rosenmüller, Leipzig

1828, consistently enumerates the congregational mosques, *madrasas*, shrines (*mas͟hhads*), pilgrimage sites (*mazārāt*) and blessed sites (*amākin mubāraka*). The centrality of these designations in al-Ẓāhirī's work and the emphasis that he places on "blessed places" indicate the contemporary importance attached to places of pilgrimage. The 6th-7th/12th-13th centuries are characterised by increased activity in the compilation of pilgrimage traditions and descriptions of pilgrimage places and the rituals and legends associated with them. These works represent a transition from an oral to a written *ziyāra* "tradition" among scholars and historians in al-S͟hām. Historians such as Ibn ʿAsākir, Muḥammad b. ʿAlī al-ʿAẓīmī (d. *ca.* 556/1161 [*q.v.*]), Yaḥyā b. Abī Ṭayyiʾ (d. *ca.* 625-30/1228/33 [see IBN ABĪ ṬAYYIʾ]), Ibn al-ʿAdīm (d. 660/1262), Ibn S͟haddād (d. 684/1285) and Ibn al-S͟hiḥna (d. 890/1485) [*q.vv.*] include in their histories detailed inventories of tombs, shrines and other monuments for the Mirdāsid, Ḥamdānid, Ayyūbid and Mamlūk periods. Their works provide significant details concerning the founding of monuments, their efficaciousness, legends associated with them, and the practices and beliefs of the common people and their encounters with the holy. Some of these traditions are based on the personal experiences of the writers or their contemporaries. Notable is the prominence accorded to *ziyāra* traditions concerning the tombs of the Family of the Prophet, his Companions and the Followers throughout these works.

Ibn ʿAsākir dedicates a number of chapters of his *Taʾrīk͟h* to places of prayer, tombs and shrines in and around Damascus to which the *ziyāra* is made. One section includes nineteen traditions concerning the burial places of prophets and Companions narrated by a number of Companions and several reports by the Damascene historian Abū Zurʿa (d. 270/894), who is critical of the authenticity of a number of tombs, stating e.g. "Regarding Mudrik b. Ziyād, I did not find any mention of him, except on the tablet on his tomb from an unverifiable source. . . ."

Like al-Harawī's *Is͟hārāt*, the works of Ibn al-ʿAdīm and Ibn S͟haddād reflect a popular level of discourse and also mention the activities of the people. Ibn al-ʿAdīm, who was a contemporary of al-Harawī, from whom he personally heard a number of accounts, devotes a chapter of his *Bug͟hyat al-ṭalab fī taʾrīk͟h Ḥalab* to "the pilgrimage sites (*mazārāt*), tombs of prophets and saints and the noble localities (*mawāṭin*) in Aleppo and its districts, which are known for the fulfilment of supplication" (ed. S. Zakkār, Beirut 1988-9, i, 459). The account includes 57 pilgrimage places for Aleppo and its districts, including accounts taken from al-Harawī and the author's father.

Ibn S͟haddād dedicates three chapters of *al-Aʿlāḳ al-k͟haṭīra* to pilgrimage sites in Aleppo, Damascus, Jordan, Palestine and Lebanon. He relies extensively on al-Harawī for Palestinian and Damascene *ziyārāt* and on Ibn al-ʿAdīm and Ibn Abī Ṭayyiʾ for Aleppan sites. The Ḥanbalī jurisprudent Muḥammad b. ʿAbd al-Hādī (d. 744/1343), who was a member of the Maḳdisī family, also composed a number of no longer extant works, including a pamphlet concerning the *ziyāra* and another on the *ḥadīt͟h* concerning the lives of the prophets and their graves. He also includes unique details concerning Ayyūbid pilgrimage sites.

Ibn Ṭūlūn (d. 953/1546 [*q.v.*]), a prolific historian and commentator on the political and social climate of Mamlūk and early Ottoman Damascus, was one of the many devout believers who made the *ziyāra* on a regular basis to tombs and shrines in his native Damascus, judging by his numerous works which mention or are devoted to Damascus' pilgrimage sites and saints, including *Mufākahat al-k͟hillān fī ḥawādit͟h al-zamān* and *al-Ḳalāʾid al-d͟jawhariyya fī taʾrīk͟h al-Ṣāliḥiyya*. Thirteen other compositions dealing with various aspects of the cult of saints are now lost but widely quoted in the aforementioned works and in his autobiography, *al-Fulk al-mas͟hḥūn fī aḥwāl Muḥammad Ibn Ṭūlūn*. Two other works survive, the first of which, *Tuḥfat al-ḥabīb fīmā warada fi ʾl-kat͟hīb* (cf. J. Sadan, *Le tombeau de Moïse à Jéricho et à Damas*, in *REI*, xlix [1981], 59-99), concerns the tombs of Moses in Damascus and Jericho, while *G͟hāyat al-bayān fī tard͟jamat al-S͟hayk͟h Arsalān* is a brief biography of a 6th/12th-century Damascene saint and a description of his burial place. Women visiting shrines prompted Ibn Ṭūlūn to write the no longer extant *al-Tawad͟jd͟juhāt al-sitt ilā kaff al-nisāʾ ʿan ḳabr al-Sitt*, against their visiting the reputed shrine of the Prophet's granddaughter Sayyida Zaynab in a village south of Damascus.

In *al-Ḳalāʾid al-d͟jawhariyya*, which he composed about the history of al-Ṣāliḥiyya [*q.v.*] outside Damascus, Ibn Ṭūlūn dedicates a chapter to its famous pilgrimage sites and mausoleums. He begins by listing a number of grottoes, caves and *miḥrāb*s, mosques and *madrasas* followed by the most important tombs for which he provides detailed biographical accounts based on those of the Maḳdisī family and others. The Maḳdisīs also composed a number of important biographical works, parts of which survive.

The first known Damascene pilgrimage guide is Ibn al-Ḥawrānī's (d. 1000/1592) *K. al-Is͟hārāt ilā amākin al-ziyārāt* (Damascus 1981), which relies upon the works of Ibn Ṭūlūn, al-Rabaʿī's *Faḍāʾil al-S͟hām* and Ibn ʿAsākir's *Taʾrīk͟h madīnat Dimas͟hḳ*. Ibn al-Ḥawrānī wrote the *Is͟hārāt* in response to a request, intending "to guide [others] to righteousness so that it will serve as an aid to the one who sets out on pilgrimage (*ṭālib al-ziyāra*), obeying the words of God the Exalted, 'Let there become of you a community that shall call for righteousness'" (Ḳurʾān, III, 104). The guide, which includes over one hundred pilgrimage sites for Damascus and outlying villages and a number of other Syrian localities like Aleppo and its surrounding villages, tombs, shrines, mosques, minarets and sacred grottoes, opens with the praise of Damascus and its congregational mosque, the traditions concerning the head of Yaḥyā b. Zakariyyāʾ [*q.v.*], the minaret where ʿĪsā will descend at the end of time and a number of individual shrines, such as the tombs of Hūd, al-Sayyida Ruḳayya and Nūr al-Dīn [*q.vv.*]. For each entry, the author provides a biography of the saint. The rest of the guide is ordered by location, beginning with the western part of the city, then proceeding to the southern, eastern and northern parts. The sixth chapter includes pilgrimage sites in the outlying villages. This is followed by a number of northern Syrian localities. Ibn al-Ḥawrānī includes pilgrimage sites on the basis of established *ziyāra* traditions, such as those found in the works of al-Rabaʿī, Ibn ʿAsākir and Ibn Ṭūlūn. The concluding chapter is devoted to *ziyāra* etiquette. According to Ibn al-Ḥawrānī, the *ziyāra* begins with the remembrance of God and the intent to perform pilgrimage. The author then indicates that the devotee reflects upon himself and his sins which prevent him from nearing God. He experiences a cathartic state in which he rebukes and scolds himself and then weeps. Then he supplicates God and reads from the Ḳurʾān, while being sincere in reaching his goal, and refrains from speaking foul words. *Ziyāra* was not only a means for fulfilment of personal supplications; the devotee was to remember God and the Afterlife, pray and read the Ḳur'ān. This is the ultimate purpose of *ziyāra*.

Ḳāḍī Maḥmūd al-ʿAdawī's (d. 1032/1623) *K. al-Ziyārāt bi-Dimashḳ* (Damascus 1956), which is an acknowledged imitation of Ibn al-Ḥawrānī's *Ishārāt*, relies upon many of the same sources and a number of literary, devotional and historical works, and mentions 98 saints' tombs and other pilgrimage sites. An emphasis on biographical details renders this a biographical work rather than a pilgrimage guide to be employed during the *ziyāra*. Al-ʿAdawī is not explicit about the purpose for which the guide is to be used. However, it may be assumed that it served a similar commemorative function to Ibn al-Ḥawrānī's *Ishārāt*, but does not stress pilgrimage etiquette.

Yāsīn al-Faraḍī b. Muṣṭafā al-Djuʿfī al-Biḳāʿī al-Ḥanafī al-Māturīdī (d. 1095/1684), the author of the guide *al-Nubdha al-laṭīfa fī 'l-mazārāt al-sharīfa* is explicit about the purpose for which devotees should use it. Al-Biḳāʿī intended that the guide be employed during pilgrimage as an aid to remembering the saints who were buried in a particular location, perhaps even suggesting that the pilgrim should visit as many pilgrimage sites as he possibly can.

During the eighteenth century, the Damascene Ṣūfī ʿAbd al-Ghanī al-Nābulusī (d. 1143?/1731 [*q.v.*]) undertook several journeys through Bilād al-Shām, Egypt and the Ḥidjāz in which he meticulously recorded details of the pilgrimage sites he visited, and in one of his several travel works, *al-Ḥaḍra al-unsiyya fī 'l-riḥla al-ḳudsiyya*, he undertook a 44-day journey from Damascus to Jerusalem in which he visited numerous shrines.

Bibliography (in addition to references given in the article): Goldziher, *Muh. Studien*, ii, 277-341, Eng. tr. Barber and Stern, *Muslim studies*, ii, 255-341 ("Veneration of saints in Islam"); J. Sourdel-Thomine, *Les anciens lieux de pèlerinage d'après les sources arabes*, in *BEO*, xiv (1954), 65-85; R.B. Serjeant, *Ḥaram and Ḥawṭah, the sacred enclave in Arabia*, in ʿA. al-Badawī (ed.), *Mélanges Taha Husain*, Cairo 1962, 41-58; M.J. Kister, *"You shall only set out for three mosques." A study of an early tradition*, in *Le Muséon*, lxxxii (1969), 173-96; Lisa Golombek, *The cult of saints and shrine architecture in the fourteenth century*, in D.K. Koyumjian (ed.), *Near Eastern numismatics, iconography, epigraphy and history. Studies in honor of George C. Miles*, Beirut 1974, 419-30; M.U. Memon, *Ibn Taimīya's struggle against popular religion, with an annotated translation of his Kitāb iqtiḍā' al-ṣirāṭ al-mustaqīm mukhālafat ahl al-jaḥīm*, The Hague 1976; N.H. Oleson, *Culte des saints et pèlerinages chez Ibn Taymiyya (661/1268-728/1328)*, Paris 1991; A. Elad, *Medieval Jerusalem and Islamic worship. Holy places, ceremonies, pilgrimage*, Leiden 1995; J. Gonnella, *Islamische Heiligenverehrung im urbanen Kontext am Beispiel von Aleppo (Syrien)*, Berlin 1995; C.S. Taylor, *In the vicinity of the righteous. Ziyāra and the veneration of Muslim saints in late medieval Egypt*, Leiden 1999; J.W. Meri, *Aspects of baraka (blessings) and ritual devotion among medieval Muslims and Jews*, in *Medieval encounters. Jewish, Christian and Muslim culture in confluence and dialogue*, v (1999).

(J.W. Meri)

2. In the central Arab lands from 1800 to the present day.

In the 19th and 20th centuries, the visitation of the tombs of saints and other holy sites has continued to be a common feature of popular religious life in Egypt, Greater Syria, ʿIrāḳ and Arabia (for Shīʿī *ziyārāt*, see 5. below). As a result of enhanced security and comfort of travel provided by modern means of transport, there has even been a remarkable increase in the number of pilgrims visiting important shrines such as that of Aḥmad al-Badawī in Ṭanṭā [*q.vv.*]. The same holds true for the *ziyāra* to the Prophet's tomb and to the old cemetery of Medina (see al-madīna and baḳīʿ al-gharḳad)—a visitation that is, of course, in most cases performed before or after the *ḥadjdj* [*q.v.*]. In this connection, it is to be noted that the destruction of tombs and shrines in Mecca, Medina and elsewhere in Arabia, at the hands of Wahhābīs [see wahhābiyya], has not in the long term resulted in a dramatic decrease of visitations to these places, at least not to the most important ones. (For a survey of the sites in Medina demolished since 1926, see e.g. Yūsuf Raghdā al-ʿĀmilī, *Maʿālim Makka wa 'l-Madīna bayn al-māḍī wa 'l-ḥāḍir*, Beirut 1997, esp. 401 ff.) However, any *ziyāra* there is to be performed, at least in principle, according to the strict rules of the Wahhābiyya and under the control of its representatives.

In other countries of the Arab East, the situation varies. For a number of reasons, including urban development measures and the confiscation of *waḳf* [*q.v.*] property by the state, many shrines (in particular the smaller ones) have become neglected or have even been demolished. Others, however, still flourish, and in fact a number of new ones have sprung up recently. Moreover, there are old shrines which, for one reason or another, have lately acquired a popularity they never had before. An interesting example of this phenomenon is the shrine of Sayyida Zaynab (*Ḳabr al-Sitt*) near Damascus, which is visited mainly, but not exclusively, by Shīʿīs (see Mervin, in *Bibl.*, and no. 25 [1996] of the journal *al-Mawsim*). In the case of Sayyida Zaynab, as well as with regard to Muslim sanctuaries in Jerusalem [see al-ḳuds], Hebron [see al-khalīl] and other *mazārāt* in Palestine (see, in particular, Canaan, in *Bibl.*), it is obvious that political circumstances, as in the past, have a considerable (positive or negative) influence on the actual performance of the *ziyārāt* and on the number of pilgrims participating.

In general, the *ziyāra* is popular especially with lower and middle-class women. Many educated Muslim men shun or even vehemently denounce all traditional forms of saint veneration, and in particular most of the *ziyāra* practices. At best, they demand that the rites be reformed according to the teachings of the Salafiyya [*q.v.*], i.e. be stripped of all words and deeds that, in their opinion, are *bidʿa* [*q.v.*].

More or less sharp criticism of what goes on at popular festivals [see mawsim and mawlid], such as prostitution and various forms of exploitation of the credulous, is to be found in modern Arabic literature. This criticism is voiced in works written by religiously conservative authors as well as by modernists and (even more so) by secularists. There are, however, many such writers who also point to the spiritual dimensions and social values which find expression in the *ziyārāt* and related practices (for Egypt, see Wielandt, in *Bibl.*).

Bibliography: L. Massignon, *Les saints musulmans enterrés à Bagdad*, in *RHR* (1908), repr. in idem, *Opera minora*, ed. Y. Moubarac, Beirut 1963, iii, 94-101; idem, *Les pèlerinages populaires à Bagdâd*, in *RMM*, vi (1908), 640-51; T. Canaan, *Mohammedan saints and sanctuaries in Palestine*, London 1927 (well-founded, detailed survey; Arabic tr. Rāmallāh 1998); J. Gaulmier, *Pèlerinages populaires à Hama*, in *BEO*, i (1931), 137-52; J.W. McPherson, *The Moulids of Egypt*, Cairo 1941; R. Kriss and H. Kriss-Heinrich,

Volksglaube im Bereich des Islam, i, *Wallfahrtswesen und Heiligenverehrung*, Wiesbaden 1960 (useful survey for Egypt, Jordan, Syria and Lebanon); E. Bannerth, *Islamische Wallfahrtsstätten Kairos*, Cairo 1973 (= Schriften des österreichischen Kulturinstituts, 2); F. de Jong, *Cairene* Ziyāra *days*, in *WI*, xvii (1976-7), 26-43; R. Wielandt, *Die Bewertung islamischen Volksglaubens in ägyptischer Erzählliteratur des 20. Jahrhunderts*, in *WI*, xxiii-xxiv (1984), 244-58; C. Mayeur, *L'intercession des saints en Islam égyptien: autour de Sayyid al-Badawī*, in *AI*, xxv (1991), 363-88; V.J. Hoffman, *Sufism, mystics, and saints in modern Egypt*, Columbia, S.C., 1995; J. Gonella, *Islamische Heiligenverehrung im urbanen Kontext am Beispiel von Aleppo (Syrien)*, Berlin 1995; S. Mervin, *Sayyida Zaynab. Banlieue de Damas ou nouvelle ville sainte chiite?*, in *Cahiers d'études sur la Méditerranée orientale et le monde turco-iranien*, no. 22 (1996), 149-62; A. Knysh, *The cult of saints and Islamic reformism in early twentieth century Ḥadramawt*, in *New Arabian Studies*, iv (1997), 139-67. (W. Ende)

3. Amongst the Copts in Egypt.

Coptic Orthodox sites for *ziyāra* can be found throughout Egypt, shaping an entirely Christian topography. The origins of sites range from the 1st to the 20th centuries. The itinerary of the Holy Family during their flight to Egypt is marked by numerous holy places. Nowadays, Copts include holy rocks and trees in their *ziyāra*, while St. Mary and Jesus became venerated in churches and monasteries built on the legendary sites. The itinerary stretches from Sakha in the north to Asyūṭ in Middle Egypt. Some noteworthy places are Musturud (where now the Church of the Virgin Mary stands), Wādī 'l-Naṭrūn (currently with four large monasteries), and Old Cairo (the churches of Abū Sardja and Muʿallaḳa and two convents for nuns). At several convents and churches, such as at Dayr Dronka and Dayr al-Muḥarraḳ near Asyūṭ, large *mawlid*s developed besides the regular *ziyāra* (Catherine Mayeur-Jaouen, *The Coptic Mouleds. Evolution of the traditional pilgrimages*, in N. van Doorn and K. Vogt, *Between desert and city. The Coptic Orthodox Church today*, Oslo 1997, 212-29).

Martyrs, saints (such as Mārī Girgīs, Abū Sayfayn, Sitt Dimyāna) and the Virgin Mary account for the majority of *ziyāra* sites, yet there are numerous local saints, some dating back to the 4th century A.D. Concurrent with the Coptic Church reform that started in the 1950s, many pilgrimage centres have been restored and re-shaped into new shrines which draw each week thousands of pilgrims who are in a process of rediscovering their Coptic heritage and history. An example of this development is the shrine of St. Menas at Maryūṭ, which was a large pilgrimage centre from the Late Roman Empire until the 9th century. In 1959 the Coptic Church built a new monastery, Dayr Abū Minā, near the site, and the relics of St. Menas were transferred from Cairo to Maryūṭ. The site gained in reputation after the remains of the popular Patriarch Kyrillos VI, who died in 1971, were laid there as well.

Concomitant with Islamic Egypt reinforcing its religious roots, Copts are purifying their *ziyāra* practices from non-Christian practices, beliefs and elements. Since the 1970s, *ziyāra* has evolved from an outing to a holy place characterised by indigenous practices, shared by Muslims and Christians alike, to a liturgical event orchestrated by the Coptic Church. Prayers are not extempore but made according to certain texts, requests made to saints go via priests and monks, *tamdjīd* (songs of praise about the saint) are sung from printed bulletins, while the *ziyāra* is supervised by church volunteers who ensure that the pilgrims obey the Church's teachings. Often a mass will be celebrated. As a result of this, the number of Muslim visitors whom these sites used to draw has drastically diminished.

An important aspect of *ziyāra* is to take home a sign of *baraka* [*q.v.*] in the shape of holy oil, a trinket with the saint's picture, or a small container with *ḥānūt* (fragrant balm that was put on the grave on the saint's day).

The goals of *ziyāra* are manifold: to pray for healing, to pronounce vows, or to deliver what was promised in an earlier vow. *Ziyāra* during *mawlids* is considered the prime time for baptising children and for exorcising evil spirits. Honouring the saint is an important aspect of *ziyāra*, thus reinforcing bonds between the living and the dead, and between the Church on earth and the Church Victorious. Churches organise bus tours to a series of sites, enabling Copts from all over Egypt to connect with each other, confirming their identity and faith.

Bibliography: J.W. McPherson, *The Moulids of Egypt. Egyptian saints' days*, Cairo 1941; G. Viaud, *Les pèlerinages coptes en Egypte*, Cairo 1979; P. Grossmann, *Abu Mina, a guide to the ancient pilgrimage center*, Cairo 1986; N.H. Biegman, *Egypt. Moulids, saints and Sufis*, London 1990; P. van Doorn-Harder, *Contemporary Coptic nuns*, Columbia, S.C. 1995, chs. 8-9; O.F.M. Meinardus, *Two thousand years of Coptic Christianity*, Cairo 1999.

(Nelly van Doorn-Harder)

4. In the Maghrib.

In 760/1359, the former vizier and scholar of Granada, Ibn al-Khaṭīb [*q.v.*], was in Marrākush where he paid a reverential visit to the sanctuary of the patron saint of the Moroccan city, Abu 'l-ʿAbbās al-Sabtī (d. 606/1205 [*q.v.*]). The Andalusī was impressed by the opulence of the sanctuary, financed by vast revenues. Daily, they normally revolved around the sum of "800 *mithkāls*" but some days could "attain or even exceed 1,000 dīnārs". Such sums of money could not fail but arouse the greed of the staff of the sanctuary and to pose problems in regard to distribution. A witness to these disputes, Ibn al-Khaṭīb saw the issues being presented before judges; the degree of opulence of the religious institution was at stake. With their gifts, the masses of pilgrims who came periodically to test the miraculous powers of the dead saint generated covetable riches. Visitors accompanied their vows with coins "deposited in chests reserved for this purpose" (al-Maḳḳarī, *Nafḥ al-ṭīb*, vii, 273). In return, it was expected that the saint would intercede with God for the fulfilment of their desires. Underlying these transactions were the God-given prerogatives apparently exercised by al-Sabtī while still alive. Dead, the saint continued to dispense his *baraka*, by virtue of the theory according to which "the miracles of saints do not disappear on their death" (Ibn Ḳunfudh, *Uns*, 6-7). This was the view commonly held in the Maghrib of the 8th/14th century: the *post mortem* miracles of Abu 'l-ʿAbbas al-Sabtī were more numerous than those that he performed in his lifetime. Having paid him a visit in 1200, Ibn al-ʿArabī (d. 638/1240 [*q.v.*]) reported on the double nature, benign and malignant, of the powers of the saint: "He made ill and he cured, he made live and made perish, gave power to certain men or deprived them of it," he asserted (*Futūḥāt*, ch. 485). Furthermore, in his lifetime, the saint had been the object of a cult associated with both "the élite" and "the masses", and his entire mystical doctrine was based on the principle of alms. After his death, his prestige increased—the city was symbolically placed under his protection—as did the number of pilgrims whose offerings made the fortune of those who managed his cult. How had these powers been acquired? Why did this human saint, first in his lifetime and subsequently after his death, become the object of a particular cult? Ibn Khaldūn gives the answer in a chapter of his *Muḳaddima*, of which a considerable part of the current historical anthropology of religious practices in the Maghrib is nothing more than a glossed version. Such saints would be included in what he says of the *fuḳahā'* and *ahl al-dīn wa 'l-ʿibāda*, who earn a great reputation, so that they are showered with presents by the pious, and become wealthy without any personal effort; they sit back, and people wonder how they have acquired such wealth and fortune (*Muḳaddima*, Eng. tr. Rosenthal, ii, 327-8, Fr. tr. Monteil, ii, 209).

Ibn Khaldūn was pointing to a phenomenon which, while quite ancient in the Maghrib, in the 6th/12th and 7th/13th centuries took on an extraordinary growth, to such an extent that it revolutionised Maghribī religiosity and gave it a new configuration. Despite the opposition of the more rigorous *ʿulamā'*, in towns as well as in the countryside, the sacred became progressively structured around a new and burgeoning social force, the saints, to whom, since the 8th/14th century, our sources have applied the term marabouts (< *murābiṭ* [see RIBĀṬ]). Whence came the power of these individuals? The answer must lie in their capacity to represent themselves as "recipients of the divine" (J. Berque), a capacity from which derives their power to dispense good fortune as well as to inflict misfortune. It also comes from their functions of patronage, of arbitration and mediation in the city. As early as the time of Ibn Khaldūn, far from merely monopolising the devotion of the common people alone, the saints who imposed themselves on rulers and on other religious scholars as redoubtable protagonists also strongly affected the modes of belief of the whole of society. Men and women, "great" and "small", sought their goodwill. How is devotion to be manifested to a patron whose benevolence is sought, other than by periodically rendering him homage? It is thus that there developed one of the most outstanding expressions of Maghribī religious life, the *ziyāra*. This would come to rival the other forms of devotional travel (*ḥādjdj*, *murābaṭa*, etc.), becoming one of the principal institutions of Maghribī devotion virtually until the mid-20th century, and persisting in certain areas even today (F. Reysoo, *Pèlerinages au Maroc*, Neuchâtel-Paris 1991).

In its nature, *ziyāra* presents a double characteristic: it can be individual or collective. It engages individuals in a personal movement as it involves groups concerned for their collective destiny. Ultimately, it evokes urban as well as rural social structures. In other words, it is unitary in its status of "distance covered", whilst it is plural or multiform in terms of its content and its usages. Men as well as women, city-dwellers as well as rustics, artisans as well as peasants, scholars as well as the illiterate, governors and governed—all contribute to making of it a ritual gesture deriving its particularity from a precise arrangement combining energy, movement, space and time and setting out the specific requirements which are to be met in each instance.

In its capacity as an individual journey, *ziyāra* was not a feature of mediaeval Maghribī religiosity. Born in the central lands of Islam around the mid-8th century, it is seen, in the Maghrib, to belong in a continuity which makes of it an eminently spiritual journey. Leaving aside this form of *ziyāra*, one may concentrate on the form that engages and sets in motion crowds and numbers. In its capacity as a collective enterprise, *ziyāra*, which is easily transformed into local pilgrimage, is definitely one of the essential elements of the cult dedicated to Maghribī saints [see WALĪ. 2.]. Although in the majority of cases this collective *ziyāra* to a saint develops on the latter's death, there are cases where it comes into being in his lifetime. The *Tashawwuf* of Ibn al-Zayyāt al-Tādilī [see TĀDLĀ] offers examples of both instances. Tracing the life of a saint of Tādlā, who died in 536/1141, this hagiographic treatise relates that "his tomb was revered, and people come even now (early 7th/13th century) in search of healing by contact with the earth that covers him" (*Tashawwuf*, 106). With regard to the famous Abū Yaʿazza Yalannūr al-Hazmīrī or al-Haskurī (d. 573/1177), we read that "people came [to him] from all countries, he nourished them [at his own expense], he gave fodder to their mounts". Such generosity was expensive. To cover it, the saint would accept alms from his "brothers in God", sc. his disciples. There were also "the residents of neighbouring villages [who] gave hospitality to those who came to visit him" when their number was too large for them to be accommodated in his *zāwiya* (*Tashawwuf*, 164).

In order to understand how a local pilgrimage came into being, it is necessary to recognise that a *mazāra* is a social invention. It is a place which, because it is endowed with a symbolic efficaciousness, crystallises the expectations and the hopes of individuals and of groups, and the greater its size, the greater the prestige radiating from the "place of pilgrimage". For this to happen, a subtle equilibrium must be established between the expectations of individuals and of groups and their fulfilment in such a manner as to replenish the source. The expectations of individuals and of groups thus have the power of life and death over places of pilgrimage. Saints can experience success in their lifetime and sink into oblivion at their death. However, one such as Abū Yaʿazza (to take an example from a rural setting), or Abu 'l-ʿAbbās al-Sabtī (to take an example from an urban setting), were revered in their lifetime, and both of these saints have continued to be the object of ritual reverence to this very day. For a *mazāra* of importance to survive, it is often necessary that the populace, the religious élite and the governing class participate in its institutionalisation. The greater the extent to which the activity of these three protagonists converges, the better the prospects of the *mazāra* to endure and to radiate across an extensive geographical area. Thus Maghribī Sharīfism, in the 9th/15th century, was broadly a phenomenon simultaneously religious and political. Also, when the body of Idrīs II, the founder of the city of Fās, was "discovered" in 1437, it is obvious that the "discoverers" had a substantial interest in restoring the prestige of the Idrīsids and their religious claims (H.L. Beck, *L'image d'Idrîs II*, Leiden 1989). Conditioned by more than a century of belief in the ancestral prestige of the *shurafā'* [*q.v.*], society readily accepted the discovery. Moving to al-Ḳayrawān, the same considerations are seen presiding over the cult of Abū Zamʿa al-Balawī, a Companion buried in Tunisian soil. The veneration offered to him seems to have been linked to the belief that he was buried with some hair of the Prophet, whose barber he was. Although it is not known when this veneration began, it is clear that it is a late phenomenon, the reason being that the exact site where the pious individual is buried is not known. The presumed site became the object of ritual interest in the 5th/11th century when a cemetery was created nearby. In the 8th/14th century, local Ṣūfism included it among pilgrimages to the most renowned sanctuaries of the town. Consecrated as an "official" *mazāra*, the presumed tomb of the saintly man was surmounted by an octagonal cupola which later was enlarged to become an architectural complex of the *zāwiya* type (S. Bergaoui, *La zâwiya Sahâbiyya de Kairouan a l'époque moderne*, in *SI*, lxxvi [1997], 103-32). Returning to Marrākus̲h̲, and moving on to the 10th/16th century, the town is seen "inventing" a pilgrimage to the tomb of the *ḳāḍī* ʿIyāḍ (d. 544/1149 [see ʿIYĀḌ B. MŪSĀ]). As to the reasons why the Moroccan city acquired a tomb four centuries after the death of its occupant, no doubt the need was felt for a man of impeccable orthodoxy to validate the ritual process which was being established under the name of *ziyāra* to the *sabʿatu rid̲j̲āl* (H. de Castries, *Les sept patrons de Marrakech*, in *Hesperis*, iv [1924], 245 ff.). Neither in his lifetime nor on his death did the theologian enjoy any particular charisma: "his tomb was little known for the place [where it was sited], was not much frequented until God revived the place though the good offices of al-Fallāḥ [a Ṣūfī saint, died in 1570]", writes the author of a biographical dictionary of the celebrities of Marrākus̲h̲ (al-Marrākus̲h̲ī, *Iʿlām*, ix, 341, quoted in K. Fekhari, *Le culte des saints à Marrakech*, Rabat 1996, 91). Examples of the "invention" of pilgrimages could be further multiplied, such as that established at the tomb of Ibn ʿAbbād al-Rundī (d. 792/1390) at Fās (P. Nwyia, *Ibn Abbâd de Ronda*, Beirut 1961, 77-80); such items constitute one of the most thoroughly documented chapters of Mag̲h̲ribī hagiography.

Before the 9th/15th century, little information is available concerning these collective pilgrimages. Only one is genuinely known of: that which was witnessed by Ibn Ḳunfud̲h̲ (d. 810/1407 [*q.v.*]) in 769/1367, when he was a judge in the land of Dukkāla, not far from the town of Aṣfī, on the Atlantic coast of Morocco. He describes it as an assemblage bringing together "an incalculable number of persons". From the information supplied it is possible to gain an impression of the sociological composition of the pilgrims; those present included *ʿulamāʾ*, Ṣūfīs, and members of the general public. Ibn Ḳunfud̲h̲ saw taking place, in the course of these proceedings, trance sessions in which sick people were encouraged to participate; they emerged, he claims, miraculously cured. This pilgrimage took place regularly, but unfortunately it is not known how and under what circumstances it came into being and who precisely was revered there. Other details, such as the question e.g. as to whether women participated in the event, are not available. It is not until the 10th/16th century that the sources begin to describe such assemblages.

Numerous *ʿulamāʾ* lent their authority to these pilgrimages. There were also many who, without denouncing the principle, deprecated the aberrations and the excesses which accompanied them. Because jurists were often called upon to make rulings on the rites involved in these pious visits, judicial material concerning the phenomenon is abundant from this period onward. The 11th/17th century, in particular, yields a rich harvest of judicial and hagiographical material. A Salafī scholar of Constantine, ʿAbd al-Karīm Lafgūn, devotes an entire work to denouncing "blameworthy innovations" (sing. *bidʿa* [*q.v.*]) in evidence in the cult of saints in his land. At the same time, he supplies a vivid portrayal of religious life in the region of Constantine. Among numerous examples, there is the following. A man acquires the reputation of a saint. He founds a *zāwiya* which resounds all day long with noisy, ecstatic seances inspired by *faḳīrs* who come, in large numbers, to congregate around the master. It is they who are responsible for the stewardship of the enterprise and they who visit tribes and villages in the locality to collect the "piety tax" (*d̲j̲ibāya*) and legal alms. The reputation of the saint is extended to cover almost the whole of the Constantine region. Each year, an immense procession (*rakb*)—the term is also used to denote the caravan of pilgrims to the Holy Places—consisting of city-dwellers, peasants and nomads traverses the land in the direction of the *zāwiya*. The pilgrims bring all kinds of offerings: "camels, horses, cattle, sheep" on the part of country people, "*rag̲h̲īfs*, pieces of cloth, money" on the part of the city-dwellers. To stimulate their pious generosity, the saint reminds them that "he who brings nothing, leaves with nothing". As a result, rather than make the pilgrimage empty-handed, the less affluent prefer to beg. But it is not only the common people who make the journey; the upper classes also come flocking to obtain the favours of the saint. They offer "horses, clothes and money" (*Mans̲h̲ūr al-hidāya*, 133-4).

At the same time, another scholar, Abu 'l-Ḥasan al-Yūsī, denounced further practices that were taking place at the eastern extremity of the Mag̲h̲rib. Analysing a venerated place in the "*ribāṭ* of Salé", he states that "it is a place of pilgrimage (*mazāra*) where people seek the *baraka* of saints who used to be there". But he adds immediately that "of the latter, in our times, it appears that only one, Yaḥyā b. Yūnus, is very well known to the public, and even he is neglected in the records. Marīnid kings are also there: they are known." And in conclusion: "All that could be mentioned as sanctifying this place besides these two elements, and which is found in certain pseudo-historic writings, is without foundation or authority" (quoted in Berque, *Al-Yousi*, Paris 1958, 60).

To give a durable framework to these local pilgrimages, the marabouts often made contractual agreements (sing. *s̲h̲arṭ*) with their flocks. Investigating, during the 1970s, what the author calls "the pilgrimage centre" of the Moroccan town of Boujad, Dale Eickelman heard it said that accords had linked the client tribes of the region to the *zāwiya* brotherhood of the S̲h̲arḳāwa since the time of the founder, Sīdī Muḥammad al-S̲h̲arḳī (d. 1010/1601) (*Moroccan Islam*, Austin, Texas 1976, 169). Credit is due to Jacques Berque for having been the first to draw attention to stipulations of this kind. From the late 1940s, he discovered among the Saksāwa of the High Atlas *s̲h̲arṭs* between tribes and local saints; an example was published in his *Structures sociales du Haut Atlas*, Paris 1955, ²1978, 278. These contractual agreements were not confined to Morocco; for some which used to be current in the central Mag̲h̲rib, i.e. in Algeria, see Houari Touati, *Entre Dieu et les hommes*, Paris 1994, 259.

Currently, some of these local pilgrimages continue to function with virtually the same degree of fervour as in former times. Such is the case of the Sbūʿ of Timimoun, which annually attracts thousands of pilgrims. But a *ṭaʿām* such as that of the Flitta—organised by the tribe in honour of its saint, Sidi M'ḥammad b. ʿŪda, who lived in the 11th/17th century—has not been held since the "Armed Islamist Groups" (GIA), fanatical adversaries of the cult of saints, destroyed this Algerian sanctuary in 1993. In the mid-1950s, it still featured among the most spectacular gatherings of the plain (E. Dermenghem describes it as "one of the finest moussems of this type" in his *Le culte des saints dans l'islam maghrébin*, Paris 1954). The same applies to that held in the High Atlas in honour of Lalla ʿAzīza, a saint of the 8th/14th century. Revisiting the site in the footsteps of Berque, twenty years later, the sociologist P. Pascon observes *en passant* that "a returning emigrant declared openly that he would not sacrifice in accordance with outdated customs . . . In May 1976, to widen the road, the great *karkūr* [*q.v.*] of Lallā ʿAzīza was pushed into a ravine by a bulldozer . . . That year, in July, there was not enough attendance to justify the slaughter of a single bull at the sanctuary of the saint" (*Structures sociales du Haut Atlas*[2]).

These examples show that all kinds of factors have combined to hasten the decline of the great ritual assemblages of the Maghrib. Some result from socio-economic transformations, others from the assimilation of the majority of the population, and yet others from new modalities of religious socialisation of which the major promoter was initially the nation state, a role adopted today by political parties in Algeria and by groups which are tolerated in Morocco but prohibited in Tunisia, all of which regard themselves as Islamist.

Bibliography: Given in the text.

(Houari Touati)

5. In Persia and other Shīʿī lands.

(a) *Shīʿī* ziyāra *connected with the* mashhad *tradition*

Shrine culture connected with a *mashhad* [*q.v.*] "place where a martyr died", is a well-established tradition in Shīʿī Islam. The concept of *shahāda* or martyrdom suffered in the "path of God" [see SHAHĪD] played an important role in the development of belief in the sanctity of the Imāms' shrines. In Shīʿī piety, all Imāms are revered as martyrs, and their tombs are sites for annual visitation by Shīʿīs, who believe that their devotion (*wilāya* [*q.v.*]) to the martyred Imāms, expressed through these pilgrimages, will win forgiveness for their sins and a share in the final victory of the messianic Imām al-Mahdī [*q.v.*]. Pious Shīʿīs also look upon the shrines as places where they can share in the Imām's sanctity.

The Shīʿī shrines are richly endowed, and lavish gifts were bestowed by various Muslim rulers, especially by Shīʿī ones. Towns grew up around them, and the sacred areas (*ḥaram*) were adorned with magnificent and costly ornamentation. All the shrines have some architectural features in common. The tomb lies in a courtyard surrounded by arched halls and cells. Its walls are resplendently decorated with coloured tiles. The entrance to the main rectangular building is through a golden outer hall. In the middle of the central golden-domed chamber lies the shrine, surrounded by a silver enclosure (*ḍharīḥ*). Two golden minarets usually flank the entrance to the shrine.

The shrines are important centres of Shīʿī learning, and important seminaries (*madrasa* [*q.v.*]) grew up around them. Every Shīʿī longs to find a last resting place in the holy precincts of the beloved Imāms, and this has resulted in the development of extensive cemeteries at all the shrines, especially at Karbalāʾ, Nadjaf, and Mashhad [*q.vv.*], and in areas near these shrines.

Of all the Imāms, it is al-Ḥusayn b. ʿAlī [*q.v.*] who enjoys the status of the "Chief of Martyrs", having suffered the torments of thirst and hunger in the desert and having been slaughtered by his enemies at Karbalāʾ. His tomb was probably the first *mashhad* in Shīʿī piety, and was regarded as holy immediately after his martyrdom in 61/680 (al-Madjlisī, *Biḥār al-anwār*, ci, *K. al-Mazār*, is a volume devoted to the merits of *ziyāra* to Karbalāʾ). The *mashhad* of ʿAlī at Nadjaf, near Kūfa, became a public shrine in the early ʿAbbāsid period (al-Shaykh al-Mufīd, *K. al-Irshād*, Tehran 1351 *sh.*/1972, i, 14). The *mashhad* at al-Kāẓimayn, near Baghdād, enshrines the tombs of al-Kāẓim and al-Djawād, the seventh and ninth Imāms. In Sāmarrāʾ, [*q.v.*] are buried al-Hādī and al-ʿAskarī, the tenth and eleventh Imāms. The eighth Imām ʿAlī al-Riḍā is buried in Sanābad, in the district of Ṭūs, around which grew up the city of Mashhad. The tombs of Fāṭima, the Prophet's daughter, and other Imāms buried in the graveyard of al-Baḳīʿ in Medina [see BAḲĪʿ AL-GHARḲAD] were levelled to the ground by the Wahhābīs in 1925. These Sunnī puritans regard the Shīʿī practice of venerating *mashhads* as polytheism (*shirk*) (Goldziher, *Muh. St.*, Eng. tr. ii, 333).

Besides the Imāms, there are numerous shrines dedicated to the ancient prophets like Adam, Noah, Jonah, and others in and around Nadjaf, and around other towns in ʿIrāḳ, Palestine, Syria, and southern Turkey. The Imāms' sons and daughters (*imāmzāda* [*q.v.*] and *sayyida* or *bībī*) also receive special reverence in the *ziyāra* tradition. Among the *imāmzādas*, the most famous are the shrines of Sayyid Muḥammad, the son of ʿAlī al-Hādī, in Balad, some 56 km/35 miles south of Sāmarrāʾ, Shāh ʿAbd al-Aẓīm al-Ḥusaynī [*q.v.*] in Rayy, and Shāh Čirāgh in Shīrāz. The very unusual *mashhad al-siḳṭ* for al-Ḥusayn's miscarried fetus is located west of Aleppo opposite Mount Djawshan, where women pray for fertility (Yāḳūt, *Buldān*, ii, 156, 308). Miraculous healing powers are attributed to all these places. Among the shrines dedicated to holy women among the *ahl-bayt* [*q.v.*] are those of Sayyida Zaynab bt. ʿAlī and Sayyida Ruḳayya bt. al-Ḥusayn in Damascus; Sayyida Zaynab and Nafīsa in Cairo; Bībī Fāṭima, daughter of Mūsā al-Kāẓim, the seventh Imām, in Ḳumm; Nardjis Khātūn, the twelfth Imām's mother, and Ḥakīma, the daughter of ʿAlī al-Hādī, the tenth Imām, in Sāmarrāʾ. In addition, the tombs of famous Shīʿī scholars are also visited in reverence for their contribution in keeping the Imāms' teachings alive. Thus in Nadjaf the tombs of Shaykh al-Ṭūsī and ʿAllāma al-Ḥillī are visited; in al-Kāẓimayn, al-Shaykh al-Mufīd and the Sharīfs al-Murtaḍā and al-Raḍī; and more recently, on the road to Ḳumm, the shrine of Āyatullāh Khumaynī [*q.v.* in Suppl.].

Besides the mausoleums there are numerous historical places connected with the events of ʿĀshūrāʾ [*q.v.*] at Karbalāʾ which are described in the manuals (*miṣbāḥ al-zāʾir* and similar titles), forming a special genre of pious literature, listing the holy places and the recommended rituals of visitation composed by prominent Shīʿī scholars (see al-Madjlisī, *op. cit.*). Kūfa boasts of several historical mosques connected with the Imāms and their prominent disciples, which draw huge crowds.

(b) *Rituals connected with* ziyāra

Ziyara to the tombs of the Shīʿī Imāms and their descendants is a religious recommendation for the Shīʿīs (Ibn Ḳawlawayh al-Ḳummī, *Kāmil al-ziyārāt*, Nadjaf 1356/1937, 294). From early days, it was common for both the Shīʿīs and Sunnīs to undertake pilgrimages to these and other shrines. Unlike the *ḥādjdj*, *ziyāra* to these shrines may be undertaken at any time, although certain days are specially recommended, and in regard to some shrines, pilgrimage is associated with a special lunar month or season of the year. Thus the *ziyāra* of Sayyida Zaynab in Cairo is performed in Radjab; whereas that of Imām al-Riḍā in Mashhad is recommended in Dhu 'l-Ḳaʿda. That of *imāmzāda* Sulṭān ʿAlī near Ḳāshān is held on the seventh day of autumn. It is only the *ziyāra* of al-Ḥusayn at Karbalāʾ that, besides on major occasions like ʿĀshūrāʾ, is recommended every Thursday evening. On these evenings, the *mashhad* is thronged with crowds of pilgrims from many lands.

The performance of *ziyāra* is regarded by the pilgrims as an act of covenant renewal between the holy person and his devotees. This is a covenant of love, sincere obedience and devotion on the part of the believers. Through *ziyāra,* one participates in the suffering and sorrows of the Prophet's *ahl al-bayt.* People who cannot undertake the arduous and expensive journey to the shrines of the Imāms can go to the wilderness, or up onto a high roof in one's house, and then turn towards the *ḳibla* and pronounce the special salutations (*ziyāra-nāma*) meant for various specific occasions. Although distinction is made between the *ziyārāt* of the Imāms and of other holy persons, Shīʿī scholars have regarded it as permissible to show all of them honour and respect by addressing them in a prescribed way, some of these salutations being narrated directly from the Imāms. However, the *ziyāra* of the Imāms is followed by two units (*rakʿa* [*q.v.*]) of worship as a gift to the Imām whose *ziyāra* is being performed. It concludes with a petition for the Prophet and his family's intercession and praise to God.

Bibliography (in addition to references in the article): Muḥammad Bāḳir al-Madjlisī, *Biḥār al-anwār*, c-ciii, *K. al-Mazār*, Tehran 1388 A.H./1968-9 (detailed description of the *ziyāra* tradition, sacred places and rituals, based on early Shīʿī sources); Goldziher, *Muh. Stud.*, ii, 277-378, Eng. tr. *Muslim studies*, ii, 255-341, London 1971, on the veneration of saints; Sh. ʿAbbās al-Ḳummī, *Mafātīḥ al-djinān*, Tehran 1381 A.H./1961-2 (concise compendium of *ziyāra* rituals throughout the lunar calendar); Hamid Algar, *Religion and state in Iran 1785-1906. The role of the Ulama in the Qajar period*, Berkeley, etc. 1969 (on the roles of Kūfa and Nadjaf in the politics of Muslim powers); Mahmoud Ayyoub, *Redemptive suffering in Islam. A study of devotional aspects of ʿAshuraʾ in Twelver Shiʿism*, The Hague 1978.

(Abdulaziz Sachedina)

6. The Turkish lands, including the Balkans and Central Asia.

In the Turkish world, the word, in its form *ziyāret*, denotes pilgrimage to and act of devotion at a saint's tomb, and is one of the words derived from this root (also *mazār, mezār, ziyāretgāh*) applied to the holy place itself. However, the names given to these holy places vary considerably according to the different regions; *tekke, türbe* in the Balkans and Turkey; *pīr, očāgh, imāmzāda* in Ādharbāydjān; *gunbez, langar, muḳaddas djāy* in Central Asia, etc. In Chinese Turkistān, the characteristic feature of a saint's tomb, sc. a banner (*ʿalam*)—a long pole surmounted by an animal's tail (*turra, tugh-i mazār*), systematically to be found close by Central Asian mausolea, but more rarely in Turkey and the Balkans—has often given its name to the *ziyāra*, sc. as *tugh-ʿalam.*

In Turkey, each Ṣūfī brotherhood used to encourage its members to make a pilgrimage to the tomb of the eponymous saint of the order or of the great *khalīfa*s. But there also existed here a pilgrimage circuit which was traditionally accomplished by the pilgrim who then desired to go to Mecca: first of all he would visit the tomb of the Prophet's Companion, Abū Ayyūb al-Anṣārī in Istanbul, and then that of the Ṣūfī Ḥādjdjī Bayrām Walī at Ankara (Hikmet Tanyu, *Ankara ve çevresinde adak ve adak yerleri*, Ankara 1967, 67). In Central Asia, given the distance from Mecca, certain *ziyāra*s functioned as substitutes for the sanctuary at the Kaʿba, and popular belief held that several pilgrimages to certain places could replace the Pilgrimage to Mecca. The most famous shrines here were the tomb of Bahāʾ al-Dīn Naḳshband at Bukhārā; the Takht-i Sulaymān at Osh in Kirghizistān, called "the Second Mecca"; and the tomb of Abū Yūsuf Hamadānī at Marw/Mari in Turkmenistān, called "the Kaʿba of Khurāsān". Also, a reproduction of the Kaʿba, which was built some years ago near the little mausoleum of Khurāsān Bābā in the Kizil Orda *oblast* of Kazakhstān, is set forth by the family of its custodians as "the Second Mecca" of the Kazakhs. In eastern Turkistān, pilgrims would in the first place make a circuit of the tombs of Satuḳ Bughra Khān at Artūsh, of Āfāḳ Khʷādja Hidāyat Allāh at Kāshghar and Isḥāḳ Walī at Yarkand. But at the present time, the great pilgrimages of Sinkiang/Xinjiang are made to the tombs of Ordām Pādishāh at Yangi Hisār and Tūyūk Khʷādjām at Turfān (see Abdürahim Häbibulla, *Uyghur etnografisi*, Shinjang Khälk Näshriyati, Ürümči, i, [1993], 349).

The curators of these holy places are either simple keepers (*türbedār*) or descendants of the saint, usually Ṣūfīs. Their main function is to act as intercessors (*shafāʿa*) for the pilgrims but they also instruct the visitors about the appropriate acts of devotion at the sites they control. Finally, they administer the alms and the offerings (money, cereals, animals, etc.), which are called, in Turkey and the Balkans, *adak, nedhir* and sometimes *niyāz* or vow. In Central Asia, one finds also the terms *sadaka* and the Arabic-Persian-Turkish compound *nadhr-niyāzmanlik.* Women, kept away from places of devotion in orthodox Islam, form the greater part of visitors to a *ziyāra*; most saints are reputed to be able to solve problems strictly affecting women (sterility, marriage, etc.) and to cure all sorts of ailments (see Liliana Masulovic-Marsol, *Tombes de saints musulmans et guérison; une approche anthropologique*, in *Cimetières et traditions funéraires dans le monde islamique*, Ankara 1996). But the reasons for pilgrimage are various, and concern men also: simple devotion, mystical interest, cures, social success, etc. The actual acts of devotion are, as a general rule, the same as those practised in the rest of the Islamic world but with some local peculiarities. Circumambulation (*ṭawāf*) is made round the tomb, habitually in an upright position but occasionally on all fours as at Ḥādjdjī Bektāsh in Anatolia, and at certain tombs is accompanied by fumigations (odoriferous and medicinal plants). *Ṭawāf* may also be made round a holy object situated near the tomb, such as a hundred-year old tree at that of Bahāʾ al-Dīn Naḳshband. Veneration may also be focused on an object other than the actual tombstone: a black stone and ram's horns at the previously-mentioned shrine; a cauldron at that of Aḥmad Yasawī at Turkistān [*q.v.*] in Kazakhstān and at Ḥādjdjī Bektāsh; and suchlike. As well as circumambulation, the pilgrim sometimes kisses the tomb or the doorstep or the sides of the door leading into the funeral chamber, or any other object connected with the saint. Another usage, especially common in the Turkish world, is to hang pieces of cloth on nearby trees or the windows of the mausoleum. One sometimes even comes across inflated sheep's skins (e.g. tomb of Mūsā Kāẓim at Khotan in eastern Turkistān). The practice of settling down in a tomb, for some hours or a whole night, is attested at several tombs. The texts read by the person filling the role of intercessor are restricted to some Ḳurʾānic sūras (generally the *Fātiḥa* and XXXVI, *Yāsīn*) and other formulae consecrated by centuries of practice, but also Persian poetry (e.g. ʿUmar Khayyām in Tādjīkistān) or Turkish chants called *gülbenk* or *terdjümān* (Ḥādjdjī Bektāsh). Certain great centres of pilgrimage (e.g. the last-named and Takht-i Sulaymān) offer, as well as the *ṭawāf*, a circuit punctuated by devotions done in grottoes, by rocks, near springs, sacred trees, etc. (e.g. at Takht-i Sulaymān; see Zaïm Khenchelaoui, *Le mythe et le culte de Salomon dans l'espace musulman*, doctoral thesis, EHESS, Toulouse 1998). Although condemned by Islamic orthodoxy, the *ziyāra* has maintained itself in the Turkish world because of its important role in popular religion. The rites of pilgrimage have admittedly undergone changes and have often disappeared round certain tombs under Marxist régimes in the Balkans, Central Asia and Sinkiang, as also in Kemalist Turkey. Also, the effects of desacralisation have deeply modified the functioning of the *ziyāra* in certain high places (e.g. at Ḥādjdjī Bayrām Walī, Takht-i Sulaymān and Āfāḳ Khʷādja). Within Turkey, with the relaxation of Kemalist doctrines since the 1950s, and since the end of Communism in the former USSR, the *ziyāra* has been reconstituted on new foundations but still connected with the old traditions. In Sinkiang, although *ziyāra* is sometimes forbidden and sometimes tolerated but still regarded with disapproval, it remains a much-followed practice in popular circles (see Th. Zarcone, *Quand le saint légitime la politique. Le mausolée de Afāq Khwādja à Kashghar*, in *Central Asian Survey* (1999).

Bibliography: F.W. Hasluck, *Christianity and Islam under the sultans*, Oxford 1929; Yusuf Ziya, *Dinî ve sirrî hayat dernek*, in *Darülfünun Ilâhiyat Fakültesi Mecmuası*, v/20 (1931); J. Castagné, *Le culte des lieux saints de l'Islam au Turkestan*, in *L'Ethnographie*, Paris (1951); J.-P. Roux, *Les traditions des nomades de la Turquie méridionale*, Paris 1970; V.N. Basilov, *Kul't svyatîkh v Islame*, Moscow 1970; G.P. Snesarev, *Khorezmskie legendî kak istočnik po istorii religioznîkh kul'-tov Sredney Azii*, Moscow 1983; T. Ataev, *Käramatli yärlär hakinda hakikat*, Ashgabat 1986; R.M. Mustafina, *Predstavleniya kul'tî, obryady u Kazakhov*, Alma Ata 1992; Baha Tanman, *Settings for the veneration of saints*, in *The dervish lodge. Architecture, art and Sufism in Ottoman Turkey*, Berkeley, etc. 1992, 141-67; Nathalie Clayer and A. Popovic, *[Le culte des saints] dans les Balkans*, and *Le culte d'Ajvatovica et son pèlerinage annuel*, in Chambert Loir and E. Guillot (eds.), *Le culte des saints dans le monde musulman*, Paris 1995; Th. Zarcone, *[Le culte des saints] en Turquie et en Asie centrale*, and *Le mausolée de Hacı Bektâsh Velî en Anatolie centrale (Turquie)*, in *ibid.*; idem, *Le mausolée de Bahâ' al-Dîn Naqshband à Bokhara (Uzbekistan)*, in *Jnal. of Turkish Studies*, xix (1995); idem, *Une route de sainteté islamique entre l'Asie centrale et l'Inde: la voie Ush-Kashghar-Srinagar, en Inde-Asie centrale. Routes du commerce et des idées*, in *Cahiers de l'Asie Centrale*, nos. 1-2 (1996), 227-54; P.B. Fenton, *Le symbolisme du rite de la circumambulation dans le judaïsme et dans l'islam, étude comparative*, in *RHR*, ccxvi/2 (1996); A. Muminov, *Veneration of holy sites of the mid-Sïrdar'ya valley. Continuity and transformation*, in M. Kemper *et alii* (eds.), *Muslim culture and Central Asia from the 18th to the early 20th centuries*, Berlin 1996; Kambar Nasriddinov, *Özbek dafn va ta'ziya marosimi*, Tashkent 1996.

(Th. Zarcone)

7. In Muslim India.

Except in the north-east of Pakistan, where it can denote the place (generally a tomb) to which pilgrimages are made, elsewhere in the Indian subcontinent the term *ziyāra* (in the form *ziyārat*) signified an actual pilgrimage. A tomb which is visited is called a *mazār*, or, if it belongs to a famous saint, a *dargāh*, i.e. a palace, since the saint is treated as the true master of the territory, like a sultan [see WALĪ. 6.]. The greatest places of pilgrimage in India are the tombs of the five great saints of the Čishtiyya brotherhood. It is said that a visit to these five tombs is worth a pilgrimage to Mecca. There are other saints, more localised but also very famous, such as Ghāzī Miyān [*q.v.*] at Bakraikh in northern India.

These visits may be made by individuals on any day, especially in the evening; individual and collective visits take place once a week, generally on a Thursday evening, or once a month. Big festivities are always organised once a year on the anniversary of the death of the saint. They are known as *ʿurs*, i.e. "(mystical) nuptials", and not *mawlid* "birth", as they are in the Arab world; they give rise to large pilgrimages where the faithful are present in great numbers. Here special attention will be paid to the great feasts in order to analyse the different elements of the pilgrimage.

Firstly, there is the journey itself, travelling from the place of residence of the pilgrim to the sanctuary and then back again. This is done, as it is for marriages, in a procession, with standard-bearers, musicians and even dancers, who are considered to be a good omen, at the front. The most famous procession in Indian history was the one to the sanctuary of Ghāzī Miyān in northern India, which was the one that the Mughal emperor Akbar (963-1014/1556-1605 [*q.v.*]) liked to watch.

Then comes the veneration of the tomb itself, when the faithful all approach one by one to honour the saint who resides there. They touch the tomb, leave perfumes and flowers there, and often make a circumambulation. This is the *ṭawāf*, which in India is often performed clockwise, considered to be a good omen for Hindus, in contrast to a counter-clockwise motion in the Arab world. This is a sign of acculturation which seems to have been only little noticed.

Then there is the transaction which takes place between the believer, the saint and God. This is the most important moment for the pilgrimage and gives rise to conflicting interpretations. The strictly orthodox view, which is expressed in the wording of the invocation, the *duʿāʾ*, demands that the offerings and prayers be addressed directly to God, beseeching Him to grant merit to the saints and the faithful. The spontaneous interpretation by the faithful is quite different; in exchange for their prayers and their offerings they invoke the intercession (*shafāʿa*) of the saints to obtain favours for themselves, which are more often of a material rather than of a spiritual nature. The Muslim conquerors used to pray for victory; today, politicians continue to come and beg for success. These transactions may take the form of vows, a sort of commercial bargaining, where the believer undertakes to perform this or that offering in return for this or that favour.

A fourth element which is not always present is communal. Animals are sacrificed in the name of the saint, or the first fruits of the harvest are offered to him, and these are then consumed in a banquet.

A fifth element, which could be termed the ecstatic, uses music and dance as a medium. Ideally, it concerns mystical chants which are performed by specially trained musicians or *kawwāls*, and they may well induce ecstatic dances. The most beautiful climax, which is repeatedly found in Indian Ṣūfism, in particular at the tomb of Muʿīn al-Dīn Čishtī at Adjmer, arises by dying from exhaustion in an ecstatic dance. These dances, however, may also change into a profane celebration with the dancers and prostitutes.

Finally, particular sanctuaries often have special features: for example, near the tomb of Bābā Farīd al-Dīn Čis̲h̲tī in Pakistan there is a "doorway to heaven", and this is open only at the annual feast. Those who pass through it are certain to enter Paradise; G̲h̲āzī Miyān cured those who were afflicted with leprosy.

Such pilgrimages allow the faithful to leave their everyday environment, to establish contact with the divine world by the intermediary of saints, and even to have a foretaste of the Hereafter through ecstasy. They return home with the hope of favours in this world and assurance for the Hereafter. Even though these great pilgrimages have borrowed Indian elements (they are often called *melā*, a fair, like the great Hindu gatherings), they still remain Islamic in their greatest features; they are focussed on the tombs of the saints and not on deities, and they appeal to the rites and mystical techniques characteristic of Muslims.

Bibliography: For a more detailed Bibl. see WALĪ. 6. For a general survey of the subject and the sources, see J.A. Subhan, *Sufism, its saints and shrines: an introduction to the study of Sufism with special reference to India*, [2]New York 1970 ([1]1938); C.W. Troll (ed.), *Muslim shrines in India. Their character, history and significance*, Dihlī 1989. Traditional Muslim views and those of the early Orientalists on pilgrimages and their timing are analysed in Garcin de Tassy, *Mémoires sur les particularités de la religion musulmane en Inde*, in *JA* (1831) ([2]Paris 1969, annotated English tr., *Muslim festivals in India*, Dihlī 1995); also in C.W. Ernst, *An Indo-Persian guide to Sufi shrine pilgrimage*, in G.M. Smith and Ernst (eds.), *Manifestations of sainthood in Islam*, Istanbul 1993, 43-67.

An ethnological analysis of pilgrimages can be found in I. Ahmad, *Ritual and religion among Muslims in India*, Dihlī 1981. For an analysis of the rituals, see M. Gaborieau, *The cult of saints among the Muslims of Nepal and Northern India*, in S. Wilson (ed.), *Saints and their cults. Studies in religious sociology, folklore and history*, Cambridge 1983, 291-308; idem, *Le culte des saints en tant que rituel: controverses juridiques*, in *Archives de sciences sociales des religions*, no. 85 (1994), 85-98.

The different places of pilgrimage in the different regions of the Indian subcontinent are treated together in D. Matringe, *Pakistan*, Gaborieau and C. Champion, *Inde* and Lyndell-Jones, *Bangladesh*, in H. Chambert-Loir and C. Guillot (eds.), *Le culte des saints dans le monde musulman*, Paris 1995, 167-234.

For detailed studies of some of the greatest pilgrimages see e.g. P.M. Currie, *The shrine and cult of Muin al-din Chishti of Ajmer*, Dihlī 1989; R.M. Eaton, *Court of man, court of god. Local perceptions of the shrine of Bâbâ Farîd, Pakpattan, Punjab*, in R.C. Martin (ed.), *Islam in local contexts*, Leiden 1982, 44-61; Gaborieau, *Légende et culte du saint musulman Ghâzî Miyân au Népal occidental et en Inde du Nord*, in *Objets et Mondes*, xv/3-4 (1975), 289-318; idem, *Les saints, les eaux et les récoltes*, dans M.A. Amir-Moezzi (ed.), *Lieux d'Islam. Cultes et cultures de l'Afrique à Java*, Paris 1996, 239-54.

(M. GABORIEAU)

8. In Indonesia.

Undertaking pilgrimages to spiritually or magically potent sites is a well-established practice in most parts of Indonesia. Spread throughout the archipelago, there are numerous sacred sites. Most of them are of local importance only but some attract visitors nationwide. Sites for *ziarah* (thus the Bahasa Indonesian form) can be divided in two main categories: graves of religious and worldly Muslim leaders such as saints, kings and high nobles; and sites that are considered laden with power due to their natural environment. The most popular Muslim saints are the *wali sanga*, the founders of Islam in Indonesia [see WALĪ. 7]. The graves of originators of *pesantren* [*q.v.*] (*kyai*) can have local fame and are visited weekly, especially by alumni and students of the *pesantren* (Z. Dhofier, *Tradisi pesantren, studi tentang pandangan hidup kiyai*, Jakarta 1985, Eng. tr. *The role of the Kiai in the maintenance of traditional Islam in Java*, Tempe, Arizona 1999). Most graves are part of a mausoleum, with the main saint in the middle and his students and family members buried around him. The reasons for undertaking a *ziarah* vary from making a request to the saint, praying to God and fulfilling a vow, to seeking blessing, power and esoteric knowledge (*ngelmu*).

Especially on Java, numerous pre-Islamic sites for *ziarah* still testify of the gradual process of Islamisation that accommodated syncretistic Javanese Hindu-Buddhist beliefs and practices (*agama jawi*). These influences on what later became orthodox Islam (*Islam santri*) shaped the customs practiced at many sites of *ziarah* (for a description of Javanese beliefs, see Koentjaraningrat, *Javanese culture*, Singapore 1985). Furthermore, pre-Islamic beliefs in the potency of certain natural areas, such as spiritually significant cosmic mountains, resulted in holy graves being placed on top of mountains. Pre-Islamic influences are especially noticeable in various architectural elements, such as the entrance gates to the graves of the *wali sanga* like Sunan Ampel and Sunan Giri in east Java and Sunan Bayat in Tembayat in central Java.

Certain locations are considered to be cosmic centres that possess the same degree of spiritual power as can be encountered in Mecca. Hence *ziarah* in the Malay world can be a substitute for those Muslims who cannot afford the *ḥadjdj* to Mecca. An example of such a centre is Mount Ciremai in Kuningan. Indonesian Muslims believe that climbing up and down this mountain three times can be considered equal to performing the Meccan Pilgrimage. Also, there are certain sites (such as Kubur Panjang at Leran near Gresik) where pilgrims go in preparation for the *ḥadjdj*.

The timing for performing a *ziarah* is determined by a complex system of the coinciding of weekly cycles based on the Muslim and the Javanese calendars. The nights prior to Fridays, when the first day of the five-day Javanese week coincides with the Muslim week of seven days (*Jumaat Kliwon*, *Jumaat Paing*, or *Jumaat Legi*), are believed to be times when the power of tombs is especially potent. On those nights, the main tombs are open, while during other days visitors can only derive blessing from the general atmosphere at mausolea. These specific times for *ziarah* are also considered the most beneficial in bringing requests for intercession to the saint. The students of a *kyai* traditionally gather at the grave of their master once a week, preferably on Thursday night. For the more Islamic Javanese pilgrims, the Eve of the first of *Sura*, the first month of the Javanese year, is the pre-eminent time to make a pilgrimage.

Customs practiced during *ziarah* also depend on the purely Islamic or purely Hindu-Javanese character of the tomb. In Imogiri (south of Yogyakarta), at the enormous mausoleum of the first Javanese Muslim kings of the Mataram empire, there are pilgrims who practice a wide range of purely Javanese practices, while others limit themselves to Islamic observances. The Javanese practices include ascetic feats and forms of Javanese meditation (*semedi* and *tapa*) in order to obtain magical power with the help of the once-powerful king, and the bringing of offerings (*sesajen*) in the form of a blessed ceremonial meal (*slamatan*). At the same time, the Muslim character of the kings might be honoured by reciting the Ḳurʾān near their graves or by performing *tahlilan*, a type of *dhikr* (for *ziarah* to Javanese-Islamic sites, see Woodward, *Islam in Java*, ch. 5; J. Pemberton, *On the subject of "Java,"* Ithaca and London 1994, ch. 7).

At the tombs of Muslim saints, it is mostly Islamic customs which prevail, such as reciting the Ḳurʾān and performing *dhikr* or *tahlilan*. Once a year, a *khaul* is held to honour the day the saint passed away or was born. This celebration may take from one day to a week and is similar to the celebration of the *mawlid* [*q.v.*] in the Middle East. Common events of the *khaul* are speeches by Islamic leaders, recitation of the Ḳurʾān, fairs and selling or distributing food. On the saint's feast day, the fabric that has covered the tomb during the past year is replaced by new cloth. Pre-Islamic customs such as drinking holy water, sprinkling flowers on the tomb and sharing a meal of blessing (*slamatan*), are tolerated at nearly all shrines. One can only approach tombs through their custodians, the *juru kunci* ("key bearers"), who guard the proper rituals to be performed during the pilgrimage. Also, they are the bearers of the saint's hagiography and of the texts of prayers and formulae in Javanese and Arabic to be presented to the saint. Local *kyai* or other Muslim officials are always in charge of the Islamic rituals, such as the perfomance of *tahlilan*.

The popularity of *ziarah* in Indonesia may also be influenced by the prevalent custom of visiting the graves (*nyekar*) of deceased relatives, which is done mostly in the week prior to the beginning of Ramaḍān. The purposes of these visits range from cleaning the graves and the recitation of religious texts for the benefit of the deceased to seeking blessings from the deceased ancestors.

Ziarah is a widespread phenomenon throughout the Malay world. Snouck Hurgronje mentioned the visiting of the tombs of kings or Muslim saints in Aceh, exclusively for the fulfillment of vows (*The Achehnese*, Leiden 1906, ii, 293). Yet many Muslim groups have considered it incompatible with orthodox Islam. In Indonesia, Muslims affiliated with the more traditional Javanese-minded organisation of *kyai*, the Nàhdatul Ulama, are in favour of performing *ziarah*, while the Reformist grouping of the Muhammadiyah reject it. The relatively small amount of literature, contemporary and historical, about the practice of *ziarah* that is available has mostly been written by Western scholars; while for Malaysia, only one major article can be mentioned, that of R.O. Winstedt, *Karamat, sacred places and persons in Malaya*, in *Jnal. of the Malayan Branch of the RAS* (1924), 264-79.

Bibliography (in addition to references in the article): M.R. Woodward, *Islam in Java: normative piety and mysticism in the sultanate of Yogyakarta*, Tucson 1989; H. de Jonge, *Heiligen, middelen en doel. Ontwikkelingen en betekenis van twee Islamitische bedevaartsorden op Java*, in W. Jansen and H. de Jonge, *Islamitische Pelgrimstochten*, Muiderberg 1991; J. Fox, *Ziarah visits to the tombs of the Wali, the founders of Islam on Java*, in M.C. Ricklefs (ed.), *Islam in the Indonesian social context*, Clayton, Victoria 1991; D.A. Rinkes, *Nine saints of Java*, Kuala Lumpur 1996 (originally 1910-11); Chen Hock Tong, *The sinicization of Malay Keramats in Malaysia*, in *JMBRAS*, lxxi/2 (1998), 29-61. (Nelly van Doorn-Harder)

9. In Central and West Africa.

Ziyāra, originally a technical term for the visitation of tombs of saintly persons, has assumed a wider meaning in Central and West Africa. Whereas the term is often used in the sense of "holy place" in parts of Muslim Asia, in the African context *ziyāra* denotes a pious visit to a *shaykh* living or dead, as well as the visit to the celebrations of a saint's life. However, there are only scanty references to *ziyāra* in the literature.

The practice of *ziyāra* has spread with the expansion of the Ṣūfī orders, particularly the Ḳādiriyya and the Tidjāniyya [*q.vv.*]. Although historical evidence is meagre, it seems that tombs became the destination of pious visits in Aïr and in the area of Timbuktu [*q.v.*, and see Kunta] in the course of the 16th century. The habit of such visits also started at the tomb of ʿUthmān b. Fūdī [*q.v.*] in Sokoto shortly after his death in 1232/1817. Probably as early as the first half of the 19th century, annual festivals were celebrated by members of both the Ḳādiriyya and the Tidjāniyya on the occasion of the *mawlid* [*q.v.*] of ʿAbd al-Ḳādir al-Djīlānī (d. 561/1166) during the month of Rabīʿ I or the *ḥawliyya* of Aḥmad al-Tidjānī (d. 1230/1815) during the month of Ṣafar. There is also evidence that performing the *ziyāra* to the Prophet's tomb at Medina was the rule for most, if not all, Africans who undertook the *ḥadjdj*.

In the 20th century, the visitation to the tombs of saints has become a common practice for many ordinary Muslims in West and Central Africa. As an example, one might point to Senegal and its Holy Cities Touba and Tivaouane, which house the tombs of Aḥmadu Bamba, founder of the Murīdiyya [*q.v.*] Ṣūfī order and al-Ḥādjdj Mālik Sy, founder of the biggest branch of the Tidjāniyya in the country [see Senegal]. However, it seems that *ziyāra*, in the sense of visiting the tomb of a holy man, is not as widespread a practice in sub-Saharan Africa as it is in the Maghrib or in Egypt, a fact strongly (and perhaps over-) emphasised by Trimingham. There are few shrines to be found in the area, and even lower is the number of tombs surmounted by a *ḳubba*. Instead of visiting the dead, intercession is sought rather from the living.

In Senegal, *ziyāra* (Wolof, *siyare*) refers to the visit to annual festivals held on the occasion of a saint's birthday, death or other significant event in his life. The locus of these visits is not necessarily the saint's tomb. Touba is the destination of the *magal*, a pilgrimage held in the month of Ṣafar to commemorate the departure of Aḥmadu Bamba to his exile in Gabon in 1895. This festival has not been without political significance in the past and has in recent years attracted more than one million people annually. Apart from the great *magal*, members of the Murīdiyya order nowadays celebrate *magal* festivities for a growing number of more or less important religious leaders. Similarly, the leaders of the Tidjāniyya order mobilise their membership to attend regular meetings known as *gamou*, a term originally applied to the *mawlid* festivities held on the Prophet's birthday. The *gamou* during the month of Rabīʿ I remains the most important event in the *ziyāra* calendar of the Senegalese Tidjāniyya, but there are now similar festivals to commemorate Tidjānī leaders throughout the year.

Owing to the lack of research, it is difficult to say anything definite on the practice of *ziyāra* in other parts of West and Central Africa. We know of guidebooks for pilgrims and travel accounts written by Nigerian scholars on visiting the Prophet's tomb at

Medina or the tomb of Aḥmad al-Tidjānī at Fās. But apart from the case of ʿUthmān b. Fūdī, there is no evidence in the literature of festivals dedicated to the memory of Nigerian holy men, although we can assume that they exist, e.g. among the Ḳādiriyya of Kano. The Hausa and speakers of other African languages use the Arabic word *ziyāra* to refer to these pious visits. In the town of Nioro du Sahel (Mali), members of religious lineages organise annual events visited by followers from far away.

Apart from the pilgrimage performed to a saint's festival, the term *ziyāra* refers also to formal visits in various social contexts. In the broadest sense, *ziyāra* is an occasion at which people pay their respects to a holy man. The motives for such pious visits might range from *tabarruk*, i.e. the wish to participate in the saint's blessing, to more concrete concerns, such as asking the saintly person for supplicatory prayers (*duʿāʾ* [*q.v.*]) or for assistance in a specific worldly matter. Women and men may seek the *shaykh*'s help to find a remedy against infertility or may just visit the *shaykh* on account of his healing power; peasants may ask the *shaykh* to drive away locusts or to pray for rain.

Another peculiarity of *ziyāra* in West Africa is the practice of offering gifts to the *shaykh*. This custom has come to be so closely associated with pious visits that in some areas the term *ziyāra* not only means "visits", but also the donations that a *shaykh* receives from his disciples in kind or in money. A religious leader might undertake a journey to "collect *ziyāra*", particularly in cases where the followers are not able to make the trip to see their *shaykh*.

Ziyāra can be described as the direct link between a living *shaykh* of a Ṣūfī order and his followers. Members of the Tidjāniyya order affiliated with the Senegalese *shaykh* Ibrāhīm Niasse (d. 1395/1975) perform the *ziyāra* on the Prophet's birthday, when huge crowds gather for celebrations at Kaolack, the home town of Niasse, and in the city of Kano. In addition, Niasse used to call upon his followers to visit him at least once a year in order to submit a donation, receiving the master's *baraka* [*q.v.*] in return. For this purpose, a date is fixed annually after the harvest, the time when the disciples from rural areas are most likely to donate large amounts of money or contributions in kind. The followers were told that *ziyāra* is the key to the gates of right guidance and well-being. The same practice is continued by leaders of the Tidjāniyya affiliated to Niasse elsewhere in sub-Saharan Africa, who use the occasion to talk and preach to their followers. More recently, the disciples of Niasse in such countries as Senegal, Gambia, Ghana, Nigeria, Cameroon and Chad have introduced a festival on 15 Radjab to commemorate Niasse's birthday.

Bibliography: P. Marty, *L'Islam au Sénégal*, ii, Paris 1917, see 42-3 for the author's theory of why Africans do not venerate dead saints; J.S. Trimingham, *Islam in West Africa*, Oxford 1959 (few references to *ziyāra*; see in particular, 88 ff.); A. Samb, *Touba et son Magal*, in *Bulletin de l'I.F.A.N.*, xxxi (1969), 733-53 (on the greatest *ziyāra* of the Murīdiyya); A.A. Batran, *Sîdî al-Mukhtâr al-Kuntî and the recrudescence of Islam in the Western Sahara and the Middle Nigeria, c. 1750-1811*, Ph.D. thesis, Univ. of Birmingham 1971 (on the Ḳādiriyya of Timbuktu); J.N. Paden, *Religion and political culture in Kano*, Berkeley 1973, see 129 on the *ziyāra* of Ibrāhīm Niasse; V. Monteil, *L'Islam noir*, [3]Paris 1980, see ch. 5; H.T. Norris, *Ṣūfī mystics of the Niger desert*, Oxford 1990 (see on Aïr, 96-7, 113 n. 69); J.O. Hunwick *et al.*, *Arabic literature of Africa*, ii, *The writings of Central Sudanic Africa*, Leiden 1995 (includes entries for pilgrims' guidebooks); L.A. Villalon, *Islamic society and state power in Senegal*, Cambridge 1995, see 163-86 on the *magal* and the *gamou* festivities; B.F. Soares, *The spiritual economy of Nioro du Sahel*, Ph.D. thesis, Northwestern University 1997, see ch. 5; C. Coulon, *The Grand Magal in Touba*, in *African Affairs*, xcviii (1999), 195-210 (on the greatest *ziyāra* of the Murīdiyya). (R. Seesemann)

10. In the Horn of Africa.

As in the rest of the Islamic world, *ziyārāt* are a common feature of Islam in the Horn of Africa. Primary and secondary source materials detailing such pilgrimages are limited; enough information exists, however, for us to draw a rough outline of these popular practices. The objects of veneration fall into roughly two categories. First are the grave sites of lineage ancestors esteemed for their position as eponymous clan founders and of traditional saints believed instrumental in the introduction of Islam to the region. The second category comprises more recent holy men associated primarily with the introduction of Ṣūfī *ṭuruḳ* [see ṬARĪḲA] in the late 19th century and venerated for their piety and direct connections with the divine. Whether seeking material assistance in this world or spiritual connection with the next, pilgrimages to the burial places of these blessed individuals play a central role in the lives of Muslims in the Horn and eastern Africa.

Among the most notable tombs belonging to the first category are those of Shaykhs Isaaq and Daarood, the eponymous founders of the Somali Isaaq and Daarood clan families, respectively. Believed to have been immigrants from southern Arabia, Somali tradition has provided both ancestors with Sharīfian credentials and sanctified their burial places as sites of annual pilgrimage. The *ziyāra* to Shaykh Isaaq's purported resting place, for instance, takes place soon after the grain harvest in the Isaaq heartland of the north. Thousands of pilgrims, primarily from the Isaaq clan as well as their client lineages, gather at the Shaykh's tomb in Mait on the northern Somali coast as well as at other shrines dedicated to him throughout the north. While taking the shape of a religious pilgrimage, as I.M. Lewis points out, the primary object of such celebrations is the reification of clan unity and social identity rather than supplication to the spirit.

The traditional burial places of holy men associated with the arrival of Islam in the Horn are also popular objects of pilgrimage. The most important sites include the tombs of Shaykh Mumin Abdullah in Bay and Shaykh Aw Barkadle near Hargeisa [*q.v.*], both located in Somalia, and the shrine of Shaykh Nūr Ḥusayn of Bale in Ethiopia. Venerated as the propagators of the true faith, they are also revered as patrons and protectors. The Somali clansmen in Bay visit Shaykh Mumin's tomb, largely in order to seek protection for their crops from predatory birds. Aw Barkhadle, renowned for destroying the evil magician Bu'ur Ba'ir, is viewed as a guarantor of fertility and guard against miscarriage. Shaykh Nūr Ḥusayn is venerated by the Oromo in Ethiopia as a general patron responsible for their overall well-being and serves as a central icon of their Muslim identity.

In addition to these sites of traditional figures, the tombs of more recent religious figures, especially those associated with the Ṣūfī movement of the late 19th and early 20th centuries, are also the objects of veneration. Tombs belonging to the primary initiators of the *ṭuruḳ* constitute the main sites of visitation, although lesser figures of each order are also frequently visited by the pious. Among the most popular sites are the graves of Shaykh ʿAbd al-Raḥmān Zaylaʿī in Kolonkool, Shaykh Uways Muḥammad al-Barāwī in Biyoole and Shaykh ʿAbd al-Raḥmān Ṣūfī in Maḳdishū, all of whom were important figures in the powerful Ḳādiriyya [*q.v.*] movement of the late 19th and early 20th centuries. Although individuals may visit the tombs of these saints for their own special intentions, the majority of pilgrims come seeking enlightenment and a spiritual closeness to the saint that in turn will place them in greater proximity to God. As one learned pilgrim to the tomb of Shaykh Uways noted, "there exists no barrier between the tomb of the Prophet and that of Uways" (ʿAbd al-Raḥmān b. ʿUmar, 155 ff.), the former being the place of closest human proximity to God. Such visits also serve as an opportunity to further an individual's own mystical knowledge by obtaining *idjāzāt* from the caretakers of each tomb, frequently the descendants of the deceased saint, for the right to recite and transmit various prayers and formulae believed to assist one on the path towards union with the divine.

The timing of pilgrimages as well as the ceremonies conducted at each varies from site to site. *Ziyārāt* to so-called "traditional" sites are frequently tied to important points in the local calendar. The pilgrimage to Shaykh Isaaq's tomb, for instance, occurs shortly after the annual grain harvest. In contrast, the annual visit to the tomb of Shaykh Mumin occurs in the spring, soon after the planting. In other cases, pilgrimages are tied to the lunar Islamic calendar. The *ziyāra* of Aw Barkhadle is held, for example, on the first Friday during the "dark period" of Djumādā I. Similarly, pilgrimages to the tombs of saints connected with the *ṭuruḳ* occur on the anniversary of each saint's death as marked on the lunar calendar. However, pilgrims, especially members of the *ʿulamāʾ*, continue to visit these sites throughout the year seeking blessings and spiritual enlightenment. An interesting combination of these two patterns occurs with the *ziyāra* connected with the tomb of Shaykh Nūr Ḥusayn of Bale. The main feast day for the saint is set on the traditional date of his birth, which is fixed on a Tuesday at the beginning of August according to the traditional Oromo calendar. The month is known in Oromifa as *jia* Shaykh Ḥusayn, or the Moon of Shaykh Ḥusayn. However, another feast day is held during the *ʿīd al-aḍḥā* during the month of Dhu 'l-Ḥidjdja coinciding with the end of the *ḥadjdj*.

Likewise, ceremonies surrounding each pilgrimage vary widely. The centerpiece of most visits is the viewing of the tomb in order to make supplications for oneself or on behalf of others. This is generally accompanied by numerous animal sacrifices and the recitation of *ḳaṣīda*s [*q.v.*] dedicated to the saint.

Visits to saints connected with the *ṭuruḳ* are largely limited to these activities, along with a heavy emphasis on sermons, religious lessons and frequent prayer. Visits to the tombs of "traditional" saints frequently include additional rituals required to complete the ceremony. At the *ziyāra* of Aw Barkhadle, for instance, a great deal of emphasis is placed on the veneration of various relics (including a gold embossed Ḳurʾān and a bed post purported to belong to the saint). A formal procession to a nearby hilltop believed to be the site of the saint's victory over the magician Bu'ur Ba'ir is the highlight of the pilgrimage, which is then completed with the performance of the *djumʿa* prayer. The pilgrimage to Shaykh Nūr Ḥusayn's tomb is even more tightly choreographed and includes numerous ceremonies that replicate elements of the pilgrimage to Mecca. Pilgrims enter the sanctuary via a gate called Bāb al-Salām, as do those who enter Mecca. They then proceed to kiss and touch a black stone known as the *darara bashu* that Nūr Ḥusayn is popularly believed to have brought from Mecca. Finally, pilgrims perform a ritual stoning of the devil in the nearby valley, Kachamsare, in imitation of the same *ḥadjdj* ritual.

Bibliography: Sh. ʿAbd al-Raḥmān b. ʿUmar, *Djawhar al-nafīs fī khawāṣṣ Shaykh Uways*, Cairo 1964; B.W. Andrzejewski, *The veneration of Sufi saints and its impact on the oral literature of the Somali people*, in *African Language Studies*, xv (1974), 15-54; U. Braukamper, *The sanctuary of Shaykh Husayn and the Oromo-Somali connections in Bale*, in *Procs. of the First International Congress of Somali Studies*, ed. H.M. Adam and Ch.L. Geshekter, Atlanta 1992; Braukamper, *Geschichte der Hadiya Süd-Äthiopiens. Von den Anfängen bis zur Revolution 1974*, Wiesbaden 1980; E. Cerulli, *Somalia. Scritti vari editi ed inediti*, 3 vols. Rome 1957, ²1959, ³1964; idem, *Note sul movimento musulmano nella Somalia*, in *RSO*, x (1923), 1-36; I.M. Lewis, *Saints and Somalis: popular Islam in a clan-based society*, London 1998; ʿUmar b. Aḥmad al-Sumayṭ, *al-Nafḥa al-shadhadhiyya min al-diyār al-Ḥaḍramiyya wa-ṭalabiyyat al-ṣawt min al-Ḥidjāz wa-Ḥaḍramawt*, privately printed Tarim 1955; Yūsuf ʿAbd al-Raḥmān (ed.), *Nuzhat al-asrār wa-ṭahārat al-aḳdār; Nisbat al-sharīf; Rabīʿ al-ḳulūb fī dhikr manāḳib al-sayyid Shaykh Nūr Ḥusayn*, Cairo 1967; and for a collection of songs in praise of the local saints of Harar, see E. Wagner, in *ZDMG*, cxxv (1975), 28-65. (S. Reese)

ZIYĀRIDS, a petty dynasty of Djīlī/Daylamī stock which ruled in the provinces at the south-eastern corner of the Caspian Sea, Ṭabaristān and Gurgān, from 319/931 to *ca.* 483/*ca.* 1090; their rise to power forms part of the general upsurge of the Daylamī peoples during the 4th/10th and early 5th/11th centuries [see DAYLAM]. In the earlier, more vital half of the dynasty's existence, members of the family were at times able to pursue independent policies, but at others, they had to acknowledge the Sāmānids [*q.v.*], and sometimes the Būyids [see BUWAYHIDS], as their suzerains; and after *ca.* 400/1011-12 they became vassals of the Ghaznawids for some 25 years and then of the Saldjūḳs. Unlike some others of the Daylamī princes of northern Persia who had inclinations towards Shīʿism, the Ziyārids were Sunnīs.

The founder of the line, Mardāwīdj b. Ziyār, claimed descent from the royal house of Gīlān. He rose to power as a mercenary commander within the vacuum of authority in northwestern Persia after the decline of direct caliphal control there, and by 322/934, shortly before his assassination, was master of Djibāl and even of Ahwāz. For details of his career, see MARDĀWĪDJ.

His brother and lieutenant, Wushmgīr, succeeded him in 323/935, and at the outset was able to hold on to Mardāwīdj's conquests in northern Persia. But after *ca.* 328/940 Ziyārid authority there was challenged by the rival Daylamī power of the Būyids, and Wushmgīr could only save his position by allying with the Sāmānids, who had ambitions of extending their control over Rayy and northern Persia; even so, he lost Ṭabaristān and Gurgān to the Būyid Rukn al-Dawla on two or three occasions. For details, see WUSHMGĪR.

When Wushmgīr died in 357/967, his eldest son Bīsutūn claimed the Ziyārid succession, but this was disputed by his younger brother Ḳābūs, who secured

Genealogy of the Ziyārid dynasty

Ziyār

Mardāwīdj (319-23/931-5)

Ẓahīr al-Dawla Wushmgīr (323-57/935-67)

Ẓahīr al-Dawla Bīsutūn (357-67/967-78)

Shams al-Maʿālī Ḳābūs (367-71/978-81, 388-402/998-1012)

Falak al-Maʿālī Manūčihr (402-20/1012-29)

Dārā

Iskandar

Anūshirwān (420-?441/1029-?1049-50)

ʿUnṣur al-Maʿālī Kay Kāwūs (441-*ca.* 480/1049-*ca.* 1087)

Gīlān Shāh (*ca.* 480-*ca.* 483/*ca.* 1087-*ca.* 1090)

the support of the Sāmānids. After a struggle, Bīsutūn gained control of Ṭabaristān and Gurgān through an alliance with the Būyids, marrying a daughter of ʿAḍud al-Dawla b. Rukn al-Dawla [*q.v.*]. On Bīsutūn's death in 367/978, Ḳābūs managed, with Būyid help, to set aside Bīsutūn's minor son and succeeded in the Ziyārid capital Gurgān. But after 369/970 Ḳābūs's relations with his protectors soured. He was ejected by a Būyid army from his principality, which was then placed under direct Būyid rule for seventeen years, whilst Ḳābūs remained an exile in Sāmānid Khurāsān. Only in 388/998 was he able to return, establishing good relations with the successor to the Sāmānids in Khurāsān, Maḥmūd of Ghazna, but ruling as an independent sovereign. For details, see ḲĀBŪS B. WUSHMAGĪR.

Ḳābūs's tyranny led to his downfall and replacement by his son Manūčihr in 402/1012, with his death in the following year. For the remaining eighty years or so of the Ziyārid dynasty's existence, the historical sources become much more sparse and then almost non-existent, and Ziyārid coins disappear after Manūčihr, so that much less is known about the later than the earlier Ziyārids. None of the later rulers reached the calibre of earlier ones like, say, Wushmgīr or Ḳābūs. Hence the dynasty lost much of its power and influence, even within the Caspian region, and never again played any role outside it. Manūčihr ruled as a tributary of Maḥmūd of Ghazna and married a Ghaznawid princess, but this did not preserve his lands from threatened ravaging by the Ghaznawid army in 419/1028 and he had to buy the troops off.

Manūčihr's young son Anūshirwān was in 420/1029 confirmed by Maḥmūd as his dead father's successor, with the requirement of continued tribute, but from 423/1032 till 431/1040 authority within the Ziyārid lands was usurped by a maternal relative of Anūshirwān's, Abū Kālīdjār b. Wayhān. Non-payment of tribute provoked a fresh Ghaznawid invasion of Gurgān and Ṭabaristān in 426/1035 until Abū Kālīdjār agreed to resume tribute to Sultan Masʿūd. Subsequently, Anūshirwān seems to have regained control in the state, but in 433/1041-2—Ghaznawid power having by now receded from Khurāsān—the Ziyārid territories were invaded by the forces of the Saldjūḳ Ṭoghrïl Beg, and the Ziyārids became tributaries of the Great Saldjūḳs.

The Ziyārids now enter their obscurest period. Anūshirwān possibly died in 441/1049-50. Yāḳūt alone mentions a certain Ḥassān as succeeding him, but this man's existence is otherwise unconfirmed. The last Ziyārids for whom we have firm information are Kay Kāwūs b. Iskandar b. Ḳābūs, the famed author of the *Ḳābūs-nāma*, named after his grandfather, who died *ca.* 480/*ca.* 1087 [see KAY KĀʾŪS], and his shadowy son Gīlān Shāh. The latter's end is wholly unknown, but he may have been overthrown by the Nizārī Ismāʿīlīs of the Elburz region, with a consequent end to the dynasty *ca.* 483/*ca.* 1090.

Bibliography: 1. Sources. For the earlier Ziyārids, these are the general chronicles for the history of northern Persia, including Masʿūdī, *Murūdj*, Miskawayh and Ibn al-Athīr, and local Caspian historians like Ibn Isfandiyār and Ẓahīr al-Dīn Marʿashī, whilst for the 5th/11th century, such early Ghaznawid sources as Gardīzī and Bayhaḳī become important.

2. Studies. The older ones by Cl. Huart, *Les Ziyârides*, in *Mém. AIBL*, xlii (1922), 357-436; E. Denison Ross, *On three Muhammadan dynasties in northern Persia in the tenth and eleventh centuries*, in *Asia Major*, ii (1925), 209-11, 221; H.L. Rabino, *L'histoire du Mâzandarân*, in *JA*, ccxxxiv (1943-5), 229-33, are now inadequate. See the specific articles on members of the dynasty mentioned above and their *Bibls.*; W. Madelung, in *Camb. hist. of Iran*, iv, 212-16; and for the later period, C.E. Bosworth, *On the chronology of the later Ziyārids in Gurgān and Ṭabaristān*, in *Isl.*, xl (1964), 25-34. For coins, see G.C. Miles, *The coinage of the Ziyārid dynasty in Gurgān and Ṭabaristān*, ANS, *Museum Notes*, 18 (1972), 119-37. For chronology and titulature, see Bosworth, *The New Islamic dynasties*, Edinburgh 1996, 166-7 no. 81.

(C.E. BOSWORTH)

ZMĀLA denotes in origin a tribe of western Algeria; secondly, a mode of semi-nomadic social organisation, illustrated notably by the celebrated community gathered round the *amīr* ʿAbd al-Ḳādir [see ʿABD AL-ḲĀDIR B. MUḤYĪ ʾL-DĪN AL-ḤASANĪ] in the middle years of the 19th century; and thirdly, inspired by ʿAbd al-Ḳādir's system and by others, under the Gallicised form *Smala*, an institutionalised strategic system adopted during the time of the French presence in Algeria.

1. The tribe of the Zmāla in history.

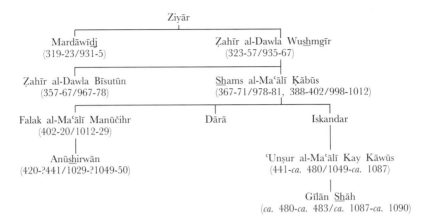

The Zmāla inhabited the lower northern slopes of the Tessāla, as well as the plain of Mlēta, traversed by the Wād Ghāsūl which separated their territory from that of the Dwāyer (Dawā'ir [*q.v.*]). It was on this plain that Dwāyer and Zmāla gathered together after the sowing season (November), before migrating with their herds to the Tessāla in March, then returning to the plain for the harvest. Their economy was of a semi-nomadic type. A tradition refers the origin of the Zmāla back to the arrival of the army of the Sultan of Morocco, Mawlāy Ismā'īl, in 1118/1707, but al-Mashrafī (12th/18th century) reckoned that Zmāla was in fact the name given to the Wnāzera, a segment of the Ulād 'Abd Allāh, of the confederation of Banū 'Āmir (Benī 'Āmer), an origin compatible with the subsequent absorption of various elements. After the capture of Oran [see WAHRĀN] in 1206/1792, Muḥammad b. 'Uthmān al-Akḥal al-Kabīr rewarded the Zmāla for their military assistance in the siege by distributing land to them and permitting their leading families to settle in the town.

In 1830, the Bey of Oran had four *aghas*. The *Agha* of the Zmāla was obliged to levy taxes on the *r'āya* (= *ra'āyā*) tribes in the territory called Ya'ḳūbiyyat al-Sharḳ, to the south-east of Mascara. In exchange for public order services, the Bey granted them the use of inalienable land (*arḍ sābga*) which could be withdrawn from them in case of disloyalty to the government.

After the fall of Algiers, Dwāyer and Zmāla, led by al-Māzarī, nephew of Muṣṭafā b. Ismā'īl, attempted reconciliation with the Sultan of Morocco. Another group, commanded by Muṣṭafā b. Ismā'īl, remained loyal to the Bey of Oran. At this time, French troops took possession of the city in a surprise attack. The locality was to remain completely isolated until the conclusion of the Desmichels Treaty on 26 February 1834. During this period, intervention by the Moroccans in Tlemcen culminated in the pillage of the city.

Rallying for the most part to 'Abd al-Ḳādir in 1833, the Zmāla participated until 1835 in his *makhzen*. Twice in 1833 a French column raided the encampments of the Zmāla at the foot of Djebel Ṭafrāwī in the mountains of the Tessāla. The Zmāla were obliged to promise to abandon 'Abd al-Ḳādir, to settle on the plain of Messergin, supply hostages and pay taxes to the French.

After the signing of the Desmichels Treaty, discord erupted between the Benī 'Āmer and the Dwāyer, who were joined by some of the Zmāla. After several battles, a segment of the latter took refuge near Mers el-Kebir. It was not until June 1251/1835 that a majority of the Dwāyer and of the Zmāla submitted definitively to French authority, signing the so-called "Fig-tree" Convention on 16 June 1835. Dwāyer and Zmāla recognised French sovereignty, accepted Muslim chieftains appointed by the Governor-General, paid an annual tribute and supplied armed contingents, guides and spies, in return for protection against attacks by neighbouring tribes, pay and provisions during campaigns, and the replacement of horses killed in action. The Zmāla returned to Oran in July 1835 with some of the Dwāyer, some of the Ghrāba and a number of black Africans, leading to the creation by the French in 1845 of an enclave known as the "Black Village".

At the time of the Mascara expedition (25 November-12 December 1251/1835) [see AL-MU'ASKAR] the Algerian camp was weakened by the defection of Muḥammad al-Māzarī, who joined the French forces at the head of a group of Dwāyer and of Zmāla. He was named *khalīfa* of the Bey of Mostaganem and *Agha* of the plain of Oran.

In March 1837 a fixed camp was established at Messergin to protect the tents of the Dwāyer and of the Zmāla. Furthermore, after the signing of the treaty of Tāfna (30 May 1837), the French element remained a minority, while more than a third of the Dwāyer and three-quarters of the Zmāla were still with 'Abd al-Ḳādir. In 1837, pay was allocated to these irregular *spahis*, generally superior to that offered by 'Abd al-Ḳādir, who sought to attract them to his side, along with the Ḳurghlān [see KUL-OGHLU], offering them employment, cattle and land. Their role was generally limited to the functions of couriers, transport, surveillance and public order, escorting and relaying of posts. Thus they provided reconnaissance for the flanks and the vanguard of the two divisions sent 18 May 1841 from Mostaganem against Tāgdemt. In September of the same year, their number rose to about a thousand.

The dispersion of the *zmāla* of 'Abd al-Ḳādir (see below, 2 (a)) took place on 16 May 1843, but the intensification of the anti-French struggle was marked in 1845 by the abandonment of Oran in one night by those of the Dwāyer and the Zmāla who had remained loyal, camping in the shelter of the French artillery.

Subsequently, the Zmāla saw their territories considerably reduced. Thus from 1846 onward, the lands of the Zmāla were included in the zone destined for colonisation, to the north of the Oran-Mascara road. Marshal Bugeaud opposed their "constriction", preferring to see them fragmented around Oran. The Zmāla were then progressively resettled in inhospitable and mountainous zones, while their population grew from 5,250 to 6,230 between 1845 and 1866. In 1867, they were divided into two principal groups: one on the southern slopes of Djebel Murdjādjo, of some 600 persons, the other on the border of the Sebkha.

Like the rest of the Algerian population, they were decimated by famines and epidemics. Their water-courses were diverted, which not only had the effect of ruining the Zmāla but also permitted seizure of the salt-pans of Arzew, vital for the economy of Oran.

Bibliography: 1. Arabic sources. 'Abd al-Ḳādir al-Mashrafī, *Bahdjat al-nāẓir fī akhbār al-dākhilīn taḥta wilāyat al-Aṣbāniyyīn bi-Wahrān min al-A'rāb ka-Banī 'Āmir*, ed. and tr. M. Bodin, *Notice historique sur les Arabes soumis aux Espagnols pendant leur occupation d'Oran*, in *RAfr.*, lxv (1924), 199, 212, 225, 243, and ed. Beirut n.d.; Ibn 'Ūda al-Māzarī, *Ṭulū' Sa'd al-Su'ūd fī akhbār madīnat Wahrān wa-makhzanihā al-usūd*, partial tr. M. Bodin, *La brève chronique du bey Hasan*, in *Bull. de la Société de Géographie d'Oran*, xliv (1924), 23-61.

2. War Ministry Archives. H 225, G. Tatareau, *Notice sur les tribus de la province d'Oran* (with map), Oran 1833; H 236, *Province d'Oran, tribus insurgées, restées fideles, tribus soumises (1845); arrêté portant organisation de la cavalerie indigène auxiliaire soldée en Algérie, sous la dénomination de Makhzen*, in *Le Moniteur Algérien*, no. 567, 30 December 1845, 1-2.

3. Military sources and accounts. L. Baudens, *Relation historique de l'expédition de Tagdempt*, in *Musée des Familles* (July 1841), 9-10, 20, 25; L. de Martimprey, *Mémoire sur l'état de la propriété territoriale dans les tribus*, in *Projets de colonisation pour les provinces d'Oran et de Constantine*, Paris 1847, 76; E.C. de Martimprey, *Souvenirs d'un officier d'état-major. Histoire de l'établissement de la domination française dans la province d'Oran, 1830-1847*, Paris 1886; E. du Martray, *En Algérie au temps d'Abd-el-Kader*, in *Carnets de la Sabretache*, xxix (1926), 398-9, 420, 460, 465, 467, 471, 480.

4. Studies. Ch. Cockenpot, *Le traité Desmichels*, Paris 1924; G. Yver, *Documents relatifs au traité de la Tafna (1837)*, Algiers 1924; art. SĪDĪ BU 'L-ʿABBĀS.

2. The mode of social organisation.

Popularised during the French invasion of Algeria under the form *smala*, the term denotes that which a person or tribe carries when in motion, i.e. all one's goods, with nothing left behind (*lā yukhalif min mālihi shay', LA, s.v. azmala*). The form given by Ibn Manẓūr, although it attests to an ancient use of the root in this sense, does not take into account a possible Berber origin. There is no reason not to envisage a hybrid. The extension of the term illustrates the fusion in operation between Berber and Arab tribes in the central Maghrib. Tribes of Arab origin moving through the Tell and the Sahara are sometimes called *zmēluya* Arabs and there exists an adjective of relation, *zmēlī*, formed on this root (e.g. among the Dwāyer).

A tribe, or a group of horsemen organised into a tribe, comes together and organises itself into a *zmāla* at a time of movement in an unsafe region or in a period of conflict. They are associated with a hostel or staging post (*ḳunāḳ, ḳnāḳ*) and placed under the authority of a holy person (*mrābeṭ = murābiṭ*) who lives in the encampment (*gaṭna*) and arbitrates cases in litigation. Responsible for the bivouac, especially from the point of view of security, he is exempt from tax. *Zmūl* horsemen patrol the roads and participate in the maintenance of order. They accompany the annual round of tax collection. Strategic roads, in particular, were dotted with these *zmāla* encampments. The horsemen were commanded by a *ḳayed ez-zmāla* endowed with a special bodyguard.

Such a type of "mobile capital" was necessary as a compromise method of gathering together the dispersed forces of Algeria to resist the French enemy. It also played a considerable role in the internal politics of the *amīr* ʿAbd al-Ḳādir.

(a) *The* zmāla *of ʿAbd al-Ḳādir*

The story of the *amīr*'s resistance to the French is told in the article ʿABD AL-ḲĀDIR B. MUḤYĪ 'L-DĪN, and only the aspects relating to his *zmāla* will be addressed in the present article.

From 1839 onwards, the *amīr* had instructed his *khalīfa*s and all the dignitaries of Mascara and of Tlemcen to leave the town and live in tents in the *zmāla*. Combatants originating from all the regions of the former Regency and influential persons from the whole of Orania, including Algerians, joined the *zmāla* on an individual basis, as did Tunisians and especially Moroccans. The *amīr* used his troops and his horses in the traditional harassment tactic of *karr wa-farr* (charge and retreat). As the French struggled to cope with an elusive enemy, warfare became total from 1841 onward.

Numerous descriptions make it possible to envisage the structure and organisation of the *zmāla* at the zenith of ʿAbd al-Ḳādir's powers. His personal tent was at the centre of his own *dawwār*, backing on one side against that of Lālla Zohra, his mother (d. 1279/1861), one of the few women venerated for her piety (*mrābṭa = murābiṭa*), and on the other that of his wife Khayra, his sister Khadīdja and his children. Adjacent to that of the *amīr* was the tent of the guests. On account of its size, the *zmāla* was a mobile city, with composition varying according to the regions traversed. This assemblage of soldiers and artisans principally comprised trades associated with the profession of arms: armourer (*shāḳmakdjī*), maker of rifle butts (*ḳondāḳdjī*), cutler (*bučāḳdjī*), blacksmith (*ḥaddād*), tailor (*khayyāṭ, ṭārzī*), saddler (*sarrādj*, particularly important), harness-maker (*brādʿī*), doctor and surgeon (*ṭabīb, djarrāḥ*), veterinarian (*ṭabīb al-ʿawd*), barbers (*berber*) and café proprietors (*ʿaskarī ḳahwādjī*).

At the time of its dispersal on 16 May 1843, near the source of the Wād Ṭāgīn, the population of the *zmāla* was estimated at between 25,000 and 60,000 persons, comprising more than 350 douars defended by 5,000 combatants (including 500 regular infantrymen and 2,000 horsemen). The nucleus extended over more than two kilometres.

A smaller structure, called *dāyra* (= *dā'ira*), was established in Morocco at the end of 1843 and served as a base for the *amīr*, despite attacks by Moroccan tribesmen and troops encouraged by France, especially after the Treaty of Tangier, completed by the Lālla Maghniyya Convention (10 September 1844 and 18 March 1845). The *dāyra* succeeded in resisting attacks until its surrender on 23 December 1847.

There exists a place called Zmāla (formerly Saint-Paul farm) in Kashrū, some 20 km to the south-east of Mascara, where ʿAbd al-Ḳādir would often spend time. Similarly, in 1840-1 there was a *zmāla* near Tāgdemt, an encampment consisting only, in the absence of the *amīr*, of a few tents pitched among the thorn bushes, this being the permanent residence of his mother, his wife and his servants.

Bibliography: 1. Arabic sources. Muḥammad b. ʿAbd al-Ḳādir al-Djazā'irī, *Tuḥfat al-zā'ir fī ta'rīkh al-Djazā'ir wa 'l-amīr ʿAbd al-Ḳādir*, Beirut 1384/1964.

2. Military sources and accounts. T.R. Bugeaud de la Piconnerie, *Mémoire ... sur la guerre dans la province d'Oran ...*, Oran 1836: Lt. Col. Daumas, *Composition et installation de la Zemala quand le terrain lui permettait de camper d'après la formation adoptée par l'émir Abd el Kader*, survey published in *Le Moniteur Algérien*, 548 (25 June 1843) and repr. Châlon-sur-Saône 1843; C. von Decker, *Algerien und die dortige Kriegführung*, Berlin 1844, partial tr. Thonissen, *Biographie d'Abd-el-Kader ...*, Anvers 1846. E. du Martray, *En Algérie au temps d'Abd el-Kader*, in *Carnets de la Sabretache*, xxix (1926), 390-428, 453-86.

3. Studies. A. Berbrugger, *Biographie d'Abd-el-Kader*, in *Le Moniteur Algerien*, 204 (6 November 1835), 3-4; idem, *Voyage au camp d'Abd-el-Kader*, in *Revue des Deux Mondes*, xv (August 1838), 455-7, and repr. Toulon 1839; M.A. de France, *Les prisonniers d'Abd-al-Kader*, Paris 1837, tr. Lady Duff Gordon, *The Prisoners of Abd el-Kader*, in *The French in Algiers*, ii, New York 1845; anon., *Renseignements historiques sur la zemala de l'émir Abd-el-Kader*, in *Le Moniteur Algérien*, 551 (10 July 1843), 2-3, 552 (15 July), 554 (25 July), 555 (29 July), 557 (10 August), 2, and repr. Paris 1843, 1845; L. Roches, *Trente-deux ans à travers l'Islam (1832-1864), l'Algérie—Abd-el-Kader*, Paris 1884-5; C. Schefer, *La "conquête totale" de l'Algérie (1839-1843). Valée, Bugeaud et Soult*, in *Revue d'Histoire des Colonies Françaises*, iv (1916), 51-3; M. Ben Cheneb, *Mots turcs et persans conservés dans le parler algérien*, Algiers 1922; E. Dermenghem, *Les souvenirs de l'émir Abdelkader dans la region de Mascara*, in *Documents algériens, série culturelle*, xxxix (1949) and *BEA*, ix (1949), 147-9; P. Fournier, *L'Etat d'Abd-el-Kader*, in *Revue d'Histoire Moderne et Contemporaine*, xiv (April-June 1967), 123-57; M. Bouayed, *Un texte précieux de l'émir Abdelkader sur l'organisation de l'Etat algérien de 1832 à 1847*, in *Promesses*, viii (1970), 40, 43-4; X. Yacono, *Les prisonniers de la smala d'Abd-el-Kader*, in *ROMM*, xv-xvi (1973), 415-34; R. Danziger, *Abd al-Qadir and the Algerians. Resistance to the French and internal consolidation*, New York and London 1977; arts. SĪDĪ BU 'L-ʿABBĀS; TANAS.

3. In the military and administrative history of French Algeria.

The concept is inseparable from French colonial strategy in Algeria, and its use involved essentially smalas of spahis and smalas of notables. From the outset of the war of conquest in Algeria of 1830, France adopted a policy of using Muslim troops raised from the country, notably the spahis, which it had employed in India during the previous century (Ar. form *ṣbāyḥī*, in Fr. *cipaye*, in Eng. *sepoy*; see SIPĀHĪ. 2 and 3). In face of the failure of the formation of regular units of zouaves and spahis recruited from the Muslims, often arising out of the infantry and cavalry contingents of the Regency, in practice not very active, inclined to rebelliousness and desertion, and expensive, the French Army took into its service the tribes of the old *ma<u>kh</u>zan* [*q.v.*] who lived in *zmāla*s, encampments with their families and herds which they left behind when called to service (see above, 2). These goums of irregular spahis (*m<u>kh</u>āzniyya*) were formed because of the insufficiency in numbers of the regular cavalry (chasseurs, hussars, chasseurs d'Afrique and regular spahis) and because of the unsuitability of this last group for reconnaissance and espionage missions and for rapid action amidst Muslim populations. This model was then applied to the regular spahis in 1834.

In the early stages of the French conquest, the function of the *a<u>gh</u>a* (who headed a *zmāla*) was maintained in order to retain the appearance of a Muslim administration over the subject people. The *a<u>gh</u>a* was specifically responsible for police functions and the collection of taxes for the occupying power, and had no role at all in the defence of the Muslim subjects. These Muslim officials were easily dismissed in case of "softness". Their jobs were progressively suppressed with the progress of colonisation, though some were kept in a purely honorific role. This was the case with the *a<u>gh</u>a* Sī Ḥamza b. Abū Bakr (b. 1859), the religious head of the Ulād Sīdī <u>Sh</u>ay<u>kh</u> who at the beginning of the 20th century exercised his authority over thirteen tribes and had at his disposal a *ma<u>kh</u>zan* and a smala; he was responsible for the docility of the Muslims of the district of Aflu, which made up, with Tiaret, the indigenous commune of Tiaret-Aflou formed in 1874, as well as for the payment of levies and taxes as representative of the captain, who was head of the Arab bureau. He received a substantial salary in addition to a share of the "Arab levy" deducted from that granted to the caïds under his orders.

Three periods can be distinguished: (1) creation of the institution for serving local needs; (2) its organisation at the level of the whole country; and (3) the failure and abandonment of the system. The installation of smalas arose in the first place as a result of local initiatives, notably by the Arab bureaux, services that were essentially charged with the transmission of orders to the Muslims and their implementation, a watch over markets and the compiling of reports of all kinds about the situation of the Muslim population (Decree of 1 February 1844, *Le Moniteur Algérien*, 593, of 10 February 1844, 1-2), and which participated in expeditions against these last. In this way was disguised an information service in the heart of the tribes in direct relation with the military command of subdivisions and divisions, thereby facilitating police and repressive duties, of which the spahis were to become the chief instrument. This took place parallel to the formation of three regiments of spahis in 1841 (one per province), into which were incorporated the effective manpower of the "gendarmes maures" when these last were dissolved.

Towards the end of 1844, a smala was created at 2.5 km/1.5 miles south of Orléansville or al-Aṣnām, meant in the first place for the spahis of the Arab bureau (*m<u>kh</u>āzniyya*), and situated close to the "penitentiary for the local population" of Lālla ʿŪda, for which it furnished Muslim prisoners. At the same time, a smala of spahis was formed a little to the west, on a site of 500 ha (1844). Finally, to strengthen the work of pacification of the Muslim population and to consolidate the north-south axis from Ténès to Orléansville, Lapasset created at the end of 1844 or beginning of 1845 a smala for the goum of the *m<u>kh</u>āzniyya* of Ténès, made up of 20 paid cavalrymen, whose chief was, however, killed in 1845. This smala was destroyed by the insurgents of Bū Maʿza in November 1845 at the time when old Ténès was attacked, and replaced in early 1846 by a centre called Smala on the plateau of the Ulād Hennī, which dominates the town of Ténès.

The spahis were formed into three regiments (of Algiers, Oran and Constantine, respectively) on 21 July 1845. This led to the creation of fixed camps where the cavalrymen making up the smala could live with their families and herds in a dual traditional way of life and a military one. Each regiment had the same structure: a regimental depôt with the general staff, and six squadrons spread over the province. Only a few places were reserved for officers, with a local rank only, from the Muslims recruited to form the troops. The red and blue uniform was inspired by local traditions, with a clear Turkish influence: a short tunic, *d<u>j</u>ābādōlī*, worn over a waistcoat; breeches ending below the knee, *serwāl*; a white *ḥāyk* worn over the shoulders and kept in place by a thick rope of camel's hair, *brīma*; and above this, a white *barnūs* covered with a red one. The definitive administrative order setting up these smalas (3 August 1850) was followed by a report on the smalas of the three regiments of spahis corresponding each one to a province.

If the formation of a *bur<u>d</u>j* allowed the families of the spahis a place of shelter in the event of a rebellion, these last were also hostages for the continued faithful allegiance of the cavalrymen when they went out on an expedition. Since it also made up an agricultural colony, a model farm for the surrounding populations, the smala eventually facilitated the introduction of new agricultural methods for the Muslim population and increased the rentable value of their cultivated land, whose industrial and commercial outlets were all in the hands of Europeans. It was above all a means to facilitate the progress of colonisation by the Muslims themselves by means of these provisional establishments, thus veiling European colonisation. The defence of the frontiers, often connected with the problems of emigration by tribes driven away by misery and various effects of the state of war against the French presence (insecurity, brigandage, etc.), also allowed a transfer of the cost of public security to the indigenous population. But the main and true aim was to recruit troops from the best Muslim cavalrymen and to tempt them with the best horses of the land, notably those of Orania, the most esteemed under the Regency, and the cheaper ones.

The use of spahis within a smala replaced the former functions of the *ma<u>kh</u>zan* of the Regency, and was to attract the sons of leading "tents" and great families (*ulād <u>kh</u>ayma kbīra* or *bayt kbīra*) which military defeat would have left unemployed, and it was also a means of utilising and remodelling the remnants of the Algerian aristocracy.

A check to this plan arose from the fact that the smalas of spahis were only recruited from the poorer rural population, who rarely had even a poor horse (*kaydār* "nag"). These men had to be equipped from top to toe, but often sold their equipment after being recruited; they were nothing but a "motley band of the lowest classes, soldiers of fortune who were dying of hunger" (Lt.-Gen. Le Pays de Bourjolly), despised by the Muslim population but nevertheless useful because of their roles as scouts and spies (*shawwāf*).

Nor did the smalas ever fulfil their agricultural role, since they only received the lands left over from colonisation and little suitable for agriculture. The precariousness of occupation of the sites allotted to the smalas is seen in the frequent displacements which took them away from urban agglomerations in a southwards direction into the tribal heartlands. These latter tribes reacted strongly, seeing these Muslim colonists as intruders on lands taken from them by force, who helped to levy taxes and impose intolerable financial demands and were the instruments of fierce repression in times of rebellion. Moreover, ruined by the occupiers, they cared little about increasing yields from ungrateful lands, often suffered misery and want and were thus forced into emigration. Hence far from being an instrument of improvement for surrounding populations, the smala was often a witness to, and at times an active agent of, the pauperisation or disappearance of those populations (a rallying-point for beggars succeeded the smala of Wād Slī). The spahis were recruited from a population often little interested in the agricultural way of life, who preferred to retain their own family plots and who rarely occupied the lands entrusted to them. In these last cases, the spahi would leave the land to be cultivated by *khmāmsa* (agricultural workers remunerated by receiving a fifth of the crop), who, having only an annual contract, were little interested in improving the traditional methods of cultivation.

In January 1871, mutinies by the smalas of Madjbar, Bū Ḥdjar, al-Ṭarf, and above all, ʿAyn Gaṭṭar, linked with the rebellion of the Ḥnēnsha, when it was announced that they were to be sent to France after the defeat of 1870, provoked a fresh repression of the Muslim population. The flight of spahis of the smala of ʿAyn Gaṭṭar with their families and herds to Tunisia sounded the knell of French projects to develop docile troops on the model of the smalas. An opinion which became more and more widespread opposed this return of lands to Muslims and advocated their opening to colonisation in order to increase their rentability, which would also allow the full imposition of taxes from which the lands had hitherto been exempt. By 1914, despite their role as foci for recruitment, the sixteen smalas which the Second Empire had bequeathed to the Third Republic had all been suppressed, except for that of Sīdī Mdjāhed in the Tāfna region, near the Moroccan frontier, to which should be added that of al-Uṭayya near Biskra, set up in 1875. This last was disbanded in 1919, and the former soon after 1930, signifying the final defeat, in face of a civilian colonisation now all-powerful, of an adaptation of Bugeaud's model of the soldier-worker, a Muslim soldier-colonist and worker in the service of France.

Bibliography: 1. War Ministry Archives, Paris. General Staff: H 226, *Règlement sur la constitution, le régime, l'administration et la comptabilité des smalas des régiments de spahis*, 1862; H 228, *Spahis, 1834-1836;* H 230 bis., *Circulaire constitutive des smalas, 3 août 1850; Rapport sur les smalas des trois régiments de spahis; Organisation des smalas, 1853-1866.*

2. Military sources and accounts. Anon., *Le général Lapasset, 1817-1864*, Paris 1898, i, 23, 26, 39-40, 111, 291; T.R. Bugeaud de la Piconnerie, *De l'établissement des troupes à cheval dans des grandes fermes*, Paris 1840, 8-9; J.A. Le Pays du Bourjolly, *Projets sur l'Algérie*, Paris 1847, 57-9.

3. Studies. F. Pharaon, *Spahis, turcos et goumiers*, Paris 1864, 1-7, 9, 15, 27, 30-1, 58, 228-9, 245; C. Rousset, *L'Algérie de 1830 à 1840*, Paris 1887, 366-7; *Journal officiel*, Documents parlementaires, 6 février 1895, Annexe 906, séance du 28 juillet 1894, XI, *Ressources territoriales à affecter à la colonisation . . .*, 54, 57-8; S. Fabre, *Monographie de la commune indigène de Tiaret-Aflou*, in *Bull. trimestriel de la Soc. de géogr. et d'archéol. d'Oran*, xxii/92 (1902), 295-6, 303; F. Mougenot, *Les smalas de l'est*, in *Bull. de la Soc. de géogr. d'Alger et de l'Afrique du Nord*, viii (1903), 97-121; R. Tinthoin, *Colonisation et évolution des genres de vie dans la région ouest d'Oran de 1830 à 1885*, Oran 1947, 38-41, 330-3; anon., *Les spahis algériens*, in *Documents algériens*, xii (1953), 207-14; X. Yacono, *Les bureaux arabes et l'évolution des genres de vie indigènes dans l'ouest du Tell algérois (Dahra, Chélif, Ouarsenis, Sersou)*, Paris 1953, 242-6; idem, *La colonisation des plaines de Chélif (de Lavigerie au confluent de la Mina)*, Algiers 1955-6, i, 285, 287, ii, 122, 166-8; A. Rey-Goldzeiguer, *Le royaume arabe. La politique algérienne de Napoléon III, 1861-1870*, Algiers 1977, 129-30, 132, 261, 352, 378.

(H. Bencheneb, shortened by the Editors)

ZONGULDAK, a port on the Black Sea coast of Turkey (lat. 41° 26' N., long. 31° 47' E.), and the chef-lieu of an *il* or province of the same name.

The town only emerged in the second half of the 19th century when coal was found in the Zonguldak-Kozlu-Ereğli area, at a convenient distance from the Black Sea (see the art. s.v. in *Yurt Ansiklopedisi, Türkiye il-il, dünü, bugünü, yarını*, x, Istanbul 1982-4). When the Ottoman navy was about to change over to steamships, a local man named Uzun Meḥmed reportedly presented Sultan Maḥmūd II with the first sacks of Zonguldak coal, and actual exploitation began in 1848 (Erol Kahveci, *The miners of Zonguldak*, in idem *et alii* (eds.), *Work and occupation in modern Turkey*, London 1996, 173-200). The mining area was linked to a pious foundation, providing revenues for the Holy Cities of Mecca and Medina (Ahmet Naim, *Zonguldak kömür havzası*, Istanbul 1934). However, between 1848 and 1865, the Ottoman authority officially in charge of the enterprise was the Khazīne-i Khāṣṣa, which transferred the actual running of the mines to English contractors. Until 1882, the sale of Ereğli-Zonguldak coal in the open market was not permitted. As a town, Zonguldak developed late; V. Cuinet records that, while *ca.* 1890 coal mining was already rather important, the only "habitation passable du lieu" was the structure housing the offices of local government (*La Turquie d'Asie*, iv, Paris 1894, 498). The population of the town in 1997 was 107,176, and that of the *il*, 612,722.

A high accident rate, low levels of production and the obligations of the Ottoman State to the Dette Ottomane after the 1875 state bankruptcy, from 1891 onwards obliged the government to resort to French investors and foreign skilled labour, and in 1896 a newly-formed company received a fifty-year concession for the exploitation of the mines and the construction of railways. Major shareholders were French, including the Banque Ottomane, but there were also Ottoman investors. Increasing involvement by Ottoman subjects, including high-level officials, prompted the late Ḥamīdian government to attempt in vain to improve the mines. In the Ottoman parliament convened after the reinstatement of the constitution, there were protests against the high transportation fees charged by the company, which apparently aimed at the ruin of its Ottoman competitors (1909) (see D. Quataert, *Social disintegration and popular resistance in the Ottoman empire, 1881-1908. Reactions to European economic penetration*, New York 1983, 41-70). It was however only in 1937 that the government of the Republic bought back the mines, with a view toward securing a national energy supply in case of war, and in 1940 the entire mining area was nationalised.

Mine labourers. Throughout the 19th century, as in earlier periods, mining was not a full-time activity but was practiced by peasants recruited for labour in the mines on a part-time basis (Suraiya Faroqhi, *Towns and townsmen of Ottoman Anatolia. Trade, crafts, and food production in an urban setting 1520-1650*, Cambridge 1984, 176-7). A law of 1867 specified that all mineworkers, except for the engineers and foremen, had to be Ottoman subjects. This same law also introduced the obligation of villagers to work in the mines; this forced labour continued until 1921. Even today, miners are largely local men, and rotational labour by part-time peasants continues, especially among hewers. However, foreign labourers, including Montenegrins, Croatians and Hungarians, as well as other qualified workers and technicians, were also imported.

Considerable labour unrest first occurred in 1908, when wage demands, fear of mechanisation and a reaction against "outside" miners brought in from Sivas, triggered a wave of strikes; Ottoman local authorities tended to support the strikers against the foreign company. In 1940 obligatory service in the mines was reintroduced, and only abolished in 1948. From 1937 and into the 1940s, prison labour was employed on a considerable scale (Kahveci, *The miners*, 183-200). Private records and memoirs document the unsanitary conditions of life in the mines, and the high incidence of diseases such as tuberculosis, typhus and intestinal ailments. Only from the 1960s onwards did the mines become a focus of organised trade union activity, with a major strike in 1965. Large-scale demonstrations sparked by a long-term decline in real wages, occurred in the early 1990s as well (see on these topics, Mübeccel Kiray, *Ereğli, ağir sanayiden önce bir sahil kasabası*, Ankara 1964; D.A. Roy, *The Zonguldak strike. A case study of industrial conflict in a developing society*, in *MES*, xii [1974], 147-85; Sina Çıladır, *Zonguldak havzasında işçi hareketlerini tarihi, 1848-1940*, Ankara 1977; T. Nichols and Erol Kahveci, *The condition of mine labour in Turkey. Injuries to miners in Zonguldak, 1942-1990*, in *MES*, xxxi [1995], 198-227; Quataert and Nadir Özbek, *The Ereğli-Zonguldak coal mines. A catalog of archival documents*, in *The Turkish Studies Assoc. Bull.*, xxiii [1999], 55-67; Quataert, *Zonguldak maden işçilerinin hayatı, 1870-1920 başlangıç niteliğinde bazı gözlemler*, in *Toplum ve Bilim*, lxxxiii [1999-2000], 80-90). After employing up to 10,000 people in 1914, and 50,000 at the peak of mining activity, the coal mines are today in crisis and scheduled for privatisation.

Fixed capital and output. Zonguldak until late into the republican period had few links to the Anatolian interior, and handled all its trade by sea. The port was constructed after 1896 by the French mining company. Railways linking the different mines to the port also were constructed, but by the beginning of the First World War, the tunnels necessary for connecting the more remote mines to the port had not as yet been dug. Coal production in the early 20th century reached 500,000 tons per year, the foreign company's share amounting to over 75%. By the terms of their contracts, all mining entrepreneurs had to offer 60% of the coal extracted to the government at prices determined by the latter. Apart from the needs of the Navy, Izmir enterprises and households also came to depend on Zonguldak coal, and there were some exports to Greece and Rumania. Yet until 1913 the foreign company was not very profitable, in part because coal seams had been poorly chosen, and management problems were rife. But impediments placed in the company's way by a government hostile to foreign control of a crucial energy source equally limited profitability.

A study published in 1995 emphasised that low investment in the mines has remained typical of the republican period as well, resulting in the widespread use of out-of-date equipment. Much of the capital invested has been derived from international sources, down to 1965, particularly funds made available under Marshall Plan auspices, more recently from the World Bank. Today, Zonguldak coal has increasingly to compete in the Turkish market against the imported item.

Other industrial towns. It is one of the peculiarities of Zonguldak province that, apart from the central city, we find two major rival towns. Karabük is of even more recent origin than Zonguldak itself, having been founded in 1939. Partly for military reasons, the steelworks established in this locality, whose construction formed a major item in the Five-Year-Plan of 1932, were built at a considerable distance from the coast, with coal brought in from Zonguldak and raw iron from distant Divriği. The other important town in the province of Zonguldak is Ereğli (Bendereğli, Karadeniz Ereğlisi), which by contrast was a small but active port as early as the 10th/16th century (Faroqhi, *op. cit.*, 110-13). Up to the 1950s, Ereğli's harbour was only suitable for small craft, and the transportation of Zonguldak coal to steamships constituted an important activity, but since 1960, Ereğli has also become the site of a large steelworks, and a modern harbour has been built.

Bibliography: Given in the article.

(Suraiya Faroqhi)

ZSITVATOROK, the name of a peace-treaty signed by the Ottomans and the Habsburgs in 1606, and so-called ever since the negotiations leading to it started on boats at the confluence of the rivers Zsitva and Danube (the literal meaning of the word being "Zsitva mouth").

The peace treaty put an end to the so-called "Long" or "Fifteen Years' War", which was begun in 1593 and renewed each year, bringing smaller or bigger successes to both sides without a final victory. The revolt led by István Bocskai against the Habsburgs helped the Ottomans to a certain extent to strengthen their sometimes rather weak positions.

First, Bocskai and the Habsburgs came to an agreement in Vienna on 9 February 1606. Three-party talks started on 29 October, when the Emperor Rudolph II was represented by Ernst Molart, the Sultan Aḥmed I by ʿAlī, the *beglerbegi* of Buda, and Bocskai by Baron István Illésházy. The treaty, to be valid for 20 years, was signed on 11 November, amended in March 1608 at (Érsek-) Újvár (Nové Zámky), and ratified by the sultan—after long consideration—on 11 October 1608.

The peace treaty stipulated, among other things,

the following: (a) it was forbidden to attack castles and take prisoners; (b) earlier captives were to be freed; (c) the Habsburg Emperor was to hand over 200,000 florins as a once-and-for-all payment; (d) castles taken in the county of Nógrád were not to be returned to the Ottomans, but Esztergom with its vicinity remained in their hands, while the future of Kanizsa and its surroundings was to be decided later; and (e) taxes were to be collected locally and handed over by village mayors.

Bibliography: G. Bayerle, *The compromise at Zsitvatorok*, in *Archivum Ottomanicum*, vi (1980), 5-53; K. Nehring, *Der Friede von Zsitvatorok*, in idem, *Adam Freiherrn zu Herbersteins Gesandtschaftsreise nach Konstantinopel* (Südosteuropäische Arbeiten 78), Munich 1983, 15-67. (G. Dávid)

ZUʿʿĀR (A., sing. *zāʿir*), lit. "rowdy, ill-behaved lads", a term used notably in the Egyptian and Syrian urban milieux during the Mamlūk and Ottoman periods, and also with the sense of "gypsies", but, rather, in an extra-urban milieu. At the present time, we have in Lebanon and Palestine *azʿar* (pl. *zuʿrān*) "vagabond, brigand". Other forms that are found include *zuʿrūr* and *zaʿir*. The Arabic dictionaries place the term under the verb *zaʿara* "to copulate, have sexual intercourse". In fact, it should be connected instead with *dhāʿir* (pl. *dhuʿʿār*) "rascal, scoundrel", itself connected with the verb *dhaʿara* "to frighten, instil fear", apparently a variant or by-form of *dāʿir* (pl. *duʿʿār*) "dirty, debauched, rotten, evil, licentious", verb *daʿara* "to smoke a great deal like green or rotten wood which refuses to burn", cf. *bayt al-diʿāra* "brothel", *daʿira* "to be immoral".

The *zuʿʿār* are often connected with the mystical *ṭuruḳ* (see E. Geoffroy, *Le soufisme en Égypte et en Syrie sous les derniers Mamelouks et les premiers Ottomans*, Damascus 1995, index s.v. *zurʿān*; A. Raymond, *Égyptiens et Français au Caire 1798-1901*, Cairo 1998, 52-9).

Words for "rascals, scoundrels" are very numerous in both the spoken and written forms of Arabic, mediaeval and modern: *al-ʿāmma* "the plebs"; *awbāsh al-nās* "the scum of the people"; *al-ʿayyārūn* [see ʿAYYĀR] "brave, swaggering youths"; *ahl al-sharr* "evildoers"; *al-djuʿaydī* "frightful, evil ones"; *djuʿaydiyya* "the populace"; *al-ghammāzūn* "those who screw up their eyes, intriguers"; *al-ghawghāʾ* "those who swarm like tiny beasts"; *ḥamalat al-silāḥ* "civilians bearing arms"; *al-ḥarāmiyya* "bastards", currently "highway bandits"; *al-ḥarāfīsh* [see ḤARFŪSH] "troubled, agitated populace" (this is sometimes written *al-kharāfīsh*, cf. a similar verb *kharbasha* "to botch something, do untidy work"); *iḥranshafa* "to prepare to fight (of a cock), to begin to pay a forfeit (of a man)"; *al-kudya* "begging", *ahl al-kudya* "vagabonds"; *man lā yamliku ḳūt laylatihi* "a person who does not possess enough to eat for a single night of his existence"; *man lā yūdjadu wa-lā yuʿrafu idhā ṭuliba* "someone who cannot be found and cannot be recognised when one looks for him"; *al-mufsadūn wa 'l-mufsidūn* "those who are corrupted and those who corrupt"; *al-murdjifūn* "agitators"; *al-mushākilūn* "footpads, highwaymen"; *al-nuhabāʾ* "those who pillage"; *al-raʿāʿ* "the mob, thieves"; *al-ramadiyya* "tramps, vagabonds"; *al-ṣaʿālīk* [see ṢUʿLŪK] "brigands, robbers"; *al-shuṭṭār* "lively, active ones"; *al-suʿāt* "the dregs of the people"; *al-sūḳa*, lit. "those led to pasture", "the flock under the ruling power", and pejoratively, "canaille"; *al-sukkāṭ* "rascals"; *al-ṭummāʿ* "those who are avid, covetous"; *yaʾkhudhūn al-khifāra* "those who run a protection racket"; *yaṭlubūn al-bāṭil wa 'l-fasād* "those who cultivate fraud and corruption (see the references to texts in Th. Bianquis, *Damas et la Syrie sous la domination fāṭimide*, i, Damascus 1989, 671 n. 1).

In effect, marginal persons were numerous in mediaeval Arab society. They involved persons who had broken with traditional family solidarity, such as villagers who had to leave their holdings which were too small to support all the young adults of the kin group and went to the towns to seek a living; former Bedouin who had been obliged to throw off tribal links after the murder of a kinsman; Kurdish bandits (*al-akrād*) driven from their mountains by hunger; and soldiers abandoned by their masters, as was often the case with black slaves purchased cheaply to act as a largely non-specialised infantry corps and then left without food or upkeep when no longer needed on the battlefield. Others fell outside such solidarity groups from birth, such as the male children of child mothers or prostitutes, often recognisable by their short *nasab*s, with *ibn* "son of" followed by the name or sobriquet of a woman. They could even come from ethnic groups who refused integration into a controlled environment, such as the Zuṭṭ [*q.v.*], buffalo herders of Indian origin installed by the Sāsānids in the 5th century in the marshlands of Lower ʿIrāḳ and then displaced by the ʿAbbāsid caliphs at the beginning of the 3rd/9th century to the plains of Antioch and Cilicia; or the Nūrīs/Nawar [see NŪRĪ], limited-ranging groups of gypsies who were blacksmiths and tinsmiths, who, still up to the 20th century, would pitch their patched and tattered tents in the Syrian steppes in the vicinity of towns, in order to hire out the charms of their wives and daughters, and who would organise entertainments in the streets with small girls and trained animals like bears, goats and monkeys. All these marginal groups might themselves create a new collective solidarity around a fictitious *nasab*, like the Banū Sāsān [*q.v.*]; see C.E. Bosworth, *The mediaeval Islamic underworld. The Banū Sāsān in Arabic society and literature*, 2 vols. Leiden 1976; K. Zakhariya, *Abū Zayd al-Sarūǧī, imposteur et mystique; relire les maqāmāt d'al-Ḥarīrī*, Damascus 2000, 121-8.

Their organised bands, *aḥzāb*, *ʿasharāt*, *ʿuṣab*, often residing near the gates either inside or outside a town, would march behind their banners to the sound of their drums and fifes (*al-ṭubūl wa 'l-zumūr*) and might be called by more glorious descriptive collective terms, such as the Muslim youths of Tinnīs, *shabāb shudjʿān* "brave youths", who in the opening years of the Fāṭimid presence regularly preyed on the rich Christian merchants, *al-aghniyāʾ al-naṣārā*, emptying their warehouses and debauching their womenfolk and daughters (see Sawīrus Ibn al-Muḳaffaʿ, *History of the Patriarchs of the Egyptian Church*, ed. and tr. A.S. Atiya *et alii*, ii/2, Cairo 1948, Ar. text 88, Eng. tr. 131-3). When they were not exterminated by the regular troops, these bands might be gradually institutionalised into urban militias, called *aḥdāth* [*q.v.*] or into confraternities, bands of *futuwwa* [*q.v.*]. See Cl. Cahen, *Mouvements populaires et autonomisme urbain dans l'Asie musulmane*, in *Arabica*, v (1958), 225-50, vi (1959), 25-56, 223-65; Bianquis, *op. cit.*, ii, 673-80; idem, *Le chevalier de la steppe, l'ânier de village, le cavalier de la citadelle: trois personnages de la transition en Syrie au XIe siècle*, in M.A. Bakhit and M.Y. Abbadi (eds.), *Bilād al-Shām during the Abbasid period*, ʿAmmān 1992, i (Ar. section), 429-44, ii (foreign languages section), 91-104; A. Havemann, *The Saljuq vizier and raʾīs in Syria. The struggle for urban self-representation*, in *IJMES*, xxi (1989), 233-42; J.M. Mouton, *Damas et son principauté sous les Saldjoukides et les Bourides, 468-549/1076-1154*, Cairo 1995; M. Yared-Riachi, *La politique extérieure de la prin-*

cipauté de Damas 468-549h/1076-1154, Damascus 1997, index at 321. Henceforth led by a *raʾīs*, they contributed towards the maintenance of order within the town and, if necessary, to its defence when it was besieged by a hostile army.

Bibliography: Given in the article; also, information kindly supplied by F. Sanagustin.

(TH. BIANQUIS)

AL-**ZUBĀRA**, a location on the north-west coast of Ḳaṭar [*q.v.*]. It was the main town on the peninsula until 1878, when it was largely destroyed. It now contains only the 1938 fort, built as a police station, and, 2 km further north, the ruins of a fortified settlement dating back to the 18th century. The surrounding land is flat, saline and barren.

In their late 17th-century migration from central Arabia, the ʿUtūb [*q.v.*] clans may have settled briefly around al-Zubāra before continuing towards present-day al-Kuwayt [*q.v.*] in the early 18th century. They included what became the early leading families in al-Kuwayt: the Āl Ṣabāḥ, the Āl D̲j̲alāhima and the Āl K̲h̲alīfa. In 1766, the Āl K̲h̲alīfa left al-Kuwayt again for al-Zubāra, shortly followed by the Āl D̲j̲alāhima. The town soon developed into a significant pearling centre and trading port, particularly after Baṣra [*q.v.*] fell to Persia in 1776. Countering a challenge to this new pre-eminence by the *s̲h̲ayk̲h̲* of Būs̲h̲ahr, the newcomers captured Baḥrayn [*q.v.*] (until then a Persian dependency) in 1783. Henceforth, the Āl K̲h̲alīfa settled on Baḥrayn, while retaining control over al-Zubāra (now increasingly eclipsed). Āl K̲h̲alīfa rule was challenged by Raḥma b. D̲j̲ābir Āl D̲j̲alāhima until his death in 1826. Thereafter, the Āl T̲h̲ānī family, based in the east of the peninsula, gradually increased its power, challenging the Āl K̲h̲alīfa's hold over al-Zubāra and north-western Ḳaṭar. Al-Zubāra at this time was described as a town of 400 houses.

The first treaty between the Āl T̲h̲ānī and Great Britain in 1868 implied Britain's right to intervene in disputes with the Āl K̲h̲alīfa. In 1873, the British Political Agent awarded the latter customary rights and access but not sovereignty over al-Zubāra. In 1878, the Āl T̲h̲ānī attacked and destroyed the town. Ḳaṭar's recognition in 1916 as a separate British protectorate failed to settle the matter. In 1937, Baḥrayn protested against a survey of the area's port potential; a section of the local Āl Naʿīm tribe sided with their traditional overlords, the Āl K̲h̲alīfa, and were attacked and defeated by the Āl T̲h̲ānī. The Āl K̲h̲alīfa imposed an embargo, which became one of the causes for the sharp decline of northern Ḳaṭar, and indeed of the whole peninsula.

In 1944 the political agent negotiated an agreement granting Baḥrayn customary and grazing rights, although tension persisted. Only in 1950 was the Baḥraynī embargo lifted when the Āl K̲h̲alīfa's right to visit was again confirmed. The following year, many of the Āl Naʿīm who had left for Baḥrayn returned. Yet in 1953 Baḥraynī maps were published claiming sovereignty over al-Zubāra, and the following year, the claim was officially revived. S̲h̲ayk̲h̲ ʿAlī Āl T̲h̲ānī in response reoccupied the fort and in 1956 added further police. In 1957, the British political agent ruled that Baḥrayn could no longer expect extraterritorial privileges in the area, thus finally establishing full effective Ḳaṭarī (Āl T̲h̲ānī) control.

During the 1980s and 1990s, the issue of al-Zubāra was raised again by Baḥrayn in the context of the other territorial disputes between the two states. When Ḳaṭar unilaterally referred the Hawar islands dispute to the International Court of Justice in 1991, Baḥrayn protested. Its 1992 offer to make a new joint submission which would include all outstanding issues—also implying al-Zubāra—was refused by Ḳaṭar.

Bibliography: Extensive mention of al-Zubāra can be found in the following: Sir Charles Belgrave, *The Pirate Coast*, Beirut 1960; A. Abu Hakima, *History of Eastern Arabia 1750-1800*, Beirut 1965; J.B. Kelly, *Britain and the Persian Gulf, 1795-1880*, Oxford 1968; R. Said Zahlan, *The creation of Qatar*, London 1979; J. Crystal, *Oil and politics in the Gulf. Rulers and merchants in Kuwait and Qatar*, new ed. Cambridge 1990; J.C. Wilkinson, *Arabia's frontiers*, London 1991; R. Schofield (ed.), *Territorial foundations of the Gulf states*, London 1994.

(G. NONNEMAN)

ZUBAYDA BT. **D̲J̲AʿFAR** b. Abī D̲j̲aʿfar al-Manṣūr [*q.v.*], Umm D̲j̲aʿfar (d. 216/831-2), wife of the caliph Hārūn al-Ras̲h̲īd [*q.v.*], mother of his successor Muḥammad al-Amīn [*q.v.*]. Her name was Amat al-ʿAzīz ("handmaid of the Almighty"), but she is known by her pet name Zubayda ("little butter ball"), given to her by her grandfather al-Manṣūr on account of her plumpness and radiant looks. Her beauty, intelligence, extravagance and generosity made her one of the most admired women in her time. She set the fashion at the caliphal court and added to its splendour by patronising scholars, poets and musicians, but she also spent fabulous sums on public works, especially in Mecca. Like her husband Hārūn al-Ras̲h̲īd, she became a literary figure, appearing in *adab* anecdotes, as also in *Alf laylā wa-laylā*.

According to Ibn al-At̲h̲īr (ed. Beirut, v, 572) Zubayda was born in 145/763, whereas earlier sources only state that she was about one year younger than Hārūn, her cousin on the paternal and maternal side, her mother Salsal being K̲h̲ayzurān's [*q.v.*] sister. Their marriage took place in 165/781-2, a happy union by all accounts, although not untroubled by rivalries and intrigues of the harem (*Ag̲h̲ānī*[3], vi, 309, ix, 88, xviii, 65, 307). In 170/787 her only child Muḥammad (al-Amīn) was born. Six months earlier, a Persian concubine had given birth to ʿAbd Allāh (al-Maʾmūn), whom Zubayda raised from infancy after his mother's death. She must have soon realised, however, that the highly intelligent, gifted ʿAbd Allāh threatened her son's succession to the caliphate. Although Muḥammad was designated caliph as early as 175/792, Hārūn's evident preference for ʿAbd Allāh and the growing rivalry between the brothers affected her increasingly in the years to come (cf. N. Abbott, *Two queens of Baghdad*, Chicago 1946, 170 ff.).

The part Zubayda played in the downfall of the Barmakids [*q.v.*] is difficult to assess (cf. Abbott, *op. cit.*, 191-200); her chief political concern remained the issue of succession. She used her Hās̲h̲imite alliances and her wealth in support of her son, who succeeded Hārūn in 193/809, but when in 195/811 an army was sent to K̲h̲urāsān against al-Maʾmūn, she urged the general ʿAlī b. ʿĪsā to treat her stepson with respect should he fall prisoner (Ṭabarī, iii, 817). During the turbulent events of the civil war, Zubayda suffered personal humiliation, first on the part of Bag̲h̲dādī rebels in 196/812, later by al-Ṭāhir's [*q.v.*] K̲h̲urāsānian troops, who were also responsible for the murder of al-Amīn in 198/813 (Ṭabarī, iii, 846, 934). Her spirit seems to have been unbroken, however. She sent placating messages to al-Maʾmūn, avowing that he was ample compensation for all her losses, and eventually effected a reconciliation (*Taʾrīk̲h̲ Bag̲h̲dād*, xiv, 433-4, no. 7802). Her quiet later years bear witness of the cordial relationship between them (cf. Abbott, *op. cit.*, 229-35).

Zubayda is commemorated for her philanthropic works, in particular the water supplies of Mecca and the pilgrim road (cf. Ibn Djubayr, *Travels*, ed. W. Wright, Leiden 1907, 208). In 193/808 she initiated an extensive system of waterworks centred around the ʿAyn Zubayda on the plane of ʿArafāt, including a subterranean aqueduct cut through the rocks at enormous costs [see MAKKA. 2]. The sources report her personal engagement in the planning and her persistence against the objections of the engineers (Wüstenfeld, *Chroniken der Stadt Mekka*, Leipzig 1858, i, 444-5; Ibn Khallikān, no. 228, tr. de Slane, i, 532). Zubayda died on 26 Djumādā I 210/10 July 831 in Baghdād. The place of her tomb is a matter of dispute (Abbott, *op. cit.*, 247-50).

Bibliography (in addition to references in the article): Balādhurī, *Futūḥ*, index; Yaʿḳūbī, Beirut 1379-1960, ii, 428, 433-34; Dīnawarī, Cairo 1960, 396; Ibn ʿAbd Rabbih, *al-ʿIḳd al-farīd*, Cairo 1962, index; Ḳālī, *Amālī*, Cairo 1344/1926, 191; Marzubānī, *Muwashshaḥ*, Cairo 1965, 538, 567; Ṣafadī, *Wāfī*, xiv, 176-8, no. 242. (RENATE JACOBI)

AL-**ZUBAYDĪ**, ABŪ BAKR MUḤAMMAD B. AL-ḤASAN (Ḥumaydī, 180) b. ʿAbd Allāh b. Madhḥidj, a well-known Arabic philologist, *faḳīh* and poet, whose great-great-great-grandfather Bishr al-Dākhil (Ibn Ḥazm, 412) had come from Ḥimṣ [*q.v.*] with the Umayyad army to al-Andalus (his genealogy goes back to the *Djāhiliyya* in Yemen). Al-Zubaydī was born in Seville *ca.* 316/928 into a scholarly family. The *ṭalab al-ʿilm* brought him to Cordova, the residence of the Umayyad caliphs, where he associated with his teachers, above all with Abū ʿAlī al-Ḳālī [*q.v.*]. The young scholar attracted the attention of the caliph al-Ḥakam II (350-66/961-76) who, when still a prince, was a great promoter of art and science. He entrusted al-Zubaydī with the education of his son Hishām, the heir to the throne. He urged him to make his knowledge available for everybody in books, similar to the way he had already shown himself as an expert in a complementary work to Sībawayhi's [*q.v.*] famous grammar, namely, his:

(1) *K. al-Istidrāk ʿalā Sībawayh fī K. al-Abniya wa 'l-ziyāda ʿalā mā awradahu fīhi muhadhdhab^an^*, additions and corrections on the structure of nouns, etc. (ed. I. Guidi, Rome 1890, repr. Baghdād *ca.* 1970; cf. *al-Mawrid*, iv/1 (1395/1975), 251-3; new ed. by Ḥannā Djamīl Ḥaddād, al-Riyāḍ 1407/1987; an excerpt is *Amthilat al-abniya fī Kitāb Sībawayhi, Tafsīr* Abī Bakr al-Zubaydī, *Sharḥ* Muḥammad Khalīfa al-Dannāʿ, Beirut 1996).

Al-Zubaydī then wrote three works, among which his biographies of grammarians and lexicographers from early times to his own days, in which he quotes his *K. al-Istidrāk* on p. 239:

(2) *K. Ṭabaḳāt al-naḥwiyyīn wa 'l-lughawiyyīn*, ed. M. Abu 'l-Faḍl Ibrāhīm, Cairo 1373/1954, ²1973, composed between the years 363/973-4 and 365/975-6. As he points out in the preface, the caliph put his personal material at his disposal, both orally and in writing (see R. Sellheim, in *Oriens*, viii [1955], 345-8). Al-Zubaydī's *Ṭabaḳāt* was used as a source by later biographers, and excerpts were made, one of which has been printed (F. Krenkow, Rome 1919).

To this period also belongs al-Zubaydī's work on "errors in language" (*laḥn* [*q.v.*]; cf. AL-ANDALUS. x) made by common people (cf. G. Krotkoff, in *Bull. of the College of Arts and Sciences, Baghdād*, ii [1957], 3-16; Sezgin, *GAS*, viii, 254-5):

(3) *K. Laḥn al-ʿawāmm*, ed. R. ʿAbd al-Tawwāb, Cairo 1964. Again, he thanks the caliph emphatically for his encouragement and assistance. Two hundred years later, Ibn Hishām al-Lakhmī [*q.v.* in Suppl.] from Seville wrote an answer to this innovative treatise (cf. D. Reig, in *SI*, lxxvii [1993], 183-9). For an excerpt from al-Zubaydī's *Laḥn*, see the introduction of the editor, his general study, called *Laḥn al-ʿāmma wa 'l-taṭawwur al-lughawī*, Cairo 1967, and his collected works *Buḥūth wa-maḳālāt fī 'l-lugha*, Cairo 1403/1982. Without examining the first edition, ʿAbd al-ʿAzīz Maṭar republished the work under the title *Laḥn al-ʿāmma*, Cairo 1981.

The third work published by al-Zubaydī at the instigation of the caliph was the highly-praised revised excerpt which he made from the first Arabic dictionary. Al-Zubaydī, too, is of the opinion that the work is only to be ascribed (*mansūb*) in its entirety to al-Khalīl b. Aḥmad [*q.v.*]. He must have finished it before the death of the caliph on 3 Ṣafar 366/1 October 976, for at the end he wishes him a long life (see further, Ḥumaydī, 47-9!):

(4) *Mukhtaṣar al-ʿAyn*, ed. Nūr Ḥāmid al-Shādhilī, 2 vols. Beirut 1417/1996 (cf. J. Kraemer, in *Oriens*, vi [1953], 207-8; Sezgin, *GAS*, viii, 52-6, 254; ʿAbd al-ʿAzīz Ibrāhīm, in *al-Mawrid*, xvii/2 [1408/1988], 196-224, xvii/3, 189-214).

Al-Zubaydī rose to become *ṣāḥib al-shurṭa* [*q.v.*], but he probably succeeded in returning to his native town Seville in the function of *ḳāḍī* only after the caliph's death and under the latter's successor, his own pupil Hishām. He died there on 1 Djumādā II/6 September 989. His son Abu 'l-Walīd Muḥammad, also one of his many pupils, died soon after 440/1048 as *ḳāḍī* in Almeria (Ḥumaydī, 36).

(5) *K. al-Wāḍiḥ fī ʿilm al-ʿarabiyya*, a highly-praised, clearly-arranged grammar, composed after the example of Sībawayhi's *Kitāb*, but shorter than others (ed. Amīn ʿAlī al-Sayyid, Cairo 1975; ed. ʿA. Khalīfa, ʿAmmān 1976; cf. Sezgin, *GAS*, ix, 250). The work seems to have circulated in various versions (*riwāyāt*), perhaps as written notes taken during lectures (*madjlis*). Partial versions may have existed before al-Zubaydī came in contact with the court.

Shorter treatises about questions concerning the *K. al-ʿAyn* may also be considered as written notes taken during lectures, also indirectly through al-Ḳālī's *K. al-Bāriʿ* [see MATHAL. iii; AL-YAZĪDĪ], and not as independent works (cf. Ḳifṭī, *Muḥammadūn*, 209; Sezgin, *GAS*, viii, 255, ix, 319), namely:

(6) *Istidrāk (?) al-ghalaṭ al-wāḳiʿ fī K. al-ʿAyn* [see LAḤN AL-ʿĀMMA];

(7) *Risālat al-intiṣār li 'l-Khalīl* (cf. Ḳifṭī, *Inbāh*, iii, 109);

(8) *al-Mustadrak min al-ziyāda fī Kitāb al-Bāriʿ ʿalā K. al-ʿAyn*;

(9) *K. Basṭ al-Bāriʿ* (cf. S.A. Bonebakker, in *Oriens*, xiii-xiv [1961], 174);

(10) *al-Radd ʿalā Ibn Masarra*, or *Hatk sutūr al-mulḥidīn* (cf. Ibn Khallikān, *s.v.*) is a treatise against the doctrines of Ibn Masarra.

Al-Zubaydī is said to have composed biographies of later jurists in Cordova:

(11) *Akhbār al-fuḳahāʾ al-mutaʾakhkhirīn min ahl Ḳurṭuba* (cf. Ḥādjdjī Khalīfa, *s.v.*).

In addition are mentioned a work on metrics:

(12) *al-Ghāya fī 'l-ʿarūḍ* (cf. Ḥādjdjī Khalīfa, *s.v.*);

(13) *al-Taḳrīẓ* (cf. Ibn Khayr, 351); and an excerpt,

(14) *Ikhtiṣār*, from al-Bukhārī's *Ṣaḥīḥ* (ms. in Tunis, see Pons Boigues, 92-3 no. 50).

Bibliography (in addition to works mentioned in the text): 1. Sources. Ibn al-Faraḍī, *T. ʿUlamāʾ al-Andalus*, Cairo 1373/1954, ii, 92 (cf. M.L. Ávila and M. Marín, in *COA*, iv (1985-7 [1989]), 41-60; Thaʿālibī, *Yatīmat al-dahr*, Cairo 1375/1956, ii, 71; Ibn Ḥazm, *Djamharat ansāb al-ʿArab*, Cairo 1382/1962, 412; Ibn Mākūlā, *Ikmāl*, Ḥaydarābād 1384/1965, iv, 221-2 (with brother and sons); Ḥumaydī, *Djadhwat al-Muktaba/is*, Cairo 1372/1952, 43-5; Fatḥ b. Khākān, *Maṭmaḥ al-anfus*, in *al-Mawrid*, x/3-4 (1402/1981), 251-4; Samʿānī, *Ansāb*, Ḥaydarābād 1386/1966, vi, 265 (with sons); Ibn Khayr, *Fahrasa*, Saragossa 1894-5 and Baghdād 1382/1963, index; Ḍabbī, *Bughyat al-multamis fī taʾrīkh ridjāl al-Andalus*, Madrid 1885, 56-7; Yāḳūt, *Udabāʾ*, vi, 518-22; Ḳifṭī, *Inbāh al-ruwāt*, Cairo 1374/1955, iii, 108-9; idem, *al-Muḥammadūn min al-shuʿarāʾ*, al-Riyāḍ 1390/1970, 207-9; Ibn Khallikān, s.v.; Ibn Saʿīd, *al-Mughrib fī ḥulā 'l-Maghrib*, ²Cairo 1964, i, 255-6; Ṣafadī, *al-Wāfī*, Istanbul 1949, ii, 351; Dhahabī, *Tadhkirat al-ḥuffāẓ*, Ḥaydarābād 1376/1957, iii, 982; idem, *al-ʿIbar*, Kuwait 1961, iii, 12; idem, *Siyar aʿlām al-nubalāʾ*, Beirut 1403/1983, xvi, 417-8; Yāfiʿī, *Mirʾāt al-djanān*, Ḥaydarābād 1338/1919, ii, 409; Ibn Farḥūn, *al-Dībādj*, Cairo 1351/1932, 263-4; Fīrūzābādī, *al-Bulgha fī taʾrīkh aʾimmat al-lugha*, Damascus 1392/1972, 218-9; Ibn Ḳāḍī Shuhba, *Ṭabaḳāt al-naḥwiyyīn wa 'l-lughawiyyīn*, Nadjaf 1974, 88-9 (with brother and sons); Suyūṭī, *Bughya*, 66-7 (Cairo 1384/1964, i, 84-5); idem, *al-Muzhir*, Cairo 1378/1958, index; Maḳḳarī, *Analectes*, ii, 320, index = *Nafḥ al-ṭīb*, Cairo 1368/1949, v, 24, 152-4, vi, 66; Ibn al-ʿImād, *Shadharāt*, iii, 94-5; Khʷānsārī, *Rawḍāt al-djannāt*, Tehran 1367/1948, 685-6; Ismāʿīl Pasha, *Hadiyyat al-ʿārifīn*, Istanbul 1955, ii, 51.

2. Studies. Brockelmann, I², 139-40, S I, 203; O. Rescher, *Abriss der arabischen Litteraturgeschichte*, Stuttgart 1933, repr. with additions, Osnabrück 1983, ii, 241-2; Ziriklī, *Aʿlām*, ⁴Beirut 1979, vi, 82; Kaḥḥāla, *Muʾallifīn*, Damascus 1379/1960, ix, 198-9; idem, *al-Mustadrak ʿalā Muʿdjam al-muʾallifīn*, Beirut 1406/1985, 625; idem, *Muʿdjam muṣannifī 'l-kutub al-ʿarabiyya fi 'l-taʾrīkh wa 'l-tarādjim wa 'l-riḥalāt*, Beirut 1406/1986, 464; M.ʿA. Mudarris, *Rayḥānat al-adab*, ²Tabrīz 1347/1968, ii, 363; G. Flügel, *Die grammatischen Schulen der Araber*, Leipzig 1862, 263-4, repr. Nendeln 1966; S. Wild, *Das Kitāb al-ʿAin und die arabische Lexikographie*, Wiesbaden 1965, index; J.A. Haywood, *Arabic lexicography*, ²Leiden 1965, 61-2 and index; N.R. ʿAzzāwī, *Abū Bakr al-Zubaydī al-Andalusī wa-āthāruhu fi 'l-naḥw wa 'l-lugha*, Baghdād 1395/1975; R. Sellheim, *Abū ʿAlī al-Qālī. Zum Problem mündlicher und schriftlicher Überlieferung*, in *Studien zur Geschichte und Kultur des Vorderen Orients (Festschrift Bertold Spuler)*, Leiden 1981, 362-74; M.L. Ávila, *Obras biográficas en el Muqtabis de Ibn Ḥayyān*, in *al-Qanṭara*, x (1989), 463-83; G. Makdisi, *The rise of humanism in Classical Islam and the Christian West*, Edinburgh 1990, index; Ṭ. ʿAlāma, *al-Ṭabaḳa wa 'l-naḥw, maʿa dirāsa li-minhadjiyyat al-nuḥāt min al-Zubaydī al-Andalusī ilā 'l-Suyūṭī al-Miṣrī*, Beirut 1992. (R. SELLHEIM)

AL-**ZUBAYR** B. AL-**ʿAWWĀM** B. KHUWAYLID, Abū ʿAbd Allāh al-Ḳurashī al-Asadī, one of the most eminent Companions of Muḥammad, known by the surname *Ḥawārī* (a Geʿez loanword) *Rasūl Allāh* ("the Disciple or Apostle of the Messenger of God"). He is one of the ten Companions to whom Paradise was promised by the Prophet (*al-ʿashara al-mubashshara* [*q.v.*] or *al-mubashsharūn al-djanna*) and a member of the *shūrā* [*q.v.*] appointed by the dying caliph ʿUmar b. al-Khaṭṭāb to elect his successor. The name al-Zubayr is derived from *al-zabr*, *ṭayy al-biʾr bi 'l-ḥidjāra*, casing of a well with stones (Ibn Durayd, *al-Ishtiḳāḳ*, 47-8) or a strong man (*LA*, s.v. *z-b-r*).

His mother, Ṣafiyya bt. ʿAbd al-Muṭṭalib b. Hāshim, was the Prophet's aunt, so that he was a cousin of Muḥammad and a nephew of his wife Khadīdja bt. Khuwaylid. A report asserts that al-Zubayr, Ṭalḥa b. ʿUbayd Allāh, ʿAlī b. Abī Ṭālib and Saʿd b. Abī Waḳḳāṣ were all born in the same year (al-Dhahabī, *Taʾrīkh*, 499). Al-ʿAwwām died when al-Zubayr was very young and he was taken into the care of his uncle Nawfal b. Khuwaylid.

Al-Zubayr was one of the earliest converts to Islam: some claim that he was the fourth or fifth male who adopted the new religion. Reports disagree concerning his age when he followed Muḥammad. The best known states that he was 16 years old at the time. Ibn Isḥāḳ attests that Abū Bakr persuaded him, together with four other future members of the *shūrā*, to embrace Islam; the version of the Zubayrīs has it that he was eight years old when he followed Muḥammad and that, when he was 12, he drew his sword to protect him and became the first person who drew a sword in the way of God; to give more credibility to this version, a report claims that he converted to Islam with ʿAlī (Ibn ʿAsākir, xviii, 344-5; al-Dhahabī, *Siyar*, i, 41, 45). The contradictions between these versions are the result of debates within Muslim society concerning the precedence claimed in adopting the new religion (*sābiḳa*), according superiority to the first converts (cf. I. Hasson, *La conversion de Muʿāwiya ibn Abī Sufyān*, in *JSAI*, xxii [1998], 214-42).

Al-Zubayr took part in the first *hidjra* and returned with the first group to Mecca when rumours spread that the Meccans had become reconciled to Muḥammad since he was ready to recognise the three goddesses, al-Lāt, al-ʿUzzā and Manāt [*q.vv.*]. Later, al-Zubayr, accompanied by his mother, migrated (*hādjara*) from Mecca to Medina.

Within the range of the institution called *al-muʾākhāt* ("brothering" [*q.v.*]), al-Zubayr was paired probably with the Awsī Salama b. Salāma b. Waḳsh or with the Khazradjī poet Kaʿb b. Mālik [*q.v.*]; earlier, in Mecca, he was paired with ʿAbd Allāh b. Masʿūd [see IBN MASʿŪD].

Al-Zubayr took part in most of the early battles. At Badr (2/624 [*q.v.*]), there were only two horsemen in the ranks of the Muslims; al-Zubayr was one of them. The Zubayrīs relate that the archangel Djibrīl and the angels who took part in this battle (Ibn Hishām, *Sīra*, ii, 285-6) wore yellow turbans like that of al-Zubayr (Ibn ʿAsākir, xviii, 353-5). At Uḥud (3/625 [*q.v.*]), the Prophet expressed his admiration for Zubayr's valour. During the Battle of the Trench (al-Khandaḳ [*q.v.*]) in 5/627, al-Zubayr was sent by the Prophet to spy on the Banū Ḳurayẓa. Muḥammad said on this occasion: "Each prophet has his true disciple, and al-Zubayr is mine" (*li-kulli nabiyy^in ḥawāriyy^un wa-ḥawāriyya al-Zubayru*; al-Wāḳidī, *al-Maghāzī*, ii, 457). Just after the Battle of al-Khandaḳ, al-Zubayr and ʿAlī organised the massacre of Banū Ḳurayẓa, carrying out the sentence pronounced by Saʿd b. Muʿādh [*q.v.*] and approved by Muḥammad (al-Wāḳidī, *al-Maghāzī*, ii, 513; al-Ṭabarī, *Taʾrīkh*, i, 1499). During the Khaybar campaign (7/628), al-Zubayr distinguished himself more than any other warrior except ʿAlī. Throughout the course of the conquest of Mecca, al-Zubayr commanded the left wing of the Muslim army. At Tabūk (9/630 [*q.v.*]), al-Zubayr held the Prophet's "greatest banner", *al-rāya al-ʿuẓmā* (al-Wāḳidī, *al-Maghāzī*, iii, 996). After Muḥammad's death, al-Zubayr took part in the battle of al-Yarmūk (15/636 [*q.v.*]) and later ʿUmar sent him with 4,000 reinforcements to support ʿAmr b. al-ʿĀṣ in the conquest of Egypt.

With such a record, it is not surprising that al-Zubayr was described as "the bravest man of Ḳuraysh" (*as͟hd͟jaʿ Ḳurays͟h*, al-Ṭabarī, ii, 805) or simply "the bravest man" (*as͟hd͟jaʿ al-nās, Ag͟hānī*, xi, 125). But in a *munāfara* (disputation over claims to nobility), Ibn ʿAbbās is said to have charged him with cowardice at the Battle of the Camel: he fled and did not attack, he fought but did not persevere (Ibn Abi 'l-Ḥadīd, ix, 327). In order to correct this impression, a pro-ʿAlid tradition claims that "he fled as a repentant and not out of cowardice".

A late report affirms that al-Zubayr served for a time as Muḥammad's secretary in the registration of the income from legal alms (*amwāl al-ṣadaḳāt*, al-Ḳalḳas͟handī, *Ṣubḥ al-aʿs͟hā*, i, 91, citing al-Ḳuḍāʿī, *ʿUyūn al-maʿārif*).

Al-Zubayr, like many other eminent Companions who opposed ʿAlī b. Abī Ṭālib before, and particularly after his proclamation as caliph, was attacked in S͟hīʿī literature (E. Kohlberg, *The attitude of the Imāmī-S͟hīʿīs to the Companions of the Prophet*, see *Bibl.*; idem, *Some Imāmī S͟hīʿī views on the Ṣaḥāba*, in *JSAI*, v [1984], 143-75). The eighth volume (in the lithographic edition) of al-Mad͟jlisī's *Biḥār al-anwār* records many such attacks; these form the main subject-matter of the S͟hīʿī literature known as *sabb al-ṣaḥāba* (cursing of the Companions). Al-Zubayr and the other leaders of the camp opposing ʿAlī in the Battle of the Camel (36/656) are designated in the S͟hīʿī tradition by the epithet *al-nākit͟hūn*, i.e. rogues, rascals, "those who broke their compact". Abū Mik͟hnaf reports that al-Zubayr was the first leader who killed Muslim captives in cold blood, *ḳatalahum ṣabr^an^* (Ibn Abi 'l-Ḥadīd, ix, 321). Nevertheless S͟hīʿī attacks on al-Zubayr are moderate in comparison with those on Ṭalḥa, ʿĀ'is͟ha, Abū Bakr, ʿUmar and others, and favourable points are mentioned. Thus it is said that, in the events which led to the election of Abū Bakr as the first caliph, al-Zubayr supported ʿAlī, together with the Banū Hās͟him and the bulk of al-Anṣār. In addition, the descriptions of the Battle of the Camel assert that al-Zubayr, despite the provocations of his son ʿAbd Allāh, did not take part in the fighting after his meeting with ʿAlī. It seems that the real reason for al-Zubayr's conduct in this battle derives from his disappointment in dropping behind Ṭalḥa in claims for the caliphate when ʿĀ'is͟ha inclined to appoint Ṭalḥa and al-Zubayr estimated that he did not have any chance to be elected caliph, even if his side won. It was thus best to leave.

The Sunnī reaction in support of al-Zubayr and other *ṣaḥāba* takes many forms. The most prevailing includes the enumeration of their virtues, *manāḳib*, and the harmonisation between Muḥammad's promise of Paradise to *al-ʿas͟hara al-mubas͟hs͟hara* and the *ḥadīt͟h* assuring Muslims who fought Muslims with Hell (Ibn ʿAsākir, xviii, 382-404; Ibn Ḥad͟jar al-Haytamī, *al-Ṣawāʿiḳ al-muḥriḳa*, 151-74). Al-Zubayr and his partners are considered as *mud͟jtahidūn* (those who strove to interpret what God wanted and what was better for Islam and the Muslims). The leaders of both camps fought *bona fide* and not for worldly gain, therefore, God will reward them in Paradise according to the Prophet's utterance "Whoever does *id͟jtihād* but errs will be rewarded; whoever does *id͟jtihād* and hits the mark, will be rewarded twice" (Abū Nuʿaym al-Iṣfahānī, *K. al-Imāma wa 'l-radd ʿalā 'l-rāfiḍa*, ed. ʿAlī al-Faḳīhī, Medina 1994, 362-81; Ibn Ḥad͟jar al-Haytamī, *Taṭhīr al-d͟janān*, Cairo 1965, 6). In order to point out al-Zubayr's abstemiousness and piety, it is reported that he had 1,000 slaves who had to pay to him a certain tribute, *ḍarība* or *k͟harād͟j*; he always gave this tribute to the poor for the sake of God; and he ceased to draw his allowance from the *dīwān* after ʿUmar's murder (Ibn ʿAsākir, xviii, 339, 343, 396-7, 399, 403).

Al-Zubayr, Ṭalḥa and ʿAlī are said to have secretly encouraged the agitation against ʿUt͟hmān, each for his own reasons, but when they felt they had lost control over events, they tried to prevent the caliph's murder, and sent their children to protect him. After ʿUt͟hmān's murder and the proclamation of ʿAlī as caliph, al-Zubayr and Ṭalḥa collaborated with ʿĀ'is͟ha against ʿAlī and declared that ʿUt͟hmān had been killed unjustly and that the new caliph was responsible for his death. They arrived in al-Baṣra, recruited an army and forced ʿAlī to fight them. The decisive Battle of the Camel took place near al-Baṣra in D͟jumādā I 36/November 656. Al-Zubayr was killed and was probably buried in Wādī al-Sibāʿ, known now as Baldat al-Zubayr, in the vicinity of al-Baṣra. He is variously reported to have died aged 64, 57 or 54.

After the *hid͟jra*, al-Zubayr had become one of the wealthiest Companions. He owned a large number of properties, including some large estates, such as al-G͟hāba in the vicinity of Medina, al-Salīla in al-Rabad͟ha; *dār al-Zubayr* and *masd͟jid al-Zubayr* in *sūḳ wardān* of al-Fusṭāṭ; and estates in Alexandria and Kūfa. Some were grants of land in Arabia from the Prophet, others were granted by ʿUt͟hmān b. ʿAffān, especially in ʿIrāḳ. His estate (*dār*) in the quarter of Banū Sulaym in al-Baṣra was vast and included markets and stores (al-Yaʿḳūbī, *Mus͟hākalat al-nās li-zamānihim*, ed. W. Millward, Beirut 1962, 13-4). In order to give an example of his fortune, it was reported that he sold one of his *dūr* for 600,000 dirhams (al-D͟hahabī, *Siyar*, i, 57).

One of his wives was Asmā' [*q.v.*], the daughter of Abū Bakr and elder half-sister of ʿĀ'is͟ha, who was known by her nickname *D͟hāt al-niṭāḳayn* ("she of the two girdles").

In the chapters on the virtues (*faḍā'il*) of the Companions, most *ḥadīt͟h* collections dedicate a section to the merits (*manāḳib* and even *faḍā'il*) of al-Zubayr (al-Buk͟hārī and al-Tirmid͟hī, *bāb manāḳib al-Zubayr*; Muslim and Ibn Mād͟ja, *bāb faḍā'il al-Zubayr*). It is said that al-Zubayr and ʿAbd al-Raḥmān b. ʿAwf obtained special permission to wear silk since they suffered from lice or scabies (*Musnad Aḥmad*, iii, 122, 127, 180, 192, 255; al-Buk͟hārī, *Ṣaḥīḥ, k. al-d͟jihād*, vi, 100-1; Muslim, *Ṣaḥīḥ, k. al-libās, bāb lubs al-ḥarīr li 'l-rad͟jul*).

The *ḥadīt͟h* corpus includes a very small number of traditions attributed to Muḥammad and cited by al-Zubayr. In addition to the "six canonical collections" (*al-kutub al-sitta al-ṣiḥāḥ*), traditions of al-Zubayr appear in many other collections, such as the *Musnad* of Aḥmad b. Ḥanbal; Aḥmad b. ʿAmr al-Bazzār, *al-Baḥr al-zak͟hk͟hār*; Abū Yaʿlā al-Mawṣilī, *al-Musnad*; ʿAbd al-Razzāḳ al-Ṣanʿānī, *al-Muṣannaf*; ʿAlī b. Abī Bakr al-Hayt͟hamī, *Mad͟jmaʿ al-zawā'id*; and al-Ṭabarānī, *al-Muʿd͟jam al-kabīr*. The Zubayrī traditionists have an explanation attributed to al-Zubayr himself, who declared that he was afraid to relate something wrong, to ascribe it to the Prophet, and then to be punished in Hell, according to the *ḥadīt͟h*: *man ḳāla ʿalayya mā lam aḳul yatabawwa' maḳʿadahu min al-nār* (Ibn ʿAsākir, xviii, 332-5).

Al-Muṣʿab al-Zubayrī (d. 236/851), a descendant of al-Zubayr, gives the names of ten of his sons in addition to several daughters. The best known are ʿAbd Allāh [*q.v.*], the first child born in the Muslim community in Medina, ʿUrwa [*q.v.*], Ḥamza, and Muṣʿab [*q.v.*]. Another descendant, al-Zubayr b. Bakkār (d. 256/870), dedicates the extant part of his *Djamharat nasab Ḳuraysh wa-akhbārihā* to al-Zubayr's offspring. Al-Zubayr is said to have given his sons the names of martyrs, *shuhadāʾ*, hoping that they would die in the service of Islam.

Bibliography: 1. Sources. Dhahabī, *Siyar aʿlām al-nubalāʾ*, ed. Shuʿayb al-Arnaʾūṭ, [3]i, 41-67; idem, *T. al-Islām*, ed. ʿUmar ʿAbd al-Salām Tadmurī, Beirut 1987 (years 11-40), 496-509; Abū Isḥāḳ al-Fazārī, *K. al-Siyar*, ed. Fārūḳ Ḥammāda, Beirut 1987, 217-8, 300-1; Ibrāhīm b. Isḥāḳ al-Ḥarbī, *K. al-Manāsik wa-amākin ṭuruḳ al-ḥadjdj*, ed. Ḥamad al-Djāsir, al-Riyāḍ 1969; Abū Bakr Ibn al-ʿArabī, *al-ʿAwāṣim min al-ḳawāṣim fī taḥḳīḳ mawāḳif al-ṣaḥāba baʿda wafāt al-nabī*, ed. Muḥibb al-Dīn al-Khaṭīb *et alii*, [5]Cairo 1408/1987-8, 151-65; Ibn ʿAsākir, *T. Madīnat Dimashḳ*, ed. Muḥibb al-Dīn al-ʿAmrawī, Beirut 1995, xviii, 332-438; Ibn Abi 'l-Ḥadīd, *Sharḥ Nahdj al-balāgha*, ed. Muḥammad Abu 'l-Faḍl Ibrāhīm, Beirut 1987, i, 331-5, ii, 166-70, vii, 33-43, ix, 113-5, 308-27; Ibn Ḥadjar al-Haytamī, *al-Ṣawāʿiḳ al-muḥriḳa fī 'l-radd ʿalā ahl al-bidaʿ wa 'l-zandaḳa*, Cairo 1313, esp. 124-35; M. Ḥamīd Allāh, *Madjmūʿat al-wathāʾiḳ al-siyāsiyya li 'l-ʿahd al-nabawī wa 'l-khilāfa al-rāshida*, [6]Beirut 1987; Ibn Ḥanbal, *K. Faḍāʾil al-ṣaḥāba*, ed. Waṣī Allāh ʿAbbās, Beirut 1983, index; idem, *K. al-Zuhd*, Cairo 1987, 179-80; Ibn Ḥazm, *Djamharat ansāb al-ʿArab*, ed. ʿAbd al-Salām Hārūn, Cairo 1962, 121-5; Ps.-Ibn Ḳutayba, *al-Imāma wa 'l siyāsa*, ed. ʿAlī Shīrī, Beirut 1990, i, 28, 42-145; Ibn Hishām, *al-Sīra al-nabawiyya*, index; Ibn al-Kalbī, *Djamharat al-nasab*, ed. Nādjī Ḥasan, Beirut 1986, 68-75 (see also W. Caskel, *Ǧamharat an-nasab*); Ibn Saʿd, iii/1, 70-80 and index; Iṣfahānī, *Aghānī*, index vols.; Masʿūdī, *Murūdj*, ed. Pellat, index; Djamāl al-Dīn al-Mizzī, *Tahdhīb al-kamāl fī asmāʾ al-ridjāl*, ed. Bashshār ʿAwwād Maʿrūf, [2]Beirut 1987, ix, 318-29; al-Muṣʿab al-Zubayrī, *K. Nasab Ḳuraysh*, ed. E. Lévi-Provençal, [3]Cairo 1982, 235-50 and index; Nasāʾī, *Faḍāʾil al-ṣaḥāba*, ed. Fārūḳ Ḥamāda, Casablanca 1984, 114-6, nos. 105-10; Suyūṭī, *Ilḳām al-ḥadjar li-man zakkā sabb Abī Bakr wa-ʿUmar*, ed. A. Arazi, in *JSAI*, (1987), 211-87, esp. editor's introd.; Ṭabarī, index; Abu 'l-ʿArab Muḥammad al-Tamīmī, *K. al-Miḥan*, ed. Yaḥyā Wahīb al-Djabbūrī, Beirut 1983, 88-96; Wāḳidī, *K. al-Maghāzī*, ed. J.M. Jones, Oxford 1966, index; Yaḥyā b. Ādam, *K. al-Kharādj*; Yaʿḳūbī, *Historiae*, index.

2. Studies. Wensinck, *Handbook*, s.v.; J. Wellhausen, *The Arab kingdom and its fall*, Calcutta 1927, index; W.M. Watt, *Muhammad at Mecca*, Oxford 1953; idem, *Muhammad at Medina*, Oxford 1956; M.A. Shaban, *Islamic history A.D. 600-750 (A.H. 132), a new interpretation*, Cambridge 1971, 34-7, 71-2; E. Kohlberg, *The attitude of the Imāmī Shīʿīs to the Campanions of the Prophet*, Ph.D diss., Univ. of Oxford 1971, unpubl.; M. Hinds, *The murder of the caliph ʿUthmān*, in *IJMES*, iii (1972), 450-69; M.G. Morony, *Iraq after the Muslim conquest*, Princeton 1984, index; H. Kennedy, *The Prophet and the age of the caliphates*, London and New York 1986, index.

(I. HASSON)

AL-ZUBAYR B. BAKKĀR B. ʿABD ALLĀH B. MUṢʿAB, Abū ʿAbd Allāh, author of *akhbār* works which combine belles-lettres and history and belong to the oldest preserved books in this field.

He was born in 172/788-9 at Medina. As a descendant of al-Zubayr b. al-ʿAwwām [*q.v.*] he was a prominent member of the illustrious Zubayrī family. When he died at Mecca in Dhu 'l-Ḳaʿda 256/October 870, he had been *ḳāḍī* of the Holy City for the previous one and a half decades. His grandfather was a close associate of the caliph al-Mahdī and was appointed governor of Medina by Hārūn al-Rashīd, and his father also was for some time governor of Medina; but al-Zubayr chose the life of a scholar. According to an account transmitted only by Ibn al-Athīr, vi, 526, he left his home town because of a quarrel with the ʿAlids. In any case, he sojourned several times at Baghdād and Sāmarrāʾ. When he came to Baghdād for the first time, probably before the death of Isḥāḳ b. Ibrāhīm al-Mawṣilī [*q.v.*] in 235/849-50, he had already produced a version of his *Djamharat nasab Ḳuraysh wa-akhbārihā* (cf. the preface of Maḥmūd M. Shākir). His appointment to the office of *ḳāḍī* of Mecca by al-Mutawakkil seems have taken place at Sāmarrāʾ in 242/856-7, and if an anecdotal report is trustworthy (*Taʾrīkh Baghdād*, vi, 469), he had become some time before that date tutor to al-Mutawakkil's son al-Muwaffaḳ [*q.v.*]. The introductory *isnād* of al-Zubayr's *Azwādj al-nabī* indicates further that he lectured in the year 246/865 at Sāmarrāʾ, and Ibn al-Nadīm, *Fihrist*, ed. Tajaddud, 123, mentions that he came to Baghdād for the last time in 253/867.

Unlike the more technically-oriented genealogical works (see, for instance, the *K. Nasab Ḳuraysh* of his uncle Muṣʿab al-Zubayrī [see MUṢʿAB]), al-Zubayr's *Djamhara* is rather a collection of *akhbār* structured in a genealogical order, and it thus develops the old narrative tradition of genealogical writing, as already reflected in the *Djamharat al-nasab* of Ibn al-Kalbī (ed. Maḥmūd Firdaws al-ʿAẓm, 3 vols. Damascus n.d. [*ca.* 1982-6] and ed. Nādjī Ḥasan, 2 vols. Beirut 1986), into a model which may be regarded a predecessor of al-Balādhurī's *Ansāb al-ashrāf*. Al-Zubayr's *Djamhara* treats the Banū Asad b. ʿAbd al-ʿUzzā b. Ḳuṣayy and centres upon the Zubayrids. In contrast to this, his *al-Akhbār al-Muwaffaḳiyyāt*, of which only a minor part is known, offers an unstructured collection including a wide range of materials current in his time. Most of the *akhbār* deal with caliphs, governors and celebrities, who are depicted in situations of social and political significance or in the context of eloquence and rhetoric art. Many of these accounts are elaborated narratives emphasising the exemplary character of the person's behaviour. Poetry plays an important role in both works. These and other works (cf. Ibn Khayr al-Ishbīlī, *Fahrasa*, 467, 499, 534), were transmitted by firmly established *riwāyāt*, the most important among them being those of al-Ḥaramī b. Abi 'l-ʿAlāʾ (*Taʾrīkh Baghdād*, iv, 390), Aḥmad b. Sulaymān al-Ṭūsī (*ibid.*, iv, 177) and Aḥmad b. Saʿīd al-Dimashḳī (*ibid.*, iv, 171). According to the anecdotally-transmitted complaints of his wife, al-Zubayr also possessed a library. Many of the titles of al-Zubayr's works listed by Ibn al-Nadīm (123) deal with the work and life of poets; none of them, however, has survived in independent transmission, although more than 600 quotations from al-Zubayr in Abu 'l-Faradj's *Aghānī* have preserved many of these materials. He is also an often-quoted authority in other works of *adab* and history, such as al-Zadjdjādjī's *al-Amālī* or al-Balādhurī's *Ansāb*, and is to be considered among the finest representatives of Classical Arabic *akhbār* literature.

Bibliography: Edited works. *Al-Akhbār al-Muwaffaḳiyyāt*, ed. Sāmī Makkī al-ʿĀnī, Baghdād 1972; *Djamharat nasab Ḳuraysh wa-akhbārihā*, ed. M.M. Shākir, i, Cairo 1381; *al-Muntakhab min Kitāb Azwādj* al-nabī, ed. Sukayna al-S̲h̲ihābī, Beirut 1403/1983, and, together with Ibn Zabāla, Azwād̲j̲ al-nabī, ed. Akram Ḍiyāʾ al-ʿUmarī, Medina 1401/1981.

2. Studies. Brockelmann, I², 146-7, S I, 215-16; Sezgin, GAS, i, 317-18, passim, see index; F. Wüstenfeld, Die Familie al-Zubeir, Göttingen 1878, 45 ff.; M. Fleischhammer, Quellenuntersuchungen zum Kitāb al-Ag̲h̲ānī, unpubl. ms. Halle 1965, 106-8; S. Leder, Prosa-Dichtung in der ak̲h̲bār-Überlieferung, in Isl., lxiv (1987), 6-41.   (S. LEDER)

ZUBDA (A.), derived from the root z-b-d with the basic meaning "foam(ing)", refers primarily to "cream (of milk), (fresh) butter", secondarily to "best part(s), essence, selection". In this transferred meaning it became a popular leading word of book titles, indicating that the work in question either encompasses the most important facts of its subject-matter (as e.g. in Zubdat al-bayān fī tadbīr amrāḍ al-insān "The essential information about the treatment of the diseases of man"; cf. Brockelmann, S II, 1031) or that it is an abridged version of some lengthier treatise (as e.g. with Zubdat al-asfār s̲h̲arḥ Muk̲h̲taṣar al-Manār "The essence of the books, Commentary upon M.M."; cf. Brockelmann, S II, 90). Occasionally the primary meaning of zubda is played upon, as e.g. in Zubdat al-ḥalab fī taʾrīk̲h̲ Ḥalab "The cream of the fresh milk; about the history of Aleppo" (Brockelmann, I, 332). Less often than zubda, its plural form zubad is used in the same way. The popularity of zubda and zubad in book titles is documented by 71 titles starting with zubda (63) or zubad (8) listed in the register of Brockelmann, S III, 1165.   (A.A. AMBROS)

ZUDJĀDJ, ZAD̲J̲ĀD̲J̲ and ZID̲J̲ĀD̲J̲ (A., sing. zud̲j̲ād̲j̲a), glass, syn. kawārīr "glass vessels, pieces of glass"; Pers. ābgīna or s̲h̲īs̲h̲a. It is mentioned in the Ḳurʾān (XXIV, 35) with the meaning of "glass container functioning as a lamp".

Glassmaking is often included in scientific works on mineralogy as a particular type of stone (see e.g. al-Bīrūnī, K. al-D̲j̲amāhir fī maʿrifat al-d̲j̲awāhir, Islamabad 1989, 191-3). In literary accounts, glass vessels and centres of glass production throughout the Islamic world are sometimes referred to, although they are invariably of generic nature. For example, Fusṭāṭ, Ṣūr, Antākiya, al-K̲h̲alīl, Ḥalab, Dimas̲h̲ḳ, Bag̲h̲dād, Ḳādisiyya, al-Baṣra, Iṣfahān, S̲h̲īrāz and Istanbul are all mentioned as glassmaking centres at various times (a survey is in Lamm 1929-30, 484-508).

Glass had been manufactured in the areas conquered by the Muslim armies for centuries, especially in Egypt and along the eastern Mediterranean coast. The "invention" of glass blowing in the 1st century B.C. had transformed this medium from an expensive, time-consuming product into an affordable, multi-purpose one. The chemistry, technology, and manipulation of glass remained unchanged in the transitional period from late Antiquity to early Islam—glassmaking being a rather traditional craft that evolved with small but steady steps in the mediaeval period. Glassmakers in the Islamic world continued to exploit artistically the wide range of available techniques of glass working, improving upon many, partially neglecting some, and reviving others. Most utilitarian objects were inflated on the blowpipe, shaped with different tools on the pontil (a solid iron rod attached to the base of the vessel after the blowpipe was cut off) and left undecorated. A large number of vessels were further manipulated with decorative effects in the so-called hot-worked technique. Designs were created applying glass trails, roundels, and splotches on the walls; patterns were impressed blow-ing the object directly in a decorated mould or making use of a tong-like tool that pressed both sides of an open-shaped vessel. The most sophisticated hot-worked objects present white trails applied in a spiral motion around the walls of a dark-coloured vessel, which are then incorporated in the surface with a rolling action against a smooth stone slab or marver, and patterned in festooned motifs with a pointed tool. This type of glass is often described as "marvered" or, better, "with marvered trails".

Cold-cut glass (glass that was abraded, incised, or cut away with hard-stone tools, rotating wheels, or drills in the lapidary technique after the vessel was shaped and left to harden and cool) was inspired by Roman and especially Sāsānid models, reaching new heights in the 4th-5th/10th-11th centuries.

The glass surface was often painted with a brush or a stylus and fired again to fix the pigments onto the surface. Early on, in the 2nd-3rd/8th-9th centuries, stained glass (usually known as "lustre-painted"), probably of pre-Islamic Egyptian origin, became popular in both Egypt and Syria. A lustrous film stained the glass surface permanently in various tones of yellow, brown, orange and red (sometimes combined) through a chemical reaction during the second firing. Difficult skills were required to control the temperature in the kiln to achieve the desired results without spoiling the shape of the re-heated vessel, skills that were perfected in the period of manufacture of enameled and gilded glass in the same areas in the 7th-8th/13th-14th centuries. Enamelled glass made under the Ayyūbids and the Mamlūks is the best known type of Islamic glass, thanks to its extraordinary polychrome appearance, the good condition of many objects, which were prized and collected through the centuries, and its technical accomplishment. Enamels, which are made of lead-rich glass pulverised and applied to the glass surface with a brush and an oily medium, and heavy gilding allowed the creation of painterly surfaces, including figural and vegetal motifs as well as calligraphic inscriptions. The texts, which often include the name of a sultan or an amīr, are extremely useful to establish the chronology of this extraordinary type of Islamic glass.

A clear art-historical development of shapes and decoration of Islamic glass is far from being entirely understood, notwithstanding the large number of extant objects and fragments. Even when it is obviously accomplished and expensive—and therefore made for wealthy clients—does glass only in rare instances include useful inscriptions, either moulded, incised or painted, that reveal the name of a patron or an artist, let alone a date. Glass was a commercial and artistic commodity across the entire Eurasian continent, shipped via land along the Silk Route and via sea on the Indian Ocean and the Mediterranean; consequently, excavated objects or vessels with a hearsay provenance were not necessarily created in the immediate vicinity. In addition, glass was traded also in the form of cullet, either as broken vessels or raw lumps, for re-melting. This simplified technology allowed fuel to be saved, but it inevitably makes the interpretation of chemical and elemental analyses a difficult task. Such lack of direct and indirect information, combined with scant and elusive original literary sources, has prevented scholars of Islamic art and of the history of glassmaking from grasping this subject thoroughly.

Carl Johan Lamm's seminal work (Lamm 1929-30, followed by the more focused Lamm 1935 and 1941) represents the only attempt to present a general study of Islamic glass thus far. The field has progressed slowly but steadily, and interest in Islamic glass has become particularly strong in the past twenty-five years. Earlier works that stimulated the recent interest in the field and are still looked upon as significant contributions—either as art-historical essays or archaeological reports—are Schmoranz 1898; Wiet 1912; Lamm 1928; Riis-Poulsen 1957; and Smith 1957, in addition to several articles that appeared in the *Journal of Glass Studies* since its first issue in 1959 (for example, Oliver 1961; Pinder-Wilson-Scanlon 1973; Bass 1984; Whitehouse 1993) and those in the *Annales* of the congresses of the *Association Internationale pour l'Histoire du Verre* since 1958.

Although time is not yet mature for a manual of Islamic glass, its general development is clear within the context of Islamic art and of mediaeval glassmaking. During the first two centuries after the advent of Islam, shapes, colours and decoration changed little from the long-established traditions of blown and hot-worked glass in the former Roman-Byzantine provinces. Bottles and perfume containers with whimsical trailed and applied decoration—among them the so-called cage flasks in the shape of quadrupeds carrying a small bottle—and moulded ribbed bowls are the most representative objects from this period. In the formerly Sāsānid area, the tradition of cold glass cutting, especially overall facets to create honeycomb patterns, probably continued during this early period, although the chronology is unclear because the majority of the extant objects show later, 3rd-4th/9th-10th-century, shapes. Relief-cut glass represents one of the best artistic achievements of the early Islamic period, the undisputed extant masterpiece being the so-called Corning Ewer in cameo glass (the decoration was achieved by partially cutting away the layer of green glass that covered the clear glass vessel; see Whitehouse 1993). Ultimately belonging to the Iranian tradition of glass cutting, this ewer is also symbolic of the transfer of techniques across the Islamic world, its shape being clearly related to Fāṭimid rock-crystal objects [see BILLAWR]. As a general statement, it can be said that a taste for colourful, textured and complex surfaces is predominant in the former Roman regions (stained- or lustre-painted glass provides a good example). Colourful *millefiori* ("thousand flowers") tiles and small vessels revived this Roman tradition in the heart of the ʿAbbāsid caliphate in the 3rd/9th century. "Scratched" or finely incised coloured objects with a wealth of geometric and vegetal motifs, probably created in the same ʿAbbāsid area, were so prized that they found their way to tombs in China (An 1991). Clear, colourless glass presenting restrained, stylised motifs belongs instead to the eastern Islamic world, with the Mesopotamian area functioning as a sort of meeting point of the two traditions. This statement, with its many exceptions, holds true also throughout the history of mediaeval Islamic glass.

That tradition played an important part in Islamic glass production is confirmed by the continuous use of many techniques throughout the mediaeval period, although shapes and details in the decoration are helpful to better understand their chronology. Functional undecorated objects (among them inkwells, alembics and scientific tools), and vessels presenting applied trails, moulded patterns, impressed motifs, marvered threads and combinations thereof, ranging from the 3rd/9th up to the 7th/13th centuries, form the bulk of glass from the Islamic lands in museums and collections worldwide, although it is not possible to select outstanding examples in the brief space assigned to this entry. About sixty circular medallions with figural motifs and, sometimes, inscriptions originally set into windows of 6th/12th-century G͟haznawid and G͟hūrid palaces in what is now Afg͟hānistān, however, deserve to be mentioned as a group that has recently come to scholarly attention, which also highlights the role of glass in architectural decoration (Field-Prostov 1942; Carboni 2001, cat. no. 73).

Enamelled and gilded glass probably originated in the Syrian region in the 6th/12th century. It was sought after by affluent merchants and rich members of the community, and also became a popular article of trade in all directions. Under the Mamlūks, not only large mosque lamps but also a profusion of secular objects include the names of sultans and *amīrs*. This is the only extant group of Islamic glass objects that provides evidence of a fervent royal and courtly sponsorship for this medium. Economic and political decline and the challenge of European trade and industry in the 9th/15th century weakened also the manufacture of enamelled glass in the Mamlūk lands. This decline in glass production, which was preceded by a similar situation in the eastern Islamic area, marks a two-century gap in our knowledge of Islamic glass, corresponding to the Tīmūrid and early Ṣafawid periods in Persia and the early Ottoman era in the former Mamlūk regions. The industry must have almost died out, although we know, for example, that glass was made in Istanbul in the 10th/16th century (Rogers 1983), until Venetian, then Bohemian, English and Dutch glass invaded the market and indirectly encouraged local production. Virtually nothing is known of Ottoman glass, but a little more about functional vessels made in Iṣfahān and S͟hīrāz under the late Ṣafawid, Zand, and Ḳād͟jār dynasties (Charleston 1974; Diba 1983; Charleston 1989). Glass manufactured in the Mug͟hal territories, instead, can be regarded as the only attempt to create artistically-motivated products (Dikshit 1969; Markel 1991; Carboni 2001, cat. nos. 104-6). Today, active but small glass factories creating vividly coloured bubbly glass, principally made with recycled cullet, can be visited throughout the Islamic world, in particular in Cairo and Damascus (see Henein 1974).

Bibliography (*JGS* stands for the *Journal of Glass Studies*): G. Schmoranz, *Altorientalische Glasgefässe*, Vienna 1898; G. Wiet, *Catalogue général du Musée Arabe du Caire. Lampes et bouteilles en verre émaillé*, Cairo 1912, repr. 1982; C.J. Lamm, *Das Glas von Samarra*, Berlin 1928; idem, *Mittelalterliche Gläser und Steinschnittarbeiten aus dem Nahen Osten*, Berlin 1929-30; idem, *Les verres trouvés à Susa*, in *Syria*, xii (1931), 358-67; idem, *Glass from Iran in the National Museum, Stockholm*, London 1935; idem, *Glass and hard stone vessels*, in *SPA*, vi, 2592-603 (glass section); idem, *Oriental glass of mediaeval date found in Sweden and the early history of lustre-painting*, Stockholm 1941; R.J. Charleston, *Types of glass imported into the Near East, some fresh examples*, in *Festschrift für Peter Wilhelm Meister*, Hamburg 1957, 245-51; P.J. Riis and V. Poulsen, *Hama, fouilles et recherches 1931-1938. Les verreries et poteries médiévales*, iv/2, Copenhagen 1957; R.W. Smith, *Glass from the Ancient World. The Ray Winfield Smith collection*, Corning 1957; P. Oliver (Harper), *Islamic relief cut glass: a suggested chronology*, in *JGS*, iii (1961), 9-29; Charleston, *The import of Venetian glass into the Near East, 15th-16th century*, in *Annales du 3e Congrès des Journées Internationales du Verre* (Damascus, Nov. 1964), Liège 1964, 158-68; *Exposition des verres syriens à travers l'histoire organisée à l'occasion du 3e Congrès des Journées Internationales du Verre au Musée

National de Damas (14-21 Nov. 1964); *Bulletin de l'Association International pour l'Histoire du Verre. Le verre en Syrie*, iii (1964); A. von Saldern, *Sassanidische und islamische Gläser in Düsseldorf und Hamburg*, in *Sonderdruck aus dem Jahrbuch der Hamburger Kunstsammlungen*, xiii (1968), 33-62; M.G. Dikshit, *History of Indian glass*, Bombay 1969; R.H. Brill, *Chemical studies of Islamic luster glass*, in R. Berger (ed.), *Scientific methods in medieval archaeology*, UCLA Center for Medieval and Renaissance Studies Contributions, iv (1970), Berkeley-Los Angeles-London, 351-77; R.H. Pinder-Wilson and G.T. Scanlon, *Glass finds from Fustat 1964-71*, in *JGS*, xv (1973), 12-30; R.J. Charleston, *Glass in Persia in the Safavid period and later*, in *AARP*, v (1974), 12-27; N.H. Henein, *Le verre soufflé en Égypte*, Institut Français d'Archéologie Orientale du Caire, Bibliothèque d'Étude, Cairo, lxii (1974), H. ʿAbd al-Khālik, *al-Zudjādj al-islāmī* (*Islamic glass*), Baghdad 1976; F. Bayramoğlu, *Turkish glass art and Beykoz-ware*, Istanbul 1976; R.H. Pinder-Wilson and W. Ezzy, *Glass*, in *The arts of Islam*, London 1976, 131-46; C. Clairmont, *Benaki Museum. Catalogue of ancient and Islamic glass*, Athens 1977; S. Fukai, *Persian glass*, Tokyo 1977; R. Hasson, *Early Islamic glass. L.A. Mayer Memorial Institute for Islamic Art*, Jerusalem 1979; *3000 Jahre Glaskunst von der Antike bis zum Jugendstil*, Lucerne 1981; S.M. Goldstein, *Islamic cameo glass*, in S.M. Goldstein, L.S. Rakow and J.K. Rakow, *Cameo glass. Masterpieces from 2000 years of glassmaking*, Corning 1982, 30-3; R.G.W. Anderson, *Early Islamic chemical glass*, in *Chemistry in Britain* (Oct. 1983), 822-23; L. Diba, *Glass and glassmaking in the eastern Islamic lands: seventeenth to nineteenth century*, in *JGS*, xxv (1983), 187-93; J.G. Kolbas, *A color chronology of Islamic glass*, in *JGS*, xxv (1983), 95-100; J.M. Rogers, *Glass in Ottoman Turkey*, in *Sonderdruck aus Istanbuler Mitteilungen, Deutsches Archäologisches Institut Abteilung Istanbul*, xxxiii (1983), 239-66; G.F. Bass, *The nature of the Serçe Limanı glass*, in *JGS*, xxvi (1984), 64-69; J. Kröger, *Glas. Islamische Kunst. Loseblattkatalog unpubliziert Werke aus deutschen Museen. Band 1. Berlin Staatliche Museen Preussischer Kulturbesitz, Museum für Islamische Kunst*, Mainz-Rhein 1984; A.H. Morton, *A catalogue of early Islamic glass stamps in the British Museum*, London 1985; H.A. Kordmahini, *Glass from the Bazargan Collection*, Iran National Museum, Tehran 1988; R.J. Charleston, *Glass*, in R.W. Ferrier (ed.), *The arts of Persia*, New Haven-London 1989, 295-305; F.H. van Doorninck, *The Serçe Limanı shipwreck: an 11th century cargo of Fatimid glassware cullet for Byzantine glassmakers*, in *I. Uluslararası Anadolu Cam Sanatı Sempozyumu 26-27 Nisan 1988/1st International Anatolian Glass Symposium, April 26-27, 1988*, Istanbul 1990, 58-63; J. An, *Dated Islamic glass in China*, in *Bulletin of the Asia Institute*, N.S., v (1991), 123-38; S. Markel, *Indian and "Indianate" vessels in the Los Angeles County Museum of Art*, in *JGS*, xxxiii (1991), 82-92; C. Meyer, *Glass from Quseir al-Qadim and the Indian Ocean trade*, Chicago 1992; K. von Folsach and D. Whitehouse, *Three Islamic molds*, in *JGS*, xxxv (1993), 149-53; D. Whitehouse, *The Corning Ewer. A masterpiece of Islamic cameo glass*, in *JGS*, xxxv (1993), 48-56; J. Allan, *Investigation into marvered glass. I*, in idem (ed.), *Islamic art in the Ashmolean Museum*, pt. 1, Oxford 1995, 1-30; J. Henderson, *Investigation into marvered glass. II*, in *ibid.*, 31-50; J. Kröger, *Nishapur. Glass of the early Islamic period*, New York 1995; R. Ward (ed.), *Gilded and enamelled glass from the Middle East*, London 1998; R.H. Brill, *Chemical analyses of early glasses*, Corning 1999; S. Carboni, *Glass production in the Fatimid lands and beyond*, in M. Barrucand (ed.), *L'Égypte fatimide, son art et son histoire*, Paris 1999, 169-77; Carboni, *Glass from Islamic lands. The al-Sabah collection*, London 2001; idem and Whitehouse, *Glass of the Sultans*, New York 2001.

(S. Carboni)

ZUHĀK, a historicised mythological tyrant of demonic nature who belonged to the Pīshdādiyān dynasty of Persian legendary history. (The form Zuhāk, if it exists at all, must be a mispronunciation of Perso-Arabic Ḍaḥḥāk, itself a re-interpretation of Middle Persian Dahāk, Avestan Azhī dahāka-, probably "snake-man"; cf. Vedic *azi-* "snake".)

According to Iranian tradition, recorded in Middle Persian, Persian and Arabic sources, Ḍaḥḥāk, also called Bīwarasp "possessor of a thousand horses", and a descendant of early Iranian world-kings, was the son of a king of the Arabs. Seduced by Satan (Ahrīman) he murdered his father, usurped his kingdom and attacked Djamshīd, the Iranian legendary king who had haughtily claimed divinity and therefore had lost the glory (*farrah*) bestowed by God on legitimate kings, seized him, had him sawed in half, captured his domain and reigned for a thousand years. His rule was characterised by severe oppression and bloodshed. Under him, drought caused famine and extreme hardship. Through Satan's machinations, two snakes grew on his shoulders. Following Satan's advice, he fed them daily with the brains of two youths to quell the torment they caused. A smith by the name of Kāwa (Kābī, in most Arabic sources) who had lost all but one of his sons to Ḍaḥḥāk's royal kitchen, made a banner of his leather apron and called upon people to rise against the tyrant. Farīdūn, a young man of royal lineage, who had been brought up in secret for fear of Ḍaḥḥāk, was sought out to head the rebellious force. He invaded the tyrant's palace, subdued him with his bull-headed mace, freed the two beauties from Djamshīd's harem whom Ḍaḥḥāk had abducted, put him in chains and sequestered him in Mount Damāwand where he will remain fettered until the restoration of the world by Soshyant, the saviour.

Azhī dahāka- (Pers. Azhdahā arabicised as Azdahāķ; see e.g. al-Ṭabarī, i, 201), the avatar of Ḍaḥḥāk, appears in the Avesta as a three-headed monster with three mouths and one thousand eyes. In Rigvedic traditions, *azi-* "snake" refers to monsters which block the passage of heavenly waters. In Middle Persian, *azhdahāg* assumes the meaning of monstrous dragons, of which the prime example is the one which is defeated and chained by Farīdūn. Rustam, the greatest warrior of Iranian legends, is said to be on his mother's side a descendant of Ḍaḥḥāk. This is supported by a tradition found in the *Mudjmal al-tawārīkh*, ed. Bahār, 25, which places the origin of Ḍaḥḥāk in the east. It seems that later on, his birth place was transferred to the deserts in the west, and in some sources, in Yaman. According to Ibn al-Balkhī (*Fārs-nāma*, ed. R. Nicholson, 11), his mother was the daughter of Djamshīd. He is one of the chief figures in the *Kūsh-nāma*, an 11th-century Persian epic in verse. Some Arabs claimed him as theirs; Abū Nuwās boasts in a line quoted by al-Ṭabarī, i, 201, of Ḍaḥḥāk's belonging to the Arab race. In a line of Abū Tammām cited by al-Thaʿālibī (*Ghurar*, 35), he is mentioned as the foremost embodiment of violence and cruelty.

Bibliography: The amplest accounts of Ḍaḥḥāk are found in Ṭabarī, i, 205-10, tr. W. Brinner, 1-7; Masʿūdī, *Murūdj*, ed. Pellat, i, § 537; *Bundahishn*, TD², 108, 209, 211, 228-9, 239, tr. T.D. Anklesaria, Bombay 1908, 137, 255, 269, 271, 273, 281, 293,

307; Balʿamī's Persian version of Ṭabarī, ed. M.T. Bahār, 132-33; Thaʿālibī, *Ghurar*, ed. H. Zotenberg, 17-35; and particularly Firdawsī, *Shāh-nāma*, ed. Khaleghi-Motlagh (Khāliḳī Muṭlaḳ), i, 55-86; Īrānshāh, *Kūsh-nāma*, ed. Dj. Matīnī, Tehran 1998; E. Yarshater, in *Cambr. Hist. Ir.*, iii/1, 372. For the development of the legend, Avestan passages and further Middle Persian sources, see P.O. Skjaervø, in *EIr*, iii, 191-9; for Ḍaḥḥāk in Persian literature, in folklore and in Armenian, see Dj. Khaleghi-Motlagh, M. Omīdsālār and J. Russell, in *ibid.*, 199-203, 203-5, 205-6, respectively.

(E. Yarshater)

ZUḤAL, the planet Saturn. The name *Zuḥal* (diptote) is said to be connected with the Arabic root *z-ḥ-l* meaning "to withdraw or become distant"; according to various lexicons (e.g. *LA, TA*), the planet takes its name from the fact that it is "far removed, in the seventh heaven". This etymology clearly postdates the knowledge among Arabic writers of Greek cosmology, for whom Saturn is the farthermost planet in the cosmos; it would have made little sense within the context of the limited astronomy of the pre-Islamic Arabs. According to the *Muḥīṭ al-muḥīṭ*, *zuḥal* was used as a metaphor for exaltedness (*ʿuluww*) as well as for being far removed; e.g., the poet al-Mutanabbī compared his patron Sayf al-Dawla's exalted state with that of *zuḥal*. Another name for Saturn found in texts from Spain and the Maghrib is *al-Muḳātil* "the warlike", just as we have there *al-Kātib* "the writer" alongside of the usual name *ʿUṭārid* [*q.v.*] for the planet Mercury (see al-nudjūm and al-Battānī, *Opus astronomicum*, i, 291). *Z-ḥ-l* does not seem to have cognates referring to Saturn in other ancient languages. (In contrast, the Akkadian name for Saturn *kajamānu* ("the steady one") evidently is the source for the Hebrew *kiyūn* (Amos v. 26) and Persian *kaywān*.)

According to ancient and mediaeval astronomy, the planets (from Greek πλανώμενοι "wanderers") are those celestial bodies that move with respect to the fixed stars as seen from the stationary Earth at the centre of the Universe. Thus in addition to our five planets observable with the naked eye (Mercury, Venus, Mars, Jupiter and Saturn), the sun and moon were considered planets as well. In Arabic, the first five, which exhibit retrograde motion in the ecliptic, were called *al-kawākib al-mutaḥayyira* ("the straying [or perplexed] stars") to distinguish them from the planets in general, which were usually referred to as *al-kawākib al-sayyāra* ("the wandering stars") [see al-nudjūm]. Following Ptolemaic cosmology, Islamic astronomers placed Saturn in the seventh and outermost planetary system of orbs (*aflāk*, sing. *falak* [*q.v.*]) between the orb of the fixed stars and Jupiter's orbs. To bring about Saturn's observed motions, three solid rotating orbs were postulated (see Fig. 1): (1) a pareclipticc (*mumaththal*) orb (centred on the Earth and in the plane of the ecliptic) whose convex (outer) surface (*muḥaddab*) was contiguous with the eighth orb of the fixed stars while its parallel concave (inner) surface (*muḳaʿʿar*) was contiguous with the convex surface of Jupiter's pareclipticc (motion equal to precessional rate of fixed stars, 1°/100 yrs.); (2) an eccentric deferent (*ḥāmil*) for the epicycle nested within the pareclipticc (mean motion in longitude of approx. 0;02°/day; eccentricity = 3 $^{5}/_{12}$ parts based on the deferent radius being 60); and (3) an epicyle (*tadwīr*), embedded within the deferent, that contained the actual planet (mean motion in anomaly of approx. 0;57°/day; radius = 6 $^{1}/_{2}$ parts). These mean motions lead to quite accurate values of 29.4 years for the mean tropical period

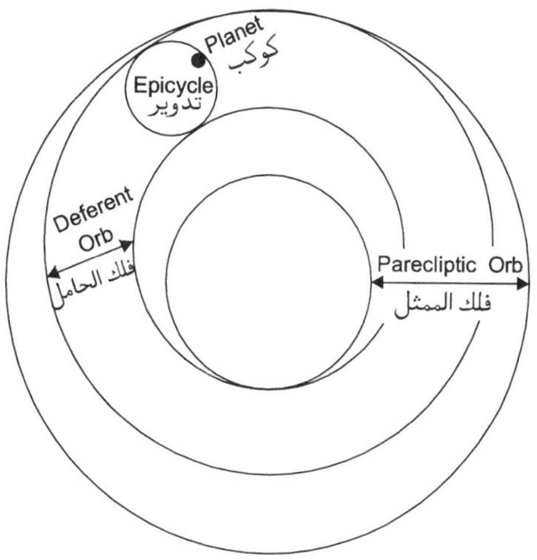

Fig. 1. Ptolemaic configuration (*hay'a*) for Venus, Mars, Jupiter and Saturn

and 1.035 years for the synodic ("anomalistic") period. Saturn's tropical period, the longest of the planets, led a number of Islamic astronomers to call for a thirty-year observational programme (see marṣad and A. Sayılı, *The observatory in Islam*, Ankara 1960, 163-6, 204, 288-9).

Ptolemy's exact values for motion in longitude and anomaly, given to six sexagesimal places, were slightly modified in various Islamic *zīdjs* [*q.v.*]. More drastic changes may be found in the precessional rate, which was given a more correct value of 1°/66 yrs. at the time of the caliph al-Maʾmūn [*q.v.*] and an even more accurate rate of 1°/70 years by the 4th/10th century. As with the other planets, Islamic astronomers proposed a number of modifications to Saturn's system of orbs to correct several non-uniform motions introduced by Ptolemy; these were considered violations of the accepted physics of the time, which required uniform circular motions in the heavens [see ʿilm al-hayʾa]. As for latitudinal motions, either above or below the ecliptic, these were brought about by inclinations of the deferent and complex motions of the epicycle (for which see Ragep, *Naṣīr al-Dīn*, i, 188-94).

Saturn's parecliptic outer surface marked the boundary between the planets and the fixed stars, and as such delimited the minimum possible size for the universe (it being unknown whether the fixed stars were all on a single orb just beyond Saturn or on multiple orbs at greater distances). Its distance from the Earth was generally given as approximately 20,000 earth radii (about 80,000,000 miles), which is of course considerably smaller than the current figure. Saturn's boundary with Jupiter was about 14,200 earth radii from the Earth, so the "thickness" (*thikhan*) of Saturn's parecliptic (equivalent to the distance occupied by its system of orbs) was 5,800 earth radii. Saturn itself, based on rather dubious observational data, was taken to be about 77 times the volume of the Earth.

Zuḥal in astrology [see minṭaḳat al-burūdj and nudjūm (aḥkām al-)].

According to a Sāsānid astrological theory, adopted by several early Islamic astrologers, Saturn-Jupiter conjunctions indicated important religious and political changes and thus provided the basis for an astrological world history [see ḲIRĀN]. Saturn is the lord of Saturday. Its two domiciles (*baytān*[i]) are Capricorn (day-house) and Aquarius (night-house); it is also the day-ruler of the third triplicity (*mut̲h̲allat̲h̲a*), consisting of Gemini, Libra and Aquarius, the night-ruler of which is Mercury. It is also the companion (*s̲h̲arīk*) of the ruler of the first *mut̲h̲allat̲h̲a* (Aries, Leo and Sagittarius). Its exaltation (*s̲h̲araf*) is in the 21st degree of Libra (20th, according to some Indian and Roman sources), and its fall (*hubūt*) is in the 21st degree of Aries. Saturn's nature is cold, dry and male, and it is characterised as black, malefic and generally of bad omen. It is called "the greater star of misfortune" (*al-naḥs al-akbar*), Mars being the lesser. They are contrasted with the two planets of good fortune, namely Jupiter and Venus [see SAʿD WA-NAḤS; AL-SAʿDĀN[i]].

In alchemy, *zuḥal* means lead.

Bibliography: In addition to references given in the article, see Bīrūnī, *K. al-Tafhīm li-awāʾil ṣināʿat al-tand̲j̲īm*, tr. R.R. Wright, London 1934 (Persian text, ed. D̲j̲alāl al-Dīn Humāʾī, Tehran 1362 *H.sh.*/1983-4); E.S. Kennedy, *A survey of Islamic astronomical tables*, in *Trans. of the American Philosophical Society*, n.s., xlvi/2 (1956), 121-77; *Ptolemy's Almagest*, tr. and annot. G.J. Toomer, New York 1984; F.J. Ragep, *Naṣīr al-Dīn al-Ṭūsī's Memoir on astronomy (al-Tadhkira fī ʿilm al-hayʾa)*, New York 1993; G. Saliba, *Arabic planetary theories after the eleventh century AD*, in *Encycl. of the history of Arabic science*, i, London-New York 1996, 58-127; Abū Maʿs̲h̲ar, *The abbreviation of the introduction to astrology*, ed. and tr. C. Burnett, K. Yamamoto and M. Yano, Leiden 1994; idem, *On historical astrology. The book of religions and dynasties (on the great conjunctions)*, ed. and tr. Yamamoto and Burnett, Leiden 2000.

(W. Hartner-[F.J. Ragep])

ZUHARA, the planet Venus. The Arabic name is derived from the root *z-h-r* meaning "to shine, be radiant", appropriate for the brightest planet whose magnitude can reach -4.4; perhaps in consequence of this, it was sometimes referred to as the white planet (*LA*). *Z-h-r* does not seem to have cognates referring to Venus in other ancient languages. Its Persian name is *(A)nāhīd*.

From Antiquity it was well known that the "morning" and "evening" stars were in fact the same planet, and that this planet, Venus, stayed fairly close (within 48°) to the sun. According to ancient and mediaeval astronomy, the planets are those celestial bodies that move with respect to the fixed stars as seen from the stationary Earth at the centre of the Universe [see on these planetary conceptions, ZUḤAL].

Following Ptolemaic cosmology, Islamic astronomers placed Venus in the third planetary system of orbs (*aflāk*, sing. *falak* [*q.v.*]) between those of Mercury and the sun. To bring about Venus's observed motions, three solid rotating orbs were postulated (see Fig. 1): (1) a parecliptic (*mumat̲h̲t̲h̲al*) orb (centred on the Earth and in the plane of the ecliptic) whose convex (outer) surface (*muḥaddab*) was contiguous with the concave surface of the sun's parecliptic while its parallel concave (inner) surface (*muḳaʿʿar*) was contiguous with the convex surface of Mercury's parecliptic (motion equal to precessional rate of fixed stars, 1°/100 yrs.); (2) an eccentric deferent (*ḥāmil*) for the epicycle nested within the parecliptic (mean motion in longitude equal to the sun's mean motion of centre, i.e. approx. 0;59°/day; eccentricity = 1 ¹/₄ parts based on the deferent radius being 60); and (3) an epicycle (*tadwīr*), embedded within the deferent, that contained the actual planet (mean motion in anomaly of approx. 0;37°/day; radius = 43 ¹/₆ parts). These mean motions lead to quite accurate values of one tropical year for the mean tropical period and 584 days for the synodic ("anomalistic") period.

Ptolemy's exact values for motion in longitude and anomaly, given to six sexagesimal places, were slightly modified in various Islamic *zīd̲j̲s* [*q.v.*]. As with the other planets, Islamic astronomers proposed a number of modifications to Venus's system of orbs to correct several non-uniform motions introduced by Ptolemy; these were considered violations of the accepted physics of the time, which required uniform circular motions in the heavens [see ʿILM AL-HAYʾA]. For precession and latitude, see ZUḤAL.

According to Ptolemy, the nearest distance to Venus, which is the same as Mercury's farthest distance, was 166 earth radii (approx. 664,000 miles); this is the distance from the Earth to the concave surface of Venus's parecliptic. Its farthest distance was 1160 earth radii (approx. 4,640,000 miles), which was the same as the Earth's nearest distance to the sun. Thus the "thickness" (*t̲h̲ik̲h̲an*) of Venus's parecliptic (equivalent to the distance occupied by its system of orbs) was 994 earth radii. These numbers, of course, depend on being able to fit the two inner planets (Venus and Mercury) between the moon and sun; as such, there were attempts to observe Venus transiting the sun, where it would thereby appear as a spot. Such observations, which were reported by a number of astronomers, would help establish that Venus was below the sun, though not definitively since it might go around the sun in its epicycle. At least one astronomer, Muʾayyad al-Dīn al-ʿUrḍī (d. 666/1266), entertained the notion that Venus might be above the sun (see B.R. Goldstein, *Some medieval reports of Venus and Mercury transits*, in *Centaurus*, xiv [1969], 49-59; idem and N.M. Swerdlow, *Planetary distances and sizes in an anonymous Arabic treatise preserved in Bodleian Ms. Marsh 621*, in *Centaurus*, xv [1970], 135-70; cf. Ragep, *Naṣir al-Dīn*, 391, 517-24). The usual volume for Venus in Islamic astronomical texts was ¹/₃₆ of the Earth's volume (Ptolemy has ¹/₄₄; see Ragep, *op. cit.*, 523).

Zuhara in astrology [see MINṬAḲAT AL-BURŪD̲J̲; NUD̲J̲ŪM (AḤKĀM AL-)].

Venus is the lord of Friday. Its two domiciles (*baytān*[i]) are Libra (day-house) and Taurus (night-house). It is the day-ruler of the second triplicity (*mut̲h̲allat̲h̲a*), consisting of Taurus, Virgo and Capricorn, the night-ruler of which is the moon, as well as day-ruler of the fourth triplicity, consisting of Cancer, Scorpio and Pisces, whose night-ruler is Mars. Its exaltation (*s̲h̲araf*) is in the 27th degree of Pisces and its fall (*hubūt*) in the 27th degree of Virgo. Venus's nature is cold and moist (phlegmatic) and female, and it is characterised as white, benefic and generally of good omen. It is called "the lesser star of good fortune" (*al-saʿd al-aṣg̲h̲ar*), Jupiter being the greater, contrasted with the two planets of misfortune, namely Saturn and Mars [see SAʿD WA-NAḤS; AL-SAʿDĀN[i]].

In alchemy, *zuhara* means copper.

Bibliography: In addition to references given in the article, see the *Bibl.* for ZUḤAL.

(W. Hartner-[F.J. Ragep])

ZUHAYR b. Abī Sulmā Rabīʿa b. Riyāḥ al-Muzanī, renowned poet of the pre-Islamic era, who, in the judgement of ancient critics, competed for first place with Imruʾ al-Ḳays and al-Nābig̲h̲a al-D̲h̲ubyānī [*q.vv.*] (Ibn Sallām, *Ṭabaḳāt fuḥūl al-s̲h̲uʿarāʾ*, ed. S̲h̲ākir, 52, 64-5; *Ag̲h̲ānī*, ix, 146-7, 158; al-Ḥuṣrī, *Zahr al-ādāb*, ed. Mubārak, 1, 90).

His father Rabīʿa belonged to the tribe of the Muzayna [*q.v.*], a minor tribe residing to the south of Medina as neighbours of the B. ʿAbd Allāh b. Ghaṭafān [*q.v.*] and of the B. Murra (an offshoot of the Ghaṭafān), his maternal uncles. Rabīʿa stayed for some time among the Banū Murra with his mother, but after a dispute over the distribution of booty following a raid, he returned with her to the Muzayna (*Aghānī*, ix, 148). However, he did not remain among them long, since in the course of a raid against the Dhubyān, the Muzayna left him behind. He returned to the Murra, settled among them and married the sister of the poet Bashāma b. al-Ghadīr, who was thus the maternal uncle of Zuhayr (*Aghānī*, ix, 157). Zuhayr was born and grew up among the Ghaṭafān, and, according to Ibn Ḳutayba (*al-Shiʿr wa 'l-shuʿarāʾ*, ed. Shakir, 137), in none of his poems does he refer to his Muzayna ancestry.

Zuhayr is classed among the *muʿammarūn*, those having a remarkably long life, and a well-known verse of the *Muʿallaḳa* (v. 47) refers to his already advanced years; in another poem, which incidentally al-Aṣmaʿī does not consider authentic (rhyme, *liyā*, al-Shantamarī, ed. Ḳabāwa no. 17, Thaʿlab, ed. Dār al-Kutub, 283-92; cf. al-ʿAynī, *al-Maḳāṣid al-naḥwiyya fī sharḥ shawāhid shurūḥ al-alfiyya*, Būlāḳ 1299, ii, 267-69) and which tells of *dahr* and the decay of human things, Zuhayr mentions the fall of al-Nuʿmān b. al-Mundhir of al-Ḥīra [see LAKHMIDS] which took place in 602. He would thus have been living at the beginning of the 7th century (R. Jacobi, *Studien zur Poetik der altarabischen Qaside*, Wiesbaden 1971, 8) and, according to the *Aghānī*, ix, 148, at 100 years old he is said to have encountered the Prophet. The *Muʿallaḳa* was composed to celebrate the end of the War of Dāḥis [*q.v.* in Suppl.] and Ghabrāʾ, between the ʿAbs and Dhubyān. This war is said to have lasted 40 years and to have continued some years after the *yawm* of Shiʿb Djabala [*q.v.*], which apparently took place around the year 550 or, according to a more widespread tradition, in the year 570. Thus the poem celebrates the end of this long war and the two chieftains of the B. Murra who concluded the peace, Harim b. Sinān and al-Ḥārith b. ʿAwf.

The *Muʿallaḳa* of Zuhayr, unlike other *muʿallaḳāt*, is linked to a specific historical episode, which it evokes: the personal exploits of an individual of Murra, al-Ḥuṣayn b. Ḍamḍam, who, having not accepted the peace accords between the two clans, killed a member of the ʿAbs. The two chieftains of Murra took responsibility for payment of the blood-price, and peace was finally concluded (*Aghānī*, ix, 148-50). This justly famous poem opens with a long *nasīb* which colourfully describes the departure of the tribe of Umm Awfā; it then passes abruptly to a paean praising the generosity of the chieftains, which is intermingled with a description of the horrors of war and the men who wage it, identified directly, without the intermediary of any comparison, with animals that need to slake their thirst with water mixed with blood and to pasture on muddy ground. The poem ends with a section composed of verses having the form of a proverb, some of which have probably been added (see M.C. Bateson, *Structural continuity in poetry*, Paris-The Hague 1970, 50; G.J.H. van Gelder, *Beyond the line*, Leiden 1982, 59).

The *dīwān* of Zuhayr has been conserved with two principal commentaries (besides the commentaries on the *Muʿallaḳa* alone; cf. in this context M. Abū Ṣūfa, *al-Ḳaṣāʾid al-ʿashr wa-maṣādir sharḥihā*, ʿAmmān 1986): the commentary of the Andalusian philologist al-Aʿlam al-Shantamarī (d. 476/1083) and the commentary of the Kūfan Thaʿlab (d. 291/904). The former, which forms part of the commentary that al-Shantamarī composed on the *dīwān* of six pre-Islamic poets, presents Zuhayr's *dīwān* according to the Baṣran *riwāya* of al-Aṣmaʿī, which has been preserved in its entirety, while citing for certain poems the likewise Baṣran *riwāya* of Abū ʿUbayda, which has been preserved in part only. This recension contains 20 poems and has been edited numerous times: by W. Ahlwardt, without commentary, London 1870, by C. Landberg, with al-Shantamarī's commentary (*Primeurs arabes*, ii, Leiden 1889) and recently by F. Ḳabāwa, Aleppo 1970. This last edition adds a *Dhayl*, which contains the poems and fragments which feature in the collections of Thaʿlab and of the Kūfan Ṣaʿūdāʾ (tutor of the children of Muḥammad b. Yazdād, vizier of al-Maʾmūn, see al-Suyūṭī, *Bughya*, i, 256, no. 476; al-Baghdādī, *Khizānat al-adab*, ed. Hārūn, v, 452, considers him "weak in grammar", but nevertheless frequently quotes his commentary). The commentary of Thaʿlab chiefly presents Zuhayr's *dīwān* according to the Kūfan *riwāya* of Abū ʿAmr al-Shaybānī, but he also collates the other Kūfan recensions (Ḥammād al-Rāwiya and al-Mufaḍḍal al-Ḍabbī) and the Baṣran recensions, cf. K. Dyroff, *Die Geschichte der Überlieferung des Zuhairdiwans*, Munich 1892, 20, and Nāṣir al-Dīn al-Asad, *Maṣādir al-shiʿr al-djāhilī*, Cairo 1956, 530-5. This collection contains 53 poems and fragments and was edited in 1944 by the Dār al-Kutub al-Miṣriyya, and in 1982 by F. Ḳabāwa. Nāṣir al-Dīn al-Asad, *op. cit.*, 526-42, and Shawḳī Ḍayf, *Taʾrīkh al-adab al-ʿarabī, al-ʿaṣr al-djāhilī*, Cairo 1960, 305-6, are of the opinion that only al-Aṣmaʿī's recension should be taken as an authentic basis for an analysis of the poetry of Zuhayr.

Early Arabic criticism attributes to Zuhayr two particular qualities: that of being born into a family of great poetical talent (Ibn al-Aʿrābī [*q.v.*], *Aghānī*, ix, 158; al-ʿAbbāsī, *Maʿāhid al-tanṣīṣ*, i, 110; Ibn Rashīḳ, *al-ʿUmda*, ii, 306; he was *rāwī* of Aws b. Ḥadjar, who had married Zuhayr's mother after the death of his father, Ibn Rashīḳ, i, 88, 99, Ḍayf, *Taʾrīkh*, 300; his maternal uncle was the poet Bashāma b. al-Ghadīr, *Aghānī*, ix, 157); and that of having worked very assiduously on the composition of his poems, something which could have required a great deal of time. Certain of the poems of Zuhayr are in fact called *ḥawliyyāt*, "poems which have been pondered over for a year" (Ibn Ḳutayba, *Shiʿr*, 78, 144). Furthermore, Zuhayr belonged to a line of poets who were in their turn transmitters (*rāwī*) of a preceding poet (Ibn Rashiḳ, i, 198, 201). Without going so far as to suppose, as Ṭāhā Ḥusayn and others after him have supposed, that "poetical schools" are involved here (M. Zwettler, *The oral tradition of classical Arabic poetry*, Columbus, Ohio 1978, 86-7; cf. also Ḍayf, *Taʾrīkh*, 306-7), it may be asserted that the poetry of Zuhayr does appear to be the fruit of a meticulous apprenticeship. According to the *khabar* of a poetical tenson or contest between Zuhayr and his son Kaʿb, transmitted only by Thaʿlab and Saʿūdāʾ (*Dīwān*, ed. Dār al-Kutub, 256-9; *Aghānī*, xv, 147-9), Zuhayr is said to have rebuked and even struck his son for composing poems before completing his education (cf. Blachère, *HLA*, 336 n. 1).

These affirmations, all of them pointing in the same direction, are reflected in the judgements of ancient critics and in their manner of citing the poetry of Zuhayr. Al-Aṣmaʿī, like his master Abū ʿAmr b. al-ʿAlāʾ, did not have a high opinion of the "slaves of poetry" (*ʿabīd al-shiʿr*), those poets whose verses are polished and refined precisely because they have been composed without recourse to natural talent (Ibn Ḳutayba, *Shiʿr*, 144, al-Djāḥiẓ, *al-Bayān wa 'l-tabyīn*, i, 206, ii, 13, in reference to al-Ḥuṭay'a, *rāwī* and disciple of Zuhayr), and for this reason he did not consider Zuhayr as a *faḥl*, preferring to him al-Nābigha al-Dhubyānī (*Fuḥūlat al-shuʿarā'*, ed. Torrey, in *ZDMG*, lvi [1911], 492; *Aghānī*, iii, 25).

On the other hand, critics of the classical epoch not only judged that this toiling over verse was a positive aspect of this poetry, but they were also often aware that this concern with form went beyond the mark of the verse taken in isolation. The expression *lā yuʿāẓilu fī/bayn al-kalām/bayn al-ḳawāfī/al-kalimatayn*, whereby ʿUmar b. al-Khaṭṭāb defined the poetry of Zuhayr (Ibn Ḳutayba, *Shiʿr*, 137-8; *Aghānī*, ix, 148; Ibn Sallām, *Ṭabaḳāt*, 63), is thus explained in the *Risāla al-Mūḍiḥa* of al-Ḥātimī (d. 388/998), ed. Nadjm, 91, as avoiding pairing words that are not of the same genus. Al-ʿAskarī (*K. al-Ṣināʿatayn*, 169) in the chapter dealing with *sū' al-naẓm*, gives a similar explanation, and adds that this defect, from which the greatest of the ancient poets were not exempt, is not to be found in the poetry of Zuhayr. At 107-8, this same critic cites an example of *madīḥ*, drawn from the *Muʿallaḳa*, in which the theme is developed over several verses, according to logical transitions which al-ʿAskarī does not fail to point out. It often happens that images or a *waṣf* are deployed over several verses which, while retaining their formal autonomy, are dependent one upon the other; Zuhayr is above all a skilled engraver, who represents both his poetical themes and his ideas by means of images which have, in every detail, a visual force.

Al-ʿAskarī also mentions other verses which are well constructed and well balanced (*Ṣināʿatayn*, 367, 401; Ibn Rashīḳ, *al-ʿUmda*, i, 333) and he underlines, several times, the formal means whereby Zuhayr surmounts the difficulties of the end of the verse and of rhyme (*Ṣināʿatayn*, 466, 468-69; Ibn Rashīḳ, *al-ʿUmda*, ii, 3) and all the critics acknowledge in him the qualities of "weightiness" and of "solidity" (Ibn Sallām, *Ṭabaḳāt*, 64; Ibn Ḳutayba, *Shiʿr*, 144). Al-Marzūḳī (*Sharḥ Dīwān al-Ḥamāsa*, 9) interprets the ancient judgement of the poetry of Zuhayr attributed to ʿUmar b. al-Khaṭṭāb ("he praised people only for the qualities that they have", Ibn Sallām, *Ṭabaḳāt*, 63) not in the moral sense but in the poetical sense of a successful description (*iṣābat al-waṣf*).

Among poetic genres, *madīḥ* is the most frequently represented (11 poems out of the 20 most positively authentic), honouring in particular the chieftains of Ghaṭafān, and this corresponds to the expressions used by tradition in defining Zuhayr as *amdaḥ al-ḳawm* (Ibn Ḳutayba, *Shiʿr*, 144) or indeed in saying that Zuhayr was *ashʿar al-nās... idhā raghiba* (judgment attributed to the grammarian Yūnus b. Ḥabīb, d. 182/798, in *Aghānī*, viii, 77; al-ʿAskarī, *Ṣināʿatayn*, 29; Ibn Rashīḳ, *al-ʿUmda*, i, 95), while recognising that he was not in thrall to the lure of gain (*ibid.*, i, 81). Numerous traditions refer to the praises addressed by Zuhayr to Harim b. Sinān as a monument *aere perennius*, while the gifts that Zuhayr received from him had been eroded by time (*Aghānī*, ix, 146); Ḳudāma b. Djaʿfar, *Naḳd al-shiʿr*, ed. Bonebakker, 33-4, cites long passages from the *madā'iḥ* of Zuhayr, to serve as an "example".

Less numerous are the *hidjā'* poems. Ibn Rashīḳ, *al-ʿUmda*, ii, 66, 171, considered that in this poetical genre Zuhayr had proved himself a stylist both caustic and pure; cf. van Gelder, *The bad and the ugly*, Leiden 1988, 16. Other poems relate to personal affairs, such as his repudiation of his first wife, Umm Awfā (*Dīwān*, al-Shantamarī, no. 16; Thaʿlab, ed. Dār al-Kutub, 342; according to al-Yazīdī, *Amālī*, 133, Muḥammad b. Ḥabīb considered these verses apocryphal), who was jealous of his second wife, the mother of Zuhayr's sons Kaʿb, Budjayr and Sālim. The last-named died young, and Zuhayr composed a *rithā'* for him (not transmitted by al-Shantamarī; *Aghānī*, ix, 157; *Dīwān*, Thaʿlab, ed. Dār al-Kutub, 340-1). Four poems deal with the theft of camels belonging to Zuhayr, and the abduction of their herdsman by a member of the Banū Asad who, as a result of some menacing verses on the part of the poet, decided to send the slave back to him (*Dīwān*, Thaʿlab, ed. Dār al-Kutub, 164-83, 300-12; al-Shantamarī, nos. 5-8; cf. al-Baghdādī, *Khizāna*, v, 453-58; according to al-Aṣmaʿī, the first of these poems was the finest *kāfiyya* in the Arabic language).

Bibliography: There hardly exists a poetical study that does not mention the poetry of Zuhayr. In addition to sources given in the article, see Wahhābī, *Marādjiʿ tarādjim al-udabā'*, iii, 139-46; Fu'ād al-Bustānī, *Zuhayr b. Abī Sulmā*, Beirut 1929; G.E. von Grunebaum, *Pre-Islamic poetry*, in *MW*, xxxii (1942), 147-53; A.J. Arberry, *The Seven Odes, the first chapter in Arabic literature*, London 1957, 90-118; M.J. Kister, *The Seven Odes*, in *RSO*, xliv (1969), 27-36; A. El-Tayib, ch. *Pre-Islamic poetry*, in *Camb. hist. of Arabic lit. Arabic literature to the end of the Umayyad period*, Cambridge 1983, 68-70; E. Wagner, *Grundzüge der klassischen arabischen Dichtung*, i, Darmstadt 1987; J.E. Montgomery, art. *s.n.*, in J.S. Meisami and P. Starkey (eds.), *Encycl. of Arabic literature*, London and New York 1998, ii, 827; Sezgin, *GAS*, ii, 118-20, ix, 255-6.

(LIDIA BETTINI)

ZUHAYR B. DJANĀB, a semi-legendary tribal leader and poet, and the eponym of a tribal group belonging to the Kalb b. Wabara [*q.v.*] who flourished in the 6th century A.D. According to some, he was in command of the whole of the Ḳuḍāʿa [*q.v.*].

Around the middle of the 6th century, Abraha [*q.v.*] put Zuhayr in charge of the two brother tribes, Taghlib b. Wā'il and Bakr b. Wā'il [*q.vv.*]. Zuhayr raided them after they had rebelled against him, taking captive Kulayb b. Rabīʿa [*q.v.*] and his brother Muhalhil. At a later stage, Zuhayr and his tribe made up for their alliance with Mecca's enemy, Abraha, by joining the *Ḥums* [*q.v.*]. Moreover, Zuhayr subdued an attempt by the Ghaṭafān [*q.v.*; see also MURRA, at Vol. VII, 629a] to establish a rival sanctuary northeast of Mecca. His action is said to have been praised by the Prophet Muḥammad.

Zuhayr is supposed to have committed suicide, when he was disobeyed, by drinking unmixed wine. Among his offspring we find Maysūn [*q.v.*] who bore for Muʿāwiya I his son Yazīd [*q.vv.*]. The prominence of Ibn al-Kalbī in the reports about Zuhayr demonstrates the latter's importance in the tribal tradition of the Kalb, and that of the Ḳuḍāʿa as a whole, for at least two centuries into the Islamic era.

Bibliography: 1. Sources. Ibn ʿAsākir, *T. Madīnat Dimashḳ*, ed. ʿU. Gh. al-ʿAmrawī, Beirut 1415/1995-, xix, 99-108; *Aghānī*[3], xix, 15-29; Abū Ḥātim al-Sidjistānī, *al-Muʿammarūn*, ed. ʿA. al-M. ʿĀmir, Cairo 1961, index.

2. Studies. H. Lammens, *Le berceau de l'Islam*, Rome 1914, 319-22; ʿĀdil ʿAṭā' Allāh al-Furaydjāt, *Zuhayr b. Djanāb al-Kalbī: akhbāruhu wa-mā tabaḳḳā min shiʿrihi*, in *MMMʿA* (Cairo), xxxviii (1994), 129-82; Sezgin, *GAS*, ii, 146; M.J. Kister, *Mecca and the tribes of Arabia*, in *Studies... in honour of David Ayalon*, ed. M. Sharon, Jerusalem and Leiden 1986, 33-57, at

43-52; M. Lecker, *The Banū Sulaym*, Jerusalem 1989, 37-41. (M. Lecker)

ZUHAYR b. **ḤARB**, Abū Khaythama al-Shaybānī al-Nasāʾī, traditionist of the early ʿAbbāsid period. He was born at Nasā in Khurāsān in 160/776-7 but lived mostly in Baghdād, dying there in Shaʿbān 234/March 849. He was amongst the seven scholars forwarded by Isḥāḳ b. Ibrāhīm to the caliph al-Maʾmūn for questioning over the createdness or otherwise of the Ḳurʾān (al-Ṭabarī, iii, 1116; see also miḥna). Regarded as a trustworthy, *thiḳa*, narrator of traditions, he was the author of a *Kitāb al-ʿIlm* (publ. Damascus 1966).

Bibliography: al-Khaṭīb al-Baghdādī, viii, 482-4 no. 4597; Ibn Abī Ḥātim, *al-Djarḥ wa ʾl-taʿdīl*, Ḥaydarābād 1952-3, i/2, 591; Ibn al-ʿImād, *Shadharāt*, ii, 80; Sezgin, *GAS*, i, 1077. (C.E. Bosworth)

ZUHAYR b. **ḲAYS** al-Balawī (b. ?, d. 76/695), Arab commander, stemming from Balī, one of the Ḳuḍāʿa [*q.v.*] tribes, of reputed Yemeni descent. Ibn Ḥadjar, *Iṣāba* i, 555-6, includes him among the Prophet's Companions and mentions his role in the conquest of Egypt, whilst al-Suyūṭī, *Ḥusn al-muḥāḍara*, i, 200, lists him as a *Ṣaḥābī* but in i, 258 as a *Tābiʿ* or Successor, showing that he belonged to the two groups.

He took part in the campaigns against the Maghrib in the time of ʿUḳba b. Nāfiʿ [*q.v.*], one of them against Surt/Syrte where, after its conquest, Zuhayr was left, together with ʿUmar b. ʿAlī al-Ḳurashī, at the head of the army; in another account, he is said to have been ʿUḳba's deputy, at the head of al-Ḳayrawān, fighting against the Berber chief Kusayla [*q.v.*] and defeating him.

Zuhayr also participated in the campaign against Ayla [*q.v.*] at the side of the governor of Egypt ʿAbd al-Raḥmān b. Djaḥdam, a partisan of the Zubayrids, against ʿAbd al-ʿAzīz b. Marwān, but ended up by coming to an agreement with the latter when Ibn al-Zubayr's influence in Egypt declined and ʿAbd al-ʿAzīz was established as *amīr* there. The latter appointed Zuhayr *amīr* of Barḳa [*q.v.*] and instructed him to attack the Byzantines. It is related that he defended himself against ʿAbd al-ʿAzīz, who retained a grudge against him from his anti-Umayyad past in Egypt and who spoke slightingly of him; Zuhayr vigorously responded that a man like himself, who had taken part in the collection of the Ḳurʾān, should not be treated humiliatingly. When a Byzantine force from Constantinople attacked Barḳa, he died valiantly with his 70 companions before the rest of the troops could come to his aid, in 76/695.

Bibliography: Ibn ʿAbd al-Ḥakam, *Futūḥ Miṣr*, ed. Torrey, 194, 198, 200, 202-3; Kindī, *Wulāt*, ed. Guest, 43-4; Ibn al-Athīr, ed. Beirut, iv, 109-10; Ibn Taghrībirdī, *Nudjūm*, i, 178, 216; Suyūṭī, *Ḥusn al-muḥāḍara*, Cairo 1387/1967, i, 200, 258; Ibn ʿIdhārī, *Bayān*, Beirut 1980, i, 32-3; Nāṣirī, *Istiḳṣāʾ*, Cairo 1312/1894, 38-42; Ziriklī, *Aʿlām*³, iii, 87-8; Kaḥḥāla, *Muʿdjam ḳabāʾil al-ʿarab*, Beirut 1985, 104-7. (R.G. Khoury)

ZUHAYR, ʿAmīd al-Dawla al-Ṣaḳlabī [see al-ṣaḳāliba], ruler of Almería middle 419-late 429/middle 1028-late 1038, originally a client (*mawlā*) of al-Manṣūr Muḥammad b. Abī ʿĀmir, the famous *ḥādjib* of al-Andalus at the end of the late 4th/10th century.

During the period of turmoil which followed the fall of the ʿĀmirids in 399/1009, a number of Ṣaḳlabī leaders left Cordova and managed to set up independent states on the eastern seaboard of Spain. Prominent among them was Khayrān, who ruled Almería (405-19/1014-28) and appointed his brother/companion (*ṣāḥib*) Zuhayr as his lieutenant in Murcia. Nominated by Khayrān as his successor in Almería, Zuhayr ruled an extensive territory extending from Almería to Játiva, Baeza and the approaches of Toledo. He even controlled Cordova itself for some fifteen months (425/1034).

Zuhayr is credited with building and later extending the great mosque of Almería and with improving the city's water supplies and fortifications. He is said to have sought, and complied with, the advice of the *fuḳahāʾ*. The description of Zuhayr by the author of the *Tibyān* as a stupid ignoramus does not accord with the accounts of Andalusian chroniclers, who speak highly of Zuhayr's piety, courage, astuteness and prudence.

Shortly after the accession of the Zīrid *amīr* of Granada Bādīs b. Ḥabūs (Ramaḍān 429/June 1038), the alliance which had existed between Zuhayr and Ḥabūs came to an end as a result of Zuhayr's alliance with Muḥammad b. ʿAbd Allāh al-Birzālī, lord of Carmona and leader of the Zanāta [*q.v.*] Berbers, traditional foes of the Ṣanhādja [*q.v.*] to which the Zīrids belonged. Zuhayr's alliance with the lord of Carmona was probably motivated by the expansionist policy of the *ḳāḍī* Muḥammad b. ʿAbbād, ruler of Seville, who in 426/1035 had installed the pseudo-Umayyad Hishām in Seville as caliph of al-Andalus. This Zuhayr and al-Birzālī adamantly refused to accept. According to the last Zīrid *amīr* of Granada, Zuhayr "on hearing of the death of Ḥabūs cast covetous eyes on Granada. He therefore marched on the city and duly encamped at a place known as Alpuente (*al-Fūnt*)" (*Tibyān*, 70, tr. 58). Having decided to open hostilities, Bādīs laid ambushes in ravines on Zuhayr's route and pulled down a bridge which the Ṣaḳlabī had to cross. On approaching the bridge, Zuhayr was set upon by Bādīs's men. At the very outset, Zuhayr's Negro detachment, some 500 strong, defected. Zuhayr himself, however, stood fast and ordered his fellow Ṣaḳāliba to engage the Granadans who, though outnumbered, routed the Ṣaḳāliba. "In the space of a single hour, it [Zuhayr's army] was routed with the loss of all its eunuchs (*khiṣyān*). Zuhayr, however, completely vanished and was not to be found either living or dead" (*Tibyān*, 70, tr. 59).

Almería was annexed, a month later, by ʿAbd al-ʿAzīz b. Abī ʿĀmir of Valencia, who acquired a huge fortune from the possessions left by "his grandfather's *mawālī*" (*Dhakhīra*, i/2, 730).

Bibliography: 1. Sources. ʿAbd Allāh b. Buluggīn, *Tibyān*, ed. A. Ṭībī, Rabat 1995, 70-71, Eng. tr. Leiden 1986, 58-9; Aḥmad b. ʿUmar al-ʿUdhrī, *Tarṣīʿ al-akhbār*, ed. A. al-Ahwānī, Madrid 1965, 83-4; Ibn Bassām al-Shantarīnī, *Dhakhīra*, ed. I. ʿAbbās, i/2, Beirut 1975, 656-63; Ibn ʿIdhārī, *Bayān*, ed. E. Lévi-Provençal, iii, Paris 1930, 168-71; Ibn al-Khaṭīb, *Aʿmāl*, ed. Lévi-Provençal, Beirut 1956, 210-5; idem, *Iḥāṭa*, ed. M.A. Enan, i, Cairo 1973, 517-20.

2. Studies. A.M. ʿAbbādī, *Los esclavos en España*, Span. tr. Madrid 1953, 16-17; Dozy, *Hist. des musulmanes d'Espagne*, Leiden 1932, index; A. Prieto y Vives, *Los Reyes de Taifas*, Madrid 1926, 34; D. Wasserstein, *The rise and fall of the Party-Kings*, Princeton 1985, index. (Amin Tibi)

ZUHAYR, al-Bahāʾ [see bahāʾ al-dīn zuhayr].

ZUHD (a.), the material and spiritual asceticism facilitating closer association with the divine.

Zuhd constitutes one of the "spiritual virtues" considered not only by the mystics, but also by a large number of believers, as essential to religious life in Islam. As such, it occupies a dominant place in the biographies of saints of the first centuries of the Hid̲j̲ra. The term embraces numerous nuances, divided between two principal meanings: on the one hand, "renunciation" in the sense of detachment, of indifference to things of this inferior world; on the other, "asceticism" in the sense of privation, mortification, tests imposed on the carnal soul (*nafs*). The two terms of Ḳurʾānic origin, *ʿābid* and *nāsik*, have often been employed as equivalents of *zāhid*, although the former (in the plural *ʿubbād*) serves to denote the devotees of God, and the latter, more specifically, the one who performs sacrifices and performs rites. *Zāhidīn* (Ḳurʾān, XII, 20), the sole occurrence of the root, describes the merchants who sold Joseph after finding him in the pit in which his brothers had thrown him, "attaching no value to him" and therefore not considering him worth keeping. Their detachment here takes on a profane sense. To denote a certain form of spiritual renunciation, the Ḳurʾān uses paraphrases, as in the verse (LVII, 23): "Do not despair in that which escapes you and do not exult in that which has been given to you." Reference could also be made to III, 14; XV, 8; XVI, 96; XVIII, 7; XX, 131; XXIII, 55, 56; XXVIII, 60, 83; XXXI, 33; XLIII, 33-5.

Literature specifically devoted to renunciation comprises, out of 63 titles listed for the period between the 2nd/8th and the 10th/16th centuries (27 of which have survived to this day), 37 works dating from the 2nd/8th and 3rd/9th centuries. Their titles include, in addition to the word *zuhd*, which appears 45 times, one instance of *taṣawwuf* (taken as a synonym of *zuhd*); two of *bukāʾ* (weeping) and *d̲h̲amm al-dunyā* (contempt for this inferior world); four of *waraʿ* (abstinence through religious scruple); and, finally, eight occurrences of *raḳāʾiḳ* (actions that elevate man), which would thus seem to be the closest equivalent, and the singular of which (*raḳīḳa*) can, as Roger Deladrière has pointed out, denote the precariousness of the life of ascetics. On the other hand, the anthology of al-Bayhaḳī (d. 458/1065 [*q.v.*]) throws light on the various nuances attributed to *zuhd* in the 4th-5th/9th-10th centuries: contentment with little (*ḳanāʿa*); isolation (*ʿuzla*); the effacement of self (*k̲h̲umūl*); opposition to the lower soul and to passion (*muk̲h̲ālafat al-nafs wa ʾl-hawāʾ*); the limitation of hopes (*ḳaṣr al-amal*); the pressure to finish works before the end of life (*al-mubādara li ʾl-ʿamal ḳabla bulūg̲h̲ al-ad̲j̲al*); zeal in obedience (*al-id̲j̲tihād fi ʾl-ṭāʿa*); safeguarding the status of a servant (*mulāzamat al-ʿubūdiyya*); scrupulous piety (*waraʿ*); and vigilant piety (*taḳwā*). Some added poverty (*faḳr*), which denotes external deprivation as much as the absence of desire for riches; the latter includes, in a spiritual sense, the absence of desire for the blessings of the other world. On the other hand, Sahl al-Tustarī (d. 283/896 [*q.v.*]) draws a clear distinction, on the basis of a prophetic tradition, between *zuhd* and *taḳas̲h̲s̲h̲uf* (mortification of the flesh).

Expressing an opinion on the subject of renunciation has never been the exclusive preserve of the Ṣūfīs. Declaring that in the *Kitāb al-Zuhd al-kabīr* of al-Bayhaḳī, it is a traditionist, Abū ʿAbd Allāh al-Ḥāfiẓ (d. 412/1021), and not a Ṣūfī who supplies most information concerning the renunciation of ascetics, mystics and gnostics, Deladrière has thrown light upon the essential role of the *ḥuffāẓ* in the elaboration of this literature. This affinity is confirmed by the fact that, in Twelver S̲h̲īʿī circles, *zuhd* was reckoned among the qualities required for the transmitter (*rāwī*) of Imāmī traditions.

The earliest works, such as those of Ibn al-Mubārak (d. 181/797 [*q.v.*]), are primarily concerned with the actions and gestures of the Prophet Muḥammad—who appears to an increasing extent, in the course of the development of mystical literature, to be the most consummate model of the "renouncer"—and of his Companions, as well as certain epigoni, the one most often cited being al-Ḥasan al-Baṣrī (d. 110/728 [*q.v.*]). The work of Ibn Ḥanbal (d. 241/855 [*q.v.*]) adds to this the renunciation practised by eleven sanctified individuals, from Adam to Jesus, and by the Umayyad caliph ʿUmar b. ʿAbd al-ʿAzīz. It is principally from the 4th/10th century onward that the leading protagonists of this literature become the mystics of the two preceding centuries: D̲h̲u ʾl-Nūn al-Miṣrī, Ibn Adham, Fuḍayl b. ʿIyāḍ, Bis̲h̲r al-Ḥāfī, Sarī al-Saḳaṭī, Yaḥyā b. Muʿād̲h̲, Sahl al-Tustarī, al-D̲j̲unayd and al-S̲h̲iblī.

Goldziher advanced the hypothesis according to which the earliest prophetic traditions, those possessing the strongest guarantee of authenticity, tended towards a rejection of *zuhd*, whereas only late forgeries endorsed or extolled it. It is in any event certain that a large number of *ḥadīt̲h̲*, corroborated by Ḳurʾān, XXV, 67, stressed the necessity of limiting the practice of asceticism and of observing a high degree of moderation.

In regard to the first four centuries of the Hid̲j̲ra, it is difficult to establish a decisive distinction between the corpus of work emanating from the Ḥanbalīs or other traditionists and that of the mystics proper. The distinction was accentuated during the Mamlūk period, at which time the Ṣūfī or the *walī* only received the epithet of *zāhid* when he had distinguished himself through extreme corporeal asceticism. E. Geoffroy has declared that at the end of this period, Ḥanbalī authors, making abundant use of the terms *zāhid* and *ʿābid*, effected a very fine demarcation between adherence to Ḥanbalism and attribution of the term Ṣūfī, especially in Syria, while in the Ottoman period there was a general rapprochement between Ḥanbalism and Ṣūfism. In practice, being an ascetic has never implied adherence to Ṣūfism, although the consensus among mystics has always stressed the importance of this quality.

For the Persian D̲j̲āmī (d. 898/1492 [*q.v.*]), who clearly differentiates *zuhd* from true Ṣūfism, "ascetics consider the beauty of the other life in the light of faith and of certitude and do not despise this inferior world, but they are still veiled by the pleasure that is afforded them by the contemplation of Paradise; on the other hand, the true Ṣūfī is separated as by a veil from these two worlds, by the vision of primordial Beauty and of eternal love" (*Nafaḥāt al-uns*, ed. Tawḥīdpūr, Tehran 1957, i, 10).

It is especially in the determination of the sphere of application of *zuhd* that the greatest differences arise. In the 2nd/8th and 3rd/9th centuries, two interpretations of the term were established: for some, it meant above all renunciation, not only of agreeable clothes, accommodation and foodstuffs, but also of comfort, sleep and all human relationships, sometimes including marriage; for others, it was a more internal and subjective asceticism, the renunciation of intentions and desires, which led to the concept of *tawakkul* [*q.v.*]. However, for many mystics, the two aspects were seen as going hand-in-hand.

Ibrāhīm b. Adham (d. 165/782 [*q.v.*]) is generally credited with a sub-division of *zuhd* into three stages, which is also found in the works of al-Sarrād̲j̲ and could emanate from a later source: (1) renunciation of the world; (2) renunciation of the joy of having devoted oneself to renunciation; and (3) the stage at which the world becomes so insignificant in the eyes of the ascetic that he is no longer interested in it. His disciple, Shaḳīḳ al-Balkhī, reckoned to be the first to have spoken of mystical states (*ʿulūm al-aḥwāl*), declares that *zuhd* constitutes the most elementary stage of those who practise sincerity (*ahl al-ṣidḳ*). It is followed by the stages of fear, of desire for Paradise, and of love of God. The beginning of *zuhd* consists in the training of the body to experience the hunger which will give release from the other preoccupations of this inferior world.

The Malāmatiyya [*q.v.*], just like the Khurāsānī spiritual leader al-Tirmidhī (d. 318/930) proposed a conception of *zuhd* which was to serve as a model for numerous mystical systems from the 3rd/9th century onward: genuine *zuhd*, that of the Prophet and of his Companions, is presented as a particular type of renunciation, which does not imply in any way a visible and material practice of asceticism, but a profound detachment, an attitude of the heart; ascetic practices may be admitted, if considered necessary, as a preparatory stage, as is affirmed, in a different context, by al-Djunayd. Such a form of renunciation presents an aspect that is entirely spontaneous, linked to a divine grace.

Abū Saʿīd al-Kharrāz (d. 286/899 [*q.v.*]) adopted the same classification as did al-Balkhī: renunciation is followed by fear, and it consists in "the progressive detachment of the heart from every desire concerning this inferior world". The "renouncers" are subdivided according to three categories: "Some act thus in order to liberate their heart from all preoccupation other than obedience to God, the mention of His name and His service; others desire, through this influence, to become light and to pass quickly over the bridge which traverses Hell, knowing that those who are weighed down will be delayed and subjected to interrogation. Finally, others act thus through the desire for Paradise. They deprive themselves of the life of this inferior world and dedicate themselves to awaiting the reward of God. But the most elevated degree of renunciation consists in consenting totally to the love of God and accepting without reserve the state of servitude by the understanding of His will" (*K. al-Ṣidḳ*, ed. ʿAbd al-Ḥalīm Maḥmūd, Cairo, 43).

For Ibn ʿAṭāʾ Allāh al-Iskandarī (d. 709/1309 [*q.v.*]), renunciation consists in liberating the heart from the love of this inferior world and from the jealousy it may feel in regard to other people and the benefits they enjoy: "O ignorant one, cease to envy the creatures of this inferior world for what they have received. Your heart is preoccupied with what they possess and you become even more ignorant than they. In fact, they are preoccupied with what they have received and you, you are preoccupied with what you have not received" (*Tādj al-ʿarūs, ʿalā hāmish al-Tanwīr*, 11).

Zuhd has gradually acquired a place in the succession of mystical stations, but differences exist between one thinker and another, although all consider it as associated with the beginning of the way.

In Twelver Shīʿī traditions, it appears to be the least of the virtues of the believer, its highest level corresponding to the lowest level of "contentment with little" (*ḳanāʿa*), while Dhu 'l-Nūn al-Miṣrī (d. 245/859 [*q.v.*]) states that the "ladder of *waraʿ* gives access to *zuhd*". For al-Dārānī (d. 205/820), spiritual heir of al-Ḥasan al-Baṣrī, the pinnacle of *zuhd* is abandonment to trust in God (*tawakkul*); it would be the same for al-Ghazālī (d. 505/1111), giving it precedence over *faḳr*. Al-Ḥakīm al-Tirmidhī considers *zuhd* as the outcome of repentance (*tawba*) and the stage preceding combat against the carnal soul (*ʿadāwat al-nafs*). We have here a stage of the heart. "The world appears worthless in the eyes of renouncers, since an invisible part has been revealed to them. They therefore do not concern themselves in the least with the subsistence that could fall to their lot, and on this matter they trust in their Lord with an utterly tranquil heart. He who does not direct his regard towards the other life and magnifies in his own eyes the life of this world, even if he is completely withdrawn from the life of here below, wears nothing but rags and eats only grass, is not a true renouncer but only a man who compels himself to renounce" (*Nawādir al-uṣūl, aṣl* 106, *fī ḥaḳīḳat al-zuhd*, Beirut, 144).

Ibn al-ʿArabī (d. 638/1240 [*q.v.*]) likewise envisages *zuhd* as one of the first stages of the way. It is situated in the wake of isolation (*ʿuzla*), of retreat (*khalwa*) and the practice of scruple (*waraʿ*). According to him, it also precedes *tawakkul*.

Thus for Muslim as well as for Christian spiritual seekers (desert anchorites and mystics), interior renunciation is held to be much more important than spectacular practices of asceticism. The latter have, however, persisted into the present day in response to precise functions, for the ascetic himself as for his entourage.

Examples of extreme mortification are not lacking among the accounts of the lives of the early Ṣūfīs; it used to be said, for example, that Shāh al-Kirmānī (d. between 270/883 and 300/912) spent forty years without sleeping; Rūzbihān Baḳlī (d. 606/1209 [*q.v.*]), told the story of a saint who had fasted totally for seventy days; Abū Saʿīd b. Abi 'l-Khayr (d. 441/1049 [*q.v.*]), a Khurāsānī Ṣūfī and disciple of al-Sulamī, practised ascetic exercises over a period of seven years, in particular the *ṣalāt maḳlūba* which consists of reciting the Ḳurʾān and praying while suspended by the feet in a dark place.

Numerous Egyptians mystics, among others, are renowned for their impressive feats of asceticism. Shaykh Murshid declared to al-Shaʿrānī that he had not eaten more than one raisin per day over a period of forty years, to the point where the skin of his stomach adhered to that of his back. Al-Sayyid al-Badawī (d. 675/1276), the famous saint of Ṭanṭā who had adopted voluntary celibacy, possessed nothing of his own and burned out his eyes by staring at the sun from his terrace, spent forty days without drinking, eating or sleeping. He never took off his clothes or his turban, waiting for them to fall to pieces by themselves. His disciples, including Abū Ṭarṭūr, were renowned for their asceticism. In this context, some mystics took it as a point of honour to surpass Jesus, regarded by the majority of Ṣūfīs as a model of poverty, of mortification and of detachment from the concerns of this world. These manifestations of the Badawiyya, as those of numerous other mystical orders, have been subjected at all times to the censure of the *ʿulamāʾ*, whose efforts have been pursued, to little effect, into the present day.

Bibliography: ʿAlḳama b. Marthad (d. 121/738), *Zuhd al-thamāniya min al-tābiʿīn*, ed. ʿAbd al-Raḥmān al-Furāwāʾī, Medina 1983; Muḥammad ʿAbd al-Raḥīm Muḥammad, *al-Zuhd li 'l-Ḥasan al-Baṣrī*, Cairo 1991; ʿAbd Allāh b. al-Mubārak, *al-Zuhd wa 'l-raḳāʾiḳ*, ed. Aʿẓamī, Beirut 1967, ed. Aḥmad Farīd, al-Riyāḍ 1995; Wakīʿ b. al-Djarrāḥ (d. 197/812), *K. al-Zuhd*, ed. al-Furāwāʾī, Medina 1984; Asad b. Mūsā = Asad al-Sunna (d. 212/827), *K. al-Zuhd*, ed. R.G. Khoury, Wiesbaden 1976; Ibn Ḥanbal, *al-Zuhd*, ed. Basyūnī Zaghlūl, Beirut 1986; *al-Waraʿ*, ed. Zaynab Ibrāhīm al-Ḳārūṭ, Beirut n.d.; Ḥammād b. al-Sārī al-Kūfī al-Tamīmī (d. 243/857), *K. al-Zuhd*, ed. ʿAbd Allāh b. Ibrāhīm al-Anṣārī, Dawḥa 1986; al-Ḥusayn b. Saʿīd al-Ahwāzī (d. 301/913), *K. al-Zuhd*, ed. Djalāl al-Dīn ʿAlī al-Ṣaghīr, Beirut 1993; Abū Bakr Aḥmad b. Abī ʿĀṣim, *K. al-Zuhd*, ed. ʿAlī ʿAbd al-Ḥamīd, Beirut 1988; Bayhaḳī, *K. al-Zuhd al-kabīr*, ed. Sh. ʿĀmir Aḥmad Ḥaydar, Beirut 1987, tr. R. Deladrière, *Bayhaḳī, l'anthologie du renoncement*, Paris 1995; Sahl al-Tustarī, *al-Muʿāraḍa wa 'l-radd ʿalā ahl al-firaḳ*, ed. Kamāl Djaʿfar, Cairo 1980, 88, 122; al-Ḥakīm al-Tirmidhī, *Manāzil al-ʿibād min al-ʿibāda*, ed. ʿAbd al-Raḥīm al-Ṣāʾiḥ, Cairo 1988, 68-72; Abū Saʿīd al-Kharrāz, *K. al-Ṣidḳ*, ed. ʿAbd al-Ḥalīm Maḥmūd, Cairo n.d., 42-5; Kulaynī, *al-Uṣūl min al-Kāfī, K. al-Īmān wa 'l-kufr, bāb dhamm al-dunyā wa 'l-zuhd fīhā*, Beirut 1985, ii, 128-37; Makkī, *Ḳūt al-ḳulūb*, i, 242-71; Ḳushayrī, *Risāla*, 67; Abū Naṣr al-Sarrādj, *al-Lumaʿ, bāb maḳām al-zuhd*, 70-2; Ghazālī, *Iḥyāʾ ʿulūm al-dīn*, iv, 154-71; Ibn al-Djawzī, *Talbīs Iblīs*, Cairo n.d., 150-60; Ibn al-ʿArabī, *Futūḥāt makkiyya*, ii, 177-8; Ibn Taymiyya (d. 729/1328), *al-Zuhd wa 'l-waraʿ wa 'l-ʿibāda, Fatāwā al-kubrā*, selections, Zarḳāʾ and ʿAmmān 1987; Ibn ʿAṭāʾ Allāh al-Iskandarī, *Tādj al-ʿarūs, ʿalā hāmish al-Tanwīr*, Cairo 1948, 11; I. Goldziher, *De l'ascétisme aux premiers temps de l'Islam*, in *RHR*, xxxvii (1898), 314-24; L. Massignon, *Essai sur les origines du lexique technique de la mystique musulmane*, [1]Paris 1954, [2]1999, 191, 212, 227; idem, *Recueil de textes inédits*, Paris 1929, 17, 146-8; P. Nwyia, *Exégèse coranique et langage mystique*, Beirut 1970, 216-24, 291; Abū Zayd ʿAlī Ibrāhīm, *Zuhd al-mudjdjān fī 'l-ʿaṣr al-ʿabbāsī*, Cairo 1986; C. Mayeur-Jaouen, *Al-Sayyid al-Badawī*, Cairo 1994, 232-5; E. Geoffroy, *Le soufisme en Égypte et en Syrie*, Damascus 1995, 287-91; Annemarie Schimmel, *Mystical dimensions of Islam*, Chapel Hill 1975, 110-24, Fr. tr. *Le soufisme ou les dimensions mystiques de l'islam*, Paris 1996, 150-62.

(Geneviève Gobillot)

ZUHDIYYA (a., pl. *zuhdiyyāt*), a pious, homiletic or ascetic poem, of the kind that flowered as a genre of Arabic poetry in the 2nd-3rd/8th-9th centuries. The noun *zuhd* [*q.v.*] denotes principally "asceticism", "renunciation (of the material world)", but the themes of the *zuhdiyya* are broader than this allows one to understand; collectively, the *zuhdiyyāt* articulate a general, God-fearing Islamic piety, exhorting mankind to be mindful of mortality and to a comportment of utter sobriety.

Though the *zuhdiyya* emerged as a distinctive genre in the early ʿAbbāsid period with the poetry of Abu 'l-ʿAtāhiya (d. 211/826 [*q.v.*]), it had its roots in an important register of pre-Islamic verse, and then, more particularly, in the pious/didactic poetry of two relatively minor Islamic poets, Sābiḳ al-Barbarī (d. 110/728) and Ṣāliḥ b. ʿAbd al-Ḳuddūs (d. 167/783-4 [*q.v.*]).

That the *zuhdiyya* was recognised in the mediaeval period as a genre in its own right can be gleaned from the divisions of poetry in *dīwān*s of individual poets (cf. Schoeler, *Einteilung*, 34 ff.). The first *dīwān* to be arranged according to theme/genre is al-Ṣūlī's (d. 335/946) recension of the *dīwān* of Abū Nuwās (d. *ca.* 198/813) which lists *zuhd* as the tenth (and final) category of poems. Ḥamza al-Iṣfahānī (d. after 350/961), for the same poet, places the *zuhdiyyāt* as the sixth of eleven categories. Subsequent *dīwān*s containing ascetic poetry are: ʿAlī b. Ḥamza al-Iṣfahānī's *dīwān* of Abū Tammām (d. *ca.* 232/845), where *zuhd* is one of eight themes; Ibn al-Muʿtazz (d. 296/908), whose *dīwān*, also arranged by al-Ṣūlī, contains a short, 10th, section on *zuhd wa-ādāb wa-shayb wa-ḥikma*; and Ṣafī al-Dīn al-Ḥillī (d. 750/1349) containing a final, 12th, section labelled *fī 'l-ādāb wa 'l-zuhdiyyāt wa-nawādir mukhtalifa* (a collection which contains few truly ascetic fragments.)

(a) *Antecedents.* The dominant thematic strain of the *zuhdiyya* is rooted in pre-Islamic poetry, particularly the elegiac tendency of much of the early corpus: the evocations of Man's mortality in a finite existence and of the despoiling effect of Time/Fate (*al-zamān/al-dahr*). In *Djāhilī* poetry, where such contemplation crystallises in aphorism, it is generally labeled *ḥikma* (lit. "wisdom") in later anthologies and manuals of poetry. *Ḥikma* penetrates and overlaps with the thematic and homiletic register of the *zuhdiyya*, which is a wisdom literature of sorts, drawing also on the *naṣāʾiḥ* of earlier poetry (cf. Muḥammad ʿAwīs, *al-Ḥikma fī 'l-shiʿr al-ʿarabī*, which symptomatically contains a section on the *zuhdiyya*).

However, pre-Islamic poetry's elegiac strain is distinct from the pessimism of *zuhd* in two fundamental respects. For it either suffuses elegies (*marāthī*), whose mood is pessimistic but whose function is nevertheless distinct from *zuhd*, or, in the poetry of *fakhr*, pessimism is transcended by the poet's enunciation of his own worth within the ethical and moral panoply of *muruwwa* (cf. Sperl, *Mannerism*, 71 ff.). Seldom, if at all, does pre-Islamic poetry give expression to the morose quietism of *zuhd*.

Insofar as his poetry contains an admixture of elegiac and religious themes, acknowledging life after death and buttressing didacticism with frequent references to the biblical prophets, the Christian poet of al-Ḥīra, ʿAdī b. Zayd (d. *ca.* 600), is viewed as the father of this genre. (Ironically, he is also described as the father of the *khamriyya* [*q.v.*] or wine poem in the genealogical histories of Arabic genres.) It is in this poet that we find the earliest significant treatment of the *ubi sunt* topos, which may have been inherited from the muse of earlier Christians of the region, but which was later Islamised in the *zuhdiyya* as a standard rhetorical feature, often stressed by passages of anaphora (the question *ayna* "where is...?" beginning a whole series of lines).

In early Islamic times, *zuhd* is understood to have been influenced largely by the ascetic teachings of al-Ḥasan of Baṣra, for whom the Prophet Muḥammad was a paragon of ascetic virtue (Hamori, 267). As an Islamic genre, the texture of the *zuhdiyya* is one rich in Ḳurʾānic allusion and quotation (*iḳtibās*); it also contains many elements of *ḥadīth*. But does Scripture support its ascetic tenor? To some extent this is certainly the case, and much can be made of verses in the Ḳurʾān which rail against human material greed (cf. e.g. XX, 131). This must be balanced, however, by an understanding of the Ḳurʾān's concomitant view of the fruits and blessing of the Earth (cf. e.g. XXXVI, 34-6). The *zuhdiyya* is an unstintingly lugubrious literature of admonishment that tends to ignore the spirit of such Ḳurʾānic verses.

(b) *Early development.* Much insight into the genre's development can be gleaned from the surviving poetry of Sābiḳ al-Barbarī (who was *imām* and *ḳāḍī* under the caliph ʿUmar II in the Syrian town of al-Raḳḳa). In his *Bayān*, al-Djāḥiẓ described (and decried) his poetry as *kulluhu amthāl*—a string of pious maxims. This is not entirely fair; indeed, some of his lengthier pieces are patterned in a way that may have influenced his successors. There is an emerging structure in his work, and some of his poetry needs to be carefully examined in the light of a variety of retrospective allusions to it in the *dīwān* of Abu 'l-ʿAtāhiya. There is a thematic consistency in his verse: addiction to this world is chided, remembrance of God is urged. A counseling temperament lends weight to such material, particularly in a poem addressed to ʿUmar b. ʿAbd al-ʿAzīz.

Whilst striking parallels between Sābiḳ and ʿAdī b. Zayd exist, Sābiḳ himself foreshadows traits of Abu 'l-ʿAtāhiya in being inventive with old motifs and transforming the semantics of the traditional lexicon of poetry. For example, *dār*, lit. "abode" (in ancient poetry, typically, the "abode of the beloved"), is made to refer to "this mortal world", and *araḳ* "insomnia", is caused not by the pains of love but by existential angst.

Abu 'l-ʿAtāhiya's *zuhdiyya* rhyming in *lām* and beginning *li-man ṭalal^un usāʾiluhu* (cf. Sperl's analysis, *Mannerism*, 82-96) bears comparison with Sābiḳ's identically rhymed *taʾawwabanī hamm^un kat͟hīr^un balābiluhu* (Kannūn, 20-2). Even more yielding is a comparison of Abu 'l-ʿAtāhiya's *lā yaʾmanu 'l-ḍahra illā 'l-k͟hāʾinu 'l-baṭiru* (*Diwan*, 153-4) with Sabiḳ's *bi-smi 'llad͟hī unzilat min ʿindihi 'l-suwaru* (Kannūn, 6-9). The metre of the two poems is identical and they clearly display an affinity with each other that is more than simply due to generic features. The first and last lines of Abu 'l-ʿAtāhiya's poem are virtual citations from Sābiḳ's, and seem to highlight the literary evocation of the earlier piece. Abu 'l-ʿAtāhiya's poem is shorter; it is also stylistically tighter, more economically structured, and more thematically homogeneous. The full literary implications of such observations require further study. The very least we can say with confidence is that Sābiḳ's poetry was in circulation during Abu 'l-ʿAtāhiya's day.

Ṣāliḥ b. ʿAbd al-Ḳuddūs was a preacher in Baṣra who edified the crowd with gnomic verse, sermons and *ḥadīt͟hs*. His poetry of *sententiae*, proverbs and *naṣīḥa* (advice) enjoyed some success, judging from the diffuse spread of his poetry in the various sources—al-Buḥturī quotes 75 verses from 35 poems (i.e. in fragmentary form in his *Ḥamāsa*). Three of his poems in particular were celebrated, his *sīniyya*, his *ḳāfiyya*, and also a *zaynabiyya*, which has also been attributed to ʿAlī. He counsels sobriety, self-control, and ascetic virtue as a guarantee for peace of mind in this world and salvation in the next. Among the qualities he extols are: faithfulness to friends, holding one's tongue, reflection before speech, avoidance of unnecessary mirth, and awareness of the fact that, even when alone, one is observed by God. One's conduct should be an exteriorisation of inner virtue. Wealth is denigrated; were it to be distributed according to intelligence, most people would be beggars. One should trust unstintingly in God (cf. Chokr, 222-4).

There is little theology in these, or in any, *zuhdiyyāt*. However, there are some attitudes that are redolent of al-Ḥasan al-Baṣrī, e.g. that of fatalistic resignation to the will of God, whilst espousing Ḳadarī views in assigning responsibility for sin (cf. Wagner, 123).

The close thematic and functional links between the *zuhdiyya* and sermon material (*waʿẓ/mawāʿiẓ*) emerge from a *ḳiṣṣat ʿAbd al-Ḳuddūs maʿa rāhib al-Sīn* attributed to him (K͟haṭīb, 93-104): it treats of the futility of existence and chides the *abnāʾ al-dunyā* for trusting too much in their lot; there are elements here of *d͟hamm al-zamān* or complaints about the corruption of the age. And finally, we find a call to repent (*tawba*). Though accused of *zandaḳa*, and eventually executed on this charge in the reign of al-Mahdī, there is no evidence of heterodoxy in his verse. The polemical/Muʿtazilī view that he was a *dahrī* dualist ignores totally his genuinely homiletic poetry which appears to be authentic (Chokr, 226-31).

(c) *Abu 'l-ʿAtāhiya.* The audience of this poet, once he came to write *zuhdiyyāt* to the exclusion of other poetry in the reign of Hārūn al-Ras͟hīd, was probably in part similar to that of Ṣāliḥ. His own views are recorded in the *Ag͟hānī*: "[*Zuhd*] does not appeal to kings, nor to transmitters of poetry, nor to students of lexical rarities; the people who really delight in it are ascetics, students of *ḥadīt͟h*, scholars of religious law, people who make a show of piety, and the common people, who most admire what they can understand" (Schoeler, *ʿAbbāsid belles-lettres*, 287-8). But if this reduces the status of his poetry on a purely linguistic level, we should be reminded of the complex literary relationships of his verse. He was a professional poet who gave himself exclusively to the *zuhdiyya* only after a conversion; in his early career he had composed in the other major genres, and he was certainly aware of the evolution of the poetic canon among his contemporaries. And it is said that he came to guard his genre jealously, warning fellow-poets from trespassing on his literary terrain (Abū Nuwās composed relatively few *zuhdiyyāt*: only 24 in the recension of al-Ṣūlī). Awareness of others—as a literary/poetic posture—is detectable in the details of his verse and in the way he constructed some of his more felicitous poems.

(d) *Structure.* Sperl has shown convincingly how individual *zuhdiyyāt* can be made up of carefully arranged and contrastive semantic, morphological and syntactical patterns. The apparent cohesion of themes in the *zuhdiyya* is achieved by more than the simple use of *anaphora* (and other types of repetition, themselves redolent of sermon material). The most visible technique is the occasional adaptation (or evocation) of the *ḳaṣīda* model.

In general, we should stress the following relatively enhanced qualities of his verse: the sometimes sustained semantic and metaphorical transformation of traditional imagery within single compositions; the tension that is sometimes felt between a purely ascetic tendency and the influence of dalliance (in its poetic manifestations)—this is more to do with (lapses of) temperament than structure; and the *zuhdiyya*'s existence virtually contiguous with the more secular, and even reprobate, genres of the Bag͟hdād circle of poets in the early ʿAbbāsid period. S.M. Stern expressed a facet of this cogently: "The worldly and other-worldly sentiments were not felt as being mutually exclusive, but as two aspects of the same conception of the world, opposing, yet at the same time counterbalancing and complementing each other. The same poet could at the same time contemplate and express both facets of his experience with equanimity. His primary and most frequently expressed attitude will be that of the enjoyment of the world; to this subject he will devote the overwhelming majority of his poetical productions. The contrary tendency will be satisfied with an occasional *zuhdiyya*, which will ultimately be inserted in his *dīwān* among other verses" (*Hispano-Arabic strophic poetry*, 81). This astute psychological evaluation further asserts the relatively subordinate status of the homiletic genre.

(e) *Later developments.* After Abu 'l-ʿAtāhiya, the *zuhdiyya* was never again so closely associated with an individual author (though mention must be made of Maḥmūd al-Warrāḳ, d. *ca.* 230/845). Yet ascetic poetry remained popular and found its way into many subsequent anthologies; fragments of ascetic poetry are quoted in Ibn Ḳutayba (d. 276/889), Ibn ʿAbd Rabbihi (d. 328/940) and al-Ibs̲h̲īhī (d. *ca.* 850/1446), to name but a few authors. In these collections, it is the affinity of this poetry with sermon material that emerges most noticeably; the literary quality of poems as a whole is almost totally ignored, and any sense of structural artifice is destroyed by their fragmentary arrangement (cf. esp. al-Buḥturī, who breaks poems down into *maʿānī*, e.g. *fi-mā ḳīla fī tawakkuʿ al-mawt wa 'l-ḥid̲h̲r minhu wa 'l-iʿdād li 'l-maʿād*, and *fi-mā ḳīla fi 'l-tuḳā wa 'l-birr*).

The survival—and certain developments—of the genre in later times are conveniently attested by Ibn Sanāʾ al-Mulk (d. 608/1211): "The *muwas̲h̲s̲h̲aḥ* treats of the same subject as the various kinds of *s̲h̲iʿr*, i.e. love, praise, mourning (*mart̲h̲iya*), invective (*hid̲j̲āʾ*) frivolity (*mud̲j̲ūn*), and asceticism (*zuhd*)" (Stern, 42). None of these ascetic *muwas̲h̲s̲h̲aḥāt* appear to survive—another marker of their minor status. However, there is some interesting evidence of the relationship between this ascetic mode and the dominant secular strain: "The special feature in these lost 'ascetic' *muwas̲h̲s̲h̲aḥ*s is that according to Ibn Sanāʾ al-Mulk they used to correspond to a given secular *muwas̲h̲s̲h̲aḥ*, i.e. that *muʿāraḍa* used to be a rule in them, applied to a special purpose; the 'ascetic' *muwas̲h̲s̲h̲aḥ* was considered as 'expiating' the sin committed through the poem which served as model" (*ibid.*, 82). This is reminiscent of the relationship one has detected between Abu 'l-ʿAtāhiya and the poetry of his libertine contemporaries (though it is not quite the same as the scorn which could be directed against the *zuhdiyya* in the form of literary lampoon: Salm al-K̲h̲āsir (d. 186/802) mocked Abu 'l-ʿAtāhiya for hypocrisy: *mā aḳbaḥa 'l-tazhīda min wāʿiẓ^{in}/yuzahhidu 'l-nāsa wa-lā yazhadu*).

Some remarks should address the survival of *zuhdiyya* once it was eclipsed by Ṣūfī poetry from the 6th/12th century onwards (a subject on which there appears to be no sustained study). The final chapter of Ibn Ḥazm's (d. 456/1054) *Ṭawḳ al-ḥamāma* contains two long poems on "the virtues of continence" (*faḍl al-taʿaffuf*). The second poem is a virtual manifesto of the *zuhdiyya* in the period of its decline, apostrophising the soul to live in *ḳunūʿ* and *tawakkul*, themes which by this time are associated more with the mystical register. In a central passage, some of the principal images of *Sūrat al-takwīr* and other sūras are woven into the text in a sustained and particularly felicitous way. We are reminded that, after Abu 'l-ʿAtāhiya, mastery of the register did not die, though no-one was ever again as prodigious, fluent and varied as he.

Finally, a fascinating permutation of the *zuhdiyya* in Arabic literary history is its role in the tale of the City of Brass in the *Arabian Nights*. This tale illustrates the survival intact of the poetry of *zuhd* right up to the pre-modern period, and evinces how Ḳurʾānic themes common to the classic *zuhdiyya* could be woven meaningfully into a narrative, delivering a richly textured message against the spiritual void of material wealth: *tazawwadū fa-inna k̲h̲ayra 'l-zādi 'l-taḳwā* (II, 197). In this story, ascetic poetry dovetails strikingly with a mystical undercurrent of the kind that had essentially displaced the *zuhdiyya* in the sphere of popular religious poetry (cf. Pinault).

With the City of Brass in mind, Allen has suggested intriguingly how this register survives in the modern period, lending a profound resonance to Ṣalāḥ ʿAbd al-Ṣabūr's celebrated poem, *al-Nās fī bilādī*.

Bibliography: S̲h̲ukrī Fayṣal, *Abu 'l-ʿAtāhiya, as̲h̲ʿāruhu wa-ak̲h̲bāruhu*, Damascus 1965; I. ʿAbbās, *S̲h̲iʿr al-K̲h̲awārid̲j̲*, Beirut n.d.; M. Ben Abdesselem, *Le thème de la mort dans la poésie arabe des origines à la fin du IIIème/IXème siècle*, Tunis 1977 (ch. X, 293-315); Muḥammad ʿAwīs, *al-Ḥikma fi 'l-s̲h̲iʿr al-ʿarabī*, Asyūṭ 1979 (esp. 185-204; contains striking samples of verse from a range of poets of the nascent Islamic period); R. Allen, *The Arabic literary heritage*, Cambridge 1998; M.A. Barānik, *Abu 'l-ʿAtāhiya*, Cairo 1947; C.H. Becker, *Ubi sunt qui ante nos in mundo fuere*, in *Aufsätze zur Kultur- und Sprachgeschichte (Ernst Kuhn Festschrift)*, Breslau 1916; J.A. Bellamy, *The impact of Islam on early Arabic poetry*, in A.T. Welch and P. Cachia (eds.), *Islam. Past influence and present challenge*, Edinburgh 1979, 141-67; L. Cheikho, *al-Anwār al-zāhiya fī Dīwān Abi 'l-ʿAtāhiya*, 2 vols. Beirut 1988; Melhem Chokr, *Zandaqa et zindīqs en Islam au second siècle de l'hégire*, Damascus 1993 (excellent bibliographic source for Ṣāliḥ b. ʿAbd al-Ḳuddūs and Abu 'l-ʿAtāhiya); M. al-Dās̲h̲, *Abu 'l-ʿAtāhiya, ḥayātuhu wa-s̲h̲iʿruhu*, Cairo 1968; Andras Hamori, *Ascetic poetry* (zuhdiyyāt), in *Camb. hist. Arab. lit., ʿAbbasid belles-lettres*, ed. Julia Ashtiany *et al.*, Cambridge 1990; M.ʿĀ.M. Ḥusayn, *D̲j̲awānib al-ʿiẓa wa 'l-ḥikma fī s̲h̲iʿr Maḥmūd al-Warrāḳ*, [Cairo] 1987; A.A. Kannūn, *Sābiḳ al-Barbarī*, Damascus 1969; M.A.A. el Kafrawy and J.D. Latham, *Perspective of Abu 'l-ʿAtāhiya*, in *IQ*, xvii (1973); P.F. Kennedy, *The wine song in Classical Arabic poetry*, Oxford 1997, chs. ii-iv; A.A. al-K̲h̲aṭīb, *Ṣāliḥ ibn ʿAbd al-Ḳuddūs al-Baṣrī*, Baṣra 1968; J.D. Martin, *The religious beliefs of Abū 'l-ʿAtāhiya according to the* zuhdīyāt, in *Trans. Glasgow Oriental Society*, xxiii (1969-70); D. Pinault, *Story-telling techniques in the Arabian Nights*, Leiden 1992, ch. iv; B. Reinert, *Die Lehre vom tawakkul in der klassischen Sufik*, Berlin 1968; O. Rescher, *Der Dīwān des Abī l-ʿAtāhiya*, i, *Die zuhdijjāt*, Stuttgart 1928; H. Ritter, *Studien zur Geschichte der islamischen Frommigkeit. i. Ḥasan al-Baṣrī*, in *Isl.*, xxi (1933), 1-83; G. Schoeler, *Die Einteilung der Dichtung bei den Arabern*, in *ZDMG*, cxxiii (1973), 9-55; M. Schwarz, *The Letter of al-Ḥasan al-Baṣrī*, in *Oriens*, xx (1967), 15-30; S. Sperl, *Mannerism in Arabic poetry*, Cambridge 1989; G. Vajda, *Les zindīqs en pays d'Islam*, in *RSO*, xvii (1938), 215-20, 225-8; E. Wagner, *Grundzüge der klassischen arabischen Dichtung*, ii, *Die arabische Dichtung in islamischer Zeit* ("Askesegedichte", 120-30), Darmstadt 1988; Maḥmūd al-Warrāḳ, *Dīwān*, ed. ʿA.R. al-ʿUbaydī, Bag̲h̲dād 1969. See also the EI^2 arts. on the *zuhhād* mentioned in the article, plus that on the important figure of Abu 'l-ʿAlāʾ al-Maʿarrī.

(P.F. KENNEDY)

ZUHRA, a clan of Ḳurays̲h̲ [*q.v.*] in Mecca, with the genealogy Zuhra b. Kilāb b. Murra b. Kaʿb b. Luʾayy b. G̲h̲ālib b. Fihr.

In pre-Islamic Mecca, the clan seems to have been prosperous, and members of it had trading connections with ʿAbd S̲h̲ams. In the factional disputes within Mecca, Zuhra were in the group led by ʿAbd Manāf, the *Muṭayyabūn* or "Perfumed Ones" [see LAʿAḲAT AL-DAM] and then in the *Ḥilf al-Fuḍūl* [*q.v.*] along with Hās̲h̲im and al-Muṭṭalib. The clan acquired Islamic kudos from the fact that the Prophet's mother Āmina bt. Wahb [*q.v.*] was from Zuhra. Early converts from the clan included ʿAbd al-Raḥmān b. ʿAwf and Saʿd b. Abī Waḳḳāṣ [*q.vv.*], but there were also opponents of Muḥammad within Zuhra (including the grandfather of the famous traditionist of Umayyad times, Ibn S̲h̲ihāb al-Zuhrī [*q.v.*], who fought on the side of Ḳurays̲h̲ against the Muslims at Badr and Uḥud), and in 8/630, after the battle of Ḥunayn, Muḥammad judged it politic to conciliate three of the leaders of Zuhra with presents of captured camels [see AL-MU'ALLAFA ḲULŪBUHUM].

Bibliography: ʿAbd Allāh Muṣʿab al-Zubayrī, *Nasab Ḳuraysh*, ed. Lévi-Provençal, 257-74; Ibn al-Kalbī-Caskel, *Ǧamharat an-nasab*, i, Tafel 4, ii, 306, 611; W.M. Watt, *Muhammad at Mecca*, Oxford 1953, 5-8, 89-90, 172; idem, *Muhammad at Medina*, Oxford 1956, 74, 375. (C.E. BOSWORTH)

AL-**ZUHRĪ**, HĀRŪN B. ʿABD ALLĀH, judge in Egypt, considered the greatest Mālikī scholar there, d. 232/846.

A native of Mecca, he came to Baghdād, but nothing is known of his activities there until al-Ma'mūn nominated him *ḳāḍī* of Egypt on 14 Ramaḍān 217/13 October 832 (al-Kindī) or a few days later (Ibn ʿAbd al-Ḥakam), where he remained in post till 13 Ṣafar 226/12 December 840. As a judge, his career was marked by innovations. He moved his seat as judge, and sat in front of the mosque in winter and in the middle of it in summer, whilst keeping a distance between himself and the faithful at prayer, as also from his own scribes and his enemies. Regarding the judicial system, on his arrival in Egypt he took personal charge of all contentious cases, visiting the scenes in question with the parties involved, e.g. in the case of *ḥubus* or pious endowments, keeping track of the income from them, and paid close attention to other things, such as the financial situation and care of orphans, etc.

Al-Zuhrī, with his strong personality, seems to have enjoyed the favour and confidence of the caliph; he would allow no-one to sit next to him, but left a place there for the caliph only. His relations with al-Ma'mūn are documented concerning the episode of the *miḥna* [*q.v.*], in 218/833, the instructions regarding which were brought by Abū Isḥāḳ b. Hārūn to the governor of Egypt at the time, Kaydur Naṣr b. ʿAbd Allāh. The latter summoned al-Zuhrī, who bowed to the caliph's orders, apparently without hesitation, followed by the majority of the *fuḳahā'*. From that time onwards, al-Zuhrī would accept attestations by witnesses only if they recognised the createdness of the Ḳur'ān, and this remained the practice in Egypt until al-Mutawakkil's accession in 232/847. He does not seem to have been ferocious against non-compliant *fuḳahā'*, since al-Muʿtaṣim is said to have sent him a letter demanding that he act more rigorously, and when he refused to act thus, the Chief Judge Aḥmad b. Abī Duwād [*q.v.*] had the caliph remove him from office in 226/840.

Al-Zuhrī left behind in Egypt an impression of honesty, acquiring only a house for himself which he sold at the end of his period of office. Al-Marzubānī attributes some poetry to him.

Bibliography: Ibn ʿAbd al-Ḥakam, *Futūḥ Miṣr*, ed. Torrey, 246-7; Kindī, *Wulāt*, ed. Guest, 443-49; Ibn Ḥadjar, *Lisān al-mīzān*, vi, 179-80; Marzubānī, *Muʿdjam al-shuʿarā'*, Cairo 1379/1960, 463; Suyūṭī, *Ḥusn al-muḥāḍara*, Cairo 1387/1967, 447; Yāfiʿī, *Mir'āt al-djanān*, ii, 107; Ibn Makhlūf al-Tūnisī, *Shadjarat al-nūr al-zakiyya fī ṭabaḳāt al-mālikiyya*, Cairo 1349/1930, 57; Ziriklī, *Aʿlām*³, ix, 41; R.G. Khoury, *Zur Ernennung von Richtern im Islam...*, in *Studien zur Geschichte und Kultur des Vorderen Orients. Festschrift B. Spuler*, Leiden 1981, 197-209; idem, *ʿAbd Allāh b. Lahīʿa, juge et grand maître de l'école égyptienne*, Wiesbaden 1986. (R.G. KHOURY)

AL-**ZUHRĪ**, IBN SHIHĀB, i.e. Abū Bakr Muḥammad b. Muslim b. ʿUbayd Allāh b. ʿAbd Allāh b. Shihāb, d. 124/742, one of the founders of Islamic tradition in the widest sense of the word. The source material about him includes both biographical data and instructive anecdotes; the latter reflect both admiration for his achievement and criticism of his links with the Umayyads and of some laxity on his part regarding the transmission of *ḥadīth*.

Al-Zuhrī's first tutor (*mu'addib*) was probably the *mawlā* [*q.v.*] Ṣāliḥ b. Kaysān al-Madanī. From ʿAbd Allāh b. Thaʿlaba b. Ṣuʿayr al-ʿUdhrī [see ʿUDHRA] (d. 87/706 or 89/708) al-Zuhrī learned the genealogy of his own clan, the Banū Zuhra. But when al-Zuhrī wanted to study *fiḳh* [*q.v.*], ʿAbd Allāh had to refer him to Saʿīd b. al-Musayyab. Later, al-Zuhrī was a student of ʿUrwa b. al-Zubayr and many others. A contemporary of his remarked that the assertive young al-Zuhrī did not outstrip his peers in knowledge; but at an assembly he would step forward from among them and present his questions, while they were held back by their youth.

Al-Zuhrī boasted of his excellent memory, but he doubtless kept records of the *ḥadīth*s transmitted to him. His colleague, Abu 'l-Zinād, a *mawlā* of the Umayyads and their official, reported that al-Zuhrī used to carry with him writing tablets and written pieces of skins (*al-alwāḥ wa 'l-ṣuḥuf*). "We used to mock him," Abu 'l-Zinād added, as if regretting the fact that he himself had not followed the same practice. This colleague was believed to have said: "We used to write down only legal matters (*al-ḥalāl wa 'l-ḥarām*), while Ibn Shihāb wrote down everything he heard." Al-Zuhrī is supposed to have widened the concept of *sunna* common to his time. One colleague of his reported that, in their quest for *sunan*, both he and al-Zuhrī recorded everything traced back to the Prophet. But al-Zuhrī went on to write down *ḥadīth* transmitted on the authority of the Prophet's Companions, while his colleague argued that such *ḥadīth* did not form *sunna*. "He succeeded," the colleague concluded, "and I failed." According to al-Zuhrī, the caliph ʿUmar II ordered him, among others, to collect the *sunan*, which were later written down in booklets [see DAFTAR] sent each to another province.

For several decades, from the days of ʿAbd al-Malik b. Marwān [*q.v.*] to those of Hishām, al-Zuhrī maintained a close relationship with the ruling house. He officiated at different periods as *ḳāḍī*, tax collector and *shurṭa* [*q.v.*] chief. Al-Dhahabī [*q.v.*] reported that al-Zuhrī had the rank of *amīr*; elsewhere al-Dhahabī said that "he had many dependants and servants, was a man of eminence, was dressed in the outfit of the *adjnād* and enjoyed high rank in the state of the Banū Umayya."

Encouraged by the ruling family, al-Zuhrī started "*ḥadīth* dictation sessions" attended by state officials. According to his own apologetic statement, he gave in to pressure from the rulers and immediately decided to hold similar sessions for scholars not affiliated with the state apparatus. One of the stimuli for the recording of *ḥadīth* is supposed to have been anti-Umayyad propaganda. Al-Zuhrī reportedly complained about ʿIrāḳī tampering with his *ḥadīth*: "We issue the *ḥadīth* [short as] a span and it returns (i.e. from ʿIrāḳ) [long as] a cubit." Al-Zuhrī is also believed to have said, "Had it not been for *ḥadīth*s which we do not know pouring upon us from the East (*al-mashriḳ*), I would not have written down, nor allowed the writing, of one single *ḥadīth*."

The dictation sessions were attended, among others, by Shuʿayb b. Dīnār or b. Abī Ḥamza al-Ḥimṣī (d. 162/778-9), a *mawlā* of the Umayyads and a scribe of Hishām [*q.v.*] who was in charge of the caliph's *nafaḳāt* [cf. DĪWĀN, at Vol. II, 323b-324a]; no wonder that <u>Sh</u>uʿayb's "books" were said to resemble the records of the state register (*tu<u>sh</u>bihu kutuba 'l-dīwān*). <u>Sh</u>uʿayb reportedly held about 1,700 of al-Zuhrī's *ḥadīth*s, and the figure gives one an idea of the amount of material processed in al-Zuhrī's sessions over the years.

In addition to *ḥadīth* and *fikh*, al-Zuhrī was also well versed in other fields of knowledge. An admiring student said about him that when he talked about eschatology (*fi 'l-targhīb* "arousing desire for Paradise"), he gave one the impression that he was only proficient in this topic, but the same happened when he talked about the prophets and the "People of the Book", or the Ḳurʾān and the *sunna*, or the Bedouin and their genealogies.

Bibliography: al-*Zuhrī* (the entry about him from Ibn ʿAsākir, *Taʾrī<u>kh</u> Madīnat Dima<u>sh</u>ḳ*), ed. Ḳūdjānī, Beirut 1402/1982; I. Goldziher, *Muslim studies*, ed. S.M. Stern, tr. C.R. Barber and S.M. Stern, London 1967-71, ii, 44-9; J. Horovitz, *The earliest biographies of the Prophet and their authors*, no. 2, in *IC*, ii (1928), 33-50; H. Motzki, *Der Fiqh des Zuhri: die Quellenproblematik*, in *Isl.*, lxviii (1991), 1-44; M. Lecker, *Biographical notes on Ibn Shihāb al-Zuhrī*, in *JSS*, xli (1996), 21-63; Ḥārith Sulaymān al-Ḍārī, *al-Imām al-Zuhrī wa-a<u>th</u>aruhu fi 'l-sunna*, Mawṣil 1405/1985.
(M. Lecker)

al-**ZUHRĪ**, Muḥammad b. Abī Bakr (thus according to Ḥusayn Muʾnis; according to the author of *al-Ḥulal al-maw<u>sh</u>iyya*, Abū ʿAbd Allāh Muḥammad b. Yaḥyā), the author of a geographical work, the *K. al-Djughrāfiya*.

This work has in the past been used by scholars who, knowing nothing about the author, have called him the "Anonymous of Almería". Al-Zuhrī appears in no biographical work, but the few personal details that can be gleaned from his book show him to have been an Andalusī of the 6th/12th century, a contemporary of al-Idrīsī, alive in 545/1150-1 and very knowledgeable about al-Andalus. His work is known under several other titles, including *K. al-Ṣafwa*, *K. al-Ṣafra* and also *K. al-Sufra*, this last seeming most appropriate ("Book of food for the traveller"). It has been edited by M. Hadj-Sadok in *BEO*, xxi (1968), 1-346, as *Kitāb al-Djaʿrāfiyya. Mappemonde du calife al-Maʾmūn reproduite par Fazārī (IIIᵉ/IXᵉ s.), rééditée et commentée par Zuhrī (VIᵉ/XIIᵉ s.)*; Hadj-Sadok used numerous mss., which have important divergences, and other copies exist, including six in Rabat libraries. The book thus seems to have enjoyed a wide diffusion, leading Muʾnis to view it as a popular guide for merchants and travellers, put together by someone without wide culture and in a fairly relaxed style. Al-Zuhrī used the word *djughrāfiya* in the sense of *mappa mundi*, and the extant text is merely the commentary on maps ignored by the copyists at the expense of the anecdotal and miraculous element [see ʿADJĀʾIB]. The *K. al-Djughrāfiya* was used by several Arabic authors; thus the anonymous *al-Ḥulal al-maw<u>sh</u>iyya* cites a passage on the Almoravids absent from the edited text.

Bibliography: E. Griffini, *Estratto della geografia de az-Zuhrī, o Anonimo de Alméria*, in *Centenario della nascita di Michele Amari*, Palermo 1910, i, 416-27; Dolors Bramón, *El mondo en el siglo XII*, Orientalia Barcinomensia, xi, Barcelona 1991; H. Muʾnis, *al-Djughrāfiya wa 'l-djughrāfiyyūn fi 'l-Andalus*, in *Rev. del. Inst. de Estudios Islámicos en Madrid*, xi-xii (1963-4), 84-120.
(Halima Ferhat)

ZŪHRĪ AḤMED EFENDI [see NEWROKOP].

ẒUHŪRĪ TURSHĪZĪ, Nūr al-Dīn Muḥammad, Persian poet, d. 1025/1616. He was born *ca.* 944/

1537 and raised in <u>Kh</u>urāsān; although most sources identify his birthplace as a village in the district of Tur<u>sh</u>īz [*q.v.*], the poet himself states that he was born in Ḳāʾin. He began his career in Yazd at the court of <u>Gh</u>iyā<u>th</u> al-Dīn Mīr-i Mīrān, where he was acquainted with the poet Waḥ<u>sh</u>ī [*q.v.*]. After spending several years in <u>Sh</u>īrāz, he migrated to India in 988/1580. Settling in the Deccan, he entered the service of the Niẓām <u>Sh</u>āhīs [*q.v.*] in Aḥmadnagar. After a brief period in the retinue of Mīrzā ʿAbd al-Raḥīm <u>Kh</u>ān-i <u>Kh</u>ānān [*q.v.*], Ẓuhūrī moved to Bidjapur *ca.* 1004/1596. He lived in this city until his death, working under the patronage of the ʿĀdil <u>Sh</u>āh [*q.v.*] Ibrāhīm II and his minister <u>Sh</u>āh Nawāz <u>Kh</u>ān. Ẓuhūrī was in contact with many of the major poets of the period, including Naẓīrī and Fayḍī. He was especially close to Malik-i Ḳummī [*q.v.*], marrying his daughter and co-writing several works with him.

During his lifetime, Ẓuhūrī was perhaps best known for his panegyric *ḳaṣīda*s, which were sometimes compared to the work of the ancient masters of the form. Though these poems were written for a wide range of patrons, including <u>Sh</u>āh ʿAbbās and the <u>Kh</u>ān-i <u>Kh</u>ānān, the majority were dedicated to Burhān Niẓām <u>Sh</u>āh II and Ibrāhīm ʿĀdil <u>Sh</u>āh II. Modern critics, however, tend to prefer Ẓuhūrī's *ghazal*s, which constitute the largest section of his *dīwān*. His *dīwān* also includes stanzaic poems and a substantial body of *rubāʿī*s. Dedicated to Burhān II, Ẓuhūrī's *sāḳī-nāma* in rhymed couplets is the longest and perhaps greatest representative of this quintessentially Ṣafawid-Mughal genre. However, it was Ẓuhūrī's prose, in particular the collection known as *Si nathr*, that exercised the greatest influence on later writers. This work consists of three introductions dedicated to Ibrāhīm II: *Dībāca-i Nawras* prefaced a collection of song lyrics written by Ibrāhīm himself in a Deccani vernacular; *Dībāca-i Gulzār-i Ibrāhīm* and *Dībāca-i <u>Kh</u>ʷān-i <u>Kh</u>alīl* both preceded collections of panegyric verse that were the joint efforts of Ẓuhūrī and Malik-i Ḳummī. These introductions were long regarded as models of rhymed, ornate prose. Several formal letters, including one addressed to Fayḍī, are also found in Ẓuhūrī's collected works. Two other prose works often attributed to Ẓuhūrī—*Pandj rukʿa* (a collection of love letters) and *Mīnā bāzār* (a description of the Bidjapur market)—are likely the work of Irādat <u>Kh</u>ān Wāḍiḥ, who died in 1128/1716 (see Ahmad, 337-52).

Bibliography: For brief biographies and a list of *tadhkira* sources, see Storey, iii, 280-1, and <u>Dh</u>. Ṣafā, *Tārī<u>kh</u>-i adabiyyāt dar Īrān*, Tehran 1364 <u>sh</u>./1985, v/2, 977-88. The most important of these sources are collected and quoted at length in A. Gulčīn-i Maʿānī, *Kārwān-i Hind*, Ma<u>sh</u>had 1369 <u>sh</u>./1990, ii, 823-38. See also Fa<u>kh</u>r al-Zamānī Ḳazwīnī, *Tadhkira-i may<u>kh</u>āna*, ed. Gulčīn-i Maʿānī, Tehran 1340 <u>sh</u>./1961, 363-412. Among the secondary sources, see M. ʿAbduʾl Ghani, *A history of Persian language and literature at the Mughal court*, Allahabad 1929-30, iii, 181-219; and Nazir Ahmad, *Zuhuri. Life and works*, Allahabad 1953, by far the most detailed and scholarly study of the poet currently available. Nazir Ahmad has also edited Ibrāhīm ʿĀdil <u>Sh</u>āh's *Kitāb-i Nawras*, Lucknow 1955. For a listing of the manuscripts of Ẓuhūrī's poetic works, see A. Munzawī, *Fihrist-i nus<u>kh</u>ahā-yi <u>kh</u>aṭṭī-yi fārsī*, iii, 1880 (*kulliyyāt*), 2419-21 (*dīwān*); and iv, 2875-77 (*sāḳī-nāma*). His *dīwān* and *sāḳī-nāma* have been lithographed in India; see *Fihrist-i kitābhā-yi čāpī-yi fārsī*, i, cols. 1554, 1571, and ii, col. 1900. For a listing of the many manuscripts and lithographs of Ẓuhūrī's authentic and putative prose works, see Storey-de Blois, iii, 281-5. In addition to the translation listed in this source, a full Persian text and English translation of Ẓuhūrī's *Si nat͟hr* can also be found in ʿAbdu'l Ghani, *History*, iii, 305-467. (P.E. Losensky)

ZULĀLĪ-yi K͟HᵂĀNSĀRĪ, Persian poet from the reign of S͟hāh ʿAbbās I [*q.v.*]. Reports on his date of death range from 1016/1607 to 1037/1627-8, but the most probable seems to be 1024-5/1615-16. Little is known about his life. He was born in K͟hᵂānsār to the northwest of Iṣfahān and divided his life between these two towns. Although reputedly quiet and retiring by nature, Zulālī had close contacts with the Ṣafawid court, particularly with Mīr Bāḳir al-Dāmād Astarābādī [*q.v.*], his principal patron.

Although Zulālī composed *g͟hazal*s and *ḳaṣīda*s, his enduring claim to fame is the collection of seven *mat͟hnawī*s, entitled *Sabʿa-yi sayyāra* ("The seven planets"). *Ḥusn-i gulzār*, written in the metre of Niẓāmī's [*q.v.*] *Mak͟hzan al-asrār*, consists of short anecdotes in a Ṣūfī-didactic framework. Of a similar structure is *S͟huʿla-yi dīdār*, in the metre of Rūmī's *Mat͟hnawī-yi maʿnawī*. The remaining five poems present continuous narratives. *Mayk͟hāna* tells the story of the legendary king D̲jams͟hīd and the discovery of wine. Zulālī's *D͟harra wa K͟hurs͟hīd* is the tale of a dust mote's love for the sun, and another allegory of mystical love appears in *Ād͟har wa Samandar*, written in the metre associated with the *Laylā wa Mad̲jnūn* romance. The *Sulaymān-nāma* narrates Solomon's love for Bilḳīs in the heroic *mutaḳārib* metre. These six *mat͟hnawī*s are all relatively short, containing 500-1,000 verses. Composed over the course of twenty years, *Maḥmūd wa Ayāz* concerns the legendary love of Sultan Maḥmūd G͟haznawī for his slave boy. It is by far Zulālī's longest work and his most sustained effort to emulate Niẓāmī's *K͟husraw wa S͟hīrīn*.

Zulālī's style is highly complex and innovative in its use of neologistic compounds and unprecedented similes and metaphors. In the opinion of most critics, his work is very uneven, with impenetrably opaque verses side-by-side with conceits of startling originality and beauty. This was apparently the result of the poet's intuitive, almost haphazard method of composition; according to Awḥadī Balyānī, he worked on all seven of his *mat͟hnawī*s simultaneously. His works were left in a state of disarray on his death, and *Maḥmūd wa Ayāz* was redacted in its final form in India. He had a great influence on the later romance tradition throughout the Persian-speaking world. Ṭug͟hrā-yi Mas͟hhadī, a poet at the court of S͟hāh D̲jahān, composed a set of prose introductions to Zulālī's works entitled *Ās͟hūb-nāma* to accompany the short introductions written by the poet himself.

Bibliography: For a list of *tad͟hkira* sources, see D͟h. Ṣafā, *Tārīk͟h-i adabiyyāt dar Īrān*, Tehran 1364 *s͟h*./1985, v/2, 965-6. The most important of these are Amīn b. Aḥmad Rāzī, *Haft iḳlīm*, ed. D̲j. Fāḍil, Tehran n.d. [1950s], ii, 484-5, and Muḥammad Ṭāhir Naṣrābādī, *Tad͟hkira-i Naṣrābādī*, ed. W. Dastgirdī, Tehran 1352 *s͟h*./1973, 230-4. Zulālī receives only passing treatment in most literary histories: see Browne, *LHP*, iv, 252, and Rypka, *Hist. of Iranian literature*, 301. Manuscripts of Zulālī's *mat͟hnawī*s are abundant, both individually and collectively; for full listings, see A. Munzawī, *Fihrist-i nusk͟hahā-yi k͟haṭṭī-yi fārsī*, under title of each work. Lithograph editions include: *Maḥmūd wa Ayāz*, Tehran 1302/1885 and 1321/1903, and *Mat͟hnawī-yi Zulālī*, Lucknow 1290/1874. A recent edition of Zulālī's six shorter *mat͟hnawī*s, prepared as a doctoral dissertation at the University of Isfahan 1374 *s͟h*./1995 by Amān Allāh ʿAlī ʿAskarī, provides the first critical edition of the poet's works. (P.E. Losensky)

ẒULM (a., verbal noun of form I), basically meaning, according to the authoritative lexicologists, "putting a thing in a place not its own" (Lane, *LA, TA*), i.e. displacement. In the moral sphere, it denotes acting in such a way as to transgress the proper limit and encroach upon the right of some other person. In common usage, *ẓulm* has come to signify wrongdoing, evil, injustice, oppression and tyranny, particularly by persons who have power and authority. Frequently it is therefore used as the antonym to *ʿadl* [*q.v.*], *inṣāf* [*q.v.*] and *ḳisṭ* and (sometimes by expressing a slightly different shade of meaning) as a synonym to *bag͟hy* (encroachment, abuse), *d̲jawr* (oppression), *fisḳ* (moral deficiency [see fāsiḳ]), *inḥirāf* (deviation), *mayl* (inclination) and *ṭug͟hyān* (tyranny). Because of its general and comprehensive meaning the root *ẓ-l-m* is current in the vocabulary of religion, theology, philosophy, ethics, law and political theory.

1. *In religion and ethics during the pre-modern period.*

The word *ẓulm* and its derivatives are found in more than 280 places in the Ḳurʾān; it can be seen as one of the most important negative value-words in the sacred book. The warnings against oppression, the admonitions against injustice and the frequent emphasis on the principles of uprightness, equity and temperance in the Ḳurʾān and the prophetic dicta must be seen mainly as a reaction against the pre-Islamic tribal society which paid little or no attention to justice. That *ẓulm* is used as a generic term becomes obvious by the semantic equivalence or close relationship between *ẓulm* and terms such as *kufr* (e.g. II, 254; IV, 168-9) [see kāfir], *s͟hirk* [*q.v.*] (e.g. II, 165; XXXI, 13), *fisḳ* (e.g. VII, 162) or *iʿtidāʾ* (transgression; e.g. V, 107); in addition, *ẓulm* is used in the sense of *d͟hanb* (offence; cf. LXV, 1; II, 35), *naḳṣ* (detriment; cf. XVIII, 33; XIX, 60) or *ḍarar* (harm; cf. II, 57). *Ẓulm* can be done to God (by man's transgressing the limits imposed by God; e.g. II, 229), to others (by going beyond the bounds of proper conduct in social life; by hurting someone seriously without any conceivable reason; e.g. XII, 75; XXI, 58-9), or even to oneself, each one of the preceding being in fact wrongdoing to oneself (*ẓulm al-nafs*): "Whoever does an injustice has wronged himself" (e.g. II, 231; III, 117; IX, 70; X, 44). The particular parameters decreed by God remain an insoluble mystery to men; sometimes, however, they are understandable in terms of the social good, e.g. when God designates usury as *ẓulm* (II, 279), or the devouring of entrusted orphan's property (IV, 2, 10), or the violation of rules concerning inheritance (IV, 11-14) and divorce (LXV, 1) prescribed by God.

The Traditions take up the warnings against the punishment of *ẓulm* in the Hereafter. Not only is the *ẓālim* himself damned but also the one who does not support the *maẓlūm* [*q.v.*] or curb the *ẓālim*. Prayers against an injust ruler will be granted in the other world; the triumph over the *ẓālim* is certain. Beside this predominant idea of compensation for *ẓulm* (an evident reflection of the historical circumstances), concrete examples of social injustice are mentioned, such as the usurpation of landed property; the delay in repayment of debts by someone who is rich enough to repay them (*maṭl al-g͟hanī*); the unjustifiable maltreatment of slaves or subjects; and the *ḳāḍī*'s unjust sentence. Only one kind of *ẓulm* is unpardonable, shirk, but the others either cannot be neglected or are excusable.

Although the Ḳur'ān affirms repeatedly that God does not do wrong (e.g. IV, 40; XVI, 33; XXIX, 40) and that He disapproves of injustice (e.g. III, 57, 140; XLII, 40), theological ethics could not be entirely divorced from the problem of theodicy or the conception of God's role in the world, and in particular, His relation to man. Therefore, two of the central theological and ethical questions were, can God do an injustice, and is there an individual responsibility for unjust acts? The Muʿtazila [*q.v.*] agreed on the premise that all God's acts are just acts, for everything done by God, including punishment for wrongdoing, is for the welfare of mankind and not for His own advantage. Following their insistence on divine justice and reason, they held that God by nature can do no injustice. Nor is it conceivable that He will ever do an injustice, because to will evil is evil. God can neither will the evil done by others nor initiate it. Whether God could be described as capable (*ḳādir*) of doing wrong and refraining from right, was, on the other hand, a highly debatable question in theological circles, including the Muʿtazila. Furthermore, divine justice meant according to the Muʿtazila that God was in some way obliged to provide "the optimum" (*al-aṣlaḥ*) for His creatures. The extreme emphasis on divine *ʿadl* and free will provoked a sharp reaction. The Ashʿariyya [*q.v.*] embraced the earlier tendency of Islam that declared God, in His unlimited omnipotence, the author of good as well as evil. All things, from human acts to natural events in the world, are the direct result of divine decree. God alone creates acts; man, however, "acquires" [see KASB] these acts and so can be deemed legally responsible for his deeds. What God does or decrees is by definition just; what He refrains from doing is unjust. Accordingly, injustice denotes actions improperly done, or done in violation of God's command.

Philosophical ethical treatises like those of Miskawayh or Naṣīr al-Dīn al-Ṭūsī [*q.vv.*] are based essentially on Greek theory, and on Plato and Aristotle in particular. As Aristotle said, justice is not a part of virtue but all virtue in its entirety; injustice as its opposite is not a portion of vice but the whole of vice. Since justice is essentially a notion of equivalence, whoever is in favour of disproportion and unequivalence is an unjust person. Injustice is the product of harm done by one man to another, either with or without intention, or it might be the result of imbalance and excess by irrational acts. Following Plato, four cardinal virtues and eight generic vices constituting either an excess or a defect in relation to the original virtues, are distinguished. Whereas justice is the most perfect virtue and the true mid-point (centre), injustice (oppression) and servility (suffering of wrong) are the extremes (peripheries). The mean is defined but not the peripheries. Analogous to the three criteria to determine justice and to ensure its application (divine law, just ruler and money), injustice is also of three types: violation of the *Sharīʿa*, repudiating the ruler's authority and violating the norms of equitable transactions involving money.

The *adab* [*q.v.*] literature scarcely deals with the conceptual aspect of justice and injustice; it essentially consists of quotations from the Ḳur'ān and *Ḥadīth*, of guidelines, general rules, anecdotes, aphorisms and poems.

Since the first *fitna*, several opposition groups (Khāridjites and [Proto-] Shīʿa [*q.vv.*]) insisted on the duty to rise against illegitimate rulers representing *djawr* and *ẓulm*, or held that if believers found themselves in the *dār al-ẓulm*, i.e. a region where a true imāmate did not prevail, it was incumbent upon them to emigrate. (For *ẓulm* and its derivatives *ẓālim* and *maẓlūm* as technical terms of Shīʿī, especially Twelver, Islam, see MAẒLŪM.) Later jurists, defining justice as protection of the *Sharīʿa*, first limited the duty of resistance to unjust rulers by possibility. Sunnī jurists since al-Ghazālī (d. 505/1111 [*q.v.*]) and Imāmī jurists, for rather different reasons and even before this, refused to permit rebellion against unjust government (in the case of the Imāmiyya, so long as the Imām was absent).

In political theory and in the Mirrors for Princes particularly, great emphasis is laid on justice: as a standard, though moral, quality demanded of the ruler and his officials, and as a guarantee for prosperity and social harmony. Nevertheless, the fear of civil war (*fitna*) and disturbance (*fasād*) leading to disorder and the need for stability finally resulted in the acknowledgement of existing power, whatever it might be. This was partly a reaction to the repeated politico-religious unrest and disorders; partly it was the result of the disagreement over who was the most excellent Imām or Sulṭān and of the absence of legal means and fixed procedures by which a tyrant could be made responsible and be deposed. (For the different functions of the *maẓālim*, see art. s.v.) Various traditions enshrining the duty of obedience to a ruler, even if unjust, and extolling the security provided by the exercise of coercive power, even if by an illegitimate ruler, as against the weakness of a just ruler which leads to anarchy, were put into circulation: "The tyranny of a sultan for forty years is preferable to the flock being left without a master for a single hour," and the like. The doctrine was evolved that, whether the ruler was good or bad, obedience to him was incumbent upon the Muslim because it was God's will that he held office. In practice, this attitude resulted in prevailing tyranny, the spread of political quietism and of the tendency to regard all authority as evil. Ibn Khaldūn (d. 808/1406 [*q.v.*]) or his follower Ibn al-Azraḳ (d. 896/1491) then contended that man is by nature oppressive and unjust.

In jurisprudence, there are two aspects of injustice, the substantive or internal aspect of law, and the procedural or external aspect. Whereas the first is measured by the adherence to the sacred law, the second or formal aspect of injustice is manifested in such corrupt practices as bribery, irregularity, inaccuracy and partiality in the application of the law, commonly named *fisḳ*.

That justice brings about prosperity, and tyranny the ruin of the country, respectively, is acknowledged by several authors. Ibn Khaldūn dedicates a whole chapter in his *Muḳaddima* to this aphorism. Attacks on property, he says, means a general destruction of the incentive to do business. Consequently, everything decays. Generally, social injustice is identified with taking property by force or unfair means, with the unjustified imposition of illegal taxes or tasks and with the use of subjects for forced labour.

Bibliography: No comprehensive and critical study or bibliography seems to have been yet undertaken. In addition to the sources already quoted above, see for the Ḳur'ān, *Concordances* of Muḥammad Fu'ād ʿAbd al-Bāḳī (in Arabic) and H.E. Kassis (in English); al-Rāghib al-Iṣfahānī, *al-Mufradāt fī gharīb al-Ḳur'ān*, ed. Muḥammad Sayyid Kaylānī, [Cairo] 1961, 315-16; T. Izutsu, *The structure of the ethical terms in the Koran*, Tokyo 1959, 152 ff.

Tradition. A.J. Wensinck, *Concordances et indices de la tradition musulmane*, Leiden 1936-88, *s.v. ẓ-l-m*, iv, 80-5; Bukhārī, *al-Adab al-mufrad*, Cairo 1979, 139-42, 193; Muḥammad b. Djaʿfar al-Kharāʾiṭī, *Masāwiʾ al-akhlāḳ wa-madhmūmuhā wa-tarāʾiḳ makrūhihā*, ed. Madjdī al-Sayyid Ibrāhīm, Cairo 1989, 217-38; Ṭabarānī, *Makārim al-akhlāḳ*, ed. Fārūḳ Ḥamāda, Casablanca 1980, 65-6, 83-4; Bayhaḳī, *al-Ādāb*, ed. Muḥammad ʿAbd al-Ḳādir Aḥmad ʿAṭāʾ, Beirut 1986, 116 ff., 124-7; *Thamānūn ḥadīth*[an] *fi 'l-ẓulm wa 'l-ẓalama wa 'l-maẓlūmīn*, ed. Djamāl ʿAbd al-Munʿim al-Kūmī and Ḥasan ʿĀshūr, Cairo 1992.

Philosophical ethics. Abū Ḥayyān al-Tawḥīdī and Miskawayh, *al-Hawāmil wa 'l-shawāmil*, ed. Aḥmad Amīn and Aḥmad Ṣaḳr, Cairo 1951, 84-8; Miskawayh, *Tahdhīb al-akhlāḳ*, ed. C.K. Zurayk, Beirut 1966, Eng. tr. idem, *The refinement of character*, Beirut 1968, Fr. tr. M. Arkoun, *Traité d'éthique*, Damascus 1969; Naṣīr al-Dīn al-Ṭūsī, *Akhlāḳ-i Nāṣirī*, ed. Mudjtabā Mīnuwī and ʿAlī Riḍā Ḥaydarī, [4]Tehran 1990, tr. G.M. Wickens, *The Nasirean ethics*, London 1964; Djalāl al-Dīn al-Dawwānī, *Akhlāḳ-i Djalālī*, Calcutta 1911, Eng. tr. W.F. Thompson, *Practical philosophy of the Muhammadan people*, London 1839; Majid Fakhry, *Ethical theories in Islam*, [2]Leiden 1994.

Theology. E.L. Ormsby, *Theodicy in Islamic thought*, Princeton, N.J. 1984; J. van Ess, *Theologie und Gesellschaft im 2. und 3. Jahrhundert Hidschra*, 6 vols., Berlin-New York 1991-7.

Adab. Ibn Ḳutayba, *ʿUyūn al-akhbār*, 4 vols., Cairo 1925-30, i, 74-9; Ibn ʿAbd Rabbih, *al-ʿIḳd al-farīd*, ed. Aḥmad Amīn and Aḥmad al-Zayn, 7 vols., Cairo 1953-65, i ([3]1965), 7 ff., 28 ff.; al-Rāghib al-Iṣfahānī, *Muḥāḍarāt al-udabāʾ*, 4 parts in 2 vols., Beirut 1961, i, 215-21; Nuwayrī, *Nihāyat al-arab fī funūn al-adab*, 31 vols., Cairo 1963-92, vi, 39 ff.; Muḥammad b. Aḥmad al-Ibshīhī, *al-Mustaṭraf fī kull fann mustaẓraf*, 2 vols., Cairo 1292/1875, i, 128-33.

Fiḳh. al-Khaṣṣāf and al-Djaṣṣāṣ, *Adab al-ḳāḍī*, ed. F.J. Ziadeh, Cairo 1979, 29 ff.; Ibn Abi 'l-Dam, *Adab al-ḳaḍāʾ*, ed. Muḥammad ʿAbd al-Ḳādir Aḥmad ʿAṭāʾ, Beirut 1987, 33 ff.; E. Tyan, *Histoire de l'organisation judiciaire en pays d'Islam*, [2]Leiden 1960, 287 ff., 433 ff.

Political thought. Thaʿālibī (?), *Tuḥfat al-wuzarāʾ*, ed. Ḥabīb ʿAlī al-Rāwī and Ibtisām Marhūn al-Ṣaffār, Baghdād 1977, 61 ff.; Ṭurṭūshī, *Sirādj al-mulūk*, ed. Muḥammad al-Fatḥī Abū Bakr, 2 vols., Cairo 1414/1994, ch. 56, pp. 591-608; Ibn Taymiyya, *al-Siyāsa al-sharʿiyya*, Cairo 1951, ch. 8, Eng. tr. Omar A. Farrukh, Beirut 1966, Fr. tr. H. Laoust, Beirut 1948; Ibn Khaldūn, *Muḳaddima*, ch. 41, ii, 93-100 (cf. Ibn Khaldūn, tr. Rosenthal, ii, 103-11); Ibn al-Azraḳ, *Badāʾiʿ al-sulk fī ṭabāʾiʿ al-mulk*, ed. ʿAlī Sāmī al-Nashshār, 2 vols., Baghdād 1977-8.

Studies. F. Rosenthal, *Political justice and the just ruler*, in *IOS*, x (1980), 92-101; S.A. Arjomand, *The shadow of God and the hidden Imam*, Chicago and London 1984; Ann K.S. Lambton, *State and government in medieval Islam*, Oxford 1981, repr. 1985; A.A. Sachedina, *The just ruler in Shiʿite Islam*, Oxford etc. 1988; U. Haarmann, *"Lieber hundert Jahre Zwangsherrschaft als ein Tag Leiden im Bürgerkrieg". Ein gemeinsamer Topos im islamischen und frühneuzeitlichen Staatsdenken*, in *Gottes ist der Orient–Gottes ist der Okzident. Festschrift für A. Falaturi*, ed. U. Tworuschka, Cologne and Vienna 1991, 262-9; Ch.E. Butterworth (ed.), *The political aspects of Islamic philosophy. Essays in honour of Muhsin S. Mahdi*, Cambridge, Mass. 1992. Different aspects are dealt with in Majid Khadduri, *The Islamic concept of justice*, Baltimore 1984; *Oxford Encyclopedia of the modern Islamic world*, ed. J.L. Esposito, Oxford and New York 1995, 4 vols., arts. (concept of) *justice, ẓulm*. (Roswitha Badry)

2. In contemporary political usage.

In the modern period, new experiences, perceptions and ideas, both at home and abroad, reshaped the theory and practice of politics in the Islamic lands. First, reports from Western lands, then the massive Western presence in the Islamic world changed Muslim perceptions of good and therefore also of bad government. The ideas and methods of the French Revolution, the German ideal of the Rechtsstaat, the example of English parliamentary government all had their impact. They were followed by such European ideas as nationalism, socialism, and the combination of the two in national socialism, each with its own definition of the functions and duties of the state, and of the circumstances when resistance to it is justified or even required.

The first external influences came from Western Europe, and the new ideal of government that they brought was that of constitutional, representative government, through elected assemblies. As good government was redefined, bad government was redefined as a departure from it. The old Islamic notions of *mashwara* and *shūrā* [*q.vv.*] were reinterpreted to provide a traditional Islamic justification for parliamentary democracy; the term *istibdād* was revived to connote autocratic personal government. As used in classical texts, it had a connotation of arbitrary and capricious rather than of illegitimate or tyrannical rule. It was used, for example, of a ruler who took decisions and actions on his own, without consulting his religious or bureaucratic advisors. In Arabic chronicles of the Mamlūk period it sometimes appears in a neutral or even in a positive sense, to indicate that one or another of contenders for power had got rid of his rivals and taken sole charge. In the 19th and 20th centuries, it came to be the term commonly used by advocates of liberal reforms to denounce the autocratic monarchs whom they wished either to restrain or to remove.

The rise of neo-Islamic movements brought a revival of the term *ẓulm*, and with it *ẓālim* and *maẓlūm*, to describe misgovernment, its practitioners and its victims. It was used in particular of rule by imperialists (understood to mean non-Muslims ruling over Muslims) and of apostates (used to condemn nominally Muslim rulers who adopt non-Muslim patterns of government and law). These terms figure prominently in the political statements of the Āyatullāh Khumaynī and more generally of the Islamic Republic of Iran, as well as of parallel movements in other Muslim countries. In the traditional Islamic world view, the converse of *ẓulm* is justice; in the democratic view, it is freedom. Modern Muslim thought and discourse reflect the meeting, and sometimes the contradictions, of the two.

Bibliography: Gudmar Aneer, *Imām Rūḥullāh Khumaini, Šāh Muḥammad Rizā Pahlavī and the religious traditions of Iran*, Uppsala 1985; B. Lewis, *The political language of Islam*, Chicago and London 1988, index s.vv. tyranny and *ẓulm*. (B. Lewis)

ZUMURRUD (a.), also Zumurrudh, the emerald, according to Islamic works on gemology, the second-best of the precious gems, after the *yāḳūt* [*q.v.*] "corundum" and before the *luʾluʾ* [*q.v.*] "pearl". The most valuable gem of the beryl group, it was often confused with *zabardjad*, the peridot, a confusion which may have started rather early. Max Bauer goes even so far as to say that in ancient times the name "emerald" was applied loosely to green gemstones in general, such as tourmaline, jasper, malachite, and others (Bauer, *Precious stones*, ii, 317).

Etymology

The *Lisān al-ʿArab* lists *zumurru<u>dh</u>* as a synonym under *zabar<u>dj</u>ad* (with the variant *zabarda<u>dj</u>*), and this is easily recognisable as a loan from Greek *smaragdos*, "emerald", probably via Aramaic (Syriac *(e)smaragda (e)zmarragda/smaragdos*). In the West, the Greek word *smaragdos* was received into Latin as *smaragdus*, which apparently developed into a Vulgar Latin form *(e)smaraldum* from which the Romance and, ultimately, the English forms derived.

Definition

Emerald ($Be_3(Al,Cr)_2 Si_6 O_{18}$) is the green variety and most valuable gem of the beryl family; it owes its verdant green colour to a trace of the chromium ion (Cr_2O_3) in its crystal structure (Webster, *Gems*, 84).

The emerald green colour ranges from dark to light. The most valuable variety is of a saturated or very deep green (*mu<u>sh</u>baʿ al-<u>kh</u>uḍra*), without any other shade of colour, with good transparency (*<u>dj</u>ayyid al-māʾiyya*).

The next in value is known as *rayḥānī*, i.e. of basil leaf colour followed by the *silḳī*, of chard green colour. The least valuable is of light green colour (*anḳaṣ <u>kh</u>uḍrat^an^*), dull or opaque (*aḳtar māʾiyyat^an^*) and with less brilliancy (*aḳall <u>sh</u>uʿāʿ^an^*).

Physical properties

The only colour of emerald (*zumurrud*) is green. It is characterised by softness (*ra<u>kh</u>āwa*) and brittleness (*ta<u>kh</u>al<u>kh</u>ul*), extreme smoothness (*malāsa*), lustre (*ṣaḳāla*) and softness (*nuʿūma*) (al-Tīfā<u>sh</u>ī, *Azhār*, 85).

The various defects that decrease the value of the stone are: freckles (*nama<u>sh</u>*), inclusions (or patches) looking like African rye (*ḥarmaliyyāt*) and white veins (*ʿurūḳ*) (al-Bīrūnī, *K. al-<u>Dj</u>amāhir*, 161). An exclusive characteristic of the *<u>dh</u>ubābī* variety of emerald is its influence on the snake's eyes, which was tested by al-Tīfā<u>sh</u>ī and found to be true (*Azhār*, 84). When an emerald of this kind is drawn near the snake's eyes, they bulge out of their sockets and burst. Other Arab gemologists made the same experiment with the *rayḥānī* and *silḳī* varieties, but the snake's eyes did not change.

Provenance

The earliest known mines of emeralds lie by the Red Sea in Egypt (Webster, *Gems*, 84). Emeralds have been found with Egyptian mummies. The appliances and tools used in the working of emerald mining have been found in the shafts of ancient mines dating back to the time of Sesostris *ca.* 1650 B.C. The ancient mines, known as those of Cleopatra, were rediscovered in 1818 by Cailliaud, a member of the expedition organised by Muḥammad ʿAlī Pa<u>sh</u>a [*q.v.*] (Webster, *Gems*, 84; Bauer, *Precious stones*, 110, 311).

Arab gemologists agree on the location of emerald mines as being in upper Egypt. Al-Ḳalḳa<u>sh</u>andī [*q.v.*] mentions that emeralds were still extracted from the mines near Ḳūṣ [*q.v.*] in Upper Egypt until the time of al-Nāṣir Muḥammad b. Ḳalāwūn [*q.v.*], but the mines were then neglected until the 9th/15th century because of high extraction costs (*Ṣubḥ*, iii, 455). Emeralds are found, according to al-Tīfā<u>sh</u>ī, embedded in a soft red earth inside the friable talc schist. They never occur in gem-gravels like rubies and diamonds, and their occurrence in Egypt is the same as that in the Ural mountains (Bauer, *Precious stones*, 310, 315). The best emeralds, which take the usual hexagonal elongated form of crystal, are extracted from the vein as one piece and called *ḳaṣaba* ("cane, filet, reed"), whilst the small ones extracted from the earth by sieving are called *faṣṣ* ("cabochon") (al-Tīfā<u>sh</u>ī, *Azhār*, 81-2). The beads cut from the small pieces are called "lentil-like" (*ʿadasiyyāt*) (*<u>Dj</u>awāhir*, 163).

Medical and magical (talismanic) uses

While al-Bīrūnī is silent as regards the practical benefits of the emerald, al-Tīfā<u>sh</u>ī (*Azhār*, 85-6), Ibn al-Akfānī (*Nu<u>kh</u>ab*, 52), Ibn al-Wardī (*<u>Kh</u>arīda*, 168) and al-Bayhaḳī (*Maʿdin al-nawādir*, 81-2) enumerate a number of what were in their time common beliefs about them, applicable to the best quality of emeralds. They say that the emerald strengthens the eyesight if one gazes at it for a long time; it guards against epilepsy if worn in a necklace or ring before the disease occurs; it saves from death if dissolved in water and drunk before the poison's effect starts; if drunk or hung externally over the liver and stomach, it stops acute dysentery, bleeding and leprosy; it repels venomous animals from the wearer; and it strengthens the teeth and the stomach if held in the mouth. Although al-Tīfā<u>sh</u>ī affirms that these benefits are exclusive to the best variety of emerald (*al-<u>dh</u>ubābī*), all varieties can be hung on the upper arm and neck for talismanic purposes, and on the thigh of a woman in labour for speeding up child delivery (*Azhār*, 86, tr. Abul Huda, 195).

Value and prices

Al-Bīrūnī discusses the prices of emeralds, relating the value in dirhams to carat weight, starting with 2,000 dirhams for 4 carats and ending with 32,000 dirhams for 21 carats (*<u>Dj</u>amāhir*, 164). The caliph al-Manṣūr bought the emerald ring known as *al-Baḥr* ("the Sea"), which weighed three *mi<u>th</u>ḳāls*, for 30,000 dīnārs (al-<u>Dj</u>āḥiẓ, *al-Tabaṣṣur bi 'l-ti<u>dj</u>āra*, 20), and al-Maʾmūn bought a piece of a *<u>dh</u>ubābī zumurrud* that weighed two *mi<u>th</u>ḳāls* for 30,000 dīnārs (al-Bayhaḳī, *Maʿdin*, 81).

Historical records

The first emeralds and other precious stones to enter the Muslim treasuries or private possessions were obtained from booty during the battles with the Sāsānids such as al-Ḳādisiyya and <u>Dj</u>alūlāʾ (15-16/635-7) and subsequent conquests.

Such emeralds were in the form of unset stones, encrustations on objects such as figurines, tables and other utensils, or carved in the shape of a spoon, a handle of a knife, a long rod, or set in jewelry as rings and strings. Encrusted and studded with emeralds and other precious stones were artifacts such as a gold figurine representing a horse, a ewer, a gold and silver table and a gold palm-tree (Ḳāḍī Ibn al-Zubayr, *Hadāyā*, §§ 180, 189, 196, 201, 209, 215).

Caskets containing large amounts of emerald stones were to be found in the treasuries of the ʿAbbāsids and in those of the Fāṭimids (*Hadāyā*, §§ 150, 346, 357, 377, 412). Al-Ra<u>sh</u>īd had an emerald rod more than one cubit long (*<u>Dj</u>amāhir*, 165; *Hadāyā*, § 28), and a similar rod was held by the Fāṭimid caliph al-Ẓāhir when he rode in processions (*<u>Dj</u>amāhir*, 165-6; *Hadāyā*, § 28). Al-Rāḍī had, like al-Ra<u>sh</u>īd, a passion for precious beautiful items made of, or studded with, precious stones, and possessed [knife] handles, one of which was of emerald (*Hadāyā*, § 244). High-ranking courtiers and officials possessed valuable emerald items also, and a concubine of Yaḥyā b. <u>Kh</u>ālid al-Barmakī is said to have given her personal physician an emerald spoon as a gift (*<u>Dj</u>amāhir*, 165).

Bibliography: 1. Sources. Ibn Māsawayh, *K. al-<u>Dj</u>awāhir wa-ṣifātuhā*, ed. ʿImād ʿAbd al-Salām Raʾūf, Cairo 1976; <u>Dj</u>āḥiẓ, *al-Tabaṣṣur bi 'l-ti<u>dj</u>āra*, ed. Ḥasan Ḥusnī ʿAbd al-Wahhāb, Cairo 1966; Ibn Ḥawḳal, *Ṣūrat al-arḍ*, Beirut 1979; Masʿūdī, *Murū<u>dj</u> al-<u>dh</u>ahab*; Bīrūnī, *K. al-<u>Dj</u>amāhir fī maʿrifat al-<u>dj</u>awāhir*,

Beirut n.d.; Tīfā<u>sh</u>ī, *K. Azhār al-afkār fī <u>dj</u>awāhir al-aḥ<u>dj</u>ār*, ed. Muḥammad Yūsuf Ḥasan and Maḥmūd Basyūnī <u>Kh</u>afā<u>dj</u>ī, Cairo 1977, tr. with comm. Samar Nadjm Abul Huda, *Arab roots of gemology–Best thoughts or the best of stones*, Lanham and London 1998; Ibn al-Akfānī, *Nu<u>kh</u>ab al-<u>dh</u>a<u>kh</u>ā'ir fī aḥwāl al-<u>dj</u>awāhir*, Cairo n.d.; Ibn al-Wardī, *<u>Kh</u>arīdat al-ʿa<u>dj</u>ā'ib wa-farīdat al-<u>gh</u>arā'ib*, ed. Maḥmūd Fā<u>kh</u>ūrī, Beirut and Aleppo n.d.; Ḳāḍī Ibn al-Zubayr [attrib.], *K. al-Hadāyā wa 'l-tuḥaf*, tr. and ann. Ghāda al-Ḥijjāwī al-Qaddūmī, *Book of gifts and rarities*, Cambridge, Mass. 1997.

2. General reference works. M. Bauer, *Precious stones*, ii, London and New York 1968; C. Cipriani, *The Macdonald encyclopedia of precious stones*, London 1986; R. Webster, *Gems. Their sources, description and identification*, London and Boston n.d.

(Ghada al-Hijjawi al-Qaddumi)

ZUMURRUD <u>KH</u>ĀTŪN, a Turkish slave, mother of the ʿAbbāsid caliph al-Nāṣir li-Dīn Allāh [*q.v.*] (575-622/1180-1225). She was politically active and continued the religious policy of her husband al-Mustaḍī' [*q.v.*] (566-75/1170-80) by favouring Ḥanbalīs, e.g. Ibn al-<u>Dj</u>awzī [*q.v.*], and interceding for them with her son. The sources praise her piety and generosity. She endowed *madrasas*, *ribāṭs* and mosques, and had a *turba* erected at the grave of the mystic Maʿrūf al-Kar<u>kh</u>ī [*q.v.*], together with a *madrasa*. On the occasion of her pilgrimage she allegedly spent 300,000 dīnārs for alms and on repairs of Meccan cisterns and water-supplies. In the year 580/1184-5 she accompanied al-Nāṣir on a politically important journey to Sāmarrā'.

When she died in <u>Dj</u>umādā I 599/Jan.-Feb. 1203, her son grieved deeply. At the funeral he preceded her bier on foot. She was transported by ship on the Tigris, all the boat people standing up in her honour (al-Ṣafadī, *Wāfī*, xiv, 213), and was buried in a *turba* built for her in her lifetime. Mourning continued for a year. Numerous elegies were composed, and her possessions, including jewels and clothes, were distributed on the caliph's order.

Bibliography: Abū <u>Sh</u>āma, *al-<u>Dh</u>ayl ʿalā 'l-Rawḍatayn*, Beirut 1974, index; Ibn al-Sāʿī, *al-<u>Dj</u>āmiʿ al-mu<u>kh</u>taṣar*, ix, ed. Muṣṭafā <u>Dj</u>awād, Ba<u>gh</u>dād 1353/1934, index; Ibn Ta<u>gh</u>rībirdī, vi, 182; A. Hartmann, *An-Nāṣir li-Dīn Allāh*, Berlin 1975, 180 and *passim*.

(Renate Jacobi)

ZŪN, <u>Zh</u>ūn, the name of a deity of the district of Zamīndāwar [*q.v.*] in eastern Af<u>gh</u>ānistān, whose shrine there figures in historical accounts of the Arabs' and Ṣaffārids' penetration of the region.

In 33/654-5 ʿAbd al-Raḥmān b. Samura, governor of Sīstān for ʿAbd Allāh b. ʿĀmir [*q.v.*], raided into Zamīndāwar and attacked the "hill of Zūn" (*<u>dj</u>abal al-Zūn*), entered the shrine and partially despoiled the idol there, telling the local *marzbān* that his sole object was to demonstrate the idol's impotence (al-Balā<u>dh</u>urī, *Futūḥ*, 394). Over two centuries later, in the accounts of the Ṣaffārid Yaʿḳūb b. al-Lay<u>th</u>'s campaigns in eastern Af<u>gh</u>ānistān, the shrine of Zūn is described as being set on a sacred mountain; the ruler there, the Zunbīl, was divine and was carried on a golden throne by twelve men (Ibn al-A<u>th</u>īr, ed. Beirut, vii, 326). Marquart located this to the northwest of the Helmand river near Bi<u>sh</u>lang. See on these events, Bosworth, *Sīstān under the Arabs, from the Islamic conquest to the rise of the Ṣaffārids (30-250/651-864)*, Rome 1968, 19, 34-6; idem, *The history of the Saffarids of Sistan and the Maliks of Nimruz (247/861 to 949/1542-3)*, Costa Mesa and New York 1994, 99 ff.

The origins and affiliations of this cult are unclear; it was clearly not Zoroastrian or Buddhist. Marquart surmised that it might have been connected with the celebrated shrine of the Sun God Āditya at Multān. Bussagli has suggested the possibility of influences from the pre-Buddhist divine monarchy of Tibet. The title of the local ruler, Zunbīl, earlier forms perhaps **Zūn-dātbar* or **Zūn-dā<u>dh</u>* [see zamīndāwar], may appear in Chinese sources as *Shun-ta*, and Christian ecclesiastical historians mention τζουνδαδέερ and *Zundaber*. See J. Marquart and J.J.M. de Groot, *Das Reich Zābul und der Gott Žūn vom 6.-9. Jahrhundert*, in G. Weil (ed.), *Festschrift Eduard Sachau*, Berlin 1915, 248-92, and the works of M. Bussagli and G. Scarcia discussed in the two books of Bosworth mentioned above. An origin in the religions of ancient Mesopotamia seems unlikely, *pace* T. Fahd, *Le panthéon de l'Arabie centrale*, Paris 1965, 199-201, nor an etymology from Greek, *pace* Wahib Atallah, *Sur un vers de Ğarīr. Etymologie de* zūn *et de* hirbi<u>d</u>, in *Arabica*, xviii (1971), 49-54.

The end of the Zunbīls and the cult of Zūn was brought about by Yaʿḳūb b. al-Lay<u>th</u>'s operations in the region from 253/867 onwards, with his killing of the Zunbīl in 237/871. Thereafter, all mention of Zūn and its devotees disappear, and we must assume that Zamīndāwar became gradually Islamised by the early 4th/10th century.

Bibliography: Given in the article.

(C.E. Bosworth)

ZUNBĪL, the putative title borne by a line of rulers in eastern Af<u>gh</u>ānistān in pre- and early Islamic times, who opposed the extension of Muslim arms into their region for some two centuries.

In the Arabic historical texts, there is uncertainty about the vocalisation of the name, with forms like *Rutbīl and *Ratbīl, etc. given. The origin of the title is quite obscure. Marquart was probably correct in seeing in it a theophoric name which included the element Zūn [*q.v.*] or <u>Zh</u>ūn, the name of the god mentioned in the Arabic sources as worshipped in the region of Zamīndāwar [*q.v.*]; but other, less plausible etymologies have been suggested such as **zanda-pīl* "furious elephant" as an epithet (Persian!) given to the ruler by the Arabs when they encountered the Zunbīl in war. The most thorough recent discussions are by M. Bussagli and G. Scarcia, especially the latter's *Ancora su «ZNBYL»*, in *AIUON*, N.S. xvi (1966), 201-5, and *Zunbīl or Zanbīl?*, in *Yádnáme-ye Jan Rypka*, Prague 1967, 41-3.

The line of Zunbīls probably arose from the time when the Southern Hephthalites [see hayāṭila] dominated Af<u>gh</u>ānistān south of the Hindu Kush and northwestern India (5th and 6th centuries). They were implacable foes of the Muslims from the time of the first Arab raids through Sīstān and Bust [*q.vv.*] in the later 7th century till the 3rd/9th century, when the campaigns of the Ṣaffārid Yaʿḳūb b. al-Lay<u>th</u> [*q.v.*] to Kābul and beyond seem to have brought the line of Zunbīls to an end, then permitting the Islamisation of eastern Af<u>gh</u>ānistān.

Bibliography: See also the references given in zūn, and especially the discussion of the title in Bosworth, *The history of the Saffarids of Sistan*, 85-6, 91-5. The course of the relations between the Zunbīls and the Muslims can be traced in the works of Marquart and de Groot and of Bosworth given in the *Bibl.* to zūn.

(C.E. Bosworth)

ZUNNĀR (a.), the girdle worn by the "Protected Peoples", *ahl al-<u>dh</u>imma* (in effect, by Jews, Christians and Zoroastrians), usually linked with the *<u>sh</u>iʿār* or *<u>gh</u>iyār* [*q.v.*], patches of varying colour worn on the *dhimmīs'* clothing to distinguish them from the Muslims. The *zunnār* was usually wider than the *minṭaḳa*, the general word for "girdle". The requirement of its usage is traditionally regarded in the sources as being part of the so-called "Covenant of ʿUmar [I]", now considered to have been a body of practices which grew up piecemeal and which did not reach full legal embodiment till the 3rd/9th century. See further DHIMMA and GHIYĀR. The term itself obviously stems from *zōnarion*, diminutive of Grk. *zōnē*, probably via Aramaic *zunnārā*; in Syriac, it denotes the girdle worn by monks. In Persian Ṣūfī poetry, it is often used for the locks of the beloved.

Bibliography: See the arts. mentioned in the text, and the references given in the *EI*[1] art. s.v.

(A.S. TRITTON*)

ZURAYʿIDS, a South Arabian dynasty of Fāṭimid allegiance (473-569/1080-1173), of Yām [*q.v.*], centred on the southern port of Yemen [see AL-YAMAN], Aden [see ʿADAN].

When the Maʿnids (Banū Maʿn), the then rulers of Aden, suspended their tribute to their masters, the Ṣulayḥids [*q.v.*] in 473/1080, al-Mukarram Aḥmad marched on Aden for the Ṣulayḥids, drove out the Maʿnids and installed as joint rulers al-ʿAbbās and al-Masʿūd, sons of one al-Mukarram b. al-Dhiʾb, in return for their previous services to the Ṣulayḥid Fāṭimid cause. Al-ʿAbbās died in 477/1084 and his son, Zurayʿ, who gave his name to the dynasty (Banū Zurayʿ), took over as joint ruler with his uncle, al-Masʿūd. The situation remained thus until 504/1101. Seeing that the Ṣulayḥids were preoccupied elsewhere, the Zurayʿids repudiated their arrangement with them, and declared themselves independent rulers of Aden.

Our sources fail us badly, for there is little information on the independent dynasty. Its early history was one of struggles between the two branches of the family and all the problems of joint rule came to the surface (see Smith, *Ayyūbids*, ii, 63, for the complete family tree). In 533/1138 ʿAlī b. Sabaʾ b. Abi ʾl-Suʿūd b. Zurayʿ assumed full power. After his death shortly afterwards, his brother, Muḥammad b. Sabaʾ took over and reinforced control over much of southern Arabia, apart from Aden. Muḥammad was appointed an official Fāṭimid *dāʿī* by the Fāṭimid caliph in Cairo. Muḥammad was able to bring much stability to the southern area of Yemen, and in 547/1152 purchased a number of fortresses to bolster his dynasty's position. He died in 548/1153 and was succeeded by his son, ʿImrān.

We know nothing of ʿImrān's reign. He died in 561/1166, and thereafter the effective control fell into the hands of Zurayʿid slave ministers. Upon the arrival in Aden in 571/1175 of the conquering Ayyūbid force coming to Yemen from Egypt [see AYYŪBIDS] in 569/1173, the ruling minister Yāsir b. Bilāl was put to death. It can be said, therefore, that the Zurayʿid dynasty was brought to an end by the Ayyūbid conquest of the country.

Bibliography: 1. Yemeni sources (relatively late and confused). ʿUmāra al-Yamanī, *Taʾrīkh al-Yaman*, in H.C. Kay, *Yaman, its early mediaeval history*, London 1892, 64-80 (Eng. tr.), 48-59 (Ar. text); ʿAbd al-Raḥmān b. ʿAlī al-Daybaʿ, *Ḳurrat al-ʿuyūn bi-akhbār al-Yaman al-maymūn*, Cairo 1977, i, 304-19; Yaḥyā b. al-Ḥusayn, *Ghāyat al-amānī fī akhbar al-ḳuṭr al-yamānī*, ed. Saʿīd ʿĀshūr, Cairo 1968, 241-84 (a Zaydī source, slightly confused).

2. Modern sources. Ḥusayn b. Fayḍ Allāh al-Hamdānī, *al-Ṣulayḥiyyūn wa ʾl-ḥaraka al-Fāṭimiyya fī ʾl-Yaman*, Cairo 1955, 345; G.R. Smith, *The Ayyūbids and early Rasūlids in the Yemen* (*GMS*, N.S. xxvi), London 1978, ii, 63-7; idem, *The political history of the Islamic Yemen down to the first Turkish invasion (1-945/622-1538)*, in W. Daum, *Yemen: 3000 years of art and civilisation in Arabia Felix*, Innsbruck and Frankfurt-am-Main 1988, 133; C.E. Bosworth, *The New Islamic dynasties*, Edinburgh 1996, 104-5 no. 46.

(G.R. SMITH)

AL-**ZURḲĀNĪ**, MUḤAMMAD B. ʿABD AL-BĀḲĪ b. Yūsuf b. Aḥmad b. Muḥammad al-Miṣrī al-Mālikī (b. 1055/1645 in Cairo, d. here 1122/1710), renowned Mālikī jurist. His forefathers came from the village of Zurḳān in the province of al-Manūfiyya in Lower Egypt. Already his father ʿAbd al-Bāḳī (d. 1099/1688; see Brockelmann, II, 414) had made a name for himself at the al-Azhar University as a jurisprudent of the Mālikī school of law; he composed a commentary on the *Mukhtaṣar* of Khalīl b. Isḥāḳ (d. 767/1365 [*q.v.*]).

Al-Zurḳānī himself was also a member of al-Azhar, where he taught *fiḳh* and *ḥadīth* until his death. Alongside commentaries on works of his predecessors among the traditionists, he became above all known far beyond the borders of Egypt as the author of a copious commentary on the *Muwaṭṭaʾ* of Mālik b. Anas [*q.v.*] with the title *Abhadj al-masālik bi-sharḥ Muwaṭṭaʾ al-Imām Mālik*, soon to be known as *Sharḥ al-Zurḳānī* (printed several times in Cairo in 4 vols.; see Sezgin, *GAS*, i, 462).

Manuscripts of his works are to be found in the Dār al-Kutub, Cairo, the library of al-Azhar, and in the Ẓāhiriyya Library, Damascus (see Kaḥḥāla, x, 124).

His *Muwaṭṭaʾ* commentary was written, according to his own indications in the preface and at the end of the work, between 1109 and 1112. He was guided by Ibn Ḥadjar al-ʿAsḳalānī's [*q.v.*] commentary on the *Ṣaḥīḥ* of al-Bukhārī. A source-analytical study of al-Zurḳānī's *Muwaṭṭaʾ* commentary has not yet been written. One may, however, consider as certain that he had direct access to the pertinent commentaries on Mālik's work, i.e. *al-Tamhīd li-mā fī ʾl-Muwaṭṭaʾ min al-maʿānī wa ʾl-asānīd* and *al-Istidhkār al-djāmiʿ li-madhāhib fuḳahāʾ al-amṣār* by the Cordovan scholar Ibn ʿAbd al-Barr [*q.v.*]. Al-Zurḳānī would have used the manuscripts of these works that are extant in the al-Azhar library. In addition to the canonical *ḥadīth* collections and *muṣannaf works*, he quotes, whether directly or not, the *K. al-Masālik fī sharḥ, Muwaṭṭaʾ Mālik* of Abū Bakr Ibn al-ʿArabī (d. 543/1148 [*q.v.*]), and the already classical biographical work on the Mālikīs by al-Ḳāḍī ʿIyāḍ b. Mūsā [*q.v.*].

The structure and the style of the work permit us to infer that we are dealing here with a handbook for teaching purposes treating the basic tenets of Mālikī law as laid out in Mālik's *Muwaṭṭaʾ* in the *riwāya* of Yaḥyā b. Yaḥyā al-Laythī [*q.v.*]; as such it was beholden to the tradition of legal and traditionist scholarship as handed down in the *madhhab*. Independent or groundbreaking comments on the legal material presented by Mālik are not to be expected in al-Zurḳānī's work.

Bibliography (in addition to references given in the article): Ziriklī, *Aʿlām*, vi, 184.

(M. MURANYI)

ZŪRKHĀNA (P), lit. "house of strength", the traditional gymnasium of Iran.

The traditional *zūrkhāna* consists of a building whose architecture recalls a public bath (*ḥammām* [*q.v.*]). Its main room is often sunken slightly below street level to provide for constant temperatures and prevent draughts that might harm the perspiring athletes, and access to it is possible only through a low door, forcing everyone to bow in respect while entering. Traditionally, admittance to the *zūrkhāna* was forbidden to women, non-Muslims, and prepubescent boys. At the centre of the room lies the *gawd*, a usually octagonal pit about a metre deep in which the exercises take place. The *gawd* is surrounded by spectator stands, behind which the walls are adorned with pictures of athletes and saints. Of particular importance is an elevated and decorated seat, the *sardam*, which is reserved for the *murshid* "guide" or "director". The *murshid*'s function is to accompany the exercises with rhythmic drumming and the chanting of verse from classical Persian poetry such as (but not limited to) Firdawsī's *Shāh-nāma* [*q.v.*] as well as poetry specific to the house of strength, most notably Mīr Nadjāt Iṣfahānī's *Gul-i kushtī* ("The Flower of Wrestling").

The standard attire for athletes is the *lung*, a cloth wrapped around the loins and passed between the legs; when wrestling, however, leather breeches (*tunbān*) are worn. The exercises take place in a standard order. After some warming up calisthenics, in the course of which one of the athletes may lift heavy wooden boards (*sang*) as he lies on his back outside the *gawd*, athletes do push-ups (*shinā*) and then swing Indian clubs (*mīl*), both exercises being accompanied by the *murshid*'s drumming and chanting. Individuals will then take turns to whirl at speed about the *gawd* (*čarkh*), and step forth to swing above their heads a heavy iron bow (*kabbāda*), on the cord of which are strung heavy rings. Until the 1940s the crowning event of a *zūrkhāna* session was wrestling (*kushtī*). With the introduction of international freestyle and graeco-roman wrestling, however, wrestling disappeared from the *gawd*. Traditional wrestling, which resembles the freestyle variety except that athletes are permitted to grab each other's breeches at the belt and at the reinforced hems, survived in a modernised form under the name of *kushtī-yi pahlawānī* ("*pahlawānī* wrestling"), but lost its organic link with the *zūrkhāna*. The loss of the institution's agonistic component lessened its attraction to young men, thus contributing to the decline of its popularity.

Traditionally, athletes were divided into a number of grades. These were, in ascending of seniority: *nawča* "novice", *nawkhʷāsta* "beginner", *pahlawān* "athlete", and, finally, each establishment's most accomplished member, the *mīyāndār*, who conducts the proceedings. Beginning in the 1940s, however, these grades gradually fell into disuse and were replaced by the standard international categories "cadet", "junior", and "senior", and, for *pahlawānī* wrestling, weight classes.

The vocabulary, rituals, ethos and grades of the *zūrkhāna* recall those of *futuwwa* [*q.v.*] and Ṣūfism [see TAṢAWWUF], but a direct filiation cannot be established. Popular religion, especially veneration of the first Shīʿī Imām, ʿAlī b. Abī Ṭālib, plays a major role in the institution, and proceedings are frequently interrupted by salvos of benediction (*ṣalawāt*). However, in the mid-20th century there were also a few Jewish and Zoroastrian *zūrkhāna*s in Tehran, Yazd and Shīrāz; their rituals were adapted accordingly.

The origins of the *zūrkhāna* are shrouded in mystery. Wrestling has an old tradition in Iran, as evinced by many episodes recounted in the *Shāh-nāma*, most famously Rustam's bout with his son Suhrāb. According to Muslim traditions, the prophets Adam, Jacob and Muḥammad, as well as ʿAlī b. Abī Ṭālib and his two sons al-Ḥasan and al-Ḥusayn excelled at it. The patron saint of *zūrkhāna* athletes (as well as Turkish wrestlers) is the 8th/14th-century Ṣūfī Pahlawān Maḥmūd of Khʷārazm, better known as Pūryā-yi Walī.

Wrestling was patronised by the Saldjūḳs, Il-Khānids, Tīmūrids and Ṣafawids, and under the latter, wrestlers were organised in a guild headed by a *pahlawān-bāshī*. But the earliest known mention of *zūrkhāna* exercises occurs in a fragment dating from the Ṣafawid era, *Ṭūmār-i Pūryā-yi Walī*. The first Western traveller to describe a *zūrkhāna* was Reinhold Niebuhr, to whom we also owe the first graphic representation of one. Beginning in the early 19th century, the Ḳādjār rulers of Iran became enthusiastic patrons of wrestling, and consequently, *zūrkhāna*s thrived. They were embedded in a town quarter's social structure and constituted an important part of community life. Some were frequented by craftsmen and tradesmen associated with the bazaar (*sūḳ* [*q.v.*]), some had a Ṣūfī membership, and still others were used by men of questionable mores on the fringes of legality, the *lūṭī*s [*q.v.*]. Later in the century, royal patronage led men of higher birth to participate in the exercises, a development that reached its peak under Nāṣir al-Dīn Shāh (*r.* 1848-96 [*q.v.*]). With the advent of the Constitutional Revolution in 1905-6, royal patronage ceased, dealing a severe blow to the houses of strength, which became once again a feature of urban lower middle-class culture. In subsequent years, the introduction of modern Western sports and physical education diminished their appeal among athletically-inclined men, while cinemas drew spectators away. *Zūrkhāna*s might have disappeared altogether, had it not been for the official millennial celebration of the poet Firdawsī's birth in 1934, on which occasion exhibitions of *zūrkhāna* exercises were held in public. They soon came to be termed *warzish-i bāstānī* "ancient sports", which implied that their origin lay in pre-Islamic times. This rendered it compatible with the official ideology of the two Pahlawī shāhs, which emphasised Iran's ancient Persian heritage at the expense of Islam. It became conventional wisdom that the *zūrkhāna*s originated in the underground resistance activities of Iranian patriots against the Arab and, later, Mongol invaders, although there is no historical evidence for this.

From 1953 to 1978 *zūrkhāna* sports were mostly under the control of Shaʿbān Djaʿfarī, who benefited from royal patronage, having been one of the ringleaders of the August 1953 riots that accompanied the military *coup d'état* that ousted the Prime Minister Muḥammad Muṣaddiḳ [*q.v.*]. The Shāh rewarded Djaʿfarī with a modern clubhouse whose *zūrkhāna* was lavish by the humble standards of traditional houses of strength. The carefully choreographed exercises performed by the members of this club became an exotic tourist attraction for visiting foreign dignitaries and celebrities, including women. Led by Djaʿfarī, *zūrkhāna* athletes performed by the hundreds in Tehran's main stadium on such occasions as the Shāh's birthday.

After the Islamic Revolution, the authorities of the Islamic Republic emphasised the Islamic character of the institution and tried to popularise it again. To attract young people, boys were permitted into the *gawd*, and a plethora of competitions are held with the aim of turning the exercises into modern sport replete with point systems, records and champions. Whether these innovations can assure the survival in the long run of the *zūrkhāna* remains to be seen.

*Zūrkhāna*s can be found in most Iranian cities. Outside Iran, they were introduced to ʿIrāḳ in the 1830s, where they existed until the 1960s. There are also *zūrkhānas* in Ādharbāydjān and Afghānistān, although their rituals differ somewhat from those found in Iran.

Bibliography: R. Niebuhr, *Reisebeschreibung*, Copenhagen 1778; M. Canard, *La lutte chez les Arabes*, in *Société historique algérienne* (ed.), *Cinquantenaire de la Faculté des Lettres d'Alger*, Algiers 1932; H. Partaw Baydā'ī Kāshānī, *Tārīkh-i warzish-i bāstānī-yi Īrān: zūrkhāna*, Tehran 1958 (fundamental: this book contains the *Ṭūmār-i Pūryā-yi Walī* and the *Gul-i kushtī*); A. Piemontese, *L'organizzazione della "Zurxâne" e la "Futuwwa"*, in *AIUON*, n.s. xiv (1964); Djamīl al-Ṭā'ī, *al-Zūrkhānāt al-Baghdādiyya*, Baghdād 1986; Ṣadr al-Dīn Ilāhī, *Nigāhī dīgar bih sunnatī kuhan: zūrkhāna*, in *Īrānshināsī*, vi (1373 *sh*./1995); Mahdī 'Abbāsī, *Tārīkh-i kushtī-yi Īrān*, 2 vols. Tehran 1374 *sh*./1995; P.L. Baker, *Wrestling at the Victoria and Albert Museum*, in *Iran JBIPS*, xxxv (1997), 73-8; Ph. Rochard, *Le "sport antique" des zurkhâne de Téhéran. Formes et significations d'une pratique contemporaine*, unpubl. PhD diss., Université Aix-Marseille I, 2000.

(H.E. Chehabi)

ZURNA, a woodwind musical instrument, the shawm, with a powerful sound, played in the open. *Zurna* (*zūrnā*) is the later Ottoman and modern Turkish spelling of the Persian and early Ottoman term *surnā* (*surnāy*), *ṣūrnā* or *ṣurnā* (*ṣurnāy*). The name spread throughout the countries of the former Ottoman empire, where it is still used in many places. In Egypt the instrument retained its traditional Arabic name *mizmār* [*q.v.*]; in Libya and Morocco it is called *ghayṭa* [*q.v.*].

The *zurna* is played with a double reed. Since the reed vibrates freely in the mouth cavity of the player, the instrument has a penetrating sound which the player cannot modify. It became the characteristic woodwind instrument of the Islamic world, played at ceremonial, military and festive occasions. In Ottoman times it served two different purposes. First, it was the prominent melody instrument of the *mehter* [*q.v.*] ensemble. Second, it was, and still is, the melody instrument of the popular pair of shawm and drum (*davul-zurna*), played mainly to accompany folk dances at festive occasions in the countryside. The folk *zurna* is characterised by a fork-shaped "spool" (*nezik*) in the head of the instrument. It was recently shown that this "ingenious invention" allows the instrument maker to fit the body of the *zurna*, in the region of the seven fingerholes and the thumbhole, with an easily made cylindrical bore instead of the traditional conical bore. It can be assumed that the fork was invented in the creative atmosphere of the Ottoman capital, from where it spread through the empire. A vivid impression of the guild of *zurna* makers and players, and of the varieties of the instrument known in 17th-century Istanbul is given by Ewliyā Čelebi.

Bibliography (in addition to the titles listed in the art. MIZMĀR): H.G. Farmer, *Turkish instruments of music in the seventeenth century. As described in the* Siyāḥat nāma *of Ewliyā Chelebī*, Glasgow 1937, 23-6; H. Sanal, *Mehter musikisi. Bestekâr mehterler – mehter havaları*, Istanbul 1964, 66-9 and *passim*; L. Picken, *Folk musical instruments of Turkey*, London 1975, 485-508; M.R. Gazimihal, *Türk nefesli çalgıları*, Ankara 1975, *passim*; Chr. Poché, art. *Zūrnā*, in *The New Grove dictionary of musical instruments*, London 1984, iii, 905-8 (with a general bibl.); J. Montagu, *The forked shawm – an ingenious invention*, in *Yearbook for Traditional Music*, xxix (1997), 74-9; U. Reinhard, *Zurna*, in *Musik in Geschichte und Gegenwart. Sachteil*, ix, Kassel 1998, cols. 2483-93 (with a special bibl. regarding Turkey).

(E. Neubauer)

AL-**ZUṬṬ**, the form in early Arabic usage for the name of a northwestern Indian people, the Jhāts [see DJĀṬ], members of whom were brought into the Persian Gulf region in the first Islamic centuries and possibly earlier.

According to al-Balādhurī, the Sāsānid emperor Bahrām V Gūr (*r.* 420-38) transported Zuṭṭ from India to Khūzistān and the Persian Gulf shores; these subsequently became Muslim and were settled by Abū Mūsā al-Ash'arī [*q.v.*] at Baṣra, being attached to the tribe of Ḥanẓala of Tamīm. At least some of them were caught up in the rebellion of Ibn al-Ash'ath [*q.v.*], and after its suppression, the governor of the East al-Ḥadjdjādj demolished their houses, deprived them of their stipends and deported a certain number. Already in Mu'āwiya's reign, the caliph had moved some of the Zuṭṭ of Baṣra and some of the Sayābidja [*q.v.*], of Malaysian origin, from Lower 'Irāḳ to the 'Amḳ near Antioch and the Cilician plain around al-Maṣṣīṣa (in 49/669 or 50/670) (al-Balādhurī, *Futūḥ*, 162, 373-4, 376-7). At the time of the Arab conquest of Sind (93/711), some of the Zuṭṭ of the Indus valley (probably including indigenous Sindīs as well as Jhāts) were transplanted by al-Ḥadjdjādj to the similar riverine environment of Lower 'Irāḳ, the Baṭā'iḥ or marshlands [see AL-BAṬĪḤA]. Both al-Walīd I and Yazīd I further moved groups of Zuṭṭ to northwestern Syria, together with water buffaloes for the hot coastal plains there (*ibid.*, 168, 376), but many Zuṭṭ clearly remained in 'Irāḳ. Whether the grandfather of the Imām Abū Ḥanīfa (d. 150/767 [*q.v.*]) named as Zūṭī in al-Khaṭīb, *Ta'rīkh Baghdād*, xiii, 324-5, came from one of the Zuṭṭ groups of Lower 'Irāḳ (Zūṭī is said to have come "from the people of Kābul" and to have been a *mawlā* of Taym Allāh b. Tha'laba of the Bakr b. Wā'il) is uncertain.

There may have been further migrations of Zuṭṭ from India to the southern provinces of Persia and to Lower 'Irāḳ during early 'Abbāsid times (al-Mas'ūdī, *Tanbīh*, 355, tr. 455). They seem to have become a turbulent element of the population in the latter region, and al-Djāḥiẓ names the *Zuṭṭ al-ādjām* "Zuṭṭ of the thickets [of the lower 'Irāḳ marshlands]" as amongst the outlaws and predatory groups with whom his beggar chief Khālid b. Yazīd had kept company (K. *al-Bukhalā'*, ed. Ḥādjirī, Cairo 1958, 49, tr. Pellat, 70). In 205/820 the caliph al-Ma'mūn had to appoint commanders for the war against the Zuṭṭ of Lower 'Irāḳ. But the troubles continued, and his successor al-Mu'taṣim had to send the veteran commander 'Udjayf b. 'Anbasa against them in 219/834; this required a campaign involving amphibious operations, and after the Zuṭṭ were subdued, 27,000 of them, including 12,000 fighting men, were reportedly in 220/835 deported to Baghdād and thence to Khānikīn [*q.v.*] on the road to Djibāl and to 'Ayn Zarba [*q.v.*] on the Byzantine frontier in Cilicia. Zuṭṭ unrest does not seem to have had the same social aspect as the rebellion of the Zandj [*q.v.*] half a century later, but may have expressed general discontent with the centralising policies of the Baghdād government; however, its exact causes and motivations are unclear (al-Ṭabarī, iii, 1044-5, 1069, 1166-70; al-Mas'ūdī, *Tanbīh*, 355-6, tr. 455-6; Ibn al-Athīr, ed. Beirut, vi, 362, 379, 389, 443-4, 446, vii, 80). The Zuṭṭ are mentioned in the late 4th/10th century, when a Būyid prince, Abū Naṣr Shāh-Fīrūz, in 390/1000 disputed control of Fārs with Bahā' al-Dawla, and gathered into his forces local groups there of Daylamīs, Zuṭṭ and Turks (Hilāl al-Ṣābi', in *Eclipse of the 'Abbasid caliphate*, iii, 349; Ibn al-Athīr, ix, 160), but thereafter, mention of the Zuṭṭ as a special group seems to fade from historical record.

De Goeje in his monograph (see *Bibl.*) endeavoured to show that those Zuṭṭ who originally settled at Baṣra, but then scattered, including by a Byzantine deportation of them from ʿAyn Zarba when this last was attacked by the Greeks, were the ancestors of a part at least of the Gypsies [for whom see ČINGĀNE; LŪLĪ; NŪRĪ]. The modern Gypsy language, of obviously northwestern Indian origin, in fact contains few words of Arabic provenance, and de Goeje's thesis remains unproven.

Bibliography (in addition to references in the article): M.J. de Goeje, *Mémoire sur les migrations des Tsiganes à travers l'Asie* (Mémoires d'histoire et de géographie orientales, no. 3), Leiden 1903, esp. 20-33; Ch. Pellat, *Le milieu baṣrien et la formation de Ǧāḥiẓ*, Paris 1953, 37-9; *EI*[1] art. *Zoṭṭ* (G. Ferrand); *EI*[2] art. DJĀṬ.

(C.E. BOSWORTH)